Musical AKAs

Assumed Names and Sobriquets of Composers, Songwriters, Librettists, Lyricists, Hymnists, and Writers on Music

Jeanette Marie Drone

The Scarecrow Press, Inc.
Lanham, Maryland • Toronto • Plymouth, UK
2007

SCARECROW PRESS, INC.

Published in the United States of America
by Scarecrow Press, Inc.
A wholly owned subsidiary of The Rowman & Littlefield Publishing Group, Inc.
4501 Forbes Boulevard, Suite 200, Lanham, Maryland 20706
www.scarecrowpress.com

Estover Road
Plymouth PL6 7PY
United Kingdom

British Library Cataloguing in Publication Information Available

Library of Congress Cataloging-in-Publication Data

Drone, Jeanette Marie, 1940–
Musical AKAs : assumed names and sobriquets of composers, songwriters, librettists, lyricists, hymnists, and writers on music / Jeanette Marie Drone.
p. cm.
Includes bibliographical references.
ISBN-13: 978-0-8108-5739-1 (hardcover : alk. paper)
ISBN-10: 0-8108-5739-1 (pbk. : alk. paper)
1. Musicians—Bio-bibliography—Dictionaries. 2. Anonyms and pseudonyms. 3. Nicknames—Dictionaries. I. Title.

ML105.D76 2006
780.92'2—dc22

2006000542

™ The paper used in this publication meets the minimum requirements of American National Standard for Information Sciences—Permanence of Paper for Printed Library Materials, ANSI/NISO Z39.48-1992.
Manufactured in the United States of America.

For my mother, Frances Rebstock Drone,
and in memory of my father, William Alexander Drone.
Thank you!

Contents

Preface: Pseudonymity in Music

In the introduction of his third edition of *Dictionary of Pseudonyms* (1998), Adrian Room discusses the various reasons literary authors use assumed names, i.e., pseudonyms pen names, noms de plume, initialisms. Using this essay as an outline, I have identified parallel examples in the field of music.

Individuals may use different names on works submitted to different publishers. In addition to using his own name, Wallingford Riegger used the following pseudonyms (see table P.1).

Table P.1. Pseudonyms of Wallingford Riegger

Assumed Names	Publishers
Edwin Farrell	Morrissey
George Northrup	Leeds
Gerald Wilfring Gore	Flammer
William Richards	Lorenz
Edgar Long	Pro Art
Walter Scotson	Witmark
John H. McCurdy	Boosey & Hawkes
Leonard Gregg	Columbia Recordings

Sometimes individuals use different names on publications submitted to a single publisher. William Arms Fisher used at least fourteen pseudonyms on titles published by Oliver Ditson, making the Ditson catalog appear more comprehensive than it really was.

There are numerous examples of individuals using different names for different musical genres. Charles N(eil) Daniels, also known as Neil Moret, used at least eight additional pseudonyms, including L'Albert on marches and Charlie Hill on western songs. Perhaps the most noted example is Vladimir Dukelsky, who composed symphonic works under his birth name and popular songs as Vernon Duke.

An assumed name can also hide the fact that a person is involved in endeavors outside his/her main career. While pursuing a career as an orchestral flutist, Otto Luening used the name James P. Cleveland to conceal the fact that he also was employed as an actor and stage manager for the Joyce English Players, and composer George Antheil wrote *Death in the Dark*, a detective novel, as Stacy Bishop.

Names are frequently changed when birth names are identified with a social condition or an ethnic group, or are difficult to pronounce, or to avoid confusion with another person with the same or similar name. During the WWI era, individuals frequently changed their German names or "Americanized" the spellings. Unquestionably, Paul Creston is easier to remember and pronounce than Giuseppe Guttoveggio. And to avoid confusion, Edward Jones added his father's given name, Stephen, as a middle name so that he would not be confused with another student who had the same name. (Later he dropped his original surname and became known as Edward Stephen[s].)

Sometimes individuals with generally common names assume a "foreign" name under the guise that "foreign is better." Sir Henry Joseph Wood was also known as Paul Klenovsky, and Ethel Liggins became Ethel Leginska.

In some cases assumed names are used to re-enforce the style or subject of a song. Cavan O'Connor wrote "My Senorita" as Jose Sabado. And then there is the delightful example of James [or Jimmy] (Francis) McHugh and Lewis Michelson's use of the names Ura Herring and Ima Fish on "Hey! You Want Any Codfish? We Only Have Mack'rel Today."

The use of a *nom de plume* on a collaborative endeavor avoids a cumbersome listing of several names. "Our Miss Gibbs" was by Cryptos—a group of lyricists and composers, including Adrien Ross [i.e., Arthur Reed Roper]; Percy Greenbank; Ivan Caryll [i.e., Felix Tilken]; and (John) Lionel (Alexander) Monckton.

Music publishers, like literary publishers, often allocate house names on "for hire" publications. Arthur P. Schmidt Co. used several house names, including W. F. Ambrosio, Ferdinand Meyer, Arthur Dana, Carl Erich, Hugh Gordon and G. P. Ritter.

Like literary critics, music critics frequently use assumed names. One of the most interesting examples is George Bernard Shaw, who wrote music criticism for *The Star* under the name Corno di Bassetto (Italian for basset horn), an instrument he described as wretched and having a peculiar watery melancholy sound.

In retrospect, several music critics who chose to write under their own names probably wished they had used assumed names. Claudia Cassidy was dubbed "Acidy Cassidy" and "Poison Pen Cassidy," William James Henderson was called "Singer's Critic and Lord High Executioner," and Henry Taylor Parker's initials H. T. P. were facetiously interpreted as "Hard to Please" and "Hell to Pay."

Assumed names are frequently found on works of parody. A contemporary example is the works of P. D. Q. Bach. Although many consider the name a pseudonym of Peter Schickele, others disagree, saying that since Schickele does not use the name as a means of concealment, it is an alter ego.

Assumed names are frequently used to obscure the sex of the composer or author. Until recent times women received less recognition for works published under their own names. Frequently a woman used initials with her surname, keeping her identity yet concealing her sex. Using the pseudonym "A Lady" identified the sex of the author/composer but masked the woman's true identity. Sometimes a minor adjustment to a given name provided a disguise, for example, Louise became Louis, and Alberta became Bert. Perhaps the most noted example in this category is Polish composer Irene Regine Wieniawska, who used the pen name Poldowski. Although men rarely assume feminine names, there are there are a few noted cases, including Septimus Winner who used the name Alice Hawthorne, and Robert A. King (originally Keiser) who composed numerous songs under the names Mary Earl, Kathleen A. Roberts, Mrs. Ravenhall, and others.

In several cases composers have assumed names of more famous composers to assure acceptance of their works. Perhaps the most noted musical hoax was perpetuated by Fritz Kreisler, who composed dozens of pieces for violin in the "olden style" which he ascribed to various 18th-century composers, including Louis Couperin, Karl von Dittersdorf, Niccolo A. Porpora, Johann Stamitz, and Antonio Vivaldi. In 1935 Kreisler finally admitted the hoax, and today the pieces are still part of the standard violin repertoire. The question remains—would they have been accepted as readily if published under Kreisler's name?

Sometimes assumed names are chosen in a sense of fun or in an attempt to be clever. Perhaps that is why Fanny J. Crosby wrote as Mrs. Nom D. Plume or why Kenneth Werner chose the name Phil Harmonic. And then there was C(yrus) Van Ness Clark and Martin Hickey, who jointly used the name Dick C. Land on "Bile Them Cabbage Down" and "Flounder Foot Polka."

Another category is described under "pseudonyms" in Nicholas Slonimsky's *Baker's Dictionary of Music* (Schirmer Books, 1977, 804). Pseudonyms can be used when ". . . a dignified composer writes undignified music." Did Slonimsky include this definition to explain his use of the pseudonyms Sol Mysnik and Nicholas Sloane? Another example in this category is Leslie Sarony [i.e., Leslie Legge Sarony Frye], who used the name Q. Kumber on "Mucking About in the Garden." And on second thought, perhaps the example of McHugh and Michelson's use of the names Ura Herring and Ima Fish, cited above, would be more appropriately be placed in this category.

A category not discussed in Room's essay is "spirit writing." In recent times the most noted examples are Clifford Enticknap, who claimed to be a "channel" for Handel's music, and Rosemary Brown, who produced hundreds of works allegedly dictated by numerous famous composers. (See Melvyn J. Willin's "Music and the Paranormal," http://www.musicpsyche.org/Journal/mp1Willin11.html [29 May 2005].)

TYPES OF PSEUDONYMS

Anagrams and reverse spellings are easily identified, for example, Cesare Meano [i.e., Marco E. Senea] and Trebor Rellim [i.e., Robert Miller]. A translated surname is another easy way to mask one's identity, for example Fredrick

Root used the surname Wurzel. The use of initials is a popular way to conceal one's identity, and although initials usually consist of the first letters of a person's given and surname, there are many examples when they stand for something completely different. For example, Jane Laurie Borthwick used the initials H. L. L., which stands for "Hymns from the Land of Luther." Nicknames are rarely chosen by an individual but rather applied by someone else. Although a nickname usually replaces an individual's given name(s), occasionally it is added to a given name (Little John, Smilin' Joe). Some nicknames identify a physical trait (Shorty, Slim, Red), while other describe a character trait (Acidy Cassidy), or identifies the instrument a person plays (Piano, Slide). Sobriquets, like nicknames, are usually applied by others and are not meant to replace a name or mask an individual's identity. In time, however, they can become a nickname, with perhaps the most noted example being "The March King"—John Philip Sousa.

Whatever the type of assumed name (legal name change, pseudonym, nickname, initials), the process of verification is usually time consuming and frequently impossible.

"O what a tangled web we weave,
When first we practise to deceive!
—Sir Walter Scott (*Marmion* Canto vi.st.17)

Acknowledgments

Special thanks to the following librarians who helped me locate sources and answered numerous e-mail messages requesting verification of names, titles, and page numbers: Alan A. Green; Thomas F. Heck; Sean W. Ferguson; C. Rockelle ("Rocki") Strader, Ohio State University; David Lasocki, Indiana University; and Laurie Eagelson, University of Arizona.

Introduction

Musical AKAs: Assumed Names and Sobriquets of Composers, Songwriters, Librettists, Lyricists, Hymnists, and Writers on Music is an index to more than 15,500 assumed names and sobriquets of approximately 9,800 music composers, songwriters, lyricists, librettists, hymnist, and writers. The term *assumed names* includes legal name changes, pseudonyms, pen names, *noms de plume*, nicknames, and initials.

Identifying assumed names is usually a complex process. General encyclopedias and dictionaries containing biographical information may include information about assumed names, but few include cross references. Likewise, biographies may contain information about an individual's assumed name(s), but in most cases the names are rarely indexed. A number of specialized indexes to pseudonymity include persons in the field of music; however, the process of locating and searching multiple sources can be extremely time consuming. Two major general sources for assumed names are *Pseudonyms and Nicknames Dictionary* (3rd ed.) (1987), *New Pseudonyms and Nicknames Dictionary* (suppl. to 3rd ed.) (1988), and Harold S. Sharp's *Handbook of Pseudonyms and Personal Nicknames* (1982). Two sources on music pseudonymity are cited in *Music Reference and Research Materials* (1997), Charles Cudworth's "Ye Old Spuriosity Shoppe, or, Put It in the Anhang," (1955), and Allan Sutton's *A Guide to Pseudonyms on American Records, 1892–1942* (1993), which is limited to performers. In the process of compiling *Musical AKAs*, two additional brief journal articles were identified: "Nom de plumes [sic] in the Musical Profession" (1889) and "The Plays the Thing" (1937).

Data for *Musical AKAs* were obtained from numerous music sources, including comprehensive and biographical dictionaries, individual biographies, journals, Internet websites, as well as print and online copyright sources. Data from copyright sources are included only for individuals identified in the sources previously identified. Individuals for whom pseudonyms were identified only in copyright sources will be included in forthcoming volumes.

The process of identifying assumed names varied, depending on the availability of cross references and indexes. Dictionaries were scanned for assumed names listed in entry headings and articles. Thousands of assumed names were identified using this "unscientific" method, but of course, it was not possible to find them all. Journal articles containing assumed names were identified using a series of keyword searches in Chadwyck-Healey's full-text databases *International Index to Music Periodicals* and *International Index to the Performing Arts*. Using the Google search site, (http://www.google.com), a series of keyword searches were used to identify Internet sources. The search process in various copyright sources is described below.

COPYRIGHT SOURCES

The following sources were used: 1) the *Catalog of Copyright Entries* (1910–1976); 2) the *Pre-1938 Pseudonyms Catalog*, located in the Library of Congress Copyright Office (Madison Bldg., Room LM-459); 3) various card catalogs located in the Copyright Office; and 4) the online database for records from 1978 forward (http://copyright.gov/records [20 May 2006]).

Search strategies for the *Catalog of Copyright Entries* (1910–1976) depended on how individual volumes are indexed. From 1910 to the mid-1940s the monthly issues are arranged alphabetically by titles, with cumulative composer indexes containing references from pseudonyms to original names. Unfortunately, only a few pseudonyms for lyricists are included in the indexes. The monthly issues of the mid to late 1940s volumes are arranged by title with annual title cumulations. Since there is no access by name, the entries were scanned to identify the character string: (pseudo). In these volumes pseudonyms for both composers and lyricists were identified. Entries in the early 1950s semi-annual volumes for published music are arranged by composer with title indexes. The corresponding semi-annual volumes for unpublished music and renewals are arranged by title, with no access by name. Pseudonyms are identified in renewal entries but not in the unpublished music entries. From the mid-1950s through 1976 the semiannual volumes are arranged by title with separate name indexes that include see references from pseudonyms to original names.

Entries in the *Pre-1938 Pseudonyms Catalog* are arranged alphabetically by pseudonym. Early entries list only the pseudonym, original name, and a copyright class letter, while later entries also include a title, year, copyright number, and sometimes information clarifying the use of the pseudonym. Since records for all types of materials, that is, monographs, dramas, music, serials, and so forth, are interfiled in the catalog, each entry was checked to identify those noted as "Class E, music"; "Class R (renewal) music"; "Class D (drama) with music"; and "Class A (books) with music."

NAMES EXCLUDED

Assumed names and sobriquets for individuals involved only in the performance of music, for example, singers, pianists, and conductors are not included. Common derivatives of forenames and nicknames, including part of an individual's forenames, for example, Little John, are incorporated into the entry of the original name when possible and are not given separate entries. Use of a second forename (the first omitted) was not considered an assumed name. Married names of women were not considered to be assumed names; however, if a married woman used a pseudonym or went by a nickname, the entry is usually under her original, that is , maiden name, with either a note or an added "assumed name" entry for her married name.

DESCRIPTION

Musical AKAs contains the following chapters: 1) sources, 2) original names (with assumed names and sobriquets), 3) assumed names and sobriquets (with references to original names), and 4) notes.

Chapter 1: Sources

Sources listed in this section are those in which assumed names and/or sobriquets were found for three or more individuals. The entries are arranged alphabetically by four character alphabetic or alpha/numeric codes derived from authors' names, titles, edition, or volume numbers. Entries for print sources include a complete bibliographic citation, and when applicable, reprint information is listed. Entries for Internet sources include website name/title, address, and date the site was last accessed. If a cited address is invalid, users are advised to use a keyword search using the original name and assumed name to locate the site or a substitute site with the same information. Notes following the citations contain explanations of volume numbers or dates added to codes and the availability of portraits.

Chapter 2: Original Names

Original names are arranged alphabetically by surname, with each entry containing the following elements: original name, dates, occupation, and alphabetic listing of assumed names/sobriquets, with each entry containing up to eight source codes.

Complete bibliographic citations for print sources are listed after four character codes for sources containing only one or two assumed names or sobriquets. Titles of works are included after copyright sources when the only means of access is by title.

Citations for Internet sources in which only one or two assumed names or sobriquets were identified include the Web address, followed by the date the site was last accessed.

"Note(s)" following an original name entry provides explanatory information and/or codes identifying sources with portraits of lesser known persons. "Note(s)" following assumed name entries provide information regarding joint pseudonyms, needed to access information in specific sources, or references to other individuals who used the same name or to chapter 4 for further explanation.

Variations in the spelling of names are incorporated in the original name entry when possible, with common derivatives and variant spellings given in brackets and unused forenames names or parts of names and/or initials given in parentheses, for example, Bates, (Otha) Ellas (or Elias); Barnes, H(oward) E(llington). In cases of variant birth/death dates, the earliest date was used, followed by a later date listed in parentheses. When possible publication dates are included as part of the entry when birth/death dates were not identified.

Types of Names

Nicknames that clearly replace forenames are entered under the surname, for example, Baker, Two Ton Dick. Those without a surname are entered in direct order, for example, Baby Duke, Cowboy Jack, Detroit Red. When it is not clear if a surname is used, entries are made under surname and also in direct order (without the surname).

Initials are entered in direct order, for exampkle, F. J. C. (i.e., Fanny J. Crosby); A. B. C. (i.e., Louis Moreau Gottschalk). Forenames followed by one or more initials are listed in direct order, for example, Roy C.

Terms of address indicating relationship or a title of position or office used with only forenames are entered in direct order, for example, Cousin Joe, Daddy Dewdrop; Dr. Zxy.

Alphabetization

Entries are alphabetized word-by-word. All letters and words are considered except those in brackets and parentheses. Surnames beginning with particles (De, La, Von, and so forth) followed by a space are alphabetized as if no space existed, for example:

De Sylva, George Gard
deThier, Henri [or Henry]
De Totis, Guiseppe
Detroit, Marcella.

Compound and hyphenated surnames are listed after the name(s) or words(s) with the same spelling of the first element. Names in which the first element is a symbol or numeral(s) are listed first; however, symbols or numerals in other positions are alphabetized as if spelled out: 1,000 (i.e., one thousand).

Other Editorial Practices

- Initial articles are inverted to last place and are ignored in alphabetization.
- Words/names containing an apostrophe are alphabetized as if the apostrophe did not exist.
- Diacritical markings are ignored for the purpose of alphabetization.
- The prefixes "Mac" and "Mc" are listed as given; with general references to the variant forms.
- "Doctor" and "Dr." are interfiled under "Doctor," and "Mister" and "Mr." are interfiled under "Mister."

Chapter 3: Assumed Names

Assumed names and sobriquets are arranged alphabetically, word-by-word, ignoring punctuation, with see references to original names listed in chapter 2. Initials are listed at the beginning of each alphabetic section. When needed, dates are included after original names to distinguish between identical or similar names.

Chapter 4: Notes

Original and assumed names are interfiled alphabetically in this section. Entries under original names include explanatory information too detailed to include in chapter 1. Entries under assumed names provide information and titles issued under a publisher's "house name."

CODA

I often wondered why someone had not compiled a dictionary or index to pseudonyms for the field of music. While working as a music librarian, I created a file of composers for whom I could not locate biographical information. Later, as I was compiling *Index to Opera, Operetta, and Musical Comedy Synopses in Collections and Periodicals* (Scarecrow Press, 1978) and *Music Theater Synopses; An Index* (Scarecrow Press, 1998), I created a second file of identified pseudonyms. The file of suspected pseudonyms continued to grow when I worked on a "name authority" contract project for OCLC. With approximately 100 identified and 150 suspected pseudonyms, I started work on *Musical AKAs*. Fortunately, ignorance is bliss—had I realized how complicated the process would be, I would have never started. This volume of *Musical AKAs* is the beginning of a project with no end. After printing the manuscript for this volume, I still have a sixteen-drawer card catalog and numerous plastic shoeboxes of index cards with thousands of assumed names identified in copyright sources.

Unfortunately there are errors in *Musical AKAs*—some are the result of mistakes in the sources indexed, and I hope only a few are the result of misinterpretation or inaccurate transcribing and keyboarding. Users are encouraged to report errors and inconsistencies and to submit additional assumed names and sobriquets (with bibliographic verification).

Jeanette M. Drone
30 August 2005

Chapter 1

Sources

SOURCES

AEIO — *aeiou encyclopedia*. Österreich Lexikon. Culture Information Center of BM:BWK. (Austrian Ministry of Education, Science and Culture. http://www.aeiou.at/aeiou.encyclop (23 Jan. 2005)

ALMC — Alm, Irene. *Catalog of Venetian Librettos at the University of California, Los Angeles*. Berkeley: University of California Press, 1993.

ALND — *Aliases, Nicknames, Legalized Names*. http://www.trussel.com/books/pseudo.htm (1 Feb. 2005)

ALMN — *Almanac of Famous People*. 6th ed. 2 vols. Detroit, Mich.: Gale, 1998.

AMEN — Amende, Coral. *Legends in Their Own Time*. New York: Prentice Hall General Reference, 1994.

AMIR — *amiright*. http://www.amiright.com/names/pseudo.shtml (1 Feb. 2005)

AMSL — American Musicological Society. *E-mail Discussion List*.

AMME — Ammer, Christine. *Unsung; A History of Women in American Music*. Westport, Conn.: Greenwood Press, 1980.

AMRG — *American Record Guide*. v. 59- , 1996- .

AMUS — *All Music Guide*. http://www.allmusic.com (30 Mar. 2005)

APPL — Appel, Bernhard. "Schumanns Davidsbund." *Archiv fur Musik-Wissenshaft* 38:1 (1981): 5+.

APSA — *A. P. Schmidt Archives*. Washington, D.C.: Library of Congress, Performing Arts Division.
Note: The "Finding Aid" for the A. P. Schmidt Archives is available at http://www.loc.gov/rr/perform/special/gd-index.html#s (June 6, 2006).

ASCA — *ASCAP Biographical Dictionary of Composers, Authors and Publishers*. New York: Thomas Y. Crowell, 1948.

ASCB — *ASCAP Biographical Dictionary of Composers, Authors and Publishers*. 2nd ed. New York: American Society of Composers, Authors and Publishers, 1952.

ASCC — *ASCAP Biograhical Dictionary of Composers, Authors and Publishers*. 1966 ed. New York: ASCAP, 1966.

ASCP — *ASCAP Biographical Dictionary*. 4th ed. New York: Bowker, 1980.

BAKE — *Baker's Biographical Dictionary of Musicians*. 7th ed. Oxford: Oxford University Press, 1984.

BAKO — *Baker's Dictionary of Opera*. Edited by Laura Kuhn. New York: Schirmer Books, 2000.

BAKR — *Baker's Biographical Dictionary of Musicians*. 8th ed. New York: Schirmer Books, 1992.

BAKT — *Baker's Biographical Dictionary of Twentieth-Century Classical Musicians*. New York: Schirmer Books, 1997.

BALT — Baltzell, W. J. *Baltzell's Dictionary of Musicians*. Boston: O. Ditson, 1911.

BAUE — Bauer, Andrew. *The Hawthorn Dictionary of Pseudonyms*. New York: Hawthorn Books, 1971.

BBDP — *Big Band Database Plus*. http://nfo.net (3 Feb. 2005)

BEAT — *Beatles Reference Library*. www.beatlesagain.com/breflib/pseudonyms.html (26 Apr. 2005)

BLIC — British Library. Integrated Catalog. http://catalogue.bl.uk (3 May 2005)

BLUE — *The Blue Pages; The Encyclopedic Guide to 78 R. P. M. Party Records*. Compiled by David Diehl. http://www.hensteeth.com (3 Feb. 2005)

Note(s): Select: "Artist Index"

BOST Bostic, Nan. Letter to Jeanette Drone. "Charles N(eil) Daniels." July 31, 1996.

BRAZ "Brazilian Music Guide." http://www.slipcue.com/music/brazil/brazilmisc.htm (Aug. 15 2005)

BROW Brown, James D. and Stephen S. Stratton. *British Musical Biography*. Birmingham: S. Stratton, 1897. (Reprint: Da Capo, 1971.)

BUL# Bull, Storm. *Index to Biographies of Contemporary Composers*. 3 vols. New York and Metuchen, N. J.: Scarecrow Press, 1964-87.

CA## *Contemporary Authors*. v. 1- . Gale Library Databases.

CANE *The Canadian Encyclopedia Encyclopedia.* http://www.canadianencyclopedia.com (31 Jan. 2005)

CART Carty, Terence John. *A Dictionary of Literary Pseudonyms in the English Language*. 2nd ed. London: Mansell, 2000.

CASS *Cassell Companion to 20th-Century Music.* Edited by David Pickering. London: Cassell, 1997. (Paperback ed., 1998.)

CCE## *Catalog of Copyright Entries*. U.S. Copyright Office. New Ser., Musical Compositions. 41 vols. Washington, D.C.: Government Printing Office, 1906-46.

Catalog of Copyright Entries. 3d Ser.: Music. 31 vols. Washington, D.C.: Government Printing Office, 1947-77.

Note(s): 20th-century dates are listed with the last 2 digits, followed by a copyright number, e.g., 1927 is CCE27 E680737. Complete 19th-century dates are listed, e.g., CCE1898.

CCME *The Comprehensive Country Music Encyclopedia*. New York: Time Books, 1994.

CCMU *Composers-Classical Music.* http://composers-classical-music.com (2 Feb. 2005)

CLAB Claghorn, Charles Eugene. *Biographical Dictionary of American Music*. West Nyack, N.Y.: Parker Publications, 1973.

CLAC Claghorn, Charles Eugene. *Women Composers and Hymnist*. Metuchen, N.J.: Scarecrow, 1984.

CLAG Claghorn, Charles Eugene. *Women Composers and Songwriters*. Lanham, MD.: Scarecrow, 1996.

CLAS ClassicThemes.com. *Arrangers/Stylists Who Made Contributions.* http://www.classicthemes.com/arrangerStylists.html (1 Feb. 2005)

CLEV Cleaver, Emrys. *Musicians of Wales*. Ruthin (Denbigh): John Jones, 1968.

CLMC ClassicThemes.com. *Mood Music Composers/Arrangers/Publishers.* http://www.classicthemes.com/moodComposers.html (1 Feb. 2005)

CLMJ ClassicThemes.com. *Composers/Arrangers Who Made Major Contributions.* http://www.classicthemes.com/majorComposers.html (28 Feb. 2005)

CLOJ ClassicThemes.com. *Those Old Commercial Jingles.* http://www.classicthemes.com/50sTVThemes/thoseOldJingles.html (28 Feb. 2005)

CLMM *Those Golden Movie Musicals*. http://www.classicmoviemusicals.com (1 Feb. 2005)

CLRA ClassicThemes.com. *Old-Time Radio: Music Theme List.* http://www.classicthemes.com/oldTimeRadioThemes/radioThemeList.html (14 May 2005)

CLTP ClassicThemes.com. *1950s TV Themes.* http://www.classictheses.com/50sTVThemes/themePages (9 Feb. 2005)

Note(s): Name of TV show after code, e.g. CLTP (Burns and Allen)

CLTV ClassicThemes.com. *1950s TV Themes—Composer List.* http://www.classicthemes.com/50sTVThemes/TVComposers.html (1 Feb. 2005)

CM## *Contemporary Musicians*. v.1-38. 1989-2002.

Note(s): CM is followed by a volume number, e.g., CM01. Entries for sobriquets listed in a table of contents include a page number, e.g., CM07 p. iii. Most entries include a portrait.

COHN Cohen, Aaron I. *International Encyclopedia of Women Composers*. 2d rev. ed. 2 vols. New York: Books & Music, 1987.

Note(s): Portraits in v. 2.

COMP *Composers.* http://www.oit.umass.edu/~shea/composers.cgi

COPL Copley, I. A.. *Music of Peter Warlock.* London: D. Dobson, 1979.

CPMS *Catalog of Printed Music Published between 1487 and 1800 now in the British Museum.* Edited by W. Barclay Squire. London: The Museum, 1912.

CPOL Library of Congress. *Copyright Monographs Database, 1978-* . http://www.copyright.gov/records/cohm.html (30 Mar. 2005).

Note(s): CPOL is followed by a registration or renewal number, e.g., CPOL PA-1-002-321, CPOL PAu-327-819, CPOL RE-240-211.

CPMU *The Catalogue of Printed Music in the British Library to 1980*. 62 vols. London: K. G. Saur, 1987.

CROA Crosby, Fanny J. *An Autobiography*. Grand Rapids, Mich.: Baker Book House, 1986.
Note(s): Reprint of: *Memories of Eighty Years*. James H. Earle, 1906. Also published as *Fanny J. Crosby, An Autobiography*. Eugene, OR: Wipf and Stock, 1999.

CSUF California State University, Fresno. *Traditional Ballad Index*. http://www.csufresno.edu/folklore/BalladIndex.html (19 Apr. 2005)

CYBH *The Cyber Hymnal*. http://www.cyberhymnal.org/bio/ (1 Feb. 2005)

DAIL *Daily Variety*. v. 1- . Hollywood, 1933- .

DANN Danner, John Howard. *The Hymns of Fanny Crosby and the Search for Assurance; Theology in a Different Key*. Ph.D. dissertation. Boston: Boston University, 1989.

DAPE *Dictionary of Anonymous and Pseudonymous English Literature*. New & engl. ed. London: Oliver and Boyd, 1926.

DAUM *A Dictionary of Australian Music*. Edited by Warren Bebbington. Melbourne: Oxford University Press, 1998.

DAVE Daverio, John. *Robert Schumann*. New York: Oxford University Press, 1997.

DAWS Dawson, Lawrence. *Nicknames and Pseudonyms*. London: George Routledge, 1908. (Reprint: Gale Research, 1974.)

DBMU *Detroit Blues Musicians*. http://www.flash.net/~dbsblues/DBS_history.htm (2 Feb. 2005)

DEAM Dearling, Robert & Cecilia. *Guinness Book of Music*. 3rd ed. Enfield: Guinness Superlatives, 1986.

DEAN Deane, Fannie Parmelee. *Nicknames and Pseudonyms of Prominent People*. New Philadelphia, Ohio: O. R. Parmelee, 1897.

DEAR Dearling, Robert. *The Guinness Book of Music Facts and Feats*. Enfield: Guinness Superlatives, 1976.

DESO De Sola, Ralph. *Abbreviations Dictionary*. Boca Raton, Fla.: CRC Press.
Note(s): DESO-7: 7th ed. "American Eponyms, Nicknames . . . ," 1986, p. 1056+; DESO-9: 9th ed. "Musical Nicknames and Superlatives," 1995, p. 1247+.

DICH Dichter, Harry and Elliott Shapiro. *Early Americn Music: Its Lure and Its Lore, 1768-1889*. New York: R. R. Bowker, 1941.

DIEH Diehl, Katharine. *Hymns and Tunes: An Index*. New York: Scarecrow, 1966.

DIMA DiMartino, Dave. *Singer-Songwriters*. New York: Billboard Books, 1994.

DOLM Dolmetsch Online. *Composers Biography*. http://www.dolmetsch.com/composers.htm (24 Feb. 2005)

DRSC *Dead Rock Stars Club, The*. http://users.efortress.com/doc-rock/deadrock.html (2 Feb. 2005)

DWCO *The Norton/Grove Dictionary of Women Composers*. Edited by Julie Anne Sadie and Rhian Samuel. New York: W. W. Norton, 1995.

EBEL Ebel, Otto, comp. *Women Composers*. Brooklyn: F. H. Chandler, 1902.

EMER Emerson, Ken. *Doo-dah; Stephen Foster and the Rise of American Popular Culture*. New York: Simon & Schuster, 1997.

ENCM *Encyclopedia of Country Music*. New York: Oxford University Press, 1998.

EPMU *Encyclopedia of Popular Music*. 3rd. ed. Edited by Colin Larkin. 8 vols. New York: MUZE, 1998.

EPON *Eponyms Dictionaries Index*. Edited by James A. Ruffner. Detroit, Mich.: Gale Research, 1977.

EPST Epstein, Dena J. *Music Publishing in Chicago before 1870; The Firm of Root & Cady, 1858-1871*. Detroit, Mich.: Information Coordinators, 1969.

ETUD "The Plays the Thing." *Etude*. 55:2 (Feb. 1937): 75-6.

ETUP "The Etude Historical Musical Portraits Series." *Etude*. 50:1-58:5 (Feb. 1932-May 1940)
Note(s): Series includes more than 4,500 portraits.

EWCY Ewen, David. *Composers of Yesterday*. New York: H. W. Wilson, 1937.

EWEC Ewen, David. *Composers Since 1900*. New York: H. W. Wilson, 1969.

EWEN Ewen, David. *American Songwriters*. New York: H. W. Wilson, 1987.

EWPA Ewen, David. *Popular American Composers*. New York: H. W. Wilson, 1962.

EWPS Ewen, David. *Popular American Composers*. Supplement 1. New York: H. W. Wilson, 1972.

FACS *Famous American Composers; The Story of American Music from Folk to Jazz*. Milwaukee: Ideal Publishing, 1977.

FAFO *Andrew Heenan's Real Names of Famous Folk*. http://www.famousfolk.com (3 Feb. 2005)

FANF *Fanfare*. v. 20- , 1996- .

FCTW *Famous Composers and Their Works*. Boston: J. B. Millet, 1891.

FINS Finson, Jon W. *The Voices That Are Gone; Themes in Nineteenth-Century American Popular Song*. Oxford: Oxford University Press, 1994.

FLIN Flint, Country Joe. *The Insider's Country Music Handbook*. Salt Lake City: Gibbs-Smith, 1993.

FULD Fuld, James J. *The Book of World-Famous Music; Classical, Popular and Folk*. 4th ed. rev. and enl. New York: Dover Publications, 1995.
Note(s): The 5th edition (2000) is identified as a "rev. and enl. edition;" however, no changes were identified in the introduction, body of the text, including musical examples, or the index.

FZSL *FZ Songlist: Composers Index*. http://globalia.net/donlope/fz/songs/composers_index.html (3 Feb. 2005)

GACC Gac, Scott. "Comrades, the Bugles Are Sounding!" *Music Research Forum* 11:2 (1996): 20-43.

GALM *Golden Age of Light Music*. http://www.guildmusic.com/light/catalogue/5112.htm (2 May 2005)

GAMM Gammond, Peter. *The Oxford Companion to Popular Music*. New York: Oxford University Press, 1991.

GANA Ganzl, Kurt. *The British Musical Theatre*. vol. 1. New York: Oxford University Press, 1986.

GANB Ganzl, Kurt. *The British Musical Theatre*. vol. 2. New York: Oxford University Press, 1986.

GAN1 Ganzl, Kurt. *The Encyclopedia of the Musical Theatre*. 2 vols. New York: Schirmer Books, 1994.

GAN2 Ganzl, Kurt. *The Encyclopedia of the Musical Theatre*. 2d ed. 3 vols. Schirmer Books, 2001.

GARR Garrett, John M. *Sixty Years of British Music Hall*. London: Chappell, 1976.

GDRM *Guide de difficultés de rédaction en musique*. http://www.mus.ulaval.ca/roberge/gdrm/01-chang.htm (5 June 2006)

GILB Gilbert, Douglas. *Lost Chords; The Diverting Story of American Popular Songs*. New York: Cooper Square Publishers, 1970.

GOLD Goldberg, Isaac. *Tin Pan Alley*. New York: John Day, 1930.

GOTE Gooch, Bryan N. S. and David Thatcher. *Musical Settings of Early and Mid-Victorian Literature*. New York: Garland, 1979.

GOTH Gooch, Bryan N. S. and David Thatcher. *A Shakespeare Music Catalogue*. Oxford: Clarendon Press, 1991.

GOTL Gooch, Bryan N. S. and David Thatcher. *Musical Settings of Late Victorian and Modern British Literature*. New York: Garland, 1976.

GOTT Gooch, Bryan N. S. and David Thatcher. *Musical Settings of British Romantic Literature*. New York: Garland, 1982.

GRAC Gracyk, Tim. *Popular American Recording Pioneers*. New York: Haworth Press, 2000.

GRAK *Tim Gracyk's Home Page*. http://www.garlic.com/~tgracyk (3 Feb. 2005)

GRAN Grant, Mark N. *Maestros of the Pen; A History of Classical Music Criticism in America*. Boston: Northeastern University Press, 1998.

GRAT Grattan, Virginia L. *American Women Songwriters; A Biographical Dictionary*. Westport, Conn.: Greenwood, Press, 1993.

GREN Greene, Frank. *Composers on Record*. Metuchen, N.J.: Scarecrow Press, 1985.

GROL *Grove Music Online*. 2nd ed. Macmillan Online Publishing.
Note(s): See also NGDJ, NGDM & NGDO.

GRV2 *Grove's Dictionary of Music and Musicians*. [2nd ed.] 5 vols. Edited by J. Al Fuller Maitland. Philadelphia: Theodore Presser, 1927.

GRV3 *Grove's Dictionary of Music and Musicians*. 3rd. ed. 6 vols. New York: Macmillan, 1935.

GRV5 *Grove's Dictionary of Music and Musicians*. 5th ed. 10 vols. New York: Macmillan, 1954.

HALL Hall, J. H. *Biography of Gospel Song and Hymn Writers*. N.Y.: Fleming H. Revell, 1914. (Reprint: AMS Press, 1971.)

HAMA Monash Music Department. *Historical Anthology of Music by Australian Women*. http://nfram.anu.edu.au/index.shtml (30 Oct. 2002)
Note(s): Notice posted: Website no longer available. (3 Feb. 2005)

HAMM Hamm, Charles. *Yesterdays; Popular Song in America*. New York: W. W. Norton, 1979.

HAMT Hamst, Olphar. *Handbook of Fictitious Names*. London. 1868. (Reprints: Gale Research,1969; P. Minet, 1971.)

HARD Hardy, Phil and Dave Laing. *The Da Capo Companion to 20th-Century Popular Music*. New York: Da Capo Press, 1995.

HARR Harrison, Nigel. *Songwriters; A Biographical Dictionary with Discographies*. Jefferson, NC: McFarland, 1998.

HARS Harris, Sheldon. *Blues Who's Who*. New Rochele, New York: Arlington House, 1979. (Reprint: DaCapo 1981.)

Note(s): Indexed in PSND; however, since entries are identified only as singers, the source was reindexed to identify individuals who also wrote songs. Contains portraits.

HARV *The Harvard Biographical Dictionary of Music*. Edited by Don Michael Randel. Cambridge, Mass.: Belknap Press of Harvard University, 1996.

HARW Harwell, Richard B. *Confederate Music*. Chapel Hill: University of North Carolina Press, 1950.

HATF Hatfield, Edwin F. *The Poets of the Church*. New York: Anson D. F. Randolph, 1884. (Reprint: Gale Research, 1978.)

HEIN Heinrich, Adel. *Organ and Harpsichord Music by Women Composers: An Annotated Catalog*. New York: Greenwood Press, 1991.

HERZ Herzaft, Gerard. *Encyclopedia of the Blues*. 2d ed. Fayetteville: University of Arkansas Press, 1997.

HESK Heskes, Irene. *Yiddish American Popular Songs 1895-1950*. Washington, D.C.: Library of Congress, 1992.

HEYT Heyter, Rauland. "Neues zur 'Cacilia; Eine Zeitschrift fur di musikalischer Welt.'" *Fontes Artis Musicae* 41:4 (1994): 340-57.
Note(s): "Pseudonyme und Initialen," pp. 356-57.

HIXN Hixon, Don L. and Don A. Hennessee. *Women in Music*. Metuchen, N. J.: Scarecrow, 1993.

HOFE Ho, Allan and Dmitry Feofanov. *Biographical Dictionary of Russian/Soviet Composers*. New York: Greenwood Press, 1989.

HOGR Hoogerwerf, Frank W. *Confederate Sheet Music Imprints*. Brooklyn, N.Y.: Institute for Studies in American Music, 1984.

HORS Horstman, Dorothy. *Sing Your Heart Out, Country Boy*. 3rd ed. Nashville: Country Music Foundation Press, 1996.

HOVL Hovland, Michael. *Musical Settings of American Poetry*. New York: Greenwood Press, 1986.

HOWD Howard, John Tasker. *Our American Music; Three Hundred Years of It*. New York: Thomas Y. Crowell, 1931.

HWOM *Hispanic World of Musicians and Actors*, by James E. Ross. http://home.earthlink.net/~jaimeeduardo/muslat.htm.

HUEV Humphreys, Maggie and Robert Evans. *Dictionary of Composers for the Church in Great Britain and Ireland*. London: Mansell, 1997.

IBIM *Internationaler Biographischer Index der Music = World Biographical Index of Music*. 2 vols. Munich: K. G. Saur, 1995.
Note(s): Extracted from K. G. Saur's "Biographical Archives." For online version see WORB.

IDBC *International Dictionary of Black Composers*. 2 vols. Chicago: Fitzroy Dearborn, 1999.
Note(s): Most entries contain a portrait.

IGER Iger, Arthur L. *Music of the Golden Age, 1900-1950 and Beyond*. Westport, CT: Greenwood Press, 1998.

IMDB *IMDb (Internet Movie Database)*. http://www.imdb.com/name/ (20 Apr. 2005)

IWWM *International Who's Who in Music and Musical Gazetteer*. 1st ed. Edited by Cesare Saerchinger. New York: Current Literature Publishing Co., 1918.

JACK Jackson, Barbara Garvey. *"Say can you deny me;" A Guide to Surviving Music by Women from the 16th through the 18th Centuries*. Fayetteville: University of Arkansas Press, 1994.

JAMU Woker, Jack, comp. *Jazz Musician Pseudonyms*. http://www16.brinkster.com/fitzgera/pseudo.htm (25 May 2005)

JASA Jasen, David A. and Gene Jones. *That American Rag; The Story of Ragtime from Coast to Coast*. New York: Schirmer Books, 2000.

JASG Jasen, David A. *Recorded Ragtime 1897-1958*. Hamden, Conn.: Archon Books, 1973.

JASN Jasen, David A. and Trebor Jay Tichenor. *Rags and Ragtime, A Musical History*. New York: Dover Publications, 1978.

JASR Jasen, David A. *Recorded Ragtime*. Hamden, Conn.: Archon Books, 1973.
Note(s): See "Composers and Their Works," pp. 111-40.

JAST Jasen, David. *Tin Pan Alley; The Composers, the Songs; the Performers and Their Times*. New York: Donald I. Fine, 1988.

JASZ Jasen, David A. and Gene Jones. *Spreadin' Rhythm Around; Black Popular Songwriters 1880-1930*. New York: Schirmer Books, 1998.

JULN Julian, John, ed. *A Dictionary of Hymnology*. Rev. ed. with new suppl. London: John Murray, 1925.
Note(s): Inconsistent use of cross reference for pseudonyms.

KICK Kick, Brent E. *The Ultimate Musician's Reference Handbook*. Anaheim Hills, CA: Centerstream, 1996.

KILG Kilgarrif, Michael. *Sing Us One of the Old Songs; A Guide to Popular Song*. Oxford: Oxford University Press, 1998.
Note(s): For revisions and additions see: http://freespace.virgin.net/m.killy/sing.html (7 Mar. 2005)

KINK Kinkle, Roger D. *The Complete Encyclopedia of Popular Music and Jazz*. 4 vols. New Rochelle, N.Y.: Arlington House, 1974.
Note(s): Biographies in vols. 2-3.

KOBW Württembergische Landesbibliothek, Stuttgart. Online. *Komponisten aus Baden und Württemberg— ein bibliographischer Lexikon*. http://www.wlb-stuttgart.de/~www/referate/musik/bw-komp.htm (2 Feb. 2005)

KOMP *Komponisten der Gegenwart im Deutschen Komponisten-Verband*. Berlin: Der Verband, 1985.
Note(s): Most entries include a portrait.

KOMS *Komponisten der Gegenwart im Deutschen Komponisten-Interessenverband*. 4. Auflag. Berlin: Deutscher Komponisten Interessenverband, 1995

KOMU Österreichische Akademie der Wissenschaften. *Kommission für Musikforschung*. Österreichisch. http://www.oeaw.ac.at/mufo/lemmata (2 Feb. 2005)

KROH Krohn, Ernst C. *Missouri Music*. New York: Da Capo, 1971.
Note(s): Original title: *A Century of Missouri Music*, St. Louis, 1924.

LAST *Lied and Art Song Texts Page*. http://www.recmusic.org/lieder (20 Jan. 2005)

LCAR# Library of Congress. *Authorities*. http://authorities.loc.gov.
Note(s): Instructions for searching are available on the homepage.

LCCC# Library of Congress. U.S. Copyright Office. Card catalogs. Madison Bldg., LM-459.
Note(s): LCCC is followed by years of a specific section of the catalog.

LCPC# Library of Congress. U.S. Copyright Office. *Pre-1935 Pseudonyms*. Card catalog. Madison Bldg., LM-459.
Note(s): LCPC is followed by a copyright number or date of cited correspondence, e.g., LCPC Efor31728 or LCPC 23 Dec. 1930.

LCRC# Library of Congress. U.S. Copyright Office. *Pre-1938 Renewals*. Card catalog. Madison Bldg., LM-459.
Note(s): LCRC is followed by year of copyright and number, e.g., LCRC11 E269470.

LCTC# Library of Congress. U.S. Copyright Office. *Music Titles Pre-1935*. Card catalog. Madison Bldg., LM-459.
Note(s): LCTC is followed by year of copyright and number, e.g., LCTC30 E17911.

LOCH Lochner, Louis P. *Fritz Kreisler*. New York: Macmillan, 1950. (Reprints: Scholarly Press, 1977, and Paganiniana Publications, 1981.)

LOVE Loveland, John. *Blessed Assurance; The Life and Hymns of Fanny J. Crosby*. Nashville, Tenn., Broadman Press, 1978.

LYMN Lyman, Darryl. *Great Jews in Music*. New York: Jonathan David, 1986.

MACE Marco, Guy A. *Encyclopedia of Recorded Sound in the United States*. New York: Garland, 1993.
Note(s): Pseudonyms listed on pp. 550-56.

MACM *The Macmillan Encyclopedia of Music and Musicians*. Compiled by Albert E. Weir. New York: Macmillan, 1938.

MAPN Marble, Annie Russell. *Pen Names and Personalities*. New York: Appleton, 1930.

MARC Marcuse, Maxwell F. *Tin Pan Alley in Gaslight*. Watkins Glen, N.Y.: Century House, 1959.

MART Martin, Deac (i.e., C[laude] T[remble]). *Deac (C. T.) Martin's Book of Musical Americana*. Englewood Cliffs, N. J.: Prentice-Hall, 1970.

MCBD Marshall's Civic Band. "Concert Band Music. Composer Index." http://skyways.lib.ks.us/orgs/mcb/Indexes/CompCB_A.htm (15 Aug. 2005)

MCCA McCarty, Clifford. *Film Composers in America; A Filmography, 1911-1970*. 2nd ed. Oxford: Oxford University Press, 2000.

MCCL McCloud, Barry. *Definitive Country; The Ultimate Encyclopedia of Country Music and Its Performers*. New York: Berkley Pub. Group, 1995.

MELL *Mellen Opera Reference Index*. 21 vols. Lewiston, N.Y.: Edwin Mellen Press, 1986-
Note(s): Volumes indexed: 1-4: *Opera Composers and Their Works*, and 5-6: *Opera Librettists and Their Works*.

METC Metcalf, Frank J. *American Writers and Compilers of Sacred Music*. New York: Abingdon Press, 1925.

METR *The Metronome*. v. 1- , 1871- .

MILL Millard, Bob. *Country Music, 70 Years of Americas Favorite Music*. New York: Harper Perennial, 1993.

MONT Mont Alto Composer File. *J. S. Zamecnik.* http://www.mont-alto.com/photoplay music//zamecnik/zamecnik.html (28 Mar. 2005)

MORI Mori, Elisabetta. *Libretti di Melodrammi e Balli del Secolo XVIII.* Firenze: Leo S. Olschki, 1984.

MOUT *The MOUTHPIECE.COM.* http://www.themouthpiece.com/vb/archiveindex.php/t-6761.html (30 June 2005)

MRAR *Musical Record and Review.* Piano music ed. & Song ed. Boston: Oliver Ditson. 1901-1902.

MRSQ *Music Reference Service Quarterly.* v.1- , 1992- .

MUAL *Music and Letters.* v. 1- , 1920- .

MUBR Dockumentation of Musical Sources . . . First Series: Musical Letters. http://www.musikerbriefe.at/schrift.asp? (7Apr. 2005)

MUCO *Musical Courier.* New York: Howard Rockwood. v. 1-163, 1880-1961.

MUHF *MusicHound Folk; The Essential Album Guide.* Detroit, Mich.: Visible Ink Press, 1998.

MUOP *Musical Opinion.* v. 1- , 1877- .

MUSA *Musical America.* v. 1-84, 1898-1964.

MUSQ *Musical Quarterly.* v. 1- , 1915- .

MUSR Musiker, Reuben and Naomi Musiker. *Conductors and Composers of Popular Orchestral Music.* Westport, CT: 1998.

MUST *Musical Times.* v. 1- , 1844- .

MUWB *MUSICWEB-International.* http://www.musicweb-international.com/index2.htm. (14 May 2005)

MWP# *Musical Woman; An International Perspective.* Vol. 1-4. Westport, Conn.: Greenwood Press, 1984-1991.
Note(s): MWP1=(1983); MWP2=(1984-1985); MWP3=(1986-1990); MWP4=(1991)

NASF Nashville Songwriters Foundation. *Hall of Fame.* http://www.nashvillesongwriters foundation.com/fame (3 Feb. 2005)

NEDM Nederlands Muziek Institut. http://www.nederlandsmuziekinstituut.nl/collecties/ (1 Feb. 2005)

NEIL Neil, Bob Joe. *Philip P. Bliss (1838-1876); Gospel Hymn Composer and Compiler.* Ed.D. dissertation. New Orleans: New Orleans Theological Seminary, 1977.

NEWB *Newberry Library Catalog of Early American Printed Sheet Music.* Boston: G. K. Hall, 1983.

NGAM *New Grove Dictionary of American Music.* 4 vols. London: Macmillan, 1986.

NGDJ *New Grove Dictionary of Jazz.* New York: St. Martin's Press, 1994.
Not(s)e: See also GROL.

NGDM *New Grove Dictionary of Music and Musicians.* 20 vols. London: Macmillan, 1980.
Note(s): See also GROL.

NGDO *New Grove Dictionary of Opera.* 4 vols. London: Macmillan, 1997.
Note(s): See also GROL.

NIEC Niecks, Frederick. *Robert Schumann.* London: J. M. Dent, 1925.

NITE Nite, Norm. *Rock On.* v. 3. New York: Harper & Row, 1985.
Note(s): Vols. 1-2 indexed in: *Pseudonyms and Nicknames Dictionary* (PSND).

NOMG *Nom de Guerre.* http://go.to/realnames (5 Feb. 2005)

NOTE *Notes; Quarterly Journal of the Music Library Association.* v.52- , 1996- .

NULM Nulman, Macy. *Concise Encyclopedia of Jewish Music.* New York: McGraw-Hill, 1975.

OB## *Obituaries in the Performing Arts.* Jefferson, N.C.: McFarland, 1994-2002.
Note(s): Numerics for specific year, e.g., OB94 = 1994; OB00 = 2000; OB01 = 2001.

OCLC# OCLC (Online Computer Library Center). *WorldCat.*
Note(s): OCLC is followed by a record accession number, e.g., OCLC 19854881.

OMUO *Oesterreichisches Musiklexikon ONLINE.* http://www.musiklexikon.ac.at/ml?frames=yes (29 Mar. 2005)

OPER *Opera Quarterly.* v. 13-18, 1996-2001.

ORBI *Organ Biography.* http://www.organ-biography.info/ (3 Feb. 2005)

ORPH Orpheus Trust. *Musicians.* http://www.orpheustrust.at/musiker.php?l=e (16 May 2005)

OSBL *Osterreichisches Biographischles Lexikon; 1815-1950.* (Online Edition) http://hw.oeaw.ac.at/oebl?frames=yes (3 Feb. 2005)

OUSH *Outer Shell (Other Music News & Views).* http://members.aol.com/outershel/artists.html (4 Feb. 2005)

PARS *Parlor Songs; 1800s-1920.* http://www.parlorsongs.com (2 May 2005)

PDMU *Public Domain Music.* http://www.pdmusic.org/index.html (3 May 2005)

PEN1 *The Penguin Encyclopedia of Popular Music.* Edited by Donald Clarke. London: Viking, 1989.
Note(s): See also MUWB.

PEN2 *The Penguin Encyclopedia of Popular Music.* 2nd ed. Edited by Donald Clark. London: Viking, 1998.
Note(s): See also MUWB.

PERF *"Perfessor" Bill Edwards.* http://www.perfessorbill.com (4 Feb. 2005)

PFSA Pfaelzer Saenger *Online: Komposisten-Daten.* http://home.t-online.de/home/pfaelzer.saenger/07/komp.htm (4 Feb. 2005)

PIAN *Piano Roll Artists.* http://www.pianola.co.nz/artists/pseudonymns.html (31 May 2005)

PIPE *Pipers Enzykopaedie des Musiktheaters.* 7 vols. Munich: Piper, 1977.

PMUC *Popular Music, 1900-1919.* Edited by Barbara Cohen-Stratyner. Detroit, Mich.: Gale Research, 1988.

PMUS *Popular Music, 1920-1979.* Revised cumulation. 3 vols. Edited by Nat Shapiro and Bruce Pollock. Detroit, Mich.: Gale Research, 1985.

PMUS# *Popular Music, 1980- .* Annual volumes. Detroit, Mich.: Gale Research, 1981- .
Note(s): Annual issues are identified by the last two digits of the year, for example, 1990 is PMUS-90, and 2000 is PMUS-00. Also 1980-89: is available as *PopularMusic, 1980-1989.* Revised cumulation, edited by Bruce Pollock. Detroit, Mich.: Gale Research, 1995.

PRAT Pratt, Waldo Selden. *The New Encyclopedia of Music and Musicians.* New York: Macmillan, 1929.

PSND *Pseudonyms and Nicknames Dictionary.* Edited by Jennifer Mossman. 3rd ed. 2 vols. Detroit, Mich.: Gale, 1987.
Note(s): Indexes over 240 sources for assumed names, initialism, nicknames, noms de plum, pseudonyms, sobriquets, and stage names. Persons identified as "composer" or "arranger" are included in the present source. A list of music sources indexed in PSDN is given at the end of this bibliography.

PSNN *New Pseudonyms and Nicknames Dictionary.* Edited by Jennifer Mossman. Supplement to 3rd ed. Detroit, Mich.: Gale, 1988.

RAGM *Ragtime MIDI Composer Index.* http://www.geocities.com/pfw8015/indices/cdef.html (3 Feb. 2005)

RAGT *Ragtime; Its History, Composers and Music.* Edited by John Edward Hassee. New York: Schirmer Books, 1985.

RECR Rees, Dafydd, and Lude Crampton. *Encyclopedia of Rock Stars.* New York: DK Publishing, 1996.

REHG Rehrig, William H. *The Heritage Encyclopedia of Band Music.* 2 vols. Columbus, OH: Integrity Press, 1991.

REHH Rehrig, William H. *The Heritage Encyclopedia of Band Music.* Supplement. Columbus, OH: Integrity Press, 1997.

RFSO *Robert Farnon Society.* http://www.rfsoc.org.uk/ (2 Apr. 2005)

RIEM *Riemann Musik Lexikon. Personenteil.* 2 vols. Mainz: B. Schott's Sohne, 1959.

RIES *Riemann Musik Lexikon. Personenteil.* Supplement. 2vols. Mainz: B. Schott's Sohne, 1972.

RILM# *RILM Abstracts of Music Literature.* Online. 1969- .
Note(s): RILM is followed by a umeric/alphabetic identifier, e.g., RILM 96-03958-ae.

ROCK *BlackCat Rockabilly Hall of Fame.* http://www.rockabillyhall.com (2 Feb. 2005)

ROGA Rogal, Samuel J., comp. *Sing Glory and Hallelujah!* Westport, Conn.: Greenwood Press, 1996.

ROGG Rogal, Samuel J. *Guide to the Hymns and Tunes of American Methodism.* New York: Greenwood Press, 1986.

ROOM Room, Adrian. *Dictionary of Pseudonyms.* 3rd. ed. Jefferson, N. C.: McFarland, 1998.

RUFF Ruffin, Bernard. *Fanny Crosby; The Hymn Writer.* Uhrichsville, Ohio: Barbour, 1995.

RUFN Ruffin, Bernard. *Fanny Crosby.* Philadelphia: Pilgrim Press, 1976.

SADC Sadie, Julie Anne. *Companion to Baroque Music.* London: J. M. Dent, 1990. (Also: Schirmer Books, 1991.)

SAMP Sampson, Henry T. *Blacks in Blackface.* Metuchen, N.J.: Scarecrow, 1980.

SCHO Scholes, Percy A. *The Mirror of Music; 1844-1944.* 2 vols. London: Novello, 1947. (Reprint: Books for Libraries Press, 1970.)

SEND Sendrey, Alfred. *Bibliography of Jewish Music.* New York: Columbia University Press, 1951.

SGMA Southern Gospel Music Association. *Hall of Fame.* http://www.sgma.org/inductees_alphabetical.htm (15 Aug. 2005)

SHAB Shaw, Arnold. *Black Popular Music in America.* New York: Schirmer Books, 1986.

SHAD Shaw, Arnold. *Dictionary of American Pop/Rock.* New York: Schirmer Books, 1982.

SHAP *Hal Shaper Collection; A Personal Collection of Memorabilia of the Great Songwriters of the 20th Century.* http://www.themusikmakers.com/shaper/Introduction.htm (4 Oct. 2002)

SHMM *Sheet Music Magazine.* Standard Piano/Guitar Ed. Dec. 1986- .
Note(s): SHMM is followed by (month/year): page number.

SHMP *Sheet Music Plus.* http://www.sheetmusicplus.com (16 May 2005)

SIFA Sifakis, Carl. *The Dictionary of Historic Nicknames.* New York: Facts on File, 1984.

SISO *Singer/Songwriter Directory.* http://singer-songwriter.com/alpha/home.html (5 Feb. 2005)

SLON Slonimsky, Nicolas. *Lexicon of Musical Invective.* 2nd ed. New York: Coleman-Ross, 1965. (Reprint: Norton, 1965.)

SMIN Smith, Norman E. *March Music Notes.* Lake Charles, LA.: Program Notes Press, 1986.

SONG *Song Index.* http://www.chartwatch.co.uk/TopTen/songs/songndxA.htm (7 Feb. 2005)

SONN Sonneck, Oscar George Theodore. *Catalogue of Opera Librettos Printed before 1800.* 2 v. Washington: G. P. O., 1914. (Reprints: Burt Franklin, 1967; Johnson Reprint, 1968.)

SOTH Southern, Eileen. *Biographical Dictionary of Afro-American and Africian Musicians.* Westport, Conn.: Greenwood Press, 1982.

SPIE Spiegl, Fritz. *Music Through the Looking Glass.* London: Routhledge & Kegan Paul, 1984.

SPTH Spaeth, Sigmund. *A History of Popular Music in America.* New York: Random House, 1948. (Reprints: Phoenix House, 1960; Random House, 1967.)

SQWB Squire, William Barclay. *Catalogue of the King's Music Library. Part II: Miscellaneous Manuscripts.* London: British Museum, 1929.

STAC Stambler, Irwin and Grelun Landon. *Country Music; The Encyclopedia.* New York: St. Martin's Press, 1997. (Paperback ed., 2000)

STAD Wiener Stadt-und Landesbibliothek. http://www.stadtbibliothek.wien.at (3 Feb. 2005)
Note(s): Select "Sammlungen;" then "Musik;" then "Nachlässe."

STAM Stambler, Irwin. *Encyclopedia of Pop, Rock & Soul.* Rev. ed. New York: St. Martin's Press, 1989.

STAR Starr, S. Frederick. *Bamboula!; The Life and Times of Louis Moreau Gottschalk.* New York: Oxford University Press, 1995. (Also published as: *Louis Moreau Gottschalk.* Urbana: University of Illinois Press, 2000.)

STGR Stieger, Franz. *Opernlexikon; Opera Catalogue.* 4 vols. in 11. Tutzing: Hans Schneider, 1975.

STC1 Studwell, William E. and Bruce R. Schueneman. *College Fight Songs; An Annotated Anthology.* New York: Haworth Press, 1998.

STC2 Studwell, William E. and Bruce R. Schueneman. *College Fight Songs II; A Supplementary Anthology.* New York: Haworth Press, 2001.

STUW Studwell, William E. *They Also Wrote.* Lanham, MD: Scarecrow Press, 2000.

SUPN Suppan, Wolfgang. *Das neue Lexikon des Blasmusikwesens.* Freiburg-Tiengen: Blasmusikverlag Schulz, 1994.

SUTT Sutton, Allan. *A Guide to Pseudonyms on American Records, 1892-1942.* Westport, Conn.: Greenwood Press, 1993.
Note(s): For entries in *Musical AKAs* containing a "SUTT" code, users should also consult Sutton's 2nd revised and expanded edition (2005) for additional pseudonyms.

TCAN *Twentieth Century American Nicknames.* Edited by Laurence Urdang. New York: H. W. Wilson, 1979.

TIPT Tipton, Patricia Gray. *The Contributions of Charles Kunkel to Musical Life in St.Louis.* Ph.D. dissertation. St. Louis: Washington University, 1977.

TODO *TODO Tango.* http://www.todotango.com (3 Feb. 2005)
Note(s): Select "Artists."

TPRF Theodore Presser Pseudonym File. (Photocopy of card file purchased by the author from Theodore Presser, September 1994.)

VACH Vaché, Warren W., Sr. *The Unsung Songwriters; America's Masters of Melody.* Lanham, MD: Scarecrow, 2000.

VDPS *Vernon Dalhart's Pseudonyms.* Mainspring Press.http://www.mainspringpress.com/dalhart.html (3 Feb. 2005)

VGRC National Library of Canada. *The Virtual Gramophone; Canadian Historical Sound Recordings.* National Library of Canada. http://www.nlc-bnc.ca/gramophone/src/bio.htm (3 Feb. 2003)

WARN Warner, Simon. *Rockspeak! The Language of Rock and Pop*. London: Blanford, 1996.

WASH Washington University in Saint Louis. Gaylord Music Library. *Necrology*. http://library/wustl.edu/units/music/necro (5 Feb. 2005)

WCAB *White's Conspectus of American Biography*. 2nd ed. New York: James T. White, 1937.

WEOP *Welt der Oper, Die*. http://www.operone.de (3 Feb. 2005)
Note(s): Select "Komponisten."

WHIC Whitcomb, Ian. *After the Ball; Pop Music from Rag to Rock*. Baltimore, Penguin Books, 1972.

WHIT Whiting, Steven Moore. *Satie the Bohemian*. New York: Oxford University Press, 1999.

WIEC *The Wind Ensemble Catalog*. Compiled by John A. Gillespie, Marshall Stoneham and David Lindsey Clark. Westport, CT: Greenwood Press, 1998.

WILG Williams, Gareth. *Valleys of Song; Music and Society in Wales, 1840-1914*. Cardiff: University of Wales Press, 1998.

WOAM *Women in American Music*. Compiled by Adrienne Fried Block and Carol Neuls-Bates. Westport, Conn.: Greenwood Press, 1979.

WOLL Woll, Allen. *Black Musical Theater: From "Coon Town" to "Dreamgirls."* Baton Rouge: Louisiana State University, 1989.

WORB *World Biographical Index*. Online. Munich: K. G. Saur Verlag.
Note(s): Based on the 5th ed. of World Biographical Index. For print version of musicians, composers, etc., see IBIM.

WORL *World Musicians*. Edited by Clifford Thompson. New York: H. W. Wilson, 1999.

WORT Worth, Fred L. and Steve D. Tamerius. *Elvis; His Life from A to Z*. Chicago: Contemporary Books, 1988.

YORK York, Terry Wayne. *Charles Hutchinson Gabriel (1854-1932); Composer, Author, Editor*. DMA dissertation. New Orleans: New Orleans Baptist Theological Seminary, 1985.

YORM "Nom-de plumes in the Musical Profession." *The Yorkshire Musician*. vol. 3 (1 June 1889): 175-6.

YOUN Young, Carlton R. *Companion to the United Methodist Hymnal*. Nashville: Abingdon, 1993.

SOURCES INDEXED IN *PSEUDONYMS AND NICKNAMES DICTIONARY*

Baker's Biographical Dictionary. 5th ed. New York: G. Schirmer, 1971.

Bushby, Roy. *British Music Hall*. Salem, N.H.: Paul Elik, 1976.

Case, Brian. *The Illustrated Encyclopedia of Jazz*. New York: Harmony Books, 1978.

Chilton, John. *Who's Who of Jazz*. New York: Chilton Book, 1970.

Claghorn, Charles Eugene. *Biographical Dictionary of American Music*. West Nyack, N.Y.: Parker Publishing, 1973.

Country Music Who's Who. [n.p.] Record World Publications, 1972

Ewen, David. *Musicians Since 1900*. New York: H. W. Wilson, 1978.

Ewen, David. *Popular American Composers*. 1st suppl. New York: H. W. Wilson, 1972.

Feather, Leonard. *The Encyclopedia of Jazz*. Rev. ed. New York: Horizon Press, 1960.

Feather, Leonard. *The Encyclopedia of Jazz in the Seventies*. New York: Horizon Press, 1976.

Gentry, Linnell. *A History and Encyclopedia of Country, Western and Gospel Music*. 2nd ed. Nashville: Clairmont, 1969.

International Who's Who in Music and Musicians Directory. 8th ed. Cambridge, Eng.: Melrose Press, 1977.

Leadbitter, Mike. *Nothing but the Blues*. London: Hanover Books, 1971.

Lilian Roxon's Rock Encyclopedia. New York: Grosset & Dunlap, 1971.

Miller, Paul Eduard. *Miller's Yearbook of Popular Music*. Chicago: Pem Publications, 1943.

Nite, Norman N. *Rock On*. Vol. 1. New York: Thomas Y. Crowell, 1974.

Nite, Norman N. *Rock On*. Vol. 2. New York: Thomas Y. Crowell, 1978.

Rose, Al and Edmond Souchon. *New Orleans Jazz*. Baton Rouge: Louisiana State University Press, 1978.

Shestack, Melvin. *The Country Music Encyclopedia*. New York: Thomas Y. Crowell, 1974,

Stambler, Irwin. *Encyclopedia of Pop, Rock and Soul*. New York: St. Martin's Press, 1974.

Stambler, Irwin. *Encyclopedia of Popular Music*. New York: St. Martin's Press, 1965.

Stambler, Irwin and Grelun Landon. *Encyclopedia of Folk, Country and Western Music*. New York: St. Martin's Press, 1969.

Vallance, Tom. *The American Musical*. New York: Castle Books, 1970.

Who's Who in Opera. Edited by Marion Rich. New York: Arno Press, 1976.

York, William. *Who's Who in Rock Music*. [n.p.]: Atomic Press, 1978.

Zalkin, Ronald. *Contemporary Music Almanac 1980/81*. New York: Schirmer Books, 1908.

Chapter 2

Original Names (with Assumed Names and Sobriquets)

– A –

Aaberg, Philip 1949- [composer, pianist]
Yates, Eddy *Source(s):* ASCP
Aagesen, Truid fl. 1593-1615 [composer, organist]
Malmogiensis, Trudo Haggaei *Source(s):* GROL
Sistinus, Theodoricus *Source(s):* GROL; LCAR; NGDM
Abady, H(arold) Temple 1903-1970 [composer]
Abady, Tim *Source(s):* GOTH
Abatematteo, John (Anthony) 1938- [composer, producer, arranger]
Abbott, John (Anthony) *Source(s):* CCE57; CCE62; PSND
Abbott, Alain André Yves 1938- [composer]
MacNell, Allan *Source(s):* CCE73; GOTH
Abeille, Johann Christian Ludwig 1761-1838 [composer, pianist, organist]
Abeille, Louis [or Ludwig] *Source(s):* LCAR; WORB
Abelard, Peter 1097-1142 [hymnist]
First of the Modernists *Source(s):* YOUN
Aberbach, Jean (J.) ?-1992 [composer]
Roche, Jean de la *Source(s):* MCCA
Abondante, Giulio [or Julio] fl. 1546-87 [lutenist, composer]
Abundante, Giulio *Source(s):* LCAR
Dal Pestrino, Giulio *Source(s):* GROL; NGDM; WORB
Pestrin(o) *Source(s):* GROL
Pestro, Giulio dal *Source(s):* LCAR
Abos, Geronimo 1715-1760 [composer]
Abos, Girolamo *Source(s):* BAKO; PSND
Abraham, David 1838-1905 [composer, conductor]
Braham, David [or Dave] *Source(s):* GAMM; GAN2; LCAR; NGDM
Abraham, F. [composer]
Maharba, F. *Source(s):* CPMU (publication date 1878)
Abraham, Irvin 1909- [composer, lyricist, writer, singer, actor]
Graham, Irvin *Source(s):* CCE41 #8841 E90789; CPOL RE-86-177; GOTH; PSND
Abraham, John 1774-1856 [composer, singer]
Note(s): Portrait: HAMM
Braham, John *Source(s):* BAKO; GAMM; LCAR; MACM; SPTH p. 51
Abrahams, Beatrice [composer]
Aram, Beatrice *Source(s):* COMP
Abrahams, Doris Caroline 1901-1982 (or 83) [songwriter]
Brahms, Caryl *Source(s):* CCE49-50; LCAR; ROOM
Linden, Oliver Spondee *Source(s):* LCAR
Spondee *Source(s):* LCAR
Abrahams, Maurice [or Maurie] 1883-1931 [composer, author, publisher]
Abrams, Maurice *Source(s):* ASCP; BBDP; CLAB; VACH
Abramovic, August 1830-1873 [composer]
Adelburg, August *Source(s):* OMUS
Abramovich, Aleksandr 1914-1995 [composer]
Argov, Sasha *Source(s):* GROL
Abrass, Osias Joshua 1820-1884 [composer]
Pit(z)sche *Source(s):* LCAR; SEND
Abreu, Jose Gomes de 1880-1935 [composer]
Abreu, Zeqhinha de *Source(s):* GREN
Abshire, Nathan 1913-1981 [songwriter, accordionist]
Professor Longhair of Cajun Music *Source(s):* EPMU
Acciaiuoli, Filippo 1637-1700 [composer, librettist]
Orfeo *Source(s):* STGR
Ovidio *Source(s):* STGR
Pistocchini *Source(s):* PIPE; STGR
Achleitner, Hubert 1952- [composer]
Goisern, Hubert von *Source(s):* AEIO; OMUO; http://www.hubertvongoisem.com/bio.html (4 Oct. 2002)
Achron, Isidor 1892-1948 [composer, pianist]
Dorr, Julian *Source(s):* CCE64;

http://www.webtext.library.yale.edu/xml2htm/music/ach-col.htm. (5 Oct. 2003)

Ackermann, Alexander c.1446-c.1506 [composer]
Agricola, Alexander *Source(s):* NGDM; PSND

Ackermann, Stefan 1951- [composer, music producer]
ACAMA *Source(s):* OMUO

Ackley, A(lfred) H(enry) 1887-1960 [hymnist, evangelist]
A. H. A. *Source(s):* CCE52; DIEH

Ackley, B(entley) D(eForrest) 1872-1958 [composer, hymnist, evangelist]
Note(s): Portrait: CYBH
DeForrest, Marie *Source(s):* CCE14; CCE40 #15093, 96 R86352; CYBH
Eyck, Lloyd Ten *Source(s):* CCE39 #9188, 11 R74238
Freeman, C. A. *Source(s):* CCE17 E404106; CCE45 #8173, 139 R135420
Howe, Katherine *Source(s):* CCE18 E426661; CCE45 #8173, 157 R135433
Howe, R. Ward *Source(s):* CCE43 #26336 E14920; CCE58
Howe, Ward *Source(s):* CCE43 #26336 E14920; CCE58; CCE70 R489350
Lansing, G. G. *Source(s):* CCE18 E426650; CCE45 #8173, 290 R135425

Ackoff, Robert 1942-1983 [songwriter]
Gentry, Bo *Source(s):* CCE66; CPOL RE-770-464; PMUS

Acland, Arthur Henry Dyke 1811-1857 [musician, hymnist]
Troyte, Arthur Henry Dyke *Source(s):* BROW; WORB

Acosta, Pedro Blanco 1902-1972 [bandoneonist, leader, composer]
Blanco, Pedro *Source(s):* LCAR
Note(s): Also identified as original name.
Laurenz, Pedro *Source(s):* BBDP; TODO

Acres, Harry [songwriter]
Brody, Hal *Source(s):* CCE29 Efor4503
Note(s): Also used by H(erbert) B(arber) Hedley (i.e., Herbert Hedley Barber), Stanley Lupino (i.e., Hook), John (or Jack)(Francis) Strachey, (Herbert) Desmond Carter, Jack Clarke, possibly others.

Acuff, Roy (Claxton) 1903-1992 [performer, songwriter, bandleader]
Bang Boys *Source(s):* CSUF
Jenkins, Floyd *Source(s):* PSND
Note(s): Also used by Fred Rose.
King of Country Music, The *Source(s):* FLIN; PSND; STAC
Note(s): See also Willie (Hugh) Nelson, David Gordon Kirkpatrick & Hank [i.e., Hir(i)am (King)] Williams.
King of Mountain Music *Source(s):* SHAD
King of the Hillbillies, The *Source(s):* PSND
Smoky Mountain Boy, (The) *Source(s):* FLIN; STAC

Adam, de la Halle c.1245-c.1285 [poet, composer]
Note(s): See LCAR for additional variant forms of name.
Adam, le boss *Source(s):* LCAR
Adam the Hunchback from Arras *Source(s):* LCAR
Adan le Bossu *Source(s):* LCAR; NGDM
Bossu, d'Arra *Source(s):* LCAR
D'Arras, Adam *Source(s):* LCAR; NGDM

Adamberger, Valentin 1743-1803 [composer]
Adamberger, Josef *Source(s):* WORB
Adamonti *Source(s):* IBIM; WORB

Adami (da Bolsena), Andrea 1663-1742 [singer, writer on music, composer]
Bolsena, Il *Source(s):* LCAR; NGDM
Caricle Piseo *Source(s):* NGDM

Adami, Friedrich (Wilhelm) 1816-1893 [librettist]
Frohberg, Paul *Source(s):* STGR; WORB

Adamo, Milo Angelo 1931- [composer, author, singer]
Adano, Bobby *Source(s):* ASCP; DOLM

Adamo, Salvadore 1943- [guitarist, singer, songwriter]
Adamo *Source(s):* EPMU

Adamovic, Bela 1856-1934 [composer]
Cepinski *Source(s):* OMUO

Adams, Charles R(aymond) 1915- [songwriter]
Note(s): Do not confuse with Charles Adams, pseud. of Harry Sugarman.
Stone, Charlie *Source(s):* CCE53-56
Note(s): For a list of titles, see NOTES: Stone, Charlie. Do not confuse with Charles Stone, pseud. of Sten Carlberg.

Adams, Chris 1958- [composer, author, producer]
Note(s): Do not confuse with Chris Adams [i.e., Leslie Hathaway], dramatist.
Adams, Fingers *Source(s):* ASCP; http://www.fingersmusic.com/fabio.htm (4 Oct. 2002)

Adams, Cliff 1923-2001 [songwriter, singer]
Forrest, David *Source(s):* CCE55 Efor31818; CPOL RE-143-473
Note(s): Jt. pseud.: Jack Fishman (1918 (or 19)-), Bob Brown & Frank [i.e., Francis] (Charles) Chacksfield.
Johns, Michael *Source(s):* CCE55 Efor31818; CPOL RE-143-473
Note(s): Jt. pseud.: Jack Fishman (1918 (or 19)-), Bob Brown & Frank [i.e., Francis] (Charles) Chacksfield.
King of the Jingles, The *Source(s):* MUWB
Shauna, Verity *Source(s):* CCE54; CPOL RE-141-048
Tudor, Al *Source(s):* CCE56; CPOL RE-176-207

Adams, Ernest Harry 1886-1959 [composer]
Masters, Henry Read *Source(s):* CCE35 E48666; CCE61
Meyer, Ferdinand *Source(s):* CCE28 E695112

Note(s): A. P. Schmidt house name; see NOTES: Meyer, Ferdinand.

Adams, Leonard F. 1904- [composer, author]
Adams, Chick *Source(s):* ASCB

Adams, Nehemiah 1806-1878 [hymnist]
Mahmied, S. E. *Source(s):* JULN

Adams, Oliver Edward Fox [composer, songwriter]
O. E. A. *Source(s):* CPMU (publication dates 1903-04)

Adams, Park 1930-1986 [composer, saxophonist]
Adams, Pepper *Source(s):* ASCP; CASS; CCE62; LCAR; PEN2

Adams, Stanley (Ace) 1926- [music publisher, songwriter]
Adams, A(ce) *Source(s):* CCE60; PSND

Adamski, Leon Stephen 1939- [composer, conductor, teacher]
Adams, Lee *Source(s):* ASCP; DOLM; REHH

Adamus Dorensis fl. 13th cent. [abbot, writer on music]
Adam of Dore [or Door, or Dowr] *Source(s):* MACM; WORB

Aday, Marvin Lee 1948- [singer, songwriter]
Meatloaf [or Meat Loaf] *Source(s):* CPOL PA-322-894; EPMU; LCAR

Adderley, Julian Edwin 1928-1975 [jazz musician, composer]
Adderley, Cannonball *Source(s):* EPMU; GROL; LCAR; NGAM; NGDM; PEN2
Blockbuster *Source(s):* JAMU
Brotherly, Jud *Source(s):* JAMU
Buckshot la Funke *Source(s):* GROL (see under: Smith, (Edward) Louis)
Johnson, Spider *Source(s):* JAMU
LeFonque, Buckshot *Source(s):* GROL (see under: Bradford, Marsalis)
New Bird, The *Source(s):* GROL
Peters, Ronnie *Source(s):* JAMU

Adderley, Nat(haniel) 1931-2000 [cornetist, composer]
Brotherly, Pat *Source(s):* JAMU
Little Brother *Source(s):* JAMU
Note(s): Also used by Leonard (Geoffrey) Feather & Eurreal Wilford Montgomery.

Addison, John 1920-1998 [composer]
Composer for the Angry Young Men, The *Source(s):* MUST 140:1866 (1999): 8

Addison, John Cramer c.1766-1844 [composer]
Hastings, Charles *Source(s):* CPMU

Addison, L(aidlaw) F(letcher) 1878-1949 [bandmaster, composer]
Addison, Puff *Source(s):* *Encyclopedia of Music in Canada*. 2nd ed. Toronto: University of Toronto Press, 1992.

Adekale, Toyin 1963- [singer, songwriter]
Toyin *Source(s):* EPMU

Adelberg, Jeff [or Joel] 1939- [composer]
Barry, Jeff *Source(s):* CCE59-60; LYMN

Adelburg, August 1830-1873 [violinist, composer, writer on music]
Abramovic, August *Source(s):* KOMU

Adelstein, Milton 1925-1981 [composer, arranger, pianist]
Rogers, Milt *Source(s):* ASCP; CCE59-60; CPOL RE-27-416

Adenez (le Roy) fl. early 13th cent. [troubadour, songwriter]
Adam le Roy *Source(s):* MACM; WORB

Adeniyi, Sunday 1946- [singer, composer, guitarist]
Ade, King Sunny *Source(s):* CASS; CM18; EPMU; LCAR; PEN2
Adé, Sunny *Source(s):* LCAR
King of Julu Music *Source(s):* CM18
Minister of Enjoyment, The *Source(s):* CASS

Adkinson, Harvey E. 1934- [composer]
Adkinson, Gene *Source(s):* PSND

Adlam, Basil G(eorge) [composer, author, conductor]
Adlam, Buzz *Source(s):* ASCP; CCE60-61; CLRA; LCAR; PSND
Adlam, George B. *Source(s):* CCE60

Adler, Hans 1880-1957 [poet, librettist]
Bauer, Hertha *Source(s):* STAD
Delar, H. H. *Source(s):* STAD
Erna *Source(s):* STAD
Hangleitner, Anton *Source(s):* STAD
Hayndl, Adam *Source(s):* STAD
Honso *Source(s):* STAD
Maréchal, Aristide *Source(s):* STAD
Note(s): Jt. pseud.: Rudolf Lothar [i.e., Spitzer]
Samson *Source(s):* STAD
Vulpius, Paul *Source(s):* STAD

Adler, John (Richard) [songwriter]
Twink *Source(s):* AMUS; PMUS-98

Adler, Lou 1933 (or 35)- [songwriter, producer]
Campbell, Barbara *Source(s):* PEN2; WARN
Garbo *Source(s):* CCE67 ("I Want to be Alone")
Spunky *Source(s):* CCE63 E179858 ("Honolulu Lulu")

Adnopoz, Elliott Charles 1931- [singer, songwriter, guitarist]
Elliott, Buck *Source(s):* EPMU; MCCL; MUHF; PSND
Elliott, Jack *Source(s):* LCAR; MCCL; PSND
Note(s): Do not confuse with Jack Elliott [i.e., Irwin Elliott Zucker (1927-2001)]
Elliott, Ramblin'jack *Source(s):* AMUS; EPMU; HARS; LCAR; MCCL; PEN2; PSND
Ramblin' Jack *Source(s):* LCAR

Adorian, Andrew [composer]
Arvin, Andrew *Source(s):* CCE65; CPMU

Adorni, Achille 1857-1910 [composer]
Arnould *Source(s):* MELL; STGR

Adrien, Martin Joseph 1766 (or 67)-1822 [singer, composer]
Adrien l'Aîne *Source(s):* MACM; NGDM
Andrien, Martin Joseph *Source(s):* NGDM
La Neuville, Martin Joseph *Source(s):* WORB
Neuville, Martin Joseph la *Source(s):* NGDM; WORB
Agazzari, Agostino 1578-c.1640 [composer, theorist]
Armonico Intronato *Source(s):* NGDM; SADC
Intronato, Armonico *Source(s):* NGDM; SADC
Agee, Ray(mond Clinton) 1930- [singer, songwriter]
Agee, Roy *Source(s):* HARS; LCAR
Egge, Ray *Source(s):* HARS; LCAR
Little Ray *Source(s):* HARS; LCAR
Ray, Isom *Source(s):* HARS; LCAR
Agnesi-(Pinottini), Maria Teresa (d') 1720-1795 [composer, harpsichordist, librettist]
Mainini, Francesco *Source(s):* JACK; KOMU; MELL; STGR
Note(s): Do not confuse with Francesco Mainini [or Mainio, or Majnini], Italian costume designer.
Agniello, Michele Andrea 1808-1884 [conductor, composer]
Costa, Michael *Source(s):* NGDM; ROOM
Agress, Mitchell 1910-1969 [arranger, composer, bandleader]
Ayres, Mitchell *Source(s):* KINK; LCAR
Agricola, Johann Friedrich 1720-1774 [organist, composer]
Agricola, C. F. *Source(s):* IBIM; WORB
Agricola, Giovanni Federico *Source(s):* IBIM
Olibrio, Flavio Amicio *Source(s):* BAKO; GROL; IBIM; NGDM; WORB
Agricola, Johannes c.1560-70-after 1601 [composer]
Noricus, Johannes *Source(s):* NGDM
Aguiari [or Agujari], Lucrezia 1743-1783 [composer]
Bastardella, La *Source(s):* LCAR; NGDM; PRAT; WORB
Bastardina, La *Source(s):* LCAR; NGDM
Aguilar, Jose Maria 1891-1951 [guitarist, composer]
Aguilar, Indio *Source(s):* TODO
Indio *Source(s):* TODO
Aguilar Quintanilla, Fermin [singer, songwriter]
Aguilar, Ponny *Source(s):* HWOM
Aguilera (Valadez), Alberto 1950- [singer, songwriter]
Gabriel, Juan *Source(s):* CCE77; LCAR
Juan Gabriel *Source(s):* HWOM
Note(s): Most reference sources list him under "Juan Gabriel;" however, there is evidence he uses "Gabriel" as a true surname. (HWOM)
Juanga *Source(s):* HWOM
Aguirre, Juan Guillermo 1950- [composer, author, singer]
Aguirre, Santiago *Source(s):* ASCP
Ahbez, Eden 1908 (or 12)-1995 [author, composer]
Nature Boy (from Brooklyn) *Source(s):* CCE50; PSND
Ahl, Fred Arthur 1897 (or 98)-1964 [singer, pianist, composer, arranger, author]
Gunboat Billy [or Willy] *Source(s):* GRAK; http://www.mainspringpress.com/lom0200.htm (13 June 2005)
Hall, Fred *Source(s):* ASCP; CCE23 E575821
Hall, Sugar *Source(s):* ASCP; KINK
Note(s): Also nickname of Gertrude Hall? or a jt. pseud.?
Home Towners, The *Source(s):* http://www.dismuke.org/how/prev11-02.htm (21 Mar. 2005)
Ahlberg, Gunnar 1886-1943 [composer]
Ammandt, Guy *Source(s):* GREN
Ahmonuel, Zyal 1950- [songwriter]
Anthony, Malcolm *Source(s):* ASCP
Ahnfelt, Oskar [or Oscar] 1813-1882 [hymnist]
Sweden's "Spiritual Troubadour" *Source(s):* CYBH
Aieta, Anselmo Alfredo 1896-1964 [bandoneonist, composer]
Aieta, Ricardo *Source(s):* TODO
Soles, Pepe *Source(s):* TODO
Aiken, Edmund Carl [singer, songwriter]
Shinehead *Source(s):* EPMU; LCAR
Ailbout, Hans 1879-1957 [composer, conductor, teacher]
Becker, E. *Source(s):* SUPN
Bell, (E.) *Source(s):* SUPN
Born, (E.) *Source(s):* SUPN
Boutail, Jean *Source(s):* SUPN
Brandt, E. *Source(s):* SUPN
Eilenberg, F. *Source(s):* SUPN
Ernesti, Hans *Source(s):* SUPN
Faneau, H. *Source(s):* SUPN
Ferrin, José *Source(s):* SUPN
Huber, F. K. *Source(s):* SUPN
Kösen, Konrad *Source(s):* SUPN
Lange, H. *Source(s):* SUPN
Torelli *Source(s):* SUPN
Ain, Susan 1941- [composer]
Ain, Noa *Source(s):* COHN; HIXN
Aitchison, Ivy (Janet) 1887-1971 [composer, singer, actress]
Saint Helier, Ivy *Source(s):* GAMM; GAN1; GAN2
Aitken, Florence H. [songwriter]
Note(s): Aitken for lyrics; MacRea for music
MacRea [or McRae], Gertrude *Source(s):* TPRF
Aiverum, Timothy Louis 1915 (or 16)- [jazz musician, songwriter]

Rogers, Oh Yeah *Source(s):* PSND
Rogers, Timmie *Source(s):* PSND
Akanite, Oliver Sunday 1947- [singer, composer]
De Coque, Oliver *Source(s):* PEN1
Akers, Howard E(stabrook) 1913-1984 [composer, conductor, author, educator]
Masters, Archie *Source(s):* ASCP; REHG; SUPN
Note(s): Also used by Stanley Smith-Masters.
Akpabot, Samuel Ekpe 1931- [musicologist, composer]
Ekpe, Samuel *Source(s):* WORB
Akst, Ruth Freed 1905-1989 [composer, author]
Fisher, Patty *Source(s):* ASCP
Al Farabi, Abu Nasr ?-940 [philosopher, writer on music]
Orpheus of Arabia, The *Source(s):* SIFA
Albam, Emmanuel 1922-2001 [composer, arranger]
Albam, Manny *Source(s):* PEN2; PSND
Albani, Joseph 1924-1988 [pianist, songwriter]
Albany, Joe *Source(s):* AMUS; GAMM; PEN2
Alberstein, Chava [singer, songwriter, actress]
Israels "First Lady of Folk *Source(s):* CM37 p. v
Albert, Heinrich 1604-1651 [musician, poet]
Father of German Songs *Source(s):* PSND
Vater der Deutschen Lied, Der *Source(s):* PSND
Albert, Karel 1901-1987 [composer]
Victors, Karel *Source(s):* DOLM
Alberti, Gasparo c.1480-c.1560 [composer]
Gaspar de Padua *Source(s):* NGDM
Gaspare bergomensis *Source(s):* NGDM
Albertini, Albert N(icholas) 1922- [composer, author, singer]
Alberts, Al *Source(s):* ASCP; CCE51; CCE61-62; LCAR
Albertoni, Azzo 1862- [composer, librettist]
Edelmann, Alberto [or Adolfo] *Source(s):* DOLM; IBIM; MELL; STGR; WORB
Albini, Srečko 1869-1933 [composer]
Albini, Felix *Source(s):* GAN1; GAN2; WORB
Albinoni, Tomaso Giovanni 1671-1750 (or 51) [composer]
Zuane *Source(s):* NGDM; SADC
Albuzio, Giovanni Giacopo 1536- [lutenist, viol player, composer]
Hans Jacob von Mailandt *Source(s):* NGDM
Alcock, John 1715-1806 [organist, novelist, composer]
J. A. *Source(s):* CPMS ("The Lover's Resolution")
Piper, John *Source(s):* GROL; NGDM
Alcuinus, Flaccus 753-804 [musical theorist, writer on music]
Albinus, Flaccus *Source(s):* MACM; WORB
Alden, Blanch Ray ?-1934 [pianist, composer]
Note(s): Portrait: ETUP 51:1 (Jan. 1933): 4 (see under: Dutton)
Dutton, Theodora *Source(s):* BUL3; COHN; HIXN
Alderfer, Zora Margolis 1948- [writer]
Alder, Annie *Source(s):* GOTH
Aldous, Donald William 1914- [writer on music]
Discobolus *Source(s):* ROOM
Aldrich, Richard 1863-1937 [music critic]
Sylvanus Urbanus *Source(s):* GRAN
Urbanus, Sylvanus *Source(s):* GRAN
Aldridge, Amanda (Christina Elizabeth) Ira 1866-1956 [composer, pianist]
Ring, Montague *Source(s):* BUL3; COHN; HIXN; IDBC; LCAR; SOTH
Aleotti, Raffaela-Argenta c.1570-after 1646 [organist, prioress, composer]
Note(s): May be same as Vittoria Aleotta; see LCAR
Raffaela *Source(s):* COHN; HIXN
Aletter, Wilhelm 1867-1934 [composer, teacher]
Note(s): Portrait: ETUP 50:2 (Feb. 1932): 84
Norden, Leo *Source(s):* CCE31 R14243; CCE42 #5201, 223 R104555; WORB
Tellier, A(lphonse) *Source(s):* CCE41 #30320, 47 R97882; DOLM; WORB
Thayer, Herbert Wells *Source(s):* CCE52 R93263 ("Ballade Suedoise")
Alexander, Alger(non) 1900-1954 [songwriter, singer]
Alexander, Texas *Source(s):* AMUS; CCE28 E681188; HARS; LCAR
Oliver, Kine *Source(s):* HARS
Alexander, Axel 1926- [composer]
Gawitzla, Alexander *Source(s):* PFSA
Alexander, (Mrs.) Cecil F(rances) (née Humphreys) 1818-1895 (or 96) [poet, hymnist]
Note(s): Portrait: CYBH
C. F. A. *Source(s):* PSND; LCAR
C. F. H. *Source(s):* JULN (Suppl.); LCAR
Humphreys, Fanny *Source(s):* LCAR
Alexander, David [or Dave] 1937- [singer, pianist, songwriter]
Black Ivory King *Source(s):* EPMU; LCAR
King, Black Ivory *Source(s):* LCAR
Alexander, Edna Belle [songwriter]
Belledna, Alex *Source(s):* CCE47 R17748 ("Granny"); JASZ
Note(s): Originally thought to be pseud. of her husband, Maceo Pinkard.
Alexander, Fitzroy 1926-1988 [calypso/soca artist, songwriter]
Lord Melody *Source(s):* LCAR
Note(s): Also used by John Frederick.
Melo *Source(s):* PEN2; LCAR
Melody, Lord *Source(s):* CCE60-61; CPOL RE-237-930; LCAR; PEN2; PMUS
Note(s): Also used by John Frederick.

Alexander, Fred 1910- [violinist, producer, composer]
Alessandro *Source(s):* MUWB
Alexander, John (Marshall), Jr. 1929-1954 [pianist, singer, composer]
Ace, Johnny *Source(s):* EPMU; HARR; KICK; LCAR; NGAM; PEN2; WORT
Alexander, John David 1954- [singer, songwriter, guitarist]
Anderson, John *Source(s):* LCAR; MCCL
Alexander, Meyer [composer]
Alexander, Jeff *Source(s):* CLTP ("The Millionaire")
Alexander, William Lindsay 1808-1884 [minister, poet]
W. L. A. *Source(s):* JULN
Alexeiev, Konstantin (Sergeievich) 1863-1938 [actor, opera director, writer on theater]
Stanislavsky, Konstantin (Sergeievich) *Source(s):* BAKO; BAKR; LCAR
Alexiou, Haris [or Charis] [singer, songwriter]
Haroula *Source(s):* http://shopping.yahoo.com/shop?d=product&id=1927120090 (4 Oct. 2002)
Alfidi, Giuseppe Arturo 1949- [composer, conductor, pianist]
Alfidi, Joseph [or Joey] *Source(s):* ASCC
Alfieri, Pietro 1801-1863 [musicologist, composer]
Geminiani, Alessandro *Source(s):* PRAT; WORB
Alfieri-Adler, Moritz [music critic, musician]
Alfieri, Max *Source(s):* WORB
Alford, Harry L(aForrest) 1883-1939 [composer]
Ford, Al J. *Source(s):* CCE17 E406152 ("Battle Hymn: Unto Death")
LaForrest, Harry *Source(s):* BAKR; REHH
Alford, John 1939- [singer, songwriter]
Allison, John *Source(s):* EPMU (see under: Allisons)
Ali, Hasaan ibn 1931- [pianist, composer]
Hassan *Source(s):* PSND
Alin, Morris 1905-1985 [author, lyricist, publicist]
Allen, Morrie [or Morris] *Source(s):* ASCP; CCE60; PSND
Alison, Richard fl. 1592-1609 [composer]
Gent. Practitioner in the Art of Musicke *Source(s):* NGDM
Alkalaj, Lucia 1928- [composer, pianist]
Alcalay, Luna *Source(s):* OMUO
Allacci, Leone 1586-1669 [musicologist]
Allatius, Leo *Source(s):* LCAR; MACM
Allazzi, Leone *Source(s):* LCAR; WORB
Allais, Alphonse 1854-1905 [musician, critic]
Sarcey *Source(s):* WHIT p. 82+
Note(s): Allais' nickname after he mocked Francisque Sarcey.
Allamby, Darrell [songwriter]
Allamby, Delite *Source(s):* SONG; http://www.radio101.it/soul/nartists/1000/a82.htm (23 Oct. 2002)
Allard, Joseph 1873-1947 [fiddler, composer]
Prince of the Violoneaux, The *Source(s):* VGRC
Allard, Louis Alexandre Didier 1821-1893 [producer]
Cantin, Louis *Source(s):* GAN2
Allegri, Lorenzo c.1573-1648 [composer, lutenist]
Lorenzino, todesco del liuto *Source(s):* NGDM
Tedeschino *Source(s):* LCAR
Note(s): See also Giovanni Battista Gigli.
Tedesco, Il *Source(s):* NGDM
Note(s): See also Johann Paul Agidius Schwartzendorf.
Allen, Elizabeth Ann (Chase) (née Akers) 1832-1911 [poet, newspaper woman]
Author of Rock Me to Sleep *Source(s):* LCAR
Percy, Florence *Source(s):* HOGR; PSND; WORB
Allen, Euphemia (Amelia) 1861-1949 [composer]
DeLulli, Arthur *Source(s):* FULD p. 70; HIXN; PERF
de Zulli, Arthur *Source(s):* PERF
Lulli, Arthur de *Source(s):* CLRA; PERF
Zulli, Arthur de *Source(s):* PERF
Allen, Fulton 1907 (or 08)-1941 [singer, guitarist, songwriter]
Brother George *Source(s):* HARS; LCAR
Note(s): See also Walter Brown McGhee & George Liberace.
Fuller, Blind Boy *Source(s):* CM20; EPMU; HARS; LCAR
Note(s): See also Walter Brown McGhee.
Allen, H. (of Birmingham) [composer]
Nellah *Source(s):* CPMU ("Die Ringelblumen Walzer" (1849))
Note(s): Possible pseud.
Allen, Harley 1930-1993 [singer; guitarist, songwriter]
Allen, Red *Source(s):* EPMU; LCAR; MCCL
Note(s): Also used by Henry (James) Allen, Jr.; see following entry.
Allen, Henry (James), Jr. 1908-1967 [composer, trumpeter, bandleader, singer]
Allen, Red *Source(s):* ASCP; CASS; EPMU; GAMM; KINK; LCAR; PEN2; PSND
Note(s): Also used by Harley Allen; see preceding entry.
Allen, Kathryn Louise 1942-1986 [singer, songwriter]
Wolf, Kate *Source(s):* HARR; MUHF
Allen, Marie (née Townsend) 19th cent. [composer]
Townsend, Mansfield *Source(s):* EBEL; IBIM; STGR
Allen, Rex (Elvey) 1920 (or 24)-1999 [singer, songwriter, actor]
Arizona Cowboy, The *Source(s):* AMUS; PSND
Cactus Rex *Source(s):* PSND
Mister Cowboy *Source(s):* ALMN; PSND; STAC

Allen, Robert 1927-2000 [songwriter]
America's Most Popular Songwriter *Source(s):* SHMM (Jan./Feb. 2001): 67 (port.)
Allen, Stephen [or Steve] (Valentine Patrick William) 1921-2000 [entertainer, composer, author]
Best Allen since Fred, The *Source(s):* PSND
Fitch, Jeremy *Source(s):* CCE68; CPOL RE-726-967
Hammer, Buck *Source(s):* CCE59; CPOL RE-337-788; NGAM
Jackson, Mary Anne *Source(s):* CCE60; CPOL RE-366-445; NGAM
Stevens, William Christopher *Source(s):* LCAR; PSND
Steverino *Source(s):* PSND
That Ad Glibber *Source(s):* PSND
Valentino, Marcel *Source(s):* CPOL RE-781-177
Allen, Thomas [or Thos] S. 1876-1919 [composer, lyricist]
Stevens, Al *Source(s):* CCE32
Source(s): http://home.rochester.rr.com/wurlitzer/50index.html (16 May 2005)
Allen, Thomas Sylvester 1931-1988 [singer, songwriter, percussionist]
Allen, Papa Dee *Source(s):* NOMG
Allihn, Heinrich 1841-1910 [musicologist]
Anders, Fritz *Source(s):* LCAR; PSND
Allison, Joe (Marion) 1924-2002 [songwriter, producer, DJ]
Jamboree Joe *Source(s):* DRSC; NASF
Uncle Joe *Source(s):* DRSC; NASF
Note(s): See also Al(fred A.) Bernard.
Allman, Michael L(ee) 1911-1989 [composer, author]
Allman, Lee *Source(s):* ASCP; CCE41 #33223 Eunp264484
Allman, Miguel *Source(s):* CPOL RE-414-066
Lee, Michael *Source(s):* CCE44 #26770 Eunp384287
Almeida, Eumir(e) Deodato 1942- [singer, composer, arranger]
Deodato *Source(s):* AMUS; EPMU; NOMG
Almqvist, Carl Jonas Love [or Ludwig] 1793-1866 [author, journalist, composer]
C. J. L. A *Source(s):* PSND
Gustavi *Source(s):* GROL; NGDM
Westermann, Professor *Source(s):* PSND
Almroth, Kunt O. W. 1900-1971 [composer]
K. O. W. A. *Source(s):* GREN
Aloma, Harold David 1908- [composer, author]
Aloma, Hal *Source(s):* ASCC; CCE49 E42295
Alpert, Herb(ert) 1935 (or 37)- [trumpeter, bandleader, composer, producer]
Alpert, Dave *Source(s):* CPOL RE-654-127
Alpert, Dore *Source(s):* NOMG; http://www.spaceports.com/~spike3/collect.htm (15 Sept. 2003)
Alpert, Herman 1916- [bass, arranger]
Alpert, Trigger *Source(s):* CCE43 #2838 E110892; PSND
Alpert, Randy (C.) [songwriter]
Badazz, Randy *Source(s):* CPOL PA-76-161; PMUS; SONG
Altenberg, Michael 1584-1640 [composer, clergyman, schoolmaster]
M. A. *Source(s):* IBIM
Orlandus Thuringiae *Source(s):* NGDM
Thuringiae, Orlandus *Source(s):* NGDM
Althans, Kurt Karl 1931- [composer]
Kalas *Source(s):* PFSA
Althouse, Monroe A. 1853-1924 [composer, conductor]
Reading March King *Source(s):* SMIN
Altshul(er), Joseph 1839-1908 [cantor, composer, teacher]
Slonimer, Yoshe [Yossi] *Source(s):* NULM
Altschuler, Sydell [composer]
Lee, Sydney *Source(s):* CLTP (Tarzan (cartoon)); CLTV
Altwerger, John 1919-1990 [saxophonist, composer, bandleader]
Auld, George [or Georgie] *Source(s):* KINK; LCAR
Alvarez, Jorge Antonio c.1969- [songwriter]
Freestyle King *Source(s):* EPMU
Kurious *Source(s):* EPMU
Alvarez, Lissette [singer, songwriter, actress]
Lissette *Source(s):* HWOM
Alvin, Dave 1955- [singer, songwriter, guitarist]
Rockabilly "King of California" *Source(s):* CM17 p. v
Amadei, Filippo c.1670-c.1730 [violoncellist, composer]
Amadio, Pippo *Source(s):* NGDM
Mattei, Filippo *Source(s):* BAKO; BAKR; NGDM
Note(s): Incorrect name listed in Mattheson's *Critica musica.*
Pippo, (Signor) *Source(s):* BAKO; BAKR; NGDM; SADC
Amalie Marie Friederike Augusta, Princess of Saxony 1794-1870 [author, composer]
Heiter, A(malie) *Source(s):* BAKR; DWCO; GROL; JACK; LCAR
Serena, A(malie) *Source(s):* DWCO; JACK; LCAR
Ambros, August Wilhelm 1816-1876 [music historian, critic, pianist, composer]
Note(s): Portrait: *Neue Musik-Zeitung* (13 June 1902): 424
Flamin *Source(s):* NGDM; WORB
Ambrosius of Milan 333?-397
Ambrose, Saint *Source(s):* ROGG
Father of Christian Hymnology, The *Source(s):* PSND (see under: Ambrose, Saint)
Note(s): See also St. Hilary, Bishop of Portiers.

Father of Church Song *Source(s):* ROGG
Saint Ambrose *Source(s):* ROGG
Amburgey, Irene 1921- [singer; songwriter]
Barn Dance Sweethearts *Source(s):* AMUS; EPMU; MCCL
Note(s): Jt. pseud. with husband: James Carson [i.e., James William Roberts]
Carson, Martha *Source(s):* AMUS; CCE52-53; CPOL RE-80-276; EPMU; MCCL
Cosse, Irene (Amburgey) *Source(s):* RE-117-392; LCCC 1955-70 E87483
Franklin, Bobbie *Source(s):* CPOL RE-31-102
Amici, Antonio 1864- [guitarist, teacher, composer]
Toto *Source(s):* http://www.weinklang.de/Lexikon.web/lex.html (4 Feb. 2004)
Ammirati, John Lewis 1944- [composer, author]
Lonesome John *Source(s):* ASCP
Amner, Ralph ?-1663 (or 64) [composer]
Bull Speaker, The *Source(s):* PSND
Amos, Myra Ellen 1963 (or 64)- [singer, songwriter]
Amos, Tori *Source(s):* ALMN; CM12; EPMU; HARR; KICK; LCAR; PEN2
Tori *Source(s):* LCAR
Amper, Quirin 1908-1989 [composer]
Remar, Peer *Source(s):* CCE56-59; CCE60; KOMP; PFSA
Zebisch, Toni *Source(s):* CCE55; CCE67
Amper, Quirin, Jr. 1935- [composer]
Frantzen, E. *Source(s):* KOMS; PFSA
Amposah, Daniel 1934- [singer, composer, guitarist]
Konimo *Source(s):* PEN1
Amu, Ephraim 1899-1995 [musicologist]
Father of Ghanian Musicology, The *Source(s):* PSNN
Ana, Francesco d' c.1460-1502 (or 03) [composer, organist]
Bossinensis, Francicus *Source(s):* GRV3
Dana, Francesco (de) *Source(s):* LCAR; WORB
F. V. *Source(s):* NGDM
Varoter, Francesco *Source(s):* NGDM
Veneto, Francesco *Source(s):* LCAR
Venetus, Franciscus *Source(s):* LCAR; NGDM
Anastasi, Philip (J.) [singer, arranger]
Parrish, Dean *Source(s):* CCE65; PMUS
Ancillon, Charles (d') 1659-1715 [composer]
Ollincan, C. d' *Source(s):* http://www.linmpi.mpg.de/~kopp/disc/index4m.html (4 Feb. 2004)
Anders, John Frank 1907- [composer, author, singer]
Anders, Andy *Source(s):* ASCP; CPOL PAu-151-474
Dersan, Jon *Source(s):* ASCP; CCE64; CPOL RE-113-782
Francis, Bennie *Source(s):* ASCP
Andersen, Lale c.1911-1972 [songwriter]
Wilke, Nic(ola) *Source(s):* CCE53; CCE61-62; PMUS
Williams *Source(s):* CCE58
Willms, (Friedrich) *Source(s):* CCE58; CCE60
Anderson, Alpharita Constantia 1947- [singer, songwriter, producer]
Esete *Source(s):* ALMN; CM10
Ganette *Source(s):* ALMN; CM10
Marley, (Mrs.) Rita *Source(s):* ALMN; CM10
Anderson, Cecil 1906-1968 [composer, calypso singer]
Duke of Iron *Source(s):* CCE57; LCAR; PSND
Anderson, Chris [composer, arranger]
Anderson, Whitey *Source(s):* MOMU
Anderson, Gary 1939- [composer]
Bonds, Gary U. S. *Source(s):* ALMN; EPMU; PEN2; ROOM; YORK
Anderson, John W. 1936 (or 37)- [poet, songwriter, singer]
KaSandra, Dobanian King *Source(s):* CPOL PAu-992-787
KaSandra, John *Source(s):* CPOL RE-775-169; LCAR; PSND
Anderson, Keith 1944- [singer, songwriter]
Andy, Bob *Source(s):* EPMU; PEN1
Anderson, Leroy 1908-1975 [composer, arranger, conductor]
Note(s): Portrait: EWPA
Red Headed Brier Hopper *Source(s):* SUTT
Anderson, Roberta Joan 1943- [singer, songwriter]
Mitchell, Joni *Source(s):* CASS; CM02; CM17; DIMA; EPMU; LCAR; PEN2
Anderson, (Evelyn) Ruth 1928- [composer, author]
Bennett, Robert Russell *Source(s):* BUL3
Note(s): Used on orchestrations for NBC-TV, 1960-66. Do not confuse with Robert Russell Bennett (1894-1981).
Anderson, Stikkan 1931-1997 [producer, songwriter]
Anderson, Stig (Arne) *Source(s):* CCE56; EPMU
Istan, Afgan *Source(s):* CCE56
Rossner, Stig *Source(s):* CCE61; CCE64
Anderson, William (Alonzo) 1916-1981 [composer, trumpeter]
Anderson, Cat *Source(s):* ASCP; EPMU; KINK; LCAR; PEN2; SOTH
Anderson, (James) William [or Bill], (III) 1937- [singer; songwriter]
Pat Boone of Country Music, The *Source(s):* ALMN
Whisperin(g) Bill *Source(s):* ALMN; FLIN
Anderson, William Henry 1882-1955 [composer, singer, choir director]
Anderson, Wallace *Source(s):* LCAR
Bilencko, Michel *Source(s):* LCAR
Garland, Hugh *Source(s):* BUL3; CCE48; GOTH; GOTT; GREN; LCAR

Anderton, Stephen P(hilbin) 1874-1947 [composer]
Leigh, Ralph *Source(s):* TPRF
Andolfo, Franco 1938- [composer, pianist, guitarist]
Vecio, El *Source(s):* KOMP; PFSA
Andrade, Daniel (Raye) 1929- [singer; guitarist; songwriter]
Andray, Danny Raye *Source(s):* CCE Eunp (year not noted)
Hank the Drifter *Source(s):* CCE62; EPMU; LCAR; MCCL; STAC
Andrade, Djalmi de 1923-1987 [composer, guitarist]
Cruz, José Luiz Oliveira *Source(s):* GREN
Oliviera Cruz, Luiz *Source(s):* GREN
Sete, Bola *Source(s):* CCE62; CM26; GREN
André, Jean Baptiste (Andreas) 1823-1882 [pianist, composer]
Saint Gilles, A. de *Source(s):* LCAR
Andreas de Florentia ?-c.1415 [composer, organist]
Andrea de' Servi, Frate *Source(s):* NGDM; RIES
Andrea degli Organi *Source(s):* NGDM; RIES
Andrea di Giovanni, Fra *Source(s):* NGDM; RIES
Andreini, Giovanni Battista 1576 (or 78)-1654 [actor, dramatist, poet]
Lelio *Source(s):* NGDM
Note(s): See also Francesco Riccoboni (the younger) & Luigi [or Louis] (Andrea) Riccoboni.
Andreoli, Peter 1941- [singer, songwriter]
Anders, Pete *Source(s):* CPOL PA-743-465; PSND
Andreozzi, Gaetano 1775-1826 [composer, singing teacher]
Jommellino, (Gaetano) *Source(s):* NGDM
Andrews, Chris [singer, songwriter]
Andrews, Tim *Source(s):* EPMU
Andrews, Curcy H., Jr. 1940- [composer, author]
Andrews, Bud *Source(s):* ASCP
Andrews, Herbert Kennedy 1904-1965 [writer on music, organist, composer]
H. K. A. *Source(s):* CPMU
Andrews, Mark [composer, organist]
Note(s): Do not confuse with Mark Andrews who used the pseud.: Sisqó.
Flivver, A. *Source(s):* CCE46 R3259 ("A Ford Song")
Andrews, Mark (Althavan) 1977- [singer, songwriter]
Note(s): Do not confuse with Mark Andrews who used the pseud.: A Flivver.
Sisqó *Source(s):* AMIR; AMUS; LCAR; PMUS-00
Andrews, R. Hoffmann (the younger) [arranger]
R. H. A. *Source(s):* CPMU
Andrews, Richard 1831-1909 [pianist, composer]
Hoffman, Richard *Source(s):* PSND
Note(s): Also used by Everett Ascher.
Andries, Franzleo 1912-1979 [composer]
Gedarro, Carlos *Source(s):* CCE54 E85170; CPOL RE-719-690
Grundhoff, Walter *Source(s):* CCE54-56; CPOL RE-97-529
Harden, Michael *Source(s):* CCE53-54; CPOL RE-94-678; PFSA
Hoff, André *Source(s):* CCE53-55
Note(s): Also jt. pseud.: Kurt (August Karl) Feltz
Korten, Hans *Source(s):* CCE53-54; CCE56-57; CCE60-62; CPOL RE-81-687
Note(s): Also jt. pseud. with Kurt (August Karl) Feltz.
Kronberger, Heini *Source(s):* CCE54-55
Luardo, Martino *Source(s):* CCE55 Efor32860; CPOL RE-183-282
Andriessen, Jurriaan 1925-1996 [composer]
De Mandelieu, Maurice *Source(s):* http://www.musicprint.nl/catalog540_1.html
Andrykowski, Robert (Charles) 1961- [singer, songwriter]
Daniel, Davis *Source(s):* AMUS; CPOL PA-1-002-321
Andrzejewski, Marek 1924- [composer]
Markowski, Andrzej *Source(s):* BUL2; NGDM
Anelli, Angelo 1761-1820 [librettist]
Fifferi, Lauro *Source(s):* GROL; NGDO; STGR
Goro, Menucci di *Source(s):* MELL
Landi, Marco *Source(s)*: GROL; MELL; NGDO; PIPE; STGR
Latanzio, P. *Source(s)*: GROL; NGDO
Liprandi, Nicolo *Source(s)*: GROL; MELL; NGDO; PIPE; SONN; STGR
Menucci, Tomasso *Source(s)*: GROL; NGDO
Scannamata, Giordano *Source(s):* MELL
Scannamato, Giovanni *Source(s)*: GROL; NGDO; STGR
Scopabirba, Gasparo *Source(s)*: GROL; NGDO
Anet, Jean-Jacques-Baptiste 1676-1755 [violinist, composer]
Baptiste *Source(s):* NGDM; SADC; WORB
Angeli, Francesco Maria 1632-1697 [composer]
Rivotorto, Il *Source(s):* GROL; NGDM
Note(s): See also Angelo DeAngelis.
Angerer, Rudolf 1918- [composer, pianist]
Orbeck, Rudi *Source(s):* KOMP; PFSA
Schoenau, Gerd *Source(s):* KOMP; PFSA
Angiolini, (Domenico Maria) Gasparo 1731-1803 [choreographer, dancer, composer]
Gasparini, Angelo *Source(s):* DOLM; GROL; LCAR; NGDM; RIES
Anglin, Jack 1916-1963 [singer, songwriter]
Johnnie & Jack *Source(s):* MCCL
Note(s): Jt. pseud.: Johnnie Robert Wright.
Angster, Manfred 1951- [composer]
Fred, Charly *Source(s):* KOBW
Animuccia, Giovanni 1500?-1571 [composer]
Father of the Oratorio, The *Source(s):* PSND
Note(s): See also Giacomo Carissimi.

Annibale 1527?-1575 [organist, composer]
Padovano, Il *Source(s):* BAKE; PSND
Anson, Robert (C.) 1946- [songwriter]
Lincoln, Phil(amore) *Source(s):* CPOL PAu-327-819; PMUS
Antes, John [or Johann] 1740-1811 [composer]
A*T*S, Giovanni *Source(s):* AMSL (12 Jan. 2004)
Note(s): Karl Kroger reported A*T*S was used on "Three Trios for 2 vlns. and cello. He probably did this because, as an ultrapious member of the Moravian community at Fulneck, near Leeds, England, he thought it inappropriate to publish secular music under his own name."
Antheil, George 1900-1959 [pianist, composer, author]
Note(s): Portraits: EWEC; Whitesitt (see below)
Bad Boy of Music, The *Source(s):* PSND
Bishop, Stacey *Source(s):* NGDM; PSNN
Note(s): Used on mysteries.
Desage, Marcel *Source(s):* Whitesitt, Linda. *The Life and Music of George Antheil*. Ann Arbor: UMI Research Press, 1983.
Exponent of Futurism, The *Source(s):* PSND; SIFA
Anthony, Bert R. 1923- [composer]
Note(s): Portrait: ETUP 50:2 (Feb. 1932): 84
Blake, Milton D. *Source(s):* CCE46 R4116; TPRF
Emerson, Stewart B. *Source(s):* CCE49 R48612 ("Little Drummer Boy")
Anthony, Malcolm 1950- [composer, author]
Ahmonuel, Zyal *Source(s):* ASCP
Antico, Andrea c.1480-1539 [composer, music printer]
Note(s): See LCAR for additional variant forms of name.
Abbate, Anthoine dell' *Source(s):* OCLC 1299770
Antiquus, Andreas *Source(s):* BAKE; LCAR
Antonini, Raymond 1922- [bandleader, trumpeter; songwriter]
Anthony, Ray *Source(s):* ALMN; KINK; LCAR; PEN2; STUW
Antunes, Arnaldo [singer, lyricist]
Calvin Johnson of Sao Polo, The *Source(s):* BRAZ
Anzelwitz [or Anzelvitz], Benjamin [or Bernard] 1891-1943 [violinist, composer, bandleader]
Bernie, Ben [or Bernard] *Source(s):* GAMM; KINK; LCAR; PSND; STUW
Green, Ben *Source(s):* PMUS
Note(s): Do not confuse with Benny Green (1963-) or Benny Green [i.e., Bernard Green] (1927-)
Old Maestro, The *Source(s):* PSND; Bryan, Al & James V. Monaco. "Hold Your Horses." New York: Leo Feist, 1932. (port. on cover)
Anzengruber, Ludwig 1839-1889 [author]
Gruber, Ludwig *Source(s):* PIPE; WORB
Momus *Source(s):* PIPE
Note(s): Also used by Nicholas Currie.
Apel, Matthäus 1594-1648 [poet, composer]
Löw, Matthias Appeles de *Source(s):* WORB
Löwenstern, Matthäus Apelles von *Source(s):* NGDM
M. A. v. L. *Source(s):* CPMU; WORB
Apell, David August von 1754-1832 [composer, author]
Capelli, (David August von) *Source(s):* CPMU; IBIM; NGDM; NGDO; PIPE; RIES; WORB
Apollino, Salvatore [composer]
Ignorate all'oscuro, (Il Sig.) *Source(s):* ALMC
Apostel, Hans Erich 1901-1972 [composer]
Hanslickianer, A *Source(s):* GROL
Note(s): Called himself.
Post, Lea *Source(s):* GDRM; GROL
Appelbaum, Willi 1893-1988 [musicologist]
Apel, Willi [or Willy] *Source(s):* CPMU; LCAR
Appignani, Adelaide (Orsola) 1807-1884 [pianist, conductor, composer]
Asperi, Ursula *Source(s):* COHN; DWCO; HIXN
Aspri, Orsola *Source(s):* COHN; DWCO; HIXN
Applebaum, Stan(ley) (Seymour) 1922- [composer, arranger, conductor, author]
Baum, Stanley *Source(s):* CCE45 #8290 E409776
Keith, Robert *Source(s):* LCAR; PSND
Lebaum, Stanley *Source(s):* CCE56
Mann, Rita *Source(s):* CCE57
Seymour, Cy *Source(s):* CCE62 Eunp741524 ("Nobdy's Home")
Note(s): Do not confuse with Cy Seymore [i.e., William C. Polla]
Aprile, Giuseppe 1732-1813 [castrato, composer]
Sciroletto *Source(s):* GROL; LCAR; RIES
Scirolino *Souce(s):* GROL; LCAR
Note(s): See also Gregorio Sciroli.
Sciorolo *Source(s):* GROL
Apthorp, William Foster 1848-1913 [music critic, lexicographer]
Boston's Musical Brahmin *Source(s):* GRAN
Aptowitzer, Arlen 1920- [music critic, composer]
Walter, Arlen *Source(s):* ORPH
Aquino, Frank J(oseph) 1906-1997 [composer, conductor]
Kane, Bernie *Source(s):* ASCP; CCE39 #6602 Eunp188428; DOLM
Araujo Yong, Maria Guadalupe 1958- [singer, songwriter]
Gabriel, Ana *Source(s):* HWOM
Archer, Michael (Eugene) 1974- [singer, songwriter, multi-instrumentalist]
D'Angelo *Source(s):* EPMU; LCAR; PMUS-00

Archilei, Vittoria (née Concarini) 1550-c.1620 [lutenist, composer]
Romanina, La *Source(s):* COHN; GREN; HIXN; SADC
Ardoin, Amedee c.1896- [singer, songwriter, accordionist]
Tite Negre *Source(s):* MCCL
Arefece, Antonio 1685-1734 [composer]
Orefice, Antonio *Source(s):* PIPE; WORB
Arellano, George Isidro 1923- [composer, educator, singer]
Arno, George *Source(s):* ASCP; CCE59
Arena, Philopina [or Filippina] (Lida) 1968- [singer, songwriter]
Arena, Tina *Source(s):* CM21; EPMU
Argumédez, Camilo Luis 1945- [singer, bandleader, composer]
Azuquita, Camilo *Source(s):* EPMU; PEN2
Ariosti, Attilio (Malachia [or Clementi]) 1666-1729 [composer, monk]
A. A. *Source(s):* CPMS
Attilio *Source(s):* LCAR
Ottavio, (Frate) *Source(s):* LCAR; NGDM; SADC
Ariosti, Giovanni Battista 1668- [musician, composer]
Odoardo *Source(s):* GROL
Arkell, Reginald 1882-1959 [lyricist, author]
Arkell, Billy *Source(s):* GAN1; GAN2
Arkin, Alan (Wolf) 1934- [actor, director, composer, singer]
McArkin, Alan *Source(s):* CCE64
Short, Roger *Source(s):* PSNN
Arluck, Hymen 1905-1986 [composer, pianist, arranger]
Note(s): Portraits: EWEN; JAST
America's Great Unknown Songwriter *Source(s):*http://www.icce.rug.nl/~soundscapes/DATABASES/TRA/Did_he_write_that.html (4 Oct. 2002)
America's Second Stephen Foster *Source(s):* LYMN
Arlen, Harold *Source(s):* ALMN; EPMU; EWEN; GAMM; GAN2; KINK; LCAR; VACH
Arluk, Chaim *Source(s):* ALMN
Paul, Walter *Source(s):* CCE72 R532531
Armbuster, Robert 1896-1994 [composer, conductor, pianist]
Bergman, Henri *Source(s):* RPRA
Summers, Robert *Source(s):* RPRA
Waldron, Gene *Source(s):* RPRA
Armenteros, Alfredo 1928- [trumpeter, composer, arranger, bandleader]
Armenteros, Chocolate *Source(s):* EPMU; PEN2
Chocolate, Monsieur *Source(s):* LCAR
Monsieur Chocolate *Source(s):* LCAR

Armitage, Ella Sophia 1841-1931 [hymnist]
E. S. A. *Source(s):* JULN (Appendix)
Armitage, Reginald Moxon 1898-1954 [composer, lyricist, organist, publisher]
Gay, Noel *Source(s):* EPMU; GAN1; GAN2; GROL; HARR; KILG; LCAR; NGDM
Hill, Stanley *Source(s):* GROL; PMUS
Noel *Source(s):* CCE52
Armstrong, (Daniel) Louis 1900 (or 01)-1971 [trumpeter, composer, singer]
Ambassador Satch *Source(s):* GROL
Ambassador with a Horn, The *Source(s):* OUSA
America's Ambassador of Good Will *Source(s):* PSND
Armstrong, King *Source(s):* TCAN
Armstrong, Louie *Source(s):* PSND
Armstrong, Pops *Source(s):* NGDJ; PSND
Armstrong, Satchmo *Source(s):* LCAR
Dippermouth *Source(s):* CASS; GROL; NGDJ
Einstein of Jazz, The *Source(s):* PSND
Gatemouth *Source(s):* TCAN
Notes(s): See also Clarence Brown.
Pops *Source(s):* GROL
Satchelmouth *Source(s):* CASS; GROL; KINK; NGDJ; NGDM
Satchmo *Source(s):* CASS; GROL; KINK; NGDJ; NGDM; TCAN
Armstrong, Henry W. 1879-1951 [songwriter, pianist, singer]
Armstrong, Harry *Source(s):* LCAR; PSND
Arnaud, Delmic [songwriter]
Daz Dat Nigga *Source(s):* AMUS; PMUS-95
Arnaud, François 1721-1784 [writer on music]
Gluckists' High Priest *Source(s):* GROL
St. Paul of the Gluck Religion, The *Source(s):* GROL
Arnaud, Noel 1904-1991 [director, arranger]
Arnaud, Léo *Source(s):* MOMU
Arne, Thomas Augustine 1710-1778 [composer]
Note(s): Portraits: CYBH; EWCY
Greatest English Composer after Handel, The *Source(s):* PSND
Arner, Betty Anne J. 1940- [author, hymnist]
Campion, Joan *Source(s):* CLAC
Arnheim, Gus 1897-1955 [bandleader, composer]
Old Colonel, The *Source(s):* PSND
Arnold, Bernard 1915-2004 [composer, author]
Arnold, Buddy *Source(s):* ASCP; CLTP ("Jimmy Durante Show")
Arnold, (Richard) Edward [or Eddie] 1918- [singer; songwriter]
Heinz Fifty-Seven Singer, A *Source(s):* STAC
Note(s): Arnold's description of the various types of songs he sings.

Tennessee Plowboy, The *Source(s):* BAKR; FLIN; MCCL; PEN2; SHAD; STAC
Arnold, Franz 1878-1960 [librettist]
Luschansky, Josef *Source(s):* WORB
Arnold, Ignaz (Theodor) Ferdinand (Cajetan) 1774 (or 79)-1812 [author, musicologist]
Gall, Joseph *Source(s):* WORB
Arnold, James 1901-1968 (or 69) [singer, guitarist, songwriter]
Arnold, Kokomo *Source(s):* HARS; HERZ; LCAR; WORT
Gitfiddle Jim *Source(s):* HARS; HERZ; LCAR
Arnold, John Henry 1887-1956 [organist, composer]
J. H. A. *Source(s):* CPMU
Arnol'd, Yury (Karlovich) 1811-1898 [writer on music, composer]
Carlini, Carlo *Source(s):* GROL
Harmonin *Source(s):* GROL
Karlovich, Karl *Source(s):* GROL
Meloman *Source(s):* GROL
Smeliy, Karl *Source(s):* GROL
Yu, A. *Source(s):* GROL
Arnondrin, Sidney (J.) 1901-1948 [clarinetist, composer]
Arodin, Sidney (J.) *Source(s):* LCAR; NGDJ
Arnone, Dominick L. 1920- [composer, guitarist]
Arnone, Don L. *Source(s):* ASCP
Arola, Lorenzo 1892-1924 [bandoneonist, arranger, composer]
Arolas, Eduardo *Source(s):* LCAR; TODO
Tiger of the Bandoneon, The *Source(s):* BBDP; TODO
Tigre del Bandoneon, El *Source(s):* BBDP; TODO
Arouet, François-Marie 1694-1778 [writer]
Note(s): See LCAR for additional pseudonyms & sobriquets.
Dulaurens *Source(s):* PIPE
Voltaire *Source(s):* GOTH; SADC; SONN
Arpa, Giovanni Leonardo dell' c.1525-1602 [composer]
Note(s): See LCAR for additional variant spellings.
Dell'Arpa, Giovanni Leonardo *Source(s):* WORB
Gian, dell'Arpa *Source(s):* LCAR
Gian Leonardo, dell'Arpa *Source(s):* LCAR
Mollica, Gian Leonardo *Source(s):* WORB
Arquette, Cliff(ord) 1905-1974 [comedian, pianist, composer, songwriter]
Weaver, Charley *Source(s):* IMDB
Arriaga (y Balzola), Juan Crisóstomo (Jacobo Antonio) de 1806-1826 [composer]
Spanish Mozart, The *Source(s):* GROL; PSND
Arrigo fl. 1350 [composer]
Henricus *Source(s):* GROL; NGDM
Arrigoni, Giovanni Giacomo 1597-1675 [organist, composer]
Affettuoso, L' *Source(s):* GROL; NGDM
Note(s): See also Mariano Tantucci.
Arrington, Joseph [or Joe], (Jr.) 1933-1982 [singer, composer]
Hazziez, Joseph [or Yusef] *Source(s):* AMUS; FAFO; HARR
Tex, Joe *Source(s):* EPMU; GAMM; HARR; LCAR; PMUS; PSND
Arrollado, J. L. [composer]
Ledesma, Jose *Source(s):* REHG
Arshawsky, Arthur Jacob 1910-2004 [bandleader, clarinetist, composer, arranger]
King of the Clarinet *Source(s):* WHIC
Note(s): See also Isadore Simon Phillips.
Shaw, Artie *Source(s):* BAKR; CM08; EPMU; GAMM; KINK; LCAR; STUW; VACH
Artale, Giuseppe 1628-1679 [librettist]
Erranti (de Napoli) *Source(s):* ALMC
Arthur, Reg [composer]
Paul, Keith *Source(s):* MUWB
Artola, Héctor 1903-1982 [bandoneonist, leader, arranger]
Artola, Quico *Source(s):* TODO
Quico *Source(s):* TODO
Artusi, Giovanni Maria c.1540-1613 [writer on music, theorist, composer]
Antonio Brassino da Todi *Source(s):* GROL; NGDM; RILM 92-02017-ae
Note(s): Possible pseud.
Baccino, Antonio *Source(s):* WORB
Braccino, Antonio *Source(s):* WORB
Ottuso, L' *Source(s):* GROL
Note(s): See also Antonio Goretti.
Todi, Antonio Brassino da *Source(s):* GROL; NGDM; RILM 92-02017-ae
Arundel, E. H. [composer]
E. H. A. *Source(s):* CPMU (publications dates: 1876-77)
Arutyun, Sayadyan 1712-1795 [poet, composer]
Sayat'-Nova *Source(s):* HOFE
Arvey, Verna 1910-1987 [pianist, conductor, librettist]
Note(s): Married name: Mrs. William Grant Still.
Smith, Maryon *Source(s):* http://www.uark.edu/libinfo/speccoll/still/still2aid.html (4 Oct. 2002)
Arvonio, Robert Anthony 1941- [composer, author, singer]
Arvon, (Bobby) *Source(s):* ASCP; CCE70; CPOL RE-771-237
Asafiev, Boris Vladimirovich 1884-1949 [composer, writer on music]
Note(s): See LCAR for variant forms of given name.

Glebov, Igor *Source(s):* BAKR; GOTH: GROL; NGDM
Aschenbrenner, Paul 1891-1958 [conductor, pianist, songwriter]
Ash, Paul *Source(s):* PSND
Ascher, Everett 1936- [composer]
Aster, Ed *Source(s):* ASCP
Hoffman, Richard *Source(s):* ASCP
Note(s): Also used by Richard Andrews.
Morton, Frank *Source(s):* ASCP; CCE60-61
Ashbaugh, Marvin 1914-1974 [composer]
Ash, Marvin *Source(s):* JASG; JASR
Asher, John Symon 1943- [bassist, pianist, songwriter]
Bruce, Jack *Source(s):* EPMU; LCAR
Ashley, John [or Josiah] c.1780- after 1834 [bassoonist, singer, songwriter]
Ashley of Bath *Source(s):* NGDM
Ashton, Winifred 1885-1965 [novelist, writer on music]
Dane, Clemence *Source(s):* LCAR
Ashwell, Benjamin George 1906-1976 [composer]
Posford, George *Source(s):* GAMM; MUSR; MUWB; REHH
Ashworth, Ernest 1928- [songwriter]
Worth, Billy *Source(s):* AMUS; CCE60; CCME; PMUS
Aškerc, Anton 1856-1912 [author]
Gorazd *Source(s):* PIPE
Askew, John 1936 (or 41)- [singer, songwriter]
Gentle, Johnny *Source(s):* EPMU; LCAR
Aspinall, C. C. [composer]
Tovey, Cécile *Source(s):* OCLC 48703243
Assandra, Caterina c. 1580- [composer]
Alessandra, Caterina *Source(s):* DWCO; LCAR
Note(s): Do not confuse with 18th cent. composer Caterina Allesandra.
Astley, Edward Thomas 1922-1998 [lyricist]
Astley, Ted *Source(s):* BBDP
Aston, Anthony [or Tony] c.1682-c.1753 [actor, singer, author, composer]
Medley, Mat(thew) *Source(s):* LCAR; MELL; SONN; STGR
Aston, C. [composer]
C. A. *Source(s):* CPMU (publication date 1905)
Astorga, Emanuele (Gioacchino Cesare Rincón) d' 1681-1755 (or 56) [composer]
Chiaro, Giuseppe del *Source(s):* NGDM; NGDO
Astruc, Gabriel (David) 1864-1938 [lyricist]
Surtac *Source(s):* WHIT
Atchison, Shelby David 1912-1982 [singer; guitarist, songwriter]
Atchison, Tex *Source(s):* MCCL
Atinsky, Jerry 1917- [composer, author]
Allen, Jerry *Source(s):* ASCP; CCE63
Atkins, Chester [or Chet] (Burton) 1924-2001 [guitarist, composer, singer]
Adkins, Chet *Source(s):* CCE75
Country Gentleman, (The) *Source(s):* PSND
Note(s): See also Carl Smith.
Mr. Guitar *Source(s):* AMEN; CM05; CM26; FLIN; PSND; STAC (see under: Carmer, Floyd)
Note(s): See also Jerry (Reed) Hubbard.
Atkins, Jeffrey [rapper, songwriter]
Ja Rule *Source(s):* AMUS; CM36
Atkinson, A. K. 1922- [composer]
Salim, Ahmad Khatab *Source(s):* PSND
Atkinson, Dorothy 1893- [poet, writer, composer]
D'Orme, Valerie *Source(s):* COHN; HIXN
Fife, Duncan *Source(s):* COHN; HIXN
Gower, Beryl *Source(s):* COHN; HIXN
Langham, Beryl *Source(s):* COHN; HIXN
Attanasio, Don(ald Joseph) 1938- [composer, author]
Christopher, Don *Source(s):* ASCP; CCE60-61; CCE66-67
Atterberg, Kurt M(agnus) 1887-1974 [engineer, composer, conductor, critic]
Note(s): Portrait: ETUP 58:6 (June 1940): 426
Richard Strauss of Sweden, The *Source(s):* Haas, Karl. "Adventures in Good Music; Mystery Composer Quiz" PBS Radio (12 June 2001)
Attwater, John Post 1862- [composer, hymnist]
North, Frank *Source(s):* JULN p. 1607
Auber, Daniel François Esprit 1782-1871 [composer]
Note(s): Portraits: ETUP 50:2 (Feb. 1932): 84; EWCY
Father of French Opera *Source(s):* http://www.rgrossmusicauthograph.com/composers50.html (4 Oct. 2002)
Note(s): See also Jean [i.e., Giovanni] Battista Lully [i.e., Lulli]
Lamare, (Jacques-)Michel Hurel de *Source(s):* GROL; http://www.stratsplace.com/rogov/prolific_french_comp.html (18 Mar. 2005)
Note(s): In GROL entry for cellist Jacques-Michel Hurel de Lamare (1772-1823), ". . . Lamare's name remained prominent as Auber's *nom de plume* for a number of cello compositions . . ."
Prince of the *Opéra-comique* *Source(s):* EWCY
Aubert, Albert 19th cent. [author]
Hazard, Désiré *Source(s):* PIPE; PSND
Note(s): Jt. pseud.: Paul Bocage & Octave Feuillet.
Aubert, Jacques 1689-1753 [violinist, composer]
Vieux, Le *Source(s):* BAKE; HARV
Auer, Josef 1928- [composer]
Auer, Pepsi *Source(s):* PSND
Auge, Henry J., Jr. 1930?-1983 [songwriter]
Auge, Bud *Source(s):* CCE64; PSND

Augustin, John Alcée 1838-1888 [lyricist]
Ye Tragic *Source(s):* HOGR
Note(s): Possible pseud.; "Short Rations."
Auinger, Franz Joseph Maria 1956- [composer, conceptual artist]
Auinger, Sam *Source(s):* OMUO
Aulich, Bruno 1902- [writer on music]
Boesting, Alfred *Source(s):* DOLM; RIES
Auracher, Harry 1888-1960 [composer, conductor]
Archer, Harry *Source(s):* CASS; EPMU; GAN1; GAN2; KINK; PSND
Kent, Richard *Source(s):* CCE58 R211207 ("Those Mem'ry Bells")
Note(s): Also used by Mirrie (Irma) Soloman.
Lounsbury, Walter *Source(s):* CCE32 E27805; CCE58
Aureli, Aurelio fl. 1652-1708 [librettist]
Imperfetti *Source(s):* ALMC
Auserón, Santiago [songwriter, musician]
Juan Perro *Source(s):* http://www.electroduendes.net/al.asp?idp=148 (5 Feb. 2005)
Austerlitz, Frederick 1899-1987 [dancer, actor, composer]
Astaire, Fred *Source(s):* EPMU; GAMM; GAN2; KINK
Austin, Frederick [composer]
Barclay, Martin *Source(s):* GREN
Note(s): Possible pseud.
Austin, H. R. [composer]
Dana, Arthur *Source(s):* CCE41 #34957 E97028; CCE70 R486280
Note(s): A. P. Schmidt house name; see NOTES: Dana, Arthur.
Austin, John 1613-1669 [composer, hymnist]
Birchley, William *Source(s):* CYBH; HATF; WORB
Catholick Gentleman *Source(s):* LCAR
Cavalier in Yorkshire, A *Source(s):* HATF
Person of Quality *Source(s):* LCAR
Authors, Barrie 1933- [arranger, songwriter, music publisher]
Barrie, J. J. *Source(s):* EPMU; WARN
Autry, (Orvon) Gene 1907 (or 08)-1998 [singer, songwriter, actor]
America's Favorite Cowboy *Source(s):* PSND
America's Favorite Singing Cowboy *Source(s):* MILL
America's Number One Singing Cowboy *Source(s):* MILL
Clayton, Bob *Source(s):* IMDB; MACE; SUTT
Dobbs, Johnny *Source(s):* http://www.nationalcowboymuseum.org/research/r_a_rao.html (17 June 2005)
Dodds, Johnny *Source(s):* IMDB; http://www.nationalcowboymuseum.org/research/r_a_rao.html
Hardy, John *Source(s):* SUTT
Hatfield, Overton *Source(s):* http://www.nationalcowboymuseum.org/research/r_a_rao.html
Hill, Sam *Source(s):* MACE; SUTT
Note(s): Do not confuse with Sam Hill [i.e., (James) Fletcher Henderson]; (SUTT).
Johnson, Gene *Source(s):* MACE; SUTT
Keene, Charles *Source(s):* MACE
Long Brothers *Source(s):* http://www.nationalcowboymuseum.org/research/r_a_rao.html
Long, Tom *Source(s):* MACE; SUTT
Oklahoma's Singing Cowboy *Source(s):* PSND; STAC
Oklahoma's Yodeling Cowboy *Source(s):* CM25; FLIN; PSND
Original Singing Cowboy, The *Source(s):* CM25
Note(s): See also Carl T. Sprague.
Silver-Screen's First Singing Cowboy, The *Source(s): Current Biography* (1999): 639
Singing Cowboy, The *Source(s):* ALMN; PSND
Note(s): See also Edgar D(ean) Glosup & James [or Jimmy] Clarence Wakeley.
Smith, Jimmie *Source(s):* SUTT
Note(s): Do not confuse with Jimmy Smith, country-style harmonica player.
Avenarius, Tony [or Toni] 18??- [composer]
Hafermann, Antonius *Source(s):* http://www.carolinaclassical.com/faust (9 Jan. 2005)
Avery c.1470?-c.1543? [composer]
Burton, Avery *Source(s):* GROL; NGDM
Avraamov, Arseny Mikhaylovich 1886-1944 [composer, theorist, music critic]
Ars *Source(s):* GDRM; GROL
Axton, Hoyt (Wayne) 1938-1999 [singer, guitarist, songwriter, actor]
Hammer Hand *Source(s):* FLIN
Ayer, Silas, H. [composer]
Reya, Silas *Source(s):* PMUS-80-89; REHG
Ayerst, David 1904- [historian, author]
Pennyless, D. M. *Source(s):* GROL; PIPE
Note(s): Jt. pseud.: Michael (Kemp) Tippet & Ruth Pennyman.
Ayinde, Sikiru 1948- [singer, composer]
Barrister, Sikiru Ayinde *Source(s):* PEN2
Fuji, Mr. *Source(s):* LCAR
Mr. Fuji *Source(s):* LCAR
Ayler, Albert 1936-1970 [saxophonist, composer]
Little Bird *Source(s):* CM19
Note(s): Also used by James [or Jimmy] (Edward) Heath.
Ayre, Ivor c.1894-1977 [pianist, composer]
Ayre, Jack *Source(s):* VGRC

Ayrton, William 1777-1853 [journalist, music critic]
Friend of the Family, A *Source(s):* CART
Azerbayev, Kenen 1884-1976 [composer, singer]
Bala-aqyn *Source(s):* GROL
Azevedo, Luiz Heitor Corrêa de 1905-1992 [writer on music]
Heitor, Luiz *Source(s):* LCAR
Aziz, Khalid Yasin Abdul 1940-1978 [organist, composer]
Yasin, Khalid *Source(s):* PSND
Note(s): Listed as original name.
Young, Larry *Source(s):* AMUS
Aznar, Abel (Mariano) 1913-1983 [musician, lyricist]
Aznar, Faro *Source(s):* TODO
Faro *Source(s):* TODO
Aznavourian, (Shanaur) Varenagh 1924 (or 25)- [singer, songwriter, actor]
Aznavour, Charles *Source(s):* BAKO; CASS; HARD; HARR; LCAR; PEN2
Frank Sinatra of France *Source(s):* http://www.franceway.com/w3/amazon/frenchsingers.html (6 Oct. 2002)
French Sinatra *Source(s):* http://www.losthighways.org/aznavouri.html (2 Oct. 2002)
Note(s): See also (Gilbert) François (Léopold) Silly.
Azor, Hurby [songwriter]
Azor, Lovebug *Source(s):* SONG
Fingerprints *Source(s):* CPOL PA-459-199
Invincibles *Source(s):* CPOL PA-459-196
Azpilcueta, Martin (de) 1492?-1586 [writer on music]
Note(s): See LCAR for variant spellings.
La Navarrus *Source(s):* WORB
Navarro, Martin *Source(s):* LCAR
Navarrus, (Martinus) *Source(s):* NGDM; WORB
Azzara, (Bennie) Anthony 1910-2001 [composer, author, singer]
Martini, Bennie *Source(s):* ASCP; CCE36 Eunp126530; CCE50-51

– B –

Baaren, Kees van 1906-1970 [composer, teacher]
Barney, Billy *Source(s):* GROL
Babbitt, Milton 1916- [composer]
Electronic Music Man, The *Source(s):* PSND
Babcock, Edward Chester 1913-1990 [composer]
Note(s): Portraits: EWEN; JAST; SHMM (Mar./Apr. 1993): [5-6]
Architect of Melody *Source(s):* ALMN
Van Heusen, James [or Jimmy] *Source(s):* ALMN; EPMU; HARR; LCAR; NGDM; PEN2; VACH
Vitale, Carmen *Source(s):* CPOL RE-194-330
Williams, Arthur *Source(s):* CCE54-55
Babell, William c.1690-1723 [harpsichordist, composer, arranger, violinist, organist]
W. B. *Source(s):* CPMU ("Marian's Charms Wound My Heart")
Note(s): Probable initials of Babell.
Babich, Herman Bernard 1917- [composer, arranger]
Babit, Hi [or Hy] *Source(s):* ASCP; CCE35 Eunp111123; CCE73
Bacalov, Luis Enríquez 1933- [composer, conductor]
Bacalof, Luis *Source(s):* BBDP; LCAR
Enriquez, Luis *Source(s):* CCE62
Luis Enriquez *Source(s):* CCE62
Note(s): Do not confuse with Luis Enrique [i.e., Luis Enrique Mejía López]
Bacchini, Giovanni Maria fl. 1588-1605 [singer, composer, theorist]
Note(s): First name incorrectly given as Girolamo.
Fra Teodoro del Carmine *Source(s):* GROL
Baccio, Fiorentino 1474-1539 [composer, organist, singer]
Bartolomeo (degli Organi) *Source(s):* GROL; LCAR
Bach, Heinrich (Freiherr von) 1835-1915 [composer]
Molbe, H(einrich) *Source(s):* COMP; MACM
Bach, Johann Christian 1735-1782 [composer]
Christel *Source(s):* GROL
English Bach, The *Source(s):* PSND
London Bach, The *Source(s):* BAKE; PSND; SIFA
Milan Bach, The *Source(s):* PSND; SIFA
Milanese Bach, The *Source(s):* PSND
Bach, Johann Christoph Friedrich 1732-1795 [composer]
Bückeburg Bach, The *Source(s):* BAKE; PSND; SADC
Bach, Johann Sebastian 1685-1750 [composer]
Father of Modern Piano Music, The *Source(s):* PSND
Galileo of Music, The *Source(s):* http://news.bbc.co.uk/hi/english/static/events/millennium/apr/guest2.stm (7 Oct. 2002)
Godfather of Western Music *Source(s):* http://news.bbc.co.uk/hi/english/static/events/millennium/apr/guest2.stm
Man, The *Source(s):* GROL
Note(s): Nickname used by Samuel Wesley. See also Hugo Wilhelm Friedhofer.
Newton of Music *Source(s):* http://news.bbc.co.uk/worldservice/programmes/composer.shtml (7 Oct. 2002)
Old Wig, The *Source(s):* SIFA
Our Apollo *Source(s):* GROL

Pinnacle of the Baroque *Source(s):* DESO-9
Saint Sebastian *Source(s):* GROL
Bach, Carl [or Karl] Philipp Emanuel 1714-1788 [composer]
Berlin Bach, The *Source(s):* BAKE; PSND
Father of the Sonata *Source(s):* http://www.ubmail.ubalt.edu/~pfitz/play/ref/sonatas.htm (7 Oct. 2002)
Hamburg Bach, The *Source(s):* BAKE; PSND
Bach, Michael 1958- [cellist, composer]
Bachtischa, Michael Bach *Source(s):* DOLM
Bach, Wilhelm Friedman 1710-1784 [composer]
Halle Bach, (The) *Source(s):* BAKR; SADC
Bacharach, Burt (F.) 1929- [composer, pianist]
Note(s): Portraits: EWEN; LYMN
Father of the New Sound, The *Source(s):* PSND
Legendary Tunesmith *Source(s):* CM20 p. v
Music Man of the 1970s, The *Source(s):* SIFA
Bache, Francis Edward 1833-1858 [composer, pianist]
Habec, Franz *Source(s):* CPMU
Bachimont, Henri 1864-1925 [composer]
Bresles, Henri *Source(s):* CCE39 #21731, 97 R77309; IBIM; MACM
Bachman, Martha Jean 1924- [composer, author]
Adams, Marty *Source(s):* ASCP
Nameth, Martha J. *Source(s):* ASCP
Bachmann, Erich 1926- [composer]
Masens, Piere *Source(s):* PFSA
Bachus, Wolfgang 1954- [composer]
Mr. Happy Music *Source(s):* PFSA
Bacilly, Bénigne (de) c.1625-1690 [singing teacher, composer]
B. D. B. *Source(s):* CPMU; GRV3
Bacon, Fred(erick) J. 1871-1948 [banjoist, arranger, composer]
Anderson, Ernie *Source(s):* MACE
Bacon, Mary Schell Hoke 1870-1934 [author, journalist, musician]
Bacon, Dolores *Source(s):* LCAR
Marbourg, Dolores *Source(s):* IBIM; LCAR; WORB
Bacon, Richard MacKenzie 1776-1844 [music critic]
Musical Student, A *Source(s):* CART
Bacon, W. Garwood, Jr. 1920- [composer, author, singer]
Rogers, Wayne *Source(s):* ASCP
Woods, Billy *Source(s):* CCE56 Eunp
Bacri, Edmond (David) 1920-2003 [singer, lyricist]
Marnay, Eddy [or Eddie] *Source(s):* BBDP; CCE53-56; CPOL RE-732-981
Marney, Eddy *Source(s):* CCE72-74
Badalamenti, Angelo (Daniel) 1937- [composer]
Badale, Andy *Source(s):* ASCP; CCE72-74; LCAR; MOMU
Daniel, John *Source(s):* CPOL RE-766-667
Bader, Ernst (Johannes Albert) 1914- [cabaret artist, lyricist]
Glückmann, Hans *Source(s):* CCE53 Efor19737
Note(s): Jt. pseud.: F(ranz) J(osef) Breuer.
Göhler, (Peter) *Source(s):* CCE55-58; CCE61; CCE67; CPOL RE-200-940; RIES
Heiden, Günther *Source(s):* CCE52-55
Marécheaux *Source(s):* CCE53; CCE55
Badi, Paolo Emilio mentioned 1689 [librettist]
Infecondo *Source(s):* ALMC
Note(s): See also Antonio Papi.
Umorista *Source(s):* ALMC
Badoaro, Giacomo 1602-1654 [librettist]
Assicurato, Academico Incognito *Source(s):* ALMC
Incognito *Source(s):* ALMC
Badura, Jens-Dieter 1935- [composer]
Kosta, Fred *Source(s):* PFSA
Melan, Frank *Source(s):* KOMP; PFSA
Baer, Nicolaus [composer]
Brumnitzius, Nocturnus *Source(s):* CPMS
Baganier, Janine 1924- [pianist, violinist, composer]
Anoka, Freddie *Source(s):* COHN; HIXN
Bagdasarian, Ross 1919-1972 [composer, author, actor]
Seville, David *Source(s):* ASCP; EPMU; HARR; LCAR; PEN2; ROOM; STUW
Bagge, Charles Ernest, Baron de 1722-1791 [violinist, teacher, composer]
Ernest, Charles *Source(s):* MACM
Bagliacca, Pietro Antonio [writer]
Camidio Matiaglauro *Source(s):* SONN
Matiaglauro, Camidio *Source(s):* SONN
Bahn, Adolf 1813-1882 [actor, playwright]
Prix, Adalbert *Source(s):* PIPE
Note(s): Jt. pseud.: Johann Christoph Grünbaum.
Bahr, Carlos Andrés 1902-1984 [lyricist, author]
Alfas *Source(s):* CCE49; CCE56
Bahr, Alfa *Source(s):* TODO
Bahr, Luke *Source(s):* TODO
Huerta, Juan de la *Source(s):* CCE56
Bahr, Robert 1920-1980 [composer, bandleader]
Bahr, Bert *Source(s):* OMUO
Bailey, Erastus [or Rasie] Michael 1939- [singer; songwriter]
Bailey, Razzy [or Rasie] *Source(s):* EPMU; MCCL
Bailey, Winston [or Wilston] late 1930s- [calypsonian, soca artist, composer]
Bassman, The *Source(s):* http://www.tobago.hm/gen-peop.htm (7 Oct. 2002)
Mighty Shadow *Source(s):* PEN2
Shadow *Source(s):* LCAR; http://www.tobago.hm/gen-peop.htm
Shadow, Mighty *Source(s):* PEN2
Bailleux, François 1817-1866 [composer]
B***, (Monsieur) *Source(s):* CPMU

Baine, John 1957- [poet]
Attila the Stockbroker *Source(s):* EPMU
Baines, William 1899-1922 [composer, pianist]
Note(s): Portrait: ETUP 50:3 (Mar. 1932): 160
Erich, Carl *Source(s):* CCE32 E31792; CCE61 (or 62)
Note(s): A. P. Schmidt house name; see NOTES: Erich, Carl.
Baiocchi, Regina A. Harris 1956- [author, poet, composer]
Ginann *Source(s):* LCAR; http://www.leonarda.com/compb.html (30 Oct. 2002)
Baker, Edythe Ruth 1895-1965 [pianist, composer]
Kansas City Virtuoso, The *Source(s)*: http://www.geocities.com/BourbonStreet/Delta/5253/ragtimewomen.html (7 Oct. 2002)
Baker, Harold 1914-1966 [composer, author, trumpeter]
Baker, Shorty *Source(s):* ASCP; CCE60; LCAR
Baker, James Britt 1913 (or 17)-1972 [singer; yodeler, songwriter, guitarist]
Britt, Elton *Source(s):* AMUS; EPMU; KINK; MCCL
Highest Yodeler in the World, The *Source(s):* MCCL
Sky High Yodeler, The *Source(s):* MCCL
World's Highest Yodeler, The *Source(s):* AMUS
Baker, John S. [composer]
Stamford, John J. *Source(s):* KILG
Note(s): Possible pseud.
Baker, Lee, Jr. 1933- [singer, guitarist, songwriter]
Brooks, Lonnie *Source(s):* HARS; http://www.geocities.com/bourbonstreet/delta/195/lonniebrooks-interview.html (6 Oct. 2003)
Guitar Jr. [or Junior] *Source(s):* HARS; http://www.geocities.com/bourbonstreet/delta/195/lonniebrooks-interview.html
Note(s): See also Luther Johnson, Jr.
Baker, McHouston 1925- [singer, guitarist, songwriter]
Baker, Guitar *Source(s):* EPMU; PSND
Baker, Mickey *Source(s):* HARS; PEN2; WARN
Gibson, S. *Source(s):* CCE57; CCE61
McHouston, Ed *Source(s):* HARS
Baker, Norman (Dale) 1918-2002 [composer, conductor]
Baker, Buddy *Source(s):* CCE54-55; DRSC; LCAR; PSND
Note(s): Do not confuse with trombonist Buddy Baker.
Baker, Ransford 1917- [guitarist, singer, songwriter]
Baker, Kidd *Source(s):* EPMU
Baker, Richard (Evans) 1916-1975 [composer, author, pianist]
Baker, Dick Two Ton *Source(s):* CCE54; CCE62
Baker, Two Ton *Source(s):* ASCP; CCE54
Merry Music Maker *Source(s):* LCAR

Bakfark, Bálint (Valentin) 1507-1576 [lutenist, composer]
Note(s): See LCAR for variant forms of name.
Greff Bakafart, Valentin *Source(s):* LCAR; NGDM
Little Hungarian, The *Source(s):* GROL
Wegrzynek *Source(s):* GROL
Balassoni, Luigi Paulino 1924- [drummer, composer, arranger]
Belli, Remo *Source(s):* PSND
Bellson, Louis [or Louie] (Paul) *Source(s):* EPMU; KINK; NGAM; PEN2
Blue Bells *Source(s):* JAMU
Leonardo da Vinci of the Drums, The *Source(s):* PSND
Vinci of the Drums, The *Source(s):* PSND
Balay, Guillaume 1871-1943 [composer]
Bailey, G(eorge) *Source(s):* REHH; SUPN
Note(s): Misprint on "Diadem of Gold" (Paxton 1953) (REHH).
Baldini, Guglielmo [fictitious composer]
Source(s): GROL
Baldwin, John 1946- [songwriter]
Jones, John Paul *Source(s):* CCE75; LCAR; PMUS
Note(s): See PMUS for list of songs. Also used by Joseph [or Joe] (M.) Davis.
Balenovic, Draga 1947- [singer, writer, composer]
Goldberg, Sonja *Source(s):* COHN; HIXN
Balent, Andrew 1934- [composer]
Fitzgerald, Warren *Source(s):* REHH
Rush, Leonard *Source(s):* REHH
Balestreri, Violet(ta) 1913-2000 [composer, pianist, teacher]
Archer, Violet *Source(s):* DWCO (port.); LCAR
Baline, Israel 1888-1989 [songwriter]
Note(s): Portraits: EWEN; EWPA; LYMN
All-American Composer, The *Source(s):* FACS
American Troubadour *Source(s):* Jablonski, Edward. *Irving Berlin; American Troubadour*. New York: Henry Holt, 1999.
America's Master Songwriter *Source(s):* http://www.encyclopedia.com/html/B/BerlinI1.asp (7 Oct.2002)
Note(s): See also Thomas [or Tom] Jefferson Scott.
Baline, Izzy *Source(s):* GAMM; NGAM
Berlin, Irving *Source(s):* ALMN; EPMU; GAMM; HARR; KINK; NGAM; NGDM
Dean of American Songwriters *Source(s):* PARS
King of Ragtime, The *Source(s):* PSND; SHAB p. 56; SHAD
Note(s): See also Scott Joplin.
Last of the Troubadours, The *Source(s):* PSND
May, Ren G. *Source(s):* RAGM; SPTH p. 383
Most Successful Songwriter of All Times, The *Source(s):* SPTH p. 465

Balinton, Umpeylia Marsema 1935- [singer, songwriter]
DeSanto, Sugar Pie *Source(s):* EPMU; ROOM
Little Miss Sugar Pie *Source(s):* EPMU; ROOM
Balkin, Alfred 1931- [composer, author, lyricist]
Blake, Alan *Source(s):* ASCP
Ball, David 1959- [singer, songwriter]
Human Jukebox *Source(s):* AMUS
Note(s): See also Mike Post.
Ball, Edward 1792-1873 [dramatist, librettist]
Fitzball, Edward *Source(s):* CART; GROL; LCAR; NGDO; PIPE
Terrible Fitzball, The *Source(s):* GROL; NGDO
Ball, Eric 1903-1989 [composer]
John, Walter *Source(s):* SUPN
Ball, Ernest R. 1878-1927 [composer, singer]
Note(s): Portraits: ETUP 50:3 (Mar. 1932): 160; EWEN; EWPA
American Tosti, The *Source(s):* MARC p. 347; PSND; SPTH p. 351
Christie, George *Source(s):* CCE38 R68553; CCE41 #15894, 418 R93616
Note(s): Do not confuse with George (N.) Christy [i.e., Harrington] (1827-1868).
Llab, E. R. *Source(s):* MARC p. 347; MART p. 140
Llab, Roland E. *Source(s):* CCE48 R40045; SPTH p. 334
Ball, Reginald 1943- [singer, songwriter]
Presley, Reg *Source(s):* HARR; NOMG
Ballard, Clint(on) C(onger), Jr. 1931- [composer, author, producer]
Porter, B. L. *Source(s):* ASCP
Ballard, Francis Drake 1899-1960 [composer, writer]
Note(s): Death date frequently listed incorrectly as 1926. (STUW)
Ballard, Pat *Source(s):* CCE28 E699913; CCE55; LCAR; PSND; STUW
Beal, Hefty *Source(s):* CCE57
Ballard, Louis W(ayne) 1931- [composer, author, producer]
Ergo Sum *Source(s):* CPOL PAu-1-190-534
Grand Eagle *Source(s):* GROL
Honganozhe *Source(s):* GROL
Hunka No-Zhe *Source(s):* BAKR
Miami, Joe *Source(s):* ASCP; CCE66; GROL
Sum, Ergo *Source(s):* CPOL PAu-1-190-534
Balmer, Charles 1817-1892 [organist, conductor, composer, publisher]
Berg, T. Van *Source(s):* GROL; KROH; NGAM
Lange, Charles *Source(s):* GROL; KROH; LCAR; NGAM
Leduc, Alphonse *Source(s):* GROL; KROH; LCAR; NGAM
Mayer, T. *Source(s):* GROL
Meyer, T. *Source(s):* KROH; LCAR; NGAM
Remlab, Charles *Source(s):* GROL; KROH; LCAR; NGAM
Rider, F. B. *Source(s):* KROH; LCAR; NGAM
Ryder, F. B. *Source(s):* GROL
Schumann, August *Source(s):* GROL; KROH; LCAR; NGAM
Van Berg, T. *Source(s):* LCAR
Werner, Henry *Source(s):* GOTH; GROL; KROH; LCAR; NGAM
Baltazar, Johannes ?-1501 (or 02) [composer]
Johannes le Petit *Source(s):* LCAR; NGDM
Ninot le Petit *Source(s):* LCAR; NGDM
Baltzer, Thomas c.1630-1663 [violinist, composer]
Swede, The *Source(s):* NGDM; SADC
Balzar, Eduard 1815 (or 17)-1893 [actor, playwright]
Liebold, Eduard *Source(s):* PIPE
Balzary, Michael 1962- [actor, composer]
Flea *Source(s):* LCAR; PMUS-95; SONG
Bamberger, Ludwig 1892-1969 [author]
Berger, Ludwig *Source(s):* PIPE
Gottfried, Heinrich *Source(s):* PIPE
Banash, Joseph 1910- [composer, songwriter, author]
King, J. J. *Source(s):* CCE61
King, Joseph [or Joe] *Source(s):* CCE61-65
King, Triston [or Tristan] *Source(s):* CCE41 #48668 E278378; CCE45
Nash, B. A. *Source(s):* ASCC; CCE41 #34399 Eunp266498
Banchieri, Adriano (Tomaso) 1568-1634 [organist, composer, writer]
Adriano da Bologna *Source(s):* RIES; SADC; WORB
Attabalippa del Peru *Source(s):* GROL; RIES
Note(s): On nonmusic works.
Dissonante, Il *Source(s):* BAKE; GROL; RIES
Scaligeri della Fratta, Camillo *Source(s):* BAKR; GROL; IBIM; RIES; SADC; STGR; WORB
Note(s): On nonmusic works.
Banck, Karl [or Carl] 1809 (or 11)-1899 [singing teacher, composer[
de Knapp *Source(s):* NGDM v. 16 p. 836
Serpentinus *Source(s):* DAVE; PSND
Bandeira, Manuel 1886-1968 [poet, songwriter]
Pia, Manduca *Source(s):* CCE76; http://www.jazzreview.com/cdreview.cfm?ID=2624 (1 Nov. 2002)
Bandrowski-Sas, Alexander 1860-1913 [singer, librettist, translator]
Barski, Aleksander *Source(s):* NGDM; NGDO
Brandt, Aleksander *Source(s):* NGDM; NGDO
Bánffy, (Count) (Domokoso Pál) Miklós 1874-1950 [opera director, designer, writer]
Kisbán, Miklós *Source(s):* GROL; NGDO
Myll, Ben *Source(s):* LCAR

Banks, Louis [pianist, composer]
Godfather of Jazz in India, The *Source(s):* http://www.dissidenten.com/louis (7 Oct. 2002)
Banta, Frank (Edgar) 1897-1968 [composer, pianist]
Andrews, Jimmy *Source(s):* JASG; JASN; JASR; RAGM
Kahler, Hunter *Source(s):* http://www.stompoffrecords.com/albums1300/1322.html (5 Nov. 2002)
Note(s): Possible pseud.
Bantock, Granville (Ransom) 1868-1946 [composer]
Note(s): Portraits: ETUP 50:3 (Mar. 1932): 160; EWEC; MUSQ 4:3 (1918): 333+
Graban *Source(s):* GANA p. 687; GROL; KILG; NGDO
Banwart, Jakob 1609-c.1657 [composer]
Avia, Jacob *Source(s):* GROL; NGDM
Note(s): Possible pseud.
Baptiste, John Phillip 1931- [singer, songwriter]
Phillips, Phil *Source(s):* EPMU; PSND
Barabeichik, Ishok Israelevich 1891 (or 93)-1953 [conductor, composer]
Dobrovel, Issay (Alexandrovich) *Source(s):* BAKT
Dobrowe(i)n, Issay (Alexandrovich) *Source(s):* BAKR; BAKT
Baravalle, Robert 1891- [author]
Burg, Hermann *Source(s):* WORB
Barbandt, Carl [composer]
C. B. *Source(s):* CPMU (publication date 1759-60)
Barbarino, Bartolomeo ?-after 1640 [composer]
Pesarino, Il *Source(s):* GROL; NGDM; SADC; WORB
Barbauld, Anna Laetitia (née Aikin) 1743-1825 [hymnist]
B—d *Source(s):* JULN
Barber, Herbert Hedley 1890-1931 [pianist, songwriter]
Brody, Hal *Source(s):* EPMU (see under: Strachey, Jack); GAN1; GAN2
Note(s): Also used by John [or Jack] (Francis) Strachey, Stanley Lupino [i.e., Hook], (Herbert) Desmond Carter, Harry Acres, Jack Clarke & possibly others.
Hedley, H(erbert) B(arber) *Source(s):* GAN2
Barbetta, Giulio Cesare c.1540-after 1603 [lutenist, composer]
Padoano *Source(s):* NGDM
Barbier, Frédéric E(tienne) 1829-1889 [composer]
Stephan, Moniseur *Source(s):* MELL; STGR
Barbieri, Leandro J. 1934- [saxophonist, composer]
Barbieri, Gato *Source(s):* LCAR; NGDJ; PEN2
Barbosa, Domingos Caldas 1738-1800 [librettist, poet]
Lerendo Secinantino *Source(s):* WORB
Secinuintino, Lerendo [or Lereno] *Source(s):* LCAR; LOWN
Barbosa, Lourenco da Fonseca 1904- [composer]
Capiba *Source(s):* CCE67-68; LCAR; RILM 88 06675-rr & 88-06766-bm
Barbour, Robert (MacDermot) 1910-1964 [playwright, lyricist]
MacDermot, Robert *Source(s):* CCE66; PSND
Barco, Miguel del 1938- [organist, composer]
Gallego, Miguel del *Source(s):* ORBI
Barczewski, Wolfgang 1937- [composer]
Baki, Wolf *Source(s):* KOMS; PFSA
Heymes, B. B. *Source(s):* KOMS; PFSA
Note(s): Jt. pseud.: Günther Birner.
Bardet, René [composer]
Valentini, Orlando *Source(s):* COMP
Vollenweider, Andreas *Source(s):* COMP
Bardi, Agustin 1884-1941 [violinist, pianist, composer]
Bardi, Mascotita *Source(s):* TODO
Mascotita *Source(s):* TODO
Bardi, Giovanni de, Count of Vernio 1534-1612 [literary critic, poet, playwright, composer]
Puro, Il *Source(s):* NGDM
Bare, Robert [or Bobby] (Joseph) 1935- [singer, songwriter]
Parsons, Bill *Source(s):* MCCL; NGAM
Bargon(e), (Frédéric) Charles (Pierre Edouard) 1876-1957 [librettist]
Note(s): See LCAR for nonmusic-related pseuds.
Farrère, Claude *Source(s):* LOWN; WORB
Barham, Richard Harris 1788-1845 [lyricist]
Ingoldsby, Thomas *Source(s):* BLIC; LCAR
Baring-Gould, Sabine 1834-1924 [cleric, writer, hymnist]
Note(s): Portrait: CYBH
S. B. G. *Source(s):* CART
Barkan, Stanley Howard 1936- [composer, author]
Hendrix, Sonny *Source(s):* ASCC; CCE63
Barletta, Alejandro 1925- [composer, bandoneonist]
Father of the Classical Bandoneon, The *Source(s):* http://www.ksanti.net/free-reed/history/bandoneon.html (20 May 2006)
Barnard, Charlotte Alington (née Pye) 1830-1869 [songwriter]
Note(s): Married name: Mrs. Charles Barnard. Portrait: CYBH.
Bell, (Mrs.) C. *Source(s):* CCE55
Claribel *Source(s):* BAKR; CART; CCE55; GAMM; HAMM; KILG
Barnard, D'Auvergne 1867- [composer]
Barth, Otto *Source(s):* CCE40 #25244, 1 R89024; CCE42
Clothilde *Source(s):* BALT; CCE38 R67537; CPMU
Dawson, Shiel *Source(s):* CCE44 #20615, 41 R123593
Devaux, Jules *Source(s):* CCE39 #9188, 110 R74201; CCE50 R65892 ("Scene de ballet")

Edwards, Julian *Source(s):* CCE45 #8173, 45 R135280; LCCC 1938-45 (see reference)
Note(s): Do not confuse with comic opera composer (George) Julian Edwards (1855-1910); see NOTES: Edwards, Julian.
Foster, Francis *Source(s):* CCE55 R161594 9 ("Thoughts at Eventide")
Reger, Carl *Source(s):* CCE32 R22584
Scott, Stuart *Source(s):* CCE52 R88311 ("Chant san paroles")
Tonelli, Carlo *Source(s):* CCE39 #9188, 680 R74219; CCE41 #30320, 445 R97942

Barnard, Ernest [composer]
Loreto, Vittore *Source(s):* CCE43 #15773, 303 R116997; CPMU; GOTH

Barnard, George D(aniel) 1858-1933 [composer]
Daniels, C. F. *Source(s):* CCE30 R7485 ("Estella") & CCE30 R7481 ("The Rose Waltz")
Note(s): Initial "C" may be a typographical error.
Daniels, G. F *Source(s):* REHG; SUPN; TPRF
Eaton, M. B. *Source(s):* CCE26 R35607; REHG; SUPN; TPRF
Note(s): Also used by George D. Hofmann & Will(iam H.) Scouton; see NOTES: Eaton, M. B.
Hazel, Ed(ward) *Source(s):* REHG; SUPN; TRPF
Note(s): Also used by George D. Hoffmann & William H. Scouton; see NOTES: Hazel, Ed(ward).
McQuaide, George *Source(s):* REHH; SUPN; TRPF
Russell, Edward *Source(s):* REHG; SUPN
Williams, S. H. *Source(s):* CCE28 R43776

Barnes, Clifford (Paulus) 1897-1967 [composer]
Bennett, Paul *Source(s):* CCE55-56
Britten, Roger *Source(s):* CCE55; REHG; SUPN
Eller, William *Source(s):* CCE56; CPOL RE-187-391
Fernandez, Jose *Source(s):* CCE55
Marteau, Marcel *Source(s):* CCE54-55

Barnes, Edwin Shippen 1887-1958 [composer]
Note(s): Portraits: CYBH; ETUP 50:3 (Mar. 1932): 160; MUSA 36:4 (29 July 1922): 15
Nomabama, Adam *Source(s):* TPRF
Note(s): Jt. pseud.: Thomas Tertius Nobel, Harry Alexander Matthews & John Sebastian Matthews.

Barnes, F. J. [songwriter]
Westbar, F. R. *Source(s):* OCLC 48709633
Note(s): Probable jt. pseud.: R(obert) P. Weston.

Barnes, Fae [or Faye] 1899 (or 1900)- [singer, songwriter, pianist]
Jones, Maggie *Source(s):* AMUS; GRAT; HARS
Texas Nightingale, The *Source(s):* AMUS; HARS
Note(s): See also Beulah Thomas.

Barnes, H. E. [composer]
Note(s): May be H(oward) E(llington)?
Barney, H. *Source(s):* SUPN

Barnes, H(oward) E(llington) 1909- [composer]
Note(s): Do not confuse with Howard Barnes (1929-)
Baines, Boogie *Source(s):* CCE62
Boswell, Dick *Source(s):* CCE51; CPOL RE-19-804
Note(s): Jt. pseud.: Harold (Cornelius) Fields & Joseph (Dominic) Roncoroni.
Carson, Milton *Source(s):* CCE51; CCE57; CCE59; CLTP ("Destiny"); CPOL RE-328-995
Note(s): Jt. pseud.: Harold (Cornelius) Fields & Joseph (Dominic) Roncoroni.
Clancy, Joe *Source(s):* CCE51; CPOL RE-19-019
Note(s): Jt. pseud.: Harold (Cornelius) Fields & Robert [or Bob] (Saul) Musel.
Feahy, Michael *Source(s):* CCE50-52
Note(s): Jt. pseud.: Harold (Cornelius) Fields & Joseph (Dominic) Roncoroni.
Hagen, Larry *Source(s):* CCE52; CPOL RE-32-129
Note(s): Jt. pseud.: Harold (Cornelius) Fields & Joseph (Dominic) Roncoroni.
Hollander, Hugo *Source(s):* CCE50-51; CCE56
Note(s): Jt. pseud.: Harold (Cornelius) Fields & Joseph (Dominic) Roncoroni.
Jerome, John *Source(s):* CCE51; CCE54; CCE56; CPOL RE-23-625
Note(s): Jt. pseud.: Harold (Cornelius) Fields & Joseph (Dominic) Roncoroni.
King, Garland *Source(s):* CCE52; CPOL RE-67-016
Note(s): Jt. pseud.: Harold (Cornelius) Fields & Joseph (Dominic) Roncoroni.
Kordah, Tibor *Source(s):* CCE52
Note(s): Jt. pseud.: Harold (Cornelius) Fields & Joseph (Dominic) Roncoroni.
Lawrence, Steve *Source(s):* CCE50-51
Note(s): Jt. pseud.: Harold (Cornelius) Fields & Joseph (Dominic) Roncoroni.
Leclair, Jean *Source(s):* CCE49
Note(s): Jt. pseud.: Harold (Cornelius) Fields & Joseph (Dominic) Roncoroni.
Lorraine, Sam *Source(s):* CCE56-57
Note(s): Jt. pseud.: Harold (Cornelius) Fields & Joseph (Dominic) Roncoroni.
Miguel, Guido *Source(s):* CCE51-52; CPOL RE-46-898
Note(s): Jt. pseud.: Harold (Cornelius) Fields, Joseph (Dominic) Roncoroni & William [or Bill] McGuffie.
Pasquale, Dino *Source(s):* CCE50
Note(s): Jt. pseud.: Harold (Cornelius) Fields & Joseph (Dominic) Roncoroni.
Sherman, Charles *Source(s):* CCE50-51
Note(s): Jt. pseud.: Harold (Cornelius) Fields & Joseph (Dominic) Roncoroni.
Stultz, Herman *Source(s):* CCE50-51
Note(s): Jt. pseud.: Harold (Cornelius) Fields & Joseph (Dominic) Roncoroni.

Wayne, Elmer *Source(s):* CCE54
Note(s): Jt. pseud.: Harold (Cornelius) Fields & Joseph (Dominic) Roncoroni.
Young, Charles *Source(s):* LCCC 1955-70
Note(s): Jt. pseud.: Harold (Cornelius) Fields & Joseph (Dominic) Roncoroni.

Barnet, Charles [or Charlie] (Daly) 1913-1991 [bandleader, saxophonist, composer]
Barnet, Mad Mab *Source(s):* KINK; PSND
Bennet(t), Dale *Source(s):* BBDP; MUWB

Barnett, Clara Kathleen 1844-1931 [singer, writer, composer]
Note(s): Portrait: ETUP 55:8 (Aug. 1937): 544
Doria, Clara *Source(s):* CART; COHN; GOTH; HIXN; LCAR; PSND; WORB
Rogers,.(Mrs.) Clara Kathleen *Source(s):* CLAB; COHN; HIXN; LCAR

Barnett, Jeannette [composer]
Barnes, Janet *Source(s):* GACC p. 29

Barnett, John 1802-1890 [composer]
Father of English Opera, The *Source(s):* CLAB (see under: Rogers, Clara Katheleen Barnett)
Note(s): See also Henry Purcell.

Barnett, Michael 1881-1936 [composer]
Bernard, Mike *Source(s):* JASA; JASN p. 290; JASR; SUTT
Ragtime King, The *Source(s):* RAGM
Note(s): See also Gene Greene.

Barnett, Samuel 1863-1927 [comedian, writer]
Bernard, Sam *Source(s):* GAN1; GAN2

Barnhill, Joe Bob [composer, author, arranger]
Roberts, Billy Joe *Source(s):* ASCP

Barnhouse, Charles Lloyd 1865-1929 [composer, music publisher, bandmaster]
Fisk, Jim *Source(s):* MCBD; NGAM; REHG; SMIN; SUPN
Laurens, A. M. *Source(s):* NGAM; REHG; SMIN; SUPN

Barnhum, H. B. 1936- [singer, arranger, bandleader]
Barnum Wonder Boy, The *Source(s):* PSND

Baron, Maurice 1889-1964 [composer, conductor]
Aborn, Morris *Source(s):* BAKE; LCAR
Delille, Francis *Source(s):* BAKE; LCAR
Tremblay, Alice *Source(s):* BAKE; LCAR

Baroni, Eleanora 1611-1670 [composer]
Adrianetta, L' *Source(s):* COHN; HIXN; JACK

Baroni, Vasco (Peter) 1910-1985 [composer, arranger]
Baron, Vic *Source(s):* ASCP; CCE42 #32017 Eunp299538; CCE64; CCE71 R503167

Barr, Raphael L. 1912-1983 [composer, arranger, pianist]
Barr, Ray *Source(s):* ASCP

Barra, Hotinet fl. 1510-23 [composer, singer]
Barat, Jehan *Source(s):* GROL

Barraud, Jean 1885- [composer]
Bartaud, Jean *Source(s):* BUL1

Barraza Rodríguez, Francisco Javier [singer, songwriter]
Barraza, Pancho *Source(s):* http://www.vistausa.com/portatas/Barraza.htm (5 Feb. 2005)
Barraza, Pepe *Source(s):* http://www.vistausa.com/portatas/Barraza.htm

Barre, Ernst 1843-1916 [author, jurist]
Ursinus *Source(s):* PIPE; WORB

Barrell, Edgar Alden, Jr. mentioned 1910 [composer, lyricist]
Note(s): Portraits: ETUP 50:3 (Mar. 1932): 160; MRAR (Choir ed.) (July 1901): 1
Barrell, Alden *Source(s):* TPRF
Claverley, Emmett *Source(s):* TPRF
Ferrarai, A. Fontata *Source(s):* TPRF
Janvier, Jeffreys *Source(s):* TPRF
Livingston, Audrey *Source(s):* CCE31 ("In a Canoe"); TPRF
Note(s): Also used by Ellen Cowdell.
Smith, Walter B. *Source(s):* TPRF
Williams, Vincent *Source(s):* CCE32 ("Aubade"); TPRF

Barrera, Rodolfo [singer, guitarist, songwriter]
Nava *Source(s):* HWOM

Barrett, John C(harles, Jr.) 1953- [producer, singer, songwriter]
Child, Desmond *Source(s):* CCE73; HARR

Barrett, Roger (Keith) 1946- [singer, songwriter]
Barrett, Syd *Source(s):* ALMN; AMUS; EPMU; HARR; PEN2

Barrett, Stephen 1855- [songwriter, singer, businessman]
Barrett, Lester *Source(s):* GAN2 (see under: Stuart, Leslie)

Barrett, Thomas Augustine 1864-1928 [composer]
Note(s): Portraits: GAN2; http://www.fullerswood.fsnet.co.uk/stuart (21 Oct. 2002)
Stuart, Leslie *Source(s):* GAN2; GREN, HARR; KILG; KINK; LCAR; MUWB; NGDM
Thomas, Lester *Source(s):* CPMU; GREN; KILG; LCAR

Barrier, Eric 1963- [rapper]
B., Eric *Source(s):* LCAR
Eric B *Source(s):* EPMU

Barros (Caraballo), Alberto 1957- [trombonist, singer, composer]
Note(s): Do not confuse with Alberto Borges de Barros (1917-)
Conejo, El *Source(s):* EPMU

Barrow, Jama(a)l 1979- [songwriter]
Shyne *Source(s):* LCAR; PMUS-00

Barry, Charles Ainslie 1830-1915 [writer on music, composer]
C. A. B. *Source(s):* GRV3
Barson, Ben [songwriter]
Boilerhouse *Source(s):* CPOL PA-683-585; SONG
Note(s): Jt. pseud.: Andy Dean & Ben Wolff.
Barstow, Norah Lee Haymond Bradley 1898-1941 [composer]
Lee, Norah *Source(s):* ASCC
Barthe, Grat-Norbert 1828-1898 [composer]
Barthe, A(drien) *Source(s):* LCAR; STGR
Barthélemon, Maria (née Young) c.1749-1799 [composer, singer]
Barthélemon, Polly *Source(s):* DWCO
Barthelson, (Helen) Joyce (Holloway) 1900-1986 [composer]
Bartlett, John *Source(s):* CCE74
Dickinson, Richard *Source(s):* CCE59 E131485; CCE61 E156404; CPOL RE-353-096
Note(s): Jt. pseud.: Walter (Charles) Ehret.
Drake, Janet *Source(s):* CCE62 E162273; CCE63 E170546
Note(s): Jt. pseud.: Walter (Charles) Ehret.
Martin, Jean *Source(s):* CCE57 E106595; CCE60 E146280 & E139122; CCE63 E172264
Note(s): Jt. pseud.: Walter (Charles) Ehret. "Descant High; Descant Low," "Big Rock Candy Mountain," "More Descants High and Low." Also used by Marcel Stellman.
Norman, William *Source(s):* CCE70s?
Bartles, Alfred Howell 1930- [composer, author, violoncellist]
Howell, Gene Mac *Source(s):* ASCP; LCAR
Bartók, Béla 1881-1945 [composer]
Aldebaran *Source(s):* OCLC #30372531
Nyugat *Source(s):* RILM 77-05072-ap
Bartoli, Amedeo mentioned 1917-25 [composer]
Barmede, Atoli *Source(s):* MELL; STGR; WORB
Tobarmè, Adelio *Source(s):* MELL; STGR
Bartoli, Erasmo 1606-1656 [composer, singer]
Padre Raimo *Source(s):* GROL
Raimo, (Padre) *Source(s):* GROL; NGDM
Bartolomeo (Torre), Carlo mentioned 1674 [librettist]
Rorobella, Marco Ettore *Source(s):* GROL
Barton, Ben 1900-1989 [composer]
Bruce, Gary *Source(s):* ASCP; CCE56; CCE59; CCE67; CPOL RE-48-829
Barton, Bernard 1784-1849 [hymnist]
Note(s): Portrait: CYBH
Quaker Poet, The *Source(s):* CYBH; GOTT; JULN; ROGG
Barton, Billy [songwriter]
Grimes, B. *Source(s):* PMUS
Barton, Horace Percival 1872-1951 [organist, composer]
Kleinjan *Source(s):* http://sacomposers.up.ac.za/barton_horace.htm (26 July 2005)
Bartzsch, Franz 1947- [composer]
Matthi, Daniel *Source(s):* KOMS; PFSA
Baruch, Löb 1786-1837 [author]
Baruch, Louis *Source(s):* LCAR; PIPE
Börne, Ludwig *Source(s):* LCAR; PIPE
Baryphonus, Henricus 1580 (or 81)-1655 [writer on music, composer]
Grobstimm, Heinrich *Source(s):* IBIM; NGDM; WORB
Pipegrop, Heinrich *Source(s):* IBIM; NGDM; WORB
Bascomb, Wilbur Odell 1916-1972 [trumpeter, bandleader, composer]
Bascomb, Dud *Source(s):* AMUS; EPMU
Basevi, Marco [composer]
Marco, Leo de *Source(s):* STGR
Basie, William (Allen) 1904-1984 [pianist, bandleader, arranger]
Bailey, Bill *Source(s):* JAMU
Basie, Count *Source(s):* EPMU; KINK; NGAM; PEN2; PSND; SHAD; VACH
Charming, Prince *Source(s):* JAMU
Holy Main, The *Source(s):* PSND
Jump King, The *Source(s):* PSND
Kid from Red Bank, The *Source(s):* VACH
Prince Charming *Source(s):* JAMU
Basile, Adriana Baroni c.1580-1640 [guitarist, harpist, singer, composer]
Bella Adriana, La *Source(s):* MWP3
Basile, Giovanni Battista [or Giambattista] 1566-1632 [poet, writer, librettist]
Abbattutis, Gian Alesio *Source(s):* GROL; PIPE
Pigro, Il *Source(s):* GROL
Basile, Gloria Vitanza 1929- [author, composer]
Morgan, McKayla (K.) *Source(s):* CCE59; PSND
Morgan, Michaela (K.) *Source(s):* CCE60; CCE62; PSND
Basquiet, Jean Michel 1960- [artist, composer]
Rammelzee *Source(s):* EPMU
Bassani, Giovanni Battista c.1650-1716 [composer]
Morte *Source(s):* ALMC
Bassano, Lodovico ?-1593 [lutenist, composer]
Lo *Source(s):* NGDM
Lodwick, Mr. *Source(s):* NGDM
Basselin, Olivier 1350?-1418 [poet]
Anacreon of His Day, The *Source(s):* PSND
Father of Bacchanalian Poetry, The *Source(s):* PSND
Father of the Vaudeville, The *Source(s):* PSND
French Drunken Barnaby *Source(s):* PSND
Joyous Father of the Vaudeville, The *Source(s):* PSND
Pere Joyeux du Vaudeville, Le *Source(s):* PSND

Basset, Charles 1822-1869 [librettist]
Adrien-Robert B. *Source(s):* MELL
Robert, Adrian *Source(s):* LCAR; WORB
Bassford, William Kipp [or Kapp] 1839-1902 [composer, pianist, organist]
Basswood, W. K. *Source(s):* DIEH
Bassi, Ercole [librettist]
Vasai, Ercole *Source(s):* MELL
Bastar, Francisco Angel 1936-1994 [percussionist, bandleader, composer]
Kako *Source(s):* EPMU; PEN2; ROOM
Baste, Eugène Pierre 1810-1887 [librettist]
Grangé, Eugène *Source(s):* LCAR; MELL
Basterra, Horatio 1914-1957 [poet, lyricist]
Sanguinetti, Horacio *Source(s):* TODO
Bastida, Gustavo Adolfo Dominguez 1836-1870 [author, poet, translator]
Bécquer, Gustavo Adolfo *Source(s):* LCAR
Dominguez Bastida, Gustavo Adolfo *Source(s):* LCAR
Rodríguez, Adolfo *Source(s):* LOWN; PIPE
Note(s): Jt. pseud.: Ramón Rodríguez Correa.
Bastini, Vincentio c.1529-1591 [composer]
Vincenzo di Pasquino *Source(s):* NGDM
Batchelder, James [composer]
Note(s): Probably James Carroll Batchelder (1850-), singer, teacher, song-composer.
Gordon, Hope *Source(s):* CPMU
Bate, (Rev.) Henry 1745-1824 [writer]
Dudley, (Sir) Henry Bate *Source(s):* LCAR; SONN
Bates, (Otha) Ellas [or Elias] 1928- [singer, songwriter, guitarist]
500 Per Cent More Man *Source(s):* HARS; PSND
Black Gladiator, The *Source(s):* HARS; PSND
Bo Diddley *Source(s):* LCAR
Diddley, Bo *Source(s):* ALMN; AMUS; CASS; CM03; EPMU; HARD; HARS; PSND
McDaniel, Ellas [or Elias] *Source(s):* ALMN; CASS; CM03; EPMU; HARD; HARS; PSND
Note(s): Name change when adopted c.1934.
Mister Jungle Man *Source(s):* CASS
Originator, The *Source(s):* ALMN
Bates, J. [composer]
Setab, J. *Source(s):* CPMU (publication date 1803)
Bates, Kathleen Doyle 1948- [composer, author, singer]
Bates, Bobo *Source(s):* ASCP
Bates, Leon 1960- [pianist, composer]
Bates, Django *Source(s):* AMUS; EPMU; LCAR
Bates, William fl. c.1750-80 [composer, singer, teacher]
Catch, Jack *Source(s):* LCAR; NGDM; STGR
Bath, John 1915-2004 [composer, editor]
Barnett, John *Source(s):* MCCA

Báthory-Kitsz, Dennis 1949- [composer, photographer]
Note(s): For pseuds. used on commercial and technical works, see: http://www.maltedmedia.com/people/bathory/bathres.html#psc (5 Mar. 2006)
Cowell, D. B. *Source(s):* DOLM
Denes, Báthory *Source(s):* DOLM
Gesamte, Kalvos *Source(s):* DOLM
Kynans, Brady *Source(s):* DOLM
Maussade, Orra *Source(s):* DOLM
Shadé, Grey *Source(s):* http://www.maltedmedia.com/people/bathory/bathres.html#psc
Zondrios, Kalvos *Source(s):* DOLM
Bathurst, William Hiley 1796-1877 [poet, hymnist]
Note(s): Portrait: CYBH
Bath *Source(s):* JULN
W. H. B. *Source(s):* PSND
Batka, Otto Barry 1906-1966 [pianist, composer, arranger]
Barry, Otto *Source(s):* OMUO
Baton, René 1879-1940 [conductor, composer]
Note(s): Portrait: ETUP 55:6 (June 1937): 356
Rhené-Baton *Source(s):* BAKO; CPMU; GREN; MACM
Batt, David 1958- [singer, songwriter, guitarist]
Sylvian, David *Source(s):* NOMG
Batt, Malcolm John [composer]
Malcolm, John *Source(s):* CCE54; MUWB; RFSO
Battavio, Margaret 1948- [songwriter]
March, Little Peggy *Source(s):* EPMU; ROOM
Batteau, Dwight Wayne, Jr. 1948- [composer, singer]
Batteau, Robin *Source(s):* ASCP; CPOL PA-191-180
Battle, Edgar (William) 1907-1977 [instrumentalist, composer, arranger]
Battle, Puddinghead *Source(s):* AMUS
Battle, Roger *Source(s):* CCE67
Battu, Léon 1829-1857 [librettist]
Dubois, Jules *Source(s):* LOWN; MELL
Note(s): Jt. pseud.: Michel Carré (the elder).
Batty, Christopher 1715-1797 [hymnist]
C. B. *Source(s):* LCAR; PSND
Bauch, Ludwig Julius 1811-1879 [actor, playwright]
Julius, Ludwig [or Louis] *Source(s):* PIPE
Bauchwitz, Peter 1953- [composer]
Bancroft(-Price), Peter *Source(s):* KOMS; PFSA
Baudouin, Jean Marie Theodore [librettist]
Aubigny, (B(audouin)) d' *Source(s):* LCAR; STGR
Bauer, Alfons 1920- [composer]
Kraus, Fritz *Source(s):* CCE60-62; KOMP; PFSA
Bauer, Emilie Frances 1865 (or 67)-1926 [pianist, critic, editor, composer]
DiNogero, Francesco [or Francisco] *Source(s):* COHN; HIXN

Manolito, E. *Source(s):* CCE44 #26477, 1117 R125911
Nogero, Francesco [or Francisco] di *Source(s):* AMME; COHN; HIXN
Bauer, Julius 1853-1941 [author]
Bauer, Gyula *Source(s):* PIPE
Spavento, Don *Source(s):* PIPE
Bäuerle, (Andreas) Adolf 1786-1859 [author, playwright]
Horn, Otto *Source(s):* PIPE; WORB
Bauernfeld, Eduard von 1802-1890 [playwright, poet]
Rusticocampius, Feld *Source(s):* LCAR
Baughman, Leon Everette 1948- [singer, songwriter]
Everette, Leon *Source(s):* AMUS; MCCL
Baumann, Eric 1962- [composer]
Loh, F(erdinand) *Source(s):* OCLC 43192137
Baumbach, Rudolf 1840-1905 [author]
Bach, Paul *Source(s):* PIPE; WORB
Baumgardtner, Claude Chalmers 1883-1942 [journalist, songwriter]
Coxie *Source(s):* PSND
Baungros, Irene [composer]
Hale, (Mrs.) Philip *Source(s):* EBEL; MACM
Renné, Victor *Source(s):* EBEL; MACM
Bawden, William Carlile 1857- [composer]
Vernon, Carlile *Source(s):* MACM
Bawr, Alexandrine Sophie de 1733-1860 [pianist, author, singer, composer]
Baur, Mme. de *Source(s):* COHN; HIXN
François, M. *Source(s):* COHN; HIXN
M***, *** *Source(s):* LCAR
Madame *** *Source(s):* LCAR
Madame de B*** *Source(s):* LCAR
Saint-Simon, Comtesse de *Source(s):* COHN; HIXN
Bax, (Sir) Arnold Edward Trevor 1883-1953 [composer, author]
Note(s): Portraits: MUOP 51:608 (May 1928): 789; MUSA 35:26 (Apr. 1922): 5
Diarmid *Source(s):* LCAR; ROOM
McDermott, Dermot *Source(s):* ROOM
Musician, A *Source(s):* CART
O'Byrne, Dermot *Source(s):* CART; GOTH; GOTT; GROL; NGDM; ROOM
Note(s): On literary works.
Baxter, Clarice Howard 1898-1972 [songwriter]
Baxter, Ma *Source(s):* PSND; SGMA (port.)
Baxter, J(essie) R(andall), (Jr.) 1887-1960 [songwriter]
Baxter, Pap *Source(s):* PSND
Baycock, Frederick 1913-1970 [organist, producer, composer]
Bayer, Frederick *Source(s):* MUWB
Boyce, Frederick *Source(s):* MUWB
Desslyn, Guy *Source(s):* MUWB
Field, William *Source(s):* MUWB
Bayer, Johann Gottfried Eduard 1822-1908 [guitarist, composer]
Caroli, A. *Source(s):* KOBW; http://www.tabulatura.com/spguac.htm (13 Apr. 2005)
Bayer, Karl ?-1888 [librettist]
Ruff, Karl *Source(s):* STGR
Bayly, (Nathaniel) Thomas Haynes 1795 (or 97)-1839 [novelist, songwriter]
B *Source(s):* CART
Mortimer, Philip *Source(s):* KILG ("She Wore a Wreath of Roses")
Note(s): Jt. pseud.?: Joseph Philip Knight.
Q in the Corner *Source(s):* CART; GOTT; LCAR; PSND
T. H. B. *Source(s):* CART
Bazan, David [singer, songwriter, guitarist]
Pedro the Lion *Source(s):* http://members.tripod.com/~thrust_2/april=01.html (7 Oct. 2002)
Bazelon, Irwin (A.) 1922-1995 [composer]
Bazelon, Buddy *Source(s):* LCAR
Graham, Budd *Source(s):* CCE65-66; CPOL RE-613-915; LCAR
Bazylik, Cyprjan [or Cyprian] c.1535-c.1600 [writer, poet, composer, printer]
Basilicus, Ciprianus *Source(s):* NGDM
Ciprianos Sieranensis *Source(s):* NGDM
Cyprian z Sieradza *Source(s):* LCAR; NGDM
Beach, Albert A(skew) 1924-1997 [composer, lyricist]
Wilson, Lee *Source(s):* ASCP; CCE55-56; CPOL RE-181-132; PMUS
Beach, Priscilla A. [composer]
Beach, Alden *Source(s):* COHN; HIXN
Beale, (Thomas) Willert 1828-1894 [composer, lawyer, writer on music]
Maynard, Walter *Source(s):* BROW, CART; CPMU; GOTH; LCAR; WORB
Beals, Ella Middaugh 1856- [writer on music, teacher]
Clarke, Helena *Source(s):* MACM
Beard, Leslie Lois 1950- [composer, author, singer]
Chain, Leslie *Source(s):* ASCP; CPOL PAu-6-431
Beaser, Norma Jean 1938- [singer, songwriter]
Norma Jean *Source(s):* AMUS
Beau, Henry John 1911-1987 [composer, arranger]
Beau, Heinie *Source(s):* ASCP
Beauharnais, Hortense Eugénie de 1783-1837 [author, composer]
Hortense, Queen, consort of Louis Bonaparte, King of Holland *Source(s):* LCAR
Hortense reine de Hollande *Source(s):* DWCO (port.); WORB
Reine Hortense, La *Source(s):* GRV3
Beaulieu, Donald George 1939- [composer, author]

Baloo, Sam (Spunky) *Source(s):* ASCP
Beaulieu, Sam *Source(s):* CPOL PAu-25-064
Beaulieu, Maurice Joseph 1920-1978 [composer, banjoist, guitarist]
Bolyer, Maurice Joseph *Source(s):* BUL3
King of the Banjo *Source(s):* CANE
Beaume, (Louis) Alexandre [or Alexander] 1827-1909 [librettist]
Beaumont, Alexandre [or Alexander] *Source(s):* GAN1; GAN2; GOTH; LCAR
Beaumont, (Captain) Alex(ander) S. 1848-1913 [patron of the arts, composer, publisher]
Woolhouse, Charles *Source(s):* MUWB
Beausseron, Giovanni [or Johannes] ?1475-1542 [composer]
Bonnevin, Giovanni [or Johannes] *Source(s):* GROL; WORB
Beck, Franz Ignaz 1734-1809 [composer, conductor, violinist, organist]
Dissepolo di Stamitz *Source(s):* NGDM
Beck, Johann Baptist 1881-1943 [musicologist]
Beck, Jean *Source(s):* LCAR; NGAM
Becker, Adolf 1870-1941 [composer]
Ballini *Source(s):* SUPN
Becker, Frank 1963- [composer]
Velhagen, Roger *Source(s):* KOMP; PFSA
Becker, Karl Heinz 1917-1988 [composer]
Ralphs, H. *Source(s):* CCE62; KOMP; PFSA
Becker, Tobias 1958- [composer]
Noiz, Nick *Source(s):* PFSA
Svensson *Source(s):* KOMS; PFSA
Becker, Werner 1943- [composer]
Ventura, Anthony *Source(s):* PFSA
Beckhard, Robert L. 1917- [composer]
Collins, Walter *Source(s):* CCE52-55; CPOL RE-181-265
Dawson, Mark *Source(s):* CCE53-55; CPOL RE-30-384
Dawson, Robert L. *Source(s):* CCE56
Gray, Philip *Source(s):* CCE53-58; CCE59-63; CPOL RE-30-375
Note(s): Also used by Jess Perlman.
Holmes, Lee *Source(s):* CCE52-55; CCE57-58; CPOL RE-100-675
Palmer, Edward *Source(s):* CCE57; CCE59-60
Roberts, Carl *Source(s):* CCE58-59
Scott, Frederic C. *Source(s):* CCE58
Snow, Daniel *Source(s):* CCE56; CCE58
Stevens, Paul *Source(s):* CCE54-61; CPOL RE-181-227
Stevens, Philip *Source(s):* CCE53-56
Stone, Peter *Source(s):* CCE52-60; CCE62-64; CPOL RE-5-567
Stone, Robert L. *Source(s):* Source not recorded
Townsend, Mark *Source(s):* CCE52-61; CPOL RE-30-374
Beckwith, John (Christmas) 1750-1809 [composer, organist]
Beckwith, Christmas *Source(s):* LCAR; NGDM
Beckwith of Norwich, Dr. *Source(s):* GOTH
Beddie, George 1857- [musician, composer, journalist]
Delamaine, Charles L. *Source(s):* IBIM; WORB
Beddome, Benjamin 1717-1795 [hymnist, composer]
Note(s): Portrait: CYBH
B. B. *Source(s):* JULN
Bedyngham, Johannes [or John] ?-1459? [composer]
Longstrides *Source(s):* DEA3
Beeks, Clarence 1922-1981 [singer, composer]
King Pleasure *Source(s):* CCE64; LCAR; PSND
Beer, Friedrich 1794-1838 [composer]
Berr, Friedrich *Source(s):* LCAR; REHG
Beer, Gustav(e) 1888-1954 [author, playwright]
Wheatley, G. W. *Source(s):* LCAR; PIPE; WORB
Beer, Jakob Liebmann 1791-1864 [composer]
Billig, Julius *Source(s):* PIPE; Warrach, John. *Carl Maria von Weber.* 2nd ed. Cambridge: Cambridge University Press, 1976, p. 104
Note(s): Also used by (Jacob) Gottfried Weber.
Father of Grand Opera *Source(s):* MUWB
Meyerbeer, Giacomo *Source(s):* BAKO; NGDM; NGDO
Philodikaios *Source(s):* PIPE; Warrach, p. 104
Note(s): Also used by (Jacob) Gottfried Weber.
Beer, Johann 1652 (or 55)-1700 [author, composer; conductor]
Bähr, Johann *Source(s):* LCAR; WORB
Behrens, Johann *Source(s):* LCAR; WORB
Expertus Rupertus Ländler, bauer von Adlersee *Source(s):* LCAR
Jucundus Jucudissimus *Source(s):* LCAR
Rebhu, Jan *Source(s):* BAUE; LCAR; PSNN
Sambelle, Francisco *Source(s):* PSNN
Ursinus, (Johann) *Source(s):* LCAR; RIEM; WORB
Ursus *Source(s):* BAKE; MACM; RIEM
Willenhag, Wolfgang von *Source(s):* BAUE; PSNN
Zendorius a Zendoriis *Source(s):* BAUE; PSNN
Beer, Otto Fritz 1910- [journalist, novelist, translator, music critic]
Ronnert, Erik *Source(s):* KOMU
Beethoven, Ludwig van 1770-1827 [composer]
Beethovenian *Source(s):* EPON
Best of the Bonn Boys *Source(s):* DESO-9
Creator, The *Source(s):* PSND
Father of Romanticism *Source(s):* MUWB
Great Mogul of Music, The *Source(s):* PSND
Man Who Freed Music, The *Source(s):* PSND
Rodomant *Source(s):* PSND
Spangol, Der *Source(s):* PSND
Spangy *Source(s):* PSND
Spaniard, The *Source(s):* PSND

Beffroy de Reigny, Louis Abel 1757-1811 [playwright, author, composer]
Cousin Jacques *Source(s):* CPMU; GROL; LCAR; NGDM; NGDO; PIPE; SONN; STGR
Le Cousin-Jacques *Source(s):* LCAR
Begleiter, Lionel 1930-1999 [composer, lyricist]
Bart, Lionel *Source(s):* ALMN; EPMU; GAMM; GAN1; GAN2; LCAR; PEN2
Nebbish, Ocher *Source(s):* EPMU (see under: Cogan, Alma)
Behm, Eduard 1862-1946 [composer]
Draude, M. B. *Source(s):* COMP; HEIN; KOBW
Edwards, Rolf *Source(s):* COMP; HEIN; KOBW
Behr, F(ranz) 1837-1898 [composer]
Aachen, Hans von *Source(s):* GREN
Bachmann, Georges *Source(s):* BAKR; MACM; REHG; SUPN
Cooper, William *Source(s):* BAKR; BALT; MACM; SUPN; TPRF; WORB
Note(s): Also used by Will(iam Cooper) Glenn.
D'Orso, Francesco *Source(s):* TPRF
Godard, Charles *Source(s):* CPMU; TPRF
Morely, Charles BAKR; ETUD; MACM; SUPN; TPRF; WORB
Orso, Francesco d' *Source(s):* BAKR; BALT; REHH; SUPN; WORB
Smith, Edwin *Source(s):* CPMU; GOTH; GREN
Note(s): Do not confuse with Edwin Smith, publications 1950-54 (London: Novello).
Behunin, Les(lie Merrill, Jr.) 1936- [composer, guitarist]
Merrill, Buddy *Source(s):* ASCP
Merrill, Les *Source(s):* CCE74
Beiderbecke, Leon Bismark 1903-1931 [cornetist, composer]
Beiderbecke, Bix *Source(s):* BAKR; LCAR
Beil, Peter 1937- [composer]
Karrasch, Tom *Source(s):* CCE68; KOMP; KOMS; PFSA
Beissel, Konrad ?-1768 [philosopher]
Friedsamer, (Konrad) *Source(s):* CPMU; WORB
Peysel, Conrad *Source(s):* WORB
Bekker, Okko 1947- [composer]
Kahn, Tro *Source(s):* KOMP; KOMS; PFSA
Belafonte, Harold [or Harry] (George) 1927- [singer, songwriter, actor]
Bell, Raymond *Source(s):* CCE61; CCE63; CPOL RE-441-009; LCAR
Restless Troubadour, The *Source(s):* PSND
Thomas, Harry *Source(s):* CCE53-54; CPOL RE-88-051
Note(s): Jt. pseud.: Millard Thomas. Also used by Reginald Thomas Broughton.
Belasco, David 1853-1931 [actor, playwright]
James, David *Source(s):* PIPE; WORB

Belcher, Frank H. [songwriter]
Note(s): Dates possibly 1869-1947.
Roma *Source(s):* BLIC; CPMU (publication dates 1895-99)
Belcher, Supply 1752-1836 [composer, tunebook compiler]
Handel(l) of Maine, The *Source(s):* GROL; PSND
Belgiojoso, Baldassare de ?-1587 [violinist, composer]
Baltazarini (da Beligioiso) *Source(s):* LCAR; NGDM
Beaujoyeux, Balthasar de *Source(s):* LCAR; NGDM
Bélime, Jean 1891-1976 [writer on music, composer]
Coeuroy, André *Source(s):* BAKO; BUL1; LCAR; NGDM
Bell, Nancy R. E. Meugens ?-1933 [writer on music]
Anvers, N. d' *Source(s):* SEND
D'Anvers, N. *Source(s):* SEND
Bell, Vincent [or Vinnie] [guitarist; arranger]
Spaceman Vinnie *Source(s):* *Guitar Player* 31:326:1 (Feb. 1997): 33
Superguitarist *Source(s):* *Guitar Player* 31:326:1 (Feb. 1997): 33
Bellak, James fl. 1849-1864 [composer]
Bellak, Ja's *Source(s):* LCAR
Bellak, James Blumtal [composer, author]
Blumtal, James *Source(s):* PSND
Bellard, Mary Rosezla 1971- [accordionist, singer, songwriter]
Ledet, Rosie *Source(s):* LCAR
Sweetheart of Zydeco, The *Source(s):* http://www.satchmo.com/nolavl/noladir.htm (6 Oct. 2002)
Bellec, Alain 1925 (or 35)- [composer, lyricist]
Barriere, Alain *Source(s):* CCE62; PSNN
Belline, Mary L. 1920- [composer, author]
Bell, Louise *Source(s):* ASCP; CCE58
Bello, Circo 1869- [composer]
Clirb, Eolo *Source(s):* MELL
Bellucci Laslandra, Mario 1902- [musicologist]
Macculi, Libero *Source(s):* WORB
Bellusci, Anthony [or Tony] (J.) 1936- [singer, accordionist, songwriter]
Bellus, Tony *Source(s):* CCE59-60; EPMU
Belobersycky, Paul Rennée 1972- [singer, songwriter]
Brandt, Paul *Source(s):* CM22; EPMU; LCAR
Belville, Edward 1858-1929 [composer]
Jakobowsky [or Jakobowski], Edward *Source(s):* GAN2; GOTH; GREN; MARC; MELL
Ben-Yaacov, Gabriel 1923-1948 [composer]
Jacobson, Gabriel *Source(s):* BUL1
Benatzky, Rudolf Josef Frantisek 1884-1957 [composer, lyricist]
Benatzky, Ralph *Source(s):* CASS; GAMM; GAN2

Bender, Erich 1913- [composer, conductor]
Pallet, Christian *Source(s):* CCE73-74
Pallet, Olaf *Source(s):* CCE76
Skalden, Olaf *Source(s):* CCE76; KOMP; KOMS; PFSA
Bender, Peter 1943- [composer]
Wyoming, Pete *Source(s):* KOMS; PFSA
Bendl, Karel 1838-1897 [composer, conductor]
Bendelssohn *Source(s):* GROL
Podskalsky, Karel *Source(s):* GDRM; GROL
Benedetti, Pietro c.1585-1649 [composer, journalist]
Invaghito, (L') *Source(s):* GROL; IBIM; WORB
Note(s): See also Tomasso Pecci & Mariano Tantucci.
Benedict, Julius 1804-1885 [conductor, composer, author]
Maledünntus Wagner, der Weberjunge *Source(s):* APPL p. 12
Bénédictus, Louis 1850- [composer]
Grallon, Bihn *Source(s):* WHIT
Note(s): Possible pseud.
Beneš, Jára 1897-1949 [composer]
Brandt, Peter *Source(s):* KOMU
Beneš, Karel Josef 1896-1969 [author]
Jizersky, Karel *Source(s):* PIPE
Benitez, John 1957- [singer, songwriter]
Benitez, Jellybean *Source(s):* PSND; WARN
Jellybean *Source(s):* LCAR
Benitez, José Antonio [composer, songwriter]
Adrián, (P.) *Source(s):* HWOM
Benjamin, Arthur 1893-1960 [composer, pianist]
Brisbane, Alan *Source(s):* MUWB
Starstruck *Source(s):* MUWB
Benjamin, Walter 1892-1940 [author]
Ackerman, A. *Source(s):* WORB
Ardor *Source(s):* PIPE; WORB
Bei, Anni M. *Source(s):* WORB
Conrad, C. *Source(s):* WORB
Holz, Detlef *Source(s):* LCAR; WORB
Mabinn, E. J. *Source(s):* WORB
Pan-ya-ming *Sources(s):* LCAR
Stemflinger, K. A. *Source(s):* WORB
Bennert, Julius Eduard 1856- [musicologist]
Schleicher, Erasmus *Source(s):* WORB
Bennet, C(harles) W(illiam) 1849-1926 [composer]
Harold, Fr. *Source(s):* CCE42 #24219, 121 R106724; TPRF
Bennet, Emile J. [arranger]
E. J. B. *Source(s):* CPMU (publication date 1923)
Bennet, Théodore 1841-1886 [pianist, composer]
Ritter, Théodore *Source(s):* BAKO; BALT; CPMU; GOTH; MACM; MELL
Bennett, David (D.) 1892-1990 [composer]
North, Norman *Source(s):* CCE68; REHG; SUPN
Bennett, Emma Marie 1824-1895 [pianist, writer, composer]
Brissac, Jules *Source(s):* COHN, CPMU; DWCO; GOTH; GROL; HIXN
MacFarren, Mrs. John *Source(s):* COHN; DWCO; GROL; HIXN
Bennett, Harry Rodney 1890-1948 [poet, lyricist]
Barrie, Royden *Source(s):* CCE51 R73634 ("I Heard You Singing"); KILG; LAST
Bennett, J. S. L(ionel) D. [arranger, composer]
Dampier, L. *Source(s):* CPMU; GOTT
Bennett, Theron C(atlin) 1879-1937 [composer]
Note(s): Portrait: JASA
Barney and Seymore *Source(s):* JASA; LCAR; PERF
Cross, R. L. *Source(s):* RAGM ("Bud Ray")
Note(s): Possible pseud.
Florence, George E. *Source(s):* JASA; PERF; RAGM
Raymond, Bruce *Source(s):* JASN
Bennett, William Cox 1820-1895 [songwriter]
Song-Writer, A. *Source(s):* CART
Bennett, William Sterndale 1816-1875 [composer]
English Mendelssohn, The *Source(s):* ETUP 50:4 (Apr. 1932): 236 (port.)
Benny, Benjamin Michel 1919-1975 [trumpeter, composer]
Harris, Benny *Source(s):* LCAR
Harris, Little Benny *Source(s):* NGDJ
Little Benny *Source(s):* LCAR
Benoit, Camille 1851-1923 [composer, writer on music]
Claes, Balthazar *Source(s):* GROL
Benoit, Pierre Léonard Léopold 1834-1901 [composer, conductor, teacher]
Note(s): Portrait: ETUP 50:4 (Apr. 1932): 236
Benoit, Peter *Source(s):* PSND
Benskin, Anthony [librettist, composer]
Rhesus *Source(s):* MUWB
Benzin, Winfried 1925- [composer]
Zimmermann, Winfried *Source(s):* KOMS; PFSA
Beolco, Angelo c.1502-1542 [playwright, actor, songwriter]
Ruz(z)ante *Source(s):* LCAR; NGDM
Berbert, Edith [songwriter]
Burt, Ed *Source(s):* HORS
Berckman, Evelyn Domenica 1900-1978 [author, composer]
Wade, Joanna *Source(s):* PSND
Berdan, Harry B. [songwriter]
Braisted, Harry *Source(s):* CCE25 R32063; SPTH p. 293
Berg, Christopher 1949- [composer, pianist]
American Hugo Wolf *Source(s):* http://www.daringdiva.com/cat/PnBi3.html (7 Oct. 2002)
Berg, George c.1730-c.1770 [composer, organist]
Scotland, John *Source(s):* CPMU ("Lightly Tread")

Note(s): Possible pseud.? In OCLC 43201004: "John Scotland" is sometimes attributed to Purcell; however, Franklin B. Zimmerman, in his *Henry Purcell; An Analytical Catalogue of His Music* (London Macmillan, 1963), ascribes the work to Michael Wise.

Berg, Samuli Kustaa 1803-1852 [author]
Kallio *Source(s):* LCAR

Bergen, A. [librettist]
George, Wilh. *Source(s):* STGR

Berger, Albin 1955- [composer]
Manoa, Chris *Source(s):* PFSA

Berger, Henry 1844-1929 [composer, conductor]
Hawaiian Musikmeister, The *Source(s):* SIFA

Berger, Karl Philipp 1793-1853 [singer, playwright]
Lattner, K. Ph. *Source(s):* PIPE; WORB

Bergersen, Edith 1925- [writer on music]
Baldwin, Edda *Source(s):* CCE51-52
Borroff, (Mrs.) Edith *Source(s):* NGDM

Bergh, Arthur 1882-1962 [violinist, conductor, composer]
Note(s): Do not confuse with Arthur F. Bergh (1912-); see next entry. Portrait: ETUP 50:4 (Apr. 1932): 236.
Arthur, Gerald *Source(s):* CCE19 E444123; CCE46 R10740
Gordon, Curtis *Source(s):* CCE19 E444666; CCE48 R25852 ("Go to It")
Hampton, Roxanne *Source(s):* CCE52 R92187 ("Dark Hawaiian Eyes")
Note(s): Also used by Joseph [or Joe] (M.) Davis.
Hill, A. L. *Source(s):* CCE19 E458091
Hill, Arthur (M.) *Source(s):* CCE47 R16316 ("Far East"); CCE50 R59648 ("Say It with Kindness")
Lamont, A. B. *Source(s):* CCE48 R34154 ("Rose of Atholone")
Peck, Gerald *Source(s):* CCE19 E458551; CCE47 R16315 ("Yokohama")
Roberts, Steve L. *Source(s):* CCE52 R98752 ("I'm Gonna Be for Myself")
Note(s): Also used by J. Russell Robinson.
Someone *Source(s):* CCE19 E442155
Stevens, Robert L. *Source(s):* CCE51 R76935 ("You and I")

Bergh, Arthur F. 1912- [composer]
Note(s): Do not confuse with Arthur Bergh (1882-1962); see preceding entry.
Duncan, Hal *Source(s):* CCE56
Keys, Buddy *Source(s):* CCE56

Berghorn, Alfred Maria 1911-1978 [composer]
Lepinski, Gerhard *Source(s):* BUL3

Bergier, Ungay [fictitous composer]
Source(s): GROL

Bergman, Dewey 1900 (or 02)- [composer, author, arranger]
Osborne, Don *Source(s):* ASCP; CCE52-55; CPOL RE-43-058
Turner, Al *Source(s):* CCE55

Bergman, Hjalmar (Fredrik Elgérus) 1883-1931 [author]
Brate, Holger *Source(s):* PIPE
Swedish Dickens, The *Source(s):* WORB

Bergmann, Walter Georg(e) ?-1988 [composer, arranger]
Walker, T. S. *Source(s):* CCE54; CPMU; GOTH

Bergström, Gurli Maria 1905-1982 [composer]
Gullmar, Kai *Source(s):* CCE37 Efor51148; CCE52; GREN

Berkeley, Lennox 1903-1989 [composer]
Timotheus *Source(s):* MUWB

Berladsky, Leonide Simeonovich 1902-1988 [violinist, composer, bandleader, actor]
Belasco, Leon *Source(s):* CLMM

Berlanga de Duero, Soria 1586-1651 [composer]
Isla, (Diego) Cristóbal de *Source(s):* NGDM

Berlin, Boris 1907-2001 [teacher, composer]
London, Lawrence *Source(s):* CANE
Saint-Jean, René *Source(s):* CANE

Berlind, Samuel 1910- [composer, author]
Berlind, Guy *Source(s):* ASCB

Berling, Thomas 1773-1823 (or 26) [actor, author]
B——g *Source(s):* PIPE

Berlinger, Milton 1908-2002 [author, comedian, author, composer]
Berle, Milton *Source(s):* ASCP; KINK; PSND
Boy Wonder, The *Source(s):* PSND
Mr. Television *Source(s):* PSND
Thief of Bad Gags, The *Source(s):* PSND
Uncle Miltie *Source(s):* PSND

Berlioz, Hector 1803-1869 [composer]
Creator of Program Music, The *Source(s):* PSND
Ducré, Pierre *Source(s):* GOTH; GOTT; NGDM
Father of Modern Orchestration *Source(s):* www.elibron.com/english/other/item_detail.phtml?msq_id=60106 (20 Apr. 2005)
Note(s): See also Franz Joseph Haydn.
Father of the Orchestra *Source(s):* http://trfn.clpgh.org/free-reed/essays/bergquistseat.html (7 Oct. 2002)
Note(s): See also Franz Joseph Haydn.
Robespierre of Music, The *Source(s):* SLON
Note(s): See also Gabriel Urbain Fauré.

Berlipp, Friedel 1900 (or 21)- [composer, arranger, conductor]
Lipman(n), Berry *Source(s):* CCE60; CCE64; CCE68; KOMP; KOMS; PFSA
Poll, Peter *Source(s):* CCE73 Efor164785

Berman, Syd [songwriter]
Browne, Lester *Source(s):* CCE46 Efor308
Note(s): Jt. pseud.: Harold (Cornelius) Fields.
Bermann, Joseph 1810-1886 [art and music dealer]
Phisemar, Benno *Source(s):* STAD
Bermann, Moritz 1823-1895 [author, composer, historian]
Mormann, Bert. *Source(s):* IBIM; WORB
Mühlfeld, Louis *Source(s):* IBIM; WORB
Zimmermann, B. *Source(s):* IBIM; WORB
Bernadetti, Ernest Marco 1884-1959 [composer]
Burnett, Ernie *Source(s):* REHH
Bernard ?-1350 [monk, bishop, writer on music]
Barlaam *Source(s):* NGDM
Bernard, Al(fred A.) 1887 (or 88)-1949 [composer, actor, author]
Anderson, Bert *Source(s):* CCE51 R75997 ("Eva,Won't You Roll Your big Eyes?")
Bennett, John *Source(s):* MACE
Note(s): Also used by Arthur Fields [i.e., Abe Finkelstein]
Boy from Dixie, The *Source(s):* GRAC
Clare, Jack *Source(s):* GRAC; MACE
Dalbert and Banning *Source(s):* GRAC
Note(s): Jt. pseud.: Vernon Dalhart [i.e., M(arion) T(ry) Slaughter]
Moore, Buddy *Source(s):* MACE
Sanborn, Dave *Source(s):* MACE
Simpson, Al *Source(s):* MACE
Sims, Skeeter *Source(s):* GRAC
Uncle Joe *Source(s):* MACE
Note(s): See also Joe (Marion) Allison.
White, Slim *Source(s):* MACE; http://www.mainspring.com/BSpseudo.html (13 June 2005)
Bernard, Clem(ent) [songwriter]
Bernard, Adrien *Source(s):* CCE70 R486152
Note(s): Jt. pseud.: Desmond Cox [i.e., Adrian Keuleman] & Harold Elton Box.
Brown, Clarrie *Source(s):* CCE40 #28606 Efor63379; CCE67
Cameron, David *Source(s):* CCE52 Efor16476 & Efor14922
Murphy, Pat *Source(s):* CCE52; CPOL RE-75-687
Pitt, Arthur *Source(s):* CCE51 Efor6599 ("Two Little Men in a Flying Saucer")
Note(s): Jt. pseud.: Eric Spear.
Bernard, Guy (Charles) 1907- [composer]
Delapierre, (Guy) Bernard *Source(s):* PIPE; WORB
Bernard, J. [composer]
Dranreb, J. *Source(s):* CPMU (publication date 1849)
Bernard, Josef Karl 1780 (or 81)-1850 [author]
Flaxius *Source(s):* PIPE
Bernard of Morlaix fl. early 12th cent. [hymnist]
Note(s): See LCAR for variant forms of name.
Bernard of Cluny *Source(s):* CYBH
Bernard, Paul 1866-1947 [playwright, librettist]
Bernard, Tristan *Source(s):* GAN1; GAN2; LCAR; WORB
Bernard, Pierre Joseph (Justin) 1708-1775 [librettist]
Gentil-Bernard *Source(s):* LCAR; PIPE; SONN
Bernardini, Marcello 1730-40-after 1800 [composer, librettist]
Capua, (Marcello di) *Source(s):* GREN, MORI; NGDM
Marcello da Capua *Source(s):* IBIM; MORI; NGDM; NGDO; SONN
Bernardino mentioned 1518 [composer]
Note(s): Do not confuse with Bernardino (1419-1445), organist, known as Il Tedesco.
Piffero, Il *Source(s):* IBIM; WORB
Bernardoni, Pietro Antonio 1672-1714 [librettist]
Cromiro Dianio *Source(s):* GROL
Dianio, Cromiro *Source(s):* GROL
Bernbrun, Karl (Andreas) 1787 (or 89)-1854 [librettist]
Carl, Karl [or Carl] *Source(s):* GOTH; LCAR; STGR
Karl, Karl *Source(s):* LCAR
Berndt, Julia Helen 1905-1988 [composer, author]
King, Bonnie B. *Source(s):* ASCP; CCE61-62
Bernhard, Christoph 1627 (or 28)-1692 [music theorist, composer, singer]
C. B. *Source(s):* NGDM
Bernhardt, Clyde Edric Barron 1905-1986 [singer, trombonist, songwriter]
Barron, Ed *Source(s):* HARS
Bernhart, Martha Ann 1922- [composer, author]
Hubble, Martie *Source(s):* ASCP
Bernhuber, Ludwig 1899-1945? [composer, singer]
Bernauer, Ludwig *Source(s):* OMUO
Bernier, Alfred 1896-1953 [musicologist, composer]
Bernal, J. *Source(s):* CANE
Bernikoff, Morris 1920- [author, lyricist, educator]
Morris, Bernard *Source(s):* ASCP; CCE57-58; CCE66-68
Bernini, Giovanni Filippo [librettist]
Parnasso, Felice *Source(s):* LOWN
Note(s): Probable pseud.
Berno, (Abbott) of Reichenau ?-1048 [writer on church music]
Bernardus (of Reichenau) *Source(s):* LCAR; NGDM
Berns, Bert(rand) (Russell) 1929 (or 31)-1967 [producer, songwriter]
Byrd, Russell *Source(s):* LCAR
Russell, Bert *Source(s):* CCE60-64; MUWB; PEN2; SONG
Bernstein, Arturo 1882-1935 [musician, composer]
Alemán, El *Source(s):* TODO

Bernstein, Elmer 1922-2004 [composer]
Bernstein West *Source(s):* http://www.playbill.com/news/article/87965.html (3 Feb. 2005)
Note(s): Nickname signifies he was the Bernstein who worked on the west coast.
Bernstein(-Porges), Elsa 1866-1925 [playwright]
Rosmer, Ernst *Source(s):* GROL; NGDO; ROOM
Bernstein, F(lorence) G. [composer]
Amber, Florence *Source(s):* CCE38 D60509 ("Some Call It Chance"); TPRF
Bernstein, Louis [songwriter]
Note(s): Do not confuse with Louis Bernstein [i.e., Leonard Berstein (1918-1990)]
Berni, Lew *Source(s):* CCE23 E570981
Slovinsky, Joseph *Source(s):* CCE23 E570981
Bernstein, Louis 1918-1990 [composer, conductor]
Note(s): Do not confuse with Louis Bernstein [nd], see above. Portraits: EWEN; EWPA; JAST
Amber, Lenny *Source(s):* CCE70; NGAM; PIPE
America's Greatest Composer *Source(s):* http://cms.westport.k12.ct.us/cms/mc/music/composers.html (7 Oct. 2002)
Note(s): See also Charles Edward Ives, George Gershwin [i.e., Jacob Gershvin] & Charles Puerner.
Bernstein, Leonard *Source(s):* CM02; GAN2; MACE; PIPE
Note(s): Name changed at age 16.
Berquist, Bernard H. 1903-1962 [composer, author]
Berquist, Whitey *Source(s):* ASCP
Berridge, John 1716-1793 [hymnist]
Old Everton *Source(s):* CYBH (port.); HATF
Berrsche, Alexander 1883-1940 [writer on music, critic]
Lösch, Alexander *Source(s):* MACM; WORB
Berry, Charles Edward Anderson 1926- [singer, composer]
Berry, Chuck *Source(s):* EWEN (port.); PSND
Father of Rock 'n' Roll, The *Source(s):* PSND
Note(s): See also Arthur Crudup, William [or Bill] (John Clifton) Haley, (Jr.), Charles Hardin Holley, Johnnie Johnson & Elvis A(a)ron Presley.
Greatest of the Rock 'n' Rollers, The *Source(s):* SHAD
Greatest Rock Lyricist This Side of Bob Dylan, The *Source(s):* SHAD
Poet Laureate of Rock 'n' Roll, The *Source(s):* SHAD (see under: Jordan, Louis)
Poet Laureate of Teenage Rock *Source(s):* SHAD
Berry, Dennis (Alfred) 1921-1994 [composer]
Dennis, Peter *Source(s):* CCE56-57; GALM; MUWB; RFSO
Kenbury, Charles *Source(s):* GALM; RFSO
Rodney, Michael *Source(s):* GALM; RFSO
Sharp, Jack *Source(s):* CCE47
Sterling, Frank *Source(s):* GALM; RFSO
Berry, Leon (Brown) 1908 (or 10)-1941 [saxophonist, composer]
Berry, Chu *Source(s):* JASZ; KINK; LCAR
Brown, Leon *Source(s):* LCAR
Bertati, Giovanni 1735-1815 [librettist]
Scoteo, Pietro *Source(s):* STGR
Berté, Heinrich 1857 (or 58)-1924 [composer, arranger]
Berté, Harry *Source(s):* GAN2; LCAR
Berteau, Martin 1708 (or 09)-1771 [violoncellist, composer]
Note(s): See LCAR for variant forms of surname.
Martino, Sgr. *Source(s):* SADC
Bertelli, Rino [or Rono] [librettist]
Libero Sentri *Source(s):* STGR
Sentri, Liberto *Source(s):* STGR
Bertha, Sándor 1843-1912 [composer, pianist, writer on music]
Alexandre de- *Source(s):* GROL
Berthier, Jeanne-Marie 1877-1970 [singer, author]
Bathori, Jane *Source(s):* BAKO; CCE55; LCAR
Bertie-Marriott, Clement 1848- [journalist, writer on music]
Albert, d' *Source(s):* OPER 12:3 (1996)
D'Albert *Source(s):* OPER 12:3 (1996)
Bertin, Jean-Honoré 1768?-1843 [violinist, composer]
Dilloy, Bertin *Source(s):* PIPE
Bertin, Pierre 1899-1979 [singer, writer on music]
Note(s): Do not confuse with Pierre Bertin [i.e., Pierre Dupont (1891-1984)], actor, playwright.
Bernac, Pierre *Source(s):* BAKO; BAKR
Bertini, Enrico 1862- [composer]
Cinerini, Berto *Source(s):* STGR
Bertini, Henri(-Jerome) 1798-1876 [composer]
Bertini le Jeune *Source(s):* PSND
Berto, Augusto Pedro 1889-1953 [bandoneonist, composer, leader]
El Oso *Source(s):* TODO
Oso, El *Source(s):* TODO
Bertram, Robert Aitken 1836- [hymnist]
R. A. B. *Source(s):* JULN
Bertrami, José Roberto 1946- [keyboardist, writer, producer]
Ze Roberto *Source(s):* PEN2
Berwald, Franz 1796-1868 [composer]
Schubert of the North *Source(s):* Hyperion CDA67081/2
Note(s): See also Carl Loewe
Besly, Edward M. [composer]
M. B. *Source(s):* CPMU (publication date 1922)
Besly, Maurice 1888-1945 [conductor, composer]
Allington, Rex *Source(s):* MUWB

Bessat, Charles 1871-1917 [lyricist, composer]
Blès, Numa *Source(s):* WHIT; WORB
Bessem, Elizabeth Prudence Manga 1948- [singer, composer, pianist]
Manga, Bebe *Source(s):* PEN1
Bessières, Emile G. 1860- [author]
Darval, Emile Germain *Source(s):* IBIM; WORB
Bester, Henry Lee 1933-1989 [harmonica player, songwriter]
Edwards, Charles *Source(s):* LCAR
Good Rockin' Charles *Source(s):* HARS; LCAR
Beswick, Harry 1868- [journalist, author]
Bezique *Source(s):* PIPE
Busy Bee *Source(s):* PIPE
Egerton, Randolph *Source(s):* PIPE
Betti(no), Stefano fl. 1562-65 [composer]
Fornarino, Il *Source(s):* IBIM; NGDM; WORB
Betulius, Sigmund 1626-1681 [poet, playwright]
Birken, Sigmund von *Source(s):* LCAR; NGDM; PIPE
Floridan *Source(s):* LCAR; NGDM
Beuler, Jacob 1796-1873 [songwriter]
Beulah, Jacob *Source(s):* KILG
Note(s): Frequent variant spelling.
Beuselinck, Paul Oscar 1944 (or 45)- [singer, actor, producer, author]
Nicholas, Paul *Source(s):* GAN2
Bevan, Clifford James 1934- [composer]
Kronk, Josef *Source(s):* CPMU
Bevan, Leonard Francis [composer]
Smith, Lance *Source(s):* CPMU (publication date 1923)
Bevel, Charles William 1938- [composer, author, singer]
Bevel, Mississippi *Source(s):* ASCP
Beyle, (Marie) Henri 1783-1842 [writer, critic]
Alceste *Source(s):* GROL
Bombet, César *Source(s):* GROL; NGDM; NGDO; RIEM
Bombet, L(ouis)-A(lexander)-C(ésar) *Source(s):* NGDM; PIPE; ROOM
De Stendhal *Source(s):* DAWS
Stendhal *Source(s):* GROL; NGDM; NGDO; PIPE; RIEM; ROOM
Bez, Helmut 1930- [author]
Berg, A. *Source(s):* PIPE
Biaggi, Girolamo Alessandro 1819-1897 [composer, music critic]
Albano, Ippolito d' *Source(s):* GROL; MACM; NGDO
Biagi, Rodolfo 1906-1969 [pianist, leader, composer]
Brujas, Manos *Source(s):* TODO
Manos Brujas *Source(s):* TODO
Biancardi, (Nicolò) Sebastiano 1679-1741 [librettist]
Lalli, (Benedetto) Domenico *Source(s):* GROL; LOWN; MELL; NGDM; NGDO; PIPE; SONN
Ortanio *Source(s):* ALMC; SONN
Bianchini, Domenico c.1510-c.1576 [lutenist, composer]
Rossetto, Il *Source(s):* LCAR; NGDM; WORB
Note(s): See also Antonio Bis(s)oni.
Rosso, Il *Source(s):* LCAR; NGDM; WORB
Veneziano, Bianchini *Source(s):* LCAR
Bianchini, Francescho fl. 1547-48 [lutenist, composer]
Blanchin, François *Source(s):* LCAR; NGDM
Biancolelli, Pierre François 1680-1734 [librettist]
Dominique, (Pierre François Biancolelli) *Source(s):* LCAR; MELL
Bibalitsch, Antonio 1922- [composer]
Bibalo, Antonio (Gio) *Source(s):* BAKE; PSND
Bichsel, Jacob 1931- [composer]
Bikayo, Les *Source(s):* REHG; SUPN
Bick, Eva [composer]
Bickvor *Source(s):* GREN
Bick, Herman c.1900- [bandleader, arranger, pianist]
Berlin, Ben *Source(s):* CCE42; NGDJ
Bideu, Louis 1919-2000 [composer, author, comedian]
Bedell, Lew *Source(s):* EPMU
Billie Joe (and the Checkmates) *Source(s):* EPMU
Chandler, R. W. *Source(s):* CCE64
Hunter, B(illy) J(oe) *Source(s):* ASCP (see under: Bedell); CCE67-68; EPMU
Bidgood, Henry [or Harry] (James) 1898-1957 [accordionist, band leader, songwriter]
Biddy, Hal *Source(s):* CCE54-55; CPOL RE-181-862
Casselden, James *Source(s):* CCE52; CPOL RE-61-287
Porto, Don *Source(s):* BBDP; http://www.accordions.com/index/art/bands.shtml (14 May 2005)
Rossini *Source(s):* BBDP; http://www.accordions.com/index/art/bands.shtml
Scala, Primo *Source(s):* BBDP; CCE51; CCE65; CPOL RE-34-967
Sylva, Lew *Source(s):* http://www.expectingrain.com/dok/who/s/scalaprimo.html (14 May 2005)
Bieber, C(aroline) F(rances) Egon 1887- [composer]
Cöln, Geno von *Source(s):* GOTH; MACM; STGR
Biedermann, Felix 1870-1928 [librettist, lyricist]
Dörmann, Felix *Source(s):* FULD; GAN1; GAN2; LOWN; MACM; PIPE
Biehl, Albert 1833 (or 35)-1899 [composer]
Erich, Carl *Source(s):* CCE21 R19423
Note(s): A. P. Schmidt house name; see NOTES: Erich, Carl.

Bieler-Wendt, Helmut 1956- [composer]
H. B.-W *Source(s):* KOMS
Bielinski, C(lifford) Martin 1921- [composer, arranger, guitarist]
Belan, Cliff *Source(s):* ASCC; CCE57-58
Bierbower, Elsie 1889-1956 [actress, singer, songwriter]
Bierbauer, Elsie *Source(s):* PSND
Janis, Elsie *Source(s):* GAN2; GRAT; PSND
Little Elsie *Source(s):* GAN2; GRAT; PSND
Petite Elsie, La *Source(s):* GAN2
Sweetheart of the A. E. F., The *Source(s):* PSND
Bierey, Gottlob Benedikt 1772-1840 [composer]
Rossini von Nowgorod *Source(s):* APPL p. 12
Biermann, Rémon 1935- [composer]
Antwerpen, Leopold *Source(s):* KOMP; KOMS; PFSA
Monster, Mac *Source(s):* KOMP; KOMS; PFSA
Namib, Swako *Source(s):* KOMP; KOMS; PFSA
Biferi, Francesco [musicologist]
Figlio, Il *Source(s):* WORB
Note(s): See also Nicolas Dôthel.
Bigard, Albany [or Alban] (Leon) 1906-1980 [composer, clarinetist, bandleader]
Note(s): In KINK & GAMM given name: Leon Albany.
Bigard, Barney *Source(s):* ASCP; BAKR; EPMU; GAMM; KINK
Bigeou, Esther c.1895-c.1936 [singer, dancer, songwriter]
Creole Songbird, The *Source(s):* HARS
Girl with the Million Dollar Smile, The *Source(s):* HARS
Biggs, Edward Smith ?-c.1820 [composer, pianist, teacher]
E. S. B. *Source(s):* CPMU
Bihan, Angelika 1837- [author, musician]
Jäger, Angelika *Source(s):* IBIM; WORB
Bilik, Jerry (Hanchrow) 1933- [composer, arranger, conductor]
Gerrard, William *Source(s):* ASCP; HOVL; REHG; SMIN; SUPN
Note(s): Do not confuse with Will Gerard, [i.e., William B. Jacobs.]
Bilk, Bernard Stanley 1929- [clarinetist, composer, bandleader]
Bilk, Acker *Source(s):* AMUS; NOMG; PEN2; PMUS-99
Billig, (Julius Karl) Gustav 1813-1888 [author, playwright]
Hufnagl, Max *Source(s):* PIPE
Netz, Paul *Source(s):* PIPE
Spinalba, C. *Source(s):* PIPE
Spindler, Alexander *Source(s):* PIPE
Billings, William ?-1800 [tanner, composer]
Father of American Music *Source(s):* MUWB
Note(s): See also Benjamin Carr & Charles Edward Ives.
Billingsley, Derrell L. 1940- [composer, author]
Todd, D. S. *Source(s):* ASCP; CCE75
Binetti, Giovanni 1882- [novelist, composer]
Dottor Gibin *Source(s):* IBIM; WORB
Fancelle, J. *Source(s):* CCE34 Efor33747
Fancello, Giovanni Battista di *Source(s):* IBIM; WORB
Gibin, Dottor *Source(s):* IBIM; WORB
Réjard, Victon *Source(s):* IBIM; WORB
Binge, Ronald 1910-1979 [songwriter]
Folia, Renato *Source(s):* CCE48
Rinaldo, F. *Source(s):* www.hallowquest.cm/compositions.htm (18 Apr. 2005)
Rosen, Abner C. *Source(s):* CCE55 Efor20980
Note(s): Jt. pseud.: A(nnuzio) P(aolo) Mantovani.
Bingham, Graham Clifton 1859-1913 [writer]
Bird, Cockiolly *Source(s):* GOTH
Cockiolly Bird *Source(s):* GOTH
Bingham, Hiram 1789-1863 [hymnist]
Binamu *Source(s):* CYBH
Bingham, William L., Jr. 1945- [composer, author, singer]
Bingham, Bing *Source(s):* ASCP; CPOL PA-510-407
Binkerd, Gordon (Ware) 1916-2003 [composer]
Ware, Gordon *Source(s):* HOVL
Binks, E. [composer]
Bergholt, Ernest *Source(s):* CPMU (publication date 1885)
Binney, Thomas 1789-1874 [hymnist]
A. Balance Esq., of the Middle Temple *Source(s):* CART
Congregational Nonconformist, A *Source(s):* CART
Fiat Justitia *Source(s):* CART
Search, John *Source(s):* CART
Binns, John c.1744-1796 [bookseller, dictionary compiler]
Hoyle, John *Source(s):* GROL; NGDM
Binzer, August Daniel 1793-1868 [philosopher, musician, journalist]
Beer, A. D. *Source(s):* IBIM; LCAR; WORB
Pinzer, August Daniel *Source(s):* IBIM; WORB
Biondi, Giovanni Battista fl. 1605-30 [composer]
Cesna, Giovanni Battista *Source(s):* LCAR; NGDM; WORB
Biondo, Rose Leonore Victoria 1931- [composer, author]
Bond, Vee *Source(s):* CCE59
Dale, Vikki *Source(s):* ASCP; CCE58-59
Birch, Peter 1940- [composer, author, singer]
Bell, Peter *Source(s):* ASCP
Lynn, Johnny *Source(s):* ASCP

Bird, Frederic(k) Mayer (or Meyer) 1838-1908 [cleric, hymnologist]
Timsol, Robert *Source(s):* CART; LCAR
Birnbach, (Joseph Benjamin) Heinrich 1793-1879 [writer on music, teacher]
B-h *Source(s):* HEYT
Birner, Günther 1937- [composer]
Apple, Jan *Source(s):* KOMS; PFSA
Clavito, Dona *Source(s):* KOMS
Heymes, B. B. *Source(s):* KOMS; PFSA
Note(s): Jt. pseud.: Wolfgang Barczewski.
Birtles, Frank 1920-1991 [singer, author]
Langdon, Michael *Source(s):* BAKO
Bisaccioni, (Conte) Maiolino 1582-1663 [dramatist]
Zorzisto, Luigo *Source(s):* SONN
Bischoff, Joh. Herm. Christian 1851- [librettist]
Bischoff, Karl *Source(s):* STGR; WORB
Bischoff, Melchior 1547-1614 [clergyman, hymnist, composer]
Episcopus, Melchior *Source(s):* NGDM
Bishop, (Sir) Henry R(owley) 1786-1855 [composer]
Note(s): Portrait: GRV3
English Mozart, The *Source(s):* NGDM; PSND
Note(s): See also Samuel Wesley.
Bishop, Walter, Jr. 1927- [composer, pianist, writer on jazz]
Bishop, Bish *Source(s):* LCAR; PSND
Bis(s)oni, Antonio 1698- [composer]
Rossetto, Il *Source(s):* SONN; WORB
Note(s): See also Domenico Bianchini.
Biss, Thomas 1934- [composer]
Deverenx, Peter *Source(s):* BUL3
Bissari, Pietro Paolo fl. 1640-1660 [guitarist, poet, dramatist]
Olympico *Source(s):* ALMC; SONN
Rincor(a)to, Academico (Olimpico) *Source(s):* ALMC; SONN
Bisson, Whelock Alexander [songwriter]
Fetchit, Stepin *Source(s):* CCE53 Eunp331608; CCE58-59 CCE62
Note(s): Also used by Lincoln (T(heodore Monroe Andrew)) Perry; see NOTES: Fetchit, Stepin.
Stepin Fetchit *Source(s):* CCE55; CCE59
Note(s): Also used by Lincoln (T(heodore Monroe Andrew)) Perry.
Bittong, Franz 1842-1904 [librettist]
Stern, Oskar *Source(s):* STGR
Bizet, Alexandre César Léopold 1838-1875 [composer]
Note(s): Registered name.
Betzi, Gaston de *Source(s):* WEOP
Bizet, Georges *Source(s):* NGDM
Note(s): Baptismal name.
Black, Dorothy 1914- [translator]
Albertyn, Dorothy *Source(s):* PIPE
Black, Kitty *Source(s):* PIPE
Black, Gloria 1944- [composer, author, singer]
Black, Rosebud *Source(s):* ASCP
Black, Stanley 1913- [composer]
Dean, Colin *Source(s):* MUWB
Blackman, Garfield 1941-2000 [soca artist, composer]
Lord Shorty *Source(s):* PEN2
Ras Shorty *Source(s):* PEN2
Shorty, Lord *Source(s):* PEN2
Blackman, Michael Bruce 1946- [lyricist, singer]
Marion, Karl *Source(s):* ASCP
Blackmar, A(rmand) E(dward) 1826-1888 [composer, arranger, music publisher]
Note(s): Portrait: ETUP 58:6 (June 1940): 426
Armand *Source(s):* HARW p. 135; *Dictionary of Louisiana Biography*. New Orleans: Louisiana Historical Assoc., 1988.
Coach, S. Low *Source(s): Dictionary of Louisiana Biography.*
Diamonds, Ducie *Source(s): Dictionary of Louisiana Biography.*
Muse, A. E. A. *Source(s): Dictionary of Louisiana Biography.*
Noir, A. *Source(s):* GROL; HARW p. 103 & 111; HOGR; NGAM
Pindar, A. *Source(s): Dictionary of Louisiana Biography.*
Schwartz *Source(s): Dictionary of Louisiana Biography.*
Voice of the South, The *Source(s):* PSND
Ye Comic *Source(s):* HOGR; *Dictionary of Louisiana Biography.*
Blackmore, Amos, (Jr.) 1934-1998 [singer, harmonica player, songwriter]
Little Giant of the Blues, The *Source(s):* HARS
Wells, Amos *Source(s):* HARS; LCAR
Wells, Junior *Source(s):* HARD; LCAR
Wells, Little Junior *Source(s):* HARS; LCAR
Blackston, Harvey 1927- [harmonica player, singer, songwriter]
Harmonica Fats *Source(s):* AMUS
Blackstone, Gerald 1936- [lyricist]
Black, Don *Source(s):* GAN2
Blackwell, Francis Hillman 1903-1954 (or 62?) [singer, guitarist, songwriter]
Black, Frankie *Source(s):* HARS
Blackwell, Scrapper *Source(s):* AMUS; HARS
Blackwell, Otis 1931-2002 [songwriter, pianist]
Davenport, John *Source(s):* PEN2; SONG; WORT
Blackwell, Robert A. 1918 (or 22)-1985 [composer, arranger, producer]

Blackwell, Bumps *Source(s):* EPMU; HARD; HARR; PEN2
Blaikley, Alan 1940- [songwriter]
Blaikley, Howard *Source(s):* BLIC; CCE65 Efor108895
Note(s): Jt. pseud.: Ken Howard.
Blair, Timothy 1967- [rapper]
Dog, Tim *Source(s):* EPMU
Blake, David 1970- [rapper]
DJ Quik *Source(s):* EPMU
Blake, George M. 1912- [composer, organist]
Troutman, John *Source(s):* ASCP
Blake, James Hubert 1883-1983 [pianist, composer, songwriter]
Note(s): Portraits: EWEN; WOLL p. [59] (with Noble (Lee) Sissle)
Blake, Eubie *Source(s):* BAKR; CM19; EWEN; HARR; NGDM; PEN2; PSND; SUTT
Note(s): Eubie Blake and His Orchestra also recorded as Blake's Jazzone Orchestra; Ben Martin and His Orchestra; and Dick Robertson and His Orchestra (see SUTT).
Blake, Robert *Source(s):* SUTT
Bluke, Ruby *Source(s):* SUTT
Elder Statesman of Ragtime *Source(s):* CM19
Martin, Ben *Source(s):* SUTT
Robertson, Dick *Source(s):* SUTT
Blakely, Ezra Lee, Jr. 1945- [songwriter]
RaSun, Eomot *Source(s):* http://www.analogueproductions.com (2 Nov. 2003)
Blanc, Claude 1854-1900 [composer]
Claudius *Source(s):* BALT
Blanc de Fontbelle, Cecile 1892- [conductor, composer]
Waldin, Hugues *Source(s):* COHN; HIXN
Blanc-Francart, Hubert 1967- [songwriter]
BoomBass, Pigalle *Source(s):* CPOL PA-699-044; SONG
Blanchard, Donald F. 1914- [singer, songwriter]
Blanchard, Red *Source(s):* CCE47; EPMU; MCCL
Blanchard, Maryanne 1945- [singer, keyboardist, songwriter]
Morgan, Misty *Source(s):* CCE71; NOMG
Blanckenmüller, Johannes 1496-1570 [poet, composer]
Walter, Johann(es) *Source(s):* BAKR; GROL
Walther, Johann(es) *Source(s):* BAKR; GROL
Bland, James A(llen) 1854-1911 [songwriter, minstrel performer]
Note(s): Portraits: ETUP 57:7 (July 1939): 431; EWEN; EWPA; HAMM
America's Forgotten Negro Minstrel *Source(s):* PSND
Idol of the Halls, The *Source(s):* JASZ; SHAB p. 32
Negro "Stephen Foster," The *Source(s):* ETUP 57:7 (July 1939): 431
Prince of Negro Songwriters, The *Source(s):* JASZ; MARC p. 21; PSND; SIFA
World's Greatest Minstrel Man, The *Source(s):* SHAB p. 32
Bland, Milton 1936- [arranger, composer, saxophonist]
Big Jox *Source(s):* CCE60
Higgins, Monk *Source(s):* CCE62; EPMU; PSND
Bland, Robert Calvin 1930- [singer, instrumentalist, songwriter]
Bland, Bobby (Blue) *Source(s):* HARS; LCAR
Soul Man, The *Source(s):* HARS
Blanes (Cortés), Camilio 1946- [singer, songwriter]
Sesto, Camilo *Source(s):* HWOM; LCAR
Blangenois, Jules 1870-1957 [composer]
Jemy, Banon *Source(s):* BUL3; SUPN
Blankfield, Peter 1946- [singer, songwriter]
Wolf, Peter *Source(s):* EPMU; HARR
Blasser, Gustav 1857-1942 [conductor, composer]
Augustin, G. B. *Source(s):* HEIN; PIPE
Blau, Alfred 1845-1896 [librettist]
Baül *Source(s):* PIPE
Blau, Édouard 1836-1906 [librettist, playwright]
Stanislas-Viateur *Source(s):* NGDO; PIPE
Blau, Eric 1921- [author, lyricist, film producer]
Blau, Milton *Source(s):* LCAR; PSND
Blaukopf, Ehepaar Kurt 1914-1999 [musicologist, music sociologist]
Wind, Hans E. *Source(s):* OMUO
Blaylock, Travis (L.) 1934- [singer, harmonica player, songwriter]
Harmonica Slim *Source(s):* HARS; LCAR
Note(s): See also James Moore.
Slim, H. *Source(s):* CCE60
Blaze, François Henri Joseph 1784-1857 [critic, librettist, composer]
Castiblazades *Source(s):* NGDM
Note(s): Term for Castil-Blaze's "modifications" of operas of several composers.
Castil-Blaze, (François Henri Joseph) *Source(s):* GROL; LCAR; NGDM; NGDO; PIPE
Generali *Source(s):* CPMU; OCLC 27692383
Singier, Alexis *Source(s):* GROL
xxx *Source(s):* NGDM
Blaze (de Bury), (Ange) Henri 1813-1888 [critic, poet, journalist]
Langenais, F. de *Source(s):* RILM 95-15505-ap
Werner, Hans *Source(s):* RILM 95-15505-ap; WORB
Note(s): Also used by Henri-Sebastien Blaze?
Blaze, Henri-Sebastian 1763-1833 [novelist, composer]
Werner, Hans *Source(s):* GDRM; GROL
Note(s): Also used by (Ange) Henri Blaze (de Bury)?

Bleiweiss, Peter R(ichard) 1944- [composer, author]
 Blythe, P(eter) Richard *Source(s):* ASCP; CCE66
 Peters, Ricci *Source(s):* CCE59-60; CCE62
 Puzzy Fuppy *Source(s):* CCE67
Blenkinsopp, Edwin Clennell Leaton 1819- [hymnist]
 E. L. B. *Source(s):* JULN
 L. B. B. *Source(s):* JULN
Blesh, Rudolph [or Rudi] (Pickett) 1899-1985 [writer on music]
 Dean of Ragtime Historians *Source(s):* RAGT p. 178-9
Blevins, Ruby(e) (Rebecca) 1912 (or 14)-1996 [singer, guitarist; songwriter, yodeler]
 Montana, Patsy *Source(s):* CCME; CM38; GRAT; HARS; KINK; MUHF; PEN2; SUTT
 Rose, (Mrs.) Ruby(e) B. *Source(s):* ASCP; CCE56
 Yodeling Cowgirl, (The) *Source(s):* GRAT; HARS
Blewitt, Jonathan 1782-1853 [composer]
 Bolsover, Colonel *Source(s):* GOTH
Blige, Mary Jane c.1971- [singer, songwriter]
 Inventor of New Jill Swing, The *Source(s):* CM15
 Queen of Hip-Hop Soul *Source(s):* CM15 p. v
Blinn, Hans 1925- [composer]
 Landauer, Hannes *Source(s):* PFSA
Bliss, P(hilip) P. 1838-1876 [composer, hymnist, singer]
 Note(s): One source lists original first name as Phil(l)ipp, explaining he separated the final "p" of his given name to create a middle initial. Another source cites a letter Bliss wrote in which he used the initials "P. P., Jr." and "P. P., Sr.," suggesting the elder Bliss' middle name was possibly "Paul". Do not confuse with his son, P(hilip) Paul (1872-1933); see next entry. Portraits: CYBH; HALL; http://www.gbgm-umc.org/churches/DesertFoothillsAZ/PPBLISS (7 Oct. 2002)
 Basso, Pro Phundo *Source(s):* CPMU; NEIL p. 80
 Bee, Pee Pee *Source(s):* NEIL p.11
 P. P. B. *Source(s):* NEIL p. 141+
 Phanciful Phil *Source(s):* NEIL p. 114
 Pro Phundo Basso *Source(s):* NEIL p. 80
Bliss, P(hilip) Paul 1872-1933 [composer, organist, music editor]
 Note(s): Do not confuse with his father, P(hilip) P. Bliss (1838-1876); see preceding entry. Portrait: ETUP 50:4 (Apr. 1932): 236.
 Abbey, W. F. *Source(s):* CCE45 #12811, 44 R136238
 Abel, J. T. *Source(s):* CCE46 R4782 ("My God, My Father. . .")
 Abner, J. E. *Source(s):* CCE44 #51525, 199 R133566
 Acton, E. R. *Source(s):* CCE46 R10229 ("Silvery Sails")
 Acton, O. E. *Source(s):* CCE46 R10227 ("Halloween")
 Benito, Pedro *Source(s):* CCE44 #46708, 419 R133295
 Berg, W. T. *Source(s):* CCE21 E520758; LCCC48 R38559
 Bittle, (R.) Clifford *Source(s):* CCE43 #3437, 444 R114793; CCE44 #14418, 15 R123145
 Bliss, Paul *Source(s):* CCE45 R140396; CCE47 R9504 ("Fourth of July")
 Brechelt, L. *Source(s):* CCE43 R115284; CCE52 R92092 ("Valley of Memory")
 Brice, Max *Source(s):* CCE41 #20979, 1009 R93946
 Bruce, Wallace *Source(s):* CCE18 D19868; LCCC46 R4778 ("Uncle Sam's Boys in Camp")
 Bueno, L. *Source(s):* CCE48 R33291 ("Night in Granada")
 Burton, R. O. *Source(s):* CCE46 R13547 ("Apple Blossoms")
 Cawood, John *Source(s):* CCE44 #51525, 151 R133565
 Chalfant, Scott *Source(s):* CCE47 R21722 ("Pom-Pom")
 Clark, H. R. *Source(s):* CCE44 #46708, 494 R133303
 Crammond, C. C. *Source(s):* CCE44 #46708, 482 R133300
 Craven, J. E. *Source(s):* CCE47 R22505 ("White Lady")
 Cross, R. B. *Source(s):* CCE45 #12811, 356 R136240
 Davies, Evan *Source(s):* CCE48 R29168 ("In Hanging Gardens")
 Davies, G. W. *Source(s):* CCE44 #51525, 221 R133564
 Dodds, L. B. *Source(s):* CCE42 #34788, 155 R109693
 Ely, S. N. *Source(s):* CCE44 R133299
 Emerson, J(ohn) *Source(s):* CCE42 #34788, 469 R109559
 Felix, Paul *Source(s):* CCE34 R29120; CCE35 R35425; CCE36 #3270, 320 R41742; TPRF
 Finn, I. D. *Source(s):* CCE47 R9510 ("Whispering")
 Frame, A. B. *Source(s):* CCE47 R9511 ("Expectancy")
 Franklyn, John *Source(s):* CCE43 #7207, 87 R115287
 Frazier, A. G. *Source(s):* CCE44 R133299 ("Buccaneers")
 Gardner, J. J. *Source(s):* CCE41 #9124, 479 R91625
 George, W. M. *Source(s):* CCE46 R10202 ("Buttercups")
 Graham, M. E. *Source(s):* CCE19 E462645; CCE47 R19878 ("Blessed Are They That Mourn")
 Haendel, L. L. *Source(s):* CCE41 #20979, 471 R93947
 Harkness, M. B. *Source(s):* CCE47 R9505 ("The Indian Scout")
 Harper, W. J. *Source(s):* CCE46 R10223 ("The King of Love")
 Hawthorne, Seymore [or Seymour] *Source(s):* CCE28 R3902; CCE38 R64288; TPRF

Note(s): Jt. pseud: Andrew J. Boex.
Howard, Wilson G. *Source(s):* CCE46 R10495 ("Night and Day, My Love for You"); CCE47 R19875
Hume, Bryn *Source(s):* CCE36 #3270, 97 R41404; TPRF
Iroquois, John *Source(s):* LCCC56 R177161
James, H. E. *Source(s):* CCE46 R10228 ("Cobwebs")
James, R. E. *Source(s):* CCE47 R9504 ("Awakening")
Johns, J. A. *Source(s):* CCE40 #15093, 822 R86360
Johns, J. H. *Source(s):* CCE42 #34788, 387 R109562
Knight, J. M. *Source(s):* CCE48 R38557 ("Hunting Song")
Kotte, Frank *Source(s):* CCE41 #9124, 283 R91627
Langey, N. J. *Source(s):* CCE47 R9503 ("Summer Voices")
Larkin, R. E. *Source(s):* CCE46 R10225 ("Jerusalem the Golden")
Lind, E. L. *Source(s):* CCE43 #2707, 415 R115286
Lord, Marion *Source(s):* CCE41 #9124, 192 R91626
Loring, Lina *Source(s):* LCCC55 R162314 ("Molly Be Jolly")
Lyon, M. J. *Source(s):* CCE47 R22502 ("Pipes of Spring")
Macdonald, A. G. *Source(s):* CCE44 #46708, 181 R133301
Marvin, J. A. *Source(s):* CCE47 R9561 ("Sleep, Comrades Sleep")
Mayor, Edouard *Source(s):* CCE41 #9124, 505 R91622
Mayor, F. S. *Source(s):* CCE47 R19876 ("Water-Fall")
Mellon, R. K. *Source(s):* CCE29 E7090; TPRF
Milton, J. G. *Source(s):* CCE46 R10036 ("Crown Him")
Moore, A. N. *Source(s):* CCE52 R92093 ("A Riddle")
Moorman, J. M. *Source(s):* CCE48 R36981 ("Three Sicilian Scenes")
Newton, Edward [or Eddie] *Source(s):* CCE43 #3437, 121 R114412; CCE44 R124605
Osborne, A. E. *Source(s):* CCE46 R10222 ("I Lay My Sins on Jesus")
Perkins, M. O. *Source(s):* CCE47 R22504 ("Pixie Band")
Prindle, G. F. *Source(s):* CCE44 #46708, 495 R133297
Rankin, W. S. *Source(s):* CCE46 R10226 ("I Heard the Voice of Jesus Say")
Redmon, J. Lindsay *Source(s):* CCE40 #11969, 153 R84612
Rich, F. E. *Source(s):* CCE41 #20979, 304 R93949
Rolfsen, A. H. *Source(s):* CCE41 #9124, 217 R91628
Sanderson, G. R. *Source(s):* CCE44 #51525, 492 R133294
Savage, I. B. *Source(s):* CCE47 R9506 ("Song of the Knight")
Seymour, H. *Source(s):* CCE39 #9188, 344 R74148
Smithers, Ralph *Source(s):* CCE46 R4784 ("Twilight in the Forest")
Smithson, S. A. *Source(s):* CCE44 #46708, 319 R133296
Stanton, Frank *Source(s):* CCE33 R23248 ("What's the Use of Sighin'")
Note(s): Not indexed; author of lyrics; see entry #4656, 684.
Starr, G. G. *Source(s):* CCE42 #34788, 73 R109558
Stewart, M. A. *Source(s):* CCE43 #7207, 302 R115285
Strietel, Edward *Source(s):* CCE46 R10429 ("Battle Hymn of the Republic," arr.)
Sweet, G. A. *Source(s):* CCE43 #3437, 234 R114414
Tandrop, A. R. *Source(s):* CCE48 R38558 ("Greet We the Springtime")
Tracy, E. C. *Source(s):* CCE48 R36984 ("Six Sunny Rhymes from Childhood")
Trapp, D. A. *Source(s):* CCE40 #11969, 582 R84609
Turner, Franklin *Source(s):* CCE52 R95232 ("Echoes of Woodlands")
Ulmer, F. E. *Source(s):* CCE48 R38560 ("Bells")
Wessel, Henry *Source(s):* CCE41 #9124, 92 R91621
West, B. E. *Source(s):* CCE41 #20979, 829 R93948
Wilkins, F. E. *Source(s):* CCE40 #11969, 403 R84608
Willis, J. A. *Source(s):* CCE46 R4779 ("Meadow Waltz")
Worthing, Richard *Source(s):* CCE42 #34788, 84 R109694
Young, G(eo.) R. *Source(s):* CCE47 R9508 ("Our Nation"); CCE48 R38556 ("Gipsy Hands")

Blitz, Leo(nard) 1901- [songwriter]
Note(s): The following names are listed as pseuds. of Leo Towers [i.e., Blitz]
Blessing, Harry *Source(s):* CCE58 R223086
Brown, Al *Source(s):* CCE64 R330847 ("Back in Those Old Kentucky Days")
Note(s): Jt. pseud.: Harry Leon [i.e., Sugarman] & Harry Leader [i.e., Henry Lebys]
Goldman, Sid *Source(s):* CCE36 Efor46327; CCE63; CCE64
Guillard, Michael *Sources(s):* CCE35 Efor39938
Note(s): Jt. pseud.: Harry Leon [i.e., Sugarman] & Rodd Arden [i.e., Dave Silver]
Jackman, Leo *Source(s):* CPOL RE-262-207
Note(s): Jt. pseud.: James [or Jimmy] Campbell & Jack Pickering.
Kingsley, Arthur *Source(s):* CCE58
Note(s): Also used by Thomas Edward Bulch.
Lennard, Jack *Source(s):* CCE64 R333473
Manners, David *Source(s):* CCE57; CPOL RE-257-861
Note(s): Jt. pseud.: Peter Yorke & James [or Jimmy] Campbell.
Marlo, Ferdi *Source(s):* CCE59 R300393; LCPC letter cited (23 Sept. 1932)

Note(s): "House name" of Keith, Prowse. Also used by Ralph (T.) Butler & possibly others; see NOTES: Marlo, Ferdi.
Marlo, Verdi *Source(s):* CCE59 R229672 ("Lovely Little Soul"); LCPC
Note(s): Given name probably a typographical error.
Marlow, Roy *Source(s):* CCE59 R234725 ("Five Minutes to Tweleve"); LCPC
Martin, Carrol *Source(s):* CCE50 Efor3153 ("The Happiest Days of Your Life")
Scholl, Fred *Source(s):* CCE59 R229689 ("One Little Hour with You"); LCPC
Summers, Joan *Source(s):* CCE53
Note(s): Jt. pseud.: Michael Carr [i.e., Maurice Alfred Cohen]
Towers, Leo *Source(s):* CCE37 Efor51137; CCE48; CCE64
Wilson, Arthur *Source(s):* CCE36 Efor46990; CCE64
Note(s): Jt. pseud.: Ralph (T.) Butler.
Bloch, Ernest 1880-1959 [composer]
Note(s): Portraits: HOWD; LYMN
First Great Composer of Modern Jewish Music *Source(s):* LYMN
Bloch, Ernst 1885-1977 [philosopher, author]
Note(s): Portrait: HOWD
Jahraus, Karl *Source(s):* PIPE
Kuerz, Jakob *Source(s):* PIPE
Bloch, Ray 1902 (or 03)-1982 [composer]
Llewellyn, Ray *Source(s):* CLMJ ("Science Fiction Theater")
Note(s): Also used by others; see NOTES: Llewellyn, Ray.
Blom, Eric Walter 1888-1959 [music critic, writer]
Farr, Sebastian *Source(s):* CART
Blomsedt, Armas Jussi Veikko 1908-1985 [composer, conductor]
Jalas, (Armas) Jussi (Veikko) *Source(s):* BUL1; BUL3; LCAR
Blood, Lizette Emma 1857 (or 58)-1913 [pianist, composer]
Note(s): Portrait: ETUP 54:10 (Oct. 1936): 606
Evarts, Ralph *Source(s):* CCE26 R32603
Ferrati, E. *Source(s):* CCE27 R42096
Harriman, Arthur *Source(s):* CCE34 R42094
Johannsen, Otto *Source(s):* TPRF
Orth, (Mrs.) L(izette) E(mma) *Source(s):* HIXN
Bloom, John Hague 1805-1873 [composer]
Haghe, J. *Source(s):* CPMU
Hague, John *Source(s):* CPMU
Bloom, Milton 1906- [composer, trumpeter, pianist]
Bloom, Mickey *Source(s):* ALMN; ASCC
Bloom, Sol 1870-1949 [songwriter]
Fitz, Albert H. *Source(s):* KILG
Bloomgarten, Solomon 1870-1927 [lyricist]
Jehoash *Source(s):* HESK
Yehoash *Source(s):* HESK
Blount, Herman 1914-1993 [keyboardist, bandleader, composer]
Note(s): In ROOM (see under: Sun Ra)
Blount, Sonny *Source(s):* LCAR; NGAM
Bourke, Sonny *Source(s):* LCAR; ROOM
Father of Intergalactic Music, The *Source(s):* http://www.phaelos.com/body_970722.htm (7 Oct. 2002)
Lee, Herman *Source(s):* LCAR; ROOM
Lee, Sonny *Source(s):* ROOM
Mr. Mystery *Source(s):* ROOM
Mystery, Mr. *Source(s):* ROOM
Ra, Sun *Source(s):* PSND; PEN2
Sony'r Ra, (Le [or La]) *Source(s):* PSND; PEN2
Sun Ra *Source(s):* CASS; CM05; EPMU; LCAR; NGAM; ROOM
Blum, Hans 1928- [composer]
Bensberg, Jack *Source(s):* CPOL RE-805-613
Valentino, Henry *Source(s):* PFSA
Blumberg, Herz 1902- [musicologist]
Blumberg, Harry *Source(s):* WORB
Blume, David Nason 1931- [composer, author, pianist]
King, T. S. *Source(s):* ASCP
Blumenreich, Heinrich 1877-1940 [librettist]
Reichert, Heinz *Source(s):* GAN1; GAN2; MACM; NGDO
Blumenthal, M. L. [singer, songwriter, music publisher]
Bloom, Marty *Source(s):* JASA p. 134
Blumenthal, Sandro 1874-1919 [composer]
Blumanns, Leonhard *Source(s):* COMP
Blumer, Rodney Milnes 1936- [music critic]
Milnes, Rodney *Source(s):* NGDO
Blümml, Emil Karl 1881-1925 [writer on music]
Giglleithner, K(arl) *Source(s):* LCAR; OMUO
Blumson, Peter [songwriter]
Dello, Pete *Source(s):* CCE67-68; CPOL RE-713-534; SONG
Blunt, Arthur Cecil 1843 (or 44)-1896 [songwriter, actor]
Cecil, Arthur *Source(s):* CPMU; KILG; LCAR; ROOM
Bluth, Frederick L. [writer]
Toby *Source(s):* GOTH
Blyth, David R(adford) 1884- [author, lyricist]
Radford, Dave *Source(s):* ASCA; CCE47 R16023 ("Sleepy Hollow Days")
Bobillier, Antoinette Christine Marie 1858-1918 [musicologist]

Brenet, Michel *Source(s):* BAKE; LCAR; MACM; NGDM
Bobrow, Laura J. 1928- [composer, author, singer]
Bee, Laurie *Source(s):* ASCP
Bocage, Paul 19th cent. [author]
Hazard, Désiré *Source(s):* PIPE; PSND
Note(s): Jt. pseud.: Albert Aubert & Octave Feuillet.
Boccherini, Giovanni Gastone 1742-1798 [librettist, dancer]
Argindo Bolimeo *Source(s):* GROL
Bolimeo, Argindo *Source(s):* GROL
Boccherini, (Ridolfo) Luigi 1743-1805 [composer, violoncellist]
Bouqueriny *Source(s):* NGDM
Giovannino del Violoncello *Source(s):* GROL
Note(s): See also Giovanni Battista Costanzi.
Haydn's Wife *Source(s):* NGDM; SIFA
Bochmann, Werner 1900-1993 [composer]
Cortez, Miguel *Source(s):* KOMP; KOMS; PFSA; SUPN
Bock, Fred 1939-1998 [composer; arranger, music publisher]
Roberts, Jason *Source(s):* ASCP; GOTT; LCAR
Bock, Ida 1872(or 75)- [author; librettist]
Paracelsus *Source(s):* MELL; WORB
Troll, Inga *Source(s):* WORB
Bock, Johann Christian 1724-1785 [playwright]
Freyenburg *Source(s):* PIPE; WORB
Bockelmann, Udo Jürgen 1934- [composer, singer]
Jürgen(s), Udo *Source(s):* CCE63; OMUO; PFSA
Bockshorn, Samuel (Friedrich) 1628-1665 [conductor, composer]
Capricornus, Samuel Friedrich *Source(s):* MACM; NGDM; PRAT
Bocquillon, Guillaume Louis 1781-1842 [musician, composer]
Wilhelm, Guillaume Louis *Source(s):* BAKE; IBIM; RIEM; WORB
Boedijn, Gerard(us Hendrik) 1893-1972 [composer]
Harvay, Jack *Source(s):* SUPN
Harvey, Jack *Source(s):* CCE61; REHG; WIEC
Boer, Eduardo de 1957- [composer]
Comitas, Alexander *Source(s):* LCAR; REHH; http://www.comitas.org/biography.html (15 Oct. 2002)
Boethius, Anicius Man(l)ius Severinus c.470-524 [philosopher]
Captain in Music, The *Source(s):* PSND; TCAN
Last of the Romans, The *Source(s):* PSND
Prince in Music, The *Source(s):* PSND; TCAN
Boex, Andrew J. [composer]
Note(s): Portrait: APSA
Bücher, Ernst *Source(s):* CCE29 R3553; TPRF
Gabriel, Raoul *Source(s):* CCE26 R33564; CCE28 R3596; TPRF
Hawthorne, Seymore [or Seymour] *Source(s):* CCE28 R3902; CCE38 R64288; TPRF
Note(s): Jt. pseud.: P(hilip) Paul Bliss.
Lemain, Victor *Source(s):* CCE28 R3238-9; TPRF
Vilbac, Remi *Source(s):* TPRF
Bogan, Lucille (née Anderson) 1897-1948 [singer, songwriter]
Jackson, Bessie *Source(s):* HARS; NOMG
Boggs, Mattie E. [songwriter]
Goss, Mattie E. *Source(s):* STC1
Note(s): Incorrect surname listed in some sources.
Boguslawski, Wojciech 1757-1829 [singer, writer, actor, producer]
Father of Polish Opera, The *Source(s):* GRV5 (see under: Elsner, Ksawery Józef)
Note(s): See also Stanislaus Moniuszko.
Böhm, Karl [or Carl] 1844-1920 [composer]
Note(s): Do not confuse with Karl Böhm (1894-1981); see next entry. Portrait: ETUP 50:5 (May 1932): 314.
Cooper, Henry *Source(s):* GREN; HEIN; REHG; SUPN
Böhm, Karl 1894-1981 [conductor, writer on music]
Note(s): Do not confuse with Karl Böhm (1844-1920); see previous entry.
Rubahn, Gerd *Source(s):* MACE p. 555
Böhm, Martin 1844-1912 [librettist]
Braun, Gustav *Source(s):* STGR; WORB
Hildebrandt, Emil *Source(s):* STGR; WORB
Böhm, Werner 1941- [composer]
Wendehals, Gottlieb *Source(s):* PFSA
Bohme, David (M.) 1916-2004 [composer, author]
Romaine, David [or Dave] *Source(s):* ASCP; CCE61; CCE67-68; CPOL RE-737-525
Bohn, Rudolf [or Rudolph] 1919-1979 [composer]
Bean, Rubino Roger *Source(s):* KOMS; PFSA
Beran, Carl [or Karl] *Source(s):* CCE58; CCE61
Bohn, Walter Moro [or Morrow] 1939- [guitarist, composer]
Bohn, Buddy (Moro) *Source(s):* ASCP; CCE68
Moro *Source(s):* CM38
Note(s): Also used by Emilian Leuthard & Bartolomeo Ratti.
Bohrmann, Heinrich 1837-1908 [playwright]
Bohrmann-Riegen *Source(s):* GAN2; PIPE
Note(s): Jt. pseud.: Julius Nigri von Sankt Albino.
Bohse(-Talander), August 1661-1740 [singer, composer, jurist]
Talander *Source(s):* IBIM; LCAR; WORB
Boieldieu, François Adrien 1775-1834 [composer]
Note(s): Portrait: EWCY
N*** *Source(s):* CPMU ("Ce front si pur aù regne la décence")
Note(s): Jt. pseud.: Etienne Nicolas Méhul, Rodolphe Kreutzer & Nicolas Isouard.

Boigas, Francisco Fernandez 19th cent. [poet]
Dulce, Curro *Source(s):* LAST
Boisselot, Paul 1848-1918 [librettist]
Dubois, Paul *Source(s):* LOWN; MELL
Note(s): Jt. pseud.: Charles Louis Étienne Nuitter [i.e., Charles Louis Étienne Truinet]. Also used by Clive Richardson on "Shadow Waltz."
Boisvallée, François de 1929-1974 [composer]
Duclos, Pierre *Source(s):* GREN; LCAR
Boito, Arrigo (Enrico) 1842-1918 [librettist, composer, poet, critic]
Note(s): Portrait: EWCY
Gorrio, Tobia *Source(s):* CCE57; GROL; NGDM; NGDO
Bojič, Milutin 1892-1917 [author]
Čidi, Arda *Source(s):* PIPE
Jovan, Otac *Source(s):* PIPE
Boland, François 1929- [composer, pianist]
Boland, Francy *Source(s):* EPMU; PSND
Bolling, Claude 20th cent. [composer]
Bolling, Klaus *Source(s):* PSND
Bolotin, Michael 1953 (or 54)- [singer, songwriter]
Bolton, Michael *Source(s):* CM04; DIMA; EPMU
Bolton, Andre [songwriter]
Dre, L. A. *Source(s):* PMUS-90
Bolton, (St. George) Guy Reginald 1884-1979 [actor, librettist]
Trevelyan, R. B. *Source(s):* GAN2
Bolz, Harriett 1909-1995 [composer, author, pianist]
Hallock *Source(s):* OCLC 7714869
Bonagura, Michael John, Jr. 1953- [composer, author, singer]
Brook, Michael *Source(s):* CPOL PA-326-155
Martial, Michael *Source(s):* ASCP
Bonano, Joseph 1904-1972 [composer, conductor, trumpeter]
Bonano, Sharkey *Source(s):* ASCP
Bonar, Horatius 1808-1889 [hymnist]
Note(s): Portrait: CYBH
Prince of Scottish Hymn-writers, The *Source(s):* Smith, H. Augustino. *Lyric Religion, the Romance of Immortal Hymns*. London: Fleming H. Revell, 1931.
Sweet Singer of Scotland, The *Source(s):* Ryden, E. E. *Story of Christian Hymnody*. Rock Island, Ill: Augustana Press, 1959.
Bonaventura 1221-1274 [friar, hymnist]
Doctor Seraphicus *Source(s):* CYBH (port)
Bond, Cyrus Whitfield 1915-1978 [singer, songwriter, actor]
Bond, Johnny *Source(s):* CCME; EPMU; HARD; MCCL; NASF; PEN2; WORT
Kenton, Jimmy *Source(s):* CCE75
Note(s): Possible pseud.? Listed as pseud. of Johnny Bond.
Whitfield, Cyrus *Source(s):* EPMU
Whitfield, Johnny *Source(s):* EPMU
Bondineri, Michele 1750- [composer]
Bondi, Neri *Source(s):* SONN
Bondy, Fritz 1888-1980 [author]
Leslie, Thomas *Source(s):* PIPE
Scarpi, N. O. *Source(s):* LCAR; PIPE; WORB
Bonelli, Luigi c.1893-1954 [librettist]
Cetoff, Sternberg Wassili *Source(s):* PIPE; WORB
Clurgi *Source(s):* MELL; PIPE; STGR
Bongiovi, John 1962- [guitarist, singer, songwriter]
Bon Jovi, Jon *Source(s):* HARR; PFSA; ROOM
Bongo, Kanda 1955- [singer, composer]
Kanda Bongo Man *Source(s):* PEN2
Boniface, Joseph Xavier 1798-1865 [dramatist; librettist]
Note(s): See LCAR for additional literary pseuds.
Saintine, (Joseph Xavier) *Source(s):* BAUE; LCAR; PIPE; PSND; STGR; WORB
Xavier *Source(s):* LCAR; PIPE; PSND; STGR
Bonis, Mél(anie) (Hélène) 1858-1937 [composer]
Note(s): Mélanie also abbeviated: Mel. Portrait: DWCO
Domange, (Madame) Albert *Source(s):* DWCO; MACM; TPRF
Mel-Bonis *Source(s):* BAKR; DWCO; GROL; HEIN; LCAR
Bonis, Novello (de) fl. 1675-1681 [librettist]
Sonnolento Tassista *Source(s):* ALMC p. 877; NGDO
Bonn, Franz 1830-1894 [jurist, author]
Mieris, Franz von *Source(s):* PIPE; WORB
Münchberg, Franz von *Source(s):* PIPE; WORB
Rachwitz, Franz Freiherr von *Source(s):* PIPE; WORB
Bonnachon, Louis-Henri 1784-1836 [writer]
Henry, Louis *Source(s):* GOTH
Bonnal, (Joseph) Ermend 1880-1944 [organist, composer]
Ermend-Bonnal *Source(s):* RIES
Marylis, Guy *Source(s):* CCE58; GDRM; GROL
Bonnemère (de Chavigny), Léon Eugène 1843- [composer, author]
Dinant, L. de *Source(s):* IBIM; WORB
Kerbiniou, Yves de *Source(s):* IBIM; WORB
Lionel *Source(s):* CCE51 ("Le roi Pandore")
Bonner, Carey 1858 (or 59)-1938 [minister, composer]
Note(s): Portrait: CYBH
Bailey, E. Rawdon *Source(s):* CYBH; HUEV
Bryce, A. *Source(s):* CYBH; HUEV
Byrne, Nora C. E. *Source(s):* CYBH; HUEV
Harding, R. Y. *Source(s):* HUEV
Muller, Hermann von *Source(s):* HUEV
Newton, Frank Ernest *Source(s):* HUEV

Vincent, Edwyn *Source(s):* HUEV
Bonner, Francis Musgrave 1834-1888 [composer, arranger, conductor]
Musgrave, Frank *Source(s):* GAN2
Bonner, Weldon (H. Philip) 1932-1978 [singer, guitarist, songwriter]
Barner, Juke Boy *Source(s):* HARS
Bonner, Juke Boy *Source(s):* AMUS; HARS; LCAR
One Man Trio, The *Source(s):* PSND
Bono, Salvatore 1935-1998 [singer, songwriter]
Barnum, H. B. *Source(s):* CCE62
Bono, Sonny *Source(s):* EPMU; HARR; KICK; PMUS; ROOM; YORK
Caesar *Source(s):* EPMU
Christy, Don *Source(s):* EPMU; ROOM; YORK
Christy, S(onny) *Source(s):* CCE58; CCE60; EPMU
Cristy, S. *Source(s):* CCE66
Note(s): Typographical error?
Sommers, Ronnie *Source(s):* EPMU; YORK
Bontempi, Francesco 1957- [songwriter]
Checco *Source(s):* SONG
Marrow, Lee *Source(s):* http://www.womrecords.it/bontempi.htm (20 Oct. 2003)
Bonvin, Ludwig 1850-1939 [composer, musicologist]
De'Sierre, Georges *Source(s):* NGAM
Rainer, J. B. *Source(s):* NGAM
Siders, B. von *Source(s):* NGAM
Boone, Charles Eugene 1934- [singer, songwriter]
Boone, Pat *Source(s):* ASCP; EPMU; MCCL; PEN2
Good Elvis, The *Source(s):* CM13
King of Poppish Rock 'n' Roll, The *Source(s):* EPMU (see under: Todd, Nick)
Boone, Clara Lyle 1927- [publisher, teacher, composer]
DeBohun, Lyle *Source(s):* BUL2; CCE74; COHN; GOTH; HIXN
Boone, John William 1864-1927 [pianist, composer]
Boone, Blind *Source(s):* IDBC ; JASN; KROH p. 143; NGAM
Boorman, Arthur 1896-1954 [actor, songwriter]
Risco, Arthur *Source(s):* GAN2
Boosey, (Beatrice) Joyce 1898- [pianist, composer]
Phillan, Eustace *Source(s):* CCE50 R65544 ("Evening Over the Forest"); COHN; HIXN
Booth-Clibhorn, Catherine 1860-1955 [hymnist]
Maréchale, (La) *Source(s):* LCAR
Boott, Francis 1813-1904 [composer]
Aldrich, F. B. *Source(s):* HOVL
F. B. *Source(s):* DICH; HOVL; LCAR
Telford *Source(s):* CLAB; GOTT; IBIM; LCAR; MACM; WORB
Boray, William 1953- [singer, songwriter]
Deville, Mink *Source(s):* HARR
Deville, Willy *Source(s):* AMUS
Borg, Oscar 1851-1930 [bandmaster, composer]
March King of Norway *Source(s):* SMIN
Borgh, Ted 1927- [composer]
Molda, Ralf *Source(s):* KOMP; PFSA
Borgman, Eino Mauno 1896-1973 [composer]
Linnala, Eino Mauno (Aleksanteri) *Source(s):* BUL2; DEA3
Borgudd, Tommy 1946- [musician, composer]
Borgudd, Slim *Source(s):* PSND
Borisoff, Alexander 1902-early 1980s [composer, author, cellist]
Alexander, Alex *Source(s):* MCCA
Borisoff, Leonard 1942- [film music critic, composer]
Barry, Len *Source(s):* CCE68; CCE70; ROOM
Borry, Len *Source(s):* CCE76
Bornet, Francois 1915- [composer, singer]
Bornet, Fred *Source(s):* ASCC
Bornschein, Franz (Carl) 1879-1948 [composer, violinist, conductor]
Note(s): Portraits: ETUP 50:5 (May 1932): 314; MUSA 30:26 (25 Oct. 1919): 17
Fairfield, Frank [or Franz] *Source(s):* CCE36 E54958-59; LCAR; NAGM
Note(s): Also used by Samuel Liddle.
Börnstein, Heinrich (Karl) 1805-1892 [actor, author]
Berge, Walter von *Source(s):* PIPE
Germamer, H. *Source(s):* PIPE
Borodin, Alexander 1833-1887 [composer]
Sunday Composer, A *Source(s):* http://www.virginiasymphony.org/Sept14-02.html (7 Oct. 2002)
Note(s): Called himself.
Borowitz, Abram Solman 1910-1985 [author, librettist, composer]
Burrows, Abe [or Abram] (Solman) *Source(s):* EPMU; GAMM; GAN1; GAN2; PIPE
Honest Abe *Source(s):* GAMM
Börschel, Erich 1907-1988 [composer]
Brodersen, Eric *Source(s):* KOMS; PFSA
Haller, Fred *Source(s):* CCE55; KOMS; PFSA; REHG; REHH; RIES; SUPN
Lattmann, Heinz *Source(s):* KOMS; PFSA
Borthwick, Jane Laurie 1813-1897 [composer, hymnist]
H. L. L. *Source(s):* COHN; CYBH; HIXN; ROOM
Note(s): H. L. L. = "Hymns from the Land of Luther."
Bortniansky, (Stepanovich) Dmitri 1752-1825 [composer]
Note(s): Portrait: ETUP 58:6 (June 1940): 426
Russian Palestrina, The *Source(s):* PSND

Borzage, Donald Dan 1925- [composer, teacher]
Bennett, Don *Source(s):* CCE60
Daniels, Don *Source(s):* ASCP (see reference)
Boster, Bob [composer, multi-media artist]
Meridies, Mr. *Source(s):* http://detritus.net/contact/rumori/3/author.html (7 Oct. 2002)
Bostick, Calvin T. 1928- [composer, author, pianist]
Bostic, C(al) *Source(s):* ASCC; CCE62; CCE64-65
Botkin, Vasily Petrovich 1812-1869 [writer, critic]
Fortepianov [or Forte'pyanov], Vasily *Source(s):* GROL; NGDM
Botsford, George 1874-1949 [songwriter, music publisher]
Becker, Will(iam) (H.) *Source(s):* JASA (port.)
Böttcher, Martin 1927- [composer, conductor, arranger]
Thomas, Michael *Source(s):* CCE54; CCE61; KOMP; KOMS; PFSA; RIES
Bottesini, Giovanni 1821-1889 [bassist, conductor, composer]
Paganini of the Double Bass *Source(s):* GROL
Bötticher, Hans (Gustav) 1883-1934 [kabarettist, poet]
Hester, Gustav *Source(s):* LCAR
Ringelnatz, Joachim *Source(s):* LCAR
Bottrigari, Ercole 1531-1612 [music theorist, composer, architect]
Benelli, Alemanno *Source(s):* BAKR; GROL; MACM
Note(s): Anagram of Anniballe Melone.
Botwinik, B. [writer on music]
Note(s): This may be Barnett (or Berl) Botwinik, 1885-1945.
Pero *Source(s):* SEND
Boucher, Eric 1958- [songwriter]
Biafra, Jello *Source(s):* AMUS; EPMU
Boucher, Lydia 1890-1971 [composer]
Marie Therese, (Sister) *Source(s):* BUL3
Boucheron, René Maximilian 1846-1896 [librettist]
Boucheron, Maxime *Source(s):* GAN2
Boulanger, Marie-Juliette (Olga) 1893-1918 [composer]
Boulanger, Lili *Source(s):* BAKR; LCAR
Boulanger, Robert Francis 1940- [composer, author, singer]
Trevor, Van *Source(s):* ASCP; CCE64
Boulogne, Joseph (de) 1739 (or 45)-1799 [composer, violinist]
Saint-Georges, (Joseph Boulogne), Chevalier de *Source(s):* IDBC; SOTH
Bourdonneau, André 1874-1945 [author, librettist]
Barde, André *Source(s):* GAN1; GAN2; WORB
Bourgeois, Karl 1904-1982 [composer]
Burgwart, Karl *Source(s):* REHG; SUPN
Bourke, Pieter [compser, percussionist, audio engineer]
Soma *Source(s):* MOMU
Snog and Black Lung *Source(s):* MOMU
Bourlin, Antoine Jean (André) 1752-1828 [writer]
Dumaniant, Antoine Jean *Source(s):* MELL; PIPE; SONN
Bourne, (Mrs.) [songwriter]
Grazia, E. N. *Source(s):* CPMU; GOTH
Note(s): Publication dates 1852-1894 (CPMU)
Bourne, Hugh 1772-1852 [hymn book editor, hymnist]
H. B. *Source(s):* JULN (Appendix)
Boursiquot, Dionysius Lardner 1820 (or 22)-1890 [actor dramatist; librettist]
Boucicault, Dion(ysus Lard(n)er) *Source(s):* GAN1; GAN2; LCAR; WORB
Lardner, Dionysius *Source(s):* MELL; NGDO
Morton, Lee *Source(s):* NGDO
Bovy, Antoine Nicolas Joseph [or Giuseppe] 1808-1868 [violinist, composer, actor]
Bovery, J(ules) *Source(s):* BAKE; GOTT; IBIM; MACM
Bowden, Arthur 1900-1982 [comedian, singer, composer]
Askey, Arthur *Source(s):* GAMM
Bowen, M. [composer, songwriter]
Fultoni, M. *Source(s):* CCE14 E347156; CPMU
Bower, Maurice [or Maury] (Donald) 1922- [composer, conductor, publisher]
Bower, Bugs *Source(s):* ASCP; CCE50; CCE62; LCAR
Bowers, Bryan Benson 1940- [singer songwriter, instrumentalist]
King of the Autoharp *Source(s):* MCCL
Bowers, Robert Hood 1877-1941 [composer, conductor]
Bowers, Robin Hood *Source(s):* KINK; LCAR; PSND
Bowland, Derek 1966- [rapper]
Derek B. *Source(s):* EPMU; http://www.discogs.com/artist/Derek+B (25 Jan. 2005)
EZQ *Source(s):* EPMU; http://www.discogs.com/artist/Derek+B
Bowles, William Lisle 1762-1850 [clergyman, poet]
Note(s): See PSND for additional nonmusic-related pseudonyms.
Fabius *Source(s):* GOTT
Macleod, (Dr.) Archibald, The Late *Source(s):* GOTT
Bowman, Don 1937- [singer, songwriter, guitarist]
World's Worst Country Singer *Source(s):* MCCL
World's Worst Guitar Picker, The *Source(s):* MCCL
World's Worst Guitarist, The *Source(s):* PSND
Bowman, Norma Jean 1937- [songwriter, singer, guitarist]

Pruett, Jeanne *Source(s):* CCME; ENCM; LCAR; MCCL

Box, Harold Elton 1903-1981 [songwriter]
Bernard, Adrien *Source(s):* CCE70 R486152
Note(s): Desmond Cox [i.e., Adrian Keuleman] & Clem(ent) Bernard.
Boccolosi, Harry *Source(s)* CCE40 #19415 Efor63075; CCE67; LCCC 1938-45 (reference card)
Note(s): Jt. pseud.: Desmond Cox [i.e., Adrian Keuleman], Harry Leon [i.e., Sugarman] & Domonic [or Don] Pelosi.
Dévereux, Jules *Source(s):* CCE40 #18216 Efor62825; LCCC 1938-45 (reference card)
Note(s): Jt. pseud.: Harry Leon [i.e., Sugarman], Domonic [or Don] Pelosi & Desmond Cox [i.e., Adrian Keuleman]
Fraser, Gordon *Source(s):* CCE40 #25023 Efor63262; CCE67; LCCC 1938-45 (reference card)
Note(s): Jt. pseud.: Harry Leon [i.e., Sugarman], Desmond Cox [i.e., Adrian Keuleman] & Dominic [or Don] Pelosi.
Fuertes, Pedro *Source(s):* CCE43 #46647 Efor68713 ("Serenade to a Dream")
Note(s): Jt. pseud.: Desmond Cox [i.e., Adrian Keuleman]
Heatherton, Fred *Source(s):* CCE45 #13436 Efor70306 ("Dreams of Yesterday"); CPOL RE-7-846
Note(s): Jt. pseud.: Desmond Cox [i.e., Adrian Keuleman] & Lewis Ilda [i.e., Irwin Dash]
Jones, Hirem *Source(s):* CCE36 Efor43964; CCE64 R334070
Note(s): Jt. pseud.: Ralph (T.) Butler, Paddy [i.e., John GodfreyOwen] Roberts & C(harles) J(oseph) Edwards.
Morrow, Morton *Source(s):* CCE63-64; CCE70 R484404
Note(s): Jt. pseud.: Desmond Cox [i.e., Adrian Keuleman] & Paddy [i.e., John Godfrey Owen] Roberts.
Perch, Polly *Source(s):* CCE34 Efor37471 ("Scratch-A-Poll-Polly")
Note(s): Jt. pseud.: Desmond Cox [i.e., Adrian Keuleman], Ralph (T.) Butler & C(harles) J(oseph) Edwards
Spade, Jack *Source(s):* CCE44 Efor 70219; KILG
Note(s): Jt. pseud.: Desmond Cox [i.e., Adrian Keuleman] & Ilda Lewis [i.e., Irwin Dash]
Young, Errol *Source(s):* CCE45 Efor70638 ("I'm Happy in Rags")
Note(s): Jt. pseud.: Desmond Cox [i.e., Adrian Keuleman]

Boyd, Edward [or Eddie] Riley 1914-1994 [singer, pianist, songwriter]
Boyd, Ernie *Source(s):* HARS; PEN2
Boyd, Little Eddie *Source(s):* HARS; PEN2
Little Eddie *Source(s):* LCAR

Boyd, William [or Bill] 1910-1977 [singer, guitarist, actor, songwriter]
Boyd, Cowboy Rambler *Source(s):* CCE42 #28295 E105339
Boyd, Rambler *Source(s):* CCE42 #28238 E105949
Cowboy Rambler, The *Source(s):* PSND; STAC

Boyd, Willie 1946-1990 [singer, guitarist, songwriter]
Gitry, Willie *Source(s):* EPMU; HARS
Note(s): Possible original name.
Harris, Hi Tide *Source(s):* CCE77; EPMU; HARS

Boyle, (Miss) [composer]
Alexandrina, (Sister) *Source(s):* CPMU (publication date 1915)
S. A. *Source(s):* CPMU (publication date 1915)

Bozzola, Luigi [librettist]
Mari, Mario *Source(s):* STGR

Braccini, Roberto 1755 (or 56)-1791 [composer]
Braccini, Luigi *Source(s):* NGDM

Braccioli, Grazio 1682-1752 [librettist]
Nigello Preteo *Source(s):* GROL

Brace, Seth Collins 1811- [minister, hymnist]
C. *Source(s):* JULN (Appendix); ROGG

Bracegirdle, Nicholas [or Nick] [songwriter]
Chicane *Source(s):* AMUS; LCAR; PMUS-00

Brack, Hans-Heinrich 1950- [singer, songwriter]
Brack, John *Source(s):* EPMU; MCCL
Mr. Swiss Country *Source(s):* EPMU; MCCL

Braconnier, Jean ?-c.1512 [singer, composer]
Lourdault *Source(s):* GROL; NGDM

Bradford, James 1954- [singer, songwriter, actor]
Nail, Jimmy *Source(s):* NOMG

Bradford, John Milton 1919-1998 [composer, author, singer]
Levinson, John M. *Source(s):* ASCP

Bradford, (John Henry) Perry 1893-1970 [composer, pianist]
Note(s): Portraits: JASZ (with W(illiam) C(hristopher) Handy); SAMP (with Jeanette Bradford)
Bradford, Mule *Source(s):* CASS; EPMU; GROL; LCAR; NGDJ; PSND
Henry, John *Source(s):* PMUS
John Henry *Source(s):* PMUS
Note(s): Also used by Joel Machado.

Bradford, Sylvester Henry 1942- [composer, author]
Brad, Lester *Source(s):* CCE55
Thompson, Ann *Source(s):* ASCP
Thompson-Lester, Andy *Source(s):* CCE55 Eunp

Bradley, (Revd.) Edward 1827-1889 [lyricist]
Bede, Cuthbert *Source(s):* KILG; LCAR

Bradley, Graham 1945- [composer]
Bonney, Graham *Source(s):* CCE66; PFSA
Bradshaw, Harriet [composer]
Wahsdarb, Teirrah *Source(s):* CPMU (publication dates 1858-59)
Bradshaw, Myron Carlton 1905 (or 08)-1958 [composer, author, singer]
Bradshaw, Tiny *Source(s):* ASCP; CPOL RE-133-999; LCAR
Bradshaw, Susan 1931- [composer, pianist]
Zak, Pyotr *Source(s):* SPIE
Note(s): Fictitious composer. Jt. pseud.: Hans Keller.
Bradsworth, Samuel [composer, songwriter]
Note(s): Publication dates for the following: 1896.
Bardows, M. S. [or T. S.] *Source(s):* CPMU
Morenzi, E. H. *Source(s):* CPMU
Rowdemath, Bláus *Source(s):* CPMU
Braga, Roberto Carlos 1941 (or 43)- [composer, singer]
Carlos, Roberto *Source(s):* CCE66-68; HWOM; PEN2
Roberto Carlos *Source(s):* HWOM; LCAR
Bragg, (Steven) William [or Billy] 1957- [singer, songwriter]
Bard of Barking, The *Source(s):* EPMU; LCAR
Brahinsky, Mani Leib 1883-1953 [lyricist]
Mani-Leib *Source(s):* HESK; LCAR
Brahms, Johannes 1833-1897 [composer]
Brahmsian *Source(s):* EPON
Kreisler, Johannes, (Jr.) *Source(s):* GROL; RILM 88-03503-as
Marks, G. W. *Source(s):* GOTH; GROL; NGDM
Note(s): Aug. Cranz house name.
Scoundrel Brahms *Source(s):* SIFA
Bramston, Richard c.1485-1554 [church musician, composer]
Smyth, Richard *Source(s):* NGDM
Branca, Giovanni Giacomo c.1620-after 1694 [violinist, composer]
Jacamo violino *Source(s):* GROL
Brand, Adolph Johannes 1934-1990 [jazz pianist, composer]
Brand, Dollar *Source(s):* CCE64; HARD; PEN2; PSND
Dollar Brand *Source(s):* LCAR
Ibrahim, Abdullah *Source(s):* CM24; EPMU; HARD; LCAR; PEN2
Brand, Michael 1814 (or 15)-1870 [composer, music critic]
Mosonyi, Mihály *Source(s):* BAKO; BAKR; LCAR; NGDM; NGDO; PIPE
Brandenburg, Helmuth 1928- [composer]
Freeman, Kookie *Source(s):* KOMS; PFSA
Brandmayer, Rudolf [or Dolf] 1913- [composer]
Brieg, Axel *Source(s):* KOMP; KOMS
Lezza, Carlo *Source(s):* KOMP; KOMS; PFSA
Slan, Jack *Source(s):* CCE74; KOMS; PFSA
Branen, Jeff T. 1872-1927 [author, publisher]
Grant and Graham *Source(s):* CCE22 E532788
Note(s): Jt. pseud.: Frederick G. Johnson.
Jeffries, T. B. *Source(s):* CCE47 R15440 ("Bring Back My Heart"); PMUS-00
Nenarb, Jeff T. *Source(s):* CCE43 #25483, 452 R118615; SPTH p. 395
Brannum, Hugh Roberts 1910-1987 [composer, author, singer]
Brannum, Lumpy *Source(s):* PSND
Jeans, Mr. Green *Source(s):* PSND
Uncle Lumpy *Source(s):* PSND
Branscombe, Gena 1881-1977 [composer, pianist]
Note(s): Portraits: APSA; DWCO
Allison, Adrian *Source(s):* CCE30 Eunp27004; STRN
Tenney, (Mrs.) John F. *Source(s):* STRN
Brase, Fritz 1884-1940 (or 41) [composer]
Castro, R. *Source(s):* SUPN
Bratman, Carroll Charles 1906-1984 [composer]
Carol, Gary *Source(s):* ASCP; CCE68
Bratton, John W(alter) 1867-1947 [composer]
Stratton, Frank *Source(s):* CCE37 R49703
Walter, J. B. *Source(s):* CCE37 R55600
Note(s): Also used by William Arms Fisher.
Brault, (Robert) Victor 1899-1963 [singer, conductor, teacher, composer]
Winter, Laurent *Source(s):* CANE
Braun, Karl Johann, Ritter von Braunthal 1802-1866 [author, librettist]
Charles, Jean *Source(s):* LCAR; OMUO
Bräutigam, Willi 1943- [composer]
Astor, Tom *Source(s):* PFSA
Bray, Mike 1951- [songwriter, singer]
Accrington, Stanley *Source(s):* EPMU; ROOM
Breen, May Singhi 1891-1970 [composer, author]
DeRose, (Mrs.) Peter *Source(s):* ASCB; KINK
Rosa, Malia *Source(s):* ASCB; CCE50-51
Sweethearts of the Air *Source(s):* JASZ; KINK; TCAN
Note(s): Jt. sobriquet with husband: Peter DeRose.
Ukelele Lady, The *Source(s):* ASCP; KINK
Breeze, Lionel 1909 (or 10)-1989 [composer]
Llewellyn, Ray *Source(s):* CLTV
Note(s): Pseud. of Lyn Murray [i.e., Lionel Breeze] & others; see NOTES: Llewellyn, Ray.
Lyn *Source(s):* CLRA
Murray, Lyn *Source(s):* CLOJ; CLRA
Breitenbach, Alfred 1875-1942 [composer, lyricist, publisher]
Note(s): With the exception of "Fred Fischer" & "Al Bryan," the names listed below were identified as pseuds. of "Fred Fisher."

Bryan, Al *Source(s):* PMUS-00
Fischer, Fred *Source(s):* EWEN; NGAM
Fisher, Fred *Source(s):* GAMM; PMUS-00
Hancock, John *Source(s):* CCE58; CCE62 R293912; CCE63 R324261
Jones, Tom *Source(s):* CCE63 R309226
Roaming Ranger, The *Source(s):* CCE62 R295085
Summey, Reid *Source(s):* CCE64; CPOL RE-574-290

Breitenfeld, Paul Emil(e) 1924-1977 [composer, saxophonist]
Desmond, Paul *Source(s):* BAKR; EPMU; LCAR; PSND; REHG

Breitengraser, Wilhelm c.1495-1542 [composer]
Breyttengraser, Guilelmus *Source(s):* REIM

Breitner, Burghard 1884- [writer]
Sturm, Bruno *Source(s):* STGR; WORB

Breker, Gerhard 1942- [composer]
Breck, Freddy *Source(s):* PFSA

Brendel, Georg Christoph 1668-1772 [theologian, poet, organist]
Chrysostomus, Polycarp *Source(s):* IBIM; LCAR; WORB
Lethander *Source(s):* IBIM; LCAR; WORB
Pantophilus, Gratian *Source(s):* IBIM; WORB
Rhinelota, Hypocritasm *Source(s):* IBIM; WORB

Brentano(-von Arnim), Anne Elisabeth [or Bettina] 1785 (or 88)-1859 [composer, singer, author]
Arnim, Bettina von *Source(s):* WORB
Note(s): Married name.
Beor, Beans *Source(s):* GROL; MUST 139:1861 (1998): 18
Bettina *Source(s):* MUST 139:1861 (1998):18; WORB
Bor, Beans van *Source(s):* JACK

Bresnan, Catharine Mary 1904- [lyricist, writer]
Canty, Cathal *Source(s):* PSND

Breuer, F(ranz) J(osef) [composer]
Fleury, Jeannette *Source(s):* CCE74
Glückmann, Hans *Source(s):* CCE53 Efor19737
Note(s): Jt. pseud.: Ernst (Johannes Albert) Bader.
Junghans, Heinz *Source(s):* CCE55-58
Triberg, Klaus *Source(s):* CCE52 Efor14600; KOMP; PFSA
Note(s): Jt. pseud.: Käte Kongsbak-König & Friedrich [or Fritz] Schlenkermann.

Breuer, Wolfgang 1938- [composer]
Kelin, Eric *Source(s):* BUL3

Breuker, Willem 1944- [composer]
Godfather of Dutch Improvisational Music, The *Source(s):* http://www.musicwords.nl/appellation.eng.htm (7 Oct. 2002)

Brewer, Jehoi(a)da 1752-1817 [minister, hymnist]
Note(s): Portrait: CYBH
Sylvestris *Source(s):* CYBH; JULN

Brewster, Henry B(ennet) 1850-1908 [author]
Leforestier, H. B. *Source(s):* PIPE

Brian, William 1876-1972 [composer, hymnist]
Brian, Havergal *Source(s):* LCAR; MUWB; ROOM
Note(s): Adopted "Havergal" sometime in the 1890s (LCAR)
H. B. *Source(s):* MUWB
La main gauche *Source(s):* MUWB
Main gauche, La *Souce(s):* MUWB
Wassail *Source(s):* MUWB

Bridge, Frank 1879-1841 [composer, violist, conductor]
More, John L. *Source(s):* BLIC ("The Turtle's Retort;" arr.)

Bridge, (Sir) (John) Frederick 1844-1924 [organist, composer, author]
Westminster Pilgrim, A *Source(s):* Bridge, Frederick. *A Westminster Pilgrim*. London: Novello, 1918.

Bridgeman, Earl Thomas 1950- [singer, songwriter]
Thomas, Earl *Source(s):* EPMU

Bridges, Robert Seymour 1844-1930 [poet]
Note(s): Portrait: CYBH
R. B *Source(s):* CPMU

Bridges, (Claude) Russell 1941 (or 42)- [singer, guitarist, songwriter]
Chameleon *Source(s):* http://leonrussellrecords.com/Leon%20bio.htm (9 Oct. 2003)
Note(s): See also Herbert [or Herbie] Jeffrey Hancock.
Master of Space and Time *Source(s):* DIMA
Roselle, Leroy *Source(s):* http://www.geocities.com/SunsetStrip/Birdland/4631/leonfaq.htm (3 Jan. 2005)
Russell, Leon(ard) *Source(s):* AMUS; CCE66; LCAR; PMUS
Wilson, Hank *Source(s):* LCAR; NGAM; NOMG
Note(s): In NGAM listed as pseud. of Leon Russell. Used on country recording.

Bridgetower, George Augustus Polgreen 1779-1860 [composer]
Abyssinian Prince, The *Source(s):* PSND

Briggs, Kevin [songwriter]
Briggs, She'kspere *Source(s): Music Connection* 24:15 (2000): 17
She'kspere *Source(s): Music Connection* 24:15 (2000): 17

Bright, Gerald 1904-1974 [composer, arranger, pianist, organist]
Geraldo, (M.) *Source(s):* CCE37 Efor47426; CCE61; LCAR; MUWB

Brignole, Rosa (B(eata)) 1903 (or 08)- [composer, author]
Ivanoff, Rose *Source(s):* ASCP

Brine, Mark Vincent 1948- [composer, author, singer]
Frost, Jack *Source(s):* ASCP; CPOL PA-70-453

Note(s): Also used by Harold G. Frost, Charles Degesco, E. Clinton Keithley & Bob Dylan, [i.e., Robert Allen Zimmerman]
Wild Blue Yodeler, The *Source(s):* http://www.wildoatsrecords.com/FeaturedArtists.html (7 Oct. 2002)
Brisman, Heskel 1923- [composer, teacher, editor]
Britt, Ben *Source(s):* ASCP
Haskell, Burt *Source(s):* ASCP
Britten, Benjamin [songwriter]
Note(s): Do not confuse with Benjamin Britten (1913-1976).
Campbell, Grace *Source(s):* KILG ("Jessie's Dream" (1858))
Britten, Emma Hardinge 1823-1899 [composer, songwriter]
Reinhold, Ernest *Source(s):* PSND
Britton, Thomas 1643 (or 44)-1714 [coal seller, musician, antiquarian]
Musical Small-Coal Man, The *Source(s):* DAWS; GRV3
Brixi, Václav Norbert 1739-1803 [organist, composer]
Brixi, Hieronymus *Source(s):* LCAR
Brixi, Jeronym *Source(s):* GROL; LCAR; NGDM
Jeronym *Source(s):* LCAR; NGDM
Broad, William Michael 1955- [singer, songwriter]
Idol, Billy *Source(s):* CM03; HARR; RECR; WORL
Broadus, Calvin 1971- [rapper; songwriter]
Snoop Doggy Dog *Source(s):* FAFO; PMUS-95; RECR
Brochowska, Pauline Marie Julie 1794-1850 [author, librettist]
Theophania, (Lina) *Source(s):* STGR; WORB
Brocht, Harley F. [composer]
Barton, Glen *Source(s):* JASA; JASN; RAGM
Note(s): Also used by Gustav Klemm.
Brocker(t), Mary Christine 1957- [singer, songwriter]
Lady T. *Source(s):* PMUS
Marie, Tenna [or Teena] *Source(s):* EPMU; PMUS
Tenna Maria *Source(s):* NOMG; PMUS
Brockman, James 1866-1967 [composer]
Brachman, James *Source(s):* CCE31 R14755
Kellette, John W(illiam) *Source(s):* BLIC; KILG
Note(s): Also jt. pseud.: Nathaniel (Hawthorne) Vincent.
Kenbrovin, Jaan *Source(s):* CCE47; CCE50; KILG; LCAR; SPTH p. 413; STUW
Note(s): Jt. pseud.: Nathaniel (Hawthorne) Vincent & James Kendis.
Brockway, Howard 1870-1951 [composer, pianist]
Kmita, Andrei *Source(s):* RPRA
Sterling, Al *Source(s):* RPRA
Brockway, Jennie M(ary) 1886?- [composer, author]
Owen, Mary Jane *Source(s):* CCE42 #25456 Eunp300959; CCE48; PSND
Brodszky, Miklós 1905-1958 [composer, songwriter]
Brodszky, Nicholaus [or Nikolaus] *Source(s):* GAN1; GAN2; LCAR; STUW
Brody, David S(eymour) 1955- [composer, author]
Dartos, Tunica *Source(s):* ASCP
Brogue, Roslyn 1919- [composer]
Philomela *Source(s):* OCLC 36974275
Bronfin, Filipp Markovic 1879-1935 [musicologist]
Fin *Source(s):* WORB
Broniewski, Wladyslaw 1897 (or 98)-1962 [author]
Czamara *Source(s):* PIPE
Orl *Source(s):* PIPE
Orlik *Source(s):* LCAR; PIPE
Brontë, Anne 1820-1849 [author, hymnist]
Note(s): Portrait: CYBH. Used other pseuds.; see literary sources.
Bell, Acton *Source(s):* ALNA; CYBH; LCAR; PIPE
Brooke, Frances (née Moore) 1724-1789 [author]
Note(s): See PSND for additional nonmusic-related pseudonyms.
Singleton, Mary *Source(s):* PIPE; WORB
Brooke, Stopford Augustus 1832-1916 [minister, hymnist]
Note(s): Portrait: CYBH
B. *Source(s):* JULN
Brooks, Anne Sooy 1911- [composer, singer]
Savoy, A(nne) *Source(s):* CCE58-61; CCE68; PSND
Brooks, Douglas (Jackson) 1956- [singer, songwriter, multi-instrumentalist]
Stone, Doug *Source(s):* ALMN; CM10; MCCL
Brooks, Elmore 1918-1963 [singer, songwriter, guitarist]
James, Elmo *Source(s):* CCE60; HARS
James, Elmore *Source(s):* CM08; HARR; LCAR
Note(s): Do not confuse with Elmore James, Jr. [i.e., Iverson Minter]
James, Joe Willie *Source(s):* HARS
Brooks, Harold (Floyd) 1932-1974 [saxophonist, composer]
Brooks, Teeny *Source(s):* EPMU
Brooks, Tina *Source(s):* CCE60-61; EPMU; GROL
Brooks, Phillips 1835-1893 [minister, hymnist]
Note(s): Portrait: CYBH
Greatest American Preacher of the 19th Century, The *Source(s):* CYBH
Broonzy, William Lee Conley 1893-1958 [singer, guitarist, songwriter]

Blues Boy Bill *Source(s):* HARS; LCAR; PSND
Broomsley, Big Bill *Source(s):* HARS; LCAR; PSND
Broonzy, Big Bill *Source(s):* CLAB; CM13; EPMU; HARS; LCAR; PSND; SUTT
Chicago Bill *Source(s):* HARS; LCAR; PSND
Hunter, Slim *Source(s):* HARS; LCAR; PSND
Johnson, Big Bill *Source(s):* HARS; LCAR; PSND
Little Sam *Source(s):* HARS; LCAR; PSND
Little Son *Source(s):* HARS; LCAR; PSND
Natchez *Source(s):* HARS; LCAR; PSND
Sampson, Sammy *Source(s):* HARS; LCAR; PSND
Smith, Howlin(g) *Source(s):* SUTT

Broschi, Carlo 1705-1782 [singer, composer, poet]
Farinelli [or Farinello] *Source(s):* GREN; KOMU; LCAR; NGDM; SADC
Note(s): Incorrectly listed in *Bielefelder Catalogue* as composer of "Idaspe," which is actually by his brother, Riccardo Broschi (1703-1756). (GREN)

Brossard, Sebastien de 1655-1730 [priest, theorist, composer]
Fontaines, Robsard des *Source(s):* GROL

Brost, Raymond 1896-1970 [songwriter]
Henderson, Ray(mond) *Source(s):* BAKR; EPMU; EWEN (port); GAN2; HARR; LCAR; NGDM

Brouck, Jacob(us) de fl. 1568-83 [singer, composer]
Prugg, Jacob de *Source(s):* GROL; LCAR

Brough, (Robert) Barnabus 1828-1860 [burlesque writer, satirist]
Brothers Brough *Source(s):* LCAR
Brough Brothers *Source(s):* LCAR
Burgh, Barnard *Source(s):* GAN2 (see under: Brough, Lionel)
Woodensconce, Papernose, Esq. *Source(s):* CART

Broughton, Reginald Thomas 1890-1941 [composer]
Thomas, Harry *Source(s):* JASA; JASG; JASN p. 295; JASR
Note(s): Also used as a jt. pseud. by Harold [or Harry] (George) Belafonte & Millard Thomas.

Brounoff, Platon G. 1863-1924 [composer, teachetr, conductor, music critic]
Sharp, B. A. *Source(s):* CART; LCAR

Brouquières, Jean 1923-1994 [composer]
Briver, John *Source(s):* REHH; SUPN

Browder, Thomas August Darnell 1950 (or 51)- [singer, producer, songwriter]
Creole Kid *Source(s):* LCAR
Darnell, August *Source(s):* CCE78; HARR

Browder, William [or Bill] 1944- [singer, songwriter]
Browser, Bill *Source(s):* NITE
Note(s): Incorrect spelling of surname.
Good Shepherd, The *Source(s):* FLIN
Sheppard, T. G. *Source(s):* CCME; FLIN; MCCL; PSND; STAC
Stacy, Brian *Source(s):* MCCL; PSND

Brown, Adeline E. [composer, author]
Brown, Pat *Source(s):* ASCC

Brown, Albert Joseph c.1968- [singer, songwriter]
Sure!, Al B. *Source(s):* CM13

Brown, Alonzo [rapper]
Mr. Hyde *Source(s):* EPMU

Brown, Angela Laverne c.1965- [singer, songwriter]
New Soul Queen *Source(s):* CM37
Stone, Angie *Source(s):* CM37

Brown, Anthony Graham 1954- [singer, songwriter, actor]
Brown, T. Graham *Source(s):* CCME; EPMU; FLIN; LCAR; MCCL; STAC
His T-Ness *Source(s):* FLIN

Brown, Bertrand 1888-1964 [composer]
Note(s): Portrait: ETUP 50:6 (June 1932): 390
Bertrand-Brown *Source(s):* LCAR; TPRF

Brown, Bob 1937?- [songwriter]
Forrest, David *Source(s):* CCE55 Efor31818; CPOL RE-143-473
Note(s): Jt. pseud.: Jack Fishman (1918 (or 19)-), Cliff Adams & Francis (or Frank) (Charles) Chacksfield.
Johns, Michael *Source(s):* CCE55 Efor31818; CPOL RE-143-473
Note(s): Jt. pseud.: Jack Fishman (1918 (or 19)-), Cliff Adams, & Francis (or Frank) (Charles) Chacksfield.
Steele, Jack *Source(s):* CCE56; CPOL RE-176-207
Wilson, Grant *Source(s):* CCE 54; CPOL RE-141-048

Brown, Chuck [bandleader, performer, songwriter]
Godfather of Go-Go, The *Source(s):* http://www.weta.org/fm/features/audio/arts/0042.html (7 Oct. 2002)

Brown, Clarence 1924-2005 [singer, instrumentalist, songwriter]
Gatemouth *Source(s):* LCAR
Note(s): See also (Daniel) Louis Armstrong.
Brown, Gatemouth *Source(s):* CM11; HARS

Brown, Cleo(patra) 1903 (or 09)-1995 [singer, composer]
Brown, C. Patra *Source(s):* PSNN

Brown, Frank 1916-2002 [music critic]
Blake, David *Source(s):* http://www.ahram.org.eg/2000/500/profile.htm (25 Feb. 2005)

Brown, Frederic [composer]
Goldstein, J. *Source(s):* GOTH

Brown, Gavin 1901-1970 [actor, singer, composer]
Gordon, Gavin *Source(s):* PSND

Brown, George W. [songwriter]
Persley, George W. *Source(s):* SPTH p. 198

Brown, Ginnette Patricia 1953- [singer, songwriter]
Brown, Ginny *Source(s):* MCCL
Little Ginny *Source(s):* MCCL
Brown, Henry 1906- [singer, pianist, songwriter]
Note(s): Do not confuse with guitarist Henry "Hi" Brown.
Brown, Papa *Source(s):* HARS
Charles, Henry *Source(s):* HARS
Brown, Henry Albert c.1864-1925 [composer, conductor]
Godin, Felix *Source(s):* MUWB; http://www.fullerswood.fsnet.co.uk/godin.htm (30 Mar. 2003)
Lorraine, Victor *Source(s):* TPRF
Brown, Ignatio Herb 1896-1964 [songwriter, pianist, music publisher]
Brown, Nacio Herb *Source(s):* EWEN (port.); HARR; NGAM
Brown, James 1928 (or 33)- [singer, songwriter]
Note(s): Records indicate Brown was born in 1928; however, he claims it was 1933.
Biggest Cat, The *Source(s):* PSND
Cultivated Catfish, The *Source(s):* PSND
Explosive Mr. Brown, The *Source(s):* PSND
Godfather of Soul, The *Source(s):* AMUS; EPMU; PSND
Grandfather of Soul, The *Source(s):* WORT
Hardest Working Man in Show Business, The *Source(s):* AMUS; EPMU
King of Soul, The *Source(s):* PSND
Note(s): See also Solomon Burke.
King of Soul Music, The *Source(s):* PSND; WORT
Minister of the New New Super Heavy Funk, The *Source(s):* EPMU
Mr. Dynamite *Source(s):* AMUS; CLAB; PSND; SHAD; WORT
Notes(s): See also Elvis A(a)ron Presley.
Original Disco Man, The *Source(s):* PSND
Soul Brother Number 1 *Source(s):* AMUS; PSND; SHAD; WORT
Brown, Jameson 1952 (or 53)- [singer, songwriter, guitarist]
Brown, Junior *Source(s):* CM15; ENCM
Brown, Jonathan C. [composer]
Frogworth, A. C *Source(s):* GOTH
Brown, Lee 1919-1980 [singer, songwriter, author]
Brown, Babs *Source(s):* LCAR
Gonzales, Bab *Source(s):* LCAR; PEN2
Gonzales, Ricardo *Source(s):* PEN2
Singh, Ram *Source(s):* PEN2
Brown, Mary E. [organist, pianist, songwriter]
Brown, Mae *Source(s):* RAGT p. 97
Brown, Nacio Herb, Jr. 1921-2002 [songwriter, music publisher]
Porter, Nacio *Source(s):* CCE57
Brown, Obadiah Bruen 1829-1901 [composer, organist, conductor]
Leslie, Ernest *Source(s):* LCAR; MACM
Mayer, Ferdinand *Source(s):* LCAR
Meyer, Ferdinand *Source(s):* CCE12 R3520; MACM; NEWB; WCAB 12:256
Note(s): A. P. Schmidt house name; see NOTES: Meyer, Ferdinand.
Brown, Olive 1922-1982 [singer, songwriter]
Foxy GGM [i.e., Great-Grandmother] *Source(s):* HARS
New Empress of the Blues *Source(s):* HARS
Princess of the Blues, The *Source(s):* HARS
Brown, Paul 1920- [composer, author, singer]
Page, Paul *Source(s):* ASCP
Brown, Ricardo 1972- [songwriter]
Kalhoon *Source(s):* AMUS
Kingpin, The *Source(s):* AMUS
Kurupt *Source(s):* AMUS; PMUS-00
Young Gotti *Source(s):* AMUS
Brown, Richard c.1880-1937 [singer, guitarist, songwriter]
Brown, Rabbit *Source(s):* HARS; LCAR
Brown, Robert 1910-1966 [singer, washboard player, songwriter]
Note(s): Do not confuse with Robert Brown (1927-1975); see next entry.
Brown, Washboard Sam *Source(s):* CCE46unp; CCE74
Ham Gravy *Source(s):* EPMU; HARS; LCAR
Shufflin' Sam *Source(s):* EPMU; HARS; LCAR
Note(s): Do not confuse with Shufflin Sam [i.e., Clarence Todd]
Washboard Sam *Source(s):* AMUS; CCE74; EPMU; HARS; LCAR; PMUS-93
Note(s): Do not confuse with Washboard Sam [i.e., Albert Johnson]
Brown, Robert 1927-1975 [singer, guitarist, songwriter]
Note(s): Do not confuse with Robert Brown (1910-1966); see previous entry.
Babe, Smoky *Source(s):* LCAR
Smoky Babe *Source(s):* HARS
Brown, Roy James 1925-1981 [singer, pianist, songwriter]
Brown, Good Rockin *Source(s):* HARS
Brown, Tommy *Source(s):* HARS
Brown, Rosemary (née Dickeson) 1916-2001 [teacher, composer medium]
Bach, Johann Sebastian (Spirit) *Source(s):* http://www.romana_Lamburg.de/RosemaryBrownE.htm (13 May 2005)
Beethoven, Ludwig van (Spirit) *Source(s):* http://www.romana_Lamburg.de/RosemaryBrownE.htm

Brahms, Johannes (Spirit) *Source(s):* http://www.romana_Lamburg.de/RosemaryBrownE.htm
Chopin, Frederic (Spirit) *Source(s):* http://www.romana_Lamburg.de/RosemaryBrownE.htm
Debussy, Claude (Spirit) *Source(s):* http://www.romana_Lamburg.de/RosemaryBrownE.htm
Liszt, Franz (Spirit) *Source(s):* http://www.romana_Lamburg.de/RosemaryBrownE.htm
Mozart, (Johann Chrysostom) Wolfgang Amadeus (Spirit) *Source(s):* http://www.romana_Lamburg.de/RosemaryBrownE.htm
Rachmaninoff, Sergei (Spirit) *Source(s):* http://www.romana_Lamburg.de/RosemaryBrownE.htm
Schubert, Franz Peter (Spirit) *Source(s):* http://www.romana_Lamburg.de/RosemaryBrownE.htm
Schumann, Robert (Spirit) *Source(s):* http://www.romana_Lamburg.de/RosemaryBrownE.htm

Brown, Samantha 1964- [singer, songwriter]
Brown, Sam *Source(s):* EPMU

Brown, T. J. [composer]
Bordonel, T. J. *Source(s):* CPMU (publication dates 1893-1910)

Brown, Timothy [rapper]
Father *Source(s):* AMUS; EPMU
Father MC *Source(s):* AMUS
McFather *Source(s):* EPMU

Brown, William 1928- [composer, pianist, flutist]
Brown, Sonny *Source(s):* CLAB

Browne, Charles F(arrar) 1834-1967 [songwriter, publisher]
Ward, Artemus *Source(s):* KILG; Tawa, Nicholas E. *High-Minded and Low-Down*. Boston: Northeastern University Press, 2000, 86.

Browne, Clyde Jackson 1948- [singer, songwriter]
Brown, Jackson *Source(s):* WARN

Browne, Diane Gale 1954- [composer, author, singer]
Browne, Daisy *Source(s):* ASCP

Browne, Ernest D. 1900-1968 [composer]
Rose, Irving *Source(s):* ASCC; CCE62

Browne, Harriet Mary ?-1858 [composer]
Brown, Miss *Source(s):* NGAM
Note(s): Do not confuse with Augusta Browne.
Sister of Mrs. Hemans *Source(s):* LCAR

Browne, Henry 1861-1952 [composer]
Rafferty, Pat *Source(s):* CPMU; KILG

Browne, Lindsay 1915- [music critic]
L. B. *Source(s):* DAUM

Brownold, Fred 1907- [composer]
Browne, Ted *Source(s):* JASAp. 321; JASG; JASR

Brownsmith, (Reginald) Douglas [arranger]
Belton, John *Source(s):* RFSO
Note(s): Jt. pseud.: Anthony [or Tony] Lowry.

Brownstein, Louis 1893-1958 [lyricist, producer, publisher]
Brown, Lew *Source(s):* CASS; EWEN (port.); GAMM; GAN1; GAN2; HARR

Brownstein, Samuel Hyman 1905-1992 [composer, author]
Brownee, Zing *Source(s):* ASCP; CCE68

Broza, Elliot Lawrence 1925- [bandleader, composer, arranger]
Drew, Dan *Source(s):* JAMU
Lawrence, Elliot(t) *Source(s):* CCE47; EPMU; GAMM; KINK; LCAR; NGDJ

Broze, Wayne Douglas 1954- [songwriter]
Douglas, Wayne *Source(s):* CPOL PAu-1-848-484; CPOL PAu-2-082-082
Note(s): Also used by Walter (Charles) Ehret, Edward J. Penney, Jr. & Fred Weber. Do not confuse with singer Wayne Douglas [i.e., Doug Sham] (1941-1999).

Brucato, Charles R. [composer]
Burke, Charles *Source(s):* CLTP ("CBS Movie Theme")

Bruce, (William) Ed(win, Jr.) 1940- [singer, songwriter]
Tennessean, The *Source(s):* MCCL

Bruce, Ervin 1932- [singer, songwriter]
Bruce, Vin *Source(s):* MCCL
King of the Cajuns *Source(s):* MCCL

Bruchhäuser, Wilfred Wolfgang 1932- [composer]
Titori, Erwin *Source(s):* KOMP; KOMS; PFSA

Bruck, Arnold von c.1500-1554 [composer]
Bruges, Arnold de *Source(s):* BAKR
Flamengo, Arnoldo *Source(s):* BAKR

Bruck, Jerry 1935- [recording engineer, writer on music]
Jerard, Walter *Source(s):* AMRG 64:2 (Mar.-Apr. 2001): 127

Brucker, Raymond (Philippe Auguste) 1800-1875 [author]
Raymond, Michel *Source(s):* LCAR; PIPE
Note(s): Jt. pseud.: Michel Masson [i.e., Auguste Michel Benoît Gaudichot-Masson]

Bruckner, (Josef) Anton 1824-1896 [composer]
Wagner of the Symphony *Source(s):* www.charlottesymphony.org/2005/program_notes_1.asp (8 Apr. 2005)
Wagnerian Symphonist *Source(s):* http://www.electic.kennett.net/ABruckner/debate.htm (20 Oct. 2003)

Brugk, Hans Melchoir 1909- [composer]
Furtner, (Joachim) *Source(s):* BUL3; KOMS; SUPN
Brügmann, Walther 1884-1945 [author]
Walther, Erich *Source(s):* PIPE
Note(s): Jt. pseud.: (Erich) Moritz Rappaport.
Bruhns, George Frederick William 1874-1963 [composer, conductor, piano]
Bruhns, Arthur *Source(s):* ASCC
Brun-Lavainne, Elie Benjamin Joseph 1791-1875 [musician, journalist, historian]
Wallon, Rodeur *Source(s):* IBIM; WORB
Bruna, Pablo 1611-1679 [organist, composer]
Ciego de Daroca, El *Source(s):* NGDM; SADC
Brunke, Wolfram 1938- [composer]
Pacific, Gary *Source(s):* KOMS; PFSA
Bryant, (Thomas) Hoyt 1908- [singer, songwriter]
Bryant, Slim *Source(s):* CCE47-49; ENCM; EPMU; LCAR; PSND
Jethro *Source(s):* CCE50
Bryant, (Ivy) James [or Jimmy] 1925-1980 [singer, songwriter]
Fastest Guitar in the Country, The *Source(s):* MCCL
Bryant, Raphael 1931- [pianist, composer]
Bryant, Ray *Source(s):* LCAR; NGDJ
Brygann, Ernst 1905- [composer]
Eck, Tobias *Source(s):* KOMP; PFSA
Bryson, Peapo 1951- [singer, songwriter, producer]
Bryson, Peabo *Source(s):* CM11
King of the Balladeers *Source(s):* CM11
Brzowska-Mejean Jadwiga 1830-1886 [pianist, composer]
Jagiello, Jadwiga *Source(s):* HIXN
Bubier, George Burden 1823- [hymnist]
B. *Source(s):* JULN
Bucalossi, Brigata (Procida Leonardo) 1862-1924 [actor, composer, conductor]
Brigata, (B.) (Sig.) *Source(s):* GANA p. 388
Bucalossi, (Procida) Ernest (Luigi) 1863-1933 [actor, musical director, composer]
Elton, Ernest *Source(s):* GAN1; GAN2
Bucalossi, Procida (Joseph Henry Edwards) 1838-1918 [composer, conductor, arranger]
Valentine, C(harles) *Source(s):* BLIC; GAN1; GAN2
Buchanam, Manley Augustus [singer, songwriter]
Big Youth *Source(s):* PEN2
Buchhalter, Simon 1881-1955 [pianist, composer]
Bucharoff, Simon *Source(s):* BAKR; BUL2; NGDO
Buchholz, Karl 1901- [composer]
Buchholz, Charlie *Source(s):* KOMP; PFSA
Buchner, Hans 1483-1538 [organist, composer]
Hans von Constanz *Source(s):* NGDM; WORB
Buchtel, Forrest (Lawrence) 1899-1996 [composer, educator]
Buck, Lawrence *Source(s):* ASCP; CCE53-54; LCAR; REHG; SUPN
Laurence, Victor *Source(s):* CCE62; LCAR
Lawrence, Victor *Source(s):* ASCP; REHG; SUPN
Buchwald, Martyn J(erel) 1942 (or 43)- [singer, songwriter]
Balin, Marty *Source(s):* BAKR; CCE66; EPMU; HARR
Buck, Edward Eugene 1885-1957 [lyricist, writer, director]
Buck, Gene *Source(s):* GAMM; LCAR
Buck, (Sir) Percy Carter 1871-1947 [writer on music, editor, organist]
P. C. B. *Source(s):* CPMU
Buckingham, Bonnie 1923 (or 24)- [singer, songwriter, guitarist]
Guitar, Bonnie *Source(s):* CCE57; CCE64; EPMU; MCCL; PEN1
Tutmarc, (Mrs.) Bonnie *Source(s):* CCE65; EPMU
Buckley, Frederick 1833-1864 [composer, violinist]
Bull(e), Ole, Jr. *Source(s):* OCLC 42607657
Master Ole Bull *Source(s):* LCAR
Ole Bull *Source(s):* LCAR
Buczkowna, Kazimiera Zofia 1940- [composer]
Buczek, Barbara *Source(s):* BAKR
Buday, Albert 1939-2001 [music critic]
Buday, Don *Source(s):* OB01
Budden, William fl. c.1795 [hymnist]
W. B. *Source(s):* JULN
Buford, George 1929- [singer, harmonica player, songwriter]
Buford, Mojo *Source(s):* LCAR
Mojo *Source(s):* HARS
Waters, Muddy, Jr. *Source(s):* HARS
Bugatti, Dominic [songwriter]
Dukes *Source(s):* EPMU
Note(s): Jt. pseud.: Frank Musker.
Bugg, Catharine Smiley 1864?-1946 [singer, composer, author]
Cheatham, Kitty *Source(s):* PSND
Buhre, Werner (Bernhard Hermann) 1901-1980 [translator]
Neuner, Robert *Source(s):* PIPE
Buie, Perry C. [songwriter]
Buie, Buddy *Source(s):* CCE68; PMUS
Bukorester, Adolf 1848- [librettist]
Just, A. *Source(s):* STGR; WORB
Bulch, Thomas Edward 1860-1930 [composer, arranger]
Abbott, Lempriere *Source(s):* SMIN
Father of Australian Band Movement, The *Source(s):* SMIN
Godfrey, Arthur *Source(s):* SMIN
King, Hall *Source(s):* SMIN
Kingsley, Arthur *Source(s):* SMIN
Note(s): Also used by Leo(nard) Blitz.
Lacosti, Eugene *Source(s):* SMIN

Laski, Henry *Source(s):* SMIN
Mills, Kerry *Source(s):* SMIN
Note(s): Also used by Frederick Allen Mills.
Parker, Godfrey *Source(s):* SMIN
Vallinare, Paul *Source(s):* SMIN
Bull, Ole (Bornemann) 1810-1880 [violionist, composer]
Musician, The *Source(s):* PSND
Paganini of the North *Source(s):* http://www.wisc.edu/wisconsinpress/books/0294.html (28 Mar. 2003)
Bull, Sverre Hagerup 1892-1976 [composer]
Helle, Finn *Source(s):* BUL1; BUL2; http://home.hccnet.nl/h.g.van.der.linden/projects/tagore/tagore.html (1 Dec. 2003)
Bullington, James Wiley 1933- [composer, author]
Edwards, Jimmy *Source(s):* ASCP; CCE57
Bullock, Annie [or Anna] Mae 1938- [singer, songwriter, actress]
Turner, Tina *Source(s):* CLAG; LCAR
Bullock, Jack A(rlen) 1929- [composer]
Cook, Paul *Source(s):* REHG; SUPN
Note(s): In REHH works by Cook [i.e., Bullock] are listed incorrectly in the entry for Jay Bocook.
Bülow, Hans von Guido 1830-1894 [conductor, pianist, music director]
Peltast *Source(s):* RIEM; WORB
Solinger, W. *Source(s):* RIEM; WORB
Bulsara, Farokh [or Frederick] 1946- [singer, songwriter]
Mercury, Freddie *Source(s):* HARR; LCAR; PSND; WARN
Bulwer-Lytton, Edward Robert 1831-1891 [statesman, poet]
Bruce, Edward *Source(s):* GOTE
Caxton, Pisistratus *Source(s):* GOTE
Meredith, Owen *Source(s):* GOTH; LCAR; PSND; WORB
New Timon, The *Source(s):* PSND
Temple, Neville *Source(s):* WORB
Trevor, Edward *Source(s):* PSND
Bümler, Georg Heinrich 1669-1745 [singer, composer, theorist]
Archimedes *Source(s):* GROL
Bummerl, Franz 1927- [composer]
Bottner, (Claus) *Source(s):* KOMP; KOMS; PFSA; REHH; SUPN
Bumpus, Mary Frances [or Francis] 1848 (or 49)-1912 [composer]
Note(s): Portraits: DWCO; ETUP 50:2 (Feb. 1932): 84
Allitsen, (Mary) Frances *Source(s):* CPMU; DWCO; GOTH; GROL; KILG; NGDM
Bunce, Corajane (Diane) 1919- [composer, author, singer]
Ward, Diane *Source(s):* ASCC; CCE59
Bunch, William 1902-1941 [singer, pianist, songwriter]
Devil's Son-in-Law, The *Source(s):* AMUS; HARS
High Sheriff from Hell, The *Source(s):* HARS
Wheatstraw, Peetie [or Pete] *Source(s):* AMUS; HARS; LCAR
Note(s): Do not confuse with Little Peetie Wheatstraw [i.e. Andrew Hogg]
Bundrick, John [keyboardist, singer, songwriter]
Bundrick, Rabbit *Source(s):* YORK
Rabbit *Source(s):* CCE71; LCAR
Note(s): Also used by John(ny) Cornelius Hodges.
Buneken, Adolf 1894- [composer]
Roland, Marc *Source(s):* MACM
Bunge, Rudolf 1836-1907 [author]
Rudolf, B(runo) *Source(s):* PIPE
Bunn, Alden 1924-1977 [singer, guitarist songwriter]
Baum, Allen *Source(s):* HARS
Bunn, Allen *Source(s):* HARS
Tarheel, Slim *Source(s):* HARS; LCAR
Buns, Benedictus 1642-1716 [organist, composer]
Benedictus a Sancto Josepho *Source(s):* NGDM
Grand Carme *Source(s):* GRV3
Bunting, William Maclardie 1805-1866 [minister, hymnist]
Alec *Source(s):* CYBH
Buntrock, Martin 1954- [composer]
Marvin, Ron *Source(s):* KOMS; PFSA
Bunyan, John [composer]
J. B. *Source(s):* CPMU (publication date 1686)
Bunz, Hans-Günther 1925- [composer]
Machauer, Bob *Source(s):* KOMP; KOMS; PFSA
Stetten, Jack *Source(s):* KOMS
Buonavita, Antonio mentioned 1589-1609 [organist, composer]
Bientina, Il *Source(s):* NGDM
Burdon, Eric 1941- [singer, songwriter]
Black Singer Trapped Inside a White Skin, A *Source(s):* CM14
Burgartz, Alfred 1890-1950 [writer on music]
Holtmont, Alfred *Source(s):* PIPE
Burgdorf, James Alan 1953- [composer, author, singer]
James, Alan *Source(s):* ASCP
Burger, David Mark 1950- [composer, author, singer]
Masters, David *Source(s):* ASCP
Burgeson, Avis Marguerite 1895-1985 [hymnist]
Note(s): Married name: Christiansen.
Anson, Christian B. *Source(s):* CYBH
Reid, Constance B. *Source(s):* CYBH
Burgess, Alexander 1807-1886 [violinist, poet, dancing master]
Poute *Source(s):* IBIM; WORB

Burgess, Marlena 1944- [singer, songwriter]
Shaw, Marlena *Source(s):* PSND
Burghardt, Victor 1937- [composer]
Bogart, Ric *Source(s):* KOMS; PFSA
Burgie, Irving Louis 1924- [lyricist, composer]
Burgess, Irving *Source(s):* CPOL RE-224-613
Burgess, Lord *Source(s):* CCE57; CPOL RE-224-613; SOTH
Burgie, Irvine *Source(s):* LCAR
Lord Burgess *Source(s):* LCAR; SOTH
Burgstahler, Elton E. [composer]
Rau, Earl *Source(s):* CCE68; HOVL; LAST
Burke, John(ny) 1908-1964 [lyricist]
Note(s): Portrait: EWEN
D'Lorah, Juan y *Source(s):* CCE61 R280175 ("La Cucaracha"); CCE62; LCCC 1955-70 (reference)
Note(s): Also used by Harold Spina in the same motion picture, but not as a jt. pseud.
Rogan, K. C. *Source(s):* CCE53-55; PMUS
Note(s): Jt. pseud.: Harold Spina.
Burke, Joseph [or Joe] A. 1884-1950 [composer, pianist]
Note(s): Do not confuse with Joe Burke [i.e., Charles N(eil) Daniels] or Joseph Francis Burke (1914-1980), see next entry. See STUW for a list of Burke's songs.
Alexandre, Josef *Source(s):* CCE57
Note(s): Jt. pseud.: Al(exander) Dubin.
Burke, Joseph Francis 1914-1980 [songwriter, arranger, conductor]
Note(s): Do not confuse with Joseph [or Joe] A. Burke (1884-1950); see previous entry, or Joe Burke [i.e., Charles N(eil) Daniels]
Burke, Sonny *Source(s):* ASCP; CCE49; CCE55; EPMU; KINK; VACH
Fadden, Bill *Source(s):* CCE55-56
Burke, Michael [songwriter]
Carnaby *Source(s):* CCE65; PMUS
Starr, Diggy *Source(s):* CPOL PAu-1-998-576
Burke, Solomon 1935 (or 36)- [singer, songwriter]
King of Soul *Source(s):* EPMU
Note(s): See also James Brown.
Wonder Boy Preacher, The *Source(s):* EPMU; PSND; SHAD
Burland, Granville (A.) 1927- [songwriter]
Burland, Sascha *Source(s):* CCE60-62; CCE65-67; PMUS
Burleigh, Cecil (Edward) 1885-1980 [composer, violinist, educator]
Note(s): Portraits: CYBH; ETUP 50:6 (June 1932): 390; HOWD
Booth, Albert J. *Source(s):* PSND
Burt, Caleb *Source(s):* PSND
Dayton, (Captain) Will *Source(s):* PSND
No Name *Source(s):* PSND
Burley, Daniel Gardner 1907-1971 [editor, musician, composer]
DeLeighbur, Don *Source(s):* PSND
Burnard, (David) Alex(ander) 1900-1971 [composer, teacher]
Phyllander *Source(s):* CPMU; http://www.nla.gov.au/music/symphlist (7 Oct. 2002)
Sebastion *Source(s):* http://www.nla.gov.au/music/symphlist
Burnand, Arthur Bransby 1859-1907 [composer, pianist, writer on music]
Note(s): Portrait: ETUP 56:10 (Oct. 1939): 630 (see under Anton Strelezki)
Chandon, Theo *Source(s):* CCE16 R8914 ("Old Love Song," soprano or baritone)
Note(s): Also used by Frank Lynes.
Esipoff, Stepán [or Stephen] *Source(s):* CPMU; GOTH; IBIM; MACM; TPRF; WORB
Strelezki, Anton *Source(s):* CPMU; GOTH; IBIM; IWWM; MACM; TPRF; WORB
Note(s): Used in bulletin issued by Theodore Presser. Extensive list of works in CPMU. Also used by Charles Kunkel. "A. Strelezki" & Charles J. Roberts [i.e., Charles Kraushaar]
Burnard, Francis Cowley 1836-1917 [humorist, burlesque writer, editor of *Punch*]
Note(s): Portrait: GAN2
Baron of Burlesque *Source(s):* GAN2
Note(s): See also H(enry) J(ames) Byron.
Bounceycore, Dion *Source(s):* CART
Britain's Baron of Burlesque *Source(s):* GAN2
Note(s): See also H(enry) J(ames) Byron.
Colvin, Cecil *Source(s):* CART
Dendron, (Miss) Rhody *Source(s):* CART
Fictor No Go *Source(s):* CART
One Who Has Done It and Can Do It Again *Source(s):* CART
Weeder *Source(s):* CART
Burnett, Chester Arthur 1910-1976 [singer, songwriter]
Big Foot *Source(s):* HARS
Bull Crow *Source(s):* HARS
Howlin' Wolf *Source(s):* AMUS; CM06; EPMU; GAMM; HARR; HARS; LCAR; RECR
Note(s): See also John T. Smith.
Premiere Man of American Music *Source(s):* CM06
Walking Encyclopedia of the Blues *Source(s):* SIFA
Wolf, The *Source(s):* RECR
Wolf, Howlin' *Source(s):* RECR
Burnett, Earl [composer]
Lebieg, Earl *Source(s):* CCE50 R70230 ("Sleep"); CCE56; CLTP ("Fred Waring Show")
Note(s): Jt. pseud.: Adam Geibel.

Burnett, Joseph Henry 1948- [singer, songwriter, actor]
Bone, Jon T. *Source(s):* CCE67
Burnett, T-Bone *Source(s):* CM13; DIMA; EPMU; HARR; MUHF; PEN2
Coward Brothers *Source(s):* AMUS
Note(s): Jt. pseud.: Elvis Costello [i.e., Declan Patrick (Aloysius) McManus]
Burnett, Nathan James 1812-1853 [violinist, composer, singer]
Sporle, Nathan James *Source(s):* BROW; GOTE; LCAR; WORB
Burnette, Jonathan [or Johnny] 1953- [songwriter]
Burnette, Rocky *Source(s):* EPMU; WARN
Burnette, Lester Alvin 1911-1967 [actor, songwriter, singer]
Burnette, Frog *Source(s):* PSND
Burnette, Smiley *Source(s):* ENCM; EPMU; LCAR; PSND
Frog, The *Source(s):* MCCL
Poor Man's Bob Hope, The *Source(s):* MCCL
Burns, Eddie 1928-1983 [singer, guitarist, songwriter]
Big Ed *Source(s):* DBMU; HARS; LCAR
Burns, Guitar *Source(s):* DBMU; HARS
Burns, "Little" Eddie *Source(s):* DBMU; HARS
Country Boy Eddie [or Eddy] *Source(s):* LCAR
Pickens, Slim *Source(s):* DBMU; HARS
Slim Pickens *Source(s):* DBMU; HARS
Swing Brother *Source(s):* DBMU; HARS; LCAR
Burns, Felix (the Elder) [composer]
Lacoste, Leona *Source(s):* CPMU (publication dates 1891-1906)
Burns, Kenneth C. 1920-1989 [singer, composer, comedian]
Note(s): Portraits: (with Henry D. Haynes) CCME; MILL
Burns, Jethro *Source(s):* CCE50; LCAR; MCCL
Crown Princes of Country Music *Source(s):* MUHF
Note(s): Jt. sobriquet: Henry D. Haynes.
Jethro(w) *Source(s):* CCE50; CCE54-55; EPMU; MUHF
Note(s): Performed as: Homer [i.e., Henry D. Haynes] & Jethro.
Burns, Raymond 1954 (or 55)- [bandleader, songwriter]
Captain Sensible *Source(s):* EPMU
Burns, Robert 1759-1796 [poet, lyricist, farmer]
Mossgiel, Rab *Source(s):* PSND
Burns, Wilfred 1917-1990 [composer, actor]
Earley, Robert *Source(s):* CCE54-55; CPOL RE-126-629; CPOL RE-221-024; RFSO
Sharples, Robert [or Bob] *Source(s):* CLTP ("Truth or Consequences" (Quiz Show)); RFSO
Note(s): "Bob Sharples" also used by Robert Frederick Standish.
Burnside, Ernest 1951- [composer]
Burnside, Jack (E.) *Source(s):* KOMS; PFSA
Burnstein, George 1919 (or 20)-1985 [singer, writer on music]
Burnnon, Gerge *Source(s):* LCAR
Burnson, George *Source(s):* LCAR
London, George *Source(s):* LCAR; RIES
Burrard, William Dutton 1861-1938 [soldier, poet, songwriter]
Aramis *Source(s):* CART; IBIM; WORB
Burrell, Bishop [songwriter]
Slick *Source(s):* PMUS-93
Stick *Source(s):* CPOL PA-670-263
Burrell, Herman Davis, II 1940- [pianist, composer]
Burrell, Dave *Source(s):* EPMU; LCAR; PEN2
Burrell, Orville (Richard) 1968- [songwriter, performer]
Pupa Rico *Source(s):* AMUS
Shaggy *Source(s):* AMIR; AMUS; CM37; PMUS-00
Burrell, Stanley (Kirk) 1962 (or 63)- [rapper, dancer, songwriter]
Hammer *Source(s):* EPMU
Hammer, M. C. *Source(s):* EPMU; HARD; RECR; WORL
Note(s): M. C. = Master of Ceremonies (LCAR).
Burroughs, Bob (Lloyd) 1937- [composer, teacher, writer on music]
Davidson, Robert *Source(s):* ASCP; CCE66; CCE73
Unknown, Arthur *Source(s):* CCE71
Burroughs, Earl S. 1940- [composer, author, singer]
Hammer, Jack *Source(s):* ASCP; REHH
Burrow, Robert Foster [composer]
Dumah *Source(s):* CPMU (publication date 1882)
Burse, Charlie 1901-1965 [singer, guitarist, songwriter]
Burse, Uke *Source(s):* HARS
Ukelele Kid *Source(s):* HARS
Burshtein, Peisach [or Pesach] 1896-1986 [songwriter]
Burstein, Paul *Source(s):* HESK
Burstein, John 1949- [composer, educator]
Goodbody, Slim *Source(s):* ASCP; LCAR
Slim Goodbody *Source(s):* LCAR
Burton, Claude E(dward Cole-Hamilton) 1869- [lyricist]
C. E. B. *Source(s):* GANB
Touchstone *Source(s):* GANB; LCAR
Note(s): Also used by Hector (Willoughby) Charlesworth & author E(lbert) Herring (1777-1876) (see LCAR).
Burton, John, (Jr.) 1803-1877 [hymnist]
Essex, J. B. *Source(s):* CYBH; JULN

Busbice, Bernarr (G(raham)) 1933-2003 [singer, songwriter]
Busby, Buzz *Source(s):* CCE54; CCE60; LCAR; MCCL
Note(s): See also William B. Busby.
Ham and Scam *Source(s):* MCCL
Note(s): Jt. pseud.: Pete Pike.
Busby, William B. [composer]
Busby, Buz *Source(s):* CCE61
Note(s): See also Bernarr (G(raham)) Busbice.
Busch, Ferdinand 1924- [composer]
Dinan, Fred *Source(s):* KOMP; KOMS; PFSA
Buschel, Ben-Zion 1926- [composer]
Orgad, Ben-Zion *Source(s):* BUL1; BUL2
Bush, Alan 1900-1995 [composer]
Underwood, Dudley *Source(s):* MUWB
Busch, Louis F(erdinand) 1910-1979 [composer, author, conductor]
Note(s): Potraits: JASA; SHMM (May/June 1992): 62
Carr, Fingers *Source(s):* ASCP; EPMU; GROL; JASA; JASN; JASR; PEN2
Carr, Joe Fingers *Source(s):* ASCP; EPMU; GROL; JASA; JASN; JASR; PEN2
Hamilton/Leland *Source(s):* PERF
Note(s): Pseud. of Busch?
Bushby, Evelyn Frances [composer, songwriter]
Francis, Evelyn *Source(s):* CPMU; GOTT
Note(s): Publication dates 1895-1914 (CPMU)
Busnach, William (Bertrand) 1932-1907 [playwright]
Abou-Djenach *Source(s):* PIPE
Busoni, Dante Michelangelo Benventuo 1886-1924 [composer, pianist, critic]
Busoni, Ferruccio *Source(s):* MACE p. 84; NGDO
Fioresucci, Bruno *Source(s):* GDRM; GROL; NGDO
Busse, Christoph 1947- [composer]
Rocco, Robert *Source(s):* PFSA
Butcher, Jack [singer, songwriter]
Barlow, Jack *Source(s):* CCE68; EPMU; MCCL
Fenster, Zoot *Source(s):* MCCL
Butler, A. L. 1933- [composer, author]
Butler, Pete *Source(s):* ASCP
Butler, E. G. ?-1941 [songwriter]
Forrester, Noel *Source(s):* KILG
Butler, George 1936-2005 [singer, guitarist, songwriter]
Butler, Wild Child *Source(s):* DRSC; HARS; LCAR
Butler, Henry ?-1652 [violinist, composer]
Botelero, Enrique *Source(s):* DEA3; NGDM; SADC
Butler, Henry W. 1919-1998 [author, librettist]
Butler, Bill *Source(s):* ASCP
Butler, Jerry 1939- [singer, songwriter]
Iceman, The *Source(s):* MUWB; SHAD
Note(s): See also Al(bert) Collins.
Butler, Ralph (T.) 1886- [songwriter]
Butler, Wright *Source(s):* CCE56 R169029 ("Ever So Goosey")
Note(s): Jt. pseud.: Julian Wright.
Clark, Cumberland *Source(s):* CCE52 R90197 ("The Ogo Pogo")
Cloff, Albert *Source(s):* CCE29 Efor2992
Note(s): Jt. pseud.: Julian Wright.
Green, Sam *Source(s):* CCE56 Efor41560
Hardy, Norman *Source(s):* CPOL RE-32-465
Note(s): Also used as jt. pseud. with Arthur Strauss: CCE51 Efor11539.
Jones, Hirem *Source(s):* CCE36 Efor43964
Note(s): Jt. pseud.: Harold Elton Box, Paddy [i.e., John Godfrey Owen] Roberts & C(harles) J(oseph) Edwards.
Kelvin, Andrew *Source(s):* CCE53 Efor22528; CPOL RE-99-930
Marlo, Ferdi *Source(s):* CCE60; LCPC letter cited (23 Sept. 1932)
Note(s): Keith, Prowse "house name" for lyricists. Also used by Leo Towers [i.e., Leo(nard) Blitz] & possibly others; see NOTES: Marlo, Ferd.
Perch, Polly *Source(s):* CCE34 Efor37471 ("Scratch-A-Poll Polly")
Note(s): Jt. pseud.: Harold Elton Box, Desmond Cox [i.e., Adrian Keuleman] & C(harles) J(oseph) Edwards
Stanley, Eugene *Source(s):* CCE62 R304036
Note(s): Jt. pseud.: S(tanley) J. Damerell [i.e., Jack Stevens] & Tolchard (B.) [i.e., Syndey] Evans.
Steinway, Henry *Source(s):* CCE53; CCE55 Efor38173; CPOL RE-173-686
Wallis, C. Jay *Source(s):* CCE30 Efor8733; LCPC letter cited (4 Jan. 1930)
Note(s): Jt. pseud.: Julian Wright, Gustave Krenkel & C(harles) J(oseph) Edwards.
Wilson, Arthur *Source(s):* CCE36 Efor46990 ("Binkie's Lullaby"); CCE64; LCPC
Note(s): Jt. pseud.: Leo Towers [i.e., Leo(nard) Blitz]
Butler, Richard W(illiam) 1844-1928 [dramatist, critic]
Cardos *Source(s):* GANA
Note(s): Jt. pseud.: H(enry) Chance Newton; however, in LCAR listed as pseud. of Newton only.
Henry, Richard *Source(s):* GANB; LCAR
Note(s): Jt. pseud.: H(enry) Chance Newton.
Richard-Henry *Source(s):* LCAR
Note(s): Jt. pseud.: H(enry) Chance Newton.
Butler, Robert Charles Walter Henry [composer]
Trelba, Marco *Source(s):* CPMU (publication dates 1909+)

Butler, Samuel 1835-1902 [author, painter, composer]
Cellarius *Source(s):* LCAR
Owen, John Pickard *Source(s):* IBIM
Butler, Terrance [or Terence] 1949- [composer, bassist]
Butler, Geezer *Source(s):* IMDB
Butterfield, Christopher (James Agnew) 1952- [composer]
Foote, Isabel *Source(s):* http://composers21.com/compdocs/butterfc.htm (23 Sept. 2002)
Butters, Francis 1867-1961 [playwright]
Neilson, Francis *Source(s):* PIPE; PSND
Rhadamanthus *Source(s):* PIPE; PSND
Savage, Adam *Source(s):* PIPE; PSND
Buus, Jacques [or Jacob] (de) c.1510-1565 [organist, composer]
Note(s): See LCAR for additional variant spellings.
Bohusius, Jacobus *Source(s):* RIEM
Buus, Giacques *Source(s):* LCAR
Buys, Jacob *Source(s):* WORB
Fiamengo, Iaches de Guant *Source(s):* LCAR
Jachet de Gaund *Source(s):* RIEM
Paus, Jacob van *Source(s):* LCAR
Buys, Peter 1881-1964 [composer]
Brent, Paul *Source(s):* REHG; SUPN
Byard, John A., Jr. 1922- [pianist, composer, saxophonist]
Byard, Jaki *Source(s):* NGDJ; PEN2; PSND
Byers, William [or Billy] (Mitchell) 1927- [trombonist, conductor, arranger]
Mond, Lex *Source(s):* JAMU
Bygraves, Walter (William) 1922- [singer, songwriter, actor]
Bygraves, Max *Source(s):* EPMU; PSND
Clayton, Kay *Source(s):* CCE53
Irwin, Roy *Source(s):* CCE54
Portway, Al(f) *Source(s):* CCE58-59
Byles, Alannah c.1958- [singer, songwriter]
Myles, Alannah *Source(s):* CM04
Byles, Keith 1948- [performer, songwriter]
Byles, Chubby *Source(s):* EPMU
Byles, Junior *Source(s):* EPMU
King, Chubby *Source(s):* EPMU
Byrd, Henry Roeland 1918-1980 [singer, pianist, songwriter]
Bach of Rock, The *Source(s):* PEN2
Boyd, Robert *Source(s):* HARS
Byrd, Bald Head *Source(s):* HARS
Byrd, Fess *Source(s):* HARS; PEN2
Byrd, Roy *Source(s):* AMUS; HARS; LCAR; PEN2
Dr. Longhair *Source(s):* PSND
Fess; Master of New Orleans Rock 'n' Roll *Source(s):* PEN2
Little Loving Henry *Source(s):* PSND
Longhair, Dr. *Source(s):* PSND
Longhair, Professor *Source(s):* AMUS; CM06; HARS; PEN2
Loving Little Henry *Source(s):* HARS
Master of New Orelans Rock 'n' Roll *Source(s):* PEN2
Professor Longhair *Source(s):* EPMU; LCAR; PEN2
Byrd, James Thomas 1904- [composer]
Byrd, Bretton *Source(s):* BBDP; MUWB
Byrd, Robert (James) 1930 (or 32)-1990 [singer, songwriter]
Day, Bobby *Source(s):* LCAR; NOMG; PEN2
Byrd, William 1543-1623 [composer]
Father of Music, The *Source(s):* PSND
Note(s): See also Johannes Mauduit & Giovanni Pierluigi da Palestrina.
Byrem, Jill Lynne 1946 (or 48)- [singer, songwriter]
Country Music's Janis Joplin *Source(s):* FLIN
Croston, Jill *Source(s):* EPMU
Dalton, Lacy J. *Source(s):* EPMU; HARR; MCCL; PSND
Lady Outlaw *Source(s):* FLIN
Note(s): See also Miriam Johnson.
Byrom, John 1691 (or 92)-1763 [author, hymnist]
Note(s): Portrait: CYBH
Dr. B. *Source(s):* JULN
Shadow, John *Source(s):* HATF
Byron, George Gordon Noël 1788-1824 [poet]
Note(s): See PSND & LCAR for additional nonmusic-related pseudonyms.
Hornem, Horace, Esq. *Source(s):* GOTT; GROL (see under: "Waltz")
Byron, H(enry) J(ames) 1834 (or 35)-1884 [author]
Note(s): Portrait: GAN2
Baron of Burlesque *Source(s):* GAN2
Note(s): See also Francis Cowley Burnand.
Britian's Baron of Burlesque *Source(s):* GAN2
Note(s): See also Francis Cowley Burnand.

– C –

Caballero, Manuel Fernández 1835-1906 [composer, conductor]
Burillo, Florentino *Source(s):* GDRM; GROL; NGDO
Cabot, Eliza Lee 1787-1860 [author, hymnist]
E. L. C. *Source(s):* JULN
Follen, (Mrs.) Eliza Lee *Source(s):* JULN
Cabral, Manuel M(edeiros) 1915- [composer]
Kaye, Manny *Source(s):* CCE55
Schreibe, Emanuel von *Source(s):* BUL3; CCE66
Von Schreibe, Emmanuel *Source(s):* CCE66-68

Cabridens, Marcel (Eugène Henri) 1900-1978 [librettist, lyricist]
Cab, Marc(h) *Source(s):* CCE34; CCE55-56; CCE60
Marc-Cab *Source(s):* CCE56 Efor48516; CCE66; CCE68; GAN2
Cacavas, John 1930- [composer]
Constantine, John *Source(s):* REHH
Flanders, David *Source(s):* REHH
Maki, Theodore *Source(s):* REHH
Markham, Seth *Source(s):* CCE61; CPOL RE-422-975; REHH
Note(s): Also used by Wilfred [or Bill] (Lawshe) Holcombe.
Winter, Mark *Source(s):* LCCC 1955-70 (see reference); REHH
Caccini, Francesca 1587-c.1640 [composer, organist, singer, poet]
Cecchina, La *Source(s):* BAKO; BAKR; IBIM; NGDM; NGDO; SADC; WORB
Raffaelli, Francesca *Source(s):* NGDO
Signorini(-Malaspina), Francesca (Caccini) *Source(s):* DWCO; NGDO
Caccini, Giulio (Romolo) 1550 (or 51)-1618 [composer, singer]
Benedetto giorno *Source(s):* GROL; LCAR
Giulio Romano *Source(s):* BAKO; BAKR; MACM; MELL; NGDM
Kachchini, Dzh(ulio) *Source(s):* LCAR
Romano, Giulio *Source(s):* BAKO; BAKR; MACM; MELL; NGDM; PIPE
Caccini, Settimia 1591-c.1638 [singer, composer]
Flora, La *Source(s):* DWCO; NGDM; SADC
Caddell, Cecilia Mary ?-1877 [hymnist]
C. M. C. *Source(s):* JULN
Cade, Salome Thomas 1867- [singer, composer]
Thomas, Clayton *Source(s):* CCE31 R13891; IBIM; WORB
Cadicamo, Enrique Domingo 1900-1999 [poet, writer]
Luna, R(osendo) *Source(s):* CCE63-64; DOLM; TODO
Luzzi, Yino *Source(s):* TODO
Cadman, Charles Wakefield 1881-1946 [composer]
Note(s): Portraits: EWEC; HOWD
Wakefield, Charles C. *Source(s):* GREN
Cadoret, Charlotte 1908- [composer]
Jean du Sacre Coeur, (Soeur) *Source(s):* BUL3
Caedmon 7th cent. [poet]
Father of English Song, The *Source(s):* PSND
Caesar, Isidore 1895-1996 [lyricist]
Note(s): Portraits: EWEN; EWPA; OB96
Caesar, Irving *Source(s):* EWEN; GAN2; GOTH; HARR; OB96; PIPE; PSND
Julius *Source(s):* CCE21 E505074; PSND
Martin, Lem *Source(s):* CCE60
Caf(f)aro, Pasquale 1706-1787 [composer]
Caffarelli *Source(s):* GRV3
Caffariello *Source(s):* PIPE
Cattaro *Source(s):* PIPE
Caffot, Sylvère (Victor Joseph) 1903-1993 [composer]
Sylviano, René *Source(s):* CCE52-61; http://www.musimem.com/caffot.htm (23 Apr. 2005)
Cage, John (Milton), Jr. 1912-1992 [composer]
Father of Musical Dissonance, The *Source(s):* PSND
Father of Musical Nonsense, The *Source(s):* PSND
Caiani, Joseph (Jack, Jr.) 1929- [composer, conductor, arranger]
Cain, Joe *Source(s):* ASCC; CCE62-63
Caicedo, José Harb(e)y [singer, songwriter]
Harvey, Kike *Source(s):* LCAR; PEN2
Caillard, Vincent (Henry Penalver) 1856-1930 [songwriter]
Schoenbach, J. *Source(s):* CPMU
Cailliet, Lucien 1897-1984 9 (or 85) [composer, arranger, conductor, clarinettist]
Girard, Jaques *Source(s):* CCE55
Stokowski, Leopold *Source(s):* GROL
Note(s): While a member of the Philadelphia Orchestra some of Cailliet's arrangements were listed and performed as arrangements of Stokowski. (GROL)
Cain, Jacqueline Ruth 1928- [pianist, composer, singer]
Jackie *Source(s):* PEN2
Cain, Noble 1896-1977 [composer, lyricist]
Note(s): Portrait: ETUP 58:7 (July 1940): 498
Ayers, Albert *Source(s):* CCE49-50; CCE55
Barton, Robert (L.) *Source(s):* CCE41 #46454 E99302; CCE69 R453475
Bick, Charles *Source(s):* CCE49; CCE52 E67577; CCE55
Caddo, Lawrence *Source(s):* CCE52 E60203; CPOL RE-75-888
Castelton, Margery *Source(s):* CCE46 E8583; CCE55
Caswell, Edward *Source(s):* CCE75 R600908
Clement, Clare *Source(s):* CCE39 #22802; CCE46 E1646; CCE54; CPOL RE-400-556
Collinger, E. H. *Source(s):* CCE42 #4108 E97534; CCE68 R445686
Corelli, E. *Source(s):* CCE61
Cosman, William *Source(s):* CCE48; CCE75 R600905
Davies, Owen *Source(s):* CPOL RE-449-680
Davis, Owen *Source(s):* CCE62
Edmiston, James *Source(s):* CCE59
Edwards, Cameron *Source(s):* CCE47; CCE63 E171931; CPOL RE-6-278
Note(s): "Oh, Clap Your Hands" (CCE47)

Farnes, Ellsworth *Source(s):* CCE47; CCE61-62; CPOL RE-180-999
Note(s): "All People That on Earth" (CCE47)
Forest, John *Source(s):* CCE52; CCE61; CPOL RE-449-667; GOTH; GOTT
Grayson, Charles *Source(s):* CCE59; CCE68 R426958; CCE71 R497881
Haney, Alice *Source(s):* CCE69 R460646
Haney, Lawrence (W.) *Source(s):* CCE69 R460644; CCE70 R487527
Hess, J. R. *Source(s):* CCE68 R462464
Hollis, C(harles) A. *Source(s):* CCE59; CCE61-64; CPOL RE-6-277
Justis, Walter *Source(s):* CCE68 R446801; CCE70 R483456
Lamont, A. R. *Source(s):* CCE59 CCE68 R426959
Lamont, Arthur (R.) *Source(s):* CCE67; CCE68 R426968
Lloyd, Joseph M. *Source(s):* CCE68
Lynn, Martha *Source(s):* CCE75 R600908
Manney, E. *Source(s):* CCE69 R466546
Manten, (E.) *Source(s):* CCE E186036; CPOL RE-586-104
Masterson, Eric *Source(s):* CCE46 E8581 & E9740; CCE55; CCE73 R558266
Matterling, George *Source(s):* CCE68 R426969; CCE71 R497881
Middleton, Carl *Source(s):* CCE46 E8584; CCE55; CCE73 R558269
Miller, Spence *Source(s):* CPOL RE-6-280
Morey, Elizabeth *Source(s):* CCE74
Morley, Eleanor *Source(s):* CCE46 E8585; CCE55; CCE73 R558270; CCE75 R600908
Morris, Clifford *Source(s):* CCE70 R487529
Moulton, Amy *Source(s):* CCE61; CPOL RE-180-996
Moulton, Ann *Source(s):* CCE61
Moulton, Charles *Source(s):* CCE42 #17017-19 E10368-70; CCE61; CPOL RE-400-535
Moulton, James *Source(s):* CPOL RE-400-556
Moulton, Joseph *Source(s):* CCE42 #17017-19 E10368-70; CCE55
Nims, Willa *Source(s):* CCE75
Noyes, Alfred *Source(s):* CCE55
Scott, Alfred *Source(s):* CCE49; CCE55; CPOL RE-27-288
Simes, Lee *Source(s):* CCE68 R446802; CCE70 R483457
Simes, Robert Lee *Source(s):* CCE70 R483457
Southey, Amy *Source(s):* CCE42 #22770-72 E102154-56; CCE69 R461702
Southey, Eric *Source(s):* CCE41 #31900 E95942; CCE42 #22770-72 E102154-56; CCE68 R448630
Spiro, Vincent *Source(s):* CCE52 E60484; CCE54-55; CPOL RE-75-886
Townsend, Louise (Mabelle) *Source(s):* CCE46 E8584; CCE55; CCE73 R668269
Valinoff, George *Source(s):* CCE75
Vhladof, A. *Source(s):* CCE41 #16491 E92684
Wainrow, Philip *Source(s):* CCE49; CCE55
Wallinger, Laird *Source(s):* CCE49; CCE55
Walton, Frederick *Source(s):* CCE49; CCE52 E67581; CCE55
Warmsen, E. A. *Source(s):* CCE70 R486802
Waverly, Jules *Source(s):* CCE51; CCE55
Wells, Channing *Source(s):* CCE74
Winter, Charles *Source(s):* CCE41 #31841 E96824; CCE42 #47485 E109271; CCE68 R44578
Woodward, Lynn *Source(s):* CCE61-62; CCE64; CPOL RE-6-281

Cairon, Claude Antoine Jules 1827-1882 [journalist, librettist, producer]
Noriac, Jules *Source(s):* GAN1; GAN2

Calabro, John A(nthony) 1909- [composer, author]
Cale, John(ny) *Source(s):* ASCP; CCE55-56; CCE60

Calace, Nicola [mandolin player, composer]
Paganini of the Mandolin *Source(s):* http://www.calace.it/storia.htm (6 Oct. 2003)
Note(s): See also David (Jay) Grisman.

Calandro, Nicola 1715-1759 (or 60) [composer]
Frascia, (Il) *Source(s):* ALMC; GROL; IBIM; SONN; WORB

Calegari, Cornelia 1644-1662? [composer, singer, organist]
Calegari, Maria Cattarina *Source(s):* HEIN; NGDM
Divina Euterpe, La *Source(s):* HEIN; HIXN

Caletti-Bruni, Pier Francesco 1602-1676 [composer]
Cavalli, Pier Francesco *Source(s):* LCAR; NGDM; NGDO; ROOM; SONN

Calhoun, Cora 1887-1972 [pianist, composer]
Austin, Lovie *Source(s):* CLAG; EPMU

Caliste, Jean 1943- [singer, songwriter]
Knight, Jean *Source(s):* PSND

Callcott, William Hutchins 1807-1882 [songwriter, arranger]
W. H. C. *Source(s):* CPMU

Callender, George (Sylvester) 1918-1992 [instrumentalist, songwriter]
Callender, Red *Source(s):* AMUS; CCE70 R488013; CLAB; EPMU

Callison, Jo Ann 1938- [composer, singer]
Smith, Jennie *Source(s):* ASCP

Calliste, Leroy 1941- [calypsonian, songwriter]
One of the Kings of Soca *Source(s):* AMUS
Stalin, Black *Source(s):* AMUS; PEN2

Calloway, Cab(ell), III 1907-1994 [bandleader, singer, composer]
Dean of American Jive *Source(s):* CM06
Hi-de-ho Man, The *Source(s):* GROL
King of Hi-de-ho *Source(s):* CASS

Mac Neil, N. *Source(s):* CCE77
Mister Hi-de-ho *Source(s):* LCAR
Neil, N. Mac *Source(s):* CCE78 R667979
Camarata, Salvador 1913-2005 [composer, arranger, conductor]
Camarata, Toots [or Tutti] *Source(s):* ASCC; BAKR; EPMU; MUSR
Odette, Dee *Source(s):* CCE55; CPOL RE-153-628
Camati, Maria 18th cent. [harpsichordist, singer, composer]
Farinetta, La *Source(s):* COHN; HIXN
Camerlo, Louis 1929- [stage manager, producer]
Erlo, Louis *Source(s):* PIPE
Cameron, (George) Basil 1884-1975 [conductor]
Hindenberg, Basil *Source(s):* BAKR
Cameron, Dan(iel) (A.) 1880-1963 [journalist, writer on music, choirmaster]
Brandt, Alan *Source(s):* CANE
Simon, the Jester *Source(s):* CANE
Campbell, Alexander 1764-1824 [writer, music-master]
Dunne-Wassail *Source(s):* DAWS
Campbell, Archie James 1914-1987 [singer, songwriter, comedian]
Country George Burns *Source(s):* MCCL
Campbell, Bek David 1970- [singer, songwriter, guitarist]
Beck *Source(s):* LCAR; NOMG
Hansen, Beck *Source(s):* LCAR; NOMG
Campbell, Cecil Bustament 1938- [singer, guitarist, songwriter]
Buster, Prince *Source(s):* NOMG
Campbell, Buster *Source(s):* http://www.mp3.com/Prince-Buster/artists/46344/biography.html (6 Feb. 2006)
Prince Buster *Source(s):* LCAR
Campbell, Edith (May [or Mary]) 1912- [hymnist]
Crosby, Claire *Source(s):* CCE46 E8696 ("The Babe in Bethelehem's Manger"); TPRF
Campbell, Glen (Travis) 1936- [singer, songwriter]
Rhinestone Cowboy, The *Source(s):* FLIN
Note(s): See also David Allan Coe.
Campbell, Georgina May 1862-1938 [singer, actor, composer]
Note(s): Portrait: VGRC
Campbell, Ada May *Source(s):* GRAK; VGRC
Note(s): First given name often listed incorrectly as Ada.
Irwin, May *Source(s):* REHG; SUTT
Note(s): Stage name.
Campbell, Henry [songwriter]
Campobello, Enrico *Source(s):* CPMU ("Forget Thee" (1876))
Campbell, Henry M. [songwriter]
Oméga, Carlo *Source(s):* CCE15 E361262 ("Viva California")
Campbell, James [or Jimmy] 1906-1967 [singer, songwriter]
Note(s): In STUW original name: James Alexander Balfour Campbell Tyrie & indexed under "Tyrie." Since not verified in second source, entry under "Tyrie" is listed below as a variant form.
Connelly, Jay *Source(s):* CCE51 R82789
Note(s): Jt. pseud.: Reg(inald) Connelly; "She's Far too Good for Me."
Gibson, Don *Source(s):* CCE51 R80600
Note(s): Jt. pseud.: Reg(inald) Connelly; "I'm Just Wild Over Dancing."
Jackman, Leo *Source(s):* CPOL RE-262-207
Note(s): Jt. pseud.: Jack Pickering & Leo Towers [i.e., Leo(nard) Blitz]
King, Irving *Source(s):* CCE41 #29397 Efor65188; FULD p. 498; PMUS; PSNN; STUW
Note(s): Jt. pseud.: Reg(inald) Connelly.
Manners, David *Source(s):* CCE57; CPOL RE-257-861
Note(s): Jt. pseud.: Peter Yorke & Leo Towers [i.e., Leo(nard) Blitz]
Tyrie, James Alexander Balfour Campbell *Source(s):* STUW
Note(s): Identified and indexed as original surname in STUW.
Vincent, Ray *Source(s):* CPOL RE-49-299
Note(s): Jt. pseud.: Reg(inald) Connelly.
Campbell, Margaret Cockburn (née Malcolm) ?-1841 [hymnist]
M. C. C. *Source(s):* JULN
Campbell, Mary M. [songwriter]
M. M. C. *Source(s):* CPMU
Campbell, Michael [composer]
Finley, Antor Dismuk (1812-1815) *Source(s):* OCLC 41228703
Note(s): Jt. pseud.: Frank Morelli & Harry Searing.
Campbell, Milton (James) 1934- [singer, guitarist, songwriter]
Little Milton *Source(s):* AMUS; CCE74; HARS; PSND
Campbell, Philip 1936- [singer, songwriter]
Sherrill, Billy *Source(s):* EPMU; HARR
Campbell, Roslyn [songwriter]
Danju, Ras *Source(s):* BLIC
Campbell, Sanford Brunson 1884-1952
Ragtime Kid, The *Source(s):* JASA p. 5
Campbell, Thomas 1777-1844 [poet]
Bard of Hope, The *Source(s):* PSND
Patriae, Amator *Source(s):* GOTT
Campbell, William Jr. 1947- [instrumentalist, singer, songwriter]
Campbell, Junior *Source(s):* HARR
Campion (Records)
Hasefeld, Anton *Source(s):* AMRG 60:4 (1997): 52
Note(s): "House name" used by Czech composers.

Campion, François c.1685-1747 [composer, theorist]
Carbassus, Monsieur l'abbe *Source(s):* GROL
Monsieur l'abbe Carbassus *Source(s):* GROL
Campo, Conrado del 1876-1953 [conductor, composer]
Spanish Strauss, The *Source(s):* GRV5
Canaro, Francisco 1888-1964 [violinist, composer]
Canaro, Pirincho *Source(s):* BBDP (port.); TODO
Candeille, Amelie-Julie 1767-1834 [actress, singer, composer]
Simons, Julie *Source(s):* MUWB
Candoli, Walter Joseph 1923- [trumpeter, composer, arranger]
Candoli, Pete *Source(s):* KINK; PSND
Chesterfield, Cootie *Source(s):* JAMU
Canis, Corneille c.1510-1554 (or 61) [composer]
Hondt, Corneille de *Source(s):* IBIM; RIEM; WORB
Cannon, Anthony J. 1855-1891 [actor, singer, producer]
Note(s): Portrait: HAMM (with Ned [i.e., Edward] Harrigan)
Hart, Tony *Source(s):* GAN1; GAN2; HAMM; SPTH p. 179
Nonpareils, The *Source(s):* SPTH p. 179, 181
Note(s): Jt. pseud.: Edward [or Ned] Harrigan.
Cannon, Gus 1883 (or 85)-1979 [instrumentalist, songwriter]
Banjo Joe *Source(s):* HARS; LCAR
Cannon, Hubert 1934- [saxophonist, composer]
Cannon, Ace *Source(s):* MCCL
Cannon, Murray Franklin 1947- [composer]
Cannon, Buddy *Source(s):* ASCP; CPOL PA-3-744
Cano Vega, Ambrosio [singer, songwriter]
Chalinillo *Source(s):* HWOM; LCAR
Capdevila, Josep 1964- [singer, songwriter]
Dalma, Sergio *Source(s):* HWOM; http://TODOmusica.org/famosos.com/topic106.html (5 Feb. 2005)
Capeci, Carlo Sigismondo 1652-1728 [librettist, playwright]
Olbiano, Metisto *Source(s):* GROL; LCAR; MORI
Capellan, Richard Victor 1943- [composer, author, singer]
Martin, Rick *Source(s):* ASCP; CPOL PAu-156-188
Capitanelli, Arnold Joseph, Jr. 1932- [composer, author, singer]
Jay, Arnold *Source(s):* ASCP
Capli, Erdogan 1926- [composer]
Capali, Pasha *Source(s):* ASCP; PSND
Caponi, Aldo 1938- [actor, composer]
Backy, Don *Source(s):* CCE63-64; CCE67-68; CCE73; NOMG
Backy, Doug *Source(s):* CCE77
Donbacky *Source(s):* CCE63-65
Caponi, Jacopo 1832?-1908 [writer on music, journalist]
Folchetto *Source(s):* GROL
Caporuscio, Aldo (Nova) 1956- [singer, songwriter, guitarist]
Nova, Aldo *Source(s):* AMUS
Caposella, Carolee 1943-2002 [composer, author]
Caposella, Cappy *Source(s):* DRSC
Cappellini, Phill(ip) Thomas 1930- [author, lyricist]
Thomas, Phill(ip) *Source(s):* ASCP (see reference); CCE61-62
Caproli, Carlo c.1615-c.1692 [composer, violinist, organist]
Caproli del Violino *Source(s):* GRV5; SADC
Carlo del Violino *Source(s):* LCAR
Note(s): See also Carlo Francesco Cesarini & Carlo Mannelli.
Carluccio del Violino *Source(s):* PIPE; WORB
Del Violino, Carlo *Source(s):* LCAR
Violino, Il *Source(s):* IBIM; NGDO; WORB
Note(s): See also Camillo Cortellini.
Violino, Carlo del *Source(s):* LCAR
Note(s): See also Carlo Francesco Cesarini & Carlo Mannelli.
Capurro, Alfredo 1914-1992 [actor, singer, author]
Drake, Alfred *Source(s):* EPMU; GAN2
Capus, Alfred Vincent 1858-1922 [author, journalist]
Canalis *Source(s):* PIPE
Graindorge *Source(s):* PIPE; WORB
Carastathis, Nicholas Sam 1922- [composer, conductor]
Carras, Nicholas [or Nick] *Source(s):* ASCP; CLTP ("Loretta Young Show #2")
Cárdenas Pinelo, Augusto 1905-1932 [singer, songwriter, guitarist]
Cárdenas, Guty *Source(s):* HWOM
Cardier, Glenn c.1950- [singer, songwriter]
Hill, Sydney *Source(s):* DAUM
Riff Raff *Source(s):* DAUM
Cardon, Ronald 1929- [composer]
Rodenhof, Guy *Source(s):* REHH
Carducci, Giosuè 1835 (or 36)-1907 [poet, musicologist]
Enotrio Romano *Source(s):* WORB
Rendel, Romilde *Source(s):* CCE55
Romano, Enotrio *Source(s):* LCAR
Caresana, Cristoforo c.1640-1709 [organist, singer, composer]
Veneziano, Il *Source(s):* SADC
Carey, Alice 1820-1871 [poet, hymnist]
Jean Ingelow of America, The *Source(s):* PSND
Lee, Patty *Source(s):* PSND

Carey, George Saville 1743-1807 [dramatist, songwriter, actor]
Tell-Truth, Paul *Source(s):* CART; LCAR
Carey, Henry c.1689-1743 [dramatist, poet, songwriter]
Note(s): Portrait: GRV3 v.2
Bounce, Benjamin *Source(s):* CART; CPMU; GOTH; GROL; NGDM; PSND; SADC
Carini, Sig(nor) *Source(s):* CART; CPMU; GOTH; GROL; NGDM; SADC
J. W. *Source(s):* CART
Nehemiah Dim-Eye *Source(s):* CUDW
Secretary to Ye Fiz-Gig Club *Source(s):* CUDW
Single, Humphrey *Source(s):* LCAR
Single, John, of Grey's Inn *Source(s):* CART
Waters, John *Source(s):* PSND
Carisio, Giovanni c.1627-1687 [composer]
Cieco, Il *Source(s):* NGDM; STGR
Note(s): See also Antonio (C.) Valente.
Orbino, Il *Source(s):* NGDM; STGR; WORB
Carissimi, Giacomo 1604-1674 [composer]
Father of the Oratorio *Source(s):* EWCY
Note(s): See also Giovanni Animuccia.
Carl, M. [composer]
Carlo *Source(s):* GOTH
Carl, Robert 1902-1987 [composer]
Gilhaus, (H.) *Source(s):* KOMP; PFSA
Roberts, Franz *Source(s):* KOMP; PFSA
Carlberg, Sten 1925- [songwriter]
Roland, Sten *Source(s):* CCE52-53; CPOL RE-27-123
Stone, Charles *Source(s):* CCE52-55; CPOL RE-53-912; CPOL RE-122-82
Note(s): Do not confuse with Charlie Stone [i.e., Charles R(aymond) Adams]
Carleton, Charles (Nicholas) 1871-1941 [actor, singer, librettist, lyricist]
Carle, Richard (E.) *Source(s):* GAN2; LCAR
Carlin, Sidney (Alan) 1925- [arranger]
Eden, Rock *Source(s):* CCE59 E135120
Wilson, Paul *Source(s):* CCE71; LCCC63 E178023
Note(s): Also used by Paul Sterrett; see NOTES: Wilson, Paul.
Carlisle, Cliff(ord Raymond) 1904-1983 [singer, songwriter, guitarist]
Carlisle, Bill *Source(s):* DRSC
Clifford, Bob *Source(s):* MCCL
Greene, Amos *Source(s):* DRSC
Lonesome Hobo, The *Source(s):* Carlisle, Cliff. "The Lonesome Hobo." Chicago: M. M. Cole. (port.)
Yodelin' Hobo *Source(s):* NGAM
Carllile, Kenneth (Ray) 1931-1987 [guitarist, songwriter]
Carllile, Thumbs *Source(s):* CCE62; MCCL; PSND
Carlone, Francis N(unzio) 1903-2001 [pianist, bandleader, composer]
Note(s): Portrait: OB01
Carle, Frankie *Source(s):* ASCP; OB01; PEN2; STUW; SUTT; VACH
Carle, Smiling Frankie *Source(s):* CCE34; CCE36
Woods, Sherman *Source(s):* CCE55; CCE60
Carlos, Roberto 1941- [songwriter]
Godfather of Brazilian Rock & Roll *Source(s):* http://www.slipcue.com/music/brazil/brazilmisc.html (4 Oct. 2002)
Carlos, Walter [songwriter]
Note(s): Do not confuse with Walter Carlos (1939-).
Gold, Billy *Source(s):* CCE29 E4646
Carlos, Walter 1939- [composer, engineer]
Note(s): Do not confuse with Walter Carlos [nd] who used the pseud., Billy Gold.
Carlos, Wendy *Source(s):* DWCO; HIXN; PEN2
Carmelo Augusto, José Francisco 1975- [singer, songwriter]
José Joel *Source(s):* HWOM
Pepito (Pepito) *Source(s):* HWOM
Sosa, José *Source(s):* HWOM
Sosa, Pepe *Source(s):* HWOM
Carmichael, Howard Hoagland 1899-1981 [composer, singer, actor]
Note(s): Portraits: EWEN; SHMM (Feb. 1987): 1, 8-9 & cover
Carmichael, Hoagy *Source(s):* CM27; EPMU; KINK; MUSR; NGAM; PEN2; VACH
Hoagland, Howard *Source(s):* MUSR p. 326
Webb, Malcolm *Source(s):* SUTT
Note(s): Hoagy Carmichael & Six Other Fellows recorded as: Malcolm Webb and His Orchestra.
Carmichael, Ralph 1927- [composer, producer, music publisher]
Calle, Rico *Source(s):* CLTV
Carolan, Turlough 1670-1738 [songwriter, harper]
Last of the Irish Bards, The *Source(s):* GRV5; PSND
O'Carolan, Turlough *Source(s):* BAKR; GRV5
Carpenter, Alicia 1930- [composer, author]
Smith, Alice *Source(s):* ASCP
Carpenter, John(ny) 1948- [composer, author, producer, actor]
Armitage, Frank *Source(s):* LCAR
Chance, James T. *Source(s):* LCAR
Chance, John T. *Source(s):* LCAR
Haight, Rip *Source(s):* LCAR
Master of the Horror Film *Source(s):* http://www.senseofcinema.com/contents/directors/03/carpenter.html (14 Mar.2005)
Quatermass, Martin *Source(s):* LCAR
Carpenter, Juanita Robins 1923- [composer, author]
Styles, Beverly *Source(s):* ASCP
Carr, Benjamin 1768 (or 69)-1831 [publisher, composer, organist]

Note(s): Portraits: ETUP 58:7 (July 1940): 498; HAMM; HOWD
Case, B. Source(s): BROW
Note(s): Misprint on "Spanish Melody," acscribed to Carr.
Father of American Music Source(s): MUWB
Note(s): See also William Billings & Charles Edward Ives.
Father of Philadelphia Music Source(s): NGDM
Carr, F(rank) Osmond 1858-1916 [composer]
Neville, Oscar Source(s): GANA
Carr, Leroy 1905-1935 [pianist, singer, songwriter]
Johnson, Blues Source(s): HARS
Carr, Thomas [arranger]
T. C. Source(s): DICH ("Star-Spangled Banner;" arr. (1814))
Carr, Thomas William 1830- [minister, hymnist]
T. W. C. Source(s): JULN
Carradine, John Arthur 1936- [actor, composer, author]
Carradine, David Source(s): PSNN
Carré, Michel (the elder) 1819-1872 [librettist]
Dubois, Jules Source(s): LOWN; MELL
Note(s): Jt. pseud.: Léon Battu.1
Carroll, Carroll [songwriter]
Oberdorfer, Theodore Eugene Sources: CLRA
Note(s): Possible jt. pseud.: John Scott Trotter.
Carroll, Earl 1892-1948 [songwriter]
Earl, Carl Source(s): GAN1; GAN2
Carroll, John [songwriter]
Brannigan, Dr. Source(s): PSND
Carruthers, John (Tiplady) 1836-1895 [violinist, composer]
Carrodus, John (Tiplady) Source(s): BAKR; LCAR
Carte, Richard D'Oyly 1844-1901 [impressario, composer]
Note(s): Portraits: ETUP 53:4 (Apr. 1935): 197; GAN2
D'Oyly-Carte, Richard Source(s): LCAR
Lynn, Mark Source(s): GANA; MUWB
Carter, Alfred T. B. [composer]
Derfla, Rétrac B. T. Source(s): CPMU (publication date 1853)
Carter, Barry Eugene 1944 (or 45)-2003 [singer, composer, producer, arranger]
Lee, Barry Source(s): GROL (see under: White, Barry)
Maestro of Love Source(s): WORL (see under: White, Barry)
Pied Piper of Love, The Source(s): PSND (see under: White, Barry)
West, Gene Source(s): http://members.chello.nl/p.klein6/Html/barry_white_profile.htm (18 May 2005)
White, Barry Source(s): LCAR
Note(s): Also used by Robert (Charles) Kingston.
Carter, Bennett L(ester) 1907-2003 [composer, arranger, saxophonist]
Carter, Benny Source(s): NGDM; PEN2; PSND; STUW; VACH
Carter, King Source(s): PSND; STUW
Carton, Billy Source(s): JAMU
Clump, Clarence Source(s): JAMU
Elder Statesman of Jazz, The Source(s): PSND
Gomez, Johnny Source(s): CCE68; CCE77; CPOL RE-6-602
King, The Source(s): EPMU
Note(s): See also Elvis A(a)ron Presley.
Lee, L. Source(s): JAMU
Carter, (Herbert) Desmond 1895-1939 [lyricist]
Brody, Hal Source(s): EPMU; GAN2
Note(s): Jt. pseud.: H(ubert) H(edley) Barber, Stanley Lupino [i.e., Hook], John [or Jack] (Francis) Strachey, Harry Acres, Jack Clarke & possibly others.
Carter, D'Wayne [songwriter, performer]
Lil' Wayne Source(s): AMUS; PMUS-00
Carter, Elizabeth 1717-1806 [composer]
Harlowe, Clarissa Source(s): JACK
Carter, Elliott 1908- [composer]
Dean of American Composers Source(s): http://www.arts.wisc.edu/news.html?get=7254 (4 Oct. 2002)
Carter, Levester 1920-2002 [guitarist, singer, songwriter]
Big Lucky Source(s): CCE64
Carter, Big Lucky Source(s): DRSC; EPMU
Carter, Shawn (C.) 1970- [songwriter; performer]
Jay-Z Source(s): AMIR; CPOL PA-996-553; PMUS-00
Carter, Wilf(red Arthur Charles) 1904-1996 [singer, guitarist, songwriter]
Balladeer of the Golden West Source(s): http://personal.inet.fi/koti/joutsi/LPmisc.html (6 Oct. 2002)
Montana Slim Source(s): ALMN; AMUS; CCE66; CCME; CLAB; NASF; STAC
Cartier, Henri ?-1899 [composer]
Raymond, Henri Source(s): STGR
Cartier, Marguerite (Marie Alice) 1918- [composer, violinist, teacher]
Jacques-Rhene, Sister Source(s): COHN (port.); HIXN
Rhene-Jacques, (Sister) Source(s): COHN; HEIN; HIXN
Carver, Cynthia May 1903-1980 [singer, songwriter]
Cousin Emmy Source(s): MCCL
First Hillbilly Star to Own a Cadillac Source(s): MCCL

Casadesus, Francis [or François] Louis 1870-1954 [composer]
Note(s): Francis, along with his brothers, Henri Gustave & Marius Robert Max collaborated in faking works by the following composers.
Bach, Karl Philipp Emanuel *Source(s):* DEA3 p. 94, 112
Handel, Georg Friedrich *Source(s):* DEA3 p. 94, 112
Casadesus, Henri Gustave 1879-1947 [composer, violist]
Note(s): See: Casadusus, Francis [or François] Louis.
Casadesus, Marius Robert Max 1892-1981 [composer, violinist]
Bach, Johann Christian *Source(s):* http://www.casadesus.com/english/famille/Marius_F.html (13 May 2005)
Mozart, (Johann Chrysostom) Wolfgang Amadeus *Source(s):* http://www.casadesus.com/english/famille/Marius_F.html
Casales, Ugo [composer]
Cazalès, Guy de *Source(s):* MELL; STGR
Casati, Girolamo [or Gerolamo] c.1590-after 1657 [composer, organist]
Filago, (Il) *Source(s):* NGDM; WORB
Cascales, John 1911-1968 [instrumentalist, composer, bandleader]
Richards, Johnny *Source(s):* AMUS; EPMU; KINK; PSND
Case, John, M. D. [composer]
Jo. CA *Source(s):* CPMS (publication date 1588)
Casembroot, J. L. 1866-1899 [musicologist]
Florestan *Source(s):* WORB
Note(s): See also Robert Schumann.
Casey, Harry Wayne 1951- [singer, songwriter, arranger]
K. C. *Source(s):* NOMG; PSND
Cash, John(ny) (R.) 1932-2003 [singer, songwriter]
Note(s): Portrait: EWEN
Cash, King Johnny *Source(s):* PSND
Hag, The *Source(s):* PSND
King of Country and Western Music, The *Source(s):* PSND
Man in Black, The *Source(s):* AMEN; CM17; FLIN; PSND
Casimiro da Silva, Joaquim 1808-1862 [composer]
Casimiro Júnior, Joaquim *Source(s):* NGDM
Cason, James E(lmore) 1939- [composer; singer]
Cason, Buzz *Source(s):* ASCP; CCE63; EPMU
Miles, Garry *Source(s):* EPMU
Caspelherr, Günther 1942- [composer]
Gabriel, Gunter *Source(s):* PFSA
Cassell, Alphonsus [composer, lyricist]
Arrow *Source(s):* EPMU; LCAR
Calypso Monarch of Montserrat *Source(s):* EPMU
Cassidy, Claudia 1899-1996 [performing arts critic]
Acidy Cassidy *Source(s):* GRAN
Cassidy, Acidy *Source(s):* GRAN
Cassidy, Poison Pen *Source(s):* MWP1
Poison Pen Cassidy *Source(s):* MWP1
Cassidy, David 1950- [actor, singer, songwriter]
Jackson, Blind Lemon *Source(s):* DAIL (31 Aug. 1993): 3
Cassirer, Fritz 1871-1926 [conductor, writer on music]
Leopold, Friedrich *Source(s):* BAKE
Casson, Reg(inald) H(epworth) 1896- [composer, arranger]
Pana, E. S. *Source(s):* CCE50; http://www.guildmusic.com/light/catalogue/5113.htm (14 May 2005)
Cassone, Michael, Jr. 1938- [composer, singer]
Michaels, Mike *Source(s):* ASCP
Cassotto, Walden Robert 1936-1973 [singer, composer, actor]
Darin, Bobby *Source(s):* CM04; EPMU; GAMM; HARR; STAM
Castaldo, Lee 1915-1991 [trumpeter, bandleader, arranger]
Castle, Lee *Source(s):* PEN2
Castelli, Ignaz Franz 1781-1862 [librettist, editor, playwright]
Cif Charon der Höhlenzote *Source(s):* APPL p.12
Fatalis *Source(s):* KOMU; PIPE
Kosmas *Source(s):* KOMU; LCAR; PIPE
Rosenfeld *Source(s):* KOMU; LCAR; PIPE
Stille, C. A. *Source(s):* KOMU; LCAR; PIPE
Castellon, Augustin 1912-1990 [composer, guitarist]
Niño de Sabicas *Source(s):* LCAR
Sabicias, (Niño) *Source(s):* CCE62; GREN; LCAR
Castleman, Robert (Lee) [songwriter]
Kass, R. L. *Source(s):* AMUS; PMUS-99
Castleman, William Allen [composer]
Allen, Billy *Source(s):* IMDB; MCCA
Williams, Allen *Source(s):* IMDB
Castling, Harry 1865-1933 [songwriter]
Fordykern, S. V. *Source(s):* KILG
Maceo, Nat *Source(s):* KILG
Casto, John Wheaton 1879-1950 [composer]
Kastowsky, Jean *Source(s):* SUPN
Caston, Leonard 1917-1987 [guitarist, pianist, songwriter]
Baby Doo *Source(s):* HARS
Baby Duke *Source(s):* HARS
Caston, Baby Doo *Source(s):* HARS; LCAR
Castro, Antonio [or Tony] 1977- [singer, songwriter]
Tonny Tún Tún *Source(s):* HWOM
Castro, Christian 1974- [singer, songwriter]
Cristian *Source(s):* LCAR

Castro, Eduardo de Sá Pereira de 1828-1872 [author]
Scaliger *Source(s):* MELL
Solinas, Alma *Source(s):* MELL
Note(s): Jt. pseud.: Luigi Conforti.
Castro, Francisco José de fl. 1695-1708 [composer]
Accademico Formato *Source(s):* GROL; LCAR
Note(s): See also D. Marcheselli.
Casulana, Maddalena c.1540-after 1583 [composer, singer]
Mezari, Maddalena *Source(s):* NGDM
Note(s): May be married name; see NGDM.
Caswall, Edward 1814-1878 [hymnist]
Note(s): Portrait: CYBH
Quiz *Source(s):* CART; LCAR
Sciblerus Redivivus *Source(s):* CART; CYBH; LCAR
Caton, Lauderic (Rex) 1910-1999 [guitarist, arranger]
Rix, Lawrence *Source(s):* GROL; JAMU
Catrufo, Gioseffo [or Giuseppe] 1771-1851 [composer]
Spagnoletto *Source(s):* GROL
Note(s): See also Francisco Javier Garcia (Fajer).
Catsos, Nicholas A. 1912-2000 [composer, author]
Brooks, Russ *Source(s):* CCE75
Dixon, George *Source(s):* CCE74
Garett, Gary *Source(s):* CCE53 Eunp; CCE73 R557406
Gregg, Joseph [or Joe] *Source(s):* CCE77; CPOL RE-52-120; CPOL RE-13-910
Harris, Nick *Source(s):* CCE57-58; CPOL RE-245-120
Price, Will *Source(s):* CCE49; CCE76; CPOL RE-13-927
Rice, Will *Source(s):* CPOL RE-52-009
Note(s): Typographical error?
Romero, Garêt *Source(s):* CCE43 #25467 Eunp338718; CCE73
Romero, Gary *Source(s):* ASCP; CCE47; CCE59-60; CPOL RE-80-922
Cattanach, James 1779?-1839? [violinist, composer]
McIntosh, James *Source(s):* IBIM; WORB
Cattigno, Francesco 1782-1847 [musical director, composer]
Catugno, Francesco *Source(s):* MACM
Note(s): Frequent incorrect spelling of surname.
Cauvin, Jean 1509-1564 [theologian]
Calvin(ius), Jean *Source(s):* RIEM; WORB
Cavallari, Ascanio 1544-1590 [cornetist, composer]
Ascanio del Cornetto *Source(s):* NGDM
Cornetto, Ascanio del *Source(s):* NGDM
Del Cornetto, Ascanio *Source(s):* NGDM
Trombetti, Ascanio *Source(s):* BAKR; NGDM
Cavallari, Girolamo 1557-1624 [composer]
Trombetti, Girolamo *Source(s):* NGDM
Cavallini, Ernesto 1807-1874 [clarinetist, composer]
Paganini of Clarinetists *Source(s):* http://www.clarinet.ch/cd/cd1.asp (12 Oct. 2002)
Cavanaugh, Robert Barnes [composer, author, educator]
Barnes, Bosby *Source(s):* ASCP; CPOL PAu-15-551
Cavazzoni, Marco Antonio c.1490-c.1570 [composer]
Marco Antonio da Bologna *Source(s):* WORB
Marco Antonio da Urbino *Source(s):* WORB
Caveirac, Jean Novi de 1713-1782 [composer]
Visigoth *Source(s):* CPMS
Caverhill, William Melville 1910-1983 [dramatist, lyricist]
Melville, Alan *Source(s):* CART; GAN1; GAN2
Cavoukian, Raffi 1948- [singer, songwriter]
Raffi *Source(s):* ALMN; CCE73; CM08
Cazalis, Henri 1840-1909 [lyricist]
Caselli, J. *Source(s):* LCAR
Lahor, J(ean) *Source(s):* BLIC; WORB
Ceballo, Kevin [singer, composer]
Kevin *Source(s):* HWOM
Cecchi d'Amico, Giovanna 1914- [playwright; translator]
Cecchi d'Amico, Suso *Source(s):* LCAR; PIPE
Cecco, Arturo de [composer]
Argentier, P. *Source(s):* STGR
Note(s): "Testagru" (1907)
Cecconi-Bates, Augusta 1933- [composer]
Calla, Arna *Source(s):* OCLC 32531508
Celiano, Livio 1557-1629 [poet, author]
Grillo, Angelo *Source(s):* LAST
Cellamare, Rosalino 1953 (or 54)- [singer, actor, songwriter]
Ron *Source(s):* EPMU
Cere, Edvige C. [composer, teacher]
Cere, Addie *Source(s):* ASCP; CPOL PAu-2-500-890
Černohorsky, Bohuslav Matej 1684-1742 [monk, organist, composer]
Bach of Bohemia *Source(s):* BAKR
Boëmo, Padre *Source(s):* GRV3
Father of Bohemian Music *Source(s):* BAKR
Note(s): See also Bedrich Smetana
Cervenka, Christine 1956- [singer, songwriter]
Exene *Source(s):* LCAR
Cervenka, Exene *Source(s):* AMUS; PMUS-00
Cervetto, James 1682-1783 [violoncellist, composer, conductor]
Note(s): "'Cervetto' points to a translation of the German-Jewish name of Hirschel." (GRV2) Father of James Cervetto (1747-1837); see next entry.
Bassevi, Giacomo *Source(s):* WORB
Cervetto, Giacob(b)o (Bas(s)evi) *Source(s):* CPMU; GRV3; GRV5

Cervetto, Giacomo *Source(s):* WORB
Cervetto the Elder *Source(s):* GRV3; GRV5
G. B. C. *Source(s):* CPMU
Vecchio, Il *Source(s):* NGDM; WORB
Note(s): See also G. Sirazi & Dario Varotari.
Cervetto, James 1747-1837 [violoncellist, composer]
Note(s): Son of James Cervetto (1682-1783); see previous entry. Portrait: Straeten, E. v. D. *History of the Violoncello.* (GRV3)
Cervetto, Jasper *Source(s):* NGDM
Note(s): Incorrect given name; however, in Eitner's *Quellen-Lexikon* identified as possibly his son. (NGDM)
Cervetto the Younger *Source(s):* GRV3; GRV5
Giovane, Il *Source(s):* WORB
Matchless Cervetto, The *Source(s):* NGDM
Cesari, Orfelio [or Elio] [composer]
Orfelius *Source(s):* CCE63 Efor96928; CPOL RE-436-430
Renis, Tony *Source(s):* CCE62; CCE63; CPOL RE-455-486; PMUS
Tonyrenis *Source(s):* CCE63 Efor94196; CCE65; CPOL RE-508-572
Cesarini, Carlo Francesco c.1664-c.1730 [composer, violinist]
Carlo del Violino *Source(s):* NGDM; SADC; WORB
Note(s): See also Carlo Caproli & Carlo Mannelli.
Violino, Carlo del *Source(s):* NGDM; WORB
Note(s): See also Carlo Caproli & Carlo Mannelli.
Cesario, Victor L(ouis) 1931- [composer, author]
Caesar, Vic *Source(s):* ASCP; CCE74; CPOL PAu-1-140-311
Cesti, Pietro 1623-1669 [composer]
Note(s): Baptismal name.
Cesti, Antonio *Source(s):* BAKR; GROL; NGDO
Cesti, Marc'Antonio *Source(s):* BAKR; GROL
Note(s): Incorrect given names in early reference sources.
Glory and Splendour of the Secular Stage, The *Source(s):* NGDO
Cesti, Remigo c.1635-1710 (or 11) [composer, organist]
Remigo, Don *Source(s):* GROL; NGDO
Cevenini, Camillo 1607 (or 08)-1676 [composer, singer]
Operoso, L' *Source(s):* NGDM
Chabania, Jacinto 1908-c.1961 [reeds player, singer, arranger]
Blake, Jerry *Source(s):* KINK
Chabanon, Michel Paul Gui de 1730-1792 [composer]
M. de C*** *Source(s):* CPMS
Chabrier, (Alexis-)Emannuel 1841-1894 [composer]
Ange du cocasse, L' *Source(s):* http://www2.hyperion-records.co.uk/notes/67133.html (4 Oct. 2003)
Angel of Comedy, The *Source(s):* http://www2.hyperion-records.co.uk/notes/67133.html
Chachkes, Maurice 1907-1964 [composer]
Maurice, Cecil *Source(s):* ASCP
Chacksfield, Francis [or Frank] (Charles) 1914-1995 [composer, conductor]
Forrest, David *Source(s):* CCE55 Efor31818; CPOL RE-143-473
Note(s): Jt. pseud.: Cliff Adams, Bob Brown & Jack Fishman (1918 (or 19)-).
Johns, Michael *Source(s):* CCE55 Efor31818; CPOL RE-143-473
Note(s): Jt. pseud.: Cliff Adams, Bob Brown & Jack Fishman (1918 (or 19)-).
Layman, Jan *Source(s):* CCE53-55; CPOL RE-99-928
Patacano, Martino *Source(s):* CPOL RE-259-300; PSNN
Paticano, Martino *Source(s):* RFSO
Senicourt, Roger *Source(s):* CCE58; CPOL RE-328-187; PSNN; RFSO
Chadwick, George Whitefield 1854-1931 [composer]
Note(s): Portraits: ETUP 50:7 (July 1932): 460; HOWD
Pillar of the Boston Classicists *Source(s):* http://www.classicalhall.org/bio1.asp?Iname=Chadwick (4 Oct. 2002)
Chaigneau, Suzanne 1875- [violoncellist, translator, music critic]
Francoeur, S. *Source(s): American Music Teacher* 47:5 (1998): 23
Chakmakjian, Alan Hovhaness 1911-2000 [composer]
Hovhaness, Alan *Source(s):* LCAR; NGAM; NGDM
Challoner, Neville Butler 1784-after 1835 [harpist, composer, conductor]
Butler, Neville Challoner *Source(s):* BLIC
Neville, C. *Source(s):* CPMU
Chambers, Herbert Arthur 1880- [composer, arranger]
H. A. C. *Source(s):* CPMU
Chambers, James (E.) 1948- [singer, composer]
Cliff, Jimmy *Source(s):* ALMN; CASS; CM08; EPMU; HARR; PEN2; PSND
Chambers, Stephen Alexander 1940-1988 [composer]
Hakim, Talib Rasul *Source(s):* BAKR; BUL3; GREN; IDBC; LCAR; PSND
Chambray, Louis François 1737-1807 [composer]
Fakaerti, Sgr. *Source(s):* GROL; NGDM
Ratisbonne, George de *Source(s):* GROL; NGDM
Champagne, Gil(l)es (Maurice) H(erve) 1929- [composer]
Champagne, Champ *Source(s):* CCE62; PSND
Champein, Stanislas 1753-1830 [composer]
Zuccarelli, (Signor) *Source(s):* LOWN; STGR

Champion, Harry 1866-1941 [composer, singer]
Conway, Will *Source(s):* GARR
Champion, Jacques before 1555-1642 [keyboardist, composer]
Chapelle, La *Source(s):* NGDM
Champion, Thomas ?-c.1580 [composer]
Mithou *Source(s):* CPMU; NGDM; WORB
Note(s): See also Jean Daniel.
Champney, H. d'A. [composer]
H. d'A. C. *Source(s):* CPMU
Chamsa, Chakim-sade 1889-1929 [author]
Nijasi *Source(s):* PIPE
Chapeau, Armand [librettist]
Desverges, (M.) *Source(s):* LCAR; LOWN
M.*** *Source(s):* LCAR (see note)
Chapelle, Paul Aimé 1806 (or 08)-1890 [librettist]
Auvray *Source(s):* WORB
Laurencin, M. *Source(s):* LOWN; MELL; STGR; WORB
Laurencin, Paul Aimé *Source(s):* WORB
Léonard *Source(s):* WORB
Lucy *Source(s):* WORB
Chapin, Harry 1942-1981 [singer, songwriter, guitarist]
One Man Cyclone, The *Source(s):* PSND
Chaplin, Charles [or Charlie] (Spencer) 1889-1977 [actor, composer]
Funniest Man in the World, The *Source(s):* PSND
Little Tramp, The *Source(s):* PSND
Spencer, Charlie *Source(s):* REHH
Twentieth Century Moses *Source(s):* PSND
Chapman, Anzentia Igene Perry 1849-1889 [hymnist]
Chapman, Angie *Source(s):* CYBH
Chapman, Melissa Carol 1958- [singer, songwriter]
Chapman, Cee Cee *Source(s):* MCCL
Chapman, Philip 1940- [trumpeter, guitarist, composer]
Lesh, Phil *Source(s):* EPMU; ROOM
Chapman, W. Granville [composer]
Hart, David *Source(s):* http://www.guildmusic.com/light/catalogue5115.htm (17 Aug. 2005)
Chap(p)onnier, Alexandre 1793-1852 [author]
Paulyanthe *Source(s):* PIPE
Polyanthe *Source(s):* PIPE
Char, Friedrich Ernst 1865-1932 [composer, conductor]
Char, Fritz *Source(s):* PSND
Charlap, Morris (Isaac) 1928-1974 [composer]
Charlap, Moose *Source(s):* ASCP; CCE52; CCE56
Charles, Leslie Sebastian 1950- [singer, songwriter]
Ocean, Billy *Source(s):* CASS; HARR; NOMG; ROOM
Spade, Joshua *Source(s):* ROOM
Spade, Sam *Source(s):* RECR; ROOM
Charlesworth, Hector (Willoughby) 1872-1945 [writer, critic, editor] Touchstone *Source(s):* CANE
Note(s): Also used by Claude E(dward Cole Hamilton) Burton & author E(lbert) Herring (1777-1876) (see LCAR).
Charriére, Isabella (Agneta Elisabeth) de 1740-1805 [composer, writer]
Note(s): See LCAR for variant name forms.
Abbe de La Tour *Source(s):* PSND
Charriere, Sophie de *Source(s):* JACK
Zélide *Source(s):* PSND
Zuylen, Belle van *Source(s):* JACK
Chase, George (W.) [composer, actor]
Chee, Lem *Source(s):* CCE61
Note(s): Possible pseud.?
Mahl, Franz *Source(s):* CLTV; IMDB
Reynolds, Michael *Source(s):* http://wald.heim.at/redwood/510196/soundtracks/P9FSM.html (25 May 2005)
Chatman, John Len 1915-1988 [singer, pianist, songwriter]
Chatman, Peter *Source(s):* AMUS; EPMU; PSND
Leroy *Source(s):* HARS; PSND
Memphis Slim *Source(s):* AMUS; EPMU; HARS; PSND; SHAD
Note(s): See also Charles Edward Davenport.
Chatmon, Armenter 1893-1964 [singer, instrumentalist, songwriter]
Carter, Bo *Source(s):* AMUS; HARS; PSND
Chatmon, Bo *Source(s):* HARS; PSND
Chatrian, Pierre Alexandre 1826-1890 [librettist]
Erckmann-Chatrian, (MM) *Source(s):* LOWN; WORB
Note(s): Jt. pseud.: Emile Erckmann.
Chatterton, Thomas 1752-1770 [poet]
Note(s): See PSND for additional nonmusic-related pseudonyms.
Asaphides *Source(s):* GOTT
D.B. *Source(s):* GOTT
Rowley, Thomas *Source(s):* GOTT; PSND; WORB
Chaumont, Lambert c.1630-1712 [composer]
Frère Lambert de St. Théodoré *Source(s):* GROL
Note(s): Called himself.
Chauvier, Serge 1943- [composer, singer]
Lama, Serge *Source(s):* CCE65; CCE68; GOTH
Chauvin, Louis 1881-1908 [composer, pianist]
King of Ragtime Players *Source(s):* JASN (port)
Chavero, Héctor (Roberto) 1908-1992 [singer, poet]
Chavero, Mario *Source(s):* CCE55; GREN
Note(s): Listed as original name.
Yupanqui, Atahualpa *Source(s):* HWOM; LCAR

Chavis, Wilson (Anthony) 1930-2001 [zydeco artist, songwriter]
Chavis, Boozoo *Source(s):* CM38; EPMU; MUHF; *Washington Post* (7 May 2001): B6
Creole Cowboy, The *Source(s):* CM38; EPMU
Checchi, Eugenio 1838-1932 [music critic, journalist]
Caliban *Source(s):* LCAR; PIPE
Calibano, Didimo *Source(s):* PIPE
Tom *Source(s):* GROL (see under: Criticism); LCAR; PIPE
Chedeville, Espirit Philippe 1696-1762 [composer]
Chédeville l'aîné *Source(s):* LCAR
Note(s): Called himself.
Chédeville, le cadet *Source(s):* LCAR
Cheeks, Julius 1929-1981 [singer, songwriter]
Cheeks, June *Source(s):* PSNN
Cheeseman, James Russell 1937- [composer]
Davis, Rusty *Source(s):* ASCP
Chelius, Oskar von 1859-1923 [composer]
Berger, Siegfried *Source(s):* PSND; STGR
Chenier, Clifton 1925-1987 [singer, instrumentalist, songwriter]
King of the South, The *Source(s):* HARS
King of Zydeco *Source(s):* CM06 p. v; HARS
Note(s): See also Alton Rubin.
Chennevière, Daniel 1895-1985 [composer, author, poet]
Note(s): Portrait: ETUP 55:10 (Oct. 1937): 628
Rudhyar, Dane *Source(s):* BAKR; BUL1; BUL2; NGDM; PSND; RIEM
Cherniavskii, A(leksandr) 1871-1942 [songwriter]
Zorin, A. *Source(s):* OCLC 29698035
Cherubini, Maria Luigi Carlo Zenobio Salvatore 1760-1842 [composer]
Italian Mozart, The *Source(s):* PSND
Chesham, Edward Mills [composer, arranger]
Mills, Edward *Source(s):* CPMU (publication dates 1878-1912)
Chessler, Shirley 1923- [composer, author]
Chessler, Deborah *Source(s):* ASCP
Chester, Harriet Mary (née Goff) 1830?- [translator]
H. M. C. *Source(s):* JULN
Chevalet, Émile 1813-1894 [journalist, author, librettist]
Rossi, Emile *Source(s):* LCAR
Théols *Source(s):* LCAR; PIPE; WORB
Chevalier, Albert (Onesime Britannicus Gawtheveoyd Louis) 1861-1923 [comedian, singer, writer]
Albert the Great *Source(s):* CASS
Coster's Laureate, The *Source(s):* CASS
Kipling of the Music Hall *Source(s):* CASS
Old Dutch *Source(s):* CASS
Chevalier, Auguste 1873-1956 [composer]
Ingle, Charles *Source(s):* CPMU; GREN; KILG

Chevrier, F. A. de [composer]
M. C*** *Source(s):* CPMS (publication date 1760)
Chezy, Wilhelmine Christine von 1783-1856 [author, librettist]
Chezy, Helmina von *Source(s):* LCAR
Helmina *Source(s):* PSNN
Chi Kim Hugnh Ma 1945- [singer, composer, lyricist]
Hoàng Oanh *Source(s):* OCLC 42516834
Chiabrano, Carlo (Giuseppe Valentino) 1723-after 1752 [violinist, composer]
Note(s): Mistakenly referred to as: Carlo Francesco Chiabrano, since frequently confused with violinist Felice (i.e., Francesco) Chabran (1756-1824). (GROL)
Chabran, Charles *Source(s):* GROL
Chabran, Francesco *Source(s):* LCAR; MACM; WORB
Note(s): Mistakenly referred to by this name. (GROL)
Chiabrano, (Gaspare Giuseppe) Gaetano 1825-c.1800 [violoncellist, conductor]
Chabran, Gaetano *Source(s):* GROL
Capperan *Source(s):* GROL
Note(s): Possibly the same person.
Chiabrera, Gabriello 1552-1638 [poet, librettist]
Savonese, Il *Source(s):* NGDM; NGDO
Chianco, Bernard V. 1932- [composer]
Sea, Bernie *Source(s):* ASCP
Chiari, Pietro 1712-1785 [librettist]
Criptonide, Egerindo *Source(s):* GROL
Chiarini, Pietro c. 1717-after 1765 [composer, pianist]
Brescianino, Il *Source(s):* PIPE; RIEM
Chiaula, Mauro c.1544-c.1603 [composer]
DaPalermo, Mauro *Source(s):* NGDM
Palermitano, Mauro *Source(s):* NGDM
Panormitano, Mauro *Source(s):* NGDM
Chichester, George Forrest, Jr. 1915-1999 [lyricist, composer]
Note(s): Portrait: EWEN
Forrest, Chet *Source(s):* GAMM; GAN1; GAN2; STUW
Forrest, George (Chichester, Jr.) *Source(s):* EWEN; GAMM; GAN1; GAN2; OB99; STUW
Chicurel, Alberto Hemsi 1897-1975 [composer, conductor, ethnomusicologist]
Hemsi, Alberto *Source(s):* LYMN
Chin, Albert Valentine [guitarist, songwriter, singer]
Chin, Tony *Source(s):* EPMU
Chinelli, Giovanni Battista 1610-1677 [composer]
Occhialino, L' *Source(s):* NGDM
Chipolone, Nunzio 1922- [composer, author, singer]
Blaine, Chip *Source(s):* ASCP; CPOL Pau-337-637

Chipperfield, Frederich 1904-1977 [composer]
Addinsell, Richard *Source(s):* MOMU
Chirico, Andrea [or Alberto] de 1891-1952 (or 56) [composer, writer, visual artist]
Savinio, Alberto *Source(s):* BUL2; MELL; NGDM; RIES; WORB
Chladni, Ernst Florens Friedrich 1756-1827 [physicist, writer on acoustics]
Father of Modern Acoustics *Source(s):* GRV2
Monochord der Tongrübler *Source(s):* APPL
Choate, Donald (W(illiam)) 1933- [songwriter]
Wayne, Don *Source(s):* CCE66-68; CCE73-75; NASF
Chop, Max (Friedrich Julius Theodor) 1862-1929 [composer, writer on music]
Charles, M(onsieur) *Source(s):* MACM; PIPE; PRAT
Chopin, Frederic 1810-1849 [composer]
Boldest and Proudest Poetic Spirit of the Times, The *Source(s):* GRV3 p. 634 col. 1
Most Polish of Polish Composers, The *Source(s):* Jarecki, Tadeudsz. *The Most Polish of Polish Composers: Frederic Chopin 1910-1849.* New York, 1949.
Pichon, M. *Source(s):* http://www.geocities.com/dambi/english/right.htm (2 Feb. 2005)
Note(s): Used on mock newspaper, "Kurier Szafarsi," sent to his parents.
Poland's Greatest Composer *Source(s):* http://www.cyberessays.com/Arts/31.htm (29 Sept. 2003)
Chorley, Henry Fothergill 1808-1872 [music critic, translator]
Note(s): Portrait: CYBH
Begging-Letter Writer, A *Source(s):* CART
Bell, Paul *Source(s):* CART; DAWS; LCAR
H. F. C. *Source(s):* CART
Mute, A *Source(s):* CART
R. O. D. H. F. *Source(s):* CART
Sharp *Source(s):* CART
Tartini's Familiar *Source(s):* CART
Chotoosingh, Mario [songwriter]
Silky *Source(s):* PMUS-96
Chotzinoff, Samuel 1889-1964 [accompanist, music critic]
Note(s): Portrait: ETUP 58:7 (July 1940): 498
Chotzie *Source(s):* GRAN
Toscanini Cultists, The *Source(s):* GRAN p. 275
Note(s): Jt. sobriquet: Lawrence Gilman & Bernard H. Haggin.
Choudard, P(ierre) J(ean) B(aptiste) 1746-1806 [playwright, singer, actor]
Desforges *Source(s):* PIPE
Choudens, Antony 1849-1902 [composer]
Bérel, Antony *Source(s):* CPMU; GOTH; MELL
Choudens, Paul de 1850-1925 [playwright, music publisher]
Bérel, P(aul) *Source(s):* LOWN; PIPE; STGR
Chowdhury, Robindra Shankar 1920- [satarist, composer]
Godfather of World Music *Source(s):* http://www.ravishankar.org/home_frames.html (3 Oct. 2002)
Shankar, Ravi *Source(s):* MUWB; PEN2
Chrisman, Paul Woodrow 1949- [singer, fiddler, songwriter]
King of the Cowboy Fiddlers *Source(s):* EPMU; http://www.ridersinthesky.com (4 Oct. 2002)
Paul, Woody *Source(s):* CCE78; EPMU; http://www.ridersinthesky.com
Christensen, Axel (W.) 1881-1955 [composer, pianist, editor]
Czar of Ragtime *Source(s):* JASA pp. 124 & 128 (port.)
Christian, Arlester 1943-1971 [songwriter]
Dyke *Source(s):* EPMU
Christian, Garrison 1955- [singer, songwriter]
Christian, Garry *Source(s):* EPMU
Christiansen, Larry A. 1941- [composer]
Johnstone, Gordon *Source(s):* CCE77; GOTH
Note(s): Also used by Joseph Sween(e)y.
Christoff, Vincent 1905- [composer]
Crombruggen, Paul van *Source(s):* GOTH
Chryssomallis, Yanni 1954- [composer, keyboardist]
New Age Keyboard Maestro *Source(s):* CM11 p.vii
Yanni *Source(s):* CM11; EPMU
Chusid, Irwin [author, radio commentator, music historian]
McDavid, Pal *Source(s):* http://raymondscott.com/Biblio.htm (1 Feb. 2005)
Cianchettini, Clelia (Veronica Elizabeth?) 1779-1833 [composer]
Campanile, (Madame) *Source(s):* JACK
Cibber, Colley 1671-1757 [actor, playwright]
Gabriel, Colley *Source(s):* PIPE
Note(s): In PIPE "Gabriel" is listed as original surname?
Gavardo, Gavardo da *Source(s):* PIPE.
King Coll(ey) *Source(s):* PSND
King of Dullness, The *Source(s):* PSND
King of Dunces, The *Source(s):* PSND
Spagnolet of the Theatre, The *Source(s):* PSND
Cicatello, Frank Domenick 1911-1991 [composer, author]
Jacey, Frank *Source(s):* ASCP
Ciccone, Madonna Louise Veronica 1958 (or 59)- [singer, actress, songwriter]
Madonna *Source(s):* ALMN; CM04; CM16; GRAT; HARR; PSND; WARN; WORL

Material Girl *Source(s):* ALMN
Queen of Pop, The *Source(s):* http://www.dotvsdot.com/vs/0/236.html (4 Oct. 2002)
Ciceu, Eugen 1940-1997 [composer]
Cicero, Eugen *Source(s):* KOMS; PFSA
Cicognini, Alessandro 1906-1995 [composer]
Icini, (C.) *Source(s):* CCE55-58; CCE77; CLTV; CPOL RE-163-059
Cicognini, Giacinto Andrea 1606-c.1650 [playwright, librettist]
Instancabile *Source(s):* ALMC
Ciminella, Christina Claire 1964- [singer, songwriter, guitarist, actress]
Judd, Wynonna *Source(s):* MCCL
Wynonna *Source(s):* MCCL
Cioroiu, Alexandru Sorin 1941- [composer]
Moga, Sorin *Source(s):* ASCP
Cipollone, Alfonso 1843-1926 [composer]
Dana, Arthur *Source(s):* CCE36 R46750
Note(s): A. P. Schmidt house name; see NOTES: Dana, Arthur.
Leonardi, A. *Source(s):* CCE39 #12613, 32 R73920
Leonardi, L. *Source(s):* CCE39 R78515-17 & R78522 ("Le Debut du jeune pianiste")
Cipretti, Pietro [librettist]
Appatista (Fiorentina) *Source(s):* ALMC
Ciummei, Alfredo 1867-1921 [composer]
Donizetti, Alfredo *Source(s):* BAKO; BAKR; MACM
Civinini, Guelfo 1873-1954 [author, journalist]
Accard *Source(s):* PIPE; WORB
Baccellino *Source(s):* WORB
Cellini, Baccio *Source(s):* PIPE; WORB
Ciù *Source(s):* WORB
Mouscardin *Source(s):* WORB
Pilusky *Source(s):* WORB
Cizos, Victor 1830-1882 [composer, conductor]
Cheri, Victor *Source(s):* MACM
Clapham, Emma 1830- [hymnist]
E. C. *Source(s):* JULN
Clapp, Charles 1899-1962 [composer, author, conductor]
Clapp, Sunny *Source(s):* ASCP; LCAR; PSND
Clapp, Eric (Patrick) 1945- [guitarist, singer, songwriter]
Clapton, Eric *Source(s):* AMUS; CM01; CM11; EPMU; GROL; STAM
Clapton, Slowhand *Source(s):* EPMU
Clayton, Eddie *Source(s):* BEAT
Slowhand *Source(s):* GROL; SHAD
x-sample *Source(s):* http://www.imusic.com/showcase/rock/ericclapton.html (4 Oct. 2002)
Clapp, Henry, Jr. 1814-1875 [writer on music]
Figaro *Source(s):* STAR p. 217
King of Bohemia *Source(s):* STAR p. 216
Clare, Edward ?-1869 [author, composer]
Smart, Grenville *Source(s):* CPMU; GOTT; HUEV
Clare, John (Lester) 1940- [writer on jazz]
Brennan, Gail *Source(s):* DAUM; LCAR
Clare, Sidney 1892-1972 [songwriter]
Song Writers on Parade *Source(s):* CCE29 E2978; CCE32 Eunp56182
Note(s): Jt. pseud.: Percy Wenrich, Charles Tobias, Al(bert) Sherman, Al(an) Lewis, (T.) Murray Mencher & Vincent Rose.
Clark see also *Clarke*
Clark, Allan 1907- [composer, author, piano]
Morrison, Alex *Source(s):* ASCP; CCE74-75
Clark, C(yrus) Van Ness 1894- [composer]
Henderson, Frame *Source(s):* CCE72 R537905; CCE73
Note(s): Jt. pseud.: Martin Hickey.
Land, Dick C. *Source(s):* CCE72 R537636-38
Note(s): Jt. pseud.: Martin Hickey.
Ness, Clarke Van *Source(s):* CCE72 R537908
Van Ness, Clarke *Source(s):* CCE73-74; LCAR
Whipple, Zeb *Source(s):* CCE72-74
Clark, Conrad Yeatis 1931-1963 [pianist, composer]
Clark, Sonny *Source(s):* EPMU; PSND
Clark, Frederick Horace 1860-1917 [pianist, teacher, writer on music]
Damian, Leo Saint *Source(s):* MACM
Saint [or St.] Damian, Leo *Source(s):* LCAR; MACM
Steiniger, C. *Source(s):* MACM
Clark(e), Harold E(ugene) 1941- [singer, songwriter]
Clark(e), Gene *Source(s):* DIMA; PMUS
Clark(e), Harry D. [songwriter]
Hymn Singer *Source(s):* OCLC 12414039
Clark, Petula (Sally Olmen [or Olwen]) 1932- [singer, composer]
Grant, Al *Source(s):* http://www.petulaclark.net.pccompositions.html (2 Sept. 2003)
Jones, Peggy *Source(s):* CPOL RE-59-337
Clark, Raymond LeRoy 1917-2000 [singer, songwriter]
Clark, Slim *Source(s):* LCAR
Clark, Yodeling Slim *Source(s):* MCCL
Clark, Roy (Linwood) 1933- [singer, songwriter, instrumentalist]
Superpicker *Source(s):* FLIN
Clarke see also *Clark*
Clarke, (Harold) Allan 1942- [songwriter]
Ransford, (L.) *Source(s):* BLIC; *Goldmine* 28:12:571 (14 June 2002): 70
Note(s): Jt. pseud.: Graham Nash & Tony (Christopher) Hicks.

Clarke, Cuthbert 1869-1953 [composer]
MacKenzie, Cyril Claude *Source(s):* CCE46 R13294 ("Naomi"); CCE48 R30032
Olsen, Elric *Source(s):* CCE42 #29091, 679 R108581; CCE50 R13928 ("Queen of the Plains")
Olsen, Elsie *Source(s):* CCE44 R133399; KILG
Peschokov, Igor *Source(s):* CCE45 #55029, 576 R141868
Clarke, Henry Leland 1907-1977 [composer, scholar]
Fairbanks, J(onathan) *Source(s):* GACC p. 29; GROL; LCAR; NGAM
Note(s): On works composed for the Composers Collective of New York.
Clarke, J. F. [composer, pianist]
Percival, Frank *Source(s):* YORM p. 175
Clarke, Jack [songwriter]
Brody, Hal *Source(s):* CCE29 Efor4503
Note(s): Jt. pseud. H(ebert) B(arber) Hedley [i.e., Herbert Hedley Barber, Stanley Lupino [i.e., Hook], John [or Jack] (Francis) Strachey, Harry Acres, (Herbert) Desmond Carter & possibly others.
Clarke, Kenneth [or Kenny] (Spearman) 1914-1985 [drummer, bandleader, composer]
Clarke, Klook *Source(s):* GROL; NGDM; PSND
Klook-Mop *Source(s):* GROL
Salaam, Liaqat Ali *Source(s):* GROL; NGDM; PSND
Clarke, Mary Elizabeth [composer]
Barrett, Meredith *Source(s):* MWP2 p. 436
Grant, Lawrence *Source(s):* MWP2 p. 436
Note(s): Also used by Lawrence A. Hostetler; see LCAR.
Clarke, Moussa [songwriter]
Moose *Source(s):* SONG
Clarke, Rebecca (Thacher) 1886-1979 [composer, arranger, violist]
Note(s): Married name: Mrs. James Friskin.
Trent, Anthony *Source(s):* BUL3; COHN; GOTH; GREN; HIXN
Clarke, Sonia [songwriter]
Sonique *Source(s):* CPOL PA-980-631; PMUS-00
Clarke, William Horatio 1840-1913 [organist, composer, writer on music]
Believer in the Internal Evidence of Divine Revelation, A *Source(s):* CART
Claudel, Paul (Louis Charles Marie) 1868-1955 [author]
Delachapelle *Source(s):* PIPE
Claudius, Georg Karl 1757-1815 [librettist]
Ehrenberg, Franz *Source(s):* SONN; STGR; WORB
Claudius, Matthias 1740-1815 [writer on music]
Asmus *Source(s):* LCAR; PIPE; WORB
Wandsbeker Bote *Source(s):* LCAR; PIPE
Claussen, Raelene (C(laire)) 1939 (or 40)- [composer, author, singer]
Raney, Sue *Source(s):* ASCC; CCE58; CCE61; EPMU
Clayton, Lee T. 1942- [singer, songwriter, guitarist]
Outlaw's Outlaw, The *Source(s):* MCCL
Note(s): See also Billy Schatz.
Clayton, Peter Joe 1898-1947 [singer, songwriter]
Blues Doctor, The *Source(s):* HARS
Clayton, Doc(tor) *Source(s):* CCE73 R564065; HARS
Cleighton, Peter *Source(s):* HARS
Clayton, Wilbur D(orsey) 1911-1991 [trumpeter, composer, arranger]
Clayton, Buck *Source(s):* ASCP; CASS; CCE73; EPMU; GAMM; KINK; PEN2
Durante, John *Source(s):* JAMU
Cleaver, H. Robinson [lyricist]
King, Roy *Source(s):* PMUS
Note(s): Also used by Roy Crimmins.
Clegg, Johnny 1953- [singer, songwriter]
White Zulu, The *Source(s):* CM08
Clemens, Lucinda [writer on music]
Hockley, Nancy *Source(s):* CANE
Clement, Jack 1931 (or 32)- [songwriter, bandleader]
Cowboy, The *Source(s):* PSND; WORT
Cowboy Jack *Source(s):* NASF; PSND; WORT
Clément, Jacob [or Jacques] c.1500-c.1557 [composer]
Clemens non Papa *Source(s):* MACM; NGDM
Master of Counterpoint, The *Source(s):* PSND
Clementi, Muzio 1752-1832 [composer, pianist]
Father of the Pianoforte, The *Source(s):* MUWB; SPIE
M. C., (Signor) *Source(s):* CPMU
Clements, Arthur fl. 1876-1884 [writer]
Hue and Eye *Source(s):* GANA
Note(s): Jt. pseud.: Frederick Hay.
Clements, Vassar Carlton 1928- [instrumentalist, singer, composer]
"Count Basie" Fiddle Player *Source(s):* http://www.vassarclements.com/bio.html (4 Oct. 2002)
Country Isaac Stern *Source(s):* http://www.vassarclements.com/bio.html
Father of Hillbilly Jazz *Source(s):* http://www.vassarclements.com/bio.html
"Miles Davis" of Bluegrass *Source(s):* http://www.vassarclements.com/bio.html
Philosopher Fiddler, The *Source(s):* MCCL
Superbow *Source(s):* MCCL; PSND
Vassar the Master *Source(s):* http://www.vogagemagazine.com/vassar
Clements, Zeke 1911-1994 [singer, songwriter, instrumentalist]
Alabama Cowboy, (The) *Source(s):* MCCL; PSND

Clemons, Clarence 1942- [saxophonist, singer, songwriter]
King of the World, The *Source(s):* CM07
Master of Disater, The *Source(s):* CM07
Clerc, Charles (Louis) 1879-1959 [songwriter]
Borel-Clerc, Ch(arles) *Source(s):* BAKR; CCE48-49; SMIN
Clerico, Francesco c.1755-c1838 [librettist]
Quirino, F. C. Accdemico *Source(s):* MORI; NGDO
Clery, W. E. fl. 1883-99 [critic]
Fryers, Austin *Source(s):* GANA
Cless, Johann fl. 1587 [composer]
Hanoius *Source(s):* GROL
Cleveland, James 1931-1991 [clergyman, singer, composer]
Crown Prince of Gospel, The *Source(s):* AMEN; CM01
King of Gospel Music, The *Source(s):* AMEN; CM01
Note(s): See also Cleophus Robinson.
Clifford, Doug(las) R. 1945- [composer, author, singer]
Clifford, Cosmo *Source(s):* ASCP; LCAR (see note)
Clifford, Hubert John 1904-1959 [composer, conductor]
Note(s): Used pseudonyms (DOLM); however, to date, only one identified.
Sarsfield, Michael *Source(s):* DOLM; MUWB
Clifford, Reese Francis, III 1942- [singer, songwriter]
Clifford, Buzz *Source(s):* EPMU; PSND
Clifton, Henry Robert 1831 (or 32)-1872 [author, composer, singer]
Clifton, Harry *Source(s):* BROW; GAMM; LCAR
Clinton, Larry 1909-1985 [composer, arranger, trumpeter]
Carlson, Lee *Source(s):* LCAR
Carlson, Lenny *Source(s):* LCAR
Dipsy Doodler, The *Source(s):* PSND
Closson, Ernest 1870-1950 [historian, critic, folk music authority]
Antoine, Paul *Source(s):* BAKE; PRAT; WORB
Clough-Leighter, Henry 1874-1956 [composer]
Note(s): Portraits: APSA; ETUP 50:8 (Aug. 1932): 532; MUSA 30:6 (7 June 1919): 23
Carvel, Robert *Source(s):* CCE35 R36072; CCE47 R16703 ("O Lamb of God, I Come")
H. C.-L. *Source(s):* CCE64 R351670 ("For a Last Good Night")
Humphries, Charles *Source(s):* CCE30 R11822
Koppitz, Louis *Source(s):* CCE49; GOTH
Lichter, Hans *Source(s):* CCE30 R10413; TPRF
Ries, Hugo *Source(s):* CCE43 #48398, 4 R120889
West, John E. *Source(s):* CCE35 R36072

Clouser, Lionel R(andolph) 1910-1942 [composer, conductor, arranger]
Rand, Lionel *Source(s):* ASCP; CCE41 #1726 E90040; CCE65; CCE68
Clutsam, George Howard 1866-1951 [composer, pianist, critic]
Aubry, Paul *Source(s):* CPMU; GROL; PIPE
Harrington, Robert *Source(s):* CPMU; GROL; PIPE
Iseledon, H. S. *Source(s):* GROL; PIPE
Latour, Georges *Source(s):* CCE34 R31316; CPMU; GROL; PIPE
Mervyn, Mat *Source(s):* CCE50 R62456 ("Gipsy Croon Song"); PIPE
Mustal, Ch. G. *Source(s):* CPMU; GROL; PIPE
Coates, Carroll 1929- [composer, lyricist, producer]
Lloyd, Ashton *Source(s):* ASCP
Coates, Eric 1886-1957 [composer, violist]
Arnold, Jack *Source(s):* BLIC; CCE51 R83681 ("Different Somehow")
Father of British Light Music *Source(s):* http://www.mfiles.co.uk/Composers/Eric-Coates.htm (26 Apr. 2005)
King of Light Music *Source(s):* MUWB
Uncrowned King of Light Music *Source(s):* CASS
Coates, Thomas 1818-1885 [bandmaster, composer]
Father of Band Music in America, The *Source(s):* http://www.eastonband.org/History.htm (4 Oct. 2002)
Note(s): See also D(avid) W(allis) Reeves.
Cobb, George L(inus) 1886-1942 [composer]
Note(s): Portrait: JASA
Boulton, John *Source(s):* CCE45 #63817, 460 R143451
Fenton, Bernard *Source(s):* CCE46 R12254 ("Rainbow"); CCE47 R9312 ("June Moon")
Gordon, Leo *Source(s):* CCE45 #22283,71 R137101; JASA
Hamilton, Ted *Source(s):* CCE45 #63817, 162 R144154; CCE47 R20111
Note(s): "Someday You'll Want Me Too" (CCE47) Also used by Edward Leslie Hamilton.
Linwood, Roy *Source(s):* CCE46 R6982 ("Beautiful Girl of Somewhere")
Raymond, Jack *Source(s):* CCE46 R6982 ("Beautiful Girl of Somewhere")
Strong, Elizabeth *Source(s):* CCE45 #55029, 836 R142410; CCE47 R25215
Taylor, Allen *Source(s):* CCE47 R22251
Temple, Harry *Source(s):* CCE45 #63817, 358 R144369
Wegman, Frank *Source(s):* CCE45 #55029, 292 R143547; CCE46 R13709
Note(s): "Dance of the Morning Glories" (CCE46)
Cobb, Will D. 1876-1930 [songwriter]
Note(s): Do not confuse with Willie Cobbs (1940-); see following entry.

Hilliard, Harry *Source(s):* CCE28 R45847
Watson, Whitford *Source(s):* CCE35 R37984
Cobbs, Willie 1940- [singer, guitarist, songwriter]
Note(s): Do not confuse with Will D. Cobb (1876-130); see preceding entry.
Willie C *Source(s):* HARS
Cochevelou, Alan [or Alain] 1944- [multi-instrumentalist, arranger]
Stivell, Alan *Source(s):* CCE68; CCE71-74; LCAR; MUHF
Cochran, Garland (Perry) 1935- [singer, songwriter]
Cochran, Hank *Source(s):* CCME; ENCM; EPMU; MCCL; NASF; PEN2; WORT
Cochran, William Wesley 1910-1958 [pianist, songwriter]
Cornell, Wes *Source(s):* BLUE
Cockburn, Alicia 1713-1794 [songwriter, poet]
Rutherford, Alison *Source(s):* PSND
Cockburn, Bruce 1945- [singer, songwriter, guitarist]
Rocker with a Mission, A *Source(s):* CM08
Cocker, John Robert 1944- [singer, songwriter]
Cocker, Joe *Source(s):* LCAR; PEN2
Cockram, Edward Purcell ?-1932 [composer]
Purcell, Edward Cockram *Source(s):* MUWB
Cocq, Rosine de 1891-1977 [composer]
Mirédo, Jean *Source(s):* NEDM
Coe, David Allan 1939- [musician, songwriter]
Mysterious Rhinestone Cowboy, The *Source(s):* FLIN; MCCL; PSND
Rhinestone Cowboy, The *Source(s):* MCCL
Note(s): See also Glen (Travis) Campbell.
Coe, Matthew 1957-1988 [guitarist, saxophonist, songwriter]
Slingsby, Xero *Source(s):* EPMU
Coenen, Paul Franz 1908- [composer]
Westring *Source(s):* KOMP; PFSA
Coffin, Lucius Powers 1864-1928 [actor, composer]
Whiting, Stanley *Source(s):* PSND
Cogane, Nelson 1902-1985 [composer]
Miller, Jack *Source(s):* CLRA; CLTP ("Aldrich Family")
Cohan, George M(ichael) 1878-1942 [actor, songwriter, playwright]
Note(s): Originally surname: Cohen. Portraits: EWEN; EWPA
Broadway, Mr. *Source(s):* PSND
Father of American Musical Comedy, The *Source(s):* FACS
Father of Musical Comedy *Source(s):* http://www.theatrehistory.com/american/cohan001.html (4 Oct. 2002)
Note(s): See also James T. Tanner.
George, Uncle *Source(s):* PSND
King of Broadway, The *Source(s):* PSND
Man Who Owned Broadway, The *Source(s):* PSND
Mr. Broadway *Source(s):* PSND
Prince of Broadway, The *Source(s):* PSND
Prince of the American Theater, The *Source(s):* PSND
Song and Dance Man, A *Source(s):* SPTH p. 344
Note(s): Called himself.
Uncle George *Source(s):* PSND
"Yankee-doodle-boy" of the American Stage *Source(s):* GAN2
Yankee Doodle Dandy, (The) *Source(s):* CM07 p.v; PSND
Cohen, Arthur C.
Arthur, C. M. *Source(s):* TPRF
King, Arthur C. *Source(s):* TPRF
Cohen, Daniel (Kelly) 1946- [composer, author]
Kelly, C(asey) *Source(s):* ASCP; CCE75-76; CPOL PA-138-595
Cohen, (Stuart) David 1941-1982 [singer, songwriter, guitarist]
Blue, David *Source(s):* CCE66; EPMU; HARR; PEN2
Cohen, Elizabeth 1916 (or 19)- [lyricist, playwright, screenwriter]
Comden, Betty *Source(s):* CLMM; GRAT; LCAR; PSND
Cohen, Frieda P. C. 1879- [playwright, composer, educator]
Hall, (Mrs.) Frieda P. C. *Source(s):* IBIM; WORB
Langly, Paul *Source(s):* IBIM; WORB
Potter, O. L. *Source(s):* IBIM; WORB
Cohen, Henri [or Henry] 1806 (or 08)-1880 [composer, musicologist]
Coen, Enrico *Source(s):* STGR
Note(s): Typographical error?
Cohen, Carlo Enrico *Source(s):* MELL
Cohen, Hermann 1821 (or 29)-1871 [pianist, composer]
Note(s): Do no confuse with Hermann Cohen, 1842-1918, writer on music.
Augustin Marie (du Tres Saint Scarement), père *Source(s):* LCAR; MACM
Hermann, (Carlo) *Source(s):* MACM, MELL
Cohen, Isidore (de Lara) 1858-1935 [composer, pianist]
De Lara, Isidore *Source(s):* BAKR; GOTH; MACM; NGDO; PIPE
Lara, Isidor de *Source(s):* IWWM; PIPE
Solla, Isidor *Source(s):* PIPE
Cohen, Joseph 1918- [composer, author]
Cowen, Joe *Source(s):* ASCP; CCE59
Cohen, Judy Kay(e) 1952- [singer, songwriter, guitarist]
Newton, Juice *Source(s):* CM37; PEN2
Cohen, Kalman 1917-2001 [composer, songwriter]
Mann, Kal *Source(s):* CCE53-56; DRSC; OB01 (port.)

September, Anthony *Source(s):* CPOL RE-233-750; MUWB; SONG
Note(s): "Butterfly" was written by Bernie Lowe & Kal Mann [i.e., Kalman Cohen] & credited to Anthony September [i.e., Anthony [or Tony] Mammarella] (MUWB).
Sheldon, Jon *Source(s):* CPOL RE-250-249
Cohen, Lane Nathan 1951- [composer, author]
Nathan, Lane *Source(s):* ASCP (see reference)
Cohen, Leonard 1934- [singer, songwriter, novelist]
Bard of the Bedsits *Source(s):* CASS
Cohen, Martin [songwriter]
Coleman, Marty *Source(s):* CCE63; CCE67; PMUS
Cohen, Maurice Alfred 1904 (or 05)-1968 [songwriter, pianist]
Note(s): The following are listed as pseuds. of Michael Carr.
Bereford, Maurice *Source(s):* CCE35 Efor41339; CCE61
Carr, Michael *Source(s):* CASS; CCE50; CPOL RE-18-629; GAMM; GREN; HARR; ROOM
Chalmers, Cy *Source(s):* CPOL RE-248-483; CPOL RE-257-858
Note(s): Jt. pseud.: Norman Newell.
Curroy, Mort *Source(s):* CCE34 Efor34120
Note(s): Jt. pseud.: Ivor Moreton, Bill Currie & Harry Roy [i.e., Harry Lipman]
Day, Ken *Source(s):* CCE52
Mahon, George *Source(s):* CCE74
Miller, Mel *Source(s):* CCE53 E70447; CCE53; CPOL RE-86-281
Note(s): Also Jt. pseud.: Peter Hart [i.e., Hargreaves]
Summers, Joan *Source(s):* CCE53
Note(s): Jt. pseud.: Leo Towers [i.e., Leo(nard) Blitz]
Cohen, Mosco 1904-1985 [writer on music]
Carner, Mosco *Source(s):* LCAR
Cohen, Robert 1912-1981 [conductor, writer on music]
Lawrence, Robert *Source(s):* BAKO; PIPE
Cohen, Samuel 1913-1993 [lyricist, singer]
Note(s): Portraits: EWEN; SHMM (June/July 1988): 28-9 & cover
Burton, Fred *Source(s):* CCE40 #28449 Eunp229812
Note(s): "That's the Way They Jitter Down in Georgia" Possible pseud.? (Published: Brooklyn).
Cahn, Sammy *Source(s):* ALMN; CM11; EPMU; EWEN; GAN2; HARR; LCAR; PSND
Kahn, Sam(my) *Source(s):* LCAR
Cohen, Theodore Charles 1928- [vibraphonist, composer, arranger]
Charles, Teddy *Source(s):* EPMU; KINK; LCAR; NGDJ; PSND
Jinx Jingles *Source(s):* JAMU
Jingles, Jinx *Source(s):* JAMU
Kahn, Stix *Source(s):* JAMU
Cohn, Al(vin Gilbert) 1925-1988 [saxophonist, arranger, composer]
Horowitz, Ike *Source(s):* JAMU
Cohn, Chester 1896- [composer]
Conn, Chester *Source(s):* BBDP; CCE53-55
Neuman, M. *Source(s):* CCE37 E60278
Cohn, (Dr.) Felix fl. c.1886 [composer]
Felix, C. *Source(s):* MELL; STGR
Cohn, Gregory Phil 1919-1991 [composer, author, organist]
Lane, Walter *Source(s):* ASCP
Note(s): Also used by Chester Nordman.
Cohn, Irving 1898-1961 [composer, lyricist]
Conn, Irving *Source(s):* FULD
Cohner, György 1868-1920 [composer, conductor]
Jarno, Georg *Source(s):* BAKO; GAN1; GAN2; WEOP
Cohon, Baruch Joseph 1926- [composer, author, singer]
Cohon, Barry *Source(s):* ASCP
Colamosca, Frank O(ctavius) 1910-1984 [composer, author, pianist]
Cole, Frank *Source(s):* ASCP; CCE55 Eunp
Colantuoni, Alberto 1880-1959 [librettist]
Aliaga, S. *Source(s):* OCLC 28015645
Colbert, Warren Ernest 1929- [composer, author]
Warren, Dane *Source(s):* ASCP; CCE75
Colchester, (Lady) [songwriter]
Me *Source(s):* CPMU (publication date 1838)
Cole, Edward William 1832-1918 [composer, editor, aranger]
Cristabel *Source(s):* http://www.lib.monash.edu.au/exhibitions/music/xmusiccat.html (4 Oct. 2002)
Cole, Edwin Lemar 1916-1964 [pianist, composer, bandleader]
Cole, Buddy *Source(s):* CCE64; KINK
Cole, Isaac 1927-2001 [pianist, composer]
Cole, Ike *Source(s):* LCAR; OB01
Cole, John William 1867-1946 [composer]
Colaza, Juan de *Source(s):* CCE31 Efor18372; REHH
Cole, Nathaniel Adams 1919-1965 [pianist, singer, actor, composer]
Calvert, Lord *Source(s):* JAMU; LCAR
Cole, Nat King *Source(s):* NGAM; SOTH
Lord Calvert *Source(s):* JAMU; LCAR
Guy, Aye *Source(s):* JAMU
Laguana Eddie *Source(s):* JAMU
Nadine, Shorty *Source(s):* JAMU
Nature Boy *Source(s):* JAMU
Schmaltz, Sam *Source(s):* JAMU
Cole, Robert [or Bob] (Allen) 1868 [or 69]-1911 [songwriter, actor, director, producer]
Cole and Johnson Brothers *Source(s):* GAN1; GAN2

Note(s): Jt. pseud.: James Weldon Johnson & J(ohn) Rosamond Johnson.
Handy, Will *Source(s):* BAKR; GAN1; GAN2; IDBC; JASZ
Note(s): Jt. pseud.: James Weldon Johnson & J(ohn) Rosamond Johnson.
Wayside, (Willie) *Source(s):* JASN; JASZ
Note(s): Stage name.
Colebault, Jacques 1483-1559 [composer]
Collebaudi, Jachet *Source(s):* CPMU
Jachet (of Mantua) *Source(s):* CPMU
Jacquet (of Mantua) *Source(s):* NGDM
Coleman, Ervan F. [composer]
Coleman, Bud *Source(s):* CCE64; PMUS
Coleman, Gary 1947-1994 [instrumentalist, singer, producer, songwriter]
B. B. *Source(s):* AMUS
Coleman, B. B. *Source(s):* AMUS; LCAR
Coleman, Gordon 1930- [composer]
Langford, Gordon *Source(s):* MUWB
Coleridge, Samuel Taylor 1772-1834 [poet, philosopher, critic]
Note(s): Portraits: EWCY; EWEC. See PSND for additional nonmusic-related pseudonyms & sobriquets.
Cordomi *Source(s):* GOTT
G.A.U.N.T. *Source(s):* GOTT
Hiawatha Man, The *Source(s):* Self, Geoffrey. *The Hiawatha Man*. Brookfield, VT: Ashgate, 1995.
Coleridge-Taylor, Gwendolen 1903-1998 [composer, conductor]
Note(s): Portrait: DWCO
Coleridge-Taylor, Avril *Source(s):* DWCO; GROL; IDBC
Riley, Peter *Source(s):* CCE48; DWCO; IDBC
Coles, Bramwell 1887-1960 [composer]
March King of the Salvation Army *Source(s):* SMIN
Coles, Dennis [songwriter, performer]
Ghostface Killah *Source(s):* AMIR; PMUS
Killah, Ghostface *Source(s):* LCAR
Starks, Tony *Source(s):* LCAR
Colette, Sidonie Gabrielle Claudine 1873-1954 [author, music critic]
Colette(-Willy) *Source(s):* ROOM
Note(s): Used hyphenated form until 1916.
Gauthiers-Villars, Sidonie Gabriel *Source(s):* ROOM
Willy *Source(s):* ROOM
Note(s): Also used by her husband, Henri Gauthier-Villars.
Willy, Colette *Source(s):* LCAR
Colin, Bernard 1931-1891 [actor, songwriter, dramatist]
Florence, William J(ames) [or J(ermyn)] *Source(s):* ALMN
Colleran, William D. 1925- [singer, writer on music]
Martin, Mac *Source(s):* EPMU
Collette, W(illiam) M(arcell) 1921- [reeds, composer, arranger, jazz historian]
Andrews, Andy A. *Source(s):* CCE59
Collette, Buddy *Source(s):* ASCP; EPMU; GAMM; KINK; LCAR; NGDJ; PEN2
Colley, Sarah Ophelia 1912-1996 [comedienne, singer, author]
Cannon, Sarah Ophelia *Source(s):* LCAR; STAC; WORT
Minnie Pearle *Source(s):* CM03; LCAR; PSND; STAC
Pearle, Minnie *Source(s):* EPMU; LCAR; PSND; STAC; WORT
Phel *Source(s):* PSND
Queen of Country Comedy, The *Source(s):* PSND; WORT
Collin du Bocage, Louis Jacques Marie 1893-1952 [playwright, librettist]
Verneuil, Louis *Source(s):* GAN1; GAN2
Colling, Elizabeth 19th cent. [hymnist]
Mawr, Eta *Source(s):* LCAR; PSND
Collins, Al(bert) 1932-1993 [guitarist, singer, songwriter]
Collins, Chocolate *Source(s):* CCE60; CPOL RE-296-858
Iceman, (The) *Source(s):* AMUS; CM19
Note(s): See also Jerry Butler.
Inventor of the Cool Sound *Source(s):* http://www.tovvund.net/guitar/Booklists/Albert_Collins.asp (4 Oct. 2002)
Master of the Telecaster, The *Source(s):* AMUS; http://www.tovvund.net/guitar/Booklists/Albert_Collins.asp
Razor Blade, The *Source(s):* AMUS; http://www.tovvund.net/guitar/Booklists/Albert_Collins.asp
Collins, Dorothy Ann 1933-1995 [keyboardist, composer]
Collins, Dolly *Source(s):* PEN2
Collins, Lawrence Albert 1944- [singer, songwriter]
Collins Kids *Source(s):* ENCM; MCCL
Note(s): Jt. pseud.: Lorrie [i.e., Lawrencine May] Collins.
Collins, Lawrencine May 1942- [singer, songwriter]
Collins Kids *Source(s):* ENCM; MCCL
Note(s): Jt. pseud.: Lawrence Albert Collins.
Collins, Lorrie *Source(s):* MCCL
Collins, Louis (Bo) 1932-1995 [singer, guitarist, songwriter]
Bo, Mister *Source(s):* HARS
Mr. Bo *Source(s):* EPMU; LCAR
Collins, Mary Ellen 1941- [composer]
Collins, Mitzie *Source(s):* GOTH

Collins, Miguel [songwriter]
Sizzla *Source(s):* EPMU
Collins, P. F. [writer]
Percy the Poet *Source(s):* http://www.csufresno.edu/folklore/ballads/FaE218.html (15 Oct. 2003)
Collins, William 1951- [singer, songwriter, bass guitarist]
Bootsy *Source(s):* LCAR
Note(s): See also A(nnie) S. Potter.
Bootzilla *Source(s):* CM08
Collins, Bootsy *Source(s):* CM08; NGAM
Number-One Funkateer *Source(s):* CM08 p. v
Collins, William Francis
Emerson, Francis *Source(s):* TPRF
Poe, Penelope *Source(s):* TPRF
See, W. F. *Source(s):* TPRF
Colloredo, Giovanni Battista mentioned 1645 [librettist]
Cratisto, Jamejo *Source(s):* LCAR; LOWN
Jamejo, Cratisto *Source(s):* LCAR; MELL
Colman, George, Jr. 1762-1836 [playwright]
Note(s): See PSND for additional nonmusic-related pseudonyms.
Griffinhoof, Arthur (of Turnham Green) *Source(s):* DAPE; GOTT; LCAR; WORB
Colmer, Graham John 1887-1957 [playwright, lyricist]
John, Graham *Source(s):* CCE62; GAN1; GAN2; PSND
Colombier, Michel 1939- [composer, arranger, conductor]
Godfather of Fusion *Source(s):* http://www.airrecords.com/colombier.htm (15 Oct. 2002)
Colombrito, Philip 1915-2005 [composer, author, singer]
Brito, Phil *Source(s):* ASCC; LCAR
Colon (Roman), William [or Willie] (Anthony) 1950- [bandleader, composer, arranger]
Malo, El *Source(s):* GROL; LCAR (see note)
Colonna, Giovanni Ambrosio fl. 1616-27 [guitarist, printer, composer]
Stampadorino, Lo *Source(s):* GROL; NGDM; WORB
Coltrane, John William 1926-1967 [saxophonist, bandleader, composer]
Blue Train *Source(s):* JAMU
Coltrane, Trane *Source(s):* PSND
Trane *Source(s):* www.allaboutjazz.com/php/article.php?id=1403 (17 Mar. 2004)
Columbo, Ruggiero de Rudolpho 1908-1934 [singer, actor, composer]
Columbo, Russ *Source(s):* CASS; GAMM; PSNN; STUW; SUTT
Romeo of Radio, The *Source(s):* PSND; PSNN
Columbus, Ferdinand 1488-1539 [bibliophile, music collector]
Colón, Fernando *Source(s):* LCAR; NGDM
Colvig, Vance D. 1892-1967 [actor, songwriter]
Colvig, Pinto *Source(s):* PSND
Dean of Hollywood Voice Men, The *Source(s):* PSND
Colvin, Douglas Glenn 1952-2002 [bassist, singer, songwriter]
King, Dee Dee *Source(s):* DRSC; LCAR
Ramone, Dee Dee *Source(s):* DRSC; LCAR
Colvin, Shanna 1956 (or 58)- [singer, guitarist, songwriter]
Colvin, Shawn *Source(s):* KICK; PEN2; RECR
Combs, Sean 1970- [producer, singer, songwriter]
Combs, Puffy *Source(s):* CM25; EPMU
P. Diddy *Source(s):* LCAR
Puff Daddy *Source(s):* CM25; EPMU
Puffy *Source(s):* LCAR
Comini, Railberto 1907- [composer, conductor, author, photographer]
Comini, Tino *Source(s):* ASCC; CCE60
Compère, Louis c.1445-1518 [composer]
Compère, Loyset *Source(s):* BAKE; GRV5; LCAR
Conant, Grace Wilber 1858-1948 [hymnist]
Ponsonby, A. B. *Source(s):* CYBH
Concina, Roberto 1963?- [DJ, producer, songwriter]
Milani, Roberto *Source(s):* AMUS; http://maks.www6.50megs.com/dance/miles.htm (18 Oct. 2002)
Miles, Robert *Source(s):* AMUS; SONG; http://maks.www6.50megs.com/dance/miles.htm
Concordel, Claude Marie [composer]
Dominique, Claude *Source(s):* GOTH
Conder, (Joan) Elizabeth (née Thomas) [hymnist]
Codner, Elizabeth *Source(s):* HATF; ROGG
Note(s): Common mispelling of name.
E. *Source(s):* JULN
Conder, Josiah 1789-1855 [hymn book editor, hymnist]
C. *Source(s):* JULN
Condon, Albert Edwin 1904-1973 [composer,conductor]
Condon, Eddie *Source(s):* ASCP
Conegliano, Em(m)anuele 1749-1838 [librettist, poet]
Da Ponte, Lorenzo *Source(s):* ALMN; BAKO; BAKR; GOTH; NGDO; PIPE
Conetta, Lewis D. 1927- [composer, author, producer]
Carey, Lew(is) *Source(s):* ASCP; GREN
Note(s): Do not confuse with Lewis Carey [i.e., Lucie Johnstone]
Conforti, Luigi 1854 (or 57)-1907 [author, poet]
Solinas, Alma *Source(s):* MELL

Note(s): Jt. pseud.: Scaliger [i.e., Eduardo de Sá Pereira de Castro]
Confrey, Edward Elzear 1895-1971 [composer, bandleader, pianist]
Note(s): Portraits: JASA; JASN
Confrey, Zez Source(s): CASS; GAMM; HARR; KINK; PEN2; SUTT
O'Keefe, Jimmy Source(s): GRAK; SUTT
Palmer, Dick Source(s): JASG; SUTT
Palmer, Vi Source(s): JASG; SUTT
Note(s): Also used by Willie Eckstein.
Conin, Henri 1856-1926 [pianist, conductor, songwriter]
Goublier, Gustave Source(s): CCE32 R2075; GAN1; GAN2
Goublier, Henri Source(s): CCE46 R7487 ("La Demoiselle du printemps")
Connelly, Reg(inald) 1895-1963 [songwriter]
Connelly, Jay Source(s): CCE51 R82789 ("She's Far too Good for Me")
Note(s): Jt. pseud.: James [or Jimmy] Campbell.
Gibson, Don Source(s): CCE51 R80600 ("I'm Just Wild Over Dancing")
Note(s): Jt. pseud.: James [or Jimmy] Campbell.
King, Irving Source(s): FULD p. 498; PMUS; PSNN; STUW
Note(s): Jt. pseud.: James [or Jimmy] Campbell.
Michael, Patrick Source(s): CCE61; CPOL RE-429-414
Michel, Pat Source(s): CPOL RE-34-970
Vincent, Ray Source(s): CPOL RE-49-299
Note(s): Jt. pseud.: James [or Jimmy] Campbell.
Wedgwood, John Source(s): CCE57-58; CPOL RE-407-262
Connor, Ingram Cecil, III 1946-1973 [songwriter, singer]
Note(s): In EPMU given names: Cecil Ingram.
Godfather of Country/Rock Music, The Source(s): SISO
Note(s): See also Chris(topher) Hillman.
Grandfather of Country/RockMusic Source(s): http://www.dizzyrambler.com (4 Oct. 2002)
Parsons, Gram Source(s): ALMN; CASS; CM07; DIMA; GAMM; HARR; MCCL; PEN2
Connor, Joseph Patrick 1895-1952 [composer]
Connor, Father Source(s): CCE63
Connor, Pierre Norman Source(s): ASCP; VACH
Norman, Pierre Source(s): CCE48; CCE50; CCE63; VACH
Openshaw, John Source(s): ASCP
Conray, Will 1865 (or 66)-1941 (or 42) [songwriter]
Champion, Harry Source(s): KILG
Conseil, Jean 1498-1535 [composer]
Consilium, Johannes Source(s): GREN; LCAR; NGDM
Constantinidis, Yannis 1903-1984 [composer]
Yannidis, Costas Source(s): GROL
Conti, Giovanni 1882-1957 [journalist, critic, author]
Ignoto, (Un) Source(s): OCLC 29069875; WORB
Contursi, Jose Maria 1911-1972 [poet, lyricist]
Contursi, Katunga Source(s): TODO
Katunga Source(s): TODO
Converse, Charles C(rozat) 1832-1918 [composer, lawyer]
Note(s): Portraits: CYBH; ETUP 50:9 (Sept. 1932): 608
Nevers, C. O. Source(s): CART; IBIM; WCAB 8:449; WORB
Reden, Karl Source(s): BAKR; CART; CYBR; IBIM; ROGG
Revons, E. C. Source(s): CART; IBIM; WCAB 8:449; WORB
Conzelmann, Hans 1920-1993 [composer]
Eric, Hans Source(s): BUL3; CPOL RE-230-858; KOMP; KOMS; PFSA
Menzing, Walter Source(s): KOMP; KOMS
Cook, David (Albert) 1947- [singer, songwriter]
Essex, David Source(s): EPMU; HARR; PSND
Cook, J. Lawrence ?-1976 [pianist, arranger, author]
Baxter, Ted Source(s): PIAN
Note(s): Also used by Max Kortlander & Lees S. Roberts.
Dean of the Piano Roll Source(s): BBDP
Doyle, Pep Source(s): PIAN
Laney, Sid Source(s): GROL (see under: QRS); PIAN
Mr. Piano Roll Source(s): GROL (see under: QRS)
Osborne & Howe Source(s): PIAN
Note(s): Also used by Max Kortlander.
Redding, Walter Source(s): PIAN
Note(s): Also used by Peter Wendling.
Scott & Watters Source(s): PIAN
Note(s): Also used by Max Kortlander.
Scott, Harold Source(s): PIAN
Note(s): Also used by Max Kortlander.
Watters, Jeff Source(s): PIAN
Note(s): Also used by Max Kortlander.
Cook, Quentin 1963- [guitarist, singer, composer, techno artist]
Cook, Norman Source(s): EPMU; LCAR
Fatboy Slim Source(s): EPMU (see under: Beats International); LCAR; PMUS-00; SONG
Fried Funk Food Source(s): LCAR
Mighty Dub Katz Source(s): LCAR
Pizzaman Source(s): EPMU (see under: Beats International); LCAR
Cook, Roger 1940- [singer, songwriter]
Cookaway, Roger Source(s): CCE72 Efor158841
Note(s): Jt. pseud.: Roger Greenaway.
Jonathan Source(s): EPMU; GAMM; PSND
Note(s): "David and Jonathan," songwriting team with Roger Greenaway.

Two Rogers *Source(s):* SHAP
Note(s): Jt. pseud.: Roger Greenaway.
Cook(e), Sam(uel) 1931 (or 35)-1964 [singer, songwriter]
Cook, Dale *Source(s):* CASS; GROL
Father of Soul *Source(s):* CASS
Note(s): See also Ray Charles Robinson.
Cook, William Mercer 1869-1944 [composer, conductor]
Note(s): Portraits: ETUP 58:7 (July 1940): 498; JASZ; SAMP
Barber, Barney *Source(s):* JASZ
Note(s): Possible pseud.; Cook is listed as original copyright owner.
Cook, Mercer *Source(s):* CCE31
Cook, Will Marion *Source(s):* JASZ; LCAR
Note(s): Sometime after 1888 he adopted his mother's middle name, Marion, as his own.
Marion, Will *Source(s):* CCE41 #34470, 160 R97515; JASZ; LCAR
Mercer *Source(s):* CCE31 Eunp41405; CCE31Eunp41406; CCE31Eunp45656
Note(s): "It Won't Be Long," "Life," & "My Gal's Gone"
Mercer, Will(iam) *Source(s):* GAN1; GAN2; NGDO
Cook, William (John) 1908 (or 09)-1987 [writer]
Tudor, Anthony *Source(s):* GOTH; LCAR
Cooke, Charles L. 1881 (or 91)-1958 [pianist, composer]
Cook, Doc *Source(s):* EPMU; LCAR; NGDJ
Cooke, Henry ?-1672 [soldier, composer]
Cooke, Captain *Source(s):* GRV3
Cooke, James Francis 1875-1960 [composer, organist, writer on music]
Note(s): Portrait: ETUP 50:9 (Sept. 1932): 608
Eastman, A. J. *Source(s):* TPRF
J. F. C. *Source(s):* LCCC1938-41 ("Christmas Song for a New World")
Media, Jay *Source(s):* LCPC; TPRF
Ribert, Jean *Source(s):* TPRF
Sherman, Carol *Source(s):* CCE44 #35637, 178 R129820; TPRF
Stearns, Herbert *Source(s):* TPRF
Tilford, Williams Robert *Source(s):* TPRF
Cooke, Matthew 1761?-1829 [organist, composer]
M. C. *Source(s):* CPMU
Cooke, (Mrs.) Philip Warren
Mohr, Halcher *Source(s):* TPRF
Cooke, Thomas (Simpson) 1703-1756 [journalist, author]
Cooke, Hesiod *Source(s):* PSND
Scriblerus, Tertius *Source(s):* BAKR; NGDO; PSND; SONN
Cooke, William 1821- [author, hymnist, editor]
A. C. C. *Source(s):* JULN
Note(s): A. C. C. = A Chester Canon.
Cooley, Donnell Clyde 1910-1969 [fiddler, songwriter, actor]
Cooley, Spade *Source(s):* BAKR; CCE45; CCE56; EPMU; LCAR; MUHF
King of Western Swing *Source(s):* BAKR; EPMU
Note(s): See also (James) Robert [or Bob] Wills.
Coon, Carleton A. 1894-1932 [drummer, vocalist, composer]
Old Right Hander, The *Source(s):* PSND
Cooper, Adeline Maxwell [songwriter]
A. M. C. *Source(s):* CPMU (publications 1855-60)
Cooper, Dale T. 1918-1977 [singer, fiddler, songwriter]
Cooper, Stoney *Source(s):* LCAR; STAC
Cooper, John c.1570-1626 [composer, violist, lutenist, teacher]
Note(s): Portrait: CYBH
Coperario, John [or Giovanni] *Source(s):* GROL
Coprario, John [or Giovanni] *Source(s):* BAKE; MACM; NGDM
Cowper, John *Source(s):* NGDM
Note(s): Possible original name.
Cooper, Myrtle Eleanor 1913-1999 [singer, songwriter]
Note(s): Portraits: CCME; MILL
Belle of the Barn Dance *Source(s):* STAC
Lulu Belle and Scotty *Source(s):* CCE38 E68367; CCME; EPMU; STAC
Note(s): Jt. pseud. with husband Scotty Wiseman.
Radio Queen *Source(s):* MCCL
Sweethearts of Country Music, The *Source(s):* EPMU; STAC
Note(s): Jt. pseud. with husband Scotty Wiseman.
Wiseman, (Mrs.) Myrtle Eleanor *Source(s):* OB99; STAC
Cooper, Walter Thomas Gaze 1895-1981 [composer]
Cooper, Gaze *Source(s):* http://www.kith.org/jimmosk/barnett.html (15 Aug. 2005)
GC *Source(s):* http://www.kith.org/jimmosk/barnett.html
Slavensky, Ivan *Source(s):* http://www.kith.org/jimmosk/barnett.html
Cooper, Wilma Lee (née Leary) 1921- [singer, guitarist, songwriter]
First Lady of Bluegrass *Source(s):* STAC
Lee, Wilma *Source(s):* CCE76
Coote, Frederick A(lfred) 1897-1985 [composer]
Note(s): Portrait: BBDP
Dorel, Francis *Source(s):* CCE41 #50454, 110 R101944; CCE46 #26447, 239 R125027

Copas, Lloyd (Estel) 1913-1963 [singer, songwriter]
Copas, Cowboy *Source(s):* CCE53; CCE67; EPMU: MCCL; PEN2
Cope, Charles Elvey ?-1943 [organist, composer, writer]
C. E. C. *Source(s):* CART
Cope, Julian 1957- [singer, songwriter]
Gordan, Rabbi Joseph *Source(s):* MUWB
Last Remaining Great English Eccentric of Rock, The *Source(s):* CM16
Cope, LaForrest [songwriter]
Cope, La La *Source(s):* PMUS
Copeland, Berniece Rose
Bennett, Alexander *Source(s):* TPRF
Copeland, Stewart 1952- [drummer, composer]
Kant, Klerk *Source(s):* LCAR
Kent, Klark *Source(s):* CM14; LCAR
Klark Kent *Source(s):* EPMU
Copelon, Allan 1924-1973 [songwriter, author]
Sherman, Allan *Source(s):* CA101; EPMU
Copland, Aaron 1900-1990 [composer]
Dean of American Music *Source(s):* http://www.dl.ket.org/humanities/music/Copland.htm (4 Oct. 2002)
Note(s): See also Walter Johannes Damrosch, Victor Herbert & Paul Whiteman.
Dean of America's Composers, The *Source(s):* PSND
Kid from Brooklyn, The *Source(s):* PSND
Note(s): See also Neil Diamond.
Shrewd Investor of Pennies *Source(s):* SLON
Symbol of America Music *Source(s):* LYMN
Coppersmith, Barbara Carole 1925- [composer, pianist]
Carroll, Barbara *Source(s):* PSND
Coppuck, Amelia (Ball) 1819-1852 [songwriter]
Amelia *Source(s):* Wetzel, Richard D. *The Musical Life and Times of William Cumming Peters.* Warren, Mich.: Harmonie Park Press, 2000, 111.
Welby, Mrs., of Kentucky *Source(s):* LCAR
Corbett, Samuel 1852- [composer]
Leum'as, Tebro'c *Source(s):* CPMU
Corcoran, Gerard 1943- [singer, songwriter]
Ford, Gerry *Source(s):* MCCL
Cordier, Jacques 1580-1653 [violinist, dancing master, composer]
Bocan *Source(s):* MACM
Bochan *Source(s):* IBIM; MACM; WORB
Bocquain *Source(s):* MACM
Bocquam *Source(s):* MACM
Corea, Armando Anthony 1941- [pianist, composer, arranger]
Corea, Chick *Source(s):* BAKR; EPMU; LCAR; NGDJ; PEN2
Corelli, Arcangelo 1653-1713 [composer]
Arcangelo bolognese *Source(s):* GROL; PSND
Archangelo *Source(s):* PSND
Arcimelo *Source(s):* DEAR
Bolognese, Il *Source(s):* GROL
Note(s): See also Marc'Antono Sportonio.
Erimanteo, Arcomelo *Source(s):* GROL
Riccoleno, Gallario *Source(s):* LCAR
Cormon, Eugéne 1811-1903 [librettist]
Piestra, Pierre Étienne *Source(s):* LCAR
Cornelius, Carter ?-1991 [songwriter]
Israel, Prince Gideon *Source(s):* EPMU (see under: Cornelius Brothers and Sister Rose)
Cornet, Michael Josef Anton 1793-1860 [singer, music critic]
Cornet, Julius *Source(s):* PIPE
Cornock, Sidney W(arren) 1885?-1954 [songwriter]
Curtis, Billy *Source(s):* CCE55 Eunp; PSND
Cornu, Francis c.1809- [playwright]
Francis *Source(s):* LCAR; PIPE; PSND
Cornuel, Jean c.1435-1499 [composer]
Saupiquet *Source(s):* NGDM
Sot *Source(s):* NGDM
Thérouanne *Source(s):* NGDM
Tribot *Source(s):* NGDM
Verjus(t) *Source(s):* NGDM
Note(s): Do not confuse with Verius, Flemish Kapelmeiser of Margaret of Parma.
Corréard, Eugène 1834-1906 [poet, musician]
Dalzac, Eugène *Source(s):* IBIM; WORB
Corrette, Michel 1707-1795 [organist, composer, teacher, arranger]
Zipoli *Source(s):* http://www.zipoli.it/history/00.htm (15 Mar. 2005)
Corri, Philip Antony 1784-1832 [composer, singer]
Clifton, Arthur *Source(s):* GOTH; GOTT; GREN; METC; MUWB; NGDO; WORB
Corsetti, Francesco 1700-1774 [writer, poet, theologian, translator]
Agieo, Oresbio *Source(s):* GROL (see under: Brown, John (1715-1766))
Oresbio Agieo *Source(s):* GROL
Corsi, Gian Franco 1923- [writer]
Zeffirelli, Franco *Source(s):* GOTH
Corsi, Giuseppe 1630-1690 [composer]
Celano *Source(s):* BAKR
Cortellini, Camillo c.1560-1630 [composer]
Violino, Il *Source(s):* NGDM
Note(s): See also Carlo Caproli.
Corvo, Niccolò mentioned 1707-1709 [author]
Mercotellis, Agasippo *Source(s):* GROL; NGDO
Note(s): Possible pseud. See also G(iuseppe) Martoscelli.

Cory, Adela Florence 1865-1904 [poet, lyricist]
Note(s): Married name: Mrs. General Nicholson.
Hope, Laurence *Source(s):* FULD; KILG; ROOM; WORB
Cory, W. J. ?-1910 [songwriter]
Adew *Source(s):* KILG
Note(s): Jt. pseud.: Evelyn Woodhouse, T. L. Mitchell-Innes & Algernon Drummond.
Costantakos, Chris Anastasios 1924- [composer, author, violinist]
Duke, Charles *Source(s):* ASCP
Costanzi, Giovanni Battista 1704-1778 [composer, violoncellist]
Giovanni da Roma *Source(s):* GROL; NGDM
Giovannino del Violoncello *Source(s):* GROL; NGDM; SADC
Note(s): See also (Ridolfo) Luigi Boccherini.
Costanzo, Jack J(ames) 1922 (or 24)- [composer]
Bongo, Mr. *Source(s):* ASCP
Mr. Bongo *Source(s):* ASCP
Costello, Billy [songwriter]
Austed, I. Felix *Source(s):* CCE26 E645453
Red Pepper Sam *Source(s):* SUTT
Côte, Hélène 1888- [composer]
Marie-Stéphane, (Soeur) *Source(s):* BUL3
Cottle, Joseph 1770-1853 [poet, bookseller, publisher]
Constantius *Source(s):* CART; JULN
Cottle, Marilyn 1933- [composer, author]
Welch, (Mrs.) Marilyn *Source(s):* ASCC
Welch, Mitzie *Source(s):* ALMN
Cotton, Charles 1630-1687 [poet, burlesque writer, translator]
One Who Never Trangressed Before *Source(s):* CART
Philo-Britanniae *Source(s):* CART
Piscator *Source(s):* CART
Viator *Source(s):* CART
Cotton, James [or Jimmy] 1935- [singer, instrumentalist, songwriter]
Denim, Joe *Source(s):* HARS; LCAR
Cottrau, Théodore 1827-1879 [composer]
Martelli, Entalindo *Source(s):* MACM
Country, Wayne [singer, songwriter]
Country, Jayne *Source(s):* EPMU
Courage, Alexander M. [composer]
Courage, Sandy *Source(s):* CLTP ("Brothers Brannagan")
Courcelle, Francesco c.1702-1778 [composer]
Corselli, Francesco *Source(s):* BAKO; BAKR; LCAR
Courteville, Raphael ?-1772 [organist, composer, political pamphleteer]
Court-evil *Source(s):* GROL
Courteville, Junior *Source(s):* GROL
Freeman, R. *Source(s):* LCAR
Courtois, Bernard c.1826-c.1870 [composer]
Bernardin *Source(s):* MELL
Coutagne, Henri ?-1896 [composer, writer on music]
Claes, Paul *Source(s):* MACM
Coutts, W. G. fl. 1875 [writer on music]
Ithuriel *Source(s):* BROW; GOTT; IBIM; WORB
Couture, Guillaume [or William] 1851-1915 [teacher, composer, critic]
Symphony *Source(s):* CANE
Couyba, Charles (Maurice) 1866-1931 [teacher, poet, lyricist]
Boukay, Maurice *Source(s):* LCAR; WHIT; WORB
Coward, Noel (Pierce) 1899-1973 [playwright, composer, actor]
Note(s): Portrait: SHMM (Apr./May 1983): 8+ & cover
Master, The *Source(s):* CASS
Whittlebot, Hernia *Source(s):* CART; LCAR; PSND
Cowdell, Ellen [composer]
Baird, Alan *Source(s):* TPRF
Livingston, Audrey *Source(s):* HIXN
Note(s): Also used by Edgar Alden Barrell, Jr.
Cowell, Henry 1897-1965 [composer, pianist, writer]
Dixon, Harry *Source(s):* NGAM
Godfather of American Experimental Music *Source(s):* http://www.multiculturalmedia.com/sfnm.html (15 Oct. 2002)
Cowen, Frederic Hymen 1852-1935 [pianist, conductor, composer]
Note(s): Portrait: ETUP 50:9 (Sept. 1932): 608
English Schubert, The *Source(s):* NGDM
Cowper, William 1731-1800 [poet, hymnist]
Alethes *Source(s):* CART
G. G. *Source(s):* CART
Indagator *Source(s):* CART
Ironside, Christopher *Source(s):* CART
Omega *Source(s):* CART
P. P. *Source(s):* CART
T. *Source(s):* CART
T. H. *Source(s):* CART
W. *Source(s):* CART
Well-Wisher to the New Translation, A *Source(s):* CART
Cox, Malik (Deshawn) [rapper, songwriter, actor]
Memphis Bleek *Source(s):* CPOL PA-1-011-880; LCAR; PMUS-00
Coypeau, Charles 1605-1677 [poet, lutenist]
Note(s): Baptismal name
Assoucy, Charles Coypeau d' *Source(s):* LCAR; SADC
Dassoucy, Charles *Source(s):* LCAR; SADC
Singe de Scarron, Le *Source(s):* WORB

Cozanet, Albert 1870-1938 [writer on music]
D'Udine, Jean *Source(s):* PSND
Udine, Jean d' *Source(s):* BAKE
Cozerbreit, Isaac 1893-1978 [composer, violinist, pianist]
Williams, Charles *Source(s):* EPMU; GALM; MUWB; RFSO
Crabb, Cecil Duane 1890-1953 [composer, publisher]
Crabb, Cece *Source(s):* JASA p. 15 & 378
Crabbé, Armand (Charles) 1883-1947 [singer, writer on music]
Morin, Charles *Source(s):* GROL; NGDO
Crabbe, George 1754-1832 [clergy man, poet]
Note(s): See PSND for additional nonmusic-related pseudonyms and sobriquets.
Ebbaac, G. *Source(s):* GOTT
Ebbare, G. *Source(s):* GOTT
Poet of the Poor, The *Source(s):* HATF
Craddock, Vincent Eugene [or Eugene Vincent] 1935-1971 [singer, songwriter, guitarist]
Vincent, Gene *Source(s):* CASS; LCAR; NOMG
Craddock, William [or Billy] Wayne 1939- [singer, songwriter, guitarist]
Craddock, Crash *Source(s):* AMUS; LCAR; MCCL
Mr. Country-Rock *Source(s):* AMUS; MCCL
Craddy, Peter (Haysom) [composer]
Haysom, Peter *Source(s):* CCE60; CPOL RE-332-067; GREN; MUWB
Warr, James *Source(s):* CCE62-63
Craig, Carl 1969- [DJ; techno composer, producer]
69 *Source(s):* AMUS; CM19; EPMU
BFC *Source(s):* CM19; EPMU
Detroit Techno *Source(s):* CM19
Innerzone Orchestra *Source(s):* AMUS; CM19; GROL
Paperclip People *Source(s):* AMUS; CM19; GROL
Psyche *Source(s):* CM19; EPMU; GROL
Sixty-nine *Source(s):* CM19; EPMU
Turntable Wizard *Source(s):* CM19
Craig, Denise 1939- [author, songwriter, singer]
LaSalle, Denise *Source(s):* EPMU
Cramer, Charles [composer]
Remarc, Carl [or Charles] *Source(s):* CPMU (publication date 1874)
Cramer, Floyd 1933-1997 [pianist, organist, songwriter]
Mr. Keyboards *Source(s):* STAC
Cramer, Johann [or John] Baptist 1771-1858 [composer, publisher]
Note(s): Portraits: EWCY; MUST (1 Oct. 1902) Supl. "He supplied so much music for the dilettante that . . . his name [i.e., Cramer] was used in France as a pseudonym for musical trifles." (GROL)
Glorious John *Source(s):* SPIE
Cramolini, Ludwig 1805 (or 08)-1884 (or 86) [librettist]
Wilke *Source(s):* STGR
Crampton, Thomas 1817-1885 [composer, organist, editor]
Bernhardt, J. Karl *Source(s):* YORM
Cranz, Oskar [or Oscar] ?-1929 [music publisher, composer]
Tosca, Antonio *Source(s):* CCE22 E552879; CCE50 R2907
Toska, Anton *Source(s):* BAKE
Craps, Ernest (Jean) 1903-1992 [saxophonist, arranger, composer]
Bee, David *Source(s):* CCMU; CPOL RE-23-623
Sparks, Ernest [or Ernie] *Source(s):* AMUS
Note(s): Identified as origianal name.
Travo, Manuel *Source(s):* GROL
Crawford, Benny [or Bennie] R(oss, Jr.) 1934- [saxophonist, pianist, composer]
Crawford, Hank *Source(s):* CCE64; CLAB; EPMU
Crawford, Jesse 1895-1962 [pianist, composer, organist]
Chapman, Joseph *Source(s):* CCE51 R7326 ("For You, Just You")
Poet of the Organ, The *Source(s):* PSND
Crawford, Robert (MacArthur) 1899-1961 [singer, author, composer, conductor]
Flying Baritone, The *Source(s):* GROL; SMIN
Crawford, Ruth (Porter) 1901-1953 [composer]
Note(s): Portraits: DWCO; Gaume (see below)
Karlan, Fred *Source(s):* CCE27 E661285; Gaume, Matilda. *Ruth Crawford Seeger; Memoirs, Memories, Music*. Metuchen, N. J.: Scarecrow, 1986, 52.
Porter, Ruth *Source(s):* Gaume, p. 235 note 2
Seeger, (Mrs.) Ruth Crawford *Source(s):* Gaume
Crawford, William 1848-1878 [composer, pianist]
Ashton, Frank B. *Source(s):* BROW; WORB
Rookford, Rudolph *Source(s):* BROW; CPMU; WORB
Crawley, C. E. [composer]
Corelli, C. *Source(s):* CPMU (publication date 1905)
Crayton, Connie Curtis 1914-1985 [singer, instrumentalist, songwriter]
Crayton, Pee Wee *Source(s):* HARS; LCAR
Homer the Great *Source(s):* HARS
Creatore, Luigi (Federico) 1920 (or 21)- [composer]
Hughes, L. *Source(s):* CCE58
Hugo & Luigi *Source(s):* CCE62
Note(s): Jt. pseud.: Hugo (Emil) Peretti.
Lawrence, Fred *Source(s):* CCE55
Note(s): Also used by James (Conrad) O'Keefe & Lester O'Keefe.
Limber, Jack *Source(s):* CCE56 Eunp
Luigi *Source(s):* CCE63 E178914

Note(s): "Hello Heartache, Goodbye Love"
Markwell, Mark *Source(s):* PMUS
Note(s): Jt. pseud.: Hugo (Emil) Peretti.
Paul, Victor *Source(s):* CCE58
Cregg, Hugh Anthony, III 1950 (or 51)- [singer, songwriter, harmonica player]
Lewis, Huey *Source(s):* CM09; HARS; LCAR
Creglianovich, G(iovanni) mentioned 1806 [writer]
Tindar(i)o, Dalmiro *Source(s):* GOTH
Creme, Lawrence 1947- [guitarist, singer, songwriter]
Creme, Lol *Source(s):* HARR
Cremer, H(ans) M(artin) 1890-1953 [playwright]
Martins, C. R. *Source(s):* LCPF Efor32242; PIPE
Crémieux, Hector Jonathan 1828-1892 [playwright, librettist]
Arcy, Paul d' *Source(s):* GROL; NGDO
Note(s): Jt. pseud.: Ludovic Halévy.
Lange, Adolphe *Source(s):* STGR
Note(s): Jt. pseud.: Ludovic Halévy.
Crimmins, Roy 1929- [trombonist, writer on music]
King, Roy *Source(s):* GROL
Note(s): Also used by H. Robinson Cleaver.
Cripps, Bruce 1941- [guitarist,songwriter]
Welch, Bruce *Source(s):* HARR
Criscuolo, James Michael 1930- [composer, author, singer]
Savoy, James *Source(s):* ASCP; CCE68
Crisp, Donald [songwriter]
Note(s): May be Donald Crisp (1880-1974), actor/director. Address in copyright files: 1853 Vista, Hollywood, Calif.
Crisp, Helen *Source(s):* CCE41 #9124, 628 R92898; CCE42 #14692, 184 R105114; TPRF
Note(s): Listed on both copyright records as a pseud.; "The Spring Has Come" (CCE41) & "Everything Sings of You" (CCE42).
Crist, (Lucien) Bainbridge 1883-1969 [composer]
Note(s): Portraits: ETUP 50:9 (Sept. 1932): 608; MUSA 33:2 (2 Apr. 1921): 9
Pottersdale, Tom *Source(s):* CCE22 E539527; CCE54; TPRF
Croal, George 1811-1907 [composer, pianist]
Zotti, Carlo *Source(s):* BROW; CPMU; GOTT; KILG; WORB
Croce, Giovanni (della) c.1557-1609 [priest, composer]
Archimusico of San Marco *Source(s):* GRV2
Chiozzotto, Il *Source(s):* BAKR; LCAR; MACM; NGDM
Ioanne(a) Cruce Clodiensis *Source(s):* NGDM
Crockett, Effie I. 1857-1940 [composer, pianist]
Canning, Effie I. *Source(s):* COHN; FULD; GRAT; HIXN; LCAR
Croger, Frederick Julian mentioned 1880 [poet]
Blake, Douglas *Source(s):* CPMU
F. J. C. *Source(s):* CPMU (publication date 1892)
Lorenzi, Leo *Source(s):* CPMU
Milltown, Mable *Source(s):* CPMU ("My Aunt's Mistake")
Note(s): Probable pseud.
Croisilles, H. 1886- [writer on music]
Malherbe, H(enry) *Source(s):* GROL
Croke, Leo T. [composer]
Claff, Lionel *Source(s):* MUWB
Crombruggen, Paul van 1905- [poet]
Christoff, Vincent *Source(s):* CCE51; RILM 69-03999-ap
Croom-Johnson, Austen [or Austin] (Herbert) 1909?-1964 [composer]
Austen, Eric *Source(s):* CCE57; MUWB
Note(s): Jt. pseud.: Eric Siday.
Cobb, Joe *Source(s):* CCE38 E73373l; CCE65-66
Johnson, Ginger *Source(s):* CCE53 Eunp; CCE50; CLOJ
Crosby, Fanny [i.e., Frances] J(ane) 1820-1915 [poet, hymnist]
Note(s): Portraits: CYBH & monographic sources listed below.
Source(s): CYBH; RUFN
Source(s): CYBH; RUFF p. 96
* *Source(s):* CYBH; RUFF p. 96
*** *Source(s):* CYBH
A *Source(s):* JULN
A. A. F. *Source(s):* DIEH ("Not, But Christ Be Honored")
Note(s): Presumed pseud.
Adrienne, Cora *Source(s):* CYBH; RUFN
Alstyne, Fannie Jane *Source(s):* CYBH
America's Blind Poet *Source(s):* Ryden, E. E. *Story of Christian Hymnody*. Rock Island, Ill.: Augustana Press, 1959.
Andrew, (Mrs.) E. A. *Source(s):* CROA; CROH
Andrews, A. E. *Source(s):* CYBH
Apple, James *Source(s):* CROA; CYBH; LOVE
Armstrong, Alice *Source(s):* CYBH; RUFN
Atherton, Rose *Source(s):* CROA; CYBH; HALL
Aunt Fanny *Source(s):* RUFF p. 7
Bell, Carrie *Source(s):* CYBH; RUFN
Bethune, Catherine *Source(s):* CYBH; RUFN
Black, James (L. [or M.]) *Source(s):* CROA; CROH; CYBH; RUFN
Blain, Henrietta *Source(s):* CROH
Blair, Henrietta (E.) *Source(s):* CROA; CYBH; HALL
Blind Girl, The *Source(s):* RUFF p. 47
Blind Poetess, The *Source(s):* RUFF p. 38
Booth, Florence *Source(s):* CROA; CYBH; LOVE
Bourne, (Mrs.) S. K. *Source(s):* JULN (Appendix II)
Bruce, Charles *Source(s):* CROA; CROH CYBH;
Bruce, Robert *Source(s):* CROA; CYBH; LOVE
Note(s): Also used by Robert B. Wright

Burns, Charles *Source(s):* CROA; CROH CYBH;
C *Source(s):* JULN
Carleton, Mary *Source(s):* CROA
Carlston, Mary *Source(s):* CYBH
Carlton, Leah *Source(s):* CROA; HALL; JULN p. 205; LOVE
Children's Friend, The *Source(s):* CYBH; RUFF p. 96
Church, Fannie *Source(s):* CYBH
Craddock, Eleanor *Source(s):* CYBH; RUFN
Cuyler, Lyman (G.) *Source(s):* CROA; CROH; CYBH
D. D. *Source(s):* CYBH
D. D. A. *Source(s):* RUFN
D. D. R. *Source(s):* CYBH
Dale, Ella *Source(s):* CROA; CYBH; HALL; JULN; YOUN
Dayton, Flora *Source(s):* CYBH; RUFN
Douglas, Ellen *Source(s):* JULN
Note(s): Also used by Ira David Sankey
Edmonds, Lizzie *Source(s):* CYBH
Edmunds, Lizzie *Source(s):* RUFN
Edwards, Lizzie *Source(s):* CLAC (see reference); CROA; CYBH; HALL
Eliot, James *Source(s):* CROA; CYBH; LOVE
F. *Source(s):* JULN
F. A. N. *Source(s):* CYBH; JULN; RUFF p. 96
F. C. *Source(s):* CCE41 E95250; DANN; JULN; ROGA
F. J. C. *Source(s):* CCE41 E95250; CYBH; DANN; JULN; ROGA
F. J. V. A. *Source(s):* CYBH; LOVE
F. J. V. J. *Source(s):* JULN
Fannie *Source(s):* CYBH; JULN; RUFF p. 96
Fanny *Source(s):* CYBH; JULN
Forest, (Mrs.) Edna *Source(s):* CYBH; RUFN
Forrest, (Mrs.) Edna *Source(s):* CYBH; RUFN
Frances, Carrie *Source(s):* CYBH
Frances, Grace (J.) *Source(s):* CROA; CYBH; HALL; JULN p. 385; RUFN
Frances, Lillian G. *Source(s):* CYBH; RUFN
Frances, S. Trevor *Source(s).* CYBH
Frances, V(ictoria) *Source(s):* CYBH; CROA; DANN
Francis, Grace J. [or I.] *Source(s):* CROH; DANN; ROGA
Francis, Victoria *Source(s):* DANN; ROGA
G. W. W. *Source(s):* CYBH
Garnet(t), Jennie *Source(s):* CROA; CROH; CYBH
Glenn, (Mrs.) Jen(n)ie *Source(s):* CROA; CYBH; JULN
Gould, Frank *Source(s):* CROA; CROH; CYBH; RUFN
Grace, J. Frances *Source(s):* JULN p. 446
Grinley, (Mrs.) Kate *Source(s):* CROA; CYBH; JULN; YOUN
Harmon, Ruth *Source(s):* CROA; CYBH; LOVE
Hawthorne, Carrie *Source(s):* CYBH
Hope, Frances *Source(s):* CROA; CYBH; LOVE
Hops, Frances *Source(s):* CYBH
Hymn Queen *Source(s):* CYBH; http://www.nyise.org/fanny/bios.html (4 Oct. 2002)
J. C. F. *Source(s):* DANN; JULN
J. F. O. *Source(s):* CYBH
J. V. C. *Source(s):* DIEH ("All Ye Saints of Light")
Note(s): Presumed pseud.
J. W. W. *Source(s):* CYBH; RUFF p. 96; RUFN
James, Annie *Source(s):* CYBH
James, Mary *Source(s):* CYBH
James, Sarah *Source(s):* CYBH
Jenny [or Jenna] V. *Source(s):* CYBH; JULN
Judson, Myra *Source(s):* CROA; CROH; CYBH
L. L. A. *Source(s):* CYBH; RUFF p. 96
Lankton, Martha (J.) *Source(s):* CROA; CYBH; LOVE
Lincoln, H. N. *Source(s):* CYBH; RUFF p. 96; RUFN
Lindsay, W. Robert *Source(s):* CROA; CYBH; LOVE
Lowry, Minnie B. *Source(s):* CYBH; RUFN
Marion, Maud(e) *Source(s):* CROA; CYBH; HALL; RUFF p. 96
Martin, S *Source(s):* CROA; DANN; DIEH
Martin, Sallie [or Sally] *Source(s):* CROA; CYBH; DANN; DIEH
Martin, Sam *Source(s):* CROA; CYBH; LOVE
Matthews, Rose *Source(s):* JULN (see reference)
Miller, Laura *Source(s):* CROA CYBH;
Modern Saint Cecelia *Source(s):* RUFF p. 7
Monteith, A(lice) *Source(s):* CROA; CYBH; DANN; ROGA
Park, Edna L. *Source(s):* CYBH
Plume, (Mrs.) N. D. *Source(s):* JULN (see reference)
Prentice, (Mrs.) L. C. *Source(s):* CYBH; RUFN
Smiling, (Mrs.) Kate *Source(s):* CYBH; RUFN
Smith, Sallie A.[or E.] *Source(s):* CYBH
Smith, Sally (M.) *Source(s):* CLAC; CROA; CROH
Smith, Sam *Source(s):* CROA; CYBH; LOVE
Song Bird in the Dark, The *Source(s):* http://www.nyise.org/fanny/songbird.html (4 Oct. 2002)
Sterling, J. L. *Source(s):* CYBH; DANN
Sterling, Julia *Source(s):* CROA; CYBH; DANN
Sterling, Ryan *Source(s):* CYBH
Sterling, Victoria *Source(s):* CYBH
Stewart, Victoria *Source(s):* CROA; CROH; CYBH;
Stirling, Julia *Source(s):* CROH
Stirling, Victoria *Source(s):* CROH
Stuart, Victoria *Source(s):* DANN
Taylor, Ida Scott *Source(s):* CYBH
Thresher, (Mrs.) J. B. *Source(s):* JULN (see reference)

Tilden, Louise W. *Source(s):* CYBH; RUFF p. 96
Tilden, Mary *Source(s):* CYBH
V., (Miss) [or (Mrs.)] *Source(s):* JULN
V. A. *Source(s):* JULN
V., Jenny *Source(s):* CYBH
Van A., (Mrs.) *Source(s):* CYBH; RUFF p. 96
Van Alstyne, (Mrs.) Alexander *Source(s):* CYBH; LOVE
Van Alstyne, (Mrs.) Fanny *Source(s):* NGAM
Viola (V. A.), (Miss) *Source(s):* CYBH; JULN; YOUN
Wallace, Zemira *Source(s):* CROA; CYBH
Wilson, (Mrs.) C(arrie) M. *Source(s):* CROA; CYBH; HALL; RUFN

Crosby, Harry Lillis 1904-1977 [singer, songwriter, actor]
Ageless Troubador, The *Source(s):* PSND
Brill, Bill *Source(s):* CCE53 ("Tenderfoot")
Note(s): Possible pseud.? (Published: Longridge Music (Los Angeles).
Crosby, Bing *Source(s):* ASCB; KINK; PSND; STUW
Crosbyana *Source(s):* source not recorded
Note(s): Term for Crosby memorabilia.
Der Bingle *Source(s):* CASS; PSND
Groaner, The *Source(s):* PSND
Hope's Diamond *Source(s):* PSND
King Bing *Source(s):* PSND
King of All Media *Source(s):* http://www.kcmetro.cc.mo.us/pennvalley/biology/lewis/crosby/bcvidbio.htm (4 Oct. 2002)
King of Christmas *Source(s):* Brennan, John Vincent. *Bing Crosby; King of Christmas.* 2000.
Lucky Bing *Source(s):* PSND
Mousetrap Builder, The *Source(s):* PSND
Mr. Take It Easy *Source(s):* PSND
Old Dad *Source(s):* PSND
Old Groaner *Source(s):* CASS; PSND
Sportsman, The *Source(s):* PSND
Sweet Singer for All Seasons *Source(s):* http://www.kcmetro.cc.mo.us/pennvalley/biology/lewis/crosby/timeobit.htm (4 Oct. 2002)

Crosby, Ronald Clyde 1942- [singer, songwriter, guitarist]
Crosby, Paul *Source(s):* MUHF; PEN1; PMUS; ROOM
Note(s): Also known as; listed as original name in PEN1; PMUS; ROOM.
Ferris, Jerry *Source(s):* LCAR; MCCL
Jacky Jack (Double Trouble) *Source(s):* AMUS; LCAR
Snowdrift, J. J. *Source(s):* LCAR
Walker, Jerry Jeff *Source(s):* AMUS; CM13; DIMA; LCAR; MCCL; NGAM; PSND
Walker, Scamp *Source(s):* LCAR

Cross, Frank L(eroy) 1904-2001 [lyricist, author]
Teasdale, Dana *Source(s):* CCE64 E189900
Tillman, James *Source(s):* CCE65; CCE67 E226948
Velmont, James *Source(s):* ASCP

Cross, Marilyn Margaret 1953- [singer, songwriter]
Cline, Tammy *Source(s):* MCCL; PEN2
Tiny Pocket Dynamo, A *Source(s):* MCCL

Crosse, (William) Mentor 1866- [composer, teacher]
Note(s): Portrait: ETUP 50:10 (Oct. 1932): 686
Kreutzer, Karl *Source(s):* TPRF
LaCroix *Source(s):* TPRF

Crossley, William Tetley 1867- [composer, organist]
Idle Ben *Source(s):* CART

Crothers, Benjamin Sherman (Louis) 1910-1986 [composer, author, singer]
Crothers, Scatman *Source(s):* ASCP; CPOL RE-211-422; LCAR
Scatman *Source(s):* LCAR

Crouch, Frederick (William) Nicholls 1808-1896 [violoncellist, singer, composer]
Nicholas, François *Source(s):* CPMU

Crow(e), Francis Luther 1905-1980 [singer, songwriter]
Note(s): See MARE & SUTT for joint pseuds. on recordings with Carson J(ay) Robison & Vernon Dalhart [i.e., M (arion) T(ry) Slaughter]. For additional pseuds., see SUTT 2nd ed. (2005)
Adams, Joe *Source(s):* MARE; SUTT
Bell, Eddie *Source(s):* SUTT
Billings, Bud *Source(s):* LCAR; MARE; SUTT
Birmingham Bud (& His Uke) *Source(s):* MARE; SUTT
Blanchard, Dan *Source(s):* MARE; SUTT
Calhoun, Jeff *Source(s):* MARE; SUTT
Note(s): Also used by Vernon Dalhart [i.e., M(arion) T(ry) Slaughter] & Arthur Fields [i.e., Abe Finkelstein]. See SUTT for recording label information.
Carson, Cal *Source(s):* SUTT
Note(s): Also used by Carson J(ay) Robison; see SUTT for additional information.
Cook, Tom *Source(s):* MARE; SUTT
Crow, Frank *Source(s):* LCAR
Crow, Phil *Source(s):* http://www.geocities.com/acuvar/frankluther.html (15 Oct. 2003)
Daniels, Walter *Source(s):* MARE; SUTT
Dixon, Martin *Source(s):* SUTT
Note(s): Also use by Vernon Dalhart [i.e., M(arion) T(ry) Slaughter]
Evans, Francis *Source(s):* MARE
Jackson, Happy *Source(s):* SUTT
Luther, Francis *Source(s):* MARE; PEN2 (see under Robison, Carson J.); SUTT
Note(s): In PEN2 see under: Robison, Carson J.
Luther, Frank *Source(s):* EPMU; HARD; MCCL

Porter, Dave *Source(s):* http://www.geocities.com/acuvar/frankluther.html (15 Oct. 2003)
Thompson, Bud *Source(s):* MARE; SUTT
Weary Willie *Source(s):* MACE
Note(s): Possible pseud. Also used by Jack [i.e., Jacob] Kaufman & Carson J(ay) Robison
Wiggins, Pete *Source(s):* MARE; SUTT
Crowders, (Ernest) Reuben 1865-1909 [singer, songwriter, entertainer]
Note(s): Portraits: JASZ; SAMP; WOLL
Crowdus, Reuben *Source(s):* LCAR
Fields, William *Source(s):* Hare, Maud (Cuny). *Negro Musicians and Their Music.* Washington D. C.: Associated, 1936. (Reprint: Da Capo, 1974)
Note(s): Listed as original name of Ernest Hogan.
Greatest of All Colored Showmen, The *Source(s):* JASZ
Hogan, Ernest *Source(s):* FINS p. 229; LCAR; NGAM; SHAB p. 30
Unbleached American, The *Source(s):* JASZ; WOLL p. 2
Crowest, Frederick J(ames) 1850-1927 [writer on music, organist, choir master]
Note(s): Portrait: ETUP 50:10 (Oct. 1932): 686
Vitton, Arthur *Source(s):* BROW; HUEV; MACM
Crowne, John ?-1703 [dramatist, songwriter]
J. C. *Source(s):* CART
Crudup, Arthur 1905-1974 [singer, guitarist, songwriter]
Big Boy *Source(s):* LCAR
Note(s): Also used by Gustavo Roy Diaz & Richard Henry.
Crudup, Big Boy *Source(s):* AMUS; EPMU; HARR; HARS; LCAR; PSND; RECR; STAM
Crudup, Percy (Lee) *Source(s):* HARS; LCAR; PSND; RECR
Crudux, Art *Source(s):* HARS; LCAR; PSND
Crump, Arthur *Source(s):* HARS; LCAR; PSND
Father of Rock 'n' Roll *Source(s):* PSND; SHAD; STAM
Note(s): See also Charles Edward Anderson Berry, William [or Bill] (John Clifton Haley, (Jr.), Charles Hardin Holley, Johnnie Johnson & Elvis A(a)ron Presley.
James, Elmer *Source(s):* EPMU; HARS; LCAR; PSND
Jones, Elmore *Source(s):* RECR
Cruikshank, George L(ouis) Zalva 1895-1951 [composer, arranger]
Zalva, George L. *Source(s):* CCE51-52; CPMU
Crump, Jess(i)e 1906- [singer, pianist, organist, songwriter]
Crump, Tiny *Source(s):* HARS; LCAR
Crupe, Jessie Wanda 1919- [singer, songwriter]
Country Music's Royal Couple *Source(s):* MCCL
Note(s): Jt. sobriquet with husband: Doc Williams [i.e., Andrew John Smik, Jr.]
Williams, Chickie *Source(s):* MCCL
Csermák, Antol [or Anthony] György [or George] 1771-1822 [composer, violinist]
Dluik und Royhans, Elder d' *Source(s):* LCAR
Luid, Edler von *Source(s):* MACM
Noble of d'Dluik and Rouhans *Source(s):* GRV5
Rohan, Edler von *Source(s):* MACM
Csmarich, Rudolf 1884-1943 [composer]
Thom, Andreas *Source(s):* LCAR; STAD
Cube, Felix Eberhard von 1903-1988 [composer]
Quast, Peter *Source(s):* KOMP; PFSA
Cubières(-Dorat de Palmézeaux), Michel de 1752-1820 [writer]
Castel-Vadron, P. Ignace de *Source(s):* GOTH
Maribarou, M. de *Source(s):* GOTH
Palmézeaux *Source(s):* PSND
Cuchetti, Richard Frank 1937- [composer, author, producer]
Conti, Dick *Source(s):* ASCP; CPOL PA-240-819
Cuffia, Carlo [composer]
Thurner, Philippe *Source(s):* STGR v. 4/pt. 1, p. 161
Cuffley, Edwin John [composer]
Ouestman, Théodore *Source(s):* CPMU (publication dates: 1857-60)
Cugat de Bru y Deulofeo, Francisco de Asis Javier 1900-1990 [bandleader, composer]
Cugat, Xavier *Source(s):* GAMM
Cugie *Source(s):* PSND
Guy Lombardo of Latin Music, The *Source(s):* PSND
Rhumba King, The *Source(s):* PSND
Culbertson, Roy Frederich 1946- [composer, author, singer]
Brano, Roscoe *Source(s):* ASCP
Eff, Roy *Source(s):* ASCP
Culp, Napoleon Brown Goodson 1929- [singer, songwriter]
Brown, Napoleon *Source(s):* LCAR
Brown, Nappy *Source(s):* LCAR
Cummings, Robert 1966- [songwriter, performer]
Straker, Rob *Source(s):* AMIR
Zombie, Rob *Source(s):* AMIR; AMUS; LCAR; PMUS-00
Cunio, Angelo 1833-1891 [pianist, composer, teacher]
Everard, S. *Source(s):* IBIM; WORB
Kuhn, Gustav *Source(s):* IBIM; WORB
Silvani, Leo *Source(s):* IBIM; WORB
Cunningham, Allan 1784-1842 [writer, poet, songwriter]
C *Source(s):* CART
Hid-Allan *Source(s):* CART
MacRobin, Mark *Source(s):* CART

Cunningham, John William 1780-1861 [poet, hymnist]
Vicar of Harrow, The *Source(s):* HATF
Victor of Wrexhill, The *Source(s):* HATF
Curet (Alonso), Catalino 1926-2003 [composer, songwriter]
Curet (Alonso), Tite *Source(s):* LCAR; WASH
Curnutt, John Paul 1939- [composer, author, singer]
Paul, John *Source(s):* ASCP (see reference); CCE68
Currie, Bill [songwriter]
Curroy, Mort *Source(s):* CCE34 Efor34120
Note(s): Jt. pseud.: Michael Carr [i.e., Maurice Alfred Cohen], Ivor Moreton & Harry Roy [i.e., Lipman]
Currie, Nicholas 1960- [singer, songwriter]
Momus *Source(s):* AMUS; LCAR; ROOM
Note(s): Also used by Ludwig Anzengruber.
Curtis, Eddie 1927-1983 [composer, arranger, singer]
Curtis, King *Source(s):* CPOL RE-59-288; LCAR
Note(s): Also used by (King) Curtis Ousley.
Curtis, Memphis (E.) *Source(s):* CPOL RE-59-288; CPOL RE-319-451; LCAR
Curtis, Tex *Source(s):* ASCP; CPOL RE-180-652; LCAR
Jackson, Sonny *Source(s):* JAMU
Curwen, John Spencer 1847-1916 [musician, publisher]
J. S. C. *Source(s):* CPMU
Cusack, Margaret Anna 1829-1899 [composer]
Cusack, Mary Francis *Source(s):* LCAR
Mary F(rancis) Clare, (Sister) *Source(s):* COHN; HIXN
Cushman, Abbie ?-1940 [music critic]
Boswell, (Mrs.) *Source(s):* GRAN
Finck, Abbie *Source(s):* GRAN
Note(s): Married name: Mrs. Henry T. Finck.
Czernik, Willy (Hermann) 1901 (or 04)- [composer, conductor]
Werly, C. *Source(s):* CCE56; RIES; SUPN

– D –

Dabney, Ford (T.) 1883-1958 [composer, conductor]
Eporu & Yenbad *Source(s):* PERF
Note(s): Jt. pseud.: James Reese Europe.
Yenbad, Eporue *Source(s):* SHAB
Note(s): Jt. pseud.: James Reese Europe.
Dach, Simon 1605-1659 [author, poet]
Chasmindo *Source(s):* PSND
Memel, Chasmindo von *Source(s):* PIPE
Philison *Source(s):* PIPE
Sichamond *Source(s):* PIPE; PSND
Weitemher, Chasmindo von *Source(s):* PIPE
Dacres, Desmond 1941 (or 42)- [singer, songwriter]
Dekker, Desmond *Source(s):* EPMU; LCAR; PSND; RECR
D'Adda, Cassano 1807-1875 [contralto, composer]
Brambilla, Marietta *Source(s):* CLAG; LCAR
Daffan, Theron Eugene 1912-1996 [guitarist, songwriter]
Brown, Frankie *Source(s):* CCE70 R485784; CCME; MCCL; NGAM
Daffan, Ted *Source(s):* CCME; ENCM; EPMU; MCCL; NASF; NGAM; SUTT
Dahlander, Nils-Bertil 1928- [composer, teacher]
Dale, Bert *Source(s):* ASCP
Dahms, Walter 1887-1973 [writer on music, critic]
Armando, Walter Gualtério *Source(s):* BAKE; LCAR; PIPE
Dahn, (Ludwig Julius) Felix 1834-1912 [author, historian]
Sophus, Ludwig *Source(s):* PIPE
Daignault, Pierre 1925- [actor, folksinger, writer on music]
Saurel, Pierre *Source(s):* CANE
Daigneux, Josef André 1915-1966 [composer]
Jad, Willy *Source(s):* SUPN
D'Ailly-Vaucheret, Achille [librettist]
Henry, Marc *Source(s):* LOWN
Dairo, I(saiah) K(ehinde) 1930- [bandleader, composer, accordionist]
Father of Juju Music *Source(s):* EPMU
Dalayrac, Nicolas(-Marie) 1753-1809 [composer]
Note(s): Portrait: ETUP 50:10 (Oct. 1932): 686
Alayrac, Citoyen d' *Source(s):* LCAR
Alayrac, Nicolas d' *Source(s):* LCAR; WORB
D-DO *Source(s):* WIEC
Dal***, M. *Source(s):* CPMU; LCAR
Tallirak *Source(s):* WIEC
Dalbotten, Charles Eric 1922- [composer]
Dalbotten, Ted *Source(s):* GOTH
Dale, Charles [songwriter]
Avon Comedy Four *Source(s):* CCE45 #6317, 2033 R142579
Note(s): Jt. pseud.: Harry Goodwin, Irving [i.e., Isidore] Kaufman & Joe Smith.
Daley, Earl 1958- [singer, songwriter]
Earl Sixteen *Source(s):* EPMU
Dalla Casa, Girolamo ?-1601 [composer]
Note(s): Dates also listed: 1567-1584
Girolamo da Undine *Source(s):* MACM; NGDM; WORB
Dall'Angelo, Giacomo mentioned 17th cent. [librettist]
Assicurato, L' *Source(s):* SONN
Dall'Aquila, Marco c.1480-1538 [lutenist, composer]
Adler, Marx von *Source(s):* LCAR; NGDM

Dallas, Fred Doble 1938- [singer, songwriter]
Dallas, Rex *Source(s):* DAUM
Dallas, J. J. 1853-1915 [writer]
Llad, S. A. *Source(s):* GANA
Dallin, Sarah [songwriter]
Bananarama *Source(s):* CPOL PA-343-491; SONG
Note(s): Jt. pseud.: Siobhan Fahey & Keren Woodward.
Dallion, Susan (Janet) 1957- [singer, songwriter, guitarist]
Sioux, Siouxsie *Source(s):* NOMG
Sioux, Susan Janet Dallion *Source(s):* NOMG
Siouxsie Sioux *Source(s):* CLAG; NOMG
Dalmaine, Cyril 1904-1986 [composer]
Barrington, Jonah *Source(s):* ORBI
Dalmau, Jaime Texidor 1884-1957 [composer]
Texidor, Jaime *Source(s):* REHG
Note(s): Originally thought to be pseud. of Reginald (Clifford) Ridewood.
Dal Pozzo, Vincenzo fl. c.1585-1612 [composer]
Puteus, Vincentius *Source(s):* NGDM
Dalton, Kathleen I. P. 1900-1943 [composer]
Pickhardt, Ione *Source(s):* HIXN; TPRF
Daly, Joseph Michael 1883-1968 [composer]
O'Connor, Laurence B. *Source(s):* JASA p. 322
Daly, Lawrence [composer, lyricist]
Lawrence, Paul *Source(s):* OCLC 37474468
Note(s): Jt. pseud.: Paul Daly.
Daly, Paul [composer, lyricist]
Lawrence, Paul *Source(s):* OCLC 37474468
Note(s): Jt. pseud.: Lawrence Daly.
Daman, Guilleaume c.1540-1591 [organist, composer]
Damon, William *Source(s):* LCAR; RIEM; WORB
Damanski, Josef 1858- [composer]
Diamand, Josef *Source(s):* SUPN
Damico, Frank James 1909-?1991 [composer, arranger]
Denning, Frank *Source(s):* ASCP; CCE41 #32549 E95856; CCE65-68; CCE74-76
Talley, Frank *Source(s):* ASCP
Dammas, Hellmuth Carl 1816-1885 [writer, composer, singer]
Hellmuth, Karl *Source(s):* IBIM; WORB
Steffens, Feodor *Source(s):* IBIM; MACM; WORB
Dammert, Hansjorg [composer]
Jordan, Robert *Source(s):* Antheil, George. *Bad Boy of Music*. Hollywood: Samuel French, 1990, 181.
Damp, Artur 1858- [composer]
Sander, Rolf *Source(s):* REHH; SUPN
Damrosch, Walter Johannes 1862-1950 [composer, conductor, educator]
Note(s): Portraits: ETUP 56:2 (Feb. 1938): cover; *American Music Lover* 5:6 (Oct. 1939): cover
Damrosch, Papa *Source(s):* GRAN
Dean of American Music, The *Source(s):* PSND
Note(s): See also Aaron Copland, Victor Herbert & Paul Whiteman.
Old English Composer of the XXth Century, An *Source(s):* CCE39 #4739 AA293086
W. M. G. D. *Source(s):* MUST 138:1853 (1997): 15
Note(s): W. M. G. D. = Wally Mollycoddle God Damrosch.
Dana-Danilowski, Wladyslaw 1902-2000 [composer, arranger, conductor]
Dan, W(l.) *Source(s):* CCE40 #39135 Eunp23958; CCE62; CCE70 R483560
Dana Walt(er) *Source(s):* BUL2; CCE34 Efor36115; CCE66
Danilowski, Wladyslaw *Source(s):* LCAR
Dance, James 1722-1774 [actor, playwright]
Love, James *Source(s):* LCAR; PIPE; PSND
Scriblerus Maximus *Source(s):* PSND
Dancourt, Florent Carton 1661-1725 [actor, playwright]
Teniers of Comedy, The *Source(s):* PSND
Dancy, Charles (E.) [composer]
Note(s): Dates may be: 1915-1995. Portrait: ETUP 50:10 (Oct. 1932): 686
Irving, L. *Source(s):* CCE42 #5201, 671 R102522; CPMU; TPRF
Danczak, Jul(ius) 1919- [composer]
Oden, Pat *Source(s):* KOMS
Daneau, Nicolas (Adolphe Gustave) 1866-1944 [composer]
Dani, N. *Source(s):* REHH; SUPN
Daneau, Suzanne 1901-1971 [pianist, composer]
Lalain, Luc *Source(s):* COHN; HIXN
Danek, Wojciech (Adalbert) c.1760- [violist, composer]
Dankowski, Wojciech (Adalbert) *Source(s):* GRV5; LCAR
Danforth, Percy (O.) 1900-1992 [musician, writer on music]
Mr. Bones *Source(s):* http://www.andy fronthall.com/drums.html (15 Aug. 2005)
D'Angelo, Gaetano 1957- [actor, composer, musician]
D'Angelo, Nino *Source(s):* MOMU
Danican, François-André 1727-1795 [author, composer]
Philidor, François-André *Source(s):* BAKR
Danican, Jean c.1620-1679 [composer]
Philidor, Jean *Source(s):* BAKR
Daniel, Francisco (Alberto Clemente) Salvador 1831-1871 [musicologist, composer, music critic]
Daniel, Salvador *Source(s):* BAKR; LCAR
Salvador-Daniel, (Francisco) *Source(s):* BAKR; LCAR; RIES
Sidi-Mahabul *Source(s):* GROL; NGDM

Daniel, George 1789-1864 [poet]
Pindar, Peter *Source(s):* LCAR; OCLC 34074676
Note(s): See also C. F. Lawler & John Wolcot.
Daniel, Jean c.1480-c.1550 [composer, organist, poet]
Mithou *Source(s):* NGDM
Note(s): See also Thomas Champion.
Daniel, Stefan 1955- [composer]
Daniels, Stevie *Source(s):* KOMP; PFSA
Daniell, Charles Addison [composer]
Addison, D. C. *Source(s):* HOVL
Danielou, Alain 1907-1994 [musicologist, author]
Sharan, Shiva *Source(s):* LCAR; WORB
Shiva Sharan *Source(s):* LCAR; PSNN; WORB
Daniels, Charles N(eil) 1878-1943 [composer, songwriter]
Note(s): Original family surname: O'Daniels? Portraits: JASA; JASN
Bertrand, Paul *Source(s):* BOST; CCE31 R14754
Note(s): Used on: "White Slave" (1903), "An Autumn Wooing" (1905) and "Say You Forgive Me (1905).
Burke, Joe *Source(s):* BOST
Note(s): ASCAP incorrectly identified as pseud. of Daniels. Nan G. Bostick explained, "A sheet music dealer friend knows the Joe Burke family and was able to confirm that the two works Villa Moret published by Joe Burke were, in fact, Joseph A. Burke pieces. The family was upset to learn ASCAP claimed Burke as Daniels so let's not perpetuate any errors (or hard feelings)." (Letter to Jeanette Drone, 29 Aug. 2003)
Carter, Sidney *Source(s):* BOST; CCE58 R226796; JASN
Note(s): Used on lyrics, 1903-25.
Hill, Charlie *Source(s):* BOST; CCE30 E18883; JASN
Note(s): On "western" titles published after 1930.
Jones, La Monte C. *Source(s):* BOST; JASN
Note(s): Used while at Remick (1903-12).
L'Albert *Source(s):* BOST; CCE34 R29510; JASN; RAGM
Note(s): Used 1903-16, mostly on marches.
Lamar, Cyrille *Source(s):* BOST
Note(s): "My Pearl of Honolulu" ASCAP listed Cyrille Lamar as a pseud. of Daniels; however, Nan G. Bostick suspects Lamar "was an actual, though mysterious, person." (Letter to the author, 29 Aug. 2003)
Lemare, Jules *Source(s):* BOST; CCE58 R226796; CCE60; JASN
Moret, Neil *Source(s):* BOST; JASA; JASN; KINK; LCAR
Rockman, Sidney *Source(s):* LCPF letter cited (18 Sept. 1929)
Strauss, Julian *Source(s):* BOST
Note(s): Only work composed under this name: "It's a Joy to Say Good Evening" (1910); on other works Strauss is listed as arranger.
Dankin, Gerald 1954- [keyboardist, songwriter]
Dammers, Jerry *Source(s):* HARR
Dankworth, John(ny) 1927- [clarinetist, saxophonist, arranger, composer, bandleader]
Nameless, Virgil *Source(s):* JAMU
Note(s): Also used by Tommy Whittle.
D'Annunzio, Gabriele 1863-1938 [author]
Debrando da Parma, Il *Source(s):* GROL
Note(s): See also Ildebrando Pizzetti.
Danoff, Mary Catherine 1944- [composer, singer]
Nivert, Taffy *Source(s):* ASCP; CPOL RE-653-070
Danowski, Conrad John 1950- [composer, author, singer]
Taylor, Conrad *Source(s):* ASCP; CPOL PA-22-065
Dant, Charles G(ustave) 1907-1999 [composer, conductor, author]
Call, Gus *Source(s):* CCE55; CCE60; CPOL RE-409-937
Dant, B(ud) *Source(s):* ASCP; BBDP; CCE57; CCE60; CPOL RE-211-983; LCAR
Kiefer, J. *Source(s):* ASCP
McIntyre, Maile *Source(s):* CCE61
Dant, June Anne 1918- [composer, author]
Stebbins, J. A. *Source(s):* ASCP; CCE68
Dantas (Filho), José de Sousa 1921-1962 [poet, composer]
Dantas, Zé *Source(s):* LCAR
Zé Dantas *Source(s):* LCAR; RILM 89-07380-bm
D'Antuono, Vincent Joseph 1940- [composer]
Anthony, Vince *Source(s):* ASCP; CCE72; CPOL PAu-83-210
Dapeer, Harry (Ellis) 1911-2001 [composer, author, publisher]
Dupree, Harry *Source(s):* ASCP; CCE64; CCE70 R490850; CPOL RE-119-612
Darby, Theodore [or Teddy] (Roosevelt) 1902 (or 06)- [singer, guitarist, pianist, songwriter]
Darby, Blind Blues *Source(s):* HARS; LCAR
Darby, Blind Teddy *Source(s):* LCAR
Turner, Blind Squire *Source(s):* HARS; LCAR
Darch, Robert R(ussell) 1920-2002 [pianist, composer]
Note(s): Portrait: JASA
Darch, Ragtime Bob *Source(s):* CCE62; JASA p. 313
Johnny Appleseed of Ragtime *Source(s):* http://www.ratimers.org/reviews/Darch%songs.html (1 Aug. 2005)
Darewski, Hermann E(dward) 1883-1947 [composer, bandleader]
Barrie, Neville *Source(s):* CCE34 Efor34363; CCE61
D'Hermann, E. *Source(s):* CPMU

Spence, J. C. *Source(s):* CCE32 Efor34886; CCE61 R279651
Darewski, Josef Adolf c.1888-1964 [producer]
Rolls, Ernest C. *Source(s):* GAN2 (see under: Darewski, Hermann (Edward))
Darley, George 1795-1846 [poet, playwright, author]
Note(s): See PSND for additional nonmusic-related pseudonyms.
Belvoir, Richard *Source(s):* GOTT
Crayton, Geoffrey, Jr. *Source(s):* PSND
G. D. *Source(s):* PSND
Lacy, John *Source(s):* GOTT; PSND
Penseval, Guy *Source(s):* GOTT; PSND
Darling, John Augustus 1835-1912 [artillery major, composer]
Mignon, August *Source(s):* IBIM; WORB
Darmanin, Joseph 1927- [composer, arranger, pianist]
London, Joe *Source(s):* ASCP; LCAR
Dash, Irwin 1892-1984 [songwriter, publisher]
Barricini, D. *Source(s):* CCE48; CCE75
Heatherton, Fred *Source(s):* CCE45 #13436 Efor70306 ("Dreams of Yesterday"); CPOL RE-7-846
Note(s): Pseud. of Ilda Lewis [i.e., Irwin Dash]. Jt. pseud.: Desmond Cox [i.e., Adrian Keuleman], Harold Elton Box.
Ilda, Lewis *Source(s):* CCE46 E1328 ("Just a Little Fond Affection"); CPOL RE-29-593; KILG
Lewis, Ilda *Source(s):* KILG p. 524 (see under: Spade, Jack)
Spade, Jack *Source(s):* CCE44 Efor70219; KILG
Note(s): Jt. pseud.: Desmond Cox [i.e., Adrian Keuleman] & Harold Elton Box.
Daspuro, Nicolo 1853-1941 [journalist, librettist]
Suardo, P. *Source(s):* CCE52; LOWN; MELL; PIPE; WORB
Daudet, (Louis Marie) Alphonse 1840-1897 [author]
Baptistet *Source(s):* PSND
French Dickens, The *Source(s):* PSND
Froisart, Jean *Source(s):* PIPE; PSND
Gaston, Marie *Source(s):* PSND
L'Isle, Jehan de *Source(s):* PIPE; PSND
Tartarin *Source(s):* PSND
Daugherty, Patrick Dale 1947- [composer, author, singer]
Daugherty, Dirty *Source(s):* ASCP
Daum, Norbert 1948- [composer]
Apolleon *Source(s):* KOMS; PFSA
Thumb, T. T. *Source(s):* KOMS; PFSA
Wesling, Bob *Source(s):* KOMS; PFSA
Dauphin, Léopold 1847-after 1900 [composer]
Pimpinelli *Source(s):* WHIT
Daus, Avraham 1902-1974 [composer, conductor]
Da-Oz, Ram *Source(s):* BAKR; NGDM
Davantes, Pierre 1525-1561 [inventor of neumonics for memorizing music]
Antesignan, Pierre d' *Source(s):* LCAR; NGDM; WORB
Davaux, Jean Baptiste 1742-1822 [composer]
Father of the Rondo, The *Source(s):* PSND
Pere aux Rondeaux, Le *Source(s):* PSND
Rondo, Father *Source(s):* PSND
Davenport, Charles Edward 1894-1955 [composer, pianist]
Bat "The Hummingbird" *Source(s):* HARS; LCAR; PSND; SUTT
Note(s): See also James Robinson.
Davenport, Cow-Cow *Source(s):* AMUS; EPMU; HARR; HARS; LCAR; KINK; PEN2; SUTT
Georgia Grinder *Source(s):* HARS; LCAR; PSND; SUTT
Hamilton, George *Source(s):* HARS; LCAR; PSND; SUTT
Memphis Slim *Source(s):* HARS; PSND
Note(s): See also Peter Chatman [i.e., John Len Chatman]
Davey, Marie [or Minnie] Augusta 1864-1932 [librettist]
Fiska, Minnie Maddern *Source(s):* LCAR; MELL
Maddern, Minnie *Source(s):* LCAR
David, Domenico ?-1698 [librettist]
Cedreatico, Osiro *Source(s):* GROL
Osiro Cedreatico *Source(s):* GROL
David, Gary 1935- [composer]
Da'oud, Gary *Source(s):* ASCP
David, Thomas 1942- [singer, songwriter, guitarist]
Roe, Tommy *Source(s):* NOMG
David, Worton 1874-1940 [songwriter]
Grey, Lilian *Source(s):* CCE43 #18474, 167 R117307; CCE46 R12831 ("How Can My Heart Forget")
Note(s): Also used by Lil(l)ian S(hirley) David.
McCarthy, Gene *Source(s):* CCE44 #35637, 567 R130258; CCE45 #40244 R14007
Note(s): Jt. pseud.: Lawrence Wright.
O'Neil, Douglas *Source(s):* CCE45 #63817, 1263 R141900
Note(s): Jt. pseud.: Lawrence Wright.
Shirley-Ospen, David *Source(s):* CCE44 #35637, 827 R130039
Note(s): Jt. pseud.: Lilian Shirley [i.e., Lawrence Wright] & R. Penso.
Stanley, Wynn *Source(s):* CCE47 R19993 ("I'm in Love with Selina"); KILG
Davidson, Christopher (John) 1948 (or 50)- [singer, songwriter]
Burgh, Chris de *Source(s):* FAFO

De Burgh, Chris *Source(s):* EPMU; HARR; PEN2; ROOM
Davidson, Russell Edward 1946- [composer, lyricist, singer]
Day, Rusty *Source(s):* ASCP
Davies, Alice Maude 1859-1938 [pianist, composer]
Note(s): Portraits: DWCO; ETUP 57:2 (Feb. 1939): 74. Wife of André Messager.
Davies, Dotie *Source(s):* DWCO; GROL; HIXN
Temple, Hope *Source(s):* GREN; GROL; HIXN; KILG
Davies, David Ivor 1893-1951 [actor, playwright, lyricist]
Note(s): Portrait: ETUP 54:9 (Sept. 1936): 534
L'Estrange, David *Source(s):* CART; GANB
Novello, Ivor *Source(s):* CART; CASS; EPMU; GAN1; GAN2; HARR; NGDO; PEN2
Uncrowned King of Ruritania, The *Source(s):* SHAP
Davies, Frances (Jean(ne)) 1883-1952 [singer, author]
Note(s): Portrait: ETUP 50:2 (Feb. 1932): 84
Alda, Frances *Source(s):* BAKO; BAUE; MACM; ROOM; SUTT
Davies, Harry Parr 1914-1955 [composer]
Burnay, Carlos *Source(s):* CCE52; CCE54; CPOL RE-74-736
Williams, Frank *Source(s):* CCE52; CPOL RE-74-709
Note(s): Also used by Richard Fote & Vernon Dalhart [i.e., M(arion) T(ry) Slaughter]
Davies, Ifor 1955- [singer, songwriter, composer]
Davies, Iva *Source(s):* EPMU
Icehouse *Source(s):* http://www.centrohd.com/bio/bio13/iva_davies_b.htm (8 Feb. 2006)
Davies, Richard 1833-1877 [lyricist, librettist]
Mynyddog *Source(s):* CYBH; KILG; LCAR; MELL
Davies, Samuel 1723-1761 [hymnist]
Note(s): Portrait: CYBH
S. D. *Source(s):* JULN
Davies, Willia m Henry 1911- [composer, author, pianist]
Henry, Will *Source(s):* ASCP
Davis, Albert Oliver 1920- [composer]
Hanson, Eric *Source(s):* CCE54-55; REHH; SUPN
Note(s): Also used by Elizabeth Wahr & Carl (F.) Ludwig; see NOTES: Hanson, Eric.
Harris, Jay *Source(s):* CCE55 E93029
Davis, Bertha Ruth 1906- [songwriter]
Davis, Bert *Source(s):* CCE53 Eunp
Collins, Billy *Source(s):* CCE50-51; CPOL RE-48-685
Gibson, Glenn *Source(s):* CCE52; CPOL RE-56-929
Richards, Howard *Source(s):* CPOL RE-59-138
Snow, Phoebe *Source(s):* CCE51; CPOL RE-37-800
Note(s): Also used by Phoebe Laub(e).
Davis, Betty Jack [singer, songwriter]
Davis Sisters, The *Source(s):* CCE54
Note(s): Jt. name: Skeeter Davis [i.e., Mary Frances Penick]. (No relation; high school friend)
Davis, Carl Estes, Jr. 1920- [conductor, arranger]
Davis, Bus(ter) *Source(s):* CCE44 #33424 Eunp387001; PIPE; PSND
Davis, Charles I. [composer]
Sivad, C. I. *Source(s):* BLIC (publication date 1912)
Davis, Clarice Ryall [songwriter]
Note(s): Publications dates: 1908-1913.
Orme, Destian *Source(s):* CPMU
Ryall, Orme *Source(s):* CPMU
Davis, Douglas E. 1966- [rapper]
Fresh, Doug E. *Source(s):* CPOL PA-975-447; EPMU
Davis, Elizabeth [librettist]
Note(s): Married name: Mrs. Leslie Kondorossy.
Hall, Shawn *Source(s):* GROL; NGDO
Davis, Gussie Lord 1863-1899 [author, comedian, songwriter]
Cincinnati's Only Colored Author and Comedian *Source(s):* SHAB p. 30
Davis, Hammie 1908-1984 [singer, instrumentalist]
Nickerson, Hammie *Source(s):* HARS
Nixon, Hammie *Source(s):* HARS
Davis, Jackson 1920- [composer, pianist, organist]
Davis, Jackie *Source(s):* PSND
Davis, James [or Jimmie] 1853-1907 [librettist, lyricist, playwright]
Hall, Owen *Source(s):* GAN1; GAN2; GROL; LCAR; LOWN; PIPE; PSND; WORB
Halle, Howen *Source(s):* LCAR
Davis, James [or Jimmie] (Houston) 1902-2000 [singer, songwriter, politician]
Note(s): Portraits: OB00; SGMA
Louisiana's Singing Governor *Source(s):* LCAR
Singing Governor *Source(s):* NGAM; NOTE 57:4 (June 2001): 865; OB00
Davis, Joseph [or Joe] (M.) 1896-1978 [composer, author, publisher]
Note(s): Dates on publications seem to indicate only one person used the name "Joe Davis;" however, it is possible there is a second person. Until more information is available the pseudonyms found for Joseph and Joe Davis are listed below.
Bacon, Leslie *Source(s):* CCE68; CLRA
Baker, Ward *Source(s):* CCE43 #943 Eunp321730; CCE70 R478508 & R480456
Beacon, Leslie *Source(s):* CCE41 #32249 E96515; CCE70 R494344; CLRA
Body, E. V. *Source(s):* CCE52 R92060 ("Lighning Express"); CCE57-58
Burns, Allen *Source(s):* CCE62
Contreras, Romulo *Source(s):* CCE59 E136444 ("I Don't Know What To Do")

Hampton, Roxanne *Source(s):* CCE51 R74759; CCE51 R76936
Note(s): "When It's Love Time in Hawaii" & "Honolulu Rose" Also used by Arthur Bergh.
Hardin, Lane *Source(s):* CCE62
Hardin, Lillian *Source(s):* CCE49 R55836; CCE51 R75056
Note(s): "My Sweet Smellin' Man" (CCE49) & "New Orleans Stomp" (CCE51)
Harris, Bill *Source(s):* CCE61
Jones, John Paul *Source(s):* CCE61
Note(s): Also used by John Baldwin.
Kuster, Richard *Source(s):* CCE61
Lowe, Harry *Source(s):* CCE61
Palalaiki, John *Source(s):* CCE52 R99302 ("Sunny Smiles of Hawaii")
Scott, Emporia "Lefty" *Source(s):* CCE43 #21853 Eunp33974; CCE70 R494343
Smith, Joe *Source(s):* CCE62
Note(s): Also used by Joseph Souter, Jr.
South, Georgia *Source(s):* CCE40 #24599 Eunp225793; CCE67
Steinberg, Rubin *Source(s):* CCE61
Svenson, Sven *Source(s):* CCE63 E176473; CPOL RE-507-790
Wood, Jack *Source(s):* CCE54 R136634 ("Fickle Mama Blues")

Davis, Josh 1973- [rapper]
DJ Shadow *Source(s):* EPMU; LCAR

Davis, Katherine K(ennicott) 1892-1980 [composer, pianist]
A. E. A. *Source(s):* CCE43 #45182 E118480 ("Jesus, Sleeping in the Manger"); CCE69
Brown, Bob *Source(s):* CCE21 E509769 ("Autumn")
Cowley, John *Source(s):* CCE50; CCE65; CCE68; WOAM
Goodhall, Clare *Source(s):* CCE51; GOTH; TPRF
Jahr, H. N. *Source(s):* CCE67 R419054
K. K. D. *Source(s):* CCE49 ("The Mill Wheel")
Moore, Michael *Source(s):* CCE68; LCCC70 R487526
Robertson, C. R. W. *Source(s):* CCE42 #27582-83 E105701; WOAM

Davis, Larry 1936-1994 [singer, instrumentalist, songwriter]
Davis, Totsy *Source(s):* HARS

Davis, Louis, Jr. [composer, keyboardist, recording executive]
Davis, Chip *Source(s):* CM04; LCAR

Davis, Mary Lee [songwriter]
Davis, Mama *Source(s):* PSND

Davis, Miles (Dewey), (III) 1926-1991 [composer, bandleader]
Henry, Cleo *Source(s):* PMUS; Carr, Ian. *Miles Davis; The Definitive Biography*. New York: Thunder's Mouth Press, 1998, 55.
Evil Genius of Jazz *Source(s):* Carr p. 172 (see above)
Prince of Darkness *Source(s):* NGDJ
Note(s): See also Louis [or Lewis] (Allen) Firbank.

Davis, Morris 1941 (or 42)- [singer, guitarist, songwriter]
Davis, Mac (Scott) *Source(s):* NOMG; STAM
Davis, Scott *Source(s):* STAM
Song Painter, (The) *Source(s):* CASS; WORT

Davis, Moses 1972- [songwriter]
Beenie Man *Source(s):* AMUS; LCAR; PMUS-00
Sivad, Sesom *Source(s):* CCE53 Eunp
Note(s): Probable pseud.

Davis, Percival [or Percy] 1887-1941 [lyricist]
Davis, Clifford *Source(s):* PIPE; PSND
Note(s): Listed as original name.
Grey, Clifford *Source(s):* CCE48 R35470; CCE52-53; EPMU; GAN1; GAN2; PIPE; PSND
Note(s): In PIPE & PSND see under: Davis, Clifford.
Grey, Percival *Source(s):* LCCC 1955-70 (see reference)

Davis, Roquel 1932-2004 [songwriter, record producer]
Carlo, T(yran) *Source(s):* CCE58; PSND; WASH
Davis, Billy *Source(s):* AMUS; WASH

Davis, Rosalind [playwright, composer]
Rosalind *Source(s):* PSND

Davis, Walter 1912-1963 [singer, pianist, songwriter]
Note(s): Do not confuse with Walter Davis, Jr. (1932-), contemporary jazz pianist.
Hooker Joe *Source(s):* HARS

Davis, William Strethen 1918-1995 [organist, pianist, arranger]
Davis, Will Bill *Source(s):* LCAR; NGDJ

Davison, Lita 1927- [composer, author, singer]
DeSaxe, Serena *Source(s):* ASCP
Shaw, Serena *Source(s):* ASCP

Davison, Sid (I)., (Jr.) 1941- [composer, author, singer]
Diamond, Dave *Source(s):* ASCP; CCE61-62

Davison, W. R. [composer]
Nosivad, W. R. *Source(s):* CPMU (publication date 1912)

Dawes, William 1840-1897 [songwriter]
Goff, Lijer *Source(s):* KILG

Dawkins, James [or Jimmy] (Henry) 1936- [singer, guitarist, songwriter]
Dawkins, Fast Fingers *Source(s):* HARS
Fast Fingers *Source(s):* LCAR

Dawson, Herbert (Henry) 1913- [singer, songwriter]
Dawson, Craig *Source(s):* CCE54-55
Dawson, Smoky *Source(s):* CCE47; CCE53-55; DAUM; EPMU

Dawson, Peter (Smith) 1882-1961 [singer, songwriter]

Allison, Peter [or Petter] *Source(s):* CCE34 Efor5677; CPMU; Glennon, James. *Australian Music and Musicians*. Adelaide: Rigby, 1968.
Ambassador of Song *Source(s): Fifty Years of Song* [sound recording] (EMI OXLP 7661-70)
Ballad King, The *Source(s):* DAUM
Baxter, Geoffrey *Source(s):* Glennon (see above)
Danby, Frank *Source(s):* KILG p.175; Glennon (see above)
Davies, Fred *Source(s):* MACE
Dawson, Leonard *Source(s):* KILG p. 175; MACE
Flint, Arnold *Source(s):* Glennon (see above)
Grant, Hector *Source(s):* KILG p. 175; MACE; Glennon (see above)
McCall, J. P(etter) *Source(s):* CART; CASS; CPMU; DAUM; KILG; LCAR; Glennon (see above)
Munday, Gilbert *Source(s):* Glennon (see above)
Osborne, James *Source(s):* MACE
Strong, Will *Source(s):* KILG p. 175; MACE; Glennon (see above)
Toms, Denton *Source(s):* Glennon (see above)
Weber, Charles *Source(s):* CCE45 #35888, 389 R139279
Welsh, George *Source(s):* MACE

Dax, Esteven 1888-1956 [composer]
Darcis, G. *Source(s):* REHH
D'Arsdorf, Jean *Source(s):* REHH
Selz, Bob *Source(s):* REHH

Day, Bob 1942- [singer, songwriter]
Allison, Bob *Source(s):* EPMU (see under: Allisons)

Day, Frederick E(dward) (Montagu) 1878-1975 [songwriter]
Dawlish, Peter *Source(s):* CCE50 R65811 ("Little June Rose")
Montagu(e), Edward [or Eduard] *Source(s):* BLIC; CCE32 R19861; CCE52-54; KILG
Terego, Al *Source(s):* CCE48; CCE50-52; CCE55-56; CCE70 R484369

Deacon, Charles [composer]
Dare, Cyril *Source(s):* CPMU (publication dates 1892-1909); TPRF

Déaddé, Edouard 1820-1872 [librettist]
D. A. D. *Source(s):* LCAR; STGR
Saint-Yves *Source(s):* LCAR; LOWN; STGR

Deal, Robert (Alan) 1955 (or 56)- [guitarist, songwriter]
Mars, Mick *Source(s):* AMUS; NOMG

Dean, Andy [songwriter]
Boilerhouse *Source(s):* CPOL PA-683-585; SONG
Note(s): Jt. pseud.: Ben Barson & Ben Wolff.

Dean, Celia [composer]
Naed, Alice *Source(s):* CPMU (publication dates 1862-64)

Dean, Jimmy 1928- [singer, songwriter]
Long Tall Texan *Source(s):* CASS

Dean, William [or Billy] Harold 1962- [singer, guitarist, songwriter]
Billy the Kid *Source(s):* STAC

De Angelis, Alfredo 1912-1990 (or 92) [pianist, leader, composer]
Colorado, El *Source(s):* TODO

DeAngelis, Angelo ?-c.1825 [composer]
Rivotorto *Source(s):* NGDM
Note(s): See also Francesco Maria Angeli.

DeanThorne, Donald James 1901-1967 [pianist, composer, arranger]
Denville, Eric *Source(s):* GALM; RFSO
Leserve, August *Source(s):* GALM; RFSO

Deason, Muriel (Ellen) 1918 (or 19)- [singer, songwriter, guitarist]
Note(s): In MCCL given names: Ellen Muriel.
Queen of Country Music *Source(s):* AMUS; CASS; CM06; EPMU; STAC
Note(s): See also Virginia Wynette Pugh & Loretta Webb.
Wells, Kitty *Source(s):* AMUS; CASS; CLAG; CM06; EPMU; GRAT; MCCL; NGAM; STAC

Debaro, Charlotte 1911- [composer]
Rozman, Sarah *Source(s):* BUL2

DeBoeck, Marcel 1921- [composer]
Rial, Marc *Source(s):* REHH

Debussy, Claude 1862-1918 [composer]
Croche, (Monsieur) *Source(s):* CASS; GROL; ROOM
Dieubussy *Source(s):* SLON
Father of Musical Impressionism, The *Source(s):* http://www.losangeles.com/music/notes6.html (15 Oct. 2002)
Father of Musical Modernism *Source(s):* http://members.ozemail.com.au/~caveman/Debussy/lisguide.htm (15 Oct. 2002)

Décarie, Reine 1912- [composer]
Johane d'Arcie, (Soeur) *Source(s):* BUL3

DeCesare, Stephen [composer, singer]
King of Schmaltz *Source(s):* http://www.meetthecomposer.org/contacts.htm (12 Mar. 2005)

Decius, Nikolaus fl. 1485-1546 [cantor, composer]
Degius, Nikolaus *Source(s):* NGDM; WORB
Hofe, Nikolaus *Source(s):* NGDM; WORB
Nickel von Hof *Source(s):* NGDM
Tech (a Curia), Nikolas *Source(s):* NGDM; WORB

Decker, Henry 1860-1922 [composer, publisher]
Dacre, Harry *Source(s):* CPMU; FULD; GAMM; KILG; MARC p. 136
Note(s): In GREN & CPMU, listed as pseud. of Frank Dean [i.e., Henry Decker]
Dean, Frank *Source(s):* FULD; GAMM; KILG

Decker, Karl von 1784-1844 [librettist]
Thale, Adalbert vom *Source(s):* STGR; WORB

Deckers, J(e)anine 1933-1985 [singer, songwriter]

Luc Dominique *Source(s):* LCAR
Luc-Gabrielle, (Sister) *Source(s):* CASS; LCAR
Singing Nun, The *Source(s):* CASS; LCAR
Sister Smile *Source(s):* LCAR
Soeur Sourire *Source(s):* CCE62; LCAR

DeCollibus, Nicholas 1913- [composer, conductor, violinist]
Nicholas, Don *Source(s):* ASCP; CCE76

DeCormier, Robert 1922- [composer, arranger, conductor]
Corman, Bob *Source(s):* CCE58; CPOL RE-349-652; LCAR

DeCosta, Joan 1930- [singer, songwriter]
Shaw, Joan *Source(s):* PSND

Decourcelle, Paul 1854- [composer]
Tellam, Heinrich *Source(s):* GREN

Decourcelle, Pierre 1856-1926 [author]
Choufleury *Source(s):* PIPE

DeCourcy, Richard 1743-1803 [cleric, hymnist]
Good Vicar, The *Source(s):* CART

Decsey, Ernst (Heinrich Franz) 1870-1941 [legal scholar, music critic]
Heinrich, Franz *Source(s):* AEIO

Dedekind, Constantin Christian 1628-1697 [poet, composer, singer, publisher]
Note(s): "K. g. P." or "K. S. C" listed after Dedekind's name refers to "Kurfürstlicher gekrönter Poet" & "Kurf Sächsischer Concertmeister."
C. Chr. D. *Source(s):* CPMU
Con Cor D(en) *Source(s):* GROL; NGDM; SADC
Concord *Source(s):* NGDM

Dedrick, Lyle T. 1918- [trumpeter, arranger, composer]
Dedrick, Rusty *Source(s):* KINK; LCAR; NGDJ

Deeley, Francis [or Frank] Arthur 1868-1927 [actor, producer]
Curzon, (Sir) Frank *Source(s):* GAN1; GAN2; WORB

Dees, Rigdon Osmond, III 1950- [singer, songwriter]
Dees, Rick *Source(s):* EPMU; PSND

De Filippi, Amedeo 1900- [composer, author, conductor]
Corio, Jose *Source(s):* CCE59
Hodgson, Daniel *Source(s):* CCE70 R478908 ("Three Marches of American Revolutionary Days")
Molin, Rafael *Source(s):* CCE58
Rader, Michael *Source(s):* CCE57
Rives, Este *Source(s):* CCE58
Ross, Donald *Source(s):* CCE57
Silva, Hector *Source(s):* CCE57
Weston, Philip *Source(s):* BUL2; BUL3; CCE42 #35689 E107265; CPMU; LCAR

De Filippis, Melchiorre 1825-1895 [composer]
Delfico, Melchiorre *Source(s):* MELL

Defilló, Pau Carlos Salvador 1876-1973 [violoncellist, composer]
Casals, Pablo *Source(s):* BAKR; BAKT; LCAR

DeFossa, François 1775-1849 [guitarist, composer]
Haydn of the Guitar *Source(s):* http://www.orphee.com/defossa/mexico.htm (9 Apr. 2005)

Defossez, René 1905-1988 [composer, conductor]
Chamare *Source(s):* NGDO

De Franco, Boniface (Ferdinand Leonardo) 1923- [composer, conductor, clarinetist]
De Franco, Buddy *Source(s):* EPMU, LCAR
Ferdinand, Buddy *Source(s):* ASCP

Dégas (Liorat), Georges 1837-1898 [accountant, librettist, lyricist]
Armand *Source(s):* LCAR
Note(s): Also used by A(rmand) E(dward) Blackmar.
Liorat, Armand *Source(s):* GAN1; GAN2; LOWN; MELL; WORB

Degenhardt, (Hans) Jürgen 1930- [author]
Hardt, H(ans) *Source(s):* CCE55; PIPE

Degesco, Charles [lyricist]
Frost, Jack *Source(s):* CCE43 #24678 E114336
Note(s): Also used by Mark Vincent Brine, Harold G. Frost, E. Clinton Keithley & Bob Dylan [i.e., Robert Allen Zimmerman]

DeGrandis, Vincenzo 1577-1646 [composer, singer]
Romano, Il *Source(s):* GROL; NGDM; SADC
Note(s): See also Tommaso Mariani.

DeGranier (de Cassagnac), Jean (Adolphe Alfred) 1890-1976 [songwriter, performer]
Saint-Granier *Source(s):* CCE30 Efor13387; GAN1; WORB

Degraw, Jimmy Dwaine 1936- [composer, author, singer]
Lawton, Jimmy *Source(s):* ASCP

DeGresac, Frederique Rosine 1866-1943 [librettist]
DeGresac, Fred *Source(s):* http://www.musicals101.com/who29.htm (18 May 2005)

De Guzman, Josie [composer, singer]
Motzan, Otto *Source(s):* PARS

Dehm, Dieter 1950- [composer]
Lerryn *Source(s):* LCAR; PFSA

Dehn, Siegfried Wilhelm 1799-1858 [theorist, music librarian, editor]
Note(s): Portrait: ETUP 50:11 (Nov. 1932): 762
S. W. D.—n *Source(s):* HEYT

Deighton, John Henry 1940- [singer, songwriter]
Farlowe, Chris *Source(s):* LCAR; RECR

Deimel, Hans 1957- [composer]
Jack 'n' Bob *Source(s):* KOMS; PFSA

Dejardin, Joseph [composer]
D***, (Monsieur) *Source(s):* CPMU (publication date 1844)

De Jong, John 1945- [singer, bandleader, songwriter]
Young, Johnny *Source(s):* EPMU

De Koven, (Henry Louis) Reginald 1859-1920 [composer]
 Note(s): Portraits: EWCY; EWEN; EWPA; GAN1
 Grand Seigneur *Source(s):* MARC p. 307
Delagaye, Georges 1937- [composer]
 Felser, René *Source(s):* KOMS; PFSA
 Pinot, Claude *Source(s):* KOMS; PFSA
De La Mare, Walter (John) 1873-1956 [author]
 Ramal, Walter *Source(s):* CCE29 Efor6684; PSND
Delaney, Francis Edward 1936- [composer, author, singer]
 DePadua, Anthony *Source(s):* ASCP
Delaney, William (M.) [composer; songbook editor]
 Wildwave, Willie *Source(s):* SPTH p. 220 & 242
DeLange, Edgar 1904-1949 [bandleader, lyricist, arranger]
 DeLange, Eddie *Source(s):* KINK; LCAR
De la Ramé(e), (Maria) Louise 1839-1908 [author, librettist]
 Ouida *Source(s):* LCAR; LOWN
DeLaughter, Hollis R(udolph) 1939- [singer, songwriter]
 Lane, Red *Source(s):* CCE66-68; ENCM; EPMU; MCCL; NASF; PMUS
Delaunay, Charles 1911-1988 [writer on music, producer]
 Chadel, H. P. *Source(s):* GROL
Delbecque, Laurent 1905-1992 [composer]
 Darling, John (A.) *Source(s):* CCE61; REHG; REHH; SUPN
Delbos, Louise Justine 1910-1959 [violinist, composer]
 Delbos, Claire *Source(s):* BUL3; COHN; HIXN
DeLeo, Lionardo Oronzo Salvatore 1694-1744 [composer]
 Leonardo, Leo *Source(s):* PSND
DeLeone, Francesco B(artolomeo) 1887-1948 [composer, conductor, pianist, editor]
 Note(s): Portrait: ETUP 50:11 (Nov. 1932): 686
 Lyons, Frank *Source(s):* TPRF
 Paridon, Roxana *Source(s):* CCE40 #21595 E85656; TPRF
De l'Epine, Francesca Margherita c.1683-1746 [librettist, singer]
 Greber's Peg *Source(s):* SADC
 Hecate *Source(s):* SADC
 Margarita *Source(s):* LCAR; LOWN
Delestre-Poirson, Charles Gaspard 1790-1859 [author]
 Saint-Marc, Amédée de *Source(s):* LCAR
 Note(s): Jt. pseud.: (Augustin) Eugène Scribe & Anne Honoré Joseph Duveyrier
Delfino, Enrique Pedro 1895-1967 [pianist, composer, actor]
 Delfy *Source(s):* CCE53-56; CCE65; LCAR; TODO
DelGiudice, Gaetano Maria 1888- [composer]
 Mauro d' Amalfi *Source(s):* IBIM; WORB
Delgrosso, Jean Ann 1938- [composer]
 Allen, Lauri *Source(s):* ASCP; CCE66
Delibes, (Clement Philibert) Leo 1836-1891 [composer]
 Delbes, Eloi *Source(s):* GDRM; GROL
Delius, Fritz Albert Theodore 1862-1934 [composer]
 Delius, Frederick *Source(s):* BAKR
Dellafield, Henry 1883-1957 [composer]
 Antoine, Frere *Source(s):* CPOL RE-86-541
 DuSacre-Cour, Sister M. *Source(s):* CPOL RE-199-389
 King, Stanford *Source(s):* CCE65-66; CCE68
 Martin, Elizabeth Blackburn *Source(s):* CPOL RE-161-528
 Maxim, George Pratt *Source(s):* CCE67 R414717
 Mays, Grace *Source(s):* CCE67 R415334
 Richter, Carl (Arthur) *Source(s):* CCE63; CCE67-68; CPOL RE-5-573; GOTH
 Note(s): Listed as original name in GOTH
 Rolfe, Walter *Sourc(s):* CCE66
 Saint Gaston, Sister M. *Source(s):* CPOL RE-199-392
 Spindle, Louise Cooper *Source(s):* CPOL RE-86-540
 Thal, Jeanette (D.) *Source(s):* CCE63; CCE67-68; CPOL RE-86-552; CPOL RE-143-282
Della [or Delle] Grazie, Gisella 1868- [librettist; composer]
 Raedzielg, Gisella *Source(s):* COHN; STGR
Della Salla, Josquino 1527-c.1597 [composer]
 Giusquino *Source(s):* WORB
 Salèm, Josquino *Source(s):* NGDM; WORB
 Note(s): Possible other name.
 Salèpico, Josquino *Source(s):* WORB
Della Valle, Pietro 1586-1652 [author, poet, writer on music, composer]
 Pellegrino, Il *Source(s):* GROL; NGDM
 Note(s): See also Orazio [or Horatio] Modiana.
Dellger, Michael Laurence [lyricist, drummer]
 Bemis, Big Ben *Source(s):* ASCP
De Long, Frank 1886-1952 [songwriter]
 Coburn, Richard *Source(s):* KILG
 Long, Frank de *Source(s):* FULD
Delores, José Silvestre de los 1836?-1918 [musician, composer]
 White, Joseph *Source(s):* LCAR; PSND
DeLoriea, Marybelle C(ruger) 1917-1985 [composer, author]
 Odell, Mamie *Source(s):* ASCP
Delp, Fred (B.) [singer, songwriter]
 Fishbone Fred *Source(s): Washington Post* (8 Sept. 1997): C5
Del Parral, Antonio [arranger]
 Boss, Al *Source(s):* OCLC 43300622
Del Riego, Teresa (Clotilde) 1876-1968 [pianist, singer, violinist, composer]

Note(s): Portrait: ETUP 50:11 (Nov. 1932): 762
Allwyn, John *Source(s):* CCE51 R74096 ("The Southern Shepherd")
Lang, Mark *Source(s):* CCE65
Leadbetter, Teresa *Source(s):* LCAR
Leadbitter, Teresa *Source(s):* CCE29 E11906; CCE65
Lemaitre, Francois *Source(s):* CCE38 R65453
March, Noel *Source(s):* CCE48; CCE58
Del Santo, Dan ?-2001 [guitarist, singer, composer]
Blues Demon, The *Source(s):* DRSC
Delusse, Charles 1731-after 1774 [composer]
D. L. *Source(s):* LCAR
Lusse, Charles de *Source(s):* CPMU; LCAR
M. de L** *Source(s):* CPMU
Delvicario, Silvio Patrick 1921-2002 [composer]
Vicar, Del *Source(s):* ASCP; CCE58
Delyssee, Jean 1894-1976 [composer, harpsichordist, pianist]
Roesgen-Champion, Marguerite *Source(s):* BUL2; LCAR
Demaio, James Paul 1913-1991 [composer, author]
Paul, Jimmy *Source(s):* ASCP; CPOL PAu-192-047
Demandowski, Axel 1867-1929 [librettist]
Delmar, Axel *Source(s):* STGR; WORB
Demarco, Rosalinda Jill 1950- [composer, author, singer]
Janns, Rose *Source(s):* ASCP
Johns, (Rosalinda) Jill *Source(s):* ASCP; CPOL PAu-263-377
DeMasi, Francesco 1930- [composer]
Mason, Frank *Source(s):* PSND
Demeter, Dimitrije [or Demetrius] 1811-1872 [author]
Afratinovic *Source(s):* LCAR; PIPE
Dempsey, James E. 1876-1918 [composer, author, singer]
Ford, Powell I. *Source(s):* ASCP; CCE42 #34788, 286 R110434
Grayson, Paul *Source(s):* ASCP
Note(s): Also used by James R(amsey) Murray.
Dempwolff, Horst 1915-1983 [composer]
Michell, Andreas *Source(s):* KOMP; KOMS; PFSA
Mico, Fen *Source(s):* KOMP; KOMS; PFSA
De Muyt, Aimé 1923- [composer]
Baker, Dave *Source(s):* REHH, SUPN
DeNaut, George Matthew [or Mathews] 1915-1999 [conductor, bassist, arranger]
DeNaut, Jud *Source(s):* ASCC; CPOL RE-342-784
Denemy, Ernest 1891(or 92)-1948 [singer, composer]
Note(s): Portrait: ETUP 57:1 (Jan. 1939): 2. Illegitimate son of Richard Anton Tauber. Original surname was Denemy; later used his mother's married name, Seiffert, before assuming his father's name. (See LCAR)
Seiffert, Ernst *Source(s):* BAKR; GAMM
Tauber, Richard *Source(s):* BAKR; GAMM; LCAR
Denis, (Johann) Michael (Kosmas Peter), (S. J.) 1729-1800 [author, hymnist]
Sined, der Barde *Source(s):* KOMU; LCAR
Denneé, Charles (Frederick) 1863-1946 [composer, teacher]
Note(s): Portraits: APSA; ETUP 50:11 (Nov. 1932): 762; MUWO (Mar. 1903): 47
Keppe(l), Franz *Source(s):* CCE17 R10406-8
Meyer, Ferdinand *Source(s):* LCPC 25156
Note(s): A. P. Schmidt house name; see NOTES: Meyer, Ferdinand.
Denni, Martha (Gwynne) 1882-1949 [actress, lyricist]
Denni, Gwynne *Source(s):* CCE44 #35526 E123798; CCE61
Gwynne, Martha *Source(s):* CCE44 #35526 E123798; PSND
Dennis, William [or Willie] [rapper]
Willie D *Source(s):* AMUS; EPMU
Densmore, John 1945- [songwriter]
Doors, The *Source(s):* GOTT; PEN2; PMUS
Note(s): Jt. pseud.: James (Douglas) Morrison, Robert Krieger & Raymond (Daniel) Manzarek.
Dente, Pietro 1879- [composer]
Dentella *Source(s):* IBIM; WORB
Denton, Sandra (or Sandy) 1969- [songwriter]
Pepa *Source(s):* EPMU; LCAR; PMUS-96; RECR
Depaolis, Leone F. 1916- [composer, author, violinist]
Allen, Leone Perry *Source(s):* CCE74; CPOL PA-318-913
Beaulieu, Toni [or Tony] *Source(s):* ASCP; CCE73-74
Depenheuer, Walter 1951- [composer]
Lindenthal, Bert *Source(s):* PFSA
Derleth, Julia 1896- [pianist, writer, composer]
Bezdek, Jan *Source(s):* COHN; HIXN
Bezdek, Sister John Joseph *Source(s):* COHN; HIXN
De Rogati(s), Francesco Saverio 1745-1827 [author, poet]
Genesio, Argisto *Source(s):* PIPE; PSND
Ginesio, Argesio *Source(s):* GROL
De Rose, Peter 1900-1953 [composer]
Havlin, Will *Source(s):* CCE57-58
Sweethearts of the Air *Source(s):* JASZ; KINK; TCAN
Note(s): Jt. sobriquet with wife: May Singhi Breen.
Desbuissons, Michel Charles 1520-before 1573 [composer]
Flandrus insulanus *Source(s):* MACM
Descartes, René 1596-1650 [philosopher, writer on music]
Note(s): See LCAR for variant forms of name.

Cartesio *Source(s):* LCAR
Cartesius, Renatus *Source(s):* MACM; WORB
Deschamps, Luis [songwriter]
Papo MC *Source(s):* HWOM
Déschán, Ludwig 1848- [librettist]
Sendach, Ludwig *Source(s):* STGR; WORB
De Schrijver, Karel 1908-1992 [composer]
Paresco, Jimmy *Source(s):* REHH; SUPN
Prago, Helmut *Source(s):* SUPN
Desessart, Fréderic [composer]
F. D*** *Source(s):* CPMS (Publication date 1732)
Des Granges, Louis Anthony 1935- [composer]
Granger, Lou *Source(s):* ASCP; CCE62-63
Granges, Lou *Source(s):* CCE47; CCE64
Louis, Des *Source(s):* CCE61
Desjardins, Louis-Edouard 1837-1919 [physician, folklorist, composer]
Ancien maitre de chapelle *Source(s):* CANE; LCAR
Bon vieux temps *Source(s):* CANE; LCAR
L. E. D. *Source(s):* CPMU
Deslouges, Philippe c.1565-before 1552 [composer]
Verdelot Philippe *Source(s):* LCAR
Verdelotto *Source(s):* LCAR
Desmarets, Henri 1661-1741 [composer, musician]
Goupillier *Source(s):* MACM
DeSmet, Jean 1885-1954 [composer]
DeSmetsky, Jean *Source(s):* REHG; SMIN
De Smet, Robin John 1935- [composer, teacher, music editor]
Jones, Stanley *Source(s):* CPMU
Desnoyers, Louis (Claude Joseph Florence) 1805-1868 [librettist]
Derville, (Henri-Louis) *Source(s):* LCAR; STGR; WORB
Desprez, Frank 1853-1916 [writer]
Soulbieu, F. *Source(s):* GANA
De Sylva, George Gard 1895-1950 [lyricist, librettist, film & stage producer]
Note(s): Portraits: EWEN; SHMM (Mar./Apr. 1944): 2 & cover
De Sylva, B. G. *Source(s):* CASS; CCE29 E2065; EWEN
De Sylva, Buddy *Source(s):* EPMU; EWEN; GAMM; HARD; HARR; KINK
Detroit, Marcella [singer, songwriter]
Levy, Marcy *Source(s):* PEN2 (see under: Shakespears Sister)
Détroyat, (Pierre) Léonce 1829-1898 (political officer, author]
Bourgneuf, L. de *Source(s):* PIPE
Deuringer, Hubert [or Herbert] (Martin) 1924- [composer]
Ensor, James (Herb) *Source(s):* CCE67; CCE73
Hellstern, Klaus *Source(s):* CCE55-59; RIES
Schäfer, Herbert M. *Source(s):* CCE56
Deutsch, Ernst 1870-1941 [writer on music]
Decsey, Ernst *Source(s):* WORB
Deutsch, Friedrich 1902-1991 [musicologist, critic]
Dorian, Frederick *Source(s):* BAKT; KOMU; LCAR; RIES; WORB
Deutsch, Max Leo 1893-1944 [poet, playwright]
Gerold, Fritz *Source(s):* PIPE
Deutschendorf, Henry John, Jr. 1943-1997 [singer, actor, composer]
Denver, John *Source(s):* CASS; CM01; CM23; DIMA; GAMM; HARR; MCCL; PEN2
Tom Sawyer of Rock, The *Source(s):* CM01; PSND
Deutscher, Karlheinz 1946- [singer, composer]
Baby Champ *Source(s):* http://www.stars-on-7-inch.com/index_d/deutscher_drafti.htm (15 Oct. 2002)
Boland, Dave *Source(s):* PFSA
Deutscher, Drafi *Source(s):* PFSA
Funkel, Lars *Source(s):* CCE73; CCE75 Efor175235
Gebegern, Kurt *Source(s):* PFSA
Goldberg, Jack *Source(s):* PFSA
Goldbird, Jack *Source(s):* CCE75 Efor174708; CCE76 Efor185458
Jensen, Karin *Source(s):* CCE76 Efor183127
Kurt gives gladly *Source(s):* http://www.arte-tv.com/thema/19970607/dtext/bios/deutscher.html (15 Oct. 2002)
Masquerade *Source(s):* http://www.stars-on-7-inch.com/index_d/deutscher_drafti.htm
Mr. Walkie Talkie *Source(s):* http://www.stars-on-7-inch.com/index_d/deutscher_drafti.htm
Mixed Emotions *Source(s):* CCE73
Pitter, Harold *Source(s):* CCE75 Efor175234
Usedom, Hecktor von *Source(s):* PFSA
Vaplus, Renata *Source(s):* CCE76 Efor185458; CPOL PA-8-579
Deutz, Magnus 1828-1883 (or 84) [composer, pianist, critic]
Magnus, (Désiré) *Source(s):* CPMU; GOTH; IBIM; MACM; STGR; WORB
Devall, Arthur Henry [composer]
A. H. D. *Source(s):* CPMU (publication date 1919)
DeVere, Margie Ann 1922- [fiddle player, composer]
Fiddlin' Kate *Source(s):* LCAR
Warren, Fiddlin' Kate *Source(s):* EPMU; MCCL
De Vito, Albert (Kenneth) 1919-1999 [composer, educator, author]
Allen, Charles *Source(s):* GREN; LCAR
Note(s): Also used by Howard Stube.
Lisbon, Kenneth *Source(s):* CCE60; CCE62; GREN; LCAR
Rogers, Kenneth *Source(s):* CCE60; CCE62 E162026; GREN; LCAR
Saunders, Kenneth *Source(s):* CCE63

DeWar, Ted Royal 1904- [composer]
Royal, Ted *Source(s):* CCE54; CCE63; CCE68; REHG
De Witt, Louis O. 1853- [composer]
Engle, Carl *Source(s):* REHG; SUPN
DeWolf, Michael 1500?-1567 [composer]
Lupus, Michael *Source(s):* BAKE; PSND
Deybrook, L(arry) M(itchell) 1910-1976 [composer, author]
Dey, Larry *Source(s):* ASCP; CCE57-58; CCE64
Deycks, Friedrich [writer on music]
D. *Source(s):* HEYT
Dks *Source(s):* HEYT
Ds, (Dr.) *Source(s):* HEYT
Dezède, Florine c.1766-1792 [librettist]
D. Z., (Mademoiselle) *Source(s):* CPMU; STGR
Dezède, Nicolas 1740(?)-1792 (or 95) [composer]
D. Z., (Monsieur) *Source(s):* CPMU; LCAR; NGDO; STGR
Desaides, Nicolas *Source(s):* LCAR; SONN
Zéde, (Monsieur) *Source(s):* CPMU
d'Haese, Dirk Hippoliet Ambrosius 1960- [composer]
Ase, Dirk d' *Source(s):* OMUO
Diabaté, Toumani 1965- [composer]
Prince of the Kora, The *Source(s):* PEN2
Diamond, Neil (Leslie) 1941- [singer, songwriter]
Kid from Brooklyn, The *Source(s):* PSND
Note(s): See also Aaron Copland
Pursuer of Beautiful Noise *Source(s):* LYMN
Diasio, Daniel J(oseph, Jr.) 1941- [composer, author]
Danny Dee *Source(s):* CCE60
Lyons, Dan D. *Source(s):* ASCP
Diaz, R(afael) J(osé) 1955- [singer, songwriter, actor]
Rafael José *Source(s):* HWOM
Diaz Herrera, Carlos Arturo 1933- [singer, songwriter]
Diaz, Santander *Source(s):* CCE67; HWOM
Dibango, Emmanuel 1933- [singer, composer, arranger]
Dibango, Manu *Source(s):* PEN2
Dibbs, Jr. *Source(s):* CCE73 Efor38109
Dibble, Scott [singer, songwriter, guitarist]
Watertown *Source(s):* http://cmi.canoe.ca/JamMusicPopEncycloPagesD/dibble_scott.html (15 Oct. 2002)
Dibdin, Charles 1745-1814 [playwright, actor, composer]
Note(s): Portrait: GRV3 v. 2
Bard of the British Navy, The *Source(s):* PSND; SIFA
Castigator *Source(s):* CART
True Laureate of England, The *Source(s):* PSND; SIFA
Tyrtaeus of the British Navy, The *Source(s):* PSND
Dibdin, Thomas J(ohn) 1771-1841 [playwright, songwriter, actor]
Merchant, Mr. (T.) *Source(s):* CART; ROOM
Pitt, Thomas Dibdin *Source(s):* KILG
Di Biase, Edoardo J(ames) 1924- [composer, arranger, violinist]
David, Vincent *Source(s):* ASCC; BUL3; CCE61-65; LCAR
Dichler-Sedlacek, Erika 1929- [pianist, composer]
Spenger, M. T. *Source(s):* COHN; HIXN
Dichmont, William 1882-1943 [organist, violinist, composer, conductor]
Lowell, Frances *Source(s):* CANE
Rutherford, Arthur *Source(s):* CANE
Dick, Derek William 1958- [singer, songwriter]
Fish *Source(s):* EPMU; LCAR; NOMG; PMUS
Dickens, Charles (John Huffam) 1812-1870 [author]
Note(s): See PSND for additional nonmusic-related pseudonyms.
Boz *Source(s):* PIPE
Dickens, James Cecil 1925- [singer, guitarist, songwriter]
Dickens, Little Jimmy *Source(s):* EPMU; FLIN; MCCL
Jimmy the Kid *Source(s):* AMUS
Singing Midget, The *Source(s):* FLIN
Tater *Source(s):* FLIN
Dickerson, Patricia Gail 1948- [singer, songwriter, producer]
Davies, Gail *Source(s):* AMUS; CM38; ENCM; MCCL
Dickey, Richard Scott 1956- [composer, author, arranger]
Estes, Richard *Source(s):* ASCP
Dickson, Ellen Elizabeth 1819-1878 [composer, lyricist]
Dolores *Source(s):* COHN; DWCO; GROL; HAMT; HOVL; MACM
Dickson, Mary Hannah 1885-1956 [composer]
Note(s): Married names: Brahe, later Morgan. Portrait: HAMA
Banks, Mervyn *Source(s):* DAUM; LCAR
Brahe, May Hannah *Source(s):* DWCO; LCAR
Crichton, Donald *Source(s):* DAUM; DWCO; LCAR
Crichton, Jean *Source(s):* HAMA
Dickson, Stanley *Source(s):* DAUM; DWCO; LCAR
Dodd, Alison *Source(s):* DAUM; DWCO; LCAR
Douglas, Stanton *Source(s):* DAUM; DWCO; LCAR
Faulkner, Eric *Source(s):* DAUM; DWCO; LCAR
Fox, Wilbur B. *Source(s):* DAUM; DWCO; LCAR
George, Harold *Source(s):* CCE48; CCE70 R492131; HAMA
Lovell, Henry *Source(s):* DAUM; DWCO; LCAR
Lucas, Jean *Source(s):* HAMA
Lucas, Margaret *Source(s):* CCE76; HAMA

Morgan, Hannah May *Source(s):* CCE51 R74098 ("Are You London?"); HAMA
Percival, Gladys *Source(s):* HAMA
Pointer, George *Source(s):* CCE51 R74098 ("Are You London?"); DAUM; DWCO; LCAR
Didymus fl. late 1st cent. [music theorist]
Chalcenterus *Source(s):* GROL
Chalkenteros *Source(s):* GROL
Diefenthaler, Margaret Kissinger [pianist, composer]
Dee, Margaret *Source(s):* COHN; HIXN
Diernhammer, Carlos 1931- [composer]
Convent, Peter *Source(s):* KOMP; KOMS; PFSA
Rodriguez, Carlos *Source(s):* CCEC58
Sidney, Sid *Source(s):* KOMP; KOMS; PFSA
Diestelhorst, H. Jean 1904-1980 [singer, composer, music publisher]
Note(s): Mrs. John Kirby.
Dale, Jean(ie) *Source(s):* KROH p. 144; LCAR; PSND
Dietger c.1050-1120 [monk, theorist]
Theogerus (von Metz) *Source(s):* LCAR; MACM
Dietz, Howard 1896-1983 [author, lyricist, librettist]
Howard, Dick *Source(s):* ASCP; CCE57; PMUS; STUW
Diez, Stephan 1954- [composer]
Kristan, Anton *Source(s):* KOMP; KOMS; PFSA
DiFiglia, Michael 1943-1987 [choreographer, director]
Bennett, Michael *Source(s):* GAN2; LCAR
Diggs, Robert 196?- [songwriter, performer]
Abbott, (The) *Source(s):* AMUS; LCAR
Digital, Bobby *Source(s):* LCAR
Prince Rakeem *Source(s):* AMUS
RZA *Source(s):* AMUS; LCAR; PMUS-00
Rzarector, The *Source(s):* AMUS; LCAR
Steels, Bobby *Source(s):* AMUS; LCAR
Di Giovanni, Rocco 1924- [composer, author]
Di Giovanni, Rob *Source(s):* CCE47 Eunp
Johnson, Rock *Source(s):* ASCP; CCE65-67; CPOL RE-670-193
Roberts, Bob *Source(s):* CCE56 Eunp
DiGiuseppe, Severino 1919- [composer, author]
D'Joseph, Jac *Source(s):* ASCP
Dill, Horace Eldred 1924- [singer, songwriter]
Dill, Danny *Source(s):* EPMU; MCCL; NASF
Dill, Jack 1889-1939 [songwriter]
Zany, King *Source(s):* CCE21 E520693; CCE52 R97197 ("Wa-Wa-Waddle Walk"); PMUS
DiLorenzo, Randy Paul 1952- [composer, author, singer]
Loren, Randy *Source(s):* ASCP
Dilthey, Wilhelm (Christian Ludwig) 1833-1911 [philosopher, writer on music]
Elkan, K(arl) *Source(s):* GROL; NGDM
Hoffner, Wilhelm *Source(s):* LCAR
Welden, Friedrich *Source(s):* GROL; NGDM
Dimant, Lear [songwriter, performer]
DJ Lethal *Source(s):* AMIR; CPOL PA-1-021-059; PMUS-00
DiMucci, Dion (Francis) 1939- [singer, songwriter]
Dion *Source(s):* ASCP; CM03; LCAR; PSND; STAM
Dinapoli, Mario John 1914- [composer, author, pianist]
Dinapoli, Mike *Source(s):* ASCP; CCE53
Dinarte, Silvio [or Sylvio] 1843-1899 [composer]
Elysio, Flavio *Source(s):* CPMU
Dingemann, Gustav 1915-1988 [composer]
Corn-Corn *Source(s):* PFSA
DiNicola, Joseph 1940- [singer, songwriter]
Dee, Joey *Source(s):* CCE61-62; ROOM; STAM
Dinino, Louis (Lee) 1928- [composer]
Dino Guitar *Source(s):* CCE65
Guitar, Dino *Source(s):* CCE65
Lee, Loye *Source(s):* ASCP
DiRobbio, Armando 1914 (or 15)-1999 [composer]
Al-Dero *Source(s):* CCE65
Dero, Al *Source(s):* ASCP; CCE61; CPOL PA-659-273
Di Sarli, Carlos 1900 (or 03)-1960 [pianist, leader, composer]
Señor del Tango, El *Source(s):* TODO
Disher, Maurice Willson 1893-1969 [theater critic]
Pry, Mr. *Source(s):* CART
Sly, Christopher *Source(s):* CART
Note(s): Also used by James Edward Neild.
Dishinger, Ronald C(hristian) [composer]
Post, S. *Source(s):* http://www.medicimusic.com (16 Oct. 2002)
Vedeski, Anton *Source(s):* http://www.medicimusic.com
Dixon, Eugene 1937- [singer, songwriter]
Chandler, Gene *Source(s):* AMUS; CCE64; CCE67; HARR; PMUS; RECR
Dixon, Floyd 1929- [singer, pianist, songwriter]
Note(s): Do not confuse with others named Floyd Dixon who worked in Texas & Florida clubs during the 1950s-60s (see EPMU).
Dixon, Skeet *Source(s):* HARS; PSND
Riggins, J. Junior *Source(s):* EPMU
Dixon, I. [hymnist]
I. D. *Source(s):* JULN
Dixon, James 1915-1992 [composer, bandleader]
Dixon, Willie *Source(s):* LCAR; PSND
Dixon, Maxwell [rapper]
Grand Puba *Source(s):* AMUS; EPMU
Djemil, Enyss 1917- [violinist, conductor, poet, composer]
Demillac, Francis-Paul *Source(s):* LCAR
Dobbin, Frederick John 1841-1922 [dancer, choreographer]
D'Auban, (Frederick) John *Source(s):* GAN2

Dober, Conrad K. 1891-1938 [composer]
Note(s): Portrait: EWEN
Conrad, Con *Source(s):* CASS; CPMU; EWEN; GAN1; GAN2; HARR; KINK; STUW; VACH
Dobey *Source(s):* http://freespace.virgin.net/m.killy/sing.html (7 Mar. 2005)
Döblin, Alfred 1878-1957 [author]
Poot, Linke *Source(s):* LCAR; PIPE
Dobnek, Johannes 1479-1552 [music theorist, composer]
Cochlaeus, (Johannes) *Source(s):* BAKR; MACM; NGDM
Dobree, Henrietta Octavia (née De Lisle) 1831-1894 [hymnist]
E. O. D. *Source(s):* CYBH
O. E. D. *Source(s):* JULN (Appendix)
Dobrovolny, Frantisek 1890-
Dobro, Frank *Source(s):* http://www.stiefelbein.via.at (port) (16 Oct. 2002)
White Godfather of Black Music, The *Source(s):* http://www.geocities.com/pawisi/link.html (16 Oct. 2002)
Dobrzynski, Walter (Max) 1908- [composer, trombonist, arranger]
Dobschinski, Walter (Max) *Source(s):* LCAR
Telke, (Max) *Source(s):* KOMP; KOMS; PFSA; RIEM; RIES
Dodd, J. D. 1944- [composer, author, singer]
Larrin, Jay *Source(s):* ASCP; CPOL PA-73-310
Dodd, Ken(neth) 1927 (or 29)- [comedian, singer]
Chuckabutty, Professor Yaffle *Source(s):* EPMU
Doddridge, Philip 1702-1751 [minister, hymnist]
Note(s): Portrait: CYBH
D. *Source(s):* JULN
Minister in the Country *Source(s):* LCAR
Dodge, J(ohn) W(ilson) 1873-1925 [composer, singer]
Note(s): Portrait: ETUP 51:1 (Jan. 1933): 4
Britton, David *Source(s):* TPRF; http://www.ibiblio.org/ccer/1924d1.htm
Perry, Chester *Source(s):* CCE51 R78288 ("Miss Caruthers Returns")
Note(s): Jt. pseud.: May Hewes Dodge.
Dodge, May Hewes [composer, violinist, pianist]
Note(s): Portrait: ETUP 51:1 (Jan. 1933): 4
Perry, Chester *Source(s):* CCE51 R78288 ("Miss Caruthers Returns")
Note(s): Jt. pseud.: J(ohn) W(ilson) Dodge.
Dodwell, Samuel [composer]
Phelps, Bernard *Source(s):* CCE24 R27893; CPMU (publication dates 1897-1915)
Doelle, Franz 1883-1965 [composer]
Doelle, Hans *Source(s):* KOMS
Doga, Eugeniu 1937- [composer]
Moldova's Greatest Composer *Source(s):* http://welcome-moldova.com/articles/eugeniu-dogma.shtml (22 Oct. 2003)
Dogan, James 1947-2002 [keyboardist, songwriter]
Dogan, King Sweets *Source(s):* DRSC; http://www.satchmo.com/nolavl/rip2002.html (22 Oct. 2003)
Doinet, Alexis-Victoire 1819-1886? [poet]
Flock, Toby *Source(s):* LAST
Dolan, Charles P. [composer]
Nalod, Charles *Source(s):* REHG
Doldinger, Klaus 1936- [composer]
Nero, Paul *Source(s):* PFSA; RIEM
Note(s): Also used by Kurt Polnarioff.
Dolin, Lynn Marie 1948- [composer, author, singer]
Mann, Lynn *Source(s):* ASCP
Dollison, Maurice [or Morris], (Jr.) 1941- [guitarist, singer, composer]
McCall, Cash *Source(s):* AMUS; CCE68; EPMU; ROOM
Domagalla, Herbert 1916- [composer]
Domus, Peter *Source(s):* CCE68; KOMP; KOMS; PFSA; SUPN
Domenico, Gerhard 1963- [composer]
Angelo, Ninode *Source(s):* PFSA
Domingues, Henrique Foreis 1908-1980 [composer, singer]
Almirante *Source(s):* LCAR; RILM 91-07640-bm
Domino, Antoine 1928- [singer, pianist, songwriter]
Domino, Fats *Source(s):* CM02; EPMU; EWEN (port.); HARR; HARS ; PSND; STAM
Dommnici, Itek 1920- [scriptwriter, lyricist]
Diamond, A. L. *Source(s):* CPOL PAu-33-709
Diamond, Al *Source(s):* ASCP
Diamond, I(sadore) [or I(sidore)] A. L. *Source(s):* PIPE; PSND
Donaggio, Giuseppe 1941- [composer]
Donaggio, P(ino) *Source(s):* CCE61; LCAR; NOMG
Donahue, John Joseph 1888 (or 92) -1930 [actor, dancer, singer, librettist]
Donahue, Jack *Source(s):* GAN2
Donald, Duckworth Bruce Andrew 1951-1984 [singer, songwriter]
Donald, Duck *Source(s):* MCCL
Donegan, Anthony [or Tony] (James) 1931-2002 [singer, songwriter]
Donegan, Lonnie *Source(s):* EPMU; LCAR; MCCL; RECR; WORT
Irish Hillbilly, The *Source(s):* EPMU; MCCL
King of Skiffle Music *Source(s):* EPMU; MCCL
Donez, Ian 1891- [composer, author]
Inez, Dolly *Source(s):* ASCB
Donisthorpe, Ida Margaret Loder 1873- [poet, songwriter]
Pansy *Source(s):* CART

Donnelly, Richard 1892- [songwriter]
Adams, Charles *Source(s):* CCE53
Note(s): Jt. pseud.: Harry Sugarman
Malloy, Mark *Source(s):* CCE51-52; CCE53 Efor22644
Malloys, The *Source(s):* CCE53
Note(s): Jt. pseud.: Mark Malloy [i.e., Richard Donnelly], Harry Sugarman & Charles Henry Forsythe.
Dörflinger, Kurt 1910-1986 [composer]
Collano *Source(s):* KOBW; KOMS; SUPN
Dorfman, Helen Horn 1913-1968 [composer, author, teacher]
Dorfman, Pretty Penny *Source(s):* ASCP
Pretty Penny *Source(s):* CCE61-62; CCE66
Dorham, McKinley Howard 1924-1972 [trumpeter, singer, composer]
Dorham, Kenny *Source(s):* LCAR; PEN2; PSND
Durham, Kenny *Source(s):* LCAR
Doriano, Cleofante [librettist]
Papi, A. *Source(s):* NGDO
Döring, Wilhelm 1887- [composer]
Ringler, Franz *Source(s):* KOBW; OCLC 41887024
Dorn, Heinrich (Ludwig Egmont) 1800 (or 04)-1892 [conductor, composer, critic]
Note(s): Portrait: ETUP 50:12 (Dec. 1932): 877
Music Director, The *Source(s):* NGDM v. 16, p. 833
Dorn, Veeder Van 1946- [composer, author]
Broma, Carleton *Source(s):* ASCP
Conga, Stu *Source(s):* ASCP
Roper, Steve *Source(s):* ASCP
Dorner, Karl 1778-1866 [author, musician]
Markwort, Johann Christian *Source(s):* IBIM; WORB
Doro, Grace 1912-1980 [composer, author]
Lee, Lora *Source(s):* ASCP
Doroshuk, Igor Fedorovich 1904- [composer]
Belza, Igor Fedorovich *Source(s):* BUL2
Dorsey, Bertha (Annabelle) (Gay) 1946-1986 [singer, songwriter]
Falls, Ruby *Source(s):* MCCL
Gay, Bert *Source(s):* CCE55 Eunp; CCE56 Eunp
Gerro, Carol [or Caron] *Source(s):* CCE57-59
Dorsey, Thomas A(ndrew) 1899-1993 [singer, songwriter, pianist]
Source(s): Portrait: HARS
Barrelhouse Tommy *Source(s):* HARS; PEN2; PSND
Dorsey, Georgia Tom *Source(s):* LCAR
Father of Gospel Music *Source(s):* CASS; http://afgen.com/gospel1.html (16 Oct. 2002)
Father of Modern Gospel Music, The *Source(s):* CM11; PSND; SIFA
Georgia Tom *Source(s):* BAKR; CM11; HARS; IBDC; LCAR; PEN2; PSND; SUTT
Memphis Jim *Source(s):* HARS; PSND
Memphis Mose *Source(s):* HARS; IDBC; PSND
Our Irving Berlin *Source(s):* SHAB p. 210; SHAD
Railroad Bill *Source(s):* HARS; IDBC; PSND
Ramsey, George? *Source(s):* HARS; PSND
Smokehouse, Charley *Source(s):* HARS; PSND; SUTT
T. D. *Source(s):* PSND
Texas, Tommy *Source(s):* HARS; PSND
Dôthel, Nicolas [or Niccolò] 1721-1810 [oboist, composer]
Note(s): Identifying Dôthel's works is difficult since James Oswald used an annagram of his name (i.e., Dottel Figlio) on works published in London. (GROL)
Figlio, Il *Source(s):* GROL
Note(s): See also Francesco Biferi.
Dougherty, Genevieve 1888- [composer, author]
Dougherty, Jennie *Source(s):* ASCC; LCCC 1946-54 (see reference)
Douglas, Charles (Laplante) 1956- [composer, singer]
Laplante, Charles *Source(s):* ASCP; CCE78; CPOL PAu-268-408
Douglas, John (Henry) [songwriter]
Hutchinson, Jill *Source(s):* BLIC; CCE53
Douglas, Lizzie 1896 (or 97)-1973 [singer, songwriter, guitarist]
Douglas, Kid *Source(s):* DBMU; HARS; LCAR
Douglas, Minnie *Source(s):* DBMU; HARS; LCAR
Gospel Minnie *Source(s):* DBMU; HARS; LCAR
McCoy, Minnie *Source(s):* DBMU; HARS; LCAR
Memphis Minnie *Source(s):* CM25; DBMU; EPMU; GRAT; HARS; LCAR; MUHF
Texas Tessie *Source(s):* DBMU; HARS; LCAR
Dovenmühle, Richard von der 1920- [composer]
Horn, Roman *Source(s):* CCE64; CCE67
Kuhn, Karl *Source(s):* CCE54-56
Lindt, Rudi *Source(s):* CCE55-58; CPOL RE-300-188; PFSA
Dowell, Horace Kirby 1904-1974 [composer, conductor, saxophonist]
Dowell, Saxie *Source(s):* ASCB; KINK; LCAR; VACH
Downey, (Sean) Morton 1901 (or 02)-1985 [singer, composer, author]
Golden Voiced Irish Tenor, The *Source(s):* PSND
Irish Nightingale, The *Source(s):* PSND
Irish Thrush, The *Source(s):* PSND
Irish Troubadour, The *Source(s):* PSND
Morton, James *Source(s):* MACE p. 554
Downey, (Sean) Morton, Jr. 1933-2001 [composer, author, singer, TV personality]
Downey, Shawn *Source(s):* CCE59
Finch, Calvin *Source(s):* ASCP; CCE60

Mort the Mouth *Source(s): Columbus Dispatch* (Obituary) (13 Mar. 2001)
Downey, Raymond J(oseph) 1912 (or 14)-1993 [composer, author]
Wells, Roy *Source(s):* ASCP; CCE52; CCE61; PSND
Downing, Denis J. 1871?-1909 [journalist, songwriter]
Dick, Dr. *Source(s):* PSND
Dr. Dick *Source(s):* PSND
Dozier, Lamont 1941- [songwriter, record producer]
Anthony, Lamont *Source(s):* EPMU; NGAM
Davis, Lamont *Source(s):* CCE62
H-D-H *Source(s):* LCAR; KICK; SHAD; SOTH
Note(s): Jt. pseud.: Eddie Holland & Brian Holland.
Holland-Dozier-Holland *Source(s):* CM05; EPMU; LCAR; PEN2
Note(s): Jt. pseud.: Eddie Holland & Brian Holland.
Wayne, Edith *Source(s):* http://www.expansionrecords.com/genjohnson.htm (18 May 2005)
Note(s): Jt. pseud.: Eddie Holland & Brian Holland.
Drabek, Kurt 1912- [composer, conductor, accordionist]
Blanchard, Pierre *Source(s):* PFSA; PIPE
Draghi, Antonio 1634 (or 35)-1700 [composer]
Tychian, Joh. Antonio *Source(s):* STGR
Draghi, Giovanni Battista 1710-1736 [composer]
Pergolesi, Giovanni Battista *Source(s):* BAKR; ROOM
Dragon, Daryl 1942- [musician, songwriter]
Captain, The *Source(s):* ALMN; LCAR
Drake, Arthur [composer]
Collard, Arthur *Source(s):* CPMU (publication date 1875)
Drake, Jimmy 1912-1968 [singer, songwriter]
Norvus, Nervous *Source(s):* LCAR; PSND
Drane, Augusta Theodosia 1823-1894 [hymnist]
Frances Raphael, Mother *Source(s):* DIEH; JULN (Suppl.)
Draper, Bourne Hall 1775-1843 [hymnist]
B. H. D. *Source(s):* CYBH
Draper, Farrell H(al) 1923-2003 [singer, guitarist, songwriter]
Draper, Freckles *Source(s):* MCCL
Draper, Rusty *Source(s):* CCE47; LCAR; MCCL
O'l Redhead *Source(s):* MCCL
Singing Emcee *Source(s):* MCCL
Note(s): See also Richard [or Dick] (Alan) Unteed.
Drawbaugh, Jacob W(ilber Jr.) 1928-2000 [composer, author]
Runningbrook, Jim *Source(s):* ASCP
St Onge, Bill *Source(s):* ASCP; CCE57-58
Dräxler, Karl (Ferdinand) 1806-1879 [composer, author]
Claudius, F. C. *Source(s):* LCAR
Claudius, Fr. *Source(s):* LCAR
Klinger, K. L. W. *Source(s):* IBIM; PIPE; WORB
Manfred *Source(s):* IBIM; LCAR; PIPE; WORB
Drayton, William 1959- [songwriter]
Flav, Flavor *Source(s):* LCAR
Flavor Flav *Source(s):* PMUS-90
Drdova, Marie 1889-1970 [composer]
Constans, Constantin *Source(s):* COHN; HIXN
Dreiser, (John) Paul, (Jr.) 1857 (or 58)-1906 [songwriter; publisher; performer]
Note(s): Portraits: BBDP; EWEN; HAMM
Dresser, Paul *Source(s):* BAKR; EWEN; GROL; HARR; KINK; LCAR; VACH
Dressler, Rudolf 1932- [composer, arranger, violinist]
Wiedensal, Uz *Source(s):* BUL3; KOMS; PFSA
Dreves, Guido Maria 1854-1909 [author, composer]
Ulrich von (der) Uhlenhorst *Source(s):* RIEM; WORB
Drexler, Werner 1928- [composer]
Cavallo, Rico *Source(s):* CCE73 Efor165427; CCE76 Efor181485
Duehrer, Walter *Source(s):* CCE76 Efor182279; CCE77 Efor186722
Impertro, Herman *Source(s):* CCE77 Efor186722
Jungert, Werner *Source(s):* CCE61; CCE65; CCE73 Efor165308; KOMS; PFSA
Kent, Roy *Source(s):* CCE67-69; CCE73 Efor165429; CPOL RE-686-954
Kingman, Tony *Source(s):* CCE73
Note(s): Possible typographical error.
Marco, Ralph *Source(s):* CCE73 Efor165303; KOMS; PFSA
Mellini, Peter *Source(s):* CCE73 Efor165306; CCE76 Efor182292
Ringman, Tony *Source(s):* CCE73 Efor165428; CCE77 Efor186726
Dreyfus, Max 1874-1964 [publisher, songwriter]
Note(s): Portrait: SHMM (May/June 1991): 7
Dean of the Music Publishing Business *Source(s):* MARC p. 403
Eugene, Max C. *Source(s):* CCE30 R8256; CCE30R9932; GOLD; SPTH p. 336
Drimcov, Serhij Prokopovyc 1867-1937 [composer, folklorist]
Drimcenko *Source(s):* WORB
Drischel, Peter 1942- [composer]
Peters, Frank *Source(s):* PFSA
Tex, Pete *Source(s):* PFSA
Drocos, Jean fl. early 12th cent. [author, composer]
Dreux, Jean *Source(s):* LYMN
Obadiah the Proselyte *Source(s):* LYMN
Drogin, Barry 1960- [composer]
Skeer, Baruch *Source(s):* http://www.geocities.com/bdrogin/biography.html (16 Oct. 2002)

Droogenbroeck, Jan van 1835-1902 [author, translator]
Ferguut, Jan *Source(s):* LOWN; PIPE; WORB
Drozdowski, Jan 1857 (or 58)-1917 (or 18) [pianist, teacher, writer on music]
Jordan, J(an) (D.) *Source(s):* BAKE; GROL; MACM
Druckman, Ervin M(aurice) 1919-1998 [composer, lyricist]
Note(s): Portrait: EWEN
Drake, Ervin *Source(s):* BBDP; EWEN; IGER; STUW
Morris, Arnold *Source(s):* CCE40 #36518 E88640; CCE68
Druckman, Milton 1916- [songwriter]
Carroll, Harry *Source(s):* CCE32 Eunp60441
Drake, Milton *Source(s):* BBDP (port.); CCE32 Eunp60441
Kent, Walter *Source(s):* CCE32 Eunp60441; CCE32 Eunp31090
Drummond, Algernon [songwriter]
Adew *Source(s):* KILG
Note(s): Jt. pseud.: Evelyn Woodhouse, T. L. Mitchell-Innes & W. J. Cory.
Drusky, Roy (Frank) 1930- [singer, songwriter]
Perry Como of Country Music, The *Source(s):* AMUS
Drysdale, Janey C. [writer, lyricist]
Doune, Ercil *Source(s):* PSND
Dubin, Al(exander) 1891-1945 [composer]
Alexandre, Josef *Source(s):* CCE57
Note(s): Jt. pseud.: Joseph [or Joe] A. Burke.
Dubinsky, Matthew D(avid) 1928- [composer, author]
Dubey, Matt *Source(s):* CCE53-56; PSND
Dubuclet, Laurent 1866-1909 [composer]
Buck, Larry *Source(s):* JASA p. 321
Du Camp, Alphonse 1840-1901 [writer]
Van den Camp, Ferdinand *Source(s):* GOTH
Du Camp Guillebert, Pierre fl. 1534-1555 [singer, composer]
D'Auxerre, Pierre *Source(s):* NGDM
Ducander, Sten Carl 1923- [composer]
Kosta, Ensio *Source(s):* PSND
Dučicć, Jovan 1871 (or 74)-1943 [author, critic]
Divo *Source(s):* PIPE
Ranko *Source(s):* PIPE
Ducis, Benedictus c.1490-1544 [composer]
Benedict(us) *Source(s):* LCAR
Duch, Benedict(us) *Source(s):* BAKE
Dux, Benedictus *Source(s):* GROL; IBIM; WORB
Hartogs, Benoit *Source(s):* WORB
Herzog, Benedikt [or Benedictus] *Source(s):* GROL; IBIM; WORB
Dudley, Leon 1892-1988 [pianist, composer]
Corfiensis, Kaikhosru Catamontanus *Source(s):* LCAR
Sorabji, Kaikhosru Shapurji *Source(s):* NGDM; RIEM; ROOM
Dudley, Walter Bronson 1877-1944 [playwright, lyricist]
Dudley, Bide *Source(s):* ASCP
Duffy, Stephen 1960- [singer, songwriter]
Duffy, Tin Tin *Source(s):* LCAR; WARN
Dugend, Herta 1915-1980 [composer]
Dugend, Enno *Source(s):* KOMP
Duggan, Joseph Francis 1817-1894? [composer]
Beyer, Fred *Source(s):* CPMU; GOTH
Note(s): Do not confuse with Ferdinand Beyer.
Dujardin, Marrianus de c.1460-1529 [composer]
Orto, Marbrianus de *Source(s):* NGDM
Dujmic, Hansi 1956- [composer]
Dew Mitch *Source(s):* KOMU
Mitch, Dew *Source(s):* KOMU
Duke, George Mac 1946- [composer, singer]
Gonga, Dawillie *Source(s):* ASCP
Dukelsky, Vladimir 1903-1969 [composer]
Note(s): Portraits: EWEN; SHMM (Oct. 1986): 38
Duke, Vernon *Source(s):* EPMU; EWEN; GAN2; GROL; NGAM; NGDM; VACH
Ivin, Ivan *Source(s):* Duke, Vernon. *Passport to Paris.* Boston: Little, Brown, 1955, p. 78.
Jekyll and Hyde of Music, The *Source(s):* Duke, Vernon. *Passport to Paris,* p. [3]
Lane, Alan *Source(s):* Duke, Vernon. *Passport to Paris,* p. 78.
Two-Headed Janus of Music, The *Source(s):* Duke, Vernon. *Passport to Paris,* p. [3]
Dula, Henry 1920- [writer]
Palmer, Lynn *Source(s):* GOTH
Dulichius, Philipp(us) 1562-1631 [composer]
Pomeranian Lassus, The *Source(s):* GROL
Teilich, Philipp *Source(s):* LCAR; NGDM
Dumais, Joseph [composer]
DuMay, D'Amour *Source(s):* CPMU (publication date 1914)
Dumont, Charles Frédéric 1916- [composer]
Dalmonte, Carlos *Source(s):* CCE57-58
Dumont, Cecil *Source(s):* CCE51
Dumont, Cedric *Source(s):* CCE53-55
Vanberg, Charles *Source(s):* CCE57-58; CCE60-61; SUPN
Vonberg, Fritz *Source(s):* CCE51; CCE55; CCE58; SUPN
Dumont, Jules Victor Alexandre 1828-1890 [actor, director, producer]
Brasseur, Jules (Victor Alexandre) *Source(s):* GAN2
Dunbar, Lowell Charles 1952- [drummer, songwriter]
Dunbar, Sly *Source(s):* LCAR
Dunbar, Paul Laurence 1872-1906 [poet, author]
Negro Poet Laureate, The *Source(s):* JASZ p. 82

Duncan, Harry (A.) [songwriter]
Duncan, Slim *Source(s):* CCE52; PMUS
Duncan, Ronald (Frederick Henry) 1914-1982 [poet, dramatist]
Bishop of Marsland *Source(s):* PIPE; PSND
Major-General of Marsland *Source(s):* PIPE; PSND
Duncan, Rosetta 1900-1959 [actress, singer, composer]
Topsy *Source(s):* PSND
Dunham, Elmer Lewis 1914-1990 [trumpeter, composer, singer]
Dunham, Sonny *Source(s):* KINK
Dunham, William (D.) 1910-2001 [composer, lyricist, scriptwriter]
Dunham, By *Source(s):* ASCP; CCE55-56; CLTP ("Flipper"); CPOL RE-161-511
Dunkerley, William Arthur 1852-1941 [hymnist]
Dcenham, John *Source(s):* OCLC 36786944
Oxenham, John *Source(s):* CYBH; DIEHL; HUEV
Ross, Julian *Source(s):* CYBH
Dunlap, William 1766-1839 [theater manager, playwright]
Note(s): Portrait: Mates, Julian. *America's Musical Stage*. Westport, CT: Greenwood, 1985.
American, An *Source(s):* PSND
Note(s): See also Joseph Hopkinson.
America's First Professional Playwright *Source(s):* PSND
Author of "The Archers" *Source(s):* MAPN; PSND
Author of "The Father" *Source(s):* MAPN; PSND
Citizen of New York *Source(s):* PSND
Father of American Drama, The *Source(s):* PSND; SIFA
Father of the American Stage *Source(s):* PSND
Dunlop, Isobel 1901-1975 [violinist, composer]
Skelton, Violet *Source(s):* BUL3; COHN; HIXN
Dunn, Sara(h) 1884-1955 [singer, songwriter]
Blues Sensation from the West, The *Source(s):* HARS
Johnson, Margaret *Source(s):* HARS
Note(s): Do not confuse with Margaret Johnson, singer/pianist (Kansas City, MO).
Martin, Sara(h) *Source(s):* GRAT; HARS
Queen of the Blues, The *Source(s):* HARS
Note(s): See also Ruth Lee Jones, Ethel Howard, Koko Taylor [i.e., Cora Walton] & Victoria [or Vicky] (Regina) Spivey.
Roberts, Sally *Source(s):* HARS
Dunstall, Ernest [songwriter]
Rickard, Manny *Source(s):* CCE58
Note(s): Jt. pseud.: Dorothy [i.e., Edna May] Squires.
Dunstaple, John 1370?-1453 [mathematician, composer]
Dunstable, John *Source(s):* PSND

Dúo Vital, Arturo Isidro 1901-1964 [composer]
Duval *Source(s):* http://www.nelsonalfonso.com/sgae/autor/18/contenido.asp (28 Sept. 2003)
Dupin, Paul 1865-1949 [composer]
Lothar, Louis *Source(s):* DEAR; PSND
Duplany, Claude Marius 1850-1896 [author, producer, actor]
Marius, Claude *Source(s):* CPMU
Marius, Mons(ieur) *Source(s):* GAN2
Dupont, Louisa [or Louise] 1913-1998 [singer, songwriter]
Barker, Blue Lu [or Lou] *Source(s):* HARS; LCAR
Barker, (Mrs.) Louisa *Source(s):* LCAR; OB98
Blue, Lu *Source(s):* HARS; OB98
Lu Blue *Source(s):* HARS; LCAR
Dupont, Pierre 1891-1984 [actor, playwright]
Bertin, Pierre *Source(s):* LCAR; PIPE
Note(s): Do not confuse with Pierre Bertin (1899-1979), singer, writer on music, who used the name Pierre Bernac.
Duport, (Nicolas) Paul 1798-1866 [dramatist]
Paulin *Source(s):* PIPE
Duppler, Gerald L. [songwriter]
Tucker, Tommy *Source(s):* CCE62 R290989 ("I Love You, Oh How I Love You"); CCE63-64
Note(s): Do not confuse with Tommy Tucker (1908-). Also used by Robert Higgenbotham (CCE62).
Dupree, William Thomas 1910-1992 [singer, songwriter, guitarist]
Brother Blues *Source(s):* AMUS; CM12; HARS
Champion Jack *Source(s):* http://www.cascadeblues.org/History/ChampionJack.htm (16 Oct. 2002)
Collins, Big Tom *Source(s):* CM12; HARS
Note(s): Also used by Walter Brown McGhee.
Dupree, Champion Jack *Source(s):* CM12; EPMU; HARS; PEN2
Johnson, Blind Boy *Source(s):* CM12; HARS
Johnson, Meathead *Source(s):* AMUS; CM12; HARS
Jordan, Willie *Source(s):* CM12; HARS
Lightnin' Jr. *Source(s):* AMUS; CM12; HARS
Durán Díaz, Gilberto Alejandro 1919-1989 [composer]
Duran, Alejo *Source(s):* IDBC
Durand, Annie 1905-1961 [composer, accordionist]
Parlando Rubato *Source(s):* www.batango.com/spotlight/dale_meyer_.php (14 Mar. 2005)
Note(s): Also used by Dale A. Meyer.
Rubato, Parlando *Source(s):* www.batango.com/spotlight/dale_meyer_.php (14 Mar. 2005)
Duranowsky, Auguste Frédéric c.1770- [composer, violinist]

Durand, Auguste Frédéric *Source(s):* CCE39 #28591 E79024; GRV3; MACM
Durante, James [or Jimmy] (Francis) 1893-1980 [actor, comedian, pianist, songwriter]
Ragtime Jimmy *Source(s):* JAST
Note(s): See also James (V.) Monaco.
Schnoz *Source(s):* CASS; KINK
Schnozzle *Source(s):* CASS
Schnozzola *Source(s):* CASS; KINK
Durell, Edward Henry 1810-1887 [lawyer, writer on music]
Didimus, (H.) *Source(s):* LCAR; STAR p. 130
D'Urfey, Thomas 1653-1723 [playwright, poet, songwriter]
Catcall, (Sir) Critic *Source(s):* CART
D'Uffey, Mr. *Source(s):* CART; LCAR; PSNN
Gabriel, John *Source(s):* PSNN
John, Gabriel *Source(s):* CART
Poet Stutter *Source(s):* CART
T. D., (Gent) *Source(s):* LCAR; PSNN
T. D'U. *Source(s):* PSNN
Duronceray, Marie Justine Benoîte 1727-1772 [singer, actress, dramatist]
Chantilly, (Mlle.) *Source(s):* NGDM
Favart, Marie Justine Benoîte *Source(s):* NGDM
Dusch, Alexander von 1789-1876 [jurist, cellist, writer on music]
Unknown, The *Source(s):* Warrack, John. *Carl Maria von Weber.* 2nd ed. Cambridge: Cambridge University Press, 1976, p. 104.
Düsing, Bernhard 1916- [composer]
Viersen, Arne *Source(s):* BUL3
Dussek, Franz Joseph 1766- [violinist, composer]
Cormundi, Francesco *Source(s):* IBIM; WORB
Dussek, Franz Benedikt *Source(s):* WORB
Duthoit, W(illiam) J(ames) 1885-1966 [composer]
Note(s): In REHG given names: James William; verified OCLC as: W. J.
Dawson, Billy *Source(s):* CCE38 Efor54582 ("Samum"); LCCC 1938-45 (see reference)
Dawson, W. J. *Source(s):* CCE50-51; REHG
Duval, Gabrielle [composer]
Gabrielle D. *Source(s):* CPMU (publication date 1916)
Duval, Georges (J.) 1847-1919 [author]
Rieux, Claude *Source(s):* LCAR; PIPE; WORB
Tabarin *Source(s):* WORB
Duval, Paul Alexandre Martin 1855-1906 [poet, journalist]
Note(s): Some sources lists given names: Martin Paul Alexander.
Bretonne, Raitif de la *Source(s):* WORB
La Bretonne, Raitif de *Source(s):* WORB
LeLorrain, Jacques *Source(s):* CCE34 R29242
Lorrain, Jean *Source(s):* LCAR; LOWN; WORB
Raitif de la Bretonne *Source(s):* WORB
Duverger, Marie Elizabeth 1761-after 1795 [harpist, composer]
Cléry, Mme *Source(s):* LCAR
Duv**, (Mlle.) *Source(s):* DWCO
Duveyrier, Anne Honoré Joseph 1787-1865 [dramatist, librettist]
Mélesville *Source(s):* CPMU; LCAR; MACM; MELL; NGDO; PIPE
Saint-Marc, Amédée de *Source(s):* LCAR
Note(s): Jt. pseud.: (Augustin) Eugène Scribe & Charles Gaspard Delestre-Poirson.
Dvořák, Antonín 1841-1904 [composer]
Composer from Bohemia, The *Source(s):* PSND
Divorceshack *Source(s):* GRAN
Note(s): James G. Huneker's pun on Dvořák's name.
Old Borax *Source(s):* PSND
Dwight, John Sullivan 1813-1893 [music critic, publisher]
Note(s): Portraits: ETUP 51:1 (Jan. 1933): 4; GRAN
Archdeacon of Music *Source(s):* GRAN
Dictator of Musical Boston *Source(s):* STAR p. 161
Father of American Musical Magazines *Source(s):* GRAN
Founding Father of American Musical Magazines *Source(s):* GRAN
J. S. D. *Source(s):* PSND
Dwight, Reginald Kenneth 1947- [singer, pianist, composer]
John, Elton (Hercules) *Source(s):* CM20; DIMA; EPMU; GAMM; HARR; KICK; LCAR
Rocket Man, The *Source(s):* CM20
Tripe, S. *Source(s):* CCE77
Note(s): Pseud. of Elton John [i.e., Reginald Kenneth Dwight]
Dwight, Timothy 1752-1817 [author, hymnist]
Dw *Source(s):* JULN
Dwyer, Everald 1972- [rapper]
Daddy Rings *Source(s):* EPMU
Dykema, Peter W(illiam) 1873-1951 [composer]
Note(s): Portrait: Birge, Edward. *History of Public School Music in the United States*, p. 250.
Peters, William D. *Source(s):* CCE74
Pierre, William *Source(s):* CCE65 R365514-15
Scott, W. D. *Source(s):* CCE65 R3365514-15
Williams, D. P. *Source(s):* CCE65 R3365514-15

– E –

Eager, Mary Ann [composer, author]
Eager, Molly *Source(s):* ASCC; CPOL RE-388-570
Eaglin, Ferd [or Fird], (Jr.) 1936- [guitarist, singer, songwriter]

Eaglin, Blind Snook(s) *Source(s):* HARS; LCAR; PEN2
Eaglin, Ford *Source(s):* HARS; LCAR
Eaglin, Snook(s) *Source(s):* HARS; LCAR; PEN2
Eames, Juanita (Masters) c.1905- [pianist, composer]
Masters, Juan *Source(s):* BUL3; CCE66; COHN; HIXN
Eanes, Homer Robert, (Jr.) 1923-1995 [singer, songwriter]
Bluegrass Balladeer, The *Source(s):* EPMU
Eanes, (Smilin') Jim *Source(s):* EPMU; MCCL
Earle, Steve 1955- [guitarist, songwriter, singer, actor]
Bubba *Source(s):* EPMU
Easton, Amos 1905-1968 [guitarist, singer, songwriter]
Armstrong, Shelley *Source(s):* HARS; LCAR
Bumble Bee Slim *Source(s):* AMUS; EPMU; HARS; LCAR; SHAB p. 116
Eaton, Gerald [singer, songwriter]
Church, Jarvis *Source(s):* http://www.mp3.com/jarvis-church/artists/483918/biography.html (15 Aug. 2005)
Ebeling, Elisabeth 1828-1905 [librarian, literary critic]
Ebeling-Filhés, E. B. *Source(s):* PIPE
Note(s): Jt. pseud.: Bertha Lehman (née Filhés).
Ling, C(hrist) *Source(s):* LCAR; PIPE; WORB
Ebenspanger, Pavao 1903-1941 [musicologist, composer]
Markovac, Pavao [or Paul] *Source(s):* OMUO
Ebersberg, Ottokar Franz 1833-1886 [author]
Berg, O. F. *Source(s):* AEIO; STAD
Eberst, Isaac Juda 1770 (-81)-1850 [composer, teacher]
Offenbach(er, Der) *Source(s):* NGDM (see under: Offenbach, Jacques)
Offenbach, Isaac *Source(s):* LCAR
Eberst, Jacob 1819-1880 [composer]
Note(s): Portraits: GAN2; LYMN
Eberst, Jacques *Source(s):* LCAR
King of Operetta *Source(s):* LYMN
Lange *Source(s):* PIPE
Levy, Jacques *Source(s):* LCAR
Mozart of the Champs-Elysées *Source(s):* MUWB
Offenbach, Jacques *Source(s):* GAN1; GAN2; NGDM
Ebert, Heinz (Helmut(z)) 1911- [composer]
Olivar, Ralf *Source(s):* CCE66-67; KOMP; KOMS; PFSA; REHG; SUPN
Ebsen, Christian (Rudolph [or Rudolf]), (Jr.) 1908-2003 [songwriter, actor, author]
Ebsen, Buddy *Source(s):* ASCP; KINK; LCAR
Eckelmann, Otto 1922- [composer]
Campe, Ronald *Source(s):* CCE65; KOMS; PFSA
Eckhardt, Fritz 1907-1995 [actor, playwright]
Norman, F. E. *Source(s):* PIPE
Paul, Franz *Source(s):* PIPE
Ecking, Samuel 1757-1785 [hymnist]
S. E-k—g *Source(s):* JULN
Eckstein, Maxwell 1905-1974 [composer]
Note(s): Portrait: ETUP 1:3 (Mar. 1933): 148
Carter, David *Source(s):* CCE57-60
Carter, John David *Source(s):* CCE57-60
Ellsworth, Mark *Source(s):* CCE53; CCE55; CCE59-60
Littoff, Maxim *Source(s):* CCE30 E13771; CCE57; GOTH
Eckstein, Pavel 1911-2000 [music critic, author, administrator]
Slezák, Petr *Source(s):* GROL
Eckstein, William Clarence 1914-1993 [singer, bandleader, composer]
Eckstine, Billy *Source(s):* LCAR; PFSA
Mr. B. *Source(s):* LCAR
Eckstein, Willie 1888-1963 [pianist, songwriter]
Note(s): Portrait: JASA
Boy Paderewski, The *Source(s):* VGRC
Mr. Fingers *Source(s):* VGRC
Palmer, Vi *Source(s):* VGRC
Note(s): Also used by Zez [i.e., Edward Elzear] Confrey.
World's Foremost Motion Picture Interpreter, The *Source(s):* VGRC
Eddis, Ellen [hymnist]
E. E. *Source(s):* JULN
Note(s): Probably wife of Edward William Eddis. In his: *Hymns for the Use of the Churches.*
Edelmann, Rudi 1948- [composer]
Morgan, Manfred *Source(s):* PFSA
Edelstein, Walter 1903-1992 [composer, violinist]
Eddy, Walter *Source(s):* ASCP; CCE77
Ederer, Josef 1932- [composer]
Ederer, Pepe *Source(s):* PFSA
Pit *Source(s):* CCE63 Efor91134; KOMS; PFSA
Till, Rocky *Source(s):* CCE73-74; PFSA
Edinger, Eddie Ross [composer]
Black Face *Source(s):* CCE27 E535648
Ross, Black Face Eddie *Source(s):* JASG; JASR
Ross, Eddie *Source(s):* CCE30 Eunp29219-20; JASG; JASR
Edison, Harry (E.) 1915-1999 [composer, trumpeter, bandleader]
Edison, Sweets *Source(s):* ASCP; CCE60; KINK; LCAR
Sweets *Source(s):* CCE74
Edler, Robert 1912- [composer]
Orrel, Max *Source(s):* KOMP
Edmonds, Kenneth 1959- [songwriter, singer]
Architect of Early 1990s Black Pop *Source(s):* CM12 p.v

Babyface *Source(s):* CM12; CPOL PA-722-435; EPMU; HARD; HARR; LCAR
Edstrom, Everett 1915-2000 [conductor, music publisher]
Note(s): For explanation of how the following names were used, see http://www.halleonard.com, (select: "About Us")
Edstrom, Leonard *Source(s):* http://www.halleonard.com (6 Oct. 2002)
Leonard, Hal *Source(s):* http://www.halleonard.com
Note(s): See also Harold Edstrom.
Edstrom, Harold [composer, music publisher]
Note(s): For explanation of how the following names were used, see http://www.halleonard.com, (select: "About Us")
Edstrom, Hal *Source(s):* MCBD; http://www.halleonard.com (6 Oct. 2002)
Leonard, Hal *Source(s):* REHG; http://www.halleonard.com
Note(s): See also Leonard Edstrom.
Edwards, C(harles) J(oseph) [songwriter]
Ferguson, Harry *Source(s):* CCE32 Efor23919; CCE59
Jones, Hirem *Source(s):* CCE36 Efor43964
Note(s): Jt. pseud.: Harold Elton Box, Paddy [i.e., John Godfrey Owen] Roberts & Ralph (T.) Butler.
Lang, Carl *Source(s):* CCE28 E685937; CCE55 R151262 ("Kow-Tow")
Lloyd, George *Source(s):* LCPC Efor28676 & Efor28780; CCE60
Note(s): For titles of works composed under joint pseuds., See NOTES: Lloyd, George.
Perch, Polly *Source(s):* CCE34 Efor37471 ("Scratch-A-Poll-Polly")
Note(s): Jt. pseud.: Harold Elton Box, Desmond Cox [i.e., Adrian Keuleman] & Ralph (T.) Butler.
Seeley, Philip *Source(s):* CCE58; LCPC letter cited (4 Jan. 1930)
Wallis, C. Jay *Source(s):* CCE30 Efor8733; LCPC letter cited (4 Jan. 1930)
Note(s): Jt. pseud.: Julian Wright, Ralph (T.) Butler & Gustav Krenkel.
Edwards, Clifton (A.) 1895-1971 [ukulele player, singer, songwriter]
Note(s): Several sources list first given name as Clifford.
Clifford, Ed *Source(s):* MACE; SUTT
Note(s): Also used by Vernon Dalhart [i.e., M(arion) T(ry) Slaughter]
Clifton, Edward *Source(s):* MACE; SUTT
Harris, Harry *Source(s):* SUTT (2nd ed.)
Note(s): Also used by Vernon Dalhart [i.e., M(arion) T(ry) Slaughter]
Ike *Source(s):* SUTT
Spencer, Samuel *Source(s):* MACE; SUTT
Note(s): Also used by Arthur Fields [i.e., Abe Finkelstein]
Ukulele Ike *Source(s):* CASS; EPMU; GAMM; KINK; MACE; PEN2; SUTT
Edwards, David 1915- [guitarist, songwriter, singer]
Edwards, Honeyboy *Source(s):* HARS; LCAR
Honey Eddy [or Eddie] *Source(s):* HARS
Honey, Mr. *Source(s):* HARS
Honeyboy *Source(s):* HARS
Mr. Honey *Source(s):* HARS
Edwards, Eric (Charles) 1910-2005 [singer, songwriter]
Alberta Slim *Source(s):* CPOL RE-100-032; http://www.albertaslim.com (17 Jan. 2005)
Hank Snow of the Prairies *Source(s):* http://www.albertaslim.com
Slim, Alberta *Source(s):* http://www.albertaslim.com
Yodeling Cowboy, The *Source(s):* http://www.albertaslim.com
Note(s): See also James [or Jimmie] (Charles) Rodgers.
Edwards, Frenchy 1929-1997 [singer, songwriter]
Edwards, Stoney *Source(s):* AMUS; EPMU; MCCL
Edwards, Joe [or Jody] 1895 (or 97)-1967 [entertainer, songwriter]
Butterbeans *Source(s):* CCE31 Eunp49869; LCAR
Note(s): See also Wilson Wesley.
Edwards, Butterbeans *Source(s):* LCAR; PSND
Edwards, Melinda [songwriter]
Fisher, Edward *Source(s):* CCE73; CCE74 E333224
Greyson, Norman LCCC77 E363002 & E366500
Note(s): Jt. pseud.: Walter (Charles) Ehret; see NOTES: Greyson, Norman.
Edwards, Thomas Jay 1954- [composer, author, singer]
Edwards, Tex *Source(s):* ASCP
Edwards, Webley Elgin 1902-1977 [composer, author]
Kalapana, John *Source(s):* ASCP
Edwards, Wilfred 1938 (or 40)-1992 [singer, songwriter]
Edwards, Jackie *Source(s):* EPMU; HARD; PEN2
Original Cool Ruler, The *Source(s):* EPMU
Egli, David Christian 1937- [lyricist]
Christian, David *Source(s):* ASCP (see reference)
Dias, David Vaz *Source(s):* ASCP
Egnatzik, Joseph (P.) 1920-1983 [composer, author, bassist]
Nelson, Sandy *Source(s):* ASCP; CCE59-60
Egstrom, (Norma) Dolores 1920-2002 [singer, actress, composer]

Lee, Peggy *Source(s):* BAKR; CM08; EPMU; GAMM; GRAT; KINK; LCAR; PSND
Melton, Susan *Source(s):* http://www.geocities.com/~peggyfan/gb0003.html (6 Oct. 2002)
Queen of American Pop Music, The *Source(s):* PSND
Eguchi, Gengo [composer]
Eguchi, Yoshi *Source(s):* REHH
Ehrenberg, Siegfried 1847-1897 [author, translator]
Carlotta, (Dr.) C(arl) *Source(s):* LOWN
Ehrenhaus, Martin 1858- [writer on music]
Erhardt, Otto *Source(s):* MUBR
Ehrenreich, Rudolph 1936- [composer, saxophonist]
Ehrenreich, Teddy *Source(s):* OMUO
Ehret, Walter (Charles) 1918- [composer]
Alexandrov, Feodor *Source(s):* CCE63 E1733535; CPOL RE-524-089 & RE-623-707
Note(s): Jt. pseud.: Elmer (F(ranklin)) Kinsman.
Barlow, (S.) Stephen *Source(s):* CCE63 E180306; CCE64 E252731; CCE67
Barrie, Walter *Source(s):* CCE58; CCE59 E128570; CPOL RE-287-590
Bergstrom, Eric *Source(s):* CCE67 E226320
Brooks, Byron *Source(s):* CPOL RE-360-401
Brulovsky, Nicolai *Source(s):* CCE63 E173351; CCE65 E210708; CPOL RE-520-038
Note(s): Jt. pseud.: Elmer (F(ranklin)) Kinsman.
Cable, Howard LCCC72 E304063
Note(s): Possible pseud. On publication: "Howard Cable, arranger," on copyright application: "arr. Walter Ehret."
Carlton, John *Source(s):* CCE58; CCE60; CPOL RE-296-436
Note(s): Also jt. pseud. with several individuals; see NOTES: Carlton, John.
Chambers, Robert *Source(s):* CCE61; CCE63 E171094
Note(s): Also jt. pseud. with several individuals; see NOTES: Chambers, Robert.
Charles, Gregg *Source(s):* CCE60 E145307-8; CCE65
Note(s): Jt. pseud.: Elmer (F(ranklin)) Kinsman.
Chase, Paul *Source(s):* CCE77 E376630
Churchill, Kenneth *Source(s):* CCE54 E82287; CPOL RE-129-278
Note(s): Jt. pseud.: John Raymond. "April Is in My Mistress' Face" CCE54 E83112; "Crucifixus" (Bach, S232) CCE54 E82287; "Hospodi pomiui" (Lvov) CCE54 E77945. Do not confuse with Kenneth Churchill (works published by C. F. Summy)?
Cramer, John *Source(s):* CCE56, CCE58-60; CCE65; CPOL RE-208-495
Creston, William *Source(s):* CCE61 E149158 ("Heavenly Sight")
Note(s): Also used as jt. pseud.: Elmer (F(ranklin)) Kinsman; for titles see: Kinsman
Cummings, David *Source(s):* CCE57 E110652; CCE58 E119160; CPOL RE-259-302
Davids, Dean *Source(s):* CCE52-53; CCE56-59; CCE61-64; CPOL RE-144-832
Davis, Lee *Source(s):* CCE77 E376462
Dickinson, Richard *Source(s):* CCE59 E131485; CCE61 E156404; CPOL RE-353-096
Note(s): Jt. pseud.: (Helen) Joyce (Holloway) Barthelson.
Douglas, Wayne *Source(s):* CCE55; CCE57-64
Note(s): Also used by Douglas Wayne Broze, Edward J. Penney, Jr. & Fred Weber; see NOTES: Douglas, Wayne. Do not confuse with singer Wayne Douglas [i.e., Doug Sham] (1941-1999).
Drake, Janet *Source(s):* CCE62 E162273; CCE63 E170546
Note(s): Jt. pseud.: (Helen) Joyce (Holloway) Barthelson.
Dunsmore, William *Source(s):* CCE62; CCE65 E202870; CCE67; CCE73 E314041
Elkins, Charles *Source(s):* CPOL RE-352-924
Note(s): Jt. pseud.: Elmer (F(ranklin)) Kinsman.
Ellison, Glenn *Source(s):* CCE57 E112814; CPOL RE-265-892
Field, Robert *Source(s):* CCE64 E92237; CCE65 E200175; CPOL RE-529-377
Note(s): Also jt. pseud.: Ivan Trusler; "Requiem, op. 48" (Faure) CPOL RE-483-993.
Follett, Charles *Source(s):* CCE62-64
Note(s): Also jt. pseud.: Elmer (F(ranklin)) Kinsman; see NOTES: Follett, Charles.
For(r)ester, Roger *Source(s):* CCE64 E183602; CCE65 E198177; CCE74 E328151
Granville, Roger *Source(s):* CCE58; CCE64-65; CCE67 E230177; CPOL RE-308-696
Greyson, Norman *Source(s):* LCCC77 E66315, E376450 & E363002
Note(s): Also jt. pseuds.: Harry Robert Wilson & also Melinda Edwards; see NOTES: Greyson, Norman.
Hardwicke, Arthur *Source(s):* CCE67 E226233; CPOL PA-18-319
Harper, Richard *Source(s):* CPOL RE-357-886
Hastings, Paul *Source(s):* CPOL RE-291-334; LCCC58 E14629
Note(s): Also jt. pseud.: Elmer (F(ranklin)) Kinsman; see NOTES: Hastings, Paul.
Hilton, Arthur *Source(s):* LCCC 1955-70 (see reference)
Note(s): Also jt. pseud. with several individuals; see NOTES: Hilton, Arthur.
Holloway, Jay *Source(s):* CCE56 E102084
Hornibrook, Wallace *Source(s):* CPOL RE-452-368

Jüngst, Hugo *Source(s):* CCE58 E211810; CCE66
Kenwal, Ernest *Source(s):* CCE55 E86929 ("Jacob's Ladder")
Note(s): Jt. pseud.: Kenneth Walton.
Kingsbury, John *Source(s):* CCE75 E336240; CPOL PA-3-425; LCAR
Kingsley, Lorrain *Source(s):* CCE55; CPOL RE-147-540; LCCC54 E83762
Knight, Gerald *Source(s):* CCE64; CCE65 E208707; CCE66 E224154
Note(s): Jt. pseud.: Harry R. Wilson.
Kolar, Andreas *Source(s):* CCE64 E189208 & E189211
Note(s): Jt. pseud.: Elmer (F(ranklin)) Kinsman.
Martin, Jean *Source(s):* CCE65 E201152 & E197311 & E199771
Note(s): "Three Cowboy Songs" & "3 Thanksgiving Hymns" & "3 Easter Hymns" Also jt. pseud.: (Helen) Joyce Barthelson; for titles see: Barthelson. Also used by Marcel Stellman.
Martin, Walter *Source(s):* CCE61 E159611
Martin, William *Source(s):* CCE59-60; CCE62; CCE66-67; CPOL RE-335-162
Milanov, Dimitri *Source(s):* CCE63 172850; CPOL RE-520-041; CPOL RE-624-260
Note(s): Jt. pseud.: Elmer (F(ranklin)) Kinsman.
Morris, William *Source(s):* CCE60 E145309; CCE64 E189207; CCE64 E189209; CCE65 E203609
Note(s): Jt. pseud.: Elmer (F(ranklin)) Kinsman. Do not confuse with William Morris, author of lyrics for "The Shepherd's Story," (music by Clarence Dickson) (renewal 1960) & composer/lyricist of "Two Sides to Every Story."
Norton, Wallace *Source(s):* CCE56-58; CPOL RE-259-319
Pace, Warren *Source(s):* CCE61 E150579; CPOL RE-448-377
Preston, Robert *Source(s):* CCE64 E220963; CCE74 E335514; CCE76 E350279
Richardson, John (A.) *Source(s):* CCE67 E245895; CCE71 E289124; CCE76E359632
Riggs, Edward *Source(s):* CPOL RE-299-473
Note(s): Jt. pseud.: Edward Ryglewicz.
Robinson, Allan *Source(s):* CCE59 E128522
Romaine, Earl *Source(s):* CPOL RE-360-392
Sawhill, Philip *Source(s):* CCE76 E370069
Schmidt, Marie *Source(s):* CCE66-67
Shaw, Roger *Source(s):* CPOL RE-353-359
Sokolov, Ivan *Source(s):* CCE63 E173694; CPOL RE-524-385
Note(s): Jt. pseud.: Elmer (F(ranklin)) Kinsman.
Spence, Robert *Source(s):* CPOL RE-360-394
Spencer, William *Source(s):* CCE58; CPOL RE-308-427
Note(s): Jt. pseud.: Lee Kjelson.
Steele, Paul *Source(s):* CCE56; CCE58-60
Stockton, Robert *Source(s):* CPOL RE-360-394; CCE74 E334583
Sumner, Robert *Source(s):* CCE60 E146491; CCE62 E167968
Thompson, David *Source(s):* CCE59 E130565; CPOL RE-291-321 & 322; CPOL RE-291-326
Note(s): Also jt. pseud.: Harold (Stillwill) Stark; see NOTES: Thompson, David.
Thompson, Ronald *Source(s):* CCE59; CCE61 E162284 & E1622831; CCE62
Note(s): Jt. pseud.: Kenneth Walton.
Wadsworth, Charles *Source(s):* CCE67 E233073
Warren, Thomas *Source(s):* CCE60 E137945
Williamson, Warren *Source(s):* CCE60; CCE66 E233280; CCE67 E238144
Note(s): Also jt. pseud.: Elmer (F(ranklin)) Kinsman; see NOTES: Williamson, Warren.
Windsor, Richard *Source(s):* CPOL RE-357-879
Wright, Richard *Source(s):* CPOL RE-360-383

Ehrlinger, Hans 1931- [composer]
Erlando, J. *Source(s):* KOMP
Flat, G. *Source(s):* KOMP; PFSA

Eibenschütz, Julius 1875- [librettist, composer]
Evelyn, Julius *Source(s):* IBIM; STGR; WORB

Eimer, A(ugust) C(harles) 1845- [composer, organist]
Remie, A. (C.) *Source(s):* CCE12 E299635; KROH p. 124; LCAR

Einhorn, Barbara (Belle) 1922- [writer, producer, songwriter]
Belle, Barbara *Source(s):* CCE44 #7086 Eunp364873; CCE72 R532369; GRAT

Eisen, Paul Stanley 1952- [singer, songwriter]
Stanley, Paul *Source(s):* HARR

Eisenschitz, Friedrich 1881- [librettist]
Pal, Friedrich *Source(s):* STGR

Eisler, Lawrence 1919 (or 20)- [author, actor, playwright]
Lawrence, Eddie *Source(s):* ASCP; CPOL Pau-1-589-040; LCAR

Eisner, Betty Grover 1915-2004 [psychologist, author, lyricist]
Rev. B. *Source(s):* CCE75; PSND
Reverend B. *Source(s):* CCE76

Ekberg, Ulf [songwriter]
Buddha *Source(s):* SONG
Ekberg, Buddha *Source(s):* CPOL
Ekberg, Joker *Source(s):* CPOL
Joker *Source(s):* CPOL PA-663-100

Elam, Dave Alexander 1938- [pianist, composer]
Alexander, Dave *Source(s):* EPMU

Elam, Keith [songwriter, performer]
Guru *Source(s):* AMIR; CPOL PA-954-757; LCAR; PMUS-00

Elbogen, Friedrich 1854-1909 [composer]
Lorrow, Friedrich *Source(s):* COMP

Eler(s), Franz after 1500-1590 [teacher, composer]
Ulisseus *Source(s):* NGDM
Elgar, (Sir) Edward 1857-1934 [composer]
Britain's Greatest Composer *Source(s):* http://www.geocities.com/hansenk69/conclusion.html (28 Sept. 2003)
Edu *Source(s):* http://www.music.pomona.edu/orchestra/ELG_EN12.HTM (3 Feb. 2005)
England's Greatest Composer *Source(s):* http://www.stratford.co.uk/elgar/elgar.html (7 Oct. 2002)
Note(s): See also Henry Purcell & (Sir) Arthur S(eymour) Sullivan.
Francke, Gustav *Source(s):* BLIC
Figurehead of Music in England *Source(s):* SIFA
Mardon, Richard *Source(s):* http://www.hyperion.records.co.uk/notes/67019.html (17 Nov. 2002)
One of the Seven Humbugs of Christendom *Source(s):* SIFA
Queen Victoria's Favorite Composer *Source(s):* PSND; SIFA
Elias, Salomon fl. c.1274 [monk, writer on music]
Salomonis *Source(s):* BAKE
Elizabeth, Queen of Romania 1843-1916 [librettist]
Carmen Sylva *Source(s):* ROOM
Laroc, P. de *Source(s):* MELL
Sylva, Carmen *Source(s):* LCAR; LOWN
Ellerbock, Charles [composer]
C. E. *Source(s):* SPTH p. 144+ ("Maryland, My Maryland" (orig. 1861 ed.))
Ellidge, Robert (Wyatt) 1945- [singer, songwriter]
Wyatt, Robert *Source(s):* CM24; DIMA; PEN2
Ellingford, Herbert Frederick 1876-1966 [composer, author, organist]
Winter, Herbert *Source(s):* PSND
Ellington, Edward Kennedy 1899-1974 [composer, bandleader, pianist]
Note(s): Portraits: CM02; EWEN
Ellington, Duke *Source(s):* CASS; CM02; EPMU; EWEN; HARR; IDBC; KINK; NGDM
Elliott, Alonzo 1891-1964 [composer, author, publisher]
Note(s): Portraits: ETUP 58:2 (Feb. 1940): 79; ETUP 58:8 (Aug. 1940): 570
Elliott, Zo *Source(s):* ASCC; FULD; GOTL; LCAR; SMIN
Elliott, Charlotte 1789-1871 [poet, hymnist]
Note(s): Portrait: CYBH
C. E. *Source(s):* JULN; PSND
Carefree Charlotte *Source(s):* http://www.workersforjesus.com/just.htm (3 Feb. 2005)
Florenz *Source(s):* LCAR
Lady, A *Source(s):* PSND
Note(s): Also used by Stephen Collins Foster, Ann Home & Julia Ward Howe.
Elliott, Ebeneezer 1781-1849 [hymnist]
Corn Law Rhymer *Source(s):* LCAR; ROGG
Elliott, John (B.) 1907- [composer, author]
Moon, Jack *Source(s):* ASCP; CCE59; CCE62; CCE65-66
Elliott, Marion [singer, songwriter]
Poly Styrene *Source(s):* EPMU
Styrene, Poly *Source(s):* AMUS
Elliott, Marjorie (Reeve) 1890-1980 [composer, author]
Fay, Sinclair *Source(s):* ASCP; CCE54-56
Reeve, Billy *Source(s):* CCE43 #45047 Eunp35649; CCE60; CCE62
Reeve, Fox *Source(s):* ASCP; CCE53-55; CCE58-60
Takeda, Ayo *Source(s):* CCE57; CCE59
Elliott, Melissa 1972- [songwriter, composer, talent scout]
Elliott, Misdemeanor *Source(s):* EPMU
Elliott, Missy *Source(s):* LCAR
Missy *Source(s):* CPOL PA-1-066-672
Elliott, Percy 1871-1932 [composer, violinist, composer, conductor]
Bush, Walter *Source(s):* CCE44 #35637, 1017 R131638; MUWB
Newark, Godfrey *Source(s):* CCE49 R4277 ("Camouflage"); MUWB
Ellis, Donald Johnson 1934- [composer]
Johnson, Donald *Source(s):* BUL3
Ellis, Royston 1941- [writer on music]
Devine, Raynard *Source(s):* LCAR
Tresillian, Richard *Source(s):* CART
Ellis, Russell E. [composer, lyricist]
King, Tyrone *Source(s):* TPRF
Note(s): On lyrics.
Ellis, Seger 1904 (or 06)-1995 [singer, pianist, songwriter]
Note(s): Verified in KINK as a songwriter.
Blue, Bud *Source(s):* Tosches, Nick. *Where Dead Voices Gather*. Boston: Little, Brown, 2002.
Haddon, Charles *Source(s):* SUTT
Hays, Charles *Source(s):* SUTT
Houston, Harry *Source(s):* Tosches, Nick. (see above)
Lisle, Ernest *Source(s):* SUTT
Staiger, Arthur *Source(s):* SUTT
Terry, Arthur *Source(s):* SUTT
Thorne, Norman(d) *Source(s):* SUTT
Ellis, Vesphew Benton 1917-1988 [clergyman, songwriter]
Note(s): Portrait: SGMA
Benton, Hugh *Source(s):* CCE51
Ellis, Vep *Source(s):* CCE51; PSND

Ellis, Wilbert Thirkield 1914-1977 [pianist, songwriter]
Big Boy *Source(s):* HARS
Big Chief *Source(s):* HARS
Ellis, Big Boy *Source(s):* HARS
Ellis, Big Chief *Source(s):* HARS; LCAR
Ellison, Byrwec [writer on music]
Bündler, David *Source(s):* NOTE 52:4 (1996): 1230
Ellmenreich, Albert 1816-1905 [composer]
Ehrich, M. L. *Source(s):* MELL; STGR
Ellwood, Florence [composer]
Natalie *Source(s):* BLIC; CPMU; OCLC 48701505
Elsbeth, Thomas ?-after 1624 [composer]
Neapolitanus Francus *Source(s):* GROL
Note(s): Called himself.
Elsmo, Ralph Norman 1919-1992 [composer, author]
Norman, Rolf *Source(s):* ASCP
Elson, Louis (Charles) 1848-1920 [music critic,author]
Note(s): Portrait: ETUP 51:2 (Feb. 1933): 78
American Critic with the Most Citations in Slonimsky's *Lexicon of Musical Invective* *Source(s):* GRAN
Embree, Charles B., Jr. 1919- [composer, author]
Embree, Riff *Source(s):* ASCP
Emetz, Joana 1945- [composer]
Joana *Source(s):* PFSA
Emmett, Dan(iel Decatur) 1815-1904 [entertainer, composer]
Note(s): Portraits: EWEN; EWPS; HOWD
Blossom, Jerry *Source(s):* LCAR; STUW
Dixie, Jr. *Source(s):* LCAR; STUW
Emmit, Old Dan D. *Source(s):* SPTH p. 94; STUW
Father of "Dixie," The *Source(s):* PSND
Father of the Minstrel Show, The *Source(s):* EWEN; STUW
Young Dixie *Source(s):* Title page of "Way Down in Dixie"
Ende, Harald 1929- [composer]
Hitman, Harold *Source(s):* KOMP; PFSA
Enders, Karl ?-1627 [composer]
Andreae, Carolus *Source(s):* NGDM
F. C. A.. *Source(s):* NGDM
Note(s): Initials for: Frater Carolus Andrae.
Endsley, Gerald [writer on music, conductor, composer, arranger]
St. James, Melvyn *Source(s):* http://www.dmamusic.org/tromba (23 Mar. 2005)
EnEarl, William Allan 1946- [composer, author, singer]
Earl, Billy *Source(s):* ASCP; CCE59-60
Enescu, Georges 1881-1955 [composer]
Romania's Greatest Composer *Source(s):* http://www.bbc.co.uk/radio3/classical/profiles/enescu.shtml (26 Sept. 2003)

Engel, Alexander 1868 (or 69)-1940 [playwright]
Cavoret, Alfred *Source(s):* PIPE
Mira, Paul *Source(s):* PIPE
Engel, Carl 1883-1944 [musicologist, librarian, composer]
Note(s): Portraits: ETUP 51:3 (Mar. 1933): 148; MUSA 34:6 (4 June 1921): 25. Do not confuse with Carl Engel (1818-1882) musical historiographer.
Angeli, Carlo d' *Source(s):* CCE39 #15639, 501 R76489
Carle, Glen *Source(s):* CCE39 #15693, 501 R76489
East, Milford *Source(s):* CCE58 R207106 ("Sleepers Awake! A Voice Is Sounding")
Jefferson, Munrow *Source(s):* CCE42 #7833 E101484
Kamoto, Igushi *Source(s):* LCPC letter cited (25 Oct. 1934)
Kingsley, Rutherford *Source(s):* CCE45 #40244, 103 R140052; CCE50 R61702 ("Five Basque Noëls")
Marshall, John *Source(s):* LCPC letter cited (25 Oct. 1934)
Martel, John *Source(s):* CCE47 R9025 ("Love Lights")
Melville, E. B. *Source(s):* CCE49 R41829 ("Bless the Lord")
Mitchell, Humphrey *Source(s):* LCPC letter cited (25 Oct. 1934)
Perrin, Jacques *Source(s):* CCE44 #51525, 114 R133548; LCAR
Spear, Howard *Source(s):* LCPC E483160
Spier, Howard *Source(s):* LCPC letter cited (25 Oct. 1934)
Warren, P(eter) C(onway) *Source(s):* CCE48 R38393 ("Six Songs"); CCE48 R38391 ("Spring Song")
West, George *Source(s):* CCE47 R15419 ("Bird Song"); LCPC letter cited (25 Oct. 1934)
Engel, Detlev 1936-1985 [composer]
Boettcher, Gerd *Source(s):* PFSA
Engel, Hartmut 1961- [composer]
Engel, Valentine *Source(s):* KOMS; PFSA
Engel (de Jánosi), Josef [or Joseph] 1851- [writer on music]
Sinoja, J. E. (de) *Source(s):* LCAR; SEND; WORB
Engel, Julius (Dimitrievich) 1868-1927 [composer, arranger]
Engel, Joel *Source(s):* LCAR; LYMN
Engel, Y(uly) *Source(s):* LCAR; LYMN
Engel, Louis [music critic]
L. E. *Source(s):* PSND
Engel, Noel Scott 1943- [singer, songwriter]
Walker, Scott *Source(s):* EPMU; HARR; LCAR
Engelhardt, Karl August 1768-1834 [poet]
Roos, Richard *Source(s):* LAST
Engelmann, Gabriele 1924- [composer]
Schneider, Gaby *Source(s):* KOMS

Engelmann, H(ans) 1872-1914 [composer]
Note(s): Portraits: ETUP 50:12 (Dec. 1932): 848; ETUP 51:3 (Mar. 1933): 148
Boysen, Alice *Source(s):* CCE40 #15093, 535 R8306
Engel, Heinrich *Source(s):* CCE29 R2180; TPRF
Garland, A. *Source(s):* CCE38 R63159; CCE46 R11902 ("Two Christmas Melodies"); TPRF
Godfrey, D. S. *Source(s):* CCE47 R19635 ("Iola Gavotte"); TPRF
Holcombe, L. V. *Source(s):* CCE28 R42912; TPRF
Lindsay, Charles *Source(s):* CCE35 R35244; TPRF
Renard, Pierre *Source(s):* CCE35 R35970; TPRF
Wolf, Carl *Source(s):* CCE35 R35365; TPRF
Engelmann, Johann Christoph 1754-1815 [violinist, actor, singer, composer]
Kaffka, Johann Christoph *Source(s):* BAKO; GOTH; IBIM; MACM; NGDO; SONN; WORB
Kawka, Johann Christoph *Source(s):* BAKO; IBIM; MACM
Engelmann, Joseph 1720-1796 [violinist, composer]
Kaffka, Joseph *Source(s):* MACM
Engelmann, Wilhelm 1752-1806 [violinist, composer]
Kaffka, Wilhelm *Source(s):* MACM
Kawka, Wilhelm *Source(s):* WORB
Engländer, Ludwig 1853-1914 [composer]
American Strauss *Source(s):* WCAB 14:518
Engländer, Richard 1859-1919 [author]
Altenberg, Peter *Source(s):* LCAR; PIPE
English, Thomas Dunn 1819-1902 [poet, lyricist]
Note(s): See LCAR for nonmusic-related pseudonyms.
Brigadier *Source(s):* MAPN
C. B. *Source(s):* MAPN
Herbert, Francis *Source(s):* MAPN
Eno, Brian 1948- [composer, producer]
Note(s): See CM08 for complete listing of Eno's given names.
Creator of Ambient Music, The *Source(s):* CM08 p. v
Inventor of Ambient, The *Source(s):* http://news.bbc.co.uk/hi/english/static/events/millennium/apr/guest2.stm (6 Oct. 2002)
Enright, Edmund 1976- [singer, songwriter]
Mundy *Source(s):* EPMU
Enticknap, Clifford 1920- [composer, composer medium]
Handel, Georg Frederick (Spirit) *Source(s):* DEAR3 p. 226
Entner, Josef 1897-after1950 [playwright, translator]
Brodecký *Source(s):* PIPE
Enzler, Josef 1884-1976 [composer]
Seffel, X. *Source(s):* REHH; SUPN
Eoff, Kenneth Dale, Jr. 1951- [singer, songwriter]
Dale, Kenny *Source(s):* MCCL
Epae, Nicholas 1932-1994 [singer, songwriter]
Epae, Jay *Source(s):* DRSC
Ephrem Syrus c.309-373 [preacher, poet]
Lyre of the Holy Spirit, The *Source(s):* GROL
Epin de Groot, Else-Antonia van 1919- [composer]
Laren, Derek *Source(s):* BUL3 (see under: Groot, Epen de); GREN
Epps, Clarence Bradley 1905-1972 [choreographer, teacher]
Bradley, Buddy *Source(s):* GAN2
Epshtein, Michail Semjonowitsch 1903-1949 [author]
Golodny, Michail *Source(s):* LCAR; PIPE
Epstein, Judith Sue 1947- [poet, songwriter]
Judy Sue *Source(s):* PSND
Epstein, Melvin 1923-1998 [pianist, arranger, composer]
Jackson, Shoeless Joe *Source(s):* JAMU
Powell, Mel *Source(s):* AMUS; EPMU; LCAR; NGDJ
Erbe, Raimond 1932- [composer]
Simon, Frank *Source(s):* KOMS; PFSA
Erby, John J. 1902- [instrumentalist, songwriter]
Seymour, George *Source(s):* HARS
Singing Pianist, The *Source(s):* HARS
Smith, Guy *Source(s):* HARS
Suddoth, J. Guy *Source(s):* HARS
Erckmann, Emile 1822-1899 [librettist]
Erckmann-Chatrian, (MM) *Source(s):* LCAR; LOWN; WORB
Note(s): Jt. pseud.: Pierre Alexandre Chatrain.
Erdoedy, Luisa (Countess) (née Drasche-Wartingerg) 1853- [pianist, composer]
Lios *Source(s):* COHN; HIXN
Erhardt, Siegfried (Marian Johann) 1907- [composer]
Erard, Jean *Source(s):* CCE49-50; RIES
Erickson, Roger Kynard 1947- [singer, songwriter]
Erickson, Roky *Source(s):* CM16; EPMU; LCAR
Erlanger, Frédéric d' 1868-1943 [composer]
Note(s): Portrait: *Musical Standard* (14 Mar. 1903)
Regnal, Frédéric *Source(s):* CPMU; GROL; MACM; NGDM; NGDO; PIPE; STGR
Ringel, Federico *Source(s):* MACM
Erlanger, Ludwig (von) 1862- [composer, librettist]
Langer, R. *Source(s):* MACM; STGR; WORB
Erlank, Willem Jacobus du Plooy [composer]
Eitemal *Source(s):* CPMU (publication date 1932); LCAR
Erlebach, Rudy 1894-1955 [pianist, composer]
Herzog, Dorothy *Source(s):* http://www.player-care.com/rollhist.html (18 June 2005)
Erler, Hermann 1844-1918 [composer]
Morley, Charles *Source(s):* COMP
Reichel, Bernhard *Source(s):* COMP
Scherz, Ernst *Source(s):* COMP

Ernst(-Meister), A(delheid) S(iegrid) 1929- [composer, pianist, conductor]
Meister, Siegrid *Source(s):* BUL3; HIX
Ernst, II, Duke of Saxe-Coburg-Gotha 1818-1893 [author]
E. H. z S. (C. G.) *Source(s):* CPMU
N. von K. *Source(s):* MELL
Wernhard, Otto *Source(s):* MELL
Ertegun, Ahmet (Munir) 1923- [songwriter, producer]
Greatest Rock and Roll Mogul in the World *Source(s):* CM10; PSNN
Nugetre, (A.) *Source(s):* CCE55-56; CCE63; PSNN; SHAB p. 185; WARN
Ervin, Difosca 1939-1995 [singer, songwriter]
Irwin, Big Dee *Source(s):* AMUS; EPMU
Erwin, George 1913-1981 [composer, trumpeter, bandleader]
Dooley, "Big Jeb" *Source(s):* JAMU
Erwin, Pee Wee *Source(s):* ALMN; ASCP; CCE62; KINK; LCAR
Irwin, Pee Wee *Source(s):* LCAR
Escajadillo, Alejandro 1969- [singer, songwriter, leader]
Syntek, Aleks *Source(s):* HWOM
Escardot, L. 1865- [playwright, composer]
Karr y de Alfonsetté, Carmen *Source(s):* COHN (addendum); HIXN
Eschborn, Georgine Christine M. 1828-1911 [singer, composer]
Eschorn, Nina *Source(s):* http://www.theatrelibrary.org/sibmas/idpac/europe/des026.html (1 Feb. 2005)
Koenneritz, Nina von *Source(s):* http://www.theatrelibrary.org/sibmas/idpac/europe/des026.html
Escobar, Pedro de c.1465-1535 [composer, singer]
Porto, Pedro do *Source(s):* LCAR
Puerto, Pedro del *Source(s):* LCAR
Escovedo, Sheila 1959- [singer, drummer, songwriter]
Sheila E. *Source(s):* CM03; EPMU; STAM
Escudier, Marie-Pierre Pascal 1809 (or 11)-1880 [music publisher, political writer]
Note(s): Used pseuds.; to date, only the following name identified.
Diplomate, Un *Source(s):* GROL
Eskelin, Rodney [singer, songwriter]
Keith, Rodd *Source(s):* http://www.observer.com/pages/story.asp?ID=6959 (10 Oct. 2003)
Espe, Walter 1895- [composer]
Corzilius, Victor *Source(s):* MACM
Espero, Ignacio Fernandez *see* Fernandez Espero, Ignacio
Espina, Angel Beaunoni 1923- [singer, composer, actor, poet]
Espina, Noni *Source(s):* PSND; WORB
Espósito, Genaro Ricardo 1886-1944 [bandoneonist, guitarist, pianist, composer]
Tano Genaro, El *Source(s):* TODO
Espre, Andrus 1956 (or 57)-1999 [accordionist, singer, songwriter]
Jocque, Beau *Source(s):* AMUS; LCAR; MUHF; OB99
Esquivel, Juan Garcia c.1919-2002 [pianist, composer, arranger}
Godfather of Lounge *Source(s):* http://www.citybeat.com/archives/1996/issue231/cover12.html (6 Oct. 2002)
Esrum-Hellerup, Dag Henrik [fictitious composer] *Source(s):* GROL
Essex, Frederick 1875?-1951 [composer, actor]
Whitlock, Billy *Source(s):* PSND
Esterhazy, (Countess) Alexandrine c.1849-1919 [composer, librettist]
Ertis *Source(s):* COHN; HIXN; MELL; STGR
Esteves, Erasmo 1941- [lyricist]
Carlos, Erasmo *Source(s):* CCE66-68; PEN2 (see under: Carlos, Roberto)
Erasmo *Source(s):* LCAR
Esteves, Joseph [or José], (Jr.) 1921-1988 [bandleader, arranger, pianist]
Loco, Joe *Source(s):* AMUS; CCE54; CCE63; PEN2; PSND
Eszterházy von Galántha, Paul 1635-1713 [composer]
Estores de Galanta *Source(s):* IBIM; WORB
Otto *Source(s):* IBIM; WORB
Etheridge, Melissa (Lou) 1961- [singer, songwriter]
Female Bruce Springsteen *Source(s):* CM16
Ettema, Theo 1906-1991 [composer]
Dean, Folk *Source(s):* NEDM
Etzel, Hans Joachim 1925- [composer]
Etzel, Roy *Source(s):* KOMP; KOMS
Europe, James Reese 1881-1919 [bandleader, songwriter]
Note(s): Portrait: JASZ
Eporu & Yenbad *Source(s):* PERF
Note(s): Jt. pseud.: Ford (T.) Dabney.
Yenbad, Eporue *Source(s):* SHAB
Note(s): Jt. pseud.: Ford (T.) Dabney.
Evans, David 1874-1948 [organist, composer]
Arthur, Edward *Source(s):* CPMU; HUEV
Evans, David [or Dave] 1961- [songwriter]
Edge, (The) *Source(s):* AMUS; PMUS-95; PMUS-00
Evans, Ernest 1941- [songwriter, singer]
Checker, Chubby *Source(s):* ASCP; CASS; CCE64; LCAR; SOTH
Twist King, The *Source(s):* WHIC (see under Checker)

Evans, George 1870-1915 [composer, entertainer]
Evans, Honey Boy *Source(s):* FULD; KINK; MARC p. 169; SPTH; STUW
Honey Boy *Source(s):* LCAR
Evans, Hal [songwriter]
Henley, Peter *Source(s):* MUWB
Evans, James Harrington 1785-1849 [vicar, hymnist]
Alix *Source(s):* JULN
Evans, Jonathan 1748 (or 49)-1809 [clergyman, hymnist]
Foleshill *Source(s):* JULN
J. E., (Coventry) *Source(s):* JULN
Evans, (Harry) Lindley 1895-1982 [pianist, composer]
Mr. Melody Man *Source(s):* Glennon, James. *Australian Music and Musicians.* Adelaide: Rigby, 1968.
Evans, Louis 1912-1972 [composer, author, music publisher, recording producer]
Evans, Redd *Source(s):* ASCC; LCAR; STUW
Evans, Mary Ann [or Marian] 1819-1880 [author]
Note(s): See PSND for additional nonmusic-related pseudonyms.
Cross, Mary Ann [or Marian] *Source(s):* GOTE; LCAR
Eliot, George *Source(s):* GOTE; LCAR; PSND
Evans, Merle (Slease) 1891 (or 94)-1987 [composer, cornetist]
Gabriel of the Circus *Source(s):* SMIN
Toscanini of the Big Top *Source(s):* REHG; SMIN
Will Rogers of the Cornetists *Source(s):* SMIN
Evans, Paul Wesley 1907-1977 [cornetist, composer, arranger]
Evans, Doc *Source(s):* EPMU; LCAR
Evans, Sydney 1901-1978 [songwriter]
Chard, Evan *Source(s):* CCE36 Efor41419; CCE63
Evans, Tolchard (B.) *Source(s):* CASS; HARD; HARR; MUWB
Stanley, Eugene *Source(s):* CCE62 R304036
Note(s): Jt. pseud.: Ralph (T.) Butler & S(tanley) J. Damerell [i.e., Jack Stevens]
Evans, William [or Bill] 1920 (or 21)- [saxophonist, composer, author]
Constantino, Monroe "Bones" *Source(s):* GROL
Gentle Joe *Source(s):* GROL
Lateef, Yusef (Abdul) *Source(s):* CM16; EPMU; LCAR; NGDJ; PEN2
Evans, William Robert, III 1940- [composer, arranger]
Evans, Butch *Source(s):* ASCP; CPOL PAu-421-081
Evans, Yasmin 1963- [singer, songwriter]
Yazz *Source(s):* EPMU; LCAR
Everett, Augusta F. H. [songwriter]
A. F. H. E. *Source(s):* CPMU (publication date 1909)
Everett, Mark (Oliver) 1963- [singer, songwriter]
E *Source(s):* CPOL PA-563-240; NOMG
Evert, Johannes 1888-1945 [composer]
Sykes, John *Source(s):* SUPN
Verta, Jose *Source(s):* SUPN
Eville, Vernon [composer]
Note(s): ETUP 51:3 (Mar. 1933): 148
Reinhardt, Ed *Source(s):* TPRF
Ewart, Florence Maud(e) (née Donaldson) 1864-1949 [composer]
Note(s): Used additional pseuds., various combinations of her name; however, only the following identified.
Alden, Sonia *Source(s):* DWCO; GROL; NGDO
Ewing, Donald Ralph 1964 (or 65)- [singer, songwriter]
Ewing, Skip *Source(s):* AMUS; ENCM; EPMU; MCCL
Ewing, Montague (George) 1890-1957 [composer, composer]
Note(s): Portrait: ETUP 51:3 (Mar. 1933): 148
Avon, Rex *Source(s):* CCE40 #25109 Efor63273
Carrington, Herbert *Source(s):* CCE32
Chaventre, Pierre *Source(s):* CCE34 Efor34210
Clark, Olive *Source(s):* CCE53; CCE62 Efor27604
Hoffman, Paul *Source(s):* CCE34 Efor35519; CCE59
Myers, Sherman *Source(s):* CCE65; GAMM; MUWB; REHH
Reid, Buddy *Source(s):* CCE59
Solano, R(amon) *Source(s):* CCE37 Efor46595; CCE53; CCE64
Vaughan, Hilary *Source(s):* CCE60
Exposito, Homero 1918-1987 [poet, lyricist]
Exposito, Mimo *Source(s):* TODO
Mimo *Source(s):* TODO
Eybel, Joseph Valentin (Sebastian) 1741-1805 [author]
Meisel *Source(s):* PIPE
Reiner *Source(s):* PIPE
Eyherabide, Carlos Alberto 1923-1989 [singer, author, composer]
Adrian, Eduardo *Source(s):* TOGO

– F –

Fabbri, Filippo (Ortensio) [librettist]
Scirtoriano, Alindo *Source(s):* MORI
Fabbrini, Giuseppe ?-1708 [composer, organist]
Armonico, L' *Source(s):* GROL; NGDM
Faber, Frederick William 1814-1863 [cleric, hymnist]
Note(s): Portrait: CYBH
Parish Priest, A. *Source(s):* CART
Faber, Heinrich before 1500-1552 [rector, music theorist, composer]

Fabri, Henrici *Source(s):* LCAR
Lichtenfels, Hainrich *Source(s):* GROL; LCAR; NGDM
Fabri, Annibale Pio 1697-1760 [singer, composer]
Balino, (Annibale Pio) *Source(s):* GRV5; MACM; NGDM
Fabricus-Bjerre, Bent 1924- [pianist, composer]
Bjorn, Frank *Source(s):* CCE62-63; EPMU
Fabric, Bent *Source(s):* CCE63; EPMU; LCAR
Graves, Bert *Source(s):* CCE63-64
Fagan, Gideon 1904-1980 [composer, arranger, conductor]
Diggenjof [or Diggenhof], (Albert) *Source(s):* CCE52; CCE57; MUSR
Fagan, Thomas O. 1936- [composer, singer]
Dell, Tommy *Source(s):* ASCP
Fagan, Dell *Source(s):* CCE62
Fagas, James [or Jimmie] 1924-1982 [composer, conductor, arranger]
Phagas, Dimitmos *Source(s):* ASCP
Fagenson, Donald c.1952?- [singer, songwriter, bassist]
Was, Don(ald) *Source(s):* CM21; LCAR; PEN2; PMUS; WARN
Fago, (Francesco) Nicola 1677-1745 [composer, teacher]
Tarantino, Il *Source(s):* LCAR; MACM; MELL; NGDM; PSND; STGR
Fago, Pasquale c.1740-1794 [composer]
Tarantino, Pasquale *Source(s):* NGDM
Fahey, John (Aloysius) 1939-2001 [guitarist, composer]
Blind Joe Death *Source(s):* PEN1; *Guitar Player* 30:321:9 (1996): 46
Blind Thomas *Source(s):* LCAR (see note)
Death, Blind Joe *Source(s):* PEN1; *Guitar Player* 30:321:9 (1996): 46
Fahey, Siobhan 1957- [singer, songwriter]
Bananarama *Source(s):* CPOL PA-343-491; SONG
Note(s): Jt. pseud.: Sarah Dallin & Keren Woodward.
Shakespears Sister *Source(s):* PEN2
Fahy, Francis Arthur 1854-1935 [poet, author, songwriter]
Dreoilin *Source(s):* PSND
Fairchild, Edgar 1898 (or 99)-1975 [composer, pianist, conductor]
Fairchild, Cooky *Source(s):* PSND
Faith, Percy 1908-1976 [pianist, arranger]
Mars, Peter *Source(s):* CCE78 R675210; CLAS
Note(s): In a renewal record for "Theme for Colgate Song Contest" Peter Mars is listed as a pseud. of Percy Faith; however, Faith experts feel it is an error.
Falco, Michele (de) 1688?-after 1732 [composer]
DeFalco, Michele *Source(s):* WORB
Melfiche, Cola *Source(s):* MELL; NGDM; WORB
Falconi(o), Placido c.1530-after 1600 [composer]
Falconio d'Asola *Source(s):* IBIM; WORB
Monacho Cassinensi Euphemiano *Source(s):* GRV3
Falk, Dieter 1959- [composer, publisher]
Baer, Herman de *Source(s):* KOMS; PFSA
Falk, Johannes Daniel 1768-1826 [author, publisher, teacher]
Ostsee, Johannes von der *Source(s):* PIPE
Von Der Oster, Johannes *Source(s):* PSND
Falla, Manuel de 1876-1946 [composer]
Spanish Gershwin, The *Source(s):* CASS
Fallet, Ed(o)uard Marius 1904- [writer on music]
Domusbricenis *Source(s):* WORB
Familia, Alfonso [singer, songwriter]
Familia, Pochy *Source(s):* HWOM
Fanch, James 1704-1767 [minister, hymnist]
F. *Source(s):* JULN
Fanciulli, Giuseppe 1881-1951 [composer]
Chichibio *Source(s):* WORB
Gapone, Maestro *Source(s):* STGR
Fane, John 1784-1859 [soldier, diplomat, musician]
Note(s): Portrait: ETUP 51:4 (Apr. 1933): 222
Burghersh, Lord *Source(s):* GOTH; LCAR; NGDM
Officer Employed in His Army, An *Source(s):* CART
Westmoreland, (John Fane), Earl of *Source(s):* GOTH; NGDM
Faning, Joseph Eaton 1850-1927 [composer]
E. F. *Source(s):* CPMU
Fanning, Cecil 1883-1931 [singer, composer]
Poet Singer of Ohio, The *Source(s):* ETUP 51:4 (Apr. 1933): 222 (port)
Faracchio, John Joseph, Jr. 1912?-2004 [singer, songwriter]
Farrow, Johnny *Source(s):* DRSC
Farfaro, Nicolò ?-before 1647 [humanist, writer on music]
Mazzaferro, Giorgio *Source(s):* GDRM; GROL; NGDM
Farjeon, (Eve) Annabel 1919- [ballet critic, author]
Jefferson, Sarah *Source(s):* PSND
Farmer, Marjorie 1921- [composer]
Connor, Mary *Source(s):* CCE78; CPOL PA-4-981
Dingwag, Brob *Source(s):* CPOL TX-601-562
Ericson, Julia *Source(s):* CPOL PA-151-988
Note(s): Jt. pseud.: James (Franklin) Leisy.
Farmer, J. M. *Source(s):* CPOL RE-236-142
Goose, M. *Source(s):* CCE61
Hunter, Ima Spouse *Source(s):* CPOL RE-249-064
J. M. *Source(s):* CCE64; CCE66-68; CPOL RE-249-064
Lambert, Jack *Source(s):* CCE78; CPOL PA-1-542
Merman, Joyce *Source(s):* CCE74; CCE78; CPOL RE-249-064

Morgan, John A. *Source(s):* CCE77
Wright, Stella *Source(s):* CPOL PA-52-002
Farnon, Dennis 1923- [instrumentalist, arranger, composer]
Gerard, Paul *Source(s):* CCE71; MUWB
Miller, Chris *Source(s):* CCE58
Farnon, Robert [or Bob] (Joseph) 1917-2005 [composer, conductor, arranger]
Dean of Light Music Composers *Source(s):* http://www.classicthemes.com/LMHOF.shtml (4 Oct. 2002)
Jensen, Ole *Source(s):* RFSO
Note(s): Possibly used by other conductors.
Light Music's Greatest Living Legend *Source(s):* RFSO
Farr, Michael (George) 1941-1996 [songwriter]
Leander, Mike *Source(s):* CCE66-67; OB96; PMUS; ROOM
Farr, Thomas Hubert 1903-1980 [singer, songwriter, fiddler, guitarist]
Farr, Hugh *Source(s):* LCAR; MCCL
Farrell, Michael John 1845-1901 [singer, lyricist]
Farrell, Hastings Gilbert *Source(s):* GARR
Macdermott, G. H. *Source(s):* GARR
Fascinato, Arthur L. 1915-1994 [arranger, conductor, pianist]
Fascinato, Jack *Source(s):* CLTP ("Ding Dong School"); IMDB
Fass, Bernard [or Bernie] 1932- [composer, author]
Halsman, David *Source(s):* ASCP; CCE68
Taylor, Bernie *Source(s):* ASCP; CCE68; CCE73-74
Faster, Oscar 1854-1931 [composer, conductor]
Note(s): Portrait: ETUP 51:5 (May 1933): 292
Fetrás, Oscar *Source(s):* GREN; LCAR; NGDM; SUPN; WORB
Johann Strauss of North Germany *Source(s):* ETUP 51:5 (May 1933): 292
Fauré, Gabriel Urbain 1845-1924 [composer]
Robespierre *Source(s):* CASS; GROL; NGDM
Note(s): See also Hector Berlioz.
Favart, Charles Simon 1710-1792 [librettist, playwright]
***, Mr. *Source(s):* OCLC 22394760 ("La fée urgele")
Matthews *Source(s):* NGDM, v. 6 p. 438
Favourite, Larry Lee 1939?-2001 [songwriter]
Lee, Larry *Source(s):* CCE75-76; *Country Music International* 8:8 (Aug. 2001): 10
Fawcett, John 1739 (or 40)-1817 [hymnist]
Note(s): Portrait: CYBH
Christopholus *Source(s):* HATF
Fawkes, Walter (or Wally) (Ernest) 1924- [clarinetist, cartoonist]
Trog *Source(s):* GROL
Feather, Leonard (Geoffrey) 1914-1994 [writer on jazz, composer, arranger]
Chavarria, Angelo *Source(s):* CCE62
Guerrero, Luciano *Source(s):* CCE62
Jackson, LeRoy *Source(s):* CCE62 ("Whisper Not")
Note(s): Also used by John Kinyon.
Little Brother *Source(s):* JAMU
Note(s): Also used by Nat(haniel) Adderley & Eurreal Wilford Montgmery.
Lopes, Papa *Source(s):* CCE62
Machado, Jack *Source(s):* CCE62
Moore, Billy *Source(s):* GROL
Note(s): Do not confuse with Billy [i.e., William] Moore (1917-1987), arranger, pianist.
Quintana, Carlos *Source(s):* CCE62
Febland, Nicholas 1960- [keyboardist, composer]
Land, Jon *Source(s):* EPMU
Fede, Johannes c.1415-?1477 [composer]
Sohier, Jean [or Johannes] *Source(s):* NGDM; WORB
Fedeli, Carlo ?-1686 [composer]
Saion(i), Carlo *Source(s):* WORB
Sajon, (Carlo) *Source(s):* ALMC; MELL
Note(s): See also Ruggiero Fedeli.
Fedeli, Giuseppe fl. 1680-1733 [composer, trombonist]
Saggione, Giuseppe *Source(s):* NGDM; WORB
Saggione, Joseph *Source(s):* LCAR
Saggione venetiano *Source(s):* NGDM
Fedeli, Ruggiero c.1655-1722 [composer, conductor]
Sajon *Source(s):* ALMC
Note(s): See also Carlo Fedeli.
Sogino *Source(s):* ALMC
Federer, Ralph 1906-1971 [composer, pianist, teacher]
Note(s): Portrait: ETUP 58:8 (Aug. 1940): 570
West, Morgan *Source(s):* TPRF
Federici, Vincenzo 1764-1826 [composer]
Marchi, Antonio *Source(s):* MELL
Federico, Gen(n)aro Antonio ?-c. 1743 [librettist]
Nelli, Jacopo Anigoti *Source(s):* STGR
Feigenbaum, Benjamin 1860-1932 [songwriter]
Feigenbaum, Ziske *Source(s):* HESK
Feinberg, Samuel 1902-1989 [composer, pianist]
Note(s): Portraits: ETUP 51:4 (Apr. 1933): 222; EWEN
Crooning Composer, The *Source(s):* PSND
Fain, Sammy *Source(s):* EPMU; EWEN; GAMM; GAN1; GAN2; HARR; LCAR; PEN2
Note(s): See SUTT for a list of jt. pseuds. with Artie Dunn on recordings.
Feind, Barthold 1678-1721 [poet, librettist, lawyer]
Aristobulos Eutropius *Source(s):* MELL; NGDM, NGDO; PIPE
Wahrmund *Source(s):* NGDM, NGDO; PIPE
Feinstein, Buddy 1912-1998 [singer, dancer, lyricist]
Feyne, Buddy *Source(s):* http://buddyfeyne.com/history.html#20 (21 Dec. 2004)

Felber, Rudolph 1891- [composer, author, playwright]
Fuerb, Raoul *Source(s):* PSND
Feld, Mark 1947-1977 [singer, composer]
Bolan, Marc *Source(s):* CASS; EPMU; GAMM; HARR; LCAR; PEN2; ROOM
Bowland, Mark *Source(s):* ROOM
Godfather of Glam Rock, The *Source(s):* http://www.superscript.co/uk/marchome/lists.html (6 Oct. 2002)
Note(s): See also David Bowie [i.e., David Robert (Hayward) Jones]
Riggs, Mark *Source(s):* ROOM
Tyler, Toby *Source(s):* EPMU; RECR; ROOM
Felder, Jerome (Solon) 1925-1991 [songwriter]
Pomus, Doc *Source(s):* CM14; EPMU; HARR; PEN2
Pomus, Jerome *Source(s):* PEN2; PMUS
Feldman, Al(exander) 1915- [songwriter]
Alexander, Van *Source(s):* EPMU; LCAR; PMUS; PSNN
Feldman, Joshua 1922-1980 [composer, arranger]
Fielding, Jerry *Source(s):* KINK; PSND
Feldner, Roberta Emily 1939- [lyricist, singer]
Carr, Roberta *Source(s):* ASCP
Stuart, Roberta *Source(s):* ASCP
Feldstein, Saul 1940- [composer, author, teacher]
Feldstein, Sandy *Source(s):* ASCP; LCAR
Felgen, Camillo 1920- [composer]
Nicolas, (Jean) *Source(s):* CCE60-63; PFSA
Felix, Margery [or Marjorie] Edith 1907- [composer, writer on music]
Consey, Jill *Source(s):* BUL3; COHN; HIXN
Conway, Jill *Source(s):* CCE56
Dawe, Margery *Source(s):* BUL3; CCE67-68; COHN; CPMU; HIXN
Medway, Carol *Source(s):* BUL3; COHN; HIXN
Fellows, Floyd George 1907-1982 [composer, author]
Frank, George *Source(s):* ASCP
Fellows, John ?-1785 [hymnist]
F—s *Source(s):* JULN
Philanthropos *Source(s):* LCAR; PSND
Note(s): See also Richard Pockrich.
Fels, Joachim 1823-1871 [composer, music critic, teacher]
Hagen, Teodor *Source(s):* MACM; WORB
Felton, William M. 1887- [songwriter]
Note(s): Portrait: ETUP 51:4 (Apr. 1933): 222
Borne, Francis *Source(s):* CCE41 #14246 E92054; TPRF
Hodson, William *Source(s):* CCE41 #14246 E92054; TPRF
Sears, Billy *Source(s):* CCE60
Felts, (Albert) Narvel 1938- [singer, songwriter, guitarist]
Narvel the Marvel *Source(s):* MCCL
Feltz, Kurt (August Karl) 1910-1982 [author, music publisher, librettist]
Bartels, Johnny *Source(s):* CCE54-58; CPOL RE-242-066; PIPE; RIES
Clemens, Paul *Source(s):* CCE52; CPOL RE-108-940
Hahnen, Josef *Source(s):* CCE54-55; CPOL RE-94-677
Hauer, Charlie *Source(s):* CCE54-55
Hennerich, Harry CCE54; CCE55 Efor38524
Hoff, André *Source(s):* CCE52-55; CPOL RE-55-962
Note(s): Jt. pseud.: Franzleo Andries.
Korten, Hans *Source(s):* CCE53-54; CCE56-57; CCE60-62
Note(s): Jt. pseud.: Franzleo Andries.
Plaschky, Hanno *Source(s):* CCE54-55; CPOL RE-183-282
Schönauer, Leopold *Source(s):* CCE54-55
Stein, Walter *Source(s):* CCE50; CCE55
Villinger, Axel *Source(s):* CCE54-55
Fennell, Frederick 1914-2004 [conductor, educator, writer on music]
Godfather of Wind Bands, The *Source(s):* http://www.econcertband.com/fanfare/jul-94.html (6 Oct. 2002)
Fenster, Harry 1919- [composer, author, singer]
Fenster, Tex *Source(s):* ASCP
Fequa, Carl [composer]
Carlton, Carl *Source(s):* http://www.angelfire.com/tx/masonmusic/marchwrite.html (6 Oct. 2002)
Note(s): See under: "March Composers."
Ferguson, Maynard 1928- [trumpeter, bandleader, composer, arranger]
Brown, Tiger *Source(s):* JAMU
Maynard, Buddy *Source(s):* JAMU
Fermoselle, Juan de 1468-1529 (or 30) [poet, dramatist, composer]
Encina, Juan del *Source(s):* NGDM
Fernández, Jorge Renales 1916-1983 [author]
Campos, Jorge *Source(s):* LCAR; PIPE
Fernández, Juan Carlos [singer, songwriter, guitarist]
Rabito *Source(s):* HWOM
Fernández Esperón, Ignacio 1894-1968 [composer]
Nacho, Tata *Source(s):* BUL3; CCE73 R559968; GREN; HWOM; LCAR
Fernandez Ortiz, Benito Antonio 1901-1983 [singer, guitarist; songwriter]
Saquito, Nico *Source(s):* EPMU; LCAR
Fernbach, Johannes 1926-2004 [composer, conductor]
Fehring, Johannes *Source(s):* CCE50; CCE57; OMUO; PFSA, RIES

Ferneyhough, Brian (John Peter) 1943- [composer]
Godfather of the "New Complexity" Movement
Source(s): http://www.geocities.com/SoHo/Den/2293/ferneyhough.html (6 Oct. 2002)
Ferrand, Humbert 1805-1868 [writer; librettist]
Arandas, George *Source(s):* GOTH
Ferrari, Benedetto 1603 (or 04)-1681 [composer; librettist]
Benedatto da Parma *Source(s):* NGDM
Benedetto dalla Tiorba *Source(s):* WORB
Dalla Tiorba *Source(s):* BAKO; BAKR; MACM; PSND
Ferrari dalla Tiorba, (Benedetto) *Source(s):* LCAR; NGDM; NGDO; SADC
Valentini, F. *Source(s):* STGR
Ferrari, Girolamo 1599-after 1664 [composer]
Girolamo, da Mondondone *Source(s):* LCAR
Hieronimo, de Mondondone *Source(s):* LCAR
Ferrazano, Anthony Joseph 1937 (or 38)-2001 [composer, author, pianist]
Ferris, Anthony J. *Sources(s):* CCE59
Zano, (A(nthony)) (J(oseph)) *Source(s):* ASCP; BUL3; CCE59; CCE63; DRSC
Ferreira, Jorge [composer, singer]
Canario (del amargue) *Source(s):* HWOM
Note(s): See also José Alberto Justiniano.
Ferri Llopis, Luis Manuel 1946-1973 [singer, songwriter]
Bravo, Nino *Source(s):* HWOM; http://www.ninobravo.com (24 Feb. 2005)
Ferté, E. Joubert de la [composer]
E. J. De La F. *Source(s):* CCE15 E351520; CPMU
Fett, Armin 1911- [composer]
Lüders, Hans *Source(s):* CCE53; KOMPS; PFSA
Feuchtwanger, Lion (Jacob Arje) 1884-1958 [author; playwright]
Wetcheek, J. L. *Source(s):* PIPE; PSND
Feuillet, Octave 1821-1890 [author]
Hazard, Désiré *Source(s):* PIPE; PSND
Note(s): Jt. pseud.: Paul Bocage & Albert Aubert.
Fiallo, David [singer, songwriter]
Ángel del amargue, El *Source(s):* HWOM
Fibich, Zděnek 1850-1900 [composer]
Note(s): Portraits: ETUP 55:5 (May 1933): 202; EWCY
Mihuczeni, Giovanni *Source(s):* GROL
Fickl, Paul 1943- [composer, arranger]
Fields, Paul *Source(s):* OMUO
Fiedler, Friedrich 1859-1917 [playwright; translator]
Alm *Source(s):* PIPE
Flider *Source(s):* PIPE
Florian *Source(s):* PIPE
Note(s): Also used by Paul Flem(m)ing.
Field, Henry Ibbot 1797-1848 [pianist, compser]
Field of Bath *Source(s):* GRVN
Field, John 1782-1837 [composer]
Note(s): Portraits: ETUP 38:3 (Mar. 1940): 154; EWCY; GRV3 v. 1
Field, Russian *Source(s):* PSND
Russian Field *Source(s):* PSND
Fielding, Henry 1707-1754 [burlesque writer, novelist, essayist]
Note(s): See PSND for additional pseudonyms and sobriquets.
Adams, Abraham *Source(s):* CART
C. and L. *Source(s):* CART
Drawcansir, (Sir) Alexander Knt., Censor of Great Britain *Source(s):* CART; LCAR
Grub, Stephen *Source(s):* CART
Gulliver, Lemuel, (Poet Laureate to the King of Lilliput) *Source(s):* CART; LCAR; PSND
Keyber, Mr. Conny *Source(s):* CART; LCAR
Lover of His Country, A. *Source(s):* CART
P. H. I. Z. C. G. S. *Source(s):* CART
Pasquin *Source(s):* CART
Philalethes *Source(s):* CART
Sans Esprit, Monsieur *Source(s):* CART
Scriblerus Secundus, (H) *Source(s):* CART; PSND; ROOM; SONN
Secundus, Scriblerus *Source(s):* LCAR
Trott-Plaid, John *Source(s):* CART
Vinegar, (Capt.) Hercules, (of Hockley in the Hole) *Source(s):* CART; LCAR; PSND
Fields, Arthur B. 1889-1965 [composer, author, agent]
Note(s): Do not confuse with Arthur Fields [i.e., Abe Finkelstein], 1888-1953, composer, author, actor. See editions of *ASCAP Dictionary* for songs by Arthur B. (Buddy) Fields.
Fields, Buddy *Source(s):* ASCP; CCE31 E23097; LCAR; VACH
Fields, Eddie ?-1962 [songwriter, singer]
Three Rascals, The *Source(s):* KILG
Note(s): Jt. pseud.: Charles O'Donnell & Benjamin Levin.
Fields, Harold (Cornelius) 1919- [songwriter]
Boswell, Dick *Source(s):* CCE51; CPOL RE-19-804
Note(s): Jt. pseud.: Joseph (Dominic) Roncoroni & H(oward) E(llington) Barnes.
Browne, Lester *Source(s):* CCE46 Efor308
Note(s): Jt. pseud.: Syd Berman.
Carmencito *Source(s):* CCE54; CPOL RE-81-686
Note(s): Jt. pseud.: Joseph (Dominic) Roncoroni.
Carson, Milton *Source(s):* CCE51; CCE57; CLTP ("Destiny"); CPOL RE-328-995
Note(s): Jt. pseud.: Joseph (Dominic) Roncoroni & H(oward) E(llington) Barnes.
Charles, Frank *Source(s):* CCE52
Clancy, Joe *Source(s):* CCE51; CPOL RE-19-019
Note(s): Jt. pseud.: H(oward) E(llingon) Barnes & Robert [or Bob] (Saul) Musel.

Cornelius, Harold *Source(s):* CCE53-54; CPOL; CPOL RE-282-082
Duke, Jerry *Source(s):* CCE58; CPOL RE-282-084
Note(s): Jt. pseud.: Robert Halfin & Joseph (Dominic) Roncoroni.
Feahy, Michael *Source(s):* CCE50-52
Note(s): Jt. pseud.: Joseph (Dominic) Roncoroni & H(oward) E(llington) Barnes.
Greer, David *Source(s):* CCE57-58; CCE60-62; CPOL RE-81-703
Note(s): Jt. pseud.: Joseph (Dominic) Roncoroni.
Hagen, Larry *Source(s):* CCE52; CPOL RE-32-129
Note(s): Jt. pseud.: Joseph (Dominic) Roncoroni & H(oward) E(llington) Barnes.
Hollander, Hugo *Source(s):* CCE50-51; CCE56
Note(s): Jt. pseud.: Joseph (Dominic) Roncoroni & H(oward) E(llington) Barnes.
Jerome, John *Source(s):* CCE51; CCE54; CCE56; CPOL RE-23-625
Note(s): Jt. pseud.: Joseph (Dominic) Roncoroni & H(oward) E(llington) Barnes.
King, Garland *Source(s):* CCE52; CPOL RE-67-016
Note(s): Jt. pseud.: Joseph (Dominic) Roncoroni & H(oward) E(llington) Barnes.
Kordah, Tibor *Source(s):* CCE52
Note(s): Jt. pseud.: Joseph (Dominic) Roncoroni & H(oward) E(llington) Barnes.
Lawrence, Steve *Source(s):* CCE50-51
Note(s): Jt. pseud.: Joseph (Dominic) Roncoroni & H(oward) E(llington) Barnes.
Leclair, Jean *Source(s):* CCE49
Note(s): Jt. pseud.: Joseph (Dominic) Roncoroni & H(oward) E(llington) Barnes.
Lorraine, Sam *Source(s):* CCE56-57
Note(s): Jt. pseud.: Joseph (Dominic) Roncoroni & H(oward) E(llington) Barnes.
Miguel, Guido *Source(s):* CCE51-52; CPOL RE-46-898
Note(s): Jt. pseud.: Joseph (Dominic) Roncoroni, H(oward) E(llington) Barnes & William [or Bill] McGuffie.
O'London, Cornelius *Source(s):* CCE63
O'London, Harold *Source(s):* CCE65
Pasquale, Dino *Source(s):* CCE50
Note(s): Jt. pseud.: Joseph (Dominic) Roncoroni & H(oward) E(llington) Barnes.
Rossiter, (John) Simon *Source(s):* CCE58; CPOL RE-282-085
Note(s): Jt. pseud.: Robert [or Bob] Halfin & Joseph (Dominic) Roncoroni.
Sherman, Charles *Source(s):* CCE50-51
Note(s): Jt. pseud.: Joseph (Dominic) Roncoroni & H(oward) E(llington) Barnes.
Stultz, Herman *Source(s):* CCE50-51
Note(s): Jt. pseud.: Joseph (Dominic) Roncoroni & H(oward) E(llington) Barnes.
Wayne, Elmer *Source(s):* CCE54
Note(s): Jt. pseud.: Joseph (Dominic) Roncoroni & H(oward) E(llington) Barnes.
Young, Charles *Source(s):* LCCC1955-70
Note(s): Jt. pseud.: Joseph (Dominic) Roncoroni & H(oward) E(llington) Barnes.

Fields, Herbert 1897-1958 [author, librettist]
Fieldsieff, Herbert *Source(s):* Hyland, William G. *Richard Rodgers*. New Haven: Yale University Press, 1998, 49.
Lorenz, H(erbert) R(ichard) *Source(s):* NGAM; Hyland p. 27 (see above)
Note(s): Jt. pseud.: Richard (Charles) Rodgers & Lorenz (Milton) Hart.

Fields, Joanna 1960- [American music promoter]
Stingray, Joanna *Source(s):* PSNN

Fields, Richard 1942-2000 [singer, songwriter]
Fields, Dimples *Source(s):* PMUS; WARN

Fierstein, Ronald K. 1950- [composer, singer]
Arbuckle, Ronnie *Source(s):* ASCP; CCE75

Figlia, Giacinto [or Giorgio] Wallington 1924-1993 [pianist, composer]
Wallington, George (Lord) *Source(s):* EPMU; NGDJ; PSND
Wallington, Lord *Source(s):* NGDJ

Figuereo, José Manuel [composer, songwriter]
Joan Sebastian *Source(s):* HWOM

Figuš-Bystrý, Viliam 1875-1937 [composer]
Bystrý, Ján *Source(s):* WEOP

Filip, Paul Francis 1917-1999 [composer, author]
Grade, Francis *Source(s):* ASCP

Filiskos, Spyridon 1861-1917 [composer]
Samara(s), Spiro *Source(s):* BAKR; GOTH; LCAR

Fillmore, (James) Henry 1881-1956 [composer, arranger, bandmaster]
Note(s): Portrait: JASA
Beans, Gus *Source(s):* GROL; NGAM; REHG; SMIN; SUPN
Bennett, Harold *Source(s):* GROL; NGAM; REHG; SMIN; SUPN
Clements, John *Source(s):* CCE56 R168593 ("Take Time for Prayer"); LCAR
Father of the Trombone Smear *Source(s):* http://www.gabbf.com/weird.html (6 Oct. 2002)
Fillmore, Sally *Source(s):* MCBD
Hall, Ray *Source(s):* GROL; NGAM; REHG; SMIN; SUPN
Harfley, Harry *Source(s):* BUL3
Note(s): Typographical error; should be Hartley.
Hartley, Harry *Source(s):* GROL; NGAM; REHG; SMIN; SUPN
Hayes, Al *Source(s):* GROL; NGAM; REHG; SMIN; SUPN

Huff, Will *Source(s):* GROL; REHG; SMIN; Bierley, Paul E. *Music of Henry Fillmore and Will Huff.* Columbus, OH: Integrity Press, 1982, 144+.
Note(s): Do not confuse with Will Huff (1875-1942).
J. H. F. *Source(s):* CCE27 R41021 ("America for Christ")
LeSaint, Louis *Source(s):* CCE48 R29661 ("Christ's Everlasting Gospel;" in: *Hymns for Today*)
Mason, Sam *Source(s):* CCE48 R35347 ("Does Jesus Know")
Moore, Henrietta *Source(s):* GROL; NGAM; REHG; SMIN; SUPN
Filsfils, Octave 1880-1970 [composer]
Tony, Max *Source(s):* SUPN
Finck, Henry Gottlob 1854-1926 [music critic, journalist, author]
Note(s): Portraits: GRAN; MUAM 44:25 (9Oct. 1926); MUWO (Aug. 1902): 89
Agent of Massenet, The *Source(s):* GRAN
Finck, Henry Theophilus *Source(s):* GRAN
Note(s): Changed middle name to sound less Teutonic.
Old Guard, The *Source(s):* GRAN p. 59
Note(s): Jt. sobriquet: William James Henderson & Henry (Edward) Krehbiel.
Old Guard's Glad Evangel, The *Source(s):* GRAN
Finco, Giuseppe Francesco 1769-1836 [composer]
Farineli, Giuseppe (Francesco) *Source(s):* BAKO; GOTH; LCAR; NGDM; NGDO; PIPE; ROOM
Fink, (Christian) Gottfried Wilhelm 1783-1846 [theogian, writer on music, composer]
Chief Organ Blower Kniff, Leader of the Opposition *Source(s):* NGDM
Knif *Source(s):* NGDM
Palestrina der Besenbinder *Source(s):* APPL
Fink, Janis Eddy 1951- [singer, songwriter]
Ian, Janis *Source(s):* CM05; CM24; DIMA; EPMU; HARR; MUHF; PSND; RECR
Finkelman, Harry 1914-1968 [composer, trumpeter, conductor]
Elman, Harry *Source(s):* EPMU; PSND
Elman, Ziggy *Source(s):* EPMU; GAMM; KINK; LCAR; LYMN; PSND
Finkelstein, Abe 1888-1953 [composer, lyricist, singer, comedian]
Note(s): The following names are listed as pseuds. of Arthur Fields [i.e., Abe Finkelstein]
For 70+ additional pseuds. see Allan Sutton's *Pseudonymns on Records, 1892-1942.* 2nd rev. & expanded ed., p. 375. See MACE & SUTT (& SUTT 2nd ed.) for jt.performing pseuds. with Fred Hall, Charles Harrison, Irving Kaufman & Jack Kaufman. Do not confuse with Arthur B. Fields, aka Buddy Fields (1889-1965).
Adler, Salmo *Source(s):* CCE26 E636107 ("She's One of the Many Who Took the Wrong Rose")
Allen, Craig *Source(s):* SUTT
Andrews, Jim *Source(s):* MACE; SUTT
Note(s): Also used by Irving [i.e., Isidore] Kaufman.
Baker, Donald *Source(s):* KILG; MACE; SUTT
Baldwin, Arthur *Source(s):* MACE; SUTT
Bennett, John *Source(s):* GRAC
Note(s): Also used by Al(fred A.) Bernard.
Bernie, D. Bud *Source(s):* MACE; SUTT
Britt, Addy [or Andy] *Source(s):* PSNN; SUTT
Britten, Ford *Source(s):* MACE; SUTT
Bronson, George *Source(s):* MACE; SUTT
Note(s): Also used by Irving [i.e., Isidore] Kaufman.
Buckley, Eugene *Source(s):* PSNN; SUTT
Calhoun, Jeff *Source(s):* MACE; SUTT
Note(s): Also used by Vernon Dalhart [i.e., M(arion) T(ry) Slaughter] & Frank Luther [i.e., Francis Luther Crow(e)]. See SUTT for recording label information.
Clarke, Billy *Source(s):* SUTT
Note(s): Also used by Irving [i.e., Isidore] Kaufman.
Cole, Rex *Source(s):* SUTT
Cole, Sam *Source(s):* SUTT
Crane, Harry *Source(s):* MACE; PSNN; SUTT
Cummings, James *Source(s):* GRAC
Note(s): Also used by Vernon Dalhart [i.e., M(arion) T(ry) Slaughter]
Dale, Charles *Source(s):* MACE; SUTT
Dale, Walter *Source(s):* MACE; PSNN; SUTT
Dexter, Charles *Source(s):* MACE; PSNN; SUTT
Donovan, Hugh *Source(s):* MACE; SUTT
Note(s): Also used by Vernon Dalhart [i.e., M(arion) T(ry) Slaughter]
Edwards, Billy *Source(s):* MACE; PSNN; SUTT
Edwards, Thomas *Source(s):* MACE; SUTT
Note(s): Also used by singer Elliott Shaw.
Elliott, Joseph *Source(s):* MACE; SUTT
Note(s): Also used by Vernon Dalhart [i.e., M(arion) T(ry) Slaughter] & others; see MACE.
Evans, Frank *Source(s):* MACE; SUTT.
Note(s): Also used by Vernon Dalhart [i.e., M(arion) T(ry) Slaughter]. Carson J(ay) Robison used the pseud. Frank(lin) Evans.
Fields, Arthur *Source(s):* MACE; SUTT p. 101
Note(s): Stage name.
French, George *Source(s):* MACE; SUTT
Gent & Wheeler *Source(s):* SUTT
Grant, Arthur *Source(s):* SUTT
Graves, Harold *Source(s):* http://www.mainspring.com/BSpseudo.html (13 June 2005)
Gray, Henry *Source(s):* MACE; SUTT
Herold, Francis *Source(s):* MACE; SUTT
Higgins, Si *Source(s):* SUTT
Hilly, Dan *Source(s):* MACE; SUTT
Hobbs, Herb *Source(s):* MACE; SUTT

Holton, Larry *Source(s):* MACE; SUTT
Hunter, James *Source(s):* MACE; SUTT
Note(s): Also used by Gustav(e) Saenger.
Kern, Jimmy *Source(s):* MACE; SUTT
King, Henry *Source(s):* MACE; SUTT
Lewis, William *Source(s):* MACE; SUTT
Lincoln, Mac *Source(s):* SUTT
Litchfield, Ben *Source(s):* SUTT
Note(s): Also used by Vernon Dalhart [i.e., M(arion) T(ry) Slaughter]
Lone Star Ranger *Source(s):* MACE
Note(s): Also used by singer John I. White & possibly Vernon Dahlhart [i.e., M(arion) T(ry) Slaughter]
Mack, Arthur *Source(s):* MACE; SUTT
Mack, Eugene *Source(s):* GRAC
Note(s): Also used by R(ichard) G. Grady.
Mander, Ambrose *Source(s):* MACE; SUTT
Martin, Jack *Source(s):* MACE; SUTT
Meadows, Arthur *Source(s):* MACE; SUTT
Mr. X *Source(s):* KILG; MACE; SUTT
Note(s): Also used by Vernon Dalhart [i.e., M(arion) T(ry) Slaughter] and also Irving [i.e., Isidore] Kaufman.
Norton, Walter *Source(s):* MACE; SUTT
O'Brian, Padric *Source(s):* MACE; SUTT
Ramsey, Jack *Source(s):* GRAC
Randall, Roy *Source(s):* MACE; SUTT
Richards, Charles *Source(s):* MACE; SUTT
Ryan, Jimmy *Source(s):* MACE; SUTT
Seelig, Arthur *Source(s):* MACE; SUTT
Note(s): Also used by Irving [i.e., Isidore] Kaufman.
Sloane, John *Source(s):* MACE; SUTT
Sparrow, The *Source(s):* GRAK; http://www.mainspringpress.com/lom0200.html (13 June 2005)
Note(s): See also Slinger Francisco.
Spencer, Ernie *Source(s):* MACE
Spencer, Samuel *Source(s):* MACE; SUTT
Note(s): Possible pseud. Also used by Cliff(ord) (A.) Edwards.
Stewart, Cliff *Source(s):* MACE; SUTT
Note(s): Also used by Vernon Dahlert [i.e., M(arion) T(ry) Slaughter] & possibly others.
Stone, Fred *Source(s):* MACE; SUTT
Thomas, Bob *Source(s):* MACE; SUTT
Note(s): Also used by Vernon Dalhart [i.e., M(arion) T(ry) Slaughter]
Trevor, Bert *Source(s):* SUTT
Veteran, Vel *Source(s):* KILG; PSNN; SUTT
Note(s): Also used by others; including Vernon Dalhart [i.e., M(arion) T(ry) Slaughter] & Irving [i.e., Isidore] Kaufman.
White, Billy *Source(s):* SUTT
Wood, Robert *Source(s):* MACE; SUTT
Note(s): Also used by Irving [i.e., Isidore] Kaufman & also by Dick Robertson.

Finkelthaus, Gottfried 1614-1657 [singer, lawyer, composer]
Federfechter, Gregorius von Lützen *Source(s):* IBIM; WORB

Finzi, Ida 1869-1948 [librettist]
Haydée *Source(s):* LOWN; MELL; WORB
Signora in grigio, La *Source(s):* WORB

Fiorente, Arnaldo Benito 1938- [composer]
Blumel, Arno *Source(s):* PFSA

Fiorito, Ted 1900-1971 [songwriter]
Rito, Ted Fio *Source(s):* BBDP; CLMM; LCAR
White, Eddie *Source(s):* CCE21 E524776

Firbank, Louis [or Lewis] (Allen) 1942 (43 or 44)- [singer, songwriter, guitarist]
Firbank, Butch *Source(s):* PSND
King Freak of New York, The *Source(s):* PSND
King of Decadence, The *Source(s):* PSND
Prince of Darkness, The *Source(s):* PSND
Note(s): See also Miles (Dewey) Davis, (III).
Reed, Lewis Allen *Source(s):* DIMA; EPMU
Note(s): Listed as original name in DIMA..
Reed, Lou *Source(s):* CM01; EPMU; PEN2; PIPE; PSND

Firth, Everett J(oseph) 1930- [composer, timpanist]
Firth, Vic *Source(s):* ASCP; CCE64; LCAR

Fischer, Ernest 1900-1975 [composer]
Fisher, Ernest *Source(s):* PIPE; SUPN
MacFarren, (John) *Source(s):* PIPE; SUPN

Fischer, Georg c.1610-after 1635 [composer, organist]
Piscator, Georg *Source(s):* NGDM

Fischer, Jan Frank 1921- [composer]
Fiser, J. F. *Source(s):* GOTH

Fischer, Johann 1930- [composer]
Fischer, Andy *Source(s):* PFSA

Fischer, Larry 1945- [singer, songwriter]
Fischer, Wild Man *Source(s):* EPMU; LCAR; PSND

Fischer, Otokar 1883-1938 [author]
Frey, Otokar *Source(s):* PIPE
Skála, Otakar *Source(s):* LCAR

Fišer, Jan 1896-1963 [composer]
Kvetoň *Source(s):* BUL3

Fish, James [composer]
Mann, Rawden de *Source(s):* CPMU (publication date 1912)

Fisher, Doris 1915-2003 [composer, singer]
Wise, Penny *Source(s):* http://www.reviewjournal.com/lvrj_home/2003/Jan-24-Fri-2003/news/20542558.html (10 Feb. 2005)

Fisher, Ethel [composer]
Barto, Gustave *Source(s):* CCE20 E483362
Du Bois, Herman *Source(s):* CCE23 E554123
DuFrerre, M. *Source(s):* CCE15 E362154

Frampton, Ray Ross *Source(s):* CCE22 E52996
Lamont, Henriot *Source(s):* LCPC
Lamont, Lois *Source(s):* CCE19 E449746
Lorraine, Frank *Source(s):* CCE19
Muehling, Carl [or Karl] *Source(s):* CCE15 E372563; CCE16 E379014
Navarre, Jean *Source(s):* CCE22 E543267
Note(s): Also used by Carl Wilhelm Kern.
Nielson, Raymond *Source(s):* CCE23 E543262
Norworth, Max *Source(s):* CCE21 E525741

Fisher, Geoffrey Francis 1887-1972 [hymnbook editor]
G. F. F. *Source(s):* CPMU

Fisher, George Clinton 1907-1984 [singer, songwriter, actor]
Fisher, Shug *Source(s):* MCCL
Judd, Aaron *Source(s):* MCCL

Fisher, Marvin 1916-1993 [composer, pianist, arranger]
Davis, Don *Source(s):* ASCP; CCE51; CCE55
Davis, Lefty *Source(s):* CCE57

Fisher, Reuben 1923- [composer, lyricist]
Fisher, Ruby *Source(s):* ASCC; CCE58; CCE61; CPOL RE-518-897

Fisher, William Arms 1861-1948 [composer, music editor, writer on music]
Note(s): Portraits: ETUP 51:5 (May 1932): 292; MRAR (Nov. 1901): 27
Armstrong, Robert *Source(s):* LCCC47 R14579 ("Welcome to Wilson")
Ashford, Robert *Source(s):* CCE46 ("Goodbye My Laddie"); LCAR; TPRF
Campbell, Colin *Source(s):* CCE40 #22693, 168 R87431
Canfield, Arthur B. *Source(s):* CCE51 R75856 (*Ditson's Music Writer and Speller*)
Confield, Arthur B. *Source(s):* LCAR; TPRF
Favilli, Mario *Source(s):* CCE37 R60621; LCAR
Kiehl, Heinrich *Source(s):* CCE28 R243; CCE31 R11911; LCAR; TPRF
Lacy, Caleb *Source(s):* LCAR; TPRF
Mackenzie, Malcolm *Source(s):* CCE45 R145362 ("My Bit-of-a-Girl")
O'Kelley, Shane *Source(s):* LCAR; TPRF
Randolph, John Carroll *Source(s):* CCE31 E20636-37; TPRF
W. A. F. *Source(s):* CPMU ("Feed My Sheep")
Note(s): Probably William Arms Fisher.
Walter, J. B. *Source(s):* CCE45 #63817, 623 R145364 ("We're with You Boys. . . .")
Note(s): Also used by John W(alter) Bratton.
Watson, Wilbur *Source(s):* CCE45 #63817, 561 R145391 ("God Bless Him! My Boy")
Wilmans, Wilman *Source(s):* LCAR

Fishman, Jack 1918 (or 19)- [songwriter]
Note(s): Published works were copyrighted by several "foreign" publishers; unpublished works were copyrighted by companies in London. Could not verify as the same person as Jack Fishman (1920-). Do not confuse with Jack Fishman (aka Jay Fishman) (1927-).
Boule, Henri *Source(s):* CCE56 Eunp447897
Note(s): Copyrighted by B. Feldman, Co. Ltd.
David, Joan *Source(s):* CCE52 Efor16698
Forrest, David *Source(s):* CCE55 Efor31818; CPOL RE-143-473
Note(s): Jt. pseud.: Cliff Adams, Bob Brown & Francis (or Frank) (Charles) Chacksfield.
Foss, Richard *Source(s):* CCE57 Efor52090
Note(s): Jt. pseud.: Norman [or Norrie] (William) Paramor.
Hall, Margaret *Source(s):* CPOL RE-99-892; LCCC53 Efor18798
Note(s): Jt. pseud.: Peter Hart [i.e., Hargreaves]
Hamilton, Lloyd *Source(s):* CCE56 Efor45878
Heywod, Phil *Source(s):* CPOL RE-257-859; LCCC57 Efor23175
Holiday, Alan *Source(s):* CCE54 Efor30215; CCE55
Jack, Peter *Source(s):* CCE76 R32139
Jackson, Lillibet *Source(s):* CCE52; CCE55; CPOL RE-72-629
Johns, Michael *Source(s):* CCE55 Efor31818; CPOL RE-143-473
Note(s): Jt. pseud.: Cliff Adams, Bob Brown & Francis (or Frank) (Charles) Chacksfield.
Kahn, Larry *Source(s):* CCE55 Efor37069; LCCC61 Efor26655
Lee, Alex *Source(s):* CCE57 Efor23232; CPOL RE-234-588; CPOL RE-235-144
Note(s): "Steady as a Rock" & "The Sham Rock." Also used by Norman (William) [or Norrie] Paramor.
Manilla, Tony *Source(s):* CCE53 Efor21119; CCE56; CPOL RE-117-492
Note(s): Also jt. pseud.: Cyril Stapleton; and also jt. pseud.: Clare Shardlow; see NOTES: Manilla, Tony.
Masters, Alex *Source(s):* CCE58 Efor47025; LCCC57 E23956
Mitchell, Michael *Source(s):* CPOL RE-214-755
Parigini, Salvador *Source(s):* CCE54 Efor30215; CCE55
Reisdorff, Emile *Source(s):* CPOL RE-114-494; LCCC54 Efor19892
Note(s): Jt. pseud.: Peter Hart [i.e., Hargreaves]
Reynolds, Brian *Source(s):* CCE55 Efor31819; CPOL RE-143-474
Richmond, Ralph *Source(s):* CCE53 Efor19033; CPOL RE-81-068
Robbins, Michael *Source(s):* CCE58 Efor56583
Sigara, Georges *Source(s):* CCE54 Efor29679; CCE55; CPOL RE-141-049

Stowe, Michael *Source(s):* CCE55 Eunp408493
Note(s): Copyrighted by Bluebird Music Co. (London)
Street, Leonard *Source(s):* CPOL RE-114-500; LCCC54 Efor20150
Note(s): Jt. pseud.: Peter Hart [i.e., Hargraves]
Terry, Sue *Source(s):* CCE59 Eunp564715; CPOL RE-350-155
White, Sam *Source(s):* CCE56 Efor46906
Fishman, Jack 1920- [journalist, composer, lyricist]
Note(s): Could not verify as the same person as Jack Fishman (1918 (or 19)- . Do not confuse with Jack Fishman (aka Jay Fishman) (1927-).
Gilman, J. D. *Source(s):* LCAR
Note(s): Jt. pseud.: Douglas Orgill.
Fishman, Jack 1927- [songwriter]
Note(s): Do not confuse with Jack Fishman (1918 (or 19)-) or Jack Fishman (1920-).
Bonni, Ed *Source(s):* CCE77
Fenton, Jack *Source(s):* CCE60-61
Fisherman, Jack *Source(s):* CPOL PAu-272-210
Fisherman, Jay *Source(s):* CPOL PAu-272-210
Fishma, Jack *Source(s):* CPOL PAu-103-474
Fishman, Jay *Source(s):* CPOL PAu-403-366; CPOL Txu-499-989
Hurricane, David G. *Source(s):* CPOL PAu-166-197
Parson, Charlotte *Source(s):* CCE65 Eunp869077; CCE66
Note(s): Do not confuse with Charlotte Parsons (CCE65); works copyrighted by Murbo Pub. & Bright Tunes?
Rockefella, David *Source(s):* CCE65 Eunp860856; CPOL RE-615-495
Fite, Wendell [songwriter, performer]
DJ Hurricane *Source(s):* AMIR; AMUS; CPOL Pau-2-008-334; PMUS-00
Fitz, Walter 1921- [composer]
Raffay, Ina *Source(s):* KOMP; PFSA
Wolperting, Paul *Source(s):* KOMP; PFSA
Fitzpatrick, Michael G. [arranger]
Fitzgerald, M. J. *Source(s):* SPTH p. 244 ("Boston Burglar" (arr.))
Fitzwygram, Augusta Catherine [composer]
Note(s): Married name: (Lady) A. C. Baker.
A. C. F. *Source(s):* CPMU (publication date 1953)
Minima *Source(s):* BLIC; CPMU
Flannery, William Jerome 1865-1932 [songwriter]
Jerome, William [or Billy] *Source(s):* GAN1; GAN2
Fläschner, Peter 1950- [composer]
Glide, Merlin *Source(s):* KOMS
Flavigny, Marie (Catherine Sophie), (Comtesse D'Agoult) 1805-1876 [writer]
Agoult, Marie Catherine Sophie de Flavigny, Comtesse d' *Source(s):* LCAR
Stern, Daniel *Source(s):* LCAR; ROOM; WORB
Fleagle, J(acob) (Roger) 1906-1992 [guitarist, arranger]
Di Gras, M. *Source(s):* CCE59
Fleagle, Brick *Source(s):* ASCP; CCE60-61; LCAR
Fleet, George Rutland 1853-1922 [actor, singer, librettist]
Barrington, Rutland *Source(s):* GAMM; GAN1; GAN2; WORB
Flegenheimer, Edmond 1874-1963 [author]
Fleg, Edmond *Source(s):* PIPE; WORB
Fleischmann, Aloys (George) 1910-1992 [composer]
Ó Rónáin, Muiris *Source(s):* GROL; LCAR; MUWB
Ronan, Maurice *Source(s):* MUWB
Fleitman, Alexander O(scar) 1924- [composer, author, singer]
Foster, Al *Source(s):* ASCP; CCE57; CCE63
Flem(m)ing, Paul 1609-1640 [poet]
Anacreon of Germany, The *Source(s):* PSND
Florian *Source(s):* PIPE
Note(s): Also used by Friedrich Fiedler.
German Herrick, The *Source(s):* PSND
Herrick of Germany, The *Source(s):* PSND
Flemmer, Christian 1640-1697 [author, poet]
Fidamor *Source(s):* PIPE
Fletcher, Julia Constance 1858-1938 [author]
Dudu *Source(s):* PIPE; PSND
Fleming, George *Source(s):* PIPE; PSND
Florence [composer]
Ecnerolf *Source(s):* BLIC; CPMU (publication date 1905)
Flores, Celedonio (Esteban) 1896-1947 [poet, lyricist]
Cele *Source(s):* CCE41 #19322 Efor64281; CCE55; CCE62
Negro Cele, El *Source(s):* TODO
Flores Pereyra, Jesús Francisco 1930-1997 [singer, songwriter]
Michel, Paco *Source(s):* HWOM
Flores Rivera, Salvador 1920-1987 [singer, songwriter]
Flores, Chava *Source(s):* HWOM; LCAR
Floridia (Napolino), Pietro 1860-1932 [composer]
Note(s): Portrait: ETUP 51:6 (June 1933): 364
Abbott, Leslie W. *Source(s):* CCE19 E457283; CCE47 R18364 ("Hudson River Waltz"); TPRF
Florio, Andrea Nicola 1927-1998 [composer, author]
Raven Grey Eagle *Source(s):* ASCP
Florio, Zackie Cooper 1912-1987 [composer, author]
Cooper, Zack [or Zackie] *Source(s):* ASCP (see reference)
Flory, Meredith I. 1926- [saxophonist, screenwriter, arranger]
Flory, Med *Source(s):* CCE60; EPMU; LCAR
Flotard, Eugène 1821- [poet, librettist]
Dartol, F. *Source(s):* OCLC 21811713

Flotow, Friedrich von 1812-1883 [composer]
Marckwordt, Ferdinand *Source(s):* GROL; LOWN; PIPE
Note(s): On translations of his "Veuve Grapin" & Grisar's "L'Eau Merveilleuse."
Flournoy, Roberta Jean 1927-2003 [composer, author]
Jiroudek, Roberta *Source(s):* CPOL PAu-885-165
Philpott, Dixie *Source(s):* CPOL RE-209-848
Randle, Dodie *Source(s):* ASCP; CPOL PAu-883-165
Flower, Amelia Matilda [piano, composer]
Fleur, M. *Source(s):* COHN; HIXN
Flower, Eliza 1803-1846 [composer]
E. F. *Source(s):* CPMU
Floyd, Frank 1908-1984 [singer, guitarist, songwriter]
Floyd, Rambling King *Source(s):* HARS
Harmonica Frank *Source(s):* HARS; LCAR
Silly Kid, The Source*(s):* HARS
Floyd, Stafford Marquette 1951- [composer, author]
Elliott, Braxton *Source(s):* ASCP
Flurie, Edward (Cletus) 1943- [singer, songwriter]
Edwards, Bud *Source(s):* CCE63
Rambeau, Eddie *Source(s):* CCE62; CCE67; EPMU; PMUS; PSND; ROOM
Fock, Dirk 1886-1973 [composer, conductor]
Note(s): Portrait: ETUP 51:6 (June 1933): 364
Foch, Dirk *Source(s):* BAKR; BUL3; LCAR
Fody, (Helene) Ilona 1920- [composer, pianist, author]
Ilona *Source(s):* CCE60; CCE62
Jacob, Helen *Source(s):* ASCP; COHN; HIXN
Foerster, Josef Bohuslav 1859-1951 [composer, writer, teacher]
-ter *Source(s):* GROL ("Narodni listy")
Essex *Source(s):* GROL
Griffith *Source(s):* GROL
Triste, Felix *Source(s):* GROL
Fogel, Wes(ley) 1940-1996 [producer, songwriter]
Farrell, Wes *Source(s):* CCE60-61; DRSC
Fok, Carolyn [composer]
Cyrnai *Source(s): Keyboard* 23:252:4 (1997): 13
Folasade, Helen 1959- [singer, songwriter]
Adu, (Mrs.) Helen *Source(s):* CM02; CM37
Sade *Source(s):* CM02; EPMU; HARR
Foley, Clyde (Julian) 1910-1968 [singer, songwriter]
Foley, Red *Source(s):* CASS; ENCM; EPMU; KINK; LCAR; MCCL; STAC
Fomin, Wasily 1902-1983 [composer]
Fomeen, Basil *Source(s):* EPMU; LCAR
Fook, Omar Lye 1969- [singer, songwriter, producer]
Omar *Source(s):* EPMU
Foote, Arthur (William) 1853-1937 [composer, organist, pianist, theorist]
Note(s): Portraits: APSA; ETUP 51:6 (June 1933): 364; GRV3 (American Suppl.); HOWD
Erich, Carl *Source(s):* GROL; NGAM
Note(s): A. P. Schmidt house name; see NOTES: Erich, Carl.
Meyer, Edward *Source(s):* ETUD
Meyer, Ferdinand *Source(s):* CCE16 R8839; GROL; NGAM
Note(s): A. P. Schmidt house name; see NOTES: Meyer, Ferdinand.
Foote, John Howard 1833-1896 [music dealer; poet]
Pearlfisher *Source(s):* WORB
Forbes, Roy 1953- [singer, songwriter]
Bim *Source(s):* LCAR; NOMG
Ford, Aleck 1899-1965 [harmonica player, singer, songwriter]
Note(s): Ford is his mother's surname (HARS).
Big Skol *Source(s):* JAMU
King of the Harmonica *Source(s):* HARS
Little Boy Blue *Source(s):* AMUS; CM09; HARS
Miller, Aleck *Source(s):* CM09; HARS; LCAR
Miller, Rice *Source(s):* CM09; EPMU; HARS; LCAR
Miller, Willie *Source(s):* HARS
Sib *Source(s):* HARS
Williams, Willie *Source(s):* HARS
Williamson, Sonny Boy *Source(s):* AMUS; EPMU; HARS; LCAR
Note(s): Also used by John Lee ("Sonny Boy") Williamson (1914-1948).
Williamson, Willie *Source(s):* CM09; HARS; LCAR
Ford, Benjamin Francis 1901-1986 [singer, songwriter]
Duke of Paducah, The *Source(s):* CCME; EPMU; MCCL
Ford, Whitey *Source(s):* CCME; EPMU; MCCL
Ford, David Everard 1797-1875 [cleric, theologian, hymnist]
Composer, A *Source(s):* CART
Ford, Ernest Jennings 1919-1991 [singer, songwriter, guitarist]
Cousin Erin *Source(s):* PSND
Ford, Tennessee Ernie *Source(s):* ASCP; CASS; ENCM; EPMU; KINK; LCAR
King of the Southern Pea Pickers, The *Source(s):* PSND
King of the Tennessee Pea Pickers, The *Source(s):* PSND
Mister Country Music *Source(s):* CASS
O' Pea Picker, The *Source(s):* FLIN
Old Pea Picker *Source(s):* MCCL
Ford, Murray ?-1932 [songwriter]
Le Breton, John *Source(s):* KILG
Le Breton, Thomas *Source(s):* KILG
Ford, Young 1877-1955 [singer, songwriter]
Ford, Harry *Source(s):* KILG p. 198

Forman, David [singer, songwriter]
Little Isidore *Source(s):* http://www.littleisidore.com/largo.htm (6 Oct. 2002)
Formey, Alfred 1844-1901 [librettist]
Schlicht, Ernest *Source(s):* LOWN; MELL; OCLC 17591849; STGR
Fornaciari, Aldelmo 1956- [guitarist, songwriter]
Fornaciari, Sugar *Source(s):* CPOL PA-800-169
Fornaciari, Zucchero *Source(s):* CPOL PA-720-960
Zucchero *Source(s):* AMUS; CPOL PA-800-166; EPMU
Forrest, Thomas 1747-1825 [composer]
Barton, Andrew *Source(s):* GREN; LCAR; Vernon, Grenville. *Yankee Doodle-Doo.* New York: Benjamin Blom, 1972, 16.
Note(s): Probable pseud ; also possible pseud. of John Leacock (p. 25).
Forsblad, Leland 1922- [composer]
Oliver, Rick *Source(s):* REHG; SUPN
Forston, Jeffrey [rapper]
Def Jef *Source(s):* EPMU; LCAR
Forsyth, Christina 1825-1859 [songwriter]
C. F. *Source(s):* JULN; LCAR
Forsyth, Wesley Octavius 1859-1937 [composer, teacher, critic]
Krueger, Carl *Source(s):* CANE
Forsythe, Charles Henry 1892-?1981 [songwriter]
LeRoyal, A. *Source(s):* CCE51 Efor7685; CPOL RE-24-659
Malloys, The *Source(s):* CCE53
Note(s): Jt. pseud.: Harry Sugarman & Mark Malloy [i.e., Richard Donnelly]
Fort, Eleanor H(ankins) 1912 (or 14)- [composer, singer]
Fort, Hank *Source(s):* CCE39 #7164 Eunp187901; CCE64; PSND
McAuliffe, Eleanor H. *Source(s):* CCE64; CCE66
Fortescue, John Henry 1923-1976 [singer, guitarist, songwriter]
Guitar Shorty *Source(s):* HARS
Note(s): Do not confuse with blues guitarist Guitar Shorty [i.e., David Kearney], (1939-).
Kearney, David William *Source(s):* HARS
Note(s): Possible pseud.
Fortini, James 1926- [composer, author, singer]
Note(s): Do not confuse with his son; see following entry.
Covais, Jack *Source(s):* ASCP
James, Pete *Source(s):* ASCP; CPOL SR-41-507
Walker, Jimmy *Source(s):* ASCP
Note(s): Also used by Earnest Earl Walker.
Fortini, James Timothy Peter (Spider) 1958- [composer, author]
Note(s): Do not confuse with his father; see preceding entry.
James, Pete, Jr. *Source(s):* ASCP
Fortner, Arnold [songwriter]
Fortner, Red *Source(s):* PMUS
Foscarini, Giovanni Paolo fl. early 1600s [composer, guitarist, lutenist, theorist]
Academico Caliginoso, L' *Source(s):* CCE54 E206151; LCAR
Caliginoso, Il *Source(s):* WORB
Furioso, Il *Source(s):* CCE65 E2061511; CPMU; GROL; LCAR; NGDM
Foster, Catherine [hymnist]
C. F. *Source(s):* DIEH; PSND
Foster, Leroy 1923-1958 [percussionist, guitarist, songwriter]
Baby Face (Leroy) *Source(s):* HARS; LCAR
Delta Joe *Source(s):* JAMU
Note(s): Also used by Albert Luandrew.
Foster, Myles Birket 1851-1922 [composer, organist]
Note(s): Portrait: ETUP 51:6 (June 1933): 364
M. B. F. *Source(s):* DIEH ("Medford")
Note(s): Presumed initials of Foster.
Foster, Olive (Leonard) 1819-1881 [poet, hymnist]
O. L. F. *Source(s):* PSND
Foster, Paula 1944- [composer, author, singer]
Hartford, Chapin *Source(s):* ASCP
Foster, Stephen Collins 1826-1864 [composer]
Note(s): Portraits: EWEN; MUCO 100:12 & 13 (Mar. 1930) (14-page pictorial biography)
American Ballad Composer *Source(s):* DESO7
America's First Composer *Source(s):* FACS
America's First Songwriter *Source(s):* http://www.ifilm.com/product/film_info/0,3699,2397442,00.html (2 Oct. 2002)
America's Troubadour *Source(s):* PSND
Byerly, William *Source(s):* EMER p. 214+ ("The Crystal Schottisch")
Note(s): Probable pseud.
Christy, E(dwin) P(earce) *Source(s):* METC
Notes(s): Not a pseud. Christy paid Foster in order to claim authorship of "The Old Folks at Home," (1851); however, royalties were received by Foster. Portrait: HOWD; also title page of 1st ed. (1852) of the work with Christy's name as composer.
Crookshank, Wm. Cullen *Source(s):* EMER p. 169+, 240 ("Once I Loved Thee Mary Dear")
Foster, L. C. *Source(s):* DICH ("Open Thy Lattic Love" (1884))
Note(s): Misprint of initials.
Lady, A. *Source(s):* EMER p. 158 & 169 ("My Hopes Have Departed Forever")
Note(s): Also used by Charlotte Elliott, Ann Home & Julia Ward Howe.
Moore, Milton *Source(s):* EMER; SPTH p. 108 ("I Would Not Die in Spring Time")

Foster, Winston 1956- [DJ, lyricist]
"King" Yellowman *Source(s):* http://www.artistonly.com/yellhm.htm (6 Oct. 2002)
Yellowman *Source(s):* AMUS; EPMU; http://www.artistonly.com/yellhm.htm
Fote, Richard 1932- [composer]
Williams, Frank *Source(s):* REHH
Note(s): Also used by Vernon Dalhart [i.e., M(arion) T(ry) Slaughter] & Harry Parr Davies.
Fotinakis, Dorothy Owens 1912-2002 [composer, author]
Fotine, Dorothy *Source(s):* ASCP
Fotinakis, Lawrence Constantine 1911-1990 [composer, author]
Fotine, Larry *Source(s):* ASCP; CLTP ("Border Patrol"); LCAR
Foulds, John Herbert 1880-1939 [composer]
Deva *Source(s):* http://www.bluntinstrument.org.uk/foulds/archive/bms10.htm (26 Apr. 2005)
Fourneau, Léon 1867-1953 [composer, author]
Xanrof, (Léon) *Source(s):* BAKO; GAMM; GAN1; GAN2; KILG; LCAR; WHIT
Fournier, Marcel (Paul) 1863 (or 65)- [librettist]
Marcelles, Paul *Source(s):* STGR; WORB
Vély, Adrien *Source(s):* OCLC 21820261
Fournier, Robert B. [songwriter]
King, Bob *Source(s):* CCE59; CCE65-66
Note(s): "Baby This Is Love" & "That Crazy Rock" (both CCE59); "Gone Again" & "So Ashamed" (both CCE65) & "Thumbs Down Baby You'd Better Not Wait" (CCE66). Do not confuse with Bob King [i.e., Robert (A(dolph)) Keiser]
Fowler, Charles [composer]
Relwoff, Charles *Source(s):* CPMU (publication date 1873)
Fox, Charles H. 19th cent. [song compiler]
Bust, Urastix *Source(s):* PSND
Fox, Charles Richard Jeremy 1921-1991 [writer on jazz]
Jeremy, Richard *Source(s):* CART
Fox, Eldridge (L.) 1936-2002 [singer, songwriter, pianist]
Foxy *Source(s):* DRSC; SGMA (port.)
Fox, Roy [songwriter]
Note(s): Probably not Roy Fox (1901-1982)?. (See next entry)
Booth, Dorothy *Source(s):* CCE31 Efor23289 ("Consolation" London: Peter Music)
Madison, Gary *Source(s):* CCE55 Efor38470 ("Birthday Waltz" London: Arcadia Music)
Marsh, Cliff *Source(s):* CCE56 Efor41704 ("All for the Sake of Love" London: Polyphone Music)
Fox, Roy 1901-1982 [bandleader, cornetist, author]
Note(s): Probably not Roy Fox [nd]?. (See preceding entry)
Whispering Cornetist, The *Source(s):* GROL
Fragny, Robert de 1894- [composer]
Proton de la Chapelle, (Robert) *Source(s):* BUL2
Fraieli, Loreto 1910-1998 [composer, author]
Crane, Jimmie *Source(s):* ASCP; CCE76-77; LCAR
França, Fernando de Assis 1967-1997 [songwriter, bandleader]
Science, Chico *Source(s):* LCAR; OB97
Francavilla, Joseph [or Joe] [singer, songwriter]
Villa, Joe *Source(s):* PSND
Francesco (Canova) da Milano 1497-1543 [composer, lutenist]
Divino, Il *Source(s):* http://www.hoasm.org/IVE/Milano.html (6 Oct. 2002)
Francesco del Liuto *Source(s):* GROL
Franchetti, Alberto 1860-1942 [composer]
Note(s): Portraits: ETUP 51:7 (July 1933): 434; MUCO (Apr. 1902): 1
Meyerbeer of Modern Italy, The *Source(s):* GRV3
Tito *Source(s):* GROL
Franchi, Ferdinand 1920- [composer]
Eifel, Ferdinand [or Ferdi] *Source(s):* PFSA
Franchi, Nando *Source(s):* PFSA
Franchi-Verney, Giuseppe Ippolito 1848-1911 [composer, writer on music, lawyer]
Valetta, Ippolito *Source(s):* BAKE; PRAT
Franchini, Anthony Joseph 1898-1997 [composer, author, music teacher]
Ball, Mel *Source(s):* ASCP; CCE57; LCAR
Zachary, Tony *Source(s):* ASCP; LCAR
Francis, Cleve(land), (Jr.) 1945- [singer, songwriter, cardiologist]
King of Hearts, The *Source(s):* MCCL
Note(s): See also Elvis A(a)ron Presley.
Francisco, Slinger 1935- [singer, composer, bandleader]
King Sparrow *Source(s):* CCE59
Little Sparrow *Source(s):* GROL
Note(s): See also Edith Giovanni Gasson.
Mighty Sparrow, (The) *Source(s):* CCE59-63; EPMU; GROL
Sparrow *Source(s):* LCAR
Note(s): Also used by Arthur Fields [i.e., Abe Finkelstein]
Franck, César 1822-1890 [composer]
Father of French Organ Music *Source(s):* MUWB
Great Old Man *Source(s):* MUWB
Francoeur, François (*le cadet*) 1698-1787 [violinist, composer]
Franker, Fransua *Source(s):* LCAR
Petits violins, Le *Source(s):* GROL
Note(s): Jt. sobriquet: François Rebel (*le fils*).

Francoeur, Louis-Joseph 1738-1804 [violinist, composer, conductor, editor]
Francoeur Neveu *Source(s):* NGDM; NGDO
François, Samson 1924-1970 [pianist, composer]
Note(s): Entry in BUL3 is under Samson, François.
Samson-François *Source(s):* BUL3; NGDM
Franconero, Constance [or Concetta] (Rosa Marie) 1938- [composer, singer, publisher]
Francis, Connie *Source(s):* ASCP; GAMM; LCAR
Frangkiser, Carl (Moerz) 1894-1967 [composer]
Akron, Philip *Source(s):* REHG; SMIN; SUPN
Allen, Stuart *Source(s):* REHG; SMIN
Arberine, G. S. *Source(s):* REHG; SMIN; SUPN
Band King, The *Source(s):* SMIN
Chandler, A. *Source(s):* CCE68; REHG; SMIN; SUPN
Collins, W. C. *Source(s):* REHG; SMIN; SUPN
Darman, Arthur S. *Source(s):* REHG; SMIN
Deniston, Paul *Source(s):* CPOL RE-11-535; REHG; SMIN; SUPN
Desmond, Walter *Source(s):* REHG; SMIN; SUPN
Elsen, C. *Source(s):* REHG; SMIN; SUPN
Evans, J. *Source(s):* REHG; SMIN; SUPN
Farrell, James *Source(s):* REHG; SMIN; SUPN
Fenshaw, Larry *Source(s):* REHG; SMIN; SUPN
Fontaine, E. *Source(s):* SUPN
Gilbert, Austin *Source(s):* REHG; SMIN; SUPN
Goldrin, Carl *Source(s):* CCE53
Goldrin, Ernesto *Source(s):* REHG; SMIN; SUPN
Graham, Arthur *Source(s):* REHG; SUPN
Note(s): "Sorority Sue" (1941). Another composer with this name also wrote for the same publisher, i.e., Boosey & Hawkes. (REHG)
Graham, W(alter) *Source(s):* CCE55; REHG; SMIN; SUPN
Holland, Teddy *Source(s):* REHG; SMIN; SUPN
Kay, Fred *Source(s):* SMIN; SUPN
King, George S. *Source(s):* REHG; SMIN
Klay, Raymond *Source(s):* REHG; SMIN; SUPN
Leoni, Chester *Source(s):* CCE67; REHG; SMIN; SUPN
Lorenz, Luther *Source(s):* REHG; SMIN; SUPN
Loss, Bernard *Source(s):* REHG; SMIN
Manton, Howard *Source(s):* REHG; SMIN; SUPN
Marlowe, David *Source(s):* REHG; SMIN; SUPN
Noble, Eric *Source(s):* REHG; SMIN
North, Frederick *Source(s):* REHG; SMIN; SUPN
Payne, Walter *Source(s):* REHG; SMIN
Perry, A. J. *Source(s):* REHG; SMIN; SUPN
Rayner, Edward *Source(s):* CCE46 E10702 ("High Vision"); REHG; SMIN
Raynor, Edward *Source(s):* REHG; SMIN
Roncal, Simeon *Source(s):* SMIN
Safroni, Leonard *Source(s):* REHG; SMIN; SUPN
Sanford, M. *Source(s):* REHG; SMIN; SUPN
Seldon, M. *Source(s):* REHG; SMIN; SUPN
Severn, Arthur *Source(s):* REHG; SMIN; SUPN
Sills, John Muir *Source(s):* REHG; SMIN; SUPN
Stevens, T. R. *Source(s):* REHG; SMIN; SUPN
Tufilli, W. *Source(s):* CCE46 E9194; REHG; SMIN
Walton, Henry *Source(s):* REHG; SMIN; SUPN
Welden, L. W. *Source(s):* REHG; SMIN; SUPN
Weldon, L. W. *Source(s):* REHG; SMIN; SUPN
Williams, Diane *Source(s):* REHG; SMIN; SUPN
Williams, M(argaret) *Source(s):* REHG; SMIN
Williams, W. *Source(s):* SUPN
Young, Lolita *Source(s):* REHG; SMIN
Frank, Dave [songwriter]
Knarf, Rex *Source(s):* OCLC 24477273
Frank, J. Ludwig
Jacobs, Franz *Source(s):* TPRF
Frank, Marco 1881-1961 [composer]
Fränkl, Markus *Source(s):* KOMU; OMUO
Ratzes *Source(s):* KOMU; OMUO
Frank, Ruth Verd 1899-1977 [composer, author, teacher]
Uhl, Ruth *Source(s):* ASCP
Frankel, Harry 1888-1948 [singer, songwriter]
Henderson, Frank *Source(s):* SUTT
Singin' Sam *Source(s):* CCE60; LCAR; SUTT
Note(s): See also Sam Steven.
Frankenberg, Franz 1919- [composer]
Finten, John *Source(s):* KOMS; PFSA
Wiesner, Fred *Source(s):* KOMS; PFSA
Frankenburger, Paul 1897-1984 [composer]
Ben-Haim, Paul (Shaul) *Source(s):* BAKR; BUL1; GOTH; LCAR; NGDM; NULM (port.); PSND
Frankenstein, Alfred 1906-1981 [music critic]
Frankenstein, Maestro *Source(s):* GRAN
Franklin, Aretha 1942- [singer, songwriter]
First Lady of Soul *Source(s):* CASS; CM17
Lady Soul *Source(s):* PSND; SHAD
Queen of Soul *Source(s):* CASS; GRAT; PSND
Soul, Lady *Source(s):* PSND
Franklin, Edward Lamonte 1928-1975 [singer, guitarist, songwriter]
Franklin, Guitar Pete *Source(s):* LCAR
Franklin, Pete *Source(s):* HARS
Guitar Pete *Source(s):* HARS; LCAR
Franklin, Malvin Maurice 1899-1981 [composer, author, pianist]
Giraldi, Georgis *Source(s):* ASCP
White, Wilkie *Source(s):* ASCP
Franz, (Maria) Marlen(e) 1922- [composer]
Maria-Marlen *Source(s):* CCE51
Marlen, Marie *Source(s):* CCE51
Olden, Stefan *Source(s):* CCE54-61
Note(s): Also possible pseud. of Walter Franz.
Franz, Walter 1921- [composer]
Brennes, Alan *Source(s):* KOMS; PFSA
Flip, Richard *Source(s):* CCE58; CCE60; CCE62

Olden, Stefan *Source(s):* CCE60
Note(s): Possible pseud. Also used by (Maria) Marlen(e) Franz.
Ritter, Helmut *Source(s):* CCE60
Frasi, Felice 1805 (or 06)-1879 [author, pianist, producer]
Franzini, Ottavio *Source(s):* MELL
Frauenberger, P. Ernst, OSB 1769-1840 [composer]
Arnusto *Source(s):* OMUO
Donnamontano *Source(s):* OMUO
Donnamonte *Source(s):* OMUO
Mannthaler *Source(s):* OMUO
Frear, Robin (James) 1889-1952 [pianist, composer, producer]
Heath, Bobby *Source(s):* PSND
Frederick, Donald R. 1917-2000 [composer]
Arick, Ron *Source(s):* ASCP
Frederick, John 1936-2004 [musician, songwriter]
Abdullah, Mohammed *Source(s):* DRSC
Lord Melody *Source(s):* DRSC
Note(s): Also used by Fritzroy Alexander.
Melody, Lord *Source(s):* DRSC
Note(s): Also used by Fritzroy Alexander.
Fredericks(-Williams), Henry St. Claire, (Jr.) 1940 (or 42)- [singer, songwriter]
Mahal, Taj *Source(s):* AMUS; HARS; LCAR; MUHF; PEN2
Taj Mahal *Source(s):* CCE65; CM06; EPMU; LCAR; PEN2
Fredericks, Julian
Maurel, Philippe *Source(s):* TPRF
Freed, Albert (James) 1921-1965 [DJ, songwriter]
Black Jack *Source(s):* CCE56 Eunp
Note(s): Possible pseud.? Listed as pseud of Alan Freed.
Freed, Alan *Source(s):* http://www.alanfreed.com (15 Oct. 2002)
Freed, Richard (Donald) 1928- [music critic]
Clay, Priam *Source(s):* BAKT
Philipp, Gregor *Source(s):* BAKT
Turner, Paul *Source(s):* BAKT
Freedman, M. Claire 1948- [composer, author]
Sunshine, Madeline *Source(s):* ASCP
Freedman, David 1916-2002 [songwriter]
Mann, David *Source(s):* BBDP
Freeman, Harry Lawrence 1869-1954 [composer]
Colored Wagner, The *Source(s):* PSNN
Freeman, Lawrence 1906-1991 [composer, conductor, saxophonist]
Freeman, Bud *Source(s):* ASCP; BAKR; EPMU; KINK; LCAR
Freeman, Philip 1818-1875 [poet]
P. F. *Source(s):* JULN (Suppl.)
Freeth, John 1730-1808 [poet, songwriter]
Birmingham Poet, The *Source(s):* PSND
Free, J(ohn) *Source(s):* LCAR
Freese, Louis [songwriter]
Dr. Freeze *Source(s):* PMUS-93
Freeze, Dr. *Source(s):* PMUS-93 ("Gangsta," "I Ain't Goin' Out Like That" & "Insane in the Brain")
Note(s): Also used by Elliot Straite.
Freese, Louis 1971- [composer]
B Real *Source(s):* LCAR
Frei, Robert 1927- [composer]
Roccard, Ken *Source(s):* SUPN
Freiburger, Earl M. fl. 1915-17 [composer]
Friberger, E. M. *Source(s):* REHH
Note(s): Variant spelling on some publications.
Freinsberg, J(ean) A(dam) G(uillaume) fl. 1702-39 [organist, harpsichordist, composer]
Guilain, Jean Adam Guillaume *Source(s):* LCAR; NGDM
French, George fl. 1950s [composer]
French, Gerry [or Garry] *Source(s):* MUWB
French, Percy 1854-1920 [poet]
Ali Baba *Source(s):* FULD
Frere, W(alter) H(oward) 1863-1938 [hymnbook editor]
W. H. F. *Source(s):* CPMU
Fresedo, Osvaldo Nicolás 1897-1984 [bandoneonist, director, composer]
Pibe de La Paternal, El *Source(s):* TODO
Freudenthaler, Erland Maria 1963- [composer]
Hijland van Vreugdedal *Source(s):* OMUO
Freund(t), Cornelius [or Kornelius] c.1535-1591 [composer, singer]
Bonamicus, Cornelius *Source(s):* LCAR; NGDM; WORB
C. F. *Source(s):* WORB
Freund, Hermann 1871-1943 [producer, librettist]
Haller, Hermann *Source(s):* GAN1; GAN2; LCAR; MACM; WORB
Freund, Walter Jakob 1926- [saxophonist, composer, arranger]
Freund, Joki *Source(s):* NGDJ
Freundlich, Ralph B. 1912-1997 [composer, flutist, guitarist]
Friendly, Ray *Source(s):* ASCP; CCE76
Frič, Josef Václav 1829-1890 [librettist]
Mostecký, H(ynek) *Source(s):* GROL; PIPE
Fricsay, Richard 1867-1945 [composer]
Vsacan, R. F. *Source(s):* SUPN
Frida, Emil Bohušlav 1853-1912 [poet; playwright; librettist]
Vrchlický, Jaroslav *Source(s):* GOTH; LCAR; LOWN; MELL; PSND; WORB
Friedhofer, Hugo Wilhelm 1902-1981 [composer]
Boss, The *Source(s):* PSND
Note(s): See also Bruce (Frederick Joseph) Springsteen.

Fox, The *Source(s):* PSND
Note(s): See also George Dale Williams.
Man, The *Source(s):* PSND
Note(s): See also Johann Sebastian Bach.
Friedl, Franz (Richard) 1892-1977 [composer, conductor]
Renée, Jacques *Source(s):* PIPE
Williams, Stanley *Source(s):* PIPE
Friedman, Alfred 1921- [composer, conductor]
Reed, Alan *Source(s):* GROL
Reed, Alfred *Source(s):* GROL
Friedman, Leo 1869-1927 [songwriter]
Bell, Victor *Source(s):* CCE16 E388519 ("Robin Redbreast's Return")
Kimball, F. R. *Source(s):* CCE16 E389215
Note(s): Also used by Henry S. Sawyer & Frank K. Root; see NOTES: Kimball, F. R.
Friedman, Maurice Herman 1905-?1984 [composer, author]
Frey, Maurice *Source(s):* ASCP
Friedman, Murray *Source(s):* ASCP
Friedman(n), Richard (F.) 1944- [singer, songwriter, actor, music critic, novelist]
Frank Zappa of Country Music, The *Source(s):* AMUS
Friedman, Kinkstah *Source(s):* LCAR
Friedman, Kinkster *Source(s):* LCAR
Friedman(n), Kinky *Source(s):* AMUS; EPMU; HARR; LCAR; MCCL; PEN2
Kinkstah, The *Source(s):* LCAR (see note)
Friedman, Theodore (Leopold) 1891 (or 92)-1971 [bandleader, clarinetist, composer]
Note(s): In GAMM original surname: Freedman.
Hamlet of the Halls, The *Source(s):* PSND
High-hat Tragedian of Song, The *Source(s):* CASS; PSND
Lewis, Ted *Source(s):* ASCP; CASS; GAMM; JASR; KINK; LCAR; PSND; STUW
Lonely Troubadour, The *Source(s):* PSND
Medicine Man for Your Blues, The *Source(s):* PSND
Top Hatted Tragedian of Jazz, The *Source(s):* PSND
Friedmann, Heinrich 1866- [composer, publisher]
Mannfred, Heinrich *Source(s):* CCE41 #38162, 229 R99456; WORB
Melba, Artur *Source(s):* WORB
Peters, C. *Source(s):* WORB
Peters, V. *Source(s):* REHG
Werner, Heinrich *Source(s):* WORB
Friedrich, Horst-Bernd 1955- [composer]
Fisher, Marc *Source(s):* KOMS; PFSA
Hardt, Steven *Source(s):* PFSA
Friedrich(-Feska), Kurt 1882-1955 [librettist]
Freksa, Friedrich *Source(s):* LOWN; WORB

Fries, William [or Bill] (D.) 1928 (or 29)- [singer, songwriter, clarinetist]
McCall, C. W. *Source(s):* CCME; EPMU; HARR; MCCL; PSND
Friml, (Charles) Rudolf 1879-1972 [composer, pianist]
Note(s): Original spelling of surname: Frimel. Portraits: APSA; EWEN
Freeman, Roderick *Source(s):* GROL; LCAR; NGAM; NGDM; NGDO; PIPE
Frith, Jeremy Webster 1949- [guitarist, composer]
Frith, Fred *Source(s):* LCAR
Orville Wright of Deconstructive Guitaring, The *Source(s):* CM19
Fritsch, Johannes Georg(e) 1941- [composer]
Jonas, Gregor *Source(s):* BUL3
Frixer, Alessandro Maria 1741-1825 [composer]
Fridzeri, Alexandre Marie Antoine *Source(s):* STGR
Frizeri, Alessandro Maria *Source(s):* LCAR
Frizzell, David Mark 1959- [singer, songwriter]
Frizzell, Crockett *Source(s):* http://www.crockettfrizzell.com/crockettbio.html (6 Oct. 2002)
Frizzell, William O(rville) 1928-1975 [singer, guitarist, songwriter]
Frizzell, Lefty *Source(s):* EPMU; FLIN; HARR; LCAR; MCCL; MUHF; PSND; STAC
Frohloff, Erich Carl 1921- [composer]
Götz, Norbert *Source(s):* KOMP; KOMS; PFSA
Frontiere, Dominic 1931- [composer]
Llewellyn, Ray *Source(s):* CLTV
Note(s): Also used by others; see NOTES: Llewellyn, Ray
Frosch, Johann c.1480-1533 [theologian, composer, theorist]
Rana, Johann *Source(s):* IBIM; NGDM; WORB
Frost, Frank Otis 1936-1999 [singer, instrumentalist, songwriter]
Mighty King, The *Source(s):* NOTE 57:4 (June 2001): 871
Rhythm and Blues King, The *Source(s):* HARS
Frost, Harold G. 1893-1959 [composer, author]
Frost, Jack *Source(s):* ASCP; CCE22 E546891; CCE51; CCE54; LCAR
Note(s): Also used by Mark Vincent Brine, Charles Degesco, E. Clinton Keithley & Bob Dylan [i.e., Robert Allen Zimmerman]
Frotzler, Karl 1873-1960 [composer]
Auer, Karl *Source(s):* MELL; STGR
Note(s): Also used by Heribert Raich.
Frugoni, Carlo Innocente 1692-1768 [writer, librettist]
Eginetico Comante *Source(s):* SONN
Fruth, Willi 1925- [composer]
Bennett, Steve *Source(s):* KOMP; KOMS; PFSA

Fry, Aaron [composer]
Phrei, Aaron *Source(s):* CPMU (publication dates 1840-43)
Fry, Charles William 1838-1882 [conductor, hymnist]
Note(s): Portraits: CYBH; HOWD
First Bandmaster of the Salvation Army *Source(s):* CYBH
Fry, William H(enry) 1813-1864 [composer, music critic]
Note(s): Portraits: ETUP 51:7 (July 1933): 434; HOWD
America's First Serious Native-Born Orchestral Composer *Source(s):* GRAN
Father of American Opera, The *Source(s):* PSND
Note(s): See also George Gershwin [i.e., Jacob Gershwin] & Kurt Weill.
Virgil Thomson of the Mid-1800s, The *Source(s):* GRAN
Frye, Leslie Legge Sarony 1897-1985 [songwriter]
Frye, Howard *Source(s):* CCE60
Kumber, Q. *Source(s):* CCE56 R176557 ("Mucking About the Garden")
Sarony, Leslie *Source(s):* ROOM
Two Leslies, The *Source(s):* CCE37 Efor49196 ("Dart Song")
Note(s): Jt. pseud.: Leslie Holmes.
Venton & Reef *Source(s):* CCE62 ("Don't Be Surprised")
Note(s): Jt. pseud.: Leslie Holmes.
Frypès, Karel (Vladimir) 1876-1929 [writer]
Novohradský, V. *Source(s):* GOTH; PIPE
Podhorský *Source(s):* PIPE
Sokolov, Vladimir *Source(s):* PIPE
Vlad *Source(s):* PIPE
Fuchs, Frank 1909-1965 [composer, conductor]
Fox, Frank *Source(s):* OMUO
Fuchs, Ignacije [or Ignaz] 1819-1854 [composer]
Lisinski, Vatroslav *Source(s):* BAKO; BAKR; LCAR; MACM; MELL; NGDM; NGDO
Fuchs, Louis 1856-1928 [librettist]
Renard, A. *Source(s):* STGR
Fuchs, Lukas 1922- [composer, conductor, pianist]
Foss, Lukas *Source(s):* BUL1; LCAR; LYMN; NGDM; WORB
Fuchs, Melchoir c.1570-1615 [composer, writer on music]
Vulpius, Melchoir *Source(s):* BAKR; NGDM
Fucik, Julius (Arnost Vilém) 1872-1916 [bandmaster, composer]
Czech March King *Source(s):* http://www.militarymusic.com/200203.htm (25 Feb. 2005)
Fuhrmann, Martin Heinrich 1669-c.1740 [choir master, author]
Frankenberg, Innocentius *Source(s):* IBIM; WORB
Frischmuth, Markus Hilarius *Source(s):* IBIM; WORB
Leuthold *Source(s):* IBIM; WORB
Liebhold *Source(s):* IBIM; WORB
Wagschal, Gerechte *Source(s):* IBIM; WORB
Fuiks, Lewis J(ohn) 1893-1962 [composer, pianist]
Arden, Victor *Source(s):* JASA; JASG; JASN; LCAR; PIAN; SUTT
King of the Piano Roll *Source(s):* PIAN
Fujisawa, Mamoru 1950- [composer]
Hisaishi, Joe *Source(s):* MOMU
Fulcher [composer, arranger]
Note(s): May be John Fulcher (1830-1893).
Rehlcuf *Source(s):* CPMU
Fuld, Leo 1913- [singer, songwriter]
King of Yiddish Music, The *Source(s):* http://henkbrower.tripod.com/fuld01.htm (port.) (6 Oct. 2002)
Fulkerson, Daniel B. [songwriter]
Boone, D. Danny *Source(s):* CCE64; PMUS
Fuller, Jess(i)e 1896-1976 [songwriter, singer, guitarist]
Fuller, Lone Cat *Source(s):* CASS; HARS; LCAR; PEN2; PSND
Fulson, Lowell 1921-1999 [singer, guitarist, songwriter]
Fulsom, Lowell *Source(s):* HARS; LCAR
Tulsa Red *Source(s):* HARS
Fulterman, Martin 1946- [composer]
Snow, Mark *Source(s):* http://geocities.com/ngxfiles/biography.html (28 Feb. 2005)
Fulton, Rosswell Henry 1929- [composer, author]
Fulton, Lucky *Source(s):* ASCP; CPOL TX-4-115-307
Fumet, Dynam-Victor 1867-1949 [composer, writer]
Dynam(ite) *Source(s):* GROL
Fumet, Dynamite *Source(s):* GROL
Funk, Joseph 1779-1862 [songwriter]
Father of Song in Northern Virginia *Source(s):* http://fasola.org/bibliography/wbib.html (6 Oct. 2002)
Furlanetto, Bonaventura 1738-1817 [composer, conductor]
Musin *Source(s):* MACM; NGDM; STGR; WORB
Furnier, Vincent (Damon) 1948- [singer, songwriter, bandleader]
Cooper, Alice *Source(s):* EPMU; GAMM; HARR; LCAR; PEN2; STAM
Godfather of Shock Rock, The *Source(s):* http://www.suite/101.com/article.cfm/9756/59820 (6 Oct.2002)
Furtwangler, Virginia W(alsh) 1932- [author, educator, songwriter]
Copeland, Ann *Source(s):* PSNN
Furze, Jessie (Lilian) 1903-1984 [composer, pianist]
Bowditch, Janet *Source(s):* DWCO; GROL
Dalebury, Jill *Source(s):* DWCO; GROL

Fussan, Werner 1912-1986 [composer]
Hansen, Werner *Source(s):* KOMS; PFSA
Fusz, János 1777-1819 [composer]
Fuss, Johann Evangelist *Source(s):* CCMU; LCAR
Futch, Edward Garvin 1944- [singer, songwriter]
Raven, Eddy *Source(s):* ASCP; CCME; ENCM; EPMU; MCCL; PEN2
Fuzet, Germain Antoine Agricol 1812-1886 [composer]
Imbert *Source(s):* IBIM; WORB
Fyodorov, Fyodor Augustovich 1860-1936 [oboist, conductor, composer]
Niman, Fyodor Augustovich *Source(s):* HOFE

– G –

Gabail, Mercedes 1903-1985 [composer]
Jacobs, Al *Source(s):* WORT
Gabilondo Soler, Francisco (José) 1907-1990 [composer, writer, singer]
Cri-Cri *Source(s):* HWOM; LCAR
Gabilondo, Pancho *Source(s):* HWOM
Grillito Cantor, (El) *Source(s):* LCAR
Gabriel, Charles H(utchinson) 1856-1932 [composer, hymnist]
Note(s): Do not confuse with his son, Charles Hutchinson, Jr. (1893-1934). Portraits: CYBH; HALL; YORK
Adams, Carrie B. *Source(s):* LCPC R21171
Allen, T. R. *Source(s):* CCE40 #25244, 26 R88837; YORK
Briel, H. G. *Source(s):* YORK
Bright, (Rev.) H. E. *Source(s):* CCE41 #26816, 126 R96744; YORK
Brown, C. S. *Source(s):* CCE45 #8173, 17 R135168 ("The Blood Cleanseth Me")
Brown, M. S. *Source(s):* CCE50 R61047 ("Jesus Will Be with Me"); YORK
Brown, Mary *Source(s):* CCE50 R61043 ("Bless the Lord"); YORK
Note(s): Do not confuse with Mary Brown, author of the 1st stanze of the hymn, "It May Not Be on the Mountain's Height." (YORK p. 159-60)
Burns, Robert *Source(s):* CCE33 R2712 ("Forever and Ever")
C. H. G. *Source(s):* CCE25 R33151 ("Are You Ready"); CCE41 R98541 ("Reaping Time Comes")
Crane, F. R. *Source(s):* YORK
Crosby, George H. *Source(s):* CCE28 R42452
DeYoe, A. S. *Source(s): Source(s):* CCE28 R43697
Dingman, (Mrs.) W. H. *Source(s):* CCE40 #39050, 118 R92286
Elliott, M(artin) A. *Source(s):* CCE30 R7693; YORK
Emerson, C. D. *Source(s):* CCE28 R42459; YORK
Fischer, Carl *Source(s):* CCE33 R27153; CCE40 #25244, 236 R88855; CCE42 #19091, 228 R108773; CCE44 #51525, 94 R133919; CCE41 #34470, 165 R98508; YORK
Note(s): The fact there was a Carl Fischer Publishing Co. added to the effectiveness of this pseud.; it also caused confusion; see NOTES: Fischer, Carl.
Ford, J(ay) A. *Source(s):* CCE31 R15703; YORK
Foster, E(van) S. *Source(s):* CCE27; LCPC A968248; YORK
Gabriel-Shelly *Source(s):* CCE30 E12153; CCE47 E12153
Note(s): Jt. pseud.: Harry Shelly
Gabriel, Vera G. *Source(s):* CCE26 R33151
H. A. H. *Source(s):* CCE25 E619326 ("Little Beam of Light"); YORK
Hains, Ben *Source(s):* CCE28 R43698
Henry, H. A. *Source(s):* CCE23 R23817; CCE28 R42463; CYBH; YORK
Henry, Hazel A. *Source(s):* CCE46 R8363 ("Some Day Dear")
Homer, Charlotte G. *Source(s):* CCE28 R43026; CYBH; GROL; YORK
Howard, Jean *Source(s):* CCE40 #15093, 414 R85665; YORK
Irving Berlin of Gospel Song, The *Source(s):* Brockett, Clyde W. "The Operettas of Charles Hutchinson Gabriel," in *Music and Culture in America; 1861-1918.* Edited by Michael Saffle. New York: Garland, 1998, p. 339.
Jackson, (Dr.) S. B. *Source(s):* CCE28 R42460; CYBH; YORK
Jacson, S. B. *Source(s):* CCE42 #24219, 1178 R107996 ("Send the Message")
Note(s): Typographical error?
Jesreal, A(dolph) *Source(s):* CCE28 R42436; CCE31 R13375
Johnson, Julia *Source(s):* CCE30 R10144
Jordon, H. C. *Source(s):* CCE40 #25244, 262 R88858; YORK
Junior, C. H. *Source(s):* CCE39 R52218 ("His Name Forever")
Junior, H. C. *Source(s):* CCE39 R85221; CCE40 #15093, 3412 R85221; YORK
Lighthall, W. M. *Source(s):* CCE33 R27373 ("He Knows Me By My Name")
Lockwood, Torrence (E.) *Source(s):* CCE32 R21288
M. A. E. *Source(s):* CCE30 R74509 ("Remember Jesus")
McAuley, N(eal) A. *Source(s):* CCE28 R43699; CCE42 #24219, 144 R107800
Oliver, A. (O.) *Source(s):* CCE40 #11969, 410 R84644; YORK
Ree, Jennie *Source(s):* CCE30 R10375; YORK

Savage, J. R. *Source(s):* CCE31 R15618; CCE40 #15093, 1304 R86395
Tiballs, John *Source(s):* CCE27 R40098
Note(s): Also used by E(dmund) S(imon) Lorenz; see NOTES: Tiballs, John.
Ward, D. C. *Source(s):* CCE21 E505150; YORK
Webb, B. F. *Source(s):* CCE40 R92283
Webb, F. R. *Source(s):* CCE42 #24219, 224 R107845; YORK
Williams, J. C. *Source(s):* CCE40 #39050, 449 R91164; YORK
Williams, O(ran) (A.) *Source(s):* CCE28 Index; CCE30 R10111
X. X. X. *Source(s):* CCE31 R13427 ("Bethlehem's Cherub")

Gabriel (de Lurieu), Jules-Joseph 1792-1869 [playwright]
Jules *Source(s):* PIPE
Sapajou, M. *Source(s):* PIPE

Gabriel, (Mary Ann) Virginia 1825-1877 [composer]
Gabrielle *Source(s):* LCAR
March, Mary Ann Virginia *Source(s):* KILG

Gabrieli, Andrea c.1533-1585 (or 86) [composer]
Andrea di Cannaregio *Source(s):* BAKR

Gabrieli, Giovanni c.1553-1612 [composer]
Father of Orchestration, The *Source(s):* DEAR; SPIE

Gabrielli, Domenico 1651-1690 [violoncellist, composer]
Menghino del Violoncello, Il *Source(s):* BAKR; MELL
Mingàn dal viulunzaal *Source(s):* BAKR; SADC
Mingein dal viulunzel *Source(s):* GROL
Minghino dal Violoncello *Source(s):* GROL; NGDM; WORB

Gadd, Paul 1940 (or 44)- [singer, songwriter]
Bucket, Rubber *Source(s):* CM19
Glitter, Gary *Source(s):* CM19; EPMU; LCAR; PEN2
Monday, Paul *Source(s):* CM19; PEN2
Raven, Paul *Source(s):* CM19; PEN2
Rubber Bucket *Source(s):* CM19
Russell, Paul *Source(s):* CM19

Gade, Niels, W. 1817-1890 [composer]
Father of Danish Music *Source(s):* MUWB

Gaeta, Giovanni 1884-1961 [composer]
Mario, E. (A.) *Source(s):* CCE53-57; GREN; LCAR

Gafori, Franchino 1451-1522 [theorist, composer]

Gafarov Ilham Baba 1964- [composer]
Azmanli *Source(s):* http://composers.aznet.org/composers/composers-g.htm (7 Oct. 2002)

Gafori, Franchino 1451-1522 [writer on music, theorist, composer]
Gaf(f)urius, Franchinus *Source(s):* LCAR

Gagliano, Marco da 1582-1643 [composer]
Affannato, L' *Source(s):* GROL
Zanobi, Marco *Source(s):* GROL
Note(s): Erronously identified as Gagliano.

Gagnon, Blanche 1867-1951 [writer on music]
Amicus *Source(s):* CANE
Note(s): See also Peter Dodds McCormick.
Bibliophile *Source(s):* CANE
Frimaire *Source(s):* CANE
Manrésien *Source(s):* CANE

Gaillard, Bulee 1916-1991 [singer, songwriter, guitarist]
Gaillard, Slim *Source(s):* BBDP; CASS; EPMU; HARR; KINK; LCAR; PEN2
Slim and Slam *Source(s):* http://www.pocreations.com/slimarticle.htm
Note(s): Jt. pseud.: Slam [i.e., Leroy Elliot] Stewart.

Gaines, LaDonna [or Donna] Andrea [or Adrian] 1948- [singer, songwriter]
Disco Queen *Source(s):* CASS
Dummer, Donna *Source(s):* CM12
Note(s): Typographical error?
Summer, Donna *Source(s):* CASS; CLAG; LCAR; NGAM

Gajkovic, Dusan 1931- [trumpeter, composer]
Goykovich, Dusko *Source(s):* PSND

Galambos, Benjamin 1814-1851 [composer, librettist, dramatist]
Egressy, Béni *Source(s):* MELL; NGDM; OMUO; PIPE

Galán Blanco, Francisco 1906-1988 [orchestra leader, songwriter]
Galán, Pacho *Source(s):* CCE61-62; HWOM
Pacho *Source(s):* CCE61-62; HWOM
Note(s): See also Juan (Felix) Maglio.

Galás, Dimitria Angeliki Elena 1955- [singer, composer]
Galás, Diamánda *Source(s):* GROL
Zina, Miss *Source(s):* GROL

Galbraith, Gordon 1930- [composer, author, singer]
Bell, George *Source(s):* CCE64
Young, Gordon *Source(s):* ASCP; CCE60

Gales, Manuel 1968- [guitarist, singer, songwriter]
Future of Blues Guitar, The *Source(s):* AMUS
King, Little Jimmy *Source(s):* AMUS

Gallego Sánchez, Luis ?-1992 [singer, songwriter]
Rey, Luis(ito) *Source(s):* HWOM

Gallimore, Rosan(ne) 1941- [singer, songwriter]
McGowan, (Mrs.) Annie *Source(s):* AMUS; EPMU
Rattlesnake Annie *Source(s):* AMUS; EPMU; MCCL

Gallot, Antoine ?-1647 [lutenist, composer]
Gallot d'Angers *Source(s):* LCAR; MACM; NGDM
Vieux Gallot *Source(s):* LCAR; NGDM

Gallot, Jacques (de) ?-1685 (or 90) [lutenist, composer]
Gallot de Paris *Source(s):* MACM

Gallot, le vieux *Source(s):* LCAR
Vieux Gallot de Paris *Source(s):* NGDM
Gallus, Joannes fl. mid 16th cent. [composer]
Note(s): See LCAR for additional variant forms of name.
Jahn, Maistre *Source(s):* NGDM
Jean, (Maître) *Source(s):* CPMU; LCAR
Le Cocq, Jehan *Source(s):* NGDM
Lecocq, Maistre Jhan *Source(s):* GROL; WORB
Gálszécsy és Butykai, Ákos 1871-1935 [composer, pianist]
Buttykay, Ákos *Source(s):* BAKO; GAN1; GAN2
Galucki, Michael [librettist]
Kryukov, A. *Source(s):* LOWN
Note(s): Probable pseud.
Galuppi, Antonio ?-c.1780 [librettist]
Liteo, Ageo *Source(s):* ALMC; LCAR; MORI; NGDO; SONN
Galuppi, Baldassare 1706-1785 [composer, conductor]
Baldissera *Source(s):* NGDO
Buranello, Il *Source(s):* ALMC; GROL; LCAR; MELL; NGDM; NGDO; PIPE; SADC
Father of Opera Buffa, The *Source(s):* http://www.xrefer.com/entry504220 (6 Oct. 2002)
Note(s): See also Carlo Goldoni.
Gamble, Kenneth [or Kenny] 1943- [songwriter, producer]
Gamble and Huff *Source(s):* LCAR (see note); NGAM
Note(s): Jt. pseud.: Leon Huff.
Ganassi (dal Fontego), Sylvestro [or Silvestro] di 1492-mid 1500s [instrumentalist, writer on music]
Silvestro del cornetto *Source(s):* GROL
Note(s): Possible nickname.
Gandonnière, Almire 1814- [journalist, author]
Goulet, Baron Paul *Source(s):* PIPE
Loué, Philibert *Source(s):* PIPE
Mortimer, (Sir) Henry *Source(s):* PIPE
Tom-Ponce *Source(s):* PIPE
Gannon, James Kimball 1900-1974 [author, lyricist]
Gannon, Kim *Source(s):* ASCP; CCE66; IGER; LCAR; STUW; VACH
Henning, Robert *Source(s):* CCE40 #40414 E89565; CCE68
Gänsbacher, Johann Baptist 1778-1844 [composer]
Triole *Source(s):* GRV2 (v. 5, p. 642, col. 1); Warrack, John. *Carl Maria von Weber.* 2nd ed. Cambridge: Cambridge University Press, 1976, p. 104.
Gant, Cecil 1913-1951 [singer, pianist, songwriter]
Carr, Gunter Lee *Source(s):* HARS; LCAR
GI Sing-Sation, The *Source(s):* HARS
García (Bautista), Braulio A. [singer, songwriter]
Braulio *Source(s):* HWOM; LCAR
Garcia (Fajer), Francisco Javier 1730 (or 31)-1809 [composer]
Españoleto, El *Source(s):* LCAR
Garcia, Padre *Source(s):* PSND
Spagnoletto, Il *Source(s):* NGDM; NGDO; STGR
Note(s): See also Gioseffo [or Giuseppe] Catrufo.
Garcia, José Maurício Nunes 1767-1830 [composer]
José Maurício (Nunez) *Source(s):* LCAR; NGDM; WORB
García Peña, Jesús Arturo 1932- [singer, songwriter]
Gareña, Mario *Source(s):* HWOM
Gardiner, William 1770-1853 [business man, music editor, composer]
Dilettante, A. *Source(s):* CART
Leicester, W. G. *Source(s):* BROW; CYBH; NGDM
Paxton *Source(s):* HUEV
W.G., of Leicester *Source(s):* CPMS
Note(s): Probable initials of Gardiner; "Ah Well A-Day" (1795?).
Gardner, Charles A. ?-1924 [composer, lyricist]
Gardner, Karl *Source(s):* PSND
Gardner, Kay 1941- [composer, flutist, conductor]
Child, C(osmos) W(onder) *Source(s):* CCE74; DWCO
Cosmos Wonder-Child *Source(s):* CCE74; DWCO
Wonder Child *Source(s):* CCE74
Gardner, Maurice 1909-2002 [composer, author, conductor, arranger]
Gardano, Alessandro *Source(s):* ASCP; CCE72; LCAR; REHG
Norman, Robert *Source(s):* ASCP; CCE52; CCE60; LCAR; REHG
Pollack, Martin *Source(s):* ASCP; LCAR; REHG; SUPN
Talmage, Gerald *Source(s):* CCE64
Note(s): Typographical error?
Thomas, Trinidad *Source(s):* CCE57
Tolmage, Gerald *Source(s):* ASCP; CCE52-53; CCE61; LCAR; REHG
Trinidad, Pete *Source(s):* CCE57
Gardner, William 1930- [arranger, composer]
Hope, Peter *Source(s):* MUWB
Garelli Della Morea, Vincenza, (Countess de Cardenas) 1859-after 1924 [pianist, composer]
Della Morea, Centa *Source(s):* DWCO; GROL; MACM (see under: Morea)
Gareth, Benedetto c.1450-1514 [poet, singer, musician]
Cariteo, Il *Source(s):* LCAR; WORB
Chariteo, Il *Source(s):* LCAR; NGDM
Chariteus *Source(s):* NGDM
Garret, Benet *Source(s):* LCAR
Garfield, Henry 1961- [singer, songwriter, actor]
Post-punk Generation's Prophet of Rage, The *Source(s):* CM11

Primal Scream Personified, A *Source(s):* CM11
Punk's Poet Laureate *Source(s):* CM11
Rollins, Henry *Source(s):* CM11; LCAR; PEN2
Garfunkel, Art(thur Ira) 1941- [singer, songwriter, actor]
Note(s): Portrait: LYMN (with Paul Frederick Simon)
Garr, Artie *Source(s):* http://www.songfta.com/bio.htm (6 Oct. 2002)
Graph, Tom *Source(s):* CCE58; PSND
Tom and Jerry *Source(s):* EPMU; PSND; SHAD
Note(s): Jt. pseud.: Paul Frederick Simon.
Garland, Mary Magdalene 1880-1960 [singer, songwriter, political activist]
Female Leadbelly, A *Source(s):* MCCL
Jackson, Aunt Molly *Source(s):* EPMU; GRAT; LCAR; MCCL
Garland, Walter [composer]
Garland, Hank *Source(s):* CLTP ("Ozark Jubilee")
Garlow, Clarence Joseph 1911-1986 [singer, instrumentalist, songwriter]
Bon-Ton *Source(s):* CCE55 Eunp
Garlow, Bon Ton *Source(s):* AMUS; HARS
Parran *Source(s):* HARS
Garnett, Leroy 1958- [composer]
Garnett, Blind *Source(s):* PSNN
Garre, (Edmée) Sophie 1775-1819 [composer]
Sophie G....., (Mme.) *Source(s):* CPMU
Garreta, Juli(o) 1875-1925 [composer]
Wagner of the Sardana, The *Source(s):* NGDM
Garrett, James Allen 1937-1998 [composer]
Garbáge, Hauloff *Source(s):* http://org.tntech.edu/tuba/pierre.htm (18 Mar. 2005)
Garbáge, Pierre *Source(s):* *TUBA* 26:1 (1998): 21; http://org.tntech.edu/tuba/pierre.htm
Gilfish, Trident "Gigger" *Source(s):* http://org.tntech.edu/tuba/pierre.htm
Raton, Rodente (Mousey) *Source(s):* http://org.tntech.edu/tuba/pierre.htm
Garrett, Samuel (M.) fl. 20th cent. [composer, lyricist]
Mills, Hank *Source(s):* CCE60; CCE65-68; PMUS; PSNN
Garrett, Thomas 1939- [composer, arranger]
Garrett, Snuff *Source(s):* MOMU
Garriguenc, Rene 1908-1998 [composer]
Garriguenc, Aime *Source(s):* CLTP ("Line-Up")
Garrity, Eddie [composer]
Banger, Ed *Source(s):* BLIC
Garsi, Santino (da Parma) 1542-1604 [lutenist, composer]
La Garsa *Source(s):* LCAR (see note); NGDM
Valdes *Source(s):* LCAR (see note); NGDM; WORB
Garza, José Francisco [singer, songwriter, radio announcer]
Garza, Pepe *Source(s):* HWOM
Gaskill, Clarence 1892-1947 [songwriter]
Alexander, (Alton) *Source(s):* CCE64; CCE67; CPOL RE-656-029; LCAR
Gasbrit, Obie *Source(s):* CCE31 Eunp33773
Grant C. E. *Source(s):* CCE65; CCE73
Grant, Cal *Source(s):* CCE61
Melody Monarch *Source(s):* VACH
Morris-Gilbert, (A.) *Source(s):* CCE65
Gasparini, Francesco 1668-1727 [composer, teacher]
Ericreo *Source(s):* GROL
Gasparus fl. 16th cent. [composer]
Kindmann *Source(s):* IBIM; WORB
Gassion, Edith Giovanna 1915-1963 [songwriter]
Little Sparrow *Source(s):* PSND
Note(s): See also Slinger Francisco.
Little Sparrow of Paris, The *Source(s):* CASS; PSND
Piaf, Edith *Source(s):* BAKR; CASS; CPMU; EPMU; LCAR; PSND
Piaf, Môme *Source(s):* FULD
Sparrow, Kid *Source(s):* PSND
Gassmann, Alfred Leonz 1876-1962 [composer]
Rhyn, Hans am *Source(s):* SUPN
Gaste, Louis (Felix-Marie) 1908-1995 [guitarist, songwriter]
Gaste, Lou Lou *Source(s):* CCE74; DRSC
Gaston-Danville, Berthe [librettist]
Rosenval *Source(s):* BLIC; LCAR
Gately, Frances Sabine 1893- [organist, pianist, composer]
Rose of Jesus, (Sister) *Source(s):* COHN; HIXN
Gätjens, Manfred 1926- [composer]
Mayn, Manni *Source(s):* PFSA
Meyn, Manni *Source(s):* KOMP; KOMS; PFSA; SUPN
Gatlif, Michael Dahmani 1948- [actor, writer, composer]
Gatlif, Tony *Source(s):* MOMU
Gatta, Antonio fl. 1763-1771 [librettist]
Niceno, Faresio *Source(s):* MORI; NGDO
Gatterman, Eugen Ludwig 1886- [author, composer]
Corvin, Eugen Alban *Source(s):* PSND
Renner, A. M. *Source(s):* PSND
Gatti, Théobalde di c.1650-1727 [composer, bass viol player]
Théobald(e) *Source(s):* NGDM; SONN
Gaucquier, Alard (Dunoyer du) c.1534-c.1582 [composer]
Du Gaucquier, Alard *Source(s):* IBIM; WORB
Dunoyer du Gaucuier, Alard *Source(s):* WORB
Nicaeus, Alardus *Source(s):* WORB
Nuceus, (Alardus) *Source(s):* IBIM; MACM; WORB
Gaudichot-Masson, Auguste Michel Benoît 1800-1883 [author]
Masson, Michel *Source(s):* LCAR; PIPE
Michel-Masson, M. *Source(s):* LCAR

Raymond, Michel *Source(s):* LCAR; PIPE
Note(s): Jt. pseud.: Raymond (Philippe Auguste) Brucker.
Gaudlitz, Gottlieb 1694-1745 [vicar, musician]
Taube, Christian Friedric *Source(s):* IBIM; WORB
Gaul, Harvey B(artlett) 1881-1945 [composer, organist, critic]
Note(s): Portrait: ETUP 51:9 (Sept. 1933): 568
Balkie Gregoire *Source(s):* CCE40 #6270 E82184; CCE67 R402362
Deems, Will *Source(s):* CCE62 R291252; GOTH; LCAR; NGAM
Demann, Ernest *Source(s):* CCE64 R333055
Douglas(s), Jessie *Source(s):* CCE34 E41218; CCE64 R331075
Jenks, Lester *Source(s):* CCE21 E513304; GOTH; LCAR; NGAM
Mapleson, Anne *Source(s):* CCE34 E41216; CCE62 R291251
Poole, Joe *Source(s):* CCE59
Wellings, Monte *Source(s):* CCE57; GOTH; LCAR; NGAM
Gaultier, Denis [or Denys] 1597-1672 [composer, lutenist]
Note(s): Portrait: ETUP 51:9 (Sept. 1933): 568
Gaultier de Paris *Source(s):* LCAR; NGDM
Gaultier le jeune *Source(s):* LCAR; NGDM
Gaultier, Ennemond [or Eunémond] 1575-1651 [composer, lutenist]
Gaultier de Lyon *Source(s):* LCAR (see note); NGDM
Vieux Gaultier, Le *Source(s):* LCAR (see note); NGDM
Gaultier, Racine 1817-1863 [pianist, composer]
Prudent, Emile Beunie *Source(s):* IBIM; WORB
Gauntlett, Henry John 1805-1876 [composer, organist, hymnbook editor]
Father of Church Music, The *Source(s):* CYBH
Note(s): See also Thomas Tallis.
H. J. G. *Source(s):* CPMU
Gauterius de Castello Rainardi 12th cent. [composer]
Gauthier of Chateaurenard *Source(s):* NGDM
Gauthier, Paul-Marcel 1910 [folklorist, singer, actor, composer]
Purlenne, Jean-Baptiste *Source(s):* CANE; LCAR
Gauthier-Villars, Henri 1859-1931 [music critic, playwright]
Max, Willy *Source(s):* LCPC Afor20123; PIPE
Ouvreuse du Cirque (d'Eté), L' *Source(s):* BAKR; WHIT; WORB
Tinan, Jean de *Source(s):* LCAR
Note(s): Ghost writer for Willy [i.e., Henri Gauthier-Villars]
Willy *Source(s):* BAKR; MACM; PIPE; WHIT; WORB
Note(s): Also used by his wife: Sidonie Gabrielle Claudine.
Gautier, François 1876-1950 [singer, composer]
Franz, Paul *Source(s):* NGDO
Note(s): Also used by A(nnuzio) P(aolo) Mantovani.
Gautier, Jacques late 1500s.-before 1660 [lutenist, composer]
Gautier d'Angleterre *Source(s):* NGDM; SADC
Gautier, Pierre 1599-after 1638 [composer, lutenist]
Gautier de Rome *Source(s):* GROL
Gautier d'Orleans *Source(s):* GROL
Gautier, Pierre c.1642-1696 [composer, organist]
Gautier de Marseille *Source(s):* GROL; LCAR; NGDO
Pierre de Marseille *Source(s):* WORB
Gavoty, Bernard (Georges Marie) 1908-1981 [critic, writer on music, organist]
Clarendon *Source(s):* GROL; LCAR; RIES; WORB
Gaye, Marvin (Pentz) 1939?-1984 [singer, composer, producer]
Mr. Midnight *Source(s):* PSND
Prince of Motown, The *Source(s):* PSND
Gaze, Hermann Otto 1908-1967 [composer]
Gaze, Heino *Source(s):* CCE53; RIES
Golden, Charles *Source(s):* CCE55 Efor36144; CPOL RE-108-940
Husarek, Jan *Source(s):* CCE55
Shield, J. *Source(s):* CCE56
Ticco, Ramon *Source(s):* CCE55
Timm, Toni *Source(s):* CCE53-56
Gearhart, Livingston 1916-1996 [composer]
Coole, Orlando *Source(s):* CCE62; GOTH
Gearinger, Lemuel Cyrus 1894-1984 [composer, author]
Hale, Mark *Source(s):* ASCP
Gebauer, Benny 1939- [composer]
Romain, Jacques *Source(s):* KOMP; KOMS
Gebler, Tobias Philipp von 1720-1786 [author, public official]
Cornatus *Source(s):* PIPE
Geehl, Henry Ernest 1881-1961 [songwriter]
Fraser, Dennise *Source(s):* CCE57; CCE64
Gheel, Henry *Source(s):* CCE54
Keller, Oscar *Source(s):* CPMU
Vaughan, Lynn *Source(s):* CCE33 Efor30525 ("Sailing")
Gehlhaar, Rolf (Rainer) 1943- [composer]
Godfather of Electronic Music *Source(s):* http://www.ecamltd.com/kodjabashiapages/nkprofile.html(6 Oct. 2002)
Note(s): See also Lev Sergievitch Termen.
Geibel, Adam 1855-1933 [composer, conductor, organist]

Note(s): Portraits: CYBH; ETUP 51:9 (Sept. 1933): 568; MUCO (20-27 Dec. 1899)
Adams, Arthur *Source(s):* CCE40 #11969, 222 R81713
Lebieg, Earl *Source(s):* CCE50 R70230 ("Sleep"); CCE56; CLTP ("Fred Waring Show"); JASA
Note(s): Jt. pseud.: Earl Burnett.
Linders, Karl *Source(s):*CCE17 E398512
Taylor, Walter G. *Source(s):* CCE42 #24219, 353 R17945
Tyler, Walter G. *Source(s):* CCE38 R63345; CCE42 #24219, 353 R107945; CCE66
Tyler, Walter J. *Source(s):* CCE38 R71204
Note(s): Possible misprint, i.e., J instead of G.
Geiringer, Hilda 1898-1977 [composer]
Note(s): Do not confuse with Hilda Güden, later Geiringer, 1917-1988.
Gerrick, Hilda *Source(s):* OMUO
Harald, Harry *Source(s):* OMUO
Geisel, Theodore Seuss 1904-1991 [author, artist, songwriter]
LeStieg, Theodore *Source(s):* LCAR; PSND
Seuss, Dr. *Source(s):* CCE52; CCE66; LCAR; PSND
Geist, Byron [songwriter]
Hilton, Arthur *Source(s):* LCCC1955-70 (see reference)
Note(s): Jt. pseud: Walter (Charles) Ehret. Ehret also used as jt. pseud. with other individuals; see NOTES: Hilton, Arthur.
Geitz, Karl Heinrich 1903- [organist, choral director, writer on music]
Zilak, Gert *Source(s):* MACM
Gelinek, Hermann Anton 1709-1779 [monk, violinist, composer]
Cervetti, Herman (Anton) *Source(s):* MACM; PRAT; WORB
Gellers, Irving 1907- [composer, arranger, conductor]
Carroll, Irv *Source(s):* ASCB
Gelück, Kurt 1927- [composer]
Parker, John *Source(s):* CCE74; KOMP; PFSA
Gem, Louis Adolphe 1824-1901 [playwright, librettist]
Jaime, (Louis) (Adolphe) *Source(s):* GAN1; GAN2; LCAR
Gemperle, Karl 1853-1934 [actor, librettist]
Lindau, Karl [or Carl] *Source(s):* GAN1; GAN2; OMUO
Genet, Elzéar c.1470-1548 [composer, singer]
Carpentras(so), (Il) *Source(s):* DAWS; LCAR; MACM; NGDM; WORB
Curpentrus *Source(s):* MACM
Genzale, John (Anthony, Jr.) 1954-1991 [singer, songwriter]
Thunders, Johnny *Source(s):* CCE73; HARR
Notes(s): Do not confuse with Johnny Thunder [i.e., Gil Hamilton]
Georgantones, Jimmy P. 1939 (or 40)- [composer, music producer]
George, Jimmy *Source(s):* ASCP; CPOL PAu-1-915-102
George III, King of Great Britain 1738-1820 [monarch, songwriter]
Barmard, Mr. *Source(s):* OCLC 43215409
George Konrad, Prince of Prussia 1826-1902 [librettist]
Conrad, G. *Source(s):* MELL
Georgiou, Steven [or Stephen] Demetri 1947 (or 48)- [singer, pianist; songwriter, guitarist]
Islam, Yusef [or Yusuf, or Yosef] *Source(s):* ALMN; CASS; CM03; PSND
Stevens, Cat *Source(s):* ALMN; CM03; CPMU; DIMA; EPMU; HARR; MUHF; PEN2
Geppert, Christopher 1951- [singer, guitarist, songwriter]
Cross, Christopher *Source(s):* ALMN; EPMU; HARD; HARR; STAM
Gerak, Berrie Lee 1942- [composer, songwriter]
Christopher, Berrie *Source(s):* ASCP
Gerant, John [actor, stage manager]
Sugarman, Jacob *Source(s):* GANA p. 807
Note(s): Possible jt. pseud.: Frederick Mantell & Henry S. Ugar.
Gerard, (Marie) Paul Émile 1850-1932 [playwright]
Sylvane, André *Source(s):* GAN1; GAN2; LCAR
Gerbert, Franz Dominik Bernhard 1720-1791 [writer on music]
Gerbert, Martin, OSB *Source(s):* http://ezines.onb.ac.at:8080/moravec/pub/schr/2164.htm (14 Oct. 2003)
Gerhard (Ottenwaelder), Robert(o) 1896-1970 [composer]
Serrallonga, Juan *Source(s):* GDRM; GROL; NOTE 51:1 (1994): 89
Gerich, Valentine 1898-1975 [composer, accordionist]
Valentine, Val *Source(s):* PSND
Gericke, Wilhelm 1845-1925 [conductor, composer]
Note(s): Portrait: ETUP 51:9 (Sept. 1933): 568
Ecker, Wenzel *Source(s):* MACM
Gerlach, (Stephen) Nicholas [or Nick] [songwriter]
Kincaid, Jesse Lee *Source(s):* CCE65; CCE68; PMUS
Gerlich, Clara 1887-1974 [singer, pianist, songwriter, author]
Note(s): Portrait: ETUP 51:3 (Mar. 1933): 148 (see under Edwards)
Edwards, (Mrs.) Clara *Source(s):* GRAT
Haig(h), Bernard *Source(s):* ASCP; BUL3; COHN; CPOL RE-462-980; HIXN; LCAR

Percy, Alexander *Source(s):* CCE65
Percy, William Alexander *Source(s):* CCE51 R75040 ("The Little Shepherd's Song")
Gershenson, Joseph E. [conductor, composer]
Sanford, Joseph G. *Source(s):* http://entertainment.msn.com/celebs/celeb.aspx?mp=b&c=53036 (2 Nov. 2003)
Gershman, Howard Elliott 1950 (or 51)-1991 [author, lyricist, director]
Ashman, Howard (Elliott) *Source(s):* GAN1; GAN2
Gershvin, Israel 1896-1983 [lyricist]
Note(s): Portraits: EWEN; EWPA
Francis, Arthur *Source(s):* CCE47 R17377; GAN1; GAN2; GROL; PIPE
Note(s): Do not confuse with Art Francis [i.e., Joseph Francis Otto]
Gersh *Source(s):* PSND
Gershwin, Bruskin *Source(s):* PSND
Gershwin, Ira *Source(s):* GAN1; GAN2
Jackson, Arthur *Source(s):* BBDP
Gershvin, Jacob 1898-1937 [composer]
Note(s): Portraits: EWEN; EWPA
America's Greatest Composer *Source(s):* http://www.ffaire.com/gershwin (6 Oct. 2002)
Note(s): See also Leonard [i.e., Louis] Bernstein, Charles Edward Ives & Charles Puerner.
Baker, James *Source(s):* PSND
Father of American Opera *Source(s):* http://www.ndr.de/bigband/disco/weill100.htm (6 Oct. 2002)
Note(s): See also William Henry Fry & Kurt Weill.
Gershwin, George *Source(s):* GAN1; GAN2
Great "Jazz Emancipator," The *Source(s):* FACS
Mr. Big of Tin Pan Alley *Source(s):* PSND
Murtha, Fred *Source(s):* PSND
Wynn, Bert *Source(s):* PSND
Wynn, George *Source(s):* Jablonski, Edward. *Gershwin Remembered*. Portland, OR: Amadeus Press, 1992, 16.
Gersov, Viktor Aleksandrovich 1899-1952 [composer]
Oranski, Viktor Aleksandrovich *Source(s):* BUL1
Gerstenberg, Heinrich Wilhelm von 1737-1823 [author, critic]
Madsen, Ohle [or Ole] *Source(s):* PIPE; WORB
Gertz, Irving 1915- [composer]
Gordon, Melvyn Lenard *Source(s):* CLTP ("Adventures of Kit Carson")
Note(s): Composed music for the publisher David M. Gordon under the names listed below, as did Dave Kahn, William Lava, Leo(n) Klatzkin, Joseph [or Joe] Mullendore & possibly others. See also David M. Gordon.
Gordon, Melvyn Lenard *Source(s):* CLTP ("Adventures of Kit Carson")
Lenard, Melvyn *Sources(s):* CLMC
Gervays, Gervasius de Anglia 14-15th cent. [composer]
Jervays, (Mr.) *Source(s):* GRV5; http://www.hoasm.org/IIIC/Jervajs.html (16 Oct. 2003)
Gesner, Clark 1938-2002 [composer, author]
Gordon, John *Source(s):* ASCP; LCAR; PIPE
Gesualdo, Carlo c.1561-1613 (or 14) [composer]
Pilonij, Giuseppe *Source(s):* IBIM; WORB
Principe di Venosa *Source(s):* IBIM; WORB
Venosa, Carlo Gesualdo da *Source(s):* WORB
Venosa, Prince of *Source(s):* SADC
Ghestem, Paulette [composer]
Soleil, Didier *Source(s):* CCE60-61; CCE66-68; GOTH
Ghignone, Giovanni Pietro 1702-1774 [violinist, composer]
Note(s): Italian violinist active in France.
Dernier Roy des violins *Source(s):* GROL
Guignon, Jean Pierre *Source(s):* LCAR
Roi des violons (et ménétries) *Source(s):* GROL
Ghiselin, Johannes [or Jean] fl. early 16th cent. [composer]
Ghisling, Johann *Source(s):* LCAR; WORB
Verbo(n)net, (Johannes) *Source(s):* NGDM; RIEM; WORB
Giacobbe, Nello 1940- [composer, author, singer]
Rossano, Nino *Source(s):* ASCP
Giacomini, Bernardo 1536-1563 (or after) [composer]
Gentilhuomo Fiorentino *Source(s):* NGDM
Giacosa, Giuseppe 1847-1906 [librettist, playwright]
Ranfagni, Enrico *Source(s):* MELL
Giancursio, Joseph 1921-1987 [composer, teacher, instrumentalist]
Cursio, Jan *Source(s):* ASCP; CPOL PAu-82-477
Giangreco, Thomas 1911-2001 [composer, author]
Greco, Tommy *Source(s):* ASCP; CCE42 #52380 Eunp318873
Giani, Romualdo 1868-1931 [writer on music]
Pagano, L. *Source(s):* GROL; NGDM
Giannini, Giovanni Matteo mentioned 1667-1693 [librettist]
Disinvolto *Source(s):* ALMC
Pacifico *Source(s):* ALMC
Simpatico *Source(s):* ALMC
Giannini, Guglielmo 1891-1960 [journalist, playwright]
Vario, Alberto *Source(s):* PIPE
Zorro *Source(s):* LCAR; PIPE; WORB
Giasson, Paul Emile 1921-1996 [composer, author, publisher]
Paulson, Guy *Source(s):* ASCP
Gibaldi, Louis M(ilo) 1951- [composer, author, singer]
Cutler, Jesse *Source(s):* ASCP; CCE74; CPOL PAu-883-834

London, Lou *Source(s):* CCE66; CCE72; CCE74
Smith, Milo *Source(s):* CPOL RE-755-749
Gibb, Michelle 1969- [singer, songwriter]
Princess Sharifa *Source(s):* EPMU
Gibbons, Irene 1895 (or 96)-1977 [singer, songwriter]
Dixie Nightingale, The *Source(s):* HARS
Henderson, Catherine *Source(s):* HARS; SUTT
Queen of the Moaners, The *Source(s):* HARS
Note(s): See also Clara Smith
Taylor, Eva *Source(s):* HARS; LCAR; SUTT
Williams, Irene *Source(s):* HARS; LCAR; SUTT
Gibbons, Orlando 1583-1625 [composer]
Note(s): Portrait: CYBH
English Palestrina, The *Source(s):* PSND
Gibbs, Henry Charles Hamilton 1879-1942 [journalist, librettist, playwright]
Hamilton, Cosmo *Source(s):* CART; GAN1; GAN2
Gibson, Clifford 1901-1963 [singer, guitarist, songwriter]
Gibson, Grandpappy *Source(s):* HARS; LCAR
Sluefoot, Joe *Source(s):* HARS; LCAR
Gieseking, Walter 1895-1956 [pianist, composer]
Giese, Willking *Source(s):* http://www.klavier.it/pianisti/gieseking-eng.htm (26 Apr. 2005)
Giesen, Willy 1911-1981 [composer]
Gollmann, Werner *Source(s):* PFSA
Gigli, Giovanni Battista ?-after 1692 [composer]
Tedeschino, Il *Source(s):* GROL; NGDM; WORB
Note(s): See also Lorenzo Allegri.
Gigli, Girolamo 1660-1721 (or 22) [poet, author]
Amaranto Sciaditico *Source(s):* SONN
Lilio, Girolamo *Source(s):* SONN
Sciadatico, Amaranto *Source(s):* MELL
Gignoux, Régis 1878-1931 [author, critic]
Montbars, Georges *Source(s):* PIPE
Gilbert, Cary (Grant) 1942-1993 [songwriter]
Hippy *Source(s):* AMUS; DRSC
Gilbert, E. Ouseley [composer]
Valmency, Edgar de *Source(s):* CCE33 Efor30525; CPMU
Gilbert, Henry F(ranklin Belknap) 1868-1928 [composer]
Note(s): Portraits: ETUP 51:10 (Oct. 1933): 640; EWCY; MUAM 34:9 (June 25, 1921): 17
Belknap, Frank *Source(s):* GROL; NGAM
Gilbert, Ronnie [singer, songwriter]
Campbell, Paul *Source(s):* PMUS
Note(s): Pseud. of The Weavers [i.e., Gilbert, Lee Hays, Pete(r R.) Seeger & Fred Hellerman]
Six, Tom *Source(s):* CCE58; CCE66
Note(s): Jt. pseud.: Lee Hays, Pete(r R.) Seeger & Fred Hellerman.
Weavers, The *Source(s):* PMUS
Note(s): Jt. pseud.: Lee Hays, Pete(r R.) Seeger & Fred Hellerman.
Gilbert, William Schwenk 1836-1911 [librettist, lyricist, playwright]
Note(s): Portrait: GAN1 v. 1 p. 540
B *Source(s):* PSNN
Bab *Source(s):* GANA; GAN1; GAN2; PSND
Gilbertian *Source(s):* EPON
King of Topsy-Turvydom, The *Source(s):* http://www.historcooperative.com (23 Oct. 2002)
LaTour, Tomline *Source(s):* PSND; ROOM
Tomline, F. L(atour) *Source(s):* CART; GANA p. 15; PSND
Gilfilen, Seely John 1923-2004 [composer, pianist]
Seely, John *Source(s):* DRSC
Gilkinson, Donald Mitchell 1950- [composer]
Mitchell, Don(nald) *Source(s):* ASCP; CCE74
Gilkyson, Hamilton Henry 1916-1999 [songwriter, singer]
Gilkyson, Terry *Source(s):* AMUS; CLAB; LCAR; OB99; PEN2
Gill, Ralph 1919- [composer, singer]
Gill, Rusty *Source(s):* ASCC; TCAN
Gill, William (Fearing) 1844-1917 [playwright, journalist]
Manchester, George *Source(s):* GANA p. 559
Note(s): Probable pseud.
Gille, Philippe Émile François 1831-1901 [playwright, librettist]
Argus *Source(s):* PIPE
Gillespie, John (Birks) 1917-1993 [trumpeter, bandleader, composer]
Berks, John *Source(s):* JAMU
Birks, John *Source(s):* JAMU
Bopstein, B. *Source(s):* http://www.tonyscott.it/from_the_beginning.htm (19 May 2005)
Burk, John *Source(s):* JAMU
Diz *Source(s):* SHAD
Gabriel *Source(s):* JAMU
Gates, Hen *Source(s):* JAMU
Note(s): Also used by Jimmy Forman.
Gillespie, Dizzy *Source(s):* CASS; CM06; EPMU; GAMM; IDBC; KINK; PEN2
Goldberg, Izzy [or Izzie] *Source(s):* JAMU
Kildare, John *Source(s):* JAMU
Gillette, Leland James 1912-1981 [composer, author]
Bergdahl, Edith [or Enid] *Source(s):* ASCP; PSND
Lee, Jimmy *Source(s):* ASCP
Patrick, Kirk *Source(s):* ASCP; CCE57; CPOL RE-108-978
Note(s): Also used by H(olbert) [or H(allbert)] H(ill) Kirkatrick & Harold William Kirpatrick, (Jr.).
Gillham, Art 1895-1961 [composer, pianist, singer]
Barrel House Pete *Source(s):* SUTT
Thomas, Fred *Source(s):* SUTT
Whispering Pianist, (The) *Source(s):* PSND; SUTT
Gillham, Richard [composer]

Mählig, Ricardo *Source(s):* CPMU (publication dates 1869-1905)
Gillum, William McKinley 1904-1966 [singer, harmonica player, songwriter]
Gillum, Jazz *Source(s):* HARS; LCAR
McKinley, Bill *Source(s):* HARS; LCAR
Gilman, Hazel Inez 1904- [composer, songwriter]
George, Gil *Source(s):* ASCP; REHH
Gilman, Lawrence 1878-1939 [music critic]
Toscanini Cultists, The *Source(s):* GRAN p. 275
Note(s): Jt. sobriquet: Bernard H. Haggin & Samuel Chotzinoff.
Gilmore, Jimmie Dale 1945- [singer, guitarist, songwriter]
Father of Western Beat, The *Source(s):* STAC
Sagebrush Poet, The *Source(s):* STAC
Gilmore, Joseph H(enry) 1834-1918 [hymnist]
Contoocock *Source(s):* YOUN
Gilmore, Patrick Sarsfield 1829-1892 [composer, bandmaster]
Note(s): Portraits: ETUP 51:10 (Oct. 1933): 640; ETUP 53:4 (Apr. 1934): 217
Father of Military Bands *Source(s):* http://www.newadvent.org/cathen/06561a.htm (6 Oct. 2002)
Father of the Modern American Concert Band *Source(s):* SMIN
Lambert, Louis *Source(s):* GROL; NGAM; REHH; STUW
Note(s): Probable pseud.?
Gilson, Paul 1865-1942 [composer]
Note(s): Portrait: ETUP 51:10 (Oct. 1933): 640. Do not confuse with Paul Gilson (1927-); see following entry.
Father of Belgian Wind Music, The *Source(s):* REHH
Gilson, Paul 1927- [composer]
Note(s): Do not confuse with Paul Gilson (1865-1942); see preceding entry.
Francy, Paul *Source(s):* CCE50
Ginder, Richard 1914- [author, composer]
McGlynn, Christopher *Source(s):* PSND
Monday, Michael *Source(s):* PSND
Ginsberg, Sol(ly) 1885-1963 [composer]
Violinsky, (Solly) *Source(s):* ASCP; CCE20 E475583; JASA; LCAR; PSND
Ginsburg [or Ginzburg], Lucien 1928-1991 [singer, songwriter]
Dirty Old Man of Popular Music, The *Source(s):* BBDP
Gainsbourg, Serge *Source(s):* CCE66; HARD; ROOM; PFSA
Gainsbourg, Steve *Source(s):* PSNN
Grix, Julien *Source(s):* http://www.rfimusique.com (19 May 2005)
Ginzburg, Aleksandr Arkad'evich 1919-1977 [actor, scriptwriter, composer, singer]
Arkadevich, Alexander *Source(s):* LCAR
Galich, Aleksandr Arkad'evich *Source(s):* HOFE; LCAR
Gioconda, Carmen Manteca 1936- [guitarist, singer, composer]
Carmen Marina *Source(s):* BUL3; COHN; HIXN
Giordani, Felice [or Felix] 1880- [librettist]
Felix, G. *Source(s):* MELL; STGR
Giordani, Giuseppe 1743 (or 44)-1798 [composer]
Giordan(i)ello *Source(s):* BAKO; GOTH; MACM; NGDO; PIPE; PSND; SONN
Giorgetti, Ferdinando 1796-1867 [composer, violinist]
Tedescone *Source(s):* GROL
Giornovichi, Giovanni Mane 1745-1804 [violinist, composer]
Cernovichi, Giovanni Marie *Source(s):* IBIM; WORB
Erratic Star, The *Source(s):* PSND
Garnovik, Giovanni Marie *Source(s):* IBIM; WORB
Jarnovic, Ivan Mane *Source(s):* LCAR
Jarnovik, Mr. *Source(s):* LCAR
Jarnowick, (Giovanni Mane) *Source(s):* IBIM; PSND; WORB
Giovanni da Cascia fl. 1340-50 [composer]
Giovanni de Florentia *Source(s):* NGDM
Giovanonne, Anthony J(ohn) 1923- [composer, author, accordionist]
Johnson, Chatta *Source(s):* ASCC; CCE57; CCE60
Girard, Harry [composer]
Kemp, Victor *Source(s):* CCE29 R5973; CPMU (publication dates 1900-03)
Giraut, de Bornelh c.1140-c.1200 [Troubadour poet, composer]
Maestre del trobadors *Source(s):* NGDM
Girman, John W(illiam) 1893- [composer]
Germaine, Jack *Source(s):* CCE37 Eunp145657; http://music.library.edu/wma/resources/wiscomp.htm (26 Feb. 2005)
Girouix(-West), Julie 1961- [composer]
West, J. A. *Source(s):* REHH
Gisinger, Albert 1919- [composer, musician]
Milano, U. *Source(s):* OMUO
Note(s): Also used by Hugo Müller
Gist, Kenneth [or Kenny] (G.), Jr. 1944- [songwriter]
O'Dell, Kenny *Source(s):* EPMU; HARR; NASF; PMUS; PSND; ROOM
Gittler, Morris 1904-1959 [lyricist]
Note(s): Portrait: EWEN
Gordon, Mack *Source(s):* BBDP; CASS; EPMU; GAMM; HARR
Giugno, Karl 1818-1891 [librettist]
Bruno, Karl *Source(s):* OMUO; PIPE; STGR
Juin, Karl *Source(s):* OMUO; PIPE; STGR; WORB

Giuliani, Francesco fl. 1619-29 [composer]
Cerato (d'Arzignano Vicentio), Il *Source(s):* GROL; IBIM; MACM; NGDM; WORB
Giuliani, Mauro 1781-1829 [guitarist, composer]
Paganini of the Guitar, The *Source(s):* http://www.telare.com/gscripts/title.asp?gsku=0525 (25 Sept. 2003)
Note(s): See also (Joseph) Fernando (Macari) Sor.
Giusberti, Giulio fl. late 16th cent. [monk, organist, composer]
Eremita, Giulio *Source(s):* GRV3; IBIM; MACM; WORB
Giuvo, Nicolà [or Nicolò] c.1680-after 1748 [librettist]
Eupidio Siriano *Source(s):* GROL
Siriano, Eupidio *Source(s):* GROL
Gjellerup, Karl Adolph 1857-1919 [author]
Epigonos *Source(s):* PIPE
Gladshtayn, Yísra'el 1907-1950 [composer]
Gladstein, Israel *Source(s):* LCAR
Gladstone, Israel *Source(s):* CCE23 E577815; HESK; LCAR
Glady, Tom 1911-1977 [composer]
Schaefer, Herman *Source(s):* REHG
Glahé, Will(y Karl-Adolf) 1902-1989 [composer]
Erpel, (Karl) *Source(s):* CCE55-59; CCE61-63; CPOL RE-295-287; PFSA
Höfgen, Willy *Source(s):* CCE54; CPOL RE-94-677
Wills, Carlo *Source(s):* CCE55
Glas, Jan Roelof van der 1879-1972 [composer]
Duverre, Jean *Source(s):* CCE58; SUPN
Glaser, Thomas P(aul) 1933- [singer, songwriter, guitarist]
Glaser, Tompall *Source(s):* CCE60; CCE62; LCAR; MCCL
Great Tompall, The *Source(s):* MCCL
Glaser, Victoria Merrylees 1918- [composer, author, teacher]
Copenahgen, A. *Source(s):* ASCP
Hanleigh, Faith *Source(s):* CPOL RE-313-353
Glasenap, Joachim von fl. 17th cent.? [bookseller, composer]
Erwachsende, Der *Source(s):* IBIM
Glass, Philip 1937- [composer]
Godfather of Minimalist *Source(s):* http://www.filmscoremonthly.com/articles/1999/24_Aug—Asian_Scores.asp (6 Oct. 2002)
Glassey, Patrick Francis 1844- [minstrel performer, author]
Leon, Francis *Source(s):* GAN2
Only Leon, The *Source(s):* GAN2
Glassmacher, Joseph F(rancis) 1912-1990 [composer]
Francis, J. F. *Source(s):* CCE20 E488702; CCE42 #5201, 867 R102480; TPRF
Francis, Jay *Source(s):* CCE27 E678059
Glassmacher, William [lyricist]
Francis, William *Source(s):* CCE20 E488702
Glazunov, Aleksandr Konstantinovich 1865-1936 [composer]
Little Glinka, The *Source(s):* CASS
Russian Mendelssohn *Source(s):* CASS
Gleason, Herbert John 1916-1987 [comedian, actor, composer]
Fat One, The *Source(s):* PSND
Gleason, Jackie *Source(s):* EPMU; PSND
Great One, The *Source(s):* NOMG; PSND
Mr. Saturday Night *Source(s):* PSND
Gledhill, John Patrick Stanford 1939- [composer, teacher]
Stanford, Patric *Source(s):* NGDM
Gleich, Ferdinand Theodor 1816-1898 [composer, author]
Giltersberg, Konstantin von *Source(s):* IBIM; WORB
Gleich, Friedrich 1782-1842 [author]
Peter der Ameisenbär *Source(s):* APPL p. 10
Gleich, Josef Alois 1772-1841 [novelist, playwright]
Bergenstamm *Source(s):* PIPE
Blum, Adolf [or Adolph] *Source(s):* PIPE
Dellarosa, Ludwig *Source(s):* PIPE
Kramer, Alois *Source(s):* PIPE
Walden, Heinrich *Source(s):* PIPE
Glembotzki, Reinhold 1939- [composer]
Bow, Glenn *Source(s):* KOMS; PFSA
Glenn, Fareil 1949- [composer, author]
Sanders, Fareil *Source(s):* ASCP
Glenn, Will(iam Cooper) 1957-2001 [violinist, pianist, guitarist, songwriter]
Cooper, William *Source(s):* http://guitarbands.de/willglenn.html (30 Oct. 2002)
Note(s): Also used by F(ranz) Behr.
Glinka, Michael Ivanovitch 1803-1857 [composer]
Father of Russian Music *Source(s):* AMEN; BAKE
Father of Russian Opera *Source(s):* http://www.fineartprimer.net/opera_main_page.htm (6 Oct. 2002)
Prophet-Patriach of Russian Music, The *Source(s):* GRV3
Glinski, Mateusz [or Matteo] 1892-1976 [music critic, conductor, composer]
Hercenstein, Matteo *Source(s):* NGDM
Glogau, Henrik ?-1877 [librettist]
Logau, Gotthold *Source(s):* LOWN; MELL
Glossop, Augustus Henry 1852-1896 [impresario, author]
Harris, Augustus *Source(s):* GAN2; LCAR
Glossop, Charles Robert 1853-1897 [director, stage manager]
Harris, Charles *Source(s):* GAN2
Note(s): Do not confuse with Charles K(assell) Harris (1867-1930).

Glosup, Edgar D(ean) 1907-1999 [singer, actor, songwriter]
Dean, Eddie *Source(s):* AMUS; ASCP; EPMU; MCCL; NOMG
Singing Cowboy *Source(s):* MCCL
Note(s): See also (Orvon) Gene Autry & James [or Jimmy] Clarence Wakeley.
Glosup, Lorene St. Clare (Donnelly) 1911-2002 [composer]
Dean, Dearest *Source(s):* ASCP; CCE55
Dean, Lorene *Source(s):* ASCP
Glover, Charles Joseph, (Jr.) 1951- [composer, author, singer]
Strange, Justin *Source(s):* ASCP; CPOL PAu-34-910
Glover, Charles William 1806-1863 [composer, arranger, violinist]
Gantier, Felix *Source(s):* CPMU; OCLC 48091367
Glover, Henry (Bernard) 1921-1991 [producer, songwriter, arranger]
Bernard, Henry *Source(s):* CPOL RE-23-266; http://www.ualr.edu/~kuar/littlewillie.html (6 Oct. 2002)
Gluck, Christoph Willibald 1714-1787 [composer]
Armonide Terpsicoreo *Source(s):* GROL
Gluckists *Source(s):* EPON
Note(s): Used to identify persons siding with Gluck in the "l'querelle célèbre" with Piccinni.
Hercules of Music, The *Source(s):* PSND; SIFA
Michel Angelo of Music, The *Source(s):* PSND
Terpsicoreo, Armonide *Source(s):* GROL
Glücksmann, Heinrich 1864-1947 [writer on music]
Fortunatus, Hermann Heinrich *Source(s):* MUBR
Goad, Dorothy LaVern 1915-1967 [singer, songwriter]
Girls of the Golden West, The *Source(s):* MCCL
Note(s): Jt. pseud.: Millie Good [i.e., Mildred Fern Goad]
Good, Dolly *Source(s):* MCCL
Goad, Mildred Fern 1913-1993 [singer, songwriter]
Girls of the Golden West, The *Source(s):* MCCL
Note(s): Jt. Pseud.: Dolly Good [i.e., Dorothy LaVern Goad]
Good, Millie *Source(s):* MCCL
Gobbaerts, Jean Louis 1835-1886 [composer, pianist]
Note(s): Portrait: ETUP 56:10 (Oct. 1938): 630 (under Streabbog)
Bachmann, G. *Source(s):* TPRF
Lecocq, Maurice *Source(s):* CPMU; LCAR
Levi, (Ludovic) *Source(s):* ETUD; GOTH; MACM
Ludovic, (G.) *Source(s):* CPMU; ETUD; GOTH
Streabbog, L(ouis) (S.) *Source(s):* CPMU; ETUD; GOTH; LCAR; MACM
Gobbi, Alfredo Julio Floro 1912-1965 [violinist, composer, arranger]
Romantic Violin of Tango, The *Source(s):* TODO
Godard d'Ancour (de Saint-Just), Claude 1769-1826 [dramatist]
Saint-Just, (Claude) *Source(s):* PIPE; SONN
Goddard, Geoff 1938-2000 [pianist, composer]
Hollywood, Anton *Source(s):* DRSC
Goddard, Leroy (A.) 1915-1991 [composer, author]
Penny, Lee *Source(s):* ASCP; CCE40 #927 Eunp212110; CCE68
Goddard, Stuart (Leslie) 1954- [songwriter]
Ant, Adam *Source(s):* EPMU; HARD; HARR; LCAR; PEN2; PMUS-95
Godebrye, Jacob 1445?-1529 [composer, singer]
Godebrie, Jacques *Source(s):* PSND
Jacotin *Source(s):* NGDM; PRAT
Godecharle, Eugene Charles Jean 1742-1814 [violinist, composer]
Godchalk, Eugene Charles Jean *Source(s):* MACM
Godfrey, Kevin Paul 1959 (or 60)-1997 [singer, songwriter]
Epic Soundtracks *Source(s):* LCAR
Soundtracks, Epic *Source(s):* AMUS; WASH
Gody, Alcayaga Lucila 1889-1957 [poet]
Mistrail, Gabriela *Source(s):* PSND
Goehr, Walter 1903-1960 [conductor, composer, arranger]
Note(s): Portrait: *Allgemeine Musik-Zeitung* 51:23/24 (12 June 1925): 525+
Perosa, H. *Source(s):* CCE36 Index
Note(s): Jt. pseud.: Harry Peros; "Alpine Valse."
Walter, G(eorg(e)) *Source(s):* CCE38 Efor53226; CPMU; LCAR; MUWB; NGDM; PIPE
Goemans, Pieter (Willem) 1925-2004 [composer]
Shott, Peter *Source(s):* CCE56; CCE58-59; http://www.flairck.com/eenmans.php (9 June 2005)
Goerdeler, Richard [composer]
Bechter, Karl *Source(s):* CCE25 R29208; ETUD; TPRF
Forest, Edwin D. *Source(s):* CCE25 R29217; TPRF
Henning, Anton *Source(s):* CCE23 R23050
Howard, W. E. C. *Source(s):* CCE26 R33290; TPRF
Keller, Arthur *Source(s):* TPRF
Mueller, August *Source(s):* CCE24 R26290
Müller, August *Source(s):* CCE26 R33276; TPRF
Gogg, Dieter 1938-2000 [composer, author]
Busch, Robert *Source(s):* OMUO
Goings, Jimmy 1955- [songwriter]
Sata Esmeralda *Source(s):* CPOL SR-2-941; NITE
Goitein, George (G.) 1914-1994 [composer, teacher]
Gorody, George *Source(s):* ASCP; CCE60
Gojkovic, Dusan 1931- [composer, trumpeter]
Dusko *Source(s):* KOMP; PFSA
Gojkovic, Dusko *Source(s):* LCAR
Golby, Philip [songwriter]
Goldberg, Phil *Source:* PMUC

Gold, Glenn Herbert 1932-1982 [pianist, composer, author, broadcaster]
Note(s): An asterisk (*) following names indicates an assumed alter ego.
Gould, Glenn (Herbert) *Source(s):* LCAR
Note(s): Family surname changed in 1939 or 40.
Haig-Guinness, Duncan* *Source(s):* http://www.collectionscanada.ca/glenngould/m23-305.2-e.html
Hochmeister, Herbert von* *Source(s):* http://www.collectionscanada.ca/glenngould/m23-305.2-e.html
Klopweisser, (Dr.) Karlheinz* *Source(s):* http://www.collectionscanada.ca/glenngould/m23-305.2-e.html
Krankmeister, Wolfgang von* *Source(s):* http://www.collectionscanada.ca/glenngould/m23-305.2-e.html
Last Puritan, The *Source(s):* NOTE 50:3 (1994): 1017
Lemming, S. F., M. D.* *Source(s):* http://www.collectionscanada.ca/glenngould/m23-305.2-e.html
Price-Davies, (Sir) Humphrey* *Source(s):* http://www.collectionscanada.ca/glenngould/m23-305.2-e.html
Slutz, Theodore* *Source(s):* http://www.collectionscanada.ca/glenngould/m23-305.2-e.html
Twitt-Thornwaite, (Sir) Nigel* *Source(s):* http://www.collectionscanada.ca/glenngould/m23-305.2-e.html
Gold, Jacob 1921-1992 [composer, singer, author]
Gold, Jack *Source(s):* ASCC; CCE52-53
Gold, Joe (D.) 1922- [composer]
Danel, J. Gordon *Source(s):* ASCP; CCE65-68
Goldbaum, Friedrich 1903- [composer]
Douce, Tilly *Source(s):* CCE62
Freed, Fred *Source(s):* CCE47; CCE52; CCE68; REHG
Goldberg Doris 1880-1928 [singer, songwriter, actress]
Bayes, Nora *Source(s):* CASS; GRAT; GREN; JAST; KINK NGAM
Greatest Single Woman Singing Comedienne in the World, The *Source(s):* GRAT
Wurzburger Girl, The *Source(s):* SPTH p. 305
Goldberg, Erwin 1920- [composer]
Gilboa, Jacob *Source(s):* OMUO
Goldberg, Harry 5/24/1912- [composer, drummer, teacher]
Note(s): Do not confuse with Harry Goldberg (5/1/1910-); see following entry.
Gold, Hal *Source(s):* ASCP
Note(s): "It's the Little Things," "Who Put the Law in Mother-in-Law" & "Hello Mr. Snow Man"
Goldberg, Harry 5/1/1910- [composer, author]
Note(s): Do not confuse with Harry Goldberg (5/24/1912-); see preceding entry.
Gordon, Hal *Source(s):* ASCP
Note(s): See list of works in ASCP.
Goldbogen, Avrom Hirsch 1907-1958 [producer]
Goldbogen, Michael *Source(s):* LCAR
Todd, Michael *Source(s):* GAN2; LCAR
Golden, William Lee, Jr. 1959- [singer, songwriter, instrumentalist]
Golden, Rusty *Source(s):* MCCL
Goldenfodim, Abraham 1840-1908 [playwright, composer]
Goldfaden, Abraham *Source(s):* LYMN
Goldenring, Stefania 1885-1920 [translator]
Roskoschny *Source(s):* PIPE
Goldhahn, Richard T(homas) 1915-2003 [composer, author, singer]
Thomas, Dick *Source(s):* ASCP (see reference); CCE61; CCE73
Goldman, Kurt fl. 1897-1907 [composer]
Margis, Gaston *Source(s):* MELL; STGR
Goldman, Richard Franko 1910-1980 [composer]
Fuller, Richard Alan *Source(s):* CCE55
Goldner, Ernest (Siegmund) 1921-1999 [composer, conductor, arranger]
Note(s): Portrait: EWPS
Ernest, J. J. *Source(s):* CCE76; NGAM
Gold, Ernest *Source(s):* BAKR; BUL3; CCE67-68; GOTH; LCAR; LYMN; OMUO
Ingersoll, Byron M. *Source(s):* CCE67; NGAM
Note(s): Pseud. of Ernest Gold [i.e., Ernest (Siegmund) Goldner]. Also jt. pseud.: Alex(ander) Kramer, Robert (B.) Sour, Don McCray, Hy(man) Zaret & Zoe Voeth [i.e., Parenteau] (CCE68 R426470).
Phillips, Olga *Source(s):* CCE41 #9694 E92199; CCE68; NGAM
Goldoni, Carlo 1707-1793 [playwright, librettist]
Calindo Grolo *Source(s):* PIPE; SONN
Cardoni, Sogol *Source(s):* DEA3
Clog, Aldimiro *Source(s):* DEA3
Colodisce, Logolcardoni *Source(s):* ALMC; GROL
Crolo, Calindo *Source(s):* ALMC
Father of Modern Comedy *Source(s):* NGDM
Father of Modern Italian Comedy *Source(s):* NGDM
Father of Opera Buffa *Source(s):* DEA3
Note(s): See also Baldassare Galuppi.
Fegejo, Polisse(n)o *Source(s):* ALMC; GROL; LCAR; MELL; MORI; NGDO; PIPE
Feglio, Polisseno *Source(S):* DEA3
Glodoci, Loran *Source(s):* PIPE; SONN
Grolo, Calindo *Source(s):* PIPE; SONN
Italian Molière, The *Source(s):* PSND

Loran Glodoci *Source(s):* SONN
Molière of Italy, The *Source(s):* PSND
Goldschmidt, Berthold 1903-1996 [composer]
Squirrel *Source(s):* MUWB
Goldschmidt, Georg 1516-1571 [poet]
Fabricius, Georg *Source(s):* NGDM
Goldsen, Michael H. 1912- [composer, lyricist]
Goldsen, Mickey *Source(s)* CCE68; CCE70 R475874
Graham, H. *Source(s):* CCE66
Graham, Steve *Source(s):* ASCP; CCE41 #49663 E99032; CPOL RE-211-352; PMUS
Lee, Vernon *Source(s):* ASCP
Note(s): Also used by Violet Paget.
Stevens, Graham *Source(s):* CCE68
Goldsmith, Hilliard Oliver Claude 1918-1971 [songwriter, publisher]
Hilliard, Bob *Source(s):* CCE 49-56; PSND
Goldsmith, Jerrald [or Jerry] 1909-2004 [composer]
Hennagin, Michael *Source(s):* CLTP ("Black Saddle"); IMDB
Note(s): Incorrectly reported pseud. Composer Michael [later Marijo] Hennagin(-Mazur), 1936-1993, was Goldsmith's brother-in-law. (http://www.filmscoremonthly.com/articles/2003/26_Nov—The_Real_Michael_Hennagin_Story.asp (17 May 2005)
Goldstein, Harvey 1944- [composer, bassist]
Brooks, Harvey *Source(s):* ASCP; CCE66; LCAR
Goldstein, Julius 1901-1981 [pianist, conductor, writer on music]
Herford, Julius *Source(s):* BAKT; NGAM
Goldstein, Mikhail 1768-1846 [composer]
Note(s): Do not confuse with Mikhail Emmanuiloch Goldstein (1917-1989); see following entry.
Ovsianiko-Kulikovskii, Nikolai Dmitrievich *Source(s):* GREN
Note(s): Name invented to deceive Soviet Music Publishing House.
Goldstein, Mikhail Emmanuilovich 1917-1989 [composer, musicologist]
Note(s): Do not confuse with Mikhail Goldstein (1768-1864); see preceding entry.
Mykhajlowsky, Mykhajlo *Source(s):* GROL; KOMP; KOMS
Goldwin, John c.1667-1719 [organist, composer]
Golding, John *Source(s):* IBIM; NGDM
Goletz, Philipp Simon 1954- [composer]
Balth, Willy *Source(s):* KOMS; PFSA
Simon, Philipp *Source(s):* PFSA
Goller, Vinzenz 1873-1953 [composer]
Berchthal, Hans von *Source(s):* BUL3; LCAR; OMUO
Gómez, Edgar 1971- [singer, songwriter, actor]
Cezán, Marcelo *Source(s):* HWOM
Gómez Llunas, Jordi 1978- [songwriter, singer]
Jordi *Source(s):* HWOM
Goni, Peña y 1846-1896 [critic, composer]
Tio Gilena, El *Source(s): Inter-American Music Review* 14:2 (1995): 110
Gonk, Terry [songwriter, guitarist]
Clapton, Richard *Source(s):* DAUM
Gonsalves, John P(ires) 1925-1998 [composer, author, singer]
Gonsalves, Joli *Source(s):* ASCC; CCE59-60
Joli *Source(s):* CCE60; CCE65
Gonzaga, Luiz, Jr. 1945-1991 [composer, singer]
Gonzaguinha *Source(s):* BRAZ
Gonzaga do Amaral, Francisca Edviges 1847-1935 [composer]
Gonzaga, Chiquinha *Source(s):* IDBC; LCAR
Gonzalez, Aaron Ruben 1908-1990 [composer, author, pianist]
Ganz, Aaron *Source(s):* ASCP
Ruben, Aaron *Source(s):* ASCP (see reference)
Gonzalez, Antonio 1949- [composer]
Laru, Tony *Source(s):* CCE78; GOTH
Gonzalez, Kenny [singer, songwriter]
Gonzalez, Dope *Source(s):* LCAR
Vega, Little Louie *Source(s):* SONG
González (Salazar), Ricardo [songwriter, singer]
Cepillin *Source(s):* HWOM
Goodendag, Johann 15th cent. [monk, composer]
Bonadies *Source(s):* MACM
Goodhart, A(rthur) M(urray) 1905-1955 [composer, arranger]
A. M. G. *Source(s):* CPMU
Goodhart, Al *Source(s):* GOTL
Goodman, Alfred (Grant) 1920-1999 [composer, arranger, musicologist]
Gilford, Fred *Source(s):* BUL3; CCE60; KOMP; KOMS; PFSA
Goodman, Benjamin [or Benny] (David) 1909-1986 [bandleader, clarinetist, songwriter]
B. G. *Source(s):* PSND
Jackson, John *Source(s):* PSND
Jackson, Shoeless John *Source(s):* JAMU
King of Swing *Source(s):* PSND; SHAD
Magnetic Killer-Diller of the "Licorice Stick" (Clarinet) *Source(s):* Slominsky, Nicholas. *Music since 1900.* New York, Schirmer, 1944, p. 94.
Goodman, Richard John 1944- [composer, singer]
Supa, Richard *Source(s):* ASCP; CCE73; CCE78
Goodrich, A(lfred) J(ohn) 1847 (or 48)-1920 [composer]
Note(s): Portrait: ETUP 51:11 (Nov. 1933): 728
Richgood, J. A. *Source(s):* TPRF

Goodson, Willie Madison 1907-1974 [singer, pianist, songwriter]
Pierce, Billie *Source(s):* GRAT
Goodwin, Charles D. 1929- [composer, author]
Goodwin, Doug *Source(s):* PSND
Goodwin, Charles Wycliffe 1817-1878 [historian, archeologist]
Noverari *Source(s):* BLIC; CPMU; WORB
Goodwin, Harry [composer]
Avon Comedy Four *Source(s):* CCE45 #6317, 2033 R142579
Note(s): Jt. pseud.: Charles Dale, Irving [i.e., Isidore] Kaufman & Joe Smith.
Goold-Verschoyle, H(amilton) F(rederick) S(tuart) 1874-1942 [composer]
G. V. *Source(s):* CPMU
Gordigiani, Giovanni Battista 1795-1871 [singer, composer, teacher]
Italian Schubert, The *Source(s):* GROL; PSND
Gordigiani, Luigi 1806-1860 [pianist, composer]
Fürstenberger, von *Source(s):* DEA3; GRV5
Zeuner *Source(s):* DEA3; GRV5
Gordon, Ben (B.) 1912- [composer, author, singer]
Gordon, Richard *Source(s):* CPOL RE-54-786
Meadows, Fred *Source(s):* ASCP; CCE51; CCE60; CCE68; CPOL RE-15-990
Gordon, David M. [composer, publisher]
David, G. *Source(s):* CLMC
Layne, Ruth *Source(s):* CLMC
Lenard, Melvyn *Source(s):* CLMC
Note(s): On music Gordon published. Also used by Irving Gertz, Dave Kahn, Leo(n) Klatzkin, William Lava, Joseph [or Joe] Mullendore & possibly others.
Marilyn, Jay *Source(s):* CLMC
Music, David *Source(s):* CLMC
Gordon, Marie [playwright]
Bergen, Alexander *Source(s):* PIPE
Calafati, Marie *Source(s):* PIPE
Saphir, Marie *Source(s):* PIPE
Stein, Max *Source(s):* PIPE
Gordon, William Marvin 1947- [composer, author, singer]
Gordon, Flash *Source(s):* ASCP; CPOL PA-16-052
Gordy, Berry, Jr. 1929- [songwriter]
Bear, The *Source(s):* CCE70
Note(s): Possible pseud.? Composer listed: Berry Gordy IV.
Corporation, The *Source(s):* HARR; PMUS
Note(s): Jt. pseud.: Fred(erick) [or Freddie] Perrin, Alphonso James Mizell & Deke Richards.
Father of the Motown Sound *Source(s):* http://www.planetpapers.com/Assets/1909.php (6 Oct. 2002)
Gordy, Kenneth [or Kennedy] 1964- [singer, songwriter]
Gordy, Rock *Source(s):* NITE
Rockwell *Source(s):* EPMU; NITE
Gordy, Robert [singer, actor, music publisher]
Kayli, Bob *Source(s):* PSND
Goreed, Joseph 1918-1999 [singer, pianist, songwriter]
Williams, Joe *Source(s):* CM11; HARS; OB99
Note(s): Also used by Joe McCoy. Do not confuse with ("Big") Joe Lee Williams (1903-).
Williams, Jumpin Joe *Source(s):* HARS; OB99
Gorelick, Kenneth 1956- [saxophonist, composer]
G., Kenny *Source(s):* LCAR
Kenny G *Source(s):* CM14; LCAR
Goretti, Antonio c.1570-1649 [music patron, composer]
Ottuso, L' *Source(s):* NGDM; SADC
Note(s): See also Giovanni Maria Artusi.
Gorey, Edward (St. John) 1925-2000 [author, illustrator]
Blutig, Eduard *Source(s):* LCAR; PIPE
Dogyear, Drew *Source(s):* LCAR; PIPE
Dowdy, (Mrs.) Regera *Source(s):* LCAR; PIPE
Dyrge, Waredo *Source(s):* PSND
Edgy, Wardore *Source(s):* LCAR; PIPE
Gewe, Raddory *Source(s):* LCAR; PIPE
Gore, D. Awdrey *Source(s):* PSND
Grewdead, Roy *Source(s):* PIPE
Grode, Redway *Source(s):* LCAR; PIPE
Mude, O. *Source(s):* LCAR; PIPE
Phypps, Hyacinthe *Source(s):* PSND
Pig, Edward *Source(s):* LCAR; PIPE
Rewdgo, Dreary *Source(s):* PSND
Ward, E. D. *Source(s):* LCAR; PIPE
Weary, Ogdred *Source(s):* LCAR; PIPE
Weedy, Garrod *Source(s):* LCAR
Wodge, Dreary *Source(s):* LCAR; PIPE
Wryde, Dogyear [or Dogear] *Source(s):* LCAR; PIPE
Gori, Antonio Francesco 1691-1757 [librettist]
Campalto *Source(s):* ALMC
Indiferente, L' *Source(s):* ALMC
Rigo, Antonio *Source(s):* PIPE
Rinio, Goanto *Source(s):* ALMC; PIPE; WORB
Scordato, Infelicio *Source(s):* ALMC
Gornetzky, Daniel Jason 1896-1990 [composer, author, producer]
Note(s): Portraits: EWEN; EWPA
Gorney, Jay *Source(s):* BBDP; REHH; ROOM
Jason, Daniel *Source(s):* CPOL RE-333-360; LCAR; REHG; ROOM
Gosdin, Vern(on) 1934- [singer, guitarist, songwriter]
Voice, The *Source(s):* FLIN; MCCL

Gosenpud, Abram Akimowitsch 1908- [writer on music, librettist]
Akimow *Source(s):* RIES
Gosting, Richard (Frank) 1941-2003 [composer, lyricist, singer]
St. John, Dick *Source(s):* ASCC; CCE60; CCE67; CPOL RE-521-080; PMUS
Gotowski, Harry 1951- [composer]
Novice, Larry *Source(s):* KOMS; PFSA
Gotthard, J(ohann) P(eter) (Pazdirek) 1839-1919 [composer]
Pazdírek, Bohumil *Source(s):* GOTT; LCAR
Pazdírek, J(ohann) (P.) *Source(s):* KOMU; LCAR
Göttig, Willy Werner 1891-1980 [music & theater librettist, critic]
Thyrolf, Guido *Source(s):* PIPE; WORB
Gottlieb, Heinrich Suso Johannes 1861-1928 [composer, violinist]
Noren, Heinrich G(ottlieb) *Source(s):* BAKE; LCAR; OMUO
Gottlieb, Susan 1957 (or 58)- [singer, songwriter]
Phranc *Source(s):* MUHF
Gottschald, Ernest [or Ernst] 1826- [writer on music]
Elterlein, Ernst von *Source(s):* BALT; LCAR; MACM; WORB
Gottschalk, Heinz-Jürgen 1948- [composer]
Gotte *Source(s):* PFSA
Vargis, Axel *Source(s):* KOMS; PFSA
Gottschalk, Louis Moreau 1829-1869 [composer]
Note(s): Portraits: ETUP 51:12 (Dec. 1933): 797; HOWD; STAR
A. B. C. *Source(s):* STAR p. 263; Doyle, John J. *Louis Moreau Gottschalk.* Detroit: Information Coordinators, 1982.
Automation Pianist, The *Source(s):* STAR p.253
Ernest, Paul *Source(s):* GROL; NGAM; STAR
Future King of Pianists, The *Source(s):* PSND
Godschack, Mr. *Source(s):* STAR p. 83
Jem Baggs *Source(s):* STAR p. 322+
Litti, Oscar *Source(s):* GROL; NGAM; STAR
Octaves, Seven *Source(s):* GROL
Prince of the Piano-Forte, The *Source(s):* PSND
Seven Octave(s) *Source(s):* GROL; NGAM; STAR
Gottschalk von Limburg ?-1098 [monk, writer of sequences]
Godescalcus, Lintpurgensis *Source(s):* NGDM
Gottschall, (Karl) Rudolf von 1823-1909 [author, dramatist]
Rudolf Carl *Source(s):* PIPE
Götz, Karl 1922- [composer]
Bergner *Source(s):* CCE62
Brugner, Joe *Source(s):* CCE58-59; CCE65 Efor105636
Burgner, (Joe) *Source(s):* CCE60-61; CCE63-64; LCAR; PFSA; RIES

Götze [or Goetze], Auguste 1840-1908 [singer, composer, writer on music]
Weimar, Auguste *Source(s):* COHN; HIXN
Goucher, Joseph Nelson 1894 (or 95)-1976 [composer, lyricist, playwright]
Dowling, Eddie *Source(s):* GAMM; KINK
Gouffé, Armand 1775-1845 [singer, composer, dramatist, vaudevillian]
Armand-Gouffé *Source(s):* LCAR
Bandy Legged *Source(s):* PSND
Panard of the 19th Century, The *Source(s):* PSND
Gouge, George ?-1730? [composer]
Gorge, Mr. *Source(s):* GOTH
Goudge, Mr. *Source(s):* GOTH
Goulart, Simon 1543-1628 [music publisher, writer]
Mongard, Louis *Source(s):* GROL
Goulden, Eric 1954?- [singer, songwriter]
Wreckless, Eric *Source(s):* CPOL PA-62-498; LCAR; WARN
Gourdine, Anthony 1940 (or 41)- [singer, songwriter]
Little Anthony *Source(s):* CCE59; LCAR; NOMG
Gourrier, John (Fred) 1941- [singer, songwriter]
Fred, J(ohn) *Source(s):* CCE65; CCE68; LCAR; NOMG
John Fred *Source(s):* CCE68
Govsky, John M. 1921- [composer]
Sky, Jack *Source(s):* ASCP
Gow, Neil [or Niel] 1727-1807 [composer, violinist]
King of Scotch Fiddlers, The *Source(s):* PSND
Gowans, Arthur Bradford 1903-1954 [instrumentalist, arranger]
Gowans, Brad *Source(s):* PSND
Grabowski, Gerd 1949- [composer]
Anderson, G. G. *Source(s):* PFSA
Grace, Grace [composer]
G. G. *Source(s):* CPMU (publication date 1861)
Poole, Naida *Source(s):* CCE23 E559283
Grace, Harvey 1874-1944 [organist, writer on music, editor]
Feste *Source(s):* GROL; SCHO p. 757
Gradenwitz, Peter Werner Emanuel 1910-2001 [composer, musicologist]
Grando, Piet *Source(s):* WORB
Vernon, Peter *Source(s):* CCE55-56
Grady, R(ichard) G. [composer]
Barrett, Bessie *Source(s):* CCE41 #20979, 289 R94957; CCE42 #29092, 108 R109338
Bartell, Henry *Source(s):* CCE39 #333235, 147 R77975
Bowen, George *Source(s):* CCE16 E389213; CCE44 #35637, 931 R130402
Gradi, R. G. *Source(s):* CCE40 #39050, 151 R91147; TPRF

Hudson, Violet *Source(s):* CCE39 #33235, 418 R77978
Jennings, Will *Source(s):* CCE16 E388516
Mack, Eugene *Source(s):* CCE40 #19376, 35 R88088
Note(s): Also used by Arthur Fields [i.e., Abe Finkelstein]
Moulton, Victor *Source(s):* CCE39 #33235, 335 R77998; JASA
Graeffer, Anton 1784- [composer]
Thyss, Peregrinus *Source(s):* IBIM; WORB
Graff, Sigmund 1898-1979 [author]
Frenzel, Georg *Source(s):* PIPE
Gräffer, Franz (Arnold) 1785-1852 [author, playwright]
Böttiger, J. L. *Source(s):* PIPE
Contée, F. H. *Source(s):* PIPE
Fergar, E. F. *Source(s):* WORB
Fergar, F. E. *Source(s):* PIPE
Rittgräff, A. E. *Source(s):* PIPE
Vaillant, D. F. *Source(s):* PIPE
Graham, Lloyd M. 1889- [author, composer, painter]
Keypton *Source(s):* PSND
Grahm, K. 1958- [singer, songwriter]
Roots, Levi *Source(s):* EPMU
Grain, (Richard) Corney 1844 (or 45)-1895 [entertainer, author, composer]
Corney, Richard *Source(s):* GAMM; KILG; ROOM
Grainger, (George) Percy (Aldridge) 1882-1961 [composer, pianist, editor]
Note(s): Portraits: ETUP 51:12 (Dec. 1933): 797; HOWD
Grainger, Perks *Source(s):* SPIE
Joyous Musician, The *Source(s):* PSND
Regniarg, Ycrep *Source(s):* CPMU; NGDM
Grainger, Porter [songwriter, writer]
Brooks, George *Source(s):* CCE51 R87431 ("Don't Know and Don't Care Blues")
Note(s): Also used by (James) Fletcher Henderson.
Foster, Jimmy *Source(s):* CCE51 R87433 ("He's Mine, All Mine")
Gray, Billy *Source(s):* CCE52 R89714 ("Steel Drivin' Sam")
Grey, Harold *Source(s):* CCE51 R87432; Peterson, Bernard L. *Early Black American Playwrights and Dramatists*. New York: Greenwood Press, 1990.
Grammatico, Lou 1950- [singer, songwriter]
Gramm, Lou *Source(s):* CCE77; HARR
Granade, John A(dam) 1763?-1805 (or 07) [hymnist, composer]
J. A. G. *Source(s):* METC
Wild Man (of the Woods, The) *Source(s):* LCAR; METC
Grandi, Alfredo mentioned 1893 [composer]
Walter *Source(s):* STGR
Grandjean, Moritz Anton 1820 (or 21)-1885 [playwright]
Herbert, M. G. *Source(s):* PIPE; WORB
Grandval, Marie Felicie Clémence de Reiset, vicomtesse de 1830-1907 [composer]
Note(s): See LCAR for variant forms of name.
Blagy, Caroline *Source(s):* LCAR
Valgrand, Celemence *Source(s):* LCAR
Granito, Carmine 1945- [songwriter]
Dante, Ron(nie) *Source(s):* CCE64; EPMU; ROOM
Grannis, S(idney) M(artin) 1827 (or 30)-1907 [songwriter]
Note(s): See also: http://members.aol.com/Jerund/nov01.html (31 Jan. 2005)
Crannis, S. M. *Source(s):* LCAR
Note(s): May be typographical error on "Do They Miss Me at Home" (Ditson).
Grannis, Mrs. S. M. *Source(s):* SPTH p. 130
Note(s): The 1856 edition of "Sparking (on a) Sunday Night" credited to Mrs. S. M. Grannis.
Markstein, S. *Source(s):* SPTH p. 130
Note(s): First 1855 edition of "Sparking (on a) Sunday Night" credited to S. Markstein.
Sparker, A. *Source(s):* SPTH p. 130
Note(s): Second 1855 edition"Sparking (on a) Sunday Night" credited to A. Sparker.
Granom, L(ewis) C(hristian) A(ustin) c.1725-1791 [composer, flutist]
L. G. *Source(s):* CPMU
Grant, Amy (Lee) 1960 (or 61)- [singer, songwriter]
First Lady of Contemporary Christian Music, The *Source(s):* AMEN; MCCL
Madonna of Contemporary Gospel, The *Source(s):* PSND
Madonna of Gospel Music, The *Source(s):* WORL
Michael Jackson of Christian Music, The *Source(s):* PSND
Sweetheart of Gospel, The *Source(s):* PSND
Grant, Harold [composer]
René, Henri *Source(s):* CLTP ("Wagon Train")
Note(s): Also used by Manfred [or Manford] Kirchstein.
Grant, Robert 1778-1838 [hymnist]
D. R. *Source(s):* CYBH
E.—Y. (D. R.) *Source(s):* CYBH; JULN
Grant-Schaeffer, G(eorge) A(lfred) 1872-1939 [composer]
Note(s): Portraits: APSA; ETUP 51:12 (Dec. 1933): 797
Stanley, Herbert *Source(s):* CCE34; TPRF
Gratton, Joseph Thomas Hector 1900-1970 [composer, conductor, arranger, pianist]
Marcato, Ben *Source(s):* BUL3; CANE
Graubins, Jekabs 1886-1961 [composer, educator, ethnomusicologist]
Arnolds, J. *Source(s):* WORB

Graupner, (Johann Christian) Gottlieb 1767-1836 [composer, publisher, teacher]
Father of American Orchestral Music, The Source(s): PSND; SIFA
Father of Negro Songs, The Source(s): PSND; SIFA
Gravenites, Nick 1938- [singer, songwriter]
Greek, The Source(s): PSND
Graves, Burkett (K.) 1925- [singer, composer]
Dobro Virtuoso, The Source(s): MCCL
Graves, (Uncle) Josh Source(s): EPMU; LCAR; MCCL
Graves, Robert (Ranke) 1895-1985 [writer; lyricist]
Doyle, John Source(s): BLIC; GOTH; LCAR
Gray, Claude (N.) 1932- [singer, songwriter, guitarist]
Tall Texan, The Source(s): AMUS; MCCL; PSND
Note(s): See also William [or Billy] (Marvin) Walker.
Gray, Dulcie (Winifred Catherine) 1919 (or 20)- [novelist, actress]
Chester, Alan Source(s): GANB
Gray, Henry 1925- [singer, organist, pianist, songwriter]
Little Henry Source(s): HARS
Gray, John Baker (Timothy) 1949- [composer, author, singer, arranger]
Note(s): Do not confuse with John Barker Gray (1927-).
Gray, Jack Source(s): CCE53 E72818; LCAR
Gray, Timothy Source(s): ASCP; CCE60; CPOL RE-371-63; LCAR
Mann, Gerry Source(s): CCE53 Efor18795; CPOL RE-99-890
Gray(-Bey), Michael Ashley 1947- [author, lyricist]
Bey, Mickey Source(s): ASCP
Gray, Terius [rapper, songwriter]
Juvenile Source(s): AMUS; LCAR; PMUS-99
Gray, William B. c.1868?-1932 [songwriter]
Glenroy, William B. Source(s): CCE21 R18992; KILG; LCAR; SPTH p. 271
Note(s): In LCAR, see: Spaulding, George L.
Graziano, Caesar Franklin 1904-1989 [composer, author, teacher]
Frankie, Lou Source(s): ASCP; CCE64
Graziano, Frankie C. Source(s): CCE64
Graziano, Generoso 1915-1976 [composer, arranger, bandleader]
Gray, Jerry Source(s): BBDP; GAMM; KINK; LCAR; NGDJ; STUW
Graziolli, Giovanni [writer]
Schizza Source(s): SONN
Greatorex, Henry Wellington 1813-1858 [hymnist, compiler]
H. W. G. Source(s): METC
Greco, Armando 1926- [pianist, singer, songwriter]
Greco, Buddy Source(s): ALMN; AMUS; EPMU; HARD; KINK; PEN2
Greco, Vicente 1888-1924 [bandoneonist, bandleader, composer]
Garrote Source(s): BBDP; TODO
Gredy, F(riedrich) M(elchior) [librettist, writer on music, translator]
Friedrich, M. G. Source(s): LCAR; LOWN; MELL
M.G. F(r. in H.) Source(s): HEYT
Green, Barry [producer, singer, songwriter]
Blue, Barry Source(s): CCE77; HARR; SONG
Note(s): Also used by Ronald Roker.
Green, Benny 1963- [pianist, composer]
Note(s): Do not confuse with Ben Green [i.e., Benjamin [or Bernard] Anzelwitz] or Benny Green [i.e., Bernard Green] (1927-), see following entry.
Prototypical Modern Jazzman, The Source(s): CM17
Green, Bernard 1927-1998 [saxophonist, writer on music]
Green, Benny Source(s): PSND
Note(s): Do not confuse with Ben Green [i.e., Benjamin [or Bernard] Anzelwitz] or Benny Green (1963-); see preceding entry.
Green, Clarence 1929-1988 [singer, pianist, songwriter]
Note(s): Do not confuse with Clarence Green, 1937-1997, singer, guitarist.
Green, Candy Source(s): HARS
Green, Galveston Source(s): HARS
Green, Cornelius 1928-1995 [singer, guitarist, pianist, songwriter]
Lonesome Sundown Source(s): HARS; LCAR
Sundown, Lonesome Source(s): LCAR
Green, Douglas B. 1946- [singer, writer on music]
Idol of American Youth, The Source(s): http://www.ridersinthesky.com/html/riders2.htm (6 Oct. 2002)
Ranger Doug Source(s): AMUS; EPMU (see under: Riders in the Sky); LCAR
Green, (Ian) Ernest Gilmore 1912-1988 [pianist, composer, arranger]
Evans, Gil Source(s): BUL3; CM17; EPMU; GAMM; KINK; LCAR; NGDM; PEN2
Svengali Source(s): CASS
Note(s): Also used by Theodore [or Teddy] Pendergrass.
Green, Hazel 1954- [singer, songwriter]
Lynch, Claire Source(s): EPMU
Green, Henry Hawes (Craven) 1837-1910 [playwright]
Craven, Hawes Source(s): PIPE
Green, John(ny) (W(aldo)) 1908-1989 [songwriter]
Evergreen, Johnny Source(s): VACH
Green, Norman G. 1907-1975 [singer, guitarist, songwriter]
Green, Slim Source(s): HARS

Guitar Slim *Source(s):* HARS
Note(s): See also Eddie Jones, Alexander T. Seward & Raymond Maurice Otey. Also used by guitarist James Stephens (1915-).
Slim *Source(s):* CCE71
Note(s): See also Harry Clarence McAuliffe.

Green, Phil(ip) 1911-1982 (or 83) [arranger, composer, conductor]
Belmonte, José *Source(s):* CCE53 Efor19327; CPOL RE-97-962; EPMU; GROL; RFSO
Caroli, Vic *Source(s):* CCE57; CPOL RE-239-160
Note(s): Jt. pseud.: Norman [or Norrie] (William) Paramor.
Carter, Perry *Source(s):* CCE49 Efor13526; CCE76
Cortez, Pepe *Source(s):* CCE53
Duke, Louis(e) *Source(s):* EPMU; RFSO
Felipe, Don *Source(s):* CCE50-51; EPMU; LCAR; MUWB; RFSO
Juarez, Miguel *Source(s):* CC57; CPOL RE-239-163
Note(s): Jt. pseud.: Norman [or Norrie] (William) Paramor.
Kawaha, Eddie *Source(s):* CCE57; CPOL RE-239-182
Note(s): Jt. pseud.: Norman [or Norrie] (William) Paramor.
Lamarr, Ricardo *Source(s):* RFSO
Mann, Dorothy *Source(s):* CCE50; CCE55; CPOL RE-29-589
Mann, John *Source(s):* CCE53; CPOL RE-99-890
Note(s): Also used by John R. Mangini.
McCarthy, Joseph *Source(s):* CCE45 Efor70366
Mercado, Manuel *Source(s):* CCE57; CPOL RE-239-159
Note(s): Jt. pseud.: Norman [or Norrie] (William) Paramor.
Miguel, Don *Source(s):* RFSO
Nicolson, Ross *Source(s):* CCE57; CPOL RE-239-161
Note(s): Jt. pseud.: Norman [or Norrie] (William) Paramor.
Paloma, Vincente *Source(s):* CCE57; CPOL RE-244-066
Note(s): Jt. pseud.: Norman [or Norrie] (William) Paramor.
Peters, Douglas *Source(s):* CCE49 Efor13526 ("I'd Give the World to You, Sweetheart")
Pilgrim, The *Source(s):* CCE53; CCE55; CPOL RE-97-963
Note(s): See also Frances McCollin.
Ramirez, Luiz *Source(s):* CCE57; CPOL RE-244-066
Note(s): Jt. pseud.: Norman [or Norrie] (William) Paramor.
Starr, Peter *Source(s):* CCE52; LCCC 1948-54 (see reference)
Note(s): Jt. pseud.: Norman Newell.
Temple, John *Source(s):* CPOL RE-114-509
Todd, Earl *Source(s):* CCE57; CPOL RE-239-180
Note(s): Jt. pseud.: Norman [or Norrie] (William) Paramor.
Toohey, Patrick *Source(s):* CCE55
Valentine, Sim *Source(s):* CCE57; CPOL RE-239-179
Note(s): Jt. pseud.: Norman [or Norrie] (William) Paramor.
Voglio, Emelio *Source(s):* CCE57; CPOL RE-239-162
Note(s): Jt. pseud.: Norman [or Norrie] (William) Paramor.

Greenaway, Roger 1938- [singer, songwriter publisher]
Cookaway, Roger *Source(s):* CCE72 for158841
Note(s): Jt. pseud.: Roger Cook.
David *Source(s):* EPMU; GAMM; PSND
Note(s): "David and Jonathan," songwriting team with Roger Cook.
Two Rogers *Source(s):* SHAP
Note(s): Jt. pseud.: Roger Cook.

Greenbank, Henry [or Harry] H(arveston) [or H(ewetson)] 1865 (or 66)-1899 [librettist, lyricist]
Carlton, Henry [or Harry] *Source(s):* GANA p. 624; GAN1
Carlton, Sydney *Source(s):* GAN2 (see under: "Monte Carlo"); KILG

Greenbank, Percy 1878-1968 [librettist, lyricist]
Cryptos *Source(s):* GANA ("Our Miss Gibbs")
Note(s): Jt. pseud. of lyricists & composers: of Ivan Caryll [i.e., Félix Tilken], Adrian Ross [i.e., Arthur Reed Ropes], (John) Lionel (Alexander) Monckton & James T(olman) Tanner.

Greenbaum, Peter (Allen) 1946- [singer, guitarist, songwriter]
Green, Peter *Source(s):* EPMU; HARR; LCAR; PEN2; ROOM
Wizard *Source(s):* EPMU; ROOM
Note(s): See also Chris (Richard) Wilson.

Greenberg, Norman 1930- [composer, recording artist]
Greene, Norman *Source(s):* ASCP; CCE53

Greenberg, Susan M. 1944- [composer, author, singer]
Green, Maxie *Source(s):* ASCP

Greenblatt, Lewis 1949- [actor, director, writer, composer]
Furey, Lewis *Source(s):* MOMU

Greene, Gene [singer, songwriter]
Ragtime King, The *Source(s):* GRAK; Tosches, Nick. *Where Dead Voices Gather.* Boston: Little, Brown, 2001, p. 44.
Note(s): See also Michael Barnett.

Greene, Jack (Henry) 1930- [singer, guitarist, songwriter]

44-5967 ML105 2006-542 CIP

Drone, Jeanette Marie. **Musical AKAs: assumed names and sobriquets of composers, songwriters, librettists, lyricists, hymnists, and writers on music.** Scarecrow, 2007. 645p bibl afp ISBN 0810857391, $100.00: ISBN 9780810857391, $100.00

Drone (independent scholar) offers a most useful guide to assumed names used by composers, lyricists, and writers about music. The author of *Musical Theater Synopses* (CH, Mar'99, 36-3656), *Index to Opera, Operetta, and Musical Comedy Synopses in Collections and Periodicals* (1978), and various other bibliographical publications, she has gathered data from many standard music reference works, stories, biographies, electronic databases, and Web sources. Chapters range from one that lists a person's real or original name with alternate names and nicknames, to another listing the various assumed names referenced to the real ones. A chapter titled "Notes" pulls together the many in-house pseudonyms used by American music publishers. Drone's work of examining the *Catalog of Copyright Entries* (in all of its manifestations) is unique, and indicates a new area of musical research regarding the output of American music publishers during the past century. Only a portion of the author's work in progress is incorporated into this book. Besides proper names, Drone lists various catchphrases attached to a personality. Inclusion of such names will be useful to reference staff needing an authoritative source when confronted with a question regarding, for instance, the "Songbird of the South" (Gertrude Malissa Nix Rainey) or

Continued

Drone, Jeanette Marie

"Singing Brakeman" (Jimmie Rodgers). This is an entertaining, delightful, and utilitarian tool. **Summing Up:** Recommended. Reference collections supporting researchers at all levels.—*C. A. Kolczynski, Boston Public Library*

Jolly Giant *Source(s):* PSND
Jolly Green Giant, The *Source(s):* AMUS; MCCL; STAC
Greene, Martha 1869-1926 [composer, organist, conductor]
Stair, Patty *Source(s):* CLAG
Greening, Karen Lynn 1962- [singer, songwriter]
Aaron, Lee *Source(s):* AMUS; EPMU
Greenleaf, George William 1867-1930 [director, choreographer]
Ellison, Sydney *Source(s):* GAN2 (port.)
Greenstein, Michael Harvey [composer]
Harvey, Michael *Source(s):* GOTH
Greenwald, Bernard 1908-1975 [composer, conductor, arranger]
Green, Bernard *Source(s):* CCE63; CPOL RE-579-143; CLRA
Green, Bernie *Source(s):* CLMC; CLRA
Greenwald, M(artin) [composer, conductor, arranger]
Aldrich, F. *Source(s):* CCE36 R46107
C. M. C. *Source(s):* LCPC (no other information)
Howard, George Elbert *Source(s):* CCE37 R49043-44
Lichner, P. *Source(s):* CCE37 R49304
Lichner, R. *Source(s):* CCE37 R49307
Martaine, G. *Source(s):* CCE37 R49998; CCE41 #20979, 251 R96462
Martin, G. *Source(s):* CCE40 #11969, 56 R84548
Paloverde, M. *Source(s):* CCE47 R24885 ("Valse Serenade")
Reed, H. *Source(s):* CCE37 R49301
Sisters of St. Joseph *Source(s):* CCE37 R49290
Stoughton, R. *Source(s):* CCE36 R46109
Note(s): Do not confuse with R(oy) S(paulding) Stoughton.
Streabbog, M. *Source(s):* CCE37 R49306
Vogt, Carl *Source(s):* CCE35 E48126
Note(s): Also used by Lee Orean Smith; see NOTES: Vogt, Carl.
Wolpaw, Sarah *Source(s):* CCE40 #11969, 34 R84542
Greenwich, Ellie 1940- [singer, songwriter, record producer]
Gaye, Ellie *Source(s):* AMUS; EPMU; GROL
Gregg, Hubert Robert Harry 1914 (or 16)- [actor, writer, composer]
Marotte, Jean Paul *Source(s):* CART
Gregori, (Primo) Giovanni [or John] 1924 (or 28)- [violinist, composer, bandleader]
Gregory, John(ny) *Source(s):* MUSR; PSND
Ricco, Nino *Source(s):* MUSR
Gregorios the Protopsaltes ?1778-1821 [composer, scribe]
Levite, The *Source(s):* GROL
Gregory, Edmund 1925-1989 [saxophonist, composer, bandleader]
Shihab, Sahib *Source(s):* EPMU; KINK; LCAR; PSND
Gregson, Edward 1945- [composer]
Eaves, Robert *Source(s):* MOUT; http://www.bandsman.co.uk/brass007/msg00271.htm (June 2005)
Grein, Louis 1872-1933 [music critic]
Green, L. Dunton *Source(s):* BAKE
Grenzebach, Herbert 1897- [composer]
Borders, Herbert *Sourc(s):* CCE34 Efor34698; CCE55; CCE68
Stamer, Borders *Source(s):* KOMP; PFSA
Greppi, Giovanni 1751-1811 [author]
Florimondo Ermionéo *Source(s):* SONN
Grétry, André Ernest Modeste 1741-1813 [composer]
Note(s): Portrait: EWCY
Moliere of Music, The *Source(s):* PSND; SIFA
Grétry, Angélique-Dorothée-Lucie 1772-1790 [composer]
Grétry, Lucille *Source(s):* BAKE
Greulich, Carl Wilhelm 1796-1839 [musician]
Amphion *Source(s):* APPL p. 10
Greville, Ursula 1894-1991 [poet]
Agrell, Margery *Source(s):* LAST
Grey, Alan 1909- [composer, pianist, author]
Grey, Lanny *Source(s):* ASCA ; CCE60
Grey, Frank H(erbert) 1883-1951 [composer, conductor, publisher]
Note(s): Portrait: ETUP 52:1 (Jan. 1934): 4
Beatty, John *Source(s):* CCE59; TPRF
Bickford, Herbert *Source(s):* CCE57
Cariljo, Jose Fernandez *Source(s):* CCE59 R238285; TPRF
Clafflin, Don(ald) *Source(s):* CCE59 R235365; CCE61 R271557; TPRF
Coleman, Byron *Source(s):* TPRF
DaViego, Emilio *Source(s):* CCE59; TPRF
Dunn, Joe *Source(s):* CCE58
Fletcher, Joseph *Source(s):* CCE67 R407066
Fogers, Calvin *Source(s):* TPRF
Francis, Herbert *Source(s):* CCE37 E6244; CCE64 R338556
François *Source(s):* CCE33 E34364; CCE60 R250055
Grau, Frank *Source(s):* CCE29 E6862; CCE56 R174448 ("In the Land of Buddha")
Grau, Franz *Source(s):* CCE29 E10066; CCE29E6018; CCE29 E8297
Grévé, François *Source(s):* LCPC E66672 ("Isle of Cuba")
Gwinn, Francis *Source(s):* CCE57
Gwynn, Francis *Source(s):* CCE30 E13789; CCE57
Hildreth, R. E. *Source(s):* CCE33 R25036 ("Elaine Out on a Frolic"); CCE35 R49728

Leonard, Emil *Source(s):* CCE59 R248424; TPRF
Locke, Harold *Source(s):* CCE61 R270542; TPRF
Martin, Gertrude R. *Source(s):* CCE61
Mathis, Jules *Source(s):* CCE51; CCE59; TPRF
Mattheson, John Somers *Source(s):* CCE59 R240310; TPRF
Maxfield, Stanley *Source(s):* CCE61 R279095
Oyett, Dayne *Source(s):* CCE30 E18989; CCE57 R201749; CCE59
Renton, Victor *Source(s):* CCE59 R247811; TPRF
Rogers, Calvin *Source(s):* TPRF
Stocking, Elaine *Source(s):* CCE28 E698099; TPRF
Thomson, R. J. *Source(s):* CCE59; TPRF
Tscherinoff, Feodor *Source(s):* CCE59 R238282; TPRF
Warren, Cecil *Source(s):* CCE61 279093
White, Herbert *Source(s):* CCE35 E47474; CCE62 R300810

Grice, Gary [songwriter, performer]
GZA *Source(s):* AMUS; LCAR
Genius *Source(s):* AMUS; PMUS-00
Head, The *Source(s):* LCAR
Justice *Source(s):* LCAR
Maxamillion *Source(s):* LCAR

Grieg, Edvard Hagerup 1843-1907 [composer]
Chopin of the North *Source(s):* Slonimsky, Nicolas. *Music Since 1900.* New York: Schirmer, 1994, p. 73
Creator of Norwegian Music *Source(s):* Haas, Karl. *Adventures in Good Music.* PBS Radio (14 Aug. 2001)
Norway's Greatest Composer *Source(s):* http://www.mnc.net/norway/EHG.htm (6 Oct. 2002)

Grier, James [or Jimmie] W. 1902-1959 [saxophonist, composer, arranger]
Griff, Ray *Source(s):* MCCL
Host to the Cost, The *Source(s):* PSND

Griffes, Charles T(omlinson) 1884-1920 [composer]
Note(s): Portrait: ETUP 52:1 (Jan. 1934): 4
American Impressionist *Source(s):* http://www.findagrave.com/pictures/20131.html (6 Oct. 2002)
Tomlinson, Arthur *Source(s):* CCE18 E425620; NGAM

Griffin, Alsie 1912-1958 (or 59) [singer, songwriter]
Griffen, Alsie *Source(s):* MCCL
Griffen, Rex *Source(s):* MCCL
Griffin, Rex *Source(s):* ENCM

Griffin, Howard [songwriter]
Griffin, Curley *Source(s):* PMUS

Griffin, James [or Jimmy] (Arthur) 1943-2005 [singer, songwriter]
James, Arthur *Source(s):* CPOL RE-777-793; PSND

Griffin, Mark c.1957- [rapper, songwriter]
MC 900 Foot Jesus *Source(s):* CM16

Griffin, William, Jr. 196?- [lyricist]
Rakim *Source(s):* AMIR; CPOL PA-978-909; EPMU; PMUS-92; LCAR

Grill, Anton 1869-1943 [composer]
Grill, Andrew *Source(s):* REHH

Grillaert, Octave 1905-1979 [composer]
Beider, Joe *Source(s):* CCE49
King, Harry *Source(s):* CCE51-52; CCE60; REHH

Grillo, (Don) Angelo 1550 (or 57)-1629 [monk, poet]
Celiano, Livio *Source(s):* GROL; LCAR

Grillparzer, Franz 1791-1871 (or 72) [dramatist]
Roller der Unbegreifliche *Source(s):* APPL p. 12

Grimaldi, John 1952- [singer, harmonica player, songwriter]
Studebaker John *Source(s):* AMUS

Grimaldi, Stephanie 1965- [singer, songwriter]
Stephanie *Source(s):* CLAG

Grimm, C(arl) W(illiam) 1863-1952 [composer]
Note(s): Portrait: ETUP 52:1 (Jan. 1934): 4
Rochelle, Robert *Source(s):* CCE47 R14588 ("Prairie Pictures for Piano"); TPRF

Grimm, Friedrich Melchior, Freiherr von 1723-1807 [critic, journalist]
Fracescus de Paula *Source(s):* NGDM; PSND
Johannes Neopomucenus *Source(s):* NGDM
Tyran de Blanc *Source(s):* PSND
Waldstorch, Gabriel *Source(s):* NGDM

Grimm, Friedrich-Karl 1902- [composer]
Cavallesco, Enrico *Source(s):* BUL3; MUBR; RIES; WORB

Grinsted, William Stanley 1868-1910 [singer, songwriter]
Blackburn, Howard *Source(s):* GRAC
Lambert, Fred *Source(s):* GRAC
Poppin, D. H. *Source(s):* GRAC
Stanley, Frank C. *Source(s):* GRAC; LCAR; MACE
Williams, George S. *Source(s):* GRAC

Griselle, Thomas (Ellwood) 1893-1955 [composer]
Ellwood, Albert *Source(s):* CCE30 E15279
Note(s): Jt. pseud.: Victor Young.

Grisman, David (Jay) 1945- [mandolinist, singer, composer]
Note(s): Portrait: MUHF
Dawg *Source(s):* MUHF
Grisman, Dawg *Source(s):* LCAR; MCCL
Paganini of the Mandolin, The *Source(s):* MCCL; MUHF
Note(s): See also Nicola Calace.

Griswold, (Mrs.) (E. W.) 1860-? [hymnist]
Paulina *Source(s):* CYBH; NEIL p. 28
Note(s): According to Elias Nason "Paulina" was a pseud. of Mrs. P. P. Bliss [i.e., Lucy J(ane) Young]; however, Major D. W. Whittle said it was the pseud. of Mrs. Griswold.

Griswold, Mary Caroline mentioned 1864 [poet]

Carrie *Source(s):* OCLC 40717122; WORB
Note(s): Possible pseud.
Gritti, L. L. Ubaldi [fictitious music historian]
Note(s): Anagram of Wilibald Gurlitt (1889-1963). *Source(s):* GROL
Grob, Anita Jean 1927- [composer, author, arranger]
Kerr, Anita *Source(s):* ASCP
Grofé, Ferdé [i.e., Ferdinand] (Rudolph von) 1892-1972 [composer, arranger]
Father of Arranging, The *Source(s):* BBDP
Grogan, Joanne 1938- [pianist, songwriter]
Bracken, Joanne *Source(s):* CLAG; PEN2
Groh, Otto Emmerich 1905-1978 [playwright, theatrical director]
Kahr, Erik *Source(s):* PIPE
Kahr, R. *Source(s):* CCE51
Grohmann, Karl 1870- [singer, operatic impressario, composer]
Greve, Karl *Source(s):* MACM
Gronnenrade, Charles Gui Xavier Van [composer]
Blois, (M.) De *Source(s):* CPMU (publication date 1776)
Groote, Alianus de fl. 15th cent. [singer, poet, composer]
Alain *Source(s):* MACM
Gross, Franz 1876 (or 77)-1930 [composer, librettist]
Richtoff, Franz *Source(s):* PIPE
Gross, Leon T. 1912-1973 [singer, pianist, songwriter]
Archibald *Source(s):* HARS; LCAR
Archie Boy *Source(s):* HARS
Gross, Pierre 1823 (or 24)-1867 [music educator]
Cronthal, William *Source(s):* WORB
Grossel, Ira 1918-1961 [actor, singer, songwriter]
Chandler, Jeff *Source(s):* ASCP; LCAR
Grossman, Arthur 1894-1973 [film producer, lyricist, composer]
Freed, Arthur *Source(s):* BBDP (port.); CASS; EPMU; GAMM; HARD; HARR
Grossman(n), Ludwik 1835-1915 [composer, conductor]
Hurejszol, W. *Source(s):* WEOP
Grosz, Wilhelm [or Will] 1894-1939 [composer, conductor, pianist]
Georg, Hans *Source(s):* CCE31 Efor19698
Grant, Will *Source(s):* CCE50
Krüger, Wilhelm *Source(s):* CCE33 Efor30743
Milos, Andre *Source(s):* CCE63 R316892 ("When Budapest Was Young"); GROL; OMUO
Williams, Hugh *Source(s):* ASCP; BBDP; GROL; NGDM; OMUO; STUW; VACH; WORT
Grothe, Wilhelm 1830-1892 [actor, author]
Ehtorg, Carl *Source(s):* PIPE
Grey, Carl *Source(s):* PIPE
Rittberg, Hugo von *Source(s):* PIPE; WORB
Grothoff, Curtis Eugene, II 1938- [composer, author, singer]
Abraham, Johnny *Source(s):* ASCP
Grou, Lucien ?-1927 [arranger]
Flagny, Lucien de *Source(s):* MACM
Grubb, Alfred
Fletcher, Alfred *Source(s):* TPRF
Gruenberg, Janeta 1926- [composer]
Negrano Schori, Jenny *Source(s):* BUL3
Gruenberg, Louis 1883 (or 84)-1964 [music publisher]
Note(s): Portraits: ETUP 52:1 (Jan. 1934): 4; HOWD
Edwards, George *Source(s):* GROL; MELL; NGAM; NGDO; PIPE; WORB
Pennington, John *Source(s):* NGAM
Gruenthal, Joseph 1910- [composer, pianist]
Dean of Composers *Source(s):* http://www.jpost.com/Editions/2000/10/02/Culture/Music.13082.html (6 Oct. 2002)
Note(s): Sobriquet of Josef Tal [i.e., Joseph Gruenthal]
Tal, Josef [or Joseph] *Source(s):* BAKR; BAKO; BUL1; BUL2; LYMN; NULM (port.); PIPE
Grünbaum, Johann Christopher 1785-1870 [singer, composer]
Prix, Adalbert *Source(s):* PIPE
Note(s): Jt. pseud.: Adolf Bahn.
Grundland, Frederick [or Fritz] 1914- [composer]
Grant, Freddy *Source(s):* CCE43 #9517 Efor67994; CCE52-56; REHG
Gründler, Kurt 1927-1986 [accordionist, composer]
Clark, Curt *Source(s):* OMUO
Grundman, Clare (Ewing) 1913-1996 [composer]
Griffin, Henry *Source(s):* CCE61
Guermo, Carlos *Source(s):* CCE62
Grunert, Alfons 1920- [composer]
More, Arno *Source(s):* KOMP; PFSA
Myk, John *Source(s):* CCE66-68; KOMP; KOMS; PFSA
Grünwald, Alfred 1884 (or 86)-1951 [librettist, lyricist]
Wald, A. G. *Source(s):* GAN2; LCAR; NGDO
Gryce, G(eorge) G(eneral) 1925-1983 [composer, arranger, saxophonist]
Gryce, Gigi *Source(s):* EPMU; LCAR
Quism, Basheer *Source(s):* NGDJ; LCAR
Sears, Lee *Source(s):* http://www.fantasyjazz.com/catalog/gryce_g_cat.html (28 Mar. 2005)
Gualzetti, G. A. [librettist]
Eriso *Source(s):* LOWN
Guaragna, Salvatore 1893-1981 [composer]
Note(s): Portrait: EWEN
Father of the Hollywood Musical, The *Source(s):*http://www.dantealighieri.net/cambridge/Amlita_music.html (15 Oct. 2002)

Forgotten Man of American Music, The *Source(s):* PSND
Herschel, Henry *Source(s):* CCE27 E672224
Warren, Hal *Source(s):* LCAR
Warren, Harry *Source(s):* ALMN; CASS; GAMM; PEN2; PIPE; PSND; VACH
Guaraldi, Vince(nt) (Anthony) 1928-1976 [pianist, composer]
Reformed Boogie-Woogie Piano Player, A *Source(s):* http://www.fantasyjazz.com/html/guaraldi_bio.html (6 Oct. 2002)
Guardino, Louis Joseph 1923-1968 [composer, author, singer]
Gardner, Lou *Sources(s):* ASCP
Guariglia, Georgio 1917- [pianist, composer, conductor]
Greeley, George (Henry) *Source(s):* MUSR
Guastavino, Carlos 1912-2000 [composer, pianist]
Argentine Schubert, The *Source(s):* http://muse.jhu.edu/journals/latin_american_music_review/v024/24.1kulp.html (1 May 2005)
Schubert of the Pampas, The *Source(s):* http://muse.jhu.edu/journals/latin_american_music_review/v024/24.1kulp.html
Gubenko, Julius (Herbert) 1924- [composer, conductor, vibraphonist]
Gibbs, Terry *Source(s):* ASCP; KINK; LCAR
Guckenheimer, Fritz 1906-1989 [composer, clarinetist, business executive]
Gump, Richard (Benjamin) *Source(s):* ASCP; CPMU
Gudenberg, E(rich) Wolff von 1883-1955 [composer]
Anders, Erich *Source(s):* CCE42 #14692, 645 R105290; GOTH; PFSA
Gudmundsdottir, Bjõrk 1965- [songwriter]
Bjõrk *Source(s):* PMUS-95; WARN
Ice Princess of Ireland, The *Source(s):* LCAR
Ice Queen, The *Source(s): Time* (Special issue: "Music Goes Global") 158:14 (Fall 2001): 48 (port.)
Guerra, Marcelino 1912-1996 [singer, songwriter]
Guerra, Rapindey *Source(s):* LCAR; *Latin Beat Magazine* 10:3 (2000): 30+
Marcelino *Source(s):* LCAR
Rapindey *Source(s):* LCAR
Guerrazzi, Francesco Domenico 1804-1873 [statesman, author]
Gualandi, Anselmo *Source(s):* PIPE; PSND
Guerrero, Eduardo 1916 (or 17)-2005 [singer, songwriter]
Guerrero, Lalo *Source(s):* WASH; http://markguerrero.net/8.php (19 May 2005)
Father of Chicano Music *Source(s):* WASH; http://markguerrero.net/8.php
Guerrini, Olindo 1845-1916 [librettist]
Note(s): See LCAR for additional nonmusic-related pseudonymns.
Stecchetti, Lorenzo *Source(s):* LCAR; LOWN; WORB
Guesnon, George 1907-1968 [singer, instrumentalist, songwriter]
Banjo King of the Southland, The *Source(s):* HARS
Gayno, Creole (George) *Source(s):* HARS
Guesnon, Creole *Source(s):* HARS; LCAR
Guesnon, Curly *Source(s):* HARS
Guetfreund, Peter c.1570-1625 [singer, composer]
Bonamico, Pietro *Source(s):* NGDM; RIES; SADC
Gugler, Bernhard (von) 1812-1880 [teacher, author]
Bernhard, G. *Source(s):* PIPE
Guglielmi, (Pietro) Carlo c.1763-1827 [composer]
Guglielmini *Source(s):* GRV3; LCAR
Guglielmi, L(o)uis 1916-1991 [composer]
Guillaume, Louis *Source(s):* FULD
Louiguy, (Bravo) *Source(s):* BBDP; CCE47-48; CCE65-66; CPOL RE-25-360; FULD
Guichard, Henri c.1660-after 1728 [librettist, architect]
Hérapine, Sieur d' *Source(s):* NGDM; SADC
Guido d' Arezzo [or Aretino] c.997-c.1050 [monk, reformer of musical notation]
Guido Aretinus *Source(s):* BAKE
Guidonian *Source(s):* EPON
Guittone, Fra *Source(s):* GRV3; PSND
Guy of Arezzo *Source(s):* GRV3
Guido, Giovanni Antonio late 17th cent.-after 1728 [violinist, composer]
Antonio, (Mr.) *Source(s):* NGDM
Guido, Juan Bautista 1898-1945 [musician, leader, composer]
Lecherito, El *Source(s):* TODO
Guidry, Robert Charles 1938 (or 39)- [singer, songwriter]
Charles, Bobby *Source(s):* CCE64; EPMU; PEN2; ROOM
Guilielmus de Francia fl. last half 14th cent. [composer]
Guiglielmo di Santo Spirito, Frate *Source(s):* LCAR; NGDM
Guimãraes, João Teixeira 1883-1947 [guitarist, composer]
Pernambuco, Joao *Source(s):* LCAR; RILM 88-06552-rr
Guisinger, Earl C(halmers) 1904-1992 [engineer, songwriter]
Singer, Guy *Source(s):* ASCP; CCE52; CCE61-62; PSND
Guitry, Alexandre Georges Pierre 1885-1957 [author, actor]

Guitry, Sacha *Source(s):* GAN1; GAN2; LCAR; MELL
Guiu, José Melis 1920- [composer, pianist, conductor]
Giui, José Melis *Sourc(s):* CLTP ("Jack Paar Tonight Show")
Note(s): Incorrect spelling of surname?
Melis, José *Source(s):* ASCC; CLTP ("Jack Paar Tonight Show"); PSND
Gula, William 1911- [composer]
Gale, Bill [or William] *Source(s):* CCE65-66; CCE68; CLTP ("Blue Ribbon Bouts")
Gulda, Friedrich 1930-2000 [flutist, singer, composer]
Golowin, Albert *Source(s):* GROL
Guldener [librettist]
Labeský *Source(s):* FANF 20:4 (1997): 91
Gullidge, (W.) Arthur 1909-1942 [bandmaster, composer]
Greendale, Arthur (W.) *Source(s):* SMIN; SUPN
Gulyayvev, Aleksandr Pavlovich 1908-1998 [composer]
Grin, A. P. *Source(s):* http://www.chessville.com/chessprints/20040314.htm (31 May 2005)
Gum(m), Albert 1878-1956 [songwriter, music publisher]
Note(s): Portrait: EWEN
Rezlit, Albert *Source(s):* CCE30 R6481
Von Tilzer, Albert *Source(s):* BAKR; EPMU; GROL; HARR; NGDM; VACH
Gum(m), Harold [or Harry] 1872-1946 [songwriter]
Note(s): Portraits: EWEN; JAST
Crawford, Stanley *Source(s):* CCE46 R6568 ("Chinese Chop Sticks")
King of American Popular Music *Source(s):* SHMM 2:3 (Mar. 1978): 4
Man Who Launched a Thousand Hits, The *Source(s):* GROL
Mr. Tin Pan Alley *Source(s):* SHMM 2:3 (Mar. 1978): 5
Von Tilzer, Harry *Source(s):* BAKR; EPMU; GROL; HARR; NGDM; VACH
Gumbinsky, Wilbur [lyricist]
Gumm, Wilbur *Source(s):* BBDP
Gund, Robert 1865-1927 [composer]
Gound, Robert *Source(s):* LCAR
Gundel, Vilem 1912- [composer]
Gunovsky, Vilem *Source(s):* PSND
Gunia, Paul Vincent 1950- [composer]
Vincent, Paul *Source(s):* KOMS; PFSA
Gunter, Sidney Louie, Jr. 1925- [singer, songwriter]
Gunter, Hardrock *Source(s):* AMUS; CCE53; CLAB; LCAR; MCCL
Günther, Franz Hermann 1824-1871 [composer]
Herther, F. *Source(s):* STGR; WORB
Guppy, Shusha 1940- [songwriter, singer, author]
Shusha *Source(s):* EPMU
Gürsch, Günther Gerhard 1919- [composer]
Guerez, Juan *Source(s):* CCE56; KOMP; KOMS; PFSA
Kleve-Gürsch *Source(s):* CCE51-52
Gustafson, Howard J(oseph) 1915-2004 [composer, author, pianist]
Howard, Bart *Source(s):* ASCP; CCE54-55; CCE61; DRSC; LCAR
Gutenberg von Weigolshausen 1640-1725 [composer]
Prendcourt, "Captain" (François de) *Source(s):* GROL; NGDM
Gutesha, Mladen 1923- [composer, arranger]
Bauer, Gerd *Source(s):* CCE57; CCE59; RIES
Guthrie, Leon Jerry 1915-1948 [singer, songwriter]
Guthrie, Jack *Source(s):* ENCM; MCCL
Guthrie, Thomas Anstey 1856 (or 57)-1934 [songwriter]
Anstey, F. *Source(s):* KILG; LCAR
Guthrie, Woodward [or Woody, or Woodie] (Wilson) 1912-1967 [singer, songwriter]
Note(s): Portrait: EWEN
Godfather of Folk, The *Source(s):*OUSH
Original Folk Hero, The *Source(s):* *Evansville Courier & Press* (22 Nov. 2000): C7
Gutiérrez, Javier [songwriter, arranger]
Mala Fe *Source(s):* HWOM
Gutierrez, Luis Eduardo Aute 1943- [composer]
Aute, L. E. *Source(s):* PMUS
Gutiérrez Grillo, Francisco Raúl 1908-1984 [composer, author, singer]
Grillo, Frank (R.) *Source(s):* LCAR
Grillo, Machito *Source(s):* CCE45 #51750 Eunp445950; PEN2
Machito *Source(s):* LCAR
Gutierrez-Najera, Manuel 1859-1895 [author; writer on music]
Crysantema *Source(s):* LCAR
Duque, Job *Source(s):* LCAR
Job Duque *Source(s):* LCAR
Mr. Can-Can. *Source(s):* RILM 96-15086-ap
Gutman, Adam 1916-2003 [violinist, composer]
Adams, George *Source(s):* http://www.cjc.ca/template.php?actin=archives&Type=1&Language=EN&REc=432 (18 June 2005)
Gutsche, Romeo Maximilian (Eugene Ludwig) 1907- [composer]
Gutchë, Gene *Source(s):* BAKR; CCE63; CCE65-66
Regus *Source(s):* CCE65; CCE67
Guttivergi, Giuseppe 1906-1985 [composer]
Creston, Paul *Source(s):* BUL1; BUL3; LCAR; NGAM

Guttmann, Alfred (Grant) 1920- [composer, arranger]
Goodman, Alfred (Grant) *Source(s):* BAKO; BAKR; BUL2; NGDO
Manfield, Fred *Source(s):* CCE40 #36163 Eunp237654
Guttmann, Artur 1891-1945 [conductor, composer]
Erwin, Otto *Source(s):* OMUO
Kulm, Otto Erwin *Source(s):* PIPE; WORB
Guttman, Therese 1899- [musicologist]
Gosztonyi, Tera *Source(s):* WORB
Guttmann, Hermann 1848-1908 [artist, composer]
Evander, H. *Source(s):* IBIM; WORB
Gutzeit, Erich 1898-1973 [composer]
Honky, Jam(e)s *Source(s):* GREN; RIES; SUPN
Gutzkow, Karl (Ferdinand) 1811-1878 [author]
Bulwer, E. L. *Source(s):* PIPE
Guy, George 1936- [singer, guitarist, songwriter]
Buddy Boy *Source(s):* HARS
Guy, Buddy *Source(s):* HARS; LCAR; MUHF
Guy, Helen 1858-1936 [songwriter]
Note(s): Portrait: ETUP 52:3 (Mar. 1934): 144
Hardelot, Guy d' *Source(s):* BAKR; KILG (see under: Rhodes, Helen); LCAR
Rhodes, Helen (Guy) *Source(s):* BAKR; LCAR
Rhodes, (Mrs.) W. I. *Source(s):* BAKR
Guy, Rose Marie (neé Mazetta) 1925- [composer, actress, singer]
Rose Marie *Source(s):* ASCP; LCAR
Guyot [de Châtelet], Jean 1512-1588 [composer]
Castileti, (Johannes [or Jean]) *Source(s):* BAKR; LCAR; MACM; OMUO; WORB
Du Châtelet, Jean *Source(s):* BAKR; LCAR; WORB
Guidonius, Jean *Source(s):* WORB
Guyoz, Jean *Source(s):* WORB
Guzmán Yañez, Enrique [songwriter, singer]
Edson *Source(s):* HWOM
Fato *Source(s):* HWOM; LCAR
Guzmán, Fato *Source(s):* HWOM
Negro Fato *Source(s):* HWOM
Guzzo, Francis 1939- [singer, songwriter]
Ford, Frankie *Source(s):* EPMU
King of Swamp Pop Music *Source(s):* http://museum.lamarpa.edu/fford.html (11 Jan. 2005)
New Orleans Dynamo *Source(s):* http://frankieford.com (11 Jan. 2005)
Gwynn Williams, W(illiam) S(idney) 1896- [composer, author, conductor]
Gwynn o'r Llan *Source(s):* CLEV
Gyldmark, Hugo 1899-1971 [composer]
Lindquist, Gosta *Source(s):* CCE60
Merriman, Sid *Source(s):* REHH (see under: Svanesøe, Robert); http://www.mic.dk/music/compidx.htm (6 Oct. 2003)
Zerine *Source(s):* CCE37 Efor48588 ("Flodhestens byrllup")
Gyldmark, Sven Rudolf S. 1904-1981 [composer]
Bonandoni, G. *Source(s):* REHH
Lacome, J. *Source(s):* REHH
O'Brien, Spike *Source(s):* CCE37 Efor8588; REHH
Gyrowetz, Adalbert 1763-1850 [lawyer, composer. conductor]
Notarsch Sakramensky *Source(s):* APPL p. 12

– H –

Haass, Hans 1877-1955 [composer, pianist]
Black, Sidney *Source(s):* RPRA
Dark, Henry *Source(s):* RPRA
Fox, Edward *Source(s):* RPRA
Note(s): Also used by Ira B(ishop) Wilson.
Fox, Felix *Source(s):* RPRA
Hare, John *Source(s):* RPRA
Häuser [or Haeuser], Hans *Source(s):* CCE54; RPRA
Johnson, Edward *Source(s):* RPRA
Keller, F. *Source(s):* RPRA
Maison, Jean *Source(s):* RPRA
Milner, George *Source(s):* RPRA
Renner, Hans *Source(s):* RPRA
Sommer, Hans *Source(s):* RPRA
Note(s): Also used by Hans Friedrich August Zincken.
Haberfield, Edwin 1925- [singer, guitarist, songwriter]
Ranger, Shorty *Source(s):* EPMU
Shorty Ranger *Source(s):* LCAR
Habermann, Philipp 1552-1618 [composer, organist]
Avenarius, Philipp *Source(s):* LCAR; NGDM
Habicht, Emma [writer on music]
C. E. H., (Mrs.) *Source(s):* EBEL
Note(s): "Recollections of Chopin"
Hackh, Otto (Christoph) 1852-1917 [composer, pianist]
Dana, Arthur *Source(s):* CCE24 R27747
Note(s): A. P. Schmidt house name; see NOTES: Dana, Arthur.
Haddakin, Edward 1906-1969 [ballet critic]
Coton, A. V. *Source(s):* PIPE
Haensch, Gerhard Delle 1926- [composer]
Landy, Manuel *Source(s):* KOMP; KOMS; PFSA; RIES
Safir, Tim *Source(s):* KOMP; KOMS; PFSA
Haenschen, Walter (G(ustave)) 1889-1980 [composer, conductor, pianist, arranger]

Coombs, Norman *Source(s):* CCE50 R61885 ("In the Land of Smiling Waters")
Note(s): Jt. pseud.: James (Conrad) O'Keefe. Also used by (Alfreda) Theodora Strandberg.
Crane, Paul *Source(s):* CCE48 R31584 ("Crying for You")
Crossing, Cyril *Source(s):* CCE52 R96103 ("Rio"); LCPC E616656
Dupont, Paul *Source(s):* BBDP; CCE49 R53483 ("La Rosita"); CCE52; STUW
Note(s): Possible pseud.; also possible pseud. of J(ohn) S(tepan) Zamecnik.
Edwards, J. Walter *Source(s):* CCE49 R53715 ("Two Tiny Bits of Heaven's Blue")
Fenton, Carl *Source(s):* CCE49 R48147 ("Stamboola"); GRAC; GRAK; STUW
Note(s): Used by Haenschen before 1927; afterwards used by Reuben Greenberg & assumed as his legal name in 1932. (GRAK)
Haenschen, Gus(tave) *Source(s):* ASCP; CCE48; CCE50; CCE53; CPOL RE-68-994
Holliday, Walter *Source(s):* BBDP; GRAC; STUW
Huntley, Austin *Source(s):* CCE50 R63437 ("Japanese Moon")
Note(s): Jt. pseud.: James (Conrad) O'Keefe. Also used by Theodore (F.) Morse.
Jaxon, Frank *Source(s):* CCE50 R56320 ("Black Eyed Blues")
Kendall, Don *Source(s):* CCE50 R57889
Note(s): Jt. pseud.: James (Conrad) O'Keefe. Also used by Jules Hurtig, Theodore (F.) Morse, Lester O'Keefe; see NOTES: Kendall, Don.
Lanum, Howard *Source(s):* CCE51 R74017 ("Down by the Wishing Well")
Preston, John *Source(s):* CCE52 R95204 ("Memories of a Rose")
Standish, Clinton *Source(s):* CCE49 R53716 ("Gray Morn")
Stuart, Allan *Source(s):* CCE52 (Index)
Note(s): Pseud. of Haenschen; however, in entry says pseud. of Paul Dupont, which is a pseud. of Haenschen. Also used by Lester O'Keefe.
Wilson *Source(s):* CCE50 R58712 ("The Land of Broken Dreams")
Wynburn, Raymond *Source(s):* CCE54 R123527 ("Adorable")
Note(s): Jt. pseud.: James (Conrad) O'Keefe.

Haesche, William Edwin 1867-1929 [composer]
Note(s): Portrait: ETUP 52:2 (Feb. 1934): 72
Hedden, Edwin *Source(s):* TPRF

Haga, Frederick Wallace 1874-1958 (or 59) [composer, violinist, publisher]
Note(s): The following names are listed as pseudonyms of Fred(ederick W.) Hager.
Belmont, Chas. W. *Source(s):* CCE50 R68122 ("The Trail of Love")
Note(s): Jt. pseud.: Justin Ring [i.e., Ringleben]
Gates, Clifford G. *Source(s):* CCE49 R53750 ("My Heart Is Waiting")
Note(s): Jt. pseud.: Justin Ring [i.e., Ringleben]
Hager, Fred(erick W.) *Source(s):* GRAC
Megar, Fay *Source(s):* CCE47 R17365 ("Babetto")
Note(s): Jt. pseud.: John Meyer.
Milo-Rega *Source(s):* CCE47 R18168
Note(s): Jt. pseud.: Justin Ring [i.e., Ringleben]
Rega, F. Wallace *Source(s):* CCE41 #17736 E93719; CCE45 #26143, 295 R137770
Rega, Milo *Source(s):* CCE47 R19471 ("Here's the Keys Boys, To Our Town"); GRAC
Regal, F. Wallace *Source(s):* CCE41 #17736 E93719; CCE45 #26143, 295 R137770
Ring-Hager *Source(s):* CCE50 R57846 ("Down Where I Belong")
Note(s): Jt. pseud.: Justin Ring [i.e., Ringleben]
Sheridan, Andy *Source(s):* CCE51 R80492 ("Honolulu Nights")
Note(s): Jt. pseud.: Justin Ring [i.e., Ringleben]
Taylor, Ruby *Source(s):* CCE49 R43587
Note(s): Jt. pseud.: Justin Ring [i.e., Ringleben]
Verdin, Henri [or Henry] *Source(s):* CCE48 R26106 ("A-La-Paree")
Note(s): Jt. pseud.: Justin Ring [i.e., Ringleben]

Hagen, J(ohn) M(ilton) 1892-1977 [composer, author]
DeNegah, Juan *Source(s):* CCE38 Eunp162744 ("My Gal Carmine"); CCE65
Hagen, Milt *Source(s):* CCE49 R50568 ("After All These Years")
Mayfield, Menlo *Source(s):* CCE27 E670621; CCE51 R76308 ("Swanee Blossoms")
Paris, Dick *Source(s):* CCE17 E409227
Sherwin, Sterling *Source(s):* ASCP; CCE39 AA294133; CCE70 R481416; LCAR

Hagert, Thornton 1930- [trumpeter, bandleader, writer on ragtime]
Hagert, Tony *Source(s):* JASN p. xi

Haggard, Merle (Ronald) 1937- [singer, guitarist, songwriter]
Note(s): Portrait: EWEN
Godfather of Country Music *Source(s):* http://www.lasvegasnv.com/brett/1020021a.htm (31 Jan. 2005)
Hat, The *Source(s):* FLIN; PSND
Okie from Muskogee, The *Source(s):* PSND
Stranger, The *Source(s):* PSND

Haggin, Bernard H. 1900-1987 [music critic]
Toscanini Cultists, The *Source(s):* GRAN p. 275
Note(s): Jt. sobriquet: Samuel Chotzinoff & Lawrence Gilman.
Ty Cobb of Music Critics, The *Source(s):* GRAN

Hägglund, Joel (Em(m)anuel) 1879-1915 [labor leader; poet, composer]
Haaglund, Joel *Source(s):* HARD; ROOM
Hill, Joe *Source(s):* HARD; MRSQ 7:3-4 p. 10; PSND; ROOM; SIFA
Hillstrom, Joe(l) *Source(s):* PSND; ROOM
Hillstrom, Joseph *Source(s):* ALMN; HARD; LCAR
Man Who Never Died, The *Source(s):* PSND; SIFA
Hahnel, Johannes c.1490-after 1520 [composer, theorist]
Note(s): Probable original name.
Alectorius, Johannes *Source(s):* GROL
Galliculus, Johannes *Source(s):* GROL
Haidenko, Igor 1961- [composer]
Kosenko *Source(s):* http://ukrainianchoir.co.uk/pages/IgorGaidenko.htm (10 Feb. 2005)
Kytasty, Hryhory [or Grygory] *Source(s):* http://ukrainianchoir.co.uk/pages/IgorGaidenko.htm
Hainsworth, Edward James [composer]
Saint James, Vivian *Source(s):* CPMU (publication date 1908)
Hainworth, Robert [composer]
R. H. *Source(s):* CPMU (publication date 1861)
Halaczinsky, Rudolf 1920- [composer]
Theal, Rolf *Source(s):* BUL3; KOMS; PFSA
Hale, Irene Baumgras c.1860- [composer]
Note(s): Married name: Mrs. Philip Hale.
René, Victor *Source(s):* COHN; HIXN
Hale, Mary Whitwell 1810-1862 [author, hymnist]
Y. L. E. *Source(s):* JULN
Note(s): Last letter of each part of name.
Hale, Nathaniel (D(awayne)) 1969- [songwriter, performer]
Nate Dogg *Source(s):* AMIR; AMUS; CPOL PA-1-104-961; PMUS-00
Hale, Philip 1854-1934 [organist, music critic]
Note(s): Portrait: ETUP 52:2 (Feb. 1934): 72
Artist in Prose, An *Source(s):* GRAN
Auntie Hale *Source(s):* GRAN
Hale, Auntie *Source(s):* GRAN
J. S. Bach of Program Annotators, The *Source(s):* GRAN
Maestro of the Program Notes, The *Source(s):* GRAN
Philip the Great *Source(s):* GRAN
Philip the Terrible *Source(s):* GRAN
Hale, Sarah J(osepha) (Buell) 1788-1879 [author, editor]
S. J. H. *Source(s):* FULD ("Mary Had a Little Lamb")
Hale-Monro, John Robert 1902-1959 [actor, singer, author, producer]
Hale, Sonnie *Source(s):* EPMU
Halévy, (Jacques-François-)Fromental 1799-1862 [composer]
Note(s): Portraits: ETUP 52:2 (Feb. 1934): 72; EWCY
Alberti *Source(s):* GROL; NGDM; NGDO; STGR
Halévy, Ludovic 1834-1908 [librettist, lyricist]
Arcy, Paul d' *Source(s):* NGDO
Note(s): Jt. pseud.: Hector Jonathan Crémieux.
Lange, Adolphe *Source(s):* STGR
Note(s): Jt. pseud.: Hector Jonathan Crémieux.
Mel and Hal *Source(s):* GAN2 (see under: Meilhac, Henri)
Note(s): Jt. nickname: Henri Meilhac.
Servières, Jules *Source(s):* GAN1; GAN2; NGDM; NGDO; PIPE
Haley, William [or Bill] (John Clifton), (Jr.) 1925-1981 [singer, songwriter]
B. H. Sees Combo *Source(s):* ROCK
Clifton, Johnny *Source(s):* ROCK
Daddy of Rock and Roll, The *Source(s):* Swenson, J. *Bill Haley; The Daddy of Rock and Roll.* 1982.
Father of Rock 'n' Roll, The *Source(s):* CM06
Note(s): See also Charles Edward Anderson Berry, Arthur Crudup, Charles Hardin Holley, Johnnie Johnson & Elvis A(a)ron Presley.
Gregory, Scott *Source(s):* ROCK
Original King of Rock and Roll, The *Source(s):* ROCK
Halfin, Robert [or Bob] [songwriter]
Duke, Jerry *Source(s):* CCE58; CPOL RE-282-084
Note(s): Jt. pseud.: Harold (Cornelius) Fields & Joseph (Dominic) Roncoroni.
Ross, David *Source(s):* CCE59; CPOL RE-344-757
Note(s): Jt. pseud.: Harold Irving [i.e., Harold Shaberman] & Ralph Ruvin.
Rossiter, (John) Simon *Source(s):* CCE58; CPOL RE-282-088
Note(s): Jt. pseud.: Harold (Cornelius) Fields & Joseph (Dominic) Roncoroni.
Williams, Ross *Source(s):* CCE58
Halikiopolos Nicolaos 1795-1872 (or 73) [composer, theorist, teacher]
Mantzaros, Nicholaos *Source(s):* NGDM
Hall, Fred(erick) Fifield 1878-1956 [composer]
Note(s): Used more than 30 pseudonyms; however, only the following have been identified.
Brand, Georges *Source(s):* DAUM
Dare, Anthony *Source(s):* DAUM
Maynard, Doris *Source(s):* CCE27 E663040
Morel, Gabriel *Source(s):* DAUM
Stanton, Albert *Source(s):* CCE27 E663472
Hall, Gertrude 1912- [composer, author]
Hall, Sugar *Source(s):* ASCC; CCE61-62
Note(s): Also nickname of Fred Hall [i.e., Fred Arthur Ahl] or a joint pseud.?
Hall, Helen [composer, author, singer]
Hall, Teddy *Source(s):* ASCC; CPOL RE-121-893

Hall, James Faye 1922-1984 [singer, songwriter, pianist]
Hall, Roy *Source(s):* HARD; MCCL
Hall, Joseph Lincoln 1866 (or 68)-1930 [composer, editor]
Note(s): Portraits: CYBH; ETUP 52:2 (Feb. 1934): 72; HALL
Clare, Howard *Source(s):* CCE27 R42067; CCE28 R42833
Clifton, Maurice A. *Source(s):* CCE26 R35719; CCE28 R42685; CYBH
Judson, Alfred *Source(s):* CCE34 R34019; CCE41 #15894, 216 R93474
Lacey, Herbert J. *Source(s):* CCE33 R23173; CCE47 R24512 ("Keep In Step"); CCE67
Lacey, R. J. *Source(s):* CCE32 R18080
Linwood, Arthur *Source(s):* CCE34 R29456
Robertson, Wilfred *Source(s):* CCE37 R56743; CCE39 #6152, 223 R72767
Stephens, H. G *Source(s):* CCE37 R49335
Willard, Clyde *Source(s):* CCE41 #45056 E99504; CCE61 R286087; http://www.ibiblio.org/ccer1925d4.htm (8 Jan. 2005)
Wilton, Arthur *Source(s):* CCE28 R4507; CCE61; CCE64 R332508
Hall, (Christopher) Newman 1816-1902 [hymnist]
Hall, Erkenvkv *Source(s):* LCAR
N. H. *Source(s):* LCAR
Hall, R(obert) B(rowne) 1858-1907 [composer, cornetist, conductor]
Note(s): Portrait: ETUP 52:2 (Feb. 1934): 72
Maine's Own March King *Source(s):* http://www.mta.link75.org/music/rbh/bardwell.html (10 Feb. 2002)
March King of New England, The *Source(s):* http://www.angelfire.com/tx/masonmusic/marchwrite.html (10 Feb. 2002)
New England March King *Source(s):* SMIN
Hall, Richard (Melville) 1965- [composer, DJ]
Moby *Source(s):* AMIR; AMUS; CM17; LCAR; PMUS-00
Hall, Thomas 1936- [singer, songwriter, guitarist, author]
Hall, Tom T *Source(s):* LCAR
Mark Twain of Country Music *Source(s):* PEN2; PSND
Nashville Storyteller *Source(s):* CASS; PEN2
Poet from Nashville, The *Source(s):* PSND
Poet of Nashville *Source(s):* CASS
Storyteller, The *Source(s):* CM04; CM26; FLIN; MCCL; PSND; STAC
Hall, Wendell (Woods) 1896-1969 [composer, singer]
Radio Red *Source(s):* MACE; SUTT
Red Headed Music Maker, The *Source(s):* CASS; KINK; MACE p. 389; PSND
Red Masked Baritone *Source(s):* MACE
Singing Xylophonist, The *Source(s):* PARS
Hallé, Karl [or Carl] 1819-1895 [pianist, conductor, compiler]
Note(s): Portrait: ETUP 52:2 (Feb. 1934): 72
Hallé, (Sir) Charles *Source(s):* BAKE; MACM
Haller, Hanne 1950- [composer]
Echner, Hansi *Source(s):* PFSA
Haliver, Joan *Source(s):* CPOL PA-371-508
Halletz, Erwin 1922 (or 23)- [composer, bandleader]
Begonha, Alberto *Source(s):* CCE55; CCE59
Kracher, Sepp *Source(s):* CCE55; CCE59
Lehmann, Alfons *Source(s):* CCE54; CCE58
Roulette, Rene *Source(s):* CCE53; PFSA; REHG; RIES; SUPN
Schöll, Peter *Source(s):* CCE55; CCE58; CCE60
Spiller Walter *Source(s):* CCE53-54; CCE56; CCE58
Truxa, Konstantin *Source(s):* CCE58-60
Hallis, B. Edward [composer]
Maurice, Victor *Source(s):* JASA p. 322
Hallmann, Paul 1600-1650 [composer, poet]
P. H. *Source(s):* IBIM; WORB
Hallowell, Russ(ell F.) 1897-1965 [composer, author]
Stewart, Gene *Source(s):* ASCC
Halper, Leivick 1888-1962 [lyricist]
Leivick, H(alper(n)) *Source(s):* HESK; WORB
Halt, Hugo 1878- [composer]
Trossbach, Hans *Source(s):* PFSA
Haltenberger, Johann Nikolaus 1748-1780 [composer]
Haltenberger, Bernhard *Source(s):* NGDM
Montenelli, Bernardo *Source(s):* NGDM
Ham, John Lee 1946- [singer, songwriter]
Lee, Johnny *Source(s):* AMUS; MCCL
Note(s): Also used by John Lee Hooker.
Hamácek, Joseph [or Josef] 1824-1876 [composer, conductor]
Nesvadba, Joseph *Source(s):* MACM
Hamblen, (Carl) Stuart 1908-1989 [singer, songwriter, guitarist]
Cowboy Joe *Source(s):* MCCL
Donner, Dave *Source(s):* MCCL
Hamburger, Michel 1947-1992 [guitarist, songwriter]
Berger, Michel *Source(s):* CCE67; EPMU; LCAR
Hursel, Michel *Source(s):* EPMU; LCAR
Michelberger *Source(s):* CCE68; CCE73 Efor166439
Hamel, Peter Michael 1947- [composer]
Henrich, Gabriel *Source(s):* PFSA
Henrich, Michael *Source(s):* KOMS
Hamill, Chris(topher) 1958- [composer]
Limahl *Source(s):* AMUS; FZSL
Hamilton, Al(bert) 1903- [songwriter]

Notes(s): Do not confuse with Johnny Thunders [i.e., John (Anthony) Genzale, (Jr.)
Kent, Al *Source(s):* CCE66-67; CPOL RE-697-497; PMUS
Hamilton, Clarence G(rant) 1865-1935 [composer]
Note(s): Portrait: ETUP 52:3 (Mar. 1934): 144
Grant, Cecil *Source(s):* CCE49 R48350; LCAR; TPRF
Hamilton, Edward Leslie 1937- [composer, author, singer]
Hamilton, Ted *Source(s):* ASCP; CPOL RE-822-862
Note(s): Also used by George L. Cobb
Hamilton, Eugene [songwriter]
Savoy, Ronnie [or Ronny] *Source(s):* CCE65-66; CPOL RE-601-281; PMUS
Hamilton, Foreststorn 1921- [drummer, composer, conductor]
Chico the Cat *Source(s):* EPMU; PSND
Drummer X *Source(s):* JAMU
Hamilton, Chico *Source(s):* ASCC; EPMU; LCAR; TCAN
Hamilton, George 1901-1957 [composer, conductor]
Hamilton, Spike *Source(s):* ASCC; CCE27 E671889; VACH
Hamilton, Gil 1941- [singer, songwriter]
Thunder, Johnny *Source(s):* AMUS; EPMU
Note(s): Do not confuse with Johnny Thunders [i.e., John (Anthony) Genzale, (Jr.)
Hammerich, Asger 1843-1923 [composer]
Hamerik, Asger *Source(s):* BAKR; LCAR; MACM; WORB
Hammerich, Ebbe 1898-1951 [composer, conductor]
Hamerik, Ebbe *Source(s):* BAKR
Hammerschmid, Hans 1930- [composer]
Stuck, Harvey *Source(s):* CCE66-67; KOMP; KOMS; PFSA
Hammerschmidt, Andreas 1611 (or 12)-1675 [musician, composer
A. H. *Source(s):* IBIM; WORB
Ham., A(nd.) *Source(s):* IBIM; WORB
Hammerstein, Oscar (Greeley Clendenning), II 1895-1960 [lyricist]
Note(s): Portraits: ETUP 52:3 (Mar. 1934): 144; EWEN
Barnum of Opera, The *Source(s):* SCHO p. 263
Gilbert and Sullivan of Broadway *Source(s):* Hyland, William G. *Richard Rodgers*. New Haven: Yale University Press, 1998, 236
Note(s): Jt. sobriquet: Richard (Charles) Rodgers.
Showmen of the Century *Source(s):* *Time.* (Special Issue). (8 June 1998)
Note(s): Jt. sobriquet: Richard (Charles) Rodgers.
Team from Siam *Source(s):* Hyland p. 203 (see above)
Note(s): Jt. sobriquet: Richard (Charles) Rodgers.
Hammett, Paul D(ean) 1915-1989 [composer, author, singer]
Case, Justin *Source(s):* ASCP; CCE68; CCE72
Hammond, John (Henry), Jr. 1910-1987 [music critic, producer]
Johnson, Henry *Source(s):* PSND
Note(s): Also used by Walter Brown McGhee.
Hammond, Roy Charles 1943- [singer, songwriter]
Roy C. *Source(s):* AMUS; EPMU
Hammond, Samuel Leroy ?-1864 [lyricist]
Wildwood, Charlie *Source(s):* HOGR; OCLC 23478575
Hamper, Stephen John 1958 (or 59)- [singer, songwriter, guitarist, critic]
Childish, Billy *Source(s):* NOMG
Hamper, W. [composer]
Repmah, W. *Source(s):* CPMU (publication date c.1800)
Hampton, Lionel (Leo) c.1909-2002 [bandleader, composer, vibraphonist, pianist]
Ell, Ly N. *Source(s):* JAMU
Hamp *Source(s):* KINK
Hampton, Locksley (Wellington) 1932- [trombonist, composer, arranger]
Hampton, Slide *Source(s):* CCE 60-61; EPMU; NGDJ; PEN2
Hanaford, J. H. 1819- [hymnist]
J. H. H. *Source(s):* JULN (Appendix)
Hancock, George 1945- [singer, songwriter, guitarist]
Hancock, Butch *Source(s):* EPMU; HARR; PEN2
Hancock, Herbert [or Herbie] Jeffrey 1940- [pianist, composer]
Chameleon, The *Source(s):* Shipton, Alyn. *Jazz Makers; Vangards of Sound.* New York: Oxford University Press, 2002, p. 201.
Note(s): See also (Claude) Russell Bridges.
Mwandishi *Source(s):* GROL; PEN2; PSND
Hancock, James S. 1910- [songwriter]
Harper, Jimmy *Source(s):* CPOL RE-142-554; KILG
Handel, Georg Friedrich 1685-1759 [composer]
Bold Briareus *Source(s):* PSND
Briareus of Music, The *Source(s):* PSND
Dear Saxon, The *Source(s):* PSND
Handelian *Source(s):* EPON
Monarch of the Musical Kingdom, The *Source(s):* PSND
Orpheus of the Eighteenth Century, The *Source(s):* PSND
Saxon Giant, The *Source(s):* PSND
Thunderbolt, The *Source(s):* PSND; SIFA
Handl, Adam mentioned 1561 [composer]
Galliculus *Source(s):* WORB

Handy, W(illiam) C(hristopher) 1873-1958 [composer]
Note(s): Portraits: CM07; EWEN; JAST; JASZ (and with Perry Bradford)
Father of the Blues, The *Source(s):* CASS; CM07; IDBC; PSND; SIFA; SMIN
Legendary Sire of the Blues *Source(s):* CM07 p. v
Hanisch, Carl c.1780-after 1854 [actor, author]
Elpons, W. [or E.] d' *Source(s):* PIPE
Hankerson, Alvin 1923-1995 [guitarist, singer, songwriter]
Guitar Nubbit *Source(s):* EPMU
Nubbit *Source(s):* EPMU
Hanley, James F. 1892-1942 [composer, librettist, lyricist]
Calhoun, John C. *Source(s):* CCE45 #4114, 552 R134256
Note(s): Jt. pseud.: Ballard MacDonald.
Nye, Hal *Source(s):* CCE49 R41733 ("Moonlight and Honeysuckle")
Hansell, John [lyricist]
Ansell, J. *Source(s):* SPTH p. 83
Hansen, Edgar 1876-1944 [composer]
Ragde, Fritz *Source(s):* KOBW
Hansen, Edward Duane 1937- [lyricist, producer]
Duane, Eddy *Source(s):* ASCP (see reference)
Hansen, Jurij 1938- [author, composer]
Moskvitin, Jurij *Source(s):* PSND
Hansen, Lawrence (William) 1905-1968 [composer, author, publisher]
Hansen, Bill *Source(s):* ASCP; CCE61; LCAR
Wood, Dale *Source(s):* CCE47-48; CCE73 R555819
Note(s): Do not confuse with (Charles) Dale Wood (1934-), composer of "Sing a Joyful Song. . . ." (CCE51 E7387)
Hanslick, Eduard 1825-1904 [music critic, musicologist]
Note(s): Portrait: ETUP 52:3 (Mar. 1934): 144
Renatus *Source(s):* NDGM
Hanson, Alfred E. 1923- [composer, author]
Hanson, Bud *Source(s):* ASCP
Hanson, Ethwell Idair 1893- [composer, author, pianist]
Hanson, Eddy *Source(s):* ASCP; CCE60; JASA p. 319
Hänssler, Friedrich 1892-1972 [composer]
Berger, Hans Ludwig *Source(s):* PFSA
Hansson, Stig (Axel) 1900-1968 [composer]
Note(s): See Alf Henrikson's poem about Hansson's pseudonyms in: Sandberg, Sven-Oloff. *Säg det i toner*. Stockholm: Sveriges radio, 1969, p. 15-6.
Björke, E(inar) *Source(s):* CCE30 Efor14150; GREN; LCAR; Sandberg (see above)
Boucher *Source(s):* Sandberg (see above)
Bramsen, Willy *Source(s):* Sandberg (see above)
Bright, W. *Source(s):* Sandberg (see above)
Brown & Ehrlich *Source(s):* Sandberg (see above)
Carlberg, Bengt *Source(s):* Sandberg (see above)
Hammar, Stig *Source(s):* Sandberg (see above)
Hannel, Sigurd *Source(s):* Sandberg (see above)
Hermann, Otto *Source(s):* Sandberg (see above)
J. S. *Source(s):* LCAR
Note(s): Initials: Jules Sylvain. (see below)
Johnson, Jack *Source(s):* Sandberg (see above)
Landahl, Sven *Source(s):* Sandberg (see above)
Larento, Jean *Source(s):* Sandberg (see above)
Larsson I Hult *Source(s):* Sandberg (see above)
Laytons, Nick *Source(s):* Sandberg (see above)
Lebedjeff, Peter *Source(s):* CCE29 Efor7601; CCE31; Sandberg (see above)
Louis, Frank *Source(s):* Sandberg (see above)
McCoy, Jim *Source(s):* Sandberg (see above)
Rahman, Emil *Source(s):* Sandberg (see above)
Reimer, Edward *Source(s):* Sandberg (see above)
Segnitz, Emil *Source(s):* Sandberg (see above)
Sinclair, Stephen *Source(s):* Sandberg (see above)
Stig *Source(s):* CCE74
Sylvain *Source(s):* LCAR
Sylvain, Jules *Source(s):* BUL2-3; GREN; LCAR; LCPC letter (17 July 1929); Sandberg (see above)
Sylvan, Sixten *Source(s):* BUL3
Widman, Eugen *Source(s):* Sandberg (see above)
Zerol, Vačlav *Source(s):* Sandberg (see above)
Hanvey, Fioan 1959- [singer, composer, painter]
Friday, Gavin *Source(s):* MOMU
Hardegen, (Count) Julius 1834-1867 [pianist, composer]
Egghard, Jules [or Julius] *Source(s):* BAKR; CPMU; MACM
Hardegg, Julius *Source(s):* CPMU (listed as original surname); RIEM
Hardenberg, Georg Friedrich Philipp von 1772-1801 [author, hymnist]
Novalis *Source(s):* CYBH; JULN; LCAR; PIPE; RIES
Hardin, Louis (Thomas) 1916-1999 [composer, author]
Arno, Joe *Source(s):* CCE55 Eunp
Moondog *Source(s):* ASCP; CCE62; LCAR; PEN2
Viking of Sixth Avenue *Source(s):* NOTE 56:4 (2000): 918
Harding, Gladwyn E(dward) [songwriter]
Harding, Chuck *Source(s):* CCE44 #50886 Eunp398967; PMUS
Harding, Lavere 1917-1965 [pianist, arranger, composer]
Harding, Buster *Source(s):* EPMU; KINK; LCAR; NGDJ
Hardwick, Archer (F.) 1918-1999 [composer]
Archer, George *Source(s):* ASCB

Hardwick, J. A. 1815-1886 [composer]
Dagonet *Source(s):* KILG ("England for the English")
Note(s): Also used by George R(obert) Sims.
Hardy, Antonio (M.) 1968 (or 69)- [singer, songwriter]
Kane, Big Daddy *Source(s):* CM07; EPMU; LCAR
Note(s): "Kane" is an acronym for "King Asiatic Nobody's Equal."
Hardy, H. E. 1869-1946 [hymnist]
Father Andrew *Source(s):* DIEH
Hare, Nicholas 1940- [arranger, composer]
Asher, Colin *Source(s):* MUWB
Harford, Frederick Kill 1832-1906 [songwriter]
Fritz *Source(s):* CPMU
Hargreaves, James [songwriter]
Magini *Source(s):* KILG
Hargreaves, Peter [composer]
Benson, Jimmy *Source(s):* CPOL RE-122-863
Hall, Margaret *Source(s):* CPOL RE-99-892; LCCC53 Efor18798
Note(s): Jt. pseud.: Peter Hart [i.e., Hargreaves] & Jack Fishman (1918 (or 19)-).
Hart, Peter *Source(s):* CCE74; CPOL RE-37-074 & RE-260-445
Miller, Mel *Source(s):* :CPOL RE-86-281
Note(s): Jt. pseud.: Michael Carr [i.e., Maurice Alfred Cohen]
Reisdorff, Emile *Source(s):* CPOL RE-114-494; LCCC54 Efor19892
Note(s): Jt. pseud.: Jack Fishman. (1918 (or 19)-).
Street, Leonard *Source(s):* CPOL RE-114-500; LCCC54 Efor21050
Note(s): Jt. pseud.: Jack Fishman. (1918 (or 19)-).
Hargreaves, Robert [composer]
LeRoy, Henri *Source(s):* LCPC Efor34210
Reaves, Erell *Source(s):* CCE60
Note(s): Jt. pseud.: S(tanley) J. Damerell [i.e., Jack Stevens]
Häring, (George) Wilhelm (Heinrich) 1798-1871 [poet, librettist]
Alexis, Willibald *Source(s):* LCAR; NIEC p. 78; STGR
Harington see also *Harrington*
Harington, Henry 1727-1816 [physician, composer]
H. H. *Source(s):* CPMU; WORB
Harkness, Arma Leveretta [or Loretta] 1864- [composer, violinist]
Note(s): Married name: Hoffmann.
Senkrah, Arma *Source(s):* AMME; LCPC; PRAT
Harley, Harold 1860-1937 [actor, songwriter]
Ambient, Mark *Source(s):* GAN2
Harling, Peter 1928- [composer]
Galatis, Hagen *Source(s):* PFSA
Harney, Ben(jamin) R(obertson) 1871 (or 72)-1938 [composer]
Father of Ragtime *Source(s):* SHAB p. 50
Jazz Originator *Source(s):* http://freepages.genealogy.rootsweb.com/~harney2/Ben_R.htm (6 Oct. 2002)
Ragtime's Father *Source(s):* http://freepages.genealogy.rootsweb.com/~harney2/Ben_R.htm
Harper, M(aurice) C(oe) 1903-1992 [composer, author, singer]
Harper, Redd *Source(s):* ASCP; CCE54-55; CLAB; LCAR
Harper, William 1904- [songwriter]
Harper, James [or Jimmy] *Source(s):* KILG
Harrell, Andre c.1959- [rapper]
Dr. Jeckyll *Source(s):* EPMU
Harrhy, Edith 1893-1969 [composer]
Note(s): Portrait: HAMA. Married name: Daly.
Carlo, Monty *Source(s):* HAMA
Errhy-Daly, E. *Source(s):* HAMA
Greville, Dorothy *Source(s):* CCE50; CCE62; HAMA
Jeffries, Roy *Source(s):* CCE50; HAMA
Steuart, Geoffrey *Source(s):* CCE48; CCE52
Stewart ,Geoffrey *Source(s):* HAMA
Trevor, Ann *Source(s):* HAMA
Wales, Evelyn *Source(s):* CCE53; HAMA
Wood, Ethel *Source(s):* HAMA
Harries, Heinrich 1762-1802 [writer, musician]
St. Hilaire *Source(s):* IBIM; WORB
Harrigan, Edward [or Ned] 1844 (or 45)-1911 [playwright, actor, producer]
Note(s): Portraits: GAN2; HAMM (with Tony Hart [i.e., Anthony J. Cannon])
America's Dickens *Source(s):* http://www.newworldrecords.org/linernotes/80265.pdf (6 Mar. 2003)
Nonpareils, The *Source(s):* SPTH p. 170, 181
Note(s): Jt. pseud.: Tony Hart [i.e., Anthony J. Cannon]
Pete *Source(s):* SPTH p. 179
Harrington see also *Harington*
Harrington, Eddy 1935- [singer, guitarist, songwriter]
Chief, The *Source(s):* AMUS
Note(s): See also Elvis A(a)ron Presley.
Clearwater, Eddy *Source(s):* AMUS; HARS
Guitar Eddy *Source(s):* AMUS; HARS
Harrington, George N. 1827-1868 [comedian, vocalist]
Christy, George (N.) *Source(s):* IBIM; LCAR; PSNN; SPTH p. 90
Note(s): Do not confuse with composer George Christie [i.e., Ernest R. Ball]
Harris, Bernard Wilfred 1917-1990 [composer]
Burns, Wilfred *Source(s)*: BBDP; CCE49-55
Harris, Charles K(assell) 1867-1930 [composer, music publisher]

Note(s): Portraits: HAMM; JAST
Charles K. *Source(s):* WHIC p. 4
Father of Tin Pan Alley *Source(s):* SHMM 2:3 (Mar. 1978): 4
Master of the Sentimental Ballad *Source(s):* PARS
King of Tear Jerkers, The *Source(s):* PARS
Tin Pan Alley's First Million Copy Seller *Source(s):* JAST (caption under portrait)

Harris, Christopher 1907- [librettist]
Fry, Christopher *Source(s):* MELL

Harris, Clement 1871-1897 [composer]
Clemris *Source(s):* BLIC; CPMU

Harris, Cuthbert 1870-1932 [composer]
Note(s): Portrait: ETUP 52:4 (Apr. 1934): 212
Cumberland, Gladys *Source(s):* CCE51 R75425 ("Jack and the Beanstalk")
Dale, Herbert *Source(s):* CCE37 E59620; CCE64; CCE73
Duval, Paul *Source(s):* CCE51 R75116; TPRF
Flavell, Gerald *Source(s):* CCE50 R63333 ("The Farewell")
Maundrell, Gerald *Source(s):* TPRF
Meredith, Claude *Source(s):* TPRF
Moran, Edward *Source(s):* CCE29 E8548
Valdemar, Paul *Source(s):* TPRF
Vaughan, Graham *Source(s):* CCE50 R70695-96; TPRF

Harris, Don 1935 (or 38)-1999 [singer, songwriter, guitarist]
Harris, Sugarcane *Source(s):* HARS; LCAR; OB99

Harris, Edward P. 1923-1953 [singer, guitarist, songwriter]
Carolina Slim *Source(s):* EPMU; HARS; LCAR
Country Paul *Source(s):* EPMU; HARS; LCAR
Georgia Pine *Source(s):* HARS; LCAR
Jammin' Jim *Source(s):* EPMU; HARS; LCAR
Lazy Slim Jim *Source(s):* EPMU; HARS; LCAR

Harris, Eleanora 1915-1959 [singer, songwriter]
Note(s): For explanation of names, see Clarke, Donald. *Wishing on the Moon*: New York: Viking, 1994.
Fagan, Eleanor *Source(s):* AMUS; EPMU
First Lady of the Blues *Source(s):* CASS
Holiday, Billie *Source(s):* CASS; EPMU; GRAT; NGAM; TCAN
Lady (Day) *Source(s):* CASS; EPMU; NGAM; SHAD; TCAN

Harris, Emmylou 1947- [singer, guitarist, songwriter]
Cajun Queen *Source(s):* FLIN

Harris, Estella 1896-1986 [singer, guitarist; songwriter]
Yancey, (Mrs.) Estella *Source(s):* GRAT; HARS
Yancey, Mama *Source(s):* GRAT; HARS

Harris, Frederick c.1866-1945 [music publisher, composer]
Heller, Maxime *Source(s):* CANE; CC37 R52013 ("Sunset on the St. Lawrence")
Note(s): Harris "composed the melody . . . which he whistled to an arranger." (The arranger is not identified) (see CANE). A later copyright record & other sources identify Maxime Heller as a pseud. of Charles Arthur Rawlings. See also: Rawlings, Charles Arthur.

Harris, George F(rederick) 1796-1867 [organist, composer]
Nordmann, Rudolph [or Rudolf] *Source(s):* BROW; CPMU; GOTH; LCAR; WORB

Harris, H. 19th cent. [songwriter]
Looker Out, A *Source(s):* PSND

Harris, James [or Jimmy] (D.) 1921-1990 [singer, harmonica player, songwriter]
Cadillac Jake *Source(s):* HARS
Harris, Shakey Jake *Source(s):* AMUS
Shakey Jake *Source(s):* EPMU; HARS; LCAR

Harris, James [or Jim], III 1956- [songwriter, producer]
Jam, Jimmy *Source(s):* CPOL PA-323-112; NOMG; PMUS-92

Harris, LeRoy Ellsworth 1898-1979 [composer]
Note(s): Portrait: ETUP 52:4 (Apr. 1934): 212
Harris, Roy *Source(s):* ALMN; BAKR
Walt Whitman of American Music, The *Source(s):* PSND

Harris, Lilly C. 19th cent. [hymnist]
Chrysanthea *Source(s):* PSND

Harris, Robert P. 1878-1936 [playwright, lyricist, composer]
Armstrong, Paul *Source(s):* CCE33 Efor28899; CCE60-61
Note(s): Pseud. of Robert P. Weston [i.e., Harris]. Jt. pseud.: Bert [i.e., Albert George] Lee.
Lincoln, Elmer *Source(s):* CCE32 Efor24411; CCE58-59
Note(s): Pseud. of Robert P. Weston [i.e., Harris]. Jt. pseud.: Bert [i.e., Albert George] Lee.
Molloy, Mary *Source(s):* CCE49 R45281 ("The Fairy Boat")
Note(s): Pseud. of Robert P. Weston [i.e., Harris]. Jt. pseud.: Bert [i.e., Albert George] Lee.
Weston, Robert P. *Source(s):* GAN2; PSND
Wheeler, Burt *Source(s):* CCE47 R18907 ("I Know")
Note(s): Pseud. of Robert P. Weston [i.e., Harris]

Harris, Shawntae 1974- [songwriter]
Da Brat *Source(s):* AMUS; CPOL PA-954-039; PMUS-97; PMUS-00

Harris, Victor F(rancis) 1911- [composer, author]
Harris, Eddie (V.) *Source(s):* ASCP; CCE62

Harris, Wynonie 1915-1969 [singer, percussionist, songwriter]

Mississippi Mockingbird, The *Source(s):* HARS
Mr. Blues *Source(s):* AMUS; HARS
Note(s): See also Arnold Dwight Moore.
Peppermint Cane *Source(s):* HARS
Harrison, George 1943-2001 [singer, songwriter]
Angel Misterioso, L' *Source(s):* BEAT
Beatles, The *Source(s):* http://www.beatlesstory.com (4 May 2005)
Note(s): With: John (Winston) Lennon; (James) Paul McCartney & Richard Starkey.
George H. *Source(s):* BEAT
Georgeson, Hari *Source(s):* BEAT
Harisein, Jai Raj *Source(s):* BEAT
Harrison, Carl *Source(s):* http://www.macca.l-org/hariontour/haripseud.htm (23 May 2005)
Harrysong, George *Source(s):* BEAT
O'Hara-Smith, George *Source(s):* http://www.deep-purple.net/othernews/harrison.htm (1 May 2005)
Son of Harry *Source(s):* BEAT
Traveling Wilburys *Source(s):* WILB
Note(s): With: Jeff Lynne, Roy (Kelton) Orbison, Tom Petty & Bob Dylan [i.e., Robert Allen Zimmerman]
Wax, Artur *Source(s):* http://www.macca.l-org/hariontour/haripseud.htm
Wilbury, Nelson *Source(s):* WILB
Wilbury, Spike *Source(s):* WILB
Harrison, Jane S. [composer]
J. S. H. *Source(s):* CPMU (publication date 1868)
Harrison, Susan [or Susie] Frances (née Riley) 1859-1935 [composer, author]
King, G(ilbert) R. *Source(s):* COHN; DWCO; GROL
Medusa *Source(s):* GROL
Seranus *Source(s):* COHN; DWCO; GROL; HIXN
Harrison, Vernon 1925-1992 [singer, pianist, songwriter]
Boogie Woogie Red *Source(s):* DBMU; HARS
Piano Red *Source(s):* DBMU; HARS
Note(s): See also William Lee Perryman.
Harshman, Robert 1944- [singer, songwriter]
Hart, Bobby *Source(s):* CCE64-65; CCE67; PMUS
Hart, Cynthia Mary Kathleen [composer, author]
Felby, Celeta *Source(s):* ASCP; CPOL PA-35-727
Fraser, Kathleen *Source(s):* CPOL PAu-59-500
Grove, Cynthia Mary Kathleen *Source(s):* CPOL PA-35-727
Hart, Joseph 1712-1768 [hymnist]
H—t *Source(s):* JULN
Hart, Lorenz (Milton) 1895-1943 [lyricist, librettist]
Boys from Columbia, The *Source(s):* Hyland, William G: *Richard Rodgers*: New Haven: Yale University Press, 1998, 117
Note(s): Jt. sobriquet: Richard (Charles) Rodgers.
Gilbert and Sullivan of America *Source(s):* SPTH p. 449 & 544
Note(s): Jt. sobriquet: Richard (Charles) Rodgers.
Hart, Larry *Source(s):* GOTH; PIPE
Hartachenko, Lorenz *Source(s):* Hyland p. 49
Kron, William *Source(s):* CCE60
Lorenz, H(erbert) R(ichard) *Source(s):* NGAM; Hyland, William G. *Richard Rodgers*. New Haven: Yale University Press, 1998, 27.
Note(s): Jt. pseud.: Richard (Charles) Rodgers & Herbert Fields.
Shelly of America *Source(s):* Furia, Philip. *The Poets of Tin Pan Alley*. New York: Oxford University Press, 1990, p. 5.
Hart, Lucille 1917- [composer, author]
Hart, Babe *Source(s):* ASCP; CCE49
Hart, Moss 1904-1961 [playwright, lyricist, composer]
Conrad, Robert Arnold *Source(s):* PIPE; PSND
Harthan, Hans 1855-1936 [composer]
Note(s): Portrait: ETUP 52:4 (Apr. 1934): 212
Anhart, J. *Source(s):* TPRF
Hartley, Fred 1905-1980 [songwriter]
Burns, Jim *Source(s):* CCE67
Taylor, Iris *Source(s):* CCE67; CCE73; MUWB
Wallace, Raymond *Source(s):* CCE40 #14853 Efor62487
Note(s): Jt. pseud.: Billy [i.e., Willis Wilfred] Reid, Fred Hartley & Huntley Trevor.
Hartley, Hal 1959- [composer, keyboardist]
Rifle, Ned *Source(s):* DAIL (18 June 1998); LCAR
Hartmann, Emma Sophie Amalie (née Zinn) 1807-1851 [composer]
Palmer, F(rederick) (H.) *Source(s):* COHN; CPMU; DWCO; GROL; HIXN; MUWB
Hartmann, (Jean-François-Romain) Georges 1843-1900 [librettist]
Germont, Henri *Source(s):* STGR
Note(s): Typographical error?
Grémont, Henri *Source(s):* GROL; LOWN; MELL; NGDO; PIPE
Hartmann, Otto B. 1939- [composer]
Batanoff, Grischa *Source(s):* KOMS; PFSA
Silfer, Ben *Source(s):* KOMS; PFSA
Waldorff, Peter *Source(s):* KOMS; PFSA
Wolfmann, Bernhard *Source(s):* KOMS; PFSA
Hartmann, Thomas (Alexandrovich) de 1886-1956 [composer, conductor]
Kross, Thomas *Source(s):* CCE57; http://webtext.library.yale.edu/xml2.htm (6 Oct. 2002)
Hartsough, Palmer 1844-1932 [singer, hymnist]
Uncle Frank *Source(s):* CYBH
Hartung, Philipp Christopher (Johann) 1706-1776 [writer on music]
Humanus, P. C. *Source(s):* CPMU; LCPC; MACM

Hartusch, Mireille 1906-1996 [actress, singer, composer]
Mireille *Source(s):* CCE47; CCE57; CCE67; CPOL RE-339-869; PEN2; ROOM
Hartwell-Jones, William P(rice) 1871- [composer]
Note(s): Portrait: ETUP 52:4 (Apr. 1934): 212
Hamilton, Gray *Source(s):* BALT; CPMU
Harvey, Lucy Quinn 1932- [composer, author, singer]
Quinn, Adelle *Source(s):* ASCP
Harwell, William Earnest 1918- [composer, author]
Harwell, Ernie *Source(s):* ASCP; CPOL TX-3-054-411
Hasenöhrl, Franz 1885-1970 [teacher, composer]
Bunny-Ears *Source(s):* http://fuguemasters .com/strauss.html (16 Mar. 2005)
Note(s): Not a pseud.; merely a translation of surname.
Höhrl, Franz *Source(s):* LCAR; OMUO; RIES; STAD
Hasse, Johann Adolf 1699-1783 [composer]
Note(s): Portrait: ETUP 52:4 (Apr. 1934): 212
Caro Sassone, Il *Source(s):* PSND; STGR
Divine Saxon, The *Source(s):* YORM p. 176 (see "Answers to Correspondents")
Padre della music *Source(s):* MUWB
Sassone, Il *Source(s):* ALMC; PSND
Hasslinger von Hasslinger, Johannes (Nepomuk), Freiherr von 1822-1898 [composer]
Hager, Johann(es) *Source(s):* GOTH; IBIM; MACM; STGR
Hässy, Günter 1944- [composer]
Henrici, Gabriel *Source(s):* KOMP; KOMS; PFSA
Hastings, Horace Lorenzo 1831-1899 [hymnist]
H. *Source(s):* JULN
Hastings, Julian 1947- [singer, songwriter]
Hastings, Pye *Source(s):* HARR
Hastings, Ross (Ray) 1915- [composer]
Fortune, Joe *Source(s):* ASCP; CCE64-65; SUPN
Schrammel, Oscar *Source(s):* CCE65 E197675; CCE66
Hastings, Thomas 1784 (or 87)-1872 [composer, hymnist]
Note(s): The following are possible pseudonyms Portraits: CYBH; ETUP 52:4 (Apr. 1934): 212
Carmeni *Source(s):* METC
Kl—f *Source(s):* METC
Zol—ffer *Source(s):* METC
Hatch, Anthony [or Tony] (Peter) 1939- [songwriter]
Anthony, Hatch *Source(s):* CPOL RE-397-653; PMUS
Anthony, Mark *Source(s):* CCE61; CCE62; CCE65; PMUS
Note(s): "Tell All the World," (CCE61), "Happiness Tree," & "Keep on Walkin"(both CCE62). Also used by Mark Anthony Traversion, Jr.
Mr. and Mrs. Music *Source(s):* DAUM
Note(s): Jt. pseud.: Jackie Trent.
Nightingale, Fred *Source(s):* AMUS; EPMU
Hatch, F(rederic) L. ?-1926 [composer, publisher, editor]
Note(s): Portrait: ETUP 52:4 (Apr. 1934): 212
Bonner, Carl *Source(s):* TPRF
Mathews, Edouard *Source(s):* CCE28 E681104
Hatch, Provine, Jr. 1921-2003 [harmonica player, songwriter]
Little Hatch *Source(s):* AMUS; EPMU
Little Walter, Jr. *Source(s):* EPMU
Note(s): See also George Smith.
Hatcher, Charles 1942- [singer, songwriter]
Starr, Edwin *Source(s):* CCE66; EPMU; LCAR
Hatfield, Alfred Griffith 1848-1921 [minstrel performer, manager, author]
Field, Al G. *Source(s):* NGAM
Hatfield, Edwin Francis 1807-1883 [hymnist]
E. F. H. *Source(s):* JULN
Hatton, John Liptrott 1809-1886 [composer]
Note(s): Portrait: ETUP 52:4 (Apr. 1934): 212
Czabeck *Source(s):* PIPE
Czapek, P. B. *Source(s):* BAKO; CPMU; GOTH; GROL; HUEV; MACM; PIPE; WORB
Hauck, Wenzel 1801-1834 [musician]
Beethoven *Source(s):* APPL p. 10
Hauer, Georg [or Hugó] 1857-1941 [playwright, author, composer]
Verö, György *Source(s):* GAN1; GAN2; MACM
Hauerbach, Otto (Abels) 1873-1963 [lyricist, libretttist]
Note(s): Portrait: EWEN
Harbach, Otto *Source(s):* BAKR; BBDP; EPMU; EWEN; GAN2; HARR; ROOM
Haug, (Johann Christoph) Friedrich 1761-1829 [author]
Frauenlob (der Jüngere) *Source(s):* LCAR; PIPE; WORB
Hophthalmos, (Friedrich) *Source(s):* LCAR; PIPE; WORB
Haughton, Aaliyal Dana 1979-2001 [singer, songwriter]
Aaliyah *Source(s):* LCAR; OB01 (port.)
Hauntreuter, Erasmus c.1525-1586 [music editor, composer, teacher]
Rothenbucher, Erasmus *Source(s):* GROL; NGDM
Hauptmann, Elisabeth 1897-1973 [author, translator]
Diesterhorst, Josefine *Source(s):* http://www .lwl.org/literaturkommision1biblio/haupmann/ bio.htm (6 Apr. 2005)
Lane, Dorothy *Source(s):* http://www .lwl.org/literaturkommision1biblio/haupmann/ bio.htm

Ux, Catherine *Source(s):* http://www.lwl.org/literaturkommision1biblio/haupmann/bio.htm
Hauschild, Richard Curtis 1949- [author, lyricist]
Hauschild, Bulldog *Source(s):* ASCP
Hausdorff, Felix 1868-1942 [author, poet]
Mongre, Paul *Source(s):* LAST
Hausenstein, Wilhelm 1882-1957 (or 59) [essayist, fine art & literary critic]
Arbruster, Johann *Source(s):* PIPE; WORB
Armbruster, Johann *Source(s):* PIPE
Bergmann, Rosso *Source(s):* PIPE
Hausey, (Elton) Howard ?-1994 [songwriter]
Bradhouse *Source(s):* CCE63
Crockett, Howard *Source(s):* CCE77; EPMU
Perkins, Norma *Source(s):* CCE58
Hausskeller, Simon before 1500-1544 [cantor, composer]
Cellarius Simon *Source(s):* RIEM
Keller, Simon *Source(s):* WORB
Häussler, Gerhardt 1932- [composer]
Romanini, J. L. *Source(s):* KOMS; PFSA
Hautcousteaux, Arthur c.1590-c.1654 [composer, singer]
Aux-Costeaus, Artus *Source(s):* LCAR; NGDM; WORB
Haviland, Frederick Benjamin 1868-1932 [publisher]
Worth, George T. *Source(s):* JAST
Note(s): Jt. pseud.: Patrick Howley.
Hawker, Kenneth 1942- [songwriter]
Carter-Lewis *Source(s):* CCE63; EPMU; PMUS
Note(s): Jt. pseud.: John Shakespeare.
Lewis, Ken *Source(s):* CCE77; EPMU
Hawkins, (Sir) Anthony Hope 1863-1933 [author, dramatist]
Hope, Anthony *Source(s):* DAWS; LCAR
Hawkins, Coleman (Randolph) 1904-1969 [songwriter]
Bean *Source(s):* EPMU; GROL; LCAR; SHAD
Hawk *Source(s):* EPMU; LCAR; SHAD
Note(s): See also Harold Franklin Hawkinsm & J(oseph) B(enjamin) Hutto & Jerry Lee Lewis.
Hawkins, Delmar Allen 1938- [singer, guitarist, songwriter]
Hawkins, Dale *Source(s):* KICK; LCAR
Hawkins, Erskine (Ramsey) 1913 (or 14)-1993 [trumpeter, bandleader, songwriter]
Twentieth-Century Gabriel, (The) *Source(s):* ALMN; CASS; CM19; EPMU
Hawkins, George E.
Ellsworth, George *Source(s):* TPRF
Hawkins, Harold Franklin 1921-1963 [singer, songwriter]
Eleven and a Half Yards of Personality *Source(s):* MCCL
Hawk, The *Source(s):* PEN2
Note(s): See also Coleman (Randolph) Hawkins (see LCAR), J(oseph) B(enjamin) Hutto & Jerry Lee Lewis.
Hawkins, Hawkshaw *Source(s):* AMUS; CCME; MCCL; PEN2
Hawkins, Hester Periam (née Lewis) [hymnist]
H. P. H. *Source(s):* JULN (Suppl.)
Hawkins, Jalacy (J.) 1929-2000 [singer, saxophonist, songwriter]
Note(s): Portrait: OB00
Clown Prince of Rock and Roll, The *Source(s):* PSND
Hawkins, Jay *Source(s):* HARS; OB00
Hawkins, Screamin' Jay *Source(s):* CM08; EPMU; HARD; HARR; HARS; PEN2
Hawkins, (Sir) John 1719-1789 [writer on music]
Note(s): Portrait: ETUP 52:5 (May 1934): 272
Fiddling Knight, The *Source(s):* DAWS
Hawkins, Lamont [songwriter, performer]
4-Bar Killer *Source(s):* AMUS
Baby U *Source(s):* AMUS
Four Bar Killer *Source(s):* AMUS
Golden Arms *Source(s):* AMUS
Luck Hands *Source(s):* AMUS
U-God *Source(s):* AMIR; PMUS-00
Hawkins, Walter [guitarist, singer, songwriter]
Hawkins, Buddy Boy *Source(s):* EPMU; LCAR
Haworth, Roger A. 1939- [composer, author, pianist]
Haworth, Rajah *Source(s):* ASCP; CPOL PAu-29-068
Haxthausen, Aurore M. G. Ch. von 1836-1888 [writer, composer]
G******** *Source(s):* COHN; HIXN
Kuhlman, Clara *Source(s):* COHN; HIXN
Hay, Edward Norman 1889-1943 [composer, critic]
Rathcol *Source(s):* GROL
Hay, Frederick [writer]
Hue and Eye *Source(s):* GANA p. 108
Note(s): Jt. pseud.: Arthur Clements.
Hay, George Dewey 1895-1968 [editor, reporter, announcer, radio executive]
Solemn Ol' [or Old] Judge, The *Source(s):* AMUS; MCCL; PSND; STAC
Haydn, (Franz) Joseph 1732-1809 [composer]
Doktor der Tonkunst *Source(s):* GROL (see section 4)
Father of Instrumentation *Source(s):* http://classicalmus.hispeed.com/articles/haydn.html (6 Oct.2002)
Father of Modern Orchestration *Source(s):* www.music-opera.com/site_english/ville_wien_e.html (19 Apr. 2005)
Note(s): See also Hector Berlioz.

Father of Orchestral Music, The *Source(s):* PSND
Father of the Orchestra *Source(s):* http://classicalmus.hispeed.com/articles/haydn.html
Note(s): See also Hector Berlioz.
Father of the String Quartet *Source(s):* MUWB; http://classicalmus.hispeed.com/articles/haydn.html
Father of the Symphony, The *Source(s):* GROL; PSND; SPIE
Haydn, Papa *Source(s):* PSND; SPIE
Haydnesque *Source(s):* MUWB
Haydnverein *Source(s):* EPON
Inventor of the Symphony *Source(s):* http://www.newadvent.org/cathen/07158b.htm (6 Oct. 2002)
Most Prolific Symphonist *Source(s):* DESO-9

Hayes, Clarence Leonard 1908-1972 [singer, banjoist, songwriter]
Hayes, Clancy *Source(s):* AMUS; EPMU; PEN2; VACH

Hayes, Edward Brian 1935-1973 [multi-instrumentalist, arranger, composer]
Hayes, Tubby *Source(s):* AMUS; EPMU

Hayes, Isaac 1942- [singer, songwriter, producer]
Black Moses *Source(s):* ALMN; CASS; IDBC; PSND
First King of Rap, The *Source(s):* IDBC
Hayes, Sack *Source(s):* ALMN
Shaftmeister *Source(s):* IDBC
Three Dimensional Man, The *Source(s):* IDBC

Hayes, Larry R(ay) 1940- [composer]
Ray, Larry *Source(s):* CCE62-64; PSND

Hayes, Philip 1738-1797 [composer, organist, singer]
Chaise, Fill *Source(s):* GROL

Hayes, Theodore, Jr. 1951- [composer, author, singer]
Osaze, Ted Ernest *Source(s):* ASCP

Hayes, William 1708-1777 [composer]
Gentleman in London *Source(s):* PSND

Hayford, George W. [composer]
Drofyah, Michael *Source(s):* CPMU (publication date 1908)

Haym, Nicolo [or Nicholas] Francesco [or Francis] 1678 (or 79)-1729 [composer]
Aimo, Nicolo Francesco *Source(s):* MACM; LCAR; WORB

Hayman, Richard Warren Joseph 1920- [composer, conductor, arranger]
Daly, M. E. *Source(s):* ASCP; GREN
Howard, Ray *Source(s):* ASCP; GREN
Savage, Richard *Source(s):* ASCP; GREN

Haynes, Cornell, (Jr.) [songwriter, performer]
Nelly *Source(s):* AMIR; AMUS; PMUS-00

Haynes, Henry D. 1917 (or 20)-1971 [guitarist, lyricist]
Note(s): Portraits: (with Kenneth C. Burns) CCME; MILL
Crown Princes of Country Music *Source(s):* MUHF
Note(s): Jt. sobriquet: Kenneth C. Burns.
Haynes, Homer *Source(s):* BBDP; LCAR
Homer *Source(s):* BBDP; CCE54-55; EPMU; MUHF
Notes(s): Performed as: Homer and Jethro [i.e., Kenneth C. Burns]

Hays, Doris Ernestine 1941- [composer, pianist, mixed media artist]
Hays, Sorrel *Source(s):* BAKT; LCAR

Hays, Lee 1914-1981 [singer, songwriter]
Campbell, Paul *Source(s):* PMUS
Note(s): Pseud. of The Weavers [i.e., Hayes, Ronnie Gilbert, Pete(r R.) Seeger & Fred Hellerman]
Six, Tom *Source(s):* CCE58; CCE66
Note(s): Jt. pseud.: Ronnie Gilbert, Fred Hellerman & Pete(r R.) Seeger.
Weavers, The *Source(s):* PMUS
Note(s): Jt. pseud.: Ronnie Gilbert, Fred Hellerman & Pete(r R.) Seeger.

Hays, Will(iam) S(hakespeare) 1837-1907 [songwriter, journalist]
Note(s): Portraits: HAMM; PDMU
Blossom, Jerry *Source(s):* LCAR; PDMU
Note(s): Also used by Dan(iel Decatur) Emmett?
Hale, Wil P. *Source(s):* PDMU
Note(s): Possible pseud.
Nobody *Source(s):* PDMU
Note(s): Possible pseud.
Old Rye *Source(s):* PDMU
Percy, Allan *Source(s):* PDMU
Note(s): Possible pseud.
Somebody *Source(s):* PDMU
Note(s): Possible pseud.

Hayward-Jones, David Robert (1947-) *see* Jones, David Robert (Hayward)

Haza, Jeannette von [writer on music]
Paris, Heinrich *Source(s):* HEYT

Hazelwood, Ellmer Clayton 1903-1990 [author, lyricist]
Hazelwood, Clate *Source(s):* ASCP

Headland-Stevens, Aimée [composer]
Dale, Sheila *Source(s):* CPMU (publication date 1915)

Heard, Richard Martin 1936- [composer, author]
Devereaux, Richmond *Source(s):* ASCP

Hearn(e), Mary Ann(e) 1834-1909 [writer, hymnist, composer]
Farningham, Marianne *Source(s):* CART; COHN; CYBH (port.); HIXN; LCAR; ROOM; WORB
Hope, Eve *Source(s):* CART

Hearne, Michael 1966- [composer]
Finn, Mickey *Source(s):* EPMU

Heath, Frederick 1935 (or 39)-1966 [singer, songwriter]
Kidd, Johnny *Source(s):* CCE63; HARD; LCAR; PEN2
Heath, (Walter) Henry 1890-1965 [composer]
Heath, Hy *Source(s):* ASCC; CCE45 #14295 E129851; CCE54-56
Heath, James C. 1959- [singer, songwriter, guitarist]
Heat, Rev. Horton *Source(s):* AMUS; NOMG
Heath, James [or Jimmy] (Edward) 1926- [flutist, composer, arranger]
Heath, Little Bird *Source(s):* GROL
Little Bird *Source(s):* GROL
Note(s): Also used by Albert Ayler.
Heath, John [composer]
Nice, W. *Source(s):* CPMU (publication dates 1891-95)
Heathcote, William Beadon 1812 (or 13)-1862 [editor]
W. B. H. *Source(s):* CPMU
Heber, Reginald 1783-1826 [prelate, hymnist]
Christian Atticus, The *Source(s):* PSND
R. *Source(s):* JULN
Hébertot, Jacques 1886-1970 [author]
Daviel, André *Source(s):* LAST
Heckel-Kotrusz, Josef 1866-1943 [composer]
Dolph-Heckel, Josef *Source(s):* STAD
Hedberg, Frans (Theodor) 1828-1908 [playwright, author]
Block, Palle *Source(s):* PIPE; PSND
Heddenhausen, Friedel-Heinz 1910- [composer, conductor]
Calenberg, Wolf *Source(s):* KOMP; PFSA; PIPE
Hedley, H(ubert) B(arber) [composer]
Brody, Hal *Source(s):* CCE29 Efor4503; EPMU; GANZ
Note(s): Jt. pseud.: Stanley Lupino [i.e., Hook], (Herbert) Desmond Carter, Harry Acres, John [or Jack] Strachey, Jack Clarke & possibly others.
Heed, J(ohn) C(lifford) 1862-1908 [composer, teacher, cornetist]
March Wizard, The *Source(s):* SMIN
Heerringen, Gustav von 1800-1851 [librettist]
Wodomerius, Ernst *Source(s):* LOWN; WORB
Héger, Attila [composer, songwriter]
d'Or, Laren *Source(s):* http://www.memi.com/update/interviews/heger_en.html (6 Oct. 2002)
Norder, Al *Source(s):* http://www.memi.com/update/interviews/heger_en.html
Hegeus, Gabor 1948-1990 [composer, singer, guitarist, producer]
Gabor, B. B. *Source(s):* GOTH; NOMG
Heidegger, Johann [or John] Jakob [or James] 1666-1749 [impressario, librettist]
Swiss Count, The *Source(s):* GRV3
Heider, Joachim 1944- [composer, pianist]
Khan, Alfie *Source(s):* PFSA
Heifetz, Jascha 1901-1987 [violinist, composer]
Hoyl, Jim *Source(s):* CCE47-48; LCAR
Heinrich, A. [librettist]
Beckmann, Adele *Source(s):* LOWN; STGR
Heinrich, Anton [or Anthony] Philip 1781-1861 [banker, organist, composer]
Note(s): Called himself Anthony after arriving in America.
Apostle of the American Composer, An *Source(s):* HOWD p. 687
Beethoven of America *Source(s):* http://www.geometry.net/composers/heinrich_anthony_philip.php (6 Oct. 2002)
Beethoven of Kentucky, The *Source(s):* http://www.newmusicbox.org/page.nmbx?id=54tp04 (6 Apr. 2005)
Beethoven of Louisville *Source(s):* http://www.ulib.iupui.edu/kaade/merrill/lesson15.html (6 Apr. 2005)
Heinrich, Father *Source(s):* METC
Loghouse Composer *Source(s):* PDMU
Heinrich, Peter Franz 1911- [composer]
Pedro, El *Source(s):* CCE52; KOMS; PFSA
Heins, Carl 1859-1923 [composer, music publisher]
Note(s): Portrait: ETUP 52:4 (Apr.. 1934): 212
Cobb, Frank *Source(s):* CCE25 E621473
Karoly, H. *Source(s):* TPRF
Heins, Francis Donaldson 1878- [organist, composer]
Heins, Donald *Source(s):* IBIM; WORB
Heins, Nicholas 1839- [composer]
N. H. *Source(s):* CPMU
Note(s): Probable initials of Heins; "The Lou Polka" (c.1870).
Heinz, Jerome (Albert Link) 1921-2003 [singer, writer on music]
Hines, Jerome *Source(s):* BAKR; BAKT; BUL3; CCE67; PIPE
Heiss, Hermann 1897-1966 [composer, teacher]
Frauenfelder, Georg *Source(s):* OMUO; SUPN
Heiss, John Stanger 1871(or 72)-1936 [actor, singer, lyricist, librettist]
Asche, Oscar *Source(s):* CASS; EPMU; GAMM; GAN1; GAN2
Held, Jan Theobald 1770-1851 [composer, singer, physician]
Orebsky, Jan *Source(s):* RIES; http://www.opera-rkm.cz/ce/ce_2.asp (26 Mar. 2003)
Held, Ludwig 1837-1900 [author, librettist]
Herger, Karl *Source(s):* PIPE; STGR

Helfman, Donald Elliott 1926-1984 [instrumentalist, singer, composer]
Elliott, Don *Source(s):* CCE60-62; KINK; LCAR
Heller, Franz 1946- [composer]
Heller, André *Source(s):* PFSA
Heller, Joachim 1518-1590 [mathematician, astronomer, composer, poet]
Hellerus Leucopetraeus *Source(s):* NGDM
Heller, Max [songwriter]
Heller, M. P. *Source(s):* OCLC 15431453
Note(s): Jt. pseud.: Paul Heller.
Heller, Paul [songwriter]
Heller, M. P. *Source(s):* OCLC 15431453
Note(s): Jt. pseud.: Max Heller.
Heller, Stephen (István) 1813 (or 14)-1888 [pianist, composer]
Note(s): Portraits: ETUP 47:6 (June 1929): 429+; EWCY
Jeanquirit *Source(s):* GROL; NGDM
Hellerman, Fred 1927- [composer, author, singer]
Barnes, David *Source(s):* CCE58
Brooks, Fred *Source(s):* ASCP; CCE54; CCE60
Note(s): Also used by Porter Grainger.
Campbell, Paul *Source(s):* PMUS
Note(s): Jt. pseud. of The Weavers [i.e., Hellerman, Lee Hays, Pete(r R.) Seeger & Ronnie Gilbert]
Harmon, Frank *Source(s):* CCE55; CCE60
Hill, Bob *Source(s):* LCAR
Note(s): Also used by Robert [or Bob] (Ernest) Miller.
Six, Tom *Source(s):* CCE58; CCE66
Note(s): Jt. pseud.: Lee Hays, Pete(r R.) Seeger & Ronnie Gilbert.
Weavers, The *Source(s):* PMUS
Note(s): Jt. pseud.: Lee Hays, Pete(r R.) Seeger & Ronnie Gilbert.
Hellmesberger, Josef 1855-1907 [composer]
Note(s): Do not confuse with Joseph Hellmesberger (1828-1893).
Hellmesberger, Pepi *Source(s):* GAN2; LCAR
Helm, Everett (Burton) 1913-1999 [composer, writer on music]
Beech, Vernon *Source(s):* CPOL RE-34-086
Helyer, Edmund Victor [composer]
Helyer, Jack *Source(s):* CPMU; GOTH
Hemachandra, Neal [composer]
Hope, Claude *Source(s):* CCE57-60; GOTH
Hempel, Rolf 1926-1976 [composer]
Lemberg, Paul *Source(s):* CCE61-62; CCE65-68; KOMS; PFSA
Henderson, (James) Fletcher (Hamilton), (Jr.) 1897 (or 98)-1952 [bandleader, songwriter, arranger]
Note(s): For pseudonyms on recordings of Henderson & his orchestra, see SUTT).
Big Band's Black Man, The *Source(s):* SIFA
Brooks, George *Source(s):* IDBC; PMUS
Note(s): Also used by Porter Grainger.
Henderson, Smack *Source(s):* CASS; CM16; IDBC; KINK; PMUS; PSND
Hill, Sam *Source(s):* SUTT
Note(s): Also used by (Orvan) Gene Autry.
Taylor, Emmett *Source(s):* SUTT
Henderson, Gilbert [composer]
Wells, Gilbert *Source(s):* KILG
Henderson, Joe 1920-1980 [pianist, composer]
Heywood, Ron *Source(s):* CCE53 Efor19033; CPOL RE-81-068
Mr. Piano *Source(s):* EPMU
Henderson, John William 1910- [singer, instrumentalist, songwriter]
Homesick James *Source(s):* EPMU (see under: Williamson, James); HARS; LCAR
Homesick Jick *Sopurce(s):* LCAR
Jick (and His Trio) *Source(s):* HARS; LCAR
Williamson, Homesick James *Source(s):* HARS; LCAR
Williamson, James *Source(s):* HARS; LCAR
Williamson, John A. *Source(s):* HARS; LCAR
Henderson, Lyle Russell Cedric 1918-2005 [pianist, conductor, composer, arranger]
Ferguson, Sydney *Source(s):* PSND; TCAN
Henderson, Skitch *Source(s):* BAKR; EPMU; KINK; PEN2; PSND; TCAN
Henderson, Norman [songwriter]
Norman, José *Source(s):* CCE66-67; PMUS
Henderson, William James 1855-1937 [author, journalist, music critic]
Old Guard, The *Source(s):* GRAN p. 59
Note(s): Jt. sobriquet: Henry (Edward) Krehbiel & Harry Theophilus [i.e., Gottlob] Finck
Singer's Critic and Lord High Executioner *Source(s):* GRAN p. 86
Hendleman, George (Joseph) 1920-1997 [arranger, composer, pianist]
Handy, George (Joseph) *Source(s):* AMUS; KINK; NGDJ
Hendricks, Doyle Floyd 1936- [singer, songwriter]
Holly, Doyle *Source(s):* MCCL
Hendricks, Frederick Wilmoth 1901-1973 [composer, author]
Houdini, King *Source(s):* CCE62; PSND
Houdini, Wilmouth *Source(s):* ASCP; PSND
Hendrix, John(ny) Allen 1942-1970 [singer, songwriter, guitarist]
Black Elvis, The *Source(s):* SHAD
Heavy Metallurgist Par Excellence, The *Source(s):* SHAD (see under: Heavy Metal Rock)
Hendrix, James Marshall *Source(s):* HARS; RECR
Note(s): Renamed at age 4.
Hendrix, Jimi [or Jimmy] *Source(s):* HARR; RECR
James, Jimmy *Source(s):* HARS; SHAD
Wild Man of Pop, The *Source(s):* PSND

Heney, R. W. [composer]
Leyland, Reginald *Source(s):* CPMU (publication dates 1876-1919)
Henning, Karl Prescott 1960- [composer, lyricist]
D'ash, K. Aaron *Source(s):* OCLC 40387544
Henrich, C. W. [composer]
Feldman(n), J. *Source(s):* LCPC; TPRF
Lambrecht, Eugene *Source(s):* CCE25 R30929; TPRF
Marchelle, Carl *Source(s):* CCE25 R30928; TPRF
Moeller, Alois *Source(s):* CCE25 R30933; TPRF
Obeloff, Ivan *Source(s):* CCE25 R30935; TPRF
Rompini, Servatins *Source(s):* CCE25 R30930; TPRF
Stanford, J. S. *Source(s):* CCE25 R30934; TPRF
Weber, E. S. *Source(s):* LCPC; TPRF
Henrici, Christian Friedrich 1700-1764 [poet, dramatist, librettist]
Picander *Source(s):* GROL; MACM; NGDM; PIPE; RIEM; SADC; WORB
Henrikson, Alice 1906- [composer]
Lebeau, Alice *Source(s):* CCE77; GREN
Henry, Anthony 1965- [rapper]
Tippa Irie *Source(s):* EPMU
Henry, Clarence 1937- [singer, songwriter]
Frogman, (The) *Source(s):* EPMU; PEN2; SHAD; SIFA
Henry, Frogman *Source(s):* LCAR
Henry, Richard 1921-2004 [singer, composer, guitar]
Big Boy *Source(s):* DRSC
Note(s): See also Arthur Crudup.
Henry, Big Boy *Source(s):* DRSC
Henschke, Alfred 1890 (or 91)-1928 [librettist]
Klabund *Source(s):* CCE54; LCAR; LOWN
Hense, Werner 1934- [composer]
Tennberg, Werner *Source(s):* KOMP; KOMS; PFSA
Hensley, William Paden 1909-1991 [singer, drummer, songwriter]
Washboard Willie *Source(s):* DBMU; HARS
Henson, Herbert Lester 1925?- [singer, songwriter]
Cousin Herb *Source(s):* CCE53; CLAB
Henson, Cousin Herb *Source(s):* CCE54
Héon, Paul [writer, critic]
Barl(l)et, Paul *Source(s):* WHIT
Hepburn, Thomas Charles [composer]
Blondello *Source(s):* CPMU
Herbert, Christopher 1956- [soca/calypso artist, composer]
Tambu *Source(s):* LCAR; PEN2
Herbert, Victor 1859-1924 [composer, conductor]
Note(s): Portraits: ETUP 58:2 (Feb. 1940): 78; EWEN; HOWD; METR 12:2 (1894): cover
American Music Master, The *Source(s):* PSND; TCAN
Dean of American Music, The *Source(s):* CLMM
Note(s): See also Aaron Copland, Walter Johannes Damrosch & Paul Whiteman.
MacClure, Noble *Source(s):* CCE42 #14692, 777 R105720 ("Valse a la mode"); PDMU
Roland, Frank *Source(s):* CCE31 R14457; SPTH p. 326
Herbst, Johann Andreas 1588-1666 [theorist, composer, violinist]
Note(s): Portrait: ETUP 52:6 (June 1934): 332
Autumnus, Johann Andreas *Source(s):* IBIM; NGDM; WORB
J. A. H. *Source(s):* IBIM; WORB
Herchenbach, Robert 1934- [composer]
Bacher, Bert *Source(s):* CCE57; CCE63; KOMP; KOMS; PFSA
Hering, Genevieve (Lillian) 1926- [singer, pianist, arranger]
Southern, Jeri *Source(s):* EPMU; LCAR
Hering, Hans 1909-1971 [composer, conductor]
Note(s): The following are listed as pseudonyms of Hans Carste.
Carste, Hans *Source(s):* PFSA
Fanta, Josef *Source(s):* CCE54-55; PFSA
Tareno, Salvadore *Source(s):* PFSA
Winther, Bob *Source(s):* CCE60-61; CPOL RE-315-007; PFSA
Herman, Aladore 1870-1951 [producer]
Woods, A(lbert) H(erman) *Source(s):* GAN2
Herman, Nikolaus [or Nicolaus] 1500-1561
N. H. *Source(s):* CPMU
Herman, Sam [composer]
Steiner, Herbert *Source(s):* JASA p. 322
Herman(n), Woodrow Charles 1913-1987 [folksinger, songwriter]
Note(s): In PSND & ASCP middle name: Wilson.
Boy Wonder (of the Clarinet), The *Source(s):* CM13; GAMM; PSND
Herman, Woody *Source(s):* CPMU; NGAM
Hermann, Willy 1868- [composer, conductor]
Note(s): Portrait: ETUP 52:6 (June 1934): 332
Dana, Arthur *Source(s):* CCE23 E566189; CCE28 E111
Note(s): A. P. Schmidt house name; see NOTES: Dana, Arthur.
Hermannus, Contractus 1013-1054 [monk, composer, instrument maker, etc.]
Contractus, Hermannus *Source(s):* LCAR; NGDM
Herman the Cripple *Source(s):* LCAR
Hermann der Lahme *Source(s):* LCAR; NGDM
Hermann von Reichenau *Source(s):* LCAR; NGDM
Hermant, Charles Joseph 1815-1858 [poet, singer]
Mitaine *Source(s):* IBIM; WORB
Hermant, Constant 1823-1903 [composer, violinist]
Herman(n), Adolf [or Adolphe] *Source(s):* GREN; MACM
Hermil, (Ange) Édouard 1833-1898 [actor, playwright]
Milher, (Ange) Édouard *Source(s):* GAN2; LCAR; PIPE; WORB

Hernaman, Claudia Frances (née Ibotson) 1838-1898 [hymnist]
C. F. H. *Source(s):* JULN
Hernandez Gonzalez, Gabriel [writer on music]
Montillana, J. de *Source(s): Inter-American Music Review* 16:1 (1997): 92
Herold, (Louis Joseph) Ferdinand 1791-1833 [composer]
Landriani *Source(s):* http://www.answers.com/topic/louis-joseph-ferdinand-herold (7 July 2005)
Herold, Helmuth 1928- [composer]
Halloway *Source(s):* KOMS; PFSA
Herpin, (Clara Adele) Luce 1825-1914 [author]
Perey, L(ucien) *Source(s):* LCAR; OCLC 46722739
Herrera, Humberto (Angel) 1900-1981 [composer, author, conductor]
D'Umberto, Angelo *Source(s):* ASCP; CCE73
Herr, Hubert *Source(s):* CCE65
Reemhber, Arthur O. *Source(s):* ASCP; CCE59-60
Herrmann, Georg 1871-1963 [singer, writer on music]
Armen, Georg *Source(s):* STGR; WORB
Armin, Georg *Source(s):* BAKR; IWWM
Herrmann, Georg 1904-1989 [composer]
Godfrée *Source(s):* PFSA
Herschell, Esther (née Fuller-Maitland) [hymnist]
Anonymous *Source(s):* JULN (Appendix) (publication date 1827)
Herschmann, Erik 1944- [composer]
Silvester, Eric *Source(s):* PSFA
Herscovici, Filip 1906-1989 [composer]
Herschkowitz, Philip *Source(s):* PFSA
Hersh, Donald (Lee) 1936- [musicologist]
Harrán, Don *Source(s):* NGDM
Herterich, Robert S. 1915-2004 [organist, pianist, arranger]
Pewrattler *Source(s):* http://www.organ.co.uk/pages/reviews/ok15.html (1 July 2005)
Herz, Heinrich [or Henri] 1803 (or 06)-1888 [pianist, composer, teacher]
Note(s): Portrait: ETUP 52:6 (June 1934): 332
H*** *Source(s):* CPMU
Vulcan Pianist *Source(s):* STAR p. 124
Herz, Maria (née Bing) 1878- [pianist, composer]
Herz, (Dr.) Albert *Source(s):* COHN; HIXN
Note(s): Used husband's name.
Herzberg, Gary Allan 1967-Allan [singer, songwriter, guitarist, actor]
Allan, Gary *Source(s):* MCCL
Herzel, Carl [or Karl] (Heinrich) [librettist]
Carlo *Source(s):* LCAR; OCLC 38679146
Note(s): Also used by M. Carl.
Karlo *Source(s):* MELL
Herzl, Ludwig 1872-1939 [gynecologist, author, playwright]
Herzer, Ludwig *Source(s):* GAN1; GAN2; GROL; LCAR; OMUO; PIPE
Heseltine, Philip (Arnold) 1894-1930 [composer, writer on music]
Note(s): Portraits: COPL; ETUP 52:6 (June 1934): 322; http://www.peterwarlock.org (6 Oct. 2002)
Beldamandis, Prosdocimus de *Source(s):* COPL
Note(s): Used name of Italian theorist (c.1375-1428).
Cambrensis *Source(s):* COPL
Cattley, Mortimer *Source(s):* COPL
Criticus, Apparatus *Source(s):* COPL
Cynimbo, Jerry *Source(s):* COPL
Gogo, Bulgy *Source(s):* COPL
Larent, Barbara C. *Source(s):* COPL
Noolas, Rab *Source(s):* CART; COPL; LCAR
Palimpsest, Huanebango Z. *Source(s):* COPL
Scacabarozus, Obricus *Source(s):* COPL
Warlock, Peter *Source(s):* CART; COPL; GROL; LCAR; NGDM
Westcott, A. Whyte *Source(s):* COPL
Wood, Peter *Source(s): Frederick Delius and Peter Warlock; A Friendship Revealed.* Ed. by Barry Smith. Oxford, Oxford University Press, 2000, 408.
Hess, David (Alexander) 1936- [composer, author, singer]
Hill, David *Source(s):* ASCP; CCE57-60; LCAR; WORT
Hess, Reimund 1935- [composer]
Hen(n)inger, Ralf *Source(s):* CCE66-67; KOMP; KOMS; PFSA
Parkman, Franky *Source(s):* CCE73 Efor165307; KOMP; KOMS; PFSA
Hess, Theodore 1875-1940 [librettist]
Halton, Theo(dore) *Source(s):* MACM
Hesse, August Wilhelm 1805-1864 [librettist]
Wages, J. Ch. *Source(s):* STGR
Hester, Wesley 1933- [composer, author, singer]
Hester, Hal *Source(s):* ASCP; LCAR
Heuchelin, Christian before 1640-after 1680 [author]
Lisander *Source(s):* PIPE
Heugel, Henri Georges 1844-1916 [music publisher, writer on music]
Moréno, Henri *Source(s):* PIPE
Heun, Hans 1920-1991 [composer]
Lones, Larry *Source(s):* GREN
Hewitt, Eliza Edmunds (Stites) 1851-1920 [hymnist]
Note(s): Portrait: CYBH
Edmunds, Lidie H. *Source(s):* CYBH
Hewitt, Lida *Source(s):* RUFF p. 151
Hewitt, Horatio Dawes ?-1894 [composer, critic]
Stulwitt, R. H. *Source(s):* TPRF
Note(s): Jt. pseud.: R(obert) M(orrison) Stults.

Hewitt, John (Henry) Hill 1801-1890 [composer, poet, music teacher]
Note(s): Portraits: EWEN; EWPA; HAMM; PARS
Alpha *Source(s):* PDMU
Bard of the Stars and Bars *Source(s):* HARW p. 26
Father of American Ballad and Poetry, The *Source(s):* HARW; PSND
Father of the American Ballad *Source(s):* HOWD p. 174
J. H. H. *Source(s):* NEWB ("The Minstrels Returned from War")
Nunns, John F. *Source(s):* STUW
Raymond, Eugene *Source(s):* HARW; HOGR; PARS; STUW; WORB
Stewart, J. J. *Source(s):* PARS
Willis, J. H. *Source(s):* STUW
Hewson, Paul (David) 1960- [singer, songwriter]
Bono (Vox) *Source(s):* LCAR; PMUS-95; PMUS-97; SONG; WORL
Vox, Bono *Source(s):* NOMG
Heybourne, Ferdinando c.1558-1618 [composer]
Richardson, Ferdinand *Source(s):* MACM; NGDM
Heyden, Sebald(us) mentioned 1660 [hymnist]
S. H. *Source(s):* CPMU; WORB
Note(s): Probable initials of Heyden.
Heyer, Walter 1914-1989 [composer]
Steeven, (Jan) *Source(s):* CCE59; CCE62-63; KOMS; PFSA
Heyl, Manfred 1908- [composer]
Eridanus *Source(s):* KOMP; KOMS; PFSA
Heyne, Christian Leberecht 1751-1821 [composer]
Wall, Anton *Source(s):* CPMU; OCLC 38645377
Heynicke, Kurt 1891-1985 [author]
Uhlenbruck, Christian *Source(s):* PIPE
Hickenlooper, Lucy [or Lucie] (Mary Olga Agnes) 1882-1948 [pianist, music critic, teacher]
Note(s): Portraits: ETUP 55:11 (Nov. 1937): 700; GRAN
Samaroff, Ogla *Source(s):* AMME; GRAN; LCAR; MWP3
Stokowski, (Mrs.) Ogla *Source(s):* AMME; GRAN; LCAR
Hickey, Martin [songwriter]
Henderson, Frame *Source(s):* CCE72-73
Land, Dick C. *Source(s):* CCE72 R537636-38
Note(s): Jt. pseud. C(yrus) Van Ness Clark.
Hicks, Otis V. 1913-1974 [singer, guitarist, songwriter]
Lightnin' Slim *Source(s):* DBMU; HARS
Hicks, Robert 1902-1931 [singer, guitarist, songwriter]
Barbecue Bob *Source(s):* HARS
Hicks, Thomas 1936- [singer, songwriter, actor]
Bennett, Jimmy *Source(s):* CCE58-59; CPOL RE-285-490; LCAR; SONG
Steele, Tommy *Source(s):* CCE67; FAFO; GAN1; GAN2; LCAR
Hicks, Tony (Christopher) 1945- [songwriter]
Ransford, (L.) *Source(s):* BLIC; *Goldmine* 28:12:571 (14 June 2002) p. 70
Note(s): Jt. pseud.: Graham Nash & Harold Allan Clarke.
Higginbotham, Irene (Evelyn) 1918- [pianist, composer]
Jones, Hart *Source(s):* BUL3; COHN; HIXN
Padellan, (Mrs.) Moetahar *Source(s):* BUL3
Higginbotham, Robert 1933-1982 [singer, pianist, songwriter]
Tucker, Tee *Source(s):* http://members.tripod.com/SoulfulKindaMusic/ttucker.htm (4 Sept. 2003)
Tucker, Tommy *Source(s):* AMUS; CCE62
Note(s): "I Can't Stand the Way You Tease," "Just for a Day" & "Shut Up" (all CCE62). Do not confuse with Tommy Tucker (1908-). Also used by Gerald L. Duppler (CCE62).
Higgins, Elbert 1944- [singer, songwriter]
Higgins, Bertie *Source(s):* ALMN
Higginson, Agnes fl. 1900 [poet]
O'Neill, Moira *Source(s):* LAST
Higginson, Doris 1937-2004 [singer, songwriter]
Payne, (Doris) *Source(s):* AMUS; CCE65; EPMU
Troy, Doris *Source(s):* AMUS; EPMU; HARD; KICK; ROOM
Higginson, J(oseph) Vincent 1896-1994 [composer, organist, teacher]
Anthony Cyril, (Brother) *Source(s):* LCPC (Letter from J. Fischer cited); CCE37 Eunp152845
De Brant, Cyr *Source(s):* ASCP; CART; CCE37 Eunp152845; LCAR
Edwards, J. V. *Source(s):* LCPC E44204 ("Hail! Jaspers, Hail!")
Higgs, Blake Alphonso 1917- [calypso singer, songwriter]
Blake, Blind *Source(s):* CCE52; CCE55
Note(s): See also Arthur Phelps.
Blind Blake *Source(s):* CCE52; CCE55; LCAR
Note(s): See also Arthur Phelps.
Higgs, Joe 1940-1999 [composer]
Father of Reggae Music *Source(s):* http://www.bobmarley.freeserve.co.uk/joehiggs.htm (6 Oct. 2002)
Note(s): See also Robert [or Bob] Nesta Marley.
Godfather of Reggae *Source(s):* http://www.artistonly.com/wailso.htm (6 Oct. 2002)
Highwater, Jamake (Mamake) 1942- [writer on music]
Marks, J. *Source(s):* LCAR
Hildebrand, Ernst 1918-1986 [composer]
Brandeau *Source(s):* KOMP; REHH; SUPN

Hildegard of Bingen 1098-1179 [composer]
God's Little Feather *Source(s):* http://stthomasirondequoit.com/SaintsAlive/id233.htm (6 Oct. 2002)
Note(s): Called herself.
Hildesheim, Ferdinand 1811-1885 [composer, conductor]
Hiller, Ferdinand *Source(s):* PSND
Hill, Alfred Hawthorne 1925-1992 [comedian, songwriter]
Hill, Benny *Source(s):* EPMU
Hill, Bertha 1905-1950 [singer, lyricist]
Hill, Chippie *Source(s):* GRAT; HARS; LCAR; PMUS
Hill, James Edward 1921-1994 [singer, songwriter, performer]
Hill, Eddie *Source(s):* ENCM
Hill, Smilin' Eddie *Source(s):* ENCM
Hill, Lester [or Leslie] 1921-1957 [singer, instrumentalist]
Be-Bop Boy, The *Source(s):* AMUS; EPMU
Chicago Sonny Boy *Source(s):* HARS
Lewis, Johnny *Source(s):* HARS
Little Joe *Source(s):* HARS
Louis, Joe (Hill) *Source(s):* AMUS; EPMU; HARS
Peption Boy, The *Source(s):* HARS
Hill, Mildred 1859-1916 [author, writer on music]
Tonsor, Johann *Source(s):* hjttp://www.kellyjanetorrance.com/archives/2002_11.html (27 Feb. 2003)
Hill, William [or Billy] (J(oseph)) 1899-1940 [songwriter, pianist, violinist]
Brown, George (W. [or F. or R]) *Source(s):* BBDP; CCE58-61; HARS; LCAR; PMUS
Note(s): Do not confuse with George Brown (1919-).
Hillmacher, Lucien Joseph Edouard 1860-1909 [composer]
Hillermacher, P(aul) L(ucien) *Source(s):* LCAR; MELL; NGDM; NGDO; PRAT
Notes(s): Jt. pseud.: Paul Joseph Guillaume Hillemacher.
Hillemacher, Paul Joseph Guillaume 1852-1933 [composer]
Hillermacher, P(aul) L(ucien) *Source(s):* LCAR; MELL; NGDM; NGDO; PRAT
Note(s): Jt. pseud.: Lucien Joseph Edouard Hillmacher.
Hillhouse, Augustus Lucas 1792-1859 [author, translator, hymnist]
Auguste, Monsieur *Source(s):* HATF
Monsieur Auguste *Source(s):* HATF
Hilliam, B(entley) C(ollingwood 1890-1968 [composer, author]
Flotsam, Mr. *Source(s):* CART; CCE31 Efor20964; GAMM; ROOM
Hillman, Chris(topher) 1942 (or 44)- [singer, songwriter]
Godfather of Country-Rock *Source(s):* MCCL
Note(s): See also Ingram Cecil Connor, III.
Hillman, Roscoe V(anos) 1910- [composer, author, teacher]
Hillman, Roc *Source(s):* ASCP; CCE41 #3986 E90346
Hills, George [composer]
Lindenblauer, Carl *Source(s):* CPMU (publication dates 1854-69)
Hills, Robert P(ennock), Jr. 1932- [composer, business executive]
Harper, R(ussell) Paul *Source(s):* CCE66-67; REHG; SMIN; SUPN
Himan, Alberto 1855- [songwriter]
Berti, Henry *Source(s):* GOLD; LCAR
Hyman, Alberto *Source(s):* LCAR
Hime, (Miss) L. [composer]
L. H., (Miss) *Source(s):* CPMU (publication date 1805)
Himmer-Perez, Arturo 1948- [composer]
Santis, Carlos de *Source(s):* KOMS; PFSA
Hindemith, Paul 1895-1963 [composer]
Baule *Source(s): Selected Letters of Paul Hindemith.* Ed. & trans. by Geoffrey Skelton. New Haven: Yale University Press, 1995.
Merano, Paul *Source(s):* PIPE; RILM 92-12577-ap
Paul the Musician *Source(s): Selected Letters* (see above), 88
Semischăcksbier *Source(s): Selected Letters* (see above), ix
Yijak *Source(s): Selected Letters* (see above), 47
Hinderer, Everett (Roland) 1914-2002 [composer, author, singer]
Cook, Shorty *Source(s):* ASCP; CCE47; CCE52
Hinds, Horace 1951- [singer, songwriter]
Andy, Horace *Source(s):* EPMU; LCAR
Andy, Sleepy *Source(s):* EPMU
Hines, Brian (Arthur) 1944- [singer, songwriter, guitarist]
Laine, Denny *Source(s):* AMUS; EPMU; NOMG; PEN2
Hines, Earl Kenneth 1903 (or 05)-1983 [composer, author, pianist]
Hines, Fatha *Source(s):* ASCP; EPMU; NGDM; PEN2; VACH
Hinojosa, Letitia [or Leticia] 1955- [singer, songwriter, guitarist]
Hinojosa, Tish *Source(s):* AMUS; MCCL
Hinsdale, Grace Webster (née Haddock) 1833-1902 [hymnist]
Farin *Source(s):* DIEH; JULN (Suppl.)
Hinstein, Gustav 1902- [composer]
Schlemm, Gustav Adolf *Source(s):* BUL1; BUL2
Hintz, Ewaldt 1613-1668 [organist, composer]
Ewaldt *Source(s):* LCAR; NGDM
Hirai, Kozaburo 1910- [composer]
Hirai, Yasuki *Source(s):* GREN

Hirsch, Franz 1878-1960 [actor, playwright, producer]
Arnold, Franz *Source(s):* GAN1; GAN2
Note(s): Do not confuse with actor/playwright Ernest Arnold (GAN2)
Hirsch, Louis A(chille) 1881-1924 [songwriter]
Note(s): Portrait: EWEN
Hiller, Louis Hirsch *Source(s):* LCAR; STGR
Hirsch, Robert Franz Richard 1883- [composer]
Hernried *Source(s):* WORB
Hirschbach, Hermann 1812-1888 [composer, violinist]
Largo, Henry *Source(s):* GOTH
Hirschfeld, Leo [or Ludwig] 1869-1924 [librettist]
Feld, Leo *Source(s):* LCAR; LOWN; MACM; PIPE; WORB
Hinzelmann, Hans Heinz *Source(s):* LOWN; MELL
Note(s): Jt. pseud.: Leo Feld [i.e., Hirschfeld] & Karl Michael von Levetzow.
Hirschfeld, Louis von [composer]
Robert, Louis *Source(s):* MELL; STGR
Hirschfeld, Victor 1858 (or 60)-1940 [journalist, librettist]
Léon, Victor *Source(s):* GAN1; GAN2; LCAR; LOWN; MELL; NGDO; PIPE; RIES
Leonard, Victor *Source(s):* PIPE
Hirschmann, Henri (Louis) 1872 (or 73)-1961 [composer]
Herblay, K. *Source(s):* GAN1; GAN2; LCAR; MELL; RIEM; STGR; WORB
Hirt, Al(ois Maxwell) 1922- [trumpeter, bandleader, songwriter]
Jumbo *Source(s):* PSND
Round Mound of Sound *Source(s):* CM05
Note(s): See also Kenny Price.
Trumpeting Behemoth *Source(s):* PSND
Hoar, Robert Crosby 1954- [singer, songwriter]
Crosby, Bob *Source(s):* CCE73-74; CCE77-78
Crosby, Rob *Source(s):* AMUS; CCE75; EPMU; MCCL
Hobbs, Rebecca [or Becky] (Ann) 1950- [singer, songwriter, pianist]
Beckaroo *Source(s):* MCCL
Hobsbawm, Eric (John Ernest) 1917- [historian, author, writer on music]
Newton, Francis *Source(s):* LCAR; NOTE 50:2 (1993): 612
Hobson, Frederick Leslie 1855-1892 [actor, burlesque writer]
Note(s): Portrait: GAN2
Hobbs, Owen *Source(s):* LCAR
Leslie, Fred(erick) *Source(s):* CART; GAN2; LCAR; WORB
Note(s): Do not confuse with Fred (A.) Leslie [i.e., Frederick William Daniel Stoneham (1882-1969)], dancer, actor, choreographer.
Torr, A. C. *Source(s):* CART; GAN1; GAN2; GANA; KILG; LCAR
Hochberg, Hans Heinrich, (Bolko Graf von XIV) 1843-1926 [theatre director, composer]
Note(s): Portrait: ETUP 51:8 (Aug. 1934): 448
Franz, J(ohann) H(einrich) *Source(s):* GROL; IBIM; MACM; NGDM; PSND
Hochberg, Isidore 1896 (or 98)-1981 [lyricist, producer]
Note(s): Portraits: EWEN; EWPA
Harburg, E(dgar) Y. *Source(s):* ASCC; CASS; EWEN; GAN1; GAN2; PEN2
Harburg, Yip(sel) *Source(s):* ASCC; BBDP; CASS; EWEN; GAN1; GAN2; HARR
Hochkirch, Franz von 1886- [writer, critic]
Loë, Franz von *Source(s):* SONN
Hocmelle, Pierre Edmond 1824-1895 [organist, critic, composer]
Bussy, Edmond de *Source(s):* MACM
Hodder-Williams, (John) Christopher (Glazebrook) 1926 (or 27)- [author, songwriter]
Brogan, James *Source(s):* LCAR; PSND
Hodeir, André 1921- [composer, arranger, violinist, writer on music]
Laurence, Claude *Source(s):* CCE50-52; GROL
Lawrence, Claude *Source(s):* BBDP; NGDJ
Hodge, Harry Baldwin Hermon 1872-1947 [composer, writer]
Langa Langa *Source(s):* CART
Hodges, John 1821-1891 [minstrel performer, songwriter]
White, Cool *Source(s):* FINS p. 191; LCAR; SPTH p. 100+
Hodges, John(ny) Cornelius 1907-1970 [saxophonist, songwriter]
Harjes, J. *Source(s):* JAMU
Harvey *Source(s):* JAMU
Hodges, Jeep *Source(s):* GROL; PEN2
Hodges, Rabbit *Source(s):* GROL; PEN2
Hodges, Squatty Roo *Source(s):* PEN2
Porter, Cue *Source(s):* JAMU
Rabbit *Source(s):* LCAR
Note(s): Also used by John Bundrick
Hödl, Karl Johann 1909- [actor, author]
Holt, Hans *Source(s):* PIPE
Hoérée, Arthur Charles Ernest 1897-1986 [composer, writer on music]
Lipton, Pedro *Source(s):* GOTH
Hofferer, Margaretha Maria Elisabeth 1923- [composer]
Komposch, Gretl *Source(s):* OMUO
Hoffman, Al 1902-1960 [songwriter, author]
Downs, Jerry *Source(s):* KINK; http://

www.webwaymonsters.com/song.shtml (25 June 2005)

Hoffman, James Senate 1922-1992 [composer, author, singer]
Landon, Buddy *Source(s):* ASCP; CPOL RE-744-531
Lang, Scott *Source(s):* CCE53

Hoffmann Balenovic, Draga 1947- [composer]
Balena, Draga *Source(s):* KOMS

Hoffmann, Eduard 1829 (or 30)-1898 [violinist, composer]
Reményi, Ed(o)uard *Source(s):* BAKR; IBIM; LCAR; NGDM

Hoffmann, Ernst Theodore Wilhelm 1776-1822 [composer, music critic]
Note(s): Portrait: EWCY
Amadeus *Source(s):* BAKR; PSND
Dori, Giuseppo *Source(s):* GROL
Hoffmann, E(rnst) T(heodor) A(madeus) *Source(s):* BAKR
Kreisler, Johannes (Kapellmeister) *Source(s):* BAKR; MACM
Vollweiler, A. *Source(s):* GROL

Hoffmann, Hans 1859-1912 [author, librettist]
Brenta, Emil *Source(s):* PIPE
Falzari, Felix *Source(s):* LOWN; MELL; PIPE; WORB

Hoffmann, Heinrich 1809-1894 [author]
Gastfenger, Polykarpus *Source(s):* PIPE
Heulenburg, Heulalius von *Source(s):* PIPE
Kinderlieb, Heinrich *Source(s):* PIPE
Kinderlieb, Reimerich *Source(s):* PIPE
Struwwell, Peter *Source(s):* LCAR; PIPE
Zweibel *Source(s):* PIPE

Hoffmann, Heinrich August 1798-1874 [poet, librarian, musicologist]
Hoffman von Fallersleben *Source(s):* BAKE; MACM

Hoffmann(-Harnish), (Friedrich) Wolfgang 1893-1965 [author, theatrical producer)
Lindroder, Wolfgang *Source(s):* PIPE

Hoffmayr, Carl c1905-1965 [reeds, arranger, bandleader]
Hoff, Carl *Source(s):* KINK; LCAR

Hofhaimer, Paul(us von) 1459-1557 [composer, organist]
Hans *Source(s):* IBIM; WORB
Hoffheymer, Paul *Source(s):* IBIM; WORB
Johann Paul *Source(s):* IBIM; WORB
Magister Paulus *Source(s):* IBIM; WORB
P. H. *Source(s):* IBIM; WORB

Hofmann, George D. [composer]
Eaton, M. B. *Source(s):* TPRF
Note(s): Also used by George D(aniel) Barnard & Will(iam H.) Scouton; see NOTES: Eaton, M. B.

Hofmann, Josef (Casimir) 1876-1957 [pianist, composer, inventor]
Note(s): Portraits: ETUP 52:7 (July 1934): 392; *Keyboard Classics* (Sept./Oct. 1983): 4+. Inventor of shock absorbers, air springs & other automobile appliances.
Dvorsky, M(ichel) *Source(s):* BAKR; BUL1; GROL; LCAR; NGAM; NGDM

Hofmannsthal, Hugo von 1874-1929 [poet, dramatist, librettist]
Hofmann, Elder von *Source(s):* PSND
Loris *Source(s):* AEIO; PSND
Melikow, Loris *Source(s):* AEIO; PSND
Morren, Theophil *Source(s):* AEIO; LCAR; PSND
O'Hagan, Archibald *Source(s):* PSND
Poet of a Doomed Austria, The *Source(s):* SIFA

Hogberg, Sven Ake [multi-instrumentalist, singer, arranger]
Burnette, Legendary Hank C. *Source(s):* EPMU
Legendary Hank C. Burnette *Source(s):* EPMU

Hogg, Andrew 1914-1960 [singer, guitarist, pianist, songwriter]
Hogg, Smok(e)y *Source(s):* CCE52-53; HARS; LCAR
Wheatstraw, Little Peetie *Source(s):* HARS
Note(s): Do not confuse with Peetie [or Pete] Wheatstraw [i.e., William Bunch]

Hogg, James 1770-1835 [poet]
Craig, J. H. *Source(s):* LCAR
Ettrick Shepherd, The *Source(s):* CCE64; GOTH; GOTT; LCAR; WORB

Hohl, Daryl Franklin 1948 (or 49)- [songwriter]
Hall, Daryl *Source(s):* HARD; HARR

Hohu, Martha Poepoe 1907-2004 [conductor, composer, arranger, organist]
Auntie Martha *Source(s):* DRSC

Holberg, Ludvig 1684-1754 [author, historian]
Note(s): See PSND & LCAR for nonmusic-related sobriquets & pseudonyms
Klimius, Nicolas *Source(s):* LCAR; PSND
Mikkelsen, Hans *Source(s):* LCAR; PIPE; PSND

Holbrooke, Joseph [or Josef] (Charles) 1878-1958 [composer]
Note(s): Portrait: ETUP 52:8 (Aug. 1934): 448
Brook, Harold *Source(s):* SHMP
Hanze, Jean *Source(s):* BLIC; CPMU
Meredith, Evan *Source(s):* CPMU

Holcomb, Densile 1923-1999 [singer, songwriter, guitarist]
Curly Dan *Source(s):* CCE66-68; MCCL

Holcombe, Wilfred (Lawshe) 1924- [composer, arranger]
Holcombe, Bill *Source(s):* REHG
Lawshe, Wilfred *Source(s):* REHG; SUPN
Markham, Seth *Source(s):* SUPN
Note(s): Also used by John Cacavas.
Tompkins, Wes *Source(s):* REHG; SUPN

Holden, Charles [songwriter]
Andre, Carl *Source(s):* CCE51 R75108 ("Moonlight Revels"); TPRF
Holden, Oliver 1765-1831 (or 34) [composer, author]
Note(s): Portraits: CYBH; ETUP 52:8 (Aug. 1934): 448
Citizen of Massachusetts, A *Source(s):* CART; PSNN
Holder, John (Wesley) c.1939- [singer; guitarist, songwriter]
Holda, Ramjohn *Source(s):* CCE60
Holder, Ram (John) *Source(s):* HARS
Holder, Neville 1946 (or 50)- [singer, songwriter, guitarist]
Holder, Noddy *Source(s):* HARR; LCAR; NOMG
Holder, William 1616-1697 (or 98) [clergyman, mathmatician, composer]
Mr. Snub-Dean *Source(s):* GROL
Hölderlin, (Johann Christian) Friedrich 1770-1843 [poet]
Scardanelli *Source(s):* GROL
Holiday, Harold [pianist, songwriter]
Black Boy Shine *Source(s):* AMUS; EPMU; LCAR
Shine, Black Boy *Source(s):* LCAR
Hollaender, Victor [or Viktor] (Hugo) 1866-1940 [composer, conductor]
Note(s): ETUP 52:8 (Aug. 1934): 448
Del Tolverno, Arricha *Source(s):* LCAR
Tolreno, Arricha del *Source(s):* PFSA
Tolveno, Arricha del *Source(s):* BAKE; GROL; LYMN; WORB
Victor, Hollis *Source(s):* CCE39 #33235, 163 R79023
Holland, Brian 1941- [songwriter]
Brianbert *Source(s):* CCE61 ("You'll Be Sorry Someday")
H-D-H *Source(s):* KICK; SHAD; SOTH
Note(s): Jt.pseud.: Eddie Holland & Lamont Dozier.
Holland-Dozier-Holland *Source(s):* CM05; EPMU; PEN2
Note(s): Jt.pseud.: Eddie Holland & Lamont Dozier.
Wayne, Edith *Source(s):* http://www.expansionrecords.com/genjohnson.htm (18 May 2005)
Note(s): Jt.pseud.: Eddie Holland & Lamont Dozier.
Holland, Eddie 1939- [songwriter]
H-D-H *Source(s):* KICK; SHAD; SOTH
Note(s): Jt.pseud.: Brian Holland & Lamont Dozier.
Holland-Dozier-Holland *Source(s):* CM05; EPMU: KICK; PEN2
Note(s): Jt.pseud.: Brian Holland & Lamont Dozier.
Wayne, Edith *Source(s):* http://www.expansionrecords.com/genjohnson.htm
Note(s): Jt.pseud.: Brian Holland & Lamont Dozier.
Holland, Kwamé [rapper, arranger]
Kwamé *Source(s):* EPMU
Hollander, Christian Janssone c.1520-1570 [composer]
Janssone, Christian *Source(s):* IBIM; WORB
Holley, Charles Hardin 1936-1959 [composer, singer, guitarist]
Father of Rock 'n' Roll, The *Source(s):* http://www.virtualubbock.com/home.html (6 Oct. 2002)
Note(s): See also Charles Edward Anderson Berry, Arthur Crudup, William [or Bill] (John) Haley, Johnnie Johnson & Elvis A(a)ron Presley.
Father of Texas Rock 'n' Roll, The *Source(s):* MCCL (see under: VanZandt, Townes)
Holly, Buddy *Source(s):* CASS; CM01; DIMA; EPMU; HARR; MCCL; PEN2; REHH
Hollingsworth, Stanley 1924- [composer]
Hollier, Stanley *Source(s):* BAKT; BUL3; CCE53
Hollombe, Daniel Ephriam 1957- [composer, author]
Hollodan, Damaskas *Source(s):* ASCP
Holman, Willis Leonard H. 1927- [composer, conductor]
Holman, Bill *Source(s):* LCAR; SUPN
Holme, (Sir) Randle Fynes Wilson 1864-1957 [solicitor, Wagnerian writer]
Fynes, Randle *Source(s):* CART
Holmes, Augusta Mary Anne 1847-1903 [composer]
Note(s): Portraits: COHN; DWCO; ETUP 52:8 (Aug. 1934): 448
Zenta, Herman(n) *Source(s):* GROL; IBIM; MACM; MELL; STRN; WORB
Zeuta, Hermann *Source(s):* PIPE; STRN
Holmes, Edward 1797-1859 [writer on music, composer]
Musical Professor, A *Source(s):* CART
Holmes, Ethel Clive fl. 1894 [composer]
Clive, Ethelbert *Source(s):* CANE
Holmes, Joe 1897-1949 [singer, guitarist; harmonica player, songwriter]
Blind Lemon's Buddy *Source(s):* HARS; LCAR
Hill, King Solomon *Source(s):* EPMU; HARS; LCAR
Note(s): Also reported but unconfirmed pseud. of Joe Lee Williams.
Holmes, Leslie [songwriter]
Two Leslies, The *Source(s):* CCE37 Efor49196 ("Dart Song")
Note(s): Jt. pseud.: Leslie Sarony [i.e., Leslie Legge Sarony Frye]
Venton & Reef *Source(s):* CCE62 ("Don't Be Surprised")
Note(s): Jt. pseud.: Leslie Sarony [i.e., Leslie Legge Sarony Frye]
Holmes, M. C.
Saroni, M. *Source(s):* TPRF
Holmes, Odetta 1930- [singer, songwriter, guitarist]

Felious, Odetta *Source(s):* CM07
Gordon, (Mrs.) Odetta *Source(s):* BAKE; CM07
Odetta *Source(s):* CM07; PEN2; PSND
Holness, Winston 1951- [singer, DJ, arranger]
Holness, Niney *Source(s):* EPMU
Observer, The *Source(s):* EPMU
Holoubek, Karl 1907-1983 [composer]
Loubé, Charles *Source(s):* CCE65; OMUO
Holst, Eduard [or Edward] 1843-1899 [compose, actor, dancing master]
Note(s): Portrait: ETUP 52:8 (Sept. 1934): 448
Novara, Léon *Source(s):* TPRF
Holt, Simeon ten 1923- [composer, pianist]
Kockyn *Source(s):* BUL3
Holte, Patricia Louise 1944- [singer, songwriter, actress, bandleader]
LaBelle, Patti *Source(s):* CM08; LCAR; NOMG
Holtei, Karl von 1798-1880 [author]
Hudltei, Schirmherr der Abruzzen *Source(s):* APPL p. 12
Holtzman(n), Wilhelm 1532-1576 [translator]
Xylander, Wilhelm *Source(s):* LCAR; MACM; WORB
Holvay, James [songwriter]
Harris, Jimmy *Source(s):* CE66-67; PMUS
Holyroyd, Ethel Mary [songwriter]
Cookridge, John (Michael) *Source(s):* CCE61-62; CPMU
Hölzel, Johann [or Hans] 1957 (or 58)-1998 [singer, songwriter]
Falco *Source(s):* EPMU; LCAR; NOMG; OB98
Homann-Webau, Otto 1877- [composer]
Hove, E. *Source(s):* KOBW
Home, Ann(e) 1742-1821 [poet]
Note(s): See also LCAR for additional pseudonyms.
Lady, A *Source(s):* CPMS ("Genie of the Mountains of Balagete")
Note(s): Also used by Charlotte Elliott, Stephen Collins Foster & Julia Ward Howe.
Homola, Bernhard 1894-1960 [composer, conductor]
Hohenberg, Franz *Source(s):* PIPE
Hone, William 1780-1842 [author]
Cecil, John *Source(s):* LCAR
Logic, Lay *Source(s):* CPMU; OCLC 45646371
Note(s): Probable pseud.
Hood, Margaret Chalmers 1825-1902 [hymnist]
M. C. H. *Source(s):* JULN (Suppl.)
M. C. W. *Source(s):* JULN (Suppl.)
Wilson, (Mrs.) Margaret Chalmers *Source(s):* JULN (Suppl.)
Hood, Thomas 1799-1845 [writer]
Incog. *Source(s):* GOTH
Hook, George Barry 1884-1962 [comedian, author]
Lupino, Barry *Source(s):* GAN2 (see under: Lupino, Stanley)
Hook, Stanley 1894-1942 [comedian, author]
Brody, Hal *Source(s):* EPMU; GANZ
Note(s): Jt. pseud.: (Herbert) Desmond Carter, H(ubert) B(arber) Hedley, John [or Jack] (Francis) Strachey, Harry Acre, Jack Clarke & possibly others.
Lupino, Stanley *Source(s):* GAN2
Hooker, John Lee 1917 (or 20)-2001 [guitarist, singer, songwriter]
Birmingham Sam (and His Magic Guitar) *Source(s):* AMUS; EPMU; HARS; LCAR
Blues Giant, The *Source(s):* http://www.angelfire.com/mn/coasters/great.html (6 Oct. 2002)
Boogie Man, (The) *Source(s):* AMUS; EPMU; HARS; LCAR
Booker, John (Lee) *Source(s):* AMUS; DBMU; EPMU; LCAR
Cooker, John Lee *Source(s):* DBMU; EPMU; HARS
Delta, John *Source(s):* AMUS; DBMU; EPMU; HARS; LCAR
Dr. Boogie *Source(s):* http://www.island.net/~blues/hooker.html (6 Oct. 2002)
Docter Feelgood *Source(s):* ALMN; CM01
Note(s): See also William Lee Perryman.
Feelgood, Doctor *Sources(s):* ALMN; CM01
Note(s): See also William Lee Perryman.
Godfather of the Blues *Source(s):* CM01; WORL
Greatest Blues Singer of the World *Source(s):* http://www.angelfire.com/mn/coasters/great.html
Note(s): See also Alonzo Johnson & Elizabeth Smith.
Hook, The *Sources(s):* ALMN; CM01
Iron John *Source(s):* http://www.angelfire.com/mn/coasters/great.html
John, Delta [or Delton] *Source(s):* AMUS; YORK
King of the Boogie, (The) *Source(s):* ALMN; WORL
King of the Endless Boogie, The *Source(s):* AMUS; PSND
Lee, Johnny *Source(s):* AMUS; DBMU; EPMU; HARS
Note(s): Also used by John Lee Ham.
Legendary King of the Blues, The *Source(s):* http://www.geocities.com/pawisi/link.html (6 Oct. 2002)
Little Pork Chops *Source(s):* AMUS
Po' Slim *Source(s):* http://www.angelfire.com/mn/coasters/great.html
Texas Slim *Source(s):* AMUS; CCE60; DBMU; EPMU; HARS; LCAR
Texas Sun *Source(s):* YORK
Williams, Johnny *Source(s):* AMUS; DBMU; EPMU; HARS; YORK

Note(s): Do not confuse with Johnny Williams, guitarist, or Robert Warren who also used the name Johnny Williams.
World's Greatest Blues Singer, The *Source(s):* http://w1.191.telia.com/~u19104970/johnnielee.html (6 Oct. 2002)
Hooper, R. S. [songwriter]
Little, Eric *Source(s):* CCE51 R78149 ("My Time Is Your Time"); PMUS
Hooven, Joseph (D(avis)) 1907- [songwriter]
Davis, Jeff(ery) *Source(s):* BLIC; CCE52-54; CPOL RE-24-781
Note(s): Do not confuse with Jeff Davis (1917-), composer of "Et bailler et dormir" (CCE53)
Hooven, Marilyn (K.) 1924- [songwriter]
Evans, Jody *Source(s):* BLIC; CCE52-54; CPOL RE-24-782
Hoover, Willis David 1909 (or 12)- [composer, author, singer]
Hoover, Bill *Source(s):* ASCP; CPOL RE-726-816
Hopkins, Charles Jerome 1836-1898 [composer, musician]
Hopkins, Edward Jerome *Source(s):* BAKE; NGDM; WORB
Note(s): Incorrect given name.
Hopkins, Harry Walter mentioned 1895 [composer]
Rodney, Paul *Source(s):* CPMU
Hopkins, John Henry, Jr. 1820-1891 [composer]
J. H. H. *Source(s):* DIEH
Hopkins, Sam 1912-1982 [singer, songwriter, guitarist]
Hopkins, Lightnin' *Source(s):* AMUS; CCE66; CM13; EPMU; HARD; HARS; MUHF
Hopkins, Smith Anderson 1920-1999 [songwriter, author, singer]
Hopkins, Little Hop *Source(s):* ASCP
Hopkinson, Francis 1737-1791 [composer, author, signer of the Declaration of Independence]
Note(s): Portraits: HAMM; HOWD. See LCAR for additional pseuds & sobriquets.
First Native Composer *Source(s):* HOWD
Hopkinson, Joseph 1770-1842 [lawyer, songwriter]
American, An *Source(s):* CART
Note(s): See also William Dunlap.
Hopp, Friedrich (Ernst) 1789-1869 [author, actor]
Cäsar, Julius *Source(s):* GAN2 p. 1978
Hopp, Julius 1819-1885 [translator]
Louis, D. *Source(s):* OCLC 4411080
Horchak, George 1937- [songwriter]
Darrick, George *Source(s):* CCE57
Darrow, George *Source(s):* CCE64-65
Dollar, Johnny *Source(s):* CCE65; PAu-170-324
Note(s): Do not confuse with singer-songwriter John(ny) (Washington) Dollar, Jr. (1933-1986).
Horgan, Richard Cornelius 1867-1941 [librettist, director]
Hurgon, Austen A. *Source(s):* GAN1; GAN2
Horn, August 1825-1893 [composer, arranger]
Corno *Source(s):* CPMU
Note(s): Probable pseud.
Horn, Charles Edward 1786-1849 [composer, singer]
Note(s): Portrait: ETUP 52:9 (Sept. 1934): 506
Flaccus *Source(s):* LCAR
Lady C. S. *Source(s):* SPTH p. 52 ("On the Banks of Allan Water")
Note(s): Possible pseud.
Hornbostel, August Gottlieb 1786-1838 [author]
Alberti, Heinrich *Source(s):* PIPE
Bohl, O. Ernest *Source(s):* PIPE
Horne, Richard Henry 1802-1884 [author, editor, poet]
Note(s): See PSND & LCAR for additional nonmusic-related pseudonyms.
Cutwalter, (Sir) Julius *Source(s):* GOTE; LCAR
Fairstar, (Mrs.) *Source(s):* GOTE; LCAR; PSND
Horne, Richard Hengist *Source(s):* GOTE; LCAR; WORB
Horneman, Christian Frederik Emil 1840 (or 41)-1906 [composer]
Note(s): Used pseuds on arrangements & potpourris (GROL); however none identified. Portrait: ETUP 52:9 (Sept. 1934): 506
Hornsby, Joseph Leith 1907-1984 [composer, author]
Thornsby, Lee *Source(s):* ASCP
Horowitz, Caroline 1902 (or 09)-1994 [composer]
Howard, Carolyne *Source(s):* ASCP; CCE52; CCE74; REHG
Horowitz, Richard (Michael) 1949- [composer]
Ztiworoh, Drahcir *Source(s):* NGAM
Horowitz, Ted [singer, songwriter]
Chubby, Popa *Source(s):* AMUS
Popa Chubby *Source(s):* LCAR
Horowitz, Vladimir 1902-1989 [pianist, composer, transcriber]
Demeny *Source(s):* http://web.telia.com/~u85420275/transcriptions.htm (6 Apr. 2005)
Note(s): Possible pseud.
Horsdal, Valdemar 1946- [guitarist, pianist, singer, songwriter]
Valdy *Source(s):* NOGM
Horsley, William 1774-1858 [glee writer]
Note(s): Portrait: ETUP 52:9 (Sept. 1934): 506
W. H. *Source(s):* CPMU
Horton, John(ny) (Gale) 1925 (or 29)-1960 [singer, guitarist, songwriter]
Singing Fisherman, The *Source(s):* FLIN; MCCL; PSND; SHAD; STAC

Horton, (George) Vaughn 1911-1988 [composer, arranger, author]
Evans, Willie *Source(s):* CCE56; CPOL RE-728-161
Pietro, George *Source(s):* CCE74
Stone, Wilbur *Source(s):* CCE56
Vaughn, George *Source(s):* CCE78 R671049; CLTP ("Ozark Jubilee"); PMUS
Horton, Walter 1917-1981 [singer; harmonica player, songwriter]
Big Walter *Source(s):* HARS
Note(s): See also Walter Travis Price & George Smith.
Horton, Shakey *Source(s):* HARS; LCAR
Mumbles *Source(s):* HARS; LCAR
Shakey Walter *Source(s):* HARS
Tangle Eye *Source(s):* HARS; LCAR
Horvath, Geza 1868-1925 [songwriter]
Note(s): Portrait: ETUP 52:9 (Sept. 1934): 506
Holzer, Julius *Source(s):* CCE48 R27820 ("Czardas Scene"); TPRF
Hoschke, Gerhard 1918- [composer]
Holger, Gerd *Source(s):* KOMS
Höslinger, Clemens 1933- [music critic, author]
Herbst, Christian *Source(s):* OMUO
Hostasch, Josef 1864-1943 [playwright, librettist]
Horst, Julius *Source(s):* GAN1; GAN2; LCAR; OMUO; PIPE; WORB
Hostetler, Lawrence A. 1903- [writer on dance]
Grant, Lawrence *Source(s):* LCAR
Note(s): Also used by Mary Elizabeth Clarke.
Stetler, Lawrence *Source(s):* LCAR
Hothby, John c.1410-1487 [writer on music, theorist, composer]
Note(s): See LCAR for additional variant forms of name.
Hobby, (Friar) John *Source(s):* GRV3
Octobi, Johannes *Source(s):* CCE64
Otobi, Giovanni *Source(s):* NGDM
Otteby, John *Source(s):* IBIM; WORB
Hotmann, Nicholas ?-1663 [bass violist, composer]
Otteman, Nicholas *Source(s):* NGDM
Hotteterre, Jacques(-Martin) 1674-1763 [teacher, composer, writer on music]
Romain, Le *Source(s):* GROL; NGDM; SADC
House, Eddie James, Jr. 1902- [guitarist, singer, songwriter]
House, Son *Source(s):* SHAB p. 108
Houston, Gilbert (Vandine) 1918-1961 [singer, songwriter]
Houston, Cisco *Source(s):* MCCL
Hovey, Nilo W(ellington) 1906-1986 [composer]
Dana, Leroy *Source(s):* CCE53; CCE55; LCAR; REHG
Hovsepian, Vanig (Rupen) 1918-2002 [composer, arranger, guitarist]
Van Lake, Turk *Source(s):* CCE59; LCAR; NGDJ; PSND
Howard, Ethel 1896-1977 [singer, actress, songwriter]
America's Foremost Ebony Comedienne *Source(s):* HARS
Baby Star *Source(s):* HARS; SIFA
Bronze Raquel Welch, The *Source(s):* PSND
Ebony Nora Bays, The *Source(s):* HARS
Jones, Mamie *Source(s):* HARS; SUTT
Original Dinah, The *Source(s):* HARS
Pryor, Martha *Source(s):* HARS
Note(s): Do not confuse with Martha Pryor, white vaudeville singer of 1920s.
Queen of the Blues, The *Source(s):* PSND
Note(s): See also: Ruth Lee Jones, Victoria [or Vicky] (Regina) Spivey, Sara(h) Dunn & Koko Taylor [i.e., Cora Walton]
Sweet Mama Stringbean *Source(s):* CASS; HARS
Tawny Yvete Guilbert, The *Source(s):* PSND
Waters, Ethel *Source(s):* CASS; GRAT; HARS
Howard, Harlan (Perry) 1929-2002 [songwriter]
Dean of Nashville Songwriters, The *Source(s):* DRSC
King of Country Singers, The *Source(s):* PSND
Mr. Songwriter *Source(s):* DRSC; http://www.harlanhoward.com/bmi.html (6 Oct. 2002)
Songwriter's Songwriter, The *Source(s):* MILL
Howard, Joseph E(dgar) 1878-1961 [singer, actor, songwriter]
Note(s): Death date sometimes given incorrectly as 1921 (STUW)
Great Howard, The *Source(s):* STUW
Howard, Ken 1939- [songwriter]
Blaikley, Howard *Source(s):* BLIC; CCE65 Efor108895
Note(s): Jt. pseud.: Alan Blaikley.
Howard, Robert [singer, songwriter, guitarist]
Dr. Robert *Source(s):* LCAR; NOMG
Robert, Dr. *Source(s):* LCAR; NOMG
Howarth, Elgar 1935- [composer, conductor, arranger, trumpeter]
Lear, W. Hogarth *Source(s):* GROL; MUWB; SUPN
Howarth, Ellen C(lementine) (née Doran) 1827-1899 [songwriter]
Enoch, Frederick *Source(s):* SPTH p. 596
Howe, Julia Ward 1819-1910 [writer, social reformer]
Note(s): Portraits: ETUP 52:9 (Sept. 1934): 506; HOWD
Lady, A. *Source(s):* CART ("Passion Flowers")
Note(s): Also used by Charlotte Elliott, Stephen Collins Foster & Ann Home.

Howell, Frederick Albert 1845-1886 [vocalist, songwriter]
Albert, Frederick *Source(s):* IBIM; WORB
Howell, Joshua Barnes 1888-1966 [singer, guitarist, songwriter]
Howell, Peg Leg *Source(s):* EPMU; HARS; LCAR
Howg, Kimberlee 1968- [singer, songwriter]
Lyle, Kami *Source(s):* EPMU
Howley, Patrick 1870-1918 [publisher]
Worth, George T. *Sources(s):* JAST
Note(s): Jt. pseud.: Frederick Benjamin Haviland.
Howson, E(dmund) W(hytehead) 1855-1905 [author, lyricist]
E. W. H. *Source(s):* CPMU (publication date 1897)
H(e)rdlicka, Bohdan 1840-1904 [librettist; playwright]
Taube, Theodore *Source(s):* GANA p. 531; KOMU; LCAR; STAD; STGR
Hrncirík, Peter 1939- [composer, conductor]
Ciri, Peter *Source(s):* OMUO
Hubay, Karl 1828-1885 [violinist, composer]
Huber, Karl *Source(s):* STGR; WORB
Hubbard, Gregg [guitarist, songwriter]
Hubbard, Hobie *Source(s):* STAC (see under: Brown, Sawyer)
Hubbard, Jerry (Reed) 1937- [singer, songwriter]
Alabama Wild Man, The *Source(s):* ALMN; FLIN; MCCL; PSND
Guitar Man, The *Source(s):* AMUS; MCCL
Mr. Guitar (Man) *Source(s):* FLIN; MCCL; PSND
Note(s): See also Chester [or Chet] (Burton) Atkins.
Reed, Jerry *Source(s):* ALMN; CASS; ENCM; EPMU; GAMM; HARR; LCAR; MCCL
Huber, Eugen 1858-1937 [violinist, composer]
Hubay, Jeno *Source(s):* PSND
Szalana, Hubay von *Source(s):* PSND
Huber, Hans 1852-1921 [composer]
Father of Swiss Music *Source(s):* WOSU (FM), Ohio State University (13 Sept. 2002)
Hubert, Stephen Fitch 1950-2005 [composer, guitarist]
Gray, Stephen Mark *Source(s):* DRSC
Sparks, Stevie *Source(s):* DRSC
Stevie Guitar *Source(s):* DRSC
Hucbald (of Saint Amand) c.840-930 [monk, theorist]
Hugbaldus *Source(s):* BAKE
Ubaldus *Source(s):* BAKE
Uchubaldus *Source(s):* BAKE
Hucknall, Mick 1960- [singer, songwriter]
Hucknall, Red *Source(s):* WARN
Hucko, Michael Andrew 1918-2003 [composer, clarinetist]
Hucko, Peanuts *Source(s):* ASCP; CCE73; LCAR
Hucks, William Richard, Jr. 1922- [composer, author, conductor]
Hughes, Dickson *Source(s):* ASCP; CCE63
Hudnall, Floris M. 1899?-1950 [composer, conductor]
Le Barron, Betty *Source(s):* PSND
Hudson, Saul 1965- [songwriter, guitarist]
Slash *Source(s):* AMUS; LCAR; PMUS-99
Hudspeth, William G(reg) [composer, author, singer]
Williams, Greg *Source(s):* ASCP; CCE67; CCE71
Hueffer, Francis 1843 (or 45)-1889 [music critic]
Note(s): Portrait: ETUP 52:10 (Oct. 1934): 570
Musical Critic, A *Source(s):* CART
Huerta, Baldemar G(arza) 1936 (or 37)- [singer, songwriter]
Bebop Kid, El *Source(s):* NGAM
Chicano Elvis Presley *Source(s):* NGAM
Fender, Fred(dy) [or Freddie] *Source(s):* AMUS; EPMU; HWOM; MCCL; NGAM; NOMG; PEN2
Little Bennie *Source(s):* HWOM; LCAR
Medina, Eddie *Source(s):* HWOM; LCAR
Wayne, Scotty *Source(s):* HWOM; LCAR
Huerter, Charles (Joseph) 1885-1974 [composer]
Note(s): Portrait: ETUP 52:10 (Oct. 1934): 570
Harles, C. *Source(s):* ETUD; TPRF
Huessman, Roelof [or Rudolf] 1442 (or 43)-1485 [lutenist, composer, philosopher]
Agricola, Rodolphus *Source(s):* GRV3; LCAR; WORB
Father of German Humanism *Source(s):* LCAR
Hueston, Billy 1896-1957 [composer, author, publisher]
Morgan, Bruce *Source(s):* ASCP
Huff, Leon 1942- [songwriter]
Gamble and Huff *Source(s):* LCAR (see note); NGAM
Note(s): Jt. pseud.: Kenneth [or Kenny] Gamble.
McGriff, Ralston *Source(s):* CCE64
Hughes, Arthur W(ellesley) 1870-c.1950 [composer]
Arthurs, H. W. *Source(s):* CANE; SMIN
Gilson, O. A. *Source(s):* SMIN; SUPN
Note(s): Used the name of the director of the Robbins Brothers Circus Band on "Robbins Brothers Triumphal March" (SMIN).
Wellesley, Arthur *Source(s):* CANE; CCE28 R45107; SMIN
Hughes, Capt. (of Vicksburg) [composer]
Signiago, J. Augustine *Source(s):* Root, Deane L. *American Popular Stage Music*. Ann Arbor: UMI Research Press, 1981, 209.
Hughes, Everette I(shmael) 1908 (or 09)-1995 [songwriter, singer, fiddler]
Hughes, Billy *Source(s):* CCE43 #4728 Eunp323619; ENCM

Hughes, Humphrey Vaughan 1889-1974 [musicologist, historian]
Hughes, Anselm *Source(s):* CPMU; NGDM
Hughes, John Ceiriog 1832-1887 [poet, librettist, folk musicologist]
Ceiriog *Source(s):* KILG; ROOM; WILG
Hughes, Patrick Cairns 1908-1987 [critic, composer, conductor, writer on music]
Cairns, Paddy *Source(s):* CCE55
Hughes, Spike *Source(s):* CCE55; CPMU; EPMU; GROL; LCAR; NGDM; PEN2; PSND
Mike *Source(s):* GROL; PSND; WHIC
Note(s): Used on reviews in *Melody Maker.*
Hughes, Philippa Swinnerton 1824-1917 [composer]
P. S. H. *Source(s):* CPMU
Hughes, Robert J(ames) 1916-1999 [composer, author, conductor]
Denton, James *Source(s):* ASCP; CCE54; CCE64-65; LCAR
Johnson, John *Source(s):* ASCP; LCAR
Maffatt, James *Source(s):* ASCP; LCAR
Moffatt, James *Source(s):* CCE67-68
Hughes, Russell Meriwether 1898-c.1980? [dancer, writer on dance]
La Meri *Source(s):* PIPE; PSND
Meri, La *Source(s):* PIPE; PSND
Hugo, Prinz zu Hohenohe-Õhringen 1816-1897 [composer]
Siebeneicher *Source(s):* WIEC
Hugo, Volker 1954- [composer]
Checker, Tex *Source(s):* KOMS; PFSA
Hull, Dorothy Spafard 1924- [composer, teacher, pianist]
Danzig, Dorothy *Source(s):* ASCP
Hullah, John Pyke 1812-1884 [organist, musicologist, composer]
Note(s): Portraits: CYBH; ETUP 52:10 (Oct. 1934): 570
I. H. *Source(s):* CART
J. H. *Source(s):* CART
Organist to the Fraternity, The *Source(s):* CART
Hüller, Johann Adam 1728-1804 [composer]
Hiller, Johann Adam *Source(s):* BALT; GRV3
Hulme, Ronald 1933- [composer]
Hamilton, Russ *Source(s):* BLIC; CCE61-62; CPOL RE-256-296; EPMU
Hume, Oscar Carl 1891-1957 [composer]
Karp, Karl *Source(s):* CCE24 E589818; PSND
Hume, Paul (Chandler) 1915-2001 [music critic]
Note(s): Portrait: GRAN
Eight-Ulcer on a Four-Ulcer Job (or Pay), An *Source(s):* GRAN; SIFA
Humfeld, Charles fl. 1910 [composer]
Humpy *Source(s):* JASN
Musical Architect, The *Source(s):* JASN
Hummel, Bertold 1925- [composer]
Martin, Nico *Source(s):* RIES
Hummel, Johann Nepomuk 1778-1837 [pianist, composer]
Ehrenmitglied der Gesellschaft *Source(s):* APPL p. 10
Hummel, Silas Early 1861-1931 [composer]
Oldsi *Source(s):* SMIN
Humperdinck, Engelbert 1854-1921 [composer]
Modern Wagner, The *Source(s):* PSND; SIFA
Humphreys, Henry S(igurd) 1909- [composer, editor, arranger]
Rauscher, Enrico *Source(s):* CCE53; CCE57-58; LCAR
Rauscher, Henry (Humphreys) *Source(s):* CCE64; GOTT; LCAR; MELL
Rauscher, Henry (Sigurd) *Source(s):* CCE58-59
Rauscher, Sigurd *Source(s):* CCE33 E37981; CCE58-59
Humphries, (John) Barry 1934- [author]
Everage, (Dame) Edna *Source(s):* CPMU; LCAR
Hundertmark, Lothar 1902-1985 [composer]
Lothar, Mark *Source(s):* NGDO; PIPE
Huneker, James Gibbons 1857-1921 [journalist, author, music critic]
Note(s): Portraits: ETUP 52:2 (Feb. 1934): 73; ETUP 52:10 (Oct. 1934): 570; GRAN
Bolshevik of the Bozart *Source(s):* GRAN
Critic of the Seven Arts *Source(s):* Schwab, A. T. *James Gibbons Huneker: Critic of the Seven Arts.* Stanford, 1963.
Garrulous Steeplejack of the Arts *Source(s):* GRAN p. 105
Gilded Age Gadfly *Source(s):* GRAN p. 105
Greatest of American Critics *Source(s):* GRAN p. 125
Lucullan Raconteur, The *Source(s):* GRAN p. 115
Melomaniac, The *Source(s):* GRAN
Old Fogy *Source(s):* BAKE; GRAN p. 109
Pianist manqué, pianophile non pareil *Source(s):* GRAN p. 111
Raconteur, The *Source(s):* GRAN p. 118
Steeplejack (of the Arts) *Source(s):* GRAN p. 105
Hungerford, Bruce 1922-1977 [pianist, photographer, archeologist]
Hungerford, Leonard *Source(s):* BAKE
Hunkemöller, Paul 1939- [composer]
Nuh, Rello Mek *Source(s):* KOMS; PFSA
Hunold, Christian Friedrich 1680 (or 81)-1721 [writer, poet, librettist]
Menantes *Source(s):* GROL; LCAR; LOWN; NGDM; PIPE; RIEM; SADC; SONN

Hunsecker, Ralph Uriah 1914-1995 [composer, author, singer]
Blane, Ralph *Source(s):* CCE62; CPOL RE-629-470; GAMM; STUW; VACH
Hunt, G(eorge) W(illiam) 1839?-1904 [organist, pianist, songwriter]
Hunt, Jingo *Source(s):* GARR; KILG p. [386]
Kipling of the Halls *Source(s):* http://www.incunabulabooks.com/ibrfathh.htm (15 Apr. 2005)
Mark Twain of the Music Halls, The *Source(s):* GARR
Hunt, Hubert Walter 1865-1945 [organist; arranger]
H. W. H. *Source(s):* CPMU
Hunt, James Henry Leigh 1784-1859 [author, poet]
Note(s): See PSND for additional nonmusic-related pseudonyms.
Brown, Harry *Source(s):* GOTE
Hunt, Vanzula Carter 1909- [composer, singer]
Hunt, Van *Source(s):* PSNN
Hunter, Alberta 1895-1984 [singer, songwriter]
Alix, May *Source(s):* EPMU; GROL; HARS; JASZ p. 271; MACE
Note(s): Also was used by 1. (Liza) May [or Mae] Alix (c.1902-), singer, aka "The Queen of the Night Clubs;" 2. Edna Hicks [i.e., Edna Landreaux] (see under Landreaux); and 3. singer Edmonia Henderson (1895-1924), aka "Ethel Clark" & "Babe Johnson." (SUTT)
America's Foremost Brown Blues Singer *Source(s):* HARS
Beatty, Josephine *Source(s):* EPMU; GROL; HARS; JASZ p. 271, LCAR; MACE
Note(s): Also used by Eva Taylor.
Marian Anderson of the Blues *Source(s):* HARS
Prime, Alberta *Source(s):* MARE
Roberts, Helen *Source(s):* HARS; JASZ p. 271
Hunter, Florence M. L. [songwriter]
F. M. L. H. *Source(s):* CPMU (publication date 1921)
Hunter, James George 1918-1996 [composer, pianist, singer]
Rowles, James [or Jimmy] (George) *Source(s):* PEN2; ROOM
Hunter, Jason [songwriter, performer]
Deck *Source(s):* LCAR
Fifth Brother *Source(s):* LCAR
Fingers, Rollie *Source(s):* AMUS
Inspectah Deck *Source(s):* AMIR; AMUS; LCAR; PMUS-00
Rebel-INS *Source(s):* AMUS; LCAR
Rollie Fingers *Source(s):* AMUS
Hunter, Joseph [or Joe] 1914-1974 [singer, songwriter, pianist, record producer]
Baron of the Boogie *Source(s):* SHAB p. 178
Hunter, Ivory Joe *Source(s):* CLAB; SHAB p. 178
Hupfauf, John Peregrin 1856-1889 [composer, teacher]
Peregrinus *Source(s):* OMUO
Note(s): Also used by Theodor Reuss.
Hupton, Job 1762-1849 [hymnist]
Note(s): All the following on contributions to *Gospel Magazine.*
A——y *Source(s):* JULN
Note(s): A——y = Ashby.
Ebenezer *Source(s):* JULN
Note(s): Also used by Richard Lee.
Eliakim *Source(s):* JULN
J. H——n *Source(s):* JULN
Hurtig, Jules 1867-1928 [songwriter]
Kendall, Don *Source(s):* CCE49 R54019-20
Note(s): Jt. pseud.: Theodore (F.) Morse. Also used by Walter Haenschen, James (Conrad) O'Keefe & Lester O'Keefe; see NOTES: Kendall, Don.
Hurvitz, Sandy (E.) [songwriter]
Mohawk, Essra *Source(s):* CCE75-76; DIMA
Hus-Desforges, Pierre Louis 1773-1838 [cellist, composer]
Desforges, Citoyen *Source(s):* BAKE
Jarowick *Source(s):* PSND
Husadel, Hans Felix 1897-1964 [composer, conductor]
Frankenstein, Lutz *Source(s):* GREN
Husch, R(ichard) G(erard) 1876-1948 [lyricist]
Gerard, Richard (H.) *Source(s):* LCAR; MRSQ å(7:3-4): 6; PSND; STUW
Husk, William Henry 1814-1887 [music scholar]
Sylvestre, Joshua *Source(s):* LCAR
Note(s): Joint pseud.: William Sandys.
Husky, Ferlin 1927- [singer, guitarist, songwriter]
Crum, Simon *Source(s):* AMUS; CCME; EPMU; MACE p. 331
Preston, Terry *Source(s):* AMUS; CCME; MACE p. 331; PEN2
Terry, Tex *Source(s):* http//www.ferlinhusky.com (20 Feb. 2007)
Husson, Alfred [songwriter]
Nossuh, Alfred *Source(s):* CPMU (publication date 1879)
Husson(-Fleury), Jules F(rançois) F(élix) 1821-1889 [writer on music]
Champfleury, Jules F(rançois) F(élix) *Source(s):* GROL; LCAR; PIPE
Fleury, Jules F(rançois) F(élix) *Source(s):* GROL; LCAR; PIPE
Hutcheson, Francis 1720 (or 21)-1784 [composer, violinist]
Ireland, Francis *Source(s):* BROW; GROL; IBIM; MACM; NGDM
Hutcheson, Ronita Marlene 1945- [composer, singer]
Bell, Roni *Source(s):* ASCP
Hutchinson, Leslie 1907- [songwriter]

Hall, Thomas *Source(s):* CCE52 Efor11249; CPOL RE-27-362
Note(s): Jt. pseud.: Norman [or Norrie] (William) Paramor.
Jones, Obadiah *Source(s):* CCE52 Efor11250; CPOL RE-27-362
Note(s): Jt. pseud.: Norman [or Norrie] (William) Paramor & Lew Jacobson.
Hutchison, (David) Warner 1930- [composer]
Hudson, Walter *Source(s):* ASCP; REHG; SUPN
Hutchison, William M(arshall) 1854-1933 [composer, publisher, songwriter]
Marshall, William *Source(s):* GANA; MUWB
Note(s): Name used for music publishing activities.
Meissler, Josef *Source(s):* BLIC; CPMU; GOTH
Mount, Julian *Source(s):* CPMU; GANA; GOTH; GOTT; MUWB
Saint Quentin, Edward *Source(s):* BLIC; STGR
Note(s): Possible pseudonym? Also used by Alfred William Rawlings. See NOTES: Saint Quentin, Edward.
Hutt, Samuel 1940- [singer, songwriter]
Wangford, Hank *Source(s):* WARN
Hutterstrasser, Karl 1863-1942 [composer, piano maker]
Verney, Charles *Source(s):* AEIO; STGR; WORB
Hutto, J(oseph) B(enjamin) 1926-1983 [singer, guitarist, songwriter]
Hawk, The *Source(s):* PSND
Note(s): See also Coleman (Randolph) Hawkins (see LCAR), Harold Franklin Hawkins & Jerry Lee Lewis.
Hyde, Abby Bradley 1799-1872 [hymnist]
Hyde *Source(s):* JULN
Hyman, Jeffrey 1951-2001 [singer, songwriter]
Ramone, Joey *Source(s):* WASH
Hyman, John Wigginton 1899-1977 [composer, conductor, cornetist]
Wiggs, Johnny *Source(s):* AMUS; CCE65; NGDJ; PSND
Hyman, Richard [or Dick] (R(oven)) 1927- [composer, pianist, arranger, conductor]
Note(s): Portraits: JASN; SHMM (Nov. 1984): 19
Charleston, Arthur *Source(s):* CCE58; CCE67; JASN
Chord, Rip *Source(s):* PERF; http://myweb.tiscali.co.uk/rbaldrock/light/index.html (18 May 2005)
Feldman, Tony *Source(s):* CCE58; CCE68
Gaines, J. *Source(s):* CCE58; JASN; JAST; JASZ
Gregory, Rod *Source(s):* JAMU; http://myweb.tiscali.co.uk/rbaldrock/light/index.html
Knox, Willie "The Rock" *Source(s):* JASN; PERF
Lowman, Richard *Source(s):* JAMU
O'Toole, Knuckles *Source(s):* JASN; PERF
Note(s): Also used by pianist William [or Billy] Rowland (c.1910-1985)
Phillips, Carter *Source(s):* CCE57-58
Roven, Richard *Source(s):* GROL
Ryan, Slugger *Source(s):* JASN; PERF
Schwartz, Jack *Source(s):* CCE58; CCE62; CCE68; JASN
Smith, Puddinhead *Source(s):* PERF; http://myweb.tiscali.co.uk/rbaldrock/light/index.html
Note(s): Also used by pianist William [or Billy] Rowland (c.1910-1985)
Willie the Rock *Source(s):* http://myweb.tiscali.co.uk/rbaldrock/light/index.html

– I –

Iannelli, Richard 1949- [author, playwright, songwriter]
Wagner, Denson *Source(s):* PSNN
Ibermann, Barry 1942- [songwriter, singer]
Note(s): Portrait: CM30
Mann, Barry *Source(s):* CCE57-59; CM30; PSND
Ibert, Jacques (François Antoine Marie) 1890-1962 [composer]
Note(s): Portrait: ETUP 52:11 (Nov. 1934): 634
Berty, William *Source(s):* GROL
Ibsen, Henrik (Johan) 1828-1906 [dramatist]
Note(s): See LCAR for variant forms of name.
Bjarme, Byrnjolf *Source(s):* PIPE; PSND
Father of Modern Drama, The *Source(s):* PSND
Ierace, Dominic 1943- [songwriter]
Iris, Don(nie) *Source(s):* KICK; NITE; PMUS
Iglesias, Enrique 1975- [singer, songwriter]
Martinez, Enrique *Source(s):* http://www.enriqueiglesias.com (6 Oct. 2002)
Iglesias, Julio 1943- [singer, songwriter]
New Valentino, The *Source(s):* Gott, Steve. *Julio Iglesias; The New Valentino.* Port Chester, NY: Cherry Lane Books, 1985. (ports.)
Spanish Frank Sinatra, The *Source(s):* PSND
Spanish Sinatra, The *Source(s):* PSND
Valentino of the 80's, The *Source(s):* PSND
Ignatius 1729-1780 [writer, composer]
God's Image Cut in Ebony *Source(s):* Hare, Maude (Cuney). *Negro Musicians and Their Music.* Washington D.C.: Associated Publishers, 1936. (Reprint: Da Capo, 1974)
Sancho, (Charles) Ignatius *Source(s):* LCAR; Hare (see above)
Ihlau, Fritz 1909-1995 [composer]
Langen, Fred *Source(s):* BUL3; KOMP; KOMS; PFSA; RIES; SUPN
Ihme, Hans-Friedrich 1940- [composer]
Haupt, Gerhard *Source(s):* KOMS; PFSA

Ijames, Mary Tunstall 1894-1963 [songwriter, actress]
Sunshine, Marion *Source(s):* ASCP; GRAT; LCAR; ROOM
Illing, Heinz 1920 (or 23)-1989 [composer]
Torsten, Peter *Source(s):* CCE53; KOMP
Tursten, Peter *Source(s):* PFSA
Illouz, Elizabeth 1926- [composer, teacher]
Jolas, Betsy *Source(s):* BAKO; BAKR; CPMU
Imhoff, Petrus 1470-1534 [composer]
Note(s): Probable name.
Alamire, Petrus *Source(s):* DOLM
Impey, Margaret [translator, arranger]
Mairead Na Clarsaich *Source(s):* BLIC; CPMU (publication date 1971)
Inabnett, Marvin 1938- [composer, author, singer]
Ingram, M(arvin) *Source(s):* ASCC; CCE60
Indy, (Paul Marie Théodore) Vincent d' 1851-1931 [composer, pianist]
Note(s): Portrait: ETUP 52:11 (Nov. 1934): 634
Stepfather of Dissonance *Source(s):* SLON
Inglis, Alexander Wood [composer]
Selva, Alessandro *Source(s):* CPMU (publication date 1878)
Inglis, Charlotte H. [hymnist]
C. H. I. *Source(s):* JULN
Inglis, Robert 1913- [composer, conductor]
Inglez, Roberto *Source(s):* LCAR; MUSR
Ingoldsby, Richard 1788-1845 [poet]
Barham, Thomas *Source(s):* LAST
Inkermann, (C.) Otto 1821-1862 [author, playwright]
Sternau, C. O. *Source(s):* PIPE; WORB
Insanguine, Giacomo (Antonio Francesco Paolo Michele) 1728-1795 [composer, teacher]
Monopoli, (Giacomo) *Source(s):* BAKR; MACM; LCAR; NGDM; NGDO; SONN; STGR
Instone, Anthony (Gordon) 1944- [composer, producer]
Macaulay, Tony *Source(s):* EPMU; HARD; HARR
Iraschek, Ronald Frederic 1956- [composer, author]
Rocket, Ronnie *Source(s):* OMUO
Urini, Ron *Source(s):* OMUO
Ireland, John (Nicholson) 1879-1962 [composer]
Note(s): Portraits: MUOP 45:539 (Aug. 1922); *The Music Teacher* 14:8 (June 1922): 465+
Royce, Turlay *Source(s):* CCE38 R69754; MUWB; Craggs, Stewart. *John Ireland*. Oxford: Clarendon Press, 1993, 24+.
Ireson, John Balfour 1937- [composer, singer]
Balfour, John *Source(s):* CCE65
Wilder, John *Source(s):* ASCP
Iriarte, Tomás (de) 1750-1791 [poet, dramatist]
Cisneros, Francisco Augustí de *Source(s):* LCAR
Imareta, Tirso *Source(s):* DEA3

Irving, Michael Clement 1937- [composer, arranger]
Gibbs, Mike *Source(s):* EPMU; GAMM; ROOM
Irving, Washington 1783-1859 [author]
Note(s): See PSND & LCAR for additional nonmusic-related pseuds. & sobriquets.
Agapida, Antonio *Source(s):* LCAR; PIPE
Crayon, Geoffrey *Source(s):* LCAR; PIPE; PSND
Father of American Literature *Source(s):* PSND; ROOM p. 27
Handiside, Mr. *Source(s):* ROOM p. 27
Knickerbocker, Diedrich *Source(s):* LCAR; PIPE; PSND; ROOM p. 27
Oldstyle, Jonathan *Source(s):* PIPE; PSND; ROOM p. 27
Irwin, Robin Lee 1953- [singer, songwriter]
Lee, Robin *Source(s):* MCCL
Isaac, Heinrich c.1450-1517 [composer]
Note(s): For additional variant forms, see LCAR.
Arrighus *Source(s):* BAKE
Arrigo d'Ugo *Source(s):* NGDM
Arrigo il Tedesco *Source(s):* NGDM
Arrigo, Tedesco *Source(s):* BAKE; LCAR
Belga, Heinricus Isaac *Source(s):* LCAR
Brabantius, Henricus Isaac *Source(s):* LCAR
Isaac, Merle (John) 1898-1996 [composer, arranger]
Leland, Robert *Source(s):* CCE45 #8594 E128792
Merle, J(ohn) *Source(s):* ASCP; CCE66; REHG; SUPN
Monroe, Margrethe *Source(s):* CCE39 #23239 E78657; CCE66
Pulaski, John *Source(s):* CCE45 #10931 E128789
Suranov, Alex *Source(s):* CCE45 #11730 E128790
Isaacs, Al(vin) K(aleolani) 1904-1984 [composer, author, singer]
Kaleolani, Al(vin) *Source(s):* ASCP; CCE68; CCE74
Isaacs, Claude Reese 1901-1953 [composer, author, teacher]
Reese, Claude *Source(s):* ASCP (see reference); CCE50-54
Isaacs, Rufus [composer]
Essex, Kenneth *Source(s):* GALM; RFSO
Dwyer, Derek *Source(s):* GALM; RFSO
Hale, Howitt *Source(s):* GALM; RFSO
Vane, Claude *Source(s):* GALM; RFSO
Isham, John c.1680-1726 [organist, composer]
Isum, John *Source(s):* GRV3; IBIM; WORB
Ishitsuji, Keiichi 1927- [composer]
Kawabe, Koichi *Sources(s):* SUPN
Iskowitz, Edward Israel 1892-1964 [singer, actor, author, lyricist]
Note(s): Portrait: LYMN
Banjo Eyes *Source(s):* EPMU; PEN2; PSND
Cantor, Eddie *Source(s):* EPMU; GAMM; KINK; LCAR; PEN2; PSND
Iskowitz, Iss *Source(s):* PSND

Itzkowitz, Isidore Israel *Source(s):* GAMM; GAN2; LCAR; LYMN; PEN2
Kanter, Isidore *Source(s):* LYMN
Isouard, Nicolas 1775-1818 [composer]
Note(s): Portrait: ETUP 52:11 (Nov. 1934): 634
N*** *Source(s):* CPMU ("Ce front si pur aù regne la décence")
Note(s): Jt. pseud.: Etienne Nicolas Méhul, François Adrien Boieldieu & Rodolphe Kreutzer.
Nicolò (de Malte) *Source(s):* BAKR; GROL; MACM; MELL; NGDM
Israel, Isaac ?-1987 [composer, conductor]
Searelle, (W(illiam)) Luscombe *Source(s):* GANA p. 202; MUWB; WORB
Ivanov, Mikhail Mikhailovich 1859-1935 [composer, conductor, teacher]
Note(s): Portrait: ETUP 52:11 (Nov. 1934): 634
Ippolitov-Ivanov, Mikhail Mikhailovich *Source(s):* BAKO; BAKR; NGDO
Note(s): Name altered to distinguish from Michael Ivanov (1849-1927), music critic.
People's Artist of the Republic *Source(s):* BAKR; PSND (see under: Ippolitov-Ivanov)
Ivanovich, Cristoforo 1628-1689 [librettist, theatre chronicler]
Sirena, Urbano *Source(s):* ALMC
Ives, Burl(e Icle Ivanhoe) 1909-1995 [arranger, folksinger]
Ivanhoe, Burl Icle *Source(s):* LCAR
McGehen, Ken *Source(s):* CCE56 Eunp; CCE64
Note(s): Also used by Helen Swann.
Renaissance Man *Source(s):* MUHF
Ives, Charles Edward 1874-1954 [composer]
American Father of Musical Modernism *Source(s):* http://www.usc.edu/dept/polish_music_PMJ/issue/4.1.01/paderewskipoems.html (6 Oct. 2002)
America's Greatest Composer *Source(s):* http://www.geometry.net/composers/ives_charles.php (6 Oct. 2002)
Note(s): See also Leonard [i.e., Louis] Bernstein, George Gershwin [i.e., Jacob Gershvin] & Charles Puerner.
Danbury's Most Famous Composer *Source(s):* http://www.geometry.net/composers/ives_charles.php (6 Oct. 2002)
Father of American Music *Source(s):* http://www.housatonic.org/ives.html (30 Oct. 2002)
Note(s): See also William Billings & Benjamin Carr.
Most Original Composer of 20th Century Music, The *Source(s):* PSND
Thomas Jefferson and Abraham Lincoln of American Music *Source(s):* DESO-7
Ivey, Artis Leon, Jr. 1963- [singer, songwriter]
Coolio *Source(s):* LCAR; NOMG
Ivry, Paul Xavier Désiré, marquis d' 1829-1903 [composer]
Ivry, Richard, marquis d' *Source(s):* LCAR
Yrvid, Richard *Source(s):* GOTH; IBIM; LCAR; PRAT
Iwaszkiewicz, Jaroslaw 1894-1979 (or 80) [author]
Eleuter *Source(s):* LCAR; PIPE; WORB
Iza Zamácola, Juan Antonio 1756-1826 [folklorist, historian]
Don Preciso *Source(s):* LCAR; WORB
Preciso, Don *Source(s):* GROL; LCAR
Zamácola, Juan Antonio *Source(s):* LCAR

–J –

Jackson, Alan (Eugene) 1958- [singer, songwriter]
Country Music's New Heartthrob *Source(s):* CM07
Jackson, Charlie ?-1938 [singer, guitarist, songwriter]
Note(s): Do not confuse with Charlie Jackson, guitarist with Tiny Parham Band.
Carter, Charlie *Source(s):* HARS
Jackson, Papa Charlie *Source(s):* LCAR
Jackson, Frankie 1893 (or 95)- [singer, composer, comedian]
Cotton Thomas *Source(s):* LCAR
Jaxon, Frankie *Source(s):* NGDJ
Jaxon, Half Pint *Source(s):* HARS; KINK; NGDJ
Jaxson, Frankie *Source(s):* NGDJ
Thomas, Cotton *Source(s):* KINK; SUTT
Jackson, George Pullen 1874-1953 [musicologist, songwriter]
Black Giant of White Spirituals, The *Source(s):* PSND; SIFA
Jackson, Judge *Source(s):* PSND; SIFA
Jackson, Greig Stewart 1918-2003 [bassist, songwriter]
Jackson, Chubby *Source(s):* ASCP; KINK; LCAR; NGDJ
Jackson, Henry R(ootes) 1820-1898 [songwriter]
Jackson, General "Stonewall" *Source(s):* HOGR ("My Wife and Child")
Note(s): Erroneously attributed to General T. J. Jackson.
Jackson, Stoney *Source(s):* CCE64
Jackson, Jane 1834-1907 [pianist, composer]
Note(s): Married name: Roeckel, (Mrs.) Joseph Leopold.
DeSivrai, Jules *Source(s):* BROW; COHN; CPMU; HIXN
Sivrai, Jules de *Source(s):* GOTH; WORB
Jackson, Jerome Louis 1942- [singer, songwriter]
Jackson, J. J. *Source(s):* NOMG

Jackson, Kevin Anthony 1967- [singer, songwriter]
Sanchez *Source(s):* CM38; LCAR
Jackson, Melvin 1915-1976 [singer, guitarist, songwriter]
Jackson, Lil' Son *Source(s):* AMUS; HARS; LCAR
Jackson, Little Son *Source(s):* LCAR
Jackson, Michael Joseph 1958- [singer, songwriter, producer]
Bray, Bill *Source(s):* PSND
Jacko *Source(s):* PSND
King of Pop *Source(s):* CM17
King of Rock and Pop, The *Source(s):* http://www.bbc.co.uk/dna/h2g2/A537662 (12 Mar. 2005)
Little Prince of Soul, The *Source(s):* PSND
Peter Pan of Pop, The *Source(s):* PSND
Jackson, Milt(on) 1923-1999 [vibraphonist, composer]
Bags *Source(s):* CASS; NGAM; NGDM; OB99
Brother Soul *Source(s):* JAMU; http://www.jazzcanadiana.on.ca/trivia1a.htm (5 Nov. 2002)
Jackson, Bags *Source(s):* LCAR
Jackson, O'Shea 1969- [songwriter]
Ice Cube *Source(s):* LCAR; PMUS-97; PMUS-00
Jackson, Thomas Gregory 1947- [singer, songwriter]
James, Tommy *Source(s):* HARR; NOMG
Jackson, Wanda (Lavonne) 1937- [singer, songwriter, guitarist]
Favorite Female Country Music Singer (of Scandinavia) *Source(s):* MCCL
Queen of Rock 'n' Roll *Source(s):* MCCL
Jackson, Warren George Harding Lee 1907- [singer, guitarist, songwriter]
Jackson, Lee *Source(s):* HARS
Lee, Warren *Source(s):* HARS
Jackson, William 1730-1803 [composer]
Jackson of Exeter *Source(s):* CART; NGDO; PSND
Nettle, H(umphrey) *Source(s):* CART; PSND
Jackson, William 1815- [organist, conductor, composer]
Jackson of Masham *Source(s):* GRV2
Jackson, William Henry [composer]
Nosjack *Source(s):* CPMU (publication date 1904)
Jackson, Willis 1932-1987 [saxophonist, composer]
Jackson, Gator(tail) *Source(s):* LCAR; PEN2; MUWB
Jacob, Nath. 1835-1916 [librettist]
Anders, N. J. *Source(s):* STGR
Jacobs, Al(bert) T. 1903- [composer, author]
Gabril, Mercedes *Source(s):* ASCP; REHG
Jackson, Tex *Source(s):* CCE75 R600892
Jacobs, James Henry [composer]
Henri, Jacques *Source(s):* CPMU
Jacobs, Manuel [writer on music]
Terpander *Sources:* http://www.musicweb.uk.net/rawsth/turner.htm (30 Sept. 2003)
Jacobs, Marion Walter 1930-1968 [singer, guitarist, songwriter]
Jacobs, Little Walter *Source(s):* LCAR
Little Walter (J.) *Source(s):* HARS; LCAR
Note(s): Also used by singer Walter J. Westbrook.
Jacobs, William B. 1941- [composer, author, actor]
Gerard, Will *Source(s):* ASCP
Note(s): Do not confuse with William Gerrard, pseud. of Jerry H(anchrow) Bilik.
Jacobsen, Colin 1937- [singer, songwriter, music publisher]
Joye, Col *Source(s):* CCE59; EPMU; ROOM
Jacobson, Lew 1911- [songwriter]
Jones, Obadiah *Source(s):* CCE52 Efor11250
Note(s): Jt. pseud.: Norman [or Norrie] (William) Paramor & Leslie Hutchinson.
Jacobson, Maurice 1896-1976 [composer, publisher]
Bateson, John *Source(s):* CCE59; CCE61; GOTE; GOTH; GOTT
Jacoby, Heinrich 1909-1990 [composer, violist, conductor]
Jacoby, Hanoch *Source(s):* BUL2; CCE54
Jacopone da Todi c.1230-1306 [hymnist]
Jacopo Benedicti *Source(s):* CYBH
Jacquot, Charles Jean Baptiste 1812-1880 [writer on music]
Kervan, Armal de *Source(s):* LCAR
Mirecourt, Eugène de *Source(s):* PIPE; SEND
Jadassohn, Salomon 1831-1902 [teacher, theorist, composer]
Lübenau, L. *Source(s):* MACM
Jaeggi, Stephen 1903-1957 [bandmaster, teacher, composer]
Band King of Switzerland *Source(s):* SMIN
Jaëll, Alfred 1832-1882 [pianist, composer]
Pianiste voyageur, Le *Source(s):* BAKE
Jaffé, Moritz 1834-1925 [composer]
Morja, (B.) *Source(s):* MELL; SEND
Jagelka, Charles 1923-1997 [guitarist, composer]
Wayne, Charles *Source(s):* KINK
Wayne, Chuck *Source(s):* LCAR
Jäger, Raimund 1961- [composer, lyricist]
Tschacko *Source(s):* OMUO
Jagermeier, Otto [fictitious composer]
Source(s): GROL
Jagger, Michael Philip 1943- [singer, songwriter, guitarist]
Jagger, Mick *Source(s):* PSND
Phelge, Nanker *Source(s):* PSND
Note(s): Jt. pseud.: Keith Richards.
Jahn, Fritz 1914-1988 [composer]
Jay, Fred *Source(s):* PFSA

Jahnen, Gerd [or Gerhard] 1920- [composer]
Parker, Charles *Source(s):* CCE60; KOMP; KOMS; PSFA
Note(s): Do not confuse with Charles [or Charlie] Parker (1920-1955).
Jakabfi, Viktor 1883-1921 [composer]
Jacobi, Viktor *Source(s):* GAN2
Jakobovits [or Jacobowicz], Béla 1871-1943 [librettist, lyricist]
Jenbach, Béla *Source(s):* GAN1; GAN2; LCAR; OMUO; WORB
Jallais, Amédée (Jean Baptiste Font-Réaux) de 1888-1965 (or 66) [author, literary critic]
Réaux, Jean de *Source(s):* LCAR; PIPE
James, Arthur Keedwell Harvey 1875-1917 [playwright, author]
Craven, Arthur Scott *Source(s):* PIPE; WORB
James, Cheryl 1969- [songwriter]
Salt *Source(s):* EPMU; PMUS-96; RECR
James, Ian (Ellis) 1952- [composer, producer]
Black, William Electric *Source(s):* CCE78; GOTH; LCAR
James, J. [composer]
Gwenynen Arfon *Source(s):* CPMU (publication date 1911)
James, James 1833-1902 [composer]
Iago ap Ieuan *Source(s):* LCAR; ROOM
James, Mary D(agworthy) 1810-1883 [hymnist]
Aaron of the 19th-century Wesleyan/Holiness Movement *Source(s):* http://www.messiah.edu/WHWC/satisfd.htm (6 Oct. 2002)
James, Nehemiah (Curtis) 1902-1969 [singer, songwriter, guitarist, pianist]
James, Skip *Source(s):* AMUS; EPMU; HARR; HARS; HERZ; MUFH; PSND
James, Richard D(avid) 1971 (or 72)- [composer, disc jockey]
AFX *Source(s):* CM14; GROL
Aphex Twin *Source(s):* AMUS; CM14; EPMU; GROL; LCAR
Blue Calx *Source(s):* GROL
Caustic Window *Source(s):* CM14; GROL
Dice Man *Source(s):* GROL
Midi Circus' Trapeze Artist, The *Source(s):* CM14
Polygon Window *Source(s):* EPMU; GROL
Power-Pill *Source(s):* GROL
Q-Chastic *Source(s):* GROL
Soit-P. P. *Source(s):* GROL
James, Sylvester 1946 (or 47)-1988 [singer, arranger]
Blue, Ruby *Source(s):* EPMU
Sylvester *Source(s):* EPMU; LCAR
Jameson, Robert 1947- [composer]
James, Bobby *Source(s):* CCE63
Note(s): Possible pseud.
Jamgochian, Robert *Source(s):* ASCP; CCE75
Jameson, Stephen 1949- [singer, songwriter]
Javells *Source(s):* EPMU
King, Nosmo *Source(s):* EPMU
Note(s): Also used by Samuel Vernon Watson.
Jan, Hermann Ludwig 1851-1908 [writer on music, novelist]
Hermann, Ludwig *Source(s):* WORB
Janeczek, Johannes Ludwig 1879-1955 [author, journalist, librettist]
Johannes, Ludwig *Source(s):* OMUO
Janiczek, Julius 1887-1956 [teacher, editor of folksong collections]
Hensel, Walther *Source(s):* BAKT; MACM; RIEM
Janke, Zikmund 1865-1918 [author]
Dvorský, Z. *Source(s):* PIPE
Janovický, Karel 1930- [composer]
Simsa, B. *Source(s):* BUL2
Jansen, Kurt 1918- [composer]
Tonius, Ralph *Source(s):* KOMS; PFSA
Janson, Hugh Michael 1936-2000 [composer, pianist]
Janson, Spike *Source(s):* ASCP
Janssen, Jacobus Hubertus Maria 1930- [composer]
Jaroc *Source(s):* SUPN
Jarczyk, Herbert 1913-1968 [composer]
Jerkins, Joe *Source(s):* KOMP; KOMS; PFSA
Jarczyk, Maximilian (Michael) Andreas 1906-1988 [composer, music publisher]
Jantzen, Max *Source(s):* PIPE; http://www.cyranos.ch/smjary-e.htm (25 Apr. 2005)
Janzen, Max *Source(s):* KOMP; KOMS; PFSA
Jary, Michael *Source(s):* CCE51-59; KOMP; KOMS; PFSA; PIPE; RIES
Leeds, Jacky [or Jackie] *Source(s):* KOMP; KOMS; PFSA; PIPE
Jarnowick, Giovanni Mane 1745-1804 [violinist, composer]
Giornovichi, Giovanni Mane *Source(s):* BAKE; BAKR; LCAR
Jarre, Jean Michel (Andre) 1948- [composer]
Godfather of Techno, The *Source(s):* http://www.library.tudelft.nl/~blouw/interv/jarre/jarre1.html (6 Oct. 2002)
Jaxtheimer, Gerald 1959- [composer]
Schaller, Werner *Source(s):* KOMS; PFSA
Jay, Harriet 1863-1932 [actress, dramatist]
Marlowe, Charles *Source(s):* GANB; LCAR
Note(s): Author of: *Strange Adventures of Miss Brown.* Also used by Charles A Margulis.
Jaycock, Alan [composer]
Clare, Alan *Source(s):* MUWB
Jedlitzková, Maria 1887-1982 [singer, author]
Jeritza, Maria *Source(s):* BAKR; WORB
Jefferson, Clarence 1897-1929 (or 30) [guitarist, singer, songwriter]

Bates, (Deacon) L. J. *Source(s):* HARS; SUTT
Blind Lemon *Source(s):* HARS; LCAR
Brown, Elder J. C. *Source(s):* HARS
Jefferson, Blind Lemon *Source(s):* CASS; EPMU; HARS
Jefferson, Lemon *Source(s):* HARS

Jeffrey, Alan [actor, writer, songwriter]
Thicke, Alan *Source(s):* NOMG

Jeffries, Herb(ert Jeffrey) 1916 (or 17)- [singer, actor, songwriter]
Bronze Buckaroo, The *Source(s):* PSND

Jehin, François 1839-1899 [violinist, composer]
Jehin-Prume *Source(s):* BAKE

Jelinek, Hanuš [or Johann] 1901-1969 [composer, teacher]
Elin, Hanns *Source(s):* CCE58; GROL; KOMU; LCAR; NGDM; PIPE

Jelínek, Hanu? 1878-1944 [author, literary historian]
Otakar, Jean *Source(s):* PIPE

Jellinek, George 1919- [writer on music, radio announcer]
Note(s): Portrait: http://www.wned.org/radio/fm/default.asp (6 Oct. 2002)
Mr. Opera *Source(s):* http://www.wned.org/radio/fm/default.asp
Summertime's "Mr. Opera" *Source(s):* http://www.wned.org/radio/fm/default.asp

Jenkins, Bill 1956- [guitarist, singer, composer, bandleader]
Dennis the Menace of Jazz, The *Source(s):* PEN2

Jenkins, David 1848-1915 [critic, composer]
Kaiser of the Cymanfa, The *Source(s):* WILG

Jenkins, Gus 1931-1985 [singer, pianist, songwriter]
Jinkins, Gus *Source(s):* HARS
Little Temple *Source(s):* HARS
Pharoah, Jaarone *Source(s):* HARS
Young Wolf, The *Source(s):* HARS

Jenkins, Harold (Lloyd) 1933-1993 [singer, songwriter, guitarist]
Best Friend a Song Ever Had, The *Source(s):* MCCL
Great Man of Country Music *Source(s):* MCCL
Hatako-Chtokchito-A-Yakni-Toloa *Source(s):* MCCL
Note(s): Honorary Choctaw chief title.
High Priest *Source(s):* ALMN; FLIN; PSND
High Priest of Country Music, The *Source(s):* ALMN; FLIN; PSND
Twitty, Conway *Source(s):* AMUS; BAKR; CM06; EPMU; FLIN; LCAR; MCCL; NGAM

Jenkins, John 1770-1829 [musicologist]
Ifor Ceri *Source(s):* ROOM

Jenkins, John P(ickens) 1916-1984 [singer, guitarist, songwriter]
Jenkins, Bobo *Source(s):* CCE54; HARS; LCAR

Jenkins, Louis 1947- [composer, author]
Jenkins, Woody *Source(s):* ASCP

Jennens, Charles 1700-1773 [author, librettist]
Soliman the Magnificant *Source(s):* PSND

Jenney, Truman Elliott 1910-1945 [trombonist, composer, bandleader]
Jenney, Jack *Source(s):* CLRA; KINK; LCAR

Jennings, Waylon [actually Wayland] (Arnold) 1937-2002 [singer, songwriter]
Jennings, Hoss *Source(s):* MCCL
Man Called Hoss, A *Source(s):* EPMU
Outlaw, The *Source(s):* CCME; PSND

Jenny, Marie-Cécile 1923- [violinist, conductor, composer]
Jenny, (Sister) Leonore *Source(s):* COHN; HEIN; HIXN
Lopwegen, Benedikt *Source(s):* COHN; HEIN; HIXN

Jensen, Harry 1911-1980 [composer]
Berg, Gøsta *Source(s):* CCE47; CCE64; http://www.mic.dk/music/compidx.htm (6 Oct. 2003)
Ulrik, Sven *Source(s):* CCE64; GOTH; http://www.mic.dk/music/compidx.htm

Jenssen, Geir [composer]
Biosphere *Source(s):* http://www.grove.nl/cd/4/49883.html (6 Oct. 2002)
Bleep *Source(s):* http://www.grove.nl/cd/4/49883.html

Jepps, Dudley [composer]
Powell, Dudley *Source(s):* GANA

Jerger, Alois 1889-1976 [composer]
Jerger, Alfred *Source(s):* OMUO

Jerningham, Charles Edward Wynne 1854-1921 [author, composer]
Marmaduke *Source(s):* CART

Jeschke, Ernst 1892 (or 95)-1962 [singer, composer, lyricist]
Arnold, Ernest *Source(s):* AEIO; DOLM; OMUO; STAD

Jessye, Eva Alberta 1895-1992 [composer, poet, journalist]
Note(s): Portrait: ETUP 5:12 (Dec. 1934): 698
Dr. of Determination *Source(s):* PSND

Jesus Maria, Carlos de 1713-1747 [composer]
Maia Croesser, Luís da *Source(s):* LCAR

Jewell, Fred(erick Alton) 1875-1936 [composer, conductor, publisher]
Wells, J. E. *Source(s):* LCAR; MCBD; NGAM; REHG; SMIN

Jhan c.1485-1538 [composer]
Maistre Jahn *Source(s):* GROL

Jiménez, Leonardo 1939- [accordionist, songwriter]
Flaco, El *Source(s):* EPMU
Jiménez, Flaco *Source(s):* EPMU; LCAR; PEN2

Jiménez Salazar, Diego 1968- [singer, songwriter]
Cigala *Source(s):* HWOM
Diego el Cigala *Source(s):* HWOM; LCAR
Dieguito (el Cigala) *Source(s):* HWOM; LCAR

Jirasek, Franz Josef 1875- [journalist, composer]
Hain, Erlefried *Source(s):* IBIM; WORB
Jírovec, Vojtěch Matayás 1763-1850 [composer, conductor]
Gyrowetz, Adalbert (Mathias) *Source(s):* BAKO; BAKR; LCAR
Joachimson, Felix 1902- [librettist]
Jackson, Felix *Source(s):* LCAR; PSNN
Jobim, Antonio Carlos 1927-1994 [composer, lyricist, pianist]
Brazil, Tony *Source(s):* JAMU
George Gershwin of Brazil *Source(s):* AMUS
Jobim, Tom *Source(s):* LCAR; PEN2
Jobski, Bernhard 1946-1987 [composer]
Sisteron, Marc *Source(s):* KOMP; KOMS; PFSA
Joel, William [or Billy] (Martin) 1949- [singer, songwriter]
Martin, Bill *Source(s):* CASS; PSND
Note(s): Also used by William (W.) MacPherson & William Wylie.
Piano Man *Source(s):* CASS
Joensson, Hans 1913- [composer]
Song, Peter *Source(s):* PFSA
Johannes de Garlandia fl. c.1240 [music theorist; writer on music]
Gallicus, Johannes *Source(s):* LCAR
Johannes Gallicus *Source(s):* NGDM
Johannes Primarius *Source(s):* GRV3
Johannes the Great *Source(s):* GRV3
John, of Garland *Source(s):* LCAR
Primarius *Source(s):* GRV3
Johannes de Olomons, Magister fl. early 15th cent. [music theorist]
Scholasticus de Casteliono *Source(s):* GROL
Johansen, David 1950- [singer, songwriter, actor]
Poindexter, Buster *Source(s):* LCAR; NOMG
Johansen, (David) Johan 1919-1999 [composer, organist, music critic]
Kvandal, (David) Johan *Source(s):* BAKO; BAKR; BAKT; LCAR
Johanson, Ernest R(obert) 1928- [composer, music director]
Hanson, Jo *Source(s):* ASCP; CCE58; CCE67
John, Oscar [composer]
Sam & John *Source(s):* SUTT
Note(s): Jt. pseud.: Sam Theard.
Johner, Franz-Xaver Karl 1874-1955 [composer, music scholar]
Johner, Dominic(us) *Source(s):* LCAR
Johnes, (Miss) [composer]
Branwen *Source(s):* CPMU (publication date 1860)
Johnova, Miroslava 1894-1973 [composer, pianist]
Cord, Mira *Source(s):* DWCO; GROL
Kord, Mira *Source(s):* BUL3; COHN; GREN; HEIN; HIXN
Vorlová, Sláva *Source(s):* BAKR; COHN; GROL; http://www.kapralova.org/VORLOVA.htm (12 Mar. 2005)
Johnsen, Stanley Allen 1955- [composer, author, singer]
Johnsen, Skip *Source(s):* ASCP
Johnson, Albert J. 1910-1984 [reeds, composer, arranger]
Johnson, Budd *Source(s):* CCE62; EPMU; PEN2; PSND
Note(s): Do not confuse with Buddy [i.e., Woodrow (Wilson)] Johnson (1915-1977).
Johnson, Albertus Wayne 1942- [composer, singer]
Wayne, Alan *Source(s):* ASCP
Johnson, Alonzo 1899-1970 [singer, instrumentalist, songwriter]
Note(s): Some sources incorrectly cite birth date as 1889.
Johnson, Lonnie *Source(s):* HARS; LCAR
Jordan, Jimmy *Source(s):* HARS
Note(s): Do not confuse with Lonnie Johnson, blues pianist from the Midwest.
Jordan, Tom *Source(s):* HARS
World's Greatest Blues Singer, The *Source(s):* HARS
Note(s): See also John Lee Hooker & Elizabeth Smith.
Johnson, Ann M. 1921- [composer, author]
Rogers, Ann *Source(s):* ASCP
Johnson, Charles L(eslie) 1876-1950 [composer, pianist]
Note(s): Portraits: JASA; JASN; JAST; PERF
Ballard, Eugene E(dgar) *Source(s):* CCE25 E622574; REHH
Birch, Raymond *Source(s):* GROL; JAVA; JASR; LCAR; NGAM; REHH; SUPN
Earnist, Ethel *Source(s):* GROL; JASA; LCAR; NGAM
Leslie, Herbert *Source(s):* CCE45 #6387, 1293 R145104; GROL; LCAR; NGAM
Moore, Moran *Source(s):* NGAM
Woods, Fannie B. *Source(s):* GROL; JASA; LCAR; NGAM
Note(s): Incorrectly identified as pseud. of Charles L. Johnson. For a biography & port. of Fannie B. Woods (1892-1974), see PERF.
Johnson, Charles LaVere 1910-1983 [multi-instrumentalist, composer]
LaVere, Charles [or Charlie] *Source(s):* EPMU
Johnson, Clair W. 1902- [composer]
Ogden, Gene *Source(s):* CCE52-53; CCE55; SUPN
Johnson, Earl (Silas) 1934-2003 [singer, guitarist, songwriter]
Note(s): Do not confuse with Earl Johnson, rock guitarist (1932-)
King, Earl *Source(s):* AMUS; CCE63; LCAR; NOMG; WASH

Johnson, Francis H(all) 1888-1970 (or 71) [conductor, composer]
World Greatest Choir Director, The *Source(s):* PSNN
Johnson, Frederic Ayres 1876-1926 [composer]
Ayres, Frederic *Source(s):* BAKR; LCAR; PSND
Johnson, Frederick G. [songwriter]
Grant and Graham *Source(s):* CCE22 E532788
Note(s): Jt. pseud.: Jeff T. Branen
Howard, Jack *Source(s):* CCE23 E576000
Johnson, Ida R. 1866-1926 [librettist, lyricist]
Young, Rida Johnson *Source(s):* GAN1; GAN2; LCAR
Johnson, J. C. 1896-1981 [songwriter, conductor, author, pianist]
Burke, Harry *Source(s):* LCAR; PMUS
Crawford, James *Source(s):* CCE58; CPOL RE-181-794
Jay Cee *Source(s):* GROL
Johnson, Jay Cee *Source(s):* GROL
Johnson, James 1948- [singer, songwriter, producer, guitarist]
Note(s): Do not confuse with James Johnson (1902-1969)
James, Rick *Source(s):* AMUS; CM02; EPMU; HARR; PSND; RECR
Johnson, James (J.) 1902-1969 [singer, pianist, songwriter]
George, Shorty *Source(s):* HARS; http://www.bluesworld.com/OTHERPRE.htm (3 Mar. 2003)
Johnson, Stump *Source(s):* HARS; LCAR; http://www.bluesworld.com/OTHERPRE.htm
Little Man *Source(s):* HARS; http://www.bluesworld.com/OTHERPRE.htm
Roberts, Snitcher *Source(s):* HARS; http://www.bluesworld.com/OTHERPRE.htm
Shorty George *Source(s):* HARS; http://www.bluesworld.com/OTHERPRE.htm
Johnson, James [or Jimmy, or Jimmie] (P(rice)) 1891 (or 94)-1955 [pianist, composer]
Note(s): Portraits: JASN; SHMM (Oct. 1985): 7
Brute, The *Source(s):* Vance, Joel. *Fats Waller; His Life and Times.* Chicago: Contemporary Books, 1977, p. 33.
Father of Stride Piano *Source(s):* AMUS; IDBC; JASN; RAGT p. 166
Grandfather of Hot Piano *Source(s):* CM16; IDBC
Jackanapes *Source(s):* Kirkeby, Ed. *Ain't Misbehavin'; The Story of Fats Walle.* New York: Dodd, Mead, 1966 p. 53.
Three Wise Men of Harlem Hot Piano, The *Source(s):* Vance (see above), p. 34
Note(s): Jt. sobriquet: Thomas Wright Waller & William [or Willie] (Henry Joseph Berthol Bonaparte) Smith.
Johnson, James Louis 1924-2001 [trombonist, composer, orchestrator]
Johnson, J(ay) J(ay) *Source(s):* EPMU; IDBC; LCAR; NGAM; NGDM; OB01
Peters, Hunt *Source(s):* JAMU
Siegel, C. C. *Source(s):* JAMU
Johnson, James Weldon 1871-1938 [poet, lyricist, writer on music, teacher]
Note(s): Portrait: CYBH
Cole and Johnson Brothers *Source(s):* GAN1; GAN2
Note(s): Jt. pseud.: James Weldon Johnson & Robert [or Bob] (Allen) Cole.
Handy, Will *Source(s):* BAKR; GAN1; GAN2; JASZ; KILG
Note(s): Jt. pseud.: James Weldon Johnson & Robert [or Bob] (Allen) Cole.
Johnson, John Harold [songwriter]
Reine, Johnny *Source(s):* CPOL RE-55-758; PMUS
Johnson, J(ohn) Rosamond 1873-1954 [composer, teacher]
Note(s): Portraits: CYBH; JASZ; WOLL
Cole and Johnson Brothers *Source(s):* GAN1; GAN2
Note(s): Jt. pseud.: James Weldon Johnson & Robert [or Bob] (Allen) Cole.
Handy, Will *Source(s):* BAKR; GAN1; GAN2; JASZ; KILG
Note(s): Jt. pseud.: James Weldon Johnson & Robert [or Bob] (Allen) Cole.
Writer of the Black National Anthem, The *Source(s):* PSN
Johnson, Johnnie [or Johnny] 1924- [composer]
Father of Rock and Roll *Source(s):* http://www.johnnie.com/news.html (6 Oct. 2002)
Note(s): See also Charles Edward Anderson Berry, Arthur Cudup, William [or Bill] (John) Haley, Charles Hardin Holley & Elvis A(a)ron Presley.
Goode, Johnnie B. *Source(s):* http://www.johnnie.com/news/html
Johnson, Karl Emil Georg 1891-1964 [actor, songwriter]
Note(s): In PSND middle name cited: Gerhard.
Gerhard, Karl *Source(s):* LCAR; PSND
Johnson, Larry 1953- [songwriter]
Starr, Maurice *Source(s):* PMUS-80-84
Johnson, Lucius Brinson 1934-1976 [singer, guitarist, songwriter]
Johnson, Georgia Boy *Source(s):* HARS
Johnson, Luther *Source(s):* HARS
Note(s): Do not confuse with Luther Johnson, Jr. (1939-).
Johnson, Snake (Boy) *Source(s):* HARS
King, Luther *Source(s):* HARS
Little Luther *Source(s):* HARS
Johnson, Lula (Grace) 1930 (or 32)- [singer, songwriter]
Howard, Jan *Source(s):* AMUS; MCCL

Johnson, Luther, Jr. 1939- [singer, guitarist, songwriter]
Note(s): Do not confuse with Luther [i.e., Lucius Brinson] Johnson (1934-1976).
Black Jr. *Source(s):* HARS
Guitar Jr. [or Junior] *Source(s):* HARS; LCAR
Note(s): See also Lee Baker, Jr.
Johnson, Guitar Junior *Source(s):* LCAR
Little Jr. *Source(s):* HARS
Note(s): See also Herman Parker.

Johnson, Malcolm 1902- [pianist, composer, bandleader]
Johnson, Johnny *Source(s):* KINK

Johnson, Margaret (Ellen) 1923 (or 25)-1967 [author, singer, pianist]
Robbins, Corky *Source(s):* ASCP; CCE52-53

Johnson, Marguerite (Annie) 1928- [poet, singer, songwriter, actress]
Angelou, Maya *Source(s):* LCAR; *Oxford Companion to Twentieth-Century Literature in English*. New York: Oxford University Press, 1996.

Johnson, Mary (née Smith) 1905-1970? [singer, songwriter]
Johnson, Signifyin (Mary) *Source(s):* GRAT; HARS; LCAR

Johnson, (Karen) Michelle 1962- [singer, songwriter]
Shocked, Michelle *Source(s):* CM04; EPMU; HARR; LCAR; MUHF; PEN2

Johnson, Michelle [or Me'shell] (Lynn) 1968 (or 70)- [bassist, singer, songwriter]
Ndegé-Ocello, Me'shell *Source(s):* ALMN; CLAG; CM18; LCAR

Johnson, Miriam 1943 (or 47)- [singer, pianist, songwriter]
Colter, Jessi *Source(s):* EPMU; FLIN; LCAR; MCCL; PEN2; PSND; STAC
Eddy, Miriam *Source(s):* AMUS; LCAR; PEN2; PSND
Lady Outlaw *Source(s):* FLIN
Note(s): See also Jill Lynne Byrem.
Preacher's Daughter *Source(s):* FLIN

Johnson, Norman 1944- [singer, songwriter]
Johnson, General *Source(s):* HARR

Johnson, Oliver [or Ollie] 1892-1954 [singer, instrumentalist, songwriter]
Johnson, Dink *Source(s):* HARS; LCAR

Johnson, Raymond [songwriter]
Johnson, Aimee *Source(s):* STC1

Johnson, Robert [singer, singer, hymnist]
Johnson, Captain *Source(s):* CYBH

Johnson, Robert (Leroy) 1911-1938 [singer, guitarist, songwriter]
Father of Modern Rock and Roll *Source(s):* http://www.geocities.com/abexile/rjohnson.html (6 Oct. 2002)
King of the Delta Blues Singers *Source(s):* CM06; IDBC; SHAD
Spencer, R(obert) L. *Source(s):* http://www.shs.starkville.K12.ms.us/mswm/MSWritersAndMusicians/musicians/Johnson.html (6 Oct. 2002)

Johnson, Samuel c.1698-c.1773 [burlesque writer, dancing master]
Johnson, Maggotty *Source(s):* SADC

Johnson, Simone 1970- [rapper]
Love, Monie *Source(s):* EPMU

Johnson, (Mrs.) William [composer]
Amateur *Source(s):* CPMU (publication dates c.1835)

Johnson, William [or Billy] (Francis) ?-1916 [comedian, singer, dancer,songwriter]
Note(s): Portrait: JASZ
Flimflammer, (Jim) *Source(s):* JASN; JASZ
Johnson, Woodrow (Wilson) 1915-1977 [bandleader, composer, arranger]
Johnson, Buddy *Source(s):* AMUS; ASCP; GAMM; KINK
Note(s): Do not confuse with Budd [i.e., Albert J.] Johnson (1910-1984).

Johnston, Eleanor [or Ellie] 1940- [singer, songwriter]
Lane, Cristy *Source(s):* AMUS; LCAR; MCCL
Stoller, Ellie *Source(s):* LCAR

Johnston, Horace Eugene 1927-2001 [author, librettist, painter, dancer]
Everett, Horace *Source(s):* LCAR
Johns, Erik *Source(s):* LCAR

Johnstone, Arthur Edward 1860-1944 [composer, teacher]
Butler, Clarence *Source(s):* http://webtext.library.yale.edu/xml2html/music/ksw-s1f.htm (30 Sept. 2003)

Johnstone, Lucie [composer]
Carey, Lewis *Source(s):* CPMU (publication dates 1906-1919)
Note(s): Do not confuse with Lew(is) Carey [i.e., Lewis D. Conetta]

Johnstone, Maurice 1900-1976 [composer, arranger, journalist]
Bowden, David *Source(s):* MUWB

Joiner, Alvin (Nathaniel, Jr.) [songwriter, performer]
Xzibit *Source(s):* AMIR; AMUS; CPOL PA-1-073-515; PMUS-00

Jojič, Boris 1933- [composer]
Joy, Bee *Source(s):* KOMS

Jommelli, Niccolò 1714-1774 [composer]
Note(s): Portraits: ETUP 52:12 (Dec. 1934): 698; EWCY
Eteoclide, Anfione *Source(s):* GROL
Italian Gluck, The *Source(s):* BAKO; BAKR
Valentino *Source(s):* GRV3; MELL

Jonas, Justus 1493-1555 [theologian, hymnist]
Koch, Jost *Source(s):* NGDM
Jones, Albert 1939- [composer, author, lyricist]
Trebla Seno J. *Source(s):* ASCP
Jones, Andrew (Bennie), (Jr.) [singer, guitarist, songwriter]
Jones, Jr. Boy *Source(s):* AMUS
Junior [or Jr.] Boy *Source(s):* CCE74
Jones, Arthur [composer]
Phillips, Barbara *Source(s):* BLIC ("Regrets," (A. Rothham, 1916))
Jones, Arthur Barclay 1869-1943 [composer]
Barclay, Arthur *Source(s):* BAKR; CPMU
Jones, Booker T. 1945 (or 46)- [pianist, singer, songwriter]
Booker T. *Source(s):* YORK
Jones, (William) Carmell 1936-1996 [trumpeter, composer]
Lawrence, Kansas *Source(s):* JAMU
Jones, David Robert (Hayward) 1947- [singer, composer, actor]
Note(s): Surname also given: Hayward-Jones. Portrait: CM23
Bowie, David *Source(s):* CM23; DIMA; EPMU; GAMM; HARR; LCAR; PEN2
Chameleon of Pop *Source(s):* CM23
Glam-Rock Godfather, The *Source(s):* OUSH
Godfather of Glam-Rock, The *Source(s):* http://www.cnn.com/SHOWBIZ/Music/9809/29/davidbowie (6 Oct. 2002)
Note(s): See also Marc Bolan [i.e., Mark Feld]
King of Glitter Rock, The *Source(s):* PSND
Stardust Kid, The *Source(s):* PSND
Stardust, Ziggy *Source(s):* PSND; WARN
White Duke, The *Source(s):* WARN
Jones, Eddie 1926-1959 [singer, guitarist, songwriter]
Guitar Slim *Source(s):* AMUS; HARS; LCAR; YORK
Note(s): See also Norman G. Green, Alexander T. Seward & Raymond Maurice Otey. Also used by guitarist James Stephens (1915-).
Jones, Guitar Slim *Source(s):* HARS; PMUS; YORK
Jones, Edward 1752-1824 [harper, historian, composer]
Note(s): Do not confuse with Edward Jones (1822-1885); see following entry.
Bardd y Brenin *Source(s):* GROL; LCAR; NGDM; WILG
King's Bard, The *Source(s):* GROL; LCAR; NGDM
King's Poet, The *Source(s):* WILG
Jones, Edward (Stephen) 1822-1885 [minister, composer]
Note(s): Entries in BROW; IBIM; ROOM are under: Stephen, Edward. Do not confuse with Edward Jones (1752-1824); see preceding entry. Added "Stephen," his fathers given name.
Jones, Stephen *Source(s):* HUEV; NGDM
Note(s): Assumed his father's Christian name to avoid confusion with another student
Stephen(s), Edward (Jones) *Source(s):* GROL; NGDM
Note(s): Later surname was omitted & he became known as Edward Stephen(s).
Tanymarian, (Edward) *Source(s):* GROL; HUEB; NGDM; WILG; WORB
Jones, Edward German 1862-1936 [composer, conductor]
Note(s): Portraits: ETUP 51:9 (Sept. 1933): 568; *Musical Standard* (5 Apr. 1902)
German, (Sir) Edward *Source(s):* BAKO; EPMU; GAMM; GAN1; GAN2; GOTH; NGDM; PIPE
German, J. E(dward) *Source(s):* NGDM
Note(s): On early compositions.
Jones, Everett LeRoi [originally Leroy] 1934- [writer on jazz, playwright, poet]
Baraka, (Imamu) Amiri *Source(s):* LCAR; NGDJ; PSND
Jones, George (Glen(n)) 1931- [singer, guitarist, songwriter]
Crown Prince of Country Music, The *Source(s):* AMEN
Jones, No Show *Source(s):* MCCL
Jones, Possum *Source(s):* MCCL
Jones, Thumper *Source(s):* AMUS; MCCL; PSND
No Show Jones *Source(s):* MCCL; MUHF
Possum, The *Source(s):* AMEN; AMUS; FLIN; MUHF; PSND
Rolls Royce of Country Music, The *Source(s):* AMEN
Rolls Royce of Country Singers *Source(s):* MCCL; MUHF; PSND
Smith, Hank *Source(s):* MCCL
Jones, Gomer L(lewellyn) [or Llewellyn Gomer] 1911- [composer]
Gomer, Llewellyn *Source(s):* CCE44 #9764 E119171; CCE53; CPOL RE-67-793; GOTH
Jones, Graham 1961- [songwriter]
Eyton, Andrew *Source(s):* BLIC
Jones, Griffith Hugh 1849-1919 [composer]
Argon, Gutyn *Source(s):* CYBH
Jones, Griffith Rhys 1834-1897 [blacksmith, conductor]
Caradog *Source(s):* WILG; *Music and British Cultures, 1785-1914.* Oxford: Oxford University Press, 2000. (port.)
Jones, Isaiah, Jr. 1940- [composer, author, pianist]
DeVall, Don E. *Source(s):* CCE65-66
Jones, Ike *Source(s):* ASCP
Jones, Isham (Edgar) 1894-1956 [composer, conductor]
Note(s): Portrait: EWPA
Composer's Composer, The *Source(s):* PSND

Covington, Allan H. *Source(s):* CCE23 E553162
Hale, Jimmy *Source(s):* SUTT
Note(s): The Isham Jones Orchestra recorded under the name: Jimmy Hale Orchestra.

Jones, John 1810-1869 [poet]
Note(s): Do not confuse with John Jones (1825-1887) or John Jones (1924-64); see the two following entries.
Talhaiarn *Sources:* KILG; LCAR

Jones, John 1825-1887 [songwriter]
Note(s): Do not confuse with John Jones (1924-64) or John Jones [nd], aka Talhaiarn; see the preceding and following entries.
Fychan, Idris *Source(s):* KILG

Jones, John 1924-1964 [songwriter]
Note(s): Do not confuse with John Jones (1825-87) or John Jones [nd], aka Talhaiam; see the two preceding entries.
Little Johnny *Source(s):* HARS

Jones, Joseph David 1827-1870 [composer]
Gwalchmai *Source(s):* CYBH

Jones, Kenneth Eugene 1942- [composer]
Jones, Bucky *Source(s):* ASCP; CPOL PA-10-633

Jones, Kimberly (Denise) 1975- [songwriter, performer]
Lil' Kim *Source(s):* AMIR; LCAR; PMUS-00

Jones, Lewis Ellis 1865-1936 [hymnist]
Edgar, Lewis *Source(s):* CYBH
Lewis, Edgar *Source(s):* CYBH
Slater, Mary *Source(s):* CYBH

Jones, Lillie Mae 1929 (or 30)- [songwriter]
BeBop Betty *Source(s):* EPMU
Bette BeBop *Source(s):* EPMU
Betty BeBop *Source(s):* EPMU; LCAR
Carter, Betty (Be-Bop) *Source(s):* EPMU; GRAT; LCAR; PSND
Carter, Lorene *Source(s):* GRAT; LCAR; PSND
Carter, Lorraine *Source(s):* EPMU; LCAR
Jones, Betty *Source(s):* LCAR
Redding, Betty *Source(s):* LCAR
Redding, Lillie Mae *Source(s):* LCAR

Jones, Lindley A(rmstrong) 1911-1965 [composer, conductor, drummer]
Jones, Spike *Source(s):* ALMN; AMEN; ASCP; NGDM; PEN2
King of Corn, The *Source(s):* ALMN; NGDM

Jones, Louis M(arshall) 1913-1998 [banjo player, songwriter]
Jones, Grandpa *Source(s):* AMUS; CCE54-56; CCE61-62; EPMU; MUHF; PSND
Young Singer of Old Songs, The *Source(s):* EPMU; MUHF

Jones, Michael 1959- [songwriter]
Kashif *Source(s):* AMUS; PMUS-80
Saleem, Kashif *Source(s):* AMUS

Jones, Nasir (Bin Olu Dara) 1973- [songwriter, performer]
Nas *Source(s):* AMIR; AMUS; CPOL PA-843-898; PMUS-00
Nasty Nas *Source(s):* AMUS

Jones, Nicholas (Allen) 1969- [songwriter, bandleader]
Wire, Nick(y) *Source(s):* AMIR; CPOL PA-593-577; SONG

Jones, Paul [guitarist, singer, songwriter]
Jones, Wine *Source(s):* AMUS; LCAR

Jones, Paul Laurence 1962- [songwriter]
Laurence, Paul *Source(s):* PMUS-85

Jones, Quincey Delight 1933- [composer, arranger]
Man Behind the Music, The *Source(s):* PSND
Q *Source(s):* CM20; PSND

Jones, Rickie Lee 1954- [singer, songwriter]
Duchess of Coolsville, The *Source(s):* ALMN

Jones, Robert Carroll 1931- [composer, teacher]
Carroll, Bob *Source(s):* ASCP (see reference)

Jones, Robert Elliott 1909-2000 [trumpeter, arranger]
Jones, Jonah *Source(s):* AMUS; EPMU; PSND

Jones, Ruth Lee 1924-1963 [singer, songwriter]
Queen of the Blues *Source(s):* CASS; HARS; SHAD
Note(s): See also Sara(h) Dunn, Ethel Howard, Koko Taylor [i.e., Cora Walton] & Victoria [or Vicky] (Regina) Spivey.
Queen of the Jukeboxes, The *Source(s):* PSND; SHAB; SHAD
Washington, Dinah *Source(s):* CASS; GRAT; HARS; LCAR; SHAB; SHAD

Jones, S. [composer]
Presbyter *Source(s):* CPMU (publication date 1919)

Jones, Sam(uel) 1924-1981 [bassist, composer]
Jones, Home *Source(s):* GROL

Jones, Stephen [or Steven] 1962- [singer, songwriter]
Baby Bird *Source(s):* AMUS; LCAR
Note(s): Originally the alias of Steven Jones; later the name of a full band.

Jones, Teren Delvon 1972- [rap musician]
Del Da Lench Mob *Source(s):* EPMU
Del Tha Funky Homosapien *Source(s):* EPMU

Jones, Thompson E(rnest) 1831-1895 [librettist]
Thompson, Alfred *Source(s):* GAN1; GAN2; GANA

Jones, William 1726-1800 [curate, composer, writer]
Jones of Nayland *Source(s):* GRV2
Jones, Trinity *Source(s):* GROL

Jonnie, Curtis 1946- [singer, songwriter, TV host]
Shingoose *Source(s):* AMUS; NOMG

Joplin, Janis 1943-1970 [singer, lyricist]
Pearl *Source(s):* PSND; SHAD
Queen of Rock *Source(s):* SHAD

Joplin, Scott 1868-1917 [composer]
Note(s): Portrait: JASN
Father of Ragtime Music *Source(s):* http://www.lasallehs.org/culture/martinez.html (21 Oct. 2002)
Joplinesque *Source(s):* JASN p. 129
King of Ragtime, The *Source(s):* PSND; SHAD; SIFA; SMIN
Note(s): See also Israel Isador Baline.
King of Ragtime Composers, The *Source(s):* PSND; SHAD; SIFA; SMIN
King of Ragtime Writers *Source(s):* JASN; RAGT p. 117
King of the Ragtime Writers *Source(s):* FACS
Jordan, Brad(ley) [songwriter, performer]
Akshen *Source(s):* AMUS
Scarface *Source(s):* AMUS; PMUS-00
Jordan, E. [composer]
Caber, C *Source(s):* GOTH
Jordan, Esteban Steve 1938 (or 39)- [accordionist, songwriter]
Jimmy Hendrix of the Accordian *Source(s):* AMUS
Parche, El *Source(s):* LCAR
Jordan, Etterlene 1955- [songwriter]
DeBarge, Bunny *Source(s):* PMUS
Jordan, Harry C. [composer]
Beaumont, H. *Source(s):* CCE25 E616285; TPRF
Jordan, Irving Sidney 1922- [pianist, composer]
D. J. *Source(s):* CCE66
Jordan, Duke *Source(s):* AMUS; CCE61; EPMU; PEN2
Jordan, Leroy 1948- [composer, singer]
Jordan, Lonnie *Source(s):* ASCP; PMUS
Jorden, Terry 1942-2004 [singer, producer, songwriter]
Day, Terry *Source(s):* IMDB; PEN2
Melcher, Terry *Source(s):* IMDB; PEN2
Jory, Sarah 1969- [guitarist, singer, songwriter]
Princess of the Pedal Steel, The *Source(s):* MCCL
Joseph, Daniel 1950- [composer, author, publisher]
Sullivan, Dane *Source(s):* ASCP
Joseph of Thessalonica [hymnist]
Joseph of the Stadium *Source(s):* CYBH (see under: Joseph the Hymnographer)
Joseph, Pleasant 1907-1989 [singer, guitarist, pianist, songwriter]
Brother Joshua *Source(s):* EPMU; HARS
Cousin Joe [or Joseph] *Source(s):* EPMU; HARS
Joe, Cousin *Source(s):* LCAR
Pleasant, Cousin Joe *Source(s):* HARS
Pleasant Joe *Source(s):* EPMU; HARS
Smiling Joe *Source(s):* HARS; LCAR
Joseph the Hymnographer ?-883 [hymnist]
Menaea *Source(s):* CYBH
Josephs, Wilfred 1927-1997 [composer]
Nelson, Maynard *Source(s):* MUWB
Wylam, Wilfred *Source(s):* GANB; MUWB
Josquin Desprez c.1440-1521 [composer]
Beethoven of the 16th Century *Source(s):* http://chorusamerica.org/vox_article_recordings.shtml (6 Apr. 2005)
Father of Modern Harmony, The *Source(s):* DAWS; PSND
Jodocus a Prato *Source(s):* NGDM
Jodocus Pratensis *Source(s):* NGDM
Josse *Source(s):* NGDM
Juschino *Source(s):* NGDM
Josquin, Jan fl. 1561-63 [theorist]
Boleslavensis, Johannes Josquinus *Source(s):* GROL
Jouy, (Victor Joseph) Etienne (de) 1764-1846 [playwright, librettist]
DeJouy, Victor Joseph Etienne *Source(s):* LCAR; PSND
Etienne *Source(s):* PSND
Jouy, Stephano *Source(s):* LCAR
Zh(i)ui *Source(s):* LCAR
Joyce, Archibald 1873-1963 [composer]
A. D. *Source(s):* CCE49 R54489 ("Jelly Jimmy")
Donaldson, Arthur *Source(s):* CCE49 R47966 ("Mr. Misery"); CCE51 R78644 ("You 'Op It")
Dzhois, A. *Source(s):* LCAR
English Waltz King, The *Source(s):* GALM; RFSO
Waltz King *Source(s):* MUWB
Note(s): See also Wayne (Harold) King, Johann (Baptist) Strauss, (Sr.) (1804-1849) & Johann (Baptist) Strauss, (Jr.) (1825-1899).
Joyce, James 1771-1850 [hymnist]
J. J. *Source(s):* JULN
Judd, Diana Ellen 1946- [singer, songwriter, author, actress]
Judd, Naomi *Source(s):* LCAR; MCCL
Judkins, Steveland 1950- [singer, songwriter]
Hardaway, Steveland *Source(s):* LCAR
Morris, Steveland *Source(s):* LCAR
Wonder, Little Stevie *Source(s):* LCAR
Wonder, Stevie *Source(s):* LCAR
Judson, Edward Zane Carrol 1822 (or 23)-1886 [author, hymnist]
Buntline, Ned *Source(s):* LCAR
King of the Dime Novel *Source(s):* http://www.geocities.com/Wellesley/Veranda/6898.indexp5.html (21 Oct. 2002)
Judson, Emily (née Chubbuck) 1817-1854 [author, hymnist]
Note(s): See LCAR for additional nonmusic-related sobriquets.
Forester, Fanny *Source(s):* CLAC; JULN

Julien, Herbert 1749-1811? [violinist, composer]
Navoigille (the younger) *Source(s):* MACM; NGDM; NGDO
Jullien, Louis (George) Antoine (Jules) 1812-1869 [composer, conductor]
Note(s): Original surname was Julien with 36 forenames, (see DEA3 or GROL). Used many of his forenames as pseudonyms; however, only those listed below were verified. Portraits: HOWD; MUOP 51:612 (Sept. 1928): 1171
Albert, Rock *Source(s):* REHG; SUPN; Carse, Adam. *The Life of Jullien*. Cambridge: W. Heffer, 1971.
Jullienesque *Source(s):* Carse (see above)
Note(s): Term used to describe Jullien's eccentricity, mock solemnity, etc.
Mons, (The) *Source(s):* PRAT; Carse p. 102-3 (see above)
Noe-Jean *Source(s):* Carse p. 107 (see above)
Paganini of the Alps, The *Source(s):* NGDM; SPIE
Roch-Albert *Source(s):* CPMU; NGDM; Carse (see above)
Jungk, Klaus 1916- [composer]
Niklas, Ferry *Source(s):* BUL3; CCE55; KOMP; KOMS; PFSA
Junker, Otto fl. 1914-1920 [composer]
Gaze, Otto *Source(s):* MELL; STGR
Junkert, Ludwig 1920- [composer]
Altis, Ludo *Source(s):* REHG; SUPN
Junsch, William Colin 1912- [composer, conductor]
D'Arcy, Colin *Source(s):* CCE55-56; LCCC 1946-54 (see reference)
Young, Billy *Source(s):* ASCC (see under: D'Arcy, Colin)
Juon, Pavel [or Pual] (Fedorovich) 1872-1940 [composer]
Note(s): Portraits: ETUP 53:1 (Jan. 1935): 2; *Musical Standard* (2 May 1903) & (22 Oct. 1927)
Russian Brahms, The *Source(s):* NGDM
Note(s): See also Nikolai Medtner & Sergey (Ivanovich) Taneev.
Jupe, Eberhard 1943- [composer]
Jersey, Mel *Source(s):* KOMS; PFSA
Jupp, Eric [songwriter]
Ricardo *Source(s):* CCE55
Teufel, Erik *Source(s):* CCE53
Note(s): Jt. pseud.: Arthur Strauss.
Juraschek, Ernst Friedrich Wilhelm 1875-1941 [playwright; director]
Welish, Ernst *Source(s):* GAN2
Jurgens, Dick (Henry) 1910 (or 11)-1995 [trumpeter, composer, bandleader]
Jurgens, Sonny *Source(s):* BBDP; STUW
Justiniano, José Alberto 1958- [singer, arranger]
Alberto, José *Source(s):* LCAR
Canario, El *Source(s):* EPMU; LCAR
Note(s): See also Jorge Ferreira.
Justis(s), William [or Bill] (E(verette?)), (Jr.) 1926 (or 27)-1982 [composer]
Everette, Bill *Source(s):* CCE61; CCE67; PMUS
Napier, James *Source(s):* CCE61
Zucker, Otto *Source(s):* PMUS; PSNN

– K –

Kaan, Eduard 1826- [librettist]
Dorn, Eduard *Source(s):* STGR; WORB
Kabas(s)elé (Tshamala), Joseph 1930-1983 [singer, composer, bandleader]
Father of Modern Zairean Music, The *Source(s):* EPMU
Father of Rhumba, The *Source(s):* AMUS
Grand(e) Kallé, (The) *Source(s):* EPMU; LCAR
Jeef, Kalle *Source(s):* PSND
Kalé *Source(s):* LCAR
Kare *Source(s):* LCAR
Kaderschafka, Franz R. 1952- [composer]
Snowbird, Frank *Source(s):* KOMS; PFSA
Kador, Ernest, Jr. 1936-2001 [singer, lyricist]
Emperor of the World *Source(s):* LCAR
Note(s): Called himself.
K-Doe, Ernie *Source(s):* CM36; HARD; LCAR; OB01
Kaempfert, Bert(hold) 1923-1980 [arranger]
Bones, M(ark) *Source(s):* CCE59-61
Kaempfert, Flip *Source(s):* CLAS
Kaempfner, Bernhard (Heinrich) 1874- [songwriter]
Skutecky, B. K. *Source(s):* MACM; WORB
Kaflún, Israel 1910-1990 [violinist, composer]
Kaplún, Raul *Source(s):* TODO
Kahakalau, Robert 1922- [composer, arranger]
Carter, Bob *Source(s):* KINK
Kahlenbach, Hermann 1929- [composer]
Danka, Fide *Source(s):* KOMP; KOMS; PFSA; REHH; SUPN
Kahlert, August 1807-1864 [writer on music]
Pfeffel *Source(s):* APPL p. 10
Kahn, Dave 1910- [songwriter]
Note(s): Kahn composed music for publisher David M. Gordon under the names listed below, as did William Lava, Irving Gertz, Leo(n) Klatzkin, Joseph [or Joe] Mullendore & possibly others. See also David M. Gordon.
Gordon, Melvyn Lenard *Source(s):* CLMC
Lenard, Melvyn *Source(s):* CLMC
Kahn, Gerald Freedmann [composer, songwriter]
Trelawny, Jack *Source(s):* CPMU (publication dates 1914-20)

Kahn, Gus 1886-1941 [singer, lyricist]
Keyes, Gilbert *Source(s):* CCE50 R61164 ("Birdie"); PMUS; PSNN
Van, Gus *Source(s):* PSNN
Kahn, Norman 1923 (or 24)-1953 [drummer, arranger, composer]
Kahn, Tiny *Source(s):* GROL; KINK; LCAR; NGDJ; PEN2
Kaiser, (Henri) Alfred (de) 1872-1917 [composer, librettist]
De Keyser, Alfred *Source(s):* BAKE
Keyser, Alfred de *Source(s):* CPMU; LOWN (col. 1302, note 1)
Kaiser, Hermann 1889-1978 [music critic, theater historian]
Ginster, Theodor *Source(s):* PIPE; WORB
Kaiser, (Johann) Rudolf 1919- [composer]
Resiak, J. R. *Source(s):* CCE56; REHH
Kaiserman, Mauricio [or Morris] Albert(o) 1951 [or 52]- [singer, composer]
Albert(o), Morris *Source(s):* CCE73 Efor165462; EPMU; KICK; PSND
Kalakaua, David (King of Hawaii) 1836-1891 [composer]
Figgs *Source(s):* http://www.hawaiimusic museum.org/forum/songs/tp119.html (6 Oct. 2002)
Kalaš, Julius 1902-1967 [composer]
Kassal, Luis *Source(s):* PIPE
Kalberg, Eelke [songwriter]
Kalmani *Source(s):* PMUS-00
Kalina z Choteriny, Matous 1516-1566 [humanist, poet, composer]
Collinus, Matthaeus *Source(s):* NGDM
Kalisch, A(lfred) 1863-1933 [journalist, music critic]
Crescendo *Source(s):* PSND; ROOM
Staccato *Source(s):* PSND; ROOM
Kalischer, Alfred Chrislieb Salomon Ludwig 1842-1909 [musicologist, editor]
Note(s): Portrait: ETUP 53:1 (Jan. 1935): 2
Christlieb, Alfred *Source(s):* SEND
Kalischnig, Walter 1926- [composer]
Bolina, F. *Source(s):* SUPN
Lingo, Vic(tor) *Source(s):* CCE64-65; REHG; SUPN
Kallwitz, Seth 1556-1615 [composer, cantor, writer]
Calvisius, Sethus *Source(s):* BAKR; MACM; WORB
Kalmanoff, Martin 1920- [composer, author, pianist, conductor, critic]
Claron, Henri *Source(s):* CCE60
Kenwood, Marty *Source(s):* ASCP; CCE48; CCE73 R554819; HOVL
Kamakaeha, Liliu (Loloku Walania) 1838-1917 [composer]
Note(s): Birth name: LCAR; Portrait: CYBH
Aorena, (Mme.) *Source(s):* COHN; DWCO; HIXN (see under: Liliuokalani, Queen of Hawaii
Kamaka'eha Paki, Lydia *Source(s):* NGAM
Liliuokalani, Queen of Hawaii *Source(s):* LCAR
Paki, Lydia *Source(s):* LCAR
Note(s): Baptized, legal name.
Kamenetzky, Jacob 1888-196? [arranger]
Kammen, Jack *Source(s):* HESK
Kamenetzky, Joseph 1888-195? [arranger]
Kammen, Joseph *Source(s):* HESK
Kamienski, Lucian [or Lucjan] 1885-1964 [composer, writer on music]
Dolega-Kamienski *Source(s):* BAKR; PRAT
Kammler, Ewald 1940- [composer]
Sandner, Rolf *Source(s):* PFSA
Stanberg, Ed *Source(s):* PFSA
Kämpf, Armin 1926- [composer]
Kennen, Frank *Source(s):* KOMS; PFSA
Kane, Kieran 1949- [singer, songwriter]
Note(s): Portrait: CCME (with Jamie O'Hara)
O'Kanes, The *Source(s):* AMUS; CCME; MCCL; MUHF
Note(s): Jt. pseud.: Jamie O'Hara.
Kann, Hans 1927- [composer, pianist]
Gilbert, Jacques *Source(s):* OMUO
Lachner, Robert *Source(s):* OMUO
Papuschek, Veit *Source(s):* OMUO
Pomeisl, Willibald *Source(s):* OMUO
Kano, Jason [singer, songwriter]
Kane, DJ *Source(s):* HWOM
Kanzus, Kanzus, J. [composer]
Kansas *Source(s):* FZSL
Kaonohi, David [composer, conductor]
Pineapple, Johnny *Source(s):* ASCP
Kaplan, Alan Kevin [composer]
Kevin, Alexander *Source(s):* GANB
Kaplan, Saul 1912-1997 [composer, pianist, arranger, movie producer]
Chaplin, Saul *Source(s):* CASS; EPMU; GAMM; IGER; STUW
Kaplan, Sol 1919-1990 [conductor, composer, pianist]
Krandel, Sol *Source(s):* LCAR; MCCA
Lee, Lester *Source(s):* CCE41 #27873 E95653; CCE68
Norris, John F. *Source(s):* CPOL RE-116-059
Kaplan, Stephen Hanan 1947- [composer]
Hanan, Stephen *Source(s):* GOTH
Kapp, David [or Dave] 1904-1976 [songwriter]
Hold, Alan *Source(s):* CCE64
Holt, Alan *Source(s):* CCE57; CPOL RE-263-858
Howell, Dan *Source(s):* CPOL RE-82-876; PMUS
Howell, Dave *Source(s):* CPOL RE-32-812
Leader, Dave K. *Source(s):* CCE61; CPOL RE-400-605
Leader, Mickey *Source(s):* CCE48; CCE75
Ruth, Michael *Source(s):* CPOL RE-400-606

Kapp, Paul 1907-1984 [composer, author, producer]
Atkinson, Geoffrey *Source(s):* CCE66
Batsford, J. Tucker *Source(s):* ASCP
Boyd, Mullen *Source(s):* ASCP
Hardt, Dick *Source(s):* CCE51; CCE54; CCE61; CPOL RE-221-351
Hardt, Richard *Source(s):* ASCP; CCE49-50
Richards, Happy *Source(s):* CCE51; CPOL RE-5-914
Karg(-Elert), Sigfrid 1877-1933 [composer, organist, theorist]
Oberndorf, Teo von *Source(s):* CCE42 #5201, 354 R102303; LCAR
Kark, Frederik 1869- [composer]
Dannenberg, Fr. *Source(s):* GREN
Dufort, Charles *Source(s):* GREN
Zeilbeck, E. *Source(s):* GREN
Karlsson, Karl 1892 (or 93)-1966 [composer, accordionist]
Jularbo, Carl *Source(s):* GREN
Károlyi, Mária 1909- [author]
Károlyi, Amy *Source(s):* PIPE
Karpeles, (Julius) Max (Heinrich) 1850-1921 [author, music critic, librettist]
Deutlich, Jeremias *Source(s):* AEIO; GROL; PIPE
Kalbeck, Max *Source(s):* AEIO
Karr y de Alfonsetti, Carmen 1865- [playwright, composer]
Escardot, L. *Source(s):* COHN; HIXN
Kartner, Pierre 1935- [composer]
Abraham, Vader *Source(s):* LCAR
Vad(d)er, Abraham *Source(s):* PFSA
Kasha, Phyllis L. [author, lyricist]
Lorraine, Phyllis *Source(s):* CCE61
Phillips, Lorraine *Source(s):* ASCP
Kashereffsky, William 1923- [percussionist, composer, conducter]
Kraft, William *Source(s):* BAKE
Kashkin, Nikolay (Dmitriyevich) 1939-1920 [music critic, teacher]
Dmitriyev, N. *Source(s):* GROL; NGDO
Kaskel, (Baron) Karl (von) 1866-1943 [composer]
Note(s): Portrait: ETUP 53:1 (Jan. 1935): 2
Korla, Karl *Source(s):* LCAR
Lasekk, Charles *Source(s):* CPMU
Katt, Friedmann 1945- [organist, composer]
Frenzel, Franz Xaver *Source(s):* OMUO
Katz, Benjamin 1915- [composer, author, singer]
Kaye, Benny *Source(s):* ASCP; CCE57-61
Katz, Erich 1900-1973 [songwriter]
Cates, Eric M. *Source(s):* LCAR; OCLC 29415946
Katz, Harold (H.) 1921- [composer]
Carr, Harold *Source(s):* CCE53
Karr, Harold *Source(s):* CCE53-56; CCE60; PSND
Katz, Josef P. [writer on music]
Kamerton *Source(s):* SEND
Katz, Richard [or Dick] (Aaron) 1924- [pianist, arranger, producer]
Richard, Bill *Source(s):* JAMU
Katzenstein, Julius 1890-1946 [writer on music]
Kastein, Josef [or Joseph] *Source(s):* LCAR; SEND
Kauders, Albert 1854-1912 [composer, music critic]
Anders, K. *Source(s):* OMUO
Kauer, Guenther M(ax) 1921-1983 [composer]
Kauer, Gene *Source(s):* ASCP; CCE56; CCE62; CLTP ("Wide Wide World")
Kauffman, Helen Reed [poet, songwriter]
Hammond, Kate *Source(s):* ASCC; CCE57; CCE64
Kauffmann, Leo Justinius 1901-1944 [composer]
Justmann, Ralf *Source(s):* COMP; KOBW
Kaufman, Barbara 1912- [violinist, composer]
Dor, Daniela *Source(s):* BUL3; CCE53-55; COHN; HIXN
Dor, Dany *Source(s):* CCE56 Eunp
Kaufman, Isidore 1890-1976 [singer, songwriter]
Note(s): The following names are listed as pseuds. of Irving [i.e., Isidore] Kaufman.
Andrews, Jim *Source(s):* GRAC; MACE
Note(s): Also used by Abe Finkelstein.
Avon Comedy Four *Source(s):* CCE45 #63817, 2033 R142579
Note(s): Jt. pseud.: Joe Smith, Harry Goodwin & Charles Dale.
Beaver, George *Source(s):* GRAC; GRAK
Beaver, Harry *Source(s):* MACE
Beaver, Henry *Source(s):* GRAK
Brady, Harry *Source(s):* GRAC
Bronson, George *Source(s):* MACE
Note(s): Also used by Arthur Field [i.e., Abe Finkelstein].
Brown, Arthur *Source(s):* MACE
Note(s): Also used by Arthur Wilson.
Burton, Sammy *Source(s):* MACE
Note(s): Possible pseud.
Charles, Harold *Source(s):* MACE
Christy, Frank *Source(s):* MACE
Clark(e), Billy *Source(s):* GRAC
Note(s): See also Arthur Fields [i.e., Abe Finkelstein] who used the pseud. Billy Clarke.
Cobbin, Ned *Source(s):* CSUF
Confidential Charlie *Source(s):* GRAC; GRAK; MACE
Note(s): Also used by Ernest Hare.
Craig, Allen *Source(s):* MACE
Crane, George *Source(s):* MACE
Dickson, Charles *Source(s):* GRAC
Edwards, Tom *Source(s):* GRAC; MACE
Epstein, George *Source(s):* MACE
Flynn, Jimmy *Source(s):* GRAC; MACE
Frawley, Tom *Source(s):* GRAC; MACE
Harper, Billy *Source(s):* MACE

Harris, David *Source(s):* MACE
Note(s): Also Vernon Dalhart [i.e., M(arion) T(ry) Slaughter] & others.
Harris, Frank *Source(s):* GRAC; MACE
Hollis, Frank *Source(s):* GRAC
Irving Henry *Source(s):* MACE
Irving, John *Source(s):* MACE
Jordan, Allan *Source(s):* GRAC
Kaufman, Irving *Source(s):* CCE51 R79666 ("Kune Jine"); GRAC
Kay, Ilo *Source(s):* CCE54-55; CCE57-58; CCE61-64
Killeen, Pete *Source(s):* GRAC; GRAK; MACE
Loew, Jack *Source(s):* MACE
Note(s): Possible pseud. See also Jack [i.e., Jacob] Kaufman.
Macy, Ed *Source(s):* http://bixbeiderbeck.com/bixdisco/bixdisco1927.doc (25 Apr. 2005)
Note(s): Possible pseud.
Mark, Freddie *Source(s):* MACE
Mister X *Source(s):* GRAC
Note(s): Also used by Arthur Fields [i.e., Abe Finkelstein] & Vernon Dalhart [i.e., M(arion) T(ry) Slaughter] & possibly others.
Mitchell, Sidney *Source(s):* MACE
Neville, Tom *Source(s):* MACE
Parsons, Happy Jim *Source(s):* MACE
Patti, Orville *Source(s):* MACE
Post, Irving *Source(s):* MACE
Note(s): Possible pseud.
Seelig, Arthur *Source(s):* GRAC
Note(s): Also used by Arthur Fields [i.e., Abe Finkelstein]
Taylor, Noel *Source(s):* GRAC, GRAK; MACE
Topping, Harry *Source(s):* http://www.jabw.demon.co.uk/rpmboth.htm (21 Oct. 2002)
Van Tuyl, Vincent *Source(s):* GRAC
Vaughn, Charles *Source(s):* GRAC
Veteran, Vel *Source(s):* GRAC
Note(s): Also used by Arthur Fields [i.e., Abe Finkelstein] & Vernon Dalhart [i.e., M(arion) T(ry) Slaughter] & possibly others.
Watt, Brian *Source(s):* GRAK; MACE
Winters, Horace *Source(s):* MACE
Wood, Robert *Source(s):* GRAC
Note(s): Also used by Arthur Fields [i.e., Abe Finkelstein] & Dick Robertson.
Woolfe, Walter *Source(s):* MACE
Young, Marvin *Source(s):* GRAC; GRAK; MACE

Kaufman, Jacob [singer, songwriter]
Note(s): The following names are listed as pseuds. of Jack [i.e., Jacob] Kaufman.
Dalton, Jack *Source(s):* MACE
Green, Bert *Source(s):* GRAC p. 210; MACE
Hershfield, Harry *Source(s):* SUTT (2nd ed.)
Holmes, Dick *Source(s):* MACE
Kaufman, Jack *Source(s):* CCE51 R77784 & R79666; GRAC; MACE
Note(s): "There Never Was a Girl Like Marry" & "Kune Jine" (both CCE51)
Loew, Jack *Source(s):* MACE
Note(s): Possible pseud. See also Irving [i.e., Isidore] Kaufman.
Martin, Happy *Source(s):* MACE
Shea, Jack *Source(s):* MACE
Weary Willie *Source(s):* MACE
Note(s): Possible pseud. See also Carson J(ay) Robison & Francis Luther [i.e., Francis Luther Crow(e)]
White, Jerry *Source(s):* MACE

Kaufman, Martin Ellis 1899- [composer, author, conductor]
Kaufman, Whitey *Source(s):* ASCP; CCE63; TCAN
W. K. *Source(s):* CCE63 Eunp774911 ("Merry Christmas")

Kaufman, Seymour 1929-2004 [songwriter, pianist]
Note(s): Portraits: EWEN; GAN1; SHMM (Mar./Apr. 1989): cover, 4+.
Coleman, Cy *Source(s):* BAKR; EPMU; EWEN; GAN1; GAN2; NGDO; PEN2; PIPE

Kaufmann, Fritz Mordechai 1888-1912 [writer on music]
Barber, Pinkus *Source(s):* SEND
Pinkus Barber *Source(s):* SEND

Kaufmann, Walter (E.) 1907-1984 [composer, conductor, musicologist]
Day, Sonny *Source(s):* CCE53 Eunp; CCE57; CCE61
Jares, Vaclav *Source(s):* CCE53 Eunp; http://www.music.indiana.edu/collections/Kaufmann/biograph.html (6 Oct. 2002)
Walter, Kenneth *Source(s):* http://www.music.indiana.edu/collections/Kaufmann/biograph.html

Kaun, Hugo 1863-1932 [composer]
Note(s): Portraits: ETUP 53:1 (Jan. 1935): 2; MUCO (21 Nov. 1900): 1
Bold, Ferdinand *Source(s):* TPRF; http://csumc.sisc.edu/exhibit/MusicTour/GAMClassical.htm (18 June 2005)
Frascard, Emile *Source(s):* CCE23 E555527; CCE50 R62244 ("Call of the Sylphs")

Kavetzky, Samuel [composer]
Bedrokowetzky *Source(s):* SEND

Kaye, Jules Leonard 1918-2002 [songwriter, record producer]
Kaye, Buddy *Source(s):* DRSC; LCAR; PSND
Note(s): Also used by L. L. Kipp.

Kaye, Leonard Jay 1946- [composer, author, guitarist]

Cromwell, Link *Source(s):* ASCP
Kazee, Buell (Hilton) 1900-1976 [singer, composer]
Epitome of the Kentucky Mountain Songster *Source(s):* EPMU
Greatest White Male Folk Singer in the United States, The *Source(s):* EPMU
Kazoreck, Hildegard 1911- [composer]
Dewitz, Hildegard *Source(s):* BUL3; COHN; HIXN
Monti, Diana *Source(s):* BUL3; COHN; HIXN
Keating, John Henry 1870-1963 [composer]
Keating, Jack *Source(s):* CCE27 R37487
Udall, Lyn *Source(s):* ASCP; CCE30 R9971; REHH; ROOM
Keats, Frederick A. 1899- [composer]
Note(s): Portrait: ETUP 53:1 (Jan. 1935): 2
Douglas, John *Source(s):* TPRF
Keats, John 1795-1821 [poet]
Note(s): See PSND for additional nonmusic-related pseudonyms.
Caviare *Source(s):* GOTT; PSND
S.Y. *Source(s):* GOTT
Keefer, Arrett (Marwood) 1913-1967 [songwriter]
Keefer, Rusty *Source(s):* CCE53-54; CCE64; PMUS; SONG
Keen, John 1945-2002 [singer, songwriter, drummer]
Keen, Speedy *Source(s):* DRSC; EPMU
Keiser, Reinhard 1674-1739 [composer]
Cesaro, Renato *Source(s):* PIPE
Cesaro, Rinardo *Source(s):* LCAR
Keiser, Robert (A(dolph)) 1861 (or 62)-1932 [composer, songwriter]
Note: In the Copyright Renewal File there is a note under "King, Robert A." citing a 1 Feb. 1929 letter stating that Robert A. Keiser changed his name at the time of the World War. However, in STUW: "There is some opinion that Keiser was his real name, but there is substantial evidence that King is his birth name." According to Spaeth (p. 411), it is impossible to know the extent of Keiser/King's works since many ". . . appeared anonymously, representing hack jobs for various publishers." Portraits: JAST; *The Gem Dance Folio for 1913.* New York: Shapiro, 1914(?) (cover)
Abtler, F. *Source(s):* CCE31 R13722
Andrews, Champs L. *Source(s):* CCE33 R23391
Beatrice, F. *Source(s):* CCE30 R7710; CCE31 R13717
Bitner, Ed. F. *Source(s):* CCE30 R8987
Braunbach, Helena [or Helene] *Source(s):* CCE33 R23389
Brinkman, Paul *Source(s):* CCE33 R23390
Burgheim, G. J. *Source(s):* CCE30 R7722
Burgheim, J. J. *Source(s):* CCE31 R13726
Calhoun, Clayton *Source(s):* CCE46 R6145
Calhoun, John Clayton *Source(s):* CCE18 E431091; CCE46 R4953 ("The Beast of Berlin")
Chapin, Betty *Source(s):* CCE25 E621412 ("The Convict and the Rose")
Note(s): Jt. pseud.: Ballard MacDonald
Clifford, Park *Source(s):* CCE30 R8988
Corinne, J. *Source(s):* CCE30 R7719; CCE31 R13718
Dewey, W. L. *Source(s):* CCE30 R7716; CCE31 R13714
Earl, Mary *Source(s):* ASCP; CCE26 E636648; GILB p.324; MARC p. 60; STUW
Note(s): "Beautiful Ohio" See NOTES: Keiser/King, Robert (A(dolph)).
Fisher, J. Arthur *Source(s):* CCE33 R23394
Grey, Vivian *Source(s):* GILB p. 323-4; SPTH p. 336
Note(s): See NOTES: Keiser/King, Robert (A(dolph)).
Haley, Ed *Source(s):* MARC p. 60; MART p. 140; SPTH p. 233; STUW
Note(s): Possible pseud. of Robert A. King [i.e.,Keiser]; see NOTES: Keiser/King, Robert (A(dolph)).
Hickman, Elmore *Source(s):* CCE33 R23392
Hills, F(rank) *Source(s):* CCE30 R7708; CCE31 R13724
Hughes, Rob *Source(s):* CCE26 E633031
Jonas, Julius *Source(s):* CCE30 R7449
Keiser, Mrs. *Source(s):* GREN; REHG
Kennedy, H(arriet) *Source(s):* CCE30 R7709; CCE31 R13712; CCE33 R23388
Kennedy, May *Source(s):* CCE30 R7721;CCE30 R8983
King, A. R. *Source(s):* CCE31 R13716
King, Bob *Source(s):* CCE27 E678665; MARC p. 60; SPTH p. 313
Note(s): Do not confuse with Bob King [i.e., Robert B. Fournier], composer of "Baby This Is Love" & "That Crazy Rock" (both CCE59)
King, Bobo *Source(s):* PSND; STUW; TCAN
King, Mary *Source(s):* CCE46 R12235 ("Beautiful Ohio")
Note(s): "Beautiful Ohio" Typographical error? Should be Mary Earl?
King, R. A. K. *Source(s):* CCE30 R7447
King, Robert (A.) *Source (s):* CCE29 E9833; JASA
King, Robert Keiser *Source(s):* GAMM; LCPF (explanation of name change)
King, S. A. R. *Source(s):* CCE30 R7721
Kingsley, Robert *Source(s):* CCE27 E679596; CCE55 R52038 ("The Bright Sherman Valley")
Kingsley, Robie *Source(s):* CCE27 E679596
Klein, David *Source(s):* CCE30 R7448
Lester, Ida *Source(s):* CCE30 R7715
May, H. I. *Source(s):* CCE30 R7721
Metzger, A. *Source(s):* CCE30 R8991
Moho-Nali, (Chief) *Source(s):* CCE33 R23202

Montaine, A. R. *Source(s):* CCE31 R13711 ("Up in a Swing")
Note(s): May be misprint, i.e., "A.R." instead of "R.A"?
Montaine, R. A. *Source(s):* CCE30 R7724; CCE31 R13711
Morgan, J. P. *Source(s):* CCE30 R7717 ("The Cricket's Parade")
Note(s): See NOTES: Keiser/King, Robert (A(dolph)).
Moskowitz, R. A. *Source(s):* CCE31 R13721; CCE39 R7714
Quinn, H. L. *Source(s):* CCE33 R23204
Ravenhall, Mrs. *Source(s):* ASCP; MARC p. 60; REHG; STUW
Ravenhall, R. A. *Source(s):* GREN; REHG
Richmond, M. *Source(s):* CCE30 R7712; CCE31 R13713
Roberts, K(athleen) A. *Source(s):* CCE29 R2492; CCE36
Rogers, Cameron *Source(s):* CCE33 R23396
Roosevelt, T(homas) *Source(s):* CCE30 R7711; CCE30 R13710; *Sonneck Society Bulletin* (15:1): 7+.
Note(s): "Under the Stars and Stripes" See NOTES: Keiser/King, Robert (A(dolph)).
Rowenhall, Mrs. *Source(s):* GAMM
Sen, Yama *Source(s):* CCE30 R7705
Seymour, S. *Source(s):* CCE30 R7706
Smith, Sol *Source(s):* CCE30 R7713; CCE31 R13725
Stanley, F. *Source(s):* CCE30 R7707
Tobani, (H.) *Source(s):* CCE30 R7718; CCE31 R13728
Troja, Vallaire *Source(s):* CCE33 R23387
Walker, Bertram *Source(s):* CCE30 R8989
White, Alice *Source(s):* CCE20 E494849; CCE26 E637851; CCE48 R38737 ("Remember Me")
Williams, B. *Source(s):* CCE05 C96728; CCE33 R23203
Williams, George B. *Source(s):* CCE33 R23203
Wilson, R. A. *Source(s):* ASCP; GREN; REHG; SPTH p. 218 & 233; STUW
Write, Alice *Source(s):* CCE17 E464756; CCE47 R21957
Note(s): Typographical error?

Keith, Benjamin F(ranklin) 1846-1914 [vaudeville impresario]
Father of Vaudeville *Source(s):* JAST

Keithley, E. Clinton 1880-1955 [songwriter]
Frost, Jack *Source(s):* CCE44 #46708, 560 R128338; CCE44 #31175, 405 R128336; CCE44 #31175, 1156 R128337
Note(s): "When the Moon Shines Down in Old Alaska . . . ," "In the Heart of an Irish Rose" & "What Would I Do Without You." Also used by Mark Vincent Brine, Charles Degesco, Harold G. Frost & Bob Dylan [i.e., Robert Allen Zimmerman]

Kéler, Adalbert Paul von 1820-1882 [composer, conductor]
Béla, Kéler *Source(s):* CCE15 E376444
Kéler, Béla (Albrecht Pál) *Source(s):* NGDM
Kéler-Béla *Source(s):* BAKE; CCE37; CCE56

Kellem, Milton 1911-1992 [composer, author]
Craig, Jimmy *Source(s):* ASCP; CCE55
Hodes, Sophie *Source(s):* ASCP
Jane, Vicki *Source(s):* CCE55-56

Keller, Edward McDonald 1897-1974 [composer]
Archer, P. T. *Source(s):* CCE48; REHG; SUPN
Cole, Addison B. *Source(s):* CCE49
Elliot, Z. G. *Source(s):* REHG
Keller, Don *Source(s):* CCE48; CCE54; REHH
Lee, Pat *Source(s):* CCE48; CCE50; REHG; SUPN
March King of the West *Source(s):* REHG
McDonald, Ed *Source(s):* REHH
Rossi, Ray *Source(s):* REHH
Thomas, Z. G. *Source(s):* CCE52; REHG; SUPN

Keller, Fortunato 1690-1757 [composer]
Chelleri, Fortunato *Source(s):* BAKO; BAKR; CCMU; IBIM; WORB

Keller, Hans [composer]
Zak, Pyotr *Source(s):* SPIE
Note(s): Fictitious composer. Jt. pseud.: Susan Bradshaw.

Keller, James Walter 1936- [author, songwriter]
Keller, Jack *Source(s):* ASCP

Kelley, Arthur 1924- [singer, guitarist, songwriter]
Kelley, Guitar *Source(s):* HARS; LCAR

Kelly, Claude Arundale [composer]
Arundale, Claude *Source(s):* CPMU (publication dates 1898-1922); GREN

Kelly, Montgomery Jerome 1910-1971 [trumpeter, arranger, conductor]
Kelly, Monty *Source(s):* MUSR

Kemmler, Hubert 1961- [composer]
KaH, Hubert *Source(s):* PFSA

Kemp, Robert C. 1820-1897 [hymnist, composer]
Note(s): Portrait: ETUP 53:2 (Feb. 1935): 66
Kemp, Father *Source(s):* LCAR; METC; PRAT

Kemp, Victor 1875- [composer]
Girard, Harry *Source(s):* CPMU

Kempen, Hendrik Willem van 1899-1984 [composer]
Carf, Henri *Source(s):* http://www.muziekgroep.nl/componisten/componist.html?zknm=CARF%20HENRI (21 Oct.2002)

Kempenfelt, Richard 1718-1782 [naval officer, hymnist]
Philotheorus *Source(s):* CYBH (port.)

Kendis, James 1883-1946 [songwriter]
Bush, Billy *Source(s):* CCE58 R222959; CCE64
Chouder, Clem *Source(s):* CCE50 R61662 ("Boodle-um Boo")

James, Charles *Source(s):* CCE42 #5201, 984 R102643; CPOL RE-414-270
Kenbrockovitch, Ivan *Source(s):* CCE46 R10091 ("Bull-sheviki"); STUW
Kenbrovin, Jaan *Source(s):* BLIC; CCE46 E8232; KILG; LCAR; SPTH p. 413; STUW
Note(s): "I'm Forever Blowing Bubbles" (1918) Also jt. pseud.: Nathaniel (Hawthorne) Vincent & James Brockman.
Kendis, Sonny *Source(s):* CCE62; CPOL RE-14-886
Minnesota, Paul *Source(s):* CCE46 Eunp; CCE73
Ort, E. Rose Reese *Source(s):* CCE46 R10088 ("Naughty, Naughty, Daddies")

Kendricks, John Henry 1927-2003 [singer, songwriter]
Ballard, Hank [or Henry] *Source(s):* WASH

Kennedy, Mary Ann [singer, songwriter]
Kennedy Rose *Source(s):* AMUS; EPMU
Note(s): Jt. pseud.: Pam Rose

Kenton, Stan(ley Newcomb) 1911-1979 [bandleader, pianist, composer, arranger]
Canyon, Steve *Source(s):* JAMU
Standhim, Kant *Source(s):* JAMU
Stanton, Ken *Source(s):* JAMU

Kenyon, C(harles) F(rederick) 1879 (or 81)-1926 [music critic, writer on music]
Cumberland, Gerald *Source(s):* BAKE; LCAR

Kerkhof, Ernst van der 1964- [keyboardist, singer, songwriter]
Case, Alan *Source(s):* http://www.dprp.vuurwerk.n./reviews/9805.htm (6 Oct. 2002)

Kern, Carl Wilhelm 1874 (or 75)-1945 [composer, pianist, editor, organist, teacher]
Note(s): Portraits: ETUP 56:1 (Jan. 1938): 59; http://library.wustl.edu/units/music/coll/cwkern.html (6 Oct. 2002)
Becht, C. *Source(s):* CCE25 E604826
Faerber, Fr. *Source(s):* LCAR
Fordell, Lucien *Source(s):* CCE25 E554222
Foster, Kenneth *Source(s):* LCAR
Hefner, Carl *Source(s):* CCE37 R49150
Hoffmeister, Ludwig *Source(s):* CCE39 #33235, 13 R77980
Humes, Doris Grace *Source(s):* TPRF
Kleinmichel *Source(s):* CCE36 E59142 ("Primary Studies")
Kraskorr, Ivan *Source(s):* TPRF
Martin, J. D(ouglas) *Source(s):* CCE38 R71387; CCE39 #33235, 95 R77981
Navarre, Jean *Source(s):* LCAR
Note(s): Also used by Ethel Fisher.
Navarro, Jean *Source(s):* CCE34 R33066; LCAR
Neruda, (Vlademir de) *Source(s):* LCAR
Renk, Ludwig *Source(s):* CCE45 #4114, 388 R133938; KROH p. 124; LCAR
Ryder, Dudley *Source(s):* CCE36 R48548; LCAR
Note(s): Also used by Chester Nordman.

Kern, James King 1906-1985 [composer]
Kyser, Kay *Source(s):* REHH

Kern, Jerome David 1885-1945 [composer]
Note(s): Portraits: EWEN; LYMN; SHMM (Mar. 1986): 3, 6 & cover
Dean of America's Show Music Composers, The *Source(s):* PSND
Father of Modern American Theater Music *Source(s):* LYMN
Father of the American Musical *Source(s):* MRSQ 3/1: 22
King of the American Musical Theater, The *Source(s):* PSND
Musical Clothier—Nothing More or Less *Source(s):* http://www.nytimes.com/learning/general/onthisday/bday/0127.html (6 Oct. 2002)
Note(s): Called himself.

Kershaw, A. [composer]
Wahsreka *Source(s):* CPMU (publication date 1899)

Kershaw, Doug(las James) 1936- [singer, songwriter, fiddler]
Crazy Cajun, The *Source(s):* MCCL
Louisiana Man *Source(s):* NGAM

Kerzanet, Jean André Léon Louis [composer]
Valmer, Michel *Source(s):* GOTH

Kessler, Richard 1875-1960 [playwright]
Richards, Friedrich *Source(s):* PIPE
Rössler, Hans *Source(s):* PIPE

Kessler, Robert von 1906- [composer, arranger]
Winterberger, (Martin) *Source(s):* CCE62; CCE65; iCCE68; RIES

Kestner, Felicitas 1911- [composer]
Kukuck, Felicitus *Source(s):* RIES

Kestner, H. [songwriter]
H. K. *Source(s):* CPMU (publication date 1846)

Kestner, John Nelson 1935- [composer, author, director]
Clifton, John *Source(s):* ASCP

Ketèlbey, Albert William 1875-1959 [composer]
Note(s): Portraits: ETUP 53:2 (Feb. 1935): 66; MUOP 52:618 (Mar. 1929): 531
Aston, (A.) William *Source(s):* CPMU; GOTH; GROL; LCAR; REHH; SUPN
Note(s): There is no substance to the story that Ketelbey's original surname was "Aston." (REHH); however, in EPMU entry is under "Aston."
Basque, Andre (de) *Source(s):* GROL; LCAR; SUPN
Charlton, Dennis *Source(s):* CCE76; GROL
Clifford, Raoul *Source(s):* CPMU; GOTH; GROL

DeBasque, Andre *Source(s):* REHH; SUPN
Kaye, Geoffrey *Source(s):* CPMU; GOTH; LCAR; SUPN
Keye, Geoffrey *Source(s):* GROL; LCAR
Vodorinski, Anton *Source(s):* CPMU; GOTH; GROL; KILG; LCAR; NGDM; SUPN

Kethe, William ?-1608? [author, hymnist]
Ke., W. *Source(s):* FULD ("Foure")
Kith, Wylliam [or Wyllyam] *Source(s):* HATF; LCAR
Kythe, William *Source(s):* HATF

Ketten, Henri 1848-1883 [composer]
Valerio *Source(s):* GREN

Ketterer, Ella 1889-1972 [composer]
Note(s): Portrait: ETUP 53:2 (Feb. 1935): 66
Scott, Ann *Source(s):* TPRF

Keuleman, Adrian 1903-1966 [songwriter]
Barnard, B(arney) *Source(s):* CCE35 Efor47889; CCE36 Efor41342
Bernard, Adrien *Source(s):* CCE70 R486152
Note(s): Jt. pseud.: Harold Elton Box & Clem(ent) Bernard.
Boccolosi, Harry *Source(s):* CCE40 #19415 Efor63075; CCE67; LCCF 1938-45 (reference card)
Note(s): Jt. pseud.: Harold Elton Box, Harry Leon [i.e., Sugarman] & Domonic [or Don] Pelosi.
Cox, Desmond *Source(s):* CCE50-51; LCCF 1946-54 (see reference citing 6/29/51 letter)
Dévereux, Jules *Source(s):* CCE40 #18216 Efor62825; LCCF 1938-45 (reference card)
Note(s): Jt. pseud.: Harry Leon [i.e., Sugarman], Harold Elton Box & Domonic [or Don] Pelosi.
Fellows, Reginald *Source(s):* CCE67
Fraser, Gordon *Source(s):* CCE40 #25023 Efor63262; CCE67; LCCF 1938-45 (reference card)
Note(s): Jt. pseud.: Harold Elton Box, Harry Leon [i.e., Sugarman] & Domonic [or Don] Pelosi.
Fuertes, Pedro *Source(s):* CCE43 #46647 Efor68713 ("Serenade to a Dream")
Note(s): Jt. pseud.: Harold Elton Box.
Heatherton, Fred *Source(s):* CCE45 #13436 Efor70306 (Dreams of Yesterday"); CPOL RE-7-846
Note(s): Jt. pseud.: Harold Elton Box & Lewis Ilda [i.e., Irwin Dash]
Morrow, Morton *Source(s):* CCE49-51; CCE63-64; CCE70 R484404
Note(s): Jt. pseud.: Harold Elton Box & Paddy [i.e., John Godfrey Owen] Roberts.
Perch, Polly *Source(s):* CCE34 Efor37471 ("Scratch-a-Poll-Polly")
Note(s): Jt. pseud.: Ralph (T.) Butler , Harold Elton Box & C(harles) J(oseph) Edwards.
Spade, Jack *Source(s):* CCE44 Efor70219; KILG
Note(s): Jt. pseud.: Harold Elton Box & Ilda Lewis [i.e., Irwin Dash]
Young, Errol *Source(s):* CCE45 Efor70638 ("I'm Happy in Rags")
Note(s): Jt. pseud.: Harold Elton Box.

Khadzhibekov, Taghi-zade 1912-1984 [conductor, composer]
Niyazi *Source(s):* BAKT

Khan, Faiyaz (Hus(s)ain) 1881-1950 [singer, composer]
Piya, Prem *Source(s):* GROL
Prem Piya *Source(s):* GROL

Khan, Hidayat 1917- [composer, conductor]
Ayaz *Source(s):* KOMS; PFSA

Khaury, Herbert 1932?-1996 [entertainer, songwriter]
Note(s): Surname also given as: Kauhry.
Castle, Vernon *Source(s):* http://www.tinytim.org/articles/magazines/phtplay_august_1968.html (20 July 2005)
Dell, Rollie *Source(s):* http://www.tinytim.org/articles/magazines/phtplay_august_1968.html
Dover, Darry *Source(s):* BBDP
Love, Larry *Source(s):* BBDP
Swink, Emmett *Source(s):* http://www.tinytim.org/articles/magazines/phtplay_august_1968.html
Tiny Tim *Source(s):* BBDP; CCE68; FAFO; LCAR

Kherlakian, Gérard Daniel 1941- [composer]
Gerard, Danyel *Source(s):* PFSA

Khu(-Elefteriadis), Emilios 1880 (or 85)-1935 [composer]
Mussorgsky of Greece, The *Source(s):* GROL
Riadis, Emil(ios) *Source(s):* BAKR; LCAR; MACM; RIEM

Kiemle, Hans Dieter 1939- [composer]
H. D. K. *Source(s):* KOMS

Kierland, Joseph Scott 1932- [author, playwright, lyricist]
Scott, Joseph *Source(s):* ASCP

Kiesekamp, Hedwig 1844-1919 [poet]
Rafael, L(udwig) *Source(s):* LAST

Kiesewetter, Hartmut 1937- [composer]
Kingston, Hardy *Source(s):* KOMS; PFSA

Kiesewetter, Raphael-Georg 1773-1850 [musicologist, writer on music]
Balthesar *Source(s):* RILM 74-00451-ap
Leduc, A. C. *Source(s):* RILM 82-03593-ap
Note(s): Presumed pseud.; however, in RILM 74-0051-ap listed as possible pseud. of Peter Lichtenthal.

Kieswetter, Rob [singer, songwriter]
Birdman, Bobby *Source(s):* http://www.hushrecords.com/bobbybird.html (2 Nov. 2003)

Kiesow, Walter 1905-1965 [composer]
Tix, Ben *Source(s):* SUPN
Walters, Will *Source(s):* SUPN

Kiessling, Heinz 1926- [songwriter, arranger, pianist]
Mondstein, Christian *Source(s):* CCE57-58; CCE60-61; NGDM; PFSA; RIES
Kilcher, Jewel 1974- [singer, songwriter]
Jewel *Source(s):* CM25; LCAR
Kilgore, David [guitarist, songwriter]
Night Owl *Source(s):* http://www.geocities.com/heinzart.geo/songwriters.htm (5 Oct. 2003)
Kill, Ignaz [writer on music]
JK *Source(s):* HEYT
Killen, W(illiam) D. 1932- [music publisher, songwriter, producer]
Killen, Buddy *Source(s):* CCE73; MCCL; PMUS; PSND
Killette, Ronald B. [songwriter]
Trail, Buck *Source(s):* CCE68; PMUS
Kilmister, Ian Fraiser 1945- [singer, songwriter]
Kilmister, Lemmy *Source(s):* BLIC
Lemmy *Source(s):* EPMU (see under: Motörhead); LCAR
Kimbro, John M. 1929- [author, playwright, composer]
Note(s): For literary pseuds., see LCAR & *Contemporary Authors.*
Allyson, Kym *Source(s):* PSND
Note(s): On music.
Kimbrough, Lottie 1900- [singer, guitarist, songwriter]
Beaman, (Mrs.) Lottie *Source(s):* AMUS; EPMU; HARS; LCAR
Brooks, Jennie *Source(s):* EPMU; HARS; LCAR
Brown, Lottie *Source(s):* EPMU; HARS; LCAR
Cary, Clara *Source(s):* EPMU; HARS; LCAR
Everson, Lottie *Source(s):* EPMU; HARS; LCAR
Johnson, Martha *Source(s):* EPMU; HARS; LCAR
Kansas City Butterball, The *Source(s):* AMUS; EPMU; HARS; LCAR
Kimbrough, Lena *Source(s):* EPMU; HARS; LCAR
Moran, Mae *Source(s):* EPMU; HARS; LCAR
Kimmel, Edwin Howard 1926- [composer, author]
Kain, Eddie *Source(s):* ASCP
Kind, (Johann) Friedrich 1768-1843 [author]
Oscar *Source(s):* PIPE
Oskar *Source(s):* WORB
Kinder, Ralph 1876-1952 [composer, organist]
Note(s): Portrait: ETUP 53:2 (Feb. 1935): 66
Kirkland, Ralph *Source(s):* TPRF
Ralph, Kirkland *Source(s):* CCE41 #44409, 13 R101031; CCE42 #29091, 506 R109148
Kindler, Dietmar [or Dittmar] 1935- [composer]
Bredow, Horst *Source(s):* CCE67; CCE73 Efor165428; KOMS; PFSA

King, Albert 1903-1943 [composer, pianist, singer]
King, Jack *Source(s):* ASCP
King, C. Dudley 1914-1982 [conductor, composer, arranger]
King, Pete *Source(s):* MUSR
King, Claude 1933-1983 [singer, songwriter, guitarist, actor]
Wolverton Mountain Man, The *Source(s):* MCCL
King, Frank H. 1847?-1900 [composer]
Note(s): Husband of Rive-King. Do not confuse with Frank King, pseud. of Julius Frank (Anthony) Kuczynski.
Rive-King, Julie *Source(s):* DWCO
Note(s): See NOTES: Rive-King, Julie.
King, Karl L(awrence) 1891-1971 [composer]
Note(s): Portrait: ETUP 58:8 (Aug. 1940): 570
America's Other "March King" *Source(s):* http://www6.semo.edu/news/nr/archive/pr101899.html (12 Oct. 2002)
Note(s): See also E(dward) T(aylor) Paull.
Lawrence, Carl *Source(s):* CCE39 #12615, 15 R73782; REHG; SMIN
King, Kenneth 1944- [songwriter, producer, broadcaster]
King, Jonathan *Source(s):* CASS; LCAR
King, Matthew Peter 1733-1823 [composer, theorist]
Author of The Siege of Valenciennes *Source(s):* LCAR
King, Master *Source(s):* NGDM
King, Oliver (A.) 1855-1923 [composer]
Note(s): Portrait: ETUP 53:2 (Feb. 1935): 66
King in C, A *Source(s):* SCHO
Rex *Source(s):* SCHO
King, Reginald (Claude McMahon) 1904-1991 [composer]
Andrew, Rex *Source(s):* http://www.bardic-music.com/king.htm (16 May 2005)
Arnold, Clifford *Source(s):* http://www.bardic-music.com/king.htm
Stevens, Hal *Source(s):* http://www.bardic-music.com/king.htm
King, Riley B. 1925- [singer, guitarist, songwriter]
Ambassador of the Blues *Source(s):* HERZ
Beale Street Blues Boy *Source(s):* AMEN; AMUS; EPMU
Blues Boy *Source(s):* AMEN; HARS
Blues Boy from Beale Street *Source(s):* AMEN; HARS
Blues Boy King *Source(s):* EPMU
Bossman of the Blues, The *Source(s):* AMEN; HARS
Boy from Beale Street, The *Source(s):* AMEN; HARS
King, B. B. *Source(s):* AMUS; CM24; EPMU; HARS; HERZ; RECR

King, Blues Boy *Source(s):* AMUS; CM24; EPMU; HARS; HERZ; RECR
King of the Blues, The *Source(s):* AMEN; CM24; HARS
Note(s): See also McKinley Morganfield.
King, Robert [songwriter]
Note(s): Probably not Robert (A.) King [i.e., Robert (A(dolph)) Keiser] since all of his works in CCE30 are renewals
Pelling, George *Source(s):* CCE30 E16640; CCE57 ("Meeting and Parting")
King, Robert [or Bob] [songwriter]
Note(s): Do not confuse with Robert (A.) King [i.e., Keiser, Robert (A(dolph))]
King, Victor *Source(s):* CCE59 E126528 ("Boppin Bobbie Jean")
King, Stanford 1912- [composer, teacher]
Lane, Vernon *Source(s):* CCE40 #36891 E89386; CCE41 #3461 E90068; TPRF
Parsons, Spencer *Source(s):* CCE58; CPOL RE-308-416; TPRF
Stevens, Milo *Source(s):* CCE49-50; TPRF
King, Wayne (Harold) 1901-1985 [clarinetist, bandleader, composer]
Waltz King, The *Source(s):* EPMU; PSND; SIFA; VACH
Note(s): See also Archibald Joyce, Johann (Baptist) Strauss, (Sr.) (1804-1849) & Johann (Baptist) Strauss, (Jr.) (1825-1899).
Kingsbury, George, (Jr.) 1926- [singer, songwriter, guitarist]
Roberts, Kenny *Source(s):* CCE51; MCCL
Kingsford, Charles 1907-1996 [composer, conductor, music therapist]
Cohen, Charles (James) *Source(s):* ASCP; CCE60-61; LCAR
Kingsley, Charles 1819-1875 [author, poet]
Note(s): Portrait: CYBH. See PSND & LCAR for additional nonmusic-related pseudonyms.
Lot, Parson *Source(s):* GOTE; LCAR; PSND
Kingsley, Gershon 1925- [composer, conductor]
Perrey-Kingsley *Source(s):* LCAR
Note(s): Jt. pseud.: Jean-Jacques Perrey.
Kingston, Mary [composer]
Marielli, M. *Source(s):* CPMU (publication dates 1805-35); JACK
Kingston, Robert (Charles) [composer]
White, Barry *Source(s):* CCE58-59; CLTP ("Mary Hartman")
Note(s): Also used by Barry Eugene Carter.
Kinkel, Johanna (née Mockel) 1810-1858 [composer, writer, pianist, teacher]
Mathieux, Johanna *Source(s):* GROL
Kinsey, Lester 1927-2001 [singer, songwriter, guitarist]
Kinsey, Big Daddy *Source(s):* HERZ; LCAR
Kinsman, Elmer (F(ranklin)) [composer]
Alexandrov, Feodor *Source(s):* CCE63 E1733535; CPOL RE-524-089 & RE-623-707
Note(s): Jt. pseud.: Walter (Charles) Ehret.
Blaine, (G.) Gordon *Source(s):* CCE61; CCE63 E178475; CPOL RE-448-387 & RE-478-271
Brulovsky, Nicolai *Source(s):* CCE63; CPOL RE-520-038
Note(s): Jt. pseud.: Walter (Charles) Ehret.
Carlton, John *Source(s):* CPOL RE-435-675 & RE-435-677
Note(s): Jt. pseud.: Walter (Charles) Ehret. Ehret also used as jt. pseud. with other individuals; see NOTES: Carlton, John.
Chambers, Robert *Source(s):* CCE58; CCE61-62; CCE64
Note(s): Jt. pseud.: Walter (Charles) Ehret. Ehret also used as jt. pseud. with other individuals; see NOTES: Chambers, Robert.
Charles, Gregg *Source(s):* CCE65
Note(s): Jt. pseud.: Walter (Charles) Ehret.
Creston, William *Source(s):* CCE62 E162285 ("Ah, Love, But a Day"); CCE62 E166286 (" Nobody Coming to Marry Me")
Note(s): Jt. pseud.: Walter (Charles) Ehret;
Elkins, Charles *Source(s):* CPOL RE-360-376
Note(s): Jt. pseud.: Walter (Charles) Ehret.
Follett, Charles *Source(s):* CCE62-64
Note(s): Jt. pseud.: Walter (Charles) Ehret; see NOTES: Follett, Charles.
G. G. B. *Source(s):* CPOL RE-529-786
Hastings, Paul *Source(s):* CPOL RE-335-410 & RE-335-412
Note(s): Jt. pseud.: Walter (Charles) Ehret; see NOTES: Hastings, Paul.
Kinsman, Frank(lin) *Source(s):* LCCF65 E218775; CPOL RE-511-591
Note(s): Do not confuse with (J.) Franklin Kinsman who used the pseud. Neal W. Kent.
Kolar, Andreas *Source(s):* CCE64 E189208 & E189211
Note(s): Jt. pseud.: Walter (Charles) Ehret.
Manning, Frank *Source(s):* CCE63 E180303; CPOL RE-529-785
Milanov, Dimitri *Source(s):* CCE63 E172850; CPOL RE-520-041; CPOL RE-624-260
Note(s): Jt. pseud.: Walter (Charles) Ehret.
Morris, William *Source(s):* CCE60; CCE64 E189207 & E189209; CCE65 E203609
Note(s): Jt. pseud.: Walter (Charles) Ehret. Do not confuse with William Morris, author of words for "This Shepherd's Story," (music by Clarence

Dickinson (1960 renewal)) & composer/lyricist of "Two Sides to Every Story."
Newcombe, Jeffery *Source(s):* CCE67
Sokolov, Ivan *Source(s):* CCE63 E173694; CPOL RE-524-385
Note(s): Jt. pseud.: Walter (Charles) Ehret.
Wentworth, Robert *Source(s):* CPOL RE-360-449
Williamson, Warren *Source(s):* CCE60; CCE66 E233280; CCE67 E238144
Note(s): Jt. pseud.: Walter (Charles) Ehret; see NOTES: Williamson, Warren.

Kinsman, (J.) Franklin [songwriter]
Note(s): Do not confuse with Frank(lin) Kinsman, i.e., Elmer (F(ranklin)) Kinsman.
Kent, Neal W. *Source(s):* CCE61 E153222 ("Rejoice, Ye Pure in Heart")

Kinyon, John L(eroy) 1918-2002 [composer]
Barrett, Charles *Source(s):* REHH
Gable, Cora *Source(s):* REHG; SMIN; SUPN
Jackson, Leroy *Source(s):* CCE54; CCE60; LCAR; REHG; SMIN; SUPN
Note(s): For a list of titles under this name, see REHG & REHH. Also used by Leonard Feather.
Lauder, Dale *Source(s):* LCAR; REHG; SMIN; SUPN
MacBeth, James *Source(s):* LCAR; REHG; SMIN; SUPN
Menz, J(ohn) *Source(s):* LCAR; REHG; SMIN; SUPN
North, Carolina *Source(s):* SMIN
Piato, A. R. *Source(s):* SMIN
Powers, Robert *Source(s):* LCAR; REHG; SMIN; SUPN
Reynolds, Peter *Source(s):* REHG; SMIN
Smith, M. M. *Source(s):* REHG; SUPN
Stanton, V. *Source(s):* LCAR; REHG; SUPN
Tyler, Clark *Source(s):* LCAR; REHG; SMIN; SUPN
Waltzer, B. A. *Source(s):* REHG; SUPN

Kipp, L. L. [composer]
Note(s): L. L. Kipp might be a pseud. of Jules Leonard Kaye?
Kaye, Buddy *Source(s):* CLTP ("Little Audrey (cartoon)" and "Little Lulu")
Note(s): Also used by Jules Leonard Kaye.

Kirby, Fred 1910-1996 [singer, songwriter]
Carolina Cowboy, The *Source(s):* MCCL
Victory Cowboy *Source(s):* MCCL

Kirby, Sylvia (Jane) 1956- [singer, songwriter, artist]
Sylvia *Source(s):* MILL; (port); MCCL
Note(s): Also used by Richard Kountz & Sylvia Vanderpool Robinson.

Kirchgässner, Helmut 1927- [composer, arranger]
Mordent, Jerry *Source(s):* CCE77; KOMP; KOMS; PFSA

Kirchlehrer, Ferenc 1791-1868 [violinist, author]
Hegyaljai *Source(s):* PIPE

Kirchstein, Harold Manfred [or Manford] 1906-1993 [composer]
Grant, Harold (M.) *Source(s):* CCE49-50; CCE73 R557411
René, Henri *Source(s):* CCE73 R564771; KOMP; LCAR; PFSA; RIES
Note(s): Also used by Harold Grant.

Kirk, Edward N. [clergyman, songwriter]
Note(s): Birth date may be 1782.
New England Pastor, A. *Source(s):* DAPE ("Songs for Social and Public Worship" (1863))

Kirk, Ronald T(heodore) 1936-1977 [multi-instrumentalist, composer]
Kirk, Rahsaan Roland *Source(s):* BAKE; CCE74; CLAB; LCAR; PEN2
Kirk, Roland *Source(s):* BAKE; LCAR; PSND
Rahsaan *Source(s):* LCAR

Kirkland, Eddie 1928- [singer, guitarist, songwriter]
Blues Man, The *Source(s):* HARS; LCAR
Note(s): See also Roosevelt Sykes.
Kirk, Eddie *Source(s):* HARS; HARS; LCAR

Kirkland, Mike James 1946- [composer, singer]
Kirkland, Bo *Source(s):* ASCP

Kirkpatrick, David Gordon 1927-2003 [singer, songwriter, guitarist]
Australia's King of Country Music *Source(s):* http://www.big.goldenguitar.com.au/Guitar.html (6 Oct. 2002)
Dusty, Slim *Source(s):* DAUM; EPMU; MCCL; PEN2
King of Country Music, The *Source(s):* MCCL
Note(s): See also Roy (Claxton) Acuff, Willie (Hugh) Nelson & Hank [i.e., Hir(i)am (King)] Williams.

Kirkpatrick, H(olbert) [or H(allbert)] H(ill) [composer]
Patrick, Kirk *Source(s):* CCE57; CPOL RE-108-978
Note(s): Also used by Harold William Kirpatrick, (Jr.) & Leland James Gillette.

Kirkpatrick, Harold William, (Jr.) [composer]
Patrick, Kirk *Source(s):* CCE65
Note(s): Also used by H(olbert) [or H(allbert)] H(ill) Kirkpatrick & Leland James Gillette.
Patrick, Toad Kirk *Source(s):* CCE53

Kirkup, James (Falconer) 1918 (or 29?)- [author, literary scholar]
Falconer, James *Source(s):* PIPE; PSND
James, Andrew *Source(s):* PIPE; PSND
Jun, Terahata *Source(s):* PSND
Shigeru, Tsuyuki *Source(s):* PSND
Summerforest, Ivy B. *Source(s):* PIPE; PSND

Kisielewski, Stefan 1911-1991 [author, composer]
Holynska, Julia *Source(s):* http://www.brum2000.swinternet.co.uk/kiesiel (1 Nov. 2002)

Kisiel, (Teodor Klon) *Source(s):* LCAR; PSND
Klon, Teodor *Source(s):* http://wiem.onet.l/wiem/ooofbf.html (29 Oct. 2002)
Stalinski, Tomasz *Source(s):* LCAR; http://wiem.onet.l/wiem/ooofbf.html
Kisowski, Karl 1864- [composer]
Kaes, Karl *Source(s):* SUPN
Kees, Karl *Source(s):* SUPN
Kjelson, Lee 1926- [composer]
Carlton, John *Source(s):* CCE60; CPOL RE-38-977
Note(s): Jt. pseud.: Walter (Charles) Ehret. Ehret also used as jt. pseud. with other individuals; see NOTES: Carlton, John.
Spencer, William *Source(s):* CCE58; CPOL RE-308-427
Note(s): Jt. pseud.: Walter (Charles) Ehret.
Kjerulf, Charles Theodor Martin 1858-1919 [composer]
Kok, Jens *Source(s):* http://www.mic.dk/music/compidx.htm (6 Oct. 2003)
Klackel, Stephan 1753-1788 [violinist, composer]
Patan *Source(s):* MACM
Klatzkin, Leo(n) 1914-1992 [composer, arranger]
Lenard, Melvyn *Source(s):* CLTP ("Racket Squad," opening theme)
Notes(s): Composed music for publisher David M. Gordon under this name as did William Lava, Irving Gertz, Dave Kahn, Joseph [or Joe] Mullendore & possibly others. See also David M. Gordon.
Klaus, Gerhard 1929- [composer]
Weiss, Lutz *Source(s):* KOMS; PFSA
Klebba, Werner 1885- [composer]
Fanta, Will *Source(s):* REHH; SUPN
Klebe, Hans Werner 1907- [composer]
Kleve *Source(s):* KOMP; KOMS
Klecki, Paul 1900-1973 [conductor, composer]
Kletzki, Paul *Source(s):* BAKE; LCAR
Kleiber, Carlos 1930-2004 [conductor, composer[
Keller, Karl *Source(s):* GDRM
Klein, Bernhard (Joseph) 1793-1832 [composer]
Note(s): Portrait: ETUP 53:3 (Mar. 1935): 132
Palestrina of Berlin *Source(s):* NGDM
Klein, Carole 1941 (or 42)- [singer, songwriter]
King, Carole *Source(s):* BAKR; CASS; CM06; DIMA; EPMU; HARR; KICK; PEN2
Klein, Fritz Heinrich 1892-1977 [composer]
Heautontimorumenos *Source(s):* OMUO
Klein, Gene 1949- [singer, songwriter, actor]
Simmons, Gene *Source(s):* LCAR; NOMG
Whitz, Chaim *Source(s):* NOMG
Note(s): Possible pseud.?
Klein, Gideon 1919-1945 [composer, pianist]
Note(s): Used pseuds. (BAKT); however, to date only one identified.
Vránek, Karel *Source(s):* GROL
Kleinbard, Annette 1940- [guitarist, singer, songwriter]
Connors, Carol *Source(s):* CCE61-62; WORT
Kleindienst, Hans 1876-after 1907 [author]
Moisson, A. *Source(s):* PIPE
Kleine, Werner 1907- [composer]
Helbig, Michael *Source(s):* CCE56-64; CCE68; RIES
Kleinmeijer, Henk [composer]
Henski [or Hensky], J. *Source(s):* REHG; SUPN
Jorna, Stephen *Source(s):* SUPN
Manninger, Fr. *Source(s):* SUPN
Klemm, Gustav 1897-1947 [composer, conductor, critic]
Note(s): Portraits: ETUP 53:3 (March 1935): 132; ETUP 53:12 (Dec. 1935): 703
Barton, Glen *Source(s):* CCE44 #49947 E126948; CCE51; TPRF
Note(s): Also used by Harley F. Brocht.
Marshall, David *Source(s):* TPRF
Tall, Victor *Source(s):* CCE72 R536575
Klickmann, F(rank) Henri 1885-1966 [composer, arranger, accordionist]
Note(s): Portrait: JASA
Camini, Bruno *Source(s):* CCE54; REHH
Carreno, Roberto *Source(s):* CCE42 #52458 E110072; CCE48; CPOL RE-31-253; REHH
Clique, Henry *Source(s):* REHH
Gossette, Jean *Source(s):* CCE41 #31709 E96119; CCE47-48; CCE68
Hendrowski, Frank *Source(s):* (not recorded)
Orlando, Sal *Source(s):* CCE62
Reynolds, Frank *Source(s):* CCE41 #47874, 112 R101211
Speroy, Robert *Source(s):* CCE77; CCE78 R674825
Stanley, Arnold *Source(s):* CCE53; CCE55
Stoner, M. S. *Source(s):* CCE46 E10049 ("Something Tells Me")
Kling, Heywood [composer]
Kling, Woody *Source(s):* CLTP ("Jimmy Durnate Show")
Klingenbrunner, Wilhelm 1782-1864 [composer]
Blum, Wilhelm *Source(s):* OMUO
Klinger, Gustav(e) 1854 (or 56)-1922 [playwright, journalist]
Buchbinder, Bernhard (Ludwig) *Source(s):* GAN1; GAN2; WORB
Klinkhammer, Stefan 1935- [composer]
Koblenzer, Jacques *Source(s):* KOMP; PFSA
St. August, John *Source(s):* KOMP; PFSA
Klitzsch, Karl Emanuel 1812-1889 [conductor, composer]
Kronach, Emanuel *Source(s):* BAKE; MACM; MELL; PRAT
Kloeren, Lothar 1928- [composer]
Daxson, (Nils) *Source(s):* CCE65; KOMP; PFSA

Klohr, John N(icholas) 1869-1956 [composer]
Note(s): Portrait: ETUP 53:3 (Mar. 1935): 132
Nichols, John *Source(s):* TPRF
Klose, Othmar 1889-1970 [pianist, conductor, composer]
Fred P. *Source(s):* OMUO
Kluczko, John(ny) 1912-1977 [arranger, composer]
Watson, John(ny G.) *Source(s):* STUW; VACH
Klug, Geraldine Dolores 1915- [composer, author, performer]
Kaye, Gerry *Source(s):* ASCP
Klüter, Willy 1955- [composer]
Werdenfels *Source(s):* KOMS; PFSA
Kmoch, Frantisek 1848-1912 [composer]
Father of Czech Band Music *Source(s):* SMIN
Father of the Czech Wind Band *Source(s):* REHG
Knabl, Rudolf [or Rudi] 1912- [composer]
Blank, Rolf *Source(s):* CCE64; KOMP; KOMS; PFSA
Knauff, John 1879-1959 [actor, composer, lyricist]
Godfrey, John *Source(s):* CCE44 #46708, 188 R133164
Norton, James *Source(s):* SUTT
Note(s): In SUTT given name in index: Jack.
Norworth, Jack *Source(s):* CASS; GAMM; NGAM; SUTT
Knauth, Robert Franz 1815-1892 [songwriter, writer on music]
Note(s): Portraits: ETUP 51:7 (July 1933): 434; EWCY
Franz, Robert *Source(s):* BAKR; ETUD; EWCY; NGDM; PRAT
Note(s): Adopted middle name as surname in 1847.
Janina, Olga de *Source(s):* IBIM; WORB
Knecht, Justin Heinrich 1752-1817 [writer on music, composer]
Baal, Johannes *Source(s):* PFSA
Pater Marianus, OSB *Source(s):* PFSA
Kneissler, Hipp. 1831-1883 [librettist]
Nessl, Erich *Source(s):* STGR
Knigge, Adolf Franz Friedrich Ludwig, Freiherr von 1752-1796 [author, musician]
Meywerk, J. C. *Source(s):* IBIM; WORB
Noldman, Benjamin *Source(s):* IBIM; WORB
Philo *Source(s):* LCAR
Wurmbrand, Joseph von *Source(s):* IBIM; WORB
Knigge, (Baron) Wilhelm 1827-1888 [composer]
Polack-Daniels, (B.) *Source(s):* MELL; STGR
Knight, Gladys (M.) 1944- [singer, lyricist]
Knight, Maria *Source(s):* ASCP
Knight, Joseph Philip 1812-1887 [composer]
Mortimer, Philip *Source(s):* CPMU; CYBH; DEA2; GOTH; GOTT; KILG
Note(s): Jt. pseud.?: Thomas Hay(n)es Bayly.
Knight, Vick (Ralph, Sr.) 1908-1984 [author, composer, writer]
Fell, Tom *Source(s):* ASCP; CCE55; CCE57
Knittelmair, Lambert 1769-1845 [composer]
L. K. *Source(s):* CPMU
Knobel, Theo 1906- [composer, conductor]
Alden, H. C. *Source(s):* CE55-59; CCE61-64; RIES
Knoblauch, Edward 1874-1945 [author, playwright]
Knoblock, Edward *Source(s):* GAN1; GAN2; LCAR; WORB
Knobloch, Fred [songwriter]
S-K-O *Source(s):* EPMU
Note(s): Jt. pseud.: Thom Schuyler & Paul Overstreet.
Knöpler, Paul 1879-1967 [composer, librettist]
Knepler, Paul *Source(s):* GAN1; GAN2; LCAR
Knorr, Iwan [or Ivan] (Otto Armand) 1853-1916 [composer, writer, teacher]
Note(s): Portrait: ETUP 53:3 (Mar. 1935): 132
Armand, I. [or J.] O. *Source(s):* GROL; MACM; MELL; WORB
Knowles, Norman George 1938- [composer, manager]
Kaaihue, Norman K. *Source(s):* CCE73 R559991
Kaye, Norman *Source(s):* ASCP
Kobylinsky, Lev L'vovich 1889-1947 [poet]
Ellis *Source(s):* LAST
Kočevar, Ferdo 1833-1878 [author]
Žavčanin *Source(s):* PIPE
Koch, Jodocus 1493-1555 [theologian, hymnist]
Jonas, Justus *Source(s):* NGDM; WORB
Koch, Jürgen 1946- [composer]
Bendt, Oliver *Source(s):* PFSA
Köchel, Jürgen (Arthur) 1925- [librettist]
Morgener, Jörg *Source(s):* PIPE; *Tempo* (No. 194): 27
Kochmann, Spero 1889- [composer]
Calmon, Theo *Source(s):* REHH; SUPN
Castaldo, S. *Source(s):* LCPC letter cited (23 Dec. 1930); REHH; SUPN
Kochnitzky, Léon 1892-1965 [poet, musician]
Uccle, Giraud d' *Source(s):* PIPE
Kochno, Boris Jewgenjewitsch 1903 (or 04)-1990 [impressario, librettist, writer on ballet]
Sobeka *Source(s):* LCAR; PIPE
Koãvara, Franz 1730-1791 [composer]
Kotzwara, Franz *Source(s):* BAKE; LCAR
Koczalski, Ra(o)ul (Armand George) 1884-1948 [pianist, composer]
Armando, George *Source(s):* LCAR; MELL
Armando, Jerzy *Source(s):* WORB

Koda, Michael (John) 1948-2000 [guitarist, writer on music, singer, songwriter]
Koda, Cub *Source(s):* EPMU; LCAR; OB00; PSND
Koelling, Karl (W. P.) 1831-1914 [composer]
Note(s): Portrait: ETUP 53:3 (Mar. 1935): 132
King, Carl *Source(s):* CCE38 R64270
Kling, Carl *Source(s):* CCE39 #9188, 405 R73708; TPRF
Koepke, Paul 1918-2000 [composer]
Montrose, Geoffrey *Source(s):* TPRF
Satterlee, Arthur *Source(s):* TPRF
Koepke, Ulrich 1910- [composer, writer on music]
Kopka, Ulrico *Source(s):* KOMP; KOMS; LCAR; PFSA
Koester, Willy 1902-1950 [composer]
Coster, Willy *Source(s):* REHG; SUPN
Kohlenegg, Leopold [or Leonhard] (Karl) Kohl von 1831 (or 34)-1875 (or 76) [librettist]
Henrion, Poly *Source(s):* LCAR; LOWN; MELL; STGR
Köhler, Johannes Robert 1933- [composer]
Cooler, Jean *Source(s):* KOMP; KOMS; PFSA
Kohlmann, Clarence (E.) 1891-1944 [composer]
Note(s): Portraits: ETUP 50:10 (Oct. 1932): 702; ETUP 53:4 (Apr. 1935): 194
Keating, Lawrence *Source(s):* CCE39 #34975 E80215; TPRF
Smith, Kenneth E. *Source(s):* TPRF
Kohlmeyer, Robert 1961- [composer]
Roko *Source(s):* KOMS; PFSA
Kohn, Bernhard mentioned 1938 [composer]
Karbach, Friedrich *Source(s):* WORB
Kohn, Hersch 1888-1959 [composer]
Leopoldi, Hermann *Source(s):* PFSA; RIES
Kohn, Karl Ferdinand 1833-1884 [musician, composer]
Konradin, (Karl Ferdinand) *Source(s):* IBIM; KOMU; STGR; WORB
Kokinacis, Alexander 1917-1996 [composer, author]
Alexander, Nick *Source(s):* ASCP; CCE60; CCE76
Kolditz, Hans 1923- [composer]
Hermann, Hans *Source(s):* SUPN
Kabec, Vlad *Source(s):* KOMP; KOMS; PFSA; SUPN
Sorbon, Kurt *Source(s):* KOMP; KOMS; PFSA; SUPN
Trèvés, Jean *Source(s):* KOMP; KOMS; PFSA; REHG; SUPN
Kollarz, Ludwig 1924- [clarinetist, pianist, arranger]
Kollarz, Wicky *Source(s):* OMUO
Kollo, Willi (Arthur) 1904-1988 [librettist, composer, music publisher]
Allan, Edgar *Source(s):* CCE26 E639370; KOMS; PFSA; PIPE
Allen, Edgar *Source(s):* LCAR; PFSA
Hinterstübl, Alois *Source(s):* CCE34 Efor35554
Kollodzieyski, Elimar Walter 1878-1940 [composer, publisher]
Kollo, Walter *Source(s):* BAKR; GAN1; GAN2; LCAR; MELL; NGDO; PIPE
Kollontay [or Kollontai] (Yermolayev), Mikhail Georgiyevich 1952- [composer]
Nosenko, Ye. *Source(s):* GROL
Ye. Nosenko *Source(s):* GROL
Kolodin, Robert 1932- [composer, singer]
Kole, Robert *Source(s):* ASCP; CCE75
Kolpenitzki, Max 1905-1998 [author]
Colby, Max *Source(s):* PIPE; WORB
Colpet, Max *Source(s):* LCAR; PIPE; WORB
Kolpe(t), Max *Source(s):* LCAR; PIPE; WORB
Komarova-Stasova, Varvara Dmitrievna 1862-1943 [writer on music]
Kareni, V(l) *Source(s):* GROL; LCAR
Komensky, Jan Amos 1592-1670 [theologian, hymnologist, teacher]
Comenius, Johann Amos *Source(s):* GROL; RIES
Kondau, Alex [guitarist, songwriter, actor]
One Man Army *Source(s):* AMUS
One Man Battalion *Source(s):* EPMU
One Man Thousand *Source(s):* AMUS; EPMU
Kone, Seydou 1953- [singer, composer]
Blondy, Alpha *Source(s):* EPMU; PEN1
Kongsback-König, Käte 1895- [songwriter]
Triberg, Klaus *Source(s):* CCE52 Efor14600; KOMP; PFSA
Note(s): Jt. pseud.: Friedrich [or Fritz] Schlenkermann & F(ranz) J(osef) Breuer.
Königsperger, Johann Erhard 1708-1769 [composer]
Königsperger, Marianus *Source(s):* LCAR; NGDM
Koning, Victor 1842 (or 43)-1894 [playwright]
Polichinelle *Source(s):* PIPE
Koningsberger, Hans 1924- [author, playwright, lyricist]
Kong *Source(s):* LCAR
Koning, Hans *Source(s):* ASCP; CPOL TX-794-418; LCAR
Koninsky, Sadie 1879-1952 [composer, arranger, pianist]
Hartman, Jerome *Source(s):* CPMU
Johnson, Julius K. *Source(s):* PERF
Note(s): Also the name of Los Angeles organist of the 1920s-30s.
Konjovič, Petar Božinski 1883-1970 [composer]
Božinski, P. K. *Source(s):* WEOP
Könnemann, Artur (Eduard Theophil) 1861- [composer]
Neustein, Rudolf *Source(s):* KOBW
Konte, Frank (Earl) 1947- [composer]
Konte, Skip *Source(s):* ASCP

Kopasz, Paul [singer, songwriter]
Paul K. *Source(s):* AMUS; EPMU
Köpfel, Wolfgang 1487-1541 [hymnist]
Capito, Wolfgang Fabricius *Source(s):* CYBH
Kopff, Pierre Albert 1846-1907 [composer]
Benfeld *Source(s):* IBIM; WORB
Koplow, Donald Howard 1935- [singer, songwriter]
Howard, Don *Source(s):* CCE53; EPMU
Koppitz, Arthur 1876-1923 [composer]
Hohenstein, Arthur *Source(s):* MACM
Korb, Nathan 1917-2002 [composer]
Lemarque, Francis *Source(s):* CCE48-59; CPOL RE-339-867; DRSC; LCAR; RIES
Korn, Selig(mann) 1803 (or 04)-1850 [author, writer on music]
Nork, F(r.) *Source(s):* LCAR
Korner, Alexis (Andrew Nicholas) 1928-1984 [guitarist, bandleader, writer]
Father of the British Blues *Source(s):* CASS; SHAD
Note(s): See also John Mayall.
Father of the British Blues Revival *Source(s):* CASS, SHAD
Grandfather of British R & B *Source(s):* SHAD (see under: Guv-nor, The)
Guv-nor, The *Source(s):* SHAD
Kornfeld, J. [composer]
Note(s): If Jakob Kornfeld, dates are 1848-1936.
Trifolium *Source(s):* CPMU
Note(s): Jt. pseud.: Louis Samson & Carli [or Karl] Zoeller.
Korngold, Erich Wolfgang 1897-1957 [composer]
Note(s): Portraits: ETUP 53:4 (Apr. 1935): 194; LYMN
Modern Mozart, The *Source(s):* PSND; SIFA
Schott, Paul *Source(s):* NGDM; PIPE; ROOM
Note(s): Jt. pseud.: Julius Korngold.
Korngold, Julius 1860-1945 [composer]
Schott, Paul *Source(s):* NGDM; PIPE; ROOM
Note(s): Jt. pseud.: Erich Wolfgang Korngold.
Kornstein, Egon (F.) 1891-1987 [violinist, musicologist, music librarian]
Kenton, Egon (F.) *Source(s):* BAKR; NGDM
Kornweibel, Albert H. 1892-1980 [music critic]
Fidelio *Source(s):* DAUM
Korny *Source(s):* DAUM
Kortchmar, Daniel [or Danny] 1946- [guitarist, songwriter]
Kootch, Danny *Source(s):* AMUS; EPMU; LCAR
Kortlander, Max 1890-1961 [composer, pianist]
Note(s): Portrait: JASN. Used additional pseuds.?
Baxter, Ted *Source(s):* BBDP; JASN; PIAN
Note(s): On piano rolls; however, not all rolls credited to Ted Baxter are necessarily by Kortlander. Also used by Lee S. Roberts & J. Lawrence Cook.
Osborne & Howe *Source(s):* PIAN
Note(s): Also used by J. Lawrence Cook.
Scott & Watters *Source(s):* PIAN
Note(s): Also used by J. Lawrence Cook.
Scott, Harold *Source(s):* PIAN
Note(s): Also used by J. Lawrence Cook.
Watters, Jeff *Source(s):* BBDP; PIAN
Note(s): Also used by J. Lawrence Cook.
Kosakowski, Wenceslaus (Walter) 1911-1989 [composer, author, banjoist]
King, Walter *Source(s):* ASCP; CCE52; CCE60; CCE67
Waters, Winslow *Source(s):* ASCP
Koschinsky, Fritz 1903-1969 [composer]
Hassler, Karl *Source(s):* PFSA
Miller, Francis D. *Source(s):* CCE63; CCE68; CCE73 Efor166485
Wood Thomas F. *Source(s):* CCE63; CCE65; CCE67
Köselitz, (Johann) Heinrich 1854-1918 [writer, composer]
Gast, Peter *Source(s):* BAKR; GOTT; LCAR; MACM; NGDM; PIPE; PRATT; PSND
New Mozart, A *Source(s):* NGDM
Kosma, Joseph 1905-1969 [composer]
Note(s): Kosma's film music was written under pseudonyms or anonymously (GROL). To date only one pseud. has been identified.
Moqué, Georges *Source(s):* http://www.francehongrie13.org/1999/kosma.htm (30 Mar. 2003)
Kossmaly, Karl [or Carl] 1812-1893 [conductor, composer, writer on music]
Orpheus *Source(s):* APPL p. 10
Note(s): Also used by John Joseph Woods.
Köstelbauer, Hans 1915-1979 [composer, conductor]
Hagen, Hans *Source(s):* OMUO
Kosterlitz, Hermann 1905-1988 [author, film producer]
Koster, Henry *Source(s):* LCAR; PIPE; PSND
Kostia, Karl 1832-1907 [playwright, journalist]
Costa, Karl *Source(s):* GAN1; GAN2; PIPE
Kostraba, Daniel 1924- [bandleader, trumpeter, arranger]
Terry, Dan *Source(s):* PSND
Kötscher, Edmund 1909-1990 [composer]
Calligos, M. *Source(s):* CCE55
Corny, Eddy *Source(s):* CCE55
Maler, H. *Source(s):* CCE59
Mariani, M(ario) *Source(s):* CCE59-61; KOMP; PFSA
Kotter, Anthonius Julius Hendrikus 1906- [teacher, composer]
Kotter, Ton *Source(s):* SMIN
Kötzler, Joseph Christoph 1800-1872 [pianist, teacher, composer]
Kessler, Joseph Christoph *Source(s):* BAKR; LCAR

Kountz, Richard 1896-1950 [composer]
Note(s): Portraits: ETUP 50:9 (Sept. 1932): 622; ETUP 53:4 (Apr. 1935): 194
Adams, Ralph *Source(s):* TPRF
Barr, G. Alexander *Source(s):* CCE57
Bellaire, R(aymond) E(arl) *Source(s):* CCE57
Cass, Alfred *Source(s):* TPRF
Collins, John B. *Source(s):* CCE22 E548378
Davidson, Ellsworth *Source(s):* TPRF
Dermott, Ralph *Source(s):* TPRF
Fall, Albert *Source(s):* CCE26 E635690
Grant, Allan P. *Source(s):* TPRF
Hall, Alfred *Source(s):* TPRF
Hanson, Mark *Source(s):* CCE21 E522795; CCE22 E54290
Hirtz, Leo *Source(s):* TPRF
Hodgson, Albert *Source(s):* TPRF
Lavita, Selma *Source(s):* CCE31 E26891; CCE58
Markley, Hubert *Source(s):* CCE28 E699385
Ostro, Paolo *Source(s):* CCE22 E541838
Paolo, Francesco *Source(s):* CCE22 E546894
Potter, Paul *Source(s):* CCE36 #26314 E57553
Potter, William *Source(s):* CCE36; TPRF
Purcell, Gilbert *Source(s):* CCE56 R174791 ("Why Should It Matter"); CCE76
Rafael, Walter *Source(s):* CCE31 E26343; CCE57
Spark, Elton *Source(s):* TPRF
Spencer, R. *Source(s):* TPRF
Sylvia *Source(s):* CCE29 E7552; CCE57 ("Lilac")
Note(s): Also used by Sylvia Kirby & Sylvia Vanderpool Robinson.
Tchervanow, Ivor *Source(s):* CCE49; CCE55
Vladinoff, Alex *Source(s):* TPRF
Wick, Eugene *Source(s):* TPRF
Wright, Basil *Source(s):* CCE67
Koussevitzky, Fabien 1891 (or 93)-1967 [composer]
Note(s): Portrait: ETUP 58:2 (Feb. 1940): 87
Sevitzky, Fabien *Source(s):* BAKR; BUL2; LCAR; MACM
Kovac, Roland 1927- [composer]
Elger, Bob *Source(s):* BUL3; RIES
Kovalyov, Marian [or Maryan] Viktrovich 1907-1971 [composer]
Kova(l), Marian [or Maryan] (Victorovitch) *Source(s):* BUL1; LCAR; ROOM
Kovalev, Marian [or Maryan] *Source(s):* BUL1
Kovarovic, Karel 1862-1920 [composer, conductor]
Note(s): Portrait: ETUP 53:4 (Apr. 1935): 194
Biset, C. *Source(s):* BAKO; BAKR
Forgeron(-Maréchal), Charles *Source(s):* IWWM; PRAT; STGR
Héral, (J.) *Source(s):* BAKO; BAKR; RIEM
Marcéchal, (Charles) *Source(s):* STGR v.4/pt.1
Zamrzla *Source(s):* STGR v.4/pt.1
Kowalchyk, Luba 1958- [singer, songwriter, instrumentalist]
Luba *Source(s):* LCAR; NOMG
Kowalski, Július 1912- [composer, teacher]
Dominik, Alexander *Source(s):* NGDM
Kozáky, Istaván 1903-1986 [composer, author]
Cosacchi, Stephan *Source(s):* PFSA
Kozeschnik, Josef 1913-1969 [composer, singer]
Kozi, Pepi *Source(s):* OMUO
Kozlov, Alexey 1935- [saxophonist, bandleader, composer]
Godfather of Russian Jazz Rock *Source(s):* http://www.jazz.ru/eng/default.html (select Kozlov) (6 Oct. 2002)
Krah, Earl E(dward) 1921-1997 [composer, author]
Richards, Eddie *Source(s):* ASCP; CCE60-61
Krakauer, Erich 1887- [composer, pianist, songwriter]
Cleve, Erich *Source(s):* MACM; WORB
Kralik (von Meyrswalden), Richard 1852-1934 [author, composer]
Roman *Source(s):* OMUO
Kramar, František (Vinzez) 1759-1831 [composer]
Krommer, Franz *Source(s):* FANF 20:1 (1996): 216; LCAR; WORB
Kramer, Alex(ander) 1903-1998 [composer, author, pianist]
Ingersoll, Byron M. *Source(s):* CCE68 R426470
Note(s): Jt. pseud.: Ernest Gold [i.e., Ernest (Siegmund) Goldner], Zoe Voeth [i.e., Parenteau], Hy(man) Zaret, Robert (B.) Sour & Don McCray.
Remark, A(xel) *Source(s):* CCE41 #36640 E96509; CCE68 R446839
Krammer, Vilmos 1859-1923 [theater manager]
Karczag, Wilhelm *Source(s):* GAN2
Krangel, David 1923- [lyricist, librettist]
Craig, David *Source(s):* LCAR; PSND
Krasnow, Herman(n) 1910-1984 [composer]
Dee, Lillian *Source(s):* CCE53
Gale, Stephen *Source(s):* ASCP; CCE51; CCE58
Herschel, Lee *Source(s):* CCE54; CCE57
Kay, Herschel *Source(s):* CCE55
Kay, Hershy *Source(s):* CCE55
Krasnow, Hecky *Source(s):* ASCP; CCE57; CCE59
Mann, Steve *Source(s):* ASCP; CCE53
Kraszewski, Józef Ignacy 1812-1887 [author]
Boleslawita, (Bohdan) *Source(s):* LCAR; PIPE; PSND
Pasternak, K(leofas) F(akund) *Source(s):* PIPE; PSND
Krauledat, Joachim (Fritz) 1944- [singer, songwriter, guitarist]

Kay, John *Source(s):* CCE73-74; CPOL RE-667-796; LCAR; NOMG
Kraus, Heinrich 1932- [author]
Hischuk, Rainer *Source(s):* PFSA
Kraus, Joseph Martin 1756-1792 [composer]
Greatest Unknown Composer of All Time *Source(s):* http://members.tripod.com/~Classical_Mike/MisterA/kraus.htm (26 Sept. 2003)
Swedish Mozart *Source(s):* NOTE 57:1 (2000): 112
Krause, Andreas 1952- [composer]
Martin, Andreas *Source(s):* PFSA
Kraushaar, Charles 1868-1957 [composer]
Note(s): In 1900 Kraushaar changed his name to Charles J. Roberts. The following names are listed as pseudonyms of Charles J. Roberts.
Akimenko, Ivan *Source(s):* CCE29 E7363
Allison, Robert *Source(s):* CCE39 #36400, 272 R80335
Clarke, Elizabeth *Source(s):* CCE29 E3378
Göndör, Károly *Source(s):* CCE29 E7365
Gray, Alfred *Source(s):* CCE29 E3379
Hodges, A. R. *Source(s):* CCE40 #28290 E87080
Note(s): Possible pseud.?
Nield, Ernest *Source(s):* CCE20 E3377; LCPC letter cited (14 Mar. 1929)
Pestalozza, A. *Source(s):* CCE36 R44720
Pickett, R. E. *Source(s):* CCE36 E56260
Roberto, Carlos *Source(s):* CCE29 E7364; CCE39 #21731, 21R77438
Roberts, Charles J. *Source(s):* CCE28 R45052; LCPC letter cited (14 Mar. 1929); SUPN
Strebor, J. C. *Source(s):* CCE29 E7213 ("Alberta")
Strelezki, A. *Source(s):* CCE36 R42163 ("Happy Days" arr. orchestra)
Note(s): Works with the pseud. "Anton Strelezki" and published by Kunkel Bros. are by Charles Kunkel. "Anton Strelezki" also used by Arthur Bransby Burnand.
Taylor, Frances *Source(s):* CCE29 E4010; LCPC letter cited (20 Apr. 1929)
Note(s): "Progressive Rhythmic Band Music Folio"
Ward, Burt *Source(s):* CCE51 R81493
Wiegand, Henry *Source(s):* CCE29 E3380
Kraushaar, Raoul 1908-2001 [composer]
Rogers, Stanley C. *Source(s):* MCCA
Stanley, Ralph *Source(s):* MCCA
Kraus-Hübner, Hans 1941- [composer]
Forland, Art *Source(s):* KOMS; PFSA
Kraussold, M. [writer on music]
M. K. *Source(s):* HEYT
Krausznai-Kraus, Mihály 1897-c.1940-5 [composer]
Krausz, Michael *Source(s):* GANZ
Kraut, Johann c.1570-1634 [composer, poet]
Brassicanus, Johannes *Source(s):* GROL; NGDM
Krehan, Hermann 1905- [author, playwright]
Crayon, H. M. *Source(s):* PIPE
Krehbiel, Henry (Edward) 1854-1923 [music critic, writer on music]
Note(s): Portraits: ETUP 53:4 (Apr. 1935): 194; GRAN; GRV3 American Suppl.
Gaslight Era Dean of New York Music Critics, The *Source(s):* GRAN
Krehbiel, Pop *Source(s):* GRAN
Old Guard, The *Source(s):* GRAN p. 59
Note(s): Jt. sobriquet: Henry Theophilus [i.e., Gottlob] Finck & William James Henderson.
Pontiff of Music Wisdom, The *Source(s):* GRAN
President, The *Source(s):* GRAN
Kreisler, Fritz [i.e., Friedrich](-Max) 1875-1962 [violinist, composer]
Note(s): After Kreisler announced he had used the names of the composers listed below on some of his compositions, the works were indentified as ". . . in the style of. . . ."
Cartier, Jean Baptiste *Source(s):* LOCH
Couperin, Louis *Source(s):* LOCH
Dittersdorf, Karl von *Source(s):* LOCH
Francoeur, François *Source(s):* LOCH
Lanner, Joseph *Source(s):* LOCH
Martini, Giambattista *Source(s):* LOCH
Porpora, Niccolo A. *Source(s):* LOCH
Pugnani, Gaetano *Source(s):* LOCH
Stamitz, Johann *Source(s):* LOCH
Vivaldi, Antonio *Source(s):* LOCH
Kreitzberg, Yasha [or Jacob] ?-1959 [composer]
Saxon, Jack *Source(s):* CCE66; HESK; LCPC letter cited (16 Mar. 1935)
Kremenliev, Boris (Angeloff) 1911-1988 [composer, musicologist]
Angeloff, Boris *Source(s):* RIES
Krenek, Ernst 1900-1991 [composer]
Donaldson, Dewey *Source(s):* Stewart, John L. *Ernst Krenek*. Berkeley: University of California Press, 1991.
Kshenek, E(rnst) *Source(s):* LCAR
Winsloe, Thornton *Source(s):* LCAR
Krenkel, Gustav [composer]
Note(s): In LCAR and MACM (cited in LCAR) Gustave Krenkel is listed as a pseud. of Alfred William Rawlings; however, since this information was not verified in an additional independent source, Krenkel is listed as a separate entry.
Clare, Georgiana *Source(s):* CPMU
Day, Valentine Elizabeth *Source(s):* CPMU
Fleur, Marcel *Source(s):* CPMU
Girdlestone, Victor *Source(s):* CPMU
St. Juste, Edouard *Source(s):* TPRF
Stroud, Sidney *Source(s):* CPMU

Wallis, C. Jay *Source(s):* CCE30 Efor8733; LCPC letter cited (4 Jan. 1930)
Note(s): Jt. pseud.: C(harles) J(oseph) Edwards, Ralph (T.) Butler & Julian Wright.
Werner, Otto *Source(s):* CPMU; TPRF
Krenn, Hans 1854-1943 [composer]
Gotthardi, G. *Source(s):* OMUO
Krentzlin, H. Richard 1864-1956 [composer, pianist]
Erich, Carl *Source(s):* LCPC E51573
Note(s): A. P. Schmidt house name; see NOTES: Erich, Carl.
Krentzlin, Rich *Source(s):* CCE32 E18270
Richter, Ernst *Source(s):* CCE33 R27299
Voigt, Fred [or Ferd.] *Source(s):* CCE13 E325117; CCE41 #9124, 342 R92368
Krettly, Grégoire(-Elie) 1922- [composer, conductor]
Calvi, Gérard *Source(s):* BUL2; CCE55; CPOL RE-525-692; GOTH; PIPE; PSNN; REHH
Calvi, Jean *Source(s):* CCE55
Kreuder, Peter 1905-1981 [composer, pianist]
Peter Pan *Source(s):* CCE55; CCE68; OMUO; PIPE
Note(s): Also used by Gosta Stevens.
Pan, Peter *Source(s):* CCE57; CPOL RE-185-333; KOMP; KOMS; PFSA
Solecki, Adam *Source(s):* KOMS; PFSA
Kreusch, Edmund [or Eduard] 1862-1922 [librettist, composer]
Robert, C. E. *Source(s):* MELL; STGR
Kreutzer, Rodolphe 1766-1831 [composer]
Note(s): Portrait: ETUP 53:5 (May 1935): 299
N*** *Source(s):* CPMU ("Ce front si pur aù regne la décence")
Note(s): Jt. pseud.: Etienne Nicolas Méhul, François Adrien Boieldieu & Nicolas Isouard.
Krička, Jaroslav 1882-1969 [composer]
Note(s): Portrait: ETUP 53:5 (May 1935): 299
Munk, J. *Source(s):* GROL
Note(s): Jt. pseud.: P(etr) Krick.
Krička, P(etr) 1884-1949 [poet, translator, teacher]
Munk, J. *Source(s):* GROL
Note(s): Jt. pseud.: Jaroslav Kricka.
Krieg, Richard Charles 1919- [composer, author]
Charles, Dick *Source(s):* ASCP; CCE46 E7248; LCAR
Krieger, Johann Philipp 1649-1725 [organist, composer]
Father of the New Cantata *Source(s):* BAKO
Krieger, Robert [or Robby, or Robbie] 1946- [songwriter, guitarist]
Doors, The *Source(s):* GOTT; PEN2; PMUS
Note(s): Jt. pseud.: James (Douglas) Morrison, John Densmore & Raymond (Daniel) Manzarek.
Krikorian, Steve 1950- [singer, songwriter]
K., Tonio *Source(s):* PMUS-96; ROOM
Tonio K. *Source(s):* PMUS-96; ROOM
Krinitz, Elise (von) 1830-1896 [writer on music]
Mouche *Source(s):* LCAR
Selden, Camil(l)e *Source(s):* HIXN; LCAR; SEND
Krno, Miloš 1922- [author]
Note(s): Portrait: CYBH
Blesk, Miloš *Source(s):* PIPE
Kroeger, E(rnest) R(ichard) 1862-1934 [composer]
Schott, Maurice *Source(s):* TPRF
Kroeger, William E.
Hilliard, Hal *Source(s):* TPRF
Kröger, Willi 1903-1968 [composer, pianist, conductor]
Buva, Ernesto *Source(s):* RIES
Hass, Willi *Source(s):* RIES
Krogmann, Carrie W(illiam(s)) 1863-1943 [composer]
Note(s): Portrait: ETUP 53:5 (May 1935): 299
Ducelle, Paul *Source(s):* AMME; BUL3; ETUD; HIXN
Hope, Victor *Source(s):* AMME; CCE24 E541525; HIXN
Kay, Caro *Source(s):* CCE24
Kent, Julian *Source(s):* CCE23 E555152; HIXN
Kleber, Carl *Source(s):* AMME; CCE32; HIXN
Williams, Carol *Source(s):* CCE24 R26949
Krohn, Ernst (Ludwig) 1858 (or 60)-1930 [pianist, conductor, composer, organist]
West, Francis *Source(s):* KROH p. 133
Krohn, Max 1886-1988 [composer, editor]
Note(s): Portrait: ETUP 53:5 (May 1935): 299
Loor, Max van *Source(s):* PFSA
Krok, Edward 1959- [composer]
Simoni, Edward *Source(s):* PFSA
Krome, Herman(n) (Friedrich) 1888-1955 [composer]
Huntley, James *Source(s):* CCE28 E684126
Lustig, Hermann *Source(s):* CCE29 E2337
Marriot *Source(s):* CCE30 E14400
Ralph, Fred *Source(s):* CCE30 Efor14422; CCE65 Efor29837; RIES
Krone, Beatrice Perham 1901-2000 [author, school music authority, composer]
Krones, The *Source(s):* CCE43 #30403 E115832; CCE61-62
Note(s): See also Max (T.) Krone.
Krone, Max (Thomas) 1901-1970 [author, editor, school music authority, composer]
Note(s): Portrait: 53:5 (May 1935): 299
Krones, The *Source(s):* CCE43 #30403 E115832; CCE61-62
Note(s): See also Beatric Perham Krone.
Spencer, Guy *Source(s):* CCE43 #11231 E112833; CCE70 R483464
Kronke, Emil 1865-1938 [composer, pianist]
Note(s): Portrait: ETUP 53:5 (May 1935): 299

Armand, René *Source(s):* CCE45 #55029, 416 R141971; CCE51 R74923 ("Evening Spell"); CPMU
Note(s): In CCE45 & CPMU listed under Oscar Kronke.
Clarke, Emile *Source(s):* CCE51R86464 ("Under the Silvery Moon")
Clarke,Oscar *Source(s):* CCE50 R59481 ("The Sunshine of Thy Smile")
Kronke, Oscar *Source(s):* CPMU
Note(s): Entered as original name.
Nawrazek, E. *Source(s):* CCE22 E540834; CCE50 R63598 ("Animato")
Roloff, Alec *Source(s):* CPMU
Note(s): Listed under Oscar Kronke.

Krow, Josef Theodor 1797-1859 [singer, composer]
Workinski *Source(s):* BAKE

Krüger, Eduard 1807-1885 [writer on music]
Dr. P. *Source(s):* GROL
Schnell, F. *Source(s):* GROL

Kruglikov, Semon Nikolayevich 1851-1910 [music critic, teacher]
Note(s): Wrote criticism under pseuds. (GROL); to date none indentified.

Krumbein, Maurice 1908-1982 [composer, author, conductor]
Carter, Ray *Source(s):* ASCP; CCE66; CLTP ("Ellery Queen, The Adventures of"); LCAR

Krumpholtz, Fanny 1785?-c.1823 [composer, harpist]
Esprit, Charlotte *Source(s):* COHN; HIXN; JACK
Note(s): Listed as possible pseud. (JACK).
Pittar, (Mrs.) Isaac *Source(s):* JACK

Krunnfusz, Gordon 1931- [composer, author, organist]
Jones, Gordon G. *Source(s):* ASCP

Krupp, D. Dudley 1894- [composer, radiologist]
Manners, Dudley *Source(s):* ASCC; CCE31 Eunp34786

Kruse, Georg 1830-1908 [librettist]
Silesius *Source(s):* STGR

Krzysniowski, Felix [composer]
Felix, Karl *Source(s):* STGR

Kübel, Josef 1900-1980 [composer]
Ming, Felix *Source(s):* KOMP

Kubelik, Jan 1880-1940 [violinist, composer]
Note(s): Portrait: ETUP 53:5 (May 1935): 299
Polgar, (Janos) *Source(s):* PSND; SCHO p. 353n

Kubka, František 1894-1969 [author, journalist]
Buk, K. *Source(s):* PIPE

Kücken, Friedrich Wilhelm 1810-1882 [composer]
Note(s): Portrait: ETUP 53:5 (May 1935): 299
Haydn *Source(s):* APPL p. 10

Kuczynski, Julius Frank (Anthony) 1914-2000 [songwriter, singer, bandleader, publisher]
Frank, J. L. *Source(s):* STUW
Note(s): Possible pseud.
King, Frank(ie) *Source(s):* CLAB; EPMU; PEN2; STUW
Note(s): Do not confuse with Frank H. King, husband of Julie Rive-King.
King, Pee Wee *Source(s):* ENCM; EPMU; HARR; MCCL; NGAM; OB00; STAC

Kudera, Lottie A. 1920- [composer, author]
Harp, Nola Jay *Source(s):* ASCP
Kota, Lu *Source(s):* ASCP

Kufferath, Maurice 1852-1919 [writer on music, cellist, conductor]
Reymont, Maurice *Source(s):* BAKE; LCAR; MACM; PIPE

Kugler, Franz (Theodore) 1808-1858 [art scholar, author]
Erwin, Franz Theodor *Source(s):* PIPE; WORB

Kuhlau, Friedrich Daniel Rodolph 1786-1832 [composer]
Note(s): Portrait: ETUP 53:5 (May 1935): 299
Beethoven of the Flute, The *Source(s):* PSND; SIFA; SPIE

Kuhmärker, Leonard Karl 1911-1993 [composer]
Märker, Leonard Karl *Source(s):* OMUO

Kuhn, Johann 1660-1722 [organist, writer on music]
Kuhnau, Johann *Source(s):* BAKR; LCAR

Kuhnert, Christian 1952- [composer]
Kuno *Source(s):* KOMS; PFSA

Kujawa, Robert V(alentine) 1925- [composer, author, music]
Kames, Bob *Source(s):* ASCP; CCE76; LCAR

Kukoff, Benjamin 1933- [songwriter, actor]
Kukoff, Bernie *Source(s):* ASCP

Kulke, Eduard 1831-1897 [essayist, dramatist, music critic]
Leipenburg, Eduard *Source(s):* OMUO
Lipiner, Eduard *Source(s):* OMUO

Kullmann, Wilton 1926- [composer]
Heliandos, Lucky *Source(s):* KOMP; KOMS; PFSA; REHH

Kumar, Dileep 1956- [composer, keyboardist]
Rahman, A. R. *Source(s):* MOMU
Rahman, Allahrakha *Source(s):* MOMU

Kummer, Hermann Gabriel 1928- [organist, composer]
Michel, Josef *Source(s):* ORBI

Kunel, Oscar [or Oskar] Friedrich 1851-1901 [librettist]
Walther, Oscar [or Oskar] *Source(s):* LOWN; MELL; WORB

Kunitz, Richard (E.) 1919-1986 [banker, composer]
Evans, Richard *Source(s):* ASCC; CCE60-62

Kunkel, Charles 1840-1923 [composer, publisher]
Note(s): Called "Karl" in his youth. Portrait: ETUP 53:5 (May 1935): 299

Anscheetz, Otto *Source(s):* CCE12 E278385
Arndt, Frank *Source(s):* CCE18 E424817
Auchester, Charles *Source(s):* CCE12 R3252-53
Bagwill, Olive Bradley *Source(s):* CCE18 E437992
Beckman, August J. *Source(s):* CCE16 R8045
Beethoven, Ludwig van *Source(s):* LCPC
Note(s): See NOTES: Kunkel Brothers.
Behr, Francois *Source(s):* CCE15 R6830
Behr-Sidus *Source(s):* CCE21 R9191-93
Benbow, Edward *Source(s):* CCE21 R19189
Bendel, Franz *Source(s):* CCE14 R5774
Bingham, Lena M. *Source(s):* CCE12 E283081
Blumenschein, W. L. *Source(s):* CCE17 R9720
Blumenthal, Jacques *Source(s):* CCE15 R6828
Boone, John W. *Source(s):* CCE21 R18413
Note(s): Name used with permission? See NOTES: Kunkel Brothers.
Brown, Fleta Jan *Source(s):* CCE12 E275431 ("Would You Like Me Better If My Eyes Were Blue?")
Note(s): Name used with permission? See NOTES: Kunkel Brothers.
Bryant, Tilghman A. *Source(s):* CCE21 E500406
Bundy, Jerry *Source(s):* CCE08 E171252; CCE10 E231106
Burke, Lora Miller *Source(s):* CCE22 E530715
Carlin, Regina M. *Source(s):* CCE21 R19194
Note(s): Name used with permission? See NOTES: Kunkel Brothers.
Carter, Christine Nordstrom *Source(s):* CCE12 E285091
Note(s): Name used with permission? See NOTES: Kunkel Brothers.
Drysale, E. M. *Source(s):* CCE15 R7289
Eichelberger, O. B. *Source(s):* CCE11 E274420; CCE13 E323418
Eilenburg, R. *Source(s):* CCE15 R6825
Elbrecht, William *Source(s):* CCE12 E284592
Freistat, Frank *Source(s):* CCE13 E311659
Grand, Steinway *Source(s):* CCE07 C138930 ("Up and Down on the Ebony")
Green, James *Source(s):* CCE12 E283082
Greene, Gallant *Source(s):* CCE21 E500407
Grieg, E. *Source(s):* CCE13 R4857
Note(s): "Norwegian Bridal Procession" See NOTES: Kunkel Brothers.
Hale, Ernest Wilbur *Source(s):* CCE17 E409398
Hartt, LeRoy *Source(s):* CCE09 E222521; CCE10 E238440; TIPT
Haydn, Joseph *Source(s):* CCE15 R6827 ("Perpetual Motion")
Note(s): See NOTES: Kunkel Brothers.
James, William W. *Source(s):* CCE18 E437991
Jensen, Adolf *Source(s):* CCE14 R5625
Johnson, Floy Mae *Source(s):* CCE21 E500408
Jones, A. M. *Source(s):* CCE12 E275429
Keller, Olive Robinson *Source(s):* CCE18 E437993
Ketterer, E(ugene) *Source(s):* CCE13 R4786; CCE15 R6826
Kimmel, Stanley *Source(s):* CCE11 E257050
Lezzi, G. *Source(s):* CCE15 R7330
Liszt, Franz *Source(s):* CCE10 E228394; CCE14 R5626; CCE16 R8047
Note(s): "Dance of the Butterflies," "Serenade" & "Fantasie" See NOTES: Kunkel Brothers.
Loeffler, R. *Source(s):* CCE15 R6824
Looney, Charlotte *Source(s):* CCE18 E429875
M. Seraphina, (Sister) *Source(s):* CCE12 E292610
Martin, Jennie (L.) *Source(s):* CCE14 E349693; CCE14 E349694
Melnotte, Claude *Source(s):* CCE12 R3317; CCE13 E304667; KROH; TIPT
Mitchell, Belle D. *Source(s):* CCE09 E217205
Moszkowski, M(oritz) *Source(s):* CCE20 R16754; CCE21 R18411
Note(s): Name used without permission. See NOTES: Kunkel Brothers.
Myers, Paul P. *Source(s):* CCE12 E278383 & E292612
Nordstrom, Christine (Carter) *Source(s):* CCE12 E278383 & E285091
Note(s): Name used with permission? See NOTES: Kunkel Brothers.
O'Bryan, Callie H. *Source(s):* CCE10 223199; CCE12 E278709
O'Keefe, James (C.) *Source(s):* CCE12 E299848; CCE14 E352360; CCE21 E502985
Note(s): Name used with permission? See NOTES: Kunkel Brothers.
Paul, Jean *Source(s):* CCE13 R4134; KROH; TIPT
Pavoni, Emelyn *Source(s):* CCE14 E530714; CCE21 E502983-86
Preyer, C. A. *Source(s):* CCE16 R7933
Rive-King, Julie *Source(s):* CCE12 R2959; CCE14 R5337
Note(s): Name used with permission. See NOTES: Kunkel Brothers.
Roads, E. Clyde *Source(s):* CCE10 E247155; CCE12 E279345
Rosellen, H. *Source(s):* CCE13 R4858
Rubinstein, Anton *Source(s):* CCE11 E252406; CCE15 R6829
Note(s): "Lichtertanz der braute von Kaschmir" (CCE15) See NOTES: Kunkel Brothers.
Sargent, J. B. *Source(s):* CCE12 E283083
Saulnier, Thelerise *Source(s):* CCE20 E46661
Schubert, Franz *Source(s):* CCE15 R6823 ("Valse Caprice")
Note(s): See NOTES: Kunkel Brothers.
Schweer, Richard M. *Source(s):* CCE18 E437990

Seraphina, Sister *Source(s):* CCE12 E292610
Sidus, Carl *Source(s):* CCE10 E241604; CCE11 R2358; KROH
Sisson, C. T. *Source(s):* CCE16 R8053
Stone, Mary A. *Source(s):* CCE10 E226922
Strauss, Richard *Source(s):* CCE09 E222328 ("Standchen")
Note(s): See NOTES: Kunkel Brothers.
Strelezki, Anton *Source(s):* CCE13 R4855 ("Mazeppa")
Note(s): Kunkel Brothers publications with this name are by Charles Kunkel. Also used by Arthur Bransby Burnand. "A. Strelezki" used by Charles J. Roberts [i.e., Charles Kraushaar]
Wolff, Bernhard *Source(s):* CCE15 R6831

Kunkel, Jacob 1846-1882 [composer, publisher, pianist]
Rive-King, Julie *Source(s):* CCE12 E284569; CCE21 R18252; CCE36 E55034
Note(s): Name used with permission; see NOTES: Kunkel Brothers.

Kunz, Alfred 1906- [composer]
Kunz, Fred Charly *Source(s):* KOMP; KOMS; PFSA

Kupelwieser, Josef [poet, librettist]
Leks, Blasius *Source(s):* MUST 140:1866 (1999): 34

Kupferberg, Tuli Naphtali 1923- [author, singer, songwriter]
Kupferberg, Tuli *Source(s):* CA13; RECR (see under: Fugs, The)

Kurc, Adolf 1913-1993 [composer]
Courts, Eddy *Source(s):* ASCP; LCAR

Kurtz, Em(m)anuel [or Manny] 1911-1984 [lyricist, composer, arranger]
Note(s): Portrait: BBDP
Curtis, Mann *Source(s):* ASCP; PMUS; STUW; VACH; WORT
Kaye, Camille *Source(s):* CCE57
Manheim, Curt *Source(s):* CCE68
Nuell, Kurt *Source(s):* CCE56 Eunp

Kurz, Johann Joseph Felix von 1717-1783 (or 84) [librettist, singer, actor]
Bernardon *Source(s):* LCAR; SONN; STGR

Kushner, Morris Hyman 1912-1997 [songwriter]
Note(s): Portraits: EWEN; SHMM (Mar./Apr. 1990): 4+, 55 & cover
Lane, Burton *Source(s):* BAKR; CCE55 E87511; LCAR; NGDM; PEN2
Levy, Burton *Source(s):* LCAR; OB97; REHH

Küster, Herbert 1909-1986 [composer]
Bertus, Bert *Source(s):* PFSA; RIES
Roeper, Ernst *Source(s):* PFSA; RIES

Küster, Hermann 1817-1878 [composer]
Küster, Lehmann *Source(s):* GOTH

Kutschenreuter, Erhard 1873-1946 [choirmaster, composer]
Kutsch, Erhard *Source(s):* MACM

Kuula, Toivo (Timoteus) 1883-1918 [composer]
Finland's Schubert *Source(s):* WOSU-FM (6 June 2002)

Kuyumzhi, Vasily Andreyevich 1872 (or 73)-1964 [composer, teacher]
Zolotaryov, Vasily Andreyevich *Source(s):* HOFE; LCAR

Kuznetsov, Konstantin Alexeyevich 1883-1853 [musicologist]
Alexeyev, K. *Source(s):* NGDM
Smis, A. K. *Source(s):* NGDM

Kuznetsova, Zhanna [or Zhanetta] (Aleksandrovna) 1937- [composer]
Strella,Yevgenia *Source(s):* HOFE p. 647

Kynaston, Herbert 1809-1878 [clergyman, hymnist]
H. K. *Source(s):* PSND

– L –

Labaigt, Laurent 1859-1942 [poet]
Rameau, Jean *Source(s):* WHIT; http://ecrivosges2st.fr/pseudos_r.htm (6 Dec. 2003)

Labarre, Théodore François Joseph 1805-1870 [harpist, composer]
Note(s): Portrait: ETUP 53:6 (June 1935): 322
Berry, Théodore François Joseph *Source(s):* GROL; PIPE

LaBeff, Thomas Paulsley 1935- [singer, songwriter]
LaBeef, Sleepy *Source(s):* LCAR; MCCL; ROCK (port.)

Laber, Richard [composer]
Baler, Robert *Source(s):* REHG

Labey, Marcel 1875-1968 [composer]
Note(s): Birth date in MACM: 1887?
Sohy, Charles *Source(s):* CCE50 R60844; MACM
Note(s): "Thème varié" (CCE50)

LaBour, Fred 1948- [singer, bassist, songwriter]
Too Slim *Source(s):* EPMU; http://www.ridersinthesky.com (ports.) (4 Oct. 2002)

Laborde, Jean Benjamin de 1734-1794 [composer]
Note(s): Portrait: ETUP 53:6 (June 1935): 322
D. L. B. *Source(s):* CPMU
Mr. xxx *Source(s):* CPMU

Labrousse, Fabrice 1856-1921 [playwright]
Carré, Fabrice *Source(s):* GAN1; GAN2

Labrunie, Gérard 1808-1855 (or 56) [librettist, writer, translator]
Aloysius *Source(s):* PIPE
Bengland, de *Source(s):* PIPE
Beugland *Source(s):* LCAR
Cadet-Roussel *Source(s):* LCAR
Gérard de Nerval *Source(s):* NGDO
Gracian *Source(s):* PIPE

Nerval, Gérard de *Source(s):* NGDO; WORB
Pilgrim, Lord *Source(s):* PIPE
Puycousin, Edouard de *Source(s):* LCAR
Lachoff, Sol(omon) 1911-1991 [composer]
Lake, Sol *Source(s):* ASCP; CCE60-62
Lackritz, Steven (Norman) 1934-2004 [saxophonist, composer]
Lacy, Steve *Source(s):* CM23; EPMU; GREN; LCAR; NGDJ; PEN2
Lacombe (d'Estalenx), Paul Jean Jacques 1838-1920 [composer]
Paolo, L. *Source(s):* SUPN
Lacout, Marie Madeleine Sophie 1855- [composer]
Darvey, Abel *Source(s):* IBIM; WORB
Lacquemant, Jean c.1622-1681 [composer, violinist]
DuBuisson, (Burgeois de Paris) *Source(s):* http://jonathan.dunford.free.fr/html/dubuisso.htm (2 May 2005)
Lacy, Catherine J. [songwriter]
Delcy, Catherine J. *Source(s):* CPMU (publication dates 1847-48)
Lacy, Michael Rophino 1795-1867 [violinist, composer]
Petit Espagnol, Le *Source(s):* NGDM
Young Spaniard, The *Source(s):* NGDM
Ladowski, Kazimierz 1824-1871 [violinist, composer]
Lada, Kazimierz *Source(s):* GROL; NGDM
Lagoanère, Oscar de 1853-1918 [composer, conductor]
Thierry *Source(s):* PIPE
La Greca, Antonio 1631-1668 [composer]
Fardiola, Il *Source(s):* GROL; IBIM; LCAR; WORB
La Greca, Antonia *Source(s):* COHN; HIXN; JACK
Note(s): Incorrectly identified as a woman in COHN & HIXN; see JACK p. 425.
Lain, John A. [composer]
McLain, Johnny *Source(s):* MUWB
Lake, Harold [composer]
Harford, Harold *Source(s):* KILG
Lake, Henrietta 1909-2001 [actress, composer]
Note(s): See IMDB for additional stage names.
Sothern, Ann *Source(s):* CLTP ("Ann Sothern Show"); LCAR
Lake, M(ayhew) L(ester) 1879-1955 [composer, conductor, editor]
Note(s): Portrait: ETUP 53:6 (June 1935): 322
Baker, Ralph *Source(s):* CCE45 #57074 E135952
Beaulac, Mayhew *Source(s):* CCE43 #30169, 63 R119187
Brockton, Lester *Source(s):* CPOL RE-923; GROL; PARS; REHG; SMIN; SUPN
Byers, Alfrey *Source(s):* PARS; REHG
DeVille, Paul *Source(s):* CCE28 E6948772-73; PARS
Note(s): "The Eclipse," banjo; "The Eclipse," saxophone. Also used by Henry Jean Prendiville.
DuLac, Paul *Source(s):* PARS; REHG
Edwards, Charles *Source(s):* PARS; REHG
Note(s): See also Henry Lee Bester.
Hall, George *Source(s):* CCE45 #57074 E135952
Hall, Robert *Source(s):* PARS; REHG
Lake, Mike *Source(s):* LCAR; SMIN
Lester, William *Source(s):* PARS; REHG
Lakond, Wladimir before 1910- [translator]
Note(s): Dates may be: 1898-1979.
Lake, Walter *Source(s):* CCE68; LCAR; PIPE
Laks, Szymon [or Simon] 1901-1983 [composer, violinist, teacher]
Axel, Robert *Source(s):* http://www.musiciansgallery.com/start/societies/viktor_ullmann_foundation.html (17 May 2005)
Lorent, André *Source(s):*http://www.musiciansgallery.com/start/societies/viktor_ullmann_foundation.html
Lalande, Michel-Richard de 1657-1726 [composer]
Note(s): Portrait: ETUP 53:5 (June 1935): 322
Latin Lully *Source(s):* NGDM; SADC
Lamare, Hilton (Napoleon) 1910-1988 [guitarist, composer, singer]
Lamare, Nappy *Source(s):* ASCP; KINK; NGDJ
Lamb, Charles 1775-1834 [author, poet]
Note(s): See PSND for additional nonmusic-related pseudonyms.
Burton Junior *Source(s):* GOTT; PSND
Elia *Source(s):* GOTT
Lambert, Emily 1838-1912 [actress, author]
Note(s): Probable surname. Portrait: GAN2
Soldene, Emily *Source(s):* GAN2
Lambert, W. [composer]
Bertlam, Wilfred *Source(s):* CPMU (publication date 1912)
Lambertus, Magister fl. c.1270 [music theorist]
Pseudo-Aristoteles *Source(s):* NGDM
Lamburn, Maria [performer, composer]
Madalena *Source(s):* http://www.cadenza.org/musicians/compose.htm (6 Oct. 2002)
La Menthe, Ferdinand Joseph 1885-1941 [pianist, bandleader, composer]
Creator of Jazz, The *Source(s):* http://www.holeintheweb.com/drp/bhd/Ragtime.htm (6 Oct. 2002)
King of New Orleans Jazz *Source(s):* CM07 p. v
King of Piano, A *Source(s):* http://www.abebooks-author.co.uk/Author/292487/Morton+Jelly+Roll.html (12 Mar. 2005)
Lamothe, Ferdinand Joseph *Source(s):* LCAR
Note(s): Variant form of surname.
Lemott, Ferdinand Joseph *Source(s):* LCAR
Note(s): May be original surname?
Mister Jelly Lord *Source(s):* Shipton, Allyn. *Jazz*

Makers; Vangards of Sound. New York: Oxford University Press, 2002, p. 17.
Morton, Ferdinand Joseph *Source(s):* TCAN
Morton, Fred *Source(s):* http://mmd.foxtail.com/Archives/Digests/199807/1998.07.25.12.html (3 Mar. 2003)
Morton, Jelly Roll *Source(s):* CM07; EPMU; GAMM; IDBC; JASA; KINK
Mouton, Ferdinand *Source(s):* LCAR
World's Greatest Hot Tune Writer, The *Source(s):* Shipton, Allyn. *Jazz Makers* (see above), p. 17
Note(s): Signed himself.

LaMotta, Frank Joseph 1904-1989 [composer, songwriter]
LaMarr, Frank *Source(s):* ASCP; CCE43 #42485 Eunp351971

LaMotta, Wilbur L. 1919-1980 [composer, author, teacher]
LaMotta, Bill *Source(s):* ASCP; CPOL PA-1-193; LCAR

Lamotte, Franz [or François] ?1751-1780 [violinist, composer]
Young Englishman, The *Source(s):* GROL

La Motte-Fouqué, Friedrich Heinrich Karl, Freiherr de 1777-1843 [author]
Fouqué, Friedrich *Source(s):* PIPE
Note(s): Entered under this name.
Frank, A. L. T. *Source(s):* PIPE
Pellegrin *Source(s):* PIPE

Lampe, J(ens) Bodewalt 1869-1929 [composer]
Note(s): Portrait: PERF
Danmark, Ribe *Source(s):* CCE39 #21731, 410 R78220; JASA; JASN p. 293; PERF
Ribe, Danmark *Source(s):* CCE37 R60188

Lamprecht, Hermann 1913- [composer]
Berlá, Hemmy *Source(s):* KOMP; PFSA

Lanaro, Luigi 1911- [writer on music]
Luila *Source(s):* WORB

Lancaster, Mary Ann Elizabeth (née Shorey) 1851- [hymnist]
Shorey, L. *Source(s):* CYBH; JULN

Lanciano, Cristoforo da 1837-1905 [composer, organist]
Cipollone, Mattia *Source(s):* MELL; WORB

Lanctin, Charles François Honoré 1758 (or 59)-1822 [composer]
Duquesnoy, Charles (François Honoré) *Source(s):* IBIM; MACM; NGDO; STGR

Landauer, Erich 1912-1993 [conductor, writer on music]
Leinsdorf, Erich *Source(s):* BAKT; LCAR; PSNN

Landesberg, Alexander 1848-1916 [author, editor, critic]
Rechberg, Otto *Source(s):* LCAR; STGR
Note(s): Jt. pseud.: Leo Stein [i.e., Rosenstein]

Landini, Francesco c.1325-1397 [composer, poet, organist]
Cechus de Florentia *Source(s):* LCAR; NGDM
Cieco, Francesco *Source(s):* WORB
Cielo, Il *Source(s):* DEAR
Francesco Cieco *Source(s):* PSND
Francesco degli Organi *Source(s):* LCAR; PSND; WORB

Landon, Letitia Elizabeth (née Maclean) 1802-1838 [author, poet]
English Sappho, The *Source(s):* PSND
L. E. L. *Source(s):* CPMU; GOTE; PSND; WORB
Ross, Sheridan *Sources(s):* GOTH
Note(s): Possible pseud.; listed as pseud. of Miss Maclean.

Landowski, F. L. 1922- [composer]
Derives, Jean *Source(s):* BUL2
Lancen, Jean Serge *Source(s):* BUL1

Landreaux, Edna 1895-1925 [singer, pianist, songwriter]
Alix, Mae *Source(s):* HARS; SUTT
Note(s): Do not confuse with (Liza) May [or Mae] Alix (c.1902-), aka "The Queen of the Night Clubs." The name "May Alix" was used by Alberta Hunter (1895-1984) (see entry under Hunter) and also by singer Edmonia Henderson (1895-1924), who also used the names "Ethel Clark" & "Babe Johnson." (SUTT).
Hicks, Edna *Source(s):* HARS; LCAR ; SUTT
Vivian, Lila *Source(s):* HARS; SUTT

Landu, M'Pongo 1956- [singer, composer]
Love, M'Pongo *Source(s):* PEN2
Voix du Ziare, La *Source(s):* PEN2

Lane, James A. 1924-1997 [singer, guitarist, songwriter]
Rogers, Jimmy *Source(s):* CCE73; HARS; LCAR; OB97

Lane, James W(eldon) 1958- [composer, author, singer]
Spiro, Demon *Source(s):* ASCP; CCE60-61; CCE66-67

Lane, Robert William 1916-1983 [guitarist, singer, songwriter]
Great Doctor Robert Morton(The World's Greatest Hypnotist), The *Source(s):* EPMU
Great Morton, The *Source(s):* EPMU
Morton, Bob *Source(s):* EPMU
Morton, Robert *Source(s):* EPMU
Morton, Tex *Source(s):* EPMU
Yodelling Boundary Rider, The *Source(s):* EPMU

Lanfranchi Rossi, Carlo Giuseppi fl. c1750-c.1800 [dramatist]
Argolide, Egisippo *Source(s):* LCAR; WORB
Egisippo Argolide *Source(s):* LCAR; SONN

Lang, Andreas 1965- [pianist, singer, composer]
Lang, Andy Lee *Source(s):* OMUO

Lang, Isaac 1891-1950 [poet, playwright]
Goll, Yvan *Source(s):* PIPE; PSND
Lassang, Iwan *Source(s):* LCAR; PSND
Lazang, Iwan *Source(s):* LCAR; PIPE
Longeville, Jean *Source(s):* LCAR; PIPE
Thor, Tristian *Source(s):* PIPE; PSND
Torsi, Tristian *Source(s):* PIPE; PSND
Lang, Johann 1955- [singer, composer]
Lang, Hansi *Source(s):* OMUO
Lang, Philip J(oseph) 1911-1986 [composer]
Dean of American Orchestration, The *Source(s):* REHH
Langdon, Chauncy 1764-1830 [lawyer, song compiler]
Philo, Musico *Source(s):* LCAR; Hamm, Charles. *Yesterday's Popular Songs in America.* New York: Norton, 1979, p. 94.
Langdon, Richard 1730-1803 [composer, organist]
R. L. *Source(s):* CPMS ("Old England's Glory Revived")
Note(s): Probable initials of Langdon.
Langdon, Verne Loring 1941- [composer, author]
Bork, J. S. *Source(s):* ASCP
Lange, Robert John 1949- [songwriter, producer]
John-Lane, Robert *Source(s):* CPOL PA-703-472
Lange, Mutt *Source(s):* LCAR; PMUS-96; SONG
Langer, Alfons 1908- [composer]
Jindra, Alfons *Source(s):* GREN
Langer, Anton 1824-1879 [librettist]
Juxinger, Jodocus *Source(s):* STGR
Langer, Victor 1842-1902 [composer]
Tisza, Aladár *Source(s):* PRAT
Langestraat, Willy 1914- [composer]
Laguestra *Source(s):* SUPN
Langeveld(t), Joris [or Georg] van 1487-1558 [dramatist, humanist, composer]
Lankveld, Georg van *Source(s):* WORB
Macropedius, Georg(ius) *Source(s):* IBIM; LCAR; RIEM
Lang-Hyde, John Reginald 1899-1990 [dramatist, poet]
Hyde, Lewis *Source(s):* GOTL
Langkammer, Margarethe 1866-1922 [librettist]
Nordmann, Richard *Source(s):* STGR; WORB
Langlé, Honoré François Marie de 1741-1807 [composer, theorist]
Fontenelle of Music, (The) *Source(s):* GROL; STGR
Langlois, Louis 1862-1945 [composer]
Deladrèvre *Source(s):* REHH
Langrishe, May Katherine 1879- [pianist, composer]
May, Orchard *Source(s):* COHN; HIXN
Lan-Hochbrunn, Paul Eugen Josef von An der 1863-1914 [conductor, composer, organist]
Hartmann, Pater *Source(s):* BAKE; LCAR
Hartmann, Paul *Source(s):* LCAR

Lanier, Sidney 1842-1881 [poet, flutist, composer, music critic]
Note(s): Portrait: ETUP 53:7 (July 1935): 385
Musical Matthew Arnold of the Confederacy *Source(s):* GRAN
Lanier, Verdell 1957- [composer, pianist, arranger]
Norman, Constance *Source(s):* ASCP
La Pier(r)e, Cherilyn 1946- [singer, songwriter, actress]
Cher *Source(s):* LCAR; STAM
Sarkisian, Cherilyn *Source(s):* LCAR
Lara, Augustín 1896-1970 [composer, poet, conductor]
Lara, Maria Teresa *Source(s):* CCE63-66; LCAR
Note(s): Wrote several songs under his sister's name.
Larco, Isabel Granda 1911?-1983 [songwriter]
Granda, Chabuca *Source(s):* LCAR; PSND
LaRocca, Dominick James 1889-1961 [composer, author, performer]
Assassinator of Syncopation *Source(s):* TCAN
LaRocca, Nick *Source(s):* ASCB; CCE37 E60475; PERF; LCAR
LaRoche, Paul [composer]
Brule' *Source(s):* LCAR; http://www.sidecanyon.com/features/namusic7.htm (21 Oct. 2002)
Native American Yanni, The *Source(s):* http://www.sidecanyon.com/features/namusic7.htm
Larosch, German Avgustovich 1845-1904 [music critic, composer]
Note(s): Portrait: http://www.tchaikovsky.host.sk/New%20Page%201.htm (21 Oct. 2002)
Laroche, Herman *Source(s):* NGDM
Nelyubov, L. *Source(s):* NGDM
Larrouy, Maurice 1882-1939 [author]
Milan, René *Source(s):* LCAR; PIPE; WORB
Y *Source(s):* LCAR; PIPE
Larsen, Søren 1962- [composer]
Hyldgaard, Søren *Source(s):* MOMU
Lartigue, Alfred Charlemagne 1815?-1883 [physician, dramatist]
Delacour, Alfred (Charlemagne) *Source(s):* GAN1; GAN2; LOWN; MELL; WORB
Delacour, M. *Source(s):* LCAR
La Rue, Pierre de 1455?-1518 [composer]
Note(s): See LCAR for variant forms of name.
Petern van Straeten *Source(s):* LCAR; NGDM
Petrus la Vic *Source(s):* LCAR
Petrus Platensis *Source(s):* LCAR
Piero delapiazza *Source(s):* LCAR
Plansis, Petrus *Source(s):* LCAR; NGDM
Lascombe, George 1879-1927 [lyricist]
Villard *Source(s):* FULD p. 426
Lasha, William B. 1929- [flutist, composer]
Lasha, Prince *Source(s):* CCE62-63; PEN1

Lasker, (Ignaz) Julius 1811-1876 [author]
Sincerus, (Julius) *Source(s):* PIPE; WORB
Lassus, Roland de 1532-1594 [composer]
Belgian Orpheus, The *Source(s):* DEA3; DEAR
Lassus, Orlando di *Source(s):* LCAR
Last, Hans 1929- [conductor, composer, arranger]
Hansi *Source(s):* EPMU
Last, James *Source(s):* CASS; CCE67-68; EPMU; KOMP; KOMS; RIES
Stahl, Hans *Source(s):* CCE60
Last, Werner 1926-1982 [composer]
Herlow, Jan *Source(s):* CCE64
Warner, Kai *Source(s):* CCE71; PFSA
Laszky, Julius Albert 1867-1935 [composer, educator]
Laszky, Béla *Source(s):* WORB
Latey, Keith P(armeter) 1896-1987 [composer]
Logan, John P. *Source(s):* CCE53; REHG; SUPN
Latham, Lance Brenton 1894-1985 [hymnist]
Latham, Doc *Source(s):* CYBH (port.)
Lathbury, Mary Ann [or Artemesia] 1841-1913 [hymnist]
Note(s): Portrait: CYBH
M. A. L. *Source(s):* DIEH ("Take Thou the Heart")
Note(s): Presumed iniatials of Lathbury.
Poet Laureate of Chautauqua *Source(s):* CYBH
LaTorraca, Gerard (A.) 1935- [composer, author, pianist]
Lambert, Jerry *Source(s):* ASCP; CCE68; CCE72
Latourelle, James 1835-1908 [composer, director]
Little Jimmy *Source(s):* PSND
La Tourrasse, André de 1910-1968 [librettist]
Orgeval, François d' *Source(s):* PIPE
Latrobe, Christian Ignatius 1758-1836 [composer]
C. I. L. T. *Source(s):* CPMU
Lätus, Georg 1500-c.1560 [composer]
Frölich, Georg *Source(s):* IBIM; WORB
Laub(e), Phoebe 1952- [singer, songwriter]
Snow, Phoebe *Source(s):* CM04; EPMU; LCAR; PEN2
Note(s): Also used by Bertha Ruth Davis.
Laube, Heinrich (Rudolf Constanz) 1806-1884 [librettist]
Campo, H. *Source(s):* PIPE; STGR
Lauder, (Sir) Harry (Maclennan) 1870-1950 [singer, comedian, composer, author]
'Braid Scotsman *Source(s):* Baker, Dale & Larry F. Kinner. *The Sir Harry Lauder Discography.* Metuchen, N. J.: Scarecrow, 1990, xiii.
Great Scot *Source(s):* Irving, Gordan. *Great Scot; The Life Story of Sir Harry Lauder, Legendary Laird of the Music Hall.* London: Frewin, 1968.
Knight of the Realm *Source(s):* PARS
Laird of the Halls, The *Source(s):* PSND
Valiant Minstrel *Source(s):* Malvern, Gladys. *Valiant Minstrel.* New York: J. Messner, 1943.
Laufer, Jake [singer, songwriter]
Godfather of Folk Disco, The *Source(s):* http://singer-songwriter.com/genre/pop/pop31.html (6 Oct. 2002)
Laurencin d'Armond, Ferdinand Peter Graf 1819-1890 [music critic]
Philokales *Source(s):* OMUO
Laurendeau, Louis-Philippe 1861-1916 [composer, arranger, writer]
Note(s): Portrait: METR 11:3 (Mar. 1985): cover
Kent, H. R. *Source(s):* LCAR
Laurent, Paul *Source(s):* LCAR; NGAM; REHG; SMIN
Lorendo, L. P. *Source(s):* CCE39 #25855, 22 R78589
Reeves, G. H. *Source(s):* CCE37 R59349; LCAR; NGAM; REHG; SMIN
Note(s): Do not confuse with D(avid) W(allis) Reeves, march composer & bandmaster.
Laurentius, von Schnüffis 1633-1702 [singer, songwriter]
Martin, Johann *Source(s):* LCAR; MACM
Laurenzi, Filberto 1619 (or 20)-after 1659 [composer, singer]
Laurenti(is), Filbertus [or Filberto] (de) *Source(s):* LCAR; NGDO; WORB
Lausen, John R. 1911-1995 [trumpeter, composer, bandleader]
Lawson, John R. *Source(s):* KINK
Lawson, Yank *Source(s):* KINK; NGDJ; ROOM
Lautenschläger, Willi 1880-1949 [composer]
Armándola, J(osé) *Source(s):* CCE50; CCE59; GREN; REHH
Haller, Edwin *Source(s):* GREN
Nippon, A. *Source(s):* GREN
Turmer, Udo *Source(s):* GREN
Wanson, James *Source(s):* GREN
Lauzières(-Thémines), Achille de 1818-1894 [librettist]
De Leone, Andrea de *Source(s):* PIPE
Leone, Andrea de *Source(s):* STGR
Lava, William 1911-1971 [songwriter]
Note(s): Composed music for publisher David M. Gordon under the names listed below, as did Dave Kahn, Irving Gertz, William Lava, Leo(n) Klatzkin, Joseph [or Joe] Mullendore & possibly others. See also David M. Gordon.
Gordon, Melvyn Lenard *Source(s):* CLMC
Lenard, Melvyn *Source(s):* CLMC
Laval Soza, Denise Lillian 1977- [singer, songwriter]
Nicole *Source(s):* HWOM
Note(s): Also used by Nicole Seibert; do not confuse with Nicole (Wray) or Nicole (McCloud)
Lavan, Henry Robert Merrill 1921-1998 [composer, lyricist]
Levan, Henry Robert Merrill *Source(s):* EWEN; LCAR
Merrill, Robert [or Bob] *Source(s):* CASS; EWEN; EWPA; GAN1; GAN2; HARR; PIPE
Stryker, Paul *Source(s):* GAN2; LCAR

LaVoie, (Roland) Kent 1943- [singer, songwriter]
Lobo *Source(s):* CCE72-74; EPMU; HARR; PEN2; PSND; WARN
Lavoriel, Ludwing [singer, songwriter]
Bombón *Source(s):* HWOM
Law, (William) Arthur 1844-1913 [playwright]
Cromer, Wes(t) *Source(s):* GAN1; GAN2; GANA p. 124
Lawes, Henry 1596-1662 [composer]
Cavalier Songwriter *Source(s):* Spink, Ian. *Henry Lawes; Cavalier Songwriter*. New York: Oxford University Press, 2000.
Tuneful Harry *Source(s):* PSND
Lawlars, Ernest 1900-1961 [singer, guitarist, songwriter]
Little Son Joe *Source(s):* HARS; LCAR
Son Joe *Source(s):* HARS
Lawler, C. F. 1728-1819 [author, poet]
Pindar, Peter *Source(s):* LCAR; ROOM
Note(s): Also used by George Daniel & John Wolcot.
Lawrence, Cornelius C. 1902-1981 [composer, author, publisher, actor]
Lawrence, Neil *Source(s):* ASCA; ASCC
Lawrence, Wilma Sue 1951- [songwriter]
Braddock, Sparky *Source(s):* PMUS
Sparky *Source(s):* CCE78
Lawrie, Marie MacDonald MacLaughlin 1948- [singer, actress, songwriter]
Lulu *Source(s):* EPMU; LCAR; PSND
Layer, Wolfgang 1948- [composer]
Alvirez, Gilberto *Source(s):* PFSA
Eik, Florian *Source(s):* PFSA
Korg, Roland *Source(s):* PFSA
Lazarides, Kostas 1949- [songwriter]
Kostas *Source(s):* ENCM
Lazarus, Gustav 1861-1920 [composer]
Note(s): Portrait: ETUP 53:7 (July 1935): 385
Laroso, Gustavo *Source(s):* CCE48 R33783 ("Fireside Story"); TPRF
Lazarus, Lazar 1934- [composer, pianist, musicologist]
Sitsky, Larry *Source(s):* DAUM
Lazeroff, Bernard 1921- [pianist, arranger, bandleader]
Leighton, Bernie *Source(s):* KINK
Lazzari, Josef Fortunat Silvester 1857 (or 60)-1944 [composer]
Lazzari, Sylvio [or Silvio] *Source):* OMUO; RIES
Leacock, John 1729-1802 [composer, silversmith]
Barton, Andrew *Source(s):* Vernon, Grenville. *Yankee Doodle-Doo*. New York: Benjamin Blom, 1972, 25.
Note(s): Possible pseud. Also possible pseud. of Thomas Forrest (Vernon p. 16)
Leader, Joyce Rona [composer]
Budtree, Red *Source(s):* CCE68
Note(s): Jt. pseud.: Harry Leader [i.e., Henry Lebys]
Gray, Rona *Source(s):* CPOL RE-644-785
LeBeau, Robert, Jr. [singer, songwriter]
New Orleans Beau *Source(s):* http://www.illinoistimes.com/8_15_02/nowplaying.html (6 Oct. 2002)
Lebègue, Nicolas c.1631-1702 [composer, organist, harpsichordist]
Note(s): The following names are probable pseuds.
Mr. Noel *Source(s):* GROL
Noel, (Mr.) *Source(s):* GROL
Lebesque, Octave 1857-1933 [librettist]
Montogueil, Georges *Source(s):* LOWN; MELL; WORB
Lebstock, Jack [songwriter]
Grayson, Jack *Source(s):* EPMU
Lebys, Henry 1906-1987 [songwriter, arranger, bandleader]
Note(s): The following names are listed as pseuds. of Harry Leader [i.e., Henry Lebys]
Brown, Al *Source(s):* CCE64 R330847
Note(s): Jt. pseud.: Harry Leon [i.e., Sugarman] & Leo Towers [i.e., Leo(nard) Blitz]
Budtree, Red *Source(s):* CCE68
Note(s): Jt. pseud.: Rona Gray [i.e., Joyce Rona Leader]
Cugaro, Georges *Source(s):* CCE50 Efor2175; CCE77
Leader, Harry *Source(s):* MUWB
Mason, John *Source(s):* CCE50
Primo, Jose *Source(s):* CCE53; CPOL RE-63-950
Ribana, Lena *Source(s):* CCE66-67; CPOL RE-644-785
Roberts, Martin *Source(s):* CCE51; CPOL RE-32-459
Rose, Mel *Source(s):* http://www.dismuke.org/how/prev3-04.html (29 July 2005)
Wain, D. *Source(s):* CCE63; CPOL RE-520-390
Lechner, Leonard c.1553-1606 [composer, music editor]
Athesinus, (Leonardus) *Source(s):* GROL
Leclair, Jean Marie 1697-1764 [composer, violinist]
Note(s): Portraits: ETUP 53:7 (July 1935): 385; EWCY
Corelli of France *Source(s):* EWCY
Leclerc, Germaine Ortala [composer]
Grigor, Nico *Source(s):* http://www.mergetel.com/~geostan/music.html (14 Mar. 2005)
Leclère, (Arthur Justin) Léon 1874-1966 [poet, painter, musician]
Klingsor, Tristan (L.) *Source(s):* GROL; LCAR; PSND; WORB
Leclère, Tristan *Source(s):* LCAR; LCCC 1955-70 (see reference)
Le Clerq, Arthur 1891-1976 [songwriter]
Clare, Arthur *Source(s):* CCE63; KILG
Henley, A. W. D. *Source(s):* KILG
Kenley, Peter *Source(s):* KILG

Leigh, Arthur *Source(s):* KILG
Milner, Ralph *Source(s):* KILG
Leclerq, Louis 1828- [author, writer on music]
Celler, Ludovic *Source(s):* LCAR; MACM; WORB
Lecocq, (Alexandre) Charles 1832-1918 [composer]
Note(s): Portrait: ETUP 53:8 (Aug. 1935): 441
Alcindor *Source(s):* STGR; WORB
Note(s): Jt. pseud.: Isidore Edouard Legouix & (Louis Auguste Joseph) Florimond Ronger.
Lecuona, Ernesto 1896-1963 [composer]
Cuba's Greatest Composer *Source(s):* http://ourworld.compuserve.com/homepages/mrbart (26 Sept. 2003)
Ledbetter, Huddie (William) 1885-1949 [singer, guitarist, songwriter]
Boyd, Walter *Source(s):* NGDM; SOTH
King of the 12 String Guitar Players *Source(s):* CM06 p. vi; HARS; SHAD
Leadbelly *Source(s):* AMUS; CM06; EPMU; HARR; HARS; NGAM; PSND; SHAD
Newman, Joel *Source(s):* PMUS; PSND
Lederer, Viktor [or Victor] 1881- [author, writer on music]
Gaerber, Siegwart *Source(s):* LCAR; WORB
Gerber, Siegwart *Source(s):* REIM
Ledesma, Mariano Rodriguez de 1779-1847 [composer]
M. de L. *Source(s):* CPMU
Ledóchowska, Maria T(h)eresa 1863-1922 [author, librettist]
Africanus *Source(s):* STGR; WORB
Afrykanin *Source(s):* STGR
Halka, Aleks *Source(s):* STGR; WORB
Leduc, P. [composer]
Claude, H. *Source(s):* TPRF
Lee, Albert George 1880-1946 [songwriter, actor]
Armstrong, Paul *Source(s):* CCE33 Efor28899; CCE60-61
Note(s): Jt. pseud.: R(obert) Weston [i.e., Robert P. Harris].
Curtis, Con *Source(s):* CCE68 R438781
Note(s): Jt. pseud.: Jack Waller & Joseph A(lbert) Tunbridge.
Lee, Bert *Source(s):* GAN1; GAN2
Lee, Herbert *Source(s):* KILG
Lincoln, Elmer *Source(s):* CCE32 Efor24411; CCE58-59
Note(s): Jt. pseud.: R(obert) Weston [i.e., Robert P. Harris].
Molloy, Mary *Source(s):* CCE49 R45281 ("The Fairy Boat")
Note(s): Jt. pseud.: R(obert) Weston [i.e., Robert P. Harris].
Shaw, Damon *Source(s):* CCE41 #29129 Efor65280; CCE68 R438781
Note(s): Jt. pseud.: Jack Waller & Joseph A(lbert) Tunbridge.
Whalen, Nat *Source(s):* CCE47 R20126 ("Buttercups and Daisies")
Lee, Edward O'Sullivan 1941- [arranger, producer]
Lee, Bunny *Source(s):* LCAR; NOMG
Striker *Source(s):* NOMG
Lee, Jonathan Butler 1947- [composer, author]
Lee, Jack *Source(s):* ASCP
Lee, Louis Leoni [composer]
Devereaux, J. L. *Source(s):* IBIM; WORB; YORM
Lee, Mary Emily Frances fl. 1950 [pianist, writer]
Lee, Cecile *Source(s):* CART
Lee, Richard [hymnist]
Ebenezer *Source(s):* HATF
Note(s): On contributions to *Evangelical Magazine.* Also used by Job Hupton.
Leemann, Max 1932- [composer]
Abel, Lex *Source(s):* REHH; SUPN
Leenen, Ullrich Jakob 1964- [composer]
Ulli *Source(s):* KOMS; PFSA
Lees, Frederick Eugene John 1928- [writer, critic, lyricist]
Lees, Gene *Source(s):* NGDJ
Morgan, Max *Source(s):* LCAR
Leeson, Jane E(liza) 1807 (or 08)-1881 (or 82) [hymnist]
J. E. L. *Source(s):* JULN
M. L. *Source(s):* JULN
Leest, Antonius Maria van 1897-1970 [composer]
Arioste, Paul *Source(s):* REHH; SUPN
Carpelle, Giulli *Source(s):* REHH; SUPN
Courtois, Jules *Source(s):* REHH; SUPN
Lenselink, W. A. *Source(s):* REHH; SUPN
Mècené, Maurice *Source(s):* REHH; SUPN
Serveau, Armand *Source(s):* REHH; SUPN
Splendeur, Andre *Source(s):* REHH; SUPN
Leeuw, Antonius Wilhelmus Andrianus 1926-1996 [composer]
Leeuw, Ton *Source(s):* LCAR
Leeuwen, Simon Petrus van 1879-1950 [composer]
Simonis, P. *Source(s):* SUPN
Lefèbvre, Françoise (M.) 1912- [lecturer, composer]
Paduc(c)i, (A(ndré)) *Source(s):* BUL1; COHN; HEIN; HIXN
Paul du Crucifix, (Sister) *Source(s):* BUL1; COHN; HEIN; HIXN
Lefèvre (d'Etaples), Jacques c.1450-1536 [theologian, humanist, music theorist]
Faber Stapulensis, Jacobus *Source(s):* NGDM; http://www.encyclopedia.com/browse/browse-Fa.asp (6 Oct. 2002)
Lefrancq, Pierre 1889- [composer]
D'Aragon, Alexandre *Source(s):* BUL1
LeGarde, Edward [or Ted] 1931- [singer, songwriter, guitarist]

Australia's Yodelling Stockmen *Source(s):* MCCL
LeGarde Twins, The *Source(s):* MCCL
Note(s): With Thomas LeGarde.
LeGarde, Thomas 1931- [singer, songwriter, guitarist]
Australia's Yodelling Stockmen *Source(s):* MCCL
LeGarde Twins, The *Source(s):* MCCL
Note(s): With Edward [or Ted] LeGarde.
Leglaire, Sophia 1915-1999 [author, lyricist]
Leglaire, Sonny *Source(s):* ASCP; CPOL RE-256-544
Legouix, Isidore Edouard 1834-1916 [composer]
Alcindor *Source(s):* STGR; WORB
Note(s): Jt. pseud.: Alexander Charles Lecocq & (Louis Auguste Joseph) Florimond Ronger.
Legoux, (Baroness) Julie 1842 (or 43)-1891 [composer]
Des Roches, Gilbert *Source(s):* COHN; HIX; LCAR
Roches, Gilbert des *Source(s):* COHN; HIXN
Le Grand, Maurice (Etienne) 1872 (or 73)-1934 [librettist]
Franc-Nohain(e) *Source(s):* LCAR; LOWN; MACM; MELL; NGDO; WHIT
Legrense, Johannes c.1415-1473 [humanist, theorist]
Carthesiensis *Source(s):* GRV3
Gallius, Johannes *Source(s):* LCAR
Johannes Gallius *Source(s):* NGDM
Johannes Mantuanus *Source(s):* NGDM
Mantuanus, Johannes *Source(s):* LCAR
Lehman, Evangeline 1896-1975 [composer]
Manley, Richard *Source(s):* CCE39 E79848; TPRF
Lehmann, Amelia 19th cent. [arranger, composer]
Note(s): Married name: Mrs.Rudolph Lehmann.
A. L. *Source(s):* COHN; CPMU; HIXN; LCAR
Lehmann, Bertha (née Filhés) 1819-after 1887 [author]
Berthold(-Filhés), B. *Source(s):* WORB
Ebeling-Filhés, E. B. *Source(s):* PIPE
Note(s): Jt. pseud.: Elisabeh Ebeling.
Lehmann, Eitel 1902-1986 [composer]
Eitel, Paul *Source(s):* KOMP; KOMS; PFSA
Lehmann, Elizabeth Nina Mary Frederika 1862-1918 [composer, singer, pianist, teacher]
Note(s): Portraits: DWCO; ETUP 53:8 (Aug. 1935): 441; *The Musician* (Nov. 1900): 337. Married name: Mrs. Herbert Bedford.
Lehmann, Liza *Source(s):* GAMM; GAN1; GAN2
Lehms, Georg Christian 1684-1717 [poet, librettist]
Palidor *Source(s):* GROL
Lehner, Fritz 1872- [composer]
Frenelle, Jules *Source(s):* STGR
Lehrer, Leibush 1887-1964 (or 65) [lyricist]
Magister, L. *Source(s):* HESK
Lehrman, Theodore Howard 1929- [composer, author, singer]
Lawson, Tedd *Source(s):* ASCP; CPOL PAu-36-690
Lehto, Lassi [composer, multi-instrumentalist]
Tenor, Jimi *Source(s):* http://www.jimitenor.com (6 Oct. 2002)
Leib, Joseph 1900-1993 [lyricist, writer on music]
Note(s): Born in Lithuania, settled in Shreveport, LA, and changed name to "Parrish;" (SHAP).
Leib, Bell *Source(s):* PMUS
Note(s): Jt. pseud.: Benny Bell [i.e., Benjamin Samberg]
Pardette, Neil *Source(s):* CCE50 R56597 ("I Never Miss the Sunshine I'm So Use to the Rain")
Parrish, Mitchell *Source(s):* PMUS ("The Blond Sailor")
Reed, Jacqueline *Source(s):* CCE57
Note(s): See index; not listed in entry.
Leiber, Jerry 1933- [lyricist]
Glick, Elmo *Source(s):* CCE60; GROL; PMUS; SONG
Note(s): Jt. pseud.: Mike Stroller.
Peters, Jed *Source(s):* CCE67
Note(s): Jt. pseud.: Mike Stroller.
Leichtentritt, Hirsch 1874-1951 [composer, music critic, musicologist]
Leichtentritt, Hugo *Source(s):* WORB
Leidzén, Erik William Gustav 1894-1962 [composer, arranger, conductor, educator]
Note(s): In REHG: Recent investigations indicate Leidzen possibly ghost-wrote many of Ernest William's pieces.
Kelly, William *Source(s):* LCAR; REHG
Stebbins, George *Source(s):* LCAR; REHG; SUPN
Note(s): "The Happy Farmer Joins the Navy." Do not confuse with George Coles Stebbins (1846-1945), composer of "Take Time to Be Holy."
Leighton, James Albert 1877-1964 [songwriter]
Leighton, Bert *Source(s):* ASCP
Leinati, Carlo Ambrogio c.1645-c.1710 [violinist, composer, impressario]
Gobbo della Regina, Il *Source(s):* BAKO; BAKR; NGDM
Hunchback, The *Source(s):* MACM
Lonati, Carlo Ambrogio *Source(s):* BAKO; BAKR; LCAR; NGDM
Queen's Hunchback, The *Source(s):* BAKO; BAKR
Leip, Karl Hermann Gottfried 1893-1983 [author]
Leip, Hans *Source(s):* PIPE
Li-Shan-Pe *Source(s):* PIPE
Leiserowitz, Jacob [or Yaakov] 1893-1965 [lyricist]
Brisker, Yankele *Source(s):* HESK
Leisy, James (Franklin) 1927-1989 [songwriter, author]
Ericson, Julia *Source(s):* CPOL PA-151-988; PSNN
Note(s): Jt. pseud.: Marjorie Farmer.
Lynn, Frank *Source(s):* CCE61 E158323; LCAR; PSND
Note(s): Also used by Joseph (Moiseyevich) Schellinger.

Leitch, Donovan (Phillip) 1943 (or 46)- [singer, songwriter]
Britain's Answer to Bob Dylan *Source(s):* EPMU
British Dylan, The *Source(s):* CASS
Donovan *Source(s):* ALMN; CASS; CM09; DIMA; EPMU; HARR; PEN2; PSND
Leitner, Herbert 1954- [composer, musician]
Mr. Herb *Source(s):* OMUO
Lelewel, Joachim [folk song collector]
Dolega-Chodakowski, Zorian *Source(s):* GROL
Lemacherier, Guillaume fl. 1418-56 [composer]
Legrant, Guillaume *Source(s):* NGDM
Lemaire, Joseph c.1820-1883 [singer, composer]
Darcier, Joseph *Source(s):* IBIM; WORB
Lemle, Sebastian fl. 1600-50? [composer]
Agnelli, Sebastian *Source(s):* WORB
Lämblein, Agnelli *Source(s):* IBIM; WORB
Lemoine, Achille(-Philibert) 1813-1895 [editor, composer]
Heintz *Source(s):* IBIM; WORB
Lemoine, Louise Françoise 1810 (or 19)-1889 [composer, singer]
Puget, Loisa *Source(s):* MELL; WORB
Lemon, Laura (Gertrude) 1866-1924 [composer, pianist]
Fleming, Austin *Source(s):* CANE
Macdonald, Ian *Source(s):* CANE
Lemonnier, Guillaume Antoine 1721 (or 31)-1797 [writer, librettist]
De Vaux *Source(s):* MELL
Vaux, de *Source(s):* SONN
Lemons, Overton Amos 1913-1966 [singer, songwriter, guitarist]
Note(s): In PSND given name: Amos Overton.
Lewis, Smiley [or Smiling] *Source(s):* AMUS; HARS; NGAM
Lemont, Cedric Wilmot 1879-1954 [organist, composer]
Note(s): Portrait: ETUP 53:8 (Aug. 1935): 441
Saxon, Cedric *Source(s):* TPRF
Lénéka, André 1859-1937 [librettist]
Delormeil *Source(s):* LOWN; MELL
Lengsfelder, Hans 1903-1979 [composer, author, recording executive]
Brehm, Günther *Source(s):* CCE58; GREN; REHG
Felder, Hans *Source(s):* GREN
Lenk, Harry *Source(s):* ASCP; CCE70 R488501; GREN; REHG
Peters, John *Source(s):* CCE58 E122581; CCE60; CPOL RE-308-685
Ross, Rusty *Source(s):* CCE54
Lengyel, Cornel Adam 1915-2003 [music critic, author, translator]
Adam, Cornel *Source(s):* LCAR; PIPE

Lennon, John (Winston) 1940-1980 [singer, songwriter, guitarist, pianist]
Beatcomber *Source(s):* BEAT
Beatles, The *Source(s):* http://www.beatlesstory.com (4 May 2005)
Note(s): With: George Harrison, (James) Paul McCartney & Richard Starkey.
Dr. Dream *Source(s):* BEAT; PSND
Ghurkin, (Rev.) Fred *Source(s):* BEAT; PSND
Ghurkin, (Rev.) Thumbs *Source(s):* BEAT; PSND
Johnson, (Hon.) John St. Jon *Source(s):* PSND
Kundalini, Kaptain *Source(s):* BEAT; PSND
McDougal, Dwarf *Source(s):* BEAT; PSND
Nohnn, Joel *Source(s):* PSND
O'Boogie, (Dr.) Winston *Source(s):* PSND
O'Cean, John *Source(s):* BEAT; PSND
O'Ghurkin, (Dr.) Winston *Source(s):* BEAT; PSND
O'Reggae, (Dr.) Winston *Source(s):* PSND
Renon, Jon *Source(s):* LCAR
Silver, Johnny *Source(s):* BEAT
Note(s): Possible pseud.?
Torment, Mel *Source(s):* BEAT; PSND
Lenoir, J. B. 1929-1967 [singer, guitarist, songwriter]
Lenore, J. B. *Source(s):* HARS
Lenz, Albert 1903- [composer]
Lé, Bert *Source(s):* KOMP; KOMS; PFSA
Lenz, Johann Reinhold von 1778-1854 [singer, author]
Kühne, (Reinhold) *Source(s):* PIPE; WORB
Leo, Leonardo (Oronzo Salvatore de) 1694 (or 95)-1744 [composer]
Ladel, Onorio *Source(s):* STGR; WORB
Leon, Jack [conductor, arranger, conductor]
Jerome, Joy *Source(s):* MUWB
Léonard(us) (le père) mentioned 17th cent. [composer]
Nervius *Source(s):* WORB
Note(s): Do not confuse with Leonard(us) Nervius [i.e., Corneilli Musel]
Leonard, Lionel Frederick 1881-1954 [playwright]
Lonsdale, Frederick *Source(s):* CART; GAN1; GAN2; PIPE
Leonard, Nellie Mabel 1875-1956 [musician, writer]
Stuart, Fay *Source(s):* CART
Leonard, Roger [guitarist, composer]
Leonard, Deke *Source(s):* EPMU; http://www.geocities.com/Nashville/Stage/8089/Deke2.htm#Biog (14 Dec. 2003)
Leonarda, Anna Isabella 1620-1704 [composer]
Musa Novarese, La *Source(s):* GROL; RIES
Leoncavallo, Ruggerio 1857-1919 [composer, librettist]
Cavallo, Roger Leon *Source(s):* OMUO
Perterfoff, L. *Source(s):* OMUO

Leoni, Franco 1864 (or 65)-1949 [composer, conductor]
Note(s): Portrait: ETUP 53:8 (Aug. 1935): 441
Chewski, C. *Source(s):* PIPE; STGR v. 4/pt.1; WEOP; WORB
Gournard, P. *Source(s):* MELL; STGR v. 4/pt.1; WEOP
Lewis, Frances *Source(s):* PIPE; WEOP; WORB
Leopold, Isaiah Edwin 1886-1966 [actor, songwriter, librettist]
Clown Prince of Comedy *Source(s):* PSND
Fire Chief, The *Source(s):* PSND
Greatest Visual Comedian of Our Day, The *Source(s):* http://timstvshowcase.com/edwynn.html (6 Oct. 2002)
Perfect Fool, The *Source(s):* GAN1; GAN2; PSND
Wynn, Ed *Source(s):* GAN1; GAN2; PSND; WORB
Lepage, Albert (Aahemar) 1920- [arranger, trumpeter]
Page, Bert *Source(s):* CCE59; CCE61
Paige, Bert *Source(s):* CCE52-53; CCE60-68; MUSR p. 264
L'Epine, Ernest Louis Victor Jules 1826-1893 [composer, poet, dramatist]
Le Hestre, Pierre *Source(s):* IBIM; WORB
Manuel, E(rnest) *Source(s):* IBIM; PIPE; ROOM; WORB
Note(s): Do not confuse with French poet/dramatist Eugenè Manuel (1823-1901).
Quatrelles *Source(s):* IBIM; LCAR; NGDO; PIPE; WORB
Lepschies, Karl 1921- [composer]
Horner, Friedrich *Source(s):* BUL3
Le Querrec, Anatole Charles 1875 (or 76)-1957 [author, playwright]
Mirande, Yves *Source(s):* GAN1; GAN2; WORB
LeRoy, Jehan c.1430-c.1485 [composer]
Regis, Johannes *Source(s):* LCAR; NGDM
Leroyer, Pierre 1918-1983 [songwriter, novelist]
Deland, Pierre *Source(s):* CPOL RE-66-195
Delanoe, Pierre *Source(s):* CCE56-68; CCE60-62; CPOL RE-339-933; LCAR
Lanoé, Pierre (de) *Source(s):* CCE50-52; CCE55-56
Noe, Pierre De La *Source(s):* CCE58
Lertzman, Carl Myron 1908-1982 [songwriter, author]
Monosha, Coleman *Source(s):* ASCP; CPOL RE-50-674
Leskow, Nikolai Semenovich 1831-1895 [author]
Stebnizki, (N.) *Source(s):* PIPE; PSND
Lessnau, Robert G(erald) 1938-2001 [composer, author, performer]
Laurel, Bob(by) *Source(s):* ASCP; CCE59; CCE61
Lester, Sidney [writer]
Steer, L. E. *Source(s):* GANA
Lesur, Daniel Jean Yves 1908-2002 [composer, teacher]
Daniel-Lesur, (Jean-Yves) *Source(s):* BAKO; MACM; NGDM; NGDO
Létang, P. E. [author]
Marville *Source(s):* WEOP
Leucks, Gottlieb 1893-1951 [conductor, composer]
Leux, Leo *Source(s):* CCE57; CCE63; MACM; RIES
Leuthard, Emilian 1919- [composer]
Moro *Source(s):* REHH
Note(s): Also used by Walter Moro [or Morrow] Bohn & Bartolomeo Ratti.
Leutwiler, Toni 1923- [composer, conductor]
Wyler, Tom *Source(s):* RFSO; RIES
Leuven, Adolphe (Ribbing) de 1800-1884 [librettist, director]
Adolphe (de L.) *Source(s):* LCAR; LOWN; NGDO
Granval, (Adolphe) *Source(s):* GDRM; GROL; NGDO
Grenvallet, (Adolphe?) *Source(s):* GDRM; GROL; NGDO
Ribbing, (Count) Adolph(e) *Source(s):* GROL; LCAR; NGDO
Leveen, Raymond 1893-1984 [author, lyricist]
Ledeen, Raymond *Source(s):* ASCP
Leventhal, Herbert 1914-1991 [composer, author]
Leighton, Herb *Source(s):* ASCP; CCE49-50; CCE65-66
Leventhal, Ronald 1927- [composer, author, arranger]
Lee, Ronny *Source(s):* ASCP; CCE67
Levetzow, Karl Micha(e)l von 1871-1945 [author, librettist]
Hinzelmann, Hans Heinz *Source(s):* LOWN; MELL
Note(s): Jt. pseud.: Leo Feld [i.e., Leo [or Ludwig] Hirschfeld]
Karlev, M. *Source(s):* LOWN; MELL
Levey, Harold [composer]
Leeds, Harold *Source(s):* CLTP ("Armstrong Circle Theatre")
Levi see also *Levy*
Levi, Sigmund 1821-1884 [pianist, teacher, editor, writer on music]
Note(s): Surname frequently given: Levy.
Lebert, Sigmund *Source(s):* BAKE; LCAR
Levi, Zhul (Efraim) 1930- [composer]
Levi, Jul(es) *Source(s):* BUL3; LCAR
Levin, Benjamin 1903-1977 [songwriter, singer, actor]
Bonn, Issy *Source(s):* EPMU; KILG; ROOM
Leven, Benny *Source(s):* EPMU; KILG; ROOM
Three Rascals, The *Source(s):* KILG
Note(s): Jt. pseud.: Eddie Fields & Charles O 'Donnell.
Levin, Joseph A. 1917-1999 [composer, arranger, author, editor]

Brok, Ervin *Source(s):* CCE57-58
Lane, Joe *Source(s):* CCE55; CCE77; CPOL RE-278-458
Lane, John *Source(s):* CCE54-55; CCE57-62; CPOL RE-173-633; LCAR
Lone, John *Source(s):* CCE73; CPOL RE-174-215
Love, John *Source(s):* CPOL RE-293-637
Nelson, David *Source(s):* CCE56; CCE58; CPOL RE-276-551
Note(s): Also used by David Nelson Miller.

Levin, Mikhail [or Michel] 1894- [composer]
Michelet, Michel *Source(s):* BAKR; CCE58-59; HOFE

Levin, Morris Albert 1900-1988 [composer]
Nevin, Mark *Source(s):* ASCP

Levine, Abe [i.e., Abraham] (Lewis) 1915-2001 [composer, author, singer]
Levine, Al *Source(s):* ASCP; CCE26 Eunp7306
Vine, Lee *Source(s):* CCE66
Note(s): Possible pseud.?

Levins, Marc(k) 1903-1967 [conductor, composer]
Lavry, Marc *Source(s):* MACM

Levinsky, Kermit [composer]
Leslie, Kermit *Source(s):* CLRA

Levinsky, Walter 1929-1999 [composer, conductor, arranger, clarinetist]
Leslie, Walter *Source(s):* ASCP; CCE55; CCE57

Levinson, Jerome [or Jerry] 1909-1987 [composer, songwriter]
Livingston, Jerry *Source(s):* ALMN; BBDP; HARR; KINK; ROOM; VACH

Levinson, Robert (Wells) 1922-1998 [composer, author, lyricist, drummer]
Jehrom, Robert *Source(s):* CPOL RE-29-363
Jerome, Robert *Source(s):* CPOL RE-16-182
Roberts, Wellesley *Source(s):* CPOL RE-16-178
Wells, Robert [or Bob] *Source(s):* IGER; LCAR; MRSQ 4:4 (1999): 13; STUW

Levisalles, Eric 1955- [composer, record producer]
Levi, Eric *Source(s):* MOMU

Levise, William, Jr. 1945- [singer, songwriter, bandleader]
Godfather of Motor City Rock and Roll, The *Source(s):* CM11
King of White Soul, The *Source(s):* CM11
Master of Blue-Eyed Rhythm and Blues, The *Source(s):* CM11
Ryder, Mitch *Source(s):* CCE67; CM11; CM23; PMUS

Levisohn, Winifred 1914-1983 [pianist, composer]
Atwell, Winifred *Source(s):* GAMM

Levy see also *Levi*

Levy, Angelina 1850-1878 [songwriter]
Angelina *Source(s):* CPMU; HAMT; PSNN
Goetz, (Mrs.) Angelina *Source(s):* PSNN

Levy, David 1913-2000 [author, lyricist]
Little, Don *Source(s):* ASCP; CLTP ("Appointment with Adventure"); CPOL RE-160-198

Lévy, (Charles) Emile 1837-1915 [composer, conductor, pianist]
Parisian Waltz King *Source(s):* GAMM; NGDM
Waldteufel, (Charles) Emile *Source(s):* GAMM; LYMN; NGDM
Note(s): Brother of Léon Lévy (1832-1884) who also used the name Waldteufel.
Waltz King of France *Source(s):* LYMN

Levy, Henry 1812 (or 13)-1900 [composer, pianist, singer]
Russell, Henry *Source(s):* PSND
Note(s): Also used by Henry Russell Olson.

Levy, Henry J. 1927(or 28)-2001 [saxophonist, composer, arranger]
Levy, Hank *Source(s):* EPMU; LCAR

Levy, Jacques Francois Fromental-Èlie 1799-1862 [composer]
Halévy, Fromental *Source(s):* ALMN; BAKR; ROOM
Levy, Elias *Source(s):* LCAR

Levy, Jules 1838-1905 [cornetist, composer]
Cornet King *Source(s):* http://www.harrogate.co.uk/harrogate-band/misc10.htm (2 Oct. 2003)
Paganini of the Cornet *Source(s):* http://www.harrogate.co.uk/harrogate-band/misc10.htm
World's Greatest Cornetist *Source(s):* http://www.harrogate.co.uk/harrogate-band/misc10.htm
Note(s): See also Joseph [or Joe] Oliver.

Levy, Julius 1831-1914 [author, poet]
Rodenberg, Julius *Source(s):* PIPE

Lévy, Léon 1805-1859 [librettist]
Note(s): Do not confuse with Léon Lévy (1832-1884)
Brunswick, (Léon-Lévy) *Source(s):* GROL; LCAR; NGDO; PIPE
Lhérie, (Léon) *Source(s):* GROL; LCAR; NGDO; PIPE

Lévy, Léon 1832-1884 [composer]
Note(s): Do not confuse with Léon Lévy (1805-1859)
Waldteufel *Source(s):* GAMM; NGDM
Note(s): See under: Waldteufel [originally Lévy], Charles Emile.
Waldteufel, Léon *Source(s):* GAMM; NGDM

Lévy, Louis 1801-1884 [composer]
Note(s): Father of (Charles) Emile and Léon Levy.
Waldteufel, Louis *Source(s):* GAMM; NGDM
Levy, Marcella 1959- [singer, songwriter]
Detroit, Marcella *Source(s):* AMUS; EPMU; PMUS-92

Levy, Michel Maurice 1883-1965 [composer]
Betove *Source(s):* BAKE; BUL3; CCE49 E54899

Levy, R(ichard) fl. 1891-1922 [composer]
Haller, Richard *Source(s):* MELL; STGR
Levy, Richard Johann 1885-1980 [conductor, music director]
Lert, Richard Johann *Source(s):* WORB
Lévy, Roland Alexis Manuel 1891-1966 [composer, writer on music]
Manuel, Roland *Source(s):* CCE47 R8907 ("Idylles"); CCE62; MELL
Roland-Manuel, (Alexis) *Source(s):* BAKO; BUL1; CPMU; MELL; NGDM; RIEM
Lévy, Victor 1808-1845 [playwright, author, theatrical producer]
Lhérie, Victor *Source(s):* PIPE
Lewald, (Johann Karl) August 1792-1861 [author, actor]
Kindermann, Hans *Source(s):* PIPE
Sonnabend, Tobias *Source(s):* PIPE
Waller, Kurt *Source(s):* PIPE
Lewandowski, Lazarus (Eliezer) 1821 (or 23)-1894 [composer, conductor]
Note(s): Portrait: ETUP 53:9 (Sept. 1935): 498
Lewandowski, Louis (Eliezer) *Source(s):* LCAR; LYMN
Lewandowski, Leopold 1931-1996 [composer, violinist, conductor]
Polish Strauss *Source(s):* http://www.usc.edu/dept/polish_music/PMJ/issue/6.1.03/Fuks.html (17 May 2005)
Leweck, Gustav Wilhelm 1847-1915 [songwriter, singer, actor]
Williams, Gus *Source(s):* FINS p. 300; NGAM
Note(s): Also used by Howard Stube.
Lewin, Gustav 1869-1938 [composer]
Haupt, Franz *Source(s):* COMP
Lewin, Michael Sultan 1885-1961 [songwriter, dramatist]
Furber, Douglas *Source(s):* CART
Lewis, Al(an) 1901-1967 [songwriter, author, publisher]
Allen, Lew *Source(s):* CCE57
Flint, Jimmy *Source(s):* CCE57
Lewis, Sherman *Source(s):* CCE30 E12899; CCE57
Note(s): Jt. pseud.: Al(bert) Sherman.
Picker, Tom *Source(s):* CCE35 R304058
Note(s): Jt. pseud.: Al(bert) Sherman & Abner Silver.
Roberts, John *Source(s):* CCE57
Song Writers on Parade *Source(s):* CCE32 Eunp56182
Note(s): Jt. pseud.: Percy Wenrich, Sidney Clare, Charles Tobias, Al(bert) Sherman, (T.) Murray Mencher & Vincent Rose.
White, Norman *Source(s):* CCE57
Note(s): Jt. pseud.: Al(bert) Sherman.
Wilson, Walter *Source(s):* CCE35 R304057
Note(s): Jt. pseud.: Al(bert) Sherman & Abner Silver.
Lewis, Al 1924- [writer of children's songs, TV producer, accordionist]
Uncle Al *Source(s):* LCAR
Lewis, Al(bert John, Sr.) 1936- [accordionist, singer, composer]
Rapone, Al *Source(s):* AMUS; CCE75; CCE77; LCAR
Lewis, Bridges George McGibbon [songwriter, producer]
Andre, Charles *Source(s):* CCE56; CPOL RE-321-269
Lange, Lee *Source(s):* CPOL RE-55-758; http://www.hallowquest.com/compositions.htm (13 May 2005)
Lewis, Bunny *Source(s):* CCE53; CCE56; CPOL RE-122-863
May, Johnny *Source(s):* CCE53-56; CPOL RE-98-472
McGibbon, Bridges George *Source(s):* CPOL RE-141-010
Lewis, Clarence [composer]
Blast, C. L. *Source(s):* FZSL
Lewis, Little Junior *Source(s):* FZSL
Lewis, Harold [composer]
Lewis, Lefty *Source(s):* CCE57; CCE64; PMUS
Lewis, Howell Elvet 1860-1953 [hymnist]
Elfed *Source(s):* CCE49; CCE77; CYBH
Lewis, Hubert Brad 1932- [singer, songwriter]
Lewis, Hugh X. *Source(s):* MCCL
Lewis, Jerrold 1928- [composer]
Bock, Gustav *Source(s):* PFSA
Lewis, Jerry Lee 1935- [singer, pianist, songwriter]
Hawk, The *Source(s):* MCCL
Note(s): See also Coleman (Randolph) Hawkins, Harold Franklin Hawkins & J(oseph) B(enjamin) Hutto.
Killer, The *Source(s):* CCME; MCCL; STAC; PSND
Survivor, The *Source(s):* MCCL
Lewis, Leon 1890-1961 [composer, conductor, pianist]
Bloom, A. Leon *Source(s):* ASCP
Lewis, Matthew Gregory 1775-1818 [poet, playwright; author]
Lewis, Monk *Source(s):* GOTT; LCAR; PIPE; PSND
Lewis, McCartha (Sandy) 1940- [soca artist, songwriter]
Calypso Rose *Source(s):* LCAR; PEN2
Crusoe Kid *Source(s):* PEN2
Lewis, Meade (Anderson) 1905-1964 [composer, pianist]
Duke of Luxembourg, The *Source(s):* PSND
Lewis, Lux *Source(s):* ASCP; CCE44 #34438 E124396; EPMU
Seward, Hatch *Source(s):* MACE; SUTT
Lewis, T. C. [arranger]
T. C. L. *Source(s):* CPMU (publication date 1843)

Lewis, Walter 1893-1981 [singer, guitarist, songwriter]
Lewis, Furry *Source(s):* CM26; HARS; LCAR; PSND
Lewis, (William) Morgan (Jr.) 1906-1968 [composer]
Lewis, Buddy *Source(s):* PSND
Lewis, William Richards 1829?-1884 [vocalist, composer]
Richards, W. H. *Source(s):* IBIM; WORB
Lewis, William Sebastian 1914-1994 [pianist, bandleader, arranger]
Lewis, Sabby *Source(s):* NGDJ
Lewysohn, Hugo 1874-1933 [composer]
Leonard, Hugo *Source(s):* MACM; REHH; WORB
Lewysohn, Rudolf 1878-1960 [composer, pianist, singer, author]
Nelson, Rudolf *Source(s):* GAN2; LCAR; PFSA; PIPE; WORB
Leybourne, George 1842-1884 [singer, songwriter, author]
Lion Comique *Source(s):* FULD p. 230
Saunders, Joe *Source(s):* FULD p. 230
Leykauf, Walter Heinz 1942- [composer]
Guley, Heinz *Source(s):* CCE63
Patrizius *Source(s):* PFSA
Leyla Hanim(efendi) 1850-1936 [composer, pianist, author]
Saz, Leylâ *Source(s):* COHN; HIXN; LCAR
Leyva González, Alejandro [singer, songwriter]
Ley Alejandro *Source(s):* HWOM
L'Henoret, Louise 1865-1942 [composer]
Legru, (Mrs.) Louise *Source(s):* IBIM; WORB
Urgel, Louis *Source(s):* CCE50 R59994 ("Le Loup et l'agneau"); IBIM; LCAR; WORB
L'Heureux, David Charles 1948 (or 56?)- [composer, author, singer]
Larue, D. C. *Source(s):* ASCP; CPOL SR-42-441
Larue, David *Source(s):* CCE76
Libbach, Roland 1914- [composer]
Lingen, Rolf van *Source(s):* OMUO
Libbey, Delores R. 1919- [composer, author]
Libbey, Dee *Source(s):* ASCP
Rohde, Q'Adrianne *Source(s):* CCE73
Liberace, (Wladziu Valentino) 1919-1987 [pianist, entertainer, composer]
Busterkeys, Walter *Source(s):* BAKE; GROL; LCAR; PSND
Liberace, Lee *Source(s):* LCAR
Liberace, Walter *Source(s):* LCAR
Mr. Showmanship *Source(s):* http://www.tripadvisor.com/Attraction_Review-g45963-d102882-Reviews-Liberace_Museum_Las_Vegas_Nevada.html (6 Oct. 2002)
Rhinestone Rubinstein, The *Source(s):* PSND
Liberace, George 1911-1983 [songwriter]
Brother George *Source(s):* PSND
Note(s): See also Fulton Allen (see LCAR) & Walter Brown McGhee.
Rosen, Maury *Source(s):* CCE68
Libert, Gualterius fl. 1423-1428 [composer]
Libert, Reginaldus *Source(s):* MACM
Liberti, Gualtero *Source(s):* LCAR
Lichtenstein, Zvi [or Tsvi] 1933-1966 [composer, writer on music]
Snunit, Zvi [or Tsvi] *Source(s):* BUL1; BUL2
Lichtenthal, Peter [writer on music]
Leduc, A. C. *Source(s):* RILM 74-00451-ap
Note(s): Possible pseud.; however, RILM 82-03593 gives as presumed pseud. of Raphael-Georg Kiesewetter.
Liddle, Samuel 1867 (or 68)-1951 [songwriter]
Bloye, Richard *Source(s):* CCE44 #51525, 367 R133448
Boyle, Richard *Source(s):* CCE44 #31175, 531 R128692
Fairfield, Frank *Source(s):* CCE31 R13896
Note(s): Also used by Franz (Carl) Bornschein.
Grayling, Gerald *Source(s):* CCE42 #53636, 326 R113922
Lid(e)l, Andreas c.1740-c.1788 [baryton & viola da gamba player, composer]
Lidl, Anton *Source(s):* LCAR
Note(s): Incorrect given name in numerous biographical sources.
Lieb, Ziskind R. 1930- [composer, arranger]
Lieb, Dick *Source(s):* ASCP; CPOL RE-195-245
Lieberman, Ernest Sheldon 1930- [composer, author, singer]
Sheldon, Ernie *Source(s):* ASCP (see reference)
Lieberson, Goddard 1911-1977 [recording executive, composer, music critic]
Sebastian, John *Source(s):* GROL; NGAM
Lieberstein, Marcus Edward 1933- [composer, author]
Lieber, Doodles *Source(s):* ASCP
Liebling, Georg(e) 1865-1946 [pianist, composer]
Note(s): Portraits: ETUP 53:9 (Sept. 1935): 498; MUCO (10 May 1899)
Myrot, André *Source(s):* BAKE; BAKT; LCAR
Liedbeck, Sixten [composer]
Norman, Charles *Source(s):* CLTP ("Foreign Intrigue")
Liénard, A(lbert) 1875-1927 [librettist]
Payen, L(ouis) *Source(s):* LCAR; MELL; WORB
Liessmann, Erich 1948- [composer]
Frankfurter, Jean *Source(s):* CCE73 Efor164774; KOMP; KOMS; PFSA

Ligeti, Gyorgy 1923- [composer]
Beethoven of the 20th Century Avant-Garde
Source(s): http://www.andante.com/article/article.cfm?id=24244 (7 Apr. 2005)
Liggins, Ethel 1886-1970 [composer, pianist, teacher]
Note(s): Portraits: DWCO; ETUP 37:5 (May 1919): 271; ETUP 53:8 (Aug. 1935): 441
Leginska, Ethel *Source(s):* AMME; BAKO; BAKR; BUL3; COHN; GREN
Liggins, Joseph [or Joe] (C.) 1915-1987 [pianist, composer, singer]
Honeydripper, The *Source(s):* KINK
Note(s): See also Roosevelt Sykes.
Lightfoot, Alexander 1924-1971 [singer, harmonica player, songwriter]
Little Papa Walter *Source(s):* HARS
Littlefoot, George *Source(s):* HARS
Lightfoot, Papa (George) *Source(s):* HARS; http://www.bluesworld.com/1128.html (16 Dec. 2003)
Papa George *Source(s):* HARS
Lightfoot, Gordon Meredith 1938- [singer, songwriter]
Sullivan, Charles *Source(s):* http://www.rhino.com/Features/liners/75802lin4.html (24 Oct. 2003)
Lijnschooten, Hendrikus [or Henk] (Cornelius) van 1928- [composer, conductor, educator]
Delft, Michel van *Source(s):* REHG; http://home.planet.nl/~henk.lijns (29 Sept. 2003)
Huggens, Ted *Source(s):* REHG; SMIN; http://home.planet.nl/~henk.lijns
Van Delft, Michael *Source(s):* SMIN
Lillenas, Haldor 1885-1959 [composer, hymnist]
Note(s): Portrait: CYBH
Golden, Rose *Source(s):* CCE39 #23128 E77363; CCE45
Golden, Virginia Rose *Source(s):* CCE51 R74849 ("His Name Is Engraved on My Heart"); CYBH
Gray, Laverne *Source(s):* CYBH
Grey, Laverne *Source(s):* CCE43 #2702, 381 R115681; CCE64
Hainsworth, Richard *Source(s):* CCE27 E660551; CCE52 R99054; CYBH
Lines, Rev. H. N. *Source(s):* CYBH
Linn, Lora *Source(s):* CCE62 E167390
Olson, H. *Source(s):* CCE44 #26477, 18 R125148
Whitmore, Robert *Source(s):* CCE30 E15121; CCE43 #17210 E113531; CYBH
Winters, Ferne *Source(s):* CYBH
Lillie, H. W. R. [composer]
H. W. R. L. *Source(s):* CPMU (publication date 1935)
Lima Meneses, Jorge (Duilio) 1940 (or 42)- [singer, composer, violinist]
Ben, Jorge *Source(s):* CCE70 Efor34760; LCAR; PMUS; PSNN
Lincke, Joseph 1783-1837 [violoncellist, composer]
Zunftmeister Violoncello *Source(s):* GRV3
Lincoln, Harry J. 1878-1937 [composer, arranger]
Note(s): There is considerable confusion concerning Lincoln's use of pseudonyms. He used the names of several composers, including Charles Sweeley & members of the Vandersloot family, and he also sold some of his compositions that subsequently were published under the names of the purchasers. (REHG p. 460+) Portrait: JASA
Casale, Thomas (B. [or (D)]) *Source(s):* LCAR; REHG; SUPN
Crosby, Ben E. *Source(s):* LCAR; REHG; SUPN
Dempsey, James L. *Source(s):* CCE46 R7792; CCE47 R17975
Note(s): "I'll Do the Same As My Daddy" (CCE46) &"Beautiful Girl" (CCE47)
Edwards, Raymond *Source(s):* CCE41 #30320, 620 R97186; CCE42 #24219, 410 R107496
Fischler, H(arry) A(ugustus) *Source(s):* JASA; PERF
Note(s): Incorrectly reported as a pseud. of Lincoln. Harry Augustus Fischler (1879-) was a composer and manager of Vandersloot Music. (PERF)
Furman-Mulliner, I. *Source(s):* CCE36 R48777; CCE52 R90777 ("Silent Persuasion")
Halls, J. C *Source(s):* CCE36 R48776; JASA
Harlin, James L. *Source(s):* CCE44 #46708, 327 R131774; REHG; SUPN
Jay, Harry *Source(s):* CCE57; CCE64; LCAR; REHG; SUPN
Kiefer, Joseph *Source(s):* CCE50 R58986 ("Plume of Purity")
Losch, Abe *Source(s):* JASA; LCAR, PARS; REHG; SUPN
Loveland, Carl (L.) *Source(s):* CCE37 R54481; REHG; SUPN
Rimert, Gay A. *Source(s):* CCE48 R32714 ("Jolly Cobbler")
Sarver, Lillian H. *Source(s):* CCE47 R19212
Sweeley, Charles C. *Source(s):* CCE28 R45816 (Orig.: 1901 #9756); CCE37 E60485; JASA; SPTH
Note(s): For works Lincoln published under Sweeley's name; see NOTES: Sweeley, Charles C.
Vandersloot, C(aird) M. *Source(s):* CCE31 R16727; CCE41 #47874, 185 R101601; LCAR; REHG
Note(s): Copyright records indicate Vandersloot is a pseud. of Lincoln.
Vandersloot, Carl D. *Source(s):* CCE45 #22283, 198 R137222; LCAR; REHG

Note(s): Carl D. Vandersloot (1898-1963) was a composer, ". . . but it is believed none of his works were published for band." (REHG p.461). (*Author's note:* copyright record for R137222 indicates Carl D. Vandersloot is a pseud. of Lincoln.)
Vandersloot, F(rederick) W(illiam) *Source(s):* CCE46 R7794; CCE48 R33856-57; CCE64 R344069; LCAR; REHG
Note(s): Copyright records indicate F. W. Vandersloot is a pseud. of Lincoln.
Warner, J. M. *Source(s):* CCE39 #21731, 210 R77201
Westover, Jessie *Source(s):* CCE47 R19209 ("National Conclave")
Williams, Frederick *Source(s):* CCE52 R90782 ("Contentment")

Lind, Bob 1942 (or 44)- [singer, songwriter]
New Bob Dylan, The *Source(s):* EPMU
Note(s): See also Loundon Wainwright, III.

Linda, Josef 1789-1834 [author, journalist]
Mitrovský *Source(s):* PIPE; RIEM

Lindberg, Armas (Emanuel) 1884-1959 [composer, musicologist]
Launis, Armas (Emanuel) *Source(s):* BAKO; BAKR; BUL1; BUL2; LCAR; NGDO; PSND

Lindberg, Charles Arthur 1932- [singer, songwriter]
Feathers, Charles *Source(s):* WORT
Hooper, Jess *Source(s):* WORT
Morgan, Charlie *Source(s):* WORT

Lindblad, Adolf Fredrik 1801-1878 [composer, teacher]
Note(s): Portrait: ETUP 53:9 (Sept. 1935): 498
Father of Swedish Song, The *Source(s):* http://www.toccata.nu/komp/lindblad.html (6 Oct. 2002)
Swedish Schubert *Source(s):* MACM; http://www.toccata.nu/komp/lindblad.html

Lindemann, Wilhelm 1882-1941 [composer]
Alfredo, Wald *Source(s):* REHG; SUPN
Bollman(n), Fritz(e) *Source(s):* CCE38 Efor5265; REHG; SUPN
Eckstein, Ernest *Source(s):* REHG; SUPN
Komzak, C. *Source(s):* REHG; SUPN

Lindemayr, Kajetan Benedikt Maximilian 1723-1783 [dramatist]
Lindemayr, Maurus *Source(s):* AEIO

Linden, David Gysbert (van der) 1913 (or 15)-1999 [composer, conductor, arranger]
Bain, Guy *Source(s):* MUSR
Note(s): Actually Guy Bain is a pseud. of Van Beuningen, a wealthy Hollander who paid Linden for composing and conducting. (MUSR)
Blene, Gerard *Source(s):* MUSR
DeCarlo, Daniel *Source(s):* MUSR
Gysberet, David *Source(s):* MUSR
Linden, Dolf van der *Source(s):* LCAR; RFSO
Lynn, Van *Source(s):* BUL3; LCAR; MUSR
Pinto, Alex *Source(s):* MUSR
Van der Linden, Dolf *Source(s):* MUSR
Van der Linden, Dorf *Source(s):* EPMU
Van der Lynn, Dorf *Source(s):* BUL2

Linder, Anton 1874-1929 [author]
Aubecq, Pierre d' *Source(s):* PIPE

Lindfors, Juhani 1893- [composer]
Pohjanmies, Juhani *Source(s):* BUL3

Lindow, G(abrielle?) [songwriter]
Wodnil, Gabrielle *Source(s):* CPMU (publication date 1908)

Lindquist, Orville A(lvin) 1873- [composer]
Note(s): Portrait: ETUP 53:10 (Oct. 1935): 567
Tieman, John *Source(s):* TPRF

Lindroth, Ernst Fred(e)rik 1889-1960 [composer, pianist]
Linko, Ernest (Fredrik) *Source(s):* BUL1; BUL2; DEA3; LCAR

Lindsay, Bryan (Eugene) 1931- [composer, author, teacher]
Lynd, Gene *Source(s):* ASCP; CCE63; CCE65

Lindsay, D'Auvergne Sharon 1904 (or 10)-1963 [actress, songwriter]
Lynn(e), Sharon (E.) *Source(s):* LCAR; PSND

Lindsay, (John) Maurice 1918- [critic, author, poet]
Brock, Gavin *Source(s):* PIPE

Linekar, Thomas Joseph 1858-1918 [conductor, composer, organist]
Berenger, Raymond *Source(s):* ORBI
Berenger, Thomas Joseph *Source(s):* HUEV

Lingenfelder, Hans 1946- [composer]
King, Ricky *Source(s):* PFSA

Linick, Michael 1963?-2003 [drummer, radio host, music critic]
Dee, Mikey *Source(s):* WASH

Link, Dorothy 1900- [composer, author]
Dick, Dorothy *Source(s):* ASCP; CCE53; CPOL RE-247-630

Linkey, Harry 1896-1956 [songwriter]
Alton, John *Source(s):* CCE49; CCE75
Link, Harry *Source(s):* BBDP

Linley, George 1798-1865 [composer]
Burton, Baylis *Source(s):* CPMU

Lione, John [songwriter]
Martin, Trade *Source(s):* CCE61-62; PMUS

Lipatti, Constantin 1917-1950 [pianist, composer]
Lipatti, Dinu *Source(s):* LCAR; NGDM
Ripatti, Dinu *Source(s):* LCAR

Lipkin, Stephen [or Steve] Barri [or Barry] 1941 (or 42)- [composer, author, singer]

Barri, Steve *Source(s):* ASCP; CCE61-62
Fantastic Baggys *Source(s):* AMUS
Note(s): Jt. pseud.: Phil(lip Gary) Schlein.
Grass Roots, The *Source(s):* AMUS
Note(s): Jt. pseud.: Phil(lip Gary) Schlein.
Lipman, Harry 1900-1971 [bandleader, saxophonist, composer]
Curroy, Mort *Source(s):* CCE34 Efor34120
Note(s): Jt. pseud.: Michael Carr [i.e., Maurice Alfred Cohen], Bill Currie & Ivor Moreton.
Roy, Harry *Source(s):* EPMU; LCAR; MUWB; ROOM
Lipman, Samuel 1934-1994 [music critic, pianist, teacher]
Postmodern Neo-Arnoldian *Source(s):* GRAN
Lipman, Walter [composer]
Shannon, Walter *Source(s):* CCE11 E243654; JASA p. 322
Lipscomb(e), Richard [or Dickey] 1936- [singer, songwriter]
Lee, Cowboy *Source(s):* AMUS; EPMU; HARS
Lee, Dickey [or Dickie] *Source(s):* AMUS; CCME; EPMU; MCCL; PSND
Lipsius, (Ida) Marie 1837-1927 [writer on music, translator]
Note(s): Portrait: ETUP 53:10 (Oct. 1935): 567
La Mara *Source(s):* GROL; LCAR; NGDM
Note(s): See also Gertrud(e Elizabeth) Schmelling.
Liptzin, Samuel 1893- [lyricist]
Note(s): For additional nonmusic-related pseudonyms, see LCAR.
Liptsin, Sem *Source(s):* LCAR
Onkel Sam *Source(s):* LCAR; SEND
Uncle Sam *Source(s):* LCAR
Lisbona, Edward 1915-1989 [composer, author, pianist]
Miller, Eddie *Source(s):* WORT
Note(s): Also used by Edward Raymond Müller.
Miller, Eddie Piano *Source(s):* ASCP; WORT
Miller, Piano *Source(s):* PSND
Lishin, Grigory Andreyevich 1854-1888 [pianist, critic, composer]
Nivlyansky, Grigory Andreyevich *Source(s):* HOFE
Lisinski, Ignaz Fuchs 1819-1854 [composer]
Lisinski, Vatroslav *Source(s):* LCAR; OMUO
Liszt, Franz 1811-1886 [composer, pianist]
Absentee Father of "Gypsy Music" *Source(s):* http://www.ce-review.org/01/13/damon13.html (6 Oct. 2002)
King of Pianist *Source(s):* GROL
Lisztian *Source(s):* EPON
Paganini of the Piano *Source(s):* http://pianoeducation.org/pnoliszt.html (11 Apr. 2005)
Snob Out of Bedlam, A *Source(s):* SLON
Liter, Monia 1905-1988 [composer, arranger, conductor, pianist]
Amado, Antoio *Source(s):* MUWB
Hamilton, Paul *Source(s):* MUWB
Mason, Squire *Source(s):* MUWB
Lithgow, Alex F. 1870-1929 [composer, bandleader]
March King of the Antipodes *Source(s):* SMIN
Little, Dudley Richard 1930- [composer, pianist, singer]
Lee, Fletcher *Source(s):* ASCP; CCE60
Little, Big Tiny *Source(s):* ASCP; LCAR
Little, Tiny *Source(s):* CCE60; CCE62; LCAR
Little, John (Leonard) 1900-1956 [entertainer, singer, composer]
Little, Jack *Source(s):* LCAR
Little, Little Jack *Source(s):* CCE52; LCAR; PSND; VACH
Radio's Cheerful Little Earful *Source(s):* PSND
Little, V(ivian?) G(ray?) [composer, editor]
V. G. L. *Source(s):* CPMU (publication date 1952)
Littledale, Richard Frederick 1833-1890 [hymnist; translator]
Note(s): The following are in: *People's Hymnal* (1867)
A. L. P. *Source(s):* CYBH; JULN
Note(s): A. L.P. = A London Priest
B. T. *Source(s):* CYBH; JULN
Note(s): Initials for his former address.
D. L. *Source(s):* CYBH; JULN
Note(s): D. L. = Dr. Littledale
F. *Source(s):* JULN
Note(s): F = Frederick
F. R. *Source(s):* JULN
Note(s): F. R. = Frederick Richard
L. *Source(s):* JULN
Note(s): L = Littledale
P. C. E. *Source(s):* CYBH; JULN
Note(s): P. C. E = Priest of the Church of England
P. P. Bk. *Source(s):* JULN
Note(s): P. P. Bk. = Priest's Prayer Book
Liverpool, Hollis Urban Lester 1941- [songwriter, teacher, author]
Chalkdust, Mighty *Source(s):* LCAR; PEN2
Chalkie *Source(s):* LCAR; PEN2
Mighty Chalkdust *Source(s):* LCAR
Livi, Ivo [or Yvo] 1921-1991 [composer]
Montand, Yves *Source(s):* LCAR; PFSA
Livingston, (Jay) Harold 1915-2001 [composer]
Note(s): Portrait: OB01
Last of the Great Songwriters, The *Source(s):* *Evansville Courier & Press.* (18 Oct. 2001): A5
Levinson, Jay *Source(s):* CCE65; CCE70 R478747
Levison, Jay *Source(s):* CCE65; CCE68
Livison, Jay *Source(s):* CCE68
Livingston, Joseph A(nthony) 1906-1957 [saxophonist, arranger, composer]
Livingston, Buddy *Source(s):* CCE63
Livingston, Fud *Source(s):* ASCP; CCE47; CCE68; EPMU; JASA p. 319; NGDJ; VACH

Livingston, Neville O'Reilly 1947- [singer, songwriter]
Livingston, Bunny *Source(s):* LCAR
Wailer, Bunny *Source(s):* CM11; LCAR ; ROOM
Livotovsky, Warren 1947-2003 [singer, songwriter, guitarist]
Zevon, Warren *Source(s):* HARR
Zevotovsky, Warren *Source(s):* http://morris2k.cti.depaul.edu/zevon/wz_triv_key.html (5 Feb. 2005)
Llado, George [rapper]
DJ Scratch on Galaxy *Source(s):* EPMU (see under: Dr. Jeckyll and Mr. Hyde)
Lloyd, A(lbert) L(ancaster) 1908-1982 [singer, journalist, broadcaster, folklorist]
Lancaster, Albert *Source(s):* http://cjtm.icaap.org/content/27/27_gregory.html (25 Apr. 2005)
Lloyd, Bert *Source(s):* http://cjtm.icaap.org/content/27/27_gregory.html
Lloyd, John c.1475-1523 [priest, composer]
Floyd, John *Source(s):* NGDM
Lloyd Webber, Andrew 1948- [composer]
"Sir Arthur Sullivan" of the Rock Age, The *Source(s):* EPMU
Lloyd Webber, William (Southcombe) 1914-1982 [composer]
Chapel, Clive *Source(s):* FANF 20:1 (1996): 356 ("Explanation")
Wade, Peter *Source(s):* CCE59
Webber, Lloyd *Source(s):* CPOL RE-585-632
Lobo, Duarte 1565-1646 [composer]
Lupus, Edwardus *Source(s):* BAKE; GROL; NGDM; RIEM; SADC
Locke, Sam 1917-1998 [playwright, screenwriter]
Malcolm, David *Source(s):* *Dramatist* 1:3 (1999): 3
Lockhart, John Gibson 1794-1854 [author, critic]
Note(s): See PSND & LCAR for additional nonmusic-related pseudonyms.
Lauerwinkle, Baron *Source(s):* GOTT
Scott, James, Esq. *Source(s):* GOTT
Wastle, William *Source(s):* GOTT; PSND
Locklin, Lawrence Hankins 1918- [singer, songwriter]
Locklin, Hank *Source(s):* CCE47 Eunp; MCCL
Locknane, Clement 1880-1940 [composer, arranger]
C. L. *Source(s):* CPMU
Lockton, Edward F. 1876-1940 [composer, lyricist]
Ashleigh Denis *Source(s):* CCE47 R24233
Bayliss, Richard *Source(s):* CCE65
Gilmour, Rex *Source(s):* CCE32 Efor23432; CCE59
Malone, Ronald *Source(s):* CCE52 R89894 ("They Are Only Drifting Clouds")
Mansfield, Richard *Source(s):* CCE52 R98825 ("Pals of Yesterday")
Rendall, John *Source(s):* CCE50 R70061 ("I Came To Your Garden")
Tesehemacher, Edward *Source(s):* CCE30 R10085; CPMU; KILG; LCPC letter cited (25 Jan. 1920)
Wilford, C. *Source(s):* HAMA (see under: Brahe, May) ("Listen Mary")
Loden, James (H.) 1929- [singer, guitarist; songwriter]
James, Sonny *Source(s):* AMUS; CCME; EPMU; MCCL; MILL; PSND; STAC
Jimmie L *Source(s):* CCE62; CCE64 E185140
Loden, Sonny *Source(s):* FLIN
Southern Gentleman, The *Source(s):* AMUS; EPMU; FLIN; MCCL; MILL; PSND; STAC
Lodge, John 1801-1873 [poet, composer]
Ellerton, John Lodge *Source(s):* BAKR; BROW; GOTH; HOVL; LCAR; NGDM
Loeb-Evans, M(atilee) [composer]
Note(s): Portrait: ETUP 55:4 (Apr. 1937): 216
Preston, (Mrs.) M(atilee) L(oeb) *Source(s):* CCE40 #15093, 807 R86690; TPRF
Loeillet, Jean Baptiste 1680-1730 [composer, harpsichordist]
Note(s): Do not confuse with Jean Baptiste Loeillet (1688-c.1720).
John Loeillet of London *Source(s):* NGDM
Loeillet of London, John *Source(s):* NGDM
Loeillett, Jean Baptiste 1688-c.1720 [composer]
Note(s): Do not confuse with Jean Baptiste Loeillet (1680-1730).
Loeillet de Gant *Source(s):* NGDM; SADC
Loes, Harry Dixon 1892-1965 [songwriter]
Barnett, Leonard C(ecil) *Source(s):* CCE52; CCE64-64; CPOL RE-66-939
Bartells, (H(arold) D(eKoven)) *Source(s):* CCE71 R505900; CE75-76; CYBH
Bartels, Henry *Source(s):* CCE75
Burton, Clark W. *Source(s):* CCE62
Daniels, Harriet L. *Source(s):* CCE50 R61648 ("Who Is the King of Glory?")
Deal, (Harold) *Source(s):* CCE54; CCE62-63; CPOL RE-495-104; CYBH
Gilbert, E. K. *Source(s):* CCE49 E41147
H. D. L. *Source(s):* CCE60; CCE63-64
Hanson, Daniel Lee *Source(s):* CCE58; CCE61-64; CPOL RE-448-118
R. D. L. *Source(s):* CCE64 ("There is an Easter"?)
Shoar(b)ley, D. R. *Source(s):* CCE50 R61649 ("Only the Love of Jesus"); CCE55
Loesser, Frank Henry 1910-1969 [composer, lyricist]
Note(s): Portrait: EWEN
Army's One Man Hit Parade, The *Source(s):* PSND; SIFA
G. I.'s Own Songwriter, The *Source(s):* PSND; SIFA
Loewe, Carl 1796-1869 [composer]
Schubert of the North *Source(s):* http://www.loewe-duo.de/lowe-duo-ld-cd/ld-cd1.html (9 Apr. 2005)
Note(s): See also Franz Berwald.

Loewe, Frederick 1904-1988 [composer]
Loewe, Fritz *Source(s):* EWEN (port.); PSND
Loewe, Hilde 1895-1976 [pianist, composer]
Love, Henry *Source(s):* OMUO
Loewenstein, Herbert 1908- [musicologist]
Avenary, Hanoch *Source(s):* BAKR; NGDM; NULM
Loewy, Salomon 1804-1890 [cantor, composer]
Father of Modern Synagogue Music *Source(s):* http://www.britannica.com (12 Apr. 2005)
Levy, Salomon *Source(s):* LYMN
Sulzer, Salomon *Source(s):* LYMN; http://www.britannica.com
Löffler, Edmund 1900- [composer]
Relfel, Hans *Source(s):* SMIN; SUPN
Löffler, Willi 1915- [composer]
Cosmar, Harold *Source(s):* KOMP; KOMS; PFSA; REHG; SUPN
Lofgren, Nils 1951- [singer, songwriter, guitarist]
Lefty *Source(s):* ALMN
Lofthouse, Charles (Thornton) 1895-1974 [composer, organist, harpsichordist]
Charles, L. *Source(s):* CCE67; PMUS; PSNN; SPTH p. 486
Lofton, Clarence 1887-1957 [singer, pianist, songwriter]
Clemens, Albert *Source(s):* HARS; LCAR
Lofton, Cripple Clarence *Source(s):* HARS; LCAR
Logroscino, Nicola (Bonifacio) 1698-1765 (or 67) [composer]
Croscino, Niccolò *Source(s):* SONN
Dio dell'Opera Buffa, Il *Source(s):* PSND
Löhmer, Klaus 1949- [composer]
Garry, Tom *Source(s):* KOMS; PFSA
Löhner(-Beda), Fritz 1883-1942 [librettist; satirical writer, lawyer]
Beda, (Fritz) *Source(s):* CCE37 Efor49418; GAN2; GANA; LCAR; PIPE; PMUS
Löhner, Beda *Source(s):* GROL; NGDO
Lõhr, Hermann 1871-1943 [composer]
Note(s): Portrait: ETUP 53:11 (Nov. 1935): 696
Grau, Leonard *Source(s):* CPMU
Gray, Leonard *Source(s):* CCE51 R82415 ("Jackanapes")
Lombardo, Carlo 1869-1959 [composer, librettist, impresario]
Bard, Léon *Source(s):* GREN; LCAR; PIPE; RIES; WORB
Leplanc *Source(s):* GREN; PIPE; RIES; WORB
Lomuto, Francisco (Juan) 1893-1950 [pianist, director, composer]
Laguna, Pancho *Source(s):* BBDP; TODO
Lomuto, Pancho *Source(s):* BBDP
Long, Andy Iona 1902-1966 [composer]
Iona, Andy *Source(s):* ASCC; CCE68; LCAR
Longbrake, Arthur 1881-1953 [songwriter]
Arzonia, Joe *Source(s):* JAST; KILG; SPTH p. 346
Lookofsky, Michael 1949- [keyboardist, songwriter]
Brown, Hash *Source(s):* http://orbita.starmedia.com/~revolutionfanzine/English/special01.html (6 Nov. 2002)
Brown, Mike [or Michael] *Source(s):* CCE66-68; PMUS; http://orbita.starmedia.com/~revolutionfanzine/English/special01.html (6 Nov. 2002)
Loomis, Harvey Worthington 1865-1930 [composer, writer]
Note(s): Portrait: ETUP 53:10 (Oct. 1935): 567
Edwards, Frank *Source(s):* HOVL
Graham, Robert Z. *Source(s):* HOVL
Leroux, Paul *Source(s):* HOVL
Scollard, Walter F. *Source(s):* GOTH; HOVL
Lopez, Francisco 1916-1995 [dentist, songwriter]
Lopez, Francis *Source(s):* CCE60; GAN1; GAN2; LCAR
López, Israel 1918- [arranger, composer, multi-instrumentalist]
Cachoa *Source(s):* CCE64 E189592 ("Centro San Agustin"); LCAR
López, Cachoa *Source(s):* CM14; EPMU; PEN2
López Tejera, Luis 1914- [composer]
Maravilla, (L(o)uis) *Source(s):* CCE64-65; LCAR; GREN
Lopiano-Pomar, Agostino [librettist]
Marlago *Source(s):* STGR
Löprich, Mario 1944- [composer]
Mann, Martin *Source(s):* PFSA
Loquin, Antole 1834-1903 [composer, writer on music]
Lavigne, Paul *Source(s):* IWWM; MACM
Sevin, Louis *Source(s):* LCAR
Ubaldi *Source(s):* LCAR
Loraine, Alan 1921-1995 [composer]
Victory, Gerard *Source(s):* BAKR; BAKT
Lorenz, Adolf 1826-1900 [jurist, musician]
Lenz, Adolf *Source(s):* IBIM; WORB
Lorenz, E(dmund) S(imon) 1854-1942 [composer]
Note(s): Portraits: CYBH; ETUP 53:10 (Oct. 1935): 567; HALL
Cameron, Alicia *Source(s):* CCE35 (Index); LCPC
Creswell, John D. *Source(s):* CCE31 D28111; CCE32 #5201,926 R102716
Edwards, L. S. *Source(s):* CYBH
Fritsche, Ivan *Source(s):* CCE35 (Index); LCPC
Mund, E. D. *Source(s):* CCE32 R17318; CYBH
Ramler, A. J. *Source(s):* CCE30 Eunp13169; CCE51 R7561 ("Mother's Old-Fashioned Flowers")

Tibballs, John *Source(s):* CCE23 R23277; CCE26 R32567
Note(s): Also used by Charles H. Gabriel; see NOTES: Tibballs, John.
Tolliver, H. *Source(s):* CCE35 (Index); LCPC
Lorenz, Ellen Jane 1907-1997 [organist, writer, composer]
Boalt, John E. *Source(s):* CCE58-59; CCE64; CPOL RE-361-285
E. J. L.
Note(s): Used on reviews.
Hadler, Rosemary *Source(s):* BUL3; CCE52; COHN; CPOL RE-147-306; HIXN; WOAM
James, Allen *Source(s):* ASCP; BUL3; COHN; CPOL RE-408-105; HIXN; PSND; WOAM
Note(s): Do not confuse with Allan James, pseud. of Allan James Crawford (CCE57).
Jerome, Peter *Source(s):* CCE76; WOAM
Kumler, Carol *Source(s):* CCE55-56; CPOL RE-188-021
Porter, Ellen Jane *Source(s):* WOAM
Note(s): Married name: Mrs. James Porter.
Porter, L. N. *Source(s):* CCE65; CCE68
Porter, Walter *Source(s):* CCE63 ("Tidings of Comfort and a Joy"); CPOL RE-515-823
Note(s): Jt. pseud.: Forrest G. Walter.
Williams, Elton J. *Source(s):* CCE38 E66340 ("The Old Barn Dance")
Note(s): Jt. pseud.: Ira B(ishop) Wilson.
Lorenzen, Lorenz 1660-1722 [composer, hymnist]
Laurenti, Laurentius *Source(s):* CYBH
Lorenzini fl. c.1570 [lutenist, composer]
Cavalier du Luth *Source(s):* NGDM
Eques (Auratus) Romanus *Source(s):* NGDM
Knight of the Lute *Source(s):* NGDM
Loriti, Heinrich, of Glarus 1488-1563 [musical theorist, writer on music]
Glarean, Heinrich (Loriti) *Source(s):* BAKE; LCAR
Glareanus, Henricus (Loritus) *Source(s):* BAKE; LCAR
Loritus, Henricus *Source(s):* BAKE; LCAR
Lösch, Alexander 1883-1940 [writer on music]
Berrsche, Alexander *Source(s):* MUBR; PIPE
Lotterer, Gustav 1906- [composer]
Brooklyn, Bill *Source(s):* SUPN
Dawitt, Tom *Source(s):* REHG
Note(s): Possible pseud.? In REHG the SUPN source is listed as a reference; however, in SUPN Dawitt is not listed as a pseud. for Lotterer; however, the following reference is included in the entry: Suppan, *Repertorium de Märsche für Blasorchester,* Teil I (Tutzing: Hans Schneider, 1982): 57: Dawitt, Tom (Ps. für Gustav Lotterer, *1906). Also used by Otto Nitze.
Lottimer, Edmund 1951?- [songwriter]
Lottimer, Ebb *Source(s):* PSND
Loubega, David 1975- [songwriter]
Bega, Lou *Source(s):* LCAR; PMUS-00
Loud, Emily L. 19th cent. [composer]
Ell *Source(s):* COHN; HIXN
Loudermilk, Charlie (Elzer) 1927- [singer, songwriter, guitarist]
Louvin Brothers *Source(s):* EPMU; LCAR
Note(s): Jt. pseud.: Ira Lonnie Loudermilk.
Louvin, Charlie *Source(s):* CCE52-57; CCE60-62; EPMU; MCCL; NASF
Wooten, Jerry *Source(s):* CCE71
Loudermilk, Ira Lonnie 1924-1965 [singer, songwriter, mandolin player]
Louvin Brothers *Source(s):* EPMU; LCAR
Note(s): Jt. pseud.: Charlie (Elzer) Loudermilk.
Louvin, Ira *Source(s):* CCE52-57; CCE62; EPMU; MCCL; NASF
Loudermilk, John D. 1934- [singer, composer]
Note(s): Portrait: EWPS
Dee, Johnny *Source(s):* CCE57; MCCL; PSND
Johnny D. *Source(s):* EPMU
Sneezer, Ebe *Source(s):* MCCL
Louveau, Fernand ?-1914 [producer, director]
Samuel, Fernand *Source(s):* GAN2
Love, Geoff(rey) 1917-1991 [composer, arranger, conductor]
Jamieson *Source(s):* CCE54
Mandingo *Source(s):* http://users.skynet.be/dada/disq/y/99a.htm (30 June 2005)
Manuel *Source(s):* BBDP; MUSR
Love, Luther Halsey, (Jr.) 1904-1981 [composer, violinist]
Love, Ludy *Source(s):* CCE46 Eunp; CCE60; CCE60-61
Van Love, Ludy *Source(s):* ASCP
Love, William Edward 1806-1867 [composer]
Polyphonist, The *Source(s):* SCHO p. 514
LoVecchio, Francesco [or Francis] Paolo [or Paul] 1913- [singer, actor, composer, author]
Laine, Frankie *Source(s):* CASS; GAMM; KINK; LCAR
Lover, Samuel 1797-1868 [novelist, poet, songwriter]
Note(s): Portrait: HAMM
Jove's Poet *Source(s):* PSND
Trovato, Ben *Source(s):* PSND; ROOM
Lovetti, Gemignano 1573-1616 [composer]
Capilupi, Gemignano *Source(s):* DEA3; NGDM
Lövgren, Kent [rapper, songwriter]
Melodie MC *Source(s):* EPMU
Lovullo, Anthony 1932- [composer, accordionist]
Lovello, Tony *Source(s):* ASCP

Lowe, Bernie 1918?-1993 [songwriter]
September, Anthony *Source(s):* MUWB
Note(s): "Butterfly" was written by Bernie Lowe & Kal Mann [i.e., Kalman Cohen] & credited to Anthony September [i.e., Anthony [or Tony] Mammarella].
Lowe, Earl c.1950- [singer, songwriter]
Little Roy *Source(s):* EPMU
Lowe, Edward ?-1682 [composer, organist]
E. L. *Source(s):* CPMS ("A Short Direction for the Performance of Cathedrall Service")
Lowe, Jeffery 1968- [songwriter]
Yak *source(s):* CPOL PAu-2-262-770
Note(s): Do not confuse with Al Yak [i.e., John(ny) (Arthur) Brandon.
Lowell, James Russell 1819-1891 [songwriter]
Note(s): Portrait: CYBH
Biglow, Hosea *Source(s):* SPTH p. 594
Meliboeus-Hipponax *Source(s):* LCAR
Wilbur, Homer *Source(s):* LCAR
Löwenbach, Jan 1880-1972 [librettist]
Budin, J. L. *Source(s):* GROL; NGDO
Löwenfeld, Peter Erwin 1882-1949 [conductor, composer[
Devinal, Prof. *Source(s):* OMUO
Lendvai [or Lendvay], (Peter) Erwin *Source(s):* LCAR; OMUO
Lowenstein, Emanuel [composer]
Lowe, E. *Source(s):* TPRF
Lowers, Wilma Ann 1924- [singer, songwriter]
Wilma Ann *Source(s):* MCCL (see under: Curly Dan & Wilma Ann)
Lowrie, Randolph W. 1839-1913 [hymnist]
R. W. L. *Source(s):* JULN (Suppl.)
Lowry, Anthony [or Tony] [composer, arranger]
Belton, John *Source(s):* RFSO
Note(s): Jt. pseud.: (Reginald) Douglas Brownsmith.
Crantock, (Peter) *Source(s):* RFSO
Note(s): Jt. pseud.: Clive Richardson.
Howard, Frank *Source(s):* CPOL RE-104-369
Notes(s): Also used by Delos Gardner [or Gardiner] Spalding.
Löwy, Heinrich 1860-1927 (or 29) [musicologist, writer on music]
Rietsch, Heinrich *Source(s):* NGDM; WORB
Loxhay, Simon c.1550-1611 [composer]
Lohet, Simon *Source(s):* LCAR; NGDM
Loyacano, Stephen J(acob) 1926- [composer, author]
Lord, Stephen *Source(s):* ASCP; CCE64-65
Loy, S. J. *Source(s):* ASCP
Loyau, George Etienne 1835-1898 [journalist, folk-song writer]
Chanson, George *Source(s):* DAUM; LCAR
Old Explorer *Source(s):* LCAR
Remos *Source(s):* DAUM; LCAR

Luandrew, Albert 1907-1995 [singer, organist, pianist, songwriter]
Delta Joe *Source(s):* AMUS; HARS
Note(s): Also used by Leroy Foster.
Doctor Clayton's Buddy *Source(s):* AMUS; EPMU; HARS
Sunnyland Slim *Source(s):* AMUS; CCE68; EPMU; HARS
Lubbe, Kurt 1888- [composer]
Korden, Emilio *Source(s):* GREN
Stafford, Frank *Source(s):* CCE30 Efor14402; GREN; MELL
Lubin, Napoléon-Antoine-Eugene 1805-1850 [composer]
Saint-Lubin, León de *Source(s):* GREN
Lubomirski, Wladyslaw 1866-1934 [composer]
Lirski, W. *Source(s):* PIPE
Lucas, Christopher Norman 1912-1970 [composer, author, conductor]
Davis, Norman *Source(s):* ASCP; CCE63
Lucas, Edward Verrall 1868-1938 [lyricist]
Mark, F. W. *Source(s):* GANB; KILG
Lucas, Eugene 1900-1972 [singer, composer, lyricist]
Austin, Gene *Source(s):* AMUS; CASS; EPMU; GAMM; PSND
Blue Ridge Duo *Source(s):* SUTT
Note(s): Jt. pseud.: George Reneau.
Collins, Bill *Source(s):* SUTT; http://www.bluegrassmessangers.com/master/cindy11.html (9 Apr. 2005)
Voice of the Southland, the *Source(s):* PSND
Whispering Tenor, The *Source(s):* PSND
Lucas, Sharalee 1949- [songwriter, author, singer]
Sharalee *Source(s):* ASCP; CCE75
Lucca, Enrique Arsenio, Jr. 1946- [pianist, arranger]
Lucca, Papo *Source(s):* EPMU
Lucciola, John (S., Jr.) 1926-1989 [composer, author]
Luce, Johnnie *Source(s):* ASCP; CCE58; CCE63; CCE67-68
Lüderwald, George Ernst 1765-1835 [composer]
Lange, (Georg) Ernst *Source(s):* SONN; STGR; WORB
Ludovicus Sanctus 1304-1361 [theorist]
Ludwig van Kempen *Source(s):* GROL
Socrates *Source(s):* GROL
Ludwig, Carl (F.) 1893-1982 [music publisher, composer, arranger]
Gliwudski, S. *Source(s):* CCE51 R72992 ("Prelude to an Imaginary Dream")
Hanson, Eric *Source(s):* CCE62-63; CCE65 E206037; CPOL RE-645-623
Note(s): Also used by Albert Oliver Davis & Elizabeth Wahr; see NOTES: Hanson, Eric.
Nagy, Ferenz *Source(s):* CCE52; CCE63
Ludwig, Doris (Adell) 1923- [organist, pianist, composer]

Baradaprana, P(ravrajika) *Source(s):* CCE63; COHN; HIXN
Ludwig, Joachim (Carl Martin) 1933- [composer]
Luckner, Lutz *Source(s):* BUL3; CCE65; GREN
Luening, Otto 1900-1996 [composer]
Cleveland, James P. *Source(s):* Hartsock, Ralph. *Otto Luening*. New York: Greenwood Press, 1991.
Note(s): Stage name as actor & manager, 1918-19.
Lühe, Willibald von der
Juvenalis *Source(s):* DAVE
Rentmeister Juvenal *Source(s):* DAVE
Lukačić, Ivan 1585-1648 [composer]
Lucacih, Giovanni *Source(s):* RIEM
Lulier, Giovanni (Lorenzo) c.1650-early 18th cent. [violoncellist, composer]
Giovanni del Violone *Source(s):* GROL; NGDM; SADC; WORB
Lulli, Giovanni Battista 1632-1687 [composer, dancer, instrumentalist]
Bouffon Odieux, Le *Source(s):* PSND
Coeur Bas, Le *Source(s):* PSND
Coquin Tenebreux, Un *Source(s):* PSND
Father of French Dramatic Music *Source(s):* DEAN
Father of French Opera *Source(s):* http://www.site-moliere.com/resources/lully.html (6 Oct. 2002)
Note(s): See also Daniel François Esprit Auber.
Hateful Clown, The *Source(s):* PSND
Lully, Jean Baptiste *Source(s):* LCAR; PSND
Signor Chiacchiarone, Il *Source(s):* GROL
Lumley, Benjamin 1812-1875 [attorney, opera impresario; author]
Hermes *Source(s):* CART; LCAR
Levy, Benjmin *Source(s):* GROL; PIPE
Lumpkin, (Elgin) 1975- [songwriter, singer]
Giuwine *Source(s):* AMIR; AMUS; LCAR; PMUS-00
Lunde, Lawson 1935- [composer, pianist]
Lunde, Lonny *Source(s):* ASCP
Lunn, William Arthur Brown ?-1879 [musician, author]
Wallbridge, Arthur *Source(s):* BROW; CPMU
Lunny, Donal 1947- [guitarist, producer, director]
Quincy Jones of Irish Music, The *Source(s):* MUHF
Lünstedt, Dieter 1945- [composer]
Hendrik, Tony *Source(s):* CCE68; KOMP; KOMS
Lupino, Henry George 1892-1959 [actor, singer, librettist]
Lane, Lupino *Source(s):* EPMU; GAMM; LCAR
Lupino, Nipper *Source(s):* EPMU
Lure, Artur (Sergeievich) 1892-1966 [composer]
Lourié, Arthur Vincent *Source(s):* BAKO; BAKT; LCAR
Lureman, Hermann Thomas 1890-1965 [composer]
Herthorn, Paul *Source(s):* CCE57; REHH; SUPN
Lusitano, Vicente before 1525-after 1553 [composer, theorist]
Vicente (de Olivença) *Source(s):* GRV3; LCAR
Lussi, Marie 1892-1968 [composer, author]
Mitale, Mari *Source(s):* ASCP; LCAR
Lustig, Jacob Wilhelm 1706-1796 [organist, composer, writer]
Wohlgemuth, Conrad *Source(s):* GROL; NGDM; SADC
Lustig-Prean, Karl 1892-1965 [theatre director, writer on music, journalist]
Janischfeld, Erwin von *Source(s):* OMUO
Lutkin, Peter C(hristian) 1858-1931 [composer, organist, conductor, educator]
Note(s): Portrait: ETUP 53:11 (Nov. 1935): 675
Jones, John *Source(s):* CCE(33?) R25289
Note(s): Also used by Elvis A(a)ron Presley.
Lutoslawski, Witold 1913-1994 [composer]
Derwid *Source(s):* CCE61; GROL
Lutter, Howard 1889-1959 [pianist, composer]
Albertson, Lester *Source(s):* PIAN
Note(s): Possible pseud.
Gregory, Stuart *Source(s):* PIAN
Kornbau, Wilhelm *Source(s):* PIAN
Note(s): Possibly Lutter's birth name?
Spencer, John *Source(s):* PIAN
Note(s): Possible pseud.
Luttrell, Joyce Reba 1934- [guitarist, singer, songwriter]
Rambo, Dottie *Source(s):* CLAG; SGMA (port)
Lutyens, Elizabeth 1906-1983 [composer]
Milhoff *Source(s):* http://music.acu.edu/www/iawm/articles/june96/robinsen.html (6 Oct. 2002)
Lutz, Wilhelm 1904-1982 [composer]
Lechner, Lothar *Source(s):* BUL3; CCE61-63; KOMP; PFSA; RIES
Lux, Lillian Sylvia [or Susan] 1918-2005 [composer, author, actress]
Amber, Lili *Source(s):* ASCP
Burnstein, Lillian *Source(s):* ASCP
Luypaerts, Guy 1917- [composer, conductor]
Lupar, Guy *Source(s):* MUSR
Lvov, Eugene 1883-1919 [composer, pianist]
Onégin, Eugene *Source(s):* BAKE (see under: Onégin, Sigrid)
Lwowczyk, Marcin [or Martin(us)] c.1530-1589 [composer]
Leoploita, Marcin [or Martin(us)] *Source(s):* LCAR; RIEM
Lyall, Jack [composer]
Chambers, Robert *Source(s):* CCE58 E120520
Note(s): Jt. pseud.: Walter (Charles) Ehret. Ehret also used as jt. pseud. with other individuals; see NOTES: Chambers, Robert.

Hilton, Arthur *Source(s):* LCCC 1955-70 (see reference)
Note(s): Jt. pseud.: Walter (Charles) Ehret. Ehret also used as jt. pseud. with other individuals; see NOTES: Hilton, Arthur.
Lyde, Cecil Orlando 1948- [composer, author, singer]
Lyde, Cisco *Source(s):* ASCP
Lyden, John (Joseph) 1956- [songwriter]
Rotten, Johnny *Source(s):* CPMU; LCAR; ROOM
Lyn(h)am, Ray c.1951- [singer, songwriter, guitarist]
Great Irish Hope of Country Music, The *Source(s):* MCCL
Lynch, Thomas Toke [or Took] 1818-1871 [author, hymnist]
Note(s): Portrait: CYBH
Dissenting Minister, A *Source(s):* PSNN
Long, Silent *Source(s):* CART; PSND
Lyne, Clifton [librettist]
Clifton, Lewis *Source(s):* GANA p. 396
Lyne, Joseph Leycester 1837-1908 [composer; hymnist, monk]
Brother I(gnatius) O(rdinis) S(ancti) B(enedicti) *Source(s):* LCAR
Ignatius, (Father) (O. S. B.) *Source(s):* CPMU; LCAR
Lynes, Frank 1858-1913 (or 14) [composer, organist]
Note(s): Portraits: APSA; ETUP 53:11 (Nov. 1935): 675
Burg, Alfred *Source(s):* CCE28 R45936, R45937 & R5939
Chandon, Theo *Source(s):* CCE18 R11700 (Orig.: CCE1891 #1322)
Note(s): "Old Love Song," arr. for piano. Also used by Anton Strelezki [i.e., Arthur Bransby Burnand]
Dana, Arthur *Source(s):* CCE32 R19182
Note(s): A. P. Schmidt house name; see NOTES: Dana, Arthur.
Erich, Carl *Source(s):* CCE32 R20355
Note(s): A. P. Schmidt house name; see NOTES: Erich, Carl.
Lynas, F. *Source(s):* GOTH
Note(s): Possible pseud.
Meyer, Ferdinand *Source(s):* CCE38 R65801-6
Note(s): A. P. Schmidt house name; see NOTES: Meyer, Ferdinand.
Lynn, Audrey 1906-1995 [organist, composer]
Leaf, Ann *Source(s):* ASCP; DeLong, Thomas. *Radio Stars*. Jefferson, N.C.: McFarland, 1996.
Little Organ Annie *Source(s):* DeLong (see above)
Mighty Mite of the Organ *Source(s):* DeLong (see above)
Lynn, Lonnie Rashied [or Rashid, or Rasheed] c.1971- [rapper, songwriter]
Common (Sense) *Source(s):* AMIR; EPMU; PMUS-00
Note(s): Originally known as Common Sense (LCAR)
Lynne, Jeff 1947- [composer, producer, singer]
Traveling Wilburys *Source(s):* http://www.wilburys.info/faq.html (2 May 2005)
Note(s): With: George Harrison, Roy (Kelton) Orbison, Tom Petty & Bob Dylan [i.e., Robert Allen Zimmerman]
Wilbury, Clayton *Source(s):* http://wilburys.info/instrav.html (2 May 2005)
Wilbury, Otis *Source(s):* http://wilburys.info/instrav.html
Lynsey, Rubin 1950- [singer, songwriter]
Lynsey, De Paul *Source(s):* SONG
Lyon, David Norman 1938- [composer]
Norman, Leo *Source(s):* BUL3; RIES
Lyon, Myer 1751-1791 (or 97) [hymnist]
Leoni *Source(s):* CYBH; GRV3
Lyon, Robert Hunter [arranger]
R. H. L. *Source(s):* CPMU (publication date 1847)
Lyons, Austin 1955- [soca artist, songwriter]
Blue Boy *Source(s):* PEN2
Superblue *Source(s):* PEN2
Lyons, Joseph Callaway 1930- [composer, author, arranger]
Lyons, Jodie *Source(s):* ASCP
Lyons, Lorenzo 1807-1886 [translator]
Laiana, Makua *Source(s):* CYBH
Lysniansky, Benjamin 1924- [composer]
Lees, Benjamin *Source(s):* BAKO; BAKR; LCAR
Lytle, Donald (Eugene) 1938 (or 41)-2003 [singer, guitarist, bandleader, songwriter]
Ohio Kid, The *Source(s):* FLIN; MCCL; PSND
Paycheck, Johnny [or John Austin] *Source(s):* CCME; ENCM; EPMU; MCCL; NGAM; PEN2
Working Man's Hero, The *Source(s):* FLIN
Young, Donny [or Donnie] *Source(s):* ENCM; FLIN; MCCL; NGAM; PSND; STAC
Lyttelton, Humphrey 1921- [bandleader, trumpeter, author]
Humph *Source(s):* CASS

– M –

Maal, Baaba 1953- [singer, songwriter, guitarist]
Nightingale, The *Source(s):* CM37
Maasland, Arie 1907 (or 08)-1980 [composer]
Malando, (A.) *Source(s):* CCE50; CCE64; REHH; SUPN
Maass, Arlene Fournier 1940- [author, lyricist, singer, pianist]
Maass, Charlee *Source(s):* ASCP; LCAR

Mabon, Willie 1925-1985 [singer, pianist, songwriter]
Big Willie *Source(s):* HARS
Mac see also *Mc*
Macarthy, Harry B. 1834-1888 [actor, singer, songwriter]
Arkansas Comedian, The *Source(s):* HAMM; HARW p. 56
National Poet of the South *Source(s):* HARW p. 58
Maccari, Giacomo fl. late 17th cent. [composer]
Vandini, Lotavio *Source(s):* SONN
Note(s): Possible pseud. Anagram of Antonio Vivaldi, but probably not a pseud. of Vivaldi.
Macchia, Frank 1958- [composer, recording producer]
Maximum, Frankie *Source(s):* http://www.littleevilthings.com/Maximum (16 Oct. 2002)
MacColl, Ewan 1915-1989 [composer, guitarist, playwright]
Miller, James [or Jimmie] *Source(s):* CASS; LCAR
MacColl, Kristy c.1960- [singer, songwriter]
Dorothy Parker of Pop, The *Source(s):* CM12
Doubt, Mandy *Source(s):* MUWB
Mandy Doubt *Sources(s):* htttp://powersurf.esmartweb.com/deadmisc.htm (4 Feb. 2005)
MacCormack, Cecil Bunting 194?- [singer, composer]
Mack, Bunny *Source(s):* PEN2
MacCulloch, James Monteath [composer]
Note(s): Publication dates 1884-69.
Monteath, James *Source(s):* CPMU
Saint-Blane, James *Source(s):* CPMU
MacDermott, Michael Terry [singer, songwriter]
Terry, Michael *Source(s):* NOMG
MacDonald, Ballard 1882-1935 [songwriter]
Calhoun, John C. *Source(s):* CCE45 #4114, 552 R134256
Note(s): Jt. pseud.: James F. Hanley
Camdon, Al D. *Source(s):* CCE39 #18200, 388 R76918; CCE49 R41733
Note(s): "Moonlight and Honeysuckle" (CCE49)
Camdon, Dal *Source(s):* CCE26 E637850
Chapin, Betty *Source(s):* CCE25 E621412 ("The Convict and the Rose")
Note(s): Jt. pseud.: Robert A. King [i.e., Keiser]
MacDonald, Georgi(n)a [composer, arranger]
Campbell, Misses *Source(s):* CCE16 E379535; LCAR
Note(s): Jt. pseud.: Amourette Miller.
M. A. C. *Source(s):* CPMU (publication dates: 1902-05)
Misses Campbell *Source(s):* LCAR
MacDonald, Malcolm 1948- [music critic, journalist]
MacDonald, Calum *Source(s):* LCAR

MacDowell, Edward (Alexander) 1860-1908 [composer]
Thorn(e), Edgar *Source(s):* CPMU; GOTH; GROL; LCAR; NGDM
Note(s): On op. 1-7; see NGDM work list. Do not confuse with Edgar Thorne, pseud. of Marie E. Merrick or E. Thorne, pseud. of Ernst Roth.
MacEachern, Malcolm 1884-1945 [singer, writer]
Jetsam, Mr. *Source(s):* CART; CCE66
Macero, Attilio Joseph 1925 (or 30)- [saxophonist, composer, producer]
Macero, Teo *Source(s):* EPMU; LCAR; PEN2
Macfadyen, D. [composer]
Note(s): Probably Dugald Macfadyen; mentioned 1880-85.
D. M. *Source(s):* CPMU
MacFarlane, Elaine 1942- [songwriter]
MacFarlane, Spanky *Source(s):* AMIR; NOMG
Macfoy, Emmanuel Kayasi 1948- [composer, author]
Oju, Abeodun *Source(s):* ASCP
MacGregor, Irvin T(homas) 1915- [composer, author, teacher]
MacGregor, Scotty *Source(s):* ASCP; CCE53; CCE58; CCE61
MacGregor, J(ohn) Chalmers 1903- [composer]
MacGregor, Chummy *Source(s):* ASCP; CCE31 Eunp35022; CCE61; CCE70 R494267
Machado, Joel 1962- [singer, songwriter
John Henry *Source(s):* http://www.maxpages.com/texasthunder (6 Oct. 2003)
Note(s): Also used by (John Henry) Perry Bradford.
Texas Thunder *Source(s):* http://www.maxpages.com/texasthunder
Machlis, Joseph 1906-1998 [writer on music, composer]
Manners, Jonathan *Source(s):* CCE57
Selcamm, George *Source(s):* GROL; PIPE
MacInnis, (Murdoch) Donald 1923- [composer, author, teacher]
Garland, Donald *Source(s):* ASCP; LCAR
Sinnicam, Don *Source(s):* ASCP; LCAR
MacIntosh, Winston (Hubert) 1944-1987 [singer, songwriter]
Tosh, Peter *Source(s):* CASS; CM03; LCAR
Mack, Bill 1929- [songwriter]
Midnight Cowboy, The *Source(s):* ENCM
Mack, Edward 1826-1882 [composer]
Mackay, E. *Source(s):* CCE41 R96822 ("Pearl Waltz"); TPRF
Max *Source(s):* http://www.bluecurl.com/ncbbp/entry_list.asp?cat=&pos=11 (19 June 2005)
Note(s): Probable pseud. "The Bat and the Ball Song"

Mackay, Charles 1814-1889 [journalist, songwriter]
Grimbosh, Herman *Source(s):* CART
Wagstaffe, John, Esq., of Wilby Grange *Source(s):* CART
Mackay, Ronald 1941-1993 [composer, pianist]
Mikhashoff, Yvar *Source(s):* BAKT; LCAR
Mackeben, Theo 1897-1953 [composer, pianist, conductor]
Marck, Robert *Source(s):* CCE55; CCE73
Morris, John *Source(s):* OMUO
Roberts, Red *Source(s):* OMUO; PIPE
MacKellar, Thomas 1812-1899 [business man, author, poet]
TAM *Source(s):* JULN
Mackie, James 1944- [composer]
Auralis *Source(s):* http://www.sibeliusmusic.com/cgi-bin/whichstore.pl?url=abademusic (10 Feb. 2005)
Mackie, William H. 1859?-1929 [composer]
Beyer, F. *Source(s):* MCBD; REHG; SUPN
Mackie-Beyer, W. H. *Source(s):* REHG; SUPN
MacKinlay, (Mrs.) J. 1850-1904 [composer]
Sterling, Antoinette *Source(s):* COHN; HIXN; STRN
MacKintosh, Robert c.1745-1807 [violinist, composer]
Red Rob *Source(s):* GRV3
Maclean, Alexander [or Alick] Morvaren 1872-1936 [composer]
God of Scarborough, The *Source(s):* MUWB
Morvaren, Alexander *Source(s):* MELL
MacLean, Dougie [i.e., Douglas] 1954- [singer, songwriter]
Scotland's Premier Folk Singing Troubadour *Source(s):* MUHF
MacLean, Walter Arthur 1852-1921 [journalist, author, librettist]
Potter, Paul M(eredith) *Source(s):* GAN2
MacNamara, Francis [or Frank] 1811- c.1868 [poet]
Frank the Poet *Source(s):* DAUM
Meredith, J. Frank the Poet *Source(s):* LCAR
Macpherson, James 1736-1796 [author]
Ossian *Source(s):* FANF 23:2 p. 313; PIPE
MacPherson, William (W.) [songwriter]
Martin, Bill *Source(s):* CCE63; LCPC letter cited [nd]; PMUS-93
Note(s): Also used by William [or Billy] (Martin) Joel & William Wylie.
MacRae, Fred A(ylor) 1929- [composer, singer, record producer]
MacRae, Johnny *Source(s):* ASCP; CCE62; PMUS
Macy, J(ames) C(artwright) 1845-1918 [songwriter]
Note(s): Portraits: ETUP 58:9 (Sept. 1940): 640; MRAR (Piano Ed.) (Aug. 1901): 2
C. J. M. *Source(s):* CCE12 R3733 ("Good-bye My Little Lady . . .")
Note(s): Typographical error?
Cartwright, C. M. *Source(s):* CCE13 R4777
Coe, Collin *Source(s):* CCE13 R4773; Jones, F. O. *A Handbook of American Music and Musicians*. New York: DaCapo, 1971.
Fiorin(i), C. *Source(s):* CCE10 R1055; CCE17 R9346 & R9348
Hatton, Chester *Source(s):* CCE19 R13203
J. C. M. *Source(s):* CCE18 R11776; CPMU
Marion *Source(s):* CCE15 R7073; Jones (see above)
Rosabel *Source(s):* CCE13 R4026; CCE21 R19012; Jones (see above)
Simpkins, Polly *Source(s):* CCE30 R7942; TPRF
Madden, Henri 1698-1748 [composer, conductor, theorist]
Madin, Henri *Source(s):* LCAR; MACM
Madelaine, Etienne Jean Baptiste Nicolas 1801-1868 [musician, writer]
LaMadelaine, Stéphen de *Source(s):* IBIM; LCAR; WORB
Madeloni, Frank (J.) 1951- [songwriter]
Slick, Earl *Source(s):* CPOL PA-116-863; LCAR; PMUS-85
Mader, Rezsõ 1856-1940 [composer, conductor]
Note(s): Portrait: ETUP 53:12 (Nov. 1935): 696
Mader, Raoul *Source(s):* GAN1; GAN2
Mäder, Wolfgang 1924- [composer]
Maduro, Franco *Source(s):* KOMP; KOMS; PFSA
Novello, Andy *Source(s):* KOMP; KOMS; PFSA
Portner, Lennie *Source(s):* KOMP; KOMS; PFSA
Stephan, Georg *Source(s):* CCE68
Madrazo (y Hahn), Federico (Carlos) de 1880-1935 [painter, musician, librettist]
Madrazo, Coco *Source(s):* PIPE
Magee, Benjamin Rush 1956?-2003 [composer, lyricist, actor]
Magee, Rusty *Source(s):* WASH
Maggini, Armande Jeanne [composer]
Altaï, Armande *Source(s):* GOTH
Maggio, Luigi fl. 1922-23 [composer]
Gisma, Giulio *Source(s):* MELL; STGR
Maghett, Sam(uel) 1937-1969 [singer, guitarist, songwriter]
Good Rocking Sam *Source(s):* HARS; LCAR
Magic Sam *Source(s):* HERZ; LCAR
Magic Singing Sam *Source(s):* HARS; LCAR
Maglio, Juan (Felix) 1880-1934 [bandoneonist, leader, composer]
Maglio, Pacho *Source(s):* BBDP; TODO
Pacho *Source(s):* CCE44 #6864 Efor68983; LCAR; TODO
Note(s): See also Francesco Galán Blanco.
Magno (Pereira), Basilio [songwriter]
Irving Berlin of India *Source(s):* http://www.goa-worldnet/basilio-magno (16 Oct. 2002)

Royal Song Writer, The *Source(s):* http://www.goa-worldnet/basilio-magno
Magnoni, Bruce [or Bruno] Albert 1922- [composer]
Diamond, Max *Source(s):* CCE50-51
Magnoni, Edrich *Source(s):* CCE5?
Note(s): Jt. pseud.: Stanley Smith-Masters.
Magoon, Eaton (Harry), Jr. 1922- [composer]
Magoon, Bob *Source(s):* ASCC; LCCC 1946-54 (see reference)
Mahler, Gustav 1860-1911 [composer]
Song Symphonist, The *Source(s):* PSND
Summer Composer, A *Source(s):* http://www.andante.com/profiles/Mahler/symph2.cfm (16 Oct. 2002)
Note(s): Called himself.
Mahler-Kalkstein, Menahem 1908-1995 [composer, arranger]
Avidom, Menahem *Source(s):* BAKR; BUL1; NGDM; NGDO; NULM (port)
Kalkstein, Menahem *Source(s):* BAKO; BAKT
Mahoney, Edward 1949- [singer, songwriter]
Money, Eddie *Source(s):* AMUS; CM16; DIMA; NITE
Mahoney, Elizabeth (née Symons) 1911- [dancer, writer on ballet]
Mara, Thalia *Source(s):* CART
Mahr, Curt 1907-1978 [composer]
Ernest, K. *Source(s):* KOMS; PFSA
Mahr, Herman Carl 1901-1964 [composer, arranger]
Mahr, Curley *Source(s):* ASCP; CCE39 #23463 E77087
Mai, Siegfried 1927- [composer]
Glück, Mathias *Source(s):* KOMS; PFSA
Wagner, Norbert *Source(s):* KOMS; PFSA
Maillard, Jean 1926- [musicologist, writer on music]
Morel, Octave *Source(s):* RIES
Mainwaring, Edward Stewart [songwriter]
Stewart, Ed *Source(s):* CPMU
Maiorana, Victor (E.) 1897-1964 [composer, pianist, organist]
Lamont, Victor *Source(s):* ASCP; CCE44 #6728 E120711; CCE54 E82325; REHG
Note(s): Also used by Floyd J. St. Clair.
Maitland, Robert c.1847-1907 [actor, writer, composer]
Mansell, Richard *Source(s):* GAN2
Maitre, Suzanne Gabrielle [composer]
De Maistre, Sylvie *Source(s):* GOTH
Majewki, Hans-Martin 1911-1977 [composer]
Troysen, Jan *Source(s):* BUL3; KOMP; KOMS; PFSA; RIES
Majo, (Gian) Francesco (de) 1732-1770 [composer]
Note(s): Portrait: ETUP 54:1 (Jan. 1936): 2
Ciccio di Majo *Source(s):* BAKO; BAKR; MACM; NGDM; PSND
Major, J. [composer]
Amateur *Source(s):* CPMU ("From Thy Roseate Bow'rs, Aurora" (1795))
Majors, Margaret Allison 1913-1972 [composer, pianist, teacher]
Bonds, Margaret Allison *Source(s):* GROL
Notes(s): Used her mother's maiden name.
Majowski, Ernest 1916- [composer]
Arimont, Jean *Source(s):* GOTH; KOMP; SUPN
Majo, Ernest *Source(s):* GOTH; SUPN
Sloma, Ernst *Source(s):* SUPN
Makarov, N(ikolai) P(etrovich) 1810-1890 [lexicographer, writer on music]
Trechzvevdockin, Ghermochen *Source(s):* http://www.geocities.com/Broadway/Alley/1154/grist.html (4 Feb. 2005)
Makem, Tommy 1932- [folksinger, singer]
Bard of Armagh *Source(s):* http://www.wfma.net/makem.htm (28 Feb. 2004)
Godfather of Irish Music, The *Source(s):* http://www.wfma.net/makem. htm
Makiadi, L'Okanga La Ndju Pene Luambo 1938-1989 [guitarist, songwriter, bandleader]
Franco *Source(s):* BAKR; LCAR; PEN2
Makkey, Peter 1949- [composer]
Maffay, Peter *Source(s):* PFSA
Maldonado, Ricardo [or Richard] (Ray) 1945- [bandleader, composer, instrumentalist]
Ray, Ricardo [or Richie] *Source(s):* CCE66-67; EPMU; PEN2
Malenfant, Anna 1902 (or 05)-1988 [singer, composer]
Lebrun, Marie *Source(s):* CCE58; HIXN
Malerba, Ricardo Francisco 1905-1974 [bandoneonist, leader, composer]
Demar, Luz *Source(s):* TODO
Maleta, Kiamuangana 1944- [singer, composer]
Verckys *Source(s):* PEN1
Malijewski, Peter Martin 1946- [composer, author, pianist]
Martin, (Kepha) Peter *Source(s):* ASCP; CCE75; CPOL SRu-257-036
Note(s): Also used by Nixon Waterman.
Mallian, Julien de 1848-1904 [playwright]
Julien *Source(s):* PIPE
Mallis, Constantine Alexander (Hadji [or Hagi]) 1914-1995 [composer]
Caliban, Cain *Source(s):* CCE74
Los Angeles, Alex *Source(s):* GOTH
Oberon, Rex *Source(s):* CCE74; GOTH
Puck, Guy *Source(s):* CCE74; GOTH
Malone, Terwilliger [pianist, composer]
Malone, Thumbs *Source(s):* PERF; RAGM

Mammarella, Anthony [songwriter]
September, Anthony *Source(s):* MUWB; PSND
Note(s): "Butterfly" was written by Bernie Lowe & Kal Mann [i.e., Kalman Cohen] & credited to Anthony September [i.e., Anthony [or Tony] Mammarella. (MUWB)
Manaois, Joseph (Anthony, Jr.) 1903- [composer, conductor]
Don Jose *Source(s):* ASCC; CCE56 Eunp
Mance, Julian Clifford, Jr. 1928- [pianist, composer; writer on music]
Mance, Junior *Source(s):* CCE60; LCAR; PEN2
Mancini, Enrico Nicola 1924-1994 [conductor, composer, arranger, pianist]
Mancini, Hank *Source(s):* CLMC
Mancini, Henry *Source(s):* CLMJ
Mandell, Pete ?-1963 [composer]
Russell, Phil *Source(s):* JASG; JASR
Mandel'shtam, Valentina Iosifovna 1888-1968 [singer, composer]
Ramm, Valentina Iosifovna *Source(s):* HOFE
Mandlick, H(ugo) 1822- [librettist]
Merlin, Hugo *Source(s):* STGR; WORB
Manelli, Francesco 1594 (or 95)-1667 [composer, singer, poet]
Fasolo, Il *Source(s):* GROL; LCAR; NGDM; NGDO; SADC
Note(s): Possible pseud.
Manera, Jesus Franco 1930- [composer, film director, writer]
Franco, Jesus *Source(s):* NOMG
Manganella, Renato Eduardo 1877 (or 80)-1939 [author, librettist]
D'Ambra, Lucio *Source(s):* CCE60; LCAR; MELL
Mangeshkar, Lata 1929- [singer, composer]
Anandghan *Source(s):* GROL
Mangini, John R. [composer]
Mann, John(ny) *Source(s):* http://www.classicthemes.com/StudioLogos.shtml (28 Feb. 2005)
Note(s): Also used by Phil(ip) Green.
Mangrum, James Leslie 1948- [singer, songwriter]
Dandy, Jim *Source(s):* NOMG
Mank, Charles 1902- [composer, author, singer]
Mank, Chaw *Source(s):* ASCP; CCE44 #40442 E125577
Mann, Robert E. 1902-1978 [composer]
Mann, Bert *Source(s):* ASCP
Mann, Stephen Follett 1945- [composer, arranger]
Diamond, Cliff *Source(s):* ASCP; CCE68
Mannelli, Carlo 1640-1697 [composer, violinist, singer]
Carlino *Source(s):* WORB
Carlo del Violino *Source(s):* LCAR; NGDM; SADC
Note(s): See also Carlo Francesco Cesarini & Carlo Caproli.
Carluccio di Pamfilio *Source(s):* LCAR; NGDM; SADC; WORB
Mannes, Leo (Ezekiel) 1911-2000 [singer, songwriter]
Charles, Susanne *Source(s):* CCE55 Eunp
Craddock, Zeke *Source(s):* BBDP; MCCL
Emmet, Leo *Source(s):* CCE55 Eunp
Jewish Hillbilly, The *Source(s):* BBDP
Manners, Craddock *Source(s):* http://www.harrynilsson.com/misc-3943-21808.html (6 Apr. 2005)
Manners, Zeke *Source(s):* ASCP; BBDP; EPMU; LCAR; MCCL; OB00; PSND
Manney, Charles Fonteyn 1872-1951 [composer, arranger]
Note(s): Portraits: ETUP 51:1 (Jan. 1933): 21; ETUP 53:12 (Dec. 1935): 696
Austin, Robert E. *Source(s):* CCE30 E19778; CCE57
C. F. M. *Source(s):* CPMU; LCAR
Clemson, Carl *Source(s):* CCE48 R33726 ("Dreaming Alone in the Twilight")
Doran, Jack *Source(s):* CCE45 #63817, 623 R145364
Moore, Hartley *Source(s):* CCE25 E617461
Westbrook, Arthur *Source(s):* CCE29 R3919
Manone, Joseph 1904-1982 [composer, lyricist, conductor]
Note(s): Orginally surname was Mannone.
Barbecue Joe & His Hot Dogs *Source(s):* SUTT
Manone, Jimmy *Source(s):* CCE65
Manone, Wingy *Source(s):* ASCP; EPMU; KINK; LCAR; SUTT
O'Capri *Source(s):* CCE66
Williams, Speed *Source(s):* SUTT
Note(s): Speed Williams Orchestra, on recordings by Wingy Manone & his orchestra.
Manschinger, Kurt 1902-1968 [conductor, composer, critic]
Vernon, Ashley *Source(s):* BAKO; BAKR, BAKT; BUL3; CCE73
Mansfield, Joseph 1889 (or 90)-1971 [actor, author]
Little Joey *Source(s):* GAN2
Santley, Joseph *Source(s):* GAN2
Note(s): Do not confuse with Joseph H. Santly (1886-1962), composer of "Hawaiian Butterfly."
Mansfield, Orlando Augustine 1863-1936 [composer, organist, writer]
Note(s): Portrait: ETUP 54:1 (Jan. 1936): 2
Adlam, Sofie N. *Source(s):* BAKE; MACM
Liemann, Oscar *Source(s):* BAKE; MACM
Mantell, Frederich [actor]
Sugarman, Jacob *Source(s):* GANA p. 807

Note(s): Possible jt. pseud.: John Gerant & Henry S. Ugar.
Mantovani, A(nnuzio) P(aolo) 1905-1980 [composer]
Cortesi, Paolo *Source(s):* CCE50; CCE55
Faye, Roy *Source(s):* CCE56; CPOL RE-290-635; http://www.hallowquest.com (18 Apr. 2005)
Fossello, Ivan *Source(s):* http://www.hallowquest.com
Note(s): Incorrectly reported as a pseud. of Mantovani.
Franz, Paul *Source(s):* CCE55 Efor38028; http://www.hallowquest.com
Note(s): Do not confuse with singer Paul Franz [i.e., François Gautier] (1876-1950).
Gandino, Leonelleo *Source(s):* http://www.guildmusic.com/light/catalogue/5110.htm (14 May 2005)
King of Light Orchestra Music *Source(s):* http://www.hallowquest.com
Lambrecht, P(aul) *Source(s):* CCE54; CCE58; CPOL RE-135-856; http://www.hallowquest.com
Manilla, Pedro *Source(s):* CCE66 R384886; CPOL RE-249-953; http://www.hallowquest.com
Note(s): Also jt. pseud.: Angelo F. Piccioni; see NOTES: Manilla, Pedro.
Mantovani, (Albert) *Source(s):* LCCC 1955-70 (see reference) Efor34168
Monty, Paul *Source(s):* http://www.guildmusic.com/light/catalogue/5110.htm
Moss, Jack *Source(s):* CCE54; CCE55 Efor28957
Moss, Ken *Source(s):* CPOL RE-4-147
Paolito, Francesco *Source(s):* CCE33 Efor30289; LCCC60 R253971
Note(s): Jt. pseud.: Angelo F. Piccioni.
Remy, Paul *Source(s):* CCE74; http://www.hallowquest.com
Rosen, Abner, C. *Source(s):* CCE55 Efor20980
Note(s): Jt. pseud.: Ronald Binge.
Trapani, T(ulio) *Source(s):* CPOL RE-285-440; http://www.hallowquest.com
Trevor, Mike *Source(s):* CCE55; CPOL RE-169-702; http://www.hallowquest.com
Manussi-Montesole, Ferdinand 1839-1908 [librettist]
Mai, Fritz *Source(s):* WORB
May, Fritz *Source(s):* STGR
Manza, Luigi mentioned 1700 [composer, poet]
Mancia, Luigi *Source(s):* WORB
Manzarek, Raymond (Daniel) 1935 (or 43)- [songwriter, pianist]
Doors, The *Source(s):* GOTT; PEN2; PMUS
Note(s): Jt. pseud.: James (Douglas) Morrison, John Densmore & Robert Krieger.
Manzione, Homero Nicolás 1905 (or 07)-1951 [poet, lyricist]
Barbeta *Source(s):* TODO
Manzi, Barbeta *Source(s):* TODO
Manzi, Homero *Source(s):* CCE53 Efor20357; TODO
Maphis, Otis Wilson 1912-1986 [guitarist, songwriter]
Maphis, Joe *Source(s):* LCAR; PEN2
Mr. and Mrs. Country Music *Source(s):* PEN2
Note(s): Jt. sobriquet with wife Rose Lee Schetrompf (1922-). See also John(ny) (R.) Mosby (with wife Jonie Mosby [i.e., Janice Irene Shields]).
Mapleson, James Henry 1830-1901 [singer, violinist, author, librarian]
Colonel, The *Source(s):* BAKE; NGDM
Mapleson, Colonel *Source(s):* BAKE; NGDM
Mariana, Enrico *Source(s):* BAKE; NGDM
Maraffi, Lewis Frederick [composer, author, conductor]
Maraffi, Fritz *Source(s):* ASCP
Maragowsky, Jacob Samuel 1856-1943 [cantor, composer, choir director]
Rovno, Zeidel *Source(s):* NULM (port.)
Marazzoli, Marco c.1602-1662 [composer, singer, harpist]
Marco dell'Arpa *Source(s):* NGDM; NGDO; SADC; WORB
Marburg, William August 1931- [singer, guitarist, songwriter]
Clifton, Bill *Source(s):* AMUS; MCCL
Marcano, Neville 1915 (or 16)-1993 [calypso writer, singer]
Growling Tiger (of Calypso) *Source(s):* AMUS; PEN2
Tiger, Growling *Source(s):* PEN2
Tiger, Siparia *Source(s):* PEN2
Marcarian, Henri 1935-1985 [singer, songwriter]
Aryan, Marc *Source(s):* DRSC
Marcelli, Vincenzo [composer]
Illecram [or Ille Cram] *Source(s):* DEAR
Marcellino, Maurice 1913-1997 [singer, composer]
Marcellino, Muzzy *Source(s):* OB97
Marcello, Alessandro 1684-1750 [composer, poet]
Strinfalico, Eterio *Source(s):* BAKE; CPMU; NGDM; PIPE; PSND; SADC
Marcello, Benedetto 1686-1739 [lawyer, writer on music, theorist]
Sacreo, Driante *Source(s):* NGDM; SADC
Marcheselli, D. [composer]
Accademico Formato *Source(s):* DEAR
Note(s): See also Francisco José de Castro.
Marchionne, L(ouis) C(ésar) 1841-1898 [composer]
Desormes, L(ouis) C(ésar) *Source(s):* CCE64; CPMU; GOTH; LCAR; MACM

Marco Antonio Girolamo mentioned 1543 [composer]
Urbino, l' *Source(s):* WORB
Marcolongo, Hèctor Domingo 1906-1987 [poet, singer, actor, leader]
Marcó, Hèctor *Source(s):* CCE71; TODO
Marcucci, Carlos 1903-1957 [bandoneonist, composer]
Pibe de Wilde, El *Source(s):* TODO
Marcus, Ahron [or Aaron] 1843-1916 [writer on music]
Verus *Source(s):* LCAR; SEND
Marcus, Greil 1945- [rock critic]
Christian, T. M. *Source(s):* http://www.snopes2.com/music/artists/masked.htm (16 Oct. 2002)
Marcuse, Albrecht [or Albert] 1920-2001 [composer, actor]
Note(s): Original spelling of surname: Marküse. Portrait: OB01
Alvis *Source(s):* CCE64 Efor105162; CCE65
Alvys *Source(s):* CCE67-68; CCE70
Birkhofer, Toni *Source(s):* CCE32 Efor23089
Hague, Albert (M.) *Source(s):* CCE67; GAN2; OB01
Hague, Bert *Source(s):* CCE40 #2658 Eunp212004
Marbot, Rolf *Source(s):* CCE30 Efor14511; CCE50-55; CPOL RE-394-631
Mare, Polignano 1928 (or 29)-1994 [singer, lyricist]
Modugno, Domenico *Source(s):* WORT
Marek, Czeslaw Jósef 1891-1985 [composer]
Mat, Mark *Source(s):* BUL3
Marenzio, Luca 1553-1599 [composer]
Divine Composer, The *Source(s):* http://www.uwgb.edu/ogradyt/ls1/madrigal.htm (7 May 2005)
Sweetest Swan (of Italy) *Source(s):* DEA3; http://www.uwgb.edu/ogradyt/ls1/madrigal.htm
Mareo, Eric 1843-1916 [composer]
Marsden, Evan *Source(s):* CPMU
Maretzek, Max 1821-1897 [violinist, composer, conductor]
Maretzek the Magnificent *Source(s):* STAR p. 121
Opera Manager, (An) *Source(s):* PSND
Margules, Michael J(ay) [composer]
Jay, Michel *Source(s):* BLIC; CPOL PA-180-301
Margulis, Charles A. 1903-1967 [composer]
Marlowe, Charles *Source(s):* ASCP; REHG
Note(s): Also used by Harriet Jay.
Margulois, David 1911 (or 12)-2000 [theatrical producer]
Note(s): Portrait: OB00
Abominable Showman, The *Source(s):* Kissel, Howard. *David Merrick; The Abominable Showman.* New York: Applause, 1993.
Barnum of Broadway Producers, The *Source(s):* PSND
Merrick, David *Source(s):* EPMU; GAN2; OB00; PSND
Maria Antonia Walpurgis 1724-1780 [composer, librettist]
Note(s): Portraits: DWCO; ETUP 54:1 (Jan. 1936): 2
Arcada, Ermelinda Talea Pastorella *Source(s):* COHN; HIXN
D***, (Madame) *Source(s):* JACK
E. T. P. A. *Source(s):* BAKR; COHN; CPMU; HIXN; JACK; PIPE
Note(s): E. T. P. A. = Ermelinda Talea Pastorella Arcada.
Ermelinda Talea (Pastorella Arcada) *Source(s):* BAKR; COHN; HIXN; SONN
Mariana, Tommaso fl. 1728-39 [librettist]
Romano *Source(s):* GROL
Note(s): See also Vincenzo DeGrandis.
Mariani, Giovanni Lorenzo 1722-1793 [composer]
Acrejo, Mirtindo *Source(s):* GROL
Mirtindo Acrejo *Source(s):* GROL
Marichal, Kalimba [singer, songwriter]
Kalimba *Source(s):* HWOM
Marie, Gabriel (Prosper) 1852-1928 [composer]
Gabriel-Marie *Source(s):* CCE56; GREN; LCAR
Marin Rosario, Fernando Luis 1930- [bandleader, composer, producer]
Rosario, Willie *Source(s):* EPMU; LCAR; PEN2
Marinan, Terrence Richard 1967- [composer, singer]
Richards, Terry *Source(s):* ASCP
Marino, Rinaldo R. 1916-1963 [composer]
Martin, Lennie *Source(s):* ASCC; CCE57; CCE60-61
Marinovici, Cesar 1949- [composer]
Marino, Caesar *Source(s):* KOBW; KOMS
Markalous, Bohumil 1882-1952 [author]
John, Jaromír *Source(s):* PIPE
Markantonatos, David [songwriter]
Marks, David *Source(s):* CCE68; PMUS
Markaritzer, Erich 1914-1982 [conductor, composer]
Maritz, Ferry *Source(s):* OMUO
Markevitch, Igor 1912-1983 [composer]
Igor the Second *Source(s):* AMRG 61:2 (1998): 57
Little Igor *Source(s):* AMRG 61:2 (1998): 57
Markowitz, Ernest H. 1919-1995 [playwright, producer]
Martin, Ernest (H.) *Source(s):* GAN2; LCAR; PIPE
Markowitz, Richard (Allen) 1926-1994 [composer, arranger]
Allen, Richard [or Dick] *Source(s):* ASCC; ASCP
Markowski, Andrzej 1924-1986 [conductor, composer]
Andrzejewski, Marek *Source(s):* NGDM; RIES
Marks, Edward B. 1865-1945 [music publisher, lyricist]
Note(s): Portrait: JASA

Bennett, Mack E. *Source(s):* CCE59
Edwards, Mack B. *Source(s):* CCE59
Edwards, Mark B. *Source(s):* CCE23 R25166; CCE27 R42099
Markham, Edward *Source(s):* CCE70 R475691
Marks, Elias J. 1880-1960 [composer, author, singer]
Dawson, Eli *Source(s):* ASCP
Marley, David 1968- [singer, songwriter]
Crown Prince of Reggae *Source(s):* ALMN
Marley, Ziggy *Source(s):* ALMN; CM03; EPMU
Marley, Robert [or Bob] Nesta 1945-1981 [singer, guitarist; songwriter]
Father of Reggae Music *Source(s):* SHAB p. 265
Note(s): See also Joe Higgs.
King of Reggae, The *Source(s):* CM03; PSND
Marley, B. B. *Source(s):* PSND
Marley, King *Source(s):* PSND
Martell, Bobby *Source(s): Goldmine*. 27:14:547 (13 July 2001): 14
Poor Man's Pope *Source(s):* CASS
Reggae King *Source(s):* SHAB p. 268
Reggae Master, The *Source(s):* PSND
Reggae Musician, The *Source(s):* PSND
Selassie, Berhane *Source(s):* Davis, Stephen. *Bob Marley*. Rochester, VT: Schenkman Books, 1990, 240.
Marmarosa, Michael 1925 (or 26)-2002 [pianist, composer, bandleader]
Marmarosa, Dodo *Source(s):* KINK; LCAR
Marmer, Merrill D. 1925-2002 [writer, lyricist, producer]
Marmer, Mike *Source(s):* DRSC
Marpurg, Friedrich Wilhelm 1718-1795 [composer, critic]
Note(s) Portrait: ETUP 54:1 (Jan. 1936): 2
Metaphrastes, Simeon *Source(s):* GRV3; LCAR; WORB
Marrero, Marta 1969- [singer, songwriter]
Martika *Source(s):* AMUS; EPMU
Marrou, Henri Irenee 1904-1977 [writer on music]
Davenson, Henri *Source(s):* RILM 71-00257-bf
Marrow, Tracy c.1958- [rapper, actor]
Ice-T *Source(s):* AMUS; CPOL PA-900-324; EPMU
Raps "Original Gangster" *Source(s):* CM07 p. v
Marsand, Luigi 1769-1841 [composer]
Ex Monaco *Source(s):* WIEC
Marschal(l)-Loepke, Grace 1895- [pianist, composer]
Note(s): Portraits: APSA; ETUP 50:9 (Sept. 1932): 608; ETUP 54:1 (Jan. 1936): 2
Clough-Leighter, Grace (Marshall) *Source(s):* CCE42 #5201, 42 R94696; CCE47 R17662; STRN
Note(s): Married name: Mrs. Henry Clough-Leighter.
Cotton-Marshall, Grace *Source(s):* HIXN
Leighton, Grace *Source(s):* HIXN
Marschal(l)-Loepke, Gloria *Source(s):* CCE41 #9124, 44 R92882; MACM; TPRF
Marshall, Gloria *Source(s):* CCE42 #5201, 42 R94696; CCE47 R17662
Marshall, Grace *Source(s):* HIXN
Marshall-Zoepke, C. *Source(s):* HIXN
Marsh, John 1752-1828 [composer]
Sharm *Source(s):* DEAM; MUWB
Marshall, Alice Smith 1867-1957 [writer on music, composer]
Barringer, Barbara *Source(s):* http://www.collectionscanada.ca/4/7/m15-416-e.html (19 June 2005)
Marshall, David [composer]
Beethoven, Loosewig von *Source(s):* REHH
Marshall, J. Herbert [composer]
Stanislaus, Henri *Source(s):* CPMU; GOTH; GOTT
Marshall, Madeleine [translator]
Jones, Graham *Source(s):* LOWN
Marsollier des Vivetiéres, Benoît-Joseph 1750-1817 [author, dramatist]
D G N *Source(s):* GROL; NGDO
Du Grand Nez *Source(s):* GROL; NGDO
Marszalek, Franz 1900-1975 [conductor, composer]
Katt, Maurus *Source(s):* CCE56; CCE59
Sanders, Herr *Source(s):* PIPE
Marteau, Franz Xaver 1741-1817 [cellist, composer]
Hammer, (Franz) Xaver *Source(s):* DEAR; LCAR
Martelli, Giovanni Battista mentioned 1564 [composer]
Martello da Monteleone *Source(s):* IBIM; WORB
Martello [or Martelli], Pier Jacopo 1665-1727 [librettest, dramatist, essayist]
Dianidio, Mirtillo *Source(s):* GROL
Martens, Adolphe-Adhemar-Louis-Michel 1898-1962 [playwright, author]
Costenoble, Philostène *Source(s):* PIPE
De Ghelderode, Michel *Source(s):* PIPE
Ghelderode, Michel de *Source(s):* PIPE
Martin, Barbara Anne 1943- [composer, author]
Martin, Bobbi *Source(s):* ASCP; CCE58
Martin, C(laude) T(remble(y)) [writer on music]
Martin, Deac *Source(s):* CCE51; CCE68; MART
Martin, Charles (Henri) 1917-1974 [fashion designer, composer]
Esterel, (Jacques) *Source(s):* CCE55-57; CPOL RE-243-636; PSND
Martin, Easthope 1882-1925 [composer]
Morrow, John *Source(s):* CCE51 R78148 ("The Sweetest Call"); CPMU
Martin, Hugh Whitfield 1874-1952 [singer, composer]
Martin, Riccardo *Source(s):* BAKR; BAKT; NGAM
Martin, Richard *Source(s):* BAKT

Martin, Johannes 1633-1702 [composer, poet, novelist]
Laurentius von Schnüffis *Source(s):* NGDM; RIEM; WORB
Martin, John 1950- [guitarist, songwriter]
Martin, Moon *Source(s):* AMUS; EPMU
Martin, Judith [or Judy] 1914- [composer]
Mary Norbert, (Sister) *Source(s):* BUL3; CCE54
Martin, Lecil T(ravis) 1931-1999 [singer, songwriter]
America's Favorite Hobo *Source(s):* AMUS; MCCL
Boxcar Willie *Source(s):* AMEN; AMUS; EPMU; MCCL
Martin, Marty *Source(s):* CCE61; EPMU; MCCL
Singing Hobo, The *Source(s):* AMEN
World Ambassador for the Hobos *Source(s):* MCCL
Martin, Lloyd 1916-1976 [saxophonist, arranger, composer]
Martin, Skip(py) *Source(s):* KINK; NGDJ
Martin, Olin E. 1904-1982 [composer, author, singer]
Martin, Freddy [or Freddie] *Source(s):* ASCP; CCE64
Martin, Ray(mond) 1918-1988 [songwriter, arranger, conductor]
Armstrong, Chris *Source(s):* CCE51-52; CPOL RE-26-652; RFSO
Cadbury, Buddy *Source(s):* CPOL RE-98-159; RFSO
Note(s): Jt. pseud.: Marcel Stellman.
Getwald, Hans *Source(s):* RFSO
Gotwald, Hans *Source(s):* CCE54
Hennessy, Ian *Source(s):* CCE55-56; CPOL RE-152-200
Note(s): Jt. pseud.: Norman [or Norrie] (William) Paramor.
Latimer, Gus *Source(s):* CCE53; CPOL RE-86-291; RFSO
Mortimer, Buddy *Source(s):* CCE53-54; CPOL RE-96-842
Mortimer, Gus *Source(s):* CCE54; CPOL RE-138-359
Nelson, Harry *Source(s):* RFSO
Powell, Lester *Source(s):* BBDP; CCE57 Efor23395; CLMC; CPOL RE-242-181; RFSO
Ross, Marshall *Source(s):* CCE53-54; CCE60 E144334; RFSO
Ross, Martin *Source(s):* CCE52; CCE54
Simmonds, Tony *Source(s):* BBDP; CLMC; CPOL RE-4-750; RFSO
Sueree, Ricardo *Source(s):* CCE55; CCE58 E115988
Suerte, Ricardo *Source(s):* CCE57; CPOL RE-181-881; RFSO
Willet(t)-Robinson, James *Source(s):* CCE53 Efor18116; CPOL RE-95-421
Note(s): Jt. pseud.: Norman [or Norrie] (William) Paramor.
Martin, Robert 1898-1982 [composer]
Cower, James *Source(s):* REHH; SUPN

Martin, Roberta Faye E. [songwriter]
Note(s): Dates may be 1907-1969.
Brown, Faye E. *Source(s):* FULD
Martín y Soler, Vicente 1754-1806 [composer]
Martini, Ignaz *Source(s):* NGDM; NGDO
Martini, Vincenzo *Source(s):* NGDM; NGDO
Spagnuolo, Lo *Source(s):* NGDM; NGDO
Valenziano, Il *Source(s):* NGDM
Martínez, Anna Katharina von 1744-1812 [singer, pianist, composer]
Martínez, Marianne von *Source(s):* BAKR; RIEM
Martinez, José 1890-1939 [pianist, composer]
Gallego, El *Source(s):* TODO
Martínez, Mariano [or Marianito] (A(lberto)) 1918- [composer, leader]
Mores, Mariano [or Marianito] *Source(s):* CCE66; CCE77-78; CPOL RE-124-576; TODO
Martinez, Peter Anthony 1951- [composer]
Anthony, Peter *Source(s):* CCE75; CPOL PAu-127; GOTH
Martini, Giovanni Battista [or Giambattista] 1706-1784 [pedagogue, writer on music, composer]
Note(s): Portrait: EWCY
Amphion, Aristoxenos *Source(s):* BAKR
Anfioneo, Aritosseno *Source(s):* BAKR
Martini, Padre *Source(s):* BAKR; LCAR; NGDO; PIPE
Martino, Donald (James) 1931 (or 32)- [composer]
Vincent, Jimmie *Source(s):* AMRG 61:5 (1998): 188; http://www.dantalian.com/jazz.html (15 June 2005)
Martinu, Bohuslav 1890-1959 [composer]
Century's Best "Unknown" Symphonist, The *Source(s):* http://www.amazon.com/exec/obidos/ts/features/2883/103-6354329-1775816 (16 Oct. 2002)
Concerto Grosso Type, A *Source(s):* see above
Note(s): Called himself.
Martl, Anton [or Toni] 1916- [composer]
Tomar, André *Source(s):* KOMP; KOMS; PFSA
Martoscelli, G(iuseppe) mentioned 1714 [poet, librettist]
Mercotellis, Agasippo *Source(s):* LOWN; WORB
Note(s): See also Niccolò Corvo.
Martyn-Green, William 1899-1975 [actor, singer, writer on music, screenwriter]
Green, Martyn *Source(s):* Oliviero, Jeffrey. *Motion Picture Players Credit*. Jefferson, N.C.: McFarland, 1991.
Marulli, Domenico mentioned 1808 [composer]
Nusco, Vincenzo *Source(s):* IBIM; STGR; WORB
Marvin, Frank(ie) James 1904-1988 [singer, songwriter, guitarist, actor]
Wallace, Frankie *Source(s):* MCCL
Marvin, John(ny) (Senator) 1897 (or 98)-1944 (or 45) [singer, songwriter]

Duke & His Uke *Source(s):* MACE; SUTT
Duke, Henry (& His Uke) *Source(s):* MACE; SUTT
Duke Honey (& His Uke) *Source(s):* SUTT
Hancock, Billy *Source(s):* MACE
Honey Duke and His Uke *Source(s):* MCCL
Lane, Jace & (His Uke) *Source(s):* MACE; SUTT
Lonesome Singer of the Air, (The) *Source(s):* PSND
MacDonald & Broons *Source(s):* SUTT
May, Jimmy *Source(s):* MACE; SUTT
Price, Jimmy [or Jimmie] *Source(s):* SUTT
Note(s): Do not confuse with Jimmie Price [i.e., John I. White]
Robbins & Uke *Source(s):* SUTT
Spence, Elton *Source(s):* MACE
Ukulele Ace, (The) *Source(s):* PSND
Wallace, Ken *Source(s):* MACE

Marx, (Adolph) Arthur 1888-1964 [composer, comedian, harpist]
Marx, Harpo *Source(s):* ASCP; CCE62

Marzian, Al(bert) F. c.1878-? [publisher, composer]
Janza, Mark *Source(s):* PERF; http://members.tripod.com/roseleafrag/02-08.html (5 Nov. 2002)

Masalin, Armas Toivo Valdemar 1885-1960 [composer]
Maasalo, Armas Toivo Valdemar *Source(s):* BUL2; WORB

Mascari, Joseph Rocco 1922- [composer, author]
Mascari, Red *Source(s):* ASCP; CCE61; CCE73

Maschek, Adrian Mathew 1918-1993 [composer, author]
Brannon, Bob *Source(s):* ASCP
Powers, Rod *Source(s):* ASCP

Maschwitz, (Albert) Eric 1901-1969 [lyricist, librettist]
Martin, Earl *Source(s):* CCE58-59
Marvell, Holt *Source(s):* CART; EPMU; GAN2; GANB; LCAR; PMUS

Mascolino, Dolores (Abigail) 1916-1983 [lyricist]
Haskin, Abby *Source(s):* ASCP; CCE63

Mašek, Karel 1867-1922 [librettist]
Presto, Fa *Source(s):* PIPE

Masgani, Pietro 1863-1945 [composer]
Sarcanti, Pigmeo *Source(s):* http://www.operaitaliana.com/autori/biografia.asp?ID=20 (17 May 2005)

Masikini, Abeti 1951-1994 [singer, songwriter]
Abeti *Source(s):* GROL

Mason, Gladys Amy 1899- [teacher, composer]
Kendal, Sydney *Source(s):* BUL1; BUL2; COHN; HEIN; HIXN

Mason, Lowell 1792-1872 [hymnist]
Note(s): Portraits: CYBH; ETUP 54:2 (Feb. 1936): 107
Father of American Church Music, The *Source(s):* CYBH; PSND

Mason, William 1724 (or 25)-1797 [cleric, dramatist, hymnist, musician]
Gentleman of Cambridge, A *Source(s):* CART
MacGreggor Arthur, of Knightsbridge Esq. *Source(s):* CART
MacGreggor, Malcolm *Source(s):* CART; CYBH

Massara, Giuseppe Previde 1931- [composer]
Massara, Pino *Source(s):* CCE63-64; GOTH

Massaro, Salvatore 1902-1933 [guitarist, songwriter, bandleader]
Dunn, Blind Eddie *Source(s):* JAMU
Dunn, Blind Willie *Source(s):* GROL; LCAR; PSND; SUTT
Lang, Ed(die) *Source(s):* ASCP; EPMU; GROL; LCAR; PSND

Massé, Felix Marie 1822-1884 [composer]
Massé, Victor *Source(s):* BAKO; BAKR; NGDM; PIPE

Massenet, Jules (Émile Frédéric) 1842-1912 [composer]
Belle-soeur de Bizet, La *Source(s):* GROL
Fille de Gounod, La *Source(s):* GROL
Massenetique Bizet *Source(s):* GROL

Massett, Stephen C. 19th cent. [author, composer]
Pipes, Jeemes (of Pipesville) *Source(s):* PSND

Massey, Lucy Fletcher 19th cent. [hymnist]
Same Compiler, The *Source(s):* PSND

Massucci, Josephine (née Vicari) 1930-2004 [author, lyricist, actor]
Carey, Josie *Source(s):* ASCP (see under: Vicari); CLTP ("Children's Corner")

Mastandrea, Carmine Niccolo 1913-1981 [violinist, conductor, arranger]
Mastren, Carmen *Source(s):* EPMU

Mathei, Nicolas Savini fl. 1401-36 [composer]
Campli, Ricci de Nucella *Source(s):* GROL
Nocella *Source(s):* GROL
Nucella *Source(s):* GROL
Ricci de Nucella Campli *Source(s):* GROL

Mathers, Marshall (Bruce), III 1974- [rapper]
Eminem *Source(s):* CM28; LCAR
Shady, Slim *Source(s):* LCAR

Matheson, Herbert [composer]
Mackenzie, Herbert *Source(s):* BLIC (publication dates 1915-19)

Matheus de Perusio ?-1418 [composer]
Matteo da Perugia *Source(s):* RIEM

Mathews, James Snookie 1919- [composer, author]
November, Johnny *Source(s):* ASCP

Mathews, Max V. 1926- [computer scientist, researcher]
Father of Computer Music, The *Source(s):* http://www.csounds.com/mathews (16 Oct. 2002)

Mathews, W(illiam) S(mythe) B(abcock) 1837-1912 [critic, writer on music]
Note(s): Portraits: ETUP 54:2 (Feb. 1936): 107; ETUP 58:4 (Apr. 1940): 228

Dean of American Music Critics, The *Source(s):* GRAN p. 109
Mathieson, Murray 1911-1975 [songwriter, conductor]
Mathieson, Muir *Source(s):* BBDP
Mathieu, (René) André (Rodolphe) 1929-1968 [pianist, composer]
Quebec Mozart *Source(s):* RFSO
Mathieu, Michel Julien 1740-after 1777 [composer, violinist, writer]
Lépidor *Source(s):* GROL; IBIM; STGR; WORB
Matlick, Jay Jeffries 1941- [lyricist]
Jeffries, Jay *Source(s):* ASCP; CPOL PAu-136-112
Matlock, Julian C(lifton) 1907-1978 [clarinetist, composer, bandleader]
Matlock, Bud *Source(s):* CCE61
Matlock, Matty *Source(s):* AMUS; ASCP; CCE59; JASA p. 312; KINK
Matos Rodríguez, G(h)erardo (Hernáu) 1897-1948 [pianist, composer, journalist]
Becho *Source(s):* TODO
Rodríguez, Becho *Source(s):* TODO
Matousek, Raymond Anthony 1926- [composer, author]
Mathews, Ray *Source(s):* CCE47; ASCP
Matsumoto, Masao 1915- [composer]
Matsumoto, Kazuyosi *Source(s):* GREN
Matteo, Gianni [librettist]
Teomagnini, Ignatio *Source(s):* ALMC
Mattes, Wilhelm [or Willy] 1916-2002 [composer, conductor]
Wildman, Charles *Source(s):* CCE51-52; CCE60-61; KOMP; KOMS; PFSA; PIPE
Wilström, Kalle *Source(s):* CCE50; CCE55
Mattheson, Johann 1681-1764 [composer; music critic, singer, theorist]
Aristoxenus, (der juengere) *Source(s):* CPMU; PIPE
Mattheus, Bernd 1953- [author, translator]
Hühnermann, Eike *Source(s):* PIPE
Kapralik, Elena *Source(s):* PIPE
Loechler, Franz *Source(s):* PIPE
Matthews, Ann c. 1920- [singer, broadcaster, songwriter]
Jones, Ann *Source(s):* ENCM; LCAR
Kate Smith of the West *Source(s):* ENCM
Matthews, C(harles) G. [songwriter]
Hews, Lee *Source(s):* CCE55 Eunp
Matthews, Red (Chuck) *Source(s):* CCE60-61; CCE64; PMUS
Matthews, Denise [singer, lyricist]
Vanity *Source(s):* AMUS; EPMU; LCAR
Matthews, Harry Alexander 1879-1973 [composer]
Note(s): Portrait: ETUP 54:2 (Feb. 1936): 107
Nomabama, Adam *Source(s):* TPRF
Note(s): Jt. pseud: Edwin Shippen Barnes, Thomas Tertius Noble & Johann Sebastian Matthews.
Matthews, John Henry 1859-1953 [priest, composer]
Hugely, J. de *Source(s):* HUEV
Matthews, John Sebastian 1870-1934 [composer]
Note(s): Portrait: ETUP 54:2 (Feb. 1936): 107
Nomabama, Adam *Source(s):* TPRF
Note(s): Jt. pseud: Edwin Shippen Barnes, Thomas Tertius Noble & Harry Alexander Matthews.
Matyszkowicz, Adam 1940- [pianist, composer]
Makowicz, Adam *Source(s):* LCAR; PEN2
Mauduit, Johannes 1557-1627 [composer]
Father of Music *Source(s):* GROL
Note(s): See also William Byrd & Giovanni Pierluigi da Palestrina.
Maughn, Don(ald) 1943- [singer, songwriter]
Fardon, Don *Source(s):* AMUS; EPMU; PSND
Maule, Leroy Ernest 1904- [composer, author, teacher]
Maule, Abe *Source(s):* ASCP
Mauriat, Paul 1925- [conductor, composer, arranger]
Roma, Del *Source(s):* BBDP
Maury, (Henry) Lowndes 1911-1975 [composer]
Maury, Lou *Source(s):* CCE55; LCAR; PSND
Mautner, Jerome (Nathan) 1913- [composer, pianist, singer]
Blake, Don *Source(s):* CC53 Eunp
Marlowe, Jerry *Source(s):* ASCC; CCE47 Eunp
Maxwell, Eddie 1912-1999 [author, songwriter, actor]
Cherkose, Eddie *Source(s):* ASCP; CCE66; CCE68
Edwards, Steven *Source(s):* CCE49
Maxwell, Francis (Kelly) 1729-1782 [writer on music]
Maxwell, John *Source(s):* GRV3; IBIM; WORB
May, Ralph 1944- [guitarist, singer, songwriter]
McTell, Ralph *Source(s):* CASS; HARD; HARR; LCAR; PEN2; PFSA
May, Robert Arden 1948- [composer, author]
January, Herb *Source(s):* ASCP
Mayall, John 1933 (or 34)- [singer, instrumentalist, songwriter]
Father of British Blues, The *Source(s):* EPMU; HARS; SHAD
Note(s): See also Alexis (Andrew Nicholas) Korner.
Grandfather of British Rock, The *Source(s):* PSND; SHAD
Maybrick, Michael 1844-1913 [composer, singer, organist]
Note(s): Portrait: ETUP 50:2 (Feb. 1932): 84
Adams, Stephen *Source(s):* CPMU; HARR; KILG; LCAR; MACM; REHG; YORM

Mayer, Anne (Elinor) Wolbrette 1913- [composer]
Brett, Anne *Source(s):* CCE46 Eunp; STRN
Mayer, Brüder Hans 1886-1958 [composer, pianist]
May, Brüder *Source(s):* OMUO
Mayer, Jakab Gyula 1858-1925 [conductor, composer]
Major, (Jakab) Gyula *Source(s):* BAKR; BAKT (see under: Major, Ervin)
Mayer, Johann(es) (?Adolf) 1886 (or 91)-1959 [composer, songwriter]
Adams, Mac *Source(s):* CCE40 #20802 Efor63042 ("King Canute")
MacAyn *Source(s):* CCE33 Efor29004
May, Hans *Source(s):* GAN1; GAN2; GLAM; MACM; RIES
Percy *Source(s):* CCE30 Efor9427 ("Uber'n Sonntag, Lieber Schatz")
Mayer, Werner 1901-1983 [composer]
Egk, Werner *Source(s):* BAKR; PIPE; SPIE
Mayerl, William [or Billy] (Joseph) 1902-1959 [pianist, composer]
Note(s): Portrait: JASN
Darr, Robert *Source(s):* CCE50; CPOL RE-11-469
Windeatt, George *Source(s):* CCE66
Mayhew, Wendell [singer, arranger]
Mayhew, Gus *Source(s):* PSNN
Mayr, Johann Simon 1763-1845 [composer]
Father of Italian Opera, The *Source(s):* http://www.guildmusic.com/catalog/gui7168z.htm (16 Oct. 2002)
Mayrhofer, Frieder 1940- [author, editor, composer]
Palmström, Jo *Source(s):* KOBW
Mayzel', Boris Sergeyevich 1907-1986 [composer]
Ksentitsky, Boris *Source(s):* GROL
Mazaurek, Georg fl. c.1847 [composer]
Macourek, Georg *Source(s):* STGR
Mazlen, Henry G(ershwin) 1912-1983 [composer, author, publisher]
Gershwin, Henry *Source(s):* ASCP; CCE60-62
Lewisohn, Arthur *Source(s):* ASCP
Mbarga, Nicholas 1950-1997 [singer, composer]
Mbarga, Prince Nico *Source(s):* AMUS; PEN2
Mboyo, M'bilia 1959- [singer, composer]
Bel, M'bilia *Source(s):* AMUS; PEN2
Mc see also *Mac*
McAlpin, Vernice Johnson 1918-1980 [songwriter]
McAlpin, Vic *Source(s):* NASF
McAnally, Lyman, Jr. 1957 (or 59)- [singer, songwriter, producer]
McAnally, Mac *Source(s):* CCME; EPMU; LCAR; MCCL; PEN2
McAuliffe, Harry C(larence) 1903 (or 04)-1966 [singer, songwriter]
Big Slim (The Lone(some) Cowboy) *Source(s):* CCE66; EPMU; LCAR; MCCL
Lone Cowboy *Source(s):* LCAR
McAuliffe, Big Slim *Source(s):* CCE39 #13822 Eunp19234
Slim *Source(s):* LCAR
Note(s): Also used by Norman G. Green.
McBeth, W(illiam) Francis 1933- [composer]
Manchester, William F. *Source(s):* http://bandchat.org/archives/jun_24dec4%5E1998/0043.html (31 Jan. 2005)
McBrien, Roger Ralph 1943- [composer, singer]
McBrien, Rod *Source(s):* ASCP; CPOL RE-693-236
McCain, Jerry 1930- [singer, instrumentalist, songwriter]
McCain, Boogie *Source(s):* AMUS; HARS
McCall, William 1812-1888 [hymnist, translator]
Tait, Gilbert *Source(s):* JULN (Appendix.)
McCallum, Colin Whitton 1852-1945 [entertainer, songwriter]
Coborn, Charles [or Charlie] *Source(s):* CPMU; PSND
Comic of the Day, The *Source(s):* PSND
Father of the Profession *Source(s):* PSND
McCarthy, Charles J. 1903-1960 [composer, author, pianist]
McCarthy, Pat *Source(s):* ASCP
McCarthy, Herbert 1872-1947 [comedian, dramatist, lyricist]
Darnley, J. Herbert *Source(s):* KILG
Dearnley, Herbert *Source(s):* MUWB
McCartney, (James) Paul 1942- [lyricist, guitarist, singer]
Beatles, The *Source(s):* http://www.beatlesstory.com (4 May 2005)
Note(s): With: George Harrison, John (Winston) Lennon & Richard Starkey.
Fireman, (The) *Source(s):* LCAR
Martin, Billy *Source(s):* BEAT
Ramon, Paul *Source(s):* BEAT; PSND; WARN
Thrillington, Percy ("Thrills") *Source(s):* BEAT
Twin Freaks *Source(s):* http://excite.contactmusic.com (8 July 2005)
Vermouth, Apollo C. *Source(s):* BEAT; PSND; WARN
Webb, Bernard *Source(s):* AMIR; PSND; WARN
McCartney, Peter Michael 1944- [songwriter, author, photographer]
McGear, Mike *Source(s):* EPMU; PSND
McClain, Charlotte Denise 1956- [singer, songwriter]
McClain, Charly *Source(s):* AMUS; MCCL
McClaskey, Harry Haley 1882-1941 [singer, lyricist, music publisher]
Note(s): Portrait: GRAK; VGRC
Alexander, Alfred *Source(s):* GRAK

Barr, Harry *Source(s):* GRAK
Burr, Henry *Source(s):* GRAK; LCAR; VGRC
Forbes, Lou *Source(s):* http://www.vghf.com/Inductees/peerless_quartet.htm (28 May 2005)
Gillette, Henry *Source(s):* GRAK
Gillette, Irving *Source(s):* GRAK
Haley, Harry *Source(s):* GRAK
King, Al *Source(s):* GRAK
Note(s): Also used by Alvin K. Smith. Do not confuse with singer/guitarist Albert King [i.e., Albert Nelson (1923-1992)]
Knapp, Frank *Source(s):* GARK
McClaskey, Shamus *Source(s):* GRAK
Rice, Robert *Source(s):* GRAK

McClean, Walter Arthur 1852-1921 [journalist, playwright, librettist]
Potter, Paul M(eredith) *Source(s):* GAN1; GAN2

McClintic, Lambert Gerhardt, Jr. 1946- [composer, author, singer]
McClintic, Gar(r)y *Source(s):* ASCP; CPOL PAu-171-830

McClintock, Harry (K(irby)) 1882-1957 [singer, songwriter]
Haywire Mac *Source(s):* AMUS; CCME; LCAR; MCCL; PSND; STUW
Lazy Larry *Source(s):* VDPS
Note(s): Also possible pseud. of Vernon Dalhart [i.e., M(arion) T(ry) Slaughter] & Carson J(ay) Robison.
Mac *Source(s):* AMUS; CCE29 E2929; CCE60-61; SUTT
McClintock, Mac *Source(s):* CCME; MCCL; STUW
Radio Mac *Source(s):* AMUS; CCME; SUTT

McClinton, Delbert 1940- [singer, instrumentalist, songwriter]
King of the White Texas Bluesmen *Source(s):* CM14; STAC

McClinton, O(bie) B(urnett) 1940-1987 [singer, songwriter]
Chocolate Cowboy, The *Source(s):* MCCL; PEN2

McClymont, Jepther 1974- [singer, songwriter]
Luciano *Source(s):* EPMU; LCAR
Stepper, John *Source(s):* LCAR

McCollin, Frances 1892-1960 [organist, pianist, composer, conductor]
Note(s): Portraits: COHN; ETUP 54:3 (Mar. 1936): 192
Alfred *Source(s):* COHN; HEIN; HIXN
Atticus *Source(s):* COHN; HEIN; HIXN
Awbury *Source(s):* COHN; HEIN; HIXN
Canonicus *Source(s):* COHN; HEIN; HIXN
Garrett *Source(s):* COHN; HEIN; HIXN
Karlton *Source(s):* COHN; HEIN; HIXN
Mayfair *Source(s):* COHN; HEIN; HIXN
Pastor *Source(s):* COHN; HEIN; HIXN
Pilgrim *Source(s):* COHN; HEIN; HIXN
Note(s): See also Phil(ip) Green.
Selin *Source(s):* COHN; HEIN; HIXN
Wendel *Source(s):* COHN; HEIN; HIXN
Wheelwright *Source(s):* COHN; HEIN;HIXN

McCollum, Robert Lee 1909-1967 [singer, guitarist, songwriter]
McCoy, Robert Lee *Source(s):* AMUS; HARS
Nighthawk, Robert *Source(s):* AMUS; HARS
Pettie's Boy *Source(s):* AMUS; HARS
Ramblin' Bob *Source(s):* AMUS; HARS

McConathy, Osbourne 1875-1947 [composer]
Note(s): Portraits: ETUP 54:3 (Mar. 1936): 182; Birge, Edward Bailey. *History of Public School Music in the United States.*
Aubert, Celia *Source(s):* CCE34 E42999; CCE61
Boykin, Edward C. *Source(s):* http://www.kingkong.demon.co/uk/ccer/pseuds.htm (9 Jan. 2005)

McCord, William (Patrick, Jr.) 1944- [singer, songwriter]
Vera, Billy *Source(s):* AMUS; ASCP; CCE62; DIMA; EPMU

McCormick, Peter Dodds 1834-1916 [composer]
Amicus *Source(s):* CCE43 #43114 Efor68780; GREN; NOMG
Note(s): See also Blanche Gagnon.

McCosh, Dudley H(untington) 1881-1929 [composer]
Huntington, Dudley *Source(s):* REHG
Leighton, M. *Source(s):* REHG
Raymond, Richard *Source(s):* REHG

McCoy, Joe 1905-1950 [guitarist, singer, songwriter]
Big Joe *Source(s):* LCAR
Georgia Pine Boy *Source(s):* HARS; LCAR
Hallelujah Joe *Source(s):* HARS; LCAR
Hamfoot Ham *Source(s):* HARS; LCAR
Kansas Joe *Source(s):* HARS; LCAR
McCoy, Big Joe *Source(s):* HARS
McCoy, Wilber [or Wilbur] *Source(s):* LCAR
Note(s): Wilber [or Wilbur] may have been McCoy's original given name? (LCAR, see note)
Mississippi Mudder *Source(s):* HARS; LCAR
Note(s): Also used by Charles McCoy (1909-1950).
Mud Dauber Joe *Source(s):* HARS; LCAR
Wilber, Bill *Source(s):* HARS
Williams, Joe *Source(s):* LCAR
Note(s): Do not confuse with Joe Williams (1918-).

McCoy, Paul Bunyan 1930- [composer, author]
McCoy, Bullfighter *Source(s):* ASCP

McCoy, Robert Jesse 1910- [singer, pianist, songwriter]
McCoy, Cyclone *Source(s):* HARS
McCoy, Robert Edward *Source(s):* HARS

McCray, Don [songwriter]
Bandler, George *Source(s):* CCE41 #32549 E95856; CCE68 R436298
Note(s): Jt. pseud.: Robert (B.) Sour.
Ingersoll, Byron M. *Source(s):* CCE41 #5570 Eunp241929; CCE68 R426470
Note(s): Jt. pseud.: Ernest Gold [i.e., Ernest (Siegmund) Goldner], Alex(ander) Kramer, Hy(man) Zaret, Robert (B.) Sour & Zoe Voeth [i.e., Parenteau]
Roberts, Don *Source(s):* CCE40 #21606 E85787; CCE67
Note(s): Jt. pseud.: Robert (B.) Sour.
McCreery, Walker William, 3rd 1921- [composer, author]
McCreery, Bud *Source(s):* ASCP; BBDP; CCE43 #21757 Eunp339428; PSND
McCrohan, Dennis Eugene 1943- [singer, songwriter, guitarist]
Bonfire, Mars *Source(s):* CPOL PA-40-239; NOMG
DelFlamingo, Rolando *Source(s):* CPOL PA-42-723
Edmonton, (Dennis) *Source(s):* CCE65-67; CPOL RE-605-427; CPOL RE-605-433
McCurry, Clarence Earl 1895- [singer, guitarist, songwriter]
Ashley, Thomas Clarence *Source(s):* PSND
McCutchan, Robert G(uy) 1877-1958 [composer, hymnologist]
Porter, John *Source(s):* CCE61-62; CYBH; ROGG
McCutcheon, John 1952- [multi-string instrumentalist, composer]
Virginia's Rustic Renaissance Man *Source(s):* MUHF
McCutcheon, Minnie L(ouise) Perkins 1941- [composer, singer, actress]
Grant, Micki *Source(s):* CCE60; CLAG; DWCO; LCAR
McDaniel, Hattie 1895-1952 [singer, actress, songwriter]
Beulah *Source(s):* PSND
Colored Sophie Tucker, The *Source(s):* HARS
Female Bert Williams, The *Source(s):* HARS
Hi-Hat Hattie *Source(s):* HARS
McDaniel, Luke 1927-1992 [songwriter]
Daniels, Jeff *Source(s):* ROCK
Lee, Earl *Source(s):* ROCK
McDonald, Barbara 1906-1989 [singer, songwriter]
Miki *Source(s):* MCCL
McDonald, Enos (William) 1915-1968 [singer, songwriter, guitarist]
McDonald, Skeets *Source(s):* AMUS; CCE51; EPMU; MCCL; PSND
McDonald, Ian Matthews 1946- [singer, songwriter]
Matthews, Iain *Source(s):* AMUS; EPMU; PSND
McDonnell, James 1961- [songwriter]
Phantom, Slim Jim *Source(s):* PMUS-85
McDow, William Dayton 1930- [composer, singer]
McDow, Peevy *Source(s):* ASCP
McDuffy, Eugene 1926- [organist, composer, bandleader]
McDuff, (Brother) Jack *Source(s):* AMUS; PEN2; PSND
McElheney, Jane 1834-1874 [writer on music]
Note(s): Do not confuse with conceptual artist Jane McElheney [i.e., Theresa Pendelbury] (LCAR)
Alastor *Source(s):* STAR p. 252
Clare, Ada *Source(s):* LCAR; STAR p. 252
Queen of Bohemia *Source(s):* STAR p. 246
McEnery, David [or Dave] L(argus) 1914-2002 [songwriter, singer]
Red River Dave *Source(s):* ASCP; CCE66; EPMU; LCAR; MCCL
Red Ryders *Source(s):* CCE62
McEnery, Velma Lee 1929- [composer, author, singer]
Reynolds, Lee *Source(s):* ASCP
McEntire, Reba 1954 (or 55)- [singer, songwriter, actress]
Queen of Country *Source(s):* FLIN
McEuen, John 1945- [strings, singer, composer]
String Wizard, The *Source(s):* AMUS
McEwen, (Sir) John Blackwood 1868-1948 [composer, teacher]
Note(s): Portrait: ETUP 54:3 (Mar. 1936): 182
Moore, Park *Source(s):* CCE38 R65352
Park, Moore *Source(s):* CPMU
McGeachy, Iain 1948- [singer, songwriter]
Martyn, John *Source(s):* EPMU
McGhee, Granville H. 1918-1961 [singer, guitarist, songwriter]
McGhee, Globetrotter *Source(s):* HARS; LCAR
McGhee, Stick(s) *Source(s):* CCE55; HARS; JASZ p. 322; LCAR
McGhee, Walter Brown 1915-1996 [singer, guitarist, songwriter]
Blind Boy Fuller #2 *Source(s):* MUHF
Brother George *Source(s):* HARS
Note(s): See also Fulton Allen (see LCAR) & George Liberace.
Collins, Big Tom *Source(s):* HARS; OB96
Note(s): Also used by William Thomas Dupree.
Fuller, Blind Boy (No. 2) *Source(s):* AMUS; EPMU; HARS
Johnson, Henry *Source(s):* HARS
Note(s): Also used by John (Henry) Hammond, Jr.
McGhee, Brownie *Source(s):* AMUS; CCE60; EPMU; HARS; LCAR; MUHF
Spider Sam *Source(s):* HARS; OB96
Tennessee Gabriel *Source(s):* HARS
Williams, Blind Boy *Source(s):* HARS; OB96

McGilvra, Douglas 1945- [composer]
Oaks, Brian *Source(s):* GOTH
McGinn, Matt 1928-1977 [singer, composer]
Scottish King of Folk, The *Source(s):* DRSC
McGonigal, Alexander Andrew 1915-1999 [composer, author]
Derr, Zan *Source(s):* ASCP; CPOL PAu-769-930
McGovern, James 1862-1943 [actor, author]
Powers, James [or Jimmy] T. *Source(s):* GAN2
McGowan, John W. 1894-1977 [actor, librettist]
McGowan, Jack *Source(s):* GAN2
McGowen, Frank(lin) S(immons) [composer, author, teacher]
Carroll, Richard *Source(s):* ASCP
McGranahan, James 1840-1907 [hymnist]
Note(s): Portraits: CYBH; HALL
G. M. J. *Source(s):* CYBH; DIEH; ROGA
Sea, M. A. *Source(s):* CCE27 R40250
McGrath, (David) Fulton 1907-1958 [composer, author, pianist]
McGrath, Fidgey *Source(s):* ASCP
McGregor, Dion 1922- [lyricist, actor]
Bradford, David *Source(s):* http://www.aspma.com/dion/chapters/6.htm (3 Mar. 2004)
McGregor, Edward 1873-1917 [singer, writer]
Note(s): Possible original name; given in *New York Times* obituary (MUHF).
Happy Tramp, The *Source(s):* MUHF
Wills, Louis Magrath *Source(s):* MUHF
Wills, Nat M. *Source(s):* MUHF
McGuffie, William [or Bill] 1927- [composer]
Maertek, Raphael *Source(s):* CCE52; CCE55
Miguel, Guido *Source(s):* CCE51-52; CPOL RE-46-898
Note(s): Jt. pseud.: Harold (Cornelius) Fields, Joseph (Dominic) Roncoroni & H(oward) E(llington) Barnes.
McGuinn, James [or Jim] (Joseph) 1942- [guitarist, singer, songwriter]
McGuinn, Roger *Source(s):* CCE67; DIMA; EPMU; HARR; LCAR
McHugh, James [or Jimmy] (F(rancis)) 1894 (or 95)-1969 [songwriter, pianist, music publisher]
Francis, James *Source(s):* CCE55
Herring, Ura *Source(s):* CCE51 R80940
Note(s): "Hey! You Want Any Codfish? We Only Have Mack'rel Today"
McIntire, Dennis (Keith) 1944- [music historian, lexicographer]
Dennisimo *Source(s):* BAKT
McIntosh, Lonnie 1941- [guitarist, singer, songwriter]
Mack, Lonnie *Source(s):* AMUS; CCE63-64; CM37; NOMG
McIntosh, Rigdon (McCoy) 1836-1899 [composer, publisher]
LaRoche, Emilius *Source(s):* CLAB; CYBH
McIntosh, Winston (Hubert) 1944-1987 [singer, composer]
Tosh, Peter *Source(s):* AMUS
McIntyre, Natalie 1970- [songwriter, performer]
Gray, Macy *Source(s):* AMIR; AMUS; PMUS-00
McKagan, Michael 1964- [bassist, songwriter]
McKagan, Duff *Source(s):* EPMU; LCAR
McKalip, M(ansell) B(rown) 1915- [composer]
McKay, Todd *Source(s):* ASCP; CCE39 #31120 Eunp 404920; CCE55-57; CCE60
McKelvy, James (M(illigan)) 1917-2003 [choral director, music publisher]
Foster, Mark *Source(s):* RILM 82094949-ap
Hopkins, Paul *Source(s):* CCE62 E161629
Johnson, Scott *Source(s):* CCE64 E195478; CPOL PA-197-106
Kiser, Max *Source(s):* CCE62; CCE63 E180694
Stroud, Ray *Source(s):* CCE62; CCE64
Weaver, Edward *Source(s):* CCE62-64; CPOL PA-187-880
McKenzie, Roger [songwriter]
Wildchild *Source(s):* LCAR; SONG
Note(s): Do not confuse with The Wild Child [i.e., Roger Dean Miller]
McKie, Harry 1854-1901 [actor, composer]
Monkhouse, Harry *Source(s):* GAN1; GAN2
McKinley, Mabel 1879-1937 [songwriter]
Baer, (Mrs.) Mabel *Source(s):* CCE32 R20484; SPTH
Grey, Vivian *Source(s):* CCE32 R20484; CPMU; KILG
Note(s): For a list of works, see CPMU. In SPTH p. 336: Grey's "Anona" was written by Robert A. King [i.e., Keiser]. See NOTES: Keiser/King, Robert (A(dolph)), "Grey, Vivian."
McLaren, Malcolm 1946- [singer, songwriter, producer]
P. T. Barnum of Modern Rock, The *Source(s):* CM23
McLaughlin, John 1942- [composer]
Hall, A(lbert) *Source(s):* BLIC
Mahavishnu *Source(s):* LCAR
McLean, Alexandra Elene 1947 (or 48)-1978 [singer, songwriter]
Denny, Sandy *Source(s):* EPMU; HARR; PEN2
McLean, Don 1945- [singer, songwriter, guitarist, poet]
Hudson River Troubadour *Source(s):* MCCL
McLean, John Lenwood, (Jr.) 1932- [saxophonist, composer]
Ahmed, Omar *Source(s):* GROL; LCAR
Kareem, Abdul *Source(s):* GROL; LCAR
McLean, Jackie *Source(s):* PEN2
McLellan, Charles Morton Stewart 1865-1916 [author, librettist]
Morton, Hugh *Source(s):* GAN1; GAN2; KILG; LCAR; MARC p. 200; MELL; SPTH p. 380

McLeod, James (P.) 1912- [composer, arranger]
McLeod, Red *Source(s):* ASCP; CCE54; CCE61; LCAR; STC1
Peters, Jacob *Source(s):* CCE61
McLeod, Odell 1916-2003 [singer, songwriter]
Odell, Mac *Source(s):* MCCL; MUWB
Old Country Boy *Source(s):* MUWB
McLoughlin, Mark 1966- [singer, songwriter]
Pellow, Marti *Source(s):* NOMG
McMahon, Andrew 1926- [singer, guitarist, songwriter]
Blueblood *Source(s):* CCE73; LCAR
McMahon, Blueblood *Source(s):* HARS
McManus, Declan Patrick (Aloysius) 1954 (or 55)- [rock singer, songwriter]
Costello, D. P. *Source(s):* AMUS
Costello, Elvis (Patrick) *Source(s):* AMUS; BAKR; CASS; CM12; EPMU; HARR; PEN2; WARN
Coward Brothers *Source(s):* AMUS; LCAR
Note(s): Jt. pseud.: T Bone [i.e., Joseph Henry] Burnett.
Imposter, The *Source(s):* WARN
Napoleon Dynamite *Source(s):* WARN
McMillan, Alec ?-1919 [jurist, writer, composer]
Buchanan, Alstair *Source(s):* CART
McNair, T. [songwriter]
Monch, Pharoahe *Source(s):* PMUS-00
McNally, Leonard 1752-1820 [barrister, dramatist, government agent]
Barrister of the Inner Temple *Source(s):* CART
MacHumbug, Leonard *Source(s):* CART
Plunder *Source(s):* CART
McNamara, Charles F. [songwriter]
Weil, Milton *Source(s):* MART p. 140 ("Just a Dream of You, Dear")
Note(s): Possible pseud.
McNaught, W(illiam) G. 1849-1918 [arranger]
Note(s): Portrait: ETUP 54:3 (Mar. 1936): 182
McN., W. G. *Source(s):* CPMU
McNeil, James [composer]
Whistler, Cadet *Source(s):* DICH ("Westpoint" (1852))
McNeil, Stephen 1907-1980 [composer, author, teacher]
Spaulding, Jack *Source(s):* ASCP; CCE56 Eunp
Stecman, Phil *Source(s):* ASCP
McNeish, Peter 1955- [singer, songwriter]
Shelley, Pete *Source(s):* EPMU; HARR
McNulty, Frank Fremont 1923- [composer, author, producer]
Curtis, Bob *Source(s):* CCE56 Eunp
Freeman, Scott *Source(s):* ASCP; CCE58
Fremont, Frank *Source(s):* CCE56; CCE58
McPhail, Lindsey 1895-1965 [composer, pianist]
Hubert, Harry *Source(s):* JASG
McPhee, Colin (Carhart) 1900-1964 [composer, pianist, ethnomusicologist]
Mercure *Source(s):* Oja, Carol J. *Colin McPhee; Composer in Two Worlds*. Washington D.C.: Smithsonian Institution Press, 1990, 166. (ports.)
McPherson, Richard C(ecil) 1883-1944 [composer]
Note(s): Portraits: JASN; JASZ
Mack, Cecil *Source(s):* JASN; JASZ; KINK; LCAR; SOTH; STUW
McPherson, Warner (Hensley) 1938- [singer, songwriter]
Mack, Warner *Source(s):* AMUS; CCME; ENCM; EPMU; MCCL; PEN2
McShann, James Columbus 1909- [pianist, bandleader, songwriter]
McShann, Hootie *Source(s):* KINK; LCAR
McShann, Jay *Source(s):* LCAR; PEN2
McTell, Willie Samuel 1901-1959 [singer, instrumentalist, songwriter]
Note(s): See below, note under: McTier, Eddie.
Barrelhouse Sammy *Source(s):* CM17; HARS; LCAR
Blind Doogie *Source(s):* CM17; HARS; LCAR
Blind Sammy [or Sammie] *Source(s):* ALMN; CM17; EPMU; HARS; LCAR; SUTT
Blind Willie *Source(s):* CM17; HARS; LCAR
Georgia Bill *Source(s):* ALMN; CM17; EPMU; HARS; LCAR; SUTT
Glaze, Red Hot Willie *Source(s):* CM17; HARS; LCAR
Hot Shot Willie *Source(s):* CM17; HARS; LCAR
McTell, Blind Willie *Source(s):* ALMN; CM17; HARS; LCAR
McTier, Eddie *Source(s):* HARS; LCAR
Note(s): Original name? On death records & gravestone.
Pig 'n' Whistle Red *Source(s):* CM17; HARS; LCAR
Red Hot Willie *Source(s):* CM17; HARS; LCAR
Meano, Cesare 1899-1957 [librettist]
Senea, E. Marco *Source(s):* LCPC letter cited (11 July 1936); NGDM (see under: Rocca, L.)
Meares, Richard fl. c.1715 [composer]
Philharmonica, (Mrs.) *Source(s):* DWCO
Mebarak (R(ipoll)), Shakira Isabel 1977- [singer, songwriter]
Latin Madonna *Source(s):* *Today Show.* (28 Nov. 2001)
Shakira *Source(s):* AMUS; HWOM; LCAR
Medley, Samuel 1738-1799 [hymnist]
Note(s): Portrait: CYBH
S. M. *Source(s):* JULN
Medoff, Samuel 1912-1991 [songwriter]
Manning, Dick *Source(s):* EPMU; ROOM
Manning, Samuel *Source(s):* EPMU
Medtner, Nikolai 1879 (or 80)-1951 [composer]
Note(s): Portrait: ETUP 54:3 (Mar. 1936): 182
Russian Brahms, The *Source(s):* PSND

Note(s): See also Paul [i.e., Pual] (Fedorovich) Juon & Sergey (Ivanovich) Taneev.
Meehan, Daniel 1942- [drummer, songwriter]
Meehan, Tony *Source(s):* NOMG
Meehan, Martha 1923- [composer, author, pianist]
Carol, Marty *Source(s):* ASCP; CPOL PAu-271-993
Carolin, Martha *Source(s):* ASCP
Meek, Robert (George) 1929-1967 [producer, songwriter]
Baker, Robert *Source(s):* CPOL RE-466-471
Crosley, Robert *Source(s):* CPOL RE-505-097
Duke, Robert *Source(s):* CPOL RE-505-097 & RE-286-999
Jacobs, Peter *Source(s):* CCE (date not recorded)
Meek, Joe *Source(s):* CPOL RE-553-958; PEN2
Meeropol, Abel 1903-1986 [composer, lyricist, educator]
Allan, Lewis *Source(s):* ASCP; CCE40 #4407 E82732; CLTP (Tennessee Ernie Ford Show); LCAR
Meester, Louis de 1904-1987 [composer]
Master, Louis *Source(s):* http://www.cebedem.be/composers/de_meester_louis/en.html (11 May 2005)
Megerle, Julius 1837-1890 [librettist]
Feld, Julius *Source(s):* STGR; WORB
Megson, Neil (Andrew) 1950- [singer, songwriter]
Orridge, Genesis *Source(s):* WARN
P-Orridge, Genesis *Source(s):* LCAR; PSND
Mehlich, Ernst 1888-1977 [conductor]
Gagnier, Paul *Source(s):* PIPE; WORB
Mehring, Walter 1896-1981 [author]
Beppo *Source(s):* CCE60
Glossator *Source(s):* PIPE
Méhul, Etienne Nicolas 1763-1817 [composer]
Fiorillo *Source(s):* PIPE
N*** *Source(s):* CPMU ("Ce front si pur aù regne la décence")
Note(s): Jt. pseud.: François Adrien Boildieu, Rodolphe Kreutzer & Nicolas Isouard.
Mei, Girolamo 1519-1594 [humanist, writer on music]
Peretola, Decimo Corinella da *Source(s):* GROL
Meier, Klaus 1932- [composer]
Cornell, Klaus *Source(s):* BUL2; BUL3; WIEC
Meier-Böhme, Alfons 1897-1969 [composer]
Monder, Alf *Source(s):* SUPN
Meilhac, Henri 1831-1897 [playwright, librettist]
Baskoff, Ivan *Source(s):* PIPE; PSND
Mel and Hal *Source(s):* GAN2
Note(s): Jt. nickname: Ludovic Halévy.
Talin *Source(s):* LCAR
Meinecke, Christopher 1782-1850 [composer, organist]
Meinecke, Charles *Source(s):* METC
Meister, Karl (August) 1903-1986 [composer]
Axolot(l) *Source(s):* BUL3; GREN
Meister, Titus *Source(s):* KOMS
Meister, Theo(dore) (H(enry)) 1940- [composer, author, recording producer]
Daryl(l), Ted *Source(s):* ASCP; CCE64-66; CCE72-75
Mejia, Gerardo, (III) 1965- [rapper, songwriter]
Gerardo *Source(s):* EPMU; LCAR; PMUS-91
Mejía López, Luis Enrique [singer, songwriter]
Luis Enrique *Source(s):* HWOM
Note(s): Do not confuse with Luis Enrique [i.e., Luis Enríquez Bacalov]
Principe de la salsa, El *Source(s):* HWOM
Melaro, H(orton) J(erome) M(artin) 1928- [composer, author, producer, lawyer]
Jerome, Horton *Source(s):* CCE68
Melaro, Jerry *Source(s):* ASCP
Melaro, Speed *Source(s):* ASCC
Meliš, Emanuel (Anton) 1831-1916 [writer on music]
Zminský, Emanuel *Source(s):* NGDM; OMUO
Melkikh, Dmitry Mikheyevich 1885-1943 [composer, writer on music]
Iglintsev, Yu *Source(s):* GROL
Mellema, Cornelis Marten 1911-1986 [composer]
Marga, Fred *Source(s):* SUPN
Mellenbruch, Giles Edward 1911- [composer, author, trumpeter]
Giles, Johnny *Source(s):* ASCP; CCE59-60
Mellencamp, John (J.) 1951- [songwriter, performer]
Note(s): Changed given middle name to "Cougar" in 1983 & dropped it in 1989 (LCAR).
Cougar, John(ny) *Source(s):* ASCP; CM02; HARD; LCAR
Little Bastard *Source(s):* http://www.mellencamp.com/albums/cuttinheads/review.html (16 Oct. 2002)
Mellencamp, Cougar *Source(s):* CM02
Mellor(s), John (Graham) 1952 (or 53)-2002 [songwriter, singer]
Strummer, Joe *Source(s):* HARR; LCAR; NOMG; PMUS
Meltzer, Richard Bruce 1945- [author, singer, DJ]
Vom, Mr. *Source(s):* ASCP
Melville, George S. [composer]
Silverstone, Mendel *Source(s):* CPMU
Menard, D(oris) L(eon) 1932- [singer, songwriter]
Cajun Hank Williams *Source(s):* AMUS; MUHF
Williams, Cajun Hank *Source(s):* AMUS; ENCM
Mencher, (T.) Murray 1898 (or 1904)- [composer, pianist]
Murray, Ted *Source(s):* ASCC; CCE42 #44418 E108667; GOTE; VACH
Song Writers on Parade *Source(s):* CCE32 Eunp56182
Note(s): Jt. pseud.: Sidney Clare, Charles Tobias,

Al(bert) Sherman, Al(an) Lewis, Percy Wenrich & Vincent Rose.
Mencken, H(enry) L(ouis) 1880-1956 [reporter, book & music critic]
Note(s): ETUP 54:5 (May 1936): 277. See PSND for additional pseudonyms & sobriquets.
America's First Satirist *Source(s):* GRAN
Maestro of the Bozart *Source(s):* GRAN
Sage of Baltimore *Source(s):* GRAN
Menckin, Thomas 1550-1611 (or 12) [composer]
Mancinus, Thomas *Source(s):* BAKR; LCAR; NGDM; RIEM
Mendelsohn, Oscar (Adolf) 1896-1978 [author, composer]
Milsen, Oscar *Source(s):* BUL1; BUL2; BUL3; PSND
Mendelssohn(-Bartholdy), Felix 1809-1847 [composer]
Meritis, F(elix) *Source(s):* DAVE p. 115; PSND
Mozart of the Nineteenth Century, The *Source(s):* GROL; PSND
Mozart of the Romantic Era *Source(s):* MUWB
Mendes, Sergio 1941- [composer, arranger, pianist, bandleader]
Brazil's Emperor of Easy Listening *Source(s):* BRAZ
Mendizábal, Rosendo (Cayetano) 1868-1913 [composer, pianist]
Rosendo, (A.) Anselmo *Source(s):* TODO; http://www.fnartes.gov.ar/mendiz (16 Oct. 2002)
Mendoza, Lydia 1916- [guitarist, songwriter]
Alondra de la Frontera, La *Source(s):* AMUS; PEN2
Lark of the Border, The *Source(s):* PEN2
Mendoza, Peter Hygham 1902-1968 [songwriter]
Venning, Peter *Source(s):* AMUS; VACH
Menezes, A. Cardosa de 1849-1915 [composer]
Freza, A. *Source(s):* NOTE 57:1 (2000): 79
Ménissier, Constant before 1790-after 1844 [playwright]
Benezech, A. *Source(s):* PIPE
Constant *Source(s):* LCAR; PIPE
Menke, Joe 1925- [composer]
Homsen, Joe *Source(s):* CCE5-59; CCE63-65; KOMP; KOMS
Menotti, Gian Carlo 1911- [composer]
Ghigi, Alearco *Source(s):* CCE59
Note(s): On English translation of "Maria Golovin."
Renaissance Man of the Theater *Source(s):* http://www.schirmer.com/comosers/menotti/essay.html (28 Oct. 2002)
Wizard of the Opera *Source(s):* PSND
Mensah, E(mmanuel) T(ettah) 1919-1996 [singer, composer, trumpeter, bandleader]
Father of Modern Highlife *Source(s):* AMUS
King of Highlife, The *Source(s):* PEN2
Mentner, Karl c.1800-1860 [composer]
Blasius Wind *Source(s):* WIEC
Wind, Blasius *Source(s):* WIEC
Merath, Siegfried 1928- [composer]
Korff, Paul *Source(s):* CCE55; RIES
Tannwald, Peter *Source(s):* RIES
Mercadante, Giuseppe Saverio Raffaele 1795-1870 [composer]
Grand Old Man of Neapolitan Music, The *Source(s):* GROL
Mercadante, Francesco Saverio *Source(s):* GOTH; LCAR
Mercadante, Xavier *Source(s):* LCAR
Mercandetti, P(ietro) 1773-1832 (or 33) [composer]
Generali, Mercandetti *Source(s):* BAKR
Generali, Pietro *Source(s):* BAKR; GOTH; LCAR; MACM; PIPE; WORB
Mercer, John(ny) (H(erndon)) 1909-1976 [lyricist, composer]
Bard from Savannah *Source(s):* http://www.johnnymercer.com/yesterday.htm (16 Oct. 2002)
Mercer, John(ny) (H(erndon)) 1909-1976 [lyricist, composer]
Bard from Savannah *Source(s):* http://www.johnnymercer.com/yesterday.htm (16 Oct. 2002)
Keith, Jack *Source(s):* http://www.johnnymercer.com/have.htm
Mercer, Joe *Source(s):* CPOL RE-286-195
Mercier, Jean *Source(s):* CCE59
Moore, Joe *Source(s):* CCE60; PMUS; http://www.johnnymercer.com/yesterday.htm
Moore, John C., Jr. *Source(s):* CPOL RE-286-172
Mercer, W(illiam) Elmo 1932- [composer, author]
Johnson, Mark *Source(s):* ASCP; CCE67
Meredith, I(saac) H(ickman) 1872-1962 [composer, hymnist, publisher]
Note(s): Portrait: CYBH
Ackley, C(harles) C. *Source(s):* CCE28 R45215; CCE37 R55770
Edwards, Broughton *Source(s):* CCE43 #9781, 12 R116366; CCE52 R97964
Grantley, Arthur *Source(s):* CCE30 E17344; CCE48-49
Kennedy, Bruce *Source(s):* CCE30 E14422
Mergot, Franciscus fl. 1560-76 [singer, composer]
de Novo Portu *Source(s):* GROL
Francisco de Novo Portu *Source(s):* GROL; NGDM
Novo Portu, (Francisco) De *Source(s):* GROL; NGDM
Mérimée, Prosper 1803-1870 [author]
Des Quarante, Un *Source(s):* PSND
Estrange, Joseph l' *Source(s):* LCAR; PIPE; PSND
Gazul, Clara *Source(s):* PIPE; PSND
Maglanowich, Hyacinthe *Source(s):* PSND
Merion, Charles M. ?-1896 [songwriter]
Cassidy, James *Source(s):* KILG
Merkl, Adolf 1876-1918 [librettist, translator, director]
Mérei, Adolf *Source(s):* GAN2

Merlo, Alessandro c.1530-after 1594 [composer, singer, viol player]
Allessandro della Viola *Source(s):* MACM; NGDM
Cesare, Don Giulio *Source(s):* MACM
Romano, Alessandro *Source(s):* MACM; NGDM; RIEM
Viola, Alessandro della *Source(s):* RIEM
Merlotti, Claudio 1533-1604 [organist; composer, publisher]
Claudio da Correggio *Source(s):* GROL; RIEM
Note(s): Called himself.
Corregias, Claudius *Source(s):* MACM; NGDM; WORB
Da Corregio, Claudio *Source(s):* BAKT
Merulo, Claudio *Source(s):* GROL; MACM; NGDM; RIEM; WORB
Merulus, Claudis *Source(s):* GROL
Merrick, Mahlon (Le Grande) 1900-1969 [composer, arranger]
Kosloff, Lou *Source(s):* CLTV
La Grande, Gene *Source(s):* CCE55; CLTP ("Burns and Allen"); CLTV
Note(s): Probably jt. pseud. with his wife, Grace Merrick, who used the stage name "Gene."
Sweeten, Claude *Source(s):* CLTV
Merrick, Marie E. [composer]
Thorn(e), Edgar *Source(s):* COHN; HIXN; MACM
Note(s): "Amourette," "Forgotten Fairy Tale," & "Six Fancies." Also used by Edward McDowell; & Ernst Roth used the pseud.: E. Thorne.
Merrill, Abraham D(own) 1796-1878 [revivalist, composer]
Merrill, Father *Source(s):* METC
Merriweather, Major 1905-1953 [singer, pianist, composer]
Big Maceo *Source(s):* HARS; HERZ; LCAR
Merriweather, Maceo *Source(s):* HARS; LCAR
Merseburger, Carl Wilhelm 1816-1885 [writer on music]
Frank, Paul *Source(s):* LCAR; SEND
Mersenne, Marin 1588-1648 [mathematician, philosopher]
Note(s): Portrait: ETUP 54:3 (Mar. 1936): 182
Sermes, Sieur de *Source(s):* CPMS ("Traite de l'Harmonie Universelle")
Sieur de Sermes *Source(s):* RIEM
Mersey, Robert 1917- [composer]
Ross, Spencer *Source(s):* RFSO
Mertel, Elias c.1561-1626 [composer]
E. M. O. *Source(s):* IBIM
Mertelius, Elias *Source(s):* LCAR
Messina, Antonio 1945- [composer]
Rosaryo *Source(s):* KOMS; PFSA
Messina, Sylvester J. 1917-1982 [composer, author]
Mess, Sylvio J. *Source(s):* CPOL PAu-343-586
Messina, Chico *Source(s):* ASCP
Messina, Sylvio J. *Source(s):* CPOL PAu-343-586
Messner, Georg 1871-1933 [composer]
Erich, Georg *Source(s):* SUPN
Mestépès, Eugène 1820-1875 [playwright]
Gaston *Source(s):* PIPE
Mestrini, Freek 1946- [composer]
Fremes, Marco *Source(s):* SUPN
Metcalf, Leon (Vinnedge) 1899-1993 [composer]
Noel, F. E. *Source(s):* CCE59; REHG; SUPN
Vitelle, Vincent *Source(s):* REHG; SUPN
Vitello, Leo *Source(s):* REHG; SUPN
Métoyen, Jean-Baptiste(-Jacques) 1733-1822 [composer, bassonist, serpent player]
Melophile *Source(s):* GROL
Metzler, Johann Georg 1770-1833 [playwright; geologist]
Giesecke, (Sir) Charles Lewis *Source(s):* LCAR (see note)
Giesecke, Karl [or Carl] Ludwig *Source(s):* GOTH; LCAR; PIPE; WORB
Meuer, Louis F. 1883-1915 [composer]
Muir, Lewis F(rank) *Source(s):* JASN; JAST; REHH
Meves, Augustus [composer]
A. M. *Source(s):* CPMU (publication date 1842)
Mey, Reinhard 1942- [composer]
Mey, Frédéric *Source(s):* PFSA
Yondraschek, Alfons *Source(s):* PFSA
Meybrunn, Franz Josef 1902-1975 [composer]
Vorbach, Klaus *Source(s):* SUPN
Meyer, Dale Arthur 1948-2002 [composer]
Parlando, Rubato *Source(s):* http://batango.com/spotlight/dale_meyer.php (14 Mar. 2005)
Rubato Parlando *Source(s):* http://batango.com/spotlight/dale_meyer.php
Note(s): Also used by Annie Durand.
Meyer, David Harold 1931-1980 [author, lyricist, actor]
Janssen, David *Source(s):* ASCP
Meyer, Ernst Hermann 1905-1988 [composer, musicologist]
Baker, Peter *Source(s):* GROL; LCAR
Meyer, Friedrich 1915-1993 [composer]
Oltmann, Bert *Source(s):* KOMP; PFSA
Meyer, John [songwriter]
Megar, Fay *Source(s):* CCE47 R17365 ("Babetto")
Note(s): Jt. pseud.: Fred(rick W.) Hager [i.e., Frederick Wallace Haga]
Meyer, Leopold von 1816-1883 [pianist, composer]
De Meyer, Leopold *Source(s):* LCAR; STAR
Lion Pianist *Source(s):* STAR
Monster Pianist *Source(s):* STAR
Meyer, (Benjamin) Wilhelm 1831-1898 [pianist, composer]

Rémy, W. A. *Source(s):* BAKO; GROL; MACM; NGDM; PSND; WORB
Meyer, Wolfgang 1929- [composer]
Hansen, Hans *Source(s):* KOMS; PFSA
Wolf, Thomas *Source(s):* KOMS; PFSA
Meyer-Förster, Wilhelm 1862-1934 [author]
Gregorow, Samar *Source(s):* PIPE
Meyer-Kundt, Heinz 1925- [composer]
Glissando *Source(s):* KOMP; PFSA
Meyerowitz, Hans-Hermann 1913-1998 [composer, teacher]
Meyerowitz, Jan *Source(s):* BAKT
Meymott, Frederick William [composer]
Wilhelm, Friedrich *Source(s):* CPMU (publication dates 1846-47)
Mezari, Mad(d)alena c.1540- [composer]
Casulana, (Maddalena) *Source(s):* LCAR; MACM; WORB
M'Glashan, Alexander ?-1797 [violinist, compiler of Scottish airs]
M'Glasan, King *Source(s):* GRV3
Miani, Marco [librettist]
Battochio, Arlequin *Source(s):* ALMC
Vovi, Montebaldo *Source(s):* ALMC
Michael, Marc (Antoine Amédée) 1812-1868 [dramatist]
Marc-Michel *Source(s):* PIPE
Michalski, Karl [or Carl] 1911- [composer]
Carl, Michael *Source(s):* CCE63; CCE66; KOMP; KOMS; PFSA
Michel, (Charles Victor) Arthur 1821-1870 [violinist, dancer, composer]
Saint-Léon, (Charles Victor) Arthur *Source(s):* LCAR; MACM; NGDM; NGDO; PIPE
Michel, Georges Ephraim 1866-1890 [librettist, poet]
Mikhaël, E(phraim) *Source(s):* LCAR; LOWN; WORB
Micheli, Romano c.1575-1659 [composer, critic]
Kesperle, Filippo *Source(s):* GROL (see under: De Grandis, Vincenzo)
Note(s): Possible pseud.
Michels, Wolfgang [singer, guitarist, composer, lyricist]
Percewood, Mike *Source(s):* http://www.wolfgang-michels.de/b/bio-90-e.html (16 Oct. 2002)
Michelson, Lewis [songwriter]
Fish, Ima *Source(s):* CCE51 R80940 ("Hey! You Want Any Codfish? We only have. . .")
Michi, Orazio 1591 (or 95)-1641 [harpist; composer]
Della'Arpa, (Orazio) *Source(s):* BAKR; LCAR; NGDM
Michon, Pierre 1610-1684 (or 85) [writer on music]
Bourdelot, Pierre *Source(s):* NGDM; WORB
Mied(c)ke, Karl August 1804-1880 [conductor, composer, pianist]
Krebs, Karl August *Source(s):* BAKR; MACM; NGDM; OMUO
Mielenz, Hans 1909- [composer]
Rambo, Peter *Source(s):* BUL3; KOMP; KOMS; PFSA; RIES; SUPN
Mielichhofer, Ludwig 1814-1892 [journalist, music critic]
Lattecort, Norbet *Source(s):* OMUO
Migliavacca, Augusto 1838-1901 [composer, violinist]
Cieco di Parma *Source(s):* WORB
Migliavacca, Giovanni Ambrogio [or Giannambrogio] c.1718-1787 [librettist]
Filodosso *Source(s):* NGDO
Mignone, Francisco (Paulo) 1897-1986 [composer, conductor]
Note(s): Portrait: ETUP 54:4 (Apr. 1936): 198
Bororó, Chico *Source(s):* GROL; LCAR; NGDO
Spano, Tito *Source(s):* CCE29 Eunp6336; LCPC letter cited (12 Jan. 1929)
Mihailovitch, Boris 1891-1963 [producer, composer]
Morros, Boris *Source(s):* BBDP; LCAR
Mihalovic, Franz 1907- [composer]
Mirac, Frank *Source(s):* KOMP; PFSA
Mihalovich, Ödön Péter József de 1842-1929 [composer, producer]
Mihalovich, Edmund von *Source(s):* BAKR
Mihevec, Jurij [or Jury] 1805-1882 [composer]
Micheuz, Georg(es) *Source(s):* GOTH; STGR v. 4/pt.1
Mika, Rudolf [or Rolf] 1955- [composer]
Bandini, Arturo *Source(s):* PFSA
Milakowski, Pinchas [writer on music]
Yimuheli, S. *Source(s):* SEND
Milanollo, Maria 1832-1948 [violinist]
Staccato, Mlle. *Source(s):* GROL; MWP3
Milanollo, Theresa (Domenica Maria) 1827-1904 [violinist, composer]
Adagio, Mlle. *Source(s):* GROL; HEIN; MWP3
Parmentier, Mme. *Source(s):* HEIN
Mildbrand, Hans 1896- [composer]
Milton, Percy *Source(s):* CCE68; KOMP
Miles, C(harles) (John) A(ustin) 1868-1946 [composer]
Note(s): Portraits: CYBH; ETUP 54:4 (Apr. 1936): 198
Payn, A(nn) A(iken) *Source(s):* ASCP; CCE32 R18140; CCE64; GREN
Payn, G. W. *Source(s):* ASCP; CCE58; CCE64; GREN
Shelley, Mary C. *Source(s):* CCE32 R18258; GREN
Miles, George (Allen) 1946 (or 48)- [drummer, singer, writer]
Miles, Buddy *Source(s):* ASCP; CPOL RE-834-763
Miles, George H(enry) 1824-1871 [author]
Halphin, E(a)rnest *Source(s):* HOGR; LCAR

Miles, Luke 1925-1987 [singer, songwriter]
Long Gone *Source(s):* CCE68
Miles, Long Gone *Source(s):* CCE60; HARS
Milette, Juliette 1900-1992 [organist, teacher, composer]
Henri de la Croix, (Sister) *Source(s):* COHN; HEIN
Rose de Montroy *Source(s):* CANE
Sister Henri-de-la-Croix *Source(s):* CANE
Miley, James Wes(t)ley 1903-1932 [trumpeter, composer, bandleader]
Miley, Bub(ber) *Source(s):* CLAB; KINK
Milhaud, Darius 1892-1974 [composer]
Communist Traveling Salesman *Source(s):* SLON
Jacarémirim *Source(s):* http://danielthompson.com/Texts/Le_Boeuf/oeuf.pt.30.htm (7 July 2005)
Militiades, George 1909-1965 [composer, arranger, instrumentalist, singer]
Melachrino, George *Source(s):* EPMU; ROOM
Milkey, Edward T(albert) 1908-1993 [composer, teacher]
Albert, Martin *Source(s):* ASCP
Talbert, Ted *Source(s):* ASCP; CCE42 #11797 Eunp290004
Millar, Ronald (Graeme) 1919- [dramatist, librettist, actor]
Jowett, John *Source(s):* GAN2; GANB p. 550
Millard, James Elwin 1823-1894 [vicar, hymnist]
J. E. M. *Source(s):* JULN
Millenet, Johann Heinrich 1785-1858 (or 59) [librettist]
Tenelli, M. *Source(s):* LOWN; STGR; WORB
Miller, Albert 1912-1977 [singer, writer, actor]
Mills, Alan *Source(s):* LCAR
Miller, Amourette [songwriter]
Campbell, Misses *Source(s):* CCE16 E379535; LCAR
Note(s): Jt. pseud.: Georgi(n)a MacDonald.
Misses Campbell *Source(s):* LCAR
Miller, Betty Lou 1942- [singer, songwriter, actress]
Smith, Margo *Source(s):* EPMU; LCAR; MCCL
Tennessee Yodeler, The *Source(s):* MCCL
Miller, Craig c.1971- [rapper]
KAM *Source(s):* EPMU
Miller, David Nelson 1955- [composer]
Nelson, David *Source(s):* REHH
Note(s): Also used by Joseph A. Levin.
Miller, Edward 1731-1807 [organist, composer, writer on music]
Professor of Music, A *Source(s):* CART
Miller, J(oseph) D(elton) 1922-1996 [producer, songwriter]
Miller, Jay *Source(s):* CPOL RE-11-409; ENCM
Miller, James [songwriter]
Rim *Source(s):* BLIC; CPMU (publication dates 1900-05)
Miller, James (Henry) 1915-1989 [singer, songwriter, author]
MacColl, Ewan *Source(s):* CASS; EPMU; GAMM; PEN2; ROOM
Miller, Joseph 1915- [composer, author, singer]
Miller, Taps *Source(s):* ASCP; CCE73 R560108
Miller, Myrna Joy 1941- [singer, songwriter]
Miller, Jody *Source(s):* MCCL
Miller, Paul D. 1970- [DJ; writer on music]
DJ Spooky (That Subliminal Kid) *Source(s):* EPMU; LCAR
Miller, Percy 1970- [songwriter, rapper]
Master P *Source(s):* AMIR; AMUS; LCAR; PMUS-00
Miller, Perry 1941 (or 44)- [singer, songwriter]
Young, Jesse Colin *Source(s):* CCE67; DIMA; EPMU; HARR; LCAR
Miller, Robert [or Bob] (Ernst) 1889 (or 95)-1955 [singer, songwriter, music publisher]
Note(s): See SUTT for a list of joint pseuds. on recordings with Barney Burney, Charlotte Miller & various ensemble groups.
Adams, A. J. *Source(s):* CCE60; CCE64
Barnes, Bill *Source(s):* SUTT
Barnett, Curt *Source(s):* CCE76
Burnett, Bob *Source(s):* PSND
Carter, Floyd *Source(s):* SUTT
Darnell, Shelby *Source(s):* CCE46 E7193; CCE51; CCE60; CPOL RE-1-449; HORS
Dees, Ashley *Source(s):* CCE53
Divina, Eleanor [or Elly] *Source(s):* CCE32 Eunp63201; CCE59
Ferguson, Bob *Source(s):* CCE63-64; LCAR; PSND; SUTT
Hill, Bob *Source(s):* SUTT
Hucklenutt, Inky *Source(s):* CCE44 #11671 E121635; CCE47
Kackley, Robert [or Bob] *Source(s):* CCE60; CCE64; PSND
Koa, Ken *Source(s):* CCE60
Mills, Bob *Source(s):* CCE50
Palmer, Bill *Source(s):* LCAR; PSND; SUTT
Palmer, Bob *Source(s):* SUTT
Rellim, Trebor *Source(s):* CCE50 R60402; CCE60; CCE64; EPMU (see under: Carson Jenny Lou)
Suede, Vasca *Source(s):* CCE70 R488028
Wilson, Lawrence *Source(s):* CCE46 E10368; CCE50; CCE62; CCE64; CPOL RE-2-701
Miller, Roger Dean 1936-1992 [singer, songwriter, composer]
King of the Road, The *Source(s):* MCCL; SHAD
Wild Child, The *Source(s):* MCCL
Note(s): Do not confuse with Wildchild [i.e., Roger McKenzie]

Miller, Ron D(ean) 1954 (or 55)- [composer, author, singer]
Rhodes, Grayson *Source(s):* ASCP
Miller, Seymour 1908-1971 [composer, author]
Miller, Sy *Source(s):* ASCP
Miller, Steven Paul 1952- [singer, songwriter, guitarist]
Miller, Buddy *Source(s):* CM31; LCAR
Miller, Thomas 1949- [composer, singer, guitarist]
Verlaine, Tom *Source(s):* AMUS; EPMU
Miller, Zyshonne 1980- [songwriter, performer]
Miller, Silkk *Source(s):* PMUS-99
Silkk the Shocker *Source(s):* AMIR; AMUS: PMUS-00
Millet, Kadish 1923- [composer, author, publisher]
Millet, Kay *Source(s):* ASCP; CCE60
Millico, Giuseppe 1730 (or 39)-1802 [singer, composer]
Moscovita, Il *Source(s):* IBIM; WORB
Milligan, Archibald 1848- [violinist, composer]
Volti, Carl *Source(s):* CPMU; IBIM; WORB
Millinder, Lucius (Venable) 1900 (or 13)-1966 [composer, bandleader, actor]
Leroy, Lecius *Source(s):* CCE51; CCE55; CPOL RE-11-366
Millinder, Lucky *Source(s):* AMUS; CCE60; GROL; NOMG; PMUS
Mills, Frederick Allen 1869-1948 [composer, author, violinist, publisher]
Note(s): Portrait: JAST
Cakewalk King, The *Source(s):* Zimmerman, Dick. "Kerry Mills; The Cakewalk King. *Rag Times.* 30:6 (Mar. 1997): 1+.
Mills, Kerry *Source(s):* ASCP; BAKR; CCE31 R15528; JAST; LCAR; STUW
Note(s): Also used by Thomas Edward Bulch.
Morin, Pierre *Source(s):* CCE44 #2888, 312 R121462
St. Clair, Avery *Source(s):* CCE44 #2888, 46 R121463
Mills, Irving 1894-1985 [songwriter]
Primrose, Joe *Source(s):* CCE57-58; PMUS; http://www.bscjb.com/arrange.htm (3 May 2005)
Winn, Jack *Source(s):* http://bixography.com/images/78labels.htm (29 Aug. 2003)
Mills, Josefa Primo 1938- [author, teacher, graphic artist]
Mills, Pepa *Source(s):* ASCP
Mills, Paul 1921- [composer, author]
Ricks, Lee *Source(s):* ASCP; CCE57; CCE68; LCAR
Minasi, Carlo [composer]
Nava, Franz *Source(s):* http://www.maccan-duet.com/merris/bibliography/english-tutors.htm (2 Feb. 2005)
Note(s): Possible pseud. of Minasi or someone with whom he collaborated. See Edward Francis Rimbault.
Mineo, Attilio 1918- [composer, conductor, arranger]
Mineo, Art *Source(s):* ASCP; CCE61
Miner, Lawrence A.. 1943- [composer, author, publisher]
Thomas, Larry *Source(s):* ASCP
Mingus, Charles 1922-1979 [bassist, composer]
Fingus, "Baron" *Source(s):* JAMU
Jazz's Angry Man *Source(s):* PSND
Mingus, Baron *Source(s):* CM10
Minkus, Aloysius Ludwig 1826 (or 27)-1890 [violinist, composer]
Minkus, Léon *Source(s):* BAKR; LCAR; PSND
Minogue, Dennis (Michael) 1941- [composer, author, singer]
Balladeer of Baseball, The *Source(s):* http://metrostarrecords.com/artists/terrycashman/press.htm (16 Oct. 2002)
Baseball's Hit Man *Source(s):* http://metrostarrecords.com/artists/terrycashman/press.htm
Cashman, (Terry) *Source(s):* ASCP; CCE73 E313598; EPMU; LCAR; PMUS
Roame, Dennis *Source(s):* CCE65
Minot, Elizabeth [composer]
Pierce, Bertha *Source(s):* GOTE
Minter, Iverson 1936- [singer, guitarist, composer]
Bey, Iverson *Source(s):* HARS
Cryin' Red *Source(s):* HARS
Fuller, Playboy *Source(s):* HARS; HERZ
Fuller, Richard Lee *Source(s):* HARS
Fuller, Rocky *Source(s):* HARS; LCAR
Guitar Red *Source(s):* HARS; HERZ
James, Elmore, Jr. *Source(s):* HARS
Note(s): Do not confuse with Elmore James (1918-1963).
Louisiana Red *Source(s):* EPMU; HARS; HERZ; LCAR
Note(s): Do not confuse with Louisiana "Guitar" Red [i.e., Cardell Boyette] (LCAR)
Minter, Red *Source(s):* HARS
Rockin' Red *Source(s):* HARS
Walkin' Slim *Source(s):* HARS
Mioduszewski, Michal Marcin 1787-1868 [priest, editor of religious songs]
X. M. M. M. *Source(s):* CPMU (see: M., X. M. M.)
Miranda, Ralph [songwriter]
Note(s): Possibly Ralph F(rank); see following entry.
Duke, Bobby *Source(s):* CCE63 ("Lavender Lace" & "Simon Says")
Miranda, Ralph F(rank) [songwriter]
Note(s): See also preceding entry.
Miranda, Bob *Source(s):* CCE63; CCE66; PMUS
Mirelli, Francesco 1866- [composer]
Teora, Francesco di *Source(s):* STGR

Mirikitani, Alan Masao 1955- [composer, author, singer]
BB Chung King *Source(s):* CPOL PA-706-180
King, BB Chung *Source(s):* CPOL PA-706-780
Tani, Al *Source(s):* ASCP; CPOL PA-706-780
Miro, Enrique 1879-1950 [composer, conductor, critic]
Miro, Henri *Source(s):* VGRC
Miron(-Michrovsky), Issachar 1919 (or 20)- [composer, conductor]
Michrovsky, Stefan *Source(s):* ASCP; REHG
Miron, Tsipora 1923- [organist, pianist, composer]
Moore, Thelma *Source(s):* ASCP; COHN; HIXN
Miskulin, Joseph [or Joey] (Michael) 1949- [singer, songwriter, accordionist]
Cow Polka King *Source(s):* MCCL
Crown Prince of the Accordian *Source(s):* MCCL
Joey, the Cowpolka King *Source(s):* http://www.riders of the sky.com (16 Oct. 2002)
Misraki [or Misrachi], Paul 1908-1998 [author, songwriter, composer]
Thomas, Paul *Source(s):* LCAR; http://ufoinfo.com/news/misraki.html (16 Oct. 2002)
Missa, Edmond(-Jean-Louis) 1861-1910 [composer]
Note(s): Do not confuse with Edmond Jean Missa (1925-); see following entry.
Michel, Marius *Source(s):* GREN
Missa, Edmond Jean 1925- [songwriter]
Note(s): Do not confuse with Edmond [or Edmund] Missa (1861-1910); see preceding entry.
Aliprandi, Paul *Source(s):* CCE53-55; CCE57; CCE62
Rignac, Jean *Source(s):* CCE51
Mitchell, Brian c.1970- [rapper]
Darkman *Source(s):* EPMU
Mitchell, Bruce Douglas 1950- [poet]
Mitchell, Waddie *Source(s):* AMUS; MCCL
Mitchell, D(onald) G(rant) 1822-1908 [critic]
Marvel, I(k(e)) *Source(s):* HAMT; LCAR; WORB
Opera Goer, An *Source(s):* HAMT
Timon, John *Source(s):* HAMT; WORB
Mitchell, Oliver 1875-1945 [acrobat, theater manager, writer]
Morosco, Oliver *Source(s):* GAN2
Mitchell-Innes, T. L. [transcriber]
Adew *Source(s):* KILG
Note(s): Jt. pseud.: Evelyn Woodhouse, Algernon Drummond & W. J. Cory.
Mitchnick, Irwin 1928- [composer, arranger]
Leigh, Mitch *Source(s):* CASS; EPMU; GAMM; GAN1; GAN2; NGDO
Miti, Pompilio ?-1766 [librettist]
Brillante Pecoraro della Selva *Source(s):* ALMC
Graziano Cimbaloni *Source(s):* ALMC
Ronzello, Itmipolimipo *Source(s):* ALMC
Mitnik, Bernardo 1933- [composer, lyricist, singer, actor]
Chameleon in Tango Color, A *Source(s):* TODO
Navarro, Chico *Source(s):* TODO
Miyahara, Teiji 1899 (or 1900)- [composer]
Ikebe, Yoshitaro *Source(s):* BUL1
Mizell, Alphonso James [songwriter]
Corporation, The *Source(s):* PMUS
Note(s): Jt. pseud.: Fred(erick) [or Freddie] Perren, Deke Richards & Berry Gordy, Jr.
Mizell, Fonce *Source(s):* LCAR; PMUS
Moderne, Jacques fl. 1523-1556. [publisher, composer]
Grand Jacques *Source(s):* NGDM; WORB
Pinguento *Source(s):* NGDM
Modiana, Orazio [or Horatio] fl. before 1625 [composer]
Pellegrino, Il *Source(s):* GROL
Note(s): See also Pietro Della Valle.
Moeckel, Charles 1926- [composer, singer]
Frankenstein *Source(s):* OMUO
Moeran, E(rnest) J(ohn) 1894-1950 [composer]
England's Lost Composer *Source(s):* http://www.moeran.co.uk (16 Oct. 2002)
Moesser, (Karl-)Peter 1915- [composer]
Gunther, Lex *Source(s):* CCE56 Eunp
Lex, (Günter) *Source(s):* CPOL RE-200-954; RIES
Moffitt, De Loyce W(hite) 1906-1976 [composer, conductor]
Moffitt, Deke *Source(s):* ASCP; CCE42 #15239 E103518; CCE51; CCE67
Mogeta, Charles Octave 1815-1875 [librettist]
Féré, Octave *Source(s):* LOWN
Mohaupt, Franz 1854-1916 [composer, teacher]
Schelmerding, Ernst *Source(s):* KOMU; OMUO; PFSA
Mohr, Fritz 1926-1988 [composer]
Starfield, Glenn *Source(s):* CCE59; KOMP; KOMS; PFSA
Mohr, Karel 1873-1845 [conductor, composer, writer]
Moor, Karel *Source(s):* BAKO
Möhrenschlager, Theo 1917- [composer, conductor]
Möhrens, Theo *Source(s):* RIES
Moineaux, Joseph Désiré 1815 (or 25)-1895 [law stenographer, playwright]
Moinaux, Jules *Source(s):* GAN1; GAN2
Moir, James [or Jim] (Roderick) 1959- [writer, actor, composer]
Reeves, Vic *Source(s):* IMDB
Mojžiš, Stanislav 1883-1967 [librettist]
Lom, Stanislav *Source(s):* LOWN; MELL
Mokesch, Günter 1959- [singer, composer]
Mo *Source(s):* OMUO
Mokry, Jarmil Michael 1921-1997 [composer, conductor, musicologist]

Burghauser, Jarmil (Michael) *Source(s):* BAKO
Hajku, Michal *Source(s):* http://www.musica.cz/comp/burghauser.htm (5 June 2006)
Mole, Irving Milfred 1898-1961 [trombonist, composer]
Mole, Miff *Source(s):* NGDM
Molenaar, Pieter Jan 1907-1979 [composer]
Rochon, J. *Source(s):* SUPN
Molijn, Sebastian [songwriter]
Pronti *Source(s):* PMUS-00
Molina, Arturo, Jr. 1964- [rapper]
Frost *Source(s):* AMUS; EPMU
Kid Frost *Source(s):* AMUS; EPMU
Molino, Antonio c.1495-after 1571 [actor, poet, composer, conductor]
Blessi, Manoli *Source(s):* CPMU; GROL; NGDM; RIES
Burchiella, (Il) *Source(s):* NGDM; RIES
Möller, Ale [songwriter]
Godfather of Contemporary Swedish Folkmusic, The *Source(s):* http://www.bahnhof.se/~kario/ale.html (16 Oct. 2002)
Moller, Joachim (à) 1546-1610 [composer, organist]
Burck, Joachim (à) *Source(s):* BAKR; GROL; LCAR; NGDM; WORB
Mollica, Giovanni Leonardo c.1525-1602 [harpist, composer, actor]
Arpa, Giovanni Leonardo dell' *Source(s):* LCAR; LYMN
Gian Leoardo, dell'Arpa *Source(s):* LCAR; NGDM; WORB
Giovanni Leonardo, dell'Arpa *Source(s):* LCAR; NGDM; WORB
Moman, Lincoln (W.) 1936- [guitarist, songwriter]
Moman, Chips *Source(s):* CCE60-61; HARR
Mombach, Israel Lazarus 1813-1880 [singer, composer]
Mombach, Julius L. *Source(s):* IBIM; WORB
Monaco, James (V.) 1885-1945 [composer]
Ragtime Jimmy *Source(s):* CASS; PSND
Note(s): See also James [or Jimmy] (Francis) Durante.
Monardo, Meco 1939- [trombonist, arranger]
Meco *Source(s):* AMUS; EPMU; PSND; WARN
Monari, Bartolomeo fl. ?1670-1707 [composer, organist]
Monarino *Source(s):* NGDM
Monckton, (John) Lionel (Alexander) 1861-1924 [composer; lyricist]
Note(s): Portrait: GAN2
Cryptos *Source(s):* GANA ("Our Miss Gibbs")
Note(s): Jt. pseud. of lyricists & composers: of Ivan Caryll [i.e., Félix Tilken], Adrian Ross [i.e., Arthur Reed Ropes], Percy Greenbank & James T(olman) Tanner.
Mayne, Leslie *Source(s):* GAN1; GAN2; KILG; REHG; SUPN
Monda, Richard 1952- [singer, songwriter]
Daddy Dewdrop *Source(s):* EPMU; LCAR; PSND
Mondello, Nuncio 1910 (or 12)-1992 [reeds player, singer, songwriter]
Mondello, Toots *Source(s):* KINK; LCAR
Moneta, Giuseppe 1761- [composer]
Fiorentino *Source(s):* SQWB
Note(s): See also Francesco Maria Veracini.
Money(-Coutts), Francis Burdett (Thomas Nevill) 1852-1923 [poet, librettist]
Latymer, Lord *Source(s):* NGDO; WORB
Mountjoy *Source(s):* GROL; LCAR
Mongredier, Augustus [composer]
A. M. *Source(s):* CPMU (publication date 1861)
Moniuszko, Stanislaus 1820-1872 [composer]
Father of Polish Opera *Source(s):* http://www.moniuszko.art.pl/eng (16 Oct. 2002)
Monk, Thelonious (Sphere) 1917 (or 20)-1982 [jazz pianist; composer]
High Priest of Bob, The *Source(s):* PSND; TCAN
Monleone, Domenico 1875-1942 [composer]
Stolzing, W(alter) (di) *Source(s):* BAKR; BAKT; GROL; NGDO; STGR v. 4/pt.1
Monnais, (Guillaume) Édouard (Désiré) 1798-1868 [writer on music, journalist]
Smith, Paul *Source(s):* LCAR; PIPE; WORB
Monroe, Vaughn (Wilton) 1911 (or 12)-1973 [songwriter, bandleader]
Moore, Wilton *Source(s):* CCE48-50; STUW
Monroe, William [or Bill] (Smith) 1911-1996 [singer, songwriter, mandolin player]
Note(s): The names identified below from CPOL & CCE are possible pseuds.
Ahr, Joe *Source(s):* CPOL RE-154-232
Father of Blue Grass, The *Source(s):* AMEN; FLIN; MCCL; MILL; PSND; STAC
Father of Country Music, The *Source(s):* AMEN
Note(s): See also James [or Jimmy] (Charles) Rodgers & Hank [i.e., Hir(i)am (King)] Williams.
Mauldin, Bessie *Source(s):* CCE77 (see Index)
Monroe, Melissa *Source(s):* CCE78 R682033 (see Index)
Mr. Bluegrass *Source(s):* FLIN
Smith, J(ames) W. *Source(s):* CCE77 (see Index)
Monroy, Victor [singer, songwriter]
Monroy, Chicles *Source(s):* HWOM
Monsell, John Samuel Bewley 1811-1875 [cleric, hymnist]
Doctor, The *Source(s):* CART
Note(s): See also Ramazini [or Ramathan] Mtoro Ongala.
Old Vicar, The *Source(s):* CART

Monsigny, P(ierre) A(lexandre) 1729-1817 [composer]
Note(s): Portraits: ETUP 54:5 (May 1936): 328; EWCY
French Sacchini, The *Source(s):* GRV3
Mr. M****y *Source(s):* CPMU
Montagney, Alexandre Joseph 1815-1845 [violinist, composer]
Artôt, (Alexandre) Joseph (Montagney) *Source(s):* NGDM; WORB
Montagney, Charles H. N. 1810-1854 [composer]
Artot, Charles Henri Napoléon *Source(s):* IBIM; WORB
Montagney, Jean D. 1803-1887 [composer]
Artot, Jean Désiré *Source(s):* LCAR; IBIM; WORB
Montagney, Maurice 1772-1829 [composer]
Artot, Maurice *Source(s):* NGDM
Montalant, Laure-Cinthie 1901-1863 [singer, composer]
Cint, Mlle. *Source(s):* BAKE
Damoreau, Laure-Cinthie *Source(s):* BAKE
Montana, Vince, Jr. 1928- [composer, arranger, conductor]
Godfather of Disco, The *Source(s):* http://www.disco-hall-of-fame.com/producers.htm (16 Oct. 2002)
Father of the "Philly Sound" *Source(s):* http://pages.prodigy.net/giantgen1 (16 Oct. 2002)
Montani, Pietro 1895-1967 [composer, author]
Bergmann, Phantasius *Source(s):* RIEM
Raggi, Peter Seak *Source(s):* RIEM
Seak, Peter *Source(s):* CCE58; CCE61; CPOL RE-454-963
Monte, Marisa 1967- [singer, songwriter]
Madonna of Brazil, The *Source(s):* CM38
Monte, Philippe [or Filippo] de 1521-1603 [composer]
Philippe de Mons *Source(s):* LCAR
Montefiore, Tomasso (Mosè) 1855-1933 [composer, writer on music]
Puck *Source(s):* PIPE
Montella, Giovan(ni) Domenico c.1570-1607 [composer, lutenist, organist]
Mico *Source(s):* LCAR
Montella, Mico *Source(s):* LCAR
Montenegro, Hugo 1925-1981 [composer, arranger, conductor]
Quad Father, The *Source(s):* CM18
Monteverdi, Claudio 1567-1643 [composer]
Father of Opera *Source(s):* http://www.kdfc.com/classical/baroque.shtml (16 Oct. 2002)
Music's Prophet *Source(s):* DEAR
Wagner of the Sixteenth Century *Source(s):* http://www.usc.edu/dept/polish_music (9 Apr. 2005)
Montgomery, (Robert) Bruce 1921-1978 [author, organist, composer]
Crispin, Edmund *Source(s):* LCAR; MUWB; PSND; ROOM
Montgomery, Charles F. 1930- [composer, arranger, pianist, vibraphonist]
Montgomery, Buddy *Source(s):* LCAR; PSND
Montgomery, Eurreal Wilford 1906-1985 [singer, composer]
Little Brother *Source(s):* CCE67-68
Note(s): Also used by Nat(haniel) Adderley & Leonard (Geoffrey) Feather.
Montgomery, Little Brother *Source(s):* CCE67; CM26; HARS; LCAR; PEN2
Montgomery, James 1771-1854 [journalist, poet, hymnist]
Note(s): Portrait: CYBH
Poet, A *Source(s):* CART; LCAR
Positive, Peter *Source(s):* CART; GOTH; GOTT
Silvertongue, Gabriel *Source(s):* CART; GOTH; GOTT
Montgomery, Merle 1904-1986 [composer, author]
Campbell, Alan *Source(s):* ASCP; CCE51
Campbell, Aline *Source(s):* BAKE; BUL3; COHN; HEIN; HIXN; LCAR; NGAM
Montgomery, Paul 1924-2002 [TV show host, pianist, composer]
Uncle Paul *Source(s):* DRSC
Montiel, Urbano Gomez 1926- [author, lyricist]
Gomez, Urbano *Source(s):* ASCP
Moodnick, Ronald 1924- [actor, composer]
Note(s): Portrait: GAN2 v. 3 p.1533
Moody, Ron *Source(s):* GAN1; GAN2
Moody, Charles Harry [or Henry] 1874-1965 [organist, composer, conductor]
Brayton, Coulthard *Source(s):* CART; HUEV; MACM
Moody, Tom fl. c.1836 [songwriter]
Ball, T. *Source(s):* Levy, L. *Flashes of Merriment.* Norman: University of Oklahoma, 1971.
Moody, Walter (R.) [songwriter]
Douglas, Ken *Source(s):* CCE66
Waters, Douglas *Source(s):* CPOL RE-768-863
Wood, Ken *Source(s):* CCE57-61; CPOL RE-187-514; PMUS
Moorat, Joseph (Samuel Edward) 1864-1938 [composer]
Ward, Joseph S. *Source(s):* CPMU; GOTH; NGDM
Moore, Alex(ander Herman) 1899-1989 [singer, pianist, harmonica player, songwriter]
Chittlins, Papa *Source(s):* HARS

Moore, Whistling Alex *Source(s):* AMUS; HARS; LCAR
Papa Chittlins *Source(s):* HARS
Moore, Arnold Dwight 1913-2004 [singer, songwriter]
Mr. Blues *Source(s):* PSND
Note(s): See also Wynonie Harris.
Moore, Dwight Gatemouth *Source(s):* LCAR
Moore, Gatemouth *Source(s):* HARS; PSND; WASH
More, Eldermo *Source(s):* PSND
Moore, (Annie) Aubertine (Woodward) 1841-1929 [writer on music, music educator]
Forestier, Auber *Source(s):* CART; HIXN; LCAR
Moore, Barry 1955- [singer, songwriter, guitarist]
Bloom, Luka *Source(s):* AMUS; CM14; MUHF
Moore, Charles Garrett Ponsonby 1910-1989 [financier, opera administrator]
Drogheda, 11th Earl of *Source(s):* NGDO; WORB
Moore, Christopher Andrew 1945- [singer, songwriter, guitarist]
Moore, Christy *Source(s):* PEN1
Moore, Dudley (Stuart John) 1935-2002 [actor, pianist, composer]
Cuddly Dudley *Source(s):* PSND
Megamidget, The *Source(s):* PSND
Wee Wonder, The *Source(s):* PSND
Moore, Eloise Irene 1929- [composer, author, guitarist]
Moore, Evalyn *Source(s):* ASCP
Moore, Trudy *Source(s):* ASCP
Trudy, Evalyn *Source(s):* ASCP
Moore, G(eorge) W(ashington) 1820-1909 [singer, songwriter]
Moore, Pony *Source(s):* KILG; LCAR (see notes)
Moore, James 1924-1970 [harmonica player, singer, songwriter]
Harmonica Slim *Source(s):* AMUS; EPMU; HARS; PEN2
Note(s): See also Travis (L.) Blaylock.
Harpo, Slim *Source(s):* AMUS; EPMU; HARR; HARS; PEN2
Slim Harpo *Source(s):* AMUS
Moore, Kevin 1952- [guitarist, singer, songwriter]
Keb' Mo' *Source(s):* AMUS; EPMU
Moore, Luella Lockwood 1864-1927 [composer]
Arlington, Marion *Source(s):* PARS
Moore, Phil & Beth *Source(s):* PARS
Moore, Melvin James 1934-2000 [singer, songwriter]
Broxton, Melvin *Source(s):* DRSC
Johnny Flamingo *Source(s):* DRSC
Moore, Monette 1902-1962 [singer, songwriter]
Girl of Smiles, The *Source(s):* HARS
Mayes, Ethel *Source(s):* HARS
Potter, Nettie *Source(s):* HARS
Smith, Susie *Source(s):* AMUS; HARS
White, Grace *Source(s):* HARS
Moore, Thomas 1779-1852 [poet]
Note(s): See LCAR & PSND for additional nonmusic-related pseudonyms. Portraits: CYBH; ETUP 54:5 (May 1936): 328.
Brown, Thomas (the younger) *Source(s):* GOTE; LCAR; PSND
Little, Thomas (Moore) *Source(s):* BLIC; CPMU; GOTE; PSND
T. M. *Source(s):* CPMU
T. M. L. *Source(s):* BLIC; CPMU
Moore, Warren (Thomas) 1938 (or 39)- [singer, songwriter]
Moore, Pete *Source(s):* ASCP; PSND
Moore, Winston (Lee) 1919-1966 [singer, songwriter]
Willet(t), Slim *Source(s):* AMUS; CCE52-54; MCCL; PSND
Moorhead, Scott 1966-1997 [singer, songwriter, guitarist]
Buckley, Jeff *Source(s):* PEN2
Moorlampen, Franz Peter 1954- [composer]
O'Melley, Howard *Source(s):* PFSA
Morais, Antonio Maria Araujo de 1921-1964 [composer]
Antonio Maria *Source(s):* LCAR
Maria, Antônio *Source(s):* CCE59; GREN
Morales (Sanabia), Norberto 1911-1964 [pianist, bandleader, composer]
Morales, Noro *Source(s):* EPMU; PEN2
Moran, Michael 1794?-1846 [composer, singer, poet]
Last Gleeman, The *Source(s):* PSND
Zozimus *Source(s):* PSND
Morandi, Giovanni 1777-1856 [composer]
Moraine, Jean *Source(s):* STGR; WORB
Morandus, Joannes *Source(s):* LCAR
Morcour, ? de [composer]
Note(s): Publication dates 1885-1886.
*** *Source(s):* CPMU
Courmor *Source(s):* CPMU
Moré (Gutiérrez), Bartolomé Maximiliano 1919-1963 [singer, composer, arranger]
Barbaro del Ritmo, El *Source(s):* PEN2
Moré, Beny *Source(s):* AMUS; PEN2
Moreau, Charles François (Jean) Baptiste 1783-1832 [playwright]
Commagny, Moreau de *Source(s):* LCAR; PIPE
Moreau, de Commagny *Source(s):* LCAR
Morei, Michal Giuseppi 1695?-1767 [writer on music]
Rofeatio, M. *Source(s):* NGDM v. 1, p. 34
Moreira, Airto (Guimova) 1941- [percussionist, singer, songwriter]
Airto *Source(s):* LCAR; YORK

Moreira, Gilberto Passos 1942- [singer, songwriter]
Gil, Gilberto *Source(s):* LCAR
Gilberto, Gil *Source(s):* CCE66-68; ROOM; WARN
Moreira de Castro, Carlos 1902-1999 [songwriter]
Cachaça, Carlos *Source(s):* LCAR
King of Samba *Source(s):* http://www.britannica.com/eb/aricle?eu=367114 (30 Oct. 2002)
Note(s): See also José Babosa [or B(atista)] Silva.
Morell, Thomas 1781-1840 [hymnist]
M. *Source(s):* JULN
Morelli, Frank [composer, bassoonist]
Finley, Antor Dismuk (1812-1815) *Source(s):* OCLC 41228703
Note(s): Jt. pseud.: Michael Campbell & Harry Searing.
Moreton, Ivor [songwriter, pianist]
Curroy, Mort *Source(s):* CCE34 Efor34120
Note(s): Jt. pseud.: Michael Carr [i.e., Maurice Alfred Cohen], Bill Currie & Harry Roy.
Moretti, Felice 1791-1863 [composer]
Davide, da Bergamo, padre *Source(s):* LCAR
Morgan, George (Thomas) 1924 (or 25)-1975 [singer, guitarist, songwriter]
Candy Kid, The *Source(s):* AMUS; FLIN; MCCL
Tennessee George *Source(s):* MCCL
Morgan, Loretta Lynn 1959- [singer, songwriter]
Morgan, Lorrie *Source(s):* AMUS; FLIN; LCAR
Morgan, Roberto Orlando 1865-1956 [composer]
Ingram, John *Source(s):* GREN
Valère *Source(s):* GREN
Morgan, W(illiam) Astor 1890- [singer, teacher, composer]
Stor, Jean *Source(s):* CCE43 #13328 E112952; CCE48; LCAR; MACM
Morganfield, McKinley 1915-1983 [singer, songwriter, guitarist]
Boss Man *Source(s):* PSND
Carter, James 'Sweet Lucy' *Source(s): Blues & Gospel Records, 1890-1943*. 4th ed. Oxford: Clarendon Press, 1997.
Carter, Sweet Lucy *Source(s): Blues & Gospel Records* (see above)
Father of Chicago Blues *Source(s):* SHAB p. 173
King of Chicago Blues *Source(s):* PSND; SHAB p. 173
King of the Blues *Source(s):* CM24
Note(s): See also Riley B. King.
Living Legend, The *Source(s):* HARS; PSND
Muddy Waters *Source(s):* EPMU
Rivers, Dirty *Source(s):* JAMU
Waters, Muddy *Source(s):* AMUS; CM24; HARR; HARS; LCAR; PEN2; PSND; SHAB
Morgio, George A. 1942- [composer]
Thatcher, Noel *Source(s):* ASCP; CCE68
Morhange, Charles-Henri-Valentin 1813-1888 [pianist, composer]
Note(s): "Henri" is incorrect; not on his birth certificate and he never used the name. (LCAR)
Alkan, Charles-Henri-Valentin *Source(s):* CPMU; GROL; LYMN; MACM; NGDM
Morhange, Napoléon Alexandre 1826- [pianist, composer]
Alkan, Napoléon Alexandre *Source(s):* IBIM; MACM; WORB
Morin, Jean Baptiste 1677-1745 [composer]
Pioneer Composer of the French Cantata *Source(s):* GROL
Morin, Léopold [or Léo-Pol] 1892-1941 [author, composer, pianist, music critic]
Callihou, James *Source(s):* GROL; PSND
Morin, Paul fl. c.1879 [composer]
Moreno, Paul *Source(s):* STGR
Morissette, Alanis (Nadine) 1974- [singer, songwriter, dancer]
Alanis *Source(s):* NOMG
Moritz, (Landgrave of Hessen-Kassel) 1572-1632 [composer]
Moritz der Gelehrte *Source(s):* LCAR; NGDM; SADC
Morny, Charles (Auguste Louis) Joseph de 1811-1865 [librettist]
Saint-Rémy, M. de *Source(s):* CPMU; LCAR; MELL; PIPE
Morphis, Robert C. 1948- [composer, author, singer]
Twine, Bobby *Source(s):* ASCP
Morra, Egidio 1906-1994 [composer, trombonist]
Morra, Gene *Source(s):* ASCP
Morrell, Thomas 1703-1784 [cleric, writer, librettist for Handel oratorios]
T. M. *Source(s):* CART
Morricone, Ennio 1928- [composer, conductor]
Dansavio *Source(s):* CCE62
Nichols, Leo *Source(s):* BBDP; CM15; http://www.morricone.de/biographie.htm (16 Oct. 2002)
Piovanti, Nicola *Source(s):* CM15; http://www.italia.rai.it/eng/principal/topics/bio/piovani.htm (14 Mar. 2005)
Note(s): The name "Nicola Piovanti" was incorrectly reported in biographcical sources as a pseud. of Ennio Morriconel. See the Nicola Piovani (1946-) website listed above.
Savio, Dan *Source(s):* BBDP; http://www.morricone.de/biographie.htm
Morris, Charles 1745-1838 [poet, songwriter]
Morris, Captain *Source(s):* PSND
Morris, James C(orbett) 1907-1998 [folklorist, songwriter]
Bard of the Ozarks, The *Source(s):* PSND
Driftwood, Jimmy *Source(s):* CCME; ENCM; EPMU; HARD; LCAR; MCCL; OB98; PEN2

Morris, Lawrence D. 1947- [cornetist, composer]
Morris, Butch *Source(s):* LCAR; PEN2
Morris, Reginald Owen 1886-1948 [composer, writer on music]
Bugsworthy, Nicholas *Source(s):* GOTT
Morris, Valentine [composer]
Note(s): Publication dates 1847-88.
Churchhill, Charles *Source(s):* CPMU
Hoechst, Carl *Source(s):* CPMU
Morrison, George Ivan 1945- [singer, songwriter]
Belfast Cowboy *Source(s):* CASS
Morrison, Van *Source(s):* ALMN; BAKR; CASS; CM24; DIMA; HARR; LCAR; PEN2
Morrison, James (Douglas) 1943-1971 [singer, songwriter]
Doors, The *Source(s):* GOTT; PMUS; SHAD
Note(s): Jt. pseud.: John Densmore, Robert Krieger & Raymond (Daniel) Manzarek.
Lizard King, The *Source(s):* ALMN; SHAD
Morriss, Ralph Alexander 1952- [composer, author, singer]
Morriss, Randy *Source(s):* ASCP
Morrissey, Steven Patrick 1959- [singer, songwriter]
Morrissey *Source(s):* CM10; EPMU; LCAR
Morse, Theodore (F.) 1873 (or 74)-1924 [composer, publisher]
Fitzgerald, Lawrence *Source(s):* CCE49 R44504
Huntley, Austin *Source(s):* CCE51 R73744 ("My Alltyme Girl")
Note(s): Also used as jt. pseud. by Walter (G(ustave)) Haenschen & James (Conrad) O'Keefe.
Kendall, Don *Source(s):* CCE50 R63624; CCE49 R54019; CCE49 R54020
Note(s): Used by Morse alone & jt. pseud.: Jules Hurtig. Also used by Walter (G(ustave)) Haenschen, James (Conrad) O'Keefe & Lester O'Keefe; see NOTES: Kendall, Don.
Martin, Fred'k *Source(s):* CCE49 R44493
Winchester, Tom *Source(s):* CCE51 R75981 ("My Sugar Man")
Note(s): Jt. pseud.: Spencer Williams.
Mortelmans, Lodewijk 1868-1952 [conductor, teacher, composer]
Prince of Flemish Song *Source(s):* BAKT
Mortimer, Al [composer]
Jerome, Henry *Source(s):* CLTP ("Winky-Kink and You"); CLTV
Mortimer, Harry 1902-1992 [composer, conductor]
Martyn, Rodney *Source(s):* CCE56; CCE58
Moreton, H. R. *Source(s):* CCE52-53
Seymour, Frank *Source(s):* CCE53; CPMU
Note(s): Jt. pseud.: Stanley Smith-Masters.
Mortjé, Arnold [or Adolphe] 1843-1885 [journalist, critic, librettist]
Domino, Un *Source(s):* PIPE
Frou-Frou *Source(s):* PIPE
Gringoire *Source(s):* PIPE
Monsieur de l'Orchestre, (Un) *Source(s):* GAN1; GAN2; PIPE
Note(s): See also Miguel Zamacoïs.
Mortier, Arnold *Source(s):* GAN1; GAN2; LCAR; PIPE
Parlotte, Monsieur de la *Source(s):* PIPE
Vert-Vert *Source(s):* PIPE
Morton, George 1942- [singer, songwriter]
Morton, Shadow *Source(s):* AMUS; EPMU; PEN1; PSND; WARN
Mosby, John(ny) (R.) 1933- [singer, songwriter, bandleader]
Mr. & Mrs. Country Music *Source(s):* LCAR; MCCL
Note(s): With wife, Jonie Mosby [i.e., Janice Irene Shields]. See also Otis Wilson Maphis (with wife Rose Lee Schetrompf).
New Sweethearts of Country Music, The *Source(s):* LCAR' MCCL
Note(s): With wife, Jonie Mosby [i.e., Janice Irene Shields]
Mosch, Ernst 1925-1999 [composer]
Zittner, Wenzel *Source(s):* KOMP; KOMS; PFSA; SUPN
Moscheles, Ignaz 1794-1870 [pianist, teacher, composer]
Note(s): Forename "Isaak-Ignaz" occasionally listed in modern publications, but never used by Moscheles professionally. (LCAR)
Tasto der Kälberfuß *Source(s):* APPL p. 12
Moseley, James Orville 1909-1994 [composer, author, teacher]
Moseley, Job *Source(s):* ASCP
Mosely, Lawrence Leo 1905-1981 [trombonist, composer, singer]
Mosely, Snub *Source(s):* ASCP; CCE60; NGDJ
Mosenthal, Salomon Hermann (von) 1821-1877 [dramatist, librettist]
Lechner, Friedrich *Source(s):* OMUO
Moses, Eleaza Aaron ?-1922 [writer, critic, composer]
Mordred *Source(s):* GANA p. 706; PIPE
Morton, Edward A. *Source(s):* GANA; PIPE
Moshinski, Albert 1925- [director]
Marre, Albert *Source(s):* GAN2
Mosko, Stephen L. 1947 (or 48)- [composer]
Mosko, Lucky *Source(s):* BAKT; LCAR (see note)
Mosley, Tim(othy) 1971- [songwriter, performer]
Timbaland *Source(s):* AMIR; AMUS; CPOL PA-1-066-672; PMUS-00
Mosmans, Alphonse Willem Josef 1872- [music publisher, composer]
Claessens, Arthur *Source(s):* MACM

Moss, E(llsworth) F(rancis) 1904-1985 [composer, author, teacher]
Ellsworth *Source(s):* CCE75-77
Richards, (Don) Rube *Source(s):* ASCP; CCE49; CCE63
Moss, Eugene 1906 (or 14)-1984 [singer, guitarist, songwriter]
Miller, Jim *Source(s):* HARS
Moss, Buddy *Source(s):* HARS; LCAR
Moten, Bennie 1894-1935 [bandleader, composer. pianist]
Godfather of Kansas City Jazz *Source(s):* http://www.kcstar.com/projects/jazz/stories/jazzbio.htm (16 Oct. 2002)
Motz-Rappaport, Erich [librettist]
Walter, Erich *Source(s):* LOWN
Moul, Alfred mentioned 1882-1888 [composer, author, musicial]
Keston, Felix *Source(s):* CPMU; OCLC 49358249
Yvolde *Source(s):* BLIC; CPMU
Moultrie, Gerard 1829-1885 [clergyman, hymnist, translator]
D P *Source(s):* JULN
Note(s): D P = Desiderius Pastor
Desiderius Pastor *Source(s):* JULN; PSND
G. M. *Source(s):* JULN
M. *Source(s):* JULN
N. N. F. *Source(s):* JULN
Moultrie, Mary Dunlop 1837-1866 [hymnist]
M. D. M. *Source(s):* JULN
Mouzo, Teodoro José 1905- [lyricist]
Isusi *Source(s):* http://www.elportaldeltango.com/english (28 July 2005)
Moyet, Genevieve 1961- [singer, songwriter]
Moyet, Al(l)ison *Source(s):* NOMG
Moyne, Jean Baptiste 1751-1796 [composer]
Lemoyne, Jean Baptiste *Source(s):* IBIM; NGDM; SONN; WORB
Mozart, Franz Xaver Wolfgang 1791-1844 [pianist, composer]
Mozart, Wolfgang Amadeus *Source(s):* BAKR; RIEM
Note(s): Frequently referred to by his father's name.
Mozart, Maria Anna 1751-1829 [pianist, composer]
Mozart, Nannerl *Source(s):* DWCO; JACK
Nannerl *Source(s):* AEIO
Mozart, Wolfgang Amadeus 1756-1791 [composer]
Father of Modern Music, The *Source(s):* PSND
Note(s): See also Arnold Schoenberg.
Masonic Composer *Source(s):* DESO-9
Mozart, Wolferl *Source(s):* PSND
Mozartian *Source(s):* EPON (Suppl. 1984)
Raphael of Music, The *Source(s):* PSND; SIFA
Raphael of Opera, The *Source(s):* PSND
W. A. M****t *Source(s):* CPMU

Mravik, Edward E. 1917-2005 [composer, author, singer]
Hawk, Eddie *Source(s):* ASCP
Mug, (Sister) Mary Theodosia 1860-1943 [composer]
Maery, H(elen) *Source(s):* CCE41 #49460 E98992; HIXN; LCPC letter cited (13 Feb 1931)
Mühlbauer, Hans Heinz 1922- [composer]
Arland, Rolf *Source(s):* CCE56-58; KOMP; KOMS; PFSA; RIES
Birk, Lothar *Source(s):* CCE66
Mühle, Nicolaus c.1750- [composer, conductor]
Mile (musikdirektor) *Source(s):* SONN
Muhlenberg, William Augustus 1796-1877 [cleric, hymnist]
Note(s): Portrait: CYBH
Catholicus *Source(s):* CART
One of the Memorialists *Source(s):* CART
Mulder, Johannes Hermanus 1894-1989 [composer]
Mulder, Herman *Source(s):* PSND
Mullen, Adelaide fl. c.1883 [singer, composer]
King, Wilton *Source(s):* COHN; HIXN; MACM
Mullen, Frederic [composer]
Note(s): In LCAR and MACM (cited in LCAR) Frederic Mullen is listed as a pseud. of Alfred William Rawlings; however, since this information was not verified in a second independent source, Mullen is listed as a separate entry.
Adam, Léon *Source(s):* CCE49 R48690 ("Wonderland"); CCE57-58; CPMU
Ashton, John *Source(s):* CPMU
Burgess, Cyril *Source(s):* CPMU
Carton, Philippe *Source(s):* CCE40 #7317, 313 R81153; CPMU; MUWB
Durand, Emil *Source(s):* CPMU
Le Clercq, Jean *Source(s):* CPMU
Lemieun, Anton *Source(s):* CCE12 E290906
Lemieux, Anton *Source(s):* CPMU
Lémune, Gaston *Source(s):* CPMU
Lépine, Maurice *Source(s):* CPMU
Lescaut, Pierre *Source(s):* CPMU; MUWB
Lesonné, Bertrand *Source(s):* CPMU
Lind, Gustave *Source(s):* CCE44 #26477, 496 R127377; CPMU; GOTH
Lund, Gustav *Source(s):* MUWB
Morel, Jean *Source(s):* BLIC; CCE50 R71710 ("Annette"); CPMU; MUWB
Neat, John *Source(s):* MUWB
Norman, Noel *Source(s):* MUWB
Thorne, Cyril *Source(s):* CCE50 R71453 ("Charlie Chaplin"); CPMU
Vardon, Paul *Source(s):* CPMU
Winlaw, Maurice *Source(s):* MUWB

Mullendore, Joseph [or Joe] 1914-1990 [composer, pianist]
Lee, George *Source(s):* CLTP ("Annie Oakley")
Note(s): "House name," MUTEL [i.e., MUsic for TELevision]. Also used by Herb Taylor.
Lenard, Melvyn *Source(s):* CLTP ("Racket Squad," closing theme 2)
Note(s): Composed music for the publisher David M. Gordon under this name as did William Lava, Irving Gertz, Dave Kahn, Leo(n) Klatzkin & possibly others. See also David M. Gordon.
Sanns, Ray *Source(s):* CPOL RE-88-871
Salon, Joseph *Source(s):* CLTP
Note(s): "House name," MUTEL [i.e., MUsic for TELevision]. Also used by Herb Taylor.

Müller(-Guttenbrunn), Adam 1852-1923 [author, critic]
Gerhold, Franz Josef *Source(s):* PIPE
Ignotus *Source(s):* PIPE
Michel, Vetter *Source(s):* PIPE

Müller, Edward Raymond 1911-1991 [clarinetist, composer]
Miller, Eddie *Source(s):* EPMU
Note(s): Also used by Edward Lisbona.

Müller, Ernest (Louis [or Ludwig]) 1740-1811 [composer, flautist]
Grascinsky, Ernest Louis *Source(s):* CPMU; LCAR; NGDM v.12 p. 769; STGR
Krasinsky, Ernest Louis *Source(s):* CPMU; GROL; LCAR; NGDM v.12 p. 769; STGR
Note(s): May be original name, although A. Choron, in *Dictionnaire historique des musiciens* (Paris: 1810-11), maintained Krasinsky was a pseud. (see GROL; NGDM)
Miller, Krazinsky *Source(s):* LCAR
Miller, M. *Source(s):* LCAR

Müller, Fidel 1627-1685 [composer]
Molitor, Fidel *Source(s):* NGDM

Müller, Georg Gottfried 1762-1821 [minister, violinist, composer]
Godfrey, George *Source(s):* BAKE; LCAR (see note)

Müller, Günther 1933- [composer]
Maredo, José *Source(s):* KOMP; PFSA
Whiteman, Roy *Source(s):* KOMP; PFSA

Müller, H. C. 1959- [composer]
mylla, h. c. *Source(s):* KOMS

Müller, Hugo 1917- [composer]
Milano, U. *Source(s):* SUPN
Note(s): Also used by Albert Gisinger.
Milhard, Hough *Source(s):* SUPN

Muller, Jacob 1889-1980 [composer]
Millar, Jack *Source(s):* SUPN

Müller, Johann Adam 1730-1773 [cleric, composer]
Molitor, Alexius *Source(s):* NGDM

Müller, Johann Aug(ust) (Karl) 1838-1900 [librettist]
Weller, A. *Source(s):* STGR

Müller, Johann Baptist 1799-1863 [teacher, singer, composer]
Moser, Johann Baptist *Source(s):* OMUO; WORB

Müller, Josef Ferdinand 1818-1895 [theater director, actor, composer]
Nesmüller, Josef Ferdinand *Source(s):* OMUO

Müller, Marcellus 1845?- [composer]
Wilhelm *Source(s):* MELL; STGR; WORB

Müller, Rainer 1941- [composer]
Kieselst(e)in, Reiner *Source(s):* KOMP; KOMS; PFSA
Miller, Ray *Source(s):* KOMP; KOMS; PFSA
Weingeist, Reiner *Source(s):* KOMP; KOMS; PFSA

Müller, Rolf-Hans 1928-1990 [composer]
Baum, Hans *Source(s):* KOMS

Müller, Valentin 1637-1713 [composer]
Molitor, Valentin *Source(s):* NGDM

Müller, Werner [or Warner] 1920-1998 [composer, conductor, arranger, trombonist]
Buchholz, Hans *Source(s):* CCE61; CCE65; CPOL RE-541-299
Buchholz, Heinz *Source(s):* CCE62-64; CLTP ("Wendy and Me"); KOMS; PFSA
Buchholz, Horst *Source(s):* CCE63
Santos, Ricardo *Source(s):* MUSR
Ullmer *Source(s):* KOMP; KOMS; PFSA

Mullican, Aubrey Wilson 1909-1967 [pianist, singer, songwriter]
Burns, Morry *Source(s):* CCE75-76
King of the Hillbilly Piano Players *Source(s):* CCME; SHAD; STAC
Mullican, Moon *Source(s):* AMUS; CCME; CLAB; STAC

Mullins, Margaret Olive 1915- [composer]
Hubick, (Mrs.) Margaret Olive *Source(s):* COHN; HIXN
Lovell, Katherine *Source(s):* COHN; GOTH; HIXN

Münch-Bellinghausen, Eligius Franz Joseph 1806-1871 [composer, writer on music]
Halm, Friedrich *Source(s):* LCAR; MUBR

Münchheimer, Adam 1830-1904 [composer]
Minhejmer, Adam *Source(s):* NGDM; STGR

Muniz, Marco Antonio 1968 (or 69)- [singer, songwriter, actor]
Anthony, Marc *Source(s):* CM19; LCAR
Marc Anthony *Source(s):* HWOM
Marco *Source(s):* HWOM
Note(s): See also Marco [or Mike] Wolff.

Munkel, Heinz 1900-1961 [composer]
Broel, Heinz *Source(s):* BUL3

Munkittrick, Howard (Talbot) 1865-1928 [composer, conductor]

Talbot, Howard *Source(s):* BAKO; CPMU; KILG; LCAR; MACM; PIPE; REHG; ROOM
Munn, Colin 1964- [guitarist, singer, songwriter]
James, Colin *Source(s):* AMUS; LCAR
Munn, William O. 1902- [songwriter]
Bruce, Richard L. *Source(s):* TPRF
Clay, Stephen *Source(s):* CCE45 #55708 E136670; CCE72
Douglas, Martin *Source(s):* CCE56 E102480; CCE59 E126314
Fariss, Michael *Source(s):* CCE45 #40515 E133817; CCE64 E188708; CPOL RE-589-183
Kahali, Vaslav *Source(s):* CCE70 R48753
Medlock, Thomas *Source(s):* CCE43 #2795 E110127; CCE70 R495361
Nobles, Oliver *Source(s):* CCE66; CCE67 R402616
Muñoz Salazar, Mario 1923- [singer, percussionist, composer]
Papaíto *Source(s):* EPMU; PEN2
Munro, Hector Hugh 1870-1916 [author]
Saki *Source(s):* CCE78; LCAR; *Washington Post* (9 Feb. 1996): H7
Murden, Eliza Crawley ?-c.1848 [poet, composer]
Lady, of Charleston, S. C. *Source(s):* JACK; LCAR
Muren, Zeki 1933-1996 [composer, singer, actor]
Sanat Gunesi *Source(s):* GROL
Murgi, Gino (Giuseppe) 1866- [composer]
Nelson, William *Source(s):* MELL; WORB
Muris, Johannes de c.1300-c.1351 [music theorist, astonomer, mathematician]
De Francia *Source(s):* PSND
Normanus *Source(s):* PSND
Mürmann, Wolfgang 1944- [composer]
Mike Moore Company *Source(s):* KOMS
Murphey, Michael Martin 1945- [singer, songwriter, guitarist]
Cosmic Cowboy *Source(s):* MCCL
Murphy, Lyle 1908-2005 [arranger, composer, saxophonist]
Murphy, Spud *Source(s):* EPMU; KINK; NGDJ
Murphy, Melvin E(dward) A(lton) 1915-1987 [composer, arranger, singer, trombonist]
Murphy, Turk *Source(s):* AMUS; CASS; CLAB; JASR; KINK; LCAR; TCAN
Murphy, Robin Williams, III 1949- [singer, songwriter, guitarist]
Williams, Robin *Source(s):* MCCL
Murphy, Rose 1913-1989 [pianist, singer, composer]
Note(s): Do not confuse with fiddler & accordionist Rose Murphy (1900-).
Chee-Chee Girl, The *Source(s):* KINK; LCAR (see note)
Murray, James R(amsey) 1841-1905 [composer]
Note(s): Portraits: CYBH; ETUP 54:7 (July 1936): 404; HALL
Ahrem, Jacques *Source(s):* TPRF
Cameron, Owen *Source(s):* TPRF
Grayson, Paul *Source(s):* TPRF
Note(s): Also used by James E. Dempsey.
Mackenzie, Murray *Source(s):* TPRF
Ong, Oliver *Source(s):* TPRF
Roe, Stafford *Source(s):* TPRF
Winthrop, (J. R.) *Source(s):* CCE12 R2503; TPRF
Murrell, Irene Janet 1936- [composer, author, pianist]
Castle, Irene *Source(s):* ASCP
Murrells, Joseph 1904- [author, songwriter]
Morellio, Joe *Source(s):* CCE49; CCE59
Temple, Edith *Source(s):* CCE45 #63075 Efor70947; CCE51-53; CPOL RE-138-925; PSND
Note(s): Do not confuse with Edith Temple, 19th-20th cent. composer.
Murschhauser, Franz Xaver Anton 1663-1738 [composer, theorist]
F. X. A. M. *Source(s):* CPMU
Musard, Philippe 1792 (or 93)-1859 [conductor, arranger]
Lord of Quadrilles and Galops *Source(s):* Carse, Adam. *Life of Jullien*. Cambridge: W. Heffer, 1951.
Musard, Great *Source(s):* Carse (see above)
Musard, Napoleon *Source(s):* Carse (see above)
Père Musard, Le *Source(s):* Carse (see above)
Roi des quadrilles, Le *Source(s):* BAKR
Muse, Lewis Anderson c. 1896- [singer, instrumentalist, songwriter]
Muse, Rabbit *Source(s):* HARS
Musel, Corneilli c.1585-1652 [composer]
Nervius, Leonard(us) *Source(s):* NGDM
Note(s): Do not confuse with Nervius [i.e., Léonard(us) le père]
Musel, Robert [or Bob] (Saul) 1909-1999 [lyricist]
Note(s): Portrait: BBDP
Carlisle, Jack *Source(s):* CPOL RE-308-027
Clancy, Joe *Source(s):* CPOL RE-19-019
Note(s): Jt. pseud.: H(oward) E(llington) Barnes & Harold (Cornelius) Fields.
Lopez, Roberto *Source(s):* CCE45 #60692 Efor70588; CCE72
Musker, Frank [songwriter]
Dukes *Source(s):* EPMU
Note(s): Jt. pseud.: Dominic Bugatti.
Mussulli, Henry W. 1917-1967 [reeds player, arranger, composer]
Mussulli, Boots *Source(s):* KINK; LCAR
Musychenko, Gavriil Vakulovich 1847-1903 [composer]
Musicescu, Gavriil *Source(s):* ROOM
Mütter, Herbert George 1965- [trombonist, composer]
Mütter, Bertl *Source(s):* OMUO

Muzáková, Johana (Rottová) 1830-1899 [librettist]
Svétlá, Karolina *Source(s):* LCAR; LOWN
Myddleton, William [or Arnold] H. 1873-1950 [composer, conductor, dramatist]
Middleton, Arnold H. *Source(s):* CPMU
Middleton, Arnold Safroni *Source(s):* SMIN; http://www.rapc.co.uk/history/imperial_echoes.htm (16 Oct. 2002)
Middleton, William H. *Source(s):* REHG; REHH
Safroni, Arnold *Source(s):* CPMU; REHG; REHH; SMIN
Myers, Charles [writer on music, editor]
MacSherry, Les *Source(s):* MUOP 121:1413 (1998): 190
Myers, Dwight 1967- [songwriter]
Heavy D. *Source(s):* CPOL PA-1-054-198; PMUS-96; LCAR
Myers, James E(dward) 1919-2001 [composer, author, music publisher]
DeKnight, Jimmy *Source(s):* ASCP; CCE51-56; CPOL PA-302-325; GOTH; OB01; ROCK
Myers, Louis 1929-1994 [singer, guitarist, songwriter]
Meyers, Louie *Source(s):* HARS
Myers, Richard 1949- [singer, songwriter, journalist]
Note(s): Do not confuse with Richardson Myers, composer, producer (1901-).
Hell, Richard *Source(s):* EPMU; LCAR; PEN2; ROOM
Myers, Richardson 1901- [composer, producer]
Note(s): Do not confuse with Richard Myers, singer, songwriter, (1949-).
Myers, Richard *Source(s):* PSND
Myers, Sharon [or Sherry] (Lee) 1944- [singer, songwriter]
Dain, Sharon Lee *Source(s):* http://www.swinginchicks.com/jackie_deshannon.htm (12 Jan. 2005)
Note(s): Incorrect listing of surname.
Dee, Jackie *Source(s):* CCE58
DeShannon, Jackie *Source(s):* CCE60-62; DIMA; GRAT; KICK; WORT
Jackie Lee *Source(s):* http://www.swinginchicks.com/jackie_deshannon.htm
Shannon, Jackie *Source(s):* http://www.swinginchicks.com/jackie_deshannon.htm
Sherry Lee *Source(s):* http://www.swinginchicks.com/jackie_deshannon.htm
Myles, Billy 1934-1976 [guitarist, composer]
King, Freddie [or Freddy] *Source(s):* EPMU; ROOM
Myrick, David Luke 1916-1972 [singer, songwriter, guitarist]
Man with a Million Friends, (The) *Source(s):* EPMU; MCCL; PSND
Tyler, (T.) Texas *Source(s):* AMUS; CCE58-59; CCME; EPMU; MCCL; PSND; STAC
Mysliveček, Josef 1737-1781 [composer]
Note(s): See LCAR for variant spellings of name.
Boëmo, Il (divino) *Source(s):* ALMC; GROL; MACM; NGDM; RIEM
Divino Boëmo, Il *Source(s):* BAKR; GROL; NGDM
Venatorini, Il *Source(s):* BAKR; MACM; NGDM; RIEM
Mysliwec, Karl Maria 1876-1956 [composer]
Jäger, Karl Maria *Source(s):* OMUO

– N –

Nachtigall, Othmar [or Ottmar] 1487-1537 [theorist, composer, organist]
Luscinius, Othmar [or Ottomar(us)] *Source(s):* IBIM; LCAR; MACM; NGDM; WORB
Progneus, Ottomar *Source(s):* IBIM; WORB
Nadel, Warren 1930- [composer, author, dentist]
Starr, Randy *Source(s):* ASCP; CCE57-60; CCE64; CPOL RE-670-681
Nagle, William S. [composer]
Note(s): Portrait: ETUP 54:7 (July 1936): 404
Averell, Philip *Source(s):* TPRF
Nakamura, Sawako 1931- [composer]
Kawai, Sawako *Source(s):* BUL3; COHN; HIXN
Nakat, Lothar 1925- [composer]
Gigg, Ulli *Source(s):* CCE67; KOMP; KOMS; PFSA
Sky, Benny *Source(s):* KOMP; KOMS; PFSA
Nanton, Joseph [or Joe] 1904-1946 [trombonist, composer]
Irish, Joseph N. *Source(s):* LCAR
Note(s): Possibly original name.
Nanton, Sam *Source(s):* LCAR
Nanton, Tricky Sam *Source(s):* KINK; LCAR
Napier, M. [composer]
Reipan, M. *Source(s):* CPMU (publication date 1869)
Narholz, Gerhard 1937- [composer, arranger, conductor]
Candler, Norman *Source(s):* KOMP, KOMS; OMUO; PFSA
Prennessel, Peter *Source(s):* CCE56
Sieben, Otto *Source(s):* KOMP; OMUO; PFSA; RIES
Narmore, Edgar Eugene 1944- [composer, author, actor]
High, Miles *Source(s):* ASCP
Nasca, Carlos D. 1873-1936 [music publisher, composer]
Gaucho Relámpago, El *Source(s):* TODO
Naschitz, Theodor 1859-1930 [composer]
Nachèz, Tivadar *Source(s):* CPMU; LCAR
Nasco, Jan [or Giovanni] c.1510-1561 [composer]
Metre Gian *Source(s):* LCAR; NGDM

Naselli, Diego mentioned 1748 [composer]
Lasnel(l), Egidio *Source(s):* GROL; IBIM; MELL; STGR; WORB
Na(i)sh, Francis (Henry) ?-1899 [singer, teacher, composer]
Novara, Franco [or Franke] *Source(s):* CPMU; IBIM; WORB
Nash, Graham 1942- [singer, songwriter]
Ransford, (L.) *Source(s):* BLIC; *Goldmine.* 28:12:571 (14 June 2002): 70
Note(s): Jt. pseud.: (Harold) Allan Clarke & Tony (Christopher) Hicks.
Nash, Lemoine 1898-1969 [singer, banjoist; guitarist, songwriter]
Banjo Boy, The *Source(s):* HARS
Nash, Lemon *Source(s):* DRSC; HARS
Nathan, David [composer]
British Ambassador of Soul *Source(s):* http://www.davidnathan.com/indexDN.html (11 Oct. 2002)
Nathan, Isaac 1790 (or 92)-1864 [composer]
Australia's First Composer *Source(s):* NGDM (see under: "Australia" [bibliography])
Father of Australian Music *Source(s):* NGDM (see above)
I. N. *Source(s):* CPMU ("Princely Strangers")
Note(s): Probable pseud.
Natividad Martinez, José 1959- [bandleader, composer, arranger]
Nati *Source(s):* EPMU; PEN2
Naty *Source(s):* PEN2
Natsume, Koyoko 1915- [composer]
Watari, Koyoko *Source(s):* COHN; HIXN
Nauenburg, Gustav 1803-1863 [singer, teacher, writer on music]
St-z, Carl *Source(s):* HEYT
Naumann, Johann Gottlieb 1741-1801 [composer, poet]
Naumann, G(iovanni) A(madeo) *Source(s):* LCAR; MELL
Naumann, Johann Amadeus *Source(s):* WORB
Navarro, Autlan de 1947- [bandleader, guitarist, songwriter]
Devadip *Source(s):* LCAR
Santana, Carlos *Source(s):* WORL
Navarro Moreno, José de Jesús 1913- [singer, lyricist]
Navarro, Chucho *Source(s):* HWOM
Navoigille, Guillaume (Julien) c.1745-1811 [composer]
Julien, G. *Source(s):* MELL
Ndonfeng, Samuel Thomas 1952- [singer, composer]
Thomas, Sam Fan *Source(s):* EPMU
N'Dour, Youssou 1959- [singer, composer]
Petit Prince de Dakar *Source(s):* PEN2
Neal, Raful 1936- [singer, composer, harmonica player]
Little Walter of Louisiana *Source(s):* HERZ
Neale, J(ohn) M(ason) 1818-1866 [author, poet, hymnist, translator]
Note(s): Portrait: CYBH
Aurelius Gratianus *Source(s):* CART
Gratianus, Aurelius *Source(s):* CART; PSNN
J. M. N. *Source(s):* LCAR; PSND
O. A. E. *Source(s):* JULN
Priest of the Church of England, A *Source(s):* CART; LCAR
Priest of the Diocese, A *Source(s):* CART; LCAR
Priest of the English Church, A *Source(s):* CART
Two Priests of the Church of England *Source(s):* PSNN
Neat(e), John ?-1949 [composer]
Norman, Victor *Source(s):* CCE34 Efor32725
Ray, Lil(l)ian *Source(s):* CCE35 Efor4141; CCE67; GREN
Nedrow, John W(ilson) 1912- [singer, lyricist]
Worden, Willey *Source(s):* ASCP; CCE67
Needham, William Horace Thomas 1837-1927 [comedian, author, lyricist]
Lingard, W(illiam) H(orace) *Source(s):* GAN2 (port.)
Neefe, Christian Gottlob 1748-1798 [composer]
Fenee *Source(s):* http://www.musicologie.org/theses/neefen.html (3 Feb. 2005)
Nefedov, Alexandra Doris 1944-1969 [composer]
Alexandra *Source(s):* PFSA
Neff, Lyle Kevin 1959- [composer, arranger, writer on music]
Lyle, Kevin *Source(s):* http://copland.udel.edu/~lneff/vita.html (15 Aug. 2005)
Negelein, Christoph Adam 1656-1701 [musician, poet]
Celadon *Source(s):* IBIM; WORB
Negri, Cesare (de') c.1535-1604 [dancing master; writer on dance]
Trombone, Il *Source(s):* LCAR; MACM; NGDM; WORB
Neidlinger, W(illiam) H(arold) 1863-1924 [organist, conductor, composer]
Note(s): Portraits: CYBH; ETUP 54:7 (July 1936): 404; MUWO 3:6 (1903): 102
Heinrich, C(arl) *Source(s):* CCE35 R35653; TPRF
LeFevre, Achille *Source(s):* CCE35 R35601; CPMU; TPRF
Starr, T(homas) B(ristol) *Source(s):* CCE35 R35655; ETUD; TPRF
Neild, James Edward 1824-1906 [forensic pathologist, drama & music critic]

Jacques *Source(s):* DAUM
Sinapsis *Source(s):* http://www.chs.unimelb.edu.au/programs/jnmhu/umfm/biogs/FM00016b.htm (1 Aug. 2005)
Sly, Christopher *Source(s):* http://www.chs.unimelb.edu.au/programs/jnmhu/umfm/biogs/FM00016b.htm
Notes(s): Also used by Maurice Willson Disher.
Tahite *Source(s):* DAUM

Nelhams, Terence 1940- [singer, author, financial consultant]
Faith, Adam *Source(s):* EPMU; LCAR

Nelke, Herman 1889-1968 [actor, director, producer, author]
Lindsay, Howard *Source(s):* GAN2

Nelson, Albert 1923-1992 [singer, songwriter, guitarist]
King, Albert *Source(s):* CM02; WASH

Nelson, Benjamin Earl 1938- [singer, songwriter]
King, Ben E. *Source(s):* EPMU; LCAR; PEN2; PSND

Nelson, Betty Mae 1921?-2001 [songwriter, singer, actress]
Nelson, Portia *Source(s):* WASH

Nelson, Eric Hilliard 1940-1985 [singer, songwriter, actor]
Nelson, Rick *Source(s):* CM02; EPMU; LCAR; MCCL; RECR

Nelson, Harrison D. 1925-1999 [singer, songwriter]
Harris, Peppermint *Source(s):* HERZ; LCAR; OB99
Peppermint Harris *Source(s):* CCE61; LCAR

Nelson, Harry Edward 1941-1994 [composer, singer]
Bo Pete *Source(s):* http://www.nationmaster.com/encyclopedia/Harry-Nilsson (19 May 2005)
Nilsson, Harry *Source(s):* ALMN; CASS; CM10; DIMA; EPMU; GAMM; HARR; PEN2

Nelson, Iromeio 1902-1974 [singer, pianist, songwriter]
Nelson, Romeo *Source(s):* HARS; LCAR

Nelson, Lucille 1894-1970 [singer, songwriter]
Baker, Fanny *Source(s):* HARS
Blues Singer Supreme, The *Source(s):* HARS
Cameo Girl, The *Source(s):* HARS
Chicago Cyclone *Source(s):* HARS
Georgia Peach *Source(s):* HARS
Note(s): See also Richard [or Ricardo] Wayne Penniman.
Harlem's Favorite *Source(s):* HARS
Hegamin, Lucille *Source(s):* HARS; LCAR

Nelson, Oswald George 1906-1975 [bandleader, songwriter, actor]
Andrews, Barney *Source(s):* SUTT
Briggs, Arnold *Source(s):* SUTT
Burton, Dick *Source(s):* SUTT
Nelson, Ozzie *Source(s):* KINK; LCAR; PEN1

Nelson, Prince Rogers 1958- [singer, songwriter, guitarist, arranger]
AFKAP *Source(s):* WORL
Note(s): AFKAP = Artist Formerly Known as Prince
Artist, The *Source(s):* WORL
Artist Formerly Known as Prince *Source(s):* LCAR
Camille *Source(s):* BLIC; WARN
Christopher *Source(s):* WARN; http://www.biography.ms/Prince_(artist).html (18 May 2005)
Coco, Joey *Source(s):* WARN; http://www.biography.ms/Prince_(artist).html
His Royal Badness *Source(s):* PSND; http://www.biography.ms/Prince_(artist).html
Kid, The *Source(s):* PSND; WARN
Nevermind, Alexander *Source(s):* PMUS-85; WARN
Prince *Source(s):* CM01; CM14; KICK; HARR; LCAR; PEN2; PSND; WORL
Purple One, The *Source(s):* http://www.biography.ms/Prince_(artist).html
Skipper *Source(s):* PSND
Spooky Electric *Source(s):* WARN
Starr, Jamie *Source(s):* PSND; WARN; http://www.biography.ms/Prince_(artist).html
TAFKAP *Source(s):* CM14; LCAR
Note(s): TAFKAP = The Artist Formerly Known as Prince.
The Artist Formerly Known as Prince
Tracy, Christopher *Source(s):* WARN; http://www.biography.ms/Prince_(artist).html
Victor *Source(s):* WARN
Note(s): Also used by Percy Bysshe Shelley.

Nelson, Ron(ald J.) 1929- [composer]
Quintessential American Composer, The *Source(s):* http://www.referencrecordings.com/DallasWind.HTML (24 Oct. 2002)

Nelson, Sidney 1800-1862 [composer, publisher]
Sydney, Nelson *Source(s):* CPMU

Nelson, Willie (Hugh) 1933- [singer, guitarist, songwriter]
King of Country Music, The *Source(s):* PSND
Note(s): See also Roy (Claxton) Acuff, David Gordon Kirkpatrick & Hank [i.e., Hir(i)am (King)] Williams.
King of Progressive Country *Source(s):* SHAD (see under: "Nashville Outlaws")
Nelson, Abbott Willie *Source(s):* PSND
Nelson, Country Willi *Source(s):* PSND
Outlaw, The *Source(s):* CCME; FLIN
Redheaded Stranger, The *Source(s):* FLIN; WORT
Shakespeare of Country Music *Source(s):* FLIN

Nembri, Octavianus 1584-1648 (or 49) [composer]
Nembri, Damianus *Source(s):* NGDM

Nemtzow, Lisa 1952- [composer]
Nemzo, Lisa *Source(s):* ASCP
Nenna, Pomponio 1556-1618 [composer]
Cavaliere Cesareo, Il *Source(s):* GRV3
Nenning, Johann 1615-1685 [composer, organist]
Pater a Monte Carmelo *Source(s):* NGDM
Spiridion, (Pater a Monte Carmelo) *Source(s):* LCAR; NGDM
Nerijnen, Jan van 1935- [composer]
Nimbly, John *Source(s):* SUPN
Seeker, David *Source(s):* SUPN
Taler, Werner *Source(s):* SUPN
Nesmith, Michael 1942- [songwriter]
Blessing, Michael *Source(s):* http://www.breaktv.com/pages/monkee_bio_mike.html (11 Oct. 2002)
Nez *Source(s):* http://www.breaktv.com/pages/monkee_bio_mike.html
One with the Hat, The *Source(s):* http://www.breaktv.com/pages/monkee_bio_mike.html
Smart Monkee, The *Source(s):* MUHF
Nestler, Fritz 1893-1988 [composer]
Fertö, Fritz *Source(s):* OMUO
Neto, Laurindo José de Araujo Almeida Nobrega 1917-1995 [guitarist, composer, arranger]
Aldeen, Ned *Source(s):* CCE63
Almeida, Laurindo *Source(s):* LCAR
Almedia, Lindo *Source(s):* LCAR
Lindo *Source(s):* LCAR
Portch, Al *Source(s):* JAMU
Note(s): Also used by James Stagliano.
Netzel, Laura Constance (née Pistolekors) 1839-1927 [composer, pianist]
Lago, (Miss) *Source(s):* COHN; DWCO; HEIN; HIXN
Netzle, Klaus 1926- [composer]
Larson, Claude *Source(s):* KOMP; KOMS; PFSA
Larson, Ewald *Source(s):* CCE65
Nishadba, Gyan *Source(s):* LCAR
Neuberger, Jean (Bernard Daniel) 1891-1976 [composer, author]
Note(s): In GREN surname given: Neuburger.
Lenoir, Jean *Source(s):* CASS; CCE65; GAMM; GREN; PFSA; RIES
Neugarten, Zvi Herbert 1912- [composer]
Nagan, Tsevi *Source(s):* LCAR
Nagan, Zvi Herbert *Source(s):* BUL2; BUL3
Neukomm, Sigismund (Ritter von) 1778-1858 [composer, pianist]
Note(s): Portrait: ETUP 54:8 (Aug. 1936): 468
King of Brummagem *Source(s):* GRV3; SCHO
Neumann, Emil 1836-1922 [singer, composer]
Bliemchen *Source(s):* MACM
Neumann, Ferenc 1878-1952 [playwright]
Molnár, Ferenc *Source(s):* GAN2
Neumeyer, Heike 1963- [composer]
Grand, June *Source(s):* PFSA
Neumeyer, Peter Alexander 1926- [composer]
Alexander, Peter *Source(s):* PFSA
Neupert, Fritz 1893-1943 [violinist, composer]
Newport, Fred *Source(s):* PIPE
Neužil, František 1907-1995 [author]
Jezer, Fráňa *Source(s):* WEOP
Nevin, (Dale) Arthur (Finley) 1871-1943 [composer, conductor, ethnomusicologist]
Note(s): Portrait: ETUP 54:8 (Aug. 1936): 468
Dale, Arthur *Source(s):* GROL
Nevin, Ethelbert (Woodbridge) 1862-1901 [composer]
Note(s): Portraits: ETUP 53:4 (Apr. 1935): 201; ETUP 54:2 (Feb. 1936): cover; EWCY; HOWD
Woodbridge, (Ethelbert) *Source(s):* ETUD; GOTH; TPRF
Nevin, Gordon Balch 1892-1943 [composer]
Note(s): Portraits: ETUP 54:8 (Aug. 1936): 468; MUSA 33:16 (12 Feb. 1921): 25
Allen, Ben D. *Source(s):* CPMU; TPRF
Shadwell, William B. *Source(s):* CCE27 E660763
Newbury, Milton S(im), (Jr.) 1940-2002 [singer, songwriter, guitarist]
Little White Wolf, The AMUS
Newbury, Mickey *Source(s):* ENCM; EPMU; HARR; MCCL; PEN2
Newcomer, John T. 1875-1954 [composer]
Hall, John T. *Source(s):* MCBD; REHG; SHMP; SUPN
Newell, Joseph Edward 1843- [composer, organist]
Murretti, Carlo *Source(s):* CPMU; GOTH
Podesta, Nicola *Source(s):* CPMU; GOTH
Newell, Norman 1919-2003 (or 04) [composer, lyricist, producer]
Baron, Ray *Source(s):* CCE58
Blake, Garry *Source(s):* CPOL RE-305-674
Boyd, Robin *Source(s):* CCE56; CPOL RE-199-454
Burke, Dave *Source(s):* CCE50
Chalmers, Cy *Source(s):* CPOL RE-248-483
Note(s): Jt. pseud.: Michael Carr [i.e., Maurice Alfred Cohen]
Clifford, Collin *Source(s):* CCE52-53; CPOL RE-75-999
Collins, Ray *Source(s):* CCE54; CCE67; CPOL 75-731; CPOL RE-76-044
Lane, David *Source(s):* CCE57; CPOL RE-222-106
Martin, Ray *Source(s):* CPOL RE-76-044
Moran, John *Source(s):* CCE51-53; CCE60; CPOL RE-72-628
Ray, David *Source(s):* CCE56; CCE59; CPOL RE-222-106
Richards, Baker *Source(s):* CCE58
Richards, Baker, and Ross *Source(s):* CPOL RE-314-284

Richards, Ross *Source(s):* CCE58
Rivers, Ken *Source(s):* CPOL RE-305-651
Starr, Peter *Source(s):* CCE52; LCCC 1948-54 (see reference)
Note(s): Jt. pseud.: Phil(ip) Green.
West, David *Source(s):* CCE60; CPOL RE-457-933

Newlon, Richard [composer]
Newlon, Jack *Source(s):* CLTP ("Ernie Kovacs Show")

Newman, Alfred 1900 (or 01)-1970 [composer]
Godfather of Celluloid Music *Source(s):* http://www.bbc.co.uk/dna/h2g2/A610804 (24 Oct. 2002)
Newman, Pappy *Source(s):* BBDP

Newman, Anthony 1941- [composer, harpsichordist, pianist]
Hip Harpsichordist, The *Source(s):* PSND

Newman, Barbara Belle 1922- [composer, author, producer]
Ogal, T. F. *Source(s):* ASCP

Newman(n), Gary 1944- [singer, songwriter]
Mark Twain of Rock *Source(s):* CASS
Newman, Randy *Source(s):* CASS; HARD

Newman, Jimmy C.[actually Yves] 1927- [singer, guitarist, songwriter]
Note(s): Adopted middle initial "C" which stands for "Cajun."
Alligator Man, Mr. *Source(s):* STAC
Cajun King *Source(s):* MCCL
Mr. Alligator Man *Source(s):* STAC

Newton, H(enry) Chance 1854-1931 [critic, dramatist, lyricist]
Carados *Source(s): Source(s):* GANB; KILG; LCAR
Note(s): In GANA incorrectly given as jt. pseud.: Richard W(illiam) Butler?
Gawain *Source(s):* KILG
Henry, Richard *Source(s):* GANA; GANB; KILG
Note(s): Jt. pseud.: Richard W(illiam) Butler.
Richard-Henry *Source(s):* LCAR
Note(s): Jt. pseud.: Richard W(illiam) Butler.

Newton, John 1725-1807 [hymnist, clergyman]
Great Blasphemer, The *Source(s):* http://www.gospelcom.net/chi/GLIMPSEF/Glimpses/glmps028.shtml (11 Oct. 2002)
Omicron *Source(s):* CYBH
Young Whitefield *Source(s):* http://www.ccel.org/ccel/eee/files/newton.htm (5 Feb. 2005)

Newton, (Mrs.) William Edward fl. 1870 [composer]
Mirana *Source(s):* CPMU; GOTT; HOVL

Ngcukana, Ezra (Nyaniso) 1954- [saxophonist, composer]
Pharoah *Source(s):* GROL

Niccolò, de Francesco ?-1362 (or 63) [composer]
Gherardello, da Firenze *Source(s):* LCAR

Nice, Steven 1951- [singer, songwriter]
Harley, Steve *Source(s):* AMUS; HARR; LCAR; NOMG

Nichol, Henry Ernest 1862-1928 [hymnist]
Sterne, Colin *Source(s):* CYBH (port.); DIEH; ROGG

Nicholas, Kasanda Wa Mikalay 1939-1985 [guitarist, composer]
Dr. Nico *Source(s):* PEN2
Nico, Dr. *Source(s):* MUWB; PEN2

Nichols, (Ernest) Loring 1905-1965 [composer; conductor, cornetist]
Loring, Ernest *Source(s):* LCAR
Nicholas, Red *Source(s):* AMUS; ASCP; EPMU; KINK; LCAR; SUTT; WIEC

Nicks, Stephanie (Lynn) 1948- [singer, songwriter]
Nicks, Stevie *Source(s):* ALMN; AMUS; CM02; CM25; DIMA; EPMU; HARR; PMUS

Nicolai, Bruno 1926-1991 [composer, conductor]
Leonhardt, Hans Günther *Source(s):* http://marchese-desade.org/musica/musica.html (6 Jan. 2005)

Nicolai, (Christoph) Friedrich 1732 (or 33)-1811 [editor, author, music historian]
Neuber, Christian Ludwig *Source(s):* WORB
Seuberlich, Daniel *Source(s):* CPMS; CPMU; WORB

Nicolaie, Louis François 1811-1879 [librettist, conductor]
Clairville (the younger) *Source(s):* CPMU; GAN2; GANA; MELL; NGDO
Clairville, Louis François *Source(s):* WORB
Clairville, M. *Source(s):* LCAR

Niday Canaday, Edna Veronica 1907-1991 [composer, author]
Abbott, Eve *Source(s):* ASCP; CPOL TXu-8-929
Canaday, Veronica *Source(s):* ASCP
Gentry, Will *Source(s):* PAu-47-001

Nieberding, William Joseph 1948- [composer, singer]
Denton, Will *Source(s):* ASCP

Nieblich, Werner Julius Gottfried 1907-1969 [musicologist, music critic, novelist]
Rehberg, Hans Peter *Source(s):* WORB

Niederbremer, Artur 1924-2003 [composer, songwriter, publisher]
Arnie, Ralf *Source(s):* CCE56-62; CPOL RE-200-943; http://www.gema.de/engl/communication/news/n167/kurzmeldungen.shtml (11 May 2005)
Arnie, Rolfe *Source(s):* CCE56-63
Bremer, Rolf *Source(s):* CCE55
Rasch, (Dieter) *Source(s):* CCE56-60; KOMP; KOMS; RIES; SUPN
Valentin, Peter *Source(s):* CCE55

Niedhammer, Ronald Edward 1930- [composer, author, singer]
Nelson, Ronnie *Source(s):* ASCP; CPOL PAu-74-625
Niedola, E. K. 19th cent. [pianist; composer]
Kompánski, Eugène *Source(s):* CPMU (publication date 1887)
Nielebock, Hermann 1888-1954 [composer]
Niel, Herms *Source(s):* SUPN
Nieman, Alfred 1913- [composer, pianist]
Legray, Robert *Source(s):* GOTH
Merlin, Alfred *Source(s):* CCE52
Nierow, (Peter) Bernard 1934- [pianist, composer, conductor]
Nero, Peter (Bernard) *Source(s):* CCE61-62; CM19; PEN1
Niessen, Josef 1922- [composer]
Daffodil, Dave *Source(s):* PFSA
Nieuwenhove, Ernest Alfons Van 1880-1968 [composer, pianist]
Agrèves, Ernest d' *Source(s):* CCE42; GREN
Nieuwenhuysen, Jean Nicolas Gustave (van) 1812-1862 [librettist]
Vaëz, Gustave *Source(s):* LCAR; LOWN; MELL
Waëz, Gustave *Source(s):* LCAR
Nieuwland, Rens 1953- [composer, guitarist]
Newland, Rens *Source(s):* OMUO
Nigri von Sankt Albino, Julius 1849-1895 [author]
Bohrmann-Riegen *Source(s):* PIPE
Note(s): Jt. pseud.: Heinrich Bohrmann.
Riegen, J. *Source(s):* GAN1; GAN2 (see under: Bohrmann, Heinrich); PIPE
Nigro, Laura 1947-1997 [singer, songwriter]
Nyro, Laura *Source(s):* DIMA; EPMU; HARR; LCAR; PEN2; PSND
Nikitich, Vladamir 1958- [producer, songwriter]
Afanasieff, Walter (N.) *Source(s):* CM26
Nikolowsky, Anton(y) 1855-1916 [librettist]
Antony, F(riedrich) *Source(s):* GAN1; GAN2; STGR; WORB
Nilles, Brad 1951- [composer, author, guitarist]
Nilles, Catfish *Source(s):* ASCP
Nini, Achinoam 1969- [songwriter]
Noa *Source(s):* LCAR; http://www.multimania.com/achinoam (11 Oct. 2002)
Nirella, Vincent Daniel 1873-1956 [composer]
Pittsburgh's March King *Source(s):* SMIN
Nite, Norman N. [writer on music]
Mr. Music *Source(s):* LCAR
Note(s): See also Jerry (P.) Osborne.
Nitrollando, Peter, Jr. 1942- [pianist, singer, composer]
Bataan, Joe *Source(s):* CCE68; MUWB; PEN2
Nitze, Otto (Max) 1924-1988 [composer]
Dawitt, Tom *Source(s):* KOMS; REHH; SUPN
Note(s): Also used by Gustav Lotterer?
Nitzelberger, Moritz Georg 1840 (or 41)-1904 [librettist, lyricist]
West, Moritz *Source(s):* GAN1; GAN2; LOWN; MELL; PIPE; WORB
Witzelsberger, Moritz Georg *Source(s):* MACM
Note(s): Incorrect spelling of surname.
Nitzsche, Bernard (Alfred) 1937-2000 [composer, arranger, producer]
Nitzsche, Jack *Source(s):* HARD; LCAR; NOMG; OB00; PEN2
Nix, Willie 1922- [singer, guitarist, songwriter]
Memphis Blues Boy *Source(s):* HARS; LCAR
Njurling, Sten 1892-1945 [composer]
Borganoff, Igor *Source(s):* GREN
Winter, Fred *Source(s):* GREN
Noack, Armona A., (Jr.) 1930-1978 [singer, songwriter]
Note(s): In EPMU given name: De Armand.
Noack, Eddie *Source(s):* ENCM; EPMU; MCCL; PSND
Wood, Tommy *Source(s):* MCCL; PSND
Noack, Walter 1900- [composer]
Dillinger, Paul *Source(s):* KOMP; PFSA; SUPN
Noak, Herbert 1898- [composer]
Cowler, Jim *Source(s):* CCE55; CCE57; PFSA
Henderson, Herbert *Source(s):* PFSA
Kauler, Herbert *Source(s):* CCE34 Efor30981; PFSA
Noble, Ray(mond) (Stanley) 1903-1978 [composer]
Chadwick, Donald *Source(s):* CCE59
Norman, Reginald *Source(s):* http://www.jabw.demon.co.uk/discuss02.htm (15 Aug. 2005)
Stanley *Source(s):* CCE59 ("Resolutions for 1932")
Noble, Reginald [or Reggie] 196?- [songwriter, performer]
Redman *Source(s):* AMIR; AMUS; LCAR; PMUS-00
Noble, Thomas Tertius 1867-1953 [composer, organist]
Note(s): Portraits: CYBH; ETUP 54:8 (Aug. 1936): 468
Nomabama, Adam *Source(s):* TPRF
Note(s): Jt. pseud: Edwin Shippen Barnes, Harry Alexander Matthews & Johann Sebastian Matthews.
Nobles, Clarence Robert 1908-1980 [singer, songwriter, poet]
Nolan, Bob [or Robert] *Source(s):* AMUS; CANE; LCAR
Nolan, (Sister) Aloysius [songwriter]
Kerr, Robert Nolan *Source(s):* CCE37 E60776; CCE57; TPRF
Nolte, Roy E. 1896-1979 [songwriter]
Note(s): Portrait: ETUP 54:9 (Sept. 1936): 534
Dahl, Wilbur *Source(s):* CCE58

Norman, Edward W. *Source(s):* CCE32 E27966; CCE51; CCE59; CPOL RE-4-464
Wahl, Wilbur *Source(s):* CCE58-59
Nonn, Karl-Heinz 1956- [composer]
Nonka, Friedel *Source(s):* KOMP; PFSA
Nono, Luigi 1924- [composer]
Jaja Luigi *Source(s):* SPIE
Luigi Jaja *Source(s):* SPIE
Noonan, Robert (A.) 1949- [singer, songwriter]
Nile, Willie *Source(s):* DIMA
Norden, Hugo (Svan) 1909-1986 [composer]
Dana, Arthur *Source(s):* CCE53 E73009; CPOL 102-185
Note(s): A. P. Schmidt house name; see NOTES: Dana, Arthur.
Erich, Carl *Source(s):* CCE48 E27205
Note(s): A. P. Schmidt house name; see NOTES: Erich, Carl.
Gordon, Hugh *Source(s):* CCE45 E136108
Note(s): A. P. Schmidt house name; see NOTES: Gordon, Hugh.
Parkman, Harold *Source(s):* CCE45 E136207; CCE64; CPOL RE-102-256
Nordlander, Bert Carsten 1905- [composer]
Carsten, Bert *Source(s):* CCE31 Eunp44256; GREN
Nordman, Chester 1895-1073 [songwriter]
Belmont, Eric *Source(s):* CCE46 E11259; CCE47
Lane, Walter *Source(s):* CCE53; CCE55
Note(s): Also used by Gregory Phil Cohn.
Otis, Stephen *Source(s):* CCE52-53; CCE55
Ryder, Dudley *Source(s):* CCE51 E58451; CCE55
Note(s): Also used by Carl Wilhelm Kern.
Norman, Don(ald) [songwriter, performer]
Storball, Don *Source(s):* PSND
Norman, John [hymnist]
Norman *Source(s):* JULN (Appendix)
Norman, Larry [songwriter]
Father of Christian Rock, The *Source(s):* http://www.zapcom.net/~glade/writers.html (Oct. 24 2002)
Norman, Leo [composer]
Lyon, David *Source(s):* MUWB
Normand, Théodule Elzéar Xavier 1812-1887 (or 88) [organist, editor, writer on music]
Huysman, Théodule *Source(s):* LCAR
Nisard, Théodore *Source(s):* BAKR; GROL; LCAR; MACM; NGDM; WORB
Torf, Théodule-Eléazar-Xavier *Source(s):* LCAR
North, Edith 1903-1988 [singer, songwriter]
Allen, Maybelle *Source(s):* HARS
Johnson, (Mrs.) Edith *Source(s):* HARS; LCAR
North, Hatti(e) *Source(s):* HARS
North, Francis 1637-1685 [musician, writer on music, lawyer]
Guilford, Baron [or Lord] *Source(s):* MACM; SADC; WORB
Northey, Carrie 1866 (or 69)-1937 [composer, singer]
Note(s): Portrait: ETUP 55:8 (Aug. 1937): 544
Roma, Cara *Source(s):* KILG; LCAR; MACM; NGAM; STGR
Norville, (J.) Kenneth 1908- 1999 [composer, conductor, vibraphonist]
Kenny, Ken *Source(s):* JAMU
Mr. and Mrs. Swing *Source(s):* EPMU
Note(s): Jt. pseud. with wife: Mildred Bailey.
Norvo, Kenneth *Source(s):* CCE63; EPMU; KINK; LCAR
Norvo, Red *Source(s):* ASCP; BAKE; CCE63; CM12; LCAR
Noseda, Aldo 1852-1916 [music critic]
Misovulgo, Il *Source(s):* GROL; WORB
Notari, Angelo 1566-1663 [composer]
Negligente, Il *Source(s):* GROL
Nothdorf, Georg 1934- [composer]
Feuer, Axel *Source(s):* KOMP
Notker, (Balbulus) c.840-912 [monk, composer, writer on music]
Balbulus (the Stammerer) *Source(s):* LCAR; MACM; NGDM
Novak, Edmund 1912- [composer]
Glad, Sven *Source(s):* KOMP; PFSA
Novo, Salvador 1904-1974 [critic]
Santana, Jorge *Source(s):* RILM 96-07733-ap
Nowlan, George 1925- [trumpeter, singer, songwriter]
Davis, Danny *Source(s):* AMUS; CCE59-60; MCCL
Nürnberg, Karlheinz 1918-1999 [composer]
Nuernberg, Carlo Enrico *Source(s):* BUL3
Nusbaum, Nathaniel Richard 1913-2000 [writer]
Nash, Nathaniel Richard *Source(s):* GOTH
Nušić, Branislav 1864-1938 [author]
Akiba, Ben *Source(s):* PIPE; PSND
Nussbaum, Horst 1940- [composer]
White, Jack *Source(s):* CCE73 Efor164984; PFSA
Nützlader, Rudolf 1885- [composer]
Cordy, Harry *Source(s):* OMUO
Nwapa, Alban [rapper]
Dr. Alban *Source(s):* EPMU
Nys, Carl Augustin Léon de 1917- [musicologist]
Boncourt, Charles Marie de *Source(s):* WORB

– O –

Oberdörffer, Manfred 1944- [composer]
Tony *Source(s):* PFSA
Õberg, Ludwig Theodore 1820-1860 [author]
Ståhl, Axel Iwar *Source(s):* CPMU

Oberstein, Eli ?-1960 [songwriter]
Lewis, Pat *Source(s):* PMUS
O'Brien, Cyril C(ornelius) 1906-1994 [author, composer]
Wilson, Crane *Source(s):* PSND
O'Brien, Daniel Webster 1833-1875 [songwriter, performer]
Bryant, Dan *Source(s):* FINS p. 287; NGDM
O'Brien, Dion 1934- [singer, composer]
Springfield, Tom *Source(s):* AMUS; GAMM; HARR
O'Brien, James Nagle 1848-1879 [songwriter]
Shamus *Source(s):* IBIM; WORB
O'Carolan, Turlough 1670-1738 [harper, composer]
Note(s): It is not clear which name form is the original.
Carolan, (Turlough [or Terence]) *Source(s):* BAKE; LCAR; PEN2
Occhelli, William Wilhelm 1762-1826 [singer, composer, theatre director]
Kelly, William Wilhelm *Source(s):* OMUO
O'Kelly, William Wilhelm *Source(s):* OMUO
Occramer, Marycoo 1746-1826 [composer]
Gardner, Newport *Source(s):* SOTH; WORB
O'Ceallaigh, Thomas [librettist]
O'Kelly, Thomas *Source(s):* LOWN
Ochs, Phil 1940-1976 [singer, songwriter]
Bob Dylan's Greatest Rival *Source(s):* EPMU
Lute the Drifter *Source(s):* Cohen, David. *Phil Ochs; A Bio-bibliography*. Westport, Conn: Greenwood Press, 1999.
Outlaw, The *Source(s):* Cohen (see above)
Train, John Butler *Source(s):* Cohen (see above)
Train, Lute *Source(s):* Cohen (see above)
Ockeghem, Johannes c.1410-1497 [composer]
Prince of Music *Source(s):* http://www.grainger.de/music/composers/ockeghem.html (11 Oct. 2002)
Prince of Musicians *Source(s):* http://www.chantboy.com.lionheart/ockeghem.htm (11 Oct. 2002)
Ockenfels, Helmut 1937- [composer, pianist]
Cadler *Source(s):* KOMS; PFSA
O'Connor, Chris c.1965- [singer, songwriter, multi-instrumentalist]
Primitive Radio Gods *Source(s):* EPMU (see under: Primitive Radio Gods)
O'Connor, Edward [composer]
Granfield, Arthur Travis [or Traves] *Source(s):* CCE46 R3929; CCE47 R17598; TPRF
Note(s): "Blue Bell Waltz" (CCE46) & "Arabella" (CCE47)
O'Connor, M. [songwriter]
Cincinnatus *Source(s):* http://memory.loc.gov/ammem/smhtml/sm1870authindex1.html (11 Oct. 2002) ("The Way To Be Happy")
O'Connor, (Rev.) Norman 1922?-2003 [pianist, DJ, writer on music]
Jazz Priest, The *Source(s):* WASH
O'Daniel, Wilbert Lee 1890-1969 [songwriter, businessman, politician]
O'Daniel, Pappy *Source(s):* LCAR; MCCL
Oddone Sulli-Rao, Elisabetta 1878-1972 [composer, organist, writer on music]
Eliodd *Source(s):* HIXN; RIES
Oden, James Burke 1903 (or 05)-1977 [singer, pianist, songwriter]
Big Bloke *Source(s):* HARS; LCAR
Burke, James *Source(s):* LCAR
Oden, Old Man *Source(s):* HARS; LCAR
Oden, St. Louis Jimmy *Source(s):* LCAR
Poor Boy *Source(s):* HARS; LCAR
St. Louis Jimmy *Source(s):* CCE64-66; HARS
Odington, Walter fl. 1298-1316 [music theorist, writer on music]
Walter of Evesham *Source(s):* BAKR; Scholes, Percy A.. *Oxford Companion to Music*. 10th ed. London: Oxford University Press, 1974.
Odom, Andrew 1936-1991 [singer, songwriter]
BB Jr. *Source(s):* HARS; LCAR
Big Voice *Source(s):* HARS; LCAR
Blues Boy *Source(s):* HARS
Little BB *Source(s):* LCAR
Odom, King *Source(s):* PSND
Odom, Moonhead *Source(s):* PSND
Odom, Voice *Source(s):* HARS
O'Donnell, Charles 1886-1962 [songwriter, singer]
Three Rascals, The *Source(s):* KILG
Note(s): Jt. pseud.: Eddie Fields & Benjamin Levin.
O'Dowd, George Alan 1961- [singer, songwriter]
Boy George *Source(s):* AMUS; EPMU; GAMM; PEN2
Dust *Source(s):* BLIC
Oehlschägel, (Franz) Joseph [or Johann] 1724-1788 [composer, organist, organ builder]
Lohelius, Joannes [or Johann] *Source(s):* NGDM; WORB
Oeser, Fritz 1911-1982 [musicologist, editor]
Friedrich, Paul *Source(s):* PIPE; RILM 94-14496-ap
O'Farrill, Arturo 1921-2001 [composer, arranger, trumpeter, bandleader]
O'Farrill, Chico *Source(s):* ASCP; CM31; EPMU; LCAR; NGDJ; OB01; PEN2
O'Flynn, Honoria 1909- [composer, author, publisher]
Mack, Noreen *Source(s):* ASCP
Oganesyan [or Oganesian], Edgar (Sergey) 1930- [composer]
Hovhannessian, Edgar (Sergey) *Source(s):* NGDM; NGDO
Oganyan, Aleksandr 1889-1932 [teacher, theorist, composer]
Oganezashvili, Sasha *Source(s):* GROL

Ogle, Charles H. [composer]
Elgo, Carl *Source(s):* CPMU (publication date 1881)
O'Gwynn, James Leroy 1928- [singer songwriter]
Smilin' Irishman of Country Music, The *Source(s):* AMUS; MCCL
O'Hagan, John 1822-1890 [jurist, songwriter]
Cuilluim, Sliabh *Source(s):* CART
O'H., J. *Source(s):* WORB
Wilhelmina, Carolina (Amelia) *Source(s):* CART
Ohana, Maurice 1913-1992 [composer, pianist]
Note(s): Because of superstition, Ohana gave his birth date as 1914; (see Rae p. [1]).
French Joseph Conrad, A. *Source(s):* Rae, Caroline. *The Music of Maurice Ohana*. Burlington, VT: Ashgate, 2000.
O'Hara, Jamie 1950- [singer, songwriter, guitarist]
Note(s): Portrait: CCME (with Kieran Kane)
O'Kanes, The *Source(s):* AMUS; CCME; MCCL; MUHF; MUWB
Note(s): Jt. pseud.: Kieran Kane.
O'Hara, John (Henry) 1905-1970 [author]
Delaney, Francy *Source(s):* PIPE; PSND
Voice of the Hangover Generation, The *Source(s):* PSND
O'Hare, William Christopher [composer]
Father of Ragtime in Shreveport, The *Source(s):* http://home.earthlink.net/~ephemeralist/ohare.html (11 Oct. 2002)
Shreveport's Father of Ragtime *Source(s):* http://home.earthlink.net/~ephemeralist/ohare.html
O'Hea, Miss ?-1880 [composer]
Norton, Elena *Source(s):* CPMU; WORB
Ohl, Ferris [songwriter]
Hilton, Arthur *Source(s):* LCCF 1955-70 (see reference)
Note(s): Jt. pseud.: Walter Ehret. Ehret also used as jt. pseud. with other individuals; see NOTES: Hilton, Arthur.
Öhquist, Johannes 1861-1949 [poet]
Habermann, Wilhelm *Source(s):* LAST
O'Keefe, James (Conrad) 1892-1942 [composer, author, movie director]
Coombs, Norman *Source(s):* CCE50 R61885 ("In the Land of Smiling Waters")
Note(s): Jt. pseud.: Walter (G(ustave)) Haenschen. Also used by (Alfreda) Theodora Strandberg.
Drew, Don *Source(s):* CCE52 R96103 ("Rio")
Note(s): Also used by Lester O'Keefe.
Hare, Leslie *Source(s):* CCE26 E641233
Note(s): Also used by Lester O'Keefe?
Huntley, Austin *Source(s):* CCE50 R63437 ("Japanese Moon")
Note(s): Jt. pseud.: Walter (G(ustave)) Haenschen. Also used by Theodore (F.) Morse.
Kendall, Don *Source(s):* CCE50 R56321; CCE50 R57889
Note(s): Jt. pseud.: Walter Haenschen. Also jt. pseud.: Lester O'Keefe. Also used by Jules Hurtig & Theodore (F.) Morse; see NOTES: Kendall, Don.
Lawrence, Fred *Source(s):* CCE55 R146576 (Orig.: 1928 E666851) ("Honolulu Moon")
Note(s): Jt. pseud.: Lester O'Keefe. Also used by Luigi (Federico) Creatore.
Olcott, Herbert *Source(s):* CCE52 R95204
Rix, Jonathan, Jr. *Source(s):* CCE62; CCE67
Spencer, Eugene *Source(s):* CCE52 R96547 ("Just a Bundle of Sunshine")
Wynburn, Raymond *Source(s):* CCE54 R123527 ("Adorable")
Note(s): Jt. pseud.: Walter (G(ustave)) Haenschen.
O'Keefe, Lester 1896-1977 [composer, author, librettist, actor]
Drew, Don *Source(s):* CCE52 R94804 "("Just a Bundle of Sunshine")
Note(s): Also used by James (Conrad) O'Keefe.
Ford, Tom *Source(s):* ASCP; CCE56 R171834 ("Moonlight on the Mississippi"); CCE57-58
Note(s): Also used by George Dale Williams.
Granville, Laurence *Source(s):* CCE61
Hare, Leslie *Source(s):* CCE26 E640350; CCE53 R122526 ("Tell Me You Love Me")
Note(s): Also used by James (Conrad) O'Keefe?
Kendall, Don *Source(s):* CCE50 R56321
Note(s): Jt. pseud.: James (Conrad) O'Keefe. Also used by Walter Haenschen, Jules Hurtig & Theodore (F.) Morse; see NOTES: Kendall, Don.
Lawrence, Fred *Source(s):* CCE28 E666851; CCE55 R146576 ("Honolulu Moon")
Note(s): Jt. pseud.: James (Conrad) O'Keefe; Also used by Luigi (Federico) Creatore.
Mason, Ted *Source(s):* CCE57
O'Hara, Leslie *Source(s):* CCE26 E640350
Oliver, Frank *Source(s):* CCE50 R61882 ("Dreamy Lotus Land")
Stuart, Allan [or Allen] *Source(s):* CCE52-53; CCE57-59; CCE61; CPOL RE-68-994
Note(s): Also used by Walter (G(ustave)) Haenschen.
Okoh, Nicolette c.1964- [singer, songwriter]
Nicolette *Source(s):* AMUS; EPMU
Olcott, Chancellor John 1858 (or 60)-1932 [actor, singer, songwriter]
Note(s): Portraits: ETUP 54:9 (Sept. 1936): 534; EWPA; SHMM (Mar. 1985): 6
American Musical Leprechaun, An *Source(s):* SHMM (Mar 1985): 6
Chancellor, John *Source(s):* GAMM; REHH
Note(s): Listed as original name.
Olcott, Chauncey *Source(s):* ALMN; BBDP; GAN2; PSND, SPTH p. 296; STUW; SUTT

Oldenburg, Elimar Anton Günther Friedrich Herzog von 1844-1895 [author, composer]
Friedrich, G. *Source(s):* OMUO
Günther, Anton *Source(s):* OMUO
Maler, J. *Source(s):* OMUO
Oldham, (Dewey) Lindon, Jr. [songwriter, organist]
Note(s): In EPMU given names: Lindon Dewey.
Oldham, Spooner *Source(s):* AMUS; EPMU; HARR; PMUS
O'Leary, Joseph ?-1845 [journalist, songwriter]
Reporter, A *Source(s):* CART
Oliphant, Carolina 1766-1845 [poet, songwriter]
B. B. *Source(s):* CART
Bogan of Bogan, (Mrs.) *Source(s):* CART
Nairne, Baroness *Source(s):* CART; WORB
S. M. *Source(s):* CART
Oliphant, Thomas 1799-1873 [composer, writer on music, editor]
Sackbut, Solomon *Source(s):* CART; GROL
Tomasi, B. *Source(s):* YORM
Oliphant, William 1906-1981 [singer, composer, bandleader]
Osborne, Will *Source(s):* KINK
Oliva, Francesco c.1669-c.1730 [poet, librettist]
Antegnano, Acanlede *Source(s):* GROL
Bettona, V. *Source(s):* MELL
Bottone, Velardino *Source(s):* MELL
Viola, Ciccio *Source(s):* GROL; MELL; WORB
Oliveira, Agenor de 1908-1980 [composer]
Cartola *Source(s):* BRAZ
Oliveira, Paulo Benjamin de 1901-1949 [writer on music]
Portela, Paulo de *Source(s):* LCAR; RILM 80-01216-bm; RILM 80-03546-bm
Oliven, Fritz 1874-1956 [lyricist, librettist]
Rideamus *Source(s):* GAN1; GAN2; LCAR; MELL; PIPE; RIES; STGR; WORB
Oliver, Joseph [or Joe] 1885-1938 [composer, bandleader, cornetist]
Note(s): See SUTT for a list of jt. pseudonyms on recordings.
Oliver, King *Source(s):* AMUS; CM15; GROL; KINK; LCAR; PSND; SOTH; VACH
Papa Joe *Source(s):* PSND
World's Greatest Cornetist *Source(s):* CM15
Oliver, Melvin James 1910 (or 11)-1988 [trumpeter, singer, composer, arranger]
Oliver, Sy *Source(s):* CASS; EPMU; KINK; LCAR; PEN2; STUW
Oliver-Sletten, Madra Imogene [composer, author, teacher]
Sletten, M. Rix *Source(s):* ASCP
Olivers, Thomas 1725-1799 [hymnist]
O. *Source(s):* JULN
Olman, Abraham [or Abe] 1888-1984 [composer, pianist, lyricist]
Note(s): Portrait: "Oh Johnny, Oh Johnny," Foster Music, 1917 (cover)
Beecher, Claire *Source(s):* CCE55 Eunp
Knowles, Marie *Source(s):* CCE45, #319 R140584
Malone, Bea *Source(s):* CCE55 Eunp
Mandell, Roger *Source(s):* CCE60; CPOL RE-167-107
Manlowe, Arthur *Source(s):* JASA p. 322
Olsen, Carl Christian 1864-1929 [composer]
Olsen, Lejre *Source(s):* REHH
Olson, Henry Russell 1913-1968 [composer, author, pianist]
Russell, Henry *Source(s):* ASCC; CCE41 #16355 E93761; CLRA; CPOL RE-168-189
Note(s): Also used by Henry Levy.
Olson, Michael 1945- [songwriter]
Michaels, Lee *Source(s):* AMUS; CPOL RE-775-008; PMUS
Olson, Robert G. 1913- [composer, editor, teacher]
Clarke, Edward R. *Source(s):* CCE60
Roberts, Jon *Source(s):* ASCP; CCE53-55
Rollins, Glenn *Source(s):* ASCP; CCE57
Note(s): In CCE57 listed as pseud. of Mrs. Robert G. Olson
O'Madden, Shane [composer, singer]
Govinda *Source(s):* http://mkmk.cm/kozlovsky/other_reviews_govinda.htm (11 Oct. 2002)
O'Mahoney, Sean [author]
Dean, John Hugh *Source(s):* GANB
Hugh, John *Source(s):* CCE66
Ondrasik, John 1968- [singer, pianist, satirist, commentator]
FFF *Source(s):* http://www.dawsoncreekmusic.com/artists/fiveforfighting (11 Oct. 2002)
Fighting for Five *Source(s):* CM36; http://www.dawsoncreekmusic.com/artists/fiveforfighting
Ondřiček, Emanuel 1880-1958 [violinist, composer]
Ploris *Source(s):* GROL
O'Neal, Johnny [songwriter]
Brother Bell *Source(s):* BLIC
Oneglia, Mario F(rancesco) 1927- [composer, trumpeter, educator]
Ornell, Marty *Source(s):* ASCP
O'Neill, Florence 1868- [songwriter]
Dasher, Dick *Source(s):* IBIM; WORB
O'Neill, John Robert 1823-1860 [writer]
Vamp, Hugo *Source(s):* CPMU; GOTH; LCAR
Ongala, Ramazini [or Ramathan] Mtoro 1947- [singer, songwriter]
Doctor, The *Source(s):* EPMU
Note(s): See also John Samuel Bewley Monsell.
Ongala, Remmy *Source(s):* AMUS; EPMU; LCAR

Ono, Yoko 1933- [composer]
High Priestess of the Happening, The *Source(s):* GROL
Onslow, George 1784-1853 [composer]
French Beethoven, The *Source(s):* MUWB
Note(s): See also (Charles) Camille Saint-Saëns.
Orbison, Roy (Kelton) 1936-1988 [singer, songwriter, guitarist]
Note(s): Portraits: EWPS; SHMM (March/April 1991): 22
Big O, The *Source(s):* MCCL
Greatest Singer in the World, The *Source(s):* MCCL
Traveling Wilburys *Source(s):* http://wilburys.info/faq.html (2 May 2005)
Note(s): With: George Harrison, Jeff Lynne; Tom Petty & Bob Dylan [i.e., Robert Allen Zimmerman]
Wilbury, Lefty *Source(s):* http://wilburys.info/instrav.html (2 May 2005)
Ord Hume, J(ames) 1864-1932 [composer]
German, William *Source(s):* SMIN
Lafont, Jacques *Source(s):* SMIN
Ordnung, Rudolf (August) 1904-1978 [composer]
Bartolli, Mario *Source(s):* CCE54
Berold, Karl *Source(s):* CCE59; CPOL RE-315-012
Bertolli, Mario *Source(s):* CCE54
Buna, Vaga *Source(s):* CCE51
Ingelhoff, Peter *Source(s):* CCE35 Efor40091; CCE51; CPOL RE-103-032; OMUO
Lüders, Jan *Source(s):* CCE54; CCE56
O'Reilly, Alton 1962- [rapper]
Chicken Chest *Source(s):* EPMU
Orem, Preston Ware 1865-1938 [organist, music editor, composer]
Note(s): Portrait: ETUP 54:10 (Oct. 1936): 606
Albert, Fabian d' *Source(s):* TPRF
D'Albert, Fabian *Source(s):* TPRF
Mero, P. W. *Source(s):* LCCC 1946-54 (see reference)
Mero, W. P. *Source(s):* CCE39 #2968, 402 R7189; TPRF
Orgill, Douglas 1922- [journalist, novelist, historian]
Gilman, J. D. *Source(s):* LCAR
Note(s): Jt. pseud.: Jack Fishman (1920-).
Orling, Hans G(eorg) 1911- [composer]
Peters, W(ilhelm) *Source(s):* CCE54
Peters, Wilm *Source(s):* CCE60-62; CCE65; RIES
Orloff, Peter 1944- [composer]
Merlin, Peter *Source(s):* KOMS; PFSA
Ornadel, Cyril 1924- [composer]
Anderson, Simon *Source(s):* GOTH
Ornstein, Leo 1893-2002 [composer]
Note(s): Portrait: ETUP 54:10 (Oct. 1936): 606
Vannin *Source(s):* http://www.newmusicbox.org/page.nmbx?id=36fp17 (24 Feb. 2005)
Ornstein, Ota 1912 (or 13)- [composer]
Hruby, K. *Source(s):* GOTL; PSND
Ornest, Ota *Source(s):* GOTL; PSND
O'Rourke, Edmund (Falconer) 1814-1879 [actor, dramatist]
Falconer, Edmund *Source(s):* CPMU; KILG; LCAR; LOWN; MELL
O'Rourke, William Michael 1794-1847 [violinist, composer]
Rooke, William Michael *Source(s):* LCAR; NGDM
Orpheus of Thrace
Father of Song *Source(s):* DEAN
Orr, Buxton Daeblitz 1924-1977 [composer]
Daeblitz, Louis *Source(s):* CCE58; CPMU
Orr, Robert (Kemsley) 1909- [composer, teacher]
Orr, Robin *Source(s):* LCAR; NGDM; NGDO
Orshan, Nate [songwriter]
Nato *Source(s):* http://www.together.net/~nato (11 Oct. 2002)
Orsini [or Orsino], Flavio 1620-1698 [librettist]
Filosinavoro *Source(s):* GROL
Orsomando, Giovanni 1895- [composer]
Grand Old Man of Italian Band Music *Source(s):* SMIN
Orth, John (Carl) 1850-1932 [pianist, teacher, composer]
Note(s): Portraits: ETUP 54:10 (Oct. 1936): 606; MRAR (Piano Ed.) (Dec. 1901): 1
Bonaldi, G. *Source(s):* CCE25 E626455; CPMU
Opper, Paul *Source(s):* CCE26 R36257; TPRF
Orth, Emil *Source(s):* CCE25 R29600; TPRF
Ortiz Barrionuevo, (Angel) Ciriaco 1905 (or 08)-1970 [bandoneonist, director, composer]
Barrionuevo, Ciriaquito *Source(s):* TODO
Ciriaquito *Source(s):* TODO
Ortiz de Landazury Yzarduy, Enrique 1967- [singer, songwriter, instrumentalist]
Bunbury, Enrique *Source(s):* HWOM
Ortiz Ruiz, Luis Esteban 1949- [trumpeter, arranger, composer]
Or, Luis "Perico" *Source(s):* PEN2
Perico *Source(s):* LCAR; http://home.coqui.net/perico/page1.html (2 Sept. 2003)
Ortolani, Riz(iero) 1925 (or 31)- [composer, conductor]
Artison *Source(s):* CCE67
Higgins, Roger *Source(s):* http://members.tripod.de/Andimandi/R_Ortolani.htm (11 Oct. 2002)
Orton, Irving [composer]
Llewellyn, Ray *Source(s):* CLTV
Note(s): Possible pseud. Also used by others; see NOTES: Llewellyn, Ray.
Ortwein, Carlernst 1916-1986 [composer, pianist]
Odd, Conny *Source(s):* BUL2; BUL3; LCAR; PIPE; RIES
Ory, Edward 1886-1973 [composer, author, conductor, trombonist]
Ory, Kid *Source(s):* AMUS; ASCP; EPMU; KINK; PSND

Osborn, Arthur H. 1884-1965 [songwriter]
Osborn, Rag(s) *Source(s):* LCAR; SPTH p. 357; STC1
Osborne, James [or Jimmie], Jr. 1923-1957 [singer, songwriter, guitarist, DJ]
Kentucky Folk Singer, The *Source(s):* ENCM; MCCL
Osborne, Jerry [writer on music]
Mr. Music *Source(s):* http://www.jerry osborne.com/jobio.htm (11 Oct. 2002)
Osbourne, John (Michael) 1948 (or 49)- [singer, songwriter]
Osbourne, Ozzy *Source(s):* AMUS; CM03; EPMU; NOMG; PMUS-00; RECR
Oscher, Paul 1950- [harmonica player, songwriter, pianist, guitarist]
Brooklyn Slim *Source(s):* http://www.bluenight .com/BluesBytes/fk0997.html (11 Oct. 2002)
O'Shaughnessy, Richard Michael 1811-1899 [violinist, conductor, composer]
Levey, Richard Michael *Source(s):* BAKR; LCAR; MACM; STGR; WORB
Note(s): Do not confuse with Richard Johann Levey, aka Richard Johann Lert.
O'Shaughnessy, William Charles 1837-1894 [composer, conductor]
Levey, William Charles *Source(s):* IBIM; WORB
Osser, Abraham [or Abe] Arthur 1914- [composer]
Osser, Glenn *Source(s):* ASCP; CCE55; CLTP ("Alcoa Hour"); REHH
Ost, Roberts 1951- [composer, author]
Roberts, Jerry *Source(s):* ASCP
Oste da Reggio mentioned 1554 [composer]
Reggio, Oste da *Source(s):* WORB
Spirito l'Hoste *Source(s):* IBIM; WORB
Ostendorf, Jens-Peter 1944- [composer]
Oswald, Max *Source(s):* PIPE
Osterberg, James Newell 1947- [singer, songwriter]
Godfather of Punk (Rock) *Source(s):* AMUS; CM23; EPMU; GROL
Iggy Pop *Source(s):* AMUS; CASS; GROL
Pop, Iggy *Source(s):* CM01; CM23; DIMA; EPMU; NGAM; PEN2; PMUS-96
Stooge, Iggy *Source(s):* HARR; PEN2; WORL
Östergren, Carl Ludvig 1842-1881 [poet]
Fjalar *Source(s):* LAST
Osterwälder, Rolf E(rich) 1922- [composer, bandleader]
Osterwald, Hazy *Source(s):* LCAR; PFSA
Ostoya-Kondrack, Michael 1902-1984 [composer]
Kondrack, Michel *Source(s):* WEOP
Konrad *Source(s):* WEOP
Ostrom, Henry 1862-1941 [minister, hymnist]
Whitcomb, George Walker *Source(s):* CYBH
Ostrow, Edward Carol 1948-2004 [guitarist, singer, songwriter]
Ottenstein, Eddy *Source(s):* DRSC
Ostrus, Merrill (J.) 1919- [composer]
Barnes, Joe *Source(s):* CCE57
Staton, Merrill *Source(s):* ASCC; CCE57; CCE60; CCE67
O'Sullivan, (Mrs.) Denis [writer]
Bidwell, Patrick *Source(s):* GANA p. 875
O'Sullivan, Dennis Patrick Terence Joseph 1906-1971 [composer, pianist]
Sullivan, Joe *Source(s):* LCAR
O'Sullivan, Ray(mond) 1946- [singer, songwriter]
Note(s): Portrait: http://www.gosullivan.com (11 Oct. 2002)
O'Sullivan, Gilbert *Source(s):* CASS; DIMA; EPMU; LCAR; PEN2
Oswald, James 1710 (or 11)-1769 [composer, arranger, cellist, music publisher]
Dottel Figlio *Source(s):* GROL
Figlio, Dottel *Source(s):* GROL
Note(s): Used an anagram of composer & flute virtuoso Dôthel, Nicolas (1721-1810) as a pseud.
Rizzio, David *Source(s):* http://www.dundeecity .gov.uk/centlib/wrighton/jos.htm (17 Mar. 2005)
Note(s): Oswald used the name of Mary Queen of Scots' secretary, David Rizzio [or Riccio] (c.1533-1566).
Oswald, John ?-1769 (or 93) [writer]
Otway, Sylvester *Source(s):* SONN; WORB
Otcasek, Richard 1949- [singer, songwriter]
Ocasek, Ric *Source(s):* DIMA
Otey, Raymond Maurice [songwriter]
Guitar Slim *Source(s):* CCE66; CCE68
Note(s): See also Norman G. Green, Eddie Jones & Alexander T. Seward. Also used by guitarist James Stephens (1915-).
Ots, Charles 1776-1845 [teacher, composer]
Chorasselt *Source(s):* NGDM
Otten, Hans 1905-1942 [composer]
Ruland, Alexander *Source(s):* GREN
Otten, Heinz 1931- [composer]
Arlac, (Gil) *Source(s):* KOMP; KOMS; PFSA
Ballang, Ary *Source(s):* KOMP; KOMS; PFSA
Ottenheimer, Paul 1873-1951 [conductor, composer]
Pawel, Dick *Source(s):* PIPE
Otto, Joseph Francis 1889- [composer, author, publisher]
Francis, Art *Source(s):* ASCP; CCE58; CCE64
Note(s): Do not confuse with Arthur Francis [i.e., Ira Gershwin, i.e., Israel Gershvin].
Francis, Otto *Source(s):* CCE62

Ottoboni, Pietro 1667-1740 [librettist]
C. P. *Source(s):* GROL
Cardinale Pietro *Source(s):* GROL
Crateo *Source(s):* GROL
Craeto Ericincio *Source(s):* GROL
Crateo Pradelini *Source(s):* GROL; NGDO; RILM 88-02465
Ericincio, Craeto *Source(s):* GROL
Fanatical Music Lover, A *Source(s):* GROL
P. C. *Source(s):* GROL
Pradelini, Crateo *Source(s):* MELL; NGDO
Otway [composer]
Yawto *Source(s):* CPMU; OCLC 47876888
Ousley, (King) Curtis 1934-1971 [songwriter, saxophonist]
Curtis, King *Source(s):* AMGB; CCE68; CM17; HARD; LCAR; PMUS; PSND
Note(s): Also used by Eddie Curtis.
King Curtis *Source(s):* CCE60-61; LCAR
Ouvarard, René 1624-1694 [theorist, writer on music, musician]
Du Reneau, (René) *Source(s):* GROL; NGDM; SADC
Ovanessian, Raymond Henri 1904-1968 [songwriter, writer]
Vincy, Raymond *Source(s):* CCE46 Efor2438; CCE53-56; GOTH
Ovcharov, Jascha 1914-1997 [composer, film maker, book illustrator]
Note(s): In LCAR original name listed in a note.
Delano, Jack *Source(s):* NGAM
Joaquín *Source(s):* LCAR
Overstake, (Virginia) Lucille 1915-1978 [singer, songwriter]
Carson, Jenny Lou *Source(s):* EPMU; MCCL
Lee, Lucille *Source(s):* MCCL
Radio Chin-up Girl, The *Source(s):* MCCL
Overstreet, Paul 1955- [songwriter]
S-K-O *Source(s):* EPMU
Note(s): Jt. pseud.: Thom Schuyler & Fred Knobloch.
Overstreet, Thomas [or Tommy] (Cary, II) 1937- [singer, songwriter, guitarist]
Tommy Dean from Abilene *Source(s):* AMUS; MCCL
Oviedo, Gilberto 1934 (or 37)- [songwriter, guitarist]
Oviedo, Papi *Source(s):* EPMU; LCAR
Papi Oviedo *Source(s):* LCAR
Owen, Alan (Edgar) 1908- [composer, BBC music producer]
Langford, Alan *Source(s):* CCE61-65; CCE67-68; CPOL RE-391-191; MUWB
Owen, Bill 1914 (or 15)-1999 [actor, writer]
Rowbotham, Bill *Source(s):* GANB; LCAR
Owen, David 1720-1749 [harpist, composer]
Dafy Y Garreg Wen *Source(s):* BROW; IBIM; WORB
Owen, John 1821-1883 [singer, composer, teacher]
Alaw, Owain *Source(s):* LCAR
Owain, Alaw *Source(s):* KILG; ROOM
Owen, Mary Jane 1886- [composer, author]
Brockway, Jennie M. *Source(s):* ASCP
Owen, Reg [composer, arranger]
Owen, Eric *Source(s):* MUWB
Note(s): Jt. pseud.: Eric Siday.
Somers, Glen *Source(s):* CCE60
Owen, William 1813-1893 [hymnist]
Prysgol *Source(s):* CYBH
Owens, A(l) L. 1930- [songwriter, singer]
Owens, Doodle *Source(s):* ENCM; WORT
Owens, Alvis Alan 1948- [singer, songwriter, guitarist]
Alan, Buddy *Source(s):* CCE72-72; EPMU; MCCL
Owens, Alvis Edgar, Jr. 1929-2006 [singer, songwriter]
Edgar, Al *Source(s):* CCE57
Note(s): Possible pseud.? (Entry under Owens, A. E., Jr.)
Owens, Buck *Source(s):* CM02; ENCM; HARR; MCCL; REHH
Owens, D(oye) [or Doie] H(ensley) 1892-1962 [composer, author, singer]
Original Texas Ranger, The *Source(s):* AMUS; NASF
Owens, Tex *Source(s):* AMUS; ASCC; ENCM; EPMU; MCCL; NASF
Owens, Dana (Elaine) 1970- [rapper, actress]
Latifah, (Queen) *Source(s):* AMUS; PMUS-91
Queen Latifah *Source(s):* EPMU; PMUS-91
Queen of Rap *Source(s): Sixty Minutes* (TV) (10 Oct. 2004)
Rap's First Lady *Source(s):* EPMU
Owenson, Sydney c.1783-1859 [author, composer]
Morgan, Lady (Sydney) *Source(s):* BROW; LCAR; WORB
Owston, Charles [or Chuck] 1942- [composer, author, singer, guitarist]
Owston, Snake *Source(s):* ASCP
Oxilia, Angelo Agostino Adolfo 1889-1917 [author, journalist]
Oxilia, Nino *Source(s):* LCAR; PIPE
Ozen, Barbara Lynn 1942- [singer, guitarist; songwriter]
Lynn, Barbara *Source(s):* AMUS; EPMU; NOGM; ROOM

– P –

Paap, Wouter (Ernest) 1908-1981 [writer on music, composer]
Schelp, Arend *Source(s):* GROL
Werker, Gerard *Source(s):* GROL

Paasch, Leopold (Wolfram) 1912-1988 [composer]
Needen, Frank *Source(s):* CCE54-55; KOMP; KOMS; PFSA
Pabst, Harry ?-1924 [arranger]
Note(s): Portrait: ETUP 54:9 (Sept. 1936): 534
Franz, Albert *Source(s):* CCE43 #3437, 547 R114391; TPRF
Pace, Adger McDavid 1882-1959 [hymnist]
Note(s): Portrait: SGMA
Glenn, Millard A. *Source(s):* CYBH
Huff, Charles H. *Source(s):* CYBH
Mayfield, Audalene *Source(s):* CYBH
Wallington, Fay *Source(s):* CYBH
Pache, Johannes 1857-1897 [composer, cantor]
Böhme, Max *Source(s):* PFSA
Pachler, F(aust(us)) 1819-1891 (or 92) [librettist]
Paul, E. *Source(s):* STGR ("Kaiser Max un sein . . . .")
Pacini, Andrea c.1690-1764 [singer, composer]
Lucchesino, Il *Source(s):* NGDM; NGDO; PIPE
Pack, Loye Donald 1900-1941 [singer, songwriter]
Cowboy Loye *Source(s):* EPMU; MCCL
Padavona, Ronald c.1940- [singer, multi-instrumentalist, songwriter]
Dio, Ronnie (James) *Source(s):* CCE62; EPMU
Padbrué, David Janszoon c.1553-1635 [composer, singer, lute player]
David, Mr. *Source(s):* NGDM
Mr. David *Source(s):* NGDM
Paderewski, Ignace Jan 1860-1941 [pianist, composer]
Lion of Paris *Source(s):* http://info-poland/classroom/paderewski/tg.html (12 Apr. 2005)
Paemurru, Elze Janova 1917- [composer, pianist]
Aarne, Els *Source(s):* BUL3; COHN; GREN; HIXN; HOFE
Pa(e)ffgen, Christa 1938-1988 [songwriter, singer, actress]
Nico, (Krista) *Source(s):* CCE68; CCE75; LCAR; NOMG
Paganini, Nic(c)olò 1782-1840 [violinist; composer]
Devil, The *Source(s):* SIFA
Liszt of the Violin, The *Source(s):* SPIE
Page, Arthur James 1846-1916 [composer, organist]
Hall, Coldham *Source(s):* CPMU
Page, N(athaniel) Clifford 1886-1956 [composer, music editor]
Note(s): Portrait: ETUP 54:11 (Nov. 1936): 678
Danforth, N. P. *Source(s):* CCE29 E8242
La Meda, A. *Source(s):* CCE37 R49179; TPRF
Remington, J. (H.) *Source(s):* CCE34 R32034
Simonton, Danforth *Source(s):* CCE36 Index; TPRF
Page, Oran Thaddeus 1908-1954 [singer, trumpeter, songwriter]
Page, Hot Lips *Source(s):* HARS; LCAR
Page, Lips *Source(s):* LCAR
Papa Snow White *Source(s):* HARS
Page, Sydney Hubert [composer]
Rose, Fabian *Source(s):* CCE30 R6404; CPMU (publication dates 1887-1915)
Pagenstecher, Bernard 1907-2003 [composer]
Bredt, James *Source(s):* ASCP; CCE66; CCE68
Bredt, Peter *Source(s):* CCE53 Eunp
Yale, Bernie *Source(s):* CCE40 #32124 E87575; CCE67
Paget, Violet 1856-1935 [author, critic]
Lee, Vernon *Source(s):* LCAR; RILM 95-15449-dd
Note(s): Also used by Michael H. Goldsen.
Pagoli, Bernardo (di Benedetto) 1490-1548 [composer, singer]
Pisano, Bernardo *Source(s):* BAKR; LCAR; NGDM
Paigne, Mme. 1827- [composer]
Silni, Max *Source(s):* COHN; HIXN; MELL; STGR
Pain, Jeff(rey) Robert [singer, guitarist, songwriter]
Dicken *Source(s):* CCE76
Pain, Dicken *Source(s):* NOMG
Paine, Thomas 1773-1811 [songwriter, poet]
Menander (Apollo) *Source(s):* CART
Paine, Robert Treat *Source(s):* CART; CLAB; LCAR; SPTH
Note(s): To avoid confusion with the more famous Thomas Paine, name changed to that of the poet's father, signer of the Declaration of Independence.
Pairman, Mark [guitarist, songwriter]
Marx, Gary *Source(s):* AMUS (see under: Eldritch, Andrew); http://hem.passagen.se/kruse/sisters/members (6 Oct. 2002)
Paladino, Gelsa Theresa 1944- [composer, author, teacher]
Palad, Gelsa *Source(s):* ASCP
Palao, Gelsa *Source(s):* CCE71; CPOL PA-463-082
Palao, Jelsa *Source(s):* CPOL PA-463-084
Palazzi, Giovanni fl. 1718-1749 [librettist]
Lizzapa, Diomedo *Source(s):* ALMC
Palestrina, Giovanni Pierluigi da 1525 (or 26)-1594 [composer]
Father of Music, The *Source(s):* PSND
Note(s): See also William Byrd & Johannes Mauduit.
Giannetto *Source(s):* GROL; NGDM
Michel Angelo of the Lyre, The *Source(s):* PSND; SIFA
Petraloysio, Giovanni *Source(s):* GROL; NGDM
Petraloysius, Joannes *Source(s):* GRV3
Praenestinus, (Petrus Aloysius) *Source(s):* GRV3
Prenestino, Giovanni Pierlugi da *Source(s):* NGDM
Prince of Music, The *Source(s):* PSND
Note(s): See also Johannes Ockeghem.
Princeps Musicae *Source(s):* DAWS;

http://www.hitsquick.com/music/cdx/309140 (12 Oct. 2002)
Savior of Church Music, The *Source(s):* PSND
Palladino, Ralph Francis 1938- [composer, singer]
Dino, Ralph *Source(s):* ASCP; CPOL PA-250-434
Pallant, Walter 1858 (or 59)-1904 [dramatist]
Palings, Walter *Source(s):* GANA p. 608; PIPE
Palmer, Alan 1949-2003 [singer, songwriter]
Britains Leading "Blue-Eyed Soul" Singer *Source(s):* EPMU
Palmer, Robert *Source(s):* EPMU; HARR; LCAR; NOMG
Palmer, Anna Campbell 1854-1928 [journalist, librettist]
Archibald, (Mrs.) George *Source(s):* CART; WORB
Palmer, Cedric King 1913-1999 [composer]
Bana, Da Paula *Source(s):* CCE48-50
Diamondez *Source(s):* CCE50
Henry, Wyn *Source(s):* CCE52
Kane, Peter *Source(s):* CCE50-51; CCE53; CCE63
Note(s): Also used by Joseph (Louis) E(dmund) Zerga.
Krotsch, Niklas *Source(s):* CCE40 #19605 Efor62677
MacKane, William *Source(s):* CCE56
North, Richard *Source(s):* CCE51; CCE53
Palmer, King *Source(s):* CCE48-49; CCE53-55; CPOL RE-400-407; LCAR
Palmer, Phoebe (Worrell) 1807-1874 [hymnist]
Moses of the 19th-century Wesleyan/Holiness Movement *Source(s):* http://www.messiah.edu/WHWC/satisfd.htm (12 Oct. 2002)
Palmer, William Henry 1830-1878 [composer, magician]
Heller, Robert *Source(s):* CPMU; IBIM; LCAR; WORB
Palmieri, Carlos Manuel, Jr. 1927-1988 [pianist, bandleader, arranger, composer]
Palmieri, Charlie *Source(s):* LCAR; PEN2
Palmieri, Eduardo [or Edward, or Eddie] 1936- [pianist, bandleader, composer, arranger]
El Loco *Source(s):* GROL
Latin Sun King, The *Source(s):* CM15
Loco, El *Source(s):* GROL
Sun of Latin Music *Source(s):* GROL
Palotta, Matteo 1688-1758 [composer]
Palermitano, Il *Source(s):* LCAR; NGDM; WORB
Panormitano, Il *Source(s):* LCAR; NGDM; RIEM; WORB
Palumbo, Camille Marie 1930- [composer, author, singer]
Evans, Jean M(arie) *Source(s):* ASCP; CCE45 #46516 Eunp428953
Pamphili, Benedetto 1653-1730 [librettist]
Larisseo, Fenicio *Source(s):* GROL
Panfili, (Cardinal) Benedetto *Source(s):* LCAR
Panard, Charles-François 1694-1765 [poet, playwright, songwriter]
Father of Modern French Songs, The *Source(s):* PSND
La Fontaine of the Vaudeville, The *Source(s):* PSND
Panayiotou, Georgios (Kyriacos) 1963-1998 [composer, singer]
Michael, George *Source(s):* CASS; CM09; DIMA; EPMU; GAMM; HARR
Pancani, Arrigo mentioned 1916 [composer]
Florian, Henry *Source(s):* IBIM; STGR v. 4/pt.1; WORB
Pancieri, Giulio mentioned 1687 [librettist]
Carenpi, Louigi *Source(s):* ALMC p. 875
Rincepa, Luigio *Source(s):* ALMC p. 875
Pancoast, Asa 1905-1991 [composer, organist]
Pancoast, Ace *Source(s):* TCAN
Pandel, Ted [or Tex] 1935- [composer]
Praxiteles *Source(s):* ASCC; ASCP; PSND
Pandrich, John Alan 1935- [folk music specialist, lecturer]
Handle, Johnny *Source(s):* EPMU
Panella, Frank A. 1878-1953 [composer]
March King of Pittsburgh *Source(s):* SMIN
Panico, Frank [composer]
Panico, Porky *Source(s):* CLTP ("Siskel & Ebert"); LCAR
Panofka, Heinrich 1807-1887 [violinist]
Viotti *Source(s):* APPL p. 10
Pantano, John [composer]
Pantano-Salsbury *Source(s):* ASCP; LCAR
Note(s): Jt. pseud.: Ron(ald Foster) Salsbury.
Paolella, Alfred 1905 (or 06)- [guitarist, composer, bandleader]
James, Freddy *Source(s):* CCE55-59; CCE63; CCE66-67; PMUS; PSND
Note(s): In CCE & PMUS listed as pseud. of Teddy Powell [i.e., Alfred Paolella]
James, Marguerite *Source(s):* CCE55-56; CCE58
Powell, Teddy *Source(s):* KINK; PSND
Papadopoulos, Joannes c.1280-c.1365 [singer, composer]
Note(s): "Although his surname has been given as Papadopoulos in some sources there is no reason to believe that he is of Greek origin. . . ." (BAKR)
Koukouzeles, Joannos *Source(s):* GROL; NGDM
Second Source of Greek Music, The *Source(s):* LCAR
Paparella, Attilio 1874-1944 [conductor, composer]
Parelli, Attilio *Source(s):* BAKO; BAKT; GREN; RIEM
Papathanassiou, Evangelos (Odyssey) 1943 (or 44)- [keyboardist, composer]
Beckermann, Denny *Source(s):* http://www.vangeliscollector.com/music_mariangela.htm (19 May. 2005)

Note(s): Possible pseud.
Broadbaker, Richard *Source(s):* http://www.vangelismovements.com/odyssey.htm (19 May 2005)
Mama O *Source(s):* http://www.vangeliscollector.com/music_mamao.htm (19 May 2005)
Tchaikovsky of the Keyboards, The *Source(s):* http://www.cinephiles.net/cgi-bin/storephp?ASIN=B00000G42 (9 Apr. 2005)
Vangelis *Source(s):* CASS; CM21; EPMU; PSNN; RECR; REHH
Papi, Antonio mentioned 1844 [librettist]
Cleofonto Doriano *Source(s):* SONN
Doniano, Cleofanto *Source(s):* ALMC
Doriano, Cleofanto *Source(s):* ALMC; GROL; MORI; SONN
Infecondo *Source(s):* ALMC
Note(s): See also Paolo Emilio Badi.
Quirino *Source(s):* ALMC
Papin da Mantova mentioned 1512 [composer]
Dionisio *Source(s):* IBIM; WORB
Papirofsky, Yosi [or Joseph] 1921-1991 [stage manager, producer]
Papp, Joseph *Source(s):* GAN2; LCAR
Paquet, Pierre 1904-1965 [trumpeter, composer, arranger]
Packay, Peter *Source(s):* CCE30 Efor14153; NGDJ
Paradossi, Giuseppe [composer]
Troili *Source(s):* GROL
Paramor, Norman [or Norrie] (William) 1913 (or 14)-1979 [songwriter, arranger]
Note(s): The following are listed as pseuds. of Norrie Paramor. Portraits: MUSR; RFSO
Caroli, Vic *Source(s):* CCE57; CPOL 239-160
Note(s): Jt. pseud.: Phil(ip) Green.
Carter, Noel *Source(s):* CCE56; CPOL RE-214-755
Eily, Jerry *Source(s):* CCE57 Efor23232; CPOL RE-235-144
Foss, Richard *Source(s):* CCE57
Note(s): Jt. pseud.: Jack Fishman (1918 (or 19)-).
Goulan, Douglas *Source(s):* CCE59; CPOL RE-335-091
Gustard, Jim *Source(s):* CCE59 Eunp565281; CPOL RE-319-827
Hale, Charles *Source(s):* CCE56 Efor45878
Hall, Thomas *Source(s):* CCE52 Efor11249; CPOL RE-27-362
Note(s): Jt. pseud.: Leslie Hutchinson.
Hennessy, Ian *Source(s):* CCE55-56; CPOL RE-152-200
Note(s): Jt. pseud.: Ray(mond) Martin.
Holloway, Milt *Source(s):* CCE53 Efor18799
Jones, Obadiah *Source(s):* CCE52 Efor11250
Note(s): Jt. pseud.: Leslie Hutchinson & Lew Jacobson.
Juarez, Miguel *Source(s):* CCE57; CPOL RE-239-163
Note(s): Jt. pseud.: Phil(ip) Green.
Kawaha, Eddie *Source(s):* CCE57; CPOL RE-239-182
Note(s): Jt. pseud.: Phil(ip) Green.
Lee, Alex *Source(s):* CCE59 ("Connemara"); CPOL RE-321-269
Note(s): Also used by Jack Fishman (1918 (or 19)-).
Mercado, Manuel *Source(s):* CCE57; CPOL RE-239-159
Note(s): Jt. pseud.: Phil(ip) Green.
Morris, Ronnie *Source(s):* CCE52 Efor12243; CCE53; CPOL RE-72-628
Needersohn, Jacob *Source(s):* CCE61; CPOL RE-429-356
Nicolson, Ross *Source(s):* CCE57; CPOL RE-293-161
Note(s): Jt. pseud.: Phil(ip) Green.
Norman, Sidney [or Sydney] *Source(s):* CCE55 Efor37221; CPOL RE-143-485; CPOL RE-149-657
Norman, Stanley *Source(s):* CCE54-55
Pace, Graham *Source(s):* CCE57 Efor48940
Paloma, Vincente *Source(s):* CCE57; CPOL RE-244-066
Note(s): Jt. pseud.: Phil(ip) Green.
Peters, Teddy *Source(s):* CCE53 Efor23319; CPOL RE-104-378
Ramirez, Luiz *Source(s):* CCE57; CPOL RE-244-066
Note(s): Jt. pseud.: Phil(ip) Green.
Seener, Joseph *Source(s):* CCE58; CCE59 Efor65275; CPOL RE-340-724
Steiger, Hans *Source(s):* CCE58 Efor60850; CPOL RE-293-341
Todd, Earl *Source(s):* CCE57; CPOL RE-239-180
Note(s): Jt. pseud.: Phil(ip) Green.
Valdez, Miguel *Source(s):* CCE59 Eunp584777; CPOL RE-321-690
Valentine, Sim *Source(s):* CCE57; CPOL RE-239-179
Note(s): Jt. pseud.: Phil(ip) Green.
Verney, Sammy *Source(s):* CCE54 Efor23992; CPOL RE-100-620
Voglio, Emelio *Source(s):* CCE57; CPOL RE-239-162
Note(s): Jt. pseud.: Phil(ip) Green.
Willet(t)-Robinson, James *Source(s):* CCE53 Efor18116; CPOL RE-95-421
Note(s): Jt. pseud.: Ray(mond) Martin.
Parent, Lionel 1905-1980 [author, composer]
Lasalle, José *Source(s):* VGRC
Sauvé, Georges *Source(s):* VGRC
Parenteau, Zoe 1914-1990 [composer, author, singer]
Day, Nellie *Source(s):* CCE41 #17147 E93765 ("Gone But Not Forgotten")
Ingersoll, Byron M. *Source(s):* CCE41 #5570 Eunp241929; CCE68 R426470
Note(s): Jt. pseud.: Ernest Gold [i.e., Ernest (Siegmund) Goldner], Alex(ander) Kramer,

Hy(man) Zaret, Robert (B.) Sour & Don McCray.
Kramer, (Mrs.) Zoe *Source(s):* ASCP; STUW
Voeth, Zoe *Source(s):* CCE41 #5570 Eunp241929 (Renewal: CCE68 R426470)
Note(s): "Zoe Voeth [i.e., Joan Whitney (actually Zoe Parenteau)]" is listed as one of the joint composers using the pseud. Bryon M. Ingersoll.
Whitney, Joan *Source(s):* ASCP; CCE68 R426470; STUW
Note(s): Also listed as pseud. of Zoe Voeth [i.e., Parenteau].

Pargeter, Maude [composer]
Pargeter, Wyatt *Source(s):* COHN; HIXN; MACM

Parham, Hartzell Strathdene 1900-1943 [pianist, composer, bandleader]
Parham, Tiny *Source(s):* KINK; LCAR

Paris, Ella Hudson fl. early 20th cent. [translator, composer]
Hualalai *Source(s):* COHN; HIXN

Paris, Twila 1958- [singer, songwriter]
Modern-Day Hymn-Writer, The *Source(s):* AMUS; CM16

Parker, Alfred Thomas [composer, arranger]
Bernard, Roy *Source(s):* CPMU
Boriwsky, Michael *Source(s):* CPMU
Deacon, Francis *Source(s):* CPMU
English, Jack *Source(s):* BLIC; CPMU
Hugo, Gabriel *Source(s):* CPMU
Jungmann, Felix *Source(s):* CPMU
Kuelm, Ludwig von *Source(s):* CPMU
Thomas, Alfred *Source(s):* CPMU

Parker, Charles [or Charlie] (Christopher, Jr.) 1920-1955 [saxophonist, composer, bandleader]
Note(s): Do not confuse with composer Charles Parker [i.e., Gerd [or Gerhard] Jahnen] (1920-).
Bird *Source(s):* LCAR
Can, Charlie *Source(s):* PFSA
Note(s): Typographical error?
Chan, Charlie *Source(s):* LCAR
Mozart of Jazz *Source(s):* CM05
Parker, Bird *Source(s):* KINK; NGDM; PSND
Parker, Yardbird *Source(s):* CM05; KINK; NGDM; PSND
Yardbird *Source(s):* LCAR

Parker, Henry Taylor 1867-1934 [performing arts critic]
H. T. P. *Source(s):* GRAN
Note(s): H. T. P = Hard to Please [or] Hell to Pay
Hard to Please *Source(s):* GRAN
Note(s): Facetious interpretation of initials, H. T. P.
Hell to Pay *Source(s):* GRAN
Note(s): Facetious interpretation of initials, H. T. P.

Parker, Herman 1932-1971 [singer, harmonica player, songwriter]
Little Junior *Source(s):* LCAR
Note(s): See also Luther Johnson, Jr.
Parker, Junior *Source(s):* LCAR
Parker, Little Junior *Source(s):* HARS; LCAR

Parker, Katherine Mary [songwriter]
K. M. P. *Source(s):* CPMU

Parker, Lawrence Krisna 1965- [rapper]
KRS-1 [or One] *Source(s):* CPOL PA-943-761; EPMU

Parker, Ramona [rapper]
Melodie, (Ms) *Source(s):* EPMU
Ms Melodie *Source(s):* EPMU

Parker, Terrance [techno composer]
Seven Grand Housing Authority *Source(s):* AMUS; EPMU

Parks, J(ames) A(sher) 1863- [composer, arranger]
Grey, Gerald *Source(s):* OCLC 21288944; http://216.170.15.163/japarks/cl.html (2 May 2005)

Parlow, Edmund 1855- [composer]
Note(s): Portait: ETUP 54:11 (Nov. 1936): 678
Erich, Carl *Source(s):* CCE41 #47874, 91 R101523
Note(s): A. P. Schmidt house name see NOTES: Erich, Carl.
Erich, F. *Source(s):* CCE27 E672117 ("When Johnny Comes Marching Home")
Giuliani, Alfred *Source(s):* TPRF
Meyer, Ferdinand *Source(s):* CCE15 E368280; CCE42 R113368
Note(s): A. P. Schmidt house name see NOTES: Meyer, Ferdinand.

Paroisse-Pougin, François-Auguste-Arthur 1834-1921 [writer on music, violinist]
Avril, Octave d' *Source(s):* WORB
Benoiton, Fanfan *Source(s):* WORB
Dax, Paul *Source(s):* PIPE, WORB
Gray, Maurice *Source(s):* WORB
Horner, Auguste *Source(s):* WORB
Pougin, Arthur *Source(s):* WORB

Parr, Harriet 1828-1900 [poet, hymnist]
Lee, Holme *Source(s):* HATF; LCAR; WORB

Parratt, (Sir) William 1841-1921 (or 24) [organist, teacher, composer]
Note(s): Portrait: ETUP 54:11 (Nov. 1936): 678
W. P. *Source(s):* CPMU

Parrott, (Horace) Ian 1916- [composer]
Karnak *Source(s):* MUWB

Parrott, Thom [or Tom] 1944- [singer, songwriter]
Dawes, T. O. *Source(s):* http://www.geocities.com/parrottsongs/bio.html (2 Jan. 2004)

Parry, Charles Clinton [composer]
Hirsch, Carl *Source(s):* CPMU (publication date 1867)

Parry, Charles Hubert Hastings 1848-1918 [composer
Note(s): Portraits: ETUP 54:11 (Nov. 1936): 678; EWCY; GRV3 v. 4
Greatest English Composer since Purcell *Source(s):* EWCY

Parry, John c.1710-1782 [harpist, collector of Welsh melodies]
Note(s): Do not confuse with John Parry (1776-1851); see following entry.
Parry, Blind *Source(s):* WILG
Parry, Ddall *Source(s):* NGDM; WILG
Parry, John 1776-1851 [instrumentalist, composer, conductor]
Note(s): Portraits: In his: *The Welsh Harper*. London: D'Almaine. 2v. Do not confuse with John Parry (c.1710-1782); see preceding entry.
Bardd Alaw *Source(s):* BAKE; GOTT; MACM; NGDM; WILG
Parry, Joseph 1841-1903 [composer]
Note(s): Portraits: CYBH; ETUP 54:11 (Nov. 1936): 678
Lad from Merthyr, The *Source(s):* CLEV
Lightning Composer, The *Source(s):* CLEV
Pencerdd America *Source(s):* CPMU; NGDO
Parry, Joseph Haydn 1864-1894 [composer, teacher]
Parry, John Haydn *Source(s):* WORB
Partch, Harry 1901-1974 [composer, performer, instrument maker]
Composer Seduced into Carpentry, A *Source(s):* http://www.computermusic.org/array.php?artid=51 (12 Oct. 2002)
Note(s): Called himself.
Hobo Composer *Source(s):* DESO-9
Philosophic Music Man, A *Source(s):* http://www.musichello.com/em/magazin.html (12 Oct. 2002)
Note(s): Called himself.
Pirate, Paul *Source(s):* Gilmore, Bob. *Harry Partch*. New Haven: Yale University Press, 1998, 60.
Partridge, (Mrs.) F. J. fl. c. 1860? [hymnist]
F. J. P. *Source(s):* JULN (Suppl.)
Partridge, Sybil F. ?-1920 [hymnist]
Mary Xavier, Sister *Source(s):* CYBH; DIEH
S. M. X. *Source(s):* CYBH
Sister Mary Xavier *Source(s):* CYBH
S. N. D. *Source(s):* DIEH
Note(s): Probable pseud.; S. N. D. = Sister of Notre Dame
Pascal, Jean-Jacques 1944- [songwriter]
Danel, Pascal *Source(s):* CCE66-67; EPMU
Pascal, Tabu 1940- [singer, composer, bandleader]
Ley, Tabu *Source(s):* EPMU
Rochereau *Source(s):* EPMU; PEN2
Tabu Ley *Source(s):* PEN2
Pascha, Edmund 1714-1772 [composer]
Ostern, Claudianus *Source(s):* DEA3; LCAR
Pasculli, Antonino [or Antonio] 1842-1924 [oboist, composer]
Paganini of the Oboe *Source(s):* http://idrs.colorado.edu/Publications/DR/DR10.3/DR10.3.Rosset.html (10 Feb. 2004)
Pasino [or Pasini], Stefano c.1625-after 1679 [organist, composer]
Ghizzolo *Source(s):* GROL; NGDM; WORB
Note(s): Do not confuse with Giovanni Ghizzolo.
Pasqualigo, Benedetto fl. 1706-1734 [librettist]
Animosi (di Venezia) *Source(s):* ALMC
Fesanio, Merindo *Source(s):* ALMC; MELL; NGDO; SONN
Merindo Fesanio *Source(s):* SONN
Pasqualini, Marc(o)'Antonio 1614-1691 [castrato, composer]
Malagigi *Source(s):* NGDO
Streviglio *Source(s):* PIPE; WORB
Pasquini, Bernardo 1637-1710 [composer]
Azetiano, Protico *Source(s):* GROL
Protico *Source(s):* http://www.fathom.com/feature/35186 (5 Apr. 2005)
Pasquini, Giovanni Claudio 1695-1763 [librettist, poet]
Migontidio, Trigenio *Source(s):* GROL
Passailaigue, Thomas E. 1932- [singer, composer, lyricist]
Bethancourt, T. Ernesto *Source(s):* PSND
Paisley, Tom *Source(s):* PSND
Pasle, Tom *Source(s):* CCE67
Passeri, Mariangiola [librettist]
Dianea, Gelmarania *Source(s):* MORI
Pastorius, John Francis 1951-1987 [bassist, composer]
Pastorius, Jaco *Source(s):* LCAR; PEN2
Patáky, Hubert 1892-1953 [composer]
Pàta, Huért *Source(s):* BUL2; CCE30 Efor11406; CCE57
Paterson, A(ndrew) B(arton) 1864-1941 [songwriter, author]
Banjo, The *Source(s):* KILG; PMUS; PSND
Paterson, Banjo *Source(s):* CCE60; FULD; PMUS; PSND
Paterson, Jimmy Dale 1935- [singer, songwriter]
Patterson, Pat *Source(s):* CLAB; PSND
Paterson, Robert Roy 1830-1903 [composer, music publisher]
Perrot, Pierre *Source(s):* CPMU
Stella, Alfred *Source(s):* BROW; CPMU; GROL; NGDM
Stella, Fra. *Source(s):* CPMU
Pathorne, Ella Baber [writer on music]
Porchea, Paul *Source(s):* OPER 13:3 (1997): 58
Patrick, Johnny [composer]
Aardvark, Aaron *Source(s):* http://www.sub-tv.co.uk/atvstartups.asp (12 Oct. 2002)
Note(s): Possible pseud.
Patrick, Kentrick c.1940- [singer, songwriter]

Lord Creator *Source(s):* EPMU; http://www.geocities.com/SunsetStrip/Disco/6032/LordCreator.htm (2 Feb. 2004)
Prodigal Creator *Source(s):* http://www.geocities.com/SunsetStrip/Disco/6032/LordCreator.htm
Patrick, Richard mentioned 1616-25 [vicar, composer]
Patrick, Nathan(iel) *Source(s):* IBIM; WORB
Patrignani, Giuseppe 1706-1724 [poet, composer]
Presepi, Presepio *Source(s):* IBIM; WORB
Patterson, Ian (Hunter) 1939 (or 46)- [singer, songwriter]
Hunter, Ian *Source(s):* CPOL RE-778-388; DIMA
Patton, Charley [or Charlie] 1887-1936 [singer, guitarist, songwriter]
Founder of the Delta Blues *Source(s):* CM26 (see under: Hooker, John Lee)
Masked Marvel, The *Source(s):* HARS; LCAR
Original King of the Delta Blues *Source(s):* AMUS
Peters, Charley *Source(s):* HARS; LCAR
Pätzold, Günter 1915- [composer]
Holstein, Peer van *Source(s):* KOMP; PFSA
Pauck, Heinz [or Heinrich] 1904- [dramatist]
Schürhoff, Christian *Source(s):* PIPE
Vivier, Carl-Wilhelm *Source(s):* PIPE
Paucker, Alexander 1905-1972 [composer]
Chagrin, Francis *Source(s):* BBDP; GOTE; GOTH; MUWB; RFSO; WIEC
Pauling, Clarence 1928-1995 [producer, singer]
Paul, Clarence *Source(s):* AMUS; EPMU
Paulirinus, Paulus 1413-after 1471 [writer on music]
Paulus de Praga *Source(s):* NGDM
Zidek, Paulus *Source(s):* NGDM
Paull, E(dward) T(aylor) 1858-1924 [composer]
Note(s): Portrait: PERF
America's Other "March King" *Source(s):* PARS
Note(s): See also Karl L. King.
New March King *Source(s):* PARS
Paulou, Andreas 1903-1968 [composer]
Anthias, Teukros [or Teferos] *Source(s):* CPMU; LCAR
Paulsen, James Joseph 1943- [singer, songwriter, guitarist, actor]
Sun, Joe *Source(s):* CCE78; EPMU; MCCL
Paulton, Edward A(ntonio) 1866-1939 [lyricist, dramatist]
Lowe, Edward *Source(s):* GAN2 (see under: Paulton, Harry)
Tedde, Mostyn *Source(s):* GAN2 (see under: Paulton, Harry); GANA p. 284
Paumgarten, Karl (von) 1854-1911 [composer]
Thul, Friedrich von *Source(s):* MELL; STGR; SUPN
Pavlov, Matvei 1888-1963 [composer, conductor]
Azancheev *Source(s):* http://www.talismusic.org/programs.html (2 May 2005)
Pawel, Piotr 1947- [composer]
Koprowski, Peter Paul *Source(s):* BUL3
Paxton, George 1916?- [songwriter]
Eddy, George *Source(s):* CCE61-63; PMUS
Payne, Jimmy *Source(s):* CCE61
Payne, Albert 1842-1921 [publisher, writer on music, singer]
Ehrlich, A. *Source(s):* LCAR; MACM; PRAT
Payne, Leon (Roger) 1917-1969 [singer, songwriter, guitarist]
Rogers, Rock *Source(s):* MCCL; NASF
Texas Blind Hitchhiker *Source(s):* MCCL
Pearl, Leo J. 1901(or 07)-1977 [composer, author]
Pearl, Lee *Source(s):* ASCP
Pearlman, Sheridan [composer, arranger]
Haskell, Jimmie *Source(s):* CLTP ("Ozzie & Harriet, The Adventures of")
Pearsall, Robert Lucas (de) 1795-1856 [composer]
Note(s): Prefix "de" added after his death (LCAR)
Berthold, G. *Source(s):* CPMU; GOTH; GOTT; GREN
R. L. P. *Source(s):* CPMU
Pearson, C(harles) E(dmund) [playwright]
Edmund, Charles *Source(s):* GANA p. 656
Pearson, Columbus Calvin, Jr. 1932-1980 [pianist, composer, arranger]
Calvin, Columbus *Source(s):* LCAR
Pearson, Duke *Source(s):* CCE60; EPMU; GROL; NGDJ; PEN2
Pearson, Henry Hugh 1815-1873 [composer]
Note(s): Portrait: ETUP 55:2 (Feb. 1937): 72
Mannsfeldt-Pierson, E. E. *Source(s):* CPMU; GOTH; GROL; NGDO
Mansfeldt, Edgar *Source(s):* GROL; MACM; NGDM, NGDO
Pierson, Heinrich Hugo *Source(s):* BAKO; CPMU; GOTH; GROL; NGDM; NGDO
Pease, Frederick Taylor 1939- [composer, teacher, drummer]
Pease, Ted *Source(s):* ASCP; CPOL Pau-733-142; LCAR
Peay, Benjamin (Franklin) 1931-1988 [singer, songwriter]
Benton, Brook *Source(s):* CM07; HARD; HARR; KICK; PEN2
Pecci, Tommaso 1576-1604 (or 06) [composer, poet]
Invaghito, (L') *Source(s):* GRV3; IBIM; WORB
Note(s): See also Pietro Benedetti & Mariano Tantucci.
Pechey, Archibald Thomas 1876-1961 [author]
Cross, Mark *Source(s):* LCAR
Valentine *Source(s):* GANB; KILG; LCAR
Pechová, Jindriska 1837 (or 47)-1926 [librettist]
Krásnohorská, Eliska *Source(s):* LOWN; NGDO
Pechstein, George P.
Lavain, George *Source(s):* TPRF

Peck, George Washington 1817-1859 [music critic]
Bigly, Cantell A. *Source(s):* GRAN; LCAR; PSND
Pedersen, Chuck [composer, songwriter, performer]
S.O.C. 7 *Source(s):* http://www.scifi.com/sfw/issue115/sound.html (12 Oct. 2002)
Pedersen, Jens Wilhelm 1939- [composer, arranger]
Fuzzy *Source(s):* GOTH; http://www.fuzzy.dk (12 Oct. 2002)
Pedrini, Teodorico 1671-1746 [composer]
Nipredi *Source(s):* DEA3; LCAR
Pedroski, Walter J. 1948- [composer, singer]
Pedroski, Lefty *Source(s):* ASCP; CCE63
Pedruska, David Darwin 1928-2003 [singer, songwriter]
Dudley, Dave *Source(s):* CCE55; CCME; EPMU; MCCL
Father of Truck Driving Songs *Source(s):* MCCL
High Priest of Diesel Country *Source(s):* MCCL
Peers, Frank 1874- [lyricist, composer, entertainer]
Leo, Frank *Source(s):* PSND
Peery, Rob Roy 1900-1973 [composer]
Note(s): Portrait: ETUP 54:12 (Dec. 1936): 749
Carleton, Bruce *Source(s):* CCE54; CCE58; CCE60; CPOL RE-315-976
Cassell, Caroline *Source(s):* TPRF
Christopher, William *Source(s):* CCE66
Ellis, Lee *Source(s):* CCE50-51; CPOL RE-5-508; TPRF
Peeters, Antonius 1957- [composer]
Peeters, Toni *Source(s):* KOMS
Peeters, (C(ornelius)) M(arcel) 1926- [composer]
Laine, Peter *Source(s):* CCE59-63; CCE66-67; REHH
Peirson, Eliza O. [author]
Aliqua *Source(s):* JULN
Peitl, Paul 1853- [librettist]
Günther, Paul *Source(s):* STGR
Mannsberg, Paul *Source(s):* WORB
Peleg, Frank 1910-1968 [composer, harpsichordist, pianist, conductor]
Pelley, Frank *Source(s):* BUL1; LYMN
Pollak, Frank *Source(s):* BUL3; LCAR; NGDM
Pelilli, Lino Ennio 1902- [composer]
Alloris, Tristano d' *Source(s):* WORB
Tristano d'Alloris *Source(s):* WORB
Pellegrin, Simon Joseph 1663-1745 [poet, playwright, librettist]
Barbier, Mlle. *Source(s):* GROL; NGDO
Note(s): Originally identified as pseud. of Pellagrin, but later identified as Maria-Anne Barbier, (c.1670-1745), dramatist, who may have collaborated with Pelligren.
Desmarets, Chevalier *Source(s):* STGR
La Roque, (Sieur de) *Source(s):* GROL; NGDO; STGR
La Serre *Source(s):* GROL; NGDO; PIPE
Pellegrini, Ferdinando c.1715-c.1766 [composer]
Note(s): Pellegrini published works of Galuppi & Rutini as his own in a set of harpsichord sonatas (op. 2). "Doubt has been cast upon other of his works, too . . ." (DEA3)
Galuppi, Baldassare *Source(s):* DEA3
Rutini, Ferdinando *Source(s):* DEA3
Pelletier, Frédéric [or Fred] 1870-1944 [choirmaster, critic, composer, physician]
Siffadaux, Remi *Source(s):* CANE
Pelosi, Domonic [or Don] 1895- [songwriter]
Boccolosi, Harry *Source(s):* CCE40 #19415 Efor63075; CCE67; LCCC 1938-45 (reference card)
Note(s): Jt. pseud.: Harold Elton Box, Desmond Cox [i.e., Adrian Keuleman] & Harry Leon [i.e., Sugarman]
Dévereux, Jules *Source(s):* CCE40 #18216 Efor62825; LCCC 1938-45 (reference card)
Note(s): Jt. pseud.: Harold Elton Box, Desmond Cox [i.e., Adrian Keuleman] & Harry Leon [i.e., Sugarman]
Fraser, Gordon *Source(s):* CCE40 #25023 Efor63262; CCE67; LCCC 1938-45 (reference card)
Note(s): Jt. pseud.: Harold Elton Box, Desmond Cox [i.e., Adrian Keuleman] & Harry Leon [i.e., Sugarman]
Gordon *Source(s):* CCE40 #4560 Efor61710 ("Home Again"); CCE67
Hardy *Source(s):* CCE66
Hart, Don *Source(s):* CCE68
McClure *Source(s):* CCE38 Efor54242; CCE55 ("Pardon My Tears"); CCE68
Pelosi, Noel *Source(s):* CCE66; CCE68
Pelovitz, Morton Herbert 1925-1983 [composer, bassist]
Herbert, Mort *Source(s):* LCAR; PSND
Peña, José Antonio late 1960s- [singer, composer]
Peña, Miles *Source(s):* HWOM; PEN2
Pendergast, Jonathan Barry 1933- [composer, arranger, conductor, trumpeter]
Angelo, Michael *Source(s):* LCAR
Barry, John *Source(s):* CASS; CM29; EPMU; LCAR
Pendergrass, Theodore [or Teddy] 1950 (or 51)- [singer, composer]
Svengali *Source(s):* PEN2; PSND
Note(s): Also used by (Ian) Ernest Gilmore Green.
Teddy Bear *Source(s):* CASS; PEN2; PSND
Penick, Mary Frances 1931 (or 32)-2004 [singer, songwriter]
Davis Sisters, The *Source(s):* CCE54
Note(s): Jt. name: Betty Jack Davis (no relation; high school friend).
Davis, Skeeter *Source(s):* CM15; EPMU; GRAT; MCCL

Peniston, Cecelia 1969- [singer, dancer, songwriter]
Peniston, Ce Ce *Source(s):* EPMU
Penn, William H. [songwriter]
Hewitt, William *Source(s):* CCE46 R5846 ("Little Italy"); CCE47 E23563 (" Will You Remember")
Lewis & Williams *Source(s):* CCE48 R39267
Note(s): Jt. pseud.: Domenico Savino.
Penney, Edward J., Jr. [songwriter]
Douglas, Wayne *Source(s):* CCE67 Eunp990861
Note(s): Also used by Douglas Wayne Broze, Walter (Charles) Ehret & Fred Weber; see NOTES: Douglas, Wayne. Do not confuse with singer Wayne Douglas [i.e., Doug Sham] (1941-1999).
Douglass, Don *Source(s):* CCE65 Eunp914404 & Eunp918348
Penniman, Richard [or Ricardo] Wayne 1932 (or 35)- [singer, pianist, songwriter]
Note(s): Given names "Richard Wayne" appear on birth certificate (WORL)
Bronze Liberace, The *Source(s):* PSND; WHIC
Georgia Peach, The *Source(s):* PSND
Note(s): See also Lucille Nelson.
Handsomest Man in Rock & Roll *Sources:* CM01
King of Rock and Roll, The *Source(s):* BAKR; PSND
Little Richard *Source(s):* BAKR; CM01; EPMU; HARS; PSND; RECR; WORL
Queen of Rock and Roll, The *Source(s):* PSND
Pennington, Ramon [or Ray] (Daniel) 1933- [singer, songwriter, guitarist]
Starr, Ray *Source(s):* CCE61; CCE63; MCCL
Pennington, Wallace Dan(iel) 1941- [songwriter]
Penn, Dan *Source(s):* CCE60; EPMU; HARD; HARR; PMUS; ROOM
Penny, Herbert Clayton 1918-1992 [singer, songwriter]
Penny, Hank *Source(s):* LCAR; MCCL
That Plain Ol' Country Boy *Source(s):* MCCL
Pennyman, Ruth before 1910- [librettist]
Pennyless, D. M. *Source(s):* GROL; PIPE
Note(s): Jt. pseud.: Michel (Kemp) Tippett & David Ayerst.
Penso, R. [songwriter]
Shirley-Ospen, David *Source(s):* CCE44 #35637, 827 R130039
Note(s): Jt. pseud.: Lilian Shirley [i.e., Lawrence Wright] & Worton David.
Penz, Ignatz von 1759-1822 [composer]
Walter, Ignatz *Source(s):* SONN
Perazzo, Joseph William 1943- [composer, singer, guitarist]
West, Joseph William *Source(s):* ASCP
Percy, Marvin (Karlton) 1925- [singer, songwriter]
Rainwater, Marvin *Source(s):* CCME; ENCM; EPMU; MCCL; PEN2
Peretti, Hugo (Emil) 1918-1986 [songwriter]
Dane, Bob *Source(s):* CCE58
Evans, H. *Source(s):* CCE58; CPOL RE-198-782
Hugo *Source(s):* CCE63 E178914 ("Hello Heartache, Goodbye, Love")
Hugo & Luigi *Source(s):* CCE62 ("I'll Take You Home"); CCE67 ("Rome Aventure")
Note(s): Jt. pseud.: Luigi Creatore.
Markwell, Mark *Source(s):* CCE58-59; PMUS
Note(s): Jt. pseud.: Luigi Creatore.
Orlando, Johnny *Source(s):* CCE56
Pereyra, Eduardo 1900-1973 [pianist, composer]
Chón, El *Source(s):* TODO
Cooper, Ray *Source(s):* TODO
Pérez, Adolfo 1897-1977 [bandoneonist, leader, composer]
Pocholo *Source(s):* TODO
Pérez, Ernesto [singer, songwriter]
Chapo (de Sinaloa), (El) *Source(s):* HWOM; LCAR
Pérez, Héctor (Juan) 1946-1993 [singer, composer]
Cantante, El *Source(s):* EPMU
Lavoe, Héctor *Source(s):* EPMU; PEN2
Singer of Singers and Improviser of Improvisers, The *Source(s):* PEN2
Perez Meza, Luis 1917-1981 [singer, songwriter]
Trovador del campo, El *Source(s):* HWOM
Perez Prado, Domasco [or Damasco] 1916 (or 22)-1989 [bandleader, arranger, composer]
King of the Mambo *Source(s):* EPMU; SHAD
Note(s): See also Ernesto Antonio Puente, (Jr.).
Mambo King, The *Source(s):* PSND
Note(s): See also Ernesto Antonio Puente, (Jr.).
Prado, Perez *Source(s):* LCAR
Rey del Mambo, El *Source(s):* PSND
Pérez Zúñiga, Juan 1860-1908 [writer, musician]
Sursum Corda *Source(s):* IBIM; WORB
Peri, Jacopo 1561-1633 [composer, singer, instrumentalist]
Zazzerino, Il *Source(s):* BAKO; BAKR; GROL; IBIM; MACM; NGDM; NGDO; PIPE
Perkings, Carl (Lee) 1932-1998 [singer, composer, guitarist]
Note(s): Perkings on birth certificate.
King of Rockabilly *Source(s):* MCCL
One String Perkins *Source(s):* MCCL
Perkins, Carl (Lee) *Source(s):* GAMM; PEN2; RECR
Rockin' Guitar Man, The *Source(s):* MCCL
Perkins, Joe Willie 1913- [singer, guitarist, pianist, songwriter]
Perkins, Pinetop *Source(s):* HARS
Perkins, Thomas (Wayne) 1940-1971 [guitarist, songwriter, producer]
Wayne, Thomas *Source(s):* EPMU

Perkins, Tony [bassist, songwriter]
Lennon, Martin Luther *Source(s):* http://www.westnet.com/consumable/1997/02.03/revmll.html (12 Oct. 2002)
M. L. L. *Source(s):):* http://www.westnet.com/consumable/1997/02.03/revmll.html
Perkinson, Coleridge Taylor 1932-2004 [composer, conductor]
Perk *Source(s):* DRSC
Perks, William 1936- [songwriter]
Wyman, Bill *Source(s):* AMUS; EPMU
Perlman, George 1915- [composer, author]
Perle, George *Source(s):* PSND
Perlman, Jess 1891-1988 [author, translator]
Gray, Philip *Source(s):* PIPE; PSND
Note(s): Also used by Robert L. Beckhard.
Peropota, Joseph Michael [composer]
Perry, Joe *Source(s):* CCE30 Eunp20690; JASA p. 322
Peros, Harry [songwriter]
Perosa, H. *Source(s):* CCE36 ("Alpine Valse"); LCPC
Note(s): Jt. pseud.: Walter Goehr.
Rutland, Lou *Source(s):* CCE30 Efor14734
Perrault, Charles 1628-1703 [author]
Note(s): See PSND for nonmusic-related sobriquets.
Darmancour, P. *Source(s):* PIPE
Perren, Fred(erick) [or Freddie] [songwriter, arranger, author]
Corporation, The *Source(s):* PMUS
Note(s): Jt. pseud.: Alphonso James Mizell, Deke Richards & Berry Gordy, Jr.
Perrey, Jean-Jacques [composer]
Leroy, Jean Marcel *Source(s):* CLTP ("The Joker's Wild")
Perrey-Kingsley *Source(s):* LCAR
Note(s): Jt. pseud.: Gershon Kingsley.
Perriere-Pilte, Anais (née Marcelli) 1836-1878 [composer]
Anaide, Marulli *Source(s):* COHN; DWCO; HIXN
Perrin, Etienne Bernard Auguste 1807-1838 [singer, composer]
Chevalier-Perrin *Source(s):* PIPE; WORB
Thenard, (Etienne Bernard Auguste) *Source(s):* PIPE; WORB
Perronnet, Amélie (Bernoux) 1831-1903 [composer, librettist]
Bernoux, Léon *Source(s):* COHN; GREN; HIXN; MELL
Perry, Clifford Albyn 1891-1937 [actor, composer]
Cliff, Laddie *Source(s):* NOMG; ROOM
Perry, Lincoln (T(heodore Monroe Andrew)) 1892-1985 [actor, dancer, songwriter, comedian]
Note(s): In some sources birth date: 1902.
Cool, Mr. *Source(s):* CCE65
Cousin Lincoln *Source(s):* CCE74
Fetchit, Stepin *Source(s):* CCE45 #52928Eunp433549; PSND; WORT
Note(s): Also used by Whelock Alexander Bisson; see NOTES: Fetchit, Stepin.
Mr. Cool *Source(s):* CCE65
Skeeter *Source(s):* ROOM
Stepin Fetchit *Source(s):* CCE65; PSND
Note(s): Also used by Whelock Alexander Bisson; see NOTES: Fetchit, Stepin.
White Man's Negro *Source(s):* PSND
Perry, Phil(ip) B(utler) 1859-1953 [music publisher, composer]
Butler, M. W. *Source(s):* CCE29 R3507; LCAR; MRSQ (1:1): 30
Holcombe, G. *Source(s):* LCAR; MRSQ (1:1): 30+
Lela *Source(s):* CCE12 R2463 ("Frost Crystals Waltz")
Perry, Rainford Hugh 1936- [producer, arranger, songwriter]
Perry, Lee *Source(s):* EPMU; GROL
Perry, Scratch *Source(s):* EPMU; LCAR
Scratch *Source(s):* GROL; LCAR
Upsetter, The *Source(s):* EPMU; LCAR
Perry, Sam A. [harmonica player, author]
Harmonica Bill *Source(s):* www.ibiblio.org/ccer/1925d2.htm (4 Jan. 2005)
Perryman, Rufus G. 1892-1973 [singer, keyboardist, songwriter]
Detroit Red *Source(s):* DBMU; HARS
Speckled Red *Source(s):* AMUS; DBMU; HARS
Perryman, William [or Willie] Lee 1911 (or 13)-1985 [singer, pianist, songwriter]
Dr. Feelgood *Source(s):* AMUS; EPMU; HARS
Note(s): See also John Lee Hooker.
Feelgood, Dr. *Source(s):* AMUS; HARS
Note(s): See also John Lee Hooker.
Mr. Boogie 'n' Blues *Source(s):* HARS
Piano Red *Source(s):* AMUS; EPMU; HARS; LCAR; PEN2
Note(s): See also Vernon Harrison.
Pers, Dirck Pietersz(oon) 1581-1662 [writer, publisher, editor]
Dirck van Embden *Source(s):* NGDM
Doretheos a Bemdba *Source(s):* NGDM
Theodorus Petrejus *Source(s):* NGDM
Persson, Harry (Arnold) 1920-1971 [bandleader, arranger, saxophonist]
Arnold, Harry *Source(s):* CCE54; CCE60; NGDJ
Bie(-Persson), Nils *Source(s):* CCE48; CCE53; CPOL RE-53-910
Persson, Nils Birger *Source(s):* CCE49; CCE51
Valesca, José *Source(s):* CCE47; CCE50
Peschek, Alfred 1929- [composer]
Bertrand, Michel *Source(s):* BUL3

Peshkov, Aleksei Maksimovich 1868-1936 [librettist]
Note(s): See LCAR for variant forms of name.
Gorki, Maxim *Source(s):* LCAR; PIPE
Gorky, Maksim *Source(s):* LCAR; LOWN
Petelin, Jakob 1550-1591 [composer]
Note(s): Probable original name; see LCAR for variant forms of name.
Carniolanus, Jacobus *Source(s):* LCAR
Gallus, Jacobus *Source(s):* LCAR; NGDM
Handl, Jacob *Source(s):* BAKR; LCAR
Peter, Nicol. Friedr. 1827-1900 [composer]
Kühner *Source(s):* STGR
Peters, Werner 1954- [composer]
Petersburg *Source(s):* KOMS; PFSA
Peters, W(illiam) C(umming) 1805-1866 [composer, music publisher]
Cumming, William *Source(s):* LCAR; Wetzel, Richard D. *The Musical Life and Times of William Cumming Peters*. Warren, Mich.: Harmonie Park Press, 2000, 1 (note 1)
Peterson, Leland Arnold 1911- [composer, author]
Peterson, Ernie *Source(s):* ASCP
Peterson, Marvin (Hannibal) 1948- [trumpeter, composer]
Hannibal *Source(s):* LCAR
Lokumbe, Hannibal *Source(s):* LCAR
Peterson, Walter [songwriter]
Kentucky Wonder Bean, The *Source(s):* Peterson, Walter. "Mountain Ballads and Old-Time Songs." Chicago, M. M. Cole. (port. on cover)
Petit, Jean-Claude 1943- [composer]
Esmeralda, Santa *Source(s):* MOMU
Petite, (E.) Dale 1926- [composer, author]
Price, Darryl *Source(s):* ASCP; CCE55 Eunp
Petkere, Bernice 1906-2000 [pianist, songwriter]
Queen of Tin Pan Alley *Source(s):* BBDP
Petrassi, Goffredo 1904-2003 [composer]
Father of Contemporary Italian Music *Source(s):* MUWB
Petrie, H(enry) W. 1857 (or 68?)-1925 [composer]
Note(s): Portrait: ETUP 55:1 (Jan. 1937): 3
Wilde(r)mere, Henry *Source(s):* CCE45 #4114, 421 R134044; TPRF
Wil(l)trie, H. B. *Source(s):* CCE38 E67235
Note(s): Jt. pseud.: Ira B(ishop) Wilson.
Petrococchino, Dimitri 1874-1943 [author, playwright]
Armont, Paul *Source(s):* GAN1; GAN2; WORB
Petrosellini, Giuseppe 1727-after 1797 [writer]
Ensildo Prosindio *Source(s):* SONN
Prosindio, Ensildo *Source(s):* ALMC; SONN
Sellini, Pietro *Source(s):* SONN
Note(s): Not a pseud.; printer's error.
Petrović, Milorad 1875-1921 [author]
Seljanćica *Source(s):* PIPE
Pettigrew, Leola (B.) 1893- [singer, actress, songwriter]
Coleman, Nancy *Source(s):* SUTT
Coot(s) *Source(s):* HARS
Grant, Coot *Source(s):* BBDP; EPMU; GRAT; HARS
Grant, Cutie *Source(s):* BBDP
Grant, Leola (B.) *Source(s):* EPMU; GRAT; HARS
Hunter, Patsy *Source(s):* EPMU; HARS
Wilson, (Mrs.) Leola (B.) *Source(s):* EPMU; HARS; SUTT
Pettis, Coleman, Jr. c.1935-1988 [guitarist, composer]
Alabama Junior *Source(s):* EPMU
Daddy Rabbit *Source(s):* EPMU
Pettis, Alabama *Source(s):* EPMU
Pettis, Daddy Rabbit *Source(s):* AMUS
Pettis, Junior *Source(s):* EPMU
Rabbit, Daddy *Source(s):* EPMU
Pettman, E. [arranger]
E. P. *Source(s):* CPMU (publication dates 1902-07)
Petty, Tom 1950- [guitarist, songwriter, singer]
Traveling Wilburys *Source(s):* WILB
Note(s): With: George Harrison, Jeff Lynne, Roy (Kelton) Orbison & Bob Dylan [i.e., Robert Allen Zimmerman.
Wilbury, Charlie T(ruscott), Jr. *Source(s):* WILB
Wilbury, Muddy *Source(s):* WILB
Petz, Manfred 1932- [guitarist, singer, lyricist]
Quinn, Freddy *Source(s):* EPMU
Peuerl, Paul 1570-after 1625 [organist, organ builder, composer]
Bäwerl, Paul *Source(s):* BAKR; LCAR
Beurlin, Paul *Source(s):* BAKR; LCAR; WORB
Payerl, Paul *Source(s):* LCAR
Peyron, Albertina Fredrika 1845-1922 [pianist, composer]
Ika *Source(s):* COHN; HIXN
Pfeferstein, John 1906-1984 [playwright, lyricist, composer]
Murray, John *Source(s):* PSND
Pfeiffer, Karl ?-1831 [librettist]
Schmidt, Fr. Georg *Source(s):* GROL (see under: Spohr, Luis); LOWN; PIPE
Pfeiffer, Marie V. [composer]
Fifer, Max *Source(s):* http://www.memory.loc.gov/cgi-bin/query (12 Oct. 2002)
Pferdemenges, Maria Pauline Augusta 1872- [organist, pianist, composer]
Pery, M. *Source(s):* COHN; HEIN; HIXN
Pfeuffer, Walter 1893-1969 [composer]
Fellow, Frank *Source(s):* SUPN

Pflüger, Andreas B. 1941- [composer]
Benedict, Andy *Source(s):* http://composers21.com/compdocs/pflugera.htm (30 Apr. 2005)
Pfohl, Albrecht 1950- [composer]
Al-Obo *Source(s):* PFSA
Pfundheller, Josef 1813-1889 [librettist]
Mareller, J. C. *Source(s):* STGR
Note(s): Jt. pseud.: Carl [or Karl] Elmar [i.e., Karl Swiedack]
Phaneuf, Albert 1919-1978 [composer, organist]
Dela, Maurice *Source(s):* BAKR; CCE65; CCE68
Phelps, Arthur c.1880-1935 [singer, guitarist, composer]
Note(s): For conflicting reports regarding original surname (HARS). Portrait: HARS
Blake, Arthur *Source(s):* IDBC; LCAR
Blake, Blind *Source(s):* AMUS; HARS; IDBC; LCAR; SUTT
Note(s): See also Blake Alphonso Higgs.
Blind Arthur *Source(s):* HARS; LCAR
Blind Blake *Source(s):* HARS; LCAR
Note(s): See also Blake Alphonso Higgs.
Gorgeous Weed *Source(s):* HARS; LCAR
James, Billy *Source(s):* HARS; LCAR
King of Ragtime Guitar, The *Source(s):* http://www.garlic.com/~tgracyk/blake1.htm (9 Oct. 2003)
Martin, Blind George *Source(s):* HARS; LCAR
Martin, George *Source(s):* HARS
Master of Ragtime Guitar, The *Source(s):* http://www.torvund.net/guitar/Booklists/Blind_Blake.asp (12 June 2003)
Ragtime Guitar's Foremost Fingerpicker *Source(s):* http://www.yazoobluemailorder.com/yaz1068.htm (12 June 2003)
Weed, Gorgeous *Source(s):* HARS
Phile, Philip 1734-1793 [violinist, composer]
Fyles, Philip *Sources:* BAKE; NGAM
Pfiel, Philip *Source(s):* NGAM
Pheil *Source(s):* DICH (see under: Phile, Philip) ("The Presidents March")
Phyla, Philip *Source(s):* BAKE
Phyles, Philip *Sources:* NGAM
Philipp, Adolf 1864-1936 [composer, playwright, actor, producer]
Note(s): Since a another Adolf Philipp was operating out of Hamburg around the same time, it is difficult to establish credit for his early German works. (GAN2)
Briquet, Jean *Source(s):* CCE38 R64183; GAN2; GROL; NGAM
German Harrigan, The *Source(s):* GAN2
Hervé, Paul *Source(s):* CCE38 R64183; GAN2; GROL; NGAM
Schumacher, F. *Source(s):* GAN2
Philipp, Isidor (Edmond) 1863-1958 [arranger, composer, pianist]
Note(s): Portraits: ETUP 55:1 (Jan. 1937): 3; MRAR (Oct. 1902): 36; MUWO (1903, #7): 113
Edmonde, Philipp *Source(s):* WORB
Phitt, Sam *Source(s):* GOTH; WORB
Philips, Peter 1560 (or 61)-1628 [composer, organist]
Filippo, Pietro *Source(s):* IBIM; WORB
Phillips, Alfred [composer]
Note(s): Publication dates 1890-1941.
Kingsmill, Leigh *Source(s):* CPMU; OCLC 48704533
Sarakowski, G. *Source(s):* CPMU
Phillips, Bruce (U.) 1935- [singer, songwriter, storyteller]
Golden Voice of the Great Southwest, The *Source(s):* MUHF
Phillips, Utah *Source(s):* EPMU; MUHF
Phillips, Harvey G. 1929- [tubist, writer on music]
Iacocca of the Tuba *Source(s):* http://www.windsongpress.com/musicians/phillips/phillips.html (28 Mar. 2003)
Mr. Tuba *Source(s):* http://www.windsongpress.com/musicians/phillips/phillips.html
Paganini of the Tuba *Source(s):* http://www.windsongpress.com/musicians/phillips/phillips.html
Tuba Meister *Source(s):* http://www.windsongpress.com/musicians/phillips/phillips.html
Phillips, Isadore Simon 1907-1973 [clarinettist, bandleader, composer, arranger]
King of the Clarinet *Source(s):* PSND
Note(s): See also Artie Shaw[i.e., Arthur Jacob Arshawsky]
Phillips, Sid *Source(s):* NGDJ; PEN1
Simon, Isadore *Source(s):* REHH
Note(s): Typographical error; original surname missing.
Phillips, James John 1902- [songwriter]
Johns, Leo *Source(s):* LCCC 1955-70 (see reference); SHAP
Note(s): Jt. pseud.: Marcel Stellman.
Phillips, Karma *Source(s):* CCE64
Price, Arthur *Source(s):* CCE56; CPOL RE-259-366
Turner, James John *Source(s):* CCE54-55; CPOL RE-218-466
Turner, John *Source(s):* CCE51-58; CCE61 ("Bella, Bella Marie"); CPOL RE-219-587
Note(s): Also used by John(ny) Tucker.
Phillips, Jane Josephine [songwriter]
Eryl, Blanche *Source(s):* CPMU (publication date 1900)
Phillips, Jason (T.) [songwriter, performer]
Jadakiss *Source(s):* AMUS; CPOL PA-1-071-515; PMUS-00

Phillips, Leslie 1962- [singer, songwriter, guitarist]
Burnett, Sam *Source(s):* LCAR
Phillips, Sam *Source(s):* CM12
Phillips, Paul [songwriter, publisher]
Driver 67 *Source(s):* EPMU
Phillips, Philip 1834-1895 [teacher, hymnist, singing evangelist]
Note(s): Portraits: CYBH; ETUP 55:1 (Jan. 1937): 3; HALL
Singing Pilgrim, The *Source(s):* HALL; JULN (Appendix)
Phillips, Ramsay 1919-1998 [songwriter]
Ames, Ramsay *Source(s):* LCAR; NOMG
Phillips, Stu(art John Tristram) 1933- [singer, songwriter, guitarist]
Western Gentleman, (The) *Source(s):* MCCL
Phillips, Teddy (Steve) 1913 (or 16)-2001 [composer, author, conductor]
Simms, T(eddy) *Source(s):* ASCP; CCE54-56; CPOL RE-208-250
Sims, Teddy *Source(s):* CPOL RE-57-999
Phillips, W. Compton [composer]
Forestier, Leonard *Source(s):* CPMU (publication date 1892)
Phillips, William [or Bill] (Clarence) 1936 (or 38)- [singer, songwriter, guitarist, actor]
Phillips, Tater *Source(s):* MCCL
Phillips, William Lovell 1816-1860 [composer, singer, violoncellist, organist]
Lovell, Philip *Source(s):* CPMU; GOTT; IBIM
Philpott, George Vere Hobart 1867-1926 [author; librettist, songwriter]
Bauer, Wright *Source(s):* PSND
Hobart, George V(ere) *Source(s):* GAN1; GAN2; PSND; WORB
Note(s): In PSND listed as original name.
Lott, Noah *Source(s):* PSND
McHugh, Hugh *Source(s):* GAN1; GAN2; PSND
Phipps, Joyce Irene 1910-1979 [actress, author, songwriter]
Grenfell, Joyce *Source(s):* EPMU; GAMM
King, Jan *Source(s):* CCE74 R582407
Piani, Giovanni Antonio 1678 (or 80)-after 1757? [violinist, composer]
Desplanes, Giovanni [or Jean] (Antoine) *Source(s):* MACM; SADC
Planes, Giovanni des *Source(s):* WORB
Piastro, Josef 1889-1964 [violinist, composer]
Borissoff *Source(s):* BAKE; RIEM
Piazza, Giovanni Battista fl. 1628-33 [composer]
Ongaretto, L' *Source(s):* GROL; NGDM; WORB
Piazzolla, Astor 1921-1992 [bandoneonist, pianist, composer, arranger]
Father of the New Tango *Source(s):* http://www.bmc.hu/bmcrecords/piazzolla/more.htm (12 Oct. 2002)
King of the Tango *Source(s):* http://www.cybozone.com/fg/quattro.html (12 Oct. 2002)
Picardo, Thomas (R., Jr.) 1942- [songwriter, record producer]
West, T. P. *Source(s):* CCE67-68; CCE73 E313598
West, Thomas [or Tommy] *Source(s):* CCE76; EPMU (see under: Cashman and West); PMUS
Note(s): Also used by Joseph Schreyvogel.
Picariello, Frederick [or Frederico] A(nthony) 1939 (or 40)- [composer, author, singer]
Cannon Boom-Boom *Source(s):* LCAR
Cannon, Freddy *Source(s):* AMUS; ASCP; CCE64-65; EPMU; PEN2
Carmen, Fred *Source(s):* CCE58
Kaplan, C. *Source(s):* CCE63
Karmon, Freddy *Source(s):* AMUS; PEN2
Last Rock 'n' Roll Star *Source(s):* EPMU
Piccini, Giulio 1849-1915 [writer on music]
Jarro *Source(s):* GROL; LCAR; LOWN; NGDO; WORB
Piccinni, (Vito) Niccolò (Marcello Antonio Giacomo) 1728-1800 [composer]
Note(s): Portrait: ETUP 55:2 (Feb. 1937): 72
Piccinnist *Source(s):* BAKR; EPDI; NGDM
Note(s): Term used to identify persons siding with Piccinni in the "l'querelle célèbre" with Gluck.
Piccioni, Angelo F. [songwriter]
Manillo, Pedro *Source(s):* CCE60; CCE65 R359686
Note(s): Jt. pseud.: A(nnuzio) P(aolo) Mantovani; see NOTES: Manillo, Pedro.
Paolito, Francesco *Source(s):* CCE33 Efor30289; CCE60 R253971
Note(s): Jt. pseud.: A(nnuzio) P(aolo) Mantovani.
Piccioni, Piero 1921- [composer]
Morgan, Piero *Source(s):* CCE51; MOMU; PSND
Piccolomini, Theodore (Auguste Maria Joseph) 1835-1902 [songwriter]
Nemo *Source(s):* KILG
Pontet, Henry Theodore *Source(s):* GOTH; KILG
Picher, Anna B. [writer on music, museum curator]
Wey, Auguste *Source(s): Inter-American Music Review* 16:2 (2000): 53
Pichot, Guillermo 1916- [songwriter]
Note(s): Do not confuse with Guillermo Juan Robstiano Pichot (1893-1959); see following entry.
Guillermo *Source(s):* CCE54
Pichot, Guillermo Juan Robustiano 1893-1959 [poet, playwright, journalist]
Note(s): Do not confuse with Guillermo Pichot (1916-); see preceding entry.
Pelay, Ivo *Source(s):* TODO

Pickar, Arnold fl. 1444-1480 [composer]
Note(s): The following are possible pseuds.
Biquardus *Source(s):* GROL
Picard *Source(s):* GROL
Wiqwardus *Source(s):* GROL
Pickering, Jack [songwriter]
Jackman, Leo *Source(s):* CPOL RE-262-207
Note(s): Jt. pseud.: Leo Towers [i.e., Leo(nard) Blitz] & James [or Jimmy] Campbell.
Pickett, Bobby 1940- [singer, songwriter, author, actor]
Pickett, Boris *Source(s):* EPMU; PSND
Pickett, Wilson 1941- [singer, songwriter]
Wicked (Pickett), The *Source(s):* ALMN; PSND
Pidoux, Madeline mentioned 1875 [writer on music]
Hermann, Jacques *Source(s):* EBEL; MACM; WORB
Piedrahita Gaviria, Luis Javier 1950- [singer, songwriter]
Fausto *Source(s):* HWOM
Pierce, Paula Wahl [composer]
LaValle, Paul *Source(s):* CCE47 R9405 ("Dance of the Rubber Dolls")
Note(s): Also used by Joseph Usifer.
Piermarini, Clito L. 1927- [composer, teacher]
Marini, Peer *Source(s):* ASCP
Piesker, Rüdiger 1923- [conductor, composer]
Cardello, Rolf *Source(s):* CCE64 Efor97714; CCE67; CPOL RE-523-927; RIES
Note(s): Also used by Hans (-Artur) Wittstatt.
Rolf, Cardello *Source(s):* CCE63
Rothmann, Paul *Source(s):* CCE64 Efor10245; CCE67
Piestre, Pierre-Étienne 1810 (or 11)-1903 [playwright; librettist]
Cormon, Eugène *Source(s):* NGDO; PIPE; WORB
Pietragrua, Carlo (Luigi) 1692-1773 [composer, singer]
Grau, Carlo (Luigi) *Source(s):* LCAR; NGDO; SONN
Pietro, Mario de [composer]
Revel, Louis *Source(s):* JASG; JASR
Pietsch, Rainer 1944- [composer]
Gernreich, Daniel *Source(s):* KOMP; KOMS; PFSA
Pietzsch, Gerhard (Wilhelm) 1904-1979 [writer on music]
Wiebenga, Wiarda *Source(s):* PIPE
Piffett, Etienne mentioned 1750 [violinist, composer]
Big Nose *Source(s):* MACM
Grand Nez, Le *Source(s):* WORB
Pigna, Alessandro 1857-1928 [composer]
Passagni, Leandro *Source(s):* MELL; STGR; WORB
Pike, Harry Hale 1874- [composer]
Note(s): Portraits: ETUP 55:1 (Jan. 1937): 3; MRAR (Choir Ed.) (July 1902): 1
Durant, Christine *Source(s):* TPRF
Hale, H. P. *Source(s):* CCE35 #19704, 139
Pike, Pete [songwriter]
Ham and Scam *Source(s):* MCCL
Note(s): Jt. pseud.: Bernarr (G(raham)) Busbice.
Pilati, Auguste 1810-1877 [composer, dramatist]
Julian, Th. *Source(s):* STGR
Juliano, A(uguste) *Source(s):* CPMU; IBIM; MACM; WORB
Ruytler *Source(s):* IBIM; MELL; STGR; WORB
Wolfart *Source(s):* MACM
Pilderwasser, Joshua Samuel 1888-1952 [songwriter, arranger]
Weisser, Samuel *Source(s):* BUL3; HESK; NULM (port.)
Pillois, Jacques 1877-1935 [composer]
Desky, Jacques *Source(s):* BAKE; LCAR
Pinard, Lancelot (Victor) 1902-2001 [composer, author, singer]
Lancelot, Sir *Source(s):* ASCP; CCE57-58; CCE64-66; OB01
Sir Lancelot *Source(s):* CCE65-66
Pinatel, Albert mentioned 1900 [editor, composer]
Saint-Kopp *Source(s):* IBIM; WORB
Pincherle, Alberto 1907-1990 [author, critic]
Moravia, Alberto *Source(s):* OCLC 25726546; WORB
Pincus, Barry Allen [or Alan] 1946- [singer, songwriter]
Manilow, Barry *Source(s):* ALMN; CM02; DIMA; EPMU; GAMM; HARR; KICK
Nose, The *Source(s):* CASS
Pincus, Herman 1905- [composer, author]
Herman, Pinky *Source(s):* ASCP; CCE57; CCE60
Pindell, Annie Pauline 1834-1901 [singer, songwriter]
Black Nightingale, The *Source(s):* PSNN
Note(s): See also Gertrude (Malissa Nix) Pridgett.
Nightingale of the Pacific *Source(s):* PSNN
Pindemon(t)e, Giovanni 1751-1812 [librettist]
Acanzio, Eschillo [or Eschibo] *Source(s):* MELL; STGR
Pinder, Harold [composer]
Rednip *Source(s):* CCE20 E491511; JASA p. 322
Pine, Arthur 1917-2000 [composer, author]
Richards, Jay *Source(s):* ASCP; CCE59-60
Pinello (di Ghirardi), Giovanni Battista c.1554-1587 [composer, singer]
Binellus (de Gerardis), Giovanni Battista *Source(s):* NGDM
Nobile Genovese *Source(s):* NGDM
Note(s): Called himself.
Pinggèra, Karl Ludwig 1930-1987 [composer]
Malco, Lu(i) *Source(s):* KOMP; PFSA

Pingoud, Ernest 1887-1942 [composer, music critic]
Bolshevist of Music *Source(s):* AMRG 61:3 (1998): 164
Ilari, Lauri *Source(s):* http://www.fimic.fi/fimic.nsf?open (26 Apr. 2005)
Loke, Jonny *Source(s):* http://www.fimic.fi/fimic.nsf?open
Pinkard, Maceo 1897-1962 [composer, lyricist, bandleader]
Belledna, Alex *Source(s):* CCE46 R6726 ("Granny"); JASZ
Note(s): Originally thought to be pseud.of Pinkard, and he did not deny it; however, later determined to be pseudonym of his wife; see Edna Belle Alexander. (JASZ p. 185-6)
Pinkus, Alwin Oskar 1891-1945 [writer on music, conductor, composer]
Alwin, Karl (Oskar) *Source(s):* BAKT
Pintacuda, Salvatore 1901?- [musicologist]
Rabula *Source(s):* WORB
Pirckmayer, Georg(e) 1918-1977 [composer]
Pier, George *Source(s):* BUL2; BUL3; CCE64; GREN; RIES
Pirola, Carlo 1945- [composer]
Picarband *Source(s):* REHH
Pirrotta, Antonio 1908-1998 [musicologist]
Pirrotta, Nino *Source(s):* BAKR; NGDO
Pisari, Pasquale 1725-1778 [composer]
Palestrina of the 18th Century, The *Source(s):* BAKR
Pischinger, Hans 1884-1966 [composer]
Pless, Hans *Source(s):* BLIC; BUL3; GOTH; RIES
Pistocchi, Francesco Antonio Ma(ssi)miliano 1659 (or 60)-1717 (or 26) [composer, singer]
Pistocchino, Il *Source(s):* BAKO; BAKR; NGDM; NGDO; PIPE; SONN; WORB
Pistocco *Source(s):* NGDO; PIPE
Pistritto, John 1920-1997 [composer, author, singer]
Tritt, Johnnie *Source(s):* ASCP
Pitman, Ambrose 1763-1817 [poet, composer, editor]
Epigram, Ephraim, Esq. *Source(s):* PSNN
Young Gentleman of Seventeen, A *Source(s):* LCAR; PSNN
Pitney, Gene (Francis Alan) 1941- [songwriter, singer]
Brian, Billy *Source(s):* NGAM; http://www.classicbands.com/pitney.html (12 Oct. 2002)
Pittaluga, Egidio [or Eligio] [composer]
Egidio da Tempo *Source(s):* STGR v. 4/pt.1
Tempo, Egidio da *Source(s):* STGR v. 4/pt.1
Pittana, Luigi 1821-1891 [composer]
Cuoghi, L. *Source(s):* MELL; STGR
Pixérécourt, René Charles Guilbert de 1773-1844 [librettist, dramatist]
Corneille of the Boulevards, The *Source(s):* GROL

Pizzetti, Ildebrando 1880-1968 [composer, conductor, critic]
Note(s): Portraits: EWEC; MUCO 98:12 (21 Mar. 1929): 8
Debrando da Parma, Il *Source(s):* GROL
Note(s): See also Gabriele D'Annunzio.
Ildebrando da Parma *Source(s):* GROL; IBIM; NGDO; PIPE; WORB
Parma, Ildebrando da *Source(s):* CPMU; NGDM; NGDO; PIPE
Pizzi, Emilio 1862-1940 [composer]
Paul, Vera *Source(s):* PIPE
Pizzi, (Giuseppe) Gioacchino 1716-1790 [librettist]
Amarinzio, Nivildo *Source(s):* GROL; MORI; NGDO; SONN
Giovacchino *Source(s):* GROL
Planard, François Antoinde Eugène 1783-1853 [librettist]
Castel *Source(s):* MELL
Eugène *Source(s):* LCAR
Planquette, (Jean) Robert (Julien) 1848-1903 [composer]
Turlet, A. *Source(s):* SUPPN (see reference)
Plautzius, Gabriel ?-1641 [composer]
Carniolus *Source(s):* GROL
Playford, Henry 1657-c.1707 [composer, music publisher]
H. P. *Source(s):* CPMU; LCAR
Merryman, Dr. *Source(s):* CART; LCAR
Pleskow, Raoul 1931- [composer, teacher]
Mozart of Contemporary Music *Source(s):* http://gram.main.nc.us/~bhammel/MUSIC/pleskow.html (7 Apr. 2005)
Plessow, Erich 1899- [composer]
Estvilla, Manuel *Source(s):* CCE32 E for26624; CCE60; GREN
Lesso-Valero, P. *Source(s):* CCE32 Efor26624; GREN
Walter, Ewald *Source(s):* CCE60; CCE62; GREN
Willis, Edward *Source(s):* GREN
Plieksan, Janis 1865-1929 [poet, librettist]
Rainis, Janis *Source(s):* LCAR; LOWN; MELL; ROOM
Plomer, William (Charles Franklin) 1903-1973 [author]
Arfey, William d' *Source(s):* PIPE
Plumlovský, Ignác 1703-1759 [composer]
Alanus, Pater *Source(s):* NGDO
Plumstead, W. H. mentioned 1827-56 [composer, arranger]
W. H. P. *Source(s):* CPMU
Plunkett, Mert(on) (Wesley) 1888-1966 [composer, conductor]
Cap Mert *Source(s):* VGRC
Plüter, Lothar 1927- [composer]
Wendra, Hans *Source(s):* BUL3

Pockrich, Richard 1690-1759 [musician, inventor of musical glasses]
Philanthropos *Source(s):* CART ("The Temple-Oge Ballad")
Note(s): See also John Fellows.
Podewils, Torsten Hünke von 1909- [composer]
Hünke, Torsten *Source(s):* KOMS
Torsten, Hünke *Source(s):* KOMS
Poenitz, Franz 1850-1913 [composer]
Benizzo, Franc. *Source(s):* GREN
Pohl, Baruch 1838-1896 (or 97) [composer]
Pollini, Bernhard *Source(s):* RIEM; WORB
Pohl, Richard 1826-1896 [writer on music; critic, translator]
Hoplit *Source(s):* BAKR; GROL; IBIM; KOBW; NGDO; WORB
Note(s): On critical writings.
Richard, Jean *Source(s):* IBIM; WORB
Poindexter, (Clarence) Albert 1902 (or 05)-1984 [singer, songwriter, guitarist]
Dexter, Al *Source(s):* ALMN; AMUS; EPMU; HARD; HARR; KINK; MCCL; NASF
Poinsinet de Sivry, Louis 1733-1804 [dramatist]
Beaupré, Cadet de *Source(s):* PIPE
Polewheel fl. 1650-60 [musician, composer]
Paulwheel *Source(s):* NGDM
Wheeler, Paul *Source(s):* NGDM
Note(s): Possibly Polewheel.
Polfus(s), Lester (William) 1915- [singer, guitarist, songwriter, inventor]
Godfather of the Electric Guitar, The *Source(s):* http://www.jazzreview.com/corners.cmf?CurrentPage=2 (12 Oct. 2002)
Hot Rod Red *Source(s):* PSND
Leslie, Paul *Source(s):* JAMU
Paul, Les *Source(s):* ALMN; CCE53-56; CLAS; CM02; LCAR; PSND; STAC
Rhubarb Red *Source(s):* PSND; SHAD; STAC
Polidoro, Federigo (Idomeneo) 1845-1903 [lecturer, writer on music]
Acuto *Source(s):* PRAT
Polla, William C. 1876-1939 [composer]
Edwards, Powell *Source(s):* CCE66
Powell, W(illiam) C. *Source(s):* CCE33 R20373; JASA p. 322; JASN; JASR; PARS
Seymore, Cy *Source(s):* JASA p. 322
Note(s): Do not confuse with Cy Seymour [i.e., Stan(ley) (Seymour) Applebaum]
Pollak, Franz 1870-1938 [composer]
Haper, C. *Source(s):* SUPN
Robert, Fred *Source(s):* SUPN
Volkwarth *Source(s):* SUPN
Pollard, Josephine 1834-1892 [hymnist]
J. P. *Source(s):* JULN
Pollock, Muriel 1895-1971 [composer, pianist, organist]
Donaldson, Molly *Source(s):* CCE66; CCE68 R449621; LCAR
Donnadieu,Yvonne *Source(s):* CCE58
Pollock, Molly *Source(s):* RAGT p. 162
Polnarioff, Kurt 1917-1958 [violinist, composer, bandleader]
Nero, Paul *Source(s):* KINK
Note(s): Also used by Klaus Doldinger.
Ponce, Manuel (Maria) 1882-1949 [composer, pianist, critic]
Weiss, Sylvius Leopold *Source(s):* http://emedia.leeward.hawaii.edu/frary/ponce_pastiches4.htm (1 Nov. 2002)
Pond, Paul (Adrian) [singer, songwriter]
Jones, Paul *Source(s):* CCE64-65; CPOL RE-576-551; NOMG
Poniatowski, Joseph Michel Xavier François Jean 1816-1873 [composer, conductor]
Monte-Rotondo, Prince *Source(s):* GOTT; IBIM; WORB
Ponsa, Maria Luisa 1878-1919 [pianist, composer]
D'Orsay, M. L. *Source(s):* COHN; HIXN
Ponsonby, Eustace ?-1924 [author, actor, songwiter]
Ponsonby, Scroby *Source(s):* GANA p. 872
Pontelibero, Ferdinando 1770-1835 [violinist, composer]
Ajutantini, (Ferdinando) *Source(s):* GROL; MACM
Pontet, Henry Theodore 1835 (or 40?)-1902 [songwriter]
Piccolomini, M. *Source(s):* CPMU; GANA p. 202; OCLC 49409510
Ponti, Andrea mentioned 1914 [composer]
D'Ontana, Pier *Source(s):* IBIM; WORB
Pontifex, Clara de 1807-1876 [writer, composer]
Chatelain, Clara (de) (Pontigny) *Source(s):* WORB
Wray, Leopolf *Source(s):* CART; IBIM; LCAR; PSND; WORB
Ziska, Leopoldine *Source(s):* IBIM; WORB
Pook, Jocelyn [composer]
Mead, Abigail *Source(s):* http://www.filmscoremonthly.com/articles/1999/18_June-Film_Score_Friday.asp (30 Sept. 2003)
Poole, Barry [songwriter]
Judd, Cledus 'T,' (No Relation) *Source(s):* AMUS; EPMU
Note(s): Added "No Relation" to his name to make clear his lack of connection to Wynonna & Naomi Judd (AMUS).
Pope, Kelvin [calypso/soca artist, composer]
Duke, Mighty *Source(s):* PEN2
Mighty Duke *Source(s):* PEN2
Popelka, Joachim 1910-1965 [composer, conductor]
Jakob, Peter Michael *Source(s):* PIPE

Popp, Wilhelm 1828-1903 [composer]
Note(s): Portrait: ETUP 55:3 (Mar. 1937): 144
Albert(i), Henry *Source(s):* GREN; IBIM; WORB
Popper, David 1843-1913 [cellist, composer]
Paganini of the Cello *Source(s):* http://www.violoncellosociety.org/inaugral.htm (11 Feb. 2004)
Note(s): See also Adrien François Servais.
Popy, Francis 1874-1928 [composer]
Staz, H(enry) *Source(s):* GREN; REHH; SMIN; SUPN
Poquelin, Jean-Baptiste 1622-1673 [playwright, actor]
Molière, (Jean Baptiste) *Source(s):* NGDM; NGDO; RIEM; WORB
Poritzky, Ruth 1902- [composer]
Porita, Ruth *Source(s):* MACM; WORB
Porpora, Nichola (Antonio) 1686-1768 [composer]
Patriarch of Harmony, The *Source(s):* PSND
Pörschmann, Walter 1903-1959 [composer]
Domingues, Alberto *Source(s):* RIES
Porter, Cole 1893-1964 [composer, lyricist]
Note(s): Portrait: EWEN
Adlai Stevenson of Songwriters, The *Source(s):* SIFA
Elegant Hoosier Tunesmith, The *Source(s):* PSND; SIFA
Juggernaut of American Song *Source(s):* CM10 p. vi
Porter, Curtis 1929- [saxophonist, composer]
Hadi, Shafi *Source(s):* EPMU; LCAR
Porter, Darryl Porter 1976- [songwriter]
Harmonic, Phil *Source(s):* PA-1-098-186
Note(s): Also used by Kenneth Werner.
Porter, Mitchell 1915- [composer]
Mitchell, Teepee *Source(s):* CCE43 #33398 E115899; CCE50-51; PMUS
Porter, Robert Morris 1924- [composer, arranger, singer]
Gatsby, Paco *Source(s):* ASCP
Posegga, Hans 1917-2002 [composer]
Marbeck, Ernst *Source(s):* CCE59; KOMP; KOMS; PFSA
Poser, Hans 1917-1970 [composer]
Tannenberg, Wolfgang *Source(s):* CCE54; KOMS; PFSA
Possendorf, Hans 1883-1956 [librettist]
Mahner-Mons, Hans *Source(s):* LCAR; LOWN; PIPE; WORB
Post, Alan [singer, songwriter]
Horvath, Alan *Source(s):* http://www.alanhorvath.com (port.) (12 Oct. 2002)
Postil, Leland M(ichael) 1945- [composer, producer, musician]
Human Jukebox *Source(s):* *Today Show* (NBC) (8 Oct. 2002)
Note(s): See also David Ball.
King of Television Themes, The *Source(s):* CM21 p. vi
Post, Mike [or Michael] *Source(s):* CCE62; CCE73; CLTV; CM21
Poswiansky, Benno 1890- [composer, writer on music]
Bardi, Benno *Source(s):* BUL1; BUL2; GOTH; WORB
Pot(ts), Victor Léon 1869-1913 [composer, pianist, variety artist]
Fragson, (Harry) [or (Henry)] *Source(s):* CASS; CCE37 R57761; GAMM; LCAR
Frogson *Source(s):* LCAR; WHIT
Music Hall Shakespeare, The *Source(s):* http://www.ibiblio.org/folkindex/m14.htm (4 Feb. 2005)
Potts, Harry (Vince Philip) *Source(s):* GANA; ROOM
Pothumus, Ann 1929-1974 [composer]
Lee, Roy Asher *Source(s):* SUPN
Potter, A(nnie) S. [songwriter]
Bootsy *Source(s):* CCE27 E664008; PMUS
Note(s): Also used by William Collins; see LCAR.
Potter, Anice 1873-1964 [pianist, composer]
Note(s): Portraits: APSA; ETUP 57:2 (Feb. 1939): 74
Stockton, Morris *Source(s):* BUL3; COHN; HIXN; LCAR
Terhune, Anice *Source(s):* COHN; HIXN
Note(s): Married name: Terhune, Mrs. Albert.
Poueigh, Jean (Marie Octave Géraud) 1876-1958 [critic, composer]
Note(s): Portrait: ETUP 55:3 (Mar. 1937): 144
Séré, Octave *Source(s):* BAKR; BUL3; GROL; MACM; NGDM
Pound, Ezra ((Weston) Loomis) 1885-1972 [poet, composer, music critic]
Atheling, William *Source(s):* GROL; LCAR; NGAM; NGDO
Dias, B. H. *Source(s):* GDRM
Poet of Titchfield Street, The *Source(s):* LCAR
Venison, Alfred *Source(s):* http://www.galegroup.com/free_resources/poets/bio/pound_e.html
Poupard, Henri-Pierre 1901-1989 [composer]
Note(s): In BAKT orig. given name: Jean Pierre.
Sauguet, Henri *Source(s):* BAKO; BAKR; BUL1; GOTH; NGDM; PIPE; RIES
Pourtalès, Guido James de 1881-1941 [writer on music]
Pourtalès, Guy de *Source(s):* BAKE
Powell, Altivia Edwards 1924- [singer, columnist]
Left Bank Mother Confessor, The *Source(s):* PSND
Powell, Buttercup *Source(s):* PSND
Powell, Christopher Bolland 1937- [composer]
Powell, Kit *Source(s):* WIEC

Powell, Clive 1943- [singer, pianist, composer]
Fame, Georgie *Source(s):* CASS; EPMU; GAMM; LCAR
Powell, David 1934- [composer, author, singer]
David, David *Source(s):* ASCP
David, Will *Source(s):* ASCP
Powell, Earl 1924-1966 [pianist, composer]
Powell, Bud *Source(s):* KINK; LCAR; PEN2
Powell, Everard Stephen, Sr. 1907-1976 [jazz clarinetist; composer]
Karweem, Musheed *Source(s):* TCAN
Powell, Rudy *Source(s):* TCAN
Powell, George (Henry) 1880-1951 [lyricist]
Asaf, George *Source(s):* FULD p. 419; KILG; PDMU
Powell, Jack 1941- [composer, author, singer]
Hawkins, Jason *Source(s):* ASCP
Powell, John 1882-1963 [pianist, composer]
Brockwell, Richard *Source(s):* http://www.composersrecordings.com/cd/704.html (12 Oct. 2002)
Powers, Chester [or Chet] 1943-1994 [songwriter]
Farrow, Jesse Oris *Source(s):* AMUS
Valenti, Dino *Source(s):* SONG; http://www.power-pro.com/DinoValentiBio.html (12 Oct. 2002)
Pozar, Robert F. 1941- [composer]
Pozar, Cleve F. *Source(s):* BUL3; LCAR
Pozo (y Gonzales), Luciano 1915-1948 [drummer, singer, composer]
Chano *Source(s):* CCE42 #5541 E101417
Pozo, Chano *Source(s):* PEN2; LCAR
Prather, Ida 1889 (or 96)-1967 [singer, songwriter]
Note(s): In JASZ & SUTT see under: Cox, Ida.
Bradley, Velma *Source(s):* HARS; JASZ p. 271
Cox, Ida *Source(s):* EPMU; GRAT
Lewis, Kate *Source(s):* HARS; JASZ p. 271; SUTT
Powers, Julia *Source(s):* HARS; JASZ p. 271; SUTT
Powers, Julius *Source(s):* HARS; SUTT
Sepia Mae West, The *Source(s):* HARS
Smith, Jane *Source(s):* HARS; JASZ p. 271; SUTT
Uncrowned Queen of the Blues, The *Source(s):* HARS
Pratoneri, Gaspero fl. 1566-c.1595 [composer]
Spirito (da Reggio) *Source(s):* NGDM; WORB
Pratt, Charles E. 1841-1902 [composer, arranger]
Note(s): Do not confuse with Charles Edward Pratt (1845-1898), author on bicycles (STUW).
Fulmer, H. J. *Source(s):* HAMM; KILG; MARC p. 47; SPTH p.224; STUW
Wood, J. T. *Source(s):* HAMM; KILG; SPTH p. 224
Wood-Fulmer *Source(s):* MARC p. 47; SPTH p.224
Pratt, Charles Trowbridge 1892-1978 [composer]
Haubiel, Charles Trowbridge *Source(s):* BAKO; BAKR; LCAR; NGDO
Pratt, Paul (Charles) 1890-1948 [composer, pianist, conductor]
Parnell, Paul *Source(s):* JASN (port.); NGAM
Predamosche, Verdacchio [pseud.] [writer]
Note(s): Orignial name unknown.
Satirico, Il *Source(s):* SONN
Pregarty, John M. 1873-1931 [actor, composer]
Lloyd, Evans *Source(s):* PSND
Preisner, Zbigniew 1955- [composer]
Van den Budenmayer *Source(s):* GROL
Preissler, Joseph 1906-197? [composer]
Boldi, Giuseppe *Source(s):* GREN; http://www.accordions.com/preissler/homepage.htm (6 Nov. 2002)
Preissová, Gabriela (née Sekerová) 1862-1946 [author]
Klos, Richard *Source(s):* PIPE
Preiss, Gabriele *Source(s):* LCAR
Turková, Marie *Source(s):* PIPE
Prendergast, John Barry 1933- [composer, bandleader]
Angelo, Michael *Source(s):* LCAR
Barry, John *Source(s):* BBDP; GAMM; HARD; HARR
Prendiville, Henri Jean 1848-1910 [composer]
DeVille, Paul *Source(s):* REHG; SUPN
Note(s): Also used by M(ayhew) L(ester) Lake.
Hatton, Gus *Source(s):* REHG
Henri, Jean *Source(s):* REHG
Henry, Carl *Source(s):* REHG
Lange, Paul *Source(s):* REHG; SUPN
Prendiville, Harry *Source(s):* http://wurlitzer-rolls.com/index1.html (30 Dec. 2004)
Prentice, Charles W(hitecross) 1898-1967 [composer, conductor]
Mallory, Charles *Source(s):* CCE39 #38557 Efor61140
Prentice, Jock *Source(s):* CPOL RE-99-909; PIPE; PSND
Prerauer, Curt [author]
Prerauer, CM *Source(s):* BEBD
Note(s): Jt. pseud.: with wife, Maria Prerauer.
Prerauer, Maria (née Wolkowsky) [music critic, singer]
Marietta *Source(s):* BEBD
Prerauer, CM *Source(s):* BEBD
Note(s): Jt. pseud. with husband, Curt Prerauer.
Prescott, Norman [or Norm] 1927-2005 [composer, author, producer]
Michael(s), Jeff *Source(s):* ASCP; CCE76; CLTP ("Tarzan (Cartoon Series)")
Presley, Elvis A(a)ron 1935-1977 [singer, guitarist, songwriter]
Alan *Source(s):* WORT; Pierce, Patricia Jobe. *The Ultimate Elvis*. New York: Simon & Schuster, 1994, 412.

Note(s): Code name at Graceland.
Atomic-Powered Singer, The *Source(s):* Coffey, Frank. *The Complete Idiot's Guide to Elvis*. New York: Alpha Books, 1997, 263; Pierce (see above)
Big El *Source(s):* Pierce (see above)
Bunting *Source(s):* Pierce (see above)
Burroughs, John *Source(s):* WORT
Note(s): Incorrect spelling of code name: Jon Burrows. In WORT listed under "Jon."
Burrows, (Dr. [or Colonel]) Jon, (Jr.) *Source(s):* WORT; Coffey (see above); Pierce (see above)
Note(s): FBI code name. In WORT listed under "Jon."
Buttons *Source(s):* Pierce (see above)
Carpenter, Dr. [or Colonel] John *Source(s):* WORT
Note(s): Code name. Do not confuse with John Carpenter (1948-), film director.
Cat, The *Source(s):* Pierce (see above).
Chief, The *Source(s):* Pierce (see above)
Note(s): See also Eddy Harrington.
Country Cat, The *Source(s):* PSND; Pierce (see above)
Crazy Cat *Source(s):* Pierce (see above)
E. P. *Source(s):* Pierce (see above)
Elvis the Pelvis *Source(s):* CM01; PSND; Coffey (see above); Pierce (see above)
Elvisology *Source(s):* Coffey (see above)
Note(s): Term for historical and statistical information about life & career of Presley.
Father of Rock 'n' Roll *Source(s):* CM01; PSND
Note(s): See also Charles Edward Anderson Berry, Arthur Crudup, William [or Bill] (John Clifton) Haley, (Jr.), Charles Hardin Holley & Johnnie Johnson.
Fire Eyes *Source(s):* Pierce (see above)
Heartbreak Kid, The *Source(s):* PSND
Hillbilly Bopper *Source(s):* Pierce (see above)
Hillbilly Cat, (The) *Source(s):* PSND; SHAD; WORT; Coffey (see above); Pierce (see above)
Hillbilly Frank Sinatra *Source(s):* Pierce (see above)
Hillbilly on a Pedestal *Source(s):* PSND
Jones, John *Source(s):* WORT (see undercode name: John Jones)
Note(s): Also used by Peter C(hristian) Lutkin.
Kid with the Sideburns, The *Source(s):* Coffey (see above)
King, The *Source(s):* CM01; PSND; WORT; Coffey (see above); Pierce (see above)
Note(s): See also Bennett L(ester) Carter.
King of Country, The *Source(s):* Pierce (see above)
King of Hearts, The *Source(s):* Pierce (see above)
Note(s): See also Cleve(land) Francis, (Jr.).
King of Love, The *Source(s):* Pierce (see above)
King of Pop Rock, The *Source(s):* Pierce (see above)
King of Rock 'n' Roll, The *Source(s):* PSND; Coffey (see above); Pierce (see above)
King of Swoon, The *Source(s):* Pierce (see above)
King of Western Bop, The *Source(s):* Coffey (see above); Pierce (see above)
King of Western Pop *Source(s):* SHAD
Memphis Flash, The *Source(s):* Coffey (see above); Pierce (see above)
Memphis Mesmerizer, The *Source(s):* PSND
Mr. Dynamite *Source(s):* WORT p. 27 (see under: Brown, James); Pierce (see above)
Mr. Obscene *Source(s):* Pierce (see above)
Mr. Rhythm *Source(s):* Pierce (see above)
Note(s): See also (Zeffrey) Andre Williams.
Mr. Safety *Source(s):* Pierce (see above)
Mr. Wiggle and Shake *Source(s):* Pierce (see above)
Operation Elvis *Source(s):* Coffey (see above)
Note(s): Name of U.S. Army's measures to protect Presley.
Pelvie *Source(s):* Pierce (see above)
Pelvis, The *Source(s):* PSND
Pelvis Elvis *Source(s):* Pierce (see above)
Poor Man's Liberace *Source(s):* Pierce (see above)
Pretzel, Elvis *Source(s):* Pierce (see above)
Reclusive Howard Hughes of Pop Music, The *Source(s):* MILL
Sir Swivel Hips *Source(s):* Pierce (see above)
Sivle Yelserp *Source(s):* WORT
Note(s): Code for Presley.
Swivel Hips *Source(s):* PSND
Tiger *Source(s):* Coffey p. 218 (see above); Pierce (see above)
Tiger Man *Source(s):* Coffey p. 218 (see above); Pierce (see above)
Whirling Dervish of Sex *Source(s):* Pierce (see above)
Wiggle Hips *Source(s):* Pierce (see above)

Presser, Theodore 1848-1925 [music publisher, composer]
Note(s): Portraits: ETUP 51:10 (Oct. 1933): 641; MUSA 43:3 (7 Nov. 1925): 31
Landmann, B. *Source(s):* TPRF
LeHache, W. *Source(s):* CCE34 R28886; TPRF

Presser, William (Henry) 1916-2004 [composer]
Brook, John *Source(s):* CCE60 E146983
Fortino, Mario *Source(s):* CCE60 E146984; OCLC 23275209
Hill, Henry *Source(s):* CCE61
Humphrey, Ralph *Source(s):* CCE60 E146985
Kulaak, Tom *Source(s):* CCE61 E154018
Ward, Paul *Source(s):* CCE61 E154020; OCLC 22945679

Preston, A. [composer]
Lara, Adelina de *Source(s):* CPMU (publication date 1892)

Preston, John F. [writer]
Goldberg, Max *Source(s):* GANA p. 965 & 991

Prestopnik, Irving Henry 1912-1949 [clarinetist, saxophonist, arranger]

Faz *Source(s):* GROL
Fazola, Butch *Source(s):* GROL
Fazola, Irving *Source(s):* GROL
Price, Kenny 1931-1987 [singer, songwriter, instrumentalist]
Round Mound of Sound, (The) *Source(s):* MCCL
Note(s): See also Al(ois Maxwell) Hirt.
Price, Ray (Noble) 1926- [singer, guitarist, bandleader, songwriter]
Cherokee Cowboy, The *Source(s):* FLIN; MCCL; STAC
Price, Thomas Gwallter 1829-1869 [lyricist]
Cuhelyn *Source(s):* KILG
Price, Walter Travis 1917- [singer, keyboardist, songwriter]
Big Walter *Source(s):* HARS
Note(s): Also used by Walter Horton & George Smith.
Thunderbird from Coast to Coast, The *Source(s):* PSND
Prichystal, Joseph 1874-1858 [composer]
Pécsi, Josef [or Joseph] *Source(s):* CCE32 (Index); LCPC letter cited (5 Nov. 1932); REHG; SUPN
Pridgett, Gertrude (Malissa Nix) 1886-1939 [singer, songerwriter]
Note(s): Portraits: CCM23; JASZ
Black Nightingale, The *Source(s):* TCAN
Note(s): See also Annie Pauline Pindell.
Golden Necklace of the Blues, The *Source(s):* TCAN
Mama Can Can *Source(s):* TCAN
Mother of the Blues, The *Source(s):* AMUS; CLAB; EPMU
Paramount Wildcat, The *Source(s):* TCAN
Patterson, Lila *Source(s):* SUTT; TCAN
Rainey, Gertrude *Source(s):* AMUS; CASS; CLAG; EPMU; GRAT
Rainey, Ma *Source(s):* AMUS; CASS; CLAG; CM23; EPMU; GRAT
Smith, Anne *Source(s):* SUTT; TCAN
Songbird of the South *Source(s):* TCAN
Prilipp, Camille c.1810- [composer, author]
Schubert, C(amille) (A.) *Source(s):* CPMU; OCLC 48904044; TPRF
Prince, Harold (S(mith)) 1928- [producer]
Prince, Hal *Source(s):* GAN2 (port.); LCAR
Prine, John 1946- [singer, songwriter]
Latterday Bob Dylan, A *Source(s):* MILL
New Dylan, The *Source(s):* MUHF
Note(s): See also Bruce Springsteen.
Rumpled, Left-Over Everly Brother, A *Source(s):* MILL
Prinz, Heinrich Ludwig 1910- [composer]
Heinzelmann, Heinz *Source(s):* CCE58-65; CPOL RE-318-647; RIES
Ludwig, (Hein) *Source(s):* CCE63-65; CPOL RE-522-308; RIES
Pritchett, James A(rthur) 1909- [songwriter]
Smith, Arthur Q. *Source(s):* CCE54-55; CCE75; EPMU (see under: Eanes, Jim)
Note(s): Do not confuse with "Fiddlin'" Arthur Smith or Arthur "Guitar Boogie" Smith.
Pritkin, Ron(ald P.) 1920- [composer]
Terry, Ron *Source(s):* ASCC; CCE57
Priwin, Andreas (Ludwig) 1929- [pianist, conductor, composer]
Flickreiter, Art *Source(s):* JAMU
Previn, André (George) *Source(s):* BAKO; BUL3; CASS; CM15; LCAR
Procacci, Giuseppe 1888- [librettist]
Dupain George *Source(s):* WORB
Reni, Paolo *Source(s):* WORB
Prochazka, Ladislav, Freiherr von 1872-1936 [composer]
Prokop, Ladislav *Source(s):* MACM
Procházka, Rudolf, Freiherr von 1864-1936 [jurist, writer on music, composer]
Elms, Leon *Source(s):* KOMU; OMUO
Procter, Adelaide Ann(e) 1825-1864 [poet, hymnist]
Berwick, Mary *Source(s):* CART; CLAC; CYBH; WORB
Procter, Bryan Waller 1787-1874 [poet, songwriter]
Bethel, J. *Source(s):* CART
Cornwall, Barry *Source(s):* CART; GOTT; KILG; LCAR; MACM; ROOM
E. E. *Source(s):* CART
J. B. *Source(s):* CART
Jessamine, James *Source(s):* CART
S *Source(s):* CART
Proffitt, Josephine (née Moore) 1914-1967 [songwriter]
Dee, Sylvia *Source(s):* ASCC; CCE68; GRAT; LCAR; WORT
DeSylva, Joe *Source(s):* CCE42 #1052 E100315
Faison, Josephine *Source(s):* WORT
Prokofiev, Serge 1891-1953 [composer]
Fortissimist *Source(s):* SLON
Tchaikovsky of the 20th Century *Source(s):* http://www.finarticles.com/cf_dls/Pl/search.jhtml?isp (11 Apr. 2005)
White Negro *Source(s):* Duke, Vernon, *Passport to Paris.* Boston: Little, Brown & Co., 1955, p. 24.
Proton de la Chapelle, Robert 1894- [composer]
Fragny, Robert de *Source(s):* BUL2; WORB
Pruvost, François [or Francis] 1885- [composer]
Pearly, Fred *Source(s):* CCE48; CCE51 R77448 ("Les Ananas")
Pryor, Arthur Willard 1870-1942 [trombonist, bandleader, composer]

Note(s): Portrait: ETUP 55:4 (Apr. 1937): 216
Paganini of the Trombone *Source(s):* http://www.fromefestival.co.uk/reviews2.html (11 Feb. 2004)
Willard, Milton *Source(s):* Frizane, Daniel E. *Arthur Pryor (1870-1942); American Trombonist, Bandmaster, Composer.* D.M.A. thesis. University of Kansas, 1984, 148 & 154.
Pryor, James Edward 1921- [singer, instrumentalist, songwriter]
Pryor, Bubba *Source(s):* HARS
Pryor, Snooky *Source(s):* HARS
Psalmon, Frederick ?-1928 [composer]
Lambert, E. Frank *Source(s):* KILG
Ptacek, Rainer 1954-1997 [singer, guitarist, songwriter]
Rainer *Source(s):* PEN2
Puccini, Giacomo 1858-1924 [composer]
Tear Jerker Composer *Source(s):* DESO-9
Puco, Philip V. [or Milo] 1926-2004
Note(s): Social Security Death Index: middle initial V.
Milo, Phil *Source(s):* ASCP; CCE72-73
Pudraska, Darwin David 1928-2003 [singer, songwriter, DJ]
Dudley, Dave *Source(s):* CCE52; WASH
Puente, Ernesto Antonio, (Jr.) 1920 (or 23)-2000 [bandleader, multi-instrumentalist, composer]
Note(s): Portrait: OB00
King of Latin Jazz, The *Source(s):* http://www.jazzhall.org/jazz.cgi?$MEMORIAM (12 Oct. 2002)
King of the Mambo *Source(s):* SHAD
Note(s): See also Domasco [or Damasco] Perez Prado.
King of the 1950s Mambo Craze *Source(s):* CM14
Mambo King, The *Source(s):* EPMU
Note(s): See also Domasco [of Damasco] Perez Prado.
Puente, Ernestito *Source(s):* PEN2
Puente, Tito *Source(s):* CM14; EPMU; GAMM; LCAR; OB00; PEN2; WORL
Rey (del timbal), El *Source(s):* HWOM; PEN2
Puerner, Charles 1849-1905 [composer]
America's Greatest Composer *Source(s):* METR 11:5 (May 1895) (port. on cover)
Note(s): See also Leonard [i.e., Louis] Bernstein, George Gershwin [i.e., Jacob Gershvin] & Charles Edward Ives.
Armand, Charles *Source(s):* METR 11:5 (May 1895): 5; REHG; SUPN
Puerto, Diego del fl. early 16th cent. [music theorist]
Didacus a Portu *Source(s):* NGDM
Pugh, Virginia Wynette 1942-1998 [singer, songwriter, guitarist]
Edith Piaf of Country America, The *Source(s):* STAC
First Lady of Country Music *Source(s):* CASS; CM24; FLIN; MCCL; OB98
Note(s): See also Loretta Webb.
Heroine of Heartbreak *Source(s):* CM02; FLIN
Queen of Country Music *Source(s):* CASS; MCCL
Note(s): See also Muriel (Ellen) Deason & Loretta Webb.
Wynette, Tammy *Source(s):* CM02; CM24; FLIN; LCAR; MCCL; OB98; STAC
Pugliese, Carlos Anibal 1944- [composer, author, singer]
Tonto, Charlie *Source(s):* ASCP
Pugno, (Stéphane) Raoul 1852-1914 [composer, pianist, organist]
Note(s): Portraits: ETUP 55:4 (Apr. 1937): 216; MUWO (Jan. 1903): 9
Richard, Franz *Source(s):* GAN1; GAN2; MELL
Richard, Max *Source(s):* GAN1; GAN2; MELL
Pulejo, Giuseppe 1941- [composer]
Bepy *Source(s):* KOMS
Pulitzer, Walter 1878-1926 [journalist, composer, author]
Pulitzer, Joseph *Source(s):* IBIM; WORB
Punturero, Armando Francisco 1917-1983 [bandoneonist, composer, director]
Pontier, Armando *Source(s):* CCE54 Efor25135; TODO
Purcell, E. B. [songwriter]
Purcell, Buzz *Source(s):* STC2
Purcell, Henry 1658-1695 [composer]
Note(s): Portrait: EWCY
England's Greatest Composer *Source(s):* http://www.henningk.locke.com/seiten/e/elinks.html (7 Oct. 2002)
Note(s): See also (Sir) Edward Elgar & (Sir) Arthur S(eymour) Sullivan.
Father of Anglican Church Music, The *Source(s):* PSND
Father of English Music *Source(s):* EWCY
Note(s): See also Thomas Tallis.
Father of English Opera *Source(s):* http://www.fineartprimer.net/opera_main_page.htm (21 Oct. 2002)
Note(s): See also John Barnett.
Scotland, John *Source(s):* OCLC 43201004 ("Glee a 3 voci" ("Lightly Tread 'Tis Hallowed Ground")
Note(s): Pseud. sometimes attributed to Henry Purcell; however, F. B. Zimmerman, in his *Henry Purcell; An Annotated Catalogue of His Music,* ascribes the work to Michael Wise. In CPMU the same work by "John Scotland" is listed under George Berg.
Purdom, John Mace 1913-1980 [singer, songwriter, guitarist]
Masters, Johnnie *Source(s):* AMUS; MCCL
Pusch, Klaus-Werner 1949- [composer]
Paddy *Source(s):* PFSA

Putman, Claude, Jr. 1930- [singer, songwriter]
Putman, Curly *Source(s):* CCE68; ENCM; EPMU; MCCL; NASF; PMUS
Putnam, Belinda [composer]
Clark, Valerie [or Valarie] *Source(s):* CLTP ("Lunch with Soupy Sales")
Pütz, Eduard [or Eddy] 1911-2002 [composer]
Mertens, E. *Source(s):* KOMP; PFSA
Pütz, Johannes 1926-1971 [conductor, composer]
Stockhold, Hans *Source(s):* CCE67; RIES
Puyol, Léon Pierre [or Pierre-Louis] Édouard 1865 (or 67)-1932 [author, librettist, lyricist]
Flers, P(ierre)-L(ouis) *Source(s):* GAN1; GAN2; GOTH
Pye, Kellow John 1812-1901 [pianist, composer]
K. J. P. *Source(s):* GOTE ("What Does Little birdie Say?")
Note(s): Possible intials of Pye.
Pyekoon, Margaret 1898-1992 [actress, lyricist]
Picon, Molly *Source(s):* BBDP; LCAR

– Q –

Quaciari, Gene L(ouis) 1950- [composer, author, producer]
Louis, Gene *Source(s):* ASCP
Quas *Source(s):* CCE67
Quaites, Terrance 1976- [singer, composer, rapper]
Squeeze *Source(s):* IMDB
TQ *Source(s):* IMDB
Quantz, Johann Joachim 1697-1773 [composer, flautist, writer on music, flute maker]
Neologos *Source(s):* GROL
Note(s): Possible pseud.
Quantz, Willibald 1905-1980 [composer]
Costino, M(arcel) *Source(s):* CCE55-58; CCE61-62; PFSA; RIES
Hansen, Rolf *Source(s):* CCE52; CCE54; PFSA; RIES
Quarles, Charles ?-c.1727 [organist, composer]
Mr. Charles Late Organist at York *Source(s):* NGDM
Note(s): Possibly Charles Quarles.
Quatrocchio, Susan Kay 1950- [singer, songwriter, guitarist, actress]
Note(s): Given names verified: LCAR
Quatro, Suzi *Source(s):* NOMG
Quelle, Ernst-August 1931- [composer, pianist]
Arno, Ernst *Source(s):* KOMP; KOMS; PFSA; RIES
Sono, Enrico *Source(s):* KOMP; KOMS; PFSA
Stanway, Bob *Source(s):* KOMP; KOMS; PFSA
Queyroul, Henri (Antoine Alexis Siméon) 1857-1921 [lyricist, librettist]
Kéroul, Henri (Antoine Alexis Siméon) *Source(s):* GAN1; GAN2; WORB
Quian (Manguito), Romón [composer, bandleader, producer]
Monguito, 'El Unico' *Source(s):* MUWB; PEN2
Unico, El *Source(s):* PEN2
Quidant, Joseph 1815-1893 [pianist, composer]
Quidant, Alfred *Source(s):* MACM
Quigley, Edwin Olin, Jr. 1886-1955 [music critic]
Downes, (Edwin) Olin *Source(s):* GRAN (port.)
Exhortationist of the *New York Times* *Source(s):* GRAN
Sibelius's Apostle *Source(s):* RILM 94-07264-bm
Quigley, Michael [composer]
Doric, Caesar *Source(s):* http://www.mjq.net/music/music.htm (7 Oct. 2002)
Quivalos, Miklos *Source(s):* http://www.mjq.net/music/music.htm
Quinn, James J(oseph?), (Jr.) 1936- [composer]
Quinn, J. Mark *Source(s):* CCE63; CCE66; CCE68; GOTH
Quintanilla (Pérez), A(be) B. [songwriter, producer]
Quintanilla, Phat Kat *Source(s):* HWOM
Quirk, Henry fl. c.1880 [songwriter]
O'Cuirc, Henry *Source(s):* IBIM; WORB

– R –

Raab, Harry 1914-1991 [pianist, singer, songwriter]
Gibson, Harry *Source(s):* EPMU; LCAR; ROOM
Harry the Hipster *Source(s):* CCE57
Hipster, The *Source(s):* EPMU; ROOM
Rabbenius, Raphael [writer on music]
Carsellini, Fabio *Source(s):* SEND (see entry 495)
Rabe, Gerhard 1944- [composer]
Zybal, Roman *Source(s):* KOMP; KOMS
Rabinovitz, Menashe 1899-1968 [musicologist, teacher, composer]
Ravina, Menashe *Source(s):* BUL3; NULM
Rabinowitz, Irving [composer]
Binny *Source(s):* IMDB
Robbin, Irving *Source(s):* CLTP ("ABC Wide World of Sports")
Rabinowitz, Solomon 1859-1916 [lyricist, poet, humorist]
Aleichem, Sholom *Source(s):* FAFO; HESK; LCAR; WORB
"Mark Twain" of Yiddish Music *Source(s):* http://www.radiohazak.com/Yiddish.html (7 Oct. 2002)
Scholem Aleichem *Source(s):* LCAR; PIPE
Racheck, Andrew (J.) 1929- [songwriter]
Rehak, Bud *Source(s):* CCE61-62; PMUS

Rachele, Luigi [composer]
Elechar, Luigi *Source(s):* MELL; STGR
Jambo *Source(s):* STGR ("La figlia di Jorio" (1904))
Rachell, James 1910-1997 [guitarist, singer, songwriter]
Blues Mandolin Man *Source(s):* Congress, Richard. *Blues Mandolin Man; The Life and Music of Yank Rachell.* Jackson: University of Mississippi, 2001.
Poor Jim *Source(s):* PSND
Rachell, Yank *Source(s):* AMUS; EPMU; HARS; LCAR; OB97; PEN2
Rachmaninoff, Sergei 1873-1943 [composer]
Mr. C# Minor *Source(s):* http://www.musicweb.uk.net/classrev/2002/Jan02/Rachmaninov-Marsher.htm (14 Oct. 2003)
Rackstraw, W(illiam) S(myth) [or Smith] 1823-1895 [pianist, composer, writer on music]
Rockstro, William S(myth) [or Smith] *Source(s):* CPMU; MACM; LCAR; NGDM; PSND
Raddick, Henry [book reviewer, composer; literary hoaxer]
Note(s): Raddick may be a pseud.; see: http://www.museumofhoaxes.com/hoax,weblog/comments/509 (30 Jan. 2006)
Lloyd-Webber, Andrew *Source(s):* http://www.theregister.co.uk/2002/07/03/lloyd_webber_web_hoaxer_unmasked (28 Feb. 2005)
Radecki, Sigismund (Arnold Ottokar) von 1891-1970 [author, singer]
Homunculus *Source(s):* LCAR; PIPE
Räder, Gustav (Adolf) 1810 (or 11)-1868 [librettist]
Emden *Source(s):* PIPE: STGR
Radocchia, Emil(io Joseph) 1932- [composer, conductor, percussionist]
Richards, Emil *Source(s):* ASCP; CCE62
Radomski, James 1932 (or 39)- [composer, lyricist, librettist, actor]
Rado, James *Source(s):* ASCP; CCE58; CCE67-68; LCAR
Radomski, Mikolaj fl. early 15th cent. [composer]
Nicolaus de Radom *Source(s):* GROL; LCAR
Raff, (Joseph) Joachim 1822-1882 [composer]
Börner, Arnold *Source(s):* STRINGS (May-June, 2001): 92; http://www.raff.org/author.htm (18 May 2005)
Raffles, Thomas 1788-1863 [minister, author, hymnist]
T. R. *Source(s):* JULN
Ragsdale, (Harold) Ray 1939- [singer, songwriter, instrumentalist]
Stevens, (Harold) Ray *Source(s):* CM07; CCE65; EPMU; FLIN; HARR; LCAR; MCCL
Rahim, Emmanuel (Khaliq) 1934- [composer, arranger]
Amalbert, (Emmanuel) Juan (Khaliq) *Source(s):* ASCP; CCE67
Raiani, Al(bert George) 1917-1962 [composer, author, teacher]
Rainy, Al(bert) *Source(s):* ASCP; CCE53-55; CCE60
Raich, Heribert 1939- [composer]
Asten, J(org) *Source(s):* REHG; SUPN
Auer, K(arl) *Source(s):* REHG; SUPN
Note(s): Also used by Karl Frotzler.
Berg, Thomas *Source(s):* REHG; SUPN
Ezl, M(anfred) *Source(s):* REHG; SUPN
Raida, Karl Alexander 1852-1923 [composer, conductor]
Adair, Charles *Source(s):* PIPE
Bell, Jonny *Source(s):* PIPE
Raimondi, Pietro [ficticious composer]
Source(s): GROL
Raines, Frank 1901-1973 [producer]
Littler, Prince *Source(s):* GAN2 (see under: Littler, Emile)
Raines, (Sir) Norman 1903-1985 [producer]
Littler, Emile *Source(s):* GAN2
Rajonsky [or Rajonski], Milton Michael 1924-1994 [composer, arranger, trumpeter]
Brown, Boots *Source(s):* CPOL Vau-105-822; JAMU
Elder Statesman, The *Source(s):* PSND
Jolly Roger *Source(s):* JAMU
Modern King of Swing, The *Source(s):* PSND
Prince, The *Source(s):* JAMU
Rogers, Milton M(ichael) *Source(s):* ASCP; KINK; PSND
Note(s): Do not confuse with Milt Rogers [i.e., Milton Adelstein]
Rogers, Shorty *Source(s):* BAKR; EPMU; GAMM; HARD; LCAR; NGDM; OB94; PEN2
Short, Roger *Source(s):* JAMU
Rakemann, Louis 1840-1895 [teacher, organist]
Walt *Source(s):* DAVE
Rakotondrasoa, Justin 1964- [valiha player, songwriter]
Valin, Justin *Source(s):* EPMU
Ralf-Kreymann, Richard 1891- [composer]
Daylight, Richard Ralf *Source(s):* KOBW
Ralph, J(ames)
Primcock, A. *Source(s):* GROL; NGDO; OPER 17:2 (Spring 2001): 188
Ralph, Katherine [or Kate] (née Roberts) 19th cent. [pianist, composer]
Morfida *Source(s):* COHN; HIXN
Ram, Samuel 1907 (or 08)-1991 [composer, producer, violinist]
Adams, Jeff *Source(s):* CCE68
Hicks, Clay *Source(s):* CCE77

Paul, Lynn *Source(s):* ASCP; STUW
Ram, Buck *Source(s):* ASCP; HARR; LCAR; STUW
Rand, Ande *Source(s):* ASCP; STUW
Rameau, Jean Philippe 1683-1764 [composer]
Newton of Harmony, The *Source(s):* PSND
Ramey, Patricia (Lee) 1957 (or 58)- [singer, songwriter, guitarist]
Loveless, Patty *Source(s):* ALMN; CM05; LCAR; MCCL; PEN2
Ramirez, Louis 1938-1993 [songwriter, arranger]
Genio de la Salsa, El *Source(s):* EPMU; PEN2
Ramirez, Roger (J.) 1913-1994 [pianist, organist, composer]
Ramirez, Ram *Source(s):* CCE70 R48570; EPMU; LCAR; NGDJ; OB94
Ramistella, John 1942- [singer, songwriter]
Rivers, Johnny *Source(s):* AMUS; EPMU; HARD; PSND
Ramsey, Leo Dupree, Jr. [rapper]
Kool Rock Jay *Source(s):* EPMU
Ramthor, Horst 1915-1993 [composer]
Tardieu, Marcel *Source(s):* CCE57; KOMP; KOMS; PFSA
Randall, James R(yder) 1839-1908 [poet, journalist, songwriter]
Baltimorean in Louisiana, A *Source(s):* CPMU; FULD p. 357
Klubs *Source(s):* HARW p. 56; HOGR; OCLC 30454553
Note(s): Possible pseud.
Randazzo, Alessandro Carmelo 1935?-2003 [songwriter]
Randazzo, Teddy *Source(s):* WASH
Randolph, Homer Louis, (III) 1926 (or 27)- [saxophonist, composer]
McMillan, E. R. *Source(s):* http://www.vigotone.com/vigotone/vigotone134notes.htm (28 Jan. 2004)
Note(s): Possible pseud.
Mr. Saxophone *Source(s):* EPMU
Randolph, Boots *Source(s):* AMUS; EPMU; LCAR; MCCL
Randolph, Randy *Source(s):* MCCL
Randolph, Jane Cary Harrison 1891-1953 [poet, teacher, writer]
Randolph, Cary (H.) *Source(s):* KROH p. 153; LCAR
Randolph, Patricia 1944- [singer, songwriter, pianist, guitarist]
Sledd, Patsy *Source(s):* MCCL
Randon (de Saint-Amand), Gabriel 1867-1933 [poet, composer]
Rictus, Jehan *Source(s):* LCAR; WHIT; WORB
Rands, William Brightly 1823-1882 [essayist, hymnist, writer for children]
Note(s): See LCAR for additional sobriquets.
Browne, Matthew *Source(s):* CART; LCAR; WORB
Brute of a Husband, A. *Source(s):* CART
Clarke, George H. *Source(s):* CART
Doudney, M. A. *Source(s):* CART
Fieldmouse, Timon *Source(s):* CART
H. H. *Source(s):* CART
Holbeach, Henry *Source(s):* CART; LCAR; WORB
Hunter, A *Source(s):* CART
Irreconcilable, An *Source(s):* CART
Political Dissenter, A *Source(s):* CART
Richardson, Henry S. *Source(s):* CART
Talker, T(homas) *Source(s):* CART; LCAR
Ranieri, Giovanni Simone c.1590-1649 [composer, singer]
Mi fiolo *Source(s):* NGDM
Rankin, Jeremiah Eames 1828-1904 [hymnist]
Jeremy, R. E. *Source(s):* CYBH
Rankin, R. S. 1933- [singer, guitarist, songwriter]
Little T-Bone *Source(s):* HARS
Note(s): Also used by Roy Gaines.
Walker, T-Bone, Jr. *Source(s):* HARS; LCAR
Rankin, Roger Hogan 1924- [singer, songwriter]
Rankin, Dusty *Source(s):* DAUM
Rankl, Karl 1898-1968 [composer]
Francis, Charles *Source(s):* MUWB
Ransford, Edwin 1805-1876 [violinist, composer, actor]
Aquila *Source(s):* BLIC; BROW; CPMU
Ranucci, Renato 1912-1991 [comedian, songwriter, singer, dancer, author]
Matibor *Source(s):* CCE63
Note(s): Possible pseud.?
Rascel, R(enato) *Source(s):* CCE51; CCE63; CPOL RE-129-001; LCAR; PMUS; PSND
Ranyard, Ellen (Henrietta) (née White) 1810 (or 11)-1879 [hymnist]
L. N. R. *Source(s):* JULN (Appendix); LCAR
Rappaport, (Erich) Moritz 1877-1943? [author]
Walther, Erich *Source(s):* PIPE; RAGM
Note(s): Jt. pseud.: Walther Brügmann.
Rashkow, Michael (Harris) [songwriter, singer]
Harris, Mikie *Source(s):* CCE68
Lendell, Michael [or Mike] *Source(s):* CCE66-67; PMUS
Rasley, John M. 1913-1998 [composer, author, conductor]
Davenport, Scott *Source(s):* CCE73
Davis, Kevin Clark *Source(s):* CCE63-65; CPOL RE-515-822
Johnston, Randolph *Source(s):* ASCC; CCE60; CCE64; CCE68
MacRoberts, Keith *Source(s):* CCE59; CCE68; CPOL RE-363-496
Martens, Richard Alan *Source(s):* CCE61; CCE65 E197735

McCall, Craig *Source(s):* CCE75-76
McCall, John *Source(s):* CCE78
Montgomery, Kent *Source(s):* CCE75-76
Rathgeber, George 1869-1946 [composer]
Werner, Max *Source(s):* KOBW
Ratti, Bartolomeo 1565-1634 [composer, singer, organist]
Moro, Il *Source(s):* NGDM; WORB
Note(s): See also Emilian Leuthard & Walter Moro [or Morrow] Bohn.
Rauch, Alfred 1909-1997 [poet]
Hasselbach, (Sepp) *Source(s):* CCE54-59; CPOL RE-321-268; RIES
Rauch, Fred *Source(s):* CCE55; CPOL RE-1-203
Rautenberg, Theo *Source(s):* RIES
Raupach, Christoph 1686-1744 [organist, composer, writer on music]
Veritophilus *Source(s):* NGDM; RIEM (see reference)
Raupach, Ernst Benjamin Salomo 1784-1848 (or 52) [dramatist, librettist]
Hirsemenzel, Lebrecht *Source(s):* NGDM; PIPE
Leutner, Emil *Source(s):* PIPE
Rausch, Frederick fl. 1732-1803 [hymnist]
F. R. *Source(s):* DICH
Ravel, Maurice (Joseph) 1875-1937 [composer]
Gallic Muse, The *Source(s):* PSND
Master of Music *Source(s):* PSND
Rara *Source(s):* PSND
Riquet, Gomex le *Source(s):* PSND
Swiss Watchmaker (of Music), The *Source(s):* http://www.wgms.com/composer-ravel.shtm
Ravenscroft, Thomas 1592?-1635? [editor, composer, theorist]
T. R. *Source(s):* CART; CPMU
Ravn, Hans Mikkelsen 1610-1663 [music theorist, theacher]
Corvinus, Johann(es) (Michaelii) *Source(s):* MACM; NGDM
Rawlings, Alfred William 1860-1917 (or 24) [composer]
Note(s): In LCAR only a death date (1917) is given; however, in DEA2 Rawlings' grandson reports the dates: 1860-1924.
Conyers, Leslie *Source(s):* CPMU; DEA2
Dressler, Max *Source(s):* CCE48 R37616 ("Razeler's"); CPMU; DEA2
Dumas, Gustave *Source(s):* CCE49 R47930 ("Fontainebleau"); CPMU; DEA2
Dwyer, Pete *Source(s):* DEA2
Fare, Florence *Source(s):* CCE37 R57503 ("Starlit Tide"); CCE62; CPMU; DEA2
Note(s): Also used by Theodore Moses Tobani.
Fortescue, Edith *Source(s):* CCE41 #44409, 236 R100163; CCE48 R35362; CPMU; DEA2
Note(s): In CCE41 listed as pseud. of Edwin St. Quentin [i.e., Alfred William Rawlings]
Gordon, Stanley *Source(s):* BLIC; CCE41 #44409, 372 R100162 ; CCE48 R35368; CPMU; DEA2
Note(s): In CCE41 listed as pseud. of Edwin St. Quentin [i.e., Alfred William Rawlings]
Henry, Hamilton *Source(s):* CPMU; DEA2
Hope, Marcus *Source(s):* DEA2
Jasper, Louis *Source(s):* DEA2
Krenkel, Gustaf *Source(s):* LCAR; MACM (cited in LCAR)
Note(s): Since Krenkel was not verified as a pseud. of A. W. Rawlings in a second source, it is listed as a separate entry, with several pseuds.
Lemoine, Felix *Source(s):* CCE41 #44409, 195 R1000165; CCE48 R37628; CPMU; DEA2
Note(s): In CCE41 listed as pseud. of Edwin St. Quentin [i.e., Alfred William Rawlings]
Melrose, Gladys *Source(s):* CCE48 R35377 ("Gates of Eternal Dawn"); DEA2
Morris, Guy *Source(s):* CPMU; DEA2
Mullen, Frederic *Source(s):* LCAR; MACM (cited in LCAR)
Note(s): Since Mullen was not verified as a pseud. of A. W. Rawlings in a second source, it is listed as a separate entry, with several pseuds.
Natale, Tito *Source(s):* DEA2
Peronne, Paul *Source(s):* DEA2
Note(s): Also used by Ernest Reeves.
Perrion, Paul *Source(s):* DEA2
Rawlings, Charles Arthur *Source(s):* LCAR; MACM
Source(s): C. A. Rawlings incorrectly listed as a pseud. of A. W. Rawlings in LCAR & MACM.
Schafer, Christian *Source(s):* CCE62
Saint [or St.] Quentin, Edward *Source(s):* BLIC; CCE37 R57504; CPMU; DEA2; GOTH
Note(s): "The Bells of Saint Mary's" (BLIC)
Saint [or St.] Quentin, Edwin *Source(s):* CCE41
Note(s): In CCE41 listed as pseud. of Edwin St. Quentin [i.e., Alfred William Rawlings]
St. Quentin, G. de *Source(s):* CPMU, DEA2
Stephano, Charles *Source(s):* CPMU; DEA2
Stephanoff, Ivan *Source(s):* CCE48 R35373 ("Bulgarian Patrol"); CPMU; DEA2
Tchakoff, Ivan *Source(s):* CCE62; CPMU; DEA2
Tchatchkoff, A de *Source(s):* DEA2
Templeman, Horace *Source(s):* CCE49 R47914 ("In Yonder Deep"); DEA2
Therese, Jules *Source(s):* CPMU; DEA2
Tomlinson, John William *Source(s):* DEA2; DEAR
Tree, Lionel *Source(s):* CCE48 R35375 ("Give Me Your Hearts"); CPMU; DEA2

White, Constance (V.) *Source(s):* CCE48 R35367 ("Dream Boat"); CPMU; DEA2
Wyman, Sydney (L.) *Source(s):* DEA2; DEAR
Zaffira, Leon *Source(s):* CCE50 R57878 ("Italian Suite")

Rawlings, Charles Arthur 1857-1919 [composer]
Note(s): Charles Arthur Rawlings is listed incorrectly as a pseud. of Arthur William Rawlings in LCAR & MACM.
Augarde, Hayd(o)n *Source(s):* CPMU; DEA2
Augarde, Jean *Source(s):* CCE44 #31175, 535 R128184; CPMU; DEA2
Bartelet, Jeanne *Source(s):* CCE43 #25483, 314 R118689; CPMU; DEA2; GOTT
Blanc, Paul *Source(s):* DEA2
Bonheur, Emile *Source(s):* DEA2
Bonheur, F. *Source(s):* DEA2
Bonheur, Georges *Source(s):* DEA2
Bonheur, Isidore *Source(s):* CPMU; DEA2
Bonheur, Otto *Source(s):* CPMU; DEA2
Bonheur, Theo(dore) *Source(s):* CPMU; DEA2; GOTH; GOTT; KILG
Note(s): Listed incorrectly as a pseud. of Alfred William Rawlings in LCAR & MACM.
Bonté, Emile *Source(s):* CCE44 #31175, 956 R129366; CPMU; DEA2; TPRF
Brandon, Faulkner *Source(s):* CCE38 R66797; CPMU; DEA2; TPRF
Brandon, Louis *Source(s):* DEA2; DEAR
Bronté, Emil *Source(s):* CCE42 #5201, 1049 R103905; CPMU; DEA2
Cambon, Jules *Source(s):* CCE45 #12811, 421 R136183
Carolon, Paul *Source(s):* DEA2
Clermont, Henri *Source(s):* CCE43 #9781, 23 R116402; DEA2
Cons, Auguste *Source(s):* CCE38 R66796; CPMU; DEA2
Courtenay, Clifford *Source(s):* CCE47 R22234 ("Boys of the Ocean Blue")
Delacassa, Eugene *Source(s):* DEA2; DEAR
Delaporte, Paul *Source(s):* CPMU; DEA2
Delcasse, Leo *Source(s):* DEA2; DEAR
Dore, Eileen *Source(s):* CPMU; DEA2
Douste, Jean *Source(s):* CCE41 #30320, 198 R97553; CPMU; DEA2
Dupré, Den(n)is *Source(s):* CCE40 #32380, 181 R83390; CCE40 #22693 , 540 R87506; DEA2
Note(s): Listed incorrectly as a pseud. of Alfred William Rawlings in LCAR & MACM.
DuTerrail, Leon *Source(s):* CPMU
Ellis, Seymour *Source(s):* CCE37 R57506; CPMU; DEA2
Faulkne *Source(s):* GOTT
Genèe, Paul *Source(s):* DEA2
Graham, Robert *Source(s):* CPMU; DEA2
Gresham, John *Source(s):* CCE44 #31175, 978 R129365; CPMU; DEA2
Heller, Maxime *Source(s):* CCE38 R66800; CCE38 R71102; DEA2; TPRF
Note(s): "Africana" & "Sunset on the Saint Lawrence" (both CCE38). In CCE37 R52013 ("Sunset on the St. Lawrence") Maxime Heller is listed as pseud. of Frederick Harris. (See also: Harris, Frederick).
James, Emerson *Source(s):* CCE37 R57505; CPMU; DEA2
Lamara, François *Source(s):* CPMU
Leigh, Harrington *Source(s):* CPMU; DEA2
Lemara, François *Source(s):* DEA2
Le Page, Carolan *Source(s):* DEA2
Loewe, Gilbert *Source(s):* CCE41 #44409, 128 R100687; CPMU; DEA2
Martino, Angelo *Source(s):* DEA2; DEAR
Menier, Alphonse *Source(s):* CPMU; DEA2
Nita *Source(s):* BLIC; CPMU; DEA2
Perrier, Paul *Source(s):* CCE38 R67501; CPMU; DEA2
Pontin, Maxime *Source(s):* CPMU; DEA2
Rawling, Elsie *Source(s):* DEA2
Rawlings, Abe *Source(s):* DEA2
Rawlings, Horatio E. *Source(s):* DEA2
Rawlings, Wellington *Source(s):* CCE41 #44409, 62 R100689; CPMU; DEA2
Reubins, Carl *Source(s):* DEA2
Rey, Vernon *Source(s):* CPMU
Ritz, Carl *Source(s):* CCE41 #30320, 164 R97552; CPMU; DEA2
Rubens, Carl *Source(s):* CPMU; DEA2
Sachs, Edward *Source(s):* CPMU; DEA2
Sachs, Emil(e) *Source(s):* CPMU; DEA2; TPRF
Sachs, Hans *Source(s):* DEA2
Seymour, Ralph *Source(s):* CPMU; DEA2
Straus, Herman *Source(s):* DEA2; DEAR
Telma, Maurice *Source(s):* CCE38 R66798; CPMU; DEA2; GOTH; LCPC letter cited (5 June 1936)
Temple, Gordon *Source(s):* CPMU; DEA2; GOTT
Terail, Leon du *Source(s):* DEA2
Terrier, Paul *Source(s):* DEA2; DEAR
Thome, Thomas *Source(s):* DEA2; DEAR
Vere, Claude de *Source(s):* CPMU; DEA2
Verne, H. *Source(s):* CPMU; DEA2
Verne, Oscar *Source(s):* CPMU; DEA2; ORBI; TPRF
Vincent, Beryl *Source(s):* CPMU; DEA2
West, Sydney [or Sidney] *Source(s):* CPMU; DEA2
Williams, Christine *Source(s):* CPMU; DEA2
Yorkston, James *Source(s):* CPMU
Note(s): Pseud. of Theodore Bonheur [i.e., Charles Arthur Rawlings]

Rawson, George 1807-1889 [solicitor, hymnist]
G. R. *Source(s):* CYBH; JULN
Leeds Layman, A *Source(s):* CYBH; PSNDn
Rawsthorne, Alan 1905-1971 [composer]
Pandora *Source(s):* GOTH
Ray, Anthony (L.) 1963 (or 64)- [rap musician, composer]
Mixalot, Sir *Source(s):* NOMG
Sir Mix-A-Lot *Source(s):* LCAR
Ray, Harmon 1914- [singer, songwriter]
Peetie's Buddy *Source(s):* LCAR
Peetie Wheatstraw's Buddy *Source(s):* HARS; LCAR
Ray, Herman *Source(s):* HARS; LCAR
Ray, Robert J(ames) 1919-2003 [composer, author, violinist]
Ray, Buddy *Source(s):* ASCC; CCE41 #35770 Eunp268111
Ray, (Lyman) Wade 1916-1998 (or 99) [singer, fiddler, guitarist, songwriter]
Youngest Violin Player in the World, The *Source(s):* AMUS; MCCL
Raymond, Harold (Newell) 1884-1957 [composer, author, publisher]
Newell, Roy *Source(s):* ASCP; CCE37 E59652; CCE63; CCE68
Ramondo, Paul *Source(s):* CCE64
Raymond, John [composer]
Churchill, Kenneth *Source(s):* CPOL RE-129-278
Note(s): Jt. pseud.: Walter (Charles) Ehret.
Raymond, Lupe Victoria Yoli 1939-1992 [singer, composer]
La Lupe *Source(s):* LCAR; PEN2
La Yi Yi Yi *Source(s):* LCAR; PEN2
Lupe, La *Source(s):* PEN2
Raymond, Rossiter Worthington 1840-1918 [hymnist]
Gray, Robertson *Source(s):* CYBH (port.)
Raymonde, Lucille Marie [singer, songwriter, guitarist]
Note(s): Married name: Savoie.
Starr, Lucille *Source(s):* AMUS; MCCL
Razafinkeriefo, Andreamenentania Paul 1895-1973 [singer, lyricist]
Note(s): Portrait: RASZ
Cook, J. L(awrence) *Source(s):* CCE75; CPOL RE-166-805
Cook, James *Source(s):* CCE24 E597418
Cook, James Ballou *Source(s):* CPOL RE-166-251
Cook, James Daniel *Source(s):* CCE77 R66464
Cook, James Joseph *Source(s):* CPOL RE-113-812
Cook, James V. *Source(s):* CPOL RE-567-586
Cook, Jean Lawrence *Source(s):* CPOL RE-277-997
Cook, Jim *Source(s):* CPOL RE-397-969
Cooke, James Francis *Source(s):* CCE75
Crooning Andy *Source(s):* PSND
LaDuke, Andrea *Source(s):* CCE73 R561421
Raz *Source(s):* HARR
Razaf, Andy [or Andrea] *Source(s):* EPMU; GAMM; HARR; PEN2; PSND; SOTH; VACH
Razafkevifo, Andrea P. *Source(s):* RAGM
Razz, A(ndrea) *Source(s):* CCE20 E470945
Smith, Dan *Source(s):* SUTT
Thompson, Johnny *Source(s):* http://newarkwww.rutgers.edu/ijs/bc/song2.htm (18 May 2005)
Razzi, Giovanni 1531-1611 [theologian, music editor, composer]
Razzi, Silvano *Source(s):* LCAR
Serafino *Source(s):* NGDM
Rea, Chris 1951- [singer, songwriter]
British Bruce Springsteen *Source(s):* CM12
Reader, (William Henry) Ralph 1903 (or 04)- 1982 [lyricist, producer, actor]
Note(s): Name verified: LCAR. Portrait: BBDP
Henry, William *Source(s):* GANB
Rover, A. Holborn *Source(s):* BBDP; CCE37 Efor51084-5; CCE63
Reader, Sadenia 1959- [singer, songwriter]
Reader, Eddi *Source(s):* PEN2
Reardon, Francis [or Frank] C(ornelius) 1925- [composer, author, singer]
Cross, Vernon *Source(s):* ASCP
Rebel, François (*le fils*) 1701-1775 [violinist, composer]
Petits violins, Le *Source(s):* GROL
Note(s): Jt. sobriquet: François Francoeur (*le cadet*).
Rebennack, Malcolm [or Mac] (John) 1940 (or 41)- [singer, songwriter]
Creaux, John *Source(s):* CCE67
Dr. John (The Night Tripper) *Source(s):* AMUS; DIMA; EPMU; HARR; LCAR
John, Dr. *Source(s):* LCAR
Night Tripper *Source(s):* AMUS
Rebhuhn, Paul c.1500-1546 [drammatist, musician]
P. R. *Source(s):* IBIM; WORB
Perdix, Paul *Source(s):* IBIM; WORB
Raphun, Paul *Source(s):* WORB
Rebling, Eberhard (Gerhard) 1911- [pianist, writer on music]
Gerhard, (Dr.) E. *Source(s):* LCAR; RIES
Noorden, (Dr.) P. van *Source(s):* RIES
Rebner, Wolfgang E(duard) [or E(dward)] 1910-1993 [composer, pianist]
Riesser, Klaus *Source(s):* PFSA
Rechtman, Mordechai 1926- [composer]
Shemer, Naomi *Source(s):* BUL3
Redbourn(e), William James 1857-1943 [dancer, choreographer]
Warde, Willie *Source(s):* GAN2

Redcliffe, Frederick J. [composer]
Carter, Stanley *Source(s):* CCE25 R32063; GREN; SPTH p. 293
Redd, Freddie 1928- [pianist, composer]
Ching, I *Source(s):* JAMU
Reddall, James William 1870-1964 [scenic artist, dancer, choregrapher]
Royce, Edward *Source(s):* GAN2
Reddell, Isaac Hadley [songwriter]
Caasi, Lledder Yeldah *Source(s):* CPMU
Note(s): Possible pseud.
Redding, David 1945- [guitarist, songwriter]
Redding, Noel *Source(s):* EPMU (see under: Fat Mattress)
Redding, Edward C(arolan) 1915 (or 17)-1984 [composer, lyricist]
Redding, Bud *Source(s):* ASCP; PSNN
Redding, Ottis 1941-1967 [singer, songwriter]
King of Soul Singers, The *Source(s):* PSND
Mister Pitiful *Source(s):* SHAD
Reddy, Helen 1941 (or 42)- [singer, songwriter, actress]
Queen of Housewife Rock *Source(s):* ALMN
Redwine, Wilbur (C.) 1926- [composer, author, pianist]
Redwine, Skip *Source(s):* ASCP; CPOL RE-728-947
Reed, Andrew 1787-1862 [clergyman, hymnist]
Note(s): Portrait: CYBH
Douglas *Source(s):* PSND
Rees, W. T. [composer, conductor]
Alaw Ddu *Source(s):* WILG
Rees, William 1902-1883 [preacher, poet, hymnist]
Hiraethog, Gwilym *Source(s):* CYBH
Reeve-Jones, Alan Edmond 1914- [author, lyricist]
Allen, Edmund *Source(s):* PSND
Lunchbasket, Roger *Source(s):* PSND
Reeves, D(avid) W(allis) 1838-1900 [composer, band director]
Note(s): Do not confuse with G. H. Reeves [i.e., Louis-Philippe Laurendeau]
Father of Band Music in America *Source(s):* http://www.mmbmusic.com/info/BrassPerc.pdf (7 Oct. 2002)
Note(s): See also Thomas Coates.
Father of Band Music in the U. S. A., The *Source(s):* SMIN
Reeves, Ernest [songwriter]
Note(s): Publication dates 1895-1933. (Author's note: Since no biographical information was found for Reeves, and since Alfred William Rawlings reportedly used "Paul Peronne," is it possible "Ernest Reeves" is a pseud. of Rawlings?)
Cameron, Allan R. *Source(s):* BLIC; CPMU
Dubois, René *Source(s):* CPMU
Marsden, Frank *Source(s):* CPMU
Peronne, Paul *Source(s):* CCE29 Efor6806; CPMU ("On Wings of Memory" (pub. 1926))
Note(s): Also used by Alfred William Rawlings.
Scott, Fabian *Source(s):* CPMU
Verré, Léon *Source(s):* CPMU
Wood, Gladys A. *Source(s):* CPMU
Reeves, Franklin Delano 1933 (or 34)- [singer, guitarist; songwriter]
Dean Martin of Country Music, (The) *Source(s):* MCCL; STAC
Reeves, Del *Source(s):* AMUS; EPMU; MCCL; PEN2; STAC
Reeves, Goebel (Leon) 1899-1959 [singer, songwriter]
George Riley, the Yodeling Rustler *Source(s):* AMUS; PSND
Riley, George, the Yodeling Rustler *Source(s):* MCCL
Texas Drifter, The *Source(s):* AMUS; MCCL; PSND
Reeves, James [or Jimmy] (Travis) 1923 (or 24)-1964 [singer, guitarist, songwriter]
Bimbo Boy *Source(s):* PSND
Gentleman Jim *Source(s):* FLIN
Reggio, Emilo mentioned 1928 [librettist]
Nelson, Will. *Source(s):* STGR
Reggio, Pietro Francesco 1632-1685 [composer, singer, lutenist]
Genovese, Il *Source(s):* RIES
Regis, Johannes c.1425-c.1496 [composer]
Leroy, Jehan *Source(s):* LCAR; NGDM
Regnault, Pierre c.1490-after 1561 [composer]
Sandrin, (P(ierre)) *Source(s):* CCE63; GROL; LCAR; NGDM; RIES
Régnier, Henri (François Joseph de) 1864-1936 [author]
Vignix, Hugues *Source(s):* PIPE
Reibold, Bruno [composer]
Gordon, Hugh *Source(s):* TPRF
Note(s): A. P. Schmidt "house name;" see NOTES: Gordon, Hugh.
Reich, Stephen [or Steve] (Michael) 1936- [composer]
America's Greatest Living Composer *Source(s):* http://www.yale.edu/opa/v29.n15/story20.html (26 Sept. 2003)
Father of "DJ Culture," The *Source(s):* http://www.users.bigpond.com/apertout/Reich.htm (18 May 2005)
Reichard(t), Johann Friedrich 1752-1814 [composer, political writer; writer on music]
Note(s): Portraits: FCTW v. 2 p. 581; *Allgemeine Musikzeitung* (21 Nov. 1902): 789
Frei, J. *Source(s):* GROL
Trahcier *Source(s):* CPMU; GOTH; RILM 96-03958-ae
Reichel, Karl Heinz 1912 (or 17)- [composer]
Martin, Karl CCE53; CCE72-73; PFSA; RIES

Reichenthal, Ralph 1901-1942 [composer, arranger, pianist]
Rainger, Ralph *Source(s):* GAMM; HARR; JASA; JASR; NGAM; SPTH p. 472
Reichman, Harold [or Harry] 1895-1972 [composer, pianist, singer, actor]
Richman, Harry, (Jr.) *Source(s):* EPMU; GAMM; KINK; LCAR; STUW
Reichner, (S(amuel)) Bickley 1905-1989 [composer, author, publisher]
Bickley *Source(s):* CCE45 #12358 E128610
Bix *Source(s):* CCE55 Eunp
Reichner, Bix *Source(s):* ASCP; LCAR; VACH; WORT
Reid, (General) Iohn [or John] 1721-1807 [composer]
I. R. *Source(s):* CPMU; WIEC
J. R. *Source(s):* CPMU; WIEC
Reid, Willis Wilfred 1910- [composer, author]
Makuakane *Source(s):* CCE72-73; CPOL PAu-420-690
Reid, Billy *Source(s):* ASCP; CCE62; CPOL PAu-203-404
Reid, Makaakane *Source(s):* CPOL PAu-651-440
Reid, Makuakane (Billy) *Source(s):* CPOL Pau-376-969;
Wallace, Raymond *Source(s):* CCE40 #14853 Efor62487
Note(s) Jt. pseud.: Billy [i.e., Willis Wilfred] Reid, Fred Hartley & Huntley Trevor.
Reilly, Jack 1932- [pianist, teacher, writer on music]
Petrahn, Sean *Source(s):* GROL
Reimann, Heinrich 1850-1906 [organist, writer on music, composer]
Reinhardt, Eric(h) *Source(s):* GDRM; GROL
Reindl, Max 1922- [poet, composer]
Gaston, Hannes *Source(s):* CCE56-57; PFSA; RIES
Reinecke, Carl Heinrich Carsten 1824-1910 [composer, teacher, pianist, conductor]
Note(s): Portraits: ETUP 55:6 (June 1937): 356; EWCY; MUWO (June 1903): 6
Carsten, (Carl) Heinrich *Source(s):* GROL; LCAR
Reinhard, Kurt 1914-1979 [ethnomusicologist, composer]
Beydemüller, Georg *Source(s):* GROL
Reinhardt, Helmut 1920- [composer]
Ben, Oliver *Source(s):* CCE59-60; CCE62; KOMP; PFSA
Hallesch, Günther *Source(s):* CCE63
Reinhardt, Jean Baptiste 1910-1953 [composer, guitarist, bandleader]
Reinhardt, Django *Source(s):* CCE54; CM07; EPMU; KINK; LCAR; PEN2; PFSA
Reipsch, Horst 1925- [composer]
Laiser, Martin *Source(s):* KOMP; KOMS; PFSA
Norstad, Olaf *Source(s):* KOMP; KOMS; PFSA
Sharkow, Bud *Source(s):* KOMP; KOMS; PFSA
Reiset, Gustave Armand Henri (Comte de) 1821-1905 [composer]
Jesper *Source(s):* IBIM; MELL; WORB
Tesier *Source(s):* IBIM; MELL; WORB
Reiset, Marie (Félicie Clémence) 1828-1907 [composer]
Blangy, Caroline *Source(s):* COHN, DWCO; GROL; HIXN; LCAR; PIPE
Grandval, Marie (Félice Clémence), Viacomtesse de *Source(s):* GROL; LCAR
Reiset, Maria Felicita *Source(s):* DWCO; GROL
Reiset de Tesier, Maria *Source(s):* GROL
Valgrand, Clémence *Source(s):* COHN; DWCO; GROL; HIXN; LCAR; MELL; PIPE
Reisinger, Oskar 1908-1985 [composer]
Oskar, Manfred *Source(s):* KOMS; RIES
Wenzel, Hesky *Source(s):* CCE53; KOMP; PFSA; RIES
Reiss, Isaac 1885-1943 [composer]
Nadir, (Isaac) Moishe *Source(s):* LCAR; SEND
Reith, Dieter 1938- [composer]
Dico, Rosh *Source(s):* KOMP; PFSA
Rider, Nicky *Source(s):* KOMP; PFSA
Rosh, Dico *Source(s):* PFSA
Reizenstein, Elmer Leopold 1892-1967 [author]
Rice, Elmer *Source(s):* MELL; PIPE; WORB
Reizenstein, Franz (Theodor(e)) 1911-1968 [composer, pianist]
Rayston, Frank *Source(s):* BUL3; CCE52
Rellstab, (Heinrich Friedrich) Ludwig 1799-1860 [music critic, poet, librettist]
Note(s): Portrait: ETUP 55:6 (June 1937): 356
L. R. *Source(s):* HEYT
Spreesprung der Kühne *Source(s):* APPL
Zuschauer, F(reimund) *Source(s):* GROL; NGDO; WORB
Remeš, B [author, librettist]
Kazničov, B. *Source(s):* GROL; MELL
Rémy d'Auxerre fl. 862-c.900 [writer on music]
Remigius Altisiodoresis *Source(s):* MACM; NGDM
Renard, (Pierre) Jules 1864-1910 [author]
Draner *Source(s):* PIPE; PSND; http://www.ulg.ac.be/wittert/fr/don/draner.html (6 Feb. 2004)
René, Natalia Petrovna 1907-1977 [writer on ballet]
Roslavelva, Natalia *Source(s):* ROOM
Reneau, George [songwriter, singer]
Blue Ridge Duo *Source(s):* SUTT
Note(s): Jt. pseud.: Gene Austin [i.e., Eugene Lucas]
Reneau, Bud *Source(s):* PMUS
Renner, Josef, (Jr.) 1868-1934 [composer]
Sephner, Otto *Source(s):* COMP

Renosto, Paolo 1935-1988 [composer]
Lesiman *Source(s):* http://www.scorebaby.com/soundlibrary.html (7 Oct. 2002)
Renz-Herzog, Wolf 1924- [composer]
Tichy *Source(s):* SUPN
Repilado (Muñoz), (Máximo) Francisco 1907-2003 [instrumentalist, songwriter]
Segundo, Company *Source(s):* HWOM; LCAR
Resinarius, Balthasar c.1485-1544 [composer]
Hartzer, Balthasar *Source(s):* IBIM; LCAR; NGDM
Resnick, Leon 1923- [composer, violinist]
Resnick, Lee *Source(s):* PSND
Respighi, Ottorino 1879-1936 [composer]
Strauss of Italy, The *Source(s):* DEAR
Rettenbacher, Johann Anton 1939-1989 [composer]
McCorn, John *Source(s):* KOMP; PFSA
Retter, Louis 1869- [pianist, conductor, composer, publisher]
Becker, Jean *Source(s):* KROH p. 103; LCAR
De Bar, Emile *Source(s):* KROH p. 106; LCAR
Keil, Th(eodore) *Source(s):* KROH p. 114; LCAR
Listeman, Arthur *Source(s):* KROH p. 117; LCAR
Nord, Lucy *Source(s):* KROH p. 120; LCAR
Sontag, Carl *Source(s):* KROH p. 128; LCAR
Réty, Charles 1826-1895 [music critic, theater director]
Darcours, Charles *Source(s):* MACM
Reubrecht, Albert 1920- [composer]
Baxter, Albert *Source(s):* CCE76
Baxter, Francis *Source(s):* CCE60-61; CCE64-65; GOTH
Vermeer, Roger *Source(s):* CCE58-59; CCE62; CCE64; CCE68
Reuss, Bernd 1961- [composer]
Royce *Source(s):* PFSA
Reuss, Theodor 1855-1923 (or 24) [journalist, author]
Merlin, Brother *Source(s):* PSND
Merlin Peregrinus *Source(s):* LCAR
Peregrinus *Source(s):* PIPE
Note(s): Also used by John Hupfauf.
Theodore, Charles *Source(s):* PSND
Reussner, Esaias 1636-1679 [composer]
E. R. *Source(s):* IBIM; WORB
Reuter, Florizel von 1890-1985 [violinist, composer]
Paganini, Nic(c)olò (Spirit) *Source(s):* DEAR p. 225
Reuter, Friedrich Otto 1863-1924 [hymnist]
Reuter, Fritz *Source(s):* CYBH
Reuther, Franz 1941- [composer]
Farian, Frank *Source(s):* KOMP; KOMS; PFSA
Rexroth-Berg, (Carl) Natanael 1879-1957 [composer]
Berg, Carl Natanael *Source(s):* NGDM
Berg, Natanael *Source(s):* NGDM
Rey, Cemal Resid 1904-1985 [conductor, pianist]
Cemal Resit *Source(s):* LCAR
Djemal Réchid *Source(s):* LCAR
Réchid, Djemal *Source(s):* MELL
Rey, Louis-Etienne-Ernest 1823-1909 [composer, critic]
Reyer, Ernest *Source(s):* BAKR; EWCY (port.); GROL; LCAR; MELL; PSND
Reynolds, Antony 1921- [pianist, writer on music, composer, conductor, broadcaster]
Hopkins, Antony *Source(s):* BAKR; BUL1; GOTH; ROOM
Reynolds, Malvina 1900-1978 [songwriter, political activist]
Singing Grandmother, The *Source(s):* PSNN
Reynolds, Wynford Herbert 1899-1958 [composer, conductor]
Raeburn, Hugh *Source(s):* CCE44 #13844 Efor69016; CCE71; MUWB
Reynoldson, (Mary) Caroline 1827-1882 [soprano, teacher, composer]
Richings, (Mary) Caroline *Source(s):* BAKR; NGDO
Reys, Jakub c.1555-c.1605 [lutenist, composer]
Note(s): See LCAR for variant name forms.
Jacques le Polonois *Source(s):* GROL; LCAR
Polak, Jakub *Source(s):* GROL; LCAR
Rhein, Eduard 1900-1993 [author]
Hellborn, Klaus *Source(s):* PIPE
Hellmer, Klaus *Source(s):* PIPE; LCAR
Horster, Hans Ulrich *Source(s):* PIPE; LCAR
Hülsen, Adrian *Source(s):* PIPE
Rheinhardt, Paul Gustav 1853- [librettist]
Dormann, Franz *Source(s):* MELL
Rhinow, Hans-Joachim 1921- [composer]
Harvest, Frank *Source(s):* KOMS; PFSA; SUPN
Rhode, Max 1884-1945 [composer]
Royer, G(unter) *Source(s):* GREN; REHG; SUPN
Royer, Max *Source(s):* LCAR
Rhodes, Andrew Jackson [songwriter]
Rhodes, Jack *Source(s):* NASF
Rhodes, Orville J. 1930- [guitarist, composer]
Rhodes, Red *Source(s):* AMUS; MCCL; PSND
Rhodes, Samuel 1900-1977 [composer]
Kershaw *Source(s):* REHH
Rhodes, William Barnes 1772-1826 [banker, burlesque writer, dramatist]
Crambo, Cornelius *Source(s):* CART; WORB
Rhys, Horton 1823-1876 [actor, writer]
Imported Sparrow *Source(s):* WORB
Price, Morton *Source(s):* CPMU; LCAR
Rhys, Philip ap fl. 1545-60 [composer, organist]
Ap Rhys, Philip *Source(s):* LCAR
Phillip of Poles, Mr. *Source(s):* NGDM
Ribon, Paul 1865-1917 [librettist]
Basset, Serge *Source(s):* LOWN
Riccati, (Count) Giordano 1709-1790 [mathematician, music theorist, architect]
Callistamio, Erbistide *Source(s):* NGDM

Ricciardello, Joseph (A.) 1911- [composer]
Ricardel, Joe *Source(s):* ASCA; CCE40 #1095 Eunp211116; CCE55; CCE64
Riccio, Teodore [or Teodoro] c.1540-c.1600 [composer]
Brixianus Italus *Source(s):* NGDM
Ricciotti, Carlo c.1681-1756 [violinist, publisher, composer]
Bacciccia *Source(s):* LCAR; NGDM; SADC; WORB
Bachiche, Charles *Source(s):* LCAR; SADC
Riccoboni, Francesco (Antonio Valentino) (the younger) 1707-1772 [author]
Lelio, *fils* *Source(s):* LCAR; SONN
Note(s): See also Luigi [or Louis] (Andrea) Riccoboni & Giovanni Battista Andreini.
Riccoboni, Luigi [or Louis] (Andrea) 1676-1753 [actor, author, translator]
Lelio *Source(s):* GROL; LCAR; PSND
Note(s): See also Francesco Riccoboni (the younger) & Giovanni Battista Andreini.
Rice, Al(an Richard) 1904- [singer, writer, actor]
Dunck, Professor *Source(s):* MCCL
Rice, Thomas Dartmouth 1808-1860 [minstrel showman, lyricist]
Note(s): Portrait: HAMM
Father of American Minstrelsy, The *Source(s):* CLAB; LCAR; SHAB p. 19
Rice, Daddy *Source(s):* CLAB; NGAM; SHAB p. 19
Rice, Jim Crow *Source(s):* CLAB
Rich, Charlie [or Charley] 1932-1995 [singer, pianist, songwriter]
Kenton, Charlie *Source(s):* EPMU
Sheridan, Buddy *Source(s):* LCAR
Silver Fox, The *Source(s):* AMUS; CM03; EPMU; FLIN; MCCL; PSND; SHAD
Richard, Willie 1936-1989 [guitarist, songwriter, singer]
Lanchan, Hip *Source(s):* EPMU
Linkchain, Hip *Source(s):* AMUS; EPMU; LCAR
Richards, Deke [songwriter]
Corporation, The *Source(s):* PMUS
Note(s): Jt. pseud.: Fred(erick) [or Freddie] Perren, Alphonso James Mizell & Berry Gordy, Jr.
Richards, Henry Brinley 1817 (or 19)-1885 (or 89) [pianist, composer]
Note(s): Portrait: ETUP 55:6 (June 1937): 356
Emmelar *Source(s):* DIEH
Luini, Carl *Source(s):* CPMU; GROL
Richards, Herbert [composer]
Peterson, H. *Source(s):* JASG; JASR
Richards, Keith 1943- [songwriter, singer, guitarist]
Note(s): Also used surname: Richard; see LCAR for explanation.
Phelge, Nanker *Source(s):* PSND
Note(s): Jt. pseud.: Michael [or Mick] (Philip) Jagger.
Rock's Original Bad Boy *Source(s):* CM10 p. vi
Rock's Ultimate Bad Boy *Source(s):* CM10
Richardson, C(larence) C(lifford) 1918- [singer, guitarist, songwriter]
Richardson, Peg *Source(s):* HARS
Richardson, Clive 1909-1998 (or 99) [composer, pianist]
Crantock, (Peter) *Source(s):* CPOL RE-56-825; RFSO
Note(s): Also jt. pseud.: Anthony [or Tony] Lowry.
Dubois, Paul *Source(s):* MUWB; RFSO
Note(s): "Shadow Waltz" Also used as a jt. pseud. by Paul Boisselot & Charles Louis Etienne Nuitter [i.e., Truinet]
Richardson, J(iles) P(erry) 1930 (or 32)-1959 [singer, songwriter]
Big Bopper, (The) *Source(s):* CASS; KICK; LCAR; PEN2; PSND
Richardson, Jape *Source(s):* LCAR; PSND
Richardson, Jaye P. *Source(s):* PEN2; ROOM
Richardson, Randell 1921- [author, singer]
Reade, Regina *Source(s):* ASCC
Rogers, Rosalind *Source(s):* ASCC
Richelot, Gustave 1844-1924 [composer]
Simia, G. R. *Source(s):* MACM; WORB
Richman, David Alan 1947- [composer, author, entertainer]
Richards, Dave *Source(s):* ASCP; CCE66
Richmond, Howard S. [lyricist, music publisher]
Cavanaugh, Jessie *Source(s):* CCE57; CCE59-61; CPOL 163-977; PMUS
Richter, Ada A. [composer, author, arranger]
Note(s): Portrait: ETUP 55:7 (July 1937): 479
Arnold, Hugh *Source(s):* ASCP; CCE39 #35090 E79842; CCE67
Moore, Wilma *Source(s):* ASCP; CCE52-53
Richter, Franz 1920- [composer]
Herf, Franz *Source(s):* SUPN
Richter, Fred 1909- [composer]
Mons, Peter *Source(s):* KOMP
Richter, Heinrich Friedrich Wilhelm mentioned 1812 [theorist]
Amadeus Autodidactos *Source(s):* RILM 94-11738-ap
Autodidactos, Amadeus *Source(s):* GROL; RILM 94-11738-ap
Richter, Amadeus Friedrich *Source(s):* RILM 94-11738-ap
Richter, Johann 1878- [composer]
Richardy, Johann *Source(s):* SUPN
Richter, Johann Paul Friedrich 1763-1825 [writer on music, poet, novelist]
Hasus, J(ohann) P(aul) F(riedrich) *Source(s):* WORB
Paul, Jean *Source(s):* CCE55; GROL; LCAR; NGDM; PIPE; WORB
Note(s): Also used by Charles Kunkel.

Richter, Rudolf 1894-1984 [translator]
Tiel, Walter *Source(s):* PIPE
Ricketts, (Major) Frederick Joseph c.1880-1945 [composer]
Alford, Kenneth J. *Source(s):* BAKT; GAMM; GREN; GROL; KILG; LCAR; REHG; SUPN
Britain's March King *Source(s):* http://www.concordband.org/pr20020614.html (7 Oct. 2002)
British March King *Source(s):* SMIN
March King of Great Britain *Source(s):* http://www3.sk.sympatico.ca/elect/scb/notes.html (7 Oct. 2002)
Richards, W. V. *Source(s):* GAMM
Ricketts, Joe *Source(s):* REHH
Ricketts, R(andolph) R(objent) 1884-1966 [composer]
Stanley, Leo *Source(s):* REHG; SMIN; SUPN (see under: Ricketts, Fred)
Ricordi, Giulio 1840-1912 [composer, publisher]
Note(s): Portrait: ETUP 55:7 (July 1937): 479
Burgmein, J. *Source(s):* BAKR; CCE19 E460056; CPMU; GROL; LCAR; PIPE
Grubmeini, J. *Source(s):* CPMU; GROL; LCAR; REHG
Ridenhour, Carlton D(ouglas) 1960- [songwriter]
Chuck D. *Source(s):* AMUS; EPMU; PMUS-90
Ridewood, Reginald (Clifford) 1907-1942 [composer]
Texidor, Jaime *Source(s):* REHG
Note(s): Originally thought to be a pseud. of Ridewood on "Amparita Roca"; however, now known to be by Jaime Texidor Dalmau (see REHG).
Ridgely, Richard (P.) 1910-1979 [composer, conductor, musician]
Ricardo, Don *Source(s):* ASCC; CCE55 Eunp
Ridges, E(dward) W(avell) [composer]
Wavell, Edward *Source(s):* CPMU (publication dates 1915-16); LCPC E367193
Rie, Therese (née Herz) 1878 (or 79)-1934 [journalist, author]
Andro, L. *Source(s):* PIPE
Riedl, Jósef Anton 1927- [composer]
Mann, Józef *Source(s):* PIPE; RIES
Riegger, Wallingford (Constantin) 1885-1961 [composer]
Farrell, Edwin *Source(s):* BUL1; BUL2; GROL; LCAR; NGAM
Gore, Gerald (Wilfring) *Source(s):* BUL1; BUL2; CCE38 E69937; GROL; GOTH; LCAR; NGAM
Gore, Wilfring *Source(s):* (source not recorded)
Gregg, Leonard *Source(s):* BUL1; GROL; LCAR; NGAM
Griegg, Leonard *Source(s):* BAKR
Note(s): Typographical error?
Long, Edgar *Source(s):* BUL1; CCE49; GROL; LCAR; NGAM
McCurdy, John H. *Source(s):* BUL1; BUL2; GROL; LCAR; NGAM
Northup, George *Source(s):* BUL1; GROL; LCAR; NGAM
Richard, J. C. *Source(s):* GACC p. 29
Richards, S. C. *Source(s):* LCAR
Richards, William *Source(s):* BUL1; GROL; LCAR; NGAM
Scotson, Walter *Source(s):* BUL1; BUL2; CCE65-66; GROL; LCAR; NGAM
Sedgwick, Robert *Source(s):* BUL1; BUL2; BAKR; CCE46 E2387
Z. G. *Source(s):* GOTH
Riemann, (Karl Wilhelm Julius) Hugo 1849-1919 [pianist, writer on music, musicology]
Note(s): Portrait: ETUP 55:7 (July 1937): 479
Ries, Hugibert *Source(s):* GDRM; GROL; MACM
Riepel, Joseph [or Josef] 1708 (or 09)-1782 [writer on music]
Ipleer, Joseph *Source(s):* RIES
Leiper, Joseph *Source(s):* RIES
Perile, Joseph *Source(s):* RIES
Riese, Wilhelm Friedrich c.1820-1879 [librettist]
Friedrich, W(ilhelm) *Source(s):* LCAR; LOWN; MELL; NGDO; WORB
Rieu, André c.1950- [composer]
Note(s): Do not confuse with conductor André Rieu (1917-)
New Waltz King *Source(s):* CM26
Pied Piper of Light Classical Music *Source(s):* CM26
Schmaltz of Waltz *Source(s):* CM26
Waltzmeister *Source(s):* CM26
Rieux, Claude 1847-1919 [journalist, author, playwright]
Duval, Georges *Source(s):* GAN1; GAN2; LCAR; LOWN
Riggs, John Frederick 1941- [composer, author]
Country Kojac *Source(s):* ASCP
Righetti, Carlo 1828 (or 30)-1906 [journalist, novelist, comedic playwright]
Arrighi, Cletto *Source(s):* LCAR; STGR; WORB
Rihovský, Vojtěch 1871-1950 [composer]
Dubsky, V. R. *Source(s):* OMUO
Riis, Donald L. 1938- [composer, author]
Howard, Johnny *Source(s):* ASCP
Rijke, Cornelius Herminus 1888-1975 [composer]
Cori, (C. J. N.) *Source(s):* REHG; SUPN
Ridée, Charl. H. *Source(s):* SUPN
Riley, Doug(las Brian) 1945- [composer, arranger, pianist]
Dr. Music *Source(s):* CANE
Riley, James 1922-1993 [composer]
O'Reilly, Séamas *Source(s): Music Research Forum* 8/9 (1993-4)

Riley, Terry 1935- [composer]
Father of Minimalism *Source(s):* http://www.geometry.net/composers/riley_terry.php (29 Sept. 2002)
Godfather of Minimalism *Source(s):* http://www.aac.pref.aichi.jp/english/bunjyo/event/PReport-e/99/99-09cms.html (29 Sept. 2002)
Note(s): See also LaMonte Young.
Poppy Nogood *Source(s):* http://www.phoenixnewtimes.com/issues/2001-05-10/music.html (29 Sept. 2002)

Rillé, Laurent (François Anatole) de 1828-1915 [composer]
Méroff *Source(s):* GREN

Rimbaud, Robin 1964 (or 69)- [electronic music composer]
Scanner *Source(s):* AMUS; CCMU

Rimbault, Edward Francis 1816-1876 [composer]
Nava, Franz *Source(s):* CPMU; HAMT; PSND
Note(s): See also Carlo Minasi.

Rimmer, William 1862-1936 [composer, teacher, conductor]
Denne, Heather *Source(s):* SMIN
Henschel, Kenneth *Source(s):* SMIN
Hessler, Carl *Source(s):* SMIN
Laurent, Michael *Source(s):* SMIN
LeDuc, F. *Source(s):* SMIN
Verner, E. *Source(s):* SMIN

Rimoli, Francisco Bautista 1903-1938 [writer, composer]
Linyera, Dante *Source(s):* http://www.elportaldeltango.com/english (28 July 2005)

Rimskij-Korsakov, Andrej Nikolaevic 1878-1940 [musicologist]
Guliver *Source(s):* WORB

Rinaldi, Nino Rota 1911-1979 [composer]
Godfather of Film Composers, The *Source(s):* http://search.npr.org/cf/cmn/cmnpd01fm.cfm?PrgDate=04%2F25/%2F2001&PrgID=4 (7 Oct. 2002)
Rota, Nino *Source(s):* BAKO; BAKR; GOTH; LCAR; PIPE
Rotta, Nino *Source(s):* LCAR
Note(s): From 1930s-90s, film music credited to Nino Rotta.

Rines, Joseph [or Joe] 1902-1986 [bandleader, jingle composer, producer]
Ryan, John *Source(s):* BBDP; BLUE

Ringgenberg, Jörg 1943- [composer]
Berg, George F. *Source(s):* REHH; SUPN
Monti, Francesco *Source(s):* REHH; SUPN

Ringleben, Justin, Jr. 1876-1962 [composer]
Belmont, Chas. W. *Source(s):* CCE50 R68122 ("The Trail of Love")
Note(s): Jt. pseud.: Justin Ring [i.e., Ringleben, Jr.] & Fred(erick W.) Hager [i.e., Haga]
Gates, Clifford G. *Source(s):* CCE49 R53750 ("My Heart Is Waiting")
Note(s): Jt. pseud.: Justin Ring [i.e., Ringleben, Jr.] & Fred(erick W.) Hager [i.e., Haga]
Kelly, Margie *Source(s):* CCE51 R86220 ("Happy")
Note(s): Pseud. of Justin Ring [i.e., Ringleben, Jr.]
LeBris, Marion (E.) *Source(s):* CCE45 #57584 E136375; CCE46 E3187
Milo, (Justin) *Source(s):* CCE48 R40374
Milo-Rega *Source(s):* CCE47 R18168
Note(s): Jt. pseud.: Justin Ring [i.e., Ringleben, Jr.] &Fred(erick W.) Hager [i.e., Haga]
Mulligan, Arizona *Source(s):* CCE47; CCE76
Ring, Justin *Source(s):* CCE30 R9185; JASA p. 322; LCAR; SUTT p. 103
Ring-Hager *Source(s):* CCE50 R57846 ("Down Where I Belong")
Note(s): Jt. pseud.: Justin Ring [i.e., Ringleben, Jr.] & Fred(erick W.) Hager [i.e., Haga]
Sheridan, Andy *Source(s):* CCE51 R80492 ("Honolulu Nights")
Note(s): Jt. pseud.: Justin Ring [i.e., Ringleben, Jr.] & Fred(erick W.) Hager [i.e., Haga]
Taylor, Ruby *Source(s):* CCE49 R43587
Note(s): Jt. pseud.: Justin Ring [i.e., Ringleben, Jr.] & Fred(erick W.) Hager [i.e., Haga]
Verdin, Henry [or Henri] *Source(s):* CCE48 R26106 ("A-La-Paree")
Note(s): Jt. pseud.: Justin Ring [i.e., Ringleben, Jr.] & Fred(erick W.) Hager [i.e., Haga]

Rinne, Hanno 1955- [composer]
Rodger *Source(s):* PFSA
Roger *Source(s):* KOMS
Zasta *Source(s):* KOMS

Rintel, Wilhelm 1818-1899 [composer]
Litner, W. *Source(s):* GOTH; MELL

Rinuccini, Ottavio 1562-1621 [librettist, poet]
Sonnacchioso, Il *Source(s):* GROL; NGDM

Rios, Christopher 1971-2000 [songwriter, rapper]
Big Pun(isher) *Source(s):* AMIR; AMUS; LCAR; PMUS-00
Pun *Source(s):* LCAR

Ripa, Alberto da 1529-1551 [composer, lutenist]
Montovano, Alberto *Source(s):* BAKE; LCAR; MACM; WORB

Ripley, Lynn (Annette) 1947 (or 48)- [singer, songwriter]
Twinkle *Source(s):* AMUS; CCE65; EPMU

Rische, Quirin 1903-1989 [composer]
Zimmer, Friedrich *Source(s):* KOMP; PFSA

Risser, Bryce Nathan 1943- [composer, author, singer]
David, Nathan *Source(s):* ASCP

Rist, Johann 1607-1667 [theologian, poet, composer]
Note(s): Portrait: CYBH
Armatus, Baptista *Source(s):* WORB
Daphnis, (aus Cimbrien) *Source(s):* CPMU; WORB
Palatin *Source(s):* WORB
Rüstige, Der *Source(s):* GROL; NGDM; WORB
Ritchie, Jean 1922- [singer, songwriter]
Hall, Than *Source(s):* http://www.mudcat.org/thread.cfm?threadid=38580 (2 May 2005)
Ritchie, Robert (James) 1971- [songwriter, performer]
Kid Rock *Source(s):* AMIR; AMUS; PMUS-00
Ritenour, John David 1950- [composer, author, guitarist]
Ritenour, Jay *Source(s):* ASCP
Ritenour, Lee 1952- [guitarist, songwriter]
Captain Fingers *Source(s):* ALMN; CM07; LCAR
Fingers, Captain *Source(s):* ALMN
Ritter, Alexander 1833-1896 [composer, violinist, conductor, poet]
Note(s): Portrait: ETUP 55:8 (Aug. 1937): 544
Ritter, Sascha *Source(s):* PIPE
Ritter, Karl 1899-1970 [conductor, composer]
Poor, Hans *Source(s):* LCAR
Ritter, Maurice Woodward 1905 (or 06)-1974 [singer, composer, actor]
Note(s): Given names also listed: Woodward Maurice
Ritter, Tex *Source(s):* CM37; EPMU; FLIN; KINK; MCCL; MUHF; NASF; STAC
Texas Cowboy, (The) *Source(s):* FLIN; NASF; STAC
Ritter, Peter 1763-1846 [violoncellist, composer]
P. R. *Source(s):* CPMU ("Gesellschaftslied, gesungen bie Schleifung")
Note(s): Probable pseud.
Rittman, Gertrude [composer, arranger]
Rittman, Trude *Source(s):* PSND
Ritz, J. H. fl. c.1720 [organist, composer]
J. H. R. *Source(s):* IBIM; WORB
Rivani, Antonio 1629-1686 [theorist]
Ciecolino *Source(s):* SADC
Rivas Avila, Manuel 1913-1990 [singer, songwriter]
Rivas, Wello *Source(s):* HWOM
Rivelli, Pauline 1939- [composer, writer on music]
Mercurio, Paul *Source(s):* ASCP
Rosina, Rose *Source(s):* ASCP
Rivera, Ismael 1931-1987 [singer, bandleader, composer, producer]
Maelo *Source(s):* LCAR
Sonero Mayor, El *Source(s):* LCAR; PEN2
Rivera Castillo, Efrain 1925-1978 [bandleader, singer, composer, multi-instrumentalist]
Rey de(l) Trabalengua, El *Source(s):* EPMU; PEN2
Rivera, Mon *Source(s):* EPMU; LCAR; PEN2
Tongue Twister King, The *Source(s):* EPMU
Rizzi, Ferrante [songwriter]
Giuglini, Signor *Source(s):* CPMU
Robarge, John F(rederick) 1922- [singer, songwriter]
Roe, Tex *Source(s):* CCE63; CCE74; CLAB
Robbins, Clarence A(aron) 1888-1949 [songwriter]
Robbins, Tod *Source(s):* STC1; STC2
Robbins, Hargus (Melvin) 1938- [pianist, composer, singer]
Robbins, Pig *Source(s):* AMUS; MCCL; STAC
Roberds, Fred A(llen) 1941- [composer, author, singer]
Roberds, (Ian) Smokey *Source(s):* ASCP; CCE64; CCE66; PMUS
Robert le Pelé 1415-1478 [composer]
Robinet de la Magdalaine *Source(s):* NGDM
Rubinet [or Rubinus] *Source(s):* NGDM
Roberts, Aldwyn [or Aldwin] 1922-2000 [singer, composer]
Note(s): Portrait: OB00
Grand Master of Calypso *Source(s):* OB00
Kitch *Source(s):* MUWB; PEN2
Kitchener, Lord *Source(s):* CCE56; CM29; LCAR; MUWB; OB00; PEN2; WORL
Lord Kitchener *Source(s):* LCAR
Road March King of the World *Source(s):* MUWB
Young Kitchener *Source(s):* LCAR
Roberts, Arthur 1852-1933 [author, music hall comedian]
Nunn, Payne *Source(s):* GANA
Roberts, Charles Luckey(e)th 1887-1968 [composer, conductor, pianist]
Note(s): Portraits: HARR; JASN; PERF; SHMM (July/Aug. 1990): 24
Roberts, Luck(e)y *Source(s):* EPMU; HARR; JASN; LCAR; NGAM; PEN2; SUTT; VACH
Roberts, Howard (Mancel) 1919-1992 [guitarist, teacher, writer on guitar]
Fender, Gib *Source(s):* JAMU
Roberts, James Martin 1889 (or 90)-1932 [composer, pianist]
Note(s): Portrait: "The Entertainer's Rag." Chicago: Forster Music, 1912 (cover)
California Ragtime King, The *Source(s):* JASA p. 188
Roberts, Jay *Source(s):* JASA p. 309; PERF
Roberts, James William 1918- [singer, songwriter]
Barn Dance Sweethearts *Source(s):* EPMU
Note(s): Jt. pseud. with wife: Martha Carson [i.e., Irene Amburgey]
Carson, James *Source(s):* CCE47; EPMU; MCCL
Roberts, John [or Jack] (Isaac) [composer]
Di Cappo (?) *Source(s):* MUWB
Kaps, Karl *Source(s):* CCE19 E446418; CPMU; MUWB; RFSO

Roberts, John 1822-1877 [hymnist, composer, conductor]
Note(s): Portrait: CYBH
Apostle of the Sacred Music of Wales, The *Source(s):* CLEV
Gwyllt, Ieua(n) *Source(s):* CYBH; GROL; NGDM; ROOM; WILG
Ieuan Gwyllt *Source(s):* CYBH; GROL; NGDM; ROOM; WILG
Roberts, John Godfrey Owen 1909- [singer, songwriter, lawyer]
Bobo, Juan *Source(s):* CCE54; CPOL RE-127-661
Godfrey, Bob *Source(s):* CCE52-53; CPOL RE-66-079
Jones, Hirem *Source(s):* CCE36 Efor43954
Note(s): Jt. pseud.: Ralph (T.) Butler, Harold Elton Box & C(harles) J(oseph) Edwards.
Morrow, Morton *Source(s):* CCE49; CCE51; CCE63-64; CCE70 R484404
Note(s): Jt. pseud.: Harold Elton Box, Desmond Cox [i.e., Adrian Keuleman] & C(harles) J(oseph) Edwards.
Roberts, Paddy *Source(s):* CCE52-56; CPOL RE-170-853
Roberts, John Henry 1848-1924 [composer, musician]
Pencerdd Gwynedd *Source(s):* LCAR; WORB
Roberts, Kenny 1927- [singer, songwriter]
America's Number One Yodeler *Source(s):* CCME
Roberts, Lee S. 1884-1949 [songwriter]
Note(s): ETUP 55:9 (Sept. 1937): 556
Baxter, Ted *Source(s):* CCE51 R74018 ("Wow")
Note(s): Also used by J. Lawrence Cook & Max Kortlander.
Kendall, Al M. *Source(s):* CCE48 R29082 ("I Love You Dear")
Roberts, Leland *Source(s):* CCE33 R27542
Roberts, Samuel 1800-1885 [minister, hymnist, translator]
S. R. *Source(s):* JULN
Roberts, William (Amos) 1868-1959 [music critic, journalist, organist]
Note(s): Portraits: ETUP 54:8 (Sept. 1936): 468; *The Music Bulletin* 8:6 (June 1926): 168+
Cecil, Hugh Mortimer *Source(s):* LCAR
Dean of British Critics *Source(s):* GRAN p. 179
England's Most Distinguished Music Critic *Source(s):* GRAN p. 283 note
Newman, Ernest *Source(s):* BAKO; BAKR; GROL; LCAR; NGDM; NGDO; PIPE
Onlooker *Source(s):* CART
Roberts, William Morgan 1853-1923 [composer, critic]
W. M. R. *Source(s):* CPMU (publication dates 1891-1907)
Robertson, Ben 1871-1938 [composer]
Harney, Ben *Source(s):* REHH
Robertson, Dick 1903- [singer, songwriter, bandleader]
Carroll, Roy *Source(s):* SUTT
Dickson, Bob *Source(s):* SUTT
Dix, Bobby *Source(s):* SUTT
Dixon, Bob *Source(s):* SUTT
Fenwyck, Jerry *Source(s):* SUTT
Hughes, Phil *Source(s):* SUTT
Leighton, Chester *Source(s):* SUTT
Roberts, Ben *Source(s):* SUTT
Wood, Robert *Source(s):* SUTT
Note(s): Also used by Arthur Fields [i.e., Abe Finkelstein] & Irving [i.e., Isidore] Kaufman.
Robertson, George (Austin), Jr. 1945- [composer, author, singer]
Roberts, Austin *Source(s):* ASCP; CCE68; CCE76
Robertson, Thomas Morgan Dolby 1958- [singer, songwriter]
Dolby, Thomas *Source(s):* CM10; DIMA; EPMU; HARR; LCAR; PEN2; RECR
Robertsson, Arturi 1903- [composer]
Rope, Arturi *Source(s):* BUL2
Robey, Don (D.) 1903 (or 04)-1975 [songwriter, recording executive]
Malone, D(eadric) *Source(s):* CM11 (see under: Brown, Clarence "Gatemouth"); http://www.houstonbluessociety.org/donrobey.html (7 Oct. 2002)
Robillard, Michael 1948- [composer]
Robillard, Duke *Source(s):* EPMU; LCAR
Robineau, Alexandre Louis Bertrand 1746-1823 [author; librettist; translator]
Beaunoir, (Madame) de *Source(s):* LCAR; LOWN; SONN; WORB
Robinson, Cleophus 1932- [clergyman, singer, songwriter, radio & TV artist]
King of Gospel Music *Source(s):* PSND
Note(s): See also James Cleveland.
Robinson, Edward Alfred 1921- [composer, author, arranger]
Belefan, Sam *Source(s):* ASCP
Robinson, Fenton 1935-1997 [guitarist, singer, songwriter]
Mellow Blues Genius, The *Source(s):* AMUS
Robinson, J. Russel(l) 1892-1963 [pianist; songwriter, vocal coach, music publisher]
Note(s): Portraits: JASA; JASN
Hooven, Joe *Source(s):* CCE33 E34605; JAST; PMUS; STUW
Hoven, Joe *Source(s):* CPOL RE-3-451; CPOL RE-13-223
Roberts, Steve L. *Source(s):* CCE52 R96546 ("What-Cha-Call-'Em Blues")

Note(s): Also used by Arthur Bergh.
Russell, Joe *Source(s):* CCE68
White Boy with the Colored Fingers, The *Source(s):* JAST
Robinson, J. Watts [composer]
Cadet *Source(s):* DICH ("Westpoint" (1852))
Robinson, James 1903-1957 [singer, pianist, songwriter]
Bat the Humming-Bird *Source(s):* AMUS; HARS
Note(s): See also Cow Cow [i.e., Charles Edward] Davenport.
Robinson, Bat ("The Hummingbird") *Source(s):* AMUS; HARS
Robinson, Jimmie [or Jimmy] Lee 1931-2002 [songwriter]
Aliomar, J.L. Latif *Source(s):* BBDP; DRSC
Robinson, Lonesome *Source(s):* BBDP
Robinson, L(ouis) C(harles) 1915-1976 [singer, instrumentalist, songwriter]
Robinson, Good Rockin' *Source(s):* HARS
Robinson, Martin D(avid) 1925-1982 [singer, guitarist, songwriter]
Note(s): Portraits: EWEN; EWPS
David, Martin *Source(s):* CCE63
Mr. Teardrop *Source(s):* CCME; FLIN; PSND
Robbin(s), Marty *Source(s):* CM09; CCME; EPMU; HARR; LCAR; PSND
Robertson, Martin David *Source(s):* CASS; NGAM
Note(s): Incorrect surname.
Teardrop, Mr. *Source(s):* CCME; FLIN; PSND
Robinson, Mary (Darby) 1758-1800 [actress, author, poet]
Note(s): See PSND & LCAR for additional nonmusic-related pseudonyms.
Bramble, Tabitha *Source(s):* GOTT; LCAR
Perdita *Source(s):* GOTT; LCAR; PSND
Robinson, Paul [songwriter, producer]
Boom, Barry *Source(s):* EPMU
Robinson, Pete(r) 1962- [singer, songwriter]
Marilyn *Source(s):* LCAR; SONG; http://www.sbu.ac.uk/stafflag/marilyn.html (21 Oct. 2002)
Robinson, Ray Charles 1930 (or 32)-2004 [pianist, singer, songwriter]
Brother Ray *Source(s):* Charles, Ray. *Brother Ray; Ray Charles' Own Story*. 1978.
Charles, Ray *Source(s):* BAKR; CASS; CM24; HARS; IDBC; LCAR; PEN2; SOTH
Father of Soul *Source(s):* SHAD
Note(s): See also Sam(uel) Cook(e).
Genius (of Soul), The *Source(s):* AMEN; HARS; PEN2
Senior Diplomat of Soul, The *Source(s):* PSND
Robinson, Robert 1735-1790 [author, hymnist]
Carbonell, Lewis *Source(s):* CART; LCAR
R—n *Source(s):* JULN
R. R. *Source(s):* LCAR
Robinson, Sylvia Vanderpool 1936- [singer, songwriter]
Sylvia *Source(s):* PSND
Note(s): Also used by Sylvia Kirby & also Richard Kountz.
Robinson, William, (Jr.) 1940- [singer, songwriter, producer]
Greatest Living Poet in America, The *Source(s):* PSND
Robinson, Smokey *Source(s):* ALMN; CASS; CM01; EPMU; HARR; LCAR; PEN2; PSND
Robinson, (Sir) William Cleaver Francis 1834-1897 [music patron, composer]
Hope, Owen *Source(s):* GROL
Robison, Carson J(ay) 1890-1957 [songwriter, singer, guitarist]
Note(s): Portrait: CCME. For listing of jt. pseuds. with Frank Luther [i.e., Francis Luther Crow(e)], Vernon Dalhart [i.e., M(arion) T(ry) Slaughter] & Phil Crow, see MACE, SUTT.
America's First Cowboy Radio Singer *Source(s):* http://library.pittstate.edu/spcoll/ndxrobison.html (7 Oct. 2002)
Andrews, Maggie (A.) *Source(s):* CCE55 R45644 ("The Gambler's Dying Words"); MCCL
Billings, Joe *Source(s):* MACE; PSNN; SUTT
Carson, Cal *Source(s):* MACE; SUTT
Note(s): Also used by Frank Luther [i.e., Francis Luther Crow(e)]. See SUTT for additional information.
Clark, James *Source(s):* MACE; SUTT
Evans, Frank(lin) *Source(s):* MACE; SUTT
Note(s): Frank Evans also used by Arthur Fields [i.e., Abe Finkelstein] & Vernon Dalhart [i.e., M(arion) T(ry) Slaughter]
Faber, Ed *Source(s):* MACE; SUTT
Granddaddy of the Hillbillies *Source(s):* http://www.kfdi.com/pages/61258.asp (7 Oct. 2002)
Jones, Harry *Source(s):* MACE; SUTT
Kansas Jaybird *Source(s):* MUHF; NASF
Lamkin, Marjorie *Source(s):* CSUF
Lazy Larry *Source(s):* VDPS
Note(s): Also possible pseud. of Vernon Dalhart [i.e., M(arion) T(ry) Slaughter] & Harry (K(irby)) McClintock.
Leavitt, Bob *Source(s):* SUTT
McAfee, Carlos B. *Source(s):* CCE52 R92185 ("Dear, Oh Dear"); http://library.pittstate.edu/spcoll/ndxrobison.html (7 Oct. 2002)
Note(s): Do not confuse with Carlos McAfee [i.e., M(arion) T(ry) Slaughter]
Mitchell, John T. *Source(s):* CCE70 R490125; http://library.pittstate.edu/spcoll/ndxrobison.html (7 Oct. 2002)

Robbie *Source(s):* http://www.geocities.com/acuvar/fankluther.html (9 Oct. 2003)
Robison, Charles *Source(s):* NASF
Samuels, Claude *Source(s):* MACE; SUTT
Smith, Travelin' Jim *Source(s):* CSUF
Tuttle, Frank *Source(s):* SUTT
Note(s): Also used by Vernon Dalhart [i.e., M(arion) T(ry) Slaughter]
Weary Willie *Source(s):* MACE
Note(s): Possible pseud. See also Jack [i.e., Jacob] Kaufman & Francis Luther [i.e., Francis Luther Crow(e)]
Wells, Charley *Source(s):* MACE

Robison, Willard 1894-1968 [songwriter, pianist]
Howe, Paul *Source(s):* SUTT

Robjohn, W(illiam) J(ames) 1843-1920 [composer, choral, conductor, teacher]
Florio, Caryl *Source(s):* BAKE; LCAR; MACM; MELL; NGAM; NGDM

Robledo, Melchor c.1510-1586 [composer, church musician]
Robledillo *Source(s):* GROL

Robrecht, Carl 1888-1961 [composer]
Reight, Robby *Source(s):* KOMP; KOMS; PFSA

Robson, Richard [composer]
Nosbor, Richard *Source(s):* CPMU (publication date 1904)

Robyn, Alfred George 1860-1935 [pianist, organist, conductor, composer]
Nybor, A. G. *Source(s):* KROH p. 121
Streat, Sixteenth (S.) *Source(s):* CCE16 R8177; KROH p. 130

Rochat, Andrée 1900- [pianist, composer]
Durand, Jean *Source(s):* COHN; HIXN

Rochberg, (Aaron) George 1918- [composer, writer on music]
Note(s): Portrait: LYMN
Anthony, George Walter *Source(s):* CCE52-54
Castleton, Gregory *Source(s):* CCE55; LCAR
Leader of Postmodernism *Source(s):* LYMN

Rochefort-Luçay, Claude-Louis-Marie, marquis de 1790-1871 [playwright]
Edmond *Source(s):* LCAR; PIPE
Rochefort, Armand de *Source(s):* LCAR; PIPE
Rochefort, Edmond *Source(s):* LCAR

Rochler, Jens 1959- [composer]
Bergersbacher, Andreas *Source(s):* PFSA

Rochon, Alfred 1885- [author, composer, actor, publisher]
Nohcor, Alfred *Source(s):* VGRC

Rockwell, George Noyes [composer]
Note(s): Portrait: ETUP 55:8 (Aug. 1937): 544
Rocheville, Georges de *Source(s):* CCE47 R16769 ("Frolic in the Barn"); TPRF

Rodby, Walter (A.) 1917 (or 20)- [composer, author, teacher]
Chambers, Robert *Source(s):* CPOL RE-378-986
Note(s): Jt. pseud.: Walter (Charles) Ehret. Ehret also used as a jt. pseud. with other individuals; see NOTES: Chambers, Robert.
Hilton, Arthur *Source(s):* CPOL RE-399-898; LCCC 1955-70 (see reference)
Note(s): Jt. pseud.: Walter (Charles) Ehret. Ehret also used as jt. pseud. with other individuals; see NOTES: Hilton, Arthur.
Ramsey, Norman *Source(s):* ASCP; CCE64; LCAR
Randall, Bruce *Source(s):* ASCP; CCE62; CCE65; LCAR

Rodeheaver, Homer A(lvan) 1880-1955 [evangelist; hymnist; publisher]
Note(s): Portraits: ETUP 55:8 (Aug. 1937): 544; SGMA
Old Glory Face *Source(s):* http://www.tanbible.com/tol_sng/othatwillbeglory.htm (3 Feb. 2005)
Rody *Source(s):* GRAK; TCAN

Roeder [or Röder], Martin 1851-1895 [teacher, composer, author]
Miedner, Raro *Source(s):* LCAR; MACM; NGDM; PRAT

Rodericus fl. late 14th cent. [composer]
Rodriguet de la guitarra *Source(s):* NGDM
Uciredor, (S.) *Source(s):* NGDM

Rodgers, James [or Jimmie] (Charles) 1897-1933 [singer, songwriter, guitarist]
America's Blue Yodeler *Source(s):* AMEN; EPMU; MCCL
Blue Yodeler, The *Source(s):* AMEN
Brakeman *Source(s):* ALMN; SHAD
Father of Country Music, The *Source(s):* CM03; EPMU; FLIN; MCCL; NASF; SHAB; SHAD
Note(s): See also William [or Bill] (Smith) Monroe & Hank [i.e., Hir(i)am (King)] Williams.
Godfather of Country, The *Source(s):* http://www.ocweekly.com/ink/02/42/feedback-jr.php (7 Oct. 2002)
Mississippi's Blue Yodeler *Source(s):* FLIN
Singing Breakman, The *Source(s):* AMEN; EPMU; FLIN; MCCL; SHAD; SIFA
Yodeling Cowboy, The *Source(s):* AMEN
Note(s): See also Eric (Charles) Edwards.

Rodgers, Richard (Charles) 1902-1979 [composer]
Note(s): Portaits: EWEN; EWPA; LYMN
Boys from Columbia, The *Source(s):* Hyland, William G. *Richard Rodgers*. New Haven: Yale University Press, 1998, [117]
Note(s): Jt. sobriquet: Lorenz (Milton) Hart.
Dean of American Musical Theater Composers *Source(s):* LYMN

Gilbert and Sullivan of America *Sources(s):* SPTH p. 449 & 544
Note(s): Jt. sobriquet: Lorenz (Milton) Hart.
Gilbert and Sullivan of Broadway *Source(s):* Hyland p. 236 (see above)
Note(s): Jt. sobriquet: Oscar (Greeley Clendenning) Hammerstein, II.
Lorenz, H(erbert) R(ichard) *Source(s):* NGAM; Hyland p. 27 (see above)
Note(s): Jt. pseud.: Lorenz (Milton) Hart & Herbert Fields.
Master of the Musical *Source(s): Washington Post.* (3 Nov. 2001): C01
Note(s): See also Maury Yeston.
Rodgers, Victor Herbert *Source(s):* Hyland p. 18 (see above)
Rodgersovsky, Richard *Source(s):* Hyland p. 49 (see above)
Showmen of the Century *Source(s): Time.* Special Issue. (8 June 1998)
Note(s): Jt. sobriquet: Oscar (Greeley Clendenning) Hammerstein, II.
Team from Siam *Source(s):* Hyland, 203 (see above)
Note(s): Jt. sobriquet: Oscar (Greeley Clendenning) Hammerstein, II.

Rodney, (Godfrey) Winston 1945 (or 48)- [singer, songwriter]
Burning Spear *Source(s):* EPMU; LCAR; WORL
Spear *Source(s):* LCAR

Rodomista, Vincent 1918- [composer, author, pianist]
Roddie, Vin *Source(s):* ASCP; CCE56-59; CCE61-62; CCE68

Rodriguez, Asensio Eugenio 1891-1952 [poet]
Cárdenas, Eugenio *Source(s):* TODO

Rodríguez Correa, Ramón [author]
Rodríguez, Adolfo *Source(s):* LOWN; PIPE
Note(s): Jt. pseud.: Gustavo Adolfo Dominguez Bastida.

Rodríguez, Ignacio Loyola 1911-1970 [singer, composer, bandleader]
Blind Marvel *Source(s):* http://www.afrocubaweb.com/arseniorodriguez.htm (7 Oct. 2002)
Ciego Maravillos, El *Source(s):* EPMU; PEN2
Rodríguez, Arsenio *Source(s):* PEN2

Rodriguez, Juan Raoul (Davis) 1951 (or 52)- [singer, songwriter]
Rodriguez, Johnny *Source(s):* CCME; ENCM; LCAR; PEN2; PSND
Note(s): Do not confuse with Johnny Rodriguez, Sr. (the Tito Puente band member) or his son, percussionist Johnny Rodriguez.

Rodríguez, Moisés Simons 1888 (or 90)-1945 [composer, lyricist, conductor]
Simons, Moisés *Source(s):* CCE31 E23122; FULD

Rodriguez, Pablo 1923-1972 (or 73) [singer, bandleader, multi-instrumentalist, composer]
Frank Sinatra of Latin Music, (The) *Source(s):* PSND
Rodriguez, Tito *Source(s):* EPMU; LCAR

Rodriguez, Ubaldo 1958- [singer, composer]
Rodriguez, Lalo *Source(s):* EPMU; LCAR; PEN2

Rodriguez Alvarez, Alejandro 1903-1965 [poet, playwright, screenwriter]
Casona, Alejandro *Source(s):* CCE68; LCAR; PIPE

Rodwell, George Herbert (Bonaparte) 1800-1852 [composer, playwright]
Herbert, George B. *Source(s):* CPMU; GOTT

Roeckel, Joseph Leopold 1838-1923 [teacher, composer, pianist]
Note(s): Portrait: ETUP 55:8 (Aug. 1937): 544
Dorn, Edward [or Edouard] *Source(s):* BLIC; CPMU; GOTH; GOTT; IBIM; MACM; WORB
Holm, Banner *Source(s):* COMP

Roemheld, Heinz (Heinrich) Erich 1901-1985 [composer]
Rommell, Rox *Source(s):* GROL

Roes, Carol Lasater [or Lasatir] 1905-1993 [composer, author]
Loke, Mele *Source(s):* ASCP; CPOL TX-1-241-301

Roeser, Donald (B.) 1947- [composer, author]
Dharma, Buck *Source(s):* ASCP; BLIC

Roesgen-Champion, Marguerite Sara 1894-1976 [composer]
Delysse, Jean *Source(s):* COHN; GREN; HEIN; HIXN

Roever, Uli 1938- [composer]
Bander, Till *Source(s):* KOMS; PFSA

Roffinella, Joseph 1910- [composer]
Roff, Joseph *Source(s):* BUL3; SUPN

Roger of Helmarshausen fl. 1110-1140 [author]
Theophilus *Source(s):* RILM 89-07925-ap; RILM 90-07611-ap
Note(s): Probable pseud.

Roger, Roger 1911-1995 [composer]
Note(s): Pronounced: Ro-ZHAY Ro-ZHAY.
Leuter, Cecil *Source(s):* http://www.weirdomusic.com/rogerroger.htm (17 May 2005)

Rogers, Eugene 1917-1993 [singer, songwriter]
Rogers, Smokey *Source(s):* CCE53-54; ENCM

Rogers, Fred (M(cFeely)) 1928 (or 29)-2003 [composer, author, producer]
Rogers, Mister *Source(s):* ASCP; CPOL PAu-419-878

Rogers, James H(otchkiss) 1857-1940 [composer, songwriter]
Note(s): Portraits: APSA; *American Organist* 2:1 (Jan. 1919): 14; ETUP 55:8 (Aug. 1937): 544
Bergthal, Hugo *Source(s):* CCE17 R9484; TPRF
Campion, Edward *Source(s):* CCE17 R10028; PSND

Rogers, Norman 1966- [songwriter]
Terminator X *Source(s):* CPOL PA-358-093; PMUS-90
Rogers, Sooliman Ernest c.1928-1994 [songwriter, performer]
Rogie, S. E. *Source(s):* GROL
Rogozin, Samuel [composer]
Rose, Sammy *Source(s):* CCE33 E37055; HESK; LCPC letter cited (8 July 1933)
Roh, Johann c. 1487-1547 [songwriter]
Cornu, Johann *Source(s):* CYBH
Horn, Johann *Source(s):* CYBH; DIEH
Röhl, Uwe 1925- [composer]
Nicolai, Sven *Source(s):* KOMP; KOMS; PFSA
Röhrig, Wolfram 1916- [composer, conductor]
Droysen, Wolf *Source(s):* KOMP; KOMS; PFSA
Roker, Ronald [singer, composer]
Blue, Barry *Source(s):* EPMU
Note(s): Also used by Barry Green.
Roland, Reiny 1898- [composer]
Müller, Reinhard *Source(s):* KOMP
Orlande, Pierre *Source(s):* KOMP; PFSA
Rolfe, Walter (L.) 1880-1944 [composer]
Note(s): Portrait: ETUP 55:8 (Aug. 1937): 544
Eflor, W. *Source(s):* CCE15 E370211
Forel, L(awrence) W. *Source(s):* CCE36 E53916; CCE74
Huyler, Jack *Source(s):* CCE32 Eunp53779
James, Rudolph *Source(s):* CCE31 Eunp45783
Langelle, Rae *Source(s):* CCE42 #4145 E101166
Lloyd, Lewellyn *Source(s):* TPRF
Lorenzo,W. *Source(s):* CCE68
Rolison, D(edrick) (D'Mon) 1971- [songwriter, performer]
Mack 10 *Source(s):* AMIR; AMUS; LCAR; PMUS-00
Rolland(-Max(-Dearly)), Lucien Paul Marie Joseph 1874-1943 [actor, author]
Dearly, Max *Source(s):* GAN2; LCAR; PIPE
Max-Dearly *Source(s):* PIPE
Villary, Roland *Source(s):* PIPE
Rolli, Paolo Antonio 1687-1735 [librettist, poet]
Boccardi, Michel Angiolo *Source(s):* GROL
Note(s): Do not confuse with Michelangelo Boccardi (fl. 1724-35), librettist.
Rollins, Lanier 1937- [composer, author, singer]
Edward, Jette *Source(s):* ASCP
Rollins, Theodore Walter [or Walter Theodore] 1929 (or 30)- [saxophonist, composer]
Note(s): Officially switched the sequence of given name to: Walter Theodore.
Rollins, Sonny *Source(s):* CM07; EPMU; KINK; LCAR; PEN2; PSND
Rollins, W(alter) E. 1906 (or 07)-1973 [songwriter]
Rollins, Jack *Source(s):* ASCP; CCE64; PSND; STUW
Rollinson, Thomas H. 1844-1928 [composer, cornetist, arranger]
Note(s): Portrait: ETUP 58:10 (Oct. 1940): 714
Pazdirek *Source(s):* SMIN
Rayder, J. H(enri) *Source(s):* CCE20 R17001; CPMU
Thomson, Rollin *Source(s):* REHG; SUPN
Roloff, W(olfgang) 1930- [composer]
Hausmann, W(olf) *Source(s):* CCE64
Roloff, Ronny *Source(s):* CCE62; PFSA
Roman, Johan Helmich 1694-1758 [composer]
Father of Swedish Music, The *Source(s):* NGDM; PSND; SIFA; SPIE
Note(s): See also Johann Theodor Römhild(t).
Swedish Handel, The *Source(s):* NGDM; SADC
Romberg, Sigmund 1887-1951 [composer]
Note(s): Portraits: EWEN; EWPA
American Successor to Johann Strauss *Source(s):* PSND
Rombro, Jakob [or Jacob] Borukhovich 1858-1922 [journalist, social activist, writer on music]
Krantz, Ph(ilip) *Source(s):* SEND
Rome, Harold 1908-1993 [songwriter, lyricist]
Note(s): Portraits: EWEN; EWPA
Rome, Hecky *Source(s):* Robinson, Earl & Gordon, Eric A. *Ballad of an American*. Lanham Md.: Scarecrow, 1998, 49+.
Romeo, Beresford 1963- [arranger, singer, songwriter]
Jazzie B. *Source(s):* CPOL PA-494-337; HARR
Romer, Frank [or Francis] 1810-1889 [composer]
Romère, François *Source(s):* CPMU
Römer, Gerhard Walter 1942- [composer]
Gewaro *Source(s):* KOMP; PFSA
Romer, Mary 1837-1881 [composer]
Note(s): Married name: Macklin.
Kiko, M. *Source(s):* IBIM; YORM; WORB
Romero, Roberto [singer, composer]
Allen, Roberto *Source(s):* AMUS
Allen, Tito *Source(s):* EPMU; PEN2
Elegante de la Salsa, El *Source(s):* EPMU
Römhild(t), Johann Theodor 1684-1756 [organist, composer]
Father of Swedish Music, The *Source(s):* BAKR
Note(s): See also Johan Helmich Roman.
Mielorth, Johann Theodor *Source(s):* LCAR; NGDM
Romita, Florenzo 1908- [author, musicologist]
Flos *Source(s):* WORB
Roncoroni, Joseph (Dominic) 1908- [songwriter]
Boswell, Dick *Source(s):* CCE51; CPOL RE-19-804
Note(s): Jt. pseud.: Harold (Cornelius) Fields & H(oward) E(llington) Barnes.
Carmencito *Source(s):* CCE54; CPOL RE-81-686
Note(s): Jt. pseud.: Harold (Cornelius) Fields.
Carson, Milton *Source(s):* CCE 51; CCE57; CLTP ("Destiny"); CPOL RE-328-995

Note(s): Jt. pseud.: Harold (Cornelius) Fields & H(oward) E(llington) Barnes.
Dominic, John *Source(s):* CCE49; CCE54
Duke, Jerry *Source(s):* CCE58; CPOL RE-282-084
Note(s): Jt. pseud.: Harold (Cornelius) Fields & Robert Halfin.
Feahy, Michael *Source(s):* CCE50-52
Note(s): Jt. pseud.: Harold (Cornelius) Fields & H(oward) E(llington) Barnes.
Greer, David *Source(s):* CCE57-58; CCE60-61; CPOL RE-81-703
Note(s): Jt. pseud.: Harold (Cornelius) Fields.
Hagen, Larry *Source(s):* CCE52; CPOL RE-32-129
Note(s): Jt. pseud.: Harold (Cornelius) Fields & H(oward) E(llington) Barnes.
Hollander, Hugo *Source(s):* CCE50-51; CCE56
Note(s): Jt. pseud.: Harold (Cornelius) Fields & H(oward) E(llington) Barnes.
Jerome, John *Source(s):* CCE51; CCE54; CCE56; CPOL RE-23-625
Note(s): Jt. pseud.: Harold (Cornelius) Fields & H(oward) E(llington) Barnes.
John, D(ominic) *Source(s):* CCE53-63; CPOL RE-282-082
King, Garland *Source(s):* CCE52; CPOL RE-67-016
Note(s): Jt. pseud.: Harold (Cornelius) Fields & H(oward) E(llington) Barnes.
Kordah, Tibor *Source(s):* CCE52
Note(s): Jt. pseud.: Harold (Cornelius) Fields & H(oward) E(llington) Barnes.
Lawrence, Steve *Source(s):* CCE50-51
Note(s): Jt. pseud.: Harold (Cornelius) Fields & H(oward) E(llington) Barnes.
Leclair, Jean *Source(s):* CCE49
Note(s): Jt. pseud.: Harold (Cornelius) Fields & H(oward) E(llington) Barnes.
Lorraine, Sam *Source(s):* CCE56-57
Note(s): Jt. pseud.: Harold (Cornelius) Fields & H(oward) E(llington) Barnes.
Miguel, Guido *Source(s):* CCE51-52; CPOL RE-46-898
Note(s): Jt. pseud.: Harold (Cornelius) Fields & H(oward) E(llington) Barnes & William [or Bill] McGuffie.
Pasquale, Dino *Source(s):* CCE50
Note(s): Jt. pseud.: Harold (Cornelius) Fields & H(oward) E(llington) Barnes.
Rossiter, (John) Simon *Source(s):* CCE58; CPOL RE-282-088
Note(s): Jt. pseud.: Robert [or Bob] Halfin & Harold (Cornelius) Fields.
Sherman, Charles *Source(s):* CCE50-51
Note(s): Jt. pseud.: Harold (Cornelius) Fields & H(oward) E(llington) Barnes.
Stultz, Herman *Source(s):* CCE50-51
Note(s): Jt. pseud.: Harold (Cornelius) Fields & H(oward) E(llington) Barnes.
Wayne, Elmer *Source(s):* CCE54
Note(s): Jt. pseud.: Harold (Cornelius) Fields & H(oward) E(llington) Barnes.
Young, Charles *Source(s):* LCCC 1955-70
Note(s): Jt. pseud.: Harold (Cornelius) Fields & H(oward) E(llington) Barnes.

Rones, Samuel Morris 1924- [composer]
Paul, Christopher *Source(s):* CCE55-56; REHG

Ronger, Emmanuel Florimond 1847-1926 [stage director, author, composer]
Note(s): Portrait: GAN1
Gardel-Hervé *Source(s):* GAN1; GAN2 (see under: Hervé)
Hervé, Gardel *Source(s):* GAN1; GAN2 (see under: Hervé)

Ronger, (Louis Auguste Joseph) Florimond 1825-1892 [composer, organist]
Note(s): Portrait: GAN2
Alcindor *Source(s):* STGR; WORB
Note(s): Jt. pseud.: Alexander Charles Lecocq & Isidor Edouard Legouix.
Brémond *Source(s):* MELL; PIPE; STGR
Compositeur Tocqué, Le *Source(s):* http://www.theatrehisory.com/french/operette001.html (7 Oct. 2002)
Crazy Composer, The *Source(s):* http://www.theatrehisory.com/french/operetta001.html
Father of Opera Bouffe, The *Source(s):* PSND
Heffer, Louis *Source(s):* PIPE; STGR
Hervé *Source(s):* BAKO; BAKR; GAN1; GAN2; GOTH; LCAR; PIPE; REHG
Hervé, Louis *Source(s):* BAKO; BAKR; GAN2

Ronssecy, (Madame) de [composer]
D., (Madame) *Source(s):* JACK (publications: c.1800-02)

Roobenian, Amber 1905-1980 [organist, composer]
Harrington, (Mrs.) Amber *Source(s):* ASCP; COHN; HIXN
Harrington, W. Clark *Source(s):* CCE55-56
Murdock, Jane *Source(s):* ASCP; COHN; HEIN; HIXN

Rooney, Mark [singer, percussionist, songwriter]
Reid, Antonio (M.) *Source(s):* http://today.answers.com/topic/the-deele (27 Feb. 2006)
Reid, L. A . *Source(s):* AMUS; KICK; http://today.answers.com/topic/the-deele
Note(s): Usually listed as pseud. of Antonio (M.) Reid.

Root, Frank K. [composer]
Kimball, F. R. *Source(s):* CCE26 R36067 ("Holiday March")

Note(s): Also used by Leo Friedman & Henry S. Sawyer; see NOTES: Kimball, F. R.

Root, George Frederick 1820-1895 [composer, music educator]
Note(s): Portraits: EWEN; EWPA; HOWD
G. F. R. *Source(s):* CPMU
Wurzel, G(eorge) Friedrich [or Frederick] *Source(s):* CART; CPMU; GROL; KILG; LCAR; NGAM

Ropes, Arthur Reed 1859-1933 [librettist, lyricist]
Cryptos *Source(s):* GANA ("Our Miss Gibbs")
Note(s): Jt. pseud. of lyricists & composers: Ross [i.e., Ropes], Ivan Caryll [i.e., Félix Tilken], Percy Greenbank, (John) Lionel (Alexander) Monckton & James T(olman) Tanner.
Pie, Brian *Source(s):* CART
Reed, Arthur *Source(s):* CART; CCE31 R16722; GANA
Ross, Adrian *Source(s):* CART; GAN2; GANA; KILG; LCAR; PIPE; ROOM; WORB

Roquet, Antoine-Ernest 1827-1894 [writer on music]
Thoinan, Ernest *Source(s):* BAKR; LOWN; NGDM; RIES

Rorem, Ned 1923- [composer, pianist, author]
America's Greatest Song Composer *Source(s):* http://www.newworld.org/release/october.html (29 Sept. 2003)

Rosa, Carlanonio de 1762-1847 [historian, writer on music]
Villarosa, Marchese de *Source(s):* NGDM; PRAT

Rosa, Noel 1910-1937 [composer]
Grandfather of Brazilian Popular Music *Source(s):* http://www.headsup.com/bios/lins.html (7 Oct. 2002)

Rosa, Salvator(e) 1615-1673 [painter, poet, musician]
Perditor Spina *Source(s):* NGDM
Salvatoriello *Source(s):* WORB

Rosa Suárez, Robert Edward 1970- [writer, composer, singer, poet]
Note(s): All names identified: http://www.usatoday.com/life/music/news/2004-03-22-rosa-on-the-verge_x.htm (5 Feb. 2005); additional sources listed as applicable.
Blake, Ian *Source(s):* HWOM; (See above)
Cornelius, Draco *Source(s):* (See above)
Dolores del Infante *Source(s):* HWOM
Draco, (Cornelius) *Source(s):* HWOM; (See above)
Infante, Dolores del *Source(s):* HOWM; (See above)
Rosa, Draco Cornelius *Source(s):* (See above)
Rosa, Robi (Draco) *Source(s):* HWOM; LCAR; (See above)

Roscoe, B. Jeanie 1932- [composer, teacher]
Groh, B. J. *Source(s):* ASCP

Rose, David D. 1910-1990 [orchestra leader, composer, pianist]
Note(s): Portrait: MUSR
Llewellyn, Ray *Source(s):* CLMJ; CLTP ("Highway Patrol" & "Sea Hunt")
Note(s): Also used by others; see NOTES: Llewellyn, Ray.
Wray, Havens *Source(s):* CLTP ("Bat Masterson"); CLTV

Rose, Eduard Emmerich 1902-1975 [composer]
Rosé, Alfred *Source(s):* BUL3

Rose, (Knols) Fred 1897-1954 [songwriter, singer, music publisher]
Dawson, Bart *Source(s):* MCCL; PSND
Jenkins, Floyd *Source(s):* CCE70 R479322; HORS; MCCL; PSND
Note(s): Also used by Roy (Claxton) Acuff.
Rambling Rogue *Source(s):* MCCL
Rose, Loren *Source(s):* CCE76
Song Doctor *Source(s):* http://www.angelfire.com/me2/kulacoco/rose.html (7 Oct. 2002)

Rose, George 1817 (or 18)-1882 [composer]
Sketchley, Arthur *Source(s):* KILG; LCAR

Rose, Karl August Nikolaus 1842-1889 [violinist, conductor, opera impressario]
Note(s): Portrait: ETUP 55:10 (Oct. 1937): 628
Rosa, Carl *Source(s):* BAKR; BALT; RIEM

Rose, Lewis Wolf 1887-1958 [playwright]
Rose, L. Arthur *Source(s):* GAN2

Rose, Pam [singer, songwriter]
Kennedy Rose *Source(s):* AMUS; EPMU
Note(s): Jt. pseud.: Mary Ann Kennedy.

Rose, Vincent 1880-1944 [composer, conductor, pianist]
Song Writers on Parade *Source(s):* CCE32 Eunp56182
Note(s): Jt. pseud.: Percy Wenrich, Sidney Clare, Charles Tobias, Al(bert) Sherman, (T.) Murray Mencher & Al(an) Lewis.

Rosenbaum, Hugo Waldemar 1903- [playwright, film producer]
Frank, Waldemar *Source(s):* PIPE

Rosenberg, George M. 1864-1936 [composer, arranger, publisher]
Note(s): Portrait: *Cadenza* (July 1902): 25
Rosey, George *Source(s):* CCE27 R45060; CPMU; JASR; LCAR; REHG

Rosenberg, Jerrold (Ross) 1926-1955 [composer, lyricist]
Ross, Jerry *Source(s):* CCE51; GAN1; GAN2; LCAR; PIPE; PSND

Rosenberg, Martin ?-1943 [composer, conductor]
Arguto, Rosebery d' *Source(s):* http://www.leonarda.com/compr.html (14 Mar. 2005)

Rosenberg, Wladimar [or Voldemar] 1910- [composer]
Berg-Wal *Source(s):* LCAR
Wal-Berg, (Voldemar) *Source(s):* CCE33 Efor31501; CCE58; LCAR; LCPC
Rosenberg, William Samuel 1899-1966 [lyricist, theater manager, composer]
Basement Barnum, The *Source(s):* PSND
Rose, Billy *Source(s):* EPMU; GAMM; GAN2; ROOM; VACH
Shorthand King of the World, The *Source(s):* PSNN
Rosenblatt, Ann 1908-1993 [librettist, music educator]
Ronell, Ann *Source(s):* STUW
Rosenblatt, Richard (Joel) 1942 (or 43)-2004 [songwriter]
Cordell, Ritchie *Source(s):* CCE63; CCE66-67; CPOL RE-770-464; DRSC; PMUS
Rose, Dick *Source(s):* CCE60
Rosendorff, Emil 1877- [composer, poet]
Emilchen, (R.) *Source(s):* WORB
Frodnesor, Limé *Source(s):* WORB
Linne, Emil *Source(s):* WORB
Nelsor, Fred *Source(s):* WORB
Rosen, E. *Source(s):* WORB
Rosen, Fred *Source(s):* WORB
Rosenfeld, Monroe H. 1861-1918 [composer, arranger, lyricist, journalist]
Note(s): Portraits: JAST; METR (Dec. 7, 1901): 63. Rosenfeld used pseudonyms & sometimes put novice composers' names on his own works to help them get started (JAST p. 16).
Allen, Harry *Source(s):* CCE38 R6559; NGAM
Belasco, F(rederick) *Source(s):* CCE12 R3304; FULD; GOLD; KILG; NGAM; SPTH p. 231
Heiser, F. [or E.] *Source(s):* GOLD; NGAM; SPTH p. 231
Man Who Named Tin Pan Alley, (The) *Source(s):* HARR; JAST
Monrose, Rose *Source(s):* CCE33 #4656, 348 R23091
Rosevelt, Monroe *Source(s):* GOLD
Rosie *Source(s):* (source not recorded)
Rosenfeld, Paul 1890-1946 [music critic]
Note(s): Portrait: GRAN
Huneker's Heirs *Source(s):* GRAN p. 284
Note(s): Jt. sobriquet: Carl Van Vechten.
Rosenfeld, S. 1844-1883 [librettist]
Fels, Roderich *Source(s):* LOWN; MELL; STGR; WORB
Rosenstein, Leo 1862-1920 [playwright, librettist]
Rechberg, Otto *Source(s):* STGR ("Die Lachtaube")
Note(s): Jt. pseud.: Leo Stein [i.e., Rosenstein] & Alexander Landesberg.
Stein, Leo *Source(s):* CCE54; GAN1; GAN2; LCAR; LOWN; PIPE; WORB
Note(s): Do not confuse with librettist/lyricist Leo Walther Stein (1866-1930).
Rosenstock, Sam(uel) 1896-1963 [author]
Tzara, Tristan *Source(s):* PIPE
Rosenthal, Carolyn (Paula) 1926-1981 (or 83) [lyricist]
Leigh, Carolyn *Source(s):* EWEN; GAN2; GRAT; PSND
Rosenthal, Emil von fl. 1883-90 [composer]
Rosé, Emil *Source(s):* MELL; STGR
Rosenthal, Mark (Mordecai) 1789-1948 [composer, violinist]
Rózsavölgyi, Mark *Source(s):* LCAR; LYMN
Rosenthan, Moriz 1862-1946 [pianist, composer]
Note(s): Portrait: ETUP 55:9 (Sept. 1937): 556
Little Giant of the Piano *Source(s):* BAKE
Rosenwald, Hans Hermann 1907-1973 [composer, educator]
Brady, Erwin *Source(s):* WORB
Rösler, Franz Anton c.1750-1792 [composer, double bassist]
Note(s): See LCAR for variant forms of name.
Rosetti, (Francesco) Antonio *Source(s):* BAKR; LCAR; NGDM
Rosmarin, Mathieu 1575 (or 76)-1647 [composer]
Capitán (Maestro) *Source(s):* GROL; LCAR; WORB
Maestro Capitán, El *Source(s):* BAKR; GROL; LCAR; NGDM, SADC
Romero, Mateo [or Matias] *Source(s):* BAKR; GROL; LCAR; NGDM; RIES; WORB
Rozi, Barnabé Farmian de *Source(s):* PIPE
Rosofsky, Isaac 1913-1976 [poet, broadcaster]
Nelson, Julio Jorge *Source(s):* TOGO
Rosquellas, Adolfo 1900-1964 [violinist, composer]
Pancho *Source(s):* PSND
Ross, Charles Isaiah 1925- [singer, instrumentalist, songwriter]
Flying Eagle, The *Source(s):* HARS
Ross, Doc(tor) *Source(s):* HARS
Ross, Lancelot P(atrick) 1906-1988 [composer, author, singer]
Matthews, Robert *Source(s):* CCE53
Ross, Ezry *Source(s):* CCE42 #15438 E103306
Ross, Lanny *Source(s):* ASCP; CCE61; LCAR
Ross, William G. 1881-1928 [composer]
Webster, Eric *Source(s):* CPMU
Rossana, Augustine S(amuel) 1932- [composer, author]
Asro, Gene *Source(s):* ASCP, CCE53-54
Azro, Gene *Source(s):* CCE55
Rossetti, Christina Georgina 1830-1894 [poet]
Alleyn, Ellen *Source(s):* GOTT; PSND

Rossi, G(iovanni) V(ittorio) 1577-1647 [writer on music]
 Erythraeus, J(anus) N(icius) *Source(s):* GROL; LCAR
Rossi, Luigi 1597 (or 98)-1653 [composer, librettist]
 Rubeis, Aloysius de *Source(s):* PIPE; WORB
 Rubens, Aloysius *Source(s):* MELL
 Rubeus, Aloysius *Source(s):* BAKE; WORB
Rossi, Michel Angelo 1601(or 02)-1656 [composer, violinist, organist]
 Michel Angelo del Violino *Source(s):* BAKR; LCAR; NGDM; PIPE; SADC
Rossi, Salomone 1570?-c.1630 [composer]
 Ebreo, (L') *Source(s):* BAKE; PSND
Rossignol, Félix Ludger 1839-1903 [critic, composer]
 Note(s): Portrait: ETUP 52:12 (Dec. 1934): 698
 Jennius *Source(s):* GRV3; PRAT
 Note(s): On critical writings
 Joncières, Victorin de *Source(s):* BAKR; LCAR; NGDM
Rossini, Gioachino Antonio 1792-1868 [composer]
 Lazy, The *Source(s):* SIFA
 Leading Bel Canto Composer *Source(s):* DESO-7
 Napoleon of Music, The *Source(s):* DEAR
 Schwan von Pesaro, Der *Source(s):* PSND
 Signor Crescendo *Source(s):* DEAR
 Swan of Pesaro, The *Source(s):* PSND; SPIE
Rossiter, Will 1867-1954 [songwriter, music publisher]
 Note(s): Portraits: JASA; JAST
 Beresford, Henry Wayne *Source(s):* CCE45 #35888, 31 R139482
 Chicago Publisher, The *Source(s):* JASA p. 113
 Thompson, Kathryne E. *Source(s):* CCE52 R90301 ("Waiting For You")
 Williams, Cleve *Source(s):* SHAP; http://americanhistory.si.edu/archives/d5300jbi.htm (8 Feb. 2005)
 Williams, W. R. *Source(s):* GROL; MARC p. 398; LCAR; NGDM; SPTH p. 266
Rössler, Carl 1864-1948 [singer, playwright]
 Ressner, Carl *Source(s):* PIPE
Rosso, Celeste 1926-1994 [trumpet, composer]
 Rosso, Nini *Source(s):* EPMU
Rossow, Helene von 1935-2000 [poet, writer, composer]
 Hrostwitha *Source(s):* COHN; HIXN
 Rostwitha *Source(s):* COHN; HIXN
Rostaing, Hubert 1918-1990 [clarinetist, bandleader, composer]
 Jospin, Hubert *Source(s):* LCAR
 Kalamazoo, Joe *Source(s):* JAMU
 Scott, Sonny *Source(s):* JAMU
Roth, Albert [composer]
 Byn *Source(s):* MELL; STGR
Roth, Ernst 1896-1971 [arranger, music publisher, author]
 Thorne, E. *Source(s):* CCE53-56; CCE58-59; CPOL RE-23-236; LCAR
 Note(s): Also used by Marie E. Merrick, and do not confuse with "Edgar Thorn(e)," used by Edward MacDowell.
Róthkrepf, Gábor 1797-1875 [composer, teacher]
 Mátray, Gábor *Source(s):* BAKR; LCAR
Rothmüller, Aron Marko 1908-1993 [singer, composer, writer]
 Kinor, Jehuda *Source(s):* LCAR; LYMN
Rothschild, (Baron) Henri de 1872-1947 [author]
 Fontaines, Charles de *Source(s):* WORB
 Maugars, R(ene?) *Source(s):* NGDM; STGR
 Note(s): In NGDM see under: Massenet, Jules, list of works: "Espada."
 Pascal, André *Source(s):* LCAR
Rothstein, Andy [guitarist, arranger]
 Robyns, Andy *Source(s):* http://www.guitar9.com/undiscov/8e.html (7 Oct. 2002)
Rothstein, James (Jakob) 1871- [composer]
 Pinozzi, Carlo *Source(s):* GREN; WORB
Rottenstein, Wilhelm 1883-1949 [composer, conductor]
 Redstone, Willie *Source(s):* CCE48 R34916 ("Duo de l'education incomplete"); GAN1; GAN2
Rottensteiner, Josef 1858-1925 [author, singer, librettist]
 Armin, Josef *Source(s):* OMUO
Rotter, Fritz 1900- [poet, composer]
 Günther, Friedrich *Source(s):* CCE59; CCE62; LCPC letter cited (21 Jan. 1933)
 Rotha, M. *Source(s):* CCE54-55; PMUS
 Schott, Ernst *Source(s):* CCE34 Efor33063; CCE61
 Shott, Ernst *Source(s):* CCE61
Rottmann, Eduard 1809-1843 [organist, composer]
 Rabensteiner, Eduard *Source(s):* KOMU
Rottschalk, Gregor 1945- [composer]
 Heilburg, Christian *Source(s):* CCE72; CCE77; CPOL RE-823-513; PFSA
Roucoux, (Paul) Urbain 1845-1901 [playwright, singer, songwriter]
 Burani, Paul *Source(s):* GAN1; GAN2; LCAR; LOWN; MELL
Rouget de Lisle, Claude Joseph 1760-1836 [military officer, author]
 Note(s): Portrait: ETUP 50:11 (Nov. 1932): 762. See LCAR for variant spellings of name.
 Father of the Marseillaise, The *Source(s):* PSND; SIFA
 Hix, Auguste *Source(s):* PIPE
 Tyrtaeus of France, The *Source(s):* PSND
Rourke, M(ichael) E(lder) 1867-1933 [songwriter]
 Reynolds, Herbert *Source(s):* LCAR; PARS
 Verona, Gypsy Countess *Source(s):* CCE26 E652319; CCE44 #14418, 387 R122949

Rous, Samuel Holland c.1865-1947 [singer, author]
Dudley, S. H. *Source(s):* MACE p. 218
Rousseau, Louise-Geneviève 1810-1838 [pianist, organist, composer]
La Hye, Louise-Geneviève de *Source(s):* GROL
Saint-Amans, M. Lèon *fils* *Source(s):* COHN; GROL; HEIN; HIXN
Rousseau, Marcel(-Auguste-Louis) 1882-1955 [composer]
Samuel-Rousseau, Marcel *Source(s):* BAKE; LCAR
Note(s): Added his father's given name to his surname.
Rousseau, Pierre 1889-1939 [composer]
Vellones, (Pierre) *Source(s):* CCE57-60; LCAR; RIES; WORB
Rousseau, Pierre-Joseph 1797-1849 [playwright]
Jaime, E. *Source(s):* PIPE
Note(s): Jt. pseud.: Jules Seveste.
James, Maxime *Source(s):* PIPE
Rousseau, James *Source(s):* LCAR; PIPE
Roussel, Henri c.1840?- [journalist, writer, author]
Corbulon *Source(s):* IBIM; WORB
Erville, Henri d' *Source(s):* IBIM; WORB
Vindex *Source(s):* IBIM; WORB
Routhier, (Sir) Adolphe-Basile 1839-1920 [lawyer, poet, lyricist]
Piquefort, Jean *Source(s):* http://members .tripol.com/saontario/id59.htm (19 Mar. 2005)
Rowe, William [or M. C.] [composer]
Arthurs, William *Source(s):* JASA p. 321
Rowland, Edward 1882-1955 [songwriter]
Rowland, Red *Source(s):* KILG
Rowlands, Abraham Cecil Francis Fothergill 1856-1914 [librettist, playwright]
Raleigh, Cecil *Source(s):* GAN1; GAN2; WORB
Rowlands, Fog *Source(s):* GAN2
Rowlands, William Penfro 1860-1937 [hymnist]
Pembroke *Source(s):* CYBH
Penfro *Source(s):* CYBH
Rowley, Alec 1892-1958 [composer]
Arnold, Stanley *Source(s):* CCE58; CCE73 R556491
Humbert, G(eorge) Frank *Source(s):* CCE62; CCE64; CCE67
Wade , Stuart *Source(s):* CCE48-49; CCE53-54; LCAR
Roy Diaz, Gustavo [rapper, songwriter]
Big Boy *Source(s):* HWOM; LCAR
Note(s): Also used by Arthur Crudup & Richard Henry.
Royce, James (Stanley) 1881-1946 [actor, lyricist, composer]
Nonnahs, Laurence B. *Source(s):* JASA p. 322
Shannon, J(ames) R(oyce) *Source(s):* CPOL PA-0179-435; MRSQ 4:4 p. 7; PARS; STUW
Shannon, James Stanley *Source(s):* CCE42 #29091, 479 R107517; JASA
Note(s): In JASA original name listed as James R(oyce) Shannon.
Sterling, James *Source(s):* CCE42 #24219, 1032 R107400
Sterling, Jane *Source(s):* CCE42 #24219, 276 R107399 & #24219, 1032 R107400
Sterling, Jayne *Source(s):* CCE41 #30320, 533 R95993
Waiman *Source(s):* JASA p. 322
Royer de Villerie, (Chevalier) [composer]
R****, de (Chevalier) *Source(s):* CPMU (publication date 1795?)
Royer, Robb [songwriter]
Wilson, Rob *Source(s):* PSND
Rózsa, Miklós 1907-1975 [composer]
Tomay, Nic *Source(s):* http://www.bbc.co .uk/music/profiles/roza.html (May 17 2005)
Ruault, Edouard 1921-2005 [conductor, composer, pianist]
Barclay, Eddie *Source(s):* CCE53 Efor21261; LCAR; MUSR; PSNN; WASH
Rubbra, Edmund 1901-1986 [composer]
Bruckner of the 20th Century *Source(s):* http://www.classical-composers.org/ cgi-bin/ccd.cgi?comp=rubbra (13 Apr. 2005)
Rubel, Henry Scott 1898- [clergyman, songwriter]
Raynor, Hal *Source(s):* CCE38 Eunp181064; PSND
Rubert, Johann Martin 1614 (or 15)-1680 [composer, organist]
J. M. R. *Source(s):* GROL (In Stieler's *Die gehamschte Venus* (1660))
Ruberti, Giovanni Battista [librettist]
Gnapeta *Source(s):* ALMC
Rubeus, Petrus 1374-1438 [composer, theorist]
Pietro de Rossi *Source(s):* NGDM
Rossi, Pietro de *Source(s):* WORB
Rubin, Alton (Jay) 1932-1993 [accordionist, composer]
King of Zydeco *Source(s):* EPMU; LCAR
Note(s): See also Clifton Chenier.
Rockin' Dopsie *Source(s):* EPMU
Rubin [or Ruben], Lynsey 1951- [composer, singer]
De Paul, Lynsey *Source(s):* HARR; PEN2; PSND
Rubin, Michael Stewart 1924 (or 29)-1987 [composer, lyricist]
Stewart, Michael *Source(s):* GAN1; GAN2; LCAR; ROOM
Rubini, Giovanni Battista 1795-1854 [singer, songwriter]
King of Tenors *Source(s):* PRAT
Rubinstein, Harold 1895-1974 [composer, lyricist, pianist, publisher, screenwriter]
Note(s): Portraits: EWEN; EWPA
Ruby, Harry *Source(s):* EPMU; EWEN; EWPA; GAMM; GAN1; GAN2; ROOM
Rubio (de Uscatescu), Consuelo 1927-1981 [singer, songwriter]
Chelo *Source(s):* AMUS; HWOM

Rubistein, Oscar 1914-1984 [poet, composer]
Rubens, Oscar *Source(s):* TODO
Rübner, (Peter Martin) Cornelius 1855-1929 [composer]
Note(s): Portrait: ETUP 55:10 (Oct. 1937): 628
Rybner, (Peter Martin) Cornelius *Source(s):* BAKR; LCAR; REHG
Ruck, Hermann 1897-1983 [composer]
Geyer, Hermann *Source(s):* KOBW
Rückert, Johann Michel Friedrich 1788-1866 [poet]
Raimer, Freymund *Source(s):* PIPE; WORB
Voran der Geharnischte *Source(s):* APPL p. 12
Ruderman, Seymour George 1926- [author, editor, lyricist]
Ruderman, Rudy *Source(s):* ASCC
Rudolph, Johann Joseph 1730-1812 [horn player, violinist, composer]
Rodolphe, Jean Joseph *Source(s):* BAKO; LCAR
Rudolz, Hartwig 1955- [choreographer]
Rudolz, Hardy *Source(s):* GAN2
Rueger, Christoph 1942- [composer]
Cranmer, Clemens *Source(s):* KOMP; KOMS; PFSA
Ruff, Walter F(riedrich) 1922- [composer]
Moro, G(uy) *Source(s):* CCE60-63; KOMP; KOMS; PFSA
Ruffini, Agostino 1812-1855 [author]
Carafa, Ettore *Source:* PIPE
Ruffini, Giovanni [or Giacomo] (Domenico) 1807-1881 [librettist]
Accursi, Michele *Source(s):* LCAR; LOWN; MELL
Camerano *Source(s):* LCAR
M. A. *Source(s):* LCAR
Rüger, Karl Erdmann 1783 (or 86)-1827 [singer, playwright]
Beckmann *Source(s):* PIPE
Ruggieri, Edmond (Anthony) 1907-1964 [composer, author, conductor]
Rogers, Eddy *Source(s):* ASCP; CCE54-56; CCE63
Ruggles, Charles Sprague 1876-1971 [composer]
Note(s): Portrait: ETUP 55:10 (Oct. 1937): 628
Ruggles, Carl *Source(s):* BAKT; NGDM
Ruh, Emil 1884-1946 [composer]
Bucher, A. *Source(s):* REHG; SUPN
Ruiz Alonso, Felipe 1896-1973 [composer, arranger]
Partichela, F. A. *Source(s):* Garrido, Juan S. *Historia de la Musica Popular en Mexico.* Editorial Extemporaneos, 1974, 46.
Ruiz Narváez, José Napoleón 1948- [singer, songwriter, actor]
Napoleón, Jose Maria *Source(s):* HWOM
Poeta de la cancione, El *Source(s):* HWOM
Rule, William Harris 1802-1890 [hymnist]
W. H. R. *Source(s):* HAMT
Note(s): In: *The Wesleyan Methodist Sunday Hymn-Book* (1851).
Rummel, Joseph 1818-1880 [pianist, clarinetist, composer]
Note(s): GRV3: Used pseuds; none identified.
Rummel, Walter Morse 1887-1953 [composer, pianist]
Note(s): Portrait: ETUP 55:10 (Oct. 1937): 628
Kelley, Fred *Source(s):* CPMU
Rumpel, Franz 1858-1935 [composer, conductor]
Waldegg, Franz *Source(s):* PIPE
Rumshinsky, Murray 1907-1998 [composer, author, conductor]
Rumsey, Murray *Source(s):* ASCP; CPOL PAu-585-571
Rusch, Harold (W(endel)) 1908-1997 [composer, author, arranger]
Reese, Wendel *Source(s):* ASCP; CCE61; REHG; SUPN
Wendel, James *Source(s):* CCE55
Rusch, Jerome Anthony 1943- [composer, author, trumpeter]
Rush, Jerry *Source(s):* ASCP
Ruse, Robert Louis 1919-1997 [composer, author]
Lewis, Bob *Source(s):* ASCP; CCE64
Note(s): "Men in Blue," "Through the Mists," & "Wiedersehen." Probably not Bob Lewis, composer of "My Little Woman" & "Will I Ever?"
Roberts, Lou *Source(s):* ASCP; CCE64
Rush, Otis 1934 (or 35)- [instrumentalist, songwriter]
Chicago Blues King *Source(s):* http://www.jwblues.com/OtisRush/OtisRush.htm (2 Feb. 2004)
Little Otis *Source(s):* HARS; http://bluesexpress.com/records/br_rushbio.html (2 Feb. 2004)
Rushing, James [or Jimmy] (Andrew) 1903-1972 [singer, songwriter]
Honey Bunny Boo *Source(s):* PSND
Mr. Five by Five *Source(s):* AMEN; AMUS; HARS
Ruslander, Mark 1932- [pianist, composer, political satirist]
Russell, Mark *Source(s):* CM06
Russell, Charles Ellsworth 1906-1969 [composer, clarinetist]
Russell, Pee Wee *Source(s):* AMUS; ASCP; VACH
Russell, George William 1867-1935 [hymnist, poet, journalist]
A. E. *Source(s):* DIEH; GOTL; LCAR
Russell, John(ny Bright) 1940- [singer, songwriter, guitarist]
Biggest Act in Country Music, The *Source(s):* MCCL

Russell, (Robert C.) Kennedy 1883-1954 [songwriter, conductor]
Hope, Barbara Melville *Source(s):* CCE51 R82607 ("A Caution"); CCE62
Paul, Roddie *Source(s):* CCE70 R488662
Ravini, E. *Source(s):* BLIC
Russell, Landon Ronald 1873-1938 [composer, pianist, conductor]
Note(s): Portrait: ETUP 55:9 (Sept. 1937): 566
Ronald, (Sir) Landon *Source(s):* BAKO; BAKR; MACM; MELL; REHG
Russell, (Lady) Rachel Evelyn ?-1898 [writer]
Evelyn *Source(s):* CPMU
Russell, Robert [DJ, lyricist, singer]
Brigadier Jerry *Source(s):* AMUS; EPMU; LCAR
Russell, S(idney) K(eith) 1914-1970 [composer, lyricist]
Note(s): Do not confuse with earlier songwriter Sydney King Russell.
Russell, Bob *Source(s):* ASCP; EPMU; KINK; LCAR; STUW; VACH
Note(s): Do not confuse Sydney King Russell, earlier songwriter or with later Nashville born Bobby Russell (STUW).
Russian, Irving 1911- [composer, pianist]
Russian, Babe *Source(s):* ASCP
Rüssmann, Georg(e) 1919-1986 [composer]
Barny, W(al) *Source(s):* CCE59; CCE61; KOMP; PFSA
Berkhaan, Otto *Source(s):* KOMP; PFSA
Caribez, Carlos *Source(s):* KOMP; PFSA
Hames, May *Source(s):* KOMP; PFSA
Ruthenberg, Jane Catherine [composer, author, teacher]
Martini, Catherine *Source(s):* ASCP
Rutherford, Dean 1955- [singer, songwriter]
Dillon, Dean *Source(s):* PEN2
Ruvin, Ralph [songwriter]
Ross, David *Source(s):* CCE59; CPOL RE-344-757
Note(s): Jt. peud.: Robert [or Bob] Halfin & Harold Irving [i.e., Shaberman]
Ryan, Robert Francis 1930- [composer, author]
Ryan, Rocket *Source(s):* ASCP
Ryba, Jakub [or Jakob] (Simon) Jan [or Johann] 1765-1815 [teacher, composer, writer on music]
Peace, Jakub Jan *Source(s):* NGDM
Poisson, Jakub Jan *Source(s):* NGDM
Ryballandni, Jakub Jan *Source(s):* NGDM
Rybaville, Jakub Jan *Source(s):* NGDM
Ryche, Anthonius (de) c.1470-between 1515 & 1534 [composer]
Divitis, Antonius *Source(s):* LCAR; NGDM
Le Riche, Anthoine *Source(s):* IBIM; LCAR; MACM; NGDM
Riche, Anthoine Le *Source(s):* LCAR; NGDM
Rydberg, Sam Hjalmar 1885-1956 [composer]
March King of Sweden *Source(s):* SMIN
Ryder, Mary E. 1924- [composer, author]
Candy, Mary *Source(s):* ASCP
Stiebler, Mary *Source(s):* ASCP
Rye, Sven 1926-2004 [songwriter]
Brown, Buster B. *Source(s):* ASCP
Ryglewicz, Edward [songwriter]
Riggs, Edward *Source(s):* CPOL RE-299-473
Note(s): Jt. pseud.: Walter (Charles) Ehret.
Ryskind, Morrie 1895-1985 [playwright, author, screenwriter]
Wintergreen, John P. *Source(s):* PIPE; PSNDf

– S –

Saalfield, Richard A. before 1865-after1890 [translator]
Fennimore, Robert *Source(s):* PIPE
Saalmüller, F(riedrich) 1802-1867 [journalist, poet]
Albano *Source(s):* LCAR
Rousseau, Johann Baptist *Source(s):* LCAR; PIPE
Sabatini, Enrico 1894-1961 [composer]
Remo, Nicola *Source(s):* REHH
Sabina, Karel 1813-1877 [author, journalist, librettist]
Blass, Leo(n) *Source(s):* OEAW; PIPE
Sabinský, (?Karel) *Source(s):* OEAW; PIPE
Vrána, Vojtěch *Source(s):* OEAW; PIPE
Želinský, Arian *Source(s):* OEAW
Sacchetti, Carl Salvatore 1915- [composer, author]
Setty, Carl *Source(s):* ASCP; CCE41 #33627 Eunp266720; CCE68
Sacchini, Antonio Marie Gaspare 1730-1786 [composer]
Racine of Music, The *Source(s):* PSND
Sacco, Anthony 1908-1984 [composer, author, singer]
Santos, Tony *Source(s):* ASCP
Starr, Tony *Source(s):* ASCP
Sacco, L(ugee) [or Lou(is)] (Alfredo Giovanni) 1943- [singer, songwriter]
Christie, Lou *Source(s):* CCE63; CCE65-68; LCAR; PMUS; PSND
Saddler, Joseph 1958- [rapper]
Grandmaster Flash *Source(s):* EPMU; LCAR
Sadler, Haskell Robert 1935-1994 [singer, guitarist, songwriter]
Cool Papa *Source(s):* HARS
Sadler, Cool Papa *Source(s):* LCAR
Saenger, Gustav(e) 1865-1935 [arranger, editor, composer]
Note(s): Portraits: ETUP 55:11 (Nov. 1937): 700; METR 13:11 (Nov. 1897): cover

Ambrosio, W. F. *Source(s):* CCE29 E7372; GOTH; LCAR
Note(s): C. Fisher house name; see NOTES: Ambrosio, W. F.
Beaumont, Paul *Source(s):* CCE33 R24331 ("Slumber Sweetly")
Note(s): Also used by Edward Sydney Smith.
Berton, Roland de *Source(s):* CCE33 R24039 ("Mocking Bird, op. 30 #11")
Centano, Jules *Source(s):* CCE45 #35888 R139927 ("Dance of the Hours")
DeBerton, R. *Source(s):* CCE31 E20238
Franklin, Howard *Source(s):* CCE32 E30176
Giddings, Clarice *Source(s):* CCE29 E4010
Gilmore, Joyce *Source(s):* CCE32 E33131
Graham, Eleanor *Source(s):* CCE32 E27785
Hervey, George *Source(s):* CCE33 E34199
Hill, Julie F. *Source(s):* CCE33 E34203
Holton, Albert *Source(s):* CCE33 E34200
Hunter, James *Source(s):* CCE32 E30512
Note(s): Also used by Arthur Fields [i.e., Abe Finkelstein]
Parker, Albert *Source(s):* CCE32 E30513
Phillips, Kenneth *Source(s):* CCE33 E35285
Preston, Stanley *Source(s):* CCE32 E30183
Richards, Frank *Source(s):* CCE32 E33132
Thornton, Frank *Source(s):* CCE21 E519877

Saeverud, Ketil 1939- [composer, organist, violinist]
Champion of Intuition, The *Source(s):* Reitan, L. "Ketil Hvoslef; The Champion of Intuition." *Nordic Sounds* (Sept. 1985)
Hvoslef, Ketil *Source(s):* BAKO; BAKT; LCAR

Safe, James W. [composer]
J. W. S... *Source(s):* CPMU (publication date 1851)

Safka, Melanie 1947- [singer, songwriter]
Melanie *Source(s):* CCE68; CM12; DIMA; EPMU; RECR; ROOM

Safonov, Vasily Ilich 1852-1918 [conductor, pianist, teacher, author]
Eagle of the Caucasus, The *Source(s):* GROL

Safránek, Miloš 1894-after 1935 [writer on music]
Expromptus *Source(s):* PIPE

Saidy, Fareed Milhelm 1907-1982 [journalist, librettist, author of revues]
Saidy, Fred *Source(s):* GAN1; GAN2; LCAR

St. Clair, Floyd J. 1871-1942 [composer]
Floyd, S. J. *Source(s):* REHG; SUPN
Lamont, Victor *Source(s):* CCE42 #21336 E102792 ("Love in the Moonlight")
Note(s): Also used by Victor (E.) Maiorana.
Lauver, (David) *Source(s):* CCE49; CCE57
Monroe *Source(s):* CCE57
Page *Source(s):* CCE57
Stewart *Source(s):* CCE57

St. Edmunds, John [composer]
Note(s): Could not verify as John St. Edmunds (1913-1986).
Challis, Roger *Source(s):* TPRF

St. Edmunds, John 1913-1986 [composer]
Edmunds, John *Source(s):* GROL

St. George, C. [composer]
Amateur *Source(s):* CPMU (publication date 1820)

Saint Germain, Count of ?-1784 (or 86) [courtier, composer, violinist]
Note(s): True identity not known? (See NGDM) Do not confuse with Claude Louis de Saint Germain or Robert-Francois Quesnay de Saint Germain.
Bellamare, Count *Source(s):* GROL; LCAR; NGDM
Giovanni *Source(s):* MACM; NGDM
Note(s): See NGDM or LCAR for explanation.
Ragotzy, Prince *Source(s):* GROL; LCAR; NGDM
Surmont, Count *Source(s):* GROL; LCAR; NGDM
Welldone, Count *Source(s):* GROL; LCAR; NGDM
Wundermann, Der *Source(s):* DEA3

St. Hilary, Bishop of Portiers ?-368 [hymnist]
Father of Christian Hymnology, The *Source(s):* http://www.concerthall.ca/history.html (7 Oct. 2002)
Note(s): See also Ambrosius of Milan.

Saint-Saëns, (Charles) Camille 1835-1921 [composer, pianist]
French Beethoven, The *Source(s):* http://www.gdyo.org/notes51803.htm (12 Apr. 2005)
Note(s): See also George Onslow.
French Mendelssohn, The *Source(s):* http://inkpot.com/classical/stsaensvc.html (12 Apr. 2005)
Phémius *Source(s):* PIPE; RIEM
Sannois, Charles *Source(s):* PIPE

Saint-Sévin, Joseph Barnabé 1727-1803 [composer, violinist]
Abbé, Joseph, L' *Source(s):* LCAR
Abbé, le fils, L' *Source(s):* LCAR
L'Abbé, Joseph *Source(s):* LCAR
L'Abbé, le fils *Source(s):* CPMU; GREN; LCAR; NGDM

Sainte-Beuve, Charles Augustin 1804-1869 [author]
Note(s): See PSND for nonmusic-related pseudonymns & sobriquets.
Delorme, Joseph *Source(s):* LCAR; PIPE; PSND

Sainte-Marie, Beverly 1941- [singer, composer, guitarist]
Sainte-Marie, Buffy *Source(s):* CCE65; FAFO; LCAR; WORL

Sakamaki, Ben 1921-1995 [composer, author, pianist]

Saks, Benny *Source(s):* ASCP; CCE58-59; CCE61
Saldana, Douglas 1941- [singer, songwriter, guitarist]
Doug, Sir *Source(s):* LCAR
Douglas, Sir *Source(s):* LCAR
Little Doug *Source(s):* MCCL
Sahm, Doug *Source(s):* HARR; LCAR; MCCL; PEN2
Salgado (Mejía), Fabio 1967- [singer, songwriter, guitarist]
Estéfano *Source(s):* CPOL PA-980-782; HWOM
Salieri, Antonio 1750-1825 [composer]
Don Tarar di Palmira *Source(s):* APPL p. 12
Palmira, Don Tarar di *Source(s):* APPL p. 12
Salio, Giuseppe ?-1737 [poet, librettist]
Edesimo, Evandro *Source(s):* ALCM p. 877
Sallmon, Alfred 1928- [composer]
Nomlas *Source(s):* KOMP; PFSA
Sallot, Louis [librettist]
Leloir, Louis *Source(s):* LOWN
Salomon, Jules Auguste 1830-1896 [violinist, conductor, composer]
Garcin, Jules Auguste *Source(s):* LCAR
Salomon, Karel 1897-1974 [composer]
Casal *Source(s):* KOBW
Salonen, Esa-Pekka 1958- [conductor, composer]
Great White Hope, The *Source(s):* CM16
LA's Fair-Haired Finn *Source(s):* CM16
Maestro of Change, The *Source(s):* CM16
Salsbury, Hubert Ivan 1938- [composer]
Salsbury, Sonny *Source(s):* ASCP; CPOL PA-23-053
Salsbury, Ron(ald Foster) 1950- [composer, author, singer]
Pantano-Salsbury *Source(s):* ASCP; LCAR
Note(s): Jt. pseud.: John Pantano.
Saltenburg, Heinz 1882-1948 [theatrical producer, director]
Florido *Source(s):* PIPE
Salter, G. H. [composer]
G. H. S. *Source(s):* CPMU (publication date 1925)
Salter, Hans J. 1896-1994 [composer]
King of Horror Film Music *Source(s): VideoHound's Soundtracks*. Detroit: Visible Ink, 733.
Salter, Harry *Source(s):* CLTP ("Arrow Show")
Salustri, Carlo Albert 1873-1950 [composer, critic]
Trilussa *Source(s):* GREN; LCAR; WORB
Saluzzi, Timoteo 1935- [folk musician, composer]
Saluzzi, Dino *Source(s):* EPMU; LCAR
Salvayre, Gervais-Bernard 1847-1916 [composer]
Note(s): Portrait: ETUP 55:11 (Nov. 1937): 700
Salvayre, Gaston *Source(s):* BAKR; GOTH
Salvioli, Giovanni 1814-1893 [writer on music]
Galvani, L(ivio) N(iso) *Source(s):* GROL
Lianovosani, Luigi *Source(s):* LOWN
Salviuolo, Joseph Anthony 1940- [composer, author]
Joseph, Sal *Source(s):* ASCP; CPOL RE-84-345
Salz, Herschel mentioned 1938 [stage director, author]
Saltenburg, Felix *Source(s):* PIPE; WORB
Salzmann, Siegmund 1869-1945 [novelist, playwright, librettist, theater critic]
Finder, Martin *Source(s):* CA137; PIPE
Mutzenbacher, Josefine *Source(s):* LCAR; STGR
Salten, Felix *Source(s):* CA137; LCAR; PIPE; STGR
Stol(l)berg, Ferdinand *Source(s):* LOWN; PIPE; STGR
Samberg, Benjamin 1906-1999 [songwriter]
Bell *Source(s):* CPOL PA-11-311
Bell, Benny *Source(s):* BLUE; CCE46 Eunp; CCE72 R542053; PMUS
Berg, Sam *Source(s):* CPOL TX-241-519
Bimbo, Benny *Source(s):* BLUE
Hobo Sam *Source(s):* CCE37 Eunp148165
Leib, Bell *Source(s):* PMUS
Note(s): Jt. pseud.: Mitchell Parrish [i.e., Joseph Leib]
Singing Turtle, The *Source(s):* CCE46 Eunp; CCE63 D5236 ("The Turtle Song")
Wynn, Paul *Source(s):* BLUE
Note(s): Also used by Phil Winston.
Young, Bobby *Source(s):* CCE37 Eunp148167
Sammartini, Giovanni Battista 1700 (or 01)-1775 [composer]
Milanese, Il *Source(s):* PSND
Sammartini, Giuseppe (Francesco Gaspare Melchiorre Baldassare) 1695-1750 [composer]
Londinese, Il *Source(s):* BAKR
Sampson, James 1930- [composer, teacher]
Samon, Grico *Source(s):* ASCP; CCE66
Samson, Louis mentioned 1875 [composer, conductor]
Trifolium *Source(s):* CPMU
Note(s): Jt. pseud.: Carli [or Karl] Zoeller & J. Kornfeld.
Samuda, Arthur J. D'Aguilar [composer]
A. DA S. *Source(s):* CPMU (publication date 1868)
Samudio, Domingo 1940?- [songwriter]
Sam the Sham *Source(s):* CCE67; EPMU; LCAR; PSND
Samudio, Sam *Source(s):* EPMU
Samuel, Sara [composer]
Leumas, Sara *Source(s):* CPMU (publication dates 1871-72); GOTE; OCLC 47897285
Samuel, Sealhenry (Olumide) 1963- [singer, songwriter]
Samuel, Henry *Source(s):* HARR; LCAR; SONG

Seal *Source(s):* CM14; HARR; LCAR; PEN2; PMUS-96; RECR; SONG
Note(s): See also Bernard Young.
Samuels, Jerry 1938- [songwriter, performer, recording engineer]
David, Scott *Source(s):* CCE61; PMUS; PSND; WARN
Napoleon XIV *Source(s):* EPMU; LCAR; PSND; SONG; WARN
Sims, Jerry *Source(s):* CCE59
Samuels, Milton (Isadore) 1904-1990 [composer, author]
Ross, Edward *Source(s):* ASCP; CCE42 #51294 E110373; CCE70 R476274
Ross, Mark *Source(s):* CCE53 Eunp
Spector, Jack *Source(s):* CCE61
Spector, Jay *Source(s):* CCE51
Winsten, Mark *Source(s):* CCE42 #21588 E104046
Samuelson, Julian 1878-1934 [director, producer]
Wylie, Julian *Source(s):* GAN1; GAN2
Samuelson, Morris Laurence 1880- [author, librettist]
Wylie, Lauri *Source(s):* GAN1; GAN2; PSND
San José (Sanchez), Victor Manuel 1947- [singer, songwriter]
Victor Manuel *Source(s):* HWOM
Sánchez(-Ramírez), Carlos Alberto 1971- [singer, songwriter]
Zaa, Charlie *Source(s):* HWOM
Sánchez Luna, Alfredo 1930 (or 31)-1989 [singer, songwriter]
Sadel, Alfredo *Source(s):* HWOM
Sánchez Pizarro, Alejandro 1968- [singer, songwriter, guitarist]
Sanz, Alejandro *Source(s):* HWOM; LCAR
Sánchez Pohl, Lorenzo Antonio 1969- [singer, songwriter]
Lorenzo Antonio *Source(s):* HWOM
Sanchez Saldano [or Saldana], José (del) Refugio 1921-2000 [singer, songwriter, actor]
Sanchez, Cuco *Source(s):* HWOM; OB00
Sanchez, Refugio *Source(s):* HWOM
Sancho, Ignatius 1728 (or 29)-1780 [composer]
African, An *Source(s):* GOTH
Note(s): Possible pseud.
Sandberg, Martin [songwriter, performer]
Martin(-Kilcher), Max *Source(s):* LCAR; PMUS-00
Sandell(-Berg), Karolina [or Carolina] Wilhelmina 1831 (or 32)-1903 [hymnist]
Note(s): Portrait: CYBH
Fanny Crosby of Sweden *Source(s):* YOUN
S. L. *Source(s):* CYBH
Sandell, Lina *Source(s):* YOUN
Sanders, Joseph [or Joe] (L.) 1896-1965 [pianist, composer, singer, conductor]
Old Left-Hander, The *Source(s):* KINK; VACH
Sanders, William fl. 1838-81 [minister, hymnist]
W. S. *Source(s):* JULN (Appendix)
Note(s): Collaborated with H(ugh) B(ourne).
Sanders, William (Nelson) 1939- [songwriter]
Sanders, Sonny *Source(s):* AMUS; CCE62; PMUS
Sandler, Peretz c.1853-1931 [songwriter]
Sandler, Peter *Source(s):* HESK
Sandys, William 1792-1874 [writer on music]
Sylvestre, Joshua *Source(s):* LCAR
Note(s): Jt. pseud.: William Henry Husk.
Sanguinazzo, Nicolo [composer]
Ozzaniugnas, Olocin *Source(s):* DEAR
Sankey, Ira David 1840-1908 [composer, hymnist]
Note(s): Portraits: CYBH; HALL. Do not confuse with his son, Ira Allan Sankey (1872-1915).
Dykes, Rian A. *Source(s):* CCE21 R19144
Dykes, Ryan A. *Source(s):* CCE24; RUFF p. 96
Edwards, J. E. *Source(s):* CCE20 E9510
Horton, R. D. *Source(s):* CCE20 E9500
Jones, R. Donald *Source(s):* CCE21 R18010; LCPC letter cited
Lower, Harry S. *Source(s):* CCE21 R19109
Santa Croce, Francesco c.1487-?1556 [composer, singer, priest]
Patavino, Francesco *Source(s):* NGDM
Santamaria (Rodríguez), Ramón 1922-2003 [percussionist, bandleader, composer]
Godfather of Latin Soul *Source(s):* http://www.rhino.com/features/75689p.html (7 Oct. 2002)
Santamaria, Mongo *Source(s):* EPMU; HWOM; LCAR; PEN2; PSND
Santander, Lora Flavio 1960- [composer, instrumentalist, producer]
Santander, Kike *Source(s):* HWOM
Santeul, Claude de 1628-1684 [hymnist]
Santolius Maglorianus *Source(s):* HATF
Santeu(i)l, Jean Baptiste de 1630-1697 [poet, hymnist]
Note(s): See LCAR for additional variant forms of name.
Santolius Victorinus *Source(s):* CYBH; HATF;LCAR
Victorinus Santolius *Source(s):* CYBH; LCAR
Santley, (Sir) Charles 1834-1922 [singer, composer, writer on music]
Note(s): Portrait: GRV3 v. 5
Betterton, Ralph *Source(s):* BAKO; CPMU; GROL; PRAT
Santly, Joseph H. 1886-1962 [performer, songwriter]
Note(s): Do not confuse with Joseph Santley, actor/author (1890-1971).
Santly, Banjo *Source(s):* PSND

Santoro, Paul 1915- [composer, author]
Sanders, Paul *Source(s):* ASCP
Sanviale, Jacopo Antonio 1699-1780 [writer]
Eaco Panellenio *Source(s):* SONN
Panellenio, Eaco *Source(s):* SONN
Sapelli, Luigi 1867-1936 [journalist, stage designer]
Caramba *Source(s):* LCAR; NGDO
Sapp, Allen (Dwight) 1922-1999 [composer]
Fundless, Hezekiah *Source(s):* Green, Alan. *Allen Sapp; A Bio-Bibliography.* Westport, Conn.: Greenwood Press, 1996, p.135.
Gédalge, Francois *Source(s):* Green (see above)
Meyer, Karl *Source(s):* Green (see above)
Polyalphabeticity *Source(s):* OCLC 31452766
Sebbél, S. M. Karl *Source(s):* Green (see above)
Spes *Source(s):* Green (see above)
Troisaent, Jacques Karl *Source(s):* Green (see above)
Saraceni, Raymond (R.) 1932-1996 [composer, author, arranger]
Adams, Gene *Source(s):* ASCP; CPOL RE-402-564
Saracen, Ray *Source(s):* CCE62
Saracini, Claudio 1586-1630? [singer, lutenist, composer]
Palusi, Il *Source(s):* LCAR; NGDM; SADC; WORB
Saraz, Louis 1854-1908 [composer]
Ratz, Ludro *Source(s):* STGR v. 4/pt.1
Sarcey (de Suttières), Francisque 1827 (or 28)-1899 [drama critic]
Francisque *Source(s):* LCAR (see note); PIPE
Sardinha, Anibal Augusto 1915-1955 [composer, guitarist, violinist]
Garôto *Source(s):* BLIC; CCE56; CPMU; GREN; LCAR
Sardou, Victorien [or Vittoriano] 1831-1908 [playwright]
Pélissié, Jules *Source(s):* PIPE
Sargent, Brian (Lawrence) 1927- [author, composer, educator]
Strange, N. Blair *Source(s):* PSND
Sargent, (Sir) (Harold) Malcolm (Watts-) 1895-1967 [conductor, composer, organist]
Flash Harry *Source(s):* MUWB
Sartain, John, Jr. 1912-2004 [composer, conductor, arranger, author]
Grandfather of Film Music *Source(s):* www.mfiles.co.uk/Composers/david-raskin.htm (7 Oct. 2002)
Raskin, David *Source(s):* ASCP; GAMM; KILG; LCAR; STUW
Sarti, Giuseppe 1729-1802 [composer, conductor]
Domenichino, Il *Source(s):* BAKR; WORB
Sartorio, Arnoldo 1853-1936 [composer]
Note(s): Portrait: ETUP 55:12 (Dec. 1937): 768
Abelle, Victor *Source(s):* CCE35 R39228; CCE38 R63920
Bocca, Carlotta *Source(s):* CCE43 #33680, 9 R120525
Dana, Arthur *Source(s):* CCE14 E338595
Note(s): A. P. Schmidt house name; see NOTES: Dana, Arthur.
Devrient, T. *Source(s):* WORB
Durand, Felix *Source(s):* CPMU ("Rhine Pictures"); WORB
Eckhardt, Rudolf *Source(s):* CCE40 #25244, 11 R89025
Esterbrook, Myron *Source(s):* CCE44 #26477, 156 R125413
Grooms, Calvin *Source(s):* CCE52 R98653 ("Torchlight Dance")
Note(s): Also used by Lee Orean Smith.
Hansen, Gustav *Source(s):* CCE38 R63917
Hartmann, Adolf *Source(s):* CCE42 #34788, 62 R110139
Lazare, Henri *Source(s):* CCE41 #30320, 117 R97855
Lenecke, Max *Source(s):* CCE35 R39224
Martinez, Felipe *Source(s):* CCE43 #33680, 7 R120516; CCE49 R45204
Melnik, J. *Source(s):* CCE41 #30320, 31 R97876
Meyer, Ferdinand *Source(s):* CCE12 E294101
Note(s): A. P. Schmidt house name; see NOTES: Meyer, Ferdinand.
Riviere, Ch. *Source(s):* CCE51 R87736; CCE52 R92403
Sartorius, Erasmus 1577 (or 78)-1637 [musician, author]
E. S. C. H. *Source(s):* IBIM; WORB
Satajewitsch, Alexandr Wiktorowitsch 1869-1936 [composer, musicologist]
Favello *Source(s):* RIES
Satie, (Alfred) Erik (Leslie) 1866-1925 [composer]
Godfather of Bad Boy Composers *Source(s):* http://www.rasputins.com/manifesto/archives/badboysc.html (7 Oct. 2002)
Godfather of Les Six *Source(s):* http://www.jazclass.aust.com/Satie.htm (7 Oct. 2002)
Lebeau, Virginie *Source(s):* WHIT p. 105
Note(s): Possible pseud. of Satie, Auriol or Allais, or may be a collective pseud.
Monsieur le Pavre *Source(s):* WHIT p. 92
Satis, Erit *Source(s):* SLON
Velvet Gentleman, The *Source(s):* WHIT p. 79
Satterwhite, C(ollen) G(ray) 1920-1978 [composer, author, arranger]
Note(s): In CCE63 original given name: Colin.
Satterwhite, Tex *Source(s):* ASCP; CCE62-63
Sattler, Hermann 1921- [composer]
Garwin, Joe *Source(s):* CCE65-66; GREN
Sauer, Wolfgang 1928- [composer]
Finette, Joe *Source(s):* CCE54 Efor104880; CCE59; KOMP; KOMS; PFSA
Saumell, (Robredo) Manuel 1817-1870 [composer]
Schubert of Cuba *Source(s):* STAR p. 184

Saunders, Albert Bokhare ?-1946 [composer]
Scott, Clement *Source(s):* http://www.abc.net.au/classic/daily/stories/s631386.htm (20 June 2005)
Saunders, Donald [songwriter, performer]
One Eye *Source(s):* PMUS-00
Saunders, Edward 1866-1910 [songwriter]
Deane, Charles *Source(s):* ROOM
Saunders, George Frederick 1785-1806 [violinist, pianist, composer]
Pinto, George Frederick *Source(s):* BAKR
Saunders, Joseph 1842-1884 [author, composer, singer]
Leybourne, George *Source(s):* GAMM
Saunders, Wallace [songwriter]
Saunders, Wash *Source(s):* PSND
Sauveplane, Henri (Emile) 1892-1942 [composer]
Rhyne, H. E. *Source(s):* GREN
Sauveur, Joseph 1653-1716 [acoustician, author]
Father of Musical Acoustics, The *Source(s):* http://www.schillerinstitute.org/music/rev_tuning_hist.html (7 Oct. 2002)
Savinio, Alberto 1758-1826 [singer, composer, flautist]
Chirico, Andrea (de) *Source(s):* LCAR
DeChirico, Andrea *Source(s):* IBIM; LCAR; NGDM; WORB
Savino, Domenico 1882-1973 [composer, arranger, conductor, editor]
David, M. *Source(s):* CCE20 E477055
Foresio, D. *Source(s):* CCE21 E514639
Lewis & Williams *Source(s):* CCE48 R39267
Note(s): Jt. pseud.: William H. Penn.
Mozeneiko, D. *Source(s):* CCE20 E495663
Onivas, David *Source(s):* LCAR
Onivas, Domenico *Source(s):* ASCP; CCE20 E471060; MUSR; SPTH; SUPN
Onomari, O. *Source(s):* CCE48 R36210 ("I Wonder Why!")
Whitehall, David *Source(s):* CCE56 Eunp
Sawyer, Henry S. 1864-1941 [composer, editor, arranger]
Note(s): Portrait: ETUP 55:12 (Dec. 1937): 768
Appleton, Albert *Source(s):* CCE19 E462346
Barnes, Joseph *Source(s):* CCE17 E412109; CCE18 E432851
Blackwell, Florence *Source(s):* CCE16 E390102
Bohn, Charles *Source(s):* CCE16 E388510
Browning, Timothy *Source(s):* CCE17 E407421
Carroll, Francis *Source(s):* CCE19 E462341
Collins, George *Source(s):* CCE19 E462338
DeLancey, J. *Source(s):* CCE16 E389216
Field, Wallace *Source(s):* CCE17 E412104
Gregory, Adam *Source(s):* CCE23 A759050 ("Denison's Descriptive Music Book")
Kaylor, Roy *Source(s):* CCE19 E462491
Kimball, F. R. *Source(s):* CCE22 E55419; CCE37 R57997 ("Keep Step March")
Note(s): Also used by Leo Friedman & Frank K. Root; see NOTES: Kimball, F. R.
LaRue, Edgar *Source(s):* CCE19; CCE45 #35888, 261 R139815
LeGrand, Herbert *Source(s):* CCE21 E520283
Manning, Franklyn *Source(s):* CCE18 E436147
Montague, James *Source(s):* CCE17 E412105
O'Malley, James *Source(s):* CCE19 E42076
Preston, Adam *Source(s):* CCE16 E390162; CCE18 E435141
Spencer, Harold *Source(s):* CCE16 E390101; CCE37 R57988; TPRF
Wallace, Elmer *Source(s):* CCE20 E490092
Weston, Morris *Source(s):* CCE16 E390164
Sayer, Gerard (Hugh) 1948- [singer, songwriter]
Sayer, Leo *Source(s):* AMUS; CASS; DIMA; HARR; LCAR; PEN2; PSND
Sbarbaro, Antonio [or Anthony] 1897-1969 [composer, drummer]
Spargo, Tony *Source(s):* ASCP; CCE54
Scaduto, Matilda Genevieve 1925-2003 [songwriter]
Bryant, Felice *Source(s):* WASH
Scafone, Jack (Dominic), (Jr.) 1936- [singer, songwriter]
Scott, Jack *Source(s):* AMUS; EPMU; HARR; LCAR, PEN2; PSND
Scaggs, William Royce 1944- [singer, songwriter]
Scaggs, Boz *Source(s):* AMUS; CM12; DIMA; HARR; NOMG; PEN2; WORL
Scanlan, William J(ames) 1856-1898 [singer, songwriter]
Irish Tenor *Source(s):* MARC p. 18
J. S. *Source(s):* SPTH p. 217
Note(s): On 1st ed. of "Jim Fisk;" later ed. had complete signature.
Temperance Boy Songster, The *Source(s):* MARC p. 18; SPTH p. 216
Scarborough, C(larence) [songwriter]
Scarborough, Skip *Source(s):* CCE73; PMUS; PSNN
Scarlatti, Alessandro 1659-1725 [composer]
Founder of Modern Opera, The *Source(s):* PSND
Founder of Neapolitan Opera, The *Source(s):* GROL
Terpandro *Source(s):* http://www.fathom.com/feature/35186 (5 Apr. 2005)
Scarlatti, (Giuseppe) Dominico 1685-1757 [composer, organist]
Escarlate [or Escarlati], Domingo *Source(s):* LCAR
Mimmo *Source(s):* RIEM

Scarlatti, Giuseppe c.1718 (or 23)-1777 [composer]
Maestro il cappella napolitano *Source(s):* NGDM
Scarpa, Eugenia 1886-1961 [composer, singer, pianist]
Sadero, Geni *Source(s):* GOTH; GREN; LCAR
Scarpa, Salvatore 1918- [composer, author, conductor]
Donson, Don *Source(s):* ASCP
Scarpari, Pietro mentioned 1722 [composer]
Dall'Oglio *Source(s):* GROL (see under: Dall'Oglio, Domenico)
Note(s): Do not confuse with Domenico Dall'Oglio (c.1700-1764).
Scarron, Paul 1610-1660 [poet, author, playwright]
Creator of Burlesque Poetry in France, The *Source(s):* PSND
Father of French Burlesque, The *Source(s):* PSND
Invalid Laureate, The *Source(s):* PSND
Schack, Benedikt 1758-1826 [singer, composer]
Cziak, Benedict *Source(s):* LCAR; SONN
Zák, Benedikt *Source(s):* IBIM; LCAR; NGDM; WORB
Schack, Carsten [songwriter, performer]
Soulshock *Source(s):* PMUS-00
Schaefer, Hermann 1911-1977 [composer]
Glady, Tom *Source(s):* REHH; SUPN
Schaeffer, Don(ald) 1935-1991 [composer]
Note(s): In REHH see under: Schaefer, Don.
Burgess, Andrew *Source(s):* CCE73; REHH
Dupre, Robert *Source(s):* REHH
Morris, Albert *Source(s):* CCE72-73; REHH
Note(s): Do not confuse with Albert Morris, composer of "Ghetto Life."
Paulson, Joseph *Source(s):* REHH
Pharmer, Henry *Source(s):* CCE68; CCE73; REHH
Schaeffer, Pierre 1910-1995 [composer]
Godfather of *music concrète*, The *Source(s):* http://www.hyperreal.org/intersection/zines/est/intervs/henry.html (7 Oct. 2002)
Inventor of Music Concrète, The *Source(s):* http://csunix1.lvc.edu/~snyder/em/schaef.html (7 Oct. 2002)
Schäfer, Johannes 1957- [composer]
Babtist, Jean Frederic *Source(s):* KOMP; KOMS; PFSA
Schaff, Sylvia 1916- [composer, author]
Brooks, Valerie *Source(s):* ASCP; CCE57-58
Schäffer, Johann Wilhelm ?-c.1700 [composer]
J. W. S. *Source(s):* CPMU ("Himlische Nachtigall . . ." (1684))
Note(s): Probable initials of Schäffer
Schalin, Adalbert 1902- [composer]
Edwards, Joe *Source(s):* CCE57; CCE60; RIES
Schall, Friedrich 1924- [composer]
Rhomberg, Kurt *Source(s):* KOMP; PFSA
Schanfield, Lewis Maurice 1867-1941 [comedian, producer]
Fields, Lew *Source(s):* GAN2
Schanppecher, Melchior c.1480- [theorist]
Malcior de Wormatia *Source(s):* NGDM
Schantz, David Mathew 1953- [composer, author]
Chance, David *Source(s):* ASCP; CPOL SR-16-422
Schanz, Julius 1828-1902 [author]
Schanz, Uli *Source(s):* PIPE; WORB
Scharf-Bauer, Martina 1958- [composer]
Merit Aton *Source(s):* OMUO
Schatt, Ronald 1927-1996 [songwriter, saxophonist, bandleader]
Gellar, Jack *Source(s):* CCE68; CPOL RE-740-769; PMUS; SONG
Scott, Ronnie *Source(s):* LCAR
Schatz, Billy 1942- [singer, guitarist, songwriter]
Clayton, Lee *Source(s):* STAC
Outlaw's Outlaw, The *Source(s):* STAC
Note(s): See also Lee T. Clayton.
Schatzell, Pauline von 1812- [singer, composer]
Marxhausen, P. F. *Source(s):* COHN; HIXN
Schaub, Siegmund Ferdinand 1880-1965 [critic, teacher, composer]
Schuab, Hans Ferdinand *Source(s):* BAKT
Schauer, Ferencz 1851- [composer]
Sárosi, Ferencz *Source(s):* STGR
Scheepers-Van Dommelen, Maria 1892- [singer, composer]
Scapus, Mit *Source(s):* COHN; HIXN
Scheffel, Konrad [or Conny] 1931- [composer]
Tiselius, Lars [or Lara] *Source(s):* CCE64; CPOL RE-584-686; KOMP; PFSA
Scheffer, Johannes 1909- [arranger, composer]
Scheffer, Pi *Source(s):* CCE52; SMIN
Vlieger, Jan de *Source(s):* CCE53; CCE56
Scheffler, Johann(es) 1624-1677 [poet, hymnist]
Note(s): Portrait: CYBH
Angelus Silesius, (Johann) *Source(s):* CCE53; CCE55; HATF; LCAR; NGDM
Schlesischer Bote *Source(s):* LCAR (see note)
Silesian Angel *Source(s):* LCAR (see note)
Silesius Angelus *Source(s):* CYBH
Scheidl-Hutterstrasser, Lili [or Lily] 1882-1942 [composer]
Hans, Lio *Source(s):* AEIO; COHN; HIXN; LCAR; MACM
Schein, Johann Hermann 1586-1630 (or 31) [composer]
Note(s): Portrait: CYBH
Heischermann, Jonah *Source(s):* IBIM; WORB
Hohenrasenn, Joachim *Source(s):* IBIM
Silvanus, Jacchus Heremias *Source(s):* IBIM; WORB
Silvanus, Menalca *Source(s):* IBIM

Scheltobrjuchow, Alexander (Konstantinovich) 1852- [jurist, dramatist]
Note(s): In IWWM origianl surname: Sheltobriuchov.
Mignard, Alexander *Source(s):* IWWM; MELL; STGR; WORB
Schenckendorff, Leopold (Adalbert Günther Heinrich von) 1909-1988 [composer]
Ernst, Günther *Source(s):* CCE36 Efor42599; CCE52-55; KOMP; PFSA
Hiller, Frank *Source(s):* CCE56; KOMP; PFSA
Hillmer, Frank *Source(s):* CCE56; PFSA
Tamp, Peter *Source(s):* CCE55; KOMP; PFSA
Schenker, Heinrich 1868-1935 [pianist, theorist, composer]
Niloff, Arthur *Source(s):* KOMU; OEAW; OMUO
Schibilsky, Klaus 1940- [composer]
Hansen, Michael *Source(s):* KOMS; PFSA
Schickele, Peter (Johann) 1935- [composer, entertainer]
Bach, P. D. Q. *Source(s):* BAKR; CM05; GOTH
Becker, William *Source(s):* ASCP; CCE67
Schickele, René (Marie Maurice Armand) 1883-1940 [author]
Sascha *Source(s):* PIPE
Schickeneder, Johann Joseph [or Jakob] 1751-1812 [librettist, actor]
Schikaneder, Emanuel *Source(s):* ALMN; RIEM
Schiemanowsky, Max 1882- [songwriter]
Lengard, Max *Source(s):* MACM; WORB
Schiessler, Sebastian Wil(l)ibald 1791-1867 [composer, writer on music]
Hilarius, Justus *Source(s):* SEND
Schifrin, Boris (C(laudio)) 1932- [pianist, composer, arranger]
Schifrin, Lalo *Source(s):* BBDP; CASS; CCE61-62; LCAR; PEN2
Schiller, Henry Carl 1807-1871 [librettist, writer on dramatic arts]
Gray, Anthony *Source(s):* CART
H. Carl S. *Source(s):* CART
Schilling, (Friedrich) Gustav 1766-1839 [author]
Note(s): Do not confuse with Gustav Schilling (1803-1881); see following entry.
Kuckuck (der Junger), Zebedäus *Source(s):* PIPE; WORB
Kukuk, Zebedäus *Source(s):* WORB
Schilling, Gustav 1803-1881 [writer on music, educator]
Note(s): Do not confuse with (Friedrich) Gustav Schilling (1766-1839); see preceding entry.
Deceased, The *Source(s):* IBIM; WORB
Hermit of Iowa, The *Source(s):* IBIM; WORB
Schillinger, Joseph (Moiseyevich) 1895-1943 [theorist, composer]
Lynn, Frank *Source(s):* GROL; LCAR
Note(s): Also used by James (Franklin) Leisy.
Schindler, Fritz 1871-1924 [composer]
Walden, Otto van *Source(s):* PFSA
Schindler, Hans 1889-1969 [composer, conductor]
Glombig, Eberhard *Source(s):* PIPE
Reuter, Hans *Source(s):* WORB
Reuter, Winston *Source(s):* WORB
Winston *Source(s):* WORB
Schink, Johann Friedrich [or Gottfried] 1755-1835 [playwright, librarian]
Grillengroll, Fritz *Source(s):* PIPE
Schinzel, Antonio 1945- [composer]
Anders, Christisan *Source(s):* PFSA
Schipa, Raffaele Attilio Amadeo 1888 (or 89)-1965 [singer, composer]
Note(s): Portrait: ETUP 56:1 (Jan. 1938): 45
Schipa, Tito *Source(s):* BAKE; LCAR
Schippers, Willem Theodoor 1942-1964 [singer, songwriter]
Schippers, Wim T. *Source(s):* LCAR
Schlächter, Karl 1804-1876 [writer on music, actor]
Haffner, Carl *Source(s):* LCAR; RIES
Schlechter, Karl *Source(s):* LCAR; RIES
Schlecker, Max 1930- [music publisher]
Schleo *Source(s):* PSND
Schleich, Ernst 1894- [composer]
Byrd, Ch(arlie) *Source(s):* CCE44 Efor14269; CCE49-52
Note(s): Also used by Alexander Thomason.
De Riviera, (E. de) *Source(s):* CCE49-50; CCE55
Ring, Bo *Source(s):* CCE49
Riviera, (E. De) *Source(s):* CCE49-50; CCE55
Schleiffarth, George (Maywood) 1848-1921 [composer, music publisher]
Maywood, George *Source(s):* CCE23 R24004; CPMU; LCAR
Schlein, Phil(lip Gary) 1944- [singer, guitarist, songwriter]
Fantastic Baggys *Source(s):* AMUS; EPMU
Note(s): Jt. pseud.: Stephen [or Steve] (Barri [or Barry]) Lipkin.
Grass Roots, The *Source(s):* AMUS
Note(s): Jt. pseud.: Stephen [or Steve] (Barri [or Barry]) Lipkin.
Sloan, P. F. *Source(s):* AMUS; CCE72; EPMU
Schlemm, Gustav Adolf 1902- [conductor, composer]
Hinstein, Gustav *Source(s):* RIEM
Schlenkermann, Friedrich [or Fritz] 1907-1988 [composer]
Kerman *Source(s):* CPOL RE-293-381; KOMP; PFSA
Triberg, Klaus *Source(s):* CCE52 Efor14600; KOMP; PFSA

Note(s): Also jt. pseud.: F(ranz) J(osef) Breuer & Käte Kongsbak-König.
Schlesinger, Bruno Walter 1876-1962 [conductor, composer]
Walter, Bruno *Source(s):* BAKR; LCAR; NGDM; RIEM
Schlesinger, Leontine 1889-1974 [actress, director]
Sagan, Leontine *Source(s):* GAN2
Schli(e)nger, Leon (Xavier) 1922-2002 [songwriter]
Regney, Noel *Source(s):* CCE55-56; IMDB; WASH
Schliepe, Ernst (Heinrich) 1893-1961 [composer, conductor, writer on music]
Heidrich, Gustav *Source(s):* PIPE
Schmadtke, Harry 1929- [composer]
Donerus, Bernd *Source(s):* KOMP; KOMS; PFSA
Schmelling, Gertrud(e Elisabeth) 1749 (or 50)-1833 [composer]
La Mara *Source(s):* JACK
Note(s): See also (Ida) Marie Lipsius.
Mara, (Gertrud Elisabeth) *Source(s):* JACK; LCAR; MWP1 p. 335
Schmid, Eduard Hermann Wilhelm 1890-1966 [author]
Edschmid, Kasimir *Source(s):* PIPE
Schmid, Matthias 1801-1886 [conductor, composer]
Müller, Adolf *Source(s):* BAKR; GAN1; LCAR; RIES
Note(s): Do not confuse with Adolf Müller (1839-1901).
Schmid, Adolf *Source(s):* LCAR
Schmid, Peter 1633-1679 [composer, organist]
Fabricius, Werner *Source(s):* DIEH
Schmidseder, Ludwig 1904-1971 [composer]
Fabro, Louis *Source(s):* GREN; PFSA; RIEM
Schmidt, (Johann) Caspar [or Kaspar] 1806-1856 [author]
Stirner, Max *Source(s):* LCAR; PIPE
Schmidt, Gerd [composer, arranger]
Dokin, Ralph *Source(s):* CCE60-68; CCE73 Efor166714; CPOL RE-648-471; RIES
Starek, Bill *Source(s):* CCE68
Schmidt, Gerhard [composer]
Zeeden, Peter *Source(s):* CCE 63-64; CPOL RE-541-304
Note(s): Also used by Robby Schmitz; see NOTES: Zeeden, Peter.
Schmidt, Jochen 1955- [composer]
Schmidt-Breitbach, Ernst *Source(s):* KOMP; PFSA
Schmidt, Johann Christoph 1712-1795 [organist, composer]
Smith, John Christopher *Source(s):* BAKR; LCAR; NGDM
Schmidt, Peter 1587-1651 [theologian, lutenist, composer]
Fabricius, Petrus *Source(s):* LCAR; NGDM
Schmidt, Ralf 1960- [composer]
Falkenberg, IC *Source(s):* PFSA
Schmidt, Walter 1907- [composer]
Walter, Fried *Source(s):* BUL3; CCE66; CPMU; RIES; SUPN
Schmidt, Wilhelm 1924- [composer]
Hrabe, Billy *Source(s):* KOMP; PFSA
Schmidt-Binge, Walter 1931-1988 [composer]
Schmidt, Christel *Source(s):* KOMS
Schmidt-Gent(n)er, Willy 1894-1964 [composer]
Fred, Will *Source(s):* CCMU; PFSA
Schmidt-Hanson, Hans 1912- [composer]
Hanson, Hanno *Source(s):* CCE58; KOMP; KOMS; PFSA
Schmit, Jean-Pierre 1904- [musicologist]
Schmit, Jempy *Source(s):* PSND
Schmitt, Alois 1851-1906 [composer]
Czanyi *Source(s):* COHN; HIXN
Schmitt, Gerhard 1964- [composer]
Tanbür, Jon *Source(s):* KOMS; PFSA
Schmitz, Josef 1901-1991 [composer]
Ring, Peter *Source(s):* KOMP; PFSA
Schmitz, Jupp *Source(s):* CCE54; PFSA
Schmitz, Robby 1925- [composer]
Norge, Bert *Source(s):* KOMP; KOMS
Zeeden, Peter *Source(s):* CCE77 Efor186727
Note(s): Also used by Gerhard Schmidt; see NOTES: Zeeden, Peter.
Schnakenburg, Margarethe 1901-1988 [playwright]
Maximowna, Ita *Source(s):* PIPE
Schneegass, Klaus-Peter 1962- [composer]
Nevini, Nero *Source(s):* KOMS
Schneider, Adalbert 1859- [author; librettist]
Schnitter, Adalbert (Virgil Ambrosius) *Source(s):* STGR; WORB
Schneider, Dorothy Fay 1932- [author, lyricist]
Schneider, Dolli *Source(s):* ASCP
Schneider, Erasmus 1577 (or 78)-1637? [writer on music]
Sartorius, Erasmus *Source(s):* PRAT; RIEM
Schneider, F. Louis [composer, arranger]
Taylor, F. Louis *Source(s):* CPMU (publication dates 1926-27)
Schneider, Hans 1906- [composer]
Heider, Johannes *Source(s):* CCE35 Efor40091
Note(s): Possible pseud.?
Landor, Fred *Source(s):* CCE61 E78654
Lauterbach, Karl *Source(s):* CCE60 Efor74207 & Efor74312; CCE64
Lund, Peter *Source(s):* BUL3; CCE55; CCE67
Schneider, Louis [or Ludwig] (Wilhelm) 1805-1878 [librettist]
Both, L. W. *Source(s):* LOWN; MELL; PIPE; STGR

Schneider, M(anfred) 1953- [composer]
Gontard, Manfred *Source(s):* CCE59
McMillan, Steve *Source(s):* KOMS; PFSA
Schneider, Paul 1569-1609 [organist, composer]
Sartorius, Paul *Source(s):* BAKR; GROL; NGDM
Schneickher, Paul *Source(s):* GROL; NGDM
Schneider, Willy 1907-1983 [composer]
Burger, Matthias *Source(s):* KOBW; LCAR; RIES; SUPN
Schnyder von Wartensee, Xaver 1786-1868 [composer, writer on music]
S. v. W. *Source(s):* HEYT
Schoeck, Othmar 1886-1957 [composer]
Swiss Schubert *Source(s):* ETUP 56:2 (Feb. 1938): 86 (port.)
Schoenberg, Alfred 1868-1949 [composer, author]
Shean, Al *Source(s):* CLMM (port.); LCAR
Schoenberg, Arnold 1874-1951 [composer]
Apostle of Atonality *Source(s):* PSND
Copernicus of Music *Source(s):* PSND
Father of Modern Music *Source(s):* http://www.usc.edu/isd/archives/schoenberg/videv014.htm (7 Oct. 2002)
Note(s): See also Wolfgang Amadeus Mozart.
Father of Negative Music, The *Source(s):* http://www.dovesong.com/positive_music/schonberg.asp (7 Oct. 2002)
Father of Twelve Tone Music, The *Source(s):* PSND
Godfather of Atonal Music *Source(s):* http://www.urthona.com/previous_issue.htm (7 Oct. 2002)
Leader of Cacophonists, The *Source(s):* SLON
Musical Von Tirpitz of Germany, The *Source(s):* SLON
Schön-bug *Source(s):* SLON
Twelve-Tone Oddity *Source(s):* PSND
Schoenberg, Gertrud (née Kolisch) c.1894-1967 [librettist]
Blonda, Max *Source(s):* GROL; LCAR; NGDM; NGDO; PIPE; ROOM
Schoenefeld, Henry 1857-1936 [composer]
Note(s): Portrait: ETUP 5:2 (Feb. 1938): 68
Cimadori, Robert *Source(s):* CCE39 #9188, 639 R73541
Ellis, Norton *Source(s):* TPRF
Schoenfeld, William C(harles) 1893-1969 [composer, author, conductor]
Blake, Lowell *Source(s):* ASCP; CCE57; CCE60
Conrad, Hugh *Source(s):* ASCP; CCE61-62; CCE65-66; CPOL RE-246-112
Field, William C. *Source(s):* CCE55
Scholze, Johann Sigismund 1705-1750 [poet, musical anthologist]
Sperontes *Source(s):* BAKR; CPMU; LCAR; MACM; NGDM; RIEM
Schön, Eduard (Ritter von) 1825-1879 [lawyer, composer, theorist]
Engelsberg, E(duard) S(chön) *Source(s):* AEIO; GOTH; MACM; PFSA; OMUO; PRAT
Schonberg, Harold (Charles) 1915-2003 [author, music critic]
Callender, Newgate *Source(s):* http://www.blogofdeath.com/archives/000184.html (15 Aug. 2005)
Note(s): Used on reviews of mysteries & thrillers.
Schönfeld, Friedhelm 1938- [composer]
Berger, Fred *Source(s):* KOMS; PFSA
Schonsleder, Wolfgang 1570-1651 [writer on music]
Decorus, Volupius *Source(s):* http://www.musiklant-tirol.at/html/musikgeschichte/mg_kloster.html (30 Sept. 2003)
Volupius Decorus *Source(s):* http://www.musiklant-tirol.at/html/musikgeschichte/mg_kloster.html
Schönwald, Albert 1878-1942 [violoncellist, composer]
Siklós, Albert *Source(s):* BAKT; NGDM; ROOM
Schöpff, Friedrich Wilhelm Traugott 1826-1916 [poet]
Neun, Wilfried von der *Source(s):* LAST
Schori, Fritz 1887-1971 [composer]
Duroc, A(chilles) *Source(s):* REHG; SMIN; SUPN
Forster, M. H. *Source(s):* REHG; SMIN; SUPN
Friederich, J(ohann) *Source(s):* REHG; SMIN; SUPN
Marquis, J *Source(s):* REHG; SMIN; SUPN
Meister, J. *Source(s):* REHG; SMIN; SUPN
Note(s): "Le Grenadier du Caucase" is credited to J. Meister; however, it is actually by Georges Meister (1848-1902). (SMIN)
Schori, Hans 1915- [composer]
Renez, H. *Source(s):* REHG; SMIN
Note(s): Son of Fritz Schori (see under: Schori, Fritz).
Schorlemmer, Erna von 1875- [composer]
Chaloix, Erny *Source(s):* COHN; HIXN
Schramm, Rudolf (R. A.) 1902-1981 [composer, author, conductor]
Marsh, Rudy *Source(s):* ASCP
Schrank, Ludwig 1828-1905 [composer]
Mannsfeld, Louis *Source(s):* KOMU
Schreiber, Aloys (Wilhelm) 1761-1841 [author, historian]
Sirius *Source(s):* PIPE
Schreibman, Alexander 1910-1997? [composer, arranger]
Small, Allan *Source(s):* ASCP; CCE41 #2314 E90302; CCE52; CCE68; LCAR
Schreyber, Heinrich c. 1492-1525 (or 26) [mathematician, musical theorist]
Grammateus, Henricus *Source(s):* NGDM

Henricus Scriptoris Efordensis *Source(s):* NGDM
Scriptoris, Grammateus *Source(s):* WORB
Schreyvogel, Joseph 1768-1832 [librettist]
West, C(arl) A(ugust) *Source(s):* LOWN; PIPE
West, Thomas *Source(s):* PIPE
Note(s): Also used by Thomas (R.) Picardo, (Jr.).
Schröder, Gertrud 1848- [composer]
Parpart, Gertrud *Source(s):* IBIM; WORB
Tiefenborn, Irma von *Source(s):* IBIM; WORB
Schröder, Heinz 1911- [composer]
Thass, Peter *Source(s):* CCE52; KOMP; KOMS; PFSA
Schrody, Eric 1970- [rapper, songwriter]
Everlast *Source(s):* CM27; EPMU; LCAR
Schrody, Everlast *Source(s):* PMUS-99
Schröpfer, William Arthur 1908-1962 [actor, writer]
Macrae, Arthur *Source(s):* GAN2
Schröter, Corona Wilhelmine Elizabeth 1751-1802 [composer, actress, artist, singer]
Note(s): Portrait: ETUP 56:3 (Mar. 1938): 138
C. S***, Mselle *Source(s):* JACK
Schubert, Franz Peter 1808-1878 [composer]
Bertl *Source(s):* GRV3; RILM 91-0414-ap
Canevas *Source(s):* RILM 91-0414-ap
Holzhacker *Source(s):* Steblin, Rita. *Die Unsinngesellschaft Franz Schubert, Leopole Kupelwieser und ihr Freundeskreis.* Wien: Böhlau, 1998.
Note(s): Code in newsletter, *Archiv des Menschlichen Unssins* (1817-18).
Indefatigable Song Composer, An *Source(s):* GROL
Juan de la Cimbala *Source(s):* Steblin (see above)
Note(s): Code in newsletter *Archiv des Menschlichen Unssins* (1817-18)
Kanevas *Source(s):* GRV3
Prince of Lyrists *Source(s):* DEAN
Schwammerl *Source(s):* GRV3; RILM 91-0414-ap; SPIE
Tyrann, Der *Source(s):* RILM 91-0414-ap
Tyrant, The *Source(s):* GRV3
Volker der Minstrel *Source(s):* RILM 91-0414-ap
Schubert, Hans 1905-1980 [composer]
Sanders, Béla *Source(s):* PFSA
Steinhorst, Werner *Source(s):* CCE51
Schuckett, Ralph Dion 1948- [composer, author]
Ralph, Ralph J. *Source(s):* ASCP
Schudson, Howard (M.) 1942- [composer]
David, Hod *Source(s):* ASCP; CCE67; CCE73
Schuette, Conrad Herman Louis 1843-1926 [hymnist, translator]
C. H. L. S. *Source(s):* JULN
Schüldkraut, Naftule 1885-1982 [clarinetist, composer, arranger, conductor]
Note(s): Birth date sometimes listed as 1899. Portrait: ETUP 56:5 (May 1938): 280
Shilkret, Nat(haniel) *Source(s):* EPMU; GRAC
Schulhoff, Ervin [or Erwin] 1894-1942 [pianist, composer]
Hanell, George *Source(s):* PIPE
Petr, Hanuš *Source(s):* PIPE
Schultheiss, Michael 1571-1621 [composer, organist, music theorist]
Praetorius, Michael *Source(s):* BAKR; PIPE; ROOM
Schultze, Michael *Source(s):* BAKR; ROOM
Schultz, Ella Georgiyevna 1846-1926 [composer, ethnomusicologist]
Adayevskaya, Ella Georgiyevna *Source(s):* GROL
Schultze, Kristian 1945- [composer]
Wladi *Source(s):* KOMP; KOMS; PFSA
Schultze, Norbert (Arnold Wilhelm Richard) 1911-2002 [composer, actor, author]
Iversen, Henri *Source(s):* BUL3; NGDM; PIPE
Kornfeld, Peter *Source(s):* BUL3; NGDM; PIPE
Norbert, Frank *Source(s):* BUL3; NGDM; PIPE
Schulz, B. Eduard 1813-1842 [author, poet]
Ferrand, Edouard *Source(s):* LAST
Schulz, Christian Waldemar 1966- [composer]
Walden, Chris *Source(s):* KOMS; PFSA
Schulz(e), Gottschalk 1528-1573 [music educator]
Praetorius, Gottschalk *Source(s):* MACM
Schulz, Hans 1948- [composer]
Delmount, Ronny *Source(s):* KOMP; KOMS; PFSA
Schultzieg, Tex *Source(s):* KOMP; KOMS; PFSA
Schulz-Clahsen, Johann *Source(s):* KOMS
Schulz(e), Hieronymus 1560-1629 [organist, composer, music editor]
Praetorius, Hieronymus *Source(s):* BAKR; WORB
Schulz, Janine 1939- [composer]
Terlojian *Source(s):* KOMP
Schulz-Reichel, Fritz 1912-1990 [composer]
Crazy (Otto) *Source(s):* KOMP; MUWB; PERF; PFSA
Otto der Schrage *Source(s):* PERF
Schräge Otto, (Der) *Source(s):* KOMP; PFSA
Schulze, Fritz *Source(s):* CCE59
Schulze, Friedrich August 1770-1849 [librettist]
Helldunkel, Hans *Source(s):* PIPE
Innocenz *Source(s):* PIPE
Jeremias *Source(s):* PIPE
Laun, Friedrich *Source(s):* LCAR; LOWN; PIPE; WORB
Spiess, Chr(istian) H(einrich) *Source(s):* PIPE
Teutobald *Source(s):* PIPE
Wohlgemuth, Felix *Source(s):* PIPE
Schulze, Klaus 1947- [musician, composer, producer]
Wahnfried, Richard *Source(s):* http://www.klaus-schulze.com/faq.htm (15 Aug. 2005)

Schulze-Gerlach, Hartmut 1948- [composer]
Muck *Source(s):* PFSA
Raiker, Thommy *Source(s):* PFSA
Schulzova, A(nežka) 1868-1905 [librettest, writer on music, critic]
Richter, C(arl) L(udwig) *Source(s):* GROL (see Fibich, Zděnko); PIPE
Schumann, Joachim 1958- [composer]
Schumann, Joschi *Source(s):* KOMS
Schumann, Robert 1810-1856 [composer]
Note(s): There is no evidence his middle name was Alexander. (GROL)
Eusebius *Source(s):* NIEC; Taylor, Ronald. *Robert Schumann*. New York: Universal Books, 1982, 103.
Florestan *Source(s):* NIEC; Taylor (see above)
Note(s): See also J. L. Casembroot.
Fridolin *Source(s):* NIEC
Raro, Meister *Source(s):* Taylor (see above)
Note(s): Thought by some to be the name Schuman used to refer to Friedrich Wieck; however, others think it refers to Schumann. (See also: Wieck, Friedrich)
Robert of the Mulde *Source(s):* Taylor (see above)
Skuländer, (Robert) *Source(s):* GROL; Taylor (see above)
Schumann, Walter Robert 20th cent. [composer]
Schumann, Robert *Source(s):* CCE41 #14527 E91935 ("Talking to the Wind")
Note(s): Not a pseud. Do not confuse with Robert Schumann (1810-1856).
Schuster, Ira 1889-1945 [composer, author, pianist, publisher]
Siras, Jack *Source(s):* CCE61-62; CPOL RE-422-602
Siras, John *Source(s):* ASCP; CCE46 E10201; LCAR; PMUS
Schütt, Eduard 1856-1933 [composer]
Note(s): Portrait: ETUP 56:3 (March 1938): 131
Clairlie, Arnolde *Source(s):* GREN; LCAR
Marling, Henri [or Henry] *Source(s):* CCE22 E527969; GREN; LCAR
Schütte, Werner 1901-1934 [composer]
Rauls, Mac *Source(s):* MACM
Schütz, Alfred 1910- [composer]
Longin, Fred *Source(s):* KOMP; KOMS
Schütz, (George) Gabriel 1633-1710 [composer, viol player]
G. (G.) S. *Source(s):* IBIM; WORB
Schütz, Heinrich 1585-1672 [composer]
Father of German Music, The *Source(s):* MUWB; PSND
Sagittarius, (Henricus) *Source(s):* CPMU; NGDM; PIPE; PSND; ROOM
Schützer, János 1910-1980 [writer on music]
Weissmann, John *Source(s):* BAKR

Schuyler, Thom 1952- [songwriter]
S-K-O *Source(s):* EPMU
Note(s): Jt. pseud.: Fred Knobloch & Paul Overstreet.
Schwab, Bonifacius 1611-1661 (or later) [composer, organist]
Schwab, Felician *Source(s):* NGDM; WORB
Schwab, Karl Heinz 1924- [composer]
Bendix, Ralph *Source(s):* PFSA
Jung, Eckehard *Source(s):* CCE66
Schwabacher, Henri Simon 1875-1937 [librettist]
Duvernois, Henri *Source(s):* LOWN; WORB
Schwandt, Wilbur (Clyde) 1904-1998 [composer, arranger]
Swan, Don *Source(s):* ASCP; CCE63; CCE68; LCAR
Schwanzara, Hans 1897- [composer]
Schanara, Hans *Source(s):* BUL3
Schwartz, Andreas (Scotus) ?-mid. 16th cent. [composer]
A. S. *Source(s):* WORB
Francus, Andreas *Source(s):* IBIM; WORB
Scotus, Andreas Francus *Source(s):* IBIM; WORB
Skotus, Andreas *Source(s):* IBIM; WORB
Schwartz, Jacob Lawrence 1912- [composer, lyricist]
Note(s): Portraits: SHMM (Sept./Oct. 1992): 2 & cover; SHMM (Nov./Dec. 1992): 2
Lawrence, Jack *Source(s):* PSND
Schwartz, Jerome Lawrence 1915-2004 [playwright, author]
Lawrence, Jerome *Source(s):* LCAR; PIPE
Lorens, G'erom *Source(s):* LCAR
Schwartz, Richard 1928- [trumpeter, arranger, bandleader]
Sutton, Dick *Source(s):* PSND
Schwartzdorf, Jacob (S.) 1909-1994 [composer, conductor, arranger, music director]
Blackton, Jay (S.) *Source(s):* LCAR; OB94; PSND
Schwarz, Brinsley [singer, guitarist, songwriter]
Rankin, Billy *Source(s):* NOMG
Schwarz, Louis fl. 1915-20 [composer]
Sandow, Ludwig *Source(s):* MELL; STGR
Schwarzendorf, Johann Paul Agidius 1741-1816 [organist, teacher, composer]
Martini il Tedesco *Source(s):* CPMU; LCAR; NGDM; NGDO; PSND
Martini, Jean Paul Egide *Source(s):* BAKO; BAKR; LCAR; NGDM; NGDO; PSND
Martin, Johann Paul Aegidius *Source(s):* BAKR; LCAR; NGDM; NGDO
Tedesco, Il *Source(s):* PSND
Note(s): See also Lorenzo Allegri.
Schwarzerd, Philipp 1497-1560 [poet, theologian, writer on music]
Didymus Faventinus *Source(s):* LCAR

Faventinus, Didymus *Source(s):* LCAR; WORB
Melanc(h)thon, Philipp *Source(s):* GROL; LCAR; NGDM
Praeceptor Germaniae *Source(s):* GROL; LCAR; NGDM
Schwarzmeier, Gustl 1922- [composer]
Gast, Willy *Source(s):* CCE56 Efor40169 ("Lorencita")
Romba, Ralph *Source(s):* CCE56; CPOL RE-443-309; KOMP; KOMS
Schwarzwald, Arnold 1918-1997 [composer]
Hughes, Arnold *Source(s):* ASCP; CCE54-56
Schweher, Kryštop [or Christoph] 1520-1593 [poet, composer]
Hecyrus, Christoph *Source(s)* NGDM; WORB
Schweinsberg, Franz Johann 1835-1913 [pianist, violinist, composer]
Renaud, G. *Source(s):* http://www.leonarda.com/cdindex.html (3 Jan. 2005)
Schwerdtfeger, E. Anne 1930- [composer, music educator]
Mary Ernest, O.P., (Sister) *Source(s):* HIXN
Schwichtenberg, Wilbur 1912-1989 [bandleader, trombonist, composer]
Bradley, Will *Source(s):* EPMU; GAMM; KINK; LCAR; PEN2
Schwieger, Jakob 1624-c.1667 [poet]
Filidor, der Dorfferer *Source(s):* CPMS; WORB
Flüchtige, Der *Source(s):* GROL; WORB
Schwingenhammer 1761-1830 [librettist]
Lamartelière *Source(s):* STGR
Schwitters, Kurt (Hermann Eduard Karl Julius) 1887-1948 [author, artist]
Pfitzer, Gustav *Source(s):* PIPE
Sciacca, Anthony 1921- [reeds, composer, bandleader]
Sciacca, Scott *Source(s):* CCE46 Eunp
Scott, Tony *Source(s):* EPMU; KINK; LCAR; PSND
Sciapiro, Michel 1891-1962 [composer, author]
Fielding, Michael *Source(s):* ASCP; CCE43 #4645 E111597; LCAR
Michel, Chester *Source(s):* CCE35 E47968
Michel, Don *Source(s):* CCE33 Eunp79806
Scibona, Jorge 1931- [composer, guitarist]
Morel, Jorge *Source(s):* ASCP; CPOL RE-384-995
Sciroli, Gregorio 1722-after 1781 [composer]
Scirolino, Il *Source(s):* GROL
Note(s): See also Giuseppe Aprile.
Scott, Charles P(hillip) [composer]
Note(s): Portrait: APSA
Dana, Arthur *Source(s):* CCE28 R69
Note(s): A. P. Schmidt house name; see NOTES: Dana, Arthur.
Erich, Carl *Source(s):* CCE30 R11705
Note(s): A. P. Schmidt house name; see NOTES: Erich, Carl.
Gordon, Hugh *Source(s):* LCCC46 E4776
Note(s): A. P. Schmidt house name; see NOTES: Gordon, Hugh.
Meyer, Ferdinand *Source(s):* CCE30 R11695
Note(s): A. P. Schmidt house name; see NOTES: Meyer, Ferdinand.
Phillips, Charles *Source(s):* CCE30 R10793
Ritter, G. P. *Source(s):* CCE26 R35790 ("Maryland, My Maryland")
Note(s): Also used by G. F. Suck; see NOTES: Ritter, G. P.
Scott, Cyril (Meir) 1879-1970 [composer, poet]
English Debussy, The *Source(s):* Self, Geoffrey. *Light Music in Britain Since 1870; A Survey.*
Aldershot: Ashgate, 2001, 157.
Father of British Modern Music, The *Source(s):* http://www.xrefer.com/entry/245085 (7 Oct. 2002); http://members.iinet.au/~nickl/composer.html (7 Oct. 2002)
Scott, James (Sylvester) 1885-1938 [composer, pianist]
Crown Prince of Ragtime *Source(s):* IDBC
Little Professor, The *Source(s):* http://www.grainger.de/music/composers/scottj.html (6 Mar. 2003)
Scott, Robert [or Bobby] William 1937-1990 [pianist, singer, composer, arranger]
Kirkland, Robert *Source(s):* CLTP ("NBC Color Movies")
Scott, Thomas [hymnist]
Sc*tt, Dr. *Source(s):* JULN
Scott, Thomas [or Tom] Jefferson 1912-1961 [composer, singer]
American Troubadour, The *Source(s):* PSND
Note(s): See also Irving Berlin [i.e., Israel Isador Baline]
Scott, (Sir) Walter 1771-1832 [author, poet]
Note(s): Portrait: CYBH. See PSND & LCAR for non-music related pseudonyms.
Cleishbotham, Jedediah *Source(s):* GOTT; LCAR; PSND
Clutterbuck, Captain (Cuthbert) *Source(s):* GOTT; PSND
Scott-Gatty, (Sir) Alfred 1847-1918 [composer]
Note(s): Portrait: ETUP 51:9 (Sept. 1933): 568
Gatty, Alfred Scott *Source(s):* CPMU; LCAR
Vaughan, Comyn *Source(s):* CPMU
Scouton, Will(iam H.) 1853-1940 [composer]
Eaton, M. B. *Source(s):* TPRF
Note(s): Also used by George D(aniel) Barnard & George D. Hofmann; see NOTES: Eaton, M. B.
Hazel, Edward *Source(s):* CCE30 #33420, 70 R11817; TPRF

Note(s): Also used by George D(aniel) Barnard see NOTES: Hazel, Edward.
Scribe, (Augustin) Eugène 1791-1861 [librettist]
Creator of Grand Opera *Source(s):* DEA3 p. 141
Félix, M. *Source(s):* LCAR
Saint-Marc, Amédée de *Source(s):* LCAR
Note(s): Jt. pseud.: Charles Gaspard Delestre-Poison & Anne-Honoré Joseph Duveyrier.
Scruggs, Irene 1901- [singer, songwriter]
Brown, Chocolate *Source(s):* HARS
Little Sister *Source(s):* HARS
Nolan, Dixie *Source(s):* HARS
Scruggs, Mary Elfrieda 1910-1981 [pianist, composer, arranger]
Burleigh, Mary Lou *Source(s):* PSND
Burley, Mary Lou *Source(s):* PSND
Queen of Jazz, The *Source(s):* PSND
Williams, Mary Lou *Source(s):* BAKR; CASS; EPMU; GRAT; IDBC; PEN2; PSND
Winn, Mary Elfrieda *Source(s):* PSND; VACH
Winn, Mary Lou *Source(s):* PSND
Seals, Dan (Wayland) 1948 (or 50)- [singer, songwriter]
England Dan *Source(s):* CM09; EPMU
Seals, Frank (Junior) 1942-2004 [singer, songwriter, guitarist]
Seals, Son *Source(s):* HARS; LCAR
Searing, Harry [composer]
Finley, Antor Dismuk (1812-1815) *Source(s):* OCLC 41228703
Note(s): Jt. pseud.: Michael Campbell & Frank Morelli.
Seaton, Harris 1944- [singer, songwriter]
Seaton, B. B. *Source(s):* EPMU
Seaton, Bibby *Source(s):* EPMU
Seay, John Allan, Jr. 1940- [singer, songwriter]
Sea, Johnny *Source(s):* CCE59; MCCL
Singing Sea, The *Source(s):* MCCL
Sebastiani, Franco 1918-1996 [composer]
Spier, Robby *Source(s):* CCE58-59; CPOL RE-678-812; KOMP; KOMS; PFSA
Sebenico, (Domenico) Giovanni c.1640-1705 [composer, organist, singer]
Master of Italian Music *Source(s):* NGDM
Sebus, Ludwig 1925- [composer]
Ossen, Lutz *Source(s):* KOMP; KOMS; PFSA
Sechler, John Ray 1919- [singer, songwriter, guitarist]
Sechler, Curly *Source(s):* LCAR; MCCL
Sechter, Simon 1788-1867 [composer, organist, theorist, conductor]
Note(s): Portrait: ETUP 56:4 (Apr. 1938): 210
Heiter, Ernst *Source(s):* MACM; MELL; STGR
Seckles, Bernhard 1872- [composer]
Note(s): Portrait: ETUP 56:4 (Apr. 1938): 210
Bernhard, S. *Source(s):* TPRF
Sedlmayr, Artur 1918- [composer]
Rua, Hans *Source(s):* KOMP; KOMS; PFSA; RIES
Seeger, Charles (Louis) 1886-1979 [musicologist, composer, writer on music]
Sands, Carl *Source(s):* BAKR; GACC p. 29; GROL; LCAR; NGAM
Note(s): Name on works composed for the Composer Collective of New York.
Seeger, Pete(r R.) 1919- [singer, songwriter]
America's Tuning Fork *Source(s):* CASS; CM38; PSND; SIFA
Bowers, Pete *Source(s):* PSND
Campbell, Paul *Source(s):* PMUS
Note(s): Pseud. of The Weavers, i.e., Seeger, Ronnie Gilbert, Lee Hays & Fred Hellerman.
Folk Music Icon *Source(s):* CM38 p. vi
Reincarnated Troubadour, The *Source(s):* PSND
Six, Tom *Source(s):* CCE58; CCE66
Note(s): Jt. pseud.: Ronnie Gilbert, Lee Hays & Fred Hellerman.
Thomas Jefferson of Folk Music, The *Source(s):* PSND; SIFA
Weavers, The *Source(s):* PMUS
Note(s): Jt. pseud.: Lee Hays, Fred Hellerman & Ronnie Gilbert.
Seeger, Robert [or Bob] (Clark) 1945- [singer, songwriter]
Godfather of Nofrills Rock Music, The *Source(s):* CM15
Seelos, Ambros 1935- [composer]
Brosi, Bernt *Source(s):* KOMS; PFSA
Monty, Carlo *Source(s):* KOMS; PFSA
Seeman, Arthur 1861- [composer]
Nautilus, A. *Source(s):* COMP
Sefardi, Jehiel Nahmany 1841-1906 [violinist, writer on music, composer]
Consolo, Federico *Source(s):* LYMN
Segalen, Victor 1878-1919 [writer on music]
Anély, Max *Source(s):* LCAR
Max-Anely *Source(s):* RILM 95-09350-bm
Segni, Julio [or Giulio] 1498-1561 [organist, composer]
Biondin *Source(s):* GROL; LCAR; NGDM
Julio [or Giulio] da Modena *Source(s):* BAKR; LCAR; MACM; NGDM; RIEM
Segrest, Fred(erick) 1926- [singer, songwriter, guitarist]
Hart, Freddie *Source(s):* EPMU; FLIN; MCCL
Mr. Easy Lovin *Source(s):* FLIN
Seib, Valentin 1925- [composer]
Mardi, H. J. *Source(s):* KOMP; PFSA
Seiber, Mátyás (George) 1905-1960 [composer, teacher]

Matthis, G(eorge) S. *Source(s):* CCE36 Efor46307; CCE64-65; CPMU; DEA3
Seibert, Nicole 1964- [composer]
Nicole *Source(s):* PFSA
Note(s): Also used by Denise Lillian Laval Soza; do not confuse with Nicole (Wray) or Nicole (McCloud)
Seidel, (George Lucas) Emil 1864-1947 [composer]
Ledies, Jean *Source(s):* JASA p. 322
Seidl, Johann Gabriel 1804-1875 [author]
Communis, Meta *Source(s):* LCAR; PIPE; WORB
Ledie, Emil *Source(s):* LCAR; PIPE
Seidler, Alan [composer]
Tom Lehrer of the Seventies, The *Source(s):* http://www.alanseidler.com/pages/bio.html (6 Mar. 2005)
Seidman, William 1953- [composer, author, guitarist]
Sideman, William *Source(s):* ASCP
Seigenthaler, William Robert 1934- [composer, author]
Trebor, Robert *Source(s):* ASCP
Seigle, Fred Elton 1931-1960 [composer, conductor]
Elton, Fred *Source(s):* ASCP
Seitz, Ernest (Joseph) 1892-1978 [pianist, songwriter]
Roberts, Raymond *Source(s):* CANE
Seitz, Roland F(orrest) 1867-1946 [composer]
Parade Music Prince *Source(s):* SMIN
Seldon, Albert Wiggin 1922- [composer, lyricist]
Selden, Albert *Source(s):* PSND
Seligmacher, Moritz 1895-1956 [composer]
Silverson, Sam *Source(s):* PFSA
Selinsky, Wladimir 1910-1984 [composer, conductor, violinist]
Sills, Ward *Source(s):* CCE61; CLTP ("Clock, The")
Selvaggio, John R(alph) [singer, lyricist]
Carlo, Johnny *Source(s):* ASCP; CCE58; CCE60
Semere, Charles Gabriel [composer]
Gabriel, Charles *Source(s):* CCE42 #18377 Eunp292765 ("We Are Fighting for Liberty")
Note(s): Do not confuse with Charles H(utchinson) Gabriel.
Semien, (Ivory) Lee 1931- [singer, drummer, songwriter]
King Ivory Lee *Source(s):* HARS
Lee, Ivory *Source(s):* HARS
Lee, King Ivory *Source(s):* HARS
Semien, Sidney 1938-1998 [singer, guitarist, songwriter]
Count Rockin' Sydney *Source(s):* HARS
Rockin' Sidney [or Sydney] *Source(s):* EPMU; HARS; LCAR
Simien, Sidney *Source(s):* HARS
Note(s): Incorrect spelling of surname.
Sendel, Erich 1917-1988 [composer]
Moran, Fred *Source(s):* KOMP; KOMS; PFSA
Picket, Ticky [or Tichy] *Source(s):* CCE75 Efor178654; CPOL RE-760-319 & RE-760-320
Note(s): In CPOL Picket is listed as pseud. of Fred Moran.
Senf, H(einrich) C(hristian) L(ebrecht) ?-1793 [poet, composer]
Filidor *Source(s):* WORB
H. C. F. *Source(s):* WORB
Senfl, Ludwig c.1486-1542 (or 43) [composer]
Note(s): Portraits: ETUP 56:4 (Apr. 1938): 210; Matthews, J. E. *Handbook of Musical History*. London: H. Grevel, 1898, 74.
L. S. *Source(s):* CPMU
Seredy, J(ulius) S. 1874-1946 [composer]
Ambrosio, W. F. *Source(s):* CCE41 #21449 E94722 & E9204
Note(s): C. Fisher house name; see NOTES: Ambroisio, W. F.
Collier, Franklin *Source(s):* CCE44 #31631 E124025
Deery, S. *Source(s):* CCE37 E60331; CCE48 E25298, E25299, E26521, E26524, E26526 & E26527
Dersey, S. J. *Source(s):* CCE35 E47017
Fields, Jules *Source(s):* CCE39 #24405 E77820
Gaylord, A. F. *Source(s):* CCE43 #11022 E113022; CCE74
Kent, H. R. *Source(s):* CCE42 #11836 E100678; CCE48-49
Note(s): Also used by Paul Sterrett and Louis-Philippe Laurendeau; see NOTES: Kent, H. R.
Pearson, E. M. *Source(s):* CCE42 #45550 E108771
Price, S. J. *Source(s):* CCE38 E66505; CCE40 #23421 E86568; CCE65
Seredy, Jules *Source(s):* CCE38 E67732
Sermisy, Claudin [or Claude] de 1490-1562 [composer]
Claudin *Source(s):* IBIM; WORB
Sermon, Erick 1968- [rapper]
E Double *Source(s):* AMUS
EPMD *Source(s):* AMUS; EPMU
Note(s): Jt. pseud.: Parrish Smith.
Erick and Parrish Making Dollars *Source(s):* AMUS; EPMU
Note(s): Jt. pseud.: Parrish Smith.
Green-Eyed Bandit *Source(s):* AMUS
MC Grand Royal *Source(s):* AMUS
Servais, Adrien François 1807-1866 [violoncellist, composer]
Paganini of the'Cello, The *Source(s):* PRAT
Note(s): See also David Popper.
Servoz, Harriet 1885-1939 [composer]
Samama, Azuma *Source(s):* COHN; HIXN

Setaro, Pete(r) (D(onald)) 1922 (or 24)- [composer, author]
Baxter, Larry *Source(s):* ASCP; CCE55; CPOL RE-286-773
Farnsworth, Larry *Source(s):* CCE59
Settelmeyer, Hermann Josef 1939- [composer]
Deutsch, Peter *Source(s):* PFSA
Settle, Lee Edgar 1882-1949 [composer]
Settle, Jelly *Source(s):* JASA p. 314 (port.)
Severinsen, Carl H(ilding) 1927- [trumpeter, composer, bandleader]
Severinsen, Doc *Source(s):* ASCP; CM01; LCAR
Severn, Edmund 1862-1942 [composer]
Note(s): Portraits: ETUP 56:4 (Apr. 1938): 210; METR 19:4 (Apr. 1903): 19 (with bio.)
Ambrosio, W. F. *Source(s):* CCE37 (Index)
Note(s): C. Fisher house name; see NOTES: Ambrosio, W. F.
Severson, Edward Louis, III 1964 (or 66)- [singer, lyricist]
Crazy Eddie *Source(s):* IMDB
Mueller, Edward [or Eddie] *Source(s):* IMDB; LCAR
Turner, Jerome *Source(s):* IMDB
Vedder, Eddie *Source(s):* ALMN; IMDB; LCAR; NOMG
Seveste, Jules 1846-1871 [playwright, actor, producer]
Herbel *Source(s):* PIPE
Jaime, E. *Source(s):* PIPE
Note(s): Jt. pseud.: Pierre-Joseph Rousseau.
Sewall, Frank 1837-1915 [composer]
F. S. *Source(s):* CPMU ("The Welcome")
Note(s): Probably Sewall.
Seward, Alexander T. 1902-1972 [singer, guitarist, songwriter]
Blues Boy *Source(s):* HARS; LCAR
Note(s): See also Riley B. King & Andrew Odom.
Blues King *Source(s):* HARS; LCAR
Georgia Slim *Source(s):* HARS; LCAR
Guitar Slim *Source(s):* HARS; LCAR
Note(s): See also Eddie Jones, Norman G. Green & Raymond Maurice Otey. Also used by guitarist James Stephens (1915-).
Seward, Slim *Source(s):* HARS; LCAR
Seward, Benjamin fl. 1750? [hymnist]
B. S. *Source(s):* JULN
Seyfried, Ignaz (Xaver) von 1776-1841 [conductor, composer, writer on music]
Krug, Dr. S. *Source(s):* HEYT
Philomusos, Amadeus *Source(s):* HEYT
Sfrd. *Source(s):* HEYT
Seymour, Albert [composer]
Schaefer, Christia(n) *Source(s):* CCE45 #16981, 328 R136337; CPMU (publication dates 1929-63)
Seymour, George F(rancis) A(lexander) (Earl of Yarmouth) [librettist, lyricist, pianist]
Hope, Eric *Source(s):* GANA p. 1055
Yarmouth, George Francis Alexander *Source(s):* CPMU (publication dates 1886-1905)
Seymour, Mary Alice Ives 1837-1897 [educator, musician, author]
Hensel, Octavia *Source(s):* LCAR
Shaberman, Harold 1924- [composer]
Irvin, Harold *Source(s):* CCE54; CPOL RE-64-227
Irving, Harold *Source(s):* CPOL RE-167-40
Ross, David *Source(s):* CCE59; CPOL RE-344-757
Note(s): Jt. pseud.: Robert [or Bob] Halfin & Ralph Ruvin.
Shackley, Frederick (Newell) 1868- [composer, organist]
Note(s): Portrait: ETUP 56:5 (May 1938): 280
Newell, Frederick *Source(s):* TPRF
Shad, Bob [songwriter]
Ellen, Robert *Source(s):* PSND
Shade, Will 1898-1966 [singer, guitarist, songwriter]
Brimmer, Son *Source(s):* HARS
Shafer, Matt(hew) 1974?- [songwriter, performer]
Uncle Kracker *Source(s):* AMIR; AMUS; LCAR; PMUS-00
Shafer, Sanger D. 1934- [songwriter]
Shafer, Whitey *Source(s):* CCME; ENCM; LCAR
Shaffer, Lloyd (M.) 1901-1999 [composer, conductor]
Loyd, Marc *Source(s):* CCE52
Moreno, Marcos *Source(s):* ASCP; CCE61; CPOL RE-461-754
Shaftel, Arthur [or Artie] 1916- [composer, author]
Arthur, Bob(b) *Source(s):* ASCP; CCE47; LCAR; PMUS
Shaftel, Selig (Sidney) 1913- [composer, author, singer]
Almeda, Margarite *Source(s):* CPOL RE-21-542
Skylar, Sunny [or Sonny] *Source(s):* ASCP; CCE43 #10173 E113490; CCE55; LCAR; STUW
Vaughn, Michael *Source(s):* CPOL RE-137-559
Shakespeare, John 1942- [singer, songwriter]
Carter, John *Source(s):* CCE73; EPMU; HARR
Carter-Lewis *Source(s):* CCE63; EPMU; PMUS
Note(s): Jt. pseud.: Kenneth Hawker.
Shallman, Morty [singer, songwriter]
Ashbury, Andrew *Source(s):* http://www.morty.org/pages/890263/index.htm (24 Oct. 2003)
Shank, Clifford (Everett, Jr.) 1926- [instrumentalist, composer]
Legge, Bud *Source(s):* JAMU
Shank, Bud *Source(s):* ASCP; CCE64; LCAR; PEN2; PSND
Spelvin, George *Source(s):* JAMU

Shapcote, Emily Mary (née Steward) 1828-after 1885? [hymnist]
E *Source(s):* JULN (Suppl.)
Shapiro, Beverly Myers [author, singer, actor]
Janis, Beverly *Source(s):* ASCP
Shardlow, Clare [songwriter]
Manilla, Tony *Source(s):* CPOL RE-364-775
Note(s): Jt. pseud.: Jack Fishman (1918 (or 19)-). Fishman also used as jt. pseud. with Cyril Stapleton; see NOTES: Manilla, Tony.
Sharp, Martha [songwriter]
Posey, Sandy *Source(s):* EPMU; ROOM
Note(s): Incorrectly identified as a pseud. of Martha Sharp, who is an executive at Warner brothers in Nashville. (http://www.poparchives.com.au/feature.php?id=161 (30 Mar. 2005)
Sharp, Robert Louis, Jr. 1924- [composer, author, singer]
Jones, Agnes *Source(s):* ASCP; CCE63; PMUS
Sharp, William 1855-1905 [composer]
MacLeod, Fiona *Source(s):* KILG; LCAR; LOWN; PIPE; ROOM
Sharpe, Alexander J(ohn) 1814-1890 [philologist, mathematician, writer on music]
Ellis, Alexander J(ohn) *Source(s):* BAKR; NGDM; RIEM
Sharpe, Joseph 1876 (or 77)-1943 [composer]
Oakley, Olly *Source(s):* JASG; JASR
Sharples, Winston S., Jr. [composer]
Singleton, Win *Source(s):* CLTP ("Mighty Hercules")
Shaver, Floyd Herbert 1905-1995 [composer, dancer, pianist]
Shaver, Buster *Source(s):* ASCP
Shavers, Charlie [i.e., Charles] (James) 1917-1971 [trumpeter, composer, arranger]
Enlovely, Swede *Source(s):* JAMU
Kidde, Chuck *Source(s):* JAMU
Schmaltz, Joe *Source(s):* JAMU
Shaw, George Bernard 1856-1950 [playwright, author, critic]
Corno di Bassetto *Source(s):* LCAR; NGDM; ROOM
Note(s): Criticism in: *The Star,* 1888-90.
Don Giovanni *Source(s):* GROL; NGDM
Note(s): Nickname.
Lee, George John Vandeleur *Source(s):* NGDM; ROOM
Note(s) Wrote musical criticisms in: *The Hornet* as "ghost" for Lee.
Lee, Vandeleur *Source(s):* NGDM; ROOM
Ribbonson, Horatio *Source(s):* CART
S. *Source(s):* CART
Shaw, Gerald 1911- [songwriter]
Rübel, Ernst *Source(s):* CCE59
Note(s): Jt. pseud.: Stanley Masters [i.e., Smith-Masters]
Shaw, Martin (Fallas) 1875-1958 [composer]
Note(s): Portrait: CYBH
B. E. L. *Source(s):* CCE25 E630430 ("The Night is Ended and Morning Nears")
M. S. *Source(s):* CPMU
M. W. V. R. S. *Source(s):* DIEH ("Cobbold")
Note(s): Jt. pseud.: Ralph Vaughan Williams.
Shaw, Oliver 1776 (or 79)-1848 (or 49) [singer, songwriter]
Blind Singer, The *Source(s):* PSND
Shaw, Robert 1908-1985 [singer, pianist, songwriter]
Shaw, Fud *Source(s):* HARS
Shayne, J. H. [songwriter]
Shayne, Freddie *Source(s):* PMUS
Shayne, Larry 1909-1996 [composer, publisher]
Joseph, Ray *Source(s):* ASCP; CCE51; CCE68; PMUS
Shearing, George 1919- [pianist, leader, composer]
Johnson, Phil *Source(s):* JAMU
Shearouse, Florine W(hiteurst) 1898- [lyricist]
Ashby, Florine *Source(s):* CCE53-54; CCE62; PSND
Stuart, Flo *Source(s):* CCE59
Sheff, Robert Nathan 1945- [composer, keyboardist]
Tyranny, "Blue" Gene *Source(s):* BAKR; LCAR; NGAM
Shelley, Percy Bysshe 1792-1822 [poet]
Note(s): See PSND & LCAR for additional nonmusic-related pseudonyms.
Victor *Source(s):* GOTT
Note(s): Also used by Prince Rogers Nelson.
Shelly, Harry (Rowe) 1858- [composer]
Note(s): Portrait: ETUP 56:5 (May 1938): 280
Gabriel-Shelly *Source(s):* CCE30 E12153; CCE47 E12153
Note(s): Jt. pseud.: Charles H. Gabriel.
Shelton, Julia (née Finley) 1835?- [poet, author]
Lorrimer, Laura *Source(s):* HOGR; WORB
Shelton, Larry Zane 1950- [composer, author, singer]
Who, Ziggy *Source(s):* ASCP
Shelton, Travis [songwriter]
Carlton, John *Source(s):* CPOL RE-163-333
Note(s): Jt. pseud.: Walter (Charles) Ehret. Ehret also used as jt. pseud. with other individuals; see NOTES: Carlton, John.
Noble, Arthur *Source(s):* CCE58
Shemer, Naomi 1930-2004 [composer]
First Lady of Israeli Song *Source(s):* LCAR
National Poet, (The) *Source(s):* GROL
Sheng, Zongliang 1955- [composer, pianist]
Chinese Bartók, The *Source(s):* MUWB
Sheng, Bright *Source(s):* MUWB

Shenshin, Afanaskii Afanas'evich 1820-1892 [writer]
Fet, A. A. *Source(s):* GOTH
Shepard, Ollie Imogene 1933- [singer, songwriter]
Shepard, Jean *Source(s):* LCAR; MCCL
Shepard-Hayward, Mae [composer]
Bergere, Lucile *Source(s):* TPRF
Shephard, Frederick Edward 1891-1949 [producer, author]
Shephard, (F.) Firth *Source(s):* GAN2
Shepherd, Berisford 1917- [drummer, arranger]
Shepherd, Shep *Source(s):* BAKR; CCE58; LCAR; NGDJ
Shepherd, Horace [composer]
Pastore, Escaro *Source(s):* RFSO
Sheppard, Henry Fleetwood 1824?-1901 [composer]
H. F. S. *Source(s):* CPMU
Sheppard, James ?-1970 [singer, songwriter]
Shep *Source(s):* PSND
Sheppard, Eightbass *Source(s):* CCE61; CPOL RE-451-189
Sheppard, Shane *Source(s):* CCE62; CPOL RE-475-321
Sheppard, Josephte Desbarats [pianist, composer]
Canadian Lady, The *Source(s):* http://www.carleton.ca/carletonsound/cscd1006.html (25 July 2005)
Note(s): Possible pseud.?
Shere, Charles 1935- [composer, music critic]
Remolif, Charles *Source(s):* GROL
Sherer, Michael before 1546-c.1607 [composer, organist]
Tonsor, Michael *Source(s):* NGDM
Sheridan, Helen Selina 1807-1867 [composer, playwright]
Blackwood, (Mrs.) Price *Source(s):* LCAR; SPTH p. 87
Dufferin (and Clandeboye), Helen Selina *Source(s):* LCAR
Note(s): Married name.
Gushington, Impulsia *Source(s):* CART; COHN; HIXN; LCAR
Sherman, Al(bert) 1897-1973 [songwriter]
Clifford, Jack *Source(s):* CCE57
Jefe, E. L. *Source(s):* CCE70; CPOL PAu-148-841
Lewis, Sherman *Source(s):* CCE30 E12899; CCE57
Note(s): Jt. pseud.: Al(an) Lewis.
Picker, Tom *Source(s):* CCE62 R304058
Note(s): Jt. pseud.: Al(an) Lewis & Abner Silver.
Sherman, Tobe *Source(s):* CCE26 Index; LCPC 1926
Note(s): Jt. pseud.: Charles Tobias.
Song Writers on Parade *Source(s):* CCE32 Eunp56182
Note(s): Jt. pseud.: Percy Wenrich, Sidney Clare, Charles Tobias, Al(an) Lewis, (T.) Murray Mencher & Vincent Rose.
White, Norman *Source(s):* CCE57
Note(s): Jt. pseud.: Al(an) Lewis.
Wilson, Walter *Source(s):* CCE62 R304057
Note(s): Jt. pseud.: Al(an) Lewis & Abner Silver.
Shewell, George Dunbar ?-1938 [composer]
Note(s): Portrait: ETUP 58:10 (Oct. 1940): 714
Austin, Martin *Source(s):* TPRF
Shiflett, Bobby [songwriter]
Alamantra *Source(s):* SISO; http://www.alamantra.org/review01.htm (27 Jan. 2005)
Shilston, Alfred Edward [composer]
Grey, Langford *Source(s):* CPMU (publication dates 1886-99)
Shin, John Bush, III 1935- [singer, songwriter, guitarist]
Bush, Johnny *Source(s):* AMUS; MCCL
Country Caruso, The *Source(s):* MCCL
Shiner, Merv(in) 1921- [singer, guitarist, songwriter]
Shiner, Nurv *Source(s):* NOMG
Shines, John Ned 1915-1992 [singer, guitarist, songwriter]
Little Wolf *Source(s):* HARS
Shoe Shine Johnny *Source(s):* AMUS; HARS
Shinhoster, Jonathan [songwriter, performer]
J-Shin *Source(s):* PMUS-00
Shipley, Daniel 1945- [singer, songwriter, guitarist]
Brannon, R. C. *Source(s):* EPMU; MCCL
Shmulewitz, Solomon 1868-1943 [composer]
Small, Sol(oman) *Source(s):* CCE22 E529907; HESK; LCAR; LCPC letter cited [nd]; SEND
Shneour, Zalman c.1885-1959 [poet; lyricist]
Shneyer, S. *Source(s):* HESK
Short, Annabelle (Macauly Allen) 1930- [singer, songwriter, actress]
Lynch, Annabelle *Source(s):* CLAG; LCAR
Ross, Annie *Source(s):* CLAG (see under: Lynch); LCAR; PEN2; PSND
Short, J. D. 1902-1962 [singer, instrumentalist, songwriter]
Note(s): No given names; only initials.
Carter, Spider *Source(s):* LCAR
Note(s): Possible pseud.
Floyd, Ell-Zee *Source(s):* LCAR
Note(s): Possible pseud.
Hanen, R. T. *Source(s):* LCAR
Note(s): Probable pseud.
Neckbones *Source(s):* LCAR
Note(s): Probable pseud.
Short, Jaydee *Source(s):* AMUS; HARS; LCAR
Short, Jelly Jaw *Source(s):* AMUS; HARS; LCAR
Stone, Joe *Source(s):* LCAR
Note(s): Probable pseud.
Shortridge, E. L. [arranger]

E. L. S. *Source(s):* CPMU (publication dates 1885-99)
Shostakovich, Dmitri Dmitryevich 1906-1975 [composer]
Beethoven of the 20th Century *Source(s):* http://musicinwords.free.fr/dschlife.htm (6 Apr. 2005)
Hero of Socialist Labor, The *Source(s):* PSND
Showalter, Max 1917-2000 [actor, composer, producer]
Adams, Casey *Source(s):* LCAR; PSND
Shower, Hudson 1919- [singer, guitarist, songwriter]
Note(s): Some sources incorrectly give orig. surname: Showers.
Little Hudson *Source(s):* AMUS; HARS
Shrivall, Richard [composer]
Shrivalli, Ricardo *Source(s):* CPMU (publication dates c.1840-1876)
Shrubsole, William, Jr. 1759-1829 [hymnist]
Note(s): Do not confuse with composer William Shrubsole, 1760-1806.
Junior *Source(s):* JULN
Probus *Source(s):* HATF; JULN
W. S. *Source(s):* HATF
Shukotoff, Arnold 1909-1989 [composer, writer, editor, music executive]
Shaw, Arnold *Source(s):* BAKR; CCE41 #36612 Eunp261980; CCE69 R46007
Sloan, Ken *Source(s):* ASCP; CCE52; CCE58; LCAR
Note(s): Pseud. of Arnold Shaw [i.e., Shukotoff].
Shulman, Edward 1918-1986 [composer, singer, bandleader]
Shu, Eddie *Source(s):* KINK; LCAR; PSND
Shuree, Eddie *Source(s):* LCAR
Sibelius, Jean [originally Johan] (Christian Julius) 1865-1957 [composer]
Composer of a Jigsaw Puzzle That Dropped from Heaven *Source(s):* http://inkpot.com/classical/bkphaidonsib.html (7 Oct. 2002)
Note(s): Called himself.
Sibeliomania *Source(s):* GRAN (see under: Quigley, Edwin Olin, Jr.)
Note(s): Term used to describe Olin Downes' enthusiam for Sibelius' music.
Sibelius, Janne *Source(s):* GROL
Sibirá (Puig), José 1882-1980 [musicologist, writer on music]
Ribó, Jesús A. *Source(s):* GROL; LCAR
Sibson, E. [songwriter]
Cympson, Edward *Source(s):* CPMU (publication dates 1874-1900)
Sichart, René Reinhold 1946- [composer]
Rendall *Source(s):* KOMP; KOMS; PFSA
Siday, Eric ?-1976 [composer]
Austen, Eric *Source(s):* CCE57; MUWB
Note(s): Jt. pseud.: Austen [or Austin] (Herbert) Croom-Johnson.
Owen, Eric *Source(s):* MUWB
Note(s): Jt. pseud.: Reg Owen.
Sidow c.1700-c.1754 [songwriter]
Seedo, Mr. *Source(s):* BAKR; NGDM
Siebach, Konrad 1912-1995 [bassist, teacher, editor]
Spitzbarth *Source(s):* GDRM; GROL
Siede, Ludwig 1888-1956 [composer]
Sentis *Source(s):* SUPN
Siegmeister, Elie 1909-1991 [composer]
Swift, L. E. *Source(s):* GACC p. 29; GROL; LCAR; NGAM
Note(s): On works for Composers Collective of New York.
Siemon, Carl (W.) 1918-2003 [composer, organist, teacher]
Simone, Carl *Source(s):* ASCP; CCE63
Sienkiewicz, Henryk (Adam Aleksandr Pius) 1946-1916 [author]
Litwos *Source(s):* PIPE; PSND
Sievey, Chris [singer, songwriter]
Sidebottom, Frank *Source(s):* WARN
Sifler, Paul John 1911-2001 [composer, choral director, organist]
Pablo, Juan *Source(s):* ASCP
Sigismondo da Jenne c.1580-1629 [composer]
Nobile Palermitano *Source(s):* http://www.carpediem-records.de/en/cielo/sigismondo.htm (7 Oct. 2002)
Sigismondo d'India *Source(s):* WORB
Sigler, Walter 1941- [singer, songwriter]
Sigler, Bunny *Source(s):* AMUS; EPMU; HARR
Sigman, Carl 1909-2000 [composer, author, lawyer]
Note(s): Portrait: OB00
Barnes, Jessie *Source(s):* ASCP; SHAP; http://www.majorsongs.com/cd09.htm (25 Mar. 2005)
Burke, Lee *Source(s):* ASCP; SHAP
Lee, Craig *Source(s):* ASCP; CCE68; SHAP
Signaigo, J(oseph) Augustine 1835-1876 [author]
Hughes, Capt. *Source(s):* HOGR; OCLC 23152556 ("Dixie, the Land of King Cotton")
Sikorski, Józef 1813 (or 15)-1896 [critic, composer]
Dudaszek, Orfeusz *Source(s):* PIPE
Gólka, Apollin *Source(s):* PIPE
Melomański, Telephon *Source(s):* PIPE
Silberg, Rubin [composer; lyricist]
Berg, Rudolf *Source(s):* HESK
Silberstein, Rhéa [composer]
Silberta, Rhéa *Source(s):* SEND

Silly, (Gilbert) François (Léopold) 1927-2001 [composer, singer]
Note(s): Portrait: OB01
Bécaud, Gilbert *Source(s):* BUL3; CASS; EPMU; GAMM; HARD; HARR; OB01
French Sinatra, The *Source(s):* http://www.worldalmanac.com/200201WAE-Newsletter.htm (7 Oct. 2002)
Note(s): See also (Shanaur) Varenagh Aznavourian.
Monsieur 100,000 Volts *Source(s):* CASS
Silva, Horace (Ward Martin Tavares) 1928- [pianist, bandleader, composer]
Silver, Horace *Source(s):* GROL; NGDJ
Silva, Ismael [composer]
Soul of Samba, The *Source(s):* http://www.artistdirect.com/music/artist/card/0,,684730,00.html 22 Oct. 2003)
Silva, José Barbosa [or B(atista)] (da) 1893-1930 [pianist, composer]
King of Samba, The *Source(s):* http://www.artistdirect.com/music/artist/card/0,684730,00.html (30 Oct. 2002)
Note(s): See also Carlos Moreira de Castro.
Sinho *Source(s):* CCE61; LCAR; RILM 84-02146-bf
Zezinho *Source(s):* CCE63 Efor95849
Silvani, Francesco c.1660-between 1728-44 [librettist]
Valsini, F(rancesco) *Source(s):* ALMC; MELL; NGDM; NGDO; PIPE; SONN; STGR
Silver, Abner 1899-1966 [songwriter]
Picker, Tom *Source(s):* CCE62 R304058
Note(s): Jt. pseud.: Al(an) Lewis & Al(bert) Sherman.
Wilson, Walter *Source(s):* CCE62 304057
Note(s): Jt. pseud.: Al(an) Lewis & Al(bert) Sherman.
Silver, Charles L. 1948- [author, lyricist]
Wolfsilver, C. L. *Source(s):* ASCP
Silver, Dave 1905- [songwriter]
Arden, Rod(d) *Source(s):* CCE52-56; CPOL RE-63-953; CPOL RE-174-060
Guillard, Michael *Source(s):* CCE35 Efor39938
Note(s): Jt. pseud.: Leon Harry [i.e., Sugarman] & Leo Towers [i.e., Leo(nard) Blitz]
Silver, Richard L. 1955- [writer]
Revlis, Earl *Source(s):* CCE78; GOTH
Silverberg, Frederick (Irwin) 1936- [composer, author, pianist]
Silver, Fred(erick) *Source(s):* ASCP; CCE61; GOTH
Silverman, Belle Miriam 1939- [singer, author, opera administrator]
Bubbles *Source(s):* BAKO
Sills, Beverly *Source(s):* BAKO
Silverstein, Herman 1910-1984 [composer, lyricist]
Silvers, Doc *Source(s):* ASCP; CCE66-68
Silvers, Herman *Source(s):* CCE65-68
Silverstein, Shel(by) 1932-1999 [author, illustrator, composer]
Uncle Shelby *Source(s):* CART; PSND
Silvestrino, Francesco fl. c.1540-50 [composer]
Chechin *Source(s):* NGDM; WORB
Simmen, Hans Georg 1918-2004 [writer on jazz]
Simmen, Johnny *Source(s):* NGDJ; WASH
Simmonds, Selina 1849-1889 [actress, singer, author]
Dolaro, Dolly *Source(s):* GAN1; GAN2
Dolaro, Selina *Source(s):* GAN1; GAN2; WORB
Simmons, Earl 1970- [rapper, songwriter]
DMX *Source(s):* AMIR; AMUS; CM25; CPOL PA-1-034-561; PMUS-00
Dark Man X *Source(s):* AMUS; CM25
Simmons, Mac(k) 1934-2000 [singer, harmonica player, songwriter]
St. Louis Mac *Source(s):* HARS
Simmons, Little Mac(k) *Source(s):* HARS
Sims, Mac *Source(s):* HARS
Simms, Leonce Errol 1881-1951 [actor, director, choreographer]
Errol, Leon *Source(s):* GAN2
Simon, Abraham 1897-1957 [composer, drummer, bandleader]
Lyman, Abe *Source(s):* KINK; REHH
Simon, George (T(homas)) 1912-2001 [author, lyricist, record producer]
Note(s): Used pseudonyms on writings in *Metronome*. (GROL) To date only one identified.
Pincus, Buck *Source(s):* ASCP; CCE49; CCE55-56
Simon, Gus(tav(e)) [or Augustus] (Edward) 1879-1945 [composer, entertainer, music publisher]
Note(s): Portraits: EWEN; EWPA
Edwards, Gus *Source(s):* BBDP; EWEN; EWPA; GAMM; LYMN; STUW
Edwards, Simon *Source(s):* PSND
Pied Piper of Broadway *Source(s):* MARC p. 273 (see under: Edwards, Gus)
Star Maker, The *Source(s):* PSND
Note(s): From title of screen biography.
Whitmore, Will *Source(s):* CCE28 R45897
Simon, Louise Marie 1903-1990 [composer]
Arrieu, Claude *Source(s):* BUL3; COHN (port.); DWCO (port.); GOTH; GREN; HEIN; HIXN
Simon, Paul Frederick 1941- [singer, songwriter]
Note(s): Portrait: LYMN (with Art Garfunkel)
Kane, Paul *Source(s):* PSND
Landis, Jerry *Source(s):* CCE58; PSND
Tom and Jerry *Source(s):* EPMU; PSND; SHAD
Note(s): Jt. pseud.: Art Garfunkel.
Simon, Waldemar 1919- [composer]
Brilland, Robert *Source(s):* KOMS; PFSA
Felten, Jean *Source(s):* KOMS; PFSA

Sarabin, Franz *Source(s):* KOMS; PFSA
Werlin, Paul *Source(s):* CCE64-65; KOMP; PFSA
Simon, William Louis 1920-2000 [composer, author, saxophonist]
Lewis, Bill *Source(s):* ASCP; CCE56 Eunp
Nomis, Lou *Source(s):* ASCP; CCE53
Simonetti, Ted Eddy 1904- [composer, author]
Eddy, Ted *Source(s):* ASCP (see reference)
Simoni, Pascal 1908- [playwright, composer]
Bastia, Pascal *Source(s):* CCE62; CCE72 R541440; GAN1; GAN2; WORB
Paris, Irving *Source(s):* CCE57; GAN1; GAN2
Simoni, Renato 1875-1952 [critic, playwright, librettist]
Kambo, S. *Source(s):* MELL
Turno *Source(s):* GROL; NGDO; PIPE
Simonini, Josef 1901-1982 [composer]
Thaler, Sepp *Source(s):* SMIN
Simonson, Britt [lyricist]
Harlen, Jack *Source(s):* CCE62; PMUS
Simonson, Ernest Lowell 1953- [composer, arranger, pianist]
Simonson, Si *Source(s):* ASCP
Simper, Caleb 1856 (or 57)-1942 [composer]
Clare, Edwin [or Edwyn] A. *Source(s):* CPMU; TPRF
Simpson, Eugene Thamon 1932- [composer, teacher, singer]
Thamon, Eugene *Source(s):* ASCP (see reference)
Simpson, Jane Cross 1811-1886 [hymnist]
Gertrude *Source(s):* CART; ROOM
Simpson, Joseph 1934- [singer, songwriter]
Simpson, Red *Source(s):* CCE63-64; CCME; EPMU; MCCL
Suitcase Red *Source(s):* EPMU
Sims, Albert Ernest 1896-1981 [composer]
Sims, George *Source(s):* REHH
Note(s): Commonly known as George.
Sims, George R(obert) 1847-1922 [dramatist]
Dagonet *Source(s):* KILG ("Billy's Rose" & others, see p. 522)
Note(s): Also used by J. A. Hardwick.
Daubigny, Delacour *Source(s):* GANA p. 192
Sims, John Haley 1925-1985 [saxophonist, composer]
James, Jesse *Source(s):* JAMU
Sims, Zoot *Source(s):* LCAR
Zoot, Jack *Source(s):* JAMU
Sims, Peter 1938- [composer]
LaRoc(c)a, Pete(r) *Source(s):* CCE68; CCE73; PSND
Simsa, B. 1930- [composer]
Janovicky, Karel *Source(s):* BUL1
Singer, André 1907-1996 [composer]
Ross, Alexander *Source(s):* GOTH
Sipes, Leonard Raymond 1930-2000 [singer, songwriter, guitarist, clergyman]
Collins, Tommy *Source(s):* AMUS; CCE66-68; CCME; EPMU; MCCL; NASF; OB00; PEN2
Sirazi, G. [composer]
Vecchio, Il *Source(s):* DEAR
Note(s): See also James Cervetto (1682-1783) & Dario Varotari.
Širca, Friderik 1859-1948 [composer]
Savin, Risto *Source(s):* LCAR
Schirza, Friederich (Elder) von *Source(s):* MACM; MELL; WORB
Note(s): Listed as original name.
Sissle, Noble (Lee) 1889-1975 [singer, lyricist, bandleader]
Note(s): Portrait: EWEN; WOLL p. [59] (with Eubie [i.e., James Hubert] Blake)
Black, Willie *Source(s):* SUTT
Brown, Willie *Source(s):* PSND; SUTT
Garnett, Jim *Source(s):* SUTT
Graham, Leonard *Source(s):* SUTT
Johnson, Lee *Source(s):* SUTT
Skelton, (Sir) John 1831-1897 [writer]
Shirley *Source(s):* JULN (Suppl.)
Skingle, Kenneth Thomas 1924-1997 [saxophonist, composer, bandleader]
Graham, Kenny *Source(s):* EPMU; PEN2
Skinner, James 1909-1979 [singer, songwriter, guitarist]
Kentucky Colonel, The *Source(s):* MCCL
Skinner, James Scott 1843-1927 [violinist, composer, dancing teacher]
Strathspey King, The *Source(s):* GROL
Skriabin, Nikolai (Mikhailovich) 1886-1966 [composer]
Nolinsky, N(ikolai Mihalovich) *Source(s):* BUL1; LCAR
Slater, David Dick 1869-1942 [organist, teacher, composer]
Note(s): Portrait: ETUP 56:6 (June1938): 388
Ambroise, Paul *Source(s):* CANE; CPMU; TPRF
Aubry, Leon *Source(s):* CANE
Hunt, Erland *Source(s):* CANE
Meredyth, Jean *Source(s):* CCE16 E384753
Rae, Kenneth *Source(s):* CANE; CPMU; TPRF
Slater, Edward 1844-1920 [composer]
Barri, Odoardo *Source(s):* GAMM; GANA; GOTE; KILG; MUWB; REHH
Slater, (John) Joseph [or Joe] 1872-1926 [composer, lyricist, publisher]
DePinna, Herbert *Source(s):* http://www.antiqbook.com/boox/dac/books80000.shtml (24 Mar. 2005)
DeWitt, Maurice *Source(s):* http://www.users.bigpond.net.au/dacapo/auspiano.html (24 Mar. 2005)

LeBert, Sam *Source(s):* http://www.booksandcollectibles (24 Mar. 2005)
LeRoy, Felix *Source(s):* DAUM; http://www.antiqbook.com/boox/dac/books80000.shtml

Slaughter, M(arion) T(ry) 1883-1948 [singer, songwriter]
Note(s): Portraits: CCME; MILL; VDPS. The following are pseudonyms of Vernon Dalhart, Slaughter's professional name that he took from the towns of Vernon and Dalhart Texas. For additional pseuds. see Allan Sutton's *Pseudonymns on Records, 1892-1942.* 2nd rev. and expanded ed. For jt. pseudonyms on recordings, see MACE, SUTT & VDPS.
Ahearn, James *Source(s):* VDPS
Ahern, James *Source(s):* MACE; SUTT
Albin, Jo(h)n *Source(s):* VDPS; www.pandlantiques.com/tidverdalhart.htm (19 Apr. 2005)
Allen, Mack *Source(s):* KINK; MACE; MCCL; PEN2; STAC; SUTT
Allen, Mark *Source(s):* SUTT
Ballard, Wolfe *Source(s):* MACE; MCCL; SUTT
Belmont, James *Source(s):* VDPS
Benson, George *Source(s):* VDPS
Blake, Harry *Source(s):* VDPS
Britt, Harry *Source(s):* VDPS
Burton, Billy *Source(s):* SUTT
Note(s): Not confirmed, see VDPS. Also used by singer Charles Harrison (see MACE).
Calhoun, Jeff *Source(s):* KINK; MACE; MCCL; STAC; SUTT
Note(s): Also used by Frank Luther [i.e., Francis Luther Crow(e)] & Arthur Fields [i.e., Abe Finkelstein] See SUTT for recording label information.
Calhoun, Jess *Source(s):* MACE; SUTT
Cannon, Jimmy *Source(s):* MACE; SUTT
Cantrell, Jimmy *Source(s):* http://www.geocities.com/robtmorca (7 Oct. 2002)
Carver, Al *Source(s):* AMUS; KINK; MCCL
Clifford, Ed *Source(s):* VDPS
Note(s): Also used by Cliff(ord) Edwards.
Country's First Hack *Source(s):* STAC
Cramer, Al *Source(s):* MACE; PEN2; SUTT
Note(s): Not confirmed, see VDPS
Craver, Al *Source(s):* CCE27 E670797; MACE; PEN2; SUTT
Cullen, Harry *Source(s):* SUTT (2nd ed.)
Cummings, James *Source(s):* MACE; SUTT
Note(s): Also used by Arthur Fields [i.e., Abe Finkelstein]
Dalbert and Banning *Source(s):* GRAC p. 45
Note(s): Jt. pseud.: Al(fred A.) Bernard.
Dalbert, Frank *Source(s):* VDPS
Dale, Vernon *Source(s):* AMUS; MCCL
Dalhart, Frank *Source(s):* http://www.geocities.com/robtmorca
Dalhart, Vernon *Source(s):* EPMU; KINK; LCAR; MACE; MCCL; PEN2; STAC; SUTT p. 100
Dall, Cernon [or Vernon?] *Source(s):* www.pandlantiques.com/tidverdalhart.htm
Dalton, Charles *Source(s):* MACE; SUTT
Dell, Vernon *Source(s):* MACE; SUTT
Dixon, Martin *Source(s):* MACE; SUTT
Note(s): Also used by Frank Luther [i.e., Francis Luther Crow(e)]
Donovan, Hugh *Source(s):* http://www.geocities.com/robtmorca
Note(s): Also used by Arthur Field [i.e., Abe Finkelstein]
Elliott, Joseph *Source(s):* MACE; MCCL; SUTT
Note(s): Also used by Arthur Field [i.e., Abe Finkelstein] & others; see MACE.
Eustic, Richard *Source(s):* VDPS
Evans, Frank *Source(s):* AMUS; MCCL; PEN2; SUTT
Note(s): Also used by Arthur Field [i.e., Abe Finkelstein]. "Frank(lin) Evans" used by Carson J(ay) Robison.
Evans, Hal *Source(s):* MACE; SUTT
Notes(s): Not confirmed, see VDPS.
Ford, Clifford *Source(s):* VDPS
Fuller, Jeff *Source(s):* MACE; SUTT
Note(s): Not confirmed, see VDPS.
Fuller, Jep *Source(s):* MACE; MCCL; SUTT
Gordon, Albert *Source(s):* http://www.geocities.com/robtmorca
Grandfather of Country Music, The *Source(s):* http://www.stardayrecords.com/HallofFame/HallofFame_2.htm (30 Oct. 2002)
Gray, Leslie *Source(s):* http://www.geocities.com/robtmorca
Harris, David *Source(s):* MACE; SUTT
Note(s): Also used by Irving [i.e., Isidore] Kaufman & others; see MACE.
Harris, Harry *Source(s):* MACE; MCCL; SUTT
Note(s): Also used by Clifton (A.) Edwards.
Harris, Henry *Source(s):* MACE; SUTT
Hayes, Lou *Source(s):* MACE; SUTT
Harold, Francis *Source(s):* http://www.geocities.com/robtmorca
Henry, Earl *Source(s):* SUTT (2nd ed.)
Holmes, Fern *Source(s):* VDPS
Note(s): Also used by others.
Hull, Howard *Source(s):* VDPS
Hutchinson, Frank *Source(s):* http://www.pandlantiques.com/tidverdalhart.htm (25 Apr. 2005)

Kincaid, Joe *Source(s):* MACE; SUTT
Notes(s): Not confirmed, see VDPS.
King, Fred *Source(s):* MACE; MCCL; SUTT
Lane, Louis *Source(s):*
http://www.geocities.com/robtmorca
Lattimer, Hugh *Source(s):* AMUS; MACE; MCCL
Lazy Larry *Source(s):* VDPS
Note(s): Not confirmed; also used by Carson J(ay) Robison & Harry (K(irby)) McClintock.
Litchfield, Ben *Source(s):* http://www.geocities.com/robtmorca
Note(s): Also used by Arthur Fields [i.e., Abe Finkelstein]
Little, Tobe *Source(s):* AMUS; KINK; MACE; MCCL; SUTT
Lone Star Ranger, The *Source(s):* AMUS; MACE; MCCL
Note(s): Possible pseud.; Also used by Arthur Fields [i.e., Abe Finkelstein] & John I. White.
Massey, Bob *Source(s):* MACE; MCCL; SUTT
Massey, Guy *Source(s):* MACE; MCCL; PEN2; SUTT
McAfee, Billy *Source(s):* MACE; MCCL
Note(s): Not confirmed; see VDPS.
McAfee, Bob *Source(s):* http://www.pandlantiques.com/tidverdalhart.htm
McAfee, Carlos *Source(s):* MCCL
Note(s): Do not confuse with Carlos B. McAfee [i.e., Carson J(ay) Robison]
McLaughlin, George *Source(s):* MACE; MCCL; SUTT
Notes(s): Not confirmed; see VDPS.
Mr. X *Source(s):* MACE; SUTT
Note(s): Also used by Arthur Fields [i.e., Abe Finkelstein] & Irvin [i.e., Isidor] Kaufman.
Mitchell, Warren *Source(s):* MACE; SUTT
Moore, Harry A. *Source(s):* MACE; SUTT
Note(s): Also used by singer Charles Harrison.
Morbid, George *Source(s):*
http:www.pandlantiques.com/tidverdalhart.htm
Morris, James *Source(s):* MACE; SUTT
Notes(s): Incorrectly reported? See VDPS.
Morse, Dick *Source(s):* SUTT
Nelson, Charles *Source(s):* http://www.geocities.com/robtmorca
O'Hara, Gwyrick *Source(s):* http://www.geocities.com/robtmorca
Peters, Sam *Source(s):* MACE; SUTT
Notes(s): Not confirmed; see VDPS.
Raymond, Harry *Source(s):* MACE; SUTT
Sam, the Barbasol Man *Source(s):* STAC
Scott, Henry *Source(s):* MACE; SUTT
Note(s): Reported, not confirmed, see VDPS. Also used by singer William Robyn.
Sears, Joseph *Source(s):* VDPS
Shaw, Eddie *Source(s):* VDPS
Smith, Joseph *Source(s):* http://www.geocities.com/robtmorca
Smith, Josephus *Source(s):* MACE; SUTT
Stewart, Cliff *Source(s):* MACE; SUTT
Note(s): Also used Arthur Fields [i.e., Abe Finkelstein] & possibly others; see MACE.
Stone, Edward *Source(s):* MACE; SUTT
Note(s): Also used by singer Charles Hart? See MACE
Stone, Howard *Source(s):* http://www.pandlantiques.com/tidverdalhart.htm
Stuart, Billy *Source(s):* MACE; MCCL; SUTT
Terry, Bill *Source(s):*
http://www.geocities.com/robtmorca
Terry, Will *Source(s):* MACE; SUTT
Texas Tenor, The *Source(s):* http://www.geocities.com/robtmorca
Thomas, Bob *Source(s):* VDPS
Note(s): Also used by Arthur Field [i.e., Abe Finkelstein]
Thompson, Fred *Source(s):* VDPS
Toomey, Welby *Source(s):* VDPS
Note(s): Incorrctly cited as pseud. of Dalhart. Welby Toomey was an actual performer from Kentucky.
Turner, Allen *Source(s):* MACE; SUTT
Note(s): Also used by others? See MACE
Turner, Billy *Source(s):*
www.pandlantiques.com/tidverdalhart.htm
Turner, Sid *Source(s):* AMUS; MACE; MCCL; SUTT
Tuttle, Frank *Source(s):* MACE; SUTT
Note(s): Also used by Carson J(ay) Robison.
Vernon, Bill(y) *Source(s):* KINK; MACE; MCCL; PEN2; SUTT
Vernon, Herbert *Source(s):* MACE; SUTT
Notes(s): Not confirmed, see VDPS.
Vernon, Will *Source(s):* MACE; SUTT
Notes(s): Not confirmed, see VDPS.
Veteran, Vel *Source(s):* MACE; SUTT
Notes(s): Incorrectly reported? See VDPS. Also used by Arthur Fields [i.e., Abe Finkelstein] & Irving [i.e., Isidore] Kaufman.
Watson, Tom *Source(s):* KINK; MACE; MCCL; STAC; SUTT
West, Charles *Source(s):* VDPS
White, Bob *Source(s):* AMUS; KINK; MACE; MCCL; STAC; SUTT
White, George *Source(s):* MACE; SUTT
Note(s): Also used by Frank Marvin (see MACE) & George Weitz.
White, Robert *Source(s):* MACE; SUTT
Whitlock, Walter *Source(s):* MACE; SUTT

Williams, Frank *Source(s):* SUTT
Note(s): Also used by Richard Fote & Harry Parr Davies.
Woods, George *Source(s):* MACE; SUTT
Slezinger, Herbert Edwin 1918-1986 [composer, author, singer]
Murray, Bert *Source(s):* ASCP; CCE59; CCE66-68; CPOL PAu-63-324
Murray, Herbert Edwin *Source(s):* CCE56
Slifka, Lewis 1920- [songwriter, singer]
Spence, Lew *Source(s):* ASCC
Sloman, Jane 1824-1850 [composer, pianist]
Torry, Sloman *Source(s):* DWCO
Slonimsky, Nicholas 1894-1995 [musicologist, conductor, composer]
Note(s): Portrait: ETUP 56:6 (June 1938): 388
Mysnik, Sol *Source(s):* HOFE; Slonimsky, Nicholas. *Music Since 1900.* New York: Schirmer, 1994.
Sloane, Nicholas *Source(s):* CCE25 E 605217 ("Puzzler's Paradise")
Slowitzky, Michael 1893-1962 [composer, conductor, violinist]
Edwards, Michael *Source(s):* ASCC; LCAR
Marcus, M. S. *Source(s):* CCE22 E540661; LCPC letter cited (7 Nov. 1933)
Slye, Leonard (Franklin) 1911-1998 [singer, songwriter, actor]
King of the Cowboys, The *Source(s):* CM09; CM24; ENCM; MCCL; PEN2; PSND; STAC
Last of the Silver Screen Cowboys *Source(s):* STAC
Rogers, Roy *Source(s):* CM09; ENCM; EPMU; KINK; LCAR; MCCL; PEN2; PSND; STAC
Slye, Len *Source(s):* CCE37 E60145; LCAR
Weston, Dick *Source(s):* CM24; LCAR; PSND
World's Top Boots and Saddle Star *Source(s):* PSND
Smegergill, William fl. 1615-1667 [lutenist, composer]
Caesar, William *Source(s):* MACM; NGDM
Smetana, Bedřich 1824-1884 [composer]
Father of Bohemian Music *Source(s):* Haas, Karl. *Adventures in Good Music.* PBS Radio (June 2001)
Note(s): See also Bohuslav Matej Cernohorsky.
Father of Czech Music *Source(s):* http://www.hearts-ease.org/cgibin/conservatory_index.cgi?ID=132 (8 Oct. 2002)
Father of Folk Opera *Source(s):* Haas, Karl. *Adventures in Good Music.* PBS Radio (June 2001)
Father of the Czech Nationalist School of Composition, The *Source(s):* PSND
Smik, Andrew John, Jr. 1914- [singer, songwriter]
Country Music's Royal Couple *Source(s):* MCCL
Note(s): Jt. sobriquet with wife: Chickie Williams [i.e., Jessie Wanda Crupe]
Williams, Doc *Source(s):* CCE60; CCE62; CCME; EPMU; MCCL; PSND
Note(s): Do not confuse with country singer Curly "Doc" Williams (1913-1970).
Smiles, Frank 1848- [vocalist, writer on music]
Quatremayne, Frank *Source(s):* BROW; WORB
Smit, Leo 1900-1943 [composer]
Fox, Leo *Source(s):* http://www.claudel.club.fr/Smit/index.html (2 May 2005)
Smith, A. Corbett [composer]
Tyrrold, Aston *Source(s):* CPMU (publication dates 1911-17)
Smith, Alfred Jesse 1941- [composer, author, singer]
Wood, Brenton *Source(s):* ASCP; CPOL Pau-151-606
Smith, Alvin K. 1926- [singer, songwriter]
King, Al *Source(s):* HARS; LCAR
Note(s): Also used by Harry Haley McClaskey. Do not confuse with singer/guitarist Albert King [i.e., Albert Nelson (1923-1992)]
Smith, Antonio [composer]
Awankana *Source(s):* http://www.schott-music.com/artist/show,1109.html (19 June 2005)
Smith, Arthur 1921-1973 [songwriter, guitarist, bandleader]
Smith, Guitar Boogie *Source(s):* CCME (port.); CLAB; MCCL; PSND
Smith, Austin Alfred 1884-1971 [actor, writer, director]
Melford, Austin *Source(s):* GAN2
Smith, Beth
Dubin, Bettie *Source(s):* TPRF
Smith, Blaine 1915- [singer, songwriter, guitarist]
Virginian Folk Singer, The *Source(s):* MCCL
Smith, C. U. (née Garfield) 1901- [author, poet, composer]
Crow Bait, Ophelia Mae *Source(s):* ASCP
Crowbate, Ophelia Mae *Source(s):* ASCP; PSND
Smith, Carl 1927- [singer, songwriter, guitarist]
Country Gentleman, (The) *Source(s):* MCCL
Note(s): See also Chester [i.e., Chet] (Burton) Atkins.
Mr. Country *Source(s):* AMUS
Smith, Charles William (of Liverpool) [composer]
Fontaine, Charles *Source(s):* CPMU (publication dates 1886-1910)
Smith, Cherry George 1956- [singer, songwriter]
Lynn, Cheryl *Source(s):* PSND
Smith, Christopher Alan 1947- [composer, author, singer]
Rock, Chris *Source(s):* ASCP
Smith, Cladys 1908-1991 [trumpeter, composer]
Smith, Jabbo *Source(s):* CCE64; EPMU; LCAR
Smith, Clara c.1894-1935 [singer, pianist, songwriter]
Green, Violet *Source(s):* HARS
Queen of the Moaners, The *Source(s):* HARS
Note(s): See also Irene Gibbons.

Smith, Jolly Clara *Source(s):* HARS
World's Champion Moaner, The *Source(s):* HARS
Smith, Clarence 1904-1929 [singer, songwriter, pianist]
Smith, Pinetop *Source(s):* CLAB; HARS; KINK; LCAR; NGDM; PSND; STUW
Smith, Clarence Edward 1940- [guitarist, singer, songwriter]
Rhodes, Sonny *Source(s):* AMUS; EPMU; ROOM
Smith, Clifford 1945- [composer, author, pianist]
Note(s): Do not confuse with Clifford Smith (1971-); see following entry.
Prometheus Gemini *Source(s):* ASCP
Smith, Clifford 1971- [songwriter, performer]
Note(s): Do not confuse with Clifford Smith (1945-); see preceding entry.
Method Man *Source(s):* AMUS; CPOL PA-1-034-561; PMUS-00
Smith, (Mrs.) Crafton E. [composer]
Lever, Sydney *Source(s):* CPMU (publication dates 1882-90); OCLC 49330183
Smith, Edward Sydney 1839-1889 [composer, pianist]
Beaumont, Paul *Source(s):* CPMU; MACM; REHH
Note(s): Also used by Gustave Saenger.
Delacour, Victor *Source(s):* CPMU; LCPC
Smith, Elizabeth 1894-1937 [singer, songwriter]
Empress of the Blues *Source(s):* CASS; CM03; HARS; LCAR (see note); SHAD
Smith, Bessie *Source(s):* CASS, CM03; HARS; LCAR
World's Greatest Blues Singer, The *Source(s):* SHAD
Note(s): See also John Lee Hooker & Alonzo Johnson.
Smith, Florence Beatrice 1887-1953 [pianist, singer, composer]
Note(s): Portrait: ETUP 54:11 (Nov. 1936): 749
Jay, Vee *Source(s):* CCE45 #27937 Eunp430048; LCAR
Price, (Mrs.) Florence Beatrice *Source(s):* IDBC; LCAR
Vee Jay *Source(s):* IDBC; LCAR
Smith, Frances Octavia 1912-2001 [actress, singer, lyricist]
Bitts, Frances O. *Source(s):* CCE68
Evans, Dale *Source(s):* ENCM; EPMU; GRAT; PSND
Queen of the Cowgirls *Source(s):* GRAT; PSND
Queen of the West, The *Source(s):* GRAT; PSND
Rogers, Dale Evans *Source(s):* GRAT; LCAR; PSND
Smith, Lucille Wood *Source(s):* Phillips, Robert W. *Roy Rogers*. Jefferson, NC: McFarland, 1995.
Note(s): Possibly original name? Name on Uvalde County, TX, birth record.
Smith, Frank Dymond [lyricist, arranger]
Blackaller, Richard *Source(s):* CPMU (publication date 1908)
Smith, Garnett c.1967- [singer, songwriter]
Garnett, Silk *Source(s):* EPMU
Silk Garnett *Source(s):* EPMU
Smith, George 1851-1914 [actor, playwright]
Note(s): Do not confuse with George Smith (1924-1983); see following entry.
Melford, Mark *Source(s):* GAN2 (see under: Melford, Austin); LCAR
Smith, George 1924-1983 [singer, harmonica player, songwriter]
Note(s): Do not confuse with George Smith (1851-1914); see preceding entry.
Allen, George *Source(s):* AMUS; HARS
Big Walter *Source(s):* AMUS; HARS
Note(s): See also Walter Horton & Walter Travis Price.
Harmonica King *Source(s):* AMUS; HARS
Hip Cat *Source(s):* PSND
Little Walter, Junior *Source(s):* AMUS; HARS
Note(s): See also Provine Hatch, Jr.
Smith, Harmonica *Source(s):* AMUS; HARS
Smith, Harry B(ache) 1860-1936 [lyricist, librettist]
Note(s): Portrait: JASZ
America's Leading Librettist *Source(s):* PSND
Grant, Richard *Source(s):* JASZ
Smith Brothers *Source(s):* MARC p.374
Note(s): Nickname for Harry B. Smith & Robert B. Smith.
Tyler, Walter *Source(s):* LCPC D71971
Note(s): Possible pseud. Do not confuse with Walter J. [or G.] Tyler, pseud. of Adam Geibel.
Smith, Henry Partridge [composer]
Partridge, Henry *Source(s):* CPMU (publication date 1909)
Smith, Hezekiah Leroy Gordon 1909-1965 (or 67) [violinist, singer, composer]
Smith, Stuff *Source(s):* CLAB; KINK; PEN2; SHAB; VACH
Smith, Houston 1910-1995 [composer, arranger, pianist]
Smith, Howdie *Source(s):* ASCP; CCE60-62
Smith, James [or Jim] 1935- [singer, songwriter, actor]
Dale, Jim *Source(s):* BBDP; www.filmbug.com/db/260413 (30 July 2005)
Smith, James Marcus 1938- [singer, songwriter]
Powers, Jett *Source(s):* RECR; WORT
Proby, P. J. *Source(s):* AMUS; CLAB; RECR; ROOM; WORT
Smith, James Todd 1968 (or 69)- [rapper, songwriter]

L. L. Cool J. *Source(s):* CPOL PA-706-414; EPMU; HARR; LCAR
Note(s): L. L. Cool J. = Ladies Love Cool James.
Smith, Jewel Fay 1943-2005 [singer, songwriter]
Girl Hero *Source(s):* MCCL
Smith, Sammi *Source(s):* DRSC; MCCL
Smith, Joe [composer]
Avon Comedy Four *Source(s):* CCE45 #6317, 2033 R142579
Note(s): Jt. pseud.: Charles Dale, Harry Goodwin & Irving [i.e., Isidore] Kaufman.
Smith, John Barto, Jr. 1963- [composer, pianist, conductor]
Barto, Tzimon *Source(s):* BAKT; LCAR
Smith, John Henry 1940- [guitarist, songwriter]
Big Bad Smitty *Source(s):* EPMU
Smith, John T. 1890-1940 [guitarist, singer, songwriter]
Howlin(g) Wolf *Source(s):* AMUS; LCAR; PSND
Note(s): See also Chester Arthur Burnett.
Smith, Funny Papa *Source(s):* AMUS; PSND
Smith, Funny Paper *Source(s):* LCAR
Smith, Howlin' *Source(s):* PSND
Smith, Joseph C(oleman) 1934- [singer, author]
Knight, Sonny *Source(s):* CCE65-66; EPMU; LCAR; ROOM
Smith, Joseph Leopold 1881-1952 [composer]
Smith, Leo *Source(s):* GOTH; GOTT
Smith, Kevin [songwriter]
Note(s): Do not confuse with Kevin Smith (1961-), aka Lovebug Starski; see following entry.
Smith, Gulliver *Source(s):* EPMU
Smith, Kevin 1961- [DJ, rapper]
Note(s): Do not confuse with Kevin Smith, aka Gulliver Smith; see preceding entry.
Lovebug Starski *Source(s):* EPMU
Starski, Lovebug *Source(s):* LCAR
Smith, Kirk 1970- [singer, songwriter]
Franklin, Kirk *Source(s): Current Biography* 61:3 (2000): 49
Smith, Lani 1934- [organist, composer]
Broughton, Edward *Source(s):* CCE76-77; ORBI
Note(s): Do not confuse with Edward Broughton (1923-).
Paxton, David *Source(s):* ORBI
Ritter, Franklin *Source(s):* ORBI
Smith, Lawrence Rackley 1932- [composer]
Rackley, Laurence *Source(s):* ASCP; REHG
Smith, Lee Orean 1874-1942 [composer, arranger]
Note(s): Portrait: MUTR (Dec. 7, 1901): 80
Chevalier, Francois *Source(s):* REHG
Grooms, Calvin *Source(s):* CCE32 E27908; GOTH; REHG
Note(s): To date all titles identified by Calvin Groom are by Lee Orean Smith except for "Torchlight Dance" which is by Arnoldo Sartorio.
Lamont, Leopold *Source(s):* CCE38 E73242; REHG
Lee, Maurice *Source(s):* CCE38 E67427; REHG
Lee, Orrie *Source(s):* CCE38 E66822; CCE41 #29959 E95719; CCE68
Obrero, Leon *Source(s):* REHG
Orrie, Lee *Source(s):* CCE42 #41879 E107465
Santos, Jose *Source(s):* REHG
Vogt, Carl *Source(s):* CCE37 (Index)
Note(s): Also used by M(artin) Greenwald; see NOTES: Vogt, Carl.
Smith, Leonard B(ingley) 1915-2002 [composer, conductor, cornetist]
America's Premier Cornet Soloist *Source(s):* REHG
Bingley, Richard *Source(s):* ASCP
Hemingway, Chas *Source(s):* ASCP
Schubert, Emile H. *Source(s):* ASCP
Smith, Max(well) c.1947- [singer, songwriter]
Romeo, Max *Source(s):* EPMU
Smith, Michael W(hitaker) 1958- [singer, songwriter, keyboardist]
True Renaissance Man of Contemporary Christian Music, A *Source(s):* CM11
Smith, Mike D. [songwriter]
Pyramid *Source(s):* http://www.sundclick.com/mikedsmith (23 June 2005)
Smith, Mira ?-1989 [guitarist, studio engineer, songwriter]
Grace Tennessee and Her Guitar *Source(s): Guitar Player* 31:331:7 (1997): 86
Tennessee, Grace *Source(s): Guitar Player* 31:331:7 (1997): 86
Smith, Moses 1932- [singer, harmonica player, songwriter]
Smith, Whispering *Source(s):* HARS
Smith, Norman (Arnold) 1923- [singer, songwriter, producer]
Smith, Hurricane *Source(s):* AMIR; CCE74
Smith, Parrish 1968- [rapper]
EPMD *Source(s):* EPMU
Note(s): Jt. pseud.: Erick Sermon.
Erick and Parrish Making Dollars *Source(s):* EPMU
Note(s): Jt. pseud.: Erick Sermon.
PMD *Source(s):* LCAR
Smith, Patricia [or Patti] (Lee) 1946- [singer, songwriter]
Godmother of Punk, The *Source(s):* OUSH
Poet Princess of Rock *Source(s):* CASS
Smith, Rebecca Carlene 1955- [singer, songwriter]
Carter, Carlene *Source(s):* EPMU; MCCL
Smith, Reginald (Leonard) 1936 (or 39)- [singer, songwriter]

Dazzling All Night Rock Show *Source(s):* RECR
Manston, Frere *Source(s):* CCE68 Efor131089; CPOL RE-740-776; PMUS
Patterson, Reg *Source(s):* EPMU
Shannon *Source(s):* RECR
Wilde, Marty *Source(s):* EPMU; MUWB; RECR
Smith, (W(illiam)) Renwick [songwriter]
Madison, Maury *Source(s):* CCE27 R673409; SPTH p. 465
Smith, Robert B. 1875-1851 [librettist, lyricist]
Note(s): Portrait: JAST
Bruce, Richard *Source(s):* CCE47 R21714; GAN2 (see under: Herbert, Victor)
Note(s): "Somewhere I Know There's a Girl for Me"
Smith Brothers *Source(s):* MARC p. 374
Note(s): Nickname for Harry B. Smith & Robert B. Smith.
Smith, Robin Peter 1943- [singer, songwriter]
St. Peters, Crispian *Source(s):* CCE65; EPMU
Smith, Rodney 1860-1947 [hymnist]
Smith, Gipsy *Source(s):* CCE25 E609679; DIEH; LCAR
Smith, Steven [or Stephen] Paul 1969-2003 [singer, songwriter, guitarist]
Smith, Elliott *Source(s):* LCAR; WASH
Smith, Talmadge (G.) 1909-1971 [saxophonist, arranger, composer]
Smith, Tab *Source(s):* KINK; LCAR; NGDJ
Smith, Timothy [singer, songwriter]
Smith, TV *Source(s):* EPMU
Smith, Trevor 1972- [songwriter, performer]
Busta Rhymes *Source(s):* AMIR; AMUS; CPOL PA-1-045-017; LCAR; PMUS-00
Ryhmes, Busta *Source(s):* LCAR
Smith, Trixie 1895-1943 [singer, songwriter, actress]
Ames, Tessie *Source(s):* HARS
Lee, Bessie *Source(s):* HARS
Southern Nightingale, The *Source(s):* HARS
Smith, William 1878-1948 [composer]
Mackenzie, Gordon *Source(s):* CCE44 #35637, 1307 R129744; GREN
Smith, William 20th cent. [songwriter]
Smith, Smitty *Source(s):* PSND
Smith, William [or Willie] (Henry Joseph Berthol Bonaparte) 1897-1973 [composer, pianist]
Note(s): Portrait: JASN
Lion, The *Source(s):* CCE62; CCE65; JASN
Smith, Lion *Source(s):* CCE62
Smith, Willie "the Lion" *Source(s):* AMUS; JASA
Three Wise Men of Harlem Hot Piano, The *Source(s):* Vance, Joel. *Fats Waller; His Life and Times*. Chicago: Contemporary Books, 1977, p. 34.
Note(s): Jt. sobriquet: Thomas Wright Waller & James [or Jimmy, or Jimmie] (P(rice)) Johnson.
Willie the Lion *Source(s):* ASCP; SHAD; TCAN
Smith-Masters, Stanley 1902 (or 03)- [composer]
Hood, Philip *Source(s):* CPOL RE-255-823
Magnoni, Edrich *Source(s):* CCE5?
Note(s): Jt. pseud.: Bruce [or Bruno] Albert Magnoni.
Man of Brass *Source(s):* RFSO
Masters, Archie *Source(s):* CCE55
Note(s): Also used by Howard E(stabrook) Akers.
Masters, Stanley *Source(s):* CCE55
Masters, Van *Source(s):* CCE53
Rübel, Ernst *Source(s):* CCE59
Note(s): Jt. pseud.: Stanley Masters [i.e., Smith-Masters] & Gerald Shaw.
Seymour, Frank *Source(s):* CCE52; CPMU
Note(s): Jt. pseud.: Harry Mortimer.
Siebert, Edrich *Source(s):* CCE53; CCE60; CPMU; CPOL RE-105-869; GREN; REHG
Smolens, Jay 1927- [music critic, editor]
Harrison, Jay *Source(s):* PSND
Smothers, Otis 1929-1993 [singer, guitarist, songwriter]
Smothers, Smokey *Source(s):* HARS
Note(s): Do not confuse with Little Smokey Smothers, guitarist.
Snow, Clarence Eugene 1914-1999 [singer, songwriter]
Hank, the Singing Ranger *Source(s):* MCCL
Hank, the Yodeling Ranger *Source(s):* CCE44 #21307 Efor69377; CCE70 R476351
Singing Ranger, (The) *Source(s):* CASS; CCE57; LCAR; PEN2; SHAD
Snow, Hank *Source(s):* BAKR; CASS; ENCM; HARR; KINK; LCAR; MCCL; OB99
Yodeling Ranger *Source(s):* MCCL
Snow, William [singer, songwriter]
Wons, Mailliw *Source(s):* PSND
Snyder, Clifford Gilpin 1917-1985 [bandleader, songwriter, music publisher, author]
Stone, Cliffie *Source(s):* CCE52; CCME; EPMU; LCAR; MCCL; PEN1; STAC
Stonehead, Cliffie *Source(s):* CCME
Sobolewski, J(ohann) F(riedrich) E(duard) 1808-1872 [conductor, composer, music critic]
Note(s): Portrait: http://library.wustl.edu/units/music/spec/sobolowski.html (8 Oct. 2002)
Feski, J. *Source(s):* http://library.wustl.edu/units/music/spec/sobolowski.html
Fesky, J. *Source(s):* HEYT
Hahnbüchn, M. *Source(s):* http://library.wustl.edu/units/music/spec/sobolowski.html
J. F. *Source(s):* HEYT
Sobolewski, Edward *Source(s):* PSND

Sobredo Galanes, Evangelina 1948-1976 [singer, songwriter, guitarist]
Cecilia *Source(s):* CCE75-76; HWOM;
Note(s): See also Clara Josephine Wieck.
Södersten, (Axel) Gunno 1920- [composer, organist]
Gess *Source(s):* BUL3; RIES
Sogomonian, (Sogomon Gevorkovich) 1869-1935 [ethnomologist, composer, conductor]
Komitas, (Sogomon) *Source(s):* BAKR; NGDM; ROOM
Vardapet, Komitas *Source(s):* GROL
Vartabed, Gomidas *Source(s):* GROL
Soifer, Alexis [or Isadore] 1910-1991 [composer]
Note(s): Internet sources identify given name: Alexis; LCAR identifies: Isadore.
North, Alex *Source(s):* CLMC; www.music-finder.net/band_9707_1.php (30 July 2005)
Sokal'sky, Pyotr Petrovich 1832-1887 [composer, critic, folksong collector]
Fagot *Source(s):* GROL; NGDM
Solberg, David (Richard) 1943- [singer, songwriter, actor]
Soul, David *Source(s):* EPMU; LCAR
Soldano, Anthony 1927- [composer, author, conductor]
Dano, Tony *Source(s):* ASCP
Soler, Enrique Llácer 1934- [percussionist, composer]
Regoli, Enrique *Source(s):* NGDJ
Soler (i Hubert), Frederic 1839-1895 [librettist]
Pitarra, Seraif *Source(s):* GROL; LCAR; WORB
Solin, Vaclav fl. 1561-64 [writer on music]
Josquin, Jan *Source(s):* GROL
Note(s): Possible pseud. Also used by Johannes Josquinus Boleslavensis.
Soliva, Antonio [musician, clergyman]
Note(s): The following is supposed pseud. of Soliva; however, more likely anagram of Francesco Antonio Tullio.
Cinéo, Filostrato Lucano *Source(s):* SONN
Filostrato Lucàno Cinnéọ *Source(s):* SONN
Solman, Alfred 1868-1937 [composer]
Fredericks, Alfred *Source(s):* CCE37 R58591
Lazzare, Paul de *Source(s):* CPMU; TPRF
Wallace, Paul *Source(s):* CCE36 (Index)
Soloman, Mirrie (Irma) 1892-1986 [composer]
Note(s): Rowena Pearce (University of Melbourne) identified several pseudonyms on published works.
Carlos, Manuel *Source(s):* CCE57
Herd, Graeme *Source(s):* CCE42 #43471 Efor67565; CCE56-57
Hill, (Mrs.) Mirrie *Source(s):* Pearce (see above)
Kent, Richard *Source(s):* Pearce (see above)
Note(s): Also used by Harry Archer [i.e., Auracher]
Moore, Adam *Source(s):* CCE57
Rea, Robert *Source(s):* CCE59
Wills, Reginald *Source(s):* CCE42 #43471 Efor67565
Solomon, Emma 1855-1935 [producer, composer]
Madame *Source(s):* GAN2
Melnotte, Violette *Source(s):* GAN2
Solomon, Fred(erick Charles) 1852-1924 [author, director, composer, director]
Solomon, Fritzy *Source(s):* GAN2
Solomon, Herbert (Jay) 1930- [composer, instrumentalist]
Mann, Herbie *Source(s):* LCAR; PSND
Solomons, Nate E. [composer]
Thane, Logan *Source(s):* JASA p. 322
Somers, Andrew James 1942- [guitarist, songwriter]
Summers, Andrew [or Andy] (James) *Source(s):* ALMN; CM03
Somerset, Henry Richard Charles 1849-1932 [songwriter]
Lord Henry *Source(s):* PSND
Somerset, Mary Hurd [composer]
Somerset, Maud *Source(s):* GOTH
Somis, (Giovanni) Lorenzo 1688-1775 [violinist, composer]
Ardy *Source(s):* GROL; LCAR
Somis, Ardy *Source(s):* NGDM
Sommerfeld, Willy 1904- [composer]
Feld, W. S. *Source(s):* BUL3; http://www.luise-berlin.de/Ehrung/s/sommerfeld_willy.htm (8 Oct. 2002)
Sommerlatte, Ulrich 1914- [composer, conductor]
Staal, Oliver *Source(s):* GREN, RIES
Somoza, Oscar Emilio Léon 1945- [singer, bassist, composer]
D'Léon, Oscar *Source(s):* PEN2
Sondheim, Stephen Joshua 1930- [composer, lyricist]
Note(s): Portraits: CM08; EWEN
Broadway's Brightest Hope *Source(s):* CM08
Ria Nido, Esteban *Source(s):* CCE66; CPOL RE-653-818
Sonenscher, Dave 1947- [songwriter]
Bourne, Carol *Source(s):* CCE57; CCE66
Lloyd, George *Source(s):* CCE33 Efor28901 & Efor29862
Note(s): For titles of works composed under joint pseuds., See NOTES: Lloyd, George.
Sonn, Dave *Source(s):* LCCC 1955-70 R159867
Sonneborn, Günter 1921- [composer]
Gronau, Thomas *Source(s):* CCE62-65; KOMP; KOMS; PFSA; RIES
Krassin, Peter *Source(s):* KOMP; KOMS; PFSA
Sonnenberg, Michael 1820-1898 [pianist, composer]
Bergson, Michael *Source(s):* LYMN

Sonnenfeld, Adolf Gustaw 1837-1914 [conductor, violinist, composer]
Note(s): For source with additional pseuds., see note 20 in the PMJ article cited below.
Adolfson, (Adolf Gustaw) *Source(s):* GROL; NGDM; PIPE
Polish Offenbach *Source(s):* http://www.usc.edu/dept/polish-music?PMJ/issue/6.1.03/Werb.html (14 May 2005)

Sonyer, Tomàs 1762-1821 [composer, teacher]
Sogner, Tommaso *Source(s):* NGDM

Sor, (Joseph) Fernando (Macari) 1778-1839 [composer, guitarist]
Beethoven of Guitar *Source(s):* http://www.laphouse.com/Music/English/jtMusic_E.htm (6 Apr. 2005)
Paganini of the Guitar *Source(s):* http://www.laphouse.com/Music/English/jtMusic_E.htm
Note(s): See also Mauro Giuliani.

Sorabji, Dudley Leon 1892-1988 [composer]
Sorabji, Kaikhosru Shapurji *Source(s):* CCMU; DDEA3

Sore, Martin 1486-1556 [writer on musical theory]
Agricola, Martin *Source(s):* IBIM; NGDM; WORB

Soter, Oswald 1925- [composer]
Ossi *Source(s):* KOMP; KOMS; PFSA
Soter, Dyck *Source(s):* KOMP; KOMS; PFSA

Soubies, (Émile Jean) Albert 1846-1918 [music historian, critic]
Lamange, B. de *Source(s):* GROL
Lomagne, B. de *Source(s):* MACM; PIPE

Souchon, Edmond, (Jr.) 1897-1968 [guitarist, author]
Souchon, Doc *Source(s):* GROL
Tuig, R. A. *Source(s):* GROL

Soulage, Marcelle Fanny Henriette 1894- [pianist, critic, composer]
Note(s): Portrait: ETUP 56:7 (July 1938): 480
Sauval, Marc *Source(s):* BUL3; COHN; HIXN; LCAR

Soulier, Jean Pierre 1755-1812 [singer, composer]
Solié, (Jean Pierre) *Source(s):* LCAR; PRAT

Sour, Robert (B.) [songwriter]
Note(s): Birth date may be 1925.
Bandler, George *Source(s):* CCE68 R436298; CPOL RE-192-918
Note(s): Jt. pseud.: Don McCray.
Bonham, Victor *source(s):* CPOL RE-177-062
Fitzgerald, John *Source(s):* CPOL RE-116-220
Ingersoll, Byron M. *Source(s):* CCE41 #5570 Eunp241929; CCE68 R426470
Note(s): Jt. pseud.: Ernest Gold [i.e., Ernest (Siegmund) Goldner], Alex(ander) Kramer, Hy(man) Zaret, Don McCray & Zoe Voeth [i.e., Parenteau]
Roberts, Don *Source(s):* CCE40 #21606 E85787; CCE67; CPOL RE-252-513
Note(s): Jt. pseud.: Don McCray.
Rogers, Gerald *Source(s):* CPOL RE-118-568
Scofield, Geraldine *Source(s):* CCE41 #16418 E93743; CCE68
Thomas, Peter *Source(s):* CCE40 #40990 E89820; CCE67-68

Sousa, John Philip 1854-1932 [composer, bandmaster]
Note(s): Portraits: HOWD; Bierley (see below). Sigmund Spaeth reports John Philip Sousa was the son of Antonio So, a Spanish trombonist in the United States Marine Band, who reputedly added the letters U. S. A.. to his surname. (SPTH p. 245)
King of the Concert Band *Source(s):* SMIN
March King, The *Source(s):* BAKT; NGDM; PSND; WCAB 9:386
Ochs, Sigismund *Source(s):* Bierley, Paul E. *John Phlip Sousa; American Phenomenan*. New York: Appleton-Century-Crofts, 1973, 67-9.
Note(s): George Frederich Hinton, Sousa Band publicity manager, originated an "S. O., U. S. A." cognomen which still persists." The full name changed, depending on the country where the band was performing. (Bierley p. 68)
Ogden, Sam *Source(s):* Bierley (see above)
Otz, Siegfried *Source(s):* Bierley (see above)
Oulette, S. *Source(s):* Bierley (see above)
Philipso, John *Source(s):* Bierley (see above)
S. O., U. S. A. *Source(s):* Bierley (see above)

Souter, Joseph, Jr. 1940- [songwriter]
South, Joe *Source(s):* CCE58-59; CCE61; EPMU; NASF; PMUS
Note(s): Also used by Joseph [or Joe] (M.) Davis.

South, Edward [or Eddie] (Otha) 1904-1962 [violinist, composer]
Doughtery, Bill *Source(s):* GROL

Southard, Mary Ann 1926- [composer, author]
Annabel *Source(s):* CCE66
Rome, J. Gus *Source(s):* ASCP
Singer, Amy *Source(s):* ASCP

Sovine, Woodrow Wilson 1918-1980 [singer, guitarist; bandleader, songwriter]
King of the Big Rigs, The *Source(s):* FLIN
Red Head, (The) *Source(s):* MCCL
Sovine, Red *Source(s):* AMUS; EPMU; FLIN; LCAR; MCCL; PEN1; STAC

Sowande, Fela 1905-1978 [composer]
High Priest of Music, The *Source(s):* PSND

Spaeth, Sigmund Gottfried 1885-1965 [writer on music]
Note(s): Portrait: ETUP 56:7 (July 1938): 480

Tune Detective, The *Source(s):* GRAN; MARC p. 208; PSND
Spagnoetti (della Diana), Paolo (Ludovico) 1773-1834 [violinist, composer]
Espagnoletto *Source(s):* GROL
Spalding, Delos Gardner [or Gardiner] 1833-1884 [musician, composer]
Delos *Source(s):* EPST
Howard, Frank *Source(s):* EPST; IBIM; PARS; WORB
Note(s): Anthony [or Tony] Lowry.
Martindale, J. F(rank) *Source(s):* CLAB
Spalding, Walter R(aymond) 1865-1962 [composer, author]
Note(s): Portrait: ETUP 56:7 (July 1938): 480
Throckmorton, Alexander *Source(s):* CCE18 E426230
Span(n), Norman [composer, singer]
King Radio *Source(s):* CCE57; CCE62; LCAR; PSND
Radio (Calypso Singer) *Source(s):* LCAR
Spangenberg, Wolfhart before 1570-1636 [theologian, writer on music, composer]
Andropediacus, Lycosthenes Psellionoros *Source(s):* GROL; NGDM; WORB
Wartlolf *Source(s):* WORB
Sparks, Harry H. fl. 1900-10 [music publisher, composer]
Herbert, Harry *Source(s):* CANE
Note(s): Possible pseud.
Spaulding, G(eorge) L(awson) 1864-1921 [composer, music publisher]
Bergmann, Karl *Source(s):* CCE37 R56335 & R58056
Ellis, Joseph *Source(s):* CCE21 E515500; CCE47 R19606 ("Dainty Dorothy"); TPRF
Flynn, Joseph *Source(s):* LCCC 1938-45 (see reference)
Graham, George *Source(s):* LCCC 1938-45 (see reference)
Lamb, Harry *Source(s):* LCAR
Lamb, Henry *Source(s):* CCE21 R18992, R18993 & R18999; LCAR; SPTH p. 265 & 271
Lawson, Paul *Source(s):* CCE37 R56271; CCE47 R20475; TPRF
Rowe, Daniel *Source(s):* CCE39 #2968, 504 R72279; CCE47 R24926; TPRF
Spenser, G(eorge) *Source(s):* CCE44 #31175, 34 R128466; TPRF
Vincent, Wallace *Source(s):* CCE40 #19376, 176 R88167
Spazier, Johann Gottlieb Karl 1761-1805 [writer on music, songwriter]
Pilger, Karl *Source(s):* PRAT; RIEM
Spear, Eric 1908- [composer]
Pitt, A(rthur) *Source(s):* CCE51 Efor6599; GOTH
Note(s): Also jt. pseud.: Clem(ent) Bernard; "Two Little Men in a Flying Saucer" (CCE51).
Spechtshart, Hugo c.1286-1359 (or 60) [music theorist, composer]
Hugo von Reutlingen *Source(s):* MACM; NGDM; RIEM
Spector, Lona [songwriter]
Stevens, Lona *Source(s):* CCE61-62; CCE65; PMUS
Spector, Phil(ip Harvey) 1940- [songwriter, record producer]
First Tycoon of Teen, The *Source(s):* CASS; PSND
Speer, Daniel 1636-1707 [composer, music theorist, author]
Asne de Rilpe *Source(s):* GROL
Deutscher Spaniol in Griechenland *Source(s):* GROL
Res Plena Dei *Source(s):* GROL
Rutge, Daniel *Source(s):* GROL; NGDM
Note(s): Possible pseud.
Simplicissimus *Source(s):* CPMU; LCAR
Note(s): "Musicalisch türkischer Eulenspiegel" Also used by Hans Richard Weinhöppel.
Spencer, Hubert [composer, conductor]
Spencer, Glenn *Source(s):* CLTP ("Last Word, The")
Spencer, Joyce Ann 1945- [composer, author, singer]
Street, Joye *Source(s):* ASCP
Spencer, Richard [or Dick] ?-1915 [banjoist, composer]
Spence, Dick *Source(s):* http://www.whitetreeaz.com/vintage/brit4.htm (28 Mar. 2005)
Spencer, Vern(on H(arold)) 1908-1974 [songwriter]
Note(s): Portrait: ETUP 56:8 (Aug. 1938): 543
Spencer, Tim *Source(s):* CCE63; CCE71 R503355; NASF; PMUS; PSNN
Spielman(n), Fred(eric) 1906-1997 [composer]
Fels, Maru *Source(s):* CCE50; CCE55
Spielman, Fritz *Source(s):* ASCP
Spiess, Otto 1955- [composer]
Style, Johnny *Source(s):* PFSA
Spikes, Benjamin F. 1888-1982 [composer]
Spikes, Reb (Benjamin) *Source(s):* EPMU; JASA p. 319
Spikes, Red *Source(s):* CCE47 Eunp
Spillman, Barbara 1927- [singer, songwriter]
Dane, Barbara *Source(s):* GRAT
Spina, Harold 1906-1997 [songwriter]
D'Lorah, Juan y *Source(s):* CCE61 R280175 ("La Cucaracha"); LCCC 1955-70 (see reference)
Note(s): Name also used by John(ny) Burke in the same motion picture; not a joint pseudonym.
Phillipps, Marty *Source(s):* CCE74 Eunp472241
Rogan, K. C. *Source(s):* CCE63-55; PMUS
Note(s): Jt. pseud.: John(ny) Burke.
Spinner, Harold *Source(s):* CCE60
Thomas, E. D. *Source(s):* CCE55-56; LCCC 1955-70 (see reference)

Spinola, Giovanni Andrea mentioned 1655 [librettist, poet]
Pisani, Giovanni Aleandro *Source(s):* NGDO
Spitzer, Cordelia [author, lyricist]
Note(s): Dates may be: 1910-1999.
Nelson, Dyer *Source(s):* ASCP
Spitzer, Louis 1853-1894 [violoncellist, composer]
Hegyesi, Louis *Source(s):* BAKR; MACM
Spitzer, Rudolf 1865-1942 (or 43) [author, critic]
Lothar, Rudolf *Source(s):* BAKE; LCAR; MELL; PIPE
Maréchal, Aristide *Source(s):* STAD
Note(s): Jt. pseud.: Hans Adler.
Spitzmüller(-Harmersbach), Alexander (von) 1894 (or 96)-1962 [composer]
Cartier, Jean *Source(s):* BUL3; GROL; LCAR; RIEM
Spivak, Nissan 1824-1906 [cantor, choir director, composer]
Nissi Belzer *Source(s):* NULM
Nissi Berdichever *Source(s):* NULM
Nissi Kishinever *Source(s):* NULM
Spivey, Victoria [or Vicky] (Regina) 1906-1976 [singer, songwriter]
Her Majesty the Queen *Source(s):* CCE67
Lucas, Jane *Source(s):* HARS; LCAR
Queen, The *Source(s):* CCE61-62; HARS
Queen of the Blues *Source(s):* HARS
Note(s): See also Ruth Lee Jones, Sara(h) Dunn, Ethel Howard & Koko Taylor [i.e., Cora Walton]
Queen, V. *Source(s):* CCE62
Spohr, Louis [actually Lud(e)wig] 1784-1859 [composer]
Father of Musical Goodwill *Source(s):* http://www.geometry.net/composers/spohr_louis_pages_no_3.php (8 Oct. 2002)
Spoliansky, Mischa [or Michail] (Pawlowitsch) 1898- [composer, pianist, conductor]
Billing, Arno *Source(s):* PIPE
Galento, Toni *Source(s):* PIPE
Sponga, Francesco 1570-1641 [composer, organist, priest]
Usper, Francesco *Source(s):* LCAR; NGDM; RIES
Note(s): Adopted surname of his patron.
Spontini, Gasparo [or Gaspare] (Luigi Pacifico) 1774-1851 [composer, conductor]
Napoleon of Opera, The *Source(s):* PSND; SIFA
Sporck, Ferdinand von 1848-1928 [librettist]
Morolf, Ferdinand *Source(s):* PIPE; WORB
Sportonio, Marc'Antono c.1631-after 1680 [castrato, composer]
Bolognese, Il *Source(s):* NGDM; SADC
Note(s): See also Arcangelo Corelli. Do not confuse with Giovanni Francesco Grimaldi (Il Bolognese), stage designer & architect.
Sprague, Carl T. 1895-1978 [singer, songwriter, guitarist]
First Cowboy Singer on Record, (The) *Source(s):* MCCL
Original Singing Cowboy, The *Source(s):* PSND
Note(s): See also Gene (Orvon) Autry.
Sprague, Doc *Source(s):* MCCL
Sprecher, Gunther William 1924- [composer, pianist, conductor]
Gunther, William *Source(s):* ASCP; BUL2
Springer, A(braham) L(eon) 1911-1994 [composer, author, actor]
Fuchs, Leo *Source(s):* ASCP, CCE76; HESK
Springsteen, Bruce (Frederick Joseph) 1949- [singer, guitarist, songwriter]
Note(s): Portraits: CM25; EWEN
Boss, The *Source(s):* ALMN; CASS; SIFA; WARN
Note(s): See also Hugo Wilhelm Friedhofer.
Brooce *Source(s):* WARN
Future of Rock 'n' Roll *Source(s):* CASS
New Dylan, The *Source(s):* CASS; CM25
Note(s): See also John Prine.
Springthorpe, Richard Lewis 1949- [singer, songwriter]
Note(s): In DAUM original surname: Sprengthorpe.
Springfield, Rick *Source(s):* CM09; DAUM; DIMA; EPMU; HARR; LCAR
Spross, Charles Gilbert 1874-1961 [composer, pianist, organist]
Note(s): Portraits: ETUP 54:12 (Dec. 1936): 58; ETUP 56:8 (Aug. 1938): 543
Philip(p)e, Jean *Source(s):* CCE45 #12811, 36 R135354; ETUD
Philips, Jean *Source(s):* TPRF
Note(s): Typographical error?
Rauch, Karl *Source(s):* CCE45 #8173, 19 R13538; ETUD; TPRF
Worthington, William *Source(s):* CCE47 R16615 ("Chimes of St. Cecilia"); ETUD; TPRF
Squarcialupi, Antonio 1416-1480 [organist, composer]
Note(s): See LCAR for variant forms of the following.
Antonio de [or di] Bartolomeo *Source(s):* NGDM; WORB
Antonio degli Organi *Source(s):* BAKR; NGDM
Antonio del Bessa *Source(s):* BAKR; NGDM
Squires, Edna May 1918-1998 [singer, songwriter]
Blair, William *Source(s):* CCE53
Moore, Emily Jane *Source(s):* CCE53
Rickard, Manny *Source(s):* CCE58
Note(s): Jt. pseud.: Ernest Dunstall.
Squires, Dorothy *Source(s):* EPMU
Warwick, Harold *Source(s):* CCE58
Westwood, Pat *Source(s):* CCE58; CCE62; CCE66
Srb, Josef 1836-1904 [writer on music]
Debrnov, Josef *Source(s):* PIPE

St. *see* Saint
Stabile, Theresa Maria 1916 (or 19)-2002 [singer, songwriter]
Dawn, Dolly *Source(s):* ASCC; EPMU; KINK; LCAR
Stace, Wesley Harding 1965- [singer, songwriter]
Harding, John Wesley *Source(s):* CM06; LCAR
Stahl, Georg 1907-1969 [composer]
Gesta *Source(s):* REHH; SUPN
Staigers, Charles Delaware 1899-1950 [composer, cornetist]
Staigers, Del *Source(s):* GREN
Stainer, John 1840-1901 [musicologist, composer]
Note(s): Portraits: ETUP 56:8 (Aug. 1938): 543; EWCY; MRAR (June 1901): 41
J. S. *Source(s):* CPMU
Stairs, Louise E. 1892-1975 [organist, pianist, composer]
Note(s): Portrait: ETUP 56:8 (Aug. 1938): 543
Forrest, Sidney *Source(s):* CCE41 #19466 E92988; COHN; HIXN
Stallman, Lou [songwriter]
Think *Source(s):* EPMU
Stamford, John J. 1840-1899 [songwriter, music hall manager]
Baker, John S. *Source(s):* KILG
Note(s): Possible pseud.
Stamm, Werner 1912- [composer]
Baum *Source(s):* KOMP; PFSA
Starow *Source(s):* KOMP; PFSA
Stamper, Wallace Logan 1930- [singer, songwriter]
Stamper, Pete *Source(s):* CLAB
Stampiglia, Silvio 1664-1725 [librettist]
Licurio, Palemone *Source(s):* ALCM; GROL; MORI; NGDM; NGDO; SONN
Palemone Licurio *Source(s):* GROL; NGDM
Stamponi, Héctor Luciano 1916-1997 [pianist, composer, arranger]
Chupita *Source(s):* TODO
Stamponi, Chupita *Source(s):* TODO
Standing, Francis [or Frank] (H.) 1845-1904 [singer, actor, lyricist]
Celli, Frank H(ubert) *Source(s):* GAN2; http://freespace.virgin.net/m.killy/sing.html#LYRC (5 Jan. 2005)
Standish, Robert Frederick 1913- [pianist, conductor, arranger]
Sharples, Robert [or Bob] *Source(s):* MUSR; RFSO
Note(s): Also used by Wilfred Burns.
Stanford, Charles Villiers 1852-1924 [composer, teacher, conductor]
Note(s): Portraits: ETUP 56:8 (Aug. 1938): 543; EWCY; GRV3 v. 4
Drofnatzki, Karel *Source(s):* CCE61; CCMU; CPMU; LCAR
Stanford, Trevor H(erbert) 1925 (or 27)-2000 [pianist, composer]
Conway, Russ *Source(s):* DRSC; EPMU; GAMM; LCAR; MUWB; OB00; ROOM
Griffiths, Bob *Source(s):* CCE57; CPOL RE-257-858
Prince Charming of Pop, The *Source(s):* DRSC
Stanford, Terry *Source(s):* CPOL RE-222-106
Stanley, Terry *Source(s):* CCE56; CPOL RE-222-105
Stange, John William 1860-1917 [librettist]
Stange, Stanislaus *Source(s):* GAN2
Stanke, Willi 1907- [composer, conductor]
Forster, (Walter) *Source(s):* CCE68; RIES
Foster, Walter *Source(s):* CCE66
Stanley, Charles c.1821- [merchant, hymnist]
Note(s): Portraits: CYBH; *Music and Letters* 2:2 (Apr. 1921)
C. S. *Source(s):* JULN (Appendix)
Sabine, Charles *Source(s):* JULN (Appendix)
Stanley, James 1930- [composer]
Hall, James *Source(s):* GREN
Staples, Roebuck 1914 (or 15)-2000 [singer, songwriter, guitarist]
Staples, Pop(s) *Source(s):* AMUS; CM11; LCAR
Stapleton, Cyril 1914-1974 [composer]
Hamilton, Clyde *Source(s):* CCE54-58; CCE61; CPOL RE-109-511; RFSO
Manilla, Tony *Source(s):* CCE59
Note(s): Jt. pseud.: Jack Fishman (1918 (or 19)-). Fishman also used as jt. pseud. with Clare Shardlow; see NOTES: Manilla, Tony.
Shaftesbury, Bill *Source(s):* CCE60; CPOL RE-397-656
Starcher, Oby Edgar 1906-2001 [singer, songwriter]
Starcher, Buddy *Source(s):* EPMU; LCAR; MCCL
Stark, Etilmon Justus [composer]
Manchester, Bud *Source(s):* JASA; JASN p. 295; RAGM
Stark, Harold (Stillwell) [composer]
Carlton, John *Source(s):* CCE59; CPOL RE-296-436
Note(s): Jt. pseud.: Walter (Charles) Ehret. Ehret also used as jt. pseud. with other individuals; see NOTES: Carlton, John.
Hilton, Arthur *Source(s):* LCCC 1955-70
Note(s): Jt. pseud.: Walter (Charles) Ehret. Ehret also used as jt. pseud. with other individuals; see NOTES: Hilton, Arthur.
Thompson, David *Source(s):* CCE59; CPOL RE-275-409; CPOL RE-335-409
Note(s): Jt. pseud.: Walter (Charles) Ehret; "Then Round about the Starry Throne." Ehret also used this pseud. (not a jt. pseud.); for a list of titles, see: Ehret, Walter (Charles).
Stark, Humphrey John 1856-1932 [organist, composer]
Stewart, Humphrey John *Source(s):* LCAR; ORBI

Stark, John (Stillwell) 1841-1927 [music publisher]
Note(s): Portait: JASA
Evangelist for Ragtime, The *Source(s):* JAST p. 29
Ligato, O. B. *Source(s):* GROL
Wezbrew, L. C. *Source(s):* GROL
Starkey, James (Sullivan) 1879-1958 [poet]
O'Sullivan, Seumas *Source(s):* CCE48-49; LCAR; PSND
Starkey, Richard 1940- [drummer, singer, composer]
Beatles, The *Source(s):* http://www.beatlesstory.com (4 May 2005)
Note(s): With: George Harrison; John (Winston) Lennon & (James) Paul McCartney.
Dyke, Roy *Source(s):* BEAT
R. S. *Source(s):* PSND
Richie *Source(s):* PSND
Shears, Billy *Source(s):* PSND
Snare, Richie *Source(s):* BEAT; PSND
Starr, Ringo *Source(s):* CASS; CM10; GAMM; LCAR; PSND; WORL
Starkie, Walter Fitzwilliam 1894-1976 [writer on music]
Gualterio, Don *Source(s):* RIES
Starominsky, Mordechai 1916-1994 [composer, teacher]
Seter, Mordecai *Source(s):* BUL1; BUL2; LCAR; LYMN; NULM
Stástný-Pokorný, Jarosalv 1952- [composer]
Graham, Peter *Source(s):* GROL; LCAR; *Czech Music* 5 (1997): 6
Statham, Francis Reginald 1844-1908 [journalist, poet, composer]
A.B.C. *Source(s):* CART
F. R. *Source(s):* CART
Reynolds, Francis *Source(s):* CART
South African, A *Source(s):* CART
True Liberal, A *Source(s):* CART
Statham, (F(rank)) Leslie 1905 (or 06)-1974 [composer]
Steck, Arnold *Source(s):* CCE49-50; CPOL RE-238-675; REHG; RFSO; SUPN
Staton, Harry M. [composer]
Roger, Rulof *Source(s):* TPRF
Staton, Merrill 1919-2000 [author, singer, conductor]
Ostrus, Merrill *Source(s):* ASCP
Steagall, Russell (Don) 1937- [singer, guitarist, songwriter, actor]
Cowboy Poet of Texas *Source(s):* AMUS
Don, Russell *Source(s):* CCE61-62
Steagall, Red *Source(s):* AMUS; CCME; EPMU; LCAR; MCCL; PEN2; PSND
Stebbins, George C(oles) 1846-1945 [composer, hymnist]
Note(s): Portraits: CYBH; ETUP 56:8 (Aug. 1938): 543; HALL
Coles, George *Source(s):* GROL; NGAM
Note(s): Hymns include: "Jesus My All to Heaven Come" (aka "Duane Street") (see ROGG). Do not confuse with (Rev.) George Coles, 1792-1858 (composer, editor of *New York Christian Advocate* and *Sunday School Advocate*).
Coles, S. G. *Source(s):* CCE16 R8011
Martin, W. S. *Source(s):* CCE12 E289566
Steele, Anne 1716 (or 17)-1778 [poet, hymnist]
Theodosia *Source(s):* CART; COHN; CYBH; HIXN; LCAR; ROOM
Steele, Henry [composer]
Snappy Dan *Source(s)* JASG; JASR
Steele, Louis (Thornton) 1911-2002 [composer, author, advertising executive]
Steele, Ted *Source(s):* ASCP; CCE54
Steffan, Ernst 1890-1967 [pianist, conductor, composer]
Helm, Ernst *Source(s):* PIPE
Steffani, Agostino 1654-1728 [composer]
Note(s): Portrait: ETUP 56:9 (Sept. 1938): 558
Piva, Gregorio *Source(s):* GROL; RILM 81-00488-ae; WORB
Note(s): Assumed the name of his copyist.
Steffen, Harro 1920- [composer]
Patten, Jim *Source(s):* CCE59; CCE61-62; KOMS
Reinhard, Bernd *Source(s):* CCE55-59; CCE68; KOMS; PFSA
Steffen, Wolfgang 1923- [composer]
Eberhardt, Wolfgang *Source(s):* RIES
Wolfgang, Eberhardt *Source(s):* CCE56; GREN
Steffkin, Theodore ?-1673 [viol player, composer]
Stoeffken, Ditrich *Source(s):* GREN; LCAR; NGDM
Stefopulos, Giorgos before 1890-after 1917 [librettist]
Osfikos, Agnis *Source(s):* PIPE
Steibelt, Daniel 1765-1823 [pianist, composer]
Note(s): Passed off other composers' works as his own, sometimes thinly arranged. (DEA3 p. 123) Composers not identified.
Stein, Herman 1915- [composer, arranger]
Gulliver, Andrew *Source(s):* ASCP
Stein, Julius Kerwin 1905-1994 [composer]
Note(s): Portraits: EWEN; EWPA; SHMM (Jan./Feb. 1989): [2]-9 & cover
Kerwin, Jules *Source(s):* Taylor, Theodore. *Jule; The Story of Composer Jule Styne*. New York: Random, 1979, p. [37]
Styne, Jule *Source(s):* ALMN; BAKR; CASS; CM21; EPMU; EWEN; EWPA; GAN2
Styne(e)se *Source(s):* Taylor, p. 8 (see above)
Note(s): Term to describe Styne's verbal shorthand.
Stein, Ronald 1930-1988 [composer, conductor, pianist, author]

Lowry, Mark *Source(s):* MCCA
Morand, Leonard *Source(s):* MCCA
Steinberg, Louis 1898-1969 [bandleader, composer, arranger, pianist]
Stone, Lew *Source(s):* CASS; GAMM; ROOM
Steingass, Helmut 1947- [composer]
Heli *Source(s):* KOMS; PFSA
Steingräber, Theodor Leberecht 1830-1904 [publisher, composer]
Note(s): Portrait: ETUP 56:9 (Sept. 1938): 558
Damm, Gustav *Source(s):* CPMU; GROL; LCAR; MACM; NGDM
Steinmann, Heinrich Ferdinand 1806-1872 [musicologist, writer on singing]
Mannstein, Heinrich Ferdinand *Source(s):* LCAR; PRAT; SEND; WORB
Steinwert von Soest, Johannes 1448-1506 [singer, composer, poet]
Grummelgut, Johannes *Source(s):* IBIM
Johann, von Soest *Source(s):* LCAR
Susato, Johannes de *Source(s):* BAKR; IBIM; WORB
Sust, Johannes von *Source(s):* WORB
Stella, Scipione c.1558-1622 [organist, composer, priest]
Pietro Paolo, Don *Source(s):* LCAR
Stellman, Marcel 1925- [lyricist, record producer]]
Cadbury, Buddy *Source(s):* CPOL RE-98-159
Note(s): Jt. pseud.: Ray(mond) Martin.
DaCintra, Ruy *Source(s):* CCE57 Efor53522; CPOL RE-259-142
Johns, Leo *Source(s):* LCCC 1955-70 (see reference); SHAP
Note(s): Jt. pseud.: James John Phillips.
Martin, Gene *Source(s):* CCE58
Note(s): Stellman's given name listed: Maurice.
Martin, Jean *Source(s):* CCE56
Note(s): Also used as a jt. pseud. by Joyce Barthelson & Walter (Charles) Ehret.
Martyn, Gene *Source(s):* CCE55-56; CCE58; CPOL RE-285-440; SHAP
Morgan, Guy *Source(s):* CPOL RE-366-756; LCCC60 Efor73745
Stelzer-Palm, Joachim 1920- [composer]
Brunn, Veit *Source(s):* KOMP
Moelber, Chr. *Source(s):* KOM
Stengler, Gustave P. Cercello fl. 1892-98 [composer]
Stengler, August *Source(s):* REHH
Stennet, Joseph 1663-1713 [cleric, hymnist]
Note(s): Portrait: CYBH
I. S. *Source(s):* JULN
J. S. *Source(s):* CART; JULN
Stennett, Samuel 1727 (or 28)-1795 [hymnist]
Note(s): Portrait: CYBH
S—t *Source(s):* JULN

Stenvall, Aleksis 1834-1872 [poet]
Kivi, Aleksis *Source(s):* LAST
Stephens, Ward 1872-1940 [composer, conductor]
Note(s): Portraits: APSA; ETUP 56:9 (Sept. 1939): 558; MUCO 100:20 (17 May 1930): [5]
The following are listed as pseudonyms of Ward-Stephens.
Delafield Olga *Source(s):* TPRF
Du Parc, Leon *Source(s):* CCE49 R43851
Note(s): "Closer L'Adoree de Mon Coeur"
Sawyer, Joan *Source(s):* CCE41 #30320, 14 R98074(3) ("Sawyer Maxixe")
Ward-Stephens *Source(s):* CCE59; CCE66; CPMU; LCAR; MACM; TPRF
Warrick, Vaughan *Source(s):* CCE36 E55399
Stephenson, B(enjamin) C(harles) 1838-1906 [author, librettist]
Rowe, B(olton) *Source(s):* GAN1; GAN2; GANA p. 40; LCAR; MELL
Stephenson, Rowland c.1790-1843 [composer]
Standish, Orlando *Source(s):* NGDM
Standish, Rowland *Source(s):* NGDM
Stept, Sam(uel) H. 1897-1964 [composer, publisher, accompanist]
Leslie, Vincent *Source(s):* CCE52 R94554 ("Darktown Nurmi")
Stern, Elsie Jean 1898-1953 [composer, author, journalist]
Elsie, Jean *Source(s):* CCE47-48; PSND; WORB
Stern, Ernesta de Hierschel [librettist]
Star, Maria *Source(s):* LOWN; MELL; STGR
Stern, Henry R. 1874-1966 [composer, publisher]
Henry, S. R. *Source(s):* ASCP; CCE28 R45902; JASG; JASR; REHG
Stern, Richard 1874-1967 [composer, teacher]
Stöhr, Richard *Source(s):* ORPH
Sterrett, Paul [composer]
Kent, H. R. *Source(s):* CPOL RE-225-009; LCCC 1955-70 letter cited. (28 June 1956)
Note(s): Also used by J(ulius) S. Seredy & Louis-Philippe Laurendeau; see NOTES: Kent, H. R.
Wilson, Paul *Source(s):* CCE61 A525332
Note(s): "Short-cut Tenor Banjo Method." Also used by Sidney (Alan) Carlin; see NOTES: Wilson, Paul.
Sterzel, Alexander C. 1967- [composer]
Axes *Source(s):* KOMS; PFSA
Stevens, Alfred Peck 1840-1888 [composer]
Dashon, Algie *Source(s):* GARR
Great Vance, The *Source(s):* GARR
Vance, Alfred Glenville *Source(s):* GARR; GOTE
Stevens, Casandra (Mayo) ?-1966 [composer, author, dancer]
Mayo, Cass *Source(s):* ASCP; CCE55 Eunp

Stevens, Gosta ?-1970 [composer]
Note(s): The following pseud. also used by Peter Kreuder.
Pan, Peter *Source(s):* CCE50 ("Sonoras Varbukette," pianoalbum nr. 28)
Peter Pan *Source(s):* CCE50
Stevens, Jack ?-1951 [songwriter]
Damerell, S(tanley) J. *Source(s):* KILG; WHIC
Mer(r)ell, Stan *Source(s):* CCE36 Efor41419; CCE63; LCPC letter cited (16 July 1936)
Noel, Kay *Source(s):* CCE34 Efor34210
Reaves, Erell *Source(s):* CCE60
Note(s): Jt. pseud.: Robert Hargreaves.
Stanley, Eugene *Source(s):* CCE62 R304036
Note(s): Jt. pseud.: Ralph (T.) Butler & Tolchard (B.) [i.e., Sydney] Evans.
Stanley, Robert *Source(s):* CCE60
Stevens, (Paul) James 1930- [composer]
James, Paul *Sources(s):* GOTH; GOTT; RIES
Note(s): Also used by James Paul Warburg.
Stevens, Sam 1939?-1984 [singer, songwriter]
Elvis Presley of the Gypsies, The *Source(s):* PSND
King of Gypsy Music, The *Source(s):* PSND
Singing Sam *Source(s):* PSND
Note(s): See also Harry Frankel.
Stevens, Yvette Marie 1953- [singer, songwriter]
Kahn, Chaka *Source(s):* CLAG; CM09; LCAR
Little Aretha *Source(s):* CM09
Stevenson, George John 1818-1888 [bookseller, educator, hymn compiler]
G. J. S. *Source(s):* JULN
Stevenson, Louis C(harles), (III) 1949- [singer, songwriter]
Stevenson, B. W. *Source(s):* AMIR; CCE76; LCAR; PEN1
Stevenson, William [arranger]
Stevenson, Mickey *Source(s):* EPMU; WARN
Steventon, G. H. 1914-1992 [composer]
Steventon, Steve *Source(s):* ASCP; CCE62
Stewart, Cal(vin) (Edward) 1856-1919 [singer, songwriter, instrumentalist]
Uncle Josh *Source(s):* MCCL
Steward, F. M. [composer]
Stresa, F. M. *Source(s):* CPMU (publication dates 1883)
Stewart, Henry (Ellis) 1921 (or 23)-2003 [singer, songwriter, instrumentalist]
Stewart, Red(d) *Source(s):* CCE54-54; CCE62; CCME; LCAR; MCCL; NASF
Stewart, Herbert 1836-1898 [songwriter]
Hall, Frank *Source(s):* KILG; LCAR
Stewart, Humphrey John 1854 (or 56)-1932 [composer]
Note(s): Portrait: ETUP 56:9 (Sept. 1938): 558
Walter Damrosch of the Pacific Coast, The *Source(s):* PSND
Stewart, Joan Beatrice [composer, teacher, singer]
Grey, Ginger *Source(s):* ASCP
Stewart, Leroy Elliott 1914-1987 [bassist, composer, author]
Slim and Slam *Source(s):* http://www.allaboutjazz.com/nickname.htm (23 June 2005)
Note(s): Joint pseud.: Slim [i.e., Bulee] Gaillard.
Stewart, Slam *Source(s):* ALMC; ASCP; KINK; LCAR
Stewart, Sylvester 1944- [singer, songwriter, keyboardist]
Godfather of Psychedelic Funk *Source(s):* SHAB p. 259
Sly *Source(s):* SHAB p. 259
Stone, Sly *Source(s):* CASS; CM08; HARR; LCAR; WORL
Stone, Sylvester *Source(s):* SHAB p. 259
Stewart, William, Jr. 1907-1967 [cornetist, DJ, critic]
Half-Valve *Source(s):* JAMU
Stewart, Rex (William) *Source(s):* AMUS; LCAR
Steyer, Matej Vaclav 1630-1692 [hymnologist]
M. S. S. J. *Source(s):* CPMU
Stich, Johann [or Jan] Wenzel [or Václav] 1746-1803 [horn player, composer]
Punto, Giovanni *Source(s):* BAKR; GROL; LCAR; MACM; NGDM
Stiegele, Georg 1859-1930 [singer, songwriter]
Stigelli, Giorgio *Source(s):* BAKE; LCAR
Stieler, Caspar [or Kaspar] (von) 1632-1707 [poet, playwright, composer]
C. S. *Source(s):* GROL ("Die geharnschte Venus . . ." (1660))
Filidor, (der Dorfferer) *Source(s):* CPMU; GROL
Spate, Der *Source(s):* GROL; LCAR
Stiles, Leslie 1876-c.1940 [lyricist]
Style, Leslie *Source(s):* KILG
Still, William Grant 1895-1978 [composer, arranger]
Note(s): Portrait: ETUP 56:9 (Sept. 1938): 558
Dean of Afro-American Composers, The *Source(s):* BAKE; PSND
Dean of America's Negro Composers *Source(s):* http://www.public.coe.edu/wcb/students/bsheldon/bsheldon.html (8 Oct. 2002)
Dean of Black Classical Composers, The *Source(s):* SIFA
Grant, Willy M. *Source(s):* IDBC
Harlem Renaissance Man *Source(s):* NOTE 58:1 (Sept. 2001): 103-4
Stillingfleet, Benjamin 1702-1771 [librettist, natural historian]
Blue-stocking, The *Source(s):* CART
Krantzovius, Irenaeus *Source(s):* CART; LCAR

Stingle, David Elliot 1948- [composer, author]
Elliott, David *Source(s):* ASCP
Stirling, Peter Lee 1942- [singer, songwriter]
Boone, Daniel *Source(s):* PSND
Stirrat, William Albert 1919-2004 [electrical engineer, songwriter, composer]
Zaret, Hy [or Hi] *Sources(s):* CPOL Pau-404-550 & RE-274-348
Note(s): Do not confuse with songwriter Hy(man) Zaret (1907-); see NOTES: Zaret, Hy.
Stitcher, L(ionel) Michael 1940- [songwriter]
Murray, Mitch *Source(s):* CCE62-63; PMUS
Stites, E(dgar) P(age) 1836-1921 [hymnist]
Note(s): Portrait: CYBH
Page, Edgar *Source(s):* CCE39 #18200, 154 R6956; CCE68; CYBH
Stiles, E. P. *Source(s):* DIEH
Note(s): Printng error; not a pseud.
Stocker, Stelle (née Prince) 1858- [composer, educator]
Omesquawigishigoque *Source(s):* IBIM; WORB
Red Sky Lady *Source(s):* IBIM; WORB
Stöckigt, Siegfried 1929- [composer]
Carell, Rainer *Source(s):* BUL3
Stoddard, I(saiah) T. [composer]
I. T. S. *Source(s):* DICH ("Hard Cider Quick Step" (1840))
Stoeckart, Jan 1927- [composer]
Faust, Willy *Source(s):* REHG
Milray, Peter *Source(s):* REHG
Staffaro, Jules *Source(s):* CCE73 Efor166295; SONG
Steffaro, Julius *Source(s):* REHG
Tromberg, Jack *Source(s):* REHG; *International Who's Who in Music*. 10th ed. 1985
Trombey, Jack *Sources):* REHG
Stojanovic, Stevan 1956-1914 [composer, folklorist]
Mokranjas, Stevan *Source(s):* RIEM; ROOM
Stokem, Johannes de c.1445-1501 [composer]
Pratis, Johannes de *Source(s):* NGDM
Prato, Johannes de *Source(s):* LCAR; NGDM
Stokowski, Leopold (Antoni Stanislaw Boleslawowicz) 1882-1977 [conductor, composer]
Stokes, Leopold *Source(s):* ROOM
Note(s): Questionable pseud.
Štolcer, Josip 1896-1955 [composer, teacher]
Slavenski, Josip *Source(s):* BAKR; BUL2; CPMU; RIES
Stolzer, Josip *Source(s):* LCAR
Note(s): Changed spelling of surname c.1930.
Stoll, Dennis Gray 1912-1987 [writer on music]
Craig, Denys *Source(s):* CART; PSND
Stoller, Mike 1933- [songwriter]
Glick, Elmo *Source(s):* CC60; CCE63; GROL; PMUS; SONG
Note(s): Jt. pseud.: Leiber, Jerry.
Peters, Jed *Source(s):* CCE63; CCE67
Note(s): Jt. pseud.: Leiber, Jerry.
Stolz, Robert 1880 (or 82)-1975 [composer]
Note(s): Portrait: ETUP 58:10 (Oct. 1940): 714
Bonelli, Gino *Source(s):* CCE31 Efor21339; CCE55-58; LCAR
Ostwig, Hans *Source(s):* CCE55-56
Weinhausen, Fritz *Source(s):* CCE55
Stone, J(ohn) S(aville) [composer]
Stein, J(ohann) S(aville) *Source(s):* CPMU (publication dates 1856-84)
Stone, Jesse (A.) 1901-1999 [pianist, arranger, composer, bandleader]
Calhoun, Charles [or Chuck] (E.) *Source(s):* AMUS; BBDP; GROL; IDBC; LCAR
Stone, Joseph T. [composer]
Pietra, Giuseppe T. *Source(s):* CPMU (publications 1855-60)
Stone, Kurt 1911-1989 [composer, music editor]
Sterne, Kenneth *Source(s):* ASCP; CCE65-66
Stone, Norman Millard, Jr. 1946- [composer, author]
Stone, Butch *Source(s):* ASCP
Stone, Roberta Russell Summers 1886- [composer]
Heath, Egdon *Source(s):* http://sfpl.lib.ca.us/librarylocations/main/art/nocacomposers.htm (15 Aug. 2005)
Stoneman, Ernest (V.) 1893-1968 [singer, songwriter, multi-instrumentalist]
Stoneman, Pop *Source(s):* LCAR; MCCL; PSND
Stonum, Harry F(rancis) 1924-2001 [composer, author]
Stone, Harry *Source(s):* ASCP; CCE55; CCE65
Stopford-Harrison, Ian George 1931- [singer, songwriter]
Ford, Clinton *Source(s):* EPMU
Storck, Karl G(ustav) L(udwig) 1873-1920 [writer on music, critic, editor]
Note(s): Portrait: ETUP 56:10 (Oct. 1938): 630
Murbach, Hans *Source(s):* GROL
Störrle, Heinz 1933- [composer]
Lester, Marc *Source(s):* KOMP; KOMS; PFSA
Story, Carl (Moore) 1916-1995 [singer, songwriter, guitarist]
Father of Bluegrass Gospel *Source(s):* MCCL
Stott, Walter [or Wally] 1923 (or 24)- [clarinetist, composer, arranger]
Morley, Angela *Source(s):* GALM; LCAR; MUSR; RFSO
Morley, Jeff *Source(s):* GALM; RFSO
Norman, John *Source(s):* MUSR
Stotz, Albert 1864- [composer]
Lainz, Albert zur *Source(s):* IBIM; WORB
Stoughton, R(oy) S(paulding) 1884-1953 [composer]
Note(s): Portrait: ETUP 56:10 (Oct. 1938): 630. Do not

confuse with R. Stoughton [i.e., M(artin) Greenwald]
Dana, Arthur *Source(s):* CCE40 #13350 E84210
Note(s): A. P. Schmidt house name; see NOTES: Dana, Arthur.
Stout, Herbert E(ugene) 1905- [composer, businessman]
Stout, Bert *Source(s):* CCE55; CCE62; PSND
Strachey, John [or Jack] (Francis) 1894-1972 [songwriter]
Brody, Hal *Source(s):* EPMU; GAN2
Note(s): Jt. pseud.: Harry Acres, Jack Clarke, H(ubert) B(arber) Hedley, Stanley Lupino [i.e., Hook], (Herbert) Desmond Carter & possibly others.
Stracke, Hans Richard 1932- [composer]
Wooker, W. *Source(s):* PFSA
Stracke, Win 1908- [singer, guitarist, songwriter]
Chicago's Minstrel *Source(s):* SHAD
Straesser, Joseph Willem Frederik 1934- [composer]
Straesser, Joep *Source(s):* PSND
Straite, Elliot [songwriter]
Dr. Freeze *Source(s):* PMUS-91 ("I Wanna Sex You Up")
Note(s): Also used by Louis Freese.
Freeze, Dr. *Source(s):* PMUS-91
Note(s): Also used by Louis Freese.
Strandberg, Karl Vilhelm August 1818- [author]
Qualis, Talis *Source(s):* PIPE
Qvalis, Talis *Source(s):* PIPE
Strandberg, (Alfreda) Theodora 1883 (or 90)-1953 [lyricist, music publisher]
Bradford, Bessie *Source(s):* CCE34 R31717
Coombs, Norman *Source(s):* CCE51 R73744 ("My Alltyme Girl")
Note(s): Also used as a jt. pseud. by James (Conrad) O'Keefe & Walter (G(ustave)) Haenschen.
Esrom, D. A. *Source(s):* ASCP; CLAB; LCAR; NGAM; PERF; STUW
Morse, Dolly *Source(s):* ASCP; CLAB; FULD; LCAR; NGAM
Morse, (Mrs.) (Alfreda) Theodora *Source(s):* ASCP; FULD; NGAM
Terriss, Dorothy *Source(s):* ASCP; CLAB; FULD; KILG; LCAR; NGAM; PERF
Terriss, Theodora *Source(s):* STUW
Strange, Joe [songwriter]
Dorset, Ray *Source(s):* BLIC
Stransky, Otto 1889-1932 [composer]
Strasser, Viktor Eugene *Source(s):* STGR
Strasser, Hugo 1922- [composer]
Molldorf, Tino *Source(s):* KOMP; PFSA
Staab, Hugo *Source(s):* CCE55; CCE57
Staab, Kurt *Source(s):* CCE67; KOMP; PFSA
Strauss, Arthur 1901(or 10)- [songwriter]
Hardy, Norman *Source(s):* CCE51 Efor11539; CPOL RE-29-654
Note(s): Jt. pseud.: Ralph (T.) Butler.
Teufel, Erik *Source(s):* CCE52
Note(s): Jt. pseud.: Eric Jupp.
Warren, Mark *Source(s):* CCE50
Strauss, Eduard 1835-1916 [composer, conductor, violinist]
Note(s): Portraits: ETUP 56:10 (Oct. 1938): 630; METR 17:4 (Apr. 1901): 23
Stylish Edi *Source(s):* GROL
Strauss, Franz (Joseph) 1822-1905 [horn, composer]
Note(s): Portrait: ETUP 56:10 (Oct. 1938): 630
Joachim of the Horn *Source(s):* SPIE
Strauss, Isaac 1806-1888 [conductor, composer, violinist]
Strauss de Paris *Source(s):* AMRG 59:5 (1996): 235
Strauss, Johann (Baptist), (Sr.) 1804-1849 [composer, conductor]
Note(s): Portrait: ETUP 56:10 (Oct. 1938): 630
Emperor of the Waltz *Source(s):* PSND
Note(s): See also Johan (Baptist) Strauss, Jr. (1825-1899)
Father of the Waltz, The *Source(s):* BAKE; PSND
King of the Waltz *Source(s):* PSND
Note(s): See also Johann (Baptist) Strauss, (Jr.) (1825-1899).
King of Three-Quarter Time, The *Source(s):* http://www.teachwithmovies.org/biography-heritabe-list..htm (8 Oct. 2002)
Musical Chameleon, A *Source(s):* GROL
Waltz King, The *Source(s):* PSND
Note(s): See also Johann (Baptist) Strauss, (Jr.) (1825-1899), Archibald Joyce & Wayne (Harold) King.
Strauss, Johann (Baptist), (Jr.) 1825-1899 [composer]
Note(s): Portrait: ETUP 56:10 (Oct. 1938): 630
Emperor of the Waltz *Source(s):* PSND
Note(s): See also Johann (Baptist) Strauss (1804-1849).
King of the Waltz *Source(s):* PSND
Note(s): See also Johann (Baptist) Strauss (1804-1849).
Napoleon of the Waltz *Source(s):* DESOL-9
Schani *Source(s):* PSND
Waltz King, The *Source(s):* BAKE; PSND
Note(s): See also Johann (Baptist) Strauss, (1804-1849), Archibald Joyce & Wayne (Harold) King.
Strauss, Johann 1866-1939 [composer]
Third, The *Source(s):* PSND
Strauss, Josef 1827-1870 [composer]
Schubert of the Waltz, The *Source(s):* http://www.philorch.org/styles/poa02e/www/prognotes_30031231.html (9 Apr. 2005)
Strauss, Richard 1864-1949 [composer]
Heldenleben, Ein *Source(s):* PSND
Maeterlinck of Music, The *Source(s):* SLON
Master of the Orchestra *Source(s):* PSND
Munich's Favorite Son *Source(s):* PSND

Richard II *Source(s):* SPIE
Richard the Second *Source(s):* SPIE
Stravinsky, Igor Fedorovich 1882-1971 [composer]
Cave Man of Music, A *Source(s):* SLON
Little Giant of Twentieth Century Music, The *Source(s):* PSND; SIFA
Modernsky *Source(s):* SPIE
Musical Giant, The *Source(s):* PSND; SIFA
Strayhorn, William [or Billy] (Thomas) 1915-1967 [composer, pianist, lyricist]
Strayhorn, Swee'Pea *Source(s):* CM13; LCAR; PEN2; PSND; TCAN
Strays *Source(s):* CM13; PEN2
Swee' Pea *Source(s):* KINK; PEN2
Weely *Source(s):* CM13
Strecker, Ludwig 1883-1978 [librettist, music publisher]
Note(s): Portrait: ETUP 56:10 (Oct. 1938): 630
Andersen, Ludwig *Source(s):* CCE60-61; CPMU; GROL; LCAR; NGDO; PIPE
Street, King Malachi 1933-1978 [singer, songwriter, guitarist]
Street, Mel *Source(s):* EPMU; LCAR; MCCL
Streeter, Roberta [or Bobbie] (Lee) 1944- [singer, songwriter]
Gentry, Bobbie *Source(s):* ALMN; ENCM; LCAR; MCCL; MILL; WORT
Street, Bobbie *Source(s):* HARD; PSND
Strickland, Lily 1887-1958 [composer, songwriter]
Note(s): Portrait: ETUP 56:10 (Oct. 1938): 630
Anderson, (Mrs.) Lily *Source(s):* BAKR; LCAR
DeLongpré, Michael *Source(s):* BAKR; CCE29 E4161; CCE57; LCAR
Strittmatter, Fred 1923-1985 [composer]
Königsdorfer, Ludwig *Source(s):* KOMP; KOMS
Tornow, Fred *Source(s):* KOMP; KOMS; PFSA
Strobl, Heinz [composer, multi-instrumentalist]
Gandalf *Sourc(s):* LCAR
Strohbach, Siegfried 1929- [composer, organist]
Durian, Tim *Source(s):* PFSA
Strohmeyer, Green 1956- [songwriter, singer, guitarist]
Gartside, Green *Source(s):* NOMG
Stromberg, John 1853-1902 [composer]
Stromberg, Honey *Source(s):* BBDP; CLAB; EWPA (port.)
Strother, Cynthia 1935- [singer, songwriter]
Bell, Cynthia *Source(s):* BBDP
Strothotte, Maurice Arnold 1865-1937 [violinist, conductor, composer]
Arnold, Maurice *Source(s):* BAKO; BAKR; IDBC; MACM
Stroud, Henry Charles 1826-1888 [singer, songwriter]
Henry, Chaplin *Source(s):* BROW; IBIM; WORB
Strozzi, Barbara 1619-1667 [composer, singer]
Valle, Barbara *Source(s):* DWCO (port.); LCAR
Strozzi, Giulio 1583-1652 [librettist, poet, dramatist]
Zorzisto, Luigi *Source(s):* ALCM; NGDM; NGDO
Strube, Erna 1944- [composer]
Fleming, Joy *Source(s):* PFSA
Strübe, Hermann 1879-1960 [author, painter]
Bay, F. A. *Source(s):* CCE35 Efor41973
Burte, Hermann *Source(s):* CCE46 D40959; LCAR; PIPE; WORB
Strúby, H. *Source(s):* CCE32 Efor23789
Zergo, Fred *Source(s):* CCE32 Efor23789
Struisky, Dmitry Yuryevich 1806-1856 [violinist, critic, composer]
Trilunny *Source(s):* HOFE
Strunck, Nicolas Adam 1640-1700 [composer]
Archdiavolo *Source(s):* PSND
Strunk, Gilbert 1933-1974 [guitarist, songwriter, author]
Turner, Gil *Source(s):* AMUS; EPMU; ROOM
Strunk, Justin Roderick, Jr. 1936-1981 [singer, songwriter, banjo player, actor]
Strunk, Jud *Source(s):* AMUS; MCCL; PSND
Strzelecki, Henry (P.) 1939- [composer, author]
Wallis, Hank *Source(s):* ASCP; CCE66; CCE68
Stuart, Thomas Gilmore 1948- [composer, author, singer]
Toboggan, Christopher *Source(s):* ASCP
Stuart-Bergström, Elsa Marianne 1889-1970 [pianist, critic, composer]
Kaimen *Source(s):* BUL3; COHN; HIXN
Stube, Howard 1890 (or 95)- [composer]
Allen, Charles *Source(s):* CCE54-55; CCE57-59; CPOL RE-160-064; CPOL RE-259-283
Note(s): Also used by Albert (Kenneth) DeVito.
Carboni, Luigi *Source(s):* CCE55 E89598; CPOL RE-157-282
Howard, Bill *Source(s):* CPOL RE-85-615
Masetti, Carlos *Source(s):* CCE54-56
Milano, Tony *Source(s):* CCE61-62; CPOL RE-435-690
Reyna, Ricardo *Source(s):* CCE55 E86575; CCE56-57
Reyna, Roberta *Source(s):* CPOL RE-405-326; RE-405-327
Reyna, Roberto *Source(s):* CCE61; CCE63; CPOL RE-461-850 & RE-461850
Solak, Ted W. *Source(s):* CCE54
Williams, Gus *Source(s):* CCE52; CCE54-56
Note(s): Also used by Gustave Wilhelm Leweck.
Stuck, Jean-Baptist(e) 1680-1755 [violoncellist, composer]
Baptiste, M. *Source(s):* GROL
Baptistin, Jean *Source(s):* GROL; LCAR; NGDM

Bat(t)istin, Jean *Source(s):* GROL; GRV3; LCAR; NGDM
Florentin *Source(s):* GROL; NGDM
Stulberger, James [songwriter]
Curtiss, J(immy) *Source(s):* CCE61;CCE65-68; PMUS
Evans, Jimmy *Source(s):* CCE58
Stull, Donald Earl 1927- [composer, author, singer]
Freesoil, Mason *Source(s):* ASCP
Stults, R(obert) M(orrison) 1861-1823 [composer]
Note(s): Portrait: ETUP 56:11 (Nov. 1938): 702
Dale, Norwood *Source(s):* CCE43 #25483, 370 R118508; CPMU; LCAR
LaFiere, R. M. *Source(s):* TPRF
Lee, Marion A. *Source(s):* TPRF
Morrison, R. S. *Source(s):* CCE40 #7317, 137 R81255; TPRF
Ray, Roland *Source(s):* TPRF
Schick, Hans *Source(s):* CCE45 #22283 R137446; TPRF
Stulwitt, R. H. *Source(s):* TPRF
Note(s): Jt. pseud.: Horatio Dawes Hewitt.
Sture, Thomas Charles 1944- [keyboardist, composer]
Constanten, Tom *Source(s):* PEN2
Hill, Thomas Charles Sture *Source(s):* PEN2
Note(s): Name changed when his mother remarried.
Suard, Jean Baptiste Antoine 1735-1817 [author, critic]
Anononyme de Vaugirard, L' *Source(s):* GROL; NGDM
Suarez Gomez, Julian-Mario 1907-1982 [composer]
Dunn, Peter *Source(s):* BUL3
Subirá (Puig), José 1882-1980 [musicologist, writer on music]
Ribó, Jesús A. *Source(s):* GROL; LCAR; PIPE; RIEM
Subotnick, Joan (née Lotz) 1947- [composer, vocalist]
LaBarbara, Joan *Source(s):* DWCO
Sucher, Bernardo Mendel 1913-1971 [pianist, composer]
Sucher, Manuel *Source(s):* TODO
Suck, G. F. [composer]
Peuret, O. *Source(s):* CCE12 R3527
Philipp(e), Geo(rge) *Source(s):* CCE09 R319; CCE11 #30364, 51 R2342
Note(s): "Gavotte" (CCE09) & "Song of Summer Birds" ("CCE11)
Ritter, G. P. *Source(s):* CCE15 R7138 & R7146
Note(s): Also used by Charles P(hillip) Scott; see NOTES: Ritter, G. P.
Tadell, I. *Source(s):* CCE09 R282
Sudds, William F. 1843-1920 [composer]
Note(s): Portraits: ETUP 56:11 (Nov. 1938): 702; MRAR (Piano ed.) (Apr. 1901): 1
Wilhelm, S. F. *Source(s):* CCE40 #15093, 594 R85528; TPRF
Sudhalter, Richard M(errill) 1938- [writer on jazz, trumpeter]
Napoleon, Art *Source(s):* GROL; LCAR; PSND
Suesse, (Nadine) Dana 1909 (or 11)-1987 [pianist, composer]
Girl Gershwin *Source(s):* GROL
Sugarman, Harry 1901-1972 [songwriter]
Note(s): In CCE76 original surname listed as "Suzamon;" however, since "Suzamon" was not verified in a second source, it is listed below as a variant form.
Adams, Charles *Source(s):* CCE53 ("You're as Sweet Today as Yesterday")
Note(s): Jt. pseud.: Richard Donnelly. Do not confuse with Charles R(aymond) Adams (1915-) who used the pseud. Charlie Stone.
Boccolosi, Harry *Source(s):* CCE40 #19415 Efor63075; CCE67; LCCC 1938-45 (reference card)
Note(s): Pseud. of Harry Leon [i.e., Sugarman]. Jt. pseud.: Harold Elton Box, Desmond Cox [i.e., Adrian Keuleman] & Domonic [or Don] Pelosi.
Brown, Al *Source(s):* CCE64 R330847 ("Back in Those Old Kentucky Days")
Notes(s): Pseud. of Harry Leon [i.e., Sugarman]. Jt. pseud.: Leo Towers [i.e., Leo(nard) Blitz] & Harry Leader [i.e., Henry Lebys]
Burken, Al *Source(s):* CCE58 R223086 ("Sleepy River")
Note(s): Pseud. of Harry Leon [i.e., Sugarman]
Clayton, John *Source(s):* CCE48; CCE55; CCE75 R608418
Cox *Source(s):* LCPC36 Efor46327 ("The Girl That Broke My Heart")
Dévereux, Jules *Source(s):* CCE40 #18216 Efor62825; LCCC 1938-45 (reference card)
Note(s): Pseud. of Harry Leon [i.e., Sugarman]. Jt. pseud.: Harold Elton Box, Desmond Cox [i.e., Adrian Keuleman] & Domonic [or Don] Pelosi.
Fraser, Gordon *Source(s):* CCE40 #25023 Efor63262; CCE67; LCCC 1938-45 (reference card)
Note(s): Pseud. of Harry Leon [i.e., Sugarman]. Jt. pseud.: Harold Elton Box, Desmond Cox [i.e., Adrian Keuleman] & Domonic [or Don] Pelosi.
Goodchild, Alan *Source(s):* CCE56; CPOL RE-259-366
Guillard, Michael *Source(s):* CCE35 Efor39938
Note(s): Pseud. of Leon Harry [i.e., Sugarman] Jt. pseud.: Leo Towers [i.e., Leo(nard) Blitz] & Rod(d) Arden [i.e., Dave Silver].
Jordan, Alvin *Source(s):* CCE59 R229672 ("Lonely Little Soul")

Note(s): Pseud. of Harry Leon [i.e., Sugarman]
Kay, Bob *Source(s):* CCE36 Efor46327; CCE64 R337150
Leon *Source(s):* LCPC36 Efor46327 ("The Girl That Broke My Heart")
Note(s): Also used by Marie Emmanuel Guillaume Théaulon (de Lambert).
Leon, Harry *Source(s):* CCE36 Efor42311; CCE37 Efor47195; CCE54-55; CPOL RE-29-603
Leon, Noel *Source(s):* CCE64; CCE68
Note(s): Pseud. of Harry Leon [i.e., Sugarman]
Leon, Sally *Source(s):* WHIC p. 191
Note(s): Nickname of Harry Leon [i.e., Sugarman]
Malloys, The *Source(s):* CCE53
Note(s): Jt. pseud.: Charles Henry Forsythe & Mark Malloy [i.e., Richard Donnelly]
Mitchell *Source(s):* CCE38 Efor54242; CCE66 ("Pardon My Tears"); CCE68
Noel, Art *Source(s):* CCE37 Efor51243; CCE55-56; CCE62; CPOL RE-32-461; LCAR
Note(s): Pseud. of Harry Leon [i.e., Sugarman]
Stein, Lew *Source(s):* CCE48 Efor8677; CCE55
Stern, Lew *Source(s):* CCE75
Note(s): Pseud. of Harry Leon [i.e., Sugarman]
Summers, Gene *Source(s):* CCE59 R234725 ("Five Minutes to Twelve")
Note(s): Pseud. of Harry Leon [i.e., Sugarman]
Suzamon, Harry *Source(s):* CCE76 R624014 & R624018 & R625162
Note(s): Original surname?
Walters *Source(s):* CCE40 #4560 Efor61710; CCE67
Zimmermann, Karl *Source(s):* CCE59 R229689 ("One Little Hour With You")
Note(s): Pseud. of Leon Harry [i.e., Sugarman]

Suiter, Arlendo D. 1919-2005 [composer]
Suiter, Don *Source(s):* PSND

Sukman, Frances Paley 1910-1990 [composer, author]
Frances, Lee *Source(s):* ASCP
Paige, Frances *Source(s):* ASCP

Sullivan, (Sir) Arthur S(eymour) 1842-1900 [composer, conductor]
England's Greatest Composer *Source(s):* http://homepages.ihug.co.nz/~melbear/obituary.html (8 Oct. 2002)
Note(s): See also Edward Elgar and Henry Purcell.

Sullivan, Gala 1939- [composer, author, publisher]
Harris, Gale S. *Source(s):* ASCP
Spain, Verna Gale *Source(s):* ASCP

Sullivan, Joseph [composer]
Navillus, (Nace) *Source(s):* CCE19 E458558; CPMU

Sullivan, V. P. [composer]
Southey, Phimon L. *Source(s):* HOVL

Sülwald, Paul (Heinrich) 1907- [music publisher, author]
Fried, Enns [or Enna] *Source(s):* CCE65-66; PIPE
Kaiser, Karl Heinz *Source(s):* CCE54

Sulzböck, Toni 1922- [composer]
Buchner, Toni *Source(s):* CCE56-57; KOMP; PFSA

Sulzer, David Louis 1956- [composer, violinist]
Soldier, Dave *Source(s):* GROL

Sulzer, Salomon 1804-1890 [cantor, composer]
Note(s): Portrait: ETUP 56:11 (Nov. 1938): 702
Father of the Modern Cantorate, The *Source(s):* NULM

Suma, Yosaku 1907- [composer]
Akashi, Hiroshi *Source(s):* REHH
Nanumi, Tomio *Source(s):* REHH
Tsukigi, Hiroshi *Source(s):* REHH

Sumner, Gordon (Matthew) 1951- [singer, songwriter]
Sting *Source(s):* ALMN; BAKR; CM02; CM19; DIMA; EPMU; LCAR

Sung-Tai, Kim 1907- [composer, conductor]
Naksok *Source(s):* PSND

Suppan, Albert 1914- [composer]
Alberts, A. *Source(s):* CCE59; KOMP; PFSA

Suratno, Nano 1944- [composer]
Nano S. *Source(s):* BAKO

Suskind, Milton 1898-1975 [composer, pianist, conductor]
Baronoff, Sascha *Source(s):* RPRA
Bert, Corrine de *Source(s):* RPRA
Note(s): Also used by pianist Adam Carroll.
Cooke, Herbert *Source(s):* RPRA
Fairchild, Edgar *Source(s):* RPRA
Lavarro, Enrico *Source(s):* RPRA
Lefevre, Henri *Source(s):* RPRA
Shipman, Harry *Source(s):* RPRA
Note(s): Also used by pianists Adam Carroll, Herbert Clair & Angelico Valerio.

Süss, Bruno (Richard) 1863 (or 65)-1938 [singer, pianist, violinist, composer, critic]
Heydrich, Bruno *Source(s):* MACM; http://www.historylearningsite.co.uk/reinhard_heydrich.htm (5 Apr. 2005)

Süssmayr, Franz Xaver 1766-1803 [composer]
Dolcevillico, Francesco Saverio *Source(s):* GROL; LCAR; NGDM; PIPE

Sutton, David C., Sr. 1925- [composer, author, singer]
Crockett, David *Source(s):* ASCP (see reference)

Svarda, William Ernest 1941- [composer, trombonist, arranger]
Svarda, Buddy *Source(s):* ASCP; LCAR

Svensson, Reinhold 1920-1968 [pianist, composer, arranger]
Olson, Hammond *Source(s):* JAMU
Ragtime Reinhold *Source(s):* JAMU; NGDJ

Svevo, Italo 1861-1928 [writer on music]

Samigli, Ettore *Source(s):* GROL; NGDO
Schmitz, Ettore *Source(s):* LCAR; WORB
Svoboda, Václav Alois 1791-1849 [author, translator]
Navarovský, V. *Source(s):* PIPE
Swaby, Horace 1953-1999 [keyboardist, composer]
Pablo, Augustus *Source(s):* EPMU; LCAR
Rockers *Source(s):* LCAR
Swann, Donald (Ibrahim) 1923-1994 [pianist, composer, entertainer]
Tablet, Hilda *Source(s):* PSND
Swann, Helen [songwriter]
Ives, Helen *Source(s):* CCE64
McGehen, Ken *Source(s):* CCE63 Eunp785226 & Eunp784585-6
Note(s): Also used by Burl Ives.
Swartz, Herbert 1926- [composer, author]
Herbert, Herbie *Source(s):* ASCP
Sweatman, Wilbur C. (S.) 1882-1961 [bandmaster, composer, clarinetist]
Sweatman, Sweat *Source(s):* PSNN
Sween(e)y, Joseph 1876-1926 [composer]
Johnstone, Gordon *Source(s):* CCE49 R43614 ("Thank God the Drums Are Silent"); TPRF
Note(s): Also used by Larry A. Christiansen.
Swiedack, Karl 1815-1888 [actor, playwright, journalist]
Elmar, Carl [or Karl] *Source(s):* LCAR; PIPE
Mareller, J. C. *Source(s):* STGR
Note(s): Jt. pseud.: Josef Pfundheller.
Swift, James Frederick 1847-1931 [composer, vocalist]
Marks, Godfrey *Source(s):* BROW; CPMU; FULD; IBIM; REHH; WORB
Swift, Jonathan 1667-1745 [author]
Note(s): See LCAR & PSND for additional nonmusic-related pseudonyms.
Bickerstaff, Isaac *Source(s):* PIPE
Swofford, William Oliver 1945- [singer, songwriter]
Oliver *Source(s):* PSND
Swybbertszon, Jan Pieterszoon 1562-1621 [composer]
Phoenix of Music *Source(s):* GRV3
Pieterszoon, Jan *Source(s):* PSND
Sweelinck, Jan Pieterszoon *Source(s):* BAKR
Sykes, Bishop Milton 1928-1994 [singer, songwriter, actor]
Bishop, Bob *Source(s):* EPMU; MCCL
Freedom, John *Source(s):* MCCL
Sykes, Bobby *Source(s):* CCE65 E202270; EPMU; MCCL
Sykes, Ethelred Lundy [songwriter]
Sykes, Epp *Source(s):* STC2
Sykes, Roosevelt 1906-1983 (or 84) [singer, pianist, songwriter]
Bey, Roosevelt Sykes *Source(s):* HARS; LCAR; NGAM; PSND
Blues Man, The *Source(s):* HARS; PSND
Note(s): See also Eddie Kirkland
Bragg, Dobby *Source(s):* AMUS; HARS; LCAR; PEN2; PSND
Honeydripper, The *Source(s):* AMUS; CM20; EPMU; HARS; LCAR; NGAM; PEN2; PSND
Note(s). See also Joseph [or Joe] (C.) Liggins.
Johnson, Easy Papa *Source(s):* AMUS; HARS; NGAM; PEN2; PSND
Kelly, Willie *Source(s):* AMUS; HARS; NGAM; PEN2; PSND; SUTT
St. Louis Johnny *Source(s):* http://afgen.com/blusroot.html (25 Jan. 2005)
Sykes, Rosy *Source(s):* PEN2
Sylvester, Joshua 1832-1873 [hymn book compiler]
Note(s): See LCAR for additional nonmusic-related pseudonyms
Hotten, John Camden *Source(s):* LCAR; WORB
Szabados, György 1930- [pianist, composer]
Godfather of the Hungarian Modern Jazz Scene *Source(s):*http://www.allabout.com/reviews/r0201_146.htm (8 Oct. 2002)
Szathmary, Irving [songwriter, arranger, conductor]
Szath-Myri, (Irving) *Source(s):* BBDP; LCAR
Szathmary, William 1924- [entertainer, composer]
Dana, Bill [or William] *Source(s):* CCE61-62; CCE65-66; IMDB
Jiménez, José *Source(s):* IMDB
Ryder, Tex S. *Source(s):* LCAR
Szatmárnémeti, Gábor 1911-1985 [composer, writer on music]
Darvas, Gábor *Source(s):* LCAR; PIPE
Steinberger, Gábor *Source(s):* LCAR; PIPE
Szekeres, Ferenc [or François] 1896- [composer]
Evans, Hardy *Source(s):* SEND
Papai, François *Source(s):* CCE52-53
Sekerech, François *Source(s):* CCE58
Szendrei, Aladár 1884-1976 [conducor, composer, musicologist]
Note(s): Portraits: ETUP 58:10 (Oct. 1940): 714; NULM
Sendrey, Alfred *Source(s):* BAKO; BAKR; LCAR; PSND
Szenkar, Claudio 1940- [composer]
Song Team *Source(s):* KOMP; PFSA
Szirmai, Albert 1880-1967 [composer, publisher]
Pace, Richard *Source(s):* CPOL RE-46-911
Sinclair, Al *Source(s):* CPOL RE-46-171
Sirmay, Albert *Source(s):* GAN2; GROL; LCAR; NGDM
Szulc, Jósef [or Joseph] Zygmunt [or Sigismond] 1875-1956 [composer, conductor, pianist]
Sulima, Jan *Source(s):* CCE12 E270214; GROL

Szymanowski, Karol 1882-1937 [composer]
Elpinor *Source(s):* http://www.chandos.net/news/NRDetails/NRdetailsCHAN%2010016.asp (18 Mar. 2005)

– T –

Tabksblat, Alexander 1921- [conductor, composer]
Tarski, Alexander *Source(s):* PSND
Tabourot, Jehan [or Jean] 1519-1595 [cleric, writer on music]
Arbeau, Thoinot *Source(s):* BAKR; NGDM; WORB
Tabrar, Joseph 1857-1931 [songwriter]
Latterday G. W. Hunt, A *Source(s):* GARR
Tagger, Theodore 1891-1958 [playwright]
Bruckner, Ferdinand *Source(s):* GOTH; LCAR; WORB
Tagi-zade-Hajibeyov, Nijazi Zul'fugarovich 1912-1984 [conductor, composer]
Nijazi *Source(s):* HOFE; NGDM; NGDO
Tagliafico, Joseph (Dieudonné) 1821-1900 [composer]
De Rez *Source(s):* GROL
Retr *Source(s):* STGR
Retz de *Source(s):* GROL; NGDM; WORB
Tagliaferro, Joseph (Dieudonné)
Note(s): Variant spelling of surname.
Taillefesse, (Marcelle) Germaine 1892-1983 [composer]
Note(s): Portrait: ETUP 57:1 (Jan. 1939): 2
Tailleferre, Germaine *Source(s):* BAKO; BAKR; LCAR
Tajani Mattone, Ida mentioned 1928 [pianist, singer, composer]
Dino, Jani(t)a *Source(s):* COHN; HIXN
Takahshi, Masanori 1953- [composer]
Kitarô *Source(s):* CM36; EPMU; LCAR
Talbot, Charles Remington 1851-1891 [author, clergyman]
Brownjohn, John *Source(s):* LCAR; PIPE; PSND
John, John Brown *Source(s):* PSND
Magnus, Merriweather *Source(s):* LCAR; PIPE
Merriweather, Magnus *Source(s):* PSND
Talent, Leo (Robert) 1906-1997 [author, composer, lyricist]
Winters, Jack *Source(s):* ASCP; CCE57-58; CCE67
Tallarico, Steven [or Stephen] (Victor) 1948- [singer, songwriter]
Tyler, Steve(n) *Source(s):* CCE73; HARR; LCAR; NOMG
Tallis, Thomas 1510?-1585 [composer]
Father of Church Music *Source(s):* http://www.signumrecords.co.uk/catalogue/sigcd001 (6 Oct. 2002)
Note(s): See also Henry John Gauntlett.
Father of English Cathedral Music, The *Source(s):* PSND
Father of English Music, The *Source(s):* PSND
Tamagni, Giovanni [librettist]
Acconziano, Amone *Source(s):* MELL; STGR
Tamayo y Baus, Manuel 1829-1898 [playwright]
Estébanez, Joaquín *Source(s):* LCAR; PIPE
Tamburini, Giuseppe fl. 1668-78 [composer, organist]
Bagnacavallo, Giuseppe da *Source(s):* NGDM
Baldrati, Bartolomeo *Source(s):* NGDM
Tammlaan, Evald 1904-1945 [author]
Jänkimees *Source(s):* PIPE
Stein, Evald *Source(s):* PIPE
Taneev, Sergey (Ivanovich) 1856-1915 [composer]
Note(s): Portraits: ETUP 57:1 (Jan. 1939): 2; EWCY; MUSQ 13:4 (Oct. 1927): 540+
Russian Brahms, The *Source(s):* GROL
Note(s): See also Paul [i.e., Pual] (Fedorovich) Juon & Nikolai Medtner
Tanner, Edward Everett, III 1921-1976 [author]
Dennis, Patrick *Source(s):* CCE62-63; LCAR; PIPE; PSND
Rowans, Virginia *Source(s):* LCAR; PIPE; PSND
Tanner, James Gideon 1885-1960 [singer, songwriter, fiddle player]
Tanner, Gid *Source(s):* MCCL
Tanner, James T(olman) 1858-1915? [librettist]
Cryptos *Source(s):* GANA ("Our Miss Gibbs")
Note(s): Jt. pseud. of lyricists & composers: Adrian Ross [i.e., Arthur Reed Ropes], Percy Greenbank; Ivan Caryll [i.e., Félix Tilken] & (John) Lionel (Alexander) Monckton.
Father of Musical Comedy, The *Source(s):* PSND
Note(s): See also George M(ichael) Cohan.
Leader, James *Source(s):* GAN2; PSND
Tañón, Olga 1967- [singer, songwriter]
Merengue Queen, The *Source(s):* CLAG
Queen of Puerto Rican Merengue Music *Source(s):* LCAR
Tansley, Alfred [composer]
Nizel, A. *Source(s):* CPMU (publication date 1877)
Tantucci, Mariano fl. 1599-1603 [musician, poet]
Affettuoso *Source(s):* GRV3; IBIM
Note(s): See also Giovanni Giacomo Arrigoni.
Invaghito, L' *Source(s):* IBIM; WORB
Note(s): See also Tommaso Pecci & Pietro Beneditti.
Tanturi, Ricardo 1905-1973 [pianist, leader, composer]
Caballero del Tango, El *Source(s):* TODO
Tanzer, William 1700-1783 [organist, composer, writer on music]
Tans'ur, William *Source(s):* BAKR; NGDM

Tapia Alcázar, Sylvia [singer, songwriter]
Prisma *Source(s):* HWOM
Tapper, Thomas 1864-1958 [teacher, editor, writer on music]
Note(s): Portraits: APSA; ETUP 57:1 (Jan. 1939): 2
Alden, Ruth *Source(s):* CCE45 #3437, 587 R114407; TPRF
Taralsen, Peer Helge [composer, guitarist]
Gynt, Peer *Source(s):* http://www.guitarsite.com/newsletters/010205/8.shtml (6 Oct. 2002)
Note(s): Also used by Nikolay Sergeyevich Zhilyayev.
King of the Mountain Blues *Source(s):* http://www.guitarsite.com/newsletters/010205/8.shtml
Taravel, Antoine 1863 (or 65)-1927 [poet, composer, singer]
Privas, Xavier *Source(s):* IBIM; MACM; WORB
Tardieu, Jean 1903-1995 [author]
Trevoux, Daniel *Source(s):* PIPE
Targett-Adams, Philip 1951- [guitarist, composer]
Manzanera, Phil *Source(s):* EPMU; LCAR
Tarnowski, (Count) Wladyslaw 1841-1878 [pianist, composer, poet]
Bulawa, Ernest *Source(s):* GROL
Tarraschuk, Dovid 1897-1989 [clarinetist, composer]
Tarras, Dave *Source(s):* LCAR
Tarrega(-Eixea), Francisco 1852-1909 [composer, guitarist]
Father of the Modern Guitar *Source(s):* MUWB
Sarasate of the Guitar *Source(s):* REHH
Tartini, Giuseppe 1692-1770 [violinist, composer, theorist]
Note(s): Portrait: ETUP 57:1 (Jan. 1939): 2
Master of the Nations, The *Source(s):* SIFA
Tarver, James L. 1916- [composer]
Walker, Richard *Source(s):* CCE52; REHG; SUPN
Tasca, Pier Antonio 1864-1934 [composer]
Anthony *Source(s):* PIPE; PRAT; STGR
D'Ant(h)ony *Source(s):* PIPE; WORB
Tasso, Torquato 1544-1595 [poet, courtier]
Pentito, Il *Source(s):* NGDM
Tassy, Tamas 1920- [composer]
Legrady, Thomas Theodore *Source(s):* PSND
Thomas, Ted *Source(s):* PSND
Tate, Arthur F(rank) 1880-1950 [composer]
Note(s): Portrait: ETUP 57:1 (Jan. 1939): 2
Fothergill, Frank *Source(s):* GREN
Marat, Jean *Source(s):* CCE49 R47382 ("Forest Dreams")
Tate, Maggie 1888-1976 [singer, author]
Teyte, (Dame) Maggie *Source(s):* BAKO
Tate, Phyllis (Margaret Duncan) 1911-1987 [composer]
Janos *Source(s):* GROL
Morelle, Max *Source(s):* CCE71; GROL
Taubenhaus, Eugene 1909- [songwriter]
Doyle, Gene *Source(s):* PSND
Tauber, Werner 1934- [composer]
Poetzsch, Werner *Source(s):* KOMP; KOMS; PFSA
Taubman, Otto 1859-1929 [arranger]
Nambuat *Source(s):* SHMP
Note(s): Also used by Horst Taubmann.
Taubmann, Horst 1912-1991 [composer, conductor, music critic]
Nambuat *Source(s):* PIPE
Note(s): Also used by Otto Taubman.
Taufstein, (Alexander) Louis [or Ludwig] 1870-1942 [playwright]
Clifford, J. S. *Source(s):* PIPE
Kolloden *Source(s):* PIPE
Taylor, Andrew William Harvey 1959- [singer, songwriter]
Eldritch, Andrew *Source(s):* AMUS; http://hem.passagen.se/kruse/sisters/members (6 Oct. 2002)
Taylor, Ann 1782-1852 [hymnist]
A. *Source(s):* JULN
A. T. *Source(s):* JULN
Gilbert, Ann *Source(s):* JULN
Taylor, Arthur 1903- [singer, pianist, songwriter]
Taylor, Montana *Source(s):* HARS; LCAR
Taylor, (Joseph) Deems 1885-1966 [composer; music critic]
Note(s): Portraits: ETUP 57:1 (Jan. 1939): 2; HOWD
Great Communicator, The *Source(s):* GRAN p.174
Smeed *Source(s):* PSND; TCAN
Taylor, Eddie 1923-1985 [singer, guitarist, songwriter]
Taylor, Playboy *Source(s):* HARS
Taylor, Harold [or Harry] 1918-1986 [singer, songwriter, guitarist]
Williams, Buddy *Source(s):* EPMU; MCCL
Yodeling Jackaroo, The *Source(s):* MCCL
Taylor, Helen ?-1943 [lyricist, translator]
Note(s): In HAMA see under: Brahe, May.
Bingham, H. *Source(s):* HAMA
Ellacott, S(ydney) *Source(s):* HAMA
Marvell, J. *Source(s):* HAMA
Stuart, Kathleen *Source(s):* HAMA
Taylor, Herb [composer]
Lee, George *Source(s):* CLRA; CLTP ("Cowboy G-Men")
Note(s): "House name," MUTEL [i.e., MUsic for TELevision]. Also used by Joseph [or Joe] Mullendore.
Solon, Joseph *Source(s):* CLTP ("Cowboy G-Men" & "Sky King")

Note(s): "House name," MUTEL [i.e., MUsic for TELevision]. Also used by Jospeh [or Joe] Mullendore.

Taylor, Isidore Justin Sévérin 1789-1879 [author]
Raimond *Source(s):* LCAR (see note); PIPE

Taylor, J(ohn) S(iebert) 1869-1948 [composer]
J. S. *Source(s):* REHG
Taylor, J. C. Bert *Source(s):* REHG
Note(s): Not a true pseud.; name mistakenly interpreted.

Taylor, James [or Jim] 1945- [composer]
Rolyat, Majo *Source(s):* KOMS

Taylor, James Vernon 1948- [singer, songwriter]
Sweet Baby James *Source(s):* ALMN

Taylor, Jane 1783-1824 [poet, hymnist]
J. *Source(s):* JULN
Q. Q. *Source(s):* JULN

Taylor, Joseph [or Joe] (Carl) 1921- [singer, songwriter, guitarist]
Cowboy Auctioneer *Source(s):* CCE53 Eunp; MCCL

Taylor, Mary Virgina 1912- [composer, arranger]
Sterling, Jean *Source(s):* ASCP
Stirling, Jean *Source(s):* ASCP; HIXN
Wood, Sue *Source(s):* ASCP; HIXN
Woods, Sue *Source(s):* ASCP; HIXN

Taylor, Robert Arthur 1923- [multi-instrumentalist, composer, instrument maker]
Taylor, Tut *Source(s):* LCAR; MCCL

Taylor, Rod(erick) [poet, singer, songwriter]
Falconer, Rod(erick) *Source(s):* http://www.rollingstone.com/reviews/cd/reiew.asp?aid=67283 (22 Oct. 2003)

Taylor, Seymour (H.) 1912-2003 [author, conductor, percussionist]
Taylor, Sy *Source(s):* ASCP; CPOL PAu-90-100

Taylor, (Roland) Steve 1957- [singer, songwriter]
Evangelical Rock's Court Jester *Source(s):* CM26
Gospel Elvis Costello, A *Source(s):* CM26

Taylor, Theodore Roosevelt 1915 (or 17)-1975 [singer, guitarist, songwriter]
Taylor, Hound Dog *Source(s):* HARS; LCAR

Tchaikovskii, Modest Illich 1850-1916 [dramatist, librettist]
Gorovoy *Source(s):* GROL; NGDO

Tchaikovskii, Peter Illich 1840-1893 [composer]
B. L. *Source(s):* http://www.users.zetnet.co.uk/blangston/pitch/th187.htm (5/11/02)
Cramer, H. *Source(s):* GROL; NGDM; NGDO
Father of the Modern Ballet Score *Source(s):* MUWB
Russian Reinecke, A *Source(s):* SLON
Sinopov, P. *Source(s):* GROL; NGDM
xxx *Source(s):* MUWB

Tcherepnin, Alexander 1899-1977 [composer]
Musical Citizen of the World *Source(s):* http://www.tcherepnin.com (6 Mar. 2003)

Tedesco, Ignaz Amadeus 1817-1882 [pianist, composer]
Hannibal of Octaves, The *Source(s):* PRAT

Tedesco, Pat Louis 1934- [composer, singer]
Clayton, Steve *Source(s):* ASCP

Teitelman, Alex 1912-1974 [composer]
Tate, Hal *Source(s):* ASCC; CCE57; CCE67

Telemann, Georg Philipp 1681-1767 [composer]
G. P. T. *Source(s):* CPMU
Melande *Source(s):* CPMU
Melante *Source(s):* LCAR; PIPE
P. T. J. *Source(s):* CPMU

Tellez, Gabriel 1571?-1648 (or 58) [librettist]
Molina, Tirso de *Source(s):* LCAR; LOWN
Tirso de Molina *Source(s):* LCAR; WORB

Temkin, Harold (P.) 1949- [composer, author]
Knight, Gary *Source(s):* ASCP; CCE66-68
Temkin, Gary *Source(s):* CCE61-62
Weston, Gary *Source(s):* ASCP; CCE63

Tempelhoff, Georg Friedrich von 1737-1807 [writer on music]
G. F. T. *Source(s):* CPMS ("Gedanken über die Temperatur . . .")

Temple, Edith 19th-20th cent. [composer]
Note(s): Do not confuse with Edith Temple [i.e., Joseph Murrells].
Caballero *Source(s):* CPMU; GOTT; OCLC 49007894

Temple, Johnny [or Johnnie] 1906-1968 [singer, guitarist, songwriter]
Temple, Geechie *Source(s):* HARS; LCAR

Tenducci, Giusto [or Giustino] Ferdinando [or Fernando] c.1735-1790 [singer, composer]
Senesino, (Il) *Source(s):* GRV3; RIES; WORB
Triorchis *Source(s):* BAKR; GROL; RIES

Tener, Martin J(ack) 1935- [author, lyricist]
Martins, Jay *Source(s):* ASCP; CCE57; CCE64

Tenev, Filip Kutev 1903-1982 [composer, bandmaster]
Kutev, Filip *Source(s):* RIES

Tennant, H. M. 1891-1967 [songwriter]
Dance, Leo *Source(s):* CCE51 R78642 ("My Time Is Your Time"); PMUS

Tennent, Warren 1973- [songwriter]
Warren, Alister *Source(s):* EPMU

Tepe, Leo 1842-1929 [librettist]
Heemstede, Léon van *Source(s):* LOWN; WORB

Termen, Lev Sergeivitch 1896-1993 [inventor]
Godfather of Electronic Music, The *Source(s):* http://themigs.com/theremins.html (6 Oct. 2002)

Note(s): See also Rolf (Rainer) Gehlhaar.
Thérémin, Léon *Source(s):* BAKE; CM19; LCAR
Terpander (of Lesbo) fl. c. 675 B.C.. [musician, poet]
Father of Greek Music, The *Source(s):* PSND
Terr, Mischa Richard 1899-1987 [composer, author, actor, publisher]
Francisco, Manuel *Source(s):* ASCP; MCCA
Teri, Richard *Source(s):* MCCA
Terr, Michael *Source(s):* MCCA; PSND
Terresco, Michael *Source(s):* ASCP; MCCA
Terradellas, Domènech Miquel Bernabé 1713-1751 [composer]
Terradeglias, Domenico [or Domingo] *Source(s):* LCAR; MELL
Terranova, Joseph A. 1941- [composer, singer]
Terry, Joe *Source(s):* ASCP
Terrell, Saunders 1911-1986 [singer, harmonica player, songwriter]
Sonny T *Source(s):* HARS
Terry, Blind Sonny *Source(s):* LCAR
Terry, Saunders *Source(s):* HARS
Terry, Sonny *Source(s):* HARS; LCAR
Terry, Frances 1884-1965 [composer, pianist, teacher]
Note(s): Portrait: ETUP 57:2 (Feb. 1939): 74
Rapelje, Marie *Source(s):* TPRF
Terry, W. [songwriter]
Ward, T. *Source(s):* KILG
Note(s): Possible pseud.
Tesone, William N. 1927- [composer, author, singer]
Duke, Billy [or William] *Source(s):* ASCC; CCE61; CCE66
Tessarini, Carlo 1690-c.1766 [violinist, composer]
Carlo Tessarini il Categarreuil *Source(s):* GROL
Categarreuil, Il *Source(s):* GROL
Tessier, Albert D(enis) 1900-1996 [composer, author, pianist]
Alden, Tessie R. *Source(s):* ASCP
Dennis, Al *Source(s):* CCE42 #2333 E100981
De Tedla, Al *Source(s):* ASCP; CCE57; CCE66; CCE68
Tester, Lewis 1887-1972 [instrumentalist, songwriter]
Tester, Scan *Source(s):* EPMU; LCAR
Teupen, Jonny Wilhelm Bernhard 1923- [harpist, composer]
Valmèr, Jean Pierre *Source(s):* RIES
Teves, Leopoldo Dante [singer, songwriter]
Dan, Leo *Source(s):* HWOM; http://www.laprensahn.com/prtadas/0201/s11.htm (5 Feb. 2005)
Thackeray, William Makepeace 1811-1863 [author]
Note(s): See PSND & LCAR for additional nonmusic-related pseudonyms.
Rollicker, Harry *Source(s):* GOTE; PSND
Titmarsh, M(ichael) A(ngelo) *Source(s):* GOTE; LCAR; PSND
Thackwell, Emily M. [composer]
Monica *Source(s):* BLIC; CPMU (publications dates: 1878-82); OCLC 48703812
Thalberg, Sigismond 1812-1871 [pianist, composer]
Note(s): Portraits: ETUP 57:2 (Feb. 1939): 74; GRV3 v. 5
Attila of the Piano, The *Source(s):* PSND
Old Arpeggio *Source(s):* GROL
Pianist King, The *Source(s):* STAR p. 253
S. T - g *Source(s):* BLIC
Tharp(e), Winston (Collins) 1905-1961 [lyricist]
Tharp, Wink(e)y *Source(s):* BBDP; CCE61
Thaws, Adrian c.1967- [singer, songwriter]
Tricky (Kid) *Source(s):* ALMN, CM18; CPOL PA-1-013-546; LCAR
Thayer, Alexander Wheelock 1817-1897 [lawyer, diplomat, musical biographier]
Note(s): Portraits: ETUP 5:2 (Feb. 1939): 74; GRV3
Brown, J., The Late *Source(s):* CART
Late J. Brown, The *Source(s):* CART
Theard, Sam 1904-1982 [songwriter, dancer, comedian]
Sam & John *Source(s):* SUTT
Note(s): Jt. pseud.: Oscar John
Spo-Dee-O-Dee *Source(s):* CCE63
Theard, Lovin' Sam *Source(s):* LCAR
Theard, Spo-Dee-O-Dee *Source(s):* CCE45 #63672 Eunp451897; PSND
Théaulon (de Lambert), Marie-Emmanuel-Guillaume (-Marguerite) 1787-1841 [playwright]
Léon *Source(s):* LCAR; PIPE
Note(s): Also used by Harry Sugarman.
Theimer, Johann 1884- [composer]
Lindsay, John [or Johann] *Source(s):* REHG; SUPN
Lindsay-Thiemer *Source(s):* CCE58; CCE63
Theis, Harry 1922- [composer]
Galega, Rico *Source(s):*PFSA
Theisen, Werner 1941- [composer]
Hermanns, Werner *Source(s):* KOMP; KOMS; PFSA
Thenon, Georges 1884-1941 [author of revues, cartoonist]
Rip *Source(s):* GAN1; GAN2; LCPC D41607
Theofanidis, Iraklis [or Hercules] (B.) 1926- [composer]
Fanidi, Theo *Source(s):* ASCP; CCE57-59; CCE67-68
Theriot, Al(lison) J(oseph), (Jr.) 1922-1985 [singer, songwriter, guitarist]
Terry, Al *Source(s):* CCE54-55; CCE62; CCME; MCCL
Thern, Károly 1817-1886 [composer, conductor, pianist]
Károly, Reth N. *Source(s):* GROL

Thewlis, Stanley 1948- [instrumentalist, pianist, arranger]
Rivera, Stan *Source(s):* MUWB; PEN2
Thibault, (Jacques) Anatole-François 1844-1924 [author]
Note(s): Portrait: GRV3
France, Anatole *Source(s):* LCAR; MELL; PIPE
Gérôme *Source(s):* LCAR
Thiel, Olof 1892-1972 (or 76) [composer]
Armand, Jacques *Source(s):* GREN
Thielmans, Jean (Baptiste) 1922- [guitarist, composer]
Thielmans, Toots *Source(s):* CCE62; CM13; EPMU; KINK
Toots *Source(s):* CCE72
Thielo, Carl August 1702-1763 [composer, writer on music]
C. A. T. *Source(s):* CPMS ("Gründ-Regeln wie, . . ." (1753))
Thilo, Carolus Augustus *Source(s):* WORB
Thieme, Hermann 1924- [composer]
Hermann, E. M. *Source(s):* CCE55-56; KOMP; PFSA
Thieme, Kerstin Anja 1909- [organist, pianist, writer, composer]
Note(s): Portraits: COHN; ETUP 57:2 (Feb. 1939): 74
Thieme, Karl *Source(s):* COHN; HEIN; HIXN
Thiersch, Bertha [librettist]
Bergh, Walter *Source(s):* LOWN; MELL
Thoma, Ludwig 1867-1921 [author]
Schlemihl, Peter *Source(s):* LCAR; PIPE; WORB
Thomas, Axel 1962- [composer]
Thomas, Lexa *Source(s):* KOMS; PFSA
Thomas, Beulah 1898-1986 [singer, organist, pianist, songwriter]
Texas Nightingale, (The) *Source(s):* GRAT; HARS
Note(s): See also Fae [or Faye] Barnes.
Wallace, (Mrs.) Beulah *Source(s):* GRAT; HARS
Wallace, Sippie *Source(s):* AMUS; CM06; GRAT; HARS; LCAR
Thomas, David Wynne 1900-1983 [composer]
Wynne, David *Source(s):* BUL2; MELL; NGDM; RIES
Thomas, Ebenezer 1802-1863 [translator]
Fardd, Eben *Source(s):* KILG
Thomas, Edward 1944-1998 [songwriter, singer, guitarist]
Rabbitt, Eddie *Source(s):* CM05; LCAR; OB98; PSND
Thomas, Everald [lyricist]
Gospel Fish *Source(s):* EPMU
Thomas, George [composer]
Custer, Clay *Source(s):* GROL
Note(s): Possible pseud.
Thomas, Hans 1937- [composer]
Mindnich *Source(s):* KOMS; PFSA
Wilcox, Pat *Source(s):* KOMS; PFSA
Thomas, James (Henry) 1926-1993 [singer, guitarist, songwriter]
Thomas, Cairo *Source(s):* HARS
Thomas, Son(ny) Ford *Source(s):* AMUS; HARS; LCAR
Thomas, John 1795-1871 [teacher, writer on music]
Ieuan Ddu *Source(s):* LCAR; WILG; WORB
Thomas, John 1826-1913 [harpist, composer, writer on music]
Note(s): Portrait: *London Musical Times* (Nov. 1800): cover
Aptommas, (Mr.) *Source(s):* BAKE; HAMT
Pencerdd Gwalia *Source(s):* BAKE; GOTT; MELL; WILG
Thomas, John 1858-1944 [hymnist]
Garth, John *Source(s):* CYBH
Thomas, John Rogers 1830-1896 [singer, composer]
Osborne, Chas. *Source(s):* PDMU
Percy, Arthur *Source(s):* PDMU
Thomas, Lillian [or Lillyn] 1885-1969 [singer, songwriter]
Baker, Fannie *Source(s):* HARS
Brown, Lillian [or Lillyn] *Source(s):* HARS
Elbrown *Source(s):* HARS
Fernandez, Mildred *Source(s):* HARS
Indian Princess, The *Source(s):* HARS
Jazzbo Syncopator, The *Source(s):* HARS
Jones, Maude *Source(s):* HARS
Kate Smith of Harlem *Source(s):* EPMU; HARS
Youngest Interlocutor in the World, The *Source(s):* HARS
Thomas, Millard (J.) [songwriter]
Ott, Sam *Source(s):* CCE63
Thomas, Harry *Source(s):* CCE53-54; CPOL RE-88-051
Note(s): Jt. pseud.: Harold [or Harry] (George) Belafonte. Also used by Reginald Thomas Broughton.
Thomas, Peter 1925- [composer]
Clift, Sten *Source(s):* CCE61; CCE67; RIES
Noel, J. C. *Source(s):* RIES
Raskolikow N(ikolai) *Source(s):* CCE68; RIES
Voli, Raoul *Source(s):* CCE68; RIES
Thomas, Rebecca Carew [composer]
Carew, Lester *Source(s):* GOTT
Thomas, Russell Linwood 1935- [woodwinds, composer]
Abdul Al-Khabyyr, Al-Hajj *Source(s): Encyclopedia of Music in Canada*. 2nd ed. Toronto: University of Toronto Press, 1992.
Thomas, Todd 1968- [rapper; songwriter]
Speech *Source(s):* CPOL PA-791-436; LCAR; PMUS-92

Thomas, W(illiam) T(homas) 1794-1857 [dramatist]
Moncrieff, William Thomas *Source(s):* CPMU; LCAR; WORB
Thomas, Walter Purl 1907-1981 [instrumentalist, arranger]
Thomas, Foots *Source(s):* EPMU; GROL; LCAR; PSND
Thomason, Alexander 1925 (or 26)-1999 [composer]
Byrd, Charlie *Source(s):* ASCP
Note(s): Also used by Ernst Schleich.
Thompson, Alfonso [or Alphonso] [pianist, composer]
Thompson, Sonny *Source(s):* CCE64; PMUS
Thompson, Alma (I.) 1912-2001 [composer, author]
Androzzo, A(lma) Bazel *Source(s):* ASCP; GREN
Thompson, C. J. [composer]
Stewart, Douglas *Source(s):* CPMU ("Rally Round the Dear Old Flag" (1914))
Note(s): Do not confuse with Douglas Macdonald Stewart.
Thompson, Charles Michael (Kitteridge, IV) 1965- [singer, songwriter]
Black, Francis *Source(s):* LCAR
Black, Frank *Source(s):* CM14; LCAR
Francis, Black *Source(s):* CM14; LCAR
Thompson, Derroll Lewis 1925-2000 [singer, songwriter]
Adams, Derroll *Source(s):* EPMU; LCAR; MCCL; ROOM
Thompson, Eli, (Jr.) 1924-2005 [saxophonist, composer]
Thompson, Lucky *Source(s):* CCE47; KINK; LCAR; WASH
Thompson, Henry William 1925- [singer, songwriter, guitarist]
Hank, the Hired Hand *Source(s):* MCCL
King of Honky Tonk Swing *Source(s):* NASF
Thompson, Hank *Source(s):* CCME; LCAR; MCCL
Thompson, Jennings Lewis, Jr. 1927- [composer, author, arranger]
Thompson, Jay *Source(s):* ASCP
Thompson, (Prince) Lincoln [singer, songwriter, arranger]
Prince Lincoln *Source(s):* EPMU; LCAR
Thompson, Oscar 1887-1845 [composer]
Note(s): Portraits: ETUP 50:2 (Feb. 1932): 79; ETUP 57:3 (Mar. 1939): 146; GRAN
Poet and Seer of His Profession, The *Source(s):* GRAN
Thompson, Richard 1949- [singer, guitarist, songwriter]
Card-Carrying Guitar Hero, A *Source(s):* CM07
Delta Bluesman from Lebanon, A. *Source(s):* CM07
Sixteenth Century Jeff Beck, A *Source(s):* CM07
Thompson, Robert Scott 1959- [composer]
Fountainhead *Source(s);* http://www.aucourantrecords.com/rst/fount.htm
Thompson, Robert Wickens, II 1949- [singer, songwriter]
Thompson, Robbin *Source(s):* ASCP; CCE72; CPOL PAu-343-337
Thompson, (James) Winston 1952- [DJ, lyricist, record producer]
Doctor Alimantado *Source(s):* AMUS; EPMU; LCAR
Ital Surgeon *Source(s):* EPMU
Ital Winston *Source(s):* AMUS
Prince, Winston *Source(s):* LCAR
Winston Cool *Source(s):* AMUS
Thomsen, Christian 1904- [composer]
Adler, Agnes *Source(s):* BUL1
Heinz, Frank *Source(s):* BUL1
Thomson, Virgil (Garnett) 1896-1989 [composer, critic]
Note(s): Portrait: ETUP 57:3 (Mar. 1939): 146
Sacred Cow Sharpshooter *Source(s):* GRAN p. 226
Tribs Ageless Enfant Terrible, The *Source(s):* GRAN p. 234
Virgil of American Musical History, The *Source(s):* PSND
Thon, Franz 1910- [composer, arranger, conductor]
Kaiser, H. J. *Source(s):* CCE59
Kaiser, Joachim *Source(s):* CCE58-59; KOMP; KOMS; PFSA; RIES
Thornton, Jim [actor, songwriter]
Broadway's King of Elbow-Benders *Source(s):* MARC p. 108
Thornton, Keith 1963- [rapper]
Dr. Doom *Source(s):* LCAR
Dr. Octagon *Source(s):* EPMU; LCAR
Gerbik, Mr. *Source(s):* AMUS; EPMU
Kool Keith *Source(s):* EPMU; LCAR
Large, Poppa *Source(s):* EPMU
Reverand Tom *Source(s):* EPMU
Rhythm X *Source(s):* AMUS
Sinister 6000 *Source(s):* EPMU
Smith, Big Willie *Source(s):* EPMU
Thornton, Willie Mae 1926-1984 [singer, songwriter]
Big Mama *Source(s):* CCE68
Thornton, Big Mama *Source(s):* CCE65; CM18; HARS; LCAR; NOMG
Thorp, N(athan) Howard 1867-1940 [writer on music]
Thorp, Jack *Source(s): Songs of the Cowboys.* Applewood Books, 1908. (Reprint)
Throckmorton, James (Fron Sonny) 1941- [songwriter, singer, guitarist]
Daye, Sonny *Source(s):* CCE62-63
Throckmorton, Sonny *Source(s):* CCE74; MCCL; NASF

Thrupp, Dorothy [or Dorthea] Ann 1779-1847 [hymnist]
D. A. T. *Source(s):* CLAC; JULN
Iota *Source(s):* CLAC; CYBH
Thrupp, Joseph Francis 1827-1867 [hymnist]
J. F. T. *Source(s):* JULN
Thurston, Jane Jacquelin 1915- [author, lyricist]
Willaden, Gene *Source(s):* ASCP
Thys, Pauline-Marie-Elisa c.1836-1909 [librettist, composer]
DuCoin, M. (Mme.) *Source(s):* DWCO; LCAR
Tiberiu, Farkas 1914- [composer]
Levary, Tibor *Source(s):* PSND
Tidman, Paul Frederick 1836-1889 [author, hymnist]
Evans, Mark *Source(s):* JULN (Suppl.); WORB
Note(s): Also used by Omer Westendorf.
Tieck, (Johann) Ludwig 1773-1853 [author]
Färber, Gottlieb *Source(s):* PIPE
Lebrecht, Peter *Source(s):* PIPE
Tiemersma, Sake Lieuwe 1912-1987 [composer]
Selté *Source(s):* REHH; SUPN
Tilgham, Amelia L. [singer, songwriter]
Queen of Song, The *Source(s):* PSNN
Tilkin, Félix (Marie Henri) 1861-1921 [composer, conductor]
Note(s): Portraits: EWPA; GAN2
Caryll, Ivan *Source(s):* CPMU; EWPA; GAN1; GAN2; KILG; KINK; LCAR; NGDM
Cryptos *Source(s):* GANA ("Our Miss Gibbs")
Note(s): Jt. pseud. of lyricists & composers: Caryll [i.e.,Tilken], Adrian Ross [i.e., Arthur Reed Ropes], Percy Greenbank, (John) Lionel (Alexander) Monckton & James T(olman) Tanner.
Tilkin, John *Source(s):* KILG
Tillis, (Lonnie) Mel(vin) 1932- [singer, songwriter, multi-instrumentalist, actor, author]
Guru of Stutterers *Source(s):* MCCL
Stutterin' Boy *Source(s):* MCCL
Tillotson, Queena 1896-1951 [soprano, teacher, author]
Mario, Queena *Source(s):* BAKO; BAKT; WORB
Tilson-Thomas, Michael 1944- [pianist, conductor, composer]
Bad Boy of Conducting *Source(s):* CM24
Timmermans, Armand 1860- [composer]
Danverd, Jules *Source(s):* MELL
Timms, Herbert Philip [composer]
Logaire, S. *Source(s):* CPMU (publication dates 1897-1906)
Timpano, Paula (Francesca Ianello) 1924- [composer, author]
Frances, Paula *Source(s):* ASCP; CCE60
Paula Frances *Source(s):* CCE60
Walters, Joan *Source(s):* CCE57

Tinctoris, Johannes c.1435-1511 [music theorist, composer]
Färbers, Johannes *Source(s):* NGDM
Lateinturier, Jan *Source(s):* WORB
Vaerwere, Johannes de *Source(s):* NGDM
Tinódi, Sebestyén [or Sebastiano] 1505-10-1556 [poet, composer]
Lantos *Source(s):* NGDM
Tinter, Georg [composer]
Diogenes *Source(s):* http://www.nla.gov.au/music/symphlist/titleorder.html (7 Mar. 2005)
Tiompkin, Dmitri 1894-1979 [composer]
Llewellyn, Ray *Source(s):* CLMJ
Note(s): Possible pseud. Also used by others; see NOTES: Llewellyn, Ray.
Tippett, Michael (Kemp) 1905-1998 [composer]
Pennyless, D. M. *Source(s):* GROL; PIPE
Note(s): Jt. pseud.: David Ayerst & Ruth Pennyman.
Tishman, Fay 1913- [composer, author, playwright]
Hart, Frances *Source(s):* ASCP; CPOL TXu-616-694
Titov, Nikolay Alexeyevich 1800-1875 [composer]
Father of Russian Song, The *Source(s):* GROL; NGDM
Tittmann, Anna [writer on music]
Annesley, Charles *Source(s):* LCPC; OCLC 19854881
Note(s): Jt. pseud.: Charles (T(rowbridge)) Tittmann.
Tittmann, Charles (T(rowbridge)) 1885-1964 [writer on music]
Note(s): Portraits: ETUP 57:3 (Mar. 1939): 146; MUSA 32:25 (16 Oct. 1920): 23
Annesley, Charles *Source(s):* LCPC; OCLC 19854881
Note(s): Jt. pseud.: Anna Tittmann.
Tiverton, Viscount (Adam Edward Giffard) 1934- [playwright]
Bath, Oliver *Source(s):* GANA p. 801
Tizol, Vincente Martinez 1900-1984 [trombonist, composer]
Tizol, Joan *Source(s):* CCE65
Tizol, Juan *Source(s):* LCAR; STUW
Tobani, Theodore Moses 1855-1933 [composer, arranger]
Note(s): Portraits: ETUP 57:3 (Mar. 1939): 146; METR 15:12 (Dec. 1899): cover
Fahrbach, Phillip *Source(s):* LCPC
Fahrbach-Tobani *Source(s):* LCPC R45414 ("King of the Turf")
Fare, Florence *Source(s):* CCE19 R14525 ("Lusitania Waltz")
Note(s): Also used by Alfred William Rawlings.
Herman(n), Andrea [or Andrew] *Source(s):* GROL; LCAR; NGAM; REHG; SUPN
Morris, Joseph *Source(s):* CCE29 E6461

Moses, Theo(dore) *Source(s):* GROL; LCAR; NGAM; REHG; SUPN
Moses-Tobani, Theodore *Source(s):* LCAR; NGAM
Reed, Florence *Source(s):* GROL; LCAR; NGAM; REHG; SUPN
Wohanka, F. *Source(s):* REHG; SUPN
Tobias, Charles 1898-1970 [songwriter]
Boy Who Writes the Songs You Sing, The *Source(s):* BBDP
Note(s): Called himself.
Brothers, The *Source(s):* CCE73 R556345
Note(s): Jt. pseud.: Harry Tobias & Henry Tobias.
Lesser, S. *Source(s):* CCE57
Sherman, Tobe *Source(s):* CCE26 Index; LCPC
Note(s): Jt. pseud.: Al(bert) Sherman.
Song Writers on Parade *Source(s):* CCE32 Eunp56182
Note(s): Jt. pseud.: Percy Wenrich, Sidney Clare, Al(bert) Sherman, Al(an) Lewis, (T.) Murray Mencher & Vincent Rose.
Tobias Brothers, The *Source(s):* CCE64
Note(s): With Harry Tobias & Henry Tobias.
Tobias, Harry 1894 (or 95)-1994 [songwriter]
Note(s): Portraits: *Rag Time* 15:1 (Mar. 1981): 4; *Rag Time* 15:4 (Nov. 1981): 3;
Brothers, The *Source(s):* CCE73 R556345
Note(s): Jt. pseud.: Charles Tobias & Henry Tobias.
Last Ragtime Songwriter, The *Source(s):* Wilkes, Glen. "The Last Ragtime Songwriter; Harry Tobias." *Rag Time* 28:6 (May 1995): 3
Tobias Brothers, The *Source(s):* CCE64
Note(s): With Charles Tobias & Henry Tobias.
Tobias, Elliot *Source(s):* CCE66
Tobias, Henry 1905-1997 [songwriter]
Brothers, The *Source(s):* CCE73 R556345
Note(s): Jt. pseud.: Charles Tobias & Harry Tobias.
Tobias Brothers *Source(s):* CCE64
Note(s): With Charles Tobias & Harry Tobias.
Toch, Ernst 1887-1964 [composer]
Artok, L. *Source(s):* CCE50 R56253
Note(s): ("Copelia Suite") Schott house name? See also Lothar Windsperger.
Toché, Raoul 1850-1895 [playwright, critic]
Escopette *Source(s):* PIPE; WORB
Frimousse *Source(s):* PIPE; WORB
Tavel, Raoul *Source(s):* PIPE; WORB
Triel, Robert *Source(s):* PIPE; WORB
Toeschi, Johann (Baptist Maria) Christoph 1735-1800 [violinist, composer]
Toesca della Castellamonte, Johann *Source(s):* BAKR; LCAR
Tolbert, Campbell Arelius 1909-2000 [saxophonist, clarinetist, arranger, composer]
Tolbert, Skeets *Source(s):* DRSC
Tolbert, Gregory Jerome 1953- [composer, author, singer]
Tolbert, Geronimo *Source(s):* ASCP
Told, Franz Xaver 1792-1849 [librettist]
Wimmer, Friedrich *Source(s):* STGR
Tolstoi, Theophil [or Feofil] Matveievitch 1809-1881 [singer, composer, critic]
Rostislav *Source(s):* HOFE; MACM; PRAT
Tomadini, Jacopo 1820-1883 [composer]
Palestrina of the 19th Century, The *Source(s):* NGDM
Tomášek, Václav Jan Křtitel 1774-1850 [composer, teacher]
Dalai Lama of Music, The *Source(s):* NGDM (see under: Hanslick, Eduard)
Tomeś, František Václav 1759-1801 [instrumentalist, composer]
Flosculus [or Floskulus] *Source(s):* GROL
Tomlin, Truman (V., Sr.) 1907 (or 08)-1987 [bandleader, composer, singer]
Tomlin, Pinky *Source(s):* BBDP; CCE62; KINK; PSND; VACH
Tomlinson, Ernest 1924- [composer]
Perry, Alan *Source(s):* CCE37 E61087; CCE58; GROL, RFSO
Tomlinson, Jarrett 1952- [singer, songwriter]
Sherman, Bim *Source(s):* EPMU
To(o)ney, Lemuel Gordon 1875-1941 [singer, songwriter, actor, author]
Leonard, Eddie *Source(s):* ASCP; CASS; GAMM; SPTH p. 333; SUTT
Tonizzo, Angelo 1854- [composer]
Elias, S. *Source(s):* STGR v. 4/pt.1
Tonna, Charlotte Elizabeth (née Browne) 1790-1846 [songwriter, author]
C. E. *Source(s):* CART
Charlotte Elizabeth *Source(s):* CART; JULN; LCAR
Tonning, Merrill D. 1910-1980 [composer, author, arranger]
Merrill, Idaho *Source(s):* ASCP; CCE54; CCE61
Töpfer, Wolfgang c.1525-1589 [composer, writer on music]
Figulus, Wolfgang *Source(s):* BAKR; GROL; NGDM; WORB
Toplady, Augustus Montague 1740-1778 [cleric, hymnist]
Note(s): Portrait: CYBH
A. T. *Source(s):* HATF
Note(s): On contributions to *Gospel Magazine.*
Clerus *Source(s):* CART
Concionator *Source(s):* HATF
Hanoverian, An *Source(s):* CART; LCAR
Minimus *Source(s):* HATF
Presbyter of the Church of England *Source(s):* CART

Torch, Sidney 1908-1990 [composer, arranger, organist, conductor]
Rycoth, Denis *Source(s):* RFSO
Torke, Michael 1961- [composer]
Ravel of His Generation, The *Source(s):* http://www.ypc.org/transientglory/cd.html (13 Apr. 2005)
Torme, Mel(vin Howard) 1925-1999 [singer, songwriter, author]
Butterscotch, Mr. *Source(s):* PSND
Kid with the Gauze in His Jaws, The *Source(s):* PSND
Mr. Butterscotch *Source(s):* PSND
Velvet Fog, The *Source(s):* CM04; PSND
Wyatt, Wesley Butler *Source(s):* LCAR; PSND
Torn, David 1953- [guitarist, composer]
SPLaTTeRCeLL *Source(s):* MOMU
Törneroos, Anders 1835-1896 [author, translator]
Tuokko, (Antti) *Source(s):* PIPE; WORB
Toro Vega, Vicitor Guillermo 1933- [singer, songwriter, guitarist, producer]
Toro, Y(omo) *Source(s):* HWOM
Torres(-García), Eduardo [or Eddie] 1939- [singer, songwriter, accordonist]
Torres, Lalo *Source(s):* HWOM
Torresano, Bartolomeo c.1520-1569 [composer]
Hoste da Reggio *Source(s):* GROL
Tortamano, Nicola c.1580-1627 [composer, teacher]
Errante, L' *Source(s):* GROL
Tórtora, Genaro 1915-1998 [bandoneonist, leader, composer]
Mancione, Alberto *Source(s):* TODO
Tortoriello, Vincent Joseph 1902-1986 [tuba/double bass player, arranger]
Tarto, Joe *Source(s):* EPMU; NGDJ
Tostado, Edmundo Martinez 1923?-2004 [bandleader, composer, singer]
Tosti, Don *Source(s):* WASH
Tosti, Francesco Paolo 1846-1916 [composer]
Tito lo Posa, F. *Source(s):* http://ourworld.compuserve.com/homepages/Katzbichler_Musikverlag/K54_Drucke. html (29 Sept, 2003)
Totis, Giuseppe Domencio de 1644-1707 [librettist]
De Totis, Giuseppe Domenico *Source(s):* LCAR
Nonacrio, Filedo *Source(s):* GROL
Totis, San(dor) 1895-1970 [composer, conductor]
Dexter, Von *Source(s):* CLMC
Note(s): Incorrectly identified as pseud. of Laszlo [i.e., Totis]. Actually Von Dexter was the pseudonym of La Von Hawley Urbanski, Chicago born conductor, composer, arranger.
Kloss, Erich *Source(s):* CLMC
Laszlo, Alexander *Source(s):* CLMC
Laszlo, Sandor *Source(s):* CLMC; CLTP ("This Is Your Life")

Touchemo(u)lin, Joseph 1727-1801 [violinist, composer]
Dousmolin, Joseph *Source(s):* MACM; WORB
Tourneaux, Nicolas le 1640-1686 [author, hymnist]
N. T. P. R. *Source(s):* JULN
Tournes, Jean de 1539-1615 [humanist, printer]
Bavent, Jean *Source(s):* GROL
Tourterelle, Henri 1796-1821 [composer, publisher]
Herdlizka, Henri *Source(s):* http://persoweb.francenet.fr/~ymorin/earlykeyb.html (21 Oct. 2002)
Toussaint, Allen (R.) 1938- [composer, pianist]
Neville, Naomi *Source(s):* EPMU; IDBC
Southern Knight, A *Source(s):* IDBC
Toussaint, Clarence *Source(s):* EPMU; IDBC
Tovey, Frank 1956-2002 [singer, songwriter]
Fad Gadget *Source(s):* AMUS; EPMU; LCAR
Townley, Charles 1843-1905 [writer, dramatist]
Thorn, Geoffrey *Source(s):* CPMU; KILG
Townsend, Devin 1972- [singer, guitarist, songwriter]
Strapping Young Lad *Source(s):* EPMU
Townsend, George Henry 1801-1874 [singer, critic]
Green, John *Source(s):* HAMT; WORB
Green, Paddy *Source(s):* WORB
Townsend, Henry 1909- [singer, guitarist, songwriter]
Thomas, Henry *Source(s):* HARS
Note(s): Do not confuse with Henry "Ragtime Texas" Thomas (1874-).
Too Tight Henry *Source(s):* AMUS; HARS
Townsend, Mary Ashley (née Van Voorhis) 1832-1901 [author, poet]
Xarifta *Source(s):* LCAR; WORB
Tozzo, Vincent J. 1929-1994 [composer, author, singer]
Roma, Vinny *Source(s):* ASCP; CCE73; CPOL PAu-652-542
Trace, Al(bert) (J(oseph)) 1900-1993 [composer, author]
Dailey, Frances *Source(s):* CCE56
Hart, Bob(b) *Source(s):* ASCP; CCE49-51; CPOL RE-58-966; STUW
Watts, Clem *Source(s):* ASCP; CCE49-50; CCE68; CPOL RE-726-648; STUW
Tranovsky, Juri 1592-1637 [poet, composer]
Slavonic Luther, The *Source(s):* GROL
Tranoscius, Georg *Source(s):* GROL
Trantow, Herbert 1903- [composer]
Note(s): Portrait: ETUP 57:4 (Apr. 1939): 219
Lenk, Helmuth *Source(s):* CCE52; CCE55; KOMP; PFSA
Traoré, Boubacar 1942- [guitarist, singer, songwriter]
Kar Kar *Source(s):* CM38

Trapassi (Gallastri), Pietro Antonio 1698-1782 [author, librettist]
Artimio Corasio *Source(s):* ALMC; SONN
Artino Corasio *Source(s):* ALMC; SONN
Corasio, Artino [or Artimio] *Source(s):* ALMC; MORI; NGDO; PIPE
Metastasio, Pietro [or Pedro] *Source(s):* ALMN; BAKO; GROL; LCAR; MACM; NGDM; NGDO
Trapassi, Antonio Domenico Bonaventura *Source(s):* LCAR
Trautzl, Jan Jakub 1749-1834 [composer]
Frantzl, Jacopo *Source(s):* WIEC
Note(s): Misprint of surname.
Saputo *Source(s):* WIEC
Travers, Alison mentioned 1930 [composer]
Farrell, Toni *Source(s):* CCE50 R66422 ("The Cannibal"); GOTH; WORB
Traywick, Randy (Bruce) 1959- [singer, songwriter, guitarist]
New Crown Prince of Country Music *Source(s):* FLIN
Ray, Randy *Source(s):* EPMU
Travis, Randy *Source(s):* BAKR; CCME; CM09; EPMU; FLIN; LCAR; MCCL; STAC
Trebilco, Leonard (Charles) 1924- [composer, conductor]
Bretton, Steve *Source(s):* CCE52; CCE54 Efor28593; RFSO
Duncan, Trevor *Source(s):* CPOL RE-332-040; EPMU; GAMM; MUSR; MUWB; RFSO
Trebol fl. 14th cent. [composer]
Borlet *Source(s):* NGDM
Note(s): May be an anagram of Trebol.
Trede, Gerhard 1913- [composer]
Cavini, Victor *Source(s):* KOMS; PFSA
Tree, Joshua [singer, songwriter, arranger, conductor]
Yester, Jerry *Source(s):* EPMU; WARN
Treharne, Bryceson 1879-1948 [composer, editor, teacher]
Note(s): Portrait: ETUP 57:4 (Apr. 1939): 219
Bruce, Edgar *Source(s):* CCE66
Downing, Kenneth *Source(s):* ASCP; CCE35, E49430; CCE68
Harding, Richard *Source(s):* CCE42 #20072-73 E104159-60; CCE67-68
Marlowe, Jeffrey *Source(s):* CCE38 E66474
Mayne, Richard *Source(s):* CCE49 R48000 ("Song of the Sea Rovers")
Norman, Wayne *Source(s):* CCE45 #56020 E135083; CCE64-65
Randall, Peter *Source(s):* CCE47; CCE74
Wallis, Chester *Source(s):* CCE42 #25038 E105412; CCE60; GOTH
Treiber, Johann Philipp 1675-1727 [composer, theorist, writer]
Dionysius Trebellianus *Source(s):* GROL
Trebellianus, Dionysius *Source(s):* GROL
Treichlinger, Wilhelm (Michael) 1902-1973 [author, dramatist]
Michael, Curt *Source(s):* PIPE
Trematerra, Rinaldo 15??-1603 [harpist, singer, composer]
Rinaldo, dall'Arpe *Source(s):* CCML
Tremblay, Irene [singer, songwriter]
Aroah *Source(s):* http://epitonic.com/artists/aroah.html (1 Aug. 2005)
Trent, Charles Wilburn 1938- [multi-instrumentalist, composer]
Mr. Banjo *Source(s):* MCCL
Trent, Buck *Source(s):* MCCL
Trent, Jackie 1940- [singer, songwriter]
Mr. and Mrs. Music *Source(s):* DAUM
Note(s): Jt. pseud.: Anthony [or Tony] (Peter) Hatch.
Tretheway, Robert 1817-1878 [actor, playwright, director]
Jones, Robert *Source(s):* GAN2 (see under: Melville, Emilie)
Treu, Daniel Gottlob 1695-1749 [composer]
Fedele, (Daniele) Teofilo *Source(s):* MACM; NGDM; NGDO; RIEM; SONN; WORB
Trevelyan, Arthur 1802-1878 [composer]
Trevelyan, Beau Brummel *Source(s):* MARC p. 178
Trevino, Rick 1971- [singer, instrumentalist, songwriter]
Hispanic Garth Brooks *Source(s):* STAC
Tex-Mex Ricky Van Shelton *Source(s):* STAC
Trevor, Huntley 1881-1943 [songwriter]
Huntley, Trevor
Note(s): Incorrect form of name.
Wallace, Chester *Source(s):* CCE49; CCE76
Wallace, Raymond *Source(s):* CCE37 Efor50997; CCE60 R266896; KILG
Note(s): Also jt. pseud.: Fred Hartley & Billy [i.e., Willis Wilfred] Reid (CCE40 #14853 Efor62487).
Williams, Slade *Source(s):* CCE37 Efor50997; CCE52 R88253 ("I've Married Sunnyside Sal")
Treybenreif, Peter c.1465-c.1525 [composer]
Athesinus, Petrus Tritonius *Source(s):* LCAR
Tritonius, Petrus *Source(s):* BAKR; LCAR; NGDM
Triboulet, M. [author]
Ponteuil *Source(s):* WEOP
Trice, William [or Willie] (Augusta) 1910-1976 [guitarist, songwriter]
Trice, Welly *Source(s):* ALMN; HARS
Triebel, Jürgen 1948- [composer]
Tee, Jay *Source(s):* KOMP; KOMS; PFSA
Trinchera, Pietro mentioned 1746 [librettist]
Chirrap, Terentio *Source(s):* NGDO; SONN; WORB

Chriter, Partenio *Source(s):* NGDO
Partenio, Chriter *Source(s):* WORB
Tritto, Giacomo 1733 (or 35)-1824 [composer, teacher]
Tarentino, Il *Source(s):* IBIM; WORB
Turitto, Giacomo *Source(s):* IBIM; WORB
Troels-Lund, Troels (Frederik) 1840-1921 [dance historian]
Vedel, Poul *Source(s):* PIPE
Troili, Giuseppe fl. 1695-1706 [composer, instrumentalist]
Paradossi, Giuseppe *Source(s):* GROL; NGDM
Paradosso, Il *Source(s):* WORB
Troilo, Anibal (Carmelo) 1914-1975 [bandoneonist, bandleader, composer]
Note(s): Portrait: BBDP
Gordo, El *Source(s):* BBDP
Pichuco *Source(s):* BBDP; CCE56-57; CCE65; TODO
Troilo, Pichuco *Source(s):* TODO
Tron Dolfin, Caterina 1736-1793 [author, poet]
Nonacrina, Dorina *Source(s):* PIPE
Trotter, Henry 1855-1912 [composer]
Devoto, Howard *Source(s):* WARN
Trafford, Howard *Source(s):* WARN
Trotère, Henry *Source(s):* BAKR; KILG; LCAR; MACM; MUWB
Trotter, John Scott [composer]
Oberdorfer, Theodore Eugene *Source(s):* CLRA
Note(s): Possible jt. pseud.: Carroll Carroll.
Trouluffe, John ?-c.1473 [composer]
Treloff, John *Source(s):* LCAR
Truelove, John *Source(s):* GRV3; LCAR
Trousselle, Josef [composer]
Schumann, Ludwig *Source(s):* CPMU (publication dates 1884-94)
Truhn, Friedrich Hieronymus 1811-1886 [composer]
Mozart *Source(s):* APPL p. 10
Truinet, Charles Louis Étienne 1828-1899 [lawyer, playwright, librettist, writer on music]
Dubois, Paul *Source(s):* LOWN; MELL
Note(s): Jt. pseud.: Paul Boisselot. Also used by Clive Richardson on "Shadow Waltz."
Nuitter, Charles Louis Etienne *Source(s):* BAKR; GAN2; GROL; LCAR; MACM; NGDO; ROOM
Trümpy, Johann Balthasar 1946- [composer]
Trümpy, Balz *Source(s):* PSND
Trusler, Ivan 1925- [composer]
Chambers, Robert *Source(s):* CCE63 E177065; CPOL RE-483-993
Note(s): Jt. pseud.: Walter (Charles) Ehret. Ehret also used as jt. pseud. with other individuals; see NOTES: Chambers, Robert.
Field, Robert *Source(s):* CCE62 E160727 (CPOL RE-483-993)
Note(s): Jt. pseud.: Walter (Charles) Ehret.
Hilton, Arthur *Source(s):* LCCC 1955-70 (see reference)
Note(s): Jt. pseud.: Walter (Charles) Ehret. Ehret also used as a jt. pseud. with other individuals; see NOTES: Hilton, Arthur.
King, Thomas *Source(s):* CPOL RE-452-365
Trzcinski, Krzysztof 1931-1969 [physician, composer, pianist]
Komeda, Krzysztof *Source(s):* ASCP; GROL; LCAR; NGDJ
Trzetrzelewska, Basia c.1959- [singer, songwriter]
Basia *Source(s):* CLAG; CM05; LCAR
Tsandoulas, Gerasimos (N(icholas)) 1939- [scientist, composer]
DiArta-Angeli, F. *Source(s):* LCAR; http://www.operagreca.com (port.) (6 Oct. 2002)
Tschirch, Friedrich Wilhelm 1818-1892 [choral conductor, composer]
Note(s): Portrait: ETUP 57:5 (May 1938): 321
Czersky, Alexander *Source(s):* LCAR; MACM; PRAT; WORB
Tsveifel', Sergey Petrovich 1905-1976 [composer, conductor]
Gorchakov, Sergei (Petrovich) LCAR
Zweifel, Sergey *Source(s):* LCAR
Tubb, Ernest (Dale) 1914-1984 [singer, guitarist, composer]
E. T. *Source(s):* CCME; MCCL
Gold Chain (Flour) Troubador, The *Source(s):* MCCL; PSND
Texas Troubadour, The *Source(s):* ALMN; CM04; FLIN; MCCL; PSND; SHAD
Tubb, Talmadge [songwriter]
Talmadge, Billy *Source(s):* CCE52
Tubb, Billy *Source(s):* CCE52; CCE55; PMUS
Tucci, Joseph William 1953- [composer, author, producer]
Matthew, Eric *Source(s):* ASCP; CCE77
Tucholsky, Kurt 1890-1935 [journalist, author]
Hauser, Kaspar *Source(s):* LCAR; PIPE
Panter, Peter *Source(s):* LCAR; PIPE
Tiger, Theobald *Source(s):* CCE68; LCAR; PIPE
Wrobel, Ignaz *Source(s):* LCAR; PIPE
Tucker, John(ny) [songwriter]
Note(s): May be John A. Tucker (1896-1971), author, conductor.
Turner, John *Source(s):* CCE31 E20382; CCE58 R206564 ("Salem Town")
Note(s): Also used by James John Phillips.
Tullio, Francesco Antonio 1660-1737 [author, librettist]
Cinnéo, Filostrate Lucàno *Source(s):* MELL; SONN
Note(s): Supposed pseud. of Antonio Soliva; however, more likely anagram of Tullio.

Feralintisco, Colantuono *Source(s):* LCAR; SONN
Filostrate Lucàno Cinnéo *Source(s):* SONN
Note(s): Supposed pseud. of Antonio Soliva; however, more likely anagram of Tullio.
Tunbridge, Joseph A(lbert) 1886-1961 [composer]
Curtis, Con *Source(s):* CCE68 R438781
Note(s): Jt. pseud.: Bert [i.e., Albert George] Lee & Jack Waller.
Graham, Herbert *Source(s):* CCE47 R24451
Hope, John *Source(s):* CCE56 R164348 ("With You Beside Me")
Note(s): Jt. pseud.: Jack Waller.
Lindon, Robert *Source(s):* GANB
Note(s): Jt. pseud.: Jack Waller.
Sharon, Paul *Source(s):* CCE65 R361123
Note(s): Jt. pseud.: Jack Waller.
Shaw, Damon *Source(s):* CCE41 #29129 Efor65280; CCE68 R438781
Note(s): Jt. pseud.: Bert [i.e., Albert George] Lee & Jack Waller.
Tunnell, George 1903- [singer, songwriter]
Bon Bon *Source(s):* LCAR
Tunnell, Bon Bon *Source(s):* EPMU
Tunney, Stephen [songwriter, novelist]
Dogbowl *Source(s):* AMUS
Tunstede, Simon ?-1369 [theorist, writer on music]
Duntede, Simon *Source(s):* MACM
Friar of Bristol *Source(s):* LCAR; NGDM
Tupinambá, Marcelo 1892-1953 [composer]
King of Tanguinho *Source(s):* http://daniellathompson.com/Texts/Le_Boeuf/Doutor_Tanguinho.htm (15 Aug. 2005)
Turges, Edmund c.1440-1502 [composer]
Sturges, Edmund *Source(s):* MACM
Turmair, Johannes 1477-1534 [historian, music theorist]
Aventinus, Johannes *Source(s):* BAKR; LCAR; MACM; NGDM
Turnbull, Graham (Morrison) 1931- [composer, author, producer]
Dewar, Allison *Source(s):* ASCP
Turner, Scott *Source(s):* ASCP; CCE62; CCE68
Turnbull, Percy (Purvis) 1902-1976 [composer, pianist, editor, teacher]
Thrale, Peter *Source(s):* BLIC; GROL
Turner, Dallas (E.) 1927- [singer, songwriter]
America's Cowboy Evangelist *Source(s):* http://www.borderradioshow.com/SHOW.PDF (19 Nov. 2004)
Nevada Slim *Source(s):* EPMU; MCCL
Slim Dallas *Source(s):* CCE60
Yodel(l)in' Slim Dallas *Source(s):* EPMU; MCCL
Turner, Daniel 1710-1798 [minister, hymnist]
Candidus *Source(s):* CART
D. T. *Source(s):* JULN
Impartial Hand, An *Source(s):* CART
Senex, Theophilus *Source(s):* LCAR
Theophilus Senex, Esq. *Source(s):* CART; LCAR
Turner, John C. 1896-1949 [composer, author, pianist]
Turner, Happy *Source(s):* ASCP
Turner, Joseph Vernon 1911-1985 [singer, songwriter]
Big Vernon *Source(s):* HARS
Boss of the Blues *Source(s):* PSND; ROCK
King of the Shouters, The *Source(s):* PSND
Turner, Big Joe *Source(s):* HARS; LCAR; ROCK
World's Greatest Blues Shouter, The *Source(s):* PSND
Turner, Margaret Marian 1920-1986 [pianist, composer]
McPartland, (Mrs.) Margaret Marian *Source(s):* LCAR
Page, Marian *Source(s):* GOTH
Turner, Robert c.1587-1629 [composer, singer]
Tornar, Roberto *Source(s):* NGDM; SADC
Turpin, Thomas Milli(o)n 1873-1922 [pianist, composer]
Father of St. Louis Ragtime *Source(s):* CLAB; SHAB p. 45-6
Turrano, Joseph A. 1918-2004 [composer, author]
Turan, Jerry *Source(s):* ASCP; CCE65
Turton, Thomas 1780-1864 [clergyman, scholar, hymnist]
Cantabrigienis, Crito *Source(s):* CYBH
Crito Cantabrigienis *Source(s):* CYBH
Turton, W(illiam) H(arry) [or H(enry)] 1856-1938 [Lieut. in Royal Engineers, hymnist]
R. E. *Source(s):* CYBH; JULN
Note(s): R. E. = Royal Engineer
Tutev, Georgi (Ivanov) 1924-1999 [composer, conductor]
Ivanov, George *Source(s):* GROL; RIES
Twain, Eil(l)een 1965- [singer, songwriter]
Twain, Shania *Source(s):* ALMN; CM17
Twardy, Werner 1926-1977 [composer]
Cooper *Source(s):* CCE63 Efor90612
Monrou, Daddy *Source(s):* CCE67; PFSA; RIES
Twohy, William Humphrey [composer]
Humphrey, William *Source(s):* BLIC (publication date 1912)
Twomey, Kathleen [or Kay] Greeley 1914- [author, lyricist]
Clare, Madeline *Source(s):* CCE68
Greeley, Joe *Source(s):* CCE41 #16375 E93750; CCE68
Hill, Al *Source(s):* ASCP; CPOL RE-124-093
Madeline Clare *Source(s):* CCE41 #29076 E85850; CCE68
Twomey, M. G. *Source(s):* CPOL RE-48-638
Tyler, George Crouse 1867-1946 [producer, theatrical manager]

Seed, A. Carroway *Source(s):* OPER 17:2 (Spring 2001): 222
Tyler, Michael 1970- [songwriter, rapper]
Mystikal *Source(s):* AMIR; AMUS; LCAR; PMUS-00
Tyrwhitt-Wilson, (Sir) Gerald Hugh 1883-1950 [composer, writer, painter]
Berners, (Baron) Gerald Hugh Tyrwhitt-Wilson *Source(s):* BAKR; LCAR
Berners, Lord *Source(s):* BAKR; CART; HOVL; LCAR
Quebec, Adela *Source(s):* CART
Tysh, Fred Salo 1905-1981 [librettist]
Tisch, F. S. *Source(s):* PIPE
Tisch, Siegfried *Source(s):* PIPE
Tyszkiewicz, Jan 1927- [composer]
Tyski, Jan *Source(s):* KOMP; KOMS; PFSA

– U –

Ugar, Henry S. [actor, writer]
Sugarman, Jacob *Source(s):* GANA p. 807
Note(s): Possible jt. pseud.: Frederick Mantell & John Gerant.
Ulbrich, Siegfried 1922- [composer]
Martin, Marvin *Source(s):* PFSA, RIES
Romans, Roman *Source(s):* PFSA
Ulbrich, Friedrich *Source(s):* CCE53
Ulrich, Don(ald Eugene) 1941-1974 [singer, songwriter]
Rich, Don *Source(s):* CCE67; ENCM; MCCL
Ulrich, Jürgen 1939- [composer]
Drlač, Jan Zdeněk *Source(s):* KOMP; KOMS; PFSA
Unteed, Richard [or Dick] (Alan) 1916- [singer, songwriter, guitarist]
Singing Emcee, (The) *Source(s):* MCCL
Note(s): See also Farrell H(al) Draper.
Unterholtzer, Rupert c.1505- [composer]
Niederholtzer, Rupert *Source(s):* NGDM
Upton, George Putnam 1834-1919 [music critic, journalist]
Note(s): Portrait: ETUP 57:5 (May 1939): 321
Pickle, Peregrine *Source(s):* CART; GRAN; PSND; ROOM
Urai, Vilmos [or William] 1910-1986 [composer]
Flory, Sylvio *Source(s):* CCE57-58; CCE60-63; CPOL RE-58-885; GOTH
Livo, Marius *Source(s):* CCE45 #4342 Efor70181; CCE70 R47503
Urbach, Ernst 1872-1927 [composer]
Rubach, Ernst *Source(s):* REHG; SMIN; SUPN
Urban, Milo 1904-1982 [author]
Rovňan, Ján *Source(s):* PIPE
Urbani, Valentino fl. 1707-14 [tenor, composer]
Valentini *Source(s):* LOWN; PRAT; WORB
Urbanski, La Von Hawley 1912-1996 [composer, arranger, conductor]
Dexter, Von *Source(s):* CLTP ("This Is Your Life"); IMDB
Note(s): Incorrectly identified as pseud. of Alexander [or Sandor] Laszlo [i.e., San(dor) Totis]
Ure, James 1953- [singer, songwriter]
Ure, Midge *Source(s):* DIMA; HARR
Usifer, Joseph 1908-1997 [composer, conductor]
Lavalle, Paul *Source(s):* LCAR; REHG; SHMP
Note(s): See REHG for titles. Also used by Paula Wahl Pierce (CCE47).
Utzerath, Wolfgang 1954- [composer]
Andree, Wolf *Source(s):* KOMP; KOMS; PFSA
Uyeda, Leslie 1962- [flutist, pianist, singer, composer]
Brown, Charles *Source(s):* COHN; HIXN

– V –

Vacchelli, Giovanni Battista c.1625-after 1667 [composer, organist]
Accademico Naufragante *Source(s):* GROL
Vačkář, Dalibor C(yril) 1906-1984 (or 85) [composer, writer]
Faltis, Dalibor C. *Source(s):* BUL3; GDRM; GROL
Faltys, Pip *Source(s):* GDRM; GROL
Filip, Peter *Source(s):* GDRM; GROL
Martin, Tomáš *Source(s):* CCE59; GDRM; GROL
Raymond, Karel *Source(s):* GDRM; GROL
Vagramian, Aram 1921- [composer, conductor, pianist]
Vega, Al *Source(s):* ASCP; CCE44 #28321 Eunp380730
Val(l)adon, Eugénie-Emma [or Emma Eugénie] Rose 1837-1913 [composer, singer]
Note(s): In COHN given names: Giovanna Emma.
Thérésa *Source(s):* COHN; GREN; HIXN; LCAR; WORB
Valdés, Miguelito 1910-1978 [composer]
Babalú, Mr. *Source(s):* PEN2
Mr. Babalú *Source(s):* PEN2
Valdez, Carlos 1926- [percussionist, composer]
Valdez, Patato *Source(s):* AMUS; PEN2
Valente, Antonio (C.) fl. mid to late 16th cent. [organist, composer]
Cieco, Il *Source(s):* BAKR; WORB
Note(s): See also Giovanni Carisio.
Valenti, Dino 1943- [singer, guitarist; songwriter]
Powers, Chet [or Chester] *Source(s):* BLIC; YORK
Valentine, Robert 1674-c.1735 [flutist, composer]
Mr. Valentine at Rome *Source(s):* NGDM
Valentine at Rome, Mr. *Source(s):* NGDM
Valentini, Roberto *Source(s):* LCAR; NGDM

Valentini, Giuseppe 1681-1753 [composer, violinist]
Leupinto, Euginaspe *Source(s):* GROL
Straccioncino *Source(s):* GROL
Valenzuela, Richard (Stephen) 1940 (or 41)-1959 [singer, guitarist, songwriter]
Allens, Arvee *Source(s):* HWOM; PSND; YORK
Valens, Richard [or Ritchie] *Source(s):* EPMU; HWOM; LCAR; PSND; RECR; YORK
Valery, Joseph, Jr. 1934-1990 [singer, guitarist, composer]
Blue, Little Joe *Source(s):* AMUS; HERZ
Little Joe Blue *Source(s):* AMUS; LCAR
Valesi, Fulgentio c.1565-after 1614 [composer, printer]
Monache San Ambrosiana *Source(s):* GRV3
Valez, Lisa 1967- [singer, songwriter]
Lisa, Lisa *Source(s):* AMUS; CM23
Valianti, Joseph 1926-1985 [singer, songwriter, guitarist]
Val, Joe *Source(s):* AMUS; MCCL
Valicki, Aljaksandr 1826-1893 [singer, musicologist]
Zaljaznjak, A. *Source(s):* WORB
Valkan, Nick 1936- [composer, author, singer]
Noble, Nick *Source(s):* ASCP; CPOL PA-18-333
Valla, Domenico fl. 1600-1605 [composer]
Fattorin da Reggio *Source(s):* GROL; NGDM
Valladares, Isidro 1916- [singer, bandleader, composer, arranger]
Caraballo, Vincente *Source(s):* CCE66
King of the Merengue *Source(s):* PEN2
Ross, Vicki *Source(s):* CCE63
Valladares, Dioris *Source(s):* CCE63; PEN2
Vallance, James [or Jim] (Douglas) 1952-1999 [drummer, singer, songwriter]
Higgs, Rodney *Source(s):* CANE; CPOL PA-16-049
Vallee, Herbert Pryor 1901-1986 [singer, actor, composer]
Crooner, The *Source(s):* PSND
Prior, H. R. *Source(s):* CCE57
Vagabond Lover, The *Source(s):* CASS; PSND
Vallee, Rudy *Source(s):* ASCP; CASS; KINK; PEN2
Valoy, Ramón Orlando [singer, songwriter]
Ramón Orlando *Source(s):* HWOM
Valverde Sanjuàn, Joaquin 1875-1918 [composer]
Quinito *Source(s):* GOTH
Van Bergijk, Johannes c.1510 (to20)-1589 [teacher, publisher, music theorist]
Oridryus, Johannes *Source(s):* NGDM
Van Brockhoven, John (A.) 1854 (or 56)-1930? [conductor, composer]
Faber, Jean *Source(s):* CCE30 R7549; TPRF
Vandanberg, Harry 1947- [songwriter, guitarist]
Vanda, Harry *Source(s):* NOMG
Vanden Gheyn, Matthias 1721-1785 [carillonneur, organist, composer]
Bach of the Carillon *Source(s):* GROL
Vandernan, Thomas ?-1778 [musician, compiler]
Merriwagg, Dr. *Source(s):* BLIC; CPMS ("Splenetick Pills, or Mirth Alamode")
Van der Stucken, Frank Valentin 1858-1929 [arranger]
Valentin, Frank *Source(s):* SHMP
Van de Vate, Nancy (Jean) Hayes 1930- [composer]
Huntley, Helen *Source(s):* BUL3; CCE64; GREN; LCAR (see note); STRN
Huntley, William *Source(s):* CCE72; LCAR (see note); STRN
Van de Vinck, Hermann 1872-1939 [conductor, composer]
Finck, Herman *Source(s):* GAN2; LCAR
Van Dieren, Bernard 1887-1936 [composer]
Dean, Helen Bevan *Source(s):* LAST
Vandross, Luther 1952-2005 [singer, songwriter]
Pavarotti of Pop, The *Source(s):* PSNN
Towering Tenor, The *Source(s):* PSNN
Vangeon, Henri-Léon 1875-1944 [playwright]
Ghéon, Henri *Source(s):* MELL; PIPE
Van Leest, Antonius Maria *see* Leest, Antonius Maria van
Van Leeuwen, Simon Petrus *see* Leeuwen, Simon Petrus van
Van Steenkist, Vincent 1812-1896 [flutist, composer]
Dorus, Vincent Joseph *Source(s):* WORB
Steenkist, Vincent *Source(s):* MACM
Vanstreels, René 1925- [composer]
Mirelle, Jean *Source(s):* SUPN
Vantard, Henri (Eugene) 1887-1969 [director, author]
Varna, Henri *Source(s):* CCE48-55; CPOL RE-561-008; GAN2
Van Vechten, Carl 1880-1964 (or 66) [music critic]
Note(s): Portraits: ETUP 57:6 (May 1939); GRAN
Atlas *Source(s):* PSND
Dilettante ne plus ultras *Source(s):* GRAN p. 291
Huneker's Heirs *Source(s):* GRAN p. 284
Note(s): Jt. sobriquet: Paul Rosenfeld.
Van Vliet, Don 1941- [singer, songwriter, sculptor]
Beefheart, Captain *Source(s):* ALMN; EPMU; PSND; YORK
Captain Beefheart *Source(s):* CM10; HARR; NGAM
Spotlight Kid, The *Source(s):* PSND
Van Wedinghem, (E.) J. ?-1886(?) [composer]
Patrie, (J.) *Source(s):* MELL; STGR; WORB
Van Winkle, Harold E. 1939- [composer, author]
Van Winkle, Rip *Source(s):* ASCP; CCE65

Van Winkle, Robert [or Robbie] 1967 (or 68)- [singer, songwriter]
  Ice, Vanilla *Source(s):* PMUS
  Vanilla Ice *Source(s):* AMUS; EPMU; PMUS
Van Zandt, Steve(n) 1950- [composer, singer, producer]
  Little Steve(n) *Source(s):* AMUS; NOMG; PSND; http://www.littlesteven.com (port.) (6 Oct. 2002)
  Sugar Miami Steve *Source(s)* PEN2; PSNN
  Note(s): Called himself.
  Van Zandt, Miami *Source(s):* PEN2
Van Zandt, (John) Townes 1944-1997 [singer, songwriter]
  Father of Texas Folk *Source(s):* MCCL
  T. V. Z. *Source(s):* CCE67
Vanzo, Vittorio Maria 1862-1945 [conductor, pianist, composer]
  Canard *Source(s):* GROL
Vapnick, Isaac 1919 (or 20)-1986 [singer, music publisher]
  James, Dick *Source(s):* EPMU; PSND; ROOM
  Sheridan, Lee *Source(s):* EPMU; ROOM
  Vapnick, Richard Leon *Source(s):* PSND
Vaqueras, Beltrame [or Betrando] 1450-after 1507 [composer]
  Note(s): See LCAR for variant forms of name.
  Bernardus [or Betrando] de Brassia *Source(s):* LCAR; RIES; WORB
Varela, Ismael Héctor 1934- [poet, lyricist]
  Negro, Héctor *Source(s):* TODO
Varela, Salustiano Paco 1914-1987 [bandoneonist, arranger, composer]
  Varela, Héctor *Source(s):* TODO
Varèse, Edgard (Victor Achille Charles) 1883-1965 [composer]
  Father of Electronic Music *Source(s):* Snyder, Jeff. *Edgard Varese: Father of Electronic Music.*
Varotari, Dario 1539-1596 [librettist]
  Ardia [or Ardio] Rivarota *Source(s):* SONN
  Delfico *Source(s):* ALMC
  Rivarota, Ardio [or Ardia] *Source(s):* ALMC; SONN
  Vecchio, Il *Source(s):* WORB
  Note(s): See also James Cervetto (1682-1783) & G. Sirazi.
  Volonteroso, (Il) *Source(s):* ALMC
Vasori, Claude 1930- [composer, conductor]
  Caravelli *Source(s):* CCE67-68; CCE73 Efor 164140; CCE74-75; MUSR
  Ermino, Cucio *Source(s):* MUSR
Vaughan, Henry 1621-1695 [hymnist]
  Silurist, The *Source(s):* JULN; LCAR (see note)
Vaughan, Yvonne 1949?- [singer, songwriter]
  Note(s): Various birth dates given: 1940, 1945, 1949.
  Fargo, Donna *Source(s):* ALMN; AMUS; CCME; ENCM; EPMU; HARR; MCCL
  Silver, Yvonne Vaughan *Source(s):* CCE68
Vaughan Williams, Ralph 1872-1958 [composer]
  Bruckner of British Music, The *Source(s):* http://classicalcereview.com/rvw2.htm (13 Apr. 2005)
  M. W. V. R. S. *Source(s):* DIEH ("Cobbold")
  Note(s): Jt. pseud.: Martin Shaw.
Vaughan Williams, Ursula (Lock) 1911- [librettist]
  Wood, Ursula *Source(s):* PSND
Vaughn, Richard (S(mith)) 1919-1991 [composer, arranger, author]
  Smith, Marion *Source(s):* CCE64
  Note(s): Possible pseud.?
  Vaughn, Billy *Source(s):* CCE60; EPMU; LCAR
Veal, George 1740-1787 [writer on music; composer]
  Bicknal, John (Lawrence) *Source(s):* IBIM; WORB
  Bicknell, John Laurence *Source(s):* BROW; STGR
  Collier, Joel *Source(s):* BROW; IBIM; WORB
  Redivivus, Joel Collier *Source(s):* PSND
Vearncombe, Colin 1951- [singer, songwriter]
  Black *Source(s):* BLIC; WARN
Vega, José [singer, songwriter, author, clown]
  Remi *Source(s):* HWOM; LCAR
Veiga, Francisco 1578-1644 [composer]
  Santiago, Francisco de *Source(s):* LCAR; NGDM
Veliotes, John A(lexander) 1921- [composer, bandleader, drummer, vibraphonist]
  Godfather of R & B, The *Source(s):* http://home.bluemarble.net/~jjperry/features/otis.html (21 Oct. 2002)
  Otis, Johnny *Source(s):* CCE57-59; LCAR; PFSA
Velke, John Arthur, (II) 1930- [composer]
  Velke, Fritz *Source(s):* CCE60; CCE65-67; REHG
Veloso, Caetano (Emmanuel Viana Telles) 1942- [songwriter]
  King of Tropicalia, The *Source(s):* BRAZ
Veneziani, Carlo 1882 (or 83)-1950 [dramatist, librettist]
  Blas, Gil *Source(s):* STGR
  Gil Blas *Source(s):* STGR; WORB
  Livognol *Source(s):* WORB
Ventura, Josep [or José] (María de la Purificación) 1817-1875 [composer]
  L'avi Pep *Source(s):* GROL; NGDM
  Pep Ventura *Source(s):* GROL; NGDM
  Ventura, Pep *Source(s):* GROL; LCAR; NGDM
Veracini, Francesco Maria 1685-1750 [violinist, composer]
  Note(s): Portraits: ETUP 57:7 (July 1939): 478; EWCY
  Fiorentino, Il *Source(s):* GRV2; MACM
  Note(s): See also Giuseppe Moneta.
  Florentine, The *Source(s):* MACM

Verbeeck, Frans 1926- [composer]
Beck, R(andy) *Source(s):* CCE63; REHG; SMIN; SUPN
Fraver *Source(s):* CCE71; SMIN; SUPN
Verdi, Giuseppe 1813-1901 [composer]
Euripides of Italian Opera, The *Source(s):* PSND
Peasant from Roncole, A *Source(s):* http://www.cosmopolis.ch/english/cosmo13/verdi.htm (6 Oct. 2002)
Note(s): Called himself.
Purest Glory of Italian Genius *Source(s):* EWCY
Symbol of Italy *Source(s):* http://news.bbc.co.uk/1/hi/entertainment/1138168.stm (6 Oct. 2002)
Vergiati, Amleto (Enrique) 1910-1974 [poet]
Alvarado, Enrique *Source(s):* TODO
Centeya, Julián *Source(s):* CCE68; TODO
Grey Man of Buenos Aires, The *Source(s):* TODO
Verio, Juan fl. c.1568-78 [composer]
Juan Verio de nacion flamengo *Source(s):* GROL
Verius, (Joanne) *Source(s):* GROL; NGDM
Note(s): Do not confuse with Jean Cornuel, nicknamed Verjus(t).
Vermont, Pierre ?-1532 [composer, singer]
Vermont primus *Source(s):* NGDM
Vernizzi, Ottavio 1569-1649 [composer, organist]
Indefesso *Source(s):* GROL; LCAR; NGDM; WORB
Invernici, Ottavio *Source(s):* LCAR; WORB
Invernizzi, Ottavio *Source(s):* LCAR; WORB
Vernici, Ottavio *Source(s):* LCAR; WORB
Vernoff, Robert Arnold 1944- [composer, author, singer]
Verne, Robert [or Bob] *Source(s):* ASCP; CCE61
Verocai, Giovanni c.1700-1745 [violinist, composer]
Venizien *Source(s):* LCAR; NGDM
Veronensis, Peregrinus Cesena fl. 1494-1508 [composer]
Cesena, Peregrinus *Source(s):* NGDM
Verschueren, Marceau 1902- [composer]
Marceau, V. *Source(s):* CCE50; CCE60; GREN
Vesala, Martti Juhani 1945-1999 [drummer, composer]
Vesala, Edward *Source(s):* AMUS; EPMU; PEN2
Vesely, (Raimund) Friedrich 1900-1954 [composer, lyricist]
Raymond, Fred(dy) *Source(s):* BUL3; GAMM; GAN1; GAN2; KOMS; NGDM; PIPE
Vesque von Püttlingen, Johann Evangelist 1803-1883 [composer]
Hoven, J(ohann) [or G.] *Source(s):* BAKR; CPMU; GROL; LCAR; NGDM; NGDO; PSND
Vézina, (François) Joseph 1849-1924 [teacher, composer, instrumentalist]
Father of the Military Band in Canada *Source(s):* SMIN
Viacava, Joseph Dominique [composer]
Kaeuffer, Ollivier *Source(s):* GOTH
Vian, Boris 1920-1959 [cornetist, songwriter, jazz critic]
Sullivan, Vernon *Source(s):* CCE51; GROL
Vianna (Filho), A(lfredo da Rocha) 1897 (or 98)-1973 [composer, arranger, bandleader]
Master of Choro, The *Source(s):* BRAZ
Pixinguinha *Source(s):* CCE42 #10134 E162615; IDBC; NGDM
Viassolo, Giovan Battista 1749-1802 [dramatist]
Federici, Camillo *Source(s):* PIPE
Viau, Albert 1910-2001 [singer, teacher, composer]
Caron, Bill *Source(s):* CCE51; http://www.collectionscanada.ca/gramophne/m2-1083-e.html (18 June 2005)
Dupont, Jacques *Source(s):* CANE; http://www.collectionscanada.ca/gramophne/m2-1083-e.html
Marcil, Paul *Source(s):* http://www.collectionscanada.ca/gramophne/m2-1083-e.html
Viaud, (Louis Marie) Julien 1850-1923 [novelist, naval officer]
Loti, Pierre *Source(s):* LCAR; PIPE; ROOM
Vicars, Harold ?-1922 [composer, conductor, arranger]
Massart, Michael *Source(s):* CCE45 #63817, 1954 R146326
Moya *Source(s):* FULD; GREN; KILG; LCAR; SPTH p. 626
Shaw, Vincent *Source(s):* CCE44 #35637, 369 R131433
Vickers, James Edward 1942- [composer, author, singer]
Edward, Jimmy *Source(s):* ASCP (see reference)
Vickers, Mike [composer]
Scott, J. *Source(s):* CLTP ("This Week in Baseball")
Scott, Patrick J. O'Hara *Source(s):* CLTP ("This Week in Baseball")
Victory, (Thomas Joseph) Gerard 1921-1995 [composer]
Note(s): Portrait: www.cmc.ie/composers/victory.html (21 Oct. 2002)
Loraine, Alan *Source(s):* BUL3; RIES
Vidacovich, Irving J(ohn, Sr.) 1904-1966 [composer, author, conductor]
Cajun Pete *Source(s):* PSND
Vidacovich, Pinky *Source(s):* ASCP; CCE57; CCE61; CPOL RE-172-469
Vidale, Piero 1902-1976 [composer]
Cantico, Jose *Source(s):* REHH
Dani, S(ergio) *Source(s):* CCE56; REHH
Dany, Sergio *Source(s):* REHH
Viera Caballero, Linda 1971- [singer, songwriter]
India *Source(s):* HWOM

Vieu, Jane [or Jeanne] (Elisabeth Marie) 1871-1955 [composer]
Pierre *Source(s):* GDRM
Valette, Pierre *Source(s):* DWCO; GROL; LCAR
Vigneron-Ramakers, Christiane-Josée 1914- [organist, pianist, conductor, composer]
Delande, Jo *Source(s):* BUL3; COHN (port.); HEIN; HIXN
Villa, Ignacio 1911-1971 [singer, songwriter, pianist]
De Nieve, Bola *Source(s):* CCE59
Bola de Nieve *Source(s):* HWOM; LCAR
Nieve, Bola de *Source(s):* CC41 #30352 Efor65429; CCE59
Villa-Lobo, Heitor 1887-1959 [composer]
Villalba Filho, Epaminondas *Source(s):* CCE56; GROL; NGDO (see under: "Izaht"); Appleby, David P. *Heitor Villa-Lobos; A Bio-Bibliography.* New York: Greenwood Press, 1988.
Zé Povo *Source(s):* Appleby (see above)
Villano [or Villani], Antonio fl. 1744-67 [librettist, poet]
Lantino, Liviano *Source(s):* MELL; SONN; STGR
Liviano, Lantino *Source(s):* GROL; NGDO
Villard, J(ean) 1895 (or 96)-1982 [songwriter]
Gilles, (Jean) *Source(s):* CCE52; CCE60; CCE65; CPOL RE-15-224; PSND
Villoldo (Arroyo), Angel (Gregorio) 1861-1919 [composer, poet]
Note(s): Portraits: BBDP; TODO
Arroyo, Angel *Source(s):* BBDP; TODO
Father of the Tango *Source(s):* BBDP; TODO
Giménez, Gregorio *Source(s):* TODO
Giminz, Gregorio *Source(s):* BBDP
Gregorio, A. *Source(s):* BBDP; TODO
Pimiento, Fray *Source(s):* BBDP; TODO
Reguero, Mario *Source(s):* BBDP; TODO
Vincent, George Frederick 1855- [composer]
G. F. V. *Source(s):* CPMU
Vincent, Nathaniel (Hawthorne) 1889 (or 90)-1979 [composer, author, singer]
Kellette, John W. *Source(s):* KILG
Note(s): Jt. pseud.: James Brockman.
Kenbrovin, Jaan *Source(s):* ASCP; CCE47; CCE50-51; LCAR; SPTH p. 413; STUW
Note(s): Jt. pseud.: James Brockman & James Kendis.
Tennant, Vic *Source(s):* CCE77; CCE78 R671915
Vinard, F. N. *Source(s):* ASCP
Whelan, Ekko *Source(s):* CCE70 R481422; CPOL RE-21-657
Wilkins, Charles [or Charlie] *Source(s):* CCE73-76; CPOL RE-254-441
Vinette, Alice 1894- [composer]
Marie-Jocelyne, (Sister) *Source(s):* BUL3
Vinson, Eddie 1917-1988 [saxophonist, songwriter]
Cleanhead, Mr. *Source(s):* PSND
Mr. Cleanhead *Source(s):* PSND
Vinson, Cleanhead *Source(s):* AMUS; HARS
Vinson, Walter Jacobs 1901-1975 [guitarist, violinist, songwriter]
Jacobs, Walter *Source(s):* HARS
Vincent, Walter *Source(s):* AMUS; HARS
Vincson, Walter *Source(s):* AMUS; HARS
Vintzius, Georg fl. 1629 [composer]
G. V. O. *Source(s):* IBIM; WORB
Viola, Francesco ?-1568 [composer]
Checco, Checchin *Source(s):* LCAR
Francesco, dalla Viola *Source(s):* LCAR
Viotti, Giovanni Battista 1753-1824 [violinist, composer]
Father of Modern Violin Playing *Source(s):* PRAT
Virchi, Giovan(ni) Paolo 1552-1610 [organist, composer]
Targetti, Giovanni Paolo *Source(s):* RIES
Targhetta, (Giovanni Paolo) *Source(s):* GROL; LCAR; RIES; WORB
Vischer, Friedrich Theodor von 1807-1887 [author, philosopher]
Allegoriowitsch, Deutobald Symbolizetti *Source(s):* PIPE
Mystifizinsky *Source(s):* PIPE; WORB
Schartenmayer, Philipp Ulrich *Source(s):* PIPE; WORB
Vïschnegradsky, Ivan Alexandrovich 1893-1979 [composer]
Volney, Ivan *Source(s):* GREN
Visconti, Gasparo 1683-c.1731 [violinist, composer]
Gasparino *Source(s):* LCAR
Gasperini *Source(s):* LCAR
Vitalis, George 1895-1959 [composer, conductor]
Valente, Giorgio *Source(s):* BAKR; BAKT; BUL3
Vitols, Jazeps [or Jasep(s)] 1863-1948 [composer, teacher]
Wihtol, Joseph [or Jasep(s)] *Source(s):* BAKR; GROL; LCAR; WORB
Vitry, Philippe de 1291-1361 [composer]
Vit(t)riaco, (Philippus de) *Source(s):* BAKR; LCAR; WORB
Vittori, Loret(t)o c.1600-1670 [singer, composer, poet, librettist]
Rovitti, Olerto *Source(s):* BAKR; GROL; LCAR; MELL; NGDM; PIPE; STGR
Vivaldi, Antonio (Lucio) 1678-1741 [composer]
Idlaviv *Source(s):* NGDM
Prete Rosso, Il *Source(s):* NGDM
Red Priest, The *Source(s):* ALMN; NGDM
Vandini, Lotavio *Source(s):* ALMC; http://www.polybiblio.cm/quaritch/F667.html (21 Jan. 2005)

Note(s): See also Giacomo Maccari. Although an anagram of Antonio Vivaldi, probably not a pseudonym. (ALMC; GROL)
Vivaldian *Source(s):* GROL
Vivian, Isabella Jane (Houlton) 19th cent. [poet, composer]
I. V. *Source(s):* PSNN
Viziru, Mihail 1944- [composer]
Wolf, Mike A. *Source(s):* SUPN
Vlak, Kees 1938- [composer, conductor]
Allmand, Robert *Source(s):* http://www.mreh.ch/repetoire/komponisten_portraits.main.html (30 Oct. 2002)
Allment, Robert *Source(s):* REHG; SUPN; http://www.beueler-rheinmusikanten.de/komp.html (21 Oct. 2002)
Bösendorfer, Alfred *Source(s):* http://www.beueler-rheinmusikanten.de/komp.html
Ghisallo, Luigi di *Source(s):* http://www.beueler-rheinmusikanten.de/komp.html
Llano, (A). *Source(s):* REHG; SUPN
Ravenal, Dick *Source(s):* SUPN; http://www.beueler-rheinmusikanten.de/komp.html
Vlessing, Philip 1905-1943 [composer]
Bottle, Jack *Source(s):* NEDM
Vockerodt, Gottfried 1665-1727 [music theorist]
Herzog, Christian *Source(s):* WORB
Vogelhofer, Andreas c. 1490-c.1535 [theorist]
Ornithoparchus, Andreas *Source(s):* LCAR; NGDM
Vögely, Fritz 1876- [composer, teacher, conductor]
Rögely, Fritz *Source(s):* MACM
Vogl, Ralph Erwin 1896-1943 [composer]
Erwin, Ralph *Source(s):* BBDP; CCE55; PFSA
Wright, Harry *Source(s):* BBDP; http://world.std.com/~kcl/ralph_erwin_vogl_top.html (9 May 2005)
Vogler, George Joseph 1749-1814 [organist, composer; author]
Note(s): Portrait: ETUP 57:8 (Aug. 1939): 542
Vogler, Abt [or Abbe] *Source(s):* PSND
Vogt, A(ugustus) S(tephen) 1861-1926 [conductor, educator, organist, music critic]
Moderato *Source(s):* CANE
Voigt, James Wesley 1940- [singer, songwriter, producer]
Taylor, Chip *Source(s):* AMUS; EPMU; HARD; HARR; LCAR; PSND
Voiten, Judy (Lynn) 1936- [singer, songwriter]
Judy Lynn *Source(s):* CCE55 Eunp
Lynn, Judy *Source(s):* MCCL
Vojtech c. 956-997 [musician, composer]
Adalbert of Prague *Source(s):* NGDM; WORB
Volkart, Bettye Sue 1945- [composer, singer, teacher]
Pierce, Bettye *Source(s):* ASCP
Zoller, Bettye *Source(s):* ASCP
Volkmann, Karl Heinz 1919- [composer]
Bergson, Lars *Source(s):* BUL3; KOMS; PFSA
Vollstedt, Robert 1854-1919 [composer]
Roberti, Robert *Source(s):* GREN; SUPN
Roberts, Robert *Source(s):* SMIN
Volpane, Keith [songwriter]
Seven *Source(s):* *Evansville Courier & Press.* (24 Aug. 2000): C6
Volpato, Jack Albert 1897- [composer, author, publisher]
Val, Jack *Source(s):* ASCP
Volpe, Giovanni Battista [or Giambattista] c.1620-1691 [organist, composer]
Rovetta, G. B. *Source(s):* NGDM
Rovettino *Source(s):* MELL; NGDM; RIEM; SADC; SONN; WORB
Ruettino *Source(s):* NGDM
Vom Berg, Johann ?-1563 [music publisher]
Berg, Johann *Source(s):* LCAR
Montanus, Johann *Source(s):* LCAR; NGDM
Von an der Lan-Hochbrunn, Paul Eugen Josef *see* Lan-Hochbrunn, Paul Eugen Josef von an der
Vonderlieth, Leonore 1894 (or 96)-1943 [songwriter, singer]
Note(s): Original surname: Vonderlieth (http://archives.lincolndailynews.com/2000/May/13/ (Select "Organizations & Events" (9 Feb. 2005)). In most of the sources cited below the names are listed as pseudonyms of Vaughan De Leath. Portraits on covers: "Two Rocking Chairs," (DeLeath, 1937) & "Beside an Open Fireplace," by Paul Denniker (Santley Brothers, 1929).
Betty *Source(s):* LCPC E78007
Brown, Betty *Source(s):* AMUS; MARE; SUTT
Note(s): Possible pseud.
Brown, Lindy *Source(s):* SUTT
Note(s): Possible pseud.
Clarke, Glory *Source(s):* AMUS; MARE; SUTT
Cobb, Lotta *Source(s):* CCE38 E73373; CCE65-66
De Leath, Vaughn *Source(s):* CCE28 E699592; CCE57; CPMU; GRAC
Note(s): Surname also given as DeLeath, deLeath & de Leath.
DeLys, V. *Source(s):* CCE26 E642125
DeMarco, Angelina [or Angelino] *Source(s):* MARE; SUTT
Dwyer, Gertrude *Source(s):* AMUS; MARE; SUTT
First Lady of Radio, The *Source(s):* http://www.tracertek.com/vaughn.htm (6 Oct. 2002)
Foster, Nancy *Source(s):* AMUS; SUTT
Gear, Gloria *Source(s):* SUTT
Geer, Georgia *Source(s):* MARE; SUTT
Geer, Gloria *Source(s):* AMUS; GRAC; MARE; SUTT

Geer, Leonore *Source(s):* GRAC
Note(s): Married name (1st marriage); Mrs. Livingston Geer.
Green, Mazie *Source(s):* GRAC
Green, Sadie *Source(s):* AMUS; MARE; PSND; SUTT
Note(s): On Parlophone R-3386. Also used by Beth Challis (Parlophone R-3421 (SUTT)).
Grimes, Betty *Source(s):* MARE; SUTT
Kennedy, Jane *Source(s):* GRAC
King, Daisy *Source(s):* MARE; SUTT
Leath, Vaughn de *Source(s):* CCE18 E429503; CCE58; CPMU
Lee, Annabelle *Source(s):* CCE26 E633204; CCE28 Eunp68543
Lee, Mamie *Source(s):* AMUS; GRAC; MARE; SUTT
Lee, Mandy *Source(s):* CCE27 E678665
Lee, Virginia *Source(s):* MARE
Leith, Leonore (von der) *Source(s):* CCE27 E655383; CPMU
Mandy Lee *Source(s):* CCE27 E678665
Marco, Angelina *Source(s):* AMUS; GRAC; SUTT
Original Radio Girl, The *Source(s):* GRAC; PSND
Radio Girl *Source(s):* GRAC; MARE; SUTT
Radio's First Song Sensation *Source(s):* http://dismuke.org/Electric/March98.html (6 Oct. 2002)
Richard, Daisy *Source(s):* MARE; SUTT
Richards, Daisy *Source(s):* MARE; SUTT
Richards, Helen *Source(s):* SUTT
Note(s): Possible pseud.
Rose, Leonore *Source(s):* LCPC letter cited (9 Apr. 1937)
Note(s): "Leonore Geer has recently married & is now Leonore Rose."
Ross, Marian [or Marion] *Source(s):* AMUS; SUTT
Smith, Julia *Source(s):* SUTT
Note(s): Possible pseud.
Thompson, Madge *Source(s):* GRAC; MARE; SUTT
Vonderleath, Leonore *Source(s):* SUTT
Note(s): Listed as original spelling of surname.
Woods, Gladys *Source(s):* MARE; SUTT
Note(s): Possible pseud.

Vonficht, Bernd 1950- [composer]
Paul, Bernie *Source(s):* KOMS; PFSA

Voorlas, Lynn Connie [singer, songwriter, guitarist]
Brody, Lane *Source(s):* MCCL
Nilles, Lynne *Source(s):* MCCL

Vorobkevych, Sydir [or Sidor] (Ivanovych) 1836-1903 [composer, poet, conductor]
Mlaka, Danilo *Source(s):* LCAR

Voss, Jane 1948- [singer, songwriter]
American Piaf, An *Source(s):* MUHF

Voynich, Ethel (Lillian) (née Boole) 1864-1960 [novelist, translator, composer]
E. L. V. *Source(s):* MUWB

Vrabely, Stephanie 1849-1919 [pianist, composer, writer]
Brand-Vrabely, Stephanie *Source(s):* DWCO; LCAR; WORB
Wurmbach-Stuppach, Ernest *Source(s):* COHN; HIXN

Vuille, Georges 1875-1921 [composer, violinist]
Wille, Georg *Source(s):* WORB

Vyhnalek, Ivo 1930- [composer]
Folten, Beda *Source(s):* KOMP; PFSA
Obit, Jon E. *Source(s):* KOMP; PFSA
Pinkura, Nero *Source(s):* KOMP; PFSA

– W –

Wachsmann, Franz 1906-1967 [composer, arranger, conductor]
Ceruomo, Francesco *Source(s):* AMSL (13 Jan. 2004)
Note(s): J. Rigbie Turner reported name used on an Alfred Hitchcock film, possibly "Rebecca."
Vaksman, F. *Source(s):* LCAR
Waxman, Franz *Source(s):* BAKR; BUL3; EPMU; KINK; NGDM; ROOM

Wachtel, Robert 1947- [guitarist, producer, songwriter]
Wachtel, Waddy *Source(s):* CM26

Wade, Joseph Augustine 1796?-1845 [composer]
W *Source(s):* CART

Wadsworth, Derek 1939- [composer, arranger, conductor]
Caine, Daniel *Source(s):* http://www.tvcentury21.com/content/view/188/0 (13 June 2005)

Waganfeald, Edward James, III 1934- [composer, author]
Fields, Eddie *Source(s):* ASCP

Wagener, Hans Günter 1951- [composer]
Keybord, Richard *Source(s):* KOMP; KOMS; PFSA

Wagenleiter, Klaus 1956- [composer]
Teil, Thilo *Source(s):* KOMS; PFSA
Villani, Claudio *Source(s):* KOMS; PFSA

Wagner, (Gottlob Heinrich) Adolf 1744-1835 [translator, author]
Nym, Ralph *Source(s):* PIPE; WORB

Wagner, Artur 1891-1955 [author]
Curriander *Source(s):* PIPE
Curry *Source(s):* PIPE

Wagner, Cosima 1837-1930 [patron of the arts]
Note(s): Wife of Richard Wagner. Portrait: ETUP 57:8 (Aug. 1939): 542.
Delphic Oracle, The *Source(s):* PSND

Wagner, Josef 1922- [composer]
Rengan *Source(s):* KOMP; KOMS; PFSA
Wagner, Josef Franz 1856-1908 [composer]
Austrian March King *Source(s):* REHG
Jacoby *Source(s):* REHG
Note(s): Incorrect attribution on "Under the Double Eagle" (Smith College, 1994).
March King of Austria *Source(s):* SMIN
Wagner, Peter 1941 (or 42)- [composer]
Heinen, Peter-Rudolph *Source(s):* KOMS; PFSA
Wagner, Richard 1813-1883 [composer]
Antichrist Incarnate of Art, The *Source(s):* SLON
Beelzebub's Court Composer *Source(s):* SLON
Cagliostro of Modernity *Source(s):* SLON
Corrupter of Music *Source(s):* SLON
Cossack, The *Source(s):* MUWB
Doctor of Cacophony *Source(s):* SLON
Doktor der Kakophonie *Source(s):* SLON
Freigedank, K(arl) *Source(s):* GROL; NOTE 53:1 (1996): 41; SEND
General Director of Hell's Music *Source(s):* SLON
Geyer, Richard *Source(s):* PRAT (see under: Geyer, Ludwig Heinrich Christian (1770-1832))
Note(s): As a student he used his stepfather's surname.
Lindhorst, Richard *Source(s):* RILM 85-02890-ap
Marat of Music, The *Source(s):* SLON
Michel Angelo of Opera, The *Source(s):* PSND
Puccini of Opera, The *Source(s):* SPIE p. 29
Richard I *Source(s):* SPIE p. 244
Richard III *Souce(s):* NGDO
Richard the First *Source(s):* SPIE p. 244
Richard the Third *Source(s):* NGDO
Shakespeare of Harmony, The *Source(s):* PSND
Titan of Music, The *Source(s):* PSND
Wagneresque *Source(s):* EPON
Wagnerian *Source(s):* EPON
Wagner, Russell William 1905-1992 [composer]
Russell, William [or Bill] *Source(s):* BAKR; BAKT; LCAR; NGDJ
Wagness, Bernard 1894- [composer]
Note(s): Portrait: ETUP 58:5 (May 1940): 290
Bradford, Kenneth *Source(s):* CCE37 E63021; TPRF
Cassandra, Anne *Source(s):* CCE40 #25622 Eunp229121
Chandler, Otis *Source(s):* CCE37 E62558; TPRF
Fleming, Margaret *Source(s):* TPRF
Franklin, George C. *Source(s):* TPRF
Hastings, Martha *Source(s):* CCE41 #17002 E93906; TPRF
Hotaling, Ralph *Source(s):* CCE36 Index; TPRF
Hotchkiss, Mary W. *Source(s):* CCE37 E62559; TPRF
Langlow, Richard *Source(s):* CCE41 #197 E91215; TPRF
Mednikoff, Alexandre *Source(s):* CCE37 E63020; TPRF
Nason, David *Source(s):* CCE37 E63019; TPRF
Northrup, Willis *Source(s):* TPRF
Novarro Alberto *Source(s):* CCE40 #86449 E86449; CCE68; TPRF
Parnell, Mary *Source(s):* TPRF
Pelham, Emory *Source(s):* TPRF
Podeska, Irina *Source(s):* CCE39 #24755 E77876; TPRF
Raymaker, Hortense *Source(s):* CCE36 E56189; TPRF
Raymond, Helen *Source(s):* CCE36 E55533; TPRF
Spencer, Marian *Source(s):* CCE36 E56190 ("Happy Is the Miller Boy")
Note(s): Incorrect given name on cover; correct name ("Marvin") on page 1.
Spencer, Marvin *Source(s):* CCE36 E56190; TPRF
Note(s): See preceding entry.
Stanyar, Joseph *Source(s):* CCE35; TPRF
Stockbridge, John *Source(s):* TPRF
Tanner, Margaret P(age) *Source(s):* CCE37 E62560; TPRF
Thorne, Rosamond *Source(s):* CCE36 E55532; TPRF
Tuckerman, Patricia *Source(s):* CCE37 E63023; TPRF
Wentworth, Lois *Source(s):* CCE36 E56188; TPRF
Wagoner, Porter (Wayne) 1930- [singer, guitarist, songwriter]
Thin Man From West Plains, The *Source(s):* AMUS; FLIN
Wahr, Elizabeth 1916- [composer]
Fennell, Elizabeth (Ludwig) *Source(s):* REHH
Note(s): Married name; previous married name: Mrs. Carl F. Ludwig.
Hanson, Eric *Source(s):* CCE51; CCE55-56; REHH
Note(s): Also used by Albert Oliver Davis & Carl (F.) Ludwig; see NOTES: Hanson, Eric.
Waignein, Andre 1942- [composer]
Ares, Rob *Source(s):* REHH; SUPN
Defoort, Rita *Source(s):* REHH; SUPN
Foster, Larry *Source(s):* REHH
Gines, Ferda [or Ferde, or Frede] *Source(s):* REHH; SUPN
Gistel, Luc *Source(s):* REHH
Kernen, Roland *Source(s):* REHH
Sebregts, Ron *Source(s):* REHH
Wainwright, Loudon, III 1946- [singer, songwriter, actor]
Charlie Chaplin of Rock, The *Source(s):* CM11
New Bob Dylan, The *Source(s):* CM11
Note(s): See also Bob Lind.
Woody Allen of Folk, The *Source(s):* CM11
Wainwright, William (Mark) 1959- [writer, composer]

Orbit, William *Source(s):* EPMU; LCAR; PMUS-00; ROOM
Strange Cargo *Source(s):* LCAR
Wajditsch Verbonac von Dönhoff, Gabriel 1888-1969 [composer]
Dönhoff, Gabriel Wajditsch Verbonac von *Source(s):* BAKO; BAKR; LCAR
Senez, Camille de *Source(s):* DEAM; STGR
Wayditch, Gabriel *Source(s):* BUL3; LCAR
Wakabe, Nakasuga Kengyo 1894-1956 [musician, composer]
Miyagi, Michio *Source(s):* BAKO; GROL; NGDM
Nakasuga (Kengyo) *Source(s):* GROL
Suga, (Michio) *Source(s):* GROL; NGDM
Wakabe, Michio *Source(s):* GROL
Wakeley, James [or Jimmy] Clarence 1914-1982 [songwriter, singer]
Melody Kid, The *Source(s):* NASF
Singing Cowboy, The *Source(s):* NASF
Note(s): See also (Orvon) Gene Autry & Edgar D(ean) Glosup.
Walbert, James D. 1918- [pianist, composer]
Wizard of the Keyboard *Source(s):* SGMA (port.)
Walden, Alfred [or Arthur] J. 1867-1947 [songwriter]
Wincott, Harry *Source(s):* FULD p. 345; KILG; SPTH p. 409
Waldenmaier, A(ugust) P(eter) 1915- [composer]
Walden, Peter *Source(s):* KOMP; KOMS; PFSA
Waldman, Robert H. 1936- [composer, arranger]
Forrester, Hugh *Source(s):* ASCP
Waldmüller, Ludwig 1879- [composer]
Müller, Ludwig *Source(s):* BUL1; BUL2
Waldo, Ralph Emerson, III ?-1944 [composer, author]
Waldo, Terry *Source(s):* ASCP; JASZ p. 283; RAGT p. 203+
Waldron, Earl Malcolm 1926-2002 [pianist, composer]
Waldron, Mal *Source(s):* AMUS; PEN2
Walker, Aaron Thibeaux 1910-1975 [singer, songwriter, guitarist]
Daddy of the Blues, The *Source(s):* ALMN; CLAB; HARS
Oak Cliff T- Bone *Source(s):* CLAB; HARS
Walker, T-Bone *Source(s):* ALMN; AMUS; CLAB; CM05; EPMU; HARR; HARS; PEN2
Walker, Cindy 1925- [songwriter, singer, guitarist]
Greatest Living Songwriter of Country Music, The *Source(s):* MCCL
Walker, Earnest Earl 1915-1990 [singer, songwriter, guitarist]
Detour Man, The *Source(s):* MCCL
Walker, Jimmy *Source(s):* MCCL
Note(s): Also used by James Fortini.
Walker, G. Denholm [composer]
Reklaw, E. M. *Source(s):* CPMU (publication date 1910)
Walker, George 1873?- [dancer, actor, songwriter]
Two Real Coons, The *Source(s):* JASZ
Note(s): With Bert [i.e., Egbert] Austin Williams; billed themselves.
Walker, H. A. [composer]
Reklaw, H. A. *Source(s):* CPMU (publication date 1879)
Walker, Jeanine Ogletree 1942- [composer, author, singer]
Vick, Danny *Source(s):* ASCP; CPOL PA-227-233
Walker, Jeffrey [songwriter]
Walker, J-Dub *Source(s):* SONG; http://www.ascap.com/membership/rhythm99-2.html (7 Oct. 2002)
Walker, John(ny) (Mayon) 1929- [singer, keyboardist, songwriter]
Big Moose *Source(s):* HARS; LCAR
Bushy Head *Source(s):* LCAR
Moose John *Source(s):* HARS; LCAR
Walker, Lawrence 1907-1968 [singer, songwriter, accordionist]
King of Accordion Players *Source(s):* MCCL
Walker, Raymond 1935- [author, lyricist]
Raymond, Walker X. *Source(s):* ASCP
Walker, Weldon 1925-2002 [singer, guitarist, songwriter]
Walker, Buddy *Source(s):* DRSC
Walker, William [or Billy] (Marvin) 1929- [singer, songwriter]
Masked Singer of Country Songs, The *Source(s):* AMUS; MCCL; PSND
Tall Texan, The *Source(s):* FLIN
Note(s): See also Claude (N.) Gray.
Traveling Texan, The *Source(s):* AMUS; MCCL; PSND
Walker, William Stearns 1917- [composer, author, pianist]
Bradford, William *Source(s):* ASCP
Walker, William Vincent 1947- [violinist, composer]
Billy Bang *Source(s):* CCE73
Bang, Billy *Source(s):* CCE73; PEN2
Wallace, Chris(topher (G.)) 1972 (or 73)-1997 [rapper, songwriter]
B. I. G., (Notorious) *Source(s):* LCAR
Big *Source(s):* CPOL PA-646-393
Biggie Smalls *Source(s):* AMUS; EPMU; LCAR
Notorious B.I.G., (The) *Source(s):* AMUS; CM20; EPMU; LCAR; PMUS-96
Smalls, Biggie *Source(s):* CM20; EPMU; LCAR; PMUS-96
Wallace, Em(m)ett 1909- [entertainer, composer]
E. B. *Source(s):* LCAR

Wallace, Babe *Source(s):* CCE63-64; ; LCAR; PSND
Wallace, King Babe *Source(s):* CCE57
Wallace, Jerry 1928 (or 33)- [singer, songwriter, guitarist, actor]
Mr. Smooth *Source(s):* MCCL; PSND
Waller, Jack 1885-1957 [composer, actor, producer]
Curtis, Con *Source(s):* CCE68 R438781
Note(s): Jt. pseud.: Bert [i.e., Albert George] Lee & Joseph A(lbert) Tunbridge.
Hope, John *Source(s):* CCE56 R164348 ("With You Beside Me")
Note(s): Jt. pseud.: Joseph A(lbert) Tunbridge.
Lindon, Robert *Source(s):* GANB
Note(s): Jt. pseud.: Joseph A(lbert) Tunbridge.
Sharon, Paul *Source(s):* CCE65 R361123
Note(s): Jt. pseud.: Joseph A(lbert) Tunbridge.
Shaw, Damon *Source(s):* CCE41 #29129 Efor65280; CCE68 R438781
Note(s): Jt. pseud.: Bert [i.e., Albert George] Lee & Joseph A(lbert) Tunbridge.
Waller, Thomas Wright 1904-1943 [pianist, singer, bandleader, composer]
Note(s): Portraits: CM07; EWEN; IDBC; JASN
Big Filthy *Source(s):* Kirkeby, Ed. *Ain't Misbehavin'; The Story of Fats Waller.* New York: Dodd, Mead, 1966, p. 53.
Black Horowitz, The *Source(s):* PSND; SIFA
Brown Tom *Source(s):* CCE52 R89883 ("Strivers Row")
Note(s): Possible pseud.?
Cheerful Little Earful, The *Source(s):* Fox, Charles. *Fats Waller.* New York: A. S. Barnes, 1961, p. 45
Fats *Source(s):* Kirkeby, Ed, p. 53 (see above)
Filthy *Source(s):* Kirkeby, Ed, p. 53 (see above)
Harmful Little Armful *Source(s):* Fox, Charles, p. 45 (see above)
Maurice *Source(s):* JAMU
Three Wise Men of Harlem Hot Piano, The *Source(s):* Vance, Joel. *Fats Waller; His Life and Times.* Chicago: Contemporary Books, 1977, p. 34.
Note(s): Jt. sobriquet: James [or Jimmy, or Jimmie] (P(rice)) Johnson & William [or Willie] (Henry Joseph Berthol Bonaparte) Smith.
Wallace, Flip *Source(s):* SUTT; http://homepages.tesco.net/~stridepiano/midi files.htm (3 Mar. 2005)
Waller, Fats *Source(s):* ALMN; CM07; EPMU; HARR; IDBC; KINK; NGAM; PEN2; PSND
Wallin, Johan Olof 1779-1839 [clergyman, hymnist]
Note(s): Portrait: CYBH
David's Harp of the North *Source(s):* PSND
Wallmann, Heinrich [author]
Heinrich von der Maltig *Source(s):* MUBR
Maltig, Heinrich von der *Source(s):* MUBR
Walser, Henry Stanley 1877-1955 [composer, pianist, organist]
Stanley, W. H. *Source(s):* KROH p. 129
Walsh, Austin [songwriter]
Pollard, Thomas Leaming *Source(s):* BLIC (publication date 1916)
Walsh, Ulysses 1903-1990 [journalist, writer on music]
Burt, L. S. *Source(s):* GRAK
Dashiell, Addison *Source(s):* GRAK
Walsh, Jim *Source(s):* GRAK; LCAR
Walter, Forrest G. [composer]
Porter, Walter *Source(s):* CCE63; CPOL RE-515-823
Note(s): Jt. pseud.: Ellen Jane Lorenz.
Walter, Lothar 1943- [composer, producer]
Holm, Michael *Source(s):* EPMU; PFSA
Walters, Harold L(aurence) 1918-1984 [composer, arranger, editor]
Frank, Fred (L.) *Source(s):* LCAR; NGAM; REHG; SMIN; SUPN
Seymour, Laurence *Source(s):* SMIN
Williams, David *Source(s):* SMIN
Walther, Johann Gottfried 1684-1748 [organist, composer]
Second Pachelbel, A *Source(s):* PRAT
Walton, Cora 1935- [singer, songwriter]
Queen of Chicago Blues, The *Source(s):* PSND
Queen of the Blues *Source(s):* *Goldmine* 27:2;553, p. 14+
Note(s): See also Ruth Lee Jones, Victoria [or Vickey] (Regina) Spivey, Sara(h) Dunn & Ethel Howard.
Taylor, Koko *Source(s):* ALMN; CM10; GRAT; HARS; LCAR
Walton, Kenneth [composer]
Kenwal, Ernest *Source(s):* CCE55? E86929 ("Jacob's Ladder")
Note(s): Jt. pseud.: Walter (Charles) Ehret
Thompson, Ronald *Source(s):* CCE59; CCE61 E162284, CCE62
Note(s): Jt. pseud.: Walter (Charles) Ehret.
Walton, Leon 1936- [singer, songwriter, guitarist]
Ashley, Leon *Source(s):* EPMU; MCCL
Waltzinger, Friedrich 1894- [music publisher, critic, composer]
Santos, Fred *Source(s):* MACM
Walther, Friedrich *Source(s):* MACM
Wälzel, Camillo 1829-1895 [librettist, theater director]
Zell, F(riedrich) *Source(s):* GAN1; LCAR; MACM; NGDO; PIPE; PRAT; STGR
Wang, An-Ming [author, songwriter]
Mak, Marion Wang *Source(s):* ASCP
Wangermée, Franz 1894-1967 [composer]
Robty *Source(s):* REHH; SUPN
Wantier, Firmin 1919- [composer]
Wallis, T. *Source(s):* SUPN

Warburg, James Paul 1896-1969 [banker, lyricist]
James, Paul *Source(s):* CCE48; CCE60; GRAT; JAST; LCAR; NGAM
Note(s): Also used by (Paul) James Stevens.
Ward, Arthur Sarsfield c.1883-1959 [writer]
Rohmer, Sax *Source(s):* CPMU; GOTH; KILG; LCAR; WORB
Ward, Charles B. 1865-1917 [composer, singer, vaudevillian]
Original Bowery Boy, The *Source(s):* JASZ; REHH; VACH
Ward, Mary Ann 1930- [singer, songwriter]
Worth, Marion *Source(s):* EPMU; MCCL
Ward, Seth 1928- [singer, songwriter]
Dandy of Country Music, The *Source(s):* PSND
Dean, Jimmy (Ray) *Source(s):* FLIN; HARD; HARR; PSND; STAC
Ware, George 1829-1895 [singer, songwriter]
Old Reliable, The *Source(s):* GARR
Ware, Harriet 1877-1962 [composer, pianist]
Note(s): Portraits: ETUP 57:9 (Sept. 1939): 554; MUSA 35:19 (4 Mar. 1922): 25
Krumbhaar, (Mrs.) Harriet *Source(s):* CCE39 #9188, 786 R74506; IBIM
Warfield, Gerald [writer on music and investments]
Friedlaw *Source(s):* AMSL (11 Jan. 2004)
Note(s): In Warfield's *Layer Analysis*. E-mail from Geoffrey Chew.
Warlop, Michael 1911-1947 [violinist, composer]
Niemczyk, Waclaw *Source(s):* GROL
Note(s): Incorrectly identified as pseud. of Warlop. Waclaw Niemczyk was a violinist who recorded in Paris for the same company as Warlop, long after Warlop's death. (http://www.abar.net/fbrisupdate.html (13 May 2005)
Warman, Cy 1855-1914 [journalist, poet, writer, railroad engineer]
Bard of the Rockies, The *Source(s):* SPTH p. 269
Warner, Anna (Barlett) 1820-1915 [author, editor, hymnist]
Lothrop, Amy *Source(s):* CYBH (port.); JULN (Suppl.); ROGA; YOUN
Warner, Brian 1969- [songwriter]
Manson, Marilyn *Source(s):* LCAR
Marilyn Manson *Source(s):* PMUS-96
Warner, Onslow Boyden Waldo 1902-1988 [composer, violist]
Warner, Ken *Source(s):* LCAR; MUWB
Warner, Susan (Bogert) 1818 (or19)-1885 [author, hymnist]
Wetherell, Elizabeth *Source(s):* CYBH; LCAR; YOUN
Warnick, Henry C(lay), Jr. 1915- [composer, author, conductor]
Warnick, Buck *Source(s):* ASCP; CCE40 #34335* D39901; LCAR
Warnken, Rodney G(eorge) 1931- [composer, author]
Warren, Rod *Source(s):* ASCP; CCE57
Warnock, Amelia Beers 1878-1956 [music critic]
Note(s): Married name: Garvin.
Hale, Katherine *Source(s):* LCAR; PSND
Warnow, Harry 1908 (or 09)-1994 [composer, conductor, arranger]
Gertrude Stein of Dada Jazz, The *Source(s):* http://www.wfmu.org/irwin (31 Jan. 2005)
Scott, Raymond *Source(s):* ASCP; EPMU; EWPA (port); JASA; KINK; LCAR; PEN2;VACH
Warren, B. Elliott [composer]
B. E. W. *Source(s):* DIEH
Warren, Edward (Rudolph) 1939- [bass player, composer]
Warren, Butch *Source(s):* CCE62; LCAR; PSND
Warren, Elinor Remick 1900-1991 [composer, pianist]
Bonner, Samuel *Source(s):* CCE62; Bortin, Virginia. *Elinor Remick Warren; A Bio-bibliography.* Westport, CT: Garland, 1993.
Warrington, John(ny) (T.) 1911-1978 [composer]
Fuentes, Ramon *Source(s):* REHG; SUPN
Ingram, Ted *Source(s):* CCE63 E177200 & E177212; CPOL RE-507-439
Johnson, Warrane *Source(s):* CCE68
Johnson, Warren *Source(s):* CCE68
Sande, Gene *Source(s):* CCE68; CCE69 E258219
Ward, Russell *Source(s):* CCE65; CCE67; CPOL RE-347-444
Wasenius, Karl Fredrik [music critic]
Bis *Source(s):* http://www.helsinki-hs.net/thisweek/03082000.html (7 Oct. 2002)
Washburn, Lalomie 1941- [composer, author, singer]
Washburn, Lomi *Source(s):* ASCP
Washburne, Joseph [or Joe] (H.) 1904-1974 [composer, author, bassist, arranger, bandleader]
O'Shea, Daddy *Source(s):* CCE64
Vaschbiergn, Josef *Source(s):* CCE64
Washburne, Country *Source(s):* ASCC; CCE64; KINK; LCAR; VACH
Wassenaer, (Count) Unico Wilhelm, (graf van) 1692-1766 [nobleman, amateur composer]
Note(s): His "Concerto Armonico" was first attributed to Ricciotti & later to Pergolesi.
Pergolesi, Giovanni Battista *Source(s):* MUWB
Ricciotti *Source(s):* MUWB
Wasserzug, Hayyim 1822-1882 [cantor, composer]
Lomzer, Reb Hayyim *Source(s):* NULM
Waterbury, Jared Bell 1799-1876 [hymnist]
J. B. W. *Source(s):* JULN
Village Pastor *Source(s):* LCAR

Waterford, Charles (E.) 1919- [singer, songwriter]
Crown Prince of the Blues, The *Source(s):* CCE60; CCE63; EPMU
Waterford, Crown Prince *Source(s):* CCE60; CCE63; EPMU; LCAR
Waterman, Nixon 1859-1944 [poet, editor]
Martin, Peter *Source(s):* LCAR; MAPN
Note(s): Also used by Peter Martin Malijewski.
Waters, Horace John [composer]
Warner, Jack *Source(s):* CPMU (publication date 1940)
Watkins, Tionne 197?- [songwriter, performer]
T-Boz *Source(s):* AMIR; PMUS-00
Watkins, T-Boz *Source(s):* LCAR
Watson, Alfred Edward Thomas 1849-1922 [music and drama critic]
Rapier *Source(s):* CART; LCAR; WORB
Wrey, Peyton *Source(s):* CART
Watson, Arthel 1923- [singer, songwriter, guitarist]
Watson, Doc *Source(s):* CCME; LCAR; MCCL
Watson, Derek 1951- [singer, songwriter]
Christian, Rick *Source(s):* EPMU
Watson, Ernest 1868-1924 [composer]
Shand, Ernest *Source(s):* MUWB
Watson, John(ny) 1935-1996 [guitarist, pianist, songwriter]
Watson, Guitar *Source(s):* HARS; LCAR
Watson, Young John *Source(s):* LCAR
Watson, Rosamund (Ball) Marriott 1863-1911 [poet]
Tomson, Graham R. *Source(s):* LCAR; MRSQ 7:3/4 (1999): 5; PSND
Watson, Samuel Vernon [songwriter]
King, Nosmo *Source(s):* CPMU (publication dates 1940-42)
Note(s): Also used by Stephen Jameson.
Watson, William Michael 1840-1889 [composer, author]
Note(s): Portrait: ETUP 57:9 (Sept. 1939): 554
Favre, Jules *Source(s):* BROW; CPMU; GOTH; MACM; PRAT
Watts, Isaac 1674-1748 [educationalist, hymnist]
Note(s): Portrait: CYBH
Greatest Hymn Writer in Christian History *Source(s):* http://www.rlhymersjr.com/Articles/02-16-03EternalBlood.html (27 Jan. 2004)
Impartial Moderator, (An) *Source(s):* CART
W. *Source(s):* JULN
W. L. *Source(s):* JULN
W. S. *Source(s):* JULN
Note(s): W. S. = Watt's Sermons
Watts, John Stanley 1921 (or 22)- [singer, actor, songwriter]
Hanson, John *Source(s):* CASS; EPMU; GAMM; LCAR
Watts, Mayme 1926- [composer, author, teacher]
Price, Penny *Source(s):* ASCP
Watz, Franz 1949- [composer]
Grain, Joe *Source(s):* REHG; SUPN
Waymon, Eunice Kathleen 1933 (or 35)-2003 [composer, author, singer, pianist]
High Priestess of Soul, The *Source(s):* PSND
Simone, Nina *Source(s):* ASCP; CLAG; PEN2; ROOM; WORL
Weaver, Jesse (B. Jr.) [songwriter]
Schooly D. *Source(s):* EPMU; PMUS-96
Webb, Brenda Gail 1951- [singer, songwriter]
Crystal Gale *Source(s):* CM01; EPMU
Gale, Crystal *Source(s):* EPMU
Gatzimos, Crystal Gale *Source(s):* CM01
Gayle, Crystal *Source(s):* MCCL; STAC
Webb, Gary Anthony James 1958- [singer, songwriter, guitarist]
Godfather of Electronica, The *Source(s):* http://www.prisonmoon2002.com (3 Oct. 2002)
Numan, Gary *Source(s):* HARD; HARR; RECR
Valerium *Source(s):* RECR
Webb, Numan *Source(s):* PEN2
Webb, Loretta 1935- [singer, songwriter, guitarist]
Coal Miner's Daughter, The *Source(s):* FLIN
First Lady of Country Music, (The) *Source(s):* FLIN
Note(s): See also Virginia Wynette Pugh.
Lynn, Loretta *Source(s):* CM02; EPMU; LCAR; MCCL
Queen of Country Music, The *Source(s):* CM02; http://www.asunderpress.com/articlequeencountry.htm (1 Nov. 2002)
Note(s): See also Muriel (Ellen) Deason & Virginia Wynette Pugh.
Webb, Peggy Sue 1947- [singer, songwriter]
Peggy Sue *Source(s):* EPMU; MCCL
Webb, (Harry) Rodger 1940- [composer]
Richard, Cliff *Source(s):* CPMU; EPMU; LCAR; PFSA; RECR
Webb, William (Henry) 1909-1939 [drummer, composer, bandleader]
Webb, Chick *Source(s):* CASS; CM14; GAMM; KINK; LCAR; STUW
Webb, Willie Lee 1937- [singer, songwriter, guitarist]
Webb, Jack *Source(s):* MCCL
Webb, Jay Lee *Source(s):* MCCL
Weber, Bedrich Divis 1766-1842 [teacher, writer on music, composer]
Weber, Friedrich Dionys(us) *Source(s):* BAKR; LCAR
Weber, C(arl) Heinrich 1819- [violoncellist, composer, publisher]
Sturmeck, Heinrich [or Heinz] von *Source(s):* KROH p. 14
Weber, Henry *Source(s):* KROH p. 14

Weber, Carl Maria von 1786-1826 [composer, pianist, conductor, critic]
Agathus der Zieltreffer, Edler von Samiel *Source(s):* APPL p. 12
B. f. z. Z. *Source(s):* Warrach, John. *Carl Maria von Weber.* 2nd ed. Cambridge: Cambridge University Press, 1976, p. 104
Note(s): B. f. z. Z. = "Beharrlichkeit fuhrt zum Ziel" ("Perseverance leads to the go al")
Father of German Opera *Source(s):* MUWB
Founder of the Romantic Movement in German Music *Source(s):* PRAT
Knaster, Simon *Source(s):* Warrach, p. 104 (see above)
Note(s): Knaster is a kind of cheap tobacco; also slang for an old grumble.
M——s *Source(s):* Warrach, p. 104
Melos *Source(s):* GROL; HEYT; PRAT (see under: Weber, Gottfried)
Weber, Fred 1912- [composer]
Douglas, Wayne *Source(s):* CCE53; CCE57; CPOL RE-97-808; REHG; SUPN
Note(s): Also used by Wayne Douglas Broze, Walter (Charles) Ehret & Edward J. Penney; see NOTES: Douglas, Wayne. Do not confuse with singer Wayne Douglas [i.e., Doug Sham] (1941-1999).
Weber, (Jacob) Gottfried 1779-1839 [jurist, composer, conductor, writer on music]
Aab, (Dr.) *Source(s):* HEYT
Billig, Julius *Source(s):* Warrach, John. *Carl Maria von Weber.* 2nd ed. Cambridge: Cambridge University Press, 1976, p. 104
Note(s): Also used by Giacomo Meyerbeer [i.e., Jakob Liebmann Beer]
Dr. Zyx *Source(s):* HEYT
G. W. *Source(s):* HEYT
Gfr. W(br.). *Source(s):* HEYT
Giusto, (G.) *Source(s):* GROL; PRAT; Warrach, p. 104 (see above)
Löwen, C(arl) v. *Source(s):* HEYT
Weber, Joseph 1854-1906 [composer, violinist]
Weber, Miroslav *Source(s):* MACM
Weber, Michel 1896-1965 [composer]
Nino *Source(s):* CCE67; LCAR; MELL
Veber, Michel *Source(s):* GROL
Weber, William Jennings Bryan 1916-1979 [composer]
Weber, Ben *Source(s):* BAKR; LCAR
Wechter, Cecile Schroeder 1936- [lyricist]
Wechter, Cissy *Source(s):* ASCP
Wecker, Georg Kaspar [or Caspar] 1632-1695 [composer, organist, teacher]
G. C. W. *Source(s):* IBIM; WORB
Wedderburn, Robin [arranger, conductor]
Ecker, W. R. *Source(s):* http://www.sscot.org.uk/personnel.htm (7 Oct. 2002)
Weed, Harold Eugene 1918- [pianist, singer, composer]
Weed, Buddy *Source(s):* KINK
Weekes, Desiree [or Des'ree] 1970- [singer, songwriter]
Des'ree *Source(s):* CM15; CM24; EPMU; LCAR
Weertz, Louis Jacob 1924- [composer, arranger, pianist]
Williams, Roger *Source(s):* ASCP; CCE56-57; CCE65; CPOL RE-256-299; LCAR
Wegener, Doris 1943- [composer]
Manuela *Source(s):* PFSA
Wehner, Gerhard 1916- [composer]
Cardot, Marcel *Source(s):* CCE60-62; KOMP; PFSA
Weider, Daniel René 1982- [singer, songwriter]
Daniel René *Source(s):* HWOM
Weidig, (Alexander) Friedrich Ludwig 1791-1837 [poet]
Hesse, Friedmund *Source(s):* PIPE
Weidler, George William 1926- [songwriter, saxophonist]
Wilder Brothers *Source(s):* CCE56 Eunp
Note(s): Jt. pseud.: Walter Wolfgang Weidler & Warner Alfred Weidler.
Wilder, George *Source(s):* CCE53; CCE57; CPOL RE-132-671
Weidler, Walter Wolfgang 1923- [songwriter]
Wilder Brothers *Source(s):* CCE56 Eunp
Note(s): Jt. pseud.: George William Weidler & Warner Alfred Weidler.
Wilder, Walt(er) *Source(s):* CCE53; CCE55 Eunp; CPOL RE-132-671
Weidler, Warner Alfred 1935- [songwriter, producer]
Boniface, Al *Source(s):* CCE68
Warbucks, Bill ("Daddy") *Source(s):* CCE77 (see Index)
Warbucks, Daddy *Source(s):* CCE77 (see Index)
Wilder Brothers *Source(s):* CCE56 Eunp
Note(s): Jt. pseud.: Walter Wolfgang Weidler & George William Weidler.
Wilder, Warner *Source(s):* ASCP; CCE53; CCE61; CPOL RE-132-671
Wing, Bobby *Source(s):* CCE61
Weil, (Max) Rene 1868-1952 [librettist]
Coolus, Romain *Source(s):* LCAR; MELL
Weill, Kurt 1900-1950 [composer]
Father of American Opera *Source(s):* http://www.ndr.de/igband/disco/weill100.html (7 Oct. 2002)
Note(s): See also William Henry Fry & George Gershwin [i.e., Jacob Gershvin]
Weinberg, Charles 1889-1955 [composer, conductor]
Wynn, Charles [or Charlie] *Source(s):* ASCP; CCE57; CCE67; PSND

Weinberg, Symson [or Simson] 1909-1988 [composer, pianist, DJ]
Note(s): In ORPH given name: Samuel.
Berg, Jimmy *Source(s):* CCE52-53; KOMU; OMUO; ORPH
Danberg, Raimund *Source(s):* KOMU; OMUO
Forst-Berg, Otto *Source(s):* KOMU; OMUO
Raabe, Helmut *Source(s):* KOMU; OMUO
Weinberger, Hermann 1883-1956 [author, singer, composer]
Berg, Armin *Source(s):* OMUO
Weiner, Lazar 1897-1982 [composer, pianist, conductor]
Note(s): Portraits: ETUP 57:10 (Oct. 1939): 624; LYMN
America's Greatest Yiddish Composer *Source(s):* LYMN
Vayner, Lazar *Source(s):* LCAR
Weiner, Yehudi 1929- [composer, pianist, conductor]
Wyner, Yehudi *Source(s):* BAKR; BAKT; LCAR; PSND
Weingarten, David 1902- [composer, author, publisher]
Gardner, Dave *Source(s):* ASCP; PSND
Weinhöppel, Hans Richard 1867-1928 [composer]
Raimar, Freimund *Source(s):* PIPE
Ruch, Hannes *Source(s):* CPMU; KOBW; LCAR; PIPE; RIES
Simplicissimus *Source(s):* STGR ("Das Gespenst von Matschatsch")
Note(s): Possible pseud. Also used by Daniel Speer.
Weinlein, Josaphat 1601-1662 [musician, composer]
Pulsitiva, Johann *Source(s):* CPMU; IBIM; WORB
Weinlinus, Josaphat *Source(s):* WORB
Weinstein, Morton (Neff) 1927- [composer, author]
Neff, Morton [or Morty] *Source(s):* ASCP (see reference); CCE52-56; CPOL RE-45-558
Weintraub, (Rotkopf) Salomon 1780 (or 81)-1829 [composer]
Kaschtan *Source(s):* NULM; SEND
Weintrop, Chaim Reuben [or Reubin] 1896-1968 [actor, songwriter]
Flanagan, Bud *Source(s):* FAFO
Flanagan, Robert (Winthrop) *Source(s):* LCAR
Winthrop, Robert *Source(s):* FAFO
Weisenberg, Karl 1875-1925 [librettist]
Berg, Carl *Source(s):* PIPE
Weisman, Ben E. [songwriter]
Note(s): Do not confuse with Bernard [or Bernie] Weisman; see following entry.
Topp, Ben *Source(s):* CCE63; CPOL RE-815-005

Weisman, Bernard [or Bernie] [songwriter]
Wiseman, Ben *Source(s):* CPOL RE-46-760; CPOL RE-177-486; SONG
Note(s): Do not confuse with Ben E. Weisman; see preceding entry.
Weismann, Julia 1898- [composer]
Kempner, Julia *Source(s):* WORB
Kerr, (Mrs.) Julia *Source(s):* COHN; HIXN; MACM
Kerwey, Julia *Source(s):* CCE29 Dunp27419; COHN; HIXN; MACM
Weiss, David c.1952- [lyricist, flutist, jazz critic]
Was, David *Source(s):* CM21 (see under: Was, Don); PEN2; PMUS-83; WARN
Weiss, Erwin 1912-2004 [pianist, composer, conductor, teacher]
Falk, Peter *Source(s):* ORPH; WORB
Weiss, Peter Howard [or Howard Peter] 1927- [pianist, composer, arranger, conductor]
Howard, Peter *Source(s):* LCAR; PIPE; PSND
Weiss, Karl 1850-1901 (or 11) [librettist]
Karlweis, C(arl) *Source(s):* STGR; WORB
Weissenburg, Heinrich 1661?-1729? [soldier, composer, violinist]
Albicastro, Henricus [or Henrico] *Source(s):* BAKR; HARV; LCAR; NGDM
Weysenbergh, (Johannes) Heinrich *Source(s):* LCAR
Weissensee, Friedrich c.1560-1622 [composer, vicar]
F. W. *Source(s):* IBIM
Weisser, Joshua Samuel 1888- [composer]
Pilderwasser *Source(s):* SEND
Weisshaus, Imre 1904 (or 05)-1987 [composer, pianist, ethnomusicologist]
Arma, Paul *Source(s):* BAKR; BAKT; BUL2; LCAR; NGDM
Weitz, George 1890 (or 92)-1968 [musical stage producer, author, composer, actor]
White, George *Source(s):* BBDP; KINK
Note(s): Also used by Vernon Dalhart [i.e., M(arion) T(ry) Slaughter]
Weitz, Ted 1907- [composer, pianist, singer]
White, Ted *Source(s):* ASCP; CCE42 #30020 Eunp303855
Weitzler, Morris Martin 1916- [composer, author]
White, Marty *Source(s):* ASCP
Welby, Anna Marie (of Louisville) [poet]
Exile *Source(s):* HARW p. 138; HOGR; OCLC 18771899
Welch, M. E. A. [composer]
Delmage *Source(s):* CPMU (publication date 1914)
Welch, Sidney Lester, Jr. 1924- [composer, author]
Welch, Patrick *Source(s):* ASCP; CCE72; CPOL PAu-152-609
Weldon, Georgina (née Thomas) 1837-1914 [singer, translator]
Treherne, Georgina *Source(s):* LCAR; MACM

Weldon, Peter fl. 1797-1810 [pianist, violinist, music publisher, composer]
P. W. *Source(s):* DICH ("President Madison's March"); LCAR
Weldon, Will(iam) 1909-196? [singer, guitarist, songwriter]
Bill, Casey *Source(s):* PMUS
Casey Bill *Source(s):* LCAR; PMUS; SUTT
Hawaiian Guitar Wizard, The *Source(s):* HARS; LCAR
Kansas City Bill *Source(s):* DBMU; HARS; LCAR
Levee Joe *Source(s):* DBMU; HARS; LCAR
Weldon, Casey Bill *Source(s):* HARS; LCAR
Welk, Lawrence (LeRoy) 1903-1992 [bandleader, songwriter]
King of Musical Corn, The *Source(s):* PSND
Liberace of the Accordion, The *Source(s):* PSND
Mr. Music Maker *Source(s):* PSND
"Wunnerful" Purveyor of Champagne Music *Source(s):* CM13 p. vii
Welker, Gotthard 1920- [composer]
Klewer, Thomas *Source(s):* CCE58; CCE60; CCE65; KOMS; PFSA
Weller, John William 1958- [singer, guitarist, songwriter]
British Pop Phenomenon of the Early 80s, The *Source(s):* CM14
Weller, Paul *Source(s):* EPMU; LCAR
Weller, Wilton Frederick 1947- [singer, songwriter, guitarist]
Weller, Freddy *Source(s):* MCCL
Wellington, Larry [composer, actor]
Ellington, L. W. *Source(s):* MCCA
Wellnitz, Gerd 1928- [composer]
Cambridge, Jack *Source(s):* PFSA
Geritz, Günther *Source(s):* PFSA
Wells, John Barnes 1880-1935 [singer, songwriter]
Note(s): Portrait: ETUP 57:10 (Oct. 1939): 624
Barmes, William *Source(s):* CCE18 E433226
Note(s): Typographical error?
Barnes, William *Source(s):* KINK; SUTT
Wells, Jack *Source(s):* LCAR
Wells, Viola (Gertrude) 1902-1984 [singer, songwriter]
Ebony Stick of Dynamite, The *Source(s):* EPMU
Miss Rhapsody *Source(s):* EPMU; GRAT; HARS; LCAR
Rhapsody, Miss *Source(s):* HARS
Underhill, Viola *Source(s):* HARS
Wells, William 1907 (or 10)-1985 [trombonist, composer]
Wells, Dicky [or Dickie] *Source(s):* ASCC; KINK; LCAR; PEN2
Wembadia, Shungu 195?- [singer, composer]
Papa Wemba *Source(s):* LCAR
Wemba, Papa *Source(s):* LCAR; PEN2

Wende, Horst 1919- [composer]
Delgado, Roberto *Source(s):* CCE74; KOMP; KOMS; PFSA
Gado, Roberto del *Source(s):* CCE55-56; KOMP; KOMS
Wendling, Pete 1888-1974 [pianist, composer]
Redding, Walter *Source(s):* PIAN
Note(s): Also used by J. Lawrence Cook.
Wendlinger, Thomas 1909- [composer]
Sonnleitner, Peter *Source(s):* PFSA
Wenrich, Percy 1887-1952 [singer, composer, pianist]
Note(s): Portraits: EWPA; JASA; JASZ
Joplin Kid, The *Source(s):* GROL; NGAM; PERF
Richmond, Dolly *Source(s):* JASA p. 322
Schmidt, Karl *Source(s):* JASA p. 322
Song Writers on Parade *Source(s):* CCE32 Eunp56182
Note(s): Jt. pseud.: Sidney Clare, Charles Tobias, Al(bert) Sherman, Al(an) Lewis, (T.) Murray Mencher & Vincent Rose.
Wenyeh, Chiang 1910-1983 [composer]
Bunya, Koh *Source(s):* PFSA
Werker, Wilhelm [author, writer on music]
Ariel *Source(s):* RIEM
Werner, Christian 1962- [composer]
Steinway, Werner *Source(s):* KOMS; PFSA
Werner, Emil 1934- [composer]
Krali, Milo *Source(s):* PFSA
Werner, Erich 1909- [composer]
Sun, Pat *Source(s):* CCE56-58; KOMP; PFSA
Werner, Kenneth 1949- [composer]
Harmonic, Phil *Source(s):* GREN; LCAR
Note(s): Also used by Darryl Porter.
Wernicke, Helmuth 1909-1994 [composer]
Jens, Arthur *Source(s):* CCE55; CCE60; KOMP; KOMS; PFSA
Wertheim, Eduard 1902-1961 [composer]
Kresmer-Wertheim *Source(s):* BUL3
Weschler, Melvin Walter 1921- [composer]
Byron, Walter *Source(s):* CCE52-53; JASA p. 321; JASG; JASR
Wesley, Charles 1707-1788 [clergyman, hymnist]
Note(s): Portrait: CYBH
Bard of Epworth *Source(s):* PSND; PSNN
C. & J. W. *Source(s):* JULN
Note(s): Joint initials: John Wesley.
England's Greatest Hymn Writer *Source(s):* http://nb-soft.com/believe/txc/wesley.htm (2 Jan. 2005)
Father of Methodist Hymnody, The *Source(s):* http://ctlibrary.com/3293 (2 Jan. 2005)
Greatest Hymn Writer of All Ages, The *Source(s):* http://ctlibrary.com/3293

Hymnist of the English Revival, The *Source(s):* PSND
J. C. W. *Source(s):* JULN
Note(s): Joint initials: John Wesley.
Poet of Methodism, The *Source(s):* PSND
Poet of the Evangelical Revival, The *Source(s):* http://ctlibrary.com/3293
Sweet Bard of Methodism *Source(s):* http://www.concerthall.ca/history.html (7 Oct. 2002)
Sweet Singer of Methodism *Source(s):* http://www.eaec.org/faithhallfame/charleswesley.htm (7 Apr. 2005)

Wesley, Garret (Colley) 1735-1781 [composer, organist]
Note(s): His father's original surname: Colley.
Mornington, Garret Wesley, (Earl of) *Source(s):* LCAR; NGDM
Wellesley, Garrett *Source(s):* LCAR; NGDM

Wesley, John 1703-1791 [hymnist]
Note(s): Portrait: CYBH
C. & J. W. *Source(s):* JULN
Note(s): Joint initials: Charles Wesley.
J. C. W. *Source(s):* JULN
Note(s): Joint initials: Charles Wesley.

Wesley, Samuel 1766-1837 [composer, organist]
Note(s): Portraits: CYBH; GRV3 v. 5; MUST (1 Dec. 1902): 801
English Mozart *Source(s):* NGDM
Note(s): See also (Sir) Henry R(owley) Bishop.

Wesley, Wilson 1893-1958 [singer, songwriter]
Butterbeans *Source(s):* EPMU
Note(s): See also Joe [or Jody] Edwards.
Pigmeat Pete *Source(s):* EPMU
Wesley, Kid *Source(s):* EPMU

West, Anthonius c.1490-1547 [composer]
Musa, Anthonius *Source(s):* NGDM

West, Camille 1956- [singer, songwriter]
Suburban Mother from Hell *Source(s):* MUHF

West, George Frederick 1844-1860 [composer]
Lemoine, Frederic *Source(s):* CPMU (publications 1847-82)

West, Wesley W(ebb) 1924-2003 [singer, guitarist, composer]
West, Speedy *Source(s):* CCE57; CLAB; MCCL; WASH

Westendorf, Omer 1916-1997 [hymnist]
Evans, Mark *Source(s):* CCE62; CCE65-66; CPOL RE-525-674
Note(s): Also used by Paul Frederick Tidman.
Evers, J. Clifford *Source(s):* CCE61-62; CPOL RE-405-564; *Hymnal 1982 Companion*, v. 1
Francis, Paul *Source(s):* CCE65; CPOL RE-525-688
Solando, Anthony *Source(s):* CCE63-64; CPOL RE-563-881
Solando, Michael *Source(s):* CCE64; CCE76

Westendorf, Thomas Paine 1848?- [songwriter]
Hoosier from Plainfield, Indiana *Source(s):* MARC p. 19+ ("I'll Take You Home Again, Kathleen")
Virginian from Louisville, Ky. *Source(s):* MARC p. 19+
Note(s): Incorrect attribution for "I'll Take You Home Again, Kathleen."

Weston, Andre 1970- [rapper]
Drayz *Source(s):* EPMU (see under: Das-EFX)

Westover, Charles W(eedon) 1934 (or 39)-1990 [singer, songwriter]
Shannon, Dee [or Del(l)] *Source(s):* ALMN; CASS; CM10; DIMA; EPMU; HARR; KICK; PEN2

Wetherell, Kenneth Alwyn 1928- [composer, arranger, conductor]
Alwyn, Kenneth *Source(s):* MUWB

Wetstein, Paul (R., Jr.) 1912-1996 [pianist; composer, bandleader, arranger]
Note(s): Portrait: MUSR (see under: Weston, Paul)
Edwards, Jonathan *Source(s):* EPMU; LCAR; PSND; STUW
Father of Lounge Music, (The) *Source(s):* http://www.parabrisas.com/d_weston.html (7 Oct. 2002)
Westbar, F. R. *Source(s):* OCLC 48709633
Note(s): Probable joint pseud.: F. J. Barnes.
Weston, Paul *Source(s):* GAMM; KINK; LCAR; STUW; VACH

Wettach, (Charles) Adrien 1880-1959 [singer, songwriter]
Grock, (The World's Greatest Clown) *Source(s):* KILG (see under: Grock, A.); LCAR; PSND

Wetzker, Ingo 1934- [composer]
Insterburg, Ingo *Source(s):* PFSA

Weutz, Giulio 1912-1984 [composer]
Viozzi, Giulio *Source(s):* GROL; RIES

Weyburn, Edward Claudius 1874-1942 [choreographer, director]
Wayburn, Ned *Source(s):* GAN2; LCAR (see note)

Weymes, Wilfred Theodore 1901-1963 [violinist, composer, bandleader]
Weems, Ted *Source(s):* KINK; STUW

Weymouth, Martina (Michele) 1950- [musician, songwriter]
Weymouth, Tina *Source(s):* FAFO; PMUS; PSNN

Wheeler, Andrew Carpenter 1835-1903 [writer on music]
Crinkle, Nym *Source(s):* STAR p. 534; WORB
Mowbray *Source(s):* LCAR

Wheeler, Billy Edd 1932- [singer, songwriter, guitarist, author]
Country Music's "Renaissance Man" *Source(s):* MCCL
Thinking Man's Hillbilly, The *Source(s):* MCCL

Wheeler, James 1933- [pianist, songwriter]
Piano C. Red *Source(s):* EPMU
Wheeler, Kenneth [or Kenny] (Vincent John) 1930- [composer, trumpeter]
Keller, Weeny *Source(s):* EPMU
Wheeler, Paul fl. 1650-60 [composer]
Note(s): Possible original name.
Polewheel *Source(s):* NGDM
Whettan, Graham Dudley 1927- [composer]
Woodstock, Howard *Source(s):* MUWB
Whippo, Walter Barrows 1922- [author, lyricist]
Barrows, Walt *Source(s):* ASCP; CCE50-51
Whitaker, Alfred Hanbury [composer]
A. H. W. *Source(s):* CPMU (publication date 1843)
Whitaker, Yolanda 1971- [rapper]
Yo Yo *Source(s):* EPMU
Whitcomb, Ian (Timothy) 1941- [writer on music, composer, singer]
Bubb, Mel *Source(s):* PSND
Kingsley, Robin *Source(s):* http://www.picklehead.com/ian/bio.htm (1 Aug. 2005)
Murphy, Buck *Source(s):* PSND
Newton, Stu *Source(s):* PSND
Nouveau, Arthur *Source(s):* PSND
Whitcomb, Kenneth G(eorge) 1926- [composer, conductor, arranger, saxophonist]
Note(s): Do not confuse with Ken Whitcomb [i.e., Leonard Whitcup]
Kenny, George *Source(s):* ASCP; LCAR; PSND; REHG; SMIN; SUPN
Whitcup, Leonard 1903-1979 [songwriter]
Lennie *Source(s):* CCE26 E641353; LCPC letter cited (9 Sept. 1929)
Rand, Harry *Source(s):* CCE53 Eunp; CCE64
Whitcomb, Ken *Source(s):* CCE66 Eunp927442; CPOL RE-703-031 ("The A Team")
Note(s): "The A Team." Do not confuse with Kenneth G(eorge) Whitcomb.
White, Booker T. Washington 1906-1977 [instrumentalist, singer, songwriter]
Singing Preacher, The *Source(s):* HARS; LCAR
White, Bucca [or Bukka] *Source(s):* AMUS; EPMU; HARS; LCAR; MUHF; SHAB p. 107
White, Washington *Source(s):* HARS; LCAR
White, Charles A(lbert) 1829 (or 30)-1892 [composer]
Note(s): Portrait: ETUP 57:11 (Nov. 1939): 690
Birch, Harry *Source(s):* CCE12 R2574; PSND
Howard, Rollin *Source(s):* CCE11 E272384
Thorne, George *Source(s):* CCE13 R4948
White, Clarence C(ameron) 1880-1960 [composer]
Note(s): Portrait: ETUP 57:11 (Nov. 1939): 690
Blanco, C. *Source(s):* ETUD; TPRF
White, Cleve 1928- [singer, guitarist, songwriter]
Schoolboy Cleve *Source(s):* HARS

White, (Mrs.) E. C. C. [composer]
E. C. C. W., (Mrs) *Source(s):* JACK ("Constitutional Portuguese Air" (1826))
White, Ellerton Oswald 1917-1971 [composer, pianist]
White, Sonny *Source(s):* CLAB; LCAR
White, Erma (Marceline) 1925- [composer, author]
Angela *Source(s):* CCE64 Eunp8558
White, Angela *Source(s):* ASCP
White, Grace [composer]
Note(s): Possibly Grace White (1896-), pianist, violinist, composer.
Tyler, Chapman *Source(s):* CCE48 R27796; TPRF
White, Harold R(obert) 1872-1943 [composer]
MacMurrough, Dermot *Source(s):* CCE37 Efor47646; CCE47 R14082; GOTH
Ormsbé, Emil *Source(s):* CPMU
White, John I(rwin) 1902-1992 [singer, song compiler, mapmaker]
Lone Star Ranger, The *Source(s): Sing Out*! 41:4 (1997): 128
Note(s): Also used by Arthur Field [i.e., Abe Finkelstein] & possibly Vernon Dalhart [i.e., M(arion) T(ry) Slaughter]
Price, Jimmie *Source(s): Sing Out*! 41:4 (1997): 128
Note(s): Do not confuse with Jimmy Price [i.e., John(ny) (Senator) Marvin]
Whitey, John *Source(s): Sing Out*! 41:4 (1997): 128
White, Josh(ua) (Daniel) 1908-1969 [guitarist, singer, songwriter]
Barton, Tippy *Source(s):* HARS
Most Famous Folk Singer of His Race, The *Source(s):* PSND
Pinewood Tom *Source(s):* HARS; LCAR
Singing Christian, The *Source(s):* HARS; LCAR
White, Sylvia 1911- [composer]
Edwards, Mon *Source(s):* CCE53 Eunp
Eisenberg, (Mrs.) Sylvia White *Source(s):* ASCP
Sedores, Sil [or Syl] *Source(s):* ASCP; CCE58-61; CPOL RE-367-079
White, Terence Hanbury 1906-1964 [author]
Aston, James *Source(s):* LCAR; PIPE
White, Tony Joe 1943- [singer, songwriter, guitarist]
Swamp Fox, (The) *Source(s):* MCCL
Whiteman, Paul 1890-1967 [bandleader, composer, violinist]
Note(s): Portrait: ETUP 57:12 (Dec. 1939): 764
Dean of American Music, The *Source(s):* http://www.singers.com/jazz/vintage/modernaires.html (7 Oct. 2002)
Note(s): See also Aaron Copland, Walter Johannes Damrosch & Victor Herbert.
Dean of American Popular Music *Source(s):* PSND

King of Jazz *Source(s):* CASS; CM17; EPMU; SHAD; SPTH p. 482
Whiteman, Pops *Source(s):* PSND
Whiting, (Mrs.) G. I. [hymnist]
G. I. W. *Source(s):* JULN (publication date 1842)
Whiting, Mary Bradford [hymnist]
M. B. W. *Source(s):* JULN (publication date 1882)
Whiting, Richard 1891-1938 [pianist, composer]
Earle, R. W. *Source(s):* KROH p. 107
Whitley, Ray(mond) Otis 1901-1979 [singer, songwriter, guitarist, actor]
RKO's Singing Cowboy *Source(s):* MCCL
Whitlock, Percy (William) 1903-1946 [composer, journalist, organist]
Clark, Kenneth *Source(s):* http://www.organclub.org/newsletter03Nov.pdf (14 May 2005)
Note(s): Typographical error?
Lark, Kenneth *Source(s):* LCAR; MUWB; RFSO
Whitman, Alberta 1888?-1964 [songwriter]
Whitman, Bert *Source(s):* PMUC
Whitman, Keith (Fullerton) [composer]
Hrvatski *Source(s):* http://yod.cm/cgibi/find_selected.cgi?ITEMNO=3932&newwin=1 (7 Mar. 2005)
Whitman, Ot(t)is (Dewey, Jr.) 1924 (or 29)- [singer, songwriter, guitarist]
America's Favorite Folksinger *Source(s):* AMUS; CM19; MCCL
Smilin' Starduster, The *Source(s):* MCCL
Verified Legend, The *Source(s):* SHAD
Whitman, Slim *Source(s):* AMUS; CM19; EPMU; LCAR; MCCL; STAC
Whitman, Walt(er) 1819-1892 [poet, music critic]
America's First Opera Connoisseur *Source(s):* GRAN
Good Gray Poet, The *Source(s):* PSND
Solitary Singer *Source(s):* PSND
Whitney, Julia (A.) 1919-1965 [composer, singer]
Gay, Tandy *Source(s):* CCE60
Yulya *Source(s):* PSND
Whittern, Emerson 1884-1958 [composer]
Note(s): Portraits: ETUP 57:12 (Dec. 1939): 764; HOWD; MUSA 28:15 (10 Aug. 1918): 19
Whithorne, Emerson *Source(s):* BAKT; BUL2; BUL3; MACM; PRAT; WORB
Whittle, (Major) D(aniel) W(ebster) 1840-1901 [hymnist]
Note(s): Portraits: CYBH; HALL
D. W. W. *Source(s):* CYBH; DIEH; ROGA
Note(s): Presumed initials of Whittle on "Fierce and Wild the Storm."
El Nathan *Source(s):* CYBH; LCAR
Nathan, El(ias) *Source(s):* CYBH; HALL; JULN (Appendix); ROGA
W. L. *Source(s):* ROGA

Whitwell, O'Brien c.1870-1915 [composer]
Butler, O'Brien *Source(s):* BAKR; MACM
Whytehead, Thomas 1815-1843 [clergyman, hymnist]
Undergraduate, An *Source(s):* PSND
Wickdahl, Lillian (S.) 1893-1989 [composer, author, publisher]
Sandell, Lynn *Source(s):* ASCC; CCE40 #7328 Eunp25055; CCE63
Wickenden, Arthur
Mariette, Anton *Source(s):* TPRF
Widestedt, Ragnar 1887-1954 [composer]
Wide, Eric(h) *Source(s):* CCE50; GREN
Widman, Franklin Darryl 1950- [composer, author]
Franklin, Richard *Source(s):* ASCP
Widmann, Erasmus 1572-1634 [composer]
E. W. *Source(s):* IBIM
Widmann, Joseph Viktor 1842-1911 [author]
Helvetico, Ariosto *Source(s):* PIPE; WORB
Ludovico, Messer *Source(s):* PIPE; WORB
Widor, Charles-Marie (Jean Albert) 1844 (or 45)-1937 [organist, composer, music critic]
Aulétès *Source(s):* GROL; PRAT
Tibicen *Source(s):* PRAT
Wieck, Clara Josephine 1819-1896 [pianist, composer]
Ambrosia *Source(s):* NGDM, v. 16, p. 836
Beda *Source(s):* NGDM, v. 16, p. 836
Cecilia *Source(s):* DWCO; PSND
Note(s): See also Evangelina Sobredo Galanes.
Chiara [or Chiarina] *Source(s):* DAVE p. 115; PSND
Europe's Queen of the Piano *Source(s):* GROL
Queen of the Piano *Source(s):* DWCO; GROL
Schumann, (Mrs.) Clara Josephine *Source(s):* DAVE
Zilia *Source(s):* DAVE p. 115; NGDM v. 16, p. 836; PSND
Wieck, (Johann Gottlob) Friedrich 1785-1873 [music teacher, writer on music]
Note(s): Portrait: ETUP 57:12 (Dec. 1939): 764
Alte Schulmeister, Der [or Das] *Source(s):* GROL; NIEC p. 173; NGDM
DAS *Source(s):* GROL
Raro, Meister *Source(s):* Walker, Alan, ed. *Robert Schumann; The Man and His Music*. London: Barrie and Jenkins, 1972, p. 429.
Note(s): Some think Schumann used this name to refer to Friedrich Wieck, while others think it refers to Schumann.
Wiedenfeld, Karl 1908-1985 [composer]
Cord, M(ichael) *Source(s):* CCE58-61; KOMP; KOMS; PFSA; RIES
Wiemer, Robert Ernest 1938- [composer, author, singer]
Belasco, Keystone *Source(s):* ASCP
Wiener, Francis [or Franz] 1877-1937 [librettist; playwright]

Croisset, Francis (de) *Source(s):* GAN1; GAN2; LOWN; PIPE; WORB
Wiener, Georg 1909- [composer]
Jurk *Source(s):* LCAR
Winar, Jurij *Source(s):* BUL3
Wieniawska, Irene Regine 1880-1932 [composer]
Paul, (Lady) Dean *Source(s):* GROL; LCAR
Paul, (Lady) Irène Reine *Source(s):* CPMU; IBIM; STRN
Poldowski *Source(s):* BAKR; COHN; GROL; HIXN; LCAR; STRN
Wierzbowski, Ray(mond Lawrence) 1920- [composer, author]
Willow, Ray *Source(s):* ASCP; CCE53-54; CCE63; CCE66
Wiesengrund(-Adorno), Theodor (Ludwig) 1903-1969 [music sociologist, composer]
Adorno, (Theodor (Wiesengrund)) *Source(s):* BAKR; BAKT; HARV; LYMN; WORB
Adoruno *Source(s):* LCAR
Rottweiler, Hektor *Source(s):* GROL; WORB
Wieth-Knudsen, Knud A(sbjørn) 1878- [composer]
Knudsen, Niels A(sbjørn) *Source(s):* MACM
Wiggen, Knut 1927- [composer, teacher]
Freed, O(lov) M(artin) *Source(s):* BUL2; GROL
Libér, T. E. *Source(s):* GROL
Wiggins, Thomas (Green(e)) 1849-1908 [pianist, composer]
Note(s): Portraits: ETUP 58:8 (Aug. 1940): 517+; JASZ p. xxiv
Bethune, Thomas (Green(e)) (Wiggins) *Source(s):* IDBC; LCAR; NGAM
Blind Tom *Source(s):* IDBC; LCAR; NGAM
Green, Thomas *Source(s):* LCAR
Incredible Imitator, The *Source(s):* PSND
Messengale, C. T. *Source(s):* LCAR
Raymond, W. F. *Source(s):* LCAR
Sexalise, François *Source(s):* BAKE; LCAR
Tom *Source(s):* LCAR
Wignall, Harrison James [writer on music]
Slater, Harrison Gradwell *Source(s):* E-mail from author (16 Jan. 2004)
Wilborn, Nelson 1907-1970 [singer, songwriter]
Dirty Red *Source(s):* AMUS; HARS
Nelson, Red *Source(s):* HARS; LCAR
Red Devil *Source(s):* HARS
Red Nelson *Source(s):* HARS
Wilcock, Roland [composer]
Arnold, Walter F. *Source(s):* CPMU (publication dates 1911-16)
Wilde, Cornel (L(ouis)) 1915 (or 18)-1989 [composer, author, director]
Nelius, Louis *Source(s):* ASCP
Pascal, Jefferson *Source(s):* ASCP; CCE58
Wilder, Alec [i.e., Alexander] (Lafayette Chew) 1907-1980 [composer, arranger]
Larramie, Ace *Source(s):* CCE49; CCE55-56
Larramie, Alec *Source(s):* CCE53 Eunp
President of the Derrieregarde, The *Source(s):* PSND
Wilder, Philip van fl. early 16th cent. [composer, lutenist]
Philips, Mr. *Source(s):* GRV3
Wild(e)roe, Philip de *Source(s):* GRV3; LCAR
Wiley, Charles A. 1925- [songwriter]
Wiley, Pete *Source(s):* LCAR; STC1
Wilhelm, Elsie Lee 1935- [lyricist]
Robberts, Oriell *Source(s):* ASCP
Wilhoite, Donald McRae, Jr. 1909-1985 [composer, pianist, lyricist, singer]
Raye, Don *Source(s):* ASCP; EPMU; HARR; KINK; LCAR; STUW; VACH
Wilhousky, Peter J., Jr. 1902-1978 [composer, author, conductor]
Willoughy, Peter *Source(s):* CCE38 E68819; CCE65
Wilkin, John (William) 1946- [musician, songwriter]
Dayton, Ronnie *Source(s):* NOMG
Wilkin, Bucky *Source(s):* CCE64; CPOL PA-169-896; CPOL RE-673-293
Wilkin, Marijohn (née Melson) 1918- [singer, songwriter, pianist]
Den Mother of Nashville, The *Source(s):* MCCL
Melson, John *Source(s):* CCE56 Eunp
Wilkins, Robert Timothy 1896-1987 [guitarist, songwriter]
Keghouse *Source(s):* HARS
Oliver, Tim *Source(s):* PSND
Willaert, Adrian c.1480-1562 [composer]
Father of the Venetian School *Source(s):* MUWB
Willan, James Healey 1880-1968 [composer, teacher, organist, choirmaster]
Note(s): Portrait: ETUP 57:12 (Dec. 1939): 764
Clare, Raymond *Source(s):* GOTH; GOTT
Leigh, H. E. *Source(s):* GOTH; GOTT
Willcox, Frank [composer]
Lover, Frank *Source(s):* BLIC
Willcox, Toyah Ann 1958- [singer, songwriter, actress]
Toyah *Source(s):* HARR; LCAR
Willeby, Charles 1865- [composer]
Croone, Oliver *Source(s):* TPRF
Hay, Will *Source(s):* TPRF
Howard *Source(s):* TPRF
Nugent, Paul *Source(s):* TPRF
Ogden, Onaway *Source(s):* CPMU; TPRF
Wynne, Cuthbert *Source(s):* CCE33 R24450; TPRF
Willemetz, Albert 1887-1964 [librettist]
Metzvil *Source(s):* GROL; PIPE
Williams, Alan Robert 1910- [composer]
Alan, Robert *Source(s):* BUL1; BUL2

Williams, Alexander Balos 1906-1997 [trombonist, composer, bandleader]
Williams, Sandy *Source(s):* LCAR; MUWB
Williams, (Zeffrey) Andre 1936- [singer, songwriter, producer]
Black Godfather, The *Source(s):* http://www.furious.com/perfect/andrewilliams.html (6 Jan. 2005)
Father of Rap, The *Source(s):* AMUS
Mr. Bacon Fat *Source(s):* http://koti.mbnet.fi/wdd/andrewilliams.htm (6 Jan. 2005)
Mr. Rhythm *Source(s):* DBMU; HARS; http://www.furious.com/perfect/andrewilliams.html
Note(s): See also Elvis A(a)ron Presley.
Williams, Bacon Fat *Source(s):* DBMU; HARS; http://koti.mbnet.fi/wdd/andrewilliams.html
Williams, Aston [songwriter]
Williams, Deacon *Source(s):* CCE41 #45613 Eunp276934; PMUS
Williams, Charles Melvin 1908-1985 [composer, trumpeter, conductor]
Williams, Cootie *Source(s):* ASCP; BAKR; KINK; LCAR
Williams, Christopher a Beckett 1890-1956 [composer, journalist]
Note(s): Portraits: ETUP 57:12 (Dec. 1939): 764; *Musical Standard* (15 Feb. 1919): 59
Wood, Sinjon *Source(s):* CART; GDRM
Williams, Damon [songwriter, performer]
Damon *Source(s):* LCAR
Dangerous (Dame) *Source(s):* AMIR; PMUS-00
Williams, David (of Aberavon) [composer]
Jones, Adam *Source(s):* CPMU ("Song of the Mid Glamorgan Men" (1907))
Williams, Doc 1913-1970 [songwriter, fiddle player]
Note(s): Do not confuse with Doc Williams [i.e., Andrew John Smik, Jr.]
Williams, Curl(e)y *Source(s):* CCME; EPMU; LCAR; MCCL
Williams, Don 1939- [singer, guitarist, songwriter, actor]
Gentle Giant (of Country Music), The *Source(s):* AMUS; CCME; FLIN; MCCL; PSND
Laid Back Texan, The *Source(s):* FLIN
Mellow Balladeer, The *Source(s):* FLIN
Williams, Dorothy Snowdon 1967- [singer, songwriter, guitarist]
Williams, Dar *Source(s):* LCAR; MUHF
Williams, Egbert Austin 1874-1922 [comedian; singer, composer]
Note(s): Portraits: JASN; JAST; JASZ; WOLL (with Lottie Williams)
Austin, Bert *Source(s):* GREN; NGAM
Austin, Egbert *Source(s):* WORB
Greatest Comedian on the American Stage, The *Source(s):* PSND
King of Laughter, The *Source(s):* PSND
Pioneer Black Comedian *Source(s):* Smith, Eric Ledell. *Bert Williams: A Biography of the Pioneer Black Comedian.* McFarland, 1992.
Rogers, Duke *Source(s):* PSND
Son of Laughter *Source(s):* Rowland, Mabel. *Bert Williams; Son of Laughter*. New York: English Crafters, 1923.
Two Real Coons, The JASZ
Note(s): With George Walker; billed themselves.
Williams, Bert *Source(s):* JASZ; KINK; LCAR; PSND; SHAB p. 68; SUTT
Williams, Emery H., (Jr.) 1931- [singer, guitarist, pianist; songwriter]
Detroit Jr.[or Junior] *Source(s):* DBMU; EPMU; HARS; LCAR
Williams, Little, Jr. *Source(s):* HARS
Williams, George Dale 1916 (or 17)- [arranger, composer, bandleader]
Ford, Tom *Source(s):* CCE51 E54407; CPOL RE-25-526
Note(s): Also used by Lester O'Keefe.
Fox, The *Source(s):* KINK; PSND
Note(s): See also Hugo Wilhelm Friedhofer.
Williams, Fox *Source(s):* PSND
Williams, Gwilym E. 1887- [journalist, critic, librettist]
Brynallt *Source(s):* MELL
Williams, Hir(i)am (King) 1923-1952 (or 53) [singer, songwriter]
Drifting Cowboy, The *Source(s):* ALMN; PSND; SHAD
Father of Country Music, The *Source(s):* CASS
Note(s): See also William [or Bill] (Smith) Monroe & James [or Jimmie] (Charles) Rodgers.
First Rock 'n' Roll Singer, The *Source(s):* EPMU
Hillbilly Shakespeare, (The) *Source(s):* ALMN; CM38 p. 221; PSND; SHAD
King of Country Music, (The) *Source(s):* PSND; TCAN
Note(s): See also Roy (Claxton) Acuff, David Gordon Kirkpatrick & Willie (Hugh) Nelson.
King of Western Country Music, The *Source(s):* PSND
Luke the Drifter *Source(s):* EPMU; FLIN; LCAR; PSND; SHAD
Singing Kid, The *Source(s):* MCCL
Williams, Hank *Source(s):* ALMN; CCME; CM04; EPMU; LCAR; MCCL; PEN2; PSND
Williams, Jerry J. 1942- [singer, songwriter, producer]
Swamp Dogg *Source(s):* AMUS; EPMU; LCAR; PEN2

Williams, Joe Lee 1903-1982 [singer, instrumentalist, songwriter]
Note(s): Do not confuse with Joe Williams [i.e., James Goreed] (1918-1999).
Hill, King Solomon *Source(s):* HARS; PSND
Note(s): Reported but unconfirmed pseud. See also Joe Holmes.
Mississippi Big Joe *Source(s):* PSND
Williams, Big Joe *Source(s):* HARS; PSND
Williams, Po Jo *Source(s):* PSND

Williams, Joseph (Benjamin) 1847 (or 48)-1923 [composer]
Calmond, Mark *Source(s):* LCAR
Duchêsnes, Pierre *Source(s):* LCAR
Elliott, Lionel *Source(s):* CCE26 R34412; CCE50; LCAR
F. P. *Source(s):* CPMU ("Les Anges dans nos campagnes" & others)
Grenville, Arthur *Source(s):* LCAR
Huber, Conrad *Source(s):* LCAR
Pascal, Florian *Source(s):* GAN1; GAN2; GOTE; GOTH; GROL; NGDM
St. Maur, Emlyn *Source(s):* LCAR
Tourville, Charles *Source(s):* LCAR
Waldeck, J. B. *Source(s):* LCAR
Williams, Florian *Source(s):* LCAR

Williams, Joseph Leon 1935- [singer, instrumentalist, songwriter]
Little Papa Joe *Source(s):* HARS
Williams, Jody *Source(s):* CCE62; HARS
Williams, Sugar Boy *Source(s):* HARS

Williams, June Deniece 1951- [singer, songwriter]
Williams, Niecy *Source(s):* PSND

Williams, Morris 1809-1874 [hymnist]
Nicander *Source(s):* ROOM

Williams, Randall Hank 1949- [singer, songwriter, instrumentalist]
Bocephus *Source(s):* FLIN; MCCL
Hawkins, Thunderhead *Source(s):* http://www.countryreview.com/HankWilliamsJr. (7 Oct. 2002)
Williams, Hank, Jr. *Source(s):* FLIN; MCCL

Williams, Robert 1766-1850 [poet, hymnist]
Robert ap Gwilym Ddu *Source(s):* ROOM

Williams, Robert 1918-1999 [songwriter]
Troupe, Bobby *Source(s):* DRSC

Williams, Sarah 1841-1868 [composer]
Sadie *Source(s):* KILG

Williams, Shelton 1972- [singer, songwriter]
Williams, Hank, III *Source(s):* CM38

Williams, Sol(lie Paul) 1917-1985 [singer, songwriter, guitarist]
Man Who Sings Tobacco Best, The *Source(s):* EPMU
Williams, Jack *Source(s):* MCCL
Williams, Tex *Source(s):* CCE47; CCME; EPMU; MCCL

Williams, Spencer 1889-1965 [songwriter]
Gounod, Pierre *Source(s):* CCE59
Guillermos, S. Gualterio *Source(s):* CCE46 Efor1936
Jones, Duke *Source(s):* CCE51 R86366 ("Undertaker's Blues"); CCE52 R90612 ("Bitter Feelin' Blues")
Maguire, Hannibal *Source(s):* CCE51 R78739 ("The Duck's Quack")
Winchester, Tom *Source(s):* CCE51 R75981 ("My Sugar Man")
Note(s): Jt. pseud.: Theodore (F.) Morse.

Williams, Stanley R. 1894-1975 [clarinetist, arranger, composer; bandleader]
Williams, Fess *Source(s):* KINK; LCAR

Williams, Theodore, Jr. [songwriter]
T. V. *Source(s):* CCE63 Eunp99605 ("Soul Monkey Twist")
Vann, Teddy *Source(s):* CCE59-61; CCE68; CPOL RE-443-406; PMUS

Williams, Theodore Chickering 1855-1915 [minister, hymnist]
T. C. W. *Source(s):* JULN (Suppl.)

Williams, Thomas [song collector]
Hafrenydd *Source(s):* WILG

Williams, Victoria 1959- [singer, songwriter]
Williams, Louisiana *Source(s):* CM17

Williams (Pantycelyn), William 1717-1791 [hymnist, clergyman]
Note(s): Portrait: CYBH
Caledfryn, Gwilym *Source(s):* PSND
First Welsh Romantic Poet *Source(s):* YOUN
Watts of Wales, The *Source(s):* PSND
Williams, of Pantycelyn *Source(s):* LCAR

Williams, William A(ubrey) 1834- [composer]
Gwilym Gwent *Source(s):* CCE28 E684007; CPMU; WILG

Williams, William N(antlais) ?-before 1/28/1701 [composer]
Nantlais *Source(s):* CPMU

Williamson, Henry 1907-1962 [vaudeville dancer, singer, songwriter]
Williams, Henry *Source(s):* HARS
Williams, Rubberlegs *Source(s):* HARS

Williamson, (Mrs.) J. 19th cent. [hymnist, composer]
J. W., (Mrs.) *Source(s):* PSNN

Williamson, John Lee 1914-1948 [singer, harmonica player, lyricist]
Williamson, Sonny Boy *Source(s):* AMUS; EPMU; HARS; LCAR; NGDM
Note(s): Considered the original "Sonny Boy" Williamson. Also used by Aleck Ford & others.

Willingham, Foy 1915-1978 [singer, songwriter, guitarist; actor]
Willing, Foy *Source(s):* AMUS; CCME; MCCL
Willis, Aaron 1932- [singer, guitarist, songwriter]
Little Sonny *Source(s):* DBMU; HARS
Willis, Little Son *Source(s):* DBMU; HARS
Willis, Mac *Source(s):* LCAR
Willis, Harold 1928-1958 [singer, songwriter]
King of the Stroll *Source(s):* ASCC; PSND; SHAD; WORT
Sheik of the Blues *Source(s):* WORT (see under: Willis, Chuck)
Sheik of the Shake *Source(s):* SHAD
Willis, Chuck *Source(s):* AMUS; CCE56
Willis, James 1915-1981 [singer, songwriter]
Willis, Guy *Source(s):* CLAB
Willis, Robert L. 1934- [guitarist, songwriter]
Stoop Down Man, The *Source(s):* EPMU
Willis, Chick *Source(s):* AMUS; EPMU
Wills, Oscar 1916-1969 [guitarist, singer, songwriter]
Slim, TV *Source(s):* AMUS; LCAR
TV Slim *Source(s):* EPMU; HARS; LCAR
Wills, (James) Robert [or Bob] 1905-1975 [singer, bandleader, composer]
King of Western Swing, The *Source(s):* CM06; MCCL; NASF
Note(s): See also Donnell Clyde Cooley.
Willson, Mary Elizabeth (née Bliss) 1842-1906 [singer, songwriter]
Note(s): Sister of P(hilip) Bliss.
Jenny Lind of Sacred Melody *Source(s): American Women.* 2 v. Detroit: Gale Research, 1973.
Willson, (Robert Reiniger) Meredith 1902-1984 [composer, conductor, flutist, lyricist]
America's Music Man *Source(s):* SMIN
Iowa Toscanini, The *Source(s):* Skipper, John C. *Meredith Willson; The Unsinkable Music Man.* Mason City, Iowa: Savas Publishing Co., 2000, 31.
Mason City's Favorite Son *Source(s):* http://www.76trombones.net/News/Willson6.shtml (7 Oct. 2002)
Music Man *Source(s):* DESO-9
Reiniger, Robert *Source(s):* LCAR
Unsinkable Music Man, The *Source(s):* Skipper (see above)
Wilmann, Jacques Georges [composer]
Florencie, Jacques *Source(s):* GOTH
Wilson, Alexander Galbraith 1924- [composer, lyricist, author]
Wilson, Sandy *Source(s):* BREW; EPMU; GAN1; GAN2; LCAR; NGDM; PEN2
Wilson, Arthur 1944- [singer, songwriter]
Brown, Arthur *Source(s):* NOMG
Note(s): Also used by Isidore Kaufman.
Wilson, Chris (Richard) 1948- [composer, entertainer]
Note(s): Do not confuse with Chris Wilson [i.e., Richard Harvey Wilson]
Gandalf the Grey *Source(s):* CCE72
Grey, Gandolf [or Grandalf] T. *Source(s):* ASCP; CPOL SRu-455-282
Wiz(z)ard, The *Source(s):* CPOL PA-187-443
Note(s): See also Peter (Allen) Greenbaum.
Wilson, Clyde 1945- [singer, songwriter]
Mancha, Steve *Source(s):* CCE66-67; EPMU
Wilson, Earl (L.), Jr. 1942- [composer, author]
Wilson, Slugger *Source(s):* ASCP
Wilson, Edith 1906-1981 [singer, songwriter]
Aunt Jemima *Source(s):* HARS
Note(s): Also used by singer Tess Gardella; see MACE.
Wilson, Harry (Robert) 1901-1968 [composer, conductor, educator]
Greyson, Norman *Source(s):* CCE57; CCE62; CPOL RE-114-953; LCCC 1971-77
Note(s): Jt. pseud.: Walter (Charles) Ehret; see NOTES: Greyson, Norman.
Knight, Gerald *Source(s):* CCE65 E208707; CCE66 E224154
Note(s): Jt. pseud.: Walter (Charles) Ehret.
Mason, Geoffrey (M.) *Source(s):* CCE62; CPOL RE-478-255; CPOL RE-478-277
Reynolds, Robert *Source(s):* CCE56-57; CPOL RE-330-402
Wilson, Henry (James) Lane 1871-1915 [organist, pianist, composer, arranger]
Batten, Robert *Source(s):* CCE32 R21376; CPMU; GOTH; LCAR
Wilson, Hilda (Matilda Ellen) 1860-1918 [singer, composer, music educator]
Hope, Douglas *Source(s):* COHN; GOTH; GREN; HIXN
Wilson, Ira B(ishop) 1880-1950 [composer]
Note(s): Portraits: CYBH; ETUP 58:1 (Jan. 1940); HALL. Do not confuse with Ira Wilson, pseud. of Ottowill I. Benson.
Baldwin, Roxanna *Source(s):* CCE30 D27711
Benson, Noel *Source(s):* CCE38 E67232; CCE50, CCE55; CCE67; CPOL RE-108
Bishop, Robert *Source(s):* LCCC 1971-77 (see reference)
Bishop, Wilson *Source(s):* CCE36 E57015
Dale, Ruth *Source(s):* CCE30 D27748; CCE41 #11967* D39971; CCE47; CPOL RE-3-236
Davis, Mary Huntington *Source(s):* CCE34 E40924; CCE61
Fisher, I. B. *Source(s):* CCE37
Fisher, Miriam Lois *Source(s):* CCE34 D28428; CCE42 #34161* D76155

Fisher, Olga Jane *Source(s):* CCE62
Fox, Edward *Source(s):* CCE57
Note(s): Also used by Hans Haass.
Fox, Joseph Ed(ward) *Source(s):* CCE30 D28180; CPOL RE-1-904
Gilbert, A(rthur) Th(omas) *Source(s):* CCE35 E46344; CCE61; CPOL RE-1-918
Holton, Fred B. *Source(s):* CCE30 E14423; CCE37 R56095; CPOL RE-97; CYBH; LCAR
Lane, C(harles) F(rancis) *Source(s):* CCE31 E25341; CCE45 #719* D76387; CPOL RE-870
Lane, Emily *Source(s):* CCE47
Lighthill, Norman *Source(s):* CCE30 E13436 & D27833; TPRF
Owen, Anne *Source(s):* CCE30 E14823; CCE41 #37606* D76043
Powers, Kane *Source(s):* CCE48 R32405 ("Hail and Farewell")
Price, Benton *Source(s):* CCE34
Note(s): Also used by Roger Cole Wilson.
Williams, Elton J. *Source(s):* LCPC E66340 ("The Old Barn Dance")
Note(s): Jt. pseud.: Ellen Jane Lorenz.
Wilson, Bishop *Source(s):* CCE21 Index
Wil(l)trie, H. B. *Source(s):* CCE38 E67235
Note(s): Jt. pseud.: H(enry) W. Petrie.

Wilson, J(ames) V(ernon) [songwriter]
Wilson, Pinky [or Pinkie] *Source(s):* CCE40 #39067 E89695; CCE49 R44099; STC1; STC2

Wilson, Jane 1832?-1872 [hymnist]
Sister Beatrice *Source(s):* JULN (Suppl.)

Wilson, John 1785-1854 [author, poet]
Note(s): See PSND & LCAR for additional nonmusic-related pseudonyms.
North, Christopher *Source(s):* GOTT; LCAR; PSND

Wilson, John Anthony (Burgess) 1917-1993 [author, critic, composer]
Burgess, Anthony *Source(s):* BAKO; BAKR; BAKT; GOTH; GROL; LCAR; MUWB; PSND
Kell, Joseph *Source(s):* GOTH; LCAR; PSND

Wilson, John F(loyd) 1929- [composer, author, teacher]
Floyd, William J. *Source(s):* ASCP
West, Martin *Source(s):* ASCP; CCE68

Wilson, Johnny Ancil 1935- [composer, author]
Wilson, Peanuts *Source(s):* ASCP

Wilson, Lena c.1898-c.1939 [singer, songwriter]
Coleman, Nelly *Source(s):* HARS; LCAR

Wilson, Nathaniel 1968- [rapper, songwriter]
G Rap *Source(s):* AMUS
Kool G(enius) Rap *Source(s):* AMIR; AMUS; LCAR; PMUS-00

Wilson, Norris D. 1938- [singer, songwriter, publisher]
Wilson, Norro *Source(s):* NASF; PSND

Wilson, Richard Harvey [songwriter]
Wilson, Chris *Source(s):* CPOL
Note(s): Do not confuse with Chris (Richard) Wilson who used: Gandolf [or Grandalf] T. Grey.

Wilson, Roger Cole 1912- [composer, arranger, conductor]
Ahrens, Thomas *Source(s):* ASCP; CCE41 #11580* D39970
Cole, Adam *Source(s):* CCE47
Landon, Stewart *Source(s):* ASCP; CCE41 #11580* D39970; CCE50; CCE61;CPOL RE-1-921
Price, Anthony *Source(s):* CCE71; CCE75
Price, Benton [or Benson] *Source(s):* ASCP; CCE43 #39621 E117516; CCE61 E15383; CCE65
Note(s): Also used by Ira B(ishop) Wilson?
Price, Walter *Source(s):* ASCP; CCE46 E1852
Rogers, Lee *Source(s):* ASCP; CCE33 E34363; CCE65-66; CPOL RE-107
Stewart, Norman *Source(s):* CCE58; CPOL RE-314-969
West, Harold *Source(s):* ASCP; CCE41 #36781 E96663

Wilson, Wesley 1893-1958 [singer, keyboardist, songwriter]
Jenkins *Source(s):* AMUS; HARS
Kid Sox *Source(s):* AMUS
Pigmeat Pete *Source(s):* AMUS; HARS
Socks *Source(s):* AMUS
Wilson, Kid *Source(s):* EPMU; PSND
Wilson, Socks [or Sox] *Source(s):* AMUS; HARS

Winawer [or Winaver], Bruno 1883-1944 [author]
Winbrun, O. *Source(s):* PIPE

Wind, Charlotte 1927- [composer]
Barron, Bebe *Source(s):* BAKR (see under: Barron, Louis); DWCO

Wind, Juergen [songwriter]
Wind, Jay *Source(s):* SONG

Windisch, Thomas 1914- [composer]
Roland, Uwe *Source(s):* KOMP; KOMS; PFSA
Wanda, Mara *Source(s):* BUL3; KOMP; PFSA

Windsperger, Lothar 1885-1935 [composer, editor, teacher]
Artok, H. *Source(s):* COMP
Artok, L(eo) *Source(s):* CCE50 R61346 ("Serenade"); CCE54 R130694 ("Alter Refrain"); COMP
Note(s): Schott house name? Also used by Ernest Toch.

Wingard, James Charles 1931- [composer, author]
Wingard, Bud *Source(s):* ASCP

Winkel, Therese Emilie Henriette aus dem 1784-1867 [harpist, teacher, composer]
Comala, (Theorosa) *Source(s):* COHN; HIXN; IBIM

Winkler, Gerhard 1906-1977 [composer]
Bern, Ben *Source(s):* CCE59-60; CPOL RE-321-268; KOMP; KOMS; PFSA; RIES

Note(s): Do not confuse with Ben Bernie (1891-1943), composer, violinist.
Eremit, Paul *Source(s):* CCE56; CPOL RE-191-811
Hansen, Peter Jan *Source(s):* CCE54-55; CPOL RE-116-984
Heidemann, Jürgen *Source(s):* CCE55-56; CPOL RE-191-859
Herman, Charles *Source(s):* CCE54
Herman(n), G(erd) *Source(s):* CCE55; CPOL RE-108-905; KOMS; PFSA
Kirchner, Alex *Source(s):* CCE56; CPOL RE-191-808
Scholz, Rudi *Source(s):* CCE55
Winkler, Karl [or Carl] Gottfried Theodor 1775-1856 [poet, composer]
Faifer von Faifersberg *Source(s):* APPL p. 12
Guido *Source(s):* PIPE
Hell, Theodor *Source(s):* GROL; LCAR; LOWN; NGDM; PIPE; PSND
Winner, Joseph E(astburn) 1837-1918 [composer, music publisher]
Betta *Source(s):* NGAM; SPTH p. 173
Eastburn, (R. A.) *Source(s):* CCE56; DICH; FULD; KILG; LCAR; NGAM; SPTH p. 173
Note(s): See NOTES: Eastburn.
Winner, Septimus 1827-1902 [composer, songwriter, music publisher]
Note(s): Portraits: CYBH; ETUP 58:1 (Jan. 1940); HAMM
Alice *Source(s):* CPMU ("Linked with Many Bitter Tears" (1868))
Eastburn *Source(s):* Claghorn, C. E. *The Mocking Bird; The Life and Diary of Its Author, Sep. Winner* Philadelphia: Magee Press, 1937.
Note(s): See NOTES: Eastburn.
Guyer, Percy *Source(s):* CYBH; LCAR; NGAM; Claghorn (see above)
Guyer, Stacy *Source(s):* LCPC E251796
Hawthorne, A. W. *Source(s):* OCLC 37735698 ("The Dance of the Sprites")
Note(s): Possible pseud.
Hawthorne, Alice *Source(s):* CART; LCAR; NGAM; WCAB 1:310; Claghorn (see above)
Masen, Mark *Source(s):* CYBH; NGDM
Mason, Mark *Source(s):* LCAR; NGAM; WCAB 1:310; Claghorn (see above)
Stenton, Paul *Source(s):* CYBH; LCAR; NGAM; Claghorn (see above)
Street, Apsley *Source(s):* CCE11 R2171; LCAR; SPTH p. 599; Claghorn (see above)
Winogradsky, Bernard [or Boris] 1909-1994 [dancer, theatrical agent, producer]
Delfont, Bernard *Source(s):* GAN2; LCAR
Lord Delfont of Stepney *Source(s):* GAN2
Winston, Phil [lyricist]
Wynn, Paul *Source(s):* BLUE
Note(s): Also used by Benjamin Samberg.
Winter, Gloria Frances 1938- [songwriter]
Winter, (Sister) Miriam Therese *Source(s):* ASCP; HIXN
Winter, Johnny 1944- [singer, guitarist, songwriter]
Texas Guitar Slim *Source(s):* HARS
Winter, William 1836-1917 [lyricist]
Vale, Mark *Source(s):* LCAR; Root, Deane L. *American Popular Stage Music.* UMI Research Press, 1981, 229.
Winterfeld, David Robert 1899-1978 [playwright, composer, lyricist]
Note(s): Son of Jean Gilbert [i.e., Max Winterfeld]
Bertram, Rudolph *Source(s):* GAN2; PIPE
Buda, Karl *Source(s):* GAN2; PIPE
Gilbert, Robert *Source(s):* GAN1; GAN2; LCAR; WORB
Honer, Hans *Source(s):* PIPE
Robert, Gilbert *Source(s):* WORB
Roberts, Harry *Source(s):* WORB
Weber, David *Source(s):* LCAR; PIPE
Winter, Robert *Source(s):* LCAR (see notes)
Winterfeld, Max 1879-1942 [composer]
Note(s): Father of David Robert Winterfeld.
Gilbert, Jean *Source(s):* BAKO; CPMU; GAN1; GAN2; GROL; LCAR; NGDO; PIPE
Winters, June 1918- [composer, singer]
Whitman, Jerry *Source(s):* ASCP; CCE55 Eunp
Wintersteen, John Schaeffer 1908- [composer, author, teacher]
Winters, John (S.) *Source(s):* ASCP; CCE68; CLRA
Winthrop, Gideon William 1919- [composer, conductor, educator]
Waldrop, Gid(eon William) *Source(s):* PSND
Winzenhörlein, Heinrich Joseph 1819-1901 [singer, author, composer]
Vincent, Heinrich Joseph *Source(s):* BAKO; BAKR; MACM; MELL; PRAT; PSND
Wircker, Johann fl. 1548-72 [composer, singer, teacher]
Hymaturgis, Johann *Source(s):* NGDM
Testorius, Johann *Source(s):* NGDM
Weber, Johann *Source(s):* NGDM
Note(s): Possible variant surname.
Wirtel, Thomas Kemper 1937- [composer]
Noor, Thomas Shabda *Source(s):* CPOL PAu-2-518-390
Nur, Shabda *Source(s):* CPOL PA-236-404; GOTH
Wirth, Carel Lodewijk Willem 1841-1935 [teacher, composer]
Wirtz, Charles Louis *Source(s):* MACM
Wise, Michael 1646-1687 [musician, composer]
Scotland, John *Source(s):* OCLC 43201004
Note(s): "Glee a 3 voci" ("Lightly Tread 'Tis Hallowed Ground"). Pseud. sometimes attributed to Henry Purcell; however, F. B. Zimmerman, in his *Henry Purcell; An Annotated Catalogue of His Music* ascribes the work to Michael Wise. In CPMU: the same work by "John Scotland" is listed under George Berg.

Wise, Robert Russell 1915-1996 [guitarist, songwriter, composer]
Wise, Chubby *Source(s):* LCAR; MCCL
Wiseman, Malcolm [or Mac] (B.) 1925- [singer, songwriter, guitarist]
Voice with a Heart, The *Source(s):* CM19; MCCL
Wiseman, Scott(y) (Greene) 1909-1981 [guitarist, songwriter]
Note(s): Portraits: CCME; MILL
Lulu Belle and Scotty *Source(s):* CCME; STAC
Note(s): Jt. pseud.: with wife Myrtle Eleanor Cooper (Wiseman).
Scotty *Source(s):* EPMU; MCCL
Skyland Scotty *Source(s):* CCE63; EPMU; MCCL; NASF
Sweethearts of Country Music, The *Source(s):* EPMU; STAC
Note(s): Jt. pseud.: with wife Myrtle Eleanor Cooper (Wiseman).
Wisner, James [or Jimmy] (Joseph) 1931- [pianist, arranger, songwriter, producer]
Adams, Jason *Source(s):* CCE65
Kokomo *Source(s):* EPMU; LCAR
Whiz, The *Source(s):* http://www.rockailly.nl/references/messages/jimmy_wisner.htm (9 May 2005)
Wither, George 1588-1667 [satirist, poet, hymnist]
Britain's Remembrancer *Source(s):* CART
Free Man, though a Prisoner, A *Source(s):* CART
Witherspoon, James [or Jimmy] 1923-1997 [singer, bassist, songwriter]
Spoon, (The) *Source(s):* CM19; HARS
Wittal, Roland 1936- [composer]
Rolli, der lustige Geiger *Source(s):* KOMS; PFSA
Tempo, Fred *Source(s):* KOMS; PFSA
Wittstatt, Hans(-Artur) 1923-1988 [composer]
Cardello, Rolf *Source(s):* CCE64 Efor103668 ("Rendezvous in alt-Wien")
Note(s): Also used by Rüdiger Piesker.
Halger, Hans *Source(s):* CCE60; CCE62; KOMP; PFSA; RIES
Wittstatt, Pepe *Source(s):* CCE64
Witzleben, (Karl) August (Friedrich) von 1773-1839 [librettist]
Trömer, August von *Source(s):* WORB
Tromlitz, A(ugust) von *Source(s):* LCAR; STGR; WORB
Wodehouse, P(elham) G(renville) 1881-1975 [author, composer]
Braley, Berton *Source(s):* CCE45 #22283, 425 R137075
Brooke-Haven, P. *Source(s):* PSND
Grenville, Pelham *Source(s):* PSND
P. G. *Source(s):* BBDP
Plum, J. *Source(s):* PSND
West, C. P. *Source(s):* PSND
Williams, J. Walker *Source(s):* PSND
Windham, Basil *Source(s):* PSND
Wodehouse, Plum *Source(s):* BBDP
Wodiczka, T. mentioned 1757 [violinist, composer]
Lustig *Source(s):* MACM
Woëlfmann, Georges [composer]
Valentin, Patrice *Source(s):* CPMU (publication date 1866)
Wohl, Yehuda 1904-1988 [composer]
Bentow, Yehuda *Source(s):* BAKE
Wohlmuth, Alois 1847 (or 52)-1930 [actor, author]
Errats *Source(s):* PIPE
Wolcot, John 1738-1819 [author, poet]
Pindar, Peter *Source(s):* LCAR; PSND; ROOM; WORB
Note(s): Also used by George Daniel & C. F. Lawler.
Wolf, Aaron 1817-1870 [composer]
Berlijn, Anton *Source(s):* BAKO; BAKR
Wolf, Hans 1927- [composer]
Carvo, Erich *Source(s):* KOMP; KOMS; PFSA
Wolf, Hubert 1934-1981 [composer]
Valcek, Wenzel *Source(s):* CCE65-66; KOMS; PFSA
Wolf, Hugo 1830-1900 [composer]
Note(s): Portrait: ETUP 58:1 (Jan. 1940): 64
Fluchu *Source(s):* GROL
Richard Wagner of the Lied *Source(s):* http://www.classical.net/music/books/biography/w.html (13 Apr. 2005)
Wagner of the Lied *Source(s):* http://www.classical.net/music/books/biography/w.html
Wolf, Johann(es) Wilhelm 1817-1855 [author]
Laicus, Johann(es) *Source(s):* PIPE; WORB
Wolf, Tom [singer, songwriter, cartoonist]
Prince of Puns *Source(s):* http://www.spiritsong.com/TomWolf/bio.html (7 Oct. 2002)
Wolfe, Randy 1951-1997 [guitarist, songwriter]
California, Randy *Source(s):* EPMU; LCAR
Wolff, Ben [songwriter]
Boilerhouse *Source(s):* CPOL PA-683-585; SONG
Note(s): Jt. pseud.: Andy Dean & Ben Barson.
Wolff, Erich J(acques) 1874-1913 [composer, pianist]
Note(s): Portrait: ETUP 58:2 (Feb. 1940): 138
Wolffsgruber *Source(s):* STGR v. 4/pt.1
Wolff, Fanny c. 1890- [dancer, songwriter]
Fanchon *Source(s):* CCE50 R62576 ("Islam Greets You"); LCAR
Wolff, Georg 1924- [composer]
Woff-Zawade *Source(s):* PFSA
Wolff, Marco [or Mike] [dancer, songwriter]
Marco *Source(s):* CCE50 R62576 ("Islam Greets You"); LCAR (see under: Wolff, Fanny)
Note(s): See also Marco Antonio Muniz.
Wolfgang, Eberhardt 1923-1993 [composer]
Steffen, Wolfgang *Source(s):* GREN
Wolfson, Maxwell A(lexander) 1923-1997 [composer, author]
Jay, Mac *Source(s):* CCE65

Marc, Ronald *Source(s):* ASCP
Wolfson, Mac(k) *Source(s):* ASCP; CCE53-54; CCE65
Wolkenstein, David 1534-1592 [mathematician, composer, writer on music]
Nephelius, David *Source(s):* NGDM
Wölki, Konrad 1904-1983 [composer]
Klingemann, Klaus *Source(s):* KOMS; PFSA
Wolpe, Stefan 1902-1972 [composer]
Beethoven of Contemporary Music *Source(s):*http://gram.main.nc.us/~bhammel/MUSIC/pleskow.html (7 Apr. 2005)
Wolquier, Nicolaus c.1480-1541 [theorist, historiographer]
Volcyr, Nicolaus *Source(s):* GROL; LCAR
Wollick, Nicolaus *Source(s):* GROL; LCAR
Wong, Siu Junn 1938- [composer]
Wong, Betty Anne *Source(s):* BUL3
Wongtschowski, Adolf Friedrich 1919- [author]
Buri, Friedrich (W.) *Source(s):* PIPE
Wood, Douglas Albert 1950- [composer, producer]
McAllister David *Source(s):* ASCP; CCE76
Wood, (Sir) Henry Joseph 1869-1944 [conductor, composer, writer]
Note(s): Portraits: MUSO (Nov. 1902): 138; *Musical Standard* (27 Sept. 1902)
Klenovsky, (Paul) *Source(s):* BAKO; BREW; CASS; CPMU; LCAR; SPIE
Maker of the Proms *Source(s):* BAKO
Timber *Source(s):* BREW; CASS; GROL; SPIE
Wood, Lauren 1950- [songwriter]
Chunky *Source(s):* CPOL PA-62-349; PSNN
Wood, Mathilda Alice Victoria 1870-1922 [singer, composer, actress]
Delmere, Bella *Source(s):* HIXN
Lloyd, Marie *Source(s):* HIXN; LCAR
Wood, Ralph (Walter) 1902- [composer, businessman]
Greenwood, K. *Source(s):* NGDM
Note(s): Jt. pseud. with wife (name not given).
Wood, Ulysses Adrian 1946- [singer, songwriter, producer]
Wood, Roy *Source(s):* AMUS; EPMU; PEN1
Woodberry, Isaac Baker 1819-1858 [composer, editor, writer on music]
Note(s): Portrait: CYBH
Woodbury, Isaac Baker *Source(s):* BAKR
Woodbridge, Hudson 1904-1981 [guitarist, pianist, singer, songwriter]
Eager, Jimmy *Source(s):* HARS; LCAR; PSND
Guitar Wizard, The *Source(s):* AMUS; CM20; CM25; EPMU; HARS; PSND
Smith, Honey Boy *Source(s):* HARS; PSND
Tampa Red *Source(s):* AMUS; CM20; CM25; EPMU; HARS; LCAR; PSND
Whittaker, Hudson *Source(s):* CM25; EPMU; HARS; LCAR; PSND; ROOM
Whittaker, Tampa Red *Source(s):* CCE46 Eunp
Woodhouse, Charles (John) 1879-1939 [composer, violinist, arranger]
Note(s): In CCE44 given names: John Charles . Portrait: ETUP 58:2 (Feb. 1940): 138
Colin, Gustave *Source(s):* CCE47 R25600; CPMU
Gray, Ronald *Source(s):* CCE65 R358614
Morand, Prosper *Source(s):* CCE65 R358613
Woodhouse, Evelyn [arranger]
Adew *Source(s):* KILG
Note(s): Jt. pseud.: T. L. Mitchell-Innes, Algernon Drummond & W. J. Cory.
Woodrow, Jane (née Blair) 19th cent. [composer, music educator]
Riche, J. B. *Source(s):* HIXN
Woods, Corey 1968- [songwriter, performer]
Raekwon *Source(s):* AMIR; AMUS; PMUS-00
Woods, H. Clarence 1888-1956 [composer]
Ragtime Wonder of the South *Source(s):* PERF
Woods, Henry MacGregor 1896-1970 [composer]
Woods, Harry *Source(s):* EPMU; GAMM
Woods, John Joseph 1849-1932 [composer]
Orpheus *Source(s):* http://www.mch.govt.nz/anthem/history.htm (18 Mar. 2005)
Note(s): Also used by Karl [or Carl] Kossmaly.
Woods, Oscar 1900-c.1956 [guitarist, songwriter]
Lone Wolf, The *Source(s):* HARS
Street Rustler, The *Source(s):* HARS
Troubadour, The *Source(s):* HARS
Woods, Buddy *Source(s):* HARS; LCAR
Woodward, Case [singer, songwriter]
Case *Source(s):* CM38
Woodward, Keren [songwriter]
Bananarama *Source(s):* CPOL PA-343-391; SONG
Note(s): Jt. pseud.: Sarah Dallin & Siobhan Fahey.
Woodworth, G(eorge) Wallace 1902-1969 [conductor, organist, writer on music]
G. W. W. *Source(s):* CCE59; CPMU
Woodworth, Samuel 1785-1842 [poet, journalist]
Note(s): See LCAR for additional nonmusic-related pseuds.
Selim *Source(s):* FULD p. 413; LCAR
Wooldridge, Anna Marie 1930- [singer, songwriter, actress]
Aminata *Source(s):* CM09; NGDJ
Anna Marie *Source(s):* AMUS; CM09; EPMU; NGDJ
Lee, Gaby *Source(s):* AMUS; CM09; EPMU; NGDJ
Lincoln, Abbey *Source(s):* AMUS; CM09; EPMU; LCAR; NGDJ; PEN2
Moseka, (Aminata) *Source(s):* CM09; EPMU; GRAT; LCAR; NGDJ
Wooldridge, Gaby *Source(s):* AMUS; NGDJ

Wooley, Shelby F. 1921-2003 [singer, guitarist, songwriter, actor]
Colder, Ben *Source(s):* AMUS; ASCP; CCME; EPMU; MCCL; STAC
Wooley, Sheb *Source(s):* ASCC; CCME; EPMU; STAC
Woolnough, Peter Allen 1944-1992 [pianist, singer, songwriter]
Note(s): Some sources give original name as: Allen, Peter Woolnough.
Allen, Peter (Woolnough) *Source(s):* DIMA; EPMU; HARR
Note(s): Some sources give original name as: Allen, Peter Woolnough.
Woolsey, Mary Hale [or Maryhale] 1899-1969 [author, songwriter]
Hale, Eugenia *Source(s):* ASCP; LCAR
Hale, Mary *Source(s):* ASCP; LCAR
Snow, T(erry) *Source(s):* ASCP; CCE50 R67233 ("When It's Springtime in the Rockies"); LCAR
Woolsey, Sarah Chauncey 1835 (or 45)-1905 [poet, hymnist]
Coolidge, Susan *Source(s):* CLAC; LCAR; WORB
Worland, Bill 1921-1976 [composer, pianist]
Franks, Gordon *Source(s):* MUWB
Groves, Ron *Source(s):* MUWB
Worrell, Bernie 1945- [composer, keyboardist, singer]
Insurance Man for the Funk *Source(s):* CM11 p. vii
Worsley, John, (II) 1931- [songwriter, composer]
Vandyke, Les *Source(s):* CCE60-61; CCE63; CPOL RE-386-406; IMDB
Note(s): "Les Vandyke" is listed as a pseud. under both John Worsley & John(ny) Worth. In LCCC 1955-70 works by John Worsley under the name "Les Vandyke" were published by various companies, incl. Young-Star Music, Ltd. & Robbins, while those by "John(ny) Worth" were published by Essex Music, Ltd.
Worth, John(ny) *Source(s):* IMDB
Wradatsch, Bruno 1883-1954 [playwright]
Hardt-Warden, Bruno *Source(s):* GAN1; GAN2; WORB
Wray, Floyd Collin 1960- [singer, guitarist, songwriter]
Raye, Collin *Source(s):* LCAR; MCCL
Wray, Bubba *Source(s):* MCCL
Wray, Lincoln 1935- [musician, singer, songwriter]
Wray, Link *Source(s):* ALMN
Wreford, John Reynell (Raymond George) 1899-1881 [hymnist]
Note(s): Given names also listed: Reynell John.
J. R. W. *Source(s):* PSND
Lovering, John *Source(s):* CCE52

Wrencher, John Thomas 1923-1977 [singer, songwriter]
One Armed John *Source(s):* DBMU; HARS; LCAR
Wright, Al George 1916- [composer, author, conductor]
Stone, George *Source(s):* ASCP
Wright, Carter Land 1911-2003 [composer, vocal coach]
Kent, Gary *Source(s):* ASCP
Wright, Eric 1963-1995 [rapper]
Easy-E(ric) *Source(s):* EPMU; LCAR
Wright Erica 1971 (or 72)- [singer, songwriter]
Badu, Erykah *Source(s):* CM26; LCAR; NOMG; PMUS-00
Wright, Eugene [or Gene] (Joseph) 1923- [bassist, teacher, composer]
Senator *Source(s):* GROL
Wright, Fred Howard [composer]
Howard, Fred *Source(s):* CLRA
Wright, Henry 1852-1914 [songwriter]
Fionn *Source(s):* CPMU
Whyte, Henry *Source(s):* OCLC 43229166
Wright, John Robert, Jr. 1942- [singer, songwriter, instrumentalist]
Wright, Bobby *Source(s):* MCCL
Wright, Johnnie Robert 1914- [singer, songwriter]
Johnnie & Jack *Source(s):* MCCL
Note(s): Jt. pseud.: Jack Anglin.
Wright, Julian 1925- [songwriter]
Butler, Wright *Source(s):* CCE56 R169029 ("Ever So Goosey")
Note(s): Jt. pseud.: Ralph (T.) Butler.
Cloff, Albert *Souce(s):* CCE29 Efor2992
Note(s): Jt. pseud.: Ralph (T.) Butler.
Lloyd, George *Source(s):* CCE33 Efor28901& Efor29862; CCE60
Note(s): For titles of works composed under joint pseuds., See NOTES: Lloyd, George.
Wallis, C. Jay *Source(s):* CCE30 Efor8733; LCPC letter cited (4 Jan. 1930)
Note(s): Jt. pseud.: Ralph (T.) Butler, Gustav Krenkel & C(harles) J(oseph) Edwards.
Wright, Lawrence 1888-1964 [composer, arranger, publisher]
Ambroise, Victor *Source(s):* CCE61; CPOL RE-95-422; GAMM; GREN; REHH
Cavanagh, Kathleen *Source(s):* GREN
Edgar Wallace of Songwriters, The *Source(s):* CASS; HARD
Kerrigan, W. *Source(s):* GAMM; REHH
Leslie, Edgar *Source(s):* CCE27 E662981; CCE54 R129277 ("Are You Listening Tonight")
Lynton, Everett *Source(s):* CCE54 Efor25354; CPOL RE-33-828; GAMM; GREN; REHH

McCarthy, Gene *Source(s):* CCE45 #40244 R14007; CCE46 R 13142
Note(s): Pseud. of Horatio Nicholls, [i.e., Lawrence Wright]. Jt. pseud.: Worton David.
Nicholls, Horatio *Source(s):* BREW; CASS; CPMU; GROL; GREN; KILG; MUWB; REHH
Nicholls, J. H. *Source(s):* CCE29
O'Hagen, Betsy *Source(s):* CPMU; GREN; MUWB; NGDM; REHH
O'Hogan, Betsy *Source(s):* KILG
Note(s): Possible typographical error.
O'Neil, Douglas *Source(s):* CCE45 #63817, 1263 R141900
Note(s): Jt. pseud.: Worton David.
Paree, Paul *Source(s):* CCE65; GAMM; GREN; REHH
Shirley, Lilian *Source(s):* GAMM; GREN
Shirley-Ospen, David *Source(s):* CCE44 #35637, 827 R130039
Note(s): Jt. pseud.: Worton David, R. Penso & Lilian Shirley [i.e., Lawrence Wright]
Treynor, Betty *Source(s):* CCE59
Williams, Gene *Source(s):* CPMU; CPOL RE-65-732; GREN; MUWB; NGDM; REHH
World's Greatest Songwriter *Source(s):* WHIC p. 162
Note(s): Sobriquet for Horatio Nicholls that Lawrence Wright used when he announced his publishing firm had secured Nicholls'services. Only those in the trade knew Wright and Nicholls were the same person. (WHIC)

Wright, Lilian Cochrane 1944- [composer, author, singer]
Cochrane, Talie *Source(s):* ASCP

Wright, Marvin M. 1911- [composer, author, pianist]
Wright, Lefty *Source(s):* ASCP; LCAR

Wright, Rita 1946-2004 [singer, lyricist, songwriter]
Syreeta *Source(s):* LCAR
Wright, Syreeta *Source(s):* LCAR; PSND

Wright, Robert B. 1915- [composer, author, violinist]
Note(s): Do ot confuse with Robert C(raig) Wright (1914-), pianist, composer.
Bruce, Robert *Source(s):* ASCC
Note(s): Also used by Fanny [i.e., Frances] J(ane) Crosby.

Wright, Willard Huntington 1888-1939 [author, music critic]
Van Dine, S. S. *Source(s):* LCAR
Van Dyne, S. S. *Source(s):* GRAN

Wrisch, Gerhard 1927- [composer]
Avera, Franco *Source(s):* KOMP; PFSA
Oberpointer, F. *Source(s):* KOMP; PFSA

Wroblewski, Ptaszyn 1936- [saxophonist, composer]
Jan *Source(s):* PSND

Wuiet, Caroline 1766-1835 [pianist, novelist, composer]
Auffdiener, Caroline Wuiet, baronne *Source(s):* LCAR
Donna Elidora *Source(s):* COHN; HIXN, JACK
Elidora, Donna *Source(s):* COHN; HIXN; JACK
Réfugiée *Source(s):* LCAR
Vuiet, Caroline *Source(s):* JACK; LCAR

Wunderman, Leslie [or Lesley] (Joy) 1962- [singer, songwriter]
Dayne, Taylor *Source(s):* CM04; LCAR

Wuolijoki, Hella (Maria) (née Murrik) 1886-1954 [author]
Tervapää, Juhani *Source(s):* LCAR; PIPE
Tuli, Felix *Source(s):* PIPE

Würfel, Václav Vilem 1790-1832 [pianist, conductor, composer]
Werfel, Wenzel *Source(s):* NGDM
Würfel, Wenzel Wilhelm *Source(s):* BAKO; BAKR

Wurm, Alice 1868-1958 [pianist, teacher, composer]
Verne, Alice *Source(s):* BAKR

Wurm, Mary [or Marie] (J. A.) 1860-1938 [pianist, composer, writer on music]
Note(s): Portrait: ETUP 58:4 (Apr. 1940): 282
Verne, Mary [or Marie] (J. A.) *Source(s):* BAKR; COHN; GOTH; HIXN

Würmli, Emil 1920- [composer]
Moliveri, Emilio *Source(s):* REHH; SUPN

Wurmser, Frédéric (Robert Léopold) 1932- [musicologist]
Robert, Frédéric *Source(s):* CCE68; NGDM

Württemberg, Eberhard von 1883-1896 [composer]
Eberhard *Source(s):* STGR

Wüst, Paul c.1473-c.1540 [minstrel, composer]
Obscoenus, Paulus *Source(s):* NGDM
Wiet(ius), Paul *Source(s):* NGDM

Wüsthoff, Klaus 1922- [composer]
Jupiter, Milt *Source(s):* RIES
Note(s): Name form in biographical entry.
Milt, Jupiter *Source(s):* RIES
Note(s): See reference has "Milt" listed as the surname?
Winter, N(orbert) *Source(s):* CCE58; CCE61; CCE63; CPOL RE-313-738

Wycherley, Ronald 1940 (or 41)-1983 [singer, songwriter]
Fury, Billy *Source(s):* EPMU; NOMG
Wilberforce, Wilber *Source(s):* CCE60

Wychodil(-Hofmeister), Gert 1923- [composer]
Colter, Frank *Source(s):* CCE58; KOMP; PFSA
Hofmeister, Trude *Source(s):* CCE53; CCE60
Vychodil, V. *Source(s):* KOMP

Wilden, Gert [or Gerd] *Source(s):* CCE53-57; CCE62-65; PFSA; RIES
Wilden, Trude *Source(s):* CCE54-55
Wilton, Jerry *Source(s):* KOMP
Wychodil, Trude *Source(s):* CCE53
Wyldebore, John fl. 1497-1538 [composer]
Dygon, John *Source(s):* NGDM
Wylie, William 1938- [songwriter, music publisher]
Martin, Bill *Source(s):* EPMU; http://musiclycos.com/artist (9 Dec. 2004)
Note(s): Also used by William [or Billy] (Martin) Joel & William (W.) MacPherson.
Wyneken, Wulff 1898- [composer, conductor]
Einegg, Erich *Source(s):* MACM
Wyngaerde, Antoine de ?-1498 (or 99) [composer]
Brussel, Antoine de *Source(s):* WORB
Bruxelas, Antoine de *Source(s):* WORB
DeVigne, Antoine *Source(s):* NGDM
Wynschenk, Howard (E.) [songwriter]
Romaine, Robert *Source(s):* BLIC; CCE62-63
Wysocki, Gerd von 1930- [musician, composer]
Banter, Harald *Source(s):* CCE55-56; CCE60-61; PIPE
Guntz, Werner *Source(s):* CCE50
Wyss, Rudolf 1932- [composer]
Keysten, Ralf *Source(s):* REHH; SUPN
Wyzewski, Théodore de 1862-1917 [musicologist]
Wyzewa, Thédore de *Source(s):* BAKE; LCAR

– X –

Xenakis, Iannis 1922-2001 [composer, mathmatician]
Note(s): Portrait: OB01
Kastrounis, Konstantin *Source(s):* http://www.thewholenote.com/wholenote_mar_01/hear.html (1 Aug. 2005)
Xiao, Shuxian 1905-1991 [composer, educator]
Hsiao, Shu-sien *Source(s):* DWCO
Note(s): Variant form.

– Y –

Yablonik, Herman [or Hyman] 1903-1981 [actor, composer, playwright]
Der Payatz *Source(s):* CCE62
Payatz, Der *Source(s):* CCE62
Yablokoff, Herman *Source(s):* CCE60-61; PSND
Ziegfeld of the Jewish Stage, The *Source(s):* PSND
Yablonka, Marc (Phillip) 1950- [composer, author]
Derringer, Marc *Source(s):* CCE73-74
Younger, Marc *Source(s):* ASCP; CPOL PA-160-830
Yakimenko, Fyodor (Stepanovich) 1876-1945 [composer, pianist]
Akimenko, Fyodor (Stepanovich) *Source(s):* BAKO; BAKT; HOFE; NGDM
IAkimenko, F(edor Stepanovych) *Source(s):* LCAR
Yale, Elsie D(uncan) 1873-1956 [lyricist]
Abbott, Dorothy *Source(s):* CCE55-56; CCE58; CCE60; CPOL RE-108
Gordon, Grace *Source(s):* CCE44 !51525, 364 R133419; CCE58-59; CYBH
Leonard, Louella *Source(s):* CCE49 R4200 ("Star of the Ages")
Yamaguchi, Kazuko 1949- [composer]
Hara, Kazuko *Source(s):* COHN; HIXN
Note(s): Do not confuse with Kazuko Hara (1935-), librettist, singer & composer.
Yamashita, Tsutomu 1947- [composer, percussionist]
Yamash'ta, Stomu *Source(s):* BAKE; BAKT; BUL3; EPMU; LCAR
Yancey, Clyde A. 1912- [singer, songwriter, guitarist]
Yancey, Skeets *Source(s):* MCCL
Yancey, James [or Jim(my)] (Edward) 1894-1951 [singer, pianist, songwriter]
Father of Boogie-Woogie *Source(s):* SHAD
Yancey, Papa *Source(s):* HARS
Yankovic, Frank(ie) (John) 1915-1998 [composer, accordionist, singer]
America's Polka King *Source(s):* MCCL
Polka King *Source(s):* MCCL; OB98
Trolli, Joseph *Soure(s):* CCE46 E8913
Yarborough, William 1937 (or 39)- [singer, songwriter]
Bell, William *Source(s):* EPMU; HARD; HARR; KICK; LCAR; PEN2
Yardley, William 1849-1900 [critic, author, producer]
Bill of the Play *Source(s):* GANA (In: "Sporting Times")
Courtley, W. *Source(s):* LCAR
Wye, W. *Source(s):* LCAR
Yellen, (Jacob) Selig [or Zelig] 1892 (or 94)-1991 [lyricist, publisher]
Note(s): Portraits: EWEN; EWPA
Wellington, Guy *Source(s):* CCE49 R51371 ("If You Knew, Would You Care?")
Yellen, Jack *Source(s):* EWEN; EWPA; HESK; LCAR; PSND; STUW
Yermolayev, Mikhail 1952- [composer, pianist]
Kollontai, Mikhail *Source(s):* MUWB
Yeston, Maury 1945- [composer, lyricist, educator]
Master of the Musical *Source(s):* CM22 p. vii
Note(s): See also Richard (Charles) Rodgers.
Yoakam, Dwight 1956- [singer, songwriter, guitarist, actor]
Heir to Bakersfield, The *Source(s):* MCCL

Yoder, Paul V(an Buskirk) 1908-1990 [composer, arranger]
Griggs, Frederick *Source(s):* REHG; SUPN
Guthrie, Lester *Source(s):* REHG; SUPN
Norton, Carl *Source(s):* REHG
Porter, Charles *Source(s):* REHG
Rader, Allan *Source(s):* REHG
Scott, James A. *Source(s):* ASCP; GROL; LCAR; NGAM; REHG; SMIN; SUPN
Thomas, Max *Source(s):* ASCP; GROL; LCAR; NGAM; REHG; SMIN; SUPN
Van Buskirk, Al *Source(s):* REHG
Yoelson, Asa 1886-1950 [singer, actor, composer]
Immortal Jolson, The *Source(s):* PSND
Jolie *Source(s):* LCAR
Jolson, Al *Source(s):* EPMU; GAMM; GAN2; GROL; LCAR; PSND; SUTT; VACH
Jolson, Jolie *Source(s):* (source not recorded)
Yoffe, Solomon 1909- [composer]
Yoffe, Shlomo *Source(s):* PSND
York, Harley C. 1944- [composer, singer]
Davidson, Harley *Source(s):* ASCP
Yorke, Peter 1902 (or 03)-1966 [composer, conductor, arranger]
Denham, Barbara *Source(s):* CCE50; CCE54-55; CPOL RE-138-195
Gould, Ivor *Source(s):* SUPN
Llewellyn, Ray *Source(s):* CLMJ
Note(s): Possible pseud. Also used by others; see NOTES: Llewellyn, Ray.
Manners, David *Source(s):* CCE57; CPOL RE-257-861
Note(s): Jt. pseud.: Leo Towers [i.e., Leo(nard) Blitz] & James [or Jimmy] Campbell.
Millbank, Gordon *Source(s):* CCE35 Efor38976
Sefton, Michael *Source(s):* CCE54; CCE60; CPOL RE-139-513
Yost, Michel 1754-1786 [composer]
Michel, (J.) *Source(s):* CPMU; LCAR
Youakim, Andrew [or Andy] 1946- [songwriter]
Kim, Andy *Source(s):* CCE62-63; CCE67; CPOL RE-743-307; PMUS
Longfellow, Baron *Source(s):* CPOL RE-743-315; NOMG
Youmans, Vincent 1898-1946 [composer]
Millie *Source(s):* MUWB
Youmans, Millie *Source(s):* MUWB
Young, Alfred 1900-1975 [composer]
Brigham, Earl(e) *Source(s):* REHG; SMIN; SUPN
Young, Andre (Ramelle [or Romell]) 1965- [singer, rapper, songwriter]
Dr. Dre *Source(s):* CM15; EPMU; LCAR; PMUS-92; WORL
Phil Spector of Rap Music *Source(s):* WORL
Young, Barbara Marie 1931- [composer, singer]
Boyle, Bobbi *Source(s):* ASCP
Young, Bernard [singer, songwriter]
Seal *Source(s):* WARN
Note(s): See also Sealhenry (Olumide) Samuel.
Young, Faron 1932-1996 [singer, songwriter, guitarist, actor]
Hillbilly Heartthrob *Source(s):* AMUS
King of Country Music Fairs, The *Source(s):* MCCL
Sheriff, The *Source(s):* PSND
Singing Outlaw, The *Source(s):* EPMU
Singing Sheriff, The *Source(s):* AMUS; EPMU; FLIN; MILL; PSND
Young Sheriff, (The) *Source(s):* AMUS; EPMU; MCCL
Young, George ?-1919 [songwriter]
Pelham, Paul *Source(s):* KILG
Young, James (Osborne [or Oliver]) 1912-1984 [trombonist, singer, composer]
Young, Trummy [or Trummie] *Source(s):* ASCP; KINK; LCAR; GAMM
Young, John(ny) O. 1918-1974 [singer, guitarist, songwriter]
Young, Man *Source(s):* HARS, LCAR
Young, LaMonte 1935- [composer, saxophonist, pianist]
Godfather of Minimalism *Source(s):* http://www.turnworld.com/artists/gunther/spooky/bios.htm (7 Aug. 2005)
Note(s): See also Terry Riley.
Grandfather of Minimal Music, The *Source(s):* CM16
Young, Lucy J(ane) 1858-1875 [hymnist]
Note(s): Married name: Mrs. P(hilip) P. Bliss. Portrait: http://www.gbgm-umc.org/churches/DesertFoothillsAZ/PPBliss (7 Oct. 2002)
Paulina *Source(s):* NEIL p. 27+
Note(s): "We Are Marching to Canaan with Banner and Song" & "I Will Love Jesus and Serve Him." According to Elias Nason, "Paulina" was a pseud. of Lucy J. Young (Mrs. Bliss); however, D(aniel) W(ebster) Whittle said it was the pseud. of (Mrs.) (E. W.) Griswold.
Young, Marvin 1967- [rapper, songwriter]
Young, master of ceremonies *Source(s):* LCAR
Young, MC *Source(s):* EPMU; LCAR
Young, Maud J(eannie) (Fuller) 1826-1882 [author, songwriter]
Confederate Lady, The *Source(s):* PSNN
M. J. Y. *Source(s):* PSNN
Soldier's Friend *Source(s):* PSNN
Young, Maurice [songwriter, performer]
Trick Daddy (Dollars) *Source(s):* AMIR; AMUS; PMUS-00
Young, Neil 1945- [songwriter, singer, director]
Bluesy Bad Boy *Source(s):* CM15
Dirty Rock 'n' Roller *Source(s):* CM15

Folkie Romantic *Source(s):* CM15
Godfather of Grunge *Source(s):* AMUS; CM15
Hippie Narcissist *Source(s):* CM15
Rockabilly Hepcat *Source(s):* CM15
Shakey, Bernard *Source(s):* IMDB; PSNN
Techno-Troubadour *Source(s):* CM15
Young, Norman Russell 1946- [composer, author]
Young, Rusty *Source(s):* ASCP
Young, Victor 1900-1956 [composer, conductor, violinist, radio director]
Note(s): Born in Chicago; do not confuse with Victor Young, composer, pianist, accompanist, born Bristol, TN. Portrait: ETUP 58:4 (Apr. 1940): 282.
Alvic, Tom *Source(s):* LCPC30 E17911 ("Little Flower of Love")
Ellwood, Albert *Source(s):* CCE30 E15279; CCE58
Note(s): Jt. pseud.: Thomas (Ellwood) Griselle.
Llewellyn, Ray *Source(s):* CLMJ
Note(s): Possible pseud. Also possibly used by Ray Bloch, Dominic Frontiere, Lynn Murray [i.e., Lionel Breeze], Irving Orton, David D. Rose, Dmitri Tiompkin & Peter Yorke.
Velasky, Armon *Source(s):* CCE53 Eunp
Young, Welton [singer, songwriter]
Dean *Source(s):* PSND
Younge, William [author, actor]
Rusden, Rupert *Source(s):* GANA p. 613
Note(s): Stage name.
Yule, Joe, (Jr.) 1920- [composer, author, actor]
Greenwood, Larry *Source(s):* CCE49
Jule, Joe, Jr. *Source(s):* ROOM
Note(s): Typograpical error (?); see under Rooney, Mickey.
McGuire, Mickey (Himself) *Source(s):* CCE44 #14074; ROOM
Mick, The *Source(s):* ROOM
Rooney, Joseph Yule *Source(s):* PSND
Note(s): Listed as original name in PSND.
Rooney, Mickey *Source(s):* ASCP; EPMU; KINK; LCAR
Yul'yevich, Iosif 1886-1943 [violinist, composer]
Achron, Joseph *Source(s):* RIEM
Yvain, Maurice Pierre Paul 1891-1965 [composer]
Sautreuil, Jean *Source(s):* GAN1; GAN2; GROL
Yvoire, Claude 1913-1997 [composer]
Zinsstag, Adolf [or Dolf] *Source(s):* BUL2
Yzo, Pierre fl. c.1715-94 [composer, teacher]
Iso, Pierro *Source(s):* GROL

– Z –

Zabler, Enrico 1961- [producer, composer]
Novarini, Rico *Source(s):* http://karine.sanche.free/fr/z.html (18 Oct. 2002)
Zacharias, Helmut 1920-2002 [composer, violinist]
Thomas, Charles *Source(s):* CCE53; KOMP; KOMS; PFSA; RIES
Zacharias, Stephan 1956- [composer]
Sempty, Paul *Source(s):* KOMS; PFSA
Zacharias, Walter 1869-1931 [conductor, composer]
Zacher, Walter *Source(s):* MACM
Zadora, Michael 1882-1946 [pianist, composer, violinist]
Note(s): Portrait: ETUP 58:4 (Apr. 1940): 282
Amadis, Pierre [or Pietro, or Peter] *Source(s):* GROL; LCAR; NGDM; SEND
De Souza, Palma *Source(s):* CCE44 #7301 E120886
Gonazles, Miguel *Source(s):* CCE43 #39073 E117661
Lamare, Pierre *Source(s):* CCE30 E14069
Souza, Palma de *Source(s):* CCE44 #7301 E120886
Von Zador, Michael *Source(s):* LCAR
Zai, Michael 1953- [composer]
Zaito, Nico *Source(s):* PFSA
Zajc, Iván 1831 (or 32)-1914 [composer]
Zaytz, Giovanni von *Source(s):* BAKO; GAN1; GAN2
Zaleski, Waclaw 1799-1849 [folksong collector]
Oleska, Waclaw z *Source(s):* GROL
Zamacoïs, Miguel 1866-1955 [critic]
Monsieur de l'Orchestre *Source(s):* WHIT; WORB
Note(s): See also Arnold [or Adolphe] Mortjé.
Zamastil, Franz 1911-1986 [composer, pianist]
Grohner, Franz *Source(s):* CCE55; CCE64; OMUO
Zambaldi, Silvio 1870-1932 [librettist]
Biagio, Adagio *Source(s):* STGR
Zambon, Francis (Rodney) 1940- [singer, songwriter]
James, Mark *Source(s):* CCE67-68; MCCL; PMUS
Zamecnik, J(ohn) S(tepan) 1872-1953 [composer, conductor, violinist]
Note(s): Portraits: ETUP 58:4 (Apr. 1940): 282; JASA.; MONT
Baxter, Lionel *Source(s):* CCE38 E70271; MONT; SMIN
Berger, Leon *Source(s):* CCE50 R69311 ("Just One More Kiss")
Castro, Arturo de *Source(s):* MONT
Creighton, Robert L. *Source(s):* CCE36 E56782; CCE58; MONT; SMIN
Creighton, Robert S. *Source(s):* CCE58 E13896
Note(s): Typographical error?
DeCastro, Arturo *Source(s):* CCE42 #5201, 288 R103880
Du Pont, Paul *Source(s):* MONT
Note(s): Possible pseud.? Also used by Walter (G(ustave)) Haenschen.
Hathaway, J(ane) *Source(s):* CCE41 #26816, 327 R96975; SMIN

Hawthorne, Kathryn *Source(s):* CCE36 E56782; SMIN
Hudson, Roberta *Source(s):* CCE44 #51525, 55 R133426; SMIN
Josh, (Ted) *Source(s):* CCE18 E429393; REHG; SMIN
Josh and Ted *Source(s):* MONT
Kawelo, Ioane *Source(s):* CCE43 #30169, 3 R119221; MONT; SMIN
Lee, Dorothy *Source(s):* CCE 42 #29891, 456 R107904; MCBD; MONT; SMIN
Lowell, J. Edgar *Source(s):* CCE42 #50835, 31 R113118; MONT; SMIN
Norman, Frederick Van *Source(s):* MONT; REHG; SMIN
Raynard, Jules *Source(s):* CCE50 R69282 ("Morning Glories"); CCE58; MONT
Reynard, Jules *Source(s):* CCE36 E56782; SMIN
Scott, Gene *Source(s):* CCE50 R70139; CCE51 R76660 ("Hurdy Gurdy Blues")
Van Norman, Frederick *Source(s):* CCE36 E56782; CCE50 R6928 ("Rellection") & R69303
Vinton, Hal(l) *Source(s):* CCE38 R69531; MONT
Wellesley, Grant *Source(s):* CCE36 E56782; CCE38 E70271; CPOL RE-33-880; MONT; SMIN

Zanardi, Carlo Antonio mentioned 1875 [journalist, critic]
Carlino di Ratta, Il *Source(s):* NGDO

Zanardi, Niccolò 1661-1729 [castrato, composer]
Giovanardi, Niccolò *Source(s):* NGDO
Zanardino, Lo *Source(s):* NGDO

Zanardini, Angelo 1820-1893 [poet, librettist]
Falanca, Albino *Source(s)* GROL; MELL
Graziani, Anneldo *Source(s):* LOWN; PIPE

Zander, Frank 1942- [composer]
Sonnenschein, Fred *Source(s):* PFSA

Zander, Hans 1905-1985 [composer]
Graetsch, Hans *Source(s):* REHG; REHH; RIES; SUPN

Zander, Helmut (Gottfried) 1924-1987 [composer, conductor]
Hartel, Helmut *Source(s):* PIPE; RIES

Zanetti, Roberto 1956- [composer, singer]
Robyx *Source(s):* http://karine.sanche.free.fr/z.html (7 Oct. 2002)
Savage *Source(s):* http://karine.sanche.free.fr/z.html

Zan(n)ettini, Antonio 1648 (or 49)-1721 [composer, organist, singer]
Gian(n)ettini, Antonio *Source(s):* MELL; PRAT; SONN; WORB

Zang, Johann Heinrich 1733-1811 [composer, organist]
Forceps *Source(s):* GROL
Ighnaz *Source(s):* GROL

Zaniboni, Antonio ?-1767 [librettist]
Esterio *Source(s):* GROL; NGDO

Zaninelli, Luigi ?-2000 [composer]
Note(s): Portrait: http://www.shawneepress.com/composerprofile.html (7 Oct. 2002)
Hayward, Lou *Source(s):* REHG; SUPN; http://www.lib.usm.edu/~archives/m346text.htm
Luigi, Gian *Source(s):* CCE73; http://www.lib.usm.edu/~archives/m346text.htm (14 Mar. 2005)

Zankoff, Jordan [composer]
Christopher, J(ordan) *Source(s):* CCE66; GOTH

Zaret, Hy(man) 1907- [songwriter, publisher, author]
Note(s): Do not confuse with Hy [or Hi] Zaret [i.e., William Albert Stirrat]; see NOTES: Zaret, Hy.
Day, Jerry *Source(s):* CCE41 #9694 E92199; CCE68
Ingersoll, Byron M. *Source(s):* CCE41 #5570 Eunp241929; CCE68 R426470
Note(s): Jt. pseud.: Ernest Gold [i.e., Goldner], Alexander Kramer, Don McCray, Robert (B.) Sour & Zoe Voeth [i.e., Parenteau]

Zavarský, Ernest 1913- [musicologist, writer on music]
Záhorský, Pavol *Source(s):* GROL

Zazueta, Zachary 1983-2002 [singer, songwriter]
Noncents *Source(s):* DRSC

Zbyszewski-Olechnowska, Maria 1865- [author, composer]
Ratuld, P. *Source(s):* COHN; HIXN

Zech, Chrysogonus 1728-1804 [composer]
Tegurini, (Padre) *Source(s):* CPMU

Zehm, Friedrich 1923- [composer]
Cammin, Heinz *Source(s):* CCE72; CCE74; KOMP; PFSA
Petersen, Ralf *Source(s):* CCE68; CPOL RE-742-342
Peterson, Rald *Source(s):* CCE68

Zehnder, Johann Peter 1654-1713 (or 15) [friar, poet, composer]
Mauritius von Menzingen *Source(s):* NGDM; WORB
Note(s): Religious name.

Zehringer, Richard 1947- [singer, songwriter]
Derringer, Rick *Source(s):* PSND

Zeidler, Armin 1938- [composer]
Arnimsson, Arne *Source(s):* KOMS; PFSA
Cat-Burgdorf, Stanley *Source(s):* KOMS; PFSA
Kominiak, Ryszard *Source(s):* KOMS; PFSA

Zelkowitz, Goldie 1942- [singer, composer]
Ravan, Genya *Source(s):* LYMN

Zerezo de Tejada, Isidore Francisco Anonio de 1811-1874 [singer, composer]
Dreso *Source(s):* MELL
Lorezzo *Source(s):* MELL; STGR

Zerga, Joseph (Louis) E(dmund) 1914 (or 24)-1992 [composer, author]
Kane, Peter *Source(s):* CCE62
Note(s): Also used by Cedric King Palmer.
Kenzie, John *Source(s):* CCE65
Mateo, Pepe J. *Source(s):* CCE67
Paul, Edmund *Source(s):* ASCP; CCE60; CCE67; CPOL RE-375-247

Zeugheer, Jakob 1803 (or 05)-1865 [violinist, composer]
Herrmann, J(acob) Z(eugheer) *Source(s):* NGDM; WORB

Zeuner, Heinrich Christoph(er) 1795-1857 [organist, composer]
Zeuner, Charles *Source(s):* BAKR; LCAR; MACM; PSND

Zeyfas, Natal'ya 1947- [musicologist]
Golodnova, N. *Source(s):* GROL
Kozina, Zh. *Source(s):* GROL
Mikhaylova, N. *Source(s):* GROL

Zhasminov, (Count) Aleksei [or Alexei] 1841-1926 [librettist]
Burenin, V(iktor Petrovich) *Source(s):* LOWN; MELL

Zhilyayev, Nikolay Sergeyevich 1881-1938 [critic, composer, teacher]
Note(s): In WORB surname given as: Ziljaev
Gynt, Peer *Source(s):* GROL; WORB
Note(s): Also used by Peer Helge Taralsen.

Zhukovsky, W. A. 1783-1852 [poet]
Joukowsky, (W. A.?) *Source(s):* FULD p. 481

Zhurbin, Lev 1978- [composer]
Ljova *Source(s):* CCMU; http://ljova.com/ljova.html (20 Jan. 2005)
Zhurbin, Ljova *Source(s):* http://ljova.com/ljova.html

Ziegler, Karl 1812-1877 [poet]
Karlopago *Source(s):* LAST

Ziegler, Richard A(dam) 1945- [composer, author, singer]
Adams, Ri(t)chie *Source(s):* ASCP; CCE60; CCE64-68
Chambers, Rick *Source(s):* CCE75

Zieritz, Grete von 1899- [composer]
Hajnal *Source(s):* CCE66 Efor91012; KOMP

Zignago Alcóver, GianMarco Javier 1970- [singer, songwriter]
GianMarco *Source(s):* HWOM; http://Imiguel52.tripod.com/id5.html (5 Feb. 2005)

Zilch, Josef 1928- [composer]
Siola, Josef *Source(s):* KOMS; PFSA

Zilcher, Paul [composer]
Note(s): May be Johann Paul, 1855-1943?
Dana, Arthur *Source(s):* CCE26 E643108
Note(s): A. P. Schmidt house name; see NOTES: Dana, Arthur.

Zimmerman, Charles A. 1861 (or 62)-1916 [bandmaster, composer]
Note(s): Portrait: METR 11:8 (Aug. 1895): cover
Zimmerman, Zimmy *Source(s):* SMIN

Zimmerman, Dieter 1943-1978 [composer]
Carpenter, Cliff *Source(s):* KOMP; KOMS; PFSA

Zimmerman, Robert Allen 1941- [singer, songwriter]
Alias *Source(s):* LCAR
American Shomo Haviv, The *Source(s):* RECR
Blind Boy Grunt *Source(s):* LCAR; PSND; ROOM
Dillon, Bob *Source(s):* Heylin, Clinton. *Bob Dylan Behind the Shades*. New York: Summit Books, 1991, 27.
Dylan, Bob *Source(s):* BAKR; CM03; CM21; LCAR; PEN2; PSND; ROOM; WORL
Dylan, Lucky *Source(s):* RECR
Dylanesque *Note(s):* Term to describe works similar to those of Dylan.
Dylanologists *Source(s): Arizona Daily Star* (23 Feb. 2002)
Note(s): Term to describe persons who study and/or write about Dylan and his works.
Dylanzine *Source(s):* Wissolik, Richard David. *Bob Dylan - American Poet and Singer*. Greenburg, PA: Eadmer Press, xiv.
Note(s): Term to describe serial publications about Dylan.
Father of Folk Rock *Source(s):* SHAD
Frost, Jack *Source(s):* http://www.grammy.com/features/0215-generalfield.html (17 Nov. 2002)
Note(s): Also used by Mark Vincent Brine, Charles Degesco, Harold G. Frost & E. Clinton Keithley.
Gook, Roosevelt *Source(s):* LCAR
Grunt, Blind Boy *Source(s):* PSND; ROOM
Gunn, Elston *Source(s):* RECR p. 896 (see under: Vee, Bobby)
Johnson, Elmer *Source(s):* Heylin p. 198 (see above)
Landy, Bob *Source(s):* LCAR; ROOM
Porterhouse, Tedham *Source(s):* EPMU; LCAR; MCCL; WARN
Note(s): In EPMU & MCCL (see under: Elliott, Ramblin' Jack).
Radical Prophet of American Youth, The *Source(s):* PSND; SIFA
Song-poet of the Sixties Generation *Source(s):* CM03 p. v
Thomas, Robert Milkwood *Source(s):* LCAR; ROOM
Traveling Wilburys *Source(s):* WILB
Note(s): With: Jeff Lynne; Roy (Kelton) Orbison, Tom Petty & George Harrison.
Wilbury, Boo *Source(s):* WILB
Wilbury, Lucky *Source(s):* WARN; WILB
Youth, The *Source(s):* PSND

Zimmermann, Agnes Maria Jacobina 1847-1925 [pianist, composer]
Agnes Z. *Source(s):* IBIM
Zincken, Hans Friedrich August 1837-1922 [composer, conductor, writer on music]
Neckniz, (Hans Friedrich August) *Source(s):* MACM; MELL; STGR
Sommer, Hans *Source(s):* BAKO; BAKR; LCAR; MACM; NGDM; PFSA; WORB
Note(s): Also used by Hans Haass.
Zintel, Gabriele 1963- [composer]
Gee, Tara *Source(s):* PFSA
Zito, Salvatore (Albert) 1932 (or 33)- [composer, arranger]
Zito, Torrie (A.) *Source(s):* ASCC; CCE56
Zittel, C. Florian [lyricist]
Zit *Source(s):* CCE36 R44447; PMUC
Zittel, Zit *Source(s):* http://www.hrc.utexas.edu/research/fa/ziegfeld2.htm (7 Apr. 2005)
Zitzmann, Heinrich Gottfried 1775-1839 [poet]
Uffo von Wildingen *Source(s):* LAST
Wildingen, Uffo von *Source(s):* LAST
ZIV-TV
Note(s): Television syndication company founded by Frederic W. Ziv (1905?-2001), "Father of Syndication." The following are probable "house names" used by well-known composers who were paid less than union scale.
Carlin, Andrew *Source(s):* CLTP ("This Man Dawson")
Radford, Cliff *Source(s):* CLTP ("Rough Riders Theme")
Rondell, Adam *Source(s):* CLTP ("Lawbreakers, The")
Zmigrod, Joseph 1902-1973 [composer]
Gray, Allan *Source(s):* BLIC; BUL1; BUL2; CCE41 #37070 Efor65452
Zoder, Raimund 1882-1963 [writer on music]
Drudmair, Zeno *Source(s):* RIES
Zoeller, Carli [or Karl] 1840-1889 [composer, violist, bandmaster]
Note(s): Portrait: ETUP 58:5 (May 1940): 354
Emmerson, H. *Source(s):* CPMU
Franck, René *Source(s):* CPMU
Marteau, Léon *Source(s):* CPMU
Trifolium *Source(s):* CPMU
Note(s): Jt. pseud.: Louis Samson & J. Kornfeld.
Zoeren, Elbert van 1930-1997 [composer]
Pitt, Jack *Source(s):* NEDM
Zorn, John 1953- [saxophonist, composer, leader]
Hajime, Dekoboko *Source(s):* GROL
Tzizit, Rav *Source(s):* GROL
Zubeldia, Emiliana de 1888-1987 [composer, pianist]
Bydwealth, Emily *Source(s):* DWCO; GROL
Zuccalmaglio, Anton Wilhelm Florentin von 1803-1869 [collector or folksongs, writer on music]
St. Diamond *Source(s):* BAKR; DAVE; NIEC
Waldbrühl, Wilhelm von *Source(s):* BAKR; DAVE; LCAR; WORB
Zuccamana, Gizelle Augusta 1884 (or 87)-1981 [composer, pianist]
Armando, Jose *Source(s):* CCE76
Cassell, (Mrs.) Irwin [or Erwin] M. *Source(s):* HIXN; LCAR
Della, Ella *Source(s):* CCE46 R5937 ("Come To My House of Dreams"); HIXN; LCAR
Kiriloff, Efrem *Source(s):* SUTT
Note(s): On recordings.
Mana-Zucca *Source(s):* BAKO; BAKT; REHG
Zuccamana, Dolly *Source(s):* LCAR
Zuckermann, (Gizelle) Augusta *Source(s):* BAKT; HIXN
Zuckerman, Gussie *Source(s):* LCAR
Zuccari, Carlo 1704-1792 [violinist, composer]
Zuccherino *Source(s):* GROL
Zucker, Irwin Elliott 1927-2001 [composer, conductor, pianist]
Elliott, Jack *Source(s):* CLTP ("Lawrence Welk Show"); DRSC
Note(s): Do not confuse with Jack Elliott [i.e., Elliott Charles Adnopoz]
Elliott, John (M.) *Source(s):* CLTP ("Lawrence Welk Show")
Zudekoff, Muni [or Moe] 1919- [trombonist, composer, bandleader]
Morrow, Buddy *Source(s):* KINK; LCAR
Zulaica y Arregui, José Gonzalo 1886-1956 [organist, musicologist, composer]
Donostia, (José Antonio de) *Source(s):* BAKT; BUL1; BUL3; NGDM; WORB
José Antonio de Donostia *Source(s):* LCAR; MUWB
Jose Antonio de San Sebastian *Source(s):* LCAR; WORB
San Sebastián, Padre *Source(s):* BAKT
Zulehner, Carl [or Charles] 1770-1830 [composer]
Mozart, Wolfgang Amadeus *Source(s):* DEA3 p. 112
Note(s): Zulehner passed off his music as by Mozart.
Zulman, Ann 1912 (or 14)-1962 [composer, music educator]
Berg, H. *Source(s):* CCE52; HIXN
Zuvich, Dennis Michael 1942- [composer, singer]
Michaels, D. Z. *Source(s):* ASCP
Zwibelson, Hortense 1915- [composer, lyricist]
Belson, Hortense Gold *Source(s):* ASCP
Zwodau dei Falkenau, Egerland 1925- [composer, bandleader]
Mosch, Ernst *Source(s):* GAMM
Zwyssig, Joseph 1808-1854 [composer]
Zwyssig, Alberich *Source(s):* BAKR

Chapter 3

Assumed Names and Sobriquets (with References to Original Names)

SYMBOLS/NUMERALS

##. *See* Crosby, Fanny [i.e., Frances] J(ane)
###. *See* Crosby, Fanny [i.e., Frances] J(ane)
*. *See* Crosby, Fanny [i.e., Frances] J(ane)
***. *See* Crosby, Fanny [i.e., Frances] J(ane)
***. *See* Morcour, ? de
***, Mr. *See* Favart, Charles Simon
-ter. *See* Foerster, Josef Bohuslav
4-Bar Killer. *See* Hawkins, Lamont
69. *See* Craig, Carl
500 Per Cent More Man. *See* Bates, (Otha) Ellas [or Elias]

– A –

A. *See* Crosby, Fanny [i.e., Frances] J(ane)
A. *See* Taylor, Ann
A*T*S, Giovanni. *See* Antes, John [or Johann]
A -y. *See* Hupton, Job
A. A. *See* Ariosti, Attilio (Malachia [or Clementi])
A. A. F. *See* Crosby, Fanny [i.e., Frances] J(ane)
A. B. C. *See* Gottschalk, Louis Moreau
A.B.C. *See* Statham, Francis Reginald
A. Balance Esq., of the Middle Temple. *See* Binney, Thomas
A. C. C. *See* Cooke, William
A. C. F. *See* Fitzwygram, Augusta Catherine
A. D. *See* Joyce, Archibald
A. DA S. *See* Samuda, Arthur J. D'Aguilar
A. E. *See* Russell, George William
A. E. A. *See* Davis, Katherine K(ennicott)
A. F. H. E. *See* Everett, Augusta F. H.
AFKAP. *See* Nelson, Prince Rogers
AFX. *See* James, Richard D(avid)
A. H. *See* Hammerschmidt, Andreas
A. H. A. *See* Ackley, A(lfred) H(enry)
A. H. D. *See* Devall, Arthur Henry
A. H. W. *See* Whitaker, Alfred Hanbury
A. L. *See* Lehmann, Amelia
A. L. P. *See* Littledale, Richard Frederick
A. M. *See* Meves, Augustus
A. M. *See* Mongredier, Augustus
A. M. C. *See* Cooper, Adeline Maxwell
A. M. G. *See* Goodhart, A(rthur) M(urray)
A. S. *See* Schwartz, Andreas (Scotus)
A. T. *See* Taylor, Ann
A. T. *See* Toplady, Augustus Montague
Aab, (Dr.). *See* Weber, (Jacob) Gottfried
Aachen, Hans von. *See* Behr, F(ranz)
Aaliyah. *See* Haughton, Aaliyah Dana
Aardvark, Aaron. *See* Patrick, Johnny
Aarne, Els. *See* Paemurru, Elze Janova
Aaron, Lee. *See* Greening, Karen Lynn
Aaron of the 19th Century Wesleyan/Holiness Movement. *See* James, Mary D(agworthy)
Abady, Tim. *See* Abady, H(arold) Temple
Abbate, Anthoine dell'. *See* Antico, Andrea
Abbattutis, Gian Alesio. *See* Basile, Giovanni Battista [or Giambattista]
Abbe de La Tour. *See* Charriére, Isabella (Agneta Elisabeth) de
Abbé, Joseph L'. *See* Saint-Sévin, Joseph Barnabé
Abbé, le fils. *See* Saint-Sévin, Joseph-Barnabé
Abbey, W. F. *See* Bliss, P(hilip) Paul
Abbott, (The). *See* Diggs, Robert
Abbott, Dorothy. *See* Yale, Elsie D(uncan)
Abbott, Eve. *See* Niday Canaday, Edna Veronica
Abbott, John (Anthony). *See* Abatematteo, John (Anthony)
Abbott, Lempriere. *See* Bulch, Thomas Edward
Abbott, Leslie W. *See* Floridia (Napolino), Pietro
Abdul Al-Khabyyr, Al-Hajj. *See* Thomas, Russell Linwood
Abdullah, Mohammed. *See* Frederick, John

Abeille, Louis [or Ludwig]. *See* Abeille, Johann Christian Ludwig
Abel, J. T. *See* Bliss, P(hilip) Paul
Abel, Lex. *See* Leemann, Max
Abelle, Victor. *See* Sartorio, Arnoldo
Abeti. *See* Masikini, Abeti
Abner, J. E. *See* Bliss, P(hilip) Paul
Abominable Showman, The. *See* Margulois, David
Aborn, Morris. *See* Baron, Maurice
Abos, Girolamo. *See* Abos, Geronimo
Abou-Djenach. *See* Busnach, William (Bertrand)
Abraham, Johnny. *See* Grothoff, Curtis Eugene, II
Abraham, Vader. *See* Kartner, Pierre
Abramovic, August. *See* Adelburg, August
Abrams, Maurice. *See* Abrahams, Maurice [or Maurie]
Abreu, Zeqhinha de. *See* Abreu, Jose Gomes de
Absentee Father of "Gypsy Music". *See* Liszt, Franz
Abtler, F. *See* Keiser, Robert (A(dolph))
Abundante, Giulio. *See* Abondante, Giulio [or Julio]
Abyssinian Prince, The. *See* Bridgetower, George Augustus Polgreen
Academico Caliginoso, L'. *See* Foscarini, Giovanni Paolo
ACAMA. *See* Ackermann, Stefan
Acanzio, Eschillo [or Eschibo]. *See* Pindemon(t)e, Giovanni
Accademico Formato. *See* Castro, Francisco José de
Accademico Formato. *See* Marcheselli, D.
Accademico Naufragante. *See* Vacchelli, Giovanni Battista
Accard. *See* Civini, Guelfo
Acconziano, Amone. *See* Tamagni, Giovan Battista
Accrington, Stanley. *See* Bray, Mike
Accursi, Michele. *See* Ruffini, Giovanni [or Giacomo] (Domenico)
Ace, Johnny. *See* Alexander, John (Marshall), Jr.
Achron, Joseph. *See* Yul'yevich, Iosif
Acidy Cassidy. *See* Cassidy, Claudia
Ackerman, A. *See* Benjamin, Walter
Ackley, C(harles) C. *See* Meredith, I(saac) H(ickman)
Acrejo, Mirtindo. *See* Mariani, Giovanni Lorenzo
Acton, E. R. *See* Bliss, P(hilip) Paul
Acton, O. E. *See* Bliss, P(hilip) Paul
Acuto. *See* Polidoro, Federigo (Idomeneo)
Adagio, Mlle. *See* Milanollo, Theresa (Domenica Maria)
Adair, Charles. *See* Raida, Karl Alexander
Adalbert of Prague. *See* Vojtech
Adam, Cornel. *See* Lengyel, Cornel Adam
Adam, le boss. *See* Adam, de la Halle
Adam le Roy. *See* Adenez (le Roy)
Adam, Léon. *See* Mullen, Frederic
Adam of Dore [or Door, or Dowr]. *See* Adamus Dorensis
Adam the Hunchback from Arras. *See* Adam, de la Halle
Adamberger, Josef. *See* Adamberger, Valentin
Adamo. *See* Adamo, Salvadore
Adamonti. *See* Adamberger, Valentin
Adams, A(ce). *See* Adams, Stanley (Ace)
Adams, A. J. *See* Miller, Robert [or Bob] (Ernst)
Adams, Abraham. *See* Fielding, Henry
Adams, Arthur. *See* Geibel, Adam
Adams, Carrie B. *See* Gabriel, Charles H(utchinson)
Adams, Casey. *See* Showalter, Max
Adams, Charles. *See* Donnelly, Richard
Adams, Charles. *See* Sugarman, Harry
Adams, Chick. *See* Adams, Leonard F.
Adams, Derroll. *See* Thompson, Derroll Lewis
Adams, Fingers. *See* Adams, Chris
Adams, Gene. *See* Saraceni, Raymond (R.)
Adams, George. *See* Gutman, Adam
Adams, Jason. *See* Wisner, James [or Jimmy] (Joseph)
Adams, Jeff. *See* Ram, Samuel
Adams, Joe. *See* Crow(e), Francis Luther
Adams, Lee. *See* Adamski, Leon Stephen
Adams, Mac. *See* Mayer, Johann(es) (?Adolf)
Adams, Marty. *See* Bachman, Martha Jean
Adams, Pepper. *See* Adams, Park
Adams, Ralph. *See* Kountz, Richard
Adams, Ri(t)chie. *See* Ziegler, Richard A(dam)
Adams, Stephen. *See* Maybrick, Michael
Adan le Bossu. *See* Adam, de la Halle
Adano, Bobby. *See* Adamo, Milo Angelo
Adayevskaya, Ella Georgiyevna. *See* Schultz, Ella Georgiyevna
Adderley, Cannonball. *See* Adderley, Julian Edwin
Addinsell, Richard. *See* Chipperfield, Frederich
Addison, D. C. *See* Daniell, Charles Addison
Addison, Puff. *See* Addison, L(aidlaw) F(letcher)
Adé, King Sunny. *See* Adeniyi, Sunday
Adé, Sunny. *See* Adeniyi, Sunday
Adelburg, August. *See* Abramovic, August
Adew. *See* Cory, W. J.
Adew. *See* Drummond, Algernon
Adew. *See* Mitchell-Innes, T. L.
Adew. *See* Woodhouse, Evely
Adkins, Chet. *See* Atkins, Chester [or Chet] (Burton)
Adkinson, Gene. *See* Adkinson, Harvey E.
Adlai Stevenson of Songwriters, The. *See* Porter, Cole
Adlam, Buzz. *See* Adlam, Basil G(eorge)
Adlam, George B. *See* Adlam, Basil G(eorge)
Adlam, Sofie N. *See* Mansfield, Orlando Augustine
Adler, Agnes. *See* Thomsen, Christian
Adler, Marx von. *See* Dall'Aquila, Marco
Adler, Salmo. *See* Finkelstein, Abe
Adolfson, (Adolf Gustaw). *See* Sonnenfeld, Adolf Gustaw
Adolphe (de L.). *See* Leuven, Adolphe (Ribbing) de
Adorno, (Theodor (Wiesengrund)). *See* Wiesengrund(-Adorno), Theodor (Ludwig)

Albinus, Flaccus. *See* Alcuinus, Flaccus
Alcalay, Luna. *See* Alkalaj, Lucia
Alceste. *See* Beyle, (Marie) Henri
Alcindor. *See* Lecocq, Alexandre Charles
Alcindor. *See* Legouix, Isidore Edouard
Alcindor. *See* Ronger, (Louis Auguste Joseph) Florimond
Alda, Frances. *See* Davies, Frances (Jean(ne))
Aldebaran. *See* Bartók, Béla
Aldeen, Ned. *See* Neto, Laurindo José de Araujo Almeida Nobrega
Alden, H. C. *See* Knobel, Theo
Alden, Ruth. *See* Tapper, Thomas
Alden, Sonia. *See* Ewart, Florence Maud(e) (née Donaldson)
Alden, Tessie R. *See* Tessier, Albert D(enis)
Alder, Annie. *See* Alderfer, Zora Margolis
Aldrich, F. *See* Greenwald, M(artin)
Aldrich, F. B. *See* Boott, Francis
Alec. *See* Bunting, William Maclardie
Alectorius, Johannes. *See* Hahnel, Johannes
Aleichem, Sholom. *See* Rabinowitz, Solomon
Alemán, El. *See* Bernstein, Arturo
Aleotta, Vittoria. *See* Aleotti, Raffaela-Argenta
Alessandra, Caterina. *See* Assandra, Caterina
Alessandro. *See* Alexander, Fred
Alethes. *See* Cowper, William
Alexander, (Alton). *See* Gaskill, Clarence
Alexander, Alex. *See* Borisoff, Alexander
Alexander, Alfred. *See* McClaskey, Harry Haley
Alexander, Dave. *See* Elam, Dave Alexander
Alexander, Jeff. *See* Alexander, Meyer
Alexander, Nick. *See* Kokinacis, Alexander
Alexander, Peter. *See* Neumeyer, Peter Alexander
Alexander, Texas. *See* Alexander, Alger(non)
Alexander, Van. *See* Feldman, Al(exander)
Alexandra. *See* Nefedov, Alexandra Doris
Alexandre de. *See* Bertha, Sándor
Alexandre, Josef. *See* Burke, Joseph [or Joe] A.
Alexandre, Josef. *See* Dubin, Al(exander)
Alexandrina, (Sister). *See* Boyle, (Miss)
Alexandrov, Feodor. *See* Ehret, Walter (Charles)
Alexandrov, Feodor. *See* Kinsman, Elmer (F(ranklin))
Alexeyev, K. *See* Kuznetsov, Konstantin Alexeyevich
Alexis, Willibald. *See* Häring, (George) Wilhelm (Heinrich)
Alfas. *See* Bahr, Carlos Andrés
Alfidi, Joseph [or Joey]. *See* Alfidi, Giuseppe Arturo
Alfieri, Max. *See* Alfieri-Adler, Moritz
Alford, Kenneth J. *See* Ricketts, (Major) Frederick Joseph
Alfred. *See* McCollin, Frances
Alfredo, Wald. *See* Lindemann, Wilhelm
Ali Baba. *See* French, Percy
Aliaga, S. *See* Colantuoni, Alberto
Alias. *See* Zimmerman, Robert Allen
Alice. *See* Winner, Septimus
Aliomar, J. L. Latif. *See* Robinson, Jimmie [or Jimmy] Lee
Aliprandi, Paul. *See* Missa, Edmond Jean
Aliqua. *See* Peirson, Eliza O.
Alix. *See* Evans, James Har(r)ington
Alix, Mae. *See* Landreaux, Edna
Alix, May. *See* Hunter, Alberta
Alkan, Charles-Henri-Valentin. *See* Morhange, Charles-Henri-Valentin
Alkan, Napoléon Alexandre. *See* Morhange, Napoléon Alexandre
All-American Composer, The. *See* Baline, Israel
Allamby, Delite. *See* Allamby, Darrell
Allan, Edgar. *See* Kollo, Willi (Arthur)
Allan, Gary. *See* Herzberg, Gary Allan
Allan, Lewis. *See* Meeropol, Abel
Allatius, Leo. *See* Allacci, Leone
Allazzi, Leone. *See* Allacci, Leone
Allegoriowitsch, Deutobald Symbolizetti. *See* Vischer, Friedrich Theodor von
Allen, Ben D. *See* Nevin, Gordon Balch
Allen, Billy. *See* Castleman, William Allen
Allen, Charles. *See* De Vito, Albert (Kenneth)
Allen, Charles. *See* Stube, Howard
Allen, Craig. *See* Finkelstein, Abe
Allen, Edgar. *See* Kollo, Willi (Arthur)
Allen, Edmund. *See* Reeve-Jones, Alan Edmond
Allen, George. *See* Smith, George (1924-1983)
Allen, Harry. *See* Rosenfeld, Monroe H.
Allen, Jerry. *See* Atinsky, Jerry
Allen, Lauri. *See* Delgrosso, Jean Ann
Allen, Leone Perry. *See* Depaolis, Leone F.
Allen, Lew. *See* Lewis, Al(an)
Allen, Mack. *See* Slaughter, M(arion) T(ry)
Allen, Mark. *See* Slaughter, M(arion) T(ry)
Allen, Maybelle. *See* North, Edith
Allen, Morrie [or Morris]. *See* Alin, Morris
Allen, Papa Dee. *See* Allen, Thoma Sylvester
Allen, Peter (Woolnough). *See* Woolnough, Peter Allen
Allen, Red. *See* Allen, Harley
Allen, Red. *See* Allen, Henry (James), Jr.
Allen, Richard [or Dick]. *See* Markowitz, Richard (Allen)
Allen, Roberto. *See* Romero, Roberto
Allen, Stuart. *See* Frangkiser, Carl (Moerz)
Allen, T. R. *See* Gabriel, Charles H(utchinson)
Allen, Tito. *See* Romero, Roberto
Allens, Arvee. *See* Valenzuela, Richard (Stephen)
Allessandro della Viola. *See* Merlo, Alessandro
Alleyn, Ellen. *See* Rossetti, Christina Georgina
Alligator Man, Mr. *See* Newman, Jimmy C. [acutally Yves]
Allington, Rex. *See* Besly, Maurice

Allison, Adrian. *See* Branscombe, Gena
Allison, Bob. *See* Day, Bob
Allison, John. *See* Alford, John
Allison, Peter [or Petter]. *See* Dawson, Peter (Smith)
Allison, Robert. *See* Kraushaar, Charles
Allitsen, (Mary) Frances. *See* Bumpus, Mary Frances [or Francis]
Allman, Lee. *See* Allman, Michael L(ee)
Allman, Miguel. *See* Allman, Michael L(ee)
Allmand, Robert. *See* Vlak, Kees
Allment, Robert. *See* Vlak, Kees
Alloris, Tristano d'. *See* Pelilli, Lino Ennio
Allwyn, John. *See* Del Riego, Teresa (Clotilde)
Allyson, Kym. *See* Kimbro, John M.
Alm. *See* Fiedler, Friedrich
Almeda, Margarite. *See* Shaftel, Selig (Sidney)
Almeida, Laurindo. *See* Neto, Laurindo José de Araujo Almeida Nobrega
Almeida, Lindo. *See* Neto, Laurindo José de Araujo Almeida Nobrega
Almirante. *See* Domingues, Henrique Foreis
Al-Obo. *See* Pfohl, Albrecht
Aloma, Hal. *See* Aloma, Harold David
Alondra de la Frontera, La. *See* Mendoza, Lydia
Aloysius. *See* Labrunie, Gérard
Alpert, Dore. *See* Alpert, Herb(ert)
Alpert, Dave. *See* Alpert, Herb(ert)
Alpert, Trigger. *See* Alpert, Herman
Alpha. *See* Hewitt, John (Henry) Hill
Alstyne, Fannie Jane. *See* Crosby, Fanny [i.e., Frances] J(ane)
Altaï, Armande. *See* Maggini, Armande Jeanne
Alte Schulmeister, Der [or Das]. *See* Wieck, (Johann Gottlob) Friedrich
Altenberg, Peter. *See* Engländer, Richard
Altis, Ludo. *See* Junkert, Ludwig
Alton, John. *See* Linkey, Harry
Alvarado, Enrique. *See* Vergiati, Amleto (Enrique)
Alvic, Tom. *See* Young, Victor
Alvirez, Gilberto. *See* Layer, Wolfgang
Alvis. *See* Marcuse, Albrecht [or Albert]
Alvys. *See* Marcuse, Albrecht [or Albert]
Alwin, Karl (Oskar). *See* Pinkus, Alwin Oskar
Alwyn, Kenneth. *See* Wetherell, Kenneth Alwyn
Amadeus. *See* Hoffmann, Ernst Theodore Wilhelm
Amadeus Autodidactos. *See* Richter, Heinrich Friedrich Wilhelm
Amadio, Pippo. *See* Amadei, Filippo
Amadis, Pierre [or Pietro, or Peter]. *See* Zadora, Michael
Amado, Antonio. *See* Liter, Monia
Amalbert, (Emmanuel) Juan (Khaliq). *See* Rahim, Emmanuel (Khaliq)
Amaranto Sciaditico. *See* Gigli, Girolamo
Amarinzio, Nivildo. *See* Pizzi, (Giuseppe) Gioacchino
Amateur. *See* Johnson, (Mrs.) William
Amateur. *See* Major, J.
Amateur. *See* St. George, C.
Ambassador of Song. *See* Dawson, Peter (Smith)
Ambassador of the Blues. *See* King, Riley B.
Ambassador Satch. *See* Armstrong, (Daniel) Louis
Ambassador with a Horn, The. *See* Armstrong, (Daniel) Louis
Amber, Florence. *See* Bernstein, F(lorence) G.
Amber, Lenny. *See* Bernstein, Louis (1918-1990)
Amber, Lili. *See* Lux, Lillian Sylvia [or Susan]
Ambient, Mark. *See* Harley, Harold
Ambroise, Paul. *See* Slater, David Dick
Ambroise, Victor. *See* Wright, Lawrence
Ambrose, Saint. *See* Ambrosius of Milan
Ambrosia. *See* Wieck, Clara Josephine
Ambrosio, W. F. *See* Saenger, Gustav(e)
Ambrosio, W. F. *See* Seredy, J(ulius) S.
Ambrosio, W. F. *See* Severn, Edmund
Amelia. *See* Coppuck, Amelia (Ball)
American, An. *See* Dunlap, William
American, An. *See* Hopkinson, Joseph
American Ballad Composer. *See* Foster, Stephen Collins
American Critic with the Most Citations in Slonimsky's *Lexicon of Musical Invective*. *See* Elson, Louis (Charles)
American Father of Musical Modernism. *See* Ives, Charles Edward
American Hugo Wolf. *See* Berg, Christopher
American Impressionist. *See* Griffes, Charles T(omlinson)
American Music Master, The. *See* Herbert, Victor
American Musical Leprechaun, An. *See* Olcott, Chancellor John
American Piaf, An. *See* Voss, Jane
American Shomo Haviv, The. *See* Zimmerman, Robert Allen
American Strauss. *See* Engländer, Ludwig
American Successor to Johann Strauss. *See* Romberg, Sigmund
American Tosti, The. *See* Ball, Ernest R.
American Troubadour. *See* Baline, Israel
American Troubadour, The. *See* Scott, Thomas [or Tom] Jefferson
America's Ambassador for the Hobos. *See* Martin, Lecil Travis
America's Ambassador of Good Will. *See* Armstrong, (Daniel) Louis
America's Blind Poet. *See* Crosby, Fanny [i.e., Frances] J(ane)
America's Blue Yodeler. *See* Rodgers, James [or Jimmie] (Charles)
America's Cowboy Evangelist. *See* Turner, Dallas (E.)
America's Dickens. *See* Harrigan, Edward [or Ned]
America's Favorite Cowboy. *See* Autry, (Orvon) Gene

America's Favorite Singing Cowboy. *See* Autry, (Orvon) Gene
America's Favorite Folksinger. *See* Whitman, Ot(t)is (Dewey, Jr.)
America's Favorite Hobo. *See* Martin, Lecil T(ravis)
America's First Composer. *See* Foster, Stephen Collins
America's First Cowboy Radio Singer. *See* Robison, Carson J(ay)
America's First Opera Connoisseur. *See* Whitman, Walt(er)
America's First Professional Playwright. *See* Dunlap, William
America's First Satirist. *See* Mencken, H(enry) L(ouis)
America's First Serious Native-Born Orchestral Composer. *See* Fry, William H(enry)
America's First Songwriter. *See* Foster, Stephen Collins
America's Foremost Brown Blues Singer. *See* Hunter, Alberta
America's Foremost Ebony Comedienne. *See* Howard, Ethel
America's Forgotten Negro Minstrel. *See* Bland, James A(llen)
America's Great Unknown Songwriter. *See* Arluck, Hymen
America's Greatest Composer. *See* Bernstein, Louis (1910-1990)
America's Greatest Composer. *See* Gershvin, Jacob
America's Greatest Composer. *See* Ives, Charles Edward
America's Greatest Composer. *See* Puerner, Charles
America's Greatest Living Composer. *See* Reich, Stephen [or Steve] (Michael)
America's Greatest Song Composer. *See* Rorem, Ned
America's Greatest Yiddish Composer. *See* Weiner, Lazar
America's Leading Librettist. *See* Smith, Harry B(ache)
America's Master Songwriter. *See* Baline, Israel
America's Most Popular Songwriter. *See* Allen, Robert
America's Music Man. *See* Wilsson, (Robert Reiniger) Meredith
America's Number One Singing Cowboy. *See* Autry, (Orvon) Gene
America's Number One Yodeler. *See* Roberts, Kenny
America's Other "March King". *See* King, Karl L(awrence)
America's Other "March King". *See* Paull, E(dward) T(aylor)
America's Polka King. *See* Yankovic, Frank(ie) (John)
America's Premier Cornet Soloist. *See* Smith, Leonard B(ingley)
America's Second Stephen Foster. *See* Arluck, Hymen
America's Troubadour. *See* Foster, Stephen Collins
America's Tuning Fork. *See* Seeger, Pete(r R.)
Ames, Ramsay. *See* Phillips, Ramsay
Ames, Tessie. *See* Smith, Trixie
Amicus. *See* Gagnon, Blanche
Amicus. *See* McCormick, Peter Dodds
Aminata. *See* Wooldridge, Anna Marie
Ammandt, Guy. *See* Ahlberg, Gunnar
Amos, Tori. *See* Amos, Myra Ellen
Amphion. *See* Greulich, Carl Wilhelm
Amphion, Aristoxenos. *See* Martini, Giovanni Battista [or Giambattista]
Anacreon of Germany, The. *See* Flem(m)ing, Paul
Anacreon of His Day, The. *See* Basselin, Olivier
Anaide, Marulli. *See* Perriere-Pilte, Anais (née Marcelli)
Anandghan. *See* Mangeshkar, Lata
Ancien maître de chapelle. *See* Desjardins, Louis-Edouard
Anders, Andy. *See* Anders, John Frank
Anders, Christian. *See* Schinzel, Antonio
Anders, Erich. *See* Gudenberg, E(rich) Wolff von
Anders, Fritz. *See* Allihn, Heinrich
Anders, K. *See* Kauders, Albert
Anders, N. J. *See* Jacob, Nath.
Anders, Pete. *See* Andreoli, Peter
Andersen, Ludwig. *See* Strecker, Ludwig
Anderson, Bert. *See* Bernard Al(fred A.)
Anderson, Cat. *See* Anderson, William (Alonzo)
Anderson, Ernie. *See* Bacon, Fred(erick) J.
Anderson, G. G. *See* Grabowski, Gerd
Anderson, John. *See* Alexander, John David
Anderson, Lilly. *See* Strickland, Lily
Anderson, Simon. *See* Ornadel, Cyril
Anderson, Stig (Arne). *See* Anderson, Stikkan
Anderson, Wallace. *See* Anderson, William Henry
Anderson, Whitey. *See* Anderson, Chris
Andray, Danny Raye. *See* Andrade, Daniel (Raye)
Andre, Carl. *See* Holden, Charles
Andre, Charles. *See* Lewis, Bridges George McGibbon
Andrea de' Servi, Frate. *See* Andreas de Florentia
Andrea degli Organi. *See* Andreas de Florentia
Andrea di Cannaregio. *See* Gabrieli, Andrea
Andrea di Giovanni, Fra. *See* Andreas de Florentia
Andreae, Carolus. *See* Enders, Karl
Andree, Wolf. *See* Utzerath, Wolfgang
Andrew, (Mrs.) E. A. *See* Crosby, Fanny [i.e., Frances] J(ane)
Andrew, Rex. *See* King, Reginald (Claude McMahon)
Andrews, A. E. *See* Crosby, Fanny [i.e., Frances] J(ane)
Andrews, Andy A. *See* Collette, W(illiam) M(arcell)
Andrews, Barney. *See* Nelson, Oswald George
Andrews, Bud. *See* Andrews, Curcy H., Jr.
Andrews, Champs L. *See* Keiser, Robert (A(dolph))
Andrews, Jim. *See* Finkelstein, Abe
Andrews, Jim. *See* Kaufman, Isidore
Andrews, Jimmy. *See* Banta, Frank (Edgar)
Andrews, Maggie (A.). *See* Robison, Carson J(ay)
Andrews, Tim. *See* Andrews, Chris
Andrien, Martin Joseph. *See* Adrien, Martin Joseph

Andro, L. *See* Rie, Therese (née Herz)
Andropediacus, Lycosthenes Psellionoros. *See* Spangenberg, Wolfhart
Androzzo, A(lma) Bazel. *See* Thompson, Alma (I.)
Andrzejewski, Marek. *See* Markowski, Andrzej
Andy, Bob. *See* Anderson, Keith
Andy, Horace. *See* Hinds, Horace
Andy, Sleepy. *See* Hinds, Horace
Anély, Max. *See* Segalen, Victor
Anfioneo, Aritosseno. *See* Martini, Giovanni Battista [or Giambattista]
Ange du cocasse, L'. *See* Chabrier, (Alexis) Emmanuel
Ángel del amargue, El. *See* Fiallo, David
Angel Misterioso, L'. *See* Harrison, George
Angel of Comedy, The. *See* Chabrier, (Alexis) Emmanuel
Angela. *See* White, Erma (Marceline)
Angeli, Carlo d'. *See* Engel, Carl
Angelina. *See* Levy, Angelina
Angelo, Michael. *See* Pendergast, Jonathan Barry
Angelo, Ninode. *See* Domenico, Gerhard
Angeloff, Boris. *See* Kremenliev, Boris (Angeloff)
Angelou, Maya. *See* Johnson, Marguerite (Annie)
Angelus Silesius, (Johann). *See* Scheffler, Johann(es)
Anély, Max. *See* Segalen, Victor
Anhart, J. *See* Harthan, Hans
Animosi (di Venezia). *See* Pasqualigo, Benedetto
Anna Marie. *See* Wooldridge, Anna Marie
Annabel. *See* Southard, Mary Ann
Annesley, Charles. *See* Tittmann, Anna
Annesley, Charles. *See* Tittmann, Charles (T(rowbridge))
Anoka, Freddie. *See* Baganier, Janine
Anononyme de Vaugirard, L'. *See* Suard, Jean Baptiste Antoine
Anonymous. *See* Herschell, Esther (née Fuller-Maitland)
Ansell, J. *See* Hansell, John
Anson, Christian B. *See* Burgeson, Avis Marguerite
Anstey, F. *See* Guthrie, Thomas Anstey
Ant, Adam. *See* Goddard, Stuart (Leslie)
Antegnano, Acanlede. *See* Oliva, Francesco
Antesignan, Pierre d'. *See* Davantes, Pierre
Anthias, Teukros [or Teferos]. *See* Paulou, Andreas
Anthony. *See* Tasca, Pier Antonio
Anthony Cyril, (Brother). *See* Higginson, J(oseph) Vincent
Anthony, George Walter. *See* Rochberg, (Aaron) George
Anthony, Hatch. *See* Hatch, Anthony [or Tony] (Peter)
Anthony, Lamont. *See* Dozier, Lamont
Anthony, Malcolm. *See* Ahmonuel, Zyal
Anthony, Marc. *See* Muniz, Marco Antonio
Anthony, Mark. *See* Hatch, Anthony [or Tony] (Peter)
Anthony, Peter. *See* Martinez, Peter Anthony
Anthony, Ray. *See* Antonini, Raymond
Anthony, Vince. *See* D'Antuono, Vincent Joseph
Antichrist Incarnate of Art, The. *See* Wagner, Richard
Antiquus, Andreas. *See* Antico, Andrea
Antoine, Frere. *See* Dellafield, Henry
Antoine, Paul. *See* Closson, Ernest
Antonio, (Mr.). *See* Guido, Giovanni Antonio
Antonio Brassino da Todi. *See* Artusi, Giovanni Maria
Antonio de [or di] Bartolomeo. *See* Squarcialupi, Antonio
Antonio degli Organi. *See* Squarcialupi, Antonio
Antonio del Bessa. *See* Squarcialupi, Antonio
Antonio Maria. *See* Morais, Antonio Maria Araujo de
Antony, F(riedrich). *See* Nikolowsky, Anton(y)
Antwerpen, Leopold. *See* Biermann, Rémon
Anvers, N. d'. *See* Bell, Nancy R. E. Meugens
Aorena, (Mme.). *See* Kamakaeha, Liliu (Loloku Walania)
Ap Rhys, Philip. *See* Rhys, Philip ap
Apel, Willi [or Willy]. *See* Appelbaum, Willi
Aphex Twin. *See* James, Richard D(avid)
Apolleon. *See* Daum, Norbert
Apostle of Atonality. *See* Schoenberg, Arnold
Apostle of the American Composer, An. *See* Heinrich, Anton [or Anthony] Philip
Apostle of the Sacred Music of Wales, The. *See* Roberts, John (1822-1877)
Appatista (Fiorentina). *See* Cipretti, Pietro
Apple, James. *See* Crosby, Fanny [i.e., Frances] J(ane)
Apple, Jan. *See* Birner, Günther
Appleton, Albert. *See* Sawyer, Henry S.
Aptommas, (Mr.). *See* Thomas, John (1826-1913)
Aquila. *See* Ransford, Edwin
Aram, Beatrice. *See* Abrahams, Beatrice
Aramis. *See* Burrard, William Dutton
Arandas, George. *See* Ferrand, Humbert
Arbeau, Thoinot. *See* Tabourot, Jehan [or Jean]
Arberine, G. S. *See* Frangkiser, Carl (Moerz)
Arbruster, Johann. *See* Hausenstein, Wilhelm
Arbuckle, Ronnie. *See* Fierstein, Ronald K.
Arcada, Ermelinda Talea Pastorella. *See* Maria Antonia Walpurgis
Arcangelo bolognese. *See* Corelli Arcangelo
Archangelo. *See* Corelli, Arcangelo
Archdeacon of Music. *See* Dwight, John Sullivan
Archdiavolo. *See* Strunck, Nicolas Adam
Archer, George. *See* Hardwick, Archer (F.)
Archer, Harry. *See* Auracher, Harry
Archer, P. T. *See* Keller, Edward McDonald
Archer, Violet. *See* Balestreri, Violet(ta)
Archibald. *See* Gross, Leon T.
Archibald, (Mrs.) George. *See* Palmer, Anna Campbell
Archie Boy. *See* Gross, Leon T.
Archimedes. *See* Bümler, Georg Heinrich
Archimusico of San Marco. *See* Croce, Giovanni (della)
Architect of Early 1990s Black Pop. *See* Edmonds, Kenneth

Architect of Melody. *See* Babcock, Edward Chester
Arcimelo. *See* Corelli, Arcangelo
Arcy, Paul d'. *See* Crémieux, Hector Jonathan
Arcy, Paul d'. *See* Halévy, Ludovic
Arden, Rod(d). *See* Silver, Dave
Arden, Victor. *See* Fuiks, Lewis J(ohn)
Ardia [or Ardio] Rivarota. *See* Varotari, Dario
Ardor. *See* Benjamin, Walter
Ardy. *See* Somis, (Giovanni) Lorenzo
Arena, Tina. *See* Arena, Philopina [or Filippina] (Lida)
Ares, Rob. *See* Waignein, Andre
Arfey, William d'. *See* Plomer, William (Charles Franklin)
Argentier, P. *See* Cecco, Arturo de
Argentine Schubert, The. *See* Guastavino, Carlos
Argindo Bolimeo. *See* Boccherini, Giovanni Gastone
Argolide, Egisippo. *See* Lanfranchi Rossi, Carlo Giuseppi
Argon, Gutyn. *See* Jones, Griffith Hugh
Argov, Sasha. *See* Abramovich, Aleksandr
Argus. *See* Gille, Philippe Émile François
Arguto, Rosebery d'. *See* Rosenberg, Martin
Arick, Ron. *See* Frederick, Donald R.
Ariel. *See* Werker, Wilhelm
Arimont, Jean. *See* Majowski, Ernest
Arioste, Paul. *See* Leest, Antonius Maria van
Aristobulos Eutropius. *See* Feind, Barthold
Aristoxenus, (der juengere). *See* Mattheson, Johann
Arizona Cowboy, The. *See* Allen, Rex (Elvey)
Arkadevich, Alexander. *See* Ginzburg, Alexandr Arkad'evich
Arkansas Comedian, The. *See* Macarthy, Harry B.
Arkell, Billy. *See* Arkell, Reginald
Arlac, (Gil). *See* Otten, Heinz
Arland, Rolf. *See* Mühlbauer, Hans Heinz
Arlen, Harold. *See* Arluck, Hymen
Arlington, Marion. *See* Moore, Luella Lockwood
Arluk, Chaim. *See* Arluck, Hymen
Arma, Paul. *See* Weisshaus, Imre
Armand. *See* Blackmar, A(rmand) E(dward)
Armand. *See* Dégas (Liorat), Georges
Armand, Charles. *See* Puerner, Charles
Armand-Gouffé. *See* Gouffé, Armand
Armand, I. [or J.] O. *See* Knorr, Iwan [or Ivan] (Otto Armand)
Armand, Jacques. *See* Thiel, Olof
Armand, René. *See* Kronke, Emil
Armando, Georg. *See* Koczalski, Ra(o)ul (Armand Georg)
Armando, Jerzy. *See* Koczalski, Ra(o)ul (Armand Georg)
Armando, Jose. *See* Zuccamana, Gizelle Augusta
Armando, Walter Gualtério. *See* Dahms, Walter
Armándola, J(osé). *See* Lautenschläger, Willi
Armatus, Baptista. *See* Rist, Johann
Armbruster, Johann. *See* Hausenstein, Wilhelm
Armen, Georg. *See* Herrmann, Georg (1871-1963)
Armenteros, Chocolate. *See* Armenteros, Alfredo
Armin, Georg. *See* Herrmann, Georg (1871-1963)
Armin, Josef. *See* Rottensteiner, Josef
Armitage, Frank. *See* Carpenter, John(ny)
Armonico, L'. *See* Fabbrini, Giuseppe
Armonico Intronato. *See* Agazzari, Agostino
Armonide Terpsicoreo. *See* Gluck, Christoph Willibald
Armont, Paul. *See* Petrococchino, Dimitri
Armstrong, Alice. *See* Crosby, Fanny [i.e., Frances] J(ane)
Armstrong, Chris. *See* Martin, Ray(mond)
Armstrong, Harry. *See* Armstrong, Henry W.
Armstrong, King. *See* Armstrong, (Daniel) Louis
Armstrong, Louie. *See* Armstrong, (Daniel) Louis
Armstrong, Paul. *See* Harris, Robert P.
Armstrong, Paul. *See* Lee, Albert George
Armstrong, Pops. *See* Armstrong, (Daniel) Louis
Armstrong, Robert. *See* Fisher, William Arms
Armstrong, Satchmo. *See* Armstrong, (Daniel) Louis
Armstrong, Shelley. *See* Easton, Amos
Army's One Man Hit Parade, The. *See* Loesser, Frank Henry
Arnaud, Léo. *See* Arnaud, Noel
Arndt, Frank. *See* Kunkel, Charles
Arnie, Ralf. *See* Niederbremer, Artur
Arnie, Rolf. *See* Niederbremer, Artur
Arnim, Bettina von. *See* Brentano(-von Arnim), Anne Elisabeth [or Bettina]
Arnimsson, Arne. *See* Zeidler, Armin
Arno, Ernst. *See* Quelle, Ernst-August
Arno, George. *See* Arellano, George Isidro
Arno, Joe. *See* Hardin, Louis (Thomas)
Arnold, Buddy. *See* Arnold, Bernard
Arnold, Clifford. *See* King, Reginald (Claude McMahon)
Arnold, Ernest. *See* Jeschke, Ernst
Arnold, Franz. *See* Hirsch, Franz
Arnold, Harry. *See* Persson, Harry (Arnold)
Arnold, Hugh. *See* Richter, Ada A.
Arnold, Jack. *See* Coates, Eric
Arnold, Kokomo. *See* Arnold, James
Arnold, Maurice. *See* Strothotte, Maurice Arnold
Arnold, Stanley. *See* Rowley, Alec
Arnold, Walter F. *See* Wilcock, Roland
Arnolds, J. *See* Graubins, Jekabs
Arnone, Don L. *See* Arnone, Dominick L.
Arnould. *See* Adorni, Achille
Arnusto. *See* Frauenberger, P. Ernst, OSB
Aroah. *See* Tremblay, Irene
Arodin, Sidney (J.). *See* Arnondrin, Sidney (J.)
Arolas, Eduardo. *See* Arola, Lorenzo
Arpa, Giovanni Leonardo dell'. *See* Mollica, Giovanni Leonardo

Arrieu, Claude. *See* Simon, Louise Marie
Arrighi, Cletto. *See* Righetti, Carlo
Arrighus. *See* Isaac, Heinrich
Arrigo d'Ugo. *See* Isaac, Heinrich
Arrigo il Tedesco. *See* Isaac, Heinrich
Arrigo, Tedesco. *See* Isaac, Heinrich
Arrow. *See* Cassell, Alphonsus
Arroyo, Angel. *See* Villoldo (Arroyo), Angel (Gregorio)
Ars. *See* Avraamov, Arseny Mikhaylovich
Arthur, Bob(b). *See* Shaftel, Arthur [or Artie]
Arthur, C. M. *See* Cohen, Arthur C.
Arthur, Edward. *See* Evans, David
Arthur, Gerald. *See* Bergh, Arthur
Arthurs, H. W. *See* Hughes, Arthur W(ellesley)
Arthurs, William. *See* Rowe, William [or M. C.]
Artimio Corasio. *See* Trapassi (Gallastri), Pietro Antonio
Artino Corasio. *See* Trapassi (Gallastri), Pietro Antonio
Artison. *See* Ortolani, Riz(iero)
Artist, The. *See* Nelson, Prince Rogers
Artist Formerly Known as Prince. *See* Nelson, Prince Rogers
Artist in Prose, An. *See* Hale, Philip
Artok, H. *See* Windsperger, Lothar
Artok, L. *See* Toch, Ernst
Artok, L(eo). *See* Windsperger, Lothar
Artola, Quico. *See* Artola, Héctor
Artot, Charles Henri Napoléon. *See* Montagney, Charles H. N.
Artôt, Jean Désiré. *See* Montagney, Jean D.
Artôt, (Alexandre) Joseph (Montagney). *See* Montagney, Alexandre Joseph
Artot, Maurice. *See* Montagney, Maurice
Arundale, Claude. *See* Kelly, Claude Arundale
Arvin, Andrew. *See* Adorian, Andrew
Arvon, (Bobby). *See* Arvonio, Robert Anthony
Aryan, Marc. *See* Marcarian, Henri
Arzonia, Joe. *See* Longbrake, Arthur
Asaf, George. *See* Powell, George (Henry)
Asaphides. *See* Chatterton, Thomas
Ascanio del Cornetto. *See* Cavallari, Ascanio
Asche, Oscar. *See* Heiss, John Stanger
Ase, Dirk d'. *See* d'Haese, Dirk Hippoliet Ambrosius
Ash, Marvin. *See* Ashbaugh, Marvin
Ash, Paul. *See* Aschenbrenner, Paul
Ashbury, Andrew. *See* Shallman, Morty
Ashby, Florine. *See* Shearouse, Florine W(hiteurst)
Ashford, Robert. *See* Fisher, William Arms
Ashleigh Denis. *See* Lockton, Edward F.
Asher, Colin. *See* Hare, Nicholas
Ashley, Leon. *See* Walton, Leon
Ashley of Bath. *See* Ashley, John [or Josiah]
Ashley, Thomas Clarence. *See* McCurry, Clarence Earl
Ashman, Howard (Elliott). *See* Gershman, Howard Elliott
Ashton, Frank B. *See* Crawford, William
Ashton, John. *See* Mullen, Frederic
Askey, Arthur. *See* Bowden, Arthur
Asmus. *See* Claudius, Matthias
Asne de Rilpe. *See* Speer, Daniel
Asperi, Ursula. *See* Appignani, Adelaide (Orsola)
Aspri, Orsola. *See* Appignani, Adelaide (Orsola)
Asro, Gene. *See* Rossana, Augustine S(amuel)
Assassinator of Syncopation. *See* LaRocca, Dominick James
Assicurato, L'. *See* Dall'Angelo, Giacomo
Assicurato, Academico Incognito. *See* Badoaro, Giacomo
Assoucy, Charles Coypeau d'. *See* Coypeau, Charles
Astaire, Fred. *See* Austerlitz, Frederick
Asten, J(org). *See* Raich, Heribert
Aster, Ed. *See* Ascher, Everett
Astley, Ted. *See* Astley, Edwin Thomas
Aston, James. *See* White, Terence Hanbury
Aston, (A.) William. *See* Ketèlbey, Albert William
Astor, Tom. *See* Bräutigam, Willi
Atchison, Tex. *See* Atchison, Shelby David
Atheling, William. *See* Pound, Ezra ((Weston) Loomis)
Atherton, Rose. *See* Crosby, Fanny [i.e., Frances] J(ane)
Athesinus, (Leonardus). *See* Lechner, Leonard
Athesinus, Petrus Tritonius. *See* Treybenreif, Peter
Atkinson, Geoffrey. *See* Kapp, Paul
Atlas. *See* Van Vechten, Carl
Atomic-Powered Singer, The. *See* Presley, Elvis A(a)ron
Attabalippa del Peru. *See* Banchieri, Adriano (Tomaso)
Atticus. *See* McCollin, Frances
Attila of the Piano, The. *See* Thalberg, Sigismond
Attila the Stockbroker. *See* Baine, John
Attilio. *See* Ariosti, Attilio (Malachia [or Clementi])
Atwell, Winifred. *See* Levisohn, Winifred
Aubecq, Pierre d'. *See* Linder, Anton
Aubert, Celia. *See* McConathy, Osbourne
Aubigny, (B(audouin)) d'. *See* Baudouin, Jean Marie Theodore
Aubry, Leon. *See* Slater, David Dick
Aubry, Paul. *See* Clutsam, George Howard
Auchester, Charles. *See* Kunkel, Charles
Auer, K(arl). *See* Raich, Heribert
Auer, Karl. *See* Frotzler, Karl
Auer, Pepsi. *See* Auer, Josef
Auffdiener, Caroline Wuiet, baronne. *See* Wuiet, Caroline
Augarde, Hayd(o)n. *See* Rawlings, Charles Arthur
Augarde, Jean. *See* Rawlings, Charles Arthur
Auge, Bud. *See* Auge, Henry J., Jr.
Auguste, Monsieur. *See* Hillhouse, Augustus Lucas
Augustin, G. B. *See* Blasser, Gustav
Augustin Marie (du Très Saint Sacrement), père. *See* Cohen, Hermann
Auinger, Sam. *See* Auinger, Franz Joseph Maria

Auld, George (or Georgie). *See* Altwerger, John
Aulétés. *See* Widor, Charles-Marie (Jean Albert)
Aunt Fanny. *See* Crosby, Fanny [i.e., Frances] J(ane)
Aunt Jemima. *See* Wilson, Edith
Auntie Hale. *See* Hale, Philip
Auntie Martha. *See* Hohu, Martha Poepoe
Auralis. *See* Mackie, James
Aurelius Gratianus. *See* Neale, J(ohn) M(ason)
Austed, I. Felix. *See* Costello, Billy
Austen, Eric. *See* Croom-Johnson, Austen [or Austin] (Herbert)
Austen, Eric. *See* Siday, Eric
Austin, Bert. *See* Williams, Egbert Austin
Austin, Egbert. *See* Williams, Egbert Austin
Austin, Gene. *See* Lucas, Eugene
Austin, Lovie. *See* Calhoun, Cora
Austin, Martin. *See* Shewell, George Dunbar
Austin, Robert E. *See* Manney, Charles Fonteyn
Australia's First Composer. *See* Nathan, Isaac
Australia's King of Country Music. *See* Kirkpatrick, David Gordon
Australia's Yodelling Stockmen. *See* LeGarde, Edward [or Ted]
Australia's Yodelling Stockmen. *See* LeGarde, Thomas
Austrian March King. *See* Wagner, Josef Franz
Aute, L. E. *See* Gutierrez, Luis Eduardo Aute
Author of Rock Me to Sleep. *See* Allen, Elizabeth Ann (Chase) (née Akers)
Author of "The Archers". *See* Dunlap, William
Author of "The Father". *See* Dunlap, William
Author of The Siege of Valenciennes. *See* King, Matthew Peter
Autodidactos, Amadeus. *See* Richter, Heinrich Friedrich Wilhelm
Automation Pianist, The. *See* Gottschalk, Louis Moreau
Autumnus, Johann Andreas. *See* Herbst, Johann Andreas
Auvray. *See* Chapelle, Paul Aimé
Aux-Costeaus, Artus. *See* Hautcousteaux, Arthur
Avenarius, Philipp. *See* Habermann, Philipp
Avenary, Hanoch. *See* Loewenstein, Herbert
Aventinus, Johannes. *See* Turmair, Johannes
Avera, Franco. *See* Wrisch, Gerhard
Averell, Philip. *See* Nagle, William S.
Avia, Jacob. *See* Banwart, Jakob
Avon Comedy Four. *See* Dale, Charles
Avon Comedy Four. *See* Goodwin, Harry
Avon Comedy Four. *See* Kaufman, Isidore
Avon Comedy Four. *See* Smith, Joe
Avon, Rex. *See* Ewing, Montague (George)
Avril, Octave d'. *See* Paroisse-Pougin, François-Auguste-Arthur
Awankana. *See* Smith, Antonio
Awbury. *See* McCollin, Frances
Axel, Robert. *See* Laks, Szymon [or Simon]
Axes. *See* Sterzel, Alexander C.
Axolot(l). *See* Meister, Karl (August)
Ayaz. *See* Khan, Hidayat Inayat
Ayers, Albert. *See* Cain, Noble
Ayre, Jack. *See* Ayre, Ivor
Ayres, Frederic. *See* Johnson, Frederic Ayres
Ayres, Mitchell. *See* Agress, Mitchell
Azancheev. *See* Pavlov, Matvei
Azetiano, Protico. *See* Pasquini, Bernardo
Azmanli. *See* Gafarov Ilham Baba
Aznar, Faro. *See* Aznar, Abel (Mariano)
Aznavour, Charles. *See* Aznavourian, (Shanaur) Varenagh
Azor, Lovebug. *See* Azor, Hurby
Azro, Gene. *See* Rossana, Augustine S(amuel)
Azuquita, Camilo. *See* Argumédez, Camilo Luis

– B –

B. *See* Bayly, (Nathaniel) Thomas Haynes
B. *See* Bubier, George Burden
B. *See* Gilbert, William Schwenk
B***, (Monsieur). *See* Bailleux, François
B d. *See* Barbauld, Anna Laetitia (née Aikin)
B -g. *See* Berling, Thomas
B-h. *See* Birnbach, (Joseph Benjamin) Heinrich
B. B. *See* Beddome, Benjamin
B. B. *See* Coleman, Gary
B. B. *See* Oliphant, Carolina
BB Chung King. *See* Mirikitana, Alan Masao
BB Jr. *See* Odom, Andrew
B. D. B. *See* Bacilly, Bénigne (de)
B. E. L. *See* Shaw, Martin (Fallas)
B. E. W. *See* Warren, B. Elliott
B., Eric. *See* Barrier, Eric
BFC. *See* Craig, Carl
B. f. z. Z. *See* Weber, Carl Maria von
B. G. *See* Goodman, Benjamin [or Benny] (David)
B. H. D. *See* Draper, Bourne Hall
B. H. Sees Combo. *See* Haley, William [or Bill] (John Clifton), (Jr.)
B. I. G., (Notorious). *See* Wallace, Chris(topher (G.))
B. L. *See* Tchaikovskii, Peter Illich
B Real. *See* Freese, Louis (1971-)
B. S. *See* Seward, Benjamin
B. T. *See* Littledale, Richard Frederick
Baal, Johannes. *See* Knecht, Justin Heinrich
Bab. *See* Gilbert, William Schwenk
Babalú, Mr. *See* Valdés, Miguelito
Babe, Smoky. *See* Brown, Robert (1927-1975)
Babit, Hi [or Hy]. *See* Babich, Herman Bernard
Babtist, Jean Frederic. *See* Schäfer, Johannes
Baby Bird. *See* Jones, Stephen [or Steven]

Baby Champ. *See* Deutscher, Karlheinz
Baby Doo. *See* Caston, Leonard
Baby Duke. *See* Caston, Leonard
Baby Face (Leroy). *See* Foster, Leroy
Baby Star. *See* Howard, Ethel
Baby U. *See* Hawkins, Lamont
Babyface. *See* Edmonds, Kenneth
Bacalof, Luis. *See* Bacalov, Luis Enriquez
Baccellino. *See* Civinini, Guelfo
Bacciccia. *See* Ricciotti, Carlo
Baccino, Antonio. *See* Artusi, Giovanni Maria
Bach, Johann Christian. *See* Casadesus, Marius Robert Max
Bach, Johann Sebastian (Spirit). *See* Brown, Rosemary (née Dickeson)
Bach, Karl Phillip Emanuel. *See* Casadeus, Francis [or François] Louis
Bach of Bohemia. *See* Černohorsky, Bohuslav Matej
Bach of Rock, The. *See* Byrd, Henry Roeland
Bach of the Carillon. *See* Vanden Gheyn, Matthias
Bach, P. D. Q. *See* Schickele, Peter (Johann)
Bach, Paul. *See* Baumbach, Rudolf
Bacher, Bert. *See* Herchenbach, Robert
Bachiche, Charles. *See* Ricciotti, Carlo
Bachmann, G. *See* Gobbaerts, Jean Louis
Bachmann, Georges. *See* Behr, F(ranz)
Bachtischa, Michael Bach. *See* Bach, Michael
Backy, Don. *See* Caponi, Aldo
Backy Doug. *See* Caponi, Aldo
Bacon, Dolores. *See* Bacon, Mary Schell Hoke
Bacon, Leslie. *See* Davis, Joseph [or Joe] (M.)
Bad Boy of Conducting. *See* Tilson-Thomas, Michael
Bad Boy of Music, The. *See* Antheil, George
Badale, Andy. *See* Badalamenti, Angelo (Daniel)
Badazz, Randy. *See* Alpert, Randy (C.)
Badu, Erykah. *See* Wright, Erica
Baer, Herman de. *See* Falk, Dieter
Baer, Mabel. *See* McKinley, Mabel
Bagnacavallo, Giuseppe da. *See* Tamburini, Giuseppe
Bags. *See* Jackson, Milt(on)
Bagwill, Olive Bradley. *See* Kunkel, Charles
Bahr, Alfa. *See* Bahr, Carlos Andrés
Bahr, Bert. *See* Bahr, Robert
Bähr, Johann. *See* Beer, Johann
Bahr, Luke. *See* Bahr, Carlos Andrés
Bailey, E. Rawdon. *See* Bonner, Carey
Bailey, G(eorge). *See* Balay, Guillaume
Bailey, Bill. *See* Basie, William (Allen)
Bailey, Razzy [or Rasie]. *See* Bailey, Erastus [or Rasie] Michael
Bain, Guy. *See* Linden, David Gysbert (van der)
Baines, Boogie. *See* Barnes, H(oward) E(llington)
Baird, Alan. *See* Cowdell, Ellen
Baker, Buddy. *See* Baker, Norman (Dale)
Baker, Dave. *See* De Muyt, Aimé
Baker, Dick Two Ton. *See* Baker, Richard (Evans)
Baker, Donald. *See* Finkelstein, Abe
Baker, Fannie. *See* Thomas, Lillian [or Lillyan]
Baker, Fanny. *See* Nelson, Lucille
Baker, Guitar. *See* Baker, McHouston
Baker, James. *See* Gershvin, Jacob
Baker, John S. *See* Stamford, John J.
Baker, Kidd. *See* Baker, Ransford
Baker, Mickey. *See* Baker, McHouston
Baker, Peter. *See* Meyer, Ernst Hermann
Baker, Ralph. *See* Lake, M(ayhew) L(ester)
Baker, Robert. *See* Meek, Robert (George)
Baker, Shorty. *See* Baker, Harold
Baker, Two Ton. *See* Baker, Richard (Evans)
Baker, Ward. *See* Davis, Joseph [or Joe] (M.)
Baki, Wolf. *See* Barczewski, Wolfgang
Bala-aqyn. *See* Azerbayev, Kenen
Balbulus (the Stammerer). *See* Notker, (Balbulus)
Baldini, Guglielmo [fictitious composer]. *See* Baldini, Guglielmo [fictitious composer]
Baldissera. *See* Galuppi, Baldassare
Baldrati, Bartolomeo. *See* Tamburini, Giuseppe
Baldwin, Arthur. *See* Finkelstein, Abe
Baldwin, Edda. *See* Bergersen, Edith
Baldwin, Roxanna. *See* Wilson, Ira B(ishop)
Balena, Draga. *See* Hoffmann Balenovic, Draga
Baler, Robert. *See* Laber, Richard
Balfour, John. *See* Ireson, John Balfour
Balin, Marty. *See* Buchwald, Martyn J(erel)
Baline, Izzy. *See* Baline, Israel
Balino, (Annibale Pio). *See* Fabri, Annibale Pio
Balkie Gregoire. *See* Gaul, Harvey B(artlett)
Ball, Mel. *See* Franchini, Anthony Joseph
Ball, T. *See* Moody, Tom
Ballad King, The. *See* Dawson, Peter (Smith)
Balladeer of Baseball, The. *See* Minogue, Dennis (Michael)
Balladeer of the Golden West. *See* Carter, Wilf(red Arthur Charles)
Ballang, Ary. *See* Otten, Heinz
Ballard, Eugene E(dgar). *See* Johnson, Charles L(eslie)
Ballard, Hank [or Henry]. *See* Kendricks, John Henry
Ballard, Pat. *See* Ballard, Francis Drake
Ballard, Wolfe. *See* Slaughter, M(arion) T(ry)
Ballini. *See* Becker, Adolf
Baloo, Sam (Spunky). *See* Beaulieu, Donald George
Baltazarini (da Beligioiso). *See* Belgiojoso, Baldassare de
Balth, Willy. *See* Goletz, Philipp Simon
Balthesar. *See* Kiesewetter, Raphael-Georg
Baltimorean in Louisiana. *See* Randall, James R(yder)
Bana, Da Paula. *See* Palmer, Cedric King
Bananarama. *See* Dallin, Sarah
Bananarama. *See* Fahey, Siobhan
Bananarama. *See* Woodward, Keren

Bancroft(-Price), Peter. *See* Bauchwitz, Peter
Band King, The. *See* Frangkiser, Carl (Moerz)
Band King of Switzerland. *See* Jaeggi, Stephen
Bander, Till. *See* Roever, Uli
Bandini, Arturo. *See* Mika, Rudolf [or Rolf]
Bandler, George. *See* McCray, Don
Bandler, George. *See* Sour, Robert (B.)
Bandy Legged. *See* Gouffé, Armand
Bang, Billy. *See* Walker, William Vincent
Bang Boys. *See* Acuff, Roy (Claxton)
Banger, Ed. *See* Garrity, Eddie
Banjo, The. *See* Paterson, A(ndrew) B(arton)
Banjo Boy, The. *See* Nash, Lemoine
Banjo Eyes. *See* Iskowitz, Edward Israel
Banjo Joe. *See* Cannon, Gus
Banjo King of the Southland, The. *See* Guesnon, George
Banks, Mervyn. *See* Dickson, Mary Hannah
Banter, Harald. *See* Wysocki, Gerd von
Baptiste. *See* Anet, Jean-Jacques-Baptiste
Baptiste, M. *See* Stuck, Johann Baptist(e)
Baptistet. *See* Daudet, (Louis Marie) Alphonse
Baptistin, Jean. *See* Stuck, Johann Baptist(e)
Baradaprana, P(ravrajika). *See* Ludwig, Doris (Adell)
Baraka, (Imamu) Amiri. *See* Jones, (Everett) LeRoi [originally Leroy]
Barat, Jehan. *See* Barra, Hotinet
Barbaro del Ritmo, El. *See* Moré (Gutiérrez), Bartolomé Maximiliano
Barbecue Bob. *See* Hicks, Robert
Barbecue Joe & His Hot Dogs. *See* Manone, Joseph
Barber, Barney. *See* Cook, William Mercer
Barber, Pinkus. *See* Kaufmann, Fritz Mordechai
Barbeta. *See* Manzione, Homer Nicolás
Barbier, Mlle. *See* Pellegrin, Simon Joseph
Barbieri, Gato. *See* Barbieri, Leandro J.
Barclay, Arthur. *See* Jones, Arthur Barclay
Barclay, Eddie. *See* Ruault, Edouard
Barclay, Martin. *See* Austin, Frederick
Bard from Savannah. *See* Mercer, John(ny) (H(erndon))
Bard, Léon. *See* Lombardo, Carlo
Bard of Armagh, The. *See* Makem, Tommy
Bard of Barking, The. *See* Bragg, (Steven) William [or Billy]
Bard of Epworth. *See* Wesley, Charles
Bard of Hope, The. *See* Campbell, Thomas
Bard of the Bedsits. *See* Cohen, Leonard
Bard of the British Navy, The. *See* Dibdin, Charles
Bard of the Ozarks, The. *See* Morris, James C(orbett)
Bard of the Rockies, The. *See* Warman, Cy
Bard of the Stars and Bars. *See* Hewitt, John (Henry) Hill
Bardd Alaw. *See* Parry, John (1776-1851)
Bardd y Brenin. *See* Jones, Edward (1752-1824)
Barde, André. *See* Bourdonneaux, André
Bardi, Benno. *See* Poswiansky, Benno
Bardi, Mascotita. *See* Bardi, Agustin
Bardows, M. S. [or T. S.]. *See* Bradsworth, Samuel
Barham, Thomas. *See* Ingoldsby, Richard
Barker, Blue Lu [or Lou]. *See* Dupont, Louise [or Louisa]
Barker, Louisa. *See* Dupont, Louise [or Louisa]
Barlaam. *See* Bernard
Barl(l)et, Paul. *See* Héon, Paul
Barlow, Jack. *See* Butcher, Jack
Barlow, (S.) Stephen. *See* Ehret, Walter (Charles)
Barmard, Mr. *See* George III, King of Great Britain
Barmede, Atoli. *See* Bartoli, Amedeo
Barmes, William. *See* Wells, John Barnes
Barn Dance Sweethearts. *See* Amburgey, Irene
Barn Dance Sweethearts. *See* Roberts, James William
Barnard, B(arney). *See* Keuleman, Adrian
Barner, Juke Boy. *See* Bonner, Weldon (H. Philip)
Barnes, Bill. *See* Miller, Robert [or Bob] (Ernst)
Barnes, Bosby. *See* Cavanaugh, Robert Barnes
Barnes, David. *See* Hellerman, Fred
Barnes, Janet. *See* Barnett, Jeannette
Barnes, Jessie. *See* Sigman, Carl
Barnes, Joe. *See* Ostrus, Merrill (J.)
Barnes, Joseph. *See* Sawyer, Henry S.
Barnes, William. *See* Wells, John Barnes
Barnet, Mad Mab. *See* Barnet, Charles [or Charlie] (Daly)
Barnett, Curt. *See* Miller, Robert [or Bob] (Ernst)
Barnett, John. *See* Bath, John
Barnett, Leonard C(ecil). *See* Loes, Harry Dixon
Barney and Seymore. *See* Bennett, Theron C(atlin)
Barney, Billy. *See* Baaren, Kees van
Barney, H. *See* Barnes, H. E.
Barnum, H. B. *See* Bono, Salvatore
Barnum of Broadway Producers, The. *See* Margulois, David
Barnum of Opera, The. *See* Hammerstein, Oscar (Greeley Clandenning), II
Barnum Wonder Boy, The. *See* Barnhum, H. B.
Barny, W(al). *See* Rüssmann, Georg(e)
Baron of Burlesque. *See* Burnand, Francis Cowley
Baron of Burlesque. *See* Byron, H(enry) J(ames)
Baron of the Boogie. *See* Hunter, Joseph [or Joe] Hunter
Baron, Ray. *See* Newell, Norman
Baron, Vic. *See* Baroni, Vasco (Peter)
Baronoff, Sascha. *See* Suskind, Milton
Barr, G. Alexander. *See* Kountz, Richard
Barr, Harry. *See* McClaskey, Harry Haley
Barr, Ray. *See* Barr, Raphael L.
Barraza, Pancho. *See* Barraza Rodríguez, Francisco Javier
Barraza, Pepe. *See* Barraza Rodríguez, Francisco Javier
Barrel House Pete. *See* Gillham, Art
Barrelhouse Sammy. *See* McTell, Willie Samuel
Barrelhouse Tommy. *See* Dorsey, Thomas A(ndrew)

Barrell, Alden. *See* Barrell, Edgar Alden, Jr.
Barrett, Bessie. *See* Grady, R(ichard) G.
Barrett, Charles. *See* Kinyon, John L(eroy)
Barrett, Lester. *See* Barrett, Stephen
Barrett, Meredith. *See* Clarke, Mary Elizabeth
Barrett, Syd. *See* Barrett, Roger (Keith)
Barri, Odoardo. *See* Slater, Edward
Barri, Steve. *See* Lipkin, Stephen [or Steve] (Barri [or Barry])
Barricini, D. *See* Dash, Irwin
Barrie, J. J. *See* Authors, Barrie
Barrie, Neville. *See* Darewski, Hermann E(dward)
Barrie, Royden. *See* Bennett, (Harry) Rodney
Barrie, Walter. *See* Ehret, Walter (Charles)
Barriere, Alain. *See* Bellec, Alain
Barringer, Barbara. *See* Marshall, Alice Smith
Barrington, Jonah. *See* Dalmaine, Cyril
Barrington, Rutland. *See* Fleet, George Rutland
Barrionuevo, Ciriaquito. *See* Ortiz Barrionuevo, (Angel) Ciriaco
Barrister of the Inner Temple. *See* McNally, Leonard
Barrister, Sikiru Ayinde. *See* Ayinde, Sikiru
Barron, Bebe. *See* Wind, Charlotte
Barron, Ed. *See* Bernhardt, Clyde Edric Barron
Barrows, Walt. *See* Whippo, Walter Barrows
Barry, Jeff. *See* Adelberg, Jeff [or Joel]
Barry, John. *See* Pendergast, Jonathan Barry
Barry, Len. *See* Borisoff, Leonard
Barry, Otto. *See* Batka, Otto Barry
Barski, Aleksander. *See* Bandrowski-Sas, Alexander
Bart, Lionel. *See* Begleiter, Lionel
Bartaud, Jean. *See* Barraud, Jean
Bartelet, Jeanne. *See* Rawlings, Charles Arthur
Bartell, Henry. *See* Grady, R(ichard) G.
Bartells, (H(arold)) D(eKoven)). *See* Loes, Harry Dixon
Bartels, Henry. *See* Loes, Harry Dixon
Bartels, Johnny. *See* Feltz, Kurt (August Karl)
Bartlett, John. *See* Barthelson, (Helen) Joyce (Holloway)
Barth, Otto. *See* Barnard, D'Auvergne
Barthe, A(drien). *See* Barthe, Grat-Norbert
Barthélemon, Polly. *See* Barthélemon, Maria (née Young)
Barto, Gustave. *See* Fisher, Ethel
Barto, Tzimon. *See* Smith, John Barto, Jr.
Bartolli, Mario. *See* Ordnung, Rudolf (August)
Bartolomeo (degli Organi). *See* Baccio, Fiorentino
Barton, Andrew. *See* Forrest, Thomas
Barton, Andrew. *See* Leacock, John
Barton, Glen. *See* Brocht, Harley F.
Barton, Glen. *See* Klemm, Gustav
Barton, Robert (L.). *See* Cain, Noble
Barton, Tippy. *See* White, Josh(ua) (Daniel)
Baruch, Louis. *See* Baruch, Löb
Bascomb, Dud. *See* Bascomb, Wilbur Odell
Baseball's Hit Man. *See* Minogue, Dennis (Michael)
Basement Barnum, The. *See* Rosenberg, William Samuel
Basia. *See* Trzetrzelewska, Basia
Basie, Count. *See* Basie, William (Allen)
Basilicus, Ciprianus. *See* Bazylik, Cyprjan [or Cyprian]
Baskoff, Ivan. *See* Meilhac, Henri
Basque, Andre (de). *See* Ketèlbey, Albert William
Basset, Serge. *See* Ribon, Paul
Bassevi, Giacomo. *See* Cervetto, James (1682-1783)
Bassman, The. *See* Bailey, Winston [or Wilston]
Basso, Pro Phundo. *See* Bliss, P(hilip) P.
Basswood, W. K. *See* Bassford, William Kipp [or Kapp]
Bastardella, La. *See* Aguiari [or Agujari], Lucrezia
Bastardina, La. *See* Aguiari [or Agujari], Lucrezia
Bastia, Pascal. *See* Simoni, Pascal
Bat "The Hummingbird". *See* Davenport, Charles Edward
Bat the Humming-Bird. *See* Robinson, James
Bataan, Joe. *See* Nitrollando, Peter, Jr.
Batanoff, Grischa. *See* Hartmann, Otto B.
Bates, Bobo. *See* Bates, Kathleen Doyle
Bates, Django. *See* Bates, Leon
Bates, (Deacon) L. J. *See* Jefferson, Clarence
Bateson, John. *See* Jacobson, Maurice
Bath. *See* Bathurst, William Hiley
Bath, Oliver. *See* Tiverton, Viscount (Adam Edward Giffard)
Bathori, Jane. *See* Berthier, Jeanne-Marie
Bat(t)istin, Jean. *See* Stuck, Johann Baptist(e)
Batsford, J. Tucker. *See* Kapp, Paul
Batteau, Robin. *See* Batteau, Dwight Wayne, Jr.
Batten, Robert. *See* Wilson, Henry (James) Lane
Battle, Puddinghead. *See* Battle, Edgar (William)
Battle, Roger. *See* Battle, Edgar (William)
Battochio, Arlequin. *See* Miani, Marco
Bauer, Gerd. *See* Gutesha, Mladen
Bauer, Gyula. *See* Bauer, Julius
Bauer, Hertha. *See* Adler, Hans
Bauer, Wright. *See* Philpott, George Vere Hobart
Baül. *See* Blau, Alfred
Baule. *See* Hindemith, Paul
Baum. *See* Stamm, Werner
Baum, Allen. *See* Bunn, Alden
Baum, Hans. *See* Müller, Rolf-Hans
Baum, Stanley. *See* Applebaum, Stan(ley) (Seymour)
Baur, Mme. de. *See* Bawr, Alexandrine Sophie de
Bavent, Jean. *See* Tournes, Jean de
Bäwerl, Paul. *See* Peuerl, Paul
Baxter, Albert. *See* Reubrecht, Albert
Baxter, Francis. *See* Reubrecht, Albert
Baxter, Geoffrey. *See* Dawson, Peter (Smith)
Baxter, Larry. *See* Setaro, Pete(r) (D(onald))
Baxter, Lionel. *See* Zamecnik, J(ohn) S(tepan)
Baxter, Ma. *See* Baxter, Clarice Howard
Baxter, Pap. *See* Baxter, J(essie) R(andall), (Jr.)

Baxter, Ted. *See* Cook, J. Lawrence
Baxter, Ted. *See* Kortlander, Max
Baxter, Ted. *See* Roberts, Lee S.
Bay, F. A. *See* Strübe, Hermann
Bayer, Frederick. *See* Baycock, Frederick
Bayes, Nora. *See* Goldberg Doris
Bayliss, Richard. *See* Lockton, Edward F.
Bazelon, Buddy. *See* Bazelon, Irwin (A.)
Beach, Alden. *See* Beach, Priscilla A.
Beacon, Leslie. *See* Davis, Joseph [or Joe] (M.)
Beal, Hefty. *See* Ballard, Francis Drake
Beale Street Blues Boy. *See* King, Riley B.
Beaman, Lottie. *See* Kimbrough, Lottie
Bean. *See* Hawkins, Coleman (Randolph)
Bean, Rubino Roger. *See* Bohn, Rudolf [or Rudolph]
Beans, Gus. *See* Fillmore, (James) Henry
Bear, The. *See* Gordy, Berry, Jr.
Beatcomber. *See* Lennon, John (Winston)
Beatles, The. *See* Harrison, George
Beatles, The. *See* Lennon, John (Winston)
Beatles, The. *See* McCartney, (James) Paul
Beatles, The. *See* Starkey, Richard
Beatrice, F. *See* Keiser, Robert (A(dolph))
Beatty, John. *See* Grey, Frank H(erbert)
Beatty, Josephine. *See* Hunter, Alberta
Beau, Heinie. *See* Beau, Henry John
Beaujoyeux, Balthasar de. *See* Belgiojoso, Baldassare de
Beaulac, Mayhew. *See* Lake, M(ayhew) L(ester)
Beaulieu, Sam. *See* Beaulieu, Donald George
Beaulieu, Toni [or Tony]. *See* Depaolis, Leone F.
Beaumont, Alexandre [or Alexander]. *See* Beaume, (Louis) Alexandre [or Alexander]
Beaumont, H. *See* Jordan, Harry C.
Beaumont, Paul. *See* Saenger, Gustav(e)
Beaumont, Paul. *See* Smith, Edward Sydney
Beaunoir, (Madame) de. *See* Robineau, Alexandre-Louis-Bertrand
Beauplan, Arthur de. *See* Rousseau, Victor Arthur
Beaupré, Cadet de. *See* Poinsinet de Sivry, Louis
Beaver, George. *See* Kaufman, Isidore
Beaver, Harry. *See* Kaufman, Isidore
Beaver, Henry. *See* Kaufman, Isidore
BeBop Betty. *See* Jones, Lillie Mae
BeBop Boy, The. *See* Hill, Lester [or Leslie]
Bebop Kid, El. *See* Huerta, Baldemar G(arza)
Bécaud, Gilbert. *See* Silly, (Gilbert) François (Léopold)s
Becho. *See* Matos Rodríguez, G(h)erardo (Hernáu)
Becht, C. *See* Kern, Carl Wilhelm
Bechter, Karl. *See* Goerdeler, Richard
Beck. *See* Campbell, Bek David
Beck, Jean. *See* Beck, Johann Baptist
Beck, R(andy). *See* Verbeeck, Frans
Beckaroo. *See* Hobbs, Rebecca [or Becky] (Ann)
Becker, E. *See* Ailbout, Hans
Becker, Jean. *See* Retter, Louis
Becker, Will(iam) (H.). *See* Botsford, George
Becker, William. *See* Schickele, Peter (Johann)
Beckermann, Denny. *See* Papathanassiou, Evangelos (Odyssey)
Beckman, August J. *See* Kunkel, Charles
Beckmann. *See* Rüger, Karl Erdmann
Beckmann, Adele. *See* Heinrich, A.
Beckwith, Christmas. *See* Beckwith, John (Christmas)
Beckwith of Norwich, Dr. *See* Beckwith, John (Christmas)
Bécquer, Gustavo Adolfo. *See* Bastida, Gustavo Adolfo Dominguez
Beda. *See* Wieck, Clara Josephine
Beda, (Fritz). *See* Löhner(-Beda), Fritz
Bede, Cuthbert. *See* Bradley, (Revd.) Edward
Bedell, Lew. *See* Bideu, Louis
Bedrokowetzky. *See* Kavetzky, Samuel
Bee, David. *See* Craps, Ernest (Jean)
Bee, Laurie. *See* Bobrow, Laura J.
Bee, Pee Pee. *See* Bliss, P(hilip) P.
Beech, Vernon. *See* Helm, Everett (Burton)
Beecher, Claire. *See* Olman, Abraham [or Abe]
Beefheart, Captain. *See* Van Vliet, Don
Beelzebub's Court Composer. *See* Wagner, Richard
Beenie Man. *See* Davis, Moses
Beer, A. D. *See* Binzer, August Daniel
Beethoven. *See* Hauck, Wenzel
Beethoven, Loosewig von. *See* Marshall, David
Beethoven, Ludwig van. *See* Kunkel, Charles
Beethoven, Ludwig van (Spirit). *See* Brown, Rosemary (neé Dickeson)
Beethoven of America. *See* Heinrich, Anton [or Anthony] Philip
Beethoven of Contemporary Music. *See* Wolpe, Stefan
Beethoven of Guitar. *See* Sor, (Joseph) Fernando (Macari)
Beethoven of Kentucky, The. *See* Heinrich, Anton [or Anthony] Philip
Beethoven of Louisville. *See* Heinrich, Anton [or Anthony] Philip
Beethoven of the Flute, The. *See* Kuhlau, Friedrich Daniel Rodolph
Beethoven of the 16th Century. *See* Josquin Desprez
Beethoven of the 20th Century. *See* Shostakovitch, Dmitri Dmitryevich
Beethoven of the 20th Century Avant-Garde. *See* Ligeti, György
Beethovenian. *See* Beethoven, Ludwig van
Bega, Lou. *See* Loubega, David
Begging-Letter Writer, A. *See* Chorley, Henry Fothergill
Begonha, Alberto. *See* Halletz, Erwin
Behr, Francois. *See* Kunkel, Charles
Behr-Sidus. *See* Kunkel, Charles
Behrens, Johann. *See* Beer, Johann
Bei, Anni M. *See* Benjamin, Walter

Beider, Joe. *See* Grillaert, Octave
Beiderbecke, Bix. *See* Beiderbecke, Leon Bismark
Bel, M'bilia. *See* Mboyo, M'bilia
Béla, Kéler. *See* Kéler, Adalbert Paul von
Belan, Cliff. *See* Bielinski, C(lifford) Martin
Belasco, F(rederick). *See* Rosenfeld, Monroe H.
Belasco, Keystone. *See* Wiemer, Robert Ernest
Belasco, Leon. *See* Berladsky, Leonide Simeonovich
Beldamandis, Prosdocimus de. *See* Heseltine, Philip (Arnold)
Belefan, Sam. *See* Robinson, Edward Alfred
Belfast Cowboy. *See* Morrison, George Ivan
Belga, Heinricus Isaac. *See* Isaac, Heinrich
Belgian Orpheus, The. *See* Lassus, Roland de
Believer in the Internal Evidence of Divine Revelation, A. *See* Clarke, William Horatio
Belknap, Frank. *See* Gilbert, Henry F(ranklin Belknap)
Bell. *See* Samberg, Benjamin
Bell, (E.) —*see* Ailbout, Hans
Bell, Acton. *See* Brontë, Anne
Bell, Benny. *See* Samberg, Benjamin
Bell, (Mrs.) C. *See* Barnard, Charlotte Alington (née Pye)
Bell, Carrie. *See* Crosby, Fanny [i.e., Frances] J(ane)
Bell, Cynthia. *See* Strother, Cynthia
Bell, Eddie. *See* Crow(e), Francis Luther
Bell, George. *See* Galbraith, Gordon
Bell, Jonny. *See* Raida, Karl Alexander
Bell, Louise. *See* Belline, Mary L.
Bell, Paul. *See* Chorley, Henry Fothergill
Bell, Peter. *See* Birch, Peter
Bell, Raymond. *See* Belafonte, Harold [or Harry] (George)
Bell, Roni. *See* Hutcheson, Ronita Marlene
Bell, Victor. *See* Friedman, Leo
Bell, William. *See* Yarborough, William
Bella Adriana, La. *See* Basile, Adriana Baroni
Bellaire, R(aymond) E(arl). *See* Kountz, Richard
Bellak, Ja's. *See* Bellak, James
Bellamare, Count. *See* Saint Germain, Count of
Belle, Barbara. *See* Einhorn, Barbara (Belle)
Belle of the Barn Dance. *See* Cooper, Myrtle Eleanor
Belle-soeur de Bizet, La. *See* Massenet, Jules (Émile Frédéric)
Belledna, Alex. *See* Alexander, Edna Belle
Belledna, Alex. *See* Pinkard, Maceo
Belli, Remo. *See* Balassoni, Luigi Paulino
Bellson, Louis [or Louie] (Paul). *See* Balassoni, Luigi Paulino
Bellus, Tony. *See* Bellusci, Anthony [or Tony] (J.)
Belmont, Chas. W. *See* Haga, Frederick Wallace
Belmont, Chas. W. *See* Ringleben, Justin, Jr.
Belmont, Eric. *See* Nordman, Chester
Belmont, James. *See* Slaughter, M(arion) T(ry)
Belmonte, José. *See* Green, Phil(ip)
Belson, Hortense Gold. *See* Zwibelson, Hortense
Belton, John. *See* Brownsmith, (Reginald) Douglas
Belton, John. *See* Lowry, Anthony [or Tony]
Belvoir, Richard. *See* Darley, George
Belza, Igor Fedorovich. *See* Doroshuk, Igor Fedorovich
Bemis, Big Ben. *See* Dellger, Michael Laurence
Ben-Haim, Paul (Shaul). *See* Frankenburger, Paul
Ben, Jorge. *See* Lima Meneses, Jorge (Duilio)
Ben, Oliver. *See* Reinhardt, Helmut
Benatzky, Ralph. *See* Benatzky, Rudolf Josef Frantisek
Benbow, Edward. *See* Kunkel, Charles
Bendel, Franz. *See* Kunkel, Charles
Bendelssohn. *See* Bendl, Karel
Benedict, Andy. *See* Pflüger, Andreas B.
Bendix, Ralph. *See* Schwab, Karl Heinz
Bendt, Oliver. *See* Koch, Jürgen
Benedatto da Parma. *See* Ferrari, Benedetto
Benedetto dalla Tiorba. *See* Ferrari, Benedetto
Benedetto giorno. *See* Caccini, Giulio (Romolo)
Benedict(us). *See* Ducis, Benedictus
Benedict, Andy. *See* Pflüger, Andreas B.
Benedictus a Sancto Josepho. *See* Buns, Benedictus
Benelli, Alemanno. *See* Bottrigari, Ercole
Benezech, A. *See* Ménissier, Constant
Benfeld. *See* Kopff, Pierre Albert
Bengland, de. *See* Labrunie, Gérard
Benitez, Jellybean. *See* Benitez, John
Benito, Pedro. *See* Bliss, P(hilip) Paul
Benizzo, Franc. *See* Poenitz, Franz
Bennet(t), Dale. *See* Barnet, Charles [or Charlie] (Daly)
Bennett, Alexander. *See* Copeland, Berniece Rose
Bennett, Don. *See* Borzage, Donald Dan
Bennett, Harold. *See* Fillmore, (James) Henry
Bennett, Jimmy. *See* Hicks, Thomas
Bennett, John. *See* Bernard, Al(fred A.)
Bennett, John. *See* Findelstein, Abe
Bennett, Mack E. *See* Marks, Edward B.
Bennett, Michael. *See* DiFiglia, Michael
Bennett, Paul. *See* Barnes, Clifford (Paulus)
Bennett, Robert Russell. *See* Anderson, (Evelyn) Ruth
Bennett, Steve. *See* Fruth, Willi
Benoit, Peter. *See* Benoit, Pierre Léonard Léopold
Benoîton, Fanfan. *See* Paroisse-Pougin, François-Auguste-Arthur
Bensberg, Jack. *See* Blum, Hans
Benson, George. *See* Slaughter, M(arion) T(ry)
Benson, Jimmy. *See* Hargreaves, Peter
Benson, Noel. *See* Wilson, Ira B(ishop)
Benton, Brook. *See* Peay, Benjamin (Franklin)
Benton, Hugh. *See* Ellis, Vesphew Benton
Bentow, Yehuda. *See* Wohl, Yehuda
Beor, Beans. *See* Brentano(-von Arnim), Anne Elisabeth [or Bettina]
Beppo. *See* Mehring, Walter
Bepy. *See* Pulejo, Giuseppe

Beran, Carl [or Karl]. *See* Bohn, Rudolf [or Rudolph]
Berchthal, Hans von. *See* Goller, Vincenz
Bereford, Maurice. *See* Cohen, Maurice Alfred
Bérel, Antony. *See* Choudens, Antony
Bérel, P(aul). *See* Choudens, Paul de
Berenger, Raymond. *See* Linekar, Thomas Joseph
Berenger, Thomas Joseph. *See* Linekar, Thomas Joseph
Beresford, Henry Wayne. *See* Rossiter, Will
Berg, A. *See* Bez, Helmut
Berg, Armin. *See* Weinberger, Hermann
Berg, Carl. *See* Weisenberg, Karl
Berg, Carl Natanael. *See* Rexroth-Berg, (Carl) Natanael
Berg, George R. *See* Ringgenberg, Jörg
Berg, Gøsta. *See* Jensen, Harry
Berg, H. *See* Zulman, Ann
Berg, Jimmy. *See* Weinberg, Symson [or Simon]
Berg, Johann. *See* Vom Berg, Johann
Berg, Natanael. *See* Rexroth-Berg, (Carl) Natanael
Berg, O. F. *See* Ebersberg, Ottokar Franz
Berg, Rudolf. *See* Silberg, Rubin
Berg, Sam. *See* Samberg, Benjamin
Berg, T. Van. *See* Balmer, Charles
Berg, Thomas. *See* Raich, Heribert
Berg, W. T. *See* Bliss, P(hilip) Paul
Berg-Wall. *See* Rosenberg,Wladimir [or Voldemar]
Bergdahl, Edith [or Enid]. *See* Gillette, Leland James
Berge, Walter von. *See* Börnstein, Heinrich (Karl)
Bergen, Alexander. *See* Gordon, Marie
Bergenstamm. *See* Gleich, Josef Alois
Berger, Fred. *See* Schönfeld, Friedhelm
Berger, Hans Ludwig. *See* Hänssler, Friedrich
Berger, Leon. *See* Zamecnik, J(ohn) S(tepan)
Berger, Ludwig. *See* Bamberger, Ludwig
Berger, Michel. *See* Hamburger, Michel
Berger, Siegfried. *See* Chelius, Oskar von
Bergere, Lucile. *See* Shepard-Hayward, Mae
Bergersbacher, Andreas. *See* Rochler, Jens
Bergh, Walter. *See* Thiersch, Bertha
Bergholt, Ernest. *See* Binks, E.
Bergier, Ungay [fictitious composer]. *See* Bergier, Ungay [fictitious composer]
Bergman, Henri. *See* Armbuster, Robert
Bergmann, Karl. *See* Spaulding, G(eorge) L(awson)
Bergmann, Phantasius. *See* Montani, Pietro
Bergmann, Rosso. *See* Hausenstein, Wilhelm
Bergner. *See* Götz, Karl
Bergson, Lars. *See* Volkmann, Karl Heinz
Bergson, Michael. *See* Sonnenberg, Michael
Bergstrom, Eric. *See* Ehret, Walter (Charles)
Bergthal, Hugo. *See* Rogers, James H(otchkiss)
Berkhaan, Otto. *See* Rüssmann, Georg(e)
Berks, John. *See* Gillespie, John (Birks)
Berlá, Hemmy. *See* Lamprecht, Hermann
Berle, Milton. *See* Berlinger, Milton
Berlijn, Anton. *See* Wolf, Aaron
Berlin Bach, The. *See* Bach, Carl [or Karl] Philipp Emanuel
Berlin, Ben. *See* Bick, Herman
Berlin, Irving. *See* Baline, Israel
Berlind, Guy. *See* Berlind, Samuel
Bern, Ben. *See* Winkler, Gerhard
Bernac, Pierre. *See* Bertin, Pierre
Bernal, J. *See* Bernier, Alfred
Bernard, Adrien. *See* Bernard, Clem(ent)
Bernard, Adrien. *See* Box, Harold Elton
Bernard, Adrien. *See* Keuleman, Adrian
Bernard, Henry. *See* Glover, Henry (Bernard)
Bernard, Mike. *See* Barnett, Michael
Bernard of Cluny. *See* Bernard of Morlaix
Bernard, Roy. *See* Parker, Alfred Thomas
Bernard, Sam. *See* Barnett, Samuel
Bernard, Tristan. *See* Bernard, Paul
Bernardin. *See* Courtois, Bernard
Bernardon. *See* Kurz, Johann Joseph Felix von
Bernardus (of Reichenau). *See* Berno, (Abbot) of Reichenau
Bernardus [or Bertrando] de Brassia. *See* Vaqueras, Beltrame [or Bertrando]
Bernauer, Ludwig. *See* Bernhuber, Ludwig
Berners, (Baron) Gerald Hugh Tyrwhitt-Wilson. *See* Tyrwhitt-Wilson, (Sir) Gerald (Hugh)
Berners, Lord. *See* Tyrwhitt-Wilson, (Sir) Gerald (Hugh)
Bernhard, G. *See* Gugler, Bernhard (von)
Bernhard, S. *See* Seckles, Bernhard
Bernhardt, J. Karl. *See* Crampton, Thomas
Berni, Lew. *See* Bernstein, Louis ([nd])
Bernie, Ben [or Bernard]. *See* Anzelwitz [or Anzelvitz], Benjamin [or Bernard]
Bernie, D. Bud. *See* Finkelstein, Abe
Bernoux, Léon. *See* Perronnet, Amélie (Bernoux)
Bernstein, Leonard. *See* Bernstein, Louis (1918-1990)
Bernstein West. *See* Bernstein, Elmer
Berold, Karl. *See* Ordnung, Rudolf (August)
Berquist, Whitey. *See* Berquist, Bernard H.
Berr, Friedrich. *See* Beer, Friedrich
Berrsche, Alexander. *See* Lösch, Alexander
Berry, Chu. *See* Brown, Leon
Berry, Chuck. *See* Berry, Charles Edward Anderson
Berry, Leon. *See* Brown, Leon
Berry, Théodore François Joseph. *See* Labarre, Théodore François Joseph
Bert, Corrine de. *See* Suskind, Milton
Berté, Harry. *See* Berté, Heinrich
Berthold(-Filhés), B. *See* Lehmann, Bertha (née Filhés)
Berthold, G. *See* Pearsall, Robert Lucas (de)
Berti, Henry. *See* Himan, Alberto
Bertin, Pierre. *See* Dupont, Pierre
Bertini le Jeune. *See* Bertini, Henri(-Jerome)

Bertl. *See* Schubert, Franz Peter
Bertlam, Wilfred. *See* Lambert, W.
Bertolli, Mario. *See* Ordnung, Rudolf (August)
Berton, Roland de. *See* Saenger, Gustav(e)
Bertram, Rudolph. *See* Winterfeld, David Robert
Bertrand, Michel. *See* Peschek, Alfred
Bertrand, Paul. *See* Daniels, Charles N(eil)
Bertrand-Brown. *See* Brown, Bertrand
Bertus, Bert. *See* Küster, Herbert
Berty, William. *See* Ibert, Jacques (François Antoine Marie)
Berwick, Mary. *See* Procter, Adelaide Ann(e)
Best Allen since Fred, The. *See* Allen, Stephen [or Steve] (Valentine Patrick William)
Best Friend a Song Ever Had, The. *See* Jenkins, Harold (Lloyd)
Best of the Bonn Boys. *See* Beethoven, Ludwig van
Bethancourt, T. Ernesto. *See* Passailaigue, Thomas E.
Bethel, J. *See* Procter, Bryan Waller
Bethune, Catherine. *See* Crosby, Fanny [i.e., Frances] J(ane)
Bethune, Thomas (Green(e)) (Wiggins). *See* Wiggins, Thomas (Green(e))
Betove. *See* Levy, Michel Maurice
Betta. *See* Winner, Joseph E(astburn)
Bette BeBop. *See* Jones, Lillie Mae
Betterton, Ralph. *See* Santley, (Sir) Charles
Bettina. *See* Brentano(-von Arnim), Anne Elisabeth [or Bettina]
Bettona, V. *See* Oliva, Francesco
Betty. *See* Vonderlieth, Leonore
Betty BeBop. *See* Jones, Lillie Mae
Betzi, Gaston de. *See* Bizet, Alexandre César Léopold
Beugland. *See* Lubrunie, Gérard
Beulah. *See* McDaniel, Hattie
Beulah, Jacob. *See* Beuler, Jacob
Beurlin, Paul. *See* Peuerl, Paul
Bevel, Mississippi. *See* Bevel, Charles William
Bey, Iverson. *See* Minter, Iverson
Bey, Mickey. *See* Gray(-Bey), Michael Ashley
Bey, Roosevelt Sykes. *See* Sykes, Roosevelt
Beydemüller, Georg. *See* Reinhard, Kurt
Beyer, F. *See* Mackie, William H.
Beyer, Fred. *See* Duggan, Joseph Francis
Bezdek, (Sister) John Joseph. *See* Derleth, Julia
Bezique. *See* Beswick, Harry
Biafra, Jello. *See* Boucher, Eric
Biagio, Adagio. *See* Zambaldi, Silvio
Bibalo, Antonio (Gio). *See* Bibalitsch, Antonio
Bibliophile. *See* Gagnon, Blanche
Bick, Charles. *See* Cain, Noble
Bickerstaff, Isaac. *See* Swift, Jonathan
Bickford, Herbert. *See* Grey, Frank H(erbert)
Bickley. *See* Reichner, (S(amuel)) Bickley
Bicknal, John (Lawrence). *See* Veal, George
Bicknell, John Laurence. *See* Veal, George
Bickvor. *See* Bick, Eva
Biddy, Hal. *See* Bidgood, Henry [or Harry] (James)
Bidwell, Patrick. *See* O'Sullivan, (Mrs.) Denis
Bie(-Persson), Nils. *See* Persson, Harry (Arnold)
Bientina, Il. *See* Buonavita, Antonio
Bierbauer, Elsie. *See* Bierbower, Elsie
Big. *See* Wallace, Chris(topher (G.))
Big Bad Smitty. *See* Smith, John Henry
Big Band's Black Man, The. *See* Henderson, (James) Fletcher (Hamilton), (Jr.)
Big Bloke. *See* Oden, James Burke
Big Bopper, (The). *See* Richardson, J(iles) P(erry)
Big Boy. *See* Crudup, Arthur
Big Boy. *See* Ellis, Wilbert Thirkield
Big Boy. *See* Henry, Richard
Big Boy. *See* Roy Diaz, Gustavo
Big Chief. *See* Ellis, Wilbert Thirkield
Big Ed. *See* Burns, Eddie
Big El. *See* Presley, Elvis A(a)ron
Big Filthy. *See* Waller, Thomas Wright
Big Foot. *See* Burnett, Chester Arthur
Big Joe. *See* McCoy, Joe
Big Jox. *See* Bland, Milton
Big Lucky. *See* Carter, Levester
Big Maceo. *See* Merriweather, Major
Big Mama. *See* Thornton, Willie Mae
Big Moose. *See* Walker, John(ny) (Mayon)
Big Nose. *See* Piffett, Etienne
Big O, The. *See* Orbison, Roy (Kelton)
Big Pun(isher). *See* Rios, Christopher
Big Skol. *See* Ford, Aleck
Big Slim (The Lone(some) Cowboy). *See* McAuliffe, Harry C(larence)
Big Vernon. *See* Turner, Joseph Vernon
Big Voice. *See* Odom, Andrew
Big Walter. *See* Horton, Walter
Big Walter. *See* Price, Walter Travis
Big Walter. *See* Smith, George (1924-1983)
Big Willie. *See* Mabon, Willie
Big Youth. *See* Buchanam, Manley Augustus
Bigard, Barney. *See* Bigard, Albany [or Alban] (Leon)
Biggest Act in Country Music, The. *See* Russell, John(ny Bright)
Biggest Cat, The. *See* Brown, James
Biggie Smalls. *See* Wallace, Chris(topher (G.))
Biglow, Hosea. *See* Lowell, James Russell
Bigly, Cantell A. *See* Peck, George Washington
Bikayo, Les. *See* Bichsel, Jacob
Bilencko, Michel. *See* Anderson, William Henry
Bilk, Acker. *See* Bilk, Bernard Stanley
Bill, Casey. *See* Weldon, Will(iam)
Bill of the Play. *See* Yardley, William
Billie Joe (and the Checkmates). *See* Bideu, Louis
Billig, Julius. *See* Beer, Jakob Liebmann

Billig, Julius. *See* Weber, (Jacob) Gottfried
Billing, Arno. *See* Spoliansky, Mischa [or Michail] (Pawlowitsch)
Billings, Bud. *See* Crow(e), Francis Luther
Billings, Joe. *See* Robison, Carson J(ay)
Billy Bang. *See* Walker, William Vincent
Billy the Kid. *See* Dean, William [or Billy] Harold
Bim. *See* Forbes, Roy
Bimbo, Benny. *See* Samberg, Benjamin
Bimbo Boy. *See* Reeves, James [or Jimmy] (Travis)
Binamu. *See* Bingham, Hiram
Binellus (de Gerardis), Giovanni Battista. *See* Pinello (di Ghirardi), Giovanni Battista
Bingham, Bing. *See* Bingham, William L., Jr.
Bingham, H. *See* Taylor, Helen
Bingham, Lena M. *See* Kunkel, Charles
Bingley, Richard. *See* Smith, Leonard B(ingley)
Binny. *See* Rabinowitz, Irving
Biondin. *See* Segni, Julio [or Giulio]
Biosphere. *See* Jenssen, Geir
Biquardus. *See* Pickar, Arnold
Birch, Harry. *See* White, Charles A(lbert)
Birch, Raymond. *See* Johnson, Charles L(eslie)
Birchley, William. *See* Austin, John
Bird. *See* Parker, Charles [or Charlie] (Christopher, Jr.)
Bird, Cockiolly. *See* Bingham, Graham Clifton
Birdman, Bobby. *See* Kieswetter, Rob
Birk, Lothar. *See* Mühlbauer, Hans Heinz
Birken, Sigmund von. *See* Betulius, Sigmund
Birkhofer, Toni. *See* Marcuse, Albrecht [or Albert]
Birks, John. *See* Gillespie, John (Birks)
Birmingham Bud (& His Uke). *See* Crow(e), Francis Luther
Birmingham Poet, The. *See* Freeth, John
Birmingham Sam (and His Magic Guitar). *See* Hooker, John Lee
Bis. *See* Wasenius, Karl Fredrik
Bischoff, Karl. *See* Bischoff, Joh. Herm. Christian
Biset, C. *See* Kovarovic, Karel
Bishop, Bish. *See* Bishop, Walter, Jr.
Bishop, Bob. *See* Sykes, Bishop Milton
Bishop of Marsland. *See* Duncan, Ronald (Frederick Henry)
Bishop, Robert. *See* Wilson, Ira B(ishop)
Bishop, Stacey. *See* Antheil, George
Bishop, Wilson. *See* Wilson, Ira B(ishop)
Bitner, Ed. F. *See* Keiser, Robert (A(dolph))
Bittle, (R.) Clifford. *See* Bliss, P(hilip) Paul
Bitts, Frances O. *See* Smith, Frances Octavia
Bix. *See* Reichner, (S(amuel)) Bickley
Bizet, Georges. *See* Bizet, Alexandre César Léopold
Bjarme, Brynjolf. *See* Ibsen, Henrik (Johan)
Bjõrk. *See* Gudmundsdottir, Bjõrk
Björke, E(inar). *See* Hansson, Stig (Axel)
Bjorn, Frank. *See* Fabricus- Bjerre, Bent
Black. *See* Vearncombe, Colin
Black Boy Shine. *See* Holiday, Harold
Black, Don. *See* Blackstone, Gerald
Black Elvis, The. *See* Hendrix, John(ny) Allen
Black Face. *See* Edinger, Eddie Ross
Black, Francis *see*— Thompson, Charles Michael (Kitteridge IV)
Black, Frank. *See* Thompson, Charles Michael (Kitteridge, IV)
Black, Frankie. *See* Blackwell, Francis Hillman
Black Giant of White Spirituals, The. *See* Jackson, George Pullen
Black Gladiator, The. *See* Bates, (Otha) Ellas [or Elias]
Black Godfather, The. *See* Williams, (Zeffrey) Andre
Black Horowitz, The. *See* Waller, Thomas Wright
Black Ivory King. *See* Alexander, David [or Dave]
Black, Jack. *See* Freed, Albert (James)
Black, James (L. [or M.]). *See* Crosby, Fanny [i.e., Frances] J(ane)
Black Jr. *See* Johnson, Luther, Jr.
Black, Kitty. *See* Black, Dorothy
Black Moses, (The). *See* Hayes, Isaac
Black Nightingale, The. *See* Pindell, Annie Pauline
Black Nightingale, The. *See* Pridgett, Gertrude (Malissa Nix)
Black, Rosebud. *See* Black, Gloria
Black, Sidney. *See* Haass, Hans
Black Singer Trapped Inside a White Skin, A. *See* Burdon, Eric
Black, William Electric. *See* James, Ian (Ellis)
Black, Willie. *See* Sissle, Noble (Lee)
Blackaller, Richard. *See* Smith, Frank Dymond
Blackburn, Howard. *See* Grinsted, William Stanley
Blackton, Jay (S.). *See* Schwartzdorf, Jacob (S.)
Blackwell, Bumps. *See* Blackwell, Robert A.
Blackwell, Florence. *See* Sawyer, Henry S.
Blackwell, Scrapper. *See* Blackwell, Francis Hillman
Blackwood, (Mrs.) Price. *See* Sheridan, Helen Selina
Blagy, Caroline. *See* Grandval, Marie Felicie Clémence de Reiset, vicomtesse de
Blaikley, Howard. *See* Blaikley, Alan
Blaikley, Howard. *See* Howard, Ken
Blain, Henrietta. *See* Crosby, Fanny [i.e., Frances] J(ane)
Blaine, Chip. *See* Chipolone, Nunzio
Blaine, (G). Gordon. *See* Kinsman, Elmer (F(ranklin))
Blair, Henrietta (E.). *See* Crosby, Fanny [i.e., Frances] J(ane)
Blair, William. *See* Squires, Edna May
Blake, Alan. *See* Balkin, Alfred
Blake, Arthur. *See* Phelps, Arthur
Blake, Blind. *See* Higgs, Blake Alphonso
Blake, Blind. *See* Phelps, Arthur
Blake, David. *See* Brown, Frank
Blake, Don. *See* Mautner, Jerome (Nathan)
Blake, Douglas. *See* Croger, Frederick Julian

Blake, Eubie. *See* Blake, James Hubert
Blake, Garry. *See* Newell, Norman
Blake, Harry. *See* Slaughter, M(arion) T(ry)
Blake, Ian. *See* Rosa Suárez, Robert Edward
Blake, Jerry. *See* Chabania, Jacinto
Blake, Lowell. *See* Schoenfeld, William C(harles)
Blake, Milton D. *See* Anthony, Bert R.
Blake, Robert. *See* Blake, James Hubert
Blanc, Paul. *See* Rawlings, Charles Arthur
Blanchard, Dan. *See* Crow(e), Francis Luther
Blanchard, Pierre. *See* Drabek, Kurt
Blanchard, Red. *See* Blanchard, Donald F.
Blanchin, François. *See* Bianchini, Francescho
Blanco, C. *See* White, Clarence C(ameron)
Blanco, Pedro. *See* Acosta, Pedro Blanco
Bland, Bobby (Blue). *See* Bland, Robert Calvin
Blane, Ralph. *See* Hunsecker, Ralph Uriah
Blank, Rolf. *See* Knabl, Rudolf [or Rudi]
Blasius Wind. *See* Mentner, Karl
Blas, Gil. *See* Veneziana, Carlo
Blass, Leo(n). *See* Sabina, Karel
Blast, C. L. *See* Lewis, Clarence
Blau, Milton. *See* Blau, Eric
Bleep. *See* Jenssen, Geir
Blene, Gerard. *See* Linden, David Gysbert (van der)
Blès, Numa. *See* Bessat, Charles
Blesk, Miloš. *See* Krno, Milos
Blessi, Manoli. *See* Molino, Antonio
Blessing, Harry. *See* Blitz, Leo(nard)
Blessing, Michael. *See* Nesmith, Michael
Bliemchen. *See* Neumann, Emil
Blind Arthur. *See* Phelps, Arthur
Blind Blake. *See* Higgs, Blake Alphonso
Blind Blake. *See* Phelps, Arthur
Blind Boy Fuller #2. *See* McGhee, Walter Brown
Blind Boy Grunt. *See* Zimmerman, Robert Allen
Blind Doogie. *See* McTell, Willie Samuel
Blind Girl, The. *See* Crosby, Fanny [i.e., Frances] J(ane)
Blind Joe Death. *See* Fahey, John (Aloysius)
Blind Lemon. *See* Jefferson, Clarence
Blind Lemon's Buddy. *See* Holmes, Joe
Blind Marvel. *See* Rodriguez, Ignacio Loyola
Blind Poetess, The. *See* Crosby, Fanny [i.e., Frances] J(ane)
Blind Sammy [or Sammie]. *See* McTell, Willie Samuel
Blind Singer, The. *See* Shaw, Oliver
Blind Thomas. *See* Fahey, John (Aloysius)
Blind Tom. *See* Wiggins, Thomas (Green(e))
Blind Willie. *See* McTell, Willie Samuel
Bliss, Paul. *See* Bliss, P(hilip) Paul
Block, Palle. *See* Hedberg, Frans (Theodor)
Blockbuster. *See* Adderley, Julien Edwin
Blois, (M.) De. *See* Gronnenrade, Charles Gui Xavier Van
Blonda, Max. *See* Schoenberg, Gertrud (née Kolisch)
Blondello. *See* Hepburn, Thomas Charles
Blondy, Alpha. *See* Kone, Seydou
Bloom, A. Leon. *See* Lewis, Leon
Bloom, Luka. *See* Moore, Barry
Bloom, Marty. *See* Blumenthal, M. L.
Bloom, Mickey. *See* Bloom, Milton
Blossom, Jerry. *See* Emmett, Dan(iel Decatur)
Blossom, Jerry. *See* Hays, William Shakespeare
Blount, Sonny. *See* Blount, Herman
Bloye, Richard. *See* Liddle, Samuel
Blue, Barry. *See* Green, Barry
Blue, Barry. *See* Roker, Ronald
Blue Bells. *See* Bellson, Luigi Paulino
Blue Boy. *See* Lyons, Austin
Blue, Bud. *See* Ellis, Seger
Blue Calx. *See* James, Richard D(avid)
Blue, David. *See* Cohen, (Stuart) David
Blue, Little Joe. *See* Valery, Joseph, Jr.
Blue, Lu. *See* Dupont, Louise [or Louisa]
Blue Ridge Duo. *See* Lucas, Eugene
Blue Ridge Duo. *See* Reneau, George
Blue Ruby. *See* James, Sylvester
Blue-stocking, The. *See* Stillingfleet, Benjamin
Blue Train. *See* Coltrane, John William
Blue Yodler, The. *See* Rodgers, James [or Jimmie] (Charles)
Blueblood. *See* McMahon, Andrew
Bluegrass Balladeer, The. *See* Eanes, Homer Robert, (Jr.)
Blues Boy. *See* King, Riley B.
Blues Boy. *See* Odom, Andrew
Blues Boy. *See* Seward, Alexander T.
Blues Boy Bill. *See* Broonzy, William Lee Conley
Blues Boy from Beale Street. *See* King, Riley B.
Blues Boy King. *See* King, Riley B.
Blues Demon, The. *See* Del Santo, Dan
Blues Doctor, The. *See* Clayton, Peter Joe
Blues Giant, The. *See* Hooker, John Lee
Blues King. *See* Seward, Alexander T.
Blues Man, The. *See* Kirkland, Eddie
Blues Man, The. *See* Sykes, Roosevelt
Blues Mandolin Man. *See* Rachell, James
Blues Sensation from the West, The. *See* Dunn, Sara(h)
Blues Singer Supreme, The. *See* Nelson, Lucille
Bluesy Bad Boy. *See* Young, Neil
Bluke, Ruby. *See* Blake, James Hubert
Blum, Adolf [or Adolph]. *See* Gleich, Joseph Alois
Blum, Wilhelm. *See* Klingenbrunner, Wilhelm
Blumberg, Harry. *See* Blumberg, Herz
Blumel, Arno. *See* Fiorente, Arnaldo Benito
Blumenschein, W. L. *See* Kunkel, Charles
Blumenthal, Jacques. *See* Kunkel, Charles
Blumanns, Leonhard. *See* Blumenthal, Sandro
Blumtal, James. *See* Bellak, James Blumtal
Blutig, Eduard. *See* Gorey, Edward (St. John)
Blythe, P(eter) Richard. *See* Bleiweiss, Peter R(ichard)

Bo Diddley. *See* Bates, (Otha) Ellas [or Elias]
Bo, Mister. *See* Collins, Louis (Bo)
Bo Pete. *See* Nelson, Harry Edward
Boalt, John E. *See* Lorenz, Ellen Jane
Bob Dylan's Greatest Rival. *See* Ochs, Phil
Bobo, Juan. *See* Roberts, John Godfrey Owen
Bocan. *See* Cordier, Jacques
Bocca, Carlotta. *See* Sartorio, Arnoldo
Boccardi, Michel Angiolo. *See* Rolli, Paolo Antonio
Boccolosi, Harry. *See* Box, Harold Elton
Boccolosi, Harry. *See* Keuleman, Adrian
Boccolosi, Harry. *See* Pelosi, Domonic [or Don]
Boccolosi, Harry. *See* Sugarman, Harry
Bocephus. *See* Williams, Randall Hank
Bochan. *See* Cordier, Jacques
Bock, Gustav. *See* Lewis, Jerrold
Bocquain. *See* Cordier, Jacques
Bocquam. *See* Cordier, Jacques
Body, E. V. *See* Davis, Joseph [or Joe] (M.)
Boëmo, Il (divino). *See* Myslivecek, Josef
Boëmo, Padre. *See* Černohorsky, Bohuslav Matej
Boesting, Alfred. *See* Aulich, Bruno
Boettcher, Gerd. *See* Engel, Detlev
Bogan of Bogan, (Mrs.). *See* Oliphant, Carolina
Bogart, Ric. *See* Burghardt, Victor
Bohl, O. Ernst. *See* Hornbostel, August Gottlieb
Böhme, Max. *See* Pache, Johannes
Bohn, Buddy. *See* Bohn, Walter Moro [or Morrow]
Bohn, Charles. *See* Sawyer, Harry S.
Bohrmann-Riegen. *See* Bohrmann, Heinrich
Bohrmann-Riegen. *See* Nigri von Sankt Albino, Julius
Bohusius, Jacobus. *See* Buus, Jacques [or Jacob] (de)
Boilerhouse. *See* Barson, Ben
Boilerhouse. *See* Dean, Andy
Boilerhouse. *See* Wolff, Ben
Bola de Nieve. *See* Villa, Ignacio
Bolan, Marc. *See* Feld, Mark
Boland, Dave. *See* Deutscher, Karlheinz
Boland, Francy. *See* Boland, François
Bold Briareus. *See* Handel, Georg Friedrich
Bold, Ferdinand. *See* Kaun, Hugo
Boldest and Proudest Poetic Spirit of the Times, The. *See* Chopin, Frederic
Boldi, Giuseppe. *See* Preissler, Joseph
Boleslavensis, Johannes Josquinus. *See* Josquin, Jan
Boleslawita, (Bohdan). *See* Kraszewski, Józef Ignacy
Bolimeo, Argindo. *See* Boccherini, Giovanni Gastone
Bolina, F. *See* Kalischnig, Walter
Bolling, Klaus. *See* Bolling, Claude
Bollman(n), Fritz(e). *See* Lindemann, Wilhelm
Bolognese, Il. *See* Corelli, Arcangelo
Bolognese, Il. *See* Sportonio, Marc'Antono
Bolsena, Il. *See* Adami (da Bolsena), Andrea
Bolshevik of the Bozart. *See* Huneker, James Gibbons
Bolshevist of Music. *See* Pingoud, Ernest
Bolsover, Colonel. *See* Blewitt, Jonathan
Bolton, Michael. *See* Bolotin, Michael
Bolyer, Maurice Joseph. *See* Beaulieu, Maurice Joseph
Bombet, César. *See* Beyle, (Marie) Henri
Bombet, L(ouis)-A(lexander)-C(ésar). *See* Beyle, (Marie) Henri
Bombón. *See* Lavoriel, Ludwing
Bon Bon. *See* Tunnell, George
Bon-Ton. *See* Garlow, Clarence Joseph
Bon vieuxtemps. *See* Dejardins, Louis-Edouard
Bonadies. *See* Goodendag, Johann
Bonaldi, G. *See* Orth, John (Carl)
Bonamico, Pietro. *See* Guetfreund, Peter
Bonamicus, Cornelius. *See* Freund(t), Cornelius [or Kornelius]
Bonandoni, G. *See* Gyldmark, Sven Rudolf S.
Bonano, Sharkey. *See* Bonano, Joseph
Boncourt, Charles Marie de. *See* Nys, Carl Augustin Léon de
Bond, Johnny. *See* Bond, Cyrus Whitfield
Bond, Vee. *See* Biondo, Rose Leonore Victoria
Bondi, Neri. *See* Bondineri, Michele
Bonds, Gary U. S. *See* Anderson, Gary
Bonds, Margaret Allison. *See* Majors, Margaret Allison
Bone, Jon T. *See* Burnett, Joseph Henry
Bonelli, Gino. *See* Stolz, Robert
Bones, M(ark). *See* Kaempfert, Bert(hold)
Bonfire, Mars. *See* McCrohan, Dennis Eugene
Bongo, Mr. *See* Costanzo, Jack J(ames)
Bonham, Victor. *See* Sour, Robert (B.)
Bonheur, Emile. *See* Rawlings, Charles Arthur
Bonheur, F. *See* Rawlings, Charles Arthur
Bonheur, Georges. *See* Rawlings, Charles Arthur
Bonheur, Isidore. *See* Rawlings, Charles Arthur
Bonheur, Otto. *See* Rawlings, Charles Arthur
Bonheur, Theo(dore). *See* Rawlings, Charles Arthur
Boniface, Al. *See* Weidler, Warner Alfred
Bon Jovi, Jon. *See* Bongiovi, John
Bonn, Issy. *See* Levin, Benjamin
Bonner, Carl. *See* Hatch, F(rederic) L.
Bonner, Juke Boy. *See* Bonner, Weldon (H. Philip)
Bonner, Samuel. *See* Warren, Elinor Remick
Bonnevin, Giovanni [or Johannes]. *See* Beaussenron, Giovanni [or Johannes]
Bonney, Graham. *See* Bradley, Graham
Bonni, Ed. *See* Fishman, Jack (1927-)
Bono (Vox). *See* Hewson, Paul (David)
Bono, Sonny. *See* Bono, Salvatore
Bonté, Emile. *See* Rawlings, Charles Arthur
Boogie Man, (The). *See* Hooker, John Lee
Boogie Woogie Red. *See* Harrison, Vernon
Booker, John (Lee). *See* Hooker, John Lee
Booker T. *See* Jones, Booker T.
Boom, Barry. *See* Robinson, Paul
BoomBass, Pigalle. *See* Blanc-Francart, Hubert

Boone, Blind. *See* Boone, John William
Boone, D. Danny. *See* Fulkerson, Daniel B.
Boone, Daniel. *See* Stirling, Peter Lee
Boone, John W. *See* Kunkel, Charles
Boone, Pat. *See* Boone, Charles Eugene
Booth, Albert J. *See* Burleigh, Cecil (Edward)
Booth, Dorothy. *See* Fox, Roy ([nd])
Booth, Florence. *See* Crosby, Fanny [i.e., Frances] J(ane)
Bootsy. *See* Collins, William
Bootsy. *See* Potter, A(nnie) S.
Bootzilla. *See* Collins, William
Bopstein, B. *See* Gillespie John (Birks)
Bor, Beans van. *See* Brentano(-von Arnim), Anne Elisabeth [or Bettina]
Borders, Herbert. *See* Grenzebach Herbert
Bordonel, T. J. *See* Brown, T. J.
Borel-Clerc, Ch(arles). *See* Clerc, Charles (Louis)
Borganoff, Igor. *See* Njurling, Sten
Borgudd, Slim. *See* Borgudd, Tommy
Borissoff. *See* Piastro, Josef
Boriwsky, Michael. *See* Parker, Alfred Thomas
Bork, J. S. *See* Langdon, Verne Loring
Borlet. *See* Trebol
Born, (E.). *See* Ailbout, Hans
Borne, Francis. *See* Felton, William M.
Börne, Ludwig. *See* Baruch, Löb
Börner, Arnold. *See* Raff, (Joseph) Joachim
Bornet, Fred. *See* Bornet, Francois
Bororó, Chico. *See* Mignone, Francisco (Paulo)
Borroff, Edith. *See* Bergersen, Edith
Borry, Len. *See* Borisoff, Leonard
Bösendorfer, Alfred. *See* Vlak, Kees
Boss, The. *See* Friedhofer, Hugo Wilhelm
Boss, The. *See* Springsteen, Bruce (Frederick Joseph)
Boss, Al. *See* Del Parral, Antonio
Boss Man. *See* Morganfield, McKinley
Boss of the Blues, The. *See* Turner, Joseph Vernon
Bossinensis, Francicus. *See* Ana, Francesco d'
Bossman of the Blues, The. *See* King, Riley B.
Bossu, d'Arra. *See* Adam, de la Halle
Bostic, C(al). *See* Bostick, Calvin T.
Boston's Musical Brahmin. *See* Apthorp, William Foster
Boswell, (Mrs.). *See* Cushman, Abbie
Boswell, Dick. *See* Barnes, H(oward) E(llington)
Boswell, Dick. *See* Fields, Harold (Cornelius)
Boswell, Dick. *See* Roncoroni, Joseph (Dominic)
Botelero, Enrique. *See* Butler, Henry
Both, L. W. *See* Schneider, Louis [or Ludwig] (Wilhelm)
Böttiger, J. L. *See* Gräffer, Franz (Arnold)
Bottle, Jack. *See* Vlessing, Phillip
Bottner, (Claus). *See* Bummerl, Franz
Bottone, Velardino. *See* Oliva, Francesco
Boucher. *See* Hansson, Stig (Axel)
Boucheron, Maxime. *See* Boucheron, René Maximilian
Boucicault, Dion(ysus Lard(n)er). *See* Boursicault, Dionysus Lardner
Bouffon Odieux, Le. *See* Lulli, Giovanni Battista
Boukay, Maurice. *See* Couyba, Charles (Maurice)
Boulanger, Lili. *See* Boulanger, Marie-Juliette (Olga)
Boule, Henri. *See* Fishman, Jack (1918 (or 19)-)
Boulton, John. *See* Cobb, George L(inus)
Bounce, Benjamin. *See* Carey, Henry
Bounceycore, Dion. *See* Burnard, Francis Cowley
Bouqueriny. *See* Boccherini, (Ridolfo) Luigi
Bourdelot, Pierre. *See* Michon, Pierre
Bourgneuf, L. de. *See* Détroyat, (Pierre) Léonce
Bourke, Sonny. *See* Blount, Herman
Bourne, Carol. *See* Sonenscher, Dave
Bourne, (Mrs.) S. K. *See* Crosby, Fanny [i.e., Frances] J(ane)
Boutail, Jean. *See* Ailbout, Hans
Bovery, J(ules). *See* Bovy, Antoine Nicolas Joseph [or Giuseppe]
Bow, Glenn. *See* Glembotzki, Reinhold
Bowden, David. *See* Johnstone, Maurice
Bowditch, Janet. *See* Furze, Jessie (Lilian)
Bowen, George. *See* Grady, R(ichard) G.
Bower, Bugs. *See* Bower, Maurice [or Maury] (Donald)
Bowers, Pete. *See* Seeger, Pete(r R.)
Bowers, Robin Hood. *See* Bowers, Robert Hood
Bowie, David. *See* Jones, David Robert (Haywood)
Bowland, Mark. *See* Feld, Mark
Boxcar Willie. *See* Martin, Lecil T(ravis)
Boy Paderewski, The. *See* Eckstein, Willie
Boy from Beale Street, The. *See* King, Riley B.
Boy from Dixie, The. *See* Bernard Al(fred A.)
Boy George. *See* O'Dowd, George Alan
Boy Who Writes the Songs You Sing, The. *See* Tobias, Charles
Boy Wonder, The. *See* Berlinger, Milton
Boy Wonder (of the Clarinet), The. *See* Herman(n), Woodrow Charles
Boyce, Frederick. *See* Baycock, Frederick
Boyd, Cowboy Rambler. *See* Boyd, William [or Bill]
Boyd, Ernie. *See* Boyd, Edward [or Eddie] Riley
Boyd, Little Eddie. *See* Boyd, Edward [or Eddie] Riley
Boyd, Mullen. *See* Kapp, Paul
Boyd, Rambler. *See* Boyd, William [or Bill]
Boyd, Robert. *See* Byrd, Henry Roeland
Boyd, Robin. *See* Newell, Norman
Boyd, Walter. *See* Ledbetter, Huddie (William)
Boykin, Edward C. *See* McConathy, Osbourne
Boyle, Bobbi. *See* Young, Barbara Marie
Boyle, Richard. *See* Liddle, Samuel
Boys from Columbia, The. *See* Hart, Lorenz (Milton)
Boys from Columbia, The. *See* Rodgers, Richard (Charles)
Boysen, Alice. *See* Engelmann, H(ans)
Boz. *See* Dickens, Charles (John Huffam)

Božinski, P. K. *See* Konjovic, Petar Božinski
Brabantius, Henricu Isaac. *See* Isaac, Heinrich
Braccini, Luigi. *See* Braccini, Roberto
Braccino, Antonio. *See* Artusi, Giovanni Maria
Brachman, James. *See* Brockman, James
Brack, John. *See* Brack, Hans-Heinrich
Bracken, Joanne. *See* Grogan, Joanne
Brad, Lester. *See* Bradford, Sylvester Henry
Braddock, Sparky. *See* Lawrence, Wilma Sue
Bradford, Bessie. *See* Strandberg, (Alfreda) Theodora
Bradford, David. *See* McGregor, Dion
Bradford, Kenneth. *See* Wagness, Bernard
Bradford, Mule. *See* Bradford, (John Henry) Perry
Bradford, William. *See* Walker, William Stearns
Bradhouse. *See* Hausey, (Elton) Howard
Bradley, Buddy. *See* Epps, Clarence Bradley
Bradley, Velma. *See* Prather, Ida
Bradley, Will. *See* Schwichtenberg, Wilbur
Bradshaw, Tiny. *See* Bradshaw, Myron Carlton
Brady, Erwin. *See* Rosenwald, Hans Hermann
Brady, Harry. *See* Kaufman, Isidore
Bragg, Dobby. *See* Sykes, Roosevelt
Braham, David [or Dave]. *See* Abraham, David
Braham, John. *See* Abraham, John
Brahe, May Hannah. *See* Dickson, Mary Hannah
Brahms, Caryl. *See* Abrahams, Doris Caroline
Brahms, Johannes (Spirit). *See* Brown, Rosemary (neé Dickeson)
Brahmsian. *See* Brahms, Johannes
'Braid Scotsman. *See* Lauder, (Sir) Harry (Maclennan)
Braisted, Harry. *See* Berdan, Harry B.
Brakeman. *See* Rodgers, James [or Jimmie] (Charles)
Braley, Berton. *See* Wodehouse, P(elham) G(renville)
Brambilla, Marietta. *See* D'Adda, Cassano
Bramble, Tabitha. *See* Robinson, Mary (Darby)
Bramsen, Willy. *See* Hansson, Stig (Axel)
Brand, Dollar. *See* Brand, Adolph Johannes
Brand, Georges. *See* Hall, Fred(erick) Fifield
Brand-Vrabely, Stephanie. *See* Vrabely, Stephanie
Brandeau. *See* Hildebrand, Ernst
Brandon, Faulkner. *See* Rawlings, Charles Arthur
Brandon, Louis. *See* Rawlings, Charles Arthur
Brandt, Alan. *See* Cameron, Dan(iel) (A.)
Brandt, Aleksander. *See* Bandrowski-Sas, Alexander
Brandt, E. *See* Ailbout, Hans
Brandt, Paul. *See* Belobersycky, Paul Rennée
Brandt, Peter. *See* Benes, Jára
Brannigan, Dr. *See* Carroll, John
Brannon, Bob. *See* Maschek, Adrian Mathew
Brannon, R. C. *See* Shipley, Daniel
Brannum, Lumpy. *See* Brannum, Hugh Roberts
Brano, Roscoe. *See* Culbertson, Roy Frederich
Brandt, Peter. *See* Beneš, Jára
Branwen. *See* Johnes, (Miss)
Brasseur, Jules (Victor Alexandre). *See* Dumont, Jules Victor Alexandre
Brassicanus, Johannes. *See* Kraut, Johann
Brate, Holger. *See* Bergman, Hjalmar (Fredrik Elgérus)
Braulio. *See* García (Bautista), Braulio A.
Braun, Gustav. *See* Böhm, Martin
Braunbach, Helena [or Helene]. *See* Keiser, Robert (A(dolph))
Bravo, Nino. *See* Ferri Llopis, Luis Manuel
Bray, Bill. *See* Jackson, Michael Joseph
Brayton, Coulthard. *See* Moody, Charles Harry [or Henry]
Brazil, Tony. *See* Jobim, Antonio Carlos
Brazil's Emperor of Easy Listening. *See* Mendes, Sergio
Brechelt, L. *See* Bliss, P(hilip) Paul
Breck, Freddy. *See* Breker, Gerhard
Bredow, Horst. *See* Kindler, Dietmar [or Dittmar]
Bredt, James. *See* Pagenstecher, Bernard
Bredt, Peter. *See* Pagenstecher, Bernard
Brehm, Günther. *See* Lengsfelder, Hans
Bremer, Rolf. *See* Niederbremer, Artur
Brémond. *See* Ronger, (Louis Auguste Joseph) Florimond
Brenet, Michel. *See* Bobillier, Antoinette Christine Marie
Brennan, Gail. *See* Clare, John (Lester)
Brennes, Alan. *See* Franz, Walter
Brent, Paul. *See* Buys, Peter
Brenta, Emil. *See* Hoffmann, Hans
Brescianino, Il. *See* Chiarini, Pietro
Bresles, Henri. *See* Bachimont, Henri
Bretonne, Raitif de la. *See* Duval, Paul Alexandre Martin
Brett, Anne. *See* Mayer, Anne (Elinor) Wolbrette
Bretton, Steve. *See* Trebilco, Leonard (Charles)
Breyttengraser, Guilelmus. *See* Breitengraser, Wilhelm
Brian, Billy. *See* Pitney, Gene (Francis Alan)
Brian, Havergal. *See* Brian, William
Brianbert. *See* Holland, Brian
Briareus of Music, The. *See* Handel, Georg Friedrich
Brice, Max. *See* Bliss, P(hilip) Paul
Brieg, Axel. *See* Brandmayer, Dolf
Briel, H. G. *See* Gabriel, Charles H(utchinson)
Brigadier. *See* English, Thomas Dunn
Brigadier Jerry. *See* Russell, Robert
Brigata, (B.) (Sig.). *See* Bucalossi, Brigata (Procida Leonardo)
Briggs, Arnold. *See* Nelson, Oswald George
Briggs, She'kspere. *See* Briggs, Kevin
Brigham, Earl(e). *See* Young, Alfred
Bright, (Rev.) H. E. *See* Gabriel, Charles H(utchinson)
Bright, W. *See* Hansson, Stig (Axel)
Brill, Bill. *See* Crosby, Harry Lillis
Brilland, Robert. *See* Simon, Waldemar
Brillante Pecoraro della Selva. *See* Miti, Pompilio
Brimmer, Son. *See* Shade, Will

Brinkman, Paul. *See* Keiser, Robert (A(dolph))
Briquet, Jean. *See* Philipp, Adolf
Brisbane, Alan. *See* Benjamin, Arthur
Brisker, Yankele. *See* Leiserowitz, Jacob [or Yaakov]
Brissac, Jules. *See* Bennett, Emma Marie
Britain's Answer to Bob Dylan. *See* Leitch, Donovan (Philip)
Britain's Baron of Burlesque. *See* Burnand, Francis Cowley
Britain's Baron of Burlesque. *See* Byron H(enry) J(ames)
Britain's Greatest Composer. *See* Elgar, (Sir) Edward
Britain's Leading "Blue-Eyed Soul" Singer. *See* Palmer, Alan
Britain's March King. *See* Ricketts, (Major) Frederick Joseph
Britain's Remembrancer. *See* Wither, George
British Ambassador of Soul. *See* Nathan, David
British Bacharach. *See* Hatch, Anthony [or Tony] (Peter)
British Bruce Springsteen. *See* Rea, Chris
British Dylan, The. *See* Leitch, Donovan (Phillip)
British March King. *See* Ricketts, (Major) Frederick Joseph
British Pop Phenomenon of the Early 80's, The. *See* Weller, John William
Brito, Phil. *See* Colombrito, Philip
Britt, Addy [or Andy]. *See* Finkelstein, Abe
Britt, Ben. *See* Brisman, Heskel
Britt, Elton. *See* Baker, James Britt
Britt, Harry. *See* Slaughter, M(arion) T(ry)
Britten, Ford. *See* Finkelstein, Abe
Britten, Roger. *See* Barnes, Clifford (Paulus)
Britton, David. *See* Dodge, J(ohn) W(ilson)
Briver, John. *See* Brouquières, Jean
Brixi, Hieronymus. *See* Brixi, Václav Norbert
Brixi, Jeroným. *See* Brixi, Václav Norbert
Brixianus Italus. *See* Riccio, Teodore [or Teodoro]
Broadbaker, Richard. *See* Papathanassiou, Evangelos (Odyssey)
Broadway, Mr. *See* Cohan, George M(ichael)
Broadway's Brightest Hope. *See* Sondheim, Stephen Joshua
Broadway's King of Elbow-Benders. *See* Thornton, Jim
Brock, Gavin. *See* Lindsay, (John) Maurice
Brockton, Lester. *See* Lake, M(ayhew) L(ester)
Brockway, Jennie M. *See* Owen, Mary Jane
Brockwell, Richard. *See* Powell, John
Brodecký. *See* Entner, Josef
Brodersen, Eric. *See* Börschel, Erich
Brodszky, Nicholaus [or Nikolaus]. *See* Brodszky, Miklós
Brody, Hal. *See* Acres, Harry
Brody, Hal. *See* Barber, H(erbert) H(edley)
Brody, Hal. *See* Carter, (Herbert) Desmond
Brody, Hal. *See* Clarke, Jack
Brody, Hal. *See* Hook, Stanley Lupino
Brody, Hal. *See* Strachey, John [or Jack] (Francis)
Brody, Lane. *See* Voorlas, Lynn Connie
Broel, Heinz. *See* Munkel, Heinz
Brogan, James. *See* Hodder-Williams, (John) Christopher (Glazebrook)
Brok, Ervin. *See* Levin, Joseph A.
Broma, Carleton. *See* Dorn, Veeder Van
Bronson, George. *See* Finkelstein, Abe
Bronson, George. *See* Kaufman, Isidore
Bronté, Emil. *See* Rawlings, Charles Arthur
Bronze Buckaroo, The. *See* Jeffries, Herb(ert Jeffrey)
Bronze Liberace, The. *See* Penniman, Richard [or Ricardo] Wayne
Bronze Raquel Welch, The. *See* Howard, Ethel
Brooce. *See* Springsteen, Bruce (Frederick Joseph)
Brook, Harold. *See* Holbrook, Joseph [or Josef] (Charles)
Brook, John. *See* Presser, William (Henry)
Brook, Michael. *See* Bonagura, Michael John, Jr.
Brooke-Haven, P. *See* Wodehouse, P(elham) G(renville)
Brooklyn, Bill. *See* Lotterer, Gustav
Brooklyn Slim. *See* Oscher, Paul
Brooks, Byron. *See* Ehret, Walter (Charles)
Brooks, Fred. *See* Hellerman, Fred
Brooks, George. *See* Grainger, Porter
Brooks, George. *See* Henderson, (James) Fletcher (Hamilton), (Jr.)
Brooks, Harvey. *See* Goldstein, Harvey
Brooks, Jennie. *See* Kimbrough, Lottie
Brooks, Lonnie. *See* Baker, Lee, Jr.
Brooks, Russ. *See* Catsos, Nicholas A.
Brooks, Teeny. *See* Brooks, Harold (Floyd)
Brooks, Tina. *See* Brooks, Harold (Floyd)
Brooks, Valerie. *See* Schaff, Sylvia
Broomsley, Big Bill. *See* Broonzy, William Lee Conley
Broonzy, Big Bill. *See* Broonzy, William Lee Conley
Brosi, Bernt. *See* Seelos, Ambros
Brother Bell. *See* O'Neal, Johnny
Brother Blues. *See* Dupree, William Thomas
Brother George. *See* Allen, Fulton
Brother George. *See* Liberace, George
Brother George. *See* McGhee, Walter Brown
Brother I(gnatius) O(rdinis) S(ancti) B(enedicti). *See* Lyne, Joseph Leycester
Brother Joshua. *See* Joseph, Pleasant
Brother Ray. *See* Robinson, Ray Charles
Brother Soul. *See* Jackson, Milt(on)
Brotherly, Jud. *See* Adderley, Julien Edwin
Brotherly, Pat. *See* Adderley, Nat(haniel)
Brothers, The. *See* Tobias, Charles
Brothers, The. *See* Tobias Harry
Brothers, The. *See* Tobias, Henry
Brothers Brough. *See* Brough, (Robert) Barnabus
Brough Brothers. *See* Brough, (Robert) Barnabus

Broughton, Edward. *See* Smith, Lani
Brown, (Miss). *See* Browne, Harriet Mary
Brown, Al. *See* Blitz, Leo(nard)
Brown, Al. *See* Lebys, Henry
Brown, Al. *See* Sugarman, Harry
Brown & Ehrlich. *See* Hansson, Stig (Axel)
Brown, Arthur. *See* Kaufman, Isidore
Brown, Arthur. *See* Wilson, Arthur
Brown, Babs. *See* Brown, Lee
Brown, Betty. *See* Vonderlieth, Leonore
Brown, Bob. *See* Davis, Katherine K(ennicott)
Brown, Boots. *See* Rajonsky [or Rajonski], Milton Michael
Brown, Buster B. *See* Rye, Sven
Brown, C. Patra. *See* Brown, Cleo(patra)
Brown, C. S. *See* Gabriel, Charles H(utchinson)
Brown, Charles. *See* Uyeda, Leslie
Brown, Chocolate. *See* Scruggs, Irene
Brown, Clarrie. *See* Bernard, Clem(ent)
Brown, Elder J. C. *See* Jefferson, Clarence
Brown, Faye E. *See* Martin, Roberta Faye E.
Brown, Fleta Jan. *See* Kunkel, Charles
Brown, Frankie. *See* Daffan, Theron Eugene
Brown, Gatemouth. *See* Brown, Clarence
Brown, George W. [or F., or R.]. *See* Hill, William [or Billy] (J(oseph))
Brown, Ginny. *See* Brown, Ginnette Patricia
Brown, Good Rockin. *See* Brown, Roy James
Brown, Harry. *See* Hunt, James Henry Leigh
Brown, Hash. *See* Lookofsky, Michael
Brown, J., The Late. *See* Thayer, Alexander Wheelock
Brown, Jackson. *See* Browne, Clyde Jackson
Brown, Junior. *See* Brown, Jameson
Brown, Leon. *See* Barry, Leon (Brown)
Brown, Lew. *See* Brownstein, Louis
Brown, Lillian [or Lillyn]. *See* Thomas, Lillian [or Lillyn]
Brown, Lindy. *See* Vonderlieth, Leonore
Brown, Lottie. *See* Kimbrough, Lottie
Brown, M. S. *See* Gabriel, Charles H(utchinson)
Brown, Mae. *See* Brown, Mary E.
Brown, Mary. *See* Gabriel, Charles H(utchinson)
Brown, Mike [or Michael]. *See* Lookofsky, Michael
Brown, Nacio Herb. *See* Brown, Ignatio Herb
Brown, Napoleon. *See* Culp, Napoleon Brown Goodson
Brown, Nappy. *See* Culp, Napoleon Brown Goodson
Brown, Papa. *See* Brown, Henry
Brown, Pat. *See* Brown, Adeline E.
Brown, Rabbit. *See* Brown, Richard
Brown, Sam. *See* Brown, Samantha
Brown, Sonny. *See* Brown, William
Brown, T. Graham. *See* Brown, Anthony Graham
Brown, Thomas (the younger). *See* Moore, Thomas
Brown, Tiger. *See* Ferguson, Maynard
Brown, Tom. *See* Waller, Thomas Wright
Brown, Tommy. *See* Brown, Roy James
Brown, Washboard Sam. *See* Brown, Robert (1910-1966)
Brown, Willie. *See* Sissle, Noble (Lee)
Browne, Daisy. *See* Browne, Diane Gale
Browne, Lester. *See* Berman, Syd
Browne, Lester. *See* Fields, Harold (Cornelius)
Browne, Matthew. *See* Rands, William Brightly
Browne, Ted. *See* Brownold, Fred
Brownee, Zing. *See* Brownstein, Samuel Hyman
Browning, Timothy. *See* Sawyer, Henry S.
Brownjohn, John. *See* Talbot, Charles Remington
Browser, Bill. *See* Browder, William [or Bill]
Broxton, Melvin. *See* Moore, Melvin James
Bruce, Charles. *See* Crosby, Fanny [i.e., Frances] J(ane)
Bruce, Edgar. *See* Treharne, Bryceson
Bruce, Edward. *See* Bulwer-Lytton, Edward Robert
Bruce, Gary. *See* Barton, Ben
Bruce, Jack. *See* Asher, John Symon
Bruce, Richard. *See* Smith, Robert B.
Bruce, Richard L. *See* Munn, William O.
Bruce, Robert. *See* Crosby, Fanny [i.e., Frances] J(ane)
Bruce, Robert. *See* Wright, Robert B.
Bruce, Vin. *See* Bruce, Ervin
Bruce, Wallace. *See* Bliss, P(hilip) Paul
Bruckner, Ferdinand. *See* Tagger, Theodore
Bruckner of British Music, The. *See* Vaughan Williams, Ralph
Bruckner of the 20th Century, The. *See* Rubbra, Edmund
Bruges, Arnold de. *See* Bruck, Arnold von
Brugner, Joe. *See* Götz, Karl
Bruhns, Arthur. *See* Bruhns, George Frederick William
Brujas, Manos. *See* Biagi, Rodolfo
Brule'. *See* LaRoche, Paul
Brulovsky, Nicolai. *See* Ehret, Walter (Charles)
Brulovsky, Nicolai. *See* Kinsman, Elmer (F(ranklin))
Brumnitzius, Nocturnus. *See* Baer, Nicolaus
Brunn, Veit. *See* Stelzer-Palm, Joachim
Bruno, Karl. *See* Giugno, Karl
Brunswick, (Léon-Lévy). *See* Lévy, Léon (1805-1859)
Brussel, Antoine de. *See* Wyngaerde, Antoine de
Brute, The. *See* Johnson, James [or Jimmy, or Jimmie] (P(rice))
Brute of a Husband, A. *See* Rands, William Brightly
Bruxelas, Antoine de. *See* Wyngaerde, Antoine de
Bryan, Al. *See* Breitenbach, Albert
Bryant, Dan. *See* O'Brien, Daniel Webster
Bryant, Felice. *See* Scaduto, Matilda Genevieve
Bryant, Ray. *See* Bryant, Raphael
Bryant, Slim. *See* Bryant, (Thomas) Hoyt
Bryant, Tilghman A. *See* Kunkel, Charles
Bryce, A. *See* Bonner, Carey
Brynallt. *See* Williams, Gwilym E.
Bryson, Peabo. *See* Bryson, Peapo
Bubb, Mel. *See* Whitcomb, Ian (Timothy)
Bubba. *See* Earle, Steve

Bubbles. *See* Silverman, Belle Miriam
Buchanan, Alstair. *See* McMillan, Alec
Bucharoff, Simon. *See* Buchhalter, Simon
Buchbinder, Bernhard (Ludwig). *See* Klinger, Gustav(e)
Bucher, A. *See* Ruh, Emil
Bücher, Ernst. *See* Boex, Andrew J.
Buchholz, Charlie. *See* Buchholz, Karl
Buchholz, Hans. *See* Müller, Werner [or Warner]
Buchholz, Heinz. *See* Müller, Werner [or Warner]
Buchholz, Horst. *See* Müller, Werner [or Warner]
Buchner, Toni. *See* Sulzböck, Toni
Buck, Gene. *See* Buck, Edward Eugene
Buck, Larry. *See* Dubuclet, Laurent
Buck, Lawrence. *See* Buchtel, Forrest (Lawrence)
Bückeburg Bach, The. *See* Bach, Johann Christoph Friedrich
Bucket, Rubber. *See* Gadd, Paul
Buckley, Eugene. *See* Finkelstein, Abe
Buckley, Jeff. *See* Moorhead, Scott
Buckshot la Funke. *See* Adderley, Julian Edwin
Buczek, Barbara. *See* Buczkowna, Kazimiera Zofia
Buda, Karl. *See* Winterfeld, David Robert
Buday, Don. *See* Buday, Albert
Buddha. *See* Ekberg, Ulf
Buddy Boy. *See* Guy, George
Budin, J. L. *See* Löwenbach, Jan
Budtree, Red. *See* Lebys, Henry
Budtree, Red. *See* Leader, Joyce Rona
Bueno, L. *See* Bliss, P(hilip) Paul
Buford, Mojo. *See* Buford, George
Buger, Matthias. *See* Schneider, Willy
Bugsworthy, Nicholas. *See* Morris, Reginald Owen
Buie, Buddy. *See* Buie, Perry C.
Buk, K. *See* Kubka, František
Bulawa, Ernest. *See* Tarnowski, (Count) Wladyslaw
Bull Crow. *See* Burnett, Chester Arthur
Bull Speaker, The. *See* Amner, Ralph
Bull(e), Ole, Jr. *See* Buckley, Frederick
Bulwer, E. L. *See* Gutzkow, Karl (Ferdinand)
Bumble Bee Slim. *See* Easton, Amos
Buna, Vaga. *See* Ordnung, Rudolf (August)
Bunbury, Enrique. *See* Ortiz de Lndazury Yzarduy, Enrique
Bündler, David. *See* Ellison, Byrwec
Bundrick, Rabbit. *See* Bundrick, John
Bundy, Jerry. *See* Kunkel, Charles
Bunn, Allen. *See* Bunn, Alden
Bunny-Ears. *See* Hasenöhrl, Franz
Bunting. *See* Presley, Elvis A(a)ron
Buntline, Ned. *See* Judson, Edward Zane Carrol
Bunya, Koh. *See* Wenyeh, Chiang
Buranello, Il. *See* Galuppi, Baldassare
Burani, Paul. *See* Roucoux, (Paul) Urbain
Burchiella, (Il). *See* Molino, Antonio
Burck, Joachim à. *See* Moller, (Count) Joachim à
Burenin, V(iktor Petrovich). *See* Zhasminov, Aleksei [or Alexei]
Burg, Alfred. *See* Lynes, Frank
Burg, Hermann. *See* Baravalle, Robert
Burger, Matthias. *See* Schneider, Willy
Burgess, Andrew. *See* Schaeffer, Don(ald)
Burgess, Anthony. *See* Wilson, John Anthony (Burgess)
Burgess, Cyril. *See* Mullen, Frederic
Burgess, Irving. *See* Burgie, Irving Louis
Burgess, Lord. *See* Burgie, Irving Louis
Burgh, Barnard. *See* Brough, (Robert) Barnabas
Burgh, Chris de. *See* Davidson, Christopher (John)
Burghauser, Jarmil (Michael). *See* Mokry, Jarmil Michael
Burgheim, G. J. *See* Keiser, Robert (A(dolph))
Burgheim, J. J. *See* Keiser, Robert (A(dolph))
Burghersh, Lord. *See* Fane, John
Burgie, Irvine. *See* Burgie Irving Louis
Burgmein, J. *See* Ricordi, Giulio
Burgner, Joe. *See* Götz, Karl
Burgwart, Karl. *See* Bourgeois, Karl
Buri, Friedrich (W.). *See* Wongtschowski, Adolf Friedrich
Burillo, Florentino. *See* Caballero, Manuel Fernández
Burk, John. *See* Gillespie, John (Birks)
Burke, Charles. *See* Brucato, Charles R.
Burke, Dave. *See* Newell, Norman
Burke, Harry. *See* Johnson, J. C.
Burke, James. *See* Oden, James Burke
Burke, Joe. *See* Daniels, Charles N(eil)
Burke, Lee. *See* Sigman, Carl
Burke, Lora Miller. *See* Kunkel, Charles
Burke, Sonny. *See* Burke, Joseph Francis
Burken, Al. *See* Sugarman, Harry
Burland, Sascha. *See* Burland, Granville (A.)
Burleigh, Mary Lou. *See* Scruggs, Mary Elfrieda
Burley, Mary Lou. *See* Scruggs, Mary Elfrieda
Burnay, Carlos. *See* Davies, Harry Parr
Burnett, Bob. *See* Miller, Robert [or Bob] (Ernst)
Burnett, Ernie. *See* Bernadetti, Ernest Marco
Burnett, Sam. *See* Phillips, Leslie
Burnett, T-Bone. *See* Burnett, Joseph Henry
Burnette, Frog. *See* Burnette, Lester Alvin
Burnette, Legendary Hank C. *See* Hogberg, Sven Ake
Burnette, Rocky. *See* Burnette, Jonathan [or Johnny]
Burnette, Smiley. *See* Burnette, Lester Alvin
Burning Spear. *See* Rodney, (Godfrey) Winston
Burnnon, George. *See* Burnstein, George
Burns, Allen. *See* Davis, Joseph [or Joe] (M.)
Burns, Charles. *See* Crosby, Fanny [i.e., Frances] J(ane)
Burns, Guitar. *See* Burns, Eddie
Burns, Jethro. *See* Burns, Kenneth C.
Burns, Jim. *See* Hartley, Fred
Burns, "Little" Eddie. *See* Burns, Eddie
Burns, Morry. *See* Mullican, Aubrey Wilson

Burns, Robert. *See* Gabriel, Charles H(utchinson)
Burns, Wilfred. *See* Harris, Bernard Wilfred
Burnside, Jack (E.). *See* Burnside, Ernest
Burnson, George. *See* Burnstein, George
Burnstein, Lillian. *See* Lux, Lillian Sylvia
Burr, Henry. *See* McClaskey, Harry Haley
Burrell, Dave. *See* Burrell, Herman Davis, II
Burroughs, John. *See* Presley, Elvis A(a)ron
Burrows, Abe [or Abram] (Solman). *See* Borowitz, Abram Solman
Burrows, (Dr. [or Colonel]) Jon. (Jr.). *See* Presley, Elvis A(a)ron
Burse, Uke. *See* Burse, Charlie
Burstein, Paul. *See* Burshtein, Peisach [or Pesach]
Burt, Caleb. *See* Burleigh, Cecil (Edward)
Burt, Ed. *See* Berbert, Edith
Burt, L. S. *See* Walsh, Ulysses
Burte, Hermann. *See* Strübe, Hermann
Burton, Avery. *See* Avery
Burton, Baylis. *See* Linley, George
Burton, Billy. *See* Slaughter, M(arion) T(ry)
Burton, Clark W. *See* Loes, Harry Dixon
Burton, Dick. *See* Nelson, Oswald George
Burton, Fred. *See* Cohen, Samuel
Burton Junior. *See* Lamb, Charles
Burton, R. O. *See* Bliss, P(hilip) Paul
Burton, Sammy. *See* Kaufman, Isidore
Busby, Buz. *See* Busby, William B.
Busby, Buzz. *See* Busbice, Bernarr (G(raham))
Busch, Robert. *See* Gogg, Dieter
Bush, Billy. *See* Kendis, James
Bush, Johnny. *See* Shin, John Bush, III
Bush, Walter. *See* Elliott, Percy
Bushy Head. *See* Walker, John(ny) (Mayon)
Busoni, Ferruccio. *See* Busoni, Dante Michelangelo Benvenuto
Bussy, Edmond de. *See* Hocmelle, Pierre Edmond
Bust, Urastix. *See* Fox, Charles H.
Busta Rhymes. *See* Smith, Trevor
Buster, Prince. *See* Campbell, Cecil Bustamente
Busterkeys, Walter. *See* Liberace, (Wladziu Valentino)
Busy Bee. *See* Beswick, Harry
Butler, Bill. *See* Butler, Henry W.
Butler, Clarence. *See* Johnstone, Arthur Edward
Butler, Geezer. *See* Butler, Terrance [or Terence]
Butler, M. W. *See* Perry, Phil(ip) B(utler)
Butler, Neville Challoner. *See* Challoner, Neville Butler
Butler, O'Brien. *See* Whitwell, O'Brien
Butler, Pete. *See* Butler, A. L.
Butler, Wild Child. *See* Butler, George
Butler, Wright. *See* Butler, Ralph (T.)
Butler, Wright. *See* Wright, Julian
Butterbeans. *See* Edwards, Joe [or Jody]
Butterbeans. *See* Wesley, Wilson
Butterscotch, Mr. *See* Torme, Mel(vin Howard)
Buttons. *See* Presley, Elvis A(a)ron
Buttykay, Ákos. *See* Gálszécsy és Butykai, Ákos
Buus, Giacques. *See* Buus, Jacques [or Jacob] (de)
Buva, Ernesto. *See* Kröger, Willi
Buys, Jacob. *See* Buus, Jacques [or Jacob] (de)
Byard, Jaki. *See* Byard, John A., Jr.
Bydwealth, Emily. *See* Zubeldia, Emiliana de
Byerly, William. *See* Foster, Stephen Collins
Byers, Alfrey. *See* Lake, M(ayhew) L(ester)
Bygraves, Max. *See* Bygraves, Walter (William)
Byles, Chubby. *See* Byles, Keith
Byles, Junior. *See* Byles, Keith
Byn. *See* Roth, Albert
Byrd, Bald Head. *See* Byrd, Henry Roeland
Byrd, Bretton. *See* Byrd, James Thomas
Byrd, Ch(arlie). *See* Schleich, Ernst
Byrd, Charlie. *See* Thomason, Alexander
Byrd, Fess. *See* Byrd, Henry Roeland
Byrd, Roy. *See* Byrd, Henry Roeland
Byrd, Russell. *See* Berns, Bert(rand) (Russell)
Byrne, Nora C. E. *See* Bonner, Carey
Byron, Walter. *See* Weschler, Melvin Walter
Bystrý, Ján. *See* Figuš-Bystrý, Viliam

– C –

C. *See* Brace, Seth Collins
C. *See* Conder, Josiah
C. *See* Crosby, Fanny [i.e., Frances] J(ane)
C. *See* Cunningham, Allan
C. A. *See* Aston, C.
C. A. B. *See* Barry, Charles Ainslie
C. A. T. *See* Thielo, Carl August
C. & J. W. *See* Wesley, Charles
C. & J. W. *See* Wesley, John
C. and L. *See* Fielding, Henry
C. B. *See* Barbandt, Carl
C. B. *See* Batty, Christopher
C. B. *See* Bernhard, Christoph
C. B. *See* English, Thomas Dunn
C. Chr. D. *See* Dedekind, Constantin Christian
C. E. *See* Ellerbock, Charles
C. E. *See* Elliott, Charlotte
C. E. *See* Tonna, Charlotte Elizabeth (née Browne)
C. E. B. *See* Burton, Claude E(dward Cole-Hamilton)
C. E. C. *See* Cope, Charles Elvey
C. E. H., (Mrs.). *See* Habicht, Emma
C. F. *See* Forsyth, Christina
C. F. *See* Foster, Catherine
C. F. *See* Freund(t), Cornelius [or Kornelius]
C. F. A. *See* Alexander, (Mrs.) Cecil F(rances) (née Humphreys)
C. F. H. *See* Alexander, (Mrs.) Cecil F(rances) (née Humphreys)

C. F. H. *See* Hernaman, Claudia Frances (née Ibotson)
C. F. M. *See* Manney, Charles Fonteyn
C. H. G. *See* Gabriel, Charles H(utchinson)
C. H. I. *See* Inglis, Charlotte H.
C. H. L. S. *See* Schuette, Conrad Herman Louis
C. I. L. T. *See* Latrobe, Christian Ignatius
C. J. L. A. *See* Almqvist, Carl Jonas Love [or Ludwig]
C. J. M. *See* Macy, J(ames) C(artwright)
C. L. *See* Locknane, Clement
C. M. C. *See* Caddell, Cecilia Mary
C. M. C. *See* Greenwald, M(artin)
C. P. *See* Ottoboni, Pietro
C. S. *See* Stanley, Charles
C. S. *See* Stieler, Caspar [or Kaspar] (von)
C. S***, Mselle. *See* Schröter, Corona Wilhelmine Elizabeth
Caasi, Lledder Yeldah. *See* Reddell, Isaac Hadley
Cab, Marc(h). *See* Cabridens, Marcel (Eugène Henri)
Caballero. *See* Temple, Edith
Caballero del Tango, El. *See* Tanturi, Ricardo
Caber, C. *See* Jordan, E.
Cable, Howard. *See* Ehret, Walter (Charles)
Cachaça, Carlos. *See* Moreira de Castro, Carlos
Cachao. *See* Lopez, Israel
Cactus Rex. *See* Allen, Rex (Elvey)
Cadbury, Buddy. *See* Martin, Ray(mond)
Cadbury, Buddy. *See* Stellman, Marcel
Caddo, Lawrence. *See* Cain, Noble
Cadet. *See* Robinson, J. Watts
Cadet-Roussel. *See* Labrunie, Gérard
Cadillac Jake. *See* Harris, James [or Jimmy] (D.)
Cadler. *See* Ockenfels, Helmut
Caesar. *See* Bono, Salvatore
Caesar, Irving. *See* Caesar, Isidore
Caesar, Vic. *See* Cesario, Victor L(ouis)
Caesar, William. *See* Smegergill, William
Caffarelli. *See* Caf(f)aro, Pasquale
Caffariello. *See* Caf(f)aro, Pasquale
Cagliostro of Modernity. *See* Wagner, Richard
Cahn, Sammy. *See* Cohen, Samuel
Cain, Joe. *See* Caiani, Joseph (Jack, Jr.)
Caine, Daniel. *See* Wadsworth, Derek
Cairns, Paddy. *See* Hughes, Patrick Cairns
Cajun Hank Williams. *See* Menard, D(oris) L(eon)
Cajun King. *See* Newman, Jimmy C. [actually Yves]
Cajun Pete. *See* Vidacovich, Irving J(ohn, Sr.)
Cajun Queen. *See* Harris, Emmylou
Cakewalk King, The. *See* Mills, Frederick Allen
Calafati, Marie. *See* Gordon, Marie
Cale, John(ny). *See* Calabro, John A(nthony)
Caledfryn, Gwilym. *See* Williams (Pantycelyn), William
Calegari, Maria Cattarina. *See* Calegari, Cornelia
Calenberg, Wolf. *See* Heddenhausen, Friedel-Heinz
Calhoun, Charles [or Chuck] (E.). *See* Stone, Jesse (A.)
Calhoun, Clayton. *See* Keiser, Robert (A(dolph))
Calhoun, Jeff. *See* Crow(e), Francis Luther
Calhoun, Jeff. *See* Finkelstein, Abe
Calhoun, Jeff. *See* Slaughter, M(arion) T(ry)
Calhoun, Jess. *See* Slaughter, M(arion) T(ry)
Calhoun, John C. *See* Hanley, James F.
Calhoun, John C. *See* MacDonald, Ballard
Calhoun, John Clayton. *See* Keiser, Robert (A(dolph))
Caliban. *See* Checchi, Eugenio
Caliban, Cain. *See* Mallis, Constantine Alexander (Hadji [or Hagi])
Calibano, Didimo. *See* Checchi, Eugenio
California Ragtime King, The. *See* Roberts, James Martin
California, Randy. *See* Wolfe, Randy
Caliginoso, Il. *See* Foscarini, Giovanni Paolo
Calindo Grolo. *See* Goldoni, Carlo
Call, Gus. *See* Dant, Charles G(ustave)
Calla, Arna. *See* Cecconi-Bates, Augusta
Calle, Rico. *See* Carmichael, Ralph
Callender, Newgate. *See* Schonberg, Harold (Charles)
Callender, Red. *See* Callender, George (Sylvester)
Calligos, M. *See* Kötscher, Edmund
Callihou, James. *See* Morin, Léopold [or Léo-Pol]
Callistamio, Erbistide. *See* Riccati, (Count) Giordano
Calmon, Theo. *See* Kochmann, Spero
Calmond, Mark. *See* Williams, Joseph (Benjamin)
Calvert, Lord. *See* Cole, Nathaniel Adams
Calvi, Gérard. *See* Krettly, Grégoire(-Elie)
Calvi, Jean. *See* Krettly, Grégoire(-Elie)
Calvin, Columbus. *See* Pearson, Columbus Calvin, Jr.
Calvin(ius), Jean. *See* Cauvin, Jean
Calvin Johnson of Sao Polo, The. *See* Antunes, Arnaldo
Calvisius, Sethus. *See* Kallwitz, Seth
Calypso Monarch of Montserrat. *See* Cassell, Alphonsus
Calypso Rose. *See* Lewis, McCartha (Sandy)
Camarata, Toots [or Tutti]. *See* Camarata, Salvador
Cambon, Jules. *See* Rawlings, Charles Arthur
Cambrensis. *See* Heseltine, Philip (Arnold)
Cambridge, Jack. *See* Wellnitz, Gerd
Camdon, Al D. *See* MacDonald, Ballard
Camdon, Dal. *See* MacDonald, Ballard
Cameo Girl, The. *See* Nelson, Lucille
Camerano. *See* Ruffini, Giovanni [or Giacomo] (Domenico)
Cameron, Alicia. *See* Lorenz, E(dmund) S(imon)
Cameron, Allan R. *See* Reeves, Ernest
Cameron, David. *See* Bernard, Clem(ent)
Cameron, Owen. *See* Murray, James R(amsey)
Camidio Matiaglauro. *See* Bagliacca, Pietro Antonio
Camille. *See* Nelson, Prince Rogers
Camini, Bruno. *See* Klickmann, F(rank) Henri
Cammin, Heinz. *See* Zehm, Friedrich
Campalto. *See* Gori, Antonio Francesco

Carlberg, Bengt. *See* Hansson, Stig (Axel)
Carle, Frankie. *See* Carlone, Francis N(unzio)
Carle, Glen. *See* Engel, Carl
Carle, Richard (E.). *See* Carleton, Charles (Nicholas)
Carle, Smiling Frankie. *See* Carlone, Francis N(unzio)
Carleton, Bruce. *See* Peery, Rob Roy
Carleton, Mary. *See* Crosby, Fanny [i.e., Frances] J(ane)
Carlin, Andrew. *See* ZIV-TV
Carlin, Regina M. *See* Kunkel, Charles
Carlini, Carlo. *See* Arnol'd, Yury (Karlovich)
Carlino. *See* Manelli, Carlo
Carlino di Ratta, Il. *See* Zanardi, Carlo Antonio
Carlisle, Bill. *See* Carlisle, Cliff(ord Raymond)
Carlisle, Jack. *See* Musel, Robert [or Bob] (Saul)
Carllile, Thumbs. *See* Carllile, Kenneth (Ray)
Carlo. *See* Carl, M.
Carlo. *See* Herzel, Carl [or Karl] (Heinrich)
Carlo del Violino. *See* Caproli, Carlo
Carlo del Violino. *See* Cesarini, Carlo Francesco
Carlo del Violino. *See* Mannelli, Carlo
Carlo, Johnny. *See* Selvaggio, John R(alph)
Carlo, Monty. *See* Harrhy, Edith
Carlo Tessarini il Categarreuil. *See* Tessarini, Carlo
Carlo, T(yran). *See* Davis, Roquel
Carlos, Erasmo. *See* Esteves, Erasmo
Carlos, Manuel. *See* Soloman, Mirrie (Irma)
Carlos, Roberto. *See* Braga, Roberto Carlos
Carlos, Wendy. *See* Carlos, Walter (1939-)
Carlotta, (Dr.) C(arl). *See* Ehrenberg, Siegfried
Carlson, Lee. *See* Clinton, Larry
Carlson, Lenny. *See* Clinton, Larry
Carlston, Mary. *See* Crosby, Fanny [i.e., Frances] J(ane)
Carlton, Carl. *See* Fequa, Carl
Carlton, Henry [or Harry]. *See* Greenbank, Henry [or Harry] H(arveston) [or H(ewetson)]
Carlton, John. *See* Ehret, Walter (Charles)
Carlton, John. *See* Kinsman, Elmer (F(ranklin))
Carlton, John. *See* Kjelson, Lee
Carlton, John. *See* Shelton, Travis
Carlton, John. *See* Stark, Harold (Stillwell)
Carlton, Leah. *See* Crosby, Fanny [i.e., Frances] J(ane)
Carlton, Sydney. *See* Greenbank, Henry [or Harry] H(arveston) [or H(ewetson)]
Carluccio del Violino. *See* Caproli, Carlo
Carluccio di Pamfilio. *See* Mannelli, Carlo
Carmen, Fred. *See* Picariello, Frederick [or Frederico] A(nthony)
Carmen Marina. *See* Gioconda, Carmen Manteca
Carmen Sylva. *See* Elizabeth, Queen of Romania
Carmencito. *See* Fields, Harold (Cornelius)
Carmencito. *See* Roncoroni, Joseph (Dominic)
Carmeni. *See* Hastings, Thomas
Carmichael, Hoagy. *See* Carmichael, Howard Hoagland
Carnaby. *See* Burke, Michael
Carner, Mosco. *See* Cohen, Mosco
Carniolanus, Jacobus. *See* Petelin, Jakob
Carniolis. *See* Plautzius, Gabriel
Caro Sassone, Il. *See* Hasse, Johann Adolf
Carol, Gary. *See* Bratman, Carroll Charles
Carol, Marty. *See* Meehan, Martha
Carolan. *See* O'Carolan, (Turlough [or Terence])
Caroli, A. *See* Bayer, Johann Gottfried Eduard
Caroli, Vic. *See* Green, Phil(ip)
Caroli, Vic. *See* Paramor, Norman [or Norrie] (William)
Carolin, Martha. *See* Meehan, Martha
Carolina Cowboy, The. *See* Kirby, Fred
Carolina Slim. *See* Harris, Edward P.
Carolon, Paul. *See* Rawlings, Charles Arthur
Caron, Bill. *See* Viau, Albert
Carpelle, Giulli. *See* Leest, Antonius Maria van
Carpenter, Cliff. *See* Zimmerman, Dieter
Carpenter, Dr. [or Colonel] John. *See* Presley, Elvis A(a)ron
Carpentras(so), (Il). *See* Genet, Elzéar
Carr, Fingers. *See* Busch, Louis F(erdinand)
Carr, Gunter Lee. *See* Gant, Cecil
Carr, Harold. *See* Katz, Harold (H.)
Carr, Joe Fingers. *See* Busch, Louis F(erdinand)
Carr, Michael. *See* Cohen, Maurice Alfred
Carr, Roberta. *See* Feldner, Roberta Emily
Carradine, David. *See* Carradine, John Arthur
Carras, Nicholas [or Nick]. *See* Carastathis, Nicholas Sam
Carré, Fabrice. *See* Labrousse, Fabrice
Carreno, Roberto. *See* Klickmann, F(rank) Henri
Carrie. *See* Griswold, Mary Caroline
Carrington, Herbert. *See* Ewing, Montague (George)
Carrodus, John (Tiplady). *See* Carruthers, John (Tiplady)
Carroll, Barbara. *See* Coppersmith, Barbara Carole
Carroll, Bob. *See* Jones, Robert Carroll
Carroll, Francis. *See* Sawyer, Henry S.
Carroll, Harry. *See* Druckman, Milton
Carroll, Irv. *See* Gellers, Irving
Carroll, Richard. *See* McGowen, Frank(lin) S(immons)
Carroll, Roy. *See* Robertson, Dick
Carsellini, Fabio. *See* Rabbenius, Raphael
Carson, Cal. *See* Crow(e), Francis Luther
Carson, Cal. *See* Robison, Carson J(ay)
Carson, James. *See* Roberts, James William
Carson, Jenny Lou. *See* Overstake, (Virginia) Lucille
Carson, Martha. *See* Amburgey, Irene
Carson, Milton. *See* Barnes, H(oward) E(llington)
Carson, Milton. *See* Fields, Harold (Cornelius)
Carson, Milton. *See* Roncoroni, Joseph (Dominic)
Carste, Hans. *See* Hering, Hans
Carsten, Bert. *See* Nordlander, Bert Carsten
Carsten, (Carl) Heinrich. *See* Reinecke, Carl Heinrich Carsten
Carter, Benny. *See* Carter, Bennett L(ester)

Caviare. *See* Keats, John
Cavini, Victor. *See* Trede, Gerhard
Cavoret, Alfred. *See* Engel, Alexander
Cawood, John. *See* Bliss, P(hilip) Paul
Caxton, Pisistratus. *See* Bulwer-Lytton, Edward Robert
Cazalès, Guy de. *See* Casales, Ugo
Cecchi d'Amico, Suso. *See* Cecchi d'Amico, Giovanna
Cecchina, La. *See* Caccini, Francesca
Cechus de Florentia. *See* Landini, Francesco
Cecil, Arthur. *See* Blunt, Arthur Cecil
Cecil, Hugh Mortimer. *See* Roberts, William (Amos)
Cecil, John. *See* Hone, William
Cecilia. *See* Wieck, Clara Josephine
Cecilia. *See* Sobredo Galanes, Evangelina
Cedreatico, Osiro. *See* David, Domenico
Ceiriog. *See* Hughes, John Ceiriog
Celadon. *See* Negelein, Christoph Adam
Celano. *See* Corsi, Giuseppe
Cele. *See* Flores, Celedonio (Esteban)
Celiano, Livio. *See* Grillo, (Don) Angelo
Cellarius. *See* Butler, Samuel
Cellarius, Simon. *See* Hausskeller, Simon
Celler, Ludovic. *See* Leclerq, Louis
Celli, Frank H(ubert). *See* Standing, Francis [or Frank] (H.)
Cellini, Baccio. *See* Civinini, Guelfo
Cemal Resit. *See* Rey, Cemal Resid
Centano, Jules. *See* Saenger, Gustav(e)
Centeya, Julián. *See* Vergiati, Amleto (Enrique)
Century's Best "Unknown" Symphonist, The. *See* Martinu, Bohuslav
Cepillin. *See* González (Salazar), Ricardo
Cepinski. *See* Adamovic, Bela
Cerato (d'Arzignano Vicentio), Il. *See* Giuliani, Francesco
Cere, Addie. *See* Cere, Edvige C.
Cernovichi, Giovanni Marie. *See* Giornovichi, Giovanni Mane
Ceruomo, Francesco. *See* Wachsmann, Franz
Cervenka, Exene. *See* Cervenka, Christine
Cervetti, Herman (Anton). *See* Gelinek, Hermann Anton
Cervetto, Giacomo. *See* Cervetto, James (1682-1783)
Cervetto, Giacob(b)o (Bas(s)evi). *See* Cervetto, James (1682-1783)
Cervetto, Jasper. *See* Cervetto, James (1747-1837)
Cervetto the Elder. *See* Cervetto, James (1682-1783)
Cervetto the Younger. *See* Cervetto, James (1747-1837)
Cesare, Don Giulio. *See* Merlo, Alessandro
Cesaro, Renato. *See* Keiser, Reinhard
Cesaro, Rinardo. *See* Keiser Reinhard
Cesena, Peregrinus. *See* Veronensis, Peregrinus Cesena
Cesna, Giovanni Battista. *See* Biondi, Giovanni Battista
Cesti, Antonio. *See* Cesti, Pietro
Cesti, Marc'Antonio. *See* Cesti, Pietro
Cetoff, Sternberg Wassili. *See* Bonelli, Luigi
Cezán, Marcelo. *See* Gómez, Edgar
Chabran, Charles. *See* Chiabrano, Carlo (Giuseppe Valentino)
Chabran, Francesco. *See* Chiabrano, Carlo (Giuseppe Valentino)
Chabran, Gaetano. *See* Chiabrano (Gaspare Giuseppe) Gaetano
Chadel, H. P. *See* Delaunay, Charles
Chadwick, Donald. *See* Noble, Ray(mond) (Stanley)
Chagrin, Francis. *See* Paucker, Alexander
Chain, Leslie. *See* Beard, Leslie Lois
Chaise, Fill. *See* Hayes, Philip
Chalcenterus. *See* Didymus
Chalfant, Scott. *See* Bliss, P(hilip) Paul
Chalinillo. *See* Cano Vega, Ambrosio
Chalkdust, Mighty. *See* Liverpool, Hollis Urban Lester
Chalkenteros. *See* Didymus
Chalkie. *See* Liverpool, Hollis Urban Lester
Challis, Roger. *See* St. Edmunds, John [nd]
Chalmers, Cy. *See* Cohen, Maurice Alfred
Chalmers, Cy. *See* Newell, Norman
Chaloix, Erny. *See* Schorlemmer, Erna von
Chamare. *See* Defossez, René
Chambers, Rick. *See* Ziegler, Richard A(dam)
Chambers, Robert. *See* Ehret, Walter (Charles)
Chambers, Robert. *See* Kinsman, Elmer (F(ranklin))
Chambers, Robert. *See* Lyall, Jack
Chambers, Robert. *See* Rodby, Walter (A.)
Chambers, Robert. *See* Trusler, Ivan
Chameleon. *See* Bridges, (Claude) Russell
Chameleon, The. *See* Hancock, Herbert [or Herbie] Jeffrey
Chameleon in Tango Color, A. *See* Mitnik, Bernardo
Chameleon of Pop. *See* Jones, David Robert (Haywood)
Champagne, Champ. *See* Champagne, Gil(l)es (Maurice) H(erve)
Champfleury, Jules F(rançois) F(élix). *See* Husson(-Fleury), Jules F(rançois) F(élix)
Champion, Harry. *See* Conray, Will
Champion Jack. *See* Dupree, William Thomas
Champion of Intuition, The. *See* Saeverud, Ketil
Chan, Charlie. *See* Parker, Charles [or Charlie] (Christopher, Jr.)
Chance, David. *See* Schantz, David Mathew
Chance, James T. *See* Carpenter, John(ny)
Chance, John T. *See* Carpenter, John(ny)
Chancellor, John. *See* Olcott, Chancellor John
Chandler, A. *See* Frangkiser, Carl (Moerz)
Chandler, Gene. *See* Dixon, Eugene
Chandler, Jeff. *See* Grossel, Ira
Chandler, Otis. *See* Wagness, Bernard
Chandler, R. W. *See* Bideu, Louis
Chandon, Theo. *See* Burnand, Arthur Bransby
Chandon, Theo. *See* Lynes, Frank

Chano. *See* Pozo (y Gonzales), Luciano
Chanson, George. *See* Loyau, George Etienne
Chantilly, (Mlle.). *See* Duronceray, Marie Justine Benoîte
Chapel, Clive. *See* Lloyd Webber, William (Southcombe)
Chapelle, La. *See* Champion, Jacques
Chapin, Betty. *See* Keiser, Robert (A(dolph))
Chapin, Betty. *See* MacDonald, Ballard
Chaplin, Saul. *See* Kaplan, Saul
Chapman, Angie. *See* Chapman, Anzenta Igene Perry
Chapman, Cee Cee. *See* Chapman, Melissa Carol
Chapman, Joseph. *See* Crawford, Jesse
Chapo (de Sinaloa), (El). *See* Pérez, Ernesto
Char, Fritz. *See* Char, Friedrich Ernst
Chard, Evan. *See* Evans, Sydney
Chariteo, Il. *See* Gareth, Benedetto
Chariteus. *See* Gareth, Benedetto
Charlap, Moose. *See* Charlap, Morris (Isaac)
Charles, Bobby. *See* Guidry, Robert Charles
Charles, Dick. *See* Krieg, Richard Charles
Charles, Frank. *See* Fields, Harold (Cornelius)
Charles, Gregg. *See* Ehret, Walter (Charles)
Charles, Gregg. *See* Kinsman, Elmer (F(ranklin))
Charles, Harold. *See* Kaufman, Isidore
Charles, Henry. *See* Brown, Henry
Charles, Jean. *See* Braun, Karl Johann, Ritter von Braunthal
Charles K. *See* Harris, Charles K(assell)
Charles, L. *See* Lofthouse, Charles (Thornton)
Charles, M(onsieur). *See* Chop, Max (Friedrich Julius Theodor)
Charles, Ray. *See* Robinson, Ray Charles
Charles, Susanne. *See* Mannes, Leo (Ezekiel)
Charles, Teddy. *See* Cohen, Theodore Charles
Charleston, Arthur. *See* Hyman, Richard [or Dick] (R(oven))
Charlie Chaplin of Rock, The. *See* Wainwright, Loudon, III
Charlotte Elizabeth. *See* Tonna, Charlotte Elizabeth (née Browne)
Charlton, Dennis. *See* Ketèlbey, Albert William
Charming, Prince. *See* Basie, William (Allen)
Charriere, Sophie de. *See* Charriére, Isabella (Agneta Elisabeth) de
Chase, Paul. *See* Ehret, Walter (Charles)
Chasmindo. *See* Dach, Simon
Chatelain, Clara (de) (Pontigny). *See* Pontifex, Clara de
Chatman, Peter. *See* Chatman, John Len
Chatmon, Bo. *See* Chatmon, Armenter
Chavarria, Angelo. *See* Feather, Leonard (Geoffrey)
Chaventre, Pierre. *See* Ewing, Montague (George)
Chavero Mario. *See* Chavero, Héctor (Roberto)
Chavis, Boozoo. *See* Chavis, Wilson (Anthony)
Cheatham, Kitty. *See* Bugg, Catharine Smiley
Checco. *See* Bontempi, Francesco
Checco, Checchin. *See* Viola, Francesco
Chechin. *See* Silvestrino, Francesco
Checker, Chubby. *See* Evans, Ernest
Checker, Tex. *See* Hugo, Volker
Chédeville l'ainé. *See* Chédeville, Espirit Philippe
Chédeville, le cadet. *See* Chédeville, Espirit Philippe
Chee-Chee Girl, The. *See* Murphy, Rose
Chee, Lem. *See* Chase, George (W.)
Cheeks, June. *See* Cheeks, Julius
Cheerful Little Earful, The. *See* Waller, Thomas Wright
Chelleri, Fortunato. *See* Keller, Fortunato
Chelo. *See* Rubio (de Uscatescu), Consuelo
Cher. *See* La Pier(r)e, Cherilyn
Cheri, Victor. *See* Cizos, Victor
Cherkose, Eddie. *See* Maxwell, Eddie
Cherokee Cowboy, The. *See* Price, Ray (Noble)
Chessler, Deborah. *See* Chessler, Shirley
Chester, Alan. *See* Gray, Dulcie (Winifred Catherine)
Chesterfield, Cootie. *See* Candoli, Walter Joseph
Chevalier, Francois. *See* Smith, Lee Orean
Chevalier-Perrin. *See* Perrin, Etienne Bernard Auguste
Chewski, C. *See* Leoni, Franco
Chezy, Helmina von. *See* Chezy, Wilhelmine Christine von
Chiara [or Chiarina]. *See* Wieck, Clara Josephine
Chiaro, Giuseppe del. *See* Astorga, Emanuele (Gioacchino Cesare Rincón) d'
Chicago Bill. *See* Broonzy, William Lee Conley
Chicago Blues King. *See* Rush, Otis
Chicago Cyclone. *See* Nelson, Lucille
Chicago Publisher, The. *See* Rossiter, Will
Chicago Sonny Boy. *See* Hill, Lester [or Leslie]
Chicago's Minstrel. *See* Stracke, Win
Chicane. *See* Bracegirdle, Nicholas [or Nick]
Chicano Elvis Presley. *See* Huerta, Baldemar G(arza)
Chichibio. *See* Fanciulli, Giuseppe
Chicken Chest. *See* O'Reilly, Alton
Chico the Cat. *See* Hamilton, Foreststorn
Chief, The. *See* Harrington, Eddy
Chief, The. *See* Presley, Elvis A(a)ron
Chief Organ-Blower Kniff, Leader of the Opposition. *See* Fink, (Christian) Gottfried Wilhelm
Cielo, Il. *See* Landini, Francesco
Child, C(osmos) W(onder). *See* Gardner, Kay
Child, Desmond. *See* Barrett, John C(harles, Jr.)
Childish, Billy. *See* Hamper, Stephen John
Children's Friend, The. *See* Crosby, Fanny [i.e., Frances] J(ane)
Chin, Tony. *See* Chin, Albert Valentine
Chinese Bartók, The. *See* Sheng, Zongliang
Ching, I. *See* Redd, Freddie
Chiozzotto, Il. *See* Croce, Giovanni (della)
Chirico, Andrea (de). *See* Savino, Alberto

Chirrap, Terentio. *See* Trinchera, Pietro
Chittlins, Papa. *See* Moore, Alex(ander Herman)
Chocolate Cowboy, The. *See* McClinton, O(bie) B(urnett)
Chocolate Monsieur. *See* Armenteros, Alfredo
Chón, El. *See* Pereyra, Eduardo
Chopin, Frederic (Spirit). *See* Brown, Rosemary (née Dickeson)
Chopin of the North. *See* Grieg, Edvard Hagerup
Chorasselt. *See* Ots, Charles
Chord, Rip. *See* Hyman, Richard [or Dick] (R(oven))
Chotzie. *See* Chotzinoff, Samuel
Chouder, Clem. *See* Kendis, James
Choufleury. *See* Decourcelle, Pierre
Christel. *See* Bach, Johann Christian
Christian Atticus, The. *See* Heber, Reginald
Christian, David. *See* Egli, David Christian
Christian, Garry. *See* Christian, Garrison
Christian, Rick. *See* Watson, Derek
Christian, T. M. *See* Marcus, Greil
Christie, George. *See* Ball, Ernest R.
Christie, Lou. *See* Sacco, L(ugee) [or Lou(is)] (Alfredo Giovanni)
Christlieb, Alfred. *See* Kalischer, Alfred Chrislieb Salomon Ludwig
Christoff, Vincent. *See* Crombruggen, Paul van
Christopher. *See* Nelson, Prince Rogers
Christopher, Berrie. *See* Gerak, Berrie Lee
Christopher, Don. *See* Attanasio, Don(ald Joseph)
Christopher, J(ordan). *See* Zankoff, Jordan
Christopher, William. *See* Peery, Rob Roy
Christopholus. *See* Fawcett, John
Christy, Don. *See* Bono, Salvatore
Christy, E(dwin) P(earce). *See* Foster, Stephen Collins
Christy, Frank. *See* Kaufman, Isidore
Christy, George (N.). *See* Harrington, George N.
Christy, S(onny). *See* Bono, Salvatore
Chriter, Partenio. *See* Trinchera, Pietro
Chrysanthea. *See* Harris, Lilly C.
Chrysostomus, Polycarp. *See* Brendel, Georg Christoph
Chubby, Popa. *See* Horowitz, Ted
Chuck D. *See* Ridenhour, Carlton D(ouglas)
Chuckabutty, Professor Yaffle. *See* Dodd, Ken(neth)
Chunky. *See* Wood, Lauren
Chupita. *See* Stamponi, Héctor Luciano
Church, Fannie. *See* Crosby, Fanny [i.e., Frances] J(ane)
Church, Jarvis. *See* Eaton, Gerald
Churchhill, Charles. *See* Morris, Valentine
Churchill, Kenneth. *See* Ehret, Walter (Charles)
Churchill, Kenneth. *See* Raymond, John
Ciccio di Majo. *See* Majo, (Gian) Francesco (de)
Cicero, Eugen. *See* Ciceu, Eugen
Čidi, Arda. *See* Bojic, Milutin
Cieco, Il. *See* Carisio, Giovanni
Cieco, Il. *See* Valente, Antonio (C.)
Cieco di Parma. *See* Migliavacca, Augusto
Cieco, Francesco. *See* Landini, Francesco
Ciecolino. *See* Rivani, Antonio
Ciego de Daroca, El. *See* Bruna, Pablo
Ciego Maravillos, El. *See* Rodríguez, Ignacio Loyola
Cielo, Il. *See* Landini, Francesco
Cif Charon der Höhlenzote. *See* Castelli, Ignaz Franz
Cigala. *See* Jiménez Salazar, Diego
Cimadori, Robert. *See* Schoenefeld, Henry
Cincinnati's Only Colored Author and Comedian. *See* Davis, Gussie Lord
Cincinnatus. *See* O'Connor, M.
Cinerini, Berto. *See* Bertini, Enrico
Cinnéo, Filostrato Lucàno. *See* Soliva, Antonio
Cinnéo, Filostrato Lucàno. *See* Tullio, Francesco Antonio
Cinti, Mlle. *See* Montalant, Laure-Cinthie
Cipollone, Mattia. *See* Lanciano, Cristoforo da
Ciprianos Sieranensis. *See* Bazylik, Cyprjan [or Cyprian]
Ciri, Peter. *See* Hrncírk, Peter
Ciriaquito. *See* Ortiz Barrionuevo, (Angel) Ciriaco
Cisnéros, Francisco Augustí de. *See* Iriarte, Tomás (de)
Citizen of Massachusetts, A. *See* Holden, Oliver
Citizen of New York. *See* Dunlap, William
Ciù. *See* Civinini, Guelfo
Claes, Balthazar. *See* Benoit, Camille
Claes, Paul. *See* Coutagne, Henri
Claessens, Arthur. *See* Mosmans, Alphonse Willem Josef
Claff, Lionel. *See* Croke, Leo T.
Clafflin, Don(ald). *See* Grey, Frank H(erbert)
Clairlie, Arnolde. *See* Schütt, Eduard
Clairville (the younger). *See* Nicolaie, Louis François
Clairville, Louis François. See Nicolaie, Louis François
Clairville, M. *See* Nicolaie, Louis François
Clancy, Joe. *See* Barnes, H(oward) E(llington)
Clancy, Joe. *See* Fields, Harold (Cornelius)
Clancy, Joe. *See* Musel, Robert [or Bob] (Saul)
Clapp, Sunny. *See* Clapp, Charles
Clapton, Eric. *See* Clapp, Eric (Patrick)
Clapton, Richard. *See* Gonk, Terry
Clapton, Slowhand. *See* Clapp, Eric (Patrick)
Clare, Ada. *See* McElheney, Jane
Clare, Alan. *See* Jaycock, Alan
Clare, Arthur. *See* LeClerq, Arthur
Clare, Edwin A. *See* Simper, Caleb
Clare, Georgiana. *See* Krenkel, Gustav
Clare, Howard. *See* Hall, Joseph Lincoln
Clare, Jack. *See* Bernard, Al(fred A.)
Clare, Madeline. *See* Twomey, Kathleen [or Kay] Greeley
Clare, Raymond. *See* Willan, James Healey
Clarendon. *See* Gavoty, Bernard (Georges Marie)
Claribel. *See* Barnard, Charlotte Alington (née Pye)

Clark see also *Clarke*
Clark(e), Billy. *See* Kaufman, Isidore
Clark, Cumberland. *See* Butler, Ralph (T.)
Clark, Curt. *See* Gründler, Kurt
Clark(e), Gene. *See* Clark(e), Harold E(ugene)
Clark, H. R. *See* Bliss, P(hilip) Paul
Clark, James. *See* Robison, Carson J(ay)
Clark, Kenneth. *See* Whitlock, Percy (William)
Clark, Olive. *See* Ewing, Montague (George)
Clark, Slim. *See* Clark, Raymond LeRoy
Clark, Sonny. *See* Clark, Conrad Yeatis
Clark, Valerie [or Valarie]. *See* Putnam, Belinda
Clark, Yodeling Slim. *See* Clark, Raymond LeRoy
Clarke see also *Clark*
Clarke, Billy. *See* Finkelstein, Abe
Clarke, Edward R. *See* Olson, Robert G.
Clarke, Elizabeth. *See* Kraushaar, Charles
Clarke, Emilie. *See* Kronke, Emil
Clarke, George H. *See* Rands, William Brightly
Clarke, Glory. *See* Vonderlieth, Leonore
Clarke, Helena. *See* Beals, Ella Middaugh
Clarke, Klook. *See* Clarke, Kenneth [or Kenny] (Spearman)
Clarke, Oscar. *See* Kronke, Emil
Claron, Henri. *See* Kalmanoff, Martin
Claude, H. *See* Leduc, P.
Claudin. *See* Sermisy, Claudin [or Claude] de
Claudio da Correggio. *See* Merlotti, Claudio
Claudius. *See* Blanc, Claude
Claudius, F. C. *See* Dräxler, Karl (Ferdinand)
Claudius, Fr. *See* Dräxler, Karl (Ferdinand)
Claverley, Emmett. *See* Barrell, Edgar Alden, Jr.
Clavito, Dona. *See* Birner, Günther
Clay, Priam. *See* Freed, Richard (Donald)
Clay, Stephen. *See* Munn, William O.
Clayton, Bob. *See* Autry, (Orvon) Gene
Clayton, Buck. *See* Clayton, Wilbur D(orsey)
Clayton, Doc(tor). *See* Clayton, Peter Joe
Clayton, Eddie. *See* Clapp, Eric (Patrick)
Clayton, John. *See* Sugarman, Harry
Clayton, Kay. *See* Bygraves, Walter (William)
Clayton, Lee. *See* Schatz, Billy
Clayton, Steve. *See* Tedesco, Pat Louis
Cleanhead, Mr. *See* Vinson, Eddie
Clearwater, Eddy. *See* Harrington, Eddy
Cleighton, Peter. *See* Clayton, Peter Joe
Cleishbotham, Jedediah. *See* Scott, (Sir) Walter
Clemens, Albert. *See* Lofton, Clarence
Clemens non Papa. *See* Clément, Jacob [or Jacques]
Clemens, Paul. *See* Feltz, Kurt (August Karl)
Clement, Clare. *See* Cain, Noble
Clements, John R. *See* Fillmore, (James) Henry
Clemris. *See* Harris, Clement
Clemson, Carl. *See* Manney, Charles Fonteyn
Cleofonto Doriano. *See* Papi, Antonio
Clermont, Henri. *See* Rawlings, Charles Arthur
Clerus. *See* Toplady, Augustus Montague
Cléry, Mme. *See* Duverger, Marie Elisabeth
Cleve, Erich. *See* Krakauer, Erich
Cleveland, James P. *See* Luening, Otto
Cliff, Jimmy. *See* Chambers, James (E.)
Cliff, Laddie. *See* Perry, Clifford Albyn
Clifford, Bob. *See* Carlisle, Cliff(ord Raymond)
Clifford, Buzz. *See* Clifford, Reese Francis, III
Clifford, Collin. *See* Newell, Norman
Clifford, Cosmo. *See* Clifford, Doug(las) R.
Clifford, Ed. *See* Edwards, Clifton (A.)
Clifford, Ed. *See* Slaughter, M(arion) T(ry)
Clifford, J. S. *See* Taufstein, (Alexander) Louis [or Ludwig]
Clifford, Jack. *See* Sherman, Al(bert)
Clifford, Park. *See* Keiser, Robert (A(dolph))
Clifford, Raoul. *See* Ketèlbey, Albert William
Clift, Sten. *See* Thomas, Peter
Clifton, Arthur. *See* Corri, Philip Antony
Clifton, Bill. *See* Marburg, William August
Clifton, Edward. *See* Edwards, Clifton (A.)
Clifton, Harry. *See* Clifton, Henry Robert
Clifton, John. *See* Kestner, John Nelson
Clifton, Johnny. *See* Haley, William [or Bill] (John Clifton), (Jr.)
Clifton, Lewis. *See* Lyne, Clifton
Clifton, Maurice A. *See* Hall, Joseph Lincoln
Cline, Tammy. *See* Cross, Marilyn Margaret
Clique, Henry. *See* Klickmann, F(rank) Henri
Clirb, Eolo. *See* Bello, Circo
Clive, Ethelbert. *See* Holmes, Ethel Clive
Cloff, Albert. *See* Butler, Ralph (T.)
Cloff, Albert. *See* Wright, Julian
Clog, Aldimiro. *See* Goldoni, Carlo
Clothilde. *See* Barnard, D'Auvergne
Clough-Leighter, Grace (Marshall). *See* Marschal(l)-Loepke, Grace
Clown Prince of Comedy, The. *See* Leopold, Isaiah Edwin
Clown Prince of Rock and Roll, The. *See* Hawkins, Jalacy (J.)
Clump, Clarence. *See* Carter, Bennett L(ester)
Clurgi. *See* Bonelli, Luigi
Clutterbuck, Captain (Cuthbert). *See* Scott, (Sir) Walter
Coach, S. Low. *See* Blackmar, A(rmand) E(dward)
Coal Miner's Daughter, The. *See* Webb, Loretta
Cobb, Frank. *See* Heins, Carl
Cobb, Joe. *See* Croom-Johnson, Austen [or Austin] (Herbert)
Cobb, Lotta. *See* Vonderlieth, Leonore
Cobbin, Ned. *See* Kaufman, Isidore
Coborn, Charles [or Charlie]. *See* McCallum, Colin Whitton
Coburn, Richard. *See* De Long, Frank

Cochlaeus, (Johannes). *See* Dobnek, Johannes
Cochran, Hank. *See* Cochran, Garland (Perry)
Cochrane, Talie. *See* Wright, Lilian Cochrane
Cocker, Joe. *See* Cocker, John Robert
Cockiolly Bird. *See* Bingham, Graham Clifton
Coco, Joey. *See* Nelson, Prince Rogers
Codner, Elizabeth. *See* Conder, (Joan) Elizabeth (née Thomas)
Coe, Collin. *See* Macy, J(ames) C(artwright)
Coen, Enrico. *See* Cohen, Henri [or Henry]
Coeur Bas, Le. *See* Lulli, Giovanni Battista
Coeuroy, André. *See* Bélime, Jean
Cohen, Carlo Enrico. *See* Cohen, Henri
Cohen, Charles (James). *See* Kingsford, Charles
Cohon, Barry. *See* Cohon, Baruch Joseph
Colaza, Juan de. *See* Cole, John William
Colby, Max. *See* Kolpenitzki, Max
Colder, Ben. *See* Wooley, Shelby F.
Cole, Adam. *See* Wilson, Roger Cole
Cole, Addison B. *See* Keller, Edward McDonald
Cole and Johnson Brothers. *See* Cole, Robert [or Bob] (Allen)
Cole and Johnson Brothers. *See* Johnson, J(ohn) Rosamond
Cole and Johnson Brothers. *See* Johnson, James Weldon
Cole, Buddy. *See* Cole, Edwin Lemar
Cole, Frank. *See* Colamosca, Frank O(ctavius)
Cole, Ike. *See* Cole Isaac
Cole, Nat King. *See* Coles, Nathaniel Adams
Cole, Rex. *See* Finkelstein, Abe
Cole, Sam. *See* Finkelstein, Abe
Coleman, B. B. *See* Coleman, Gary
Coleman, Bud. *See* Coleman, Ervan F.
Coleman, Byron. *See* Grey, Frank H(erbert)
Coleman, Cy. *See* Kaufman, Seymour
Coleman, Marty. *See* Cohen, Martin
Coleman, Nancy. *See* Pettigrew, Leola (B.)
Coleman, Nelly. *See* Wilson, Lena
Coleridge-Taylor, Avril. *See* Coleridge-Taylor, Gwendolen
Coles, George. *See* Stebbins, George C(oles)
Coles, S. G. *See* Stebbins, George C(oles)
Colette(-Willy). *See* Colette, Sidonie Gabrielle Claudine
Colin, Gustave. *See* Woodhouse, Charles (John)
Collano. *See* Dõrflinger, Kurt
Collard, Arthur. *See* Drake, Arthur
Collebaudi, Jachet. *See* Colebault, Jacques
Collette, Buddy. *See* Collette, W(illiam) M(arcell)
Collier, Franklin. *See* Seredy, J(ulius) S.
Collier, Joel. *See* Veal, George
Collinger, E. H. *See* Cain, Noble
Collins, Big Tom. *See* Dupree, William Thomas
Collins, Big Tom. *See* McGhee, Walter Brown
Collins, Bill. *See* Lucas, Eugene
Collins, Billy. *See* Davis, Bertha Ruth
Collins, Bootsy. *See* Collins, William
Collins, Chocolate. *See* Collins, Al(bert)
Collins, Dolly. *See* Collins, Dorothy Ann
Collins, George. *See* Sawyer, Henry S.
Collins, John B. *See* Kountz, Richard
Collins Kids. *See* Collins, Lawrence Albert
Collins Kids. *See* Collins, Lawrencine May
Collins, Lorrie. *See* Collins Lawrencine May
Collins, Mitzie. *See* Collins, Mary Ellen
Collins, Ray. *See* Newell, Norman
Collins, Tommy. *See* Sipes, Leonard Raymond
Collins, W. C. *See* Frangkiser, Carl (Moerz)
Collins, Walter. *See* Beckhard, Robert L.
Collinus, Matthaeus. *See* Kalina z Choteriny, Matous
Cöln, Geno von. *See* Bieber, C(aroline) F(rances) Egon
Colodisce, Logolcardoni. *See* Goldoni, Carlo
Colón, Fernando. *See* Columbus, Ferdinand
Colonel, The. *See* Mapleson, James Henry
Colorado, El. *See* De Angelis, Alfredo
Colored Sophie Tucker, The. *See* McDaniel, Hattie
Colored Wagner, The. *See* Freeman, Harry Lawrence
Colpet, Max. *See* Kolpenitzki, Max
Colter, Frank. *See* Wychodil(-Hofmeister), Gert
Colter, Jessi. *See* Johnson, Miriam
Coltrane, Trane. *See* Coltrane, John William
Columbo, Russ. *See* Columbo, Ruggiero de Rudolpho
Colvig, Pinto. *See* Colvig, Vance D.
Colvin, Cecil. *See* Burnard, Francis Cowley
Colvin, Shawn. *See* Colvin, Shanna
Comala, (Theorosa). *See* Winkel, Therese Emilie Henriette aus dem
Combs, Puffy. *See* Combs, Sean
Comden, Betty. *See* Cohen, Elizabeth
Comenius, Johann Amos. *See* Komenshy, Jan Amos
Comic of the Day, The. *See* McCallum, Colin Whitton
Comini, Tino. *See* Comini, Railberto
Comitas, Alexander. *See* Boer, Eduardo de
Commagny, Moreau de. *See* Moreau, Charles François (Jean) Baptiste
Common (Sense). *See* Lynn, Lonnie Rashied [or Rashid, or Rasheed]
Communis, Meta. *See* Seidl, Johann Gabriel
Communist Traveling Salesman. *See* Milhaud, Darius
Compère, Loyset. *See* Compère, Louis
Composer, A. *See* Ford, David Everard
Composer for the Angry Young Men, The. *See* Addison, John
Composer from Bohemia, The. *See* Dvořák, Antonín
Composer of a Jigsaw Puzzle That Dropped from Heaven. *See* Sibelius, Jean [originally Johan] (Christian Julius)
Composer Seduced into Carpentry, A. *See* Partch, Harry
Composer's Composer, The. *See* Jones, Isham (Edgar)

Compositeur Tocqué, Le. *See* Ronger, (Louis Auguste Joseph) Florimond
Con Cor D(en). *See* Dedekind, Constantin Christian
Concerto Grosso Type, A. *See* Martinu, Bohuslav
Concionator. *See* Toplady, Augustus Montague
Concord. *See* Dedekind, Constantin Christian
Condon, Eddie. *See* Condon, Albert Edwin
Conejo, El. *See* Barros (Caraballo), Alberto
Confederate Lady, The. *See* Young, Maud J(eannie) (Fuller)
Confidential Charlie. *See* Kaufman, Isidore
Confield, Arthur B. *See* Fisher, William Arms
Confrey, Zez. *See* Confrey, Edward Elzear
Conga, Stu. *See* Dorn, Veeder Van
Congregational Nonconformist, A. *See* Binney, Thomas
Conn, Chester. *See* Cohn, Chester
Conn, Irving. *See* Cohn, Irving
Connelly, Jay. *See* Campbell, James [or Jimmy]
Connelly, Jay. *See* Connelly, Reg(inald)
Connor, Father. *See* Connor, Joseph Patrick
Connor, Mary. *See* Framer, Marjorie
Connor, Pierre Norman. *See* Connor, Joseph Patrick
Connors, Carol. *See* Kleinbard, Annette
Conrad, C. *See* Benjamin, Walter
Conrad, Con. *See* Dober, Conrad K.
Conrad, G. *See* George Konrad, Prince of Prussia
Conrad, Hugh. *See* Schoenfeld, William C(harles)
Conrad, Robert Arnold. *See* Hart, Moss
Cons, Auguste. *See* Rawlings, Charles Arthur
Consey, Jill. *See* Felix, Margery [or Marjorie] Edith
Consilium, Johannes. *See* Conseil, Jean
Consolo, Federico. *See* Sefardi, Jehiel Nahmany
Constans, Constantin. *See* Drdova, Marie
Constant. *See* Ménissier, Constant
Constanten, Tom. *See* Sture, Thomas Charles
Constantine, John. *See* Cacavas, John
Constantino, Monroe "Bones". *See* Evans, William [or Bill]
Constantius. *See* Cottle, Joseph
Contée, F. H. *See* Gräffer, Franz (Arnold)
Conti, Dick. *See* Cuchetti, Richard Frank
Contoocock. *See* Gilmore Joseph H(enry)
Contractus, Hermannus. *See* Hermannus, Contractus
Contreras, Romulo. *See* Davis, Joseph [or Joe] (M.)
Contursi, Katunga. *See* Contursi, Jose Maria
Convent, Peter. *See* Diernhammer, Carlos
Conway, Jill. *See* Felix, Margery [or Marjorie] Edith
Conway, Russ. *See* Stanford, Trevor H(erbert)
Conway, Will. *See* Champion, Harry
Conyers, Leslie. *See* Rawlings, Alfred William
Cook *see also* Cooke
Cook, Dale. *See* Cook(e), Sam(uel)
Cook, Doc. *See* Cooke, Charles L.
Cook, J. L(awrence). *See* Razafinkeriefo, Andreamenentania Paul
Cook, James. *See* Razafinkeriefo, Andreamenentania Paul
Cook, James Ballou. *See* Razafinkeriefo, Andreamenentania Paul
Cook, James Daniel. *See* Razafinkeriefo, Andreamenentania Paul
Cook, James Joseph. *See* Razafinkeriefo, Andreamenentania Paul
Cook, James V. *See* Razafinkeriefo, Andreamenentania Paul
Cook, Jean Lawrence. *See* Razafinkeriefo, Andreamenentania Paul
Cook, Jim. *See* Razafinkeriefo, Andreamenentania Paul
Cook, Mercer. *See* Cook, William Mercer
Cook, Norman. *See* Cook, Quentin
Cook, Paul. *See* Bullock, Jack A(rlen)
Cook, Shorty. *See* Hinderer, Everett (Roland)
Cook, Tom. *See* Crow(e), Francis Luther
Cook, Will Marion. *See* Cook, William Mercer
Cookaway, Roger. *See* Cook, Roger
Cookaway, Roger. *See* Greenaway, Roger
Cooke *see also* Cook
Cooke, Captain. *See* Cooke, Henry
Cooke, Herbert. *See* Suskind, Milton
Cooke, Hesiod. *See* Cooke, Thomas (Simpson)
Cooke, James Francis. *See* Razafinkeriefo, Andreamenentania Paul
Cooker, John Lee. *See* Hooker, John Lee
Cookridge, John (Michael). *See* Holyroyd, Ethel Mary
Cool, Mr. *See* Perry, Lincoln (T(heodore Monroe Andrew))
Cool Papa. *See* Sadler, Haskell Robert
Coole, Orlando. *See* Gearhart, Livingston
Cooler, Jean. *See* Köhler, Johannes Robert
Cooley, Spade. *See* Cooley, Donnell Clyde
Coolidge, Susan. *See* Woolsey, Sarah Chauncey
Coolio. *See* Ivey, Artis Leon, Jr.
Coolus, Romain. *See* Weil, (Max) Rene
Coombs, Norman. *See* Haenschen, Walter (G(ustave))
Coombs, Norman. *See* O'Keefe, James (Conrad)
Coombs, Norman. *See* Strandberg, (Alfreda) Theodora
Cooper. *See* Twardy, Werner
Cooper, Alice. *See* Furnier, Vincent (Damon)
Cooper, Gaze. *See* Cooper, Walter Thomas Gaze
Cooper, Henry. *See* Böhm, Karl [or Carl] (1844-1920)
Cooper, Ray. *See* Pereyra, Eduardo
Cooper, Stoney. *See* Cooper, Dale T.
Cooper, William. *See* Behr, F(ranz)
Cooper, William. *See* Glenn, Will(iam Cooper)
Cooper, Zack [or Zackie]. *See* Florio, Zackie Cooper
Coot(s). *See* Pettigrew, Leola (B.)
Copas, Cowboy. *See* Copas, Lloyd (Estel)
Cope, La La. *See* Cope, LaForrest
Copeland, Ann. *See* Furtwangler, Virginia W(alsh)
Copenahgen, A. *See* Glaser, Victoria Merrylees

Coperario, John [or Giovanni]. *See* Cooper, John
Copernicus of Music. *See* Schoenberg, Arnold
Coquin Tenebreux, Un. *See* Lulli, Giovanni Battista
Corasio, Artino [or Artimio]. *See* Trapassi (Gallastri), Pietro Antonio
Corbulon. *See* Roussel, Henri
Cord, M(ichael). *See* Wiedenfeld, Karl
Cord, Mira. *See* Johnova, Miroslava
Cordell, Ritchie. *See* Rosenblatt, Richard (Joel)
Cordomi. *See* Coleridge, Samuel Taylor
Cordy, Harry. *See* Nützlader, Rudolf
Corea, Chick. *See* Corea, Armando Anthony
Corelli, C. *See* Crawley, C. E.
Corelli, E. *See* Cain, Noble
Corelli of France. *See* Leclair, Jean Marie
Corfiensis, Kaikhosru Catamontanus. *See* Dudley, Leon
Cori, (C. J. N.). *See* Rijke, Cornelius Herminus
Corinne, J. *See* Keiser, Robert (A(dolph))
Corio, Jose. *See* De Filippi, Amedeo
Corman, Bob. *See* DeCormier, Robert
Cormon, Eugène. *See* Piestre, Pierre-Étienne
Cormundi, Francesco. *See* Dussek, Franz Joseph
Corn-Corn. *See* Dingemann, Gustav
Corn Law Rhymer. *See* Elliott, Ebeneezer
Cornatus. *See* Gebler, Tobias Philipp von
Corneille of the Boulevards, The. *See* Pixérécourt, René Charles Guilbert de
Cornelius, Draco. *See* Rosa Suráez, Robert Edward
Cornelius, Harold. *See* Fields, Harold (Cornelius)
Cornell, Klaus. *See* Meier, Klaus
Cornell, Wes. *See* Cochran, William Wesley
Cornet, Julius. *See* Cornet, Michael Josef Anton
Cornet King. *See* Levy, Jules
Cornetto, Ascanio del. *See* Cavallari, Ascanio
Corney, Richard. *See* Grain, (Richard) Corney
Corno. *See* Horn, August
Corno di Bassetto. *See* Shaw, George Bernard
Cornu, Johann. *See* Roh, Johann
Cornwall, Barry. *See* Procter, Bryan Waller
Corny, Eddy. *See* Kötscher, Edmund
Corporation, The. *See* Gordy, Berry, Jr.
Corporation, The. *See* Mizell, Alphonso James
Corporation, The. *See* Perren, Fred(erick) [or Freddie]
Corporation, The. *See* Richards, Deke
Corregias, Claudius. *See* Merlotti, Claudio
Corrupter of Music. *See* Wagner, Richard
Corselli, Francesco. *See* Courcelle, Francesco
Cortesi, Paolo. *See* Mantovani, A(nnunzio) P(aolo)
Cortez, Miguel. *See* Bochmann, Werner
Cortez, Pepe. *See* Green, Phil(ip)
Corvin, Eugen Alban. *See* Gatterman, Eugen Ludwig
Corvinus, Johann(es) (Michaelii). *See* Ravn, Hans Mikkelsen
Corzilius, Victor. *See* Espe, Walter
Cosacchi, Stephan. *See* Kozáky, Istávan
Cosman, William. *See* Cain, Noble
Cosmar, Harold. *See* Löffler, Willi
Cosmic Cowboy. *See* Murphey, Michael Martin
Cosmos Wonder-Child. *See* Gardner, Kay
Cossack, The. *See* Wagner, Richard
Cosse, Irene (Amburgey). *See* Amburgey, Irene
Costa, Karl. *See* Kostia, Karl
Costa, Michael. *See* Agniello, Michele Andrea
Costello, D. P. *See* McManus, Declan Patrick (Aloysius)
Costello, Elvis (Patrick). *See* McManus, Declan Patrick (Aloysius)
Costenoble, Philostène. *See* Martens, Adolphe-Adhemar-Louis-Michel
Coster, Willy. *See* Koester, Willy
Coster's Laureate, The. *See* Chevalier, Albert (Onesime Britannicus Gawtheveoyd Louis)
Costino, M(arcel). *See* Quantz, Willibald
Coton, A. V. *See* Haddakin, Edward
Cotton-Marshall, Grace. *See* Marschal(l)-Loepke, Grace
Cotton Thomas. *See* Jackson, Frankie
Cougar, John(ny). *See* Mellencamp, John (J.)
"Count Basie" Fiddle Player. *See* Clements, Vassar Carlton
Count Rockin' Sydney. *See* Semien, Sidney
Country Boy Eddie [or Eddy]. *See* Burns, Eddie
Country Caruso, The. *See* Shin, John Bush, III
Country Cat. *See* Presley, Elvis A(a)ron
Country Gentleman, (The). *See* Atkins, Chester [or Chet] (Burton)
Country Gentleman, (The). *See* Smith, Carl
Country George Burns. *See* Campbell, Archie James
Country Isaac Stern. *See* Clements, Vassar Carlton
Country, Jayne. *See* Country, Wayne
Country Kojac. *See* Riggs, John Frederick
Country Music's Janis Joplin. *See* Byrem, Jill Lynne
Country Music's New Heartthrob. *See* Jackson, Alan (Eugene)
Country Music's "Renaissance Man". *See* Wheeler, Billy Edd
Country Music's Royal Couple. *See* Crupe, Jessie Wanda
Country Music's Royal Couple. *See* Smik, Andrew John, Jr.
Country Paul. *See* Harris, Edward P.
Country's First Hack. *See* Slaughter, M(arion) T(ry)
Couperin, Louis. *See* Kreisler, Fritz [i.e., Friedrich](-Max)
Courage, Sandy. *See* Courage, Alexander M.
Courmor. *See* Morcour, ? de
Court-evil. *See* Courteville, Raphael
Courtenay, Clifford. *See* Rawlings, Charles Arthur
Courteville, Junior. *See* Courteville, Raphael
Courtley, W. *See* Yardley, William
Courtois, Jules. *See* Leest, Antonius Maria van
Courts, Eddy. *See* Kurc, Adolf

Cousin Emmy. *See* Carver, Cynthia May
Cousin Erin. *See* Ford, Ernest Jennings
Cousin Herb. *See* Henson, Herbert Lester
Cousin Jacques. *See* Beffroy de Reigny, Louis Abel
Cousin Joe [or Joseph]. *See* Joseph, Pleasant
Cousin Lincoln. *See* Perry, Lincoln (T(heodore Monroe Andrew))
Covais, Jack. *See* Fortini, James (1926-)
Covington, Allan H. *See* Jones, Isham (Edgar)
Cow Polka King. *See* Miskulin, Joseph [or Joey] (Michael)
Coward Brothers. *See* Burnett, Joseph Henry
Coward Brothers. *See* McManus, Declan Patrick (Aloysius)
Cowboy, The. *See* Clement, Jack
Cowboy Auctioneer. *See* Taylor, Joseph [or Joe] (Carl)
Cowboy Jack. *See* Clement, Jack
Cowboy Joe. *See* Hamblen, (Carl) Stuart
Cowboy Loye. *See* Pack, Loye Donald
Cowboy Poet of Texas. *See* Steagall, Russell (Don)
Cowboy Rambler, The. *See* Boyd, William [or Bill]
Cowell, D. B. *See* Báthory-Kitsz, Dennis
Cowen, Joe. *See* Cohen, Joseph
Cower, James. *See* Martin, Robert
Cowler, Jim. *See* Noack, Herbert
Cowley, John. *See* Davis, Katherine K(ennicott)
Cowper, John. *See* Cooper, John
Cox. *See* Sugarman, Harry
Cox, Desmond. *See* Keuleman, Adrian
Cox, Ida. *See* Prather, Ida
Coxie. *See* Baumgardtner, Claude Chalmers
Crabb, CeCe. *See* Crabb, Cecil Duane
Craddock, Crash. *See* Craddock, William [or Billy] (Wayne)
Craddock, Eleanor. *See* Crosby, Fanny [i.e., Frances] J(ane)
Craddock, Zeke. *See* Mannes, Leo (Ezekiel)
Craeto. *See* Ottoboni, Pietro
Craeto Ericincio. *See* Ottoboni, Pietro
Craeto Paradelini. *See* Ottoboni, Pietro
Craig, Allen. *See* Kaufman, Isidore
Craig, David. *See* Krangel, David
Craig, Denys. *See* Stoll, Dennis Gray
Craig, J. H. *See* Hogg, James
Craig, Jimmy. *See* Kellem, Milton
Crambo, Cornelius. *See* Rhodes, William Barnes
Cramer, Al. *See* Slaughter, M(arion) T(ry)
Cramer, H. *See* Tchaikovskii, Peter Illich
Cramer, Johann [or John] ([pseud.]). *See* Cramer, Johann [or John] Baptist
Cramer, John. *See* Ehret, Walter (Charles)
Crammond, C. C. *See* Bliss, P(hilip) Paul
Crane, F. R. *See* Gabriel, Charles H(utchinson)
Crane, George. *See* Kaufman, Isidore
Crane, Harry. *See* Finkelstein, Abe
Crane, Jimmie. *See* Fraieli, Loreto
Crane, Paul. *See* Haenschen, Walter (G(ustave))
Cranmer, Clemens. *See* Rueger, Christoph
Crannis, S. M. *See* Grannis, S(idney) M(artin)
Crantock, (Peter). *See* Lowry, Anthony [or Tony]
Crantock, (Peter). *See* Richardson, Clive
Crateo (Pradelini). *See* Ottoboni, Pietro
Cratisto, Jamejo. *See* Colloredo, Giovanni Battista
Craven, Arthur Scott. *See* James, Arthur Keedwell Harvey
Craven, Hawes. *See* Green, Henry Hawes (Craven)
Craven, J. E. *See* Bliss, P(hilip) Paul
Craver, Al. *See* Slaughter, M(arion) T(ry)
Crawford, Hank. *See* Crawford, Benny [or Bennie] R(oss, Jr.)
Crawford, James. *See* Johnson, J. C.
Crawford, Stanley. *See* Gum(m), Harold [or Harry]
Crayon, Geoffrey. *See* Irving, Washington
Crayon, H. M. *See* Krehan, Hermann
Crayton, Geoffrey, Jr. *See* Darley, George
Crayton, Pee Wee. *See* Crayton, Connie Curtis
Crazy Cajun, The. *See* Kershaw, Doug(las James)
Crazy Cat. *See* Presley, Elvis A(a)ron
Crazy Composer, The. *See* Ronger, (Louis Auguste Joseph) Florimond
Crazy Eddie. *See* Severson, Edward Louis, III
Crazy Otto. *See* Schulz-Reichel, Fritz
Creator, The. *See* Beethoven, Ludwig van
Creator of Ambient Music. *See* Eno, Brian
Creator of Burlesque Poetry in France, The. *See* Scarron, Paul
Creator of Grand Opera. *See* Scribe, (Augustin) Eugène
Creator of Jazz, The. *See* La Menthe, Ferdinand Joseph
Creator of Norweigan Music. *See* Grieg, Edvard Hagerup
Creator of Program Music, The. *See* Berlioz, Hector
Creaux, John. *See* Rebennack, Malcolm [or Mac] (John)
Creighton, Robert L. *See* Zamecnik, J(ohn) S(tepan)
Creighton, Robert S. *See* Zamecnik, J(ohn) S(tepan)
Creme, Lol. *See* Creme, Lawrence
Creole Cowboy, The. *See* Chavis, Wilson (Anthony)
Creole Kid. *See* Browder, Thomas August Darnell
Creole Songbird, The. *See* Bigeou, Esther
Crescendo. *See* Kalisch, A(lfred)
Creston, Paul. *See* Guttivergi, Giuseppe
Creston, William. *See* Ehret, Walter (Charles)
Creston, William. *See* Kinsman, Elmer (F(ranklin))
Creswell, John D. *See* Lorenz, E(dmund) S(imon)
Cri-Cri. *See* Gabilondo Soler, Francisco (José)
Crichton, Donald. *See* Dickson, Mary Hannah
Crichton, Jean. *See* Dickson, Mary Hannah
Crinkle, Nym. *See* Wheeler, Andrew Carpenter
Criptonide, Egerindo. *See* Chiari, Pietro
Crisp, Helen. *See* Crisp, Donald
Crispin, Edmund. *See* Montgomery, (Robert) Bruce

Cristabel. *See* Cole, Edward William
Cristian. *See* Castro, Christian
Cristy, S. *See* Bono, Salvatore
Critic of the Seven Arts. *See* Huneker, James Gibbons
Criticus, Apparatus. *See* Heseltine, Philip (Arnold)
Crito Cantabrigienis. *See* Turton, Thomas
Croche, (Monsieur). *See* Debussy, Claude
Crockett, David. *See* Sutton, David C., Sr.
Crockett, Howard. *See* Hausey, (Elton) Howard
Croisset, Francis (de). *See* Wiener, Francis [or Franz]
Crolo, Calindo. *See* Goldoni, Carlo
Crombruggen, Paul van. *See* Christoff, Vincent
Cromer, Wes. *See* Law, (William) Arthur
Cromiro Dianio. *See* Bernardoni, Pietro Antonio
Cromwell, Link. *See* Kaye, Leonard Jay
Cronthal, William. *See* Gross, Pierre
Crookshank, Wm. Cullen. *See* Foster, Stephen Collins
Croone, Oliver. *See* Willeby, Charles
Crooner, The. *See* Vallee, Herbert Pryor
Crooning Andy. *See* Razafinkeriefo, Andreamenentania Paul
Crooning Composer, The. *See* Feinberg, Samuel
Crosby, Ben E. *See* Lincoln, Harry J.
Crosby, Bing. *See* Crosby, Harry Lillis
Crosby, Claire. *See* Campbell, Edith (May [or Mary])
Crosby, George H. *See* Gabriel, Charles H(utchinson)
Crosby, Bob. *See* Hoar, Robert Crosby
Crosby, Paul. *See* Crosby, Ronald Clyde
Crosby, Rob. *See* Hoar, Robert Crosby
Crosbyana. *See* Crosby, Harry Lillis
Croscino, Niccolò. *See* Logroscino, Nicola (Bonifacio)
Crosley, Robert. *See* Meek, Robert (George)
Cross, Christopher. *See* Geppert, Christopher
Cross, Mark. *See* Pechey, Archibald Thomas
Cross, Mary Ann [or Marian]. *See* Evans, Mary Ann [or Marian]
Cross, R. B. *See* Bliss, P(hilip) Paul
Cross, R. L. *See* Bennett, Theron C(atlin)
Cross, Vernon. *See* Reardon, Francis [or Frank] C(ornelius)
Crossing, Cyril. *See* Haenschen, Walter (G(ustave))
Croston, Jill. *See* Byrem, Jill Lynne
Crothers, Scatman. *See* Crothers, Benjamin Sherman (Louis)
Crow Bait, Ophelia Mae. *See* Smith, C. U. (née Garfield)
Crow, Frank. *See* Crow(e), Francis Luther
Crow, Phil. *See* Crow(e) Francis Luther
Crowbate, Ophelia Mae. *See* Smith, C. U. (née Garfield)
Crowdus, Ruben. *See* Crowders, (Ernest) Reuben
Crown Prince of Country Music, The. *See* Jones, George (Glen(n))
Crown Prince of Gospel, The. *See* Cleveland, James
Crown Prince of Ragtime. *See* Scott, James (Sylvester)
Crown Prince of Reggae. *See* Marley, David
Crown Prince of the Accordian. *See* Miskulin, Joseph [or Joey] (Michael)
Crown Prince of the Blues, The. *See* Waterford, Charles (E.)
Crown Princes of Country Music. *See* Burns, Kenneth (C.)
Crown Princes of Country Music. *See* Haynes, Henry D.
Crudup, Big Boy. *See* Crudup, Arthur
Crudup, Percy (Lee). *See* Crudup, Arthur
Crudux, Art. *See* Crudup, Arthur
Crum, Simon. *See* Husky, Ferlin
Crump, Arthur. *See* Crudup, Arthur
Crump, Tiny. *See* Crump, Jess(i)e
Crusoe Kid. *See* Lewis, McCartha Sandy
Cruz, José Luiz Oliveira. *See* Andrade, Djalmi de
Cryin' Red. *See* Minter, Iverson
Cryptos. *See* Greenbank, Percy
Cryptos. *See* Monckton, (John) Lionel (Alexander)
Cryptos. *See* Ropes, Arthur Reed
Cryptos. *See* Tanner, James T(holman)
Cryptos. *See* Tilkin, Félix (Marie Henri)
Crysantema. *See* Gutierrez-Najera, Manuel
Crystal Gale. *See* Webb, Brenda Gail
Cuba's Greatest Composer. *See* Lecuona, Ernesto
Cuddly Dudley. *See* Moore, Dudley (Stuart John)
Cugaro, Georges. *See* Lebys, Henry
Cugat, Xavier. *See* Cugat de Bru y Deulofeo, Francisco de Asis Javier
Cugie. *See* Cugat de Bru y Deulofeo, Francisco de Asis Javier
Cuhelyn. *See* Price, Thomas Gwallter
Cuilluim, Sliabh. *See* O'Hagan, John
Cullen, Harry. *See* Slaughter, M(arion) T(ry)
Cultivated Catfish, The. *See* Brown, James
Cumberland, Gerald. *See* Kenyon, C(harles) F(rederick)
Cumberland, Gladys. *See* Harris, Cuthbert
Cumming, William. *See* Peters, W(illiam) C(umming)
Cummings, David. *See* Ehret, Walter (Charles)
Cummings, James. *See* Finkelstein, Abe
Cummings, James. *See* Slaughter, M(arion) T(ry)
Cuoghi, L. *See* Pittana, Luigi
Curet (Alonso), Tite. *See* Curet (Alonso), Catalino
Curly, Dan. *See* Holcomb, Densile
Curpentrus. *See* Genet, Elzéar
Curriander. *See* Wagner, Artur
Curroy, Mort. *See* Cohen, Maurice Alfred
Curroy, Mort. *See* Currie, Bill
Curroy, Mort. *See* Lipman, Harry
Curroy, Mort. *See* Moreton, Ivor
Curry. *See* Wagner, Artur
Cursio, Jan. *See* Giancursio, Joseph
Curtis, Billy. *See* Cornock, Sidney W(arren)
Curtis, Bob. *See* McNulty, Frank Fremont
Curtis, Con. *See* Lee, Albert George

Curtis, Con. *See* Tunbridge, Joseph A(lbert)
Curtis, Con. *See* Waller, Jack
Curtis, King. *See* Curtis, Eddie
Curtis, King. *See* Ousley, (King) Curtis
Curtis, Mann. *See* Kurtz, Em(m)anuel [or Manny]
Curtis, Memphis (E.). *See* Curtis, Eddie
Curtis, Tex. *See* Curtis, Eddie
Curtiss, J(immy). *See* Stulberger, James
Curzon, (Sir) Frank. *See* Deeley, Francis [or Frank] Arthur
Cusack, Mary Francis. *See* Cusack, Margaret Anna
Custer, Clay. *See* Thomas, George
Cutler, Jesse. *See* Gibaldi, Louis M(ilo)
Cutwalter, (Sir) Julius. *See* Horne, Richard Henry
Cuyler, Lyman (G.). *See* Crosby, Fanny [i.e., Frances] J(ane)
Cympson, Edward. *See* Sibson, E.
Cynimbo, Jerry. *See* Heseltine, Philip (Arnold)
Cyprian z Sieradza. *See* Bazylik, Cyprjan [or Cyprian]
Cyrnai. *See* Fok, Carolyn
Czabeck. *See* Hatton, John Liptrott
Czamara. *See* Broniewski, Wladyslaw
Czanyi. *See* Schmitt, Alois
Czapek, P. B. *See* Hatton, John Liptrott
Czar of Ragtime. *See* Christensen, Axel (W.)
Czech March King. *See* Fucik, Julius (Arnost Vilém)
Czersky, Alexander. *See* Tschirch, Friedrich Wilhelm
Cziak, Benedict. *See* Schack, Benedikt

– D –

D. *See* Deycks, Friedrich
D. *See* Doddridge, Philip
D., (Madame). *See* Ronssecy, (Madame) de
D***, (Monsieur). *See* Dejardin, Joseph
D***, (Madame). *See* Maria Antonia Walpurgis
D. A. D. *See* Déaddé, Edouard
DAS. *See* Wieck, (Johann Gottlob) Friedrich
D. A. T. *See* Thrupp, Dorothy [or Dorthea] Ann
D.B. *See* Chatterton, Thomas
D. D. *See* Crosby, Fanny [i.e., Frances] J(ane)
D. D. A. *See* Crosby, Fanny [i.e., Frances] J(ane)
D-DO. *See* Dalayrac, Nicolas(-Marie)
D. D. R. *See* Crosby, Fanny [i.e., Frances] J(ane)
D G N. *See* Marsollier des Vivetières, Benoît-Joseph
D. J. *See* Jordan, Irving Sidney
DJ Hurricane. *See* Fite, Wendell
DJ Lethal. *See* Dimant, Lear
DJ Quik. *See* Blake, David
DJ Scratch On Galaxy. *See* Llado, George
DJ Shadow. *See* Davis, Josh
DJ Spooky (That Subliminal Kid). *See* Miller, Paul D.
Dks. *See* Deycks, Friedrich
D. L. *See* Delusse, Charles
D. L. *See* Littledale, Richard Frederick
D. L. B. *See* Laborde, Jean Benjamin de
D. M. *See* Macfadyen, D.
DMX. *See* Simmons, Earl
D P. *See* Moultrie, Gerard
D. R. *See* Grant, Robert
Ds, (Dr.). *See* Deycks, Friedrich
D. T. *See* Turner, Daniel
Dw. *See* Dwight, Timothy
D. W. W. *See* Whittle, (Major) D(aniel) W(ebster)
D. Z., (Mademoiselle). *See* Dezède, Florine
D. Z., (Monsieur). *See* Dezède, Nicolas
Da Brat. *See* Harris, Shawntae
Da Correggio, Claudio. *See* Merlotti, Claudio
DaCintra, Ruy. *See* Stellman, Marcel
Dacre, Harry. *See* Decker, Henry
Daddy Dewdrop. *See* Monda, Richard
Daddy of Rock and Roll, The. *See* Haley, William [or Bill] (John Clifton) (Jr.)
Daddy of the Blues, The. *See* Walker, Aaron Thibeaux
Daddy Rabbit. *See* Pettis, Coleman, Jr.
Daddy Rings. *See* Dwyer, Everald
Daeblitz, Louis. *See* Orr, Buxton Daeblitz
Daffan, Ted. *See* Daffan, Theron Eugene
Daffodil, Dave. *See* Niessen, Josef
Dafy Y Garreg Wen. *See* Owen, David
Dagonet. *See* Hardwick, J. A.
Dagonet. *See* Sims, George R(obert)
Dahl, Wilbur. *See* Nolte Roy E.
Dailey, Frances. *See* Trace, Al(bert) (J(oseph))
Dain, Sharon Lee. *See* Myers, Sharon [or Sherry] (Lee)
Dal***, M. *See* Dalayrac, Nicolas(-Marie)
Dalai Lama of Music, The. *See* Tomášek, Václav Jan Křtitel
D'Albert. *See* Bertie-Marriott, Clement
Dalbert and Banning. *See* Bernard, Al(fred A.)
Dalbert and Banning. *See* Slaughter, M(arion)T(ry)
D'Albert, Fabian. *See* Orem, Preston Ware
Dalbert, Frank. *See* Slaughter, M(arion) T(ry)
Dalbotten, Ted. *See* Dalbotten, Charles Eric
Dale, Arthur. *See* Nevin, (Dale) Arthur (Finley)
Dale, Bert. *See* Dahlander, Nils-Bertil
Dale, Charles. *See* Finkelstein, Abe
Dale, Ella. *See* Crosby, Fanny [i.e., Frances] J(ane)
Dale, Herbert. *See* Harris, Cuthbert
Dale, Jean(ie). *See* Diestelhorst, H. Jean
Dale, Jim. *See* Smith, James [or Jim]
Dale, Kenny. *See* Eoff, Kenneth Dale, Jr.
Dale, Norwood. *See* Stults, R(obert) M(orrison)
Dale, Ruth. *See* Wilson, Ira B(ishop)
Dale, Sheila. *See* Headland-Stevens, Aimée
Dale, Vernon. *See* Slaughter, M(arion) T(ry)
Dale, Vikki. *See* Biondo, Rose Leonore Victoria
Dale, Walter. *See* Finkelstein, Abe
Dalebury, Jill. *See* Furze, Jessie (Lilian)

Dalhart, Frank. *See* Slaughter, M(arion) T(ry)
Dalhart, Vernon. *See* Slaughter, M(arion) T(ry)
Dall, Cernon [or Vernon?]. *See* Slaughter, M(arion) T(ry)
Dalla Tiorba. *See* Ferrari, Benedetto
Dallas, Rex. *See* Dallas, Fred Doble
Dall'Oglio. *See* Scarpari, Pietro
Dalma, Sergio. *See* Capdevila, Josep
Dalmonte, Carlos. *See* Dumont, Charles Frédéric
Dal Pestrino, Giulio. *See* Abondante, Giulio [or Julio]
Dalton, Charles. *See* Slaughter, M(arion) T(ry)
Dalton, Jack. *See* Kaufman, Jacob
Dalton, Lacy J. *See* Byrem, Jill Lynne
Daly, M. E. *See* Hayman, Richard Warren Joseph
Dalzac, Eugène. *See* Corréard, Eugène
D'Ambra, Lucio. *See* Manganella, Renato Eduardo
Damerell, S(tanley) J. *See* Stevens, Jack
Damian, Leo Saint. *See* Clark, Frederick Horace
Damm, Gustav. *See* Steingrãber, Theodor Leberecht
Dammers, Jerry. *See* Dankin, Gerald
Damon. *See* Williams, Damon
Damon, William. *See* Daman, Guilleaume
Damoreau, Laure-Cinthe. *See* Montalant, Laure-Cinthe
Dampier, L. *See* Bennett, J. S. L(ionel) D.
Damrosch, Papa. *See* Damrosch, Walter Johannes
Dan, Leo. *See* Teves, Leopoldo Dante
Dan, W(l.). *See* Dana-Danilowski, Wladyslaw
Dana, Arthur. *See* Austin, H. R.
Dana, Arthur. *See* Cipollone, Alfonso
Dana, Arthur. *See* Hackh, Otto (Christoph)
Dana, Arthur. *See* Hermann, Willy
Dana, Arthur. *See* Lynes, Frank
Dana, Arthur. *See* Norden, Hugo (Svan)
Dana, Arthur. *See* Sartorio, Arnoldo
Dana, Arthur. *See* Scott, Charles P(hillip)
Dana, Arthur. *See* Stoughton, R(oy) S(paulding)
Dana, Arthur. *See* Zilcher, Paul
Dana, Bill [or William]. *See* Szathmary, William
Dana, Francesco (de). *See* Ana, Francesco d'
Dana, Leroy. *See* Hovey, Nilo W(ellington)
Dana, Walter. *See* Dana-Danilowski, Wladyslaw
Danberg, Raimund. *See* Weinberg, Symson [or Simson]
Danbury's Most Famous Composer. *See* Ives, Charles Edward
Danby, Frank. *See* Dawson, Peter (Smith)
Dance, Leo. *See* Tennant, H. M.
Dandy, Jim. *See* Mangrum, James Leslie
Dandy of Country Music, The. *See* Ward, Seth
Dane, Barbara. *See* Spillman, Barbara
Dane, Bob. *See* Peretti, Hugo (Emil)
Dane, Clemence. *See* Ashton, Winifred
Danel, J. Gordon. *See* Gold, Joe (D.)
Danel, Pascal. *See* Pascal, Jean-Jacques
Danforth, N. P. *See* Page, N(athaniel) Clifford
D'Angelo. *See* Archer, Michael (Eugene)
D'Angelo, Nino. *See* D'Angelo, Gaetano
Dangerous (Dame). *See* Williams, Damon
Dani, N. *See* Daneau, Nicolas (Adolphe Gustave)
Dani, S(ergio). *See* Vidale, Piero
Daniel, Davis. *See* Andrykowski, Robert (Charles)
Daniel, John. *See* Badalamenti, Angelo (Daniel)
Daniel-Lesur, (Jean-Yves). *See* Lesur, Daniel Jean Yves
Daniel René. *See* Weider, Daniel René
Daniel, Salvador. *See* Daniel, Francisco (Alberto Clemente) Salvador
Daniels, C. F. *See* Barnard, George D(aniel)
Daniels, Don. *See* Borzage, Donald Dan
Daniels, G. F. *See* Barnard, George D(aniel)
Daniels, Harriet L. *See* Loes, Harry Dixon
Daniels, Jeff. *See* McDaniel, Luke
Daniels, Stevie. *See* Daniel, Stefan
Daniels, Walter. *See* Crow(e), Francis Luther
Danilowski, Wladyslaw. *See* Dana-Danilowski, Wladyslaw
Danju, Ras. *See* Campbell, Roslyn
Danka, Fide. *See* Kahlenbach, Hermann
Dankowski, Wojciech (Adalbert). *See* Danek, Wojciech (Adalbert)
Danmark, Ribe. *See* Lampe, J(ens) Bodewalt
Dannenberg, Fr. *See* Kark, Frederik
Danny Dee. *See* Diasio, Daniel J(oseph, Jr.)
Dano, Tony. *See* Soldano, Anthony
Dansavio. *See* Morricone, Ennio
Dant, B(ud). *See* Dant, Charles G(ustave)
Dantas, Zé. *See* Dantas (Filho), José de Souza
Dante, Ron(nie). *See* Granito, Carmine
D'Ant(h)ony. *See* Tasca, Pier Antonio
Danverd, Jules. *See* Timmermans, Armand
D'Anvers, N. *See* Bell, Nancy R. E. Meugens
Dany, Sergio. *See* Vidale, Piero
Danzig, Dorothy. *See* Hull, Dorothy Spafard
Da'oud, Gary. *See* David, Gary
Da-Oz, Ram. *See* Daus, Avraham
DaPalermo, Mauro. *See* Chiaula, Mauro
Daphnis, (aus Cimbrien). *See* Rist, Johann
Da Ponte, Lorenzo. *See* Conegliano, Em(m)anuele
D'Aragon, Alexandre. *See* Lefrancq, Pierre
Darby, Blind Blues. *See* Darby, Theodore [or Teddy] (Roosevelt)
Darby, Blind Teddy. *See* Darby, Theodore [or Teddy] (Roosevelt)
Darch, Ragtime Bob. *See* Darch, Robert R(ussell)
Darcier, Joseph. *See* Lemaire, Joseph
Darcis, G. *See* Dax, Esteven
Darcours, Charles. *See* Réty, Charles
D'Arcy, Colin. *See* Junsch, William Colin
Dare, Anthony. *See* Hall, Fred(erick) Fifield
Dare, Cyril. *See* Deacon, Charles
Darin, Bobby. *See* Cassotto, Walden Robert
Dark, Henry. *See* Haass, Hans
Dark Man X. *See* Simmons, Earl

Darkman. *See* Mitchell, Brian
Darling, John (A.). *See* Delbecque, Laurent
Darman, Arthur S. *See* Frangkiser, Carl (Moerz)
Darmancour, P. *See* Perrault, Charles
Darnell, August. *See* Browder, Thomas August Darnell
Darnell, Shelby. *See* Miller, Robert [or Bob] (Ernst)
Darnley, J. Herbert. *See* McCarthy, Herbert
Darr, Robert. *See* Mayerl, William [or Billy] (Joseph)
D'Arras, Adam. *See* Adam, de la Halle
Darrick, George. *See* Horchak, George
Darrow, George. *See* Horchak, George
D'Arsdorf, Jean. *See* Dax, Esteven
Dartol, F. *See* Flotard, Eugene
Dartos, Tunica. *See* Brody, David S(eymour)
Darval, Emile Germain. *See* Bessières, Emile G.
Darvas, Gábor. *See* Szatmárnémeti, Gábor
Darvey, Abel. *See* Lacout, Marie Madeleine Sophie
Daryl(l), Ted. *See* Meister, Theo(dore) (H(enry))
D'ash, K. Aaron. *See* Henning, Karl Prescott
Dasher, Dick. *See* O'Neill, Florence
Dashiell, Addison. *See* Walsh, Ulysses
Dashon, Algie. *See* Stevens, Alfred Peck
Dassoucy, Charles. *See* Coypeau, Charles
D'Auban, (Frederick) John. *See* Dobbin, Frederick John
Daubigny, Delacour. *See* Sims, George R(obert)
Daugherty, Dirty. *See* Daugherty, Patrick Dale
D'Auxerre, Pierre. *See* Du Camp Guillebert, Pierre
Davenport, Cow-Cow. *See* Davenport, Charles Edward
Davenport, John. *See* Blackwell, Otis
Davenport, Scott. *See* Rasley, John M.
Davenson, Henri. *See* Marrou, Henri Irenee
David. *See* Greenaway, Roger
David, David. *See* Powell, David
David, G. *See* Gordon, David M.
David, Hod. *See* Schudson, Howard (M.)
David, Joan. *See* Fishman, Jack (1918 (or 19)-)
David, M. *See* Savino, Domenico
David, Martin. *See* Robinson, Martin (David)
David, Mr. *See* Padbrué, David Janszoon
David, Nathan. *See* Risser, Bryce Nathan
David, Scott. *See* Samuels, Jerry
David, Vincent. *See* Di Biase, Edoardo J(ames)
David, Will. *See* Powell, David
Davide, da Bergamo, padre. *See* Moretti, Felice
Davids, Dean. *See* Ehret, Walter (Charles)
David's Harp of the North. *See* Wallin, Johan Olof
Davidson, Ellsworth. *See* Kountz, Richard
Davidson, Harley. *See* York, Harley C.
Davidson, Robert. *See* Burroughs, Bob (Lloyd)
DaViego, Emilio. *See* Grey, Frank H(erbert)
Daviel, André. *See* Hébertot, Jacques
Davies, Dotie. *See* Davis, Alice Maude
Davies, Evan. *See* Bliss, P(hilip) Paul
Davies, Fred. *See* Dawson, Peter (Smith)
Davies, G. W. *See* Bliss, P(hilip) Paul
Davies, Gail. *See* Dickerson, Patricia Gail
Davies, Iva. *See* Davies, Ifor
Davies, Owen. *See* Cain, Noble
Davis, Bert. *See* Davis, Bertha Ruth
Davis, Billy. *See* Davis, Roquel
Davis, Bus(ter). *See* Davis, Carl Estes, Jr.
Davis, Chip. *See* Davis, Louis, Jr.
Davis, Clifford. *See* Davis, Percival [or Percy]
Davis, Danny. *See* Nowlan, George
Davis, Don. *See* Fisher, Marvin
Davis, Jackie. *See* Davis, Jackson
Davis, Jeff(ery). *See* Hooven, Joseph (D(avis))
Davis, Kevin Clark. *See* Rasley, John M.
Davis, Lamont. *See* Dozier, Lamont
Davis, Lee. *See* Ehret, Walter (Charles)
Davis, Lefty. *See* Fisher, Marvin
Davis, Mac (Scott). *See* Davis, Morris
Davis, Mama. *See* Davis, Mary Lee
Davis, Mary Huntington. *See* Wilson, Ira B(ishop)
Davis, Norman. *See* Lucas, Christopher Norman
Davis, Owen. *See* Cain, Noble
Davis, Rusty. *See* Cheeseman, James Russell
Davis, Scott. *See* Davis, Morris
Davis Sisters, The. *See* Davis, Betty Jack
Davis Sisters, The. *See* Penick, Mary Frances
Davis, Skeeter. *See* Penick, Mary Frances
Davis, Totsy. *See* Davis, Larry
Davis, Will Bill. *See* Davis, William Strethen
Dawe, Margery. *See* Felix, Margery [or Marjorie] Edith
Dawes, T. O. *See* Parrott, Thom [or Tom]
Dawg. *See* Grisman, David (Jay)
Dawitt, Tom. *See* Lotterer, Gustav
Dawitt, Tom. *See* Nitze, Otto (Max)
Dawkins, Fast Fingers. *See* Dawkins, James [or Jimmy] (Henry)
Dawlish, Peter. *See* Day, Frederick E(dward) (Montagu)
Dawn, Dolly. *See* Stabile, Theresa Maria
Dawson, Bart. *See* Rose, (Knols) Fred
Dawson, Billy. *See* Duthoit, W(illiam) J(ames)
Dawson, Craig. *See* Dawson, Herbert (Henry)
Dawson, Eli. *See* Marks, Elias J.
Dawson, Leonard. *See* Dawson, Peter (Smith)
Dawson, Mark. *See* Beckhard, Robert L.
Dawson, Robert L. *See* Beckhard, Robert L.
Dawson, Shiel. *See* Barnard, D'Auvergne
Dawson, Smoky. *See* Dawson, Herbert (Henry)
Dawson, W. J. *See* Duthoit, W(illiam) J(ames)
Dax, Paul. *See* Paroisse-Pougin, François-Auguste-Arthur
Daxson, (Nils). *See* Kloeren, Lothar
Day, Bobby. *See* Byrd, Robert (James)
Day, Jerry. *See* Zaret, Hy(man)
Day, Ken. *See* Cohen, Maurice Alfred
Day, Nellie. *See* Parenteau, Zoe
Day, Rusty. *See* Davidson, Russell Edward

Day, Sonny. *See* Kaufmann, Walter (E.)
Day, Terry. *See* Jorden, Terry
Day, Valentine Elizabeth. *See* Krenkel, Gustav
Daye, Sonny. *See* Throckmorton, James (Fron Sonny)
Daylight, Richard Ralf. *See* Ralf-Kreymann, Richard
Dayne, Taylor. *See* Wunderman, Leslie [or Lesley] (Joy)
Dayton, Flora. *See* Crosby, Fanny [i.e., Frances] J(ane)
Dayton, Ronnie. *See* Wilkin, John (William)
Dayton, (Captain) Will. *See* Burleigh, Cecil (Edward)
Daz Dat Nigga. *See* Arnaud, Delmic
Dazzling All Night Rock Show. *See* Smith, Reginald (Leonard)
Dcenham, John. *See* Dunkerley, William Arthur
de Knapp. *See* Banck, Karl [or Carl]
de Novo Portu. *See* Mergot, Franciscus
Deacon, Francis. *See* Parker, Alfred Thomas
Deal, (Harold). *See* Loes, Harry Dixon
Dean. *See* Young, Welton
Dean, Colin. *See* Black, Stanley
Dean, Dearest. *See* Glosup, Lorene St. Clare (Donnelly)
Dean, Eddie. *See* Glosup, Edgar D(ean)
Dean, Folk. *See* Ettema, Theo
Dean, Frank. *See* Decker, Henry
Dean, H. *See* Rimmer, William
Dean, Helen Bevan. *See* Van Dieren, Bernard
Dean, Jimmy (Ray). *See* Ward, Seth
Dean, John Hugh. *See* O'Mahoney, Sean
Dean, Lorene. *See* Glosup, Lorene St. Clare (Donnelly)
Dean Martin of Country Music, (The). *See* Reeves, Franklin Delano
Dean of Afro-American Composers, The. *See* Still, William Grant
Dean of American Composers. *See* Carter, Elliott
Dean of American Jive. *See* Calloway, Cab(ell), III
Dean of American Music. *See* Copland, Aaron
Dean of American Music, The. *See* Damrosch, Walter Johannes
Dean of American Music, The. *See* Herbert, Victor
Dean of American Music, The. *See* Whiteman, Paul
Dean of American Music Critics, The. *See* Mathews, W(illiam) S(mythe) B(abcock)
Dean of American Musical Theater Composers. *See* Rodgers, Richard (Charles)
Dean of American Orchestration, The. *See* Lang, Philip J(oseph)
Dean of American Popular Music. *See* Whiteman, Paul
Dean of America's Composers, The. *See* Copland, Aaron
Dean of America's Negro Composers. *See* Still, William Grant
Dean of America's Show Music Composers, The. *See* Kern, Jerome David
Dean of American Songwriters. *See* Baline, Israel
Dean of Black Classical Composers, The. *See* Still, William Grant
Dean of British Critics. *See* Roberts, William (Amos)
Dean of Composers. *See* Gruenthal, Joseph
Dean of Hollywood Voice Men, The. *See* Colvig, Vance D.
Dean of Light Music Composers. *See* Farnon, Robert [or Bob] (Joseph)
Dean of Nashville Songwriters, The. *See* Howard, Harlan (Perry)
Dean of Ragtime Historians. *See* Blesh, Rudolph [or Rudi] (Pickett)
Dean of the Music Publishing Business. *See* Dreyfus, Max
Dean of the Piano Roll. *See* Cook, J. Lawrence
Deane, Charles. *See* Saunders, Edward
Dear Saxon, The. *See* Handel, Georg Friedrich
Dearly, Max. *See* Rolland(-Max(-Dearly)), Lucien Paul Marie Joseph
Dearnley, Herbert. *See* McCarthy, Herbert
Death, Blind Joe. *See* Fahey, John (Aloysius)
De Bar, Emile. *See* Retter, Louis
DeBarge, Bunny. *See* Jordan, Etterlene
DeBasque, Andre. *See* Ketèlbey, Albert William
DeBerton, R. *See* Saenger, Gustave
DeBohun, Lyle. *See* Boone, Clara Lyle
Debrando da Parma, Il. *See* D'Annunzio, Gabriele
Debrando da Parma, Il. *See* Pizzetti, Ildebrando
DeBrant, Cyr. *See* Higginson, J(oseph) Vincent
Debrnov, Josef. *See* Srb, Josef
De Burgh, Chris. *See* Davidson, Christopher (John)
Debussy, Claude (Spirit). *See* Brown, Rosemary (née Dickeson)
DeCarlo, Daniel. *See* Linden, David Gysbert (van der)
DeCastro, Arturo. *See* Zamecnik, J(ohn) S(tepan)
Deceased, The. *See* Schilling, Gustav (1803-1881)
DeChirico, Alberto. *See* Savinio, Alberto
Deck. *See* Hunter, Jason
De Coque, Oliver. *See* Akanite, Oliver Sunday
Decorus, Volupius. *See* Schonsleder, Wolfgang
Decsey, Ernst. *See* Deutsch, Ernst
Dedrick, Rusty. *See* Dedrick, Lyle T.
Dee, Jackie. *See* Myers, Sharon [or Sherry] (Lee)
Dee, Joey. *See* DiNicola, Joseph
Dee, Johnny. *See* Loudermilk, John D.
Dee, Lillian. *See* Krasnow, Herman(n)
Dee, Margaret. *See* Diefenthaler, Margaret Kissinger
Dee, Mikey. *See* Linick, Michael
Dee, Sylvia. *See* Proffitt, Josephine (née Moore)
Deems, Will. *See* Gaul, Harvey B(artlett)
Deery, S. *See* Seredy, J(ulius) S.
Dees, Ashley. *See* Miller, Robert [or Bob] (Ernst)
Dees, Rick. *See* Dees, Rigdon Osmond, III
Def Jef. *See* Forston, Jeffrey
DeFalco, Michele. *See* Falco, Michele (de)
Defoort, Rita. *See* Waignein, Andre
DeForrest, Marie. *See* Ackley, B(entley) D(eForrest)

De Francia. *See* Muris, Johannes de
De Franco, Buddy. *See* De Franco, Boniface (Ferdinand Leonardo)
De Ghelderode, Michel. *See* Martens, Adolphe-Adhemar-Louis-Michel
Degius, Nikolaus. *See* Decius, Nikolaus
DeGresac, Fred. *See* DeGresac, Frederique Rosine
De Jouy, Victor Joseph Etienne. *See* Jouy, (Victor Joseph) Etienne (de)
De Keyser, Alfred. *See* Kaiser, (Henri) Alfred (de)
Dekker, Desmond. *See* Dacres, Desmond
DeKnight, Jimmy. *See* Myers, James E(dward)
Del Da Lench Mob. *See* Jones, Teren Delvon
Del Tha Funky Homosapien. *See* Jones, Teren Delvon
Dela, Maurice. *See* Phaneuf, Albert
Delacassa, Eugene. *See* Rawlings, Charles Arthur
Delachapelle. *See* Claudel, Paul (Louis Charles Marie)
Delacour, Alfred (Charlemagne). *See* Lartigue, Alfred Charlemagne
Delacour, M. *See* Lartigue, Alfred Charlemagne
Delacour, Victor. *See* Smith, Edward Sydney
Deladrèvre. *See* Langlois, Louis
Delafield Olga. *See* Stephens, Ward
Delamaine, Charles L. *See* Beddie, George
DeLancey, J. *See* Sawyer, Henry S.
Deland, Pierre. *See* Leroyer, Pierre
Delande, Jo. *See* Vigneron-Ramakers, Christiane-Josée
Delaney, Francy. *See* O'Hara, John (Henry)
DeLange, Eddie. *See* DeLange, Edgar
Delano, Jack. *See* Ovcharov, Jascha
Delanoë, Pierre. *See* Leroyer, Pierre
Delapierre, (Guy) Bernard. *See* Bernard, Guy (Charles)
Delaporte, Paul. *See* Rawlings, Charles Arthur
Delar, H. H. *See* Adler, Hans
De Lara, Isidore. *See* Cohen, Isidore (de Lara)
Delbes, Eloi. *See* Delibes, (Clement Philibert) Leo
Delbos, Claire. *See* Delbos, Louise Justine
Delcasse, Leo. *See* Rawlings, Charles Arthur
Del Cornetto, Ascanio. *See* Cavallari, Ascanio
Delcy, Catherine J. *See* Lacy, Catherine J.
DeLeath, Vaughn. *See* Vonderlieth, Leonore
DeLeighbur, Don. *See* Burley, Daniel Gardner
De Leone, Andrea. *See* Lauzières(-Thémines), Achille de
Delfico. *See* Varotari, Dario
Delfico, Melchiorre. *See* De Filippis, Melchiorre
DelFlamingo, Rolando. *See* McCrohan, Dennis Eugene
Delfont, Bernard. *See* Winogradsky, Bernard [or Boris]
Delft, Michael van. *See* Lijnschooten, Hendrikus [or Henk] (Cornelius) van
Delfy. *See* Delfino, Enrique Pedro
Delgado, Roberto. *See* Wende, Horst
Delille, Francis. *See* Baron, Maurice
Delius, Frederick. *See* Delius, Fritz Albert Theodore
Dell, Rollie. *See* Khaury, Herbert
Dell, Tommy. *See* Fagan, Thomas O.
Dell, Vernon. *See* Slaughter, M(arion) T(ry)
Della'Arpa, (Orazio). *See* Michi, Orazio
Della, Ella. *See* Zuccamana, Gizelle Augusta
Della Morea, Centa. *See* Garelli Della Morea, Vincenza, (Countess de Cardenas)
Dellarosa, Ludwig. *See* Gleich, Joseph Alois
Dell'Arpa, Giovanni Leonardo. *See* Arpa, Giovanni Leonardo dell'
Dello, Pete. *See* Blumson, Peter
Delmage. *See* Welch, M. E. A.
Delmar, Axel. *See* Demandowski, Axel
Delmere, Bella. *See* Wood, Mathilda Alice Victoria
Delmount, Ronny. *See* Schulz, Hans
DeLongpré, Michael. *See* Strickland, Lily
Delorme, Joseph. *See* Sainte-Beuve, Charles Augustin
Delormeil. *See* Lénéka, André
Delos. *See* Spalding, Delos Gardner [or Gardiner]
Delphic Oracle, The. *See* Wagner, Cosima
Delta Bluesman from Lebanon, A. *See* Thompson, Richard
Delta Joe. *See* Foster, Leroy
Delta Joe. *See* Luandrew, Albert
Delta, John. *See* Hooker, John Lee
Del Tolveno, Arricha. *See* Hollaender, Victor [or Vicktor] (Hugo)
DeLulli, Arthur. *See* Allen, Euphemia (Amelia)
Del Violino, Carlo. *See* Caproli, Carlo
DeLys, V. *See* Vonderlieth, Leonore
Delysse, Jean. *See* Roesgen-Champion, Marguerite Sara
De Maistre, Sylvie. *See* Maitre, Suzanne Gabrielle
De Mandelieu Maurice. *See* Andriessen, Jurriaan
Demann, Ernest. *See* Gaul, Harvey B(artlett)
Demar, Luz. *See* Malerba, Ricardo Francisco
DeMarco, Angelina [or Angelino]. *See* Vonderlieth, Leonore
Demeny. *See* Horowitz, Vladimir
De Meyer, Leopold. *See* Meyer, Leopold von
Demillac, Francis-Paul. *See* Djemil, Enyss
Dempsey, James L. *See* Lincoln, Harry J.
Den Mother of Nashville, The. *See* Wilkin, Marijohn (née Melson)
DeNaut, Jud. *See* DeNaut, George Matthew [or Mathews]
Dendron, (Miss) Rhody. *See* Burnard, Francis Cowley
DeNegah, Juan. *See* Hagen, J(ohn) M(ilton)
Denes, Báthory. *See* Báthory-Kitsz, Dennis
Denham, Barbara. *See* Yorke, Peter
De Nieve, Bola. *See* Villa, Ignacio
Denim, Joe. *See* Cotton, James [or Jimmy]
Deniston, Paul. *See* Frangkiser, Carl (Moerz)
Denne, Heather. *See* Rimmer, William
Denni, Gwynne. *See* Denni, Martha (Gwynne)
Denning, Frank. *See* Damico, Frank James
Dennis, Al. *See* Tessier, Albert D(enis)

Dennis, Patrick. *See* Tanner, Edward Everett, III
Dennis, Peter. *See* Berry, Dennis (Alfred)
Dennis the Menace of Jazz, The. *See* Jenkins, Bill
Dennisimo. *See* McIntire, Dennis (Keith)
Dentella. *See* Dente, Pietro
Denton, James. *See* Hughes, Robert J(ames)
Denton, Will. *See* Nieberding, William Joseph
Denver, John. *See* Deutschendorf, Henry John, Jr.
Denville, Eric. *See* DeanThorne, Donald James
Deodato. *See* Almeida, Eumir(e) Deodato
DePadua, Anthony. *See* Delaney, Francis Edward
De Paul, Lynsey. *See* Rubin [or Ruben], Lynsey
DePinna, Herbert. *See* Slater, (John) Joseph [or Joe]
De Rez. *See* Tagliafico, Joseph (Dieudonné)
Der Bingle. *See* Crosby, Harry Lillis
Der Payatz. *See* Yablonik, Herman [or Hyman]
Derek B. *See* Bowland, Derek
Derfla, Rétrac B. T. *See* Carter, Alfred T. B.
Derives, Jean. *See* Landowski, F. L.
De Riviera, (E. de). *See* Schleich, Ernst
Dermott, Ralph. *See* Kountz, Richard
Dernier Roy des violins. *See* Ghignone, Giovanni Pietro
Dero, Al. *See* DiRobbio, Armando
DeRose, (Mrs.) Peter. *See* Breen, May Singhi
Derr, Zan. *See* McGonigal, Alexander Andrew
Derringer, Marc. *See* Yablonka, Marc (Phillip)
Derringer, Rick. *See* Zehringer, Richard
Dersan, Jon. *See* Anders, John Frank
Dersey, S. J. *See* Seredy, J(ulius) S.
Derville, (Henri-Louis). *See* Desnoyers, Louis (Claude Joseph Florence)
Derwid. *See* Lutoslawski, Witold
Des Quarante, Un. *See* Mérimée, Prosper
Desage, Marcel. *See* Antheil, George
Desaides, Nicolas. *See* Dezède, Nicolas
DeSanto, Sugar Pie. *See* Balinton, Umpeylia Marsema
DeSaxe, Serena. *See* Davison, Lita
Desforges. *See* Choudard, P(ierre) J(ean) B(aptiste)
Desforges, Citoyen. *See* Hus-Desforges, Pierre Louis
DeShannon, Jackie. *See* Myers, Sharon [or Sherry] (Lee)
Desiderius Pastor. *See* Moultrie, Gerard
De'Sierre, Georges. *See* Bonvin, Ludwig
DeSivrai, Jules. *See* Jackson, Jane
Desky, Jacques. *See* Pillois, Jacques
Desmarets, Chevalier. *See* Pellegrin, Simon Joseph
DeSmetsky, Jean. *See* DeSmet, Jean
Desmond, Paul. *See* Breitenfeld, Paul Emil(e)
Desmond, Walter. *See* Frangkiser, Carl (Moerz)
Desormes, L(ouis) C(ésar). *See* Marchionne, L(ouis) C(ésar)
De Souza, Palma. *See* Zadora, Michael
Desplanes, Giovanni [or Jean] (Antoine). *See* Piani, Giovanni Antonio
Des'ree. *See* Weekes, Desiree [or Des'ree]
Des Roches, Gilbert. *See* Legoux, (Baroness) Julie
Desslyn, Guy. *See* Baycock, Frederick
De Stendhal. *See* Beyle, (Marie) Henri
Desverges, (M.). *See* Chapeau, Armand
De Sylva, B. G. *See* De Sylva, George Gard
De Sylva, Buddy. *See* De Sylva, George Gard
DeSylva, Joe. *See* Proffitt, Josephine (née Moore)
DeTedla, Al. *See* Tessier, Albert D(enis)
De Totis, Giuseppe Domenico. *See* Totis, Giuseppe Demenico de
Detour Man, The. *See* Walker, Earnest Earl
Detroit Jr. [or Junior]. *See* Williams, Emery H., (Jr.)
Detroit, Marcella. *See* Levy, Marcella
Detroit Red. *See* Perryman, Rufus G.
Detroit Techno. *See* Craig, Carl
Deutlich, Jeremias. *See* Karpeles, (Julius) Max (Heinrich)
Deutsch, Peter. *See* Settelmeyer, Hermann Josef
Deutscher, Drafi. *See* Deutscher, Karlheinz
Deutscher Spaniol in Griechenland. *See* Speer, Daniel
Deva. *See* Foulds, John Herbert
Devadip. *See* Navarro, Autlan de
DeVall, Don E. *See* Jones, Isaiah, Jr.
De Vaux. *See* Lemonnier, Guillaume Antoine
Devaux, Jules. *See* Barnard, D'Auvergne
Devereaux, J. L. *See* Lee, Louis Leoni
Devereaux, Richmond. *See* Heard, Richard Martin
Deverenx, Peter. *See* Biss, Thomas
Dévereux, Jules. *See* Box, Harold Elton
Dévereux, Jules. *See* Keuleman, Adrian
Dévereux, Jules. *See* Pelosi, Domonic [or Don]
Dévereux, Jules. *See* Sugarman, Harry
DeVigne, Antoine. *See* Wyngaerde, Antoine de
Devil, The. *See* Paganini, Nic(c)olò
Deville, Mink. *See* Boray, William
Deville, Willy. *See* Boray, William
DeVille, Paul. *See* Lake, M(ayhew) L(ester)
DeVille, Paul. *See* Prendiville, Henri Jean
Devil's Son-in-Law, The. *See* Bunch, William
Devinal, Prof. *See* Löwenfeld, Peter Erwin
Devine, Raynard. *See* Ellis, Royston
Devoto, Howard. *See* Trotter, Howard
Devrient, T. *See* Sartorio, Arnoldo
Dew Mitch. *See* Dujmic, Hansi
Dewar, Allison. *See* Turnbull, Graham (Morrison)
Dewey, W. L. *See* Keiser, Robert (A(dolph))
DeWitt, Maurice. *See* Slater, (John) Joseph [or Joe]
Dewitz, Hildegard. *See* Kazoreck, Hildegard
Dexter, Al. *See* Poindexter, (Clarence) Albert
Dexter, Charles. *See* Finkelstein, Abe
Dexter, Von. *See* Totis, San(dor)
Dexter, Von. *See* Urbanski, La Von Hawley
Dey, Larry. *See* Deybrook, L(arry) M(itchell)
DeYoe, A. S. *See* Gabriel, Charles H(utchinson)
de Zulli, Arthur. *See* Allen, Euphemia (Amelia)
Dharma, Buck. *See* Roeser, Donald (B.)

D'Hermann, E. *See* Darewski, Hermann E(dward)
Diamand, Josef. *See* Damanski, Josef
Diamond, A. L. *See* Dommnici, Itek
Diamond, Al. *See* Dommnici, Itek
Diamond, Cliff. *See* Mann, Stephen Follett
Diamond, Dave. *See* Davison, Sid (I.), (Jr.)
Diamond, I(sadore) [or I(sidore)] A. L. *See* Dommici, Itek
Diamond, Max. *See* Magnoni, Bruce [or Bruno] Albert
Diamondez. *See* Palmer, Cedric King
Diamonds, Ducie. *See* Blackmar, A(rmand) E(dward)
Dianea, Gelmarania. *See* Passeri, Mariangiola
Dianidio, Mirtillo. *See* Martello [or Martelli], Pier Jacopo
Dianio, Cromiro. *See* Bernardoni, Pietro Antonio
Diarmid. *See* Bax, (Sir) Arnold Edward Trevor
DiArta Angeli, F. *See* Tsandoulas, Gerasimos (N(icholas))
Dias, B. H. *See* Pound, Ezra ((Weston) Loomis)
Dias, David Vaz. *See* Egli, David Christian
Diaz, Santander. *See* Diaz Herrera, Carlos Arturo
Dibango, Manu. *See* Dibango, Emmanuel
Dibbs, Jr. *See* Dibango, Emmanuel
Di Cappo (?). *See* Roberts, John [or Jack] (Isaac)
Dice Man. *See* James, Richard D(avid)
Dick, Dr. *See* Downing, Denis J.
Dick, Dorothy. *See* Link, Dorothy
Dicken. *See* Pain, Jeff(rey) Robert
Dickens, Little Jimmy. *See* Dickens, James Cecil
Dickinson, Richard. *See* Barthelson, (Helen) Joyce (Holloway)
Dickinson, Richard. *See* Ehret, Walter (Charles)
Dickson, Bob. *See* Robertson, Dick
Dickson, Charles. *See* Kaufman, Isidore
Dickson, Stanley. *See* Dickson, Mary Hannah
Dico, Rosh. *See* Reith, Dieter
Dictator of Musical Boston. *See* Dwight, John Sullivan
Didacus a Portu. *See* Puerto, Diego del
Diddley, Bo. *See* Bates, (Otha) Ellas [or Elias]
Didimus, (H.). *See* Durell, Edward Henry
Didymus Faventinus. *See* Schwarzerd, Philipp
Diego el Cigala. *See* Jiménez Salazar, Diego
Dieguito (el Cigala). *See* Jiménez Salazar, Diego
Diestelhorst, Josefine. *See* Hauptmann, Elisabeth
Dieubussy. *See* Debussy, Claude
Diggenjof [or Diggenhof], Albert. *See* Fagan, Gideon
Di Giovanni, Rob. *See* Di Giovanni, Rocco
Digital, Bobby. *See* Diggs, Robert
Di Gras, M. *See* Fleagle, J(acob) (Roger)
Dilettante, A. *See* Gardiner, William
Dilettante ne pus ultra. *See* Van Vechten, Carl
Dill, Danny. *See* Dill, Horace Eldred
Dillinger, Paul. *See* Noack, Walter
Dillon, Bob. *See* Zimmerman, Robert Allen
Dillon, Dean. *See* Rutherford, Dean
Dilloy, Bertin. *See* Bertin, Jean-Honoré
Dinan, Fred. *See* Busch, Ferdinand
Dinant, L. de. *See* Bonnemère (de Chavigny), Léon Eugène
Dinapoli, Mike. *See* Dinapoli, Mario John
Dingman, (Mrs.) W. H. *See* Gabriel, Charles H(utchinson)
Dingwag, Brob. *See* Farmer, Marjorie
Dino Guitar. *See* Dinino, Louis (Lee)
Dino, Jani(t)a. *See* Tajani Mattone, Ida
Dino, Ralph. *See* Palladino, Ralph Francis
DiNogero, Francesco [or Francisco]. *See* Bauer, Emilie Frances
Dio dell'Opera Buffa, Il. *See* Logroscino, Nicola (Bonifacio)
Dio, Ronnie (James). *See* Padavona, Ronald
Diogenes. *See* Tinter, Georg
Dion. *See* DiMucci, Dion (Francis)
Dionisio. *See* Papin da Mantova
Dionysius Trebellianus. *See* Treiber, Johann Philipp
Diplomate, Un. *See* Escudier, Marie-Pierre-Pascal
Dippermouth. *See* Armstrong, (Daniel) Louis
Dipsy Doodler, The. *See* Clinton, Larry
Dirck van Embden. *See* Pers, Dirck Pietersz(oon)
Dirty Old Man of Popular Music, The. *See* Ginsburg [or Ginzburg], Lucien
Dirty Red. *See* Wilborn, Nelson
Dirty Rock 'n' Roller. *See* Young, Neil
Disco Queen. *See* Gaines, LaDonna [or Donna] Andrea [or Adrian]
Discobolus. *See* Aldous, Donald William
Disinvolto. *See* Giannini, Giovanni Matteo
Dissenting Minister, A. *See* Lynch, Thomas Toke [or Took]
Dissepolo di Stamitz. *See* Beck, Franz Ignaz
Dissonante , Il. *See* Banchieri, Adriano (Tomaso)
Dittersdorf, Karl von. *See* Kreisler, Fritz [i.e., Friedrich](-Max)
Divina, Eleanor [or Elly]. *See* Miller, Robert [or Bob] (Ernst)
Divina Euterpe, La. *See* Calegari, Cornelia
Divine Composer, The. *See* Marenzio, Luca
Divine Saxon, The. *See* Hasse, Johann Adolf
Divino, Il. *See* Francesco (Canova) da Milano
Divino Boëmo, Il. *See* Mysliveček, Josef
Divitis, Antonius. *See* Ryche, Anthonius (de)
Divo. *See* Dučić, Jovan
Divorceshack. *See* Dvořák, Antonín
Dix, Bobby. *See* Robertson, Dick
Dixie, Jr. *See* Emmett, Dan(iel Decatur)
Dixie Nightingale, The. *See* Gibbons, Irene
Dixon, Bob. *See* Robertson, Dick
Dixon, George. *See* Catsos, Nicholas A.
Dixon, Harry. *See* Cowell, Henry

Dixon, Martin. *See* Crow(e), Francis Luther
Dixon, Martin. *See* Slaughter, M(arion) T(ry)
Dixon, Skeet. *See* Dixon, Floyd
Dixon, Willie. *See* Dixon, James
Diz. *See* Gillespie, John (Birks)
Djemal Réchid. *See* Rey, Cemal Resid
D'Joseph, Jac. *See* DiGiuseppe, Severino
D'Léon, Oscar. *See* Somoza, Oscar Emilio Léon
D'Lorah, Juan y. *See* Burke, John(ny)
D'Lorah, Juan y. *See* Spina, Harold
Dluik und Rouhans, Elder d'. *See* Csermák, Antol [or Anthony] György [or George]
Dmitriyev, N. *See* Kashkin, Nikolay (Dmitriyevich)
Dobbs, Johnny. *See* Autry, (Orvon) Gene
Dobey. *See* Dober, Conrad K.
Dobro, Frank. *See* Dobrovolny, Frantisek
Dobro Virtuoso, The. *See* Graves, Burkett (K.)
Dobrovel, Issay (Alexandrovich). *See* Barabeichik, Ishok Israelevich
Dobrowe(i)n, Issay (Alexandrofich). *See* Barabeichik, Ishok Israelevich
Dobschinski, Walter (Max). *See* Dobrzynski, Walter (Max)
Doctor and *Dr.* are interfiled; see also *Doktor*
Doctor, The. *See* Monsell, John Samuel Bewley
Doctor, The. *See* Ongala, Ramazini [or Ramathan] Mtoro
Dr. Alban. *See* Nwapa, Alban
Doctor Alimantado. *See* Thompson, (James) Winston
Dr. B. *See* Byrom, John
Dr. Boogie. *See* Hooker, John Lee
Doctor Clayton's Buddy. *See* Luandrew, Albert
Dr. Dick. *See* Downing, Denis J.
Dr. Doom. *See* Thornton, Keith
Dr. Dre. *See* Young, Andre (Ramelle [or Romell])
Dr. Dream. *See* Lennon, John (Winston)
Doctor Feelgood. *See* Hooker, John Lee
Dr. Feelgood. *See* Perryman, William [or Willie] Lee
Dr. Freeze. *See* Freese, Louis
Dr. Freeze. *See* Straite, Elliot
Dr. Jeckyll. *See* Harrell, Andre
Dr. John (The Night Tripper). *See* Rebennack, Malcolm [or Mac] (John)
Dr. Longhair. *See* Byrd, Henry Roeland
Dr. Music. *See* Riley, Doug(las Brian)
Dr. Nico. *See* Nicholas, Kasanda Wa Mikalay
Dr. Octagon. *See* Thornton, Keith
Doctor of Cacophony. *See* Wagner, Richard
Dr. of Determination. *See* Jessye, Eva Alberta
Dr. P. *See* Krüger, Eduard
Dr. Robert. *See* Howard, Robert
Doctor Seraphicus. *See* Bonaventura
Dr. Zxy. *See* Weber, (Jacob) Gottfried
Dodd, Alison. *See* Dickson, Mary Hannah
Dodds, Johnny. *See* Autry, (Orvon) Gene
Dodds, L. B. *See* Bliss, P(hilip) Paul
Doelle, Hans. *See* Doelle, Franz
Dog, Tim. *See* Blair, Timothy
Dogan, King Sweets. *See* Dogan, James
Dogbowl. *See* Tunney, Stephen
Dogyear, Drew. *See* Gorey, Edward (St. John)
Dokin, Ralph. *See* Schmidt, Gerd
Doktor see also *Doctor*
Doktor der Kakophonie. *See* Wagner, Richard
Doktor der Tonkunst. *See* Haydn, (Franz) Joseph
Dolaro, Dolly. *See* Simmonds, Selina
Dolaro, Selina. *See* Simmonds, Selina
Dolby, Thomas. *See* Robertson, Thomas Morgan Dolby
Dolcevillico, Francesco Saverio. *See* Süssmayr, Franz Xaver
Dolega-Chodakowski, Zorian. *See* Lelewel, Joachim
Dolega-Kamienski. *See* Kamienski, Lucian [or Lucjan]
Dollar Brand. *See* Brand, Adolph Johannes
Dollar, Johnny. *See* Horchak, George
Dolores. *See* Dickson, Ellen Elizabeth
Dolores del Infante. *See* Rosa Suárez, Robert Edward
Dolph-Heckel, Josef. *See* Heckel-Kotrusz, Josef
Domange, (Madame) Albert. *See* Bonis, Mél(anie) (Hélène)
Domenichino, Il. *See* Sarti, Giuseppe
Domingues, Alberto. *See* Pörschmann, Walter
Dominguez Bastida, Gustavo Adolfo. *See* Bastida, Gustavo Adolfo Dominguez
Dominic, John. *See* Roncoroni, Joseph (Dominic)
Dominik, Alexander. *See* Kowalski, Július
Dominique, (Pierre François Biancolelli). *See* Biancolelli, Pierre François
Dominique, Claude. *See* Concordel, Claude Marie
Domino, Un. *See* Mortjé, Arnold [or Adolphe]
Domino, Fats. *See* Domino, Antoine
Domus, Peter. *See* Domagalla, Herbert
Domusbricenis. *See* Fallet, Ed(o)uard Marius
Don Giovanni. *See* Shaw, George Bernard
Don Jose. *See* Manaois, Joseph (Anthony, Jr.)
Don Preciso. *See* Iza Zamácola, Juan Antonio
Don, Russell. *See* Steagall, Russell (Don)
Don Tarar di Palmira. *See* Salieri, Antonio
Donaggio, P(ino). *See* Donaggio, Giuseppe
Donahue, Jack. *See* Donahue, John Joseph
Donald, Duck. *See* Donald, Duckworth Bruce Andrew
Donaldson, Arthur. *See* Joyce, Archibald
Donaldson, Dewey. *See* Krenek, Ernst
Donaldson, Molly. *See* Pollock, Muriel
Donbacky. *See* Caponi, Aldo
Donegan, Lonnie. *See* Donegan, Anthony [or Tony] (James)
Donerus, Bernd. *See* Schmadtke, Harry
Dönhoff, Gabriel Wajditsch Verbonac von. *See* Wajditsch Verbonac von Dönhoff , Gabriel
Doniano, Cleofanto. *See* Papi, Antonio

Donizetti, Alfredo. *See* Ciummei, Alfredo
Donna Elidora. *See* Wuiet, Caroline
Donnadieu, Yvonne. *See* Pollock, Muriel
Donnamontano. *See* Frauenberger, P. Ernst, OSB
Donnamonte. *See* Frauenberger, P. Ernst, OSB
Donner, Dave. *See* Hamblen, (Carl) Stuart
Donostia, (José Antonio de). *See* Zulaica y Arregui, José Gonzalo
Donovan. *See* Leitch, Donovan (Phillip)
Donovan, Hugh. *See* Finkelstein, Abe
Donovan, Hugh. *See* Slaughter, M(arion) T(ry)
Donson, Don. *See* Scarpa, Salvatore
D'Ontana, Pier. *See* Ponti, Andrea
Dooley, "Big Jeb". *See* Erwin, George
Doors, The. *See* Densmore, John
Doors, The. *See* Krieger, Robert [or Robby, or Robbie]
Doors, The. *See* Manzarek, Raymond (Daniel)
Doors, The. *See* Morrison, James (Douglas)
Dor, Daniela. *See* Kaufman, Barbara
Dor, Dany. *See* Kaufman, Barbara
d'Or, Laren. *See* Héger, Attila
Doran, Jack. *See* Manney, Charles Fonteyn
Dore, Eileen. *See* Rawlings, Charles Arthur
Dorel, Francis. *See* Coote, Frederick A(lfred)
Doretheos a Bemdba. *See* Pers, Dirck Pietersz(oon)
Dorfman, Pretty Penny. *See* Dorfman, Helen Horn
Dorham, Kenny. *See* Dorham, McKinley Howard
Dori, Giuseppo. *See* Hoffmann, Ernst Theodore Wilhelm
Doria, Clara. *See* Barnett, Clara Kathleen
Dorian, Frederick. *See* Deutsch, Friedrich
Doriano, Cleofanto. *See* Papi, Antonio
Doric, Caesar. *See* Quigley, Michael
Dörmann, Felix. *See* Biedermann, Felix
Dormann, Franz. *See* Rheinhardt, Paul Gustav
D'Orme, Valerie. *See* Atkinson, Dorothy
Dorn, Eduard. *See* Kaan, Eduard
Dorn, Edward [or Edouard]. *See* Roeckel, Joseph Leopold
D'Orso, Francesco. *See* Behr, F(ranz)
Dorothy Parker of Pop, The. *See* MacColl, Kristy
Dorr, Julian. *See* Achron, Isidor
D'Orsay, M. L. *See* Ponsa, Maria Luisa
Dorset, Ray. *See* Strange, Joe
Dorsey, Georgia Tom. *See* Dorsey, Thomas A(ndrew)
Dorus, Vincent Joseph. *See* Van Steenkist, Vincent
Dottel Figlio. *See* Oswald, James
Dottor Gibin. *See* Binetti, Giovanni
Doubt, Mandy. *See* MacColl, Kristy
Douce, Tilly. *See* Goldbaum, Friedrich
Doudney, M. A. *See* Rands, William Brightly
Doug, Sir. *See* Saldana, Douglas
Doughtery, Bill. *See* South, Edward [or Eddie] (Otha)
Dougherty, Jennie. *See* Dougherty, Genevieve
Douglas see also Douglass
Douglas. *See* Reed, Andrew
Douglas, Ellen. *See* Crosby, Fanny [i.e., Frances] J(ane)
Douglas(s), Jessie. *See* Gaul, Harvey B(artlett)
Douglas, John. *See* Keats, Frederick A.
Douglas, Ken. *See* Moody, Walter (R.)
Douglas, Kid. *See* Douglas, Lizzie
Douglas, Martin. *See* Munn, William O.
Douglas, Minnie. *See* Douglas, Lizzie
Douglas, Sir. *See* Saldana, Douglas
Douglas, Stanton. *See* Dickson, Mary Hannah
Douglas, Wayne. *See* Broze, Wayne Douglas
Douglas, Wayne. *See* Ehret, Walter (Charles)
Douglas, Wayne. *See* Penney, Edward J., Jr.
Douglas, Wayne. *See* Weber, Fred
Douglass see also Douglas
Douglass, Don. *See* Penney, Edward J., Jr.
Doune, Ercil. *See* Drysdale, Janey C.
Dousmolin, Joseph. *See* Touchemo(u)lin, Joseph
Douste, Jean. *See* Rawlings, Charles Arthur
Dover, Darry. *See* Khaury, Herbert
Dowdy, (Mrs.) Regera. *See* Gorey, Edward (St. John)
Dowell, Saxie. *See* Dowell, Horace Kirby
Dowling, Eddie. *See* Goucher, Joseph Nelson
Downes, (Edwin) Olin. *See* Quigley, Edwin Olin, Jr.
Downey, Shawn. *See* Downey, (Sean) Morton, Jr. (1933-2001)
Downing, Kenneth. *See* Treharne, Bryceson
Downs, Jerry. *See* Hoffman, Al
Doyle, Gene. *See* Taubenhaus, Eugene
Doyle, John. *See* Graves, Robert (Ranke)
D'Oyly-Carte, Richard. *See* Carte, Richard D'Oyly
Dr. is interfiled with *Doctor*
Draco, (Cornelius). *See* Rosa Suárez, Robert Edward
Drake, Alfred. *See* Capurro, Alfredo
Drake, Ervin. *See* Druckman, Ervin M(aurice)
Drake, Janet. *See* Barthelson, (Helen) Joyce (Holloway)
Drake, Janet. *See* Ehret, Walter (Charles)
Drake, Milton. *See* Druckman, Milton
Draner. *See* Renard, (Pierre) Jules
Dranreb, J. *See* Bernard, J.
Draper, Freckles. *See* Draper, Farrell H(al)
Draper, Rusty. *See* Draper, Farrell H(al)
Draude, M. B. *See* Behm, Eduard
Drawcansir, (Sir) Alexander Knt., Censor of Great Britain. *See* Fielding, Henry
Drayz. *See* Weston, Andre
Dre, L. A. *See* Bolton, Andre
Dreoilin. *See* Fahy, Francis Arthur
Dreso. *See* Zerezo de Tejada, Isidore Francisco Antonio de
Dresser, Paul. *See* Dreiser, (John) Paul, (Jr.)
Dressler, Max. *See* Rawlings, Alfred William
Dreux, Jean. *See* Drocos, Jean
Drew, Dan. *See* Broza, Elliot Lawrence
Drew, Don. *See* O'Keefe, James (Conrad)

Drew, Don. *See* O'Keefe, Lester
Drifting Cowboy, The. *See* Williams, Hir(i)am (King)
Driftwood, Jimmy. *See* Morris, James C(orbett)
Drimcenko. *See* Drimcov, Serhij Prokopovyc
Driver 67. *See* Phillips, Paul
Drlač, Jan Zdeněk. *See* Ulrich, Jürgen
Drofnatzki, Karel. *See* Stanford, Charles Villiers
Drofyah, Michael. *See* Hayford, George W.
Drogheda, 11th Earl of. *See* Moore, Charles Garrett Ponsonby
Droysen, Wolf. *See* Röhrig, Wolfram
Drudmair, Zeno. *See* Zoder, Raimund
Drummer X. *See* Hamilton, Foreststorn
Drysale, E. M. *See* Kunkel, Charles
Du Grand Nez. *See* Marsollier des Vivetières, Benoît-Joseph
Duane, Eddy. *See* Hansen, Edward Duane
Dubey, Matt. *See* Dubinsky, Matthew D(avid)
Dubin, Bettie. *See* Smith, Beth
Du Bois, Herman. *See* Fisher, Ethel
Dubois, Jules. *See* Battu, Léon
Dubois, Jules. *See* Carré, Michel (the elder)
Dubois, Paul. *See* Boisselot, Paul
Dubois, Paul. *See* Richardson, Clive
Dubois, Paul. *See* Truinet, Charles Louis Étienne
Dubois, René. *See* Reeves, Ernest
Dubsky, V. R. *See* Rihovský, Vojtéch
DuBuisson, (Burgeois de Paris). *See* Lacquemant, Jean
Ducelle, Paul. *See* Krogmann, Carrie W(illiam(s))
Duch, Benedict(us). *See* Ducis, Benedictus
Du Châtelet, Jean. *See* Guyot [du Chátelet], Jean
Duchêsnes, Pierre. *See* Williams, Joseph (Benjamin)
Duchess of Coolsville, The. *See* Jones, Rickie Lee
Duclos, Pierre. *See* Boisvallée, François de
DuCoin, M. (Mme.). *See* Thys, Pauline-Marie-Elisa
Ducré, Pierre. *See* Berlioz, Hector
Dudaszek, Orfeusz. *See* Sikorski, Józef
D'Udine, Jean. *See* Cozanet, Albert
Dudley, Bide. *See* Dudley, Walter Bronson
Dudley, Dave. *See* Pedruska, David Darwin
Dudley, (Sir) Henry Bate. *See* Bate, (Rev.) Henry
Dudley, S. H. *See* Rous, Samuel Holland
Dudu. *See* Fletcher, Julia Constance
Duehrer, Walter. *See* Drexler, Werner
Dufferin (and Clandeboye), Helen Selina. *See* Sheridan, Helen Selina
D'Uffey, Mr. *See* D'Urfey, Thomas
Duffy, Tin Tin. *See* Duffy, Stephen
Dufort, Charles. *See* Kark, Frederik
DuFrerre, M. *See* Fisher, Ethel
Du Gaucquier, Alard. *See* Gaucquier, Alard (Dunoyer du)
Dugend, Enno. *See* Dugend, Herta
Duke & His Uke. *See* Marvin, John(ny) (Senator)
Duke, Billy [or William]. *See* Tesone, William N.
Duke, Bobby. *See* Miranda, Ralph
Duke, Charles. *See* Costantakos, Chris Anastasios
Duke, Henry (& His Uke). *See* Marvin, John(ny) (Senator)
Duke Honey (& His Uke). *See* Marvin, John(ny) (Senator)
Duke, Jerry. *See* Fields, Harold (Cornelius)
Duke, Jerry. *See* Halfin, Robert [or Bob]
Duke, Jerry. *See* Roncoroni, Joseph (Dominic)
Duke, Louise. *See* Green, Phil(ip)
Duke, Mighty. *See* Pope, Kelvin
Duke of Iron. *See* Anderson, Cecil
Duke of Luxembourg, The. *See* Lewis, Meade (Anderson)
Duke of Paducah, The. *See* Ford, Benjamin Francis
Duke, Robert. *See* Meek, Robert (George)
Duke, Vernon. *See* Dukelsky, Vladimir
Dukes. *See* Bugatti, Dominic
Dukes. *See* Musker, Frank
DuLac, Paul. *See* Lake, M(ayhew) L(ester)
Dulaurens. *See* Arouet, François-Marie
Dulce, Curro. *See* Boigas, Francisco Fernandez
Dumah. *See* Burrow, Robert Foster
Dumaniant, Antoine Jean. *See* Bourlin, Antoine Jean (André)
Dumas, Gustave. *See* Rawlings, Alfred William
DuMay, D'Amour. *See* Dumais, Joseph
D'Umberto, Angelo. *See* Herrera, Humberto (Angel)
Dummer, Donna. *See* Gaines, LaDonna [or Donna] Andrea [or Adrian]
Dumont, Cecil. *See* Dumont, Charles Frédéric
Dumont, Cedric. *See* Dumont, Charles Frédéric
Dunbar, Sly. *See* Dunbar, Lowell Charles
Duncan, Hal. *See* Bergh, Arthur F.
Duncan, Slim. *See* Duncan, Harry (A.)
Duncan, Trevor. *See* Trebilco, Leonard (Charles)
Dunck, Professor. *See* Rice, Al(an Richard)
Dunham, By. *See* Dunham, William (D.)
Dunham, Sonny. *See* Dunham, Elmer Lewis
Dunn, Blind Eddie. *See* Massaro, Salvatore
Dunn, Blind Willie. *See* Massaro, Salvatore
Dunn, Joe. *See* Grey, Frank H(erbert)
Dunn, Peter. *See* Suarez Gomez, Julian-Mario
Dunne-Wassail. *See* Campbell, Alexander
Dunoyer du Gaucquier, Alard. *See* Gaucquier, Alard (Dunoyer du)
Dunsmore, William. *See* Ehret, Walter (Charles)
Dunstable, John. *See* Dunstaple, John
Duntede, Simon. *See* Tunstede, Simon
Dupain George. *See* Procacci, Giuseppe
Du Parc, Leon. *See* Stephens, Ward
Dupont, Jacques. *See* Viau, Albert
Dupont, Paul. *See* Haenschen, Walter (G(ustave))
Du Pont, Paul. *See* Zamecnik, J(ohn) S(tepan)
Dupré, Den(n)is. *See* Rawlings, Charles Arthur
Dupre, Robert. *See* Schaeffer, Don(ald)

– E –

Eastburn. *See* Winner, Septimus
Eastman, A. J. *See* Cooke, James Francis
Easy-E(ric). *See* Wright, Eric
Eaton, M. B. *See* Barnard, George D(aniel)
Eaton, M. B. *See* Hofmann, George D.
Eaton, M. B. *See* Scouton, Will(iam H.)
Eaves, Robert. *See* Gregson, Edward
Ebbaac, G. *See* Crabbe, George
Ebbare, G. *See* Crabbe, George
Ebeling-Filhés, E. B. *See* Ebeling, Elisabeth
Ebeling-Filhés, E. B. *See* Lehmann, Bertha (née Filhés)
Ebenezer. *See* Hupton, Job
Ebenezer. *See* Lee, Richard
Eberhard. *See* Württemberg, Eberhard von
Eberhardt, Wolfgang. *See* Steffen, Wolfgang
Eberst, Jacques. *See* Eberst, Jacob
Ebony Nora Bays, The. *See* Howard, Ethel
Ebony Stick of Dynamite, The. *See* Wells, Viola (Gertrude)
Ebreo, (L'). *See* Rossi, Salomone
Ebsen, Buddy. *See* Ebsen, Christian (Rudolph [or Rudolf]), (Jr.)
Echner, Hansi. *See* Haller, Hanne
Eck, Tobias. *See* Brygann, Ernst
Ecker, W. R. *See* Wedderburn, Robin
Ecker, Wenzel. *See* Gericke, Wilhelm
Eckhardt, Rudolf. *See* Sartorio, Arnoldo
Eckstein, Ernest. *See* Lindemann, Wilhelm
Eckstine, Billy. *See* Eckstein, William Clarence
Ecnerolf. *See* Florence
Eddy, George. *See* Paxton, George
Eddy, Miriam. *See* Johnson, Miriam
Eddy, Ted. *See* Simonetti, Ted Eddy
Eddy, Walter. *See* Edelstein, Walter
Edelmann, Alberto [or Adolfo]. *See* Albertoni, Azzo
Eden, Hirem. *See* Rimmer, William
Eden, Rock. *See* Carlin, Sidney (Alan)
Ederer, Pepe. *See* Ederer, Josef
Edesimo, Evandro. *See* Salio, Giuseppe
Edgar, Al. *See* Owens, Alvis Edgar, Jr.
Edgar, Lewis. *See* Jones, Lewis Ellis
Edgar Wallace of Songwriters, The. *See* Wright, Lawrence
Edge, (The). *See* Evans, David [or Dave]
Edgy, Wardore. *See* Gorey, Edward (St. John)
Edison, Sweets. *See* Edison, Harry (E.)
Edith Piaf of Country America, The. *See* Pugh, Virginia Wynette
Edmiston, James. *See* Cain, Noble
Edmond. *See* Rochefort-Luçay, Claude-Louis-Marie, marquis de
Edmonde, Philipp. *See* Philipp, Isidor (Edmond)
Edmonds, Lizzie. *See* Crosby, Fanny [i.e., Frances] J(ane)
Edmonton, (Dennis). *See* McCrohan, Dennis Eugene
Edmund, Charles. *See* Pearson, C(harles) E(dmund)
Edmunds, John. *See* St. Edmunds, John (1913-1986)
Edmunds, Lidie H. *See* Hewitt, Eliza Edmunds (Stites)
Edmunds, Lizzie. *See* Crosby, Fanny [i.e., Frances] J(ane)
Edschmid, Kasimir. *See* Schmid, Eduard Hermann Wilhelm
Edson. *See* Guzmán Yañez, Enrique
Edstrom, Hal. *See* Edstrom, Harold
Edstrom, Leonard. *See* Edstrom, Everett
Edu. *See* Elgar, (Sir) Edward
Edward, Jette. *See* Rollins, Lanier
Edward, Jimmy. *See* Vickers, James Edward
Edwards, Billy. *See* Finkelstein, Abe
Edwards, Broughton. *See* Meredith, I(saac) H(ickman)
Edwards, Bud. *See* Flurie, Edward (Cletus)
Edwards, Butterbeans. *See* Edwards, Joe [or Jody]
Edwards, Cameron. *See* Cain, Noble
Edwards, Charles. *See* Bester, Henry Lee
Edwards, Charles. *See* Lake, M(ayhew) L(ester)
Edwards, Clara. *See* Gerlich, Clara
Edwards, Frank. *See* Loomis, Harvey Worthington
Edwards, George. *See* Gruenberg, Louis
Edwards, Gus. *See* Simon, Gus(tav(e)) [or Augustus] (Edward)
Edwards, Honeyboy. *See* Edwards, David
Edwards, J. E. *See* Sankey, Ira David
Edwards, J. V. *See* Higginson, J(oseph) Vincent
Edwards, J. Walter. *See* Haenschen, Walter (G(ustave))
Edwards, Jackie. *See* Edwards, Wilfred
Edwards, Jimmy. *See* Bullington, James Wiley
Edwards, Joe. *See* Schalin, Adalbert
Edwards, Jonathan. *See* Wetstein, Paul (R., Jr.)
Edwards, Julian. *See* Barnard, D'Auvergne
Edwards, L. S. *See* Lorenz, E(dmund) S(imon)
Edwards, Lizzie. *See* Crosby, Fanny [i.e., Frances] J(ane)
Edwards, Mack B. *See* Marks, Edward B.
Edwards, Mark B. *See* Marks, Edward B.
Edwards, Michael. *See* Slowitzky, Michael
Edwards, Mon. *See* White, Sylvia
Edwards, Powell. *See* Polla, William C.
Edwards, Raymond. *See* Lincoln, Harry J.
Edwards, Rolf. *See* Behm, Eduard
Edwards, Simon. *See* Simon, Gus(tav(e)) [or Augustus] (Edward)
Edwards, Steven. *See* Maxwell, Eddie
Edwards, Stoney. *See* Edwards, Frenchy
Edwards, Tex. *See* Edwards, Thomas Jay
Edwards, Thomas. *See* Finkelstein, Abe
Edwards, Tom. *See* Kaufman, Isidore
Eff, Roy. *See* Culbertson, Roy Frederich
Eflor, W. *See* Rolfe, Walter (L.)
Egerton, Randolph. *See* Beswick, Harry
Egge, Ray. *See* Agee, Ray(mond Clinton)
Egghard, Jules [or Julius]. *See* Hardegen, (Count) Julius

Egidio da Tempo. *See* Pittaluga, Egidio [or Eligio]
Eginetico, Cornante. *See* Frugoni, Carlo Innocenzo
Egisippo Argolide. *See* Lanfranchi Rossi, Carlo Giuseppi
Egk, Werner. *See* Mayer, Werner
Egressy, Béni. *See* Galambos, Benjamin
Eguchi, Yoshi. *See* Eguchi, Gengo
Ehrenberg, Franz. *See* Claudius, Georg Karl
Ehrenmitglied der Gesellschaft. *See* Hummel, Johann Nepomuk
Ehrenreich, Teddy. *See* Ehrenreich, Rudolph
Ehrlich, A. *See* Payne, Albert
Ehtorg, Carl. *See* Grothe, Wilhelm
Eichelberger, O. B. *See* Kunkel, Charles
Eifel, Ferdinand [or Ferdi]. *See* Franchi, Ferdinand
Eight-Ulcer on a Four-Ulcer Job (or Pay), An. *See* Hume, Paul (Chandler)
Eik, Florian. *See* Layer, Wolfgang
Eilenberg, F. *See* Ailbout, Hans
Eilenburg, R. *See* Kunkel, Charles
Eily, Jerry. *See* Paramor, Norman [or Norrie] (William)
Einegg, Erich. *See* Wyneken, Wulff
Einstein of Jazz, The. *See* Armstrong, (Daniel) Louis
Eisenberg, Sylvia White. *See* White, Sylvia
Eitel, Paul. *See* Lehmann, Eitel
Eitemal. *See* Erlank, Willem Jacobus du Plooy
Ekberg, Buddha. *See* Ekberg, Ulf
Ekberg, Joker. *See* Ekberg, Ulf
Ekpe, Samuel. *See* Akpabot, Samuel Ekpe
El Loco. *See* Palmieri, Eduardo [or Edward, or Eddie]
El Nathan. *See* Whittle, (Major) D(aniel) W(ebster)
El Oso. *See* Berto, Augusto Pedro
Elbrecht, William. *See* Kunkel, Charles
Elbrown. *See* Thomas, Lillian [or Lillyn]
Elder Statesman, The. *See* Rajonsky [or Rajonski], Milton Michael
Elder Statesman of Jazz, The. *See* Carter, Bennett L(ester)
Elder Statesman of Ragtime. *See* Blake, James Hubert
Eldritch, Andrew. *See* Taylor, Andrew William Harvey
Elechar, Luigi. *See* Rachele, Luigi
Electronic Music Man, The. *See* Babbitt, Milton
Elegant Hoosier Tunesmith, The. *See* Porter, Cole
Elegante de la Salsa, El. *See* Romero, Roberto
Eleuter. *See* Iwaszkiewicz, Jaroslaw
Eleven and a Half Yards of Personality. *See* Hawkins, Harold Franklin
Elfed. *See* Lewis, Howell Elvet
Elger, Bob. *See* Kovac, Roland
Elgo, Carl. *See* Ogle, Charles H.
Elia. *See* Lamb, Charles
Eliakim. *See* Hupton, Job
Elias, S. *See* Tonizzo, Angelo
Elidora, Donna. *See* Wuiet, Caroline
Elin, Hanns. *See* Jelinek, Hanuš [or Johann]
Eliodd. *See* Oddone Sulli-Rao, Elisabetta
Eliot, George -*see* Cross, Mary Ann [or Marian]
Eliot, James. *See* Crosby, Fanny [i.e., Frances] J(ane)
Elkan, K(arl). *See* Dilthey, Wilhelm (Christian Ludwig)
Elkins, Charles. *See* Ehret, Walter (Charles)
Elkins, Charles. *See* Kinsman, Elmer (F(ranklin))
Ell. *See* Loud, Emily L.
Ell, Ly N. *See* Hampton, Lionel (Leo)
Ellacott, S(ydney). *See* Taylor, Helen
Ellen, Robert. *See* Shad, Bob
Eller, William. *See* Barnes, Clifford (Paulus)
Ellerton, John Lodge. *See* Lodge, John
Ellington, Duke. *See* Ellington, Edward Kennedy
Ellington, L. W. *See* Wellington, Larry
Elliot, Z. G. *See* Keller, Edward McDonald
Elliott, Braxton. *See* Floyd, Stafford Marquette
Elliott, Buck. *See* Adnopoz, Elliott Charles
Elliott, David. *See* Stingle, David Elliot
Elliott, Don. *See* Helfman, Donald Elliott
Elliott, Jack. *See* Adnopoz, Elliott Charles
Elliott, Jack. *See* Zucker, Irwin Elliott
Elliott, John (M.). *See* Zucker, Irwin Elliott
Elliott, Joseph. *See* Finkelstein, Abe
Elliott, Joseph. *See* Slaughter, M(arion) T(ry)
Elliott, Lionel. *See* Williams, Joseph (Benjamin)
Elliott, M(artin) A. *See* Gabriel, Charles H(utchinson)
Elliott, Misdemeanor. *See* Elliott, Melissa
Elliott, Missy. *See* Elliott, Melissa
Elliott, Ramblin' Jack. *See* Adnopoz, Elliott Charles
Elliott, Zo. *See* Elliott, Alonzo
Ellis. *See* Kobylinsky, Lev L'vovich
Ellis, Alexander J(ohn). *See* Sharpe, Alexander J(ohn)
Ellis, Big Boy. *See* Ellis, Wilbert Thirkield
Ellis, Big Chief. *See* Ellis, Wilbert Thirkield
Ellis, Joseph. *See* Spaulding, G(eorge) L(awson)
Ellis, Lee. *See* Peery, Rob Roy
Ellis, Norton. *See* Schoenefeld, Henry
Ellis, Seymour. *See* Rawlings, Charles Arthur
Ellis, Vep. *See* Ellis, Vesphew Benton
Ellison, Glenn. *See* Ehret, Walter (Charles)
Ellison, Sydney. *See* Greenleaf, George William
Ellsworth. *See* Moss, E(llsworth) F(rancis)
Ellsworth, George. *See* Hawkins, George E.
Ellsworth, Mark. *See* Eckstein, Maxwell
Ellwood, Albert. *See* Griselle, Thomas (Ellwood)
Ellwood, Albert. *See* Young, Victor
Elman, Harry. *See* Finkelman, Harry
Elman, Ziggy. *See* Finkelman, Harry
Elmar, Carl [or Karl]. *See* Swiedack, Karl
Elms, Leon. *See* Procházka, Rudolf, Freiherr von
Elpinor. *See* Szymanowski, Karol
Elpons, W. [or E.] d'. *See* Hanisch, Carl
Elsen, C. *See* Frangkiser, Carl (Moerz)
Elsie, Jean. *See* Stern, Elsie Jean
Elterlein, Ernst von. *See* Gottschald, Ernest [or Ernst]

Elton, Ernest. *See* Bucalossi, (Procida) Ernest (Luigi)
Elton, Fred. *See* Seigle, Fred Elton
Elvis Presley of the Gypsies, The. *See* Stevens, Sam
Elvis the Pelvis. *See* Presley, Elvis A(a)ron
Elvisology. *See* Presley, Elvis A(a)ron
Ely, S. N. *See* Bliss, P(hilip) Paul
Elysio, Flavio. *See* Dinarte, Silvio [or Sylvio]
Embree, Riff. *See* Embree, Charles B., Jr.
Emden. *See* Räder, Gustav (Adolf)
Emerson, C. D. *See* Gabriel, Charles H(utchinson)
Emerson, Francis. *See* Collins, William Francis
Emerson, J(ohn). *See* Bliss, P(hilip) Paul
Emerson, Stewart B. *See* Anthony, Bert R.
Emilchen, (R.). *See* Rosendorff, Emil
Eminem. *See* Mathers, Marshall (Bruce), III
Emmelar. *See* Richards, Henry Brinley
Emmerson, H. *See* Zoeller, Carli [or Karl]
Emmet, Leo. *See* Mannes, Leo (Ezekiel)
Emmit, Old Dan D. *See* Emmett, Dan(iel Decatur)
Emperor of the Waltz. *See* Strauss, Johann (Baptist), (Sr.) (1804-1949)
Emperor of the Waltz. *See* Strauss, Johann (Baptist), (Jr.) (1825-1899)
Emperor of the World. *See* Kador, Ernest, Jr.
Empress of the Blues. *See* Smith, Elizabeth
Encina, Juan del. *See* Fermoselle, Juan de
Engel, Heinrich. *See* Engelmann, H(ans)
Engel, Joel. *See* Engel, Julius (Dimitrievich)
Engel, Valentine. *See* Engel, Hartmut
Engel, Y(uly). *See* Engel, Julius (Dimitrievich)
Engelsberg, E(duard) S(chön). *See* Schön, Eduard (Ritter von)
England Dan. *See* Seals, Dan (Wayland)
England's Greatest Composer. *See* Elgar, (Sir) Edward S(eymour)
England's Greatest Composer. *See* Purcell, Henry
England's Greatest Composer. *See* Sullivan, (Sir) Arthur
England's Greatest Hymn Writer. *See* Wesley, Charles
England's Lost Composer. *See* Moeran, E(rnest) J(ohn)
England's Most Distinguished Music Critic. *See* Roberts, William (Amos)
Engle, Carl. *See* De Witt, Louis O.
English Bach, The. *See* Bach, Johann Christian
English Debussy, The. *See* Scott, Cyril (Meir)
English, Jack. *See* Parker, Alfred Thomas
English Mendelssohn, The. *See* Bennett, William Sterndale
English Mozart, The. *See* Bishop, (Sir) Henry R(owley)
English Mozart. *See* Wesley, Samuel
English Palestrina, The. *See* Gibbons, Orlando
English Sappho, The. *See* Landon, Letitia Elizabeth (née Maclean)
English Schubert, The. *See* Cowen, Frederic Hymen
English Waltz King, The. *See* Joyce, Archibald
Enlovely, Swede. *See* Shavers, Charlie [i.e., Charles] (James)
Enoch, Frederick. *See* Howarth, Ellen C(lementine) (née Doran)
Enotrio Romano. *See* Carducci, Giosuè
Enríquez, Luis. *See* Bacalov, Luis Enríquez
Ensildo Prosindio. *See* Petrosellini, Giuseppe
Ensor, James (Herb). *See* Deuringer, Hubert [or Herbert] (Martin)
Epae, Jay. *See* Epae, Nicholas
Epic Soundtracks. *See* Godfrey, Kevin Paul
Epigonos. *See* Gjellerup, Karl Adolph
Epigram, Ephraim, Esq. *See* Pitman, Ambrose
Episcopus, Melchior. *See* Bischoff, Melchior
Epitome of the Kentucky Mountain Songster. *See* Kazee, Buell (Hilton)
Epstein, George. *See* Kaufman, Isidore
Eques (Auratus) Romanus. *See* Lorenzini
Erard, Jean. *See* Erhardt, Siegfried (Marian Johann)
Erasmo. *See* Esteves, Erasmo
Erckmann-Chatrian, (MM). *See* Chatrian, Pierre Alexandre
Erckmann-Chatrian, (MM). *See* Erckmann, Emile
Eremit, Paul. *See* Winkler, Gerhard
Eremita, Giulio. *See* Giusberti, Giulio
Ergo Sum. *See* Ballard, Louis W(ayne)
Erhardt, Otto. *See* Erhenhaus, Martin
Eric B. *See* Barrier, Eric
Eric, Hans. *See* Conzelmann, Hans
Erich, Carl. *See* Baines, William
Erich, Carl. *See* Biehl, Albert
Erich, Carl. *See* Foote, Arthur (William)
Erich, Carl. *See* Krentzlin, H. Richard
Erich, Carl. *See* Lynes, Frank
Erich, Carl. *See* Norden, Hugo (Svan)
Erich, Carl. *See* Parlow, Edmund
Erich, Carl. *See* Scott, Charles P(hillip)
Erich, F. *See* Parlow, Edmund
Erich, Georg. *See* Messner, Georg
Ericincio, Craeto. *See* Ottoboni, Pietro
Erick and Parrish Making Dollars. *See* Sermon, Erick
Erick and Parrish Making Dollars. *See* Smith, Parrish
Erickson, Roky. *See* Erickson, Roger Kynard
Ericreo. *See* Gasparini, Francesco
Ericson, Julia. *See* Farmer, Marjorie
Ericson, Julia. *See* Leisy, James (Franklin)
Eridanus. *See* Heyl, Manfred
Erimanteo, Arcomelo. *See* Corelli, Arcangelo
Eriso. *See* Gualzetti, G. A.
Erlando, J. *See* Ehrlinger, Hans
Erlo, Louis. *See* Camerlo, Louis
Ermelinda Talea (Pastorella Arcada). *See* Maria Antonia Walpurgis
Ermend-Bonnal. *See* Bonnal, (Joseph) Ermend
Ermino, Cucio. *See* Vasori, Claude

Erna. *See* Adler, Hans
Ernest, Charles. *See* Bagge, Charles Ernest, Baron de
Ernest, J. J. *See* Goldner, Ernest (Siegmund)
Ernest, K. *See* Mahr, Curt
Ernest, Paul. *See* Gottschalk, Louis Moreau
Ernesti, Hans. *See* Ailbout, Hans
Ernst, Günther. *See* Schenckendorff, Leopold (Adalbert Günther Heinrich von)
Erpel, (Karl). *See* Glahé, Will(y Karl Adolf)
Errante, L'. *See* Tortamano, Nicola
Erranti (de Napoli). *See* Artale, Giuseppe
Erratic Star, The. *See* Giornovichi, Giovanni Mane
Errats. *See* Wohlmuth, Alois
Errhy-Daly, E. *See* Harrhy, Edith
Errol, Leon. *See* Simms, Leonce Errol
Ertis. *See* Esterhazy, (Countess) Alexandrine
Erville, Henri d'. *See* Roussel, Henri
Erwachsende, Der. *See* Glasenap, Joachim von
Erwin, Franz Theodor. *See* Kugler, Franz (Theodore)
Erwin, Otto. *See* Guttmann, Artur
Erwin, Pee Wee. *See* Erwin, George
Erwin, Ralph. *See* Vogl, Ralph Erwin
Eryl, Blanche. *See* Phillips, Jane Josephine
Erythraeus, J(anus) N(icius). *See* Rossi, G(iovanni) V(ittorio)
Escardot, L. *See* Karr y de Alfonsetti, Carmen
Escarlate [or Escarlati], Domingo. *See* Scarlatti, (Giuseppi) Dominico
Eschborn, Nina. *See* Eschborn, Georgine Christine M.
Escopette. *See* Toché, Raoul
Esete. *See* Anderson, Alpharita Constantia
Esipoff, Stepán [or Stephen]. *See* Burnand, Arthur Bransby
Esmeralda, Santa. *See* Petit, Jean-Claude
Espagnoletto. *See* Spagnoetti (della Diana), Paolo (Ludovico)
Españoleto, El. *See* Garcia (Fajer), Francisco Javier
Espina, Noni. *See* Espina, Angel Beaunoni
Esprit, Charlotte. *See* Krumpholtz, Fanny
Esrom, D. A. *See* Strandberg, (Alfreda) Theodora
Esrum-Hellerup, Dag Henrik. [fictitious composer]
Essex. *See* Foerster, Josef Bohuslav
Essex, David. *See* Cook, David (Albert)
Essex, J. B. *See* Burton, John, (Jr.) (1803-1877)
Essex, Kenneth. *See* Isaacs, Rufus
Estébanez, Joaquín. *See* Tamayo y Baus, Manuel
Estéfano. *See* Salgado (Mejía), Fabio
Esterbrook, Myron. *See* Sartorio, Arnoldo
Esterel, (Jacques). *See* Martin, Charles (Henri)
Esterio. *See* Zaniboni, Antonio
Estes, Richard. *See* Dickey, Richard Scott
Estores de Galanta. *See* Eszterházy von Galántha, Paul
Estrange, Joseph l'. *See* Mérimée, Prosper
Estvilla, Manuel. *See* Plessow, Erich
Eteoclide, Anfione. *See* Jommelli, Niccolò
Etienne. *See* Jouy, (Victor Joseph) Etienne (de)
Ettrick Shepherd, The. *See* Hogg, James
Etzel, Roy. *See* Etzel, Hans Joachim
Eugène. *See* Planard, Françoise Antoinde Eugène
Eugene, Max C. *See* Dreyfus, Max
Eupidio Siriano. *See* Giuvo, Nicolà [or Nicolò]
Euripides of Italian Opera, The. *See* Verdi, Giuseppe
Europe's Queen of the Piano. *See* Wieck, Clara Josephine
Eusebius. *See* Schumann, Robert
Eustic, Richard. *See* Slaughter, M(arion) T(ry)
Evander, H. *See* Guttmann, Hermann
Evangelical Rock's Court Jester. *See* Taylor, (Roland) Steve
Evangelist for Ragtime, The. *See* Stark, John (Stillwell)
Evans, Butch. *See* Evans, William Robert, III
Evans, Dale. *See* Smith, Frances Octavia
Evans, Doc. *See* Evans, Paul Wesley
Evans, Francis. *See* Crow(e), Francis Luther
Evans, Frank. *See* Finkelstein, Abe
Evans, Frank(lin). *See* Robison, Carson J(ay)
Evans, Frank. *See* Slaughter, M(arion) T(ry)
Evans, Gil. *See* Green, (Ian) Ernest Gilmore
Evans, H. *See* Peretti, Hugo (Emil)
Evans, Hal. *See* Slaughter, M(arion) T(ry)
Evans, Hardy. *See* Szekeres, Ferenc [or François]
Evans, Honey Boy. *See* Evans, George
Evans, J. *See* Frangkiser, Carl (Moerz)
Evans, Jean M(arie). *See* Palumbo, Camille Marie
Evans, Jimmy. *See* Stulberger, James
Evans, Jody. *See* Hooven, Marilyn (K.)
Evans, Mark. *See* Tidman, Paul Frederick
Evans, Mark. *See* Westendorf, Omer
Evans, Redd. *See* Evans, Louis
Evans, Richard. *See* Kunitz, Richard (E.)
Evans, Tolchard (B.). *See* Evans, Sydney
Evans, Willie. *See* Horton, (George) Vaughn
Evarts, Ralph. *See* Blood, Lizette Emma
Evelyn. *See* Russell, (Lady) Rachel Evelyn
Evelyn, Julius. *See* Eibenschütz, Julius
Everage, (Dame) Edna. *See* Humphries, (John) Barry
Everard, S. *See* Cunio, Angelo
Everett, Horace. *See* Johnston, Horace Eugene
Everette, Bill. *See* Justis(s), William [or Bill] E(verette?), (Jr.)
Everette, Leon. *See* Baughman, Leon Everette
Evergreen, Johnny. *See* Green, John(ny) (W(aldo))
Everlast. *See* Schrody, Eric
Evers, J. Clifford. *See* Westendorf, Omer
Everson, Lottie. *See* Kimbrough, Lottie
Evil Genius of Jazz. *See* Davis, Miles (Dewey), (III)
Ewaldt. *See* Hintz, Ewaldt
Ewing, Skip. *See* Ewing, Donald Ralph
Ex Monaco. *See* Marsand, Luigi

Exene. *See* Cervenka, Christine
Exhortationist of the *New York Times*. *See* Quigley, Edwin Olin, Jr.
Exile. *See* Welby, Anna Marie (of Louisville)
Expertus Rupertus Ländler, bauer von Adlersee. *See* Beer, Johann
Explosive Mr. Brown, The. *See* Brown, James
Exponent of Futurism, The. *See* Antheil, George
Exposito, Mimo. *See* Exposito, Homero
Expromptus. *See* Safránek, Miloš
Eyck, Lloyd Ten. *See* Ackley, B(entley) D(eForrest)
Eyton, Andrew. *See* Jones, Graham
Ezl, M(anfred). *See* Raich, Heribert

– F –

F. *See* Crosby, Fanny [i.e., Frances] J(ane)
F. *See* Fanch, James
F. *See* Littledale, Richard Frederick
F s. *See* Fellows, John
F. A. N. *See* Crosby, Fanny [i.e., Frances] J(ane)
F. B. *See* Boott, Francis
F. C. *See* Crosby, Fanny [i.e., Frances] J(ane)
F. C. A. *See* Enders, Karl
F. D***. *See* Desessart, Fréderic
FFF. *See* Ondrasik, John
F. J. C. *See* Croger, Frederick Julian
F. J. C. *See* Crosby, Fanny [i.e., Frances] J(ane)
F. J. P. *See* Partridge, (Mrs.) F. J.
F. J. V. A. *See* Crosby, Fanny [i.e., Frances] J(ane)
F. J. V. J. *See* Crosby, Fanny [i.e., Frances] J(ane)
F. M. L. H. *See* Hunter, Florence M. L.
F. P. *See* Williams, Joseph (Benjamin)
F. R. *See* Littledale, Richard Frederick
F. R. *See* Rausch, Frederick
F. R. *See* Statham, Francis Reginald
F. S. *See* Sewall, Frank
F. V. *See* Ana, Francesco d'
F. W. *See* Weissensee, Friedrich
F. X. A. M. *See* Murschhauser, Franz Xaver Anton
Faber, Ed. *See* Robison, Carson J(ay)
Faber, Jean. *See* Van Brockhoven, John (A.)
Faber Stapulensis, Jacobus. *See* Lefèvre (d'Etaples), Jacques
Fabius. *See* Bowles, William Lisle
Fabri, Henrici. *See* Faber, Heinrich
Fabric, Bent. *See* Fabricus-Bjerre, Bent
Fabricius, Georg. *See* Goldschmidt, Georg
Fabricius, Petrus. *See* Schmidt, Peter
Fabricius, Werner. *See* Schmid, Peter
Fabro, Louis. *See* Schmidseder, Ludwig
Fad Gadget. *See* Tovey, Frank
Fadden, Bill. *See* Burke, Joseph Francis
Faerber, Fr. *See* Kern, Carl Wilhelm
Fagan, Dell. *See* Fagan, Thomas O.
Fagan, Eleanor. *See* Harris, Eleanora
Fagot. *See* Sokal'sky, Petro Petrovich
Fahrbach, Phillip. *See* Tobani, Theodore Moses
Fahrbach-Tobani. *See* Tobani, Theodore Moses
Faifer von Faifersberg. *See* Winkler, Karl [or Carl] Gottfried Theodor
Fain, Sammy. *See* Feinberg, Samuel
Fairbanks, J(onathan). *See* Clarke, Henry Leland
Fairchild, Cooky. *See* Fairchild, Edgar
Fairchild, Edgar. *See* Suskind, Milton
Fairfield, Frank [or Franz]. *See* Bornschein, Franz (Carl)
Fairfield, Frank. *See* Liddle, Samuel
Fairstar, (Mrs.). *See* Horne, Richard Henry
Faison, Josephine. *See* Profitt, Josephine (née Moore)
Faith, Adam. *See* Nelhams, Terence
Fakaerti, Sgr. *See* Chambray, Louis François
Falanca, Albino. *See* Zanardini, Angelo
Falco. *See* Hölzel, Johann [or Hans]
Falconer, Edmund. *See* O'Rourke, Edmund (Falconer)
Falconer, James. *See* Kirkup, James (Falconer)
Falconer, Roderick. *See* Taylor, Rod(erick)
Falconio d'Asola. *See* Falconi(o), Placido
Falk, Peter. *See* Weiss, Erwin
Falkenberg, IC. *See* Schmidt, Ralf
Fall, Albert. *See* Kountz, Richard
Falls, Ruby. *See* Dorsey, Bertha (Annabelle) (Gay)
Faltis, Dalibor C. *See* Vačkář, Dalibor C(yril)
Faltys, Pip. *See* Vačkář, Dalibor C(yril)
Falzari, Felix. *See* Hoffmann, Hans
Fame, Georgie. *See* Powell, Clive
Familia, Pochy. *See* Familia, Alfonso
Fanatical Music Lover, A. *See* Ottoboni, Pietro
Fancelle, J. *See* Binetti, Giovanni
Fancello, Giovanni Battista di. *See* Binetti, Giovanni
Fanchon. *See* Wolff, Fanny
Faneau, H. *See* Ailbout, Hans
Fanidi, Theo. *See* Theofanidis, Iraklis [or Hercules] (B.)
Fannie. *See* Crosby, Fanny [i.e., Frances] J(ane)
Fanny. *See* Crosby, Fanny [i.e., Frances] J(ane)
Fanny Crosby of Sweden. *See* Sandell(-Berg), Karolina [or Carolina] Wilhelmina
Fanta, Josef. *See* Hering, Hans
Fanta, Will. *See* Klebba, Werner
Fantastic Baggys. *See* Lipkin, Stephen [or Steve] (Barri [or Barry])
Fantastic Baggys. *See* Schlein, Phil(lip Gary)
Färber, Gottlieb. *See* Tieck, (Johann) Ludwig
Färbers, Johannes. *See* Tinctoris, Johannes
Fardd, Eben. *See* Thomas, Ebenezer
Fardiola, Il. *See* La Greca, Antonio
Fardon, Don. *See* Maughn, Don(ald)
Fare, Florence. *See* Rawlings, Alfred William
Fare, Florence. *See* Tobani, Theodore Moses
Fargo, Donna. *See* Vaughan, Yvonne

Farian, Frank. *See* Reuther, Franz
Farin. *See* Hinsdale, Grace Webster (née Haddock)
Farineli, Giuseppe (Francesco). *See* Finco, Giuseppe Francesco
Farinelli [or Farinello]. *See* Broschi, Carlo
Farinetta, La. *See* Camati, Maria
Fariss, Michael. *See* Munn, William O.
Farlowe, Chris. *See* Deighton, John Henry
Farmer, J. M. *See* Farmer, Marjorie
Farnes, Ellsworth. *See* Cain, Noble
Farningham, Marianne. *See* Hearn(e), Mary Ann(e)
Farnsworth, Larry. *See* Setaro, Pete(r) (D(onald))
Faro. *See* Aznar, Abel (Mariano)
Farr, Hugh. *See* Farr, Thomas Hubert
Farr, Sebastian. *See* Blom, Eric Walter
Farrell, Edwin. *See* Riegger, Wallingford (Constantin)
Farrell, Hastings Gilbert. *See* Farrell, Michael John
Farrell, James. *See* Frangkiser, Carl (Moerz)
Farrell, Toni. *See* Travers, Alison
Farrell, Wes. *See* Fogel, Wes(ley)
Farrère, Claude. *See* Bargon(e), (Frédéric) Charles (Pierre Edouard)
Farrow, Jesse Oris. *See* Powers, Chester [or Chet]
Farrow, Johnny. *See* Faracchio, John Joseph, Jr.
Fascinato, Jack. *See* Fascinato, Arthur L.
Fasolo, Il. *See* Manelli, Francesco
Fast Fingers. *See* Dawkins, James [or Jimmy] (Henry)
Fastest Guitar in the Country, The. *See* Bryant, (Ivy) James [or Jimmy]
Fat One, The. *See* Gleason, Herbert John
Fatalis. *See* Castelli, Ignaz Franz
Fatboy Slim. *See* Cook, Quentin
Father. *See* Brown, Timothy
Father Andrew. *See* Hardy, H. E.
Father MC. *See* Brown, Timothy
Father of American Ballad and Poetry, The. *See* Hewitt, John (Henry) Hill
Father of American Church Music, The. *See* Mason, Lowell
Father of American Drama, The. *See* Dunlap, William
Father of American Literature. *See* Irving, Washington
Father of American Minstrelsy, The. *See* Rice, Thomas Dartmouth
Father of American Music. *See* Billings, William
Father of American Music. *See* Carr, Benjamin
Father of American Music. *See* Ives, Charles Edward
Father of American Musical Comedy, The. *See* Cohan, George M(ichael)
Father of American Musical Magazines. *See* Dwight, John Sullivan
Father of American Opera, The. *See* Fry, William H(enry)
Father of American Opera. *See* Gershvin, Jacob
Father of American Opera. *See* Weill, Kurt
Father of American Orchestral Music, The. *See* Graupner, (Johann Christian) Gottlieb
Father of Anglican Church Music, The. *See* Purcell, Henry
Father of Arranging. *See* Grofé, Ferdé [i.e., Ferdinand] (Rudolph von)
Father of Australian Band Movement, The. *See* Bulch, Thomas Edward
Father of Australian Music. *See* Nathan, Isaac
Father of Bacchanalian Poetry, The. *See* Basselin, Olivier
Father of Band Music in America, The. *See* Coates, Thomas
Father of Band Music in America. *See* Reeves, D(avid) W(allis)
Father of Band Music in the U. S. A., The. *See* Reeves, D(avid) W(allis)
Father of Belgian Wind Music, The. *See* Gilson, Paul (1865-1942)
Father of Blue Grass, The. *See* Monroe, William [or Bill] (Smith)
Father of Bluegrass Gospel. *See* Story, Carl (Moore)
Father of Bohemian Music. *See* Černohorsky, Bohuslav Matej
Father of Bohemian Music. *See* Smetana, Bedřich
Father of Boogie-Woogie. *See* Yancey, James [or Jim(my)] (Edward)
Father of British Blues. *See* Korner, Alexis
Father of British Blues, The. *See* Mayall, John
Father of British Blues Revival. *See* Korner, Alexis
Father of British Light Music. *See* Coates, Eric
Father of British Modern Music, The. *See* Scott, Cyril (Meir)
Father of Chicano Music. *See* Guerrero, Eduardo
Father of Chicago Blues. *See* Morganfield, McKinley
Father of Christian Hymnology, The. *See* Ambrosius of Milan
Father of Christian Hymnology, The. *See* St. Hilary, Bishop of Portiers
Father of Christian Rock, The. *See* Norman, Larry
Father of Church Music, The. *See* Gauntlett, Henry John
Father of Church Music. *See* Tallis, Thomas
Father of Church Song. *See* Ambrosius of Milan
Father of Computer Music, The. *See* Mathews, Max V.
Father of Contemporary Italian Music. *See* Petrassi, Goffredo
Father of Country Music, The. *See* Monroe, William [or Bill] (Smith)
Father of Country Music, The. *See* Rodgers, James [or Jimmie] (Charles)
Father of Country Music, The. *See* Williams, Hir(i)am (King)
Father of Czech Band Music. *See* Kmoch, Frantisek
Father of Czech Music. *See* Smetana, Bedřich
Father of Danish Music. *See* Gade, Niels W.

Father of "Dixie," The. *See* Emmett, Dan(iel Decatur)
Father of "DJ Culture," The. *See* Reich, Stephen [or Steve] (Michael)
Father of Electronic Music. *See* Varèse, Edgard (Victor Achille Charles)
Father of English Cathedral Music, The. *See* Tallis, Thomas
Father of English Church Music. *See* Purcell, Henry
Father of English Music, The. *See* Tallis, Thomas
Father of English Opera, The. *See* Barnett, John
Father of English Opera. *See* Purcell, Henry
Father of English Song, The. *See* Caedmon
Father of Folk Opera. *See* Smetana, Bedřich
Father of Folk Rock. *See* Zimmerman, Robert Allen
Father of French Burlesque, The. *See* Scarron, Paul
Father of French Dramatic Music. *See* Lulli, Giovanni Battista
Father of French Opera. *See* Auber Daniel François Esprit
Father of French Opera. *See* Lulli, Giovanni Battista
Father of French Organ Music. *See* Franck, César
Father of German Humanist. *See* Huessman, Roelof [or Rudolf]
Father of German Music, The. *See* Schütz, Heinrich
Father of German Opera. *See* Weber, Carl Maria von
Father of German Songs. *See* Albert, Heinrich
Father of Ghanian Musicology, The. *See* Amu, Ephraim
Father of Gospel Music. *See* Dorsey, Thomas A(ndrew)
Father of Grand Opera. *See* Beer, Jakob Liebmann
Father of Greek Music, The. *See* Terpander (of Lesbo)
Father of Hillbilly Jazz. *See* Clements, Vassar Carlton
Father of Instrumentation. *See* Haydn, (Franz) Joseph
Father of Intergalactic Music, The. *See* Blount, Herman
Father of Italian Opera, The. *See* Mayr, Johann Simon
Father of Juju Music. *See* Dairo, I(saiah) K(ehinde)
Father of Lounge Music, (The). *See* Wetstein, Paul (R., Jr.)
Father of Methodist Hymnody, The. *See* Wesley, Charles
Father of Military Bands. *See* Gilmore, Patrick Sarsfield
Father of Minimalism. *See* Riley, Terry
Father of Modern Acoustics. *See* Chladni, Ernst Florens Friedrich
Father of Modern American Theater Music. *See* Kern, Jerome David
Father of Modern Comedy. *See* Goldoni, Carlo
Father of Modern Drama, The. *See* Ibsen, Henrick (Johan)
Father of Modern French Songs, The. *See* Panard, Charles-François
Father of Modern Gospel Music, The. *See* Dorsey, Thomas A(ndrew)
Father of Modern Harmony, The. *See* Josquin Desprez
Father of Modern Highlife. *See* Mensah, E(mmanuel) T(ettah)
Father of Modern Italian Comedy. *See* Goldoni, Carlo
Father of Modern Music, The. *See* Mozart, Wolfgang Amadeus
Father of Modern Music. *See* Schoenberg, Arnold
Father of Modern Orchestration. *See* Berlioz, Hector
Father of Modern Orchestration. *See* Haydn, (Franz) Joseph
Father of Modern Piano Music, The. *See* Bach, Johann Sebastian
Father of Modern Rock and Roll. *See* Johnson, Robert (Leroy) (1911-1938)
Father of Modern Synagogue Music. *See* Loewy, Salomon
Father of Modern Violin Playing. *See* Viotti, Giovanni Battista
Father of Modern Zairean Music, The. *See* Kabas(s)elé (Tshamala), Joseph
Father of Music, The. *See* Byrd, William
Father of Music, The. *See* Mauduit, Johannes
Father of Music, The. *See* Palestrina, Giovanni Pierluigi da
Father of Musical Acoustics, The. *See* Sauveur, Joseph
Father of Musical Comedy. *See* Cohan, George M(ichael)
Father of Musical Comedy, The. *See* Tanner, James T(olman)
Father of Musical Dissonance, The. *See* Cage, John (Milton), Jr.
Father of Musical Goodwill. *See* Spohr, Louis [actually Lud(e)wig]
Father of Musical Impressionism, The. *See* Debussy, Claude
Father of Musical Modernism. *See* Debussy, Claude
Father of Musical Nonsense, The. *See* Cage, John (Milton), Jr.
Father of Negative Music, The. *See* Schoenberg, Arnold
Father of Negro Songs, The. *See* Graupner, (Johann Christian) Gottlieb
Father of Opera. *See* Monteverdi, Claudio
Father of Opera Bouffe, The. *See* Ronger, (Louis Auguste Joseph) Florimond
Father of Opera Buffa. *See* Galuppi, Baldassare
Father of Opera Buffa. *See* Goldoni, Carlo
Father of Orchestral Music, The. *See* Haydn, (Franz) Joseph
Father of Orchestration, The. *See* Gabrieli, Giovanni
Father of Philadelphia Music. *See* Carr, Benjamin
Father of Polish Opera, The. *See* Boguslawski, Wojciech
Father of Polish Opera. *See* Moniuszko, Stanislaus
Father of Polish Theater, The. *See* Boguslawski, Wojciech
Father of Ragtime. *See* Harney, Ben(jamin) R(obertson)
Father of Ragtime in Shreveport, The. *See* O'Hare, William Christopher

Father of Ragtime Music, The. *See* Joplin, Scott
Father of Rap. *See* Williams, (Zeffrey) Andre
Father of Reggae Music. *See* Higgs, Joe
Father of Reggae Music. *See* Marley, Robert [or Bob] Nesta
Father of Rhumba, The. *See* Kabas(s)elé (Tshamala), Joseph
Father of Rock and Roll. *See* Johnson, Johnnie [or Johnny]
Father of Rock 'n' Roll, The. *See* Berry, Charles Edward Anderson
Father of Rock 'n' Roll. *See* Crudup, Arthur
Father of Rock 'n' Roll, The. *See* Haley, William [or Bill] (John Clifton), (Jr.)
Father of Rock-n-Roll, The. *See* Holley, Charles Hardin
Father of Rock 'n' Roll. *See* Presley, Elvis A(a)ron
Father of Romanticism. *See* Beethoven, Ludwig van
Father of Russian Music. *See* Glinka, Michael Ivanovitch
Father of Russian Opera. *See* Glinka, Michael Ivanovitch
Father of Russian Song, The. *See* Titov, Nikolay Alexeyevich
Father of Saint Louis Ragtime. *See* Turpin, Thomas Milli(o)n
Father of Song. *See* Orpheus of Thrace
Father of Song in Northern Virginia. *See* Funk, Joseph
Father of Soul. *See* Cook(e), Sam(uel)
Father of Soul. *See* Robinson, Ray Charles
Father of Stride Piano. *See* Johnson, James [or Jimmy, or Jimmie] (P(rice))
Father of Swedish Music, The. *See* Roman, Johan Helmich
Father of Swedish Music, The. *See* Rõmhild(t), Johann Theodor
Father of Swedish Song, The. *See* Lindblad, Adolf Fredrik
Father of Swiss Music. *See* Huber, Hans (1852-1921)
Father of Texas Folk. *See* Van Zandt, (John) Townes
Father of Texas Rock 'n' Roll. *See* Holley, Charles Hardin
Father of the American Ballad. *See* Hewitt, John (Henry) Hill
Father of the American Musical. *See* Kern, Jerome David
Father of the American Stage. *See* Dunlap, William
Father of the Blues, The. *See* Handy, W(illiam) C(hristopher)
Father of the British Blues. *See* Korner, Alexis (Andrew Nicholas)
Father of the British Blues, The. *See* Mayall John
Father of the British Blues Revival. *See* Korner, Alexis (Andrew Nicholas)
Father of the Classical Bandoneon, The. *See* Barletta, Alejandro
Father of the Czech Nationalist School of Composition, The. *See* Smetana, Bedřich
Father of the Czech Wind Band. *See* Kmoch, Frantisek
Father of the Hollywood Musical. *See* Guaragna, Salvatore
Father of the Marseillaise, The. *See* Rouget de Lisle, Claude Joseph
Father of the Military Band in Canada. *See* Vézina, (François) Joseph
Father of the Minstrel Show, The. *See* Emmett, Dan(iel Decatur)
Father of the Modern American Concert Band. *See* Gilmore, Patrick Sarsfield
Father of the Modern Ballet Score. *See* Tchaikovskii, Peter Illich
Father of the Modern Cantorate, The. *See* Sulzer, Salomon
Father of the Modern Guitar. *See* Tarrega(-Eixea), Francisco
Father of the Motown Sound. *See* Gordy, Berry, Jr.
Father of the New Cantata. *See* Krieger, Johann Philipp
Father of the New Sound, The. *See* Bacharach, Burt (F.)
Father of the New Tango. *See* Piazzolla, Astor
Father of the Oratorio, The. *See* Animuccia, Giovanni
Father of the Oratorio. *See* Carissimi, Giacomo
Father of the Orchestra. *See* Berlioz, Hector
Father of the Orchestra. *See* Haydn, (Franz) Joseph
Father of the "Philly Sound". *See* Montana, Vince, Jr.
Father of the Pianoforte, The. *See* Clementi, Muzio
Father of the Profession. *See* McCallum, Colin Whitton
Father of the Rondo, The. *See* Davaux, Jean Baptiste
Father of the Sonata. *See* Bach, Carl [or Karl] Philipp Emanuel
Father of the String Quartet. *See* Haydn, (Franz) Joseph
Father of the Symphony, The. *See* Haydn, (Franz) Joseph
Father of the Tango. *See* Villoldo (Arroyo), Angel (Gregorio)
Father of the Trombone Smear. *See* Fillmore, (James) Henry
Father of the Vaudeville, The. *See* Basselin, Olivier
Father of the Venetian School. *See* Willaert, Adrian
Father of the Waltz, The. *See* Strauss, Johann (Baptist), (Sr.) (1804-1849)
Father of Tin Pan Alley. *See* Harris, Charles K(assell)
Father of Truck Driving Songs. *See* Pedruska, David Darwin
Father of Twelve Tone Music, The. *See* Schoenberg, Arnold
Father of Vaudeville. *See* Keith, Benjamin F(ranklin)
Father of Western Beat, The. *See* Gilmore, Jimmie Dale
Fato. *See* Guzmán Yañez, Enrique
Fats. *See* Waller, Thomas Wright
Fattorin da Reggio. *See* Valla, Domenico

Faulkne. *See* Rawlings, Charles Arthur
Faulkner, Eric. *See* Dickson, Mary Hannah
Faust, Willy. *See* Stoeckart, Jan
Fausto. *See* Piedrahita Gaviria, Luis Javier
Favart, Marie Justine Benoîte. *See* Duronceray, Marie Justine Benoîte
Favello. *See* Satajewitsch, Alexandr Wiktorowitsch
Faventinus, Didymus. *See* Schwarzerd, Philipp
Favilli, Mario. *See* Fisher, William Arms
Favorite Female Country Music Singer (of Scandinavia). *See* Jackson, Wanda (Lavonne)
Favre, Jules. *See* Watson, William Michael
Fay, Sinclair. *See* Elliott, Marjorie (Reeve)
Faye, Roy. *See* Mantovani, A(nnuzio) P(aolo)
Faz. *See* Prestopnik, Irving Henry
Fazola, Butch. *See* Prestopnik, Irving Henry
Fazola, Irving. *See* Prestopnik, Irving Henry
Feahy, Michael. *See* Barnes, H(oward) E(llington)
Feahy, Michael. *See* Fields, Harold (Cornelius)
Feahy, Michael. *See* Roncoroni, Joseph (Dominic)
Feathers, Charles. *See* Lindberg, Charles Arthur
Fedele, (Daniele) Teofilo. *See* Treu, Daniel Gottlob
Federfechter, Gregorius von Lützen. *See* Finkelthaus, Gottfried
Federici, Camillo. *See* Viassolo, Giovan Battista
Feelgood, Doctor. *See* Hooker, John Lee
Feelgood, Dr. *See* Perryman, William [or Willie] Lee
Fegejo, Polisse(n)o. *See* Goldoni, Carlo
Feglio, Polisseno. *See* Goldoni, Carlo
Fehring, Johannes. *See* Fernbach, Johannes
Feigenbaum, Ziske. *See* Feigenbaum, Benjamin
Felby, Celeta. *See* Hart, Cynthia Mary Kathleen
Feld, Julius. *See* Megerle, Julius
Feld, Leo. *See* Hirschfeld, Leo [or Ludwig]
Feld, W. S. *See* Sommerfeld, Willy
Felder, Hans. *See* Lengsfelder, Hans
Feldman(n), J. *See* Henrich, C. W.
Feldman, Tony. *See* Hyman, Richard [or Dick] (R(oven))
Feldstein, Sandy. *See* Feldstein, Saul
Felious, Odetta. *See* Holmes, Odetta
Felipe, Don. *See* Green, Phil(ip)
Felix, C. *See* Cohn, (Dr.) Felix
Felix, G. *See* Giordani, Felice [or Felix]
Felix, Karl. *See* Krzysniowski, Felix
Félix, M. *See* Scribe, (Augustin) Eugène
Felix, Paul. *See* Bliss, P(hilip) Paul
Fell, Tom. *See* Knight, Vick (Ralph, Sr.)
Fellow, Frank. *See* Pfeuffer, Walter
Fellows, Reginald. *See* Keuleman, Adrian
Fels, Maru. *See* Spielman(n), Fred(eric)
Fels, Roderich. *See* Rosenfeld, S.
Felser, René. *See* Delagaye, Georges
Felten, Jean. *See* Simon, Waldemar
Female Bert Williams, The. *See* McDaniel, Hattie
Female Bruce Springsteen. *See* Etheridge, Melissa (Lou)
Female Leadbelly, A. *See* Garland, Mary Magdalene
Fender, Fred(dy) [or Freddie]. *See* Huerta, Baldemar G(arza)
Fender, Gib. *See* Roberts, Howard (Mancel)
Fenee. *See* Neefe, Christian Gottlob
Fennell, Elizabeth (Ludwig). *See* Wahr, Elizabeth
Fennimore, Robert. *See* Saalfield, Richard A.
Fenshaw, Larry. *See* Frangkiser, Carl (Moerz)
Fenster, Tex. *See* Fenster, Harry
Fenster, Zoot. *See* Butcher, Jack
Fenton, Bernard. *See* Cobb, George L(inus)
Fenton, Carl. *See* Haenschen, Walter (G(ustave))
Fenton, Jack. *See* Fishman, Jack (1927-)
Fenwyck, Jerry. *See* Robertson, Dick
Feralintisco, Colantuono. *See* Tullio, Francesco Antonio
Ferdinand, Buddy. *See* De Franco, Boniface (Ferdinand Leonardo)
Féré, Octave. *See* Mogeta, Charles Octave
Fergar, E. F. *See* Gräffer, Franz (Arnold)
Fergar, F. E. *See* Gräffer, Franz (Arnold)
Ferguson, Bob. *See* Miller, Robert [or Bob] (Ernst)
Ferguson, Harry. *See* Edwards, C(harles) J(oseph)
Ferguson, Sydney. *See* Henderson, Lyle Russell Cedric
Ferguut, Jan. *See* Droogenbroeck, Jan van
Fernandez, Jose. *See* Barnes, Clifford (Paulus)
Fernandez, Mildred. *See* Thomas, Lillian [or Lillyn]
Ferrand, Edouard. *See* Schulz, B. Eduard
Ferrarai, A. Fontata. *See* Barrell, Edgar Alden, Jr.
Ferrari dalla Tiorba, (Benedetto). *See* Ferrari, Benedetto
Ferrati, E. *See* Blood, Lizette Emma
Ferrin, José. *See* Ailbout, Hans
Ferris, Anthony J. *See* Ferrazano, Anthony Joseph
Ferris, Jerry. *See* Crosby, Ronald Clyde
Fertö, Fritz. *See* Nestler, Fritz
Fesanio, Merindo. *See* Pasqualigo, Benedetto
Feski, J. *See* Sobolewski, J(ohann) F(riedrich) E(duard)
Fesky, J. *See* Sobolewski, J(ohann) F(riedrich) E(duard)
Fess, Master of New Orleans Rock 'n' Roll. *See* Byrd, Henry Roeland
Feste. *See* Grace, Harvey
Fet, A. A. *See* Shenshin, Afanaskii Afanas'evich
Fetchit, Stepin. *See* Bisson, Whelock Alexander
Fetchit, Stepin. *See* Perry, Lincoln (T(heodore Monroe Andrew))
Fetrás, Oscar. *See* Faster, Oscar
Feuer, Axel. *See* Nothdorf, Georg
Feyne, Buddy. *See* Feinstein, Buddy
Fiamengo, Iaches de Guant. *See* Buus, Jacques [or Jacob] (de)
Fiat Justitia. *See* Binney, Thomas
Fictor No Go. *See* Burnard, Francis Cowley
Fidamor. *See* Flemmer, Christian
Fiddlin' Kate. *See* DeVere, Margie Ann
Fiddling Knight, The. *See* Hawkins, (Sir) John

Fidelio. *See* Kornweibel, Albert H.
Field, Al G. *See* Hatfield, Alfred Griffith
Field of Bath. *See* Field, Henry Ibbot
Field, Robert. *See* Ehret, Walter (Charles)
Field, Robert. *See* Trusler, Ivan
Field, Russian. *See* Field, John
Field, Wallace. *See* Sawyer, Henry S.
Field, William. *See* Baycock, Frederick
Field, William C. *See* Schoenfeld, William C(harles)
Fielding, Jerry. *See* Feldman, Joshua
Fielding, Michael. *See* Sciapiro, Michel
Fieldmouse, Timon. *See* Rands, William Brightly
Fields, Arthur. *See* Finkelstein, Abe
Fields, Buddy. *See* Fields, Arthur B.
Fields, Dimples. *See* Fields, Richard
Fields, Eddie. *See* Waganfeald, Edward James, III
Fields, Jules. *See* Seredy, J(ulius) S.
Fields, Lew. *See* Schanfield, Lewis Maurice
Fields, Paul. *See* Fickl, Paul
Fields, William. *See* Crowders, (Ernest) Reuben
Fieldsieff, Herbert. *See* Fields, Herbert
Fife, Duncan. *See* Atkinson, Dorothy
Fifer, Max. *See* Pfeiffer, Marie V.
Fifferi, Lauro. *See* Anelli, Angelo
Fifth Brother. *See* Hunter, Jason
Figaro. *See* Clapp, Henry, Jr.
Figgs. *See* Kalakaua, David, (King of Hawaii)
Fighting for Five. *See* Ondrasik, John
Figlio, Il. *See* Biferi, Francesco
Figlio, Il. *See* Dôthel, Nicolas [or Niccolò]
Figlio, Dottel. *See* Oswald, James
Figulus, Wolfgang. *See* Töpfer, Wolfgang
Figurehead of Music in England. *See* Elgar, (Sir) Edward
Filago, (Il). *See* Casati, Girolamo [or Gerolamo]
Filidor. *See* Senf, H(einrich) C(hristian) L(ebrecht)
Filidor, (der Dorfferer). *See* Stieler, Caspar [or Kaspar] (von)
Filidor, der Dorfferer. *See* Schwieger, Jakob
Filip, Peter. *See* Vačkář, Dalibor C(yril)
Filippo, Pietro. *See* Philips, Peter
Fille de Gounod, La. *See* Massenet, Jules (Émile Frédéric)
Fillmore, Sally. *See* Fillmore, (James) Henry
Filodosso. *See* Migliavacca, Giovanni Ambrogio [or Giannambrogio]
Filosinavoro. *See* Orsini [or Orsino], Flavio
Filostrato Lucàno Cinnéo. *See* Soliva, Antonio
Filostrato Lucàno Cinnéo. *See* Tullio, Francesco Antonio
Filthy. *See* Waller, Thomas Fats
Fin. *See* Bronfin, Filipp Markovic
Finch, Calvin. *See* Downey, Sean Morton, Jr. (1933-2001)
Finck, Abbie. *See* Cushman, Abbie
Finck, Henry Theophilus. *See* Finck, Henry Gottlob
Finck, Herman. *See* Van de Vinck, Hermann
Finder, Martin. *See* Salzmann, Siegmund
Finette, Joe. *See* Sauer, Wolfgang
Fingerprints. *See* Azor, Hurby
Fingers, Captain. *See* Ritenour, Lee
Fingers, Rollie. *See* Hunter, Jason
Fingus, "Baron". *See* Mingus, Charles
Finland's Schubert. *See* Kuula, Toivo (Timoteus)
Finley, Antor Dismuk. *See* Campbell, Michael
Finley, Antor Dismuk. *See* Morelli, Frank
Finley, Antor Dismuk. *See* Searing, Harry
Finn, I. D. *See* Bliss, P(hilip) Paul
Finn, Mickey. *See* Hearne, Michael
Finten, John. *See* Frankenberg, Franz
Fionn. *See* Wright, Henry
Fiorentino. *See* Moneta, Giuseppe
Fiorentino, Il. *See* Veracini, Francesco Maria
Fioresucci, Bruno. *See* Busoni, Dante Michelangelo Benventuo
Fiorillo. *See* Méhul, Etienne Nicolas
Fiorin(i), C. *See* Macy, J(ames) C(artwright)
Firbank, Butch. *See* Firbank, Louis [or Lewis] (Allen)
Fire Chief. *See* Leopold, Isaiah Edwin
Fire Eyes. *See* Presley, Elvis A(a)ron
Fireman, (The). *See* McCartney, (James) Paul
First Bandmaster of the Salvation Army. *See* Fry, Charles William
First Cowboy Singer on Record, (The). *See* Sprague, Carl T.
First Great Composer of Modern Jewish Music. *See* Bloch, Ernest
First Hillbilly Star to Own a Cadillac. *See* Carver, Cynthia May
First King of Rap, The. *See* Hayes, Isaac
First Lady of Bluegrass. *See* Cooper, Wilma Lee (née Leary)
First Lady of Contemporary Christian Music, The. *See* Grant, Amy (Lee)
First Lady of Country Music. *See* Pugh, Virginia Wynette
First Lady of Country Music, (The). *See* Webb, Loretta
First Lady of Israeli Song. *See* Shemer, Naomi
First Lady of Radio, The. *See* Vonderlieth, Leonore
First Lady of Soul. *See* Franklin, Aretha
First Lady of the Blues. *See* Harris, Eleanora
First Native Composer. *See* Hopkinson, Francis
First of the Modernists. *See* Abelard, Peter
First Rock 'n' Roll Singer, The. *See* Williams, Hir(i)ram (King)
First Tycoon of Teen, The. *See* Spector, Phil(ip Harvey)
First Welsh Romantic Poet. *See* Williams (Pantycelyn), William
Firth, Vic. *See* Firth, Everett J(oseph)
Fischer, Andy. *See* Fischer, Johann

Fischer, Carl. *See* Gabriel, Charles H(utchinson)
Fischer, Fred. *See* Breitenbach, Alfred
Fischer, Wild Man. *See* Fischer, Larry
Fischler, H(arry) A(ugustus). *See* Lincoln, Harry J.
Fiser, J. F. *See* Fischer, Jan Frank
Fish. *See* Dick, Derek William
Fish, Ima. *See* Michelson, Lewis
Fishbone Fred. *See* Delp, Fred (B.)
Fisher, Edward. *See* Edwards, Melinda
Fisher, Ernest. *See* Fischer, Ernest
Fisher, Fred. *See* Breitenbach, Alfred
Fisher, I. B. *See* Wilson, Ira B(ishop)
Fisher, J. Arthur. *See* Keiser, Robert (A(dolph))
Fisher, Marc. *See* Friedrich, Horst-Bernd
Fisher, Mirian Lois. *See* Wilson, Ira B(ishop)
Fisher, Olga Jane. *See* Wilson, Ira B(ishop)
Fisher, Patty. *See* Akst, Ruth Freed
Fisher, Ruby. *See* Fisher, Reuben
Fisher, Shug. *See* Fisher, George Clinton
Fisher, Tom. *See* Muschler, Fritz
Fisherman, Jack. *See* Fishman, Jack (1927-)
Fisherman, Jay. *See* Fishman, Jack (1927-)
Fishma, Jack. *See* Fishman, Jack (1927-)
Fishman, Jay. *See* Fishman, Jack (1927-)
Fisk, Jim. *See* Barnhouse, Charles Lloyd
Fiske, Minnie Maddern. *See* Davey, Marie [or Minnie] Augusta
Fitch, Jeremy. *See* Allen, Stephen [or Steve] (Valentine Patrick William)
Fitz, Albert H. *See* Bloom, Sol
Fitzball, Edward. *See* Ball, Edward
Fitzgerald, John. *See* Sour, Robert (B.)
Fitzgerald, Lawrence. *See* Morse, Theodore (F.)
Fitzgerald, M. J. *See* Fitzpatrick, Michael G.
Fitzgerald, Warren. *See* Balent, Andrew
Fjalar. *See* Östergren, Carl Ludvig
Flaccus. *See* Horn, Charles Edward
Flaco, El. *See* Jiminéz, Leonardo
Flagny, Lucien de. *See* Grou, Lucien
Flamengo, Arnoldo. *See* Bruck, Arnold von
Flamin. *See* Ambros, August Wilhelm
Flanagan, Bud. *See* Weintrop, Chaim Reuben [or Reubin]
Flanagan, Robert (Winthrop). *See* Weintrop, Chaim Reuben [or Reubin]
Flanders, David. *See* Cacavas, John
Flandrus insulanus. *See* Desbuissons, Michel Charles
Flash, Harry. *See* Sargent, (Sir) (Harold) Malcolm (Watts-)
Flat, G. *See* Ehrlinger, Hans
Flav, Flavor. *See* Drayton, William
Flavell, Gerald. *See* Harris, Cuthbert
Flavor Flav. *See* Drayton, William
Flaxius. *See* Bernard, Josef Karl
Flea. *See* Balzary, Michael
Fleagle, Brick. *See* Fleagle, J(acob) (Roger)
Fleg, Edmond. *See* Flegenheimer, Edmond
Fleming, Austin. *See* Lemon, Laura (Gertrude)
Fleming, George. *See* Fletcher, Julia Constance
Fleming, Joy. *See* Strube, Erna
Fleming, Margaret. *See* Wagness, Bernard
Flers, P(ierre)-L(ouis). *See* Puyol, Léon Pierre [or Pierre-Louis] Édouard
Fletcher, Alfred. *See* Grubb, Alfred
Fletcher, Joseph. *See* Grey, Frank H(erbert)
Fleur, M. *See* Flower, Amelia Matilda
Fleur, Marcel. *See* Krenkel, Gustav
Fleury, Jeannette. *See* Breuer, F(ranz) J(osef)
Fleury, Jules F(rançois) F(élix). *See* Husson(-Fleury), Jules F(rançois) F(élix)
Flickreiter, Art. *See* Priwin, Andreas (Ludwig)
Flider. *See* Fielder, Friedrich
Flimflammer, (Jim). *See* Johnson, William [or Billy] (Francis)
Flint, Arnold. *See* Dawson, Peter (Smith)
Flint, Jimmy. *See* Lewis, Al(an)
Flip, Richard. *See* Franz, Walter
Flivver, A. *See* Andrews, Mark
Flock, Toby. *See* Doinet, Alexis-Victoire
Flora, La. *See* Caccini, Settimia
Florence, George E. *See* Bennett, Theron C(atlin)
Florence, William J(ames) [or J(ermyn)]. *See* Colin, Bernard
Florencie, Jacques. *See* Wilmann, Jacques Georges
Florentin. *See* Stuck, Johann Baptist(e)
Florentine, The. *See* Veracini, Francesco Maria
Florenz. *See* Elliott, Charlotte
Flores, Chava. *See* Flores Rivera, Salvador
Florestan. *See* Casembroot, J. L.
Florestan. *See* Schumann, Robert
Florian. *See* Fiedler, Friedrich
Florian. *See* Flem(m)ing, Paul
Florian, Henry. *See* Pancani, Arrigo
Floridan. *See* Betulius, Sigmund
Florido. *See* Saltenburg, Heinz
Florimondo Ermionèo. *See* Greppi, Giovanni
Florio, Caryl. *See* Robjohn, W(illiam) J(ames)
Flory, Med. *See* Flory, Meredith I.
Flory, Sylvio. *See* Urai, Vilmos [or William]
Flos. *See* Romita, Florenzo
Flosculus [or Flokulus]. *See* Tomeš, František Václav
Flotsam, Mr. *See* Hilliam, B(entley) C(ollingwood)
Floyd, Ell-Zee. *See* Short, J. D.
Floyd, John. *See* Lloyd, John
Floyd, Rambling King. *See* Floyd, Frank
Floyd, S. J. *See* St. Clair, Floyd J.
Floyd, William J. *See* Wilson, John F(loyd)
Flüchtige, Der. *See* Schwieger, Jakob
Fluchu. *See* Wolf, Hugo
Flying Baritone, The. *See* Crawford, Robert (MacArthur)

Flying Eagle, The. *See* Ross, Charles Isaiah
Flynn, Jimmy. *See* Kaufman, Isidore
Flynn, Joseph. *See* Spaulding, G(eorge) L(awson)
Foch, Dirk. *See* Fock, Dirk
Fogers, Calvin. *See* Grey, Frank H(erbert)
Folchetto. *See* Caponi, Jacopo
Foleshill. *See* Evans, Jonathan
Foley, Red. *See* Foley, Clyde (Julian)
Folia, Renato. *See* Binge, Ronald
Folk Music Icon. *See* Seeger, Pete(r R.)
Folkie Romantic. *See* Young, Neil
Follen, Eliza Lee. *See* Cabot, Eliza Lee
Follett, Charles. *See* Ehret, Walter (Charles)
Follett, Charles. *See* Kinsman, Elmer (F(ranklin))
Folten, Beda. *See* Vyhnalek, Ivo
Fomeen, Basil. *See* Fomin, Wasily
Fontaine, Charles. *See* Smith, Charles William (of Liverpool)
Fontaine, E. *See* Frangkiser, Carl (Moerz)
Fontaines, Charles de. *See* Rothschild, (Baron) Henri de
Fontaines, Robsard des. *See* Brossard, Sebastien de
Fontenelle of Music, (The). *See* Langlé, Honoré François Marie de
Foote, Isabel. *See* Butterfield, Christopher (James Agnew)
Forbes, Lou. *See* McClaskey, Harry Haley
Forceps. *See* Zang, Johann Heinrich
Ford, Al J. *See* Alford, Harry L(aForrest)
Ford, Clifford. *See* Slaughter, M(arion) T(ry)
Ford, Clinton. *See* Stopford-Harrison, Ian Georg
Ford, Frankie. *See* Guzzo, Francis
Ford, Gerry. *See* Corcoran, Gerard
Ford, Harry. *See* Ford, Young
Ford, J(ay) A. *See* Gabriel, Charles H(utchinson)
Ford, Powell I. *See* Dempsey, James E.
Ford, Tennessee Ernie. *See* Ford, Ernest Jennings
Ford, Tom. *See* O'Keefe, Lester
Ford, Tom. *See* Williams, George Dale
Ford, Whitey. *See* Ford, Benjamin Francis
Fordell, Lucien. *See* Kern, Carl Wilhelm
Fordykern, S. V. *See* Castling, Harry
Forel, L(awrence) W. *See* Rolfe, Walter (L.)
Foresio, D. *See* Savino, Domenico
Forest, (Mrs.) Edna. *See* Crosby, Fanny [i.e., Frances] J(ane)
Forest, Edwin D. *See* Goerdeler, Richard
Forest, John. *See* Cain, Noble
Forester, Fanny. *See* Judson, Emily (née Chubbuck)
For(r)ester, Roger. *See* Ehret, Walter (Charles)
Forestier, Auber. *See* Moore, (Annie) Aubertine (Woodward)
Forestier, Leonard. *See* Phillips, W. Compton
Forgeron(-Maréchal), Charles. *See* Kovarovic, Karel
Forgotten Man of American Music, The. *See* Guaragna, Salvatore
Forland, Art. *See* Kraus-Hübner, Hans
Fornaciari, Sugar. *See* Fornaciari, Adelmo
Fornaciari, Zucchero. *See* Fornaciari, Adelmo
Fornarino, Il. *See* Betti(no), Stefano
Forrest, Chet. *See* Chichester, George Forrest, Jr.
Forrest, David. *See* Adams, Cliff
Forrest, David. *See* Brown, Bob
Forrest, David. *See* Chacksfield, Francis [or Frank] (Charles)
Forrest, David. *See* Fishman, Jack (1918 (or 19)-)
Forrest, (Mrs.) Edna. *See* Crosby, Fanny [i.e., Frances] J(ane)
Forrest, George (Chichester, Jr.). *See* Chichester, George Forrest, Jr.
Forrest, Sidney. *See* Stairs, Louise E.
Forrester, Hugh. *See* Waldman, Robert H.
Forrester, Noel. *See* Butler, E. G.
Forst-Berg, Otto. *See* Weinberg, Symson [or Simson]
Forster, (Walter). *See* Stanke, Willi
Forster, M. H. *See* Schori, Fritz
Fort, Hank. *See* Fort, Eleanor H(ankins)
Fortepianov [or Forte'pyanov], Vasily. *See* Botkin, Vasily Petrovich
Fortescue, Edith. *See* Rawlings, Alfred William
Fortino, Mario. *See* Presser, William (Henry)
Fortissimist. *See* Prokofiev, Serge
Fortner, Red. *See* Fortner, Arnold
Fortunatus, Herman Heinrich. *See* Glücksmann, Heinrich
Fortune, Joe. *See* Hastings, Ross (Ray)
Foss, Lukas. *See* Fuchs, Lukas
Foss, Richard. *See* Fishman, Jack (1918 (or 19)-)
Foss, Richard. *See* Paramor, Norman [or Norrie] (William)
Fossell, Ivan. *See* Mantovani, A(nnuzio) P(aolo)
Foster, Al. *See* Fleitman, Alexander O(scar)
Foster, E(van) S. *See* Gabriel, Charles H(utchinson)
Foster, Francis. *See* Barnard, D'Auvergne
Foster, Jimmy. *See* Grainger, Porter
Foster, Kenneth. *See* Kern, Carl Wilhelm
Foster, L. C. *See* Foster, Stephen Collins
Foster, Larry. *See* Waignein, Andre
Foster, Mark. *See* McKelvy, James (M(illigan))
Foster, Nancy. *See* Vonderlieth, Leonore
Foster, Walter. *See* Stanke, Willi
Fothergill, Frank. *See* Tate, Arthur F(rank)
Fotine, Dorothy. *See* Fotinakis, Dorothy Owens
Fotine, Larry. *See* Fotinakis, Lawrence Constantine
Founder of Modern Opera, The. *See* Scarlatti, Alessandro
Founder of Neapolitan Opera, The. *See* Scarlatti, Alessandro
Founder of the Delta Blues. *See* Patton, Charlie [or Charley]

Founder of the Romantic Movement in German Music. *See* Weber, Carl Maria von
Founding Father of American Musical Magazines. *See* Dwight, John Sullivan
Fountainhead. *See* Thompson, Robert Scott
Fouqué, Friedrich. *See* La Motte-Fouqué, Friedrich Heinrich Karl, Freiherr de
Four Bar Killer. *See* Hawkins, Lamont
Fox, The. *See* Friedhofer, Hugo Wilhelm
Fox, The. *See* Williams, George Dale
Fox, Edward. *See* Haass, Hans
Fox, Edward. *See* Wilson, Ira B(ishop)
Fox, Felix. *See* Haass, Hans
Fox, Frank. *See* Fuchs, Frank
Fox, Joseph Ed(ward). *See* Wilson, Ira B(ishop)
Fox, Wilbur B. *See* Dickson, Mary Hannah
Foxy. *See* Fox, Eldridge (L.)
Foxy GGM [Great-Grandmother]. *See* Brown, Olive
Fra Teodora del Carmine. *See* Bacchini, Giovanni Maria
Fracescus de Paula. *See* Grimm, Friedrich Melchior, Freiherr von
Fragny, Robert de. *See* Proton de la Chapelle, Robert
Fragson, (Harry) [or (Henry)]. *See* Pot(ts), Victor Léon
Frame, A. B. *See* Bliss, P(hilip) Paul
Frampton, Ray Ross. *See* Fisher, Ethel
Franc-Nohain(e). *See* Le Grand, Maurice (Etienne)
France, Anatole. *See* Thibault, (Jacques) Anatole-François
Frances, Carrie. *See* Crosby, Fanny [i.e., Frances] J(ane)
Frances, Grace (J.). *See* Crosby, Fanny [i.e., Frances] J(ane)
Frances, Lee. *See* Sukman, Frances Paley
Frances, Lillian G. *See* Crosby, Fanny [i.e., Frances] J(ane)
Frances, Paula. *See* Timpano, Paula (Francesca Ianello)
Frances Raphael, Mother. *See* Drane, Augusta Theodosia
Frances, S. Trevor. *See* Crosby, Fanny [i.e., Frances] J(ane)
Frances, V(ictoria). *See* Crosby, Fanny [i.e., Frances] J(ane)
Francesco Cieco. *See* Landini, Francesco
Francesco, dalla Viola. *See* Viola, Francesco
Francesco degli Organi. *See* Landini, Francesco
Francesco del Liuto. *See* Francesco (Canova) da Milano
Franchi, Nando. *See* Franchi, Ferdinand
Francis. *See* Cornu, Francis
Francis, Art. *See* Otto, Joseph Francis
Francis, Arthur. *See* Gershvin, Israel
Francis, Bennie. *See* Anders, John Frank
Francis, Black. *See* Thompson, Charles Michael (Kitteridge, IV)
Francis, Charles. *See* Rankl, Karl
Francis, Connie. *See* Franconero, Constance [or Concetta] (Rosa Marie)
Francis, Evelyn. *See* Bushby, Evelyn Frances
Francis, Grace J. [or I.]. *See* Crosby, Fanny [i.e., Frances] J(ane)
Francis, Herbert. *See* Grey, Frank H(erbert)
Francis, J. F. *See* Glassmacher, Joseph F(rancis)
Francis, James. *See* McHugh, James [or Jimmy] (F(rancis))
Francis, Jay. *See* Glassmacher, Joseph (Francis)
Francis, Otto. *See* Otto, Joseph Francis
Francis, Paul. *See* Westendorf, Omer
Francis, V(ictoria). *See* Crosby, Fanny [i.e., Frances] J(ane)
Francis, William. *See* Glassmacher, William
Francisco de Novo Portu. *See* Mergot, Franciscus
Francisco, Manuel. *See* Terr, Mischa Richard
Francisque. *See* Sarcey (de Suttières), Francisque
Franck, René. *See* Zoeller, Carli [or Karl]
Francke, Gustav. *See* Elgar, (Sir) Edward
Franco. *See* Makiadi, L'Okanga La Ndju Pene Luambo
Franco, Jesus. *See* Manera, Jesus Franco
Francoeur, François. *See* Kreisler, Fritz [i.e., Friedrich](-Max)
Francoeur Neveu. *See* Francoeur, Louis-Joseph
Francoeur, S. *See* Chaigneau, Suzanne
François. *See* Grey, Frank H(erbert)
François, M. *See* Bawr, Alexandrine Sophie de
Francus, Andreas. *See* Schwartz, Andreas (Scotus)
Francy, Paul. *See* Gilson, Paul (1927-)
Frank, A. L. T. *See* La Motte-Fouqué, Friedrich Heinrich Karl, Freiherr de
Frank, Fred (L.). *See* Walters, Harold L(aurence)
Frank, George. *See* Fellows, Floyd George
Frank, J. L. *See* Kuczynski, Julius Frank (Anthony)
Frank, Paul. *See* Merseburger, Carl Wilhelm
Frank Sinatra of France. *See* Aznavourian, (Shanaur) Varenagh
Frank Sinatra of Latin Music, (The) —*see* Rodriguez, Pablo
Frank the Poet. *See* MacNamara, Francis [or Frank]
Frank, Waldemar. *See* Rosenbaum, Hugo Waldemar
Frank Zappa of Country Music, The. *See* Friedman(n), Richard (F.)
Frankenberg, Innocentius. *See* Fuhrmann, Martin Heinrich
Frankenstein. *See* Moeckel, Charles
Frankenstein, Lutz. *See* Husadel, Hans Felix
Frankenstein, Maestro. *See* Frankenstein, Alfred
Franker, Fransua. *See* Francoeur, François (*le cadet*)
Frankfurter, Jean. *See* Liessmann, Erich
Frankie, Lou. *See* Graziano, Caesar Franklin
Fränkl, Markus. *See* Frank, Marco
Franklin, Bobbie. *See* Amburgey, Irene
Franklin, George C. *See* Wagness, Bernard
Franklin, Guitar Pete. *See* Franklin, Edward Lamonte
Franklin, Howard. *See* Saenger, Gustave

Franklin, Kirk. *See* Smith, Kirk
Franklin, Pete. *See* Franklin, Edward Lamonte
Franklin, Richard. *See* Widman, Franklin Darryl
Franklyn, John. *See* Bliss, P(hilip) Paul
Franklyn, Paul. *See* Linden, David Gysbert
Franks, Gordon. *See* Worland, Bill
Frantzen, E. *See* Amper, Quirin, Jr.
Frantzl, Jacopo. *See* Trautzl, Jan Jakub
Franz, Albert. *See* Pabst, Harry
Franz, J(ohann) H(einrich). *See* Hochberg, Hans Heinrich, (Bolko Graf von XIV)
Franz, Paul. *See* Gautier, François
Franz, Paul. *See* Mantovani, A(nnuzio) P(aolo)
Franz, Robert. *See* Knauth, Robert Franz
Franzini, Ottavio. *See* Frasi, Felica
Frascard, Emile. *See* Kaun, Hugo
Frascia, (Il). *See* Calandros, Nicola
Fraser, Dennise. *See* Geehl, Henry Ernest
Fraser, Gordon. *See* Box, Harold Elton
Fraser, Gordon. *See* Keuleman, Adrian
Fraser, Gordon. *See* Pelosi, Domonic [or Don]
Fraser, Gordon. *See* Sugarman, Harry
Fraser, Kathleen. *See* Hart, Cynthia Mary Kathleen
Frauenfelder, Georg. *See* Heiss, Hermann
Frauenlob (der Jüngere). *See* Haug, (Johann Christoph) Friedrich
Fraver. *See* Verbeeck, Frans
Frawley, Tom. *See* Kaufman, Isidore
Frazier, A. G. *See* Bliss, P(hilip) Paul
Fred, Charly. *See* Angster, Manfred
Fred, J(ohn). *See* Gourrier, John (Fred)
Fred P. *See* Klose, Othmar
Fred, Will. *See* Schmidt-Gent(n)er, Willy
Fredericks, Alfred. *See* Solman, Alfred
Free, J(ohn). *See* Freeth, John
Free Man, though a Prisoner, A. *See* Wither, George
Freed, Alan. *See* Freed, Albert (James)
Freed, Arthur. *See* Grossman, Arthur
Freed, Fred. *See* Goldbaum, Friedrich
Freed, O(lov) M(artin). *See* Wiggen, Knut
Freedom, John. *See* Sykes, Bishop Milton
Freeman, Bud. *See* Freeman, Lawrence
Freeman, C. A. *See* Ackley, B(entley) D(eForrest)
Freeman, Kookie. *See* Brandenburg, Helmuth
Freeman, R. *See* Courteville, Raphael
Freeman, Roderick. *See* Friml, (Charles) Rudolf
Freeman, Scott. *See* McNulty, Frank Fremont
Freesoil, Mason. *See* Stull, Donald Earl
Freestyle King. *See* Alvarez, Jorge Antonio
Freeze, Dr. *See* Freese, Louis
Freeze, Dr. *See* Straite, Elliot
Frei, J. *See* Reichard(t), Johann Friedrich
Freigedank, K(arl). *See* Wagner, Richard
Freistat, Frank. *See* Kunkel, Charles
Freksa, Friedrich. *See* Friedrich(-Freska), Kurt
Fremes, Marco. *See* Mestrini, Freek
Fremont, Frank. *See* McNulty, Frank Fremont
French Beethoven, The. *See* Onslow, George
French Beethoven, The. *See* Saint-Saëns, (Charles) Camille
French Dickens, The. *See* Daudet, (Louis Marie) Alphonse
French Drunken Barnaby. *See* Basselin, Olivier
French, George. *See* Finkelstein, Abe
French, Gerry [or Garry]. *See* French, George
French Joseph Conrad, A. *See* Ohana, Maurice
French Mendelssohn, The. *See* Saint-Saëns, (Charles) Camille
French Sacchini, The. *See* Monsigny, P(ierre) A(lexandre)
French Sinatra. *See* Aznavourian, (Shanaur) Varenagh
French Sinatra, The. *See* Silly, (Gilbert) François (Léopold)
Frenelle, Jules. *See* Lehner, Fritz
Frenzel, Franz Xaver. *See* Katt, Friedmann
Frenzel, Georg. *See* Graff, Sigmund
Frère Lambert de St. Théodoré. *See* Chaumont, Lambert
Fresh, Doug E. *See* Davis, Douglas E.
Freund, Joki. *See* Freund, Walter Jakob
Frey, Maurice. *See* Friedman, Maurice Herman
Frey, Otokar. *See* Fischer, Otokar
Freyenburg. *See* Bock, Johann Christian
Freza, A. *See* Menezes, A. Cardosa de
Friar of Bristol. *See* Tunstede, Simon
Friberger, E. M. *See* Freiburger, Earl M.
Friday, Gavin. *See* Hanvey, Fionan
Fridolin. *See* Schumann, Robert
Fridzeri, Alexandre Marie Antoine. *See* Frixer, Alessandro Maria
Fried, Enns [or Enna]. *See* Sülwald, Paul (Heinrich)
Fried Funk Food. *See* Cook, Quentin
Friederich, J(ohann). *See* Schori, Fritz
Friedlaw. *See* Warfield, Gerald
Friedman, Kinstah. *See* Friedman(n), Richard (F.)
Friedman, Kinkster. *See* Friedman(n), Richard (F.)
Friedman(n), Kinky. *See* Friedman(n), Richard (F.)
Friedman, Murray. *See* Friedman, Maurice Herman
Friedrich, G. *See* Oldenburg, Elimar Anton Günther Friedrich Herzog von
Friedrich, M. G. *See* Gredy, F(riedrich) M(elchior)
Friedrich, Paul. *See* Oeser, Fritz
Friedrich, W(ilhelm). *See* Riese, Wilhelm Friedrich
Friedsamer, (Konrad). *See* Beissel, Konrad
Friend of the Family, A. *See* Ayrton, William
Friendly, Ray. *See* Freundlich, Ralph B.
Frimaire. *See* Gagnon, Blanche
Frimousse. *See* Toché, Raoul
Frischmuth, Markus Hilarius. *See* Fuhrmann, Martin Heinrich

Frith, Fred. *See* Frith, Jeremy Webster
Fritsche, Ivan. *See* Lorenz, E(dmund) S(imon)
Fritz. *See* Harford, Frederick Kill
Frizeri, Alessandro Maria. *See* Frixer, Alessandro Maria
Frizzell, Crockett. *See* Frizzell, David Mark
Frizzell, Lefty. *See* Frizzell, William O(rville)
Frodnesor, Limé. *See* Rosendorff, Emil
Frog, The. *See* Burnette, Lester Alvin
Frogman, (The). *See* Henry, Clarence
Frogson. *See* Pot(ts), Victor Léon
Frogworth, A. C. *See* Brown, Jonathan C.
Frohberg, Paul. *See* Adami, Friedrich (Wilhelm)
Froisart, Jean. *See* Daudet, (Louis Marie) Alphonse
Frölich, Georg. *See* Lätus, Georg
Frost. *See* Molina, Arturo, Jr.
Frost, Jack. *See* Brine, Mark Vincent
Frost, Jack. *See* Degesco, Charles
Frost, Jack. *See* Frost, Harold G.
Frost, Jack. *See* Keithley, E. Clinton
Frost, Jack. *See* Zimmerman, Robert Allen
Frou-Frou. *See* Mortjé, Arnold [or Adolphe]
Fry, Christopher. *See* Harris, Christoperher
Frye, Howard. *See* Frye, Leslie Legge Sarony
Fryers, Austin. *See* Clery, W. E.
Fuchs, Leo. *See* Springer, A(braham) L(eon)
Fuentes, Ramon. *See* Warrington, John(ny) (T.)
Fuerb, Raoul. *See* Felber, Rudolph
Fuertes, Pedro. *See* Box, Harold Elton
Fuertes, Pedro. *See* Keuleman, Adrian
Fuji, Mr. *See* Ayinde, Sikiru
Fuller, Blind Boy. *See* Allen, Fulton
Fuller, Blind Boy (No. 2). *See* McGhee, Walter Brown
Fuller, Jeff. *See* Slaughter, M(arion) T(ry)
Fuller, Jep. *See* Slaughter, M(arion) T(ry)
Fuller, Lone Cat. *See* Fuller, Jess(i)e
Fuller, Playboy. *See* Minter, Iverson
Fuller, Richard Alan. *See* Goldman, Richard Franko
Fuller, Richard Lee. *See* Minter, Iverson
Fuller, Rocky. *See* Minter, Iverson
Fulmer, H. J. *See* Pratt, Charles E.
Fulsom, Lowell. *See* Fulson, Lowell
Fulton, Lucky. *See* Fulton, Rosswell Henry
Fultoni, M. *See* Bowen, M.
Fumet, Dynamite. *See* Fumet, Dynam-Victor
Fundless, Hezekiah. *See* Sapp, Allen (Dwight)
Funkel, Lars. *See* Deutscher, Karlheinz
Funniest Man in the World, The. *See* Chaplin, Charles (Spencer)
Furber, Douglas. *See* Lewin, Michael Sultan
Furey, Lewis. *See* Greenblatt, Lewis
Furioso, Il. *See* Foscarini, Giovanni Paolo
Furman-Millner, I. *See* Lincon, Harry J.
Fürstenberger, von. *See* Gordigiani, Luigi
Furtner, (Joachim). *See* Brugk, Hans Melchoir
Fury, Billy. *See* Wycherley, Ronald
Fuss, Johann Evangelist. *See* Fusz, János
Future King of Pianists, The. *See* Gottschalk, Louis Moreau
Future of Blues Guitar, The. *See* Gales, Manuel
Future of Rock 'n' Roll. *See* Springsteen, Bruce (Frederick Joseph)
Fuzzy. *See* Pedersen, Jens Wilhelm
Fychan, Idris. *See* Jones, John (1825-1887)
Fyles, Philip. *See* Phile, Philip
Fynes, Randle. *See* Holme, (Sir) Randle Fynes Wilson

– G –

G********. *See* Haxthausen, Aurore M. G. Ch. von
G.A.U.N.T. *See* Coleridge, Samuel Taylor
G. B. C. *See* Cervetto, James (1682-1783)
GC. *See* Cooper, Walter Thomas Gaze
G. C. W. *See* Wecker, Georg Kaspar [or Caspar]
G. D. *See* Darley, George
G. F. F. *See* Fisher, Geoffrey Francis
Gfr. W(br.). *See* Weber, (Jacob) Gottfried
G. F. R. *See* Root, George Frederick
G. F. T. *See* Tempelhoff, Georg Friedrich von
G. F. V. *See* Vincent, George Frederick
G. G. *See* Cowper, William
G. G. *See* Grace, Grace
G. G. B. *See* Kinsman, Elmer (F(ranklin))
G. H. S. *See* Salter, G. H.
GI Sing-Sation, The. *See* Gant, Cecil
G. I.'s Own Songwriter, The. *See* Loesser, Frank Henry
G. I. W. *See* Whiting, (Mrs.) G. I.
G. J. S. *See* Stevenson, George John
G., Kenny. *See* Gorelick, Kenneth
G. M. *See* Moultrie, Gerard
G. M. J. *See* McGranahan, James
G. P. T. *See* Telemann, Georg Philipp
G. R. *See* Rawson, George
G Rap. *See* Wilson, Nathaniel
G. (G.) S. *See* Schütz, (George) Gabriel
G. V. *See* Goold-Verschoyle, H(amilton) F(rederick) S(tuart)
G. V. O. *See* Vintzius, Georg
G. W. *See* Weber, (Jacob) Gottfried
G. W. W. *See* Crosby, Fanny [i.e., Frances] J(ane)
G. W. W. *See* Woodworth, G(eorge) Wallace
GZA. *See* Grice, Gary
Gabilondo, Pancho. *See* Gabilondo Soler, Francisco (José)
Gable, Cora. *See* Kinyon, John L(eroy)
Gabor, B. B. *See* Hegeus, Gabor
Gabriel. *See* Gillespie, John (Birks)
Gabriel, Ana. *See* Araujo Yong, María Gaudalupe
Gabriel, Charles. *See* Semere, Charles Gabriel

Gabriel, Colley. *See* Cibber, Colley
Gabriel, Gunter. *See* Caspelherr, Günther
Gabriel, John. *See* D'Urfey, Thomas
Gabriel, Juan. *See* Aguilera (Valadez), Alberto
Gabriel-Marie. *See* Marie, Gabriel (Prosper)
Gabriel of the Circus. *See* Evans, Merle (Slease)
Gabriel, Raoul. *See* Boex, Andrew J.
Gabriel-Shelly. *See* Gabriel, Charles H(utchinson)
Gabriel-Shelly. *See* Shelly, Harry (Rowe)
Gabriel, Vera G. *See* Gabriel, Charles H(utchinson)
Gabrielle. *See* Gabriel, (Mary Ann) Virginia
Gabrielle D. *See* Duval, Gabrielle
Gabril, Mercedes. *See* Jacobs, Al(bert) T.
Gado, Roberto del. *See* Wende, Horst
Gaerber, Siegwart. *See* Lederer, Viktor [or Victor]
Gaf(f)urius, Franchinus. *See* Gafori, Franchino
Gagnier, Paul. *See* Mehlich, Ernst
Gaillard, Slim. *See* Gaillard, Bulee
Gaines, J. *See* Hyman, Richard [or Dick] (R(oven))
Gainsbourg, Serge. *See* Ginsburg [or Ginzburg], Lucien
Gainsbourg, Steve. *See* Ginsburg [or Ginzburg], Lucien
Galán, Pacho. *See* Galán Blanco, Francisco
Galás, Diamánda. *See* Galás, Dimitria Angeliki Elena
Galatis, Hagen. *See* Harling, Peter
Gale, Bill [or William]. *See* Gula, William
Gale, Crystal. *See* Webb, Brenda Gail
Gale, Stephen. *See* Krasnow, Herman(n)
Galega, Rico. *See* Theis, Harry
Galento, Toni. *See* Spoliansky, Mischa [or Michail] (Pawlowitsch)
Galich, Aleksandr Arkas'evich. *See* Ginzburg, Aleksandr Arkad'evich
Galileo of Music, The. *See* Bach, Johann Sebastian
Gall, Joseph. *See* Arnold, Ignaz (Theodore) Ferdinand (Cajetan)
Gallego, El. *See* Martinez, José
Gallego, Miguel del. *See* Barco, Miguel del
Gallic Muse, The. *See* Ravel, Maurice (Joseph)
Galliculus. *See* Handl, Adam
Galliculus, Johannes. *See* Hahnel, Johannes
Gallicus, Johannes. *See* Johannes de Garlandia
Gallius, Johannes. *See* Legrense, Johannes
Gallot d'Angers. *See* Gallot, Antoine
Gallot de Paris. *See* Gallot, Jacques (de)
Gallot, le vieux. *See* Gallot, Jacques (de)
Gallus, Jacobus. *See* Petelin, Jakob
Galuppi, Baldassare. *See* Pellegrini, Ferdinando
Galvani, L(ivio) N(iso). *See* Salvioli, Giovanni
Gamble and Huff. *See* Gamble, Kenneth [or Kenny]
Gamble and Huff. *See* Huff, Leon
Gandalf. *See* Strobl, Heinz
Gandalf the Grey. *See* Wilson, Chris (Richard)
Gandino, Leonello. *See* Mantovani, A(nnuzio) P(aolo)
Ganette. *See* Anderson, Alpharita Constantia
Gannon, Kim. *See* Gannon, James Kimball
Gantier, Felix. *See* Glover, Charles William
Ganz, Aaron. *See* Gonzalez, Aaron Ruben
Gapone, Maestro. *See* Fanciulli, Giuseppe
Garbáge, Hauloff. *See* Garrett, James Allen
Garbáge, Pierre. *See* Garrett, James Allen
Garbo. *See* Adler, Lou
Garcia, Padre. *See* Garcia (Fajer), Francisco Javier
Garcin, Jules Auguste. *See* Salomon, Jules Auguste
Gardano, Alessandro. *See* Gardner, Maurice
Gardel-Hervé. *See* Ronger, Emmanuel Florimond
Gardner, Dave. *See* Weingarten, David
Gardner, J. J. *See* Bliss, P(hilip) Paul
Gardner, Karl. *See* Gardner, Charles A.
Gardner, Lou. *See* Guardino, Louis Joseph
Gardner, Newport. *See* Occramer, Marycoo
Gareña, Mario. *See* García Peña, Jesús Arturo
Garett, Gary. *See* Catsos, Nicholas A.
Garland, A. *See* Engelmann, H(ans)
Garland, Donald. *See* MacInnis, (Murdoch) Donald
Garland, Hank. *See* Garland, Walter
Garland, Hugh. *See* Anderson, William Henry
Garlow, Bon Ton. *See* Garlow, Clarence Joseph
Garnet(t), Jennie. *See* Crosby, Fanny [i.e., Frances] J(ane)
Garnett, Blind. *See* Garnett, Leroy
Garnett, Jim. *See* Sissle, Noble (Lee)
Garnett, Silk. *See* Smith, Garnett
Garnovik, Giovanni Marie. *See* Giornovichi, Giovanni Mane
Garôto. *See* Sardinha, Anibal Augusto
Garr, Artie. *See* Garfunkel, Art(hur Ira)
Garret, Benet. *See* Gareth, Bennedetto
Garrett. *See* McCollin, Frances
Garrett, Snuff. *See* Garrett, Thomas
Garriguenc, Aime. *See* Garriguenc, Rene
Garrote. *See* Greco, Vicente
Garrulous Steeplejack of the Arts. *See* Huneker, James Gibbons
Garry, Tom. *See* Löhmer, Klaus
Garth, John. *See* Thomas, John (1825-1944)
Gartside, Green. *See* Strohmeyer, Green
Garwin, Joe. *See* Sattler, Hermann
Garza, Pepe. *See* Garza, José Francisco
Gasbrit, Obie. *See* Gaskill, Clarence
Gaslight Era Dean of New York Music Critics, The. *See* Krehbiel, Henry (Edward)
Gaspar de Padua. *See* Alberti, Gasparo
Gaspare bergomensis. *See* Alberti, Gasparo
Gasparini, Angelo. *See* Angiolini, (Domenico Maria) Gaspero
Gasperini. *See* Visconti, Gasparo
Gasparino. *See* Visconti, Gasparo
Gast, Peter. *See* Köselitz, (Johann) Heinrich
Gast, Willy. *See* Schwarzmeier, Gustl
Gaste, Lou Lou. *See* Gaste, Louis (Felix-Marie)

Gastfenger, Polykarpus. *See* Hoffmann, Heinrich
Gaston. *See* Mestépès, Eugène
Gaston, Hannes. *See* Reindl, Max
Gaston, Marie. *See* Daudet, (Louis Marie) Alphonse
Gatemouth. *See* Armstrong, (Daniel) Louis
Gatemouth. *See* Brown Clarence
Gates, Clifford G. *See* Haga, Frederick Wallace
Gates, Clifford G. *See* Ringleben, Justin, Jr.
Gates, Hen. *See* Gillespie, John (Birks)
Gatlif, Tony. *See* Gatlif, Michel Dahmani
Gatsby, Paco. *See* Porter, Robert Morris
Gatty, Alfred Scott. *See* Scott-Gatty, (Sir) Alfred
Gatzimos, Crystal Gale. *See* Webb, Brenda Gail
Gaucho Relámpago, El. *See* Nasca, Carlos D.
Gaultier de Lyon. *See* Gaultier, Ennemond [or Eunémond]
Gaultier de Paris. *See* Gaultier, Denis [or Denys]
Gaultier le jeune. *See* Gaultier, Denis [or Denys]
Gauthier of Chateaurenard. *See* Gauterius de Castello Rainardi
Gauthiers-Villars, Sidonie Gabriel. *See* Colette, Sidonie Gabrielle Claudine
Gautier d'Angleterre. *See* Gautier, Jacques
Gautier de Marseille. *See* Gautier, Pierre (c.1642-1696)
Gautier de Rome. *See* Gautier, Pierre (1599-after 1638)
Gautier d'Orleans. *See* Gautier, Pierre (1599-after 1638)
Gavardo, Gavardo da. *See* Cibber, Colley
Gawain. *See* Newton, H(enry) Chance
Gawitzla, Alexander. *See* Alexander, Axel
Gay, Bert. *See* Dorsey, Bertha (Annabelle) (Gay)
Gay, Noel. *See* Armitage, Reginald Moxon
Gay, Tandy. *See* Whitney, Julia (A.)
Gaye, Ellie. *See* Greenwich, Ellie
Gayle, Crystal. *See* Webb, Brenda Gail
Gaylord, A. F. *See* Seredy, J(ulius) S.
Gayno, Creole (George). *See* Guesnon, George
Gaze, Heino. *See* Gaze, Hermann Otto
Gaze, Otto. *See* Junker, Otto
Gazul, Clara. *See* Mérimée, Prosper
Gear, Gloria. *See* Vonderlieth, Leonore
Gebegern, Kurt. *See* Deutscher, Karlheinz
Gédalge, Francois. *See* Sapp, Allen (Dwight)
Gedarro, Carlos. *See* Andries, Franzleo
Gee, Tara. *See* Zintel, Gabriele
Geer, Georgia. *See* Vonderlieth, Leonore
Geer, Gloria. *See* Vonderlieth, Leonore
Geer, Leonore. *See* Vonderlieth, Leonore
Gellar, Jack. *See* Schatt, Ronald
Geminiani, Alessandro. *See* Alfieri, Pietro
Genèe, Paul. *See* Rawlings, Charles Arthur
General Director of Hell's Music. *See* Wagner, Richard
Generali. *See* Blaze, François Henri Joseph
Generali, Mercandetti. *See* Mercandetti, P(ietro)
Generali, Pietro. *See* Mercandetti, P(ietro)
Genesio, Argisto. *See* De Rogati(s), Francisco Saverio
Genio de la Salsa, El. *See* Ramirez, Louie
Genius. *See* Grice, Gary
Genius (of Soul), The. *See* Robinson, Ray Charles
Genovese, Il. *See* Reggio, Pietro Francesco
Gent & Wheeler. *See* Finkelstein, Abe
Gent. Practitioner in the Art of Musicke. *See* Alison, Richard
Gentil-Bernard. *See* Bernard, Pierre Joseph (Justin)
Gentilhuomo Fiorentino. *See* Giacomini, Bernardo
Gentle Giant (of Country Music), The. *See* Williams, Don
Gentle Joe. *See* Evans, William [or Bill]
Gentle, Johnny. *See* Askew, John
Gentleman in London. *See* Hayes, William
Gentleman Jim. *See* Reeves, James [or Jimmy] (Travis)
Gentleman of Cambridge, A. *See* Mason, William
Gentry, Bo. *See* Ackoff, Robert
Gentry, Bobbie. *See* Streeter, Roberta [or Bobbie] (Lee)
Gentry, Will. *See* Niday Canady, Edna Veronica
Georg, Hans. *See* Grosz, Will [i.e., Wilhelm]
George Gershwin of Brazil. *See* Jobim, Antonio Carlos
George, Gil. *See* Gilman, Hazel Inez
George H. *See* Harrison, George
George, Hans. *See* Grosz, Wilhelm [or Will]
George, Harold. *See* Dickson, Mary Hannah
George, Jimmy. *See* Georgantones, Jimmy P.
George Riley, the Yodeling Rustler. *See* Reeves, Goebel (Leon)
George, Shorty. *See* Johnson, James J. (1905-1972)
George, Uncle. *See* Cohan, George M(ichael)
George, W. M. *See* Bliss, P(hilip) Paul
George, Wilh. *See* Bergen, A.
Georgeson, Hari. *See* Harrison, George
Georgia Bill. *See* McTell, Willie Samuel
Georgia Grinder. *See* Davenport, Charles Edward
Georgia Peach. *See* Nelson, Lucille
Georgia Peach, The. *See* Penniman, Richard [or Ricardo] Wayne
Georgia Pine. *See* Harris, Edward P.
Georgia Pine Boy. *See* McCoy, Joe
Georgia Slim. *See* Seward, Alexander T.
Georgia Tom. *See* Dorsey, Thomas A(ndrew)
Gérad de Nerval. *See* Labrunie, Gérard
Geraldo, (M.). *See* Bright, Gerald
Gerard, Danyel. *See* Kherlakian, Gérard Daniel
Gerard, Paul. *See* Farnon, Dennis
Gerard, Richard (H.). *See* Husch, R(ichard) G(erard)
Gerard, Will. *See* Jacobs, William B.
Gerardo. *See* Mejia, Gerardo, (III)
Gerber, Siegwart. *See* Lederer, Viktor [or Victor]
Gerbert, Martin, OSB. *See* Gerbert, Franz Dominik Bernhard
Gerbik, Mr. *See* Thornton, Keith
Gerhard, (Dr.) E. *See* Rebling, Eberhard (Gerhard)

Gerhard, Karl. *See* Johnson, Karl Emil George
Gerhold, Franz Josef. *See* Müller(-Guttenbrunn), Adam
Geritz, Günther. *See* Wellnitz, Gerd
Germaine, Jack. *See* Girman, John W(illiam)
Germamer, H. *See* Börnstein, Heinrich (Karl)
German, (Sir) Edward. *See* Jones, Edward German
German Harrigan, The. *See* Philipp, Adolf
German Herrick, The. *See* Flem(m)ing, Paul
German, J. E(dward). *See* Jones, Edward German
German, William. *See* Ord Hume, J(ames)
Germont, Henri. *See* Hartmann, Georges
Gernreich, Daniel. *See* Pietsch, Rainer
Gerold, Fritz. *See* Deutsch, Max Leo
Gérôme. *See* Thibault, (Jacques) Anatole François
Gerrard, William. *See* Bilik, Jerry (Hanchrow)
Gerrick, Hilda. *See* Geiringer, Hilda
Gerro, Carol [or Caron]. *See* Dorsey, Bertha (Annabelle) (Gay)
Gersh. *See* Gershvin, Israel
Gershwin, Bruskin. *See* Gershvin, Israel
Gershwin, George. *See* Gershvin, Jacob
Gershwin, Henry. *See* Mazlen, Henry G(ershwin)
Gershwin, Ira. *See* Gershvin, Israel
Gertrude. *See* Simpson, Jane Cross
Gertrude Stein of Dada Jazz, The. *See* Warnow, Harry
Gesamte, Kalvos. *See* Báthory-Kitsz, Dennis
Gess. *See* Södersten, (Axel) Gunno
Gesta. *See* Stahl, Georg
Getwald, Hans. *See* Martin, Ray(mond)
Gewaro. *See* Römer, Gerhard Walter
Gewe, Raddory. *See* Gorey, Edward (St. John)
Geyer, Hermann. *See* Ruck, Hermann
Geyer, Richard. *See* Wagner, Richard
Gheel, Henry. *See* Geehl, Henry Ernest
Ghelderode, Michel de. *See* Martens, Adolphe-Adhemar-Louis-Michel
Ghéon, Henri. *See* Vangeon, Henri-Léon
Gherardello, da Firenze. *See* Niccolò, de Francesco
Ghigi, Alearco. *See* Menotti, Gian Carlo
Ghisallo, Luigi di. *See* Vlak, Kees
Ghisling, Johann. *See* Ghiselin, Johannes [or Jean]
Ghizzolo. *See* Pasino [or Pasini], Stefano
Ghostface Killah. *See* Coles, Dennis
Ghurkin, (Rev.) Fred. *See* Lennon, John (Winston)
Ghurkin, (Rev.) Thumbs. *See* Lennon, John (Winston)
Gian Leoardo, dell'Arpa. *See* Mollica, Giovanni Leonardo
GianMarco. *See* Zignago Alcóver, GianMarco Javier
Gian(n)ettini, Antonio. *See* Zan(n)ettini, Antonio
Giannetto. *See* Palestrina, Giovanni Pierluigi da
Gibbs, Mike. *See* Irving, Michael Clement
Gibbs, Terry. *See* Gubenko, Julius (Herbert)
Gibin, Dottor. *See* Binetti, Giovanni
Gibson, Don. *See* Campbell, James [or Jimmy]
Gibson, Don. *See* Connelly, Reg(inald)
Gibson, Glenn. *See* Davis, Bertha Ruth
Gibson, Grandpappy. *See* Gibson, Clifford
Gibson, Harry. *See* Raab, Harry
Gibson, S. *See* Baker, McHouston
Giddings, Clarice. *See* Saenger, Gustave
Giese, Willking. *See* Gieseking, Walter
Giesecke, (Sir) Charles Lewis. *See* Metzler, Johann Georg
Giesecke, Karl [or Carl] Ludwig. *See* Metzler, Johann Georg
Gigg, Ulli. *See* Nakat, Lothar
Giglleithner, K(arl). *See* Blümml, Emil Karl
Gil Blas. *See* Veneziani, Carlo
Gil, Gilberto. *See* Moreira, Gilberto Passos
Gilbert and Sullivan of America. *See* Hart, Lorenz (Milton)
Gilbert and Sullivan of America. *See* Rodgers, Richard (Charles)
Gilbert and Sullivan of Broadway. *See* Hammerstein, Oscar (Greeley Clendenning), II
Gilbert and Sullivan of Broadway. *See* Rodgers, Richard (Charles)
Gilbert, Ann. *See* Taylor, Ann
Gilbert, A(rthur) T(homas). *See* Wilson, Ira B(ishop)
Gilbert, Austin. *See* Frangkiser, Carl (Moerz)
Gilbert, E. K. *See* Loes, Harry Dixon
Gilbert, Jacques. *See* Kann, Hans
Gilbert, Jean. *See* Winterfeld, Max
Gilbert, Robert. *See* Winterfeld, David Robert
Gilbertian. *See* Gilbert William Schwenck
Gilberto, Gil. *See* Moreira, Gilberto Passos
Gilboa, Jacob. *See* Goldberg, Erwin
Gilded Age Gadfly. *See* Huneker, James Gibbons
Giles, Johnny. *See* Mellenbruch, Giles Edward
Gilfish, Trident "Gigger". *See* Garrett, James Allen
Gilford, Fred. *See* Goodman, Alfred (Grant)
Gilhaus, (H.). *See* Carl, Robert
Gilkyson, Terry. *See* Gilkyson, Hamilton Henry
Gill, Rusty. *See* Gill, Ralph
Gilles, (Jean). *See* Villard, J(ean)
Gillespie, Dizzy. *See* Gillespie, John (Birks)
Gillette, Henry. *See* McClaskey, Harry Haley
Gillette, Irving. *See* McClaskey, Harry Haley
Gillum, Jazz. *See* Gillum, William McKinley
Gilman, J. D. *See* Fishman, Jack (1920-)
Gilman, J. D. *See* Orgill, Douglas
Gilmore, Joyce. *See* Saenger, Gustave
Gilmour, Rex. *See* Lockton, Edward F.
Gilson, O. A. *See* Hughes, Arthur W(ellesley)
Giltersberg, Konstantin von. *See* Gleich, Ferdinand Theodor
Giménez, Gregorio. *See* Villoldo (Arroyo), Angel (Gregorio)
Giminz, Gregorio. *See* Villoldo (Arroyo), Angel (Gregorio)

Ginann. *See* Baiocchi, Regina A. Harris
Gines, Ferda [or Ferde, or Frede]. *See* Waignein, Andre
Ginesio, Argesio. *See* De Rogati(s), Francesco Saverio
Ginster, Theodor. *See* Kaiser, Hermann
Giordan(i)ello. *See* Giordani, Giuseppe
Giornovichi, Giovanni Mane. *See* Jarnowick, Giovanni Mane
Giovacchino. *See* Pizzi, (Giuseppe) Gioacchino
Giovanardi, Niccolò. *See* Zanardi, Niccolò
Giovane, Il. *See* Cervetto, James (1747-1837)
Giovanni. *See* Saint Germain, Count of
Giovanni da Roma. *See* Costanzi, Giovanni Battista
Giovanni de Florentia. *See* Giovanni da Cascia
Giovanni del Violone. *See* Lulier, Giovanni (Lorenzo)
Giovanni Leonardo, dell'Arpa. *See* Mollica, Giovanni Leonardo
Giovannino del Violoncello. *See* Boccherini, (Ridolfo) Luigi
Giovannino del Violoncello. *See* Costanzi, Giovanni Battista
Giraldi, Georgis. *See* Franklin, Malvin Maurice
Girard, Harry. *See* Kemp, Victor
Girard, Jaques. *See* Cailliet, Lucien
Girdlestone, Victor. *See* Krenkel, Gustav
Girl Gershwin. *See* Suesse, (Nadine) Dana
Girl Hero. *See* Smith, Jewel Fay
Girl of Smiles, The. *See* Moore, Monette
Girl with the Million Dollar Smile, The. *See* Bigeou, Esther
Girls of the Golden West, The. *See* Goad, Dorothy LaVern
Girls of the Golden West, The. *See* Goad, Mildred Fern
Girolamo, da Mondondone. *See* Ferrari, Girolamo
Girolamo da Udine. *See* Dalla Casa, Girolamo
Gisma, Giulio. *See* Maggio, Luigi
Gistel, Luc. *See* Waignein, Andre
Gitfiddle Jim. *See* Arnold, James
Gitry, Willie. *See* Boyd, Willie
Giuglini, Signor. *See* Rizzi, Ferrante
Giui, José Melis. *See* Guiu, José Melis
Giuliani, Alfred. *See* Parlow, Edmund
Giulio Romano. *See* Caccini, Giulio (Romolo)
Giusquino. *See* Della Salla, Josquino
Giusto, (G.). *See* Weber, (Jacob) Gottfried
Giuwine. *See* Lumpkin, (Elgin)
Glad, Sven. *See* Novak, Edmund
Gladstein, Israel *see*— Gladshtayn, Yísra'el
Gladstone, Israel. *See* Gladshtayn, Yísra'el
Glady, Tom. *See* Schaefer, Hermann
Glam-Rock Godfather, The. *See* Jones, David Robert (Haywood)
Glarean, Heinrich (Loriti). *See* Loriti, Heinrich, of Glarus
Glareanus, Heinrich (Loriti). *See* Loriti, Heinrich, of Glarus
Glaser, Tompall. *See* Glaser, Thomas P(aul)
Glaze, Red Hot Willie. *See* McTell, Willie Samuel
Gleason, Jackie. *See* Gleason, Herbert John
Glebov, Igor. *See* Asafiev, Boris Vladimirovich
Glenn, (Mrs). Jen(n)ie. *See* Crosby, Fanny [i.e., Frances] J(ane)
Glenn, Millard A. *See* Pace, Adger McDavid
Glenroy, William B. *See* Gray, William B.
Glick, Elmo. *See* Leiber, Jerry
Glick, Elmo. *See* Stoller, Mike
Glide, Merlin. *See* Fläschner, Peter
Glissando. *See* Meyer-Kundt, Heinz
Glitter, Gary. *See* Gadd, Paul
Gliwudski, S. *See* Ludwig, Carl (F.)
Glodoci, Loran. *See* Goldoni, Carlo
Glombig, Eberhard. *See* Schindler, Hans
Glorious John. *See* Cramer, Johann [or John] Baptist
Glory and Splendour of the Secular Stage, The. *See* Cesti, Pietro
Glossator. *See* Mehring, Walter
Glück, Mathias. *See* Mai, Siegfried
Gluckists. *See* Gluck, Christoph Willibald
Gluckists' High Priest. *See* Arnaud, François
Glückmann, Hans. *See* Bader, Ernst (Johannes Albert)
Glückmann, Hans. *See* Breuer, F(ranz) J(osef)
Gnapeta. *See* Ruberti, Giovanni Battista
Gobbo della Regina, Il. *See* Leinati, Carlo Ambrogio
God of Scarborough, The. *See* Maclean, Alexander [or Alick] Morvaren
Godard, Charles. *See* Behr, F(ranz)
Godchalk, Eugene Charles Jean. *See* Godecharle, Eugene Charles Jean
Godebrie, Jacques. *See* Godebrye, Jacob
Godescalcus, Lintpurgensis. *See* Gottschalk von Limburg
Godfather of American Experimental Music. *See* Cowell, Henry
Godfather of Atonal Music. *See* Schoenberg, Arnold
Godfather of Bad Boy Composers. *See* Satie, (Alfred) Erik (Leslie)
Godfather of Brazilian Rock & Roll. *See* Carlos, Roberto
Godfather of Celluloid Music. *See* Newman, Alfred
Godfather of Contemporary Swedish Folkmusic. *See* Möller, Ale
Godfather of Country, The. *See* Rodgers, James [or Jimmie] (Charles)
Godfather of Country Music. *See* Haggard, Merle (Ronald)
Godfather of Country/Rock, The. *See* Connor, Ingram Cecil, III
Godfather of Country-Rock. *See* Hillman, Chris(topher)
Godfather of Disco, The. *See* Montana, Vince, Jr.
Godfather of Dutch Improvisational Music. *See* Breuker, Willem

Godfather of Electronic Music. *See* Gehlhaar, Rolf (Rainer)
Godfather of Electronic Music. *See* Termen, Lev Sergeivitch
Godfather of Electronica, The. *See* Webb, Gary Anthony James
Godfather of Film Composers, The. *See* Rinaldi, Nino Rota
Godfather of Folk, The. *See* Guthrie, Woodrow [or Woody, or Woodie] (Wilson)
Godfather of Folk Disco, The. *See* Laufer, Jake
Godfather of Fusion. *See* Colombier, Michel
Godfather of Glam Rock, The. *See* Feld, Mark
Godfather of Glam Rock, The. *See* Jones, David Robert (Hayward)
Godfather of Go-Go, The. *See* Brown, Chuck
Godfather of Grunge. *See* Young, Neil
Godfather of Irish Music. *See* Makem, Tommy
Godfather of Jazz in India, The. *See* Banks, Louis
Godfather of Kansas City Jazz. *See* Moten, Bennie
Godfather of Latin Soul. *See* Santamaria (Rodríguez), Ramón
Godfather of Les Six. *See* Satie, (Alfred) Erik (Leslie)
Godfather of Lounge. *See* Esquivel, Juan Garcia
Godfather of Minimalism. *See* Riley, Terry
Godfather of Minimalism. *See* Young, LaMonte
Godfather of Minimalist. *See* Glass, Philip
Godfather of Motor City Rock and Roll, The. *See* Levise, William, Jr.
Godfather of *music concrète*, The. *See* Schaeffer, Pierre
Godfather of Nofrills Rock Music, The. *See* Seeger, Robert [or Bob] (Clark)
Godfather of Psychedelic Funk. *See* Stewart, Sylvester
Godfather of Punk (Rock). *See* Osterberg, James Newell
Godfather of R & B, The. *See* Veliotes, John A(lexander)
Godfather of Reggae. *See* Higgs, Joe
Godfather of Russian Jazz Rock. *See* Kozlov, Alexey
Godfather of Shock Rock, The. *See* Furnier, Vincent (Damon)
Godfather of Soul, The. *See* Brown, James
Godfather of Techno, The. *See* Jarre, Jean Michel (Andre)
Godfather of the Blues. *See* Hooker, John Lee
Godfather of the Electric Guitar, The. *See* Polfus(s), Lester (William)
Godfather of the Hungarian Modern Jazz Scene. *See* Szabados, György
Godfather of the "New Complexity" Movement. *See* Ferneyhough, Brian (John Peter)
Godfather of Western Music. *See* Bach, Johann Sebastian
Godfather of Wind Bands, The. *See* Fennell, Frederick
Godfather of World Music. *See* Chowdhury, Robindra Shankar
Godfrée. *See* Herrmann, Georg (1904-1989)
Godfrey, Arthur. *See* Bulch, Thomas Edward
Godfrey, Bob. *See* Roberts, John Godfrey Owen
Godfrey, D. S. *See* Engelmann, H(ans)
Godfrey, George. *See* Müller, Georg Gottfried
Godfrey, John. *See* Knauff, John
Godin, Felix. *See* Brown, Henry Albert
Godmother of Punk. *See* Smith, Patricia [or Patti] (Lee)
God's Image Cut in Ebony. *See* Ignatius
God's Little Feather. *See* Hildegard of Bingen
Godschack, Mr. *See* Gottschalk, Louis Moreau
Goetz, Angelina. *See* Levy, Angelina
Goff, Lijer. *See* Dawes, William
Gogo, Bulgy. *See* Heseltine, Philip (Arnold)
Göhler, (Peter). *See* Bader, Ernst (Johannes Albert)
Goisern, Hubert von. *See* Achleitner, Hubert
Gojkovic, Dusko. *See* Gojkovic, Dusan
Gold, Billy. *See* Carlos, Walter ([nd])
Gold Chain Troubador, The. *See* Tubb, Ernest (Dale)
Gold, Ernest. *See* Goldner, Ernest (Siegmund)
Gold, Hal. *See* Goldberg, Harry (5/24/1912-)
Gold, Jack. *See* Gold, Jacob
Goldberg, Izzy [or Izzie]. *See* Gillespie, John (Birks)
Goldberg, Jack. *See* Deutscher, Karlheinz
Goldberg, Max. *See* Preston, John F.
Goldberg, Phil. *See* Golby, Philip
Goldberg, Sonja. *See* Balenovic, Draga
Goldbird, Jack. *See* Deutscher, Karlheinz
Goldbogen, Michael. *See* Goldbogen, Avrom Hirsch
Golden Arms. *See* Hawkins, Lamont
Golden, Charles. *See* Gaze, Hermann Otto
Golden Necklace of the Blues, The. *See* Pridgett, Gertrude (Malissa Nix)
Golden, Rose. *See* Lillenas, Haldor
Golden, Rusty. *See* Golden, William Lee, Jr.
Golden, Virginia Rose. *See* Lillenas, Haldor
Golden Voice of the Great Southwest, The. *See* Phillips, Bruce (U.)
Golden Voiced Irish Tenor, The. *See* Downey, (Sean) Morton (1901 (or 02)-1985)
Goldfaden, Abraham. *See* Goldenfodim, Abraham
Golding, John. *See* Goldwin, John
Goldman, Sid. *See* Blitz, Leo(nard)
Goldrin, Carl. *See* Frangkiser, Carl (Moerz)
Goldrin, Ernesto. *See* Frangkiser, Carl (Moerz)
Goldsen, Mickey. *See* Golsen, Michael H.
Goldstein, J. *See* Brown, Frederic
Gólka, Apollin. *See* Sikorski, Józef
Goll, Yvan. *See* Lang, Isaac
Gollmann, Werner. *See* Giesen, Willy
Golodnova, N. *See* Zeyfas, Natal'ya
Golodny, Michail. *See* Epshtein, Michail Semjonowitsch
Golowin, Albert. *See* Gulda, Friedrich
Gomer, Llewellyn. *See* Jones, Gomer L(lewellyn) [or Llewellyn Gomer]
Gomez, Johnny. *See* Carter, Bennett L(ester)

Gomez, Urbano. *See* Montiel, Urbano Gomez
Gonazles, Miguel. *See* Zadora, Michael
Göndör, Károly. *See* Kraushaar, Charles
Gonga, Dawillie. *See* Duke, George Mac
Gonsalves, Joli. *See* Gonsalves, John P(ires)
Gontard, Manfred. *See* Schneider, M(anfred)
Gonzaga, Chiquinha. *See* Gonzaga do Amaral, Francisca Edviges
Gonzaguinha. *See* Gonzaga, Luiz, Jr.
Gonzales, Bab. *See* Brown, Lee
Gonzales, Ricardo. *See* Brown, Lee
Gonzalez, Dope. *See* Gonzalez, Kenny
Good, Dolly. *See* Goad, Dorothy Lavern
Good Elvis, The. *See* Boone, Charles Eugene
Good Gray Poet, The. *See* Whitman, Walt(er)
Good, Millie. *See* Goad, Mildred Fern
Good Rockin' Charles. *See* Bester, Henry Lee
Good Rocking Sam. *See* Maghett, Sam(uel)
Good Shepherd, The. *See* Browder, William [or Bill]
Good Vicar, The. *See* DeCourcy, Richard
Goodbody, Slim. *See* Burstein, John
Goodchild, Alan. *See* Sugarman, Harry
Goode, Johnnie B. *See* Johnson, Johnnie [or Johnny]
Goodhall, Clare. *See* Davis, Katherine K(ennicott)
Goodhart, Al. *See* Goodhart, A(rthur) M(urray)
Goodman, Alfred (Grant). *See* Guttmann, Alfred (Grant)
Goodwin, Doug. *See* Goodwin, Charles D.
Gook, Roosevelt. *See* Zimmerman, Robert Allen
Goose, M. *See* Framer, Marjorie
Gorazd. *See* Aškerc, Anton
Gorchakov, Sergei (Petrovich). *See* Tsveifel', Sergey Petrovich
Gordan, Rabbi Joseph. *See* Cope, Julian
Gordo, El. *See* Troilo, Anibal (Carmelo)
Gordon. *See* Pelosi, Domonic [or Don]
Gordon, Albert. *See* Slaughter, M(arion) T(ry)
Gordon, Curtis. *See* Bergh, Arthur
Gordon, Flash. *See* Gordon, William Marvin
Gordon, Gavin. *See* Brown, Gavin
Gordon, Grace. *See* Yale, Elsie D(uncan)
Gordon, Hal. *See* Goldberg, Harry (5/1/1910-)
Gordon, Hope. *See* Batchelder, James
Gordon, Hugh. *See* Norden, Hugo (Svan)
Gordon, Hugh. *See* Reibold, Bruno
Gordon, Hugh. *See* Scott, Charles P(hillips)
Gordon, John. *See* Gesner, Clark
Gordon, Leo. *See* Cobb, George L(inus)
Gordon, Mack. *See* Gittler, Morris
Gordon, Melvyn Lenard. *See* Gertz, Irving
Gordon, Melvyn Lenard. *See* Gordon, David M.
Gordon, Melvyn Lenard. *See* Kahn, Dave
Gordon, Melvyn Lenard. *See* Lava, William
Gordon, Odettta. *See* Holmes, Odetta
Gordon, Rabbi Joseph. *See* Cope, Julian
Gordon, Richard. *See* Gordon, Ben (B.)
Gordon, Stanley. *See* Rawlings, Alfred William
Gordy, Rock. *See* Gordy, Kenneth [or Kennedy]
Gore, D. Awdrey. *See* Gorey, Edward (St. John)
Gore, Gerald (Wilfring). *See* Riegger, Wallingford (Constantin)
Gore, Wilfring. *See* Riegger, Wallingford (Constantin)
Gorge, Mr. *See* Gouge, George
Gorgeous Weed. *See* Phelps, Arthur
Gorki, Maxim. *See* Peshkov, Aleksei Maksimovich
Gorky, Maksim. *See* Peshkov, Aleksei Maksimovich
Gorney, Jay. *See* Gornetzky, Daniel Jason
Goro, Menucci de. *See* Anelli, Angelo
Gorody, George. *See* Goitein, George (G.)
Gorovoy. *See* Tchaikovskii, Modest Illich
Gorrio, Tobia. *See* Boito, Arrigo (Enrico)
Gospel Elvis Costello, A. *See* Taylor, (Roland) Steve
Gospel Fish. *See* Thomas, Everald
Gospel Minnie. *See* Douglas, Lizzie
Goss, Mattie E. *See* Boggs, Mattie E.
Gossette, Jean. *See* Klickmann, F(rank) Henri
Gosztonyi, Tera. *See* Guttman, Therese
Gotte. *See* Gottschalk, Heinz-Jürgen
Gottfried, Heinrich. *See* Bamberger, Ludwig
Gotthardi, G. *See* Krenn, Hans
Gotwald, Hans. *See* Martin, Ray(mond)
Götz, Norbert. *See* Frohloff, Erich Carl
Goublier, Gustave. *See* Conin, Henri
Goublier, Henri. *See* Conin, Henri
Goudge, Mr. *See* Gouge, George
Goulan, Douglas. *See* Paramor, Norman [or Norrie] (William)
Gould, Frank. *See* Crosby, Fanny [i.e., Frances] J(ane)
Gould, Glenn (Herbert). *See* Gold, Glenn Herbert
Gould, Ivor. *See* Yorke, Peter
Goulet, Baron Paul. *See* Gandonnière, Almire
Gound, Robert. *See* Gund, Robert
Gounod, Pierre. *See* Williams, Spencer
Goupillier. *See* Desmarets, Henri
Gournard, P. *See* Leoni, Franco
Govinda. *See* O'Madden, Shane
Gowans, Brad. *See* Gowans, Arthur Bradford
Gower, Beryl. *See* Atkinson, Dorothy
Goykovich, Dusko. *See* Gajkovic, Dusan
Graban. *See* Bantock, Granville (Ransom)
Grace, J. Frances. *See* Crosby, Fanny [i.e., Frances] J(ane)
Grace Tennessee and Her Guitar. *See* Smith, Mira
Gracian. *See* Labrunie, Gérard
Grade, Francis. *See* Filip, Paul Francis
Gradi, R. G. *See* Grady, R(ichard) G.
Graetsch, Hans. *See* Zander, Hans
Graham, Arthur. *See* Frangkiser, Carl (Moerz)
Graham, Budd. *See* Bazelon, Irwin (A.)
Graham, Eleanor. *See* Saenger, Gustave

Graham, George. *See* Spaulding, G(eorge) L(awson)
Graham, H. *See* Goldsen, Michael H.
Graham, Herbert. *See* Turnbridge, Joseph A(lbert)
Graham, Irvin. *See* Abraham, Irvin
Graham, Kenny. *See* Skingle, Kenneth Thomas
Graham, Leonard. *See* Sissle, Noble (Lee)
Graham, M. E. *See* Bliss, P(hilip) Paul
Graham, Peter. *See* Stástný-Pokorný, Jarosalv
Graham, Robert. *See* Rawlings, Charles Arthur
Graham, Robert Z. *See* Loomis, Harvey Worthington
Graham, Steve. *See* Goldsen, Michael H.
Graham, W(alter). *See* Frangkiser, Carl (Moerz)
Grain, Joe. *See* Watz, Franz
Graindorge. *See* Capus, Alfred Vincent
Grainger, Perks. *See* Grainger, (George) Percy (Aldridge)
Grallon, Bihn. *See* Bénédictus, Louis
Gramm, Lou. *See* Grammatico, Lou
Grammateus, Henricus. *See* Schreyber, Heinrich
Grand Carme. *See* Buns, Benedictus
Grand Eagle. *See* Ballard, Louis W(ayne)
Grand Jacques. *See* Moderne, Jacques
Grand, June. *See* Neumeyer, Heike
Grand(e) Kallé, (The). *See* Kabas(s)elé (Tshamala), Joseph
Grand Master of Calypso. *See* Roberts, Aldwyn [or Aldwin]
Grand Nez, Le. *See* Piffett, Etienne
Grand Old Man of Italian Band Music. *See* Orsomando, Giovanni
Grand Old Man of Neapolitan Music, The. *See* Mercadante, Giuseppe Saverio Raffaele
Grand Puba. *See* Dixon, Maxwell
Grand Seigneur. *See* De Koven, (Henry Louis) Reginald
Grand, Steinway. *See* Kunkel, Charles
Granda, Chabuca. *See* Larco, Isabel Granda
Granddaddy of the Hillbillies. *See* Robison, Carson J(ay)
Grandfather of Brazilian Popular Music. *See* Rosa, Noel
Grandfather of British R & B. *See* Korner, Alexis (Andrew Nicholas)
Grandfather of British Rock, The. *See* Mayall, John
Grandfather of Country Music, The. *See* Slaughter, M(arion) T(ry)
Grandfather of Country/Rock Music. *See* Connor, Ingram Cecil, III
Grandfather of Film Music. *See* Sartain, John, Jr.
Grandfather of Hot Piano. *See* Johnson, James [or Jimmy, or Jimmie] (P(rice))
Grandfather of Minimal Music, The. *See* Young, LaMonte
Grandfather of Soul, The. *See* Brown, James
Grandmaster Flash. *See* Saddler, Joseph
Grando, Piet. *See* Gradenwitz, Peter Werner Emanuel
Grandval, Marie (Félicie Clémence), Viacomtesse de. *See* Reiset, Marie (Félicie Clémence)
Granfield, Arthur Travis [or Traves]. *See* O'Connor, Edward
Grangé, Eugène. *See* Baste, Eugène Pierre
Granger, Lou. *See* Des Granges, Louis Anthony
Granges, Lou. *See* Des Granges, Louis Anthony
Grannis, Mrs. S M. *See* Grannis, S(idney) M(artin)
Grant, Al. *See* Clark, Petula (Sally Olmen [or Olwen])
Grant, Allan P. *See* Kountz, Richard
Grant and Graham. *See* Branen, Jeff T.
Grant and Graham. *See* Johnson, Frederick G.
Grant, Arthur. *See* Finkelstein, Abe
Grant, C. E. *See* Gaskill, Clarence
Grant, Cal. *See* Gaskill, Clarence
Grant, Cecil. *See* Hamilton, Clarence G(rant)
Grant, Coot. *See* Pettigrew, Leola (B.)
Grant, Cutie. *See* Pettigrew, Leola (B.)
Grant, Freddy. *See* Grundland, Frederick [or Fritz]
Grant, Harold (M.). *See* Kirchstein, Harold Manfred [or Manford]
Grant, Hector. *See* Dawson, Peter (Smith)
Grant, Lawrence. *See* Clarke, Mary Elizabeth
Grant, Lawrence. *See* Hostetler, Lawrence A.
Grant, Leola (B.). *See* Pettigrew, Leola (B.)
Grant, Micki. *See* McCutcheon, Minnie L(ouise) Perkins
Grant, Richard. *See* Smith, Harry B(ache)
Grant, Will. *See* Grosz, Wilhelm [or Will]
Grant, Willy M. *See* Still, William Grant
Grantley, Arthur. *See* Meredith, I(saac) H(ickman)
Granval, (Adolphe). *See* Leuven, Adolphe (Ribbing) de
Granville, Laurence. *See* O'Keefe, Lester
Granville, Roger. *See* Ehret, Walter (Charles)
Graph, Tom. *See* Garfunkel, Art(hur Ira)
Grascinsky, Ernest Louis. *See* Müller, Ernest (Louis [or Ludwig])
Grass Roots, The. *See* Lipkin, Stephen [or Steve] (Barri [or Barry])
Grass Roots, The. *See* Schlein, Phi((lip) Gary)
Gratianus, Aurelius. *See* Neale, J(ohn) M(ason)
Grau, Carlo (Luigi). *See* Pietragrua, Carlo (Luigi)
Grau, Frank. *See* Grey, Frank H(erbert)
Grau, Franz. *See* Grey, Frank H(erbert)
Grau, Leonard. *See* Lõhr, Hermann
Graves, Bert. *See* Fabricius-Bjerre, Bent
Graves, Harold. *See* Finkelstein, Abe
Graves, (Uncle) Josh. *See* Graves, Burkett (K.)
Gray, Alfred. *See* Kraushaar, Charles
Gray, Allan. *See* Zmigrod, Joseph
Gray, Anthony. *See* Schiller, Henry Carl
Gray, Billy. *See* Grainger, Porter
Gray, Henry. *See* Finkelstein, Abe
Gray, Jack. *See* Gray, John Baker (Timothy)
Gray, Jerry. *See* Graziano, Generoso
Gray, Laverne. *See* Lillenas, Haldor

Gray, Leonard. *See* Löhr, Hermann
Gray, Leslie. *See* Slaughter, M(arion) T(ry)
Gray, Macy. *See* McIntyre, Natalie
Gray, Maurice. *See* Paroisse-Pougin, François-Auguste-Arthur
Gray, Philip. *See* Beckhard, Robert L.
Gray, Philip. *See* Perlman, Jess
Gray, Robertson. *See* Raymond, Rossiter Worthington
Gray, Rona. *See* Leader, Joyce Rona
Gray, Ronald. *See* Woodhouse, Charles (John)
Gray, Stephen Mark. *See* Hubert, Stephen Fitch
Gray, Timothy. *See* Gray, John Baker (Timothy)
Grayling, Gerald. *See* Liddle, Samuel
Grayson, Charles. *See* Cain, Noble
Grayson, Jack. *See* Lebstock, Jack
Grayson, Paul. *See* Dempsey, James E.
Grayson, Paul. *See* Murray, James R(amsey)
Grazia, E. N. *See* Bourne, (Mrs.)
Graziani, Anneldo. *See* Zanardini, Angelo
Graziano Cimbaloni. *See* Miti, Pompilio
Graziano, Frankie C. *See* Graziano, Caesar Franklin [or Frankie]
Great Blasphemer, The. *See* Newton, John
Great Communicator, The. *See* Taylor, (Joseph) Deems
Great Doctor Robert Morton (— The World's Greatest Hypnotist), The. *See* Lane, Robert William
Great Howard, The. *See* Howard, Joseph E(dgar)
Great Irish Hope of Country Music, The. *See* Lyn(h)am, Ray
Great "Jazz Emancipator," The. *See* Gershvin, Jacob
Great Man of Country Music. *See* Jenkins, Harold (Lloyd)
Great Mogul of Music, The. *See* Beethoven, Ludwig van
Great Morton, The. *See* Lane, Robert William
Great Old Man. *See* Franck, César
Great One, The. *See* Gleason, Herbert John
Great Scot. *See* Lauder, (Sir) Harry (Maclennan)
Great Tompall, The. *See* Glaser, Thomas P(aul)
Great Vance, The. *See* Stevens, Alfred Peck
Great White Hope, The. *See* Salonen, Esa-Pekka
Greatest American Preacher of the 19th Century, The. *See* Brooks, Phillips
Greatest Blues Singer of the World. *See* Hooker, John Lee
Greatest Comedian on the American Stage, The. *See* Williams, Egbert Austin
Greatest English Composer after Handel, The. *See* Arne, Thomas Augustine
Greatest English Composer since Purcell. *See* Parry, Charles Hubert Hastings
Greatest Hymn Writer in Christian History. *See* Watts, Isaac
Greatest Hymn Writer of All Ages, The. *See* Wesley, Charles
Greatest Living Poet in America, The. *See* Robinson, William, (Jr.)
Greatest Living Songwriter of Country Music, The. *See* Walker, Cindy
Greatest of All Colored Showmen, The. *See* Crowders, (Ernest) Reuben
Greatest of American Critics. *See* Huneker, James Gibbons
Greatest of the Rock 'n' Rollers, (The). *See* Berry, Charles Edward Anderson
Greatest Rock and Roll Mogul in the World. *See* Ertegun, Ahmet (Munir)
Greatest Rock Lyricist This Side of Bob Dylan, The. *See* Berry, Charles Edward Anderson
Greatest Singer in the World, The. *See* Orbison, Roy (Kelton)
Greatest Single Woman Singing Comedienne in the World, The. *See* Goldberg, Doris
Greatest Unknown Composer of All Times. *See* Kraus, Joseph Martin
Greatest Visual Comedian of Our Day, The. *See* Leopold, Isaiah Edwin
Greatest White Male Folk Singer in the United States, The. *See* Kazee, Buell (Hilton)
Greber's Peg. *See* De l'Epine, Francesca Margherita
Greco, Buddy. *See* Greco, Armando
Greco, Tommy. *See* Giangreco, Thomas
Greek, The. *See* Gravenites, Nick
Greeley, George (Henry). *See* Guariglia, Georgio
Greeley, Joe. *See* Twomey, Kathleen [or Kay] Greeley
Green, Ben. *See* Anzelwitz [or Anzelvitz], Benjamin [or Bernard]
Green, Benny. *See* Green, Bernard
Green, Bernard. *See* Greenwald, Bernard
Green, Bernie. *See* Greenwald, Bernard
Green, Bert. *See* Kaufman, Jacob
Green, Candy. *See* Green, Clarence
Green-Eyed Bandit. *See* Sermon, Erick
Green, Galveston. *See* Green, Clarence
Green, James. *See* Kunkel, Charles
Green, John. *See* Townsend, George Henry
Green, L. Dunton. *See* Grein, Louis
Green, Martyn. *See* Martyn-Green, William
Green, Maxie. *See* Greenberg, Susan M.
Green, Mazie. *See* Vonderlieth, Leonore
Green, Paddy. *See* Townsend, George Henry
Green, Peter. *See* Greenbaum, Peter (Allen)
Green, Sadie. *See* Vonderlieth, Leonore
Green, Sam. *See* Butler, Ralph (T.)
Green, Slim. *See* Green, Norman G.
Green, Thomas. *See* Wiggins, Thomas (Green(e))
Green, Violet. *See* Smith, Clara
Greendale, Arthur (W.). *See* Gullidge, (W.) Arthur
Greene, Amos. *See* Carlisle, Cliff(ord Raymond)

Greene, Gallant. *See* Kunkel, Charles
Greene, Norman. *See* Greenberg, Norman
Greenwood, K. *See* Wood, Ralph (Walter)
Greenwood, Larry. *See* Yule, Joe, (Jr.)
Greer, David. *See* Fields, Harold (Cornelius)
Greer, David. *See* Roncoroni, Joseph (Dominic)
Greff Bakafart, Valentin. *See* Bakfark, Bálint (Valentin)
Gregg, Joseph [or Joe]. *See* Catsos, Nicholas A.
Gregg, Leonard. *See* Riegger, Wallingford (Constantin)
Gregorio, A. *See* Villoldo (Arroyo), Angel (Gregorio)
Gregorow, Samar. *See* Meyer-Förster, Wilhelm
Gregory, Adam. *See* Sawyer, Henry S.
Gregory, John(ny). *See* Gregori, (Primo) Giovanni [or John]
Gregory, Rod. *See* Hyman, Richard [or Dick] (R(oven))
Gregory, Scott. *See* Haley, William [or Bill] (John Clifton), (Jr.)
Gregory, Stuart. *See* Lutter, Howard
Grémont, Henri. *See* Hartmann, (Jean-François-Romain) Georges
Grenfell, Joyce. *See* Phipps, Joyce Irene
Grenvallet, (Adolphe?). *See* Leuven, Adolphe (Ribbing) de
Grenville, Arthur. *See* Williams, Joseph (Benjamin)
Grenville, Pelham. *See* Wodehouse, P(elham) G(renville)
Gresham, John. *See* Rawlings, Charles Arthur
Grétry, Lucille. *See* Grétry, Angélique-Dorothée-Lucie
Grévé, François. *See* Grey, Frank H(erbert)
Greve, Karl. *See* Grohmann, Karl
Greville, Dorothy. *See* Harrhy, Edith
Grewdead, Roy. *See* Gorey, Edward (St. John)
Grey, Carl. *See* Grothe, Wilhelm
Grey, Clifford. *See* Davis, Percival [or Percy]
Grey, Gandolf [or Gandalf] T. *See* Wilson, Chris (Richard)
Grey, Gerald. *See* Parks, J(ames) A(sher)
Grey, Ginger. *See* Stewart, Joan Beatrice
Grey, Harold. *See* Grainger, Porter
Grey, Langford. *See* Shilston, Alfred Edward
Grey, Lanny. *See* Grey, Alan
Grey, Laverne. *See* Lillenas, Haldor
Grey, Lilian. *See* David, Worton
Grey Man of Buenos Aires, The. *See* Vergiati, Amleto (Enrique)
Grey, Percival. *See* Davis, Percival [or Percy]
Grey, Vivian. *See* Keiser, Robert (A(dolph))
Grey, Vivian. *See* McKinley, Mabel
Greyson, Norman. *See* Edwards, Melinda
Greyson, Norman. *See* Ehret, Walter (Charles)
Greyson, Norman. *See* Wilson, Harry (Robert)
Grieg, E. *See* Kunkel, Charles
Griegg, Leonard. *See* Riegger, Wallingford (Constantin)
Griff, Ray. *See* Grier, James [or Jimmie] W.
Griffen, Alsie. *See* Griffin, Alsie
Griffen, Rex. *See* Griffin, Alsie
Griffin, Curley. *See* Griffin, Howard
Griffin, Henry. *See* Grundman, Clare (Ewing)
Griffin, Rex. *See* Griffin, Alsie
Griffinhoof, Arthur (of Turnham Green). *See* Colman, George, Jr.
Griffith. *See* Foerster, Josef Bohuslav
Griffiths, Bob. *See* Standord, Trevor H(erbert)
Griggs, Frederick. *See* Yoder, Paul V(an Buskirk)
Grigor, Nico. *See* Leclerc, Germaine Ortala
Grill, Andrew. *See* Grill, Anton
Grillengroll, Fritz. *See* Schink, Johann Friedrich [or Gottfried]
Grillito Cantor, (El). *See* Gabilondo Soler, Francisco (José)
Grillo, Angelo. *See* Celiano, Livio
Grillo, Frank (R.). *See* Gutiérrez Grillo, Francisco Raúl
Grillo, Machito. *See* Gutiérrez Grillo, Francisco Raúl
Grimbosh, Herman. *See* Mackay, Charles
Grimes, B. *See* Barton, Billy
Grimes, Betty. *See* Vonderlieth, Leonore
Grin, A. P. *See* Gulyayvev, Aleksandr Pavlovich
Gringoire. *See* Mortjé, Arnold [or Adolphe]
Grinley, (Mrs.) Kate. *See* Crosby, Fanny [i.e., Frances] J(ane)
Grisman, Dawg. *See* Grisman, David (Jay)
Gritti, L. L. Ubalai [fictitious composer?]. *See* Gritti, L. L. Ubalai [fictitious composer?]
Grix, Julien. *See* Ginsburg [or Ginzburg], Lucien
Groaner, The. *See* Crosby, Harry Lillis
Grobstimm, Heinrich. *See* Baryphonus, Henricus
Grock, (The World's Greatest Clown). *See* Wettach, (Charles) Adrien
Grode, Redway. *See* Gorey, Edward (St. John)
Groh, B. J. *See* Roscoe, B. Jeanie
Grohner, Franz. *See* Zamastil, Franz
Grolo, Calindo. *See* Goldoni, Carlo
Gronau, Thomas. *See* Sonneborn, Günter
Grooms, Calvin. *See* Sartorio, Arnoldo
Grooms, Calvin. *See* Smith, Lee Orean
Grove, Cynthia Mary Kathleen. *See* Hart, Cynthia Mary Kathleen
Groves, Ron. *See* Worland, Bill
Growling Tiger (of Calypso). *See* Marcano, Neville
Grub, Stephen. *See* Fielding, Henry
Gruber, Ludwig. *See* Anzengruber, Ludwig
Grubmeini, J. *See* Ricordi, Giulio
Grummelgut, Johannes. *See* Steinwert von Soest, Johannes
Grundhoff, Walter. *See* Andries, Franzleo
Grunt, Blind Boy. *See* Zimmerman, Robert Allen
Gryce, Gigi. *See* Gryce, G(eorge) G(eneral)
Gualandi, Anselmo. *See* Guerrazzi, Francesco Domenico
Gualterio, Don. *See* Starkie, Walter Fitzwilliam

Guerez, Juan. *See* Gürsch, Günther Gerhard
Guermo, Carlos. *See* Grundman, Clare (Ewing)
Guerra, Rapindey. *See* Guerra, Marcelino
Guerrero, Lalo. *See* Guerrero, Eduardo
Guerrero, Luciano. *See* Feather, Leonard (Geoffrey)
Guesnon, Creole. *See* Guesnon, George
Guesnon, Curly. *See* Guesnon, George
Guglielmini. *See* Guglielmi, (Pietro) Carlo
Guido. *See* Winkler, Karl [or Carl] Gottfried Theodor
Guido Aretinus. *See* Guido d'Arezzo [or Aretino]
Guidonian. *See* Guido d' Arezzo [or Aretino]
Guidonius, Jean. *See* Guyot [de Châtelet], Jean
Guiglielmo di Santo Spirito, Frate. *See* Guilielmus de Francia
Guignon, Jean Pierre. *See* Ghignone, Giovanni Pietri
Guilain, Jean Adam Guillaume. *See* Freinsberg, J(ean) A(dam) G(uillaume)
Guilford, Baron [or Lord]. *See* North, Francis
Guillard, Michael. *See* Blitz, Leo(nard)
Guillard, Michael. *See* Silver, Dave
Guillard, Michael. *See* Sugarman, Harry
Guillaume, Louis. *See* Guglielmi, L(o)uis
Guillermo. *See* Pichot, Guillermo
Guillermos, S. Gualterio. *See* Williams, Spencer
Guitar, Bonnie. *See* Buckingham, Bonnie
Guitar, Dino. *See* Dinino, Louis (Lee)
Guitar Eddy. *See* Harrington, Eddy
Guitar Jr. [or Junior]. *See* Baker, Lee, Jr.
Guitar Jr. [or Junior]. *See* Johnson, Luther, Jr.
Guitar Man, The. *See* Hubbard, Jerry (Reed)
Guitar, Nubbit. *See* Hankerson, Alvin
Guitar Pete. *See* Franklin, Edward Lamonte
Guitar Red. *See* Minter, Iverson
Guitar Shorty. *See* Fortescue, John Henry
Guitar Slim. *See* Green, Norman G.
Guitar Slim. *See* Jones, Eddie
Guitar Slim. *See* Otey, Raymond Maurice
Guitar Slim. *See* Seward, Alexander T.
Guitar Wizard, The. *See* Woodbridge, Hudson
Guitry, Sacha. *See* Guitry, Alexandre Georges Pierre
Guittone, Fra. *See* Guido d'Arezzo [or Aretino]
Guley, Heinz. *See* Leykauf, Walter Heinz
Guliver. *See* Rimskij-Korsakov, Andrej Nikolaevic
Gulliver, Andrew. *See* Stein, Herman
Gulliver, Lemuel, Poet Laureate to the King of Lilliput. *See* Fielding, Henry
Gullmar, Kai. *See* Bergström, Gurli Maria
Gumm, Wilbur. *See* Gumbinsky, Wilbur
Gump, Richard (Benjamin). *See* Guckenheimer, Fritz
Gunboat Billy [or Willy]. *See* Ahl, Fred Arthur
Gunn, Elston. *See* Zimmerman, Robert Allen
Gunovsky, Vilem. *See* Gundel, Vilem
Gunter, Hardrock. *See* Gunter, Sidney Louie, Jr.
Günther, Anton. *See* Oldenburg, Elimar Anton Günther Friedrich Herzog von
Günther, Friedrich. *See* Rotter, Fritz
Gunther, Lex. *See* Moesser, (Karl-)Peter
Günther, Paul. *See* Peitl, Paul
Gunther, William. *See* Sprecher, Gunther William
Guntz, Werner. *See* Wysocki, Gerd von
Guru. *See* Elam, Keith
Guru of Stutterers. *See* Tillis, (Lonnie) Mel(vin)
Gushington, Impulsia. *See* Sheridan, Helen Selina
Gustard, Jim. *See* Paramor, Norman [or Norrie] (William)
Gustavi. *See* Almqvist, Carl Jonas Love [or Ludwig]
Gutchë, Gene. *See* Gutsche, Romeo Maximilian (Eugene Ludwig)
Guthrie, Jack. *See* Guthrie, Leon Jerry
Guthrie, Lester. *See* Yoder, Paul V(an Buskirk)
Guv-nor, The. *See* Korner, Alexis (Andrew Nicholas)
Guy, Aye. *See* Cole Nathaniel Adams
Guy, Buddy. *See* Guy, George
Guy Lombardo of Latin Music, The. *See* Cugat de Bru y Deulofeo, Francisco de Asis Javier
Guy of Arezzo. *See* Guido d'Arezzo [or Aretino]
Guyer, Percy. *See* Winner, Septimus
Guyer, Stacy. *See* Winner, Septimus
Guyoz, Jean. *See* Guyot [de Châtelet], Jean
Guzmán, Fato. *See* Guzmán Yañez, Enrique
Gwalchmai. *See* Jones, Joseph David
Gwenynen Arfon. *See* James, J.
Gwilym Gwent. *See* Williams, William A(ubrey)
Gwinn, Francis. *See* Grey, Frank H(erbert)
Gwyllt, Ieua(n). *See* Roberts, John
Gwynn, Francis. *See* Grey, Frank H(erbert)
Gwynn o'r Llan. *See* Gwynn Williams, W(illiam) S(idney)
Gwynne, Martha. *See* Denni, Martha (Gwynne)
Gynt, Peer. *See* Taralsen, Peer Helge
Gynt, Peer. *See* Zhilyayev, Nikolay Sergeyevich
Gyrowetz, Adalbert (Mathias). *See* Jírovec, Vojtěch Matayáš
Gysberet, David. *See* Linden, David Gysbert

– H –

H. *See* Hastings, Horace Lorenzo
H***. *See* Herz, Heinrich [or Henri]
H—t. *See* Hart, Joseph
H. A. C. *See* Chambers, Herbert Arthur
H. A. H. *See* Gabriel, Charles H(utchinson)
H. B. *See* Bourne, Hugh
H. B. *See* Brian, William
H. B-W. *See* Bieler-Wendt, Helmut
H. C. F. *See* Senf, H(einrich) C(hristian) L(ebrecht)
H. C.-L. *See* Clough-Leighter, Henry
H. Carl S. *See* Schiller, Henry Carl
H. d'A. C. *See* Champney, H. d'A.

H-D-H. *See* Dozier, Lamont
H-D-H. *See* Holland, Brian
H-D-H. *See* Holland, Eddie
H. D. K. *See* Kiemle, Hans Dieter
H. D. L. *See* Loes, Harry Dixon
H. F. C. *See* Chorley, Henry Fothergill
H. F. S. *See* Sheppard, Henry Fleetwood
H. H. *See* Harrington, Henry
H. H. *See* Rands, William Brightly
H. J. G. *See* Gauntlett, Henry John
H. K. *See* Kestner, H.
H. K. *See* Kynaston, Herbert
H. K. A. *See* Andrews, Herbert Kennedy
H. L. L. *See* Borthwick, Jane Laurie
H. M. C. *See* Chester, Harriet Mary (née Goff)
H. P. *See* Playford, Henry
H. P. H. *See* Hawkins, Hester Periam (née Lewis)
H. T. P. *See* Parker, Henry Taylor
H. W. G. *See* Greatorex, Henry Wellington
H. W. H. *See* Hunt, Hubert Walter
H. W. R. L. *See* Lillie, H. W. R.
Haaglund, Joel. *See* Hägglund, Joel (Em(m)anuel)
Habec, Franz. *See* Bache, Francis Edward
Habermann, Wilhelm. *See* Öhquist, Johannes
Haddon, Charles. *See* Ellis, Seger
Hadi, Shafi. *See* Porter, Curtis
Hadler, Rosemary. *See* Lorenz, Ellen Jane
Haendel, L. L. *See* Bliss, P(hilip) Paul
Haenschen, Gus(tave). *See* Haenschen, Walter (G(ustave))
Hafermann, Antonius. *See* Avenarius, Tony [or Toni]
Haffner, Carl. *See* Schlächter, Karl
Hafrenydd. *See* Williams, Thomas
Hag, The. *See* Cash, John(ny) (R.)
Hagen, Hans. *See* Köstelbauer, Hans
Hagen, Larry. *See* Barnes, H(oward) E(llington)
Hagen, Larry. *See* Fields, Harold (Cornelius)
Hagen, Larry. *See* Roncoroni, Joseph (Dominic)
Hagen, Milt. *See* Hagen, J(ohn) M(ilton)
Hagen, Teodor. *See* Fels, Joachim
Hager, Fred(erick W.). *See* Haga, Fred(erick Wallace)
Hager, Johann(es). *See* Hasslinger von Hasslinger, Johannes (Nepomuk), Freiherr von
Hagert, Tony. *See* Hagert, Thornton
Haghe, J. *See* Bloom, John Hague
Hague, Albert (M.). *See* Marcuse, Albrecht [or Albert]
Hague, Bert. *See* Marcuse, Albrecht [or Albert]
Hague, John. *See* Bloom, John Hague
Hahnbüchn, M. *See* Sobolewski, J(ohann) F(riedrich) E(duard)
Hahnen, Josef. *See* Feltz, Kurt (August Karl)
Haig(h), Bernard. *See* Gerlich, Clara
Haig-Guinness, Duncan. *See* Gold, Glenn Herbert
Haight, Rip. *See* Carpenter, John(ny)
Hain, Erlefried. *See* Jirasek, Franz Josef
Hains, Ben. *See* Gabriel, Charles H(utchinson)
Hainsworth, Richard. *See* Lillenas, Haldor
Hajime, Dekoboko. *See* Zorn, John
Hajku, Michal. *See* Mokrý, Jarmil Michael
Hajnal. *See* Zieritz, Grete von
Hakim, Talib Rasul. *See* Chambers, Stephen Alexander
Hale, Auntie. *See* Hale, Philip
Hale, Charles. *See* Paramor, Norman [or Norrie] (William)
Hale, Ernest Wilbur. *See* Kunkel, Charles
Hale, Eugenia. *See* Woolsey, Mary Hale [or Maryhale]
Hale, H. P. *See* Pike, Harry Hale
Hale, Howitt. *See* Isaacs, Rufus
Hale, Jimmy. *See* Jones, Isham (Edgar)
Hale, Katherine. *See* Warnock, Amelia Beers
Hale, Mark. *See* Gearinger, Lemuel Cyrus
Hale, Mary. *See* Woolsey, Mary Hale [or Maryhale]
Hale, (Mrs.) Philip. *See* Baungros, Irene
Hale, Sonnie. *See* Hale-Monro, John Robert
Hale, Wil P. *See* Hays, Will(iam) S(hakespeare)
Halévy, Fromental. *See* Levy, Jacques Francois Fromental Èlie
Haley, Ed. *See* Keiser, Robert (A(dolph))
Haley, Harry. *See* McClaskey, Harry Haley
Half-Valve. *See* Steward, William, Jr.
Halger, Hans. *See* Wittstatt, Hans(-Artur)
Haliver, Joan. *See* Haliver, Hanne
Halka, Aleks. *See* Ledóchowska, Maria Teresa
Hall, A(lbert). *See* McLaughlin, John
Hall, Alfred. *See* Kountz, Richard
Hall, Coldham. *See* Page, Arthur James
Hall, Daryl. *See* Hohl, Daryl Franklin
Hall, Erkenvkv. *See* Hall, (Christopher) Newman
Hall, Frank. *See* Stewart, Herbert
Hall, Fred. *See* Ahl, Fred Arthur
Hall, Frieda P. C. *See* Cohen, Frieda P. C.
Hall, George. *See* Lake, M(ayhew) L(ester)
Hall, James. *See* Stanley, James
Hall, John T. *See* Newcomer, John T.
Hall, Margaret. *See* Fishman, Jack (1918 (or 19)-)
Hall, Margaret. *See* Hargreaves, Peter
Hall, Owen. *See* Davis, James [or Jimmy] (1853-1907)
Hall, Ray. *See* Fillmore, (James) Henry
Hall, Robert. *See* Lake, M(ayhew) L(ester)
Hall, Roy. *See* Hall, James Faye
Hall, Shawn. *See* Davis, Elizabeth
Hall, Sugar. *See* Ahl, Fred Arthur
Hall, Sugar. *See* Hall, Gertrude
Hall, Teddy. *See* Hall, Helen
Hall, Than. *See* Ritchie, Jean
Hall, Thomas. *See* Hutchinson, Leslie
Hall, Thomas. *See* Paramor, Norman [or Norrie] (William)
Hall, Tom T. *See* Hall, Thomas
Halle Bach, (The). *See* Bach, Wilhelm Friedman

Hallé, (Sir) Charles. *See* Hallé, Karl [or Carl]
Halle, Howen. *See* Davis, James [or Jimmie]
Hallelujah Joe. *See* McCoy, Joe
Haller, Edwin. *See* Lautenscläger, Willi
Haller, Fred. *See* Börschel, Erich
Haller, Hermann. *See* Freund, Hermann
Haller, Richard. *See* Levy, R(ichard)
Hallesch, Günther. *See* Reinhardt, Helmut
Hallock. *See* Bolz, Harriett
Halloway. *See* Herold, Helmuth
Halls, J. C. *See* Lincoln, Harry J.
Halm, Friedrich. *See* Münch-Bellinghausen, Eligius Franz Joseph
Halphin, E(a)rnest. *See* Miles, George H(enry)
Halsman, David. *See* Fass, Bernard [or Bernie]
Haltenberger, Bernhard. *See* Haltenberger, Johann Nikolaus
Halton, Theo(dore). *See* Hess, Theodore
Ham., A(nd.). *See* Hammerschmidt, Andreas
Ham and Scam. *See* Busbice, Bernarr (G(raham))
Ham and Scam. *See* Pike, Pete
Ham Gravy. *See* Brown, Robert (1910-1966)
Hamburg Bach, The. *See* Bach, Carl [or Karl] Philipp Emanuel
Hamerik, Asger. *See* Hammerich, Asger
Hamerik, Ebbe. *See* Hammerich, Ebbe
Hames, May. *See* Rüssmann, Georg(e)
Hamfoot Ham. *See* McCoy, Joe
Hamilton, Chico. *See* Hamilton, Foreststorn
Hamilton, Clyde. *See* Stapleton, Cyril
Hamilton, Cosmo. *See* Gibbs, Henry Charles Hamilton
Hamilton, George. *See* Davenport, Charles Edward
Hamilton, Gray. *See* Hartwell-Jones, William P(rice)
Hamilton/Leland. *See* Busch, Louis F(erdinand)
Hamilton, Lloyd. *See* Fishman, Jack (1918 (or 19)-)
Hamilton, Paul. *See* Liter, Monia
Hamilton, Russ. *See* Hulme, Ronald
Hamilton, Spike. *See* Hamilton, George
Hamilton, Ted. *See* Cobb, George L(inus)
Hamilton, Ted. *See* Hamilton, Edward Leslie
Hamlet of the Halls, The. *See* Friedman, Theodore (Leopold)
Hammar, Stig. *See* Hansson, Stig (Axel)
Hammer. *See* Burrell, Stanley (Kirk)
Hammer, Buck. *See* Allen, Stephen [or Steve] (Valentine Patrick William)
Hammer Hand. *See* Axton, Hoyt (Wayne)
Hammer, Jack. *See* Burroughs, Earl S.
Hammer, M. C. *See* Burrell, Stanley (Kirk)
Hammer, (Franz) Xaver. *See* Marteau, Franz Xaver
Hammond, Kate. *See* Kauffman, Helen Reed
Hamp. *See* Hampton, Lionel (Leo)
Hampton, Roxanne. *See* Bergh, Arthur
Hampton, Roxanne. *See* Davis, Joseph [or Joe] (M.)
Hampton, Slide. *See* Hampton, Locksley (Wellington)
Hanan, Stephen. *See* Kaplan, Stephen Hanan
Hancock, Billy. *See* Marvin, John(ny) (Senator)
Hancock, Butch. *See* Hancock, George
Hancock, John. *See* Breitenbach, Alfred
Handel, Georg Friedrich. *See* Casadesus, Francis [or François] Louis
Handel, Georg Friedrich (Spirit). *See* Enticknap, Clifford
Handel(l) of Maine, The. *See* Belcher, Supply
Handelian. *See* Handel, Georg Friederich
Handiside, Mr. *See* Irving, Washington
Handl, Jacob. *See* Petelin, Jakob
Handle, Johnny. *See* Pandrich, John Alan
Handsomest Man in Rock & Roll. *See* Penniman, Richard [or Ricardo] Wayne
Handy, George (Joseph). *See* Hendleman, George (Joseph)
Handy, Will. *See* Cole, Robert [or Bob] (Allen)
Handy, Will. *See* Johnson, J(ohn) Rosamond
Handy, Will. *See* Johnson, James Weldon
Hanell, George. *See* Schulhoff, Ervin [or Erwin]
Hanen, R. T. *See* Short, J. D.
Haney, Alice. *See* Cain, Noble
Haney, Lawrence (W.). *See* Cain, Noble
Hangleitner, Anton. *See* Adler, Hans
Hank Snow of the Prairies. *See* Edwards, Eric (Charles)
Hank the Drifter. *See* Andrade, Daniel (Raye)
Hank, the Hired Hand. *See* Thompson, Henry William
Hank, the Singing Ranger. *See* Snow, Clarence Eugene
Hank, the Yodeling Ranger. *See* Snow, Clarence Eugene
Hanleigh, Faith. *See* Glaser, Victoria Marylees
Hannel, Sigurd. *See* Hansson, Stig (Axel)
Hannibal. *See* Peterson, Marvin (Hannibal)
Hannibal of Octaves, The. *See* Tedesco, Ignaz Amadeus
Hanoius. *See* Cless, Johann
Hanoverian, An. *See* Toplady, Augustus Montague
Hans. *See* Hofhaimer, Paul(us von)
Hans Jacob von Mailandt. *See* Albuzio, Giovanni Giacopo
Hans, Lio. *See* Scheidl-Hutterstrasser, Lili [or Lily]
Hans von Constanz. *See* Buchner, Hans
Hansen, Beck. *See* Campbell, Bek David
Hansen, Bill. *See* Hansen, Lawrence (William)
Hansen, Gustav. *See* Sartorio, Arnoldo
Hansen, Hans. *See* Meyer, Wolfgang
Hansen, Michael. *See* Schibilsky, Klaus
Hansen, Peter Jan. *See* Winkler, Gerhard
Hansen, Rolf. *See* Quantz, Willibald
Hansen, Werner. *See* Fussan, Werner
Hansi. *See* Last, Hans
Hanslickianer, A. *See* Apostel, Hans Erich
Hanson, Bud. *See* Hanson, Alfred E.
Hanson, Daniel Lee. *See* Loes, Harry Dixon
Hanson, Eddy. *See* Hanson, Ethwell Idair
Hanson, Eric. *See* Davis, Albert Oliver

Harrysong, George. *See* Harrison, George
Hart, Babe. *See* Hart, Lucille
Hart, Bob(b). *See* Trace, Al(bert J(oseph))
Hart, Bobby. *See* Harshman, Robert
Hart, David. *See* Chapman, W. Granville
Hart, Don. *See* Pelosi, Domonic [or Don]
Hart, Frances. *See* Tishman, Fay
Hart, Freddie. *See* Segrest, Fred(erick)
Hart, Larry. *See* Hart, Lorenz (Milton)
Hart, Peter. *See* Hargreaves, Peter
Hart, Tony. *See* Cannon, Anthony J.
Hartachenko, Lorenz. *See* Hart, Lorenz (Milton)
Hartel, Helmut. *See* Zander, Helmut (Gottfried)
Hartford, Chapin. *See* Foster, Paula
Hartley, Harry. *See* Fillmore, (James) Henry
Hartman, Jerome. *See* Koninsky, Sadie
Hartmann, Adolf. *See* Sartorio, Arnoldo
Hartmann, Pater. *See* Lan-Hochbrunn, Paul Eugen Josef von An der
Hartmann, Paul. *See* Lan-Hochbrunn, Paul Eugen Josef von An der
Hartogs, Benoit. *See* Ducis, Benedictus
Hartt, LeRoy. *See* Kunkel, Charles
Hartzer, Balthasar. *See* Resinarius, Balthasar
Harvay, Jack. *See* Boedijn, Gerard(us Hendrik)
Harvest, Frank. *See* Rhinow, Hans-Joachim
Harvey. *See* Hodges, John(ny) Cornelius
Harvey, Jack. *See* Boedijn, Gerard(us Hendrik)
Harvey, Kike. *See* Caicedo, José Harb(e)y
Harvey, Michael. *See* Greenstein, Michael Harvey
Harwell, Ernie. *See* Harwell, William Earnest
Hasefeld, Anton. *See* Campion (Records)
Has(s)elbach, (Sepp). *See* Rauch, Alfred
Haskell, Burt. *See* Brisman, Heskel
Haskell, Jimmie. *See* Pearlman, Sheridan
Haskin, Abby. *See* Mascolino, Dolores (Abigail)
Hass, Willi. *See* Kröger, Willi
Hassan. *See* Ali, Hasaan ibn
Hasselbach, (Sepp). *See* Rauch, Alfred
Hassler, Karl. *See* Koschinsky, Fritz
Hastings, Charles. *See* Addison, John Cramer
Hastings, Martha. *See* Wagness, Bernard
Hastings, Paul. *See* Ehret, Walter (Charles)
Hastings, Paul. *See* Kinsman, Elmer (F(ranklin))
Hastings, Pye. *See* Hastings, Julian
Hasus, J(ohann) P(aul) F(riedrich). *See* Richter, Johann Paul Friedrich
Hat, The. *See* Haggard, Merle (Ronald)
Hatako-Chtokchito-A-Yakni-Toloa. *See* Jenkins, Harold (Lloyd)
Hateful Clown, The. *See* Lulli, Giovanni Battista
Hatfield, Overton. *See* Autry, (Orvon) Gene
Hathaway, J(ane). *See* Zamecnik, J(ohn) S(tepan)
Hatton, Chester. *See* Macy, J(ames) C(artwright)
Hatton, Gus. *See* Prendiville, Henri Jean
Haubiel, Charles Trowbridge. *See* Pratt, Charles Trowbridge
Hauer, Charles. *See* Feltz, Kurt (August Karl)
Haupt, Franz. *See* Lewin, Gustav
Haupt, Gerhard. *See* Ihme, Hans-Friedrich
Hauschild, Bulldog. *See* Hauschild, Richard Curtis
Hauser, Kaspar. *See* Tucholsky, Kurt
Hausmann, W(olf). *See* Roloff, W(olfgang)
Häusser [or Haeuser], Hans. *See* Haass, Hans
Havlin, Will. *See* De Rose, Peter
Hawaiian Guitar Wizard, The. *See* Weldon, Wil(liam)
Hawaiian Musikmeister, The. *See* Berger, Henry
Hawk. *See* Hawkins, Coleman (Randolph)
Hawk, The. *See* Hawkins, Harold Franklin
Hawk, The. *See* Hutto, J(oseph) B(enjamin)
Hawk, The. *See* Lewis, Jerry Lee
Hawk, Eddie. *See* Mravik, Edward E.
Hawkins, Buddy Boy. *See* Hawkins, Walter
Hawkins, Dale. *See* Hawkins, Delmar Allen
Hawkins, Hawkshaw. *See* Hawkins, Harold Franklin
Hawkins, Jason. *See* Powell, Jack
Hawkins, Jay. *See* Hawkins, Jalacy (J.)
Hawkins, Screamin' Jay. *See* Hawkins, Jalacy (J.)
Hawkins, Thunderhead. *See* Williams, Randall Hank
Haworth, Rajah. *See* Haworth, Roger A.
Hawthorne, A. W. *See* Winner, Septimus
Hawthorne, Alice. *See* Winner, Septimus
Hawthorne, Carrie. *See* Crosby, Fanny [i.e., Frances] J(ane)
Hawthorne, Kathryn. *See* Zamecnik, J(ohn) S(tepan)
Hawthorne, Seymore [or Seymour]. *See* Bliss, P(hilip) Paul
Hawthorne, Seymore [or Seymour]. *See* Boex, Andrew J.
Hay, Will. *See* Willeby, Charles
Haydée. *See* Finzi, Ida
Haydn. *See* Kücken, Friedrich Wilhelm
Haydn, Joseph. *See* Kunkel, Charles
Haydn, Papa. *See* Haydn, (Franz) Joseph
Haydn of the Guitar. *See* DeFossa, François
Haydnesque. *See* Haydn, (Franz) Joseph
Haydn's Wife. *See* Boccherini, (Ridolfo) Luigi
Haydnverein. *See* Haydn, (Franz) Joseph
Hayes, Al. *See* Fillmore, (James) Henry
Hayes, Clancy. *See* Hayes, Clarence Leonard
Hayes, Lou. *See* Slaughter, M(arion) T(ry)
Hayes, Sack. *See* Hayes, Isaac
Hayes, Tubby. *See* Hayes, Edward Brian
Hayndl, Adam. *See* Adler, Hans
Haynes, Homer. *See* Haynes, Henry D.
Hays, Charles. *See* Ellis, Seger
Hays, Sorrel. *See* Hays, Doris Ernestine
Haysom, Peter. *See* Craddy, Peter (Haysom)
Hayward, Lou. *See* Zaninelli, Luigi
Haywire Mac. *See* McClintock, Harry (K(irby))

Hazard, Désiré. *See* Aubert, Albert
Hazard, Désiré. *See* Bocage, Paul
Hazard, Désiré. *See* Feuillet, Octave
Hazel, Ed(ward). *See* Barnard, George D(aniel)
Hazel, Edward. *See* Scouton, Will(iam H.)
Hazelwood, Clate. *See* Hazelwood, E(lmer) Clayton
Hazziez, Joseph [or Yusef]. *See* Arrington, Joseph [or Joe], (Jr.)
Head, The. *See* Grice, Gary
Heartbreak Kid, The. *See* Presley, Elvis A(a)ron
Heat, Rev. Horton. *See* Heath, James C.
Heath, Bobby. *See* Frear, Robin (James)
Heath, Egdon. *See* Stone, Roberta Russell Summers
Heath, Hy. *See* Heath, (Walter) Henry
Heath, Little Bird. *See* Heath, James [or Jimmy] (Edward)
Heatherton, Fred. *See* Box, Harold Elton
Heatherton, Fred. *See* Dash, Irwin
Heatherton, Fred. *See* Keuleman, Adrian
Heautontimorumenos. *See* Klein, Fritz Heinrich
Heavy D. *See* Myers, Dwight
Heavy Metallurgist Par Excellence, The. *See* Hendrix, John(ny) Allen
Hébertot, Jacques. *See* Daviel, André
Hecate. *See* De l'Epine, Francesca Margherita
Hecyrus, Christoph. *See* Schweher, Kryštop [or Christoph]
Hedden, Edwin. *See* Haesche, William Edwin
Hedley, H(erbert) B(arber). *See* Barber, Herbert Hedley
Heemstede, Léon van. *See* Tepe, Leo
Heffer, Louis. *See* Ronger, (Louis Auguste Joseph) Florimond
Hefner, Carl. *See* Kern, Carl Wilhelm
Hegamin, Lucille. *See* Nelson, Lucille
Hegyaljai. *See* Kirchlehrer, Ferenc
Hegyesi, Louis. *See* Spitzer, Louis
Heidemann, Jürgen. *See* Winkler, Gerhard
Heiden Günther. *See* Bader, Ernst (Johannes Albert)
Heider, Johannes. *See* Schneider, Hans
Heidrich, Gustav. *See* Schliepe, Ernst (Heinrich)
Heilburg, Christian. *See* Rottschalk, Gregor
Heinen, Peter-Rudolph. *See* Wagner, Peter
Heinrich, C(arl). *See* Neidlinger, W(illiam) H(arold)
Heinrich, Father. *See* Heinrich, Anton [or Anthony] Philip
Heinrich, Franz. *See* Decsey, Ernst (Heinrich Franz)
Heinrich von der Maltig. *See* Wallman, Heinrich
Heins, Donald. *See* Heins, Francis Donaldson
Heintz. *See* Lemoine, Achille(-Philibert)
Heinz Fifty-Seven Singer, A. *See* Arnold, (Richard) Edward [or Eddie]
Heinz, Frank. *See* Thomsen, Christian
Heinzelmann, Heinz. *See* Prinz, Heinrich Ludwig
Heir to Bakersfield, The. *See* Yoakam, Dwight
Heischermann, Jonah. *See* Schein, Johann Hermann
Heiser, F. [or E.]. *See* Rosenfeld, Monroe H.
Heiter, A(malie). *See* Amalie Marie Friederike Augusta, Princess of Saxony
Heiter, Ernst. *See* Sechter, Simon
Heitor, Luiz. *See* Azevedo, Luis Heitor Corrêa de
Helbig, Michael. *See* Kleine, Werner
Heldenleben, Ein. *See* Strauss, Richard
Heli. *See* Steingass, Helmut
Heliandos, Lucky. *See* Kullmann, Wilton
Hell, Richard. *See* Myers, Richard
Hell, Theodor. *See* Winkler, Karl [or Carl] Gottfried Theodor
Hell to Pay. *See* Parker, Henry Taylor
Hellborn, Klaus. *See* Rhein, Eduard
Helldunkel, Hans. *See* Schulze, Friedrich August
Helle, Finn. *See* Bull, Sverre Hagerup
Heller, André. *See* Heller, Franz
Heller, M. P. *See* Heller, Max
Heller, M. P. *See* Heller, Paul
Heller, Maxime. *See* Harris, Frederick
Heller, Maxime. *See* Rawlings, Charles Arthur
Heller, Robert. *See* Palmer, William Henry
Hellerus Leucopetraeus. *See* Heller, Joachim
Hellmer, Klaus. *See* Rhein, Eduard
Hellmesberger, Pepi. *See* Hellmesberger, Josef
Hellmuth, Karl. *See* Dammas, Hellmuth Carl
Hellstern, Klaus. *See* Deuringer, Hubert [or Herbert] (Martin)
Helm, Ernst. *See* Steffan, Ernst
Helmina. *See* Chezy, Wilhelmine Christine von
Helvetico, Ariosto. *See* Widmann, Joseph Viktor
Helyer, Jack. *See* Helyer, Edmund Victor
Hemingway, Chas. *See* Smith, Leonard B(ingley)
Hemsi, Alberto. *See* Chicurel, Alberto Hemsi
Henderson, Catherine. *See* Gibbons, Irene
Henderson, Frame. *See* Clark, C(yrus) Van Ness
Henderson, Frame. *See* Hickey, Martin
Henderson, Frank. *See* Frankel, Harry
Henderson, Herbert. *See* Noack, Herbert
Henderson, Ray(mond). *See* Brost, Raymond
Henderson, Skitch. *See* Henderson, Lyle Russell Cedric
Henderson, Smack. *See* Henderson, (James) Fletcher (Hamilton), (Jr.)
Hendrik, Tony. *See* Lünstedt, Dieter
Hendrix, James Marshall. *See* Hendrix, John(ny) Allen
Hendrix, Jimi [or Jimmy]. *See* Hendrix, John(ny) Allen
Hendrix, Sonny. *See* Barkan, Stanley Howard
Hendrowski, Frank. *See* Klickman, F(rank) Henri
Hen(n)inger, Ralf. *See* Hess, Reimund
Henley, A. W. D. *See* Le Clerq, Arthur
Henley, Peter. *See* Evans, Hal
Hennagin, Michael. *See* Goldsmith, Jerrald [or Jerry]
Hennerich, Harry. *See* Feltz, Kurt (August Karl)
Hennessy, Ian. *See* Martin, Ray(mond)

Hennessy, Ian. *See* Paramor, Norman [or Norrie] (William)
Henning, Anton. *See* Goerdeler, Richard
Henning, Robert. *See* Gannon, James Kimball
Henri-de-la-la croix, Sister. *See* Milette, Juliette
Henri, Jacques. *See* Jacobs, James Henry
Henri, Jean. *See* Prendiville, Henri Jean
Henrich, Gabriel. *See* Hamel, Peter Michael
Henrich, Michael. *See* Hamel, Peter Michael
Henrici, Gabriel. *See* Hässy, Günter
Henricus. *See* Arrigo
Henricus Scriptoris Efordensis. *See* Schreyber, Heinrich
Henrion, Poly. *See* Kohlenegg, Leopold [or Leonhard] (Karl) Kohl von
Henry, Big Boy. *See* Henry, Richard
Henry, Carl. *See* Prendiville, Henri Jean
Henry, Chaplin. *See* Stroud, Henry Charles
Henry Earl. *See* Slaughter, M(arion) T(ry)
Henry, Frogman. *See* Henry, Clarence
Henry, H. A. *See* Gabriel, Charles H(utchinson)
Henry, Hamilton. *See* Rawlings, Alfred William
Henry, Hazel A. *See* Gabriel, Charles H(utchinson)
Henry, John. *See* Bradford, (John Henry) Perry
Henry, Louis. *See* Bonnachon, Louis-Henri
Henry, Marc. *See* D'Ailly-Vaucheret, Achille
Henry, Richard. *See* Butler, Richard W(illiam)
Henry, Richard. *See* Newton, H(enry) Chance
Henry, S. R. *See* Stern, Henry R.
Henry, Will. *See* Davies, William Henry
Henry, William. *See* Reader, (William Henry) Ralph
Henry, Wyn. *See* Palmer, Cedric King
Henschel, Kenneth. *See* Rimmer, William
Hensel, Octavia. *See* Seymour, Mary Alice Ives
Hensel, Walther. *See* Janiczek, Julius
Henski [or Hensky], J. *See* Kleinmeijer, Henk
Henson, Cousin Herb. *See* Henson, Herbert Lester
Her Majesty the Queen. *See* Spivey, Victoria [or Vicky] (Regina)
Héral, (J.). *See* Kovarovic, Karel
Hérapine, Sieur d'. *See* Guichard, Henri
Herbel. *See* Seveste, Jules
Herbert, Francis. *See* English, Thomas Dunn
Herbert, George B. *See* Rodwell, George Herbert (Bonaparte)
Herbert, Harry. *See* Sparks, Harry H.
Herbert, Herbie. *See* Swartz, Herbert
Herbert, M. G. *See* Grandjean, Moritz Anton
Herbert, Mort. *See* Pelovitz, Morton Herbert
Herblay, K. *See* Hirschmann, Henri (Louis)
Herbst, Christian. *See* Höslinger, Clemens
Hercenstein, Matteo. *See* Glinski, Mateusz [or Matteo]
Hercules of Music, The. *See* Gluck, Christoph Willibald
Herd, Graeme. *See* Soloman, Mirrie (Irma)
Herdlizka, Henri. *See* Tourterelle, Henri
Herf, Franz. *See* Richter, Franz
Herford, Julius. *See* Goldstein, Julius
Herger, Karl. *See* Held, Ludwig
Herlow, Jan. *See* Last, Werner
Herman(n), Adolf [or Adolphe]. *See* Hermant, Constant
Herman(n), Andrea [or Andrew]. *See* Tobani, Theodore Moses
Herman, Charles. *See* Winkler, Gerhard
Herman(n), G(erd). *See* Winkler, Gerhard
Herman, Pinky. *See* Pincus, Herman
Herman the Cripple. *See* Hermannus, Contractus
Herman, Woody. *See* Herman(n), Woodrow Charles
Hermann, (Carlo). *See* Cohen, Hermann
Hermann der Lahme. *See* Hermannus, Contractus
Hermann, E. M. *See* Thieme, Hermann
Hermann, Hans. *See* Kolditz, Hans
Hermann, Jacques. *See* Pidoux, Madeline
Hermann, Ludwig. *See* Jan, Hermann Ludwig
Hermann, Otto. *See* Hansson, Stig (Axel)
Hermann von Reichenau. *See* Hermannus, Contractus
Hermanns, Werner. *See* Theisen, Werner
Hermes. *See* Lumley, Benjamin
Hermit of Iowa, The. *See* Schilling, Gustav (1803-1881)
Hernried. *See* Hirsch, Robert Franz Richard
Hero of Socialist Labor, The. *See* Shostakovich, Dmitri Dmitryevich
Heroine of Heartbreak. *See* Pugh, Virginia Wynette
Herold, Francis. *See* Finkelstein, Abe
Herr, Hubert. *See* Herrera, Humberto (Angel)
Herrick of Germany, The. *See* Flem(m)ing, Paul
Herring, Ura. *See* McHugh, James [or Jimmy] (F(rancis))
Herrmann, J(acob) Z(eugheer). *See* Zeugheer, Jakob
Herschel, Henry. *See* Guaragna, Salvatore
Herschel, Lee. *See* Krasnow, Herman(n)
Herschkowitz, Philip. *See* Herscovici, Filip
Hershfield, Harry. *See* Kaufman, Jacob
Herther, F. *See* Günther, Franz Hermann
Herthorn, Paul. *See* Lureman, Hermann Thomas
Hervé. *See* Ronger, (Louis Auguste Joseph) Florimond
Hervé, Gardel. *See* Ronger, Emmanuel Florimond
Hervé, Louis. *See* Ronger, (Louis Auguste Joseph) Florimond
Hervé, Paul. *See* Philipp, Adolf
Hervey, George. *See* Saenger, Gustave
Herz, (Dr.) Albert. *See* Herz, Maria (née Bing)
Herzer, Ludwig. *See* Herzl, Ludwig
Herzog, Benedikt [or Benedictus]. *See* Ducis, Benedictus
Herzog, Christian. *See* Vockerodt, Gottfried
Herzog, Dorothy. *See* Erlebach, Rudy
Hess, J. R. *See* Cain, Noble
Hesse, Friedmund. *See* Weidig, (Alexander) Friedrich Ludwig
Hessler, Carl. *See* Rimmer, William

Hinzelmann, Hans Heinz. *See* Levetzow, Karl Micha(e)l von
Hip Cat. *See* Smith, George (1924-1983)
Hip Harpsichordist, The. *See* Newman, Anthony
Hippie Narcissist. *See* Young, Neil
Hippy. *See* Gilbert, Cary (Grant)
Hipster, The. *See* Raab, Harry
Hiraethog, Gwilym. *See* Rees, William
Hirai, Yasuki. *See* Hirai, Kozaburo
Hirsch, Carl. *See* Parry, Charles Clinton
Hirsemenzel, Lebrecht. *See* Raupach, Ernst Benjamin Salomo
Hirtz, Leo. *See* Kountz, Richard
His Royal Badness. *See* Nelson, Prince Rogers
His T-Ness. *See* Brown, Anthony Graham
Hisaishi, Joe. *See* Fujisawa, Mamoru
Hischuk, Rainer. *See* Kraus, Heinrich
Hispanic Garth Brooks. *See* Trevino, Rick
Hitman, Harold. *See* Ende, Harald
Hix, Auguste. *See* Rouget de Lisle, Claude Joseph
Hoagland, Howard. *See* Carmichael, Howard Hoagland
Hoàng Oanh. *See* Chi Kim Hugnh Ma
Hobart, George V(ere). *See* Philpott, George Vere Hobart
Hobbs, Herb. *See* Finkelstein, Abe
Hobbs, Owen. *See* Hobson, Fredrick Leslie
Hobby, John (Friar). *See* Hothby, John
Hobo Composer. *See* Partch, Harry
Hobo Sam. *See* Samberg, Benjamin
Hochmeister, Herbert von. *See* Gold, Glenn Herbert
Hockley, Nancy. *See* Clemens, Lucinda
Hodes, Sophie. *See* Kellem, Milton
Hodges, A. R. *See* Kraushaar, Charles
Hodges, Jeep. *See* Hodges, Cornelius
Hodges, Rabbit. *See* Hodges, John(ny) Cornelius
Hodges, Squatty Roo. *See* Hodges, John(ny) Cornelius
Hodgson, Albert. *See* Kountz, Richard
Hodgson, Daniel. *See* De Filippi, Amedeo
Hodson, William. *See* Felton, William M.
Hoechst, Carl. *See* Morris, Valentine
Hofe, Nikolaus. *See* Decius, Nikolaus
Hoff, André. *See* Andries, Franzleo
Hoff, André. *See* Feltz, Kurt (August Karl)
Hoff, Carl. *See* Hoffmayr, Carl
Hoffheymer, Paul. *See* Hofhaimer, Paul(us von)
Hoffman, Paul. *See* Ewing, Montague (George)
Hoffman, Richard. *See* Andrews, Richard
Hoffman, Richard. *See* Ascher, Everett
Hoffman von Fallersleben. *See* Hoffmann, Heinrich August
Hoffmann, E(rnst) T(heodor) A(madeus). *See* Hoffmann, Ernst Theodore Wilhelm
Hoffmeister, Ludwig. *See* Kern, Carl Wilhelm
Hoffner, Wilhelm. *See* Dilthey, Wilhelm (Christian Ludwig)
Höfgen, Willy. *See* Glahé, Will(y Karl-Adolf)
Hofmann, Elder von. *See* Hofmannsthal, Hugo von
Hofmeister, Trude. *See* Wychodil(-Hofmeister), Gert
Hogan, Ernest. *See* Crowders, (Ernest) Reuben
Hogg, Smok(e)y. *See* Hogg, Andrew
Hohenberg, Franz. *See* Homola, Bernhard
Hohenrasenn, Joachim. *See* Schein, Johann Hermann
Hohenstein, Arthur. *See* Koppitz, Arthur
Höhrl, Franz. *See* Hasenöhrl, Franz
Holbeach, Henry. *See* Rands, William Brightly
Holcombe, Bill. *See* Holcombe Wilfred (Lawshe)
Holcombe, G. *See* Perry, Phil(ip) B(utler)
Holcombe, L. V. *See* Engelmann, H(ans)
Hold, Alan. *See* Kapp, David [or Dave]
Holda, Ramjohn. *See* Holder, John (Wesley)
Holder, Noddy. *See* Holder, Neville
Holder, Ram (John). *See* Holder, John (Wesley)
Holger, Gerd. *See* Hoschke, Gerhard
Holiday, Alan. *See* Fishman, Jack (1918 (or 19)-)
Holiday, Billie. *See* Harris, Eleanora
Holland, Teddy. *See* Frangkiser, Carl (Moerz)
Holland-Dozier-Holland. *See* Dozier, Lamont
Holland-Dozier-Holland. *See* Holland, Brian
Holland-Dozier-Holland. *See* Holland, Eddie
Hollander, Hugo. *See* Barnes, H(oward) E(llington)
Hollander, Hugo. *See* Fields, Harold (Cornelius)
Hollander, Hugo. *See* Roncoroni, Joseph (Dominic)
Holliday, Walter. *See* Haenschen, Walter (G(ustave))
Hollier, Stanley. *See* Hollingsworth, Stanley
Hollis, C(harles) A. *See* Cain, Noble
Hollis, Frank. *See* Kaufman, Isidore
Hollodan, Damaskas. *See* Hollombe, Daniel Ephriam
Holloway, Jay. *See* Ehret, Walter (Charles)
Holloway, Milt. *See* Paramor, Norman [or Norrie] (William)
Holly, Buddy. *See* Holley, Charles Hardin
Holly, Doyle. *See* Hendricks, Doyle Floyd
Hollywood, Anton. *See* Goddard, Geoff
Holm, Banner. *See* Roeckel, Joseph Leopold
Holm, Michael. *See* Walter, Lothar
Holman, Bill. *See* Holman, Willis Leonard H.
Holmes, Dick. *See* Kaufman, Jacob
Holmes, Fern. *See* Slaughter, M(arion) T(ry)
Holmes, Lee. *See* Beckhard, Robert L.
Holness, Niney. *See* Holness, Winston
Holstein, Peer van. *See* Pätzold, Günter
Holt, Alan. *See* Kapp, David [or Dave]
Holt, Hans. *See* Hödl, Karl Johann
Holtmont, Alfred. *See* Burgartz, Alfred
Holton, Albert. *See* Saenger, Gustave
Holton, Fred B. *See* Wilson, Ira B(ishop)
Holton, Larry. *See* Finkelstein, Abe
Holy Main, The. *See* Basie, William (Allen)

Holynska, Julia. *See* Kisielewski, Stefan
Holz, Detlef. *See* Benjamin, Walter
Holzer, Julius. *See* Horvath, Geza
Holzhacker. *See* Schubert, Franz Peter
Home Towners, The. *See* Ahl, Fred Arthur
Homer. *See* Haynes, Henry D.
Homer, Charlotte G. *See* Gabriel, Charles H(utchinson)
Homer the Great. *See* Crayton, Connie Curtis
Homesick James. *See* Henderson, John William
Homesick Jick. *See* Henderson, John William
Homsen, Joe. *See* Menke, Joe
Homunculus. *See* Radecki, Sigismund (Arnold Ottokar) von
Hondt, Corneille de. *See* Canis, Corneille
Honer, Hans. *See* Winterfeld, David Robert
Honest Abe. *See* Borowitz, Abram Solman
Honey Boy. *See* Evans, George
Honey Bunny Boo. *See* Rushing, James [or Jimmy] (Andrew)
Honey Duke and His Uke. *See* Marvin, John(ny) (Senator)
Honey Eddy [or Eddie]. *See* Edwards, David
Honey, Mr. *See* Edwards, David
Honeyboy. *See* Edwards, David
Honeydripper, The. *See* Liggins, Joseph [or Joe] (C.)
Honeydripper, The. *See* Sykes, Roosevelt
Honganozhe. *See* Ballard, Louis W(ayne)
Honky, Jam(e)s. *See* Gutzeit, Erich
Honso. *See* Adler, Hans
Hood, Philip. *See* Smith-Masters, Stanley
Hook, The. *See* Hooker, John Lee
Hooker Joe. *See* Davis, Walter
Hooper, Jess. *See* Lindberg, Charles Arthur
Hoosier from Plainfield, Indiana. *See* Westendorf, Thomas Paine
Hooven, Joe. *See* Robinson, J. Russel(l)
Hoover, Bill. *See* Hoover, Willis David
Hoover, Joe. *See* Robinson, J. Russel(l)
Hope, Anthony. *See* Hawkins, (Sir) Anthony Hope
Hope, Barbara Melville. *See* Russell, (Robert C.) Kennedy
Hope, Claude. *See* Hemachandra, Neal
Hope, Douglas. *See* Wilson, Hilda (Matilda Ellen)
Hope, Eric. *See* Seymour, George F(rancis) A(lexander) (Earl of Yarmouth)
Hope, Eve. *See* Hearn(e), Mary Ann(e)
Hope, Frances. *See* Crosby, Fanny [i.e., Frances] J(ane)
Hope, John. *See* Tunbridge, Joseph A(lbert)
Hope, John. *See* Waller, Jack
Hope, Laurence. *See* Cory, Adela Florence
Hope, Marcus. *See* Rawlings, Alfred William
Hope, Owen. *See* Robinson, (Sir) William Cleaver Francis
Hope, Peter. *See* Gardner, William
Hope, Victor. *See* Krogmann, Carrie W(illiam(s))
Hope's Diamond. *See* Crosby, Harry Lillis
Hophthalmos, (Friedrich). *See* Haug, (Johann Christoph) Friedrich
Hopkins, Antony. *See* Reynolds, Antony
Hopkins, Edward Jerome. *See* Hopkins, Charles Jerome
Hopkins, Lightnin'. *See* Hopkins, Sam
Hopkins, Little Hop. *See* Hopkins, Smith Anderson
Hopkins, Paul. *See* McKelvy, James (M(illigan))
Hoplit. *See* Pohl, Richard
Hops, Frances. *See* Crosby, Fanny [i.e., Frances] J(ane)
Horn, Johann. *See* Roh, Johann
Horn, Otto. *See* Bäuerle, (Andreas) Adolf
Horn, Roman. *See* Dovenmühle, Rudi von der
Horne, Richard Hengist. *See* Horne, Richard Henry
Hornem, Horace, Esq. *See* Byron, George Gordon Noël
Horner, Auguste. *See* Paroisse-Pougin, François-Auguste Arthur
Horner, Friedrich. *See* Lepschies, Karl
Hornibrook, Wallace. *See* Ehret, Walter (Charles)
Horowitz, Ike. *See* Cohn, Al(vin Gilbert)
Horst, Julius. *See* Hostasch, Josef
Horster, Hans Ulrich. *See* Rhein, Eduard
Hortehse, Queen, Consort of Louis Bonaparte, King of Holland. *See* Beauharnais, Hortense Eugénie de
Hortense reine de Hollande. *See* Beauharnais, Hortense Eugénie de
Horton, R. D. *See* Sankey, Ira David
Horton, Shakey. *See* Horton, Walter
Horvath, Alan. *See* Post, Alan
Host to the Cost, The. *See* Grier, James [or Jimmie] W.
Hoste da Reggio. *See* Torresano, Bartolomeo
Hot Rod Red. *See* Polfus(s), Lester (William)
Hot Shot Willie. *See* McTell, Willie Samuel
Hotaling, Ralph. *See* Wagness, Bernard
Hotchkiss, Mary W. *See* Wagness, Bernard
Hotten, John Camden. *See* Sylvester, Joshua
Houdini, King. *See* Hendricks, Frederick Wilmoth
Houdini, Wilmouth. *See* Hendricks, Frederick Wilmoth
House, Son. *See* House, Eddie James, Jr.
Houston, Cisco. *See* Houston, Gilbert (Vandine)
Houston, Harry. *See* Ellis, Seger
Hove, E. *See* Homann-Webau, Otto
Hoven, J(ohann) [or G.]. *See* Vesque von Püttlingen, Johann Evangelist
Hovhaness, Alan. *See* Chakmakjian, Alan
Hovhannessian, Edgar (Sergey). *See* Oganesyan [or Oganesian], Edgar (Sergey)
Howard. *See* Willeby, Charles
Howard, Bart. *See* Gustafson, Howard J(oseph)
Howard, Bill. *See* Stube, Howard
Howard, Carolyne. *See* Horowitz, Caroline
Howard, Dick. *See* Dietz, Howard
Howard, Don. *See* Koplow, Donald Howard
Howard, Frank. *See* Lowry, Anthony [or Tony]

Howard, Frank. *See* Spalding, Delos Gardner [or Gardiner]
Howard, Fred. *See* Wright, Fred Howard
Howard, George Elbert. *See* Greenwald, M(artin)
Howard, Jack. *See* Johnson, Frederick G.
Howard, Jan. *See* Johnson, Lula (Grace)
Howard, Jean. *See* Gabriel, Charles H(utchinson)
Howard, Johnny. *See* Riis, Donald L.
Howard, Peter. *See* Weiss, Peter Howard [or Howard Peter]
Howard, Ray. *See* Hayman, Richard Warren Joseph
Howard, Rollin. *See* White, Charles A(lbert)
Howard, W. E. C. *See* Goerdeler, Richard
Howard, Wilson G. *See* Bliss, P(hilip) Paul
Howe, Katherine. *See* Ackley, B(entley) D(eForrest)
Howe, Paul. *See* Robison, Willard
Howe, R. Ward. *See* Ackley, B(entley) D(eForrest)
Howe, Ward. *See* Ackley, B(entley) D(eForrest)
Howell, Dan. *See* Kapp, David [or Dave]
Howell, Dave. *See* Kapp, David [or Dave]
Howell, Gene Mac. *See* Bartles, Alfred Howell
Howell, Peg Leg. *See* Howell, Joshua Barnes
Howlin' Wolf. *See* Burnett, Chester Arthur
Howlin(g) Wolf. *See* Smith, John T.
Hoyl, Jim. *See* Heifetz, Jascha
Hoyle, John. *See* Binns, John
Hrabe, Billy. *See* Schmidt, Wilhelm
Hrostwitha. *See* Rossow, Helene von
Hrubý, K. *See* Ornstein, Ota
Hrvatski. *See* Whitman, Keith (Fullerton)
Hsiao, Shu-sien. *See* Xiao, Shuxian
Hualalai. *See* Paris, Ella Hudson
Hubay, Jeno. *See* Huber, Eugen
Hubbard, Hobie. *See* Hubbard, Gregg
Hubble, Martie. *See* Bernhart, Martha Ann
Huber, Conrad. *See* Williams, Joseph (Benjamin)
Huber, F. K. *See* Ailbout, Hans
Huber, Karl. *See* Hubay, Karl
Hubert, Harry. *See* McPhail, Lindsey
Hubick, Margaret Olive. *See* Mullins, Margaret, Olive
Hucklenutt, Inky. *See* Miller, Robert [or Bob] (Ernst)
Hucknall, Red. *See* Hucknall, Mick
Hucko, Peanuts. *See* Hucko, Michael Andrew
Hudltei, Schirmherr der Abruzzen. *See* Holtei, Karl von
Hudson River Troubadour. *See* McLean, Don
Hudson, Roberta. *See* Zamecnik, J(ohn) S(tepan)
Hudson, Violet. *See* Grady, R(ichard) G.
Hudson, Walter. *See* Hutchison, (David) Warner
Hue and Eye. *See* Clements, Arthur
Hue and Eye. *See* Hay, Frederick
Huerta, Juan de la. *See* Bahr, Carlos Andrés
Huff, Charles H. *See* Pace, Adger McDavid
Huff, Will. *See* Fillmore, (James) Henry
Hufnagl, Max. *See* Billig, (Julius Karl) Gustav
Hugbaldus. *See* Hucbald (of Saint Armand)
Hugely, J. de. *See* Matthews, John Henry
Huggens, Ted. *See* Lijnschooten, Hendrikus [or Henk] (Cornelius) van
Hugh, John. *See* O'Mahony, Sean
Hughes, Anselm. *See* Hughes, Humphrey Vaughan
Hughes, Arnold. *See* Schwarzwald, Arnold
Hughes, Billy. *See* Hughes, Everette I(shmael)
Hughes, Capt. *See* Signaigo, J(oseph) Augustine
Hughes, Dickson. *See* Hucks, William Richard, Jr.
Hughes, L. *See* Creatore, Luigi (Federico)
Hughes, Phil. *See* Robertson, Dick
Hughes, Rob. *See* Keiser, Robert (A(dolph))
Hughes, Spike. *See* Hughes, Patrick Cairns
Hugo. *See* Peretti, Hugo (Emil)
Hugo & Luigi. *See* Creatore, Luigi (Federico)
Hugo & Luigi. *See* Peretti, Hugo (Emil)
Hugo, Gabriel. *See* Parker, Alfred Thomas
Hugo von Reutlingen. *See* Spechtshart, Hugo
Hühnermann, Eike. *See* Mattheus, Bernd
Hull, Howard. *See* Slaughter, M(arion) T(ry)
Hülsen, Adrian. *See* Rhein, Eduard
Human Jukebox. *See* Ball, David
Human Jukebox. *See* Postil, Leland M(ichael)
Humanus, P. C. *See* Hartung, Philipp Christopher (Johann)
Humbert, G(eorge) Frank. *See* Rowley, Alec
Hume, Bryn. *See* Bliss, P(hilip) Paul
Humes, Doris Grace. *See* Kern, Carl Wilhelm
Humph. *See* Lyttelton, Humphrey
Humphrey, Ralph. *See* Presser, William (Henry)
Humphrey, William. *See* Twohy, William Humphrey
Humphreys, Fanny. *See* Alexander, (Mrs.) Cecil F(rances) (née Humphreys)
Humphries, Charles. *See* Clough-Leighter, Henry
Humpy. *See* Humfeld, Charles
Hunchback, The. *See* Leinati, Carlo Ambrogio
Huneker's Heirs. *See* Rosenfeld, Paul
Huneker's Heirs. *See* Van Vechten, Carl
Hungerford, Leonard. *See* Hungerford, Bruce
Hunka No-Zhe. *See* Ballard, Louis Wayne
Hünke, Torsten. *See* Podewils, Torten Hünke von
Hunt, Erland. *See* Slater, David Dick
Hunt, Jingo. *See* Hunt, G(eorge) W(illiam)
Hunt, Van. *See* Hunt, Vanzula Carter
Hunter, A. *See* Rands, William Brightly
Hunter, B(illy) J(oe). *See* Bideu, Louis
Hunter, Ian. *See* Patterson, Ian (Hunter)
Hunter, Ima Spouse. *See* Farmer, Marjorie
Hunter, Ivory Joe. *See* Hunter, Joseph [or Joe]
Hunter, James. *See* Finkelstein, Abe
Hunter, James. *See* Saenger, Gustave
Hunter, Patsy. *See* Pettigrew, Leola (B.)
Hunter, Slim. *See* Broonzy, William Lee Conley

Huntington, Dudley. *See* McCosh, Dudley H(untington)
Huntley, Austin. *See* Haenschen, Walter (G(ustave))
Huntley, Austin. *See* Morse, Theodore (F.)
Huntley, Austin. *See* O'Keefe, James (Conrad)
Huntley, Helen. *See* Van de Vate, Nancy (Jean) Hayes
Huntley, James. *See* Krome, Herman(n) (Friedrich)
Huntley, Trevor. *See* Trevor, Huntley
Huntley, William. *See* Van de Vate, Nancy (Jean) Hayes
Hurejszol, W. *See* Grossman(n), Ludwik
Hurgon, Austen A. *See* Horgan, Richard Cornelius
Hurricane, David G. *See* Fishman, Jack (1927-)
Hursel, Michel. *See* Hamburger, Michel
Husarek, Jan. *See* Gaze, Hermann Otto
Hutchinson, Frank. *See* Slaughter, M(arion) T(ry)
Hutchinson, Jill. *See* Douglas, John (Henry)
Huyler, Jack. *See* Rolfe, Walter (L.)
Huysman, Théodule. *See* Normant, Théodule Elzéar Xavier
Hvoslef, Ketil. *See* Saeverud, Ketil
Hyde. *See* Hyde, Abby Bradley
Hyde, Lewis. *See* Lang-Hyde, John Reginald
Hyldgaard, Søren. *See* Larsen, Søren
Hyman, Alberto. *See* Himan, Alberto
Hymaturgis, Johann. *See* Wircker, Johann
Hymn Queen. *See* Crosby, Fanny [i.e., Frances] J(ane)
Hymn Singer. *See* Clark(e), Harry D.
Hymnist of the English Revival, The. *See* Wesley, Charles

– I –

I. D. *See* Dixon, I.
I. H. *See* Hullah, John Pyke
I. N. *See* Nathan, Isaac
I. R. *See* Reid, (General) Iohn [or John]
I. S. *See* Stennet, Joseph
I. T. S. *See* Stoddard, I(saiah) T.
I. V. *See* Vivian, Isabella Jane (Houlton)
Iacocca of the Tuba. *See* Phillips, Harvey G.
Iago ap Ieuan. *See* James, James
IAkimenko, F(edor Stepanovich). *See* Yakimenko, Fyodor (Stepanovich)
Ian, Janis. *See* Fink, Janis Eddy
Ibrahim, Abdullah. *See* Brand, Adolph Johannes
Ice Cube. *See* Jackson, O'Shea
Ice Princess of Ireland, The. *See* Gundmundsdottir, Björk
Ice Queen, The. *See* Gudmundsdottir, Björk
Ice-T. *See* Marrow, Tracy
Ice, Vanilla. *See* Van Winkle, Robert [or Robbie]
Icehouse. *See* Davies, Ifor
Iceman, The. *See* Butler, Jerry
Iceman, (The). *See* Collins, Al(bert)
Icini, (C.). *See* Cicognini, Alessandro
Idalviv. *See* Vivaldi, Antonio (Lucio)
Idle Ben. *See* Crossley, William Tetley
Idol, Billy. *See* Broad, William Michael
Idol of American Youth, The. *See* Green, Douglas B.
Idol of the Halls, The. *See* Bland, James A(llen)
Ieuan Ddu. *See* Thomas, John (1795-1871)
Ieuan Gwyllt. *See* Roberts, John (1822-1877)
Ifor Ceri. *See* Jenkins, John
Iggy Pop. *See* Osterberg, James Newell
Ighnaz. *See* Zang, Johann Heinrich
Iglintsev, Yu. *See* Melkikh, Dmitry Mikheyevich
Ignatius, (Father), (O. S. B.). *See* Lyne, Joseph Leycester
Ignorate all'oscuro, (Il Sig.). *See* Apollino, Salvatore
Ignoto, (Un). *See* Conti, Giovanni
Ignotus. *See* Müller(-Guttenbrunn), Adam
Igor the Second. *See* Markevitch, Igor
Ika. *See* Peyron, Albertina Fredrika
Ike. *See* Edwards, Clifton (A.)
Ikebe, Yoshitaro. *See* Miyahara, Teiji
Ilari, Lauri. *See* Pingoud, Ernest
Ilda, Lewis. *See* Dash, Irwin
Ildebrando da Parma. *See* Pizzetti, Ildebrando
Illecram [or Ille Cram]. *See* Marcelli, Vincenzo
Ilona. *See* Fody, (Helene) Ilona
Imareta, Tirso. *See* Iriarte, Tomás (de)
Imbert. *See* Fuzet, Germain Antoine Agricol
Immortal Jolson, The. *See* Yoelson, Asa
Impartial Hand, An. *See* Turner, Daniel
Impartial Moderator, (An). *See* Watts, Isaac
Imperfetti. *See* Aureli, Aurelio
Impertro, Herman. *See* Drexler, Werner
Imported Sparrow. *See* Rhys, Horton
Imposter, The. *See* McManus, Declan Patrick (Aloysius)
Incog. *See* Hood, Thomas
Incognito. *See* Badoaro, Giacomo
Incredible Imitator, The. *See* Wiggins, Thomas (Green(e))
Indagator. *See* Cowper, William
Indefatigable Song Composer, An. *See* Schubert, Franz Peter
Indefesso. *See* Vernizzi, Ottavio
India. *See* Viera Caballerro, Linda
Indian Princess, The. *See* Thomas, Lillian [or Lillyn]
Indiferente, L'. *See* Gori, Antonio Francesco
Indio. *See* Aguilar, Jose Maria
Inez, Dolly. *See* Donez, Ian
Infante, Dolores del. *See* Rosa Suárez, Robert Edward
Infecondo. *See* Badi, Paolo Emilio
Infecondo. *See* Papi, Antonio
Ingelhoff, Peter. *See* Ordnung, Rudolf (August)
Ingersoll, Byron M. *See* Goldner, Ernest (Siegmund)
Ingersoll, Byron M. *See* Kramer, Alex(ander)
Ingersoll, Byron M. *See* McCray, Don
Ingersoll, Byron M. *See* Parenteau, Zoe

Ingersoll, Byron M. *See* Sour, Robert (B.)
Ingersoll, Byron M. *See* Zaret, Hy(man)
Ingle, Charles. *See* Chevalier, Auguste
Inglez, Roberto. *See* Inglis, Robert
Ingoldsby, Thomas. *See* Barham, Richard Harris
Ingram, John. *See* Morgan, Roberto Orlando
Ingram, M(arvin). *See* Inabnett, Marvin
Ingram, Ted. *See* Warrington, John(ny) (T.)
Innerzone, Orchestra. *See* Craig, Carl
Innocenz. *See* Schulze, Friedrich August
Inspectah Deck. *See* Hunter, Jason
Instancabile. *See* Cicognini, Giacinto Andrea
Insterburg, Ingo. *See* Wetzker, Ingo
Insurance Man for the Funk. *See* Worrell, Bernie
Intronato, Armonico. *See* Agazzari, Agostino
Invaghito, (L'). *See* Benedetti, Pietro
Invaghito, (L'). *See* Pecci, Tommaso
Invaghito, L'. *See* Tantucci, Mariano
Invalid Laureate, The. *See* Scarron, Paul
Inventor of Ambient, The. *See* Eno, Brian
Inventor of Musique Concrète. *See* Schaeffer, Pierre
Inventor of New Jill Swing, The. *See* Blige, Mary Jane
Inventor of the Cool Sound. *See* Collins, Al(bert)
Inventor of the Symphony. *See* Haydn, (Franz) Joseph
Invernici, Ottavio. *See* Vernizzi, Ottavio
Invernizzi, Ottavio. *See* Vernizzi, Ottavio
Invincibles. *See* Azor, Hurby
Ioanne(a) Cruce Clodiensis. *See* Croce, Giovanni (della)
Iona, Andy. *See* Long, Andy Iona
Iota. *See* Thrupp, Dorothy Ann
Iowa Toscanini, The. *See* Willson, (Robert Reiniger) Meredith
Ipleer, Joseph. *See* Riepel, Joseph [or Josef]
Ippolitov-Ivanov, Mikhail Mikhailovich. *See* Ivanov, Mikhail Mikhailovich
Ireland, Francis. *See* Hutcheson, Francis
Iris, Don(nie). *See* Ierace, Dominic
Irish Hillbilly, The. *See* Donegan, Anthony [or Tony] (James)
Irish, Joseph N. *See* Nanton, Joseph [or Joe]
Irish Nightingale, The. *See* Downey, (Sean) Morton (1901?-1985)
Irish Tenor. *See* Scanlan, William J(ames)
Irish Thursh, The. *See* Downey, (Sean) Morton (1901?-1985)
Irish Troubadour, The. *See* Downey, (Sean) Morton (1901?-1985)
Iron John. *See* Hooker, John Lee
Ironside, Christopher. *See* Cowper, William
Iroquois, John. *See* Bliss, P(hilip) Paul
Irreconcilable, An. *See* Rands, William Brightly
Irvin, Harold. *See* Shaberman, Harold
Irvin, Ivan. *See* Dukelsky, Vladimir
Irving Berlin of India. *See* Magno (Pereira), Basilio
Irving Berlin of Gospel Song, The. *See* Gabriel, Charles H(utchinson)
Irving, Harold. *See* Shabermann, Harold
Irving, Henry. *See* Kaufman, Isidore
Irving, John. *See* Kaufman, Isidore
Irving, L. *See* Dancy, Charles (E.)
Irwin, Big Dee. *See* Ervin, Difosca
Irwin, May. *See* Campbell, Georgina May
Irwin, Pee Wee. *See* Erwin, George
Irwin, Roy. *See* Bygraves, Walter (William)
Iseledon, H. S. *See* Clutsam, George Howard
Iskowitz, Iss. *See* Iskowitz, Edward Israel
Isla, (Diego) Cristóbal de. *See* Berlanga de Duero, Soria
Islam, Yusef [or Yusuf, or Yosef]. *See* Georgiou, Steven [or Stephen] Demetri
Iso, Pierre. *See* Yzo, Pierre
Israel, Prince Gideon. *See* Cornelius, Carter
Israels "First Lady of Folk". *See* Alberstein, Chava
Istan, Afgan. *See* Anderson, Stikkan
Isum, John. *See* Isham, John
Isusi. *See* Mouze, Teodoro José
Ital Surgeon. *See* Thompson, (James) Winston
Ital Winston. *See* Thompson, (James) Winston
Italian Gluck, The. *See* Jommelli, Nic(c)olò
Italian Molière, The. *See* Goldoni, Carlo
Italian Mozart, The. *See* Cherubini, Maria Luigi Carlo Zenobio Salvatore
Italian Schubert, The. *See* Gordigiani, Giovanni Battista
Ithuriel. *See* Coutts, W. G.
Itzkowitz, Isidore Israel. *See* Iskowitz, Edward Israel
Ivanhoe, Burl Icle. *See* Ives, Burl(e Icle Ivanhoe)
Ivanov, George. *See* Tutev, Georgi (Ivanov)
Ivanoff, Rose. *See* Brignole, Rosa (B(eata))
Iversen, Henri. *See* Schultze, Norbert (Arnold Wilhelm Richard)
Ives, Helen. *See* Swann, Helen
Ivin, Ivan. *See* Dukelsky, Vladimir
Ivry, Richard d'. *See* Ivry, Paul Xavier Désiré, marquis d'

– J –

J. *See* Taylor, Jane
J. A. *See* Alcock, John
J. A. G. *See* Granade, John A(dam)
J. A. H. *See* Herbst, Johann Andreas
J. B. *See* Bunyan, John
J. B. *See* Procter, Bryan Waller
J. B. W. *See* Waterbury, Jared Bell
J. C. *See* Crowne, John
J. C. F. *See* Crosby, Fanny [i.e., Frances] J(ane)
J. C. M. *See* Macy, J(ames) C(artwright)
J. C. W. *See* Wesley, Charles
J. C. W. *See* Wesley, John

J. E., (Coventry). *See* Evans, Jonathan
J. E. L. *See* Leeson, Jane E(liza)
J. E. M. *See* Millard, James Elwin
J. F. *See* Sobolewski, J(ohann) F(riedrich) E(duard)
J. F. C. *See* Cooke, James Francis
J. F. O. *See* Crosby, Fanny [i.e., Frances] J(ane)
J. F. T. *See* Thrupp, Joseph Francis
J. H. *See* Hullah, John Pyke
J. H -n. *See* Hupton, Job
J. H. A. *See* Arnold, John Henry
J. H. F. *See* Fillmore, (James) Henry
J. H. H. *See* Hanaford, J.H.
J. H. H. *See* Hewitt, John (Henry) Hill
J. H. H. *See* Hopkins, John Henry, Jr.
J. H. R. *See* Ritz, J. H.
J. J. *See* Joyce, James
JK. *See* Kill, Ignaz
J. M. *See* Framer, Marjorie
J. M. N. *See* Neale, J(ohn) M(ason)
J. M. R. *See* Rubert, Johann Martin
J. P. *See* Pollard, Josephine
J. R. *See* Reid, (General) Iohn [or John]
J. R. W. *See* Wreford, John Reynell (Raymond George)
J. S. *See* Hansson, Stig (Axel)
J. S. *See* Scanlan, William J(ames)
J. S. *See* Stainer, John
J. S. *See* Stennet, Joseph
J. S. *See* Taylor, J(ohn) S(iebert)
J. S. Bach of Program Annotators, The. *See* Hale, Philip
J. S. C. *See* Curwen, John Spencer
J. S. D. *See* Dwight, John Sullivan
J. S. H. *See* Harrison, Jane S.
J-Shin. *See* Shinhoster, Jonathan
J. V. C. *See* Crosby, Fanny [i.e., Frances] J(ane)
J. W. *See* Carey, Henry
J. W., (Mrs.). *See* Williamson, (Mrs.) J.
J. W. S. *See* Safe, James W.
J. W. S. *See* Schäffer, Johann Wilhelm
J. W. W. *See* Crosby, Fanny [i.e., Frances] J(ane)
Ja Rule. *See* Atkins, Jeffrey
Jacamo violino. *See* Branca, Giovanni Giacomo
Jacarémirim. *See* Milhaud, Darius
Jacey, Frank. *See* Cicatello, Frank Domenick
Jachet (of Mantua). *See* Colebault, Jacques
Jachet de Gaund. *See* Buus, Jacques [or Jacob] (de)
Jack 'n' Bob. *See* Deimel, Hans
Jack, Peter. *See* Fishman, Jack (1918 (or 19)-)
Jackanapes. *See* Johnson, James [or Jimmy, or Jimmie] (P(rice))
Jackie. *See* Cain, Jacqueline Ruth
Jackie Lee. *See* Myers, Sharon [or Sherry] (Lee)
Jackman, Leo. *See* Blitz, Leo(nard)
Jackman, Leo. *See* Campbell, James [or Jimmy]
Jackman, Leo. *See* Pickering, Jack
Jacko. *See* Jackson, Michael Joseph
Jackson, Arthur. *See* Gershvin, Israel
Jackson, Aunt Molly. *See* Garland, Mary Magdalene
Jackson, Bags. *See* Jackson, Milt(on)
Jackson, Bessie. *See* Bogan, Lucille (née Anderson)
Jackson, Blind Lemon. *See* Cassidy, David
Jackson, Chubby. *See* Jackson, Greig Stewart
Jackson, Felix. *See* Joachimson, Felix
Jackson, Gator(tail). *See* Jackson, Willis
Jackson, General "Stonewall". *See* Jackson, Henry R(ootes)
Jackson, Happy. *See* Crow(e), Francis Luther
Jackson, J. J. *See* Jackson, Jerome Louis
Jackson, John. *See* Goodman, Benjamin [or Benny] David
Jackson, Judge. *See* Jackson, George Pullen
Jackson, Lee. *See* Jackson, Warren George Harding Lee
Jackson, LeRoy. *See* Feather, Leonard (Geoffrey)
Jackson, Leroy. *See* Kinyon, John L(eroy)
Jackson, Lil' Son. *See* Jackson, Melvin
Jackson, Lillibet. *See* Fishman, Jack (1918 (or 19)-)
Jackson, Little Son. *See* Jackson, Melvin
Jackson, Mary Anne. *See* Allen, Stephen [or Steve] (Valentine Patrick William)
Jackson of Exeter. *See* Jackson, William (1730-1803)
Jackson of Masham. *See* Jackson, William (1815-1866?)
Jackson, Papa Charlie. *See* Jackson, Charlie
Jackson, (Dr.) S. B. *See* Gabriel, Charles H(utchinson)
Jackson, Shoeless Joe. *See* Epstein, Melvin
Jackson, Shoeless John. *See* Goodman, Benjamin [or Benny] (David)
Jackson, Sonny. *See* Curtis, Eddie
Jackson, Stoney. *See* Jackson, Henry R(ootes)
Jackson, Tex. *See* Jacobs, Al(bert) T.
Jacky Jack (Double Trouble). *See* Crosby, Ronald Clyde
Jacob, Helen. *See* Fody, (Helene) Ilona
Jacobi, Viktor. *See* Jakabfi, Viktor
Jacobs, Al. *See* Gabail, Mercedes
Jacobs, Franz. *See* Frank, J. Ludwig
Jacobs, Little Walter. *See* Jacobs, Marion Walter
Jacobs, Peter. *See* Meek, Robert (George)
Jacobs, Walter. *See* Vinson, Walter Jacobs
Jacobson, Gabriel. *See* Ben-Yaacov, Gabriel
Jacoby. *See* Wagner, Josef Franz
Jacoby, Hanoch. *See* Jacoby, Heinrich
Jacopo Benedicti. *See* Jacopone da Todi
Jacotin. *See* Godebrye, Jacob
Jacques. *See* Neild, James Edward
Jacques le Polonois. *See* Reys, Jakub
Jacques-Rhene, (Sister). *See* Cartier, Marguerite (Marie Alice)
Jacquet (of Mantua). *See* Colebault, Jacques
Jacson, S. B. *See* Gabriel, Charles H(utchinson)
Jad, Willy. *See* Daigneux, Josef André

Jadakiss. *See* Phillips, Jason (T.)
Jäger, Angelika. *See* Bihan, Angelika
Jäger, Karl Maria. *See* Mysliwec, Karl Maria
Jagermeier, Otto [fictitious composer]. *See* Jagermeier, Otto [fictitious composer]
Jagger, Mick. *See* Jagger, Michael Philip
Jagiello, Jadwiga. *See* Brzowska-Mejean Jadwiga
Jahn, Maistre. *See* Gallus, Joannes
Jahr, H. N. *See* Davis, Katherine K(ennicott)
Jahraus, Karl. *See* Bloch, Ernst
Jaime, (Louis) (Adolphe). *See* Gem, Louis Adolphe
Jaime, E. *See* Rousseau, Pierre-Joseph
Jaime, E. *See* Seveste, Jules
Jaja Luigi. *See* Nono, Luigi
Jakob, Peter Michael. *See* Popelka, Joachim
Jakobowsky [or Jakobowski], Edward. *See* Belville, Edward
Jalas, (Armas) Jussi (Veikko). *See* Blomstedt, Armas Jussi Veikko
Jam, Jimmy. *See* Harris, James [or Jimmy], III
Jamboree Joe. *See* Allison, Joe (Marion)
Jambo. *See* Rachele, Luigi
Jamejo, Cratisto. *See* Colloredo, Giovanni Battista
James, Alan. *See* Burgdorf, James Alan
James, Allen. *See* Lorenz, Ellen Jane
James, Andrew. *See* Kirkup, James (Falconer)
James, Annie. *See* Crosby, Fanny [i.e., Frances] J(ane)
James, Arthur. *See* Griffin, James [or Jimmy] (Arthur)
James, Billy. *See* Phelps, Arthur
James, Bobby. *See* Jameson, Robert
James, Charles. *See* Kendis, James
James, Colin. *See* Munn, Colin
James, David. *See* Belasco, David
James, Dick. *See* Vapnick, Isaac
James, Elmer. *See* Crudup, Arthur
James, Elmo. *See* Brooks, Elmore
James, Elmore. *See* Brooks, Elmore
James, Elmore, Jr. *See* Minter, Iverson
James, Emerson. *See* Rawlings, Charles Arthur
James, Freddy. *See* Paolella, Alfred
James, H. E. *See* Bliss, P(hilip) Paul
James, Jesse. *See* Sims, John Haley
James, Jimmy. *See* Hendrix, John(ny) Allen
James, Joe Willie. *See* Brooks, Elmore
James, Marguerite. *See* Paolella, Alfred
James, Mark. *See* Zambon, Francis (Rodney)
James, Mary. *See* Crosby, Fanny [i.e., Frances] J(ane)
James, Maxime. *See* Rousseau, Pierre-Joseph
James, Paul. *See* Stevens, (Paul) James
James, Paul. *See* Warburg, James Paul
James, Pete. *See* Fortini, James (1926-)
James, Pete, Jr. *See* Fortini, James Timothy Peter (Spider)
James, R. E. *See* Bliss, P(hilip) Paul
James, Rick. *See* Johnson, James (1948-)
James, Rudolph. *See* Rolfe, Walter (L.)
James, Sarah. *See* Crosby, Fanny [i.e., Frances] J(ane)
James, Skip. *See* James, Nehemiah (Curtis)
James, Sonny. *See* Loden, James (H.)
James, Tommy. *See* Jackson, Thomas Gregory
James, William W. *See* Kunkel, Charles
Jamgochian, Robert. *See* Jameson, Robert
Jamieson. *See* Love, Geoff(rey)
Jammin' Jim. *See* Harris, Edward P.
Jan. *See* Wroblewski, Ptaszyn
Jane, Vicki. *See* Kellem, Milton
Janina, Olga de. *See* Knauth, Robert Franz
Janis, Beverly. *See* Shapiro Beverly Myers
Janis, Elsie. *See* Bierbower, Elsie
Janischfeld, Erwin von. *See* Lustig-Prean, Karl
Jänkimees. *See* Tammlaan, Evald
Janns, Rose. *See* Demarco, Rosalinda Jill
Janos. *See* Tate, Phyllis (Margaret née Duncan)
Janovicky, Karel. *See* Simsa, B.
Janson, Spike. *See* Janson, Hugh Michael
Janssen, David. *See* Meyer, David Harold
Janssone, Christian. *See* Hollander, Christian Janssone
Jantzen, Max. *See* Jarczyk, Maximilian (Michael) Andreas
January, Herb. *See* May, Robert Arden
Janvier, Jeffreys. *See* Barrell, Edgar Alden, Jr.
Janza, Mark. *See* Marzian, Al(bert) F.
Janzen, Max. *See* Jarczyk, Maximilian (Michael) Andreas
Jares, Vaclav. *See* Kaufmann, Walter (E.)
Jarno, Georg. *See* Cohner, György
Jarnovic, Ivan Mane. *See* Giornovichi, Giovanni Mane
Jarnovick, Mr. *See* Giornovichi, Giovanni Mane
Jarnowick, (Giovanni Marie). *See* Giornovichi, Giovanni Mane
Jaroc. *See* Janssen, Jacobus Hubertus Maria
Jarowick. *See* Hus-Desforges, Pierre Louis
Jarro. *See* Piccini, Giulio
Jary, Michael. *See* Jarczyk, Maximilian (Michael) Andreas
Jason, Daniel. *See* Gornetzky, Daniel Jason
Jasper, Louis. *See* Rawlings, Alfred William
Javells. *See* Jameson, Stephen
Jaxon, Frank. *See* Haenschen, Walter (G(ustave))
Jaxon, Frankie. *See* Jackson, Frankie
Jaxon, Half Pint. *See* Jackson, Frankie
Jaxson, Frankie. *See* Jackson, Frankie
Jay, Arnold. *See* Capitanelli, Arnold Joseph, Jr.
Jay Cee. *See* Johnson, J. C.
Jay, Fred. *See* Jahn, Fritz
Jay, Harry. *See* Lincoln, Harry J.
Jay, Mac. *See* Wolfson, Maxwell A(lexander)
Jay, Michel. *See* Margules, Michel J(ay)
Jay, Vee. *See* Smith, Florence Beatrice
Jay-Z. *See* Carter, Shawn (C.)

Jazz Originator. *See* Harney, Ben(jamin) R(obertson)
Jazz Priest, The. *See* O'Connor, (Rev.) Norman J.
Jazzbo Syncopator, The. *See* Thomas, Lillian [or Lillyn]
Jazzie B. *See* Romeo, Beresford
Jazz's Angry Man. *See* Mingus, Charles
Jean, (Maître). *See* Gallus, Joannes
Jean du Sacre Coeur, (Soeur). *See* Cadoret, Charlotte
Jean Ingelow of America, The. *See* Carey, Alice
Jeanquirit. *See* Heller, Stephen (István)
Jeans, Mr. Green. *See* Brannum, Hugh Roberts
Jeef, Kalle. *See* Kabas(s)elé (Tshamala), Joseph
Jefe, E. L. *See* Sherman, Al(bert)
Jefferson, Blind Lemon. *See* Jefferson, Clarence
Jefferson, Lemon. *See* Jefferson, Clarence
Jefferson, Munrow. *See* Engel, Carl
Jefferson, Sarah. *See* Farjeon, (Eve) Annabel
Jeffries, Jay. *See* Matlick, Jay Jeffries
Jeffries, Roy. *See* Harrhy, Edith
Jeffries, T. B. *See* Branen, Jeff T.
Jehin-Prume. *See* Jehin, François
Jehoash. *See* Bloomgarten, Solomon
Jehrom, Robert. *See* Levinson, Robert (Wells)
Jekyll and Hyde of Music, The. *See* Dukelsky, Vladimir
Jellybean. *See* Benitez, John
Jem Baggs. *See* Gottschalk, Louis Moreau
Jemy, Banon. *See* Blangenois, Jules
Jenbach, Béla. *See* Jakobovits [or Jacobowicz], Béla
Jenkins. *See* Wilson, Wesley
Jenkins, Bobo. *See* Jenkins, John P(ickens)
Jenkins, Floyd. *See* Acuff, Roy (Claxton)
Jenkins, Floyd. *See* Rose, (Knols) Fred
Jenkins, Woody. *See* Jenkins, Louis
Jenks, Lester. *See* Gaul, Harvey B(artlett)
Jenney, Jack. *See* Jenney, Truman Elliott
Jennings, Hoss. *See* Jennings, Waylon [acutally Wayland] (Arnold)
Jennings, Will. *See* Grady, R(ichard) G.
Jennius. *See* Rossignol, Félix Ludger
Jenny, (Sister) Leonore. *See* Jenny, Marie-Cécile
Jenny Lind of Sacred Melody. *See* Willson, Mary Elizabeth (née Bliss)
Jenny [or Jenna] V. *See* Crosby, Fannie [i.e., Frances] J(ane)
Jens, Arthur. *See* Wernicke, Helmuth
Jensen, Adolf. *See* Kunkel, Charles
Jensen, Karin. *See* Deutscher, Karlheinz
Jensen, Ole. *See* Farnon, Robert [or Bob] (Joseph)
Jerard, Walter. *See* Bruck, Jerry
Jeremias. *See* Schulze, Friedrich August
Jeremy, R. E. *See* Rankin, Jeremiah Eames
Jeremy, Richard. *See* Fox, Charles Richard Jeremy
Jerger, Alfred. *See* Jerger, Alois
Jeritza, Maria. *See* Jedlitzková, Maria
Jerkins, Joe. *See* Jarczyk, Herbert
Jerome, Henry. *See* Mortimer, Al
Jerome, Horton. *See* Melaro, H(orton) J(erome) M(artin)
Jerome, John. *See* Barnes, H(oward) E(llington)
Jerome, John. *See* Fields, Harold (Cornelius)
Jerome, John. *See* Roncoroni, Joseph (Dominic)
Jerome, Joy. *See* Leon, Jack
Jerome, Peter. *See* Lorenz, Ellen Jane
Jerome, Robert. *See* Levinson, Robert (Wells)
Jerome, William [or Billy]. *See* Flannery, William Jerome
Jeroným. *See* Brixi, Václav Norbert
Jersey, Mel. *See* Jupe, Eberhard
Jervays, (Mr.). *See* Gervays, Gervasius de Anglia
Jesper. *See* Reiset, Gustave Armand Henri (Comte de)
Jesreal, A(dolph). *See* Gabriel, Charles H(utchinson)
Jessamine, James. *See* Procter, Bryan Waller
Jethro. *See* Bryant, (Thomas) Hoyt
Jethro(w). *See* Burns, Kenneth C.
Jetsam, Mr. *See* MacEachern, Malcolm
Jewel. *See* Kilcher, Jewel
Jewish Hillbilly, The. *See* Mannes, Leo (Ezekiel)
Jezer, Fraña. *See* Neužil, František
Jick (and His Trio). *See* Henderson, John William
Jiménez, Flaco. *See* Jiménez, Leonardo
Jiménez, José. *See* Szathmary, William
Jimmie L. *See* Loden, James (H.)
Jimmy Hendrix of the Accordian. *See* Jordan, Estaban Steve
Jimmy the Kid. *See* Dickens, James Cecil
Jindra, Alfons. *See* Langer, Alfons
Jingles, Jinx. *See* Cohen, Theodore Charles
Jinkins, Gus. *See* Jenkins, Gus
Jinx Jingles. *See* Cohen, Theodore Charles
Jiroudek, Roberta. *See* Flournoy, Roberta Jean
Jizerský, Karel. *See* Beneš, Karel Josef
Jo CA. *See* Case, John, M.D.
Joachim of the Horn. *See* Strauss, Franz (Joseph)
Joan Sebastian. *See* Figueroa, José Manuel
Joana. *See* Emetz, Joana
Joaquín. *See* Ovcharov, Jascha
Job Duque. *See* Gutierrez-Najera, Manuel
Jobim, Tom. *See* Jobim, Antonio Carlos
Jocque, Beau. *See* Espre, Andrus
Jodocus a Prato. *See* Josquin Desprez
Jodocus Pratensis. *See* Josquin Desprez
Joe, Cousin. *See* Joseph, Pleasant
Joey, the Cowpolka King. *See* Miskulin, Joseph [or Joey] (Michael)
Johane d'Arcie, (Soeur). *See* Décarie, Reine
Johann Paul. *See* Hofhaimer, Paul(us von)
Johann Strauss of North Germany. *See* Faster, Oscar
Johann, von Soest. *See* Steinwert von Soest, Johannes
Johannes Gallicus. *See* Johannes de Garlandia
Johannes Gallius. *See* Legrense, Johannes
Johannes le Petit. *See* Baltazar, Johannes
Johannes, Ludwig. *See* Janeczek, Johannes Ludwig

Johannes Mantuanus. *See* Legrense, Johannes
Johannes Neopomucenus. *See* Grimm, Friedrich Melchior, Freiherr von
Johannes Primarius. *See* Johannes de Garlandia
Johannes the Great. *See* Johannes de Garlandia
Johannsen, Otto. *See* Blood, Lizette Emma
John, D(ominic). *See* Roncoroni, Joseph (Dominic)
John, Delta [or Delton]. *See* Hooker, John Lee
John, Dr. *See* Rebennack, Malcolm [or Mac] (John)
John, Elton (Hercules). *See* Dwight, Reginald Kenneth
John Fred. *See* Gourrier, John (Fred)
John, Gabriel. *See* D'Urfey, Thomas
John, Graham. *See* Colmer, Graham John
John Henry. *See* Bradford, (John Henry) Perry
John Henry. *See* Machado, Joel
John, Jaromír. *See* Markalous, Bohumil
John, John Brown. *See* Talbot, Charles Remington
John-Lane. *See* Lange, Robert John
John Loeillet of London. *See* Loeillet, Jean Baptiste (1680-1730)
John of Garland. *See* Johannes de Garlandia
John, Walter. *See* Ball, Eric
Johner, Dominic(us). *See* Johner, Franz-Xaver Karl
Johnnie & Jack. *See* Anglin, Jack
Johnnie & Jack. *See* Wright, Johnnie Robert
Johnny Appleseed of Ragtime. *See* Darch, Robert R(ussell)
Johnny D. *See* Loudermilk, John D.
Johnny Flamingo. *See* Moore, Melvin James
Johns, Erik. *See* Johnston, Horace Eugene
Johns, J. A. *See* Bliss, P(hilip) Paul
Johns, J. H. *See* Bliss, P(hilip) Paul
Johns, (Rosalinda) Jill. *See* Demarco, Rosalinda Jill
Johns, Leo. *See* Phillips, James John
Johns, Leo. *See* Stellman, Marcel
Johns, Michael. *See* Adams, Cliff
Johns, Michael. *See* Brown, Bob
Johns, Michael. *See* Chacksfield, Francis [or Frank] (Charles)
Johns, Michael. *See* Fishman, Jack (1918 (or 19)-)
Johnsen, Skip. *See* Johnsen, Stanley Allen
Johnson, Aimee. *See* Johnson, Raymond
Johnson, Big Bill. *See* Broonzy, William Lee Conley
Johnson, Blind Boy. *See* Dupree, William Thomas
Johnson, Blues. *See* Carr, Leroy
Johnson, Budd. *See* Johnson, Albert J.
Johnson, Buddy. *See* Johnson, Woodrow (Wilson)
Johnson, Captain. *See* Johnson, Robert [nd]
Johnson, Chatta. *See* Giovanonne, Anthony J(ohn)
Johnson, Dink. *See* Johnson, Oliver [or Ollie]
Johnson, Donald. *See* Ellis, Donald Johnson
Johnson, Easy Papa. *See* Sykes, Roosevelt
Johnson, Edith. *See* North, Edith
Johnson, Edward. *See* Haass, Hans
Johnson, Elmer. *See* Zimmerman, Robert Allen
Johnson, Floy Mae. *See* Kunkel, Charles
Johnson, Gene. *See* Autry, (Orvon) Gene
Johnson, General. *See* Johnson, Norman
Johnson, Georgia Boy. *See* Johnson, Lucius Brinson
Johnson, Ginger. *See* Croom-Johnson, Austen [or Austin] (Herbert)
Johnson, Guitar Junior. *See* Johnson, Luther, Jr.
Johnson, Henry. *See* Hammond, John (Henry), Jr.
Johnson, Henry. *See* McGhee, Walter Brown
Johnson, J(ay) J(ay). *See* Johnson, James Louis
Johnson, Jack. *See* Hansson, Stig (Axel)
Johnson, Jay Cee. *See* Johnson, J. C.
Johnson, John. *See* Hughes, Robert J(ames)
Johnson, (Hon.) John St. Jon. *See* Lennon, John (Winston)
Johnson, Johnny. *See* Johnson, Malcolm
Johnson, Julia. *See* Gabriel, Charles H(utchinson)
Johnson, Julius K. *See* Koninsky, Sadie
Johnson, Lee. *See* Sissle, Noble (Lee)
Johnson, Lonnie. *See* Johnson, Alonzo
Johnson, Luther. *See* Johnson, Lucius Brinson
Johnson, Maggotty. *See* Johnson, Samuel
Johnson, Margaret. *See* Dunn, Sara(h)
Johnson, Mark. *See* Mercer, W(illiam) Elmo
Johnson, Martha. *See* Kimbrough, Lottie
Johnson, Meathead. *See* Dupree, William Thomas
Johnson, Phil. *See* Shearing, George
Johnson, Randy. *See* Báthory-Kitsz, Dennis
Johnson, Rock. *See* Di Giovanni, Rocco
Johnson, Scott. *See* McKelvy, James (M(illigan))
Johnson, Signifyin (Mary). *See* Johnson, Mary (née Smith)
Johnson, Snake (Boy). *See* Johnson, Lucius Brinson
Johnson, Spider. *See* Adderley, Julien Edwin
Johnson, Stump. *See* Johnson, James (J.) (c.1905-c.1972)
Johnston, Randolph. *See* Rasley, John M.
Johnson, Warrane. *See* Warrington, John(ny) (T.)
Johnson, Warren. *See* Warrington, John(ny) (T.)
Johnstone, Gordon. *See* Christiansen, Larry A.
Johnstone, Gordon. *See* Sween(e)y, Joseph
Joker. *See* Ekberg, Ulf
Jolas, Betsy. *See* Illouz, Elizabeth
Joli. *See* Gonsalves, John P(ires)
Jolie. *See* Yoelson, Asa
Jolly Giant. *See* Greene, Jack (Henry)
Jolly Green Giant, The. *See* Greene, Jack (Henry)
Jolly Roger. *See* Rajonsky [or Rajonski], Milton Michael
Jolson, Al. *See* Yoelson, Asa
Jolson, Jolie. *See* Yoelson, Asa
Jommellino, (Gaetano). *See* Andreozzi, Gaetano
Jonas, Gregor. *See* Fritsch, Johannes Georg(e)
Jonas, Julius. *See* Keiser, Robert (A(dolph))
Jonas, Justus. *See* Koch, Jodocus
Jonathan. *See* Cook, Roger
Joncières, Victorin de. *See* Rossignol, Félix Ludger

Jones, A. M. *See* Kunkel, Charles
Jones, Adam. *See* Williams, David (of Aberavon)
Jones, Agnes. *See* Sharp, Robert Louis, Jr.
Jones, Ann. *See* Matthews, Ann
Jones, Betty. *See* Jones, Lillie Mae
Jones, Bucky. *See* Jones, Kenneth Eugene
Jones, Duke. *See* Williams, Spencer
Jones, Elmore. *See* Crudup, Arthur
Jones, Gordon G. *See* Krunnfusz, Gordon
Jones, Graham. *See* Marshall, Madeleine
Jones, Grandpa. *See* Jones, Louis M(arshall)
Jones, Guitar Slim. *See* Jones, Eddie
Jones, Harry. *See* Robison, Carson J(ay)
Jones, Hart. *See* Higginbotham, Irene (Evelyn)
Jones, Hirem. *See* Box, Harold Elton
Jones, Hirem. *See* Butler, Ralph (T.)
Jones, Hirem. *See* Edwards, C(harles) J(oseph)
Jones, Hirem. *See* Roberts, John Godfrey Owen
Jones, Home. *See* Jones, Sam(uel)
Jones, Ike. *See* Jones, Isaiah, Jr.
Jones, John. *See* Lutkin, Peter C(hristian)
Jones, John. *See* Presley, Elvis A(a)ron
Jones, John Paul. *See* Baldwin, John
Jones, John Paul. *See* Davis, Joseph [or Joe] (M.)
Jones, Jonah. *See* Jones, Robert Elliott
Jones, Jr. Boy. *See* Jones, Andrew (Bennie), (Jr.)
Jones, La Monte C. *See* Daniels, Charles N(eil)
Jones, Maggie. *See* Barnes, Fae [or Faye]
Jones, Mamie. *See* Howard, Ethel
Jones, Maude. *See* Thomas, Lillian [or Lillyn]
Jones, No Show. *See* Jones, George (Glen(n))
Jones, Obadiah. *See* Hutchinson, Leslie
Jones, Obadiah. *See* Jacobson, Lew
Jones, Obadiah. *See* Paramor, Norman [or Norrie] (William)
Jones of Nayland. *See* Jones, (Rev.) William
Jones, Paul. *See* Pond, Paul (Adrian)
Jones, Peggy. *See* Clak, Petula (Sally Olmen [or Olwen])
Jones, Possum. *See* Jones, George (Glen(n))
Jones, R. Donald. *See* Sankey, Ira David
Jones, Robert. *See* Tretheway, Robert
Jones, Spike. *See* Jones, Lindley A(rmstrong)
Jones, Stanley. *See* De Smet, Robin John
Jones, Stephen. *See* Jones, Edward (Stephen) (1822-1885)
Jones, Thumper. *See* Jones, George (Glen(n))
Jones, Tom. *See* Breitenbach, Alfred
Jones, Trinity. *See* Jones, William
Jones, Wine. *See* Jones, Paul
Joplin Kid, The. *See* Wenrich, Percy
Joplinesque. *See* Jopin, Scott
Jordan, Allan. *See* Kaufman, Isidore
Jordan, Alvin. *See* Sugarman, Harry
Jordan, Duke. *See* Jordan, Irving Sidney
Jordan, J(an) (D.). *See* Drozdowski, Jan
Jordan, Jimmy. *See* Johnson, Alonzo
Jordan, Lonnie. *See* Jordan, Leroy
Jordan, Robert. *See* Dammert, Hansjorg
Jordan, Tom. *See* Johnson, Alonzo
Jordan, Willie. *See* Dupree, William Thomas
Jordi. *See* Gómez Llunas, Jordi
Jordon, H. C. *See* Gabriel, Charles H(utchinson)
Jorna, Stephen. *See* Kleinmeijer, Henk
José Antonio de Donostia. *See* Zulzica y Arregui, José Gonzalo
José Antonio de San Sebastian. *See* Zulaica y Arregui, José Gonzalo
José Joel. *See* Carmelo Augusto, José Francisco
José Maurício (Nunez). *See* Garcia, José Maurício Nunes
Joseph of the Stadium. *See* Joseph of Thessalonica
Joseph, Ray. *See* Shayne, Larry
Joseph, Sal. *See* Salviuolo, Joseph Anthony
Josh, (Ted). *See* Zamecnik, J(ohn) S(tepan)
Josh and Ted. *See* Zamecnik, J(ohn) S(tepan)
Jospin, Hubert. *See* Rostaing, Hubert
Josquin, Jan. *See* Solin, Vaclav
Josse. *See* Josquin Desprez
Joukowsky, (W. A.?). *See* Zhukovsky, W. A.
Jouy, Stephano. *See* Jouy, (Victor Joseph) Etienne (de)
Jovan, Otac. *See* Bojić, Milutin
Jove's Poet. *See* Lover, Samuel
Jowett, John. *See* Millar, Ronald (Graeme)
Joy, Bee. *See* Jojić, Boris
Joye, Col. *See* Jacobsen, Colin
Joyous Father of the Vaudeville, The. *See* Basselin, Olivier
Joyous Musician, The. *See* Grainger, (George) Percy (Aldridge)
Juan de la Cimbala. *See* Schubert, Franz Peter
Juan Gabriel. *See* Aguilera (Valadez), Alberto
Juan Perro. *See* Auserón, Santiago
Juan Verio de nacion flamengo. *See* Verio, Juan
Juanga. *See* Aguilera (Valadez), Alberto
Juarez, Miguel. *See* Green, Phil(ip)
Juarez, Miguel. *See* Paramor, Norman [or Norrie] (William)
Jucundus Jucudissimus. *See* Beer, Johann
Judd, Aaron. *See* Fisher, George Clinton
Judd, Cledus 'T,' (No Relation). *See* Poole, Barry
Judd, Diana Ellen. *See* Judd, Naomi
Judd, Wynonna. *See* Ciminella, Christina Claire
Judson, Alfred. *See* Hall, Joseph Lincoln
Judson, Myra. *See* Crosby, Fanny [i.e., Frances] J(ane)
Judy Lynn. *See* Voiten, Judy (Lynn)
Judy Sue. *See* Epstein, Judith Sue
Juggernaut of American Song. *See* Porter, Cole
Juin, Karl. *See* Giugno, Karl
Jularbo, Carl. *See* Karlsson, Karl
Jule, Joe, Jr. *See* Yule, Joe, Jr.

Jules. *See* Gabriel (de Lurieu), Jules-Joseph
Julian, Th. *See* Pilati, Auguste
Juliano, A(uguste) P. *See* Pilati, Auguste
Julien. *See* Mallian, Julien de
Julien, G. *See* Navoigille, Guillaume (Julien)
Julio [or Giulio] da Modena. *See* Segni, Julio [or Giulio]
Julius. *See* Caesar, Isidore
Julius, Ludwig [or Louis]. *See* Bauch, Ludwig Julius
Jullienesque. *See* Jullien, Louis (George) Antoine (Jules)
Jumbo. *See* Hirt, Al(ois Maxwell)
Jump King, The. *See* Basie, William (Allen)
Jun, Terahata. *See* Kirkup, James (Falconer)
Jung, Eckehard. *See* Schwab, Karl Heinz
Jungert, Werner. *See* Drexler, Werner
Junghans, Heinz. *See* Breuer, F(ranz) J(osef)
Jungmann, Felix. *See* Parker, Alfred Thomas
Jüngst, Hugo. *See* Ehret, Walter (Charles)
Junior. *See* Shrubsole, William, Jr.
Junior [or Jr.] Boy. *See* Jones, Andrew (Bennie), (Jr.)
Junior, C. H. *See* Gabriel, Charles H(utchinson)
Junior, H. C. *See* Gabriel, Charles H(utchinson)
Jupiter, Milt. *See* Wüsthoff, Klaus
Jürgen(s), Udo. *See* Bockelmann, Udo Jürgen
Jurgens, Sonny. *See* Jurgens, Dick (Henry)
Jurk. *See* Wiener, Georg
Juschino. *See* Josquin Desprez
Just, A. *See* Bukorester, Adolf
Justice. *See* Grice, Gary
Justis, Walter. *See* Cain, Noble
Justmann, Ralf. *See* Kauffmann, Leo Justinus
Juvenalis. *See* Lühe, Willibald von der
Juvenile. *See* Gray, Terius
Juxinger, Jodocus. *See* Langer, Anton

– K –

KAM. *See* Miller, Craig
K. C. *See* Casey, Harry Wayne
K-Doe, Ernie. *See* Kador, Ernest, Jr.
Ke., W. *See* Kethe, William
K. J. P. *See* Pye, Kellow John
K. K. D. *See* Davis, Katherine K(ennicott)
Kl—f. *See* Hastings, Thomas
K. M. P. *See* Parker, Katherine Mary
K. O. W. A. *See* Almroth, Kunt O. W.
KRS-1 [or One]. *See* Parker, Lawrence Krisna
K., Tonio. *See* Krikorian, Steve
Kaaihue, Norman K. *See* Knowles, Norman George
Kabec, Vlad. *See* Kolditz, Hans
Kachchini, Dzh(ulio). *See* Caccini, Giulio (Romolo)
Kackley, Robert [or Bob]. *See* Miller, Robert [or Bob] (Ernst)
Kaempfert, Flip. *See* Kaempfert, Bert(hold)
Kaes, Karl. *See* Kisowski, Karl
Kaeuffer, Ollivier. *See* Viacava, Joseph Dominique
Kaffka, Johann Christoph. *See* Engelmann, Johann Christoph
Kaffka, Joseph. *See* Engelmann, Joseph
Kaffka, Wilhelm. *See* Engelmann, Wilhelm
KaH, Hubert. *See* Kemmler, Hubert
Kahali, Vaslav. *See* Munn, William O.
Kahler, Hunter. *See* Banta, Frank (Edgar)
Kahn, Chaka. *See* Stevens, Yvette Marie
Kahn, Larry. *See* Fishman, Jack (1918 or 19)-)
Kahn, Sam(my). *See* Cohen, Samuel
Kahn, Stix. *See* Cohen, Theodore Charles
Kahn, Tiny. *See* Kahn, Norman
Kahn, Tro. *See* Bekker, Okko
Kahr, Erik. *See* Groh, Otto Emmerich
Kahr, R. *See* Groh, Otto Emmerich
Kaimen. *See* Stuart-Bergström, Elsa Marianne
Kain, Eddie. *See* Kimmel, Edwin Howard
Kaiser, H. J. *See* Thon, Franz
Kaiser, Joachim. *See* Thon, Franz
Kaiser, Karl Heinz. *See* Sülwald, Paul (Heinrich)
Kaiser of the Cymanfa, The. *See* Jenkins, David
Kako. *See* Bastar, Francisco Angel
Kalamazoo, Joe. *See* Rostaing, Hubert
Kalapana, John. *See* Edwards, Webley Elgin
Kalas. *See* Althans, Kurt Karl
Kalbeck, Max. *See* Karpeles, (Julius) Max (Heinrich)
Kalé. *See* Kabas(s)elé (Tshamala), Joseph
Kaleolani, Al(vin). *See* Isaacs, Al(vin) K(aleolani)
Kalhoon. *See* Brown, Ricardo
Kalimba. *See* Marichal, Kalimba
Kalkstein, Menahem. *See* Mahler-Kalkstein, Menahem
Kallio. *See* Berg, Samuli Kustaa
Kalmani. *See* Kalberg, Eelke
Kamaka'eha Paki. *See* Kamakaeha, Liliu (Loloku Walania)
Kambo, S. *See* Simoni, Renato
Kamerton. *See* Katz, Josef P.
Kames, Bob. *See* Kujawa, Robert V(alentine)
Kammen, Jack. *See* Kamenetzky, Jacob
Kammen, Joseph. *See* Kamenetzky, Joseph
Kamoto, Igushi. *See* Engel, Carl
Kanda Bongo Man. *See* Bongo, Kanda
Kane, Bernie. *See* Aquino, Frank J(oseph)
Kane, Big Daddy. *See* Hardy, Antonio (M.)
Kane, DJ. *See* Kano, Jason
Kane, Paul. *See* Simon, Paul Frederick
Kane, Peter. *See* Palmer, Cedric King
Kane, Peter. *See* Zerga, Joseph (Louis) E(dmund)
Kanevas. *See* Schubert, Franz Peter
Kansas. *See* Kanzus, Kanzus, J.
Kansas City Bill. *See* Weldon, Wil(liam)
Kansas City Butterball, The. *See* Kimbrough, Lottie
Kansas City Virtuoso, The. *See* Baker, Edythe Ruth
Kansas Jaybird. *See* Robison, Carson J(ay)

Kansas Joe. *See* McCoy, Joe
Kant, Klerk. *See* Copeland, Stewart
Kanter, Isidore. *See* Iskowitz, Edward Israel
Kaplan, C. *See* Picariello, Frederick [Frederico] A(nthony)
Kaplún, Raúl. *See* Kaflún, Israel
Kapralik, Elena. *See* Mattheus, Bernd
Kaps, Karl. *See* Roberts, John [or Jack] (Isaac)
Kar Kar. *See* Traoré, Boubacar
Karbach, Friedrich. *See* Kohn, Bernhard
Karczag, Wilhelm. *See* Krammer, Vilmos
Kare. *See* Kabas(s)elé (Tshamala), Joseph
Kareem, Abdul. *See* McLean, John Lenwood, (Jr.)
Karenin, V(l). *See* Komarova-Stasova, Varvara
Karl, Karl. *See* Bernbrun, Karl (Andreas)
Karlan, Fred. *See* Crawford, Ruth (Porter)
Karlev, M. *See* Levetzow, Karl Micha(e)l von
Karlo. *See* Herzel, Carl [or Karl] (Heinrich)
Karlopago. *See* Ziegler, Karl
Karlovich, Karl. *See* Arnol'd, Yury (Karlovich)
Karlton. *See* McCollin, Frances
Karlweis, C(arl). *See* Weiss, Karl
Karmon, Freddy. *See* Picariello, Frederick [or Frederico] A(nthony)
Karnak. *See* Parrott, (Horace) Ian
Károly, Göndör. *See* Kraushaar, Charles
Karoly, H. *See* Heins, Carl
Károly Reth N. *See* Thern, Károly
Károlyi, Amy. *See* Károlyi, Mária
Karp, Karl. *See* Hume, Oscar Carl
Karr, Harold. *See* Katz, Harold (H.)
Karrasch, Tom. *See* Beil, Peter
Karr y de Alfonsetté, Carmen. *See* Escardot, L.
Karweem, Musheed. *See* Powell, Everard Stephen, Sr.
KaSandra, Dobanian King. *See* Anderson, John W.
KaSandra, John. *See* Anderson, John W.
Kaschtan. *See* Weintraub, (Rotkopf) Salomon
Kashif. *See* Jones, Michael
Kass, R. L. *See* Castleman, Robert (Lee)
Kassal, Luis. *See* Kalaš, Julius
Kastein, Josef [or Joseph]. *See* Katzenstein, Julius
Kastowsky, Jean. *See* Casto, John Wheaton
Kastrounis, Konstantin. *See* Xenakis, Iannis
Kate Smith of Harlem, The. *See* Thomas, Lillian [or Lillyn]
Kate Smith of the West. *See* Matthews, Ann
Katt, Maurus. *See* Marszalek, Franz
Katunga. *See* Contursi, Jose Maria
Kauer, Gene. *See* Kauer, Guenther M(ax)
Kaufman, Irving. *See* Kaufman, Isidore
Kaufman, Jack. *See* Kaufman, Jacob
Kaufman, Whitey. *See* Kaufman, Martin Ellis
Kauler, Herbert. *See* Noack, Herbert
Kawabe, Koichi. *See* Ishitsuji, Keiichi
Kawaha, Eddie. *See* Green, Phil(ip)
Kawaha, Eddie. *See* Paramor, Norman [or Norrie] (William)
Kawai, Sawako. *See* Nakamura, Sawako
Kawelo, Ioane. *See* Zamecnik, J(ohn) S(tepan)
Kawka, Johann Christoph. *See* Engelmann, Johann Christoph
Kawka, Wilhelm. *See* Engelmann, Wilhelm
Kay, Bob. *See* Sugarman, Harry
Kay, Caro. *See* Krogmann, Carrie W(illiam(s))
Kay, Fred. *See* Frangkiser, Carl (Moerz)
Kay, Herschel. *See* Krasnow, Herman(n)
Kay, Hershy. *See* Krasnow, Herman(n)
Kay, Ilo. *See* Kaufman, Isidore
Kay, John. *See* Krauledat, Joachim (Fritz)
Kaye, Benny. *See* Katz, Benjamin
Kaye, Buddy. *See* Kaye, Jules Leonard
Kaye, Buddy. *See* Kipp, L. L.
Kaye, Camille. *See* Kurtz, Em(m)anuel [or Manny]
Kaye, Geoffrey. *See* Ketèlbey, Albert William
Kaye, Gerry. *See* Klug, Geraldine Dolores
Kaye, Manny. *See* Cabral, Manuel M(edeiros)
Kaye, Norman. *See* Knowles, Norman George
Kayli, Bob. *See* Gordy, Robert
Kaylor, Roy. *See* Sawyer, Henry S.
Kazničov, B. *See* Remeš, B.
Kearney, David William. *See* Fortescue, John Henry
Keating, Jack. *See* Keating, John Henry
Keating, Lawrence. *See* Kohlmann, Clarence (E.)
Keb' Mo'. *See* Moore, Kevin
Keefer, Rusty. *See* Keefer, Arrett (Marwood)
Keen, Speedy. *See* Keen, John
Keene, Charles. *See* Autry, (Orvon) Gene
Kees, Karl. *See* Kisowski, Karl
Keghouse. *See* Wilkins, Robert Timothy
Keil, Th(eodore). *See* Retter, Louis
Keiser, Mrs. *See* Keiser, Robert (A(dolph))
Keith, Jack. *See* Mercer, John(ny) (H(erndon))
Keith, Robert. *See* Applebaum, Stan(ley) (Seymour)
Keith, Rodd. *See* Eskelin, Rodney
Kéler, Béla (Albrecht Pál). *See* Kéler, Adalbert Paul von
Kéler-Béla. *See* Kéler, Adalbert Paul von
Kelin, Eric. *See* Breuer, Wolfgang
Kell, Joseph. *See* Wilson, John Anthony (Burgess)
Keller, Arthur. *See* Goerdeler, Richard
Keller, Don. *See* Keller, Edward McDonald
Keller, F. *See* Haass, Hans
Keller, Jack. *See* Keller, James Walter
Keller, Karl. *See* Kleiber, Carlos
Keller, Olive Robinson. *See* Kunkel, Charles
Keller, Oscar. *See* Geehl, Henry Ernest
Keller, Simon. *See* Hausskeller, Simon
Keller, Weeny. *See* Wheeler, Kenneth [or Kenny] (Vincent John)
Kellette, John W(illiam). *See* Brockman, James

Kellette, John W(illiam). *See* Vincent, Nathaniel (Hawthorne)
Kelley, Fred. *See* Rummel, Walter Morse
Kelley, Guitar. *See* Kelley, Arthur
Kelly, C(asey). *See* Cohen, Daniel (Kelly)
Kelly, Margie. *See* Ringleben, Justin, Jr.
Kelly, Monty. *See* Kelly, Montgomery Jerome
Kelly, William. *See* Leidzén, Erik William Gustav
Kelly, William Wilhelm. *See* Occhelli, William Wilhelm
Kelly, Willie. *See* Sykes, Roosevelt
Kelvin, Andrew. *See* Butler, Ralph (T.)
Kemp, Father. *See* Kemp, Robert C.
Kemp, Victor. *See* Girard, Harry
Kempner, Julia. *See* Weismann, Julia
Kenbrockovitch, Ivan. *See* Kendis, James
Kenbrovin, Jaan. *See* Brockman, James
Kenbrovin, Jaan. *See* Kendis, James
Kenbrovin, Jaan. *See* Vincent, Nathaniel (Hawthorne)
Kenbury, Charles. *See* Berry, Dennis (Alfred)
Kendal, Sydney. *See* Mason, Gladys Amy
Kendall, Al M. *See* Roberts, Lee S.
Kendall, Don. *See* Haenschen, Walter (G(ustave))
Kendall, Don. *See* Hurtig, Jules
Kendall, Don. *See* Morse, Theodore (F.)
Kendall, Don. *See* O'Keefe, James (Conrad)
Kendall, Don. *See* O'Keefe, Lester
Kendis, Sonny. *See* Kendis, James
Kenley, Peter. *See* LeClerq, Arthur
Kennedy, Bruce. *See* Meredith, I(saac) H(ickman)
Kennedy, H(arriet). *See* Keiser, Robert (A(dolph))
Kennedy, Jane. *See* Vonderlieth, Leonore
Kennedy, May. *See* Keiser, Robert (A(dolph))
Kennedy Rose. *See* Kennedy, Mary Ann
Kennedy Rose. *See* Rose, Pam
Kennen, Frank. *See* Kämpf, Armin
Kenny G. *See* Gorelick, Kenneth
Kenny, George. *See* Whitcomb, Kenneth G(eorge)
Kenny, Ken. *See* Norville, (J.) Kenneth
Kent, Al. *See* Hamilton, Al(bert)
Kent, Gary. *See* Wright, Carter Land
Kent, H. R. *See* Laurendeau, Louis-Philippe
Kent, H. R. *See* Seredy, J(ulius) S.
Kent, H. R. *See* Sterrett, Paul
Kent, Julian. *See* Krogmann, Carrie W(illiam(s))
Kent, Klark. *See* Copeland, Stewart
Kent, Neal W. *See* Kinsman, (J) Franklin
Kent, Richard. *See* Auracher, Harry
Kent, Richard. *See* Soloman, Mirrie (Irma)
Kent, Roy. *See* Drexler, Werner
Kent, Walter. *See* Druckman, Milton
Kenton, Charlie. *See* Rich, Charlie [or Charley]
Kenton, Egon (F.). *See* Kornstein, Egon (F.)
Kenton, Jimmy. *See* Bond, Cyrus Whitfield
Kentucky Colonel, The. *See* Skinner, James
Kentucky Folk Singer, The. *See* Osborne, James [or Jimmie], Jr.
Kentucky Wonder Bean. *See* Peterson, Walter
Kenwal, Ernest. *See* Ehret, Walter (Charles)
Kenwal, Ernest. *See* Walton, Kenneth
Kenwood, Marty. *See* Kalmanoff, Martin
Kenzie, John. *See* Zerga, Joseph (Louis) E(dmund)
Keppe(l), Franz. *See* Denneé, Charles (Frederick)
Kerbiniou, Yves de. *See* Bonnemère (de Chavigny), Léon Eugène
Kerman. *See* Schlenkermann, Friedrich [or Fritz]
Kern, Jimmy. *See* Finkelstein, Abe
Kernen, Roland. *See* Waignein, Andre
Kéroul, Henri (Antoine Alexis Siméon). *See* Queyroul, Henri (Antoine Alexis Siméon)
Kerr, Anita. *See* Grob, Anita Jean
Kerr, Julia. *See* Weismann, Julia
Kerr, Robert Nolan. *See* Nolan, (Sister) Aloysius
Kerrigan, W. *See* Wright, Lawrence
Kershaw. *See* Rhodes, Samuel
Kervan, Armal de. *See* Jacquot, Charles Jean Baptiste
Kerwey, Julia. *See* Weismann, Julia
Kerwin, Jules. *See* Stein, Julius Kerwin
Kesperle, Filippo. *See* Micheli, Romano
Kessler, Joseph Christoph. *See* Kötzler, Joseph Christoph
Keston, Felix. *See* Moul, Alfred
Ketterer, E(ugene). *See* Kunkel, Charles
Kevin. *See* Ceballo, Kevin
Kevin, Alexander. *See* Kaplan, Alan Kevin
Keyber, Mr. Conny. *See* Fielding, Henry
Keybord, Richard. *See* Wagener, Hans Günter
Keye, Geoffrey. *See* Ketèlbey, Albert William
Keyes, Gilbert. *See* Kahn, Gus
Keypton. *See* Graham, Lloyd M.
Keys, Buddy. *See* Bergh, Arthur F.
Keyser, Alfred de. *See* Kaiser, (Henri) Alfred (de)
Keysten, Ralf. *See* Wyss, Rudolf
Khan, Alfie. *See* Heider, Joachim
Kid, The. *See* Nelson, Prince Rogers
Kid from Brooklyn, The. *See* Copland, Aaron
Kid from Brooklyn, The. *See* Diamond, Neil (Leslie)
Kid from Red Bank, The. *See* Basie, William (Allen)
Kid Frost. *See* Molina, Arturo, Jr.
Kid Rock. *See* Ritchie, Robert (James)
Kid Sox. *See* Wilson, Wesley
Kid with the Gauze in His Jaws, The. *See* Torme, Mel(vin Howard)
Kid with the Sideburns, The. *See* Presley, Elvis A(a)ron
Kidd, Johnny. *See* Heath, Frederick (Albert)
Kidde, Chuck. *See* Shavers, Charlie [i.e., Charles] (James)
Kiefer, J. *See* Dant, Charles G(ustave)
Kiefer, Joseph. *See* Lincoln, Harry J.
Kiehl, Heinrich. *See* Fisher, William Arms

Kieselst(e)in, Reiner. *See* Müller, Rainer
Kiko, M. *See* Romer, Mary
Kildare, John. *See* Gillespie, John (Birks)
Killah Ghostface. *See* Coles, Dennis
Killeen, Pete. *See* Kaufman, Isidore
Killen, Buddy. *See* Killen, W(illiam) D.
Killer, The. *See* Lewis, Jerry Lee
Kilmister, Lemmy. *See* Kilmister, Ian Fraiser
Kim, Andy. *See* Youakim, Andrew [or Andy]
Kimbrough, Lena. *See* Kimbrough, Lottie
Kimball, F. R. *See* Friedman, Leo
Kimball, F. R. *See* Root, Frank K.
Kimball, F. R. *See* Sawyer, Henry S.
Kimmel, Stanley. *See* Kunkel, Charles
Kincaid, Jesse Lee. *See* Gerlach, (Stephen) Nicholas [or Nick]
Kincaid, Joe. *See* Slaughter, M(arion) T(ry)
Kinderlieb, Heinrich. *See* Hoffmann, Heinrich
Kinderlieb, Reimerich. *See* Hoffmann, Heinrich
Kindermann, Hans. *See* Lewald, (Johann Karl) August
Kindmann. *See* Gasparus
King, The. *See* Carter, Bennett L(ester)
King, The. *See* Presley, Elvis A(a)ron
King, A. R. *See* Keiser, Robert (A(dolph))
King, Al. *See* McClaskey, Harry Haley
King, Al. *See* Smith, Alvin K.
King, Albert. *See* Nelson, Albert
King, Arthur C. *See* Cohen, Arthur C.
King, B. B. . *See* King, Riley B.
King, BB Chung. *See* Mirikitani, Alan Masao
King, Ben E. *See* Nelson, Benjamin Earl
King Bing. *See* Crosby, Harry Lillis
King, Black Ivory. *See* Alexander, David [or Dave]
King, Blues Boy. *See* King, Riley B.
King, Bob. *See* Fournier, Robert B.
King, Bob. *See* Keiser, Robert (A(dolph))
King, Bobo. *See* Keiser, Robert (A(dolph))
King, Bonnie B. *See* Berndt, Julia Helen
King, Carl. *See* Koelling, Karl (W. P.)
King, Carole. *See* Klein, Carole
King, Chubby. *See* Byles, Keith
King Coll(ey). *See* Cibber, Colley
King Curtis. *See* Ousley, (King) Curtis
King, Daisy. *See* Vonderlieth, Leonore
King, Dee Dee. *See* Colvin, Douglas Glenn
King, Earl. *See* Johnson, Earl (Silas)
King, Frank(ie). *See* Kuczynski, Julius Frank (Anthony)
King Freak of New York, The. *See* Firbank, Louis [or Lewis] (Allen)
King, Fred. *See* Slaughter, M(arion) T(ry)
King, Freddie [or Freddy]. *See* Myles, Billy
King, G(ilbert) R. *See* Harrison, Susan [or Susie] Frances (née Riley)
King, Garland. *See* Barnes H(oward) E(llington)
King, Garland. *See* Fields, Harold (Cornelius)
King, Garland. *See* Roncoroni, Joseph (Dominic)
King, George S. *See* Frangkiser, Carl (Moerz)
King, Hall. *See* Bulch, Thomas Edward
King, Harry. *See* Grillaert, Octave
King, Henry. *See* Finkelstein, Abe
King in C, A. *See* King, Oliver (A)
King, Irving. *See* Campbell, James [or Jimmy]
King, Irving. *See* Connelly, Reg(inald)
King Ivory Lee. *See* Semien, (Ivory) Lee
King, J. J. *See* Banash, Joseph
King, Jack. *See* King, Albert
King, Jan. *See* Phipps, Joyce Irene
King, Jonathan. *See* King, Kenneth
King, Joseph [or Joe]. *See* Banash, Joseph
King, Little Jimmy. *See* Gales, Manuel
King, Luther. *See* Johnson, Lucius Brinson
King, Mary. *See* Keiser, Robert (A(dolph))
King, Master. *See* King, Matthew Peter
King, Nosmo. *See* Jameson, Stephen
King, Nosmo. *See* Watson, Samuel Vernon
King of Accordion Players. *See* Walker, Lawrence
King of All Media. *See* Crosby, Harry Lillis
King of American Popular Music. *See* Gum(m), Harold [or Harry]
King of Bohemia. *See* Clapp, Henry, Jr.
King of Broadway, The. *See* Cohan, George M(ichael)
King of Brummagem. *See* Neukomm, Sigismund (Ritter von)
King of Chicago Blues. *See* Morganfield, McKinley
King of Christmas. *See* Crosby, Harry Lillis
King of Corn, The. *See* Jones, Lindley A(rmstrong)
King of Country, The. *See* Presley, Elvis A(a)ron
King of Country and Western Music, The. *See* Cash, John(ny) (R.)
King of Country Music, The. *See* Acuff, Roy (Claxton)
King of Country Music, The. *See* Kirkpatrick, David Gordon
King of Country Music, The. *See* Nelson, Willie (Hugh)
King of Country Music, (The). *See* Williams, Hir(i)am (King)
King of Country Music Fairs, The. *See* Young, Faron
King of Country Singers, The. *See* Howard, Harlan (Perry)
King of Decadence, The. *See* Firbank, Louis [or Lewis] (Allen)
King of Dullness, The. *See* Cibber, Colley
King of Dunces, The. *See* Cibber, Colley
King of Glitter Rock, The. *See* Jones, David Robert (Hayward)
King of Gospel Music, The. *See* Cleveland, James
King of Gospel Music. *See* Robinson, Cleophus
King of Gypsy Music, The. *See* Stevens, Sam
King of Hearts, The. *See* Francis, Cleve(land), (Jr.)
King of Hearts,The. *See* Presley, Elvis A(a)ron

King of Hi-de-ho. *See* Calloway, Cab(ell), III
King of Highlife, The. *See* Mensah, E(mmanuel) T(ettah)
King of Honky Tonk Swing. *See* Thompson, Henry William
King of Horror Film Music. *See* Salter, Hans J.
King of Jazz. *See* Whiteman, Paul
King of Juju Music. *See* Adeniyi, Sunday
King of Latin Jazz, The. *See* Puente, Ernesto Antonio, (Jr.)
King of Laughter, The. *See* Williams, Egbert Austin
King of Light Music. *See* Coates, Eric
King of Light Orchestra Music. *See* Mantovani, A(nnuzio) P(aolo)
King of Love, The. *See* Presley, Elvis A(a)ron
King of Mountain Music. *See* Acuff, Roy (Claxton)
King of Musical Corn. *See* Welk, Lawrence (LeRoy)
King of New Orleans Jazz. *See* La Menthe, Ferdinand Joseph
King of Operetta. *See* Eberst, Jacob
King of Pianist. *See* Liszt, Franz
King of Piano, A. *See* La Menthe, Ferdinand Joseph
King of Pop. *See* Jackson, Michael Joseph
King of Pop Rock, The. *See* Presley, Elvis A(a)ron
King of Poppish Rock 'n' Roll, The. *See* Boone, Charles Eugene
King of Progresssive Country. *See* Nelson, Willie (Hugh)
King of Ragtime, The. *See* Baline, Israel
King of Ragtime, The. *See* Joplin, Scott
King of Ragtime Composers, The. *See* Joplin, Scott
King of Ragtime Guitar, The. *See* Phelps, Arthur
King of Ragtime Players. *See* Chauvin, Louis
King of Ragtime Writers. *See* Joplin, Scott
King of Reggae, The. *See* Marley, Robert [or Bob] Nesta
King of Rock and Pop. *See* Jackson, Michael Joseph
King of Rock and Roll, The. *See* Penniman, Richard [or Ricardo] Wayne
King of Rock 'n' Roll, The. *See* Presley, Elvis A(a)ron
King of Rockabilly. *See* Perkins, Carl (Lee)
King of Samba. *See* Moreira de Castro, Carlos
King of Samba, The. *See* Silva, José Barbosa [or B(atista)] (da)
King of Schmaltz. *See* DeCesare, Stephen
King of Scotch Fiddlers, The. *See* Gow, Neil [or Niel]
King of Skiffle Music. *See* Donegan, Anthony [or Tony] (James)
King of Soul, The. *See* Brown, James
King of Soul. *See* Burke, Solomon
King of Soul Music, The. *See* Brown, James
King of Soul Singers, The. *See* Redding, Ottis
King of Swamp Pop Music. *See* Guzzo, Francis
King of Swing. *See* Goodman, Benjamin [or Benny] (David)
King of Swoon, The. *See* Presley, Elvis A(a)ron
King of Tanguinho. *See* Tupinambá, Marcelo
King of Television Themes, The. *See* Postil, Leland M(ichael)
King of Tenors. *See* Rubini, Giovanni Battista
King of the American Musical Theater, The. *See* Kern, Jerome David
King of the Autoharp. *See* Bowers, Bryan Benson
King of the Balladeers. *See* Bryson, Peapo
King of the Banjo. *See* Beaulieu, Maurice Joseph
King of the Big Rigs, The. *See* Sovine, Woodrow Wilson
King of the Blues, The. *See* King, Riley B.
King of the Blues. *See* Morganfield, McKinley
King of the Boogie, (The). *See* Hooker, John Lee
King of the Cajuns. *See* Bruce, Ervin
King of the Clarinet. *See* Arshawsky, Arthur Jacob
King of the Clarinet. *See* Phillips, Isadore Simon
King of the Concert Band. *See* Sousa, John Philip
King of the Cowboy Fiddlers. *See* Chrisman, Paul Woodrow
King of the Cowboys, The. *See* Slye, Leonard (Franklin)
King of the Delta Blues Singers. *See* Johnson, Robert (Leroy) (1911-1938)
King of the Dime Novel. *See* Judson, Edward Zane Carrol
King of the Endless Boogie, The. *See* Hooker, John Lee
King of the Harmonica. *See* Ford, Aleck
King of the Hillbillies, The. *See* Acuff, Roy (Claxton)
King of the Hillbilly Piano Players. *See* Mullican, Aubrey Wilson
King of the Jingles, The. *See* Adams, Cliff
King of the Mambo. *See* Perez Prado, Domasco [or Damasco]
King of the Mambo. *See* Puente, Ernesto Antonio, (Jr.)
King of the Merengue. *See* Valladares, Isidro
King of the Mountain Blues. *See* Taralsen, Peer Helge
King of the 1950s Mambo Craze. *See* Puente, Ernesto Antonio, (Jr.)
King of the Piano Roll. *See* Fuiks, Lewis J(ohn)
King of the Ragtime Writers. *See* Joplin, Scott
King of the Road, The. *See* Miller, Roger Dean
King of the Shouters, The. *See* Turner, Joseph Vernon
King of the South, The. *See* Chenier, Clifton
King of the Southern Pea Pickers, The. *See* Ford, Ernest Jennings
King of the Stroll. *See* Willis, Harold
King of the Tango. *See* Piazzolla, Astor
King of Tear Jerkers, The. *See* Harris, Charles K(assell)
King of the Tennessee Pea Pickers, The. *See* Ford, Ernest Jennings
King of the 12 String Guitar Players. *See* Ledbetter, Huddie (William)
King of the Waltz. *See* Strauss, Johann (Baptist), Sr. (1804-1949)
King of the Waltz. *See* Strauss, Johann, (Baptist), Jr. (1825-1899)

King of the White Texas Bluesmen. *See* McClinton, Delbert
King of the World, The. *See* Clemons, Clarence
King of Three-Quarter Time, The. *See* Strauss, Johann (Baptist) (1804-1849)
King of Topsy-Turvydom, The. *See* Gilbert, William Schwenk
King of Tropicalia, The. *See* Veloso, Caetano (Emmanuel Viana Telles)
King of Western Bop, The. *See* Presley, Elvis A(a)ron
King of Western Country Music, The. *See* Williams, Hir(i)am (King)
King of Western Pop. *See* Presley, Elvis A(a)ron
King of Western Swing. *See* Cooley, Donnell Clyde
King of Western Swing, The. *See* Wills, (James) Robert [or Bob]
King of White Soul, The. *See* Levise, William, Jr.
King of Yiddish Music, The. *See* Fuld, Leo
King of Zydeco. *See* Chenier, Clifton
King of Zydeco. *See* Rubin, Alton (Jay)
King, Pee Wee. *See* Kuczynski, Julius Frank (Anthony)
King, Pete. *See* King, C. Dudley
King Pleasure. *See* Beeks, Clarence
King, R. A. K. *See* Keiser, Robert (A(dolph))
King Radio. *See* Span(n), Norman
King, Ricky. *See* Lingenfelder, Hans
King, Robert (A.). *See* Keiser, Robert (A(dolph))
King, Robert Keiser. *See* Keiser, Robert (A(dolph))
King, Roy. *See* Cleaver, H. Robinson
King, Roy. *See* Crimmins, Roy
King, S. A. R. *See* Keiser, Robert (A(dolph))
King Sparrow. *See* Francisco, Slinger
King, Stanford. *See* Dellafield, Henry
King, T. S. *See* Blume, David Nason
King, Thomas. *See* Trusler, Ivan
King, Triston [or Tristan]. *See* Banash, Joseph
King, Tyrone. *See* Ellis, Russell E.
King, Victor. *See* King Robert [or Bob]
King, Walter. *See* Kosakowski, Wenceslaus (Walter)
King, Wilton. *See* Mullen, Adelaide
"King" Yellowman. *See* Foster, Winston
Kingman, Tony. *See* Drexler, Werner
Kingpin, The. *See* Brown, Ricardo
King's Bard, The. *See* Jones, Edward (1752-1824)
King's Poet, The. *See* Jones, Edward (1752-1824)
Kingsbury, John. *See* Ehret, Walter (Charles)
Kingsley, Arthur. *See* Blitz, Leo(nard)
Kingsley, Arthur. *See* Bulch, Thomas Edward
Kingsley, Lorrain. *See* Ehret, Walter (Charles)
Kingsley, Robert. *See* Keiser, Robert (A(dolph))
Kingsley, Robie. *See* Keiser, Robert (A(dolph))
Kingsley, Robin. *See* Whitcomb, Ian (Timothy)
Kingsley, Rutherford. *See* Engel, Carl
Kingsmill, Leigh. *See* Phillips, Alfred
Kingston, Hardy. *See* Kiesewetter, Hartmut
Kinkstah, The. *See* Friedman(n), Richard (F.)
Kinor, Jehuda. *See* Rothmüller, Aron Marko
Kinsey, Big Daddy. *See* Kinsey, Lester
Kinsman, Frank(lin). *See* Kinsman, Elmer (F(ranklin))
Kipling of the Halls. *See* Hunt, G(eorge) W(illiam)
Kipling of the Music Hall. *See* Chevalier, Albert (Onesime Britannicus Gawtheveoyd Louis)
Kirchner, Alex. *See* Winkler, Gerhard
Kiriloff, Efrem. *See* Zuccamana, Gizelle Augusta
Kirk, Eddie. *See* Kirkland, Eddie
Kirk, Rahsaan Roland. *See* Kirk, Ronald T(heodore)
Kirk, Roland. *See* Kirk, Ronald T(heodore)
Kirkland, Bo. *See* Kirkland, Mike James
Kirkland, Ralph. *See* Kinder, Ralph
Kirkland, Robert. *See* Scott, Robert [or Bobby] William
Kisbán, Miklós. *See* Bánffy, (Count) (Domokoso Pál) Miklós
Kiser, Max. *See* McKelvy, James (M(illigan))
Kisiel, (Teodor Klon). *See* Kisielewski, Stefan
Kitarô. *See* Takahshi, Masanori
Kitch. *See* Roberts, Aldwyn [or Aldwin]
Kitchener, Lord. *See* Roberts, Aldwyn [or Aldwin]
Kith, Wylliam [or Wyllyam]. *See* Kethe, William
Kivi, Aleksis. *See* Stenvall, Aleksis
Klabund. *See* Henschke, Alfred
Klark Kent. *See* Copeland, Stewart
Klay, Raymond. *See* Frangkiser, Carl (Moerz)
Kleber, Carl. *See* Krogmann, Carrie W(illiam(s))
Klein, David. *See* Keiser, Robert (A(dolph))
Kleinjan. *See* Barton, Horace Percival
Kleinmichel. *See* Kern, Carl Wilhelm
Klenovsky, (Paul). *See* Wood, (Sir) Henry Joseph
Kletzki, Paul. *See* Klecki, Paul
Kleve. *See* Klebe, Hans Werner
Kleve-Gürsch. *See* Gürsch, Günther Gerhard
Klewer, Thomas. *See* Welker, Gotthard
Klimius, Nicolas. *See* Holberg, Ludvig
Kling, Carl. *See* Koelling, Karl (W. P.)
Kling, Woody. *See* Kling, Heywood
Klingemann, Klaus. *See* Wölki, Konrad
Klinger, K. L. W. *See* Dräxler, Karl (Ferdinand)
Klingsor, Tristan (L.). *See* Leclère, (Arthur Justin)Léon
Klon, Teodor. *See* Kisielewski, Stefan
Klook-Mop. *See* Clarke, Kenneth [or Kenny] (Spearman)
Klopweisser, (Dr.) Karlheinz. *See* Gold, Glenn Herbert
Klos, Richard. *See* Preissová, Gabriela (née Sekerová)
Kloss, Erich. *See* Totis, San(dor)
Klubs. *See* Randall, James R(yder)
Kmita, Andrei. *See* Brockway, Harold
Knapp, Frank. *See* McClaskey, Harry Haley
Knarf, Rex. *See* Frank, Dave
Knaster, Simon. *See* Weber, Carl Maria von
Knepler, Paul. *See* Knöpler, Paul
Knickerbocker, Diedrich. *See* Irving, Washington

Knif. *See* Fink, (Christian) Gottfried Wilhelm
Knight, Gary. *See* Temkin, Harold (P.)
Knight, Gerald. *See* Ehret, Walter (Charles)
Knight, Gerald. *See* Wilson, Harry (Robert)
Knight, J. M. *See* Bliss, P(hilip) Paul
Knight, Jean. *See* Caliste, Jean
Knight, Maria. *See* Knight, Gladys (M.)
Knight of the Lute. *See* Lorenzini
Knight of the Realm. *See* Lauder, (Sir) Harry (Maclennan)
Knight, Sonny. *See* Smith, Joseph C(oleman)
Knoblock, Edward. *See* Knoblauch, Edward
Knowles, Marie. *See* Olman, Abraham [or Abe]
Knox, Willie "The Rock". *See* Hyman, Richard [or Dick] (R(oven))
Knudsen, Niels. *See* Wieth-Knudsen, Knud (A(sbjørn))
Koa, Ken. *See* Miller, Robert [or Bob] (Ernst)
Koblenzer, Jacques. *See* Klinkhammer, Stefan
Koch, Jost. *See* Jonas, Justus
Kockyn. *See* Holt, Simeon ten
Koda, Cub. *See* Koda, Michael (John)
Koenneritz, Nina von. *See* Eschborn, Georgine Christine M.
Kok, Jens. *See* Kjerulf, Charles Theodor Martin
Kokomo. *See* Wisner, James [or Jimmy] (Joseph)
Kolar, Andreas. *See* Ehret, Walter (Charles)
Kolar, Andreas. *See* Kinsman, Elmer (F(ranklin))
Kole, Robert. *See* Kolodin, Robert
Kollarz, Wicky. *See* Kollarz, Ludwig
Kollo, Walter. *See* Kollodzieyski, Elimar Walter
Kolloden. *See* Taufsten, (Alexander) Louis [or Ludwig]
Kollontai, Mikhail. *See* Yermolayev, Mikhail
Kolpe(t), Max. *See* Kolpenitzki, Max
Komeda, Krzysztof. *See* Trzcinski, Krzysztof
Kominiak, Ryszard. *See* Zeidler, Armin
Komitas, (Sogomon). *See* Sogomonian, (Sogomon Gevorkovich)
Kompánski, Eugène. *See* Niedola, E. K.
Komposch, Gretl. *See* Hofferer, Margaretha Maria Elisabeth
Komzak, C. *See* Lindemann, Wilhelm
Kondrack, Michael. *See* Ostoya-Kondrack, Michael
Kong. *See* Koningsberger, Hans
Königsdorfer, Ludwig. *See* Strittmatter, Fred
Königsperger, Marianus. *See* Königsperger, Johann Erhard
Konimo. *See* Amposah, Daniel
Koning, Hans. *See* Koningsberger, Hans
Konrad. *See* Ostoya-Kondrack, Michael
Konradin, (Karl Ferdinand). *See* Kohn, Karl Ferdinand
Konte, Skip. *See* Konte, Frank (Earl)
Kool G(enius) Rap. *See* Wilson, Nathaniel
Kool, Keith. *See* Thornton, Keith
Kool Rock Jay. *See* Ramsey, Leo Dupree, Jr.
Kootch, Danny. *See* Kortchmar, Daniel [or Danny]
Kopka, Ulrico. *See* Koepke, Ulrich
Koppitz, Louis. *See* Clough-Leighter, Henry
Koprowski, Peter Paul. *See* Pawel, Piotr
Kord, Mira. *See* Johnova, Miroslava
Kordah, Tibor. *See* Barnes, H(oward) E(llington)
Kordah, Tibor. *See* Fields, Harold (Cornelius)
Kordah, Tibor. *See* Roncoroni, Joseph (Dominic)
Korden, Emilio. *See* Lubbe, Kurt
Korff, Paul. *See* Merath, Siegfried
Korg, Roland. *See* Layer, Wolfgang
Korla, Karl. *See* Kaskel, (Baron) Karl (von)
Kornbau, Wilhelm. *See* Lutter, Howard
Kornfeld, Peter. *See* Schultze, Norbert (Arnold Wilhelm Richard)
Korny. *See* Kornweibel, Albert H.
Korten, Hans. *See* Andries, Franzleo
Korten, Hans. *See* Feltz, Kurt (August Karl)
Kösen, Konrad. *See* Ailbout, Hans
Kosenko. *See* Haidenko, Igor
Kosloff, Lou. *See* Merrick, Mahlon (Le Grande)
Kosmas. *See* Castelli, Ignaz Franz
Kosta, Ensio. *See* Ducander, Sten Carl
Kosta, Fred. *See* Badura, Jens-Dieter
Kostas. *See* Lazarides, Kostas
Koster, Henry. *See* Kosterlitz, Hermann
Kota, Lu. *See* Kudera, Lottie A.
Kotte, Frank. *See* Bliss, P(hilip) Paul
Kotter, Ton. *See* Kotter, Anthonius Julius Hendrikus
Kotzwara, Franz. *See* Kočvara, Franz
Koukouzeles, Joannos. *See* Papadopoulos, Joannes
Kova(l), Marian [or Maryan] (Victorovitch). *See* Kovalyov, Marian [or Maryan] Viktrovich
Kovalev, Marian [or Maryan] (Victorovitch). *See* Kovalyov, Marian [or Maryan] Viktrovich
Kozi, Pepi. *See* Kozeschnik, Josef
Kozina, Zh. *See* Zeyfas, Natal'ya
Kracher, Sepp. *See* Halletz, Erwin
Kraft, William. *See* Kashereffsky, William
Krali, Milo. *See* Werner, Emil
Kramer, Alois. *See* Gleich, Josef Alois
Kramer, Zoe. *See* Parenteau, Zoe
Krandel, Sol. *See* Kaplan, Sol
Krankmeister, Wolfgang von. *See* Gold, Glenn Herbert
Krantz, Ph(ilip). *See* Rombro, Jakob [or Jacob] Borukhovich
Krantzovius, Irenaeus. *See* Stillingfleet, Benjamin
Krasinsky, Ernest Louis. *See* Müller, Ernest (Louis [or Ludwig])
Kraskorr, Ivan. *See* Kern, Carl Wilhelm
Krásnohorská, Eliska. *See* Pechová, Jindriska
Krasnow, Hecky. *See* Krasnow, Herman(n)
Krassin, Peter. *See* Sonneborn, Günter
Kraus, Fritz. *See* Bauer, Alfons
Krausz, Michael. *See* Krausznai-Kraus, Mihály

Krebs, Karl August. *See* Mied(c)ke, Karl August
Krehbiel, Pop. *See* Krehbiel, Henry (Edward)
Kreisler, Johannes, (Jr.). *See* Brahms, Johannes
Kreisler, Johannes (Kapellmeister). *See* Hoffmann, Ernst Theodore Wilhelm
Krenkel, Gustav. *See* Rawlings, Alfred William
Krentzlin, Rich. *See* Krentzlin, H. Richard
Kresmer-Wertheim. *See* Wertheim, Eduard
Kreutzer, Karl. *See* Crosse, (William) Mentor
Krintz, Elsie. *See* Selden, Camille
Kristan, Anton. *See* Diez, Stephan
Krommer, Franz. *See* Kramar, František (Vinzez)
Kron, William. *See* Hart, Lorenz (Milton)
Kronach, Emanuel. *See* Klitzsch, Karl Emanuel
Kronberger, Heini. *See* Andries, Franz Leo
Krones, The. *See* Krone, Beatrice Perham
Krones, The. *See* Krone, Max (Thomas)
Kronk, Josef. *See* Bevan, Clifford James
Kronke, Oscar. *See* Kronke, Emil
Kross, Thomas. *See* Hartmann, Thomas (Alexandrovich) de
Krotsch, Niklas. *See* Palmer, Cedric King
Krueger, Carl. *See* Forsyth, Wesley Octavius
Krug, Dr. S. *See* Seyfried, Ignaz (Xaver) von
Krüger, Wilhelm. *See* Grosz, Wilhelm [or Will]
Krumbhaar, Harriet. *See* Ware, Harriet
Kryukov, A. *See* Galucki, Michael
Ksentitsky, Boris. *See* Mayzel', Boris Sergeyevich
Kshenek, E(rnst). *See* Krenek, Ernst
Kuckuck (der Junger), Zebedäus. *See* Schilling, (Friedrich) Gustav (1766-1839)
Kuelm, Ludwig von. *See* Parker, Alfred Thomas
Kuerz, Jakob. *See* Bloch, Ernst
Kuhlman, Clara. *See* Haxthausen, Aurore M. G. Ch. von
Kuhn, Gustav. *See* Cunio, Angelo
Kuhn, Karl. *See* Dovenmühle, Rudi von der
Kuhnau, Johann. *See* Kuhn, Johann
Kühne, (Reinhold). *See* Lenz, Johann Reinhold von
Kühner. *See* Peter, Nicol. Friedr.
Kukoff, Bernie. *See* Kukoff, Benjamin
Kukuck, Felicitus. *See* Kestner, Felicitas
Kukuk, Zebedäus. *See* Schilling, (Friedrich) Gustav (1766-1839)
Kulaak, Tom. *See* Presser, William (Henry)
Kulm, Otto Erwin. *See* Guttmann, Artur
Kumber, Q. *See* Frye, Leslie Legge Sarony
Kumler, Carol. *See* Lorenz, Ellen Jane
Kundalini, Kaptain. *See* Lennon, John (Winston)
Kuno. *See* Kuhnert, Christian
Kunz, Fred Charly. *See* Kunz, Alfred
Kupferberg, Tuli. *See* Kupferberg, Naphtali
Kurious. *See* Alvarez, Jorge Antonio
Kurt gives gladly. *See* Deutscher, Karlheinz
Kurupt. *See* Brown, Ricardo
Küster, Lehmann. *See* Küster, Hermann
Kuster, Richard. *See* Davis, Joseph [or Joe] (M.)
Kutev, Filip. *See* Tenev, Filip Kutev
Kutsch, Erhard. *See* Kutschenreuter, Erhard
Kvandal, (David) Johan. *See* Johansen, (David) Johan
Kvetoň. *See* Fišer, Jan
Kwamé. *See* Holland, Kwamé
Kynans, Brady. *See* Báthory-Kitz, Dennis
Kyser, Kay. *See* Kern, James King
Kytasty, Hryhory [or Grygory]. *See* Haidenko, Igor
Kythe, William. *See* Kethe, William

– L –

L. *See* Littledale, Richard Frederick
LA's Fair-Haired Finn. *See* Salonen, Esa-Pekka
L. B. *See* Browne, Lindsay
L. B. B. *See* Blenkinsopp, Edwin Clennell Leaton
L. E. *See* Engel, Louis
L. E. D. *See* Desjardins, Louis-Edouard
L. E. L. *See* Landon, Letitia Elizabeth (née Maclean)
L. G. *See* Granom, L(ewis) C(hristian) A(ustin)
L. H., (Miss). *See* Hime, (Miss) L.
L. K. *See* Knittelmair, Lambert
L. L. A. *See* Crosby, Fanny [i.e., Frances] J(ane)
L. L. Cool J. *See* Smith, James Todd
L. N. R. *See* Ranyard, Ellen (Henrietta) (née White)
L. R. *See* Rellstab, (Heinrich Friedrich) Ludwig
L. S. *See* Senfl, Ludwig
La Lupe. *See* Raymond, Lupe Victoria Yoli
La main gauche. *See* Brian, William
La Navarrus. *See* Azpilcueta, Martin (de)
La Yi Yi Yi. *See* Raymond, Lupe Victoria Yoli
L'Abbe, Joseph. *See* Saint-Sévin, Joseph Barnabé
L'Abbé, le fils. *See* Saint-Sévin, Joseph Barnabé
LaBarbara, Joan. *See* Subotnick, Joan (née Lotz)
LaBeef, Sleepy. *See* LaBeff, Thomas Paulsley
LaBelle, Patti. *See* Holte, Patricia Louise
Labeský. *See* Guldener
La Bretonne, Raitif de. *See* Duval, Paul Alexandre Martin
Lacey, Herbert J. *See* Hall, Joseph Lincoln
Lacey, R. J. *See* Hall, Joseph Lincoln
Lachner, Robert. *See* Kann, Hans
Lacome, J. *See* Gyldmark, Sven Rudolf S.
Lacoste, Leona. *See* Burns, Felix (the Elder)
Lacosti, Eugene. *See* Bulch, Thomas Edward
LaCroix. *See* Crosse, (William) Mentor
Lacy, Caleb. *See* Fisher, William Arms
Lacy, John. *See* Darley, George
Lacy, Steve. *See* Lackritz, Steven (Norman)
Lad from Merthyr, The. *See* Parry, Joseph (1841-1903)
Lada, Kazimierz. *See* Ladowski, Kazimierz
Ladel, Onorio. *See* Leo, Leonardo (Oronzo Salvatore de)

LaDuke, Andrea. *See* Razafinkeriefo, Andreamenentania Paul
Lady, A. *See* Elliott, Charlotte
Lady, A. *See* Foster, Stephen Collins
Lady. *See* Harris, Eleanora
Lady, A. *See* Home, Ann(e)
Lady, A. *See* Howe, Julia Ward
Lady C. S. *See* Horn, Charles Edward
Lady Day. *See* Harris, Eleanor
Lady, of Charleston, S(outh) C(arolina). *See* Murden, Eliza Crawley
Lady Outlaw. *See* Byrem, Jill Lynne
Lady Outlaw. *See* Johnson, Miriam
Lady Soul. *See* Franklin, Aretha
Lady T. *See* Brocker(t), Mary Christine
LaFiere, R. M. *See* Stults, R(obert) M(orrison)
Lafont, Jacques. *See* Ord Hume, J(ames)
La Fontaine of the Vaudeville, The. *See* Panard, Charles-François
LaForrest, Harry. *See* Alford, Harry L(aForrest)
La Funque, Buckshot. *See* Adderley, Julien Edwin
La Garsa. *See* Garsi, Santino (da Parma)
Lago, (Miss). *See* Netzel, Laura Constance (née Pistolekors)
La Grande, Gene. *See* Merrick, Mahlon (La Grande)
La Greca, Antonia. *See* La Greca, Antonio
Laguana, Eddie. *See* Cole, Nathaniel Adams
Laguestra. *See* Langestraat, Willy
Laguna, Pancho. *See* Lomuto, Francisco (Juan)
Lahor, J(ean). *See* Cazalis, Henri
La Hyde, Louise-Geneviève de. *See* Rousseau, Louise-Geneviève
Laiana, Makua. *See* Lyons, Lorenzo
Laicus, Johann(es). *See* Wolf, Johann(es) Wilhelm
Laid Back Texan, The. *See* Williams, Don
Laine, Denny. *See* Hines, Brian (Arthur)
Laine, Frankie. *See* LoVecchio, Francesco [or Francis] Paolo [or Paul]
Laine, Peter. *See* Peeters, (C(ornelius)) M(arcel)
Lainz, Albert zur. *See* Stotz, Albert
Laird of the Halls, The. *See* Lauder, (Sir) Harry (Maclennan)
Laiser, Martin. *See* Reipsch, Horst
Lake, Mike. *See* Lake, M(ayhew) L(ester)
Lake, Sol. *See* Lachoff, Sol(omon)
Lake, Walter. *See* Lakond, Wladimir
Lalain, Luc. *See* Daneau, Suzanne
L'Albert. *See* Daniels, Charles N(eil)
Lalli, (Benedetto) Domenico. *See* Biancardi, (Nicolò) Sebastiano
Lama, Serge. *See* Chauvier, Serge
LaMadelaine, Stéphen de. *See* Madelaine, Etienne Jean Baptiste Nicolas
Lamange, B. de. *See* Soubies, (Émile Jean) Albert
Lamar, Cyrille. *See* Daniels, Charles N(eil)
La Mara. *See* Lipsius, (Ida) Marie
La Mara. *See* Schmelling, Gertrud(e Elizabeth)
Lamara, François. *See* Rawlings, Charles Arthur
Lamare, (Jacques-)Michel Hurel de. *See* Auber, Daniel François Espirit
Lamare, Nappy. *See* Lamare, Hilton (Napoleon)
Lamare, Pierre. *See* Zador, Michael
LaMarr, Frank. *See* LaMotta, Frank Joseph
Lamarr, Ricardo. *See* Green, Phil(ip)
Lamartelière. *See* Schwingenhammer
Lamb, Harry. *See* Spaulding, G(eorge) L(awson)
Lamb, Henry. *See* Spaulding, G(eorge) L(awson)
Lambert, E. Frank. *See* Psalmon, Frederick
Lambert, Fred. *See* Grinsted, William Stanley
Lambert, Jack. *See* Farmer, Marjorie
Lambert, Jerry. *See* LaTorraca, Gerard (A.)
Lambert, Louis. *See* Gilmore, Patrick Sarsfield
Lämblein, Agnelli. *See* Lemle, Sebastian
Lambrecht, Eugene. *See* Henrich, C. W.
Lambrecht, P(aul). *See* Mantovani, A(nnuzio) P(aolo)
La Meda, A. *See* Page, N(athaniel) Clifford
La Meri. *See* Hughes, Russell Meriwether
Lamkin, Marjorie. *See* Robison, Carson J(ay)
Lamont, A. B. *See* Bergh, Arthur
Lamont, A. R. *See* Cain, Noble
Lamont, Arthur (R.). *See* Cain, Noble
Lamont, Henriot. *See* Fisher, Ethel
Lamont, Leopold. *See* Smith, Lee Orean
Lamont, Louis. *See* Fisher, Ethel
Lamont, Victor. *See* Maiorana, Victor (E.)
Lamont, Victor. *See* St. Clair, Floyd J.
Lamothe, Ferdinand Joseph. *See* La Menthe, Ferdinand Joseph
LaMotta, Bill. *See* LaMotta, Wilbur L.
Lancaster, Albert. *See* Lloyd, A(lbert) L(ancaster)
Lancelot, Sir. *See* Pinard, Lancelot (Victor)
Lancen, Jean Serge. *See* Landowski, F. L.
Lanchan, Hip. *See* Richard, Willie
Land, Dick C. *See* Clark, C(yrus) Van Ness
Land, Dick C. *See* Hickey, Martin
Land, Jon. *See* Febland, Nicholas
Landahl, Sven. *See* Hansson, Stig (Axel)
Landauer, Hannes. *See* Blinn, Hans
Landi, Marco. *See* Anelli, Angelo
Landis, Jerry. *See* Simon, Paul Frederick
Landmann, B. *See* Presser, Theodore
Landon, Buddy. *See* Hoffman, James Senate
Landon, Stewart. *See* Wilson, Roger Cole
Landor, Fred. *See* Schneider, Hans
Landriani. *See* Herold, (Louis Joseph) Ferdinand
Landy, Bob. *See* Zimmerman, Robert Allen
Landy, Manuel. *See* Haensch, Gerhard Delle
Lane, Alan. *See* Dukelsky, Vladimir
Lane, Burton. *See* Kushner, Morris Hyman

Lane, C(harles) F(rancis). *See* Wilson, Ira B(ishop)
Lane, Cristy. *See* Johnston, Eleanor [or Ellie]
Lane, David. *See* Newell, Norman
Lane, Dorothy. *See* Hauptmann, Elisabeth
Lane, Emily. *See* Wilson, Ira B(ishop)
Lane, Jace & (His Uke). *See* Marvin, John(ny) (Senator)
Lane, Joe. *See* Levin, Joseph A.
Lane, John. *See* Levin, Joseph A.
Lane, Louis. *See* Slaughter, M(arion) T(ry)
Lane, Lupino. *See* Lupino, Henry George
Lane, Red. *See* DeLaughter, Hollis R(udolph)
Lane, Vernon. *See* King, Stanford
Lane, Walter. *See* Cohn, Gregory Phil
Lane, Walter. *See* Nordman, Chester
La Neuville, Martin Joseph. *See* Adrien, Martin Joseph
Laney, Sid. *See* Cook, J. Lawrence
Lang, Andy Lee. *See* Lang, Andreas
Lang, Carl. *See* Edwards, C(harles) J(oseph)
Lang, Ed(die). *See* Massaro, Salvatore
Lang, Hansi. *See* Lang, Johann
Lang, Mark. *See* Del Riego, Teresa (Clotilde)
Lang, Scott. *See* Hoffman, James Senate
Langa Langa. *See* Hodge, Harry Baldwin Hermon
Langdon, Michael. *See* Birtles, Frank
Lange. *See* Eberst, Jacob
Lange, Adolphe. *See* Cremieux, Hector Jonathan
Lange, Adolphe. *See* Halévy, Ludovic
Lange, Charles. *See* Balmer, Charles
Lange, (Georg) Ernst. *See* Lüderwald, George Ernst
Lange, H. *See* Ailbout, Hans
Lang, Lee. *See* Lewis, Bridges George McGibbon
Lange, Mutt. *See* Lange, Robert John
Lange, Paul. *See* Prendiville, Henri Jean
Langelle, Rae. *See* Rolfe, Walter (L.)
Langen, Fred. *See* Ihlau, Fritz
Langenais, F. de. *See* Blaze (de Bury), (Ange) Henri
Langer, R. *See* Erlanger, Ludwig (von)
Langey, N. J. *See* Bliss, P(hilip) Paul
Langford, Alan. *See* Owen, Alan (Edgar)
Langford, Gordon. *See* Coleman, Gordon
Langham, Beryl. *See* Atkinson, Dorothy
Langlow, Richard. *See* Wagness, Bernard
Langly, Paul. *See* Cohen, Frieda P. C.
Lankton, Martha (J.). *See* Crosby, Fanny [i.e., Frances] J(ane)
Lankveld, Georg van. *See* Langeveld(t), Joris [or Georg] van
Lanner, Joseph. *See* Kreisler, Fritz [i.e., Friedrich](-Max)
Lanoé, Pierre (de). *See* Leroyer, Pierre
Lansing, G. G. *See* Ackley, B(entley) D(eForrest)
Lantino, Liviano. *See* Villano [or Villani], Antonio
Lantos. *See* Tinódi, Sebestyén [or Sebastino]
Lanum, Howard. *See* Haenschen, Walter (G(ustave))
Laplante, Charles. *See* Douglas, Charles (Laplante)
Lara, Adelina de. *See* Preston, A.
Lara, Isidore de. *See* Cohen, Isidore (de Lara)
Lara, Maria Teresa. *See* Lara, Augustín
Lardner, Dionysius. *See* Boursiquot, Dionysius Lardner
Laren, Derek. *See* Epin de Groot, Else-Antonia van
Larent, Barbara C. *See* Heseltine, Philip (Arnold)
Larento, Jean. *See* Hansson, Stig (Axel)
Large, Poppa. *See* Thornton, Keith
Largo, Henry. *See* Hirschbach, Hermann
Larisseo, Fenicio. *See* Pamphili, Benedetto
Lark, Kenneth. *See* Whitlock, Percy (William)
Lark of the Border, The. *See* Mendoza, Lydia
Larkin, R. E. *See* Bliss, P(hilip) Paul
Laroc, P. de. *See* Elizabeth, Queen of Romania
LaRoc(c)a, Pete(r). *See* Sims, Peter
LaRocca, Nick. *See* LaRocca, Dominick James
LaRoche, Emilius. *See* McIntosh, Rigdon (McCoy)
Laroche, Herman. *See* Larosch, German Avgustovich
La Roque, (Sieur de). *See* Pellegrin, Simon Joseph
Laroso, Gustavo. *See* Lazarus, Gustav
Larramie, Ace. *See* Wilder, Alec [i.e., Alexander] (Lafayette Chew)
Larramie, Alec. *See* Wilder, Alec [i.e., Alexander] (Lafayette Chew)
Larrin, Jay. *See* Dodd, J. D.
Larson, Claude. *See* Netzle, Klaus
Larson, Ewald. *See* Netzle, Klaus
Larsson I Hult. *See* Hansson, Stig (Axel)
Laru, Tony. *See* Gonzalez, Antonio
Larue, D. C. *See* L'Heureux, David Charles
Larue, David. *See* L'Heureux, David Charles
LaRue, Edgar. *See* Sawyer, Henry S.
LaSalle, Denise. *See* Craig, Denise
Lasalle, José. *See* Parent, Lionel
Lasekk, Charles. *See* Kaskel, (Baron) Karl (von)
La Serre. *See* Pellegrin, Simon Joseph
Lasha, Prince. *See* Lasha, William B.
Laski, Henry. *See* Bulch, Thomas Edward
Lasnel(l), Egidio. *See* Naselli, Diego
Lassang, Iwan. *See* Lang, Isaac
Lassus, Orlando di. *See* Lassus, Rolande de
Last Gleeman, The. *See* Moran, Michael
Last, James. *See* Last, Hans
Last of the Great Songwriters, The. *See* Livingston, (Jay) Harold
Last of the Irish Bards, The. *See* Carolan, Turlough
Last of the Romans, The. *See* Boethius, Anicius Man(l)ius Severinus
Last of the Silver Screen Cowboys. *See* Slye, Leonard (Franklin)
Last of the Troubadours, The. *See* Baline, Israel
Last Puritan, The. *See* Gold, Glenn Herbert
Last Ragtime Songwriter, The. *See* Tobias, Harry
Last Remaining Great English Eccentric of Rock, The. *See* Cope, Julian

Last Rock 'n' Roll Star. *See* Picariello, Frederick [or Frederico] A(nthony)
Laszky, Béla. *See* Laszky, Julius Albert
Laszlo, Alexander. *See* Totis, San(dor)
Laszlo, Sandor. *See* Totis, San(dor)
Latanzio, P. *See* Anelli, Angelo
Late, J. Brown, The. *See* Thayer, Alexander Wheelock
Lateef, Yusef (Abdul). *See* Evans, William [or Bill]
Lateinturier, Jan. *See* Tinctoris, Johannes
Latham, Doc. *See* Latham, Lance Brenton
Latifah, (Queen). *See* Owens, Dana (Elaine)
Latimer, Gus. *See* Martin, Ray(mond)
Latin Lully. *See* Lalande, Michel-Richard de
Latin Madonna. *See* Mebarak (R(ipoll)) Shakira, Isabel
Latin Sun King, The. *See* Palmieri, Eduardo [or Edward, or Eddie]
Latour, Georges. *See* Clutsam, George Howard
LaTour, Tomline. *See* Gilbert, William Schwenk
Lattecort, Norbert. *See* Mielichhofer, Ludwig
Latterday Bob Dylan, A. *See* Prine, John
Latterday G. W. Hunt, A. *See* Tabrar, Joseph
Lattimer, Hugh. *See* Slaughter, M(arion) T(ry)
Lattmann, Heinz. *See* Börschel, Erich
Lattner, K. Ph. *See* Berger, Karl Philipp
Latymer, Lord. *See* Money(-Coutts), Francis Burdett (Thomas Nevill)
Lauder, Dale. *See* Kinyon, John L(eroy)
Lauerwinkle, Baron. *See* Lockhart, John Gibson
Laun, Friedrich. *See* Schulze, Friedrich August
Launis, Armas (Emanuel). *See* Lindberg, Armas (Emanuel)
Laurel, Bob(by). *See* Lessnau, Robert G(erald)
Laurence, Claude. *See* Hodeir, André
Laurence, Paul. *See* Jones, Paul Laurence
Laurence, Victor. *See* Buchtel, Forrest (Lawrence)
Laurencin, M. *See* Chapelle, Paul Aimé
Laurencin, Paul Aimé. *See* Chapelle, Paul Aimé
Laurens, A. M. *See* Barnhouse, Charles Lloyd
Laurent, Michael. *See* Rimmer, William
Laurent, Paul. *See* Laurendeau, Louis-Philippe
Laurenti(is), Filbertus [or Filberto] (de). *See* Laurenzi, Filberto
Laurenti, Laurentius. *See* Lorenzen, Lorenz
Laurentius von Schnüffis. *See* Martin, Johannes
Laurenz, Pedro. *See* Acosta, Pedro Blanco
Lauterbach, Karl. *See* Schneider, Hans
Lauver, (David). *See* St. Clair, Floyd J.
Lavain, George. *See* Pechstein, George P.
LaValle, Paul. *See* Pierce, Paula Wahl
Lavalle, Paul. *See* Usifer, Joseph
Lavarro, Enrico. *See* Suskind, Milton
LaVere, Charles [or Charlie]. *See* Johnson, Charles LaVere
L'avi Pep. *See* Ventura, Josep [or José] (María de la Purificación)
Lavigne, Paul. *See* Loquin, Antole
Lavita, Selma. *See* Kountz, Richard
Lavoe, Héctor. *See* Perez, Héctor (Juan)
Lavry, Marc. *See* Levins, Marc(k)
Lawrence, Carl. *See* King, Karl L(awrence)
Lawrence, Claude. *See* Hodeir, André
Lawrence, Eddie. *See* Eisler, Lawrence
Lawrence, Elliot(t). *See* Broza, Elliot Lawrence
Lawrence, Fred. *See* Creatore, Luigi (Federico)
Lawrence, Fred. *See* O'Keefe, John (Conrad)
Lawrence, Fred. *See* O'Keefe, Lester
Lawrence, Jack. *See* Schwartz, Jacob Lawrence
Lawrence, Jerome. *See* Schwartz, Jerome Lawrence
Lawrence, Kansas. *See* Jones, (William) Carmell
Lawrence, Neil. *See* Lawrence, Cornelius C.
Lawrence, Paul. *See* Daly, Lawrence
Lawrence, Paul. *See* Daly, Paul
Lawrence, Robert. *See* Cohen, Robert
Lawrence, Steve. *See* Barnes, H(oward) E(llington)
Lawrence, Steve. *See* Fields, Harold (Cornelius)
Lawrence, Steve. *See* Roncoroni, Joseph (Dominic)
Lawrence, Victor. *See* Buchtel, Forrest (Lawrence)
Lawshe, Wilfred. *See* Holcombe, Wilfred (Lawshe)
Lawson, John R. *See* Lausen, John R.
Lawson, Paul. *See* Spaulding, G(eorge) L(awson)
Lawson, Tedd. *See* Lehrman, Theodore Howard
Lawson, Yank. *See* Lausen, John R.
Lawton, Jimmy. *See* Degraw, Jimmy Dwaine
Layman, Jan. *See* Chacksfield, Francis [or Frank] (Charles)
Layne, Ruth. *See* Gordon, David M.
Laytons, Nick. *See* Hansson, Stig (Axel)
Lazang, Iwan. *See* Lang, Isaac
Lazare, Henri. *See* Sartorio, Arnoldo
Lazy, The. *See* Rossini, Gioachino Antonio
Lazy Larry. *See* McClintock, Harry (K(irby))
Lazy Larry. *See* Robison, Carson J(ay)
Lazy Larry. *See* Slaughter, M(arion) T(ry)
Lazy Slim Jim. *See* Harris, Edward P.
Lazzare, Paul de. *See* Solman, Alfred
Lazzari, Sylvio [or Silvo]. *See* Lazzari, Josef Fortunat Silvester
Lé, Bert. *See* Lenz, Albert
Le Cousin-Jacques. *See* Beffroy de Reigny, Louis Abel
Leadbelly. *See* Ledbetter, Huddie (William)
Leadbetter, Teresa. *See* Del Riego, Teresa (Clotilde)
Leadbitter, Teresa. *See* Del Riego, Teresa (Clotilde)
Leader, Dave K. *See* Kapp, David [or Dave]
Leader, Harry. *See* Lebys, Henry
Leader, James. *See* Tanner, James T(olman)
Leader, Mickey. *See* Kapp, David [or Dave]
Leader of Cacophonists, The. *See* Schoenberg, Arnold
Leader of Postmodernism. *See* Rochberg, (Aaron) George

Leading Bel Canto Composer. *See* Rossini, Gioachino Antonio
Leaf, Ann. *See* Lynn, Audrey
Leander, Mike. *See* Farr, Michael (George)
Lear, W. Hogarth. *See* Howarth, Elgar
Leath, Vaughn de. *See* Vonderlieth, Leonore
Leavitt, Bob. *See* Robison, Carson J(ay)
Le Barron, Betty. *See* Hudnall, Floris M.
Le Bert, Sam. *See* Slater, (John) Joseph [or Joe]
Lebaum, Stanley. *See* Applebaum, Stan(ley) (Seymour)
Lebeau, Alice. *See* Henrikson, Alice
Lebeau, Virginie. *See* Satie, (Alfred) Erik (Leslie)
Lebedjeff, Peter. *See* Hansson, Stig (Axel)
Lebert, Sigmund. *See* Levi, Sigmund
Lebieg, Earl. *See* Burnett, Earl
Lebieg, Earl. *See* Geibel, Adam
Lebrecht, Peter. *See* Tieck, (Johann) Ludwig
Le Breton, John. *See* Ford, Murray
Le Breton, Thomas. *See* Ford, Murray
LeBris, Marion (E.). *See* Ringleben, Justin, Jr.
Lebrun, Marie. *See* Malenfant, Anna
Lecherito, El. *See* Guido, Juan Baustista
Lechner, Friedrich. *See* Mosenthal, Salomon Hermann (von)
Lechner, Lothar. *See* Lutz, Wilhelm
Leclair, Jean. *See* Barnes, H(oward) E(llington)
Leclair, Jean. *See* Fields, Harold (Cornelius)
Leclair, Jean. *See* Roncoroni, Joseph (Dominic)
Le Clercq, Jean. *See* Mullen, Frederic
Leclère, Tristan. *See* Leclère, (Arthur Justin) Léon
Le Cocq, Jehan. *See* Gallus, Jacques (de)
Lecocq, Maistre Jhan. *See* Gallus, Jacques (de)
Lecocq, Maurice. *See* Gobbaerts, Jean Louis
Ledeen, Raymond. *See* Leveen, Raymond
Ledesma, Jose. *See* Arrollado, J. L.
Ledet, Rosie. *See* Bellard, Mary Rosezla
Ledie, Emil. *See* Seidl, Johann Gabriel
Ledies, Jean. *See* Seidel, (George Lucas) Emil
Leduc, A. C. *See* Kiesewetter, Raphael-Georg
Leduc, A. C. *See* Lichtenthal, Peter
Leduc, Alphonse. *See* Balmer, Charles
LeDuc, F. *See* Rimmer, William
Lee, Alex. *See* Fishman, Jack (1918 (or 19)-)
Lee, Alex. *See* Paramor, Norman [or Norrie] (William)
Lee, Annabelle. *See* Vonderlieth, Leonore
Lee, Barry. *See* Carter, Barry Eugene
Lee, Bert. *See* Lee, Albert George
Lee, Bessie. *See* Smith, Trixie
Lee, Bunny. *See* Lee, Edward O'Sullivan
Lee, Cecile. *See* Lee, Mary Emily Frances
Lee, Cowboy. *See* Lipscomb(e), Richard [or Dickey]
Lee, Craig. *See* Sigman, Carl
Lee, Dickey. *See* Lipscomb(e), Richard [or Dickey]
Lee, Dorothy. *See* Zamecnik, J(ohn) S(tepan)
Lee, Earl. *See* McDaniel, Luke
Lee, Fletcher. *See* Little, Dudley Richard
Lee, Gaby. *See* Wooldridge, Anna Marie
Lee, George. *See* Mullendore, Joseph [or Joe]
Lee, George. *See* Taylor, Herb
Lee, George John Vandeleur. *See* Shaw, George Bernard
Lee, Herbert. *See* Lee, Albert George
Lee, Herman. *See* Blount, Herman
Lee, Holme. *See* Parr, Harriet
Lee, Ivory. *See* Semien, (Ivory) Lee
Lee, Jack. *See* Lee, Jonathan Butler
Lee, Jimmy. *See* Gillette, Leland James
Lee, Johnny. *See* Ham, John Lee
Lee, Johnny. *See* Hooker, John Lee
Lee, King Ivory. *See* Semien, (Ivory) Lee
Lee, L. *See* Carter, Bennett L(ester)
Lee, Larry. *See* Favourite, Larry Lee
Lee, Lester. *See* Kaplan, Sol
Lee, Lora. *See* Doro, Grace
Lee, Loye. *See* Dinino, Louis (Lee)
Lee, Lucille. *See* Overstake, (Virginia) Lucille
Lee, Mamie. *See* Vonderlieth, Leonore
Lee, Mandy. *See* Vonderlieth, Leonore
Lee, Marion A. *See* Stults, R(obert) M(orrison)
Lee, Maurice. *See* Smith, Lee Orean
Lee, Michael. *See* Allman, Michael L(ee)
Lee, Norah. *See* Barstow, Norah Lee Haymond Bradley
Lee, Orrie. *See* Smith, Lee Orean
Lee, Pat. *See* Keller, Edward McDonald
Lee, Patty. *See* Carey, Alice
Lee, Peggy. *See* Egstrom, (Norma) Dolores
Lee, Robin. *See* Irwin, Robin Lee
Lee, Ronny. *See* Leventhal, Ronald
Lee, Roy Asher. *See* Pothumus, Ann
Lee, Sonny. *See* Blount, Herman
Lee, Sydney. *See* Altschuler, Sydell
Lee, Vandeleur. *See* Shaw, George Bernard
Lee, Vernon. *See* Goldsen, Michael H.
Lee, Vernon. *See* Paget, Violet
Lee, Virginia. *See* Vonderlieth, Leonore
Lee, Warren. *See* Jackson, Warren George Harding Lee
Lee, Wilma. *See* Cooper Wilma Lee (née Leary)
Leeds, Harold. *See* Levey, Harold
Leeds, Jacky [or Jackie]. *See* Jarczyk, Maximilian (Michael) Andreas
Leeds Layman, A. *See* Rawson, George
Lees, Benjamin. *See* Lysniansky, Benjamin
Lees, Gene. *See* Lees, Frederick Eugene John
Leeuw, Ton. *See* Leeuw, Antonius Wilhelms Andrianus
LeFevre, Achille. *See* Neidlinger, W(illiam) H(arold)
Lefevre, Henri. *See* Suskind, Milton
LeFonque, Buckshot. *See* Adderley, Julian Edwin
Leforestier, H. B. *See* Brewster, Henry B(ennet)
Left Bank Mother Confessor, The. *See* Powell, Altivia Edwards
Lefty. *See* Lofgren, Nils

LeGarde Twins, The. *See* LeGarde, Edward [or Ted]
LeGarde Twins, The. *See* LeGarde, Thomas
Legendary Hank C. Burnette. *See* Hogberg, Sven Ake
Legendary King of Blues, The. *See* Hooker, John Lee
Legendary Sire of the Blues. *See* Handy, W(illiam) C(hristopher)
Legendary Tunesmith. *See* Bacharach, Burt (F.)
Legge, Bud. *See* Shank, Clifford (Everett, Jr.)
Leginska, Ethel. *See* Liggins, Ethel
Leglaire, Sonny. *See* Leglaire, Sophia
Legrady, Thomas Theodore. *See* Tassy, Tamas
LeGrand, Herbert. *See* Sawyer, Henry S.
Le Grande, Gene. *See* Merrick, Mahlon (Le Grande)
Legrant, Guillaume. *See* Lemacherier, Guillaume
Legray, Robert. *See* Nieman, Alfred
Legru, Louise. *See* L'Henoret, Louise
LeHache, W. *See* Presser, Theodore
Le Hestre, Pierre. *See* L'Epine, Ernest Louis Victor Jules
Lehmann, Alfons. *See* Halletz, Erwin
Lehmann, Liza. *See* Lehmann, Elizabeth Nina Mary Frederika
Leib, Bell. *See* Leib, Joseph
Leib, Bell. *See* Samberg, Benjamin
Leicester, W. G. *See* Gardiner, William
Leichtentritt, Hugo. *See* Leichtentritt, Hirsch
Leigh, Arthur. *See* LeClerq, Arthur
Leigh, Carolyn. *See* Rosenthal, Carolyn (Paula)
Leigh, H. E. *See* Willan, James Healey
Leigh, Harrington. *See* Rawlings, Charles Arthur
Leigh, Mitch. *See* Mitchnick, Irwin
Leigh, Ralph. *See* Anderton, Stephen P(hilbin)
Leighton, Bernie. *See* Lazeroff, Bernard
Leighton, Bert. *See* Leighton, James Albert
Leighton, Chester. *See* Robertson, Dick
Leighton, Grace. *See* Marshal(l)-Loepke, Grace
Leighton, Herb. *See* Leventhal, Herbert
Leighton, M. *See* McCosh, Dudley H(untington)
Leinsdorf, Erich. *See* Landauer, Erich
Leip, Hans. *See* Leip, Karl Hermann Gottfried
Leipenburg, Eduard. *See* Kulke, Eduard
Leiper, Joseph. *See* Riepel, Joseph [or Josef]
Leith, Leonore (von der). *See* Vonderlieth, Leonore
Leivick, H(alper(n)). *See* Halper, Leivick
Leks, Blasius. *See* Kupelwieser, Josef
Lela. *See* Perry, Phil(ip) B(utler)
Leland, Robert. *See* Isaac, Merle (John)
Lelio. *See* Andreini, Giovanni Battista
Lelio. *See* Riccoboni, Luigi [or Louis] (Andrea) (c.1676-1753)
Lelio, *fils*. *See* Riccoboni, Francesco (Antonio Valentino) (the younger)
Leloir, Louis. *See* Sallot, Louis
LeLorrain, Jacques. *See* Duval, Paul Alexandre Martin
Lemain, Victor. *See* Boex, Andrew J.
Lemaitre, Francois. *See* Del Riego, Teresa (Clotilde)
Lemara, Francois. *See* Rawlings, Charles Arthur
Lemare, Jules. *See* Daniels, Charles N(eil)
Lemarque, Francis. *See* Korb, Nathan
Lemberg, Paul. *See* Hempel, Rolf
Lemieun, Anton. *See* Mullen, Frederic
Lemieux, Anton. *See* Mullen, Frederic
Lemming, S. F., M. D. *See* Gold, Glenn Herbert
Lemmy. *See* Kilmister, Ian Fraiser
Lemoine, Felix. *See* Rawlings, Alfred William
Lemoine, Frederic. *See* West, George Frederick
Lemott, Ferdinand Joseph. *See* La Menthe, Ferdinand Joseph
Lemoyne, Jean Baptiste. *See* Moyne, Jean Baptiste
Lémune, Gaston. *See* Mullen, Frederic
Lenard, Melvyn. *See* Gertz, Irving
Lenard, Melvyn. *See* Gordon, David M.
Lenard, Melvyn. *See* Kahn, Dave
Lenard, Melvyn. *See* Klatzkin, Leo(n)
Lenard, Melvyn. *See* Lava, William
Lenard, Melvyn. *See* Mullendore, Joseph [or Joe]
Lendell, Michael [or Mike] —*see* Rashkow, Michael (Harris)
Lendvai [or Lendvay], (Peter) Erwin. *See* Löwenfeld, Peter Erwin
Lenecke, Max. *See* Sartorio, Arnoldo
Lengard, Max. *See* Schiemanowsky, Max
Lenk, Harry. *See* Lengsfelder, Hans
Lenk, Helmuth. *See* Trantow, Herbert
Lennard, Jack. *See* Blitz, Leo(nard)
Lennie. *See* Whitcup, Leonard
Lennon, Martin Luther. *See* Perkins, Tony
Lenoir, Jean. *See* Neuberger, Jean (Bernard Daniel)
Lenore, J. B. *See* Lenoir, J. B.
Lenselink, W. A. *See* Leest, Antonius Maria van
Lenz, Adolf. *See* Lorenz, Adolf
Leo, Frank. *See* Peers, Frank
Leon. *See* Sugarman, Harry
Léon. *See* Théaulon (de Lambert), Marie-Emmanuel-Guillaume(-Marguerite)
Leon, Francis. *See* Glassey, Patrick Francis
Leon, Harry. *See* Sugarman, Harry
Leon, Noel. *See* Sugarman, Harry
Leon, Sally. *See* Sugarman, Harry
Léon, Victor. *See* Hirschfeld, Victor
Léonard. *See* Chapelle, Paul Aimé
Leonard, Deke. *See* Leonard, Roger
Leonard, Eddie. *See* To(o)ney, Lemuel Gordon
Leonard, Emil. *See* Grey, Frank H(erbert)
Leonard, Hal. *See* Edstrom, Everett
Leonard, Hal. *See* Edstrom, Harold [or Hal]
Leonard, Hugo. *See* Lewysohn, Hugo
Leonard, Louella. *See* Yale, Elsie D(uncan)
Leonard, Victor. *See* Hirschfeld, Victor
Leonardi, A. *See* Cipollone, Alfonso
Leonardi, L. *See* Cipollone, Alfonso

Leonardo da Vinci of the Drums, The. *See* Balassoni, Luigi Paulino
Leonardo, Leo. *See* DeLeo, Lionardo Oronzo Salvatore
Leone, Andrea de. *See* Lauzières(-Thémines), Achille de
Leonhardt, Hans Günther. *See* Nicolai, Bruno
Leoni. *See* Lyon, Myer
Leoni, Chester. *See* Frangkiser, Carl (Moerz)
Leoploita, Marcin [or Martin(us)]. *See* Lwowczyk, Marcin [or Martin(us)]
Leopold, Friedrich. *See* Cassirer, Fritz
Leopoldi, Hermann. *See* Kohn, Hersch
Le Page, Carolan. *See* Rawlings, Charles Arthur
Lépidor. *See* Mathieu, Michel-Julien
Lépine, Maurice. *See* Mullen, Frederic
Lepinski, Gerhard. *See* Berghorn, Alfred Maria
Leplanc. *See* Lombardo, Carlo
Lerendo Secinantino. *See* Barbosa, Domingos Caldas
Le Riche, Anthoine. *See* Rycke, Anthonius (de)
Leroux, Paul. *See* Loomis, Harvey Worthington
Leroy. *See* Chatman, John Len
LeRoy, Felix. *See* Slater, (John) Joseph [or Joe]
LeRoy, Henri. *See* Hargreaves, Robert
Leroy, Jean Marcel. *See* Perrey, Jean-Jacques
Leroy, Jehan. *See* Regis, Johannes
Leroy, Lecius. *See* Millinder, Lucius (Venable)
LeRoyal, A. *See* Forsythe, Charles Henry
Lerryn. *See* Dehm, Dieter
Lert, Richard Johann. *See* Levy, Richard Johann
LeSaint, Louis. *See* Fillmore, (James) Henry
Lescaut, Pierre. *See* Mullen, Frederic
Leserve, August. *See* DeanThorne, Donald James
Lesh, Phil. *See* Chapman, Philip
Lesiman. *See* Renosto, Paolo
Leslie, Edgar. *See* Wright, Lawrence
Leslie, Ernest. *See* Brown, Obadiah Bruen
Leslie, Fred(erick). *See* Hobson, Frederick Leslie
Leslie, Herbert. *See* Johnson, Charles L(eslie)
Leslie, Kermit. *See* Levinsky, Kermit
Leslie, Paul. *See* Polfus(s), Lester (William)
Leslie, Thomas. *See* Bondy, Fritz
Leslie, Vincent. *See* Stept, Sam(uel) H.
Leslie, Walter. *See* Levinsky, Walter
Lesonné, Bertrand. *See* Mullen, Frederic
Lesser, S. *See* Tobias, Charles
Lesso-Valero, P. *See* Plessow, Erich
Lester, Marc. *See* Störrle, Heinz
Lester, Ida. *See* Keiser, Robert (A(dolph))
Lester, William. *See* Lake, M(ayhew) L(ester)
LeStieg, Theodore. *See* Geisel, Theodore Seuss
L'Estrange, David. *See* Davies, David Ivor
Lethander. *See* Brendel, Georg Christoph
Leumas, Sara. *See* Samuel, Sara
Leum'as, Tebro'c. *See* Corbett, Samuel
Leupinto, Euginaspe. *See* Valentini, Giuseppe
Leuter, Cecil. *See* Roger, Roger
Leuthold. *See* Fuhrmann, Martin Heinrich
Leutner, Emil. *See* Raupach, Ernst Benjamin Salomo
Leux, Leo. *See* Leucks, Gottlieb
Levan, Henry Robert Merrill. *See* Lavan, Henry Robert Merrill
Levary, Tibor. *See* Tiberiu, Farkas
Levee Joe. *See* Weldon, Wil(liam)
Leven, Benny. *See* Levin, Benjamin
Lever, Sydney. *See* Smith, (Mrs.) Crafton E.
Levey, Richard Michael. *See* O'Shaughnessy, Richard Michael
Levey, William Charles. *See* O'Shaughnessy, William Charles
Levi, (Ludovic). *See* Gobbaerts, Jean Louis
Levi, Eric. *See* Levisalles, Eric
Levi, Jul(es). *See* Levi, Zhul (Efram)
Levine, Al. *See* Levine, Abe [i.e., Abraham] (Lewis)
Levinsky, Kermit. *See* Levinsky, Walter
Levinson, Jay. *See* Livingston, (Jay) Harold
Levinson, John M. *See* Bradford, John Milton
Levison, Jay. *See* Livingston, (Jay) Harold
Levite, The. *See* Gregorios the Protopsaltes
Levy, Benjamin. *See* Lumley, Benjamin
Levy, Burton. *See* Kushner, Morris Hyman
Levy, Elias. *See* Levy, Jacques Francois Fromental Elie
Levy, Hank. *See* Levy, Henry J.
Levy, Jacques. *See* Eberst, Jacob
Levy, Marcy. *See* Detroit, Marcella
Levy, Salomon. *See* Loewy, Salomon
Lewandowski, Louis (Eliezer). *See* Lewandowski, Lazarus (Eliezer)
Lewis & Williams. *See* Penn, William H.
Lewis & Williams. *See* Savino, Domenico
Lewis, Bill. *See* Simon, William Louis
Lewis, Bob. *See* Ruse, Robert Louis
Lewis, Buddy. *See* Lewis, (William) Morgan (Jr.)
Lewis, Bunny. *See* Lewis, Bridges George McGibbon
Lewis, Edgar. *See* Jones, Lewis Ellis
Lewis, Frances. *See* Leoni, Franco
Lewis, Furry. *See* Lewis, Walter
Lewis, Huey. *See* Cregg, Hugh Anthony, III
Lewis, Hugh X. *See* Lewis, Hubert Brad
Lewis, Ilda. *See* Dash, Irwin
Lewis, Johnny. *See* Hill, Lester [or Leslie]
Lewis, Kate. *See* Prather, Ida
Lewis, Ken. *See* Hawker, Kenneth
Lewis, Lefty. *See* Lewis, Harold
Lewis, Little Junior. *See* Lewis, Clarence
Lewis, Lux. *See* Lewis, Meade (Anderson)
Lewis, Monk. *See* Lewis, Matthew Gregory
Lewis, Pat. *See* Oberstein, Eli
Lewis, Sabby. *See* Lewis, William Sebastian
Lewis, Sherman. *See* Lewis, Al(an)
Lewis, Sherman. *See* Sherman, Al(bert)

Lewis, Smiley [or Smiling]. *See* Lemons, Overton Amos
Lewis, Ted. *See* Friedman, Theodore (Leopold)
Lewis, William. *See* Finkelstein, Abe
Lewisohn, Arthur. *See* Mazlen, Henry G(ershwin)
Lex, (Günter). *See* Moesser, (Karl-)Peter
Ley Alejandro. *See* Leyva González, Alejandro
Ley, Tabu. *See* Pascal, Tubu
Leybourne, George. *See* Saunders, Joseph
Leyland, Reginald. *See* Heney, R. W.
Lezza, Carlo. *See* Brandmayer, Rudolf [or Dolf]
Lezzi, G. *See* Kunkel, Charles
Lhérie, (Léon). *See* Lévy, Léon (1805-1859)
Lhérie, Victor. *See* Lévy, Victor (1808-1845)
Li-Shan-Pe. *See* Leip, Karl Hermann Gottfried
Lianovosani, Luigi. *See* Salvioli, Giovanni
Libbey, Dee. *See* Libbey, Delores R.
Libér, T. E. *See* Wiggen, Knut
Liberace, Lee. *See* Liberace, (Wladziu Valentino)
Liberace of the Accordion, The. *See* Welk, Lawrence (LeRoy)
Liberace, Walter. *See* Liberace, (Wladziu Valentino)
Libero Sentri. *See* Bertelli, Rino [or Rono]
Libert, Reginaldus. *See* Libert, Gualterius
Liberti, Gualtero. *See* Libert, Gualterius
Lichner, P. *See* Greenwald, M(artin)
Lichner, R. *See* Greenwald, M(artin)
Lichtenfels, Hainrich. *See* Faber, Heinrich
Lichter, Hans. *See* Clough-Leighter, Henry
Licurio, Palemone. *See* Stampiglia, Silvio
Lidl, Anton. *See* Lid(e)l, Andreas
Lieb, Dick. *See* Lieb, Ziskind R.
Lieber, Doodles. *See* Lieberstein, Marcus Edward
Liebhold. *See* Fuhrmann, Martin Heinrich
Liebold, Eduard. *See* Balzar, Eduard
Liemann, Oscar. *See* Mansfield, Orlando Augustine
Ligato, O. B. *See* Stark, John (Stillwell)
Light Music's Greatest Living Legend. *See* Faron, Robert [or Bob] (Joseph)
Lightfoot, Papa (George). *See* Lightfoot, Alexander
Lighthall, W. M. *See* Gabriel, Charles H(utchinson)
Lighthill, Norman. *See* Wilson, Ira B(ishop)
Lightnin' Jr. *See* Dupree, William Thomas
Lightnin' Slim. *See* Hicks, Otis V.
Lightning Composer, The. *See* Parry, Joseph (1841-1903)
Lil' Kim. *See* Jones, Kimberly (Denise)
Lil' Wayne. *See* Carter, D'Wayne
Lilio, Girolamo. *See* Gigli, Girolamo
Liliuokalani, Queen of Hawaii. *See* Kamakaeha, Liliu (Loloku Walania)
Limahl. *See* Hamill, Chris(topher)
Limber, Jack. *See* Creatore, Luigi (Federico)
Lincoln, Abbey. *See* Wooldridge, Anna Marie
Lincoln, Elmer. *See* Harris, Robert P.
Lincoln, Elmer. *See* Lee, Albert George
Lincoln, H. N. *See* Crosby, Fanny [i.e., Frances] J(ane)
Lincoln, Mac. *See* Finkelstein, Abe
Lincoln, Phil(amore). *See* Anson, Robert (C.)
Lind, E. L. *See* Bliss, P(hilip) Paul
Lind, Gustave. *See* Mullen, Frederic
Lindau, Karl [or Carl]. *See* Gemperle, Karl
Lindemayr, Maurus. *See* Lindemayr, Kajetan Benedikt Maximilian
Linden, Dolf van der. *See* Linden, David Gysbert (van der)
Linden, Oliver. *See* Abrahms, Doris Caroline
Lindenblauer, Carl. *See* Hills, George
Lindenthal, Bert. *See* Depenheuer, Walter
Linders, Karl. *See* Geibel, Adam
Lindhorst, Richard. *See* Wagner, Richard
Lindo. *See* Neto, Laurindo José de Araujo Almeida Nobrega
Lindon, Robert. *See* Tunbridge, Joseph A(lbert)
Lindon, Robert. *See* Waller, Jack
Lindquist, Gosta. *See* Gyldmark, Hugo
Lindroder, Wolfgang. *See* Hoffmann(-Harnish), (Friedrich) Wolfgang
Lindsay, Charles. *See* Engelmann, H(ans)
Lindsay, Howard. *See* Nelke, Herman
Lindsay, John [or Johann]. *See* Theimer, Johann
Lindsay, W. Robert. *See* Crosby, Fanny [i.e., Frances] J(ane)
Lindsay-Thiemer. *See* Theimer, Johann
Lindt, Rudi. *See* Dovenmühle, Rudi von der
Lines, Rev. H. N. *See* Lillenas, Haldor
Ling, C(hrist). *See* Ebeling, Elisabeth
Lingard, W(illiam) H(orace). *See* Needham, William Horace Thomas
Lingen, Rolf van. *See* Libbach, Roland
Lingo, Vic(tor). *See* Kalischnig, Walter
Link, Harry. *See* Linkey, Harry
Linkchain, Hip. *See* Richard, Willie
Linko, Ernest (Fredrik). *See* Lindroth, Ernst (Fred(e)rik)
Linn, Lora. *See* Lillenas, Haldor
Linnala, Eino Mauro Aleksanteri. *See* Borgmann, Eino Mauno
Linne, Emil. *See* Rosendorff, Emil
Linwood, Arthur. *See* Hall, Joseph Lincoln
Linwood, Roy. *See* Cobb, George L(inus)
Linyera, Dante. *See* Rimoli, Francisco Bautista
Lion, The. *See* Smith, William [or Willie] (Henry Joseph Berthol Bonaparte)
Lion Comique. *See* Leybourne, George
Lion of Paris. *See* Paderewski, Ignace, Jan
Lion Pianist. *See* Meyer, Leopold von
Lionel. *See* Bonnemère (de Chavigny), Léon Eugène
Liorat, Armand. *See* Dégas (Liorat), Georges
Lios. *See* Erdoedy, Luisa (Countess) (née Drasche-Wartingerg)
Lipatti, Dinu. *See* Lipatti, Constantin

Lipiner, Eduard. *See* Kulke, Eduard
Lipman(n), Berry. *See* Berlipp, Friedel
Liprandi, Nicolo. *See* Anelli, Angelo
Lipton, Pedro. *See* Hoérée, Arthur Charles Ernest
Liptsin, Sem. *See* Liptzin, Samuel
Lirski, W. *See* Lubomirski, Wladyslaw
Lisa, Lisa. *See* Valez, Lisa
Lisander. *See* Heuchelin, Christian
Lisbon, Kenneth. *See* De Vito, Albert (Kenneth)
Lisinski, Vatroslav. *See* Fuchs, Ignacije [or Ignaz]
Lisle, Ernest. *See* Ellis, Seger
L'Isle, Jehan de. *See* Daudet, (Louis Marie) Alphonse
Lissette. *See* Alvarez, Lissette
Listeman, Arthur. *See* Retter, Louis
Liszt, Franz. *See* Kunkel, Charles
Liszt, Franz (Spirit). *See* Brown, Rosemary (née Dickeson)
Liszt of the Violin, The. *See* Paganini, Nic(c)olò
Lisztian. *See* Liszt, Franz
Litchfield, Ben. *See* Finkelstein, Abe
Litchfield, Ben. *See* Slaughter, M(arion) T(ry)
Liteo, Ageo. *See* Galuppi, Antonio
Litner, W. *See* Rintel, Wilhelm
Litti, Oscar. *See* Gottschalk, Louis Moreau
Little Anthony. *See* Gourdine, Anthony
Little Aretha. *See* Stevens, Yvette Marie
Little BB. *See* Odom, Andrew
Little Bastard. *See* Mellencamp, John (J.)
Little Bennie. *See* Huerta, Baldemar G(arza)
Little Benny. *See* Benny, Benjamin Michel
Little, Big Tiny. *See* Little, Dudley Richard
Little Bird. *See* Ayler, Albert
Little Bird. *See* Heath, James [or Jimmy] (Edward)
Little Boy Blue. *See* Ford, Aleck
Little Brother. *See* Adderley, Nat(haniel)
Little Brother. *See* Feather, Leonard (Geoffrey)
Little Brother. *See* Montgomery, Eurreal Wilford
Little, Don. *See* Levy, David
Little Doug. *See* Saldana, Douglas
Little, Eddie. *See* Boyd, Edward [or Eddie] Riley
Little Elsie. *See* Bierbower, Elsie
Little, Eric. *See* Hooper, R. S.
Little Giant of the Blues, The. *See* Blackmore, Amos, (Jr.)
Little Giant of the Piano. *See* Rosenthal, Moriz
Little Giant of Twentieth Century Music, The. *See* Stravinsky, Igor Fedorovich
Little Ginny. *See* Brown, Ginnette Patricia
Little Glinka, The. *See* Glazunov, Alexandr Konstantinovich
Little Hatch. *See* Hatch, Provine, Jr.
Little Henry. *See* Gray, Henry
Little Hudson. *See* Shower, Hudson
Little Hungarian, The. *See* Bakfark, Bálint (Valentin)
Little Igor. *See* Markevitch, Igor
Little Isidore. *See* Forman, David
Little Jack. *See* Little, John (Leonard)
Little Jimmy. *See* Latourelle, James
Little Joe. *See* Hill, Lester [or Leslie]
Little Joe Blue. *See* Valery, Joseph, Jr.
Little Joey. *See* Mansfield, Joseph
Little Johnny. *See* Jones, John (1924-1964)
Little Jr. *See* Johnson, Luther, Jr.
Little Junior. *See* Parker, Herman
Little, Little Jack. *See* Little, John (Leonard)
Little Loving Henry. *See* Byrd, Henry Roeland
Little Luther. *See* Johnson, Lucius Brinson
Little Man. *See* Johnson, James (J.) (c.1905-c.1972)
Little Milton. *See* Campbell, Milton (James)
Little Miss Sugar Pie. *See* Balinton, Umpeylia Marsema
Little Organ Annie. *See* Lynn, Audrey
Little Otis. *See* Rush, Otis
Little Papa Joe. *See* Williams, Joseph Leon
Little Papa Walter. *See* Lightfoot, Alexander
Little Pork Chops. *See* Hooker, John Lee
Little Prince of Soul, The. *See* Jackson, Michael Joseph
Little Professor, The. *See* Scott, James (Sylvester)
Little Ray. *See* Agee, Ray(mond Clinton)
Little Richard. *See* Penniman, Richard [or Ricardo] Wayne
Little Roy. *See* Lowe, Earl
Little Sam. *See* Broonzy, William Lee Conley
Little Sister. *See* Scruggs, Irene
Little Son. *See* Broonzy, William Lee Conley
Little Son Joe. *See* Lawlars, Ernest
Little Sonny. *See* Willis, Aaron
Little Sparrow. *See* Gassion, Edith Giovanna
Little Sparrow. *See* Francisco, Slinger
Little Sparrow of Paris, The. *See* Gassion, Edith Giovanna
Little Steve(n). *See* Van Zandt, Steve(n)
Little T-Bone. *See* Rankin, R. S.
Little Temple. *See* Jenkins, Gus
Little, Thomas (Moore). *See* Moore, Thomas
Little, Tiny. *See* Little, Dudley Richard
Little, Tobe. *See* Slaughter, M(arion) T(ry)
Little Tramp, The. *See* Chaplin, Charles (Spencer)
Little Walter (J.). *See* Jacobs, Marion Walter
Little Walter, Jr. *See* Hatch, Provine, Jr.
Little Walter, Junior. *See* Smith, George (1924-1983)
Little Walter of Louisiana. *See* Neal, Raful
Little White Wolf, The. *See* Newbury, Milton S(im), (Jr.)
Little Wolf. *See* Shines, John Ned
Littlefoot, George. *See* Lightfoot, Alexander
Littler, Emile. *See* Raines, (Sir) Norman
Littler, Prince. *See* Raines, Frank
Littoff, Maxim. *See* Eckstein, Maxwell

Litwos. *See* Sienkiewicz, Henryk (Adam Aleksandr Pius)
Liviano, Lantino. *See* Villano [or Villani], Antonio
Living Legend, The. *See* Morganfield, McKinley
Livingston, Audrey. *See* Barrell, Edgar Alden, Jr.
Livingston, Audrey. *See* Cowdell, Ellen
Livingston, Buddy. *See* Livingston, Joseph A(nthony)
Livingston, Bunny. *See* Livingston, Neville O'Reilly
Livingston, Fud. *See* Livingston, Joseph A(nthony)
Livingston, Jerry. *See* Levinson, Jerome [or Jerry]
Livison, Jay. *See* Livingston, (Jay) Harold
Livo, Marius. *See* Urai, Vilmos [or William]
Livognol. *See* Veneziani, Carlo
Lizard King, The. *See* Morrison, James (Douglas)
Lizzapa, Diomedo. *See* Palazzi, Giovanni
Ljova. *See* Zhurbin, Lev
Llab, E. R. *See* Ball, Ernest R.
Llab, Roland E. *See* Ball, Ernest R.
Llad, S. A. *See* Dallas, J. J.
Llano, (A.). *See* Vlak, Kees
Llewellyn, Ray. *See* Bloch, Ray
Llewellyn, Ray. *See* Breeze, Lionel
Llewellyn, Ray. *See* Frontiere, Dominic
Llewellyn, Ray. *See* Orton, Irving
Llewellyn, Ray. *See* Rose, David D.
Llewellyn, Ray. *See* Tiompkin, Dmitri
Llewellyn, Ray. *See* Yorke, Peter
Llewellyn, Ray. *See* Young, Victor
Lloyd, Ashton. *See* Coates, Carroll
Lloyd, Bert. *See* Lloyd, A(lbert) L(ancaster)
Lloyd, Evans. *See* Pregarty, John M.
Lloyd, George. *See* Edwards, C(harles) J(oseph)
Lloyd, George. *See* Sonenscher, Dave
Lloyd, George. *See* Wright, Julian
Lloyd, Joseph M. *See* Cain, Noble
Lloyd, Lewellyn. *See* Rolfe, Walter (L.)
Lloyd, Marie. *See* Wood, Mathilda Alice Victoria
Lloyd-Webber, Andrew. *See* Raddick, Henry
Lo. *See* Bassano, Lodovico
Lobo. *See* La Voie, (Roland) Kent
Locke, Harold. *See* Grey, Frank H(erbert)
Locklin, Hank. *See* Locklin, Lawrence Hankins
Lockwood, Torrence (E.). *See* Gabriel, Charles H(utchinson)
Loco, El. *See* Palmieri, Eduardo [or Edward, or Eddie]
Loco, Joe. *See* Esteves, Joseph [or Jose], (Jr.)
Loden, Sonny. *See* Loden, James (H.)
Lodwick, Mr. *See* Bassano, Lodovico
Loë, Franz von. *See* Hochkirch, Franz von
Loechler, Franz. *See* Mattheus, Bernd
Loeffler, R. *See* Kunkel, Charles
Loeillet de Gant. *See* Loeillet, Jean Baptiste (1688-c.1720)
Loeillet of London, John. *See* Loeillet, Jean Baptiste (1680-1730)
Loew, Jack. *See* Kaufman, Isidore
Loew, Jack. *See* Kaufman, Jacob
Loewe, Fritz. *See* Loewe, Frederick
Loewe, Gilbert. *See* Rawlings, Charles Arthur
Lofton, Cripple Clarence. *See* Lofton, Clarence
Logaire, S. *See* Timms, Herbert Philip
Logan, John P. *See* Latey, Keith P(armeter)
Logau, Gotthold. *See* Glogau, Henrik
Loghouse Composer. *See* Heinrich, Anton [or Anthony] Philip
Logic, Lay. *See* Hone, William
Loh, F(erdinand). *See* Baumann, Eric
Lohelius, Joannes [or Johann). *See* Oehlschägel, (Franz) Joseph [or Johann]
Lohet, Simon. *See* Loxhay, Simon
Löhner, Beda. *See* Löhner(-Beda), Fritz
Loke, Jonny. *See* Pingoud, Ernest
Loke, Mele. *See* Roes, Carol Lasater [or Lasatir]
Lokumbe, Hannibal. *See* Peterson, Marvin (Hannibal)
Lom, Stanislav. *See* Mojžíš, Stanislav
Lomagne, B. de. *See* Soubies, (Émile Jean) Albert
Lomuto, Pancho. *See* Lomuto, Francisco (Juan)
Lomzer, Reb Hayyim. *See* Wasserzug, Hayyim
Lonati, Carlo Ambrogio. *See* Leinati, Carlo Ambrogio
Londinese, Il. *See* Sammartini, Giuseppe (Francesco Gaspare Melchiorre Baldassare)
London Bach, The. *See* Bach, Johann Christian
London, George. *See* Burnstein, George
London, Joe. *See* Darmanin, Joseph
London, Lawrence. *See* Berlin, Boris
London, Lou. *See* Gibaldi, Louis M(ilo)
Lone Cowboy. *See* McAuliffe, Harry C(larence)
Lone, John. *See* Levin, Joseph A.
Lone Star Ranger. *See* Finkelstein, Abe
Lone Star Ranger, The. *See* Slaughter, M(arion) T(ry)
Lone Star Ranger, The. *See* White, John I(rwin)
Lone Wolf, The. *See* Woods, Oscar
Lonely Troubadour, The. *See* Friedman, Theodore (Leopold)
Lones, Larry. *See* Heun, Hans
Lonesome Hobo, The. *See* Carlisle, Cliff(ord Raymond)
Lonesome John. *See* Ammirati, John Lewis
Lonesome Singer of the Air, (The). *See* Marvin, John(ny) (Senator)
Lonesome Sundown. *See* Green, Cornelius
Long Brothers. *See* Autry, (Orvon) Gene
Long, Edgar. *See* Riegger, Wallingford (Constantin)
Long, Frank de. *See* De Long, Frank
Long Gone. *See* Miles, Luke
Long, Silent. *See* Lynch, Thomas Toke [or Took]
Long Tall Texan. *See* Dean, Jimmy
Long, Tom. *See* Autry, (Orvon) Gene

Longeville, Jean. *See* Lang, Isaac
Longfellow, Baron. *See* Youakim, Andrew [or Andy]
Longhair, Dr. *See* Byrd, Henry Roeland
Longhair, Professor. *See* Byrd, Henry Roeland
Longin, Fred. *See* Schütz, Alfred
Longstrides. *See* Bedyngham, Johannes [or John]
Lonsdale, Frederick. *See* Leonard, Lionel Frederick
Looker Out, A. *See* Harris, H.
Looney, Charlotte. *See* Kunkel, Charles
Loor, Max van. *See* Krohn, Max
Lopes, Papa. *See* Feather, Leonard (Geoffrey)
López, Cachao. *See* López, Israel
Lopez, Francis. *See* Lopez, Francisco
Lopez, Roberto. *See* Musel, Robert [or Bob] (Saul)
Lopwegen, Benedikt. *See* Jenny, Marie-Cécile
Loraine, Alan. *See* Victory, (Thomas Joseph) Gerard
Loran Glodoci. *See* Goldoni, Carlo
Lord Burgess. *See* Burgie, Irving Louis
Lord Calvert. *See* Cole, Nathaniel Adams
Lord Creator. *See* Patrick, Kentrick
Lord Delfont of Stepney. *See* Winogradsky, Bernard [or Boris]
Lord Henry. *See* Somerset, Henry Richard Charles
Lord Kitchener. *See* Roberts, Aldwyn [or Aldwin]
Lord, Marion. *See* Bliss, P(hilip) Paul
Lord Melody. *See* Alexander, Fitzroy
Lord Melody. *See* Frederick, John
Lord of Quadrilles and Galops. *See* Musard, Philippe
Lord Shorty. *See* Blackman, Garfield
Lord, Stephen. *See* Loyacano, Stephen J(acob)
Loren, Randy. *See* DiLorenzo, Randy Paul
Lorendo, L. P. *See* Laurendeau, Louis-Philippe
Lorens, G'erom. *See* Schwartz, Jerome Lawrence
Lorent, André. *See* Laks, Szymon [or Simon]
Lorenz, H(erbert) R(ichard). *See* Fields, Herbert
Lorenz, H(erbert) R(ichard). *See* Hart, Lorenz (Milton)
Lorenz, H(erbert) R(ichard). *See* Rodgers, Richard (Charles)
Lorenz, Luther. *See* Frangkiser, Carl (Moerz)
Lorenzi, Leo. *See* Croger, Frederick Julian
Lorenzino, todesco del liuto. *See* Allegri, Lorenzo
Lorenzo Antonio. *See* Sánchez Pohl, Lorenzo Antonio
Lorenzo, W. *See* Rolfe, Walter (L.)
Loreto, Vittore. *See* Barnard, Ernest
Lorezzo. *See* Zerezo de Tejada, Isidore Francisco Antonio de
Loring, Ernest. *See* Nichols, (Ernest) Loring
Loring, Lina. *See* Bliss, P(hilip) Paul
Loris. *See* Hofmannsthal, Hugo von
Loritus. *See* Loriti, Henrich, of Glarus
Lorrain, Jean. *See* Duval, Paul Alexandre Martin
Lorraine, Frank. *See* Fisher, Ethel
Lorraine, Phyllis. *See* Kasha, Phyllis L.
Lorraine, Sam. *See* Barnes, H(oward) E(llington)
Lorraine, Sam. *See* Fields, Harold (Cornelius)
Lorraine, Sam. *See* Roncoroni, Joseph (Dominic)
Lorraine, Victor. *See* Brown, Henry Albert
Lorrimer, Laura. *See* Shelton, Julia (née Finley)
Lorrow, Friedrich. *See* Elbogen, Friedrich
Los Angeles, Alex. *See* Mallis, Constantine Alexander (Hadji [or Hagi])
Losch, Abe. *See* Lincoln, Harry J.
Lösch, Alexander. *See* Berrsche, Alexander
Loss, Bernard. *See* Frangkiser, Carl (Moerz)
Lot, Parson. *See* Kingsley, Charles
Lothar, Louis. *See* Dupin, Paul
Lothar, Mark. *See* Hundertmark, Lothar
Lothar, Rudolf. *See* Spitzer, Rudolf
Lothrop, Amy. *See* Warner, Anna (Barlett)
Loti, Pierre. *See* Viaud, (Louis Marie) Julien
Lott, Noah. *See* Philpott, George Vere Hobart
Lottimer, Ebb. *See* Lottimer, Edmund
Loubé, Charles. *See* Holoubek, Karl
Loué, Philibert. *See* Gandonnière, Almire
Louiguy, (Bravo). *See* Guglielmi, L(o)uis
Louis, D. *See* Hopp, Julius
Louis, Des. *See* Des Granges, Louis Anthony
Louis, Frank. *See* Hansson, Stig (Axel)
Louis, Gene. *See* Quaciari, Gene L(ouis)
Louis, Joe (Hill). *See* Hill, Lester [or Leslie]
Louisiana Man. *See* Kershaw, Doug(las James)
Louisiana Red. *See* Minter, Iverson
Louisiana's Singing Governor. *See* Davis, James [or Jimmie] (Houston)
Lounsbury, Walter. *See* Auracher, Harry
Lourdault. *See* Braconnier, Jean
Lourié, Arthur Vincent. *See* Lure, Artur (Sergeievich)
Louvin Brothers. *See* Loudermilk, Charles (Elzer)
Louvin Brothers. *See* Loudermilk, Ira Lonnie
Louvin, Charlie. *See* Loudermilk, Charlie (Elzer)
Louvin, Ira. *See* Loudermilk, Ira Lonnie
Love, Henry. *See* Loewe, Hilda
Love, James. *See* Dance, James
Love, John. *See* Levin, Joseph A.
Love, Larry. *See* Khaury, Herbert
Love, Ludy. *See* Love, Luther Halsey, (Jr.)
Love Monie. *See* Johnson, Simone
Love, M'Pongo. *See* Landu, M'Pongo
Lovebug Starski. *See* Smith, Kevin (1961-)
Loveland, Carl (L.). *See* Lincoln, Harry J.
Loveless, Patty. *See* Ramey, Patricia (Lee)
Lovell, Henry. *See* Dickson, Mary Hannah
Lovell, Katherine. *See* Mullins, Margaret Olive
Lovell, Philip. *See* Phillips, William Lovell
Lovello, Tony. *See* Lovullo, Anthony
Lover, Frank. *See* Willcox, Frank
Lover of His Country, A. *See* Fielding, Henry
Lovering, John. *See* Wreford, John Reynell (Raymond George)
Loving Little Henry. *See* Byrd, Henry Roeland

Löw, Matthias Appeles de. *See* Apel, Matthäus
Lowe, E. *See* Lowenstein, Emanuel
Lowe, Edward. *See* Paulton, Edward A(ntonio)
Lowe, Harry. *See* Davis, Joseph [or Joe] (M.)
Lowell, Frances. *See* Dichmont, William
Lowell, J. Edgar. *See* Zamecnik, J(ohn) S(tepan)
Löwen, C(arl) v. *See* Weber, (Jacob) Gottfried
Löwenstern, Matthäus Apelles von. *See* Apel, Matthäus
Lower, Harry S. *See* Sankey, Ira David
Lowman, Richard. *See* Hyman, Richard [or Dick] (R(oven))
Lowry, Mark. *See* Stein, Ronald
Lowry, Minnie B. *See* Crosby, Fanny [i.e., Frances] J(ane)
Loy, S. J. *See* Loyacano, Stephen J(acob)
Loyd, Marc. *See* Shaffer, Lloyd (M.)
Lu Blue. *See* Dupont, Louise [or Louisa]
Luardo, Martino. *See* Andries, Franzkeo
Luba. *See* Kowalchyk, Luba
Lübenau, L. *See* Jadassohn, Salomon
Luc Dominique. *See* Decker, J(e)annine
Luc-Gabrielle, (Sister). *See* Decker, J(e)annine
Lucacih, Giovanni. *See* Lukačić, Ivan
Lucas, Jane. *See* Spivey, Victoria [or Vicky] (Regina)
Lucas, Jean. *See* Dickson, Mary Hannah
Lucas, Margaret. *See* Dickson, Mary Hannah
Lucca, Papo. *See* Lucas, Enrique Arsenio, Jr.
Lucchesino, Il. *See* Pacini, Andrea
Luce, Johnnie. *See* Lucciola, John (S., Jr.)
Luciano. *See* McClymont, Jepther
Luck Hands. *See* Hawkins, Lamont
Luckner, Lutz. *See* Ludwig, Joachim (Carl Martin)
Lucky Bing. *See* Crosby, Harry Lillis
Lucullan Raconteur, The. *See* Huneker, James Gibbons
Lucy. *See* Chapelle, Paul Aimé
Lüders, Hans. *See* Fett, Armin
Lüders, Jan. *See* Ordnung, Rudolf (August)
Ludovic, (G.). *See* Gobbaerts, Jean Louis
Ludovico, Messer. *See* Widmann, Joseph Viktor
Ludwig, (Hein). *See* Prinz, Heinrich Ludwig
Ludwig van Kempen. *See* Ludovicus Sanctus
Luid, Elder von. *See* Csermák, Antol [or Anthony] György [or George]
Luigi. *See* Creatore, Luigi (Federico)
Luigi, Gian. *See* Zaninelli, Luigi
Luigi Jaja. *See* Nono, Luigi
Luila. *See* Lanaro, Luigi
Luini, Carl —*see* Richards, Henry Brinley
Luis Enrique —*see* Mejía López, Luis Enrique
Luis Enríquez. *See* Bacalov, Luis Enríquez
Luke the Drifter. *See* Williams, Hir(i)am (King)
Lulli, Arthur de. *See* Allen, Euphemia (Amelia)
Lully, Jean Baptiste. *See* Lulli, Giovanni Battista
Lulu. *See* Lawrie, Marie MacDonald MacLaughlin
Lulu Belle and Scotty. *See* Cooper, Myrtle Eleanor
Lulu Belle and Scotty. *See* Wiseman, Scott(y) (Greene)
Luna, R(osendo). *See* Cadicamo, Enrique Domingo
Lunchbasket, Roger. *See* Reeve-Jones, Alan Edmond
Lund, Gustav. *See* Mullen, Frederic
Lund, Peter. *See* Schneider, Hans
Lunde, Lonny. *See* Lunde, Lawson
Lupar, Guy. *See* Luypaerts, Guy
Lupe, La. *See* Raymond, Lupe Victoria Yoli
Lupino, Barry. *See* Hook, George Barry
Lupino, Nipper. *See* Lupino, Henry George
Lupino, Stanley. *See* Hook, Stanley
Lupus, Edwardus. *See* Lobo, Duarte
Lupus, Michael. *See* DeWolf, Michael
Luschansky, Josef. *See* Arnold, Franz
Luscinius, Othmar [or Ottomar(us)]. *See* Nachtigall, Othmar [or Ottmar]
Lusse, Charles de. *See* Delusse, Charles
Lustig. *See* Wodiczka, T.
Lustig, Hermann. *See* Krome, Herman(n) (Friedrich)
Lute the Drifter. *See* Ochs, Phil
Luther, Francis. *See* Crow(e), Francis Luther
Luther, Frank. *See* Crow(e), Francis Luther
Luzzi, Yino. *See* Cadicamo, Enrique Domingo
Lyde, Cisco. *See* Lyde, Cecil Orlando
Lyle, Kami. *See* Howg, Kimberlee
Lyle, Kevin. *See* Neff, Lyle Kevin
Lyman, Abe. *See* Simon, Abraham
Lyn. *See* Breeze, Lionel
Lynas, F. *See* Lynes, Frank
Lynch, Annabelle. *See* Short, Annabelle (Macauly Allen)
Lynch, Claire. *See* Green, Hazel
Lynd, Gene. *See* Lindsay, Bryan (Eugene)
Lynn, Barbara. *See* Ozen, Barbara Lynn
Lynn, Cheryl. *See* Smith, Cherry George
Lynn, Frank. *See* Leisy, James (Franklin)
Lynn, Frank. *See* Schillinger, Joseph (Moiseyevich)
Lynn, Johnny. *See* Birch, Peter
Lynn, Judy. *See* Voiten, Judy (Lynn)
Lynn, Loretta. *See* Webb, Loretta
Lynn, Martha. *See* Cain, Noble
Lynn(e), Sharon (E.). *See* Lindsay, D'Auvergne Sharon
Lynn, Van. *See* Linden, David Gysbert (van der)
Lynne, Mark. *See* Carte, Richard D'Oyly
Lynsey, De Paul. *See* Lynsey, Rubin
Lynton, Everett. *See* Wright, Lawrence
Lyon, David. *See* Norman, Leo
Lyon, M. J. *See* Bliss, P(hilip) Paul
Lyons, Dan D. *See* Diasio, Daniel J(oseph, Jr.)
Lyons, Frank. *See* DeLeone, Francesco B(artolomeo)
Lyons, Jodie. *See* Lyons, Joseph Callaway
Lyre of the Holy Spirit, The. *See* Ephrem Syrus

– M –

M. *See* Morell, Thomas
M. *See* Moultrie, Gerard
M.***. *See* Chapeau, Armand
M***, ***. *See* Bawr, Alexandrine Sophie de
M. A. *See* Altenberg, Michael
M. A. *See* Ruffini, Giovanni [or Giacomo] (Domenico)
M. A. C. *See* MacDonald, Georgi(n)a
M. A. E. *See* Gabriel, Charles (Hutchinson)
M. A. L. *See* Lathbury, Mary Ann [or Artemesias]
M. A. v. L. *See* Apel, Mathäus
M. B. *See* Besly, Edward M.
M. B. F. *See* Foster, Myles Birket
M. B. W. *See* Whiting, Mary Bradford
M. C., (Signor). *See* Clementi, Muzio
M. C. *See* Cooke, Matthew
M. C***. *See* Chevrier, F. A. de
M. C. C. *See* Campbell, Margaret Cockburn (née Malcolm)
MC Father. *See* Brown, Timothy
MC Grand Royal. *See* Sermon, Erick
M. C. H. *See* Hood, Margaret Chalmers
MC 900 Foot Jesus. *See* Griffen, Mark
McN., W. G. *See* McNaught, W(illiam) G.
M. C. W. *See* Hood, Margaret Chalmers
M. D. M. *See* Moultrie, Mary Dunlop
M. de C***. *See* Chabanon, Michel Paul Gui de
M. de L. *See* Ledesma, Mariano Rodriguez de
M. de L**. *See* Delusse, Charles
M. G. F(r. in H.). *See* Gredy, F(riedrich) M(elchior)
M. J. Y. *See* Young, Maud J(eannie) (Fuller)
M. K. *See* Kraussold, M.
M. L. *See* Leeson, Jane E(liza)
M. L. L. *See* Perkins, Tony
M. M. C. *See* Campbell, Mary M.
M. S. *See* Shaw, Martin (Fallas)
M---s. *See* Weber, Carl Maria von
M. S. S. J. *See* Steyer, Matej Vaclav
M. Seraphina, (Sister). *See* Kunkel, Charles
M. W. V. R. S. *See* Shaw, Martin (Fallas)
M. W. V. R. S. *See* Vaughan Williams, Ralph
Maasalo, Armas Toivo Valdemar. *See* Masalin, Armas Toivo Valdemar
Maass, Charlee. *See* Maass, Arlene Fournier
Mabinn, E. J. *See* Benjamin, Walter
Mac. *See* McClintock, Harry (K(irby))
Macaulay, Tony. *See* Instone, Anthony (Gordon)
MacAyn. *See* Mayer, Johann(es) (?Adolf)
MacBeth, James. *See* Kinyon, John L(eroy)
MacClure, Noble. *See* Herbert, Victor
MacColl, Ewan. *See* Miller, James (Henry)
Macculi, Libero. *See* Bellucci Lasalandra, Mario
MacDermot, Robert. *See* Barbour, Robert MacDermot
Macdermott, G. H. *See* Farrell, Michael John
Macdonald, A. G. *See* Bliss, P(hilip) Paul
MacDonald & Broons. *See* Marvin, John(ny) (Senator)
MacDonald, Calum. *See* MacDonald, Malcolm
Macdonald, Ian. *See* Lemon, Laura (Gertrude)
Maceo, Nat. *See* Castling, Harry
Macero, Teo. *See* Macero, Attilio Joseph
MacFarlane, Spanky. *See* MacFarlane, Elaine
MacFarren, (John). *See* Fischer, Ernest
MacFarren, (Mrs.) John. *See* Bennett, Emma Marie
MacGregor, Chummy. *See* MacGregor, J(ohn) Chalmers
MacGregor, Scotty. *See* MacGregor, Irvin T(homas)
MacGreggor, Arthur, of Knightsbridge Esq. *See* Mason, William
MacGreggor, Malcolm. *See* Mason, William
Machado, Jack. *See* Feather, Leonard (Geoffrey)
Machauer, Bob. *See* Bunz, Hans-Günther
Machito. *See* Gutiérrez Grillo, Francisco Raúl
MacHumberg, Leonard. *See* McNally, Leonard
Mack, Arthur. *See* Finkelstein, Abe
Mack, Bunny. *See* MacCormack, Cecil Bunting
Mack, Cecil. *See* McPherson, Richard C(ecil)
Mack, Eugene. *See* Finkelstein, Abe
Mack, Eugene. *See* Grady, R(ichard) G.
Mack, Lonnie. *See* McIntosh, Lonnie
Mack, Noreen. *See* O'Flynn, Honoria
Mack 10. *See* Rolison, D(edrick) (D'mon)
Mack, Warner. *See* McPherson, Warner (Hensley)
MacKane, William. *See* Palmer, Cedric King
Mackay, E. *See* Mack, Edward
MacKenzie, Cyril Claude. *See* Clarke, Cuthbert
Mackenzie, Gordon. *See* Smith, William (1878-1948)
Mackenzie, Herbert. *See* Matheson, Herbert
Mackenzie, Malcolm. *See* Fisher, William Arms
Mackenzie, Murray. *See* Murray, James R(amsey)
Mackie-Beyer, W. H. *See* Mackie, William H.
Macleod, (Dr.) Archibald, The Late. *See* Bowles, William Lisle
MacLeod, Fiona. *See* Sharp, William
MacMurrough, Dermot. *See* White, Harold R(obert)
Mac Neil, N. *See* Calloway, Cab(ell), III
MacNell, Allan. *See* Abbott, Alain André Yves
Macourek, Georg. *See* Mazaurek, Georg
Macrae, Arthur. *See* Schröpfer, William Arthur
MacRae, Johnny. *See* MacRae, Fred A(ylor)
MacRea [or McRae], Gertrude. *See* Aitken, Florence H.
MacRoberts, Keith. *See* Rasley, John M.
MacRobin, Mark. *See* Cunningham, Allan
Macropedius, Georg(ius). *See* Langeveld(t), Joris [or Georg] van
MacSherry, Les. *See* Myers, Charles
Macy, Ed. *See* Kaufman, Isidore
Madalena. *See* Lamburn, Maria
Madame. *See* Solomon, Emma
Madame ***. *See* Bawr, Alexandrine Sophie de
Madame de B***. *See* Bawr, Alexandrine Sophie de

Maddern, Minnie. *See* Davey, Marie [or Minnie] Augusta
Madeline Clare. *See* Twomey, Kathleen [or Kay] Greeley
Mader, Raoul. *See* Mader, Rezsõ
Madin, Henri. *See* Madden, Henri
Madison, Gary. *See* Fox, Roy ([nd])
Madison, Maury. *See* Smith, (W(illiam)) Renwick
Madonna. *See* Ciccone, Madonna Louise Veronica
Madonna of Brazil, The. *See* Monte, Marisa
Madonna of Contemporary Gospel, The. *See* Grant, Amy (Lee)
Madonna of Gospel Music, The. *See* Grant, Amy
Madrazo, Coco. *See* Madrazo (y Hahn), Federico (Carlos) de
Madsen, Ohle [or Ole]. *See* Gerstenberg, Heinrich Wilhelm von
Maduro, Franco. *See* Mäder, Wolfgang
Maelo. *See* Rivera, Ismael
Maertek, Raphael. *See* McGuffie, William [or Bill]
Maery, H(elen). *See* Mug, (Sister) Mary Theodosia
Maestre del trobadors. *See* Giraut, de Bornelh
Maestro Capitán, El. *See* Rosmarin, Mathieu
Maestro il cappella napolitano. *See* Scarlatti, Giuseppe
Maestro of Change, The. *See* Solonen, Esa-Pekka
Maestro of Love. *See* Carter, Barry Eugene
Maestro of the Bozart. *See* Mencken, H(enry) L(ouis)
Maestro of the Program Notes, The. *See* Hale, Philip
Maeterlinck of Music, The. *See* Strauss, Richard
Maffatt, James. *See* Hughes, Robert J(ames)
Maffay, Peter. *See* Makkey, Peter
Magee, Rusty. *See* Magee, Benjamin Rush
Magic Sam. *See* Maghett, Sam(uel)
Magic Singing Sam. *See* Maghett, Sam(uel)
Magini. *See* Hargreaves, James
Magister, L. *See* Lehrer, Leibush
Magister Paulus. *See* Hofhaimer, Paul(us von)
Maglanowich, Hyacinthe. *See* Mérimée, Prosper
Maglio, Pacho. *See* Maglio, Juan (Felix)
Magnetic Killer-Diller of the "Licorice Stick" (clarinet). *See* Goodman, Benjamin [or Benny] (David)
Magnoni, Edrich. *See* Magnoni, Bruce [or Bruno] Albert
Magnoni, Edrich. *See* Smith-Masters, Stanley
Magnus, (Désiré). *See* Deutz, Magnus
Magnus, Merriweather. *See* Talbot, Charles Remington
Magoon, Bob. *See* Magoon, Eaton (Harry), Jr.
Maguire, Hannibal. *See* Williams, Spencer
Mahal, Taj. *See* Fredericks(-Williams), Henry St. Claire, (Jr.)
Maharba, F. *See* Abraham, F.
Mahavishnu. *See* McLaughlin, John
Mahl, Franz. *See* Chase, George
Mähllig, Ricardo. *See* Gillham, Richard
Mahmied, S. E. *See* Adams, Nehemiah
Mahner-Mons, Hans. *See* Possendorf, Hans
Mahon, George. *See* Cohen, Maurice Alfred
Mahr, Curley. *See* Mahr, Herman Carl
Mai, Fritz. *See* Manussi-Montesole, Ferdinand
Maia Crosesser, Luís da. *See* Jesus Maria, Carlos de
Main gauche, La. *See* Brian, William
Maine's Own March King. *See* Hall, R(obert) B(rowne)
Mainini, Francesco. *See* Agnesi-(Pinottini), Maria Teresa (d')
Mairead Na Clarsaich. *See* Impey, Margaret
Maison, Jean. *See* Haass, Hans
Maistre Jahn. *See* Jhan
Maitland, John. *See* Begleiter, Lionel
Majo, Ernest. *See* Majowski, Ernest
Major-General of Marsland. *See* Duncan, Ronald (Frederick Henry)
Major, (Jakab) Gyula. *See* Mayer, Jakab Gyula
Mak, Marion Wang. *See* Wang, An-Ming
Maker of the Proms. *See* Wood, (Sir) Henry Joseph
Maki, Theodore. *See* Cacavas, John
Makowicz, Adam. *See* Matyszkowicz, Adam
Makuakane. *See* Reid, Willis Wilfred
Mala Fe. *See* Gutiérrez, Javier
Malagigi. *See* Pasqualini, Marc(o)'Antonio
Malando, (A.). *See* Maasland, Arie
Malcior de Wormatia. *See* Schanppecher, Melchior
Malco, Lu(i). *See* Pinggèra, Karl Ludwig
Malcolm, David. *See* Locke, Sam
Malcolm, John. *See* Batt, Malcolm John
Maledünntus Wagner, der Weberjunge. *See* Benedict, Julius
Maler, H. *See* Kötscher, Edmund
Maler, J. *See* Oldenburg, Elimar Anton Günther Friedrich Herzog von
Malherbe, H(enry). *See* Croisilles, H.
Mallory, Charles. *See* Prentice, Charles W(hitecross)
Malloy, Mark. *See* Donnelly, Richard
Malloys, The. *See* Donnelly, Richard
Malloys, The. *See* Forsythe, Charles Henry
Malloys, The. *See* Sugarman, Harry
Malmogiensis, Trudo Haggaei. *See* Aagesen, Truid
Malo, El. *See* Colon (Ramon), William [or Willie] (Anthony)
Malone, Bea. *See* Olman, Abraham [or Abe]
Malone, D(eadric). *See* Robey, Don (D.)
Malone, Ronald. *See* Lockton, Edward F.
Malone, Thumbs. *See* Malone, Terwilliger
Maltig, Heinrich von der. *See* Wallmann, Heinrich
Mama Can Can. *See* Pridgett, Gertrude (Malissa Nix)
Mama O. *See* Papathanassiou, Evangelos (Odyssey)
Mambo King, The. *See* Perez Prado, Domasco [or Damasco]
Mambo King. *See* Puente, Ernesto Antonio, (Jr.)
Man, The. *See* Bach, Johann Sebastian
Man, The. *See* Friedhofer, Hugo Wilhelm
Man Behind the Music, The. *See* Jones, Quincy Delight

Man Called Hoss, A. *See* Jennings, Waylon [actually Wayland] (Arnold)
Man in Black, The. *See* Cash, John(ny) (R.)
Man of Brass. *See* Smith-Masters, Stanley
Man Who Freed Music, The. *See* Beethoven, Ludwig van
Man Who Launched a Thousand Hits, The. *See* Gum(m), Harold [or Harry]
Man Who Named Tin Pan Alley, (The). *See* Rosenfeld, Monroe H.
Man Who Never Died, The. *See* Hägglund, Joel (Em(m)anuel)
Man Who Owned Broadway, The. *See* Cohan, George M(ichael)
Man Who Sings Tobacco Best, The. *See* Williams, Sol(lie Paul)
Man with a Million Friends, (The). *See* Myrick, David Luke
Mana-Zucca. *See* Zuccamana, Gizelle Augusta
Mance, Junior. *See* Mance, Julian Clifford, Jr.
Mancha, Steve. *See* Wilson, Clyde
Manchester, Bud. *See* Stark, Etilmon Justus
Manchester, George. *See* Gill, William (Fearing)
Manchester, William F. *See* McBeth, W(illiam) Francis
Mancia, Luigi. *See* Manza, Luigi
Mancini, Hank. *See* Mancini, Enrico Nicola
Mancini, Henry. *See* Mancini, Enrico Nicola
Mancinus, Thomas. *See* Menckin, Thomas
Mancione, Alberto. *See* Tórtora, Genaro
Mandell, Roger. *See* Olman, Abraham [or Abe]
Mander, Ambrose. *See* Finkelstein, Abe
Mandingo. *See* Love, Geoff(rey)
Mandy Doubt. *See* MacColl, Kristy
Mandy Lee. *See* Vonderlieth, Leonore
Manfield, Fred. *See* Guttmann, Alfred (Grant)
Manfred. *See* Dräxler, Karl (Ferdinand)
Manga, Bebe. *See* Bessem, Elizabeth Prudence Manga
Manheim, Curt. *See* Kurtz, Em(m)anuel [or Manny]
Mani-Leib. *See* Brahinsky, Mani Leib
Manilla, Pedro. *See* Mantovani, A(nnuzio) P(aola)
Manilla, Pedro. *See* Piccioni, Angelo F.
Manilla, Tony. *See* Fishman, Jack (1918 (or 19)-)
Manilla, Tony. *See* Shardlow, Clare
Manilla, Tony. *See* Stapleton, Cyril
Manilow, Barry. *See* Pincus, Barry Allen [or Alan]
Mank, Chaw. *See* Mank, Charles
Manley, Richard. *See* Lehman, Evangeline
Manlowe, Arthur. *See* Olman, Abraham [or Abe]
Mann, Barry. *See* Ibermann, Barry
Mann, Bert. *See* Mann, Robert E.
Mann, David. *See* Freedman, David
Mann, Dorothy. *See* Green, Phil(ip)
Mann, Gerry. *See* Gray, John Baker (Timothy)
Mann, Herbie. *See* Solomon, Herbert (Jay)
Mann, John. *See* Green, Phil(ip)
Mann, John(ny). *See* Mangini, John R.
Mann, Józef. *See* Riedl, Jósef Anton
Mann, Kal. *See* Cohen, Kalman
Mann, Lynn. *See* Dolin, Lynn Marie
Mann, Martin. *See* Löprich, Mario
Mann, Rawden de. *See* Fish, James
Mann, Rita. *See* Applebaum, Stan(ley) (Seymour)
Mann, Steve. *See* Krasnow, Herman(n)
Manners, Craddock. *See* Mannes, Leo (Ezekiel)
Manners, David. *See* Blitz, Leo(nard)
Manners, David. *See* Campbell, James [or Jimmy]
Manners, David. *See* Yorke, Peter
Manners, Dudley. *See* Krupp, D. Dudley
Manners, Jonathan. *See* Machlis, Joseph
Manners, Zeke. *See* Mannes, Leo (Ezekiel)
Manney, E. *See* Cain, Noble
Mannfred, Henrich. *See* Friedmann, Heinrich
Manning, Dick. *See* Medoff, Samuel
Manning, Frank. *See* Kinsman, Elmer (F(ranklin))
Manning, Franklyn. *See* Sawyer, Henry S.
Manning, Samuel. *See* Medoff, Samuel
Manninger, Fr. *See* Kleinmeijer, Henk
Mannsberg, Paul. *See* Peitl, Paul
Mannsfeld, Louis. *See* Schrank, Ludwig
Mannsfeldt-Pierson, E. E. *See* Pearson, Henry Hugh
Mannstein, Heinrich Ferdinand. *See* Steinmann, Heinrich Ferdinand
Mannthaler. *See* Frauenberger, P. Ernst, OSB
Manoa, Chris. *See* Berger, Albin
Manolito, E. *See* Bauer, Emilie Frances
Manone, Jimmy. *See* Manone, Joseph
Manone, Wingy. *See* Manone, Joseph
Manos Brujas. *See* Biagi, Rodolfo
Manrésien. *See* Gagnon, Blanche
Mansell, Richard. *See* Maitland, Robert
Mansfeldt, Edgar. *See* Pearson, Henry Hugh
Mansfield, Richard. *See* Lockton, Edward F.
Manson, Marilyn. *See* Warner, Brian
Manston, Frere. *See* Smith, Reginald (Leonard)
Manten, (E.). *See* Cain, Noble
Manton, Howard. *See* Frangkiser, Carl (Moerz)
Mantovani, (Albert). *See* Mantovani, A(nnuzio) P(aolo)
Mantuanus, Johannes. *See* Legrense, Johannes
Mantzaros, Nicholaos. *See* Halikiopolos Nicolaos
Manuel. *See* Love, Geoff(rey)
Manuel, E(rnest). *See* L'Epine, Ernest Louis Victor Jules
Manuel, Roland. *See* Lévy, Roland Alexis Manuel
Manuela. *See* Wegener, Doris
Manzanera, Phil. *See* Targett-Adams, Philip
Manzi, Barbeta. *See* Manzione, Homero Nicolás
Manzi, Homero. *See* Manzione, Homero Nicolás
Maphis, Joe. *See* Maphis Otis Wilson
Mapleson, Anne. *See* Gaul, Harvey B(artlett)
Mapleson, Colonel. *See* Mapleson, James Henry

Mara, (Gertrud Elisabeth). *See* Schmelling, Gertrud(e Elisabeth)
Mara, Thalia. *See* Mahoney, Elizabeth (née Symons)
Maraffi, Fritz. *See* Maraffi, Lewis Frederick
Marat, Jean. *See* Tate, Arthur F(rank)
Marat of Music, The. *See* Wagner, Richard
Maravilla, (L(o)uis). *See* López Tejera, Luis
Marbeck, Ernst. *See* Posegga, Hans
Marbot, Rolf. *See* Marcuse, Albrecht [or Albert]
Marbourg, Dolores. *See* Bacon, Mary Schell Hoke
Marc Anthony. *See* Muniz, Marco Antonio
Marc-Cab. *See* Cabridens, Marcel (Eugène Henri)
Marc-Michel. *See* Michael, Marc (Antoine Amédie)
Marc, Ronald. *See* Wolfson, Maxwell A(lexander)
Marcato, Ben. *See* Gratton, Joseph Thomas Hector
Marceau, V. *See* Verschueren, Marceau
Marcéchal, (Charles). *See* Kovarovic, Karel
Marcelino. *See* Guerra, Marcelino
Marcelles, Paul. *See* Fournier, Marcel (Paul)
Marcellino, Muzzy. *See* Marcellino, Maurice
Marcello da Capua. *See* Bernardini, Marcello
March King, The. *See* Sousa, John Philip
March King of Austria. *See* Wagner, Josef Franz
March King of Great Britain. *See* Ricketts, (Major) Frederick Joseph
March King of New England, The. *See* Hall, R(obert) B(rowne)
March King of Norway. *See* Borg, Oscar
March King of Pittsburgh. *See* Panella, Frank A.
March King of Sweden. *See* Rydberg, Sam Hjalmar
March King of the Antipodes. *See* Lithgow, Alex F.
March King of the Salvation Army. *See* Coles, Bramwell
March King of the West. *See* Keller, Edward McDonald
March, Little Peggy. *See* Battavio, Margaret
March, Mary Ann Virginia. *See* Gabriel, (Mary Ann)Virginia
March, Noel. *See* Del Riego, Teresa (Clotilde)
March Wizard, The. *See* Heed, J(ohn) C(lifford)
Marchelle, Carl. *See* Henrich, C. W.
Marchi, Antonio. *See* Frederici, Vincenzo
Marcil, Paul. *See* Viau, Albert
Marck, Robert. *See* Mackeben, Theo
Marckwordt, Ferdinand. *See* Flotow, Friedrich von
Marco. *See* Muniz, Marco Antonio
Marco. *See* Wolff, Marco [or Mike]
Marco, Angelina. *See* Vonderlieth, Leonore
Marco Antonio da Bologna. *See* Cavazzoni, Marco Antonio
Marco Antonio da Urbino. *See* Cavazzoni, Marco Antonio
Marco dell'Arpa. *See* Marazzoli, Marco
Marcó, Hèctor. *See* Marcolongo, Hèctor Domingo
Marco, Leo de. *See* Basevi, Marco
Marco, Ralph. *See* Drexler, Werner
Marcus, M. S. *See* Slowitzky, Michael
Mardi, H. J. *See* Seib, Valentin
Mardon, Richard. *See* Elgar, (Sir) Edward
Maréchal, Aristide. *See* Adler, Hans
Maréchal, Aristide. *See* Spitzer, Rudolf
Maréchale, (La). *See* Booth-Clibhorn, Catherine
Marécheaux. *See* Bader, Ernst (Johanes Albert)
Maredo, José. *See* Müller, Günther
Mareller, J. C. *See* Pfundheller, Josef
Mareller, J. C. *See* Swiedack, Karl
Maretzek the Magnificent. *See* Maretzek, Max
Marga, Fred. *See* Mellema, Cornelis Marten
Margarita. *See* De l'Epine, Francesca Margherita
Margis, Gaston. *See* Goldman, Kurt
Mari, Mario. *See* Bozzola, Luigi
Maria, Antônio. *See* Morais, Antonio Maria Araujo de
Maria-Marlen. *See* Franz, (Maria) Marlen(e)
Marian Anderson of the Blues. *See* Hunter, Alberta
Mariana, Enrico. *See* Mapleson, James Henry
Mariani, M(ario). *See* Kötscher, Edmund
Maribarou, M. de. *See* Cubières(-Dorat de Palmézeaux), Michel de
Marie-Jocelyne, (Sister). *See* Vinette, Alice
Marie-Stéphane, (Soeur). *See* Côte, Hélène
Marie, Tenna [or Teena]. *See* Brocker(t), Mary Christine
Marie Therese, (Sister). *See* Boucher, Lydia
Marielli, M. *See* Kingston, Mary
Marietta. *See* Prerauer, Maria (née Wolkowsky)
Mariette, Anton. *See* Wickenden, Arthur
Marilyn. *See* Robinson, Pete(r)
Marilyn, Jay. *See* Gordon, David M.
Marilyn Manson. *See* Warner, Brian
Marini, Peer. *See* Piermarini, Clito L.
Marino, Caesar. *See* Marinovici, Cesar
Mario, E. (A.). *See* Gaeta, Giovanni
Mario, Queena. *See* Tillotson, Queena
Marion. *See* Macy, J(ames) C(artwright)
Marion, Karl. *See* Blackman, Michael Bruce
Marion, Maud(e). *See* Crosby, Fanny [i.e., Frances] J(ane)
Marion, Will. *See* Cook, William Mercer
Maritz, Ferry. *See* Markaritzer, Erich
Marius, Claude. *See* Duplany, Claude Marius
Marius, Mons(ieur). *See* Duplany, Claude Marius
Mark, F. W. *See* Lucas, Edward Verrall
Mark, Freddie. *See* Kaufman, Isidore
Mark Twain of Country Music. *See* Hall, Thomas
Mark Twain of Rock. *See* Newman(n), Gary
Mark Twain of the Music Halls. *See* Hunter, G(eorge) W(illiam)
"Mark Twain" of Yiddish Music. *See* Rabinovitz, Solomon
Märker, Leonard Karl. *See* Kuhmärker, Leonhard Karl
Markham, Edward. *See* Marks, Edward B.
Markham, Seth. *See* Cacavas, John

Markham, Seth. *See* Holcombe, Wilfred (Lawshe)
Markley, Hubert. *See* Kountz, Richard
Markovac, Pavao [or Paul]. *See* Ebenspanger, Pavao
Markowski, Andrzej. *See* Andrzejewski, Marek
Marks, David. *See* Markantonatos, David
Marks, G. W. *See* Brahms, Johannes
Marks, Godfrey. *See* Swift, James Frederick
Marks, J. *See* Highwater, Jamake (Mamake)
Markstein, S. *See* Grannis, S(idney) M(artin)
Markwell, Mark. *See* Creatore, Luigi (Federico)
Markwell, Mark. *See* Peretti, Hugo (Emil)
Markwort, Johann Christian. *See* Dorner, Karl
Marlago. *See* Lopiano-Pomar, Agostino
Marlen, Maria. *See* Franz, (Maria) Marlen(e)
Marley, B. B. *See* Marley, Robert [or Bob] Nesta
Marley, King. *See* Marley, Robert [or Bob] Nesta
Marley, Rita. *See* Anderson, Alpharita Constantia
Marley, Ziggy. *See* Marley, David
Marling, Henri [or Henry]. *See* Schütt, Eduard
Marlo, Ferdi. *See* Blitz, Leo(nard)
Marlo, Ferdi. *See* Butler, Ralph (T.)
Marlo, Verdi. *See* Blitz, Leo(nard)
Marlow, Roy. *See* Blitz, Leo(nard)
Marlowe, Charles. *See* Jay, Harriet
Marlowe, Charles. *See* Margulis, Charles A.
Marlowe, David. *See* Frangkiser, Carl (Moerz)
Marlowe, Jeffrey. *See* Treharne, Bryceson
Marlowe, Jerry. *See* Mautner, Jerome (Nathan)
Marmaduke. *See* Jerningham, Charles Edward Wynne
Marmarosa, Dodo. *See* Marmarosa, Michael
Marmer, Mike. *See* Marmer, Merrill D.
Marnay, Eddy [or Eddie]. *See* Bacri, Edmond (David)
Marney, Eddy. *See* Bacri, Edmond David
Marotte, Jean Paul. *See* Gregg, Hubert Robert Harry
Marquis, J. *See* Schori, Fritz
Marre, Albert. *See* Moshinski, Albert
Marriot. *See* Krome, Herman(n) (Friedrich)
Marrow, Lee. *See* Bontempi, Francesco
Mars, Mick. *See* Deal, Robert (Alan)
Mars, Peter. *See* Faith, Percy
Marschal(l)-Loepke, Gloria. *See* Marschal(l)-Loepke, Grace
Marsden, Evan. *See* Mareo, Eric
Marsden, Frank. *See* Reeves, Ernest
Marsh, Cliff. *See* Fox, Roy ([nd])
Marsh, Rudy. *See* Schramm, Rudolf (R. A.)
Marshall, David. *See* Klemm, Gustav
Marshall, Gloria. *See* Marschal(l)-Loepke, Grace
Marshall, Grace. *See* Marschal(l)-Loepke, Grace
Marshall, John. *See* Engel, Carl
Marshall, William. *See* Hutchison, William M(arshall)
Marshall-Zoepke, C. *See* Marschal(l)-Loepke, Grace
Martaine, G. *See* Greenwald, M(artin)
Marteau, Léon. *See* Zoeller, Carli [or Karl]
Marteau, Marcel. *See* Barnes, Clifford (Paulus)
Martel, John. *See* Engel, Carl
Martell, Bobby. *See* Marley, Robert [or Bob] Nesta
Martelli, Entalindo. *See* Cottrau, Théodore
Martello da Monteleone. *See* Martelli, Giovanni Battista
Martens, Richard Alan. *See* Rasley, John M.
Martial, Michael. *See* Bonagura, Michael John, Jr.
Martika. *See* Marrero, Marta
Martin, Andreas. *See* Krause, Andreas
Martin, Ben. *See* Blake, James Hubert
Martin, Bill. *See* Joel, William [or Billy] (Martin)
Martin, Bill. *See* MacPherson, William (W.)
Martin, Bill. *See* Wylie, William
Martin, Billy. *See* McCartney, (James) Paul
Martin, Blind George. *See* Phelps, Arthur
Martin, Bobbi. *See* Martin, Barbara Anne
Martin, Carrol. *See* Blitz, Leo(nard)
Martin, Deac. *See* Martin, C(laude) T(remble(y))
Martin, Earl. *See* Maschwitz, (Albert) Eric
Martin, Elizabeth Blackburn. *See* Dellafield, Henry
Martin, Ernest (H.). *See* Markowitz, Ernest H.
Martin, Freddy [or Freddie]. *See* Martin, Olin E.
Martin, Fred'k. *See* Morse, Theodore (F.)
Martin, G. *See* Greenwald, M(artin)
Martin, Gene. *See* Stellman, Marcel
Martin, George. *See* Phelps, Arthur
Martin, Gertrude R. *See* Grey, Frank H(erbert)
Martin, Happy. *See* Kaufman, Jacob
Martin, J. D(ouglas). *See* Kern, Carl Wilhelm
Martin, Jack. *See* Finkelstein, Abe
Martin, Jean. *See* Barthelson, (Helen) Joyce (Holloway)
Martin, Jean. *See* Ehret, Walter (Charles)
Martin, Jean. *See* Stellman, Marcel
Martin, Jennie (L.). *See* Kunkel, Charles
Martin, Johann. *See* Laurentius, von Schnüffis
Martin, Johann Paul Aegidius. *See* Schwarzendorf, Johann Paul Agidius
Martin, Karl. *See* Reichel, Karl Heinz
Martin, Lem. *See* Caesar, Isidore
Martin, Lennie. *See* Marino, Rinaldo R.
Martin, Mac. *See* Colleran, William D.
Martin, Marty. *See* Martin, Lecil T(ravis)
Martin, Marvin. *See* Ulbrich, Siegfried
Martin(-Kilcher), Max. *See* Sandberg, Martin
Martin, Moon. *See* Martin, John
Martin, Nico. *See* Hummel, Bertold
Martin, (Kepha) Peter. *See* Malijewski, Peter Martin
Martin, Peter. *See* Waterman, Nixon
Martin, Ray. *See* Newell, Norman
Martin, Riccardo. *See* Martin, Hugh Whitfield
Martin, Richard. *See* Martin, Hugh Whitfield
Martin, Rick. *See* Capellan, Richard Victor
Martin, S. *See* Crosby, Fanny [i.e., Frances] J(ane)
Martin, Sallie [or Sally]. *See* Crosby, Fanny [i.e., Frances] J(ane)
Martin, Sam. *See* Crosby, Fanny [i.e., Frances] J(ane)

Martin, Sara(h). *See* Dunn, Sara(h)
Martin, Skip(py). *See* Martin, Lloyd
Martin, Tomás. *See* Váčkař, Dalibor C(yril)
Martin, Trade. *See* Lione, John
Martin, W. S. *See* Stebbins, George C(oles)
Martin, Walter. *See* Ehret, Walter (Charles)
Martin, William. *See* Ehret, Walter (Charles)
Martindale, J. F(rank). *See* Spalding, Delos Gardner [or Gardiner]
Martinez, Enrique. *See* Iglesias, Enrique
Martinez, Felipe. *See* Sartorio, Arnoldo
Martínez, Marianne von. *See* Martínez, Anna Katharina von
Martini, Bennie. *See* Azzara, (Bennie) Anthony
Martini, Catherine. *See* Ruthenberg, Jane Catherine
Martini, Giambattista. *See* Kreisler, Fritz [i.e., Friedrich](-Max)
Martini, Ignaz. *See* Martín y Soler, Vicente
Martini il Tedesco. *See* Schwarzendorf, Johann Paul Aegidius
Martini, Jean Paul Egide. *See* Schwarzendorf, Johann Paul Aegidius
Martini, Johann Paul Aegidius. *See* Schwarzendorf, Johann Paul Aegidius
Martini, Padre. *See* Martini, Giovanni Battista [or Giambattista]
Martini, Vincenzo. *See* Martín y Soler, Vicente
Martino, Angelo. *See* Rawlings, Charles Arthur
Martino, Sgr. *See* Berteau, Martin
Martins, C. R. *See* Cremer, H(ans) M(artin)
Martins, Jay. *See* Tener, Martin J(ack)
Martyn, Gene. *See* Stellman, Marcel
Martyn, John. *See* McGeachy, Iain
Martyn, Rodney. *See* Mortimer, Harry
Marvel, I(k(e)). *See* Mitchell, D(onald) G(rant)
Marvell, Holt. *See* Maschwitz, (Albert) Eric
Marvell, J. *See* Taylor, Helen
Marville. *See* Létang, P.E.
Marvin, J. A. *See* Bliss, P(hilip) Paul
Marvin, Ron. *See* Buntrock, Martin
Marx, Gary. *See* Pairman, Mark
Marx, Harpo. *See* Marx, (Adolph) Arthur
Marxhausen, P. F. *See* Schatzell, Pauline von
Mary Ernest, O.P., (Sister). *See* Schwerdtfeger, E. Anne
Mary F(rancis) Clare, (Sister). *See* Cusack, Margaret Anna
Mary Norbert, (Sister). *See* Martin, Judith
Mary Xavier, (Sister). *See* Partridge, Sybil F.
Marylis, Guy. *See* Bonnal, (Joseph) Ermend
Mascari, Red. *See* Mascari, Joseph Rocco
Mascotita. *See* Bardi, Agustin
Masen, Mark. *See* Winner, Septimus
Masens, Piere. *See* Bachmann, Erich
Masetti, Carlos. *See* Stube, Howard
Masked Marvel, The. *See* Patton, Charley [or Charlie]
Masked Singer of Country Songs, The. *See* Walker, William [or Billy] (Marvin)
Mason City's Favorite Son. *See* Willson, (Robert Reiniger) Meredith
Mason, Frank. *See* DeMasi, Francesco
Mason, Geoffrey (M.). *See* Wilson, Harry (Robert)
Mason, John. *See* Lebys, Henry
Mason, Mark. *See* Winner, Septimus
Mason, Sam. *See* Fillmore, (James) Henry
Mason, Squire. *See* Liter, Monia
Mason, Ted. *See* O'Keefe, Lester
Masonic Composer. *See* Mozart, Wolfgang Amadeus
Masquerade. *See* Deutscher, Karlheinz
Massara, Pino. *See* Massara, Giuseppe Previde
Massart, Michael. *See* Vicars, Harold
Massé, Victor. *See* Massé, Felix Marie
Massenetique Bizet. *See* Massenet, Jules (Émile Frédéric)
Massey, Bob. *See* Slaughter, M(arion) T(ry)
Massey, Guy. *See* Slaughter, M(arion) T(ry)
Masson, Michel. *See* Gaudichot-Masson, Auguste Michel Benoît
Master, The. *See* Coward, Noel (Pierce)
Master, Louis. *See* Meester, Louis de
Master of Blue-Eyed Rhythm and Blues, The. *See* Levise, William, Jr.
Master of Choro, The. *See* Vianna (Filho), A(lredo da Rocha)
Master of Counterpoint, The. *See* Clément, Jacob [or Jacques]
Master of Disater, The. *See* Clemons, Clarence
Master of Italian Music. *See* Sebenico, (Domenico) Giovanni
Master of Music. *See* Ravel, Maurice (Joseph)
Master of New Orleans Rock 'n' Roll. *See* Byrd, Henry Roeland
Master of Ragtime Guitar, The. *See* Phelps, Arthur
Master of Space and Time. *See* Bridges, (Claude) Russell
Master of the Horror Film. *See* Carpenter, John(ny)
Master of the Musical. *See* Rodgers, Richard (Charles)
Master of the Musical. *See* Yeston, Maury
Master of the Nations, The. *See* Tartini, Giuseppe
Master of the Orchestra. *See* Strauss, Richard
Master of the Sentimental Ballad. *See* Harris, Charles K(assell)
Master of the Telecaster, The. *See* Collins, Al(bert)
Master Ole Bull. *See* Buckley, Frederick
Master P. *See* Miller, Percy
Masters, Alex. *See* Fishman, Jack (1918 (or 19)-)
Masters, Archie. *See* Akers, Howard E(stabrook)
Masters, Archie. *See* Smith-Masters, Stanley
Masters, David. *See* Burger, David Mark
Masters, Henry Read. *See* Adams, Ernest Harry
Masters, Johnnie. *See* Purdom, John Mace

Masters, Juan. *See* Eames, Juanita (Masters)
Masters, Stanley. *See* Smith-Masters, Stanley
Masters, Van. *See* Smith-Masters, Stanley
Masterson, Eric. *See* Cain, Noble
Mastren, Carmen. *See* Mastandrea, Carmine Niccolo
Mat, Mark. *See* Marek, Czeslaw Józef
Matchless Cervetto, The. *See* Cervetto, James (1747-1837)
Mateo, Pepe J. *See* Zerga, Joseph (Louis) E(dmund)
Material Girl. *See* Ciccone, Madonna Louise Veronica
Mathews see also *Matthews*
Mathews, Edouard. *See* Hatch, F(rederic) L.
Mathews, Ray. *See* Matousek, Raymond Anthony
Mathieson, Muir. *See* Mathieson, Murray
Mathieux, Johanna. *See* Kinkel, Johanna (née Mockel)
Mathis, Jules. *See* Grey, Frank H(erbert)
Matiaglauro, Camidio. *See* Bagliacca, Pietro Antonio
Matibor. *See* Rannucci, Renato
Matlock, Bud. *See* Matlock, Julian C(lifton)
Matlock, Matty. *See* Matlock, Julian C(lifton)
Mátray, Gábor. *See* Róthkrepf, Gábor
Matsumoto, Kazuyosi. *See* Matsumoto, Masao
Mattei, Filippo. *See* Amadei, Filippo
Matteo da Perugia. *See* Matheus de Perusio
Matterling, George. *See* Cain, Noble
Mattheson, John Somers. *See* Grey, Frank H(erbert)
Matthew, Eric. *See* Tucci, Joseph William
Matthews see also *Mathews*
Matthews. *See* Favart, Charles Simon
Matthews, Iain. *See* McDonald, Ian Matthews
Matthews, Red (Chuck). *See* Matthews, C(harles) G.
Matthews, Robert. *See* Ross, Lancelot P(atrick)
Matthews, Rose. *See* Crosby, Fanny [i.e., Frances] J(ane)
Matthi, Daniel. *See* Bartzsch, Franz
Matthis, G(eorge) S. *See* Seiber, Mátyás (George)
Maugars, R(ene?). *See* Rothschild, (Baron) Henri de
Makuakane. *See* Reid, Willis Wilfred
Mauldin, Bessie. *See* Monroe, William [or Bill] (Smith)
Maule, Abe. *See* Maule, Leroy Ernest
Maundrell, Gerald. *See* Harris, Cuthbert
Maurel, Philippe. *See* Fredericks, Julian
Maurice. *See* Waller, Thomas Wright
Maurice, Cecil. *See* Chachkes, Maurice
Maurice, Victor. *See* Hallis, B. Edward
Mauritius von Menzingen. *See* Zehnder, Johann Peter
Mauro d' Amalfi. *See* DelGiudice, Gaetano Maria
Maury, Lou. *See* Maury, (Henry) Lowndes
Maussade, Orra. *See* Báthory-Kitsz, Dennis
Mawr, Eta. *See* Colling, Elizabeth
Max. *See* Mack, Edward
Max, Willy. *See* Gauthier-Villars, Henri
Max-Anely. *See* Segalen, Victor
Max-Dearly. *See* Rolland(-Max(-Dearly)), Lucien Paul Marie Joseph
Maxamillion. *See* Grice, Gary
Maxfield, Stanley. *See* Grey, Frank H(erbert)
Maxim, George Pratt. *See* Dellafield, Henry
Maximowna, Ita. *See* Schnakenburg, Margarethe
Maximum, Frankie. *See* Macchia, Frank
Maxwell, John. *See* Maxwell, Francis (Kelly)
May, Brüder. *See* Mayer, Brüder Hans
May, Fritz. *See* Manussi-Montesole, Ferdinand
May, H. I. *See* Keiser, Robert (A(dolph))
May, Hans. *See* Mayer, Johann(es) (?Adolf)
May, Jimmy. *See* Marvin, John(ny) (Senator)
May, Johnny. *See* Lewis, Bridges George McGibbon
May, Orchard. *See* Langrishe, May Katherine
May, Ren G. *See* Baline, Israel
Mayer, Ferdinand. *See* Brown, Obadiah Bruen
Mayer, T. *See* Balmer, Charles
Mayes, Ethel. *See* Moore, Monette
Mayfair. *See* McCollin, Frances
Mayfield, Audalene. *See* Pace, Adger McDavid
Mayfield, Menlo. *See* Hagen, J(ohn) M(ilton)
Mayhew, Gus. *See* Mayhew, Wendell
Mayn, Manni. *See* Gätjens, Manfred
Maynard, Buddy. *See* Ferguson, Maynard
Maynard, Doris. *See* Hall, Fred(erick) Fifield
Maynard, Walter. *See* Beale, (Thomas) Willert
Mayne, Leslie. *See* Monckton, (John) Lionel (Alexander)
Mayne, Richard. *See* Treharne, Bryceson
Mayo, Cass. *See* Stevens, Casandra (Mayo)
Mayor, Edouard. *See* Bliss, P(hilip) Paul
Mayor, F. S. *See* Bliss, P(hilip) Paul
Mays, Grace. *See* Dellafield, Henry
Maywood, George. *See* Schleiffarth, George (Maywood)
Mazzaferro, Giorgio. *See* Farfaro, Nicolò
Mbarga, Prince Nico. *See* Mbarga, Nicholas
McAfee, Billy. *See* Slaughter, M(arion) T(ry)
McAfee, Bob. *See* Slaughter, M(arion) T(ry)
McAfee, Carlos. *See* Slaughter, M(arion) T(ry)
McAfee, Carlos B. *See* Robison, Carson J(ay)
McAllister David. *See* Wood, Douglas Albert
McAlpin, Vic. *See* McAlpin, Vernice Johnson
McAnally, Mac. *See* McAnally, Lyman, Jr.
McArkin, Alan. *See* Arkin, Alan (Wolf)
McAuley, N(eal) A. *See* Gabriel, Charles H(utchinson)
McAuliffe, Big Slim. *See* McAuliffe, Harry C(larence)
McAuliffe, Eleanor H. *See* Fort, Eleanor H(ankins)
McBrien, Rod. *See* McBrien, Roger Ralph
McCain, Boogie. *See* McCain, Jerry
McCall, C. W. *See* Fries, William [or Bill] (D.)
McCall, Cash. *See* Dollison, Maurice [or Morris], Jr.
McCall, Craig. *See* Rasley, John M.
McCall, J. P(etter). *See* Dawson, Peter (Smith)
McCall, John. *See* Rasley, John M.
McCarthy, Gene. *See* David, Worton
McCarthy, Gene. *See* Wright, Lawrence

McCarthy, Joseph. *See* Green Phil(ip)
McCarthy, Pat. *See* McCarthy, Charles J.
McClain, Charly. *See* McClain, Charlotte Denise
McClaskey, Shamus. *See* McClaskey, Harry Haley
McClintic, Gar(r)y. *See* McClintic, Lambert Gerhardt, Jr.
McClintock, Mac. *See* McClintock, Harry (K(irby))
McClure. *See* Pelosi, Domonic [or Don]
McCorn, John. *See* Rettenbacher, Johann Anton
McCoy, Big Joe. *See* McCoy, Joe
McCoy, Bullfighter. *See* McCoy, Paul Bunyan
McCoy, Cyclone. *See* McCoy, Robert Jesse
McCoy, Jim. *See* Hansson, Stig (Axel)
McCoy, Minnie. *See* Douglas, Lizzie
McCoy, Robert Edward. *See* McCoy, Robert Jesse
McCoy, Robert Lee. *See* McCollum, Robert Lee
McCoy, Wilber [or Wilbur]. *See* McCoy, Joe
McCreery, Bud. *See* McCreery, Walker William, 3rd
McCurdy, John H. *See* Riegger, Wallingford (Constantin)
McDaniel, Ellas [or Elias]. *See* Bates, (Otha) Ellas [or Elias]
McDavid, Pal. *See* Chusid, Irwin
McDermott, Dermot. *See* Bax, (Sir) Arnold Edward Trevor
McDonald, Ed. *See* Keller, Edward McDonald
McDonald, Skeets. *See* McDonald, Enos (William)
McDougal, Dwarf. *See* Lennon, John (Winston)
McDow, Peevy. *See* McDow, William Dayton
McDuff, (Brother) Jack. *See* McDuffy, Eugene
McFather. *See* Brown, Timothy
McGear, Mike. *See* McCartney, Peter Michael
McGehen, Ken. *See* Ives, Burl(e Icle) (Ivanhoe)
McGehen, Ken. *See* Swann, Helen
McGhee, Brownie. *See* McGhee, Walter Brown
McGhee, Globetrotter. *See* McGhee, Granville H.
McGhee, Stick(s). *See* McGhee, Granville H.
McGibbon, Bridges George. *See* Lewis, Bridges George McGibbon
McGlynn, Christopher. *See* Ginder, Richard
McGowan, Annie. *See* Gallimore, Rosan(ne)
McGowan, Jack. *See* McGowan, John W.
McGrath, Fidgey. *See* McGrath, (David) Fulton
McGriff, Ralston. *See* Huff, Leon
McGuinn, Roger. *See* McGuinn, James [or Jim] (Joseph)
McGuire, Mickey (Himself). *See* Yule, Joe, Jr.
McHouston, Ed. *See* Baker, McHouston
McHugh, Hugh. *See* Philpott, George Vere Hobart
McIntosh, James. *See* Cattanach, James
McIntyre, Maile. *See* Dant, Charles G(ustave)
McKagan, Duff. *See* McKagan, Michael
McKay, Todd. *See* McKalip, M(ansell) B(rown)
McKinley, Bill. *See* Gillum, William McKinley
McLain, Johnny. *See* Lain, John A.
McLaughlin, George. *See* Slaughter, M(arion) T(ry)
McLean, Jackie. *See* McLean, John Lenwood, (Jr.)
McLeod, Red. *See* McLeod, James (P.)
McMahon, Blueblood. *See* McMahon, Andrew
McMillan, E. R. *See* Randolph, Homer Louis, (III)
McMillan, Steve. *See* Schneider, M(anfred)
McPartland, Margaret Marian. *See* Turner, Margaret Marian
McQuaide, George. *See* Barnard, George D(aniel)
McShann, Hootie. *See* McShann, James Columbus
McShann, Jay. *See* McShann, James Columbus
McTell, Blind Willie. *See* McTell, Willie Samuel
McTell, Ralph. *See* May, Ralph
McTier, Eddie. *See* McTell, Willie Samuel
Me. *See* Colchester, (Lady)
Mead, Abigail. *See* Pook, Jocelyn
Meadows, Arthur. *See* Finkelstein, Abe
Meadows, Fred. *See* Gordon, Ben (B.)
Meatloaf [or Meat Loaf]. *See* Aday, Marvin Lee
Mècené, Maurice. *See* Leest, Antonius Maria van
Meco. *See* Monardo, Meco
Media, Jay. *See* Cooke, James Francis
Medicine Man for Your Blues, The. *See* Friedman, Theodore (Leopold)
Medina, Eddie. *See* Huerta, Baldemar G(arza)
Medley, Mat(thew). *See* Aston, Anthony [or Tony]
Medlock, Thomas. *See* Munn, William O.
Mednikoff, Alexandre. *See* Wagness, Bernard
Medusa. *See* Harrison, Susan [or Susie] Frances (née Riley)
Medway, Carol. *See* Felix, Margery [or Marjorie] Edith
Meehan, Tony. *See* Meehan, Daniel
Meek, Joe. *See* Meek, Robert (George)
Megamidget, The. *See* Moore, Dudley (Stuart John)
Megar, Fay. *See* Haga, Frederick Wallace
Megar, Fay. *See* Meyer, John
Meinecke, Charles. *See* Meinecke, Christopher
Meisel. *See* Eybel, Joseph Valentin (Sebastian)
Meissler, Josef. *See* Hutchison, William M(arshall)
Meister, J. *See* Schori, Fritz
Meister, Siegrid. *See* Ernst(-Meister), A(delheid) S(iegrid)
Meister, Titus. *See* Meister, Karl (August)
Mel and Hal. *See* Halévy, Ludovic
Mel and Hal. *See* Meilhac, Henri
Mel-Bonis. *See* Bonis, Mél(anie) (Hélène)
Melachrino, George. *See* Militiades, George
Melan, Frank. *See* Badura, Jens-Dieter
Melanc(h)thon, Philipp. *See* Schwarzerd, Philipp
Melande. *See* Telemann, Georg Philipp
Melanie. *See* Safka, Melanie
Melante. *See* Telemann, Georg Philipp
Melaro, Jerry. *See* Melaro, H(orton) J(erome) M(artin)
Melaro, Speed. *See* Melaro, H(orton) J(erome) M(artin)
Melba, Artur. *See* Friedmann, Heinrich
Melcher, Terry. *See* Jorden, Terry
Mélesville. *See* Duveyrier, Anne Honoré Joseph

Melfiche, Cola. *See* Falco, Michele (de)
Melford, Austin. *See* Smith, Austin Alfred
Melford, Mark. *See* Smith, George (1851?-1914)
Meliboeus-Hipponax. *See* Lowell, James Russell
Melikow, Loris. *See* Hofmannsthal, Hugo von
Melis, José. *See* Guiu, José Melis
Mellencamp, Cougar. *See* Mellencamp, John (J.)
Mellini, Peter. *See* Drexler, Werner
Mellon, R. K. *See* Bliss, P(hilip) Paul
Mellow Balladeer, The. *See* Williams, Don
Mellow Blues Genius, The. *See* Robinson, Fenton
Melnik, J. *See* Sartorio, Arnoldo
Melnotte, Claude. *See* Kunkel, Charles
Melnotte, Violette. *See* Solomon, Emma
Melo. *See* Alexander, Fitzroy
Melodie, (Ms.). *See* Parker, Ramona
Melodie MC. *See* Lövgren, Kent
Melody Kid, The. *See* Wakeley, James [or Jimmy] Clarence
Melody, Lord. *See* Alexander, Fitzroy
Melody, Lord. *See* Frederick, John
Melody Monarch. *See* Gaskill, Clarence
Meloman. *See* Arnol'd, Yury (Karlovich)
Melomaniac, The. *See* Huneker, James Gibbons
Melomański, Telephon. *See* Sikorski, Józef
Melophile. *See* Métoyen, Jean-Baptiste(-Jacques)
Melos. *See* Weber, Carl Maria von
Melrose, Gladys. *See* Rawlings, Alfred William
Melson, John. *See* Wilkin, Marijohn (née Melson)
Melton, Susan. *See* Egstrom, (Norma) Delores
Melville, Alan. *See* Caverhill, William Melville
Melville, E. B. *See* Engel, Carl
Memel, Chasmindo von. *See* Dach, Simon
Memphis Bleek. *See* Cox, Malik (Deshawn)
Memphis Blues Boy. *See* Nix, Willie
Memphis Flash, The. *See* Presley, Elvis A(a)ron
Memphis Jim. *See* Dorsey, Thomas A(ndrew)
Memphis Mesmerizer, The. *See* Presley, Elvis A(a)ron
Memphis Minnie. *See* Douglas, Lizzie
Memphis Mose. *See* Dorsey, Thomas A(ndrew)
Memphis Slim. *See* Chatman, John Len
Memphis Slim. *See* Davenport, Charles Edward
Menaea. *See* Joseph the Hymnographer
Menander (Apollo). *See* Paine, Thomas
Menantes. *See* Hunold, Christian Friedrich
Menghino del Violoncello, Il. *See* Gabrielli, Domenico
Menier, Alphonse. *See* Rawlings, Charles Arthur
Menucci, Tomasso. *See* Anelli, Angelo
Menz, J(ohn). *See* Kinyon, John L(eroy)
Menzing, Walter. *See* Conzelmann, Hans
Merano, Paul. *See* Hindemith, Paul
Mercadante, Francesco Saverio. *See* Mercadante, Giuseppe Saverio Raffaele
Mercadante, Xavier. *See* Mercadante, Giuseppe Saverio Raffaele
Mercado, Manuel. *See* Green, Phil(ip)
Mercado, Manuel. *See* Paramor, Norman [or Norrie] (William)
Mercer. *See* Cook, William Mercer
Mercer, Joe. *See* Mercer, John(ny) (H(erndon))
Mercer, Will(iam). *See* Cook, William Mercer
Merchant, Mr. (T.). *See* Dibdin, Thomas J(ohn)
Mercier, Jean. *See* Mercer, John(ny) (H(erndon))
Mercotellis, Agasippo. *See* Corvo, Niccolò
Mercotellis, Agasippo. *See* Martoscelli, G(iuseppe)
Mercure. *See* McPhee, Colin (Carhart)
Mercurio, Paul. *See* Rivelli, Pauline
Mercury, Freddie. *See* Bulsara, Farokh [or Frederick]
Meredith, Claude. *See* Harris, Cuthbert
Meredith, Evan. *See* Holbrooke, Joseph [or Josef] (Charles)
Meredith, J. Frank the Poet. *See* MacNamara, Francis [or Frank]
Meredith, Owen. *See* Bulwer-Lytton, Edward Robert
Meredyth, Jean. *See* Slater, David Dick
Mérei, Adolf. *See* Merkl, Adolf
Mer(r)ell, Stan. *See* Stevens, Jack
Merengue Queen, The. *See* Tañón, Olga
Meri, La. *See* Hughes, Russell Meriwether
Meridies, Mr. *See* Boster, Bob
Merindo Fesanio. *See* Pasqualigo, Benedetto
Merit Aton. *See* Scharf-Bauer, Martina
Meritis, F(elix). *See* Mendelssohn(-Bartholdy), Felix
Merle, J(ohn). *See* Isaac, Merle (John)
Merlin, Alfred. *See* Nieman, Alfred
Merlin, Brother. *See* Reuss, Theodor
Merlin, Hugo. *See* Mandlick, H(ugo)
Merlin Peregrinus. *See* Reuss, Theodor
Merlin, Peter. *See* Orloff, Peter
Merman, Joyce. *See* Farmer, Marjorie
Mero, P. W. *See* Orem, Preston Ware
Mero, W. P. *See* Orem, Preston Ware
Méroff. *See* Rillé, Laurent (François Anatole) de
Merrick, David. *See* Margulois, David
Merrill, Buddy. *See* Behunin, Les(lie Merrill, Jr.)
Merrill, Father. *See* Merrill, Abraham D(own)
Merrill, Idaho. *See* Tonning, Merrill D.
Merrill, Les. *See* Behunin, Les(lie Merrill, Jr.)
Merrill, Robert [or Bob]. *See* Lavan, Henry Robert Merrill
Merriman, Sid. *See* Gyldmark, Hugo
Merriwagg, Dr. *See* Vandernan, Thomas
Merriweather, Maceo. *See* Merriweather, Major
Merriweather, Magnus. *See* Talbot, Charles Remington
Merry Music Maker. *See* Baker, Richard (Evans)
Merryman, Dr. *See* Playford, Henry
Mertelius, Elias. *See* Mertel, Elias
Mertens, E. *See* Pütz, Eduard [or Eddy]
Merulo, Claudio. *See* Merlotti, Claudio
Merulus, Claudis. *See* Merlotti, Claudio

Milan, René. *See* Larrouy, Maurice
Milanese, Il. *See* Sammartini, Giovanni Battista
Milanese Bach, The. *See* Bach, Johann Christian
Milani, Roberto. *See* Concina, Roberto
Milano, Tony. *See* Stube, Howard
Milano, U. *See* Gisinger, Albert
Milano, U. *See* Müller, Hugo
Milanov, Dimitri. *See* Ehret, Walter (Charles)
Milanov, Dimitri. *See* Kinsman, Elmer (F(ranklin))
Mile (musikdirektor). *See* Mühle, Nicolaus
Miles, Buddy. *See* Miles, George (Allen)
"Miles Davis" of Bluegrass. *See* Clements, Vasser Carlton
Miles, Garry. *See* Cason, James E.
Miles, Long Gone. *See* Miles, Luke
Miles, Robert. *See* Concina, Roberto
Miley, Bub(ber). *See* Miley, James Wes(t)ley
Milhard, Hough. *See* Müller, Hugo
Milher, (Ange) Édouard. *See* Hermil, (Ange) Édouard
Milhoff. *See* Lutyens, Elizabeth
Millar, Jack. *See* Muller, Jacob
Millbank, Gordon. *See* Yorke, Peter
Miller, Aleck. *See* Ford, Aleck
Miller, Buddy. *See* Miller, Steven Paul
Miller, Chris. *See* Farnon, Dennis
Miller, Eddie. *See* Lisbona, Edward
Miller, Eddie. *See* Müller, Edward Raymond
Miller, Eddie Piano. *See* Lisbona, Edward
Miller, Francis D. *See* Koschinsky, Fritz
Miller, Jack. *See* Cogane, Nelson
Miller, James [or Jimmie]. *See* MacColl, Ewan
Miller, Jay. *See* Miller, J(oseph) D(elton)
Miller, Jim. *See* Moss, Eugene
Miller, Jody. *See* Miller, Myrna Joy
Miller, Krazinsky. *See* Müller, Ernest (Louis [or Ludwig])
Miller, Laura. *See* Crosby, Fanny [i.e., Frances] J(ane)
Miller, M. *See* Müller, Ernest (Louis [or Ludwig])
Miller, Mel. *See* Cohen, Maurice Alfred
Miller, Mel. *See* Hargreaves, Peter
Miller, Piano. *See* Lisbona, Edward
Miller, Ray. *See* Müller, Rainer
Miller, Rice. *See* Ford, Aleck
Miller, Silkk. *See* Miller, Zyshonne
Miller, Spence. *See* Cain, Noble
Miller, Sy. *See* Miller, Seymour
Miller, Taps. *See* Miller, Joseph
Miller, Willie. *See* Ford, Aleck
Millet, Kay. *See* Millet, Kadish
Millie. *See* Youmans, Vincent
Millinder, Lucky. *See* Millinder, Lucius (Venable)
Mills, Alan. *See* Miller, Albert
Mills, Bob. *See* Miller, Robert [or Bob] (Ernst)
Mills, Edward. *See* Chesham, Edward Mills
Mills, Hank. *See* Garrett, Samuel (M.)
Mills, Kerry. *See* Bulch, Thomas Edward
Mills, Kerry. *See* Mills, Frederick Allen
Mills, Pepa. *See* Mills, Josefa Primo
Milltown, Mable. *See* Croger, Frederick Julian
Milner, George. *See* Haass, Hans
Milner, Ralph. *See* Le Clerq, Arthur
Milnes, Rodney. *See* Blumer, Rodney Milnes
Milo, (Justin). *See* Ringleben, Justin, Jr.
Milo, Phil. *See* Puco, Philip V. [or Milo]
Milo-Rega. *See* Haga, Frederick Wallace
Milo-Rega. *See* Ringleben, Justin, Jr.
Milos, Andre. *See* Grosz, Wilhelm [or Will]
Milray, Peter. *See* Stoeckart, Jan
Milsen, Oscar. *See* Mendelsohn, Oscar (Adolf)
Milt, Jupiter. *See* Wüsthoff, Klaus
Milton, J. G. *See* Bliss, P(hilip) Paul
Milton, Percy. *See* Mildbrand, Hans
Mimmo. *See* Scarlatti, (Giuseppe) Domenico
Mimo. *See* Exposito, Homero
Mindnich. *See* Thomas, Hans
Mineo, Art. *See* Mineo, Attilio
Ming, Felix. *See* Kübel, Josef
Mingàn dal viulunzaal. *See* Gabrielli, Domenico
Mingein dal viulunzel. *See* Gabrielli, Domenico
Minghino dal Violoncello. *See* Gabrieli, Domenico
Mingus, Baron. *See* Mingus, Charles
Minhejmer, Adam. *See* Münchheimer, Adam
Minima. *See* Fitzwygram, Augusta Catherine
Minimus. *See* Toplady, Augustus Montague
Minister in the Country. *See* Doddridge, Philip
Minister of Enjoyment, The. *See* Adeniyi, Sunday
Minister of the New New Super Heavy Funk, The. *See* Brown, James
Minkus, Léon. *See* Minkus, Aloysius Ludwig
Minnesota, Paul. *See* Kendis, James
Minnie Pearle. *See* Colley, Sarah Ophelia
Minter, Red. *See* Minter, Iverson
Mira, Paul. *See* Engel, Alexander
Mirac, Frank. *See* Mihalovic, Franz
Mirana. *See* Newton, (Mrs.) William Edward
Miranda, Bob. *See* Miranda, Ralph F(rank)
Mirande, Yves. *See* Le Querrec, Anatole Charles
Mirecourt, Eugène de. *See* Jacquot, Charles Jean Baptiste
Mirédo, Jean. *See* Cocq, Rosine de
Mireille. *See* Hartusch, Mireille
Mirelle, Jean. *See* Vanstreels, René
Miro, Henri. *See* Miro, Enrique
Mirtindo acrejo. *See* Mariani, Giovanni Lorenzo
Misovulgo, Il. *See* Noseda, Aldo
Miss Rhapsody. *See* Wells, Viola (Gertrude)
Misses Campbell. *See* MacDonald, Georgi(n)a
Misses Campbell. *See* Miller, Amourette
Mississippi Big Joe. *See* Williams, Joe Lee
Mississippi Mockingbird, The. *See* Harris, Wynonie

Mitrovský. *See* Linda, Josef
Mixalot, Sir. *See* Ray, Anthony (L.)
Mixed Emotions. *See* Deutscher, Karlheinz
Miyagi, Michio. *See* Wakabe, Nakasuga Kengyo
Mizell, Fonce. *See* Mizell, Alphonso James
Mlaka, Danilo. *See* Vorobkevych, Sydir [or Sidor] (Ivanovych)
Mo. *See* Mokesch, Günter
Moby. *See* Hall, Richard (Melville)
Moderato. *See* Vogt, A(ugustus) S(tephen)
Modern-Day Hymn-Writer, The. *See* Paris, Twila
Modern King of Swing, The. *See* Rajonsky [or Rajonski], Milton Michael
Modern Mozart, The. *See* Korngold, Erich Wolfgang
Modern Saint Cecelia. *See* Crosby, Fanny [i.e., Frances] J(ane)
Modern Wagner, The. *See* Humperdinck, Engelbert
Modernsky. *See* Stravinsky, Igor Fedorovich
Modugno, Domenico. *See* Mare, Polignano
Moelber, Chr. *See* Stelzer-Palm, Joachim
Moeller, Alois. *See* Henrich, C. W.
Moffatt, James. *See* Hughes, Robert J(ames)
Moffitt, Deke. *See* Moffitt, De Loyce W(hite)
Moga, Sorin. *See* Cioroiu, Alexandru Sorin
Mohawk, Essra. *See* Hurvitz, Sandy (E.)
Moho-Nali, (Chief). *See* Keiser, Robert (A(dolph))
Mohr, Halcher. *See* Cooke, (Mrs.) Philip Warren
Möhrens, Theo. *See* Möhrenschlager, Theo
Moinaux, Jules. *See* Moineaux, Joseph Désiré
Moisson, A. *See* Kleindienst, Hans
Mojo. *See* Buford, George
Mokranjas, Stevan. *See* Stojanovic, Stevan
Molbe, H(einrich). *See* Bach, Heinrich (Freiherr von)
Molda, Ralf. *See* Borgh, Ted
Moldova's Greatest Composer. *See* Doga, Eugeniu
Mole, Miff. *See* Mole, Irving Milfred
Molière, (Jean Baptiste). *See* Poquelin, Jean-Baptiste
Molière of Italy, The. *See* Goldoni, Carlo
Moliere of Music, The. *See* Grétry, André Ernest Modeste
Molin, Rafael. *See* De Filippi, Amedeo
Molina, Tirso de. *See* Tellez, Gabriel
Molitor, Alexius. *See* Müller, Johann Adam
Molitor, Fidel. *See* Müller, Fidel
Molitor, Valentin. *See* Müller, Valentin
Moliveri, Emilio. *See* Würmili, Emil
Molldorf, Tino. *See* Strasser, Hugo
Molloy, Mary. *See* Harris, Robert P.
Molloy, Mary. *See* Lee, Albert George
Molnár, Ferenc. *See* Neumann, Ferenc
Moman, Chips. *See* Moman, Lincoln (W.)
Mombach, Julius L. *See* Mombach, Israel Lazarus
Momus. *See* Anzengruber, Ludwig
Momus. *See* Currie, Nicholas
Monache San Ambrosiana. *See* Valesi, Fulgentio
Monacho Cassinensi Euphemiano. *See* Falconi, Placido
Monarch of the Musical Kingdom, The. *See* Handel, Georg Friedrich
Monarino. *See* Monari, Bartolomeo
Monch, Pharoahe. *See* McNair, T.
Moncrieff, William Thomas. *See* Thomas, W(illiam) T(homas)
Mond, Lex. *See* Byers, William [or Billy] (Mitchell)
Mond, Lex. *See* Byers, William [or Billy]
Monday, Michael. *See* Ginder, Richard
Monday, Paul. *See* Gadd, Paul
Mondello, Toots. *See* Mondello, Nuncio
Monder, Alf. *See* Meier-Böhme, Alfons
Mondstein, Christian. *See* Kiessling, Heinz
Money, Eddie. *See* Mahoney, Edward
Mongard, Louis. *See* Goulart, Simon
Mongre, Paul. *See* Hausdorff, Felix
Monguito, 'El Unico. *See* Quian (Manguito), Romón
Monica. *See* Thackwell, Emily M.
Monkhouse, Harry. *See* McKie, Harry
Monochord der Tongrübler. *See* Chladni, Ernst Florens Friedrich
Monopoli, (Giacomo). *See* Insanguine, Giacomo (Antonio Francesco Paolo Michele)
Monosha, Coleman. *See* Lertzman, Carl Myron
Monroe. *See* St. Clair, Floyd J.
Monroe, Margrethe. *See* Isaac, Merle (John)
Monroe, Melissa. *See* Monroe, William [or Bill] (Smith)
Monrose, Rose. *See* Rosenfeld, Monroe H.
Monrou, Daddy. *See* Twardy, Werner
Monroy, Chicles. *See* Monroy, Victor
Mons, (The). *See* Jullien, Louis (George) Antoine (Jules)
Mons, Peter. *See* Richter, Fred
Monsieur Auguste. *See* Hillhouse, Augustus Lucas
Monsieur Chocolate. *See* Armenteros, Alfredo
Monsieur de l'Orchestre, (Un). *See* Mortjé, Arnold [or Adolphe]
Monsieur de l'Orchestre. *See* Zamacoïs, Miguel
Monsieur l'abbe Carbassus. *See* Campion, François
Monsieur le Pavre. *See* Satie, (Alfred) Erik (Leslie)
Monsieur 100,000 Volts. *See* Silly, (Gilbert) François (Léopold)
Monster, Mac. *See* Biermann, Rémon
Monster Pianist. *See* Meyer, Leopold von
Montagu(e), Edward [or Eduard]. *See* Day, Frederick E(dward) (Montagu)
Montague, James. *See* Sawyer, Henry S.
Montaine, A. R. *See* Keiser, Robert (A(dolph))
Montaine, R. A. *See* Keiser, Robert (A(dolph))
Montana, Patsy. *See* Blevins, Ruby(e) (Rebecca)
Montana Slim. *See* Carter, Wilf(red Arthur Charles)
Montand, Yves. *See* Livi, Ivo [or Yvo]
Montanus, Johann. *See* Vom Berg, Johann
Montbars, Georges. *See* Gignoux, Régis

Monte-Rotondo, Prince. *See* Poniatowski, Joseph Michel Xavier François Jean
Monteath, James. *See* MacCulloch, James Monteath
Monteith, A(lice). *See* Crosby, Fanny [i.e., Frances] J(ane)
Montella, Mico. *See* Montella, Giovan(ni) Domenico
Montenelli, Bernardo. *See* Haltenberger, Johann Nikolaus
Montgomery, Buddy. *See* Montgomery, Charles F.
Montgomery, Kent. *See* Rasley, John M.
Montgomery, Little Brother. *See* Montgomery, Eurreal Wilford
Monti, Diana. *See* Kazoreck, Hildegard
Monti, Francesco. *See* Ringgenberg, Jörg
Montillana, J. de. *See* Hernandez Gonzalez, Gabriel
Montogueil, Georges. *See* Lebesque, Octave
Montovano, Alberto. *See* Ripa, Alberto da
Montrose, Geoffrey. *See* Koepke, Paul
Monty, Carlo. *See* Seelos, Ambros
Monty, Paul. *See* Mantovani, A(nnuzio) P(aolo)
Moody, Ron. *See* Moodnick, Ronald
Moon, Jack. *See* Elliott, John (B.)
Moondog. *See* Hardin, Louis (Thomas)
Moor, Karel. *See* Mohr, Karel
Moore, A. N. *See* Bliss, P(hilip) Paul
Moore, Adam. *See* Soloman, Mirrie (Irma)
Moore, Billy. *See* Feather, Leonard (Geoffrey)
Moore, Buddy. *See* Bernard, Al(fred A.)
Moore, Christy. *See* Moore, Christopher Andrew
Moore, Dwight Gatemouth. *See* Moore, Arnold Dwight
Moore, Emily Jane. *See* Squires, Edna May
Moore, Evalyn. *See* Moore, Eloise Irene
Moore, Gatemouth. *See* Moore, Arnold Dwight
Moore, Harry A. *See* Slaughter, M(arion) T(ry)
Moore, Hartley. *See* Manney, Charles Fonteyn
Moore, Henrietta. *See* Fillmore, (James) Henry
Moore, Joe. *See* Mercer, John(ny) (H(erndon))
Moore, John C., Jr. *See* Mercer, John(ny) (H(erndon))
Moore, Michael. *See* Davis, Katherine K(ennicott)
Moore, Milton. *See* Foster, Stephen Collins
Moore, Moran. *See* Johnson, Charles L(eslie)
Moore, Park. *See* McEwen, (Sir) John Blackwood
Moore, Pete. *See* Moore, Warren (Thomas)
Moore, Phil & Beth. *See* Moore, Luella Lockwood
Moore, Pony. *See* Moore, G(eorge) W(ashington)
Moore, Thelma. *See* Miron, Tsipora
Moore, Trudy. *See* Moore, Eloise Irene
Moore, Whistling Alex. *See* Moore, Alex(ander Herman)
Moore, Wilma. *See* Richter, Ada A.
Moore, Wilton. *See* Monroe, Vaughn (Wilton)
Moorman, J. M. *See* Bliss, P(hilip) Paul
Moose. *See* Clarke, Moussa
Moose John. *See* Walker, John(ny) (Mayon)
Moqué, Georges. *See* Kosma, Joseph
Moraine, Jean. *See* Morandi, Giovanni
Morales, Noro. *See* Morales (Sanabia), Norberto
Moran, Edward. *See* Harris, Cuthbert
Moran, Fred. *See* Sendel, Erich
Moran, John. *See* Newell, Norman
Moran, Mae. *See* Kimbrough, Lottie
Morand, Leonard. *See* Stein, Ronald
Morand, Prosper. *See* Woodhouse, Charles (John)
Morandus, Joannes. *See* Morandi, Giovanni
Moravia, Alberto. *See* Pincherle, Alberto
Morbid, George. *See* Slaughter, M(arion) T(ry)
Mordent, Jerry. *See* Kirchgässner, Helmut
Mordred. *See* Moses, Eleaza Aaron
More, Arno. *See* Grunert, Alfons
Moré, Beny. *See* Moré (Gutiérrez), Bartolomé (Maximiliano)
More, Eldermo. *See* Moore, Arnold Dwight
More, John L. *See* Bridge, Frank
Moreau, de Commagny. *See* Moreau, Charles François (Jean) Baptiste
Morel, Gabriel. *See* Hall, Fred(erick) Fifield
Morel, Jean. *See* Mullen, Frederic
Morel, Jorge. *See* Scibona, Jorge
Morel, Octave. *See* Maillard, Jean
Morelle, Max. *See* Tate, Phyllis (Margaret née Duncan)
Morellio, Joe. *See* Murrells, Joseph
Morely, Charles. *See* Behr, F(ranz)
Moréno, Henri. *See* Heugel, Henri Georges
Moreno, Marcos. *See* Shaffer, Lloyd (M.)
Moreno, Paul. *See* Morin, Paul
Morenzi, E. H. *See* Bradsworth, Samuel
Mores, Marianito [or Mariano]. *See* Martínez, Marianito [or Mariano] (A(lberto))
Moret, Neil. *See* Daniels, Charles N(eil)
Moreton, H. R. *See* Mortimer, Harry
Morey, Elizabeth. *See* Cain, Noble
Morfida. *See* Ralph, Katherine [or Kate] (née Roberts)
Morgan, Bruce. *See* Hueston, Billy
Morgan, Charlie. *See* Lindberg, Charles Arthur
Morgan, Guy. *See* Stellman, Marcel
Morgan, Hannah May. *See* Dickinson, Hannah May
Morgan, J. P. *See* Keiser, Robert (A(dolph))
Morgan, John A. *See* Farmer, Marjorie
Morgan, Lady (Sydney). *See* Owenson, Sydney
Morgan, Lorrie. *See* Morgan, Loretta Lynn
Morgan, Manfred. *See* Edelmann, Rudi
Morgan, Max. *See* Lees, Frederick Eugene John
Morgan, McKayla (K.). *See* Basile, Gloria Vitanza
Morgan, Michaela (K.). *See* Basile, Gloria Vitanza
Morgan, Misty. *See* Blanchard, Maryanne
Morgan, Piero. *See* Piccioni, Piero
Morgener, Jörg. *See* Köchel, Jürgen (Arthur)
Morin, Charles. *See* Crabbé, Armand (Charles)
Morin, Pierre. *See* Mills, Frederick Allen

Moulton, Charles. *See* Cain, Noble
Moulton, James. *See* Cain, Noble
Moulton, Joseph. *See* Cain, Noble
Moulton, Victor. *See* Grady, R(ichard) G.
Mount, Julian. *See* Hutchison, William M(arshall)
Mountjoy. *See* Money(-Coutts), Francis Burdett (Thomas Money(-Coutts), Nevill)
Mouscardin. *See* Civinini, Guelfo
Mousetrap Builder, The. *See* Crosby, Harry Lillis
Mouton, Ferdinand. *See* La Menthe, Ferdinand Joseph
Mowbray. *See* Wheeler, Andrew Carpenter
Moya. *See* Vicars, Harold
Moyet, Al(l)ison. *See* Moyet, Genevieve
Mozart. *See* Truhn, Friedrich Hieronymus
Mozart, (Johann Chrysostom) Wolfgang Amadeus. *See* Casadesus, Marius Robert Max
Mozart, (Johann Chrysostom) Wolfgang Amadeus. *See* Zulehner, Carl [or Charles]
Mozart, (Johann Chrysostom) Wolfgang Amadeus (Spirit). *See* Brown, Rosemary (née Dickeson)
Mozart, Nannerl. *See* Mozart, Maria Anna
Mozart of Contemporary Music. *See* Pleskow, Raoul
Mozart of Jazz. *See* Parker, Charles [or Charlie] (Christopher, Jr.)
Mozart of the Champs-Elysées. *See* Eberst, Jacob
Mozart of the Nineteenth Century, The. *See* Mendelssohn(-Bartholdy), Felix
Mozart of the Romantic Era The. *See* Mendelssohn(-Bartholdy), Felix
Mozart, Wolferl. *See* Mozart, Wolfgang Amadeus
Mozart, Wolfgang Amadeus. *See* Mozart, Franz Xaver Wolfgang
Mozartian. *See* Mozart, Wolfgang Amadeus
Mozeneiko, D. *See* Savino, Domenico
Mr. is interfiled with *Mister*
Ms Melodie. *See* Parker, Ramona
Muck. *See* Schulze-Gerlach, Hartmut
Mud Dauber Joe. *See* McCoy, Joe
Muddy Waters. *See* Morganfield, McKinley
Mude, O. *See* Gorey, Edward (St. John)
Muehling, Carl [or Karl]. *See* Fisher, Ethel
Mueller, August. *See* Goerdeler, Richard
Mueller, Edward [or Eddie]. *See* Severson, Edward Louis, III
Mühlfeld, Louis. *See* Bermann, Moritz
Muir, Lewis F. *See* Meuer, Louis F.
Mulder, Herman. *See* Mulder, Johannes Hermanus
Mullen, Frederic. *See* Rawlings, Alfred William
Müller, Adolf. *See* Schmid, Matthias
Müller, August. *See* Goerdeler, Richard
Muller, Hermann von. *See* Bonner, Carey
Müller, Ludwig. *See* Waldmüller, Ludwig
Müller, Reinhard. *See* Roland, Reiny
Mullican, Moon. *See* Mullican, Aubrey Wilson
Mulligan, Arizona. *See* Ringleben, Justin, Jr.
Mumbles. *See* Horton, Walter
Münchberg, Franz von. *See* Bonn, Franz
Mund, E. D. *See* Lorenz, E(dmund) S(imon)
Munday, Gilbert. *See* Dawson, Peter (Smith)
Mundy. *See* Enright, Edmund
Munich's Favorite Son. *See* Strauss, Richard
Munk, J. *See* Krićka, Jaroslav
Munk, J. *See* Krićka, P(etr)
Murbach, Hans. *See* Storck, Karl G(ustav) L(udwig)
Murdock, Jane. *See* Roobenian, Amber
Murphy, Buck. *See* Whitcomb, Ian (Timothy)
Murphy, Pat. *See* Bernard, Clem(ent)
Murphy, Spud. *See* Murphy, Lyle
Murphy, Turk. *See* Murphy, Melvin E(dward) (Alton)
Murray, Bert. *See* Slezinger, Herbert Edwin
Murray, Herbert Edwin. *See* Slezinger, Herbert Edwin
Murray, John. *See* Pfeferstein, John
Murray, Lyn. *See* Breeze, Lionel
Murray, Mitch. *See* Stitcher, L(ionel) Michael
Murray, Ted. *See* Mencher, (T.) Murray
Murretti, Carlo. *See* Newell, Joseph Edward
Murtha, Fred. *See* Gershvin, Jacob
Musa, Anthonius. *See* West, Anthonius
Musa Novarese, La. *See* Leonarda, Anna Isabella
Musard, Great. *See* Musard, Philippe
Musard, Napoleon. *See* Musard, Philippe
Muse, A. E. A. *See* Blackmar, A(rmand) E(dward)
Muse, Rabbit. *See* Muse, Lewis Anderson
Musgrave, Frank. *See* Bonner, Francis Musgrave
Music, David. *See* Gordon, David M.
Music Director, The. *See* Dorn, Heinrich (Ludwig Egmont)
Music Hall Shakespeare, The. *See* Pot(ts), Victor Léon
Music Man. *See* Willson, (Robert Reiniger) Meredith
Music Man of the 1970s, The. *See* Bacharach, Burt (F.)
Musical Architect, The. *See* Humfeld, Charles
Musical Chameleon, A. *See* Strauss, Johann (Baptist) (1804-1849)
Musical Citizen of the World. *See* Tcherepnin, Alexander
Musical Clothier — Nothing More or Less. *See* Kern, Jerome David
Musical Critic, A. *See* Hueffer, Francis
Musical Giant, The. *See* Stravinsky, Igor Fedorovich
Musical Matthew Arnold of the Confederacy. *See* Lanier, Sidney
Musical Professor, A. *See* Holmes, Edward
Musical Small-Coal Man, The. *See* Britton, Thomas
Musical Student, A. *See* Bacon, Richard MacKenzie
Musical Von Tirpitz of Germany, The. *See* Schoenberg, Arnold
Musicescu, Gavriil. *See* Musychenko, Gavriil Vakulovich
Musician, A. *See* Bax, (Sir) Arnold Edward Trevor
Musician, The. *See* Bull, Ole (Bornemann)

Music's Prophet. *See* Monteverdi, Claudio
Musin. *See* Furlanetto, Bonaventura
Mussorgsky of Greece, The. *See* Khu(-Elefteriadis), Emilios
Mussulli, Boots. *See* Mussulli, Henry W.
Mustal, Ch. G. *See* Clutsam, George Howard
Mute, A. *See* Chorley, Henry Fothergill
Mütter, Bertl. *See* Mütter, Herbert George
Mutzenbacher, Josefine. *See* Salzmann, Siegmund
Mwandishi. *See* Hancock, Herbert [or Herbie] Jeffrey
Myers, Paul P. *See* Kunkel, Charles
Myers, Richard. *See* Myers, Richardson
Myers, Sherman. *See* Ewing, Montague (George)
Myk, John. *See* Grunert, Alfons
Mykhajlowsky, Mykhajlo. *See* Goldstein, Mikhail Emmanuilovich (1917-1989)
Myles, Alannah. *See* Byles, Alannah
Myll, Ben. *See* Bánffy, (Count) (Domokos Pál) Miklós
mylla, h. c. *See* Müller, H. C.
Mynyddog. *See* Davies, Richard
Myrot, André. *See* Liebling, Georg(e)
Mysnik, Sol. *See* Slonimsky, Nicholas
Mysterious Rhinestone Cowboy, The. *See* Coe, David Allan
Mystery, Mr. *See* Blount, Herman
Mystifizinsky. *See* Vischer, Friedrich Theodor von
Mystikal. *See* Tyler, Michael

– N –

N***. *See* Boieldieu, François Adrien
N***. *See* Isouard, Nicolas
N***. *See* Kreutzer, Rodolphe
N***. *See* Méhul, Etienne Nicolas
N. H. *See* Hall, (Christopher) Newman
N. H. *See* Heins, Nicholas
N. H. *See* Herman, Nikolaus [or Nicolaus]
N. N. F. *See* Moultrie, Gerard
N. T. P. R. *See* Tourneaux, Nicolas le
N. von K. *See* Ernst, II, Duke of Sax-Coburg-Gotha
Nachèz, Tivadar. *See* Naschitz, Theodor
Nacho, Tata. *See* Fernández Esperón, Ignacio
Nadine, Shorty. *See* Cole, Nathaniel Adams
Nadir, (Isaac) Moishe. *See* Reiss, Isaac
Naed, Alice. *See* Dean, Celia
Nagan, Tsevi. *See* Neugarten, Zvi Herbert
Nagan, Zvi Herbert. *See* Neugarten, Zvi Herbert
Nagy, Ferenz. *See* Ludwig, Carl (F.)
Nail, Jimmy. *See* Bradford, James
Nairne, Baroness. *See* Oliphant, Carolina
Nakasuga (Kengyo). *See* Wakabe, Nakasuga Kengyo
Naksok. *See* Sung-Tai, Kim
Nalod, Charles. *See* Dolan, Charles P.
Nambuat. *See* Taubman, Otto
Nambuat. *See* Taubmann, Horst
Nameless, Virgil. *See* Dankworth, John(ny)
Nameth, Martha J. *See* Bachman, Martha Jean
Namib, Swako. *See* Biermann, Rémon
Nannerl. *See* Mozart, Maria Anna
Nano S. *See* Suratno, Nano
Nantlais. *See* Williams, William N(antlais)
Nanton, Sam. *See* Nanton, Joseph [or Joe]
Nanton, Tricky Sam. *See* Nanton, Joseph [or Joe]
Nanumi, Tomio. *See* Suma, Yosaku
Napier, James. *See* Justis(s), William [or Bill] (E(verette?)), (Jr.)
Napoleon, Art. *See* Sudhalter, Richard M(errill)
Napoleon Dynamite. *See* McManus, Declan Patrick (Aloysius)
Napoleon XIV. *See* Samuels, Jerry
Napoleón, José Maria. *See* Ruiz Narváez, José Napoleón
Napoleon of Music, The. *See* Rossini, Giacchino (Antonio)
Napoleon of Opera, The. *See* Spontini, Gasparo [or Gaspare] (Luigi Pacifico)
Napoleon of the Waltz. *See* Strauss, Johann (Baptist), (Jr.) (1825-1899)
Narvel the Marvel. *See* Felts, (Albert) Narvel
Nas. *See* Jones, Nasir (Bin Olu Dara)
Nash, B. A. *See* Banash, Joseph
Nash, Lemon. *See* Nash, Lemoine
Nash, Nathaniel Richard. *See* Nusbaum, Nathaniel Richard
Nashville Storyteller. *See* Hall, Thomas
Nason, David. *See* Wagness, Bernard
Nasty Nas. *See* Jones, Nasir (Bin Olu Dara)
Natale, Tito. *See* Rawlings, Alfred William
Natalie. *See* Ellwood, Florence
Natchez. *See* Broonzy, William Lee Conley
Nate Dogg. *See* Hale, Nathaniel (D(awayne))
Nathan, El(ias). *See* Whittle, (Major) D(aniel) W(ebster)
Nathan, Lane. *See* Cohen, Lane Nathan
Nati. *See* Natividad Martinez, José
National Poet, (The). *See* Shemer, Naomi
National Poet of the South. *See* Macarthy, Harry B.
Native American Yanni, The. *See* LaRoche, Paul
Nato. *See* Orshan, Nate
Nature Boy (from Brooklyn). *See* Ahbez, Eden
Nature Boy. *See* Cole, Nathaniel Adams
Naty. *See* Natividad Martinez, José
Naumann, G(iovanni) A(madeo). *See* Naumann, Johann Gottlieb
Naumann, Johann Amadeus. *See* Naumann, Johann Gottlieb
Nautilus, A. *See* Seeman, Arthur
Nava. *See* Barrera, Rodolfo
Nava, Franz. *See* Minasi, Carlo
Nava, Franz. *See* Rimbault, Edward Francis

Navarovský, V. *See* Svoboda, Václav Alois
Navarre, Jean. *See* Fisher, Ethel
Navarre, Jean. *See* Kern, Carl Wilhelm
Navarro, Chico. *See* Mitnik, Bernardo
Navarro, Chucho. *See* Navarro Moreno, José de Jesús
Navarro, Jean. *See* Kern, Carl Wilhelm
Navarro, Martin. *See* Azpilcueta, Martin (de)
Navarrus, (Martinus). *See* Azpilcueta, Martin (de)
Navillus, (Nace). *See* Sullivan, Joseph
Navoigille (the younger). *See* Julien, Herbert
Nawrazek, E. *See* Kronke, Emil
Ndegé-Ocello, Me'shell. *See* Johnson, Michelle [or Me'shell] (Lynn)
Neapolitanus Francus. *See* Elsbeth, Thomas
Neat, John. *See* Mullen, Frederic
Nebbish, Ocher. *See* Begleiter, Lionel
Neckbones. *See* Short, J. D.
Neckniz, (Hans Friedrich August). *See* Zincken, Hans Friedrich August
Needen, Frank. *See* Paasch, Leopold (Wolfram)
Needersohn, Jacob. *See* Paramor, Norman [or Norrie] (William)
Neff, Morton [or Morty]. *See* Weinstein, Morton (Neff)
Negligente, Il. *See* Notari, Angelo
Negrano Schori, Jenny. *See* Gruenberg, Janeta
Negro Cele, El. *See* Flores, Celedonio (Esteban)
Negro Fato. *See* Guzmán Yañez, Enrique
Negro, Héctor. *See* Varela, Ismal Héctor
Negro Poet Laureate, The. *See* Dunbar, Paul Laurence
Negro "Stephen Foster," The. *See* Bland, James A(llen)
Nehemiah Dim-Eye. *See* Carey, Henry
Neil, N. Mac. *See* Calloway, Cab(ell), III
Neilson, Francis. *See* Butters, Francis
Nelius, Louis. *See* Wilde, Cornel (L(ouis)
Nellah. *See* Allen, H. (of Birmingham)
Nelli, Jacopo Anigoti. *See* Federico, Gen(n)aro Antonio
Nelly. *See* Haynes, Cornell, (Jr.)
Nelson, Abbott Willie. *See* Nelson, Willie (Hugh)
Nelson, Charles. *See* Slaughter, M(arion) T(ry)
Nelson, Country Willi. *See* Nelson, Willie (Hugh)
Nelson, David. *See* Levin, Joseph A.
Nelson, David. *See* Miller, David Nelson
Nelson, Dyer. *See* Spitzer, Cordelia
Nelson, Harry. *See* Martin, Ray(mond)
Nelson, Julio Jorge. *See* Rosofsky, Isaac
Nelson, Maynard. *See* Josephs, Wilfred
Nelson, Ozzie. *See* Nelson, Oswald George
Nelson, Portia. *See* Nelson, Betty Mae
Nelson, Red. *See* Wilborn, Nelson
Nelson, Rick. *See* Nelson, Eric Hilliard
Nelson, Romeo. *See* Nelson, Iromeio
Nelson, Ronnie. *See* Niedhammer, Ronald Edward
Nelson, Rudolf. *See* Lewysohn, Rudolf
Nelson, Sandy. *See* Egnatzik, Joseph (P.)
Nelson, Will. *See* Reggio, Emilo
Nelson, William. *See* Murgi, Gino (Giuseppe)
Nelsor, Fred. *See* Rosendorff, Emil
Nelyubov, L. *See* Larosh, German Avgustovich
Nembri, Damianus. *See* Nembri, Octavianus
Nemo. *See* Piccolomini, Theodore (Auguste Maria Joseph)
Nemzo, Lisa. *See* Nemtzow, Lisa
Nenarb, Jeff T. *See* Branen, Jeff T.
Neologos. *See* Quantz, Johann Joachim
Nephelius, David. *See* Wolkenstein, David
Nero, Paul. *See* Doldinger, Klaus
Nero, Paul. *See* Polnarioff, Kurt
Nero, Peter (Bernard). *See* Nierow, (Peter) Bernard
Nerval, Gérad de. *See* Labrunie, Gérard
Nervius. *See* Léonard(us) (le père)
Nervius, Leonard(us). *See* Musel, Corneilli
Neruda, (Vlademir de). *See* Kern, Carl Wilhelm
Nesmüller, Josef Ferdinand. *See* Müller, Josef Ferdinand
Ness, Clarke Van. *See* Clark, C(yrus) Van Ness
Nessl, Erich. *See* Kneissler, Hipp.
Nesvadba, Joseph. *See* Hamácek, Joseph
Nettle, H(umphrey). *See* Jackson, William (1730-1893)
Netz, Paul. *See* Billig, (Julius Karl) Gustav
Neuber, Christian Ludwig. *See* Nicolai, (Christoph) Friedrich
Neuman, M. *See* Cohn, Chester
Neun, Wilfred von der. *See* Schöpff, Friedrich Wilhelm Traugott
Neuner, Robert. *See* Buhre, Werner (Bernhard Hermann)
Neustein, Rudolf. *See* Könnemann, Artur (Eduard Theophil)
Neuville, Martin Joseph la. *See* Adrien, Martin Joseph
Nevada Slim. *See* Turner, Dallas (E.)
Nevermind, Alexander. *See* Nelson, Prince Rogers
Nevers, C. O. *See* Converse, Charles C(rozat)
Neville, C. *See* Challoner, Neville Butler
Neville, Naomi. *See* Toussaint, Allen (R.)
Neville, Oscar. *See* Carr, F(rank) Osmond
Neville, Tom. *See* Kaufman, Isidore
Nevin, Mark. *See* Levin, Morris Albert
Nevini, Nero. *See* Schneegass, Klaus-Peter
New Age Keyboard Maestro. *See* Chryssomallis, Yanni
New Bird, The. *See* Adderley, Julian Edwin
New Bob Dylan, The. *See* Lind, Bob
New Bob Dylan, The. *See* Wainwright, Loudon, III
New Crown Prince of Country Music. *See* Traywick, Randy (Bruce)
New Dylan, The. *See* Prine, John
New Dylan, The. *See* Springsteen, Bruce (Frederick Joseph)
New Empress of the Blues. *See* Brown, Olive
New England March King. *See* Hall, R(obert) B(rowne)

New England Pastor, A. *See* Kirk, Edward N.
New March King. *See* Paull, E(dward) T(aylor)
New Mozart, A. *See* Köselitz, (Johann) Heinrich
New Orleans Beau. *See* LeBeau, Robert, Jr.
New Orleans Dynamo. *See* Guzzo, Francis
New Soul Queen. *See* Brown, Angela Laverne
New Sweethearts of Country Music, The. *See* Mosby, John(ny) (R.)
New Sweethearts of Country Music, The. *See* Shields, Janice Irene (see under Mosby, John(ny) (R.))
New Timon, The. *See* Bulwer-Lytton, Edward Robert
New Valentino, The. *See* Iglesias, Julio
New Waltz King. *See* Rieu, André
Newark, Godfrey. *See* Elliott, Percy
Newbury, Mickey. *See* Newbury, Milton S(im), (Jr.)
Newcombe, Jeffrey. *See* Kinsman, Elmer F(ranklin)
Newell, Frederick. *See* Shackley, Frederick (Newell)
Newell, Roy. *See* Raymond, Harold (Newell)
Newland, Rens. *See* Nieuwland, Rens
Newlon, Jack. *See* Newlon, Richard
Newman, Ernest. *See* Roberts, William (Amos)
Newman, Joel. *See* Ledbetter, Huddie (William)
Newman, Pappy. *See* Newman, Alfred
Newman, Randy. *See* Newman(n), Gary
Newport, Fred. *See* Neupert, Fritz
Newton, Edward [or Eddie]. *See* Bliss, P(hilip) Paul
Newton, Francis. *See* Hobsbawm, Eric (John Ernest)
Newton, Frank Ernest. *See* Bonner, Carey
Newton, Juice. *See* Cohen, Judy Kay(e)
Newton of Harmony, The. *See* Rameau, Jean Philippe
Newton of Music. *See* Bach, Johann Sebastian
Newton, Stu. *See* Whitcomb, Ian (Timothy)
Nez. *See* Nesmith, Michael
Nicaeus, Alardus. *See* Gaucquier, Alard (Dunoyer du)
Nicander. *See* Williams, Morris
Nice, W. *See* Heath, John
Niceno, Faresio. *See* Gatta, Antonio
Nicholas, Don. *See* DeCollibus, Nicholas
Nicholas, François. *See* Crouch, Frederick (William) Nicholls
Nicholas, Paul. *See* Beuselinck, Paul Oscar
Nicholls, Horatio. *See* Wright, Lawrence
Nicholls, J. H. *See* Wright, Lawrence
Nichols, John. *See* Klohr, John N(icholas)
Nichols, Leo. *See* Morricone, Ennio
Nichols, Red. *See* Nichols, (Ernest) Loring
Nickel von Hof. *See* Decius, Nikolaus
Nickerson, Hammie. *See* Davis, Hammie
Nicks, Stevie. *See* Nicks, Stephanie (Lynn)
Nico, (Krista). *See* Pa(e)ffgen, Christa
Nico, Dr. *See* Nicholas, Kasanda Wa Mikalay
Nicolai, Sven. *See* Röhl, Uwe
Nicolas, (Jean). *See* Felgen, Camillo
Nicolaus de Radom. *See* Radomski, Mikolaj
Nicole. *See* Laval Soza, Denise Lillian
Nicole. *See* Seibert, Nicole
Nicolette. *See* Okoh, Nicolette
Nicolò (de Malte). *See* Isouard, Nicolas
Nicolson, Ross. *See* Green, Phil(ip)
Nicolson, Ross. *See* Paramor, Norman [or Norrie] (William)
Niederholtzer, Rupert. *See* Unterholtzer, Rupert
Niel, Herms. *See* Nielebock, Hermann
Nield, Ernest. *See* Kraushaar, Charles
Nielson, Raymond. *See* Fisher, Ethel
Niemczyk, Waclaw. *See* Warlop, Michael
Nieve, Bola de. *See* Villa, Ignacio
Nigello Preteo. *See* Braccioli, Grazio
Night Owl. *See* Kilgore, David
Night Tripper. *See* Rebennack, Malcolm [or Mac] (John)
Nighthawk, Robert. *See* McCollum, Robert Lee
Nightingale, The. *See* Maal, Baaba
Nightingale, Fred. *See* Hatch, Anthony [or Tony] (Peter)
Nightingale of the Pacific. *See* Pindell, Annie Pauline
Nijasi. *See* Chamsa, Chakim-sade
Nijazi. *See* Tagi-zade-Hajibeyov, Nijazi Zul'fugarovich
Niklas, Ferry. *See* Jungk, Klaus
Nile, Willie. *See* Noonan, Robert (A.)
Nilles, Catfish. *See* Nilles, Brad
Nilles, Lynne. *See* Voorlas, Lynn Connie
Niloff, Arthur. *See* Schenker, Heinrich
Nilsson, Harry. *See* Nelson, Harry Edward
Niman, Fyodor Augustovich. *See* Fyodorov, Fyodor Augustovich
Nimbly, John. *See* Nerijnen, Jan van
Nims, Willa. *See* Cain, Noble
Nino. *See* Weber, Michel
Niño de Sabicas. *See* Castellon, Augustin
Ninot le Petit. *See* Baltazar, Johannes
Nippon, A. *See* Lautensclāger, Willi
Nipredi. *See* Pedrini, Teodorico
Nisard, Théodore. *See* Normand, Théodule Elzéar Xavier
Nishadba, Gyan. *See* Netzle, Klaus
Nissi Belzer. *See* Spivak, Nissan
Nissi Berdichever. *See* Spivak, Nissan
Nissi Kishinever. *See* Spivak, Nissan
Nita. *See* Rawlings, Charles Arthur
Nitzsche, Jack. *See* Nitzsche, Bernard (Alfred)
Nivert, Taffy. *See* Danoff, Mary Catherine
Nivlyansky, Grigory Andreyevich. *See* Lishin, Grigory Andreyevich
Nixon, Hammie. *See* Davis, Hammie
Niyazi. *See* Khadzhibekov, Taghi-zade
Nizel, A. *See* Tansley, Alfred
No Name. *See* Burleigh, Cecil (Edward)
No Show Jones. *See* Jones, George (G(len(n))
Noa. *See* Nini, Achinoam
Noack, Eddie. *See* Noack, Armona A., (Jr.)

Nobile Genovese. *See* Pinello (di Ghirardi), Giovanni Battista
Nobile Palermitano. *See* Sigismondo da Jenne
Noble, Arthur. *See* Shelton, Travis
Noble, Eric. *See* Frangkiser, Carl (Moerz)
Noble, Nick. *See* Valkan, Nick
Noble of d'Dluik and Rouhans. *See* Csermák, Antol [or Anthony] György [or George]
Nobles, Oliver. *See* Munn, William O.
Nobody. *See* Hays, Will(iam) S(hakespeare)
Nocella. *See* Mathei, Nicolas Savini
Noe-Jean. *See* Jullien, Louis (George) Antoine (Jules)
Noe, Pierre De La. *See* Leroyer, Pierre
Noel. *See* Armitage, Reginald Moxon
Noel, (Mr.). *See* Lebègue, Nicolas
Noel, Art. *See* Sugarman, Harry
Noel, F. E. *See* Metcalf, Leon (Vinnedge)
Noel, J. C. *See* Thomas, Peter
Noel, Kay. *See* Stevens, Jack
Nogero, Francesco [or Francisco] di. *See* Bauer, Emilie Frances
Nohcor, Alfred. *See* Rochon, Alfred
Nohnn, Joel. *See* Lennon, John (Winston)
Noir, A. *See* Blackmar, A(rmand) E(dward)
Noiz, Nick. *See* Becker, Tobias
Nolan, Bob [or Robert]. *See* Nobles, Clarence Robert
Nolan, Dixie. *See* Scruggs, Irene
Noldman, Benjamin. *See* Knigge, Adolf Franz Friedrich Ludwig, Freiherr von
Nolinsky, N(ikolai Mihalovich). *See* Skriabin, Nikolai (Mikhailovich)
Nomabama, Adam. *See* Barnes, Edwin Shippen
Nomabama, Adam. *See* Matthews, Harry Alexander
Nomabama, Adam. *See* Matthews, John Sebastian
Nomabama, Adam. *See* Noble, Thomas Tertius
Nomis, Lou. *See* Simon, William Louis
Nomlas. *See* Sallmon, Alfred
Nonacrina, Dorina. *See* Tron Dolfin, Caterina
Nonacrio, Filedo. *See* Totis, Giuseppe Domenico de
Noncents. *See* Zazueta, Zachary
Nonka, Friedel. *See* Nonn, Karl-Heinz
Nonnahs, Laurence B. *See* Royce, James (Stanley)
Nonpareils, The. *See* Cannon, Anthony J.
Nonpareils, The. *See* Harrigan, Edward [or Ned]
Noolas, Rab. *See* Heseltine, Philip (Arnold)
Noor, Thomas Shabda. *See* Wirtel, Thomas Kemper
Noorden, (Dr.) P. van. *See* Rebling, Eberhard (Gerhard)
Norbert, Frank. *See* Schultze, Norbert (Arnold Wilhelm Richard)
Nord, Lucy. *See* Retter, Louis
Norden, Leo. *See* Aletter, Wilhelm
Norder, Al. *See* Héger, Attila
Nordmann, Richard. *See* Langkammer, Margarethe
Nordmann, Rudolph [or Rudolf]. *See* Harris, George F(rederick)
Nordstrom, Christine (Carter). *See* Kunkel, Charles
Noren, Heinrich G(ottlieb). *See* Gottlieb, Heinrich Suso Johannes
Norge, Bert. *See* Schmitz, Robby
Noriac, Jules. *See* Cairon, Claude Antoine Jules
Noricus, Johannes. *See* Agricola, Johannes
Nork, F(r). *See* Korn, Selig(mann)
Norma Jean. *See* Beaser, Norma Jean
Norman. *See* Norman, John
Norman, Charles. *See* Liedbeck, Sixten
Norman, Constance. *See* Lanier, Verdell
Norman, Edward W. *See* Nolte, Roy E.
Norman, F. E. *See* Eckhardt, Fritz
Norman, Frederick Van. *See* Zamecnik, J(ohn) S(tepan)
Norman, John. *See* Stott, Walter [or Wally]
Norman, José. *See* Henderson, Norman
Norman, Leo. *See* Lyon, David Norman
Norman, Noel. *See* Mullen Frederic
Norman, Pierre. *See* Connor, Joseph Patrick
Norman, Reginald. *See* Noble, Ray(mond) (Stanley)
Norman, Robert. *See* Gardner, Maurice
Norman, Rolf. *See* Elsmo, Ralph Norman
Norman, Sidney [or Sydney]. *See* Paramor, Norman [or Norrie] (William)
Norman, Stanley. *See* Paramor, Norman [or Norrie] (William)
Norman, Victor. *See* Neat(e), John
Norman, Wayne. *See* Treharne, Bryceson
Norman, William. *See* Barthelson, (Helen) Joyce (Holloway)
Normanus. *See* Muris, Johannes de
Norris, John F. *See* Kaplan, Sol
Norstad, Olaf. *See* Reipsch, Horst
North, Alex. *See* Soifer, Alexis [or Isadore]
North, Carolina. *See* Kinyon, John L(eroy)
North, Christopher. *See* Wilson, John
North, Frank. *See* Attwater, John Post
North, Frederick. *See* Frangkiser, Carl (Moerz)
North, Hatti(e). *See* North, Edith
North, Norman. *See* Bennett, David (D.)
North, Richard. *See* Palmer, Cedric King
Northrup, Willis. *See* Wagness, Bernard
Northup, George. *See* Riegger, Wallingford (Constantin)
Norton, Carl. *See* Yoder, Paul V(an Buskirk)
Norton, Elena. *See* O'Hea, Miss
Norton, James. *See* Knauff, John
Norton, Wallace. *See* Ehret, Walter (Charles)
Norton, Walter. *See* Finkelstein, Abe
Norvo, Kenneth. *See* Norville, (J.) Kenneth
Norvo, Red. *See* Norville, (J.) Kenneth
Norvus, Nervous. *See* Drake, Jimmy
Norway's Greatest Composer. *See* Grieg, Edvard Hagerup
Norworth, Jack. *See* Knauff, John

Norworth, Max. *See* Fisher, Ethel
Nosbor, Richard. *See* Robson, Richard
Nose, The. *See* Pincus, Barry Allen [or Alan]
Nosenko, Ye. *See* Kollontay [or Kollontai] (Yermolayev), Mikhail Georgiyevich
Nosivad, W. R. *See* Davison, W. R.
Nosjack. *See* Jackson, William Henry
Nossuh, Alfred. *See* Husson, Alfred
Notarsch Sakramensky. *See* Gyrowetz, Adalbert
Notorious B.I.G., (The). *See* Wallace, Chris(topher (G.))
Nouveau, Arthur. *See* Whitcomb, Ian (Timothy)
Nova, Aldo. *See* Caporuscio, Aldo (Nova)
Novalis. *See* Hardenberg, Georg Friedrich Philipp von
Novara, Franco [or Franke]. *See* Na(i)sh, Francis (Henry)
Novara, Léon. *See* Holst, Eduard [or Edward]
Novarini, Rico. *See* Zabler, Enrico
Novarro Alberto. *See* Wagness, Bernard
Novello, Andy. *See* Mäder, Wolfgang
Novello, Ivor. *See* Davies, David Ivor
November, Johnny. *See* Mathews, James Snookie
Noverari. *See* Goodwin, Charles Wycliffe
Novice, Larry. *See* Gotowski, Harry
Novo Portu, (Francisco) De. *See* Mergot, Franciscus
Noyes, Alfred. *See* Cain, Noble
Nubbitt. *See* Hankerson, Alvin
Nucella. *See* Mathei, Nicolas Savini
Nuceus, (Alardus). *See* Gaucquier, Alard (Dunoyer du)
Nuell, Kurt. *See* Kurtz, Em(m)anuel [or Manny]
Nuernberg, Carlo Enrico. *See* Nürnberg, Karlheinz
Nugent, Paul. *See* Willeby, Charles
Nugetre, (A.). *See* Ertegun, Ahmet (Munir)
Nuh, Rello Mek. *See* Hunkemöller, Paul
Nuitter, Charles Louis Etienne. *See* Truinet, Charles Louis Étienne
Numan, Gary. *See* Webb, Gary Anthony James
Number-One Funkateer. *See* Collins, William
Nunn, Payne. *See* Roberts, Arthur
Nunns, John F. *See* Hewitt, John (Henry) Hill
Nur, Shabda. *See* Wirtel, Thomas (Kemper)
Nusco, Vincenzo. *See* Marulli, Domenico
Nybor, A. G. *See* Robyn, Alfred George
Nye, Hal. *See* Hanley, James F.
Nym, Ralph. *See* Wagner, (Gottlob Heinrich) Adolf
Nyro, Laura. *See* Nigro, Laura
Nyugat. *See* Bartòk, Béla

– O –

O. *See* Olivers, Thomas
O. A. E. *See* Neale, J(ohn) M(ason)
O. E. A. *See* Adams, Oliver Edward Fox
O. E. D. *See* Dobree, Henrietta Octavia (née De Lisle)
O'H., J. *See* O'Hagan, John
O. L. F. *See* Foster, Olive (Leonard)
Ó Rónáin, Muiris. *See* Fleischmann, Aloys (George)
O' Pea Picker, The. *See* Ford, Ernest Jennings
Oak Cliff T-Bone. *See* Walker, Aaron Thibeaux
Oakley, Olly. *See* Sharpe, Joseph
Oaks, Brian. *See* McGilvra, Douglas
Obadiah the Proselyte. *See* Drocos, Jean
Obeloff, Ivan. *See* Henrich, C. W.
Oberndorf, Teo von. *See* Karg(-Elert), Sigfrid
Oberdorfer, Theodore Eugene. *See* Carroll, Carroll
Oberdorfer, Theodore Eugene. *See* Trotter, John Scott
Oberon, Rex. *See* Mallis, Constantine Alexander (Hadji [or Hagi])
Oberpointer, F. *See* Wrisch, Gerhard
Obit, Jon E. *See* Vyhnalek, Ivo
O'Boogie, (Dr.) Winston. *See* Lennon, John (Winston)
Obrero, Leon. *See* Smith, Lee Orean
O'Brian, Padric. *See* Finkelstein, Abe
O'Brien, Spike. *See* Gyldmark, Sven Rudolf S.
O'Bryan, Callie H. *See* Kunkel, Charles
Obscoenus, Paulus. *See* Wüst, Paul
Observer, The. *See* Holness, Winston
O'Byrne, Dermot. *See* Bax, (Sir) Arnold Edward Trevor
O'Capri. *See* Manone, Joseph
O'Carolan, Turlough. *See* Carolan, Turlough
Ocasek, Ric. *See* Otcasek, Richard
Occhialino, L'. *See* Chinelli, Giovanni Battista
Ocean, Billy. *See* Charles, Leslie Sebastian
O'Cean, John. *See* Lennon, John (Winston)
Ochs, Sigismund. *See* Sousa, John Philip
O'Connor, Laurence B. *See* Daly, Joseph Michael
Octaves, Seven. *See* Gottschalk, Louis Moreau
Octobi, Johannes. *See* Hothby, John
O'Cuirc, Henry. *See* Quirk, Henry
O'Daniel, Pappy. *See* O'Daniel, Wilbert Lee
Odd, Conny. *See* Ortwein, Carlernst
O'Dell, Kenny. *See* Gist, Kenneth [or Kenny] (G.), Jr.
Odell, Mac. *See* McLeod, Odell
Odell, Mamie. *See* DeLoriea, Marybelle C(ruger)
Oden, Old Man. *See* Oden, James Burke
Oden, Pat. *See* Danczak, Jul(ius)
Oden, St. Louis Jimmy. *See* Oden, James Burke
Odetta. *See* Holmes, Odetta
Odette, Dee. *See* Camarata, Salvador
Odoardo. *See* Ariosti, Giovanni Battista
Odom, King. *See* Odom, Andrew
Odom, Moonhead. *See* Odom, Andrew
Odom, Voice. *See* Odom, Andrew
O'Farrill, Chico. *See* O'Farrill, Arturo
Offenbach(er, Der). *See* Eberst, Isaac Juda
Offenbach, Isaac. *See* Eberst, Isaac Juda
Offenbach, Jacques. *See* Eberst, Jacob
Officer Employed in His Army, An. *See* Fane, John
Ogal, T. F. *See* Newman, Barbara Belle
Oganezashvili, Sasha. *See* Oganyan, Aleksandr

Ogden, Gene. *See* Johnson, Clair W.
Ogden, Onaway. *See* Willeby, Charles
Ogden, Sam. *See* Sousa, John Philip
O'Ghurkin, (Dr.) Winston. *See* Lennon, John (Winston)
O'Hagan, Archibald. *See* Hofmannsthal, Hugo von
O'Hagen, Betsy. *See* Wright, Lawrence
O'Hara, Gwyrick. *See* Slaughter, M(arion) T(ry)
O'Hara, Leslie. *See* O'Keefe, Lester
O'Hara-Smith, George. *See* Harrison, George
Ohio Kid, The. *See* Lytle, Donald (Eugene)
O'Hogan, Betsy. *See* Wright, Lawrence
Oju, Abeodun. *See* Macfoy, Emmanuel Kayasi
O'Kanes, The. *See* Kane, Kieran
O'Kanes, The. *See* O'Hara, Jamie
O'Keefe, James (C.). *See* Kunkel, Charles
O'Keefe, Jimmy. *See* Confrey, Edward Elzear
O'Kelley, Shane. *See* Fisher, William Arms
O'Kelly, Thomas. *See* O'Ceallaigh, Thomas
O'Kelly, William Wilhelm. *See* Occhelli, William Wilhelm
Okie from Muskogee, The. *See* Haggard, Merle (Ronald)
Oklahoma's Singing Cowboy. *See* Autry, (Orvon) Gene
Oklahoma's Yodeling Cowboy. *See* Autry, (Orvon) Gene
Ol' Redhead. *See* Draper Farrell H.
Olbiano, Metisto. *See* Capeci, Carlo Sigismondo
Olcott, Chauncey. *See* Olcott, Chancellor John
Olcott, Herbert. *See* O'Keefe, James (Conrad)
Old Arpeggio. *See* Thalberg, Sigismond
Old Borax. *See* Dvorák, Antonín
Old Colonel, The. *See* Arnheim, Gus
Old Country Boy. *See* McLeod, Odell
Old Dad. *See* Crosby, Harry Lillis
Old Dutch. *See* Chevalier, Albert (Onesime Britannicus Gawtheveoyd Louis)
Old English Composer of the XXth Century, An. *See* Damrosch, Walter Johannes
Old Everton. *See* Berridge, John
Old Explorer. *See* Loyau, George Etienne
Old Fogy. *See* Huneker, James Gibbons
Old Glory Face. *See* Rodeheaver, Homer A(lvan)
Old Groaner. *See* Crosby, Harry Lillis
Old Guard, The. *See* Finck, Henry Gottlob
Old Guard, The. *See* Henderson, William James
Old Guard, The. *See* Krehbiel, Henry (Edward)
Old Guard's Glad Evangel, The. *See* Finck, Henry Gottlob
Old Left-Hander, The. *See* Sanders, Joseph [or Joe] (L.)
Old Maestro, The. *See* Anzelwitz [or Anzelvitz], Benjamin [or Bernard]
Old Pea Picker. *See* Ford, Ernest Jennings
Old Reliable, The. *See* Ware, George
Old Right Hander, The. *See* Coon, Carleton A.
Old Rye. *See* Hays, Will(iam) S(hakespeare)
Old Vicar, The. *See* Monsell, John Samuel Bewley
Old Wig, The. *See* Bach, Johann Sebastian
Olden, Stefan. *See* Franz, (Maria) Marlen(e)
Olden, Stefan. *See* Franz, Walter
Oldham, Spooner. *See* Oldham, (Dewey) Lindon, Jr.
Oldsi. *See* Hummel, Silas Early
Oldstyle, Jonathan. *See* Irving, Washington
Ole Bull. *See* Buckley, Frederick
Oleska, Waclaw z. *See* Zaleski, Waclaw
Olibrio, Flavio Amicio. *See* Agricola, Johann Friedrich
Olivar, Ralf. *See* Ebert, Heinz (Helmut(z))
Oliver. *See* Swofford, William Oliver
Oliver, A. (O.). *See* Gabriel, Charles H(utchinson)
Oliver, Frank. *See* O'Keefe, Lester
Oliver, Kine. *See* Alexander, Alger(non)
Oliver, King. *See* Oliver, Joseph [or Joe]
Oliver, Rick. *See* Forsblad, Leland
Oliver, Sy. *See* Oliver, Melvin James
Oliver, Tim. *See* Wilkins, Robert Timothy
Oliviera Cruz, Luiz. *See* Andrade, Djalmi de
Ollinean, C. d'. *See* Ancillon, Charles d'
O'London, Cornelius. *See* Fields, Harold (Cornelius)
O'London, Harold. *See* Fields, Harold (Cornelius)
Olsen, Elric. *See* Clarke, Cuthbert
Olsen, Elsie. *See* Clarke, Cuthbert
Olsen, Lejre. *See* Olsen, Carl Christian
Olson, H. *See* Lillenas, Haldor
Olson, Hammond. *See* Svensson, Reinhold
Oltmann, Bert. *See* Meyer, Friedrich
Olympico. *See* Bissari, Pietro Paolo
O'Malley, James. *See* Sawyer, Henry S.
Omar. *See* Fook, Omar Lye
Omega. *See* Cowper, William
Oméga, Carlo. *See* Campbell, Henry M.
O'Melley, Howard. *See* Moorlampen, Franz Peter
Omesquawigishigoque. *See* Stocker, Stelle (née Prince)
Omicron. *See* Newton, John
One Armed John. *See* Wrencher, John Thomas
One Eye. *See* Saunders, Donald
One Man Army. *See* Kondau, Alex
One Man Battalion. *See* Kondau, Alex
One Man Cyclone, The. *See* Chapin, Harry
One Man Thousand. *See* Kondau, Alex
One Man Trio, The. *See* Bonner, Weldon (H. Philip)
One of the Kings of Soca. *See* Calliste, Leroy
One of the Memorialists. *See* Muhlenberg, William Augustus
One of the Seven Humbugs of Christendom. *See* Elgar, (Sir) Edward
One String Perkins. *See* Perkins, Carl (Lee)
One Who Has Done It and Can Do It Again. *See* Burnard, Francis Cowley
One Who Never Trangressed Before. *See* Cotton, Charles
One with the Hat, The. *See* Nesmith, Michael

Onégin, Eugene. *See* Lvov, Eugene
O'Neil, Douglas. *See* David, Worton
O'Neil, Douglas. *See* Wright, Lawrence
O'Neill, Moira. *See* Higginson, Agnes
Ong, Oliver. *See* Murray, James R(amsey)
Ongala, Remmy. *See* Ongala, Ramazini [or Ramathan] Mtoro
Ongaretto, L'. *See* Piazza, Giovanni Battista
Onivas, David. *See* Savino, Domenico
Onivas, Domenico. *See* Savino, Domenico
Onkel Sam. *See* Liptzin, Samuel
Onlooker. *See* Roberts, William (Amos)
Only Leon, The. *See* Glassey, Patrick Francis
Onomari, O. *See* Savino, Domenico
Openshaw, John. *See* Connor, Joseph Patrick
Opera Goer, An. *See* Mitchell, D(onald) G(rant)
Opera Manager, (An). *See* Maretzek, Max
Operation Elvis. *See* Presley, Elvis A(a)ron
Operoso, L'. *See* Cevenini, Camillo
Opper, Paul. *See* Orth, John (Carl)
Or, Luis "Perico." *See* Ortiz Ruiz, Luis Esteban
Oranski, Viktor Aleksandrovich. *See* Gersov, Viktor Aleksandrovich
Orbeck, Rudi. *See* Angerer, Rudolf
Orbino, Il. *See* Carisio, Giovanni
Orbit, William. *See* Wainwright, William (Mark)
Orebsky, Jan. *See* Held, Jan Theobald
Orefice, Antonio. *See* Arefece, Antonio
O'Reggae, (Dr.) Winston. *See* Lennon, John (Winston)
O'Reilly, Séamas. *See* Riley, James
Oresbio Agieo. *See* Corsetti, Francesco
Orfelius. *See* Cesari, Orfelio [or Elio]
Orfeo. *See* Acciaiuoli, Filippo
Orgad, Ben-Zion. *See* Buschel, Ben-Zion
Organist to the Fraternity, The. *See* Hullah, John Pyke
Orgeval, François d'. *See* La Tourrasse, André de
Oridryus, Johannes. *See* Van Bergijk, Johannes
Original Bowery Boy, The. *See* Ward, Charles B.
Original Cool Ruler, The. *See* Edwards, Wilfred
Original Dinah, The. *See* Howard, Ethel
Original Disco Man, The. *See* Brown, James
Original Folk Hero, The. *See* Guthrie, Woodward [or Woody, or Woodie] (Wilson)
Original King of Rock and Roll. *See* Haley, William [or Bill] (John Clifton), (Jr.)
Original King of the Delta Blues. *See* Patton, Charley [or Charlie]
Original Radio Girl, The. *See* Vonderlieth, Leonore
Original Singing Cowboy, The. *See* Autry, (Orvon) Gene
Original Singing Cowboy, The. *See* Sprague, Carl T.
Original Texas Ranger, The. *See* Owens, D(oye) [or Doie] H(ensley)
Originator, The. *See* Bates, (Otha) Ellas [or Elias]
Orl. *See* Broniewski, Waldyslaw
Orlande, Pierre. *See* Roland, Reiny
Orlando, Johnny. *See* Peretti, Hugo (Emil)
Orlando, Sal. *See* Klickmann, F(rank) Henri
Orlandus Thuringiae. *See* Altenberg, Michael
Orlik. *See* Broniewski, Waldyslaw
Orme, Destian. *See* Davis, Clarice Ryall
Ormsbé, Emil. *See* White, Harold R(obert)
Ornell, Marty. *See* Oneglia, Mario F(rancesco)
Ornest, Ota. *See* Ornstein, Ota
Ornithoparchus, Andreas. *See* Vogelhofer, Andreas
Orpheus. *See* Kossmaly, Karl [or Carl]
Orpheus. *See* Woods, John Joseph
Orpheus of Arabia, The. *See* Al Farabi, Abu Nar
Orpheus of the Eighteenth Century, The. *See* Handel, Georg Friedrich
Orr, Robin. *See* Orr, Robert (Kemsley)
Orrel, Max. *See* Edler, Robert
Orridge, Genesis. *See* Megson, Neil (Andrew)
Orrie, Lee. *See* Smith, Lee Orean
Orso, Francesco d'. *See* Behr, F(ranz)
Ort, E. Rose Reese. *See* Kendis, James
Ortanio. *See* Biancardi, (Nicolò) Sebastiano
Orth, Emil. *See* Orth, John (Carl)
Orth, L(izette) E(mma). *See* Blood, Lizette Emma
Orto, Marbrianus de. *See* Dujardin, Marrianus de
Orville Wright of Deconstructive Guitaring, The. *See* Frith, Jeremy Webster
Ory, Kid. *See* Ory, Edward
Osaze, Ted Ernest. *See* Hayes, Theodore, Jr.
Osborn, Rag(s). *See* Osborn, Arthur H.
Osborne, A. E. *See* Bliss, P(hilip) Paul
Osborne & Howe. *See* Cook, J. Lawrence
Osborne & Howe. *See* Kortlander, Max
Osborne, Chas. *See* Thomas, John Rogers
Osborne, Don. *See* Bergman, Dewey
Osborne, James. *See* Dawson, Peter (Smith)
Osborne, Will. *See* Oliphant, William
Osbourne, Ozzy. *See* Osbourne, John (Michael)
Oscar. *See* Kind, (Johann) Friedrich
Osfikos, Agnis. *See* Stefopulos, Giorgos
O'Shea, Daddy. *See* Washburne, Joseph [or Joe] (H.)
Osiro Cedreatico. *See* David, Domenico
Oskar. *See* Kind, (Johann) Friedrich
Oskar, Manfred. *See* Reisinger, Oskar
Oso, El. *See* Berto, Augusto Pedro
Ossen, Lutz. *See* Sebus, Ludwig
Osser, Glenn. *See* Osser, Abraham [or Abe] Arthur
Ossi. *See* Soter, Oswald
Ossian. *See* Macpherson, James
Ostern, Claudianus. *See* Pascha, Edmund
Osterwald, Hazy. *See* Osterwälder, Rolf E(rich)
Ostro, Paolo. *See* Kountz, Richard
Ostrus, Merrill. *See* Staton, Merrill
Ostsee, Johannes von der. *See* Falk, Johannes Daniel
Ostwig, Hans. *See* Stolz, Robert

O'Sullivan, Gilbert. *See* O'Sullivan, Ray(mond)
O'Sullivan, Seumas. *See* Starkey, James (Sullivan)
Oswald, Max. *See* Ostendorf, Jens-Peter
Otakar, Jean. *See* Jelínek, Hanuš
Otis, Johnny. *See* Veliotes, John A(lexander)
Otis, Stephen. *See* Nordman, Chester
Otobi, Giovanni. *See* Hothby, John
O'Toole, Knuckles. *See* Hyman, Richard [or Dick] (R(oven))
Ott, Sam. *See* Thomas, Millard (J.)
Ottavio, (Frate). *See* Ariosti, Attilio (Malachia [or Clementi])
Otteby, John. *See* Hothby, John
Otteman, Nicholas. *See* Hotmann, Nicholas
Ottenstein, Eddy. *See* Ostrow, Edward Carol
Otto. *See* Eszterházy von Galántha, Paul
Otto der Schrage. *See* Schulz-Reichel, Fritz
Ottuso, L'. *See* Artusi, Giovanni Maria
Ottuso, L'. *See* Goretti, Antonio
Otway, Sylvester. *See* Oswald, John
Otz, Siegfried. *See* Sousa, John Philip
Ouestman, Théodore. *See* Cuffley, Edwin John
Ouida. *See* De la Ramé(e), (Marie) Louise
Oulette, S. *See* Sousa, John Philip
Our Apollo. *See* Bach, Johann Sesbastian
Our Irving Berlin. *See* Dorsey, Thomas A(ndrew)
Outlaw, The. *See* Jennings, Waylon [actually Wayland] (Arnold)
Outlaw, The. *See* Nelson, Willie (Hugh)
Outlaw, The. *See* Ochs, Phil
Outlaw's Outlaw, The. *See* Clayton, Lee T.
Outlaw's Outlaw, The. *See* Schatz, Billy
Ouvreuse du Cirque (d'Eté), L'. *See* Gauthier-Villars, Henri
Ovidio. *See* Acciaiuoli, Filippo
Oviedo, Papi. *See* Oviedo, Gilberto
Ovsianiko-Kulikovskii, Nikolai Dmitrievich. *See* Goldstein, Mikhail (1768-1846)
Owain, Alaw. *See* Owen, John
Owen, Anne. *See* Wilson, Ira B(ishop)
Owen, Eric. *See* Owen, Reg
Owen, Eric. *See* Siday, Eric
Owen, John Pickard. *See* Butler, Samuel
Owen, Mary Jane. *See* Brockway, Jennie M(ary)
Owens, Buck. *See* Owens, Alvis Edgar, Jr.
Owens, Doodle. *See* Owens, A(l). L.
Owens, Tex. *See* Owens, D(oye) [or Doie] H(ensley)
Owston, Snake. *See* Owston, Charles [or Chuck]
Oxenham, John. *See* Dunkerley, William Arthur
Oxilia, Nino. *See* Oxilia, Angelo Agostino Adolfo
Oyett, Dayne. *See* Grey, Frank H(erbert)
Ozzaniugnas, Olocin. *See* Sanguinazzo, Nicolo

– P –

P. C. *See* Ottoboni, Pietro
P. C. B. *See* Buck, (Sir) Percy Carter
P. C. E. *See* Littledale, Richard Frederick
P. Diddy. *See* Combs, Sean
P. F. *See* Freeman, Philip
P. G. *See* Wodehouse, P(elham) G(renville)
P. H. *See* Hallmann, Paul
P. H. *See* Hofhaimer, Paul(us von)
P. H. I. Z. C. G. S. *See* Fielding, Henry
PMD. *See* Smith, Parrish
P-Orridge, Genesis. *See* Megson, Neil (Andrew)
P. P. *See* Cowper, William
P. P. B. *See* Bliss, P(hilip) P.
P. P. Bk. *See* Littledale, Richard Frederick
P. R. *See* Rebhuhn, Paul
P. R. *See* Ritter, Paul
P. S. H. *See* Hughes, Philippa Swinnerton
P. T. Barnum of Modern Rock, The. *See* McLaren, Malcolm
P. T. J. *See* Telemann, Georg Philipp
P. W. *See* Weldon, Peter
Pablo, Augustus. *See* Swaby, Horace
Pablo, Juan. *See* Sifler, Paul John
Pace, Graham. *See* Paramor, Norman [or Norrie] (William)
Pace, Richard. *See* Szirmai, Albert
Pace, Warren. *See* Ehret, Walter (Charles)
Pacho. *See* Galán Blanco, Francisco
Pacho. *See* Maglio, Juan (Felix)
Pacific, Gary. *See* Brunke, Wolfram
Pacifico. *See* Giannini, Giovanni Matteo
Packay, Peter. *See* Paquet, Pierre
Paddy. *See* Pusch, Klaus-Werner
Padellan, (Mrs.) Moetahar. *See* Higginbotham, Irene (Evelyn)
Padoano. *See* Barbetta, Giulio Cesare
Padovano, Il. *See* Annibale
Padre della music. *See* Hasse, Johann Adolf
Padre Raimo. *See* Bartoli, Erasmo
Paduc(c)i, (A(ndré)). *See* Lefebvre, Françoise (M.)
Paganini, Nic(c)olò (Spirit). *See* Reuter, Florizel von
Paganini of Clarinetists. *See* Cavallini, Ernesto
Paganini of the Alps, The. *See* Jullien, Louis (George) Antoine (Jules)
Paganini of the Cello. *See* Popper, David
Paganini of the Cello, The. *See* Servais, Adrien François
Paganini of the Cornet. *See* Levy, Jules
Paganini of the Double Bass. *See* Bottesini, Giovanni
Paganini of the Guitar, The. *See* Giuliani, Mauro
Paganini of the Guitar. *See* Sor, (Joseph) Fernando (Macari)
Paganini of the Mandolin. *See* Calace, Nicola

Paganini of the Mandolin, The. *See* Grisman, David (Jay)
Paganini of the North. *See* Bull, Ole (Bornemann)
Paganini of the Oboe. *See* Pasculli, Antonino [or Antonio]
Paganini of the Piano. *See* Liszt, Franz
Paganini of the Trombone. *See* Pryor, Arthur Willard
Paganini of the Tuba. *See* Phillips, Harvey G.
Pagano, L. *See* Giani, Romualdo
Page. *See* St. Clair, Floyd J.
Page, Bert. *See* Lepage, Albert (Aahemar)
Page, Edgar. *See* Stites, E(dgar) P(age)
Page, Hot Lips. *See* Page, Oran Thaddeus
Page, Lips. *See* Page, Oran Thaddeus
Page, Marian. *See* Turner, Margaret Marian
Page, Paul. *See* Brown, Paul
Paige, Bert. *See* Lepage, Albert (Aahemar)
Paige, Frances. *See* Sukman, Frances Paley
Pain, Dicken. *See* Pain, Jeff(rey) Robert
Paine, Robert Treat. *See* Paine, Thomas
Paisley, Tom. *See* Passailaigue, Thomas E.
Paki, Lydia. *See* Kamakaeha, Liliu (Loloka Walania)
Pal, Friedrich. *See* Eisenschitz, Friedrich
Palad, Gelsa. *See* Paladino, Gelsa Theresa
Palalaiki, John. *See* Davis, Joseph [or Joe] (M.)
Palao, Gelsa. *See* Paladino, Gelsa Theresa
Palao, Jelsa. *See* Paladino, Gelsa Theresa
Palatin. *See* Rist, Johann
Palemone, Licurio. *See* Stampiglia, Silvio
Palermitano, Il. *See* Palotta, Matteo
Palermitano, Mauro. *See* Chiaula, Mauro
Palestrina der Besenbinder. *See* Fink, (Christian) Gottfried Wilhelm
Palestrina of Berlin. *See* Klein, Bernhard (Joseph)
Palestrina of the 18th Century, The. *See* Pisari, Pasquale
Palestrina of the 19th Century, The. *See* Tomadini, Jacopo
Palidor. *See* Lehms, Georg Christian
Palimpsest, Huanebango Z. *See* Heseltine, Philip (Arnold)
Palings, Walter. *See* Pallant, Walter
Pallet, Christian. *See* Bender, Erich
Pallet, Olaf. *See* Bender, Erich
Palmer, Bill. *See* Miller, Robert [or Bob] (Ernst)
Palmer, Bob. *See* Miller, Robert [or Bob] (Ernst)
Palmer, Dick. *See* Confrey, Edward Elzear
Palmer, Edward. *See* Beckhard, Robert L.
Palmer, F(rederick) (H.). *See* Hartmann, Emma Sophie Amalie (née Zinn)
Palmer, King. *See* Palmer, Cedric King
Palmer, Lynn. *See* Dula, Henry
Palmer, Robert. *See* Palmer, Alan
Palmer, Vi. *See* Confrey, Edward Elzear
Palmer, Vi. *See* Eckstein, Willie
Palmézeaux. *See* Cubières(-Dorat de Palmézeaux), Michel de
Palmieri, Charlie. *See* Palmieri, Carlos Manuel, Jr.
Palmira, Don Tarar di. *See* Salieri, Antonio
Palmström, Jo. *See* Mayrhofer, Frieder
Paloma, Vincente. *See* Green, Phil(ip)
Paloma, Vincente. *See* Paramor, Norman [or Norrie] (William)
Paloverde, M. *See* Greenwald, M(artin)
Palusi, Il. *See* Saracini, Claudio
Pan, Peter. *See* Kreuder, Peter
Pan, Peter. *See* Stevens, Gosta
Pan-ya-ming. *See* Benjamin, Walter
Pana, E. S. *See* Casson, Reg(inald) H(epworth)
Panard of the 19th Century, The. *See* Gouffé, Armand
Pancho. *See* Rosquellas, Adolfo
Pancoast, Ace. *See* Pancoast, Asa
Pandora. *See* Rawsthorne, Alan
Panellenio, Eaco. *See* Sanviale, Jacopo Antonio
Panfili, (Cardinal) Benedetto. *See* Pamphili, Benedetto
Panico Porky. *See* Panico, Frank
Panormitano, Il. *See* Palotta, Matteo
Panormitano, Mauro. *See* Chiaula, Mauro
Pansy. *See* Donisthorpe, Ida Margaret Loder
Pantano-Salsbury. *See* Pantano, John
Pantano-Salsbury. *See* Salsbury, Ron(ald Foster)
Panter, Peter. *See* Tucholsky, Kurt
Pantophilus, Gratian. *See* Brendel, Georg Christoph
Paolito, Francesco. *See* Mantovani, A(nnuzio) P(aolo)
Paolito, Francesco. *See* Piccioni, Angelo F.
Paolo, Francesco. *See* Kountz, Richard
Paolo, L. *See* Lacombe (d'Estalenx), Paul Jean Jacques
Papa Chittlins. *See* Moore, Alex(ander Herman)
Papa George. *See* Lightfoot, Alexander
Papa Joe. *See* Oliver, Joseph [or Joe]
Papa Snow White. *See* Page, Oran Thaddeus
Papa Wemba. *See* Wembadia, Shungu
Papai, François. *See* Szekeres, Ferenc [or François]
Papaíto. *See* Muñoz Salazar, Mario
Paperclip People. *See* Craig, Carl
Papi, A. *See* Doriano, Cleofante
Papi Oviedo. *See* Oviedo, Gilberto
Papo MC. *See* Deschamps, Luis
Papp, Joseph. *See* Papirofsky, Yosi [or Joseph]
Papuschek, Veit. *See* Kann, Hans
Paracelsus. *See* Bock, Ida
Parade Music Prince. *See* Seitz, Roland F(orrest)
Paradossi, Giuseppe. *See* Troili, Giuseppe
Paradosso, Il. *See* Troili, Giuseppe
Paramount Wildcat, The. *See* Pridgett, Gertrude (Malissa Nix)
Parche, El. *See* Jordan, Estaban Steve
Pardette, Neil. *See* Lieb, Joseph
Paree, Paul. *See* Wright, Lawrence
Parelli, Attilio. *See* Paparella, Attilio
Paresco, Jimmy. *See* De Schrijver, Karel

Pargeter, Wyatt. *See* Pargeter, Maude
Parham, Tiny. *See* Parham, Hartzell Strathdene
Paridon, Roxana. *See* DeLeone, Francesco B(artolomeo)
Parigini, Salvador. *See* Fishman, Jack (1918 (or 19)-)
Paris, Dick. *See* Hagen, J(ohn) M(ilton)
Paris, Heinrich. *See* Haza, Jeannette von
Paris, Irving. *See* Simoni, Pascal
Parish Priest, A. *See* Faber, Frederick William
Parisian Waltz King. *See* Lévy, (Charles) Emile
Park, Edna L. *See* Crosby, Fanny [i.e., Frances] J(ane)
Park, Moore. *See* McEwen, (Sir) John Blackwood
Parker, Albert. *See* Saenger, Gustave
Parker, Bird. *See* Parker, Charles [or Charlie] (Christopher, Jr.)
Parker, Charles. *See* Jahnen, Gerd [or Gerhard]
Parker, Godfrey. *See* Bulch, Thomas Edward
Parker, John. *See* Gelück, Kurt
Parker, Junior. *See* Parker, Herman
Parker, Little Junior. *See* Parker, Herman
Parker, Yardbird. *See* Parker, Charles [or Charlie] (Christopher, Jr.)
Parkman, Franky. *See* Hess, Reimund
Parkman, Harold. *See* Norden, Hugo (Svan)
Parlando Rubato. *See* Durand, Annie
Parlando Rubato. *See* Meyer, Dale Arthur
Parlotte, Monsieur de la. *See* Mortjé, Arnold [or Adolphe]
Parma, Ildebrando da. *See* Pizzetti, Ildebrando
Parmentier, Mme. *See* Milanollo, Teresa (Domenica Maria)
Parnasso, Felice. *See* Bernini, Giovanni Filippo
Parnell, Mary. *See* Wagness, Bernard
Parnell, Paul. *See* Pratt, Paul (Charles)
Parpart, Gertrud. *See* Schröder, Gertrud
Parran. *See* Garlow, Clarence Joseph
Parrish, Dean. *See* Anastasi, Philip (J.)
Parrish, Mitchell. *See* Lieb, Joseph
Parry, Blind. *See* Parry, John (c.1710-1782)
Parry, Ddall. *See* Parry, John (c.1710-1782)
Parry, John Haydn. *See* Parry, Joseph Haydn (1864-1894)
Parson, Charlotte. *See* Fishman, Jack (1927-)
Parsons, Bill. *See* Bare, Robert [or Bobby] (Joseph)
Parsons, Gram. *See* Connor, Ingram Cecil, III
Parsons, Happy Jim. *See* Kaufman, Isidore
Parsons, Spencer. *See* King, Stanford
Partenio, Chriter. *See* Trinchera, Pietro
Partichela, F. A. *See* Ruiz Alonso, Felipe
Partridge, Henry. *See* Smith, Henry Partridge
Pascal, André. *See* Rothschild, (Baron) Henri de
Pascal, Florian. *See* Williams, Joseph (Benjamin)
Pascal, Jefferson. *See* Wilde, Cornel (L(ouis))
Pasle, Tom. *See* Passailaigue, Thomas E.
Pasquale, Dino. *See* Barnes, H(oward) E(llington)
Pasquale, Dino. *See* Fields, Harold (Cornelius)
Pasquale, Dino. *See* Roncoroni, Joseph (Dominic)
Pasquin. *See* Fielding, Henry
Passagni, Leandro. *See* Pigna, Alessandro
Pasternak, K(leofas) F(akund). *See* Krasewski, Józef Ignacy
Pastor. *See* McCollin, Frances
Pastore, Escaro. *See* Shepherd, Horace
Pastorius, Jaco. *See* Pastorius, John Francis
Pat Boone of Country Music, The. *See* Anderson, (James) William [or Bill], (III)
Pàta, Huért. *See* Patáky, Hubert
Patacano, Martino. *See* Chacksfield, Francis [or Frank] (Charles)
Patan. *See* Klackel, Stephan
Patavino, Francesco. *See* Santa Croce, Francesco
Pater a Monte Carmelo. *See* Nenning, Johann
Pater Marianus, OSB. *See* Knecht, Justin Heinrich
Paterson, Banjo. *See* Paterson, A(ndrew) B(arton)
Paticano, Martino. *See* Chacksfield, Francis [or Frank] (Charles)
Patriae, Amator. *See* Campbell, Thomas
Patriarch of Harmony, The. *See* Porpora, Nichola (Antonio)
Patrick, Kirk. *See* Gillette, Leland James
Patrick, Kirk. *See* Kirkpatrick, H(olbert) [or H(allbert)] H(ill)
Patrick, Kirk. *See* Kirkpatrick, Harold William, (Jr.)
Patrick, Nathan(iel). *See* Patrick, Richard
Patrick, Toad Kirk. *See* Kirkpatrick, H(olbert) [or H(allbert)] H(ill)
Patrie, (J.). *See* Van Wedinghem, (E.) J.
Patrizius. *See* Leykauf, Walter Heinz
Patten, Jim. *See* Steffen, Harro
Patterson, Lila. *See* Pridgett, Gertrude (Malissa Nix)
Patterson, Pat. *See* Paterson, Jimmy Dale
Patterson, Reg. *See* Smith, Reginald (Leonard)
Patti, Orville. *See* Kaufman, Isidore
Paul, Bernie. *See* Vonficht, Bernd
Paul, Christopher. *See* Rones, Samuel Morris
Paul, Clarence. *See* Pauling, Clarence
Paul, (Lady) Dean. *See* Wieniawski, Irene Regine
Paul du Crucifix, (Sister). *See* Lefebvre, Francoise (M.)
Paul, E. *See* Pachler, F(aust(us))
Paul, Edmund. *See* Zerga, Joseph (Louis) E(dmund)
Paul, Franz. *See* Eckhardt, Fritz
Paul, (Lady) Irène Reine. *See* Wieniawski, Irene Regine
Paul, Jean. *See* Kunkel, Charles
Paul, Jean. *See* Richter, Johann Paul Friedrich (1763-1825)
Paul, Jimmy. *See* Demaio, James Paul
Paul, John. *See* Curnutt, John Paul
Paul K. *See* Kopasz, Paul
Paul, Keith. *See* Arthur, Reg

Percy, Allan. *See* Hays, Will(iam) S(hakespeare)
Percy, Arthur. *See* Thomas, John Rogers
Percy, Florence. *See* Allen, Elizabeth Ann (Chase) (née Akers)
Percy the Poet. *See* Collins, P. F.
Percy, William Alexander. *See* Gerlich, Clara
Perdita. *See* Robinson, Mary (Darby)
Perditor Spina. *See* Rosa, Salvator(e)
Perdix, Paul. *See* Rebhuhn, Paul
Pere aux Rondeaux, Le. *See* Davaux, Jean Baptiste
Pere Joyeux du Vaudeville, Le. *See* Basselin, Oliver
Père Musard, Le. *See* Musard, Philippe
Peregrinus. *See* Hupfaur, John Peregrin
Peregrinus. *See* Reuss, Theodor
Peretola, Decimo Corinella da. *See* Mei, Girolamo
Perey, L(ucien). *See* Herpin, (Clare Adele) Luce
Perfect Fool, The. *See* Leopold, Isaiah Edwin
Pergolesi, Giovanni Battista. *See* Draghi, Giovanni Battista
Pergolesi, Giovanni Battista. *See* Wassenaer, (Count) Unico Wilhelm (graf van)
Perico. *See* Oritz Ruiz, Luis Esteban
Perile, Joseph. *See* Riepel, Joseph [or Josef]
Perk. *See* Perkinson, Coleridge Taylor
Perkins, Carl (Lee). *See* Perkings, Carl (Lee)
Perkins, M. O. *See* Bliss, P(hilip) Paul
Perkins, Norma. *See* Hausey, Howard (Elton)
Perkins, Pinetop. *See* Perkins, Joe Willie
Perle, George. *See* Perlman, George
Pernambuco, Joao. *See* Guimaraes, Joao Teixeira
Pero. *See* Botwinik, B.
Peronne, Paul. *See* Rawlings, Alfred William
Peronne, Paul. *See* Reeves, Ernest
Perosa, H. *See* Goehr, Walter
Perosa, H. *See* Peros, Harry
Perrey-Kingsley. *See* Kingsley, Gershon
Perrey-Kingsley. *See* Perrey, Jean-Jacques
Perrier, Paul. *See* Rawlings, Charles Arthur
Perrin, Jacques. *See* Engel, Carl
Perrion, Paul. *See* Rawlings, Alfred William
Perrot, Pierre. *See* Paterson, Robert Roy
Perry, A. J. *See* Frangkiser, Carl (Moerz)
Perry, Alan. *See* Tomlinson, Ernest
Perry, Chester. *See* Dodge, J(ohn) W(ilson)
Perry, Chester. *See* Dodge, May Hewes
Perry Como of Country Music, The. *See* Drusky, Roy (Frank)
Perry, Joe. *See* Peropota, Joseph Michael
Perry, Lee. *See* Perry, Rainford Hugh
Perry, Scratch. *See* Perry, Rainford Hugh
Persley, George W. *See* Brown, George W.
Person of Quality. *See* Austin, John
Persson, Nils Birger. *See* Persson, Harry (Arnold)
Perteroff, L. *See* Leoncavallo, Ruggiero
Pery, M. *See* Pferdemenges, Maria Pauline Augusta
Pesarino, Il. *See* Barbarino, Bartolomeo
Peschkov, Igor. *See* Clarke, Cuthbert
Pestalozza, A. *See* Kraushaar, Charles
Pestrin(o). *See* Abondante, Giulio [or Julio]
Pestro, Giulio dal. *See* Abondante, Giulio [or Julio]
Pete. *See* Harrigan, Edward [or Ned]
Peter der Ameisenbär. *See* Gleich, Friedrich
Peter Pan. *See* Kreuder, Peter
Peter Pan. *See* Stevens, Gosta
Peter Pan of Pop, The. *See* Jackson, Michael Joseph
Petern van Straeten. *See* La Rue, Pierre de
Peters, C. *See* Friedmann, Heinrich
Peters, Charley. *See* Patton, Charley [or Charlie]
Peters, Douglas. *See* Green, Phil(ip)
Peters, Frank. *See* Drischel, Peter
Peters, Hunt. *See* Johnson, James Louis
Peters, Jacob. *See* McLeod, James (P.)
Peters, Jed. *See* Leiber, Jerry
Peters, Jed. *See* Stoller, Mike
Peters, John. *See* Lengsfelder, Hans
Peters, Ricci. *See* Bleiweiss, Peter R(ichard)
Peters, Ronnie. *See* Adderley, Julien Edwin
Peters, Sam. *See* Slaughter, M(arion) T(ry)
Peters, Teddy. *See* Paramor, Norman [or Norrie] (William)
Peters, V. *See* Friedmann, Heinrich
Peters, W(ilhelm). *See* Orling, Hans G(eorg)
Peters, William D. *See* Dykema, Peter W(illiam)
Peters, Wilm. *See* Orling, Hans G(eorg)
Petersburg. *See* Peters, Werner
Petersen, Ralf. *See* Zehm, Friedrich
Peterson, Ernie. *See* Peterson, Leland Arnold
Peterson, H. *See* Richards, Herbert
Peterson, Rald. *See* Zehm, Friedrich
Petit Espagnol, Le. *See* Lacy, Michael Rophino
Petit Prince de Dakar. *See* N'Dour, Youssou
Petite Elsie, La. *See* Bierbower, Elsie
Petits violins, Le. *See* Francoeur, François (*le cadet*)
Petits violins, Le. *See* Rebel, François (*le fils*)
Petr, Hanuš. *See* Schulhoff, Ervín [or Erwin]
Petrahn, Sean. *See* Reilly, Jack
Petraloysio, Giovanni. *See* Palestrina, Giovanni Pierluigi da
Petraloysius, Joannes. *See* Palestrina, Giovanni Pierluigi da
Petrahn, Sean. *See* Reilly, Jack
Petrus la Vic. *See* La Rue, Pierre de
Petrus Platensis. *See* La Rue, Pierre de
Pettie's Boy. *See* McCollum, Robert Lee
Pettis, Alabama. *See* Pettis, Coleman, Jr.
Pettis, Daddy Rabbit. *See* Pettis, Coleman, Jr.
Pettis, Junior. *See* Pettis, Coleman, Jr.
Peuret, O. *See* Suck, G. F.
Pewrattler. *See* Herterich, Robert S.
Peysel, Conrad. *See* Beissel, Konrad

Pfeffel. *See* Kahlert, August
Pfiel, Philip. *See* Phile, Philip
Pfitzer, Gustav. *See* Schwitters, Kurt (Hermann Eduard Karl Julius)
Phagas, Dimitmos. *See* Fagas, James [or Jimmie]
Phanciful Phil. *See* Bliss, P(hilip) P.
Phantom, Slim Jim. *See* McDonnell, James
Pharmer, Henry. *See* Schaeffer, Don(ald)
Pharoah. *See* Ngcukana, Ezra (Nyaniso)
Pharoah, Jaarone. *See* Jenkins, Gus
Pheil. *See* Phile, Philip
Phel. *See* Colley, Sarah Ophelia
Phelge, Nanker. *See* Jagger, Michael Philip
Phelge, Nanker. *See* Richards, Keith
Phelps, Bernard. *See* Dodwell, Samuel
Phémius. *See* Saint-Säens, (Charles) Camille
Phil Spector of Rap Music. *See* Young, Andre (Ramelle [or Romell])
Philalethes. *See* Fielding, Henry
Philanthropos. *See* Fellows, John
Philanthropos. *See* Pockrich, Richard
Philharmonica, (Mrs.). *See* Meares, Richard
Philidor, François-André. *See* Danican, François-André
Philidor, Jean. *See* Danican, Jean
Philip the Great. *See* Hale, Philip
Philip the Terrible. *See* Hale, Philip
Philip(p)e, Jean. *See* Spross, Charles Gilbert
Philipp(e), Geo(rge). *See* Suck, G. F.
Philipp, Gregor. *See* Freed, Richard (Donald)
Philippe de Mons. *See* Monte, Philippe [or Filippo] de
Philips, Jean. *See* Spross, Charles Gilbert
Philips, Mr. *See* Wilder, Philip van
Philipso, John. *See* Sousa, John Philip
Philison. *See* Dach, Simon
Phillan, Eustace. *See* Boosey, (Beatrice) Joyce
Phillip of Poles, Mr. *See* Rhys, Philip ap
Phillipps, Marty. *See* Spina, Harold
Phillips, Barbara. *See* Jones, Arthur
Phillips, Carter. *See* Hyman, Richard [or Dick] (R(oven))
Phillips, Charles. *See* Scott, Charles P(hillips)
Phillips, Karma. *See* Phillips, James John
Phillips, Kenneth. *See* Saenger, Gustave
Phillips, Lorraine. *See* Kasha, Phyllis L.
Phillips, Olga. *See* Goldner, Ernest (Siegmund)
Phillips, Phil. *See* Baptiste, John Phillip
Phillips, Sam. *See* Phillips, Leslie
Phillips, Sid. *See* Phillips, Isadore Simon
Phillips, Tater. *See* Phillips, William [or Bill] (Clarence)
Phillips, Utah. *See* Phillips, Bruce (U.)
Philo. *See* Knigge, Adolf Franz Friedrich Ludwig, Freiherr von
Philo-Britanniae. *See* Cotton, Charles
Philo, Musico. *See* Langdon, Chauncy
Philodikaios. *See* Beer, Jakob Liebmann
Philokales. *See* Laurencin d'Armond, Ferdinand Peter Graf
Philomela. *See* Brogue, Roslyn
Philomusos, Amadeus. *See* Seyfried, Ignaz (Xaver) von
Philosopher Fiddler, The. *See* Clements, Vassar Carlton
Philosophic Music Man, A. *See* Partch, Harry
Philotheorus. *See* Kempenfelt, Richard
Philpott, Dixie. *See* Flournoy, Roberta Jean
Phisemar, Benno. *See* Bermann, Joseph
Phitt, Sam. *See* Philipp, Isidor (Edmond)
Phoenix of Music. *See* Swybbertszon, Jan Pieterszoon
Phranc. *See* Gottlieb, Susan
Phrei, Aaron. *See* Fry, Aaron
Phyla, Philip. *See* Phile, Philip
Phyles, Philip. *See* Phile, Philip
Phyllander. *See* Burnard, (David) Alex(ander)
Phypps, Hyacinthe. *See* Gorey, Edward (St. John)
Pia, Manduca. *See* Bandeira, Manuel
Piaf, Edith. *See* Gassion, Edith Giovanna
Piaf, Môme. *See* Gassion, Edith Giovanna
Pianist King, The. *See* Thalberg, Sigismond
Pianist manqué, pianophile non pareil. *See* Huneker, James Gibbons
Pianiste voyageur, Le. *See* Jaëll, Alfred
Piano C. Red. *See* Wheeler, James
Piano Man. *See* Joel, William [or Billy] (Martin)
Piano Red. *See* Harrison, Vernon
Piano Red. *See* Perryman, William [or Willie] Lee
Piato, A. R. *See* Kinyon, John L(eroy)
Pibe de La Paternal, El. *See* Fresedo, Osvaldo Nicolás
Pibe de Wilde, El. *See* Marcucci, Carlos
Picander. *See* Henrici, Christian Friedrich
Picarband. *See* Pirola, Carlo
Picard. *See* Pickar, Arnold
Piccinnist. *See* Piccinni, (Vito) Niccolò (Marcello Antonio Giacomo)
Piccolomini, M. *See* Pontet, Henry Theodore
Pichon, M. *See* Chopin, Frederic
Pichuco. *See* Troilo, Anibal (Carmelo)
Pickens, Slim. *See* Burns, Eddie
Picker, Tom. *See* Lewis, Al(an)
Picker, Tom. *See* Sherman, Al(bert)
Picker, Tom. *See* Silver, Abner
Picket, Ticky [or Tichy]. *See* Sendel, Erich
Pickett, Boris. *See* Pickett, Bobby
Pickett, R. E. *See* Kraushaar, Charles
Pickhardt, Ione. *See* Dalton, Kathleen I. P.
Pickle, Peregrine. *See* Upton, George Putnam
Picon, Molly. *See* Pyekoon, Margaret
Pie, Brian. *See* Ropes, Arthur Reed
Pied Piper of Broadway. *See* Simon, Gus(tav(e)) [or Augustus] (Edward)
Pied Piper of Light Classical Music. *See* Rieu, André
Pied Piper of Love, The. *See* Carter, Barry Eugene
Pier, George. *See* Pirckmayer, Georg(e)

Pierce, Bertha. *See* Minot, Elizabeth
Pierce, Bettye. *See* Volkart, Bettye Sue
Pierce, Billie. *See* Goodson, Willie Madison
Piero delapiazza. *See* La Rue, Pierre de
Pierre. *See* Vieu, Jane [or Jeanne] (Elisabeth Marie)
Pierre de Marseille. *See* Gautier, Pierre (c.1642-1696)
Pierre, William. *See* Dykema, Peter W(illiam)
Pierson, Heinrich Hugo. *See* Pearson, Henry Hugh
Piestra, Pierre Étienne. *See* Cormon, Eugéne
Pieterszoon, Jan. *See* Swybbertszon, Jan Pieterszoon
Pietra, Giuseppe T. *See* Stone, Joseph T.
Pietro de Rossi. *See* Rubeus, Petrus
Pietro, George. *See* Horton, (George) Vaughn
Pietro Paolo, Don. *See* Stella, Scipione
Piffero, Il. *See* Bernardino
Pig, Edward. *See* Gorey, Edward (St. John)
Pig 'n' Whistle Red. *See* McTell, Willie Samuel
Pigmeat Pete. *See* Wilson, Wesley
Pigro, Il. *See* Basile, Giovanni Battista [or Giambattista]
Pilderwasser. *See* Weisser, Joshua Samuel
Pilger, Karl. *See* Spazier, Johann Gottlieb Karl
Pilgrim, The. *See* Green, Phil(ip)
Pilgrim. *See* McCollin, Frances
Pilgrim, Lord. *See* Labrunie, Gérard
Pillar of the Boston Classicists. *See* Chadwick, George Whitefield
Pilonij, Giuseppe. *See* Gesualdo, Carlo
Pilusky. *See* Civinini, Guelfo
Pimiento, Fray. *See* Villoldo (Arroyo), Angel (Gregorio)
Pimpinelli. *See* Dauphin, Léopold
Pincus, Buck. *See* Simon, George (T(homas))
Pindar, A. *See* Blackmar, A(rmand) E(dward)
Pindar, Peter. *See* Daniel, George
Pindar, Peter. *See* Lawler, C. F.
Pindar, Peter. *See* Wolcot, John
Pineapple, Johnny. *See* Kaonohi, David
Pinewood Tom. *See* White, Josh(ua) (Daniel)
Pinguento. *See* Moderne, Jacques
Pinkura, Nero. *See* Vyhnalek, Ivo
Pinkus Barber. *See* Kaufmann, Fritz Mordechai
Pinnacle of the Baroque. *See* Bach, Johann Sebastian
Pinot, Claude. *See* Delagaye, Georges
Pinozzi, Carlo. *See* Rothstein, James (Jakob)
Pinto, Alex. *See* Linden, David Gysbert (van der)
Pinto, George Frederick. *See* Saunders, George Frederick
Pinzer, August Daniel. *See* Binzer, August Daniel
Pioneer Black Comedian. *See* Williams, Egbert Austin
Pioneer Composer of the French Cantata. *See* Morin, Jean-Baptiste
Piovanti, Nicola. *See* Morricone, Ennio
Pipegrop, Heinrich. *See* Baryphonus, Henricus
Piper, John. *See* Alcock, John
Pipes, Jeemes (of Pipesville). *See* Massett, Stephen C.
Pippo, (Signor). *See* Amadei, Filippo
Piquefort, Jean. *See* Routhier, (Sir) Adolphe-Basile
Pirate, Paul. *See* Partch, Harry
Pirrotta, Nino. *See* Pirrotta, Antonio
Pisani, Giovanni Aleandro. *See* Spinola, Giovanni Andrea
Pisano, Bernardo. *See* Pagoli, Bernardo (di Benedetto)
Piscator. *See* Cotton, Charles
Piscator, Georg. *See* Fischer, Georg
Pistocchini. *See* Acciaiuoli, Filippo
Pistocchino, Il. *See* Pistocchi, Francesco Antonio Ma(ssi)miliano
Pistocco. *See* Pistocchi, Francesco Antonio Ma(ssi)miliano
Pit. *See* Ederer, Josef
Pitarra, Seraif. *See* Soler (i Hubert), Frederic
Pit(z)sche. *See* Abrass, Osias Joshua
Pitt, A(rthur). *See* Spear, Eric
Pitt, Arthur. *See* Bernard, Clem(ent)
Pitt, Jack. *See* Zoeren, Elbert van
Pitt, Thomas Dibdin. *See* Dibdin, Thomas J(ohn)
Pittar, (Mrs.) Isaac. *See* Krumpholtz, Fanny
Pitter, Harold. *See* Deutscher, Karlheinz
Pittsburgh's March King. *See* Nirella, Vincent Daniel
Piva, Gregorio. *See* Steffani, Agostino
Pixinguinha. *See* Vianna (Filho), A(lfredo da Rocha)
Piya, Prem. *See* Khan, Faiyaz (Hus(s)ain)
Pizzaman. *See* Cook, Quentin
Planes, Giovanni des. *See* Piani, Giovanni Antonio
Plansis, Petrus. *See* La Rue, Pierre de
Plaschky, Hanno. *See* Feltz, Kurt (August Karl)
Pleasant, Cousin Joe. *See* Joseph, Pleasant
Pleasant Joe. *See* Joseph, Pleasant
Pless, Hans. *See* Pischinger, Hans
Ploris. *See* Ondříček, Emanuel
Plum, J. *See* Wodehouse, P(elham) G(renville)
Plume, (Mrs.) N. D. *See* Crosby, Fanny [i.e., Frances] J(ane)
Plunder. *See* McNally, Leonard
Po' Slim. *See* Hooker, John Lee
Pocholo. *See* Pérez, Adolfo
Podeska, Irina. *See* Wagness, Bernard
Podesta, Nicola. *See* Newell, Joseph Edward
Podhorský. *See* Frypès, Karel (Vladimir)
Podskalsky, Karel. *See* Bendl, Karel
Poe, Penelope. *See* Collins, William Francis
Poet, A. *See* Montgomery, James
Poet and Seer of His Profession, The. *See* Thompson, Oscar
Poet from Nashville, The. *See* Hall, Thomas
Poet Laureate of Chautauqua. *See* Lathbury, Mary Ann [or Artemesia]
Poet Laureate of Rock 'n' Roll, The. *See* Berry, Charles Edward Anderson
Poet Laureate of Teenage Rock. *See* Berry, Charles Edward Anderson

Poet of a Doomed Austria, The. *See* Hofmannsthal, Hugo von
Poet of Methodism, The. *See* Wesley, Charles
Poet of Nashville. *See* Hall, Thomas
Poet of the Evangelical Revival. *See* Wesley, Charles
Poet of the Organ, The. *See* Crawford, Jesse
Poet of the Poor, The. *See* Crabbe, George
Poet of Titchfield Street, The. *See* Pound, Ezra ((Weston) Loomis)
Poet Princess of Rock. *See* Smith, Patricia [or Patti] (Lee)
Poet Singer of Ohio, The. *See* Fanning, Cecil
Poet Stutter. *See* D'Urfey, Thomas
Poeta de la canción, El. *See* Ruiz Narváez, José Napoleón
Poetzsch, Werner. *See* Tauber, Werner
Pohjanmies, Juhani. *See* Lindfors, Juhani
Poindexter, Buster. *See* Johansen, David
Pointer, George. *See* Dickson, Mary Hannah
Poison Pen Cassidy. *See* Cassidy, Claudia
Poisson, Jakub Jan. *See* Ryba, Jakub [or Jakob] (Simon) Jan [or Johann]
Polak-Daniels, (B.). *See* Knigge, (Baron) Wilhelm
Polak, Jakub. *See* Reys, Jakub
Poland's Greatest Composer. *See* Chopin, Frederic
Poldowski. *See* Wieniawska, Irene Regine
Polewheel. *See* Wheeler, Paul
Polgar, (Janos). *See* Kubelik, Jan
Polichinelle. *See* Koning, Victor
Polish Offenbach. *See* Sonnenfeld, Adolf Gustaw
Polish Strauss. *See* Lewandowski, Leopold
Political Dissenter, A. *See* Rands, William Brightly
Polka King. *See* Yankovic, Frank(ie) (John)
Poll, Peter. *See* Berlipp, Friedel
Pollack, Martin. *See* Gardner, Maurice
Pollak, Frank. *See* Peleg, Frank
Pollard, Thomas Leaming. *See* Walsh, Austin
Pollini, Bernhard. *See* Pohl, Baruch
Pollock, Molly. *See* Pollock, Muriel
Poly Styrene. *See* Elliott, Marion
Polyalphabeticity. *See* Sapp, Allen (Dwight)
Polyanthe. *See* Chap(p)onnier, Alexandre
Polygon Window. *See* James, Richard D(avid)
Polyphonist, The. *See* Love, William Edward
Pomeisl, Willibald. *See* Kann, Hans
Pomeranian Lassus, The. *See* Dulichius, Philipp(us)
Pomus, Doc. *See* Felder, Jerome (Solon)
Pomus, Jerome. *See* Felder, Jerome (Solon)
Ponsonby, A. B. *See* Conant, Grace Wilbur
Ponsonby, Scroby. *See* Ponsonby, Eustace
Pontet, Henry Theodore. *See* Piccolomini, Theodore (Auguste Maria Joseph)
Ponteuil. *See* Triboulet, M.
Pontier, Armando. *See* Punturero, Armando Francisco
Pontiff of Music Wisdom, The. *See* Krehbiel, Henry (Edward)
Pontin, Maxime. *See* Rawlings, Charles Arthur
Poole, Joe. *See* Gaul, Harvey B(artlett)
Poole, Naida. *See* Grace, Grace
Poor Boy. *See* Oden, James Burke
Poor, Hans. *See* Ritter, Karl
Poor Jim. *See* Rachell, James
Poor Man's Bob Hope, The. *See* Burnette, Lester Alvin
Poor Man's Liberace. *See* Presley, Elvis A(a)ron
Poor Man's Pope. *See* Marley, Robert [or Bob] Nesta
Poot, Linke. *See* Döblin, Alfred
Pop, Iggy. *See* Osterberg, James Newell
Popa Chubby. *See* Horowitz, Ted
Poppin, D. H. *See* Grinsted, William Stanley
Poppy Nogood. *See* Riley, Terry
Pops. *See* Armstrong, (Daniel) Louis
Porchea, Paul. *See* Pathorne, Ella Baber
Porita, Ruth. *See* Poritzky, Ruth
Porpora, Niccolo A. *See* Kreisler, Fritz [i.e., Friedrich] (-Max)
P-Orridge, Genesis. *See* Megson, Neil (Andrew)
Portch, Al. *See* Neto, Laurindo José de Araujo Almeida Nobrega
Portela, Paulo de. *See* Oliveira, Paulo Benjamin de
Porter, B. L. *See* Ballard, Clint(on) C(onger), Jr.
Porter, Charles. *See* Yoder, Paul V(an Buskirk)
Porter, Cue. *See* Hodges, John(ny) Cornelius
Porter, Dave. *See* Crow(e), Francis Luther
Porter, Ellen Jane. *See* Lorenz, Ellen Jane
Porter, John. *See* McCutchan, Robert G(uy)
Porter, L. N. *See* Lorenz, Ellen Jane
Porter, Nacio. *See* Brown, Nacio Herb, Jr.
Porter, Ruth. *See* Crawford, Ruth (Porter)
Porter, Walter. *See* Lorenz, Ellen Jane
Porter, Walter. *See* Walter, Forrest G.
Porterhouse, Tedham. *See* Zimmerman, Robert Allen
Portner, Lennie. *See* Mäder, Wolfgang
Porto, Don. *See* Bidgood, Henry [or Harry] (James)
Porto, Pedro do. *See* Escobar, Pedro de
Portway, Al(f). *See* Bygraves, Walter (William)
Posey, Sandy. *See* Sharp, Martha
Posford, George. *See* Ashwell, Benjamin George
Positive, Peter. *See* Montgomery, James
Possum, The. *See* Jones, George (Glen(n))
Post, Irving. *See* Kaufman, Isidore
Post, Lea. *See* Apostel, Hans Erich
Post, Mike. *See* Postil, Leland M(ichael)
Post-punk Generation's Prophet of Rage, The. *See* Garfield, Henry
Post, S. *See* Dishinger, Ronald C(hristian)
Postmodern Neo-Arnoldian. *See* Lipman, Samuel
Potter, Nettie. *See* Moore, Monette
Potter, O. L. *See* Cohen, Frieda P. C.
Potter, Paul. *See* Kountz, Richard

Potter, Paul M(eredith). *See* MacClean, Walter Arthur
Potter, William. *See* Kountz, Richard
Pottersdale, Tom. *See* Crist, (Lucien) Bainbridge
Potts, Harry (Vince Philip). *See* Pot(ts), Victor Léon
Pougin, Arthur. *See* Paroisse-Pougin, François-Auguste-Arthur
Pourtalès, Guy de. *See* Pourtalès, Guido James de
Poute. *See* Burgess, Alexander
Powell, Bud. *See* Powell, Earl
Powell, Buttercup. *See* Powell, Altivia Edwards
Powell, Dudley. *See* Jepps, Dudley
Powell, Kit. *See* Powell, Christopher Bolland
Powell, Lester. *See* Martin, Ray(mond)
Powell, Mel. *See* Epstein, Melvin
Powell, Rudy. *See* Powell, Everard Stephen, Sr.
Powell, Teddy. *See* Paolella, Alfred
Powell, W(illiam) C. *See* Polla, William C.
Power-Pill. *See* James, Richard D(avid)
Powers, Chet [or Chester]. *See* Valenti, Dino
Powers, James [or Jimmy] T. *See* McGovern, James
Powers, Jett. *See* Smith, James Marcus
Powers, Julia. *See* Prather, Ida
Powers, Julius. *See* Prather, Ida
Powers, Kane. *See* Wilson, Ira B(ishop)
Powers, Robert. *See* Kinyon, John L(eroy)
Powers, Rod. *See* Maschek, Adrian Mathew
Pozar, Cleve F. *See* Pozar, Robert F.
Pozo, Chano. *See* Pozo (y Gonzales), Luciano
Pradelini, Crateo. *See* Ottoboni, Pietro
Prado, Perez. *See* Perez Prado, Domasco [or Damasco]
Praeceptor Germaniae. *See* Schwarzerd, Philipp
Praenestinus, (Petrus Aloysius). *See* Palestrina, Giovanni Pierluigi da
Praetorius, Gottschalk. *See* Schulz(e), Gottschalk
Praetorius, Hieronymus. *See* Schulz(e), Hieronymus
Praetorius, Michael. *See* Schultheiss, Michael
Prago, Helmut. *See* De Schrijver, Karel
Pratis, Johannes de. *See* Stokem, Johannes de
Prato, Johannes de. *See* Stokem, Johannes de
Praxiteles. *See* Pandel, Ted [or Tex]
Preacher's Daughter. *See* Johnson, Miriam
Preciso, Don. *See* Iza Zamácola, Juan Antonio de
Predamosche, Verdacchio [pseud.]. *See* Predamosche, Verdacchio [pseud.]
Preiss, Gabriele. *See* Preissová, Gabriela (née Sekerová)
Prem Piya. *See* Khan, Faiyaz (Hus(s)ain)
Premiere Man of American Music. *See* Burnett, Chester Arthur
Prendcourt, "Captain" (François de). *See* Gutenberg von Weigolshausen
Prendiville, Harry. *See* Prendiville, Henri Jean
Prenestino, Giovanni Pierlugi da. *See* Palestrina, Giovanni Pierluigi da
Prennessel, Peter. *See* Narholz, Gerhard
Prentice, Jock. *See* Prentice, Charles W(hitecross)
Prentice, (Mrs.) L. C. *See* Crosby, Fanny [i.e., Frances] J(ane)
Prerauer, CM. *See* Prerauer, Curt
Prerauer, CM. *See* Prerauer, Maria (née Wolkowsky)
Presbyter. *See* Jones, S.
Presbyter of the Church of England. *See* Toplady, Augustus Montague
Presepi, Presepio. *See* Patrignani, Giuseppe
President, The. *See* Krehbiel, Ernest (Edward)
President of the Derrieregarde, The. *See* Wilder, Alec [i.e., Alexander] (Lafayette Chew)
Presley, Reg. *See* Ball, Reginald
Presto, Fa. *See* Mašek, Karel
Preston, Adam. *See* Sawyer, Henry S.
Preston, John. *See* Haenschen, Walter (G(ustave))
Preston, M(atilee) L(oeb). *See* Loeb-Evans, M(atilee)
Preston, Robert. *See* Ehret, Walter (Charles)
Preston, Stanley. *See* Saenger, Gustave
Preston, Terry. *See* Husky, Ferlin
Prete Rosso, Il. *See* Vivaldi, Antonio (Lucio)
Pretty Penny. *See* Dorfman, Helen Horn
Pretzel, Elvis. *See* Presley, Elvis A(a)ron
Previn, André (George). *See* Priwin, Andreas (Ludwig)
Preyer, C. A. *See* Kunkel, Charles
Price, Anthony. *See* Wilson, Roger Cole
Price, Arthur. *See* Phillips, James John
Price, Benton. *See* Wilson, Ira B(ishop)
Price, Benton [or Benson]. *See* Wilson, Roger Cole
Price, Darryl. *See* Petite, (E.) Dale
Price-Davies, (Sir) Humphrey. *See* Gold, Glenn Herbert
Price, Florence Beatrice. *See* Smith, Florence Beatrice
Price, Jimmie. *See* White, John I(rwin)
Price, Jimmy. *See* Marvin, John(ny) (Senator)
Price, Morton. *See* Rhys, Horton
Price, Penny. *See* Watts, Mayme
Price, S. J. *See* Seredy, J(ulius) S.
Price, Walter. *See* Wilson, Roger Cole
Price, Will. *See* Catsos, Nicholas A.
Priest of the Church of England, A. *See* Neale, J(ohn) M(ason)
Priest of the Diocese, A. *See* Neale, J(ohn) M(ason)
Priest of the English Church, A. *See* Neale, J(ohn) M(ason)
Primal Scream Personified, A. *See* Garfield, Henry
Primarius. *See* Johannes de Garlandia
Primcock, A. *See* Ralph, J(ames)
Prime, Alberta. *See* Hunter, Alberta
Primitive Radio Gods. *See* O'Connor, Chris
Primo, Jose. *See* Lebys, Henry
Primrose, Joe. *See* Mills, Irving
Prince. *See* Nelson, Prince Rogers
Prince, The. *See* Rajonsky [or Rajonski], Milton Michael
Prince Buster. *See* Campbell, Cecil Bustamente
Prince Charming. *See* Basie, William (Allen)

Prince Charming of Pop, The. *See* Stanford, Trevor H(erbert)
Prince, Hal. *See* Prince, Harold (S(mith))
Prince in Music, The. *See* Boethius, Anicius Man(l)ius Severinus
Prince Lincoln. *See* Thompson, (Prince) Lincoln
Prince of Broadway, The. *See* Cohan, George M(ichael)
Prince of Darkness. *See* Davis, Miles (Dewey), (III)
Prince of Darkness, The. *See* Firbank, Louis [or Lewis] (Allen)
Prince of Flemish Song. *See* Mortelmans, Lodewijk
Prince of Lyrists. *See* Schubert, Franz Peter
Prince of Motown, The. *See* Gaye, Marvin (Pentz)
Prince of Music. *See* Ockeghem, Johannes
Prince of Music, The. *See* Palestrina, Giovanni Pierluigi da
Prince of Musicians. *See* Ockeghem, Johannes
Prince of Negro Songwriters, The. *See* Bland, James A(llen)
Prince of Puns. *See* Wolf, Tom
Prince of Scottish Hymn-writers, The. *See* Bonar, Horatius
Prince of the American Theater, The. *See* Cohan, George M(ichael)
Prince of the Kora, The. *See* Diabaté, Toumani
Prince of the *Opéra-comique*. *See* Auber, Daniel François Esprit
Prince of the Piano-Forte, The. *See* Gottschalk, Louis Moreau
Prince of the Violoneaux, The. *See* Allard, Joseph
Prince Rakeem. *See* Diggs, Robert
Prince, Winston. *See* Thompson, (James) Winston
Princeps Musicae. *See* Palestrina, Giovanni Pierluigi da
Princess of the Blues, The. *See* Brown, Olive
Princess of the Pedal Steel, The. *See* Jory, Sarah
Princess Sharifa. *See* Gibb, Michelle
Principe de la salsa, El. *See* Mejía López, Luis Enrique
Principe di Venosa. *See* Gesualdo, Carlo
Prindle, G. F. *See* Bliss, P(hilip) Paul
Prior, H. R. *See* Vallee, Herbert Pryor
Prisma. *See* Tapia Alcázar, Sylvia
Privas, Xavier. *See* Taravel, Antoine
Prix, Adalbert. *See* Bahn, Adolf
Prix, Adalbert. *See* Grünbaum, Johann Christopher
Pro Phundo Basso. *See* Bliss, P(hilip) P.
Probus. *See* Shrubsole, William, Jr.
Proby, P. J. *See* Smith, James Marcus
Prodigal Creator. *See* Patrick, Kentrick
Professor Longhair. *See* Byrd, Henry Roeland
Professor Longhair of Cajun Music. *See* Abshire, Nathan
Professor of Music, A. *See* Miller, Edward
Progneus, Ottomar. *See* Nachtigall, Othmar [or Ottmar]
Prokop, Ladislav. *See* Prochazka, Ladislav, Freiherr von
Prometheus Gemini. *See* Smith, Clifford (1945-)
Pronti. *See* Molijn, Sebastian
Prophet-Patriach of Russian Music, The. *See* Glinka, Michael Ivanovitch
Prosindio, Ensildo. *See* Petrosellini, Giuseppe
Protico. *See* Pasquini, Bernardo
Proton de la Chapelle. *See* Fragny, Robert de
Prototypical Modern Jazzman, The. *See* Green, Benny (1963-)
Prudent, Emile Beunie. *See* Gaultier, Racine
Pruett, Jeanne. *See* Bowman, Norma Jean
Prugg, Jacob de. *See* Brouck, Jacob(us) de
Pry, Mr. *See* Disher, Maurice Willson
Pryor, Bubba. *See* Pryor, James Edward
Pryor, Martha. *See* Howard, Ethel
Pryor, Snooky. *See* Pryor, James Edward
Prysgol. *See* Owen, William
Pseudo-Aristoteles. *See* Lambertus, Magister
Psyche. *See* Craig, Carl
Puccini of Opera, The. *See* Wagner, Richard
Puck. *See* Montefiore, Tommaso (Mosè)
Puck, Guy. *See* Mallis, Constantine Alexander (Haji [or Hagi])
Puente, Ernestito. *See* Puente, Ernesto Antonio, (Jr.)
Puente, Tito. *See* Puente, Ernesto Antonio, (Jr.)
Puerto, Pedro del. *See* Escobar, Pedro de
Puff Daddy. *See* Combs, Sean
Puffy. *See* Combs, Sean
Puget, Loisa. *See* Lemoine, Louise Françoise
Pugnani, Gaetano. *See* Kreisler, Fritz [i.e., Friedrich] (-Max)
Pulaski, John. *See* Isaac, Merle (John)
Pulitzer, Joseph. *See* Pulitzer, Walter
Pulsitiva, Johann. *See* Weinlein, Josaphat
Pun. *See* Rios, Christopher
Punk's Poet Laureate. *See* Garfield, Henry
Punto, Giovanni. *See* Stich, Johann [or Jan] Wenzel [or Václav]
Pupa Rico. *See* Burrell, Orville (Richard)
Purcell, Buzz. *See* Purcell, E. B.
Purcell, Edward Cockram. *See* Cockram, Edward Purcell
Purcell, Gilbert. *See* Kountz, Richard
Purest Glory of Italian Genius. *See* Verdi, Giuseppe
Purlenne, Jean-Baptiste. *See* Gauthier, Paul-Marcel
Puro, Il. *See* Bardi, Giovanni de', Count of Vernio
Purple One, The. *See* Nelson, Prince Rogers
Pursuer of Beautiful Noise. *See* Diamond, Neil (Leslie)
Puteus, Vincentius. *See* Dal Pozzo, Vincenzo
Putman, Curly. *See* Putman, Claude, Jr.
Puzzy Fuppy. *See* Bleiweiss, Peter R(ichard)
Puycousin, Edouard de. *See* Labrunie, Gérard
Pyramid. *See* Smith, Mike D.

– Q –

Q. *See* Jones, Quincey Delight
Q-Chastic. *See* James, Richard D(avid)
Q in the Corner. *See* Bayly, (Nathaniel) Thomas Haynes
Q. Q. *See* Taylor, Jane
Quad Father, The. *See* Montenegro, Hugo
Quaker Poet, The. *See* Barton, Bernard
Qualis, Talis. *See* Strandberg, Karl Vilhelm August
Quas. *See* Quaciari, Gene L(ouis)
Quast, Peter. *See* Cube, Felix Eberhard von
Quatermass, Martin. *See* Carpenter, John(ny)
Quatrelles. *See* L'Epine, Ernest Louis Victor Jules
Quatremayne, Frank. *See* Smiles, Frank
Quatro, Suzi. *See* Quatrocchio, Susan Kay
Quebec, Adela. *See* Tyrwhitt-Wilson, (Sir) Gerald (Hugh)
Quebec Mozart. *See* Mathieu, (René) André (Rodolphe)
Queen, The. *See* Spivey, Victoria [or Vicky] (Regina)
Queen Latifah. *See* Owens, Dana (Elaine)
Queen of American Pop Music, The. *See* Egstrom, (Norma) Dolores
Queen of Bohemia. *See* McElheney, Jane
Queen of Chicago Blues, The. *See* Walton, Cora
Queen of Country. *See* McEntire, Reba
Queen of Country Comedy, The. *See* Colley, Sarah Ophelia
Queen of Country Music. *See* Deason, Muriel (Ellen)
Queen of Country Music. *See* Pugh, Virginia Wynette
Queen of Country Music, The. *See* Webb, Loretta
Queen of Hip-Hop Soul. *See* Blige, Mary Jane
Queen of Housewife Rock. *See* Reddy, Helen
Queen of Jazz, The. *See* Scruggs, Mary Elfrieda
Queen of Pop, The. *See* Ciccone, Madonna Louise Veronica
Queen of Puerto Rican Merengue Music. *See* Tañón, Olga
Queen of Rap. *See* Owens, Dana (Elaine)
Queen of Rock. *See* Joplin, Janis
Queen of Rock and Roll, The. *See* Penniman, Richard [or Ricardo] Wayne
Queen of Rock 'n' Roll. *See* Jackson, Wanda (Lavonne)
Queen of Song, The. *See* Tilgham, Amelia L.
Queen of Soul. *See* Franklin, Aretha
Queen of the Blues, The. *See* Dunn, Sara(h)
Queen of the Blues, The. *See* Howard, Ethel
Queen of the Blues. *See* Jones, Ruth Lee
Queen of the Blues. *See* Spivey, Victoria [or Vicky] (Regina)
Queen of the Blues. *See* Walton, Cora
Queen of the Cowgirls. *See* Smith, Frances Octavia
Queen of the Jukeboxes, The. *See* Jones, Ruth Lee
Queen of the Moaners, The. *See* Gibbons, Irene
Queen of the Moaners, The. *See* Smith, Clara
Queen of the Piano. *See* Wieck, Clara Josephine
Queen of the West, The. *See* Smith, Frances Octavia
Queen of Tin Pan Alley. *See* Petkere, Bernice
Queen, V. *See* Spivey, Victoria [or Vicky] (Regina)
Queen Victoria's Favorite Composer. *See* Elgar, (Sir) Edward
Queen's Hunchback, The. *See* Leinati, Carlo Ambrogio
Quico. *See* Artola, Héctor
Quidant, Alfred. *See* Quidant, Joseph
Quincy Jones of Irish Music, The. *See* Lunny, Donal
Quinito. *See* Valverde Sanjuàn, Joaquin
Quinn, Adelle. *See* Harvey, Lucy Quinn
Quinn, Freddy. *See* Petz, Manfred
Quinn, H. L. *See* Keiser, Robert (A(dolph))
Quinn, J. Mark. *See* Quinn, James J(oseph?), (Jr.)
Quintana, Carlos. *See* Feather, Leonard (Geoffrey)
Quintanilla, Phat Kat. *See* Quintanilla (Perez), A(be) B.
Quintessential American Composer, The. *See* Nelson, Ron(ald J.)
Quirino. *See* Papi, Antonio
Quirino, F. C. Accdemico. *See* Clerico, Francesco
Quism, Basheer. *See* Gryce, G(eorge) G(eneral)
Quivalos, Mikolos. *See* Quigley, Michael
Quiz. *See* Caswall, Edward
Qvalis, Talis. *See* Strandberg, Karl Vilhelm August

– R –

R. *See* Heber, Reginald
R**** de, (Chevalier). *See* Royer de Villerie, (Chevalier)
R n. *See* Robinson, Robert
R. A. B. *See* Bertram, Robert Aitken
R. B. *See* Bridges, Robert Seymour
R. D. L. *See* Loes, Harry Dixon
R. E. *See* Turton, W(illiam) H(arry) [or H(enry)]
R. H. *See* Hainworth, Robert
R. H. A. *See* Andrews, R. Hoffmann (the younger)
R. H. L. *See* Lyon, Robert Hunter
RKO's Singing Cowboy. *See* Whitley, Ray(mond) Otis
R. L. *See* Langdon, Richard
R. L. P. *See* Pearsall, Robert Lucas (de)
R. O. D. H. F. *See* Chorley, Henry Fothergill
R. R. *See* Robinson, Robert
R. S. *See* Starkey, Richard
R. W. L. *See* Lowrie, Randolph W.
RZA. *See* Diggs, Robert
Ra, Sun. *See* Blount, Herman
Raabe, Helmut. *See* Weinberg, Symson [or Simson]
Rabbit. *See* Bundrich, John
Rabbit. *See* Hodges, John(ny) Cornelius
Rabbit, Daddy. *See* Pettis, Coleman, Jr.
Rabbitt, Eddie. *See* Thomas, Edward
Rabensteiner, Eduard. *See* Rottmann, Eduard
Rabito. *See* Fernández, Juan Carlos
Rabula. *See* Pintacuda, Salvatore

Rachell, Yank. *See* Rachell, James
Rachmaninoff, Sergei (Spirit). *See* Brown, Rosemary (née Dickeson)
Rachwitz, Franz Freiherr von. *See* Bonn, Franz
Racine of Music, The. *See* Sacchini, Antonio Marie Gaspare
Rackley, Laurence. *See* Smith, Lawrence Rackley
Raconteur, The. *See* Huneker, James Gibbons
Rader, Allan. *See* Yoder, Paul V(an Buskirk)
Rader, Michael. *See* De Filippi, Amedeo
Radford, Cliff. *See* ZIV-TV
Radford, Dave. *See* Blyth, David R(adford)
Radical Prophet of American Youth, The. *See* Zimmerman, Robert Allen
Radio (Calypso Singer). *See* Span(n), Norman
Radio Chin-Up Girl, The. *See* Overstake, (Virginia) Lucille
Radio Girl. *See* Vonderlieth, Leonore
Radio Mac. *See* McClintock, Harry (K(irby))
Radio Queen. *See* Cooper, Myrtle Eleanor
Radio Red. *See* Hall, Wendell (Woods)
Radio's Cheerful Little Earful. *See* Little, John (Leonard)
Radio's First Song Sensation. *See* Vonderlieth, Leonore
Rado, James. *See* Radomski, James
Rae, Kenneth. *See* Slater, David Dick
Raeburn, Hugh. *See* Reynolds, Wynford Herbert
Raedzielg, Gisella. *See* Della [or Delle] Grazie, Gisella
Raekwon. *See* Woods, Corey
Rafael José. *See* Diaz, R(afael) J(osé)
Rafael, L(udwig). *See* Kieskamp, Hedwig
Rafael, Walter. *See* Kountz, Richard
Raffaela. *See* Aleotti, Raffaela-Argenta
Raffaelli, Francesca. *See* Caccini, Francesca
Raffay, Ina. *See* Fitz, Walter
Rafferty, Pat. *See* Browne, Henry
Raffi. *See* Cavoukian, Raffi
Ragde, Fritz. *See* Hansen, Edgar
Raggi, Peter Seak. *See* Montani, Pietro
Ragotzy, Prince. *See* Saint Germain, Count of
Ragtime Guitar's Foremost Fingerpicker. *See* Phelps, Arthur
Ragtime Jimmy. *See* Durante, James [or Jimmy] (Francis)
Ragtime Jimmy. *See* Monaco, James (V.)
Ragtime Kid, The. *See* Campbell, Sanford Brunson
Ragtime King, The. *See* Barnett, Michael
Ragtime King, (The). *See* Greene, Gene
Ragtime Reinhold. *See* Svensson, Reinhold
Ragtime Wonder of the South. *See* Woods, H. Clarence
Ragtime's Father. *See* Harney, Ben(jamin) R(obertson)
Rahman, A. R. *See* Kumar, Dileep
Rahman, Allahrakha. *See* Kumar Dileep
Rahman, Emil. *See* Hansson, Stig (Axel)
Rahsaan. *See* Kirk, Ronald T(heodore)
Raiker, Thommy. *See* Schulze-Gerlach, Hartmut
Railroad Bill. *See* Dorsey, Thomas A(ndrew)
Raimar, Freimund. *See* Weinhöppel, Hans Richard
Raimer, Freymund. *See* Rückert, Johann Michel Friedrich
Raimo, (Padre). *See* Bartoli, Erasmo
Raimond. *See* Taylor, Isidore Justin Sévérin
Raimondi, Pietro. *See* Raimondi, Pietro [ficticious composer]
Rainer. *See* Ptacek, Rainer
Rainer, J. B. *See* Bonvin, Ludwig
Rainey, Gertrude. *See* Pridgett, Gertrude (Malissa Nix)
Rainey, Ma. *See* Pridgett, Gertrude (Malissa Nix)
Rainger, Ralph. *See* Reichenthal, Ralph
Rainis, Janis. *See* Plieksan, Janis
Rainwater, Marvin. *See* Percy, Marvin (Karlton)
Rainy, Al(bert). *See* Raiani, Al(bert George)
Raitif de la Bretonne. *See* Duval, Paul Alexandre Martin
Rakim. *See* Griffin William, Jr.
Raleigh, Cecil. *See* Rowlands, Abraham Cecil Francis Fothergill
Ralph, Fred. *See* Krome, Herman(n) (Friedrich)
Ralph, Kirkland. *See* Kinder, Ralph
Ralph, Ralph J. *See* Schuckett, Ralph Dion
Ralphs, H. *See* Becker, Karl Heinz
Ram, Buck. *See* Ram, Samuel
Ramal, Walter. *See* De La Mare, Walter (John)
Rambeau, Eddie. *See* Flurie, Edward (Cletus)
Ramblin' Bob. *See* McCollum, Robert Lee
Ramblin' Jack. *See* Adnopoz, Elliott Charles
Rambling Rogue. *See* Rose, (Knols) Fred
Rambo, Dottie. *See* Luttrell, Joyce Reba
Rambo, Peter. *See* Mielenz, Hans
Rameau, Jean. *See* Labaigt, Laurent
Ramirez, Luis. *See* Green, Phil(ip)
Ramirez, Luis. *See* Paramor, Norman [or Norrie] (William)
Ramirez, Ram. *See* Ramirez, Roger (J.)
Ramler, A. J. *See* Lorenz, E(dmund) S(imon)
Ramm, Valentina Iosifovna. *See* Mandel'shtam, Valentina Iosifovna
Rammelzee. *See* Basquiet, Jean Michel
Ramón Orlando. *See* Valoy, Ramón Orlando
Ramon, Paul. *See* McCartney, (James) Paul
Ramone, Joey. *See* Hyman, Jeffrey
Ramondo, Paul. *See* Raymond, Harold (Newell)
Ramone, Dee Dee. *See* Colvin, Douglas Glenn
Ramsey, George?. *See* Dorsey, Thomas A(ndrew)
Ramsey, Jack. *See* Finkelstein, Abe
Ramsey, Norman. *See* Rodby, Walter (A.)
Rana, Johann. *See* Frosch, Johann
Rand, Ande. *See* Ram, Samuel
Rand, Harry. *See* Whitcup, Leonard

Rand, Lionel. *See* Clouser, Lionel R(andolph)
Randall, Bruce. *See* Rodby, Walter (A.)
Randall, Peter. *See* Treharne, Bryceson
Randall, Roy. *See* Finkelstein, Abe
Randazzo, Teddy. *See* Randazzo, Alessandro Carmelo
Randle, Dodie. *See* Flournoy, Roberta Jean
Randolph, Boots. *See* Randolph, Homer Louis, (III)
Randolph, Cary (H.). *See* Randolph, Jane Cary Harrison
Randolph, John Carroll. *See* Fisher, William Arms
Randolph, Randy. *See* Randolph, Homer Louis, (III)
Raney, Sue. *See* Claussen, Raelene (C(laire))
Ranfagni, Enrico. *See* Giacosa, Giuseppe
Ranger Doug. *See* Green, Douglas B.
Ranger, Shorty. *See* Haberfield, Edwin
Rankin, Billy. *See* Schwarz, Brinsley
Rankin, Dusty. *See* Rankin, Roger Hogan
Rankin, W. S. *See* Bliss, P(hilip) Paul
Ranko. *See* Dučić, Jovan
Ransford, (L.). *See* Clarke, (Harold) Allan
Ransford, (L.). *See* Hicks, Tony (Christopher)
Ransford, (L.). *See* Nash, Graham
Rapelje, Marie. *See* Terry, Frances
Raphael of Music, The. *See* Mozart, Wolfgang Amadeus
Raphael of Opera, The. *See* Mozart, Wolfgang Amadeus
Raphun, Paul. *See* Rebhuhn, Paul
Rapier. *See* Watson, Alfred Edward Thomas
Rapindey. *See* Guerra, Marcelino
Rapone, Al. *See* Lewis, Al(bert John, Sr.)
Rap's First Lady. *See* Owens, Dana (Elaine)
Rap's "Original Gangster". *See* Marrow, Tracy
Rara. *See* Ravel, Maurice (Joseph)
Raro, Meister. *See* Schumann, Robert
Raro, Meister. *See* Wieck, (Johann Gottlob) Friedrich
Ras Shorty. *See* Blackman, Garfield
Rascel, R(enato). *See* Ranucci, Renato
Rasch, (Dieter). *See* Niederbremer, Artur
Raskin, David. *See* Sartain, John, Jr.
Raskolikow, N(ikolai). *See* Thomas, Peter
RaSun, Eomot. *See* Blakely, Ezra Lee Jr.
Rathcol. *See* Hay, Edward Norman
Ratisbonne, Georg de. *See* Chambray, Louis François
Raton, Rodente (Mousey). *See* Garrett, James Allen
Rattlesnake Annie. *See* Gallimore, Rosan(ne)
Ratuld, P. *See* Zbyszewski-Olechnowska, Maria
Ratz, Ludro. *See* Saraz, Louis
Ratzes. *See* Frank, Marco
Rau, Earl. *See* Burgstahler, Elton E.
Rauch, Fred. *See* Rauch, Alfred
Rauch, Karl. *See* Spross, Charles Gilbert
Rauls, Mac. *See* Schütte, Werner
Rauscher, Enrico. *See* Humphreys, Henry S(igurd)
Rauscher, Henry Humphreys. *See* Humphreys, Henry S(igurd)
Rauscher, Henry (Sigurd). *See* Humphreys, Henry S(igurd)
Rauscher, Sigurd. *See* Humphreys, Henry S(igurd)
Rautenberg, Theo. *See* Rauch, Alfred
Ravan, Genya. *See* Zelkowitz, Goldie
Ravel of His Generation, The. *See* Torke, Michael
Raven, Eddy. *See* Futch, Edward Garvin
Raven Grey Eagle. *See* Florio, Andrea Nicola
Raven, Paul. *See* Gadd, Paul
Ravenal, Dick. *See* Vlak, Kees
Ravenhall, Mrs. *See* Keiser, Robert (A(dolph))
Ravenhall, R. A. *See* Keiser, Robert (A(dolph))
Ravina, Menashe. *See* Rabinovitz, Menashe
Ravini, E. *See* Russell, (Robert C.) Kennedy
Rawling, Elsie. *See* Rawlings, Charles Arthur
Rawlings, Abe. *See* Rawlings, Charles Arthur
Rawlings, Charles Arthur. *See* Rawlings, Alfred William
Rawlings, Horatio E. *See* Rawlings, Charles Arthur
Rawlings, Wellington. *See* Rawlings, Charles Arthur
Ray, Buddy. *See* Ray, Robert J(ames)
Ray, David. *See* Newell, Norman
Ray, Herman. *See* Ray, Harmon
Ray, Isom. *See* Agee, Ray(mond Clinton)
Ray, Larry. *See* Hayes, Larry R(ay)
Ray, Lil(l)ian. *See* Neat(e), John
Ray, Randy. *See* Traywick, Randy (Bruce)
Ray, Ricardo [or Richie]. *See* Maldonado, Ricardo [or Richard] (Ray)
Ray, Roland. *See* Stults, R(obert) M(orrison)
Rayder, J. H(enri). *See* Rollinson, Thomas H.
Raye, Collin. *See* Wray, Floyd Collin
Raye, Don. *See* Wilhoite, Donald McRae, Jr.
Raymaker, Hortense. *See* Wagness, Bernard
Raymond, Bruce. *See* Bennett, Theron C(atlin)
Raymond, Eugene. *See* Hewitt, John (Henry) Hill
Raymond, Fred(dy). *See* Vesely, (Raimund) Friedrich
Raymond, Harry. *See* Slaughter, M(arion) T(ry)
Raymond, Helen. *See* Wagness, Bernard
Raymond, Henri. *See* Cartier, Henri
Raymond, Jack. *See* Cobb, George L(inus)
Raymond, Karel. *See* Vačkař, Dalibor C(yril)
Raymond, Michel. *See* Brucker, Raymond (Philippe Auguste)
Raymond, Michel. *See* Gaudichot-Masson, Auguste Michel Benoît
Raymond, Richard. *See* McCosh, Dudley H(untington)
Raymond, W. F. *See* Wiggins, Thomas (Green(e))
Raymond, Walker X. *See* Walker, Raymond
Raynard, Jules. *See* Zamecnik, J(ohn) S(tepan)
Rayner, Edward. *See* Frangkiser, Carl (Moerz)
Raynor, Edward. *See* Frangkiser, Carl (Moerz)
Raynor, Hal. *See* Rubel, Henry Scott

Rayston, Frank. *See* Reizenstein, Franz (Theodor(e))
Raz. *See* Razafinkeriefo, Andreamenentania Paul
Razaf, Andy [or Andrea]. *See* Razafinkeriefo, Andreamenentania Paul
Razafkevifo, Andrea P. *See* Razafinkeriefo, Andreamenentania Paul
Razor Blade, The. *See* Collins, Al(bert)
Razz, A(ndrea). *See* Razafinkeriefo, Andreamenentania Paul
Razzi, Silvano. *See* Razzi, Giovanni
Rea, Robert. *See* Soloman, Mirrie (Irma)
Reade, Regina. *See* Richardson, Randell
Reader, Eddi. *See* Reader, Sadenia
Reading March King. *See* Althouse, Monroe A.
Réaux, Jean de. *See* Jallais, Amédée (Jean Baptiste Font-Réaux) de
Reaves, Erell. *See* Hargreaves, Robert
Reaves, Erell. *See* Stevens, Jack
Rebel-INS. *See* Hunter, Jason
Rebhu, Jan. *See* Beer, Johann
Rechberg, Otto. *See* Landesberg, Alexander
Rechberg, Otto. *See* Rosenstein, Leo
Réchid, Djemal. *See* Rey, Cemal Resid
Reclusive Howard Hughes of Pop Music, The. *See* Presley, Elvis A(a)ron
Red Devil. *See* Wilborn, Nelson
Red Head, The. *See* Sovine, Woodrow Wilson
Red Headed Brier Hopper. *See* Anderson, Leroy
Red Headed Music Maker, The. *See* Hall, Wendell (Woods)
Red Hot Willie. *See* McTell, Willie Samuel
Red Masked Baritone. *See* Hall, Wendell (Woods)
Red Nelson. *See* Wilborn, Nelson
Red Pepper Sam. *See* Costello, Billy
Red Priest, The. *See* Vivaldi, Antonio (Lucio)
Red River Dave. *See* McEnery, David [or Dave] L(argus)
Red Rob. *See* MacKintosh, Robert
Red Ryders. *See* McEnery, David [or Dave] L(argus)
Red Sky Lady. *See* Stocker, Stelle (née Prince)
Redding, Betty. *See* Jones, Lillie Mae
Redding, Bud. *See* Redding, Edward C(arolan)
Redding, Lillie Mae. *See* Jones, Lillie Mae
Redding, Noel. *See* Redding, David
Redding, Walter. *See* Cook, J. Lawrence
Redding, Walter. *See* Wendling, Pete
Reden, Karl. *See* Converse, Charles C(rozat)
Redheaded Stranger, (The). *See* Nelson, Willie (Hugh)
Redivivus, Joel Collier. *See* Veal, George
Redman. *See* Noble, Reginald [or Reggie]
Redmon, J.Lindsay. *See* Bliss, P(hilip) Paul
Rednip. *See* Pinder, Harold
Redstone, Willie. *See* Rottenstein, Wilhelm
Redwine, Skip. *See* Redwine, Wilbur (C.)
Ree, Jennie. *See* Gabriel, Charles H(utchinson)
Reed, Alan. *See* Friedman, Alfred
Reed, Alfred. *See* Friedman, Alfred
Reed, Arthur. *See* Ropes, Arthur Reed
Reed, Florence. *See* Tobani, Theodore Moses
Reed, H. *See* Greenwald, M(artin)
Reed, Jacqueline. *See* Leib, Joseph
Reed, Jerry. *See* Hubbard, Jerry (Reed)
Reed, Lewis Allen. *See* Firbanks, Louis [or Lewis] (Allen)
Reed, Lou. *See* Firbanks, Louis [or Lewis] (Allen)
Reemhber, Arthur O. *See* Herrera, Humberto (Angel)
Reese, Claude. *See* Isaacs, Claude Reese
Reese, Wendel. *See* Rusch, Harold (W(endel))
Reeve, Billy. *See* Elliott, Marjorie (Reeve)
Reeve, Fox. *See* Elliott, Marjorie (Reeve)
Reeves, Del. *See* Reeves, Franklin Delano
Reeves, G. H. *See* Laurendeau, Louis-Philippe
Reeves, Vic. *See* Moir, James [or Jim] (Roderick)
Reformed Boogie-Woogie Piano Player, A. *See* Guaraldi, Vince(nt) (Anthony)
Réfugiée. *See* Wuiet, Caroline
Rega, F. Wallace. *See* Haga, Frederick Wallace
Rega, Milo. *See* Haga, Frederick Wallace
Regal, F. Wallace. *See* Haga, Frederick Wallace
Reger, Carl. *See* Barnard, D'Auvergne
Reggae King. *See* Marley, Robert [or Bob] Nesta
Reggae Master, The. *See* Marley, Robert [or Bob] Nesta
Reggae Musician, The. *See* Marley, Robert [or Bob] Nesta
Reggio, Oste da. *See* Oste da Reggio
Regis, Johannes. *See* LeRoy, Jehan
Regnal, Frédéric. *See* Erlanger, Frédéric d'
Regney, Noel. *See* Schli(e)nger, Leon (Xavier)
Regniarg, Ycrep. *See* Grainger, (George) Percy (Aldridge)
Regoli, Enrique. *See* Soler, Enrique Llácer
Reguero, Mario. *See* Villoldo (Arroyo), Angel (Gregorio)
Regus. *See* Gutsche, Romeo Maximilian (Eugene Ludwig)
Rehak, Bud. *See* Racheck, Andrew (J.)
Rehberg, Hans Peter. *See* Nieblich, Werner Julius Gottfried
Rehlcuf. *See* Fulcher
Reichel, Bernhard. *See* Erler, Hermann
Reichert, Heinz. *See* Blumenreich, Heinrich
Reichner, Bix. *See* Reichner, (S(amuel)) Bickley
Reid, Antonio (M.). *See* Rooney, Mark
Reid, Billy. *See* Reid, Willis Wilfred
Reid, Buddy. *See* Ewing, Montague (George)
Reid, Constance B. *See* Burgeson, Avis Marguerite
Reid, L. A. *See* Rooney, Mark
Reid, Makaakane. *See* Reid, Willis Wilfred
Reid, Makuakane (Billy). *See* Reid, Willis Wilfred

Reight, Robby. *See* Robrecht, Carl
Reimer, Edward. *See* Hansson, Stig (Axel)
Reincarnated Troubadour, The. *See* Seeger, Pete(r R.)
Reine Hortense, La. *See* Beauharnais, Hortense Eugénie de
Reine, Johnny. *See* Johnson, John Harold
Reiner. *See* Eybel, Joseph Valentin (Sebastian)
Reinhard, Bernd. *See* Steffen, Harro
Reinhardt, Django. *See* Reinhardt, Jean Baptiste
Reinhardt, Ed. *See* Eville, Vernon
Reinhardt, Eric(h). *See* Reimann, Heinrich
Reinhold, Ernest. *See* Britten, Emma Hardinge
Reiniger, Robert. *See* Willson, (Robert Reiniger) Meredith
Reipan, M. *See* Napier, M.
Reisdorff, Emile. *See* Fishman, Jack (1918 (or 19)-)
Reisdorff, Emile. *See* Hargreaves, Peter
Reiset de Tesier, Maria. *See* Reiset, Marie (Félicie Clémence)
Reiset, Maria Felicita. *See* Reiset, Marie (Félicie Clémence)
Réjard, Victon. *See* Binetti, Giovanni
Reklaw, E. M. *See* Walker, G. Denholm
Reklaw, H. A. *See* Walker, H. A.
Relfel, Hans. *See* Löffler, Edmund
Rellim, Trebor. *See* Miller, Robert [or Bob] (Ernst)
Relwoff, Charles. *See* Fowler, Charles
Remar, Peer. *See* Amper, Quiren (1908-1989)
Remarc, Carl [or Charles]. *See* Cramer, Charles
Remark, A(xel). *See* Kramer, Alex(ander)
Reményi, Ed(o)uard. *See* Hoffmann, Eduard
Remi. *See* Vega, José
Remie, A. (C.). *See* Eimer, A(ugust) C(harles)
Remigius Altisiodoresis. *See* Rémy d'Auxerre
Remigo, Don. *See* Cesti, Remigo
Remington, J. (H.). *See* Page, N(athaniel) Clifford
Remlab, Charles. *See* Balmer, Charles
Remo, Nicola. *See* Sabatini, Enrico
Remolif, Charles. *See* Shere, Charles
Remos. *See* Loyau, George Etienne
Remy, Paul. *See* Mantovani, A(nnuzio) P(aolo)
Rémy, W. A. *See* Meyer, (Benjamin) Wilhelm
Renaissance Man. *See* Ives, Burl(e Icle Ivanhoe)
Renaissance Man of the Theater. *See* Menotti, Gian Carlo
Renard, A. *See* Fuchs, Louis
Renard, Pierre. *See* Engelmann, H(ans)
Renatus. *See* Hanslick, Eduard
Renaud, G. *See* Schweinsberg, Franz Johann
Rendall. *See* Sichart, René Reinhold
Rendall, John. *See* Lockton, Edward F.
Rendel, Romilde. *See* Carducci, Giosuè
René, Henri. *See* Grant, Harold
René, Henri. *See* Kirchstein, Harold Manfred [or Manford]
René, Victor. *See* Hale, Irene Baumgras
Reneau, Bud. *See* Reneau, George
Renée, Jacques. *See* Friedl, Franz (Richard)
Renez, H. *See* Schori, Hans
Rengan. *See* Wagner, Josef
Reni, Paolo. *See* Procacci, Giuseppe
Renis, Tony. *See* Cesari, Orfelio [or Elio]
Renk, Ludwig. *See* Kern, Carl Wilhelm
Renné, Victor. *See* Baungros, Irene
Renner, A. M. *See* Gatterman, Eugen Ludwig
Renner, Hans. *See* Haass, Hans
Renon, Jon. *See* Lennon, John (Winston)
Rentmeister Juvenal. *See* Lühe, Willibald von der
Renton, Victor. *See* Grey, Frank H(erbert)
Repmah, W. *See* Hamper, W.
Reporter, A. *See* O'Leary, Joseph
Res Plena Dei. *See* Speer, Daniel
Resiak, J. R. *See* Kaiser, (Johann) Rudolf
Resnick, Lee. *See* Resnick, Leon
Ressner, Carl. *See* Rössler, Carl
Restless Troubadour, The. *See* Belafonte, Harold [or Harry] (George)
Retr. *See* Tagliaferro, Jospeh (Dieudonné)
Retz. *See* Tagliaferro, Jospeh (Dieudonné)
Reubins, Carl. *See* Rawlings, Charles Arthur
Reuter, Fritz. *See* Reuter, Friedrich Otto
Reuter, Hans. *See* Schindler, Hans
Reuter, Winston. *See* Schindler, Hans
Rev. B. *See* Eisner, Betty Grover
Revel, Louis. *See* Pietro, Mario de
Reverand Tom. *See* Thornton, Keith
Reverend B. *See* Eisner, Betty Grover
Revlis, Earl. *See* Silver, Richard L.
Revons, E. C. *See* Converse, Charles C(rozat)
Rewdgo, Dreary. *See* Gorey, Edward (St. John)
Rex. *See* King, Oliver (A.)
Rey(del timbal), El. *See* Puente, Ernesto Antonio, Jr.
Rey de(l) Trabalengua, El. *See* Rivera Castillo, Efrain
Rey del Mambo, El. *See* Perez Prado, Domasco
Rey, Luis(ito). *See* Gallego Sánchez, Luis
Rey, Vernon. *See* Rawlings, Charles Arthur
Reya, Silas. *See* Ayer, Silas, H.
Reyer, Ernest. *See* Rey, Louis-Etienne-Ernest
Reymont, Maurice. *See* Kufferath, Maurice
Reyna, Ricardo. *See* Stube, Howard
Reyna, Roberta. *See* Stube, Howard
Reyna, Roberto. *See* Stube, Howard
Reynard, Jules. *See* Zamecnik, J(ohn) S(tepan)
Reynolds, Brian. *See* Fishman, Jack (1918 (or 19)-)
Reynolds, Francis. *See* Statham, Francis Reginald
Reynolds, Frank. *See* Klickmann, F(rank) Henri
Reynolds, Herbert. *See* Rourke, M(ichael) E(lder)
Reynolds, Lee. *See* McEnery, Velma Lee
Reynolds, Michael. *See* Chase, George
Reynolds, Peter. *See* Kinyon, John L(eroy)

Reynolds, Robert. *See* Wilson, Harry (Robert)
Rezlit, Albert. *See* Gum(m), Albert
Rhadamanthus. *See* Butters, Francis
Rhapsody, Miss. *See* Wells, Viola (Gertrude)
Rhené-Baton. *See* Baton, René
Rhene-Jacques, (Sister). *See* Cartier, Marguerite (Marie Alice)
Rhesus. *See* Benskin, Anthony
Rhinelota, Hypocritasm. *See* Brendel, Georg Christoph
Rhinestone Cowboy, The. *See* Campbell, Glen (Travis)
Rhinestone Cowboy, The. *See* Coe, David Allan
Rhinestone Rubinstein, The. *See* Liberace, (Wladziu Valentino)
Rhodes, Grayson. *See* Miller, Ron D(ean)
Rhodes, Helen (Guy). *See* Guy, Helen
Rhodes, Jack. *See* Rhodes, Andrew Jackson
Rhodes, Red. *See* Rhodes, Orville J.
Rhodes, Sonny. *See* Smith, Clarence Edward (1940-)
Rhodes, (Mrs). W. I. *See* Guy, Helen
Rhomberg, Kurt. *See* Schall, Friedrich
Rhubarb Red. *See* Polfus(s), Lester (William)
Rhumba King, The. *See* Cugat de Bru y Deulofeo, Francisco de Asis Javier
Rhymes, Busta. *See* Smith, Trevor
Rhyn, Hans am. *See* Gassmann, Alfred Leonz
Rhyne, H. E. *See* Sauveplane, Henri (Emile)
Rhythm and Blues King, The. *See* Frost, Frank Otis
Rhythm X. *See* Thornton, Keith
Ria Nido, Esteban. *See* Sondheim, Stephen Joshua
Riadis, Emil(ios). *See* Khu(-Elefteriadis), Emilios
Rial, Marc. *See* DeBoeck, Marcel
Ribana, Lena. *See* Lebys, Henry
Ribbing, (Count) Adolph(e). *See* Leuven, Adolphe (Ribbing) de
Ribbonson, Horatio. *See* Shaw, George Bernard
Ribe, Danmark. *See* Lampe, J(ens) Bodewalt
Ribert, Jean. *See* Cooke, James Francis
Ribó, Jesús A. *See* Subirá (Puig), José
Ricardel, Joe. *See* Ricciardello, Joseph (A.)
Ricardo. *See* Jupp, Eric
Ricardo, Don. *See* Ridgely, Richard (P.)
Ricci de Nucella Campli. *See* Mathei, Nicolaus Savini
Ricciotti. *See* Wassenaer, (Count) Unico Wilhelm, (graf van)
Ricco, Nino. *See* Gregori, (Primo) Giovanni [or John]
Riccoleno, Gallario. *See* Corelli, Arcangelo
Rice, Daddy. *See* Rice, Thomas Dartmouth
Rice, Elmer. *See* Reizenstein, Elmer Leopold
Rice, Jim Crow. *See* Rice, Thomas Dartmouth
Rice, Robert. *See* McClaskey, Harry Haley
Rice, Will. *See* Catsos, Nicholas A.
Rich, Don. *See* Ulrich, Don(ald Eugene)
Rich, F. E. *See* Bliss, P(hilip) Paul
Richard I. *See* Wagner, Richard
Richard II. *See* Strauss, Richard
Richard III. *See* Wagner, Richard
Richard, Bill. *See* Katz, Richard [or Dick] (Aaron)
Richard, Cliff. *See* Webb, (Harry) Rodger
Richard, Daisy. *See* Vonderlieth, Leonore
Richard, Franz. *See* Pugno, (Stéphane) Raoul
Richard-Henry. *See* Butler, Richard W(illiam)
Richard-Henry. *See* Newton, H(enry) Chance
Richard, J. C. *See* Riegger, Wallingford (Constantin)
Richard, Jean. *See* Pohl, Richard
Richard, Max. *See* Pugno, (Stéphane) Raoul
Richard Strauss of Sweden, The. *See* Atterberg, Kurt M(agnus)
Richard the First. *See* Wagner, Richard
Richard the Second. *See* Strauss, Richard
Richard the Third. *See* Wagner, Richard
Richard Wagner of the Lied. *See* Wolf, Hugo
Richards, Baker. *See* Newell, Norman
Richards, Baker, and Ross. *See* Newell, Norman
Richards, Charles. *See* Finkelstein, Abe
Richards, Daisy. *See* Vonderlieth, Leonore
Richards, Dave. *See* Richman, David Alan
Richards, Eddie. *See* Krah, Earl E(dward)
Richards, Emil. *See* Radocchia, Emil(io Joseph)
Richards, Frank. *See* Saenger, Gustave
Richards, Friedrich. *See* Kessler, Richard
Richards, Happy. *See* Kapp, Paul
Richards, Helen. *See* Vonderlieth, Leonore
Richards, Howard. *See* Davis, Bertha Ruth
Richards, Jay. *See* Pine, Arthur
Richards, Johnny. *See* Cascales, John
Richards, Ross. *See* Newell, Norman
Richards, (Don) Rube. *See* Moss, E(llsworth) F(rancis)
Richards, S. C. *See* Riegger, Wallingford (Constantin)
Richards, Terry. *See* Marinan, Terrence Richard
Richards, W. H. *See* Lewis, William Richards
Richards, W. V. *See* Ricketts, (Major) Frederick Joseph
Richards, William. *See* Riegger, Wallingford (Constantin)
Richardson, Ferdinand. *See* Heybourne, Ferdinando
Richardson, Henry S. *See* Rands, William Brightly
Richardson, Jape. *See* Richardson, J(iles) P(erry)
Richardson, Jaye P. *See* Richardson, J(iles) P(erry)
Richardson, John (A.). *See* Ehret, Walter (Charles)
Richardson, Peg. *See* Richardson, C(larence) C(lifford)
Richardy, Johann. *See* Richter, Johann (1878-)
Riche, Anthoine Le. *See* Ryche, Anthonius (de)
Riche, J. B. *See* Woodrow, Jane (née Blair)
Richgood, J. A. *See* Goodrich, A(lfred) J(ohn)
Richie. *See* Starkey, Richard
Richings, (Mary) Caroline. *See* Reynoldson, (Mary) Caroline
Richman, Harry (Jr.). *See* Reichman, Harold [or Harry]
Richmond, Dolly. *See* Wenrich, Percy
Richmond, M. *See* Keiser, Robert (A(dolph))
Richmond, Ralph. *See* Fishman, Jack (1918 (or 19)-)

Richter, Amadeus Friedrich. *See* Richter, Heinrich Friedrich Wilhelm
Richter, C(arl) L(udwig). *See* Schulzova, A(nezka)
Richter, Carl (Arthur). *See* Dellafield, Henry
Richter, Ernst. *See* Krentzlin, H. Richard
Richthoff, Franz. *See* Gross, Franz
Rickard, Manny. *See* Dunstall, Ernest
Rickard, Manny. *See* Squires, Edna May
Ricketts, Joe. *See* Ricketts, (Major) Frederick Joseph
Ricks, Lee. *See* Mills, Paul
Rictus, Jehan. *See* Randon (de Saint Amand), Gabriel
Rideamus. *See* Oliven, Fritz
Ridée, Charl. H. *See* Rijke, Cornelius Herminus
Rider, F. B. *See* Balmer, Charles
Rider, Nicky. *See* Reith, Dieter
Riegen, J. *See* Nigri von Sankt Albino, Julius
Ries, Hugibert. *See* Riemann, (Karl Wilhelm Julius) Hugo
Ries, Hugo. *See* Clough-Leighter, Henry
Riesser, Klaus. *See* Rebner, Wolfgang E(duard)[or E(dward)]
Rietsch, Heinrich. *See* Löwy, Heinrich
Rieux, Claude. *See* Duval, Georges (J.)
Riff Raff. *See* Cardier, Glenn
Rifle, Ned. *See* Hartley, Hal
Riggins, J., Junior. *See* Dixon, Floyd
Riggs, Edward. *See* Ehret, Walter (Charles)
Riggs, Edward. *See* Ryglewicz, Edward
Riggs, Mark. *See* Feld, Mark
Rignac, Jean. *See* Missa, Edmond Jean
Rigo, Antonio. *See* Gori, Antonio Francesco
Riley, George, the Yodeling Rustler. *See* Reeves, Goebel (Leon)
Riley, Peter. *See* Coleridge-Taylor, Gwendolen
Rim. *See* Miller, James
Rimert, Gay A. *See* Lincoln, Harry J.
Rinaldo, dall'Arpa. *See* Trematerra, Rinaldo
Rinaldo, F. *See* Binge, Ronald
Rincepa, Luigio. *See* Pancieri, Giulio
Rincor(a)to, Academico (Olimpico). *See* Bissari, Pietro Paolo
Ring, Bo. *See* Schleich, Ernst
Ring-Hager. *See* Haga, Frederick Wallace
Ring-Hager. *See* Ringleben, Justin, Jr.
Ring, Justin. *See* Ringleben, Justin, Jr.
Ring, Montague. *See* Aldridge, Amanda (Christina Elizabeth) Ira
Ring, Peter. *See* Schmitz, Josef
Ringel, Federico. *See* Erlanger, Frédéric d'
Ringelnatz, Joachim. *See* Bötticher, Hans (Gustav)
Ringler, Franz. *See* Döring, Wilhelm
Ringman, Tony. *See* Drexler, Werner
Rinio, Goanto. *See* Gori, Antonio Francesco
Rip. *See* Thenon, Georges
Ripatti, Dinu. *See* Lipatti, Constantin
Riquet, Gomex le. *See* Ravel, Maurice (Joseph)
Risco, Arthur. *See* Boorman, Arthur
Ritenour, Jay. *See* Ritenour, John David
Rito, Ted Fio. *See* Fiorito, Ted
Rittberg, Hugo von. *See* Grothe, Wilhelm
Ritter, Franklin. *See* Smith, Lani
Ritter, G. P. *See* Scott, Charles P(hillips)
Ritter, G. P. *See* Suck, G. F.
Ritter, Helmut. *See* Franz, Walter
Ritter, Sascha. *See* Ritter, Alexander
Ritter, Tex. *See* Ritter, Maurice Woodward
Ritter, Théodore. *See* Bennet, Théodore
Rittgräff, A. E. *See* Gräffer, Franz (Arnold)
Rittman, Trude. *See* Rittman, Gertrude
Ritz, Carl. *See* Rawlings, Charles Arthur
Rivarota, Ardio. *See* Varotari, Dario
Rivas, Wello. *See* Rivas Avila, Manuel
Rive-King, Julie. *See* King, Frank H.
Rive-King, Julie. *See* Kunkel, Charles
Rive-King, Julie. *See* Kunkel, Jacob
Rivera, Mon. *See* Rivera Castillo, Efrain
Rivera, Stan. *See* Thewlis, Stanley
Rivers, Dirty. *See* Morganfield, McKinley
Rivers, Johnny. *See* Ramistella, John
Rivers, Ken. *See* Newell, Norman
Rives, Este. *See* De Filippi, Amedeo
Riviera, (E. De). *See* Schleich, Ernst
Riviere, Ch. *See* Sartorio, Arnoldo
Rivotorto, Il. *See* Angeli, Francesco Maria
Rivotorto. *See* DeAngelis, Angelo
Rix, Jonathan, Jr. *See* O'Keefe, James (Conrad)
Rix, Lawrence. *See* Caton, Lauderic (Rex)
Rizzo, David. *See* Oswald, James
Road March King of the World. *See* Roberts, Aldwyn [or Aldwin]
Roads, E. Clyde. *See* Kunkel, Charles
Roame, Dennis. *See* Minogue, Dennis
Roaming Ranger, The. *See* Breitenbach, Alfred
Robberts, Oriell. *See* Wilhelm, Elsie Lee
Robbie. *See* Robison, Carson (Jay)
Robbin, Irving. *See* Rabinowitz, Irving
Robbins & Uke. *See* Marvin, John(ny) (Senator)
Robbins, Corky. *See* Johnson, Margaret (Ellen)
Robbins, Marty. *See* Robinson, Martin D(avid)
Robbins, Michael. *See* Fishman, Jack (1918 (or 19)-)
Robbins, Pig. *See* Robbins, Hargus (Melvin)
Robbins, Tod. *See* Robbins, Clarence A(aron)
Roberds, (Ian) Smokey. *See* Roberds, Fred A(llen)
Robert, Adrien. *See* Basset, Charles
Robert ap Gwilym Ddu. *See* Williams, Robert
Robert, C. E. *See* Kreusch, Edmund [or Eduard]
Robert, Dr. *See* Howard, Robert
Robert, Fred. *See* Pollak, Franz
Robert, Frédéric. *See* Wurmser, Frédéric (Robert Léopold)

Robert, Gilbert. *See* Winterfeld, David Robert
Robert, Louis. *See* Hirschfeld, Louis von
Robert of the Mulde. *See* Schumann, Robert
Roberti, Robert. *See* Vollstedt, Robert
Roberto Carlos. *See* Braga, Roberto Carlos
Roberto, Carlos. *See* Kraushaar, Charles
Roberts, Austin. *See* Robertson, George (Austin), Jr.
Roberts, Ben. *See* Robertson, Dick
Roberts, Billy Joe. *See* Barnhill, Joe Bob
Roberts, Bob. *See* Di Giovanni, Rocco
Roberts, Carl. *See* Beckhard, Robert L.
Roberts, Charles J. *See* Kraushaar, Charles
Roberts, Don. *See* McCray, Don
Roberts, Don. *See* Sour, Robert (B.)
Roberts, Franz. *See* Carl, Robert
Roberts, Harry. *See* Winterfeld, David Robert
Roberts, Helen. *See* Hunter, Alberta
Roberts, Jason. *See* Bock, Fred
Roberts, Jay. *See* Roberts, James Martin
Roberts, Jerry. *See* Ost, Roberts
Roberts, John. *See* Lewis, Al(an)
Roberts, Jon. *See* Olson, Robert G.
Roberts, K(athleen) A. *See* Keiser, Robert (A(dolph))
Roberts, Kenny. *See* Kingsbury, George, (Jr.)
Roberts, Leland. *See* Roberts, Lee S.
Roberts, Lou. *See* Ruse, Robert Louis
Roberts, Luck(e)y. *See* Roberts, Charles Luckey(e)th
Roberts, Martin. *See* Lebys, Henry
Roberts, Paddy. *See* Roberts, John Godfrey Owen
Roberts, Raymond. *See* Seitz, Ernest (Joseph)
Roberts, Red. *See* Mackeben, Theo
Roberts, Robert. *See* Vollstedt, Robert
Roberts, Sally. *See* Dunn, Sara(h)
Roberts, (Ian) Smokey. *See* Roberds, Fred A(llen)
Roberts, Snitcher. *See* Johnson, James (J.) (c.1905-c.1972)
Roberts, Steve L. *See* Bergh, Arthur
Roberts, Steve L. *See* Robinson, J. Russell
Roberts, Wellesley. *See* Levinson, Robert (Wells)
Robertson, C. R. W. *See* Davis, Katherine K(ennicott)
Robertson, Dick. *See* Blake, James Hubert
Robertson, Martin David. *See* Robinson, Martin D(avid)
Robertson, Wilfred. *See* Hall, Joseph Lincoln
Robespierre. *See* Fauré, Gabriel Urbain
Robespierre of Music, The. *See* Berlioz, Hector
Robillard, Duke. *See* Robillard, Michael
Robinet de la Magdalaine. *See* Robert le Pelé
Robinson, Allan. *See* Ehret, Walter (Charles)
Robinson, Bat ("The Hummingbird"). *See* Robinson, James
Robinson, Good Rockin'. *See* Robinson, L(ouis) C(harles)
Robinson, Lonesome. *See* Robinson, Jimmie [or Jimmy]
Robinson, Smokey. *See* Robinson, William, (Jr.)
Robison, Charles. *See* Robison, Carson J(ay)
Robledillo. *See* Robledo, Melchor
Robty. *See* Wangermée, Franz
Robyns, Andy. *See* Rothstein, Andy
Robyx. *See* Zanetti, Roberto
Roccard, Ken. *See* Frei, Robert
Rocco, Robert. *See* Busse, Christoph
Roch-Albert. *See* Jullien, Louis (George) Antoine (Jules)
Roche, Jean de la. *See* Aberbach, Jean (J.)
Rochefort, Armand de. *See* Rochefort-Luçay, Claude-Louis-Marie, marquis de
Rochefort, Edmond. *See* Rochefort-Luçay, Claude-Louis-Marie, marquis de
Rochelle, Robert. *See* Grimm, C(arl) W(illiam)
Rochereau. *See* Pascal, Tabu
Roches, Gilbert des. *See* Legoux, (Baroness) Julie
Rocheville, Georges de. *See* Rockwell, George Noyes
Rochon, J. *See* Molenaar, Pieter Jan
Rock, Chris. *See* Smith, Christopher Alan
Rockabilly Hepcat. *See* Young, Neil
Rockabilly "King of California". *See* Alvin, Dave
Rockefella, David. *See* Fishman, Jack (1927-)
Rocker with a Mission, A. *See* Cockburn, Bruce
Rockers. *See* Swaby, Horace
Rocket Man, The. *See* Dwight, Reginald Kenneth
Rocket, Ronnie. *See* Iraschek, Ronald Frederic
Rockin' Dopsie. *See* Rubin, Alton (Jay)
Rockin' Guitar Man, The. *See* Perkings, Carl (Lee)
Rockin' Red. *See* Minter, Iverson
Rockin' Sidney [or Sydney]. *See* Semien, Sidney
Rockman, Sidney. *See* Daniels, Charles N(eil)
Rock's Original Bad Boy. *See* Richards, Keith
Rock's Ultimate Bad Boy. *See* Richards, Keith
Rockstro, William S(myth) [or S(mith)]. *See* Rackstraw, W(illiam) S(myth) [or S(mith)]
Rockwell. *See* Gordy, Kenneth [or Kennedy]
Roddie, Vin. *See* Rodomista, Vincent
Rodenberg, Julius. *See* Levy, Julius
Rodenhof, Guy. *See* Cardon, Ronald
Rodger. *See* Rinne, Hanno
Rodgers, Victor Herbert. *See* Rodgers, Richard (Charles)
Rodgersovsky, Richard. *See* Rodgers, Richard (Charles)
Rodney, Paul. *See* Hopkins, Harry Walter
Rodolphe, Jean Joseph. *See* Rudolph, Johann Joseph
Rodomant. *See* Beethoven, Ludwig van
Rodriguet de la guitarra. *See* Rodericus
Rodriguez, Adolfo. *See* Bastida, Gustavo Adolfo Dominguez
Rodriguez, Adolfo. *See* Rodríguez Correa, Ramón
Rodríguez, Arsenio. *See* Rodríguez, Ignacio Loyola
Rodríguez, Becho. *See* Matos Rodríguez, G(h)erardo (Hernáu)
Rodriguez, Carlos. *See* Diernhammer, Carlos
Rodriguez, Johnny. *See* Rodriguez, Juan Raoul (Davis)

Rodriguez, Lalo. *See* Rodriguez, Ubaldo
Rodriguez, Tito. *See* Rodriguez, Pablo
Rody. *See* Rodeheaver, Homer A(lvan)
Roe, Stafford. *See* Murray, James R(amsey)
Roe, Tex. *See* Robarge, John F(rederick)
Roe, Tommy. *See* David, Thomas
Roeper, Ernst. *See* Küster, Herbert
Roesgen-Champion, Marguerite. *See* Delyssee, Jean
Rofeatio, M. *See* Morei, Michal Giuseppi
Roff, Joseph. *See* Roffinella, Joseph
Rogan, K. C. *See* Burke, John(ny)
Rogan, K. C. *See* Spina, Harold
Rögely, Fritz. *See* Vögely, Fritz
Roger. *See* Rinne, Hanno
Roger, Rulof. *See* Staton, Harry M.
Rogers, Ann. *See* Johnson, Ann M.
Rogers, Calvin. *See* Grey, Frank H(erbert)
Rogers, Cameron. *See* Keiser, Robert (A(dolph))
Rogers, Clara Kathleen. *See* Barnett, Clara Kathleen
Rogers, Dale Evans. *See* Smith, Frances Octavia
Rogers, Duke. *See* Williams, Egbert Austin
Rogers, Eddy. *See* Ruggieri, Edmond (Anthony)
Rogers, Gerald. *See* Sour, Robert (B.)
Rogers, Jimmy. *See* Lane, James A.
Rogers, Kenneth. *See* De Vito, Albert (Kenneth)
Rogers, Lee. *See* Wilson, Roger Cole
Rogers, Milt. *See* Adelstein, Milton
Rogers, Milton M(ichael). *See* Rajonsky [or Rajonski], Milton Michael
Rogers, Mister. *See* Rogers, Fred (M(cFeely))
Rogers, Oh Yeah. *See* Aiverum, Timothy Louis
Rogers, Rock. *See* Payne, Leon (Roger)
Rogers, Rosalind. *See* Richardson, Randell
Rogers, Roy. *See* Slye, Leonard (Franklin)
Rogers, Shorty. *See* Rajonsky [Rajonski], Milton Michael
Rogers, Smokey. *See* Rogers, Eugene
Rogers, Stanley C. *See* Kraushaar, Raoul
Rogers, Timmie. *See* Aiverum, Timothy Louis
Rogers, Wayne. *See* Bacon, W. Garwood, Jr.
Rogie, S. E. *See* Rogers, Sooliman Ernest
Rohan, Edler von. *See* Csermák, Antol [or Anthony] György [or George]
Rohde, Q'Adrianne. *See* Libbey, Delores R.
Rohmer, Sax. *See* Ward, Arthur Sarsfield
Roi des quadrilles, Le. *See* Musard, Philippe
Roi des violons (et ménétries). *See* Ghignone, Giovanni Pietro
Roko. *See* Kohlmeyer, Robert
Roland, Frank. *See* Herbert, Victor
Roland-Manuel, (Alexis). *See* Lévy, Roland Alexis Manuel
Roland, Marc. *See* Buneken, Adolf
Roland, Sten. *See* Carlberg, Sten
Roland, Uwe. *See* Windisch, Thomas
Rolf, Cardello. *See* Piesker, Rüdiger
Rolfe, Walter. *See* Dellafield, Henry
Rolff, Ronny. *See* Rolff, W(olfgang)
Rolfsen, A. H. *See* Bliss, P(hilip) Paul
Roller der Unbegreifliche. *See* Grillparzer, Franz
Rolli, der lustige Geiger. *See* Wittal, Roland
Rollicker, Harry. *See* Thackeray, William Makepeace
Rollie Fingers. *See* Hunter, Jason
Rollins, Glenn. *See* Olson, Robert G.
Rollins, Henry. *See* Garfield, Henry
Rollins, Jack. *See* Rollins, W(alter) E.
Rollins, Sonny. *See* Rollins, Theodore Walter [or Walter Theodore]
Rolls, Ernest C. *See* Darewski, Josef Adolf
Rolls Royce of Country Music. *See* Jones, George (Glen(n))
Rolls Royce of Country Singers. *See* Jones, George (Glen(n))
Roloff, Alec. *See* Kronke, Emil
Roloff, Ronny. *See* Roloff, W(olfgang)
Rolyat, Majo. *See* Taylor, James [or Jim]
Roma. *See* Belcher, Frank H.
Roma, Cara. *See* Northey, Carrie
Roma, Del. *See* Mauriat, Paul
Roma, Vinny. *See* Tozzo, Vincent J.
Romain, Le. *See* Hotteterre, Jacques(-Martin)
Romain, Jacques. *See* Gebauer, Benny
Romaine, David [or Dave]. *See* Bohme, David (M.)
Romaine, Earl. *See* Ehret, Walter (Charles)
Romaine, Robert. *See* Wynschenk, Howard (E.)
Roman. *See* Kralik (von Meyrswalden), Richard
Romania's Greatest Composer. *See* Enescu, Georges
Romanina, La. *See* Archilei, Vittoria (née Concarini)
Romanini, J. L. *See* Häussler, Gerhardt
Romano, Il. *See* DeGrandis, Vincenzo
Romano. *See* Mariani, Tommaso
Romano, Alessandro. *See* Merlo, Alessandro
Romano, Enotrio. *See* Carducci, Giosuè
Romano, Giulio. *See* Caccini, Giulio (Romolo)
Romans, Roman. *See* Ulbrich, Siegfried
Romantic Violin of Tango, The. *See* Gobbi, Alfredo Julio Floro
Romba, Ralph. *See* Schwarzmeier, Gustl
Rome, Hecky. *See* Rome, Harold
Rome, J. Gus. *See* Southard, Mary Ann
Romeo, Max. *See* Smith, Max(well)
Romeo of Radio, The. *See* Columbo, Ruggiero de Rudolpho
Romère, François. *See* Romer, Frank [or Francis]
Romero, Garêt. *See* Catsos, Nicholas A.
Romero, Gary. *See* Catsos, Nicholas A.
Romero, Mateo [or Matias]. *See* Rosmarin, Mathieu
Rommell, Rox. *See* Roemheld, Heinz (Heinrich) Erich
Rompini, Servatins. *See* Henrich, C. W.
Ron. *See* Cellamare, Rosalino

Rottweiler, Hektor. *See* Wiesengrund(-Adorno), Theodor (Ludwig)
Roulette, Rene. *See* Halletz, Erwin
Round Mound of Sound. *See* Hirt, Al(ois Maxwell)
Round Mound of Sound, (The). *See* Price, Kenny
Rousseau, James. *See* Rousseau, Pierre-Joseph
Rousseau, Johann Baptist. *See* Saalmüller, F(riedrich)
Roven, Richard. *See* Hyman, Richard [or Dick] (R(oven))
Rover, A. Holborn. *See* Reader, (William Henry) Ralph
Rovetta, G. B. *See* Volpe, Giovanni Battista [or Giambattista]
Rovettino. *See* Volpe, Giovanni Battista [or Giambattista]
Rovitti, Olerto. *See* Vittori, Loret(t)o
Rovňan, Ján. *See* Urban, Milo
Rovno, Zeidel. *See* Maragowsky, Jacob Samuel
Rowans, Virginia. *See* Tanner, Edward Everett, III
Rowbotham, Bill. *See* Owen, Bill
Rowdemath, Bláus. *See* Bradsworth, Samuel
Rowe, B(olton). *See* Stephenson, B(enjamin) C(harles)
Rowe, Daniel. *See* Spaulding, G(eorge) L(awson)
Rowenhall, Mrs. *See* Keiser, Robert (A(dolph))
Rowland, Red. *See* Rowland, Edward
Rowlands, Fog. *See* Rowlands, Abraham Cecil Francis Fothergill
Rowles, James [or Jimmy] (George). *See* Hunter, James George
Rowley, Thomas. *See* Chatterton, Thomas
Roy C. *See* Hammond, Roy Charles
Roy, Harry. *See* Lipman, Harry
Royal Songwriter, The. *See* Magno (Pereira), Basilio
Royal, Ted. *See* DeWar, Ted Royal
Royce. *See* Reuss, Bernd
Royce, Edward. *See* Reddall, James William
Royce, Turlay. *See* Ireland, John (Nicholson)
Royer, G(unter). *See* Rhode, Max
Royer, Max. *See* Rhode, Max
Rozi, Barnabé Farmian de. *See* Rosoy, Barnabé Farmian de
Rozman, Sarah. *See* Debaro, Charlotte
Rózsavölgyi, Márk. *See* Rosenthal, Mark (Mordecai)
Rua, Hans. *See* Sedlmayr, Artur
Rubach, Ernst. *See* Urbach, Ernst
Rubahn, Gerd. *See* Böhm, Karl (1894-1981)
Rubato, Parlando. *See* Durand, Annie
Rubato, Parlando. *See* Meyer, Dale Arthur
Rubber Bucket. *See* Gadd, Paul
Rubeis, Aloysius de. *See* Rossi, Luigi
Rübel, Ernst. *See* Shaw, Gerald
Rübel, Ernst. *See* Smith-Masters, Stanley
Ruben, Aaron. *See* Gonzalez, Aaron Ruben
Rubens, Aloysius. *See* Rossi, Luigi
Rubens, Carl. *See* Rawlings, Charles Arthur
Rubens, Oscar. *See* Rubistein, Oscar
Rubeus, Aloysius. *See* Rossi, Luigi
Rubinet [or Rubinus]. *See* Robert le Pelé
Rubinstein, Anton. *See* Kunkel, Charles
Ruby, Harry. *See* Rubinstein, Harold
Ruch, Hannes. *See* Weinhöppel, Hans Richard
Ruderman, Rudy. *See* Ruderman, Seymour George
Rudhyar, Dane. *See* Chennevière, Daniel
Rudolf, B(runo). *See* Bunge, Rudolf
Rudolf, Carl. *See* Gottschall, (Karl) Rudolf von
Rudolz, Hardy. *See* Rudolz, Hartwig
Ruettino. *See* Volpe, Giovanni Battista [or Giambattista]
Ruff, Karl. *See* Bayer, Karl
Ruggles, Carl. *See* Ruggles, Charles Sprague
Ruland, Alexander. *See* Otten, Hans
Rumpled, Left-Over Everly Brother, A. *See* Prine, John
Rumsey, Murray. *See* Rumshinsky, Murray
Runningbrook, Jim. *See* Drawbaugh, Jacob W(ilber Jr.)
Rusden, Rupert. *See* Younge, William
Rush, Jerry. *See* Rusch, Jerome Anthony
Rush, Leonard. *See* Balent, Andrew
Russell, Bert. *See* Berns, Bert(rand) (Russell)
Russell, Bob. *See* Russell, Sidney Keith
Russell, Edward. *See* Barnard, George D(aniel)
Russell, Henry. *See* Levy, Henry
Russell, Henry. *See* Olson, Henry Russell
Russell, Joe. *See* Robinson, J. Russel(l)
Russell, Leon(ard). *See* Bridges, (Claude) Russell
Russell, Mark. *See* Ruslander, Mark
Russell, Paul. *See* Gadd, Paul
Russell, Pee Wee. *See* Russell, Charles Ellsworth
Russell, Phil. *See* Mandell, Pete
Russell, William [or Bill]. *See* Wagner, Russell William
Russian, Babe. *See* Russian, Irving
Russian Brahms, The. *See* Juon, Pavel [or Pual] (Fedorovich)
Russian Brahms, The. *See* Medtner, Nikolai
Russian Brahms. *See* Taneev, Sergey (Ivanovich)
Russian Field. *See* Field, John
Russian Mendelssohn. *See* Glazunov, Aleksandr Konstantinovich
Russian Palestrina, The. *See* Bortniansky, (Stepanovich) Dmitri
Russian Reinecke, A. *See* Tchaikovsky, Petr Illich
Rusticocampius, Feld. *See* Bauernfeld, Eduard von
Rüstige, Der. *See* Rist, Johann
Rutge, Daniel. *See* Speer, Daniel
Ruth, Michael. *See* Kapp, David [or Dave]
Rutherford, Alison. *See* Cockburn, Alicia
Rutherford, Arthur. *See* Dichmont, William
Ruthland, Lou. *See* Peros, Harry
Rutini, Ferdinando. *See* Pellegrini, Ferdinando
Ruytler. *See* Pilati, Auguste
Ruz(z)ante. *See* Beolco, Angelo
Ryall, Orme. *See* Davis, Clarice Ryall

Ryan, Jimmy. *See* Finkelstein, Abe
Ryan, John. *See* Rines, Joseph [or Joe]
Ryan, Rocket. *See* Ryan, Robert Francis
Ryan, Slugger. *See* Hyman, Richard [or Dick] (R(oven))
Ryballandni, Jakub Jan. *See* Ryba, Jakub [or Jakob] (Simon) Jan [Johannes]
Rybaville, Jakub Jan. *See* Ryba, Jakub [or Jakob] (Simon) Jan [or Johannes]
Rybner, (Peter Martin) Cornelius. *See* Rübner, (Peter Martin) Cornelius
Rycoth, Denis. *See* Torch, Sidney
Ryder, Dudley. *See* Kern, Carl Wilhelm
Ryder, Dudley. *See* Nordman, Chester
Ryder, F. B. *See* Balmer, Charles
Ryder, Mitch. *See* Levise, William, Jr.
Ryder, Tex S. *See* Szathmary, William
Rzarector, The. *See* Diggs, Robert

– S –

S. *See* Procter, Bryan Waller
S. *See* Shaw, George Bernard
S t. *See* Stennett, Samuel
S. A. *See* Boyle, (Miss)
S. B. G. *See* Baring-Gould, Sabine
Sc*tt, Dr. *See* Scott, Thomas
S. D. *See* Davies, Samuel
S. E-k—g. *See* Ecking, Samuel
Sfrd. *See* Seyfried, Ignaz (Xaver) von
S. H. *See* Heyden, Sebald(us)
S. J. H. *See* Hale, Sarah J(osepha) (Buell)
S-K-O. *See* Knobloch, Fred
S-K-O. *See* Overstreet, Paul
S-K-O. *See* Schuyler, Thom
S. L. *See* Sandell(-Berg), Karolina [or Carolina] Wilhelmina
S. M. *See* Medley, Samuel
S. M. *See* Oliphant, Carolina
S. M. X. *See* Partridge, Sybil F.
S. N. D. *See* Partridge, Sybil F.
S.O.C. 7. *See* Pedersen, Chuck
S. O., U. S. A. *See* Sousa, John Philip
S. R. *See* Roberts, Samuel
S. T - g. *See* Thalberg, Sigismond
St-z, Carl. *See* Nauenburg, Gustav
S. v. W. *See* Schnyder von Wartensee, Xaver
S. W. D—n. *See* Dehn, Siegfried Wilhelm
S.Y. *See* Keats, John
Sabicias, (Niño). *See* Castellon, Augustin
Sabine, Charles. *See* Stanley, Charles
Sabínský, (?Karel). *See* Sabina, Karel
Sachs, Edward. *See* Rawlings, Charles Arthur
Sachs, Emil(e). *See* Rawlings, Charles Arthur
Sachs, Hans. *See* Rawlings, Charles Arthur
Sackbut, Solomon. *See* Oliphant, Thomas
Sacred Cow Sharpshooter. *See* Thomson, Virgil (Garnett)
Sacreo, Driante. *See* Marcello, Benedetto
Sade. *See* Folasade, Helen
Sadel, Alfredo. *See* Sánchez Luna, Alfredo
Sadero, Geni. *See* Scarpa, Eugenia
Sadie. *See* Williams, Sarah
Sadler, Cool Papa. *See* Sadler, Haskell Robert
Safir, Tim. *See* Haensch, Gerhard Delle
Safroni, Arnold. *See* Myddleton, William [or Arnold] H.
Safroni, Leonard. *See* Frangkiser, Carl (Moerz)
Sagan, Leontine. *See* Schlesinger, Leontine
Sage of Baltimore. *See* Mencken, H(enry) L(ouis)
Sagebrush Poet, The. *See* Gilmore, Jimmie Dale
Saggione, Giuseppe. *See* Fedeli, Giuseppe
Saggione, Joseph. *See* Fedeli, Giuseppe
Saggione venetiano. *See* Fedeli, Giuseppe
Sagittarius, (Henricus). *See* Schütz, Heinrich
Sahm, Doug. *See* Saldana, Douglas
Saidy, Fred. *See* Saidy, Fareed Milhelm
Saint and *St.* are interfiled
Saint-Amans, M. Léon, *fils*. *See* Rousseau, Louise-Geneviève
Saint Ambrose. *See* Ambrosius of Milan
St. August, John. *See* Klinkhammer, Stefan
Saint-Blane, James. *See* MacCulloch, James Monteath
St. Clair, Avery. *See* Mills, Frederick Allen
Saint [or St.] Damian, Leo. *See* Clark, Frederick Horace
St. Diamond. *See* Zuccalmaglio, Anton Wilhelm Florentin von
Saint Gaston, Sister M. *See* Dellafield, Henry
Saint-Georges, (Joseph Boulogne), Chevalier de. *See* Boulogne, Joseph (de)
St. Gilles, A. de. *See* André, Jean Baptiste (Andreas)
Saint-Granier. *See* DeGranier (de Cassagnac), Jean (Adolphe Alfred)
Saint Helier, Ivy. *See* Aitchison, Ivy (Janet)
St. Hilaire. *See* Harries, Heinrich
Saint James, Melvyn. *See* Endsley, Gerald
Saint James, Vivian. *See* Hainsworth, Edward James
Saint-Jean, René. *See* Berlin, Boris
St. John, Dick. *See* Gosting, Richard (Frank)
Saint-Just, (Claude). *See* Godard d'Ancour (de Saint-Just), Claude
St. Juste, Edouard. *See* Krenkel, Gustav
Saint-Kopp. *See* Pinatel, Albert
Saint-Léon, (Charles Victor) Arthur. *See* Michel, (Charles Victor) Arthur
St. Louis Jimmy. *See* Oden, James Burke
St. Louis Johnny. *See* Sykes, Roosevelt
St. Louis Mac. *See* Simmons, Mac(k)
Saint-Lubin, León de. *See* Lubin, Napoléon-Antoine-Eugene

Saint-Marc, Amédée de. *See* Delestre-Poirson, Charles Gaspard
Saint-Marc, Amédée de. *See* Duveyrier, Anne Honoré Joseph
Saint-Marc, Amédée de. *See* Scribe, (Augustin) Eugène
St. Maur, Emlyn. *See* Williams, Joseph (Benjamin)
St Onge, Bill. *See* Drawbaugh, Jacob W(ilbur, Jr.)
St. Paul of the Gluck Religion, The. *See* Arnaud, François
St. Peters, Crispian. *See* Smith, Robin Peter
Saint Quentin, Edward. *See* Hutchison, William M(arshall)
Saint [or St.] Quentin, Edward. *See* Rawlings, Alfred William
Saint [or St.] Quentin, Edwin. *See* Rawlings, Alfred William
Staint [or St.] Quentin, G. de. *See* Rawlings, Alfred William
Saint-Rémy, M. de. *See* Morny, Charles (Auguste Louis) Joseph de
Saint Sebastian. *See* Bach, Johann Sebastian
Saint-Simon, Comtesse de. *See* Bawr, Alexandrine Sophie de
Saint-Yves. *See* Déaddé, Edouard
Sainte-Marie, Buffy. *See* Sainte-Marie, Beverly
Saintine, (Joseph Xavier). *See* Boniface, Joseph Xavier
Saion(i), Carlo. *See* Fedeli, Carlo
Sajon, (Carlo). *See* Fedeli, Carlo
Sajon. *See* Fedeli, Ruggiero
Saki. *See* Munro, Hector Hugh
Saks, Benny. *See* Sakamaki, Ben
Salaam, Liaqat Ali. *See* Clarke, Kenneth [or Kenny] (Spearman)
Saleem, Kashif. *See* Jones, Michael
Salèm, Josquino. *See* Della Sala, Josquino
Salèpico, Josquino. *See* Della Sala, Josquino
Salim, Ahmad Khatab. *See* Atkinson, A. K.
Salomonis. *See* Elias, Salomon
Salon, Joseph. *See* Mullendore, Joseph [or Joe]
Salon, Joseph. *See* Taylor, Herb
Salsbury, Sonny. *See* Salsbury, Hubert Ivan
Salt. *See* James, Cheryl
Salten, Felix. *See* Salzmann, Siegmund
Saltenburg, Felix. *See* Salz, Herschel
Salter, Harry. *See* Salter, Hans J.
Saluzzi, Dino. *See* Saluzzi, Timoteo
Salvador-Daniel, (Francisco). *See* Daniel, Francisco (Alberto Clemente) Salvadore
Salvatoriello. *See* Rosa, Salvator(e)
Salvayre, Gaston. *See* Salvayre, Gervais-Bernard
Sam & John. *See* John, Oscar
Sam & John. *See* Theard, Sam
Sam, the Barbasol Man. *See* Slaughter, M(arion) T(ry)
Sam the Sham. *See* Samudio, Domingo
Samama, Azuma. *See* Servoz, Harriet
Samara(s), Spiro. *See* Filiskos, Spyridon
Samaroff, Ogla. *See* Hickenlooper, Lucy [or Lucie] (Mary Olga Agnes)
Sambelle, Francisco. *See* Beer, Johann
Same Compiler, The. *See* Massey, Lucy Fletcher
Samigli, Ettore. *See* Svevo, Italo
Samon, Grico. *See* Sampson, James
Samson-François. *See* François, Samson
Sampson, Sammy. *See* Broonzy, William Lee Conley
Samson. *See* Adler, Hans
Samudio, Sam. *See* Samudio, Domingo
Samuel, Fernand. *See* Louveau, Fernand
Samuel, Henry. *See* Samuel, Sealhenry (Olumide)
Samuel-Rousseau, Marcel. *See* Rousseau, Marcel(-Auguste-Louis)
Samuels, Claude. *See* Robison, Carson J(ay)
San Sebastián, Padre. *See* Zulaica y Arregui, José Gonzalo
Sanat Gunesi. *See* Muren, Zeki
Sanborn, Dave. *See* Bernard, Al(fred A.)
Sanchez. *See* Jackson, Kevin Anthony
Sanchez, Cuco. *See* Sánchez Saldano [or Saldana], José (del) Refugio
Sanchez, Refugio. *See* Sánchez Saldano [or Saldana], José (del) Refugio
Sancho, (Charles) Ignatius. *See* Ignatius
Sande, Gene. *See* Warrington, John(ny) (T.)
Sandell, Lina. *See* Sandell(-Berg), Karolina [or Carolina] Wilhelmina
Sandell, Lynn. *See* Wickdahl, Lillian (S.)
Sander, Rolf. *See* Damp, Artur
Sanders, Herr. *See* Marszalek, Franz
Sanders, Béla. *See* Schubert, Hans
Sanders, Fareil. *See* Glenn, Fareil
Sanders, Paul. *See* Santoro, Paul
Sanders, Sonny. *See* Sanders, William (Nelson) (1939-)
Sanderson, G. R. *See* Bliss, P(hilip) Paul
Sandler, Peter. *See* Sandler, Peretz
Sandner, Rolf. *See* Kammler, Ewald
Sandow, Ludwig. *See* Schwarz, Louis
Sandrin, (P(ierre)). *See* Regnault, Pierre
Sands, Carl. *See* Seeger, Charles (Louis)
Sanford, Joseph G. *See* Gershenson, Joseph E.
Sanford, M. *See* Frangkiser, Carl (Moerz)
Sanguinetti, Horacio. *See* Basterra, Horatio
Sannois, Charles. *See* Saint-Saëns, (Charles) Camille
Sanns, Ray. *See* Mullendore, Joseph [or Joe]
Sans Esprit, Monsieur. *See* Fielding, Henry
Santamaria, Mongo. *See* Santamaria (Rodríguez), Ramón
Santana, Carlos. *See* Navarro, Autlan de
Santana, Jorge. *See* Novo, Salvador
Santander, Kike. *See* Santander, Lora Flavio
Santiago, Francisco de. *See* Veiga, Francisco
Santis, Carlos de. *See* Himmer-Perez, Arturo

Santley, Joseph. *See* Mansfield, Joseph
Santly, Banjo. *See* Santly, Joseph H.
Santolius Maglorianus. *See* Santeul, Claude de
Santolius Victorinus. *See* Santeu(i)l, Jean Baptiste de
Santon, Fred. *See* Waltzinger, Friedrich
Santos, Jose. *See* Smith, Lee Orean
Santos, Ricardo. *See* Müller, Werner [or Warner]
Santos, Tony. *See* Sacco, Anthony
Sanz, Alejandro. *See* Sánchez Pizarro, Alejandro
Sapajou, M. *See* Gabriel (de Lurieu), Jules-Joseph
Saphir, Marie. *See* Gordon, Marie
Saputo. *See* Trautzl, Jan Jakub
Saquito, Nico. *See* Fernandez Ortiz, Benito Antonio
Sarabin, Franz. *See* Simon, Waldemar
Saracen, Ray. *See* Saraceni, Raymond (R.)
Sarakowski, G. *See* Phillips, Alfred
Sarasate of the Guitar. *See* Tarrega(-Eixea), Francisco
Sarcanti, Pigmeo. *See* Masgani, Pietro
Sarcey. *See* Allais, Alphonse
Sargent, J. B. *See* Kunkel, Charles
Sarkisian, Cherilyn. *See* La Pier(r)e, Cherilyn
Saroni, M. *See* Holmes, M. C.
Sarony, Leslie. *See* Frye, Leslie Legge Sarony
Sárosi, Ferencz. *See* Schauer, Ferencz
Sarsfield, Michael. *See* Clifford, Hubert John
Sartorius, Erasmus. *See* Schneider, Erasmus
Sartorius, Paul. *See* Schneider, Paul
Sarver, Lillian H. *See* Lincoln, Harry J.
Sascha. *See* Schickele, René (Marie Maurice Armand)
Sassone, Il. *See* Hasse, Johann Adolf
Sata Esmeralda. *See* Goings, Jimmy
Satchelmouth. *See* Armstrong, (Daniel) Louis
Satchmo. *See* Armstrong, (Daniel) Louis
Satirico, Il. *See* Predamosche, Verdacchio [pseud.]
Satis, Erit. *See* Satie, (Alfred) Erik (Leslie)
Satterlee, Arthur. *See* Koepke, Paul
Satterwhite, Tex. *See* Satterwhite, C(ollen) G(ray)
Sauguet, Henri. *See* Poupard, Henri-Pierre
Saulnier, Thelerise. *See* Kunkel, Charles
Saunders, Joe. *See* Leybourne, George
Saunders, Kenneth. *See* De Vito, Albert (Kenneth)
Saunders, Wash. *See* Saunders, Wallace
Saupiquet. *See* Cornuel, Jean
Saurel, Pierre. *See* Daignault, Pierre
Sautreuil, Jean. *See* Yvain, Maurice Pierre Paul
Sauval, Marc. *See* Soulage, Marcelle Fanny Henriette
Sauvé, Georges. *See* Parent, Lionel
Savage. *See* Zanetti, Roberto
Savage, Adam. *See* Butters, Francis
Savage, I. B. *See* Bliss, P(hilip) Paul
Savage, J. R. *See* Gabriel, Charles H(utchinson)
Savage, Richard. *See* Hayman, Richard Warren Joseph
Savin, Risto. *See* Širca, Friderik
Savinio, Alberto. *See* Chirico, Andrea [or Alberto] de
Savio, Dan. *See* Morricone, Ennio
Savior of Church Music, The. *See* Palestrina, Giovanni Pierluigi da
Savonese, Il. *See* Chiabrera, Gabriello
Savoy, A(nne). *See* Brooks, Anne Sooy
Savoy, James. *See* Criscuolo, James Michael
Savoy, Ronnie [or Ronny]. *See* Hamilton, Eugene
Sawhill, Philip. *See* Ehret, Walter (Charles)
Sawyer, Joan. *See* Stephens, Ward
Saxon, Cedric. *See* Lemont, Cedric Wilmot
Saxon Giant, The. *See* Handel, Georg Friedrich
Saxon, Jack. *See* Kreitzberg, Yasha [or Jacob]
Sayat'-Nova. *See* Arutyun, Sayadyan
Sayer, Leo. *See* Sayer, Gerard (Hugh)
Saz, Leylâ. *See* Leyla Hanim(efendi)
Scacabarozus, Obricus. *See* Heseltine, Philip (Arnold)
Scaggs, Boz. *See* Scaggs, William Royce
Scala, Primo. *See* Bidgood, Henry [or Harry] (James)
Scaligeri. *See* Castro, Eduardo de Sá Pereira de
Scaligeri della Fratta, Camillo. *See* Banchieri, Adriano (Tomaso)
Scannamata, Giordano. *See* Anelli, Angelo
Scannamato, Giovanni. *See* Anelli, Angelo
Scanner. *See* Rimbaud, Robin
Scapus, Mit. *See* Scheepers-Van Dommelen, Maria
Scarborough, Skip. *See* Scarborough, C(larence)
Scardanelli. *See* Hölderlin, (Johann Christian) Friedrich
Scarface. *See* Jordan, Brad(ley)
Scarpi, N. O. *See* Bondy, Fritz
Scatman. *See* Crothers, Benjamin Sherman (Louis)
Schaefer, Christia(n). *See* Seymour, Albert
Schaefer, Herman. *See* Glady, Tom
Schafer, Christian. *See* Rawlings, Alfred William
Schäfer, Herbert M. *See* Deuringer, Hubert [or Herbert] (Martin)
Schaller, Werner. *See* Jaxtheimer, Gerald
Schanara, Hans. *See* Schwanzara, Hans
Schani. *See* Strauss, Johann (Baptist), (Jr.) (1825-1899)
Schanz, Uli. *See* Schanz, Julius
Schartenmayer, Philipp Ulrich. *See* Vischer, Friedrich Theodor von
Scheffer, Pi. *See* Scheffer, Johannes
Schelmerding, Ernst. *See* Mohaupt, Franz
Schelp, Arend. *See* Paap, Wouter (Ernest)
Scherz, Ernst. *See* Erler, Hermann
Schick, Hans. *See* Stults, R(obert) M(orrison)
Schifrin, Lalo. *See* Schifrin, Boris (C(laudio))
Schikaneder, Emanuel. *See* Schickeneder, Johann Joseph [or Jakob]
Schipa, Tito. *See* Schipa, Raffaele Attilio Amadeo
Schippers, Wim T. *See* Schippers, Willem Theodoor
Schirza, Friederich (Elder) von. *See* Širca, Friderik
Schizza. *See* Graziolli, Giovanni
Schlechter, Karl. *See* Schlächter, Karl
Schleicher, Erasmus. *See* Bennert, Julius Eduard
Schlemihl, Peter. *See* Thoma, Ludwig

Scott, Harold. *See* Kortlander, Max
Scott, J. *See* Vickers, Mike
Scott, Jack. *See* Scafone, Jack (Dominic), (Jr.)
Scott, James A. *See* Yoder, Paul V(an Buskirk)
Scott, James, Esq. *See* Lockhart, John Gibson
Scott, Joseph. *See* Kierland, Joseph Scott
Scott, Patrick J. O'Hara. *See* Vickers, Mike
Scott, Raymond. *See* Warnow, Harry
Scott, Ronnie. *See* Schatt, Ronald
Scott, Sonny. *See* Rostaing, Hubert
Scott, Stuart. *See* Barnard, D'Auvergne
Scott, Tony. *See* Sciacca, Anthony
Scott, W. D. *See* Dykema, Peter W(illiam)
Scottish King of Folk, The. *See* McGinn, Matt
Scotty. *See* Wiseman, Scott(y) (Greene)
Scotus, Andreas Francus. *See* Schwartz, Andreas (Scotus)
Scoundrel Brahms. *See* Brahms, Johannes
Scratch. *See* Perry, Rainford Hugh
Scriblerus Maximus. *See* Dance, James
Scriblerus Secundus, (H). *See* Fielding, Henry
Scriblerus, Tertius. *See* Cooke, Thomas (Simpson)
Scriptoris, Grammateus. *See* Schreyber, Heinrich
Sea, Bernie. *See* Chianco, Bernard V.
Sea, Johnny. *See* Seay, John Allan, Jr.
Sea, M. A. *See* McGranahan, James
Seak, Peter. *See* Montani, Pietro
Seal. *See* Samuel, Sealhenry (Olumide)
Seal. *See* Young, Bernard
Seals, Son. *See* Seals, Frank (Junior)
Search, John. *See* Binney, Thomas
Searelle, (William) Luscombe. *See* Israel, Isaac
Sears, Billy. *See* Felton, William M.
Sears, Joseph. *See* Slaughter, M(arion) T(ry)
Sears, Lee. *See* Gryce, G(eorge) G(eneral)
Seaton, B. B. *See* Seaton, Harris
Seaton, Bibby. *See* Seaton, Harris
Sebastian, John. *See* Lieberson, Goddard
Sebastion. *See* Burnard, (David) Alex(ander)
Sebbél, S. M. Karl. *See* Sapp, Allen (Dwight)
Sebregts, Ron. *See* Waignein, Andre
Sechler, Curly. *See* Sechler, John Ray
Secinuntino, Lerendo [or Lereno]. *See* Barbosa, Domingos Caldas
Second Pachelbel, A. *See* Walther, Johann Gottfried
Second Source of Greek Music, The. *See* Papadopoulos, Joannes
Secretary to Ye Fiz-Gig Club. *See* Carey, Henry
Secundus, Scriblerus. *See* Fielding, Henry
Sedgwick, Robert. *See* Riegger, Wallingford (Constantin)
Sedores, Sil [or Syl]. *See* White, Sylvia
See, W. F. *See* Collins, William Francis
Seed, A. Carroway. *See* Tyler, George Crouse
Seedo, Mr. *See* Sidow
Seeger, Ruth Crawford. *See* Crawford, Ruth (Porter)
Seeker, David. *See* Nerijnen, Jan van
Seely, John. *See* Gilfilen, Seely John
Seeley, Philip. *See* Edwards, C(harles) J(oseph)
Seelig, Arthur. *See* Finkelstein, Abe
Seelig, Arthur. *See* Kaufman, Isidore
Seener, Joseph. *See* Paramor, Norman [or Norrie] (William)
Seffel, X. *See* Enzler, Josef
Sefton, Michael. *See* Yorke, Peter
Segnitz, Emil. *See* Hansson, Stig (Axel)
Segundo, Company. *See* Repilado (Muñoz), (Máximo) Francisco
Seiffert, Ernst. *See* Denemy, Richard
Sekerech, François. *See* Szekeres, Ferenc [or François]
Selassie, Berhane. *See* Marley, Robert [or Bob] Nesta
Selcamm, George. *See* Machlis, Joseph
Selden, Albert. *See* Seldon, Albert Wiggin
Selden, Camille. *See* Krinitz, Elsie (von)
Seldon, M. *See* Frangkiser, Carl (Moerz)
Selim. *See* Woodworth, Samuel
Selin. *See* McCollin, Frances
Seljancica. *See* Petrović, Milorad
Sellini, Pietro. *See* Petrosellini, Giuseppe
Selté. *See* Tiemersma, Sake Lieuwe
Selva, Alessandro. *See* Inglis, Alexander Wood
Selz, Bob. *See* Dax, Esteven
Semischăcksbier. *See* Hindemith, Paul
Sempty, Paul. *See* Zacharias, Stephan
Sen, Yama. *See* Keiser, Robert (A(dolph))
Sendach, Ludwig. *See* Déschán, Ludwig
Senator. *See* Wright, Eugene [or Gene]
Sendrey, Alfred. *See* Szendrei, Aladár
Senea, E. Marco. *See* Meano, Cesare
Senesino, (Il). *See* Tenducci, Giusto [or Giustino] Ferdinando [or Fernando]
Senex, Theophilus. *See* Turner, Daniel
Senez, Camille de. *See* Wajditsch Verbonac von Dönhoff, Gabriel
Senicourt, Roger. *See* Chacksfield, Francis [or Frank] (Charles)
Senior Diplomat of Soul, The. *See* Robinson, Ray Charles
Senkrah, Arma. *See* Harkness, Arma Levretta [or L(e)oretta]
Señor del Tango, El. *See* Di Sarli, Carlos
Sentis. *See* Siede, Ludwig
Sentri, Liberto. *See* Bertelli, Rino [or Rono]
Sephner, Otto. *See* Renner, Josef, (Jr.)
Sepia Mae West, The. *See* Prather, Ida
September, Anthony. *See* Cohen, Kalman
September, Anthony. *See* Lowe, Bernie
September, Anthony. *See* Mammarella, Anthony
Serafino. *See* Razzi, Giovanni
Seranus. *See* Harrison, Susan [or Susie] Frances (née Riley)

Seraphina, (Sister). *See* Kunkel, Charles
Séré, Octave. *See* Poueigh, Jean (Marie Octave Géraud)
Seredy, Jules. *See* Seredy, J(ulius) S.
Serena, A(malie). *See* Amalie, Marie Friederike Augusta, Princess of Saxony
Sermes, Sieur de. *See* Mersenne, Marin
Serpentinus. *See* Banck, Karl [or Carl]
Serrallonga, Juan. *See* Gerhard (Ottenwaelder), Robert(o)
Serveau, Armand. *See* Leest, Antonius Maria van
Servières, Jules. *See* Halévy, Ludovic
Sesto, Camilo. *See* Blanes (Cortés), Camilio
Setab, J. *See* Bates, J.
Sete, Bola. *See* Andrade, Djalmi de
Seter, Mordecai. *See* Starominsky, Mordechai
Settle, Jelly. *See* Settle, Lee Edgar
Setty, Carl. *See* Sacchetti, Carl Salvatore
Seuberlich, Daniel. *See* Nicolai, (Christoph) Friedrich
Seuss, Dr. *See* Geisel, Theodore Seuss
Seven. *See* Volpane, Keith
Seven Grand Housing Authority. *See* Parker, Terrance
Seven Octave(s). *See* Gottschalk, Louis Moreau
Severinsen, Doc. *See* Severinsen, Carl H(ilding)
Severn, Arthur. *See* Frangkiser, Carl (Moerz)
Seville, David. *See* Bagdasarian, Ross
Sevin, Louis. *See* Loquin, Antole
Sevitzky, Fabien. *See* Koussevitzky, Fabien
Seward, Hatch. *See* Lewis, Meade (Anderson)
Seward, Slim. *See* Seward, Alexander T.
Sexalise, François. *See* Wiggins, Thomas (Green(e))
Seymore, Cy. *See* Polla, William C.
Seymour, Cy. *See* Applebaum, Stan(ley) (Seymour)
Seymour, Frank. *See* Mortimer, Harry
Seymour, Frank. *See* Smith-Masters, Stanley
Seymour, Georg. *See* Erby, John J.
Seymour, H. *See* Bliss, P(hilip) Paul
Seymour, Laurence. *See* Walters, Harold L(aurence)
Seymour, Ralph. *See* Rawlings, Charles Arthur
Seymour, S. *See* Keiser, Robert (A(dolph))
Shadé, Grey. *See* Báthory-Kitsz, Dennis
Shadow. *See* Bailey, Winston [or Wilston]
Shadow, John. *See* Byrom, John
Shadow, Mighty. *See* Bailey, Winston [or Wilston]
Shadwell, William B. *See* Nevin, Gordon Balch
Shady, Slim. *See* Mathers, Marshall (Bruce), III
Shafer, Whitey. *See* Shafer, Sanger D.
Shaftesbury, Bill. *See* Stapleton, Cyril
Shaftmeister. *See* Hayes, Isaac
Shaggy. *See* Burrell, Orville (Richard)
Shakespeare of Country Music. *See* Nelson, Willie (Hugh)
Shakespeare of Harmony, The. *See* Wagner, Richard
Shakespears Sister. *See* Fahey, Siobhan
Shakey, Bernard. *See* Young, Neil
Shakey Jake. *See* Harris, James [or Jimmy] (D.)
Shakey Walter. *See* Horton, Walter
Shakira. *See* Mebarak (R(ipoll)), Shakira Isabel
Shamus. *See* O'Brien, James Nagle
Shand, Ernest. *See* Watson, Ernest
Shank, Bud. *See* Shank, Clifford (Everett, Jr.)
Shankar, Ravi. *See* Chowdhury, Robindra Shankar
Shannon. *See* Smith, Reginald (Leonard)
Shannon, Dee [or Del(l)]. *See* Westover, Charles W(eedon)
Shannon, J(ames) R(oyce). *See* Royce, James (Stanley)
Shannon, Jackie. *See* Myers, Sharon [or Sherry] (Lee)
Shannon, James Stanley. *See* Royce, James (Stanley)
Shannon, Walter. *See* Lipman, Walter
Sharalee. *See* Lucas, Sharalee
Sharan, Shiva. *See* Danielou, Alain
Sharkow, Bud. *See* Reipsch, Horst
Sharm. *See* Marsh, John
Sharon, Paul. *See* Tunbridge, Joseph A(lbert)
Sharon, Paul. *See* Waller, Jack
Sharp. *See* Chorley, Henry Fothergill
Sharp, B. A. *See* Brounoff, Platon G.
Sharp, Jack. *See* Berry, Dennis (Alfred)
Sharples, Robert [or Bob]. *See* Burns, Wilfred
Sharples, Robert [or Bob]. *See* Standish, Robert Frederick
Shauna, Verity. *See* Adams, Cliff
Shaver, Buster. *See* Shaver, Floyd Herbert
Shaw, Arnold. *See* Shukotoff, Arnold
Shaw, Artie. *See* Arshawsky, Arthur Jacob
Shaw, Damon. *See* Lee, Albert George
Shaw, Damon. *See* Tunbridge, Joseph A(lbert)
Shaw, Damon. *See* Waller, Jack
Shaw, Eddie. *See* Slaughter, M(arion) T(ry)
Shaw, Fud. *See* Shaw, Robert
Shaw, Joan. *See* DeCosta, Joan
Shaw, Marlena. *See* Burgess, Marlena
Shaw, Roger. *See* Ehret, Walter (Charles)
Shaw, Serena. *See* Davison, Lita
Shaw, Vincent. *See* Vicars, Harold
Shayne, Freddie. *See* Shayne, J. H.
Shea, Jack. *See* Kaufman, Jacob
Shean, Al. *See* Schoenberg, Alfred
Shears, Billy. *See* Starkey, Richard
Sheik of the Blues. *See* Willis, Harold
Sheik of the Shake. *See* Willis, Harold
Sheila E. *See* Escovedo, Sheila
She'kspere. *See* Briggs, Kevin
Sheldon, Ernie. *See* Lieberman, Ernest Sheldon
Sheldon, Jon. *See* Cohen, Kalman
Shelley, Mary C. *See* Miles, C(harles) (John) A(ustin)
Shelley, Pete. *See* McNeish, Peter
Shelly of America. *See* Hart, Lorenz (Milton)
Shemer, Naomi. *See* Rechtman, Mordechai
Sheng, Bright. *See* Sheng, Zongliang
Shep. *See* Sheppard, James

Silly Kid, The. *See* Floyd, Frank
Silni, Max. *See* Paigne, Mme.
Silurist, The. *See* Vaughan, Henry
Silva, Hector. *See* De Filippi, Amedeo
Silvani, Leo. *See* Cunio, Angelo
Silvanus, Jacchus Heremias. *See* Schein, Johann Hermann
Silvanus, Menalca. *See* Schein, Johann Hermann
Silver Fox, The. *See* Rich, Charlie [or Charley]
Silver, Fred(erick). *See* Silverberg, Frederick (Irwin)
Silver, Horace. *See* Silva, Horace (Ward Martin Tavares)
Silver, Johnny. *See* Lennon, John (Winston)
Silver-Screen's First Singing Cowboy, The. *See* Autry, (Orvon) Gene
Silver, Yvonne Vaughan. *See* Vaughan, Yvonne
Silvers, Doc. *See* Silverstein, Herman
Silvers, Herman. *See* Silverstein, Herman
Silverson, Sam. *See* Seligmacher, Moritz
Silverstone, Mendel. *See* Melville, George S.
Silvertongue, Gabriel. *See* Montgomery, James
Silvester, Eric. *See* Herschmann, Erik
Silvestro del cornetto. *See* Ganassi (dal Fontego), Sylvestro [or Silvestro] di
Simes, Lee. *See* Cain, Noble
Simes, Robert Lee. *See* Cain, Noble
Simia, G. R. *See* Richelot, Gustave
Simien, Sidney. *See* Semien, Sidney
Simmen, Johnny. *See* Simmen, Hans Georg
Simmonds, Tony. *See* Martin, Ray(mond)
Simmons, Gene. *See* Klein, Gene
Simmons, Little Mac(k). *See* Simmons, Mac(k)
Simms, T(eddy) . *See* Phillips, Teddy (Steve)
Simon, Frank. *See* Erbe, Raimond
Simon, Isadore. *See* Phillips, Isadore Simon
Simon, Philipp. *See* Goletz, Philipp Simon
Simon, the Jester. *See* Cameron, Dan(iel) (A.)
Simone, Carl. *See* Siemon, Carl (W.)
Simone, Nina. *See* Waymon, Eunice Kathleen
Simoni, Edward. *See* Krok, Edward
Simonis, P. *See* Leeuwen, Simon Petrus van
Simons, Julie. *See* Candeille, Amelie-Julie
Simons, Moisés. *See* Rodríguez, Moisés Simons
Simonson, Si. *See* Simonson, Ernest Lowell
Simonton, Danforth. *See* Page, N(athaniel) Clifford
Simpatico. *See* Giannini, Giovanni Matteo
Simpkins, Polly. *See* Macy, J(ames) C(artwright)
Simplicissimus. *See* Speer, Daniel
Simplicissimus. *See* Weinhöppel, Hans Richard
Simpson, Al. *See* Bernard, Al(fred A.)
Simpson, Red. *See* Simpson, Joseph
Sims, George. *See* Sims, Albert Ernest
Sims, Jerry. *See* Samuels, Jerry
Sims, Mac. *See* Simmons, Mac(k)
Sims, Skeeter. *See* Bernard, Al(fred A.)
Sims, Teddy. *See* Phillips, Teddy (Steve)
Sims, Zoot. *See* Sims, John Haley
Simsa, B. *See* Janovický, Karel
Sinapsis. *See* Neild, James Edward
Sincerus, (Julius). *See* Lasker, (Ignaz) Julius
Sinclair, Al. *See* Szirmai, Albert
Sinclair, Stephen. *See* Hansson, Stig (Axel)
Sined, der Barde. *See* Denis, (Johann) Michael (Kosmas Peter), (S. J.)
Singe de Scarron, Le. *See* Coypeau, Charles
Singer, Amy. *See* Southard, Mary Ann
Singer, Guy. *See* Guisinger, Earl C(halmers)
Singer of Singers and Improviser of Improvisers, The. *See* Pérez, Héctor (Juan)
Singer's Critic and Lord High Executioner. *See* Henderson, William James
Singh, Ram. *See* Brown, Lee
Singier, Alexis. *See* Blaze, François Henri Joseph
Singin' Sam. *See* Frankel, Harry
Singing Breakman, The. *See* Rodgers, James [or Jimmie] (Charles)
Singing Christian, The. *See* White, Josh(ua) (Daniel)
Singing Cowboy, The. *See* Autry, (Orvon) Gene
Singing Cowboy. *See* Glosup, Edgar D(ean)
Singing Cowboy, The. *See* Wakeley, James [or Jimmy] Clarence
Singing Emcee. *See* Draper, Farrell H(al)
Singing Emcee, (The). *See* Unteed, Richard [or Dick] (Alan)
Singing Fisherman, The. *See* Horton, John(ny) (Gale)
Singing Governor. *See* Davis, James [or Jimmie] (Houston) (1899-2000)
Singing Grandmother, The. *See* Reynolds, Malvina
Singing Hobo, The. *See* Martin, Lecil T(ravis)
Singing Kid, The. *See* Williams, Hir(i)am (King)
Singing Midget, The. *See* Dickens, James Cecil
Singing Nun, The. *See* Deckers, J(e)anine
Singing Outlaw, The. *See* Young, Faron
Singing Pianist, The. *See* Erby, John J.
Singing Pilgrim, The. *See* Phillips, Philip
Singing Preacher, The. *See* White, Booker T. Washington
Singing Ranger, (The). *See* Snow, Clarence Eugene
Singing Sam. *See* Stevens, Sam
Singing Sea, The. *See* Seay, John Allan, Jr.
Singing Sheriff, The. *See* Young, Faron
Singing Turtle, The. *See* Samberg, Benjamin
Singing Xylophonist, The. *See* Hall, Wendel (Woods)
Single, Humphrey. *See* Carey, Henry
Single, John, of Grey's Inn. *See* Carey, Henry
Singleton, Mary. *See* Brooke, Frances (née Moore)
Singleton, Win. *See* Sharples, Winston S., Jr.
Sinho. *See* Silva, José Barbosa [or B(atista)] (da)
Sinister 6000. *See* Thornton, Keith
Sinnicam, Don. *See* MacInnis, (Murdoch) Donald
Sinoja, J. E (de). *See* Engel (de Jánosi), Josef [or Joseph]

Smith, Bessie. *See* Smith, Elizabeth
Smith, Big Willie. *See* Thornton, Keith
Smith Brothers. *See* Smith, Harry B(ache)
Smith Brothers. *See* Smith, Robert B.
Smith, Dan. *See* Razafinkeriefo, Andreamenentania Paul
Smith, Edwin. *See* Behr, F(ranz)
Smith, Elliott. *See* Smith, Steven [or Stephen] Paul
Smith, Eric. *See* Kaper, Bronislaw
Smith, Funny Paper. *See* Smith, John T.
Smith, Gipsy. *See* Smith, Rodney
Smith, Guitar Boogie. *See* Smith, Arthur
Smith, Gulliver. *See* Smith, Kevin ([nd])
Smith, Guy. *See* Erby, John J.
Smith, Hank. *See* Jones, George (Glen(n))
Smith, Harmonica. *See* Smith, George (1924-1983)
Smith, Honey Boy. *See* Woodbridge, Hudson
Smith, Howdie. *See* Smith, Houston
Smith, Howlin(g). *See* Broonzy, William Lee Conley
Smith, Howlin'. *See* Smith, John T.
Smith, Hurricane. *See* Smith, Norman (Arnold)
Smith, Jabbo. *See* Smith, Cladys
Smith, J(ames) W. *See* Monroe, William [or Bill] (Smith)
Smith, Jane. *See* Prather, Ida
Smith, Jennie. *See* Callison, Jo Ann
Smith, Jimmie. *See* Autry, (Orvon) Gene
Smith, Joe. *See* Davis, Joseph [or Joe] (M.)
Smith, John Christopher. *See* Schmidt, Johann Christoph
Smith, Jolly Clara. *See* Smith, Clara
Smith, Joseph. *See* Slaughter, M(arion) T(ry)
Smith, Josephus. *See* Slaughter, M(arion) T(ry)
Smith, Julia. *See* Vonderlieth, Leonore
Smith, Kenneth E. *See* Kohlmann, Clarence (E.)
Smith, Lance. *See* Bevan, Leonard Francis
Smith, Leo. *See* Smith, Joseph Leopold
Smith, Lion. *See* Smith, William [or Willie] (Henry Joseph Berthol Bonaparte)
Smith, Lucille Wood. *See* Smith, Frances Octavia
Smith, M. M. *See* Kinyon, John L(eroy)
Smith, Margo. *See* Miller, Betty Lou
Smith, Marion. *See* Vaughn, Richard (S(mith))
Smith, Maryon. *See* Arvey, Verna
Smith, Milo. *See* Gibaldi, Louis M(ilo)
Smith, Paul. *See* Monnais, (Guillaume) Édouard (Désiré)
Smith, Pinetop. *See* Smith, Clarence (1904-1929)
Smith, Puddinhead. *See* Hyman, Richard [or Dick] (R(oven))
Smith, Sallie A. [or E.]. *See* Crosby, Fanny [i.e., Frances] J(ane)
Smith, Sally (M.). *See* Crosby, Fanny [i.e., Frances] J(ane)
Smith, Sam. *See* Crosby, Fanny [i.e., Frances] J(ane)
Smith, Sammi. *See* Smith, Jewel Fay
Smith, Smitty. *See* Smith, William (20th cent.)
Smith, Sol. *See* Keiser, Robert (A(dolph))
Smith, Stuff. *See* Smith, Hezekiah Leroy Gordon
Smith, Susie. *See* Moore, Monette
Smith, Tab. *See* Smith, Talmadge (G.)
Smith, Travelin' Jim. *See* Robison, Carson J(ay)
Smith, TV. *See* Smith, Timothy
Smith, Walter B. *See* Barrell, Edgar Alden, Jr.
Smith, Whispering. *See* Smith, Moses
Smith, Willie "the Lion". *See* Smith, William [or Willie] (Henry Joseph Berthol Bonaparte)
Smithers, Ralph. *See* Bliss, P(hilip) Paul
Smithson, S. A. *See* Bliss, P(hilip) Paul
Smokehouse, Charley. *See* Dorsey, Thomas A(ndrew)
Smoky Babe. *See* Brown, Robert (1927-1975)
Smoky Mountain Boy, (The). *See* Acuff, Roy (Claxton)
Smooth, Mr. *See* Wallace, Jerry
Smothers, Smokey. *See* Smothers, Otis
Smyth, Richard. *See* Bramston, Richard
Snappy Dan. *See* Steele, Henry
Snare, Richie. *See* Starkey, Richard
Sneezer, Ebe. *See* Loudermilk, John D.
Snob Out of Bedlam, A. *See* Liszt, Franz
Snog and Black Lung. *See* Bourke, Pieter
Snoop Doggy Dog. *See* Broadus, Calvin
Snow, Daniel. *See* Beckhard, Robert L.
Snow, Hank. *See* Snow, Clarence Eugene
Snow, Mark. *See* Fulterman, Martin
Snow, Phoebe. *See* Davis, Bertha Ruth
Snow, Phoebe. *See* Laub(e), Phoebe
Snow, T(erry). *See* Woolsey, Mary Hale [or Maryhale]
Snowbird, Frank. *See* Kaderschafka, Franz R.
Snowdrift, J. J. *See* Crosby, Ronald Clyde
Snunit, Zvi [or Tsvi]. *See* Lichtenstein, Zvi [or Tsvi]
Sobeka. *See* Kochno, Boris Jewgenjewitsch
Sobolewski, Edward. *See* Sobolewski, J(ohann) F(riedrich) E(duard)
Socks. *See* Wilson, Wesley
Socrates. *See* Ludovicus Sanctus
Soeur Sourire. *See* Deckers, J(e)anine
Sogino. *See* Fedeli, Ruggiero
Sogner, Tommaso. *See* Sonyer, Tomàs
Sohier, Jean [or Johannes]. *See* Fede, Johannes
Sohy, Charles. *See* Labey, Marcel
Soit-P.P. *See* James, Richard D(avid)
Sokolov, Ivan. *See* Ehret, Walter (Charles)
Sokolov, Ivan. *See* Kinsman, Elmer (F(ranklin))
Sokolov, Vladimir. *See* Frypès, Karel (Vladimir)
Solak, Ted W. *See* Stube, Howard
Solando, Anthony. *See* Westendorf, Omer
Solando, Michael. *See* Westendorf, Omer
Solano, R(amon). *See* Ewing, Montague (George)
Soldene, Emily. *See* Lambert, Emily
Soldier, Dave. *See* Sulzer, David Louis
Soldier's Friend. *See* Young, Maud J(eannie) (Fuller)

Solecki, Adam. *See* Kreuder, Peter
Soleil, Didier. *See* Ghestem, Paulette
Solemn Ol' [or Old] Judge, The. *See* Hay, George Dewey
Soles, Pepe. *See* Aieta, Anselmo Alfredo
Solié, (Jean Pierre). *See* Soulier, Jean Pierre
Soliman the Magnificant. *See* Jennens, Charles
Solinas, Alma. *See* Castro, Eduardo de Sá Pereira de
Solinas, Alma. *See* Conforti, Luigi
Solinger, W. *See* Bülow, Hans von Guido
Solitary Singer. *See* Whitman, Walt(er)
Solla, Isidor de. *See* Cohen, Isidore (de Lara)
Solomon, Fritzy. *See* Solomon, Fred(erick Charles)
Solon, Joseph. *See* Taylor, Herb
Solyrn, A. *See* Salerno, Nicola
Soma. *See* Bourke, Pieter
Somebody. *See* Hays, Will(iam) S(hakespeare)
Someone. *See* Bergh, Arthur
Somers, Glen. *See* Owen, Reg
Somerset, Maud. *See* Somerset, Mary Hurd
Somis, Ardy. *See* Somis, (Giovanni) Lorenzo
Sommer, Hans. *See* Haass, Hans
Sommer, Hans. *See* Zincken, Hans Friedrich August
Sommers, Ronnie. *See* Bono, Salvatore
Son Joe. *See* Lawlars, Ernest
Son of Harry. *See* Harrison, George
Son of Laughter. *See* Williams, Egbert Austin
Sonero Mayor, El. *See* Rivera, Ismael
Song and Dance Man, A. *See* Cohan, George M(ichael)
Song Bird see also *Songbird*
Song Bird in the Dark, The. *See* Crosby, Fanny [i.e., Frances) J(ane)
Song Doctor. *See* Rose, (Knols) Fred
Song Painter, (The). *See* Davis, Morris
Song, Peter. *See* Joensson, Hans
Song-Poet of the Sixties Generation. *See* Zimmerman, Robert Allen
Song Symphonist, The. *See* Mahler, Gustav
Song Team. *See* Szenkar, Claudio
Song-Writer, A. *See* Bennett, William Cox
Song Writers on Parade. *See* Clare, Sidney
Song Writers on Parade. *See* Lewis, Al(an)
Song Writers on Parade. *See* Mencher, (T.) Murray
Song Writers on Parade. *See* Rose, Vincent
Song Writers on Parade. *See* Sherman, Al(bert)
Song Writers on Parade. *See* Tobias, Charles
Song Writers on Parade. *See* Wenrich, Percy
Songbird see also *Song Bird*
Songbird of the South. *See* Pridgett, Gertrude (Malissa Nix)
Songwriter's Songwriter, The. *See* Howard, Harlan (Perry)
Sonique. *See* Clarke, Sonia
Sonn, Dave. *See* Sonenscher, Dave
Sonnabend, Tobias. *See* Lewald, (Johann Karl) August
Sonnacchioso, Il. *See* Rinuccini, Ottavio
Sonnenschein, Fred. *See* Zander, Frank
Sonnleitner, Peter. *See* Wendlinger, Thomas
Sonnolento Tassista. *See* Bonis, Novello (de)
Sonny T. *See* Terrell, Saunders
Sono, Enrico. *See* Quelle, Ernst-August
Sontag, Carl. *See* Retter, Louis
Sony'r Ra, (Le [or La]). *See* Blount, Herman
Sophie G., (Mme.). *See* Garre, (Edmée) Sophie
Sophus, Ludwig. *See* Dahn, (Ludwig Julius) Felix
Sorabji, Kaikhosru Shapurji. *See* Dudley, Leon
Sorbon, Kurt. *See* Kolditz, Hans
Sosa, José. *See* Carmelo Augusto, José Francisco
Sosa, Pepe. *See* Carmelo Augusto, José Francisco
Sot. *See* Cornuel, Jean
Soter, Dyck. *See* Soter, Oswald
Sothern, Ann. *See* Lake, Henrietta
Souchon, Doc. *See* Souchon, Edmond, (Jr.)
Soul Brother Number 1. *See* Brown, James
Soul, David. *See* Solberg, David (Richard)
Soul, Lady. *See* Franklin, Aretha
Soul Man, The. *See* Bland, Robert Calvin
Soul of Samba. *See* Silva, Ismael
Soulbieu, F. *See* Desprez, Frank
Soulshock. *See* Schack, Carsten
Soundtracks, Epic. *See* Godfrey, Kevin Paul
South African, A. *See* Statham, Francis Reginald
South, Georgia. *See* Davis, Joseph [or Joe] (M.)
South, Joe. *See* Souter, Joseph, Jr.
Southern Gentleman, The. *See* Loden, James (H.)
Southern, Jeri. *See* Hering, Genevieve (Lillian)
Southern Knight, A. *See* Toussaint, Allen (R.)
Southern Nightingale, The. *See* Smith, Trixie
Southey, Amy. *See* Cain, Noble
Southey, Eric. *See* Cain, Noble
Southey, Phimon L. *See* Sullivan, V. P.
Souza, Palma de. *See* Zadora, Michael
Sovine, Red. *See* Sovine, Woodrow Wilson
Spaceman Vinnie. *See* Bell, Vincent [or Vinnie]
Spade, Jack. *See* Box, Harold Elton
Spade, Jack. *See* Dash, Irwin
Spade, Jack. *See* Keuleman, Adrian
Spade, Joshua. *See* Charles, Leslie Sebastian
Spade, Sam. *See* Charles, Leslie Sebastian
Spagnolet of the Theatre, The. *See* Cibber, Colley
Spagnoletto. *See* Catrufo, Gioseffo [or Giuseppe]
Spagnoletto, Il. *See* Garcia (Fajer), Francisco Javier
Spagnuolo, Lo. *See* Martín y Soler, Vicente
Spain, Verna Gale. *See* Sullivan, Gala
Spangol, Der. *See* Beethoven, Ludwig van
Spangy. *See* Beethoven, Ludwig van
Spaniard, The. *See* Beethoven, Ludwig van
Spanish Frank Sinatra, The. *See* Iglesias, Julio
Spanish Gershwin, The. *See* Falla, Manuel de

Spanish Mozart, The. *See* Arriaga (y Balzola), Juan Crisóstomo (Jacobo Antonio) de
Spanish Sinatra, The. *See* Iglesias, Julio
Spanish Strauss, The. *See* Campo, Conrado del
Spano, Tito. *See* Mignone, Francisco (Paulo)
Spargo, Tony. *See* Sbarbaro, Antonio [or Anthony]
Spark, Elton. *See* Kountz, Richard
Sparker, A. *See* Grannis, S(idney) M(artin)
Sparks, Ernest [or Ernie]. *See* Craps, Ernest (Jean)
Sparks, Stevie. *See* Hubert, Stephen Fitch
Sparky. *See* Lawrence, Wilma Sue
Sparrow, The. *See* Finkelstein, Abe
Sparrow. *See* Francisco, Slinger
Sparrow Kid. *See* Gassion, Edith Giovanna
Spate, Der. *See* Stieler, Caspar [or Kaspar](von)
Spaulding, Jack. *See* McNeil, Stephen
Spavento, Don. *See* Bauer, Julius
Spear. *See* Rodney, (Godfrey) Winston
Spear, Howard. *See* Engel, Carl
Speckled Red. *See* Perryman, Rufus G.
Spector, Jack. *See* Samuels, Milton (Isadore)
Spector, Jay. *See* Samuels, Milton (Isadore)
Speech. *See* Thomas, Todd
Spelvin, George. *See* Shank, Clifford (Everett, Jr.)
Spence, Dick. *See* Spencer, Richard [or Dick]
Spence, Elton. *See* Marvin, John(ny) (Senator)
Spence, J. C. *See* Darewski, Hermann E(dward)
Spence, Lew. *See* Slifka, Lewis
Spence, Robert. *See* Ehret, Walter (Charles)
Spencer, Charles. *See* Chaplin, Charles (Spencer)
Spencer, Ernie. *See* Finkelstein, Abe
Spencer, Eugene. *See* O'Keefe, James (Conrad)
Spencer, Glenn. *See* Spencer, Hubert
Spencer, Guy. *See* Krone, Max (Thomas)
Spencer, Harold. *See* Sawyer, Henry S.
Spencer, John. *See* Lutter, Howard
Spencer, Marian. *See* Wagness, Bernard
Spencer, Marvin. *See* Wagness, Bernard
Spencer, R. *See* Kountz, Richard
Spencer, R(obert) L. *See* Johnson, Robert (Leroy) (1911-1938)
Spencer, Samuel. *See* Edwards, Clifton (A.)
Spencer, Samuel. *See* Finkelstein, Abe
Spencer, Tim. *See* Spencer, Vern(on H(arold))
Spencer, William. *See* Ehret, Walter (Charles)
Spencer, William. *See* Kjelson, Lee
Spenger, M. T. *See* Dichler-Sedlacek, Erika
Spenser, G(eorge). *See* Spaulding, G(eorge) L(awson)
Sperontes. *See* Scholze, Johann Sigismund
Speroy, Robert. *See* Klickmann, F(rank) Henri
Spes. *See* Sapp, Allen (Dwight)
Spider Sam. *See* McGhee, Walter Brown
Spielman, Fritz. *See* Spielman(n), Fred(eric)
Spier, Howard. *See* Engel, Carl
Spier, Robby. *See* Sebastiani, Franco
Spiess, C(hristian) H(einrich). *See* Schulze, Friedrich August
Spikes, Reb (Benjamin). *See* Spikes, Benjamin F.
Spikes, Red. *See* Spikes, Benjamin F.
Spiller Walter. *See* Halletz, Erwin
Spinalba, C. *See* Billig, (Julius Karl) Gustav
Spindle, Louise Cooper. *See* Dellafield, Henry
Spindler, Alexander. *See* Billig, (Julius Karl) Gustav
Spinner, Harold. *See* Spina, Harold
Spiridion, (Pater a Monte Carmelo). *See* Nenning, Johann
Spirito (da Reggio). *See* Pratoneri, Gaspero
Spirito l'Hoste. *See* Oste da Reggio
Spiro, Demon. *See* Lane, James W(eldon)
Spiro, Vincent. *See* Cain, Noble
Spitzbarth. *See* Siebach, Konrad
SPLaTTeRCell. *See* Torn, David
Splendeur, Andre. *See* Leest, Antonius Maria van
Spo-Dee-O-Dee. *See* Theard, Sam
Spondee. *See* Abrahams, Doris Caroline
Spooky Electric. *See* Nelson, Prince Rogers
Spoon, (The). *See* Witherspoon, James [or Jimmy]
Sporle, Nathan James. *See* Burnett, Nathan James
Sportsman, The. *See* Crosby, Harry Lillis
Spotlight Kid, The. *See* Van Vliet, Don
Sprague, Doc. *See* Sprague, Carl T.
Spreesprung der Kühne. *See* Rellstab, (Heinrich Friedrich) Ludwig
Springfield, Rick. *See* Springthorpe, Richard Lewis
Springfield, Tom. *See* O'Brien, Dion
Spunky. *See* Adler, Lou
Squeeze. *See* Quaites, Terrance
Squires, Dorothy. *See* Squires, Edna May
Squirrel. *See* Goldschmidt, Berthold
St. Interfiled with *Saint*
Staab, Hugo. *See* Strasser, Hugo
Staab, Kurt. *See* Strasser, Hugo
Staal, Oliver. *See* Sommerlatte, Ulrich
Staccato. *See* Kalisch, A(lfred)
Staccato, Mlle. *See* Milanollo, Maria
Stacy, Brian. *See* Browder, William [or Bill]
Staffaro, Jules. *See* Stoeckart, Jan
Stafford, Frank. *See* Lubbe, Kurt
Ståhl, Axel Iwar. *See* Õberg, Ludwig Theodore
Stahl, Hans. *See* Last, Hans
Staiger, Arthur. *See* Ellis, Seger
Staigers, Del. *See* Staigers, Charles Delaware
Stair, Patty. *See* Greene, Martha
Stalin, Black. *See* Calliste, Leroy
Stalinski, Tomasz. *See* Kisielewski, Stefan
Stamer, Borders. *See* Grenzebach, Herbert
Stamford, John J. *See* Baker, John S.
Stamitz, Johann. *See* Kreisler, Fritz [i.e., Friedrich](-Max)
Stampadorino, Lo. *See* Colonna, Giovanni Ambrosio

Stamper, Pete. *See* Stamper, Wallace Logan
Stamponi, Chupita. *See* Stamponi, Héctor Luciano
Standberg, Ed. *See* Kammler, Ewald
Standhim, Kant. *See* Kenton, Stan(ley Newcomb)
Standish, Clinton. *See* Haenschen, Walter (G(ustave))
Standish, Orlando. *See* Stephenson, Rowland
Standish, Rowland. *See* Stephenson, Rowland
Stanford, J. S. *See* Henrich, C. W.
Stanford, Patric. *See* Gledhill, John Patrick Stanford
Stanford, Terry. *See* Stanford, Trevor H(erbert)
Stange, Stanislaus. *See* Stange, John William
Stanislas-Viateur. *See* Blau, Édouard
Stanislaus, Henri. *See* Marshall, J. Herbert
Stanislavsky, Konstantin (Sergeievich). *See* Alexeiev, Konstantin (Sergeievich)
Stanley. *See* Noble, Ray(mond) (Stanley)
Stanley, Arnold. *See* Klickmann, F(rank) Henri
Stanley, Eugene. *See* Butler, Ralph (T.)
Stanley, Eugene. *See* Evans, Sydney
Stanley, Eugene. *See* Stevens, Jack
Stanley, F. *See* Keiser, Robert (A(dolph))
Stanley, Frank C. *See* Grinsted, William Stanley
Stanley, Herbert. *See* Grant-Schaeffer, G(eorge) A(lfred)
Stanley, Leo. *See* Ricketts, R(andolph) R(objent)
Stanley, Paul. *See* Eisen, Paul Stanley
Stanley, Ralph. *See* Kraushaar, Raoul
Stanley, Robert. *See* Stevens, Jack
Stanley, Terry. *See* Stanford, Trevor H(erbert)
Stanley, W. H. *See* Walser, Henry Stanley
Stanley, Wynn. *See* David, Worton
Stanton, Albert. *See* Hall, Fred(erick) Fifield
Stanton, Frank. *See* Bliss, P(hilip) Paul
Stanton, Ken. *See* Kenton, Stan(ley Newcomb)
Stanton, V. *See* Kinyon, John L(eroy)
Stanway, Bob. *See* Quelle, Ernst-August
Stanyar, Joseph. *See* Wagness, Bernard
Staples, Pop(s). *See* Staples, Roebuck
Star Maker, The. *See* Simon, Gus(tav(e)) [or Augustus] (Edward)
Star, Maria. *See* Stern, Ernesta de Hierschel
Starcher, Buddy. *See* Starcher, Oby Edgar
Stardust Kid, The. *See* Jones, David Robert (Hayward)
Stardust, Ziggy. *See* Jones, David Robert (Hayward)
Starek, Bill. *See* Schmidt, Gerd
Starfield, Glenn. *See* Mohr, Fritz
Starks, Tony. *See* Coles, Dennis
Starow. *See* Stamm, Werner
Starr, Diggy. *See* Burke, Michael
Starr, Edwin. *See* Hatcher, Charles
Starr, G. G. *See* Bliss, P(hilip) Paul
Starr, Jamie. *See* Nelson, Prince Rogers
Starr, Lucille. *See* Raymonde, Lucille Marie
Starr, Maurice. *See* Johnson, Larry
Starr, Peter. *See* Green, Phil(ip)
Starr, Peter. *See* Newell, Norman
Starr, Randy. *See* Nadel, Warren
Starr, Ray. *See* Pennington, Ramon [or Ray] (Daniel)
Starr, Ringo. *See* Starkey, Richard
Starr, T(homas) B(ristol). *See* Neidlinger, W(illiam) H(arold)
Starr, Tony. *See* Sacco, Anthony
Starski, Lovebug. *See* Smith, Kevin (1961-)
Starstruck. *See* Benjamin, Arthur
Staton, Merrill. *See* Ostrus, Merrill (J.)
Staz, H(enry). *See* Popy, Francis
Steagall, Red. *See* Steagall, Russell (Don)
Stearns, Herbert. *See* Cooke, James Francis
Stebbins, George. *See* Leidzén, Erik William Gustav
Stebbins, J. A. *See* Dant, June Anne
Stebnizki, (N.). *See* Leskow, Nikolai Semenovich
Stecchetti, Lorenzo. *See* Guerrini, Olindo
Steck, Arnold. *See* Statham, (F(rank)) Leslie
Stecman, Phil. *See* McNeil, Stephen
Steele, Jack. *See* Brown, Bob
Steele, Paul. *See* Ehret, Walter (Charles)
Steele, Ted. *See* Steele, Louis (Thornton)
Steele, Tommy. *See* Hicks, Thomas
Steels, Bobby. *See* Diggs, Robert
Steenkist, Vincent. *See* Van Steenkist, Vincent
Steeplejack (of the Arts). *See* Huneker, James Gibbons
Steer, L. E. *See* Lester, Sidney
Steeven, (Jan). *See* Heyer, Walter
Steffaro, Julius. *See* Stoeckart, Jan
Steffen, Wolfgang. *See* Wolfgang, Eberhardt
Steffens, Feodor. *See* Dammas, Hellmuth Carl
Steiger, Hans. *See* Paramor, Norman [or Norrie] (William)
Stein, Evald. *See* Tammlaan, Evald
Stein, J(ohann) S(aville). *See* Stone, J(ohn) S(aville)
Stein, Leo. *See* Rosenstein, Leo
Stein, Lew. *See* Sugarman, Harry
Stein, Max. *See* Gordon, Marie
Stein, Walter. *See* Feltz, Kurt (August Karl)
Steinberg, Rubin. *See* Davis, Joseph [or Joe] (M.)
Steinberger, Gábor. *See* Szatmárnémeti, Gábor
Steiner, Herbert. *See* Herman, Sam
Steinhorst, Werner. *See* Schubert, Hans
Steiniger, C. *See* Clark, Frederick Horace
Steinway, Henry. *See* Butler, Ralph (T.)
Steinway, Werner. *See* Werner, Christian
Stella, Alfred. *See* Paterson, Robert Roy
Stella, Fra. *See* Paterson, Robert Roy
Stemflinger, K. A. *See* Benjamin, Walter
Stendhal. *See* Beyle, (Marie) Henri
Stengler, August. *See* Stengler, Gustave P. Cercello
Stenton, Paul. *See* Winner, Septimus
Stepfather of Dissonance. *See* Indy, (Paul Marie Théodore) Vincent d'
Stephan, George. *See* Mäder, Wolfgang
Stephan, Monsieur. *See* Barbier, Frédéric E(tienne)

Stephanie. *See* Grimaldi, Stephanie
Stephano, Charles. *See* Rawlings, Alfred William
Stephanoff, Ivan. *See* Rawlings, Alfred William
Stephen(s), Edward (Jones). *See* Jones, Edward (Stephen) (1822-1885)
Stephens, H. G. *See* Hall, Joseph Lincoln
Stepin Fetchit. *See* Bisson, Whelock Alexander
Stepin Fetchit. *See* Perry, Lincoln (T(heodore Monroe Andrew))
Stepper, John. *See* McClymont, Jepther
Sterling, Al. *See* Brockway, Harold
Sterling, Antoinette. *See* MacKinlay, (Mrs.) J.
Sterling, Frank. *See* Berry, Dennis (Alfred)
Sterling, J. L. *See* Crosby, Fanny [i.e., Frances] J(ane)
Sterling, James. *See* Royce, James (Stanley)
Sterling, Jane. *See* Royce, James (Stanley)
Sterling, Jayne. *See* Royce, James (Stanley)
Sterling, Jean. *See* Taylor, Mary Virgina
Sterling, Julia. *See* Crosby, Fanny [i.e., Frances] J(ane)
Sterling, Ryan. *See* Crosby, Fanny [i.e., Frances] J(ane)
Sterling, Victoria. *See* Crosby, Fanny [i.e., Frances] J(ane)
Stern, Daniel. *See* Flavigny, Marie (Catherine Sophie), (Comtesse D'Agoult)
Stern, Lew. *See* Sugarman, Harry
Stern, Oskar. *See* Bittong, Franz
Sternau, C. O. *See* Inkermann, (C.) Otto
Sterne, Colin. *See* Nichol, Henry Ernest
Sterne, Kenneth. *See* Stone, Kurt
Stetler, Lawrence. *See* Hostetler, Lawrence A.
Stetten, Jack. *See* Bunz, Hans-Günther
Steuart, Geoffrey. *See* Harrhy, Edith
Stevens, Al. *See* Allen, Thomas [or Thos.] (S.)
Stevens, Cat. *See* Georgiou, Steven [or Stephen] Demetri
Stevens, Graham. *See* Goldsen, Michael H.
Stevens, Hal. *See* King, Reginald (Claude McMahon)
Stevens, Lona. *See* Spector, Lona
Stevens, Milo. *See* King, Stanford
Stevens, Paul. *See* Beckhard, Robert L.
Stevens, Philip. *See* Beckhard, Robert L.
Stevens, (Harold) Ray. *See* Ragsdale, (Harold) Ray
Stevens, Robert L. *See* Bergh, Arthur
Stevens, T. R. *See* Frangkiser, Carl (Moerz)
Stevens, William Christopher. *See* Allen, Stephen [or Steve] (Valentine Patrick William)
Stevenson, B. W. *See* Stevenson, Louis C(harles), (III)
Stevenson, Mickey. *See* Stevenson, William
Steventon, Steve. *See* Steventon, G. H.
Steverino. *See* Allen, Stephen [or Steve] (Valentine Patrick William)
Stevie Guitar. *See* Hubert, Stephen Fitch
Stewart. *See* St. Clair, Floyd J.
Stewart, Cliff. *See* Finkelstein, Abe
Stewart, Cliff. *See* Slaughter, M(arion) T(ry)
Stewart, Douglas. *See* Thompson, C. J.
Stewart, Ed. *See* Mainwaring, Edward Stewart
Stewart, Gene. *See* Hallowell, Russ(ell F.)
Stewart, Geoffrey. *See* Harrhy, Edith
Stewart, Humphrey John. *See* Stark, Humphrey John
Stewart, J. J. *See* Hewitt, John (Henry) Hill
Stewart, M. A. *See* Bliss, P(hilip) Paul
Stewart, Michael. *See* Rubin, Michael Stewart
Stewart, Norman. *See* Wilson, Roger Cole
Stewart, Red(d). *See* Stewart, Henry (Ellis)
Stewart, Rex (William). *See* Stewart, William, Jr.
Stewart, Slam. *See* Stewart, Leroy Elliott
Stewart, Victoria. *See* Crosby, Fanny [i.e., Frances] J(ane)
Stick. *See* Burrell, Bishop
Stiebler, Mary. *See* Ryder, Mary E.
Stig. *See* Hansen, Stig (Axel)
Stigelli, Giorgio. *See* Stiegele, Georg
Stiles, E. P. *See* Stites, E(dgar) P(age)
Stille, C. A. *See* Castelli, Ignaz Franz
Sting. *See* Sumner, Gordon (Matthew)
Stingray, Joanna. *See* Fields, Joanna
Stirling, Jean. *See* Taylor, Mary Virgina
Stirling, Julia. *See* Crosby, Fanny [i.e., Frances] J(ane)
Stirling, Victoria. *See* Crosby, Fanny [i.e., Frances] J(ane)
Stirner, Max. *See* Schmidt, (Johann) Caspar [or Kaspar]
Stivell, Alan. *See* Cochevelou, Alan [or Alain]
Stockbridge, John. *See* Wagness, Bernard
Stockhold, Hans. *See* Pütz, Johannes
Stocking, Elaine. *See* Grey, Frank H(erbert)
Stockton, Morris. *See* Potter, Anice
Stockton, Robert. *See* Ehret, Walter (Charles)
Stoeffken, Ditrich. *See* Steffkin, Theodore
Stöhr, Richard. *See* Stern, Richard
Stokes, Leopold. *See* Stokowski, Leopold (Antoni Stanislaw Boleslawowicz)
Stokowski, Leopold. *See* Cailliet, Lucien
Stokowski, Olga. *See* Hickenlooper, Lucy [or Lucie] (Mary Olga Agnes)
Stol(l)berg, Ferdinand. *See* Salzmann, Siegmund
Stoller, Ellie. *See* Johnston, Eleanor [or Ellie]
Stolzer, Josip. *See* Stolcer, Josip
Stolzing, W(alter) (di). *See* Monleone, Domenico
Stone, Angie. *See* Brown, Angela Laverne
Stone, Butch. *See* Stone, Norman Millard, Jr.
Stone, Charles. *See* Carlberg, Sten
Stone, Charlie. *See* Adams, Charles R(aymond)
Stone, Cliffie. *See* Snyder, Clifford Gilpin
Stone, Doug. *See* Brooks, Douglas (Jackson)
Stone, Edward. *See* Slaughter, M(arion) T(ry)
Stone, Fred. *See* Finkelstein, Abe
Stone, George. *See* Wright, Al George
Stone, Harry. *See* Stonum, Harry F(rancis)
Stone, Howard. *See* Slaughter, M(arion) T(ry)

Stone, Joe. *See* Short, J. D.
Stone, Lew. *See* Steinberg, Louis
Stone, Mary A. *See* Kunkel, Charles
Stone, Peter. *See* Beckhard, Robert L.
Stone, Robert L. *See* Beckhard, Robert L.
Stone, Sly. *See* Stewart, Sylvester
Stone, Sylvester. *See* Stewart, Sylvester
Stone, Wilbur. *See* Horton, (George) Vaughn
Stonehead, Cliffie. *See* Snyder, Clifford Gilpin
Stoneman, Pop. *See* Stoneman, Ernest (V.)
Stoner, M. S. *See* Klickmann, F(rank) Henri
Stooge, Iggy. *See* Osterberg, James Newell
Stoop Down Man, The. *See* Willis, Robert L.
Stor, Jean. *See* Morgan, W(illiam) Astor
Storball, Don. *See* Norman, Don(ald)
Storyteller, The. *See* Hall, Thomas
Stoughton, R. *See* Greenwald, M(artin)
Stout, Bert. *See* Stout, Herbert E(ugene)
Stowe, Michael. *See* Fishman, Jack (1918 (or 19)-)
Straccioncino. *See* Valentini, Giuseppe
Strachey, Jack. *See* Strachey, John Francis
Straesser, Joep. *See* Straesser, Joseph Willem Frederik
Straker, Rob. *See* Cummings, Robert
Strange Cargo. *See* Wainwright, William (Mark)
Strange, Justin. *See* Glover, Charles Joseph, (Jr.)
Strange, N. Blair. *See* Sargent, Brian (Lawrence)
Stranger, The. *See* Haggard, Merle (Ronald)
Strapping Young Lad. *See* Townsend, Devin
Strasser, Viktor Eugene. *See* Stransky, Otto
Strathspey King, The. *See* Skinner, James Scott
Stratton, Frank. *See* Bratton, John W(alter)
Straus, Herman. *See* Rawlings, Charles Arthur
Strauss de Paris. *See* Strauss, Isaac
Strauss, Julian. *See* Daniels, Charles N(eil)
Strauss of Italy, The. *See* Respighi, Ottorino
Strauss, Richard. *See* Kunkel, Charles
Strayhorn, Swee'Pea. *See* Strayhorn, William [or Billy] (Thomas)
Strays. *See* Strayhorn, William [or Billy] (Thomas)
Streabbog, L(ouis) (S.). *See* Gobbaerts, Jean Louis
Streabbog, M. *See* Greenwald, M(artin)
Streat, Sixteenth (S.). *See* Robyn, Alfred George
Strebor, J. C. *See* Kraushaar, Charles
Street, Apsley. *See* Winner, Septimus
Street, Bobbie. *See* Streeter, Roberta [or Bobbie] (Lee)
Street, Joye. *See* Spencer, Joyce Ann
Street, Leonard. *See* Fishman, Jack (1918 (or 19)-)
Street, Leonard. *See* Hargreaves, Peter
Street, Mel. *See* Street, King Malachi
Street Rustler, The. *See* Woods, Oscar
Strelezki, A. *See* Kraushaar, Charles
Strelezki, Anton. *See* Burnand, Arthur Bransby
Strelezki, Anton. *See* Kunkel, Charles
Strella,Yevgenia. *See* Kuznetsova, Zhanna [or Zhanetta] (Aleksandrovna)
Stresa, F. M. *See* Steward, F. M.
Streviglio. *See* Pasqualini, Marc(o)'Antonio
Strietel, Edward. *See* Bliss, P(hilip) Paul
Striker. *See* Lee, Edward O'Sullivan
Strinfalico, Eterio. *See* Marcello, Alessandro
String Wizard, The. *See* McEuen, John
Stromberg, Honey. *See* Stromberg, John
Strong, Elizabeth. *See* Cobb, George L(inus)
Strong, Will. *See* Dawson, Peter (Smith)
Stroud, Ray. *See* McKelvy, James (M(illigan))
Stroud, Sidney. *See* Krenkel, Gustav
Strúby, H. *See* Strübe, Hermann
Strummer, Joe. *See* Mellor(s), John (Graham)
Strunk, Jud. *See* Strunk, Justin Roderick, Jr.
Struwwell, Peter. *See* Hoffmann, Heinrich
Stryker, Paul. *See* Lavan, Henry Robert Merrill
Stuart, Allan. *See* Haenschen, Walter (G(ustave))
Stuart, Allan [or Allen]. *See* O'Keefe, Lester
Stuart, Billy. *See* Slaughter, M(arion) T(ry)
Stuart, Fay. *See* Leonard, Nellie Mabel
Stuart, Flo. *See* Shearouse, Florine W(hiteurst)
Stuart, Kathleen. *See* Taylor, Helen
Stuart, Leslie. *See* Barrett, Thomas Augustine
Stuart, Roberta. *See* Feldner, Roberta Emily
Stuart, Victoria. *See* Crosby, Fanny [i.e., Frances] J(ane)
Stuck, Harry. *See* Hammerschmid, Hans
Studebaker John. *See* Grimaldi, John
Stultz, Herman. *See* Barnes, H(oward) E(llington)
Stultz, Herman. *See* Field, Harold (Cornelius)
Stultz, Herman. *See* Roncoroni, Joseph Dominic
Stulwitt, R. H. *See* Hewitt, Horatio Dawes
Stulwitt, R. H. *See* Stults, R(obert) M(orrison)
Sturges, Edmund. *See* Turges, Edmund
Sturm, Bruno. *See* Breitner, Burghard
Sturmeck, Heinrich [or Heinz] von. *See* Weber, C(arl) Heinrich
Stutterin' Boy. *See* Tillis, (Lonnie) Mel(vin)
Style, Johnny. *See* Spiess, Otto
Style, Leslie. *See* Stiles, Leslie
Styles, Beverly. *See* Carpenter, Juanita Robins
Stylish Edi. *See* Strauss, Eduard
Styne, Jule. *See* Stein, Julius Kerwin
Styne(e)se. *See* Stein, Julius Kerwin
Styrene, Poly. *See* Elliott, Marion
Suardo, P. *See* Daspuro, Nicolo
Suburban Mother from Hell. *See* West, Camille
Sucher, Manuel. *See* Sucher, Bernardo Mendel
Suddoth, J. Guy. *See* Erby, John J.
Suede, Vasca. *See* Miller, Robert [or Bob] (Ernst)
Sueree, Ricardo. *See* Martin, Ray(mond)
Suerte, Ricardo. *See* Martin, Ray(mond)
Suga, (Michio). *See* Wakabe, Nakasuga Kengyo
Sugar Miami Steve. *See* Van Zandt, Steve(n)
Sugarman, Jacob. *See* Gerant, John
Sugarman, Jacob. *See* Mantell, Frederick

Sugarman, Jacob. *See* Ugar, Henry S.
Suitcase Red. *See* Simpson, Joseph
Suiter, Don. *See* Suiter, Arlendo D.
Sulima, Jan. *See* Szulc, Jósef [or Joseph] Zygmunt [or Sigismond]
Sullivan, Charles. *See* Lightfoot, George Meredith
Sullivan, Dane. *See* Joseph, Daniel
Sullivan, Joe. *See* O'Sullivan, Dennis Patrick Terence Joseph
Sullivan, Vernon. *See* Vian, Boris
Sulzer, Salomon. *See* Loewy, Salomon
Sum, Ergo. *See* Ballard, Louis W(ayne)
Summer Composer, A. *See* Mahler, Gustav
Summer, Donna. *See* Gaines, LaDonna [or Donna] Andrea [or Adrian]
Summerforest, Ivy B. *See* Kirkup, James (Falconer)
Summers, Andrew [or Andy] (James). *See* Somers, Andrew James
Summers, Gene. *See* Sugarman, Harry
Summers, Joan. *See* Blitz, Leo(nard)
Summers, Joan. *See* Cohen, Maurice Alfred
Summers, Robert. *See* Armbuster, Robert
Summertime's "Mr. Opera". *See* Jellinek, George
Summey, Reid. *See* Breitenbach, Alfred
Sumner, Robert. *See* Ehret, Walter (Charles)
Sun, Joe. *See* Paulsen, James Joseph
Sun of Latin Music. *See* Palmieri, Eduardo [or Edward, or Eddie]
Sun, Pat. *See* Werner, Erich
Sun Ra. *See* Blount, Herman
Sunday Composer, A. *See* Borodin, Alexander
Sundown, Lonesome. *See* Green, Cornelius
Sunnyland Slim. *See* Luandrew, Albert
Sunshine, Madeline. *See* Freedman, M. Claire
Sunshine, Marion. *See* Ijames, Mary Tunstall
Supa, Richard. *See* Goodman, Richard John
Superblue. *See* Lyons, Austin
Superbow. *See* Clements, Vassar Carlton
Superguitarist. *See* Bell, Vincent [or Vinnie]
Superpicker. *See* Clark, Roy (Linwood)
Suranov, Alex. *See* Isaac, Merle (John)
Sure!, Al B. *See* Brown, Albert Joseph
Surmont, Count. *See* Saint Germain, Count of
Sursum Corda. *See* Pérez Zúñiga, Juan
Surtac. *See* Astruc, Gabriel (David)
Survivor, The. *See* Lewis, Jerry Lee
Susato, Johannes de. *See* Steinwert von Soest, Johannes
Sust, Johannes von. *See* Steinwert von Soest, Johannes
Sutton, Dick. *See* Schwartz, Richard
Suzamon, Harry. *See* Sugarman, Harry
Svarda, Buddy. *See* Svarda, William Ernest
Svengali. *See* Green, (Ian) Ernest Gilmore
Svengali. *See* Pendergrass, Theodore [or Teddy]
Svenson, Sven. *See* Davis, Joseph [or Joe] (M.)
Svensson. *See* Becker, Tobias
Svétlá, Karolina. *See* Muzáková, Johana (Rottová)
Swamp Dogg. *See* Williams, Jerry J.
Swamp Fox, (The). *See* White, Tony Joe
Swan, Don. *See* Schwandt, Wilbur (Clyde)
Swan of Pesaro, The. *See* Rossini, Gioachino Antonio
Sweatman, Sweat. *See* Sweatman, Wilbur C. (S.)
Swede, The. *See* Baltzer, Thomas
Sweden's "Spiritual Troubadour". *See* Ahnfelt, Oskar [or Oscar]
Swedish Dickens, The. *See* Bergman, Hjalmar (Fredrik Elgérus)
Swedish Handel, The. *See* Roman, Johan Helmich
Swedish Mozart. *See* Kraus, Joseph Martin
Swedish Schubert. *See* Lindblad, Adolf Fredrik
Swee' Pea. *See* Strayhorn, William [or Billy] (Thomas)
Sweeley, Charles C. *See* Lincoln, Harry J.
Sweelinck, Jan Pieterszoon. *See* Swybbertszon, Jan Pieterszoon
Sweet Baby James. *See* Taylor, James Vernon
Sweet Bard of Methodism. *See* Wesley, Charles
Sweet, G. A. *See* Bliss, P(hilip) Paul
Sweet Mama Stringbean. *See* Howard, Ethel
Sweet Singer of Methodism. *See* Wesley, Charles
Sweet Singer of Scotland, The. *See* Bonar, Horatius
Sweeten, Claude. *See* Merrick, Mahlon (La Grande)
Sweetest Swan (of Italy). *See* Marenzio, Luca
Sweetheart of Gospel, The. *See* Grant, Amy (Lee)
Sweetheart of the A. E. F., The. *See* Bierbower, Elsie
Sweetheart of Zydeco, The. *See* Bellard, Mary Rosezla
Sweethearts of Country Music, The. *See* Cooper, Myrtle Eleanor
Sweethearts of Country Music, The. *See* Wiseman, Scott(y) (Greene)
Sweethearts of the Air. *See* Breen, May Singhi
Sweethearts of the Air. *See* De Rose, Peter
Sweets. *See* Edison, Harry (E.)
Swift, L. E. *See* Siegmeister, Elie
Swing Brother. *See* Burns, Eddie
Swink, Emmett. *See* Khaury, Herbert
Swiss Count, The. *See* Heidegger, Johann [or John] Jakob [or James]
Swiss Schubert. *See* Schoeck, Othmar
Swiss Watchmaker (of Music), The. *See* Ravel, Maurice (Joseph)
Swivel Hips. *See* Presley, Elvis A(a)ron
Sydney, Nelson. *See* Nelson, Sidney
Sykes, Bobby. *See* Sykes, Bishop Milton
Sykes, Epp. *See* Sykes, Ethelred Lundy
Sykes, John. *See* Evert, Johannes
Sykes, Rosy. *See* Sykes, Roosevelt
Sylva, Carmen. *See* Elizabeth, Queen of Romania
Sylva, Lew. *See* Bidgood, Henry [or Harry] (James)
Sylvain. *See* Hansson, Stig (Axel)
Sylvain, David. *See* Batt, David
Sylvain, Jules. *See* Hansson, Stig (Axel)

Sylvan, Sixten. *See* Hansson, Stig (Axel)
Sylvane, André. *See* Gerard, (Marie) Paul Émile
Sylvanus Urbanus. *See* Aldrich, Richard
Sylvester. *See* James, Sylvester
Sylvestre, Joshua. *See* Husk, William Henry
Sylvestre, Joshua. *See* Sandys, William
Sylvestris. *See* Brewer, Jehoi(a)da
Sylvia. *See* Kirby, Sylvia (Jane)
Sylvia. *See* Kountz, Richard
Sylvia. *See* Robinson, Sylvia Vanderpool
Sylvian, David. *See* Batt, David
Sylviano, René. *See* Caffot, Sylvère (Victor Joseph)
Symbol of American Music. *See* Copland, Aaron
Symbol of Italy. *See* Verdi, Giuseppe
Symphony. *See* Couture, Guillaume [or William]
Syntek, Aleks. *See* Escajadillo, Alejandro
Syreeta. *See* Wright, Rita
Szalana, Hubay von. *See* Huber, Eugen
Szath-Myri, (Irving). *See* Szathmary, Irving

– T –

T. *See* Cowper, William
TAFKAP. *See* Nelson, Prince Rogers
TAM. *See* MacKellar, Thomas
T-Boz. *See* Watkins, Tionne
T. C. *See* Carr, Thomas
T. C. L. *See* Lewis, T. C.
T. C. W. *See* Williams, Theodore Chickering
T. D. *See* Dorsey, Thomas A(ndrew)
T. D., (Gent.). *See* D'Urfey, Thomas
T. D'U. *See* D'Urfey, Thomas
T. H. *See* Cowper, William
T. H. B. *See* Bayly, (Nathaniel) Thomas Haynes
T. M. *See* Moore, Thomas
T. M. *See* Morrell, Thomas
T. M. L. *See* Moore, Thomas
TQ. *See* Quaites, Terrance
T. R. *See* Raffles, Thomas
T. R. *See* Ravenscroft, Thomas
T. V. *See* Williams, Theodore, Jr.
TV Slim. *See* Wills, Oscar
T. V. Z. *See* Van Zandt, (John) Townes
T. W. C. *See* Carr, Thomas William
Tabarin. *See* Duval, Georges (J.)
Tablet, Hilda. *See* Swann, Donald (Ibrahim)
Tabu Ley. *See* Pascal, Tabu
Tadell, I. *See* Suck, G. F.
Tagliaferro, Joseph (Dieudonné). *See* Tagliafico, Joseph (Dieudonné)
Tahite. *See* Neild, James Edward
Tailleferre, Germaine. *See* Taillefesse, (Marcelle) Germaine
Tait, Gilbert. *See* McCall, William
Taj Mahal. *See* Fredericks(-Williams), Henry St. Claire, (Jr.)
Takeda, Ayo. *See* Elliott, Marjorie (Reeve)
Tal, Josef [or Joseph]. *See* Gruenthal, Joseph
Talander. *See* Bohse(-Talander), August
Talbert, Ted. *See* Milkey, Edward T(albert)
Talbot, Howard. *See* Munkittrick, Howard (Talbot)
Taler, Werner. *See* Nerijnen, Jan van
Talhaiarn. *See* Jones, John ([nd])
Talin. *See* Meilhac, Henri
Talker, T(homas). *See* Rands, William Brightly
Tall Texan, The. *See* Gray, Claude (N.)
Tall Texan, The. *See* Walker, William [or Billy] (Marvin)
Tall, Victor. *See* Klemm, Gustav
Talley, Frank. *See* Damico, Frank James
Tallirak. *See* Dalayrac, Nicolas(-Marie)
Talmadge, Billy. *See* Tubb, Talmadge
Talmage, Gerald. *See* Gardner, Maurice
Tambu. *See* Herbert, Christopher
Tamp, Peter. *See* Schenckendorff, Leopold (Adalbert Günther Heinrich von)
Tampa Red. *See* Woodbridge, Hudson
Tanbür, Jon. *See* Schmitt, Gerhard
Tandrop, A. R. *See* Bliss, P(hilip) Paul
Tangle Eye. *See* Horton, Walter
Tani, Al. *See* Mirikitani, Alan Masao
Tannenberg, Wolfgang. *See* Poser, Hans
Tanner, Gid. *See* Tanner, James Gideon
Tanner, Margaret P(age). *See* Wagness, Bernard
Tannwald, Peter. *See* Merath, Siegfried
Tano Genaro, El. *See* Espósito, Genaro Ricardo
Tans'ur, William. *See* Tanzer, William (Stephen)
Tanymarian, (Edward). *See* Jones, Edward (Stephen) (1822-1885)
Tarantino, Il. *See* Fago, (Francesco) Nicola
Tarantino, Pasquale. *See* Fago, Pasquale
Tardieu, Marcel. *See* Ramthor, Horst
Tareno, Salvadore. *See* Hering, Hans
Tarentino, Il. *See* Tritto, Giacomo
Targetti, Giovanni Paolo. *See* Virchi, Giovan(ni) Paolo
Targhetta, (Giovanni Paolo). *See* Virchi, Giovan(ni) Paolo
Tarheel, Slim. *See* Bunn, Alden
Tarras, Dave. *See* Tarraschuk, Dovid
Tarski, Alexander. *See* Tabksblat, Alexander
Tartarin. *See* Daudet, (Louis Marie) Alphonse
Tartini's Familiar. *See* Chorley, Henry Fothergill
Tarto, Joe. *See* Tortoriello, Vincent Joseph
Tasto der Kälberfuß. *See* Moscheles, (Isaak-)Ignaz
Tate, Hal. *See* Teitelman, Alex
Tater. *See* Dickens, James Cecil
Taube, Christian Friedric. *See* Gaudlitz, Gottlieb
Taube, Theodore. *See* H(e)rdlicka, Bohdan

Tauber, Richard. *See* Denemy, Ernest
Tavel, Raoul. *See* Toché, Raoul
Tawny Yvete Guilbert, The. *See* Howard, Ethel
Taylor, Allen. *See* Cobb, George L(inus)
Taylor, Bernie. *See* Fass, Bernard [or Bernie]
Taylor, Chip. *See* Voigt, James Wesley
Taylor, Conrad. *See* Danowski, Conrad John
Taylor, Emmett. *See* Henderson, (James) Fletcher (Hamilton), (Jr.)
Taylor, Eva. *See* Gibbons, Irene
Taylor, F. Louis. *See* Schneider, F. Louis
Taylor, Frances. *See* Kraushaar, Charles
Taylor, Hound Dog. *See* Taylor, Theodore Roosevelt
Taylor, Ida Scott. *See* Crosby, Fanny [i.e., Frances] J(ane)
Taylor, Iris. *See* Hartley, Fred
Taylor, J. C. Bert. *See* Taylor, J(ohn) S(iebert)
Taylor, Koko. *See* Walton, Cora
Taylor, Montana. *See* Taylor, Arthur
Taylor, Noel. *See* Kaufman, Isidore
Taylor, Playboy. *See* Taylor, Eddie
Taylor, Ruby. *See* Haga, Frederick Wallace
Taylor, Ruby. *See* Ringleben, Justin, Jr.
Taylor, Sy. *See* Taylor, Seymour (H.)
Taylor, Tut. *See* Taylor, Robert Arthur
Taylor, Walter G. *See* Geibel, Adam
Tchaikovsky of the Keyboards, The. *See* Papathanassiou, Evangelos (Odyssey)
Tchaikovsky of the 20th Century. *See* Prokofiev, Serge
Tchakoff, Ivan. *See* Rawlings, Alfred William
Tchatchkoff, A. de. *See* Rawlings, Alfred William
Tchervanow, Ivor. *See* Kountz, Richard
Team from Siam. *See* Hammerstein, Oscar (Greeley Clendenning), II
Team from Siam. *See* Rodgers, Richard (Charles)
Tear Jerker Composer. *See* Puccini, Giacomo
Teardrop, Mr. *See* Robinson, Martin D(avid)
Teasdale, Dana. *See* Cross, Frank L(eroy)
Tech (a Curia), Nikolas. *See* Decius, Nikolaus
Techno-Troubadour. *See* Young, Neil
Tedde, Mostyn. *See* Paulton, Edward A(ntonio)
Teddy Bear. *See* Pendergrass, Theodore [or Teddy]
Tedeschino. *See* Allegri, Lorenzo
Tedeschino, Il. *See* Gigli, Giovanni Battista
Tedesco, Il. *See* Allegri, Lorenzo
Tedesco, Il. *See* Schwarzendorf, Johann Paul Aegidius
Tedescone. *See* Giorgetti, Ferdinando
Tee, Jay. *See* Triebel, Jürgen
Tegurini, (Padre). *See* Zech, Chrysogonus
Teil, Thilo. *See* Wagenleiter, Klaus
Teilich, Philipp. *See* Dulichius, Philipp(us)
Telford. *See* Boott, Francis
Telke, (Max). *See* Dobrzynski, Walter (Max)
Tell-Truth, Paul. *See* Carey, George Saville
Tellam, Heinrich. *See* Decourcelle, Paul
Tellier, A(lphonse). *See* Aletter, Wilhelm
Telma, Maurice. *See* Rawlings, Charles Arthur
Temkin, Gary. *See* Temkin, Harold (P.)
Temperance Boy Songster, The. *See* Scanlan, William J(ames)
Temple, Edith. *See* Murrells, Joseph
Temple, Geechie. *See* Temple, Johnny [or Johnnie]
Temple, Gordon. *See* Rawlings, Charles Arthur
Temple, Harry. *See* Cobb, George L(inus)
Temple, Hope. *See* Davis, Alice Maude
Temple, John. *See* Green, Phil(ip)
Temple, Neville. *See* Bulwer-Lytton, Edward Robert
Templeman, Horace. *See* Rawlings, Alfred William
Tempo, Egidio da. *See* Pittaluga, Egidio [or Eligio]
Tempo, Fred. *See* Wittal, Roland
Tenelli, M. *See* Millenet, Johann Heinrich
Teniers of Comedy, The. *See* Dancourt, Florent Carton
Tenna Maria. *See* Brocker(t), Mary Christine
Tennant, Vic. *See* Vincent, Nathaniel (Hawthorne)
Tennberg, Werner. *See* Hense, Werner
Tennessean, The. *See* Bruce, (William) Ed(win, Jr.)
Tennessee Gabriel. *See* McGhee, Walter Brown
Tennessee George. *See* Morgan, George (Thomas)
Tennessee, Grace. *See* Smith, Mira
Tennessee Plowboy, The. *See* Arnold, (Richard) Edward [or Eddie]
Tennessee Yodeler, The. *See* Miller, Betty Lou
Tenney, (Mrs.) John F. *See* Branscombe, Gena
Tenor, Jimi. *See* Lehto, Lassi
Teomagnini, Ignatio. *See* Matteo, Gianni
Teora, Francesco di. *See* Mirelli, Francesco
Terail, Leon du. *See* Rawlings, Charles Arthur
Terego, Al. *See* Day, Frederick E(dward) (Montagu)
Terhune, Anice. *See* Potter, Anice
Teri, Richard. *See* Terr, Mischa Richard
Terlojian. *See* Schulz, Janine
Terminator X. *See* Rogers, Norman
Terpander. *See* Jacobs, Manuel
Terpandro. *See* Scarlatti, Alessandro
Terpsicoreo, Armonide. *See* Gluck, Christoph Willibald Ritter von
Terr, Michael. *See* Terr, Mischa Richard
Terradeglias, Domenico [or Domingo]. *See* Terradellas, Domènech Miquel Bernabé
Terresco, Michael. *See* Terr, Mischa Richard
Terrible Fitzball, The. *See* Ball, Edward
Terrier, Paul. *See* Rawlings, Charles Arthur
Terriss, Dorothy. *See* Strandberg, (Alfreda) Theodora
Terriss, Theodora. *See* Strandberg, (Alfreda) Theodora
Terry, Al. *See* Theriot, Al(lison) J(oseph), (Jr.)
Terry, Arthur. *See* Ellis, Seger
Terry, Bill. *See* Slaughter, M(arion) T(ry)
Terry, Blind Sonny. *See* Terrell, Saunders
Terry, Dan. *See* Kostraba, Daniel
Terry, Joe. *See* Terranova, Joseph A.
Terry, Michael. *See* MacDermott, Michael Terry

Terry, Ron. *See* Pritkin, Ron(ald P.)
Terry, Saunders. *See* Terrell, Saunders
Terry, Sonny. *See* Terrell, Saunders
Terry, Sue. *See* Fishman, Jack (1918 (or 19)-)
Terry, Tex. *See* Husky, Ferlin
Terry, Will. *See* Slaughter, M(arion) T(ry)
Tervapää, Juhani. *See* Wuolijoki, Hella (Maria) (née Murrik)
Tesehemacher, Edward. *See* Lockton, Edward F.
Tesier. *See* Reiset, Gustave Armand Henri (Comte de)
Tester, Scan. *See* Tester, Lewis
Testorius, Johann. *See* Wircker, Johann
Teufel, Erik. *See* Jupp, Eric
Teufel, Erik. *See* Strauss, Arthur
Teutobald. *See* Schulze, Friedrich August
Tex, Joe. *See* Arrington, Joseph [or Joe], (Jr.)
Tex-Mex Ricky Van Shelton. *See* Trevino, Rick
Tex, Pete. *See* Drischel, Peter
Texas Blind Hitchhiker. *See* Payne, Leon (Roger)
Texidor, Jaime. *See* Dalmau, Jaime Texidor
Texidor, Jaime. *See* Ridewood, reginald (Clifford)
Texas Cowboy, (The). *See* Ritter, Maurice Woodward
Texas Drifter, The. *See* Reeves, Goebel (Leon)
Texas Guitar Slim. *See* Winter, Johnny
Texas Nightingale, The. *See* Barnes, Fae [or Faye]
Texas Nightingale, (The). *See* Thomas, Beulah
Texas Slim. *See* Hooker, John Lee
Texas Sun. *See* Hooker, John Lee
Texas Tenor, The. *See* Slaughter, M(arion) T(ry)
Texas Tessie. *See* Douglas, Lizzie
Texas Thunder. *See* Machado, Joel
Texas, Tommy. *See* Dorsey, Thomas A(ndrew)
Texas Troubadour, The. *See* Tubb, Ernest (Dale)
Texidor, Jaime. *See* Dalmau, Jaime Texidor
Texidor, Jaime. *See* Ridewood, Reginald (Clifford)
Teyte, (Dame) Maggie. *See* Tate, Maggie
Thal, Jeanette (D.). *See* Dellafield, Henry
Thale, Adalbert vom. *See* Decker, Karl von
Thaler, Sepp. *See* Simonini, Josef
Thamon, Eugene. *See* Simpson, Eugene Thamon
Thane, Logan. *See* Solomons, Nate E.
Tharp(e), Wink(e)y. *See* Tharp(e), Winston (Collins)
Thass, Peter. *See* Schröder, Heinz
That Ad Glibber. *See* Allen, Stephen [or Steve] (Valentine Patrick William)
That Plain Ol' Country Boy. *See* Penny, Herbert Clayton
Thatcher, Noel. *See* Morgio, George A.
Thayer, Herbert Wells. *See* Aletter, Wilhelm
The Artist Formerly Known as Prince. *See* Nelson, Prince Rogers
Theal, Rolf. *See* Halaczinsky, Rudolf
Theard, Lovin' Sam. *See* Theard, Sam
Theard, Spo-Dee-O-Dee. *See* Theard, Sam
Thenard, (Etienne Bernard Auguste). *See* Perrin, Etienne Bernard Auguste
Théobald(e). *See* Gatti, Théobalde di
Theodore, Charles. *See* Reuss, Theodor
Theodorus Petrejus. *See* Pers, Dirck Pietersz(oon)
Theodosia. *See* Steele, Anne
Theogerus (von Metz). *See* Dietger
Théols. *See* Chevalet, Emile
Theophania, (Lina). *See* Brochowska, Pauline Marie Julie
Theophilus. *See* Roger of Helmarshausen
Theophilus Senex, Esq. *See* Turner, Daniel
Thérémin, Léon. *See* Termen, Lev Sergeivitch
Thérésa. *See* Val(l)adon, Eugénie-Emma [or Emma Eugénie] (Rose)
Therese, Jules. *See* Rawlings, Alfred William
Thérouanne. *See* Cornuel, Jean
Thicke, Alan. *See* Jeffrey, Alan
Thief of Bad Gags, The. *See* Berlinder, Milton
Thielmans, Toots. *See* Thielmans, Jean (Baptiste)
Thieme, Karl. *See* Thieme, Kerstin Anja
Thierry. *See* Lagoanère, Oscar de
Thilo, Carolus Augustus. *See* Thielo, Carl August
Thin Man From West Plains, The. *See* Wagoner, Porter (Wayne)
Think. *See* Stallman, Lou
Thinking Man's Hillbilly, The. *See* Wheeler, Billy Edd
Third, The. *See* Strauss, Johann (1866-1939)
Thoinan, Ernest. *See* Roquet, Antoine-Ernest
Thom, Andreas. *See* Csmarich, Rudolf
Thomas, Alfred. *See* Parker, Alfred Thomas
Thomas, Bob. *See* Finkelstein, Abe
Thomas, Bob. *See* Slaughter, M(arion) T(ry)
Thomas, Cairo. *See* Thomas, James (Henry)
Thomas, Charles. *See* Zacharias, Helmut
Thomas, Clayton. *See* Cade, Salome Thomas
Thomas, Cotton. *See* Jackson, Frankie
Thomas, Dick. *See* Goldhahn, Richard T(homas)
Thomas, E. D. *See* Spina, Harold
Thomas, Earl. *See* Bridgeman, Earl Thomas
Thomas, Foots. *See* Thomas, Walter Purl
Thomas, Fred. *See* Gillham, Art
Thomas, Harry. *See* Belafonte, Harold [or Harry] (George)
Thomas, Harry. *See* Broughton, Reginald Thomas
Thomas, Harry. *See* Thomas, Millard (J.)
Thomas, Henry. *See* Townsend, Henry
Thomas Jefferson and Abraham Lincoln of American Music. *See* Ives, Charles Edward
Thomas Jefferson of Folk Music, The. *See* Seeger, Pete(r R.)
Thomas, Larry. *See* Miner, Lawrence A.
Thomas, Lester. *See* Barrett, Thomas Augustine
Thomas, Lexa. *See* Thomas, Axel
Thomas, Max. *See* Yoder, Paul V(an Buskirk)
Thomas, Michael. *See* Böttcher, Martin
Thomas, Paul. *See* Misraki [or Misrachi], Paul

Thomas, Peter. *See* Sour, Robert (B.)
Thomas, Phill(ip). *See* Cappellini, Phill(ip) Thomas
Thomas, Robert Milkwood. *See* Zimmerman, Robert Allen
Thomas, Sam Fan. *See* Ndonfeng, Samuel Thomas
Thomas, Son(ny) Ford. *See* Thomas, James (Henry)
Thomas, Ted. *See* Tassy, Tamas
Thomas, Trinidad. *See* Gardner, Maurice
Thomas, Z. G. *See* Keller, Edward McDonald
Thome, Thomas. *See* Rawlings, Charles Arthur
Thompson, Alfred. *See* Jones, Thompson E(rnest)
Thompson, Ann. *See* Bradford, Sylvester Henry
Thompson, Bud. *See* Crow(e), Francis Luther
Thompson, David. *See* Ehret, Walter (Charles)
Thompson, David. *See* Stark, Harold (Stillwell)
Thompson, Fred. *See* Slaughter, M(arion) T(ry)
Thompson, Hank. *See* Thompson, Henry William
Thompson, Jay. *See* Thompson, Jennings Lewis, Jr.
Thompson, Johnny. *See* Razafinkeriefo, Andreamenentania Paul
Thompson, Kathryne E. *See* Rossiter, Will
Thompson-Lester, Andy. *See* Bradford, Sylvester Henry
Thompson, Lucky. *See* Thompson, Eli, (Jr.)
Thompson, Madge. *See* Vonderlieth, Leonore
Thompson, Robbin. *See* Thompson, Robert Wickens, II
Thompson, Ronald. *See* Ehret, Walter (Charles)
Thompson, Ronald. *See* Walton, Kenneth
Thompson, Sonny. *See* Thompson, Alfonso [or Alphonso]
Thomson, R. J. *See* Grey, Frank H(erbert)
Thomson, Rollin. *See* Rollinson, Thomas H.
Thor, Tristian. *See* Lang, Issac
Thorn(e), Edgar. *See* MacDowell, Edward (Alexander)
Thorn(e), Edgar. *See* Merrick, Marie E.
Thorn, Geoffrey. *See* Townley, Charles
Thorne, Cyril. *See* Mullen, Frederic
Thorne, E. *See* Roth, Ernst
Thorne, George. *See* White, Charles A(lbert)
Thorne, Norman(d). *See* Ellis, Seger
Thorne, Rosamond. *See* Wagness, Bernard
Thornsby, Lee. *See* Hornsby, Joseph Leith
Thornton, Big Mama. *See* Thornton, Willie Mae
Thornton, Frank. *See* Saenger, Gustave
Thorp, Jack. *See* Thorp, N(athan) Howard
Thrale, Peter. *See* Turnbull, Percy (Purvis)
Three Dimensional Man, The. *See* Hayes, Isaac
Three Rascals, The. *See* Fields, Eddie
Three Rascals, The. *See* Levin, Benjamin
Three Rascals, The. *See* O'Donnell, Charles
Three Wise Men of Harlem Hot Piano, The. *See* Johnson, James [or Jimmy, or Jimmie] P(rice))
Three Wise Men of Harlem Hot Piano, The. *See* Smith, William [or Willie] (Henry Joseph Berthol Bonaparte)
Three Wise Men of Harlem Hot Piano, The. *See* Wright, Thomas Wright
Thresher, (Mrs.) J. B. *See* Crosby, Fanny [i.e., Frances] J(ane)
Thrillington, Percy ("Thrills"). *See* McCartney, (James) Paul
Throckmorton, Alexander. *See* Spalding, Walter R(aymond)
Throckmorton, Sonny. *See* Throckmorton, James (Fron Sonny)
Thul, Friedrich von. *See* Paumgarten, Karl (von)
Thumb, T. T. *See* Daum, Norbert
Thunder, Johnny. *See* Hamilton, Gil
Thunderbird from Coast to Coast, The. *See* Price, Walter Travis
Thunderbolt, The. *See* Handel, Georg Friedrich
Thunders, Johnny. *See* Genzale, John (Anthony, Jr.)
Thuringiae, Orlandus. *See* Altenberg, Michael
Thurner, Philippe. *See* Cuffia, Carlo
Thyrolf, Guido. *See* Göttig, Willy Werner
Thyss, Peregrinus. *See* Graeffer, Anton
Tiballs, John. *See* Gabriel, Charles H(utchinson)
Tibbals, John. *See* Lorenz, E(dmund) S(imon)
Tibicen. *See* Widor, Charles-Marie (Jean Albert)
Ticco, Ramon. *See* Gaze, Hermann Otto
Tichy. *See* Renz-Herzog, Wolf
Tiefenborn, Irma von. *See* Schröder, Gertrud
Tiel, Walter. *See* Richter, Rudolf
Tieman, John. *See* Lindquist, Orville A(lvin)
Tiger. *See* Presley, Elvis A(a)ron
Tiger, Growling. *See* Marcano, Neville
Tiger Man. *See* Presley, Elvis A(a)ron
Tiger of the Bandonean, The. *See* Arola, Lorenzo
Tiger, Siparia. *See* Marcano, Neville
Tiger, Theobald. *See* Tucholsky, Kurt
Tigre del Bandoneon, El. *See* Arola, Lorenzo
Tilden, Louise W. *See* Crosby, Fanny [i.e., Frances] J(ane)
Tilden, Mary. *See* Crosby, Fanny [i.e., Frances] J(ane)
Tilford, Williams Robert. *See* Cooke, James Francis
Tilkin, John. *See* Tilkin, Félix (Marie Henri)
Till, Rocky. *See* Ederer, Josef
Tillman, James. *See* Cross, Frank L(eroy)
Timbaland. *See* Mosley, Tim(othy)
Timber. *See* Wood, (Sir) Henry Joseph
Timm, Toni. *See* Gaze, Herman Otto
Timon, John. *See* Mitchell, D(onald) G(rant)
Timotheus. *See* Berkeley, Lennox
Timsol, Robert. *See* Bird, Frederic(k) Mayer [or Meyer]
Tin Pan Alley's First Million Copy Seller. *See* Harris, Charles K(assell)
Tinan, Jean de. *See* Gauthier-Villars, Henri
Tindar(i)o, Dalmiro. *See* Creglianovich, G(iovanni)
Tiny Pocket Dynamo, A. *See* Cross, Marilyn Margaret
Tiny Tim. *See* Khaury, Herbert
Tio Gilena, El. *See* Goni, Peña y
Tippa Irie. *See* Henry, Anthony

Tirso de Molina. *See* Tellez, Gabriel
Tisch, F. S. *See* Tysh, Fred Salo
Tisch, Siegfried. *See* Tysh, Fred Salo
Tiselius, Lars [or Lara]. *See* Scheffel, Konrad [or Corny]
Tisza, Aladár. *See* Langer, Victor
Titan of Music, The. *See* Wagner, Richard
Tite Negre. *See* Ardoin, Amedee
Titmarsh, M(ichael) A(ngelo). *See* Thackeray, William Makepeace
Tito. *See* Franchetti, Alberto
Tito lo Posa, F. *See* Tosti, Francesco Paolo
Titori, Erwin. *See* Bruchhäuser, Wilfred Wolfgang
Tix, Ben. *See* Kiesow, Walter
Tizol, Joan. *See* Tizol, Vincente Martinez
Tizol, Juan. *See* Tizol, Vincente Martinez
Tobani, (H.). *See* Keiser, Robert (A(dolph))
Tobarmè, Adelio. *See* Bartoli, Amedeo
Tobias Brothers, The. *See* Tobias, Charles
Tobias Brothers, The. *See* Tobias, Harry
Tobias Brothers, The. *See* Tobias, Henry
Tobias, Elliot. *See* Tobias, Harry
Toboggan, Christopher. *See* Stuart, Thomas Gilmore
Toby. *See* Bluth, Frederick L.
Todd, D. S. *See* Billingsley, Derrell L.
Todd, Earl. *See* Green, Phil(ip)
Todd, Earl. *See* Paramor, Norman [or Norrie] (William)
Todd, Michael. *See* Goldbogen, Avrom Hirsch
Todi, Antonio Brassino da. *See* Artusi, Giovanni Maria
Toesca della Castellamonte, Johann. *See* Toeschi, Johann (Baptist Maria) Christoph
Tolbert, Geronimo. *See* Tolbert, Gregory Jerome
Tolbert, Skeets. *See* Tolbert, Campbell Arelius
Tolliver, H. *See* Lorenz, E(dmund) S(imon)
Tolmage, Gerald. *See* Gardner, Maurice
Tolreno, Arricha del. *See* Hollaender, Victor [or Viktor] (Hugo)
Tolveno, Arricha del. *See* Hollaender, Victor [or Viktor] (Hugo)
Tom. *See* Checchi, Eugenio
Tom. *See* Wiggins, Thomas (Green(e))
Tom and Jerry. *See* Garfunkel, Art(hur Ira)
Tom and Jerry. *See* Simon, Paul Frederick
Tom Lehrer of the Seventies, The. *See* Seidler, Alan
Tom-Ponce. *See* Gandonnière, Almire
Tom Sawyer of Rock, The. *See* Deutschendorf, Henry John, Jr.
Tomar, André. *See* Martl, Anton [or Toni]
Tomasi, B. *See* Oliphant, Thomas
Tomay, Nic. *See* Rózsa, Miklós
Tomlin, Pinky. *See* Tomlin, Truman (V., Sr.)
Tomline, F. L(atour). *See* Gilbert, William Schwenk
Tomlinson, Arthur. *See* Griffes, Charles T(omlinson)
Tomlinson, John William. *See* Rawlings, Alfred William
Tommy Dean from Abilene. *See* Overstreet, Thomas [or Tommy] (Cary, II)
Tompkins, Wes. *See* Holcombe, Wilfred (Lawshe)
Toms, Denton. *See* Dawson, Peter (Smith)
Tomson, Graham R. *See* Watson, Rosamund (Ball) Marriott
Tonelli, Carlo. *See* Barnard, D'Auvergne
Tongue Twister King, The. *See* Rivera Castillo, Efrain
Tonio K. *See* Kirkorian, Steve
Tonius, Ralph. *See* Jansen, Kurt
Tonny Tún Tún. *See* Castro, Antonio [or Tony]
Tonsor, Johann. *See* Hill, Mildred
Tonsor, Michael. *See* Sherer, Michael
Tonto, Charlie. *See* Pugliese, Carlos Anibal
Tony. *See* Oberdörffer, Manfred
Tony, Max. *See* Filsfils, Octave
Tonyrenis. *See* Cesari, Orfelio [or Elio]
Too Slim. *See* LaBour, Fred
Too Tight Henry. *See* Townsend, Henry
Toohey, Patrick. *See* Green, Phil(ip)
Toomey, Welby. *See* Slaughter, M(arion) T(ry)
Toots. *See* Thielmans, Jean (Baptiste)
Top Hatted Tragedian of Jazz, The. *See* Friedman, Theodore (Leopold)
Topp, Ben. *See* Weisman, Ben E.
Topping, Harry. *See* Kaufman, Isidore
Topsy. *See* Duncan, Rosetta
Torelli. *See* Ailbout, Hans
Torf, Théodule-Eléazar-Xavier. *See* Normand, Théodule Elzéar Xavier
Tori. *See* Amos, Myra Ellen
Torment, Mel. *See* Lennon, John (Winston)
Tornar, Roberto. *See* Turner, Robert
Tornow, Fred. *See* Strittmatter, Fred
Toro, Y(omo). *See* Toro Vega, Vícitor Guillermo
Torr, A. C. *See* Hobson, Frederick Leslie
Torres, Lalo. *See* Torres(-Garía), Eduardo [or Eddie]
Torry, Sloman. *See* Sloman, Jane
Torsi, Tristian. *See* Lang, Isaac
Torsten, Hünke. *See* Podewils, Torsten Hünke von
Torsten, Peter. *See* Illing, Heinz
Tosca, Antonio. *See* Cranz, Oskar [or Oscar]
Toscanini Cultists, The. *See* Chotzinoff, Samuel
Toscanini Cultists, The. *See* Gilman, Lawrence
Toscanini Cultists, The. *See* Haggin, Bernard H.
Toscanini of the Big Top. *See* Evans, Merle (Slease)
Tosh, Peter. *See* MacIntosh, Winston (Hubert)
Toska, Anton. *See* Cranz, Oskar [or Oscar]
Tosti, Don. *See* Tostado, Edmundo Martinez
Toto. *See* Amici, Antonio
Touchstone. *See* Burton, Claude E(dward Cole-Hamilton)
Touchstone. *See* Charlesworth, Hector (Willoughby)
Tourville, Charles. *See* Williams, Joseph (Benjamin)
Toussaint, Clarence. *See* Toussaint, Allen (R.)
Tovey, Cécile. *See* Aspinall, C. C.
Towering Tenor, The. *See* Vandross, Luther

Towers, Leo. *See* Blitz, Leo(nard)
Townsend, Louise (Mabelle). *See* Cain, Noble
Townsend, Mansfield. *See* Allen, Marie (née Townsend)
Townsend, Mark. *See* Beckhard, Robert L.
Toyah. *See* Willcox, Toyah Ann
Toyin. *See* Adekale, Toyin
Tracy, Christopher. *See* Nelson, Prince Rogers
Tracy, E. C. *See* Bliss, P(hilip) Paul
Trafford, Howard. *See* Trotter, Howard
Trahcier. *See* Reichard(t), Johann Friedrich
Trail, Buck. *See* Killette, Ronald B.
Train, John Butler. *See* Ochs, Phil
Train, Lute. *See* Och, Phil
Trane. *See* Coltrane, John William
Tranoscius, Georg. *See* Tranovsky, Juri
Trapani, T(uilio). *See* Mantovanni, A(nnuzio) P(aolo)
Trapassi, Antonio Domenico Bonaventura. *See* Trapassi (Gallastri), Pietro Antonio
Trapp, D. A. *See* Bliss, P(hilip) Paul
Traveling Texan, The. *See* Walker, William [or Billy] (Marvin)
Traveling Wilburys. *See* Harrison, George
Traveling Wilburys. *See* Lynne, Jeff
Traveling Wilburys. *See* Orbison, Roy (Kelton)
Traveling Wilburys. *See* Petty, Tom
Traveling Wilburys. *See* Zimmerman, Robert Allen
Travis, Randy. *See* Traywick, Randy (Bruce)
Travo, Manuel. *See* Craps, Ernest (Jean)
Trebellianus, Dionysius. *See* Treiber, Johann Philipp
Trebla Seno J. *See* Jones, Albert
Trebor, Robert. *See* Seigenthaler, William Robert
Trechzvevdockin, Ghermochen. *See* Makarov, N(ikolai) P(etrovich)
Tree, Lionel. *See* Rawlings, Alfred William
Treherne, Georgina. *See* Weldon, Georgina (née Thomas)
Trelawny, Jack. *See* Kahn, Gerald Freedmann
Trelba, Marco. *See* Butler, Robert Charles Walter Henry
Treloff, John. *See* Trouluffe, John
Tremblay, Alice. *See* Baron, Maurice
Trent, Anthony. *See* Clarke, Rebecca (Thacher)
Trent, Buck. *See* Trent, Charles Wilburn
Tresillian, Richard. *See* Ellis, Royston
Trevelyan, Beau Brummel. *See* Trevelyan, Arthur
Trevelyan, R. B. *See* Bolton, (St. George) Guy Reginald
Trèvés, Jean. *See* Kolditz, Hans
Trevor, Ann. *See* Harrhy, Edith
Trevor, Bert. *See* Finkelstein, Abe
Trevor, Edward. *See* Bulwer-Lytton, Edward Robert
Trevor, Mike. *See* Mantovani, A(nnuzio) P(aolo)
Trevor, Van. *See* Boulanger, Robert Francis
Trevoux, Daniel. *See* Tardieu, Jean
Treynor, Betty. *See* Wright, Lawrence
Triberg, Klaus. *See* Breuer, F(ranz) J(osef)
Triberg, Klaus. *See* Kongsbak-König, Käte
Triberg, Klaus. *See* Schlenkermann, Friedrich [or Fritz]
Tribot. *See* Cornuel, Jean
Tribs Ageless Enfant Terrible, The. *See* Thomson, Virgil (Garnett)
Trice, Welly. *See* Trice, Willam [or Willie] (Augusta)
Trick Daddy (Dollars). *See* Young, Maurice
Tricky (Kid). *See* Thaws, Adrian
Triel, Robert. *See* Toché, Raoul
Trifolium. *See* Kornfeld, J.
Trifolium. *See* Samson, Louis
Trifolium. *See* Zoeller, Carli [or Karl]
Trilunny. *See* Struisky, Dmitry Yuryevich
Trilussa. *See* Salustri, Carlo Albert
Trinidad, Pete. *See* Gardner, Maurice
Triole. *See* Gänsbacher, Johann Baptist
Triorchis. *See* Tenducci, Giusto [or Giustino] Ferdinando [or Fernando]
Tripe, S. *See* Dwight, Reginald Kenneth
Tristano d'Alloris. *See* Pelilli, Lino Ennio
Triste, Felix. *See* Foerster, Josef Bohuslav
Tritonius, Petrus. *See* Treybenreif, Peter
Tritt, Johnnie. *See* Pistritto, John
Trog. *See* Fawkes, Walter [or Wally] (Ernest)
Troili. *See* Paradossi, Giuseppe
Troilo, Pichuco. *See* Troilo, Anibal (Carmelo)
Troisaent, Jacques Karl. *See* Sapp, Allen (Dwight)
Troja, Vallaire. *See* Keiser, Robert (A(dolph))
Troll, Inga. *See* Bock, Ida
Trolli, Joseph. *See* Yankovic, Frank(ie) (John)
Tromberg, Jack. *See* Stoeckart, Jan
Trombetti, Ascanio. *See* Cavallari, Ascanio
Trombetti, Girolamo. *See* Cavallari, Girolamo
Trombey, Jack. *See* Stoeckart, Jan
Trombone, Il. *See* Negri, Cesare (de')
Trömer, August von. *See* Witzleben, (Karl) August (Friedrich) von
Tromlitz, A(ugust) von. *See* Witzleben, (Karl) August (Friedrich) von
Trossbach, Hans. *See* Halt, Hugo
Trotère, Henry. *See* Trotter, Henry
Trott-Plaid, John. *See* Fielding, Henry
Troubadour, The. *See* Woods, Oscar
Troupe, Bobby. *See* Williams, Robert
Troutman, John. *See* Blake, George M.
Trovador del campo, El. *See* Perez Meza, Luis
Trovato, Ben. *See* Lover, Samuel
Troy, Doris. *See* Higginsen, Doris
Troysen, Jan. *See* Majewki, Hans-Martin
Troyte, Arthur Henry Dyke. *See* Acland, Arthur Henry Dyke
Trudy, Evalyn. *See* Moore, Eloise Irene
True Laureate of England, The. *See* Dibdin, Charles
True Liberal, A. *See* Statham, Francis Reginald
True Renaissance Man of Contemporary Christian Music, A. *See* Smith, Michael W(hitaker)

Truelove, John. *See* Trouluffe, John
Trumpeting Behemoth. *See* Hirt, Al(ois Maxwell)
Trümpy, Balz. *See* Trümpy, Johann Balthasar
Truxa, Konstantin. *See* Halletz, Erwin
Tschacko. *See* Jäger, Raimund
Tscherinoff, Feodor. *See* Grey, Frank H(erbert)
Tsukigi, Hiroshi. *See* Suma, Yosaku
Tuba Meister. *See* Phillips, Harvey G.
Tubb, Billy. *See* Tubb, Talmadge
Tucker, Tee. *See* Higginbotham, Robert
Tucker, Tommy. *See* Duppler, Gerald L.
Tucker, Tommy. *See* Higginbotham, Robert
Tuckerman, Patricia. *See* Wagness, Bernard
Tudor, Al. *See* Adams, Cliff
Tudor, Anthony. *See* Cook, William (John)
Tuerto, El. *See* Di Sarli, Carlos
Tufilli, W. *See* Frangkiser, Carl (Moerz)
Tuig, R. A. *See* Souchon, Edmond, (Jr.)
Tuli, Felix. *See* Wuolijoki, Hella (Maria) (née Murrik)
Tulsa Red. *See* Fulson, Lowell
Tune Detective, The. *See* Spaeth, Sigmund Gottfried
Tuneful Harry. *See* Lawes, Henry
Tunnell, Bon Bon. *See* Tunnell, George
Tuokko, (Antti). *See* Törneroos, Anders
Turan, Jerry. *See* Turrano, Joseph A.
Turitto, Giacomo. *See* Tritto, Giacomo
Turková, Marie. *See* Preissová, Gabriela (née Sekerová)
Turlet, A. *See* Planquette, (Jean) Robert (Julien)
Turmer, Udo. *See* Lautenscläger, Willi
Turner, Al. *See* Bergman, Dewey
Turner, Allen. *See* Slaughter, M(arion) T(ry)
Turner, Big Joe. *See* Turner, Joseph Vernon
Turner, Billy. *See* Slaughter, M(arion) T(ry)
Turner, Blind Squire. *See* Darby, Theodore [or Teddy] (Roosevelt)
Turner, Franklin. *See* Bliss, P(hilip) Paul
Turner, Gil. *See* Strunk, Gilbert
Turner, Happy. *See* Turner, John C.
Turner, James John. *See* Phillips, James John
Turner, Jerone. *See* Severson, Edward Louis, III
Turner, John. *See* Phillips, James John
Turner, John. *See* Tucker, John(ny)
Turner, Paul. *See* Freed, Richard (Donald)
Turner, Scott. *See* Turnbull, Graham (Morrison)
Turner, Sid. *See* Slaughter, M(arion) T(ry)
Turner, Tina. *See* Bullock, Annie [or Anna] Mae
Turno. *See* Simoni, Renato
Turntable Wizard. *See* Craig, Carl
Tursten, Peter. *See* Illing, Heinz
Tutmarc, Bonnie. *See* Buckingham, Bonnie
Tuttle, Frank. *See* Robison, Carson J(ay)
Tuttle, Frank. *See* Slaughter, M(arion) T(ry)
Twain, Shania. *See* Twain, Eil(l)een
Twelve-Tone Oddity. *See* Schoenberg, Arnold
Twentieth Century Gabriel, (The). *See* Hawkins, Erskine (Ramsey)
Twentieth Century Moses. *See* Chaplin, Charles (Spencer)
Twin Freaks. *See* McCartney, (James) Paul
Twine, Bobby. *See* Morphis, Robert C.
Twink. *See* Adler, John (Richard)
Twinkle. *See* Ripley, Lynn (Annette)
Twist King, The. *See* Evans, Ernest
Twitt-Thornwaite, (Sir) Nigel. *See* Gold, Glenn Herbert
Twitty, Conway. *See* Jenkins, Harold (Lloyd)
Two-Headed Janus of Music, The. *See* Dukelsky, Vladimir
Two Leslies, The. *See* Frye, Leslie Legge Sarony
Two Leslies, The. *See* Holmes, Leslie
Two Priests of the Church of England. *See* Neale, J(ohn) M(ason)
Two Real Coons, The. *See* Walker, George
Two Real Coons, The. *See* Williams, Egbert Austin
Two Rogers. *See* Cook, Roger
Two Rogers. *See* Greenaway, Roger
Twomey, M. G. *See* Twomey, Kathleen [or Kay] Greeley
Ty Cobb of Music Critics, The. *See* Haggin, Bernard H.
Tychian, Joh. Antonio. *See* Draghi, Antonio
Tyler, Chapman. *See* White, Grace
Tyler, Clark. *See* Kinyon, John L(eroy)
Tyler, Steve(n). *See* Tallarico, Steven [or Stephen] (Victor)
Tyler, (T.) Texas. *See* Myrick, David Luke
Tyler, Toby. *See* Feld, Mark
Tyler, Walter. *See* Smith, Harry B(ache)
Tyler, Walter G. *See* Geibel, Adam
Tyler, Walter J. *See* Geibel, Adam
Tyran de Blanc. *See* Grimm, Friedrich Melchior, Freiherr von
Tyrann, Der. *See* Schubert, Franz Peter
Tyranny, "Blue" Gene. *See* Sheff, Robert Nathan
Tyrant, The. *See* Schubert, Franz Peter
Tyrie, James (Alexander Balfour) Campbell. *See* Campbell, James [or Jimmy]
Tyrrold, Aston. *See* Smith, A. Corbett
Tyrtaeus of France, The. *See* Rouget de Lisle, Claude Joseph
Tyrtaeus of the British Navy, The. *See* Dibdin, Charles
Tyski, Jan. *See* Tyszkiewicz, Jan
Tzara, Tristan. *See* Rosenstock, Sam(uel)
Tzizit, Rav. *See* Zorn, John

– U –

U-God. *See* Hawkins, Lamont
Ubalde. *See* Loquin, Antole
Ubaldus. *See* Huchbald (of Saint Armand)
Uccle, Giraud d'. *See* Kochnitzky, Léon

Uchubaldus. *See* Hucbald (of Saint Armand)
Uciredor, (S.). *See* Rodericus
Udall, Lyn. *See* Keating, John Henry
Udine, Jean d'. *See* Cozanet, Albert
Uffo von Wildingen. *See* Zitzmann, Heinrich Gottfried
Uhl, Ruth. *See* Frank, Ruth Verd
Uhlenbruck, Christian. *See* Heynicke, Kurt
Ukulele Ace, (The). *See* Marvin, John(ny) (Senator)
Ukulele Ike. *See* Edwards, Clifton (A.)
Ukelele Kid. *See* Burse, Charlie
Ukelele Lady, The. *See* Breen, May Singhi
Ulbrich, Friedrich. *See* Ulbrich, Siegfried
Ulisseus —*see* Eler(s), Franz
Ulli. *See* Leenen, Ullrich Jakob
Ullmer. *See* Müller, Werner [or Warner]
Ulmer, F. E. *See* Bliss, P(hilip) Paul
Ulrich von (der) Uhlenhorst. *See* Dreves, Guido Maria
Ulrik, Sven. *See* Jensen, Harry
Umorista. *See* Badi, Paolo Emilio
Unbleached American, The. *See* Crowders, (Ernest) Reuben
Uncle Al. *See* Lewis, Al (1924-)
Uncle Frank. *See* Hartsough, Palmer
Uncle George. *See* Cohan, George M(ichael)
Uncle Joe. *See* Allison, Joe (Marion)
Uncle Joe. *See* Bernard, Al(fred A.)
Uncle Josh. *See* Stewart, Cal(vin) (Edward)
Uncle Kracker. *See* Shafer, Matt(hew)
Uncle Lumpy. *See* Brannum, Hugh Roberts
Uncle Miltie. *See* Berlinger, Milton
Uncle Paul. *See* Montgomery, Paul
Uncle Sam. *See* Liptzin, Samuel
Uncle Shelby. *See* Silverstein, Shel(by)
Uncrowned King of Light Music. *See* Coates, Eric
Uncrowned King of Ruritania, The. *See* Davies, David Ivor
Uncrowned Queen of the Blues, The. *See* Prather, Ida
Undergraduate, An. *See* Whytehead, Thomas
Underhill, Viola. *See* Wells, Viola (Gertrude)
Underwood, Dudley. *See* Bush, Alan
Unico, El. *See* Quian (Manguito), Romón
Unknown, The. *See* Dusch, Alexander von
Unknown, Arthur. *See* Burrough, Bob (Lloyd)
Unsinkable Music Man, The. *See* Willson, (Robert Reiniger) Meredith
Upsetter, The. *See* Perry, Rainford Hugh
Urbanus, Sylvanus. *See* Aldrich, Richard
Urbino, l'. *See* Marco Antonio Girolamo
Ure, Midge. *See* Ure, James
Urgel, Louis. *See* L'Henoret, Louise
Urini, Ron. *See* Iraschek, Ronald Frederic
Ursinus. *See* Barre, Ernst
Ursinus, (Johann). *See* Beer, Johann
Ursus. *See* Beer, Johann
Usedom, Hecktor von. *See* Deutscher, Karlheinz
Usper, Francesco. *See* Sponga, Francesco
Ux, Catherine. *See* Hauptmann, Elisabeth

– V –

V. A. *See* Crosby, Fanny [i.e., Frances] J(ane)
V. G. L. *See* Little, V(ivian?) G(ray?)
V., Jenny. *See* Crosby, Fannie [i.e., Frances] J(ane)
Vad(d)er Abraham. *See* Kartner, Pierre
Vaerwere, Johannes de. *See* Tinctoris, Johannes
Vaëz, Gustave. *See* Nieuwenhuysen, Jean Nicolas Gustave (van)
Vagabond Lover, The. *See* Vallee, Herbert Pryor
Vaillant, D. F. *See* Gräffer, Franz (Arnold)
Vaksman, F. *See* Wachsmann, Franz
Val, Jack. *See* Volpato, Jack Albert
Val, Joe. *See* Valianti, Joseph
Valcek, Wenzel. *See* Wolf, Hubert
Valdemar, Paul. *See* Harris,Cuthbert
Valdes. *See* Garsi, Santino (da Parma)
Valdez, Miguel. *See* Paramor, Norman [or Norrie] (William)
Valdez, Patato. *See* Valdez, Carlos
Vladinoff, Alex. *See* Kountz, Richard
Valdy. *See* Horsdal, Valdemar
Vale, Mark. *See* Winter, William
Valens, Richard [or Ritchie]. *See* Valenzuela, Richard (Stephen)
Valente, Giorgio. *See* Vitalis, George
Valenti, Dino. *See* Powers, Chester [or Chet]
Valentin, Frank. *See* Van der Stucken, Frank Valentin
Valentin, Patrice. *See* Woëlfmann, Georges
Valentin, Peter. *See* Niederbremer, Artur
Valentine. *See* Pechey, Archibald Thomas
Valentine at Rome, Mr. *See* Valentine, Robert
Valentine, C(harles). *See* Bucalossi, Procida (Joseph Henry Edwards)
Valentine, Sim. *See* Green, Phil(ip)
Valentine, Sim. *See* Paramor, Norman [or Norrie] (William)
Valentine, Val. *See* Gerich, Valentine
Valentini. *See* Urbani, Valentino
Valentini, F. *See* Ferrari, Benedetto
Valentini, Orlando. *See* Bardet, René
Valentini, Roberto. *See* Valentine, Robert
Valentino. *See* Jommelli, Nic(c)olò
Valentino, Henry. *See* Blum, Hans
Valentino, Marcel. *See* Allen, Stephen [or Steve] (Valentine Patrick William)
Valentino of the 80's, The. *See* Iglesias, Julio
Valenziano, Il. *See* Martín y Soler, Vicente
Valère. *See* Morgan, Roberto Orlando
Valerio. *See* Ketten, Henri
Valerium. *See* Webb, Gary Anthony James

Valesca, José. *See* Persson, Harry (Arnold)
Valetta, Ippolito. *See* Franchi-Verney, Giuseppe Ippolito
Valette, Pierre. *See* Vieu, Jane [or Jeanne] (Elisabeth Marie)
Valgrand, Clémence. *See* Grandval, Marie Felicie Clémence de Reiset, vicomtesse de
Valiant Minstrel. *See* Lauder, (Sir) Harry (Maclennan)
Valin, Justin. *See* Rakotondrasoa, Justin
Valinoff, George. *See* Cain, Noble
Valladares, Dioris. *See* Valladares, Isidro
Valle, Barbara. *See* Strozzi, Barbara
Vallee, Rudy. *See* Vallee, Herbert Pryor
Vallinare, Paul. *See* Bulch, Thomas Edward
Valmency, Edgar de. *See* Gilbert, E. Ouseley
Valmèr, Jean Pierre. *See* Teupen, Jonny Wilhelm Bernhard
Valmer, Michel. *See* Kerzanet, Jean André Léon Louis
Valsini, F(rancesco). *See* Silvani, Francesco
Vamp, Hugo. *See* O'Neill, John Robert
Van, Gus. *See* Kahn, Gus
Van A., (Mrs.). *See* Crosby, Fanny [i.e., Frances] J(ane)
Van Alstyne, (Mrs.) Alexander. *See* Crosby, Fanny [i.e., Frances] J(ane)
Van Alstyne, Fanny. *See* Crosby, Fanny [i.e., Frances] J(ane)
Vanberg, Charles. *See* Dumont, Charles Frédéric
Van Berg, T. *See* Balmer, Charles
Van Buskirk, Al. *See* Yoder, Paul V(an Buskirk)
Vance, Alfred Glenville. *See* Stevens, Alfred Peck
Vanda, Harry. *See* Vandanberg, Harry
Van Delft, Michael. *See* Lijnschooten, Hendrikus [or Henk] (Cornelius) van
Van den Budenmayer. *See* Preisner, Zbigniew
Van den Camp, Ferdinand. *See* Du Camp, Alphonse
Van der Linden, Dolf. *See* Linden, David Gysbert (van der)
Van der Linden, Dorf. *See* Linden, David Gysbert (van der)
Van der Lynn, Dorf. *See* Linden, David Gysbert (van der)
Vandersloot, C(aird) M. *See* Lincoln, Harry J.
Vandersloot, Carl D. *See* Lincoln, Harry J.
Vandersloot, F(rederick) W(illiam). *See* Lincoln, Harry J.
Van Dine, S. S. *See* Wright, Willard Huntington
Vandini, Lotavio. *See* Maccari, Giacomo
Vandini, Lotavio. *See* Vivaldi, Antonio (Lucio)
Vandyke, Les. *See* Worsley, John, (II)
Van Dyne, S. S. *See* Wright, Willard Huntington
Vane, Claude. *See* Isaacs, Rufus
Vangelis. *See* Papathanassiou, Evangelos (Odyssey)
Van Heusen, James [or Jimmy]. *See* Babcock, Edward Chester
Vanilla Ice. *See* Van Winkle, Robert [or Robbie]
Vanity. *See* Matthews, Denise
Van Lake, Turk. *See* Hovsepian, Vanig (Rupen)
Van Love, Ludy. *See* Love, Luther Halsey, (Jr.)
Vann, Teddy. *See* Williams, Theodore, Jr.
Van Ness, Clarke. *See* Clark, C(yrus) Van Ness
Vannin. *See* Ornstein, Leo
Van Norman, Frederick. *See* Zamecnik, J(ohn) S(tepan)
Van Tuyl, Vincent. *See* Kaufman, Isidore
Van Winkle, Rip. *See* Van Winkle, Harold E.
Van Zandt, Miami. *See* Van Zandt, Steve(n)
Vaplus, Renata. *See* Deutscher, Karlheinz
Vapnick, Richard Leon. *See* Vapnick, Isaac
Vardapet, Komitas. *See* Sogomonian, (Sogomon Gevorkovich)
Vardon, Paul. *See* Mullen, Frederic
Varela, Héctor. *See* Varela, Salustiano Paco
Vargis, Axel. *See* Gottschalk, Heinz-Jürgen
Vario, Alberto. *See* Giannini, Guglielmo
Varna, Henri. *See* Vantard, Henri (Eugene)
Varoter, Francesco. *See* Ana, Francesco d'
Vartabed, Gomidas. *See* Sogomonian, (Sogomon Gevorkovich
Vasai, Ercole. *See* Bassi, Ercole
Vaschbiergn, Josef. *See* Washburne, Joseph [or Joe] (H.)
Vassar the Master. *See* Clements, Vassar Carlton
Vater der Deutschen Lied, Der. *See* Albert, Heinrich
Vaughan, Comyn. *See* Scott-Gatty, (Sir) Alfred
Vaughan, Graham. *See* Harris, Cuthbert
Vaughan, Hilary. *See* Ewing, Montague (George)
Vaughan, Lynn. *See* Geehl, Henry Ernest
Vaughn, Billy. *See* Vaughn, Richard (S(mith))
Vaughn, Charles. *See* Kaufman, Isidore
Vaughn, George. *See* Horton, (George) Vaughn
Vaughn, Michael. *See* Shaftel, Selig (Sidney)
Vaux, de. *See* Lemonnier, Guillaume Antoine
Vayner, Lazar. *See* Weiner, Lazar
Veber, Michel. *See* Weber, Michel
Vecchio, Il. *See* Cervetto, James (1682-1783)
Vecchio, Il. *See* Sirazi, G.
Vecchio, Il. *See* Varotari, Dario
Vecio, El. *See* Andolfo, Franco
Vedder, Eddie. *See* Severson, Edward Louis, III
Vedel, Poul. *See* Troels-Lund, Troels (Frederik)
Vedeski, Anton. *See* Dishinger, Ronald C(hristian)
Vee Jay. *See* Smith, Florence Beatrice
Vega, Al. *See* Vagramian, Aram
Vega, Little Louie. *See* Gonzalez, Kenny
Velasky, Armon. *See* Young, Victor
Velhagen, Roger. *See* Becker, Frank
Velke, Fritz. *See* Velke, John Arthur, (II)
Vellones, (Pierre). *See* Rousseau, Pierre
Velmont, James. *See* Cross, Frank L(eroy)
Velvet Fog, The. *See* Torme, Mel(vin Howard)
Velvet Gentleman, The. *See* Satie, (Alfred) Erik (Leslie)
Vély, Adrien. *See* Fournier, Marcel (Paul) Roger
Venatorini, Il. *See* Mysliveček, Josef

Veneto, Francesco. *See* Ana, Francesco d'
Venetus, Franciscus. *See* Ana, Francesco d'
Veneziano, Il. *See* Caresana, Cristoforo
Veneziano, Bianchini. *See* Bianchini, Domenico
Venison, Alfred. *See* Pound, Ezra ((Weston) Loomis)
Venizien. *See* Verocai, Giovanni
Venning, Peter. *See* Mendoza, Peter Hygham
Venosa, Carlo Gesualdo da. *See* Gesualdo, Carlo
Venosa, Prince of. *See* Gesualdo, Carlo
Venton & Reef. *See* Frye, Leslie Legge Sarony
Venton & Reef. *See* Holmes, Leslie
Ventura, Anthony. *See* Becker, Werner
Ventura, Pep. *See* Ventura, Josep [or José] (María de la Purificación)
Vera, Billy. *See* McCord, William (Patrick, Jr.)
Verbon(n)et, (Johannes). *See* Ghiselin, Johannes [or Jean]
Verckys. *See* Maleta, Kiamuangana
Verdelot, Philippe. *See* Deslouges, Philippe
Verdelotto. *See* Deslouges, Philippe
Verdin, Henri [or Henry]. *See* Haga, Frederick Wallace
Verdin, Henri [or Henry]. *See* Ringleben, Justin, Jr.
Vere, Claude de. *See* Rawlings, Charles Arthur
Verified Legend, The. *See* Whitman, Ot(t)is (Dewey, Jr.)
Veritophilus. *See* Raupach, Christoph
Verius, (Joanne). *See* Verio, Juan
Verjus(t). *See* Cornuel, Jean
Verlaine, Tom. *See* Miller, Thomas
Vermeer, Roger. *See* Reubrecht, Albert
Vermont primus. *See* Vermont, Pierre
Vermouth, Apollo C. *See* McCartney, (James) Paul
Verne, Alice. *See* Wurm, Alice
Verne, H. *See* Rawlings, Charles Arthur
Verne, Mary [or Marie] (J. A.). *See* Wurm, Mary [or Marie] (J. A.)
Verne, Oscar. *See* Rawlings, Charles Arthur
Verne, Robert [or Bob]. *See* Vernoff, Robert Arnold
Verner, E. *See* Rimmer, William
Verneuil, Louis. *See* Collin du Bocage, Louis Jacques Marie
Verney, Charles. *See* Hutterstrasser, Karl
Verney, Sammy. *See* Paramor, Norman [or Norrie] (William)
Vernici, Ottavio. *See* Vernizzi, Ottavio
Vernon, Ashley. *See* Manschinger, Kurt
Vernon, Bill(y). *See* Slaughter, M(arion) T(ry)
Vernon, Carlile. *See* Bawden, William Carlile
Vernon, Herbert. *See* Slaughter, M(arion) T(ry)
Vernon, Peter. *See* Gradenwitz, Peter Werner Emanuel
Vernon, Will. *See* Slaughter, M(arion) T(ry)
Verö, György. *See* Hauer, Georg [or Hugó]
Verona, Gypsy Countess. *See* Rourke, M(ichael) E(lder)
Verré, Léon. *See* Reeves, Ernest
Vert-Vert. *See* Mortjé, Arnold [or Adolphe]
Verta, Jose. *See* Evert, Johannes
Verus. *See* Marcus, Ahron [or Aaron]
Vesala, Edward. *See* Vesala, Martti Juhani
Veteran, Vel. *See* Finkelstein, Abe
Veteran, Vel. *See* Kaufman, Isidore
Veteran, Vel. *See* Slaughter, M(arion) T(ry)
Vhladof, A. *See* Cain, Noble
Viator. *See* Cotton, Charles
Vicar, Del. *See* Delvicario, Silvio Patrick
Vicar of Harrow, The. *See* Cunningham, John William
Vicente (de Olivença). *See* Lusitano, Vicente
Vick, Danny. *See* Walker, Jeanine Ogletree
Victor. *See* Nelson, Prince Rogers
Victor. *See* Shelley, Percy Bysshe
Victor, Hollis. *See* Hollaender, Victor [or Viktor] (Hugo)
Victor Manuel. *See* San Jose (Sanchez), Victor Manuel
Victor of Wrexhill, The. *See* Cunningham, John William
Victorinus, Santolius. *See* Santeu(i)l, Jean Baptiste de
Victors, Karel. *See* Albert, Karel
Victory Cowboy. *See* Kirby, Fred
Victory, Gerard. *See* Loraine, Alan
Vidacovich, Pinky. *See* Vidacovich, Irving J(ohn, Sr.)
Viersen, Arne. *See* Düsing, Bernhard
Vieux, Le. *See* Aubert, Jacques
Vieux Gallot. *See* Gallot, Antoine
Vieux Gallot de Paris. *See* Gallot, Jacques (de)
Vieux Gaultier, Le. *See* Gaultier, Ennemond [or Eunémond]
Vignix, Hugues. *See* Régnier, Henri (François Joseph de)
Viking of Sixth Avenue. *See* Hardin, Louis (Thomas)
Vilbac, Remi. *See* Boex, Andrew J.
Villa, Joe. *See* Francavilla, Josephe [or Joe]
Village Pastor. *See* Waterbury, Jared Bell
Villalba Filho, Epaminondas. *See* Villa-Lobo, Heiter
Villani, Claudio. *See* Wagenleiter, Klaus
Villard. *See* Lascombe, George
Villarosa, Marchese de. *See* Rosa, Carlanonio de
Villary, Roland. *See* Rolland(-Max(-Dearly)), Lucien Paul Marie Joseph
Villinger, Axel. *See* Feltz, Kurt (August Karl)
Vinard, F. N. *See* Vincent, Nathaniel (Hawthorne)
Vincent, Beryl. *See* Rawlings, Charles Arthur
Vincent, Edwyn. *See* Bonner, Carey
Vincent, Gene. *See* Craddock, Vincent Eugene [or Eugene Vincent]
Vincent, Heinrich Joseph. *See* Winzenhörlein, Heinrich Joseph
Vincent, Jimmie. *See* Martino, Donald (James)
Vincent, Paul. *See* Gunia, Paul Vincent
Vincent, Ray. *See* Campbell, James [or Jimmy]
Vincent, Ray. *See* Connelly, Reg(inald)
Vincent, Wallace. *See* Spaulding, G(eorge) L(awson)
Vincent, Walter. *See* Vinson, Walter Jacobs
Vincenzo di Pasquino. *See* Bastini, Vincentio
Vinci of the Drums, The. *See* Balassoni, Luigi Paulino

Vincson, Walter. *See* Vinson, Walter Jacobs
Vincy, Raymond. *See* Ovanessian, Raymond Henri
Vindex. *See* Roussel, Henri
Vine, Lee. *See* Levine, Abe [i.e., Abraham] (Lewis)
Vinegar, (Capt.) Hercules, (of Hockley in the Hole). *See* Fielding, Henry
Vinson, Cleanhead. *See* Vinson, Eddie
Vinton, Hal(l). *See* Zamecnik, J(ohn) S(tepan)
Viola, Allesandro della. *See* Merlo, Allesandro
Viola, Ciccio. *See* Oliva, Francesco
Viola V. A., (Miss). *See* Crosby, Fanny [i.e., Frances] J(ane)
Violino, Il. *See* Caproli, Carlo
Violino, Il. *See* Cortellini, Camillo
Violino, Carlo del. *See* Caproli, Carlo
Violino, Carlo del. *See* Cesarini, Carlo Francesco
Violinsky, (Solly). *See* Ginsberg, Sol(ly)
Viotti. *See* Panofka, Heinrich
Viozzi, Giulio. *See* Weutz, Giulio
Virgil of American Musical History, The. *See* Thomson, Virgil (Garnett)
Virgil Thomson of the Mid-1800s, The. *See* Fry, William H(enry)
Virginian Folk Singer, The. *See* Smith, Blaine
Virginian from Louisville, Ky. *See* Westendorf, Thomas Paine
Virginia's Rustic Renaissance Man. *See* McCutcheon, John
Visigoth. *See* Caveirac, Jean Novi de
Vitale, Carmen. *See* Babcock, Edward Chester
Vitelle, Vincent. *See* Metcalf, Leon (Vinnedge)
Vitello, Leo. *See* Metcalf, Leon (Vinnedge)
Vit(t)riaco, (Philippus de). *See* Vitry, Philippe de
Vitton, Arthur. *See* Crowest, Frederick J(ames)
Vivaldi, Antonio. *See* Kreisler, Fritz [i.e., Friedrich](-Max)
Vivaldian. *See* Vivaldi, Antonio (Lucio)
Vivian, Lila. *See* Landreaux, Edna
Vivier, Carl-Wilhelm. *See* Pauck, Heinz [or Heinrich]
Vlad. *See* Frypés, Karel (Vladimir)
Vlademar, Paul. *See* Harris, Cuthbert
Vladinoff, Alex. *See* Kountz, Richard
Vlieger, Jan de. *See* Scheffer, Johannes
Vodorinski, Anton. *See* Ketèlbey, Albert William
Voeth, Zoe. *See* Parenteau, Zoe
Vogler, Abt [or Abbe]. *See* Vogler, George Joseph
Voglio, Emelio. *See* Green, Phil(ip)
Voglio, Emelio. *See* Paramor, Norman [or Norrie] (William)
Vogt, Carl. *See* Greenwald, M(artin)
Vogt, Carl. *See* Smith, Lee Orean
Voice, The. *See* Gosdin, Vern(on)
Voice of the Hangover Generation, The. *See* O'Hara, John (Henry)
Voice of the South, The. *See* Blackmar, A(rmand) E(dward)
Voice of the Southland, The. *See* Lucas, Eugene
Voice with a Heart, The. *See* Wiseman, Malcolm [or Mac] (B.)
Voigt, Fred [or Ferd.]. *See* Krentzlin, H. Richard
Voix du Ziare, La. *See* Landu, M'Pongo
Volcyr, Nicolaus. *See* Wolquier, Nicolaus
Voli, Raoul. *See* Thomas, Peter
Volker der Minstrel. *See* Schubert, Franz Peter
Volkwarth. *See* Pollak, Franz
Vollenweider, Andreas. *See* Bardet, René
Vollweiler, A. *See* Hoffmann, Ernst Theodore Wilhelm
Volney, Ivan. *See* Vïschnegradsky, Ivan Alexandrovich
Volonteroso, (Il). *See* Varotari, Dario
Voltaire. *See* Arouet, François-Marie
Volti, Carl. *See* Milligan, Archibald
Volupius Decorus. *See* Schonsleder, Wolfgang
Vom, Mr. *See* Meltzer, Richard Bruce
Vonberg, Fritz. *See* Dumont, Charles Frédéric
Vonderleath, Leonore. *See* Vonderlieth, Leonore
Von Der Oster, Johanne. *See* Falk Johannes Daniel
Von Schreibe, Emmanuel. *See* Cabral, Manuel M(edeiros)
Von Tilzer, Albert. *See* Gum(m), Albert
Von Tilzer, Harry. *See* Gum(m), Harold [or Harry]
Von Zador, Michael. *See* Zador, Michael
Voran der Geharnischte. *See* Rückert, Johann Michel Friedrich
Vorbach, Klaus. *See* Meybrunn, Franz Josef
Vorlová, Sláva. *See* Johnova, Miroslava
Vovi, Montebaldo. *See* Miani, Marco
Vox, Bono. *See* Hewson, Paul (David)
Vrána, Vojtěch. *See* Sabina, Karel
Vránek, Karel. *See* Klein, Gideon
Vrchlický, Jaroslav. *See* Frida, Emil Bohuslav
Vsacan, R. F. *See* Fricsay, Richard
Vuiet, Caroline. *See* Wuiet, Caroline
Vulcan Pianist. *See* Herz, Heinrich [or Henri]
Vulpius, Melchoir. *See* Fuchs, Melchoir
Vulpius, Paul. *See* Adler, Hans
Vychodil, V. *See* Wychodil(-Hofmeister), Gert

– W –

W. *See* Cowper, William
W. *See* Wade, Joseph Augustine
W. *See* Watts, Isaac
W. A. F. *See* Fisher, William Arms
W. A. M****t. *See* Mozart, Wolfgang Amadeus
W. B. *See* Babell, William
W. B. *See* Budden, William
W. B. H. *See* Heathcote, William Beadon
W. G., of Leicester. *See* Gardiner, William

W. H. *See* Horsley, William
W. H. B. *See* Bathurst, William Hiley
W. H. C. *See* Callcott, William Hutchins
W. H. F. *See* Frere, W(alter) H(oward)
W. H. P. *See* Plumstead, W. H.
W. H. R. *See* Rule, William Harris
W. K. *See* Kaufman, Martin Ellis
W. L. *See* Watts, Isaac
W. L. *See* Whittle, (Major) D(aniel) W(ebster)
W. L. A. *See* Alexander, William Lindsay
W. M. G. D. *See* Damrosch, Walter Johannes
W. M. R. *See* Roberts, William Morgan
W. P. . *See* Parratt, (Sir) William
W. S. *See* Sanders, William (fl. 1838-81)
W. S. *See* Shrubsole, William, Jr.
W. S. *See* Watts, Isaac
Wachtel, Waddy. *See* Wachtel, Robert
Wade, Joanna. *See* Berckman, Evelyn Domenica
Wade, Peter. *See* Lloyd-Webber, William (Southcombe)
Wade, Stuart. *See* Rowley, Alec
Wadsworth, Charles. *See* Ehret, Walter (Charles)
Waëz, Gustave. *See* Nieuwenhuysen, Jean Nicolas Gustave (van)
Wages, J. Ch. *See* Hesse, August Wilhelm
Wagner, Denson. *See* Iannelli, Richard
Wagner, Norbert. *See* Mai, Siegfried
Wagner of the Lied. *See* Wolf, Hugo
Wagner of the Sardana, The. *See* Garreta, Juli(o)
Wagner of the Sixteenth Century. *See* Monteverdi, Claudio
Wagner of the Symphony. *See* Bruckner, (Josef) Anton
Wagneresque. *See* Wagner, Richard
Wagnerian. *See* Wagner, Richard
Wagnerian Symphonist. *See* Bruckner, (Josef) Anton
Wagschal, Gerechte. *See* Fuhrmann, Martin Heinrich
Wagstaffe, John, Esq., of Wilby Grange. *See* Mackay, Charles
Wahl, Wilbur. *See* Nolte, Roy E.
Wahnfried, Richard. *See* Schulze, Klaus
Wahrmund. *See* Feind, Barthold
Wahsdarb, Teirrah. *See* Bradshaw, Harriet
Wahsreka. *See* Kershaw, A.
Wailer, Bunny. *See* Livingston, Neville O'Reilly
Waiman. *See* Royce, James (Stanley)
Wain, D. *See* Lebys, Henry
Wainrow, Philip. *See* Cain, Noble
Wakabe, Michio. *See* Wakabe, Nakasuga Kengyo
Wakefield, Charles C. *See* Cadman, Charles Wakefield
Wal-Berg, (Voldemar). *See* Rosenberg, Wladimir [or Voldemar]
Wald, A. G. *See* Grünwald, Alfred
Waldbrühl, Wilhelm von. *See* Zuccalmaglio, Anton Wilhelm Florentin von
Waldeck, J. B. *See* Williams, Joseph (Benjamin)
Waldegg, Franz. *See* Rumpel, Franz
Walden, Chris. *See* Schulz, Christian Waldemar
Walden, Heinrich. *See* Gleich, Josef Alois
Walden, Otto von. *See* Schindler, Fritz
Walden, Peter. *See* Waldenmaier, A(ugust) P(eter)
Waldin, Hugues. *See* Blanc de Fontbelle, Cecile
Waldo, Terry. *See* Waldo, Ralph Emerson, III
Waldorff, Peter. *See* Hartmann, Otto B.
Waldron, Gene. *See* Armbuster, Robert
Waldron, Mal. *See* Waldron, Earl Malcolm
Waldrop, Gid(eon William). *See* Winthrop, Gideon William
Waldstorch, Gabriel. *See* Grimm, Friedrich Melchior, Freiherr von
Waldteufel. *See* Lévy, Léon (1832-1884)
Waldteufel, (Charles) Emile. *See* Lévy, (Charles) Emile
Waldteufel, Léon. *See* Lévy, Léon (1832-1884)
Waldteufel, Louis. *See* Lévy, Louis
Wales, Evelyn. *See* Harrhy, Edith
Walker, Bertram. *See* Keiser, Robert (A(dolph))
Walker, Buddy. *See* Walker, Weldon
Walker, J-Dub. *See* Walker, Jeffrey
Walker, Jerry Jeff. *See* Crosby, Ronald Clyde
Walker, Jimmy. *See* Fortini, James (1926-)
Walker, Jimmy. *See* Walker, Earnest Earl
Walker, Richard. *See* Tarver, James L.
Walker, Scamp. *See* Crosby, Ronald Clyde
Walker, Scott. *See* Engel, Noel Scott
Walker, T-Bone. *See* Walker, Aaron Thibeaux
Walker, T-Bone, Jr. *See* Rankin, R. S.
Walker, T. S. *See* Bergmann, Walter Georg(e)
Walkin' Slim. *See* Minter, Iverson
Walking Encyclopedia of the Blues. *See* Burnett, Chester Arthur
Wall, Anton. *See* Heyne, Christian Leberecht
Wallace, Babe. *See* Wallace, Em(m)ett
Wallace, Beulah. *See* Thomas, Beulah
Wallace, Chester. *See* Trevor, Huntley
Wallace, Elmer. *See* Sawyer, Henry S.
Wallace, Flip. *See* Waller, Thomas Wright
Wallace, Frankie. *See* Marvin, Frank(ie) James
Wallace, Ken. *See* Marvin, John(ny) (Senator)
Wallace, King Babe. *See* Wallace, Em(m)ett
Wallace, Paul. *See* Solman, Alfred
Wallace, Raymond. *See* Hartley, Fred
Wallace, Raymond. *See* Reid, Willis Wilfred
Wallace, Raymond. *See* Trevor, Huntley
Wallace, Sippie. *See* Thomas, Beulah
Wallace, Zemira. *See* Crosby, Fanny [i.e., Frances] J(ane)
Wallbridge, Arthur. *See* Lunn, William Arthur Brown
Waller, Fats. *See* Waller, Thomas Wright
Waller, Kurt. *See* Lewald, (Johann Karl) August
Wallinger, Laird. *See* Cain, Noble
Wallington, Fay. *See* Pace, Adger McDavid
Wallington, George (Lord). *See* Figlia, Giacinto [or Giorgio] Wallington

Watson, Doc. *See* Watson, Arthel
Watson, Guitar. *See* Watson, John(ny)
Watson, John(ny G.). *See* Kluczko, John(ny)
Watson, Tom. *See* Slaughter, M(arion) T(ry)
Watson, Whitford. *See* Cobb, Will D.
Watson, Wilbur. *See* Fisher, William Arms
Watson, Young John. *See* Watson, John(ny)
Watt, Brian. *See* Kaufman, Isidore
Watters, Jeff. *See* Cook, J. Lawrence
Watters, Jeff. *See* Kortlander, Max
Watts, Clem. *See* Trace, Al(bert J(oseph))
Watts of Wales, The. *See* Williams (Pantycelyn), William
Wavell, Edward. *See* Ridges, E(dward) W(avell)
Waverly, Jules. *See* Cain, Noble
Wax, Artur. *See* Harrison, George
Waxman, Franz. *See* Wachsmann, Franz
Wayburn, Ned. *See* Weyburn, Edward Claudius
Wayditch, Gabriel. *See* Wajditsch Verbonac von Dönhoff, Gabriel
Wayne, Alan. *See* Johnson, Albertus Wayne
Wayne, Charles. *See* Jagelka, Charles
Wayne, Chuck. *See* Jagelka, Charles
Wayne, Don. *See* Choate, Donald (W(illiam))
Wayne, Edith. *See* Dozier, Lamont
Wayne, Edith. *See* Holland, Brian
Wayne, Edith. *See* Holland, Eddie
Wayne, Elmer. *See* Barnes, H(oward) E(llington)
Wayne, Elmer. *See* Fields, Harold (Cornelius)
Wayne, Elmer. *See* Roncoroni, Joseph (Dominic)
Wayne, Scotty. *See* Huerta, Baldemar G(arza)
Wayne, Thomas. *See* Perkins, Thomas (Wayne)
Wayside, (Willie). *See* Cole, Robert [or Bob] (Allen)
Weary, Ogdred. *See* Gorey, Edward (St. John)
Weary Willie. *See* Crow(e), Francis Luther
Weary Willie. *See* Kaufman, Jacob
Weary Willie. *See* Robison, Carson J(ay)
Weaver, Charley. *See* Arquette, Cliff(ord)
Weaver, Edward. *See* McKelvy, James (M(illigan))
Weavers, The. *See* Gilbert, Ronnie
Weavers, The. *See* Hays, Lee
Weavers, The. *See* Hellerman, Fred
Weavers, The. *See* Seeger, Pete(r R.)
Webb, B. F. *See* Gabriel, Charles H(utchinson)
Webb, Bernard. *See* McCartney, (James) Paul
Webb, Chick. *See* Webb, William (Henry)
Webb, F. R. *See* Gabriel, Charles H(utchinson)
Webb, Jack. *See* Webb, Willie Lee
Webb, Jay Lee. *See* Webb, Willie Lee
Webb, Malcolm. *See* Carmichael, Howard Hoagland
Webb, Numan. *See* Webb, Gary Anthony James
Webber, Lloyd. *See* Lloyd-Webber, William (Southcombe)
Weber, Ben. *See* Weber, William Jennings Bryan
Weber, Charles. *See* Dawson, Peter (Smith)
Weber, David. *See* Winterfeld, David Robert
Weber, E. S. *See* Henrich, C. W.
Weber, Friedrich Dionys(us). *See* Weber, Bedrich Divis
Weber, Henry. *See* Weber, C(arl) Heinrich
Weber, Johann. *See* Wircker, Johann
Weber, Miroslav. *See* Weber, Joseph
Webster, Eric. *See* Ross, William G.
Wechter, Cissy. *See* Wechter, Cecile Schroeder
Wedber, Friedrich Dionys. *See* Weber, Bedrich Divis
Wedgwood, John. *See* Connelly, Reg(inald)
Wee Wonder, The. *See* Moore, Dudley (Stuart John)
Weed, Buddy. *See* Weed, Harold Eugene
Weed, Gorgeous. *See* Phelps, Arthur
Weeder. *See* Burnard, Francis Cowley
Weedy, Garrod. *See* Gorey, Edward (St. John)
Weely. *See* Strayhorn, William [or Billy] (Thomas)
Weems, Ted. *See* Weymes, Wilfred Theodore
Wegman, Frank. *See* Cobb, George L(inus)
Wegrzynek. *See* Bakfark, Bálint (Valentin)
Weil, Milton. *See* McNamara, Charles F.
Weimar, Auguste. *See* Götze [or Goetze], Auguste
Weingeist, Reiner. *See* Müller, Rainer
Weinhausen, Fritz. *See* Stolz, Robert
Weinlinus, Josaphat. *See* Weinlein, Josaphat
Weisman, Ben. *See* Weisman, Bernard [or Bernie]
Weiss, Lutz. *See* Klaus, Gerhard
Weiss, Sylvius Leopold. *See* Ponce, Manuel (Maria)
Weisser, Samuel. *See* Pilderwasser, Joshua Samuel
Weissmann, John. *See* Schützer, János
Weitemher, Chasmindo von. *See* Dach, Simon
Welby, Mrs., of Kentucky. *See* Coppuck, Amelia (Ball)
Welch, Bruce. *See* Cripps, Bruce
Welch, Marilyn. *See* Cottle, Marilyn
Welch, Mitzie. *See* Cottle, Marilyn
Welch, Patrick. *See* Welch, Sidney Lester, Jr.
Welden, Friedrich. *See* Dilthey, Wilhelm (Christian Ludwig)
Welden, L. W. *See* Frangkiser, Carl (Moerz)
Weldon, Casey Bill. *See* Weldon, Wil(liam)
Weldon, L. W. *See* Frangkiser, Carl (Moerz)
Welish, Ernst. *See* Juraschek, Ernst Friedrich Wilhelm
Well-Wisher to the New Translation, A. *See* Cowper, William
Welldone, Count. *See* Saint Germain, Count of
Weller, A. *See* Müller, Johann Aug(ust) (Karl)
Weller, Freddy. *See* Weller, Wilton Frederick
Weller, Paul. *See* Weller, John William
Wellesley, Arthur. *See* Hughes, Arthur W(ellesley)
Wellesley, Garret. *See* Wesley, Garret (Colley)
Wellesley, Grant. *See* Zamecnik, J(ohn) S(tepan)
Wellings, Monte. *See* Gaul, Harvey B(artlett)
Wellington, Guy. *See* Yellen, (Jacob) Selig [or Zelig]
Wells, Amos. *See* Blackmore, Amos, (Jr.)
Wells, Channing. *See* Cain, Noble
Wells, Charley. *See* Robison, Carson J(ay)

Wells, Dicky [or Dickie]. *See* Wells, William
Wells, Gilbert. *See* Henderson, Gilbert
Wells, J. E. *See* Jewell, Fred(erick Alton)
Wells, Jack. *See* Wells, John Barnes
Wells, Junior. *See* Blackmore, Amos, (Jr.)
Wells, Kitty. *See* Deason, Muriel (Ellen)
Wells, Little Junior. *See* Blackmore, Amos, (Jr.)
Wells, Robert [or Bob]. *See* Levinson, Robert (Wells)
Wells, Roy. *See* Downey, Raymond J(oseph)
Welsh, George. *See* Dawson, Peter (Smith)
Wemba, Papa. *See* Wembadia, Shungu
Wendehals, Gottlieb. *See* Böhm, Werner
Wendel. *See* McCollin, Frances
Wendel, James. *See* Rusch, Harold (W(endel))
Wendra, Hans. *See* Plüter, Lothar
Wentworth, Lois. *See* Wagness, Bernard
Wentworth, Robert. *See* Kinsman, Elmer (F(ranklin))
Wenzel, Hesky. *See* Reisinger, Oskar
Werdenfels. *See* Klüter, Willy
Werfel, Wenzel. *See* Würfel, Václav Vilem
Werker, Gerard. *See* Paap, Wouter (Ernest)
Werlin, Paul. *See* Simon, Waldemar
Werly, C. *See* Czernik, Willy (Hermann)
Werner, Hans. *See* Blaze (de Bury), (Ange) Henri
Werner, Hans. *See* Blaze, Henri-Sebastien
Werner, Henry. *See* Balmer, Charles
Werner, Heinrich. *See* Friedmann, Heinrich
Werner, Max. *See* Rathgeber, Georg
Werner, Otto. *See* Krenkel, Gustav
Wernhard, Otto. *See* Ernst, II, Duke of Saxe-Coburg-Gotha
Wesley, Kid. *See* Wesley, Wilson
Wesling, Bob. *See* Daum, Norbert
Wessel, Henry. *See* Bliss, P(hilip) Paul
West, B. E. *See* Bliss, P(hilip) Paul
West, C(arl) A(ugust). *See* Schreyvogel, Joseph
West, C. P. *See* Wodehouse, P(elham) G(renville)
West, Charles. *See* Slaughter, M(arion) T(ry)
West, David. *See* Newell, Norman
West, Francis. *See* Krohn, Ernst (Ludwig)
West, Gene. *See* Carter, Barry Eugene
West, George. *See* Engel, Carl
West, Harold. *See* Wilson, Roger Cole
West, J. A. *See* Girouix(-West), Julie
West, John E. *See* Clough-Leighter, Henry
West, Joseph William. *See* Perazzo, Joseph William
West, Martin. *See* Wilson, John F(loyd)
West, Morgan. *See* Federer, Ralph
West, Moritz. *See* Nitzelberger, Moritz Georg
West, Speedy. *See* West, Wesley W(ebb)
West, Sydney [or Sidney]. *See* Rawlings, Charles Arthur
West, T. P. *See* Picardo, Thomas (R., Jr.)
West, Thomas [or Tommy]. *See* Picardo, Thomas (R., Jr.)
West, Thomas. *See* Schreyvogel, Joseph
Westbar, F. R. *See* Barnes, F. J.
Westbar, F. R. *See* Weston, R(obert) J.
Westbrook, Arthur. *See* Manney, Charles Fonteyn
Westcott, A. Whyte. *See* Heseltine, Philip (Arnold)
Westermann, Professor. *See* Almqvist, Carl Jonas Love [or Ludwig]
Western Gentleman, (The). *See* Phillips, Stu(art John Tristram)
Westminster Pilgrim, A. *See* Bridge, (Sir) (John) Frederick
Westmoreland, (John Fane) Earl of. *See* Fane, John
Weston, Dick. *See* Slye, Leonard (Franklin)
Weston, Gary. *See* Temkin, Harold (P.)
Weston, Morris. *See* Sawyer, Henry S.
Weston, Paul. *See* Wetstein, Paul (R., Jr.)
Weston, Philip. *See* De Filippi, Amedeo
Weston, Robert P. *See* Harris, Robert P.
Westover, Jessie. *See* Lincoln, Harry J.
Westring. *See* Coenen, Paul Franz
Westwood, Pat. *See* Squires, Edna May
Wetcheek, J. L. *See* Feuchtwanger, Lion (Jacob Arje)
Wetherell, Elizabeth. *See* Warner, Susan (Bogert)
Wey, Auguste. *See* Picher, Anna B.
Weymouth, Tina. *See* Weymouth, Martina (Michele)
Weysenbergh, (Johannes) Heinrich. *See* Weissenburg, Heinrich
Wezbrew, L. C. *See* Stark, John (Stillwell)
Whalen, Nat. *See* Lee, Albert George
Wheatley, G. W. *See* Beer, Gustav(e)
Wheatstraw, Little Peetie. *See* Hogg, Andrew
Wheatstraw, Peetie [or Pete]. *See* Bunch, William
Wheeler, Burt. *See* Harris, Robert P.
Wheeler, Paul. *See* Polewheel
Wheelwright. *See* McCollin, Frances
Whelan, Ekko. *See* Vincent, Nathaniel (Hawthorne)
Whipple, Zeb. *See* Clark, C(yrus) Van Ness
Whirling Dervish of Sex. *See* Presley, Elvis A(a)ron
Whisperin(g) Bill. *See* Anderson, (James) William [or Bill], (III)
Whispering Cornetist, The. *See* Fox, Roy (1901-1982)
Whispering Pianist, (The). *See* Gillham, Art
Whispering Tenor, The. *See* Lucas, Eugene
Whistler, Cadet. *See* McNeil, James
Whitcomb, George Walker. *See* Ostrom, Henry
Whitcomb, Ken. *See* Whitcup, Leonard
White, Alice. *See* Keiser, Robert (A(dolph))
White, Angela. *See* White, Erma (Marceline)
White, Barry. *See* Carter, Barry Eugene
White, Barry. *See* Kingston, Robert (Charles)
White, Billy. *See* Finkelstein, Abe
White, Bob. *See* Slaughter, M(arion) T(ry)
White Boy with the Colored Fingers, The. *See* Robinson, J. Russel(l)

White, Bucca [or Bukka]. *See* White, Booker T. Washington
White, Constance (V.). *See* Rawlings, Alfred William
White, Cool. *See* Hodges, John
White Duke, The. *See* Jones, David Robert (Hayward)
White, Eddie. *See* Fiorito, Ted
White, George. *See* Slaughter, M(arion) T(ry)
White, George. *See* Weitz, George
White Godfather of Black Music, The. *See* Dobrovolny, Frantisek
White, Grace. *See* Moore, Monette
White, Herbert. *See* Grey, Frank H(erbert)
White, Jack. *See* Nussbaum, Horst
White, Jerry. *See* Kaufman, Jacob
White, Joseph. *See* Delores, José Silvestre de los
White Man's Negro. *See* Perry, Lincoln (T(heodore Monroe Andrew))
White, Marty. *See* Weitzler, Morris Martin
White Negro. *See* Prokofiev, Serge
White, Norman. *See* Lewis, Al(an)
White, Norman. *See* Sherman, Al(bert)
White, Robert. *See* Slaughter, M(arion) T(ry)
White, Sam. *See* Fishman, Jack (1918 (or 19)-)
White, Slim. *See* Bernard, Al(fred A.)
White, Sonny. *See* White, Ellerton Oswald
White, Ted. *See* Weitz, Ted
White, Washington. *See* White, Booker T. Washington
White, Wilkie. *See* Franklin, Malvin Maurice
White Zulu, The. *See* Clegg, Johnny
Whitehall, David. *See* Savino, Domenico
Whiteman, Pops. *See* Whiteman, Paul
Whiteman, Roy. *See* Müller, Günther
Whitey, John. *See* White, John I(rwin)
Whitfield, Cyrus. *See* Bond, Cyrus Whitfield
Whitfield, Johnny. *See* Bond, Cyrus Whitfield
Whithorne, Emerson. *See* Whittern, Emerson
Whiting, Stanley. *See* Coffin, Lucius Powers
Whitlock, Billy. *See* Essex, Frederick
Whitlock, Walter. *See* Slaughter, M(arion) T(ry)
Whitman, Bert. *See* Whitman, Alberta
Whitman, Jerry. *See* Winters, June
Whitman, Slim. *See* Whitman, Ot(t)is (Dewey, Jr.)
Whitmore, Robert. *See* Lillenas, Haldor
Whitmore, Will. *See* Simon, Gustav(e) [or Augustus] (Edward)
Whitney, Joan. *See* Parenteau, Zoe
Whittaker, Hudson. *See* Woodbridge, Hudson
Whittaker, Tampa Red. *See* Woodbridge, Hudson
Whittlebot, Hernia. *See* Coward, Noel (Pierce)
Whitz, Chaim. *See* Klein, Gene
Whiz, The. *See* Wisner, James [or Jimmy] (Joseph)
Who, Ziggy. *See* Shelton, Larry Zane
Whyte, Henry. *See* Wright, Henry
Wick, Eugene. *See* Kountz, Richard
Wicked (Pickett), The. *See* Pickett, Wilson
Wide, Eric(h). *See* Widestedt, Ragnar
Widman, Eugen. *See* Hansson, Stig (Axel)
Wiebenga, Wiarda. *See* Pietzsch, Gerhard (Wilhelm)
Wiedensal, Uz. *See* Dressler, Rudolf
Wiegand, Henry. *See* Kraushaar, Charles
Wiesner, Fred. *See* Frankenberg, Franz
Wiest(ius), Paul. *See* Wüst, Paul
Wiggins, Pete. *See* Crow(e), Francis Luther
Wiggle Hips. *See* Presley, Elvis A(a)ron
Wiggs, Johnny. *See* Hyman, John Wigginton
Wihtol, Joseph [or Jasep(s)]. *See* Vitols, Jazeps [or Jasep(s)]
Wilber, Bill. *See* McCoy, Joe
Wilberforce, Wilber. *See* Wycherley, Ronald
Wilbur, Homer. *See* Lowell, James Russell
Wilbury, Boo. *See* Zimmerman, Robert Allen
Wilbury, Charlie T(ruscott). *See* Petty, Tom
Wilbury, Clayton. *See* Lynne, Jeff
Wilbury, Lefty. *See* Orbison, Roy (Kelton)
Wilbury, Lucky. *See* Zimmerman, Robert Allen
Wilbury, Muddy. *See* Petty, Tom
Wilbury, Nelson. *See* Harrison, George
Wilbury, Otis. *See* Lynne, Jeff
Wilbury, Spike. *See* Harrison, George
Wilcox, Pat. *See* Thomas, Hans
Wild Blue Yodeler, The. *See* Brine, Mark Vincent
Wild Child, The. *See* Miller, Roger Dean
Wild Man of Pop, The. *See* Hendrix, John(ny) Allen
Wild Man (of the Woods, The). *See* Granade, John A(dam)
Wildchild. *See* McKenzie, Roger
Wilde, Marty. *See* Smith, Reginald (Leonard)
Wilde(r)mere, Henry. *See* Petrie, H(enry) W.
Wilden, Gert [or Gerd]. *See* Wychodil(-Hofmeister), Gert
Wilden, Trude. *See* Wychodil(-Hofmeister), Gert
Wildengen, Uffo von. *See* Zitzmann, Heinrich Gottfried
Wilder Brothers. *See* Weidler, George William
Wilder Brothers. *See* Weidler, Walter Wolfgang
Wilder Brothers. *See* Weidler, Warner Alfred
Wilder, George. *See* Weidler, George William
Wilder, John. *See* Ireson, John Balfour
Wilder, Walt(er). *See* Weidler, Walter Wolfgang
Wilder, Warner. *See* Weidler, Warner Alfred
Wildman, Charles. *See* Mattes, Wilhelm [or Willy]
Wild(e)roe, Philip de. *See* Wilder, Philip van
Wildwave, Willie. *See* Delaney, William (M.)
Wildwood, Charlie. *See* Hammond, Samuel Leroy
Wiley, Pete. *See* Wiley, Charles A.
Wilford, C. *See* Lockton, Edward F.
Wilhelm. *See* Müller, Marcellus
Wilhelm, Friedrich. *See* Meymott, Frederick William

Willie the Lion. *See* Smith, William [or Willie] (Henry Joseph Berthol Bonaparte)
Willie the Rock. *See* Hyman, Richard [or Dick] (R(oven))
Willing, Foy. *See* Willingham, Foy
Willis, Chick. *See* Willis, Robert L.
Willis, Chuck. *See* Willis, Harold
Willis, Edward. *See* Plessow, Erich
Willis, Guy. *See* Willis, James
Willis, J. A. *See* Bliss, P(hilip) Paul
Willis, J. H. *See* Hewitt, John (Henry) Hill
Willis, Little Son. *See* Willis, Aaron
Willis, Mac. *See* Willis, Aaron
Willms, (Friedrich). *See* Andersen, Lale
Willoughby, Peter. *See* Wilhousky, Peter J., Jr.
Willow, Ray. *See* Wierzbowski, Ray(mond Lawrence)
Wills, Carlo. *See* Glahé, Will(y Karl-Adolf)
Wills, Louis Magrath. *See* McGregor, Edward
Wills, Nat M. *See* McGregor, Edward
Wills, Reginald. *See* Soloman, Mirrie (Irma)
Willy. *See* Colette, Sidonie Gabrielle Claudine
Willy. *See* Gauthier-Villars, Henri
Willy, Colette. *See* Colette, Sidonie Gabrielle Claudine
Wilma Ann. *See* Lowers, Wilma Ann
Wilmans, Wilman. *See* Fisher, William Arms
Wilson. *See* Haenschen, Walter (G(ustave))
Wilson, Arthur. *See* Blitz, Leo(nard)
Wilson, Arthur. *See* Butler, Ralph (T.)
Wilson, Bishop. *See* Wilson, Ira B(ishop)
Wilson, (Mrs.) C(arrie) M. *See* Crosby, Fanny [i.e., Frances] J(ane)
Wilson, Chris. *See* Wilson, Richard Harvey
Wilson, Crane. *See* O'Brien, Cyril C(ornelius)
Wilson, Grant. *See* Brown, Bob
Wilson, Hank. *See* Bridges, (Claude) Russell
Wilson, Kid. *See* Wilson, Wesley
Wilson, Lawrence. *See* Miller, Robert [or Bob] (Ernst)
Wilson, Lee. *See* Beach, Albert A(skew)
Wilson, Leola (B.). *See* Pettigrew, Leola (B.)
Wilson, Margaret Chalmers. *See* Hood, Margaret Chalmers
Wilson, Norro. *See* Wilson, Norris D.
Wilson, Paul. *See* Carlin, Sidney (Alan)
Wilson, Paul. *See* Sterrett, Paul
Wilson, Peanuts. *See* Wilson, Johnny Ancil
Wilson, Pinky [or Pinkie]. *See* Wilson, J(ames) V(ernon)
Wilson, R. A. *See* Keiser, Robert (A(dolph))
Wilson, Rob. *See* Royer, Robb
Wilson, Sandy. *See* Wilson, Alexander Galbraith
Wilson, Slugger. *See* Wilson, Earl (L.), Jr.
Wilson, Socks [or Sox]. *See* Wilson, Wesley
Wilson, Walter. *See* Lewis, Al(an)
Wilson, Walter. *See* Sherman, Al(bert)
Wilson, Walter. *See* Silver, Abner
Wilström, Kalle. *See* Mattes, Wilhelm [or Willy]
Wilton, Arthur. *See* Hall, Joseph Lincoln
Wilton, Jerry. *See* Wycholdil(-Hofmeister), Gert
Wil(l)trie, H. B. *See* Petrie, H(enry) W.
Wil(l)trie, H. B. *See* Wilson, Ira B(ishop)
Wimmer, Friedrich. *See* Told, Franz Xaver
Winar, Jurij. *See* Wiener, Georg
Winbrun, O. *See* Winawer [or Winaver], Bruno
Winchester, Tom. *See* Morse, Theodore (F.)
Winchester, Tom. *See* Williams, Spencer
Wincott, Harry. *See* Walden, Alfred [or Arthur] J.
Wind, Blasius. *See* Mentner, Karl
Wind, Hans E. *See* Blaukopf, Ehepaar Kurt
Wind, Jay. *See* Wind, Juergen
Windeatt, George. *See* Mayerl, William [or Billy] (Joseph)
Windham, Basil. *See* Wodehouse, P(elham) G(renville)
Windsor, Basil. *See* Smith, Eli
Windsor, Richard. *See* Ehret, Walter (Charles)
Wing, Bobby. *See* Weidler, Warner Alfred
Wingard, Bud. *See* Wingard, James Charles
Winlaw, Maurice. *See* Mullen, Frederic
Winn, Jack. *See* Mills, Irving
Winn, Mary Elfrieda. *See* Scruggs, Mary Elfrieda
Winn, Mary Lou. *See* Scruggs, Mary Elfrieda
Winsloe, Thornton. *See* Krenek, Ernst
Winsten, Mark. *See* Samuels, Milton (Isadore)
Winston. *See* Schindler, Hans
Winston Cool. *See* Thompson, (James) Winston
Winter, Charles. *See* Cain, Noble
Winter, Fred. *See* Njurling, Sten
Winter, Herbert. *See* Ellingford, Herbert Frederick
Winter, Laurent. *See* Brault, (Robert) Victor
Winter, Mark. *See* Cacavas, John
Winter, (Sister) Miriam Therese. *See* Winter, Gloria Frances
Winter, N(orbert). *See* Wüsthoff, Klaus
Winter, Robert. *See* Winterfeld, David Robert
Winterberger, (Martin). *See* Kessler, Robert von
Wintergreen, John P. *See* Ryskind, Morrie
Winters, Ferne. *See* Lillenas, Haldor
Winters, Horace. *See* Kaufman, Isidore
Winters, Jack. *See* Talent, Leo (Robert)
Winters, John (S.). *See* Wintersteen, John Schaeffer
Winther, Bob. *See* Hering, Hans
Winthrop, (J. R.). *See* Murray, James R(amsey)
Winthrop, Robert. *See* Weintrop, Chaim Reuben [or Reubin]
Wiquardus. *See* Pickar, Arnold
Wire, Nick(y). *See* Jones, Nicholas (Allen)
Wirtz, Charles Louis. *See* Wirth, Carel Lodewijk Willem
Wise, Chubby. *See* Wise, Robert Russell
Wise, Penny. *See* Fisher, Doris
Wiseman, Ben. *See* Weisman, Bernard [or Bernie]
Wiseman, Myrtle Eleanor. *See* Cooper, Myrtle Eleanor
Wittstatt, Pepe. *See* Wittstatt, Hans(-Artur)

– X –

– Y –

Ye Comic. *See* Blackmar, A(rmand) E(dward)
Ye. Nosenko. *See* Kollontay [or Kollontai] (Yermolayev), Mikhail Georgiyevich
Ye Tragic. *See* Augustin, John Alcée
Yehoash. *See* Bloomgarten, Solomon
Yellen, Jack. *See* Yellen, (Jacob) Selig [or Zelig]
Yellowman. *See* Foster, Winston
Yenbad, Eporue. *See* Daubney, Ford (T.)
Yenbad, Eporue. *See* Europe, James Reese
Yester, Jerry. *See* Tree, Joshua
Yijak. *See* Hindemith, Paul
Yimuheli, S. *See* Milakowski, Pinchas
Yo Yo. *See* Whitaker, Yolanda
Yodelin' Hobo. *See* Carlisle, Cliff(ord Raymond)
Yodel(l)in' Slim Dallas. *See* Turner, Dallas (E.)
Yodeling Cowboy, The. *See* Edwards, Eric (Charles)
Yodeling Cowboy, The. *See* Rodgers, James [or Jimmie] (Charles)
Yodeling Cowgirl, (The). *See* Blevins, Ruby(e) (Rebecca)
Yodeling Jackaroo, The. *See* Taylor, Harold [or Harry]
Yodeling Ranger, The. *See* Snow, Clarence Eugene
Yodelling Boundary Rider, The. *See* Lane, Robert William
Yoffe, Shlomo. *See* Yoffe, Solomon
Yondraschek, Alfons. *See* Mey, Reinhard
Yorkston, James. *See* Rawlings, Charles Arthur
Youmans, Millie. *See* Youmans, Vincent
Young, Billy. *See* Junsch, William Colin
Young, Bobby. *See* Samberg, Benjamin
Young, Charles. *See* Barnes H(oward) E(llington)
Young, Charles. *See* Fields, Harold (Cornelius)
Young, Charles. *See* Roncoroni, Joseph (Dominic)
Young Dixie. *See* Hays, Will(iam) S(hakespeare)
Young, Donny [or Donnie]. *See* Lytle, Donald Eugene
Young Englishman, The. *See* Lamotte, Franz [or François]
Young, Errol. *See* Box, Harold Elton
Young, Errol. *See* Keuleman Adrian
Young, G(eo.) R. *See* Bliss, P(hilip) Paul
Young Gentleman of Seventeen, A. *See* Pitman, Ambrose
Young, Gordon. *See* Galbraith, Gordon
Young Gotti. *See* Brown, Ricardo
Young, Jesse Colin. *See* Miller, Perry
Young, Johnny. *See* De Jong, John
Young Kitchener. *See* Roberts, Aldwyn [or Aldwin]
Young, Larry. *See* Aziz, Khalid Yasin Abdul
Young, Lolita. *See* Frangkiser, Carl (Moerz)
Young, Man. *See* Young, John(ny) O.
Young, master of ceremonies. *See* Young, Marvin
Young, Marvin. *See* Kaufman, Isidore
Young, MC. *See* Young, Marvin
Young, Rida Johnson. *See* Johnson, Ida R.
Young, Rusty. *See* Young, Norman Russell
Young Sheriff, (The). *See* Young, Faron
Young Singer of Old Songs, The. *See* Jones, Louis M(arshall)
Young Spaniard, The. *See* Lacy, Michael Rophino
Young, Trummy [or Trummie]. *See* Young, James (Osborne [or Oliver])
Young Whitefield. *See* Newton, John
Young Wolf, The. *See* Jenkins, Gus
Younger, Marc. *See* Yablonka, Marc (Phillip)
Youngest Interlocutor in the World, The. *See* Thomas, Lillian [or Lillyn]
Youngest Violin Player in the World, The. *See* Ray, (Lyman) Wade
Youth, The. *See* Zimmerman, Robert Allen
Yrvid, Richard. *See* Ivry, Paul Xavier Désiré, marquis d'
Yu. A. *See* Arnol'd, Yury (Karlovich)
Yulya. *See* Whitney, Julia (A.)
Yupanqui, Atahualpa. *See* Chavero, Héctor (Roberto)
Yvolde. *See* Moul, Alfred

– Z –

Z. G. *See* Riegger, Wallingford (Constantin)
Zaa, Charlie. *See* Sánchez(-Ramírez), Carlos Alberto
Zachary, Tony. *See* Franchini, Anthony Joseph
Zacher, Walter. *See* Zacharias, Walter
Zaffira, Leon. *See* Rawlings, Alfred William
Záhorský, Pavol. *See* Zavarský, Ernest
Zaito, Nico. *See* Zai, Michael
Zák, Benedikt. *See* Schack, Benedikt
Zak, Pyotr. *See* Bradshaw, Susan
Zak, Pyotr. *See* Keller, Hans
Zaljaznjak, A. *See* Valicki, Aljaksandr
Zalva, George L. *See* Cruikshank, George L(ouis) Zalva
Zamácola, Juan Antonio. *See* Iza Zmácola, Juan Antonio
Zamrzla. *See* Kovarovic, Karel
Zanardino, Lo. *See* Zanardi, Niccolò
Zano, (A(nthony)) (J(oseph)). *See* Ferrazano, Anthony Joseph
Zanobi, Marco. *See* Gagliano, Marco da
Zany, King. *See* Dill, Jack
Zaret, Hy [or Hi]. *See* Stirrat, William Albert
Zasta. *See* Rinne, Hanno
Žavcanin. *See* Kočevar, Ferdo
Zaytz, Giovanni von. *See* Zajc, Iván
Zazzerino, Il. *See* Peri, Jacopo
Zé Dantas. *See* Dantas (Filho), José de Sousa
Zé Povo. *See* Villa-Lobos, Heiter
Ze Roberto. *See* Bertrami, José Roberto
Zebisch, Toni. *See* Amper, Quirin (1908-1989)
Zéde, (Monsieur). *See* Dezède, Nicolas
Zeeden, Peter. *See* Schmidt, Gerhard

Zeeden, Peter. *See* Schmitz, Robby
Zeffirelli, Franco. *See* Corsi, Gian Franco
Zeilbeck, E. *See* Kark, Frederik
Zélide. *See* Charriére, Isabella (Agneta Elisabeth) de
Želinský, Arian. *See* Sabina, Karel
Zell, F(riedrich). *See* Wälzel, Camillo
Zendorius a Zendoriis. *See* Beer, Johann
Zenta, Herman(n). *See* Holmes, Augusta Mary Anne
Zergo, Fred. *See* Strübe, Hermann
Zerine. *See* Gyldmark, Hugo
Zerol, Vačlav. *See* Hansson, Stig (Axel)
Zeuner. *See* Gordigiani, Luigi
Zeuner, Charles. *See* Zeuner, Heinrich Christoph(er)
Zeuta, Hermann. *See* Holmes, Augusta Mary Anne
Zevon, Warren. *See* Livotovsky, Warren
Zevotovsky, Warren. *See* Livotovsky, Warren
Zezinho. *See* Silva, José Barbosa [or B(atista)] (da)
Zh(i)ui. *See* Jouy, (Victor Joseph) Etienne (de)
Zhurbin, Ljova. *See* Zhrubin, Lev
Zidek, Paulus. *See* Paulirinus, Paulus
Ziegfeld of the Jewish Stage, The. *See* Yablonik, Herman [or Hyman]
Zilak, Gert. *See* Geitz, Karl Heinrich
Zilia. *See* Wieck, Clara Josephine
Zimmer, Friedrich. *See* Rische, Quirin
Zimmerman, Zimmy. *See* Zimmerman, Charles A.
Zimmermann, B. *See* Bermann, Moritz
Zimmermann, Karl. *See* Sugarman, Harry
Zimmermann, Winfried. *See* Benzin, Winfried
Zina, Miss. *See* Galás, Dimitria Angeliki Elena
Zinsstag, Adolf [or Dolf]. *See* Yvoire, Claude
Zipoli. *See* Corrette, Michel
Ziska, Leopoldine. *See* Pontifex, Clara de
Zit. *See* Zittel, C. Florian
Zito, Torrie (A.). *See* Zito, Salvatore (Albert)
Zittel, Zit. *See* Zittel, C. Florian
Zittner, Wenzel. *See* Mosch, Ernst
Zminský, Emanuel. *See* Meli(š), Emanuel (Anton)
Zol—ffer. *See* Hastings, Thomas
Zoller, Bettye. *See* Volkart, Bettye Sue
Zolotaryov, Vasily Andreyevich. *See* Kuyumzhi, Vasily Andreyevich
Zombie, Rob. *See* Cummings, Robert
Zondrios, Kalvos. *See* Báthory-Kitsz, Dennis
Zoot, Jack. *See* Sims, John Haley
Zorin, A. *See* Cherniavskii, A(leksandr)
Zorro. *See* Giannini, Guglielmo
Zorzisto, Luigi. *See* Strozzi, Giulio
Zorzisto, Luigo. *See* Bisaccioni, (Conte) Maiolino
Zotti, Carlo. *See* Croal, George
Zozimus. *See* Moran, Michael
Ztiworoh, Drahcir. *See* Horowitz, Richard (Michael)
Zuane. *See* Albinoni, Tomaso Giovanni
Zuccamana, Dolly. *See* Zuccamana, Gizelle Augusta
Zuccarelli, (Signor). *See* Champein, Stanislas
Zuccherino. *See* Zuccari, Carlo
Zucchero. *See* Fornaciari, Aldelmo
Zucker, Otto. *See* Justis(s), William [or Bill] (E(verette?)), (Jr.)
Zuckermann, (Gizelle) Augusta. *See* Zuccamana, Gizelle Augusta
Zuckermann, Gussie. *See* Zuccamana, Gizelle Augusta
Zulli, Arthur de. *See* Allen, Euphemia (Amelia)
Zunftmeister Violoncello. *See* Lincke, Joseph
Zuschauer, F(reimund). *See* Rellstab, (Heinrich Friedrich) Ludwig
Zuylen, Belle van. *See* Charriére, Isabella (Agneta Elisabeth) de
Zweibel. *See* Hoffmann, Heinrich
Zweifel, Sergey. *See* Tsveifel', Sergey Petrovich
Zwyssig, Alberich. *See* Zwyssig, Joseph
Zybal, Roman. *See* Rabe, Gerhard

Chapter 4
Notes

AMBROSIO, W. F.

"W. F. Ambrosio" is a Carl Fischer house name used on "for hire" compositions and arrangements by Gustav Saenger, J(ulius) S. Seredy and Edmund Severn.

To date the following compositions have been identified:

Saenger, Gustav

"Aida, Grand March," by Verdi; arr. W.F.A. (CCE33 R24506)
"Air de Ballett, op.18 #4," arr. W.F.A. (LCRC34 R32383)
"Angel's Serenade," arr. W.F.A. (CCE33 R24514)
"Annie Laurie," arr. W.F.A. (CCE33 R27013)
"Berceuse," by B. Godard; arr. W.F.A. (CCE33 R24509)
"Cavaleria Rusticana," by P. Mascagni; arr. W.F.A. (CCE33 R24512)
"Cavatina," arr. W.F.A. (LCRC35 R39206)
"Celebrated Nocturne," arr. W.F.A. (LCRC35 R39209)
"Cradle Song," arr. W.F.A. (CCE33 R24513)
"Danse Grotesque, op. 18, #6 ," arr. W.F.A. (LCRC34 R32384)
"Fantaisie Caprice," arr. W.F.A. (LCRC35 R39208)
"Flower Song," arr. W.F.A. (LCRC33 R24510)
"Gavotte," by J. Gossec; arr. W.F.A. (CCE37 R58499)
"Gavotte, from 'Mignon,'" by C. Thomas; arr. W.F.A. (CCE33 R24508)
"Kuiawiak," by H. Wieniawski; arr. W.F.A. (CCE33 R24511)
"Largo," by G. F. Handel; arr. W.F.A. (CCE37 R55493)
"Legends," arr. W.F.A. (LCRC35 R39210)
"Londonderry Air," arr. W.F.A. (CCE37 E62523)
"Metodo per lo studio de pianoforte," by B. Cesi; ed. & trans. W. F. A. (CCE37 R56620)
"Menuet, op. 18, #5," arr. W.F.A. (LCRC34 R32382)
"Pas de fleurs from 'Naila,'" by C. Delibes; arr. W.F.A. (CCE37 R5595)
"Pas de Sylphs.op. 18, #3," arr. W.F.A. (LCRC34 R32381)
"Poem," by Z. Fibich; arr. W.F.A. (CCE37 E63595)
"Polka Gracieuse, op. 81 #2," arr. W.F.A. (LCRC34 R32380)
"Les Rameaux," by G. Faure; arr. W.F.A. (CCE33 R25310)
"Reverie," arr. W.F.A. (LCRC35 R39207)
"Rocked in the Cradle of the Deep," arr. W.F.A. (CCE33 R25731)
"Salut d'amour," by E. Elgar; arr. W.F.A. (CCE37 R55509)
"Scene de ballet," by C. Beriot; arr. W.F.A. (CCE33 R25309))
"Simple aveu," arr. W. F. A. (LCRC35 R39205)

"Song to the Evening Star," by R. Wagner; arr. W.F.A. (CCE37 R63580)
"Spring Song," by F. Mendelssohn; arr. W.F.A. (CCE33 R25312)
"Il Trovatore, Anvil Chorus," by G. Verdi; arr. W.F.A. (CCE33 R24507)
"Valse, op. 18 #1," arr. W.F.A. (LCRC R32379)
"Wearing of the Green," arr. W.F.A. (CCE33 R25730)

Seredy, J(ulius) S.

"Blue Danube," by Johann Strauss, violin & piano; arr. W.F.A (CCE41 #21449 E94722)
"Blue Danube," by Johann Strauss, violin, cello, piano; arr. W.F.A. (CCE41 #21450 E94721)
"Practical Method for the Bassoon" (CCE41 #24941 E95204)

Severn, Edmund

"Andantino," by E. H. Lamare; arr. W.F.A. (CCE36 E58028)
"La cinquantane," by Gabriel-Marie," arr. W.F.A. (CCE36 E57309)
"Deep River, violin & piano," arr. W.F.A. (CCE36 E58029)
"Eili, Eili, violon & piano," arr. W.F.A. (CCE36 E58025)
"Hatikwoh, violin & piano," arr. W.F.A. (CCE36 E58017)
"Kol nidre, violin. & piano," arr. W.F.A. (CCE36 E58016)
"The Merry Widow," by F. Lehar; arr. W.F.A. (CCE36 E58030)
"Military March," by F. Schubert; arr. W. F. A. (CCE36 E58031)
"Poupee valsante," by E. Poldini; arr. W. F. A. (CCE36 E57308)

Additional Works by "W. F. Ambrosio"

"Aloha oe Farewell to Thee" (CCE17 E403159; CCE43 R116963)
"Carnival of Venice," arr. W. F. A. (CCE42 R111188; CCE44 R132839)
"Cavatina," by Carl Bohm; arr. W. F. A. (CCE38 R65282)
"Chant du nord," by G. Lange; arr. W. F. A. (CCE42 R110626)
"Christmas Joys in Verse & Song," arr. W. F. A. (CCE1908 C194435)
"Cellists Solo Album (CPMU; publication date :1946)
"Country Gardens; Handkerchief Dance" (CCE1933)
"Encore," violin & piano (CPMU; publication date :1945)
"Famous Waltz," violin & piano" 1926 (CPMU)
"52 Russian Folksongs," 2 violins & piano 1921 (CPMU)
"Five Characteristic Impressions, op. 102," by J. Sibelius; arr. W. F. A.. (CPMU; publication: 1925)
"Forest Whisper," violin & piano, by F. Losey; arr. W. F. A. (CCE41 R9935)
"Gavotte," by F. Gossec (CCE40 R85451)
"Hejre kati," by Jeno Hubay (CCE38 R65284)
"The Herd-girls Dream," by A. Labitsky (CCE40 R85452)
"Hungarian dance #5 & #6," by Brahms (CCE38 R65285-86)
"Impromptu and scherzo," violin & piano, by Cecil Burleigh; arr. W. F. A. (CCE38 R70416)
"Intermezzo, from 'Cavalleria Rusticana,'" by Mascagni; arr. W. F. A. (CPMU; publication date:1925)
"Love in Idleness" (CCE39 R78394)
"Meditation," violin & piano, by J. S. Bach; arr. W. F. A. (CCE38 R65287)
"Melody," by A. Rubinstein (CCE38 R65288)
"Miniature Masterpieces," violin & piano (CPMU; publication date :1939)
"Norwegian Dance op. 35 #2," arr. W. F. A. (CPMU; publication date :1929)
"Obertass Mazurka, op. 19," by Henri Wieniawski; arr. W. F. A. 1912 (CPMU)
"On Wings of Song," violin & piano, by Mendelssohn; arr. W. F. A. (CCE56 R168182)
"Operatic Favorites," arr. W. F. A. (CPMU; publication date :1913)
"Playful Rondo," by W. Green; arr. W. F. A. (CCE38 R69496)
"Religious Meditations" (CPMU; publication date :1925)
"Serenade," by Franz Drdla; arr. W. F. A. (CCE38 R65292)

"Serenade," by F. Schubert; arr. W. F. A. (CCE38 R65294)
"Souvenir," by Franz Drdla; arr. W. F. A. (CCE38 R65295)
"Twenty-five Melodious & Characteristic Studies for Violin" (CPMU; publication date :1910)
"Violin Virtuoso; A Collection" (CPMU; publication date :1924)
"Woodland Echoes," violin & piano, by Addison P. Wyman; arr. W. F. A. (CPMU)

CARLTON, JOHN

"John Carlton" is a pseudoym used by Walter Ehret alone and also as a joint pseudonym with each of the following individuals: Elmer (F(ranklin)) Kinsman, Lee Kjelson, Travis Shelton, and Harold (Stillwell) Stark.
To date the following titles have been identified:

Ehret, Walter

"Agnus Dei," by Michael Haydn; arr. J. C. (LCCF76 E361596)
"All Glory Be To God" (LCCF57 E110623)
"Five Chorales from 'St. John Passion'" by J. S. Bach; arr. J. C. (LCCF60 E137699)
"Forth from Jesse Sprang a Rose" (CPOL RE-472-666)
"God So Loved the World" (CCE76 359253)
"Great Lord God! Thy Kingdom Shall Endure" (LCCF75 E43281)
"He Watching Over Israel" (LCCF58 E119608)
"Hear Us, Lord" (CPOL RE-472-668)
"How Lovely Shines the Morning Star" (LCCF E192236)
"If By His Spirit," by J. S. Bach; arr. J. C. (CPOL RE-295-608)
"If Ye Love Me, Keep My Commandments," by T. Tallis; arr. J. C. (LCCF58 E119602)
"Is There Anybody Here?" (CPOL RE-473-075)
"Lamb of God," by G. Verdi; arr. J. C. (LCCF 1955-70 E150755)
"Lo, My Shepherd Is Divine" (CPOL RE-435-636)
"Magnificat," by J. Pachelbel; arr. J. C. (CCE77 E376584)
"Now Thank We All Our God," by J. S. Bach; arr. J. C. (CCE77 E370735-6)
"O Jesus Christ, Saviorof All" (LCCF76 361593)
"O Lord, Correct Me" (CPOL RE-435-647)
"O Rejoice, Ye Christian Loudly" (CPOL RE-576-061)
"Open the Gates of the Temple" (CPOL RE-235-985; LCCF57 E108339)
"Praise Him" (LCCF58 E121608)
"Sanctus and Hosanna," by F. Schubert; arr. J. C. (CPOL RE-376-415)
"Thou Must Leave Thy Lovely Dwelling" (CPOL RE-472-672)
"Three Chorales from the 'Saint Matthew Passion,'" by J. S. Bach; arr. J. C. (CPOL RE-235-734)
"Two Bach Chorales," by J. S. Bach; arr. J. C. (CPOL RE-473-081)
"With Joyful Voice" (LCCF75 E34481)

Kinsman, Elmer (F(ranklin)) & Walter Ehret

"The Song of Mary" (CPOL RE-435-675)
"Two Wings" (CPOL RE-435-677)

Kjelson, Lee & Walter Ehret

"Cherubim Song (CPOL RE-378-977)

Shelton, Travis & Walter Ehret

"Jesu, nimm deiner Glieden," by J. S. Bach; arr. J. C. (CCE55 E92524)
"O Rejoice, Ye Christians, Loudly" (CPOL RE-163-333)

Stark, Harold (Stillwell) & Walter Ehret

"If You Love Me Keep My Commandments" (CCE59; CPOL RE-296-436)

CHAMBERS, ROBERT

"Robert Chambers" is a pseudoym used by Walter Ehret alone and also as a joint pseudonym with each of the following individuals: Elmer (F(ranklin)) Kinsman, Jack Lyall, Walter Rodby and Ivan Trusler. To date the following titles have been identified:

Ehret, Walter

"How Lovely Shines the Morning Star" (CPOL RE-576-082)
"Now Let the Heavens be Joyful" (CCE63 E171094)
"Sing To the Lord" (LCCF69 E263864)

Kinsmanm, Elmer F(ranklin)) & Walter Ehret

"All That Has Life and Breath" (CCE60 E146631; CPOL RE-378-985)
"As Joseph Was A-Walking" (CPOL RE-295-609)
"A Babe Is Born" (CPOL RE-296-435)
"Bow Down Thy Ear O Lord" (CCE62 E162859; CPOL RE-472-663; CPOL RE-529-371)
"A Child Is Born in Bethlehem" (CCE63 E176609; CPOL RE-379-009)
"Come, Let Us All This Day" (CCE63 E176537; CPOL RE-379-007)
"Hares on the Mountains" (CPOL RE-378-983)
"Is There Anybody Here?" (CCE63 E170867; CPOL RE-473-075)
"Lord Most High" (CCE64)
"The Shepherdess" (CPOL RE-435-464; CPOL RE-473-074)
"Sing Unto the Lord Most High", by Pergolesi, arr. R. C. (CCE63 E184236; CPOL RE-575-849)
"The Song of Mary" (CPOL RE-435-675)
"To Spring" (CPOL RE-435-636)
"Two Wings" (CPOL RE-435-677)
"The World Itself is Bright and Gay" (CPOL RE-376-406)

Lyall, Jack & Walter Ehret

"Now Mine Eyes Are Grown Dim" (CPOL RE-295-235)

Rodby, Walter A. & Walter Ehret

"Let Their Celestial Concerts All Unite" (CPOL RE-378-986)

Trusler, Ivan & Walter Ehret

"On This Day To Us Is Born" (CCE63 E177065; CPOL RE529-374)

DANA, ARTHUR

"Arthur Dana" is an Arthur P. Schmidt Co house name used on "for hire" compositions and arrangements by H. R. Austin, Alfonso Cipollone, Otto (Christoph) Hackh, Willy Hermann, Frank Lynes, Hugo (Svan) Norden, Arnoldo Sartorio, Max Schultze, Charles P(hillip) Scott, R(oy) S(paulding) Stoughton, and Paul Zilcher.

To date the following titles have been identified:

Austin, H. R.

"Christ Victorious, by F. Maker, new words & adapted A. D. (CCE43 #3806 E111440; CCE70 R486280)
"Dance of the Sugar Plums" (CCE41 #34957 E97028; CCE68)
"The Glad Earth Yields, by Arthur Berridge; arr. A. D. (CCE42 #6175 E101254)
"Three Carols;" arr. A. D. (LCCF40 E88150)
"Two Responses," by J. Sibelius & P. Tchaikowsky; arr. A. D. (CCE42 #4401 E101255)

Cipollone, Alfonso

"Fairy Life" (CCE36 R46750)
"Maravilla" (CCE E341936)

Hackh, Otto (Christoph)

"At the Sea-Shore, op. 30 no. 6" (CCE24 R27744)
"Carnival Galop, op. 30 no. 2" (CCE24 R27740)
"Christmas Tree March, op. 30 no. 12" (CCE24 R27750)
"Easter Thoughts, op. 30 no. 4" (CCE24 R27742)
"Hunting Song, op. 30 no. 10" (CCE24 R27748)
"Moonlight in the Forest, op. 30, no. 8" (CCE24 R27746)
"On the Meadow, op. 30, no. 7" (CCE24 R27745)
"Returning from Vacation, op. 30, no. 9" (CCE24 R27747)
"Sleighriding, op. 30 no.1" (CCE24 R27739)
"Snowbells, op. 30 no. 3" (CCE24 R27741)
"Spring Song, op. 30 no. 5" (CCE24 R27743)
"Thanksgiving Hymn, op. 30 no. 11" (CCE24 R27749)

Hermann, Willy

"Champagne, op. 14" (CCE23 E566189)
"Evening" (CCE27 E672270)
"The Flowers All Sleep Soundly," arr. A. D. (CCE32 E27535)
"Hark! The Lark," by F. Schubert; arr. A. D. (CCE39 #3767 E74301)
"Hawthorn Blossoms" (CCE27 E672178)
"The Linden Tree," by F. Schubert; arr. A. D. (CCE28 E111)
"Vesper Hymn," by D. Bortniansky; arr. A. D. (CCE52 R98507-09)

Lynes, Frank

"Abide With Me," mixed voices (CCE37 R22950)
"Abide With Me," song (CCE32 R19182)
"Music Box, op. 135," by B. Godard; arr. A. D. (CCE26 R3248)
"On the Playground, op. 693, no. 11," by F. Behr; arr. A. D. (CCE28 R33678)
"On Vacation, op. 693, no. 2," by F. Behr; arr. A. D. (CCE28 R33679)
"Thistledown, op. 54, no. 3" (year & number not recorded)

Norden, Hugo (Svan)

"Blow, Blow, Thou Winter Wind," by. J. Sarjeant; arr. A. D. (CCE53 E73009; CPOL RE-102-185)

Sartorio, Arnoldo

"Moonlight in the Forest, op. 30, no.8" (CCE14 E338595)

Schultze, Max

"Christmas Tree March," (In: "The Seasons," no. 12) (CCE14 E338596)

Scott, Charles P(hillip)

"Arpeggio Studies, op. 27" (CCE27 R41667)
"The Butterfly (Schmellerting)," by G. Merkel, op. 81, no. 4; ed. A. D. (CCE26 R33688)
"The Dot," (In: "The Pupil's First Etude Album") (CCE28 R68)
"The Flowers All Sleep Soundly," arr. A. D., op.19, no. 1" (CCE32 E27535)
"March of the Dryads, op. 31, no. 2" (CCE24 R26262)
"The Meadow Brook, op. 4," by Gustav Wartenstein, rev. A. D. (CCE26 R35396)
"O Lord, How Happy Should We Be" (CCE24 E596495)
"Procession of the Elves, op. 31, no. 1" (CCE24 R26261)
"The Tie," (In: "The Pupil's First Etude Album") (CCE28 R69)
"The Wood Nymph's Wedding March, op. 31, no. 3" (CCE24 R26263; CCE26 R35399)

Stoughton, R(oy) S(paulding)

"Lift Up Your Hearts," by Jean Sibelius; arr. A. D. (CCE40 #13350 E84210)
"Lift Up Your Hearts," by Jean Sibelius; arr. A. D. (CCE41 #36151 E97030)
"Sleep On, op. 19, no. 3," arr. A. D. (CCE42 E101253)
"Three Carols," arr. A. D. (CCE67 R424416)

Zilcher, Paul

"In Colonial Days" (collection)
"Gossipers" (CCE26 E643111)
"A Graceful Minuet" (CCE26 E643112)
"Indian Canoe" (CCE26 E643115)
"Lovely Nancy" (CCE26 E643109)
"Minute Men" (CCE26 E643110)
"The Old Spinning Wheel" (CCE26 E643108)
"Paul Revere" (CCE26 E643114)
"Thanksgiving Song" (CCE26 E643117)
"The Wooden Cradle" (CCE26 E643113)

Additional Works by "Arthur Dana"

"Alpine Rose" (CCE08 #19127)
"Fairy Gavotte" (CCE08 #19544)
"O All Ye Works of God" (CCE46 #3724)
"Olivia, valse de salon," piano (CCE08 #20321)
"Serenade espagnole" (CCE24 E601664 #26037) (pub. by APS?)
"Wake Thou My Soul" (CCE45 E132966 #62954)

DOUGLAS, WAYNE

"Wayne Douglas" is a pseudoym used by Wayne Douglas Broze, Walter Ehret, Edward J. Penney and Fred Weber. To date the following titles have been identified:

Broze, Wayne Douglas

"Songs Written by Mark Allison & Wayne Douglas" (CPOL PAu-1-848-484)
"Wayne Douglas Collection" (CPOL PAu-2-082-082)

Ehret, Walter

"All Glory Be to God" (LCCF57 E110623)
"All Glory, Laud and Honor" (CPOL RE-642-675; LCCF60 E139883)
"All Mighty God, We Worship Thee" (LCCF64 E183331; LCCF64 E182723)
"All Night, All Day" (LCCF61 E147895; LCCF62 E162938; LCCF64 E183335; LCCF66 E215854)
"Ave Maria," by B. Amon; arr. W. D. (CCE65 E199753)
"Be Thou Exalted, by G. F. Handel; arr. W. D." (CCE75 E336794)
"Blessed Are They That Always Keep Judgement" (LCCF57 E106682)
"Bow Down Thine Ears," by P. Tchaikovsky; arr. W. D. (LCCF55 E88712)
"Bright and Joyful Is the Morn" (CCE75 E336796)
"Canon Alleluia!" (LCCF76 E350598)
"Child in the Manger" (LCCF61 E147892; LCCF62 E162784)
"Climbin' up the Mountain" (CCE65 E197313)
"Come, Ye Lowly, Come, Ye Lowly" (LCCF63 E171371)
"Come Your Hearts and Voices Raising" (LCCF74 E322847)
"Comfort, O Lord," by W. Crotch; arr. W. D. (CCE55 E88969)
"Cotton Needs Pickin'" (LCCF67 E226259)
"Crown Him with Many Crowns" (CCE63 E171359)
"Darkness Was Over All," by M. Haydn; arr. W. D. (CPOL RE-670-992; LCCF66 E216278)
"Deep River" (LCCF77 E365744)
"The Fox" (LCCF70 E271568)
"Give Praise Unto the Lord" (LCCF76 E350624)
"Glorious Be Thy Name Forever," by H. Farmer; arr. W. D. (CCE55 E88714)
"Go Where I Send Thee" (LCCF61 E147885; LCCF61 E147890)
"Hail the Holy Infant" (LCCF74 E322846)
"Help Us, O God" (LCCF76 E350599)
"Hosanna," by C. Gregor; arr. W. D. (CCE65 E201153; LCCF62 E162786; LCCF66 E212392)
"I Bow in Prayer before Thee" (LCCF70 E271569)
"In Heav'nly Love Abide" (LCCF76 E350590)
"Jesus, Word of God Incarnate," by C. Gounod; arr. W. D. (LCCF57 R105211)
"Joseph Tender, Joseph Mine" (LCCF62 E162785; CCE65 E199761)
"Katrina's Wedding Day" (LCCF61 E14876; LCCF62 E162785)
"Kyrie Eleison," by G. Palestrina; arr. W. D. (CPOL RE-676-037; LCCF66 E216277)
"Let Us Now Our Voices Raise" (LCCF76 E350594)
"The Little Pig" (LCCF70 E271567)
"The Lord Is Great" (LCCF59 E128024)
"Michael Finnigin" (LCCF76 E350596)
"Now Let Us Sing" (LCCF77 E365733)
"Now Sing in Exultation" (CPOL RE-641-159; LCCF77 E365755)
"Now Sing We Now Rejoice," by Praetorius; arr. W. D. (CCE65 E199752)
"O Who Will Come and Go with Me?" (LCCF77 E365732)
"Old Ship of Zion" (LCCF62 E162949)
"Praise Ye the Lord," by P. Ivanoff; arr W. D. (CCE55 E87742)
"Safe in Thy Manger" (LCCF74 E323405)
"Shepherds in the Fields A-Watching" (LCCF74 E322848)
"Sing Praises to God" (LCCF76 E350623)
"Souls of the Righteous ," by T. T. Noble; arr. W. D. (CCE55 E87729)
"This Is the Birthday of the Lord" (CCE75 E225802)
"To Thee in Song" (CCE63 E173676)
"Treble Chorister" (LCCF61 E150148)
"Wake Up! Jacob" (LCCF68 E240612)
"When My Rich Husband Is at Home" (LCCF63 E173639)
"When Our Lord Was Born" (LCCF70 E271565
"When the Saints Go Marching In" (CCE65 E199750
"A Zulu King" (LCCF64 E185877)

Penney, Edward J., Jr.

"Little Dreamer" (CCE66)
"Moonlight Baby" (CCE66)
"Someone Else's Arms" (CCE67 Eunp990861)

Weber, Fred

"The Belwin Band Builder" (CCE53; CCE57; CPOL RE-97-808; REHG; SUPN)

EASTBURN

"Eastburn" is a pseudoym used by Joseph E. Winner and Septimus Winner. The following titles were identified in Harry Dichter & Elliott Shapiro's *Early American Sheet Music* (New York: R. R. Bowker, 1941).

Winner, Joseph E.

"The Little Brown Jug," (Philadelphia, 1869)

Winner, Septimus

"Died in the Streets"
"Friends of Our Early Days"
"The Little Homeless One"
"Meet Me with a Kiss"
"Never Censure"
"Planchette"
"Vanished Dreams"
"Sallie of the Dell"
"We Have Met, Loved and Parted"
"When the Shadows of Evening Had Fallen"

EATON, M. B.

"M. B. Eaton" is a pseudoym used on compositions by George D(aniel) Barnard, George D. Hofmann, and Will(iam H.) Scouton.

To date the following titles have been identified:

Barnard, George D(aniel)

"Cynthia Mazurka" (CCE28 R44671; REHG)
"Imperial Overture," for orchestra (CCE26 R35607)
"Irenya Mazurka" (REHG)
"Ormaz Schottische" (REHG)
"Our Companions" (REHG)
"Rosedale Waltz," for band (CCE30 R74; REHG)
"Viva Polka" [or "Polka Viva"?] (CCE28 R44680; REHG)

Hofmann, George D.

(Identified in TPRF; however, no title(s) given.)

Scouton, Will(iam H.)

(Identified in TPRF; however, no title(s) given.)

EDWARDS, JULIAN

"Julian Edwards" is a pseudoym used by D'Auvergne Barnard on works published by B. F. Woods. To date the followining titles have been identified:
"Cuckoo in the Woods, op. 15, no. 6" (CCE45 #8173, 45, R135280)
"Evening bells, op. 15, no. 2" (CCE45 #8173, 61, R135276)
"Harvest song, op. 15, no. 7" (CCE45 #8173, 101, R135281)
"Hunter's horn, op. 15, no. 1" (CCE45 #8173, 120, R135275)
"Shadow Dance, op. 15, no. 3" (CCE45 #8173, 255, R135277)
"Six Very Easy Duets, op. 16" (CCE49 R55303)
"Twilight Story, op. 15, no. 4" (CCE45 #8173, 302, R135278)
"Woodland Frolic, op. 15, no. 5" (CCE45 #8173, 341, R135279)
"Young Warriors, op. 15, no. 8" (CCE45 #8173, 344, R135282)

ERICH, CARL

"Carl Erich" is an Arthur P. Schmidt Co. house name used on "for hire" compositions and arrangements by William Baines, Albert Biehl, Arthur (William) Foote, H. R(ichard) Krentzlin, Hugo (Svan) Norden, Edmund Parlow, and Charles P(hillip) Scott.

To date, the following compositions have been identified:

Baines, William

"Country Gardens" (CCE32 E31792; CCE62 R288404)

Biehl, Albert

"Alla Turca," by W. Mozart; arr. C. E. (CCE22 R20505)
"Bridal March, from 'Lohengrin,'" by R. Wagner; arr. C. E. (CCE22 R20502)
"Elegie," by W. Ernest, arr. C. E. (CCE22 R19906)
"Hungarian Dance," by J. Brahms; arr. C. E. (CCE23 R23675)
"Impromptu, op. 142, no. 2" by F. Schubert; arr. C. E. (CCE16 R8229)
"Invitation and Dance," by C. Weber; arr. C. E. (CCE22 R20503)
"Marche Militaire," by F. Schubert; arr. C.E. (CCE22 R19907)
"Mazurka, no. 2" (CCE23 R23676)
"Melancolia," by Prume; arr. C. E. (CCE21 R19422)
"Menuett, from 'Symphony in E-flat,'" by W. Mozart; arr. C. E. (CCE21 R19429)
"Merry Party, op. 174, no. 4," arr. C. E. (CCE25 R30700)
"Nocturne,op. 9, no. 2," by F. Chopin; arr. C. E. (CCE16 R8230)
"Radetzky March," by R. Strauss; arr. C. E. (CCE22 R20504)
"Rakoczy March," by H. Berlioz; arr. C. E. (CCE21 R19432)
"Romance," by A. Rubenstein; arr. C. E. (CCE23 R23666)
"Spanish Dance," by Moszkowski; arr. C. E. (CCE23 R23647)
"Spinnerlied, from 'Fliegende Hollander,'" by R. Wagner; arr. C. E. (CCE23 R23665)
"Turkish March," by L. Beethoven; arr. C. E. (CCE22 R20506)

Foote, Arthur

"Minuet, from 'Don Giovanni,'" by. W. A. Mozart; arr. C. E. (CCE22 R19954)
"Minuten walzer," by F. Chopin; arr. C. E. (CCE22 R19953)
"Moment musicale," by F. Schubert; arr. C. E. (CCE22 R19955)

Krentzlin, H. R(ichard)

"Minuet," by Beethoven; arr. C. E. (CCE48 R37681)

Lynes, Frank

"Intermezzo, from 'Cavaleria Rusticanna,'" by P. Mascagni; ed. C. E. (CCE32 R20355)
"O Holy Night," by Adolf Adam; arr. C. E. (CCE41 #26816, 524 R95622)

Norden, Hugo (Svan)

"Minuet in F," by Mozart; arr. C. E. (CCE48 27205)

Parlow, Edmund

"Chansons san Paroles by P. Tchaikovsky; arr. C. E. (CCE51 R80513)
"Habanera, from 'Carmen,'" by G. Bizet; arr. C. E. (CCE47 R24252)
"Humoreske, op. 111, no. 7," by A. Dvorak; arr. C. E. (CCE41# 47874, 91 R101523)
"Serenata," by M. Moszkowski; arr. C. E. (CCE22 E539809; CCE49 R49638)
"Valse Gracieuse," by P. Tchaikovsky; arr. C. E. (CCE22 E539808; CCE49 R9637)

Scott, Charles P(hillip)

"Gipsy Rondo," by J. Haydn; arr. C. E. (CCE49 R50787)
"Toreador Song, from 'Carmen,'" by G. Bizet; arr. C. E. (CCE30 R11705)

Additional Work by "Carl Erich"

"Bright Flowers" (CCE21)

FETCHIT, STEPIN

"Stepin Fetchit" is a pseudoym used by Lincoln (T(heodore Monroe Andrew)) Perry and Whelock Alexander Bisson.
To date the following compositions have been identified:

Bisson, Whelock Alexander

"Dancin' Bill Bo'jangles" (CCE55 Eunp409211)
"David Crocket Boogie, The" (CCE55 Eunp397893; CPOL RE-157-668)
"Father of the Blues" (CCE58 Eunp537387)
"(New Way) Cra-a-a-a-a-zy" (CCE53 Eunp331608; CPOL RE-95-937)
"Defiant One, The" (CCE59 Eunp565511)

Perry, Lincoln (T(heodore Monroe Andrew))

"Dig Mr. Cool" (CCE65 Eunp916030)
"Mr. Cool" (CCE65 Eunp916029)
"Puttin' It Down" (CCE45 #52098 Eunp433549)

FIELD, ROBERT

"Robert Field" is a pseudoym used by Walter Ehret alone and also as a joint pseudonym with Ivan Trusler.
To date the following titles have been identified:

Ehret, Walter

"Angelus ad pastorale cit" (CPOL RE-576-083)
"Blessed Are They" (CPOL RE-295-607)

"Confitemini Domini" (CCE64 E196123; CPOL RE-576-205)
"Four Arms, Two Necks, One Wreathing" (LCCF65 E200175)
"Hallelujah," by Handel; arr. R. F. (LCCF59 E131385)
"Hence, Care, Thou Art Too Cruel" (LCCF64 E184243)
"Hodie Christus Natus" (CCE64 E192238)
"Holy, Holy, Holy," by J. S. Bach; arr. R. F. (CPOL RE-529-377)
"Hosana to the Son of David" (LCCF64 E189991)
"Jesu, Joyaunce of My Heart" (CPOL RE-576-205)
"Jesus, Fount of Consolation" (CPOL RE-576-213)
"Jubilate Deo," by Orlando di Lasso; arr. R. F. (LCCF63 E180673)
"Lift Up Your Heads, Ye Gates" (CCE75 E337552)
"O Savior Mine, What Agony" (CPOL RE-576-214)
"O Spotless Lamb" (CPOL RE-576-209)
"Oh Lord Most Holy" (CPOL RE-576-211)
"The Sweet Bells of Christmas" (CPOL PA-3-427)
"Thou Art So Weak, So Frail, So Helpless" (CPOL PA-7-027)
"Unlatch the Bolt that Locks the Door" (CCE75 E339022
"Weep, O Mine Eyes" (CPOL RE-576-210)
"Weep, Weep, Weep, Mine Eyes" (LCCF64 E196134)

Trusler, Ivan & Walter Ehret

"Requiem, op. 48," by Faure; arr. R. F. (CPOL RE-483-993; LCCF62 E160727)

FISCHER, CARL

"Carl Fischer" is a pseudoym used by Charles H(utchinson) Gabriel on the following works:
"All Things to Me" (CCE34 R29832)
"The Cross" (CCE36 R46296)
"The Cross Will Be the Glory Song" (CCE34 R29835)
"Everything for Jesus" (CCE37 R29397)
"Eye Hath Not Seen" (CCE44 #51525, 94 R133919)
"Fight the Good Fight" (CCE36 R46200)
"Go Tell Them" (CCE34 R29405)
"The Guiding Light" (CCE34 R29830)
"He Never Broke a Promise" (CCE42 #29091, 22 R108773)
"I Tell Jesus all About It" (CCE36)
"I'm in His Hands" (CCE41 #34470, 165 R98508)
"Into Thy Hand" (CCE33 R2713)
"Jesus Is All You Need" (CCE33R27183)
"Little Evangels" (CCE34 R29404)
"Little Sowers" (CCE34 R29813)
"Lost and Found" (CCE36 R46202)
"My Hope Is Stayed on Thee" (CCE42 R108775)
"Sing the Christmas Song" (CCE40 #25244, 236 R88855; YORK)
"Singing for Jesus" (CCE34 R29820)
"Stand Fast in Jesus" (CCE37 R57882)
"'Tis Sweet to Know" (CCE33 R27374)
"Waiting for You" (CCE37 R58981)

FOLLETT, CHARLES

"Charles Follett" is a pseudoym used by Walter Ehret alone and also as a joint pseudonym with Elmer (F(ranklin) Kinsman.

To date the following titles have been identified:

Ehret, Walter

"Angels from the Realms of Glory" (LCCF67 E226238)
"Blessed Infant, Thou" (LCCF60 E146533)
"Choirs of Angels" (LCCF60 E146277; LCCF66 E215852)
"Cleanse Me" (LCCF77 E365747)
"Come to the Manager" (CCE65 E203043)
"Fare You Well" (LCCF74 E323386)
"Hark! A Thrilling Voice Is Sounding" (LCCF66 E218813)
"Hear Ye Now the Joyful Tidings" (LCCF61 E147872)
"Holy, Holy" (LCCF76 E350593)
"How Sweet Is the Voice of My Lord" (LCCF76 E350622)
"I Come to Thee, Jesus" (CCE75 E336587)
"The King of Love My Shepherd Is" (CCE75 E336800)
"The Lights Are Bright at Christmas" (LCCF73 E309801)
"The Lord is My Shepherd" (LCCF61 E147884)
"Low in the Grave He Lay" (LCCF66 E218811)
"My Song Is Love Unknown" (LCCF66 E218819)
"O Thou, Who Through This Holy Week," attributed to H. Purcell; arr. C. F. (LCCF66 E218809)
"O'er Bethlehem a Star Is Shining" (LCCF73 E311462)
"Praise Ye the Father" (LCCF61 E147881)
"Rise and Shine" (LCCF66 E215849)
"The Spell of Christmas" (LCCF67 E226241)
"Such a Gay and Happy Tune" (LCCF76 E350583)
"Then Shall the Righteous Shine Forth" (LCCF77 E365728)
"There Is a Name I Love to Hear" (LCCF77 E365727)
"Three-Part Singer" (LCCF65 E213616)
"Thy Loving Kindness" (LCCF77 E365726)
"'Tis Noel Again" (LCCF76 E350604)
"Today Above the Sky He Soared" (LCCF66 E212388)
"We Praise Thee, O God" (LCCF74 E323385)
"We Walk Through the Meadow" (LCCF76 E350615)
"Whom Did Ye See Ye Shepherds?" (LCCF74 E322843)

Kinsman, Elmer (F(ranklin)) & Walter Ehret

"Ain't It a Shame?" (CCE63 171331)
"Babylon's Falling" (CCE68 E24278)
"Come to the Manger" (CCE65 E203043; CPOL RE-653-885)
"Gloucestershire Wassail" (CCE64 E185878)
"Go Down, Moses" (CCE68 E242788)
"Goin' to Sing" (CCE62 E184037)
"His Praises We'll Sing" (CCE62 E163483; CCE64 E183327)
"In Bethlehem City" (CCE64 E185881)
"I've a Jolly Sixpence" (CCE68 E242946)
"Library of Song for Male Voices, Bks. 1-5" (CCE65 E198997, CCE65 E198913; CCE65 E201528, CCE65 E201529, CCE65 E201530)
"Listen to the Angels Shoutin'" (CCE62 E162023)
"No Hiding Place Down There" (CCE62 E162024)
"O Worship the Lord" (CCE63 E171337)
"Rise and Shine" (CCE64 E183336)
"Saviour, Like a Shepherd Lead Us" (CCE64 E183337)
"Sing, O Sing This Blessed Morn" (CCE62 E162905)
"When the Shepherds Heard the Angels" (CCE65 E199762)

GORDON, HUGH

"Hugh Gordon" is an A. P. Schmidt Co. house name used on "for hire" compositions and arrangements by Hugo (Svan) Norden, Bruno Reibold and Charles P(hillip) Scott.
To date, the following titles have been identified:

Norden, Hugo (Svan)

"Alla Marcia" (CCE46 E2929)
"Allah" (CCE47 E16638)
"Asleep in the Manger" (CCE45 E136108)
"Be Strong in the Lord" (CPOL RE-66-279)
"Blessed Be the Name of the Lord" (CPOL RE-102-159)
"Carnival of the Flowers" (CCE53 E69903)
"Come to the Luteplayers House" (CCE53 E69902)
"Enthroned in Light" (CCE53 E70501)
"Hark! The Voice of Love and Mercy" (CCE46 E1732; CCE53 E72185)
"Joyful Hearts We Bring To Thee" (CCE53 E72184)
"The Lamb" (CCE75 R608885)
"Lamb of God" (CPOL RE-102-184)
"Maestroso e scherzando, from 'Das wohltemperirte Clavier,'" by J. S. Bach; arr. H. G. (CCE53 E68565)
"O Blessed Lord, Thy Truth" (CCE53 E71693)
"Remember God's Goodness" (CCE46 E2928)

Reibold, Bruno

(Identified in TPRF; however, no title(s) given.)

Scott, Charles P(hillip)

"Be Still, Be Still" (CCE46 E4776)

GREYSON, NORMAN

"Norman Greyson" is a pseudoym used by Walter Ehret alone and also as a joint pseudonym with Melinda Edwards, and also with Harry Robert Wilson.
To date the following titles have been identified:

Ehret, Walter

"At Evening" (CCE65)
"Autumn" (CCE65)
"Dies sanctificatus" (CPOL RE-529-009)
"Echo Song" (LCCF77 E366315)
"Gloria Patri" (LCCF75 E345538)
"Hail, Hail, Play and Song" (LCCF77 E376450)
"Which Is the Properest Day to Sing?" by T. Arne; arr. N. G. (LCCF77 E363002)

Edwards, Melinda & Walter Ehret

"Farewell Song," by J. Brahms; arr. N. G. (CPOL PA-96-753)
"The Lark," by F. Mendelssohn; arr. N. G. (CPOL PA-101-788)
"The Lucky Ones," by F. Mendelssohn; arr. N. G. (CPOL PA-57-064)
"No, I Cannot Bear the Folk Who Love to Tattle" (CPOL PA-57-060)
"The Primrose" (LCCF77 E366500)

"Song of Spring," by F. Mendelssohn; arr. N. G. (LCCF77 E363002)
"Tell Me, Maiden," by Brahms; arr. N. G. (CPOL PA-91-566)
"The Trees Are Blooming in the Vale," by F. Mendelssohn; arr. N. G. (CPOL PA-59-324)

Wilson, Harry Robert & Walter Ehret

"Adoramus te," by A. Clement; arr. N. G. (CPOL RE-114-954)
"Adoramus te," by G. Corsi; arr. N. G. (CPOL RE-234-473)
"Adoramus te," by G. Palestrina; arr. N. G. (CPOL RE-234-469)
"Agnus Dei," by H. Hassler; arr. N. G. (CPOL RE-114-953)
"Agnus Dei," by T. Morley; arr. N. G. (CPOL RE-335-405)
"Ah, Love, I Laugh While Singing," by H. Hassler; arr. N. G. (CPOL RE-623-623)
"Ah, May the Sun" (CCE62 E16323; CPOL RE-488-956)
"Alas, My God," by C. Jannequin; arr. N. G. (CPOL RE-754-091)
"All Happiness Love Gives To Me" (CCE62 E162083; CPOL RE-497-664)
"All Ye People" (CCE69 E256604)
"All Ye Who Music Love" (CPOL RE-497-660)
"Almighty and Everlasting God," by O. Gibbons; arr. N. G. (CPOL 335-434)
"Almighty God Who Hast Me Brought" (CPOL RE-234-468)
"At Evening," by R. Volkmann; arr. N. G. (CCE65 E196801; CPOL RE-571-987)
"Autumn" by A. Gretchaninoff; arr. N. G. (CCE65 E196802; CPOL RE-571-988)
"Ave Maria," by J. Arcadelt; arr. N. G. (CPOL RE-114-955)
"Ave Maria," by G. Fogliano; arr. N. G. (CPOL RE-659-512)
"Ave Maria Stella" (CCE62 E163524; CPOL RE-483-668)
"Ave verum," by J. Des Pres; arr. N. G. (CPOL RE-659-520)
"Ave verum corpus" by W. Byrd; arr. N. G. (CPOL RE-335-406)
"Behold, I Shall Die This Day," by Gesualdo; arr. N. G. (CPOL RE-754-104)
"The Bells of Speyer," by L. Senfl; arr. N. G. (CPOL RE-623-621)
"Call To Remembrance" (CPOL RE-234-467)
"Call To Remembrance," by R. Farrant; arr. N. G. (CPOL RE-659-511)
"Cantate Domino" (CPOL RE-121-772)
"Cantate Domino" (CPOL RE-234-477)
"Cantata Domino" by G. Pitoni; arr. N. G. (CCE62 E162873; CPOL RE-121-774; CPOL RE-335-426)
"Cantata Domino," by H. Hassler; arr. N. G. (CPOL RE-234-477)
"Cantata Domino," by H. Schutz (CPOL RE-335-427)
"Change Me, O Heavens," by J. Wilbye; arr. N. G. (CPOL RE-659-519)
"Charm Me Asleep" (CPOL PA-57-063)
"Come, Let Us Start a Joyful Song" (CPOL RE-234-488)
"Come, Let Your Hearts be Singing" (CPOL RE-234-470)
"Come Now, Let Us Be Joyful" (CCE62; CPOL RE-497-661)
"Come, Sing This Round with Me" (CPOL RE-234-481)
"Counterpoint of the Animals" (CPOL RE-335-432)
"The Cuckoo," by L. Lemlin; arr. N. G. (CPOL RE-659-513)
"The Cuckoo Has Met His Death" (CPOL RE-754-102)
"The Dance," by F. Schubert; arr. N. G. (CCE65 E196800; CPOL RE-571-986)
"Dancing and Springing" (CPOL RE-121-766)
"The Dawn," by C. Cui; arr. N. G. (CCE65 E196799; CPOL RE-571-985)
"Echo Song," by O. Di Lasso; arr. N. G. (CPOL RE-234-494)
"Ego sum panis vivus," by W. Byrd; arr. N. G. (CPOL RE-659-517)
"The Evening," by J. Brahms; arr. N. G. (CCE65 E196798; CPOL RE-571-984)
"Exultate Deo," by A. Scarlatti; arr. N. G. (CPOL RE-335-429)
"Fair Maid, Thy Charm and Loveliness" (CPOL RE-335-430; CPOL RE-754-101)
"Fair One, Who Holds My Life," by T. Arbeau; arr. N. G. (CPOL RE-754-100)
"Farewell To the Wood," by F. Mendelssohn; arr. N. G. (CCE65 E196797; CPOL RE-572-053)
"The Fields Abroad," by T. Morley; arr. N. G. (CPOL RE-659-515)

"Fire, Fire My Heart" (CPOL RE-488-954)
"From the Depth of Sin," by W. Byrd; arr. N. G. (CPOL RE-623-620)
"The Gentle Heart," by J. Brahms; arr. N. G. (CCE65 E196796; CPOL RE-572-052)
"Gloria Patri" (CPOL RE-335-418; CPOL RE-501-987)
"Good Day My Dear" (CPOL RE-335-436 & RE-754-099)
"Happy and Gay" (CPOL RE-234-483)
"He Is Good and Handsome" (CPOL RE-335-433)
"He Who Hath Joy in Music" (CPOL RE-754-098)
"I Can Not Conceal It," by P. Certon; arr. N. G. (CPOL RE-335-424)
"I Say Adieu" (CPOL RE-623-617)
"In Autumn," by J. Brahms; arr. N. G. (CCE65 E196795; CPOL RE-572-051)
"In nomine Jesu," by J. Handl; arr. N. G. (CPOL RE-623-622)
"In Praise of Spring," by F. Mendelssohn; arr. N. G. (CCE65 E196794; CPOL RE-572-050)
"In These Delightful Pleasant Groves," by H. Purcell; arr. N. G. (CPOL RE-234-480)
"In This House of Softened Splendor" (CCE65 E196793; CPOL RE-572-049)
"Jesu, dulcis memoria," by T. DeVictoria; arr. N. G. (CPOL RE-335-428)
"Laughing So Heartely," by A. Willaert; arr. N. G. (CPOL RE-659-522)
"A Little White Hen," by A. Scandello; arr. N. G. (CPOL RE-235-980)
"Look Down, O Lord" (CCE62; CPOL RE-488-955)
"Lord, Hear My Prayer" by W. Byrd; arr. N. G. (CPOL RE-754-092)
"Lullaby, My Sweet Little Baby" (LCCF76 E353661)
"The Maiden" (CPOL PA-66-609)
"Matona, Lovely Maid," by O. Di Lasso; arr. N. G. (CPOL RE-335-437)
"May Song," by F. Mendelssohn; arr. N. G. (CCE65 E196792; CPOL RE-572-048)
"Maybe 'Tis Aye, Maybe 'Tis No" (CPOL RE-754-097)
"Morning Song," J. Brahms; arr. N. G. (CCE65 E196791; CPOL RE-572-047)
"My Bonny Lass," by T. Morley; arr. N. G. (CPOL RE-335-423)
"My Heart with Love Is Springing" (CPOL 335-404)
"My Lady, Thou Art So Fair" (CPOL RE-659-514)
"Night, Lovely Night" (CCE65 E196790; CPOL RE-572-046)
"The Nightingale" (CCE62; CPOL RE-483-667)
"Noel, a Child from Heaven Now Is Born" (CPOL RE-754-090)
"O bone Jesu" (CPOL RE-335-421; CPOL RE-624-275)
"O Come Ye Servants of the Lord," by C. Tye; arr. N. G. (CPOL RE-240-204)
"O Cross We Hail," by G. Palestrina; arr. N. G. (CPOL RE-754-093)
"O Death, I Come To Thee Now" (CPOL RE-335-419)
"O felix anima" (CCE62; CPOL RE-497-662)
"O filii et filiae," by V. Leisring; arr. N. G. (CPOL RE-240-207)
"O God of Life Above" (CPOL RE-754-094)
"O Jesu Christe" (CCE62; CPOL RE-483-666)
"O Lord God, Forgive My Sins," by O. Di Lasso; arr. N. G. (CPOL RE-754-089)
"O Lovely May," by J. Brahms; arr. N. G. (CCE65 E196789; CPOL RE-572-045)
"O magnum mysterium," by T. DeVictoria; arr. N. G. (CPOL RE-240-211)
"O Rex glorie" (CPOL RE-624-276)
"O Sacred and Holy Feast," by G. Palestrina; arr. N. G. (CPOL RE-754-095)
"O Thoughts which Tear Apart My Life" (CPOL RE-670-241)
"O'er the Mountains and the Valleys," by A. Arensky; arr. N. G. (CPOL PA-66-608)
"On This Day, Saint Joseph Brought Us," by F. Guerrero; arr. N. G. (CPOL RE-670-245)
"Plorate filii Israel," by G. Carissimi; arr. N. G. (CPOL RE-335-435)
"Popule meus," by T. DeVictoria; arr. N. G. (CPOL RE-670-242)
"The Pretty Vines and Roses" (CPOL RE-624-278)
"Psallite," by Praetorius; arr. N. G. (CPOL RE-290-205)
"Reflection," by J. Brahms; arr. N. G. (CPOL PA-57-062)
"Regina coeli," by P. Philips; arr. N. G. (CPOL RE-670-243)
"Rejoice in the Lord Always" (CPOL RE-624-277)

"Resonet in laudibus" (CPOL RE-121-771)
"The Return of Springtime," by C. LeJeune; arr. N. G. (CPOL RE-670-244)
"Share We Regrets" (CPOL RE-754-096)
"The Silver Swan" (CPOL RE-121-767)
"Since I Cannot Forget" (CPOL RE-624-279)
"Sing, Sing a Song for Me," by O. Vecchi; arr. N. G. (CPOL RE-335-431)
"The Swallow," by J. Brahms; arr. N. G. (CCE65 E196788; CPOL RE-572-044)
"Sweet Love Doth Now Invite," by J. Dowland; arr. N. G. (CPOL RE-121-768; CPOL RE-335-425)
"They Who Grieving Soweth" (CCE62; CPOL-RE-483-658)
"This Day," by A. Dvorak; arr. N. G. (CPOL RE-572-043)
"This Sweet and Lovely Siren," by G. Gastoldi; arr. N. G. (CPOL RE-659-518)
"To Yon Fair Grove" (CPOL RE-335-420)
"Tristis est anima mea," by G. Naso; arr. N. G. (CPOL RE-659-521)
"Trust," by R. Schumann; arr. N. G. (CCE65 E196786; CPOL RE-572-042)
"Up Sprang a Birch Tree," by A. Dvorak; arr. N. G. (CCE65 E196785; CPOL RE-572-041)
"Verbum caro," by G. Palestrina; arr. N. G. (CPOL RE-659-516)
"Vere languores nostros" (CPOL RE-114-958)
"We Adore Thee" (CPOL RE-754-088)
"We Be Three Poor Mariners and We Be Soldiers Three" (CPOL RE-121-763)
"Weep O Mine Eyes" (CPOL RE-240-540)
"Which Is the Properest Day?" (CPOL RE-114-958)
"While the Bright Sun" (CCE62; CPOL RE-497-663)
"Who Could be More Filled with Grief," C. Sermisy; arr. N. G. (CPOL RE-754-103)
"With Drooping Wings" (CCE62; CPOL RE-483-669)

Additional Works by "Norman Greyson"

"Grant Us Peace, O Lord," by M. Franck; arr. N. G. (CPOL PA-284-548)
"Have Mercy Upon Me, O God" (CPOL PA-142-844)
"It Was a Lover and a Lass," by T. Morley; arr. N. G. (CPOL PA-346-586)
"Kyrie elison, from Mass IV," by G. Palestrina; arr. N. G. (CPOL PA-207-873)
"O Domini Jesus Christe," by G. Palestrina; arr. N. G. (CPOL PA-346-586)
"O Sing unto the Lord," by H. Purcell; arr. N. G. (CPOL PA-43-820)

HANSON, ERIC

"Eric Hanson" is a pseudoym used by Albert Oliver Davis, Elizabeth Wahr and Carl F. Ludwig. A reference card in the Library of Congress Card File (LCCF) 1955-70 explains the usage of "Eric Hanson" in catalog records for the works of Davis and Wahr. Since Wahr requested her identity not be disclosed (26 Jume 1953 letter cited), her works are cataloged under the name "Eric Hanson, pseud.," with no mention of her name. Davis' works are cataloged under his name with information concerning the use of the pseudonym "Eric Hanson" listed in either the statement of responsibility or a note. The works listed below by Davis and Wahr were identified using these guidelines. Works composed by Carl F. Ludwig are cataloged under his name with information concerning the use of "Eric Hanson" in either the statement of responsibility or a note.

Davis, Albert Olive

"Cathedral Canyon" (published by Ludwig Music) (CCE55 E89619)
Note: In REHH listed under Elizabeth Fennell [i.e., Wahr].
"Green Meadows" (published by Ludwig Music) (CCE53 E72250)
Note: In REHH listed under Elizabeth Fennell [i.e., Wahr].
"Pleasant Valley," (published Ludwig Music) (LCCF1946-54 E79698)
"The Whistling Boy," (published Kjos) (CCE54 E79174; REHH)

Wahr, Elizabeth C.

Note: Married names: Mrs. Carl F. Ludwig (married 1955); later Mrs. Frederick Fennell (married 1986). The works listed below were published by Ludwig Music.

"Allan-a-Dale" (CCE51 E55204)
"Allegro," for oboe, violin & piano, by W. Mozart; arr. E. H. (CPOL RE-511-582)
"Bagatelle," for oboe or violin & piano, by L. Beethoven; arr. E. H. (CPOL RE-511-580)
"Ballet Music from 'William Tell,'" by G. Rossini; arr. E. H. (CCE54 E82175)
"Believe Me If All Those Endearing Young Charms," arr. E. H. (CCE52 E68561)
"Kamarinskaya," for horn & piano by P. Tchaikovsky; arr. E. H. (CPOL RE-551-581)
"Minuet and Allegretto," for oboe or violin & piano, by G. Handel; arr. E. H. (CPOL RE-511-583)
"The Oprichinik, Guard of the Czar," by P. Tchaikovsky; arr. E. H. (CCE56 E102779)
"Scherzo," for clarinet & piano, by K. Dittersdorf; arr. E. H. (CPOL RE-511-594)
"Sonata," for clarinet & piano, by A. Corelli; arr. E. H. (CPOL RE-5110595)
"A Tear," by M. Moussourgsky; arr. by Carl Ludwig & E. H. (CPOL RE-511-602)

Ludwig, Carl (F.)

"Minuet; from 'Symphony 17,'" by F. J. Haydn; arr. E. H. (CCE65 E206037; CPOL RE-645-623)
"The Music Box," by A. Liadov; arr. E. H. (LCCF1971-77 E291103)
"Sonata no. 2," for 3 trumpets & piano, arr. E. H. (LCCF1971-77 E285287)

Additional Works by "Eric Hanson"

"A Song for Daniel" (Seesaw, 1972)
"Songs of the British Isles" (Great Works, 1995) (cited REHH)
"This Empty World" (Eunp 775115)

HASTINGS, PAUL

"Paul Hastings" is a pseudoym used by Walter Ehret alone and also as a joint pseudonym with Elmer (F(ranklin)) Kinsman.
To date the following titles have been identified:

Ehret, Walter

"Angels from the Realms of Glory" (CCE58 E124629)
"For the Beauty of the Earth" (CCE58 E124626)
"Lift Up Your Heads O Ye Gates" (CCE58 E124630)
"Lo, He Comes with Clouds Descending" (LCCF58 E124625; CPOL RE-291-334)
"O Thou, Who by a Star" (LCCF58 E124631; CPOL RE-291-337)
"Unto Us A Boy Is Born" (LCCF58 E124624; CPOL RE-291-333)

Kinsman, Elmer (F(ranklin)) & Walter Ehret

"As Joseph Was A-Walking" (CPOL RE-591-511)
Note: Kinsman's given name is listed as Frank on this work.
"Come, Holy Spirit, Come" (CCE59 E128311; CPOL RE-355-412)
"Come Thou Almighty King" (CCE59 E128316; CPOL RE-335417)
"Hail the Day That Sees Him Rise" (CCE59; CPOL RE-335-410)
"Hallelujah, Jesus Lives" (CPOL RE-335-411)
"Joy Dawned Again on Easter Day" (CCE59 128512; CPOL RE-335-413)
"The King of Glory Praise" (CCE59 E128315; CPOL RE-335-416)
"Lord, in This, Thy Mercy's Day" (CCE59 E128314; CPOL RE-335-417)
"When I Survey the Wonderous" (CCE59 E128313; CPOL RE-335-413)

HAZEL, ED(WARD)

"E(dward) Hazel" is a pseudoym used by George D(aniel) Barnard and Will(iam H.) Scouton. To date the following titles have been identified:

Barnard, George D(aniel)

"Alognia March" (CCE27 R7007)
"Azalea Quadrille" (CCE26 R35605; REHG)
"Badger Tournament" (CCE57; REHG)
"Caranola Waltz" (CCE36 R43498; REHG)
"Celestial Crown" (CCE36 R43599; REHG)
"The Challenge" (REHG)
"Concentration" (REHG)
"Corinthian" (REHG)
"Eloise" (REHG)
"Elysian" (REHG)
"Excelsior" (REHG)
"Festal (Overture)" (CCE37 R58209; REHG)
"The Fillmore National" (REHG)
"Fleet Wings Galop" (CCE28 R44672; REHG)
"Floretta (Waltz)" (REHG)
"Forget Me Not" (REHG)
"Glorial" (REHG)
"Glory of Youth" (CCE57)
"The Graduate" (REHG)
"Heart Throbs" (REHG)
"The Husking Bee" (REHG)
"In Ole Kentuck" (REHG)
"Ivanhoe" (REHG)
"Konorah" (REHG)
"Little Primrose" (CCE57; REHG)
"Little Sunshine Gavotte" (REHG)
"Lone Star" (REHG)
"Myrana (Waltz)" (CCE28 R44679; REHG)
"Ni-Phrata" (REHG)
"Olive Branch" (REHG)
"Pure Gold Orchestra Folio" (CCE43 #15773, 413 R117133)
"The Regimental Prize" (REHG)
"Romola" (REHG)
"Rosalena" (REHG)
"Sambo's Birthday" (REHG)
"6th Battalion March" (CCE28 R44682; REHG)
"Sweet Memories" (CCE41 #20979, 903-4 R9657 & R96426; REHG)
"Triumph" (REHG)
"Uncle Jasper" (REHG)
"Wanda Schottische" (CCE28 R44425)

Scouton, Will(iam H.)

"Hazel's New Ideal Orchestra Book" (CCE30 #33420, 70 R11817)
"Konorah , march," for band (CCE28 R1219)
"Ornena, march," for orchestra (CCE28 R1458)
"Overture Ivanhoe," for band (CCE28 R42)
"Overture Ivanhoe," for orchestra (CCE27 R37013)

HILTON, ARTHUR

"Arthur Hilton" is a pseudoym used by Walter Ehret alone and also as a joint pseudonym with each of the following: Byron, Geist, Jack Lyall, Ferris Ohl, Walter (A.) Rodby, Harold (Stillwell) Stark and Ivan Trusler.

To date the following titles have been identified:

Ehret, Walter

"Agnus Die, from Mass 10," by A. Lotti; arr. A. H. (LCCF76 E361597)
"All My Friends Have Forsaken Me" (LCCF75 E34370)
"Allelujah," by H. Purcell; arr. A. H. (LCCF70 E270437)
"Amen" (CCE70 E270440)
"Amen," by G. Pergolesi; arr. A. H. (LCCF73 E308933)
"Arise, Ye Who Serves the Lord" (LCCF71 E292390)
"Blessed the Lord for Ever and Ever" (LCCF75 343287)
"Give Praise To Our God" (LCCF70 E281071)
"God's Son This Day To Us Is Born" (LCCF74 E323759)
"He Was Despised," by K. H. Graun; arr. A. H. (LCCF70 E280103)
"Hear My Prayer, O Lord" (LCCF73 E38935)
"Hear Our Supplication" (CCE70 E270439)
"Holy, Holy, Holy," by F. J. Haydn; arr. A. H. (LCCF74 E322758)
"Holy, Holy, Holy," by G. Rossini; arr. A. H. (CPOL PA-24-735)
"I Will Call Upon the Lord" (LCCF60 E140539)
"In Thee, O Lord, Have I Trusted" (LCCF71 E286351)
"Jesus, My Lord, My God, My All" (LCCF73 E308936)
"Keep No Silence, My Lord" (LCCF72 E306054)
"Let All That Put Their Trust in Thee," by K.Graun; arr. A. H. (LCCF70 E280765)
"Let My Prayer Come Up" (LCCF71 E286349)
"Let Thy Merciful Ears O Lord" (LCCF61 E158349)
"Lord God of Saboth," by L. Cherubini; arr. A. H. (LCCF71 E286775)
"Lord Have Mercy," by G. Pergolesi; arr. A. H. (LCCF70 E281073)
"Lord, I Beseech Thee," by A. Bruckner; arr. A. H. (LCCF74 E322754)
"Lord, Remember Not," by F. Mendelssohn; arr. A. H. (LCCF77 E364703)
"O Worship the Lord" (LCCF61 E158348)
"On Mount of Olives" (LCCF74 E325265)
"Out of the Depths," by K. Graun; arr. A. H. (LCCF70 E270436)
"People Know Thee," by E. Eberlin; arr. A. H. (LCCF74 E325264)
"Sanctus," by F. J. Haydn; arr. A. H. (LCCF61 E163270)
"Sanctus," by T. DeVictoria; arr. A. H. (LCCF72 E307234)
"Thou, Lord, Our Refuge," by F. Mendelssohn; arr. A. H. (LCCF61 E158351)
"Two Chorales," by J. S. Bach; arr. A. H. (LCCF58 E123945)
"Ye That Do Your Master's Will" (LCCF61 E158347)

Geist, Byron & Walter Ehret

"Behold the Lamb of God" (LCCF1955-70 (reference))

Jack Lyall, Jack & Walter Ehret

"O Jesus, Tender Shepherd Hear" (LCCF1955-70 (reference))

Ohl, Ferris & Walter Ehret

"Cherubim Song" (LCCF1955-70 (reference))

Rodby, Walter & Walter Ehret

"Send Forth Thy Spirit" (CPOL RE-349-898)
"To Thee, Jehovah!" (LCCF1955-70 (reference))

Stark, Harold (Stillwell) & Walter Ehret

"Emitte spiritum Tuum" (LCCF1955-70 (reference))

Trusler, Ivan & Walter Ehret

"He That Shall Endure To the End" (LCCF1955-70 (reference))

KEISER/KING, ROBERT (A(DOLPH))

In the Copyright Pre-1938 Renewal File (LCRC) under "King, Robert A." there is reference to a (1 Feb. 1929) letter which explains Robert A. Keiser changed his surname to "King" at the time of the World War. Works originally copyrighted under the name "Keiser" are in the LCRC under "King."

Earl, Mary

Keiser/King composed his most famous song, "Beautiful Ohio" under this name. The publisher Shapiro, Bernstein reported a total of $60,000 royalty payments to King. (Douglas Gilbert, *Lost Chords; The Diverting Story of American Popular Songs*. New York: Cooper Square Publishers, 1970, 324.)

Grey, Vivian

Conflicting information about the song "Anona" makes it difficult to verify if Vivian Grey is a pseudonym of Robert Keiser/King or Mabel Baer (née McKinley).

Two sources identify Vivian Grey as the pseudonymn of Mable Baer (née McKinley) as the composer:

1. The copyright renewal record for "Anona" (CCE32 R20484), and
2. The composer of "Anona" (1903) is listed as Vivian Grey, pseudonym of Mabel McKinley in *Ragtime; Its History, Composers, and Music* (Schirmer Books, 1985)

Four sources identify Vivian Grey as a pseudonym of King:

1. According to Sigmund Spaeth, Vivian Grey's "Anona" was composed by " . . . the ubiquitous Keiser-King." (Spaeth, *A History of Popular Music in America*, p. 366)
2. In King's obituary "Anona" is listed as one of King's songs. (*New York Times* (16 April 1932): 78.
3. The entry for Robert A(dolph) King in *The National Cyclopaedia of American Biography* states, "'Anona' was written for Mabel McKinley, a niece of President McKinley, while he [i.e., King] was acting as her piano accompanist."
4. Douglas Gilbert writes: "The first issues of . . ."Anona" bear the name of Vivian Grey. It was popularized by . . . Mabel McKinley, a niece of the assassinated President. When it went into the hit class, "Vivian Grey" was removed from the cover and the song attributed to Miss McKinley, who legally defended her "ownership." . . . "On the night of September 18, 1903, Doris Wilson . . . was just beginning the chorus of "Anona" when a process server stomped down the aisle waving his summons, shouting to Miss Wilson to stop. . . . The action was said to have been initiated by Miss McKinley to prevent Miss Wilson and others from singing "her" song that King wrote." (Gilbert, *Lost Chords*, 324)

Haley, Ed

"Wait Till the Clouds Roll By" and "While Strolling Through the Park One Day," which was published under the title, "The Fountain in the Park," were composed under the pseudonym "Ed Haley." Douglas Gilbert reports the actual composer is either Theodore Morse, F. B. Haviland, Robert King or Herman Snyder. "Which one of the four wrote which song no one knows and no one ever will, but "The Fountain in the Park" was dedicated to Robert (King) Keiser." (Gilbert, *Lost Chords*, 324-5). James Fuld argues that since Robert King did not renew "The Fountain in the Park" he is not the composer, also stating ". . . it would be highly unusual for the user of a pseudonym to dedicate the song to his true name." (Fuld, *The Book of World-Famous Music; Classical, Popular and Folk*, 646-7).

Roosevelt, T.

"Under the Stars and Stripes," a march by T. Roosevelt, first appeared in *Ainslee's Collection of World's Musical Masterpieces* (Century Publishing Co.). Many people thought Theodore Roosevelt composed the song since he was credited with helping to preserve music of the Indians, had a fondness for western cowboy songs and ballads, recognized the importance of John Lomax's research, and was aware of the social values of music. Margery Stomme Selden reported in her article "T. Roosevelt; Mystery Composer," (*Sonneck Society Bulletin*. 15:1, 7-11) that an anonymous correspondent at Century Publishing Co. contacted Wallace Finley Dailey, Curator of the Theodore Roosevelt Collection at Harvard University, alerting him to the fact that "Under the Stars and Stripes" was not by ex-President Theodore Roosevelt. Selden also reported information received from Kathleen Cabana of the Library of Congress Copyright Office indicating the renewal application for the work was signed by Robert A. Keiser King as author, i.e., composer.

Author's note: The copyright renewal record for "Under the Stars and Stripes" (LCRC) lists the printed initial "*T*" followed by "*homas*" penciled in. One can only imagine King's delight in issuing the work with only the initial "T," undoubtedly suspecting it would be associated with Theodore Roosevelt.

Note: The *Ainslee's Collection* included two additional works by Keiser/King: "The Fawn, Valse du Salon," by Robert A. King and "National Airs Medley, Two-Step and March" by R. Keiser.

KENDALL, DON

"Don Kendall" is a Leo Feist Co. house name used on compositions by Walter Haenschen, Jules Hurtig, Theodore Morse, James O'Keefe and Lester O'Keefe.
To date the following works have been identified:

Haenschen, Walter & James (Conrad) O'Keefe

"Indian Lullaby" (CCE50 R57889 & R57099)

Morse, Theodore

"Brass" (CCE50 R63624)

Morse, Theodore & Jules Hurtig

"Just Married" (CCE49 R54019; CCE49 R54020)

O'Keefe, James (Conrad) & Lester O'Keefe

"Bambina" (CCE56 R174190)
"Black Eyed Blues" (CCE50 R56321)"Melancholy Moon" (CCE56 R170802)

KENT, H. R.

"H. R. Kent" is a Carl Fischer house name used on compositios and arrangements by Louis-Philippe Laurendeau, J(ulius) S. Seredy and Paul Sterrett.
To date the following titles have been identified:

Seredy, J(ulius) S.

"American Patrol," by F. W. Meacham; arr. H.R.K. (CCE73 R547607)
"Arioso, from 'Cantata 1560", by J. S. Bach; arr. H.R.K. (CCE45 E132155)
Note: Arranged for several different instruments.
"The Army Air Corps" (CCE43 E116882; CCE70 R494734)
"Ballet Egytien," by A. Luigini; arr. H.R.K. (CCE72 R538775)
"The Bat," by J. Strauss; arr. H.R.K. (CCE74 R581711)
"The Caissons Go Rolling," arr. H.R.K. (CCE71 R508672)
"Carmen Fantasia," by G. Bizet; arr. H.R.K. (CCE74 R589748)
"Caucasian," by M. Ippolitov-Ivanhov; arr. H.R.K. (CCE74 R589747)

"The Conqueror," by C. Teike; arr. H.R.K. (CCE73 R542997)
"Dreams of Love," by F. Liszt; arr. H.R.K. (CCE72 R543002)
"Fantasia de concerto solo," by E. Boccalari; arr. H.R.K. (CCE 76 R625681)
"La feria," by P. Lacome; arr. H.R.K. (CCE48 E21686; CCE75 R602496)
"Irish Tune from County Derry and Shepherd's Hey," by P.Grainger; arr. H.R.K.
"La gazza ladra," by G. Rossini; arr. H.R.K. (CCE48 E28392; RCCE75 R607901)
"Let Us Have Music" (CCE42 #11836 E100678)
"Lullaby," by J. Brahms; arr. H.R.K. (CCE43 E119285)
"Orpheus Overture," by J. Offenbach; new parts by H. R. K. (CCE73 R561327)
"Over the Waves," by J. Rosas; arr. H.R.K. (CCE48 E30643)
"Pique-dance," arr. H.R.K. (CCE48 E30197)
"Poet and Peasant," arr. H.R.K. (CCE45 E128616)
"Prelude, from 'Die Meistersinger,'" by R. Wagner; arr. H.R.K. (CCE48; CCE75 R607896)
"Les Preludes," by F. Listz; new parts by H. R. K. (CCE73)
"Sakuntala Overture," by C. Goldmark; new parts by H. R. K. (CCE73 R561333)
"Slavonic rhapsody," by C. Friedeman; arr. H. R. K. (CCE73 R561325)
"Valse des fleurs, from 'Nutcracker Suite,'" by P. Tschaikowsky; new parts by H. R. K. (CCE73 R561329)
"Young Prince and the Young Princess, from 'Scheherazade,'" by Rimsky-Korsakov; arr. H. R.K. (CCE75 RH. R. K.)

Sterrett, Paul

"Der Freischütz," arr. by T. Moses-Tobani; rev. H. R. Kent (LCCF 1955-70 6/28/56 letter cited)

KIMBALL, F. R.

"F. R. Kimball" is a McKinley house name used on compositions by Leo Friedman, Frank K. Root, Henry S. Sawyer and possibly others.
To date the following titles have been identified:

Friedman, Leo

"Birds and Flowers" (CCE16 E389216)

Root, Frank K.

"Angelic Voices" (CCE10 E242817)
Note: Probably by Root; publisher is listed as Frank Root, Chicago.
"Holiday March" (CCE26 36067)

Sawyer, Henry S.

"Keep Step March" (CCE22 E5419; CCE37 R57997)

Additional Works by "F. R. Kimball"

"Hay Ride" (CCE07)
"In the Silver Moonlight" (CCE07)
"Masonic Parade" (CCE07)
"Emblem of Peace, march, piano" (CCE08)
"Gleaming Waters, piano" (CCE08)
"Warblings of the Birds, piano" (CCE08)
"Bright Star of Heaven, piano" (CCE09)
"Chanticleer, march, piano" (CCE10)

"Dreams at Sunset, piano" (CCE10)
"Love's Message, piano" (CCE10)
"Blind Man's Buff, piano" (CCE11)
"The Husking Bee, piano" (CCE11)
"Rocky Rill, piano" (CCE11)
"The Star of Hope, piano" (CCE11)
"Whispering Leaves" (CCE11)
"Hip-hip-hooray, piano" (CCE12)
"Voices of the Night" (CCE12)
"Love's Hesitation, piano" (CCE14)

KUNKEL BROTHERS (CHARLES AND JACOB)

Charles Kunkel composed under numerous *noms de plume*, including names of famous composers and noted pianists without their permission or acknowledgement. And he had no qualms about editing their works, frequently changing parts that he thought needed improvement. This was risky when he used the works of living composers; for example, Moritz Moszkowski was furious when he learned of Kunkel's "reduced" edition of his "Waltz in E major, op. 34, no. 1" and " . . . threatened to come to America and shoot the perpetrator" (Krohn, p. 211; cited in Tipton, p. 28).

On copyright records the names of several composers in the Saint Louis area are identified as pseudonyms of Charles Kunkel, including Fleta Jan Brown (1883-1938), composer, singer; John William "Blind" Boone (1864-1927), composer, pianist; Christine Nordstrom Carter, teacher, composer; (Mrs.) Regina M(ullery) Carlin, organist, singer, music supervisor, composer; Ifrenaeus D. Foulon, lawyer, editor; and James (Conrad) O'Keefe (1892-1942), composer, author, movie director. These individuals may have composed the works, or they may have given Kunkel permission to use their names. In either case, when Kunkel applied for copyright renewals, he claimed the works as his own and indicated that the other names were pseudonyms. (For additional information about the Saint Louis area composers listed above, see Krohn's *Missouri Music*.) It is not known if these individuals gave permission to use their name.

Kunkel Brothers & Julie Rive-King

The Kunkels had permission to use the name of noted pianist Julie Rive-King. She bought the compositions and in turn the Kunkels paid her royalties on the copies they sold. (Krohn p. 150) (See also NOTE: Rive-King, Julie)

The following Catalog of Copyright Entries were identified:

Kunkel, Charles

"Fragrant Breezes," transcription of Jensen's "Murmelndes, Luftchen Bluthenwind in freier Uebertrgung," by Julie Rive-King (CCE11 R2277)
"Home, Sweet Home, grand paraphrase de concert," by Julie Rive-King (CCE14 R5337)
"Nearer My God to Thee, grand paraphrase de concert," by Julie Rive-King (CCE12 R2959)"Supplication," transcription of Jensen's "Lehn 'deine Wang an meine Wang,'" by Julie Rive-King" (CCE11R2278)
"Tannhauser March," by Franz Lizst; fingered by Julie Rive-King. (CCE11 R2376)

Kunkel, Jacob

"Bubbling Spring, tone-poem characteristic," by Julie Rive-King. (CCE21 R18252)
Note: Some sources report Rive-King helped edit and revise her husband's "Bubbling Spring;" however; according to the CCE21 renewal entry Jacob Kunkel was the composer and Charles Kunkel was the editor/revisor.
"Gems of Scotland, caprice de concert," by Julie Rive-King; rev. & ed. by Carl Wilhelm Kern. (CCE36, E55034)

Sources:

Krohn, Ernest C. "The Amazing Kunkels." Chapter from an unfinished manuscript held at Gaylord Library, Washington University, Saint Louis, MO.

Krohn, Ernest C. *Missouri Music*. New York: Da Capo, 1971.
Tipton, Patricia Gray. *The Contributions of Charles Kunkel to Musical life in St.Louis*. (Ph. D. dissertation) St. Louis: Washington University, 1977.

LLEWELLYN, RAY

There is debate among experts on TV music as to whether "Ray Llewellyn" was a pseud of David D. Rose or a house name used by several composers under ZIV-TV contract for non-union projects. According to Paul Mandell the following composers working for the company during the period of the eight shows with music by "Ray Llewellyn:" Ray Bloch, Domonic Frontiere, Lynn Murray [i.e., Lionel Breeze], Irving Orton, David D. Rose, Dmitri Tiompkin, Peter Yorke, and Victor Young. (http://www.classicalthemes.com/50sTVThemes/mysteriesOfTVM.htm (3 Mar. 2005))

1949 Martin Kane—Private Eye
1953 I Led Three Lives
1954 Meet Corliss Archer (Syndicated version)
1955 Highway Patrol (Theme 1 & 2) ("Ray Llewellyn" = David D. Rose)
1955 Science Fiction Theater ("Ray Llewellyn" = Ray Bloch)
1956 Dr. Christian
1957 Sea Hunt (Ray Llewellyn" = David D. Rose)
1961 King of Diamonds

LLOYD, GEORGE

"George Lloyd" is a pseudoym used by Dave Sonenscher and Julian Wright and also by Sonenscher, Wright and C(harles) J(oseph) Edwards.

To date the following titles have been identified:

Sonenscher, Dave & Julian Wright

"I'm Coming Home to Gertrude . . . " (CCE33 Efor28901)
"Marching to a Military Band" (CCE33 Efor29862)

Sonenscher, Dave, Julian Wright, & C(harles) J(oseph) Edwards

"I'm One of the Ladsof Valencia" (CCE33 Efor28676)
"Jolly Old Ma! Jolly Old PA! (CCE33 Efor28780)

MANILLA, PEDRO

"Pedro Manilla" is a pseudonym used by A(nnuzio) P(aolo) Mantovani alone and also as a jt. pseud. with Angelo F. Picconi.

To date the following titles have been identified:

Mantovani, A(nnuzio) P(aolo)

"American Gypsy"
"Autumn Rhapsody"
"Autumn Theme"
"Blue Mantilla"
"Call of the West"
"Cuor Ingrato"
"Havana Moonlight" (CCE38 Efor54909; CCE66 R)
"In Sunny Napoli" (CCE38 Efor55556; CCE66 R)

"Lazy Gondolier" (CCE55 Efor40951)
"Madam You're Lovely" (CCE60 R243972)
"Marengo"
"Mexican Starlight"
"Phantom Wheels"
"Song of Sorrento" (CCE56 Efor40951)
"Tango De La Luna"

Mantovani, A(nnuzio) P(aolo) & Angelo F. Picconi

"Arana de la noche" (CCE63 R319101)
"Tango Romantico" (CCE38 Efor53958; CCE65 R359686)

MANILLA, TONY

"Tony Manilla" is a pseudoym used by Jack Fishman (1918 (or 19)-) alone and also as a joint pseudonym with Cyril Stapleton and also Clare Shardlow.
To date the following titles have been identified:

Fishman, Jack

"Keeping Cool with Lemonade"
"One Man and His Dog" (CPOL RE-358-105)

Fishman, Jack & Cyril Stapleton

"I Saw a Light" (CPOL RE-364-775)

Fishman, Jack & Clare Shardlow

"Let Me Take You Home Again" (CPOL RE-117-492)

MARLO, FERDI

"Ferdi Marlo" is a Sam Fox Publishing Co. house name for lyricists, including Ralph (T.) Butler and Leo Towers [i.e., Leo(nard) Blitz] and possibly others. A letter from the company, dated 23 September 1932, is cited in the LCPF: ". . . the pseudonym of Ferdi Marlo is a house name which we have given and will give to various lyrics written by authors who do not wish their name to appear on the copy . . ."
To date the following titles have been identified:

Butler, Ralph (T.)

"If You Kiss Me" (CCE60 R249648)

Towers, Leo [i.e., Leo(nard) Blitz]

"Marie, Marie" (LCCF59 R229685)
"Old Mountain Lullaby" (LCCF62 R300393)
"Sweet Lady" (LCCF59 R239973)
"Tonight You're In My Arms" (LCCF59 R229676)
"When I See You Smile, Cheri" (LCCF59 R239970)
"When The Dance Is Ended" (LCCF59 R239969)

MEYER, FERDINAND

"Ferdinand Meyer" is an Arthur P. Schmidt Co. house name used on "for hire" compositions and arrangements by Ernest Harry Adams, O(badiah) B(ruen) Brown, Charles F(rederick) Dennee; Arthur (William) Foote, Frank Lynes, Edmund Parlow, Arnoldo Sartorio, and Charles P(hillip) Scott.. To date the following "Ferdinand Meyer" compositions have been identified:

Adams, Ernest Harry

"The Pupil's Third Etude Album," selected & arr. F. M. (CCE28 E695112)
"Trills," after Bertini, by F. M. (CCE28 E695113)

Brown, O(badiah) B(ruen)

"He's Watching O'er Thy Mother" (Verified in NEWB)
"Serenade," by C. M. Widor; arr. F. M. (CCE12 R3520)
"When This War Is Over I Will Come Back to Thee" (Verified in NEWB)

Dennee, Charles F(rederick)

"The Boys before the Mast" (CCE30 R11698)
"The Defender" (CCE30 R11699)

Foote, Arthur (William)

"Agitato," by Jules Schudhoff; rev. F. M. (LCRC26 R33243)
"Air de ballet," by C. Chaminade; rev. F. M. (LCRC24 R28518)
"Always Gay," by Julius Handrock; rev. F. M. (LCRC25 R31457)
"Amoretten, op. 306," by G. Lange; rev. F. M. (LCRC26 R32678)
"Arietta, op. 97," by T. Lack; rev. F. M. (CCE15 R7063)
"At the Spinning Wheel," by J. Low; rev. F. M. (LCRC16 R8393)
"Barcarolle in F minor," by A. Rubenstein; ed. F. M. (CCE24 R27981)
"Barcarolle in G minor, op. 50," by A. Rubenstein; arr. F. M. (LCRC26 R34526)
"Buchner," by A. Emil; rev. F. M. (CCE09 R303)
"Cabaletta," by T. Lack; rev. F. M. (LCRC15 R7040)
"Le Cavalier Fantastique, op. 42, no. 1," by B. Godard; ed. F. M. (CCE29 R1866)
"Chaconne," by H. Roubier; rev. F. M. (LCRC26 R33246)
"Chaminade, serenade, op. 26" (CCE26 R33703)
"The Chase, op. 5," by J. Rheinberger; rev. F. M. (LCRC15 R7126)
"Coquetry, op. 12, no. 5," by N. von Wilm; rev. F. M. (CCE13 #24273, 19 R4807)
"Cradle Song (Wiegenlied)," by S. Heller, rev. F. M. (CCE14 R5439)
"Il Desiderio, op. 14," by H. Cramer; ed. F. M. (CCE21 R1896)
"Etude de Style, op. 14, no. 1," by H. Ravina; ed. F. M. (CCE29 R1680)
"Etude melodique, op. 130, no. 2," by J. Raff; ed. F. M. (CCE27 R41000)
"Etude Mignonne," by Eduard Schutt; rev. F. M. (CCE14 R5303)
"Evening Breezes," by F. Schubert; arr. S. Heller; rev. F. M. (LCRC23 R25413)
"Fabliau, op. 75, no. 2," by J. Raff; ed. F. M. (CCE24 R25968)
"Fairy Tale," by J. Raff; ed. F. M. (LCRC25 R30313)
"La Fontaine," by C. B. Lysberg; ed. F. M. (LCRC25 R32656)
"Gavotte, op. 62, no. 6," by X. Scharwenka; ed. F. M. (LCRC13 R4436)
"Gavotte and Menuett," by H. Reinhold; ed. F. M. (CCE15 R6371)
"Gavotte Moderne, op. 25," by B. Tours; ed. F. M. (CCE21 R19452)
"Gondolina" (CCE20 R161195)
"Hark! Hark the Lark," by F. Schubert; ed. F. M. (CCE23 25453)
"Hunting Song, op. 86, no. 3," by S. Heller; ed. F. M. (CCE29 R1867)

"Hunting Song (Jagdlied), op. 81, no. 2," by G. Merkel; ed. F. M. (CCE24 R27980)
"Idyl, op. 34, no. 4" (LCRC25 R30330)
"In the Woods (Im Walde), op. 12, no. 6," by N. von Wilm; rev. F. M. (CCE14 R5590)
"Intermezzo," by Edward Schutt; rev., F. M. (LCRC25 R30311)
"La lisonjera (The Flatterer), op. 50," by C. Chaminade; ed. F. M. (CCE24 R26911)
"Madrigal, op. 136," by T. Lack; rev. F. M. (CCE26 R33247)
"March, op. 62, no. 1," by X. Scharwenka; rev. F. M. (CCE13 R4805)
"Mazurka in A-flat, op. 11," by F. Wrede; rev. F. M. (CCE25 R31453)
"Melodie in G-flat major," by M.Moszkowski; ed. F. M. (CCE24 R26910)
"Menuet," by B. Godard; rev. F. M. (CCE16 R8399)
"Menuet, op. 126, no. 1," by J. Raff; rev. F. M. (CCE26 R33258)
"Menuet de Bergamo, op. 75," by A. Durand; rev. F. M. (LCRC17 R10929)
"Morning Song," by T. Oesten; rev. F. M. (CCE12 R2410)
"My Heart Ever Faithful," by J. S. Bach; arr. Lavignac; rev. F. M. (LCRC23 R23679)
"Neapolitan Boat-Song," by Paul Wacha; rev. F. M. (LCRC26 R33257)
"Nocturne, op. 92," by Fr. Bendel; rev. F. M. (CCE13 #25626, 3 R4840)
"Pastorale in E minor," by Domenico Scarlatti; arr. C. Tausig; fingering by F. M. (CCE15 R6905)
"Patrol of the Musketeers," by G. Bachmann; rev. F. M. (LCRC26 R33259)
"Pierrette, op. 41, no. 5," by C. Chaminade; rev. F. M. (LCRC26 R35022)
"Polka Boheme," by A. Rubenstein; rev. F. M. (LCRC23 R25452)
"Renouveau, op. 82," by B. Godard; rev. F. M. (LCRC25 R30314)
"Reverie in A-flat, op. 34, no. 5," by E. Schutt; rev. F. M. (LCRC25 R32655)
"Romance, op. 62, no. 7," by X. Scharwenka; rev. F. M. (LCRC13 R4437)
"Scherzino," by A. Emil Buchner; rev. F. M. (CCE09 R303)
"Scherzino, op. 18, no. 2," by M. Moszkowski; rev. F. M. (LCRC13 R4434)
"Scherzino, by X. Scharwenka, op. 62, no. 10; rev. F. M. (LCRC13 R4804)
"Serenade, op. 19," by O. Olsen; rev. F. M. (LCRC26 R35401)
"Serenata, op. 15, no. 1," by M. Moszkowski; rev. F. M. (LCRC26 R34527)
"Slumber Song (Schlummerlied), op. 124, no. 16," by R. Schumann; ed. F. M. (CCE24 R25908)
"The Spinning Wheel," by N. von Wilm; ed. F. M. (CCE16 R8839)
"Staccato Etude, op. 102," by C. Hause; ed. F. M. (CCE26 R33254)
"Staccato-Etude," by F. Spnidler; rev. F. M. (LCRC25 R32645)
"Swallows," by G. Bachmann; rev. F. M. (LCRC26 R33260)
"Sylvains, op. 60," by C. Chaminade; rev. F. M. (LCRC25 R30296)
"Tanz Rondo, op. 131, no. 1," by A. Biehl; rev. F. M. (LCRC25 R31450)
"Tanzweise, op. 28, no. 2," by E. Meyer-Helmund; rev. F. M. (CCE25 R30295)
"Tarantelle in A-flat major; op. 85, no.2," by S. Heller ed. F. M. (CCE21 R18732)
"Valse Arabesque, op. 82," by T. Lack; rev. F. M. (LCRC26 R35400)
"Valse Caprice," by A. Rubenstein; rev. F. M. (LCRC25 R29775)
"Valse de Salon," by Jean Vogt; rev. F. M. (LCRC25 R30312)
"Valse Lente," by Eduard Schutt; rev. F. M. (LCRC19 R14504)
"Venitienne, op. 110, no. 2," by Benjamin Godard; ed. F. M. (CCE24 R26909)
"Wolfrem's Invocation" (LCRC22 R21218)

Lynes, Frank

"Abschied und Heimkehr, op. 27" (CCE38 R 65806)
"Ankunft der gaste schellenfahrt, op. 27" (CCE38 R65802)
"Auf zum Weihnachtsbaum marsch, op. 27" (CCE38 R65803)
"Kuiawiak," by J. Wieniawski, ed. by F. M. (CCE23 R23669)
"Tanz der Alten, op. 27" (CCE38 R65805)
"Tanz der Jungen, op. 27" (CCE38 R65804)
"Weihnachtsglocken, op. 27" (CCE38 R65801)

Parlow, Edmund

"In Rank and File" (CCE42 R113368)

Sartorio, Arnoldo

"Devotion (Pensee intime), op. 26, no. 2" (CCE09 E213495)
"Happy Days (Sich selbst getreu), op. 50, no. 1" (CCE12 E294101)
"A Heart Secret (Secred de Coeur), op. 26, no. 1" (CCE09 E213495)
"Just in Time (Zur rechten zeit), op. 51, no. 3" (CCE12 E294100)
"Nothing Ventured Nothing Gained, op. 51, no. 2" (CCE12 E294102)

Scott, Charles P(hillip)

"Auf der Kirmes, op. 486, no. 5," by J. E. Hummel; arr. F.M. (CCE29 R4751)
"Berges gruss, op. 486 no. 11," by J. E. Hummel; arr. F. M. (CCE29 R4757)
"Birds of Spring (Fruhlings-sanger), op. 426," by G. Lang; rev. F. M. (CCE24 R26953)
"Capriccietto, op. 30 no. 2," by St. Niewiadomski; ed. F. M. (CCE29 R5718)
"Chant du d'Avril, op. 147," by T. Lack; ed. F. M. (CCE30 R11255)
"Chers souvenirs (Sweet Remembrance)," by G. Horvath; arr. F. M. (CCE29 R5451)
"Cradle song (Wiegenlied)," by L. Streabbog [i.e., Jean Louis Gobbaerts]; arr. F. M. (CCE24 R26952)
"La Danse de Colomine (Dance of Columbine), op. 47, no. 1," by G.Horvath; arr. F. M. (CCE29 R5450)
"Dance grotesque, op. 34, no. 6," by St. Niewiadomski; ed. F. M. (CCE30 R11697)
"Deux mazureks, op. 26," by St. Niewiadomski; ed. F. M. (CCE29 R5716)
"The Elves," by F. Behr; ed. F. M. (LCRC24 R28599)
"Gitana," by F. Behr; ed. F. M. (LCRC24 R28600)
"Glocklein im walde, op. 488, no. 1," by J. E. Hummel; arr. F. M. (CCE29 R4618)
"Gretchen's puppe, op. 486, no. 3," by J. E. Hummel; arr. F. M. (CCE29 R4749)
"Halali, op. 486, no. 9," by J. E. Hummel; arr. F. M. (CCE29 R4755)
"Humoresque, op. 34, no. 4," by St. Niewiadomski; ed. F. M. (CCE30 R11695)
"Idylle, op. 34, no. 5," by St. Niewiadomski; ed. F. M. (CCE30 R11696)
"Der Junge barde," by J. E. Hummel; arr. F. M. (CCE29 R4752)
"Der Klein Kaddet," by J. E. Hummel; arr. F. M. (CCE29 R4754)
"Krakowiak, op. 31, no. 2," by St. Niewiadomski; ed. F. M. (CCE29 R5713)
"Madrigal," by Gabriel-Marie; arr. F. M. (CCE31 R15951)
"Marche hongroise heroique, op. 48, no. 3," by G. Horvath; ed. F. M. (CCE30 R11704)
"Marquita, danse espagnole," by G. Horvath; arr. F. M. (CCE29 R5454)
"Mazurek, op. 26, no. 1," by St. Niewiadomski; ed. F. M. (CCE229 R5715)
"Mazurka galante, op. 181," by D. Krug; ed. F. M. (CCE30 R11254)
"Meditation," by Gabriel-Marie; arr. F. M. (CCE31 R15952)
"Melodie romantic, op. 30, no. 1(?); by St. Niewiadomski; ed. F. M. (CCE29 R5717)
"Merry Lads," by Th. F.Schild; arr. F. M. (CCE35 R37856)
"Mit anmuth, op. 486, no. 6," by J. E. Hummel; arr. F.M. (CCE29 R4753)
"Moment lyrique, op. 34, no. 2," by St. Niewiadomski; ed. F. M. (CCE30 R9462)
"Octave Study," by W. Mozart; arr. F.M. (In: "The Pupil's First Etude Album") (CCE28 R76)
"Polonaise, op. 30, no. 1(?)," by St. Niewiadomski; ed. F. M. (CCE29 R5714)
"Polonaise in E minor," by J. Hoffman; arr. F. M. (CCE38 R68335)
"Princesse-valse, op. 25," by W. Goldner, op. 25; ed. F. M. (CCE30 R11256)
"The Pupil's First Etude Album," arr. F. M. (CCE28 R77)
"The Pupil's Second Etude Album," arr. F. M. (CCE06 C126058; CCE33 R 26592)
"Rain (or Rein?) of Gold" (LCRC25 R30859)
"Das Rosenfest, op. 486, no. 2," by J. E. Hummel; arr. F. M. (CCE29 R4748)
"D'Schwalberlin (The Swallows), op. 65," by C. Schild; arr. F. M. (CCE29 R3261)
"Seerosen (Water-lilies), op. 482," by J. E. Hummel; arr., F. M. (CCE29 R4904)
"Senner's abschied (The Alpine Shepherd's Farewell)," by J. E. Hummel, op. 492, ed. F.M. (CCE29 R5453)

"Serenade, op. 34, no. 1," by St. Niewiadomski; ed. F. M. (CCE30 R9461)
"Serenade Slave," by St. Niewiadomski; ed. F. M. (CCE29 R5719)
"Skylark," by J. H. Wallis; rev. F. M. (CCE24 R26954)
"Soldaten-liedchen, op. 486, no. 1," by J. E. Hummel; arr. F. M. (CCE29 R4747)
"Die Sprudelnde quelle," by J. E. Hummel; arr. F. M. (CCE29 R4758)
"Tarantelle Mignonne, op. 48, no. 2," by G. Horvath; ed. F. M. (CCE30 R11703)
"To the Forest," by Th. F. Schild; arr. F. M. (CCE35 R37857)
"Two Melodies at the Same Time," (In: "The Pupil's First Etude Album") (CCE28 R70)
"Valse, op. 30, no. 4,"by St. Niewiadomski; ed. F. M. (CCE29 R5716)
"Valse gracieuse, op. 34, no. 3," by St. Niewiadomski; ed. F. M. (CCE30 R11694)
"Valse parisienne, op. 48, no. 1," by G. Horvath; ed. F. M. (CCE30 R11702)
"Veilchen am bach, op. 486, no. 10," by J. E. Hummel; arr. F. M. (CCE29 R4756)
"Wanderer's abendliedchen, op. 486, no. ?," by J. E. Hummel; arr. F.M. (CCE29 R4750)

Additional Works by "Ferdinand Meyer"

"Christmas Suite (CCE10 R1929)
"Weihnachtglocken?"
"Schlittenfahrt"
"Auf zum Weihnachtsbaum"
"Tanz der Junge"
"Tanz der Alten"
"Abschied und Heimkehr"
"Flying Leaves, op. 28" (CCE10)
"Spring's First Message"
"Violets and Forget-Me Nots"
"Elfin Dance"
"The Victor's Joy"
"Song without Words"
"L'Ingenue, Morceau a la Gavotte, op. 26" (CCE08)
"6 Melodious Studies, op. 25" (CCE08)
"At Twilight"
"First Grief"
"Coaxing"
"Fleeting Time"
"A Pleasant Fancy"
"Gracefulness"

RITTER, G. P.

"G. P. Ritter" is an Arthur P. Schmidt Co. house name used on "for hire" compositions and arrangements by Charles P. Scott and G. F. Suck.

To date the following works have been identified:

Scott, Charles P(hilipp)

Maryland, My Maryland; arr. G. P. R. (CCE26 R35790)

Suck, G. F.

"Annie Laurie," arr. G. P. R. (CCE22 R21201)
"Auld Lang Syne," arr. by G.P.R. (CCE12 R2414)
"Believe Me If All Those Endearing ...," arr. G. P. R. (CCE09 R287)
"Bridal Chorus from Lohengrin," by R. Wagner; arr. G. P. R. (CCE09 R286)

"The Brook" (CCE13 R4505)
"Capricietto" (CCE13 R4504)
"Comin' Thro'the Rye," arr. G. P. R. (CCE22 R19958)
"Constancy" (CCE17 R10195)
"Cradle Song" (CCE15 R7137)
"Cujus Animam," by G. Rossini; arr. G. P. R. (CCE11 R2460)
"Duettino" (CCE15 R7145)
"The Echo" (CCE15 R7143)
"Elisie's Delight" (CCE15 R7147)
"Epiphany" (CCE21 R19419)
"First Violet". (CCE15 R7142)
"The First Waltz" (CCE15 R7148)
"Forsaken," by T. Kaschat; arr. G. P. R. (CCE09 R288)
"Grandma's Story" (CCE15 R7139)
"Grandpa's Dance" (CCE15, R7135)
"Happy Birdling" (CCE15 R7134)
"The Happy Child" (CCE15 R7144)
"The Harp That Once Thro' Tara's Halls," arr. G. P. R. (CCE09 R307)
"How Can I Leave Thee" (CCE09 R308)
"How So Fair, from 'Martha,'" by Flotow, arr. G. P. R. (CCE09 R285)
"Huntman's Song" (CCE15 R7136)
"Hymn of Trust" (CCE20 R15068)
"In Maytime" (CCE22 R19959)
"In the Orchards" CC24 R25934)
"Katydid" (CCE24 R25938)
"The Last Rose of Summer" (CCE12 R3343)
"Menuet, op. 78," by F. Schubert; arr. G. P. R. (CCE09 R284)
"Puzzler Is My Name (Ich heiss glatteis)" (CCE11 R18965)
"A Song" (CCE21 R19418)
"Rondo-Turc" (CCE13 R1438)
"Six Miniatures, op. 172, nos. 1-6," by C. Gurlitt; arr. G. P. R. (Individual copyrights)
"Spanish Dance" (CCE15 R7138)
"Spring Song" (CCE15, R7146)
"Spring Time" (CCE15 R7138)
"Trinklied," by C. Gurlitt; arr. G. P. R. (CCE19 R14154)
"Tyrolienne" (CCE10 R584)
"Tyrolienne, from 'William Tell,'" by Rossini; arr. G. P. R. (CCE15 R6690)
"Within a Mile of Edinburgh" (CCE12 R2412)

RIVE-KING, JULIE

According to M. L. Petteys' entry on Julie Rive-King in *The Norton/Grove Dictionary of Women Composers* (New York: W. W. Norton, 1995), Julie's husband, Frank H. King, persuaded her to publish *his* works under *her* name as a way of enhancing her reputation. For the same reason the couple also allowed Kunkel Brothers (St. Louis) to publish transcriptions by Charles and Jacob Kunkel under Julie's name.

See also NOTE: Kunkel Brothers (Charles and Jacob). Details about Frank King and Julia Rive-King's financial arrangements with the Kunkel Brothers and the problems Julie encountered after her husband's death are described in M. L. Petteys' *Julie Rive-King, American Pianist*. Ph. D. Dissertation. Kansas City: University of Missouri, 1987.

SAINT QUENTIN, EDWARD

"Edward Saint Quentin is a pseudonym used by Alfred William Rawlings and possibly by William M(arshall) Hutchison.

To date, the following works have been identified:

Hutchison, William M(arshall)

"Far Away Dreams" (BLIC; CPMU)
Note: In the last section of the CPMU listing for "Saint Quentin (Edward) [i.e., Alfred William Rawlings]", there is an entry for this work with a see reference to W. M. Hutchison. Under Hutchison this work is listed as transcribed by E. St. Quentin [i.e., A. W. Rawlings]
"A Fearful Mystery," farce (performed 1886) (STGR)
"Glamour" (performed 1886) (STGR)
"They Didn't Give In," operetta (performed 1907) (STGR)

Rawlings, Alfred William

In CPMU approximately 300 titles are entered under: Saint Quentin, Edward [i.e., Alfred William Rawlings]

STONE, CHARLIE

"Charlie Stone" is a pseudonym of Charles R(aymond) Adams. To date, the following titles have been identified:
"Are You Real" (CCE54 E79233)
"Foolishly" (CCE54 E81252)
"If You Need Me" (CCE53 E73190; CPOL RE-102-781)
"I'm Gone" (CCE56 E101231)
"Ooh Ya Gotta" (CCE55 E94197)
"Rattle My Bones" (CCE56 E99444)
"Shame" (CCE54 E79232)
"That Blue-Eyed Baby of Mine" (CCE53 E73192)
"You're as Sweet Today as Yesterday" (CCE53)

SWEENEY, CHARLES

Copyright records for "The Rival King" (CCE37 E60485), "Our Band March" (CCE38 R65776) & "Lu Lu Band March" (CCE39 #21731, 205) clearly state "Charles C. Sweeley" is a pseud. of Harry J. Lincoln. The most controversial work is "Repasz Band and 2 Step." According to many sources Lincoln sold the work to Sweeley who then published the work under his name. In the original 1901 copyright record, Sweeley is listed as the composer and Lincoln the arranger; however, on the 16 August 1928 renewal card there is the penciled notation: "by Charles C. Sweeley (pseudonym of Harry J. Lincoln, arr. by H. J. L.)" (See REHG p. 460 & SMIN).

THOMPSON, DAVID

"David Thompson" is a pseudoym used by Walter Ehret alone and also as a joint pseudonym with Harold Stark.

To date the following titles have been identified:

Ehret, Walter

"Breakforth, O Beauteous Heavenly Light" (CPOL RE-291-321)
"Heavenly Father" (CCE58 E119613; CPOL RE-291-320)
"Praise Ye the Father" (CCE59 E130565)

"Sanctus and Hosanna," by W. Mozart; arr. D. T. (CCE58 E119794; CPOL RE-291-322)
"The Three Kings" (CCE58 E121250; CPOL RE-291-326)

Stark, Harold (Stillwell) & Walter Ehret

"Then Round about the Starry Throne" (CCE59 E130261; CPOL RE-335-409)

TIBALLS, JOHN

"John Tiballs" is a pseudoym used by Charles H(utchinson) Gabriel and E(dmund) S(imon) Lorenz. To date the following titles have been identified:

Gabriel, Charles H(utchinson)M

"Something for My Savior" (CCE27 R40098)
Note: Words by Jennie Wilson. Copyright date: 26 Feb. 1927. See below; same title by Lorenz.

Lorenz, E(dmund) S(imon)

"Blessed Are They" (CCE26 R34616)
"Do You Know It Just Now" (CCE27 R36911)
"He Will Have Mercy" (CCE26 32567)
"I Am the Resurection" (CCE26 R32574)
"I Will Sing" (CCE23 R23277)
"Something for My Savior" (CCE27 R37114)
Note: Words by Jennie Wilson. Copyright date: 2Feb. 1927. See above; same title by Gabriel.
"To Make Men Free" (CCE27 R37121)
"Try to Be Like Jesus" (CCE27 R37131)
"Where the Lord Leads" (CCE25 R28957)
"Yes We Will" (CCE27 R37126)

VOGT, CARL

"Carl Vogt" is a pseudoym used on compositions and arrangements by M(artin) Greenwald, Lee Orean Smith and possibly others.
To date the following titles have been identified:

Greenwald, M(artin)

"At the Country Fair" (CCE35 E48126)
"Barbara" (CCE35 E48125)
"Betty's Waltz" (CCE35 E48131)
"The Big Bass Fiddler" (CCE35 E48123)
"A Bunch of Daisies" (CCE35 E48117)
"The Dancers" (CCE35 E48127)
"Dreaming of Santa Claus" (CCE35 E48119)
"Elizabeth Waltz" (CCE35 E48132)
"The Floral Parade" (CCE35 E48118)
"A Little French Doll" (CCE35 E48137)
"Little Rondo" (CCE35 E48124)
"March of the Boy Scouts" (CCE35 E48133)

"Marche Militaire" (CCE35 E48130)
"The Meadow Brook" (CCE35 E48128)
"Morning Prayer, by L. Streabbog [i.e., Jean Louis Gobbaerts]; arr. C. V. (CCE35 E48122)
"An Old Moss Covered Church," by H. P. Hopkins; arr. C. V. (CCE35 E48135)
"On a Visit" (CCE35 E48120)
"Pretty Sunshine" (CCE35 E48121)
"School Pictures," by H. P. Hopkins; arr. C. V. (CCE35 E48134)
"Watching the Soldiers," by H. P. Hopkins; arr. C. V. (CCE35 E48136)

Smith, Lee Orean

"Shadows on the Water," by A. Loumey; arr. C. V. (CCE37 E60431-33)
Note: Editions for violin & piano, clarinet & piano, and cornet/trumpet & piano.
A piano 4-hand version is arranged by Calvin Grooms [i.e., Lee Orean Smith]. (All editions published by Century Music.)

Additional Works by "Carl Vogt"

"Boat song," saxophone (CCE26 E650372)
"Boat song," violin (CPMU)
"Dream Waltz," saxophone (CCE26 E650373)
"Easy Recreations," violin & piano (1908)
"Evening Song," violin (CPMU)
"Familiar Airs," violin (CPMU)
"Innocence," violin (CPMU)
"May Song," violin (CPMU)
"Morning Song," violin (CPMU)
"Playtime Waltz," violin (CPMU)
"Remembrance," violin (CPMU)
"Sax-o-moan" (CCE26 E650368)
"Saxonade" (CCE26 E650370)
"Saxonola" (CCE26 E650369)
"Soldiers' Song," violin (CPMU)

WILLIAMSON, WARREN

"Warren Williamson" is a pseudoym used by Walter Ehret alone and also as a joint pseudonym with Elmer (F(ranklin)) Kinsman.

To date the following titles have been identified:

Ehret, Walter

"Ev'ry Time I Feel the Spirit" (CCE67 E238144)

Kinsman, Elmer (F(ranklin)) & Walter Ehret

"Ev'ry Time I Feel the Spirit" (CC65 E203614)
"Ezekiel Saw the Wheel" (CCE65 E203616)
"He Is King of Kings" (CCE64 E184462)
"Hear the Voice of Love and Mercy" (CCE64 E184463)
"I Saw Three Ships" (CCE65 E206663)
"Poor Wayfaring Stranger" (CCE65 E203615)

Additional Works by "Warren Williamson"

"Now Hath Christ Arisen" (CPOL PA-609-881)
"Open the Gates of the Temple" (CPOL PA-570-128)

WILSON, PAUL

"Paul Wilson" is a pseudoym used on compositions and arrangements by Sidney (Alan) Carlin and Paul Sterret. To date the following titles have been identified:

Carlin, Sidney (Alan)

"Allegro Spirito," by F. J. Haydn; arr. P. W. (CPOL RE-503-406)
"Fantasia," by W. Byrd; arr. P. W. (CPOL RE-713-300)
"Finale, from 'Elijah,'" by F. Mendelssohn; arr. P. W. (CPOL RE-713-301)
"Gavotte," by G. Teleman; arr. P. W. (CPOL RE-569-525)
"Jubilation and Praise," by Vulpius; arr. P.W. (CPOL RE-713-299)
"Minuet in G," by G. Handel; arr. P. W. (CPOL RE-569-527; LCCF63 E178023)
"Scherzo, from 'Lyrical Pieces,'" by. E. Grieg; arr. P. W. (CPOL RE-449-588)
"Themes from Mendelssohn's Second Piano Concerto," arr. P. W. (CCE75 E346314)
"Two Songs," by W. Mozart; arr. P. W. (CPOL RE-503-407)

Sterret, Paul

"Short-cut Tenor Banjo Method" (CCE61 A525332)

A Zaret, Hy

According to articles in the *News Transcript* (Farmington, NJ) William Albert Stirrat used the pseudonym "Hy Zaret" in 1936 when he penned the lyrics for "Unchained Melody." At the time he was a summer scholarship student at Yaddo's Triuna Arts of the Theatre School where he met Alex North, who wrote the music. The issue of authorship was complicated by the fact that several men claimed to be Hy Zaret. (http://newstranscript.gmnews.com/news/2003/1203/Front_page/047.html; http://newstranscript.gmnews.com/news/2004/0714/Front_page/070.html [20 Mar. 2006]) *Note:* Copyright records further complicate matters since entries for "Unchained Melody" appear under William Albert Stirrat, with Hy Zaret identified as his pseudonym, and also under Hy Zaret (1907-), see CPOL records for "Unchained Melody."

ZEEDEN, PETER

"Peter Zeeden" is a pseudonym used by Gerhard Schmidt and Robby Schmitz.
To date the following titles have been identified:

Schmidt, Gerhard

"Kapt'n Jack" (CCE63 Efor94949)
"Rosen-Rosmarie" CCE64 Efor97533)
"Schotten-Twist" (CCE64 Efor99185)
"Si Pudiera, beguine" (CCE63 Efor96604)
"Tiritombablu" (CCE64 Efor103352)

Schmitz, Robby

"Swedish Summer" (CCE77 Efor186727)

References

Cudworth, Charles L. "Ye Old Spuriosity Shoppe, or, Put It in the Anhang," *Notes* 12 (September 1955): 533–53.
Duckles, Vincent H.; Reed, I; Keller, Michael A., eds. *Music Reference and Research Materials: An Annotated Bibliography.* 5th ed. New York: Schirmer Books, 1997.
Mossman, Jennifer, ed. *Pseudonyms and Nicknames Dictionary* 3rd ed. Detroit, Mich.: Gale Research, 1987.
———, ed. *New Pseudonyms and Nicknames Dictionary* Suppl. to 3rd ed. Detroit, Mich.: Gale Research, 1988.
"Nom de plumes [sic] in the Musical Profession," *The Yorkshire Musician* 3 (1 June 1889): 175–76.
"The Plays the Thing," *Etude* 55:2 (February 1937): 75–76.
Sharp, Harold S. *Handbook of Pseudonyms and Personal Nicknames* 5 vols. Metuchen, N.J.: Scarecrow Press, 1982.
Sutton, Allan. *A Guide to Pseudonyms on American Records, 1892–1942.* New York: Greenwood Press, 1993.

About the Author

Jeanette Marie Drone is a freelance educator. She received a bachelor's degree in music education and a master's degree in library science from George Peabody College for Teachers (now Peabody College of Vanderbilt University), a master's in music from The University of Michigan, and a Ph. D. in library and information science from the University of Illinois at Urbana–Champaign. Since completing a two-year postdoctoral fellowship in the OCLC Office of Research in 1988, Drone has held visiting academic appointments at schools of library/information science at the University of California, Los Angeles, University of Illinois at Urbana–Champaign, University of Oklahoma, and the University of Arizona. From 1969 through 1980 she was music librarian at Memphis State University (now University of Memphis). Her publications include *Index to Opera, Operetta and Musical Comedy Synopses in Collections and Periodicals* (Scarecrow Press, 1978), the supplement *Musical Theater Synopses; An Index* (Scarecrow Press, 1998), reports issued by the Illinois State Library, and music cataloging tools published by OCLC.